THE ZONDERVAN
ENCYCLOPEDIA
OF THE BIBLE

THE ZONDERVAN ENCYCLOPEDIA OF THE BIBLE

Volume 3
H–L

Merrill C. Tenney, General Editor / Moisés Silva, Revision Editor

Revised, Full-Color Edition

ZONDERVAN.com/
AUTHORTRACKER
follow your favorite authors

ZONDERVAN

The Zondervan Encyclopedia of the Bible
Copyright © 2009 by Zondervan
First edition copyright © 1975, 1976 by Zondervan

Requests for information should be addressed to:
Zondervan, *Grand Rapids, Michigan 49530*

Library of Congress Cataloging-in-Publication Data

    The Zondervan encyclopedia of the Bible / Moisés Silva, revision editor ; Merrill C. Tenney, general editor. — Rev. full-color ed.
        p. cm.
    Rev. ed. of: The Zondervan pictorial encyclopedia of the Bible.
    Includes bibliographical references.
    ISBN 978-0-310-24133-1 (hardcover, printed)
    ISBN 978-0-310-24136-2 (set)
       1. Bible—Encyclopedias. I. Silva, Moisés. II. Tenney, Merrill Chapin, 1904-1985. III. Zondervan pictorial encyclopedia of the Bible. IV. Title: Encyclopedia of the Bible.
    BS440.Z63 2009
    220.3—dc22
                                                                                                                                2009004956

All Scripture quotations, unless otherwise indicated, are taken from the *Holy Bible, New International Version*®. NIV®. Copyright © 1973, 1978, 1984 by International Bible Society. Used by permission of Zondervan. All rights reserved.

Any Internet addresses (websites, blogs, etc.) and telephone numbers printed in this book are offered as a resource. They are not intended in any way to be or imply an endorsement by Zondervan, nor does Zondervan vouch for the content of these sites and numbers for the life of this book.

All rights reserved. No part of this publication may be reproduced, stored in a retrieval system, or transmitted in any form or by any means—electronic, mechanical, photocopy, recording, or any other—except for brief quotations in printed reviews, without the prior permission of the publisher.

Interior design by Tracey Walker

Printed in China

09 10 11 12 13 14 15 • 23 22 21 20 19 18 17 16 15 14 13 12 11 10 9 8 7 6 5 4 3 2 1

IMAGE SOURCES

The Amman Archaeological Museum. Amman, Jordan.
Todd Bolen/www.BiblePlaces.com
The British Museum. London, England.
The Cairo Museum. Cairo, Egypt.
The Church of Annunciation Museum. Nazareth, Israel.
Direct Design. Amarillo, Texas.
The Egyptian Ministry of Antiquities.
The Ephesus Archaeological Museum. Selchok, Turkey.
The Eretz Israel Museum. Tel Aviv, Israel.
The House of Anchors. Kibbutz Ein Gev. Sea of Galilee, Israel.
International Mapping.
The Isma-iliya Museum. Isma-iliya, Egypt.
The Israel Museum, Jerusalem, courtesy of the Israel Antiquities Authority.
The Istanbul Archaeological Museum. Istanbul, Turkey.
Dr. James C. Martin.
The Jordanian Ministry of Antiquities. Amman, Jordan.
Ministero per I Beni e le Attivita Culturali—Soprintendenza Archaeologica di Roma. Rome, Italy.
Mosaic Graphics.
Musée du Louvre. Paris, France.
Phoenix Data Systems
Z. Radovan/www.BibleLandPictures.com
Reproduction of the City of Jerusalem at the time of the Second Temple—located on the grounds of the Holy Land Hotel, Jerusalem.
Sola Scriptura. The Van Kampen Collection on display at the Holy Land Experience. Orlando, Florida.
The Turkish Ministry of Antiquities. Ankara, Turkey.
The Yigal Allon Center. Kibbutz Ginosar, on the western shore of the Sea of Galilee, Israel.

ABBREVIATIONS

I. General

א	(Aleph) Codex Sinaiticus
A	Codex Alexandrinus
AASOR	Annual of the American Schools of Oriental Research
AB	Anchor Bible
ABD	*Anchor Bible Dictionary*
ABR	*Australian Biblical Review*
ad loc.	*ad locum*, at the place
AHR	*American Historical Review*
AJA	*American Journal of Archaeology*
AJP	*American Journal of Philology*
AJSL	*American Journal of Semitic Languages and Literature*
AJT	*American Journal of Theology*
Akk.	Akkadian
ANE	Ancient Near East(ern)
ANEP	*The Ancient Near East in Pictures Relating to the Old Testament*, ed. J. B. Pritchard (1954)
ANET	*Ancient Near East Texts Relating to the Old Testament*, ed. J. B. Pritchard, 3rd ed. (1969)
ANF	*Ante-Nicene Fathers*
ANRW	*Aufstieg und Niedergang der römischen Welt* (1972–)
aor.	aorist
APOT	*Apocrypha and Pseudepigrapha of the Old Testament*, ed. R. H. Charles, 2 vols. (1913)
Apoc.	Apocrypha
approx.	approximate(ly)
Aq.	Aquila
ARAB	*Ancient Records of Assyria and Babylonia*, ed. D. D. Luckenbill, 2 vols. (1926–27)
Arab.	Arabic
Aram.	Aramaic
Arch	*Archaeology*
ARM	*Archives royales de Mari*
Assyr.	Assyrian
ASV	American Standard Version
AThR	*Anglican Theological Review*
AUSS	*Andrews University Seminary Studies*
B	Codex Vaticanus
b.	born
BA	*Biblical Archaeologist*
BAR	*Biblical Archaeology Review*
BASOR	*Bulletin of the American Schools of Oriental Research*
BASORSup	*Bulletin of the American Schools of Oriental Research Supplemental Studies*
BBR	*Bulletin for Biblical Research*
BC	F. J. Foakes-Jackson and K. Lake, eds., *The Beginnings of Christianity*, 5 vols. (1920–33)
BDAG	W. Bauer, *A Greek-English Lexicon of the New Testament and Other Early Christian Literature*, 3rd ed., rev. F. W. Danker (2000)
BDB	F. Brown, S. R. Driver, and C. A. Briggs, *A Hebrew and English Lexicon of the Old Testament* (1907)
BDF	F. Blass, A. Debrunner, and R. W. Funk, *A Greek Grammar of the New Testament and Other Early Christian Literature* (1961)
BDT	*Baker's Dictionary of Theology*, ed. E. F. Harrison (1960)
BECNT	Baker Exegetical Commentary on the New Testament
BETS	*Bulletin of the Evangelical Theological Society*
BHK	*Biblia Hebraica*, ed. R. Kittel, 3rd ed. (1937)
BHS	*Biblia Hebraica Stuttgartensia*, ed. K. Elliger and W. Rudolph (1983)
Bib.	*Biblica*
BJRL	*Bulletin of the John Rylands Library*
BKAT	Biblischer Kommentar, Altes Testament
BNTC	Black's New Testament Commentaries
BRev	*Bible Review*
BSac	*Bibliotheca Sacra*
BWL	*Babylonian Wisdom Literature*, ed. W. G. Lambert (1960)
BZ	*Biblische Zeitschrift*
C	Codex Ephraemi Syri
c.	*circa*, about

CAH	*Cambridge Ancient History*
CANE	*Civilizations of the Ancient Near East*, ed. J. M. Sasson, 4 vols. (1995)
CBQ	*Catholic Biblical Quarterly*
CBSC	Cambridge Bible for Schools and Colleges
CD	Cairo: Damascus (i.e., *Damascus Document*)
cent.	century
CEV	Contemporary English Version
cf.	*confer*, compare
CGTC	Cambridge Greek Testament Commentary
ch(s).	chapter(s)
CT	*Christianity Today*
CIG	*Corpus inscriptionum graecarum*
CIL	*Corpus inscriptionum latinarum*
CIS	*Corpus inscriptionum semiticarum*
col(s).	column(s)
COS	*The Context of Scripture*, ed. W. W. Hallo, 3 vols. (1997–2002)
CRINT	Compendia rerum iudaicarum ad Novum Testamentum
D	Codex Bezae
d.	died, date of death
DAC	*Dictionary of the Apostolic Church*, ed. J. Hastings, 2 vols. (1915–18)
DBI	*Dictionary of Biblical Interpretation*, ed. J. H. Hayes, 2 vols. (1999)
DBSup	*Dictionnaire de la Bible: Supplément*, ed. L. Pirot and A. Robert (1928–)
DCG	*Dictionary of Christ and the Gospels*, ed. J. Hastings, 2 vols. (1906–08)
DDD	*Dictionary of Deities and Demons in the Bible*, ed. K. van der Toorn et al., 2nd ed. (1999)
DJD	Discoveries in the Judaean Desert
DJG	*Dictionary of Jesus and the Gospels*, ed. J. B. Green et al. (1992)
DLNT	*Dictionary of the Later New Testament and Its Developments*, ed. R. P. Martin and P. H. Davids (1997)
DNTB	*Dictionary of New Testament Background*, ed. C. A. Evans and S. E. Porter (2000)
DOTHB	*Dictionary of the Old Testament: Historical Books*, ed. B. T. Arnold and H. G. M. Williamson (2005)
DOTP	*Dictionary of the Old Testament: Pentateuch*, ed. T. D. Alexander and D. W. Baker (2003)
DOTT	*Documents from Old Testament Times*, ed. D. W. Thomas (1958)
DPL	*Dictionary of Paul and his Letters*, ed. G. F. Hawthorne et al. (1993)
DSS	Dead Sea Scrolls
E	east
EA	El-Amarna Tablets. See *Die el-Amarna-Tafeln, mit Einleitung und Erläuterung*, ed. J. A. Knudtzon, 2 vols. (1908–15; suppl. by A. F. Rainey, 2nd ed., 1978)
EBC	*The Expositor's Bible Commentary*, ed. F. E. Gaebelein et al., 12 vols. (1979–92)
EBr	*Encyclopedia Britannica*
ed(s).	editor(s), edited, edition
e.g.	*exempli gratia*, for example
EGT	*Expositor's Greek Testament*, ed. W. R. Nicoll, 5 vols. (1897–1910)
Egyp.	Egyptian
EKKNT	Evangelisch-katholischer Kommentar zum Neuen Testament
EncBib	*Encyclopaedia Biblica*, ed. T. K. Cheyne and J. S. Black, 4 vols. (1899–1903)
EncJud	*Encyclopedia Judaica*, 16 vols. (1972)
Eng.	English
ERE	*Encyclopedia of Religion and Ethics*, ed. J. Hastings, 13 vols. (1908–27)
ERV	English Revised Version
esp.	especially
ESV	English Standard Version
et al.	*et alii*, and others
ETR	*Etudes théologiques et religieuses*
ETSB	*Evangelical Theological Society Bulletin*
Euseb.	Eusebius
EvQ	*Evangelical Quarterly*
EvT	*Evangelische Theologie*
Exp	*The Expositor*
ExpTim	*Expository Times*
ff.	following (verses, pages, etc.)
FCI	*Foundations of Contemporary Interpretation*, ed. M. Silva, 6 vols. in 1 (1996)
fem.	feminine
FFB	*Fauna and Flora of the Bible*, UBS Handbook Series, 2nd ed. (1980)
fig.	figure, figurative(ly)
fl.	*floruit*, flourished
FOTL	Forms of the Old Testament Literature
ft.	foot, feet
GCS	Die griechische christliche Schriftsteller

Ger.	German
GKC	Gesenius-Kautzsch-Cowley, *Gesenius' Hebrew Grammar*, 2nd ed. (1910)
Gk.	Greek
GNB	Good News Bible
HAL	*Hebräisches und aramäisches Lexikon zum Alten Testament*, by L. Koehler et al., 5 fascicles (1967–95)
HALOT	*Hebrew and Aramaic Lexicon of the Old Testament*, by L. Koehler et al., 5 vols. (1994–2000)
HAT	Handbuch zum Alten Testament
HDB	Hastings' *Dictionary of the Bible*, 5 vols. (1898–1904); rev. ed. in 1 vol. by F. C. Grant and H. H. Rowley (1963)
Heb.	Hebrew
HGHL	*Historical Geography of the Holy Land*, by G. A. Smith, 25th ed. (1931)
Hitt.	Hittite
HibJ	*Hibbert Journal*
HJP	*A History of the Jewish People in the Time of Jesus Christ*, by E. Schürer, 5 vols., 2nd ed. (1885–90); rev. ed., *The History of the Jewish People in the Age of Jesus Christ (175 B.C.–A.D. 135)*, by G. Vermès and F. Millar, 4 vols. (1973–87)
HNT	Handbuch zum Neuen Testament
HNTC	Harper's New Testament Commentaries
HTKAT	Herders theologischer Kommentar zum Alten Testament
HTKNT	Herders theologischer Kommentar zum Neuen Testament
HTR	*Harvard Theological Review*
HUCA	Hebrew Union College Annual
IB	*Interpreter's Bible*, ed. G. A. Buttrick et al., 12 vols. (1951–57)
ibid.	*ibidem*, in the same place
ICC	International Critical Commentary
id.	*idem*, the same (as previously mentioned)
IDB	*Interpreter's Dictionary of the Bible*, ed. G. A. Buttrick, 4 vols. (1962); supplementary vol., ed K. Crim (1976)
i.e.	*id est*, that is
IEJ	*Israel Exploration Journal*
Ign.	Ignatius
illus.	illustration
impf.	imperfect
impv.	imperative
inscr.	inscription
Int	*Interpretation*
IPN	*Die israelitischen Personennamen*, by M. Noth (1928)
Iren.	Irenaeus
ISBE	International Standard Bible Encyclopedia, ed. M. G. Kyle, 4 vols. (1929); rev. ed., G. W. Bromiley, 4 vols. (1979–88)
JANESCU	*Journal of the Ancient Near Eastern Society of Columbia University*
JAOS	*Journal of American Oriental Society*
JASA	*Journal of the American Scientific Affiliation*
JB	Jerusalem Bible
JBL	*Journal of Biblical Literature*
JBR	*Journal of Bible and Religion*
JCS	*Journal of Cuneiform Studies*
JE	The Jewish Encyclopedia, ed. I. Singer, 12 vols. (1925)
JEA	*Journal of Egyptian Archaeology*
JETS	*Journal of the Evangelical Theological Society*
JJS	*Journal of Jewish Studies*
JNES	*Journal of Near Eastern Studies*
JNSL	*Journal of North Semitic Languages*
Jos.	Josephus
JPOS	*Journal of the Palestine Oriental Society*
JPS	Jewish Publication Society, *The Holy Scriptures according to the Masoretic Text: A New Translation . . .* (1945)
JQR	*Jewish Quarterly Review*
JR	*Journal of Religion*
JRS	*Journal of Roman Studies*
JSJ	*Journal for the Study of Judaism in the Persian, Hellenistic, and Roman Periods*
JSNT	*Journal for the Study of the New Testament*
JSOT	*Journal for the Study of the Old Testament*
JSP	*Journal for the Study of the Pseudepigrapha*
JSS	*Journal of Semitic Studies*
JTS	*Journal of Theological Studies*
KAI	*Kanaanäishce und aramäische Inschriften*, by H. Donner and W. Röllig, 2nd ed., 3 vols. (1966–69)
KAT	Kommentar zum Alten Testament
KB	L. Koehler and W. Baumgartner, *Lexicon in Veteris Testamenti libros*, 2nd ed. (1958; for 3rd ed., see *HAL*)

KD	C. F. Keil and F. Delitzsch, *Biblical Commentary on the Old Testament*, 25 vols. (1857–78)	NEB	New English Bible
		neut.	neuter
KEK	Kritisch-exegetischer Kommentar über das Neue Testament (= Meyer-Kommentar)	*NewDocs*	*New Documents Illustrating Early Christianity*, ed. G. H. R. Horsley and S. Llewelyn (1981–)
		NHC	Nag Hammadi Codex
KJV	King James Version	*NHL*	*Nag Hammadi Library in English*, ed. J. M. Robinson, 4th ed. (1996)
Lat.	Latin		
LCL	Loeb Classical Library	NIBCNT	New International Bible Commentary on the New Testament
lit.	literal(ly), literature		
LN	J. P. Louw and E. A. Nida, *Greek-English Lexicon of the New Testament Based on Semantic Domains*, 2 vols., 2nd ed. (1989)	NIBCOT	New International Bible Commentary on the Old Testament
		NICNT	New International Commentary on the New Testament
LSJ	H. G. Liddell, R. Scott, and H. S. Jones, *A Greek-English Lexicon*, 9th ed., with rev. supplement (1996)	NICOT	New International Commentary on the Old Testament
		NIDNTT	*New International Dictionary of New Testament Theology*
LXX	The Seventy = Septuagint		
Maj. Text	Majority Text	*NIDOTTE*	*New International Dictionary of Old Testament Theology and Exegesis*
masc.	masculine		
mg.	margin	NIGTC	New International Greek Testament Commentary
mi.	mile(s)		
MM	J. H. Mouton and G. Milligan, *The Vocabulary of the Greek Testament* (1930)	NIV	New International Version
		NIVAC	New International Version Application Commentary
MNTC	Moffatt New Testament Commentary		
MS(S)	manuscript(s)	NJB	New Jerusalem Bible
McClintock and Strong	J. McClintock and J. Strong, *Cyclopedia of Biblical, Theological, and Ecclesiastical Literature*, 12 vols. (1867–87)	NJPS	*Tanakh: The Holy Scriptures. The New JPS translation according to the Traditional Hebrew Text*
		NKJV	New King James Version
MT	Masoretic text	NLT	New Living Translation
N	north	*NovT*	*Novum Testamentum*
n.	note	NPNF	Nicene and Post-Nicene Fathers
NA	Nestle-Aland, *Novum Testamentum Graecum*	NRSV	New Revised Standard Version
		NT	New Testament
NAB	New American Bible	*NTAp*	*New Testament Apocrypha*, ed. E. Hennecke, 2 vols., trans. R. McL. Wilson (1963–65); unless otherwise indicated, references are to the rev. ed. by W. Schneemelcher, trans. R. McL. Wilson (1991–92)
NAC	New American Commentary		
NASB	New American Standard Bible		
NBD	*New Bible Dictionary*, ed. J. D. Douglas et al.; unless otherwise noted, references are to the 3rd ed. (1996)		
		NTD	Das Neue Testament Deutsch
NCB	New Century Bible	*NTS*	*New Testament Studies*
NCBC	New Century Bible Commentary	NW	northwest
NCE	*New Catholic Encyclopedia*, ed. W. J. McDonald et al., 15 vols. (1967)	*OCD*	*Oxford Classical Dictionary* (1949)
		ODCC	*Oxford Dictionary of the Christian Church*, ed. F. L. Cross and E. A. Livingstone, 3rd ed. (1997)
NCV	New Century Version		
n.d.	no date		
NE	northeast		
NEAEHL	*The New Encyclopedia of Archaeological Excavations in the Holy Land*, ed. E. Stern et al., 4 vols. (1993)	*Onom.*	Eusebius's *Onomasticon*, according to E. Klostermann, ed., *Das Onomastikon der biblischen Ortsnamen* (1904)

op. cit.	*opere citato*, in the work previously cited	SHERK	*The New Schaff-Herzog Encyclopedia of Religious Knowledge*, 13 vols. (1908–14)
orig.	original(ly)		
OT	Old Testament	SIG	*Sylloge inscriptionum graecarum*, ed. W. Dittenberger, 4 vols., 3rd ed. (1915–24)
OTL	Old Testament Library		
OTP	*Old Testament Pseudepigrapha*, ed. J. H. Charlesworth, 2 vols. (1983–85)	sing.	singular
		SJT	*Scottish Journal of Theology*
p., pp.	page, pages	SP	Sacra Pagina
pass.	passive	*ST*	*Studia theologica*
PEQ	*Palestine Exploration Quarterly*	Str-B	H. L. Strack and P. Billerbeck, *Kommentar zum Neuen Testament aus Talmud und Midrash*, 6 vols. (1922–61)
Pers.	Persian		
pf.	perfect		
PG	*Patrologia graeca*, ed. J.-P. Migne, 162 vols. (1857–96)	Sumer.	Sumerian
		s.v.	*sub verbo*, under the word
PJ	*Palästina-Jahrbuch*	SW	southwest
pl.	plural	Syr.	Syriac
PL	*Patrologia latina*, ed. J.-P. Migne, 217 vols. (1844–64)	Symm.	Symmachus
		Tac.	Tacitus
POxy	Oxyrhynchus Papyri	*TDNT*	*Theological Dictionary of the New Testament*, ed. G. Kittel and G. Friedrich, 10 vols. (1964–76)
prob.	probably		
Pseudep.	Pseudepigrapha		
ptc.	participle	*TDOT*	*Theological Dictionary of the Old Testament*, ed. G. J. Botterweck and H. Ringgren (1974–)
PTR	*Princeton Theological Review*		
RA	*Revue d'assyriologie et d'archéologie orientale*		
		TEV	Today's English Version
Rahlfs	A. Rahlfs, *Septuaginta, id est, Vetus Testamentum graece iuxta LXX interpretes*, 3rd ed. (1949)	Tg.	Targum
		Theod.	Theodotion
		THKNT	Theologischer Handkommentar zum Neuen Testament
RB	*Revue biblique*		
RE	*Realencyclopädie für protestantische Theologie und Kirche*, ed. J. J. Herzog and A. Hauck, 24 vols. (1896–1913)	*ThTo*	*Theology Today*
		TNIV	Today's New International Version
		TNTC	Tyndale New Testament Commentaries
REB	Revised English Bible	TOTC	Tyndale Old Testament Commentaries
repr.	reprint(ed)	TR	Textus Receptus
rev.	revised	trans.	translation, translator, translated
RevExp	*Review and Expositor*	*TWNT*	*Theologisches Wörterbuch zum Neuen Testament*, ed. ed. G. Kittel and G. Friedrich, 10 vols. (1932–79)
RevQ	*Revue de Qumran*		
RGG	*Die Religion in Geschichte und Gegenwart*, ed. K. Galling, 7 vols., 3rd ed. (1857–65)		
		TynBul	Tyndale Bulletin
		TZ	*Theologische Zeitschrift*
Rom.	Roman	UBS	United Bible Society, *The Greek New Testament*
RSPT	*Révue des sciences philosophiques et théologiques*		
		UF	*Ugarit-Forschungen*
RSV	Revised Standard Version	Ugar.	Ugaritic
RV	Revised Version	UM	*Ugaritic Manual*, by C. H. Gordon, 3 parts (1955)
S	south		
SacBr	A. F. Rainey and R. S. Notley, *The Sacred Bridge: Carta's Atlas of the Biblical World* (2005)	UT	*Ugaritic Textbook*, by C. H. Gordon, 3 parts (1965)
		v., vv.	verse, verses
Sansk.	Sanskrit	*VT*	*Vetus Testamentum*
SE	southeast	viz.	*videlicet*, namely
sec.	section	v.l.	*varia lectio*, variant reading

vol(s).	volume(s)
vs.	versus
Vulg.	Vulgate
W	west
WBC	Word Biblical Commentary
WEB	World English Bible
WH	B. F. Westcott and F. J. A. Hort, *The New Testament in the Original Greek*, 2 vols. (1881)
WTJ	*Westminster Theological Journal*
ZAW	*Zeitschrift für die alttestamentliche Wissenschaft*
ZDMG	*Zeitschrift der deutschen morgenländischen Gesellschaft*
ZDPV	*Zeitschrift der deutschen Palästina-Vereins*
ZNW	*Zeitschrift für die neutestamentliche Wissenschaft*
ZRGG	*Zeitschrift für Religions und Geistesgeschichte*

II. Books of the Bible
Old Testament

Gen.	Genesis
Exod.	Exodus
Lev.	Leviticus
Num.	Numbers
Deut.	Deuteronomy
Josh.	Joshua
Jdg.	Judges
Ruth	Ruth
1 Sam.	1 Samuel
2 Sam.	2 Samuel
1 Ki.	1 Kings
2 Ki.	2 Kings
1 Chr.	1 Chronicles
2 Chr.	2 Chronicles
Ezra	Ezra
Neh.	Nehemiah
Esth.	Esther
Job	Job
Ps.	Psalm(s)
Prov.	Proverbs
Eccl.	Ecclesiastes
Cant.	Canticles (Song of Songs)
Isa.	Isaiah
Jer.	Jeremiah
Lam.	Lamentations
Ezek.	Ezekiel
Dan.	Daniel
Hos.	Hosea
Joel	Joel
Amos	Amos
Obad.	Obadiah
Jon.	Jonah
Mic.	Micah
Nah.	Nahum
Hab.	Habakkuk
Zeph.	Zephaniah
Hag.	Haggai
Zech.	Zechariah
Mal.	Malachi

New Testament

Matt.	Matthew
Mk.	Mark
Lk.	Luke
Jn.	John
Acts	Acts
Rom.	Romans
1 Cor.	1 Corinthians
2 Cor.	2 Corinthians
Gal.	Galatians
Eph.	Ephesians
Phil.	Philippians
Col.	Colossians
1 Thess.	1 Thessalonians
2 Thess.	2 Thessalonians
1 Tim.	1 Timothy
2 Tim.	2 Timothy
Tit.	Titus
Phlm.	Philemon
Heb.	Hebrews
Jas.	James
1 Pet.	1 Peter
2 Pet.	2 Peter
1 Jn.	1 John
2 Jn.	2 John
3 Jn.	3 John
Jude	Jude
Rev.	Revelation

Apocrypha

1 Esd.	1 Esdras
2 Esd.	2 Esdras (= *4 Ezra*)
Tob.	Tobit
Jdt.	Judith
Add. Esth.	Additions to Esther
Wisd.	Wisdom of Solomon

Sir.	Ecclesiasticus (Wisdom of Jesus the Son of Sirach)	2 En.	2 Enoch
Bar.	Baruch	4 Ezra	4 Ezra (= 2 Esdras)
Ep. Jer.	Epistle of Jeremy	Jub.	Book of Jubilees
Pr. Azar.	Prayer of Azariah	Let. Aris.	Letter of Aristeas
Sg. Three	Song of the Three Children (or Young Men)	Life Adam	Life of Adam and Eve
		3 Macc.	3 Maccabees
		4 Macc.	4 Maccabees
Sus.	Susanna	Mart. Isa.	Martyrdom of Isaiah
Bel	Bel and the Dragon	Pss. Sol.	Psalms of Solomon
Pr. Man.	Prayer of Manasseh	Sib. Or.	Sibylline Oracles
1 Macc.	1 Maccabees	T. Benj.	Testament of Benjamin (etc.)
2 Macc.	2 Maccabees	T. 12 Patr.	Testaments of the Twelve Patriarchs
		Zad. Frag.	Zadokite Fragments

III. Pseudepigrapha

As. Moses	*Assumption of Moses*
2 Bar.	*2 Baruch*
3 Bar.	*3 Baruch*
1 En.	*1 Enoch*

Other Christian, Jewish, and Greco-Roman texts are referred to by their standard abbreviations. See, e.g., *The SBL Handbook of Style* (1999), ch. 8, appendix F, and appendix H.

THE ZONDERVAN ENCYCLOPEDIA OF THE BIBLE

Woman harvesting wheat near Bethlehem.

H. An abbreviation used to designate the Holiness Code (the legal corpus found in Lev. 17–26). See LEVITICUS, BOOK OF I; PENTATEUCH III.

Haahashtari hay´uh-hash´tuh-r*i* (הָאֲחַשְׁתָּרִי *H2028*, a gentilic form meaning "the Ahashtarite[s]"). Son of Ashhur by Naarah and a descendant of JUDAH, although the precise genealogical connection is unclear (1 Chr. 4:6). The term is probably a family name reflecting descent from an otherwise unknown person presumably named Ahashtar.

Habaiah huh-bay´yuh. See HOBAIAH.

Habakkuk, Book of huh-bak´uhk (חֲבַקּוּק *H2487*, possibly the name of a garden plant, or derived from חָבַק *H2485*, "to clasp, embrace"). The eighth book of the Minor Prophets. The name Habakkuk was interpreted by JEROME, in his prologue to the book, to mean "wrestler" (*quia certamen ingreditur cum Deo*, "because he wrestled with God"). Luther favored this derivation, which has been adopted by some later commentators. "It is certainly not unfitting, for in this little book we see a man, in deadly earnest, wrestling with the mighty problem of theodicy — the divine justice — in a topsy-turvy world" (L. E. H. Stephens-Hodge). More recent scholars relate this name to the Akkadian word for a plant, *ḫambaqūqu*, but the derivation remains uncertain.

Several legends attached themselves to the prophet Habakkuk. According to a Jewish tradition, he was the son of the Shunammite woman (see SHUNEM), who was told by ELISHA, "At this season, in due time, you shall embrace [*ḥōbeqet*] a son" (2 Ki. 4:16 NRSV); but this identification is excluded on account of the difference in time (Elisha ministered more than a century before Habakkuk). According to a second tradition, Habakkuk must be identified with the watchman referred to in Isa. 21:6; the correspondence of this passage with Hab. 2:1 is, however, superficial, and does not fit the same age and situation. In BEL AND THE DRAGON, an apocryphal addition to the book of DANIEL, it is told that the prophet Habakkuk had to bring food to Daniel in the lions' den (Bel 30–42 [LXX Dan. 14:30–42]). This interesting story, engraved on a fresco in the CATACOMBS in Rome, is also a fiction. Daniel's experience in the lions' den was about seventy years after the time of Habakkuk's activities.

We know nothing about Habakkuk apart from his name and the fact that he was called "the prophet" (Hab. 1:1; 3:1). This does not justify the charge raised by some scholars that he was an ecstatic. See PROPHETS AND PROPHECY. From Hab. 3:19b, some have deduced that the prophet "evidently was a member of the Temple choir, hence a Levite" (T. Laetsch, *The Minor Prophets* [1956], 313). The fact is, however, that the musical allusions in ch. 3 form a minor and superficial part of the prophecy, and could easily have been added to adapt this chapter for liturgical purposes (J. Ridderbos). Although nothing definitive is known of the prophet, he speaks forth in his books in such a way that one could recognize in him a man dedicated to his task to bear the sins and anxieties of his people, and to wrestle with God in prayer and through faith. The testimony of PAUL is applicable to him: "I have fought the good fight, I have finished the race, I have kept the faith" (2 Tim. 4:7).

I. Unity. A consistency of theme runs throughout the book, and accordingly most traditional scholars maintain that the prophecy must be conceived of as a whole. This does not exclude the possibility that separate passages were written down on different occasions (Van Katwyk, Aalders). According to critical scholars, the book is of composite authorship. They contend that Hab. 1:5–11, the raising up of the Chaldeans (Babylonians) to devastate the land, more or less interrupts the sequence of thought between the lamentations in 1:2–4 and 1:12–17. Some scholars (Wellhausen, Giesebrecht) delete these verses; others (Budde, Rothstein) put them after 2:4; while H. Schmidt (*ZAW* 62 [1949–50]: 52–63) suggests that 1:2–4, 12–13a, and 3:17–19 are lamentations of an individual that were added later to the scroll of Habakkuk. Conservative scholars recognize the difficulty in connection with 1:5–11, but contend that the problem can be solved by interpreting it as referring to an actual historical event (Young), or even by allowing a lapse of time between the announcement of the coming of the Babylonians and their threatening of Judah shortly after Carchemish in 605 B.C. (Van Katwyk, Aalders).

Another disputed passage is Hab. 3. This psalm is certainly somewhat different in style from the rest of the book, but this is hardly sufficient reason to deny Habakkuk's authorship. Because of the superscription, the postscript, and the word *Selah* in vv. 3, 9, 13, the opinion was long current that this psalm passed from some liturgical collection of hymns into the book of Habakkuk. According to Robert Pfeiffer, the musical terms denote a late origin for this chapter, presumably in the 4th or 3rd cent. B.C. Gleason Archer rightly observes that such an argument assumes the validity of the supposition that the musical terms in the Davidic psalms are late, and that despite Amos 6:5 and similar references, King David had nothing to do with music or song since he was a man of war. This inference, of course, is unacceptable "for those who take seriously the Biblical tradition that David was very much concerned with the writing and singing of psalms"; it follows that such musical terms constitute no evidence of late authorship (*A Survey of Old Testament Introduction*, 3rd ed. [1994], 396).

Some critical scholars reverse the argument and assume that the hymn in Hab. 3, on account of its general character, was borrowed from the book of Habakkuk for the liturgy (Duhm, Cannon, Sellin, Mowinckel). The fact that this chapter is introduced and concluded with musical terms is no reason for denying it to Habakkuk (Young, Aalders, Archer). The theme of ch. 3 is the same as that of the preceding chapters and there are also important similarities in language (cf. Young). In addition, the passage is ascribed specifically to "Habakkuk the prophet" (3:1). The absence of the third chapter in the Habakkuk Commentary found among the Dead Sea Scrolls (1QpHab) is not an argument against the unity of the book, since the Qumran commentaries in general present no continued development of thought (cf. Millar Burrows, *The Dead Sea Scrolls* [1955], 321–22). W. F. Albright's contention (in *Studies in Old Testament Prophecy*, ed. H. H. Rowley [1950], 1–18) that "The Psalm of Habakkuk," although forming a substantial unit with the rest of the book, contains reminiscences of the myth of the conflict between Yahweh and the primordial dragon (Sea or River), is interesting, but presupposes "some thirty-eight corrections of the Masoretic text," and is, therefore, hardly convincing.

II. Date. There is considerable division of opinion with regard to the date of the book of Habakkuk. The only clear historical reference is found in Hab. 1:6: "I am raising up the Babylonians." The neo-Babylonian or Chaldean empire came to prominence during the reign of Nabopolassar (625–605 B.C.), and more so later when his son Nebuchadnezzar (605–562) defeated the Egyptians at the battle of Carchemish in 605, and reestablished Babylon as the seat of world power. The raising up of the Babylonians is described in v. 5 as a marvelous work of the Lord, so wholly unexpected as to seem unbelievable to the people in their day. According to some scholars, this fact effectually disposes of the possibility of dating Habakkuk's activity as beginning in Jehoiakim's rule, when the Babylonians already had gained the world supremacy by destroying Nineveh in 612 (Laetsch, Eissfeldt, Gemser). They, accordingly, prefer a date either during the last years of Manasseh's reign (689–641), or preferably in the early years of Josiah (639–609).

The majority of scholars, however, maintain that Hab. 1:6 has reference to the Babylonians as an actual threat to Judah, and since such a threat seemed first to materialize at the battle of

The bricks used in the buildings of Nebuchadnezzar II (605–562 B.C.) usually have inscriptions with the king's names and titles. Habakkuk's prophecy that God would carry out his judgment through the Babylonians (Hab. 1:6–13) may be a reference to Nebuchadnezzar's campaign against Judah.

Carchemish, Habakkuk's activity must have been during the reign of Jehoiakim (Young, Archer, Ridderbos). Albright (in *Studies*, ed. Rowley, 2) ranges himself emphatically with this point of view, "seeing no valid reason why the book should not be treated as a substantial unit and dated between 605 and 589 B.C., i.e., between Nebuchadnezzar's decisive victory over Necho at Carchemish and the beginning of the last invasion of Judah before the end of the First Temple." This point of view is substantiated by 1:2–4, where the national depravity of the people of God is being denounced. This implies a time after the death of Josiah (609), and corresponds with the description given in Jer. 22 of the reign of Jehoiakim (608–597).

By changing the name "Babylonians" (Heb. *kaśdim* H4169, "Chaldeans") in Hab. 1:6 to read "Kittim" (*kittiyyîm* H4183, "Cypriots," i.e., "Greeks"), some scholars bring the date of the prophecy down to the time of Macedonian conquest, c. 330 B.C. (Duhm, Torrey, Procksch). According to Paul Haupt (*John Hopkins University Circular* [1920], 680ff.), the book must be dated in 161 B.C., just after the victory of Judas MACCABEE over NICANOR. This emendation, however, has no textual support.

III. Canonicity and text. The canonicity of the book of Habakkuk was never seriously questioned; it always has retained the eighth place among the twelve so-called Minor Prophets. According to Albright, "the text is in better state of preservation than often supposed, though its archaic obscurity made it somewhat enigmatic even to the earliest translators" (in *Studies*, ed. Rowley, 2). He, however, proposes some thirty-eight corrections of the MT of Hab. 3 (ibid., 10). Although some words or phrases are not easy to translate (1:3, 9; 2:5, 7, 10, 15, 19; 3:9, 11, 13, 14, 16), there is hardly any reason for altering the Hebrew text, as it is done in the RSV (1:9; 2:4, 15, 16, 17; 3:13, 14). Apart from a number of orthographical variations, the Habakkuk Commentary from Qumran has substantially the same text as that of the first two chapters of our book.

IV. Background. Habakkuk prayed and prophesied in times of crisis. Shortly before he began his ministry, the international scene was shocked by events of far-reaching import: the Assyrian empire was crushed, never to regain its power; the Egyptians, after slaying Josiah, king of Judah (609 B.C.), were themselves utterly defeated (605). The new world power, concentrated in Babylon and executed by the vigorous Nebuchadnezzar, was stretching itself across the breadth of the earth to seize habitations not their own. Within a period of approximately twenty years, the Babylonians swept over Judah in successive waves, and ultimately destroyed the country and took its inhabitants away into captivity in the years 597 and 587.

Internally, the people of God were caught up in the crises of religious and moral bewilderment. The pious King Josiah was succeeded by Jehoiakim, who "did evil in the eyes of the LORD, just as his fathers had done" (2 Ki. 23:37). The situation of depravity is described in Hab. 1:2–4 (cf. Jer. 22). The last two kings of Judah, JEHOIACHIN (597) and ZEDEKIAH (597–587), maintained the status quo, and ultimately were taken captive by the Chaldeans. In these times of national and international crisis, Habakkuk "contended with God" (Walter Lüthi).

V. Content. The book may be subdivided into six sections.

Hab. 1:1–4. The prophet cries to God because of the violence, inequity, strife, contention, and injustice he sees around him, and asks how long God would suffer it to go on unpunished. Some critics refer this passage to a heathen oppressor: the Babylonians (Giesebrecht), the Assyrians (Budde, Gemser), or even the Egyptians (G. A. Smith, who compares 1:2–4 with 2 Ki. 23:33–35). We agree with Archer (*Survey*, 396) that there is no good evidence in the text of Hab. 1:2–4 that heathen invaders are referred to; the manipulation of the law courts to favor the wealthy points to a domestic evil.

Hab. 1:5–11. God answers that he is raising up the Babylonians as his instrument of judgment, describing the fierceness of their armies and their contempt for any obstacle placed in their way.

Hab. 1:12–17. This answer plunges Habakkuk into a greater perplexity: How can a righteous God use the wicked Babylonians to punish his people, which in spite of its apostasy, is still more righteous than they are?

Hab. 2:1–4. The prophet waits upon the Lord. The answer, linked up with the history of God's divine providence, comes in the assertion that the pride of the Babylonian will be his downfall and the faith of the believer will be his salvation.

Hab. 2:5–20. A taunt-song is addressed presumably to the Babylonian king, consisting of a series of five woes against aggression (vv. 6b–8), self-assertion (vv. 9–11), violence (vv. 12–14), inhumanity (vv. 15–17), and idolatry (vv. 18–20).

Hab. 3:1–19. This psalm, voiced by the prophet, but on behalf of his people, is the "amen of faith" to the revelation of God. The prophet describes the divine manifestation in terms of a stormy theophany (3:2–15), with allusions to the mighty deeds of God in the history of the deliverance of Israel from Egypt. The impression created by this theophany is awe-inspiring (3:2, 16a). No matter what may befall them, the prophet and his people shall trust in God (3:16–19).

VI. Theology. The content of this book is characterized as an oracle or burden (Heb. *maśśāʾ* H5363; cf. Isa. 13:1; 14:28; et al.) that Habakkuk *the prophet* saw. Its purport, therefore, is to represent the word of God. It is evident, however, that the prophecy of Habakkuk has a unique form. It consists partly of lamentations that the prophet addresses to God (1:2–4, 12–17; 2:1; 3:1–19), and partly of prophetic utterances (1:5–11; 2:2–20). Archer (*Survey*, 397) rightly observes that, with the possible exception of Daniel, no other biblical author employs this particular technique. We may, however, assume that the whole content of Habakkuk's book is meant as REVELATION, as the imparting of God's message to his people.

On the material side, the content of this prophecy is characterized by the following features:

A. The prophet's orientation toward God. He calls him "LORD" (Hab. 1:2, 12; 2:2, 13–14, 16, 20; 3:2, 8, 18–19), "my God" (1:12; 3:3, 18–19), "my Holy One" (1:12; 3:3), and "O Rock" (1:12); he acknowledges him as the supreme Judge (1:2–4), as the God of the everlasting covenant (1:12), as the sovereign Ruler of all nations (1:5, 17; 2:12; 3:6, 12) and of all nature (3:3–11), the God who answers prayer (2:2), delivers his people (2:3; 3:13, 16, 18–19), determines the course of history (2:3; 3:2), and fills the earth with the knowledge of his glory (2:14).

B. The prophet's reaction against sin. Habakkuk is well aware of the sins of his people, of their political oppression, social wrongs, and prevailing manipulation of the law courts (Hab. 1:2–4). He not only observes it, but he testifies against it, and cries out to God to correct it. He also is conscious of the sins of the world power, its covetousness (1:6, 8, 9, 13–17), haughty self-assertion (1:7, 11, 16; 2:4), idolatry (2:18–19), and violence (1:17; 2:5–17).

C. The objective and subjective aspects of the prophet's message. Habakkuk called forth the judgment of the Lord first upon Judah and subsequently upon the Babylonians. This is the objective aspect of his message. In the course of time both prophecies of judgment were fulfilled. The oppressing nobilities first were taken into captivity in the two preliminary deportations of 605 and 597 B.C., and this was followed by the major deportation in 587. God indeed was not an inactive onlooker on the scene of his people. With these calamities the waiting time for the righteous remnant began (Hab. 2:2–3; 3:2). At the appointed time, the Babylonians were judged (539), and the captives of Judah were later allowed to return to the Promised Land.

The subjective aspect of Habakkuk's message is that the righteous shall live by his faith. Apart from ISAIAH (cf. Isa. 7:9; 28:16), no other prophet stressed the significance of faith and prayerful trust in such a way as did Habakkuk. Though the land may be stripped bare by the subsequent judgments of God, yet he will rejoice in the Lord (Hab. 3:17–18). The central theme of Habakkuk's prophecy, namely, that the righteous shall live by his faith (2:4), is taken up in the NT and applied in significant contexts (Rom. 1:17; Gal. 3:11; Heb. 10:38–39).

(Important commentaries include O. Happel, *Das Buch des Propheten Habackuk* [1900]; D. J. van Katwyk, *De Profetie van Habakkuk* [1912]; W. H. Ward, *A Critical and Exegetical Commentary on Habakkuk* [bound with other minor prophets], ICC [1911]; J. Trinquet, *Habaquq, Abdias, Joël* [1953]; W. Vischer, *Der Prophet Habakuk* [1958]; D. E. Gowan, *The Triumph of Faith in Habakkuk* [1976]; R. L. Smith, *Micah-Malachi*, WBC 32 [1984]; O. P. Robertson, *The Books of Nahum, Habakkuk, and Zephaniah*, NICOT [1990]; R. D. Patterson, *Nahum, Habakkuk, Zephaniah* [1991]; J. J. M. Roberts, *Nahum, Habakkuk, and Zephaniah: A Commentary* [1991]; F. F. Bruce in *The Minor Prophets: An Exegetical and Expository Commentary*, ed. T. McComiskey [1992–98], 2:831–96; K. L. Barker and W. Bailey, *Micah, Nahum, Habakkuk, Zephaniah*, NAC 20 [1998]; F. I. Andersen, *Habakkuk*, AB 25 [2001]; J. K. Bruckner, *Jonah, Nahum, Habakkuk, Zephaniah*, NIVAC [2004].

See also P. Humbert, *Problèmes du livre d'Habacuc* [1944]; W. H. Brownlee, *The Text of Habakkuk in the Ancient Commentary from Qumran* [1959]; id., *The Midrash Pesher of Habakkuk* [1979]; D. Bratcher, *The Theological Message of Habakkuk* [1984]; T. Hiebert, *God of My Victory: The Ancient Hymn of Habakkuk 3* [1986]; A. van der Wal, *Nahum, Habakkuk: A Classified Bibliography* [1988]; R. D. Haak, *Habakkuk* [1992]; G. Michael O'Neal, *Interpreting Habakkuk as Scripture: An Application of the Canonical Approach of Brevard S. Childs* [2007]; and the bibliography compiled by W. E. Mills, *Nahum-Habakkuk* [2002].)   P. A. VERHOEF

Habazziniah hab'uh-zi-ni'uh (חֲבַצִּנְיָה *H2484*, possibly "Yahweh has made me abundant [*or* joyful]"). KJV Habaziniah. Grandfather of JAAZANIAH, who was the leader of the RECABITES (Jer. 35:3).

Habbacuc. KJV Apoc. form of HABAKKUK (Bel 33–39).

habergeon hab'uhr-juhn. A sleeveless coat of mail. The term is used by the KJV a few times (Exod. 28:32 et al.). See ARMOR IV.B.

Habiru, Hapiru hah-bee'roo, hah-pee'roo. The Akkadian term *ḫabiru* (which can also be transliterated *ḫapiru*) appears in cuneiform texts dated from the 20th to the 18th centuries B.C. in southern MESOPOTAMIA, in ASIA MINOR, and in the HARAN and MARI areas. They are frequently mentioned in the TELL EL-AMARNA letters (14th cent. B.C.). In Egyptian texts they are called ʿ*apiru*, and the Ugaritic form is ʿ*apiruma*. Many scholars note the similarity

This statue of King Idrimi of Alalakh (c. 1570–1500 B.C.) contains a cuneiform inscription in which he mentions his time spent in Canaan with the Habiru.

of these forms with the Hebrew name ʿibrî H6303 and conclude that the *Habiru* are identical with the biblical Hebrews (see HEBREW PEOPLE).

The Habiru covered a geographical area much wider than that in which the biblical Hebrews moved. It may be reasoned that the people who were usually known as Israelites were at times identified as Habiru, but that this term included many other peoples of similar status as the Israelites. Note that EBER (ʿēber H6299, Gen. 10:24–25), for whom the Hebrews are traditionally named, lived eight generations before JACOB (Israel) for whom the Israelites are named. In this sense all Israelites are ʿibrîm ("Hebrews") but all Hebrews need not be Israelites.

In the nonbiblical literature of the ANE, the Habiru appear as landless individuals who live outside the established social order. They appear as mercenaries in texts from BABYLON. At NUZI they sold themselves into slavery in order to earn a living. Letters from Abdi-Hiba of Jerusalem to Akhenaten of Egypt complain that the Habiru were posing a threat to the status quo in Canaan. Some scholars see in these references the Canaanite version of the conquest of Canaan under JOSHUA.

The root from which the names Eber and Hebrew are derived conveys the idea of "crossing over." This fact has been interpreted geographically, with the thought that Eber and the Hebrews came from the region beyond the EUPHRATES River (according to others, the JORDAN). Perhaps the word was coined by the settled inhabitants who looked upon the newcomers, wherever they appeared, as "people who had crossed over" or trespassers (the Akkadian term means "fugitive" or "refugee"). The word would thus lose any ethnic significance and could be applied to any group of people who did not have land or social status within the established social order. The word *gypsy* has had a comparable history in more recent times. (If the root of Habiru/Hapiru is ʿpr, "dust," the term may have been used figuratively to indicate a low social class.)

Once ABRAHAM is named "the Hebrew" (Gen. 14:13). To his fellow prisoners, JOSEPH was "a young Hebrew" (41:12). The term *Hebrew* is typically used in contexts in which the biblical people—Israelites as they came to be called—identify themselves to, or are addressed by, foreigners. In such contexts, this presumably familiar name appears to have been a useful means of identification. The term *Habiru* thus includes the biblical Hebrews or Israelites. It includes many other peoples as well, however. (See further M. Greenberg, *The Ḫab/piru* [1955]; J. Bottéro in *Dialogues d'histoire ancienne* 6 [1980]: 201–13; O. Loretz, *Habiru-Hebräer: Eine soziolinguistische Studie*… [1984]; N. P. Lemche in *ABD*, 3:6–10; *SacBr*, 88–89.) C. F. PFEIFFER

Habor hay´bor (חָבוֹר H2466). A tributary of the EUPHRATES River, flowing through the district of GOZAN, to the banks of which SHALMANESER and SARGON transported the exiled Israelites (2 Ki. 17:6; 18:11; 1 Chr. 5:26). The river originates in the mountains of SE Turkey and is now known by the name Khabur.

Hacaliah hak´uh-li´uh (חֲכַלְיָה H2678, perhaps "wait for Yahweh" [if vocalized חַכְלְיָה]). KJV Hachaliah; TNIV Hakaliah. Father of NEHEMIAH (Neh. 1:1; 10:1).

Hachilah. See HAKILAH.

Hachmoni hak´moh-ni. See HACMONI.

Hacmoni hak´moh-ni (חַכְמֹנִי H2685, possibly "wise"; if gentilic, "Hacmonite"). Also Hachmoni; TNIV Hakmoni. **(1)** Father of JASHOBEAM; the latter was a chief officer among DAVID's mighty men (1 Chr. 11:11). However, the Hebrew expression "the son of Hacmoni" should perhaps be understood as "the Hacmonite" (cf. NIV). In the parallel passage (2 Sam. 23:8), Jashobeam is called "Josheb-Basshebeth, a Tahkemonite," probably the result of a copyist's mistake.

(2) Father of Jehiel, who was in charge of David's sons (1 Chr. 27:32); it is possible, though less likely, that here too the term should be taken as a gentilic, and the phrase rendered, "Jehiel the Hacmonite."

Hadad (deity) hay´dad. Also Adad (Akk. form), Adda (in EBLA). Although not mentioned in the Bible, this ancient Semitic god was worshiped in PALESTINE, SYRIA, and MESOPOTAMIA from about the time of ABRAHAM on (in SUMER he was known as Ishkur). Hadad was considered the son

Stela with representation of Baal-Hadad (from Ras Shamra, 15–13th cent. B.C.).

of DAGON (Dagan) in UGARIT, and he is frequently mentioned in the Ras Shamra texts as the proper name of BAAL, a storm-god who manifests himself in thunder, lightning, and rain (the name Hadad prob. means "thunderer"). Since storms are often destructive, he is asked in prayers and hymns to restrain his destructive propensities; but since storms are also bringers of beneficial rains, he is looked upon as a principle of life and fertility. He is the Baal of the FERTILITY CULTS of UGARIT and CANAAN. The thunder is his voice. He is the dying and rising god, like TAMMUZ of Mesopotamia. He is also a warrior god and is represented as a warrior standing on a bull, carrying a mace and a thunderbolt, with the horns of a bull on his helmet. He was worshiped as a warrior god particularly by the Assyrians. (See WARRIOR, DIVINE.) The monolith of SHALMANESER calls him "the god of Aleppo." The name Hadad functions as a divine element in such compound names as BEN-HADAD, HADADEZER, and HADAD RIMMON. See also HADAD (PERSON). (Cf. N. Wyatt in *UF* 12 [1980]: 375–79; J. C. Greenfield in *DDD*, 716–26; A. R. W. Green, *The Storm-God in the Ancient Near East* [2003].)

Hadad (person) hay´dad (חֲדַד H2524 [only #1 below, Gen. 25:15; 1 Chr. 1:30], possibly "sharp, fierce"; הֲדַד H2060, probably "thunderer," and perhaps an abbreviation of a compound name that included a theophoric element; see HADAD (DEITY)). **(1)** Son of ISHMAEL and grandson of ABRAHAM (Gen. 25:15 [KJV, "Hadar," following the Bomberg ed. of the Heb. text]; 1 Chr. 1:30 ["Hadar" in a few Heb. MSS]).

(2) Son of Bedad and a king of EDOM who is said to have defeated MIDIAN; his capital was Avith (Gen. 36:35–36; 1 Chr. 1:46–47). His dates are unknown.

(3) Another Edomite king of uncertain date; his capital was Pau, and the text includes a reference to his wife, Mehetabel daughter of MATRED (Gen. 36:39 ["Hadar" in most Heb. MSS]; 1 Chr. 1:50–51 ["Hadar" in a few Heb. MSS]).

(4) An Edomite prince who was an adversary of SOLOMON (1 Ki. 11:14–22, 25). After JOAB defeated the Edomites and occupied their country, Hadad was taken to Egypt as a young boy. There PHARAOH welcomed him and later gave him his wife's sister in marriage, so Hadad's son was brought up in the court of Egypt. After the death of DAVID, Hadad returned to Edom and attempted to stir up the Edomites against the rule of Solomon, apparently with some success. A. Lemaire (in *Biblische Notizen* 43 [1988]: 14–18) emends "Edom" (ʾdm) to "Aram" (ʾrm), making Hadad a descendant of HADADEZER, and argues that this proposed reading makes for a more coherent literary tradition. (See further J. R. Bartlett in *PEQ* 104 [1972]: 26–37 and in *ZAW* 88 [1976]: 205–26; E. A. Knauf in *ABD*, 3:11–12.)   S. BARABAS

Hadadezer hay´dad-ee´zuhr (הֲדַדְעֶזֶר H2061, "Hadad is help"). KJV Hadarezer (following many Heb. MSS). Son of REHOB and king of ZOBAH in ARAM, whose kingdom in the time of DAVID extended as far eastward as the EUPHRATES and as far southward as AMMON. There are three accounts in the OT of conflicts between him and David (though some scholars argue that these passages refer to only one or two distinct battles). In each, Hadadezer was defeated, and finally he was made tributary. The first is 2 Sam. 8:3–8, in which it is said that as Hadadezer went to restore his power at the Euphrates, David dealt him a severe defeat, and when the Arameans of DAMASCUS came to help him, David killed 22,000 of them. The second account, found in 2 Sam. 10:5–14, records that the Ammonites formed a league of Aramean rulers to protect them from the wrath of David, whom the Ammonites had insulted by shaving off the beards of his ambassadors (vv. 1–6). David sent JOAB against them, and they were badly beaten. The last passage, 2 Sam. 10:15–18, relates a defeat of the army of Hadadezer at HELAM under their commander SHOBACH, after which Hadadezer made peace with Israel and became subject to them. After these wars, David put a garrison in Damascus and received a tribute from Hadadezer. (See M. F. Unger, *Israel and the Arameans of Damascus* [1957], 42–48; W. Pitard, *Ancient Damascus* [1987], 90–94.) See HADAD (DEITY) and HADAD (PERSON). It should be noted that the Hadadezer (Adad-ʾidri) of CUNEIFORM texts refers to BEN-HADAD II.   S. BARABAS

Hadad Rimmon hay´dad-rim´uhn (הֲדַד־רִמּוֹן H2062; Aramean and Akkadian deities, respectively, both probably meaning "thunderer"). KJV Hadadrimmon; NRSV Hadad-rimmon. The prophet ZECHARIAH predicted, "On that day the weeping in Jerusalem will be great, like the weeping of [*or* for] Hadad Rimmon in the plain of Megiddo" (Zech. 12:11). The name is thought by some to refer to a place (JEROME actually identified it with Maximianopolis, a village near JEZREEL), possibly alluding to the mourning that took place after the death of JOSIAH (2 Ki. 23:29–30; 2 Chr. 35:20–25). Others understand Hadad Rimmon to be a dying-and-rising vegetation god whose worship involved annual ritual mourning. See HADAD (DEITY) and RIMMON (DEITY).   S. BARABAS

Hadar hay´dahr (הֲדַר H2076 [not in NIV], "splendor"). This name, a textual variant of "Hadad," occurs twice in the KJV (Gen. 25:15; 36:39; in the latter passage, NRSV has "Hadar" as well). See HADAD (PERSON).

Hadarezer hay´duhr-ee´zuhr. KJV form of HADADEZER.

Hadashah huh-dash´uh (חֲדָשָׁה H2546, "new"). A town in the lowland of the tribe of JUDAH (Josh. 15:37). Hadashah was in the same district as LACHISH and EGLON, but its location is unknown. The suggestion that it should be identified with ADASA (1 Macc. 7:40; cf. *ABD*, 3:13) cannot be sustained, either linguistically or geographically.

Hadassah huh-das´uh (הֲדַסָּה H2073, "myrtle"). The Hebrew name of ESTHER (Esth. 2:7). Hadassah was apparently her original name, that is, given to her at birth, even though she was more commonly known by the Akkadian (or Persian) name, Esther. The older view that Hadassah is the Hebrew form of the Akkadian word for "bride" (*ḥadaššatu*), a term applied to the goddess ISHTAR) has been generally abandoned.

Hadattah. See HAZOR HADATTAH.

Hades hay´deez (ᾅδης G87, etymology disputed, perhaps from the negative particle α and the verb ἰδεῖν, "[that which is] not seen," "the invisible one"). In Greek mythology, the god of the netherworld (see GREEK RELIGION AND PHILOSOPHY I.A); the term was then applied to the underworld itself, that is, the abode of the DEAD.

I. Pagan background. According to Homer, Hades was the name of both the underworld where the departed spirits dwell and the god of that underworld, also called Pluto (Pluton), the son of Chronas and Rhea. Its original genitive form, *Hadou*, that is, "of Hades," may reflect the idea that the netherworld belongs to the god Hades. This place, according to Greek mythology, was approached by crossing the River Styx, and at its entrance three judges decided the fate of the soul. (See T. Gantz, *Early Greek Myth* [1993], 70–73, 123–28.)

II. OT equivalent. Hades is the Greek term used by the SEPTUAGINT to render Hebrew SHEOL (in every instance except 2 Sam. 22:6). In the OT, Sheol was the place where the dead existed. The Hebrew concept was quite similar to that of the other peoples of the ANE. Sheol was a gloomy underworld where the godly and the ungodly dwelt together, with little distinction between them, on a level of existence far below that of life on earth. Toward the end of the OT period, there emerged a few inklings of hope for the rescue of God's people from Sheol, expressed by JOB, by DAVID, and by DANIEL (Job 19:25–27; Pss. 16:9–11; 17:15; Dan. 12:2).

III. Intertestamental developments. The literature of the intertestamental period reflects the growth of the idea of the division of Hades into separate compartments for the godly and the ungodly. This aspect of ESCHATOLOGY was a popular subject in the APOCALYPTIC LITERATURE that flourished in this period. Notable is the pseudepigraphical *1 Enoch* (written c. 200 B.C.; see ENOCH, BOOKS OF, I), which includes the description of a tour supposedly taken by ENOCH into the center of the earth. There Enoch sees four hollow places, one is for the saintly martyrs, the next for ordinary righteous people, a third for the wicked who were insufficiently punished in this life, and the final one for sinners who suffered a violent death, which apparently was a sufficient punishment for leaving them in this intermediate state forever. In another passage in Enoch, he sees at the center of the earth two places—PARADISE, the place of bliss, and the Valley of Gehinnom (HINNOM), the place of punishment.

The above illustrates that there was a general notion of compartments in Hades that developed in the intertestamental period, but that there was diversity of details regarding these compartments. Some scholars interpret this division into compartments as the result of foreign influences, such as that of Persian ZOROASTRIANISM with its pronounced DUALISM; but a more likely explanation is that the OT faith (with its strong emphasis on the justice of God leading to the blessings of the godly and the punishment of the ungodly, and with its teaching that the true meaning of life is fellowship with God) could not conceive of a common fate for the wicked and the righteous as the final word on the subject.

Whatever the original sources of this development of distinct sections in Hades, it was confirmed by the teachings of Christ. The apocalyptic literature, however, included detailed and grotesque descriptions of the nature of existence in the compartments of Hades inhabited by the damned which go far beyond a legitimate development of the faith of the OT (cf. *Sib. Or.* 2.283–310 [English trans. in *OTP*, 1:352–53]).

IV. NT usage. The Greek word *hadēs* is used only ten times in the NT (eleven times if one includes the textual variant in 1 Cor. 15:55, but the more reliable MSS have *thanate*, "O death"). The term is translated "hell" in the KJV, but the same rendering is used for *geenna* G1147 (see GEHENNA), which refers to the place of eternal punishment. The NRSV maintains the transliteration "Hades" throughout, whereas the NIV uses several renderings.

In Matt. 11:23 (and in the parallel passage, Lk. 10:15) Hades is used to describe the tragic fate awaiting unrepentant CAPERNAUM. That city will be "brought down to Hades" (NIV, "to the depths") in marked contrast to being "exalted to heaven." Apparently Hades is here considered to be a place of punishment. Christ promises that the "gates of Hades" will not prevail against his CHURCH (Matt. 16:18). Although this text has usually been interpreted otherwise (no doubt because of the influence of the rendering "hell" for Hades), the promise probably means that even death itself will not be able to prevent God's people from sharing in the victory of Christ.

Hades is also the place to which the rich man went when he was buried, in contrast to ABRAHAM'S BOSOM, to which poor Lazarus was transported by angels when he died (Lk. 16:23; NIV, "hell"). This passage (a parable by Jesus) gives far more information about Hades than any other in the NT, but to what extent the language is parabolic and to what extent it is to be taken literally is a question upon which commentators are not agreed. Hades is described here as a place of "torment" in which the wicked dwell in flames, a condition that produces "agony" and specifically a desire to have one's tongue cooled by water (v. 24). Furthermore, although presumably in a disembodied state, the rich man could "lift up his eyes" (KJV) to see those on the other side of the "great chasm"; and he believed that Lazarus could "dip the tip of his finger in water." In the parable, conversation is possible between the inhabitants of Abraham's bosom and of Hades, although no one can cross from one realm to the other. See LAZARUS AND DIVES.

Hades is mentioned twice by PETER in his sermon on the day of PENTECOST (Acts 2:27, 31; NIV, "grave"). In the first instance, Peter quotes Ps. 16:10, where Hades is a translation of Sheol, and in the second instance he applies this Psalm as a prophecy of the RESURRECTION OF JESUS CHRIST; because he rose from the dead, Christ was not detained in Hades, and thus the prophecy was fulfilled.

Finally, the word Hades is used four times in the book of Revelation. Jesus describes himself as possessing "the keys of death and Hades" (Rev. 1:18). In 6:8 John sees a pale horse whose rider is named Death, "and Hades was following close behind him." These terms are coupled two additional times: at the final judgment, "death and Hades gave up the dead that were in them" and then "death and Hades were thrown into the lake of fire" (20:13–14). This last reference apparently teaches that Hades is a temporary place that will be destroyed at the end of the world.

As one considers these instances of NT usage, there appears to be some variation in the way the term Hades is used. Sometimes it seems almost to be equated with death itself, and therefore to be the condition into which both the godly and the ungodly enter. Elsewhere it appears to be the temporary abode of the ungodly prior to the final judgment, whereas the godly go immediately to be with the Lord in glory. G. Vos seeks to solve this problem by distinguishing between Hades as a place and as a state. According to him, only the ungodly go to the place called Hades, whereas the godly go into the *state* of disembodied existence, which is designated by the same word.

Other passages of the NT are sometimes interpreted as referring to Hades, although they do not mention the word itself. According to Eph. 4:9, Christ "descended into the lower parts of the earth" (KJV), and this statement was interpreted by the church fathers and some later commentators as describing a DESCENT INTO HADES by Christ after his death. However, other commentators claim that this passage simply speaks of Christ's coming down from heaven to earth (cf. NIV). Another passage, 1 Pet. 3:19, says that Christ "went and preached to the spirits in prison"; this verse too has been interpreted by some to refer to a descent of Christ into Hades at his death. (Cf. further G. Bartle, *The Scriptural Doctrine of Hades* [1869]; J. P. Lange, *A Commentary on the Holy Scriptures: The Revelation of John* [1874], 364–77; W. O. E. Oesterley, *Immortality and the Unseen World* [1921]; J. Jeremias in *TDNT*, 1:146–49; *DDD*, 382–83; *OCD*, 661–62.)

V. The early church. Whereas the ante-Nicene fathers were somewhat vague in their statements on the subject, later theologians were in rather general agreement that believers who died before Christ were kept in Hades until Christ, after his crucifixion, descended to their abodes and brought them up to paradise, which was considered to be either a higher part of Hades or the lower regions of heaven. That part of Hades where the OT believers dwelt before Christ rescued them was later named the *Limbus Patrum*. According to the fathers, after Christ's descent into Hades, believers at death went directly to paradise, which was, however, not the highest heaven where the vision of God could be enjoyed, but was rather a place of preparation and further development, which in later Roman Catholic theology became "purgatory." The phrase "he descended into hell [Hades]" was used in Arian creeds about the middle of the 4th cent., but was not added to the APOSTLES' CREED until much later. See also CREED III.A; HELL.

H. BUIS

Hadid hay′did (חָדִיד H2531, possibly "sharp"). A town listed with LOD and ONO as having been resettled by hundreds of Jews after the EXILE (Ezra 2:33; Neh. 7:37); those returning were "descendants of the Benjamites from Geba" (Neh. 11:31–35). Hadid may have been settled first during the divided monarchy when the tribe of BENJAMIN spread to the W. It is probably to be identified with ADIDA (1 Macc. 12:38; 13:13) and with the modern el-Haditheth, about 3.5 mi. ENE of Lod (Lydda).

Hadlai had′lī (חֶדְלָי H2536, prob. "stout," fig. "successful"). Father of AMASA; the latter was a leader in the tribe of EPHRAIM during the reign of PEKAH king of Israel (2 Chr. 28:12).

Hadoram huh-dor′uhm (הֲדוֹרָם H2066, possibly "HADAD is exalted"). **(1)** Son (or descendant) of JOKTAN son of EBER (Gen. 10:27; 1 Chr. 1:21). Some scholars identify the name with Dauram, a locality in Yemen; Hadoram thus may have been the name of a S Arabian tribe (see *ABD*, 3:16).

(2) Son of TOU (Toi) king of HAMATH; he was sent by his father with presents to DAVID "to greet him and congratulate him on his victory in battle over Hadadezer, who had been at war with Tou" (1 Chr. 18:10). In the parallel passage (2 Sam. 8:10), he is called JORAM; some consider this name a textual corruption, but others interpret it as the Israelite equivalent (that is, using an abbreviated form of Yahweh rather than the pagan name Hadad; cf. A. Malamat in *JNES* 22 [1963]: 1–17, esp. 6–7).

(3) A variant form of ADONIRAM (2 Chr. 10:18).

Hadrach had′rak (חַדְרָךְ H2541, meaning unknown). TNIV Hadrak. A locality N of Israel against which ZECHARIAH prophesied (Zech. 9:1). Grouped with DAMASCUS, HAMATH, TYRE, and SIDON, Hadrach is probably the same as the Ḫatarikka mentioned in some Assyrian inscriptions. It is identified with Tell Afis, about 28 mi. SW of ALEPPO.

Hadrak had′rak. TNIV form of HADRACH.

Hadrian hay′dree-uhn. Emperor of ROME, A.D. 117–138. Publius Aelius (Traianus) Hadrianus was born, probably in Spain, in the year 76. Before he was ten years old, his father died, and the future emperor TRAJAN (a relative) became one of his guardians. His military career began during the reign of DOMITIAN, and after Trajan became emperor, Hadrian held several posts, including the governorship of SYRIA. Shortly before Trajan died, he reportedly adopted Hadrian, although it was rumored that Trajan's wife had staged the adoption after his death. In any case, Hadrian was recognized as emperor by the army and thereafter by the senate.

Hadrian's two decades of rule were uneven. He was a cultured man, devoted to Greek literature and showing great interest in philosophy, science, and architecture. The famous Hadrian's Wall, marking the frontiers of the empire in Britain, signaled an end to Roman expansion. In the year 130 Hadrian visited JUDEA and took several steps, such as banning CIRCUMCISION, that provoked Jewish sensibilities. A revolt was inevitable, and BAR KOKHBA rose against Rome in 132. By 135 the rebellion had been crushed, Jerusalem made into a Roman colony named Aelia Capitolina, and the nation of Israel brought to an end (see WARS, JEWISH). Hadrian died three years later. (See further A. R. Birley, *Hadrian: The Restless Emperor* [1997]; E. Speller, *Following Hadrian: A Second-Century Journey through the Roman Empire* [2003]; D. Danziger and N. Purcell, *Hadrian's Empire: When Rome Ruled the World* [2005]; *OCD*, 662–63.)

Haeleph hay-ee′lif (הָאֶלֶף H2030, "the ox"). A town in the tribal territory of BENJAMIN listed between ZELA and JERUSALEM (Josh. 18:28; KJV, "Eleph"). Following a SEPTUAGINT variant (*Sēlaleph* in CODEX ALEXANDRINUS), some scholars join Haeleph with the preceding word and identify Zela-Haeleph with the Zela mentioned elsewhere (2 Sam. 21:14). In any case, the location of the city is unknown.

hag, night. See LILITH.

Hagab hay′gab (חָגָב H2507, "locust"). Ancestor of a family of temple servants (NETHINIM) who returned after the EXILE with ZERUBBABEL (Ezra 2:46; 1 Esd. 5:30 [KJV, "Agaba"]; not mentioned in the parallel list, Neh. 7:48, probably because a scribe inadvertently skipped "Akkub Hagab" after writing the similar name "Hagabah").

Hagaba, Hagabah hag′uh-buh (חֲגָבָה H2509 [חֲגָבָא in Bomberg ed. at Neh. 7:48], "locust"). Ancestor of a family of temple servants (NETHINIM) who returned after the EXILE with ZERUBBABEL (Ezra 2:45 ["Hagabah"]; Neh. 7:48 [most English versions, "Hagaba," but see NJPS]; 1 Esd. 5:29 [KJV, "Graba"]). The common English spelling "Hagaba" in Nehemiah derives from a printed edition of the Hebrew Bible published in 1524–25 (cf. *BHK*), but is not supported by the MSS (curiously, the form is regarded as prob. correct by L. W. Batten, *A Critical and Exegetical Commentary on the Books of Ezra and Nehemiah*, ICC [1913], 98).

Hagar hay′gahr (הָגָר *H2057*, meaning uncertain). KJV NT Agar. The concubine of ABRAHAM and the mother of ISHMAEL. To understand the story of Hagar, it is necessary to begin ten years before she appears upon the scene, to the time when God called Abraham to leave his own country for a new land. God then promised that even though Abraham was old (seventy-five years) and childless, he would make of him a great nation (Gen. 12:1–3). After ten years of fruitless waiting for the promised son, SARAH offered to Abraham her personal Egyptian maid, Hagar (prob. acquired during their brief stay in EGYPT, Gen. 12:10–20), as a concubine in the hope of producing a son by her. The code of HAMMURABI and the NUZI tablets (which come from the region of the patriarchs although from a slightly later period) show it was customary for a childless wife to provide her husband with a concubine. If a son was born of the union, he was regarded as the child of the wife. Apparently both Abraham and Sarah were convinced that God would not give them children by Sarah, but that God's promise could be fulfilled by a son through Hagar.

Abraham followed Sarah's suggestion. Hagar conceived but then began to show contempt and disdain for her mistress in various ways, causing distress to Sarah. Bitter feelings and wounded pride caused Sarah to blame Abraham for doing what she herself had suggested (Gen. 16:5). He replied that Sarah could do anything she wanted with Hagar, her maid. Sarah decided to humble Hagar, probably by having her do menial work and live with her servants. Hagar refused to accept correction and fled from her mistress.

It may be that Hagar decided to go back to her own country, Egypt, for the angel of the Lord appeared to her not far from its border and told her to return to her mistress and submit to her. He also comforted her by adding that she would bear a son, whom she was to call Ishmael (meaning "God hears"); and he told her what kind of man he would be—a wild and lawless one, quarrelsome even with his own kindred, and that she would have innumerable descendants. Hagar's son was born when Abraham was eighty-six years old.

Fourteen years later, when Abraham was one hundred years old, and Sarah ninety, God gave them a son whom they named ISAAC. The day the child was weaned (among the Jews this was two or three years after birth), at a great feast made to celebrate the occasion, Sarah became incensed when she saw Ishmael, now a lad about seventeen years old, mocking Isaac (Gen. 21:9; the NRSV has "playing with," but the context and Gal. 4:29 indicate the meaning "mocking"; indeed, the NRSV renders the same Heb. word "jesting" in Gen. 19:14 and "insult" in 39:14, 17). Sarah told Abraham to send Hagar and Ishmael away. Abraham loved Ishmael and was therefore very unwilling to do this, but God told him to do what Sarah asked, and Abraham obeyed.

Hagar and Ishmael left the home of Abraham and went into the wilderness of BEERSHEBA. When the water they had with them gave out, Hagar placed her exhausted son in the shade of some bushes and waited for him to die. The angel of the Lord spoke to her, indicating that God had heard his cry, and showed her where there was a spring of water. He also assured her that God would make of him a great nation. Ishmael lived in the wilderness of PARAN and became an expert hunter, and his mother got for him a wife from the land of Egypt. (Some scholars believe that Hagar represents an Arabian tribal confederacy, possibly to be connected with the country of Agarrum/Gerrha in E Arabia; cf. *ABD*, 3:18–19.)

In Gal. 4:22–31 PAUL applies the story allegorically, suggesting that Hagar the bondwoman and

Hagar was sent out into the wilderness of Beersheba. (View to the SE.)

her son represent the old covenant, while Sarah and Isaac typify the grace and freedom of the new covenant. See ALLEGORY; COVENANT, THE NEW.

S. BARABAS

Hagarene, Hagarite, Hagerite hag′uh-reen, hag′uh-rit, hay′guh-rit. KJV forms of HAGRITE.

Haggadah hah′gah-dah′, huh-gah′duh (הַגָּדָה or אַגָּדָה [Aggadah], from נָגַד H5583 hiphil, "to tell, narrate"). Also Haggada, Aggada(h); pl. haggadoth, aggadoth. Traditional Jewish literature that is not legal in character; it may also refer to a specific story or lesson. Its counterpart is HALAKAH. Whereas the latter denotes authoritative rabbinic teaching in respect to the Mosaic law, especially as deposited in the MISHNAH, Haggadah is didactic discourse mainly concerned with edification. It is usually based upon homiletical exegesis and has a moral purpose in view, but the word often functions as a catch-all term to include anything nonhalakic. (See G. F. Moore, *Judaism in the First Centuries of the Christian Era: The Age of the Tannaim*, 3 vols. [1927–30], 1:161–63. On the origins of the term, the classic study is W. Bacher in *JQR* 4 [1892]: 406–29.)

The TALMUD consists of both parts: the homiletical narrative and the legal decisions supported by tradition. The midrashic literature (see MIDRASH) is mainly haggadic in the sense that it consists of homiletical exegesis reinforced by anecdotes, legends, and sayings from a variety of sources. In some pious circles there was the tendency to treat haggadic material with the same respect as the halakic teaching, an attitude criticized by Maimonides. Though part of the Jewish tradition, Haggadah has no binding authority. Many Jewish scholars hold that the haggadic literature was aimed mainly at the populace, but Montefiore believes that it was intended "for the inner smaller circles of students and disciples and for the delectation of the Rabbis themselves" (C. G. Montefiore and H. Loewe, *A Rabbinic Anthology* [1938], xvii). In modern usage, the Haggadah refers to a book that contains the story of the EXODUS and the PASSOVER ritual. (See further H. L. Strack and G. Stemberger, *Introduction to the Talmud and Midrash* [1992], 57–58 et passim.)

J. JOCZ

Haggai, Book of hag′i (חַגַּי H2516, "[born] on a feast day"). The tenth book of the Minor Prophets.

I. Background. Haggai prophesied in the period following the return of the exiles from BABYLON about 538 B.C. The conquest of Babylonia by CYRUS the Persian one year earlier made it possible for captive elements within the Babylonian population to look for liberty from enslavement. That this expectation was fully justified is indicated by the celebrated Cylinder of Cyrus, a cuneiform text that recorded the Persian conqueror's general permission to the racial minorities—previously carried captive by the Babylonian regime—to return to their homeland and begin life afresh. The cylinder reads in part, "(As to the region) from … as far as Ashur and Susa, Agade, Eshnunna, the towns Zamban, Me-Turnu, Der as well as the region of the Gutians, I returned to (these) sacred cities on the other side of the Tigris, the sanctuaries of which have been ruins for a long time, the images which (used) to live therein and established for them permanent sanctuaries. I (also) gathered all their (former) inhabitants and returned (to them) their habitations" (*ANET*, 316).

The prospect of a return to a desolate and impoverished land was by no means attractive to all of the Jews who had been in exile in Babylonia, particularly for those whose faith in the God of Israel had been shattered by the calamity of captivity. In

The Persian palace at Persepolis. During the time of Haggai, the Holy Land was ruled by the Persians.

addition, the opportunity of returning to Palestine to rebuild the ruins of the past had little practical appeal to those Jews who had managed to take advantage of the generous and rather naive Babylonians to build up prosperous commercial enterprises. In consequence, only those Jews who had caught a vision of service to God and man in the light of the promised covenant (Jer. 31:31–35; Ezek. 18:1–32) were seriously interested in the challenge inherent in restoring the years that the locusts had eaten. The enthusiasm that this remnant must have experienced at the thought of personal liberty was no doubt tempered by the sober realization that great hardships and difficulties lay ahead in the land of their forebears.

Those exiles who returned were led by descendants of the house of DAVID, the most prominent of whom were SHESHBAZZAR (possibly from the Babylonian form *Sin-aba-uṣur* or *Šamaš-aba-uṣur*) and ZERUBBABEL (Babylonian *Zēr-Bābili*). Sheshbazzar was cited as the "prince of Judah" (Ezra 1:8), and he bore the title of "governor" (5:14), presumably indicating that he was the first ruler of the Persian province of Judah. In 537 B.C., the first year of the return to Palestine, the altar of burnt offering was rebuilt, some of the ancient ceremonial rites were restored to public worship, and most important of all, the repatriated exiles laid the foundation of a new TEMPLE in the midst of ruined JERUSALEM (cf. Ezra 5:16).

As indicated above, a great many Jews who had managed to establish successful careers or business ventures in Babylonia were reluctant to abandon them for the prospects of a bleak and unpromising future in Palestine. It can be inferred, therefore, that the bulk of those who did return to Judea were sustained more by religious zeal than by material possessions. Although the sight of the ruined sanctuary in Jerusalem may well have evoked a good deal of initial compassion, the most pressing consideration for repatriates of limited means would be that of gaining as good a living as possible from the environs of the capital city. This preoccupation with the desperate struggle for existence amid unpromising surroundings seems to have taken almost all the available time and energy of the returned exiles. More seriously than this, the book of Haggai seems to indicate that the state of shock that must have accompanied these conditions had sapped the spiritual zeal of the repatriates, making them apathetic about restoring the ruined sanctuary to something of its former grandeur. Certainly there is no evidence in the prophecy of Haggai that anything more than the laying of the foundation of the new structure had been accomplished in a decade of life in Judea.

It has sometimes been supposed that, since Haggai was not mentioned until about 520 B.C. (Ezra 5:1), he had returned as an adult to Palestine with a fresh group of exiles at this period. However, there is no indication in his prophecy that such was actually the case, and in the absence of any evidence to the contrary it is legitimate to suppose that Haggai was still a child when he returned to Judea with his parents in 537.

II. Unity. The book of Haggai comprises four short oracles delivered by the prophet himself; written in the third person, they are associated with the restoration of the temple in 520 B.C. They were delivered respectively in the first day of the sixth month (Hag. 1:1), the twenty-first day of the seventh month (2:1), and the twenty-fourth day of the ninth month (2:10, 20), in the reign of DARIUS I. It has been suggested by some writers that the work proceeded from two different hands, one of which compiled the narrative material while the other assembled a small collection of oracles. Other scholars, however, have denied that the prophecy constitutes an editing of diverse sources, and have argued, from the obvious closeness of the writer to events that occurred in Judea in the time of Darius I, for the unity and historicity of the prophecy.

III. Authorship. The name Haggai may have been derived from the word for "festival," suggesting that his birth coincided with some Israelite feast. The name of his father is unknown, and there is no information available concerning the family background of the prophet or the social situation from which he came. The historical activities of Haggai are corroborated by references in Ezra (Ezra 5:1; 6:14), and his prophecy, along with that of ZECHARIAH, is of great importance as a source of information relating to the period between the return from exile and the work of EZRA and NEHEMIAH.

Those who rebuilt the temple at the time of Haggai may have harvested stone for the building from this quarry N of Jerusalem.

Some scholars have argued that, because the extant prophecy appears as résumés of addresses, the book as it stands cannot have come from the hand of Haggai, but instead was the work of a disciple or group of disciples. However, the extant form of the oracles suggests that they were written down from memory shortly after being delivered, and since the prophetic ministry of Haggai was of such short duration, it is highly unlikely that he had attracted disciples before his work was actually committed to written form. There is no element in the prophecy as it now stands that points to diversity of authorship. Indeed, the weight of internal and external evidence supports the contention that the prophet Haggai was himself the author of the work attributed to him, and that he furnished a narrative of contemporary events involving himself in an objective manner.

IV. Date. Fortunately it is possible to assign a precise date to the book without difficulty, because the various oracles are related to the reign of Darius I (522–486 B.C.). The first address, given on the first day of the sixth month, placed the beginning of the prophetic activity of Haggai in August-September of 520. His fourth oracle was delivered on the ninth day of the fourth month (November-December), shortly after the prophet Zechariah commenced his ministry.

V. Place of origin. The oracles of Haggai consistently presuppose a background of life in Judea in the period following the return of the exiles. Since the various utterances were connected with the site of the ruined temple (shortly to be restored), with the civil governor, and with the priests of the cultus, there can be no doubt that the place of origin of the prophecies was Jerusalem itself. No other location in Judea can be considered as an acceptable substitute.

VI. Destination. The words of the prophet were meant primarily for local consumption. The first oracle in particular exhorted the repatriates to rebuild the house of God in Jerusalem, whereas the second (Hag. 2:1–9) comprised a message of encouragement to the laboring populace, promising them that the fruit of their striving would attract greater honor than its renowned predecessor. The involving of the priests in the argument of the third utterance (2:10–19) again bespeaks a local situation, as does the assurance given to Zerubbabel, the civil governor of Judea, in the fourth oracle (2:20–23). From the nature of the prophetical and historical situation, it is evident that the utterances of Haggai were meant for the populace of Judea.

VII. Occasion. The specific occasion that gave rise to the various prophecies was that associated with the reconstruction of the temple about 520 B.C. on the ruins of the former site in Jerusalem. Haggai's oracles convey the impression that the enormity of the difficulties confronting the repatriated exiles had weakened their initial spiritual vision, and that whatever energies they possessed were being spent in an urgent attempt to survive physically. However, the first oracle spoke of the "paneled houses" of the returned Jews (Hag. 1:4), implying that once the bare necessities of life had been met, a spirit of apathy toward the rebuilding of the temple had set in.

As time passed without any attempt at reconstruction, the inhabitants of Jerusalem became even more dispirited, particularly when the traditions concerning the splendor and majesty of the Solomonic temple were recalled, no doubt by some elderly members of the populace who had seen it as children. The purpose of the prophecy, therefore, was to combat apathy and depression by giving inspired leadership for the actual reconstruction, along with a promise from God that the glory of the new temple would exceed that of the former. Along with these emphases came the reminder that the Jews needed to observe spiritual priorities strictly if they were to expect material prosperity and divine blessing.

VIII. Purpose. The principal aim of the oracles was to stimulate the lethargic repatriates to the rebuilding of the temple and to reorganize community life on a proper footing in terms of spiritual priorities. Because of their attitudes, the Jews of Judea were in serious danger of losing the vision of a theocratic community in which the revealed will of God would be mediated to the populace by means of a consecrated priesthood. The restored community was not meant to be just another agglomeration of citizens living in free association, but a brotherhood of the spirit, bound to one another and to God through loyalty to the divine covenant, and living as a witness of the ability of God to liberate the captive and restore the penitent to a proper place in society. In a time of considerable upheaval in the Persian empire (see PERSIA III), it was the responsibility of Haggai to assure the citizens of Jerusalem and Judea that obedience to the will of God would ensure them a period of peace and prosperity. As far as the civil and religious rulers were concerned, Haggai was at pains to make clear their place in the larger purpose of God for the theocracy by showing that God had chosen them and fitted them for their special tasks.

IX. Canonicity. The prophecy was included from the beginning in the twelve short compositions known as the Minor Prophets. Chronologically, the book of Haggai was the earliest of the three postexilic prophecies—Haggai, Zechariah, and Malachi—that dealt with the period of the restoration of the temple, and there has never been any question as to the legitimacy of its place in the canon of Hebrew Scripture. This was doubtless due in no small measure to the influence of Ezra, who attested directly to the work of Haggai. See CANON (OT).

X. Text. The Hebrew text of Haggai is in good order, although there are some corruptions (Hag. 1:7, 9, 10, 12; 2:6, 15, 17), as well as the possibility of textual dislocation (2:15–19), which may have arisen from the confusion of dates (1:15 and 2:18). The SEPTUAGINT text contains an addition in Hag. 2:9, and in other respects is an aid to the reconstruction of the MT. See TEXT AND MANUSCRIPTS (OT).

XI. Content. The prophecy can be outlined as follows:

A. The first oracle and response: a reminder to put first things first (Hag. 1:1–15).

B. A message of encouragement about the destiny of the temple (2:1–9).

C. An argument from the ritual law to show that the labor of the people will be blessed (2:10–19).

D. A special promise to Zerubbabel relating to his personal safety (2:20–23).

XII. Theology. Whereas the prophecy is historical rather than religious in character, it stands firmly in the theological tradition of EZEKIEL with regard to the development of the priestly commonwealth. This is clearly indicated by the way Haggai related the prophetic ESCHATOLOGY of salvation to the constructing of the second temple. Haggai has occasionally been criticized for upholding the "superficial view" of material prosperity automatically following the careful observance of the mechanics of cultic worship. It should be noticed, however, that like

Ezekiel, who also paid punctilious attention to the minutiae of ritual worship, Haggai stressed the correct motivation of the human spirit.

This emphasis upon priorities was a consistent element in his theology. He saw God as a wholly righteous and moral being who demanded from his covenant people complete obedience and spiritual loyalty. If they manifested his moral and ethical characteristics, they would be true witnesses to his power and would be rewarded with peace and prosperity while other nations were in the grip of turmoil. Seeking the kingdom, in the truest sense, would insure that all other necessities would be added to them, whereas a prime emphasis upon material possessions would only result in individual and community deterioration.

So far from being deficient in spirituality, Haggai furnished in his third oracle the most succinct statement to be found anywhere in the OT concerning the fact that evil is far more penetrating and diffusive than goodness. His insight constituted a lesson for the priests, whose forebears had been responsible morally and spiritually for the calamity of the exile by condoning idolatry, but it was also equally applicable to the general populace. By employing a question relating to ritual procedure, Haggai was able to make clear that even a small amount of evil requires an enormous amount of operative goodness to offset its deleterious effects.

(Important commentaries include H. G. Mitchell et al., *A Critical and Exegetical Commentary on Haggai, Zechariah, Malachi and Jonah*, ICC [1912]; R. L. Smith, *Micah-Malachi*, WBC 32 [1984]; D. L. Petersen, *Haggai and Zechariah 1–8*, OTL [1984]; P. A. Verhoef, *The Books of Haggai and Malachi*, NICOT [1987]; C. L. Meyers and E. M. Meyers, *Haggai, Zechariah 1–8*, AB 25B [1987]; H. W. Wolff, *Haggai: A Commentary* [1988]; E. H. Merrill, *Haggai, Zechariah, Malachi: An Exegetical Commentary* [1994]; J. A. Motyer in *The Minor Prophets: An Exegetical and Expository Commentary*, ed. T. McComiskey [1992–98], 3:963–1002; R. A. Taylor and R. Clendenen, *Haggai, Malachi*, NAC 21A [2004]; M. J. Boda, *Haggai, Zechariah*, NIVAC [2004]. See also J. E. Tollington, *Tradition and Innovation in Haggai and Zechariah 1–8* [1993]; J. Kessler, *The Book of Haggai: Prophecy and Society in Early Persian Yehud* [2002]; and the bibliography compiled by W. E. Mills, *Zephaniah and Haggai* [2002].)   R. K. HARRISON

Haggedolim hag′uh-doh′lim (הַגְּדוֹלִים H2045, "the great ones"). Father of ZABDIEL; the latter was a chief officer among the priests that settled in Jerusalem after the EXILE (Neh. 11:14; KJV renders, "Zabdiel, the son of *one of* the great men"). Some scholars emend the word to *haggādôl*, "the great [one]," and interpret it to mean, "the high priest" (cf. 3:1 et al. and see *ABD*, 3:23).

Haggeri hag′uh-ri. KJV form of HAGRI.

Haggi hag′ee (חַגִּי H2515, "[born] on a feast day"; gentilic חַגִּי H2515, "Haggite"). Son of GAD and eponymous ancestor of the Haggite clan (Gen. 46:16; Num. 26:15).

Haggiah ha-gi′uh (חַגִּיָּה H2517, "feast of Yahweh"). Son of Shimei and a descendant of LEVI through MERARI (1 Chr. 6:30).

Haggite hag′it. See HAGGI.

Haggith hag′ith (חַגִּית H2518, "[born] on a feast day"). One of DAVID's wives and the mother of ADONIJAH, who was born in HEBRON when David's capital was there (2 Sam. 3:4; 1 Ki. 1:5, 11; 2:13; 1 Chr. 3:2).

Hagia hay′gee-uh. See AGIA.

Hagiographa hag′ee-og′ruh-fuh. A term meaning "Sacred Writings" (from Gk. *hagios* G41 and *graphē* G1210) and applied to the third division of the Hebrew Bible, after the Law (the PENTATEUCH) and the Prophets (which includes Joshua, Judges, Samuel, and Kings, as well as Isaiah, Jeremiah, Ezekiel, and the Minor Prophets). Also known simply as the Writings or KETUBIM, this section consists of the following books: Psalms, Proverbs, Job, Song of Solomon, Ruth, Lamentations, Ecclesiastes, Esther, Daniel, Ezra, Nehemiah, and 1–2 Chronicles (in the TALMUD, the book of Ruth is put in the first place, prob. to provide the prehistory of David and to serve as an introduction to the Psalter of David, which follows).

This threefold division was already adopted about the middle of the 2nd cent. B.C., as appears from the prologue of Ecclesiasticus, which speaks of the Law, the Prophets, "and the other books of our fathers." Josephus, at the end of the 1st cent. A.D., knew of a similar division, though in the last section he places only four books (*Apion* 1.8 §§38–41). It will be noted that according to the Jewish tradition, the book of Daniel is not counted among the prophetic writings. Some argue from this fact that for Josephus the third division consisted of "hymns to God and precepts for the conduct of human life." It is suggested that the four books were Psalms, Song of Songs, Proverbs, and Ecclesiastes (cf. H. St. J. Thackeray in his edition of *Apion* for LCL, note on p. 179) and that the missing books in Josephus's list were distributed differently from the present order. In this case, Daniel may have been among the Prophets.

In the NT, in at least one passage, the threefold division occurs: "the Law of Moses, the Prophets and the Psalms" (Lk. 24:44). Whether the Psalter stands for the hagiographic literature as a whole is difficult to say. Otherwise, *hē graphē* (sing.) and *hai graphai* (pl.) each includes the whole of the OT, though occasionally reference is made to "Moses" or "the law of Moses" (Matt. 8:4; Lk. 2:22; Jn. 7:23; Acts 13:39; et al.); to the Prophets (Rom. 16:26); or to David, meaning the Psalter (Heb. 4:7). See canon (OT).   J. Jocz

Hagri hag′rī (הַגְרִי H2058, perhaps "wanderer"). The father of Mibhar, who was one of David's mighty warriors (1 Chr. 11:38; KJV, "Haggeri"). The parallel passage has "Bani the Gadite" (*bānî haggādî*, 2 Sam. 23:36), but some MSS of the Septuagint have *huios Agēri* (= *ben-hagri*, "the son of Hagri"), and this reading is adopted by the NIV (cf. further *ABD*, 4:805, s.v. "Mibhar"). P. K. McCarter (*II Samuel*, AB 9 [1984], 493–94) further emends the text so that Igal son of Nathan is described as "the commander of the army of the Hagrites." See also Hagrite.

Hagrite hag′rīt (הַגְרִי H2058, possibly "wanderer" or "descendant of Hagar"; pl. הַגְרִאִים in 1 Chr. 5:10, 19–20, but הַגְרִים in Ps. 83:6). The name of an Arabian tribe living in the region E of Gilead (some think the tribe may have been Aramean; see Aram). In the time of King Saul, the Israelites twice inflicted a crushing defeat upon them in war and seized their lands (1 Chr. 5:10, 19–22; KJV, "Hagarites"). David appointed Jaziz the Hagrite to look after his flocks (1 Chr. 27:30–31; KJV, "Hagerite"). A psalm of Asaph makes mention of them along with Moab, Edom, and the Ishmaelites, all of whom were enemies of Israel living in Transjordan (Ps. 83:6; KJV, "Hagarenes"). The ethnological relationship of the Hagrites with Hagar (Gen. 16) is uncertain. The Hagrites and other Arab tribes are mentioned in an inscription of Tiglath-Pileser III (745–727 B.C.). (See further I. Eph'al, *The Ancient Arabs: Nomads on the Borders of the Fertile Crescent, 9th–5th Centuries B.C.* [1982], 61 et passim; N. Na'aman in *VT* 38 [1988]: 71–79.)   S. Barabas

Hahiroth. See Pi Hahiroth.

Hai hī. KJV alternate form of Ai (only Gen. 12:8; 13:3).

hail, hailstones. Hail is frozen raindrops, though hailstones are often much larger than any single raindrop, sometimes reaching three or four inches in diameter and a pound or more in weight. It usually falls in the spring or summer during severe thunderstorms, when raindrops are carried upward by rising air currents and freeze in the cooling air. When the hailstones fall, they often cohere, forming solid masses, which can do great damage to crops and even endanger life.

Hailstones are not common in Palestine, but they are not unusual and can be very severe. Occasionally they take place in Egypt. Hail is often mentioned in the Bible, and always as an instrument of God's judgment. A severe hail (Heb. *bārād* H1352) was the seventh plague in Egypt (Exod. 9:18–34). It probably took place at the beginning of February, when the flax was in bloom and the barley in the ear (v. 31). Wheat, which does not ripen until about a month later, escaped (v. 32), to become later the prey of the locusts (Exod. 10:12–15). The Amorites were smitten by hailstones at Beth Horon, so that more died from the hailstones than were smitten with the sword by the Israelites (Josh. 10:11). The

Scriptures often speak of hail as a means of punishing the wicked (Isa. 28:2, 17) and as a symbol of God's anger, both in the OT (Ezek. 38:22; Hag. 2:17) and in the NT (Gk. *chalaza* G5898, Rev. 8:7; 11:19; 16:21). S. Barabas

hair. Although all mammals have hair (e.g., goats, 1 Sam. 19:13; camels, Mk. 1:6), the term is usually applied to human beings (Heb. *śēʿār* H8552 or *śaʿărâ* H8553; Gk. *thrix* G2582). The ancients usually wore the hair long, although priests, warriors, and young boys often were shaved. Boys left a side lock. Recall the long hair of Samson and Absalom. Because the hair was shaved in an initiation to a divinity in Arabia, the cutting of hair was an abomination to the Jews (Jer. 49:32). The Nazirite knew that the whole body, including the hair, belonged to God, so a razor never touched his skin until his service was ended (Num. 6:18; Jdg. 16:17). Captive women shaved their heads for purification, as did the lepers (Lev. 14:8). Priests kept their hair at a moderate length (Ezek. 44:20), but were forbidden to make tonsures (Lev. 21:5).

Baldness, except in leprosy, was not derided (Lev. 13:40) unless it was given as a curse (Isa. 3:24). Since the head held the spirit, the hair was not to be cut in times of danger, for it was considered the source of strength. By NT times, long hair was thought to be degrading to a man, but to a woman it was a source of pride (1 Cor. 11:14). Mary wiped the Lord's feet with her hair. In the Song of Solomon the hair is the veil (Cant. 4:3). Loss of hair to a woman was shameful (1 Cor. 11:6). Women were warned against elaborate hair dressing (1 Pet. 3:3).

The braided hair (a wig) on the mummy of Nedjmet, an Egyptian queen of 11th cent. B.C.

© Dr. James C. Martin. The Cairo Museum. Photographed by permission.

An assurance of safety was Jesus' word that the hairs of the head are numbered (Matt. 10:30). David felt his sins were more than the hairs of his head (Ps. 40:12). Gray hair was honored and gained in a righteous life (Prov. 20:29; Heb. *śêbâ* H8484), while white hair meant a glorious presence as of Christ himself (Rev. 1:14). Hair seldom was dyed in Palestine, but Herod is said to have dyed his black (Jos. *Ant.* 16.8.1 §233). Hair standing up is a sign of fear (Job 4:15) caused by the contraction of small muscles attached obliquely to each hair. Tearing or pulling out hair expressed deep sorrow (Isa. 15:2) or mourning for the dead, and putting ashes on the head showed shame and grief, like Tamar's desecration (2 Sam. 13:19). Anointing the head was a sign of joy (Ps. 23:5) and prosperity, but only the purest could be anointed with the sacred oil (Exod. 30:32). Good marksmen could "sling a stone at a hair and not miss" (Jdg. 20:16). R. L. Mixter

Hakaliah hak′uh-li′uh. TNIV form of Hacaliah.

Hakeldamah huh-kel′duh-muh. See Akeldama.

Hakilah huh-ki′luh (חֲכִילָה H2677). A hill in the wilderness of Judah, S of Jeshimon, where the strongholds of Horesh were located; there David took refuge when Saul pursued him (1 Sam. 23:19; 26:1). Saul pitched his camp on the hill (26:3). It is described as being within the wilderness of Ziph (23:19), which is a few miles SE of Hebron. The site has not been identified. S. Barabas

Hakkatan hak′uh-tan (הַקָּטָן H2214, "the little one"). Father of Johanan and descendant of Azgad; Johanan was one of the family heads who returned to Jerusalem with Ezra (Ezra 8:12; 1 Esd. 8:38 [KJV, "Acatan"]). According to some, the phrase *yôḥānān ben-haqqāṭān* should be rendered "Johanan the younger."

Hakkore. See En Hakkore.

Hakkoz hak′oz (הַקּוֹץ H2212, "the thorn"). KJV Koz (except in 1 Chr. 24:10). The head of a priestly family at the time of David (1 Chr. 24:10). His descendants returned from the Babylonian captivity, but could not serve because they were unable to document their claim to priestly rank (Ezra 2:61; Neh. 7:63; 1 Esd. 5:38 [KJV, "Accoz"]). One of his descendants, MEREMOTH, was involved in repairing the wall of Jerusalem (Neh. 3:4, 21).

S. BARABAS

Hakmoni hak´moh-ni. TNIV form of HACMONI.

Hakupha huh-kyoo´fuh (חֲקוּפָא H2979, "crooked"). Ancestor of a family of temple servants (NETHINIM) who returned from exile with ZERUBBABEL (Ezra 2:51; Neh. 7:53; 1 Esd. 5:31 [KJV, "Acipha"]).

Halachah. See HALAKAH.

Halah hay´luh (חֲלַח H2712). One of the places to which kings of ASSYRIA deported Israelites on the capture of SAMARIA (2 Ki. 17:6; 18:11; 1 Chr. 5:26). Halah was apparently on the way to GOZAN, but its location is uncertain. Among various proposals, one that has gained favor is Ḥalaḫḫu, the name of a town and a district NE of NINEVEH (cf. *ABD*, 3:25). The name Halah occurs also as a conjecture in the NRSV (Obad. 20, where MT *haḥēl-hazzeh*, "this company," is emended to *ḥălaḥ zeh*).

Halak, Mount hay´lak (חָלָק H2748, "smooth" or "bare"). A mountain in the NEGEV described as rising toward SEIR; it formed the southern limit of the conquests of JOSHUA (Josh. 11:17; 12:7). Many scholars identify it with Jebel Halaq, on the NW side of the Wadi Marra, and some 28 mi. SE of BEERSHEBA.

Halakah hah´lah-kah´ (הֲלָכָה, "walk, practice, ruling, law," from הָלַךְ H2143, "to go, walk, behave"). Also Halacha(h), Halakhah; pl. halakot(h), halakhot(h). This term in rabbinic studies can refer either to a specific legal ruling (in which case the word is usually lowercased) or to the general literary category of legal material, contrasted with HAGGADAH. The concept thus encompasses all the laws, ordinances, and legal decisions of the rabbis that determined the Jewish way of life—religious, social, political, and civil. It was believed by the PHARISEES and their followers that God had given to MOSES on Mount SINAI not only the written law that was embodied in the PENTATEUCH, but also a large mass of oral law which he communicated to the Jewish people and which the rabbis passed on until it was written down in the MISHNAH. See also MIDRASH.

The object of the Halakah, which involved the interpretation and the reinterpretation of the Mosaic law through a long succession of Jewish teachers from the time of EZRA onward, was to state in detail and to apply to all possible cases the principles laid down in the TORAH, and to surround it with a hedge so as to prevent transgression (cf. *m.)Abot* 1.1). These authoritative legal rulings were ostensibly the result of biblical exegesis, though some scholars argue that the Halakah developed more or less independently of Scripture and that proof texts were added subsequently to justify the decisions. The importance given to the oral law ("the tradition of the elders") had the tendency of pushing into the background Scripture itself, and it is not surprising that Jesus denounced its excesses (Mk. 7:1–13). (See G. F. Moore, *Judaism in the First Centuries of the Christian Era: The Age of the Tannaim*, 3 vols. [1927–30], 1:135–60; S. Safrai in *The Literature of the Sages: First Part*, ed. S. Safrai, CRINT 2/3/1 [1987], ch. 3; H. L. Strack and G. Stemberger, *Introduction to the Talmud and Midrash* [1992], 18–19 et passim.)

S. BARABAS

half-shekel tax. The RSV rendering of *didrachmon* G1440 (Matt. 17:24; NIV, "two-drachma tax"). See DIDRACHMA.

half-tribe of Manasseh. The part of Manasseh that settled in GILEAD and BASHAN E of the Jordan (Deut. 3:13 et al.). See MANASSEH, TRIBE OF. Like the tribes of REUBEN and GAD, the half-tribe of Manasseh was obliged to help the main body of the Hebrews in the conquest of Palestine (Josh. 1:12–18). Its clans included the descendants of MAKIR (Num. 32:39–40), who is referred to as "the ancestor of the Gileadites" (Josh. 17:1; lit., "the father of Gilead"), and the descendants of the Judahite HEZRON, who married the daughter of Makir (1 Chr. 2:21–23). The history of the half-tribe closed when they were led into captivity by TIGLATH-PILESER of Assyria (2 Ki. 15:29; 1 Chr. 5:26).

A. BOWLING

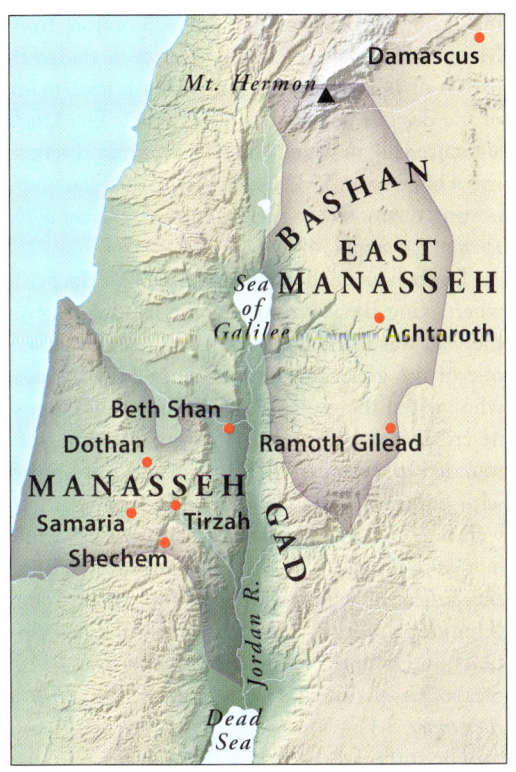

Tribe of Manasseh.

Halhul hal′huhl (חַלְחוּל *H2713*, derivation uncertain). A town in the hill country of the tribe of JUDAH, listed first in a district of six towns (Josh. 15:58). It is identified with modern Ḥalḥul, 4 mi. N of HEBRON.

Hali hay′li (חֲלִי *H2718*, "adornment"). A town in the tribal territory of ASHER, listed between HELKATH and BETEN (Josh. 19:25). The site is now identified with Khirbet Ras ʿAli (or a location nearby), some 11 mi. SSE of Acco.

Halicarnassus hal′uh-kahr-nas′uhs (Ἁλικαρνασσός). City and trading center on the coast of CARIA, in SW ASIA MINOR, opposite the island of Cos. Situated on the Ceramic Gulf astride a magnificent, natural harbor that extended on each side to fortified promontories, the city early gained great commercial importance. The surrounding country was unusually fertile and noted for its abundant olive, fig, and almond orchards.

The city was founded by Dorian colonists, but it was excluded from the confederacy of Carian states because of an ancient dispute, according to HERODOTUS (*Hist.* 1.144). It was conquered by the Persians, who allowed the city semi-autonomous rule. Because it sided with the Persians, ALEXANDER THE GREAT burned the city after a long siege, a catastrophe from which it never fully recovered. It was renowned as the birthplace of the historians Herodotus and Dionysius, and as the site of King Mausoleus's tomb, one of the seven wonders of the ancient world (from it the word *mausoleum* is derived).

Halicarnassus was one of the free cities to which the Romans sent letters in 139 B.C., proclaiming the friendship of Rome for the Jews and defending their rights (1 Macc. 15:23). According to JOSEPHUS (*Ant.* 14.10.23), the people of the city passed an ordinance in the 1st cent. B.C. that Jewish men and women should be allowed to build prayer chapels by the sea, as was their custom, to observe the SABBATH, and to perform their sacred rites. (See C. T. Newton, *Travels and Discoveries in the Levant* 4 [1865], chs. 35–41, 45; G. E. Bean, *Turkey Beyond the Maeander*, 2nd ed. [1980], ch. 9.)

A. RUPPRECHT

hall. This English term is used variously in Bible translations to render several words. For example, Samuel is said to have "brought Saul and his servant into the hall" (Heb. *liškâ H4384*, 1 Sam. 9:22; KJV, "parlor") and given him a place at the head of about thirty persons who had been invited. The nature of this room is not defined, but the Hebrew word here is also used in the OT for a chamber connected with a sanctuary (1 Chr. 9:26; 23:28; Jer. 35:2, 4; Ezek. 40:17, 38, 44–46; et al.; also for a scribe's room in the royal palace, Jer. 36:12, 20–21). It was evidently a place where worshipers ate sacrificial meals; benches would be placed on three of the walls, while the fourth opened to a courtyard.

Among the buildings SOLOMON erected after the completion of the TEMPLE was "the Hall of Pillars" (NRSV for *ʾûlām hāʿammûdîm*, 1 Ki. 7:6; NIV, "a colonnade"), the purpose of which is not stated. Apparently, one went through it to reach "the throne hall, the Hall of Justice" (NIV for the phrases *ʾûlām hakkissēʾ* and *ʾûlām hammišpāṭ*, v. 7; KJV, "a porch for the throne … *even* the porch of judgment"), where Solomon sat in judgment on

Columns in the Great Hall of Ramses II at Karnak.

makers from Babylon, and wall decorators from Media and Egypt. The walls were decorated with panels of beautifully colored glazed bricks, many of the designs being executed in relief. The king's audience hall, in which King Xerxes met Esther, was a huge room 193 ft. square, with 36 pillars supporting the roof. (See A. T. Olmstead, *History of the Persian Empire* [1948], 166–71.)

The banquet hall (Aram. *bêt mištĕyāʾ*, Dan. 5:10) where King Belshazzar saw the handwriting on the wall was in Babylon, which for centuries was one of the great cities of antiquity. Herodotus, who visited the city after its conquest by Cyrus, describes it as a great square 42 mi. in circuit, surrounded by a rampart 300 ft. high and 75 ft. broad with 100 gates of brass. Its famous hanging gardens were regarded by ancients as one of the seven wonders of the world. The city had three royal palaces, the largest of which contained the throne room (Herodotus, *Hist.* 1.178–83; cf. also the descriptions by Diodorus Siculus, *Bibl. Hist.* 2.7, 9–10; Strabo, *Geogr.* 16.1.2, 5; Q. Curtius Rufus, *Hist. of Alexander*, 5.1).

The author of the Acts of the Apostles says that when Jews in Ephesus rejected and opposed Paul's message, he left the synagogue where he had been teaching for three months and went to the "lecture hall" of Tyrannus, where the apostle taught daily for two years (Acts 19:9; Gk. *scholē G5391*, KJV, "school"). This hall was probably a part of some gymnasium, which normally included not only areas for exercise and sports, but also gardens and halls that were made use of by teachers, poets, and philosophers for giving recitations and lectures. Ephesus had at least five such gymnasiums. By some arrangement Paul obtained the use of the hall and taught there every day from late morning until the end of the afternoon.

Other relevant Greek terms include *gamos G1141*, "wedding" (rendered "wedding hall" in Matt. 22:10), *aulē G885*, "courtyard" (Mk. 15:16 et al.; KJV, "hall," identified as the Praetorium), and *akroatērion G211*, "place of hearing, auditorium" (Acts 25:23; NRSV, "audience hall"). The last reference may indicate a room used for various purposes and apparently served as a "hall of justice." It was located in the palace that Herod the Great had built in Caesarea; the Roman governors used it as their headquarters in

cases brought before him. His own palace was "set farther back" and "was similar in design" (v. 8). The exact position of these various buildings relative to each other is a matter of dispute. (See D. Ussischkin in *BA* 36 [1973]: 78–105.)

The royal palace in Susa, the winter capital of the Persian kings, included a structure called "the king's hall" (Esth. 5:1; however, the Heb. is *bêt hammelek*, "the house of the king," which is rendered "the king's palace" earlier in the same verse). In an inscription in which Darius the Great tells about the building of this palace, he recorded that wood was brought from Lebanon, Gandhara, and Carmania; gold from Sardis and Bactria; lapis lazuli and carnelian from Sogdiana; turquoise from Chorasmia; silver and ebony from Egypt; ivory from Ethiopia, Sind, and Arachosia; ornamentation for the walls from Ionia; and stone columns from Elam. Stonecutters came from Ionia and Sardis, goldsmiths from Media and Egypt, carpenters from Sardis and Egypt, brick-

Palestine. (See also J. Finegan, *Light From the Ancient Past* [1959], 224, 242–44.) S. BARABAS

Hallel halʹel (הַלֵּל, from הָלַל H2146, piel, "to praise"). Rabbinic term for several groups of psalms of praise. The expression Great Hallel usually denotes Ps. 136, though it can refer to Pss. 120–136. "Hallel" can be applied also to Pss. 146–148, but the most significant group is the Egyptian Hallel, Pss. 113–118. These psalms were recited in Jewish homes during the course of the PASSOVER observance and in public temple and synagogue services for the FEASTS of Unleavened Bread, Pentecost, Tabernacles, and Dedication. As an expression of joy, it was most appropriate for the great joyful feasts listed above. Modern Judaism has several musical settings for this Hallel. It doubtless played its customary role in the Lord's last Passover observance with his disciples, and the hymn with which the meal ended was probably either the last part of the Egyptian Hallel (Pss. 115–118) or the Great Hallel (Ps. 136). (See A. Edersheim, *The Life and Times of Jesus the Messiah* [1886], 1:230, 2:159, 533; *EncJud*, 7:1198–99.) A. BOWLING

hallelujah halʹuh-looʹyuh (הַלְלוּ [from הָלַל H2146, piel, "to praise"] and יָהּ H3363 [short form of Yahweh]; ἁλληλουϊά G252). A Hebrew expression that is invariably translated "Praise the LORD"; the corresponding Greek term in the NT is transliterated "hallelujah" (KJV, "alleluia"). In the OT text, the expression consists of two words, often hyphenated but never joined as one word. It may be that the Jews became accustomed to considering it a compound, even though it was never written as such. When it was borrowed by Greek and other languages, however, it was treated as one word. *Hallelujah*, like AMEN, has practically become a universal word. It is an acclamation of PRAISE of the highest order, praising God in man's most elegant expression in reverence, awe, and humility. Its use is limited altogether to songs of praise, appearing only in Psalms and Revelation.

Hallelujah functions as a liturgical interjection and an exclamation. As such, it is not grammatically connected with accompanying sentences, but it has vital spiritual and worshipful connections where found. Its common use was as a call to praise God at the beginning of songs and as a shout of spiritual exultation at the end. Some scholars point out that in occasional instances where it appears at the end of a Psalm, it properly belongs at the beginning of the following Psalm (see Ps. 104 and 117). In one instance, the hallelujah follows the DOXOLOGY when it logically should precede it (Ps. 106).

The expression is used sparingly in the OT, occurring only twenty-four times, and that only in the Psalms. In the Hebrew mind it probably held a certain sacred distinctiveness that restricted its frequent use. It is strictly a religious term and consequently limited to personal and congregational worship. The most prominent use of "Praise the LORD" was in the major Hebrew FEASTS, Passover, Pentecost, and Tabernacles. Psalms 105 and 106, now comprising a pair, were composed for use at one of these festivals, and at some time in their history acquired the ritual shout, "Hallelujah," employed both at the beginning and end. (Note the rearrangement suggested earlier.)

One group of psalms constitute, in Jewish liturgical tradition, the so-called Egyptian HALLEL (Pss. 113–118). These were sung not only at the three major festivals, but also at the feast of DEDICATION. At the PASSOVER, Pss. 113 and 114 were sung before the meal, and 115–118 were sung afterward (thus prob. by Jesus and his disciples at the Last Supper, Matt. 26:30). These are all "Hallelujah" hymns, with the call to "Praise the LORD" obviously intended for the beginning. It is an appropriate and effective summons to WORSHIP. During the reigns of DAVID and SOLOMON, pilgrimages to Jerusalem for celebrating the great festivals were significant national events. Anyone who has attended a mass rendition of the "Hallelujah Chorus" may visualize the ancient Hebrew songs of praise at these great feasts. All five psalms concluding the Psalter (Pss. 146–150) begin and end with "Hallelujah."

This exclamation was not limited to congregational use, however, but found expression also in personal praise. In Ps. 111:1 the soloist sang, "Praise the LORD. / I will extol the LORD with all my heart / in the council of the upright and in the assembly." Note also Ps. 146:1–2: "Praise the LORD. / Praise the LORD, O my soul. / I will praise the LORD all my life; / I will sing praise to my God as long as I live." In this passage, only the first instance of "Praise the Lord" translates Hebrew *halĕlû-yāh* (the second instance reads, *halĕlî napšî ʾet-yhwh*). The liturgical interjection apparently retained its distinctiveness even here. Moreover, the great psalmists dared to use it personally when their hearts overflowed with thanksgiving and consequent praise to the Lord.

In the NT, "hallelujah" appears four times, all in one chapter (Rev. 19:1, 3, 4, 6). As the Hebrew Psalter closes with God's chosen people singing "hallelujah," so also the NT closes with God's redeemed in heaven singing "hallelujah." John heard in the heavenly choir "what sounded like a great multitude, like the roar of rushing waters and like loud peals of thunder, shouting: 'Hallelujah!' For our Lord God Almighty reigns" (v. 6).

G. B. Funderburk

Hallohesh huh-loh´hesh (הַלּוֹחֵשׁ H2135, "the whisperer"). Father of Shallum; the latter was "ruler of a half-district of Jerusalem" in the time of Nehemiah and repaired a section of the walls of Jerusalem (Neh. 3:12; KJV, "Halohesh"). This Hallohesh is probably the same man listed among those who sealed the covenant with Nehemiah (10:24).

hallow. To render or treat as holy, to sanctify or consecrate. This English term is used over thirty times in the KJV but is less common in modern versions. It occurs seven times in the NRSV, while the NIV uses it only in the context of the Lord's Prayer (Matt. 6:9; Lk. 11:1). See consecration; dedicate; holiness; sanctification.

Halohesh. KJV form of Hallohesh.

Ham (person) ham (חָם H2769, possibly "warm, hot"). Also Cham (some older English versions). Second son of Noah and brother of Shem and Japheth (Gen. 5:32; 6:10; 7:13; 9:18, 22; 10:1, 6, 20; 1 Chr. 1:4, 8). Ham had four sons, Cush, Mizraim (Egypt), Put, and Canaan (Gen. 10:6). His descendants were spread abroad in many lands. From him and his brothers came all the nations of the earth. In the Table of Nations (Gen. 10:6–10), Ham is mentioned as the ancestor of the Egyptians and of the peoples who were under the control of Egypt in NE Africa, Arabia, and Canaan (with the exception of Nimrod). His name serves also as the patronymic of his descendants (Pss. 78:51; 105:23, 27; 106:22; possibly also 1 Chr. 4:40 [NIV, "Hamites," supplied also in v. 41], but this reference may allude to an otherwise unknown place). The term *Hamitic* was commonly used in the past to designate a group of languages in N Africa, including Egyptian, that are related to the Semitic languages (the label *Hamito-Semitic* is seldom used today by scholars, who prefer the term *Afroasiatic*; see languages of the ANE I.B).

After the flood Noah became intoxicated, and he lay in a drunken stupor in his tent. Ham entered the tent and then told his brothers what he had seen. Shem and Japheth took a robe and walking backward into the tent, so as not to look upon their father's nakedness, let it fall across their father to cover him. When Noah awoke from his stupor and learned what had happened to him and what his son Ham had done, he cursed Ham's son Canaan and said that his descendants would be the slaves of the descendants of Shem and Japheth. The story does not make clear why Noah should curse Canaan. Various explanations have been given, one of the most likely being that Canaan had done something not mentioned in the story that deserved cursing.

S. Barabas

Ham (place) ham (הָם H2154). The name of a city whose inhabitants, the Zuzites, were subdued by Kedorlaomer and his allies in the time of Abraham (Gen. 14:5). The site is usually identified with modern Tell Ham in N Jordan, about 3 mi. SSW of Irbid (Beth Arbel).

Haman hay´muhn (הָמָן H2172, possibly from Old Pers. *hamanā*, "illustrious," or *humayun*, "the great"). KJV Apoc., Aman. Son of Hammedatha and prime minister of Persia under Xerxes (Esth. 3:1 et al.). He is also called the Agagite, a name that links him with the king of the Amalekites that Saul was told to destroy (1 Sam. 15). Haman became the bitter enemy of Mordecai, the uncle of Esther, because Mordecai, being a Jew, would not prostrate himself before him like the other subjects of the king (Esth. 3:2). He therefore determined in revenge not only to kill Mordecai but also to exterminate all the Jews in the Persian empire, and received from

Xerxes a decree to do this (3:8–9). When Mordecai heard of this plot, he urged Esther, who was the queen of Xerxes, to intercede in behalf of her people (ch. 4). At a banquet to which she invited the king and Haman, Esther exposed Haman's purpose to slaughter her people. The king left the room in a rage and Haman threw himself on the queen's couch to beg for his life. Xerxes returned and, thinking that Haman was assaulting Esther, ordered his execution on the very gallows Haman had prepared for Mordecai (ch. 7). The Feast of PURIM celebrates the deliverance of the Jews from Haman's plot to kill them. (See T. C. Thornton in *JTS* 37 [1986]: 419–26.) S. BARABAS

Hamath hay´math (חֲמָת *H2828*, possibly "fortress"; gentilic חֲמָתִי *H2833*, "Hamathite"). KJV also Hemath (1 Chr. 13:5; Amos 6:14). A city of SYRIA (ARAM) c. 120 mi. N of DAMASCUS. Built on both banks of the ORONTES River, Hamath was surrounded by hills and had a warm and humid climate. The city was founded in the Neolithic period and destroyed c. 1750 B.C., probably by the HYKSOS, although there are no findings from the Hyksos period. THUTMOSE III (1502–1448) conquered the city, and during the time of Egyptian control of Syria the city prospered. Sometime before 900 B.C. it became the HITTITE capital of a small kingdom; many Hittite inscriptions have been found.

SHALMANESER III (c. 860–825 B.C.) invaded the Hittite country as far as the Mediterranean. To resist him, a league that included DAMASCUS, Israel, Hamath, and twelve kings of the coast was formed. A battle was fought at Qarqar in 854 B.C., but it must have ended indecisively, since both sides claimed the victory. Three years later Shalmaneser III was again stopped by the league, but in the eleventh year of his reign he plundered many towns of the kingdom of Hamath, although he was stopped again. He returned in the fourteenth year of his reign, and this time he conquered and broke the power of the league.

TIGLATH-PILESER III (745–727 B.C.) conquered Hamath and compelled it to pay tribute. SARGON II conquered and destroyed the city in 720 B.C. He transported peoples from a number of different territories in his kingdom, including Hamath, and settled them in the cities of SAMARIA, replacing the Israelites he had taken into captivity. These people brought with them their pagan gods (2 Ki. 17:24, 30). Among the places to which he transported Israelites was Hamath (Isa. 11:11). After Sargon's time the city seems to have become subordinate to Damascus (Jer. 49:23). There are a number of references in the OT to the Assyrian conquest of Hamath (2 Ki. 18:34; 19:13; Isa. 10:9; 36:19; 37:13; Amos 6:2). Amos calls the city Hamath the Great (Amos 6:2).

The Babylonian Chronicle records that at Hamath NEBUCHADNEZZAR overtook the Egyptians fleeing from CARCHEMISH (605 B.C.). Jeremiah and Zechariah declared that the city was doomed (Jer. 49:23; Zech. 9:2); these prophets classed the city with Arpad, Damascus, Tyre, and Sidon. Ezekiel prophesied that the land of Israel would some day extend N to Hamath (Ezek. 47:16, 17; 48:1). Later, during the Seleucid period, ANTIOCHUS IV Epiphanes renamed the city Epiphania (Jos. *Ant.* 1.6.2). Jonathan MACCABEE met the army of DEMETRIUS in the region of Hamath (1 Macc. 12:25; KJV, "Amathis").

The modern city of Hama (Ḥamah), with a population of about 65,000, is built around the tell of the ancient city. Harald Ingholt conducted excavations at Hamath in 1931–38. He discovered twelve strata of occupation from the Arabic period down to the Neolithic stratum (*Rapport préliminaire sur sept campagnes de fouilles à Hama en Syrie (1932–38)* [1940]; updates in *ABD*, 3:33–36; *NEAEHL*, 2:561–62). See also HAMATH ZOBAH; LEBO HAMATH. S. BARABAS

Hamath, entrance of. This (or a similar) expression is used by some Bible versions to render Hebrew *lĕbōʾ ḥămāt H4217*, which is better regarded as a place name, LEBO HAMATH (Num. 13:21 et al.).

Hamathite hay´muh-th*i*t (חֲמָתִי *H2833*). The Hamathites are listed as a nation descended from CANAAN (Gen. 10:18; 1 Chr. 1:16). Presumably, they were early settlers of the city of HAMATH. See also NATIONS II.A.

Hamath Zobah hay´math-zoh´buh (חֲמָת צוֹבָה *H2832*, possibly "fortress of Zobah"). A city conquered by SOLOMON, apparently near TADMOR in the region of HAMATH (2 Chr. 8:3). Some have identified Hamath Zobah with the city of Hamath itself, while others have conjectured that it is a different city also called Hamath, but situated in the territory of ZOBAH, an Aramean kingdom (see ARAM) that Assyrian records say reached as far as the EUPHRATES and in the 10th cent. was a threat to ASSYRIA. It is also possible that the double name simply indicates the extent of Solomon's conquests, that is, the combined regions of Hamath and Zobah. Finally, some have thought that the Hebrew text is corrupt (CODEX VATICANUS reads *Bai Zōba*, reflecting the name Beth Zobah, otherwise unknown).

Hammath (person) ham´ath (חַמַּת H2830, possibly "hot [spring]"). A man included in the genealogy of CALEB and described as the father of the house of RECAB; he was the ancestor of the KENITES (1 Chr. 2:55; KJV, "Hemath"). Some scholars connect, or even identify, Hammath with the city of the same name; see HAMMATH (PLACE). Others interpret the word as a common noun (cf. *ḥām* H2767, "father-in-law") and understand the verse to say that the Kenites were related by marriage to the ancestor of the Recabites (see NEB).

Hammath (place) ham´ath (חַמַּת H2829, "hot [spring]"). A fortified city in the tribal territory of NAPHTALI (Josh. 19:35). It is probably the same as HAMMON #2 (1 Chr. 6:76) and HAMMOTH DOR (Josh. 21:32). When JOSEPHUS mentions that HEROD Antipas built the city of TIBERIAS, he adds, "There is a hot spring not far from it in a village called Ammathus [*Ammathous*]" (*Ant.* 18.2.3 §36; cf. *War* 4.1.3 §11). Hammath is generally identified with the modern Ḥammam Ṭabariyeh, famous for its hot baths, c. 2 mi. S of Tiberias on the W shore of the Sea of Galilee. Archaeological work, however, has uncovered remains dating back only to the Roman period. (See M. Dothan, *Hammath Tiberias*, 2 vols. [1983–2000]; *NEAEHL*, 2:573–77. For a discussion of the "double list" of Levitical cities, see Y. Aharoni, *The Land of the Bible: A Historical Geography*, rev. ed. [1979], 116, 301–5).

Hammedatha ham´uh-day´thuh (הַמְּדָתָא H2158, possibly from Pers. *amadāta*, "strongly made," or *haomadāta*, "given by [the deity] Hama" [*ABD*, 3:38]). The father of HAMAN, who was the chief minister of XERXES and a bitter enemy of the Jews (Esth. 3:1, 10; 8:5; 9:10, 24; KJV Apoc., "Adamatha" and "Adamathus," Add. Esth. 12:6; 16:10, 17).

Hammelech ham´uh-lek. The KJV rendering of *hammelek* in two passages (Jer. 36:26; 38:6). Modern versions translate it correctly as "the king"; however, the designation "son of the king" apparently refers to a minor royal official with police duties (see R. de Vaux, *Ancient Israel* [1961], 119–20).

hammer. ANE craftsmen had available for use a wide variety of specialized hammers suited for different purposes. Hammer marks on building stones and other evidences indicate that the type of hammers available in the ancient world corresponded roughly to the types still used in the Near E today.

Hammath and Hamath.

The Hebrew term *maqqebet* H5216 refers to a relatively small tool used for driving nails and pegs (Jdg. 4:21; cf. also *halĕmût* H2153, 5:26), dressing surfaces of building stone (1 Ki. 6:7), and decorating wooden idols (Jer. 10:4; metal idols, Isa. 44:12). Another term, *paṭṭîš* H7079, is once used for the large sledge hammer used to crack boulders (Jer. 23:29) and once for a blacksmith's hammer (Isa. 41:7); it is also used figuratively of Babylon's earth-shaking role as the "hammer of the whole earth" (Jer. 50:23). A. BOWLING

Hammolecheth. See HAMMOLEKETH.

Hammoleketh ha-mol´uh-keth (הַמֹּלֶכֶת H2168, "the queen"). Also Hammolecheth. Daughter of MAKIR by his wife MAACAH and granddaughter of MANASSEH; she is described as the sister of GILEAD and as having given birth to three children (1 Chr. 7:18). A few scholars, however, have thought that the text refers to her rather as the sister of Manasseh. It has also been suggested that the word is not a proper name but a description of her role as a person of authority ("she who reigns"). Neither of these views has gained favor.

Hammon ham´uhn (חַמּוֹן H2785, possibly "hot [spring]"). (1) A town included in the boundary description of the tribe of ASHER (Josh. 19:28). The location of Hammon has been debated, but most scholars identify it with modern Khirbet Umm el-ʿAwamid in Lebanon, near Ras en-Naqurah and about 14.5 mi. NNE of Acco.

(2) A Levitical town in the tribal territory of NAPHTALI; it was assigned to the Levites descended from GERSHON (1 Chr. 6:76). This Hammon is generally identified with Hammath (Josh. 19:35) and Hammoth Dor (21:32), on the W shore of the Sea of Galilee. See further HAMMATH (PLACE).

Hammoth Dor ham´uhth-dor´ (חַמֹּת דֹּאר H2831, "hot [spring] of Dor"). A Levitical town in the tribal territory of NAPHTALI; it was assigned to the Levites descended from GERSHON (Josh. 21:32). Hammoth Dor is probably an alternate name for Hammath (Josh. 19:35) and Hammon (1 Chr. 6:76), on the W shore of the Sea of Galilee. See further HAMMATH (PLACE).

Hammuel ham´yoo-uhl (חַמּוּאֵל H2781, perhaps "god of Ham" or "Hammu is God" or "God protects"). KJV Hamuel. Son of Mishma and descendant of SIMEON through Shaul (1 Chr. 4:26).

Hammurabi ham´uh-rah´bee (Akk. *ḫammu*, from Amorite ʿ*Ammu* ["Sun" or "kinsman" or "nation"] + *rabi* ["great, vast"] or *rapi* ["healing"]; possible meanings are "[the god] Hammu is great," "vast nation," "the [divine] kinsman heals"). Also Hammurapi. This name was borne by two kings of ALEPPO in the 18th and 17th cent. B.C. (cf. the list in *CANE*, 2:1202) and by other individuals, but special importance attaches to the sixth king of the first dynasty of BABYLON, who is the subject of the present article. (Hammurabi is not mentioned in the Bible, although some have thought that he should be identified with AMRAPHEL, Gen. 14:1, 9.)

I. Political events. Hammurabi was son and successor of Sin-muballit and father of Samsuiluna. The widely accepted date for his reign is 1792–1750 B.C. (suggested alternatives include 1728–1686 [W. F. Albright] and 1642–1626 [A. Goetze]). He inherited a small kingdom centered on Babylon itself. According to the date-formulae of documents from his time and his own account of events given in the prologue to his laws, he captured the cities of Uruk and Isin in his seventh year, destroyed Malgum, warred against Emutbal, and attacked Rapiqum. The same sources state that between his 11th and 30th regnal years he was preoccupied mainly with

Hot springs at Hammath Tiberias on the W shore of the Sea of Galilee.

local affairs and the rebuilding of religious shrines, despite an uneasy truce with the neighboring city-states of Assyria and Eshnunna.

The lively correspondence from this period found at Mari throws interesting light on the relative powers and is based on information from ambassadors at the court of Babylon. An emissary of Zimri-Lim, king of Mari, wrote him saying, "There is no king who is strong by himself. Ten to fifteen kings follow Hammurabi, the governor of Babylon, a like number Rim-Sin of Larsa, a like number Ibalpiel of Eshnunna, a like number Amutpiel of Qatana, and twenty follow Yarimlim of Yamhad." In his 29th year Hammurabi won an outstanding victory over a coalition holding the E of the River Tigris, and the way was open for the attack, made two years later, against his old rival Rim-Sin, king of Larsa and Emutbal, to gain control of the southern cities. The balance of power was now drastically changed.

Assyria was soon subdued, and in this 38th year the Babylonians crushed Eshnunna by inundation due to diverted waterways. The next year his forces marched against the desert peoples to the NW and rendered the great city of Mari, about 250 mi. from Babylon, impotent by the destruction of its walls. This was to prove the northernmost limit of Babylonian conquest at this time. The period till his death in his 43rd year of reign was much occupied with resettling his new frontiers. An abundance of administrative letters and contracts reveal something of the strong character of this king, who was engaged in personal control of matters of war, diplomacy, and business, yet fond of good food, hunting, and fine buildings.

II. Economic conditions. At this time numerous contracts attest the increase in private trading, though the palace (state) played a dominant part in external dealings. The hold over the economy formally exercised by the temple was weakened by the use of manpower in cooperative projects such as harvesting and irrigation; and by royal decree fixing the prices of staple commodities, power centered in the person of the king. Access to his presence was freely accorded, and out of the many decisions made there arose a collection of legal judgments commonly called the Laws of Hammurabi.

III. Lawgiver. An 8-ft. high diorite stela surmounted with a portrait of the king receiving a scepter and ring (symbols of justice and order) from the sun-god Shamash, the divine law-giver, was found in 1901 at Susa. It had been taken there in 1160 B.C. by the Elamite Shutruk-nahhunte following a successful raid on Babylon. Fragments of other stelae and tablets bearing copies of the same text show that the monument once stood in the Esagil temple of Marduk in Babylon with copies at other centers. The prologue tells how the king had received a divine call to "make justice to shine forth in the land, to destroy the evil and the wicked, that the strong might not oppress the weak ... to give light to the land." (For an English translation of the text, see *ANET*, 163–80.)

The increasingly diverse elements within the empire required the clear definition of the rights of an individual. Manifold personal indebtedness and a large measure of dependence on slave labor provided both the reason and means of doing this. By stating the wages of agricultural and technical workers and by decreeing release from slavery or debt, the king could largely guide the whole life of the nation. This was done by a periodical decree of "righteousness" (*mesharum*). In his first full regnal year, as dated by one such decree, Hammurabi made a public pronouncement of the standard of law that would govern the religious and economic life of his peoples. This action has been compared with the so-called "reforms" by the Hebrew kings who, by restating allegiance to the law in the opening year of their rule, "did the right [*yāšār*] in the eyes of the Lord." Hammurabi's laws may well date from the beginning of his reign in part, but their final edition and compilation was undertaken toward the end of his reign, when he made a report to his god on his stewardship and exercise of "wisdom."

Two hundred eighty-two paragraphs or judgments remain, phrased in the form of a summary of the evidence followed by the brief decision. It was decided that "if a son has struck his father they shall cut off his hand" (§195). The laws are not comparable to a modern law code, the cases being grouped according to subject, though in only a few cases are they worded as general ordinances having universal application. Because of their specific reference to cases judged by the king, sometimes of an unusual nature (though background detail often is lacking to confirm this), the application of these laws rarely is reflected in the contemporary court cases or legal contracts. The latter were enacted before local judges or magistrates, some of whom sat at the city gate or "ward."

Some of the cases are similar to those recorded by earlier rulers (e.g., Lipit-Ishtar of Isin, or Bilalama [?] of Eshnunna). A few bear close resemblance to Hebrew laws, though in general the Hammurabi statutes do not deal with religious affairs. Punishments included ordeal by immersion in the river, the LEX TALIONIS, fines, restitution by labor or in kind, and death. Penalties might vary according to the class of the offender, the Babylonians being at this time divided for this purpose into "freeman" (*awēlum*), "state-dependent" (*muškenum*), and "slave" (*wardum*). The laws may be analyzed as follows:

Various offenses and crimes (§§1–25). These include false witness (cf. Deut. 5:20; 19:16–19); a charge of sorcery (cf. Deut. 18:10; Exod. 22:18); action to be taken against a corrupt judge (cf. Exod. 23:6–9; Lev. 19:15; Deut. 16:18–19). The death penalty imposed for theft or receipt of stolen property from a temple or palace (§6) contrasts with the allowance of restoration in Exod. 22:1; Lev. 6:2. The penalty for dereliction (§7) is death or restoration of the stolen property thirtyfold or tenfold (according to the status of the accused), whereas the Hebrew equivalent law requires that restoration be twofold (Exod. 22:1–4, 7) and if necessary that the thief be sold (into slavery?) to provide the means of restitution. Kidnapping (§14) is punishable by death as in the Hebrew law (Exod. 21:16; Deut. 24:7). Death is prescribed also for the theft of fugitive slaves, robbery, and looting.

Property (§§26–99) is covered with special reference to crown-tenants, absconding fief-holders, and tenant farmers. Loans of money or seed against an anticipated crop, pledges, and distraint played a dominant part in a precarious agricultural existence. However, the man who planted trees was allowed four years for them to bear fruit before repaying capital (§60). Hebrew practice was similar, save that any firstfruits in the fourth year had to be dedicated to God (Lev. 19:23–25).

Commercial law (§§100–126) related to partnerships and agencies, as well as to sales and carriage of merchandise including liquor. Cases of deposit, distraint, and slavery figure prominently, for Hammurabi legislated for an urban community that subsisted on a large body of slave labor, and debtors were more severely treated than in the Hebrew pastoral groups (cf. Exod. 23:1).

Marriage (§§127–61) cases concerned the rights of both parties, dowry settlements, bridal gifts, divorce, and matrimonial offenses. Adultery with a married woman resulted in the death penalty for both parties (as Deut. 22:22); in the case of rape, the man was executed (as 22:25). Both the Babylonian (§131) and Hebrew (Num. 5:13–22) laws sentenced the adulterous wife to trial by ordeal. A husband captured abroad (§§133–35) had his marriage safeguarded, as was the intent of the Deuteronomic prohibition of military or merchant service in the first year of married life (Deut. 24:5). The common reference to concubinage (§§144–47) and protection for the girl against divorce or reduction to slavery, except for offenses against the first wife, throw light on patriarchal practices (Gen. 16:2, 4; 21:8–14). The Babylonian laws forbid a man to put away his sick wife (§148; some interpret Deut. 24:1 as allowing for divorce in these circumstances). Incest was treated with equal severity in both societies.

Children (§§162–77). The firstborn had special rights and portion (as Deut. 15:21).

Special cases concerning women and priestesses in cloisters (§§178–84), whose support was weakened by the increase in state and private ownership of land, reveal a situation applicable to N Babylonia only at this time.

Adoption (§§185–94) included the granting of "sonship" to apprentices and the legal force of oral depositions both to adopt and disown. Violence by an unruly son was met by cutting off the offending limb (cf. Exod. 21:15).

Assault and damage to persons and property (§§195–208). This section includes harm to pregnant women (Exod. 21:22–23), a surgeon's liability in an eye operation, builders of faulty constructions, and hire of boats.

Agricultural work and offenses (§§241–67) includes a case requiring the owner of a goring ox to have been warned before further action can be taken (as in Exod. 21:28–32).

Rates and wages (§§268–77) for seasonal workers, craftsmen, hire of beasts, carts, and boats emphasize the divergences between the urban community for which these judgments were given and the conditions in early Israel.

An appendix concerning slaves (§§278–82) includes matters concerning their purchase and sale.

While similar judgments in both the Hebrew and Babylonian laws may arise from similar circumstances and a common ANE tradition, they should not be overstressed in the light of the overriding religious purpose and expression in the Hebrew legislation. (See further F. M. Böhl, *King Hammurabi of Babylon in the Setting of His Time* [1946]; G. R. Driver and J. Miles, *The Babylonian Laws* [1952]; D. J. Wiseman in *JSS* 7 [1962]: 161–72; C. J. Gadd in *CAH* 2/1, 2nd ed. [1973], 176–227; M. E. J. Richardson, *Hammurabi's Laws: Text, Translation and Glossary* [2000]; M. Van de Mieroop, *King Hammurabi of Babylon: A Biography* [2005]; *ABD*, 3:39–42; *CANE*, 2:901–15.) D. J. WISEMAN

Hamonah huh-moh′nuh (הֲמוֹנָה *H2164*, "roaring" or "horde"). The name of a city in the symbolical valley of HAMON GOG, where the defeated armies of GOG will be buried (Ezek. 39:16). The Hebrew clause in the MT (*wĕgam šem-ʿîr hămônâ*, lit., "and also the name of the city [is] Hamonah") is problematic. The NRSV and other versions read *šām H9004*, "there," instead of *šem* (construct of *šēm H9005*, "name"); the NIV apparently accepts the MT vocalization ("a town called Hamonah") but then supplies the phrase "shall be there" to clarify the meaning (TNIV similarly, "near a town called Hamonah"). Some scholars emend the text by omitting the phrase altogether (see summary of views in *ABD*, 3:42).

Hamon Gog hay′-muhn-gog′ (הֲמוֹן גּוֹג *H2163*, "horde of Gog"). The name of "the valley of those who travel east toward the Sea"; this place will be named Hamon Gog because there the forces of GOG will be destroyed and buried (Ezek. 39:11, 15). The valley is said to be "in Israel" and—if the NIV rendering "toward the Sea" is correct—probably located W of the Dead Sea (perhaps alluding to the ESDRAELON Valley). However, the NRSV translates, "the Valley of the Travelers [*hāʿōběrîm*] east of the sea" (cf. also TNIV), which suggests a place in TRANSJORDAN (unless "the sea" refers to the Mediterranean). If so, the allusion may be to the ABARIM mountain range in MOAB. Given the symbolic nature of the passage, it is likely that the prophet does not intend a specific known site. See TRAVELERS, VALLEY OF.

Hamor hay′mor (חֲמוֹר *H2791*, "[male] donkey"). The father of SHECHEM; he is called a HIVITE (Gen. 33:19; 34:2 et al.). When JACOB returned from PADDAN ARAM, he bought a piece of ground from the sons of Hamor (this plot of land would later become the burial place of JOSEPH, Josh. 24:32; regarding the apparent discrepancy in Acts 7:16 [KJV, "Emmor"], see MACHPELAH). DINAH, Jacob's daughter, was violated by Shechem, and in revenge the sons of Jacob slew Hamor, Shechem, and all the males of the city (Gen. 34). During the period of the judges, the inhabitants of the city of Shechem were called "men of Hamor" (Jdg. 9:28); they suffered a severe defeat from ABIMELECH, a ruler of the Israelites. S. BARABAS

Hamran ham′ran. See HEMDAN.

Hamuel. KJV form of HAMMUEL.

Hamul hay′muhl (חָמוּל *H2783*, possibly "spared" or "pitied"; gentilic חָמוּלִי *H2784*, "Hamulite"). Son of PEREZ, grandson of JUDAH, and ancestral head of the Hamulite clan (Gen. 46:12; Num. 26:21; 1 Chr. 2:5).

Hamutal huh-myoo′tuhl (חֲמוּטַל *H2782*, possibly "my father-in-law is dew [*or* protection]"; cf. ABITAL). The mother of JEHOAHAZ and ZEDEKIAH, kings of Judah; she was the daughter of a certain Jeremiah of Libnah and the wife of King JOSIAH (2 Ki. 23:31; 24:18; Jer. 52:1).

Hana hay′nuh. See HANAN.

Hanael han′ay-uhl. See ANAEL.

Hanameel huh-nam′ee-uhl. KJV form of HANAMEL.

Hanamel han′uh-mel (חֲנַמְאֵל *H2856*, "God is gracious"). KJV Hanameel. Son of Shallum and cousin of JEREMIAH the prophet (Jer. 32:7–9). Hanamel owned a field in ANATHOTH, and when Jerusalem was besieged, he asked Jeremiah, as nearest relative, to buy it (cf. Lev. 25:25). God had forewarned Jeremiah about this request, so the prophet bought the field to show his confidence that "Houses, fields and vineyards will again be bought in this land" (Jer. 32:15).

Hanan hay´nuhn (חָנָן H2860, "[God or Yahweh] is gracious"; short form of ELHANAN, HANANEL, HANANIAH, or JOHANAN [cf. also BAAL-HANAN and BEN-HANAN]). **(1)** Son of Shashak and descendant of BENJAMIN; listed among the heads of families who lived in Jerusalem (1 Chr. 8:23; cf. v. 28). His genealogical connection is unclear.

(2) Son of Azel and descendant of King SAUL (1 Chr. 8:38; 9:44).

(3) Son of Maacah, included among DAVID's mighty men (1 Chr. 11:43).

(4) Son of Igdaliah; Hanan is described as "the man of God" (although this epithet perhaps applies to Igdaliah), and his sons occupied a chamber in the temple into which JEREMIAH brought the family of the Recabites (Jer. 35:4; see RECAB). According to some scholars, the phrase "sons of Hanan" refers to a prophetic guild.

(5) Ancestor of a family of temple servants (NETHINIM) who returned to Palestine after the EXILE (Ezra 2:46; Neh. 7:49; called "Hana" in 1 Esd. 5:30 NRSV [KJV, "Anan"]).

(6) A Levite who helped EZRA instruct the people in the law (Neh. 8:7); he is probably the Hanan listed among the Levites who sealed the covenant (10:10). Some believe he is also the same as #9 below.

(7–8) Two leaders of the people who sealed the covenant (Neh. 10:22).

(9) Son of Zaccur; NEHEMIAH appointed him as assistant to those who were in charge of the temple storerooms (Neh. 13:13). See also #6 above.

S. BARABAS

Hananeel huh-nan´ee-uhl. KJV form of HANANEL.

Hananel, Tower of han´uh-nel (חֲנַנְאֵל H2861, "God is gracious"). KJV Hananeel. The name of a tower on the N wall of JERUSALEM, between the FISH GATE and the Tower of the HUNDRED, not far from the SHEEP GATE (Neh. 3:1; 12:39). The Tower of Hananel must have been a significant landmark, for it is mentioned in two prophetic passages that deal with the rebuilding of Jerusalem (Jer. 31:38; Zech. 14:10). Its precise location is uncertain, though some scholars believe that in the time of HEROD it was replaced by the Tower of ANTONIA (cf. M. Avi-Yonah in *IEJ* 4 [1954]: 239–48, esp. 242). See also NEHEMIAH.

Modern reconstruction of the Antonia Fortress, possibly built on the location of the Tower of Hananel. (View to the NW from the temple court.)

Hanani huh-nay´ni (חֲנָנִי H2862, "[Yahweh] is gracious"; short form of HANANIAH). **(1)** Father of the prophet JEHU (1 Ki. 16:1, 7; 2 Chr. 19:2; 20:34). Described as "the seer," Hanani rebuked King ASA for relying on the Arameans; the king "was so enraged that he put him in prison" (2 Chr. 16:7–10).

(2) Son of HEMAN, DAVID's seer (1 Chr. 25:4). Hanani and his thirteen brothers were set apart "for the ministry of prophesying, accompanied by harps, lyres and cymbal" (v. 1). When lots were cast to determine the duties of the Levitical singers, he, along with his sons and relatives, received the eighteenth lot (v. 25).

(3) One of the descendants of IMMER who agreed to put away their foreign wives in the time of EZRA (Ezra 10:20; 1 Esd. 9:21 [KJV, "Ananias"]).

(4) A brother (or relative) of NEHEMIAH who brought news to SUSA of the distressing condition of the Jews in Palestine (Neh. 1:2). He was subsequently made one of the governors of Jerusalem (7:2).

(5) A musician who took part in the dedication of the walls of Jerusalem after the return from exile (Neh. 12:36). Some have suggested that this Hanani is the same as #3 or #4 above. S. BARABAS

Hananiah han'uh-ni'uh (חֲנַנְיָה *H2863*, "Yahweh is [or has been] gracious"; cf. JEHOHANAN; JOANAN; JOHN). A popular Jewish name, especially after the EXILE. It is possible that some of the references in EZRA and NEHEMIAH treated separately in this article speak of the same individual.

(1) Son of ZERUBBABEL and father of Pelatiah and Jeshaiah (1 Chr. 3:19, 21).

(2) Son of Shashak and descendant of BENJAMIN; listed among the heads of families who lived in Jerusalem (1 Chr. 8:24; cf. v. 28).

(3) Son of HEMAN, DAVID's seer (1 Chr. 25:4). Hananiah and his thirteen brothers were set apart "for the ministry of prophesying, accompanied by harps, lyres and cymbal" (v. 1). When lots were cast to determine the duties of the Levitical singers, he, along with his sons and relatives, received the sixteenth lot (v. 23).

(4) A royal official under King UZZIAH of Judah; under his direction, Jeiel the secretary and Maaseiah the officer mustered the army (2 Chr. 26:11).

(5) Son of Azzur and a false prophet who opposed JEREMIAH (Jer. 28). A native of GIBEON, Hananiah prophesied that King JECONIAH and the Jewish captives in Babylon would soon return to Jerusalem, bringing with them the vessels of the temple that NEBUCHADNEZZAR had carried away. In reply, Jeremiah told him that he would die within the year because he had made the people believe a lie. Jeremiah's words were fulfilled when Hananiah died in the seventh month of that year.

(6) Father of a certain Zedekiah; the latter was one of the high officials of Judah under King JEHOIAKIM (Jer. 36:12).

(7) Father of Shelemiah and grandfather of Irijah (Jer. 37:13); the latter was captain of the guard and arrested JEREMIAH on the charge of intending to desert to the Babylonians.

(8) One of the companions of DANIEL; his name was changed to Shadrach by the Babylonians (Dan. 1:6–7; 1 Macc. 2:59 [KJV, "Ananias"]; 4 Macc. 16:21; 18:12). See SHADRACH, MESHACH, ABEDNEGO.

(9) One of the descendants of Bebai who agreed to put away their foreign wives in the time of Ezra (Ezra 10:28; 1 Esd. 9:29 [KJV, "Ananias"]).

(10) A perfume-maker who helped Nehemiah rebuild the wall of Jerusalem (Neh. 3:8).

(11) Son of Shelemiah; he helped repair the wall above the HORSE GATE (Neh. 3.30). This Hananiah may be the same as #10 above.

(12) Commander of the citadel in Jerusalem. Described as "a man of integrity" who "feared God more than most men do," he was appointed joint ruler of the city along with Hanani, Nehemiah's brother (Neh. 7:2).

(13) A leader of the people who sealed the covenant with Nehemiah (Neh. 10:23).

(14) Head of the priestly family of Jeremiah in the days of JOIAKIM the high priest (Neh. 12:12). He is probably the same priest who played the trumpet at the dedication of the walls of Jerusalem (v. 41).

(15) Ancestor of a Levitical family that returned from the EXILE (1 Esd. 8:48 [KJV, "Channuneus"; LXX v. 47, *Chanounaios*]; not mentioned in the parallel passage, Ezra 8:19). S. BARABAS

Hananiel huh-nan'ee-uhl. See ANANIEL.

hand. The usual Hebrew term for "hand" (*yād H3338*; Gk. *cheir G5931*) can refer to the fingers where rings are worn (Gen. 41:42) and to the wrist on which ABRAHAM's servant put the bracelets for REBEKAH (24:22; NRSV, "arms"). Generally the hand suggests power (Exod. 14:30), while the use of the word "finger" implies dexterity (Ps. 8:3), so possibly the laying on of the hand was considered a means of passing the spirit from the strong one to the recipient.

The shield was held by the left hand, but a friend stood on one's right hand to guard him on his stronger side, which an enemy was most likely to assail (Ps. 16:8; Heb. *yāmîn H3545*, "right"). The accuser also stood at one's right hand (109:6). The right hand was the point of most danger and honor, although to be on either side of Christ in his kingdom was a desirable place (Mk. 10:37; Gk. *dexios G1288*, "right," and *aristeros G754*, "left"). The left

Hand carved in ivory with depiction of the Egyptian goddess Hathor.

hand was inclined to evil (Eccl. 10:2; Heb. *śĕmōʾl* H8520, "left"), and the rejected goats were sent to the left at the glorious throne (Matt. 25:31). "On the right hand" indicated S and "on the left hand" the N (cf. Gen. 14:15).

Parts of the hand were sometimes cut off in war and brought home as symbols of victory (Jdg. 1:6). The hand also was cut off after a shameful act (Deut. 25:12; cf. the metaphorical use in Matt. 5:30). A mark on the hand was a reminder of the successful exodus from Egypt (Exod. 13:16) or a sign of ownership (Isa. 44:5). The reference to those "who cannot tell their right hand from their left" (Jon. 4:11) may allude to the innocence of children or to the poor moral sense of the Ninevites.

In idioms, the hand portrayed many activities. It could stand for the whole person as in "their hand also is with David" (1 Sam. 22:17 NRSV); "hand for hand" gave justice (Exod. 21:24); to "shake the fist" promised judgment (Isa. 10:32); to "lay the hand on" meant to injure or kill (Gen. 22:12); to "slack the hand" was to avoid duty (Josh. 10:6 KJV); to "bury the hand" is a sluggard's inertia (Prov. 19:24); to "lay your hand upon your mouth" commanded silence (Job 21:5 NRSV); and to put one's hand on the head displayed grief from injustice (2 Sam. 13:19). Washing hands could imply innocence or a shirking of responsibility, for which PILATE became infamous (Matt. 27:24). Hands were smitten together in both joy and anger (Num. 24:10) and in spiteful triumph (Nah. 3:19), and one kissed his own hands in pride (Job 31:27 NRSV). A job is begun when one "puts his hand to" it (Deut. 12:7; Lk. 9:62). One risks his own life if he puts it in his hands (1 Sam. 19:5). Hands were lifted up to bless a multitude (Lev. 9:22), and were stretched out to ask for help (Ps. 143:6). Likewise "to lift holy hands" means to beseech in prayer (1 Tim. 2:8).

Laying hands upon the head of children to give a blessing was done by both Israel and Jesus (Gen. 48:13; Matt. 19:13). Jesus also raised the daughter of JAIRUS by taking her hand (Matt. 9:25). The HOLY SPIRIT was received by the laying on of hands (Acts 8:17; 1 Tim. 4:14), but sins were transferred to a sacrificial animal in like fashion (Lev. 16:21). The Egyptians had a similar custom.

The Lord God says, "I will stretch out my hand against" the wicked (Ezek. 25:13) and to help his people (Deut. 3:24; 4:34). Jesus demonstrated his identity by showing the print of the nails in his hands (Jn. 20:27). Christian ASSURANCE is guaranteed by no one's being able to pluck the believer out of the Father's hand (10:29). The Lord Jesus, who committed his spirit into the Father's hands (Lk. 23:46), is now sitting at the right hand of God (Ps. 110:1).   R. L. MIXTER

handbreadth. This term (Heb. *ṭōpaḥ* H3256) indicates a measurement of about three inches based on the width of the hand at the base of the four fingers (cf. Vulg. *quattuor digitis* in Exod. 25:25; note also Jer. 52:21). Three handbreadths equaled a span, and six handbreadths a cubit, but the long cubit had an extra handbreadth (Ezek. 40:5). The term is used to describe equipment in the tabernacle (Exod. 25:25; 37:12) and temple (1 Ki. 7:26; 2 Chr. 4:5; future temple, Ezek. 40:43; 43:13), and metaphorically for the brevity of man's life (Ps. 39:5). See also WEIGHTS AND MEASURES I.D.   M. R. WILSON

handicraft. Most industrial products of the biblical world were produced by skilled craftsmen, though some industries, notably mining and quarrying, used unskilled, forced labor. Craft clans probably held a traditional claim to certain industries (e.g., the KENITES; see also GE HARASHIM), although individual skilled craftsmen such as BEZALEL and OHOLIAB (Exod. 36:1) are mentioned. OT craftsmen usually were free men or members of free craft clans, but by NT times "factories" manned by dozens of slaves competed with free craftsmen. Some typical crafts of the Bible are the following: carpenter, dyer, fuller, jeweler, mason, perfumer, potter, sculptor, seamstress, smith, and weaver. See CRAFTS.

A. BOWLING

handkerchief. This English term is used once to render Greek *soudarion* G5051 (from Lat. *sudarium*, "face-cloth," Acts 19:12). The reference is probably to "sweat rags" tied by PAUL about his head while active as a leather worker; these were brought to sick people in EPHESUS for healing purposes. The Greek term can also refer to the cloth used as a face or head covering (Jn. 11:44; 20:7; KJV, "napkin"), and more generally of any "piece of cloth" (Lk. 19:20). Marriage contracts of the 2nd–3rd centuries include a *soudarion* in the bride's dowry.

M. R. WILSON

handle. This English term, as noun or verb, is used variously in Bible translations to render several words and expressions, such as the Hebrew noun *kātēp* H4190 (1 Ki. 7:34; NRSV, "support"), the Hebrew verb *nûp* H5677 (Isa. 10:15 NRSV; NIV, "use"), and the Greek verb *psēlaphaō* G6027 (Lk. 24:39 KJV; NIV, "touch"). Some passages include the term "handle" as a part of an idiom (Prov. 16:20 KJV; Mk. 12:4 KJV; 2 Tim. 2:15).

handmaid. Term used by the KJV to render words that are better translated "maidservant" (NIV) or "slave-girl" (NRSV) or simply "servant" (cf. Gen. 16:1; Jdg. 19:19; Acts 2:18). These terms are sometimes used by women with reference to themselves as an expression of humility (e.g., Ruth 2:13; 1 Sam. 1:11; Lk. 1:38). See also MAID.

handpike. See ARMOR, ARMS IV.A.

hands, laying on of. A ceremony of ancient origin with different meanings, depending upon its occurrence in various contexts.

I. In relation to sacrificial procedures. The prescriptions of the Mosaic law required worshipers who brought burnt and sin offerings for sacrifice to God to lay their hands upon the animal victims before the latter were killed (Exod. 29:10; Lev. 1:4; 4:4, 24, 29, 33; 8:14; Num. 8:10, 12). It should not be assumed that this symbolic act implied a general transference of guilt from the worshiper to the victims, since this only occurred with the imposition of hands on the scapegoat on the Day of Atonement (Lev. 16:21; see ATONEMENT, DAY OF). Instead, it seems probable that the act of imposition consecrated the victim for its special task.

II. In relation to punishment. A blasphemer had the hands of witnesses laid on him before being taken away to be stoned (Lev. 24:14).

III. In association with blessing. JACOB blessed the children of JOSEPH in this way (Gen. 48:14), as Christ also blessed the children (Matt. 19:15; Mk. 10:13, 16). The invoking of a benediction upon a group involved outstretched arms, such as the priestly benedictions (Lev. 9:22) or the occasion of Christ's ascension (Lk. 24:50).

IV. In relation to healing. In the NT, the concept behind the practice seems to have been that of transferring spiritual vitality to produce a wholeness of personality in the recipient that manifested itself in physical or mental healing. Such instances included the healing of JAIRUS's daughter (Mk. 5:23), where Christ finally "took her by the hand" (5:41); the commission to the disciples that included healing (16:18); the healings occurring at CAPERNAUM (Lk. 4:40), and the restoration of the hopelessly crippled woman (13:13). In the same way, ANANIAS laid hands on PAUL to enable him to recover his sight (Acts 9:12, 17), and Paul in turn healed the father of PUBLIUS in MALTA (28:8), who seems to have been suffering from dysentery and perhaps an accompanying malaria. Healings of a general nature are described as occurring through the "hands of the apostles" (5:12 KJV), that is, through apostolic agency.

V. Gift of the Spirit. The imposition of hands also conveyed the gift of the HOLY SPIRIT (Acts 8:18–19; 19:6). The resultant manifestations of spiritual vitality were often of the external variety, such as the ability to speak in TONGUES. The denominations that justify their postbaptismal confirmation rites by reference to such passages (Heb. 6:2) clearly misunderstand the significance of the practice in the early apostolic age.

VI. Ordination rites. A special blessing was envisaged, as with the ordination of JOSHUA by MOSES as his successor (Num. 27:18, 23; Deut. 34:9). At the ceremony, Joshua was commissioned to his new task and was not given the gifts of leadership or wisdom, which he already possessed. In effect, his ordination attested to his special qualities of spirit, giving him formal authority to exercise the functions of leadership among the Israelites. The same principle applied to the Seven (Acts 6:6) and the commissioning of Paul and BARNABAS (13:3). The imparting of a SPIRITUAL GIFT is implied by Paul (1 Tim. 4:14; 2 Tim. 1:6). Paul's advice to TIMOTHY involved the restoration of penitents to leadership (1 Tim. 5:22).

(See further F. J. Foakes-Jackson and K. Lake, *The Beginnings of Christianity* 5 [1933], 121–40; A. Ehrhardt, *Journal of Ecclesiastical History* 5 [1954]: 125–38; D. Daube, *The New Testament and Rabbinic Judaism* [1956], 224–46; J. K. Parratt in *ExpTim* 80 [1969]: 210–14; D. P. Wright in *JAOS* 106 [1986]: 433–46; *ABD*, 3:47–49.)

R. K. HARRISON

Hanes hay´neez (חֵנֵס *H2805*). An Egyptian city, mentioned with ZOAN (Tanis), in a passage that condemns those who look for protection from PHARAOH (Isa. 30:4). It is probably to be identified with Heracleopolis Magna, capital of the northern part of Upper EGYPT, about 50 mi. S of MEMPHIS and just S of the Fayum. It was a city of great importance in the 25th and 26th dynasties (c. 715–600 B.C.) and during the reign of Psammetichus I (c. 660–610). It has, however, also been identified with Heracleopolis Parva in the eastern NILE delta.

S. BARABAS

hang. Death by hanging is mentioned several times in the Bible (e.g., Esth. 2:23 et al.). In the case of AHITHOPHEL (2 Sam. 17:23) and JUDAS ISCARIOT (Matt. 27:5), it was self-inflicted. In some passages, however, the terms used denote impaling, gibbeting, or CRUCIFIXION. This often was done to the corpse after death (Gen. 40:19, 22; 41:13; Deut. 21:22; Lam. 5:12) but not always. Ezra 6:11 indicates that a living man was to be impaled and left to die. PAUL asserts that Jesus became a curse by being hung upon a tree (Gal. 3:13, quoting from Deut. 21:23), his point being that Jesus bore the accursed death due to sin vicariously, so that those who deserved it could be set free.

W. A. ELWELL

hangings. This English term is used in the KJV and other versions to render two different words in the OT. Hebrew *qelaʿ H7846* (cf. Exod. 27:9–22; 38:9–18; NIV, "curtains") refers to long, heavy drapes intended to serve as walls for the court of the TABERNACLE, which measured 100 by 50 cubits (c. 150 x 75 ft.). They were hung from a rod supported by twenty pillars on the longer sides, ten pillars on the W side, and six pillars on the E side (in which was the gateway, 20 cubits in width). The hangings were to be 5 cubits (7.5 ft.) in height and woven of a finely twisted linen, unspecified as to color.

The other term, *māsāk H5009*, "screen," was a heavy drape used as the door of the outer court (where it measured 20 cubits in width); a similar curtain screened off the entrance into the Holy Place of the tabernacle itself. Both of these were gorgeously embroidered with threads of BLUE,

Reconstruction of curtain surrounding the tabernacle.

(bluish purple, a dye obtained from the murex shell), PURPLE (a deeper purple tinged with dark red, also derived from murex dye but of much higher quality and cost), and SCARLET ("crimson worm," which was a dye obtained from the *Coccus ilicis*, a worm taken from the bark of the ilex tree; its dried body yielded a powder producing a brilliant and indelible scarlet hue). These were embroidered on the finely twisted linen fabric mentioned above. It was suspended from a rod supported by four pillars filleted with silver and based on sockets of bronze (Exod. 27:16–17). The screen at the entrance to the Holy Place was supported by five pillars of ACACIA overlaid with GOLD (26:37), and attached with golden hooks. Possibly it was somewhat wider than the screen to the court. The responsibility for caring for these various hangings and drapes of the tabernacle and its court was entrusted to the Levitical family of GERSHON (Num. 3:25–26). G. L. ARCHER

Haniel han´ee-uhl. KJV alternate form of HANNIEL.

Hannah han´uh (חַנָּה *H2839*, "grace, favor" or "[Yahweh] has been gracious"; see JOANNA, JOHANAN). Favorite wife of ELKANAH and mother of SAMUEL (1 Sam. 1–2). Hannah was childless and was consequently unmercifully taunted by Elkanah's other wife, PENINNAH, who had children. Hannah prayed for a son year after year, vowing that if her prayers were answered she would give him to the Lord. One day, during the annual pilgrimage to SHILOH with Elkanah, as she prayed in the tabernacle the high priest ELI observed her lips moving and mistakenly took her to be a drunken woman. She denied the accusation and explained to him that she had been silently praying for a son.

In due time Hannah bore a son and named him Samuel. When the boy was weaned, she fulfilled her vow and took him to Shiloh, where she gave him to the Lord. In a beautiful psalm of praise to God (1 Sam. 2:1–10)—which has many echoes both in the Song of DAVID at the end of the books of Samuel (2 Sam. 22) and in the MAGNIFICAT of the Virgin Mary (Lk. 1:46–55; see MARY, MOTHER OF JESUS)—Hannah exulted in the power of Yahweh, who raises up the poor and needy, and casts down the rich. (See J. T. Willis in *CBQ* 35 [1973]: 139–54.) Hannah was in the habit of bringing to Samuel a little robe on her yearly visits to Shiloh. She later became the mother of other sons and daughters. S. BARABAS

Hannathon han´uh-thon (חַנָּתֹן *H2872*, apparently from חֵן *H2834*, "charm, favor"). A town on the N border of the tribal territory of ZEBULUN (Josh. 19:14). Located on a major highway, Hannathon is mentioned both in the TELL EL-AMARNA Tablets (14th cent. B.C.) and in the annals of TIGLATH-PILESER III (747–727 B.C.). It is identified with modern Tell el-Bedeiwiyeh, about 2 mi. W of NAZARETH.

Hanniel han´ee-uhl (חַנִּיאֵל *H2848*, "God was gracious" or "favor of God"). KJV also Haniel (1 Chr. 7:39). **(1)** Son of Ephod; he was a leader from the tribe of MANASSEH, chosen to assist in the distribution of the land (Num. 34:23).

(2) Son of Ulla and descendant of ASHER, included among the "heads of families, choice men, brave warriors and outstanding leaders" (1 Chr. 7:39–40). S. BARABAS

Hanoch hay´nok (חֲנוֹךְ *H2840*, possibly "dedicated" or "initiated" [see ENOCH]; gentilic חֲנֹכִי *H2854*, "Hanochite"). TNIV Hanok. **(1)** Son of MIDIAN and grandson of ABRAHAM by KETURAH (Gen. 25:4; 1 Chr. 1:33 [KJV, "Henoch"]). The name may be related to a location in ARABIA (cf. F. V. Winnett in *Translating and Understanding the Old Testament*, ed. H. T. Frank and W. L. Reed [1970], 192–93; I. Eph‛al, *The Ancient Arabs: Nomads on the Borders of the Fertile Crescent, 9th–5th Centuries B.C.* [1982], 231–33). Because the names of Hanoch and two of his brothers (EPHAH and EPHER) are also borne by men in three Hebrew tribes (respectively Reuben, Judah, and Manasseh) that were geographically close to Midian, some have speculated that certain Midianite clans may have been incorporated in Israel (cf. J. Skinner, *A Critical and Exegetical Commentary on Genesis*, ICC, 2nd ed. [1930], 351).

(2) Eldest son of REUBEN, grandson of JACOB, and ancestor of the Hanochite clan (Gen. 46:9; Exod. 6:14; Num. 26:5; 1 Chr. 5:3).

Hanok hay´nok. TNIV form of HANOCH.

Hanukkah hah′nuh-kuh (חֲנֻכָּה H2853, "dedication"). See DEDICATION, FEAST OF.

Hanun hay′nuhn (חָנוּן H2842, "favored"). **(1)** Son and successor of NAHASH, king of the Ammonites (2 Sam. 10:1–4; 1 Chr. 19:1–6; see AMMON). Upon the death of Nahash, DAVID sent a message of condolence to Hanun. This gesture was misinterpreted, and the messengers were grossly insulted and dishonored. The result was a war that David waged against Hanun, and the Ammonites lost their independence. David appointed the brother of Hanun, SHOBI, in his place (2 Sam. 17:27).

(2) Son of Zalaph; after the return from EXILE, he assisted in repairing the VALLEY GATE in JERUSALEM and about five hundred yards of the wall (Neh. 3:13, 30). According to some scholars, these passages refer to two different men (for a full discussion, see D. V. Edelman in *ABD*, 3:52–54). S. BARABAS

hapax legomenon hah′pahks-luh-gohm′uh-non (ἅπαξ λεγόμενον, "once said"). Pl. *hapax legomena*. This phrase is used with reference to words that occur only once in a specific document or in a larger body of literature. Because surviving Greek literature is extensive, relatively few words in the NT are not attested elsewhere. Ancient Hebrew, however, has survived almost exclusively in the books of the OT, and thus there is a large proportion of Hebrew *hapax legomena*, as well as many terms that occur only two or three times. When there is only one context (or very few) where a word appears, determining its meaning can be difficult. In addition to paying very careful attention to that context, scholars make use of other information, such as the word's likely etymology, cognate terms in related Semitic languages, the rendering of the word in the ancient versions, and interpretative comments in rabbinic literature. (See F. E. Greenspahn, *Hapax Legomena in Biblical Hebrew* [1984].)

Hapharaim haf′uh-ray′im (חֲפָרַיִם H2921, "two pits"). KJV Haphraim (some editions). A town on the frontier of the tribal territory of ISSACHAR, listed after SHUNEM (Josh. 19:19). SHISHAK (c. 918 B.C.) mentions a Hapharaim in his list of conquered towns, but this may be a different location. Biblical Hapharaim has been identified with Khirbet el-Farriyeh (prob. too far W to be included within the boundaries of Issachar), eṭ-Ṭaiyibeh (c. 7 mi. NW of BETH SHAN), and ʿAfulleh (6.5 mi. ENE of MEGIDDO and 2 mi. W of Shunem; see the discussion in Z. Kallai, *Historical Geography of the Bible* [1986], 421–24).

Hapiru. See HABIRU.

happiness. The English terms *happiness* and *happy* are used variously in Bible translations to render several words (see JOY). Of special interest is the Greek noun *makarismos* G3422, which is used only three times in the NT, all by PAUL (Rom. 4:6, 9; Gal. 4:15; the cognate adjective *makarios* G3421, "happy, blessed," occurs frequently, Matt. 5:3 et al.). This noun is most often rendered "blessing" and indicates the state of being happy. In Romans, Paul describes happiness as the state of the just: "In the same sense David speaks of the happiness of the man whom God 'counts' as just … 'Happy are they', he says, 'whose lawless deeds are forgiven … happy is the man whose sins the Lord does not count against him'" (Rom. 4:6–8 NEB). Nor is being a Jew a sole requisite for "this happiness," as seen in ABRAHAM's righteousness by faith (v. 9). The other use of "happiness" is that of an emotional experience of delight or joy in the presence of a person loved, as the Galatians' happiness in having Paul with them (Gal. 4:15). See also BEATITUDES; BLESSEDNESS. G. B. FUNDERBURK

Happizzez hap′uh-zez (הַפִּצֵּץ H2204, apparently piel form of פָּצַץ H7207 [polel, "to shatter"] with definite article). The leader of a priestly family whom DAVID appointed by lot as the head of the eighteenth division for temple duties (1 Chr. 24:15; KJV, "Aphses"). The name Happizzez may be a clan designation, possibly connected with the town of BETH PAZZEZ.

Happuch. See KEREN-HAPPUCH.

Hara hair′uh (הָרָא H2217, derivation uncertain, perhaps related to הַר H2215, "mountain"). One of the places to which TIGLATH-PILESER, the king of Assyria, exiled the tribes of Reuben, Gad, and half of Manasseh in 734–732 B.C. (1 Chr. 5:26). It is mentioned along with HALAH, HABOR, and the river Gozan—all places in N Mesopotamia. Several identifications have been proposed (cf. *ABD*, 3:57), but the name Hara is omitted in the Septuagint, and it is also missing in the Hebrew text of the parallel passages (2 Ki. 17:6; 18:11), which instead have "the towns [ʿārê] of the Medes" (LXX, *orē*, apparently reading Heb. *hārê*, "mountains"). Many scholars believe that the text in Chronicles is corrupt, and several emendations have been suggested. S. BARABAS

Haradah huh-ray′duh (חֲרָדָה *H3011*, "[place of] fear"). A camping station in the wilderness journeys of the Israelites (Num. 33:24–25). The name suggests that some otherwise unknown incident here may have caused anxiety among the people. It was located between Mount Shepher and Makheloth, but none of these sites can be identified.

Haran (person) hair′uhn (הָרָן *H2237*, possibly "mountaineer" [if derived from הַר *H2215*] or "sanctuary" [if related to a South Arabian name]; the place name Haran renders a different Hebrew word). **(1)** Son of TERAH, brother of ABRAHAM and NAHOR, and father of LOT and two daughters, Milcah and Iscah (Gen. 11:26–31). Haran died in UR before his father Terah set out to go to CANAAN.

(2) Son of CALEB by his concubine Ephah, included in the genealogy of JUDAH (1 Chr. 2:46).

(3) Son of SHIMEI and descendant of GERSHON; he was one of the Levites who headed the families of LADAN (1 Chr. 23:9).

Haran (place) hay′ruhn (חָרָן *H3059*, from Akk. *ḥarrānu*, "road" [i.e., crossroads]; Χαρράν *G5924*). Also Harran; KJV NT Charran. A city of MESOPOTAMIA situated c. 24 mi. SE of Urfa (EDESSA) on the river Balikh, a tributary of the EUPHRATES. It was an important commercial center because of its location on one of the main trade routes between Babylonia and the Mediterranean: CARCHEMISH lay some 50 mi. W, and GOZAN about the same distance E. The place name Haran is to be distinguished from HARAN (PERSON), which renders a different Hebrew word.

Excavations show that Haran flourished from at least the 3rd millennium B.C. It was conquered by SHALMANESER I in the 13th cent. B.C., and is mentioned by TIGLATH-PILESER I (c. 1115 B.C.) in a prism inscription. For a long time it was an Assyrian provincial capital, but was destroyed because of a rebellion in 763 (an event apparently referred to in 2 Ki. 19:12). It was restored by SARGON II. The last king of Assyria, Ashur-urballit, made Haran his capital in 612, after the destruction of NINEVEH by the Babylonians, but he was forced to abandon the city in 610 (see ASSYRIA AND BABYLONIA). In ancient times, and until about the 11th cent. A.D., Haran was the center of various forms of the worship of Sin, the moon-god. In Hellenistic and Roman times it was known as Carrhae. The city was then successively ruled by Nestorian Christians, Moslems, and Crusaders; today it retains the name Harran as a small Arab village in SE Turkey.

Haran was the city in which TERAH and ABRAHAM settled after leaving UR (Gen. 11:31–32), and from which Abraham set out when he journeyed to CANAAN (12:1). NAHOR, Abraham's brother, settled in Haran, and hence it is called the "city of Nahor" in the story of ISAAC and JACOB (24:10; 27:43). LABAN, the kinsman of Isaac and Jacob, lived in Haran, and it was there that Jacob stayed during his long sojourn in Mesopotamia (28:10; 29:4). Jacob fled to Haran to escape ESAU's anger (27:43), and there he met his brides (29:10–11). Ezekiel speaks of the merchants of Haran as trading with

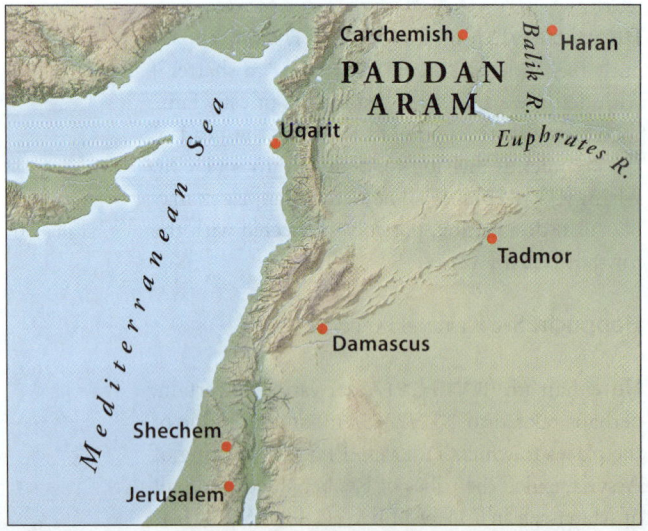

Haran.

Beehive homes from the early part of the 20th cent. now cover the village of Haran, a region once inhabited by Abraham and his ancestors. (View to the S.)

Tyre (Ezek. 27:23). (See S. Lloyd and W. Brice in *Anatolian Studies* 1 [1951]: 77–111; J. N. Postgate, "Ḫarrān," *Reallexikon der Assyriologie* 4 [1975]: 122–25; O. R. Gurney in *Ancient Anatolia*, ed. R. Matthews [1998], 163–76.)   S. Barabas

Hararite hair′uh-rīt (הֲרָרִי *H2240* [with orthographic variations], possibly "mountain dweller"). An epithet applied to two (or three) of David's heroes. Shammah son of Agee, who was one of the Three, achieved a great victory over the Philistines (2 Sam. 23:11). His name appears also in the list of the Thirty, but as the father of a certain Jonathan (2 Sam. 23:32b–33a [following the Lucianic mss of the lxx]; 1 Chr. 11:34 has Shagee instead of Shammah). Another Hararite included in the list of the Thirty is Ahiam son of Sharar (2 Sam. 23:33b; 1 Chr. 11:35 has "Ahiam son of Sacar"). The term Hararite may refer to a clan or, more probably, a location; if the latter, it may indicate a specific town (one suggestion is Aroer) or some general mountainous area (cf. English *hillbilly*).   S. Barabas

Harbona hahr-boh′nuh (חַרְבוֹנָא *H3002* and חַרְבוֹנָה *H3003*, from Pers. *kherbân*, "donkey driver"). KJV also Harbonah. One of the seven eunuchs sent by Ahasuerus king of Persia (i.e., Xerxes, who reigned 486–465 B.C.), to bring Queen Vashti to a royal feast (Esth. 1:10). It was Harbona who later suggested that Haman be hanged on the same gallows that Haman himself had erected for Mordecai (7:9).

harbor. The sheltered part of a body of water. The term is used to render Hebrew *mēzaḥ H4651* (Isa. 23:10, in an oracle concerning Tyre and Tarshish) and Greek *limēn G3348* (Acts 27:12, with reference to Fair Havens; in the NIV and other versions, the rendering "ports" in v. 2 is a contextual translation of the Greek word for "places").

hardening, spiritual. Both the OT and the NT use a variety of terms in several combinations to express the idea of stubborn human resistance to God. The Hebrew verb *qāšâ H7996* ("to be heavy, hard") and its cognate adjective can be used with spirit (e.g., Deut. 2:30, parallel verb *ʾāmēṣ H599*, "be strong"), neck (2 Chr. 30:8; see stiff-necked), heart (Exod. 7:3), face (Ezek. 2:4, Heb.), and forehead (Ezek. 3:7 NRSV; here coupled with the adjective *ḥāzāq H2617*, "firm, hard"), each combination standing for the opposition of the entire self.

Of special interest are the statements that God hardened Pharaoh's heart (Exod. 7:3; 10:1 [here *kābēd H3877*]; 14:4) and that Pharaoh hardened his own heart (Exod. 9:34–35; 13:15). Paul appeals to the SOVEREIGNTY OF GOD in discussing Pharaoh (Rom. 9:18, Gk. verb *sklērynō G5020*), although the factor of human responsibility through repeated warnings is clearly involved (cf. 1 Sam. 6:6; Rom. 1:21–25). Hardening one's heart brings punishment (Prov. 29:1), as is evident in Israel's resistance at MERIBAH (Ps. 95:8). Refusal to listen, to obey, or to be thankful characterize the hardened heart, and Israel is portrayed as a prime example of this condition (2 Ki. 17:14; Neh. 9:16–17; Heb. 3:8).

The disciples' hearts were said to be hardened or dull (Gk. *pōroō G4800*) when they failed to understand the miracle of the loaves (Mk. 6:52; 8:17). Gentile unbelievers are alienated from God because of their ignorance and hardness of heart (Eph. 4:18, noun *pōrōsis G4801*). With reference to Israel, PAUL states that while the elect obtained salvation, "the others were hardened" (Rom. 11:7; cf. v. 25; see ELECTION). Here the individuals themselves are described as being hardened, but elsewhere he says that "their minds were made dull" (2 Cor. 3:14).

H. M. WOLF

hare. A mammal of the genus *Lepus* (the most common in Palestine being *L. syriacus*), similar to the rabbit, but with longer ears and legs. The hare is mentioned in the Bible (Heb. *ʾarnebet H817*) only in two lists of unclean animals that chew the cud but do not have a split hoof (Lev. 11:6; Deut. 14:7; see UNCLEANNESS). This context of the only two occurrences was once considered contradictory, but recent work confirms the apparently strange statement. Hares, like rabbits, are now known to practice "refection": at certain times of the day, when the hare is resting, it passes droppings of different texture, which it at once eats. Thus the hare appears to be chewing without taking fresh greens into its mouth. On its first passage through the gut, indigestible vegetable matter is acted on by bacteria and can be better assimilated the second time through. Almost the same principle is involved as in chewing the cud. Hares, somewhat like the European hare or American jack rabbit (which is a true hare) but rather smaller, are found in many parts of Palestine. (See *FFB*, 39–40.)

G. S. CANSDALE

Harel hair′uhl. See ARIEL.

harem. This English term (from Arabic *ḥarim*, "forbidden") denotes the building assigned to the wives and concubines of one man; the word often refers to the women themselves. Modern versions use it as the rendering of the Hebrew phrase, *bêt-hannāšîm*, "house of the women" (Esth. 2:3, 9, 11, 13–14; the NIV uses it also in vv. 8 and 15, where the Heb. simply has *hannāšîm*, "the women"). In addition, it is possible that the expression *šiddâ wĕšiddôt*, which occurs only in Eccl. 2:8 and which perhaps means literally, "a mistress and mistresses," refers to a harem (so NIV; see discussion in *HALOT*, 1:354).

Hareph hair′if (חָרֵף *H3073*, possibly "sharp, shrewd," others "scorn[ful]" or "harvest-time, autumn" [i.e., mature]; cf. HARIPH and HARUPHITE). Son of HUR, descendant of CALEB, and "father" (i.e., founder or ruler) of BETH GADER; listed in the genealogy of JUDAH (1 Chr. 2:51).

Hareshah. See TEL HARSHA.

Hareth hair′eth. KJV form of HERETH.

Harhaiah hahr-hay′yuh (חַרְהֲיָה *H3015* [some edd., חַרְחֲיָה], derivation unknown). Father of Uzziel; the latter was one of the goldsmiths who helped to repair the walls of Jerusalem after the EXILE (Neh. 3:8). Some scholars emend the text to read "Uzziel, a son [i.e., member] of the guild [*ḥeber*] of the goldsmiths."

Harhas hahr′has (חַרְחַס *H3030*, derivation unknown). Father of Tikvah and grandfather of Shallum; the latter was "keeper of the wardrobe" and the husband of HULDAH the prophetess (2 Ki. 22:14). The name is given as HASRAH (and father of Tokhath) in the parallel passage (2 Chr. 34:22).

Har-heres. See HERES #1.

Harhur hahr′huhr (חַרְחוּר *H3028*, possibly "raven" or "[born during mother's] fever"). Ancestor of a family of temple servants (NETHINIM) who returned after the EXILE (Ezra 2:51; Neh. 7:53;

this name is missing in the parallel list, 1 Esd. 5:31 [perhaps replaced by Asur]).

Harim hair′im (חָרִם H3053, "consecrated" [see DEVOTED]). **(1)** The leader of a priestly family whom DAVID appointed by lot as the head of the third division for duties in the sanctuary (1 Chr. 24:8). He is possibly the same priest listed as the ancestor of a family of 1,017 people that returned from the Babylonian captivity with ZERUBBABEL (Ezra 2:39; Neh. 7:42; cf. 1 Esd. 5:25 [KJV, "Carme"; NRSV, "Charme"]), some of whom had married foreign wives and agreed to divorce them (Ezra 10:21). Perhaps this is the same priestly family (or a member of it also named Harim) that joined in sealing the covenant of NEHEMIAH (Neh. 10:5). However, many scholars link this passage with what may be a different priestly family whose leader was Adna (Neh. 12:15; the name REHUM in v. 3 may be a variant of Harim).

(2) Ancestor of a family of 320 people that returned from the Babylonian captivity with Zerubbabel (Ezra 2:32; Neh. 7:35). Because this list includes many geographic names, Harim here may refer to a town. Some members of this family had married foreign wives and agreed to divorce them (Ezra 10:31; called "Annan" [KJV, "Annas"] in 1 Esd. 9:32). The same family (or a member of it also named Harim) joined in sealing the covenant of NEHEMIAH (Neh. 10:27). Malkijah, a descendant of this family (or the son of the individual Harim) helped repair a section of the wall of JERUSALEM as well as the Tower of the OVENS (Neh. 3:11).

It should be noted that many scholars identify four or more different individuals (or families) by the name of Harim (cf. *ABD*, 3:60).

Hariph hair′if (חָרִיף H3040, "sharp, brisk" or "[born at] harvest-time"; cf. HAREPH, HARUPHITE). Ancestor of a family of 112 members that returned from exile with ZERUBBABEL (Neh. 7:24; called "Jorah" in Ezra 2:18 and "Arsiphurith" in 1 Esd. 5:16). The same family (or a member of it also named Hariph) joined in sealing the covenant of NEHEMIAH (Neh. 10:19).

harlot. See PROSTITUTION.

Har-magedon hahr′muh-ged′uhn. See ARMAGEDDON.

Harmon hahr′muhn (הַרְמוֹן H2236, meaning unknown). A city or region to which the powerful and unjust women of SAMARIA were to be exiled (Amos 4:3; KJV, "the palace"). No place with this name is known, and the text is widely thought to be corrupt (Gk. variants include "the mountain Remman [Rimmon]," "mount Hermon," and even "Armenia" [so Symmachus; cf. Targum and Peshitta]). Many emendations have been proposed (cf. NIV mg., "O mountain of oppression"), but none has been generally accepted.

harmony of the Gospels. An edition of the GOSPELS that seeks to show the agreement or coherence among them. Gospel harmonies may take two forms: (1) works that interweave material from all four Gospels into one chronological narrative, and (2) arrangements ("synopses") of the Gospels, especially the synoptics, in parallel columns according to some chronological scheme. The earliest harmony was Tatian's DIATESSARON, produced c. A.D. 170. Another early effort was that of an Alexandrian named Ammonius (3rd cent.), whose work is known only from citations in EUSEBIUS. The Gospels were sometimes commented on in harmonistic fashion, for example, by AUGUSTINE in his *De consensu evangelistarum libri quattuor* (c. A.D. 400).

Many new harmonies began to appear in the 16th cent. (e.g., by the German theologian A. Osiander in 1537), but the first modern work of this type, which did not necessarily assume agreement among the Gospels, was J. J. Griesbach's *Synopsis evangeliorum* (1776). During the 19th cent., similar synopses were edited by various prominent scholars, such as G. M. de Wette (1818), J. H. Friedlieb (1847), and C. von Tischendorf (1851). A. Huck's *Synopse der drei ersten Evangelien*, which first appeared in 1892 (thoroughly revised by H. Greeven, *Synopsis of the First Three Gospels: With the Addition of the Johannine Parallels*, 13th ed. [1981]) became the most widely used in modern times until the publication of *Synopsis quattuor evangeliorum* by K. Aland (15 ed., 2005), which includes material from the apocryphal and patristic literature.

The bulkier two-volume work by R. W. Funk, *New Gospel Parallels* (1985), presents sequentially each Gospel in its entirety, along with its parallels. Also distinctive in their approach are the following: R. J. Swanson, *The Horizontal Line Synopsis of the Gospels* (1975); J. B. Orchard, *A Synopsis of the Four Gospels in Greek, Arranged according to the Two-Gospel Hypothesis* (1983), and M. É. Boismard and A. Lamouille, *Synopsis graeca quattuor evangeliorum* (1986; cf. the review by J. S. Kloppenborg in *CBQ* 50 [1988]: 707–9). W. WHITE, JR.

Harnepher hahr´nuh-fuhr (חַרְנֶפֶר H3062, "Horus [an Egyptian deity] is good"). Son (or descendant) of Zophah, included in the genealogy of ASHER (1 Chr. 7:36). The name Harnepher, however, may be a clan designation or even a place name (some have speculated that it was derived from an Egyptian outpost in Palestine). It has been suggested that the genealogy was composed on the basis of taxation lists and that the names represent geographical areas inhabited by Asherite clans.

harness. This English term, as noun or verb, is used a few times in Bible translations to render several Hebrew words, such as ʾāsar H673, "tie up" (Jer. 46:4; used of hitching up chariots, 1 Ki. 18:44, and yoking cows, 1 Sam. 6:7). The KJV also uses this English word in its older sense of "armor" (1 Ki. 22:34; 2 Chr. 18:33).

Harod hair´uhd (חֲרֹד H3008, "trembling"; gentilic חֲרֹדִי H3012, "Harodite"). **(1)** A spring at which

The Harod Spring at the base of Mount Gilboa.

GIDEON encamped with his men while preparing for battle with the Midianites (Jdg. 7:1). Some have speculated that SAUL encamped at this spring (1 Sam. 29:1, "the spring in Jezreel") before his fatal battle with the PHILISTINES (cf. 31:1). Harod is generally identified with ʿEin Jalud, 9 mi. WNW of BETH SHAN.

(2) The epithet Harodite is applied to two of DAVID's mighty warriors, Shammah and Elika (2 Sam. 23:25; cf. 1 Chr. 11:27, "Shammoth the Harorite"). Some associate this name with #1 above, but many scholars believe it refers to an unrelated town also named Harod, possibly to be identified with modern Khirbet el-Ḥaredhan, c. 5 mi. SE of JERUSALEM.

Haroeh huh-roh´uh (הָרֹאֶה H2218, "the seer"). Son (or descendant) of SHOBAL, included in the genealogy of CALEB (1 Chr. 2:52); probably the same as REAIAH (1 Chr. 4:2).

Harorite hay´roh-rīt (הֲרוֹרִי H2229). Epithet applied to Shammoth, one of DAVID's mighty warriors (1 Chr. 11:27); probably the same as SHAMMAH the Harodite. See HAROD.

Harosheth Haggoyim huh-roh´shith-huh-goi´im (חֲרֹשֶׁת הַגּוֹיִם H3099, "woodland [*or* plantations] of the nations"). A Canaanite town and the home of SISERA, from which he led his forces against DEBORAH and BARAK (Jdg. 4:13), and to which his army fled after his defeat (v. 16). Some have identified it with Muḥrashti (a town in the Plain of SHARON mentioned in the TELL EL-AMARNA letters), others with modern Khirbet el-Ḥarithiyeh (c. 14 mi. SSE of Acco) or such nearby sites as Tell ʿAmr and Tell el-Harbaj. Still others think Harosheth Haggoyim was not a town at all but, as its name suggests, a general woodland region in GALILEE of the Gentiles (see Y. Aharoni, *The Land of the Bible: A Historical Geography*, rev. ed. [1979], 221) or a district in JEZREEL inhabited by foreigners (see *SacBr*, 150–51).

harp. See MUSIC, MUSICAL INSTRUMENTS IV.D.

harpoon. This English term is used to render Hebrew *śukkâ* H8496, which occurs only once (Job 41:7; KJV, "barbed irons") parallel to "fishing spears"; both weapons are said to be futile in the battle with LEVIATHAN.

Harran. See HARAN.

harrow. This English term, as a noun (referring to a heavy farm implement with sharp teeth or disks), is used by the KJV to render Hebrew *ḥāriṣ H3044* ("hoe, pick"), which occurs twice (2 Sam. 12:31; 1 Chr. 20:3). The verb *harrow* ("to break up and level the soil with a harrow") occurs as the rendering of *śādad H8440* (piel stem), a term of uncertain meaning, but clearly referring to some process of treating the soil (Job 39:10 KJV and NRSV [NIV, "till"]; Isa. 28:24 NRSV and NIV [KJV, "break the clods"]; Hos. 10:11 NRSV [KJV, "break his clods"; NIV, "break up the ground"]). The passage in Isaiah mentions "opening" the ground before harrowing and then leveling the face of it (Isa. 28:24–25). Perhaps the Hebrew term refers to pulling branches behind the PLOW to cover the seed uniformly. Some suggest that it meant cross plowing or the making of furrows. No tool resembling a harrow is known from Egypt or ancient Palestine.   H. M. WOLF

Harsha hahr′shuh (חַרְשָׁא *H3095*, possibly "deaf" or "mute"). Ancestor of a family of temple servants (NETHINIM) who returned from the EXILE (Ezra 2:52; Neh. 7:54; apparently called "Charea" in the parallel list, 1 Esd. 5:32).

Harsha, Tel. See TEL HARSHA.

hart. This English word is now a semitechnical term for the male of some DEER, usually the red deer, especially after the fifth year (the female, usually from the third year, is known as HIND). The KJV uses "hart" consistently as the rendering of Hebrew *ʾayyāl H385* (Deut. 12:15 et al.), but modern versions prefer "deer."   G. S. CANSDALE

Harum hair′uhm (חָרֻם *H2227*). Father of Aharhel and a descendant of JUDAH through ASHHUR (1 Chr. 4:8; cf. v. 5).

Harumaph huh-roo′maf (חֲרוּמַף *H3018*, "split nose" [cf. Lev. 21:18 and see FLAT NOSE]). Father of Jedaiah; the latter helped in repairing the walls of JERUSALEM in the time of NEHEMIAH (Neh. 3:10).

Haruphite huh-roo′fit (חֲרוּפִי *H3020*; cf. HAREPH, HARIPH). Epithet applied to Shephatiah, one of the warriors from BENJAMIN who joined DAVID at ZIKLAG (1 Chr. 12:5; *Ketib*, "Hariphite"). It is not clear whether the term indicates geographic origin or connection to a clan.

Haruz hair′uhz (חָרוּץ *H3027*, possibly "gold" or "diligent"). Father of MESHULLEMETH, who was the mother of AMON, king of Judah (2 Ki. 21:19). The name may be either Phoenician or Arabic (see J. A. Montgomery, *A Critical and Exegetical Commentary on the Book of Kings*, ICC [1951], 522).

harvest. The ingathering of crops was a vital part of Palestine's agrarian culture. BARLEY harvest began in mid-April along the JORDAN and about a month later in the high areas. The SICKLE was the major instrument used. During harvest time, the Jordan overflowed its banks (Josh. 3:15). Two weeks later, the WHEAT harvest began, lasting about seven weeks (Ruth 2:23). Summer fruits, such as FIGS and grapes (see VINE), were harvested in August and September. From September through the middle of November, OLIVES were gathered by beating the trees with sticks (Deut. 24:20). The drying of FLAX stalks took place in March and April (Josh. 2:6). The Gezer CALENDAR of the 10th cent. B.C. supplies valuable information concerning the dating of various harvests (see AGRICULTURE V).

The Mosaic law gave clear instructions requiring reapers to leave crops in areas of the field so that the poor and sojourners might follow them (Lev. 19:9; Ruth 2:15–16). Harvest time was characterized by intense heat, when a mist-cloud brought welcome relief (Prov. 25:13; Isa. 18:4). The joy in harvest was a highlight of the year (Isa. 9:3).

Several moral teachings are related to sowing and reaping. The law of reaping what one sows, whether righteousness (Hos. 10:12) or wickedness (Prov. 22:8), is given repeatedly; Gal. 6:7 echoes this law. Harvest is a picture of the blessing upon the returning captivity of Judah (Hos. 6:11). More frequently, the wielding of the sickle in harvest portrays the judgment upon the nations of the world

Palestinian villagers harvest wheat in the Jezreel Valley (photo taken in 1905).

(Joel 3:13). The NT repeats this image of judgment as an angel is told, "Take your sickle and reap, because the time to reap has come, for the harvest of the earth is ripe" (Rev. 14:15).

Jesus compares the harvest to the KINGDOM OF GOD, which grows by stages (Mk. 4:29). The separation of the weeds and wheat will occur at the "harvest" of the kingdom (Matt. 13:30). Christ used the harvest to represent a world of souls that is ready to be reached with the gospel. The fields are ready to be harvested, "but the workers are few" (Matt. 9:37). (See G. E. Wright, *Biblical Archaeology* [1962], 183–87.)   H. M. WOLF

Hasadiah has′uh-di′uh (חֲסַדְיָה *H2878*, "Yahweh is faithful"). **(1)** Son of ZERUBBABEL and descendant of DAVID through SOLOMON (1 Chr. 3:20), possibly born in Palestine (see HASHUBAH).

(2) Son of Hilkiah and ancestor of BARUCH (Bar. 1:1; KJV, "Asadias").

Hasenuah. KJV form of HASSENUAH.

Hashabiah hash′uh-bi′uh (חֲשַׁבְיָה *H3116*, "Yahweh has taken account"; cf. also HASHABNAH and HASHABNEIAH). **(1)** Son of Amaziah, descendant of MERARI, and ancestor of ETHAN, who was a Levite musician in the time of DAVID (1 Chr. 6:45).

(2) Son of JEDUTHUN, father of Azrikam, ancestor of Shemaiah, and a Levite musician (1 Chr. 9:14; 25:3, 19; Neh. 11:15). This Hashabiah was the head of the twelfth company of temple musicians appointed by lot under David.

(3) A ruler from HEBRON in the time of David who, along with his relatives, was "responsible in Israel west of the Jordan for all the work of the LORD and for the king's service" (1 Chr. 26:30).

(4) Son of Kemuel and an officer over the tribe of LEVI under King David (1 Chr. 27:17).

(5) A leader of the Levites in the reign of JOSIAH who gave liberally toward the sacrifices (2 Chr. 35:9; 1 Esd. 1:9 [KJV, "Assabias"]).

(6) A prominent Levite who returned from the EXILE with EZRA; he is usually associated with SHEREBIAH (Ezra 8:19; Neh. 12:24; 1 Esd. 8:48 [KJV, "Asebia"]). He was also one of the priests entrusted with the temple treasures that were brought to Jerusalem (Ezra 8:24; 1 Esd. 8:54 [KJV, "Assanias"]). Moreover, this Hashabiah may have been the same one who as "ruler of half the district of Keilah" helped to repair the wall (Neh. 3:17) and who affixed his seal to the covenant of NEHEMIAH (10:11).

(7) One of the descendants of PAROSH who agreed to divorce their foreign wives (Ezra 10:25 NRSV, following the LXX [MT, "Malkijah"]; cf. 1 Esd. 9:26, "Asibias"). See MALKIJAH ##4–6.

(8) Son of Mattaniah, descendant of Asaph, and grandfather of Uzzi; the latter was chief officer of the Levites (Neh. 11:22).

(9) Head of the priestly house of Hilkiah in the time of Joiakim the high priest (Neh. 12:21).

Hashabnah huh-shab′nuh (חֲשַׁבְנָה H3118, possibly short form of Hashabneiah, "Yahweh has taken account of me"; cf. also Hashabiah). One of the leaders of the Israelites who sealed the covenant under Nehemiah (Neh. 10:25).

Hashabneiah hash′uhb-nee′yah (חֲשַׁבְנְיָה H3119, "Yahweh has taken account of me"; cf. Hashabiah and Hashabnah). KJV Hashabniah. **(1)** Father of Hattush; the latter helped rebuild the walls of Jerusalem in the time of Nehemiah (Neh. 3:10).

(2) One of the Levites who offered prayer in the ceremonies that preceded the sealing of the covenant (Neh. 9:5). Some scholars identify him with Hashabiah #6.   S. Barabas

Hashabniah hash′uhb-ni′uh. KJV form of Hashabneiah.

Hashbaddanah hash-bad′uh-nuh (חַשְׁבַּדָּנָה H3111, derivation uncertain). KJV Hashbadana. One of the prominent men who stood near Ezra when the law was read at the great assembly (Neh. 8:4; called "Nabariah" [KJV, "Nabarias"] in the parallel, 1 Esd. 9:44).

Hashem hay′shim (הָשֵׁם H2244). A Gizonite whose sons are included among David's mighty men (1 Chr. 11:34; the expression *bĕnê hāšēm* could be read as "the sons of the name," with the possible meaning, "famous men"). Many scholars, however, emend the text by omitting "the sons of" (the previous name ends with the consonants *bny*; cf. also LXX and NRSV) and changing "Hashem" to "Jashen" (cf. 2 Sam. 23:32).

Hashmonah hash-moh′nuh (חַשְׁמֹנָה H3135, derivation uncertain). A place at which the Israelites stopped during their wilderness journey (Num. 33:29–30). It was evidently located between Mithcah and Moseroth, but the site is unknown.

Hashub. KJV alternate form of Hasshub.

Hashubah huh-shoo′buh (חֲשֻׁבָה H3112, possibly "considered [by Yahweh]" or "[highly] esteemed"; cf. Hashabiah). Son of Zerubbabel and descendant of David through Solomon (1 Chr. 3:20). Some scholars suggest that the word is not a name and emend the text to "after his return" (*ʾaḥărê šûbô*), indicating that the subsequent names refer to Zerubbabel's sons born in Palestine.

Hashum hay′shuhm (חָשֻׁם H3130, "broad nose"). **(1)** Son of Dan (Gen. 46:23 NRSV, following LXX; MT, Hushim; see also Shuham).

(2) Ancestor of a family of 223 (or 328) members who returned from the exile (Ezra 2:19; Neh. 7:22). Some members of this family had married foreign wives and agreed to divorce them (Ezra 10:33; 1 Esd. 9:33 [KJV, "Asom"]).

(3) One of the prominent men who stood near Ezra when the law was read at the great assembly (Neh. 8:4; called "Lothasubus" in the parallel, 1 Esd. 9:44). He may be the same Hashum who affixed his seal to the covenant (Neh. 10:18).

Hashupha. KJV alternate form of Hasupha.

Hasideans, Hasidim has′uh-dee′uhns, has′uh-dim (Ἀσιδαῖοι or Ἀσιδαίοι, from חֲסִידִים [pl. of חָסִיד H2883], "faithful ones, devout ones"). KJV Assideans. The term *Hasideans*—which occurs only three times, all of them in 1–2 Maccabees—refers to a group of very devout, orthodox Jews in the 2nd cent. B.C. who took part with the Maccabeans in the revolt against Antiochus Epiphanes. When Mattathias and his followers decided to fight the Seleucid ruler, "there united with them a company of Hasideans, mighty warriors of Israel, all who offered themselves willingly for the law" (1 Macc. 2:42; cf. also 7:13). They must have existed as a party before the days of the Maccabees, but nothing is said of their origin. They undoubtedly shared the beliefs and practice of other pious Jews of the time (cf. 1 Macc. 1:63; 2:34; 2 Macc. 6:18–20; Jdt. 12:2; Jos. *Ant.* 14.4.3).

After the death of Antiochus, "all the lawless and the ungodly of Israel … led by Alcimus, who wanted to be high priest" (1 Macc. 7:5), complained to the new king, DEMETRIUS, that Judas MACCABEE and his brothers had brought ruin on the land. Demetrius made ALCIMUS high priest and sent him with BACCHIDES to take vengeance, but the "Hasideans were first among the Israelites to seek peace" (7:13). Although Alcimus promised not to harm them, "he seized sixty of them and killed them in one day, in accordance with the word that was written, 'The flesh of your faithful ones [Gk. *hosios* ὅσιος, "pure, holy," a word that commonly renders Heb. *ḥāsîd*] and their blood they poured out all around Jerusalem, and there was no one to bury them'" (7:16–17, quoting Ps. 79:2–3). Elsewhere we read that, at a later time, the former high priest Alcimus reported to Demetrius: "Those of the Jews who are called Hasideans, whose leader is Judas Maccabeus, are keeping up war and stirring up sedition, and will not let the kingdom attain tranquility" (2 Macc. 14:6; quotations from NRSV).

After the revolt, the Maccabean leaders (who belonged to the priestly line but were not descendants of ZADOK) laid claim to the high priesthood, and most scholars believe that the Hasidim broke with them over this issue (see HASMONEANS). It is also widely thought that the later PHARISEES and possibly the ESSENES (whose name is perhaps derived from *ḥāsîd*) developed out of two branches of the Hasidim. (Various views are represented by the following: *HJP*, rev. ed. [1973–87], 1:145, 157; 2:400–401; P. Davies in *JJS* 28 [1977]: 127–40; R. T. Beckwith in *RevQ* 11, no. 41 [Oct. 1982]: 3–46; J. Kampen, *The Hasideans and the Origin of Pharisaism: A Study in 1 and 2 Maccabees* [1988].)

The modern Hasidim (Chasidim) constitute a Jewish sect founded by Baal Shem Tov (1698–1760) in eastern Europe. He was famed as a miracle worker and healer, and was a pious character and mystic. His teaching developed in opposition to the unbending rationalism of the TALMUD and was characterized by a joyous worship of God, religious frenzy, emotional exaltation in prayer, and communion with God through ecstasy. Learning, he taught, is not necessary to gain favor with God, for God hears the joyous prayers of the unschooled just as much as those of the learned.

The leaders of the modern Hasidim are called Zaddikim (Tzadikim). They were thought to have achieved so holy a state that they could serve as mediators between God and the common people. Their doctrines spread with great rapidity among the poor and uneducated masses, and aroused a great deal of opposition among the Talmudists, who in 1781 pronounced it a heresy. Eventually the Hasidim separated from the rest of Judaism as a distinct sect. During the first half of the 19th cent., Hasidism won over nearly half of all the Jews of the world, but with the rise of the Enlightenment in Europe its power waned. It continued, however, as a living force in eastern Europe until the Second World War. In attenuated form it still continues in Palestine, America, and other lands to which it was transplanted. In modern times it was popularized by Martin Buber. (See G. Scholem, *Major Trends in Jewish Mysticism* [1941], chs. 3 and 9; M. L. Diamond, *Martin Buber—Jewish Existentialist* [1960], 110–37; J. R. Mintz, *Hasidic People: A Place in the New World* [1992]; T. Rabinovicz, ed., *The Encyclopedia of Hasidism* [1996].)   S. BARABAS

Hasidim. See HASIDEANS, HASIDIM.

Hasmonean haz´muh-nee´uhn (from Ἀσαμοναῖος). Also Asmonaean. Name applied to a dynasty of Jewish high priests and kings, beginning with SIMON MACCABEE (who achieved political independence in 142 B.C.) and ending with the Roman occupation of Judea (63 B.C.).

   I. The Jewish war of independence
   II. The Hasmonean dynasty
      A. John Hyrcanus
      B. Aristobulus
      C. Alexander Jannaeus
      D. Alexandra
      E. Hyrcanus II
      F. Aristobulus II
   III. The intervention of the Romans

I. The Jewish war of independence. In the early days of the Maccabean Revolt, the Syrians (Seleucids) underestimated the strength of the Maccabees. With major problems in the eastern part of their empire, the Syrians were content to send minor generals and small detachments to deal with the rebellious Jews. The revolt, however, had wide popular support, with the result that Judas MACCABEE and his brothers posed a serious challenge to Syrian rule. One after another of the Syrian armies sent against the Jews suffered defeat. Judas killed the general APOLLONIUS, and another, named SERON, was routed at BETH HORON.

ANTIOCHUS Epiphanes, the Seleucid emperor, realized that he had a full-scale revolt in Judea—but his attention was diverted by another rebellion among the PARTHIANS, successors to the old Persian empire. Antiochus personally moved eastward to Parthia, leaving his general LYSIAS to handle the rebellious Jews. Lysias gathered an army of Syrians, Hellenistically minded Jews (see HELLENISM), and volunteers from neighboring countries to defeat the Jewish rebels. Nicanor, Gorgias, and Ptolemy, subordinates of Lysias, were in charge of the engagement. Judas, however, by a surprise night attack, annihilated the Syrian army and seized enormous stores of booty. This victory, at the town of EMMAUS (166–165 B.C.), opened the road to JERUSALEM for Judas and his followers.

As Judas and his army moved toward Jerusalem, MENELAUS, the high priest who had collaborated with Antiochus, fled. Judas and his followers, subsequently known as the Maccabees, entered Jerusalem and took everything except the fort known as the ACRA. They entered the temple and removed the signs of paganism that had been installed there. The altar dedicated to Jupiter (ZEUS) was destroyed, and a new altar was erected to the God of Israel. The statue of Zeus was ground to dust. Beginning with the twenty-fifth of Kislev (December), they celebrated an eight-day Feast of DEDICATION, known also as Hanukkah and as the Feast of Lights.

For about a year and a half, Judas was master of Judea. The Syrians were awaiting an opportunity to strike back, however, and Judea's neighbors proved sympathetic to the Hellenists. The Syrian general, Lysias, marched against Judea and defeated a Maccabean army at Beth Zechariah near Jerusalem. Lysias then besieged Jerusalem, hoping to starve the Maccabees into submission. During the siege, however, Lysias learned that ANTIOCH OF SYRIA, capital of the empire, was being threatened by a rival, Philip. Anxious to head N, Lysias made an offer of peace to the Jews.

In the name of Syria, Lysias offered to refrain from interference in the internal affairs of Judea. Laws against the observance of Judaism would be repealed. Menelaus would be removed from office, and the high priesthood granted to a milder Hellenist named Eliakim, or ALCIMUS. Lysias promised that Judas and his followers would not be punished. The walls of Jerusalem would be razed, however.

A provisional government in Jerusalem considered the peace terms. This council included Maccabean army officials, respected scribes and elders from the party of the Hasidim (see HASIDEANS), and orthodox Jews who had supported Judas. The promise of religious freedom satisfied a majority of the council. Judas, however, was convinced that the promise was meaningless apart from full political liberty. The appeal of peace won the day, however, and Judas was outvoted. Alcimus was installed as priest. Menelaus was executed. Judas and a few of his followers left the city.

The fears of Judas proved correct, however. Alcimus had a number of the Hasidim, the orthodox party, seized and executed. Many loyal Jews turned to Judas again, and the war was renewed. Difficulties were greater than before, however. Alcimus appealed to Syria for aid, and a sizable army was sent. The hellenizing Jews adopted a more moderate attitude and won over large segments of the followers of Judas. Left with an ill-equipped army of 800 men, Judas bravely met a large Syrian army under NICANOR. Nicanor's Day became the holiday commemorating Judas's victory on that occasion. In 161 B.C., Judas fell in battle with another Syrian

Modern reproduction of the three towers of Herod's palace in Jerusalem, one of which was named after his Hasmonean wife, Mariamne.

Prutah ("small coin") with a menorah minted at the time of Mattathias Antigonus, a Hasmonean who ruled 40–37 B.C.

general, BACCHIDES. With the death of Judas, the first phase of the Maccabean struggle ended.

Several hundred soldiers loyal to the principles of Judas fled across the Jordan River. From the standpoint of Syria, they were a band of outlaws, but to many Jews—even those who had made their peace with Alcimus—they were the true patriots. Judas's brother Jonathan became the new leader, and young Jews were constantly being attracted to their ranks.

Syria was able to gain important military victories, and the Jews were on the defensive in the years following Judas's death. In 160 B.C., however, Alcimus died, an event regarded by many as God's judgment on him for his wickedness. From 160 to 153 the Maccabees slowly regained power. Jonathan's victory came as a result of diplomacy rather than war. A pretender, Alexander Balas, claimed the Syrian throne of Demetrius II (153–152), and both claimants sought Jewish support. Demetrius freed hostages held in Syria. Both Demetrius and Balas recognized Jonathan as the leader best able to rally the Jews. The Hellenistic Jews were bypassed, and in the year 153 Balas appointed Jonathan high priest. Jonathan had no interest in either the pretender or Demetrius, but he was astute enough to play a delaying action, which ultimately proved successful. He supported Balas and made treaties with Sparta and Rome. Rome had designs on the eastern Mediterranean, and therefore had a vested interest in weakening the Seleucid empire. In 150, Demetrius was killed, and Alexander Balas emerged as king. Jonathan continued as high priest and was further designated as governor of Judea and a member of the Syrian nobility. Jonathan's brother Simon was named governor of the Philistine territory along the Mediterranean coast. The Roman senate, with an eye to the future, declared itself the friend of Judea, but no efforts were made to implement the declaration.

Jonathan's foreign policy promoted the internal prosperity of Judea. The coastal cities, ruled by Simon, were practically annexed. Trypho, a former general under Alexander Balas, set out to destroy Jonathan and force Judea back into the Syrian orbit. He was able to take Jonathan by trickery, after which Jonathan was murdered. Simon succeeded him as leader of the Maccabean forces. See SIMON MACCABEE.

Simon was advanced in years when he became ruling high priest. Syria was rent into factions, one acknowledging Demetrius II as king, the other recognizing the legitimacy of Antiochus VI, a boy under the guardianship of the ambitious TRYPHO. Trypho ultimately murdered Antiochus and took the throne for himself, reigning as the first Syrian king who did not trace his dynasty to SELEUCUS, Alexander's general who had founded the dynasty. Simon ignored Trypho, recognizing Demetrius as rightful king of Syria.

Demetrius, in return for Jewish recognition, granted the Jews full immunity from taxation. This was interpreted as an acknowledgment of independence, and it occasioned great joy among the Jews. Simon was able to starve out the Syrian garrison at the citadel in Jerusalem known as the Acra. He also occupied the cities of Joppa, Beth Zur, and Gaza. Coins were issued bearing the words, "Holy Jerusalem," "Shekel of Israel," and the year numbers, 1, 2, 3, 4, and 5.

During the period of peace that marked the priesthood of Simon, the question of the legitimacy of the Maccabean priesthood was settled. The party of the Hasidim (the pious) had recognized the rights of the family of ONIAS, the priest first deposed by Antiochus Epiphanes, as legitimate heirs to the Aaronic priesthood. The family of Onias had gone to Egypt during the Maccabean conflict, a fact that was interpreted as a renouncing of claims to the priesthood. In recognition of Simon's wise rule, a convocation of leaders in Israel named him "leader and high priest for ever, until a trustworthy prophet" should arise (1 Macc. 14:25–49). The priesthood would henceforth be hereditary in the family of Simon. Simon was the last of the sons of Mattathias. The dynasty that he founded is known as the Hasmonean dynasty, named for an ancestor of the Maccabees named Asamonaios (Jos. *Ant.* 12.6.1 §265; many scholars believe this term is derived from the place name HESHMON). Under Simon, a brother of Judas and the last of the sons of Mattathias, the concept of a hereditary ruling priesthood in the Hasmonean family was established and legitimized.

II. The Hasmonean dynasty

A. John Hyrcanus. In 135 B.C., Simon and two of his sons, Mattathias and Judas, were murdered by an ambitious son-in-law. A third son, John Hyrcanus, managed to escape and succeed Simon as hereditary head of the Jewish state. The older generation that had fought and died for religious liberty was dying out. A new generation, proud of past victories and anticipating greater successes, was in control.

Although Syria under Antiochus VII was powerful enough to have conquered Jerusalem, she offered conditional recognition to Hyrcanus. The Roman senate may have helped write the terms of recognition. Hyrcanus was to consider himself subject to Syria and to help in Syrian military campaigns when requested. He was to forfeit the coastal cities that had been annexed under Jonathan and Simon, except for JOPPA, which would serve as the port city of the Jews. The Syrians, for their part, pledged to leave Judea. As a result, the hellenizing party disappeared from the Jewish political scene.

In 128 B.C., Antiochus was killed during a Parthian campaign. From this time on Judea enjoyed de facto independence. John Hyrcanus began a policy of territorial expansion, including the reconquest of the coastal cities ceded to Syria during the early years of his reign: Hyrcanus turned southward and conquered the province known as IDUMEA. The ancient Edomites (see EDOM) had been pushed out of their territory S and E of the Dead Sea by the NABATEAN Arabs, with the result that they moved into southern Palestine, including the area S of Hebron. This is the area that came to be known as Idumea, and it was forcibly annexed to the Jewish state by John Hyrcanus.

The coastal cities linked the commercial highway through Palestine. From earliest times merchants and warriors passed N from Egypt along the coastal road leading to Syria and Mesopotamia (see VIA MARIS). Without control of commercial routes, Hyrcanus could not hope to build a major state. As soon as Syrian internal affairs made interference from the N unlikely, Hyrcanus took the coastal cities as a guarantee of the future of his state's freedom of movement.

Another ancient trade route passed S of Judea, through Idumea, to Egypt. As Hyrcanus captured this territory, he compelled the Idumeans to accept Judaism and become circumcised. This action met opposition from many of the pious Jews of his own

Greatest extent of the Hasmonean rule.

generation and has been condemned in succeeding ages. Ironically, the grandson of Mattathias forced religious conformity on a people conquered by Jewish arms (and a later Idumean "Jew," HEROD, would oppress Judea again). Some men of wealth and the aristocracy favored Hyrcanus for making possible new commercial opportunities and for annexing larger territories to be governed. Moreover, some extreme nationalists supported Hyrcanus in the interests of enhanced national glory. The mass of the population, however, did not profit from territorial expansion. They were alarmed at the growing secularism of the age. The priesthood had little semblance of a sacred office. There were practical considerations, too. Wars cost lives as well as money.

The conquest of SAMARIA by John Hyrcanus ended the Samaritan challenge to the Jewish state. Samaritans had been enemies of the Jews since the return from Babylonian exile. They had built their temple on Mount GERIZIM, their sacred mountain. Samaria fell after a siege of one year, after which the city was razed. Old animosities continued, but the Hasmonean state proved itself militarily capable of dealing with the Samaritans.

During the reign of John Hyrcanus, political parties realigned. The old party of the Hasidim, "the pious," became the party of the PHARISEES, "the separatists"—a probable reference to separation from uncleanness and defilement. It may be that the ESSENES date from the same period. Essenes were highly regarded by ancient writers such as JOSEPHUS, PHILO JUDAEUS, and PLINY the Elder. They were industrious, peace-loving, and pious. They ultimately separated themselves geographically from their countrymen, forming communal settlements such as that at QUMRAN where they attempted to cultivate their inner lives and live in total conformity to God's law (see DEAD SEA SCROLLS). Both Pharisees and Essenes continued the traditions of the Hasidim.

The old party of the Hellenists disappeared, to be replaced by the SADDUCEES, ostensibly the descendants of the priest ZADOK. As the sect developed, however, it became the party of the Jerusalem aristocracy and of the temple priesthood. John Hyrcanus began as a Pharisee, but during his reign he broke relations with the heirs of the Hasidim and espoused the cause of the Sadducees, who had a more secular and pro-Hellenistic philosophy.

The reign of John Hyrcanus was a turning point in the history of the Jews. The unity of the Hasmonean state was guaranteed. The borders of the state had been extended on every side. Although breaking with his orthodox past, Hyrcanus's life did not offend the most meticulous adherent of the law. His children, however, grew up in a palace and numbered themselves among the aristocrats. Their training was more in Greek than in Hebrew thought, and they had little sympathy for the older piety.

B. Aristobulus. The death of John Hyrcanus (104 B.C.) precipitated a dynastic struggle among his five children. His eldest son, who preferred his Greek name ARISTOBULUS to his Hebrew name Judah, emerged as victor. He cast his mother and three of his brothers into prison, where two of his brothers are thought to have starved to death, along with his mother. Another brother, Antigonus, was murdered in the palace.

Aristobulus continued the policy of territorial expansion begun by Hyrcanus. In his short reign of one year he pushed N, conquered and Judaized GALILEE, and annexed area near the Lebanon mountains. Not content with the title of high priest, Aristobulus took to himself that of king. The Hasmoneans used that title until POMPEY took Judea and made it part of the Roman empire. Aristobulus was called the phil-Hellene—the lover of Greece and things Greek. Whereas it is true that the records are prejudiced in favor of the Pharisees and against Aristobulus, it is still difficult to find anything of a positive nature in his record. Drink, disease, and the haunting fear of rebellion brought death, ending his one-year reign.

C. Alexander Jannaeus. After the death of Aristobulus, his widow, Salome ALEXANDRA, released his younger brother, Alexander, from prison, married him, and raised him to the throne.

Any who hoped for a change in policy with the accession of Jannaeus were bitterly disappointed. Alexander Jannaeus had to defend Judea against Egypt, but in the aftermath he was able to extend his territory to the Egyptian frontier and into the

Transjordan area. The size of the state he ruled compared to that of the days of David and Solomon. It incorporated the whole of Palestine with adjacent areas from the Egyptian border to Lake Huleh. Perea in Transjordan was included, as were the Philistine cities except Ashkelon. The Hasmoneans aspired to become a maritime power. Ships are depicted on coins of the period, and they are sculptured on the family tomb near Modein.

Territories incorporated into the Hasmonean kingdom were quickly Judaized. Edomites came to exercise an important place in Jewish life. Although the orthodox of Judea considered "Galilee of the Gentiles" less than wholly trustworthy, this important region became thoroughly Jewish in its life and piety. Only Samaria resisted assimilation successfully. Individual cities such as Apollonia and Scythopolis, with only a small Jewish element in their population, likewise retained their non-Jewish character.

The rift between the Pharisees and the Hasmonean leaders, first noted during the reign of John Hyrcanus, reached its climax during the reign of Jannaeus, who used foreign mercenaries to keep the Pharisees in subjection. Open rebellion broke out at a memorable Feast of Tabernacles. Jannaeus, while officiating in the temple as priest-king, showed his contempt for the Pharisees by pouring out a libation at his own feet, instead of on the altar as prescribed in the Pharisaic ritual. Enraged, the people in the temple pelted Jannaeus with the citrons that they were carrying in honor of the feast. Jannaeus called upon his soldiers to restore order, and in the process 6,000 people were killed (Jos. Ant. 13.13.5).

The result was six years of civil war. The Pharisees invited Demetrius III, the king of Syria, to aid them. In this turn of events, the spiritual descendants of the Hasidim asked the descendants of Antiochus Epiphanes to aid them against the descendants of the Maccabees. The Syrians came and, aided by the Pharisees, forced Jannaeus into hiding in the Judean hills. The Pharisees did some serious thinking, however. Fearing that the Syrians would claim Judea as the fruit of victory, and hoping that Alexander Jannaeus and his sympathizers had learned their lesson, 6,000 Pharisees deserted the Syrian army and went over to Jannaeus. With this realignment of forces, Demetrius withdrew his Syrian armies, and Alexander Jannaeus emerged as victor.

Jannaeus did not learn from his near-defeat, however. He instituted a hunt for the leaders of the rebellion and made a horrible example of those he caught. He celebrated his victory with a banquet to which the leaders of the Sadducees were invited. Josephus wrote that 800 Pharisees were crucified in the presence of the celebrating guests. While one must allow for exaggeration, Alexander Jannaeus must be considered a tyrant of the worst kind. Some feel that he was the "Wicked Priest" who, according to the DSS, persecuted the "Teacher of Righteousness." The bloody deeds of Jannaeus made compromise between Pharisees and Sadducees impossible.

One of the pious leaders of the Pharisees during the days of Alexander Jannaeus was Simon ben Shetach, the brother of his wife Alexandra. Tradition suggests that Jannaeus repented on his deathbed, instructing his wife to get rid of the Saducean advisers and reign with the aid of the Pharisees.

D. Alexandra. Salome Alexandra had been successively the widow of Aristobulus and of Alexander Jannaeus. She was nearly seventy years of age when she began to reign in her own right, and she reigned alone for seven more years. Being a woman, Salome could not officiate as high priest. She appointed her elder son, Hyrcanus II, as high priest, and assigned the military command to his brother Aristobulus II. Simon ben Shetach, Alexandra's brother, was an important spiritual force from the party of the Pharisees.

The influence of the Pharisees in the area of education was a positive one. The Sanhedrin, the Jewish Council of State, decreed that every young man should be educated. This education was primarily in the Torah — the biblical law. A comprehensive system of elementary education was developed so that the larger villages, towns, and cities of Judea could produce a literate, informed people.

The reign of Alexandra was peaceful in comparison with its predecessors. Aristobulus led an expedition against Damascus that proved futile, while a threatened invasion from Armenia was averted by diplomacy and bribes. Internal wounds were not healed, however. The Pharisees were happy in their recent recognition, but the Sadducees were resentful of the fact that they had lost power. To make matters worse, the Pharisees used their power to seek revenge for the massacre of their leaders by Alexander Jannaeus. Sadducean blood was spilt, and the makings of another civil war were developing. The Sadducees found in Aristobulus II, the younger son of Jannaeus and Alexandra, the man they would support as Alexandra's successor. He was a soldier and thus appealed to those who dreamed of imperial expansion and power. Hyrcanus II, the older brother and rightful heir, was congenial to the Pharisees. With the death of Alexandra, the partisans of the two sons faced a showdown.

E. Hyrcanus II. At the death of Salome Alexandra, her older son Hyrcanus, already serving as high priest, succeeded to the throne, unmindful of the challenge he was soon to face. Aristobulus promptly rallied the Sadducees, gained a victory near Jericho, and marched his army to Jerusalem. Hyrcanus and the Pharisees had neither enthusiasm for war nor military ability. Declaring that he never really desired the throne, Hyrcanus surrendered all his honors to Aristobulus.

F. Aristobulus II. By right of conquest and backed by the Sadducees, Aristobulus took the throne from his brother. Hyrcanus and Aristobulus vowed eternal friendship. The eldest son of Aristobulus, Alexander, married Hyrcanus's only daughter, Alexandra.

Peace between the brothers was short-lived. Hyrcanus found it advisable (or necessary) to flee to Aretas, king of the Nabatean Arabs. Antipater, an Idumean by birth, saw in Hyrcanus's position an opportunity to gain political power in Judea. Hyrcanus was persuaded that he had been defrauded of his rights to the throne by his younger brother. According to Antipater's plan, the Nabateans would come to Jerusalem, drive out the usurper, and restore Hyrcanus to his rightful position. Hyrcanus agreed to the plan, and the Nabateans marched against Jerusalem. Aristobulus, caught by surprise, shut himself up in Jerusalem, and both sides prepared for a long siege.

III. The intervention of the Romans. The battles between Aristobulus II and Hyrcanus II provided Rome with the opportunity to intervene. In 63 B.C., Pompey took Palestine. Rome probably would not have invaded Palestine if a dependable ruler had been there. As it was, Rome had a ready-made excuse to intervene in Palestinian affairs. Although the heirs of the Hasmoneans continued to serve under the Romans for a few decades, Pompey's invasion brought the Hasmonean Dynasty to a close.

(See further V. Tcherikover, *Hellenistic Civilization and the Jews* [1959]; W. Foerster, *From the Exile to Christ: A Historical Introduction to Palestinian Judaism* [1964]; D. S. Russell, *The Jews from Alexander to Herod* [1967]; *HJP*, rev. ed. [1973–87], 1:125–242; H. Jagersma, *A History of Israel from Alexander the Great to Bar Kochba* [1986]; J. Efron, *Studies on the Hasmonean Period* [1987]; D. J. Harrington, *The Maccabean Revolt: Anatomy of a Biblical Revolution* [1988]; L. L. Grabbe, *Judaism from Cyrus to Hadrian*, 2 vols. [1992]; J. H. Hayes and S. R. Mandell, *The Jewish People in Classical Antiquity: From Alexander to Bar Kochba* [1998]; J. C. VanderKam, *From Joshua to Caiaphas: High Priests after the Exile* [2004], ch. 4.)   C. F. Pfeiffer

Hasrah has′ruh (חֶסְרָה H2897, derivation uncertain). **(1)** Father of Tokhath and grandfather of Shallum; the latter was "keeper of the wardrobe" and the husband of Huldah the prophetess (2 Chr. 34:22). The name is given as Harhas (and father of Tikvah) in the parallel passage (2 Ki. 22:14).

(2) Ancestor of a family of temple servants (Nethinim) who returned with Zerubbabel from the exile (1 Esd. 5:31; LXX *Asara*, KJV "Azara"; not included in the parallel lists in Ezra and Nehemiah). Some identify him with #1 above.

Hassenaah has′uh-nay′uh (הַסְּנָאָה H2189, possibly from שָׂנֵא H8533, "to hate"). The father (or ancestor) of a family that rebuilt the Fish Gate (Neh. 3:3). Many believe, however, that Hassenaah should be understood as the definite article plus Senaah (Ezra 2:35; Neh. 7:38), which may well be a place name. If so, "the sons of Hassenaah" means perhaps "the people from the [region of] Senaah." See also Hassenuah.

Hassenuah has´uh-noo´uh (הַסְּנֻאָה H2190, possibly from שָׂנֵא H8533, "to hate"). KJV Hasenuah. Father of Hodaviah and ancestor of Sallu, from the tribe of BENJAMIN; Sallu is mentioned as one of the first to resettle in Jerusalem (1 Chr. 9:7). In a parallel list of postexilic Benjamites, Hassenuah is mentioned as father (or ancestor) of a certain Judah who was in charge of the Second District of Jerusalem (Neh. 11:9; KJV, "Senuah"). The name is possibly a variant form of HASSENAAH and SENAAH.

Hasshub hash´uhb (חַשּׁוּב H3121, "considerate" or "[highly] regarded" or "one to whom has been reckoned"). KJV also Hashub (in Nehemiah). **(1)** Son (meaning prob. a descendant) of PAHATH-MOAB; along with Malkijah son of Harim, he helped repair a section of the wall of JERUSALEM as well as the Tower of the OVENS (Neh. 3:11). He is probably the same Hasshub mentioned along with a certain Benjamin as having made repairs in front of their house (v. 23).

(2) One of the Israelite leaders who sealed the covenant in the time of EZRA (Neh. 10:23).

(3) Father of Shemaiah; the latter was a leader of the MERARI clan among the Levites and is mentioned has having settled in Jerusalem after the return from the captivity (1 Chr. 9:14; Neh. 11:15).

S. BARABAS

Hassophereth ha-sof´uh-rith (הַסֹּפֶרֶת H2191 [Ezra 2:55], "the [office of] scribe" or "the guild of scribes"; also סֹפֶרֶת H6072 [Neh. 7:57]). Ancestor of a family of SOLOMON's SERVANTS who returned after the EXILE ("Hassophereth" in Ezra 2:55; "Sophereth" in Neh. 7:57 [KJV has "Sophereth" in both passages]; "Assaphioth" in 1 Esd. 5:33 [KJV, "Azaphion"]). Because the name is feminine in form, some have thought that the reference is to a matriarchal clan descended from a female scribe (cf. *ABD*, 6:159, s.v. "Sophereth"; however, cf. the form *qōhelet* H7738, Eccl. 1:1).

Hasupha huh-soo´fuh (חֲשׂוּפָא H3102, possibly "stripped" or "prematurely born"). KJV Hashupha (in Nehemiah). Ancestor of a family of temple servants (NETHINIM) who returned after the EXILE (Ezra 2:43; Neh. 7:46; 1 Esd. 5:29 [KJV, "Asipha"]).

hat. This English term is used by the KJV and other versions to render Aramaic *karbĕlâ* H10368, which occurs only once (Dan. 3:21; NIV, "turbans"); it is listed among other articles of clothing worn by the three Hebrews in the fiery furnace. It probably means "helmet, cap" (cf. Akk. *karballatu*, "pointed caps"), although some prefer "mantle" (cf. the cognate Heb. verb *kirbēl* H4124, "to clothe, wrap," in 1 Chr. 15:27).   H. M. WOLF

Hatach hay´tak. KJV form of HATHACH.

hatchets. Possible rendering of Hebrew *kêlappôt* H3965, with reference to an implement, perhaps a type of crowbar, used by the enemy in smashing the engraved wood of the temple (Ps. 74:6; NRSV renders "hammers," but uses "hatchets" [NIV, "axes"] for the accompanying term, *kaššîl* H4172).

hate, hatred. An intense aversion or active hostility that is expressed in settled opposition to a person or thing. In ordinary OT usage, the Hebrew verb *śānēʾ* H8533 expresses the hatred that people have for their fellow human beings—a response that usually comes from anger, fear, or a sense of injury, as when Esau is said to have hated JACOB (Gen. 27:41; NIV, "held a grudge against"). In the NT, something of the same emphasis can be seen in the prophetic statement that Christ's disciples will be hated by men (Jn. 15:18–25; Gk. *miseō* G3631). The apostle PAUL condemned hatred, listing it as one of the works of the flesh (Gal. 5:20). Also, the OT includes a clear prohibition of hatred between kindred (Lev. 19:17).

There is a special and sometimes problematic usage in the OT, where God is said to love Jacob but to hate Esau (Mal. 1:2–3), to hate evildoers (Ps. 5:5), and to hate that which was evil (Prov. 6:16). The emotional connotation should be subtracted from such passages; God must not be understood to act on the human plane of anger and hostility. It must likewise be recognized that the Hebrew thought-form makes no sharp distinction between the individual and his deeds. A person in Hebrew thought is the sum total of the actions of his life, so that to say God hated a man is not to say that God was maliciously disposed toward a particular personality, but to note divine opposition to evil that was registered in that life. In connection with Esau, "hate" has a very colorless sense, being almost equivalent to the acknowledgement of a divine selectivity: Jacob he chose and Esau he rejected. God also was said to hate idolatry and false worship (Deut. 12:31; 16:22; Jer. 44:4) and even Israel's worship when it was external only (Isa. 1:14; Amos 5:21; Mal. 2:13–16).

Some OT passages intertwine God's hatred with the hatred of humans. God's enemies were the enemies of his people, and the enemies of God's people likewise became the objects of a divine hatred (Num. 10:35; Deut. 7:15; 33:11). The book of Psalms especially joined the hatred of God and his people for their mutual enemies (Pss. 68:1–2; 139:19–22).

Jesus modified the teaching of the Jews by insisting that although they had heard it said they were to love their neighbors but hate their enemies, they should rather love their enemies and do good to those who hated them (Matt. 5:43; Lk. 6:27). Jesus' words of admonition to his disciples seem strange in light of his teaching of love for enemies when he also said, "If anyone comes to me and does not hate his father and mother, his wife and children, his brothers and sisters—yes, even his own life—he cannot be my disciple" (Lk. 14:26). The key to understanding these words is found in a knowledge of Semitic thought-forms. The Semitic mind thought by the contrast of extremes, such as light and darkness, truth and falsehood, love and hate. The disciples were thus instructed not that they should have anger, or hostility, toward those nearest and dearest to them, but rather that even those nearest and dearest to them must be given second place to their loyalty and affection for Jesus. Nothing must be allowed to interfere with the disciples' commitment to the cause of Christ, especially not their own selfish desires or ambitions.

The antithesis of love to hatred is especially emphasized in the Gospel of John, which expresses a sharp Semitic juxtaposition in the imagery of light and darkness. "Everyone who does evil hates the light, and will not come into the light for fear that his deeds will be exposed" (Jn. 3:20). In the same context, it is the love of God in Jesus Christ that has become operative in the world to destroy the hatred of the light; and even though the disciples are hated by the world, they are to reveal to it the love of Christ that is stronger than hate (17:14, 20–26). See LOVE.   H. L. DRUMWRIGHT, JR.

Hathach hay′thak (הֲתָךְ H2251, possibly Persian, "good one" or "courtier"). KJV Hatach; TNIV Hathack. A EUNUCH under King XERXES assigned to attend Queen ESTHER (Esth. 4:5–6, 9–10). He served as a messenger between Esther and MORDECAI after HAMAN plotted to kill the Jews.

Hathak hay′thak. TNIV form of HATHAK.

Hathath hay′thath (חֲתַת H3171, "dread" or "weakling"). Son of OTHNIEL and grandson of Kenaz (CALEB's younger brother), included in the genealogy of JUDAH (1 Chr. 4:13).

Hatipha huh-ti′fuh (חֲטִיפָא H2640, "captured"). Ancestor of a family of temple servants (NETHINIM) who returned from the captivity (Ezra 2:54; Neh. 7:56; 1 Esd. 5:32 [KJV, "Atipha"]).

Hatita huh-ti′tuh (חֲטִיטָא H2638, meaning uncertain). Ancestor of a family of gatekeepers who returned with ZERUBBABEL from the captivity (Ezra 2:42; Neh. 7:45; 1 Esd. 5:28 [KJV, "Teta"]).

hatred. See HATE, HATRED.

Hatsi-hammenuchoth (חֲצִי הַמְּנֻחוֹת). KJV marginal reading for a Hebrew phrase that probably means "half of the Menuhoth" (1 Chr. 2:52 NRSV; KJV text, "half of the Manahethites" [similarly NIV]).

Hattaavah. See KIBROTH HATTAAVAH.

Hatti. See HITTITE.

Hatticon, Hattikon. See HAZER HATTICON.

Hattil hat′uhl (חַטִּיל H2639, possibly "talkative"). Ancestor of a family of SOLOMON's SERVANTS who returned from the captivity (Ezra 2:57; Neh. 7:59; called "Agia" [KJV, "Hagia"] in 1 Esd. 5:34).

Hattush hat′uhsh (חַטּוּשׁ H2637, meaning unknown). **(1)** Son of Shemaiah and descendant of

David through Zerubbabel and Shecaniah; he is apparently the same Hattush mentioned among the family heads who returned from the captivity (1 Chr. 3:22; Ezra 8:2; 1 Esd. 8:29 [KJV, "Lettus"]). Some scholars emend the text of Ezra to agree with the parallel in 1 Esdras ("Hattush the son of Shecaniah"), and on that basis delete from 1 Chronicles the phrase *ûbĕnê šĕma'yâ* ("and the sons of Shemaiah," which may have arisen through dittography). If so, Hattush was the brother, not the son, of Shemaiah.

(2) Son of Hashabneiah; he was one of the Israelites who helped repair the wall of Jerusalem under Nehemiah (Neh. 3:10).

(3) A priest who sealed the covenant with Nehemiah (Neh. 10:4); he is probably the same man listed among those who returned with Zerubbabel and Jeshua (12:2).

Hauran haw'ruhn (חוֹרָן H2588, derivation uncertain). A district SE of Mount Hermon, E of the Jordan and the Sea of Galilee, N of the Yarmuk River, and W of Jebel Druze. The area, which partially corresponds with biblical Bashan, is about 50 mi. square and some 2,000 ft. above sea level. It was called Auranitis in the Greco-Roman period. The many extinct volcanoes on the E and W sides of the plateau give evidence of extensive volcanic activity in prehistoric times. The fertility of the rich lava soil has made it a great grain-growing area, providing wheat for Damascus and Palestine. The district abounds in ruined cities dating back to the early Christian centuries, and everywhere there may be seen abandoned houses built entirely of black basalt. Hauran is almost treeless.

The name appears only in the book of Ezekiel, where it is mentioned as the ideal border of Canaan on the E (Ezek. 47:16, 18). The name occurs also in Egyptian texts of the 19th dynasty and in ancient inscriptions of Assyria, but not much is known about the history of Hauran beyond the 1st cent. B.C. The tribe of Manasseh settled both N and S of the Yarmuk, but in later times there were comparatively few Israelites in the land. Although Solomon taxed the region, it was seldom mastered by Israelite rulers. Alexander Jannaeus (see Hasmoneans II.C) gained control of the W part, but the Nabateans repeatedly brought it under their sway. Herod the Great included the whole of the land in his kingdom; and when he died his son Philip ruled it as a separate tetrarchy (Lk. 3:1), although it was not really Jewish. After Philip's death, Caligula bestowed it upon Herod Agrippa I, who ruled it until his death in A.D. 44, after which for nine

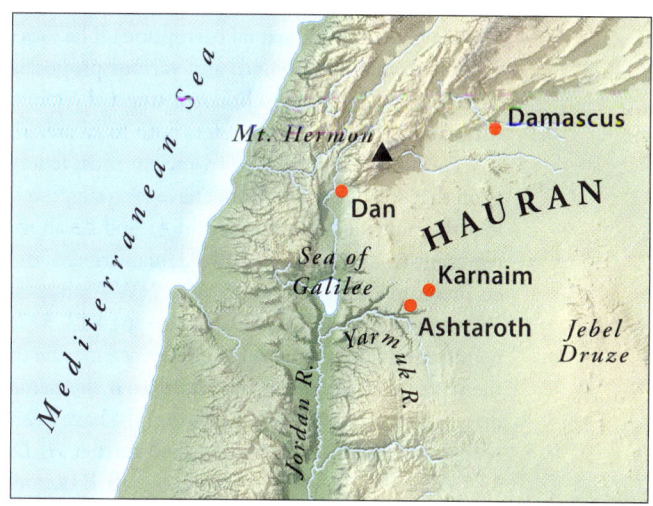

Hauran.

years it was administered by the Romans. Claudius then gave it to Herod Agrippa II, and after his death in A.D. 106 Trajan added it to the Roman province of Syria. Under the Romans, Christianity made rapid progress in the area, but in 632 the Muslim hordes from Arabia swept through the land and utterly destroyed the church. (See G. A. Smith, *The Historical Geography of the Holy Land*, 25th ed. [1931], ch. 30.)   S. Barabas

Haustafel. See Household Code.

haven. See Fair Havens.

Havilah hav'uh-luh (חֲוִילָה H2564, "sandy"). (1) Son of Cush and grandson of Ham (Gen. 10:7; 1 Chr. 1:9). His name is probably related to the geographical area discussed in #3 below.

(2) Son of Joktan, grandson of Eber, and descendant of Shem (Gen. 10:29; 1 Chr. 1:23). His name is probably related to the geographical area discussed in #3 below.

(3) A land described as being bounded by one of the four rivers of the Garden of Eden, the Pishon,

and as being rich in gold, resin, and onyx (Gen. 2:11–12; see EDEN, GARDEN OF). The region, or a different place bearing the same name, is mentioned with SHUR (prob. in N SINAI) as one of the limits of the territory of the Amalekites (25:18; see AMALEK); and SAUL is said to have defeated the Amalekites in this area (1 Sam. 15:7, though it is widely thought that Havilah here is a textual corruption). The location of Havilah is disputed, and various proposals have been made. Many scholars connect the name with Arabic *Ḥaulan*, which refers both to an area in SW ARABIA (Yemen) and to an ancient tribal federation that still lives there. Some have even suggested that the individuals mentioned in #1 and #2 above represent two branches of this Arabian tribe. Others prefer to locate Havilah in W or NW Arabia. C. Westermann (*Genesis*, 3 vols. [1984–86], 313, 527) points out that in Gen. 2:11 the reference may be to the whole Arabian peninsula and that, if the name derives from *ḥôl* H2567, "sand," it might have been used in any number of places. (See further *ABD*, 3:81–82.)   S. BARABAS

Havvoth Jair hav′oth-jay′uhr (חַוֺּת יָאִיר H2596, "villages of Jair"). KJV Havoth-jair (Num. 32:41; Jdg. 10:4), Bashan-havoth-jair (Deut. 3:14); "towns of Jair" (1 Chr. 2:23). A settlement of sixty (Josh. 13:30) villages E of the JORDAN on the border of GILEAD and BASHAN. They were taken by JAIR, the son of Segub, and named after himself (Num. 32:41; 1 Chr. 2:22), and were part of the inheritance allotted by MOSES to the half-tribe of MANASSEH. At one time they belonged to the kingdom of OG, king of Bashan (Josh. 13:29–30). Jair was able to conquer "the whole region of Argob as far as the border of the Geshurites and the Maacathites" (Deut. 3:14).

These settlements are named as part of the commissariat district of BEN GEBER, SOLOMON's purveyor in RAMOTH GILEAD, but it is not clear whether "the district of Argob in Bashan and its sixty large walled cities with bronze gate bars" (1 Ki. 4:13) refers to "the settlements of Jair" or are in addition to it. Similarly, the precise meaning of 1 Chr. 2:22–23 is uncertain: "Segub was the father of Jair, who controlled twenty-three towns in Gilead. (But Geshur and Aram captured Havvoth Jair, as well as Kenath with its surrounding settlements—sixty towns.)" It is possible that the sixty towns attributed to Jair in Josh. 13:30 include the towns originally associated with Nobah, who is said to have "captured Kenath and its surrounding settlements" (Num. 32:42). KD (*Pentateuch*, 3:305) speculate that "*Nobah* was a subordinate branch of the family of *Jair*, and the towns conquered by him were under the supremacy of Jair."

According to Jdg. 10:3–4, moreover, Havvoth Jair was the name of a group of thirty villages in Gilead ruled by the thirty sons of Jair of Gilead, one of the judges of Israel. If this passage refers to the same settlements discussed above, it may be that Jair of Gilead inherited (or otherwise took over) the sixty towns previously under Jair son of Segub and that thirty of them were controlled by his sons. But other explanations are possible. Some scholars believe that the texts reflect different and conflicting etiologies. It is also worthy of note that the term *ḥawwōt* (possibly "tent-villages") occurs only in the combination *ḥawwōt yāʾîr* (except for the associated use in Num. 32:41a), though the significance of this detail is uncertain. (See further Y. Aharoni, *The Land of the Bible: A Historical Geography*, rev. ed. [1979], 209; *ABD*, 3:82–83.)

hawk. To the ordinary person, a hawk is any small day-bird of prey (see BIRDS OF PREY). The falconer gives the name to any species he uses, while to the naturalist it means those with short rounded wings, like the sparrow hawk (Old World) and the Cooper's hawk (North America). In the Bible the term is used to render Hebrew *nēṣ* H5891, which occurs in two lists of unclean foods (Lev. 11:16; Deut. 14:15) and in a poetic passage, "Does the hawk take flight by your wisdom / and spread his wings toward the south?" (Job 39:26; the autumn migration movement is suggested, but this applies equally to many species). G. R. Driver (in *HDB* rev., 367) notes that this bird is placed in between some of the owls and takes it as a general name for small birds of prey, such as kestrel and sparrow hawk. According to *HALOT* (2:714), the Hebrew term refers to the *Falco peregrinus*; see FALCON. (The NRSV uses "hawk" also to render *qāʾat* H7684 in Isa. 34:11, but this word probably refers to the desert owl; cf. Lev. 11:18 et al. See further *FFB*, 40–41; *ABD*, 6:45–46.)   G. S. CANSDALE

hay. Grass (or other plants) cut and dried to be used as fodder. The term is used in the NIV to render the common Hebrew and Greek words for "grass" in two appropriate contexts (*ḥāṣîr* H2945, Prov. 27:25 [cf. also Isa. 15:6 KJV]; *chortos* G5965, 1 Cor. 3:12).

Hazael hay´zay-uhl (חֲזָאֵל H2599 [also חֲזָהאֵל], "God has seen"). One of the most powerful of the kings of ARAM (Syria), ruling from c. 843 to c. 796 B.C. He reigned contemporaneously with Jehoram (the last few years), Jehu, and Jehoahaz, kings of Israel, and with Jehoram, Ahaziah, Athaliah, and Joash, kings of Judah. He is first mentioned in 1 Ki. 19:15–17, where ELIJAH at Mount Horeb was told by God that he would anoint Hazael king over Aram. At this time he was a high officer in the court of BEN-HADAD II, king of Aram. On a subsequent occasion, his sick sovereign sent him to inquire of the prophet ELISHA, who was then in DAMASCUS, whether or not he would recover from his illness. To this question Elisha replied that the illness of his master was not fatal, but that he would nevertheless die; and he added that Hazael himself was to become king of Aram and would be the perpetrator of monstrous cruelties against the children of Israel. The day after Hazael reported to the king the results of his interview with Elisha, he killed him by smothering him with a wet cloth, and Hazael became king in his stead (2 Ki. 8:7–15).

Soon after, Hazael fought against the combined forces of JEHORAM and AHAZIAH at RAMOTH GILEAD (8:28, 29; 9:14, 15). He frequently defeated JEHU in battle, devastating all his country E of the Jordan from the ARNON River in the S to BASHAN in the N (10:32–33). During the reign of JEHOAHAZ, Jehu's successor, he repeatedly encroached upon the territory of Israel, which was kept from complete destruction only by God's mercy (13:3, 22–23). Hazael also moved into SW Palestine, taking GATH; he compelled the king of Judah to pay a heavy bribe for sparing JERUSALEM (12:17–18; 2 Chr. 24:23–24). It was not until the death of Hazael that Israel was able successfully to check the aggression of Aram under Ben-hadad III, the son of Hazael (2 Ki. 13:24–25).

CUNEIFORM inscriptions show that Hazael (Assyr. *Ḥazaʾ-ila*) played a large role in some of the campaigns of SHALMANESER III. In the Black Obelisk from CALAH, Shalmaneser records that in 842 B.C. he joined battle with Hazael. He claims that the Aramean king was defeated, losing 6,000 warriors, 1,121 chariots, and 470 horsemen, together with his stores, and that although Shalmaneser did not capture Damascus, he overran the Hauran and all the territory back to the Mediterranean Sea. Among his tributary kings he mentions the name of Jehu son of Omri. In another inscription Shalmaneser refers to Hazael as the "son of a nobody," and mentions that Hazael had "seized the throne" and rebelled against him. (See *ANET*, 280.)

Among the spoils taken from Damascus by Assyria, and found by archaeologists at Arslan Tash (Hadathah), were an ivory inlay from the side of a bed, with the words engraved on it, "Bar Ama to our Lord Hazael in the year …," and another ivory tablet, possibly a part of the same bed, showing in relief a god or king in Phoenician-Aramean style, which some scholars believe is actually a portrait of Hazael himself. (Cf. E. Puech in *RB* 88 [1981]: 544–62. See further E. Kraeling, *Aram and Israel* [1918], 79–83; M. F. Unger, *Israel and the Aramaeans of Damascus* [1957], 75–82, 160–63; I. M. Price et al., *The Monuments and the Old Testament* [1958], 239–41, 245, 347–49; D. W. Thomas, ed., *Documents from Old Testament Times* [1958)] 46–52, 242–50; M. Avi-Yonah, *Views of the Biblical World*, 2 [1960], 248, 264, 273; W. Pitard, *Ancient Damascus* [1987], 145–60.)

S. BARABAS

In this basalt stela of the 9th cent. B.C., known as the Tel Dan Inscription (or House of David Inscription), Hazael king of Aram boasts of having killed both a northern Israelite king and a ruler of the Davidic dynasty.

Hazaiah huh-zay′yuh (חֲזָיָה H2610, "Yahweh has seen"). Son of Adaiah, descendant of JUDAH through Shelah, and ancestor of Maaseiah; the latter was a provincial leader who settled in Jerusalem after the EXILE (Neh. 11:5).

Hazar Addar hay′zuhr-ad′uhr (חֲצַר־אַדָּר H2960, "settlement of Addar"). Also Hazar-addar. A site marking the S border of CANAAN (Num. 34:4). It was apparently between KADESH BARNEA and AZMON, but the precise location is unknown. The most common identification is modern ʿAin Qedeis (c. 51 mi. SW of BEERSHEBA). The parallel passage (Josh. 15:3) is thought by some to break up the name Hazar Addar into two, HEZRON and ADDAR; others believe that Addar and Hazar Addar are identical and to be distinguished from Hezron. (See Y. Aharoni, *The Land of the Bible: A Historical Geography*, rev. ed. [1979], 70–72.)

Hazar Enan hay′zuhr-ee′nuhn (חֲצַר עֵינָן H2966, "settlement of Enan" [in Ezekiel, חֲצַר עֵינוֹן]). Also Hazar-enan and Hazar-enon. A site marking the ideal NE boundary of Israel (Num. 34:9–10), apparently between DAMASCUS and HAMATH (Ezek. 47:17 [cf. also v. 18 RSV by emendation]; 48:1; and see HAZER HATTICON). Some scholars in the past identified it with the modern Hadr at the foot of Mount HERMON, not far from DAN (PLACE) and more than 30 mi. SW of Damascus, but now it is generally believed to be the same as Qaryatein, a full 70 mi. NE of Damascus. If the latter is correct, the envisioned territory of Israel would be almost twice as large as it was during most of its history.

Hazar Gaddah hay′zuhr-gad′uh (חֲצַר גַּדָּה H2961, "settlement of Gad"). Also Hazar gaddah. A town in the NEGEV, the extreme S of the tribal territory of JUDAH (Josh. 15:27). It is mentioned between Moladah and Heshmon, but its precise location is unknown.

Hazar-hatticon hay′zuhr-hat′uh-kon. KJV form of HAZER HATTICON.

Hazarmaveth hay′zuhr-may′vith (חֲצַרְמָוֶת H2975, "village of Maveth [death]"). Son of JOKTAN, grandson of EBER, and descendant of SHEM (Gen. 10:26;

1 Chr. 1:20). His name appears to be preserved in Arabic *Ḥaḍramaut*, applied to a S Arabian tribe and to a fruitful valley running parallel to the Arabian sea coast for about 200 mi. See SABTA. In the days of its greatest glory (5th cent. B.C. and 1st and 2nd cent. A.D.) it was the home of a great civilization, with its capital at Shabwa. (See R. A. B. Hamilton, "Six Weeks in Shabwa," *Geographical Journal* 108 [1942]: 107–23; G. C. Thompson, *The Tombs and Moon Temple of Hureidha* [1944]; W. L. Brown and A. F. L. Beeston, "Sculptures and Inscriptions from Shabwa," *Journal of the Royal Asiatic Society*, no vol. [1954]: 43–62; K.-H. Bochow and L. Stein, *Hadramaut: Geschichte und Gegenwart einer südarabischen Landschaft* [1986]; *ABD*, 3:85–86.)   S. BARABAS

Hazar Shual hay′zuhr-shoo′uhl (חֲצַר שׁוּעָל H2967, "fox habitat"). Also Hazar-shual. A village in the NEGEV, lying within the tribal territory of JUDAH, but assigned to SIMEON (Josh. 15:28; 19:3; 1 Chr. 4:28). It was resettled by the Israelites after the EXILE (Neh. 11:27). It is always mentioned in close relationship with BEERSHEBA, but its precise location is unknown.

Hazar Susah, Hazar Susim hay′zuhr-soo′suh, hay′zuhr-soo′sim (חֲצַר סוּסָה H2963 [alternate pl. form, חֲצַר סוּסִים H2964], "mare farm, horse enclosure"). Also Hazar-susah, Hazar-susim. A city in the SW part of the tribal territory of JUDAH, but assigned to SIMEON (Josh. 19:5; called "Hazar Susim" in 1 Chr. 4:31). Some scholars believe that the town was originally called SANSANNAH (listed in the parallel passage, Josh. 15:31), and that it was renamed because SOLOMON may have kept there the horses he brought from Egypt and sold to the Hittites and Syrians (1 Ki. 4:26; 9:19; 10:29). If this identification is incorrect, the location of Hazar Susah remains unknown, although some have suggested modern Sbalat Abu Susein, a short distance E of the Wadi Farʿah.

Hazar Susim. See HAZAR SUSAH.

Hazazon Tamar haz′uh-zon-tay′muhr (צְצוֹן תָּמָר H2954, "gravel terrain of Tamar [date-palm]"). KJV Hazezon-tamar; TNIV Hazezon Tamar. After KEDORLAOMER and his allies defeated the HORITES in Seir, "they turned back and went to En Mishpat (that is, Kadesh), and they conquered the whole territory of the Amalekites, as well as the Amorites who were living in Hazazon Tamar" (Gen. 14:7). This description, along with the subsequent narrative, suggests that Hazazon Tamar was located S or SW of the Dead Sea, and some scholars identify it with Tamar (1 Ki. 9:18; Ezek. 47:18–19; 48:28), which is generally thought to be modern ʿAin Ḥuṣb, c. 23 mi. SSW of the S tip of the Dead Sea. See discussion under Tamar (place). Elsewhere, however, Hazazon Tamar is identified with En Gedi (2 Chr. 20:2), which lies on the W shore of the Dead Sea, midpoint between the N and S tips. It seems unlikely, but not impossible, that Kedorlaomer fought the Amorites in En Gedi. Perhaps the name Hazazon Tamar was applied to more than one site distinguished by palm groves.

hazel. See almond (Gen. 30:37 KJV).

Hazelelponi. KJV form of Hazzelelponi.

Hazer Hatticon hay´zuhr-hat´uh-kon (חֲצַר הַתִּיכוֹן H2962, "settlement of Hatticon" or "middle court"). Also Hazar-hatticon; TNIV Hazer Hattikon. A place said to be on the border of Hauran and named among the boundaries of ideal Israel (Ezek. 47:16). It is generally thought to be a scribal error or a variant name for Hazar Enan.

Hazerim huh-zihr´im. The KJV transliteration of Hebrew ḥăṣērîm, plural form of the common noun ḥāṣēr H2958, "village" (Deut. 2:23).

Hazeroth huh-zihr´oth (חֲצֵרוֹת H2972, "settlements"). A camping station of the Israelites during their wilderness wanderings (Num. 11:35; 12:16; 33:17–18; Deut. 1:1). It was here that Aaron and Miriam quarreled with Moses regarding his marriage to a Cushite woman and his claim that God spoke only through him (Num. 12:1–15). Hazeroth is generally identified with ʿAin Khadra (Ḥudrat), some 30 mi. NE of Jebel Musa (see Sinai), on the way to Aqabah. S. Barabas

Hazezon Tamar haz´uh-zon-tay´muhr. TNIV form of Hazazon Tamar.

Haziel hay´zee-uhl (חֲזִיאֵל H2609, possibly "God has seen" or "vision of God"). Son of Shimei and a Levite descended from Gershon (1 Chr. 23:9). The text is problematic and emended by some scholars.

Hazo hay´zoh (חֲזוֹ H2605, derivation uncertain). Son of Nahor by his wife Milcah; nephew of Abraham (Gen. 22:22). The passage as a whole seems to indicate the origins of a dozen Aramean tribes (see Aram), and the name Hazo is usually associated with Assyrian Ḫazu (mentioned in an inscription of Esarhaddon), referring to a mountainous region in N Arabia.

Hazor hay´zor (חָצוֹר H2937, "enclosure"). (1) One of the southernmost towns within the tribal territory of Judah (Josh. 15:23). It was situated in the Negev, near the country of Edom (v. 21), but its precise location is unknown. See also Hazor Hadattah.

(2) An alternate name for Kerioth Hezron, also included in the list of the southernmost towns of Judah (Josh. 15:25).

(3) A town within the tribal territory of Benjamin listed among the places settled by those who

Hazor in Naphtali.

At the height of its power, Hazor in Naphtali was the largest city of ancient Israel. (View to the E.)

returned from the EXILE (Neh. 11:33). Its location is uncertain, though some have identified it with Khirbet Hazzur (some 3 mi. NW of JERUSALEM).

(4) An otherwise unknown group of desert settlements against which JEREMIAH prophesied (Jer. 49:28–33). The oracle speaks of "the kingdoms of Hazor" and associates them with KEDAR (a N Arabian tribe). Hazor is described as "a nation at ease … that has neither gates nor bars" and whose "people live alone." NEBUCHADNEZZAR king of Babylon would attack them, plundering their camels and large herds. Hazor would thus "become a haunt of jackals, a desolate place forever." Although some have thought Hazor was an Arab settlement in S Palestine, most scholars believe that the name referred to associated villages inhabited by semi-nomadic peoples in W or NW ARABIA (and Kedar may have been one of the kingdoms in the league).

(5) A city in N Palestine in the tribal territory of NAPHTALI (Josh. 11:1, 10–13, et al.). It was located c. 5 mi. SW of Lake Huleh and 10 mi. N of the Sea of Galilee. In 1928 it was identified as Tell el-Qedah by John Garstang, after he had made several trial digs. However, systematic excavation was not carried out until 1955 by Yigael Yadin (*IEJ* 6 [1956]: 120–25; 7 [1957]: 118–23; 8 [1958]: 1–14; 9 [1959]: 74–88; 19 [1969]:1–19; see also his synthesis in *NEAEHL*, 2:594–606 [includes supplement by A. Ben-Tor]). The site consists of the tell proper, measuring about 25 acres, and a "camp area" (as Garstang called it), which was actually the lower city; the latter covers about 180 acres N of the tell (it is 1,000 meters in length by 700 in width). The main "tell" was founded in the 3rd millennium, and the lower city was probably added during the HYKSOS period early in the 2nd millennium. The lower city was protected along the W wall by an earthen rampart and a deep moat. The N and E were protected by a deep glacis.

Hazor was the largest city ever built in Palestine during the biblical period, accommodating up to 40,000 inhabitants. Though the city dates back to the 3rd millennium (2700–2500 B.C.), its most flourishing era was during the 2nd millennium. It was the military and political hub of Palestine during this period, which probably explains the statement that "Hazor had been the head of all these kingdoms" (Josh. 11:10). A. Malamat (in *JBL* 79 [1960]: 12–19) argues its importance as "the western outpost of the fertile crescent" from its mention in the MARI archives. Its strategic importance was due to its location. The VIA MARIS, which runs along the S coast of Palestine, branches at

MEGIDDO. One branch continues along the northern coastline to ACCO and TYRE; the second one turns inland to Hazor and then northward to ABEL BETH MAACAH, IJON, and the Lebanese BEQAʿ. At Hazor there was a junction between this N-S road and one which crossed the JORDAN River just below Lake Huleh and went to DAMASCUS. BEN-HADAD I (c. 885 B.C.) and TIGLATH-PILESER III (733 B.C.) both invaded Palestine through this N–S route (1 Ki. 15:20 and 2 Ki. 15:29).

The downfall of the Canaanite Hazor is dated in the 13th cent. B.C., corroborating the account in Josh. 11:1–11 (although some attribute the destruction of the city to the SEA PEOPLES). JABIN, king of Hazor, formed a coalition with the kings of MADON, SHIMRON, ACSHAPH, the kings of the northern hill country and in the ARABAH S of KINNERETH and in the lowlands, to stop the advance of the Israelites. The coalition was defeated at the Waters of MEROM, and Joshua took Hazor and burned it. After its destruction, the lower city was never rebuilt, and the Israelite attempts to resettle the city during the 12th and 11th centuries were very poor and limited only to some parts of the tell. Excavations of the lower city have turned up a Canaanite temple and a small shrine. The Bible mentions a second battle between the Israelites and a Jabin of Hazor (a dynastic name?). DEBORAH and BARAK led the troops of Israel against SISERA, the captain of Jabin's army, who had 900 chariots of iron. Because of divine aid, Israel defeated the Canaanites and was relieved of the oppression under which they had suffered for twenty years (Jdg. 4–5).

The city was rebuilt in the 10th cent. by SOLOMON (c. 950 B.C.) as a fortress, evidently to protect the N entrance to Palestine. According to 1 Ki. 9:15, he utilized forced labor to build Hazor, Megiddo, and GEZER as well as other projects. The great gate found at Hazor has proven to be very similar to those at Megiddo and Gezer, suggesting even the possibility of the same architect. The city was again destroyed by fire, probably by BEN-HADAD I, c. 885 (cf. 1 Ki. 15:20). Over the next two centuries, it was rebuilt and destroyed five different times. The last city of any significance is thought to have been demolished in the campaign of TIGLATH-PILESER III in 732 (2 Ki. 15:29). In the ash layer of this level a fragment of a wine jar was found bearing the name of PEKAH. There are evidences of further resettlements during the Assyrian, Persian, and Hellenistic periods, but the citadels were quite small. W. B. COKER

Hazor Hadattah hay′zor-huh-dat′uh (חָצוֹר חֲדַתָּה H2939, "New Hazor [enclosure]"). Also Hazor-haddattah. One of the southernmost towns within the tribal territory of JUDAH (Josh. 15:25; KJV reads two names, "Hazor, Haddattah"). Several towns in the NEGEV bore the name HAZOR, but their precise locations are unknown. The second component of the name Hazor Hadattah is the Aramaic word for "new" (cf. Heb. HADASHAH), which seems unusual. Some have speculated that the town was settled by residents of Hazor in NAPHTALI who had closer contact with Aramaic-speaking populations.

Hazzelelponi haz′uh-lel-poh′ni (הַצְּלֶלְפּוֹנִי H2209, perhaps "shade my face"). KJV Hazelelponi. Daughter of ETAM, included in the genealogy of JUDAH (1 Chr. 4:3). The name is highly unusual, however, and various emendations have been proposed. For example, some have thought that the names of two different daughters have been merged. Others suggest that the name was simply Hazlel (*haṣĕlel*, "give shade") and that the second part of the word, *pônî*, is a scribal dittography (the first word in the next verse is the name *pĕnûʾēl*, Penuel; see G. N. Knoppers, *I Chronicles 1–9*, AB 12 [2005], 338).

Hazzobebah haz′oh-bee′buh (הַצֹּבֵבָה H2200, meaning uncertain). Son of KOZ, included in the genealogy of JUDAH (1 Chr. 4:8). The first syllable of the name appears to be the Hebrew definite article, and thus the NRSV and other versions render, "Zobebah." It may be the name of a clan.

he hay (הֵא, meaning uncertain). The fifth letter in the Hebrew ALPHABET (ה), with a numerical value of five. Its sound corresponds to that of English *h* (but it is usually silent at the end of a word, where it serves to represent vowel sounds).

head. Both the brain case and the face are included in the head, considered to be the seat of life or the SOUL, although the Jews regarded the

HEART as the seat of the intellect, and often used "head" (Heb. *rōʾš H8031*) to stand for the whole person (Acts 18:6, Gk. *kephalē G3051*). The word applies to animals, such as the bull's head of the burnt offering (Lev. 1:4), and to inanimate objects in phrases like, "Lift up your heads, O you gates" (Ps. 24:7), the four heads of rivers (Gen. 2:10), and the headstone (Zech. 4:7, a concept also applied to Christ, Matt. 21:42; see CORNERSTONE). Heads of animals decorated the tops of furniture in eastern homes. Early Christians preserved the head of a saint or martyr as an object of adoration which could exert miraculous power (J. A. MacCulloch in *ERE*, 6:536). The mark of the beast was put upon the FOREHEAD (Rev. 14:9).

Injury to the head was a chief form of defeating an enemy (Ps. 68:21). Decapitation, a custom likewise practiced in ASSYRIA AND BABYLONIA, added insult to injury (1 Sam. 17:51). On the other hand, anointing the head was a symbol of joy and prosperity (Ps. 23:5; Heb. 1:9), and dedication to priestly service (Exod. 29:7).

Leaders are heads: "the elders and prominent men are the head, / the prophets who teach lies are the tail" (Isa. 9:15). Christ is the HEAD OF THE CHURCH, his BODY, and of all CREATION (Eph. 1:22), every human being (1 Cor. 11:3), and of all rule and authority (Col. 2:10). The husband is the head of the woman. Because of the Greek custom of veiling of women, as opposed to the Jewish practice, PAUL urged the Corinthian women to be obedient to the local standards of decency and order, and to cover the head in worship. Men, however, pray with uncovered heads. See COVERING OF THE HEAD.

Blessing comes upon the head (Gen. 49:26), therefore the hands were laid upon it (48:17) and sins were transferred from the person to the beast by this gesture (Exod. 29:15). To "heap coals of fire on the head" meant returning good for evil (Matt. 5:44; Rom. 12:20). The Israelite swore by his head (Matt. 5:36). Covering or dusting the head or laying the hand on it signified sadness, grief, or shame (2 Sam. 13:19). To wag the head expressed derision (Mk. 15:29) and to bow down the head displayed sadness, humility, and mourning (Isa. 58:5). "Yet will I not lift up my head" is equivalent to lack of self-assertion (Job 10:15 KJV). Life gave one a hoary head along with honor and wisdom (Prov. 16:31).

R. L. MIXTER

headband. This English term is used variously by Bible versions to render several Hebrew terms, such as *šābîs H8667* (which occurs only in Isa. 3:18) and *migbāʿâ H4014* (which occurs only with reference to the headgear of priests; so NIV in Exod. 28:40 et al., where NRSV has "sashes"). See also HEADDRESS.

head covering. See COVERING FOR THE HEAD.

headdress. The ancients wore many forms of headdress. The Hebrews originally wore no covering for the head, except for special occasions, as a leather helmet in battle. Egyptian monuments show Syrian men wearing a fillet of rope or cord. Another type of headdress protected the head, neck, and shoulders from the sun, like the modern *kaffiyeh*. Assyrian sculptures show men with a TURBAN, a long cloth wound around the head (cf. Isa. 3:23 NRSV; Zech 3:5; note also the royal "diadem" in Isa. 62:3). The "hats" worn by DANIEL's friends (Dan. 3:21 KJV) were probably one kind of the conical Babylonian headdress. ANTIOCHUS Epiphanes compelled young Jewish nobles to wear a low, broad-brimmed hat associated with the Greek god HERMES (2 Macc. 4:12). Among the many types of head covering worn by men in NT times was a scarf wound around the head and hanging down over the neck. Women sometimes wore a turban. Syrian women sometimes wore a headband on the hair. Syrian sculptures show women wearing a shawl covering the whole body from the head to the ankles. The OT mentions both mantles and veils, but it is impossible to distinguish between them.

S. BARABAS

head of the church. This phrase occurs only in Eph. 5:23 (Gk. *kephalē tēs ekklēsias*), but similar expressions occur elsewhere (Eph. 1:22; 1 Cor. 11:3; and esp. Col. 1:18, *hē kephalē tou sōmatos tēs ekklēsias*, "the head of the body, the church"; see BODY OF CHRIST and CHURCH). These phrases in each case are mentioned incidentally to some other argument, such as the proper place of women in the congregation and the home, and as a phrase in a doxological context. The reference is to the lordship of Christ as the risen exalted head of the congregation of God, a figure derived from the OT (Pss. 2:7–8; 72:7, 8; Dan. 7:13, 14; et al.), and reinforced by several events in the gospel narratives (Matt. 17:1–9; Jn. 1:32–34; cf. Mk. 9:2–9; Lk. 9:28–36). The phrase appears to have been a common one in the ancient church and it is used by the Greek and Latin church fathers. In the medieval era, after the declaration of the bulla *Unam Sanctum* (A.D. 1302), such passages were assumed to increase papal power, a thesis rejected by the reformers. W. WHITE, JR.

healing, gifts of. This expression (Gk. *charismata iamatōn*) appears three times, all of them in 1 Cor. 12 (vv. 9, 28, 30). The theme of the chapter is the unity in which the "one and the same Spirit" (v. 11) distributes and administers the varieties of gifts within the one BODY OF CHRIST at CORINTH. The application is that believers, as members of the BODY OF CHRIST, have need of one another that all may benefit in the performance of particular ministries (12:4–7); therefore, they ought not to be divided by schism of any kind.

Certain gifts, such as apostleship, prophecy, and teaching (1 Cor. 12:28; cf. Rom. 12:6–8), have *modi operandi* and fulfill the normal needs of the CHURCH; others have special and exceptional functions. While they could be associated with certain members in the congregation (1 Cor. 12:30), these particular individuals are not set forth as appointed with gifts so as to become official or regular workers of miracles or healers. While PETER and PAUL (as well as PHILIP in SAMARIA) had an extensive healing ministry as recorded in the book of Acts, they were not identified as divine healers, nor is there any such designation elsewhere in Scripture. Gifts of healing were spontaneous within the assembly, and their exercise implied the rendering of service among believers. The plural "gifts of healing" suggests varieties of the sicknesses healed and the different manners in which the healings took place.

Further light is cast upon the function of these gifts in Jas. 5:13–16, where procedure is given for the corporate local church regarding those who particularly desire bodily healing. The sick (v. 14, literally, "without strength," and thus perhaps prostrate) patient is to call for the elders of the church who are to ANOINT him with OIL in the name of the Lord and pray over him. See ELDER (NT). Biblical anointing is symbolic of the HOLY SPIRIT who administers the manifestation of gifts (1 Cor. 12:8–11). Kings, high priests, and prophets were anointed with oil, which sanctified them to a special work for God. The tabernacle, the altar, the vessels, and Aaron were anointed so that they might be sanctified or consecrated (Lev. 8:10–12).

There is no suggestion in James of medicinal use of the oil, since this might have been administered by anyone beside the elders. The use of oil symbolized sanctified commitment of the sick body to the operation of the Holy Spirit's ministry, which quickens the mortal bodies of believers that they may be enabled and led to fulfill the ministry he has purposed for them as fellow heirs with Christ (Rom. 8:11–17). The promise in Jas. 5 is that the anointing of oil "and the prayer offered in faith will make the sick person well; the Lord will raise him up" (v. 15). Furthermore, believers are to confess their faults to one another and pray for one another that they may be healed, since "the prayer of a righteous man is powerful and effective" (v. 16).

Thus it appears that the suggested procedure as related to the sick who are to call for the elders of the church is not the only circumstantial manner by which God heals. God also heals as believers pray for one another; but it is the elders and not so-called "divine healers" that are to be sought when believers who are sick in body are hindered from gathering with the assembly. The prayer of faith is required; and the gift is in no way separated from the Giver, the blessing from the Blesser, or a human healer from the divine One. Sin is the greatest hindrance to the prayer of faith, whether it be in the patient or in those who pray in fellowship for him (Jas. 5:15–16). Sin is not necessarily the reason God does not heal or give the prayer of faith, since the Holy Spirit apportions his gifts to each believer individually as he wills (1 Cor. 12:11).

Closely associated with "gifts of healing" is the "working of miracles" (1 Cor. 12:10, 28–29). In the book of Acts, MIRACLES were associated with bodily healing and the casting out of evil spirits

(8:6–7; 19:11–12). These were described as "great signs and miracles" (8:13) and "extraordinary miracles" (19:11). The distinction drawn in 1 Cor. 12 may carry this connotation and imply that "gifts of healing" were relatively common in the church and were practiced according to Jas. 5:13–16 in distinction from "working of miracles." The prescription given in James suggests "gifts of healing" rather than "working of miracles" as the result of the prayer of faith.

John Calvin comments: "As the gift of healing as yet continued, he (James) directs the sick to have recourse to that remedy. It is, indeed, certain that they were not all healed; but the Lord granted this favor as often and as far as he knew it would be expedient; nor is it probable that the oil was indiscriminately applied, but only when there was some hope of restoration. For, together with the power there was given also discretion to the ministers, lest they should by abuse profane the symbol. The design of James was no other than to commend the grace of God which the faithful might then enjoy, lest the benefit of it should be lost through contempt or neglect." He adds, "For this purpose he ordered the presbyters to be sent for, but the use of the anointing must have been confined to the power of the Holy Spirit" (*Commentaries on the Catholic Epistles* [1948], 335).

Today there is a new interest and a rethinking of the entire field of Christian healing. There is no reason to believe that gifts of healing have passed from the ministry of the church. Although from the early church to modern times records of divine healing can be found, the missing ingredient is the full ministry of the church in the exercise of charismatic gifts with the proper balance and relationship of the gifts as set forth by Paul in 1 Cor. 12. (Cf. H. J. Blair, "Spiritual Healing: An Enquiry," *EvQ* 30 [1958]: 147–51; J. G. S. S. Thomson, "Spiritual Gifts," in *BDT*, 497–500.) See also SPIRITUAL GIFTS.

S. J. STOESZ

healing and health. In the Scriptures healing is the restoration to a state of health by physical means or by miracle; the methods are not necessarily mutually exclusive.

  I. Healing by physical means
 II. Healing by miracle
III. Health in pagan nations surrounding the Israelites
    A. Superstitions regarding the cause of illness
    B. Fantastic ingredients of pagan medicines
IV. Health among the Israelites
    A. Significance of the laws of the Pentateuch for Israel's health
    B. Significance of the laws of the Pentateuch to public health today

I. Healing by physical means. Healing by means of medicines and surgical appliances is supported by Scripture. Local applications of ointments and bandaging of wounds were certainly standard treatment in OT times (Isa. 1:6). Moreover, the use of a plaster made of a cake of figs to be laid upon HEZEKIAH's boil was recognized as appropriate treatment and was advocated by God's prophet (38:21). The broken arm of PHARAOH, king of Egypt, was said by the prophet to require a bandage to bind it (Ezek. 30:21). Doubtless this bandage included the application of splints, for Egyptian mummies have been found, according to A. R. Short (*The Bible and Modern Medicine* [1953], 12), with broken bones treated by splints made of the bark of trees fixed with bandages.

Reference is furthermore made to the healing BALM of Gilead (Jer. 8:22; 46:11; 51:8). Short (*The Bible and Modern Medicine*, 72) believes that this may have been of the nature of FRANKINCENSE or some similar aromatic juice from a shrub, containing benzoin, which finds medicinal use today with its pleasant odor and definite antiseptic properties. There are those who interpret Jas. 5:14 concerning the anointing with OIL as not merely referring to a religious rite, but as an injunction to accompany the prayer of faith with the application of whatever oil or balm seemed to be required in the particular instance of illness. Such applications were extensively used in Bible times, and may be regarded as similar to the present-day use of applications of oil of wintergreen to joints for rheumatic symptoms or of salve to wounds. See ANOINT.

Other than these few instances, the Bible gives little or no information regarding healing with medicines. This is no wonder, for the introduction of the great array of medicines, such as penicillin, sulfonamides, tetracyclines, insulin, and chloroquine, which are so effective today in healing and prolonging life, have all come on the scene in the past several decades.

II. Healing by miracle. Miraculous healing with or without associated use of physical means is frequently referred to in the Bible. It was performed, not as broadcast philanthropy, as Short points out, but as a SIGN. He declares that the purpose of the MIRACLES was to show that God was at work in a new way, using and accrediting his representatives so that their message might be believed. Short brushes aside the natural assumption that the ailment involved was functional or hysterical in most cases. Whereas it is true that hysteria may imitate a great variety of truly organic diseases, "We may rest assured that the man with the withered hand, the woman with the issue of blood, the woman with the bowed back presumably due to bony fusion of the vertebrae, either tuberculous or osteoarthritic; the blind people, and the lepers, cannot reasonably be written down as functional.... Cases of paralysis are occasionally functional, and there is a one-in-a-million chance that the patient who was brought by his four friends may have been an example, but it is begging the question to regard him as a case of hysterical paralysis just because he got well."

It is interesting to note that Christ in two cases (Mk. 8:23; Jn. 9:6) used saliva to anoint the patient's eyes for healing, for it parallels the fact that the Egyptians believed saliva to be a valuable remedy for blindness, and PLINY the Elder and TACITUS both voiced similar beliefs. Short conjectures that Jesus used saliva partly to strengthen their faith, and partly to teach that divine healing may go hand in hand with the use of recognized medical remedies.

III. Health in pagan nations surrounding the Israelites. The view that history books give of conquering and defeated armies is often a distorted one. Back of these conquests was often a health situation that determined the outcome of wars.

A. Superstitions regarding the cause of illness. The nations round about Israel were deeply steeped in idolatry, and they frequently blamed their diseases on evil spirits, which must be driven out by incantations or magical formulas (see DEMON; EXORCISM). Without knowledge of the one true God, such vagaries of reasoning were doubtless inevitable. Epidemics wrought havoc among these peoples, often causing them to flee their lands to get away from supposed evil spirits to which they attributed disease.

B. Fantastic ingredients of pagan medicines. The Egyptian Papyri, discovered in Thebes about 1862, furnish medical prescriptions issued in Egypt about 1552 B.C. Sometimes these prescriptions were used to repair the supposed damage caused by an evil spirit, the medicine being given after the evil spirit was exorcised. These prescriptions are, in the light of our day, a compilation of fantastic and worthless nostrums. Listed among them, as quoted by S. I. McMillen (*None of These Diseases* [1963], 11), are "lizards' blood, swine's teeth, putrid meat, stinking fat, moisture from pigs' ears, milk, goose grease, asses' hoofs, animal fats from various sources, excreta from animals including human beings, donkeys, antelopes, dogs, cats, and even flies." He further notes that to embedded splinters, worms' blood and asses' dung were applied, which doubtless resulted in a heavy toll of death from lockjaw since dung is loaded with tetanus spores. Indeed, one cannot help but wonder how these nations survived to the extent they did under such unsanitary conditions, lacking enlightened medical care. (In other respects, however, medicine in Egypt was relatively advanced; see K. R. Weeks in *CANE*, 3:1787–98.)

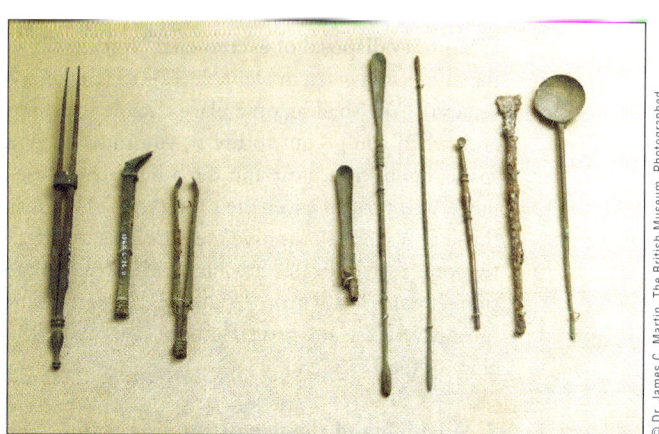

Ancient Roman medical and surgical instruments.

IV. Health among the Israelites. In striking contrast, the Israelites enjoyed comparatively good health. They had been given God's promises that, hearkening to his commandments, none of the diseases that afflicted the Egyptians would come upon them (Exod. 15:26).

A. Significance of the laws of the Pentateuch for Israel's health. In light of the fact that MOSES was instructed in all the wisdom of the Egyptians (Acts 7:22), it is amazing that none of the fanciful nostrums of the day appear in the PENTATEUCH. McMillen (*None of These Diseases*, 11–24) concludes that there is but one answer to this puzzle: that the medical instructions of the Pentateuch were actually given to MOSES by God, as he says they were. McMillen's work (a revised edition of which by D. E. Stern appeared in 2000) has been challenged by various writers. Nevertheless, it is remarkable that what Moses recorded has stood the test of time. Indeed, the mechanism by which the Jewish race has been preserved throughout the centuries is doubtless found in the sanitary measures observed by the Jews in Europe during the frightful scourges that visited Israel's neighbors in ancient and medieval times. This survival took place despite the crowded ghettos of large towns, which were full of tuberculosis. Short (*The Bible and Modern Medicine*, 38) remarks that without doubt this survival is an attestation of divine providence, whereas from a secular point of view it was rendered possible by the healthy habits of living based upon the medical instructions of the Pentateuch.

1. Sanitary disposal of excrement. Noteworthy is the instruction given in Deut. 23:12–13 (Berkeley's version), "You shall set off a place outside the camp and, when you go out to use it, you must carry a spade among your gear and dig a hole, have easement, and turn to cover the excrement." Whereas this is in a sense a primitive measure, it is an effective one that indicates advanced ideas of sanitation. It contrasts with the dumping of excrement in unpaved city streets in Europe, even up to the close of the 18th cent.

2. Washing and the use of running water. The emphasis on washing of the body and the clothes in WATER after contact with disease is worthy of comment. It is significant, too, that in some instances running water was specified (Lev. 14:50), which certainly had its advantages, not only in convenience but also in actual sanitation, since it eliminates the reuse of contaminated water. The introduction of modern plumbing has demonstrated this time and again. Concern for the purity of water supplies is notable in the OT. For example, the elders at JERICHO doubtless rightly attributed the town's epidemic to contaminated water, and so ELISHA was asked to purify it (2 Ki. 2:19–22). The discoveries of modern sanitary science as to typhoid fever, cholera, and schistosomiasis being carried by contaminated water accent the importance of these attitudes. Short refers to the Jews as a washing people and points out that PAUL knew where he was most likely to find a Jewish meeting place in PHILIPPI, because it naturally would be along the river bank where the water was.

3. Isolation and quarantine. Isolation and quarantine were imposed upon the Israelites in the Mosaic law. It is a natural corollary to the commandment to love one's neighbor as oneself. It is noteworthy that, as Short points out, the Jews escaped lightly in Italy in the 14th cent. when others died in epidemics of plague. It was rightly concluded that this might be due to their laws of uncleanness after touching dead bodies. On this basis the Jewish code was made compulsory on the whole community, and a period of forty days' quarantine (an English term derived from *quaranta*, Italian for "forty") was imposed with salutary results (Lev. 12:1–4). Today, with modern laboratory technology, it is possible to differentiate diseases more accurately and hence determine more specifically the needed period and strictness of isolation for the various diseases. For the day in which the regulations of the Pentateuch were promulgated, the blanket rules for preventing the spread of diseases served well.

4. Dietary regulations. The food laws of the Pentateuch are remarkable in the light of modern science. The restrictions regarding meats are based on two simple tests, namely, the animals suitable for human consumption must both part the hoof and chew the cud. This means that the pig and the rabbit are categorized as being unsuitable for eating. Modern parasitology has demonstrated that these animals are especially liable to infections with parasites and are safe only if well-cooked. The pig in particular is an unclean feeder, and often harbors two kinds of parasites, namely, trichina and the pork tapeworm, which are frequent causes of disease in man. These diseases still occur in the United States, although the introduction of federal meat inspection and compulsory boiling of garbage have greatly helped to reduce their incidence. In the absence of such adjuncts and good culinary apparatus, including readily available fuel for cooking (which certainly was not the case in ancient Israel), the complete avoidance of the use of these animals for food was indeed beneficial in preventing the spread of disease.

5. Dealing with bodily discharges. The method in the Pentateuch of dealing with infectious discharges has long aroused the admiration of experts in sanitation. Although not all bodily discharges are infectious, many are dangerous. To determine which of them carry diseases requires bacteriological tests that were obviously not available in Moses' day. The disposal of discharges, therefore, was based on the assumption that all were infectious in the absence of a ready means to distinguish the infectious from the noninfectious discharges. With this in view, the discharges were dealt with in a most scientific manner. It is almost surprising to find sputum mentioned as a possible vehicle of infection (Lev. 15:8), for the realization that sputum is a vehicle for the transmission of tuberculosis is usually dated to the discovery of the tubercle bacillus by Koch in modern times.

6. Cleansing after touching the dead. The regulations of the Pentateuch regarding touching dead bodies in connection with their burial specified a period of UNCLEANNESS of seven days' duration. During this time, the person involved must be isolated from others and had to perform certain acts that included bathing his body and washing his clothes. On completion of these acts and at the expiration of the time period, the unclean person was considered cleansed so that he could return to community life (Num. 19:11–22). Such precautions ought to have been considered essential for dealing with a body that had died of smallpox, plague, or other contagious diseases so rampant in those days. Modern health provisions including isolation regulations have so reduced the incidence of these diseases in America that the average individual is unaware of the real risk of these diseases spreading. Actually, they are still a menace in some parts of the world, and it is only by constant vigilance and strict enforcement of health regulations that they are kept from spreading to the United States in today's swift air travel. Application of the same regulations in death from all causes was warranted in Moses' day, since at that time methods of distinguishing between contagious diseases and other causes of death were not established on a scientific basis.

7. Sexual morality. The strict laws of the Pentateuch concerning sexual morality should not be glossed over in these days when there is so much loose talking and thinking regarding promiscuous sexual relations. These laws, and in particular the seventh commandment, if strictly observed, would put an end to the spread of venereal diseases. Sexual immorality by adults, who may be unknowingly infected with venereal disease, is no more hygienic, or permissible on a common-sense basis, than it is for a tuberculosis patient to spit his germs in public places. Not only does sexual promiscuity have dire psychological consequences, but the resulting high incidence of venereal disease is a steep price to pay. The complete cure of syphilis and gonorrhea, even with the newest and best of antibiotics, is rarely if ever absolutely sure. Often the initial symptoms respond promptly to treatment, convincing individuals that they are cured, whereas the disease may readily crop up twenty years or so later in a rapidly fatal heart condition or a severe mental disturbance, such as the general paresis of the insane caused by advanced syphilis of the brain. God knew what he was commanding when he gave the seventh commandment, and this law has not been abrogated. (See SEX.)

8. Circumcision and its timing. Some modern medical data seem to suggest that, where male CIRCUMCISION is practiced, the incidence of cancer of the male procreative organ is greatly reduced. Interestingly enough, the incidence of cancer of the female genitals, particularly of the cervix uteri (the mouth of the womb), is likewise said to be reduced where the male partner has been circumcised (see *New England Journal of Medicine* 346 no. 15 [2002]: 1105–12). Some argue that, without the foreskin, carcinogenic smegma can no longer be harbored in this location for local irritation in the male or for transmission to a female sex partner. In the light of this, circumcision of males may be regarded not only as a religious rite but also as a hygienic measure. (It should be noted, however, that in 1999 the American Academy of Pediatrics concluded that although circumcision has "some potential medical benefits," there is not sufficient data to support recommending routine newborn circumcision. According to the American Cancer Society, the evidence that circumcision reduces the risk of penile cancer is ambiguous.)

McMillen also points out that the specification in the Pentateuch of the eighth day after birth constitutes the optimum time for circumcision. After cutting off the foreskin, stanching of bleeding requires two elements to be present: (1) One of these is vitamin K, which is not formed in normal amounts in the baby's intestine until the fifth to seventh day of life. Then by the eighth day adequate amounts of vitamin K are absorbed into the blood to enhance clotting. (2) The other essential element is prothrombin. Careful investigations of the available prothrombin are charted by McMillen and show that on the third day of a baby's life the available prothrombin is only 30 percent, whereas on the eighth day it is 110 percent, after which it levels off to 100 percent. In other words, there is more prothrombin available for clotting the blood on the eighth day of life than at any other time in the whole life of the individual.

B. Significance of the laws of the Pentateuch to public health today. Modern sanitary measures have been arrived at occasionally as the outcome of research and discovery, sometimes through trial and error; but frequently these measures have been developed by reverting to the sanitary precepts of the Pentateuch, even in the absence of clear rationale for doing so. McMillen, quoting Rosen, points out that following the major plagues of the Dark Ages, including leprosy and the Black Death, which left the physicians of the day completely perplexed, order came out of chaos only when the church took over and used as its guiding principle the concept of contagion embodied in the OT. Thus, by combating leprosy, the first great feat in methodical eradication of disease was accomplished. More recently, the writer, when in China as a medical missionary, observed at first hand the decimating effects of contagious diseases such as diphtheria and scarlet fever in the absence of quarantine as it wiped out the early-school-age child population of whole villages. Amazingly, the nationals in the primitive part of the country viewed our notions of quarantine as a kind of imported Western superstition. Eventually the government public health services, organized on modern epidemic prevention principles, took over with salutary results. (Cf. P. E. Adolph, *Surgery Speaks to China* [1945], 92.)

Modern surgical procedures are largely made possible through the simple measure of washing the hands, introduced in 1847 by Semmelweis under such great protest and ridicule that it was many years before it was universally adopted. Yet the oft-repeated, almost monotonous, admonition to wash one's body with water and change the clothes as instructed in Leviticus furnishes the key to the whole matter. Before surgeons adopted these principles, the mortality following major surgical operations was exceedingly high. McMillen further points out that the New York State Department of Health became so alarmed over the spread of infections from a carrier who failed to wash his hands carefully that in 1960 the department issued a book on techniques for washing the hands, which approximates the scriptural method given in Num. 19. (For bibliography see DISEASE; MEDICINE.)

P. E. ADOLPH

health. See HEALING AND HEALTH.

heap of stones. The act of raising a heap of stones could be a symbol and reminder of a shameful act. After ACHAN and his family were stoned and burned, a pile of stones was heaped over their slain bodies (Josh. 7:26). After JOSHUA hanged the king of AI, he raised a heap of stones over his body (8:29). A similar heap of stones was raised over the body of ABSALOM, who was killed by JOAB and his

Heaps of stones are still used to mark Palestinian agricultural boundaries.

men after he had tried to seize the throne from his father DAVID (2 Sam. 18:17). A heap of stones could also symbolize a COVENANT made between two persons, as in the case of JACOB and LABAN at MIZPAH; Laban said to Jacob that the heap was a witness that neither of them would pass over it to harm the other (Gen. 31:46–52; see GALEED). Finally, piles of stones could indicate God's judgment upon a sinful city or family (Job 15:28; Isa. 37:26; Jer. 9:11; Hos. 12:11).

heart. Aside from literal references to the physical organ, the term *heart* in the Bible (Heb. *lēb* H4213 and *lēbāb* H4222; Gk. *kardia* G2840) usually refers to the "inner person," or the seat of mental functions (where one remembers, thinks), or the seat and center of all physical and spiritual life—the SOUL or MIND as the fountain of thoughts, passions, desires, affections, appetites, purposes, endeavors. See ATTITUDE. The Hebrew terms occur almost 800 times in the OT; the Greek term occurs almost 150 times in the NT. (See *NIDOTTE*, 2:749–54; *NIDNTT*, 2:180–84.)

I. Psychological definition. *Heart* denotes the essence of personality, the seat and center of all life. The psychological term of nearest equivalency to this old English word is *ego*, which represents the "I, self, person." It is that term which is formalized, as a logical necessity, to denote that "center" to which all of a person's psychological activities and characteristics refer. As such, the "heart" is probably unknowable, but the word is a natural, created, figurative expressive concept. The term was born of logical need for categorical expression, communicative clarity, and practical utility. The "human heart" represents, then, that innermost center which is of ultimate importance; that which is basic, central, substantive, and of profound essence.

II. Consistency and variety of usage. There is a consistency of treatment with all biblical uses of *heart*. The term invariably refers to that which is central. Even when the word is used as a figure of speech, expressive of things and situations apart from mankind, it denotes central location, center, or being in the midst: "Your borders are in the heart of the seas" (Ezek. 27:4 NRSV; cf. also Ps. 46:2; Matt. 12:40). The word is employed to express certain important dimensions of human beings and God's concern and dealings with them. It is used, then, to denote:

A. The "inner self" (1 Pet. 3:4; lit., "the hidden man of the heart"), that central essence of a human being with which God is primarily concerned. It is that portion or essence of men and women which God the Lord looks on, searches, and tries (1 Sam. 16:7; Prov. 10:8; Jer. 11:20; 17:10; 20:12). It is the center and source of belief and faith (Lk. 24:25; Rom. 10:10).

B. That central agency and facility within a person whereby he imagines, intends, purposes, thinks, and understands (Ezek. 13:2).
(1) Behaviors, expressions, and words have their origins there (Matt. 12:34–35; 15:18–19)
(2) Beliefs and faith center there (Lk. 24:25; Rom. 10:10).
(3) Considerations, concerns are associated (Jer. 12:11).
(4) Imaginations originate (Prov. 6:18).
(5) Inclinations are formed (Eccl. 10:2).
(6) Intents are present there (Heb. 4:12).
(7) It is very profound, deep (Ps. 64:6).
(8) Numerous devices are known to it (Prov. 19:21).
(9) Ponderings are made (Lk. 2:19).
(10) Purposes are formed (Prov. 20:5; Acts 11:23).
(11) Reflections are cogitated (1 Cor. 2:9; Rev. 18:7).
(12) Understandings (1 Ki. 3:9; Job 38:36).
(13) Will is exercised (Eph. 6:6).

C. Particular qualities of a person's character. As such, one may be seen to be or possess a "heart" that is:
(1) Double (1 Chr. 12:33).
(2) Honest and good (Lk. 8:15).
(3) Large (1 Ki. 4:29).
(4) Perfect or mature (1 Ki. 8:61; 11:4; 2 Chr. 16:9; 25:2; Ps. 101:2).
(5) Pure (Ps. 24:4; Prov. 22:11; Matt. 5:8; 1 Tim. 1:5; 2 Tim. 2:22; 1 Pet. 2:22).
(6) Single (2 Chr. 30:12; Jer. 32:39; Acts 2:46; 4:32; Col. 3:22).
(7) True (Heb. 10:22).
(8) Understanding (Job 38:36).
(9) Wise (Job 9:4).

D. That which is descriptive of a person's attitude as depicted in his actions (behavior):
(1) Despiteful, despising (Ezek. 25:15; 2 Sam. 6:16).
(2) Dull (Acts 28:27).
(3) False (Hos. 10:2).
(4) Gross (Ps. 119:70).
(5) Hard (Mk. 3:5; 16:14; Rom. 2:5).
(6) Haughty (Prov. 18:12).
(7) Impenitent (Rom. 2:5).
(8) Meek and lowly (Jesus, as self-described, Matt. 11:29–30).
(9) Searching (Jdg. 5:15, 16).
(10) Stony (Ezek. 11:19; 36:26).
(11) Subtle (Prov. 7:10).
(12) Taken away (Hos. 4:11).
(13) Whorish (Ezek. 6:9).
(14) Willing (Exod. 35:5).
(15) Wise (Prov. 10:8; 11:29; there are nearly fifty occurrences of the word in Proverbs).

E. That center, essence, and inner substance of a person that needs to be reconciled to God, redeemed; being righted with God, it may be reconciled to others. As such, the heart is described as being:
(1) Deceitful and desperately wicked (Prov. 12:20; Isa. 44:20; Jer. 17:9).
(2) Froward and proud (Ps. 101:4–5).
(3) In need of a new creation and cleansing by God (Ps. 51:10).
(4) In need of being renewed so as to know the Lord (Jer. 24:7).
(5) Set to do evil (Eccl. 8:11; 9:3).
(6) Stony, needing removal, and a new heart given in its stead (Ezek. 11:19; 18:31; 36:26).
(7) Stubborn and rebellious (Jer. 5:23).
(8) Turned by the Lord to others, otherwise to be smitten with a curse (Mal. 4:6).
(9) Wicked (Ps. 58:2).

F. The core and seat of emotions; the center of emotional reaction, feeling, and sensitivity. As such, the heart may experience or know what it is to be:
(1) Astonished (Deut. 28:28).
(2) Bitter (Ezek. 27:31).
(3) Broken (Pss. 34:18; 69:20; 147:3; Isa. 61:1).
(4) Discouraged (Num. 32:7–9).
(5) Failing (1 Sam. 17:32).
(6) Fainting (Gen. 45:26).
(7) Fearful (Isa. 21:4; 35:4).
(8) Glad (Deut. 28:47; Ps. 104:15; Prov. 24:17; 27:11).
(9) Grieved (1 Sam. 25:31; Ps. 73:21).
(10) Heavy (Prov. 12:25; 25:20; 31:6; Matt. 26:37).
(11) Joyful (Job 29:13; Eccl. 2:10).
(12) Merry (1 Sam. 25:36; 1 Ki. 21:7; Esth. 1:10; Prov. 15:13, 15; 17:22).
(13) Smitten (1 Sam. 24:5; Ps. 102:4).
(14) Trembling (Deut. 28:65).

J. M. Lower

hearth. In biblical times the hearth was a depression in the floor of a HOUSE or TENT—in the center or in a corner—and in this area FOOD was cooked, or BREAD was baked in the ashes or on hot stones. There was no chimney; smoke escaped through a door or a window. Where obtainable, wood was used as a fuel, but withered vegetation (Matt. 6:30) and dried cow and camel dung were also used (Ezek. 4:15). In the better class of houses, in the cold season, rooms were warmed by means of a brazier or firepot (Jer. 36:22–23; Zech. 12:6). The term "altar hearth" was applied to the top of the ALTAR of burnt offering (various Heb. terms are used in Lev. 6:9; Isa. 29:2; 30:14; Ezek. 43:15–16). S. Barabas

heat and cold. These words appear in the same context twice (Gen. 8:22; 31:40). A striking feature of the climate of PALESTINE is the differences in temperature within so small a country. The land can experience almost tropical heat and bitter cold, although the cold lasts only a short time. These variations are due mainly to the nearness of plains and mountains, desert and sea, and the JORDAN valley. The differences increase as one moves eastward from the Mediterranean Sea, which keeps the temperature of the maritime plain much more constant than is found in the interior of the country.

Summers in Palestine are very hot, the intense heat leading to sunstroke, and the glare of the sun to eye trouble. A possible illustration may be the small boy who cried to his father, "My head! My head!" and died on his mother's lap (2 Ki. 4:19–20). SNOW seldom falls in Palestine except sometimes in the winter months, and when it does it quickly melts. But because the cold lasts so short a time, homes are not protected against it, causing real discomfort. To keep warm, people huddled about a charcoal brazier, as Peter did in the court of the high priest (Jn. 18:18).   S. BARABAS

heath. A low-growing shrub with evergreen leaves (also known as *heather*). The term is used by the KJV twice to render Hebrew ʿarʿār H6899 (Jer. 17:6; 48:6; NIV, "bush" [in the latter passage the text can be understood differently]). Since the true heath does not grow in Palestine, the Hebrew word probably refers to the JUNIPER (*Juniperus phoenicia*), a small tree with very small scale-like leaves and round cones; it grows on the W side of the mountains of EDOM. (Cf. *FFB*, 131–32.) See also FLORA (under *Leguminosae* and *Pinaceae*).   S. BARABAS

heathen. See GENTILE, NATIONS.

heaven. The biblical doctrine of heaven has never received, from a theological standpoint, the consideration that has been given to the doctrine of HELL and eternal punishment (see PUNISHMENT, ETERNAL). W. T. Shedd, for example, assigned two pages in his 3-volume *Dogmatic Theology* (1888–94) to heaven and eighty-seven pages to eternal punishment. Richard Niebuhr, in his quite exhaustive work, *The Nature and Destiny of Man: A Christian Reinterpretation* (1941–43), gives no consideration to the matter of heaven except for a regrettable statement, "It is unwise for Christians to claim any knowledge of either the furniture of heaven or the temperature of hell" (2:294). John Baillie asks the question, "How many preachers during these last twenty-five years have dwelt on the joys of the heavenly rest with anything like the old ardent love and impatient longing, or have spoken of the world that now is as a place of sojourn and pilgrimage" (*And the Life Everlasting* [1934], 15).

Furthermore, as has been pointed out: "The rapid changes in Western civilization have subjectivized and secularized heaven. In the nineteenth century, the concept grew increasingly vague, with wide scope in meaning. Eschatology which gathered up the 'apparatus of celestial being' gave much assurance and comfort, but lacked reality. The twentieth century has been ever more devastating to the idea of heaven. The word 'heaven' has been appropriated for many purposes, and used in connection with dreams, loves, lyrics, and fiction, until now it has been deprived of meaning for much of society" (R. E. Knudsen, *Theology in the New Testament* [1964], 408).

Of the hundreds of occurrences of the word *heaven* in the English Bible, practically all render just two terms: Hebrew šāmayim H9028 (which has a dual form) and Greek *ouranos* G4041 (see *NIDOTTE*, 4:160–66; *NIDNTT*, 2:188–96). These terms, which can also be translated "sky" (cf. also Heb. šaḥaq H8836, "cloud," in Ps. 89:6 et al.), refer to that which is above earth and above human beings. Except when used figuratively, *heaven* designates one of three realms—the atmospheric space immediately above us, the stellar heavens that must ultimately embrace the universe, and heaven as the abode of God. In Catholic and medieval theology, these three realms are referred to as *coelum aqueum, coelum sidereum, coelum empyreum*. Interestingly enough, these are the three basic meanings of the word *ouranos* in Greek classical literature.

I. The atmospheric heavens. This realm includes the space that immediately surrounds the earth, the air that we breathe (in modern scientific terms, the troposphere, which does not extend more than 20 mi. above the earth; beyond it is the stratosphere). The most frequently occurring atmospheric phenomenon in the Scripture is, of course, RAIN, and also, on rare occasions, SNOW. One of the most relevant and wonderful passages embracing these matters is Isa. 55:9–11: "As the rain and the snow / come down from heaven, / and do not return to it / without watering the earth / and making it bud and flourish, / so that it yields seed for the sower and bread for the eater, / so is my word that goes out from my mouth: / It will not return to me empty, / but will accomplish what I desire / and achieve the purpose for which I sent it."

Frost also is said to be sent from heaven, and dew as well (Job 38:29; Deut. 33:13). Probably the statement regarding Yahweh casting down "great stones from heaven" at the battle of Gibeon refers to huge hailstones (Josh. 10:11 KJV; see hail). Frequently, the Bible mentions thunder from heaven (1 Sam. 2:10 et al.). Often, clouds are identified with these atmospheric heavens: "he covers the heavens with clouds, / prepares rain for the earth, / makes grass grow on the hills" (Ps. 147:8 NRSV). Clouds often have an eschatological importance, especially in relation to the second coming of Christ.

The Bible sometimes speaks of "the four winds of heaven" (Zech. 2:6; 6:5). Probably the statement that bread came down "from heaven" (Exod. 16:4; Ps. 78:24; see manna) refers to the atmospheric heavens, though it also may include the idea of bread as a gift from God. Birds of heaven, such as eagles and others, are announced in the initial account of creation (Gen. 1:26, 30; Prov. 23:5). Generally, these atmospheric phenomena point to favors bestowed upon the human race, but sometimes they embrace destructive forces, as fire and brimstone sent down upon Sodom and Gomorrah (Gen. 19:24).

II. The celestial heavens. The term *heaven*, in both the OT and NT, often refers to the vast space above, in which are included the sun, moon, the planets, and the stars. At the beginning of the creation account is the phrase, "lights in the firmament of the heavens" (Gen. 1:14 KJV [NIV, "lights in the expanse of the sky"]; cf. 15:5; Deut. 4:19 and see firmament). Repeatedly one reads, as the writer to the Hebrews states, "The heavens are the work of your hands" (e.g., Heb. 1:10; Ps. 33:6). Among the planets, Venus and Saturn are possibly referred to (Isa. 14:12; Amos 5:26); and among the so-called fixed stars, several constellations are named in the book of Job, as the Pleiades and Orion (Job 9:9; 38:31; cf. Amos 5:8). See astronomy. The Hebrew people were forbidden to worship these stellar bodies (Exod. 20:4; cf. the offering of sacrifices to the Queen of Heaven, Jer. 44:17–25) and to indulge in astrological speculations (Isa. 47:13). In such phrases as "under the whole heaven" (Dan. 7:27), the reference is to the totality of mankind.

III. Heaven as the abode of God. Although the Scriptures teach that "the heavens, even the highest heaven, cannot contain" God (1 Ki. 8:27), and that God is everywhere present in the universe, they nevertheless clearly affirm that heaven is in a particular way the habitation of God. "For this is what the high and lofty One says— / he who lives forever, whose name is holy: / 'I live in a high and holy place, / but also with him who is contrite and lowly in spirit, / to revive the spirit of the lowly / and to revive the heart of the contrite'" (Isa. 57:15; cf. 63:15).

The psalmist often used the title "Most High," especially when he wished to give thanks to God for deliverance or when appealing to him for deliverance from trouble (Pss. 7:17; 18:13; 57:2). Frequently in passages that relate to Israel and the nations round about occurs the title "The Lord, the God of heaven" (2 Chr. 36:23; Neh. 1:4, 5; Dan. 2:37, 44). Gabriel, in the annunciation to Mary, referred to Christ as "the Son of the Most High" (Lk. 1:32), and Jesus spoke of his disciples as "sons of the Most High" (6:35).

The word *heaven* as used in the Bible can refer to the atmosphere where the birds fly, or to outer space where the stars are found, or to God's abode.

Various words in the OT and NT allude to heaven by referring to God's habitation. The basic word is TABERNACLE, referring both to the tent erected by Moses and the building that the Lord set up, not man (Heb. 8:2; 9:11). The idea of God's dwelling in a TEMPLE on earth is parallel with his dwelling in heaven (1 Ki. 8:12–13). The word SANCTUARY is used in reference to God's dwelling in the tabernacle (Exod. 25:8), but also in relation to the holy place of heaven (Heb. 8:2; 9:8, 12), a similar use is found with the word DWELLING (Exod. 15:13; Ps. 33:14; cf. Isa. 63:15; Lk. 16:9).

The word that appears with greatest frequency in reference to heaven, both pointing to earthly structures and the heaven of God's abode, is the word *house*, first introduced in Gen. 28:17. This use of the term occurs some fifteen times; note especially Solomon's dedicatory prayer (and its context), where we read the great statement, "But will God really dwell on earth? The heavens, even the highest heaven, cannot contain you. How much less this temple I have built!" (1 Ki. 8:27). The same concept may be found in the Lord's famous promise regarding the many "rooms" in his Father's house (Jn. 14:2; but cf. the same Gk. word for "room," *monē* G3665, in its only other occurrence, v. 23). Another term used in reference to heaven (as well as to structures on earth) is *temple*, found even in reference to the first tabernacle (1 Sam. 1:9; 3:3). A good illustration is DAVID's statement, "In my distress I called to the LORD; / I called out to my God. / From his temple he heard my voice; / my cry came to his ears" (2 Sam. 22:7; cf. Isa. 6:1). The word *sanctuary* sometimes refers to the holiest part of the tabernacle or temple, but also to God's heavenly abode (Ps. 102:19; cf. Heb. 8:2; Rev. 3:12; et al.).

Often heaven is called the THRONE of God, both in the OT and NT (Isa. 61:1; Jer. 14:21; Matt. 5:34; and in the Apocalypse). The term GLORY often is used in reference both to the earthly tabernacle or temple and to the heavenly abode of God (Acts 7:55; 1 Tim. 3:16); the HOPE of heaven can be referred to as "the hope of glory" (Col. 1:27). Heaven can even occur as a synonym for God, as in the phrase "looking up to heaven" (Matt. 14:19; cf. Lk. 9:16). When the prodigal son said, "I have sinned against heaven," he meant that he had sinned against God (Lk. 15:18; see also Matt. 23:22; Rom. 10; et al.).

IV. The relationship of Christ to heaven. The Lord Jesus in the NT is said to have dwelt eternally in the heavens, as he himself declares in the high priestly prayer (Jn. 17:5). Compare especially John's statement that before his advent he was "in the bosom of the Father" (1:18 KJV), concerning which B. F. Westcott says that here is "the combination (as it were) of rest and motion, of a continuous relation, with the realisation of it" (*The Gospel according to St. John* [1880], 15). Repeatedly, the advent of Christ is expressed as Christ's coming down from heaven, which he himself affirmed even at the beginning of his ministry (3:13). Six times in his great discourse on the Bread of Life, the Lord referred to himself as "the bread that came down from heaven" (6:33–51). Three times in the Gospels, utterances from heaven confirmed the claims of Christ: the first at the time of his BAPTISM (Matt. 3:16–17); then in the great experience of the TRANSFIGURATION (17:5; cf. 2 Pet. 1:18); and finally at the end of his ministry (Jn. 12:28; only in the fourth gospel).

The subject of heaven is inextricably identified with the ASCENSION of Jesus Christ. The APOSTLES' CREED summarizes the NT teaching in the clause, "he ascended into heaven." This was stated by the Lord himself (Jn. 20:17) and by Luke in his account (Lk. 24:51; Acts 1:9). The event is confirmed in references in the letters of PAUL (Eph. 4:10; 1 Tim. 3:16; 1 Pet. 3:22). To ascend into heaven was to ascend to God. As K. Schilder puts it (*Heaven, What Is It?* [1950], 56): "The ascension of Christ

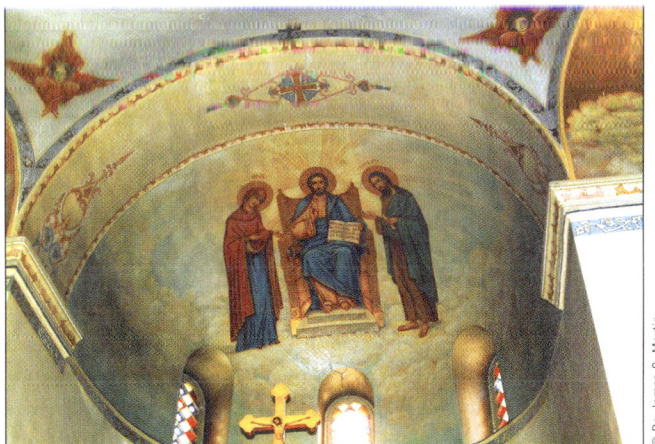

Jesus on his throne in heaven. Painting in the Russian Orthodox Church of the Ascension, Mount of Olives, Jerusalem.

is of special meaning in the history of heaven. It reveals anew that the history of heaven is closely bound up with that of the earth. The *diastase* [separation] and the conjunction are clearly revealed. For Christ withdrew from the dwelling place of his people. The Greek puts it thus: he made *diastase* between himself and them [*dieste ap' auton*, Lk. 24:51]. But there is conjunction also; Christ carried his physical body to heaven, a pledge of the coming union between heaven and earth. And he sent his Spirit as a counter pledge—the Spirit who utters that longing of men with unutterable groaning, crying out, 'How long, O Lord?' And heaven, too, awaits that consummation; the Son intercedes for the church, straining toward that end, that great moment of time. And the blessed cry out also, 'How long, how long, O Lord?' How long before we shall reach that 'moment of time when earth and heaven shall be drawn together, as they ought to be'?"

V. The present inhabitants of heaven. From ages long before the CREATION, heaven was the home of the angels. See ANGEL. Large groups of these are referred to as hosts: "Praise him, all his angels, / praise him, all his heavenly hosts!" (Ps. 148:2; cf. 103:21). The expression "the holy ones" can refer to angelic beings (Job 5:1; 15:15; Zech. 14:5). Karl Barth goes so far as to say, "A dogmatics which tried to escape the task of Angelology would be guilty of an indolent omission which might well jeopardize the whole church" (*Church Dogmatics* [1964–82], 3/3:374).

The CHERUBIM are first mentioned immediately after the FALL of the first parents. Having driven ADAM and EVE out of the Garden of Eden, God "placed on the east side of the Garden of Eden cherubim and a flaming sword flashing back and forth to guard the way to the tree of life" (Gen. 3:24; see EDEN, GARDEN OF). Apart from symbolic references, they appear especially prominent in Ezek. 10, where they are apparently to be identified with the living creatures of the first chapter. It is impossible here to interpret all the complicated details given concerning these creatures in EZEKIEL. Moorehead's comment on these supernatural beings is a model of conciseness when he says that they are "hieroglyphs of God's attributes, of the eternal forces and infinite powers of the throne of God. . . .

The execution of his will is through the power and forces which he himself has created, angels, natural law, human beings and the animal creation."

VI. The possibility of heavenly life now. At the beginning of the Lord's ministry, in the great prayer he taught his disciples, a life ruled by heaven is certainly implied: "your will be done on earth as it is in heaven" (Matt. 6:10). True servants of the Lord cannot do anything else but obey his will, as Paul himself enjoined his readers not to be men pleasers, but "slaves of Christ, doing the will of God from your heart" (Eph. 6:6). A prayer such as this, taught by the Lord Jesus, certainly must be one that can be fulfilled.

Paul in his letter to the PHILIPPIANS has one of the fullest statements regarding the present relationship to heaven to be found anywhere in the Scriptures. He connects the heavenly influence upon present life with the great truth that some day in heaven believers will be clothed in a body conformable to the glorious body of the Lord Jesus: "But our citizenship is in heaven. And we eagerly await a Savior from there, the Lord Jesus Christ, who, by the power that enables him to bring everything under his control, will transform our lowly bodies so that they will be like his glorious body" (Phil. 3:20–21). The Greek word translated CITIZENSHIP is *politeuma* G4487, which meant first of all a commonwealth or a state, and then it came to mean a colony of foreigners who, in the environment of their present residence outside of their native country, were living according to the laws of the country of which they were citizens, not according to the laws of the country in which they were living.

Heaven as the sphere of spiritual life is mentioned in COLOSSIANS. If believers have been raised together with Christ they are to "set [their] hearts on things above, where Christ is seated at the right hand of God" (Col. 3:1). In EPHESIANS, Paul declares that God has "blessed us in the heavenly realms with every spiritual blessing in Christ" (Eph. 1:3, 20; 2:6; 3:10; 6:12). The word here translated "heavenly realms" is the plural of *epouranios* G2230 (see HEAVENLY), and this particular notion of "in heavenly places" is found exclusively in this one epistle (the word is used elsewhere in reference to God [Matt. 18:35], Christ [1 Cor. 15:48–49; 2 Tim. 4:18; Heb. 11:16; 12:22], celestial bodies [1 Cor. 15:40], and heavenly things [Heb. 9:23]). Westcott's interpretation of this phrase deserves study: "… the supramundane, supra-sensual eternal order, or as we should say generally, 'the spiritual world' which is perceived by thought and not by sight. This is not distant or future but present, the scene even now of the Christian's struggle where his life is already centered and his strength is assured to him and his triumph is already realized" (*St. Paul's Epistle to the Ephesians* [1906], 7). The hope that sustains us is laid up for us in heaven (Col. 1:5). Believers "share in the heavenly calling" (Heb. 3:1), that is, they "have tasted the heavenly gift" (6:4).

VII. The rule of heaven in the Apocalypse. Except for references to the kingdom of heaven, so frequently found in the Gospel of Matthew, the word *heaven* more frequently appears in the book of Revelation than in any other successive twenty-two chapters in the Word of God—fifty-two times, to be exact. Actually, the tremendous events prophetically set forth in the Apocalypse are, as in no other book in the Bible, under the rule of heaven. The phrase "the God of heaven" occurs once (Rev. 11:13). The phenomenon most mentioned in Revelation in reference to heaven is God's "throne," which is referred to thirty-six times, from the opening paragraph of the first chapter to the initial statement of the last chapter, a concept that goes back as far as the Psalter (see Ps. 45:6 quoted in Heb. 1:8). The One seated upon the throne whom John beheld when he was taken into heaven is certainly God the Father. At the same time, John beheld a group of creatures surrounding the throne identified as twenty-four elders, each sitting upon separate thrones, of whom R. Govett (pseudonym Matheetees) says: "They are councillors of the throne; conversant with the purposes of the king and able to impart intelligence to John, as the servant of God" (*The Apocalypse* [1861], 2:21). The second group, consisting of four living creatures, "full of eyes before and behind," are probably the same as the cherubim of the OT (Ezek. 1:5–10). In addition, of course, there were multitudes of angels and (only in Rev. 14:2) "harpists playing their harps."

In Rev. 11:19 is mentioned "God's temple in heaven," where John saw the ARK OF THE COVENANT. Henry Alford (*The Greek Testament*, 4 vols. [1871–74], 4:666–67) comments: "The ark of the Covenant is seen, the symbol of God's faithfulness in bestowing grace on His people and in inflicting vengeance on His people's enemies. This is evidently a solemn and befitting inauguration of God's final judgments, as it is a conclusion of the series pointed out by the trumpets, which have been inflicted in answer to the prayers of His saints. It is from this temple that the judgments proceed forth (cf. ch. xiv. 15, 17, xv. 5 ff., xvi. 17); from His inmost and holiest place that those acts of vengeance are wrought which the great multitude in heaven recognize as faithful and true, ch. xix. 2. The symbolism of this verse, the *opening* for the first time of the heavenly temple, also indicates of what nature the succeeding visions are to be: that they will relate to God's covenant people and His dealings with them."

The angels announce the various judgments of God (Rev. 8:1—9:1; 16:1–17). It is an angel to whom was given the key to the pit of the abyss (9:1). There are also the angels who had MICHAEL as their leader in the great war in heaven (12:7–9). Angels sent from heaven are especially active in the judgments upon BABYLON (17:1; 18:1, 4, 20). The twelfth song in the book is sung by a great multitude at the time of the marriage of the Lamb (19:6–8). After John saw heaven open at the beginning of the series of judgments (4:1), he heard "the voice of many angels, numbering thousands upon thousands, and ten thousand times ten thousand" (5:11). In the final events that usher in ETERNITY, the dragon is bound and cast into the abyss by an angel coming down from heaven (10:1).

The Bible begins with God, the Creator of heaven and earth. The NT begins with One coming down from heaven to establish the kingdom of heaven and to fulfill the promise of life in heaven forever with him. Appropriately, the last book of the NT, in depicting the final and universal rebellions against Christ—participated in by men, by Satan, by Satan's angels, and by the antichrist—shows heaven and its supernatural citizens as possessing a foreknowledge of all that is to happen on earth, and supernatural power to determine the time and limitations of these outbursts, to announce and execute the judgment of God, and to participate in the final disposition of every power arraigned against God. Here is fulfilled in final and irrevocable reality the oft-heard pronouncement that all power and authority has been given to Christ. He and he alone is able to subdue all things unto himself and to bring those whom he has redeemed into their eternal habitation, which is the habitation of God. See KINGDOM OF GOD.

(Classic works on the subject include R. Baxter, *The Saints' Everlasting Rest, or a Treatise of the Blessed State of the Saints in their Enjoyment of God in Glory* [1649], in *Works of Richard Baxter* [1688]; J. Bunyan, *The Holy City; or, the New Jerusalem* [1665], in his *Works* [1853]; I. Watts, *The World to Come; or, Discourses on the Joys and Sorrows of Departed Souls at Death* 7 [n.d.]; id., *Heaven; or, An Earnest and Scriptural Inquiry into the Abode of the Sainted Dead*, 17th ed. [1848]; id., *The Heavenly Recognition*, 9th ed. [1856]; Bishop R. Mant, *The Happiness of the Blessed Considered*, 6th ed. [1853]; H. Harbaugh, *The Heavenly Home; or, the Employments and Enjoyments of the Saints in Heaven*, 9th ed. [1858]; Countess Valerie des Gasparin, *The Near and Heavenly Horizons* [1861]; F. W. Grant, *Facts and Theories as to a Future State* [1879]; D. L. Moody, *Heaven and How to Get There* [1880]; G. H. Pike, *The Heavenly World: Views of the Future Life by Eminent Writers* [1880]; S. Fallows, *The Home Beyond: Views of Heaven and Its Relation to Earth by over Four Hundred Prominent Thinkers and Writers* [1883]; T. Hamilton, *Beyond the Stars; or, Heaven, Its Inhabitants, Occupations, and Life*, 4th ed. [n.d.]; J. Paton, *The Glory and Joy of the Resurrection* [1902]; E. M. Bounds, *Heaven: A Place—A City—A Home* [1921]; A. Kuyper, *Asleep in Jesus* [1929]. More recent works include U. Simon, *Heaven in the Christian Tradition* [1958]; id., *The Ascent to Heaven* [1961]; R. Pache, *The Future Life* [1962]; W. M. Smith, *The Biblical Doctrine of Heaven* [1968]; J. Gilmore, *Probing Heaven: Key Questions on the Hereafter* [1989]; D. J. Rumford, *What about Heaven and Hell?* [2000]; E. Donnelly, *Biblical Teaching on the Doctrines of Heaven and Hell* [2001].) W. M. SMITH

Heaven, Queen of. See QUEEN OF HEAVEN.

heavenly. That which relates to HEAVEN. The relevant Greek adjectives (*ouranios G4039, epouranion G2230*) are used with reference to spiritual truths and to the divine and eternal realm. The meaning is best understood in context.

Jesus contrasted "the earthly things" (*ta epigeia*), concerning the rebirth of men on earth, with "the heavenly things" (*ta epourania*), concerning the revelation of his divine person from heaven (Jn. 3:12); the idea is somewhat abstract but not divorced from the idea of heaven as a locality. In the book of HEBREWS, the TABERNACLE is characterized as a copy and shadow of the "heavenly" sanctuary (Heb. 8:5): it contains "heavenly things," which are purified by the high priestly offering of Christ (9:23). "Heavenly" here should be associated directly with "heaven itself" and "the presence of God" (9:24).

PAUL used the phrase in three distinguishable senses. (a) The sphere of thought is *futurist eschatology* in 1 Cor. 15 where the glorious nature of the RESURRECTION bodies of believers is seen in analogy to the heavenly bodies of the stars (vv. 40, 48); as Christians have an earthly body, they shall have a "heavenly" or glorified body (v. 49; cf. v. 22; 2 Cor. 3:18). (b) In Ephesians the context is that of *"realized" eschatology:* by virtue of a present or "realized" UNION WITH CHRIST, the believer is the recipient of spiritual blessings "in the heavenly realms" (Eph. 1:3, 20). Believers are raised with Christ and made to sit "with him in the heavenly realms" (2:6); and thus united to Christ, they participate in the conquest against the principalities and powers, "the spiritual forces of evil in the heavenly realms" (6:12; 3:10). (c) Finally, the simple idea of *locale* is present in Paul's reference to heaven (Phil. 2:10) and Christ's heavenly kingdom (2 Tim. 4:18). (See *TDNT*, 5:358–42; A. T. Lincoln, *Paradise Now and Not Yet: Studies in the Role of the Heavenly Dimension in Paul's Thought with Special Reference to his Eschatology* [1981].) J. C. DEYOUNG

heavens, new. The expression "new heaven(s) and a new earth" is a technical term in the eschatological language of the Bible to define and describe the final, perfected state of the created universe. See ESCHATOLOGY. The conception of a re-created universe has its origin in the biblical account of CREATION: "In the beginning God created the heavens and the earth" (Gen. 1:1). Here the phrase "the heavens and the earth" is meant to embrace the whole of the created universe (cf. Jn. 1:2–3; see also COSMOGONY; WORLD). The creation of the universe may be defined further as a creation out of nothing (ex nihilo), and as accomplished by divine commandment. "Heavens" in the primitive worldview was meant to describe all that is above the earth — the sky with its heavenly bodies — and therefore should be distinguished from HEAVEN as the dwelling place of God that is outside the realm of the created universe. The promise of a re-creation of the heavens and the earth arises not out of some inherent lack or evil in the material universe, but because of man's sin and God's subsequent curse: "Cursed is the ground because of you" (Gen. 3:17).

The idea of a renewed or re-created universe is present in substance in many passages: Isa. 51:16; Matt. 19:28; 24:29–31, 35; Mk. 13:24–27, 31; Rom. 8:19–23; 2 Cor. 5:17; Heb. 12:26–28. Specific mention of "new heaven(s) and a new earth" is found in Isa. 65:17; 66:22; 2 Pet. 3:13; Rev. 21:1. These passages suggest the following points of interest:

God is the source of this new universe. "Behold, I will create new heavens and a new earth" (Isa. 65:17; cf. 66:22). The hope for a renewed human life and society is rooted in a new world that will be purified in a radical way by God.

God will bring the new universe into existence in the end of history. It will be the product of a purely eschatological activity and will be directly related to degeneracy in human ethical and religious life (Mk. 13:24–27; cf. Rom. 8:19–20; 2 Pet. 3:3–12) as well as accomplishment of the evangelistic task of the church (Matt. 24:14). It will be the result of catastrophic events in the created universe that are designed not to annihilate but to cleanse and purify (Mk. 13:24–27 and parallels; 2 Pet. 3:3–13). It will be brought about by a radical renovation but not by a new creation ex nihilo. Thus, Jesus spoke of the method to be used as "renewal" (*palingenesia G4098*, Matt. 19:28; KJV, "regeneration"). Likewise PETER speaks of "the restitution [*apokatastasis G640*] of all things" (Acts 3:21 KJV; NRSV, "universal restoration"), which will be in a way similar to the cleansing of the world with the flood — the world will be purged by fire (2 Pet. 3:6–7; this continuity between the present and future universe stands in contrast to the rabbinic teaching that the new heavens and new earth were created at the end of the original creation week).

The divine revelation concerning the new heavens and new earth is closely related to the theme of the NEW JERUSALEM (Rev. 21:2—22:5), which contains the motif of a new Garden of Eden (22:2). (See K. Schilder, *Heaven, What Is It?* [1950], 69–71, 113–18; U. Simon, *Heaven in the Christian Tradition* [1958], 46–51, 221–27; J. C. DeYoung, *Jerusalem in the New Testament* [1960], 152ff.)

J. C. DEYOUNG

heave offering. See SACRIFICE AND OFFERINGS IV.C.

Heber hee´buhr (חֶבֶר *H2491*, "associate, companion"; gentilic חֶבְרִי *H2499*, "Heberite"). **(1)** Son of Beriah, grandson of ASHER, and eponymous ancestor of the Heberite clan (Gen. 46:17; Num. 26:45; 1 Chr. 7:31–32).

(2) A KENITE who separated himself for a time from the main body of Kenites and settled near KEDESH, W of the Sea of Galilee (Jdg. 4:11). Heber's clan established friendly associations with JABIN king of HAZOR, who was an enemy of Israel. The king's commander, SISERA, having been defeated by BARAK, fled for refuge to Heber's settlement. Sisera went into the tent of JAEL, Heber's wife (4:17). Jael, however, betraying the alliance between Jabin and her husband, took this opportunity to kill Sisera (4:18–22; 5:24–27).

(3) Son of Mered (by the latter's Judahite wife), "father" (i.e., "ruler/founder") of SOCO, and descendant of JUDAH, although his precise genealogical connection is unclear (1 Chr. 4:18).

(4) Son of ELPAAL and descendant of BENJAMIN (1 Chr. 8:17).

(5) KJV alternate form of EBER (1 Chr. 5:13; 8:22; Lk. 3:35).

S. BARABAS

Hebrew language. A NW Semitic language spoken by the HEBREW PEOPLE. With the exception of Dan. 2–6 and portions of Ezra 4–7 (which were written in ARAMAIC), the OT was composed in Hebrew, and has been preserved in Masoretic mss, equipped with vowel-points and accents, which date from the 8th or 9th cent. A.D. See TEXT AND MANUSCRIPTS (OT). Earlier MSS of the Hebrew Bible without such vowel signs have been discovered among the DEAD SEA SCROLLS. As for extrabiblical Hebrew, very few texts composed during the biblical period are extant, but significant documents are found among the DSS, and extensive Hebrew (esp. rabbinic) literature survives dating from about A.D. 200. The correct interpretation of the OT depends on an adequate mastery of Hebrew lexicography, grammar, syntax, and style.

I. The position of Hebrew in the Semitic language group. The Semitic family of languages has traditionally been divided into E Semitic (Akkadian with its subdialects of Babylonian and Assyrian; possibly also Eblaite), S Semitic (comprising Arabic, S Arabian, and Ethiopic), and NW Semitic (comprising Canaanite and Aramaic). More recently, linguists have argued that Arabic (or N Arabian) is more closely related to the NW Semitic languages than to S Semitic, and have proposed a basic distinction between E and W Semitic, with the latter further subdivided into S Semitic (comprising S Arabian and Ethiopic) and Central Semitic (comprising N Arabian and NW Semitic). See LANGUAGES OF THE ANE II.

In either case, Hebrew clearly belongs within the Canaanite branch of NW Semitic. Canaanite also includes Moabite, which differs from Hebrew only in a few minor details, and Phoenician. The language spoken in MOAB is preserved almost exclusively in an inscription of King MESHA (see MOABITE STONE). The language of PHOENICIA was spoken in the great coastal cities of TYRE, SIDON, Berytus, Tripolis, and Byblos (see GEBAL), and in all of the colonies settled by Phoenician emigrants in Cyprus, Sardinia, Sicily, and N Africa (in which latter area regional peculiarities developed resulting in Punic). It was apparently the Phoenician alphabet that was adopted by all the Canaanite-speaking peoples, including Hebrews and Moabites, and also by the Arameans as well, no later than the the 11th cent. B.C. By this period several Semitic consonants had merged in Canaanite (e.g., $\underline{d}$ with z; $\underline{h}$ with h; $\underline{t}$ with $š$). Phoenician also developed characteristics that set it apart from Hebrew, such as the causative stem *yiphil* (Heb. *hiphil*).

Cannanite moreover would have included the languages spoken in AMMON and EDOM (both extant in a few small texts) and possibly also AMORITE (which has been preserved largely in the form of personal names). The language attested in the so-called Sinaitic inscriptions (written in a type of alphabetic script resembling hieroglyphics, and found not only in the turquoise mines of Serabit el-Khadim in the Sinai peninsula but also in Palestine) may represent a type of S Canaanite, but the interpretation of these texts is debated (cf. W. F. Albright, *The Proto-Sinaitic Inscriptions and Their Decipherment* [1966]). See ALPHABET; WRITING.

Also controversial is the placement of Ugaritic, the language spoken in Ras Shamra (ancient UGARIT). Written in a thirty-character CUNEIFORM alphabet, Ugaritic preserved most of the original Semitic phonemes that were assimilated to other phonemes in Hebrew and Phoenician. Some scholars regard it as an early form of Canaanite, but others believe it represents a distinct branch within NW Semitic. (See further Z. S. Harris, *The Development of the Canaanite Dialects* [1939]; S. Moscati et al., *An Introduction to the Comparative Grammar of the Semitic Languages* [1964]; W. R. Garr, *Dialect Geography of Syria-Palestine, 1000–586 B.C.E.* [1985]; J. Huehnergard in *CANE*, 4:2117–34.)

The lexical relationship of Hebrew to other Semitic languages deserves special attention. It is only to be expected that the other Canaanite dialects are of great importance in illuminating the grammatical and lexical usages of biblical Hebrew, although unfortunately the amount of literature in these languages is regrettably meager, with the exception of Ugaritic. The decipher-

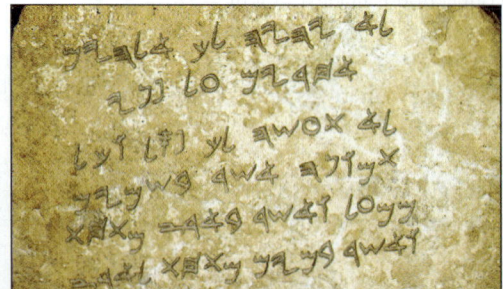

Contemporary display of the Ten Commandments in the paleo-Hebrew script.

ment and analysis of Ugaritic, totally unknown to modern scholarship until 1929, has proven to be of major importance in establishing that certain words and phrases, suspected by many OT critics of being textual errors in the Hebrew Scriptures, were in fact current back in the Mosaic period. New meanings for rare biblical words have been made available by the use of cognates in Ugaritic literature, and many obscurities thereby have been alleviated or cleared up altogether.

Another important source of information concerning the meaning of obscure biblical terms is the considerable literature preserved in Aramaic. To be sure, there is a rather limited amount of this from the OT period, largely consisting of funerary inscriptions, biographical epitaphs, governmental decrees, and a few epistles. Most of the Aramaic from intertestamental and NT times consists of the writings of Jews who were rooted in the OT tradition. The GENESIS APOCRYPHON, discovered in Qumran Cave 1, was written in the 1st cent. B.C. or earlier (in a form of Aram. separated by centuries of development from the Aram. of Daniel and Ezra); the *Targum of Onkelos* on the Pentateuch can be dated no earlier than A.D. 200, and the *Targum of Jonathan* on the Prophets somewhat later than that (see TARGUM). The Aramaic of the MIDRASH and TALMUD is later still. The Syriac Peshitta (written in an eastern dialect of Aram., and in a different form of alphabet from the "Square Hebrew" of biblical and post-biblical Aram.) can hardly be older than the late 2nd cent. A.D.

Outside the NW Semitic group, important sources of lexical data come from Akkadian (Assyro-Babylonian) literature, all of which dates back to OT times or even earlier, and some of which deals with matters discussed in the Hebrew Scriptures. Beginning with the Old Akkadian inscriptions of Sargon of Agade (c. 2200 B.C.), the first dynasty of Babylon with its Code of HAMMURABI (c. 1700), the MARI tablets from the same period, the NUZI tablets from 1500, the Old Assyrian letters and commercial documents from the Assyrian merchant colony in Cappadocia, the royal inscriptions, official annals, and business documents from the Assyrian Empire period (850–612 B.C.), and the Neo-Babylonian inscriptions and annals from the 6th cent.—all of these furnish a large body of linguistic data from which to receive help in solving lexical problems.

As far as S Semitic is concerned, there is a modest number of dedicatory, boundary-marker, and funerary inscriptions in the various dialects (SABEAN, MINEAN, Qatabanian, Ḥadramautian) of Old S Arabian. Northern Arabian material prior to Muhammad consists largely of short graffiti (Thamudic, Lihyanic, Safahitic) dating from the 1st cent. B.C. to the 4th cent. A.D. Beginning with the Koran and the early Islamic period, a tremendous wealth of vocabulary has been preserved in a Semitic dialect so conservative in character as to retain, with relatively little change, the phonology and morphology of Primitive Semitic. Literary Arabic is of major value in supplying the most likely vowel patterns for the vowelless scripts of Ugaritic, Phoenician, Old Aramaic, and even of the earliest (Mosaic) form of biblical Hebrew, which may still have retained short vowel endings on its nouns and verbs during the 2nd millennium B.C. Otherwise, one has to rely on the transcriptions of Canaanite names contained in Middle Kingdom and New Kingdom Egyptian inscriptions, and about thirty-six different Canaanite words (the so-called "Canaanite glosses") inserted into the Akkadian texts of the TELL EL-AMARNA Letters (c. 1420–1370 B.C.) in cuneiform syllabic spelling, clearly demonstrating that the short-vowel endings were still in use back in that period.

The chief extrabiblical Hebrew documents from the OT period include the following: (1) A schoolboy's exercise on a clay tablet listing the agricultural significance of the successive months

Facsimile of the *Community Rule*, an early Hebrew text from Qumran.

of the year; dated at about 925 B.C. and discovered at Gezer, it is known as the Gezer Calendar (see Agriculture V). (2) The Siloam Inscription dating from about 705 B.C. in the reign of Hezekiah, and describing the completion of the tunnel cut through from the pool of Siloam to a reservoir inside the city wall of Jerusalem. (3) The Samaritan Ostraca dating from the reign of Jeroboam II (c. 770 B.C.) and consisting of receipts for taxes paid to the royal treasury in the form of wine or oil. (4) The Lachish letters dating from about 587 B.C., discovered at Tell ed-Duweir, and consisting largely of communications from the commander of a Jewish outpost to his superior officer in the city headquarters. Apart from these are a few fragmentary lists of names, one discovered at Arad, and another found in the Qumran area, dating back to a preexilic army outpost maintained for a time in this region. These documents have served to confirm the authenticity of the OT books as written in the period to which they purport to belong (thus, the Lachish letters are strongly reminiscent of Jeremiah); but more important still, they indicate the way Hebrew was spelled in the older period, and thus give a clue as to possible ways in which copyists' errors may have arisen in the course of the transmission of the OT text.

II. Phonology. The Hebrew alphabet consists of twenty-two letters, all of which are consonants. These letters represent almost all the consonantal sounds found in English plus a number of sounds foreign to Western languages, such as the pharyngeal fricatives *ḥet* (ח) and *ʿayin* (ע), and the so-called "emphatic" consonants *ṭet* (ט), *ṣade* (צ), and *qoph* (ק). The precise pronunciation of these and other sounds in biblical times is debated. Hebrew had three sibilants: in addition to *šin* (ש, pronounced like Eng. *sh*), some kind of distinction existed between *samek* (ס = Eng. *s*) and *śin* (ש, perhaps an intermediate position between *s* and *š*). It seems clear that in the northern kingdom of the ten tribes the distinction was lost quite early; in Judah it faded away by the 6th cent., and (esp. under Aram. influence), *samekh* began to be substituted for *śin* in the spelling of words. It also should be observed that sometime after 500 B.C. the occlusives or stops *b*, *g*, *d*, *k*, *p*, and *t* (known as the *begadkephat* consonants) became spirantized after vowel sounds, that is, the flow of air was not fully obstructed (cf. Spanish *dedo*, "finger": the first *d* is pronounced as in English, but the second, which immediately follows a vowel, approximates the sound of *th* in *those*).

As for the Hebrew vocalic system, it is often described as consisting of ten vowels (*a, e, i, o, u*, each of them pronounced short or long) and two diphthongs (*ai* and *au*). This description appears to be inaccurate, however. The vowel markings used by the Tiberian Masoretes seem to indicate a sevenfold distinction in quality or timbre: *a* (*pataḥ*), *i* (*ḥireq*), *u* (*qibbuṣ*), open *e* (*segol*), close *e* (*ṣere*), open *o* (*qameṣ*), and close *o* (*ḥolem*). In this system, vowel length had no phonemic significance, although there is little doubt that, for example, the *ḥolem* and the *qameṣ* usually represent an original long *ō* and short *o* respectively, and that such length distinctions were linguistically significant in the biblical period. (See further P. Joüon and T. Muraoka, *A Grammar of Biblical Hebrew*, 2 vols. [1991], 1:34–46.) Note: in the discussion that follows, for the sake of simplicity, certain vowel distinctions are not represented in the transliteration if they do not affect the point being made.

III. Nouns. In the earliest period the Hebrew nouns, as in other Semitic languages, no doubt possessed short vowel endings: the nominative case ended in *-u*, the genitive in *-i*, and the accusative in *-a* (the feminine noun generally ended in *-atu*, *-ati*, *-ata*). The masculine plural was *-īma* for all three cases; the feminine plural was *-ātu* or *-āti*. There was also a dual number, especially for parts of the body existing in pairs (e.g., eyes, ears, wings, feet); the masculine dual ending was *-ayim*, and the feminine *-ātayim*. Already in the Mosaic period, however, the feminine long *ā* had rounded to long *ō* (the "Canaanite shift"); hence *-ōtu* in the plural and *-ōtayim* in the dual.

In the course of time the short vowel endings were dropped altogether, except that in some cases the accusative masculine *-a* was retained as a long *ā* in order to express motion toward a place (so called "*he*-directive," since this was spelled with a final silent consonant *he*), or in rare cases, a simple location (e.g., *mizbeḥāh*, "on the altar"). Unlike feminine nouns ending in accented *-āh*, the accent always fell on the penult in the case of a *he*-directive. The genitive had to be expressed by word position after the case endings were lost; that is, the possessor always followed right after the thing possessed. For example, "the word of the king" (originally *dabar hammalki*, from *dabaru* "word," and *malku* "king") was expressed *dĕbar hammelek* (the notation *ĕ* denotes the *shewa* sound or "half vowel"). Note that the definite article, "the," was expressed by *ha*- and the doubling of the first letter of the noun itself. The first member of this pair was put into what is called the "construct" state. Partly because constructs lost their short vowel endings much earlier than did the absolutes, and partly because the construct bore no principal accent (which always fell on the second noun), the constructs often differed slightly from their normal or "absolute" form. This was especially true of feminine nouns. For example, the word for "queen" was originally *malkatu*, and this became *malkāh* in the OT period; but in the case of the construct the *-t* was retained, thus "the queen of Israel" was *malkat yiśraʾel*.

In the case of the masculine plural, the ending *-ey* (*-ê*) was used for the construct; thus, from *susim*, "horses," we get *susey hammelek*, "the horses of the king." Apart from these special cases, the construct relationship was shown merely by the immediate juxtaposition of two nouns. One other important development ensued upon the loss of case endings, and that was the use of *ʾet* as an indicator of the direct object, especially if the noun object was definite (i.e., preceded by the definite article, *ha*). This was virtually obligatory in prose (although is rarely used in poetry). Thus, "The king killed the horse" would be: *qaṭal hammelek ʾet-hassus*.

As for adjectives, they were treated exactly like nouns, and originally had the same case endings. If they were attributive, they had to follow their noun rather than precede it, and they had to have the definite article if their noun did. Thus, "a good horse" was *sus ṭob*, but "the good horse" was *hassus haṭṭob*. On the other hand, if the adjective was predicate, it normally preceded the noun and was never definite: "The horse (is) good" would be *ṭob hassus*. Interestingly enough, Hebrew was the first of the Canaanite dialects to develop the definite article, probably because the definite article was used widely in colloquial Egyptian during the 18th dynasty before the Israelites migrated from Egypt to Palestine.

IV. Verbs. Unlike many Western languages such as English, the Semitic tongues appear to be less interested in time values than in *aspectual* distinctions. That is to say, verbal forms do not primarily indicate when an action took place (past, present, future) but rather the way the action is perceived or presented by the speaker (as a complete whole or as an incomplete process). In general, the Hebrew "perfect" or perfective tense (a suffix conjugation) viewed the action as complete, while the "imperfect" or nonperfective tense (a prefix conjugation) presented it as incomplete (which sometimes reflected repetitive or continual action).

As a practical matter, however, the perfect tense in narrative usually referred to past time, and the imperfect tense usually referred to present or future time. Thus, for purposes of convenience one may render the form *katab* (perf. 3rd sing. masc.) as "he wrote"; and its corresponding imperfect, *yiktob*, as "he will write" or "he writes." Such renderings always need to be verified from the context: the surrounding setting of the imperfect verb may show that it referred to action in progress in past time; correspondingly, the perfect tense was used sometimes to express the immediate past, where in English we would employ the present tense. The frequent formula, "Thus says the LORD" renders *koh ʾamar Yahweh*; the verb *ʾamar* is in the perfect because the action is viewed as a complete whole (perhaps suggesting that the prophet knows what Yahweh has said only because he has already told him). The perfect is also used occasionally to express a future action that has been foretold by the Lord as part of his divine plan—and is therefore as certain of accomplishment as if it had already taken place. In each case the context will indicate quite clearly what the temporal locus is for each verb.

Basically the same antinomy between complete and incomplete action carries over into the "consecutive" (or "conversive") tenses. Unlike other Semitic languages, Hebrew developed a specialized use of the conjunction "and." When the simple particle *wĕ-* preceded the imperfect, there was no change in its tense value; but if it was strengthened to *wa-* with the doubling of the first consonant of the verb form, then it had the effect of converting an imperfect into a perfect in its function. Thus, *yiktob* meant "he will write," but *wayyiktob* meant "and he wrote." This usage seems to have originated from an old preterite tense that had genuine time value (cf. Akk. *iprus*, "he judged"). It never had the short vowel ending of the genuine imperfect; the original conversive was *yaktub*, and the original imperfect was *yaktubu*. Since both forms became *yiktob* in the 1st millennium, the only factor showing past time was the connective particle *wa-*.

Related to this preterite conversive form is the use of the Arabic jussive after the negative *lam*. The jussive also lacked a short vowel ending; thus, Arabic *lam yaktub* meant, "he did not write." Then, by a principle of polarity (i.e., if a *waw* can change an impf. into a pf., then a *waw* should change a pf. into an impf.) the perfect conversive (or "consecutive") arose as a secondary development. Thus, *katab* means "he wrote," but *wĕkatab* means "and he will write" (or even, "that he might write"). At least 90 percent of the perfects preceded by *waw* in biblical Hebrew are converted; the remaining 5 or 10 percent can be shown from the context to be unconverted. (The interpretation of the verbal conjugations is debated, however. For a full discussion, see B. K. Waltke and M. O'Connor, *An Introduction to Biblical Hebrew Syntax* [1990], chs. 29–33.)

In addition to its indicative uses, the imperfect can function as a subjunctive or a jussive. After a *waw* (or an explicit purpose particle), the imperfect is used to express the subjunctive idea: "in order that he may write." There was also a jussive form that looked just like the indicative imperfect in the strong verb (except for the hiphil stem, where impf. *yaktib*, "he will cause to write," contrasts with the jussive *yakteh*, "let him cause to write"). But since this jussive, like the imperfect conversive, went back to an original form that lacked short-vowel endings (*yaktub*, as contrasted with the impf. *yaktubu*), distinctive jussive forms were maintained in certain types of "weak" verbs. Thus, from the verb *qum* ("arise") we have imperfect *yaqum* ("he will arise"), but jussive *yaqom* ("let him arise").

The imperative of the verb consisted of the imperfect form without the prefix. Thus, *tiktob* meant "you will write" (impf.), but *kĕtob* meant "write!" (imperative). There were two types of infinitive: (a) The infinitive construct (*kĕtob*, resembling the imperative), which could serve as a complement to a main verb, was often preceded by a preposition like *lĕ-* ("to"); it could also take suffix pronouns as its subjects or objects. (b) The infinitive absolute (*katob*), which could have no preposition before it or suffix pronoun after it, served to emphasize or extend the action of the main verb it accompanied, or else could take the place of the main verb altogether (in cases where the action was being emphasized, rather than the agent of the action).

Having discussed the function of the various tenses of the verb, we now come to an analysis of the structure of the perfect and imperfect. Semitic verbs were constructed on a skeleton consisting usually of three consonants, and indicating tense or stem by doubling one of the consonants or by the vowel pattern used with them. Given the pattern, one is able to identify the tense and stem of almost any verb. (In the examples that follow, $ā=qameṣ$, $ē=ṣere$, $ō=ḥolem$). The pattern $CāCaC$ (where C represents any radical consonant) always means the perfect active masculine 3rd person singular of that verb (thus, *kātab*, "he wrote"; *qāṭal*, "he killed"; *šāmar*, "he guarded"). The pattern $yiCCōC$ always means the imperfect 3rd masculine singular active (thus, *yiktōb*, "he will write"; *yiqṭōl*, "he will kill"; *yišmōr*, "he will guard"). The perfect tense was inflected by the addition of suffixes (thus *kātabti*, "I wrote," *kātabtā*, "you [masc.] wrote," *kātabt*, "you [fem.] wrote," etc.).

The imperfect tense was inflected by both prefixes and suffixes (also referred to as preformatives and sufformatives). For example, the masculine 3rd singular was indicated by *yi-* (*yiktōb*, "he will write"), the masculine 3rd plural by the same prefix plus suffix *-u* (*yiktĕbu*, "they will write"), the 1st singular by the prefix *ʾe-* (*ʾektōb*, "I will write"), and so on. If the root of the verb begins with a guttural (ʿ*ayin*, *hē*, *ḥet*, or even *ʾaleph*), the vowel of the preformative preserves the original short *a* (e.g., *yaʿămōd*, "he will stand," instead of *yiʿmōd*). So-called hollow verbs (which appear to be missing a middle consonant), such as *qum*, "arise," also preserve this *a*, but modified because the prefix syllable ends in a vowel (thus, *yāqum*, "he will arise").

The examples given above use verbs in their basic stem, called *qal* ("light"). In common with the other Semitic languages, however, Hebrew verbs possessed derived stems that modified the root idea in various ways. (1) The *niphal* was a conjugation or stem that put the root into a reflexive or passive meaning (the stem names are derived from the classical model verb, *pāʿal*, "to make"). (2) The *piel* involved the doubling of the middle consonant, and it either intensified the action (thus, *šibbēr*, "shatter," from *šābar*, "break"), or else it rendered the action transitive or causative. From *qādaš*, "be holy," the piel *qiddēš* meant "sanctify." Some verbs, such as *dibbēr*, "speak," nearly always occur in the piel. (3) The passive of piel was *pual*; thus, *šubbar* meant "he was shattered," and *quddaš* meant "he was sanctified." (4) The reflexive of piel was *hitpael*; thus, *hitqaddēš* meant "he sanctified himself." (5) The stem *hiphil* was primarily causative; thus, *hiktib*, "he caused to write." Some hiphils, however, were characteristic, that is, they showed some noun in action. Thus, from the noun *ʾōzen*, "ear," comes the hiphil *heʾĕzin* (note how *hi-* modifies to *he-* before a guttural), meaning "to use the ear," that is, "listen." (6) The passive form of hiphil was *hophal*; for example, *hoktab* meant "he was caused to write." Each verb might theoretically appear in seven stems (including the *qal*), but in actuality few verbs do; some of them occur in only one or two of these conjugations.

Some verbs are referred to as "weak" if any of their root consonants were subject to modification or even disappearance under certain conditions; this often resulted in alteration of the accompanying vowels. Thus, we have already seen that an initial guttural in the root would prevent the attenuation of an original short *a* to short *i* (thus, *yaʿămōd* instead of *yiʿmōd*) and would compel an original *i* to become *e* (thus, *yeḥĕzaq* instead of *yiḥzaq*). Similar changes were occasioned by a guttural in whichever position it was present in the root, whether first radical, second, or third. Then again, if the first radical was a *nun* (נ=n), this became assimilated to the middle radical whenever no vowel sound separated them; thus, *yippōl* resulted from *nāpal* ("he fell"; the unassimilated form would have been *yinpōl*). If the middle radical was *waw* or *yod*, the result was a "hollow" verb like *qum* ("arise") or *bin* ("understand"). If it was the third radical that was *waw* or *yod*, this led to alterations such as *bānāh* ("he built") from original *banaya*, or *yibneh* ("he will build") from original *yibnayu*. Or again, if the third radical was the same as the second, the two would combine to form a doubled consonant whenever there was no vowel sound in between. Thus from *sābab* ("surround") is derived *yāsōbbu* (or else, by a transfer of the doubling to the first radical, *yissĕbu*), "they will surround."

It should be added that all seven stems possessed participles; thus, from *qādaš* ("be holy") the qal participle would be *qōdēš*, the niphal *niḥdāš*, the piel *mĕqaddēš*, and so on. These participles could serve as simple adjectives (thus, *hassōpēr hakkōtēb* would be "the writing scribe"), or as relative clauses (the previous example could also be translated, "the scribe who was writing"), or as agential nouns like *kōhēn*, "priest" (from the root *khn*, which in the piel means "perform the duties of priest"), or as the predicate of a clause after a noun or pronoun subject. This last construction, known as a *present periphrastic*, was used to convey either continuous, durative action (e.g. *hassōpēr kōtēb*, "the scribe is writing") or else imminent action (e.g., *Yahweh nōtēn lākem* could mean, "Yahweh is about to give to you").

V. Pronouns. Hebrew makes use of both independent pronouns (e.g., *ʾănî* or *ʾānōkî*, "I," *ʾattāh*, "you [masc. sg.]," etc.) and pronominal suffixes. The latter can be attached to nouns (e.g., *sûsî*, "my horse," *sûsō*, "his horse," etc.) and to verbs (*qĕṭaltîhû*, "I killed him," *qĕṭaluhā*, "they killed her"). When attached to nouns, the construct form is used; thus a feminine noun like *malkāh* ("queen") shows an *-at* ending before the possessive pronoun is added ("your [masc. sg.] queen" is *malkatĕkā*). Hebrew has the demonstrative pronoun "this" (masc. sing. *zeh*), but "that" is expressed with the independent third person pronouns preceded by the article ("that king" is *hammelek hahûʾ*, lit. "the king the he"). The relative pronoun is *ʾăšer* (more rarely *še-*, esp. in poetry), although often the relative clause was expressed by a participle with the definite article (thus, *ʾĕlōhîm habbōrēʾ ʾet-hāʾāreṣ* means "God who created the earth").

VI. Word order. The normal word order of Hebrew prose was: (1) verb, (2) pronoun object or indirect object, (3) noun subject, (4) noun object. For example, "The king gave me the book" would be, *natan li hammelek ʾet-hasseper*. Any deviation from this order indicated some special emphasis. Thus, *li natan hammelek ʾet-hasseper* could be rendered, "It was to me that the king gave the book." Correspondingly, *ʾet-hasseper natan li hammelek* would suggest, "It was the book the king gave me." In poetry the same general word order prevailed, but emphasis often influenced deviations from the verb-subject-object pattern. Introductory temporal or causal phrases would of course precede the verb; likewise such conjunctions as *kî* ("when, because, if"), *ʾim* ("if"), or the relative pronoun, etc. Special emphasis also was achieved by the use of the independent pronoun with an inflected verb. Thus *ʾattâ kātabtā* would indicate, "It was you who wrote"; *ʾănî ʾădabbēr* means, "I myself will speak."

VII. Loanwords. As the Israelites came into contact with foreign cultures, they naturally tended to absorb terms from other languages, especially nouns referring to manufactured products, or technical expressions relating to weights and measures, governmental administration, or the like. There was a certain carry-over of Mesopotamian words from the time of ABRAHAM, who was an immigrant from Ur and Haran, and it is possible that the Hebrew names of the months, many of which resemble the Akkadian, were imported into the language from the beginning. Likewise terms like *hêkāl*, "temple" (Akk. *ēkallu*, which was borrowed from Sumer. *ē-gal*, "great house"), *kĕtōnet*, "linen garment, tunic" (Akk. *kitintu*), and others. There also were early borrowings from Aramaic in patriarchal times, as might be expected from Abraham's sojourn in Haran, and the marriage of ISAAC and JACOB to Aramaic-speaking wives. Note that, according to Gen. 31:47, what Jacob called in Canaanite GALEED ("witness heap") his father-in-law Laban called in Aramaic JEGAR SAHADUTHA (same meaning).

The most noteworthy assortment of loanwords comes from Egyptian during the Pentateuchal period (as was only to be expected from the Israelites' 430-year sojourn in GOSHEN). These include terms for weights and measures like *zeret*, "span" (Egyp. *ḏrt*, "hand") and *ʾêpâ*, "ephah" (Egyp. *ʾpt*), as well as other common words, such as *qemaḥ*, "flour" (Egyp. *kmḥw*, a type of bread) and *yĕʾōr*, "river" (esp. the Nile, from Egyp. *ʾ(t)rw*). During the Solomonic period, while trade relations were being carried on with India, a few words of probable Sanskrit origin were adopted (e.g., *ʾappiryōn*, "palanquin, sedan-chair," from Skt. *paryanka*, Cant. 3:9). Later on, in the 8th cent. and under the influence of Assyria, an infusion of Akkadian terms began, such as *peḥâ*, "governor" (Isa. 36:9). During the Captivity it was only to be expected that many new terms would be adopted from Babylonian, like *ʾiggeret*, "epistle" (Akk. *egirtu*), and *middâ*, "tribute" (Akk. *mandattu*). Since Aramaic displaced Hebrew as the household speech of the Jews during the captivity, one is not surprised to see a word like *ṭalal*, "cover over" (instead of the regular *ṣillēl*), as well as many others. After the Persian conquest of Babylon, numerous new words were added to the vocabulary of Hebrew, such as *dāt*, "law" (Pers. *dāta*) and *ʾappeden*, "palace" (Pers. *apadāna*).

VIII. Style. From the foregoing description of the morphology of biblical Hebrew, it will be apparent that it lacked precision in tenses such as characterize Greek, Latin, and the Indo-European languages generally. It possessed remarkable power as a medium of emotional expression and prophetic eloquence. Because of its ability to compress so much thought-content into few syllables, it possessed a dynamic, penetrative force capable of stirring the hearer to the depths of his being. It may have lacked the ability of Greek to express fine shades of meaning, and many of its key terms may be difficult to define exactly, but it possessed a remarkable ability to soar to sublimer heights in its beautiful parallelistic poetry or exalted prophetic passages than other languages could hope to attain. In sound it was unusually sonorous, more so than the other Semitic languages, because of the frequency of pretonic long syllables (a feature peculiar to Hebrew).

No translation into another tongue can do justice to the emotional intensity and rugged beauty of its verse (perhaps German comes the closest to this ideal), or duplicate its shifting moods of exaltation and pathos. Its theological vocabulary requires careful study in depth, if the overtones, undertones, and connotations are to be grasped, for these are beyond the power of even the most skillful translation to convey with any real adequacy. Truly this was a linguistic medium ideally adapted for the proclamation of God's message, so as to reach the intellect, the emotions, and the will.

(In addition to the works mentioned in the body of the article, see S. R. Driver, *A Treatise on the Use of the Tenses in Hebrew* [1881, reprinted with an introduction by W. R. Garr, 1998]; E. Y. Kutscher, *A History of the Hebrew Language* [1982]; N. Waldman, *The Recent Study of Hebrew* [1989]; A. Sáenz-Badillos, *A History of the Hebrew Language* [1996]; I. Young, ed., *Biblical Hebrew: Studies in Chronology and Typology* [2003]; G. M. Schram and P. C. Schmitz in *ABD*, 4:203–14. Though outdated in important respects, *Gesenius' Hebrew Grammar*, ed. E. Kautzsch, trans. A. C. Cowley, 2nd ed. [1910], is still widely used; more up-to-date is P. Joüon, *A Grammar of Biblical Hebrew*, trans. and rev. T. Muraoka, 2 vols. [1991; rev. one-vol. ed., 2006]. Major lexicons include BDB [1907]; *HALOT*, 5 vols. [1994]; and the extensive project headed by D. J. A. Clines and J. Elwolde, *The Dictionary of Classical Hebrew*, 8 vols. [1993–].)   G. L. ARCHER

Hebrew of the Hebrews. A phrase used by PAUL to describe himself (Gk. *Hebraios ex Hebraiōn*, Phil. 3:5). In this passage, the apostle was defending his integrity and recounting his pedigree for the benefit of his readers. In effect he was stating that he was of pure Hebrew stock and had retained the language and traditions of his ancestors, unlike some Jews who had become hellenized. The phrase involves the use of the Hebrew superlative, with a noun in special relationship to another noun (cf. "the song of songs," i.e., the most excellent song).
R. K. HARRISON

Hebrew people. Members of the nation of ISRAEL (see also JEW). The term ʿibri H6303 has traditionally been derived from EBER (ʿēber H6299), the grandson of SHEM and ancestor of ABRAHAM (Gen. 10:24; 11:16). Others have derived the term directly from the verb ʿābar H6296, "to pass, cross over, go beyond"; thus a Hebrew would be "one from the other side," that is, beyond the JORDAN (cf. Josh. 1:2 et al.) or beyond the EUPHRATES (note that the LXX renders Gen. 14:13 with *Abram tō peratē*, "Abram who crossed over," i.e., the migrant or wanderer).

Since the discovery of the TELL EL AMARNA tablets, an effort was made to identify the nationality of the HABIRU mentioned in these documents. Some have argued that this term is not the name of a people but an *appellativum* descriptive of a juridic-social position. The contexts suggest that the term refers to mercenaries. On the basis of various biblical texts (e.g., such as Exod. 21:2–6; 1 Sam. 14:21; Jer. 34:8–11, 14), G. von Rad surmises that Habiru originally described the legal position of servitude, or slavery, as opposed to *ḥopšī*, the free person. Gradually, first by outsiders and then by Israelites, the word was used as a *gentilicium*.

It is difficult to decide which opinion is right, but there is much to be said for the view that regards *hāʿibrim* as a topographical description: "those from across the Jordan." The memory of Israel's origin lingered long in Jewish tradition: "My father was a wandering Aramean" (Deut. 26:5). The land was God's gift to his people. The Psalms repeatedly refer to the miracle of the conquest. The Israelites knew themselves as Hebrews early in their history and were known as such (cf. 1 Sam. 4:6; cf. Jon. 1:9). In the NT, there is complete identification between Israelite and Hebrew (2 Cor. 11:22). The name stands as a constant reminder of the pilgrimage across the desert to the Promised Land. If this is the right interpretation, Israel's history is a paradigm of humanity at large. (See G. Dalman, *Jesus-Jeshua* [1929], 7ff.; P. K. Hitti, *History of Syria* [1951], 160–61; A. H. Van Zyl, *The Moabites* [1960], 188; D. Harden, *The Phoenicians* [1962], 116ff.; N. P.

Orthodox Jews worshipping in the synagogue at the Western Wall in Jerusalem.

Lemche in *ST* 33 [1979]: 1–23; N. Naʾaman in *JNES* 45 [1986]: 271–88.)   J. Jocz

Hebrew poetry. That the Semites in general were people of some musical ability, and that the Hebrews in particular fostered the cultural pursuits of music and poetry, will be apparent when it is realized that one-third of the Hebrew Bible was actually composed in poetic form. The wealth of poetic material that existed in the ANE has been illustrated by archaeological discoveries, some of which, such as the Ras Shamra texts (see UGARIT), have a direct bearing on the poetical material of the OT. Whereas the more obvious members of this corpus are Psalms, Proverbs, and the Song of Solomon, it also includes Lamentations, Obadiah, Micah, Nahum, Habakkuk, and Zephaniah, all of which were cast in poetic form apart from their superscriptions or titles. In addition, about one-half of Jeremiah is poetic in form, and there are also substantial segments of poetry in Job, Isaiah, Hosea, Joel, and Amos. Of all the OT writings, only Leviticus, Ruth, Ezra, Nehemiah, Esther, Haggai, and Malachi do not seem to contain lines of poetry. The three divisions of the Hebrew CANON contain poetry in progressively increasing amounts.

    I. Early studies in Hebrew poetry
    II. Parallelism
    III. Meter
    IV. Strophe
    V. Ugarit and Hebrew poetry
    VI. Varieties of Hebrew poetry
    VII. Figures of rhetoric
    VIII. Poetry in the prophets

I. Early studies in Hebrew poetry. Of those books that comprised the Writings or HAGIOGRAPHA (the third division of the Heb. canon), the books of Psalms, Proverbs, and Job were regarded by the Jews as being specifically poetical in nature, and were described by a mnemonic title, "The Book of Truth" (the consonants of the Heb. word for "truth," *ʾĕmet* H622, correspond to the initial letters of the names of those books). Christian scholars also recognized readily the poetic cast of these three compositions, but apart from such notable instances of Hebrew poetry as the Song of Moses and the Israelites (Exod. 15:1–18), the Song of Moses to Israel (Deut. 32:1–43), and the Song of Deborah and Barak (Jdg. 5:2–31), they tended to assume that the bulk of the OT narratives were uniformly written in prose.

This attitude was understandable enough in light of the fundamental differences that exist between what people in the ANE understood as poetry and what is generally implied in the Western world by that term. Occidental poetry has been influenced to a large extent by the structural forms of the classical Greek and Latin writings, where the units of speech were structured in terms of carefully accentuated lines in which rhyme was often involved. By contrast, the poetry of the ANE, and particularly that of the Hebrews, was formulated along different lines in which rhyme as such was unknown, and the structural units consisted of ideas or concepts that were set out according to a balanced arrangement of component clauses. However, the format of the Hebrew itself seldom gave any indication of a poetic structure, although some MSS of the MT arrange the text of Psalms, Proverbs, and Job in terms of poetic units. Documents discovered at Qumran (see DEAD SEA SCROLLS) have indicated that certain of the Psalms and the Song of Moses were copied in something approaching a stichometric format, but this seems to have been the exception rather than the rule in scribal practice.

Of course, from the fact that the books of Psalms, Proverbs, and Job possessed a more intricate system of punctuation in the Masoretic tradition, it is possible to argue for the existence of some awareness of poetic form among the Hebrew scribes. Nevertheless it is still true that poetic sections in the Torah and the Prophets were apparently not recognized as such by the Masoretes; or if they were, they were ignored. Equally unfortunate is the fact that, despite the wealth of classical Greek and Latin tradition in this regard, those who translated the Hebrew into the Greek and Old Latin versions were seemingly unaware of the possibility that the material with which they were working might have been cast in poetic form, an attitude that was also reflected in the Aramaic and Syriac versions of the OT books.

English translations also followed this general tradition, and even the American Standard Version of 1881 printed only the poetic books in a recognizable stichometric form. The Revised Standard Version of 1952 was the first English translation to cast all the poetic passages in the OT in a correspondingly distinctive form, which had the result of showing students of the English Bible precisely how much poetry there is in the OT Scriptures. Probably the earliest attempts to distinguish between poetry and prose structures were found in Josephus, who related that Moses had composed a song in hexameter verse in Exod. 15, and in the same meter in Deut. 32 (Jos. *Ant.* 2.16.4; 4.8.44). Of David he wrote that he composed songs and hymns to God in various meters, "some he made in trimeters and others in pentameters" (7.12.3). Philo Judaeus agreed with this general opinion, and held that Moses had learned the "lore of meter, rhythm, and harmony" from the Egyptians (*Vita Mosis* 1.5). The recognition of poetry in portions of the OT other than the Hagiographa was a distinct advance, but unfortunately it was spoiled by the application of classical analogies to poetic forms that were actually different from those of the Aegean writers. Eusebius, Jerome, and Origen were influenced by the remarks of Josephus, though Origen is supposed to have distinguished between Greek and Hebrew methods of writing pentameter and hexameter poetry.

Some medieval commentators such as Ibn Ezra and Kimchi were aware that the thoughts were frequently reproduced in parallel form in Hebrew poetry, but in general the phenomenon was either ignored or misinterpreted by Jewish and Christian exegetes. Attempts made to study Hebrew poetry dealt with the syllabic forms in terms of Greek and Latin structures, an approach that was repudiated as late as 1753 by Bishop Lowth in his *Lectures on the Sacred Poetry of the Hebrews*. In this work, he stressed the existence of *parallelism*, holding that Hebrew poetry consisted of measured lines and that the verses contained two or more elements in parallel form. Lowth distinguished between various kinds of parallelism with considerable success, and his recognition of the presence of poetry throughout the Hebrew Bible laid the foundation for subsequent studies.

His successors in the field began to apply the metric principles of different varieties of Semitic poetry to Hebrew verse, but this approach involved syllabics rather than stresses. Some investigators made the accent the basis for determining the nature of poetic sections, and although this gained the approval of English-speaking scholars, it was marred in Europe by an indulgence in textual

A Hebrew poem from Qumran known as Psalm 151.

emendation. The arrangement of Hebrew poetry in terms of strophes was pointed out by F. B. Köster, who attempted to establish the existence of several different types. Although C. A. Briggs collated the findings in relation to the studies in parallelism that had emerged from studies subsequent to those of Lowth, the next real advance came with the work of G. B. Gray (*The Forms of Hebrew Poetry* [1915]), who resolved all poetic parallelisms into complete and incomplete forms, the latter being amenable to certain variations.

II. Parallelism. The fact that this phenomenon is so fundamentally a part of Hebrew poetic forms will be sufficient to show the importance that the Semites attached to the balance of thought as distinct from mechanical concepts of meter based on sound or phonic rhythm. Whereas Hebrew poetry may, and frequently does, contain a variety of rhetorical devices that aid in the promulgation of the particular aspect of thought, these elements must now be regarded as being consistently subordinated in the minds of the writers to the expression of the thought-forms in terms of literary parallelism. This balancing of thought against thought, and word against word, was adopted from the literary culture of the ANE, but was developed by the Hebrews with great skill to the point where it surpassed similar attempts in the literature of pagan nations.

As Bishop Lowth recognized, the essential formal characteristic of Hebrew poetry is what he described as the *parallelismus membrorum*, or the counterbalancing in a verse of components of thought that manifested an internal relationship to one another. Lowth distinguished between three kinds of parallelism as follows: (1) *Synonymous*, in which the second part of a poetic verse recapitulated the thought of the first part (Isa. 1:3). (2) *Antithetic*, where the two principal parts of a verse exhibited the idea of contrast (e.g., Prov. 1:29); sometimes the same concept would be expressed first in a positive form and then in a negative form (Ps. 90:6). (3) *Synthetic*, in which the sense was developed in a continuous manner to reach its logical conclusion (Ps. 1:1–2).

Later scholars came to realize that the last of these categories was hardly parallelism in the strictest sense. They also employed the term *stichos* (Gk. *stichos*, "row" or "line") to describe individual lines of poetry. Two or three of these lines normally comprise the complete parallel form, which is marked, of course, by a proper degree of grammatical and syntactical unity. If a line is known as a *stichos* or *stich*, the half-line could be designated as a *hemistich*, although the latter term is occasionally used of the complete line also. The larger unit of two or three lines is described as a *distich* or a *tristich* respectively if whole lines are involved, or as a stich when the half-line components are regarded as hemistichs. Sometimes the two (or three) components of a Hebrew phrase are known as *bicola* (or *tricola*), but the term *colon* can be confused all too readily with the English punctuation mark of that name. The normal Hebrew poem thus consists of a series of terms that are grouped in pairs and are marked off from preceding and subsequent terms by means of major pauses, or *caesuras*. The general arrangement can be illustrated from Ps. 23:4–5 (KJV):

> Thy rod and thy staff, / they comfort me.//
> Thou preparest a table before me;/
>   in the presence of my enemies;//
> Thou anointest my head with oil,/
>   my cup overflows.//

In the above quotation, the caesura is represented by a double diagonal line, whereas the single diagonal signifies a minor pause within the pairs, represented in the citation by an antecedent comma. Quite frequently, the verse form of the English versions follows that of the MT, but this is by no means uniform.

In the light of the foregoing observations, it is possible to illustrate the various kinds of parallelism as suggested by Lowth and others. The first variety, synonymous parallelism, reproduces the same thought in successive stichoi, and is the least complex form of parallelism in Hebrew poetry. In Ps. 83:14, the first portion of the verse speaks of a fire burning the forest, a theme that is repeated quite simply in the second part in the figure of a flame setting the mountains on fire. One expression thus merely reinforces the thought of the other by the process of repetition in almost identical words and without the addition of any supplementary material. Recognition of this structural form occasionally clarifies obscure passages that could easily be misinterpreted, as with the familiar parallelism of Zech. 9:9:

> Rejoice greatly, O Daughter of Zion!
>   Shout, Daughter of Jerusalem!
> See, your king comes to you;
>   righteous and having salvation,
> gentle and riding on a donkey,
>   on a colt, the foal of a donkey.

According to some, Matthew assumed that two animals were involved, the donkey and her foal (Matt. 21:5), whereas the other three evangelists rightly discerned the synonymous parallelism involved in the citation, and consequently mentioned just one animal (however, see D. A. Carson in *EBC*, 8:438). Although in many synonymous parallelisms each term in the first stichos is matched by a corresponding term in the second, there are numerous instances where the parallels are not strictly complete, due to variations of vocabulary or rhetorical style. Moreover, it needs to be pointed out that typically the second member of the parallelism does not merely repeat the idea of the first but adds to it in some way (cf. T. Longman III in *FCI*, 171–72).

The second kind of parallelism described by Lowth as antithetic involves the two (or three) portions or members of the verse in some form of contrast. Quite often this is of a rather radical nature, as in Ps. 1:6: "For the LORD watches over the way of the righteous, / But the way of the wicked will perish." The Wisdom literature is particularly rich in such contrasts, since it frequently offered individuals a choice of two quite different courses of action: "Hatred stirs up dissension, / but love covers all wrongs" (Prov. 10:12). As with synonymous parallelism, the antithetic form can be complete or incomplete, and in addition it can express the same concept in alternate positive and negative forms.

The third variety identified by Lowth, namely synthetic parallelism, is marked by balanced stichoi in which the thought of the first is developed by the second. Although this is not actually true parallelism, the two stichoi are in fact balanced off and marked by breaks in the continuity of the thought with preceding and subsequent material. Thus the quotation from Ps. 2:3 (NRSV), "Let us burst their bonds asunder, / and cast their cords from us," exhibits a complementary balance of thought that is distinctively different from the remainder of the psalm. Even though there may not be a demonstrable parallelism of thought between the stichoi, the balance of form is seen in the pattern of recurrent major and minor stops in the poetry, and this factor has led certain scholars to describe this kind of parallelism as *formal* or *numerical*. Following the time of Lowth, further studies in Hebrew poetry described three subsidiary types of parallelism. They cannot be regarded as fundamental patterns, and seem to consist largely of variations or combinations of the three basic forms of parallelism discussed above.

Emblematic parallelism describes a situation where one stichos employed a literal or factual statement whereas the other stichos suggested a simile or a metaphor: "As the deer pants for streams of water, / so my soul pants for you, O God" (Ps. 42:1).

Climactic, or stairlike, parallelism is marked by the repetition and development of a concept in successive stichoi, perhaps involving three or more such members. It combines the principles of synonymous and synthetic parallelism to give the impression of extending the thought by recapitulation, where each stichos begins at the same place, but extends somewhat beyond its immediate precursor. An excellent example of this particular poetic pattern is Ps. 29:1–2: "Ascribe to the Lord, O mighty ones, / ascribe to the Lord glory and strength. / Ascribe to the Lord the glory due his name; / worship the Lord in the splendor of his holiness."

The final subsidiary form, known as *introverted* or *chiastic* parallelism, involves four stichoi arranged in such a manner that the first corresponds to the fourth and the second to the third in an a:b::b:a pattern. Cf. Ps. 30:8–10:

(a) To you, O Lord, I called;
    to the Lord I cried for mercy.
(b) What gain is there in my destruction,
    in my going go down into the pit?
(b) Will the dust praise you?
    Will it proclaim your faithfulness?
(a) Hear, O Lord, and be merciful to me;
    O Lord, be my help.

The researches of Gray resulted in the description of two broad classes of parallelism, the first of which was *complete*, in which every word in one stichos was balanced by an appropriate word in the other stichos, as in Isa. 1:3, where two synonymous parallelisms actually combine to form a total antithetic parallelism:

The ox knows his master,
    the donkey his owner's manger,
but Israel does not know,
    my people do not understand,

The other type of parallelism was described as *incomplete*, a designation that itself covered two subsidiary forms. One of these exhibited a pattern in which a part of the second stichos was parallel to the first: "But I will sing of your strength, / in the morning I will sing of your love" (Ps. 59:16). The other variety comprised a form in which a term was inserted in the second stichos that had no strict counterpart in the first stichos (Ps. 75:6):

No one from the east or the west
    or from the desert can exalt a man.
But it is God who judges:
    He brings one down, he exalts another.

Hebrew poetry frequently supplemented the parallelism between stichoi by means of a corresponding parallelism between distichs, resulting in what is sometimes described by scholars as *external* parallelism. An external synonymous parallel structure is found in Isa. 1:10:

Hear the word of the Lord,
    you rulers of Sodom;
listen to the law of our God,
    you people of Gomorrah!

An even more sophisticated parallelism results from an external inversion (Isa. 6:10) with reference to certain bodily organs, italicized in the following passage so that the literary pattern can be recognized with ease:

> Make the *heart* of this people calloused;
>   make their *ears* dull
> and close their *eyes*.
> Otherwise they might see with their *eyes*,
>   hear with their *ears*,
>   understand with their *hearts*,
> and turn and be healed.

It will be apparent from the foregoing that, in the hands of a competent poet, the possibilities of variation in Hebrew parallelism are virtually limitless. The concept of balance inherent in the relationship of the stichoi imposed a necessary degree of control over the composer and prevented diffuseness of style or thought while allowing sufficient freedom for an aesthetically gratifying arrangement of the constituent members. The particular degree of sophistication that marked the literary form of the finished product would naturally vary with the skill of the individual composer, but even the least proficient of these invariably produced a poem that by its elasticity and fluency outclassed the stereotyped repetitions so typical of ANE poetry in general.

III. Meter. Having emphasized the fundamental importance of parallelism in Hebrew poetry, some attention can now be given to the possibility of metrical division. Since there is no tradition of meter in the poetic compositions of the Hebrews, any conclusions that are arrived at will necessarily be by analogy from other Semitic poetry as well as by inference from the kind of balance that the stichoi themselves exhibit. A great deal of caution needs to be exercised in this matter, however, since a mechanical regularity of syllabic or accentual structure does not seem to have been a part of Hebrew poetry at any time. A warning must also be given about the use of analogy in relationship to alien poetic meters, particularly those of the classical composers, since the fundamental principle at issue in Hebrew poetry is the balance of thought. In this connection, it might be observed that although Josephus applied the concepts of classical European poetry to the writings of an ANE people, he did so to demonstrate to his Gentile readers the fact that Hebrew poetry did conform to specific structural patterns.

Having said this, it should also be remarked that the analogy between classical hexameters, pentameters, and the rhythms of the Hebrew poems should not be pressed too closely. From the evidence afforded by ANE poetic compositions generally, it is apparent that there was a freedom and a fluidity about what is described in Western thought as meter. However, it may well be that at least some of the Psalms were written with something approaching meter in mind, since certain of them were apparently meant to be sung at some stage in their history, no doubt to the accompaniment of musical instruments. Again, it may be that the dominant concern of the composer was for the beat or rhythm of the psalm rather than for the sort of metrical regularity characteristic of Greek and Latin poems. Certainly, in a heavily accented language such as Hebrew, the concept of stress was of great significance.

In 1866, J. Ley suggested that the character of a specific verse could be determined only by reference to the number of accented or stressed syllables that the verse contained. An accentual pattern could be formulated on the assumption that each major word of a stichos or distich should be assigned a numerical unit consisting of one stress. Ley observed that many of the verses of Hebrew poems consist of a three-stress stichos that was separated from a parallel two-stress stichos by means of a pause or caesura. He assigned the numerical value of 3:2 to this rhythmic pattern, and regarded it as an elegiac pentameter. Because this form occurred predominantly in Lamentations, it was given the name of *qinah* or "dirge meter" by K. Budde (Heb. *qinâ* H7806, "lament, dirge"). In one sense this designation was rather unfortunate, since subsequent studies showed that, whereas the *qinah* stresses were associated with emotional outpouring, that emotion was by no means always one of grief, as shown by its occurrence in some compositions where the theme was one of praise and gladness (Ps. 65). Concerning the unequal stresses, the 3:2 pattern is by far the most widespread in the OT. It is varied by means of 2:2 stresses, and there seem to be occasions when a 2:3 pattern is evident also.

It would appear proper to point out at this juncture that a certain degree of subjectivity attaches to the matter of assigning stresses to particular words in Hebrew poetry, and this in itself should induce caution in the application of this particular approach. Part of the problem arises from the fact that the accentual system that was devised by the Masoretes assigned one stress to each word, no matter what its length, apart from words joined together by means of the Hebrew hyphen (*maqqeph*), in which event only the last syllable of the combination was accented. However, it is not known for certain whether or not each word in Hebrew poetry actually received one stress. It may well have been that under some circumstances, two or perhaps three separate short words were treated as though they only merited one stress. Furthermore, whereas older scholars generally denied the possibility of a lengthy word receiving more than one stress, it still has to be proven that this was the invariable practice of the Hebrew poets.

Since there appears to have been an unregulated number of unstressed syllables that were permitted to occur between two stressed syllables, it seems evident that the ancient Hebrews were governed by principles that allowed them much flexibility in the matter of rhythm. The studies that led to the recognition of stress patterns in Hebrew poetry were based on the theory that it was permissible to allow one stress, or *ictus*, to each of the major words in a stichos, distich, or tristich. It seems legitimate to establish this procedure as a general principle on the analogy of other ANE compositions, particularly when the laments of the Hebrews are compared with the penitential psalms of the Babylonians, or when Hebrew poetry is compared with its Ugaritic counterparts. Once again, however, these compositions give evidence of the fluid nature of anything approaching a metrical scheme. The poetry of ancient Babylonia was characterized by a 2:2 stress pattern, although some lines contain an extra ictus to make a 3:2 or 2:3 form. Other lines seem to have the kind of stress pattern that can best be scanned as 2:2:2, or occasionally as 2:2:3. On the basis of the normal stresses in ancient Babylonian poetry, the comparative simplicity of form exhibited in Hebrew speech would suggest that the primary type of poetic line was of a 2:2 order. Although it is true that this stress arrangement is commonly found in Hebrew poems, a 3:2 form occurs even more frequently.

By far the most widely used stress scheme in OT poetry, however, is the 3:3 pattern, which is found in the poetic portions of Job, Proverbs, in the bulk of the Psalms, and in a great many prophetic oracles. It needs to be observed that however much one particular stress pattern may have been favored by an author, it was never used to the exclusion of others. The poetic literature from Ras Shamra, written in a dialect closely related to biblical Hebrew, frequently employed a 3:3 pattern as a rhythmic basis, but at the same time incorporated a great many variations. These compositions, which came from the Amarna Age and thus anteceded the bulk of Hebrew poetry, exhibit a degree of constructional freedom that should warn against expecting to find a recognizable degree of metrical regularity in Hebrew poetry. They positively preclude the emendation of the Hebrew text to make it conform to some particular metrical scheme, a practice that was popular among German scholars of an earlier generation.

In light of the available evidence, it seems clear that Hebrew poetry never possessed a mechanical regularity of a syllabic or accentual nature, and that if one is to speak of meter at all, the concept should be entertained only in terms of the rhythmical counterpart of the thought-parallelisms. There is no intrinsic evidence in the OT for meter in Hebrew poetry, a fact that was ultimately conceded by the eminent German Hebraist Bernhard Duhm. Instead of employing a term such as meter, it is probably better to think of rhythmical balance

An ancient harp depicted on the top right row from the Standard of Ur mosaic (c. 2600 B.C.). Harps and other instruments are often mentioned in biblical poetry.

based on elements of thought rather than upon strict syllabic quantities. Obviously, this approach involves considerably more subtlety than the mechanical patterns of Greek and Latin poetry, since in Hebrew poetic compositions, regularity of stress is of less significance than the regularity of balanced concepts of thought.

The situation can be summarized by presenting the three basic forms of Hebrew poetry as follows: (1) *Qinah*, the so-called "dirge-meter"—3:2 or sometimes 2:3, varied by the inclusion of 2:2 stresses. (2) *Hexameter*—3:3 or 2:2:2. (3) *Heptameter*—4:3 or 2:2:3. The use of the words *hexameter* and *heptameter* in this connection is related primarily to the sum of the stresses, and should not be interpreted in terms of Greek or Latin poetic usage.

IV. Strophe. During the last century and a half, much scholarly discussion has centered upon the question of whether it was possible to group the lines of Hebrew poetry to form stanzas or strophes. The researches of Köster in 1837 built on the foundation established by Lowth and laid great emphasis upon the strophic arrangement of Hebrew poetry. Successive scholars of the critical school held to the theory that the Psalms in particular had been arranged according to a fairly consistent strophic pattern. In those instances where this did not appear particularly evident in the Psalter, it was maintained that the original pattern had been partially obscured as the result of later liturgical glosses, and therefore needed textual emendation to make the basic form evident.

Subsequent studies took a different course by showing that the grouping of distichs and tristichs into larger poetic units cannot be demonstrated conclusively in the poetry of the OT. That such an arrangement was possible, however, is clear from the presence of *acrostic* poems, the most obvious of which is Ps. 119. In this arrangement, which is clearly rather contrived at best, the first word of the initial stanza commenced with the first consonant of the Hebrew alphabet, the first word of the second strophe with the second letter, and so on. Precisely where the idea of the acrostic arrangement originated is uncertain, but it had the undoubted value of imposing a degree of control over the vocabulary and the length of the composition, even though the final form was structurally rather artificial in nature. Psalm 119 consists of eight-distich stanzas or strophes, whereas chs. 1, 2, and 4 of Lamentations, which is also written in acrostic form, are composed of two-distich strophes (ch. 3 varies the pattern some by being made up of three-distich strophes). In Lam. 2, the alphabetic order is not followed scrupulously, since the letter *pe* comes before ʿ*ayin* instead of after it in the usual alphabetical manner. Interestingly enough, although ch. 5 contains twenty-two verses, one for each consonant of the Hebrew alphabet, there are no indications of an acrostic arrangement. Whatever the reasons for the use of an acrostic in the above compositions, it still remains true that the strophic pattern was never allowed to interfere with the sequence of the thought, a matter that was always of paramount importance. Under these circumstances it would appear that the stanza was never basic to the structure of Hebrew poetry in the sense in which it is for most modern poetical compositions.

Perhaps some sort of strophic arrangement may be indicated by the presence of a refrain, or chorus, that appears at a specific point in a psalm. Thus Ps. 46:7 and 11 have the following refrain: "The Lord Almighty is with us, / the God of Jacob is our refuge." A rather more sophisticated example of this literary device can be seen in Ps. 107, where the repeated refrain consists of two parts as follows: (a) "Then they cried to the Lord in their trouble, / and he delivered them from their distress"; (b) "Let them give thanks to the Lord for his unfailing love / and his wonderful deeds for men" (e.g., vv. 6, 8). Between these two portions of the refrain were inserted descriptions of deliverance from various perils by divine power, but the theme was handled in such a way that the poem contained strophes of quite unequal length. A more balanced arrangement was contained in Pss. 42–43, which seems to have formed a single poem and in which the refrain appears on three occasions (42:5, 11; 43:5):

> Why are you downcast, O my soul?,
> Why so disturbed within me?
> Put your hope in God,
> for I will yet praise him,
> my Savior and my God.

As well as being indicated by the presence of a recurring refrain, the end of a stanza or strophe may possibly be marked by the inclusion of the enigmatic expression *selâ* H6138. The word itself comes from a Hebrew root meaning "to cast up, raise, build a road," and occurs seventy-one times in thirty-nine Psalms as well as in Hab. 3:3, 9, 13. In normal circumstances, *selah* stands outside the balanced arrangement of the thought-form, which is indicated in most English versions either by the word being enclosed in brackets or written in italics. However, some scholars have raised doubts that the term can be considered as a valid indication of strophic arrangement, if only because the meaning of the word is still uncertain. Since it occurs in association with what have been supposed to be musical titles in some of the Psalms, some commentators think that it was a direction to the singers of the particular psalm, calling for a crescendo of voices at that particular juncture.

It may be that the translators of the SEPTUAGINT had some sort of liturgical usage in mind when they rendered the term by Greek *diapsalma*, "interlude," since an accompaniment of musical (stringed) instruments was evidently involved. Thus the Hebrew term could either indicate the "lifting up" of voices in music or in the recitation of the psalm, or the cessation of the voices and the crescendo of musical instruments. Of these two alternatives the latter seems more acceptable, for *selah* occurred generally at the end of some phase of thought in the poetry, where in recitation the voice would normally pause in any event.

It has also been suggested that *selah* directed the conductor of the temple musicians and singers to interrupt the flow of the chanting by means of a clash of cymbals or tambourines. Thus the presence of *selah* with *higgaion* (Ps. 9:16, from *hāgâ* H2047, "to moan, mutter") would seem to point to the thought of the psalm terminating in a soft whispering of stringed instruments followed at the direction of the conductor by a clash of cymbals to mark the end of the recitation.

Despite the foregoing suggestions, however, there must still remain considerable doubt whether the word *selah* was ever related to strophic arrangement in Hebrew poetry. The very fact that the term is distributed in the Psalter and Habakkuk would indicate that it can hardly be regarded as a genuine device for strophic division in more than a very few cases. If this term is not to be regarded as an indication of strophic arrangement, however, the only other hint of such a structure apart from the presence of a refrain or an acrostic form is found in the symmetrical ordering of the thought itself.

This feature may be illustrated by reference to Isaiah's Song of the Vineyard (Isa. 5:1–8), which can be divided quite naturally into four subsections consisting of two verses each, as follows: vv. 1–2, the care of the vineyard; vv. 3–4, a call for judgment between the owner and his vineyard; vv. 5–6, the destruction of the vineyard heralded; vv. 7–8, the application in parabolic form to Israel. Each subsection consists of four distichs except for the third one, which is irregular and has one tristich added to the four distichs. Although the thought of the poem can be divided in this way, there is some doubt whether a short composition of this kind would ever have been broken down into such small components, particularly since the thought-pattern of the first six verses is given unity of form and meaning by the concluding two verses. This would suggest that the composition should be considered as an integrated structure with the major pause, normally indicated by the end of a stanza, marking the completion of the poem as a unit.

By way of concluding the discussion of the possibility of strophic formulation in Hebrew poetry, mention ought to be made of a technical device to which scholars have given the name of *anacrusis*. This normally consists of a single word, such as an interrogative particle or an exclamation, that stands outside the stress-pattern of the verse in which it occurs. For example, the interrogative "why" can sometimes be removed from the text without prejudice to the rhythm of the verse, which in fact conforms to the 3:3 pattern so commonly found in Hebrew poetry (Jer. 12:1). The exclamation "how" (Lam. 1:1) can be isolated from the remainder of the verse without disrupting the stresses, which fall into the 3:2; 2:2; 2:2 pattern. The presence of such words tends to affect the whole of the passage that follows them, and not infrequently the poetic material in these sections is of a particularly expressive nature.

An earlier generation of scholars was accustomed to resort to textual emendation as a commonplace procedure to restore what was thought to have been the original strophic arrangement of certain Hebrew poems in the belief that the structure had been disrupted and obscured by such things as marginal glosses, lacunae, or displacements of the text. Such reconstructions were sometimes made on the basis of readings reflected by the LXX, but there were many other instances where they were indulged in simply as the result of subjective speculation. Since the discovery of the Ras Shamra tablets, it has now become clear that only the most cautious of textual emendations can be countenanced, since the composers of Ugaritic poetry enjoyed a liberty of literary form and a freedom from mechanical meter that positively precludes the kind of rigid patternism foisted upon the Hebrew text by some 19th-cent. scholars.

V. Ugarit and Hebrew poetry. New light has been shed since 1928 on the nature of OT poetry as the result of archaeological discoveries at Ras Shamra (UGARIT). At this site, some literary texts originating in the early 14th cent. B.C., which were written in a previously unknown language and inscribed in an unfamiliar CUNEIFORM script, were deciphered and found to have been composed in a NW Semitic dialect closely related to biblical Hebrew (see HEBREW LANGUAGE). The tablets included both prose and poetic material, the latter being of great importance for the textual study of the Psalms. Among other things, the Ugaritic poetic compositions exhibited parallelism, as can be seen from the following example: "Lo, your enemies, O Baal, / Lo, your enemies you will smite. / Lo, you will vanquish your foes."

These sentiments are remarkably similar to the thought of Ps. 92:9, and serve to illustrate the close degree of affinity that can often be seen when Ugaritic and Hebrew poetic compositions are compared. There seems to have been a common fund of linguistic expressions and literary idioms from which the two peoples drew. Thus BAAL was described as the "rider of the clouds" (cf. Pss. 68:4; 104:3) who was enthroned in the heavens (cf. Pss. 2:4; 103:19) and hurled down lightnings and thunderbolts (cf. Pss. 18:13; 77:18; 144:6). Canaanite poetry, as observed above, was based on a 3:3 stress pattern, but admitted of a great many variations. There is nothing that would indicate metrical exactitude in Ugaritic poetry, and in view of this it would hardly seem likely that the Hebrews placed any significant emphasis upon meter as such.

The Ugaritic material, however, has done an enormous amount of good in clarifying supposed textual anomalies in books such as the Hebrew Psalter. Alleged corruptions that were frequently emended by earlier scholars have now been seen to constitute genuine Canaanite grammatical and literary forms whose particular significance had been forgotten with the disappearance of Ugaritic culture. This realization has consequently prompted a much more cautious approach to the textual study of the Psalter.

VI. Varieties of Hebrew poetry. It is very difficult to maintain a formal distinction between the religious and the secular in the poetic compositions of Israel, since each tended to interpenetrate the other. The Hebrews employed their songs as expressions of or accompaniments to social activity in a manner by no means unfamiliar to other societies in a different age. One such poetic fragment is the so-called Song of the Well (Num. 21:17–18): "Spring up, O well! Sing about it, / about the well that the princes dug, / that the nobles of the people sank— / the nobles with scepters and staffs."

This utterance celebrated the way in which the well near a site called BEER was opened under the direction of the leaders of Israel. The use of the imperative form at the beginning of the poem would seem to express the concerns of those involved in digging the well that an abundant supply of water should reward their efforts. No doubt the same sentiments continued to be expressed by those who used the water of that same well in subsequent times. On such a basis there can be no thought of magic or incantation rituals associated with the task of excavation, as some have imagined.

The same would hold true for other daily activities where indulgence in song helped to make the time pass more quickly and lighten the burdens of work. Such choruses or songs (Jdg. 9:27; Isa. 16:10) were used where the harvesting of grapes was undertaken (Jer. 25:30; 48:33), and where shouts of joy accompanied the trampling of grapes in the winepresses. Quite probably, the rhythmic stresses of the songs employed on such occasions matched the pace of the work being undertaken. However, because of the scanty evidence for "work songs" as such, it is far from easy to identify them as a genuine literary category.

Some poetic fragments appear to have come from taunt or mocking songs that were credited to the activities of the "ballad singers." One particular poem (Num. 21:27–30) heaped scorn on the Moabites and taunted them in connection with the destruction of their principal cities. A fragmentary quotation from the "song of the harlot" (Isa. 23:16) was applied prophetically to the city of Tyre: "Take a harp, / walk through the city, / O prostitute forgotten; / play the harp well, / sing many a song, / so that you will be remembered." It should be noted that the "song" was not so much an actual poem recited to musical accompaniment by harlots, as in later Rome, but rather a derisive ditty mocking the efforts of an aged prostitute to attract the attention of potential clients.

There are references to drinking songs (Amos 6:4–6; Isa. 5:11–13) where the prophets were perhaps thinking of the musical entertainments that formed part of contemporary banquets. It may be that the citation, "'Let us eat and drink,' you say, / 'for tomorrow we die!'" (Isa. 22:13), expressed the general tenor of the lyrics sung on such occasions. A more optimistic form of the song declares (56:12), "'Come,' each one cries, 'let me get wine! / Let us drink our fill of beer! / And tomorrow will be like today, / or even far better.'" Aside from these two possible instances, however, no other portions of actual drinking songs have been preserved in the OT.

If it is legitimate to regard the lyrics of Song of Solomon as a collection of Israelite love poetry, then this genre would constitute yet another attestable class of Hebrew verse. From the account of the wedding of Samson (Jdg. 14:10–18), it would appear that such festivities were animated affairs at that time, during which singing and dancing were very much in evidence. The poems contained in Canticles include some that described the physical beauties of the betrothed male and female, and it may be that these were recited or chanted during the wedding festivities somewhat in the manner of the more modern Arabic *wasfs*. Perhaps the author refers to the spectacular wedding procession of King Solomon, though other sections of the book need only be regarded as celebrating the depth and beauty of true human love in the absence of a specific wedding situation (Cant. 3:6–11). If it is granted, as suggested by some scholars, that Canticles as a whole has only a rather coincidental connection with marriage celebrations, it is difficult to isolate any other wedding poetry as such from the OT narratives.

Laments were a familiar part of Israelite funerary customs, the mourning songs being sung either by the relatives and others connected with the dead person (2 Sam. 1:17; 3:33) or by professional male and female mourners (Jer. 9:16; cf. Amos 5:16–17). The sarcophagus of Ahiram from Byblos (Gebal), dated about 1200 B.C., showed realistic pictures of professional female mourners stripped to the waist, wailing, beating their breasts, and tearing their hair. The most expressive funerary dirge was that composed by David to commemorate the death of Saul and Jonathan (2 Sam. 1:19–27). It formed part of the Book of Jashar (v. 18), which was apparently a national epic set down in written form during the early monarchy. The lament was used as a training poem on the orders of David whenever the Judeans were being instructed in the arts of bowmanship.

This situation was by no means unusual in the Mycenaean Heroic Age (15th to 10th centuries B.C.), in which music, poetry, and dancing had a regular place in all programs of military training. The dirge lamented the slaying of the "glory" of Israel, lauded the virtues of the deceased, and exhorted the nation to mourn the dead heroes. The exquisite beauty and delicacy of the lament is eloquent testimony to the artistic levels that Hebrew

Illustration of mourners gathered at the tomb of Lazarus. Professional mourners often gave voice to the family's grief using funeral dirges.

poetry had attained in the days of David, and its independence of form furnishes additional assurance of authorship by the "sweet singer of Israel."

The concept of the funeral dirge was used with great effect by the preexilic prophets to convey the seriousness of the national situation to an indifferent and unheeding Israel. Perhaps the most notable literary accomplishment along these general lines is to be found in Lam. 1–2 and 4, where this style was used in allegorical fashion of Jerusalem. Chapter 5 is a psalm of lamentation for the whole nation, whereas ch. 3 contains mixed elements of lamentation.

Not unnaturally, a great deal of the ancient lyric poetry found in the OT had to do with wars and victory in battle. One form of commemoration of the mighty act of divine salvation at the time of the exodus was the Song of Miriam (Exod. 15:20–21), which was chanted to the accompaniment of tambourines and dancers: "Sing to the Lord, / for he is highly exalted. / The horse and its rider / he has hurled into the sea." In so far as this theme was echoed by the people, it comprised the genuine response in thanksgiving of those who had participated in a miracle and had witnessed the destruction of their enemies. A genuine psalm of victory is seen in the Song of Deborah (Jdg. 5:2–31), which constitutes the poetic parallel of the prose version of victory contained in the preceding chapter. Whereas it is a psalm of thanksgiving for victory, it also contains such diverse elements as confession, praise, taunting, curses, and thanksgiving.

What has been described by some scholars as the Song of the Ark (Num. 10:35–36) appears to have consisted of two shouts or rallying cries with which the ark of the covenant was greeted by Moses on its departure and return from battle: "Rise up, O Lord! / May your enemies be scattered; / may your foes flee before you," and "Return, O Lord, / to the countless thousands of Israel." These pronouncements were doubtless intended to strengthen the morale of the Israelite warriors and the nation as a whole by assuring them that the power of God was accompanying them and acting through them to secure victory over their enemies. When military success had been achieved, it was the common practice for the victors to boast of their valor, as in the ancient fragment known as the Song of Lamech (Gen. 4:23–24): "Adah and Zillah, listen to me; / wives of Lamech, hear my words. / I have killed a man for wounding me, / a young man for injuring me. / If Cain is avenged seven times, / then Lamech seventy-seven times."

The social conditions portrayed in this fragment are long antecedent to the Mosaic age, since they reflect the personal vendettas of the nomad to whom the humanitarian prescriptions of the Mosaic law were entirely unknown. In the Heroic Age the victor in battle was frequently greeted on his return with songs and dances, as were Jephthah (Jdg. 11:34) and David (1 Sam. 18:6–7). In the case of the latter the narrative has preserved the chorus of the victory chant, "Saul has slain his thousands, / and David his tens of thousands"—a tribute that did not exactly strike an endearing chord in the mind of King Saul.

Forming a poetic category of their own are the benedictions pronounced by the patriarchs, and their counterpart in the "last words of David" (2 Sam. 23:1–7). As is now well known from archaeological discoveries at Mari and Nuzi, a benediction of this kind constituted in effect a last will and testament whose stipulations and dispositions were binding upon all those concerned. Prominent in the patriarchal benedictions was a prophetic element that was frequently coupled with a penetrating character analysis of the recipients of blessing to indicate to them what prosperity or adversity they could expect in the coming days. By contrast, the "last words of David" comprise nothing more than a short personal testimony to the power of God in his life and the essential transience of those who are motivated by lesser forces.

Into yet another category came the utterances of Balaam, the talented Mesopotamian seer whom Balak of Moab had hired to curse his enemies, the Israelites. Magical texts recovered from Mari and elsewhere indicate that Balaam came within the professional classification of a master-diviner, and as such could command a high fee for his services. His pronouncements fell into a regular poetic form, one of which (Num. 24:3–9) was described by the prophetic term "oracle." Because of the character of his encounter with God, the utterances of Balaam were in the nature of benedictions, and as such have a great deal in common with the patriarchal blessings.

Whereas the psalter may properly be regarded as an anthology of Hebrew poetry, there are other lesser collections of lyrics in the OT. Lamentations and Canticles comprise complete books of poems of specific kinds, but there are still smaller poetic collections that are important, having been associated with particular historic occasions. One of these anthologies has survived in fragmentary form in early OT literature under the designation of "the Book of the Wars of the LORD" (Num. 21:14–15). The surviving portion comprises a geographical note that may have referred to battles in Transjordan: "Waheb in Suphah and the ravines, / the Arnon and the slopes of the ravines / that lead to the site of Ar / and lie along the border of Moab." This fragment gives no firm indication concerning the nature or content of the book, but from the title it may be assumed that it dealt in poetic form with the battles of the early conquest period before the main invasion of Canaan. See WARS OF THE LORD, BOOK OF THE.

The Book of Jashar, mentioned above, may have been a later counterpart of the Book of the Wars of the Lord, since it included the training poem for bowmanship originally composed by David as a lament for the death of Saul and Jonathan (2 Sam. 1:18–27). However, it is unwise to speculate about the relative dates of the two anthologies, since neither collection of poems is now extant. The Book of Jashar also included the celebrated charge of JOSHUA to the sun and moon: "'O sun, stand still over Gibeon, / O moon, over the Valley of Aijalon.' / So the sun stood still, / and the moon stopped, / till the nation avenged itself on its enemies" (Josh. 10:12–14).

No doubt there were a number of collections of poetic material of various kinds that have not survived the centuries. A record of one such collection was preserved by the Chronicler (2 Chr. 35:25), who spoke of an anthology of laments that was supposed to have contained the dirge composed by the prophet JEREMIAH at the time when King JOSIAH died. This collection has also vanished without trace. Scholars have pointed out that in general the poetry of the OT emerges either from continuous communal functions or from situations in which the material was formulated for some special historical purpose. To the former group belong most of the Psalms, particularly where the individual composition was of a devotional nature and had no particular historical associations. The latter category can be illustrated by reference to Lamentations, written as a tragic commemoration of the destruction of the theocracy.

Some of the different kinds of secular Hebrew poetry have already been discussed, including harvest songs, taunts, funeral laments, victory odes, and love lyrics. The more specifically sacred poetry, which was generally restricted to use in divine WORSHIP, fell into certain readily recognizable classes. These include prayers, songs of praise, special petitions for deliverance from sickness or enemies or both, confessions of faith in God as a contrast to the prevailing trends of polytheism, confessions of sin, imprecatory psalms that called down divine punishment on the heathen, intercession for the nation and its rulers, instructional or homiletical psalms, meditations, and psalms in praise of the Torah.

One of the more problematic classes of Hebrew poetry, known as the royal psalms, raises the question of the function of the king in relationship to the particular composition. Some scholars have gone so far as to suppose that certain of the royal psalms were used in connection with the coronation (cf. Pss. 2; 110), the marriage of the king (cf. Ps. 45), preparation for battle (cf. Ps. 20), and the victory celebrations that followed the successful conclusion of a military campaign (cf. Ps. 21). Other scholars have denied that there was ever anything approaching the modern concept of an elaborate religious ceremony at which the ruler was formally crowned, and still others have questioned whether the psalms in which God is mentioned as king should be included in the royal psalms at all.

Certain interpreters have gone to great lengths to adduce from certain of the royal psalms some evidence that would support the theory that there was an annual New Year festival in preexilic Israelite times at which God was greeted as the king who renewed his dominion by re-creating the world and life. In particular, S. Mowinckel (*Psalmenstudien*, 4 vols. [1921–24]) took the phrase "the LORD reigns," occurring in certain of the so-called "enthronement psalms" (Pss. 93:1; 97:1; 99:1; cf. 47:8; 96:10), and interpreted it to mean, "the LORD has become king" (Heb. *yhwh mālak*). For him this constituted a triumphal shout that marked the climax of an enthronement festival liturgy proclaiming the Lordship of the God of Israel for another civil year. There is no evidence, however, that such a festival ever existed at any time in Israelite life; and, in addition, the rendering "the Lord has become king" is an unnatural translation of the Hebrew, the force of which is simply "the Lord is king" or "the Lord rules." Still other interpreters of the concept of sacral kingship have maintained that the ceremonial acknowledgment of divine rule arose through metaphorical usage during the postexilic period, when kingship had been replaced by the developed theocracy. Although this may possibly have been a secondary usage of some of the royal psalms, it can hardly have been the primary one, since this particular category of poetry appears to have been preexilic in origin and to have represented the king as an individual functioning in a distinctive capacity.

VII. Figures of rhetoric. Part of the subtlety and attraction of Hebrew poetry consists in the way ordinary words are treated to heighten their general effect. To this end, several technical literary devices were employed by the ancient poets, one of the most obvious being *paronomasia,* or play on words. This is the basis of the pun, long favored among peoples in the Middle E as a refined form of HUMOR, but in the hands of such writers as the prophets the form took on a moral or an eschatological connotation. We read in Isa. 5:7 that the justice (*mišpāṭ* H5477) for which the Lord looked had been replaced by bloodshed (*mišpāḥ* H5384), and righteousness (*ṣĕdāqâ* H7407) by a cry (*ṣĕʿāqâ* H7591). The basket of summer fruit (*qayiṣ* H7811) that Amos saw in a vision reminded him that the end (*qēṣ* H7891) of the nation was at hand (Amos 8:2). Clearly this is a very powerful rhetorical device for proclaiming fundamental theological issues in memorable terms.

Another effective marshaling of words is seen in the use of *alliteration,* which groups related sounds occurring at the beginning of words or phrases. The exhortation to pray for the peace of Jerusalem (Ps. 122:6) is given emphasis by the consonance of syllables in the Hebrew, *šaʾălû šĕlôm yĕrûšālaim yišlāyû.* A related rhetorical form favored by the prophets was that of *assonance,* which placed emphasis upon the correspondence of sound in the accented vowels, particularly where pronominal and verbal suffixes were involved. Thus in Isa. 53:4–7, the permanently long vowel *û* occurs no fewer than fifteen times, strengthening by its very sound the general impression of grief and woe contained in the verses. Hebrew writers generally made use of another device, known as *onomatopoeia,* in which the sense of a word was suggested by its sound. The gutturals and labials (42:14) convey the sense of a woman groaning and catching her breath during the pangs of childbirth. These literary and rhetorical techniques went far toward replacing rhyme, which does not occur in Hebrew poetry except where the same pronominal or verbal suffix is repeated at the end of two consecutive lines. This phenomenon is rare, and in each instance it must be considered strictly accidental in nature.

VIII. Poetry in the prophets. Prophetic poetry had its roots in the specific historical situations to which the divine message was addressed, and seldom comprised a formulation of devotional poetry for its own sake. The third chapter of Habakkuk may, however, furnish an exception to this general rule. In the matter of form and technique there is no difference between prophetic and other poetry in the OT writings. What made the poetry of the prophets distinctive was the occasion to which it was directed. Thus, the taunt song was given particular force by Isaiah when directed against Babylon (Isa. 47:1–15) or against Assyria (Ashur, Isa. 37:21).

A clever parody of the funeral lament was made by Jeremiah in his dirge on the people of Judah (Jer. 9:17–22). The poem described the situation immediately preceding the downfall of the nation, and it followed the tidings of doom by describing the travails of death. Instead of contemplating a glorious future, the women would have to teach their daughters how to become professional mourners. Death was personified in the dirge as an impartial "Harvester" who gathers in small and great alike. A much shorter dirge (Amos 5:2) dealt in a similar vein with the "virgin Israel," who was hurled to the ground by death. There are other examples of prophetic laments (Ezek. 19:1–14; 26:17–18; Nah. 3:18–19). Certain prophetic utterances, including denunciations of foreign nations, were described by the Hebrew term *maśśāʾ* **H5363**, "oracle," but apart from this they had no distinctive features of form or rhythm. The prophetic writers found that they could express their message adequately by employing the traditional poetic structure as well as the normal prose forms, and it is clear that their genius as spiritual leaders in Israel arose from the content rather than the form of their poetic utterances.

Observed in retrospect, the fact that their predictions of doom were fulfilled with such finality gives added stature to the majestic poetic utterances that were declaimed so vigorously by these ancient servants of God. By contrast, the gentle, optimistic visions that saw blessing in the future for a penitent and obedient Israel carry more than a hint of sadness in their lyricism in the light of the fate which ultimately befell the Jews.

(Much of the material above is taken from R. K. Harrison, *Introduction to the Old Testament* [1969], 965–75. See further A. Condamin, *Poèmes de la Bible avec une introduction sur la strophe hébraïque* [1933]; H. Gunkel and J. Begrich, *Einleitung in die Psalmen* [1933]; C. Kraft, *The Strophic Structure of Hebrew Poetry* [1938]; T. H. Robinson, *The Poetry of the Old Testament* [1947]; N. K. Gottwald in *IDB*, 3:829–38; M. O'Connor, *Hebrew Verse Structure* [1980]; J. Kugel, *The Idea of Biblical Poetry: Parallelism and Its History* [1981]; W. G. Watson, *Classical Hebrew Poetry: A Guide to Its Techniques* [1984]; R. Alter, *The Art of Biblical Poetry* [1985]; A. Berlin, *The Dynamics of Biblical Parallelism* [1985]; J. P. Fokkelman, *Reading Biblical Poetry: An Introductory Guide* [2001]; P. van der Lugt, *Cantos and Strophes in Biblical Hebrew Poetry* [2006].)   R. K. HARRISON

Hebrews, Epistle to the. The longest of the non-Pauline letters in the NT. Traditionally it follows the thirteen letters attributed to PAUL; in the great uncials it comes between Paul's nine letters to churches and his four to individuals; in P⁴⁶ (c. A.D. 200, the oldest extant MS of the *corpus Paulinum*), it comes second among the letters addressed to churches, next after Romans. (This was its original position in the Syrian textual tradition; in the Coptic Sahidic version it follows 2 Corinthians; in the archetype of CODEX VATICANUS it followed Galatians.)

    I. Authorship
   II. Destination
  III. Occasion, purpose, and date
  IV. Outline
   V. Relation to the apostolic preaching
  VI. Argument
 VII. Canonicity and authority

I. Authorship. In spite of traditional ascriptions and brilliant guesses, the authorship of Hebrews is unknown. At ALEXANDRIA it was ascribed to Paul from the second half of the 2nd cent. onward, although difficulties in this ascription were acknowledged by CLEMENT OF ALEXANDRIA and ORIGEN: "God knows the truth of the matter," said the latter (Euseb. *Hist.* 6.25.14). TERTULLIAN (*De pudicitia* 20) ascribed it to BARNABAS. Luther's ascription to APOLLOS has commended itself to many; A. von Harnack's ascription to PRISCILLA seems to be ruled out by the masculine participle in Heb. 11:32. The author was a second-generation Christian, master of a fine literary style, quite unlike Paul's; like Apollos, he may have had an Alexandrian Jewish background and he certainly had "a thorough knowledge of the Scriptures" (Acts 18:24), which he knew in the SEPTUAGINT version and interpreted according to a creative exegetical principle.

II. Destination. The document does not name those for whom it is intended any more than the man who composed it. The title "To (the) Hebrews" goes back to the last quarter of the 2nd cent. A.D., but it cannot be determined if it corresponds to the original mind of the author or, if so, what "Hebrews" precisely means. From internal evidence it may be inferred that the recipients were Hellenistic Jews who had embraced the gospel. Gentile believers who were disposed to backslide would not be greatly moved by an argument that began, "If perfection could have been attained through the Levitical priesthood …" (Heb. 7:11); their reaction would have been "Well, we never imagined it was!" The insistence on the obsolete character of the old covenant (8:13) and encouragement to the readers to go forth to Christ "outside the camp" (13:13) would have more point if their background was Jewish, as would also the author's confidence that they would accept the authority of the OT (Gentiles who were inclined to give up the Christian faith would give up the OT with it). Where they lived cannot be conclusively decided. Jerusalem, Caesarea, Antioch, Alexandria, the Lycus valley, Ephesus, Corinth have all been suggested; but perhaps they may best be regarded as members of a house-church in Rome, the city in which knowledge of the epistle is first attested (in Clement of Rome, c. A.D. 96).

III. Occasion, purpose, and date. The people to whom the letter was sent were in danger of losing their initial enthusiasm. When first they became Christians, their exhilaration was such that they rejoiced amid persecution, endured plunder and outrage without complaint, and were unstinting in their service of fellow believers, especially those who were imprisoned. With the passing of the years their earlier zest waned. The PAROUSIA, which they had ardently expected, seemed as distant as ever; the Jewish establishment and the fellowship of the SYNAGOGUE, which they had given up for Christianity, continued to flourish and to offer the protection of a religion whose practice was licensed by the Roman state. Their original impetus slackened off; they were tempted to look backward instead of forward. Hence the urgency with which the author exhorts them, using a variety of metaphors, not to drift downstream but to row hard against the current, not to flag in the race but to persevere in faith. It may well be, as William Manson has argued, that he wanted to see them play their part in the advance of the Christian world-mission with other fellow believers instead of remaining in a backwater (*The Epistle to the Hebrews: An Historical and Theological Reconsideration* [1951], 44). To do this they must be prepared to burn their boats and sever their links with the old order. To ignore the forward call would be worse than negligence; it would be outright apostasy, turning away "from the living God" (Heb. 3:12). Against this he warns them solemnly, while at the same time he expresses his confidence that they will show themselves worthy of their first love and press on in patience and faith.

As for the date of the letter, a *terminus ad quem* is provided by the references to it in Clement of Rome (thus not later than c. A.D. 96). A *terminus a quo* is indicated in that author and readers alike received the gospel from those who had heard the Lord (Heb. 2:1–4). No completely definitive answer can be given to the question whether the letter was written before or after the destruction of the Jerusalem temple in A.D. 70. The sacrificial ritual is referred to in the present tense, and the "old covenant" under which that ritual was instituted is said to be "ready to vanish away" (8:13 RSV), but it is arguable that this is a "literary present" since the description of the ritual is based not on current practice but on the Pentateuchal prescriptions. Nevertheless, if, by the time of writing, the temple had been destroyed and the sacrifices brought to an end, this would have added such weight to the author's argument that some allusion to it, however veiled, could hardly have been avoided. Thus a date before A.D. 70 is more probable, though not certain.

If the people addressed were Roman Christians, a date not later than A.D. 64 is indicated by Heb. 12:4, "In your struggle against sin, you have not yet resisted to the point of shedding your blood." This could not have been written after the Neronian persecution. (The persecution of Heb. 10:32–34, which did not involve martyrdom, may have been connected with the expulsion of Jews from Rome in A.D. 49, mentioned in Acts 18:2.) Another chronological pointer may be the "forty years" quoted from Ps. 95:10 in Heb. 3:9, 17. The current belief in a forty-year probation at the end time to match that at the beginning of Israel's history is attested, for example, in the QUMRAN texts (DEAD SEA SCROLLS); and if a period of forty years from the death of Christ was nearing its end when the author was writing, there would be the greater relevance in his quotation of the psalm.

IV. Outline. The letter is described by the writer as a "word of exhortation" (Heb. 13:22), an expression used elsewhere of a synagogue sermon (Acts 13:15). It is, indeed, a carefully constructed homily, delivered by force of circumstances in writing instead of orally.

    A. The finality of the gospel (Heb. 1:1—2:18)
        1. God's completed revelation in the Son (1:1–4)
        2. Christ superior to angels (1:5–14)

3. First admonition: gospel and law (2:1–4)
4. Humiliation and glory of the Son of man (2:5–9)
5. The Son of man the Savior and High Priest of his people (2:10–18)

B. The true home of the people of God (3:1—4:13)
 1. Jesus superior to Moses (3:1–6)
 2. Second admonition: the rejection of Jesus more serious than the rejection of Moses (3:7–19)
 3. The true rest of God may be forfeited (4:1–10)
 4. Exhortation to attain God's rest (4:11–13)

C. The high priesthood of Christ (4:14—6:20)
 1. Christ's high priesthood an encouragement to his people (4:14–16)
 2. Qualifications for high priesthood (5:1–4)
 3. Christ's qualifications for high priesthood (5:5–10)
 4. Third admonition: spiritual immaturity (5:11–14)
 5. No second beginning possible (6:1–8)
 6. Encouragement to persevere (6:9–12)
 7. The steadfastness of God's promise (6:13–20)

D. The order of Melchizedek (7:1–28)
 1. Melchizedek the priest-king (7:1–3)
 2. The greatness of Melchizedek (7:4–10)
 3. Imperfection of Aaron's priesthood (7:11–14)
 4. Superiority of the new priesthood (7:15–19)
 5. Superior because of God's oath (7:20–22)
 6. Superior because of permanence (7:23–25)
 7. Superior because of the character of Jesus (7:26–28)

E. Covenant, sanctuary, and sacrifice (8:1—10:18)
 1. Priesthood and promise (8:1–7)
 2. The old covenant superseded (8:8–13)
 3. The sanctuary under the old covenant (9:1–5)
 4. A temporary ritual (9:6–10)
 5. Christ's eternal redemption (9:11–14)
 6. The Mediator of the new covenant (9:15–22)
 7. The perfect sacrifice (9:23–28)
 8. The old order a shadow of the reality (10:1–4)
 9. The new order the reality (10:5–10)
 10. The enthroned High Priest (10:11–18)

F. Call to worship, faith, and perseverance (10:19—12:29)
 1. Access to God through the sacrifice of Christ (10:19–25)
 2. Fourth admonition: the willful sin of apostasy (10:26–31)
 3. Call to perseverance (10:32–39)
 4. The faith of the elders (11:1–40)
  a. Prologue: the nature of faith (11:1–3)
  b. Faith of the antediluvians (11:4–7)
  c. Faith of Abraham and Sarah (11:8–12)
  d. The city of God the home of the faithful (11:13–16)
  e. Faith of the patriarchs (11:17–22)
  f. Faith of Moses (11:23–28)
  g. Faith at the exodus and settlement (11:29–31)
  h. Further examples of faith (11:32–38)
  i. Epilogue: faith's vindication comes in Christ (11:39–40)
 5. Jesus, pioneer and perfecter of faith (12:1–3)
 6. Discipline is for sons (12:4–11)
 7. Call to action (12:12–17)
 8. Earthly Sinai and heavenly Zion (12:18–24)
 9. God's voice must be heeded (12:25–29)

G. Concluding exhortation and prayer (13:1–21)
 1. Ethical injunctions (13:1–6)
 2. Examples to follow (13:7–8)
 3. The true Christian sacrifices (13:9–16)
 4. Submission to leaders (13:17)
 5. Request for prayer (13:18–19)
 6. Prayer and doxology (13:20–21)

H. Postscript (13:22–25)
 1. Personal notes (13:22–23)
 2. Final greetings and benediction (13:24–25)

V. Relation to the apostolic preaching. Because Hebrews represents a distinct school of thought within the NT, it is the more interesting to compare the GOSPEL message that is presupposed as common ground between author and readers with the message presented in other NT documents, and to discover that in basic essentials it is the same gospel.

The new age has been inaugurated; the OT prophecies have been fulfilled. "Jesus the Son of God" (Heb. 4:14) "has appeared once for all at the consummation of the ages" (9:26 ASV mg.). In his eternal being he is identified with wisdom, God's agent in the creation of the world (1:1–3; cf. Jn. 1:1–3; Col. 1:15–17; Rev. 3:14); his human descent from DAVID is implied in what is stated to be a matter of common knowledge, that he belonged to the tribe of JUDAH (Heb. 7:14). The material circumstances of his death are known (13:12); he endured it "to do away with sin" (9:26; cf. Rom. 4:25; 1 Cor. 15:3). His resurrection is assumed rather than affirmed (cf. Heb. 13:20); it is part of the general movement of his exaltation to the right hand of God, where he intercedes for his people (cf. Rom. 8:34; Phil. 2:9–11). His parousia, which is confidently expected (Heb. 10:37), will consummate his people's salvation (9:28). Meanwhile, they have received the Holy Spirit, whose presence with them is attested by his gifts "distributed according to his will" (2:4; cf. 1 Cor. 12:4–11; Gal. 3:2–5).

Ancient mosaic from a synagogue floor depicting Jewish symbols and including the seven-branched candlestick and the curtain of the temple. Hebrews states that Jesus went beyond this curtain before us and entered the Holy of Holies on our behalf (Heb. 6:19–20).

It has often been said that in Hebrews the older ESCHATOLOGY of the two ages has been combined (if not overlaid) with the Platonic scheme of the two worlds—the upper world of eternal reality and the lower world characterized by material and temporary copies of that reality. Something of this sort is indeed recognizable in Heb. 8–9, where the true abode of God is contrasted with the earthly sanctuary with its priesthood and ritual. Even for this, the author finds his text in the OT (Exod. 25:40, quoted in Heb. 8:5). He certainly shows himself familiar with the Platonic scheme, probably as mediated through PHILO JUDAEUS, but his principal category of thought in this respect is the Hebraic scheme of the two ages, modified (as by the other NT writers) in the light of the coming of Christ and God's definitive word spoken in him "in these last days" (Heb. 1:2; cf. 1 Cor. 10:11; 1 Pet. 1:20). (See C. K. Barrett, "The Eschatology of the Epistle to the Hebrews," in *The Background of the New Testament and Its Eschatology*, ed. W. D. Davies and D. Daube [1956], 363–93.)

VI. Argument. On this basis the writer establishes the finality of the gospel as God's perfect revelation. The gospel is contrasted in this regard with everything that preceded it, especially with the Levitical ritual. By emphasizing the completeness of the work of Christ and the perfection of his person, he presents the gospel as the one way that secures unimpeded access to God.

Christ, he shows, is superior to all the servants and spokesmen of God that went before him, whether human beings like Moses (Heb. 3:3) or angelic intermediaries like those through whom the law was communicated (1:4; 2:2). Christ is the SON OF GOD, his agent in creating and maintaining the universe (1:1–3), yet the One who, as SON OF MAN, submitted to humiliation and death (2:5–18). Now he is exalted above the heavens, enthroned at God's right hand as his people's representative (1:3; 4:14). This ministry is presented in terms of high priesthood, Hebrews being the only NT document that explicitly uses this language in reference to Jesus. His high priesthood is expounded partly on the basis of Ps. 110:4 (where the Davidic Messiah is acclaimed by God as "a priest forever, in the order of Melchizedek"), partly on the historical facts about Jesus. Whereas the oracle of Ps. 110:1, frequently quoted or echoed in Hebrews, is one of the commonest TESTIMONIA in the NT, the use of 110:4 is peculiar to this epistle. The MESSIAH who is acclaimed as king in 110:1 ("Sit at my right hand"), says the author, is acclaimed as priest in 110:4 (Heb. 5:6). The reference to the priestly order of MELCHIZEDEK is explained (Heb. 7) with the help of the narrative about that priest (Gen. 14:18–20), significance being found not only in what is said of him there but also in what is not said of him. This scriptural argument for Messiah's high-priestly office is reinforced by Jesus' personal qualifications to discharge that office: not only was he "holy, blameless, pure" in character (Heb. 7:26) but, having been tempted in every respect as his people are, he can sympathize with them and supply the help they need in the hour of trial (4:15–16; 5:7–10).

Jesus' intercessory ministry finds mention in the Gospels (e.g., Lk. 12:8; 22:32; Jn. 17) and Epistles (Rom. 8:34; 1 Jn. 2:1–2), but it is elaborated in a distinctive manner in Hebrews. Various arguments are adduced to show that his priesthood is not only superior to that of AARON but also belongs to a totally different order. It belongs to the new covenant foretold in Jer. 31:31–34, a covenant marked by better promises and a better hope than the old covenant of Sinai under which the Aaronic priests ministered (Heb. 7:11–19; 8:6–13). See COVENANT (OT); COVENANT, THE NEW. It is associated with a better sacrifice than any that went before (9:23) and is discharged in a better sanctuary than any of this creation (9:11). Priesthood and sacrifice are inseparable. The priests of Aaron's line repeatedly offered up animal sacrifices (7:27), notably the annual sin offering on the Day of Atonement (9:7), but these could not meet the real need of men and women (10:4). Such sacrifices could not cleanse the conscience from the defilement of SIN, which is the great barrier to fellowship with God (9:9). Christ's high-priestly ministry, however, is exercised on the basis of a real, voluntary, and effective sacrifice—"the sacrifice of himself" (9:26)—which, unlike all other sacrifices, cleanses the human conscience so that we can henceforth "serve the living God" (9:14). See SACRIFICE AND OFFERINGS.

The writer finds this perfect sacrifice predicted in Ps. 40:6–8, where a speaker, dismissing all animal sacrifice as unacceptable, dedicates his life to God for the obedient accomplishment of his will (Heb. 10:5–7). The words of the psalm are understood as the words of Christ when he comes into the world. In the "body … prepared" for him (Ps. 40:6, according to LXX) he fulfilled the will of God, in life and death alike. By this sacrifice of perfect obedience to God's will his people are once for all sanctified and given the right of access to God (Heb. 10:10, 22); by it, moreover, the new covenant is established in which God implants his law in their hearts and remembers their sins no more (10:15–18). These arguments, based on the interpretation of Scripture, were corroborated by the practical experience of a generation of believers who, since the passion and triumph of Christ, had proved in their lives the efficacy of his sacrifice and intercession. Such a sacrifice (unlike the Levitical order) required no repetition; for those who repudiated this sacrifice no further sin-offering could be available; hence the solemn warning not to spurn the Son of God and profane his covenant-blood (10:26–31).

What the readers needed in their present situation was to cultivate patient endurance and hold fast their confession to the end. They should not be discouraged by hope deferred; the coming One would come (Heb. 10:36–39). The example of faith shown by men and women who lived and died in the hope of the promise which was fulfilled in Christ, although they themselves did not witness that fulfillment, should help them (11:1–40); still more should the example of Christ's endurance nerve them to press on in the path of obedience to God and not give up the struggle (12:1–17). The familiar and congenial environment of their earlier days was vanishing, never to return; as heirs of the one unshakable kingdom they should sever the bonds that tied them to their past and go forth to Christ, embracing the stigma attached to his name, following him on the way of faith to "the city that is to come" (12:28—13:14).

VII. Canonicity and authority. Hebrews may be said to have received canonical recognition first of all when a 2nd-cent. editor (prob. in Alexandria) incorporated it into the *corpus Paulinum*. Certainly from the time of Pantaenus (c. A.D. 180) its canonicity was unanimously acknowledged by Alexandria; whatever ORIGEN's doubts on its authorship might be, he had none on its canonical quality. See CANON (NT). The example of Alexandria was followed by the eastern churches generally. EUSEBIUS of Caesarea included Hebrews (reckoned by him as a Pauline letter) among the books whose canonicity was "obvious and plain," although he did not overlook the fact that "some have set it aside on the ground that it was rejected by the Roman church as non-Pauline" (Euseb. *Eccl. Hist.* 3.3.5). EPHRAEM SYRUS (c. A.D. 350) and the other Syriac-speaking fathers accepted it without question as canonical (and as Pauline); unlike some of the CATHOLIC EPISTLES, it was included in the Peshitta (early 5th cent.) from the beginning.

In the W the situation was quite different. Although the epistle was known at Rome before the end of the 1st cent., it was not regarded as canonical there until the 4th cent., presumably because it was known not to be the work of an apostle. At last the Roman church, with no great enthusiasm, decided not to remain out of step with the eastern churches in this regard, being moved particularly by the persuasiveness of Athanasius, who spent his second exile (A.D. 340–346) in Rome. Even IRENAEUS of Lyons (c. A.D. 180), despite his belonging to proconsular Asia, had reservations about Hebrews; he may have given it a deutero-canonical

This painting in the Church of Jacob's Well (Nablus) illustrates the persecution and torture of the saints such as is described in Heb. 11.

status comparable to that of Wisdom (Euseb. *Eccl. Hist.* 5.26).

The difficulty felt by the Roman church was largely due to the tradition that linked canonical authority with apostolic authorship. Jerome and AUGUSTINE were content to accept Hebrews as a Pauline letter on this ground rather than from considerations of literary criticism. It was included in the canon promulgated by the Synods of Hippo (393) and Carthage (397) in this form: "Of Paul the apostle, thirteen epistles; of the same to the Hebrews, one."

When the question was reopened by the Reformers, the canonicity and apostolic authorship of Hebrews were clearly distinguished. Luther rejected its Pauline authorship and seemed to relegate it to a lower position because it contained, as he thought, some "wood, hay and stubble." Calvin equally denied its Pauline authorship but affirmed: "I class it without hesitation among the apostolic writings"—"apostolic" in doctrine and authority, not in authorship. Of its inherent worth he said: "There is no book of Holy Scripture which speaks so clearly of the priesthood of Christ, which so highly exalts the virtue and dignity of that only true sacrifice which he offered by his death, which so abundantly deals with the use of ceremonies as well as their abrogation, and, in a word, so fully explains that Christ is the end of the law. Let us therefore not allow the church of God or ourselves to be deprived of so great a benefit, but firmly defend the possession of it" (*Commentary on Hebrews*, trans. W. B. Johnston [1963], introduction).

It is all to the good that canonicity and authorship should be thus distinguished by the recognition of the right of an anonymous work to a place within the NT because of its essential quality. The abiding authority of the epistle can be found in its insistence on the inwardness of true religion and its relegation of externalities to a place of relative unimportance. (Even sacraments may have been included by the author among such externalities; it is not without significance that the one statement about Melchizedek in Gen. 14:18–20 to which no reference is made in Heb. 7:1–10 is his bringing forth bread and wine.) The purification that matters in the sight of God is the purification of the conscience from sin, not the removal of ritual pollution; the one sacrifice that avails in the sight of God to effect this purification is the sacrifice of an unreservedly willing and dedicated life, like that of the Isaianic Servant who spontaneously and deliberately offered himself "to take away the sins of many people" (Heb. 9:28).

No material shrine is necessary for the worship of God; the house of God, where his presence is manifested and the high-priestly ministry of the exalted Christ is discharged, is higher than the heavens in a spiritual, not in a spatial, sense, for it is identified with the fellowship of his people, if they hold fast their confidence and glorying of their hope (Heb. 3:6). No geographical city or country claims their allegiance because of some special sanctity; the once holy city was no longer such because Jesus, expelled beyond its precincts, "suffered outside the city gate" (13:12). The people of Christ must follow him as a pilgrim community, never halting in his service short of the rest that remains for them in "the city with foundations, whose architect and builder is God" (4:9; 11:10). In a changing world, where the old landmarks disappear and old standards are no longer recognized, the only constant point of reference is the unchanging, onward-moving Christ, "the same yesterday and today and forever" (13:8); the path of wisdom is to face the unknown with him. Our author anticipates Herbert Butterfield in finding here "a principle which both gives us a firm Rock and leaves us the maximum elasticity for our minds; the principle: Hold to Christ, and for the rest be totally uncommitted" (*Christianity and History* [1950], 146).

(Among older works, note A. B. Davidson, *The Epistle to the Hebrews* [1882]; B. F. Westcott, *The Epistle to the Hebrews* [1892]; A. B. Bruce, *The Epistle to the Hebrews: The First Apology for Christianity* [1889]; W. Milligan, *The Theology of the Epistle to the Hebrews* [1899]; A. Nairne, *The Epistle of Priesthood* [1913]; J. Moffatt, *A Critical and Exegetical Commentary on the Epistle to the Hebrews*, ICC [1924]. Important commentaries since 1950 include C. Spicq, *L'épître aux Hébreux* [1952]; F. F. Bruce, *The Epistle to the Hebrews*, NICNT [1964]; H. W. Montefiore, *The Epistle to the Hebrews* [1964]; O. Michel, *Der Brief an die Hebräer*, KEK, 12th ed. [1966]; P. E. Hughes, *Commentary on the Epistle to the Hebrews* [1977]; H. W. Attridge, *A Commentary on the Epistle to the Hebrews*, Hermeneia [1989]; W. L. Lane, *Hebrews*, WBC 47, 2 vols. [1991]; P. Ellingworth, *The Epistle to the Hebrews: A Commentary on the Greek Text*, NIGTC [1993]; E. Grässer, *An die Hebräer*, EKKNT 17, 3 vols. [1991–97]; D. A. deSilva, *Perseverance in Gratitude. A Socio-rhetorical Commentary on the Epistle "to the Hebrews"* [2000]; C. R. Koester, *Hebrews: A New Translation with Introduction and Commentary*, AB 36 [2001]; L. T. Johnson, *Hebrews: A Commentary* [2006]. Note also such monographs as W. Manson, *The Epistle to the Hebrews: An Historical and Theological Reconsideration* [1951]; G. Vos, *The Teaching of the Epistle to the Hebrews* [1956]; A. Snell, *New and Living Way* [1959]; S. Kistemaker, *The Psalm Citations in the Epistle to the Hebrews* [1961]; G. H. Guthrie, *The Structure of Hebrews: A Text-linguistic Analysis* [1994]; R. W. Johnson, *Going Outside the Camp: The Sociological Function of the Levitical Critique in the Epistle to the Hebrews* [2001]; P. Gray, *Godly Fear: The Epistle to the Hebrews and Greco-Roman Critiques of Superstition* [2004]; S. D. Mackie, *Eschatology and Exhortation in the Epistle to the Hebrews* [2007].)   F. F. BRUCE

Hebrews, Gospel of the. A *Gospel according to the Hebrews* is mentioned by CLEMENT OF ALEXANDRIA, who quotes from it a saying also found, with some variation, in the OXYRHYNCHUS SAYINGS OF JESUS (POxy 654) and in the Coptic *Gospel of Thomas* (logion 2; see THOMAS, GOSPEL OF). This material has led to the claim that the *Gospel of the Hebrews* was the source of the other two, but the evidence is too meager to permit far-reaching conclusions. Only fragments are extant, and it is not certain that all the fragments quoted under this or similar titles belong to the same work. The document was known also to ORIGEN, who quotes from it a statement of Jesus that his mother, the Holy Spirit, took him by one of his hairs and carried him off to Mount TABOR (a variation of the temptation story, although Tabor was traditionally the mountain of the transfiguration). Thereafter patristic testimony is highly confused.

EUSEBIUS mentions a *Gospel of the Hebrews* in which Jewish converts take special delight; he links with it a story adduced by PAPIAS, which may be the *pericope adulterae* (Jn. 7:53—8:11), and says that the book was used by Hegesippus, who also quoted some things "from the Syriac" and "from the Hebrew language" (see Euseb. *Eccl. Hist.* 3.25.5; 3.39.17; 4.22.8). Some EBIONITES used only the *Gospel of the Hebrews*, esteeming the others as of little value (ibid., 3.27.4; according to IRENAEUS, the Ebionites used only Matthew). Eusebius also mentions a Hebrew Gospel of Matthew, said to have been taken by BARTHOLOMEW to India (*Eccl. Hist.* 5.10.3). In his *Theophania*, Eusebius quotes a gospel current among the Jews in Hebrew, but gives no name. He may thus have known two documents: a Greek *Gospel according to the Hebrews* known to Clement and Origen, and before them to Papias and Hegesippus, and an Aramaic gospel known also to Hegesippus (cf. P. Vielhauer and G. Strecker in *NTAp*, 1:138).

According to EPIPHANIUS (*Pan.* 29.9.4), the Nazoreans had the Gospel of Matthew complete in Hebrew, but evidently he had not himself seen the book. Like Irenaeus, he says that the Ebionites used only the Gospel of Matthew, but he adds that they called it the *Gospel of the Hebrews* (*Pan.* 30.3.7). The documents are not identical: while for Epiphanius the *Gospel of the Nazoreans* was Matthew complete in Hebrew, that of the Ebionites was merely a "so-called Matthew," a falsified abridgment (*NTAp*, 1:141). Epiphanius is the first to identify the Nazorean *Gospel of the Hebrews* with the Hebrew "original" of Matthew, and it looks as if he has combined the statements of Irenaeus and Eusebius concerning the Ebionites. The documents appear, however, to be distinct: the Nazorean gospel he knows only by repute, the Ebionite he quotes (but for this he is the sole authority). Suspicion is cast upon his testimony by the fact that elsewhere he says that Tatian's DIATESSARON "is also called the Gospel according to the Hebrews" (*Pan.* 46.1).

Confusion is increased by JEROME, who uses various formulae to introduce his quotations: *Gospel according to the Hebrews* (seven times), *Gospel of the Hebrews* (twice), the *Hebrew Gospel* (thrice), the *Hebrew Gospel according to Matthew* (twice). He speaks of its use by the NAZARENES (the various forms of this name constitute another problem) or by the Nazarenes and Ebionites, and claims to have translated it from Hebrew into Greek and Latin. One of his quotations, however, is the statement cited above from Origen, who gives no hint that it was not already before him in Greek. After a detailed chronological review, Vielhauer concludes that the measure of confidence to be placed in Jerome's statements is very small (*NTAp*, 1:146). Jerome had only one gospel in mind, which he called the *Gospel according to the Hebrews* and identified (wrongly) with the Aramaic *Gospel of the Nazarenes*. His claims to have obtained the latter from the Nazoreans and to have translated it into Greek are open to serious question.

The problems are, therefore, (a) to determine how many documents are involved, and (b) to allocate the surviving fragments among them. Vielhauer argues cogently for three: a Greek *Gospel of the Hebrews* known already to Clement and Origen, a Greek *Gospel of the Ebionites* known only from Epiphanius (who also supplies the only extant fragments), and an Aramaic *Gospel of the Nazarenes*, attested by Hegesippus and Eusebius, Epiphanius, and Jerome. On the other hand, his allocation of the fragments may at some points be open to question. For example, M. R. James (*The Apocryphal New Testament* [1924], 1–8) distinguishes two documents, the *Gospel of the Hebrews* and that of the *Ebionites*, and assigns to the former the fragments allocated by Vielhauer to the *Gospel of the Nazarenes*; but he isolates as from a different document a Coptic fragment assigned by Vielhauer to the *Gospel of the Hebrews* (it has a partial parallel in *Epistula Apostolorum* 14, and hence, while unorthodox, is not necessarily completely heretical).

Two other fragments frequently quoted in modern literature as from the *Gospel of the Hebrews* are both assigned by Vielhauer to the *Gospel of the Nazarenes*: the note that the man with the withered hand (Matt. 12:9–13) was a mason, and Jerome's comment that it was not the veil of the temple that was rent (27:51), but the lintel that collapsed. Both, however, are introduced in terms similar to those used for fragments assigned to the *Gospel of the Hebrews*.

In the circumstances it is difficult to be certain of the character, form, and compass of these documents, and precarious in the extreme to build hypotheses upon the little that is known. All three seem to stand in some relation to Matthew, but the extent of modification or abridgement is not clear. The *Gospel of the Hebrews* is, however, commonly mentioned by the church fathers with a certain respect, and hence was not obtrusively heretical. It was probably the gospel of Jewish Christians in Egypt, distinguished by its title from the *Gospel of the Egyptians* (which *may* have been more Gnostic); but to go much further is to enter the realm of speculation. (See further *NTAp*, 1, ch. 4; *ABD*, 3:105–6.) R. McL. Wilson

Hebrews, history of the. See Israel, history of.

Hebrews, religion of the. See Israel, religion of.

Hebron (person) hee´bruhn (חֶבְרוֹן H2497, "associate, companion"; gentilic חֶבְרוֹנִי H2498, "Hebronite"). **(1)** Son of Kohath, grandson of Levi, and uncle of Moses (Exod. 6:18; Num. 3:19, 27; 1 Chr. 6:2, 18; 15:9; 23:12, 19; 24:23); eponymous ancestor of the Hebronite Levitical clan, which played an important role during the time of David (Num. 3:27; 26:58; 1 Chr. 26:23, 30–31).

(2) Son of Mareshah and great-grandson of Caleb (1 Chr. 2:42–43). The Hebrew text is difficult and variously emended. According to the Septuagint, Mareshah (not Mesha) was the firstborn of Caleb, in which case Hebron would be Caleb's grandson; according to other reconstructions, Hebron is removed from Caleb by several generations. It has also been suggested that v. 42 should be translated, "Mesha his firstborn, who was the founder of [the city] Ziph, and his son Mareshah who was the founder of [the city] Hebron"; but this interpretation is inconsistent with v. 43, which says that Hebron had four sons. Nevertheless, there may be a connection between Hebron son of Mareshah and Hebron (place).

Hebron (place) hee´bruhn (חֶבְרוֹן H2496, "association"). A city about 20 mi. SSW of Jerusalem at more than 3,000 ft. above sea level, situated between two ridges and occupying the valley between, lying somewhat WNW by ESE (today it is also known as El-Khalil). The main residential part of the city lies on the slopes of the ridges to the E and N with movement to the SW ridge and up the NE slope of Jebel er-Rumeideh, site of the ancient tell of Hebron. The present city extends N from the W end of the valley on both sides of a wide street forming the present road to Jerusalem. The city valley itself is the lower end of the Wadi Tuffaʿ (Valley of the Apples). A large number of springs and wells dot the landscape, making it certain of occupation. Two large pools with cut-stone walls are located within the city area. Apple, plum, fig, pomegranate, apricot, and nut trees are found in profusion; grapes, melons, and several vegetables are also abundant from the rich soil of valley and terrace. The principal landmark in the present city is the Ḥaram el-Khalil, the area sacred to the Arabs, covering the ancient cave of Machpelah, and Deir el-Arbaʾin, the traditional burying place of Ruth and Jesse.

Hebron is mentioned frequently in the OT, and several times its earlier name of Kiriath Arba is given (Gen. 23:2 et al.). It "had been built seven years before Zoan in Egypt" (Num. 13:22), or c.

Hebron.

1728 B.C., which is the Hyksos period. However, excavations performed in 1964–66 show that the tell on Jebel er-Rumeideh was occupied as early as c. 3300 B.C. and has enjoyed fairly continuous habitation down to the present time (P. Hammond, *American Expedition to Hebron: Preliminary Report* [1966], 1), which makes it appear that the building spoken of was a rebuilding, probably under the Hyksos, since a Middle Bronze II wall some 30 ft. wide has been uncovered at the SE corner of what was an ancient tell, now obscured by grape and olive yard terraces but with masonry outcroppings visible here and there.

Hebron is the later name for the general area (Gen. 23:19) in the days of Moses, and included Mamre, the latter traditionally located less than 2 mi. N of Hebron to the E of the Jerusalem road (the site of a temple built by Constantine to the memory of Abraham's sojourn there). Some (G. F. Moore, *A Critical and Exegetical Commentary on Judges*, ICC [1910], 23; F. Hommel, *The Ancient Hebrew Tradition* [1897], 232–234) deemed the older name Kiriath Arba to mean *tetrapolis* (fourfold city) on the grounds that the name is an anomalous Hebrew form, indicative of being a loanword, therefore not a personal name; the similarity to Arba, the father of Anak (cf. Josh. 14:15), is a coincidence and here a play on the word. What the four cities were which made up the "association" is not known except for Mamre.

The archaeology of Hebron may be summarized as follows. Evidence of Chalcolithic occupation from as early as c. 3000 B.C. was exposed at the SE angle of what should prove to be the Middle Bronze wall. Not far away under a new house to the S was found evidence of Early Bronze I habitation, but outside the Middle Bronze II wall. The latter was discovered to be c. 30 ft. broad, with a large portion of its southern face exposed to display the usual cyclopean unworked stones. The wall continued at least 330 ft. westward. Some 197 ft. northward of the Middle Bronze II wall, Iron I occupation was unearthed in a significant house of the monarchy period (11th–10th centuries). Some data may point to the invasions of Sennacherib and the destruction of the land by Nebuchadnezzar.

The next certain occupation was that of the Hellenistic period, most striking in the large pottery works, with at least two kilns at the westward end below and outside of the Middle Bronze II wall, and on the N side of the tell as well. In this area, a remarkable settling and water storage system from the Byzantine era was unearthed hardly a foot below terrace level. However, the largest amount of evidence for Byzantine occupation was unearthed below Arab remains at the eastern end of

The region of Hebron looking to the W.

er-Rumeideh some 400 ft. E of the tell. An extensive Byzantine burial ground was uncovered with typical artifacts. A later Muslim palatial house covered part of this area, and below its courtyard were found evidences of Roman occupation. All phases of Islamic occupation down to the present era were brought to light.

Abram (ABRAHAM) moved to Hebron after Lot left him (Gen. 13:18) when Mamre was known as part of Hebron, the latter being the biblical author's identification of the place by the later name. Abram built the first altar there to Yahweh. Mamre was named at this time after Mamre the AMORITE (Gen. 14:13) in league with Abram. In Abraham's ninety-ninth year, Yahweh appeared to him with the two angels "near the great trees in Mamre" (18:1). Two ancient trees in the vicinity of Hebron have been called "the oaks of Mamre," traditionally associated with Abraham: one near the traditional site of Mamre, and another on the western edge of the Wadi Tuffaʿ in the grounds of the Russian Orthodox Church. At Mamre, Abraham pled with Yahweh to spare SODOM (18:23), marking him as "the friend [Arab. *el-Khalil*] of God" (cf. Isa. 41:8; Jas. 2:23).

It was in Hebron that SARAH died (Gen. 23:2), and Abraham bought the cave of Machpelah (23:17), which was opposite Mamre, from EPHRON the HITTITE. By this time the Hittite enclaves had replaced the Amorites (cf. chs. 13–14). There was buried Sarah, and later ISAAC, REBEKAH, LEAH, and JACOB (49:31; 50:13). In the days of the exodus, spies were sent into the land and from the brook ESHCOL in Hebron took back the wondrous grapes on a staff (Num. 13:22–24). For his valor and constancy (cf. Josh. 14:9), CALEB was given the area of Hebron (14:13), but the town became one of the CITIES OF REFUGE. When SAMSON tore loose the doors of the city gate of GAZA, he carried them to Hebron (Jdg. 16:3).

DAVID settled in Hebron after the death of SAUL (2 Sam. 2:1) and from there ruled over Judah for seven and a half years before being anointed king over all Israel (5:4–5). After this, he moved to Jerusalem. However, it was from Hebron that ABSALOM launched his revolt (15:7–12), perhaps considering he would have stronger support there for his rebellion. In his own days, REHOBOAM fortified Hebron, possibly in the prospect of attack from Egypt by SHISHAK.

The next references to Hebron are from the period of the Maccabees. Judas MACCABEE defeated the Edomites who had invaded the NEGEV from EDOM and established themselves as far N as Hebron. Later, HEROD erected the enclosure (Haram) about the ancient burial place of Abraham; the "Herodian" masonry is clearly distinguishable from later work. Pilasters adorn the walls, a distinct peculiarity, and the Muslim work begins above them. Islam has made the Haram a sacred site because Muhammad is said to have passed through it on his night journey to heaven. It came into Muslim control after the Arab conquests.

In the 19th cent., Guy le Strange summarized some of the reports of ten previous visitors to Hebron, one of whom, in A.D. 1172, declared he had seen the bodies of Abraham, Isaac, and Jacob. In 1168, Hebron was made the seat of a bishopric but reverted to Arab rule in 1187 in Saladin's conquests. It was reported by Ibn Battuta that Joseph's body was moved there by 1395. Cenotaphs within the Haram are reputedly over the resting places of the bodies. History and tradition thus combine in designating this as the cave of Machpelah where Abraham and others were buried.

(See further E. Robinson and E. Smith, *Biblical Researches in Palestine*, 2 [1841], 431–46; T. Wright, ed., *Early Travel in Palestine* [1848]; F. Hommel, *The Ancient Hebrew Tradition* [1897], 232–34; L. H. Vincent in *RB* 38 [1929]: 107–10; F. F. Bishop in *IBR* 16 [1948]: 94–99; C. D. Matthews, *Palestine, Mohammedan Holy Land* [1949]; D. Maden Maundr. [1957]; D. M. Jacobson in *PEQ* 113 [1980]: 73–81; D. Jericke, *Abraham in Mamre: Historische und exegetische Studien zur Region von Hebron und zu Genesis 11,27–19,38* [2003].)

H. G. STIGERS

hedge. This noun is used by the NIV twice, in both cases with reference to thorn shrubs (Heb. *měsûkkâ* H5372, Isa. 5:5; *měsûkâ* H5004, Mic. 7:4). Verbal expressions are used figuratively to refer to God's protecting care (Job 1:10) or his constraint (3:23). The KJV uses the noun also to render Hebrew *gādēr* H1555, "stone wall" (Ps. 80:12 et al.) and Greek *phragmos* G5850 with reference to a FENCE, enclosure, or partitioning WALL (Matt. 21:33; Mk. 12:1; Lk. 14:23 [NIV, "lanes"]; Eph. 2:14).

hedgehog. An insectivorous mammal covered with dense spines. The term is used by the NRSV twice to render Hebrew *qippōd H7887* (Isa. 14:23; 34:11 [RSV, "porcupine"]; the NIV takes this term as a reference to the OWL). The hedgehog should be distinguished from the porcupine, which is the largest rodent in Palestine and may weigh over forty pounds. The powerful sharp spines, up to fifteen inches long, are modified hairs. Porcupines live in all countries where they can find rocky shelter, eating mostly roots and other vegetable matter but also some bones, and even animal remains. In most parts of their range they are considered good eating. Hedgehogs are much smaller, up to about ten inches, and they are covered above with short spines; in color they are sandy to brown. They eat a wide range of insects, as well as baby rodents, birds' eggs, small reptiles, etc., mostly at night. When alarmed they roll into a defensive ball, spines pointing outward. Three species live in Palestine, two being desert forms. (See *FFB*, 66.) G. S. CANSDALE

heel. The Hebrew word *ʿāqēb H6811* is twice used in a literal sense of ESAU's heel, which JACOB grasped while still in the womb of REBEKAH (Gen. 25:26; Hos. 12:3). Elsewhere, the term *heel* is use in a figurative sense. In the protevangelium (Gen. 3:15), God said that the seed of the woman would bruise the serpent's head, but the serpent would bruise his heel—clearly a reference to the conflict between Satan and the Son of God and the utter defeat Christ would administer to the foe responsible for his crucifixion at Calvary. The dying patriarch Jacob, when blessing his children, spoke of DAN's enemies as a rider whose horse's heel is bitten by a serpent (Dan) so that the frightened animal rears and throws his rider (Gen. 49:17). Similarly, he spoke of GAD as someone who would attack raiders "at their heels" (v. 19). JOB's friend BILDAD the Shuhite insinuated that Job was like the wicked who bring about their own destruction: "A trap seizes him by the heel" and he is caught (Job 18:9). The psalmist laments that the bosom friend whom he trusted and who dined at his table lifted his heel against him, that is, spurned him with brutal violence or perhaps kicked him when he was down (Ps. 41:9). Jesus referred to this statement at the Last Passover and applied it to himself; the bosom friend who ate with him and then betrayed him was Judas (Jn. 13:18, Gk. *pterna G4761*). S. BARABAS

Hegai heg´i (הֵגַא *H2043* and הֵגַי *H2051*, derivation uncertain). EUNUCH of King XERXES in charge of the HAREM; he was entrusted the women from whom the king intended to choose a queen to replace VASHTI (Esth. 2:3 [KJV, "Hege"], 8, 15). ESTHER quickly won Hegai's favor, and he provided her with special treatment (v. 9). Another part of the harem was the responsibility of SHAASGAZ (v. 14).

Hege hee´gee. KJV alternate form of HEGAI.

Hegemonides hej´uh-moh´nuh-deez (Ἡγεμονίδης). A Syrian officer appointed by the boy-king ANTIOCHUS V Eupator over the district from Ptolemais to Gerar at the time when the king was forced to return to ANTIOCH OF SYRIA to deal with a revolt by Philip in 162 B.C. (2 Macc. 13:24). The KJV takes the name as an adjective ("made him principal governor"), but contemporary inscriptions confirm the existence of a military commander named Hegemonides son of Zephorus.

Heglam heg´luhm (הֶגְלָם, from גָּלָה *H1655*, hiphil "to take into exile"). Son of EHUD and father of Uzza and Ahihud (1 Chr. 8:7 NRSV). The passage is difficult, however, and it is possible that a person named Heglam did not exist. The Hebrew words *wĕgērāʾ hûʾ heglām* (NRSV, "and Gera, that is, Heglam") can be rendered "and Gera, who deported them" (so NIV; cf. KJV).

heifer. See CATTLE.

heifer, red. This term (Heb. *pārâ ʾădummâ*) refers to a red-brown, unblemished, and unworked cow that was sacrificed and burned (Num. 19:1–8); its ashes were then kept "for use in the water of cleansing; it is for purification from sin" (v. 9). The cleansing in view had to do with corpse contamination (vv. 11–22). This ritual included several unusual features, such as the requirement that the slaughtering take place outside the camp (instead

Copy of a relief depicting the Carchemish Royal family (Neo-Hittite, c. 800 B.C.). Kingship was often inherited passing from father to son.

of on the ALTAR), and some scholars have argued that it should not be regarded as a SACRIFICE in the strict sense. Various interpretations, some allegorical, have been proposed regarding the details of this offering (see J. Milgrom in *VT* 31 [1981]: 62–72; R. B. Allen in *EBC*, 2:858–60). See also CLEAN; PURIFICATION; PURITY; UNCLEANNESS; WATER OF CLEANSING.

heir. A person who inherits the property of another, usually upon the latter's death. The OT includes two legislative texts pertaining to INHERITANCE (Num. 27:1–11; Deut. 21:15–17). The disposition of property by a last will and TESTAMENT is never mentioned in the OT. Before the head of a house died he gave verbal instructions about the distribution of his property, but in doing so he had to conform to the laws and customs of the time.

The FIRSTBORN son succeeded to the headship of the FAMILY and received an inheritance that was double that of each of the other brothers (Deut. 21:17). He could, however, lose this BIRTHRIGHT by surrendering it to a brother (cf. ESAU, Gen. 25:29–34) or for a serious offense (REUBEN, 35:22). The law protected him against favoritism on the part of his father (Deut. 21:15–17). There are, however, a number of cases in the OT where a younger son displaced an elder son, but these were exceptions to the ordinary law.

In the early history of Israel, the sons of concubines did not share the inheritance unless the father adopted them and made them equal in rank with the sons of his freeborn wives. SARAH objected to ISHMAEL's sharing the inheritance with her son ISAAC (Gen. 21:10). In later times this practice was not so strictly followed. Daughters did not inherit property unless there were no male heirs. If a man died without sons, the order of succession was as follows: daughter, brother(s), paternal uncle(s), nearest male relative (Num. 27:1–11).

The widow had no right to the inheritance because the property could pass outside the family. A childless widow either remained a member of her husband's family by the LEVIRATE LAW of marriage or returned to her father (Gen. 38:11; Lev. 22:13). Undoubtedly she could keep what she had contributed to the marriage and the gifts she had received from her husband. If she had grown-up children, they provided for her.

A daughter who inherited had to marry within the tribe of her father to keep the inheritance within the tribe (Num. 36:6–9). If she married outside the tribe, her inheritance was forfeited and went to the person next in succession. On occasion, however, this law seems to have been set aside (1 Chr. 2:34–36). (See further E. Neufeld, *Ancient Hebrew Marriage Laws* [1944]; R. de Vaux, *Ancient Israel: Its Life and Institutions* [1961], 53–55.)

In the NT the Greek word *klēronomos* G3101 is typically used in a special theological sense of the recipients of God's promises and of those who wait for what is promised. PAUL, especially, brings out that the heirs of the promises of salvation made to the seed of ABRAHAM, which are to be fulfilled in the messianic age, are not physical descendants of Abraham who keep the law but his spiritual descendants—those who have faith like him (Rom. 4:14; Gal. 3:29; Eph. 3:6). (See *TDNT*, 3:767–85.) S. BARABAS

Helah hee´luh (חֶלְאָה H2690, "necklace"). One of the two wives of ASHHUR (apparently founder of the town of TEKOA), who is included in the genealogy of JUDAH; she had four children (1 Chr. 4:5, 7).

Helam hee´luhm (חֵילָם H2663, meaning unknown). A town in TRANSJORDAN to which the Arameans under HADADEZER retreated after JOAB initially routed them; there they were subsequently defeated by DAVID (2 Sam. 10:16-17). This town is not mentioned elsewhere in the Hebrew OT, though the SEPTUAGINT apparently refers to it in Ezek.

47:16 (*Ēlam*) as being N of Damascus toward Hamath. Most scholars consider such a location too far N, and some identify Helam with Alema (1 Macc. 5:26; cf. *ḥlʾm* in the Egyptian Execration Texts, c. 1850 B.C.), which is modern ʿAlma in Hauran, c. 50 mi. S of Damascus and c. 35 mi. E of the Sea of Galilee. J. B. Scott

Helbah hel′buh (חֶלְבָּה *H2695*, possibly "forest" or "fruitful"). A town in the tribal territory of Asher from which Israel could not expel the Canaanites (Jdg. 1:31). Similarity in the consonants and location leads many scholars to identify Helbah with Ahlab (1:31) and Mahalab (Josh. 19:29) at Khirbet el-Maḥalib, 4 mi. NE of Tyre on the coast (but see Z. Kallai, *Historical Geography of the Bible* [1986], 222).

Helbon hel′bon (חֶלְבּוֹן *H2696*, possibly "forest" or "fruitful"). A city or region mentioned by Ezekiel in his lamentation over Tyre (Ezek. 27:18; cf. also the *Genesis Apocryphon* [1Q20] XXII, 10, which identifies Hobah as Helbon). From Helbon wine was imported to Tyre by traders of Damascus. It is probably to be identified with the Valley of Halbun, some 12 mi. N of Damascus. The area has been famous from ancient times for its fine wines, preferred even by kings (Strabo, *Geogr.* 15.3.22 [735]). J. B. Scott

Helchiah, Helchias hel-kī′uh, hel-kī′uhs. KJV alternate Apoc. forms of Hilkiah (1 Esd. 8:1; 2 Esd. 1:1).

Heldai hel′di (חֶלְדַּי *H2702*, possibly "mole"). **(1)** A descendant of Othniel from the town of Netophah who served as captain of the temple guard for the twelfth monthly course (1 Chr 27:15). He is probably the same as Heled.

(2) One of a group of Jewish exiles who brought gold and silver from Babylon to help those who had returned under Zerubbabel; from these gifts a crown was to be made for Joshua (Jeshua) the high priest (Zech. 6:10; in v. 14 the MT has *ḥēlem* [KJV, "Helem"], apparently a scribal error or an alternate name for Heldai.

Heleb hee′lib. See Heled.

Helech hee′lik (חֵילֵךְ *H2662*). TNIV Helek. A city or region that, along with Arvad (a Phoenician island town), supplied sailors and soldiers for Tyre (Ezek. 27:11). Although several identifications have been suggested, perhaps the least objectionable proposal is to equate Helech with Assyrian Ḥilakku, that is, Cilicia, in SE Asia Minor (the Cilicians were noted for their warlike character and would fit as mercenaries of Tyre). The Septuagint (*hē dynamis sou*) and the KJV ("thine army") interpret the Hebrew word not as a name but as the common noun *ḥayil H2657* with suffix (2nd person fem. sing.). This view is preferred by some scholars.

Heled hee′lid (חֵלֶד *H2699*, possibly "mold"; in 2 Sam. 23:29, most Heb. mss have חֵלֶב, possibly "fruitful"). Son of Baanah from the town of Netophah; he is included in the list of David's mighty men (2 Sam. 23:29 [KJV, NRSV, "Heleb"]; 1 Chr. 11:30).

Helek hee′lik (חֵלֶק *H2751*, "portion, lot," possibly short form of חֶלְקִיָּהוּ *H2760*, "Yahweh is my portion" [see Hilkiah]; gentilic חֶלְקִי *H2757*, "Helekite"). **(1)** Son of Gilead and great-grandson of Manasseh; eponymous ancestor of the Helekite clan (Num. 26:30). Elsewhere, however, "the sons of Helek" (Josh. 17:2, lit. trans.) are listed with other Manassite clans as receiving an inheritance W of the Jordan, in distinction from the Gileadites, who were granted territory in Transjordan.

(2) TNIV form of Helech.

Helem hee′lim (חֵלֶם *H2152*, meaning uncertain). **(1)** Son of Heber and great-grandson of Asher (1 Chr. 7:35; some edd. of RSV have the misprint "Heler"); many scholars emend the text to Hotham (on the basis of v. 32).

(2) A variant form of Heldai (Zech. 6:14 KJV and other versions, following the MT).

Heleph hee′lif (חֶלֶף *H2738*, possibly "replacement [place]" or "marsh grass [settlement]"). The (western) starting point of the southern boundary of the tribe of Naphtali (Josh. 19:33). The precise location of Heleph is uncertain, but many scholars identify it with Khirbet ʿIrbadeh, about 3 mi. NE of Mount Tabor.

Heler. See HELEM #1.

Helez hee´liz (חֶלֶץ H2742, possibly "[God/Yahweh] has rescued"). **(1)** One of DAVID's mighty men, identified as "the Paltite" (2 Sam. 23:26), meaning probably a native of BETH PELET or perhaps a descendant of PELET the Calebite; in the parallel list he is called "the Pelonite" (1 Chr. 11:27), a term of unknown derivation and maybe a scribal misspelling. He is probably the same as "Helez the Pelonite, an Ephraimite," commander of the seventh division (1 Chr. 27:10).

(2) Son of Azariah, included in the genealogy of JUDAH (1 Chr. 2:39).

Heli hee´li (Ἠλί G2459 [some editions Ἠλί or Ἠλεί], from Heb. עֵלִי H6603, possibly "lofty" or "[God/Yahweh] is high"). **(1)** Son of MATTHAT and father of JOSEPH according to Luke's GENEALOGY OF JESUS CHRIST (Lk. 3:23). Because the parallel passage lists Matthan son of Eleazar as the father of Joseph (Matt. 1:15), some regard Heli as his grandfather, perhaps corresponding to Eleazar. Others argue that Luke gives Mary's genealogy, in which case Heli is really her father, not Joseph's.

(2) KJV Apoc. form of ELI (2 Esd. 1:2).

Helias hee´lee-uhs. KJV Apoc. form of ELIJAH (2 Esd. 7:39; NRSV v. 109).

Heliodorus hee´lee-uh-dor´uhs (Ἡλιόδωρος, "gift of Helios [the sun god]"). The chief minister of King SELEUCUS IV Philopator (187–175 B.C.). He tried unsuccessfully to plunder the treasury of the temple in Jerusalem (2 Macc. 3:7–40; 4:1; 5:18). A Jew named Simon had a disagreement with the high priest ONIAS and, because he could not have his way, decided in revenge to tell Apollonius, the governor of Phoenicia and Coelesyria, that there were vast treasures in the temple in Jerusalem that could easily come into the possession of Seleucus, who was then in control of Palestine. When Apollonius reported to the king what Simon had told him, the king immediately sent Heliodorus, his chief minister, to take possession of the money.

When Heliodorus arrived, the Jews told him that the money belonged mostly to widows and orphans, who had deposited it there for safekeeping, and that it would be sacrilegious to take it. When Heliodorus entered the treasury with a bodyguard, he saw a great apparition, a rider on a magnificently caparisoned horse, and two young men, strong and splendidly dressed. The horse struck Heliodorus with its hoofs, and the young men scourged him mercilessly. His men carried him out on a stretcher sorely wounded and pled with Onias to spare his life. The high priest prayed for him, and Heliodorus recovered. After offering a sacrifice and making grateful vows to God, he returned to Syria. (The same story is told in 4 Macc. 4, but with the important difference that Seleucus sends Apollonius rather than Heliodorus to plunder the temple.)

Although he was reared with Seleucus when they were boys, in 175 B.C. Heliodorus murdered the king and attempted to seize the throne, but he was driven out by Eumenes of Pergamus and his brother Attalus. Then ANTIOCHUS IV (Epiphanes), the brother of Seleucus, ascended the throne (Appian, *Syrian Wars* 233). It was this Antiochus whose attempt to hellenize the Jews led to the Maccabean war, which ended with deliverance from Syrian control. See MACCABEE. S. BARABAS

Heliopolis hee´lee-op´uh-lis (from ἥλιος G2463, "sun," and πόλις G4484, "city"). This name occurs in the NIV as the rendering of Hebrew 'āwen H225, corresponding to Egyptian 'Iwnw (Ezek. 30:17; KJV, AVEN; NRSV, ON); in the NRSV it is used to render *bêt šemeš*, "house of the sun" (Jer 43:13; KJV "Beth-shemesh"; NIV, "the temple of the sun"). In both instances, the SEPTUAGINT has *hēliou polis*, "city of the sun," but probably to be understood as a proper name. See SUN, CITY OF THE.

Heliopolis was an ancient city in EGYPT, sacred to the sun-god RE and located in Tell el-Ḥisn, near el-Matarieh, about 10 mi. out of Cairo to the NNE. It first attained prominence in the Old Kingdom (Pyramid Age) of Egyptian history, when the pharaohs used a solar symbol for their tombs and adopted the title "Son of Re." The kings of the fifth dynasty may have come from Heliopolis as a subordinate branch of the fourth dynasty. However, the major influence of Heliopolis in Egypt was less on the political than on the religious plane. The theological system and cultic usages there elaborated profoundly influenced the religion of Egypt in general. Identified with the local creator-god Atum, Re was at the head of a "family" of nine gods (Ennead) among whom the Heliopolitan theologians skillfully included the funerary god OSIRIS, chief rival of Re in the late Old Kingdom. The main temple in Heliopolis accordingly was that of Re, or Re-Atum, the site being marked by the remains of a great enclosure and by the sole remaining obelisk of Sesostris I (c. 1900 B.C.).

Sesostris rebuilt the great temple of Re (Berlin Leather Roll; see A. de Buck in *Studia Aegyptiaca* 1 [1938]: 48–57); this was doubtless the structure at which Joseph's father-in-law POTIPHERAH (POTIPHAR) subsequently served as "priest of On" (high priest in Heliopolis?), an affiliation reflected by his name, which means "gift of Re" (Gen. 41:45, 50; 46:20). The greatest pharaohs of the New Kingdom (c. 1550–1070 B.C.) adorned the temples of Heliopolis. The works of THUTMOSE III included two well-known obelisks, now in New York and London ("Cleopatra's Needle"). Under RAMSES III, Heliopolis came second only to THEBES in its wealth of royal endowments (Papyrus Harris I). Among other edifices, obelisks were also erected by Amenhotep II, Seti I (now in Rome), and Ramses IV; these were slender, pyramidically topped shafts sacred to the sun-god.

As late as HERODOTUS, Heliopolis remained important, but thereafter sank into decline. Prior to his time three OT passages of the 8th–7th centuries B.C. appear to refer to Heliopolis. The City of Destruction in Isa. 19:18 is possibly a Hebrew pun for City of the Sun, that is, Heliopolis (see DESTRUCTION, CITY OF). Ezekiel's judgment on Egypt (Ezek. 30:17) included Aven (*ʾāwen* H225, "wickedness"), perhaps also a pun (for *ʾôn* H228, "On" or Heliopolis); its association there with Bubastis (PI BESETH) and MEMPHIS (KJV, Noph) would agree well with this identification. Similarly, Jeremiah threatened that NEBUCHADNEZZAR of Babylon would ravage Egypt's temples with fire, and "break the obelisks of Heliopolis" (Jer. 43:13 NRSV).

(See further J. H. Breasted, *Ancient Records of Egypt* [1906], 1, §§ 498–506, and 4, §§ 247–304; B. Porter and R. L. B. Moss, *Topographical Bibliography of Ancient Egyptian Hieroglyphic Texts* [1934], 4:59–65; A. H. Gardiner, *Ancient Egyptian Onomastica* [1947]: 2:144*, 146* (:400); H. Kees, *Der Götterglaube im alten Ägypten* [1956], 214–86; P. Montet, *Géographie de l'Égypte Ancienne* [1957], 1:155–71 and figs. 17–19; W. Helck, *Materialen zur Wirtschaftsgeschichte des Neuen Reiches* [1960], 1:124–30; H. Kees, *Ancient Egypt: A Cultural Topography* [1961], 147–82 et passim; A. Saleh, *Excavations at Heliopolis*, 2 vols. [1981–83].)

K. A. KITCHEN

Helkai hel′ki (חֶלְקָי H2758, short form of חִלְקִיָּהוּ H2760, "Yahweh is my portion" [see HILKIAH]). The head of a priestly house who returned from exile with ZERUBBABEL (Neh. 12:15).

Helkath hel′kath (חֶלְקָת H2762, "smooth place" or "plot of ground"). A town that served to mark the boundary of the tribal territory of ASHER (Josh. 19:25). It was one of four cities from this tribe that were assigned to the Levite family descended from GERSHON (21:31; called HUKOK in the parallel passage, 1 Chr. 6:75, probably a scribal mistake). It is first mentioned in the list of towns conquered by THUTMOSE III (c. 15th cent. B.C.). Its precise location is uncertain, but two possible identifications are Khirbet el-Harbaj, c. 12 mi. S of Acco, and Tell el-Qassis, some 5 mi. farther S and closer to the exit of the valley of ESDRAELON. (See further *ABD*, 3:125–26.)

J. B. SCOTT

Helkath Hazzurim hel′kath-haz′yoo-rim (חֶלְקַת הַצֻּרִים H2763, perhaps "field of rocks [*or* flint knives]," but meaning debated). Also Helkath-hazzurim. A place near the pool of GIBEON where twelve men under JOAB fought to the death with an equal number from ABNER's forces (2 Sam. 2:16); the precise location is unknown. It is difficult to see why the area would have been called "field of rocks" as a result of this confrontation, and various changes to the text have been proposed (see *ABD*, 3:126–27).

Helkias hel-ki′uhs. KJV Apoc. form of HILKIAH (1 Esd. 1:8).

hell. This English word (from a Germanic root meaning "concealed place" or "underworld") is used by the KJV in the OT to render Hebrew *šeʾôl* H8619

(Deut. 32:22 et al.; see SHEOL); in the NT it renders Greek *hadēs* G87 (Matt. 11:23 et al.; see HADES) and *geenna* G1147 (5:2 et al.; see GEHENNA). The NIV and other modern versions use it almost exclusively as a translation of *geenna*, which refers to the Valley of HINNOM (Wadi er-Rababi, just SW of JERUSALEM), the location of the notorious sacrificial offering by fire of children to the god MOLECH (2 Chr. 28:3; 33:6; cf. 2 Ki. 23:10; Jer. 7:32; 19:6). The apocalyptic book of *1 Enoch* states that there would be an abyss filled with fire S of Jerusalem into which ungodly Israelites would be thrown. Later the idea was extended so that this place was conceived to be the scene of fiery punishment for all of the ungodly. Still later, when the place of punishment was conceived of as under the earth, the idea of fiery torment was maintained. (The English term occurs also as part of a phrase used to render *tartaroō* G5434, "to send to hell," 2 Pet. 2:4. In Gk. mythology, Tartarus was the name of a deep abyss below Hades where the Titans were imprisoned, but in time the term became roughly equivalent to Hades.)

I. Intertestamental views. The teaching that there is a place where the ungodly are punished forever is scarcely mentioned in the OT. In the intertestamental period, however, this idea became prominent, although its acceptance by the rabbis was far from unanimous. According to the Apocryphal book of 2 Esdras (also known as *4 Ezra*; see ESDRAS, SECOND), Ezra asks if the lost soul will be tortured immediately at death or not until the renewal of the creation, to which God answers, "As the spirit leaves the body … if it is one of those who have shown scorn and have not kept the way of the Most High … such spirit shall … wander about in torment, ever grieving and sad … they will consider the torment laid up for themselves in the last days" (2 Esd. 7:7–84).

The pseudepigraphical book of *1 Enoch* gives detailed descriptions of Gehenna as a place of punishment. The PHARISEES accepted this view: according to JOSEPHUS (*War* 2.8.14), they believed that "the souls of bad men are subject to eternal punishment." Elsewhere he describes the position of the Pharisees by saying that the wicked "are to be detained in an everlasting prison." In the time just prior to the NT period, the rabbinical school of Shammai divided all men into three groups: the righteous, the wicked who are "immediately written and sealed to Gehenna," and a third group of people who "go down to Gehinnom and moan and come up again." The school of HILLEL thought that the ungodly were punished in Gehenna for a year and then annihilated, although certain especially wicked men "go down to Gehinnom and are punished there to ages of ages."

II. Teachings of Jesus. It should be noted that in the NT, *geenna* is used only in the synoptics (except for an occurrence in Jas. 3:6), and only by JESUS CHRIST. In other words, the knowledge of hell comes almost exclusively from the teachings of Christ, who spoke emphatically on the subject on a number of occasions.

(1) Jesus states that "anyone who says, 'You fool!' will be in danger of the fire of hell" (Matt. 5:22). In the context Jesus is saying that whereas the OT simply condemned murder, he has a higher demand, and the result is that expressions of anger toward one's brother can lead to the most severe punishment.

(2) According to Jesus, the punishment of hell is so severe that it would be better for a person to lose an eye or a hand rather than that these members of the body should be instruments of sins that would lead to hell. Twice he speaks about the whole body being thrown into hell (Matt. 5:29–30).

(3) Without using the word Gehenna itself, Jesus is obviously speaking of the punishment of

Some ancients believed that this cave at Caesarea Philippi (modern Panias) was an entrance into the Underworld.

hell when he says that the tree that does not bear good fruit will be cut down and "thrown into the fire" (Matt. 7:19).

(4) Part of the punishment pronounced upon the ungodly is that they will be cast out from the presence of Christ (Matt. 7:23). It is noteworthy that all of the above references come from the SERMON ON THE MOUNT.

(5) The ultimate punishment resulting from apostasy will include being consigned "outside, into the darkness, where there will be weeping and gnashing of teeth" (Matt. 8:12).

(6) Jesus states that God has the power to "destroy both soul and body in hell" (Matt. 10:28).

(7) In the parable of the tares, as well as in the parable of the nets, Jesus says that at the end of the age, sinners will be cast "into the fiery furnace, where there will be weeping and gnashing of teeth" (Matt. 13:42, 50).

(8) The ultimate punishment inflicted upon sinners is described by Jesus as being much worse than death itself, for it would be better to be drowned than to be punished for causing a child to be led astray (Matt. 18:6). Jesus then adds that it would be better to lose a limb that was the source of sinful behavior than to "be thrown into eternal fire" or "the fire of hell" (vv. 8–9). The parallel speaks of going "into hell, where fire never goes out" (Mk. 9:43), and hell is further described as the place "where their worm does not die, and the fire is not quenched" (9:48, citing Isa. 66:24).

(9) In the parable of the wedding feast, the punishment is again described as that of being "outside, into the darkness, where there will be weeping and gnashing of teeth" (Matt. 22:13).

(10) Jesus condemns the Pharisees for making their converts "twice as much a child of hell as you are" (Matt. 23:15). A little later he warns that they will not be able to "escape being condemned to hell" (v. 33).

(11) In the parable of the talents, Jesus again alludes to outer darkness and to the weeping and gnashing of teeth (Matt. 25:30), while in the parable of the sheep and the goats, Jesus says to those whom he condemns, "Depart from me, you who are cursed, into the eternal fire prepared for the devil and his angels" (25:41). Later in the same parable, Jesus describes their fate as "eternal punishment" (v. 46).

In several passages, Jesus implies that there will be degrees of punishment in hell. He speaks of hypocrites as those who will "receive the greater condemnation" (Mk. 12:40 NRSV); some "will be beaten with many blows," whereas others who have a lesser knowledge of the master's will, "with few blows" (Lk. 12:47–48). The certain conclusion from all of these passages is that Jesus taught the doctrine of hell clearly and emphatically. All but those who interpret Scripture with extreme literalism agree that this is figurative language used to describe hell, but the figures stand for the most terrible reality.

III. Writings of the apostles. As already noted, the word *hell* (Gehenna) occurs only once outside the synoptics (Jas. 3:6), but the idea of severe punishment in the world to come is taught in several passages. For example:

(1) PAUL speaks of the impending judgment of God, which will result in eternal life for those who do good, but "wrath and anger" for those who do wickedness. For the evildoer, "there will be trouble and distress" (Rom. 2:7–9).

(2) A person's appearance before the JUDGMENT SEAT of Christ will result in receiving "good or evil" depending on the actions during this life (2 Cor. 5:10). Paul sees the danger of this terrible fate as an impelling force in his ministry (v. 11).

(3) At the return of Christ, those dwelling in complacency will experience sudden destruction, "and they will not escape" (1 Thess. 5:3).

(4) At the SECOND COMING, Jesus will be "revealed from heaven in blazing fire with his powerful angels. He will punish those who do not know God and do not obey the gospel of our Lord Jesus. They will be punished with everlasting destruction and shut out from the presence of the Lord and from the majesty of his power" (2 Thess. 1:7–9).

(5) The author of Hebrews speaks of "eternal judgment" as a fundamental of the faith (Heb. 6:2), and of the threat of punishment as "a fearful expectation of judgment and of raging fire that will consume the enemies of God" (10:27). He refers to it as "much worse punishment" (v. 29 NRSV) than the death that was administered to those who broke the law of Moses.

(6) JAMES speaks of the tongue as "set on fire by hell" (Jas. 3:6).

(7) In his second epistle, Peter writes about the angels who sinned and says that God "sent them to hell [Tartarus]," a place described as "gloomy dungeons" (2 Pet. 2:4). Later in the passage, God is described as knowing how "to hold the unrighteous for the day of judgment, while continuing their punishment" (v. 9). The ungodly are like brute beasts that will be "caught and destroyed" (v. 12). "Blackest darkness is reserved for them" (v. 17).

(8) In a similar passage in Jude, it is revealed that the fallen angels have been kept by God "in darkness, bound with everlasting chains for judgment on the great Day" (Jude 6). The inhabitants of SODOM and GOMORRAH "serve as an example of those who suffer the punishment of eternal fire" (v. 7).

(9) In the book of Revelation, an angel says of those who worship the beast that "the smoke of their torment rises forever and ever" (Rev. 14:11). The place of the wicked "will be in the fiery lake of burning sulfur. This is the second death" (21:8).

These scriptural references demonstrate that the apostles followed Christ in teaching that life issues in two possible destinies, eternal blessedness or the torment of hell. The NT writers are very reserved in their descriptions of hell, especially in comparison to the contemporary extrabiblical literature, but they are clear in teaching a judgment issuing in eternal punishment. (See PUNISHMENT, ETERNAL for a discussion of the claims that the Bible teaches annihilation or universalism.)

IV. The early church. In the period immediately after NT days, the doctrine of hell was clearly taught. Many of the martyrs of that period, considering hell to be the fate of those who denied the faith, were given courage to face martyrdom by the conviction that this was the easier of the two alternatives.

In the 2nd cent., the church fathers give evidence in their writings of their convictions on the subject. For example, IGNATIUS (died A.D. 110) says, "one so defiled will go into unquenchable fire" (*Eph.* 16.2). The *Epistle of Barnabas* (c. 130) mentions "the way of eternal death with punishment" (20.1). The *Shepherd of Hermas* (c. 140) states, "those who fell into the fire and were burned are those who have departed for ever from the living God" (*Vis.* 3.7.2).

JUSTIN MARTYR (c. 110–165) states, "we are fully convinced that each will suffer punishment by eternal fire, according to the demerit of his actions" (*1 Apol.* 17.4). IRENAEUS (c. 135–200) uses the term "eternal fire" repeatedly. TERTULLIAN (c. 160–220) mentions "the greatness of the punishment which continueth, not for a long time, but forever." He is the first of the church fathers who expresses joy at the spectacle of the lost in hell, an attitude not found in the Bible, but one that became common in the Middle Ages. The early Christian theologians gave unanimous testimony in favor of the belief in hell. It was not until ORIGEN (c. 185–254), who held a number of other unbiblical views as well, that a major church teacher denied this doctrine.

In conclusion, the doctrine of hell is a thoroughly biblical doctrine. Therefore it is not surprising that in the history of theology a denial of this doctrine has often accompanied weak views of biblical inspiration. The reaction against this doctrine has, however, been partly the fault of some of its adherents who have proclaimed it in crudely literalistic terms. Thoroughgoing conservatives such as Calvin, Hodge, Strong, and Schilder have recognized the symbolic nature of the biblical terms "worm," "fire," etc. Another cause of reaction against the doctrine has been the exultant glee or other unloving attitudes held by some who have proclaimed it, but this is not a part of the biblical doctrine.

The Bible does not give the physical location of hell or anything about its furnishings, but it assures readers that those whose sins are not atoned for by Jesus Christ will receive perfect justice from God, that they will receive exactly what they deserve for all eternity, which will be a most miserable fate. This ought to be one of the impelling motives making evangelism the urgent business of all Christians.

(See further S. Bartlett, *Life and Death Eternal* [1866]; W. Shedd, *Dogmatic Theology* [1888], 2:667–754; K. Schilder, *Wat is de hel?* [1920]; W. R. Inge et al., *What Is Hell?* [1930]; J. S. Bonnell, *Heaven and Hell* [1956]; H. Buis, *The Doctrine of Eternal Punishment* [1957]; H. Blamires, *Knowing the Truth about Heaven and Hell: Our Choices and Where They Lead Us* [1988]; N. M. de S. Cameron, ed., *Universalism and the Doctrine of Hell* [1992]; W. V. Crockett et al., *Four Views on Hell* [1992]; W. Grudem, *Systematic Theology: An Introduction to Biblical Doctrine* [1994], ch. 56; C. W. Morgan and R. A. Peterson, eds., *Hell under Fire: Modern Scholarship Reinvents Eternal Punishment* [2004].)

H. Buis

Hellenism (from Ἕλλην *G1818*, "Greek"). The civilization and culture of ancient GREECE; especially, the dissemination and adoption of Greek thought, customs, and life style. It often implies the fusion of Greek and non-Greek culture. (Among classical scholars, the term *Hellenistic* is primarily a chronological designation, covering the period from Alexander to the beginnings of the Roman empire. In biblical scholarship, the term has a broader connotation and is roughly equivalent to *Greco-Roman*.)

ALEXANDER THE GREAT, who was taught by Aristotle, devoted his life to conquering the world for the spread of Greek culture. He was convinced of the superiority of the Greek way of life and carried with him on his campaigns copies of Homer's *Iliad* and *Odyssey*. In the summer of 334 B.C. he entered ASIA MINOR, and by the autumn of 333 he was already entering SYRIA and had conquered the whole of Syria and PALESTINE, and then EGYPT by the winter of 332/331. In 331 the Persian empire was in his hands. He died in 323, and the empire came into the hands of his generals. His eleven years of conquest changed the course of history, introducing a new lifestyle that affected every nation conquered, even the Jewish nation. Alexander and his successors broke down the old national, political, cultural, and religious establishment and introduced Greek culture by establishing new colonies and cities, by rapidly spreading the Koine (see GREEK LANGUAGE), and by the intermarriages of the Greeks with the Asiatics.

According to JOSEPHUS, Alexander's relationship to the Jews both in Palestine (*Ant.* 11.8.5 §§329–39) and in ALEXANDRIA (*War* 2.18.7 §§487–88; *Apion* 2.4 §35) was friendly. After Alexander's death and until 198 B.C., the Jews were under the Ptolemaic influence (see PTOLEMY). During this time they were treated with consideration, particularly in Alexandria where the Ptolemies, trying to compete with ATHENS, encouraged scholars and writers from every nation to help them achieve their goal. The Ptolemies set up the largest library in the world, founded learned societies, and established schools to teach the Greek culture and language. It was this influence that led the Alex-

Centaur wrestling with Lapith. Hellenistic culture focused on form, pleasure, and entertainment.

andrian Jews in the 3rd cent. to translate the Bible into Greek (see SEPTUAGINT).

The Ptolemaic influence over Palestine ended in 198 B.C. with their defeat by the SELEUCID empire under ANTIOCHUS the Great. The Seleucids gained control of the selection of the high priesthood, which allowed some Hellenistic influence to penetrate. However, with the Seleucids trying to force their way of life, the Jews finally resisted this influence which finally led to the Maccabean War beginning in 168 (see MACCABEE). But only three decades later John Hyrcanus (see HASMONEAN II.A) made a pact with the Seleucids, and from then on one can see some influence of Hellenism in Palestine right down to the time of the Roman occupation in 63 B.C. This influence continued with the Roman and Herodian rulers. The entrenchment of Hellenism can more readily be seen among the Alexandrian Jews, especially among some of their philosophers such as PHILO JUDAEUS, who adopted the allegorical interpretation that led to the sacrificing of the truth in the OT on the altar of pagan philosophy.

Hellenistic influence is apparent early in the church's history (in Gk. literature, the term *Hellēnistēs G1821* occurs for the first time in Acts 6:1; 9:29; 11:20; in the last passage, some early witnesses have *Hellēnas*, i.e., Greeks or Gentiles). According to Acts 6:1, there was a dispute in the Christian community at

Jerusalem between the Hebrews and the Hellenists (KJV, "Grecians"; NIV, "Grecian Jews") because the widows of the Hellenistic group were being neglected in the daily allocation from the common pool of property. Some have thought that these Hellenists were non-Jews, but (1) the context of Acts 1–5 is the spread of the church among Jews in Judea; (2) the admission of Gentiles into the church marked a new phase that begins later (chs. 10–11); (3) the subsequent conflict of the church regarding the admission of the Gentiles without circumcision (ch. 15) would have been pointless if the Gentiles were admitted in the church at its inception; and (4) the reference to Hellenists in 9:29 makes no sense if it means "Greeks," for Paul was not disputing with Gentiles in Jerusalem. Most scholars, therefore, believe that the passage refers to Jews who spoke Greek (in contrast to the "Hebrews," who spoke Hebrew or, more likely, Aramaic; for the various views, see H. J. Cadbury in *BC* 1/5 [1933], 59–74; C. F. D. Moule in *ExpTim* 70 [1958–59]: 100–102; I. H. Marshall in *NTS* 19 [1972–73]: 271–87; C. K. Barrett, *A Critical and Exegetical Commentary on the Acts of the Apostles*, ICC, 2 vols. [1994–96], 1:307–9).

These "Hellenists" were probably Jews from the Diaspora who had returned to Palestine. (See Paul; Stephen.) In the past, some scholars argued that such individuals had a liberal attitude to the adoption of Greco-Roman ways and that they would often have been in conflict with the stricter Jews native to Judea. Diaspora Jews, no doubt, were sometimes viewed with suspicion, but it is widely agreed now that the evidence does not support a sharp dichotomy between Hellenistic and "Hebraic" Jews with regard to their approach to the Mosaic law.

(See further M. Rostovtzeff, *The Social and Economic History of the Hellenistic World*, 3 vols. [1941]; S. Lieberman, *Hellenism in Jewish Palestine* [1950]; W. W. Tarn and G. Griffith, *Hellenistic Civilization*, 3rd ed. [1952]; M. Simon, *St. Stephen and the Hellenists in the Primitive Church* [1958], 1–19; A. J. Toynbee, *Hellenism: The History of a Civilization* [1959]; V. Tcherikover, *Hellenistic Civilization and the Jews* [1959]; M. Hengel, *Judaism and Hellenism*, 2 vols. [1974]; R. Bichler, *"Hellenismus": Geschichte und Problematik eines Epochenbegriffs* [1983]; A. Kuhrt and S. M. Sherwin-White, *Hellenism in the East: Interaction of Greek and Non-Greek Civilizations from Syria to Central Asia after Alexander* [1987]; F. Walbank, *The Hellenistic World*, rev. ed. [1993]; J. J. Collins and G. E. Sterling, eds., *Hellenism in the Land of Israel* [2001]; J. L. Kugel, ed., *Shem in the Tents of Japhet: Essays on the Encounter of Judaism and Hellenism* [2002]; T. Penner, *In Praise of Christian Origins: Stephen and the Hellenists in Lukan Apologetic History* [2004]; P. Green, *The Hellenistic Age: A Short History* [2007]. *ABD*, 3:127–35; *DNTB*, 164–82; *OCD*, 677–79.)

H. W. Hoehner

helmet. The head-protecting part of the soldier's armor. The walls of Karnak in Egypt show Hittites wearing helmets in the form of a skullcap. In the early history of Israel, probably only kings and prominent persons wore helmets. King Saul's armor included a helmet of bronze (Heb. *qôbaʿ* H7746, 1 Sam. 17:38), as did also that of Goliath (*kôbaʿ* H3916, 17:5). The helmet was part of the equipment of foreign troops (Jer. 46:4; Ezek. 23:24; 27:10; 38:5). King Uzziah provided his soldiers with helmets

Assyrian helmet made of iron with bronze inlay around the rim. From a palace in Nimrud (8th cent. B.C.).

(2 Chr. 26:14). The helmet worn by Assyrian and Babylonian soldiers was pointed, in contrast to the Syrian-Hittite helmet. Roman soldiers wore helmets with a crest. Helmets were usually made of leather; only in the SELEUCID period was the ordinary soldier supplied with brass helmets (1 Macc. 6:35). In the OT, the Lord is represented as wearing a helmet of salvation (Isa. 59:17); and PAUL in the NT says that the armor of the Christian too includes the helmet that symbolizes the hope of salvation (Gk. *perikephalaia G4330*, Eph. 6:17; 1 Thess. 5:8). S. BARABAS

Helon hee′lon (חֵלֹן *H2735*, "strong"). Father of ELIAB; the latter was a leader of the tribe of ZEBULUN at the time of MOSES (Num. 1:9; 2:7; 7:24, 29; 10:16).

helpmeet. This English term, meaning "helpmate," does not occur in the Bible, but apparently arose from a misunderstanding of the words, "I will make him an help meet [*i.e.*, a helper suitable] for him" (Gen. 2:18, 20 KJV). See ADAM; EVE.

helps. Aside from its occurrence in Acts 27:17 (Gk. *boētheia G1069*, "help, support"), the English plural *helps* is used by the KJV to render the plural of Greek *antilēmpsis G516*, which is found only in 1 Cor. 12:28, listed among the SPIRITUAL GIFTS God gives to the church. The RSV translates the word as "helpers," but it is questionable whether this rendering, which understands the word as a *personal* noun, can be justified ("helper" would be rather the translation of *antilēptōr*, LXX *antilēmptōr*). The word is really an abstract noun, has reference to that which the helper does, and hence should be translated "helpful deeds," "acts of aid," or "succor" (cf. NRSV, "forms of assistance").

Similarly, the other four items mentioned in the second part of this list refer to gifts and not to separate offices. Only the first three in this list of eight items are clearly officers: apostles, prophets, and teachers. The rest of the list refers to charismatic gifts that may be possessed by various officers. A Christian may hold one office and have many special gifts that he exercises in the one office. (Both the RSV and the NIV render all eight terms in personal fashion, apparently assuming that the gifts should be taken, by metonymy, as references to those who possess the gifts.) Although "helps" does not refer to a separate office, it is commonly believed that it does refer to gifts expressed more particularly in the work of deacons, while "administrations" (*kybernēseis*) refers to the gifts of elders in their ruling functions. See DEACON; ELDER (NT). However, Paul admonished the Ephesian elders to "help [*antilambanō G514*] the weak" (Acts 20:35), and he directed a similar exhortation to Christians in general (1 Thess. 5:14). (See J. Bannerman, *The Church of Christ* [1869], 2:229–30; *TDNT*, 1:375–76.) J. C. DEYOUNG

hem (of a garment). The part of the outer garment that would hang down loosely. It could be on the outer upper garment or on the lower one. The Hebrews were instructed to wear tassels on the four corners of the outer garment as a constant reminder of the commandments (Num. 15:38–39; Deut. 22:12; see FRINGE). AARON's robe was to have golden bells and pomegranates on its hem (Heb. *šûl H8767*, Exod. 28:33–34; 39:24–26). Jesus criticized the PHARISEES for their false display of piety by lengthening the TASSELS (Gk. *kraspedon G3192*, "edge, border, hem") on their garments (Matt. 23:5). However, the hem or fringe of Jesus' garment plays an important role with the hemorrhaging woman who believed that she would be healed if she could but touch the hem of his cloak; Jesus responded to her faith and granted her request (Lk. 8:43–48).

G. GIACUMAKIS, JR.

Hemam hee′muhn (הֵימָם *H2123*). Son of the clan chief Lotan and grandson of SEIR the Horite (Gen. 36:22 KJV). The NIV reads HOMAM on the basis of the parallel passage (1 Chr. 1:39), whereas the NRSV renders it HEMAN.

Heman hee′muhn (הֵימָן *H2124*). (1) Son of the clan chief LOTAN and grandson of SEIR the HORITE (Gen. 36:22 NRSV, following the LXX reading, *Aiman*). The KJV follows the MT, HEMAM, whereas the NIV has HOMAM (1 Chr. 1:39).

(2) Son (or descendant) of ZERAH and grandson (or more distant descendant) of JUDAH (1 Chr. 2:6). He is also listed as one of "the sons of Mahol" (meaning perhaps "members of the musical guild") who were regarded as wise men (1 Ki. 4:31). See DARDA; ETHAN; MAHOL.

(3) Son of Joel and grandson of Samuel; a Kohathite prophet-musician (see Kohath) whom David appointed to lead in the musical services (1 Chr. 6:33; 2 Chr. 5:12). He is usually mentioned along with Asaph and Ethan (Jeduthun): they were responsible for sounding the trumpets, the bronze cymbals, and other instruments (1 Chr. 15:17, 19; 16:41–42), and some of their sons were set apart "for the ministry of prophesying, accompanied by harps, lyres and cymbals" (25:1). Heman, also called "the king's seer," had fourteen sons and three daughters, divinely given to him "through the promises of God to exalt him" (25:4–6). The names of several of his sons are unexampled elsewhere, and some scholars have attempted to interpret the last nine as a liturgical prayer (see J. M. Myers, *1 Chronicles*, AB 12 [1965], 172–73); it may be that the names were derived from the openings (or other significant phrases) in individual psalms. Heman's descendants served during the reign of Hezekiah and Josiah (2 Chr. 29:14; 35:15).

Hemath hee′math. KJV alternate form of Hamath (1 Chr. 13:5; Amos 6:14) and Hammath (1 Chr. 2:55).

Hemdan hem′dan (חֶמְדָּן *H2777*, possibly "desirable"). Son of the clan chief Dishon and grandson of Seir the Horite (Gen. 36:26; also 1 Chr. 1:41 NIV [following a significant number of Heb. and Gk. mss], where KJV has "Amram" and NRSV "Hamran" [MT, *ḥamran*]).

hemlock. This English term can refer to any of various coniferous evergreens as well as to certain poisonous plants (genera *Conium* and *Cicuta*). It is used by the KJV in two figurative passages to render Hebrew *rō’š H8032* (Hos. 10:4; NIV and NRSV, "poisonous weeds") and *la‘ănâ H4360* (Amos 6:12; NIV, "bitterness"; NRSV, "wormwood"). According to some scholars, the first term does refer to the poison hemlock (*Conium maculatum*), which grows throughout Palestine (see FFB, 167–68). See also Gall; Poison; Wormwood.

hemorrhage. Bleeding or the flow of blood from a break in continuity of a blood vessel whether from injury or frailty of the blood vessel walls. The woman having an issue of blood twelve years (Lk. 8:43–44) probably had recurrent severe hemorrhage in connection with her menstrual flow because of a fibroid tumor in the womb, a condition readily treated today by surgery (cf. A. R. Short, *The Bible and Modern Medicine* [1953], 30–31). For further discussion, see Disease.   P. E. Adolph

hemorrhoids. See Tumor.

hen. The female of the domestic fowl (Matt. 23:27; Lk. 13:34; see Chicken; Rooster) or of various other birds. The NRSV uses water hen as the rendering of *tinšemet H9492* (Lev. 11:18; Deut. 14:16 [NIV, "white owl"]; see Owl).

Hen (person) hen (חֵן *H2835*, "gracious"). Son of a certain Zephaniah; he was one of several men to whom was given the crown that was made for Joshua (Jeshua) the high priest (Zech. 6:14; NRSV, "Josiah"). Hen was apparently another name, or perhaps a descriptive title (cf. NIV mg.) for Josiah son of Zephaniah; if so, it was in his house that the crown was made (v. 10).

Hena hen′uh (הֵנַע *H2184*, meaning uncertain). One of several Syrian city-states vanquished by Sennacherib (2 Ki. 18:34; 19:13; Isa. 37:13). The commander of the Assyrian forces, seeking to shake Hezekiah's confidence in the Lord, claimed that the gods and kings of those cities were powerless before Sennacherib. Because Hena is listed along with Hamath and Arpad (also Sepharvaim and Ivvah), it is thought to have been located in N Syria; one possible identification is modern ‘Anah (‘Ānat) on the Euphrates in Iraq, but that location may be too far E (41.5° E longitude). Some scholars, noticing that Hena and Ivvah are not mentioned in similar lists (2 Ki. 17:24; Isa. 36:19), and suspecting that they are not true geographical names, have suggested that they are pagan deities, or that the text is corrupt, or that the words should be rendered, "he has taken away and overthrown" (see *ABD*, 3:137–38).

Henadad hen′uh-dad (חֵנָדָד *H2836*, "favor of [the god] Hadad"). Father or ancestor of a family of priests who helped rebuild the temple under Zerubbabel (Ezra 3:9), assisted in repairing the wall of Jerusalem in the time of Nehemiah (Neh. 3:18, 24), and signed the covenant (10:9).

henna. A small tree (*Lawsonia inermis*, called the Egyptian privet in some quarters), common in Palestine, having privet-like leaves and masses of white or pink scented flowers that grow in clusters. The term is used twice figuratively in Song of Solomon to describe the bride (Heb. *kōper* H4110, Cant. 1:14; 4:13 [KJV, "camphire"]; cf. also 7:12 NIV mg.). The leaves of the henna, when dried and powdered, can be made into a paste that was used in the E for dyeing the toenails, fingernails, and even the soles of the feet and palms of the hands. Men colored their beards with henna and used it also to groom their horses' tails. It was a cosmetic dye much used in Egypt at the time of Moses. (Cf. *FFB*, 127–28.) See flora (under *Lithraceae*). W. E. Shewell-Cooper

Henoch hee'nuhk. KJV alternate form of Enoch (1 Chr. 1:3) and Hanoch (1:33).

Hepher (person) hee'fuhr (חֵפֶר H2918, possibly "protector"; gentilic חֶפְרִי H2920, "Hepherite"). **(1)** Son of Gilead, descendant of Manasseh, father of Zelophehad, and ancestor of the Hepherite clan (Num. 26:32; 27:1; Josh. 17:2–3). His clan may be associated with Hepher (place).

(2) Son of Ashhur (apparently founder of the town of Tekoa) by his wife Naarah; included in the genealogy of Judah (1 Chr. 4:6).

(3) A Mekerathite, included among David's mighty warriors (1 Chr. 11:36; his name is missing in the parallel list in 2 Sam. 23).

Hepher (place) hee'fuhr (חֵפֶר H2919, possibly "protector" or "[water] hole"). A Canaanite royal city whose king was defeated by Joshua (Josh. 12:17). Presumably, it was part of the "land of Hepher," which became the third administrative district under Ben-Hesed in the time of Solomon (1 Ki. 4:10). Possible identifications are el-Ifshar (c. 25 mi. NNE of Joppa and only 3 mi. from the coast) and Tell el-Muhaffar in the hill country of Manasseh (c. 2 mi. NW of Dothan and 11 mi. SSE of Megiddo). The latter view has been proposed by A. Zertal (see *ABD*, 3:138–39), who suggests that "the land of Hepher" was approximately defined by the territory belonging to the daughters of Zelophehad (Num. 27:1–11).

Hephzibah hef'zi-buh (חֶפְצִי־בָהּ H2915, "my delight is in her"). **(1)** Wife of King Hezekiah and mother of King Manasseh (2 Ki. 21:1).

(2) Symbolic name of Zion (Isa. 62:4; the NRSV translates the name, "My Delight Is in Her"). See Beulah for a brief discussion of the passage.

Heptapegon (Ἑπταπηγῶν, "Seven Fountains"). This name, first attested in the Middle Ages, is applied to an area with several springs about 2 mi. SW of Capernaum. Known today as ʿAin eṭ-Ṭabgha (in Heb., ʿEn Shebaʿ), the place was apparently referred to as Capernaum in the time of Josephus (*War* 3.10.8), no doubt because of its close connection with the town. (See *ABD*, 3:139–41; *NEAEHL*, 2:614–16.)

Herakles her'uh-kleez. Greek name of Hercules.

herald. A messenger who proclaims important news. The term is used occasionally in Bible versions to render such words as Aramaic *kārôz* H10370 (Dan. 3:4) and Greek *kēryx* G3061 (1 Tim. 2:7; 2 Tim. 1:11; this term is often translated "preacher" in 2 Pet. 2:5). In two passages (Isa. 40:9; 41:27), the NRSV uses "herald of good tidings" to render the piel participle of Hebrew *bāśar* H1413 (see gospel). A herald was usually a representative of a royal or government official having as his specific responsibility the bearing of a message. The message and whom he represented was his primary concern, and he was to remain secondary. See also preaching.

herb. This term in English refers to plants that have fragile stems (and thus usually die at the end of the growing season) or to aromatic plants used for seasoning and medicinal purposes. The word occurs frequently in the KJV with reference to vegetation generally (e.g., to render Heb. *ʿēśeb* H6912, Gen. 1:11–12 et al.), but modern versions use it sparingly, for example, with reference to the light plants gathered by a member of the company of the prophets to add flavor to the stew (Heb. *ʾōrâ*

H246, 2 Ki. 4:39), and to the garden plants that the PHARISEES tithed (*lachanon G3303*, Lk. 11:42; this Gk. term occurs also in Matt. 13:32; Mk. 4:32; Rom. 14:2). See FLORA.

Hercules huhr´kyuh-leez´. Roman name for Herakles (*Hēraklēs*), son of ZEUS by a mortal woman and the most popular of mythological Greek heroes. The name occurs in one passage in the APOCRYPHA (2 Macc. 4:18–20) in connection with the attempts of ANTIOCHUS IV Epiphanes (176–164 B.C.) to impose Hellenistic culture in Judea. See MACCABEE. JASON, who had changed his Hebrew name Joshua to this Greek form, was able to seize the high priesthood in JERUSALEM from his brother ONIAS III in 175 by allying himself to Antiochus. To further the hellenization of the city, Jason obtained the authority to form a Greek city-state within Jerusalem; here he also established a GYMNASIUM, which led to the weakening of Jewish life. See HELLENISM.

Once every four years games were held in TYRE in honor of Hercules, who was linked with the Phoenician god Melqart (Gk. *pentaetērikos* in this passage literally means "quinquennial, every five years," which reflects an inclusive method of reckoning time). Jason sent "envoys, chosen as being Antiochian citizens from Jerusalem," to represent the city and to bear silver for the sacrifice of Hercules. However, those who were bearing the tribute felt that this was an evil use of the money, so they spent it instead on shipbuilding. The story highlights Jewish resistant to Jason's Hellenistic reforms.

Some scholars, pointing out similarities between the legends regarding Herakles/Hercules and events in the life of Jesus, have argued that the Gospels may have derived from a document influenced by a Hellenistic life of the Greek hero. Others have suggested a less direct influence of "Herakles imagery" on the NT, especially the letter to the Hebrews (see D. E. Aune in *Greeks, Romans, and Christians: Essays in Honor of Abraham J. Malherbe*, ed. D. L. Balch et al. [1990], 3–19; note also his article in *DDD*, 765–71). G. GIACUMAKIS, JR.

Hercules fights the Nemean Lion (amphora from Athens, c. 520–500 B.C.).

herd. See CATTLE; SHEEP.

herdsman. KJV, "herdman." This English term is used a few times in Bible versions as the rendering of Hebrew *rōʿeh* (ptc. of *rāʿâ H8286*, Gen. 26:20 et al.), a term usually translated "shepherd" (the KJV uses "herdman" also to render other Heb. terms in Amos 1:1; 7:14). The frequent biblical references to keepers of livestock emphasize the important agricultural basis of the Palestinian economy. The herdsman's responsibility in tending his flocks was (1) to guide them to fertile areas, (2) to make sure the flocks could get to water, and (3) to protect them from wild beasts and robbers. See SHEPHERD. G. GIACUMAKIS, JR.

Heres hihr´iz (חֶרֶס *H3065*, possibly "sunny"). (1) "Mount Heres" (NRSV, "Har-heres") is mentioned, along with AIJALON and SHAALBIM, as one of the places from which the tribe of DAN could not drive out the AMORITES (Jdg. 1:34–35). It is usually identified with the town of IR SHEMESH ("city of the sun," Josh. 19:41; cf. Shaalabbin and Aijalon in v. 42), which in turn is probably the same as BETH SHEMESH ("house of the sun," Josh. 15:10 et al.), on the boundary between Judah and Dan. However, it would be unusual to call a village a *har*

H2215 ("mountain"), and some scholars prefer to identify it with a mountain range on the eastern side of the valley of Aijalon, 2 or 3 mi. SE of modern Yalo (see *ABD*, s.v. Har-heres, 3:56–57).

(2) The "Pass [*or* Ascent] of Heres" was apparently a place E of the Jordan from which GIDEON returned after defeating two kings of MIDIAN (Jdg. 8:13). The text can be interpreted differently, however (KJV translates, "before the sun was up"). If it is indeed a geographical reference, the site is unknown.

See also DESTRUCTION, CITY OF; SUN, CITY OF THE; TIMNATH HERES.

Heresh hihr′ish (חֶ֫רֶשׁ H3090, "silent, mute"). A Levite, listed among those who returned from the EXILE (1 Chr. 9:15; his name is omitted in the parallel, Neh. 11:15).

heresy. This English term is derived (through French and Latin) from Greek *hairesis* G146, which meant "a taking" or "choice," hence "opinion, way of thinking." In the Hellenistic period it came to mean "[political] preference," then "system, sect, faction." Not till the 2nd cent. A.D. did the word come to mean specifically a position or doctrine at variance with established, orthodox church doctrine (though this was a natural development from negative uses in the NT).

In the book of Acts, the word is applied to the religious "parties" of the SADDUCEES and PHARISEES (Acts 5:17; 15:5). PAUL was accused of being "a ringleader of the Nazarene sect" (Acts 24:5; cf. 24:14; 28:22). A negative element is more apparent when the apostle speaks about the "factions" present in the Corinthian church (1 Cor. 11:19 NRSV; NIV, "differences"), for in the same context he uses the stronger term *schisma* G5388, "division, split" (vv. 10, 18). Elsewhere he includes the word *hairesis* in his list of the works of the flesh (Gal. 5:20, mentioned between "dissensions" and "envy"). The NT use closest to the later technical, theological meaning is found in 2 Pet. 2:1, which states that false teachers "will secretly introduce destructive heresies, even denying the sovereign Lord who bought them—bringing swift destruction on themselves." This language implies willful departure from accepted teaching.

Even in this last reference, the negative element is borne primarily by the adjective "destructive" as well as the broader context, so the noun could be rendered simply "opinions" (so NRSV). Nevertheless, such a use leads to a semantic change whereby the term by itself indicates "wrong opinion, false teaching," as in the letters of IGNATIUS (e.g., "you all live according to truth, and no heresy dwells in you," *Eph.* 6.2; cf. *Thral.* 6.1). The term is used with this technical sense by other 2nd-cent. writers (Herm. *Sim.* 9.22.4; Justin, *1 Apol.* 26.8 et al.). Indeed, "within Christianity *hairesis* always denotes hostile societies" (*TDNT*, 1:183). (Cf. M. Simon, "From Greek *Hairesis* to Christian Heresy," in *Early Christian Literature and the Classical Greek Intellectual Tradition: In Honorem Robert M. Grant*, ed. W. R. Schoedel and R. L. Wilken [1979], 101–16; on the relationship between Judaism and early Christianity regarding the notion of heresy, see D. Boyarin, *Border Lines: The Partition of Judaeo-Christianity Divinations: Rereading Late Antique Religion* [2004].)

The church had to deal with heresy from the earliest times. Error crept into the church as it grew and larger numbers of believers attempted to understand and express their faith. Error which developed into a conscious resolute position necessitated that the church address it. Heresy thus contributed to the formation of orthodox doctrine as the defenders of the faith denounced the error and attempted to define TRUTH, or at least the limits of doctrinal truth if not the precise meaning of the truth. As the church addressed heresies like GNOSTICISM, Montanism, Monarchianism, Arianism, and others, it was forced to define the doctrine of the TRINITY. Thus doctrinal formulation came as a corrective to error.

According to some scholars, it is misleading to speak of "orthodoxy" and "heresy" in the early stages of Christianity. In an influential work published first in 1934, Walter Bauer argued that the church was at that time characterized by great diversity and that there was no unified and established norm that could help define particular movements as heretical (the 2nd ed. of his work was translated as *Orthodoxy and Heresy in Earliest Christianity*, ed. R. A. Kraft and G. Krodel [1971]). It is certainly true that we should not transfer back to the 1st and 2nd centuries the notion of an explicitly institutionalized church with well-defined theological norms; any assessment of Christianity during that period must take fully into account its variegated character and fuzzy boundaries. It would be an even greater mistake, however, to infer that the Christian communities were unconcerned about the distinction between truth and error or that no central theological commitments united the church against unacceptable teachings.

H. A. WHALEY

Hereth hihr′ith (חֲרֶת *H3101*). KJV Hareth. The name of a forest in the tribal territory of JUDAH where DAVID hid after he left his parents in MOAB for their safety (1 Sam. 22:5). Its location is unknown, though some scholars have suggested the site of Kharas because it is near KEILAH (some 18 mi. SW of Jerusalem), which was the scene of a confrontation between David and the PHILISTINES a short time later (23:1–5).

heritage. See INHERITANCE.

Hermas huhr′muhs (Ἑρμᾶς *G2254*). One of several Christians in Rome that PAUL greets by name in his letter to the church there (Rom. 16:14b; note that the KJV, following the TR, reverses the names "Hermas" and "Hermes"). It was thought by some in the ancient church that he was the author of *Shepherd of Hermas*; this work, however, was probably composed over a period of time in the 2nd cent. (see next entry). The name is possibly a short form of *Hermodōros* (cf. BDF §125.1), but see also HERMES (PERSON).

Hermas, Shepherd of huhr′muhs (Ἑρμᾶς *G2254*). A noncanonical APOCALYPTIC writing of the early church; it is the longest of all the books included among the APOSTOLIC FATHERS, and considerably longer than any book of the NT. It was apparently considered an inspired book by many early Christians, including IRENAEUS, ORIGEN, and also TERTULLIAN in his earlier years.

I. Author. The author called himself Hermas. His style indicates either Jewish origin or acquaintance with Jewish literature. He was, or had been, a slave, and was not brought up by his parents. He was married. A revelation indicated that his wife was too careless in her speech (*Vis.* 2.2.3). His children were apparently, at best, undisciplined. He had a country farm that he worked, but he was obviously not a man of great ability or talent.

II. Date and place of origin. Hermas placed at least part of his life at Rome, and some of his early visions occurred on the road to Cumae, an ancient Greek town about 12 mi. NW of Naples. The work has, then, a central Italian background.

Hermas was instructed to write some of the words revealed to him in two little books and to give one to Clement and one to Grapte (*Vis.* 2.4.3). Clement was to send his book to the foreign cities, since that was his function. Presumably the reference is to the author of the first epistle of Clement, an officer of the church at Rome, considered by later writers from Irenaeus on to have been in the succession of Roman bishops, though not in a modern sense of the term. See CLEMENTS, EPISTLES OF. Since Clement lived in Rome c. 88–97, it is probable that the early part of the *Shepherd* was written at some time during that period. On the other hand, the MURATORIAN CANON (c. A.D. 200) reads: "very recently, in our own times, in the city of Rome, Hermas wrote the Shepherd, when his brother Pius, the bishop, sat upon the chair of the city of Rome." This gives an impression of being trustworthy. Pius was a bishop in the decade beginning with the year 140. These indications are not necessarily contradictory. The *Shepherd* may well have been written in parts over a considerable period of time, which seems more likely because of its content, style, and organization.

III. Content. The *Shepherd* is almost exclusively concerned with Christian living. Its purpose was to set forth in detail the Christian virtues, that is, to indicate how the Christian should live and what he should avoid. A particular issue, referred to more than once, is the problem of sins committed after baptism. Can they be forgiven? The generally held view of sin in the 2nd cent. was so far removed from that presented in Scripture that it was commonly believed that Christians did not, ideally, sin at all after baptism. However, it was obvious that some did. Could they be granted forgiveness if they repented? Hermas reverted to this theme again and again. In general, his answer was that God was graciously granting an opportunity for repentance and forgiveness at the time at which Hermas was writing. But there would be no such opportunities in the future. This would be the last occasion that the grace of God might be expected in such an instance.

The book is divided into three sections: five *Visions*, twelve *Mandates* (commands), and ten *Similitudes* (parables). The first two are approximately of equal length, the third is much longer.

The *Visions* concerned the church. The basic form in which the church appeared is that of a tower in process of construction. Explanations were given by an old lady who also personified the church. The first woman to appear in the visions was Rhoda, who was Hermas's owner when he was a slave. Then came the old woman who personified the church. The tower, which is the church, was being built of stones, representing people. The officers—apostles, bishops, deacons, teachers—fitted easily. So did martyrs and the upright. Unbelievers and apostates were the stones that were cast away. There were seven women around the tower. They were daughters who represented the virtues of faith, continence, simplicity, knowledge, innocence, reverence, and love. The old woman, the church, appeared first as old, then as middle aged, and finally, as young and beautiful as the faith of Hermas became stronger. The fourth vision is devoted to the great beast of persecution. The world was to be destroyed by blood and fire. The fifth, which is called a revelation rather than a vision in the oldest MS, introduced the shepherd who was to give Hermas the commandments and parables. At the end of the vision he was called the angel of repentance.

The *Mandates* were not organized according to any discernible plan or developing sequence. The unity of God was stressed in the first, the seventh exhorted concerning the fear of God, and warnings against grieving the Holy Spirit were mentioned in the tenth. The ethical principles of simplicity, reverence, and innocence were commended in the second, patience in the fifth, joy in the tenth. Christian conduct was discussed by the command in the third mandate to tell the truth; in the fourth, to reject adultery and fornication; and in the eighth, to be temperate in all living. Faith, an undivided heart, and the rejection of evil desire were commended in the sixth, ninth, and twelfth commandments. The section came toward its close with the warning that if the commandments were not kept, salvation would be lost. On the other hand, resolution will make it easy to keep them.

The *Similitudes* are not a brilliant collection. They consist of exhortations containing similes and metaphors and an occasional full-story parable. The city in heaven and the city on earth were compared. The rich man is like a prolific vine that needs the support of the poor man, the elm tree, to be most useful. Budding trees are the righteous, dry trees the wicked. There is an elaborate parable of the willow tree as the law of God, with the distribution of branches from it to Christians and their varied development. There is a shepherd of luxury, clothed in yellow, and a shepherd of punishment, clothed in a white goatskin. The most extensive parable is the ninth, concerning the twelve mountains in Arcadia. They differed in color, formation, and vegetation, and represented different types of persons from good bishops and hospitable men on the one hand to apostates and blasphemers on the other. The figure of the tower, as the church, appeared again, being constructed in stages.

IV. Theology. Hermas was not a theologian. His theological statements are confused. In the parable of the field, the master, the son, and the servant (*Sim.* 5), the field is the world and the servant is said to be the Son of God (5.5.2), leaving the Son unexplained. The Holy Spirit is said to dwell in flesh and the flesh is made the Spirit's companion (5.6.6). Later, we are told that the Holy Spirit is the Son of God (9.1.1). Baptism is presented as necessary for salvation; the apostles baptized those who had died before them that they might be saved (9.16.5).

V. Ethics. The tone of the *Shepherd* is that of ASCETICISM in general, though not to the strictest degree. The twelve maidens in Arcadia were faith, temperance, power, longsuffering, simplicity, guilelessness, holiness, joy, truth, understanding, concord, and love (*Sim.* 9.15.2). A second marriage after the death of a partner was permissible but is not as virtuous as remaining unmarried (*Mand.* 4.4). Works beyond the commandments of God were possible and made one "more honorable with God" than one was "destined to be" (*Sim.* 5.3.3).

VI. Text. The *Shepherd* was written in Greek, but there is no complete Greek text available. CODEX SINAITICUS contains the text as far as *Mand.* 4.3.6. A 15th-cent. MS from Mount Athos contains most of the rest, and other incomplete texts on papyrus or parchment exist. There are two Latin and one Ethiopic versions, as well as fragments in Coptic and Persian.

(See further J. A. Robinson, *Barnabas, Hermas and the Didache* [1920]; M. Dibelius, *Der Hirt des Hermas* [1923]; W. J. Wilson in *HTR* 20 [1927]: 21–62; J. Reiling, *Hermas and Christian Prophecy: A Study of the Eleventh Mandate* [1973]; C. Osiek, *Rich and Poor in the Shepherd of Hermas: An Exegetical-Social Investigation* [1983]; J. C. Wilson, *Toward a Reassessment of the Shepherd of Hermas: Its Date and Its Pneumatology* [1993]; id., *Five Problems in the Interpretation of the Shepherd of Hermas* [1995]; E. M. Humphrey, *The Ladies and the Cities: Transformation and Apocalyptic Identity in Joseph and Aseneth, 4 Ezra, the Apocalypse and the Shepherd of Hermas* [1995]; C. Osiek, *The Shepherd of Hermas: A Commentary*, Hermeneia [1999].)   P. WOOLLEY

hermeneutics. See INTERPRETATION.

Hermes (deity) huhr′meez (Ἑρμῆς *G2258*). In Greek mythology, the son of ZEUS and Maia (a Titan nymph), known among the Romans as Mercury. He was thought of as the spirit of the *herma* ("support, cairn, stone heap"), set up as a guidepost or boundary, though it is now questioned whether the connection between the god and the cairn was original. The herm (or herma) developed into a four-cornered pillar, with a bust of the god on top and a phallus on the front. Diverse ideas were associated with him: he was ingenious, having invented the lyre the day he was born; he guided souls from earth to HADES; he became the patron of merchants, travelers, and even robbers; he was the giver of good luck, fertility, and cunning.

Hermes was best known, however, as the messenger of the gods; he was often represented with traveler's cap, winged sandals, and herald's staff. Preferring persuasion to violence, he could be viewed as the god of oratory (the term *hermeneutics* is derived from his name; see INTERPRETATION). It is this role that prompted the people of LYSTRA to iden-

This marble statue of Hermes, the protector of travelers, was used as a sacred mile stone on the roads. Roman copy of a work by the famous Greek sculptor Alkamenes (5th cent. B.C.).

tify PAUL, being "the chief speaker," with Hermes (Acts 14:12; KJV, "Mercurius"), while BARNABAS was identified with Zeus. Such a response may have as its background the story of an aged couple who lived in that general region and who entertained Jupiter and Mercury without realizing who they were (Ovid, *Metamorphoses* 8.620–724; cf. further F. F. Bruce, *The Acts of the Apostles: The Greek Text with Introduction and Commentary*, 3rd ed. [1990], 321–22; for a broader discussion, see *DDD*, 771–83). See also GREEK RELIGION; on Hermes Trismegistus, see HERMETIC WRITINGS.

Hermes (person) huhr′meez (Ἑρμῆς *G2258*). One of several Christians in Rome that PAUL greets by name in his letter to the church there (Rom. 16:14a; note that the KJV, following the TR, reverses the names "Hermas" and "Hermes"). This was a common name, especially among slaves, probably because Hermes was the god of good fortune (but see BDF §125.1). It has been suggested that possibly all five men mentioned in this verse were, or had been, slaves. One of them was named HERMAS, which may be a variant of Hermes (see C.

K. Barrett, *A Critical and Exegetical Commentary on the Epistle to the Romans*, ICC, 2 vols. [1975–79], 2:795.

Hermetic writings. A collection of religious and philosophical tractates, the main body of which is known as the *Corpus Hermeticum* (or simply *Hermetica*), probably dating around the 2nd or 3rd cent. A.D. The title of the literature is derived from the name Hermes Trismegistus (Gk. *trismegistos*, "thrice greatest"). See HERMES (DEITY). The Greek messenger of the gods had much earlier been identified with the Egyptian god Thoth, whom the Egyptians sometimes referred to as "very great-great" (see W. Scott, *Hermetica: The Ancient Greek and Latin Writings which Contain Religious or Philosophic Teachings Ascribed to Hermes Trismegistos*, 4 vols. [1924–1936], 1:4–5). The literature, which probably originated in Egypt though written in Greek, was a typical product of Hellenistic syncretism. "Hermes" thus became a suitable appellation for the figure who revealed the secrets pertaining to man's divine origin and salvation. Affinities are evident with Platonic thought, the STOICS, PHILO JUDAEUS, GNOSTICISM, the Gospel of John (with notable contrasts; see JOHN, GOSPEL OF IV.C) and the OT, on which it is, in part, dependent.

The extant material is in various forms, ranging from the discourses and dialogues of the main corpus of eighteen works to a number of fragments, some of which are in the Gnostic library of Chenoboskion (the so-called NAG HAMMADI texts; see ASCLEPIUS #2). The best-known treatise is the *Poimandres*, the first in the corpus; another significant text is entitled *Peri palingenesias* ("Concerning Regeneration").

The meaning of the name Poimandres may be "Shepherd of Man" (cf. H. Jonas, *The Gnostic Religion*, 2nd ed. [1963], 147–73) or "the knowledge of the Sun-God" (cf. Scott, *Hermetica*, 2:15–16). The latter suits the dominant theme, held in common with Gnosticism, of religion as true KNOWLEDGE. Poimandres is the spirit being who provides the information, recorded in the first tractate, on the origin of the world, the fall of man, and his restoration through knowledge. The SEPTUAGINT of Genesis is reproduced in several details, but in a totally different COSMOGONY. This cosmogony involves the successive generation of intermediary beings, which include Light (identified with Nous/Mind), the Word or Son of God, and the Demiurge, who created the world. Through desire, man, the child of God, became mortal, but through *gnosis* (knowledge) his soul may pass through the spheres to the godhead. This restoration is described in *Peri palingenesias* as a rebirth, during which the soul is cleansed from the things, characteristic of life in the material world, which were punishing him: lust, ignorance, wrath, etc. Each of these is countered by an appropriate "power" from God, who is Light and Life.

Following the conclusions of C. H. Dodd (*The Interpretation of the Fourth Gospel* [1955], 10–55 et passim) and others, it may be affirmed that the affinities with Christian thought forms, particularly those of John, need not imply dependence in either direction. The basic data of the Christian gospel concerning the atoning work of Christ are conspicuously lacking.

(See also C. H. Dodd, *The Bible and the Greeks* [1935]; A. J. Festugière, *La révélation d' Hermès Trismégiste*, 4 vols. [1944–54]; A. D. Nock and A. J. Festugière, ed./trans., *Hermès Trismégiste: Corpus Hermeticum*, 4 vols., 2nd ed. [1945–60]; G. Van Moorsel, *The Mysteries of Hermes Trismegistus* [1955]; W. C. Grese, *Corpus Hermeticum XIII and Early Christian Literature* [1979]; B. P. Copenhaver, *Hermetica: The Greek Corpus Hermeticum and the Latin Asclepius in a New English Translation, with Notes and Introduction* [1992]; T. Freke and P. Gandy, *The Hermetica: The Lost Wisdom of the Pharaohs* [1999]; *DNTB*, 482–85.)

W. L. LIEFELD

Hermogenes huhr-moj´uh-neez (Ἑρμογένης G2259, "born of HERMES"). Named with Phygelus as among the disciples in proconsular ASIA who abandoned PAUL when he rightly expected their support (2 Tim. 1:15). Some view it as a doctrinal defection; others as a refusal to testify in Paul's behalf during the second imprisonment at Rome for fear of sharing Paul's fate. The language used ("deserted me") suggests that "the defection was from Paul personally, not necessarily from the faith … but in the light of the preceding verses it may well have included a rejection of Paul's version of Christian teaching" (I. H. Marshall and P. H. Towner, *A Critical and Exegetical Commentary on the Pastoral Epistles*, ICC [1999], 717; see also W. Hendriksen, *New Testament Commentary: The Pastoral Epistles* [1957], 238–40). Hermogenes and the others stand in sharp contrast to ONESIPHORUS (v. 16). In the *Acts of Paul and Thecla*, Demas and Hermogenes are named as Paul's companions, "full of hypocrisy," when he fled to Iconium (see *NTAp*, 2:239). D. E. HIEBERT

Hermon huhr'muhn (חֶרְמוֹן H3056, possibly "place of consecration [*or* of the BAN]"). The S spur of the ANTILEBANON chain of mountains, which runs parallel to the Lebanon range and is separated from it by the valley of BEQAʿ. It is c. 9,200 ft. above sea level, the highest mountain in Syria. It can be seen from many places in PALESTINE, even from as far away as the DEAD SEA. Because snow covers it for much of the year, the Arabs call it the "gray-haired mountain" or the "mountain of the snow." The water from its melting snows flow into the rivers of N HAURAN and provide the principal source for the JORDAN River. Below the snow, the sides are covered with trees (pine, oak, and poplar) and with vineyards. Its forests contain wolves and leopards, and sometimes Syrian bears. It is not a high summit with a distinctly marked base, but a whole cluster of mountains. Its three summits are nearly equal in height and are the same distance from each other. It extends 16–20 mi. from N to S.

According to Deut. 4:9, the people of Sidon referred to Hermon as SIRION (a name that occurs elsewhere only in Ps. 29:6, but see Deut. 4:48 NRSV), whereas the AMORITES called it SENIR (1 Chr. 5:23 [which perhaps differentiates Senir, Hermon, and BAAL HERMON as three distinct peaks]; Cant. 4:8 [differentiating Senir and Hermon]; Ezek. 27:5 [the builders of TYRE made use of the pine trees from Senir]). In a textually uncertain passage, Hermon is called Mount SIYON (Deut. 4:48; KJV, "Sion"; NRSV [following the Syriac version], "Sirion").

Mount Hermon was the N boundary of the Amorite kingdom (Deut. 3:8; 4:48), and thus is said to lie in the territory of OG (Josh. 12:5; 13:11). It was the N limit of the conquests of JOSHUA (Josh. 11:17; 12:1; 13:5), and the N limit of the half-tribe of MANASSEH. The HITTITES dwelt at the foot of Hermon in the land of MIZPEH (Josh. 11:3). It is mentioned in the Bible as the N boundary of the Promised Land (Deut. 3:8). In ancient times it was

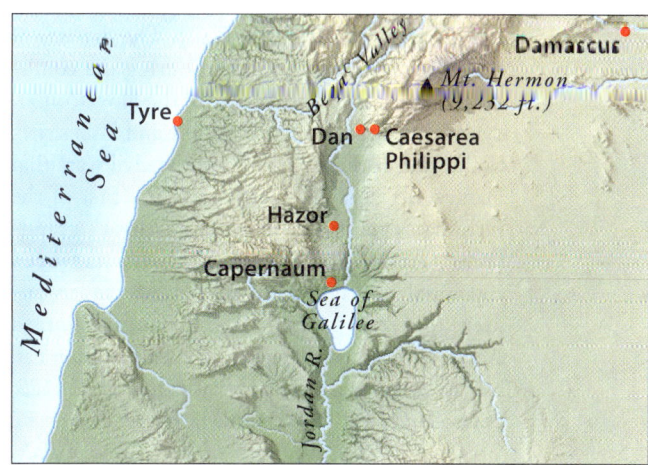

Mount Hermon, northern boundary of the Promised Land.

regarded as a sacred mountain, as its Hebrew name suggests; the alternate (or at least associated) name Baal Hermon (Jdg. 3:3) suggests that BAAL was worshiped there. Remains of shrines are found on the highest summit. It is thought by some scholars that the TRANSFIGURATION took place on Hermon. Its modern name is Jebel esh-Sheikh, "the mountain of the chief," or Jebel eth-Thalj, "mount of snow." (See further *ABD*, 3:158–60; *NEAEHL*, 2:616–18.) S. BARABAS

Hermonites huhr'muh-nīts. KJV rendering of *ḥermônîm*, plural form of *ḥermôn* H3056 (Ps. 42:7; NIV, "heights of Hermon"). See HERMON.

Herod her'uhd (Ἡρῴδης G2476; the original spelling Ἡρωίδης is found in inscriptions and papyri). The ruling dynasty in Jewish Palestine during the period of Roman domination.

    I. Background (67–47 B.C.)
   II. Herod the Great (47–4 B.C.)
       A. As governor of Galilee (47–37 B.C.)
       B. As king (37–4 B.C.)
  III. Herod's will disputed
  IV. Archelaus (4 B.C. to A.D. 6)

V. Antipas (4 B.C. to A.D. 39)
   A. His realm
   B. His rule
VI. Philip the Tetrarch (4 B.C. to A.D. 34)
VII. Agrippa I (A.D. 37–44)
VIII. Agrippa II (A.D. 50–100)

I. Background (67–47 B.C.). The dynasty of the Herods became prominent during the confusion resulting from the decline of the HASMONEAN dynasty, the transference of SYRIA and PALESTINE to the rule of the Romans, and the civil wars that marked the decay of the nation. The first of the Herodian dynasty was Herod the Great's grandfather, Antipater (or Antipas), who had been appointed governor of IDUMEA by Alexander Jannaeus (Jos. *Ant.* 14.1.3 §10). His son, also named Antipater, was considered by JOSEPHUS an Idumean by race and a man of great wealth (*War* 1.6.2 §123; cf. also *Ant.* 14.1.3 §9; Justin Martyr, *Dialogue with Trypho* 52.3; Euseb. *Hist.* 1.6.2; 1.7.11; *b. Baba Bathra* 3b–4a; *Kiddushin* 70b). The latter came into prominence after the death of ALEXANDRA, the Maccabean queen.

Alexandra's eldest son, Hyrcanus II, assumed the royal power in 67 B.C. Being a quiet and peaceful man, he was set aside by his younger brother Aristobulus after only three months' reign (Jos. *Ant.* 14.1.2 §4–7; 14.6.4 §180; *War* 1. 5.4 §§117–19). Hyrcanus, declaring that he never really had desired the throne, surrendered all his honors to Aristobulus, who became king and high priest. Although Hyrcanus and Aristobulus publicly made peace with each other, it was short lived. Antipater saw in the position of Hyrcanus an opportunity to fulfill his own dream of being a political power in Judea. It was not difficult for Antipater to persuade Hyrcanus that he had been unjustly deprived of his hereditary rights by his younger brother, and suggested he should flee to ARETAS, king of ARABIA, with a view to recovering his rightful kingdom. Thus he fled to PETRA (Jos. *Ant.* 14.1.3–4 §§8–18).

It was at this point that Rome intervened. POMPEY, the general who had been so successful in bringing the Roman power to the E, determined to act. Scaurus, one of his subordinates, felt that Pompey should support Aristobulus, who would probably be better able to pay the bribe offered by each contestant. Pompey, however, decided to side with Hyrcanus because there was evidence that Aristobulus might revolt against Rome (Jos. *Ant.* 14.3.3 §§46–47). Pompey made war against Aristobulus, besieging the Jerusalem temple for three months. When Pompey won the war, he went into the holy of holies but did not plunder it of its valuables (Jos. *Ant.* 14.4.4 §§69–72; *War* 1.6.5—1.7.6 §§133–53; Tac. *Hist.* 5.9; Livy, *Epit.* 102; Appian, *Mithridatic Wars* 106, 114; Florus, *Epit.* 1.40.30; Plutarch, *Pompey* 39; cf. Dio Cassius, *Rom. Hist.* 37.15–17). Because of Hyrcanus's loyalty, Pompey reinstated him as high priest (Jos. *Ant.* 14.4.4 §73; *War* 1.7.6 §153). Jerusalem was made a tributary of Rome and placed under Scaurus, whom Pompey made legate of the province of Syria.

Antipater proved himself useful to the Romans both in government and in their operations against the Hasmoneans. He married a woman named Cypros, daughter of an illustrious Arabian, by whom he had four sons: Phasael, Herod, Joseph, Pheroras, and a daughter, Salome (Jos. *Ant.* 14.7.3 §121; *War* 1.8.9 §181).

After Pompey was defeated by Julius CAESAR in 48 B.C. in Egypt (at Pharsalus), Hyrcanus and Antipater attached themselves to Caesar's party. Antipater had risked his life for Caesar in the fighting in Egypt the previous year. Because of this Caesar made Antipater a Roman citizen with exemption of taxes and appointed him procurator of JUDEA. Also he confirmed the appointment of Hyrcanus to the office of high priest and gave him the title of ETHNARCH of the Jews (Jos. *Ant.* 14.8.1–5 §§127–55; 14.10.2 §191; *War* 1.9.3—1.10.4 §§187–203). Immediately after, Antipater went about the country to suppress the disorders and appealed to the restless Judean population to be loyal to Hyrcanus. Although appealing to the people in this fashion, he felt that Hyrcanus was an unsuitable leader of Judea, so he took the country in his own hands and appointed his son Phasael as governor of Jerusalem and his second son Herod as governor of GALILEE (Jos. *Ant.* 14.9.1–2 §§156–58; *War* 1.10.4 §§201–3). Antipater continued his loyalty to Hyrcanus, yet it can be seen that Antipater was the power behind the throne.

II. Herod the Great (47–4 B.C.)

A. As governor of Galilee (47–37 B.C.)

1. His rule. Herod became governor of Galilee at the young age of twenty-five years. Immediately he was admired by the Galilean Jews and Roman officials in Syria because of his promptness in capturing and executing the bandit leader Ezekias and many of his followers. Some in Hyrcanus's court persuaded him that Herod was getting too powerful and that he had violated the Jewish law in the execution of Ezekias and his followers and thus should be tried before the SANHEDRIN. So Hyrcanus ordered a trial. Herod appeared not as an accused person but as a king in purple and attended by a bodyguard. Sextus Caesar, governor of Syria, ordered Hyrcanus to acquit Herod or there would be consequences following. Herod was released and fled to join Sextus Caesar at DAMASCUS. Appointed by the latter governor of COELESYRIA because of his popularity, Herod became involved with the affairs of Rome in Syria. He then began to march against Jerusalem in order to avenge himself for the insult Hyrcanus had given him but was persuaded by his father and brother to refrain from violence (Jos. *Ant.* 14.9.2–5 §§158–84; *War* 1.10.5–9 §§204–15; cf. *b. Kiddushin* 43a). All this occurred in 47 or the beginning of 46 B.C.

Caecilius Bassus, a partisan of Pompey who was Julius Caesar's foe, murdered Sextus Caesar and became the leader of Syria (Dio Cassius, *Rom. Hist.* 47.26.7—47.27.2, Livy, *Epit.* 114; Jos. *Ant.* 14.11.1 §§266ff.; *War* 1.10.10 §216f.). Antipater, a friend of Julius Caesar, sent troops under his two sons against Bassus. This minor war dragged on indecisively for about three years. After Cassius, Brutus, and their followers murdered Caesar on March 15 of the year 44 B.C., Cassius defeated Bassus and became leader of Syria. In the need of raising certain required taxes exacted by Cassius, Antipater selected Herod, Phasael, and Malichus for the job.

Because of Herod's success in collecting taxes, Cassius not only appointed him as governor of Coelesyria (as he had been under Sextus) but also promised to make him king of Judea after the war that Cassius and Brutus were fighting against Caesar and Antony. The Herodians were definitely growing in power under the Romans, and because of this Malichus, whose life Antipater had previously saved, bribed a butler to poison Antipater (43 B.C.). Finally, in revenge Herod killed Malichus by stabbing him (Jos. *Ant.* 14.11.3–6 §§277–93; *War* 1.11.2–8 §§220–35).

When Cassius had moved out of Syria to join Brutus for the campaign against Octavius and Antony, troubles caused by Hyrcanus broke out again in Judea. With some difficulty Herod quieted the revolt (43 B.C.). Hardly was this revolt crushed when another broke out. Ptolemy, the prince of the Itureans, had taken Mattathias Antigonus, son of Aristobulus, under his protection and saw a chance to use him. Herod defeated them (42 B.C.) and was received with acclamations by the people and warm congratulations by Hyrcanus (Jos. *Ant.* 14.12.1 §§297–99; *War* 1.12.2–3 §§238–40).

By this time Herod had a wife, Doris, and by her a son, Antipater. Although she is described as a native of Jerusalem, she most likely was an Idumean. But also during this time Herod became betrothed to Mariamne (MARIAMME), granddaughter of Hyrcanus II and daughter of Aristobulus's son, Alexander, and thus a niece to Antigonus,

The legacy of Herod the Great.

the rival of Herod (Jos. *Ant.* 14.12.1 §300; *War* 1.12.3 §241). This strengthened Herod's position immensely, for he would marry into the royal house of the Hasmoneans and would become the natural regent when Hyrcanus, who was growing old, should eventually pass away. Herod's betrothal to Mariamne won him, being by birth an Idumean, an acceptance in the Judean circles.

In 42 B.C. Antony defeated Cassius at PHILIPPI and then proceeded to BITHYNIA of ASIA MINOR and was met by Jewish leaders there who brought accusations against Herod and Phasael (governor of Jerusalem) to the effect that they had usurped the power of the government while leaving Hyrcanus with titular honors. Herod defended himself against the accusers with the result that the charges were neutralized (Jos. *Ant.* 14.12.2–6 §§301–23; *War* 1.12.4–6 §§242–45; Plutarch, *Antony* 24; Dio Cassius, *Rom. Hist.* 48.24; Appian, *Civil Wars* 5.4). Soon after, in the autumn of 41, when Antony had gone to Antioch, the Jewish leaders again made accusations against Herod and Phasael. Since Hyrcanus was there, Antony asked him who would be the best qualified ruler and Hyrcanus pronounced in favor of Herod and Phasael. Antony thus appointed them as TETRARCHS of Judea (Jos. *War* 1.12.5 §§243–44; *Ant.* 14.13.1 §§324–26).

2. His struggle against the Parthians. The new tetrarchs of Judea enjoyed their office for only a brief period. The next year (40 B.C.) the PARTHIANS appeared in Syria. Pacorus, a Parthian prince, joined with Antigonus in the effort to place the latter on the throne held by Hyrcanus. This move began a complicated series of incidents, and Jerusalem was eventually besieged by the invaders (Jos. *War* 1.13.2 §§250–52; cf. also 1.12.3 §240; *Ant.* 14.13.3 §335). A civil war was inevitable. There were daily skirmishes between the two forces.

As the feast of PENTECOST drew near, thousands of Jews came to Jerusalem. At this moment, a Parthian cup-bearer also named Pacorus appeared with an army and claimed to come to settle the dispute in the name of Barzaphranes, the Parthian king. Though Herod was suspicious of the proposal, Phasael and Hyrcanus decided to meet the Parthian king in Galilee. Phasael and Hyrcanus were treacherously put in chains, and simultaneously a Parthian detachment left behind in Jerusalem tried to convince Herod to accompany them outside the Jerusalem walls. Having heard of the mistreatment given to Phasael and Hyrcanus, Herod with his troops, close relatives, and Mariamne made their escape and took refuge in MASADA and then finally moved to PETRA, the capital of the NABATEAN kingdom (Jos. *Ant.* 14.13.7–9 §§352–64; *War* 1.13.6–7 §§261–64).

Meanwhile in Jerusalem the Parthians began a pillage that they extended into the other parts of Judea. Antigonus was made king (Dio Cassius, *Rom. Hist.* 48.41 [note also 48.26]; cf. Jos. *Ant.* 14.13.10 §§368–69; *War* 1.13.9 §§268–70). In order to prevent the possibility of Hyrcanus's restoration to the high priesthood, Antigonus mutilated him. Phasael died either by suicide or poisoning, or in battle (Jos. *Ant.* 14.13.10 §§365–69; *War* 1.13.10–11 §§271–73). Hyrcanus was taken to Parthia (Jos. *Ant.* 15.12.1 §12).

Malchus, the Arabian king from whom Herod had expected help, asked Herod to leave. He thus departed to Egypt and then to Rome, where he was welcomed by Antony and Octavius Caesar. After hearing Herod's story, they with the senate's confirmation designated him as king of Judea (Jos. *Ant.* 14.14.6 §§381–85; *War* 1.14.4 §§282–85; cf. also Strabo, *Geogr.* 16.2.46; Appian, *Civil Wars* 5.75; Tac. *Hist.* 5.9). This occurred in late 40 B.C. From Italy he sailed back to Ptolemais in late 40 or early 39, marched through Galilee, and then captured Joppa and finally moved to Masada where his relatives were under attack (Jos. *Ant.* 14.5.1 §§394–98; *War* 1.15.3–4 §§290–94). With the help of the Roman armies, Herod then proceeded to encamp on the W side of Jerusalem. He proclaimed that he was the lawful king and promised to forget all the past offenses against himself. Antigonus made counterproclamations, stating that Herod was a commoner and an Idumean, that is, a half-Jew, and thus not a legitimate heir to the throne.

In 38 B.C. Herod put down the guerrilla bands in Galilee. Being discontent with the slow progress, he went to Antony to get effective aid from the Romans. Thus he divided his forces and left part of them with his brother Joseph under the orders not to fight until he received reinforcements, and with the rest he went to Samosata where Antony was besieging Antiochus, king of Commagene,

The cliffs of Arbel, where Herod attacked the Sicarii (violent Jewish nationalists) who were hiding in the caves. (View to the NE, with the Sea of Galilee in the background.)

who had sided with the Parthians. Herod hoped by giving timely assistance to Antony, who had not been very successful with the siege, that Antony might help him in return. Antony was pleased with Herod's unsolicited demonstration of loyalty, and after the defeat of Samosata, he ordered one of his legates, Sossius, to use the Roman army to support Herod.

On returning to Antioch with Sossius and two legions, Herod received the bad news that his brother Joseph had been killed at Jericho, which was a result of disobedience to Herod. Finally Herod defeated the opposition in Galilee (Jos. *Ant* 14.15.8–13 §§439–64; *War* 1.16.7—1.17.7 §§320–41). Next spring (37 B.C.), the third year since he had been proclaimed king when at Rome, Herod moved his troops to Jerusalem and prepared for the siege. Having assigned his army to several tasks, he appointed his most efficient lieutenants to supervise the work while he left for Samaria to marry Mariamne, with whom he had been betrothed for about five years. This was certainly a contemptuous move against Antigonus, the uncle of Mariamne, for marrying a Hasmonean strengthened Herod's claim to the throne.

After the wedding he returned to Jerusalem. Following a long and bitter siege, Jerusalem fell and Antigonus was captured by Sossius in the summer of 37 B.C. (Jos. *Ant*. 14.16.2 §§470–80; *War* 1.18.2 §§349–52; Tac. *Hist*. 5.9; Dio Cassius, *Rom. Hist.* 19.22). One of the great problems that faced Herod was to stop the Roman allies from profaning and plundering the temple and the city of their great wealth. Herod did not want to be a king of a wilderness, and he knew that if the temple were desecrated by the Romans it would never be forgiven him by the Jews. He appealed to Sossius to prevent this pillage of the temple and city by promising a reward for each soldier as well as a sizable gift for Sossius out of his own purse. The troops were called in, the promised donation was paid, and Sossius marched away taking Antigonus to Antony in chains. According to Josephus (*Ant*. 14.16.4 §§489–90), Herod gave a large bribe to persuade the Romans to put Antigonus out of the way. It is recorded that Antigonus fell beneath the ax (Jos. *War* 1.18.3 §357; Plutarch, *Antony* 36; cf. also Dio Cassius, *Rom. Hist.* 19.22). This, of course, ends the Hasmonean rule of 129 years. Herod, therefore, ceased to be the nominee for king and became king de facto.

B. As king (37–4 B.C.). The reign of Herod is divided by most scholars into three periods: first, consolidation from 37 to 25; second, prosperity from 25 to 14; and finally, the period of domestic troubles from 14 to 4.

1. Consolidation (37–25 B.C.). This period extends from his accession as king to the death of the sons of Babas (with Costobarus, the second husband of Salome, Herod's sister), when the last male representative of the Hasmonean family was removed from his pathway. During this time of rule he had to contend with many powerful adversaries: the people and the Pharisees, the ruling class, the Hasmonean family, and Cleopatra.

The first adversaries were the people, who were under the persuasion of the PHARISEES. The Pharisees did not like Herod as their king because of his being an Idumean, a half-Jew, and a friend of the Romans. Therefore, he had to secure the obedience of the population. Those of Judea's population who opposed him were punished, while those whom he won to his side he rewarded with favors and honors (Jos. *Ant.* 15.1.1 §§2–3; *War* 1.18.4 §358).

The second of the adversaries were the aristocracy, who sided with Antigonus. Herod executed forty-five of the most wealthy and the most prominent of this class. He confiscated their properties and replenished his coffers, which had been depleted due to the payment of Sossius and his soldiers and the payment of money to Antony in order to gain a firmer hold upon him (Jos. *Ant.* 15.1.2 §§5–6, *War* 1.18.4 §359).

The third of the adversaries were the Hasmonean family. It was Alexandra, Herod's mother-in-law, who caused the most trouble. Herod needed a high priest to replace Hyrcanus. Although Hyrcanus had come back from his Parthian exile, Antigonus had mutilated him, which disqualified him to be the high priest. It is assumed, then, that Herod did not choose himself as high priest, as did Antigonus, because he was an Idumean (though he liked to be considered as of a priestly family). He wanted a high priest of insignificance and yet belonging to the Zadokite family (see ZADOK), which held the office before the Hasmoneans. This would seem to be a legitimate change. Herod found his man in Ananel (Hananeel), a priest of the Babylonian DIASPORA (Jos. *Ant.* 15.1.1–4 §§11–22).

This decision was taken as an insult by Herod's mother-in-law Alexandra, who thought it was an infringement on the Hasmonean line and felt that the position should be given to the only rightful heir, her sixteen-year-old son Aristobulus, the brother of Mariamne. She, therefore, used every conceivable means in order to secure her wishes. Particularly she wrote to CLEOPATRA urging her to exert her influence on Antony, who in turn would force Herod to appoint Aristobulus as high priest (Jos. *Ant.* 15.2.5 §§23–24). Mariamne also pled with Herod to have her brother as high priest. Thus Herod finally gave way to the petitions and set aside Ananel (which was unlawful because the high priest was to hold the office for life) and made Aristobulus high priest. He was only in his seventeenth year (c. late 36 or early 35 B.C.).

This brought peace between Herod and Alexandra but it was short lived. Herod mistrusted Alexandra and so he kept a watchful eye on her. Alexandra grew tired of this situation, and Cleopatra told her to escape with her son and come to Egypt. Two coffins were prepared for the flight from the city to the sea coast, but the scheme was betrayed. Herod allowed the scheme to be carried on and caught them in the act. Even though he overlooked the offense, he became all the more suspicious of her (Jos. *Ant.* 15.3.2 §§42–49).

When the next feast of Tabernacles was celebrated, there arose among the people a great affection for Aristobulus, who officiated. Because of Aristobulus's growth in popularity, Herod determined to get rid of this dangerous rival and enemy. After the festivities, Herod was invited by Alexandra to a feast at Jericho. Herod acted with friendliness toward Aristobulus and suggested they go swimming since the day was very hot. While swimming in a pool Aristobulus was pushed under the water, as if in sport, by some of those with him who had been bribed by Herod. He was kept down so long that he was drowned. Herod displayed the most profound grief and gave him a most magnificent funeral. No one publicly questioned the official version of the death, but Alexandra was not deceived and resolved to devote her life to revenge (Jos. *Ant.* 15.3.3–4 §§50–61; *War* 1.22.2 §437).

Since Alexandra believed Aristobulus's death to be murder, she sent a report to Cleopatra, who persuaded Antony to summon Herod for an account of such actions. Herod was under obligation to go, and, realizing that Antony could and might sentence him to death, he put Mariamne under the surveillance of his uncle Joseph, who was married to Herod's sister

(Salome), instructing him in strict secrecy that he should execute Mariamne if Herod were killed, so that she would not become someone else's lover.

By eloquence and bribery Herod persuaded Antony to free him of any charges. When Herod returned, Salome charged her husband Joseph of having unlawful intercourse with Mariamne. Herod questioned Mariamne but was satisfied with her denial. But when he learned that Mariamne knew about the secret command he had given to Joseph (who thought it was evidence of Herod's love to her), Herod believed this was a confirmation of Salome's charge and had Joseph executed without giving him an opportunity to be heard (34 B.C.). He also put Alexandra in chains and under guard, for he blamed her in part for all these troubles (Jos. *Ant.* 15.3.5–9 §§62–87; *War* 1.22.4–5 §§441–44).

The fourth of the adversaries of Herod was Cleopatra. In connection with Alexandra she made trouble for Herod. By her influence over Antony she obtained an increase of territory. Although at first he would not yield to her, finally during his expedition against Armenia (c. 34 B.C.) he was induced to give her the whole of Phoenicia, the coast of Philistia south of Eleutherus River (with the exception of the free cities of Tyre and Sidon), a portion of Arabia, and the district of Jericho with its palm trees and balsams, which was the most fertile area of Herod's kingdom (Jos. *Ant.* 15.4.1–2 §§88–96; *War* 1.18.4–5 §§360–63). Cleopatra visited the territories, and Herod, though reluctantly, received her with great honor and splendor. But when she tried to entrap Herod by her devices, he would not give in (Jos. *Ant.* 15.4.2 §§97–103).

Civil war broke out between Antony and Octavius. Herod wished to help Antony, but at the instigation of Cleopatra he was instead ordered by Antony to fight against Malchus, the Arabian king. Malchus failed to pay his tribute, and she wanted him to be punished. Actually she hoped that when the two kingdoms weakened each other, she could absorb both (Jos. *Ant.* 15.5.1 §§108–10). Initially Herod was victorious over the Arabs, but Cleopatra helped them, resulting in Herod's eventual defeat. In the spring of 31 a destructive earthquake occurred in Herod's domain costing the lives of 30,000, and when Herod sent envoys to Arabia for the purpose of making peace, the Arabians slew them. After encouraging his troops, who were despondent because of these circumstances, he attacked and defeated the Arabs and then returned home (Jos. *Ant.* 15.5.2–5 §§121–60; *War* 1.19.3–6 §§369–85).

Soon after, on 2 September 31 B.C., Antony was defeated by Octavius (later AUGUSTUS) in the Battle of Actium. This turn of events was a blow to Herod. With political skill Herod had to convince Octavius that he should be regarded as the only legitimate ruler of Judea. Since Hyrcanus II was his only possible rival, he charged Hyrcanus of plotting with the king of the Nabateans and subsequently killed him (Jos. *Ant.* 15.6.1–4 §§161–82; *War* 1.20.1 §386).

On setting out to see Octavius in Rhodes (spring, 30 B.C.), Herod thought it wise to prevent Alexandra from stirring up any revolts. He placed her and Mariamne in Alexandreion (3 mi. SW of the confluence of the Jabbok and Jordan Rivers) under the custody of his steward Joseph (not Herod's brother-in-law) and Soemus, the Iturean who was a trusted friend of Herod. He instructed them to execute the two women if Herod were to be killed and to preserve the kingdom for his sons and his brother Pheroras (Jos. *Ant.* 15.6.5 §§183–86).

At Rhodes Herod played his part skillfully. He admitted his loyalty to Antony, although actually he did not fight against Octavius because of his war against the Arabs. He showed that his loyalty would benefit Octavius, and the latter confirmed Herod in his royal rank. Herod, then, returned to

A Greek coin with the inscription ΗΡΟΔΟΥ ΒΑΣΙΛΕΩΣ ("of King Herod").

his own home. In that same summer Octavius left Asia Minor and landed on the Phoenician coast on his way to Egypt. Herod met him with great pomp at Ptolemais and gave him 800 talents and provided supplies for Octavius's soldiers during that hot season. This was appreciated by Octavius (Jos. *Ant.* 15.6.6–7 §§188–201; *War* 1.20.1–3 §§387–95).

Octavius gained control of Egypt when he defeated Antony. Antony and Cleopatra committed suicide in August of 30 B.C. Having heard this, Herod went to Egypt to congratulate Octavius and to secure a great reward for himself. Octavius gave him the title of king (Strabo *Geogr.* 16.2.46). In addition, Octavius now gave back to him not only Jericho, but also Gadara, Hippos, Samaria, Gaza, Anthedon, Joppa, and Strato's Tower (later CAESAREA; Jos. *Ant.* 15.7.3 §§215–17; *War* 1.20.3 §§396–97). Thus Herod secured much for himself.

While Herod seemed to enjoy the outward success of having his kingdom conferred to him by Octavius and of having gained control of new areas, his domestic affairs were far from peaceful. While he was at Rhodes, Mariamne found out from Soemus that Herod had ordered him and Joseph to kill her if he were killed. When Herod returned she was very unfriendly to him. Since Herod was caught between loving and hating her, his sister Salome and their mother Cypros saw their opportunity to satisfy their hatred toward Mariamne and spread slanderous stories about her which would fill Herod with hatred and jealousy at the same time. Herod would not listen to them.

Later when he returned from Egypt, after congratulating Octavius and receiving the new territories, Mariamne's attitude toward him was more irritating. Salome seized upon this opportunity by bribing Herod's butler to say that Mariamne prepared a love-potion for the king. Herod inquired with regards to the love-potion but the butler did not know. Being in an ugly mood, Herod had Mariamne's eunuch examined by torture regarding this love-potion. He also knew nothing of it but did confess of Mariamne's hatred of him because of the command he had given Soemus. Because Soemus, as well as Joseph, had betrayed his secret, Herod felt this was proof of unlawful intercourse and had Soemus immediately executed. Mariamne, after a judicial investigation, was condemned and then finally executed at the end of 29 B.C. (Jos. *Ant.* 15.7.1–5 §§202–36). Herod never sanely accepted Mariamne's death. He fell ill, and because his recovery was doubtful, Alexandra began to scheme so that if he died she would secure the throne. She tried to win over those in command of the two fortified palaces in Jerusalem. When this was reported to Herod, Alexandra was executed in the year 28 (Jos. *Ant.* 15.7.6–8 §§237–52).

After Herod recovered from his depression over Mariamne, he found occasion for further bloodshed in this period. Soon after his accession as king, he had appointed a distinguished Idumean, Costobarus, as governor of Idumea and given him his sister Salome, after putting to death her former husband Joseph (in 34 B.C.). Even during this first period Costobarus secretly conspired with Cleopatra against Herod, but Herod granted him pardon at the entreaty of Salome. However, now Salome was getting tired of her husband and so she wanted to get rid of him. She had learned that he, along with Antipater, Lysimachus, and Dositheus, was planning to revolt. As a proof of her charges she revealed that her husband had preserved the influential sons of Babas, who remained loyal to Antigonus and always spoke ill of Herod. When Herod heard this, Costobarus and his followers, whose place of concealment was betrayed by Salome, were seized and executed in 25 B.C. Herod now could console himself that all the male relatives of Hyrcanus (who could dispute the occupancy of the throne) were no longer living (Jos. *Ant.* 15.7.9–10 §§253–66). This ends the first period of Herod's reign.

2. Prosperity (25–14 B.C.). This period is marked with splendor and enjoyment, although there were moments of disturbance. The first event mentioned by Josephus regarding this period is Herod's violation of the Jewish law by his introduction of the quinquennial games in honor of Caesar and by the building of theaters, amphitheaters, and race courses for both men and horses (Jos. *Ant.* 15.8.1 §§267–76). Some time later (c. 24), Herod built for himself a royal palace and also built or rebuilt a good many fortresses and Gentile temples, including the rebuilding of Strato's Tower, which was renamed CAESAREA (Jos. *Ant.* 15.8.5—15.9.6 §§292–341).

The Hyrcania fortress, built by Herod the Great some 10 mi. SE of Jerusalem, was used to detain his political prisoners.

Herod's greatest building, of course, was the TEMPLE in JERUSALEM, work on which began c. 20 B.C. Josephus considers it the most noble of all his achievements (Jos. *Ant.* 15.11.1 §380). Rabbinic literature states: "he who has not seen the Temple of Herod has never seen a beautiful building" (*b. Baba Bathra* 4a). Also, it is suggested that it was his "atonement for having slain so many sages of Israel" (*Midr. Num.* 14:8; for a discussion of Herod's building projects, see E. Netzer in *ABD*, 3:169–72; D. W. Roller, *The Building Program of Herod the Great* [1998]). Also during this period, he took great interest in culture and surrounded himself with a circle of men accomplished in Greek literature and art. The highest offices of state were entrusted to Greek rhetoricians, one of whom, Nicolas of Damascus, was Herod's instructor in philosophy, rhetoric, and history. He was the king's adviser and figured much in Herod's dealings.

Regarding domestic affairs, late in the year 24 he married Mariamne (who will be designated as Mariamne II), daughter of Simon, a well-known priest in Jerusalem. Herod sent his two sons by Mariamne I, Alexander and Aristobulus, to Rome for their education. Augustus (Octavius's title since 27 B.C.) himself received the sons and they stayed at the house of Asinius Pollio, who professed to be one of Herod's most devoted friends. At this time Augustus gave him the territories of TRACONITIS, BATANEA, and Auranitis (HAURAN), which had been occupied by nomad robber tribes with whom the neighboring tetrarch Zenodorus had made common cause (Jos. *Ant.* 15.10.1–2 §§342–49; *War* 1.20.4 §§398–99). It is apparent that there was a friendly relationship between Caesar and Herod. Herod, undoubtedly, was considered an important king to Rome, for he kept that section of the Roman empire well in control.

Augustus came to Syria in 20 B.C. and bestowed upon Herod the territory of Zenodorus, or that which laid between Traconitis and Galilee (containing Ulatha and Paneas), and made it so the procurators of Syria had to get Herod's consent for all their actions (Jos. *Ant.* 15.10.3 §§354–60; *War* 1.20.4; cf. Dio Cassius, *Rom. Hist.* 64.7.4–6; 64.9.3). He also asked Augustus for a territory for his brother Pheroras, who was given PEREA (Jos. *Ant.* 15.10.3 §362; cf. *War* 1.24.5 §483). Because of these gracious bestowments, Herod erected a beautiful temple for Augustus in the territory of Zenodorus, near the place called Paneion (Jos. *Ant.* 15.10.3 §363; *War* 1.21.3 §§404–6).

Also at this same time Herod remitted a third of the taxes under the pretext of crop failure but actually it was to bring goodwill among those who were displeased with his emphasis on Greco-

Roman culture and religion. The remittance of taxes was effective for the most part. There seemingly was a great dissatisfaction because Herod would not allow the people to congregate for fear of a revolt. He demanded a loyalty oath by the people, but excluded Pollion the Pharisee and his disciple Samaias, as well as most of their disciples. The ESSENES did not have to submit to this oath because, according to Josephus (*Ant.* 15.10.4 §§365–72), Herod had a high regard for them. In 17 or 16 B.C., Herod made a trip to Rome to meet Augustus and fetch his two sons, who had completed their education. Upon their return to Judea, Aristobulus was married to Salome's daughter Berenice, while Alexander married Glaphyra, the daughter of Archelaus, king of CAPPADOCIA (Jos. *Ant.* 16.1.2 §§6–11; *War* 1.23.1 §§445–46).

One can conclude that the period from 25 to 14 B.C. was the most brilliant in Herod's entire reign. His building program was of great splendor and his domestic affairs were reasonably stable (until near the end of this period). Although he had some trouble within his political sphere, he had good control of his people and twice he favored them by lowering taxes (in the year 14 he reduced taxes by one-fourth, Jos. *Ant.* 16.2.5 §§64–65).

3. Domestic troubles (14–4 B.C.). Herod married a total of ten wives (Jos. *Ant.* 17.1.3 §§19–22; *War* 1.28.4 §§562–63). Herod repudiated his first wife Doris and their son Antipater when he married Mariamne I in 37 B.C., but they were allowed to visit Jerusalem during the festivals (Jos. *War* 1.22.1 §433). This Mariamne, the granddaughter of Hyrcanus, bore him five children. The two daughters were Salampsio and Cypros (Jos. *Ant.* 18.5.4 §§130–32). The youngest son died during the course of his education in Rome (Jos. *War* 1.22.2 §435). The older sons were Alexander and Aristobulus, who played an important part during this period of Herod's life. Herod married his third wife Mariamne II in late 24 B.C., and by her he had Herod (Philip). His fourth wife was a Samaritan, Malthace, by whom he had Archelaus and Antipas. His fifth wife, Cleopatra of Jerusalem, was the mother of Philip. Of the other five wives, only Pallas, Phaedra, and Elpsis are known by name, and none of these played a significant role (Jos. *Ant.* 17.1.3 §§19–22; *War* 1.28.4 §§562–63).

Herod's favorite sons were Alexander and Aristobulus, the two he had by Mariamne I. After they had returned from Rome and had married Glaphyra and Berenice respectively, troubles domestically began to come to the forefront. Salome, Herod's sister and mother of Berenice, hated these two sons and tried desperately to establish her own son. It may well be that to a certain degree the haughtiness by the two sons of Mariamne I was due to their being a part of the Hasmonean dynasty. Salome aggravated them by speaking ill of their mother, whom Herod had killed, which caused them to defend her. Salome and Pheroras (brother of Herod and Salome) reported to Herod that his life was in danger because the two sons were not going to leave the murder of their mother unavenged and that Archelaus, king of Cappadocia (father of Glaphyra), would help them reach the emperor and bring charges against their father (Jos. *Ant.* 16.3.1–2 §§66–77).

In order to provide a counterbalance to their aspirations and to show them that there might be another who could be heir to the throne, Herod recalled his exiled son Antipater. In the spring of 13 B.C., Herod sent him to Rome in the company of Agrippa (friend of Augustus), who left the E to go to Rome, so that he might present Antipater to the emperor. Instead of being a counterbalance, Antipater used every conceivable means to acquire the throne. He used slander against his two half brothers. The rift between Herod and Mariamne I's two sons became so great that Herod decided to accuse his two sons before the emperor. In 12 B.C. the two sons went with Herod and they were tried before Augustus in Aquileia. After the case was heard, Augustus was able to reconcile Herod and his sons, and having restored domestic peace, the father, the two sons, and Antipater returned home. When they arrived home, Herod named Antipater as his first successor and next after him were to be Alexander and Aristobulus (Jos. *Ant.* 16.3.3–4. 6 §§66–135; *War* 1.23.3–5 §§451–66).

Scarcely had they arrived home when Antipater, being helped by Herod's sister Salome and Herod's brother Pheroras, began to slander the two sons of Mariamne I. Alexander and Aristobulus became more decidedly hostile in their attitude. Herod became suspicious and increasingly morbid about the situation. Antipater played on Herod's fears. He even caused the friends of Alexander to be tortured so that they might confess any attempt to take Herod's life, and one friend made the admission that Alexander, with the help of Aristobulus, had planned to kill him and then flee to Rome to lay claim on his kingdom. For this Alexander was committed to prison. When the Cappadocian king Archelaus, Alexander's father-in-law, heard of this state of affairs, he began to fear for his daughter and son-in-law and thus made a journey to Jerusalem to see if there could be reconciliation. He appeared before Herod very angry over his good-for-nothing son-in-law and threatened to take his daughter back with him. Because of this Herod defended his son against Archelaus. By this sly maneuver on the part of Archelaus, he accomplished the reconciliation he desired and then returned to his home (Jos. *Ant.* 16.7.2—16.8.6 §§188–270; *War* 1.24.1—1.25.6 §§467–512). These events probably occurred in 10 B.C. Thus there was peace once again in Herod's household.

In this same period Herod had troubles with some foreign enemies and with the emperor. Syllaeus, who ruled in the place of the Arabian king Obodas and who was determinedly hostile to Herod, gave shelter to forty rebels of Traconitis and tried to relieve his country from paying a debt contracted with Herod. The latter demanded the handing over of the rebels and the payment of the debt. With the consent of the governor of Syria, Saturninus, Herod invaded Arabia and enforced his rights (c. 9 B.C.). This attack was only to be a punitive measure with no intentions of territorial gain, but Syllaeus had meanwhile gone to Rome and distorted the picture, with the result that Augustus became suspicious and intimated to Herod that their close relationship was at an end and that he would henceforth treat him no longer as a friend but as a subject. In order to justify himself, Herod sent an embassy to Rome and, when this failed, he sent a second under the leadership of Nicolas of Damascus (Jos. *Ant.* 16.9.1–4 §§271–99).

About this time, the domestic discord again came to the forefront. A certain Eurycles from Lacedemon, a man of bad character, inflamed the father against the sons and the sons against the father (Jos. *Ant.* 16.10.1 §§300–310; *War* 1.26.1–4 §§513–33; cf. also Pausanias, *Description of Greece* 2.3.5; Strabo, *Geogr.* 8.5.1; Plutarch, *Antony* 67). As other mischief-makers became involved, Herod's patience was exhausted: he put Alexander and Aristobulus into prison and complained to the emperor that they were involved in treasonable plots. Meanwhile Nicolas of Damascus had accomplished his mission and had again won over the emperor to Herod. When the messengers who were bringing the accusations of Herod reached Rome, they found Augustus in a favorable mood. The emperor gave Herod absolute power to proceed in the matter of his sons as he wished, but advised him that the trial should take place outside of Herod's territory at Berytus (Beirut), before a court of which Roman officials would form part, and to have the charges against his sons investigated by it (Jos. *Ant.* 16.10.5—16.11.1 §§320–60; *War* 1.27.1 §§534–37).

Herod accepted the advice of the emperor. Although the governor of Syria, Saturninus, and his three sons thought that Herod's sons, though guilty, should not be put to death, the court almost unanimously pronounced the death sentence. Tiro, an old soldier, publicly proclaimed that the trial had been unjust and the truth suppressed. But he and 300 others were denounced as friends of Alexander and Aristobulus and thus were put to death. Therefore, at Sebaste (Samaria), where Herod had married Mariamne thirty years before, her two sons were executed by strangling, probably in 7 B.C. (Jos. *Ant.* 16.11.2–8 §§361–404; *War* 1.27.2–6 §§538–51).

Antipater, now remaining as the sole heir and enjoying the full confidence of his father, was still not satisfied, for he wished to have the government wholly in his own hands. He held secret conferences with Herod's brother Pheroras, tetrarch of Perea, which Salome reported to her brother Herod, stating that they were contriving to kill him. Thus the relationship of Antipater and his father became strained. Antipater thus wrote his friends in Rome to ask if Augustus would instruct Herod to send Antipater to Rome. Herod sent him to Rome and designated in his will that Antipater was his successor to the throne; in the event that Antipater's death might occur before his own, Herod (Philip), son of Mariamne II, the high priest's daughter, was named as his successor.

While Antipater was in Rome, Pheroras died, and this event proved to be the seal of Antipater's fate. Freedmen of Pheroras went to Herod to relate to him that Pheroras had been poisoned and that Herod should investigate the matter more closely. It was found out that the poison was sent by Antipater with the intention not to kill Pheroras but rather that Pheroras might give it to Herod. Herod also learned from the female slaves of Pheroras's household of the complaints that Antipater had made at those secret meetings regarding the king's long life and about the uncertainties of his prospects. Consequently Herod recalled Antipater under false pretenses, and Antipater returned with no suspicion. When he arrived he was committed to prison in the king's palace and was tried the next day before Varus, the governor of Syria. In light of the many proofs against him, he could make no defense. Herod put him in chains and made a report of the matter to the emperor. This occurred c. 5 B.C.

Another plot of Antipater was unveiled and Herod desired to kill him. Herod then became very ill with a disease from which he would not recover. Therefore, he drew up a new will in which he by-passed his eldest sons, Archelaus and Philip, because Antipater had poisoned his mind against them. Instead he chose the youngest son, Antipas, as his sole successor (Jos. *Ant.* 17.2.4—17.6.1 §§32–146; *War* 1.29.1—1.32.7 §§567–646).

According to Matthew, shortly before Herod's death the MAGI came to Judea to worship the newborn king of the Jews. Herod summoned the wise men, asking them to report to him the location of the Christ child when they found him in BETHLEHEM. Being warned in a dream, the Magi did not return to Herod but departed to the E by another route. The Lord appeared to Joseph in a dream and told him to flee to Egypt because of Herod's intention to kill Jesus. They fled to Egypt and Herod killed all the male children of Bethlehem who were two years and under (Matt. 2:1–18).

Herod was now nearly seventy years old and his sickness grew worse. As news spread that he had an incurable disease, two rabbis, Judas son of Sepphoraeus and Matthias son of Margalus, stirred up the people to tear down the offensive eagle from the temple gate. Judas and Matthias argued that such an action would be pleasing to God. Herod, having heard this, seized the offenders and passed sentences of death upon them and had the principal leaders burned alive.

As Herod's disease grew worse, the baths at Callirrhoe (see ZERETH SHAHAR) no longer benefited him. When he returned to Jericho, he commanded all notable Jews from all parts of the nation to come to him, and when they arrived he shut them up in the hippodrome, summoned his sister Salome and her husband Alexas, and ordered that all these leaders should be cut down at the moment he died so that there would be a national mourning rather than a festival. At the time he was giving these instructions, he received a letter from Rome in which the emperor gave him permission to execute his son Antipater, which he did immediately. Herod again altered his will by nominating Archelaus, the older son of Malthace, as king, Antipas as tetrarch of Galilee and Perea, and Philip as tetrarch of Gaulanitis, Traconitis, Batanea, and Paneas.

Finally, on the fifth day after the execution of Antipater, Herod died at Jericho in the spring of 4 B.C. Salome and Alexas dismissed those who were summoned to the hippodrome. Then Ptolemy, who had been entrusted with the king's seal, read Herod's last will in public, and the crowd acclaimed Archelaus as their king. A pompous funeral procession accompanied the body from Jericho to the HERODIUM, where it was finally laid (Jos. *Ant.* 17.6.1—17.8.3 §§147–99; *War* 1.33.1–9 §§647–73; cf. R. K. Fenn, *The Death of Herod: An Essay in the Sociology of Religion* [1992]).

Herod's reign, if one reckons from 37 B.C., lasted thirty-three to thirty-four years. Much of his rule was characterized by violence, though in this respect other rulers were not very different from him. As a whole, he was disliked by the Jews because of his infidelity to or his unconcern for their law. Although he was the king of the Jews, many of his subjects would not characterize him as truly a Jewish king. (See further J. S. Minkin, *Herod, King of the Jews* [1936]; S. Perowne, *The Life and Times of Herod the Great* [1956]; S. Sandmel, *Herod: Profile of a Tyrant* [1967]; A. Schalit, *König Herodes: Der Mann und sein Werk* [1969]; M. Grant, *Herod the Great* [1971]; *HJP*, rev. ed. [1973–1987],

1:287–329; P. Richardson, *Herod: King of the Jews and Friend of the Romans* [1996]; E. Netzer, *The Architecture of Herod, the Great Builder* [2006].)

III. Herod's will disputed. During his life Herod had written six wills (actually, the sixth will was a set of codicils to the fifth). As mentioned above, the sixth will was made only five days before his death. Hence it needed the ratification of the emperor. So as soon as Herod died Archelaus took over the leadership, but he did not accept the title of king nor allow himself to be crowned (Jos. *Ant.* 17.8.4. §§202–3; *War* 2.1.1 §§2–3). Immediately after the Passover, Archelaus and Antipas left for Rome to dispute the wills of Herod while Philip took care of the home front. Archelaus claimed that Augustus should ratify the sixth will because it expressed Herod's desire just before he died. On the other hand, Antipas claimed that the fifth will, which already had been ratified, had greater validity, because when Herod designated Antipas as king, he was in good physical and mental health, whereas when he named Archelaus as king in the codicils, he was stricken both in mind and body and was incapable of good reasoning. To complicate the situation further, there was a revolt in Palestine while the two brothers were in Rome disputing the will. The result of this revolt was that a Jewish delegation was sent to the emperor pleading for the autonomy of the nation and for its union with the province of Syria. By now Philip had also gone to Rome.

After considerable debate and delay, Augustus decided on a compromise solution: (a) Archelaus was designated ETHNARCH, with the promise to be made king if he proved capable of that position, and was to rule over Idumea, Judea, and Samaria; (b) Antipas was made TETRARCH over Galilee and Perea; (c) and Philip was made tetrarch over Gaulanitis, Traconitis, Batanea, and Paneas (Jos. *Ant.* 17.11.4 §§317–20; *War* 2.6.3 §§93–100). Therefore, although Antipas lost claim to kingship, he prevented Archelaus from being king over the whole realm.

IV. Archelaus (4 B.C. to A.D. 6). Archelaus was born c. 22 B.C. to Herod the Great and Malthace (a Samaritan). As soon as Herod died, Ptolemy, to whom the king had entrusted his signet-ring, read the codicils that designated Archelaus as king and Philip and Antipas as tetrarchs. Although the codicils were not ratified, Archelaus assumed the leadership. The people began making demands with which Archelaus complied in order to ingratiate himself with them. There were, however, revolutionaries among the crowd who were out to revenge the blood of those whom Herod killed for cutting down the eagle from the temple gate. Archelaus, wanting to prevent an uprising of the mob at Passover, sent out an army and killed 3,000 people (Jos. *Ant.* 18.8.4—19.9.3 §§200–218; *War* 2.1.1–3 §§1–13). Consequently his rule got off to a bad start.

While on his way to Rome, another revolt broke out at Pentecost lasting about two months: the temple porticoes were burned and its treasury pillaged by the Romans. This revolt spread to the countryside of Judea as well as to Galilee and Perea (Jos. *Ant.* 17.10.2–5 §§254–72; *War* 2.3.1—2.4.1 §§40–56). Thus when Herod's sons returned to Palestine (prob. in the spring of 3 B.C.) after the trial, the situation was all but ideal for them to begin their rule.

Archelaus proceeded to treat both Jews and Samaritans with great brutality (Jos. *War* 2.7.3 §111). This unfortunate state of affairs is reflected in the NT, which relates that Joseph, after returning from the flight to Egypt, heard that Archelaus was the ruler of Judea, and being afraid to go back there, withdrew to Galilee (Matt. 2:22). Furthermore, Archelaus removed the high priest Joazar, the son of Boethus, on the pretext that he sided with the insurgents; he appointed in his stead Joazar's brother Eleazar, who in turn was later replaced by Jesus son of See (Jos. *Ant.* 17.13.1 §§339–41). Archelaus divorced his wife Mariamne to marry Glaphyra, who was the daughter of King Archelaus of Cappadocia and had formerly been married to Archelaus's half-brother, Alexander, thus transgressing the ancestral law (Jos. *Ant.* 17.13.1, 4–5 §§341, 350–53; *War* 2.7.4 §§114–16). Either or both of these last mentioned events may have caused unrest in the country, and Archelaus's methods of suppression of unrest were oppressive.

Finally in A.D. 6 Archelaus was deposed. Although there are divergencies in the accounts, it can be reasonably reconstructed. It was triggered by a formal complaint to Augustus by a delegation of Jews and Samaritans concerning Archelaus's cruelty and tyranny. The cooperation of these two communities, normally bitter enemies, indicates the seriousness of the grievances. Furthermore, Archelaus's brothers, Antipas and Philip, went to Rome to bring charges against him, presumably regarding his oversight of them, since as ethnarch he was the Roman representative for Palestine. The outcome was that Archelaus was banished to Vienna in Gaul (modern Vienne on the Rhône, S of Lyons), while Antipas and Philip retained their rule. Archelaus's domains were reduced to a province under the rule of PREFECTS or PROCURATORS (Jos. *Ant.* 17.13.1–5 §§342–55; *War* 2.7.3–2.8.1 §§111–18; Strabo, *Geogr.* 16.2.46; Dio Cassius, *Rom. Hist.* 55.27.6; see further *HJP*, rev. ed. [1973–1987], 1:353–57).

V. Antipas (4 B.C. to A.D. 39). Antipas was born c. 20 B.C. to Herod and Malthace (a Samaritan), hence was the younger full brother of Archelaus.

A. His realm. Of all the Herodians, he figures most prominently in the NT, for he was the tetrarch over Galilee and Perea, the two areas in which John the Baptist and Christ had most of their ministry. When Antipas returned from Rome to begin his rule in the domains allotted to him, he found them ravaged by the rebellion at the feast of Pentecost in 4 B.C. He had to restore order and rebuild what had been destroyed. Following in the footsteps of ALEXANDER THE GREAT and his father Herod the Great, he founded cities. He began by rebuilding SEPPHORIS, which was the largest city in Galilee as well as the capital for his domains until he built TIBERIAS. Sepphoris was probably completed c. A.D. 8–10, and it is very possible that Joseph, Mary's husband, plied his trade as a carpenter (Matt. 13:55; Mk. 6:3) during its rebuilding, since NAZARETH was only 4 mi. SSW of Sepphoris. Probably the second city to be rebuilt was Livias (or Julias) of Perea in honor of Livia, the wife of Augustus. This city was most likely completed in A.D. 13.

Tiberias should be considered one of the most important of all twelve cities built by the Herodian family, for it was the first city in Jewish history to be founded within the municipal framework of a Greek *polis*. It was built in honor of the reigning emperor, TIBERIUS. While building it, they struck upon a cemetery, which was destroyed. Antipas thus had difficulty in getting devout Jews to settle there, for they considered the city unclean. He offered free houses and lands and exemption from taxes for the first few years if anyone moved into the new city. It was completed c. A.D. 23 and became his capital.

B. His rule

1. Antipas and Archelaus. The only significant event that occurred early in Antipas's career was in A.D. 6, when he and Philip, as well as a delegation of Jews and Samaritans, went to Rome with the intention of bringing about the downfall of his brother Archelaus. In the end, Antipas remained a tetrarch but gained the dynastic title *Herod* (cf. Jos. *Ant.* 18.2.1 §26; *War* 2.9.1 §167), which was of great significance both to his subjects and to the political and social circles of the Roman world. This title given by the emperor may have been a concession in lieu of his being made king.

2. Antipas and John the Baptist. The episode for which Antipas is best remembered is his involvement in the imprisonment and death of JOHN THE BAPTIST (Matt. 14:3–12; Mk. 6:17–29; Lk. 3:19–20; Jos. *Ant.* 18.5.2 §§116–19). Antipas had married the daughter of ARETAS IV (her name is not known), a NABATEAN king, before A.D. 14. This relationship probably was instigated by Augustus, who was known to favor intermarriages among the various rulers for the sake of peace in the Roman empire. This particular alliance would have made for peace between the Jews and the Arabs; in addition, Aretas's territory served as a buffer between Rome and Parthia.

Around A.D. 29 Antipas made a journey to Rome. On his way he paid a visit to his half-brother Herod (prob. Herod Philip; see below), who apparently lived in one of the coastal cities of Palestine. Antipas fell in love with his host's wife HERODIAS, who was also his own niece. She was ambitious, and this was her opportunity to become the wife of a tetrarch. Herodias agreed to marry Antipas on his return from Rome, with the stipulation that Aretas's daughter must be ousted (Jos. *Ant.* 18.5.1 §§109–10). The latter got wind of the

Reconstructed Roman house and theater at Sepphoris, a city of Galilee rebuilt by Herod Antipas. (View to the SW.)

arrangement and consequently fled to her father. This divorce was not only a personal insult to Aretas but also a breach of a political alliance; it later led to a retaliation by Aretas.

Soon after the departure of Aretas's daughter, Antipas and Herodias were married. John the Baptist spoke boldly against this union, and consequently Antipas incarcerated him. John's denouncement was that Antipas had married his brother Philip's wife. The Mosaic law forbade the marriage of a brother's wife (Lev. 18:16; 20:21) with the exception of raising children to a deceased childless brother by LEVIRATE marriage (Deut. 25:5; Mk. 12:19). However, in Antipas's case his brother had offspring, namely, Salome; more seriously, Antipas's brother was still alive.

A problem arises over the identification of Herodias's first husband, for the Gospels state that he was Philip (Matt. 14:3; Mk. 6:17), whereas Josephus (*Ant.* 18.5.1 §109) identifies him as Herod, son of Herod the Great and Mariamne II. Many scholars think that the gospel accounts are incorrect. Since the Herodian genealogy is very complicated, they propose that Matthew and Mark confused this Herod with Philip the tetrarch, who later married Herodias's daughter Salome. However, as easy as this solution may be at first sight, it is untenable for several reasons.

(1) The Gospels would be guilty of three historical errors: (a) confusing this Herod with his half-brother Philip, (b) making Philip the tetrarch husband of Herodias instead of the husband of her daughter, and (c) identifying Salome as the daughter of Philip the tetrarch, who according to Josephus had no children. It is quite improbable that the evangelists would have committed three blunders in matters of well-known history with which they otherwise show familiarity. Such major lapses seem especially incredible when one considers that the Christian community had in its midst such individuals as JOANNA, wife of Chuza (who was Antipas's financial minister, Lk. 8:3), and MANAEN (an intimate friend of Antipas, Acts 13:1). (2) The Gospels speak of a daughter of Herodias before she was married to Antipas (Matt. 14:6, 8–11; Mk. 6:22, 24–26, 28) which harmonizes exactly with Josephus's comment that Herodias and Herod (son of Mariamne II) had a daughter named Salome (Jos. *Ant.* 18.5.4 §136). (3) The objection that Herod the Great would not have had two sons with the name Philip is untenable, for although they had the same father, they had different mothers; also, Herod the Great had two sons named Antipas/Antipater and two sons named Herod. (4) It is not unreasonable for Herodias's first husband to have a double name, namely, Herod Philip; no one

disputes that the Herod of Acts 12 is the Agrippa of Josephus or suggests that Luke confused him with Herod, king of Chalcis (similarly, Archelaus is the same as Herod Archelaus). (5) If the evangelists meant that Herodias's former husband was Philip the tetrarch, why did they not call him by that title as they had called Antipas right within that same pericope (Matt. 14:1; Mk. 6:14, 26)? Therefore, it is most reasonable to consider that the Philip in the Gospels and the Herod in Josephus to be one and the same person. In fact, to do otherwise would seem to create inextricable confusion.

Herodias was not satisfied to leave John in prison and so at a suitable time she arranged for a banquet, probably for Antipas's birthday, at Machaerus in Perea in order to get rid of John. Her daughter Salome danced before the dignitaries, and Antipas promised her with an oath that he would give her anything up to half of his kingdom. Being advised by her mother, she requested John the Baptist's head on a platter. Antipas was sorry he had made the promise under oath, but due to the presence of his underlords he had to follow through with the request. Consequently John the Baptist's ministry came to an end c. A.D. 31 or 32 (according to a different chronology, in the year 27). See chronology (NT) II.

3. Antipas and Jesus. Antipas's relationship to Jesus is seen in three episodes. (1) Antipas heard of Jesus' ministry and concluded, possibly with a note of irony, that Jesus was John the Baptist resurrected (Matt. 14:1–2; Mk. 6:14–16; Lk. 9:7–9). He had put to end one dangerous movement headed by John the Baptist, but now there appeared a still more remarkable and successful people's preacher. Hence, it was John the Baptist all over again. Antipas wanted to see Jesus but was not able to do so because he withdrew from his territories; in addition, he did not want to use force because he might rouse his people again as he had in connection with John.

(2) The second episode to be noted is when Jesus was on his final journey to Jerusalem. Some of the Pharisees came to Jesus and stated that he had better remove himself from Antipas's territories because he wanted to kill Jesus (Lk. 13:31–33). Jesus replied by saying, "Go tell that fox, 'I will drive out demons and heal people today and tomorrow, and on the third day I will reach my goal.'" In other words, Jesus would continue his ministry for a short time at least, but only after he had finished would he go to Jerusalem to perish. Antipas saw the potential danger of Christ's popular movement and wanted him to leave his domains by threatening to kill him. Antipas did not dare to use force because there was no evidence that Jesus was causing potential trouble, and the people had not forgiven Antipas for his treatment of John the Baptist whom they considered a prophet. But Jesus saw through Antipas's scheme and called him a "fox" (a weak animal that uses cunning deceit to achieve its aims), hence a crafty coward. The lion of Judah was not going to be ordered by the fox (the fox and lion often were contrasted in ancient literature). Jesus was to finish his ministry there for a short time, and though Antipas had killed John the Baptist in his territory, he did not control the fate of Jesus.

(3) The final encounter was when Jesus was tried by Antipas in the year 33 (alternately, 30). The incident is recorded in Lk. 23:6–12, and many scholars consider this pericope as legendary since it is not in the other Gospels. However, it is difficult to see any apologetic purpose for its inclusion; it was probably included because of Luke's particular interest in the Herodian house (specifically, Luke and his addressee Theophilus, who may have been a Roman officer, would have been interested in the reconciliation between Antipas and Pilate, 23:12). Since the other Gospels did not have a particular interest in the Herods, one can see the reason for the omission of this event, which adds nothing to the progression of the trial of Christ. There are some scholars who think that the source of the pericope is Acts 4:25–26 (which quotes Ps. 2:1–2), but upon close examination the opposite is true. Other scholars say that the pericope's origin is in the *Gospel of Peter*, but the parallel is not strong (in fact, the *Gospel of Peter* holds Antipas responsible for Jesus' death where there is nothing of this in Luke).

Regarding the contents of the pericope itself, Pilate sent Jesus to Antipas, who was in Jerusalem for the Passover. Pilate did not make this move out of kindness but to free himself from an awkward case: the Jews insisted on Jesus' execution but

Pilate found no guilt in him. Another reason for handing Jesus over to Antipas was for diplomatic courtesy in order to improve his relationship with Antipas, which had been strained by the Galilean massacre (Lk. 13:1) and by the incident over the votive shields being brought into Jerusalem by Pilate (Philo, *Legatio ad Gaium* 299–304). The last incident was reported by Antipas (and other Herods) to Tiberius, who ordered Pilate to remove the shields immediately. Pilate had overstepped himself and was anxious to appease. Antipas did not presume on Pilate's gesture; after mocking Jesus, he sent Jesus back. The one thing that was accomplished in this trial was the reconciliation of Antipas and Pilate.

4. Antipas and Rome. In A.D. 36 Aretas made an attack on Antipas and defeated his army. The Jews saw this defeat as a divine retribution upon Antipas for his execution of John the Baptist (Jos. *Ant.* 5.1.2 §§116–19). Tiberius ordered Vitellius, governor of Syria, to help Antipas. Before attacking Aretas, however, Vitellius and Antipas went up to Jerusalem to celebrate a feast (prob. Pentecost of 37), and while there received the news of Tiberius's death (16 March 37). Consequently, Vitellius called off his expedition against Aretas until he received commands from the new emperor, CALIGULA.

Caligula upon his accession gave his friend Agrippa I, brother of Herodias, the land of Philip as well as the tetrarchy of Lysanias with the title of king (Jos. *Ant.* 18.6.10 §§225–39). Later Agrippa went to Palestine (c. Aug. of 38). Due to Agrippa's acquisition of the title of king, Herodias prodded Antipas to go to Rome to seek the same title. Finally in 39 Antipas with Herodias went to Rome, but meanwhile Agrippa dispatched one of his freedmen to Rome to bring accusations against Antipas. As a result, Antipas was banished to exile at Lugdunum Convenarum (now Saint-Bertrand de Comminges of France). Although Herodias did not have to go into exile, she chose to follow her husband. Antipas's territories were given to Agrippa (Jos. *Ant.* 18.7.1–2 §§240–55; *War* 2.9.6 §§181–83).

(See further J. Blinzler, *Herodes Antipas und Jesus Christus* [1947]; V. E. Harlow, *The Destroyer of Jesus: The Story of Herod Antipas, Tetrarch of Galilee* [1954]; G. Schofield, *Crime before Calvary:* *Herodias, Herod Antipas, and Pontius Pilate; a New Interpretation* [1960]; F. F. Bruce in *Annual of Leeds University Oriental Society* 5 [1963–65]: 6–23; H. W. Hoehner, *Herod Antipas* [1972]; *HJP*, rev. ed. [1973–1987], 1:340–53; J. A. Darr, *Herod the Fox: Audience Criticism and Lucan Characterization* [1998]; M. H. Jensen, *Herod Antipas in Galilee* [2006].)

VI. Philip the tetrarch (4 B.C. to A.D. 34). Philip was born c 22/21 B.C. to Herod the Great and Cleopatra of Jerusalem. As a result of the debate over Herod's will, Augustus made Philip the tetrarch over the northern part of Herod the Great's domain, which included GAULANITIS, Auranitis (HAURAN), Batanea (BASHAN), TRACONITIS, Paneas, and ITUREA (Jos. *Ant.* 17.8.1 §189; 17.9.4 §319; 18.4.6 §106; 18.5.4 §136; *War* 1.33.8 §668; 2.6.3 §95; Lk. 3:1). The make-up of his subjects was primarily non-Jewish; the Syrian and Greek element was predominant, and he was the first and only Herodian to have the images of the emperor on his coins.

Philip built two cities (Jos. *Ant.* 18.2.1 §28; *War* 2.9.1 §168). He rebuilt and enlarged Paneas/Banias, the city near the source of the Jordan. He renamed it CAESAREA PHILIPPI in honor of the Roman emperor (the addition of Philippi to the name served to distinguish it from the coastal Caesarea). It is here that Jesus received PETER's confession of faith and gave the revelation of the formation of the church (Matt. 16:13–20, Mk. 8:27–30). The second city Philip rebuilt was the fishing village of BETHSAIDA (where the Jordan flows into the Sea of Galilee), which he raised to the status of a Greek *polis*. He renamed the city Julias in honor of Augustus's daughter Julia. It is here that Jesus healed the blind man (Mk. 8:22–26); and it was a desert place near Bethsaida where the feeding of the 5,000 occurred (Lk. 9:10). It may very well be that the feeding of the 4,000 also occurred in the southern portion of Philip's territory.

Philip, not being so ambitious and scheming as his brothers, ruled his domain with moderation and tranquillity. He was well liked by his subjects (Jos. *Ant.* 18.4.6 §§106–8). He married Herodias's daughter Salome, whose dances had earlier led to the execution of John the Baptist. They had no children (Jos. *Ant.* 18.5.4 §137). After Philip died in A.D. 34, Tiberius annexed his tetrarchy to Syria. When Caligula became emperor in 37, he gave Philip's territory to Agrippa I, brother of Herodias. (See further *HJP*, rev. ed. [1973–1987], 1:336–40.)

VII. Agrippa I (A.D. 37–44). Agrippa was born in 10 B.C. to Aristobulus (son of Herod the Great and Mariamne) and Berenice (daughter of Herod's sister Salome and Costobarus, Jos. *War* 1.28.1 §552; *Ant.* 19.8.2 §350). He was the brother of Herodias. Agrippa went to school in Rome and lived a careless and extravagant life, especially after his mother's death. He soon ran out of money and accumulated debts. When Tiberius's son Drusus was poisoned by Sejanus in A.D. 23, Agrippa lost the support and favor of the court and had to retire quietly to Maltha, a fortress in Idumea, leaving many angry creditors behind him in Rome (Jos. *Ant.* 18.6.1–2 §§143–47; 18.6.4 §165). Being utterly depressed over his humiliation, he contemplated suicide, but his wife Cypros pleaded with his sister Herodias for help. Antipas gave him a home, a guaranteed income, and a small civil service position as inspector of markets in Antipas's new capital Tiberias. But the new position in life did not last long. Matters came to a head one evening at Tyre during a feast when Antipas reproached Agrippa for his poverty and debts. Agrippa left and went to L. Pomponius Flaccus, legate of Syria (c. A.D. 32/33), whom he had known intimately at Rome, but soon left for Rome after they had quarreled (c. 36). He repaid old debts by incurring new ones (Jos. *Ant.* 18.6.2–3 §§148–60).

In Rome, Agrippa made friends with Gaius Caligula but was imprisoned by Tiberius because of his unwise remark (overheard by a servant) that he wished Tiberius would relinquish his throne to Gaius, who was much more capable of ruling. He remained in prison until Tiberius's death six months later (Jos. *Ant.* 18.6.4–10 §§161–236; *War* 2.9.5 §§178–80; Dio Cassius, *Rom. Hist.* 59.8.2). When Caligula became emperor, he released Agrippa and gave him a chain of gold equal in weight to the chain he had worn in prison. He also conferred upon him the region of Philip the tetrarch and the more northerly tetrarchy of Lysanias and gave him the title of king (Jos. *Ant.* 18.6.10 §237; *War* 2.9.6 §181). The Senate also conferred upon him the honorary rank of praetor (Philo, *In Flaccum* 40) and subsequently gave him consular rank (Dio Cassius, *Rom. Hist.* 60.8.2).

In late summer of 38, Agrippa went to Palestine to see his land. As noted above, his political rise led to the downfall of Antipas. Agrippa's sister Herodias prodded her husband Antipas to ask for the title of king. Because of her insistence, Antipas finally in 39 went to Rome to ask for the new title. Upon hearing this, however, Agrippa dispatched one of his freedmen, Fortunatus, to Rome to bring charges against Antipas. Agrippa's move was successful and led to Antipas's banishment; subsequently Agrippa was given the tetrarchy and property of Antipas (Jos. *Ant.* 18.7.1–2 §§240–56; *War* 2.9.6 §§181–83). In the year 41 Agrippa happened to be in Rome when Caligula was murdered, and he was helpful in the accession of CLAUDIUS, a childhood friend, to the throne (Jos. *Ant.* 19.4.1–6 §§236–73; *War* 2.11.1–4 §§204–13; Dio Cassius, *Rom. Hist.* 65.8.2). Claudius confirmed Agrippa in his rule and added Judea and Samaria to his domains, which meant that he ruled over all the territory of his grandfather Herod the Great (Jos. *Ant.* 19.5.1 §§274–75; *War* 2.11.5 §§214–15).

Agrippa I is known in the NT for his persecution of the early church in order to curry favor

Bronze coin of King Herod of Chalcis (A.D. 41–48), showing him with his brother, King Agrippa of Judea, crowning the Emperor Claudius.

of the Jews (Acts 12:1–19). He killed JAMES, the son of Zebedee, and imprisoned PETER; the latter, however, was released by an angel, and Agrippa had the sentries put to death. Agrippa died in 44 in Caesarea. According to Josephus, on the second day of a festival he appeared in the theater with a robe made wholly of silver. When the robe sparkled in the sun, the people cried out flatteries, declaring him to be a god and entreating him to have mercy upon them. While the king allowed himself to be carried away with the flatteries, he noticed an owl on a rope, which was an omen that he would die very soon. Immediately he had severe stomach pains and was carried to his house and died five days later (Jos. *Ant.* 19.8.2 §§343–52).

Luke states that Agrippa was in Caesarea sitting on the judgment seat, dressed in royal robes and addressing ambassadors from Tyre and Sidon with whom he was displeased. While speaking, the people called out stating that it was the voice of a god and not man. Immediately an angel of the Lord smote him because he did not give God the glory; and he was eaten of worms, and died (Acts 12:20–23). It may well be that Agrippa went to the festival as mentioned by Josephus and that on the second day (12:21 says on an appointed day), dressed in royal apparel, he made the oration to the ambassadors of Tyre and Sidon. Also, it could be a period of five days from the time he was smitten by an angel of the Lord until he died. Hence the two narratives can be harmonized.

His survivors were three daughters, Berenice (see BERNICE), Mariamne, and Drusilla, and a son also named Agrippa who was seventeen years of age (Jos. *Ant.* 19.9.1 §§354–55; *War* 2.11.6 §§218–20). Because Agrippa II was a minor, Agrippa I's territories were reduced temporarily to a province. (See further *HJP*, rev. ed. [1973–1987], 1:442–54; O. W. Allen, Jr., *The Death of Herod: The Narrative and Theological Function of Retribution in Luke-Acts* [1997].)

VIII. Agrippa II (A.D. 50–100). Agrippa II was the son of Agrippa I and Cypros, daughter of Phasael (Herod the Great's nephew) and Salampsio (Herod the Great's daughter; Jos. *Ant.* 18.5.4 §§130–32). Upon the death of Agrippa I, Claudius wanted to make him king over his father's territories but was persuaded by two freedmen that a youth would not be able to hold sway over a large and much-harassed kingdom. Consequently Cuspius Fadus was appointed procurator of Palestine.

In A.D. 50, two years after the death of Agrippa II's uncle and brother-in-law Herod, king of Chalcis, Claudius made Agrippa II king of Chalcis (Jos. *Ant.* 20.5.2 §104; *War* 2.12.1 §223). In 53 Claudius granted Agrippa II the tetrarchy of Philip, ABILENE (or Abila), Traconitis, and Arca (the tetrarchy of Varus) in exchange for the territory of Chalcis (Jos. *Ant.* 20.7.1 §138; *War* 2.12.8 §247). NERO became emperor in 54 and shortly after his accession he gave Agrippa the Galilean cities of Tiberias and Tarichea with their surrounding land, as well as the Perean cities of Julias (or Betharamphtha) and Abila with their surrounding land (Jos. *Ant.* 20.8.4 §159; *War* 2.13.2 §252). In appreciation for the imperial favor, Agrippa enlarged his capital city Caesarea Philippi and renamed it Neronius (Jos. *Ant.* 20.9.4 §211). So Agrippa now ruled Philip's tetrarchy with the added toparchies of Galilee and the three detached territories of Abilene, Arca, and the two middle toparchies of Perea.

Agrippa II's private life was not exemplary. His sister Bernice had become a widow after her second husband (and uncle) Herod, king of Chalcis, died in A.D. 48. From that date she lived in her brother's house. In an attempt to quiet the rumors of incest she resolved to marry Polemo of Cilicia. But she did not continue long with him and returned to Agrippa. The apparently inappropriate relationship became the common talk of Rome (Jos. *Ant.* 20.7.3 §§145–47; Juvenal, *Satires* 6.156–60).

Like his uncle Herod, king of Chalcis, Agrippa II was in control of the temple treasury and the vestments of the high priest and consequently could appoint high priests (Jos. *Ant.* 20.5.2 §103; 20.9.4 §213; 20.9.7 §222). The Romans would consult him on religious matters, and this is probably why FESTUS asked him to hear PAUL at Caesarea (A.D. 59). Agrippa was accompanied by his sister Bernice (Acts 25–26).

In May of 66, the revolution in Palestine broke out (Jos. *War* 2.14.4 §284). Agrippa attempted to stop the revolt but was unable to do so, and all through the war of 66–70 he was unhesitatingly on the side of the Romans (see WARS, JEWISH). After Nero's suicide on 9 June 68, VESPASIAN sent his son TITUS, who was accompanied by Agrippa, to pay respects to the new Emperor Galba. On the way to Rome they received the news of Galba's murder (15 January 69) and Titus returned to Palestine while Agrippa continued to Rome. After Vespasian had been elected emperor (1 July 69) by the Egyptian and Syrian legions, Agrippa returned to Palestine to take the oath of allegiance to the new emperor (Tac. *Hist.* 2.81). Agrippa continued to be with Titus, who was in charge of the war (Tac. *Hist.* 5.1) and after the conquest of Jerusalem (5 Aug 70), Agrippa was probably present at the victory celebrations over the destruction of his people (Jos. *War* 2.1.2—2.3.1 §§5–40).

Vespasian confirmed Agrippa in the possession of the kingdom he had previously governed and added new territories. In the year 75 he and his sister Bernice went to Rome where she resumed being Titus's mistress (as she had been in Palestine), which became a public scandal (Tac. *Hist.* 2.2). Titus was forced to send her away; when he became emperor (Vespasian died on 23 June 79), she returned once more to Rome, but Titus left her unnoticed (Dio Cassius, *Rom. Hist.* 56.18) and so she went back to Palestine.

Nothing further is known of Agrippa or Bernice except that he corresponded with Josephus about the *Jewish War*, praising its accuracy, and subsequently purchased a copy (Jos. *Life* 65 §§361–67; *Apion* 1.9 §§47–52). Although some hold that Agrippa II's death was c. A.D. 93 (cf. *HJP*, rev. ed. [1973–1987], 1:481), it is more probable that it was c. 100. The TALMUD (*b. Sukkah* 27a) implies that Agrippa had two wives, but Josephus gives no indication of his being married or having any children. His death marked the end of the Herodian dynasty.

(In addition to the works mentioned in the body of the article, important treatments on the Herodian family as a whole include M. Brann in *Monatsschrift für Geschichte und Wissenschaft des Judenthums* 22 [1873]: 241–56, 305–21, 345–60, 407–20, 459–74, 497–507; F. W. Farrar, *The Herods* [1898]; W. Otto, *Herodes: Beiträge zur Geschichte des letzten jüdischen Königshauses* [1913]; F. Willrich, *Das Haus des Herodes* [1929]; A. H. M. Jones, *The Herods of Judaea* [1938]; S. Perowne, *The Later Herods* [1958]; F. O. Busch, *The Five Herods* [1958]; N. Kokkinos, *The Herodian Dynasty: Origins, Role in Society and Eclipse* [1998]; J. Wilker, *Für Rom und Jerusalem: Die herodianische Dynastie im 1. Jahrhundert n. Chr.* [2007].)

H. W. HOEHNER

Herodians hi-roh′dee-uhnz (Ἡρῳδιανοί *G2477*). A party, mentioned in the Gospels, who cooperated with the PHARISEES on two different occasions in opposition to Jesus (Mk. 3:6; 12:13 [= Matt. 22:16]). Composed of the name HEROD and a common suffix, the term designates partisans of Herod the Great or his dynasty. The Herodians are named only in Matthew and Mark. JOSEPHUS uses the term *Hērōdeiōn* (*War* 1.16.6) and elsewhere speaks of *tous ta Hērōdou phronountas*, (lit., "those who mind the things of Herod"), referring to those who were favorable to Herod the Great before he became master of the whole country (*Ant.* 15.15.6), but it is doubtful that the party alluded to by Josephus should be identified with the group mentioned in the NT.

Although the NT designation evidently refers to adherents of a Herod or of the Herodian dynasty, a more specific identification is a matter of conjecture, and varied suggestions concerning them have been made: soldiers of Herod; courtiers of Herod; Jews belonging to the northern tetrarchies ruled by sons of Herod; supporters of Jewish aspirations for a national kingdom who favored Herodian rule versus direct Roman rule; political supporters of Antipas. Of these, the last is most probable and receives wide support. F. C. Grant (in *IB*, 7:683) suggests that they were "members of the Herodian party, satellites of the tetrarch Antipas, royalists who hoped for a restoration of the Herodian monarchy." Unlike the Pharisees, they were not a religious party but rather a political group concerned with the interests of the Herodian dynasty. Theologically, their membership doubtless cut across recognized party lines. They may have had Sadducean proclivities, but the Gospels never suggest that the Herodians are to be equated with the SADDUCEES. That Matt. 16:6 substitutes "Saducees" for "Herod" in Mk. 8:15 (a few MSS read "Herodians") does not establish the identity; Matthew simply omits the reference to Herod or the Herodians and names another group.

The Herodians in the gospel accounts first appear in Galilee, where they joined with the Pharisees against Jesus to attempt to destroy him (Mk. 3:6;

cf. Matt. 12:14, which omits them). The politically minded Herodians would be interested with the ecclesiastical Pharisees in preserving the status quo. During PASSION week they joined with the Pharisees in seeking to trap Jesus on the question of paying tribute (Mk. 12:13; cf. Matt. 22:17). F. V. Filson (*A Commentary on the Gospel according to St. Matthew* [1960], 234) suggests that the Herodians as supporters of Antipas were "in Jerusalem to forestall the supposed revolutionary tendencies of Jesus"; however, they would naturally have been in Jerusalem for the Passover. (See further B. W. Bacon in *JBL* 39 [1920]: 102–12; E. J. Bickerman in *RB* 47 [1938]: 184–97; H. H. Rowley in *JTS* 41 [1940]: 14–27; W. Bennett in *NovT* 17 [1975]: 9–14; W. Braun in *RevQ* 14 [1989]:75–88.) D. E. HIEBERT

Herodias hi-roh′dee-uhs (Ἡρῳδιάς *G2478*). The wife of Herod Antipas who contrived the death of JOHN THE BAPTIST (Matt. 14:3–12; Mk. 6:17–29; Lk. 3:19–20). Herodias was the daughter of Aristobulus, son of Herod the Great; her brothers were Herod Agrippa I and Herod king of Chalcis. (See HEROD, esp. sections V and VII.)

Herodias's first husband was her uncle, called Philip (Matt. 14:3; Mk. 6:17), to be distinguished from the tetrarch Philip (Lk. 3:1). JOSEPHUS (*Ant.* 18.5.1) calls her first husband "Herod," Luke gives no name, and a few ancient witnesses (D and Lat. versions in Matt. 14:3) lack the name Philip; some scholars therefore hold this name is an error, a probable confusion with that of the tetrarch. But the name Philip is clearly original in Mark and most probably also in Matthew. The argument that two sons of Herod would not both be called Philip is weakened by the fact that two of his sons were called Herod (Jos. *Ant.* 18.1.3; 18.5.4). Herodias's husband was apparently named Herod Philip, just as Antipas could also be referred to as Herod Antipas.

Herodias and her husband, by whom she had a daughter named SALOME, lived in Rome; while a guest in their home, Antipas persuaded Herodias to marry him. Antipas divorced his first wife, a NABATEAN princess, to marry Herodias. Because John the Baptist publicly denounced Antipas for marrying his brother's wife, he was imprisoned at MACHAERUS. John's bold rebuke aroused the bitter hatred of the unscrupulous Herodias. She finally managed to secure John's death by instructing her daughter, the dancing girl, to demand of Antipas the head of John on a platter. The ambitious Herodias proved the downfall of her second husband. When her brother Agrippa I was given the tetrarchy of Philip with the title of "king," Herodias persuaded the tetrarch to solicit the title for himself. The emperor instead banished Antipas to Gaul. The proud Herodias followed her husband into exile. (See further F. M. Gillman, *Herodias: At Home in That Fox's Den* [2003].) D. E. HIEBERT

Herodion hi-roh′dee-uhn (Ἡρῳδίων *G2479*). A Christian at Rome to whom PAUL sent greetings (Rom. 16:11). The apostle refers to him as his *syngenēs G5150*, meaning that he was either Paul's blood-relative or, more likely, a fellow Jew. The name suggests that he may have been a freedman of the HEROD family and perhaps a member of the household of ARISTOBULUS (v. 10). See also HERODIUM. D. E. HIEBERT

Herodium hi-roh′dee-uhm (Ἡρῴδειον). Also Herodion. One of two fortress palaces built by HEROD the Great as memorials to himself. One was on the Idumean frontier, the exact site of which is not known. The other one has been identified as modern Jebel el Fureidis, c. 8 mi. S of JERUSALEM and less than 4 mi. SE of BETHLEHEM. It was built on a mountain that was artificially heightened and had a conical shape. It was one of a chain of palace-fortresses Herod erected to protect his kingdom—some others being Alexandrium, Hyrcania, MASADA,

Aerial view of the Herodium hill fortress (looking SW).

MACHAERUS, CAESAREA, JERICHO. In the year 40 B.C., Herod had defeated at this spot PARTHIANS and Jews, and he built the citadel in memory of the great victory he achieved there (Jos. *War* 1.13.8). It was begun about 24 B.C. and completed by 15 B.C.

According to JOSEPHUS, it was encompassed with circular towers, and 200 polished marble steps led to the summit, where rich royal apartments provided both for security and beauty. At the foot of the mountain were other palaces, buildings, pools, and terraces. An aqueduct brought an abundance of water, at a vast expense, from a great way off (Jos. *Ant.* 15.9.4; *War* 1.21.10). During the Roman period it was the chief town of a toparchy (*War* 3.3.5). The fortress played a role at the time of the war in A.D. 66–70 and was one of the last refuges for the rebels (*War* 4.9.5, 9). See WARS, JEWISH.

In 1962 excavations at Herodium were begun by the Italian archaeologist Vergilio Corbo. These revealed that the site was inhabited again in the 5th cent. by some Christians. They also showed the damage that was done by the Roman siege machines. Objects found were some Greek and Hebrew OSTRACA, arrow heads, plaster wall decorations, and a Roman bath system. DEAD SEA SCROLL materials reveal that BAR KOKHBA used Herodium's installations for collecting grain for his forces. Herod's tomb has as yet not been discovered at Herodium. (See C. F. Pfeiffer, *The Biblical World* [1966], 287–89; E. Netzer, *Greater Herodium* [1981], and his summary in *ABD*, 3:176–80; *NEAEHL*, 2:618–26.)   S. BARABAS

Herodotus hi-rah´du-tuhs (Ἡρόδοτος). Born early in the 5th cent. B.C. at HALICARNASSUS (on the W coast of ASIA MINOR), Herodotus lived to see the Persians take over Ionian Greece, was expelled from his home for political reasons, wandered through much of the ancient world, and finally settled as a colonist in Thurii in Italy where he died. He is commonly referred to as the "Father of History" and is best remembered for his *Histories*: nine books dealing with the provincial history of the Persian empire, the immediate causes of the Persian-Greek war, and the actual war itself. The underlying philosophy of his work is that pride draws down the wrath of the gods, which accounts for the fact that the Persians lost the war to the numerically inferior Greeks. Although his trustworthiness has at times been disputed, Herodotus is an indispensable source of information for the ANE at the end of the OT period. (See J. L. Myres, *Herodotus: Father of History* [1953]; J. Gould, *Herodotus* [1989]; J. A. S. Evans, *Herodotus: Explorer of the Past* [1991]; *OCD*, 696–98.)   W. A. ELWELL

heron. A wading bird of the family *Ardea*; it has a long neck and long legs as well as a pointed bill. The English word occurs in two lists of unclean birds (Lev. 11:19; Deut. 14:18) as a rendering of Hebrew ʾănāpâ H649, a term that has always been in dispute (philologists can only suggest that the root may describe a bird with a beak shaped like a nose, whereas *Targum Pseudo-Jonathan* treats it as a hawk). Some scholars believe it refers to the plover or to the cormorant, but it would not be surprising if herons were listed in these passages. A dozen species live in or pass through Palestine, some of them conspicuous and in numbers; several of them are palatable when young, but their habits might class them as unclean. The most common are the gray, purple, and night herons, and the little and cattle egrets. These may all be seen at close quarters in spring in the bird sanctuaries on the Israeli coast and in the upper Jordan valley. (See *FFB*, 41.) Some have thought that Hebrew ḥăsîdâ H2884 (Lev. 11:19 et al.) means "heron," but this term probably refers to the STORK.   G. S. CANSDALE

Heshbon hesh´bon (חֶשְׁבּוֹן H3114, perhaps "reckoning, account"). A city in TRANSJORDAN, c. 15 mi. ENE of the N tip of the DEAD SEA and less than 4 mi. NE of Mount NEBO. Originally part of MOAB, it was captured by the AMORITE king SIHON, who made it his capital. Heshbon was then taken from Sihon by the Israelites under MOSES on their way to Canaan (Num. 21:25–30; Deut. 1:4; 2:24–30; et al.; see Y. Aharoni, *The Land of the Bible: A Historical Geography*, rev. ed. [1979], 200–209). It was located within the tribal territory of REUBEN on its border with GAD, and the Reubenites rebuilt it after the conquest of Canaan (Num. 32:3, 37). Apparently absorbed by the Gadites, Heshbon was then assigned to the Levites descended from MERARI (Josh. 21:39; 1 Chr. 6:81). The town subsequently must have fallen again into the hands of the

Moabites, for the prophets repeatedly mention it in their denunciations of Moab (Isa. 15:4; 16:8–9; Jer. 48:2, 34, 45; 49:3; cf. also the references to nearby MEDEBA in the MOABITE STONE, *ANET*, 320–21). In later days the HASMONEANS and HEROD the Great controlled it (Jos. *Ant.* 13.15.4; 15.8.5).

The name Heshbon is apparently preserved in the modern city of Hesban in Jordan, some 12 mi. SW of Amman. Ruins of the city, which come chiefly from the Roman period, lie on the summit of a hill and are about a mile in circuit. Nearby there is a large ruined reservoir, which may be the "pools of Heshbon" mentioned in the Song of Solomon (Cant. 7:4). Archaeological evidence, however, has led some scholars to believe that the OT site itself may be in nearby Jalul. (See R. D. Ibach, Jr., *Archaeological Survey of the Hesban Region* [1987]; A. J. Ferch et al., *Historical Foundations: Studies of Literary References to Hesban and Vicinity* [1989]; L. T. Geraty in *ABD*, 3:181–84; *NEAEHL*, 2:626–30.)   S. BARABAS

Heshmon hesh′mon (חֶשְׁמוֹן *H3132*, possibly "smooth field"). A town in the NEGEV, the extreme S of the tribal territory of JUDAH (Josh. 15:27). It was apparently near BETH PELET, but its precise location is unknown. Heshmon may have been the original home of the HASMONEANS (Jos. *Ant.* 12.6.1).

heth hayth (חֵית). Also *het* and *cheth*. The eighth letter of the Hebrew ALPHABET (ח), with a numerical value of eight. Although in modern Hebrew it is pronounced as a velar fricative ($ḫ$, consisting of a vibration of the uvula), in biblical times it was probably a pharyngeal sound ($ḥ$, a constriction of the throat muscles). These two sounds were distinct phonemes in proto-Semitic (and are preserved as such in Arabic), but they merged in Hebrew and other Semitic languages.   F. W. BUSH

Heth heth (חֵת *H3147*). Son of CANAAN, grandson of HAM, and eponymous ancestor of the HITTITES. The Hebrew form is rendered "Heth" by the KJV in all its occurrences (Gen. 10:15; 23:3–20; 25:10; 27:46; 49:32; 1 Chr. 1:13). The NRSV has the name "Heth" only in the Table of Nations (Gen. 10:15; 1 Chr. 1:13); elsewhere it renders the name as "Hittite(s)." The NIV uses "Hittite(s)" throughout. See NATIONS II.A.

Hethlon heth′lon (חֶתְלֹן *H3158*, derivation uncertain). In EZEKIEL's vision, Hethlon is one of the places marking the ideal N boundary of Israel; a road passing by it leads from the Mediterranean to LEBO HAMATH (Ezek. 47:15; 48:1). The site is unknown, though some places on the Lebanese coast have been proposed, including modern Heitela, NE of Tripoli.

hewer. This English term is used by the KJV and other translations to render the participle of Hebrew *ḥāṭab H2634*, "to cut or gather [wood]" (cf. also *ḥāṣēb H2933* and derivatives). The expression "hewers of wood" (NIV, "woodcutters") was apparently a special social classification; it was imposed on the Gibeonites, residents of four towns in the area of Jerusalem because they had tricked JOSHUA into a treaty (Josh. 9:21, 23, 27; see GIBEON). This status, which is better defined as forced labor, was not quite as degrading as slavery, but still very low on the social ladder. The Hebrews despised forced labor, as is later evidenced during the reign of SOLOMON. JOSHUA also delegated the Gibeonites to be "drawers of water" (Josh. 9:27 [NIV, "water carriers"]; cf. Deut. 29:11), which would fit with their low class status. Some of them became the later temple slaves. Not all woodcutters or woodsmen are included in this social status, for social levels change frequently in a society. Those referred to in 2 Chr. 2:10 and Jer. 46:22 are important segments of the society. With the increased construction during the united monarchy, a carpenter or craftsman would be in great demand.   G. GIACUMAKIS, JR.

Hexapla hek′suh pluh. The name (from Gk. *hex G1971*, "six") given to a six-column work produced by ORIGEN. For most of the OT, it included the Hebrew text (both in Hebrew characters and in Greek transliteration), followed by four Greek translations (Aquila, Symmachus, the LXX, and Theodotion). See SEPTUAGINT V.A.

Hexateuch hek′suh-tyook. This term (from Gk. *hex*, "six," and *teuchos*, "book") is used by some scholars as a designation for the first six books of the Bible (cf. PENTATEUCH, "five books"; TETRATEUCH, "four books"). It derives from the theory that the original compilation of books pertaining to the early background and establishment of the commonwealth of Israel included the book of Joshua, rather than Deuteronomy, as its last component, a view apparently first set forth by Alexander Geddes in 1792 (cf. E. J. Young, *Introduction to the Old Testament* [1959], 133). He felt convinced that Joshua was compiled by the same author as the preceding five books, and that it constituted "a necessary appendix to the history contained in the former books." See DEUTERONOMY; JOSHUA, BOOK OF.

This position was more fully elaborated by Friedrich Bleek in his *De libri Geneseos origine* (1836), in which he argued that after the first redaction of the "Mosaic" books in the 10th cent. B.C., a second redaction was carried through by the compiler of Deuteronomy in the late 7th cent., and this included Joshua as well. Heinrich Ewald (in his *History of the People of Israel* [1840–1845]) regarded the Hexateuch as the product of five redactions or stages of crystallization, the final stage being about 600 B.C. (he later brought the final compilation of Deuteronomy down to 500).

After enjoying great favor for a century or more, the concept of a Hexateuch began to fall out of vogue in critical scholarship. D. N. Freedman (*IDB*, 2:597) remarks: "In recent scholarship the Hexateuchal reconstruction has come under suspicion, and the Hexateuch itself has disintegrated. It is by no means certain that the sources in Joshua are the same as those in the Pentateuch. Prominent scholars have argued that J and E are not to be found in Joshua, but end substantially in the book of Numbers; that the lists in Joshua may be P-type material, but not necessarily P; and finally that Joshua in its present form is part of the great Deuteronomic history extending from Deuteronomy through 2 Kings, and does not therefore belong to a Pentateuchal complex." Thus the position of Ivan Engnell (*Old Testament Introduction* [1945]) has come to the forefront, and the present trend is to understand Genesis through Numbers as a P (priestly) complex, and Deuteronomy through 2 Kings as a D (Deuteronomistic) complex. See DEUTERONOMISTIC HISTORY.

It was only natural for adherents of the Documentary Hypothesis, who dated the earliest portions of the Pentateuch (Document J) in the 9th cent., to feel that the successful climax of the Hebrew migration from Egypt to Canaan must have been included in the Israelite tradition by that time. Yet there are absolutely compelling considerations that render the Hexateuch theory logically untenable. Foremost is the undeniable fact that the SAMARITAN PENTATEUCH, which regarded the Pentateuch as canonical, did not include Joshua with it. This is all the more significant because the SAMARITANS above all others had every reason to exalt Joshua to canonical status. It is apparent from the propagandistic insertions into the Samaritan text of the Torah that they were most concerned to prove that Mount GERIZIM, rather than Mount ZION, was the holy mountain of the Lord, and that leadership of Israel belonged to the tribe of EPHRAIM rather than to JUDAH.

Unquestionably there is much in Joshua to commend itself to Samaritan nationalism, for Joshua himself was an Ephraimite hero, and he summoned the twelve tribes to meet with him in SHECHEM, under the brow of Mount Gerizim. Furthermore, in this book is recorded the setting up of inscribed stelae containing the law of Moses in conformity to Joshua's command (Josh. 8:32), after which the solemn reading of the Torah with all its blessings and curses took place in the presence of the twelve tribes upon the slopes of Gerizim and EBAL. Despite all of these incentives to include Joshua with the Pentateuch as authoritative and canonical, the Samaritans never did so. There can be only one reason for this: at the time of the Samaritan schism it was so widely and universally known that the Pentateuch constituted a unity by itself that it was impossible to add Joshua to it, however advantageous it would have been for them to do so.

A second difficulty for the Hexateuchal theory is found in the consideration that Joshua does not purport to have been composed or compiled by Moses himself; hence it could not have been regarded as part of his legacy to the nation. Therefore, no matter how profoundly influenced in viewpoint, ideals and language the book of Joshua may have been by the Pentateuch, this must be understood as a natural consequence ensuing from Joshua's status as the successor and spiritual heir of Moses. Joshua is not at all presented as a God-inspired legislator;

he is only an executive who carries out in action the principles of the law. The book of Joshua, therefore, is not to be regarded as an integral part of the Torah. — G. L. ARCHER

Hezeki hez´uh-k*i*. KJV form of HIZKI.

Hezekiah hez´uh-ki´uh (חִזְקִיָּהוּ H2625, חִזְקִיָּה H2624 [mainly 2 Ki. 18], יְחִזְקִיָּהוּ H3491 [mainly 2 Chr. 28–33], יְחִזְקִיָּה H3490 [only Ezra 2:16; Hos. 1:1; Mic. 1:1], "Yahweh has strengthened me" or "Yahweh is my strength" [see HIZKI and HIZKIAH, cf. EZEKIEL, JEHEZKEL, JEHEZKIAH]; Ἐζεκίας G1614). Several men in the Bible are known by this name. **(1)** An ancestor of the prophet ZEPHANIAH (Zeph. 1:1 [KJV, "Hizkiah"]); possibly the same as #5, below. **(2)** The head of a family that returned from the EXILE (Ezra 2:16; Neh. 7:21; 10:17 [KJV, "Hizkijah"]; 1 Esd. 5:15; see ATER). **(3)** One of the men who stood beside EZRA when he read the law to the people (1 Esd. 9:43, called HILKIAH in Neh. 8:4). **(4)** Son of Neariah and postexilic descendant of DAVID (1 Chr. 3:23 KJV; see HIZKIAH). **(5)** Son of AHAZ, descendant of David, and king of Judah; three accounts are given of his reign (2 Ki. 18:1—20:21; 2 Chr. 29:1—32:33; Isa. 36:1—39:8). The rest of this article deals only with King Hezekiah.

    I. Chronology
    II. Historical background
    III. Hezekiah's policies
    IV. The Assyrian threat

I. Chronology. The twenty-nine-year reign of Hezekiah is best dated in the three decades 716/15 to 687/86 B.C. The extensive research on the chronology of this period by E. R. Thiele (*The Mysterious Numbers of the Hebrew Kings*, 3rd ed. [1983], ch. 9) reflects some difficulties in interpreting the dating systems during OT times and awaits further analysis. By adopting the above dates for Hezekiah, the interpretation of the biblical data and its synchronization with the chronologies of Syria, Assyria, Babylon, and Egypt seem to offer the best solution to the difficulties in the light of present knowledge. Based on this chronology, some of the important events during the lifetime of Hezekiah can be dated as follows:

740—Birth of Hezekiah
736—Ahaz begins coregency with Jotham
732—Damascus capitulates to Assyria
    —Jotham dies
    —Hoshea replaces Pekah in Samaria
727—Shalmaneser V becomes king of Assyria
723—Samaria conquered by Assyria
722—Sargon becomes king of Assyria
716/15—Ahaz dies, Hezekiah becomes king
711—Ashdod conquered by Sargon II
705—Sennacherib becomes king of Assyria
701—Hezekiah's sickness, fifteen-year extension
    —Deliverance from Assyrian pressure
    —Merodach-Baladan congratulates Hezekiah
697—Manasseh made coregent with Hezekiah
689—Babylon destroyed by Sennacherib
688—Sennacherib fails in his second threat to conquer Jerusalem

---

II. Historical background. The reign of Hezekiah can be understood better in the light of the international pressure that the Assyrian kings brought to bear upon the nation of Judah during his life (see ASSYRIA). Judah emerged as the strongest power in the heart of Palestine under UZZIAH (Azariah) during the decade from 750 to 740 B.C. Israel had enjoyed its greatest peak of economic and political prosperity under JEROBOAM II, who died in 753.

During the following three decades, revolutions and dynastic changes occurred repeatedly until SAMARIA capitulated to the Assyrians in 723 B.C. The aggressive westward move of TIGLATH-PILESER, who ruled Assyria from 745 to 727, was temporarily halted (c. 743) by a coalition in northern Syria in which Uzziah, king of Judah, participated in a battle at ARPAD. Since MENAHEM, the king of Israel, paid tribute to Tiglath-Pileser, the Assyrians did not advance southward so that Uzziah was able to maintain an anti-Assyrian policy. JOTHAM continued this policy but likely was replaced by AHAZ because the latter adopted a pro-Assyrian policy in 736/35. At the same time, PEKAH in Samaria and

Rezin in Damascus formed an alliance to resist Assyrian aggression. Ahaz triumphed in his Assyrian alliance even when the two kings of the N temporarily invaded Judah. The political involvement of Ahaz, who met the Assyrian king in Damascus when Rezin and Pekah were both dethroned, brought idolatry and paganism into the temple where God alone was to be worshiped.

By 723 B.C. Shalmaneser V had invaded Israel and conquered Samaria. Sargon II (722–705) advanced southward along the Mediterranean coast conquering Ashdod in 711. When Sennacherib came to the Assyrian throne in 705, he began the conquest of numerous cities on the coastal plain, boasting that he subjected forty-six walled cities. Although he threatened Hezekiah repeatedly, he never succeeded in conquering Jerusalem. In 701, Sennacherib's plans were abruptly terminated when he had to return to suppress a Babylonian rebellion. After destroying Babylon in 689, he may have made another attempt to suppress Hezekiah. Sennacherib never claims in his records to have conquered Jerusalem. In 681, Sennacherib was killed by two of his sons and succeeded by another son named Esarhaddon.

III. Hezekiah's policies. Religiously and politically, Hezekiah faced a kingdom in need of extensive reforms. Under Ahaz, who had defied the warnings and advice by Isaiah, idolatry had been promoted to an unprecedented degree through his alliance with Assyria. Hezekiah was not interested in currying the favor of the Assyrian kings either politically or religiously.

The Siloam Inscription, discovered in the tunnel built during the reign of Hezekiah. It describes the completion of the project, when the hewers could hear the workers on the other side.

Hezekiah reacted drastically to the idolatrous conditions that prevailed in Judah and Jerusalem. Being keenly aware that the Israelites were God's covenant people, he provided leadership as king in initiating a reform program to honor God in accordance with the Mosaic revelation. The temple in Jerusalem was reopened. The Levites were given the responsibility for repairing and renovating it so that God could again be properly worshiped. All the things associated with idolatry were removed to the brook Kidron, whereas the vessels that had been desecrated were sanctified for the temple to be used by the priests and Levites in their ministries. The initiation of sacrifices was accompanied by musical groups employing harps, cymbals, and lyres as had been the custom in the time of David. Burnt offerings were accompanied by liturgical singing in which psalms of David and Asaph were used by the participants.

With Israel having been reduced to the status of an Assyrian province, Hezekiah took advantage of the opportunity to invite the Israelites from the northern tribes to join in the celebration of the Passover in Jerusalem. Many responded to Hezekiah's invitation. Except for observing the Passover a month late to allow adequate time for preparation, the religious leaders under Hezekiah carefully followed the Mosaic instructions. The joyfulness of the celebration of this Passover had been previously exceeded only at the time when the temple had been dedicated under Solomon.

Throughout Judah, Benjamin, Ephraim, and Manasseh there were signs of religious reformation in the destruction of idols. Pillars, Asherim (see Asherah), high places, and altars were demolished throughout the land. Hezekiah himself exemplified his concern by destroying the bronze serpent Moses had erected in the wilderness (Num. 21:4–9), so that the people could no longer use it as an object of worship (see Nehushtan). Like David, Hezekiah provided leadership in organizing the priests and Levites for the regular religious services. The tithe was reinstituted and allotted to the religious leaders who devoted themselves to the service of God in accordance with the law. So generous were the contributions that all the priests and Levites had sufficient support to engage in their religious responsibilities. Plans were made to observe the feasts and seasons regularly according to the order prescribed in the law of Moses. As a whole, the religious reformation under Hezekiah was a decided success.

From the political and military perspective, Hezekiah provided equally strong leadership to Judah. When Sargon II advanced into the PHILISTINE area and captured Ashdod, international tension developed. ISAIAH dramatically warned Hezekiah and his people not to interfere with the Ashdod siege lest Jerusalem become directly involved and attacked by the Assyrians (Isa. 20:1–6). During this time, Hezekiah made extensive preparation in anticipation of Assyrian aggression. As part of his defense program he built fortifications around Jerusalem, stimulated craftsmen in the production of shields and weapons, and organized his fighting forces under combat commanders.

Realizing the importance of an adequate water supply, Hezekiah constructed a tunnel extending 1,777 ft. through solid rock from the GIHON SPRING to the SILOAM pool. The city wall was extended to enclose this vital source of water. In the area surrounding Jerusalem other sources of water were cut off as far as possible, so that the invading Assyrians would not be able to utilize them to their own advantage.

Having led his people in extensive religious and military reforms to prepare them for the impending threat of the Assyrians, Hezekiah exemplified before the nation an attitude of confidence in God. Boldly he assured them that God would sustain them to withstand the enemy who was dependent on "the arm of flesh" (2 Chr. 32:1–8).

IV The Assyrian threat. The scriptural accounts of the relationships between Judah and Assyria during the Hezekiah-Sennacherib era, the extension of Hezekiah's life, and Judah's contacts with Babylon are quite extensive and detailed, but they are not necessarily in chronological order. Exact time sequence is often omitted. Although a number of problems await solution, it seems probable that the biblical and secular accounts can be reasonably integrated by allowing for the sequence of developments in the following order.

In 705 B.C., Sennacherib faced numerous rebellions when he succeeded Sargon as king of Assyria. Babylon rebelled under MERODACH-BALADAN, who by 702 abandoned his throne to Bel-ibni. Nationalism surged in Egypt under Shabako, an Ethiopian king who founded the 25th dynasty (c. 710). Having forced Merodach-Baladan into exile, Sennacherib turned westward to subdue PHOENICIA and other coastal resistance centers, advancing to the maritime plain W of Jerusalem. By 701, he boasted about conquering forty-six walled cities and taking 200,000 captives.

From Hezekiah he exacted a heavy tribute in silver and gold and then sent representatives to Jerusalem to intimidate the king and his people (2 Ki. 18:13—19:8; Isa. 36:1—37:8). Speaking in the Hebrew language, the Assyrians warned the people that their God would not give them any more aid than the heathen gods had aided other cities in their futile resistance against Assyrian might. Hezekiah reacted in great distress, went to the temple dressed in sackcloth, and sent word to Isaiah. The latter predicted that Sennacherib would hear a rumor and suddenly return to his own land where he would die by the sword (2 Ki. 19:7). Shortly after this, Sennacherib received word that Babylon was in rebellion. Immediately he abandoned his siege of LACHISH and departed without conquering Jerusalem. In his records he merely boasts about shutting up Hezekiah like a bird in a cage.

With the Assyrian exit from Palestine, the surrounding cities and nations expressed their congratulations to Hezekiah with abundant gifts (2 Chr. 32:23). These gifts, plus the resumption of trade, ushered in a period of economic prosperity such as Judah had not enjoyed for some time.

Very likely it was in 701 B.C. that Hezekiah was seriously ill. Although warned by Isaiah to prepare for death, Hezekiah's prayer was answered in the extension of his life for a fifteen-year period as well as the promise of deliverance from the Assyrians (Isa. 38:4–6; 2 Ki. 20:1–11). The congratulations of Merodach-Baladan may have been a recognition of Hezekiah's physical recovery as well as his successful resistance to the king of Assyria. The triumph of Hezekiah's personal and national recovery was only tempered by Isaiah's prediction that subsequent to his reign Judah would be subjected to Babylonian captivity.

After a decade or more of repeated rebellions, Sennacherib destroyed Babylon in 689 B.C.

Hearing of the advance of Tirhakah, king of Ethiopia, Sennacherib may have attempted to march across the Arabian desert toward Egypt the following year. This time he sent a letter to Hezekiah (2 Ki. 19:9–34; Isa. 37:9–36). To this threat Hezekiah responded very calmly, spreading this letter out before the Lord in the temple and praying in confidence that God would deliver. From Isaiah came the message that the king of Assyria would return the way he came. Subsequently the army of Sennacherib was decimated in a miraculous manner by 185,000 men (2 Ki. 19:35–37). Probably Sennacherib returned across the desert, abandoning his hopes to conquer Hezekiah and Tirhakah. In 681, he was killed by two of his sons as had been predicted by Isaiah twenty years earlier.

Hezekiah died in 686 B.C., having enjoyed the fifteen-year extension of his life in peace and prosperity. He was succeeded by Manasseh his son, who probably had become coregent in 696. (See further J. Finegan, *Light from the Ancient Past* [1946], 170–82; W. F. Albright in *BASOR* 130 [April 1953]: 4–11; S. J. Schultz, *The Old Testament Speaks*, 4th ed. [1990], 209–15, 301–2, 311–14; I. W. Provan, *Hezekiah and the Books of Kings* [1988]; D. Bostock, *A Portrayal of Trust: The Theme of Faith in the Hezekiah Narratives* [2006]; *SacBr*, 239–45.)

S. J. Schultz

Hezion hee′zee-uhn (חֶזְיוֹן *H2611*, possibly "vision" or "lop-eared"). Father of Tabrimmon and grandfather of the Aramean king, Ben-Hadad (1 Ki. 15:18). He may be the same as Rezon (1 Ki. 11:23).

Hezir hee′zuhr (חֵזִיר *H2615*, "boar"). (1) A descendant of Aaron whose family in the time of David made up the eighteenth division of priests (1 Chr. 24:15).

(2) A leader of the people who signed the covenant of Nehemiah (Neh. 10:20).

Hezrai hez′ri. KJV form of Hezro (2 Sam. 23:35).

Hezro hez′roh (חֶצְרוֹ *H2968*, derivation uncertain). A Carmelite included in the list of David's mighty warriors (2 Sam. 23:35 [KJV, "Hezrai," following many Heb. mss]; 1 Chr. 11:37). On the tenuous grounds that Hezron was from the city of Carmel, some have speculated that he may have been a servant of Nabal who fled from his master to join David.

Hezron (person) hez′ruhn (חֶצְרוֹן *H2969*, derivation uncertain; gentilic חֶצְרוֹנִי *H2971*, "Hezronite"; Ἑσρώμ *G2272*). (1) Son of Reuben, grandson of Jacob, and eponymous ancestor of the Hezronite clan within the tribe of Reuben (Gen. 46:9; Exod. 6:14; Num. 26:6; 1 Chr. 5:3). Some scholars argue that the Reubenites were assimilated into the tribe of Judah and that these Hezronites became a Judahite clan; see #2 below.

(2) Son of Perez and grandson of Judah; father of Jerahmeel, Ram, Caleb (Kelubai), and Segub (the latter by the daughter of Makir, a Manassite, whom Hezron married at sixty); eponymous ancestor of the Hezronite clan within the tribe of Judah; and ancestor of David (Gen. 46:12; Num. 26:21; Ruth 4:18–19; 1 Chr. 2:5, 9, 18, 21, 24–25; 4:1). Hezron is included in the genealogy of Jesus Christ (Matt. 1:3; Lk. 3:33). A few textual problems in 1 Chr. 2 make it difficult to reconstruct certain details regarding Hezron's family; for example, see Abijah #3.

Hezron (place) hez′ruhn (חֶצְרוֹן *H2970*, possibly "enclosure, settlement"). A town on the S border of the tribe of Judah (Josh. 15:3). Hezron was apparently somewhere between Kadesh Barnea and Addar, but the precise location is unknown. Regarding the parallel passage (Num. 34:4), see the discussion under Hazar Addar. The town of Hezron is to be distinguished from Kerioth Hezron (Josh. 15:25), which was also in the S of Judah.

S. Barabas

Hiddai hid′i (הִדַּי *H2068*, possibly "splendor [of God]"). An Ephraimite from the ravines of Gaash, included in the list of David's mighty warriors (2 Sam. 23:30; called "Hurai" in the parallel, 1 Chr. 11:32, probably a scribal error).

Hiddekel hid′uh-kel (חִדֶּקֶל *H2538*, from Sumer. *Idigna*; cf. Akk. *Idiqlat* and Old Pers. *Tigrā*). The KJV rendering of the Hebrew name for the river Tigris (Gen. 2:14; Dan. 10:4).

Hiel hi'uhl (חִיאֵל *H2647*, possibly "brother of God" or "God lives [here]"). A man of BETHEL who in the days of King AHAB rebuilt the city of JERICHO, and the loss of whose sons, ABIRAM and SEGUB, was interpreted as the fulfillment of a curse pronounced by JOSHUA upon anyone who might rebuild the city (1 Ki. 16:34; cf. Josh. 6:26). It is uncertain whether Hiel sacrificed his sons or whether they died a natural death.   S. BARABAS

Hierapolis hi'uh-rap'uh-lis (Ἱεράπολις *G2631*, "sacred city"). A city in the Lycus Valley, part of the region of PHRYGIA in W ASIA MINOR (its only NT mention is Col. 4:13). A good contour map of Asia Minor will reveal the importance of the Lycus Valley in the communications system of the peninsula. The chief trade route from the AEGEAN to the EUPHRATES and SYRIA ran due E from EPHESUS, SMYRNA, and MILETUS, up the valley of the Maeander. The central plateau of Asia Minor had to be surmounted, and the best approach to the high country, which topped 8,500 ft., was manifestly by the gentler gradients of the river valleys. The highway ran due E until it reached the so-called Gates of Phrygia. Beyond this point, where Phrygia and CARIA met, the Maeander Valley became difficult to negotiate and the road followed the Lycus Valley, which continued its easterly direction for some distance before bending in a more northerly direction and ascending the western slopes of the plateau. It was obvious that a highway so important would attract commerce and the population that commerce and trade foster.

The three cities of the Lycus Valley are mentioned in the NT: the rich and self-conscious LAODICEA, COLOSSE, to whose church Paul wrote an important letter; and Hierapolis. The city of Hierapolis lay across the river from Laodicea, distant 6–7 mi., a subsidiary town of the great markets and banking center, a spa of importance, and perhaps a residential area. It occupied a conspicuous position on an elevated ledge of the hills with gleaming white cliffs below. The surviving ruins demonstrate what an unusual building site Hierapolis was.

The name of the city undoubtedly derived from the hot springs located there, a phenomenon always associated with the presence of a deity. Those familiar with any area of thermal activity—e.g., the Yosemite district, or preeminently the Rotorua district in New Zealand—will be familiar with the features that marked the topography of Hierapolis: the glazed terraces, the whitened banks covered with the chemical deposits of the heavily laden waters, even the Plutonium, as the vent of mephitic gas was called (the Karapiti Blowhole at

Aerial view of the theater in Hierapolis and the Lycus Valley. (View to the N.)

Wairakei in New Zealand is just such a volcanic phenomenon). The people of Laodicea were no doubt very familiar with the features of thermal activity in nearby Hierapolis. Two matters in the imagery of the apocalyptic letter to that church (Rev. 3:14–20) are based upon it. Highly emulsified and chemically charged mud is a mark of hot springs and probably formed a constituent of the salve for which the valley was known, and which provides the writer with an ironic point (see EYE-SALVE). Water "neither hot nor cold" and emetic in its quality must also have been a feature of the place (New Zealand has a similar nauseating warm soda spring near Lake Rotorua).

The church of Hierapolis was probably founded during PAUL's Ephesian ministry by that process of diffusion down the main roads that was a principle of his strategy. EPAPHRAS (Col. 4:12–13) may have been active there. Polycrates, bishop of Ephesus at the end of the 2nd cent., quotes a tradition that PHILIP ministered in this church. Also, JOHN THE APOSTLE probably served there.

In secular history, Hierapolis was the birthplace of EPICTETUS the STOIC. There was, according to inscriptions, a Jewish community. The Jews of Hierapolis appear to have been organized in trade guilds, of which those of the purple dyers and carpet makers are known. The city recognized these organizations, and also the "congregation of the Jews," which had its public headquarters and the power to prosecute for religious offenses—privileges that dated from a royal foundation by a Hellenistic king (if the word *katoikia* G3000, used in this connection, has its common significance of "colony"). The feasts of Unleavened Bread and Pentecost are mentioned in inscriptions. The information is of interest because the close neighborhood of Laodicea makes it likely that the position of Jews in Hierapolis indicates what their standing was in the larger center. (See further A. H. M. Jones, *The Cities of the Eastern Roman Provinces*, 2nd ed. [1971], 73–75; G. E. Bean, *Turkey Beyond the Maeander*, 2nd ed. [1980], ch. 20; E. Yamauchi, *The Archaeology of New Testament Cities in Western Asia Minor* [1900], ch. 11.)

E. M. BLAIKLOCK

Hiereel hi-ihr´ee-uhl. KJV Apoc. form of JEHIEL (1 Esd. 9:21).

Hieremoth hi-ihr´uh-moth. KJV Apoc. form of JEREMOTH (1 Esd. 9:27, 30).

Hierielus hi-ihr´i-ee´luhs. KJV Apoc. form of JEHIEL (1 Esd. 9:27).

Hiermas hi-uhr´muhs. KJV Apoc. form of RAMIAH (1 Esd. 9:25).

hieroglyphics. See WRITING.

Hieronymus hi´uh-ron´uh-muhs (Ἱερώνυμος, "of hallowed name"). A district governor in Palestine under ANTIOCHUS V who, with his fellow governors, harassed the Jews (2 Macc. 12:2).

Higgaion hi-gay´yon (הִגָּיוֹן H2053). A musical term of uncertain meaning, used in conjunction with *Selah* (Ps. 9:16). The Hebrew word is used three other times, once with the meaning "melody, sounding, playing" (Ps. 92:3; elsewhere "meditation, planning," Ps. 19:14, and "murmur, talk," Lam. 3:62). See MUSIC VI.D.

high (higher) gate. See UPPER GATE.

high place. The usual English rendering of Hebrew *bāmâ* H1196 (Lev. 26:30 and frequently in cultic contexts), a term that otherwise means "back" (like Ugar. *bmt* [C. H. Gordon, *Ugaritic Manual* [1955], §19.332]; cf. Deut. 33:29 NRSV) or "ridge, height" (like Akk. *bāmtu*; cf. Num. 21:28 et al.). A high place, as the term indicates, was usually an elevated geographic site (one "goes up" or "comes down" from it, 1 Sam. 9:13, 25). In the OT, the term takes on the specialized meaning of a place of WORSHIP ordinarily situated on a hill or mountain and commonly associated with false religions. Such sanctuaries could however be found at city gates (cf. 2 Ki. 23:8), which have no apparent connection with an elevated area; and some "high places" were located even in valleys (Jer. 7:31; 19:5–6; 32:35). Other Hebrew terms of comparable meaning can also be used in a cultic sense (e.g., *gaḥ* H1461, "mound," and *rāmâ* H8229, "height," in Ezek. 16:24–25, 31, 39; note also *šěpî* H9155, "barren height," Num. 23:3–4; Jer. 3:21–23; 7:29).

The selection of an elevated spot seems psychological, for this location put the worshiper above his immediate environment with its mundane associations and placed him nearer the skies, where the ultimate object of worship was believed to reside. In the plains of ancient MESOPOTAMIA, the feeling for a height for religious observances led to the construction of the staged or terraced temple tower, or ZIGGURAT. A requirement for the high place was an ALTAR, often simply made of unhewn stones, on which animal sacrifices could be slain and then offered by fire. Related to the high place was a tree or pole of wood that served as an idol or as an adjunct to worship (cf. ASHERAH). In Muslim areas, a *weli* (shrine) of a departed sheikh typically has nearby a tree to which the faithful may attach items that will bring the needs of the worshiper to the attention of the spiritual benefactor.

Frequently the high place had a stone symbol, a kind of obelisk or pillar (Heb. *maṣṣēbâ* H5167, Exod. 23:24 et al.) that also was an object of veneration or a commemorative monument. The high place could also contain images of heathen gods placed in a shrine (cf. 2 Ki. 17:29). Sometimes the high place had a basin or tank where water could be kept for ablutions or libations. In addition to violating the greatest commandment, the IDOLATRY of the high place involved the breaking of other divine laws, for the worship of certain deities demanded human sacrifice (usually of infants or children) and the celebration of rites of a sexual nature, whether religious PROSTITUTION or homosexual acts.

Several examples of these high places are known from archaeological evidence. A large oval platform measuring 8 × 10 yards and standing 6 yards high has been found at MEGIDDO. A flight of steps led up to the platform and sacrifices were obviously offered upon this shrine, which was built in the middle of the 3rd millennium B.C. Similar examples are known from Hazar (13th cent. B.C.), Nahariyah near Haifa (18th or 17th cent. B.C.), and at Malhah, SE of Jerusalem (7th–6th cent. B.C.). Among the best known examples of actual high places visible today are those of GEZER and PETRA (see R. A. S. Macalister, *The Excavation of Gezer* [1912], 2:281–411).

The Canaanites used the high places long before the Israelite conquest of the land, but the first mention of such a shrine in the Bible appears in connection with that event. The children of Israel were commanded to demolish the high places of the Canaanites, along with the idols of those people (Num. 33:52). At the same time the Lord warned the Israelites that if they disobeyed his laws he would punish them and destroy their high places and false worship (Lev. 26:30; cf. Ps. 78:58). After the destruction of SHILOH and before the building of the TEMPLE at Jerusalem, the high place was used as a site of true worship. SAMUEL blessed the offering which the people made at the high place (1 Sam. 9:12–14). When SAUL consulted Samuel, Samuel invited him to take part in the feast at the high place. On his way home, Saul was met by a band of prophets coming down from the high place of GIBEAH (10:5, 10); Saul prophesied with them and also went to the high place (v. 13).

The chronicler remarked that the tabernacle of the Lord was situated at the high place of GIBEON during the reign of DAVID (1 Chr. 16:39; 21:29; 2 Chr. 1:3–4). In the time of SOLOMON, mention is made of sacrificing at the high places, because a temple had not yet been built (1 Ki. 3:2–3). At the great high place of Gibeon, Solomon offered a thousand burnt offerings (v. 4; cf. 2 Chr. 1:3–6, 13). In his later years Solomon fell into apostasy and built high places for the Moabite CHEMOSH and the Ammonite MOLECH on the mountain E of Jerusalem (1 Ki. 11:7–8; cf. 2 Ki. 23:13). At the division of the kingdom, JEROBOAM tried to prevent the Israelites from going to Jerusalem for the religious festivals: he set up calves of gold at BETHEL and DAN (PLACE), built houses on high places, and

The "high place" at Dan.

appointed non-Levitical priests to serve at the high places (1 Ki. 12:26–32; cf. 13:33; 2 Chr. 11:15). A prophet of God predicted that the priests of the high place of Bethel would be sacrificed upon that altar and that the altar would be torn down (1 Ki. 13:2–3).

Meanwhile, in the southern kingdom there was also apostasy; during the reign of REHOBOAM, "They also set up for themselves high places, sacred stones and Asherah poles on every high hill and under every spreading tree. There were even male shrine prostitutes in the land" (1 Ki. 14:23–24). When ASA became king of Judah, he initiated many religious reforms, but "he did not remove the high places" (15:12–14). The Chronicler provides more details: "He removed the foreign altars and the high places, smashed the sacred stones and cut down the Asherah poles" (2 Chr. 14:3) and also "removed the high places and incense altars in every town in Judah" (v. 5), but "he did not remove the high places from Israel" (15:17).

In similar fashion, JEHOSHAPHAT "did what was right in the eyes of the LORD. The high places, however, were not removed, and the people continued to offer sacrifices and burn incense there" (1 Ki. 22:43). Some reforms of Jehoshaphat are indicated: "he removed the high places and the Asherah poles out of Judah" (2 Chr. 17:6; cf. 20:33). His son, the murderous JEHORAM, did what was evil and "built high places on the hills of Judah" (21:11). JOASH again did what was right, but the high places remained and the people continued to use them (2 Ki. 12:3). His son AMAZIAH followed his father's policy, with the same results (14:3–4), as did his son UZZIAH (Azariah, 15:3–4), and Uzziah's son JOTHAM (15:34–35). AHAZ, the son of Jotham, departed from his father's ways and followed the kings of Israel; he even burned his son as an offering, and sacrificed and burned incense on the high places he made in every city in Judah (16:3–4).

The fall of SAMARIA was the result of sin and was related to the worship conducted at the high places (2 Ki. 17:7–18). The Israelites built high places in all of their towns, "from watchtower to fortified city" (v. 9). "They set up sacred stones and Asherah poles on every high hill and under every spreading tree. At every high place they burned incense" and "worshiped idols" (vv. 10–12). This apostasy involved the making of an Asherah, the worship of the host of heaven, the service of BAAL, the offering of sons and daughters, and the use of divination and sorcery (vv. 16–17). The people who replaced the deported Israelites made their own gods and "set them up in the shrines the people of Samaria had made at the high places" (17:29), but they also feared the Lord and appointed priests to sacrifice for them in the shrines of the high places (v. 32).

In Judah, HEZEKIAH introduced some far-sweeping reforms; he removed the high places, breaking the pillars, cutting down the Asherah poles, and even smashing the NEHUSHTAN, the bronze serpent of the wilderness wanderings (2 Ki. 18:3–4; 2 Chr. 31:1; Isa. 36:7). MANASSEH, the son of Hezekiah, went contrary to his father's example; he rebuilt the high places his father had torn down and brought many elements of heathen religion into Judah and Jerusalem (2 Ki. 21:2–9, esp. v. 3; 2 Chr. 33:3–9, 17, 19). In the revival during the reign of JOSIAH, extensive reforms were again carried out (2 Ki. 23:4–25; 2 Chr. 34:3–7); Josiah deposed the idolatrous priests who served at the high places (2 Ki. 23:5); he defiled the high places, from GEBA to BEERSHEBA, and broke down the high places of the gates (v. 8). He defiled the high places E of Jerusalem, which Solomon had built for Ashtoreth, Chemosh, and Milcom (v. 13; cf. 1 Ki. 11:7). He utterly destroyed the high place at Bethel and burned human bones upon it (2 Ki. 23:15–16; cf. 1 Ki. 13:2).

The prophets spoke boldly against the high places, whether of Israel or the surrounding nations. Isaiah and Jeremiah mention the high places of MOAB (Isa. 15:2; 16:12; Jer. 48:35). Jeremiah refers to the high place of TOPHETH, which was built in the HINNOM Valley (Jer. 7:31), where people burned their children as offerings to Baal (19:5). Ezekiel and others also prophesied that the high places of Israel would be destroyed (Ezek. 6:3; Hos. 10:8; Amos 7:9). The prophet described the worship of the high places and made a word play on the name BAMAH (Ezek. 20:27–31). The Babylonian captivity served as a severe lesson to Israel concerning idolatry, and after that event no more is said in the Bible concerning high places.

(See further G. L. Robinson, *The Sarcophagus of an Ancient Civilization* [1930], 107–71; R. Brinker, *The Influence of Sanctuaries in Early Israel* [1946]; C. C. McCown in *JBL* 69 [1950]: 205–19; W. F. Albright, *Archaeology and the Religion of Israel*, 3rd ed. [1953], 103–7; W. Albright in *Volume du congres: Strasbourg, 1956* [1957], 242–58; S. Iwry in *JBL* 76 [1957]: 225–32; P. H. Vaughan, *The Meaning of "bāmâ" in the Old Testament* [1974]; J. T. Whitney in *TynBul* 30 [1979]: 125–47; M. D. Fowler in *ZAW* 94 [1982]: 203–13; W. B. Barrick in *ABD*, 3:196–200.)   C. E. DeVries

high priest. See PRIESTS AND LEVITES.

Hilen hi′luhn (חֵילֵן *H2664*). A Levitical town in the hill country of the tribe of JUDAH, assigned to the descendants of KOHATH (1 Chr. 6:58 [MT, v. 43], according to many Heb. MSS; the MT reads *ḥilēz*). The parallel passage has HOLON (Josh. 21:15).

Hilkiah hil-ki′uh (חִלְקִיָּה *H2759*, חִלְקִיָּהוּ *H2760*, "Yahweh is my portion"). **(1)** Son of Amzi, descendant of MERARI, and ancestor of the Levite musician ETHAN (1 Chr. 6:45).

(2) Son of HOSAH and descendant of Merari; he was a Levite gatekeeper during the time of DAVID (1 Chr. 26:11).

(3) Father of ELIAKIM, who was palace administrator under King HEZEKIAH (2 Ki. 18:18, 26, 37; Isa. 22:20; 36:3).

(4) Father of JEREMIAH the prophet and a priest in ANATHOTH (Jer. 1:1). It is often suggested that he descended from ABIATHAR, David's high priest, whom SOLOMON exiled to Anathoth for supporting ADONIJAH (1 Ki. 2:26–27).

(5) Father of GEMARIAH, who carried a message from Jeremiah to the captive Jews (Jer. 29:3).

(6) Son of Shallum (Meshullam), high priest in the time of King JOSIAH, and ancestor of EZRA; this is the Hilkiah who helped Josiah in his religious reforms and who found the Book of the Law in the temple (2 Ki. 22:4–14; 23:4; 1 Chr. 6:13; 9:11; 2 Chr. 34:9–22; 35:8; Ezra 7:1; Neh. 11:11; 1 Esd. 1:8 [KJV, "Helkias"]; 8:1 [KJV, "Helchiah"]; 2 Esd. 1:1 [KJV, "Helchiah"]; Bar. 1:7 [KJV, "Chelcias"]).

(7) One of the leaders of the priests who returned from EXILE with ZERUBBABEL and JESHUA (Neh. 12:7); his son or descendant Hashabiah later became leader of his priestly family (v. 21).

(8) One of the prominent men who stood near EZRA when the law was read at the great assembly (Neh. 8:4; called "Hezekiah" in 1 Esd. 9:43). He may be the same as #7 above.

(9) An ancestor of BARUCH, the servant of Jeremiah (Bar. 1:1; KJV, "Chelcias").

(10) The father of SUSANNA (Sus. 2, 29, 63; KJV, "Chelcias").

(11) Son of Eliab and ancestor of JUDITH (Jdt. 8:1; omitted in KJV).   S. BARABAS

hill. Natural land elevations in PALESTINE are seldom more than 3,000 ft. high, and therefore what English Bibles call "mountains" may in some other parts of the world be regarded as nothing more than high hills. Only familiarity with the geography of the land will enable the reader to know what sort of elevation is meant. Moving eastward from the Mediterranean, Palestine is divided into four main geographical divisions: the maritime plain

The hill country.

The hill country of Judah. (View to the NW toward Jerusalem.)

along the coast; the SHEPHELAH or "hill country"; the JORDAN valley; and the TRANSJORDAN plateau. Most of the country is hilly and mountainous.

The most common Hebrew term for "hill," "hill country," "mountain," or "mountain range" is *har* H2215, which occurs almost 500 times. It is often applied to ZION (Pss. 2:6; 48:2, 11). A hilly area often is identified with the designation "the hill country of" (e.g., of Judah and Israel, Josh. 11:21; of Ephraim, 17:15; of Naphtali, 20:7). Another term, *gibʿâ* H1496, which occurs more than 60 times, refers to elevated terrain in general, although never to a range of mountains (Exod. 17:9 et al.); it can also be used as a proper name (GIBEAH of Saul, 1 Sam. 11:4; 15:34; of Benjamin, 13:16). See also OPHEL.

The general Greek word for "hill" is *bounos* G1090 (only Lk. 3:5; 23:30). More frequent is *oros* G4001, which can also be rendered "hill" (e.g., Matt. 5:14), but more typically "mountain" (4:8 et al.). (See *NIDOTTE*, 1:805, 1051–54; *NIDNTT*, 3:1009–13.)   S. BARABAS

Hillel hil´uhl, hi-lel´ (הִלֵּל H2148, prob. "he has praised"). (1) Father of ABDON; the latter led Israel for eight years during the time of the judges (Jdg. 12:13, 15). See JUDGES, PERIOD OF IV.

(2) A Jewish scholar (c. 60 B.C. to A.D. 20), reputed to have played a foundational role in the development of the oral law. He and his contemporary Shammai mark the beginning of the Tannaitic period in rabbinic history (see MISHNAH), although it is difficult to determine the historical value of statements attributed to them (for a skeptical approach, cf. J. Neusner, *From Politics to Piety: The Emergence of Pharisaic Judaism* [1973], ch. 2, which popularizes parts of his earlier work, *The Rabbinic Traditions about the Pharisees before 70*, 3 vols. [1971]).

According to tradition, Hillel was head of the SANHEDRIN during part of the reign of King HEROD. A native of BABYLON, he desired earnestly to study Torah in Jerusalem under the famed teachers there. He went to Jerusalem, but because of his extreme poverty, he was not able to pay for such study. It is said that he sat upon the window to hear the words of the learned teachers, Shemaʿiah and Abtalion. One Sabbath eve as he sat on the window, the snow fell, covering him three cubits deep. In the morning Shemaʿiah asked Abtalion why the house was so dark. They then spied Hillel in the window and brought him in. Any man thinking himself too poor to study Torah was often referred to Hillel's example: "Were you poorer than Hillel?"

The legends that are told of Hillel magnify his kindness and gentleness and contrast him with his colleague, Shammai, a native Judean, who was said to be of a harsher disposition, impatient, and irascible. The personalities of Hillel and Shammai are also reflected in their interpretation of the law, Hillel being more humanitarian and liberal, Shammai more stringent and conservative. These tendencies were later reflected in the two schools associated with their names, although in many specific cases the "House of Hillel" ruled with greater stringency than that of Shammai. Especially after A.D. 70, the generally progressive school of Hillel became preeminent, thus giving direction to the course of classical Judaism.

Perhaps the best-known anecdote concerning these two rabbis concerns a heathen who went to see Shammai and stated that he would embrace Judaism provided it could be explained to him while he stood on one foot. In response, Shammai chased him out with a measuring stick, but when the man spoke to Hillel, the latter answered: "Do not do to your neighbors what is hateful to you. This is the whole law; the rest is commentary" (b. Šabb. 31a). Such moral and ethical aphorisms characterize Hillel's contribution to Pharisaic and Talmudic Judaism. To many, Hillel was a second EZRA from Babylonia, one who came to establish the law and its interpretation among the people.

Hillel is credited for having developed seven rules of biblical INTERPRETATION; these made it possible to draw from the written law logically valid principles that could be applied juridically. The most famous enactment ascribed to him was the *Prosbul*, which concerned the cancellation of debts in the sabbatical year (Deut. 15:2). Fearing the loss of their money, wealthy individuals were unwilling to lend to the poor as the sabbatical year approached. Hillel's interpretation, however, made it possible for a creditor to make the court his agent; because the debt, through this fiction, was no longer of a private nature, it could be collected even after the sabbatical year. Although such a ruling was motivated by humanitarian reasons, it allowed people to feel justified when they refused to cancel the debts owed to them.

(See further G. F. Moore, *Judaism in the First Centuries of the Christian Era: The Age of Tannaim* [1927], 1:77–82; A. Kaminka in *JQR* 30 [1939–40]: 107–22; J. Goldin in *JR* 26 [1946]: 263–77; N. N. Glatzer, *Hillel the Elder: The Emergence of Classical Judaism* [1956]; E. E. Urbach, *The Sages: Their Concepts and Beliefs*, 2 vols., 2nd. ed. [1979], 1:576–603; *HJP*, rev. ed. [1973–1987], 2:363–67; J. H. Charlesworth and L. L. Johns, eds., *Hillel and Jesus: Comparison of Two Major Religious Leaders* [1997].) W. B. COKER

hin. See WEIGHTS AND MEASURES III.A.

hind. This English term (the female of HART) is used by the KJV to render Hebrew *'ayyālâ H387* (Gen. 49:21 et al.); modern versions usually translate "doe." See DEER.

hind of the morning. The RSV rendering of *'ayyelet haššaḥar* (Ps. 22 title; NIV, "Doe of the Morning"; NRSV, "Deer of the Dawn"). This is either the name of a particular melody that was popular in the day of the psalmist and was the cue to the way the psalm should be sung, or it is some type of technical musical term. Since this is the only place the phrase occurs, it may be best to leave it untranslated (cf. KJV and NASB). See MUSIC VI.B. G. GIACUMAKIS, JR.

hinge. This English term, referring to a device that allows a DOOR or lid to turn, is used rarely in Bible versions (e.g., to render the unique Hebrew word *ṣîr H7494*, Prov. 26:14). Most of the ancient hinges were of a pivot type that would fit into a socket (cf. 1 Ki. 7:50 KJV).

Hinnom, Valley of (Ben) hin'uhm (הִנֹּם *H2183*) A valley that ran W and S of JERUSALEM, along the boundary of the tribes of JUDAH and BENJAMIN (Josh. 15:8; 18:16); the POTSHERD GATE led to it (Jer. 19:2). The valley had an evil reputation in later OT times because it was the site of TOPHETH, where parents made their children pass through the fire to BAAL and MOLECH. Kings AHAZ and MANASSEH were guilty of this horrible abomination (2 Chr. 28:3; 33:6). Isaiah refers to it, although not by name, as a place where the dead bodies of the unbelieving shall lie, and where their worm shall not die and the fire is not quenched (Isa. 66:24).

Aerial view of Jerusalem (looking NE). The Hinnom Valley lies to the W and S of the Old City.

Jeremiah predicted that God would visit the place with such awful destruction because of its wickedness that it would become known as the "Valley of Slaughter" (Jer. 7:31–34). King JOSIAH defiled this place so as to make it unfit for its idolatrous rites (2 Ki. 23:10). It became a type of sin, punishment, and misery because the bodies of dead animals and criminals were burned at its ever-burning fires. The Hebrew name *gê-hinnōm* is the origin of the term GEHENNA, which in the NT is used to designate the place of eternal punishment.

The location of the valley has been much disputed. All three of the valleys around Jerusalem have been identified with it—the KIDRON to the E, the Tyropoeon in the center, and the Wadi er-Rababi on the W. Early Jewish, Christian, and Muslim writers identified it with Kidron, but scarcely anyone does so today. Since the Tyropoeon Valley was incorporated within the city walls before the time of Manasseh, it is extremely unlikely that it could have been the place of the sacrifice of children, which must have been done outside the walls (2 Ki. 21:10–15). The Wadi er-Rababi location has the most support. It begins W of the Jaffa gate, turns S about a third of a mile, and gradually curves E to join the Kidron Valley. If Bir Ayyub is the biblical EN ROGEL (Josh. 15:7; 18:16), as seems probable, then the Wadi er-Rababi locates the Valley of Hinnom. S. BARABAS

hip. This English term is used a few times in Bible versions to render Hebrew *yārēk* H3751, which properly refers to the upper THIGH. JACOB was struck on the socket of his hip (Gen. 32:25; KJV, "the hollow of his thigh") to reduce his feeling of self-sufficiency and to make him lean upon God. This Hebrew term is used alongside another word meaning "thigh" or "leg" (*šôq* H8797) when the biblical writer says that SAMSON struck the PHILISTINES *šôq ʿal-yārēk* (Jdg. 15:8), an unusual expression that the KJV and NRSV render somewhat literally, "hip and thigh," while the NIV interprets it to mean "viciously." The NRSV also uses "hips" once to translate *motnayim* H5516 (Exod. 28:42; NIV, "waist"; see LOINS) and twice to translate the plural of *šēt* H9268 (2 Sam. 10:4; 1 Chr. 19:4; NIV, "buttocks").

hippopotamus. See BEHEMOTH.

Hirah hi´ruh (חִירָה H2669, derivation uncertain). A Canaanite man from the town of ADULLAM with whom JUDAH stayed after leaving his brothers (Gen. 38:1 NIV; according to the NRSV,

Judah "settled near" Hirah). Subsequently Hirah is described as a friend of Judah (vv. 12, 20; the LXX and the Vulg., vocalizing the Heb. differently, have "shepherd" instead of "friend"); he was sent to get back the pledge that Judah had given to a woman he thought was a prostitute (in reality, TAMAR; see vv. 13–26).

Hiram, Huram hi′ruhm, hyoor′uhm (חִירָם H2671, חִירוֹם H2670 [1 Ki. 5:10, 18; 7:40], חוּרָם H2586 [only in Chronicles]; from Phoen. אחרם, "my brother is lifted up"). To avoid confusion, the NIV uses "Hiram" for #1 below and "Huram" for #2; in the Hebrew text, however, both forms are used for both individuals.

(1) The king of TYRE in the reigns of DAVID and SOLOMON, with whom he had peaceful and friendly relations. After David captured Jerusalem and made it his capital, Hiram sent him wood, carpenters, and stonemasons to build his palace (2 Sam. 5:11). When Solomon ascended the throne, Hiram wrote to the new king expressing the hope that the long-existing friendship he had enjoyed with David would continue with Solomon. Thus Solomon asked for help in building a temple and a new palace, projects that took him twenty years to complete. Hiram sent him wood—cedar, pine, and algum—from the forests of LEBANON and all the gold he needed (1 Ki. 5:1–9; 2 Chr. 2:3–10), together with all the skilled workmen necessary for erecting and furnishing them. In return, Solomon sent him every year "twenty thousand cors of wheat as food for his household, in addition to twenty thousand baths of pressed olive oil" (1 Ki. 5:11). He also gave Hiram twenty cities in GALILEE, but when Hiram inspected them, he told Solomon he was not well pleased with them (9:10–14). When Solomon built a fleet of ships at EZION GEBER in EDOM, on the shore of the RED SEA, Hiram sent him experienced seamen to work with Solomon's men on the ships. Once every three years they brought to Solomon gold, silver, ivory, apes, and peacocks (1 Ki. 10:22; 2 Chr. 9:21).

According to JOSEPHUS (*Apion* 1.17–18), the father of Hiram was Abibalus, who had been king of Tyre before him. He also comments that Hiram and Solomon wrote many letters to each other, consulting one another on problems they had—for which Solomon had the better solutions. Josephus reports that Hiram died at the age of fifty-three, after a prosperous reign of thirty-four years. The reliability of these and other details is questioned by some scholars. (See H. J. Katzenstein, *The History of Tyre: From the Beginning of the Second Millennium B.C.E. until the Fall of the Neo-Babylonian Empire in 538 B.C.E.* [1973]; H. Donner in *Studies in the Period of David and Solomon and Other Essays*, ed. T. Ishida [1982], 205–14.)

(2) A skilled craftsman sent by King Hiram to Solomon to help him build his palace and the temple. He is also called Huram-Abi (חוּרָם אָבִי H2587, 2 Chr. 2:13 [KJV, "Huram my father"; cf. LXX]; חוּרָם אָבִיו, 4:16 [KJV, "Huram his father"]; the second element may be a title). His father was a native of Tyre of a family of craftsmen, but his mother was of the tribe of NAPHTALI (1 Ki. 14:2); according to the Chronicler, however, she was of the daughters of DAN (2 Chr. 2:13; see the discussion in R. B. Dillard, *2 Chronicles*, WBC 15 [1987], 4–5, 20–21). He was skilled in working with all sorts of materials—gold and silver, copper and iron, wood, and cloth—and was a fine engraver. Among the important metal parts of the temple and its furnishings that he made were the two bronze pillars, called Jakin and Boaz, the elaborate capitals on the pillars, the molten sea and the twelve oxen on which it rested, ten bases of bronze, ten basins of bronze, and the pots, shovels, and tossing-bowls used in the temple.   S. BARABAS

hire. See WAGES.

hireling. This English term, which today has a negative connotation (someone who does menial or even offensive work for pay), is used several times in the KJV to render Hebrew *śākîr* H8502 (Job 7:1 et al.) and Greek *misthōtos* G3638 (only Jn. 10:12–13). Modern versions prefer such renderings as "laborer" and "hired hand." See LABOR; WAGES.

hiss. To make a sharp sibilant sound (like a prolonged *s* or *sh*), an act of special meaning in many Near Eastern cultures. The English term is used by the KJV and other versions mainly to render the Hebrew verb *šāraq* H9239, "to whistle," which occurs a dozen times in the OT (Job 27:23 et al.). Because hissing is used to express derision, the NIV often renders it with "scoff" (e.g., 1 Ki. 9:8). The related noun is *šĕrēqâ H9240*, "whistling, hissing" (2 Chr. 29:8 et al.; NIV, "scorn").

history. A narrative of events or the study of the past. God often has been isolated from history or too closely linked with it. Karl Marx refused even to consider divine activity in history because history is the outcome of matter in motion. Many of the theological existentialists so link God with what they call holy history that he is uninterested in the historical events resulting from human action. Others invert biblical ideas. PROVIDENCE is replaced by progress, ETERNITY by time, and a MILLENNIUM by an earthly Utopia brought about by human activity in a secular setting. The Bible, however, links the events of SALVATION with empirically verifiable history except for CREATION (Heb. 11:3) and the final consummation of history (2 Pet. 3; see ESCHATOLOGY).

I. The Bible and the definition of history. History may be defined as events in time and space that have social significance. The Bible indicates that the coming of Christ to earth in the home of Joseph is to be linked with history (Gal. 4:4; Jn. 1:14, 18). History in this sense is absolute, occurring only once in time and space, and cannot be directly studied by the historian as the scientist can study his data.

If we follow Thucydides' use of the Greek word *historia* (from which our word *history* is ultimately derived), and consider it as the documents, remains, or relics of historical action or as research upon those events through these remains, then biblical writers think of history in this sense too. LUKE in the prologue to his gospel makes the claim that he used both secondary narratives and firsthand accounts by eyewitnesses of the life of Christ (Lk. 1:1-4). He describes how he did research upon the data to write his gospel in a manner similar to that of the modern historian. If history is defined as literary reconstruction of the past to record the events by the study of documents, Luke suggests that this is his objective. The Bible seems to emphasize history as events relating the acts of God to the acts of human beings, but history as document, research, or reconstruction is also given consideration.

II. The Bible and the writing of history. Luke and other biblical writers give attention to the method of the historian. Luke's prologue is a summary of much of what one finds concerning historical methodology in the best modern manuals on that subject. As already noted, he points out in his prologue that he used several secondary narratives of the life of Christ. His use of the word "us" (Lk. 1:1-2) and "also" (v. 3) suggests that he thought these were valid documents. Like modern historians, he emphasized his use of firsthand information of eyewitnesses. Mary's story of the birth of Christ in chs. 1-2 must have been one of these eyewitness sources. He would agree also with other biblical writers that one should have two independent witnesses to an event to confirm truth (Deut. 19:15; Jn. 8:17; 2 Cor. 13:1). His material was therefore empirical as well as revelational. Luke's use of the word *parakoloutheō G4158*, "to follow closely" (Lk. 1:3) suggests the idea of careful personal investigation of documents and eyewitnesses to reconstruct the events. The word *akribōs G209*, "exactly, accurately," also suggests his care in the testing and use of material.

The biblical writers recognized that, while God claims that some TRUTH is his alone, other truth concerning historical events has been given to us (Deut. 29:29; Amos 3:7). Luke believed that facts drawn from records of the events should be related in an orderly synthesis which would yield meaning, certainty, or truth concerning the matter under investigation (Lk. 1:4). PAUL (1 Cor. 10:6, 11) and PETER (2 Pet. 2:16) believed that a good historical reconstruction of past events should have moral value in helping one to avoid the mistakes and sins of the past. Paul also asserts that written history will have a positive function (Rom. 15:4). History in their opinion has a didactic, moral, or intellectual function in life that makes us better and wiser.

III. The Bible and the meaning of history. The historian may be scientific in his method of gathering and evaluating documentary evidence concerning past events, but engages in what is philosophic work when he asks what meanings his carefully gleaned facts have. If, as it may be defined, philosophy is an attempt to find a unifying principle by which events can be integrated and related to ultimate meaning, then the Bible is also philosophic and has an underlying philosophy of history that all the writers hold in common. Both the secular and the divine history are related to the historical process.

Some writers, such as Oswald Spengler, think of history as cyclical, deterministic, and lacking any progress. Others in the liberal tradition of the Renaissance and Enlightenment are so sure man can make progress in history by his own efforts that they replace the treadmill or cycle of history with an escalator or spiral or upward moving graph to picture their belief in progress by the efforts of perfectible human beings. Theological existentialists, who accept the universality of sin, are not so optimistic, but do have confidence that God will bring an end to history outside history. Evangelicals prefer to take their stand with the biblical writers, who were "pessimistic optimists" in their interpretation of history.

A. The source of history. Biblical writers assert that God is the source of history because he initiates it through his sovereign creative will and acts within it. Events such as the birth and resurrection of Christ are as historically verifiable as those initiated by human beings (with the exception of the creation and the consummation of history, which come to us by revelation). History is neither an evolving process in which God is imprisoned, nor the result of chance. Instead it is an act of the sovereign self-sufficient God (Gen. 1:1; Rom. 11:36). Isaiah pictures God as the Creator of heaven and earth (Isa. 40:26, 28; 42:5; 45:12). Jeremiah (Jer. 27:5) and the psalmist (Pss. 8:3, 6; 19:1; 24:1–2), as well as John (Rev. 4:11) and Paul (Acts 17:25; Rom. 1:19–21), agree with Isaiah.

Man as the chief actor on the earthly stage of history is also pictured by the biblical writers as the result of divine creativity. They did not think of him as the result of a natural process (Gen. 1:26–28; 2:7; Job 33:4; Pss. 8:5–6; 24:1; 139:14–16; Isa. 42:5; 43:7; 45:12; Jer. 27:5; Acts 17:24–26; Heb. 11:3). Man's task was to master nature for his good and the glory of God (Gen. 1:28; Ps. 8:6–8).

When speaking of CREATION, the biblical writers reveal their belief that the preexistent Christ was the divine agent of God the Father (Jn. 1:4; Col. 1:16; Heb. 1:2–3). Christ is neither an indifferent transcendent Creator nor enmeshed in pantheistic fashion in his creation. History is a linear process moving to a meaningful end under the divine guidance rather than a meaningless series of cycles or an evolutionary escalator to progress. God and Christ are also considered to be the source of moral values to enlighten conscience after the FALL (Jn. 8:9; Rom. 2:15).

This is not to say that the biblical writers ignore the role in history of secondary horizontal factors, such as geography, economics, or great individuals. They recognize the role of the economic factor in history as a secondary or contingent, but never as a final cause (Deut. 8:3; Matt. 4:4; 1 Thess. 4:11–12). These factors all have their proper subordinate role.

B. The scope of history. The biblical writers—unlike G. W. F. Hegel, who limited the divine in history to his ideal monarchical Protestant Prussian state, or K. Marx, who looked to the chosen proletariat to achieve a workers' Utopia—look upon history as a universal and unitary process that involved the human race rather than any chosen segment of it. All are linked with ADAM as the head of the race (Acts 17:26; Rom. 5:12–19).

There is, however, a clear concept of temporal dualism within history because of the entry of sin into the race by the failure of Adam and Eve in the garden. This event affected everyone, leaving human beings corrupt and sinful (Gen. 3; Ps. 51:5; Jer. 13:23; 17:9; Rom. 5:12–19; 1 Cor. 15:22). Even nature is pictured in the Bible as affected by the human failure to obey God (Gen. 3:17; Rom. 8:22–23). This sin becomes self-assertion contrary to God's will. This dualism is developed in time as some become the willing subjects of God's kingdom through faith in the incarnate Christ, whose cross offers an opportunity for grace and the destruction of the work of Satan (Jn. 1:14; 1 Jn. 3:5, 8). Others reject this proffered grace to form the earthly city. This dualism in time is temporary and is to be resolved at the end of time and history by the coming of Christ.

Human beings are not only finite (Ps. 115:16) as creatures, but also fallen and fallible. They are subjected to the pressures of Satan, the world around them, and the tendency of their fleshly nature to evil (Eph. 2:2–3; 1 Jn. 2:15–16). This tragic flaw makes human progress impossible except in limited areas of technical and scientific progress. Biblical realism is thus opposed to the optimistic monism of the Renaissance and the Enlightenment and modern liberalism. Modern history with its Stalins and Hitlers demonstrates that man can be demonic and defiant.

C. The scheme of history. (1) Paul considers the scheme, or course, or pattern of history to be controlled by the divine sovereignty (Rom. 11:36; Eph. 4:6). God is transcendent to nature but manifests his power in it as providence. His creatures profit by the uniformity of nature. Whether nature is good or bad, it is sustained in its course by divine power (Job 12:10; Col. 1:17; Heb. 1:3). Natural calamities may come, but to biblical writers they are the result of interim judgment of God in history to bring sinners to repentance (Joel 1:4; 2:23–26). Others may come because human sin violates the divine order in nature by ravishing the soil or denuding the hills of their forest cover. It is this uniformity of nature under divine providence that provides a basis for science.

(2) The Bible traces human institutions to the act of God. The FAMILY (Gen. 1:28; 2:20; Deut. 4:7–10; Matt. 19:4–6; Eph. 6:4) and human GOVERNMENT (Gen. 9:5–6; Rom. 13:1–7; 1 Pet. 2:14–17) are depicted in Scripture as gifts of God to promote orderly SOCIETY. Without them society would become hopelessly anarchic and chaotic. God also is pictured as the sovereign controller of the events of history and particularly the affairs of the three most significant groups in Scripture, the Gentile nations, the Jews, and the church (1 Cor. 10:32). DANIEL links spiritual beings with historical events in the history of nations (Dan. 10:13, 21; 12:1).

(3) Several writers express the general principle that nations operate under the sovereignty of God even though they may ignore him in their domestic and diplomatic policies (Deut. 32:8; Isa. 40:15, 28; Jer. 46:28; Dan. 2:21, 37; 4:17, 32–35; 5:21; Acts 17:26; Rom. 9:17, 22–23). Special nations are said to be under divine governance. Syria and Philistia as well as Israel have been brought to their place of habitation by the act of God (Amos 9:7). Edom is punished for her treachery toward those that were tied to her by blood (Obadiah). Ezekiel sees Egypt suffering judgment under the hand of God (Ezek. 26:10; 29:6, 13, 19; 30:4, 10, 19, 26).

Isaiah believes that God had a hand in the history of empires, such as Assyria (Isa. 10:5; 30:31; 37:36; 38:6), to effect his will. Jonah is forced to recognize the mercy of God to a repentant Nineveh, a great city of Assyria. Babylonian kings had to learn that God ruled over their nation and put them in office (Dan. 2:21, 37; 4:18, 32–35; 5:12). They were used to punish the sinful Jewish nation and to wean her finally from the worship of idols (Jer. 24:5; 25:9–12; 27:5–11; 46:13; 50:11; Dan. 9:1; Hab. 1:1–11). Babylon also was reminded that God would finally punish her for her sins after she had served his purpose (Jer. 25; 27; Hab. 2). Persia with her more tolerant policy is linked by the bibli-

Commemorative cylinder of Shamshi-Adad I (c. 1800 B.C.) that dedicates the Ishtar temple and ziggurat at Nineveh.

cal writers with the deliverance of the Jews from the Babylonian Captivity (Ezra 1:1–3; Isa. 5:11; 13:7; 44:28; 45:1). Although human leaders have freedom to act and are responsible for their actions in history, the writers of the Bible believe that God uses nations to effect his will and judges them in history. Battles such as those at Marathon and the naval defeat of the Spanish Armada, as well as the rise of the Frankish nation in western Europe and the Byzantine Empire in eastern Europe to protect the western and eastern flanks of Europe in a period of weakness, may also be illustrations of the same principles.

(4) God's control of events is especially linked with the history of the Jews, who are looked upon by the writers of the OT as God's chosen people who are to reveal his will to the nations. Their continuity and persistence as a nation makes them a problem for the modern scientific historian. The nation emerged in an interlude between about 1200 and 800 B.C. when the Egyptian and Hittite empires had fallen and the Assyrian and Babylonian empires had not yet risen. Thus Jews were not hindered in their growth to an empire under Solomon. They were said to be chosen by God (Gen. 15:13–16; Deut. 2:25; 4:34; 6:12; 7:6; 11:12; 15:6; 20:17–18; Ezek. 23:9), rescued from Egypt and brought to their land by him (Amos 9:7). God was said to be present in their dispersal and captivity in Babylon (cf. Jer. 24:5; 25:9–12; Dan. 1:2). In the light of several passages (Isa. 11:11; 27:11; Jer. 31:33, 33–37; Ezek. 37), one can well presume that these prophets would have rejoiced in the modern emergence of Israel as a nation in 1948. Perhaps the Jews' long period of being set aside as a nation in the present era (Lk. 21:24; Acts 15:14; Rom. 11:25–26) is nearing the end when God will more particularly deal with them again.

(5) NT writers affirm that God in the period of Jewish national eclipse is using the CHURCH. Peter sees the church as chosen of God and redeemed by Christ's sacrifice (1 Pet. 1:18–21). It was to proclaim Christ's grace to all (Matt. 28:18–20; Lk. 24:45–48; Acts 1:8; 2 Cor. 5), to have an impact on the culture of their day (Eph. 2:10; Tit. 3:8), to display his wisdom to the universe (Eph. 3:10), and to glorify God (Eph. 3:20) until the time of Christ's second advent.

(6) Above all, the Bible writers look upon Christ, largely ignored by classical Roman writers, as the source of all knowledge and wisdom (Col. 2:2–3). He becomes the center of linear history as well as the key to its fulfillment and consummation. Unlike the Greeks, whose leaders became gods, John and others see Christ as the God who became man in the fullness of time (Jn. 1:14; Acts 2:23; 4:28; Gal. 4:4; 1 Pet. 1:20) in order to minister to and redeem sinners by his death on the cross (Mk. 10:45). His resurrection was looked upon as a historic event that confirmed his divine origin and work (Acts 17:2, 3; Rom. 1:4; 4:25; 1 Cor. 15:3–4). God then gave to him all authority in time (Matt. 11:27–28; 28:18; Jn. 3:35; 13:3). Christ will consummate history as its Judge and the Initiator of divine rule on earth subsequent to his return to earth.

D. The solution of history. God is also linked in the Scriptures with the solution of history at its end as well as with the course of events in time. God challenges pagan gods, according to Isaiah, because they cannot foresee the end of history (Isa. 41:22; 42:9; 46:10; 48:3; cf. 2 Pet. 1:19–21). History is not deterministic cyclic recurrence lacking linear progress or a goal, nor human evolutionary progress to a human Utopia. Instead the Bible pictures history moving to linear consummation by Christ as it earlier moved toward Christ in linear centered time.

Both the OT and NT writers find the solution to the story of the Gentile nations, the Jews, and the church in the SECOND COMING of Christ to judge all three groups and to set up his kingdom prior to the eternal state. This coming is the hope of the church (Jas. 1:4; 1 Thess. 4:14–18; 1 Pet. 1:16, 19–21), which is also to be judged for reward for the work it has done for Christ (Rom. 14:10; 1 Cor. 3:11–15; 2 Cor. 5:10). The Jewish and the Gentile nations also are depicted by the writers of the Bible as undergoing judgment at the hands of Christ, to whom God has given the power to judge (Jn. 5:28–29; Acts 24:15). The proof of that power is the RESURRECTION (Acts 17:31). The principle of judgment after resurrection is set forth in Gen. 18:25; Heb. 9:27–28; 12:23. Judgment upon nations is specially mentioned by Matthew (Matt. 25:31–46).

The prophets then picture a righteous rule of Christ in history upon earth with the Jewish nation playing an important part in this period (Isa. 11; 65:17; 66:12; Dan. 2:44; Acts 15:13–17; Phil. 2:8–11). Even the Son will, when sin and death are conquered, return his rule to the Father, who will rule over all in the eternal kingdom of God (Rom. 11:36; 1 Cor. 15:24–28; Rev. 11:15; 21:14; 22:3).

This biblical conception of history does not exclude the secondary horizontal factors of history, such as geography and economics, but relates them as the ultimate cause in a vertical orientation to God. It speaks also to the problem of recurrence in history raised by the Greeks and by Spengler and to the problems of continuity and progress that seem to be the dream of modern man. Change and continuity are reconciled in the divine plan for history that is concerned both with secular and religious events without creating a dualism. Both the writers of the OT and NT emphasize eschatological linear direction in history rather than cyclical motion or an indefinite spiral of progress through human activity. God is for them the Creator, Controller, and Consummator of history. See ACTS, BOOK OF; DEUTERONOMISTIC HISTORY; GOSPELS; ISRAEL, HISTORY OF.

(Relevant studies include R. Niebuhr, *Faith and History: A Comparison of Christian and Modern Views of History* [1949]; K. Lowith, *Meaning in History* [1949]; H. Butterfield, *Christianity and History* [1950]; D. C. Masters, *The Christian Idea of History* [1962]; J. W. Montgomery, *Where Is History Going?* [1969]; R. Alter, *The Art of Biblical Narrative* [1981]; M. Stanford, *Nature of Historical Knowledge* [1986]; B. Halpern, *The First Historians: The Hebrew Bible and History* [1988]; V. P. Long, *The Art of Biblical History* [1994], reprinted in *FCI*, 281–429; Y. Amit, *History and Ideology: An Introduction to Historiography in the Hebrew Bible* [1999]; V. P. Long et al., eds., *Windows into Old Testament History: Evidence, Argument, and the Crisis of "Biblical Israel"* [2002]; J. B. Kofoed, *Text and History: Historiography and the Study of the Biblical Text* [2005].)

E. E. CAIRNS

Hittite hit′tit (חִתִּי *H3153*, cf. also בְּנֵי־חֵת, "the sons of HETH" [Gen. 23:3 et al.]; represented in cuneiform as *ḫatti*). The Hittites were an ancient Indo-European people who lived in ANATOLIA and N SYRIA. The term, however, is used in the OT to designate several peoples of differing ethnic origins.
  I. Use of the term *Hittite*
  II. The Indo-European Hittites of Asia Minor
    A. History
    B. Languages and scripts
    C. Religion and pantheon
  III. The Neo-Hittites of N Syria
  IV. Hittites in the OT
    A. Terminology
    B. Hittite influences on the literature and culture of Israel

I. Use of the term Hittite. In scholarly usage, the term *Hittite* bears at least three meanings. It can denote: (1) the aboriginal inhabitants of the central plateau of ASIA MINOR, more accurately designated as *Hattians*; (2) that branch of Indo-European immigrants that settled in central Anatolia c. 2000 B.C. and wrote in a language that they called "Nesite" (*nesumnili*); and (3) the people who lived in several large city-states of N Syria during the 1st millennium B.C., which had been vassal states of the Anatolian Hittites during the period c. 1400–1200. Some scholars designate this third group by the term *neo-Hittites*. To the Assyrians and Hebrews of the 1st millennium B.C., the term *Hittites* covered all the inhabitants of the earlier Hittite empire and its Syrian dependencies, irrespective of their linguistic or ethnic affiliation.

II. The Indo-European Hittites of Asia Minor

A. History. During the 3rd millennium B.C., central Anatolia (Asia Minor) was occupied by several small kingdoms of non-Semitic and non-Indo-European peoples. One of these, the Hattians, bequeathed their name to the large mass of Indo-European immigrants who entered Asia Minor c. 2300–2000 and soon became the dominant political power. The centers of Indo-European power during the earliest period were the cities of Nesa and Kussar, but with the eclipse of the small Hattian kingdoms c. 1750, the seat of Hittite power soon shifted (c. 1650) to the city of Hattusas. Already in the reign of Hattusilis I (c. 1650–1620), Hittite armies made forays into N Syria, where important cities such as ALALAKH,

Aleppo, and Hashshum endured their onslaught. Hittite activities in Syria and Mesopotamia at this early period were limited to raids without any attempt at consolidation of conquests or the appointment of governors or vassals. Though the Hittite raids were ephemeral, they were none the less impressive. About 1600, the successor of Hattusilis I, Mursilis I (c. 1620–1590), raided and sacked the mighty city of Babylon. The rest of the period called the "Old Kingdom" (c. 1600–1400) was marred by internal dissension and weakness in the homeland, which made any appreciable Hittite influence abroad impossible.

The revival of Hittite fortunes can be traced to the reign of an energetic monarch with the throne-name Suppiluliuma (Shuppiluliumas) I, c. 1380–1340 B.C. His reign initiated the "empire period," which lasted until the fall of Hattusas c. 1190. Suppiluliuma I began the practice of seeking to control the important, but small, city-states of N Syria by a combination of military force and astute diplomacy. He created a vast network of vassal states bound to the Hittite suzerain by treaties (see TREATY). The system was a kind of benevolent feudalism. Each vassal king was given a free hand in matters of internal rule and the guaranteed protection of his dynasty against usurpers. In turn he forswore the right to an independent foreign policy and pledged an annual delivery of tribute to the Hittite capital.

The archrivals of the Hittites in Syria were the Egyptians, who controlled most of S Syria. A military showdown was reached in 1300 B.C., when Ramses II of Egypt and his allies joined battle with Muwatallis (c. 1315–1290) and the Hittite allies in the vicinity of Kadesh on the Orontes. In traditional style, both sides vociferously claimed the victory. It appears, however, as though no appreciable amount of territory changed hands. After 1300, both powers seemed to realize increasingly their need for each other's support. In 1284, Hattusilis III of Hatti and Ramses II of Egypt concluded a treaty of mutual recognition and assistance. The new enemy of both powers was the Assyrian kingdom of Tukulti-Ninurta I.

By c. 1265, when Tudhalia (Tudhaliyas) IV began his reign, political and military pressure on Hatti came from another direction. Freebooters called the *Ahhiyawa*, who may have been an early wave of SEA PEOPLES from the Greek mainland, began harassing the western coast of Asia Minor and prompted Tudhalia to lead an army to the W c. 1230 to protect Hittite interests. Some scholars connect this pressure from the Ahhiyawa with the traditional invasion of the western coast of Asia Minor by the Achaeans at the time of the Trojan War (c. 1230–1210?). When the end finally came for the Hittite empire c. 1190 during the reign of Suppiluliuma II, the conquering hordes included another wave of Sea Peoples who likewise brought to an end the influential city-state of UGARIT.

B. Languages and scripts. The official archives of the Hittite capital city, Hattusas, contained clay tablets on which were inscribed in CUNEIFORM script documents composed in at least five distinct languages: (1) Hattic, the language of the aboriginal inhabitants; (2) Nesite, the language of the Indo-Europeans who initiated the Hittite kingdom at Hattusas; (3–4) Luwian and Palaic, Indo-European dialects closely related to Nesite; and (5) Hurrian. In addition, the most common cuneiform languages, (6) Sumerian and (7) Akkadian, were represented (see LANGUAGES OF THE ANE). Since

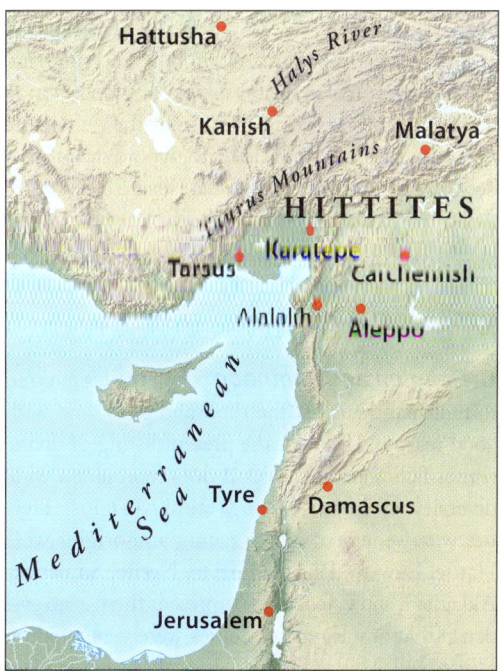

The Hittites.

Hittite pictographs. From Carchemish, 8th cent. B.C.

the vast majority of texts were written in Nesite, this language was dubbed "Hittite" and was assumed to have been the official language of the empire.

The Indo-European character of Nesite and its sister dialects is apparent not only from its vocabulary (containing words like *mekki-* "much," *pada-* "foot," *watar* "water," *eshar* "blood," *kard-* "heart," *genu-* "knee," and *pahhur* "fire"), but also from its grammatical inflection of nouns and verbs, and its pronominal forms (*kuis* "who," etc.). It is at present the oldest known written Indo-European language and has in consequence enormous value for the reconstruction of the early history and development of that language family. It appears that the Hittites and their neighbors also recorded their language in a hieroglyphic script on tablets of wood, which have not been preserved because of the perishable medium. Examples of this hieroglyphic script have been found inscribed in stone or lead from sites in Anatolia, Syria, and northern Mesopotamia. The language of these texts, though popularly referred to as "hieroglyphic Hittite," is actually closer to Luwian than to Nesite.

C. Religion and pantheon. The Hittites referred to their pantheon as "the thousand gods" and with good reason. Although the present listing of divine names falls short of 1,000, it does represent a wide diversity of linguistic and ethnic origins. Deities were venerated whose names and origins were Hattic, Luwian, Palaic, Hurrian, Nesite, Sumerian, Akkadian, and Canaanite. At present there is no evidence that any Egyptian deities were venerated on Hittite soil. Many of these deities are known only as names in a list of treaty guardians, whereas others are described in myths, rituals, and festival texts. Most of these deities are depicted in the long relief carved into the rock at the sanctuary of Yazilikaya near modern Boğazköy. Gods were worshiped in their own language by singers called "the Hurrian singer," "the Hattic singer," "the Nesite singer," etc. The male head of the pantheon was a storm deity; the female head, a solar deity. During the empire period, the HURRIAN elements in the pantheon gained the ascendancy. Each king had his own patron deity.

III. The Neo-Hittites of N Syria. The term "neo-Hittites" implies nothing with regard to continuity of language or ethnos with the Hittites of Anatolia during the 2nd millennium B.C. When the Hittite capital was destroyed by the Sea Peoples c. 1190, the only centers that remained to continue the culture of the Hittites were the important cities of Syria that had once been under their sway. It is not clear just to what extent the culture of the Hittite empire truly survived in these Syrian centers. This much is clear: (1) The old Hattic throne names borne by the Hittite emperors (Suppiluliuma, Labarnas, Muwatallis, Hattusilis) continued to be used by the kings of N Syria during the 1st millennium, for they appear in the Assyrian annals (as Sapalulme, Lubarna, Mutallu, Katuzili). (2) Many of these kings erected stone monuments bearing inscriptions in "hieroglyphic Hittite." (3) The Assyrians and Hebrews of the 1st millennium B.C. continued to refer to N Syria as Hatti and its inhabitants as "Hittites."

Among the petty kingdoms that scholars call "neo-Hittite" were: Tuwana (classical Tyana), Tunna (Tynna), Hupisna (Kybistra), Shinukhtu, and Ishtunda, all in the Taurus Mountains or on the S edge of the central plateau; Tabala (biblical TUBAL) to the NE of these, somewhere along the upper reaches of the EUPHRATES River; Milid (modern Malatya), capital of Kammanu; Marqasi (modern Marash), capital of Gurgum (both of the latter were along the upper Euphrates); to the S was the kingdom of Kummukhi (classical COMMAGENE); and still farther S the city-state of CARCHEMISH. NW of Carchemish was the kingdom of ARPAD, to the W of which, and reaching to the gulf of Alexandretta, was the state of Ya'udiya (also known as Sam'al). Occupying the Amuq plain was the kingdom of

Basalt stela of the Hittite goddess Kubaba holding a mirror and standing beneath a winged sun-disk (9th cent. B.C., from Birecik, N of Carchemish).

Hattina with its capital at Kinaluwa (biblical CAL-NEH). In the vicinity of ALEPPO was located the kingdom of Lukhut with its capital first at Aleppo itself and later at Hatarikka (biblical HADRACH). In the extreme S was the kingdom of HAMATH, and E of the Euphrates was a kingdom centered in Til-Barsip (modern Tell Ahmar). These kingdoms were by no means all continuations of Hittite vassal kingdoms during the 2nd millennium. To the contrary, with the exception of Carchemish and Aleppo, almost all of them were newly founded during the centuries that immediately succeeded the fall of Hattusas (c. 1190 B.C.). It cannot be denied, however, that they were culturally the heirs of much that is properly associated with the 2nd-millennium Hittites. In time, as the powerful neo-Assyrian armies pushed westward to the Mediterranean coast and into Asia Minor itself, these small kingdoms were—one by one—incorporated into the Assyrian empire. Culture is not subject to force of arms, and the distinctive neo-Hittite culture of these areas continued with only slight diminution down into the Hellenistic age, where traces of it appear at sites such as Nemrud Dagh.

IV. Hittites in the OT

A. Terminology

1. In the patriarchal age. The OT employs the expressions "sons of Heth" and "Hittites" synonymously. The former expression, which has reference to HETH (Gen. 10:15; 1 Chr. 1:13), the eponymous ancestor of the "Hittites," occurs only in Genesis (Gen. 10:15; 23:3, 5, 7, 10, 16, 20; 25:10; 27:46 ["daughters of Heth"]; 49:32). It is used to designate the "Hittites" only of the patriarchal age and no others. The term *ḥitti*, on the other hand, has a much broader reference and is found not only in Genesis (15:20; 23:10; et al.), but also throughout the historical and prophetical literature of the OT. With reference to the many meanings that the term *Hittite* bears in scholarly literature, it may be noted that in the OT it denotes only two groups. There is no reference in the OT under this term to the Indo-European Hittites of Asia Minor. Nor is there any allusion to the Hattians. In the OT, the term *Hittites* refers either to an ethnic group in Palestine during the patriarchal age, the period of the exodus, and the period of the conquest, or to the "neo-Hittite" peoples and kingdoms of Syria during the 1st millennium B.C.

E. Forrer (in *PEQ* no vol. [1936]: 190–209) proposed, on the basis of a cuneiform Hittite text written in the reign of Mursilis II (c. 1330 B.C.), that a group of Hittite people from the city of Kurustamma migrated into Egyptian territory (i.e., anywhere S of Kadesh on the Orontes, but prob. Palestine). There they formed an enclave and survived into biblical times. The above-mentioned text, though written c. 1330, refers to an incident that might have taken place centuries before. But the migration described would hardly have taken place as early as c. 1700 (i.e., during the patriarchal age). And even this ingenious proposal does not fully satisfy the biblical data. O. R. Gurney (*The Hittites*, 2nd ed. [1990]) presents an alternative view: that the Hattians were originally much more widespread geographically than just in central Asia Minor, and that an enclave of Hattians had lived in Palestine since prepatriarchal times. Neither of these two views can, of course, be conclusively proved.

Some scholars have seen in the account of ABRAHAM's purchase of the cave in MACHPELAH (Gen. 23) from EPHRON the Hittite a reflection of subtle distinctions of Hittite law relating to transfer of certain feudal obligations by sale of property (M. R. Lehmann in *BASOR* 129 [Feb. 1953]: 15–18; Hittite laws ##46–47 in *ANET*, 191). If this interpretation is correct, the passage would offer support to Forrer's theory (but cf. H. Hoffner in *TynBul* 20 [1969]: 27–55). Whatever the geographic origin of the "Hittites" of Palestine in the patriarchal age, it is clear that they have been thoroughly semitized, for none of their personal names can be satisfactorily interpreted as Indo-European or HURRIAN.

2. In the monarchy. During the age of the Hebrew monarchy, other "Hittites" appear in the narratives, but these are foreigners rather than aboriginal inhabitants of Palestine. They are, in fact, the "neo-Hittites" of Syria. Solomon's Hittite wives, unlike Esau's, were foreigners he married for political reasons, along with women from Egypt, Moab, Ammon, Edom, and Sidon (1 Ki. 11). The "kings of the Hittites" mentioned elsewhere (2 Ki. 7:6–7; 2 Chr. 1:17) were powerful monarchs from Syria. In this category one would wish to place URIAH the Hittite, the faithful soldier in DAVID's army. The hard core of David's army consisted of foreign mercenary troops, who were undeterred by petty local allegiances from following him without question (2 Sam. 15). Since David's northern border reached all the way to the Euphrates (8:3), it is surely likely that among his mercenaries would be a sizable number of Syrian "Hittites." And since the new bureaucracy of David's state required the service of experienced civil servants from Egypt and elsewhere (2 Sam. 8; 1 Chr. 18 [note the Egyptian name Shavsha in v. 16]), the political affairs in the new capital, Jerusalem, may also have received the council of trained bureaucrats from Syria, that is, "Hittites."

B. Hittite influences on the literature and culture of Israel. In 1954, G. Mendenhall proposed that the structure of the biblical COVENANT at Sinai be understood as preserving a very ancient TREATY form best known from, but not originating in, the Hittite suzerainty treaties with Syrian vassal states during the 2nd millennium B.C. (see *BA* 17 [1954]: 26–46, 49–76). This "form" contained the following elements: (1) a preamble; (2) a historical prologue, detailing the previous relations between the two parties to the treaty; (3) a section of stipulations, which included (a) prohibition of foreign alliances outside the Hittite orbit, (b) prohibition of hostility against another vassal of Hatti, (c) obligation to answer any call to arms issued by Hittite suzerain, (d) obligation to suppress any vicious rumors about the Hittite crown or secret plots to rebel, (e) prohibition against granting asylum to refugees from Hatti, and obligation to extradite all such fugitives to Hatti, (f) obligation to appear personally at least once a year at Hittite court with tribute; (4) a provision for depositing a copy of the treaty in the sanctuary and bringing it forth for periodic public reading; (5) lists of the gods of both the Hittite empire and the vassal state as legal witnesses and enforcers of the treaty; and (6) formulae of curses and blessings.

Each of these elements finds a striking counterpart in the OT passages relating to the Sinai covenant. Some years later, M. G. Kline (*Treaty of the Great King* [1963]) extended this comparison to the problem of the formal unity of the book of DEUTERONOMY. These theories do not presuppose a direct influence of the Anatolian Hittites on the biblical Hebrews. Rather they employ evidence from the Hittite texts to elucidate the form in which a given segment of biblical narrative might have been cast. (Kline's theory has apologetic ramifications, since, if one can demonstrate very early prototypes contemporaneous with Moses for the literary form of Deuteronomy, then there is less plausibility for certain critical views regarding the source analysis of the book and its supposed compilation as late as the reign of Josiah.)

Another portion of the biblical text where the literary form of the narrative might possibly hark back to a prototype dating from the 2nd millennium, and most familiar from Hittite texts, is the section from 1 Sam. 15 to 2 Sam. 8, which many OT source critics are accustomed to designate as the court history of David and to regard as one of the oldest portions of the OT in its present written form. This pericope, dealing as it does with the transfer of rule from SAUL, the unfit incumbent, to David as chosen of God, may well be a very early piece of dynastic justification. Political apologies that seriously attempt to justify an extraordinary transfer of power on a firm moral and theological basis are far from common in the ANE. There are, however, concrete examples of such to be found. One with many striking similarities to the court history of David is the Hittite text that E. H. Sturtevant aptly entitles "The Apology of Hattusilis" (*Hittite Chrestomathy* [1935], 43; this is a much more appropriate label than "The Autobiography of Hattusilis" used by many other Hittitologists). The text in question is certainly no autobiography, for it omits too much that is pertinent to such a literary genre and includes much that is unnecessary, placing a conspicuous emphasis at every turn on the "propagandistic" elements. The entire thrust of the document is to demonstrate that the paranoiac Urhi-Teshub (Mursilis II) was not only unable to function as a worthy ruler, but in a jealous rage actively pursued plots to murder Hattusilis III, when he suspected that the goddess ISHTAR had designated the latter to succeed him to the throne.

The similarities extend beyond mere coincidental incidents in the lives of the persons involved and point to a possible formal similarity attributable to the function of the respective documents. It is by no means suggested that the constituent episodes in the two documents were fabricated for propaganda purposes. On the contrary, such documents would depend upon the reliability of the information for their effectiveness. Nor does this theory imply that David's motives were questionable in having such a document drawn up. When David came to power, matters were unstable for many years. It was advantageous for him to have drawn up a record of the events leading up to his accession, making clear to all that he had no hand in killing Saul, that he at all times refrained from taking the initiative to drive his predecessor from the throne, and that Yahweh had been working behind the scenes from the start to place upon the throne of Israel his chosen one. If within his cabinet, or bureaucracy, there were Syrians who knew of an appropriate form in which to express this information, David would certainly have felt inclined to employ it.

A final area of possible Hittite influence on the literature and culture of Israel is the science of historiography. From the earliest periods of Sumerian and Egyptian history, documentary records were kept of important events. The lists of such events can in a very loose sense be termed HISTORY. Historical writing in the sense in which we encounter it, as in the writings of HERODOTUS ("the father of history-writing") is found in only two areas of the ANE. Only in Hatti and ancient Israel is there evidence of historical writing that probes for causes, and which seeks to express a kind of moral philosophy of history. (Cf. A. Malamat, "Doctrines of Causality in Hittite and Biblical Historiography," *VT* 5 [1955]: 1–12; A. Kammenhuber, "Die hethitische Geschichtsschreibung," *Saeculum* 9 [1958]: 136–55.) Without desiring to instigate a pan-Hittite movement in the study of ANE civilizations, some scholars have suggested an indirect influence here by the 2nd millennium culture of the Hittites upon the late 2nd millennium and early 1st millennium culture of the Hebrews.

(In addition to the works mentioned in the article, see F. F. Bruce, *The Hittites and the Old Testament* [1948]; O. Eissfeldt, *The Old Testament: An Introduction* [1965], 32–56; J. Lehmann, *The Hittites: People of a Thousand Gods* [1977]; H. Hoffner, "Histories and Historians of the Ancient Near East: The Hittites," *Or* 49 [1980]: 283–332; O. R. Gurney in *CAH* 2/1, 3rd ed. [1973], ch. 6; J. D. Hawkins in *CAH* 3/1, 2nd ed. [1982], ch. 9; J. G. Macqueen, *The Hittites and Their Contemporaries in Asia Minor*, rev. ed. [1986]; H. Hoffner in *Peoples of the Old Testament World*, ed. A. J. Hoerth et al. [1994], 127–55; T. Bryce, *Life and Society in the Hittite World* [2002]; A. Altman, *The Historical Prologue of the Hittite Vassal Treaties: An Inquiry into the Concepts of Hittite Interstate Law* [2004]; C. A. Burney, *Historical Dictionary of the Hittites* [2004]; T. Bryce, *The Kingdom of the Hittites*, new ed. [2005]; *ABD*, 3:219–33; *CANE*, 2:1067–1120, 1295–1308.)　　　　　　　H. A. HOFFNER, JR.

Hivite hiv´it (חִוִּי *H2563*, derivation uncertain). One of the names appearing in the lists of peoples dispossessed by the Israelites (Exod. 3:8, 17; 13:5; 23:23, 28; 33:2; 34:11; Deut. 7:1; 20:17; Josh. 3:10; 9:1; 11:3; 12:8; 24:11; Jdg. 3:5; 1 Ki. 9:20, cf. 2 Chr. 8:7). In the Table of NATIONS, the Hivites are included as descendants of CANAAN (Gen. 10:17). They were located in the LEBANON hills (Jdg. 3:3) and in the HERMON range (Josh. 11:3). In the reign of DAVID they are listed after SIDON and TYRE (2 Sam. 24:7), implying their location near these cities. HAMOR, the father of SHECHEM, is called a Hivite (Gen. 34:2). The inhabitants of GIBEON to the N of JERUSALEM are also identified as Hivites (Josh. 9:7; 11:19).

Many equate Hivite with HORITE, assuming an early textual corruption of the Hebrew letter *resh* (ר) to *waw* (ו). A certain ZIBEON is apparently identified both as a Hivite and as a Horite (Gen. 36:2, 20), and the SEPTUAGINT twice reads Horite where MT has Hivite (Josh. 9:7; Gen. 34:2; note also that some MSS of the LXX read Hittite for MT's Hivite in Josh. 11:3; Jdg. 3:3). Clearly these strange ethnic designations confused the scribes. It has been maintained that, since no name that closely resembles Hivite has yet been found in extrabiblical sources, the biblical name should be viewed as a corruption of Horite, and that both Hivites and Horites should be seen as groups related culturally and linguistically to the HURRIANS. (See *Die Israeliten und deren Nachbarstämme* [1906], 328–45; E. A. Speiser in AASOR 13 [1933]: 26–31; H. A. Hoffner, Jr., in *TynBul* 20 [1969], 27–37.)   H. A. HOFFNER, JR.

Hizki hiz´ki (חִזְקִי *H2623*, "[Yahweh] has strengthened me" or "[Yahweh] is my strength"; see HEZEKIAH). KJV Hezeki. Son of ELPAAL and descendant of BENJAMIN (1 Chr. 8:17).

Hizkiah hiz-ki´uh (חִזְקִיָּה *H2624*, "Yahweh has strengthened me" or "Yahweh is my strength"; see HEZEKIAH). **(1)** KJV alternate form of HEZEKIAH (Zeph. 1:1; see also Heb. text of 2 Ki. 18:1, 10, 13–16; Neh. 7:21; 10:17; Prov. 25:1). **(2)** Son of Neariah and a postexilic descendant of DAVID (1 Chr. 3:23; KJV, "Hezekiah").

Hizkijah hiz-ki´juh. KJV alternate form of HEZEKIAH (Neh. 10:17).

hoarfrost. See FROST.

Hobab hoh´bab (חֹבָב *H2463*, possibly "beloved" or "crafty"). Son of REUEL the Midianite (Num. 10:29). Reuel was another name for JETHRO, father-in-law of MOSES; Hobab was therefore the sister of ZIPPORAH and Moses' brother-in-law. Because Hobab, as a native of MIDIAN, would have been very familiar with the desert regions in the SINAI peninsula, Moses invited him to guide the Israelites in their travels. Hobab declined, for he wanted to return to his (heathen) land and family, but Moses insisted, promising to share God's blessings with him (vv. 29–32). Although Hobab's final response is not recorded, the text seems to imply that he consented; moreover, his descendants are later associated with the Israelites (Jdg. 1:16; 4:11). The latter passage raises a difficulty by referring to the KENITES as "descendants of Hobab the father-in-law of Moses" (NRSV). According to some scholars, Hobab was another name for Jethro/Reuel, but in this verse it may be better to revocalize the Hebrew *ḥōtēn H3162* ("father-in-law") to *ḥātān H3163*, a broader term that can be rendered "brother-in-law" (cf. NIV). The precise relationship between the Kenites and the Midianites is unclear; it may be that Jethro's family was a Kenite tribe that had migrated to Midian.

Hobah hoh´buh (חוֹבָה *H2551*, possibly from Egyp. *Abum*, "land of reeds"). A city or region N (lit., "left") of DAMASCUS to which ABRAHAM pursued the defeated armies of KEDORLAOMER and his allies (Gen. 14:15; called HELBON in *Genesis Apocryphon* [1Q20] XXII, 10). The location is unknown, though some have identified it with modern Ḥoba (c. 55 mi. NNW of Damascus, on the road to Palmyra/TADMOR), and others with ancient Ube/Upi, a territory of which Damascus was part (*ANET*, 329 n. 8, 477; EA, 53.27–63). See also CHOBA.

Hobaiah hoh-bay´yuh (חֲבָיָה *H2469*, "Yahweh has hidden [or protected]"). Ancestor of a postexilic family that was unable to prove its priestly descent (Ezra 2:61 [KJV, NRSV, "Habaiah"]; Neh. 7:63 [KJV, "Habaiah"]; 1 Esd. 5:38 [KJV, "Obdia"; NRSV, "Habaiah"]).   S. BARABAS

Hod hod (הוֹד H2087, "majesty, vigor"). Son of Zophah and descendant of ASHER (1 Chr. 7:37).

Hodaiah hoh-day′yuh. KJV alternate form of HODAVIAH (1 Chr. 3:24).

Hodaviah hod-uh-vi′uh (הוֹדַוְיָה H2088 [Neh. 7:43], הוֹדְוָיה H2089 [1 Chr. 5:24; 9:7; Ezra 2:40], הוֹדַוְיָהוּ H2090 [1 Chr. 3:24, *Qere*], "praise Yahweh"; cf. JUDAH and JUDITH). **(1)** A clan chief of the half-tribe of MANASSEH; he and others are described as "brave warriors, famous men, and heads of their families" (1 Chr. 5:24). Because of their unfaithfulness, however, they and their families were taken captive by the Assyrians (vv. 25–26).

(2) Son of Hassenuah and descendant of BENJAMIN; his grandson Sallu was among those who resettled in Jerusalem after the EXILE (1 Chr. 9:7; cf. vv. 1–3; apparently called "Joed" in Neh. 11:7).

(3) Ancestor of a family of Levites who returned from the exile (Ezra 2:40; 3:9 [KJV, "Judah," following MT]; Neh. 7:43 [KJV, NRSV, "Hodevah"]; apparently called "Sudias" in 1 Esd. 5:26 and "Joda" in 1 Esd. 5:58).

(4) Son of Elioenai and postexilic descendant of SOLOMON (1 Chr. 3:24 [KJV, "Hodaiah"]).

Hodesh hoh′desh (חֹדֶשׁ H2545, "new [moon]"). One of the wives of SHAHARAIM, a Benjamite; she bore him seven children (1 Chr. 8:9–10). Instead of "his wife Hodesh," some render "his new wife"; apparently he married her after divorcing Hushim and Baara (v. 8).

Hodevah hoh-dee′vuh. KJV, NRSV alternate form of HODAVIAH (Neh. 7:43).

Hodiah hoh-di′uh (הוֹדִיָּה H2091, "majesty of Yahweh"). KJV Hodijah (except 1 Chr. 4:19). **(1)** Father or ancestor of KEILAH the Garmite and ESHTEMOA the Maacathite; he is included in the genealogy of JUDAH and also identified as having married the sister of a certain Naham. Hodiah's place in the genealogy is unclear (see the textual discussion of vv. 18–19 in G. N. Knoppers, *I Chronicles 1–9*, AB 12 [2005], 341–42). To avoid this difficulty, the KJV interprets the verse to refer back to Mered, adds a pronoun, and renders, "the sons of *his* wife Hodiah." Others, also referring to Mered, emend "and the sons of the wife of Hodiah" (*ûbĕnê ʾēšet hôdiyyâ*) to "the sons of his Judean wife" (*ûbĕnê ʾištô hayĕhudiyyâ*, as in v. 18).

(2) A Levite who helped EZRA instruct the people in the law (Neh. 8:7; 1 Esd. 9:48 [KJV, "Auteas"]). He is probably the same person mentioned among those who led the people in confession and worship (Neh. 9:5) and among the Levites who signed the covenant with NEHEMIAH (10:10).

(3) Another Levite who sealed the covenant (Neh. 10:13). Some scholars emend the text to read HODAVIAH.

(4) One of the layleaders of the people who signed the covenant (Neh. 10:18).

Hoglah hog′luh (חָגְלָה H2519, "partridge"). The third of the five daughters of ZELOPHEHAD of the tribe of MANASSEH (Num. 26:33). Since Zelophehad had no sons, Hoglah and her sisters requested ELEAZAR the priest that they be allowed to inherit their father's property, and the request was granted (27:1–11; 36:11; Josh. 17:3–4). Some see a connection between her and the town of BETH HOGLAH.

S. BARABAS

Hoham hoh′ham (הוֹהָם H2097, meaning unknown). King of HEBRON during the time of JOSHUA (Josh. 10:3). Hoham formed a league with four other AMORITE kings to make war on GIBEON because its inhabitants had signed a treaty of peace with Joshua. The five kings were decisively defeated in a battle at BETH HORON, and after being shut up in a cave at MAKKEDAH in which they had taken refuge, they were put to death (vv. 4–26).

S. BARABAS

holiness. The state or quality of being morally pure and separate from evil.
  I. In the OT
     A. Vocabulary
     B. Holiness of God
     C. Holiness of God's people
     D. Holiness of times, places, and things
  II. In the NT
     A. Vocabulary
     B. Holiness of God
     C. Holiness of the church
     D. Holiness of the Christian

I. In the OT

A. Vocabulary. According to some scholars, holiness is the most typical concept in the OT faith. It is revealed chiefly in the Hebrew verb *qādaš* H7727 and its cognates (*ḥāram* H3049 and its cognates will not be considered since the underlying connotation of the BAN is largely negative; see also ACCURSED). The verb is used primarily in the piel form (*qiddaš*), which means "to pronounce, make, or treat as holy; to sanctify, consecrate." The related adjective, *qādôš* H7705, is usually translated "holy" or "sacred." Several nouns are built on the same root: *qōdeš* H7731 ("holy thing, holiness, sacredness"), *miqdāš* H5219 ("holy place, sanctuary, shrine"), *qādēš* H7728 ("consecrated person"="cult prostitute"). Forms of the root appear some 830 times in the OT, about 350 of them being in the PENTATEUCH; the cognate Aramaic *qaddîš* H10620 ("holy") occurs thirteen times in Daniel. Aside from *qādēš*, which is used in connection with heathen cults, words derived from the root *qdš* invariably are related to God as himself holy, or to people, times, places, and objects made holy because of their association with him. "No thing or person is holy in itself, but becomes holy as it is placed in relation to God" (H. Ringgren, *The Prophetical Conception of Holiness* [1948], 9).

With respect to meaning, *qōdeš* is clearly the opposite of *ḥōl* H2687, "common, profane" (1 Sam. 21:5; Ezek. 22:26; et al.). The etymology, however, is disputed. An earlier theory, ventilated by G. F. Oehler and others, assumed an affinity between the root *qdš* and *ḥādaš* H2542 (piel, "to renew"), but this connection is rejected by O. Procksch (*TDNT*, 1:89) as contrary to the Semitic laws of sound, although E. Jacob (*Theology of the Old Testament* [1958], 86) recognizes this interpretation as a possibility.

W. W. Graf von Baudissin (*Studien zur semitischen Religionsgeschichte*, 2 vols. [1876–78]) followed H. L. Fleischer in pointing to a more basic root *qd*, "to divide," and concluded that the essence of *qdš* is separation from the secular. The root would then signify "to cut off, withdraw, set apart." The nuances of "to deprive" and "to elevate" also have been attached. Although this interpretation has been adopted by many (e.g., R. Asting, J. Skinner, A. B. Davidson, W. R. Smith, O. C. Whitehouse, J. Muilenburg), others consider it unlikely (cf. *HALOT*, 3:1072). N. H. Snaith accepts Baudissin's main argument while challenging the view that the term was altogether devoid of moral content (*The Distinctive Ideas of the Old Testament* [1944], 21–50). It has been claimed that whenever this root appears in the OT, the meaning of separation is permissible, and in many cases demanded. Ringgren, on the other hand, believes that "the idea of withdrawal, or separation, is not always very prominent" (*Prophetical Conception*, 6).

To meet those who have objected that such a derivation provides an unduly negative presentation of holiness, proponents of this theory emphasize the dual nature of separation, as implying not only being cut off from the secular, but positively devoted to and destined for the service of God. W. Eichrodt considers that this latter reference is primary. O. R. Jones concludes that holiness involves separation, but rarely is to be understood as equivalent to it. Things are separate because they are holy, not holy because they are separate. Only in virtue of its relationship to God did anything become holy and thus be regarded as separate.

Another school of etymological research attempts to trace the Hebrew root to the Akkadian *qadāšu*, "clear, bright, brilliant." Supporters of this view have included W. Gesenius, A. Dillmann, T. K. Cheyne, K. Kohler, and H. Zimmern. More recently T. C. Vriezen has gone on record as conceding that this is the most plausible meaning. The idea is linked with that of fear. Some point out that the root has the double significance of shining and terrible. This notion, of course, is implied in those passages in the OT which speak of God as revealed by fire (e.g., Exod. 3:2–5; Lev. 9:24; Deut. 4:12–24; Josh. 24:19–20; Ps. 18:8–11; Isa. 4:4–5; 6:1–5; 10:17; Ezek. 1:4). F. Delitzsch took the root as indicating freedom from defect. U. Bunzel carried this approach further by stressing the element of purity involved in brightness. Procksch considers that *ṭāhôr* H3196 ("pure") is most closely related materially to *qōdeš* (the latter being the basic cultic term, while the former is ritual). Yet, he adds, "there is always an energy in the holy which is lacking in the pure or clean" (*TDNT*, 1:89).

It was no doubt with these apparently divergent theories in mind that J. Pedersen decided that "a consideration of this root ... affords no insight into the nature of holiness, since nothing is known about it except the very fact that it is used about what we call holiness" (*Israel: Its Life and Culture*, 2 vols. [1926–40], 2:264). Etymological considerations sometimes shed light on a rarely used term, but they never determine the actual meaning of a word as used by the speaker. Since the *qdš* word group is widely attested in the OT, and since its etymology remains obscure, its actual employment in the Bible itself determines its significance. A look at its occurrences in context suggests that the factor of separateness is present, but not to the exclusion of other elements, such as radiance and purity.

B. Holiness of God. The adjective *qādôš* is a distinctly religious term, and is used exclusively in relation to God. It refers either to God himself, or to what has been sanctified by him. Primarily, however, it is God who is holy (Exod. 15:11; Isa. 6:3). There is no holiness unassociated with him. Holiness is not a human quality, nor is it an impersonal concept. Its divine provenance is everywhere insisted on in the OT.

T. C. Vriezen sees holiness as "the central idea of the Old Testament faith in God" (*An Outline of Old Testament Theology*, 2nd ed. [1970], 300). Some scholars treat the entire doctrine of God in the OT under this head (e.g., J. Hänel, *Die Religion der Heiligkeit* [1931]). Perhaps Hos. 11:9 supplies the most succinct declaration of God's holiness found in the OT: "For I am God and not man—the Holy One among you." This pregnant statement lays stress (a) on the "otherness" of God, his majesty and incomparability with any created being; and (b) on his nearness and involvement in the affairs of his people, his persistent love and graciousness (cf. *HDB* rev., 387). To equate God's holiness with his transcendence and to dissociate it from his immanence is to fall short of the OT revelation. Ringgren, who interprets *qōdeš* in terms of "the wholly other," nevertheless recognizes that it includes the divine beneficence. The Holy One is also the kindly God who has chosen Israel and has mercy on his people.

The holiness of God, however, was proclaimed long before the period of the prophets. It is implicit from the earliest times. "The concept of God's sanctity is proper to Mosaic religion from its very inception as well as to pre-Mosaic religion. The prophets only stressed this truth to a greater extent in their denunciation of a cult that was wholly external" (P. Heinisch, *Theology of the Old Testament* [1955], 69).

God is described as "the Holy One of Israel." The title recurs twenty-four times in Isaiah (cf. also 2 Ki. 19:22; Job 6:10; Pss. 71:22, 78:41, 89:18, Prov. 9:10; 30:3; Jer. 50:29; 51:5; Ezek. 39:7; Hab. 1:12; 3:3). The appellation does not mean that the Holy One belongs to Israel, although strict grammar might allow such a rendering, as E. Jacob notes. He is so not because he is consecrated to Israel, but because he has consecrated Israel to himself; and Israel itself is holy only because of what God has done.

Holiness is not merely one of God's attributes. It represents his essential nature. Holiness is his selfhood. When he swears by his holiness, he swears by himself (Amos 4:2; 6:8; cf. Gen. 22:16; Pss. 89:35; 108:7). As a predicate of God, *holy* comes to mean divine, and can be employed as an adjective for God (Isa. 5:16; 6:3; Hos. 11:9; Hab. 3:3). The niphal form strongly indicates this (Ezek. 20:41; 28:22, 25; 36:23; 38:16; 39:27; cf. Num. 20:13). God's holiness is simply his self-assertion (Vriezen). It is his active self-differentiation (Brunner). As such it expresses his whole divine personality. "The 'godness' of God is highlighted by the word 'holy' when it is used in connection with him" (O. J. Baab, *The Theology of the Old Testament* [1949], 34). Holiness is what makes God who he is.

As holy he is thus unique and incomparable (1 Sam. 2:2; 6:20; Job 25:5; Isa. 40:18–20, 25–26; Hab. 3:3). God's holiness marks him off from angels (Job 4:17–18; 15:14–15; Sir. 42:17), from heathen gods (Exod. 15:11; Ps. 77:13), and from men (Job 4:17; 15:14; Eccl. 5:2). Hence unapproachability is an element that, according to J. Skinner, "is never absent from the notion" of holiness (*HDB*, 2:397). Holiness is an aspect of God's sovereignty. He is set apart from and above all other beings for the sake of manifesting himself as he is and fulfilling his magisterial purposes. "God is free of all considerations and conditions, absolutely free master of his own will, of his feelings, even of his wrath; mighty, not having any responsibility or requiring any justification, exalted over all, Lord absolutely of his resolutions and decisions and therefore to be feared absolutely. Holy is at once exalted, supreme, and fearful" (L. Koehler, *Old Testament Theology* [1957], 53).

Holiness entails power. As the Holy One, God controls all the forces of the universe. This he does, not in order to reserve tyrannical overlordship for himself, but to convey life and blessing to mankind through his chosen people Israel (Gen. 12:1–3). This integration of the divine holiness with the righteous purpose of God is a distinctive feature of the OT revelation (Exod. 3:7; Isa. 5:16). It is thus that *qōdeš* acquires an intensified moral orientation, as it is taken up into the personal being of God (*TDNT*, 1:91). God's holiness is expressed in his justice (Lev. 10:3; Num. 20:12–13; Ps. 99:3–5; Isa. 5:16; Ezek. 28:22; 38:23).

It also manifests itself in his attitude to SIN. God's holiness denotes not merely his separation from sin in the perfection of his own being, but also his abhorrence of it and hostility to it. As a "faithful God who does no wrong" (Deut. 32:4), his "eyes are too pure to look on evil" and he "cannot tolerate wrong" (Hab. 1:13). He is concerned for his holy NAME, which he cannot allow to be profaned (Ezek. 36:20–22). He vindicates his own holiness by showing his hatred of sin and cleansing his people from it (Ezek. 36:23–25). It is in the presence of God's holiness that we become aware of our sin (Isa. 6:3–8).

Hence, there is a strong connection between divine holiness and divine JUDGMENT. A holy God who abhors sin can do no other than punish it. He is "not a God who takes pleasure in evil"; with him "the wicked cannot dwell" (Ps. 5:4). Those who desecrate God's holiness must expect his displeasure (Ps. 11:5). Indeed, the holy God proves himself to be holy as he executes his judgments (Isa. 5:16). It is by his holiness that he swears that the worldly women who oppress the poor will not escape retribution (Amos 4:1–2). JOSHUA warned the people that because God was a holy God he would not forgive their transgressions while they forsook him and served idols (Josh. 24:19–20). When fire came out from the presence of the Lord to devour NADAB and ABIHU in their impiety, MOSES pointed out to AARON that the Lord had said, "Among those who approach me / I will show myself holy; / in the sight of all the people / I will be honored" (Lev. 10:3). Similarly, KORAH and his band of Levites perished because they had despised the Lord by violating his holiness (Num. 16:30).

Such judgment will be visited on nations as well as on individuals, and for the same reason. This takes place both during the course of history and at the end of history. The Holy One of Israel is like a flame that burns and devours the thorns and briers of ASSYRIA in one day (Isa. 10:17). As he summons every kind of terror to destroy the forces of GOG in the final age, he will thereby demonstrate his greatness and holiness (Ezek. 38:23).

The supreme manifestation of God's holiness, however, is in his LOVE. In this the OT prepares the way for the fuller disclosure of the divine nature in the NT. It is in the prophecy of HOSEA that "the concept of holiness takes up into itself as the fulness of deity the thought of love" (*TDNT*, 1:93). The prophet's own domestic tragedy becomes a parable of God's predicament in the face of human waywardness and sin. Hosea's readiness to love his wanton wife and restore her to himself mirrors the immeasurably more comprehensive LOVE of God for his lost children. As Procksch brings out, the opposition between the holiness of God and all that is human still remains, but is absorbed into the deeper opposition of holy love to unholy nature. What God in virtue of his holiness may do to love unholy nature, no human being may do, and therefore the antithesis between God and us consists in the very love which overcomes it (*TDNT*, 1:93). See also GOD, BIBLICAL DOCTRINE OF.

C. Holiness of God's people. The holiness of God is expressed not only in his own mighty acts both of judgment and of mercy, but is also reflected in the holiness of his people. This is what Brunner calls his transitive holiness. Israel is "holy to the Lord" (Deut. 7:6; 14:2, 21; 26:19; 28:9; Jer. 2:3), "a holy nation" (Exod. 19:6), "a holy people" (Isa. 62:12; 63:18; Dan. 12:7), "a holy seed" or "race" (Ezra 9:2; Isa. 6:13), a community of "saints" or "holy ones" (Pss. 16:3, 34:9, 89:5; Dan. 7:21, 27), "a kingdom of priests" (Exod. 19:6), "a holy congregation" (Num. 16:3).

Moses was commanded to announce to the assembled people of Israel: "Be holy because I, the

LORD your God, am holy" (Lev. 19:2). As M. Noth (*Leviticus: A Commentary*, rev. ed. [1977], 139) points out, the expression leaves it undecided whether this is a statement (lit., "You shall be holy") or a demand. Perhaps it might be concluded that with reference to Israel's position it is a statement, but with reference to Israel's character it is a demand. This dual aspect has an important bearing on the developed revelation of holiness in the NT as it applies to God's people. Israel's holiness in the first place lies in the fact that she has been set apart by God and for God, in order that she might become the instrument of his purpose in the world. She is positionally holy since she belongs to God and has been called out from among the nations to be a chosen people for his glory (Exod. 19:4; Ezek. 37:27; Hos. 2:23). In virtue of this relationship, ratified in the COVENANT, Israel is to exhibit an actual holiness in forsaking sin and following the commandments of the law. To this end the whole body of ceremonial, legal, and moral requirements was designed.

These requirements are summarized in the Holiness Code of Lev. 17–26, in which the cultic and moral elements are intermingled. The repeated theme of Lev. 19:2 serves as a text for the whole (cf. 20:7–8, 26; 21:6, 8, 15, 23). "The remarkable distinction of this collection," explains J. L. Mays, "is the passionate urgency with which it holds holiness before Israel as the essential mark of existence as the people of the Lord" (*Leviticus, Numbers* [1964], 55). The moral code includes such practical matters as honesty (19:11, 36), truthfulness (19:11), respect for parents (19:3; 20:9), respect for elders (19:32), fair treatment of servants (19:13), love for neighbors (19:13, 16–18), kindness to strangers (19:33–34), generosity to the poor (19:10, 15), help to the handicapped (19:14, 32), sexual purity (18:1–30; 20:1–21), and the avoidance of superstition (19:26, 31; 20:6, 27).

The remainder of the Holiness Code has to do with cultic regulations. These, however, must not be dismissed as of minimal importance. The ceremonial sanctity of God's people was an expression of devotion to him. When linked, as in Leviticus, with the call to personal righteousness, it had its place in the development of the religious ideal. What the prophets later repudiated was a ceremonial cult divorced from justice. The holiness of God's people

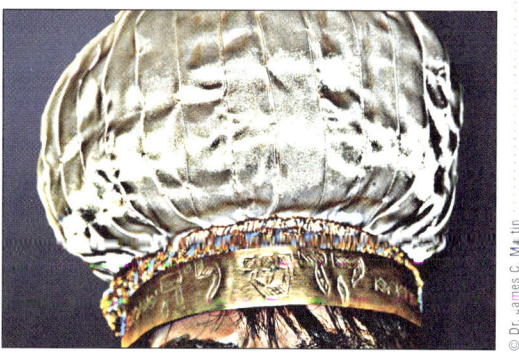

The Hebrew word for "holy" (קדש) was printed on the turban of the high priest.

was derived from their relationship to him and was originally both cultic and ethical. The two elements are often scarcely distinguishable (cf. 2 Ki. 4:9). The first requires the second. Cultic sanctity is imperfect without ethical sanctity. Cultic purity itself demands personal purity (*TDNT*, 1:92). As over against Mowinckel, who denies that the word "holy" has any predominant ethical reference in the OT, a growing consensus of scholarly opinion is inclined to reemphasize this element, while at the same time recognizing the spiritual value of the cultic.

D. Holiness of times, places, and things.
These are regarded as holy because of their association with God. They possess no inherent sacredness. They are consecrated through contact with him.

Times set apart for worship are said to be holy. Most prominent is the SABBATH or holy day (e.g., Gen. 2:3; Exod. 16:23; 20:8; Lev. 23:3, 8; Neh. 8:9–11; 9:14; 10:31; Isa. 58:13, 14). The gathering itself is described as a holy assembly (Exod. 12:1–6; Lev. 23:3–4, 7–8, 21, 24, 35; Num. 28:18, 25–26; 29:7, 12).

Places designated as holy are those where God has revealed himself or is worshiped. HEAVEN itself as the abode of God is described as holy (Deut. 26:15; 2 Chr. 30:27; Ps. 11:4; Isa. 63:15; Jer. 25:30; Jon. 2:4, 7; Mic. 1:2; Hab. 2:20; Zech. 2:13). The same adjective is applied to such earthly locations as the BURNING BUSH (Exod. 3:5), SINAI (19:11), GILGAL (Josh. 5:13–15), and the resting place of the ARK OF THE COVENANT in Jerusalem (2 Chr. 8:11). Similarly both BETHEL and Horeb (SINAI) were regarded as sacred (Gen. 28:17; 1 Ki. 19:8).

The land of promise is holy (Exod. 15:13; Ezek. 4:12–13; Hos. 9:3, 4; Amos 7:17; Zech. 2:12). The camp of the Israelites is holy (Lev. 10:4, 5; 13:6; 16:20–22; Deut. 23:14). The city of Jerusalem is holy (Neh. 11:1, 18; Ps. 46:2, 4; Isa. 48:2; 52:1–2); Zion is holy (Isa. 11:9; 27:13; 56:7).

Both the tabernacle and later the temple, with all their appurtenances, are called holy. The tabernacle itself is called a sanctuary (Exod. 38:24; Lev. 10:4). The court of the tabernacle also is called a sanctuary (Lev. 10:17–18). The tabernacle and its courts together with their contents are holy (Exod. 40:9). The first section, the outer room, is known as "the holy place" (26:33; 28:29). The second section, the inner room, is known as "the most holy" or "holy of holies" (26:33–34). The entrance to the tabernacle is holy (29:31). The temple is a holy house (1 Chr. 29:3; Pss. 5:7; 79:1; 138:2; Isa. 64:11). Its precincts share this sacredness (1 Chr. 24:5; 2 Chr. 29:7). The holy place (Ezek. 41:21, 23; 42:14; 44:27) and the most holy place (1 Ki. 6:16; 7:50; 8:6; 2 Chr. 3:8, 10; 4:22; 5:7; Ezek. 41:4) retain their distinctions.

Every item connected with the tabernacle and the temple is represented as holy: the altars of incense and burnt offering (Exod. 29:37; 30:27; 40:10), the flesh of the sacrifices (Num. 18:17; 2 Chr. 29:33; Ezek. 36:38; Hag. 2:12), the food of the sacrifices (Lev. 21:22; Num. 5:9; 18:9), the vessels for drink offerings (1 Ki. 8:4), the ark of God (Exod. 30:26; 2 Chr. 35:3), the anointing oil (Exod. 30:25; Ps. 89:20), the incense (Exod. 30:35, 37), the table (30:27), the showbread (Lev. 24:5–9; 1 Sam. 21:4), the candlestick (Exod. 30:2), the laver (30:28), the clothing of the priests (28:2; 29:29; 31:10; Ezek. 42:14), the shekel of the sanctuary (Exod. 30:13), the valuables deposited in the treasury (Josh. 6:19; 1 Ki. 7:51). In keeping with the holiness associated with the tabernacle and the temple, the priests ministering there also are regarded as sacred and for this reason were consecrated to their office (Exod. 29:1; Lev. 21:6, 23; 22:9).

No doubt this repeated emphasis in the OT on the holiness of times, places, and things belongs to the realm of the cultic rather than the moral. It is never altogether easy to disentangle these elements. While such a materialization of the holy might lend itself to abuse—such times, places, and things could be considered to possess some sanctity in themselves apart from the presence of the living God—this danger seems largely to have been avoided when his people remained faithful to him. The spreading contagion of uncleanness is not paralleled by any such uncontrolled dissemination of holiness (cf. Lev. 6:27; 22:1–9; Num. 19:11–13). When Haggai asked the priests of the return: "If a person carries consecrated meat in the fold of his garment, and that fold touches some bread or stew, some wine, oil or other food, does it become consecrated?" they were able to answer quite correctly, "No" (Hag. 2:12).

While the ethical content in the OT conception of holiness must not be underrated any more than the cultic, it is to be remembered that the overriding and determinative factor is that holiness comes from the Lord. "The uniqueness of the OT definition of holiness," declares W. Eichrodt, "lies not in its elevated moral standard, but in the personal quality of the God to which it refers" (*Theology of the Old testament*, 2 vols. [1961], 1:276).

(See further F. J. Leenhardt, *La notion de sainteté dans l'Ancien Testament* [1929]; G. Bettenzoli, *Geist der Heiligkeit. Traditionsgeschichtliche Untersuchung des QDŠ-Begriffes im Buch Ezechiel* [1979]; J. G. Gammie, *Holiness in Israel* [1989]; *ABD*, 3:237–49; *NIDOTTE*, 3:877–87.)

II. In the NT

A. Vocabulary. The concept of holiness is expressed in the NT through various terms, such as the adjectives *hosios* G4008 (e.g., of God himself, Rev. 15:4) and *hieros* G2641 (of Scripture, 2 Tim. 3:15), and the noun *hosiotēs* G4009 (Lk. 1:75; Eph. 4:24). Of greater significance, however, is the frequent adjective *hagios* G11, which recurs some 230 times, as well as several of its cognates. This adjective can be used as a substantive (e.g., of sacrificial meat, Matt. 7:6; of the sanctuary, esp. in the plural, Heb. 8:2 et al.). The expression *ho hagios*, "the Holy One," is used of God the Father in the Greek OT, but only of Christ the Son in the NT (Mk. 1:24 et al.; cf. *ton hosion sou*, Acts 2:27), unless 1 Jn. 2:20 is an exception. The plural *hoi hagioi*, "the holy ones," is used of angels (1 Thess. 3:13; 2 Thess. 1:10) and of saints, that is, Christians consecrated to God (Acts 9:13, 32; Rom. 1:7; et al.). In the Septuagint, *hagios* is consistently utilized to render the Hebrew adjective *qādôš*, and the fact that this Greek term was appropriated wholly in the interests of the OT view of holiness is determinative for NT usage.

Out of four or five Greek terms that could be rendered "holy," *hagios* is the least frequent in classical literature. The concept of holiness had to be filled with fresh content, hence, as H. Cremer saw, this Greek adjective "is one of the words wherein the radical influence, the transforming and newly fashioning power of revealed religion is most clearly shown" (*Biblico-Theological Lexicon of New Testament Greek*, 3rd ed. [1883], 35). It has a history similar to the corresponding Hebrew term. Originally it was a cultic concept, indicating that which is consecrated or devoted to or qualified to approach a deity (BDAG, 9). Its earliest established attestation is in HERODOTUS (*Hist.* 5.119), where it is used in close association with the sanctuary. It is also applied to the gods. But *hagios* does not appear to have been related to man in connection with the cultus, *hagnos* G54 being preferred for this usage (*TDNT*, 1:89).

There are indeed some few instances in the NT where the cultic sense persists. This is particularly the case in OT quotations and allusions to the former dispensation. Jerusalem is described as the holy city as in the OT (Matt. 4:5; 27:53; Rev. 11:2). The same expression is applied to the heavenly Jerusalem (Rev. 21:2, 10; 22:19). The temple is spoken of as the holy place (Matt. 24:15; Acts 6:13; 21:28). The mount of transfiguration is holy (2 Pet. 1:18). It is noticeable that all these instances are related to places rather than persons. Even in this connection, the adjective soon shades over into the fuller meaning of holy, that is, pure, perfect, worthy of God. The term is employed in this sense with reference to the law of God (Rom. 7:12), the temple of the body (1 Cor. 3:17), the temple of the church (Eph. 2:21), and the spiritual sacrifice of the Christian (Rom. 12:1).

In the great preponderance of occurrences, *hagios* is used of persons and signifies a relationship to God, who is himself holy (Jn. 17:11; 1 Pet. 1:15; Rev. 4:8). The prophets of the OT are described as holy (Lk. 1:70; Acts 3:21; 2 Pet. 3:2). John the Baptizer is "a righteous and holy man" (Mk. 6:20). The apostles are holy (Eph. 3:5). The most common reference of all is to Christians who, because of their position before God in Christ and the sanctifying work of the indwelling Spirit, are properly designated holy. This is connected closely with their calling and election (Col. 3:12; 2 Tim. 1: 9). The commandment they have received, to which obedience must be given, is holy (2 Pet. 2:21). This association between calling, commandment, and holiness is crystallized in 1 Pet. 1:15–16: "But just as he who called you is holy, so be holy in all you do; for it is written, 'Be holy, because I am holy.'"

The fact that *hagios* is the NT equivalent of *qādôš* suggests that the idea of separation and purity is carried over into a new context. It is given a reinforced ethical and spiritual cast. As applied to Christians, the term means set apart for God, reserved for his praise and service. Believers have been made holy by the saving work of Christ on the cross, which has separated them from this present evil world and transferred them into the kingdom of God's dear Son (Col. 1:13). They are continually being made holy by the work of the HOLY SPIRIT within, who enables them to respond to the NT summons to live in righteousness and purity. According to G. B. Stevens, *hagios* is "above all things a qualitative and ethical term" (*HDB*, 2:399). This is indicated by the adjectives with which it is paired: *dikaios* G1465, "righteous" (Mk. 6:20; Acts 3:14), and *amōmos* G320, "blameless" (Eph. 1:4; 5:27; Col. 1:22).

The cognate verb *hagiazō*, "to make holy," "consecrate," "sanctify," appears twenty-seven times in

Marble pig (Greek, 350–300 B.C.). The holiness of the Israelites was reflected in their diet; certain foods, such as pork, were considered "unclean."

the NT, though it is rare in extrabiblical usage. In the LXX it is the usual rendering of the root *qdš* in its verbal forms. The NT uses the verb in the sense of setting aside or rendering things suitable for ritual purposes (cf. Matt. 23:19, the altar makes the gift sacred; 1 Tim. 4:5, what is received with thanksgiving is consecrated by the Word of God and prayer). It is used also of profane things made holy by contact with the sacred (cf. Matt. 23:17, the temple makes the gold sacred). With reference to persons, the verb may signify "consecrate, dedicate, make holy," that is, "include ... in the inner circle of what is holy, in both cultic and moral associations of the word" (BDAG, 10). It is so used of the CHURCH, which Christ sanctified and cleansed "by the washing with water through the word" (Eph. 5:26), and of Christians consecrated by BAPTISM (1 Cor. 6:11).

The verb *hagiazō* also may mean "to sanctify" by the blood of sacrifice, that is, to atone for sins (Heb. 2:11; 9:13; 10:10, 14, 29; 13:12). Sometimes its significance is "to treat as holy, to reverence" (Matt. 6:9; Lk. 11:2; 1 Pet. 3:15). Its basic connotation is to consecrate or sanctify by contact with the One who alone is holy, God himself. So Christians are *hēgiasmenoi*, in a state of having been sanctified (Jn. 17:19; Acts 20:32; 26:18; Rom. 15:16; 1 Cor. 1:2). It is God who sanctifies (Jn. 17:17; 1 Thess. 5:23).

Cognate substantives are comparatively infrequent: *hagiōsynē* G43 seems to refer to holiness as a quality (Rom. 1:4; 2 Cor. 7:1; 1 Thess. 3:13); *hagiasmos* G40, holiness as a process or result, that is, "sanctification, consecration" (Rom. 6:19, 22; 1 Cor. 1:30; 1 Thess. 4:3–4, 7; 2 Thess. 2:13; 1 Tim. 2:15; Heb. 12:14; 1 Pet. 1:2); and *hagiotēs* G42, holiness as a condition or state (2 Cor. 1:12; Heb. 12:10).

The rare word *hagiōsynē* is constructed from the adjective *hagios* by extension as an abstract term of quality (cf. *dikaiosynē*, "righteousness," from *dikaios*, "righteous"). It is not found in prebiblical Greek. The three NT occurrences are all in the Pauline epistles. In Rom. 1:4, the phrase "according to [NIV, through] the Spirit of holiness" is contrasted with "according to the flesh" (v. 3; NIV, "as to his human nature"). Some take this to be an exact rendering of the Hebrew phrase for "Holy Spirit" (Ps. 51:11; Isa. 63:10–11); others argue, on the basis of the antithesis with flesh, that the reference is to Christ's own spirit (however, see T. R. Schreiner, *Romans*, BECNT [1998], 43). In 2 Cor. 7:1 Paul urges his converts to purify themselves "from everything that contaminates body and spirit, perfecting holiness out of reverence for God" (NEB, "complete our consecration"). The ethical character of *hagiōsynē* is obviously prominent here. This is equally the case in 1 Thess. 3:13, where Paul's prayer for his readers is that the Lord may strengthen their hearts so that at the PAROUSIA they may stand before God the Father "unblamable in holiness" (RSV).

The term *hagiasmos* is an active verbal noun derived from *hagiazō*; it thus implies the act of sanctifying rather than SANCTIFICATION either as a condition (*hagiotēs*) or as a quality (*hagiōsynē*). When used in a moral sense (as it is invariably), *hagiasmos* denotes a process or on occasion the result of a process. It is infrequent in the LXX and has no specific Hebrew equivalent (*TDNT*, 1:113). In the NT it is confined to the epistles and occurs mainly in the context of Gentile Christianity. The act or process of being sanctified is the will of God for Christians (1 Thess. 4:3). It is manifested in the sphere of sexual morality as the husband learns how to honor his body (or his wife; cf. NIV mg.). The opposite is "impurity" (4:7 NRSV; the term is also linked with modesty or propriety, 1 Tim. 2:15). The body, which was once employed in the service of impurity and lawlessness, now must be yielded to God in the service of righteousness, with *hagiasmos* ("a holy life," NEB) as the goal in view (Rom. 6:19). In this emancipation from sin in the service of God, the return (lit. "fruit") Christians get is holiness (Rom. 6:22). The source of such sanctification can only be the holy God: he sanctifies us in Christ, whom he has made to be our *hagiasmos* as well as our wisdom, righteousness, and redemption (1 Cor. 1:30). This work is said to be by or in the Spirit (2 Thess. 2:13; 1 Pet. 1:2). Without it no one will even see the Lord when he returns; hence, it is to be aimed at and striven for as the goal of the Christian life (Heb. 12:14).

The third noun, *hagiotēs*, is quite rare (cf. the references in BDAG, 11). As a condition or state, *hagiotēs* is an essential attribute of God which he shares in measure with his children, so that it can be said that they "share in his holiness" (Heb. 12:10; a notion virtually equivalent to "participate in the divine nature," 2 Pet. 1:4). Although this state is only consummated and perfected in glorification, the implication seems to be that already in this life believers partake of God's holiness. The other NT occurrence of the term (2 Cor. 1:12) is less certain, since most MSS have the word *haplotēs* G605 (KJV, "simplicity"; NRSV, "frankness"). This latter term is preferred by many scholars, partly because of the context (the word is paired with *eilikrineia* G1636, "sincerity"), partly because Paul does not elsewhere use *hagiotēs*. But the earliest witnesses have *hagiotēs*, which may be regarded as the more difficult reading and thus the more likely to be original (cf. NIV). The genitive "of God" is not necessarily possessive (as Procksch assumes, *TDNT*, 1:114); it may be one of origin, indicating that holiness and sincerity in the believer spring from the working of God's grace. In this case a qualitative element is also implied (cf. G. Abbott-Smith, *A Manual Greek Lexicon of the New Testament*, 3rd ed. [1937], 5).

B. Holiness of God. In the OT the holiness of God is trebled in the praises of the seraphim: "Holy, holy, holy is the LORD Almighty" (Isa. 6:3). This *trisagion* is repeated in the NT as John in his vision is permitted to hear the living creatures that surround the heavenly throne singing in ceaseless antiphon: "Holy, holy, holy, is the Lord God Almighty" (Rev. 4:8). Such a threefold reiteration, however, is not merely impressive in its effect. It is related to the TRINITY of persons in the Godhead, and this factor, implicit in the OT, is made explicit in the NT. The Son addresses the Holy Father (Jn. 17:11), he is himself the Holy Servant or Child (Acts 4:30); and the third Person of the Godhead is the Holy Spirit (Jn. 14:26). Holiness is not reserved for one but belongs to each.

1. God the Father. The number of passages in the NT in which holiness is directly attributed to God the Father is not large. It is not to be supposed that the NT regards the holiness of God the Father as of less importance than the OT, or that there is any discrepancy between what is revealed in the OT and what is revealed in the NT. On the contrary, it is in the harmony of the Testaments that one sees the reason for the comparative paucity of references. The OT itself had sufficiently established the personality and holiness of the Father. It remained for the NT to focus on the Son and the Spirit. If, however, the holiness of God the Father is seldom stated in the NT, it is everywhere presumed (*TDNT*, 1:101). Mary in her MAGNIFICAT rejoices in God her Savior: "the Mighty One has done great things for me—holy is his name" (Lk. 1:49). Whenever the Father is named, his holiness is asserted.

The teaching of Jesus is definitive. The prominence given to the hallowing of the Father's name in the initial clause of the prayer he taught his disciples is indicative of the place it held in his mind (Matt. 6:9; Lk. 11:2; see LORD'S PRAYER). In his own high priestly prayer, he addressed "the only true God" (Jn. 17:3) not simply as "Father" (vv. 1, 5, 21, 24) but as "Holy Father" (v. 11) as well as "righteous Father" (v. 25). The context in which this expression is used is most instructive. Jesus pleaded with his holy Father to keep his disciples who were to be left in the world. The basic element in God's holiness is his separation from this present evil world. W. Temple remarks that in Jn. 17:15, "where the burden of prayer is deliverance from the evil power of the world … the thought of God as wholly separate from that evil is specially appropriate. The Father is asked to grant to the disciples His own immunity from evil" (*Readings in St. John's Gospel* [1945], 318). In the conjunction of holiness and FATHERHOOD, the transcendence and immanence of God, already implied in the OT revelation of holiness, is further emphasized.

2. God the Son. In twelve NT passages, Christ is described as holy. In nine of them the adjective *hagios* is used (Mk. 1:24; Lk. 1:35; 4:34; Jn. 6:69; Acts 3:14; 4:27, 30; 1 Jn. 2:20; Rev. 3:7), and in three *hosios* (Acts 2:27; 13:5; Heb. 7:26). Before his birth, the Lord was marked out as holy. The angel announced to Mary: "The Holy Spirit will come upon you, and the power of the Most High will overshadow you. So the holy one to be born [of you] will be called the Son of God" (Lk. 1:35). The demon-possessed man in the CAPERNAUM synagogue cried out: "I know who you are—the Holy One of God" (Mk. 1:24; Lk. 4:24). There was a mortal confrontation between the Holy One and the evil one. In Jn. 6:69 there is recorded a confession of faith on the part of Simon Peter which is to be set beside that in the synoptics (cf. Mk. 8:29; Matt. 16:16). Its essence is belief, and indeed knowledge, that Jesus is the Holy One of God.

Three times in Acts—once in Peter's speech in Solomon's portico and twice in the prayer of the believers after Peter and John had been discharged by the Sanhedrin—Jesus is referred to as God's (holy) servant (Acts 3:13–14; 4:26, 30). The word in Greek is *pais* G4090, which also can mean a child. It significantly identifies Jesus with the Suffering Servant of Isaiah, and at the same time asserts his divine Sonship: both as Servant and Son, he is holy. The two verses in Acts where Christ is described as "the Holy One" (*ho hosios*) are both quotations from Ps. 16:10 (Acts 2:27; 13:35), and F. F. Bruce takes the reference in Heb. 7:26 to reflect this same usage (*The Epistle to the Hebrews*, NICNT [1964], 156).

The Holy One in 1 Jn. 2:20, by whom believers are anointed, is clearly to be regarded as the Son. If this unction is not directly connected with the Holy Spirit, but with the Lord's own messianic consecration at his baptism, now shared by all who belong to him, as C. H. Dodd believes, the identification is confirmed. The Lord of the churches is described as "holy and true" (Rev. 3:7), a title that reappears as appertaining to God the Father (6:10), and is thus a tacit acknowledgement of the Son's divinity (see DEITY OF CHRIST). Jesus is he "whom the Father has sanctified and sent into the world" (Jn. 10:36 NRSV). The holiness of the Son as it is manifested to the world is derived from that of the Father.

The holiness of the Son is exhibited in his character. He loved righteousness and hated iniquity (Heb. 1:9). Both the positive and the negative factors are essential to holiness. He refrained from evil and pursued the good. He committed no sin of any kind (1 Pet. 2:22). Although he was tempted in every respect as all human beings are, yet he remained entirely without sin (Heb. 4:15). It was because of the holiness of his nature that he was thus enabled to triumph over the evil one. His testimony was that he always did what was acceptable to his Father (Jn. 8:29). It was only by virtue of his holiness that the Lord was equipped to make the one sufficient sacrifice on the cross which would save men from their sins. Because his abhorrence of sin was so acute, he willingly turned his back on heavenly glory in order to redeem lost humanity. Only the one who knew no sin could be made sin for us (2 Cor. 5:21). Only the perfectly righteous could suffer and die for the unrighteous, that he might bring us to God (1 Pet. 3:18).

3. God the Spirit. The holiness of the Spirit is indicated by the frequent attachment of the predicate *hagios* to his name. It is not for nothing that the NT describes him predominantly as the HOLY SPIRIT. This title occurs only three times in the OT (Ps. 51:11; Isa. 63:10–11), but is found no fewer than ninety-one times in the NT. In the OT he usually is designated as "the Spirit," "the Spirit of the Lord," or "the Spirit of God." In the NT he appears simply as "the Spirit" forty-six times, as "the Spirit of God" eighteen times, and as "the Spirit of the Lord" four times. The title "Holy Spirit" is by far the most common.

It is used in the first instance to distinguish him from other spirits, especially those which are evil. "The adjective here is not merely qualitative: it is adversative" (J. J. von Allmen, *Vocabulary of the Bible* [1958], 172). The NT emphasis on the Spirit as holy marks him out as altogether unique and incomparable (Matt. 12:32; Rom. 15:16; 1 Cor. 6:19; Eph. 2:18; 2 Tim. 1:14). The qualitative aspect of the title cannot, however, be overlooked. It implies that the third Person of the Trinity shares the holiness of the godhead. The essential nature of deity belongs to the Spirit, as well as to the Father and the Son. In view of the fact that in the NT holiness is invariably personalized, the use of *hagios* in connection with the Spirit is further evidence that the Spirit is regarded as a Person rather than merely an influence.

His holiness is implicit in the fact that he is described as the Spirit of Christ (Rom. 8:9; Phil. 1:19; 1 Pet. 1:11; cf. Gal. 4:6). His work is to glorify the Son (Jn. 16:14; cf. 15:26). He fixes attention on the Savior. It is his function to cause the living Christ to dwell within the heart of the believer. As F. D. E. Schleiermacher recognized, the fruit of the Spirit is nothing less than the virtues of Christ. It is the Spirit who makes possible such conformity to the Master's image: he can do so only by reason of his holiness. None but the Holy Spirit can be the Spirit of Christ. He is holy in himself and also makes believers holy by renewing them in the likeness of their Lord.

The teaching of Jesus concerning the Spirit sufficiently substantiates his holiness. There has been a tendency on the part of some more radical scholars to discount this evidence on critical grounds. As C. K. Barrett (*The Gospel according to John*, 2nd ed. [1978], 88) insists, however, the comparative sparseness of reference is to be accounted for in terms of Jn. 7:39 — "Up to that time the Spirit had not been given, since Jesus had not yet been glorified." Even as it stands, the Lord's teaching about the Spirit clearly demonstrates his holiness. There could be no BLASPHEMY against any but a *Holy* Spirit (Mk. 3:28–30; cf. Matt. 12:31, 32; Lk. 12:10). None other than a Holy Spirit could eject demons, acting as "the finger of God" (Matt. 12:28; Lk. 11:20). Baptism into the name of the Holy Spirit, as well as of the Father and of the Son, implies that the Spirit's name is holy (Matt. 28:19).

We have seen that in the OT the holiness of God is a synonym for his power. This is made markedly apparent in the NT with reference to the Holy Spirit. T. W. Manson (*The Teaching of Jesus: Studies in Its Form and Content*, 2nd ed. [1935], 266 n. 1) maintained that "power" in Mk. 14:62 simply means God (cf. NIV, "the Mighty One"). The close association of the Spirit with power would seem to suggest that in him this power is brought directly down to earth and made available for the purposes of godly living.

C. Holiness of the church. This theme is implicit throughout the NT, although the explicit phrase "holy church" does not occur. The personal factor remains uppermost, since in the NT the CHURCH is not regarded as an organization as much as a fellowship of those who are in Christ. There is "no holy 'It,' above all no holy collective, no holy institution" (E. Brunner, *Dogmatics* [1962], 3:125). Nevertheless, "the idea of holiness remains basically communal and ecclesiastical" (Allmen, *Vocabulary*, 168). The believer is born again into the family of God and only in that family will he grow in grace. O. Cullmann can go so far as to define holiness in these terms simply as "the fact of belonging to the saints" (*Baptism in the New Testament* [1950], 53).

Byzantine mosaic depicting a queen (Church of Hagia Sophia, Istanbul); the halo has long been a symbol of holiness.

The holiness of the church is the NT equivalent for the holiness of Israel as God's people in the OT. The community of Christians constitutes the New Israel (Gal. 6:16; Eph. 2:12; Heb. 8:10). This is not merely a matter of continuity: indeed, if this were the sole consideration, it is doubtful whether the phrase New Israel should be used at all. But the determinative factor is that Christians are heirs of the new covenant in Christ Jesus, the true Messiah, in whose advent the kingdom had arrived (see COVENANT, THE NEW). Living in the last days under the rule of God and awaiting the return of Christ as judge, Christians were identified with the saints or holy ones of Dan. 7:18, 22 (and *1 En.* 38.4–5) who lived in expectation of the end. It is in this sense that the church is regarded in the NT as the New Israel. As such it shares in the holiness of God's people.

It is significant that Peter in his first letter takes the expression of Exod. 19:6 — "a kingdom of priests and a holy nation" — and transfers it to the church, adding, as if to stress the point, "a chosen people" and "a people belonging to God" (1 Pet. 2:9). Holiness is a characteristic of the church as the continuing people of God. The covenantal basis of Israel's holiness was strongly underlined in the OT (Exod. 19:5–6; Lev. 19:2; Deut. 7:6; 26:19; Ps. 89:5). In the NT the new covenant in Christ's blood shed on the cross is the ground (Jn. 17:19; Rom. 15:16; 1 Cor. 1:2; 6:11; Eph. 5:26).

Holiness is much more than a secondary feature of the church. On the contrary, it defines its very essence. Its importance is reflected in the frequency of references in the NT. The holiness of the church is alluded to in fourteen NT writings, and in seven others parallel expressions occur. As being holy, the church is the creation and possession of God. Both its inception and its survival depend on his gracious activity. The community of Christians is "a people only because he dwells within them and moves among them" (P. S. Minear, *Images of the Church in the New Testament* [1961], 69).

The idea of separation, so prominent in the OT, is carried over into the NT doctrine of the church (2 Cor. 6:14). However, the positive aspect of being set aside for God to be utilized in his service prevails over any negative exclusivism. The OT conception of property as forming an extension of personality finds its loftiest expression in the relationship between God and his people. In the NT this is intensified in respect of the church and of the Christians who compose it. The church as the BODY OF CHRIST belongs to God and becomes the vehicle of his activity in the world (1 Cor. 12:27; Col. 1:18). Similarly, the church as a dwelling place of God in the Spirit exists solely to further the ends of redemption (Eph. 2:22; 3:5–6). In order to prove an effective instrument of the gospel, the church must be holy.

Not only does the NT doctrine of the church take over and fill out the OT concept of Israel as the holy people of God: it also reinterprets the temple cultus spiritually in terms of a new sanctuary, in which Christ is both priest and sacrifice. The priests of the former dispensation who offered gifts according to the law served "a copy and shadow of what is in heaven" (Heb. 8:5). Hence, *hagios* in the NT takes on a pneumatic sense (*TDNT*, 1:106). Christ as the Holy Servant of God becomes the center of a new WORSHIP in which he is supreme. As the great High Priest in glory, he has now sat down at God's right hand, indicating that his sacrificial work is once for all complete (Heb. 7:27; 10:12). Henceforward the cultic holiness of the church is displayed in the offering of spiritual worship (Rom. 12:1) and spiritual sacrifices of praise, thanksgiving, and doing good (Heb. 13:15–16; 1 Pet. 2:5), since there is no longer any sacrifice for sin (Heb. 10:18, 26). The church reveals itself as holy by its emancipation from materialistic expressions of worship. It is significant that the temple itself is reinterpreted as the community of the Spirit (Eph. 2:19–22), and that when there is a localized reference, it is to the believer's body in which the Spirit makes his home (1 Cor. 3:16–17).

The eschatological dimension of the church's holiness must not be overlooked (see ESCHATOLOGY). As we have seen, in OT apocalyptic the holy are those who have been delivered from the domain of darkness and participate in the glory of the messianic age. According to the NT, Christians have even now entered into the FIRSTFRUITS of this blessing. They enjoy the seal of the Spirit, which is the guarantee of their INHERITANCE until they acquire full possession of it (Eph. 1:13–14). But the riches of Christ's glorious patrimony still lie in the future (Eph. 1:18). Being holy, the church is continually waiting for and hastening toward the coming of God's great day (2 Pet. 3:11–12). Its members are being built up by the word of God's grace, which is able to give them "the inheritance among all those who are sanctified" (Acts 20:32).

The eschatological, however, is never divorced from the ethical. In view of what lies in store for the church at the end, the purpose of God is "to purify for himself a people that are his very own, eager to do what is good" (Tit. 2:14). It was for this that Christ "loved the church and gave himself up for her to make her holy ... without stain or wrinkle or any other blemish, but holy and blameless" (Eph. 5:25–27). The church is betrothed to Christ, and at the parousia she is to be presented "as a pure bride to her one husband" (2 Cor. 11:2 RSV; cf. Rev. 19:7–8; 21:9).

D. Holiness of the Christian. This theme already has been dealt with in expounding the meaning of *hagios* and its cognates. We have also noted that in the NT, as in the OT, it is the intention of the holy God that his children should be holy as he is. It is the function of the Holy Spirit to effect this sanctification by conforming believers to the image of Christ. The personal manner in which the church is presented in the NT as the fellowship of Christians means that it is holy as its members are holy. We need do no more than summarize the evidence.

The most common name for Christians in the NT is *saints*. They share in the first resurrection, or new birth, and as such are regarded as holy (Rev. 20:6). They have been sanctified in Christ (Acts 20:32; 26:18; 1 Cor. 6:11; Heb. 10:10). They are holy brethren (1 Thess. 5:27), constituting a holy priesthood (1 Pet. 2:5). They have been separated from sin (1 Cor. 6:19; 2 Tim. 2:19; Tit. 2:12), and consecrated to a life of purity and godliness (Eph. 1:4; 5:27; Col. 1:22; 2 Pet. 3:11). Holiness is inseparably bound up with the Christian's calling and election (Col. 3:12; 2 Tim. 1:9; 1 Pet. 1:5). It is accomplished by the will of the Father (1 Thess. 4:3; 5:24; Heb. 10:10). Its center is Christ himself (1 Cor. 1:30) and its agent is the Holy Spirit (2 Thess. 2:13; 1 Pet. 1:2). It is connected with faith, which is at once its outcome and the ground on which it continues to operate (Acts 26:18; Eph. 1:1; Col. 1:2; 2 Thess. 1:11; Rev. 13:10). Its objective is the glory of God, both now and at the last (2 Thess. 1:10, 12).

Holiness is ultimately to be interpreted in terms of the complementary experiences of our being in Christ and Christ being in us. These two are inextricable. In the NT to be in Christ is at the same time to have Christ in us (Eph. 3:17). Any alleged UNION WITH CHRIST that fails to produce the image of Christ within is exposed as false (Rom. 8:9).

The supreme manifestation of holiness is in love. There is at once a eulogy of Christian love and a delineation of Christian holiness (1 Cor. 13). It is perfectly realized only in the man Christ Jesus. It remains nevertheless the criterion by which the believer's growth in grace is to be assessed. The essence of the divine nature is holy love. It is in this above all that as he is so are we to be in the world (1 Jn. 4:17). See SANCTIFICATION.

(See further E. Issel, *Der Begriff der Heiligkeit im Neuen Testament* [1881]; E. H. Askwith, *The Christian Conception of Holiness* [1900]; S. Neill, *Christian Holiness* [1960]; O. R. Jones, *The Concept of Holiness* [1961]; D. Peterson, *Possessed by God: A New Testament Theology of Sanctification and Holiness* [1995]; S. Hauerwas, *Sanctify Them in the Truth: Holiness Exemplified* [1998]; S. C. Barton, ed., *Holiness: Past and Present* [2003]; *ABD*, 3:249–54; *NIDNTT*, 2:223–38.)

A. S. WOOD

Holiness Code. A common designation for the legal corpus found in Lev. 17–26, thought by many to have had an independent origin; often referred to simply as H. See PENTATEUCH.

holm tree. This term is used by some English versions (based on the Vulg. *ilex*) to render Hebrew *tirzâ* H9560, which occurs only once (Isa. 44:14 [NRSV, "He cuts down cedars or chooses a holm tree or an oak"]; cf. also KJV Sus. 58 for Gk. *prinos*). The holm oak, also known as the holly oak (*Quercus ilex*), is a beautiful Mediterranean evergreen that reaches a height of 40–50 ft. (see *FFB*, 128–29). The meaning of the Hebrew word is uncertain, however, and the NIV follows the KJV in interpreting it as a reference to the CYPRESS. See also FLORA (under *Fagaceae*).

Holofernes hol´uh-fuhr´neez (Ὀλοφέρνης or Ὁλοφέρνης; cf. Ὀροφέρνης [closer to the original Persian form] in Polybius, *Hist.* 3.5.2 et al.). According to the book of JUDITH, Holofernes was the chief general of the army of NEBUCHADNEZZAR, king of Assyria (!) and second only to the king in power (Jdt. 2:4 et al.). He was commissioned by the king with the task of subjugating "the whole of the west," including Palestine. One after another, the nations fell before him; only Israel refused to yield. Holofernes besieged the Jewish town of BETHULIA, where the army of Israel was concentrated, and almost forced its capitulation, when a beautiful Jewish widow named Judith asked the Jewish leaders for permission to leave the town and see Holofernes. Permission was granted. When she appeared before the general, she told him that she had come because she knew that BETHULIA was doomed and she knew how the town could be captured easily. Holofernes fell completely under the spell of her charm and beauty and believed everything she told him. On the fourth night of her stay with him, he made a banquet to which she was invited. Holofernes got drunk, and after everyone else had left she took his sword and cut off his head, which she took in a bag to the leaders of Israel. When the Assyrians realized that their general was murdered, they were seized with panic and fled. Thus ended the Assyrian threat.

S. BARABAS

Holon hoh´lon (חֹלוֹן *H2708*, possibly "sandy"). **(1)** A town in the hill country of the tribe of JUDAH (Josh. 15:51); it was later assigned to the Levites descended from KOHATH (21:15; called HILEN in the parallel passage, 1 Chr. 6:58). The site is unknown. Some scholars have identified it with Khirbet ʿAlin, c. 11 mi. NW of HEBRON, but a location S or SW of Hebron seems more likely (Holon is associated with such towns as ANIM, DEBIR, and ESHTEMOA).

(2) A city in the plain of MOAB against which JEREMIAH pronounced judgment (Jer. 48:21). It was probably located N of the ARNON River, but the site is unknown.

Holy Ghost. See HOLY SPIRIT.

Holy of Holies. See TABERNACLE.

Holy Place. See TABERNACLE.

Holy Sepulchre, Church of the. See GOLGOTHA.

Holy Spirit. In Christian theology, the third person of the TRINITY. The OT refers to the Spirit of God (Gen. 1:2 et al.) with the Hebrew term *rûah H8120*, which often means "wind"—an invisible, irresistible power, sometimes benign and beneficial, sometimes raging and destructive (Gen. 8:1; Exod. 10:13, 19; 14:21; Num. 11:31; et al.). By analogy, the word was applied to the human breath, and since the breath is at once the evidence of animal vitality and the vehicle of thought and passion, the word means both the principle of animation and the distinctive spiritual principle in human beings (Gen. 6:17; Job 17:1; Ezek. 37:6; see SPIRIT). The OT writers also believed that man was made in the IMAGE OF GOD, that he had received his vital breath from God, and that at death, when he breathed his last, he gave his spirit back to God. Thus God is described as being or having a *rûah*, thus as being essentially Spirit, the source of that breath of life by which all living creatures are animated, and the Giver of those unique qualities that make human beings like himself.

The name Holy Spirit occurs in the OT in only two passages (Ps. 51:11; Isa. 63:10–11; lit., "Spirit of holiness"), but in the NT it is found over ninety times (the KJV renders "Holy Ghost" in almost all instances). The word for "spirit" in Greek is *pneuma G4460* (from the verb *pneō G4463*, "to breathe, blow"; cf. Jn. 3:8), which can also mean "wind, breath." The NT, moreover, includes many references to the Spirit "of God," or "of the Lord," or "of the Father," or "of Jesus," or "of the Christ" (for the last two, see Acts 16:7; Rom. 8:9; Phil. 1:19; 1 Pet. 1:11; cf. Gal. 4:6)—or simply "the Spirit." Above all, it is significant that the Spirit now receives a personal name, in anticipation of his unique historical manifestation: he is the other Comforter or PARACLETE (Jn. 14:16–26).

  I. The Spirit of God in the OT
    A. His work in general
    B. His saving work
 II. The Spirit in the NT
    A. Jesus and the Spirit
    B. The coming of the Spirit upon the disciples
    C. The Holy Spirit in the epistles of Paul
    D. The doctrine of the Spirit in the non-Pauline documents of the NT
    E. Conclusion
III. The Holy Spirit in the theology and life of the church
    A. The Holy Spirit and the Trinity
    B. The sin against the Holy Spirit
    C. The Holy Spirit and spiritual gifts
    D. The gift of tongues
    E. Baptism and the Holy Spirit
    F. The Holy Spirit and confirmation
    G. The Holy Spirit and Scripture
    H. The inward testimony of the Spirit
    I. The Holy Spirit and the mission of the church

I. The Spirit of God in the OT

A. His work in general. The Spirit of God, or the Spirit of the Lord, is repeatedly mentioned in all parts of the OT. These uses do not indicate clearly the Spirit is a person distinct from the Father and the Son. This Trinitarian meaning, which Christians commonly assume in using the term Spirit or Holy Spirit, presupposes and rests upon the events of the INCARNATION and the day of PENTECOST. In the OT, the Spirit is holy (cf. Ps. 51:11), not because he is "the Holy Spirit" in distinction to the Father and the Son, but because the Spirit pertains to God and comes from God who is holy. See HOLINESS. The Spirit of God is the divine nature viewed as vital energy. This vital energy that comes from God is related both to the world, which is his creation, and especially to humankind, the crown of creation.

As for the world of nature, in the beginning the Spirit of God brooded like a bird on the nest over the formless primeval chaos (Gen. 1:2). As a result, from chaos there emerged the cosmos. The Spirit, as the source of all energy and life, impregnated, as it were, the deep nothingness or formless void, and out of it came forth at the divine behest the vast realm of the created order. Once the CREATION has been achieved, the same Spirit conserves, renews, and withdraws life by a continuous process in the realm of nature (Job 33:4; Pss. 33:6; 104:30). Thus the OT justifies the epithet "the One who makes alive," used to describe the Spirit in the Nicene Creed (see CREED III.B).

As for human beings, their very life depends on a special impartation of the "breath [here Heb. *nĕšāmâ H5972*] of life" (Gen. 2:7), and the divine Spirit is behind all the unique powers that they possess in distinction to the animals. The Spirit, or Breath, of God is the source of human reason (Job 32:8); of endowments and gifts (Gen. 41:38; Exod. 28:3); of artistic skills, as in the case of BEZALEL (Exod. 36); of cunning in war, as exemplified in JOSHUA (Deut. 34:9); of heroism, as displayed in the Judges (Jdg. 13:25); of wisdom, as celebrated in SOLOMON (1 Ki. 3:28); of religious and ethical insights, as seen in the inspiration of the poets and prophets (Num. 11:17, Jb. 26:4[?]; 2 Sam. 23:2, 1 Ki. 22:24, Ezek. 11:5; Dan. 4:8–9); and of purity, as seen in the strength and penitence of the righteous (Neh. 9:20; Ps. 51:11; Isa. 63:10; Ezek. 36:26; Zech. 12:10).

In view of these passages, it is hardly possible to suppose that the "evil spirit" (see DEMON) sent by the Lord as a judgment upon certain wicked men (Jdg. 9:23; 1 Sam. 16:14; 18:10) is the Holy Spirit performing a mission of penal judgment. More likely, the thought is that even an evil spirit, who inspires lying or jealousy, is under God's control as his creature, and accomplishes his purposes. One is reminded of the saying of Luther, "The devil is God's devil."

B. His saving work. The strand of OT revelation that most directly anticipated the NT doctrine of the Holy Spirit tells of the Spirit's saving work. As early as the era of the judges, it is clear that salvation was wrought in Israel by the Spirit of the Lord. See JUDGES, PERIOD OF. Without previous preparation or the possibility of resistance, unknown sons of peasants were stirred up and enabled to perform mighty acts of valor by the Spirit of God. Thus Israel was delivered from her enemies (Jdg. 3:10; 11:29; 14:6; 1 Sam. 11:6). Chosen for a more lasting function, kings were anointed (1 Sam. 16:13), a rite that signified the permanent endowment of the Spirit, investing them with a sacred character (26:11).

The salvation of Israel did not depend solely upon judges and kings empowered to deliver God's people from their enemies. There were also seers and prophets, who by an equal charismatic endowment and sovereign constraint were lifted into communion with God and made interpreters of the divine will to the people. Primarily as a result of their teaching, Israel had a unique literature containing a message of judgment and salvation (2 Sam. 23:2; Ezek. 2:2; 3:12, 14; Mic. 3:8; note also the frequent use of the formula, "thus says the LORD," in Isaiah and Jeremiah).

Ancient Babylonian basalt statue of a lion devouring a man. The Spirit of God protected his people from danger, such as Daniel in the lion's den.

Earthly kings, though anointed of God, were not always faithful or able to establish peace and justice in Israel. The greatest of the prophets found the people stiffnecked and unwilling to hear (Jer. 17:19–23), and complained that none believed their message (Isa. 53:1). Therefore, to accomplish God's purpose of salvation, ultimately there must be one who would uniquely combine the roles of prophet, priest, and king, and who would be uniquely endowed with the Spirit of God, that is the MESSIAH, the Anointed One par excellence. This shoot out of JESSE's stock, this branch out of his roots (Isa. 11:1), would receive the gifts of the Spirit in their fullness (11:2; 42:1; 61:1). Thus Jesus became the ideal Prophet and King, because he was anointed with the Spirit of God above measure; this is what makes him the Christ.

The OT anticipated that when the Messiah came, the Spirit would be poured out on all flesh like the rain that gives life to the earth (Isa. 32:15), as the breath of life animated dry bones (Ezek. 37). This effusion of the Spirit would transform the hearts of the people, making them receptive to the voice of God and spontaneously obedient to his word (Isa. 59:21; Ps. 143:11). This vision of the age of the Spirit remained principally a hope, not a reality, in the history of Israel. The people rebelled and grieved God's Holy Spirit so that he was turned into their enemy (Isa. 63:10). If this hope was to be realized, it was necessary that God should do the impossible—that he should come himself in person. "Oh, that you would rend the heavens and come down, / that the mountains would tremble before you!" (Isa. 64:1). (See further L. J. Wood, *The Holy Spirit in the Old Testament* [1976]; W. Hildebrandt, *An Old Testament Theology of the Spirit of God* [1995]; *NIDOTTE*, 3:1073–78.)

The APOCRYPHA and other Jewish literature between the Testaments add nothing significant. In works that have a Palestinian origin, references to the Spirit are uncommon (but see J. R. Levison, *The Spirit in First Century Judaism* [1997]). In the Jewish Alexandrian literature, the activity of the divine Spirit is underscored particularly by associating the Spirit with wisdom, an association that culminated in the writings of PHILO JUDAEUS. The Spirit promoted clearness of vision and a capacity for an intellectual knowledge of God.

II. The Spirit in the NT

A. Jesus and the Spirit. The gospel age opened with a special moving of the Spirit. JOHN THE BAPTIST, the forerunner of the Messiah, is described as one who was filled with the Holy Spirit from his mother's womb (Lk. 1:15, 80). By the inspiration of the Spirit, SIMEON divined the presence of the Messiah in the person of the infant Jesus (Lk. 2:25). As for the Messiah himself, his mother was informed by an angel that her son would be conceived by the power of the Holy Spirit (1:35; cf. Matt. 1:18, 20). The Spirit was active in the creation of a new humanity, free from the taint of human corruption. (That which was begotten of the virgin is "holy," Lk. 1:35 NRSV.) The true immaculate conception is not that of the virgin, but of her Son. See VIRGIN BIRTH.

When Jesus was about thirty years of age, he was baptized. As he had been sanctified in his humanity at birth by the Spirit, so at his baptism he was consecrated to the office of Messiah by the same Spirit, who descended upon him in the form of a dove (Matt. 3:16; Lk. 3:22), an appropriate symbol for One who came as the "Prince of Peace." PETER was probably referring to this event when, in his first sermon to the Gentiles, he spoke of Jesus as the One whom God had anointed with the Holy Spirit and with power (Acts 10:38). The Gospel of John emphasizes the plenitude of this endowment with the Spirit: "For the one whom God has sent speaks the words of God, for God gives the Spirit without limit" (Jn. 3:34).

From the time of his baptism, the life of Jesus was filled with manifestations of the Spirit's power. Immediately after coming up out of the waters of Jordan, Jesus was driven by the Spirit into the wilderness where he encountered the tempter (Mk. 1:12–13 and parallels). In his victory as the second ADAM, the true man, he overcame the power of the Evil One by the Spirit of God. The Lord later attributed his power of EXORCISM to the Holy Spirit (Matt. 12:28). The same is true of his teaching; the Spirit had anointed him to preach good tidings to the poor and to proclaim release to the captives (Lk. 4:18).

Running through the gospel account of Jesus' public ministry are allusions to a strange power working within him. He was seized by such a sense of urgency that people thought he was beside himself (Mk. 3:21); they were impressed with the authority of his teachings (1:22); he was sometimes seemingly forgetful of bodily needs (Jn. 4:31); and some even supposed him to be demon-possessed (8:48). When the seventy returned from a successful evangelistic tour, Luke relates how Jesus rejoiced in the Holy Spirit (Lk. 10:21).

The question might well be asked, Why, if Jesus is himself God the Son, was the power of the Spirit so necessary to carry out his mission? A part of the answer must lie in the real humanity that Jesus assumed when he became incarnate (see INCARNATION). Jesus was no less a man because he was divine, as though he were divine omnipotence masquerading as human frailty. Since God had made man by his Spirit, and since man always lived in dependence upon God's Spirit, therefore Jesus, if he was one with mankind, must also have depended upon the indwelling Spirit of God. That is why, in the economy of salvation, he assumed the role of the Messiah, the One who was anointed by the Spirit of God. Yet he was also conscious of his own divine, absolute authority. Unlike the prophets in their dependence upon the Spirit, he did not say, "Thus says the LORD," but "truly, I say unto you." See DEITY OF CHRIST.

B. The coming of the Spirit upon the disciples. Jesus' reception of the Spirit is associated with his baptizing others with the same Spirit. John the Baptist said, "I would not have known him, except that the one who sent me to baptize with water told me, 'The man on whom you see the Spirit come down and remain is he who will baptize with the Holy Spirit'" (Jn. 1:33). Two events following the RESURRECTION OF JESUS CHRIST mark this extension of the messianic unction to the whole body of the disciples. The first occurred shortly after the resurrection when Jesus breathed, saying, "Receive the Holy Spirit" (Jn. 20:22). The other is the well-known descent of the Spirit at PENTECOST (Acts 2). In an effort to harmonize these two, it has been suggested that the former event is symbolic of the latter (cf. esp. the full discussion by D. A. Carson, *The Gospel according to John* [1991], 649–55). It seems preferable, however, to suppose the real communication of the Spirit when Jesus breathed on his disciples (although the Gk. simply says "he breathed," without an object), which anticipated the larger effusion of the Spirit upon the whole body of believers gathered in the upper room with the apostles on the day of Pentecost. Perhaps Jesus' breathing looked back to the original divine inbreathing of the Creator (Gen. 2:7) and symbolized the infusion of a new principle of life by the risen Lord into the redeemed race, present in embryonic form in the little band of disciples.

Whatever our understanding of Jn. 20:22, Pentecost is an event that can hardly be overemphasized: it is of the same order of importance in redemptive history as the Incarnation. The symbolism of a rushing mighty wind is clear enough in the light of the basic meaning of the Hebrew and Greek words for Spirit—not to mention Jesus' word to NICODEMUS in Jn. 3:8, which likened the Spirit to the wind that blows where it will. At the same time, there

The southern steps of the temple at Jerusalem. The apostle Peter, filled with the Holy Spirit, probably preached from these steps on the day of Pentecost.

appeared also tongues as of fire, resting upon the heads of all, possibly in fulfillment of the prediction of John the Baptist that Jesus should baptize with the Holy Spirit and with fire (Matt. 3:11; according to some, the Baptist's prediction is a reference to judgment). The tongues as of fire were distributed to indicate that none should be without his portion in this new age of the Spirit, for the same Spirit gives gifts "to each one, just as he determines" (1 Cor. 12:11). The gift of the Spirit, then, is both collective and individual, for the whole body of the church and for each individual member.

Empowered by the Spirit, the apostles began to proclaim the mighty works of God. Devout Jews from all over the Roman empire were amazed to hear these men speaking the mighty works of God in their own languages (Acts 2:7–12). In response to Peter's Spirit-inspired sermon, many were baptized, confessing Christ; thus the Christian church was born. With this Pentecostal outpouring, what may be called the "dispensation of the Spirit" began. The promise of the prophet Joel that God would pour out his Spirit upon all flesh was fulfilled (Joel 2:28–29), as was also the saying of our Lord Jesus Christ that the Holy Spirit would come to teach the disciples how they ought to speak (Mk. 13:11; Lk. 12:12). The most elaborate account of the Lord's teaching regarding the coming of the Spirit is in Jn. 14–17, where it is made plain that the primary work of the Spirit was to illumine the minds of the disciples in their teaching in order that Christ may be glorified. This is exactly what happened at Pentecost and throughout the period recorded in the book of Acts. By the preaching of the apostles through the power of the Spirit, men were everywhere convicted in respect of sin and of righteousness and of judgment (Jn. 16:8; Acts 2:37).

According to Acts, the entire historical movement, beginning at Pentecost and resulting in the founding of the church universal, took its rise from the BAPTISM OF THE HOLY SPIRIT (Acts 1:5, 8) and was under his direction and control. The presence of the Spirit became the distinctive mark of the Christian society. The Spirit directed PHILIP to the ETHIOPIAN EUNUCH and later "took Philip away" (8:29, 39). At JOPPA, the Spirit spoke to PETER and led him to CORNELIUS in CAESAREA (10:19; 11:12). The Spirit enjoined the church at ANTIOCH OF SYRIA to set apart PAUL and BARNABAS for the missionary task (13:2) and guided the church in its deliberations over the most crucial question arising out of that mission (15:29). The Spirit would not allow PAUL to enter ASIA (16:6) and warned him especially through the prophecy of AGABUS about the evil intent of the Jews in Jerusalem (20:23; 21:11). Paul told the Ephesian elders that the Holy Spirit had made them bishops to feed the church (20:28), and presumably he would have said this of all churches. Therefore, the church age may be called the age of the Spirit, and the time that preceded it may be cited as a time when the Spirit had not yet been given (Jn. 7:39). The difference between the Spirit's manifestation before and after Pentecost was so great that it is here expressed in absolute terms, though such absolutes should not be pressed literally.

C. The Holy Spirit in the epistles of Paul.

The epistles of Paul contain the fullest treatment of the doctrine of the Spirit in the NT. In harmony with the teaching of the book of Acts, which gives great prominence to the place of the Spirit, Paul associated the gift of the Spirit with spiritual power (1 Thess. 1:5), with inward joy (1:6), with moral purity (4:4–8), and with religious consecration (2 Thess. 2:13). As for the gift of prophecy, Christians were admonished neither to despise this gift, which would be to quench the Spirit (1 Thess. 5:19), nor to accept gullibly every teaching that purports to be inspired of the Spirit, when such was not the case (2 Thess. 2:1–2; see PROPHETS AND PROPHECY). Over and beyond these considerations, Paul wrote certain things about the Spirit that are not clearly expressed elsewhere and may be looked upon as new revelation. It is the Holy Spirit who bears witness to human spirits that they are God's children (Rom. 8:16), and enables them to call God their Father (Rom. 8:15; Gal. 4:6; see FATHERHOOD OF GOD). He likewise assists them in PRAYER with sighs too deep for words (Rom. 8:26).

One of the more difficult aspects of Paul's teaching about the Spirit concerns his concept of the relation of the Spirit to Christ. As will be seen later, the universal teaching of the church has always been that the Spirit is a distinct person of the Godhead, as the third member of the Holy

HOLY SPIRIT

Metal relief depicting Paul in chains laying hands on those visiting him while imprisoned in Rome.

Trinity. However, upon examination of what Paul wrote about the Spirit, it is obvious that the "metaphysical" question of how God, Christ, and the Spirit are related is not a primary concern. In Rom. 8:9–10 Paul uses the expressions "Spirit of God," "Spirit of Christ," and "Christ" as interchangeable. To "walk in the Spirit" is the same as "minding the things of the Spirit," which is the same as "being in the Spirit." All of these expressions are broadly synonymous with being "in Christ." That is to say, the Spirit is the sphere in which the believer lives, a sphere of power and newness of life where "through Christ Jesus the law of the Spirit of life set me free from the law of sin and death" (8:2).

Is the Spirit then simply the power of the risen Lord as it is manifest in the life of the Christian and in the church? One recalls Paul's words, "Now the Lord is the Spirit" (2 Cor. 3:17). Some have suggested that this sentence be reversed to read, "Now the Spirit is the Lord," and see in it an affirmation of the sovereignty and divinity of the Holy Spirit. The context, however, shows plainly that the word LORD refers to Christ. He who is Lord is himself the Spirit (see the close of v. 18). Hence it would be difficult to establish any great difference in Paul's thought between the formula "in Christ" and "in the Spirit." The Spirit is the glorified Lord, the Christ, as he is present and active in his church. But if this is the case, why did Paul invoke upon his converts "the grace of the Lord Jesus Christ, and the love of God, and the fellowship of the Holy Spirit" (2 Cor. 13:14)? Using a Trinitarian benediction, he implied there is as much of a distinction between Christ and the Spirit as there is between Christ and God his Father.

The best resolution of this difficulty is to remember that in Paul's writings the Spirit is also called the Spirit of God. "Don't you know that you yourselves are God's temple and that God's Spirit lives in you?" (1 Cor. 3:16; cf. 6:19). Paul conceived of the Spirit as the essential being of God. Where the Spirit dwells and works, God is at work, for as the spirit of man knows the things of a man, so the Spirit of God knows the things of God (1 Cor. 2:11). This does not mean that there is no distinction in his mind between God, as he has revealed himself to be the Father, and God who, as the Spirit, enables believers to cry from the depth of their hearts, "Abba, Father." No one need suppose that Paul so identified Christ and the Spirit as to make no distinction between the Lord and the One who enables believers to call Jesus Lord, that is, the Holy Spirit (1 Cor. 12:3). It is because of the oneness of the *work* of Christ and the Spirit that his language reflects an identity between them. It is a dynamic identity; it is through his Spirit that the risen Lord dwells in his church and works in people's lives. Christ may do everything that the Spirit does; and the formula "in the Spirit" can mean the same as "in Christ."

The majority of references to the Spirit in Paul's epistles are concerned with his work in the spirit of believers. When the Spirit "indwells" a Christian, there is manifest in his life the fruit of love, joy, peace, patience, kindness, goodness, faithfulness, gentleness, and self-control (Gal. 5:22–23). With these virtues and graces, which adorn the Christian life and make a person the temple of the Spirit (1 Cor. 3:16), there is the firm hope of the resurrection: "And if the Spirit of him who raised Jesus from the dead is living in you, he who raised Christ from the dead will also give life to your mortal bodies through his Spirit, who lives in you" (Rom. 8:11).

Where Paul is concerned with the work of the Spirit in the human spirit, it is not easy to determine whether the word *pneuma* refers to the Holy Spirit or to the spirit of a person under the influence of the divine Spirit. This is especially true in passages contrasting the FLESH and the Spirit. The flesh lusts against the S(s)pirit and the S(s)pirit against the flesh (Gal. 5:17). Flesh may be understood as the weak and sinful aspect of human nature, whereas spirit may be interpreted as the human spirit, empowered by the divine Spirit in its struggle against the flesh. In other words, those whose spirit struggles against the flesh are those who live "in accordance with the [Holy] Spirit, [and] have their minds set on what the [Holy] Spirit desires" (Rom. 8:5).

A similar antithesis is found in 1 Cor. 3:1–2, where Paul distinguishes between "spiritual men" and "men of the flesh." A man "of the flesh" is one who is dominated by his lower nature. The spiritual man, by contrast, is one who lives by the higher nature, the spirit, as guided and dominated by the Holy Spirit. The human spirit and the divine Spirit are one in their operation (not in their essence, for Paul is not a mystic). The "Spirit-filled" person is one in whom the Holy Spirit so assumes the ascendancy that at every point his or her life is guided and sustained by the Holy Spirit. Such a person is a citizen of that kingdom that is "righteousness and peace and joy in the Holy Spirit" (Rom. 14:17), someone who abounds in hope through the Holy Spirit (15:13).

The doctrine of Christian perfection, which is commonly regarded as the hallmark of the Wesleyan tradition, is so basic to the NT concept of the Christian life that it can be suppressed only by doing violence to the Christian message (see PERFECT). Those who feel an antipathy for all forms of "perfectionism" may indeed quote the verse, "For you died, and your life is now hidden with Christ in God" (Col. 3:3). Though the root of the tree be hid from view, the fruit is there for all to see. The same apostle admonished his readers, "Do not get drunk on wine, which leads to debauchery. Instead, be filled with the Spirit" (Eph. 5:18). If anyone is drunk, people will know it. Should they not also be able to see the difference that the Spirit makes in the life of one who is controlled, not by the destructive power of inebriation, but by the greater redemptive power of the Spirit? The note of caution that needs to be sounded is that there is no easy formula for achieving this perfection, as some who have talked about the "higher" or "victorious" Christian life have implied. Although the law of the Spirit of life in Christ Jesus has already made believers free from the law of sin and death (Rom. 8:2), there yet remains another law (7:21–22). Delivery from the strength of this subtle and sinister "law of sin" is not so instantaneous and dramatic as some teachers of perfection maintain. See SANCTIFICATION.

Another contrast beside that of "flesh" and "Spirit" is that which Paul drew between the Spirit and the letter (*gramma G1207*). Having died to the law (the written code), "we serve in the new way of the Spirit, and not in the old way of the written code" (Rom. 7:6). He styled himself a minister "of a new covenant—not of the letter but of the Spirit; for the letter kills, but the Spirit gives life" (2 Cor. 3:6). Not that the law is without spiritual worth ("the law is spiritual," Rom. 7:14), but viewed as an external code of conduct by which a person can be justified before God, it can only minister death; for the sinner, the law can bring only the knowledge of SIN, never deliverance from sin (Rom. 3:20). Viewed as the JUDAIZERS understood it, the law is in opposition to the Spirit and the Spirit to the law. He who is renewed by the Spirit and so united to Christ by faith, has died to the law as a way of salvation. Paul reminded the Galatians: "But if you are led by the Spirit, you are not under law" (Gal. 5:18).

Before leaving the teaching of Paul on the Holy Spirit, a word must be said about the Spirit and the CHURCH. The Spirit is the bond of catholic unity, which has been regarded as one of the marks of the true church (Eph. 4:3). It is helpful to associate Paul's thought here with his figure of the church as a body (1 Cor. 12:12–27; see BODY OF CHRIST). The Holy Spirit is the One who animates the body: "For we were all baptized by one Spirit into one body ... and we were all given the one Spirit to drink" (12:13). The gifts of the Spirit are for the edification of the church (14:12; see below, III.C). Christians love one another in the Spirit (Col. 1:8); they have fellowship in the Spirit (Phil. 2:1); they worship God in the Spirit (Phil. 3:3); the church is comprised of Christians who are built up together as a habitation of God in the Spirit (Eph. 2:22); thus the church becomes an epistle of Christ, written not with ink, but by the Spirit of the living God (2 Cor. 3:3).

D. The doctrine of the Spirit in the non-Pauline documents of the NT. Although the other writings in the NT speak freely of the Spirit, they add little to Paul's teaching. The author of Hebrews stressed the role of the Spirit in the inspiration of Scripture. When he quoted Scripture, he often did so as though it were the direct Word of the Spirit. The Holy Spirit is the One who says what the Scripture says, and the Scripture says what the Holy Spirit says (Heb. 3:7; 9:8; 10:15). In this light one should understand the familiar verse where the "word of God" is described in personal categories, having the power to penetrate a person's inmost being and to discern the thoughts and intents of his heart (4:12). This power is not in the WORD as such, but only as it is the Word inspired by the Spirit, and the Spirit, who inspired it, uses it as a means to convict and convert those who hear. (Note Paul's reference to the word of God as the sword of the Spirit, Eph. 6:17.) Peter reflected the same view of the Spirit's relation to Scripture when he stated that the Spirit of Christ was in the OT prophets, bearing witness both to the sufferings and coming glories of the Christ (1 Pet. 1:11). Like the author of Hebrews, PETER gave the priority, not to the human author, but to the Holy Spirit in the writing of Scripture. No prophecy ever came by the will of man, but men spoke from God being moved by the Holy Spirit (2 Pet. 1:21).

In the epistle to the Hebrews it is said of the Lord's atoning death that "through the eternal Spirit" Christ "offered himself unblemished to God" (Heb. 9:14), a phrase difficult to interpret. It is probably best understood of his own Spirit as the eternal, preexistent Son of God. Unlike the animals of ritual sacrifices, he voluntarily offered up himself, thus acquiescing in the redemptive purpose of the Father (note Paul's reference to Christ as a "life-giving spirit," 1 Cor. 15:45).

The last book of the Bible, the Apocalypse, speaks of the Spirit from the perspective of his role in OT prophecy. The author, like the prophets of old, was "in the Spirit" on the Lord's Day (Rev. 1:10), and he wrote a message in which the Spirit spoke to the churches (2:7). "The testimony of Jesus," said the angel, "is the spirit of prophecy" (19:10); that is, it was the same Spirit who inspired the prophets that enabled the angel to show John these things, and who enabled John to receive and write them; hence, the angel was John's fellow servant. The Apocalypse refers repeatedly to the "seven spirits" of God (1:4; 3:1; 4:5; 5:6). The NUMBER seven is generally understood as a symbol of the perfection of the Spirit in the plenitude of his universal efficacy in the church. This interpretation is the basis of the well-known lines of the Latin hymn *Veni, Creator Spiritus*: "Come, Holy Ghost, our souls inspire, / And lighten with celestial fire. / Thou the anointing Spirit art, / Who doest thy *seven-fold* gifts impart." The Holy Spirit not only speaks to the church, but also joins his voice with the church in calling for Christ's return (Rev. 22:17).

E. Conclusion. Scripture reveals that the Holy Spirit is divine (not a created intelligence superior to the angels and inferior to the Son, as ARIUS maintained), in some sense one with the Father and the Son, in another differing from them. In his work, the Holy Spirit is intimately involved in the creation of all things, and sustaining all things, especially those creatures in which is found the breath of life. He is also intimately involved in the redemption of humanity, being not only the author of moral purity, but the Spirit who inspired the prophets to tell of the coming Savior. It is he who in due time anointed the Savior, resting all his fullness upon him. In the last days he extended his gifts to the whole world that he might raise up a new Israel, an elect nation, the church catholic, which he empowered to bear witness to Christ, and which he leads into all truth. This is accomplished by the renewal of the hearts of individual persons, whom he indwells, making them his temple, purifying them inwardly, and identifying with them in their struggle against the world, the flesh, and the devil, and in their aspiration for God. By his mighty power, with which he raised up Jesus from the dead, he will raise up the saints in the last day, a glorious company resting from their labors, whose works shall follow after them (Rev. 14:13).

III. The Holy Spirit in the theology and life of the church. Certain questions concerning the teaching of Scripture about the Holy Spirit have been omitted or only briefly touched upon in the above survey—matters for which more especial treatment has been reserved because of their importance or difficulty, or because they are matters on which the Christian church has been divided, or concerning which it has an uncommon interest.

A. The Holy Spirit and the Trinity. In the OT, the Spirit of God is described as holy, but there is no doctrine of the Holy Spirit as the "third person of the Trinity." This mode of expression, however, has had a large and varied history in Christian theology, and it is necessary to review briefly the meaning of the phrase and seek to outline the biblical basis for a Trinitarian understanding of God.

To say that the OT contains no doctrine of the Spirit as a distinct person does not imply that the Spirit in the OT is a vague, impersonal force. The Spirit is God's Spirit, and because the God of Israel is a personal God, his Spirit is invested with personal qualities and involved in personal acts. As the living energy of a personal God, the Spirit is said to brood, rule, guide, quicken, and move. "Where can I go from your Spirit? / Where can I flee from your presence?" asked the psalmist (Ps. 139:7), implying that where God's Spirit is, there he is personally present. The Holy Spirit of God was grieved by the rebellion of Israel (Isa. 63:10).

In view of this personalistic language, the promise of Jesus that when he departed from them (Jn. 16:7), the Father would send another Comforter (PARACLETE), even the Holy Spirit (14:16, 28), is a promise in keeping with the OT teaching concerning the Spirit. Furthermore, since he had fellowship with his disciples as a person, the implication is that the Spirit, who shall take his place, must also be a person like himself. Otherwise the promise of the Paraclete would offer little comfort to the disciples in the contemplation of their Master's departure. Not that they would have had any clear understanding of these matters before Pentecost, but given that great revelational event, they were prepared by what they had learned from Jewish Scripture and the Lord himself, to regard the Spirit, not simply as God's presence, much less as some vague influence, but as a personal manifestation of God.

Hence, Peter could accuse ANANIAS of lying to the Holy Spirit, who is God (Acts 5:3–4). This side of the incarnation and Pentecost, Peter could use the term Holy Spirit as distinct from both the risen Lord, who had been taken up from them into heaven (1:9), and the Father, to whose right hand Jesus had been exalted and from whom he had received the promise of the Spirit (2:33). This same hypostatic, or personal, distinction of the Spirit appears in Paul's pronouncing of a threefold benediction upon the Corinthians: "The grace of the Lord Jesus Christ, and the love of God, and the fellowship of the Holy Spirit be with you all" (2 Cor. 13:14).

The clearest Trinitarian statement in the NT is the Lord's commission to his disciples to baptize "in the name of the Father and of the Son and of the Holy Spirit" (Matt. 28:19). One passage concerning the Spirit that has figured largely in the debate of the church is Jn. 15:26: "When the Counselor comes, whom I will send to you from the Father, the Spirit of truth who goes out from the Father, he will testify about me." As far as the doctrine of the Trinity is concerned, this passage has classically been appealed to as establishing the doctrine of the *procession* of the Holy Spirit. As the Son is "begotten of" the Father, so the universal church confesses that the Spirit "proceeds from" the Father. (Under the influence of AUGUSTINE, the Western church, both Roman Catholic and Protestant, confesses that the Spirit proceeds from the Father "and the Son" [*filioque*], but this element is not expressly stated in Scripture.)

In interpreting this text, note should be taken of the two clauses. It was the Paraclete whom the

Son would send, and it is the Spirit who proceeds from the Father. The former clause seems definitely to refer to the sending of the Spirit at Pentecost in his role, or office, as Sanctifier. Since this sending of the Spirit as the Paraclete was yet future at the time Jesus spoke, he used the future tense, referring to the Spirit as the One whom "I will send." In technical theological language, this is an "economical" clause, that is, it describes the role of the Spirit in the "economy" (plan) of redemption. The latter clause, "who goes out from the Father," describes, by contrast, the essential nature of the Spirit himself, that is, it is an "ontological" clause. The Holy Spirit is the One who eternally proceeds from the Father.

Not all scholars are agreed on this last point. Some would understand the proceeding from the Father and the future sending by the Son as both referring to the Spirit's coming at Pentecost. In this case it may be maintained (from the plainly revealed fact that the Spirit was given by the Father and the Son to the church at Pentecost) that it is proper to describe his mysterious intertrinitarian relation to the Father and the Son in an analogical way. Hence, the church speaks of his "eternal procession" from the Father and the Son after the analogy of his proceeding into the world at Pentecost from the Father and the Son.

B. The sin against the Holy Spirit. Although the NT is full of the message of mercy, pardon, and reconciliation, which is the gospel, there are some sobering statements about a "sin unto death" (1 Jn. 5:16 KJV), about insulting "the Spirit of grace" in a way that invites the divine vengeance (Heb. 10:29), about blaspheming the Holy Spirit, a sin that shall never be forgiven, neither in this world nor in the one to come (Mk. 3:28–29, and parallels). The particular offense called blaspheming against the Spirit in the Gospels is attributing Jesus' power of exorcism to BEELZEBUB, the prince of the demons, as though Jesus himself were possessed of an unclean spirit. There are many nuances of interpretation of this passage, but it surely seems that the unpardonable nature of the sin must be related to the hopeless warping and perversion of the moral nature, which would make one capable of such blindness to the truth as to attribute works of mercy having their origin in the power of God's Spirit to a diabolic source, a malignity so deep-seated as to make one insusceptible of redeeming grace. It is not clear that the church has the insight infallibly to perceive such a sin, much less the power to invoke the anathema upon it; but the warning clearly implies that a person may be guilty of such a sin and that he will surely have to reckon with God. See UNPARDONABLE SIN.

This is essentially what the apostate does when having been one of those "who have shared in the Holy Spirit, who have tasted the goodness of the word of God and the powers of the coming age," he falls away, becoming someone "who has trampled the Son of God under foot, who has treated as an unholy thing the blood of the covenant that sanctified him, and who has insulted the Spirit of grace" (Heb. 6:4–5; 10:29). The person who does this is one who says that the witness that the Spirit bears in his own soul is a lie, and he will not live by his original confession, and by his life declares that he does not believe what the Spirit says. Such a person cannot be renewed to repentance. On such a background one can appreciate a little more the seriousness of the sin of Ananias and Sapphira (Acts 5) and the swift judgment that befell them. As mentioned earlier, these statements contribute to the evidence that the Spirit is a person. One cannot sin against an influence; sin is meaningful only in the personal dimension, in the sphere of personal relationships. Since the sin against the Holy Spirit is the most aggravated form of sin, the conclusion is obvious that it is a sin against a most sacred, holy, and divine person.

C. The Holy Spirit and spiritual gifts. The word *charisma* is principally a Pauline term used technically for the gifts of the Spirit bestowed upon Christians for the edification of the church. None of the various lists in Paul's epistles is exhaustive, but by collating and combining the texts, it is possible to form an impressive list of SPIRITUAL GIFTS. Some of the gifts are connected with the proclamation of the Word and the preserving and inculcating of the truth (prophecy, Rom. 12:6; 1 Cor. 12:10; discerning of spirits, 1 Cor. 12:10; 1 Jn. 4:1; teaching, Rom. 12:7; 1 Cor. 12:28; tongues and their interpretation, 1 Cor. 12:10, 28, 30; miracles, 12:10, 28, 29; the word of wisdom and the word of knowledge, 12:8); others have to do with rendering service, some of it quite mundane in character, to the Christian brotherhood (healings, 12:9, 28, 30; governments, 12:28; helps, 12:28). The scope of these gifts illustrates that, according to the NT, the Spirit animates the whole church as a body, so that nothing is done except by his enabling power. Evidently the apostles exercised all these gifts, but Paul wrote to the Corinthians (12:4–5) as if, for the most part, gifts were distributed among the individual members of the church according to the Spirit's sovereign will (12:11), looking to the building up of the church. These gifts are to be received with thanksgiving and exercised with due consideration, but they are not abiding nor universal, as are faith, hope, and love (13:13). These normal fruits of the Spirit—"love, joy, peace, patience, kindness, goodness, faithfulness, gentleness and self-control"—make up the fullness of the Christian life (Gal. 5:22–23).

In keeping with the sovereignty of the Spirit, whom Jesus likened to the wind that "blows wherever it pleases" (Jn. 3:8), there seems to be no uniform modus operandi by which these gifts are given. In the initial outpouring of the Spirit on the day of Pentecost, as the disciples were gathered in an attitude of expectation, suddenly the Spirit came with the sound as the rushing of a mighty wind and appeared in the form of tongues as of fire resting upon each one of them (Acts 2:1–4). At another time, while Peter was preaching the Word, the Spirit fell upon the house of Cornelius (10:44). At other times, the Spirit in his charismatic manifestations comes not by the hearing of the Word but by the laying on of hands. It is especially interesting to note that in Samaria, Philip was endowed with certain *charismata* as he preached—demons were exorcised, the sick were healed (8:7–8)—yet those who believed and were baptized did not have the Spirit fall upon them until Peter and John laid hands upon them (8:17). The Spirit was similarly mediated by Paul's laying hands on twelve disciples of John the Baptist in Ephesus (19:1–7).

The laying on of hands has become the received custom in the Christian church for symbolically conveying the Spirit in confirmation and ordination, and in those communions where charismatic endowment is sought and manifested, this receiving of the gifts of the Spirit is generally accompanied by the laying on of hands. The hands have always been expressively used by men and women, and their imposition has been from ancient times a means of conveying a blessing or benediction (Gen. 48:13–16; Mk. 10:16). It is appropriate then that receiving this supreme blessing of the Spirit's presence and power should be symbolized by such an outward act. See HANDS, LAYING ON OF.

As for the range of spiritual gifts, they extend all the way from the most striking displays of power to humble and menial matters. Acts 19:12 reports healings by a touch of handkerchiefs and aprons used by the apostle Paul. Paul listed "helpers" and "administrators" among those gifted by the Spirit (1 Cor. 12:28 RSV). It does not seem, however, that any overt, miraculous endowment is necessarily involved. Rather, those in the fellowship of believers who were endowed with wisdom in practical affairs and whose spiritual strength made them a worthy example to the weak, were regarded as having received such endowments from the Spirit as a gift, to be employed in the establishing of the church.

As time passed on, the inspirational aspect of the ministry began to recede in favor of the institutional in the form of the offices of presbyter (see ELDER (NT)) and DEACON, and many of the supernatural manifestations of the Spirit disappeared altogether. There can be no doubt that this trend impoverished the Christian communities, and the struggle to keep the church from becoming a merely institutional structure within human society, with the loss of that vital inspiration that only the Spirit can give, remained a constant factor throughout the centuries of Christian history. The rise and rapid growth of Pentecostalism in modern times is a striking testimony to the need of the institutional church for spiritual renewal. Without the presence and power of the Holy Spirit, the church is simply a sociological phenomenon.

D. The gift of tongues. In the discussions of the sovereignty of the Spirit in bestowing his gifts, of the renewal of the church, and of the wide range of the charismata, no subject will more quickly reveal a difference of opinion on all these questions than that of the gift of tongues. Because of the modern recrudescence of interest in this subject, a brief discussion is necessary from the point of view of the general treatment of the doctrine of the Holy

Spirit. Some dismiss this question on the score that Paul evidently found the gift an embarrassment, placing it last in a list where apostleship was first (1 Cor. 12:28), and exhorted his readers to covet the greater gifts (12:31), saying that he would rather speak five words in church with his understanding than a thousand in a strange tongue (14:19). On the other side, however, is the obvious fact that Paul, the chief of the apostles, recognized the gift as given by the Spirit (12:11), and thanked God that he spoke in tongues more than anyone else (14:18). The gift of tongues, furthermore, was central in the Pentecostal effusion of the Spirit and the founding of the Christian church.

Whether the initial gift of tongues at Pentecost was the same as that later manifested in CORINTH, however, is not altogether clear. The same word for "tongue" (*glōssa* G1185) is used in both instances, and the same inspiration of the Spirit is presupposed. Even the same reaction on the part of unbelievers is possible. Some mockingly accused the apostles of being inebriated (Acts 2:13), and Paul feared that unbelievers would consider the Christians as lunatics (1 Cor. 14:23). There is, however, the plain testimony in Acts that the Jews of the DIASPORA heard the apostles speaking in their native dialects (Acts 2:8). Whereas the sound was described as a "tongue" from the speaker's standpoint, it was called a "language" from the hearer's standpoint. Such, however, was not the case with the glossolalia of Corinth. There the phenomenon was described as an "unknown tongue" both from the speaker's and the hearer's point of view, for an interpreter was necessary for the edification of the hearers. That Paul spoke of the ecstatic experience of tongues as praying in the spirit while the mind was "unfruitful" (1 Cor. 14:14) has led many to feel that the Corinthian gift is not "language" at all, but gibberish, though this is perhaps to use a word that is too pejorative. (Some have argued that Paul refers to unknown tongues in the sense of very obscure languages, but linguistic analysis does not support this thesis. See further discussion under TONGUES, GIFT OF.)

Unbelief will, of course, dismiss all such manifestations as mere enthusiasm, there being no need to invoke the supernatural to explain them. It must indeed be granted that the emotions are radically involved in the use of tongues, just as the glands are radically involved in the exercise of love and anger. But even as the experience of love is more than glandular secretion ("a cold sweat in propinquity"), so speaking in tongues may be more than emotion. It may be emotion evoked by the presence and power of the Holy Spirit.

The popularity of the gift both in the ancient church and in certain circles today is understandable. As a person is drawn up into an ecstasy, he feels his spirit suffused with the divine Spirit, hence he is intensely aware of being in favor with God and in closest fellowship with him. Against such a spiritual experience there is surely no law, and it is a hollow prejudice that would deny the right of a Christian thus to "speak to himself and to God" (1 Cor. 14:28). Nonetheless, the gift is obviously a showy one in public and gratifying to anyone who craves personal prominence. In his classical evaluation of the gift (chs. 12–14) Paul recognized tongues as a divine gift (12:10), and expressed gratitude for this gift in his own personal experience (14:18). Yet it is a gift by no means indispensable, and the more excellent way is the way of LOVE (12:31). Speaking in tongues without love is like "a resounding gong or a clanging cymbal" (13:1). Therefore let him who speaks in a tongue renounce all self-glorification and seek the edification of the body (14:4).

When such rules are observed, there is no reason to demean the use of tongues. It is not the presence or absence of a particular gift as much as the lack of spiritual power in the lives of individuals and the church that is at issue. This is the summons which the Pentecostal movement addresses to the whole church: Do not quench the Spirit, but earnestly desire his gifts. Where has it ever been shown that 1 Cor. 12 and 14 are for the apostolic age alone? Only let those who claim to have discovered the neglected gifts of 1 Cor. 12 and 14 not neglect the love of 1 Cor. 13, which is the best and only commendation of the Spirit-filled life. (See J. L. Sherrill, *They Speak with Other Tongues* [1964]; H. Thielicke, *Between Heaven and Earth* [1965], ch. 5.)

E. Baptism and the Holy Spirit. One reason that the church in its more institutional form has shown little interest in the demonstrative evidence of the presence of the Spirit, is that the theology of the Spirit's role in the church and the Christian life has been intimately bound up with the theology of BAPTISM. It is taught that one receives the Spirit at the time of his or her baptism and needs, therefore, no other experience of the Spirit. On first consideration this might seem anomalous, since John the Baptist expressly contrasted his baptism in water with the baptism in the Holy Spirit and in fire that his successor (Christ) would perform (Matt. 3:11 and parallels). How then can these two baptisms, which are so sharply contrasted by the Baptist, be associated in the teaching of the church?

First, it must be recognized that the prophecy of baptism in the Spirit and in fire had its fulfillment at Pentecost, when the Spirit descended upon the disciples with the manifestation of tongues as of fire (Acts 1:5). There is no reason to associate this experience in any direct way with the baptism in water, which apparently took place during the earthly ministry of Christ (Jn. 4:1). Furthermore, the outpouring of the Spirit on the household of Cornelius, identified as the baptism of the Holy Spirit by Peter (Acts 11:16), was obviously independent of their baptism in water, which took place only subsequently.

Before the relationship of the Spirit to water baptism is considered, it is necessary to determine the meaning of the expression "baptism in the Holy Spirit." Does the phrase describe a unique event at the founding of the church, or should Christians in all ages seek such an experience? In this writer's judgment, one should reserve the term "baptism in the Spirit" for the initial gift of the Spirit to the church. The phrase used both by John the Baptist (Mk. 1:8) and by the risen Lord (Acts 1:5) clearly refers to Pentecost, and Pentecost is obviously unique in redemptive history (a uniqueness that is commemorated in the Christian year in Whitsunday).

How, then, does one explain Acts 11:16, where Cornelius's house is said to have been "baptized with the Holy Spirit"? It should be noted that this incident was looked upon by Luke as unique. This is the first account of the preaching of the gospel to Gentiles, and when Peter rehearsed the affair before the Jerusalem elders, he stressed that the Holy Spirit had now fallen on the Gentiles as "on us at the beginning" (11:15). Thus Peter directly linked this outpouring of the Spirit to the first outpouring at Pentecost. His hearers recognized it as such: "So then, God has granted even the Gentiles repentance unto life" (11:18). Therefore the opening of the door of the gospel to the Gentiles was the completion of what happened at Pentecost, since it showed that not only Jews "from every nation under heaven," but Gentiles as well, are to be embraced in the blessings and privileges of the new dispensation of the Spirit. The Scriptures refer to both these events as the "baptism in the Spirit," reserving the term exclusively for these events.

The baptism in the Spirit simply describes that coming of the Spirit upon the church at the beginning in a new and permanent way, in contrast to the partial, transient, and limited manifestations of his power in the OT age. Because the Spirit has come in a final and full manifestation, he remains present in the church in all ages to bestow every spiritual gift and blessing necessary for the life and growth of the individual Christian and the ongoing of the mission of the church. Since the Spirit has thus come to abide with the church forever, Christians are bidden to "live [*lit.*, walk] by the Spirit" (Gal. 5:16), and to be "filled with the Spirit" (Eph. 5:18). They are said to have the "anointing" of the Spirit (1 Jn. 2:20–27); the Spirit is called the "guarantee" of the Christian's inheritance (Eph. 1:14). This last expression (Gk. *arrabōn* G775) refers to a "first installment" or "down payment" or "pledge," which obligates the one making it to make further payments (see EARNEST). The apostle's thought is that the Spirit is given as a first installment of the believer's inheritance in Christ.

Although baptism in the Spirit is to be distinguished from water baptism, it by no means supersedes baptism with water (as the Quakers have taught). The work of the Holy Spirit is closely related in the NT to water baptism. To begin with, the Lord, when commissioning his disciples to baptize, told them it should be "in the name ... of the Holy Spirit" (Matt. 28:19). Such a command would indicate at least this much, that the baptized Christian is placed in a relationship of dependence upon the Holy Spirit throughout the remainder of his life and consecrated to the service he inspires. Baptism itself does not effect this relationship, but there is no true baptism where this relationship between the Spirit and the one baptized is lacking.

The connection between baptism and the Spirit can be more closely defined by the account of Jesus' conversation with NICODEMUS (Jn. 3). Jesus traced the spiritual life of the individual back to its origins in the new birth effected by the Spirit. At the same time, he connected this inner renewal effected by the Spirit with water: "no one can enter the kingdom of God unless he is born of water and the Spirit" (3:5). Whereas it would be anachronistic to say that Jesus referred expressly to Christian baptism, it would be even less plausible to suppose this Scripture has nothing to do with baptism (as is done when water is allegorized to mean the "word"). The use of water for the religious purpose of ablution and cleansing, with which Nicodemus was familiar as a Jew, was subsumed into the meaning of the Christian rite of initiation by baptism.

There can be little doubt that by the time the Gospel of John was written, the phrase "to be born of water" was understood of the outward sign of baptism, while "to be born of the Spirit" referred to the inward grace that is signified. It can hardly be overemphasized, however, in the light of the long history of sacramentalism, that this distinction between the outward sign and the inward grace must be carefully maintained. The symbolism and the inner reality move along parallel lines. Therefore baptism is the appropriate symbol of the inner renewal of the Spirit, but baptism itself does not effect this renewal. The new birth is the result of a supernatural work of the Spirit in the heart (cf. Jn. 6:63). That the work of the Spirit is associated with baptism, but not dependent upon it, is seen in the several events during the early years of the church: in Acts 8:17, the Spirit is said to have come in his charismatic gifts after baptism; in 9:17, before baptism; and in 19:5–6, immediately upon baptism.

This last instance is interesting, since Paul, when he perceived that the disciples in Ephesus did not have the Spirit, raised the question of their baptism, which he would not have done had there been no connection in his mind between the two. Having asked if they had received the Spirit, and they having professed utter ignorance of the matter, he then inquired: "Into what, then, were you baptized?" (Acts 19:3 NRSV). The naturalness with which Paul associated baptism and the receiving of the Spirit is also evident from 1 Cor. 12:13: "For we were all baptized by one Spirit into one body." The Spirit is the element in which the baptism takes place, for it is he who animates the body, that is, the church, to which one is joined through baptism. Paul continued in the same verse to say, "we were all given the one Spirit to drink," which may allude to the EUCHARIST, but that seems farfetched. It is likely that the whole verse refers to baptism. Literally, Paul wrote that all were "watered" or "saturated" with the one Spirit, by which all were baptized into one body. The figure is that of being immersed in the Spirit or drinking of the Spirit as the potion of new life, which is the experience of the baptized Christian.

Another passage that possibly indicates that Paul associated the reception of the Spirit and baptism is found in his second letter to Corinth. He wrote to the Corinthians: "Now he that establisheth us with you in Christ, and anointed us, is God; who also sealed [*sphragizō* G5381] us, and gave us the earnest … of the Spirit in our hearts" (2 Cor. 1:21–22 ASV). As early as the 2nd cent., baptism was called a "seal," and it is quite possible that Paul was alluding to baptism in the figure of sealing, as that which marks, authenticates, and attests the believer's union with Christ and the reception of his Spirit in his heart.

Perhaps the closest association in Paul's epistles between the outward rite of baptism and the inward receiving of the Spirit is found in his brief letter to Titus, where the apostle says that God, because of his mercy, "saved us through the washing of rebirth and renewal by the Holy Spirit, whom he poured out on us generously through Jesus Christ our Savior" (Tit. 3:5–6). The language of "washing" is plainly an allusion to baptism, and REGENERATION refers to the new birth, a fundamental inner change that issues in a (progressive) "renewal by the Holy Spirit." If this were all that Paul ever wrote about baptism and the new birth, one might conclude that the former effects the latter. But in the larger context of his teaching on the efficacy of baptism, it is best to understand this passage in a manner that takes away neither from the meaning of the outward sign nor from the power of the Holy Spirit. Baptism is a washing of regeneration in the sense that it pertains to and sets forth, in a symbolic manner, the inward cleansing from the sin of the past, so that he who is baptized rises from the waters of baptism to a new life in Christ, here called the "renewal by the Holy Spirit." See also BAPTISM OF THE HOLY SPIRIT.

F. The Holy Spirit and confirmation. Confirmation is a rite closely related to baptism and is practiced in one form or another by many Christian churches. Because of the association between the reception of the Spirit and baptism, reflected in the Scriptures that have been discussed, in ancient times the church symbolized the receiving of the Spirit by a special rite immediately following baptism. The newly baptized confessor was "confirmed" by the laying on of hands, and his body was anointed with oil in the form of a cross on his forehead, that he might be endued with the Holy Spirit and consecrated to the spiritual priesthood of believers. This rite has been practiced down to the present time in the Eastern church. Since baptism is now commonly administered in infancy, the newborn child is anointed in token of his reception of the Spirit. In the Roman church, however, the rite of confirmation, which has attained separate status as a sacrament, is delayed until the age of puberty as "the sacrament through which the Holy Ghost comes to us in a special way to enable us to profess our faith as strong and perfect Christians and soldiers of Jesus Christ."

The Reformers minced no words in depriving this rite of its sacramental status. Luther called it "foolery and lying prattle, devised to adorn the office of the bishop that they may have at least something to do in the church." Yet, though divested of its sacramental status, some form of confirmation has been retained in those communions practicing infant baptism, as a sort of completion of that ordinance. When the question is asked what precisely the rite of confirmation signalizes, classically the answer has been given (esp. in Lutheran and Anglican circles), that it symbolizes the impartation of the Holy Spirit. This thought, included in the "Order of Confirmation" of the *English Book of Common Prayer*, has been adorned with poetic beauty in Keble's *Christian Year*. Speaking of the child about to be confirmed, he sings: "Draw, Holy Ghost, thy seven-fold veil / Between us and the fires of youth, / Breathe, Holy Ghost, thy freshening gale, / Our fevered brow in age to soothe."

Whereas it is true that in two instances in the book of Acts baptism is followed by the laying on of hands and the reception of the Spirit (Acts 8:17, the Samaritans, and 19:6, the Ephesian disciples of John), there are no other instances of this exact order of events. Furthermore, in both these instances, those who were baptized were adults confessing their faith, and the coming of the Spirit involved the use of charismatic gifts. (This is not expressly said of the Samaritans, but the response of SIMON MAGUS, as he observed the effect of the laying on of hands, implies as much.) By contrast, the present-day rite of confirmation is given to those who have been baptized as infants and it is not concerned with the exercise of the gifts of the Spirit. It is doubtful, therefore, if the view that one receives the Spirit at confirmation can be established from the NT. (See further G. W. H. Lampe, *The Seal of the Spirit: A Study in the Doctrine of Baptism and Confirmation in the New Testament and the Fathers*, 2nd ed. [1967].)

G. The Holy Spirit and Scripture. Throughout the history of the church, the written Word of God and the Spirit of God have been closely associated. The authority of the Jewish Scriptures in the apostolic church is expressly grounded in the INSPIRATION of the Spirit. David wrote the Psalms through the Spirit (Matt. 22:43; Mk. 12:36; Acts 1:16); the same is true of the prophets (Acts 28:25; 1 Pet. 1:11; 2 Pet. 1:21). The author of Hebrews is especially clear that it was the Spirit of God who spoke in Scripture (Heb. 3:7; 9:8; 10:15). The most comprehensive statement is found in 2 Tim. 3:16, which reads that all Scripture is God-breathed (*theopneustos* G2535). Often it is said that "God speaks" or "the Lord speaks" in Scripture (Mk. 12:26; Matt. 1:22). That such language is interchangeable with "the Spirit speaks" is further evidence for the full deity of the third person of the Godhead.

When Christ came, the "Word made flesh" did nothing except by the Spirit. The words that he spoke were Spirit-filled and they are life. He, in turn, promised that when he left his disciples he would send another, who would bring to their remembrance what he had said and lead them into the truth (Jn. 14:26). The church has universally understood this promise to mean that the apostles

A Greek minuscule MS of the Gospels from the 9th cent. "All Scripture is God-breathed" (2 Tim. 3:16).

were uniquely inspired by the Spirit as witnesses to Christ and as teachers of the church. The documents, therefore, that they and their associates wrote are of final authority for the church, along with the OT Scriptures.

The role of the Holy Spirit in REVELATION is summarized as follows: From the day of Pentecost onward, the Spirit assured the validity of the apostolic testimony to Jesus Christ (Acts 1:8; 2:1–2). Illumined by the Spirit, they discovered both the significance of Jesus' existence and the final meaning of the OT Scriptures that bore witness to him. This truth was the object of their witness (Acts 2:22–41), a witness that has been preserved by the church in the NT Scriptures.

H. The inward testimony of the Spirit. When it comes to authority in matters of faith, Rome appeals to the magisterium, or teaching office, of the church; the sectarians appeal to the direct inspiration of the Spirit, which tends to merge with enlightened reason or conscience, or religious ecstasy. The Protestant church appeals to Scripture alone (*sola Scriptura*). The doctrine of the inward testimony of the Spirit teaches that the same Spirit who *spoke* the Scripture *speaks* in human hearts by and with the Scripture, to confirm and seal its truths to all who believe. This inward testimony adds nothing to the written revelation, for outside of Scripture there is no revelation. But it attests the Scripture to be God's Word so that "our full persuasion and assurance of the infallible truth and divine authority of Scripture, is from the inward work of the Holy Spirit, bearing witness by and with the word in our hearts" (*Westminster Confession of Faith* 1.5).

In this regard, note should be taken of John's reference to the unction from the Holy One that Christians have, which enables them to know all things—that is, all things necessary for their salvation (1 Jn. 2:20). It seems best to understand this "unction" or "anointing" to refer to the Holy Spirit whom believers have from Christ. This anointing, wrote John, "remains in you, and you do not need anyone to teach you. But as his anointing teaches you about all things and as that anointing is real, not counterfeit—just as it has taught you, remain in him" (1 Jn. 2:27). This is said in a larger context of admonition and warning against false teachers, whom John called ANTICHRISTS, teachers who deny the Christ. As an inspired apostle, he wrote to his converts urging them to abide in the truth that they had heard from the beginning (v. 24). Significantly, he did not rely solely upon his own authority as an apostle, important as it was that he should exercise this authority by writing a letter to them. For the authentication of the truth of his teaching over against the false teaching of those whom he opposed, he appealed to the anointing that his readers had received as Christians. It is natural to understand this anointing by the Holy One as the work of the Holy Spirit. This Spirit, given by Christ, confirmed and sealed to the hearts of the Christians to whom John wrote the truth of God's Word as the apostle had taught it to them, so that there was no danger that they would succumb to false teaching. They had the anointing that enabled them to discern all things.

The word *witness* is an apt and biblical term to describe this aspect of the Holy Spirit's work, for he is the preeminent witness. As Jesus bore witness to the Father, so the Spirit bears witness to Jesus throughout Scripture. This may be the meaning of the difficult verse in 1 Tim. 3:16, which says that Jesus was "vindicated by the Spirit." That is, Jesus, who was condemned by unbelieving men and crucified, is vindicated by the witness of the Spirit that he is the Christ, as the Scriptures testify. He seals to the hearts of believers what the Scriptures say about Jesus as the Christ.

However one may interpret 1 Tim. 3:16, the importance of the Spirit's witness in our hearts, as far as Scripture is concerned, is that thereby the Bible becomes the personal address of God to the individual. Otherwise it remains a mere human book, to be read as one of the Great Books of the world, a masterpiece of literature savored for its passages of great prose. When the Spirit speaks through Scripture, one discovers that the holy history, which unfolds from the first to the second Adam, engages him in his own destiny. He stands fallen in Adam and condemned; and, by the grace of God, he stands righteous in Christ. It is this inward testimony of the Spirit that transforms the formal authority of Scripture — which the Roman Catholic Church accepted as well as the Reformers — into a material authority, so that it becomes "alive and powerful" to transform lives.

John not only associated the Spirit with the proclamation of the apostles that Jesus is the Christ, as that Word is preserved in Scripture, but also with the sacraments: "This is the one who came by water and blood — Jesus Christ. He did not come by water only, but by water and blood. And it is the Spirit who testifies, because the Spirit is the truth. For there are three that testify: the Spirit, the water and the blood; and the three are in agreement" (1 Jn. 5:6–8). This passage is notably difficult, and the detailed interpretation offers several options. It is possible that the "water" and the "blood" are an allusion to the baptism and crucifixion of Jesus. If so, it is difficult to know why Jesus' baptism and death should be mentioned in this way, unless some reference to the baptism of the faithful and their eucharistic participation in Christ's death was made, to which is enjoined the inward witness of the Spirit. When the Spirit bears witness with a person's spirit that he is a child of God, and he has the faith to confess Jesus as Lord, then the outward, sacramental signs "agree" with the inner witness of the Spirit, and the three bear a common witness to the truth.

The perennial objection to the doctrine of the inward testimony of the Spirit is that it is mere subjectivism (this doctrine was called by D. F. Strauss the "Achilles' heel" of Protestant theology). The question is pressed, how can one verify an inward experience? How do we know that we have to do with the Spirit of God, and not mere psychology? After all, people can be inwardly certain and convinced about some very uncertain and unconvincing things. John offers this answer: the way to prove a spirit, whether it be of God — for there are many false prophets in the world — is to see if one is led to confess that Jesus Christ, who came in the flesh, is of God. "By this you know the Spirit of God" (1 Jn. 4:2). The movement of the argument, then, is from the inward conviction to the outward, external, historical event of the Incarnation.

This is, indeed, an adequate criterion only for those who stand within the circle of faith. Should one press for a "neutral" criterion by which to verify the presence of the Holy Spirit in the life of the individual Christian, or the church as a whole, there can be no other than that of love. Everyone, says the apostle, who is begotten of God, loves God, for God is love. And if a believer loves God, he will love his neighbor also, for how can he hate a brother whom he has seen, and love God whom he has not seen? If he loves God, God abides in him (1 Jn. 4:7–8). There can be no doubt that this abiding presence of God in the heart and life is the presence of the Holy Spirit, for "God has poured out his love into our hearts by the Holy Spirit, whom he has given us" (Rom. 5:5). Therefore, of all the fruits of the Spirit, love is the greatest, and it is the most excellent way (1 Cor. 13).

I. The Holy Spirit and the mission of the church. God entered history in Jesus Christ; he also continued to participate in history in and through the work of the Spirit. The Acts of the Apostles are the acts of the Holy Spirit in the world. As the writer of Hebrews quotes Scripture with the words, "the Holy Spirit says," so what was accomplished in the mission of the apostolic church may be described as "that which the Holy Spirit does." This mission of the church continues and will continue until the Lord shall have conquered the last enemy, death. As Jesus' life, death, and resurrection are the content of the gospel, so it is the Holy Spirit who makes the gospel a transforming, redeeming reality in society. Were it not for the Holy Spirit, there would be no church in the world. It is the

Spirit who speaks to the church (Rev. 2:7, 11, 17, 29), and it is he who thrusts the church into the world to proclaim the gospel (Acts 13:1–4), and empowers it under all circumstances faithfully to bear this witness (Heb. 2:3–4).

(See further J. Calvin, *Institutes of the Christian Religion*, 1.7, 12; 3.1; A. Murray, *The Spirit of Christ* [1888]; G. Smeaton, *The Doctrine of the Holy Spirit* [1889]; H. B. Swete, *The Holy Spirit in the New Testament* [1910]; A. Kuyper, *The Work of the Holy Spirit* [1941]; T. Preiss, *Le témoignage intérieur du Saint-Esprit* [1946]; C. K. Barrett, *The Holy Spirit and the Gospel Tradition* [1947]; L. Berkhof, *The Doctrine of the Holy Spirit* [1964]; F. D. Bruner, *A Theology of the Holy Spirit* [1970]; M. Green, *I Believe in the Holy Spirit* [1975]; C. F. D. Moule, *The Holy Spirit* [1978]; R. B. Gaffin, Jr., in *WTJ* 43 [1980–81]: 58–78; D. A. Carson, *Showing the Spirit: A Theological Exposition of 1 Corinthians 12–14* [1987]; G. Hawthorne, *The Presence and the Power: The Significance of the Holy Spirit in the Life and Ministry of Jesus* [1991]; G. D. Fee, *Paul, the Spirit, and the People of God* [1996]; S. B. Ferguson, *The Holy Spirit* [1996]; J. McIntyre, *The Shape of Pneumatology: Studies in the Doctrine of the Holy Spirit* [1997]; M. Turner, *The Holy Spirit and Spiritual Gifts in the New Testament Church and Today* [1998]; J. Hur, *A Dynamic Reading of the Holy Spirit in Luke-Acts* [2001]; V.-M. Kärkkäinen, *Pneumatology: The Holy Spirit in Ecumenical, International, and Contextual Perspective* [2002]; F. Philip, *The Origins of Pauline Pneumatology: The Eschatological Bestowal of the Spirit upon Gentiles in Judaism and in the Early Development of Paul's Theology* [2005]; *TDNT*, 6:332–455; *NIDNTT*, 3:689–709; *ABD*, 3:260–80.) P. K. JEWETT

Homam hoh´mam (הוֹמָם H2102, derivation uncertain). Son of the clan chief LOTAN and grandson of SEIR the Horite (1 Chr. 1:39). The parallel passage reads HEMAM (Gen. 36:22 KJV; the NRSV has HEMAN, following LXX), though the NIV regards this form as an alternate of Homam and thus uses the latter in both passages.

homer. See WEIGHTS AND MEASURES III.B.

homicide. See CRIMES AND PUNISHMENTS I.B.

homosexuality. See SEX; SODOM.

honesty. See SINCERE; TRUTH.

honey. The common Hebrew term *děbaš* H1831 can refer both to the sweet fluid produced by bees from the nectar of flowers and to syrup made from

The Israelites cultivated the production of honey by encouraging bees to nest in bee-keeping jars like these (from the Hasmonean period).

fruit, such as dates and grapes (these were the only sweet food stuffs known in antiquity). The foraged honey is referred to as "from the rock" (Deut. 32:13; bees often built their combs in the crags) and "on the ground" (1 Sam. 14:25 et al.). Domestic honey from bee hives also is mentioned in the list of FIRSTFRUITS (2 Chr. 31:5). The significance of this food for the Israelites may be gauged from the characteristic description of PALESTINE as "a land flowing with milk and honey" (Exod. 3:8 and frequently). A less common term for domestic honey is *nōpet* H5885 (e.g., Ps. 19:10, which states that God's ordinances are sweeter; cf. Ps. 119:103). The Greek term for "honey" is *meli* G3510 (Matt. 3:4; Mk. 1:6; Rev. 10:9–10). See also BEE; FOOD. W. WHITE, JR.

honor. This English term is used to render various words, especially Hebrew *kābôd* H3883 (frequently "glory"; cf. also the cognate verb *kābēd* H3877 in the piel form) and Greek *timē* G5507 (verb *timaō* G5506). In antiquity, the dual concepts of honor and SHAME played a very important role in the ordering of SOCIETY (cf. J. G. Péristiany, ed., *Honour and*

Shame: The Values of Mediterranean Society [1966]), and recent scholarship has paid increasing attention to the significance of this cultural theme for biblical INTERPRETATION (e.g., J. H. Neyrey, *Honor and Shame in the Gospel of Matthew* [1998]; D. A. DeSilva, *The Hope of Glory: Honor Discourse and New Testament Interpretation* [1999]; J. H. Hellerman, *Reconstructing Honor in Roman Philippi* [2005]).

In a more general sense, honor is an enviable esteem, a valuable reward for excellence in station, character, or service. It is paid in thought, word, deed, or substance (cf. Isa. 29:13; Prov. 3:9). Primarily, God is to be honored, but all people are to "honor the Son just as they honor the Father" (Jn. 5:23; cf. Mk. 6:4). All that is sacred is to be honored, such as the SABBATH (Isa. 58:13–14) and MARRIAGE (Heb. 13:4, *timios* G5508). God declared to the Israelites that he would set them high above the nations "in praise, fame and honor" (Deut. 26:19). The Bible also mentions many individuals who were held in honor, including SAMUEL, DAVID, and JOB (1 Sam. 9:6; Ps. 4:2; Job 30:15 [Heb. *nědîbâ* H5619, NIV, "dignity"]). SOLOMON and other kings were described as having riches and honor (2 Chr. 1:12; 17:5; 18:1; 32:33; cf. Ps. 45:9). Also, "The wise inherit honor" (Prov. 3:35). See GLORY.

Paul told the Christians in Rome to pay "honor to whom honor is due" (Rom. 13:7 NRSV). The Bible is clear on who merits honor, including the list above. The fifth commandment is explicit: "Honor your father and your mother" (Exod. 20:12; Eph. 6:2–3). Jesus rebuked the PHARISEES and SCRIBES for not honoring their parents with material necessities (Matt. 15:4–6). Ancient laws pronounced the death penalty on those who dishonored parents in act or word (Exod. 21:15, 17; Lev. 20:9). PETER exhorted his readers to honor everyone, especially "the king" (i.e., the emperor, 1 Pet. 2:17), and Paul asked slaves to honor their masters (1 Tim. 6:1). (See *NIDOTTE*, 2:577–87; *NIDNTT*, 2:48–52; *DNTB*, 518–22.)   G. B. FUNDERBURK

hook. This term occurs in English Bibles as the rendering of several words, including Hebrew *wāw* H2260 (used of the gold and silver connectors or pegs from which various hangings were suspended in the TABERNACLE, Exod. 26:32 et al.) and *ḥāḥ* H2626 (used, for example, of a ring put on the nose of a captive or an animal, 2 Ki. 19:28; Ezek. 19:4; et al.). In the NT, Greek *ankistron* G45 refers to a fishhook (Matt. 17:27).

hoopoe. One of the birds that the Israelites were not to eat (Heb. *dûkîpat* H1871, Lev. 11:19; Deut. 14:18; KJV, "lapwing"). There is general agreement that the species in question is the *Upupa epops*, a quite unmistakable bird, with long curved bill, fan-like crest (erected only when settled), and very conspicuous black-and-white wing pattern seen in flight. It hunts insects in all sorts of unsavory places, taking many dung beetles and other insects, and its nest gets into the most unsanitary condition because the excreta is left in and around it. Hoopoes visit Palestine to breed and have been well known there since early times. Several Arab legends link this bird with Solomon. (See *FFB*, 42.)   G. S. CANSDALE

hope. The most common Hebrew noun for "hope" is *tiqwâ* H9536 (Ruth 1:12 et al.; note also the verbs *qāwâ* H7747 and *yāḥal* H3498, "to wait, expect, hope," Isa. 40:31; Job 6:11; et al.). In the NT this meaning is expressed with the Greek noun *elpis* G1828 (Acts 2:26 et al.) and its cognate verb *elpizō* G1827 (Matt. 12:21 et al.). Other Hebrew and Greek terms or expressions can signify attitudes that are related to hope.

  I. Definition of hope
 II. Human beings as hopeful
III. Function of hope
IV. Presence and nature of hope in the Bible
 V. Objects of hope in the Bible
   A. Earthly blessings
   B. God
   C. A new world
VI. Prominence of hope in the Bible.

I. Definition of hope. Hope has been defined as "desire accompanied by expectation." Hope, however, is not always expectant. One may have hope with little or no expectation. He may recognize the possible, though not the certain or probable, fulfillment of something. On the other hand, a person may be so confident of something that he simply expects it to happen. A better definition of hope is "an interest or desire whose fulfillment is cherished." Defining it thus, distinction can be made between strong and weak hope and between great and earnest hope. Strong hope has better grounds for believing an interest or desire will be fulfilled than a weak hope. It will be more confident and expectant. Great hope may refer to the intensity rather than to the confidence with which something is cherished, whereas earnest hope may designate the seriousness with which it is contemplated.

Hope is also to be distinguished from FAITH. They supplement each other, but are hardly identical. Hope is based on desire, facts, and rational considerations as well as, in its higher form, on faith. Faith is based not only on facts (Jer. 33:20, 25) and rational considerations (Gen. 1:1; Pss. 14:1; 19:1–4; 104; Isa. 40:12–26, 28; 41:17–20; 44:9–20; 45:2–8, 18–19; Acts 17:22–31; Rom. 1:18–23), but on a sense of God's presence in one's own life and in the life of a godly community (Isa. 12:2–6). It is also strengthened by one's personal devotion and commitment to God. Like simple expectation, faith in its certainty or confidence is apt to go beyond hope (Heb. 11:1); yet in some respects a Christian's hope is rooted in his faith and goes beyond it. It is in faith that Christ himself becomes one's hope.

II. Human beings as hopeful. Because human beings are limited in their knowledge of the future and aware of alternative eventualities, they are hope-full, for they naturally seek fulfillment and meaning in life. The STOICS, who recommended apathy as the rational way of life, still hoped to attain happiness thereby. Nietzsche held that hope was the worst of evils, because it prolongs the torment of many but his life was largely marked by hopeful efforts to interpret the world acceptably. Human beings are inherently hopeful.

III. Function of hope. Hope is not the only activating and guiding principle in human life; faith, thankfulness, intellectual curiosity, bodily desires and needs, moral ideals, social interests, and religious objectives and zeal also motivate us. Hope, however, is a major factor among them all and is intimately associated with the others. None of the other factors spur us to action without some measure of hope or certainty that our action will satisfy us in a given way. Dr. Karl Menninger (in *Pastoral Psychology* 11 [1960]: 11–24) speaks of the sustaining function of hope. Animals are known to revive quickly when given new hope but to die quickly when hopeless. Furthermore, evidence shows that helplessness and hopelessness can develop organic disease in human beings. Samuel Johnson was not far wrong when he observed that where there is no hope there can be no endeavor.

IV. Presence and nature of hope in the Bible. In view of its important function in human life, it is not surprising to find hope present in many biblical accounts long before it is mentioned by name. EVE saw that the forbidden tree was good for food and was to be desired to make her wise, and in the hope of satisfying her appetite and achieving wisdom she took of its fruit and ate (Gen. 3:6). JACOB had hope that by God granting his sons mercy Joseph might send back Simeon and Benjamin (43:14).

From these and other references it is evident that hope may lead to sin as well as to righteousness. It may err as well as guide correctly. What hope does depends on where a person seeks to find fulfillment and on what the hope is based. According to the Bible, no one should put his trust in riches (Job 31:24; Ps. 52:7; Lk. 12:13–21; 1 Tim. 6:17), or hope in men rather than God (Pss. 118:8–9; 146:3–4; Jer. 17:5–6). Reliance on idols is futile (Jer. 48:13; Hab. 2:18–19), and dependence on other nations is, to say the least, uncertain (Ps. 33:10; Isa. 19:3; 20:5–6; 31:1, 3; 37:6–7; Ezek. 29:13–16). Misplaced hope may prove false, and in some cases sinful. But it should be observed that even where an instance of hope is viewed as sinful, hope itself is nowhere in the Bible regarded as evil. Throughout the Bible, hope is considered a desirable attribute of human life. Even JOB in all his suffering does not curse hope as a cruel tantalizer, but laments the fact that his days are swifter than a weaver's shuttle and come to their end without hope (Job 7:6).

V. Objects of hope in the Bible

A. Earthly blessings. Much of the hope in the Bible has to do with personal, temporal, and earthly concerns. There is the hope of bearing children (Ruth 1:12), of finding water (Job 6:15–20), of military victory (Ps. 33:18), of receiving repayment (Lk. 6:34), of seeing a miracle performed (23:8), of being saved in a storm (Acts 27:20), of sharing a crop (1 Cor. 9:10), and of visiting someone (Rom. 15:24; 1 Cor. 16:7; 1 Tim. 3:14; 2 Jn. 12; 3 Jn. 14). Much hope in the Bible also has to do with a better adjustment to life and the world individually and collectively (Jer. 29:11; 31:17; Zech. 9:12; Jn. 5:45). In both these cases, the people's further hope is often placed in God (Ezra 10:2–4; Pss. 33:18–19; 62:5–7; 71:5; 146:5–7; Jer. 14:8, 22; Lam. 3:21–24).

B. God. Besides placing hope in God when seeking individual and collective blessings, the truly religious person also finds his highest longings and hopes directly fulfilled in God himself. Of the psalms perhaps none offer a better example than Pss. 42–43. "As the deer pants for streams of water, / so my soul pants for you, O God. / My soul thirsts for God, for the living God. / When can I go and meet with God?" (42:1–2). The writer's soul is cast down, but he enjoins it to hope in God because, he says, "I will yet praise him, my Savior and my God" (42:5). God is his "exceeding joy" (43:4 NRSV). A similar sentiment is expressed in Ps. 73, where the psalmist asks, "Whom have I in heaven but you?" and adds, "And earth has nothing I desire besides you" (73:25). Passages like these suggest a love of God with all one's heart, and with all one's soul and with all one's might (Deut. 6:5).

This God-centered attitude of the OT persists in the NT. Jesus says, "Now this is eternal life: that they know you, the only true God, and Jesus Christ, whom you have sent" (Jn. 17:3). For Paul, to live is Christ, and to depart and be with him is far better than to remain in the flesh (Phil. 1:21, 23). The peace of God is what he cherishes (4:7). John anticipates being like Jesus and seeing him as he is (1 Jn. 3:2–3).

Geerhardus Vos, in an article on "The Eschatology of the Psalter," has very aptly expressed something of the fulfillment we can find in God: "The Psalmists sometimes succeed in transporting themselves into the midst of the joy and blessedness, wherewith Jehovah himself contemplates the consummate perfection of his work. This faculty for entering into the inner spirit of God's own share in the religious process represents the highest and finest in worship; it closes the ring of religion" (*PTR* 18 [1920]: 19). Fulfillment such as this makes clear why God, or Christ, himself is the highest object of hope.

C. A new world. (1) *Scriptural statements.* Finding hope and fulfillment of life directly in God is something that occurs in the present life. In the Bible is also a vision of individual and community life that in important respects transcends our ordinary earthly existence. It is sometimes hard to distinguish between such a transcendent life and what simply is a better adjustment to life and the world. Yet it is there and repeatedly comes to clear expression. A day will come when "the Root of Jesse will stand as a banner for the peoples; the nations will rally to him, and his place of rest will be glorious" (Isa. 11:10; cf. 2:2–3). Not only shall the nations finally beat their swords into plowshares and their spears into pruning hooks (Isa. 2:4; Mic. 4:3), but even the animal kingdom will be peaceable (Isa. 11:6–9). God will create a new heaven and a new earth, and the former things shall not be remembered or come to mind (Isa. 65:17; 66:22). All flesh shall come to worship before him (66:23). See HEAVENS, NEW.

Jeremiah states that the days are coming when the Lord will make a new covenant with the house of Israel and with the house of Judah, and they shall all know him from the least to the greatest (Jer. 31:31, 34). Significantly, at the Last Supper Jesus said, "This is my blood of the covenant, which is poured out for many" (Mk. 14:24). Paul stated that "if any one is in Christ, he is a new creation" (2 Cor. 5:17). Christ rose from the dead, and because he lives his disciples will live also (Jn. 14:19). We who are in Christ are now "children of God, and what we will be has not yet been made known" (1 Jn. 3:2). "Now we know that if the earthly tent we live in is destroyed, we have a building from God, an eternal house in heaven, not built by human hands" (2 Cor. 5:1). John on Patmos "saw a new heaven and a new earth; for the first heaven and the first earth had passed away" (Rev. 21:1). He also saw a throne and he who sat upon it said, "I am making everything new" (21:5). Many other passages are relevant. See ESCHATOLOGY.

(2) *Its nature.* According to the NT, OT visions and promises find a special fulfillment in Jesus Christ, but a further fulfillment of some of them (as well as of new promises) awaits the future. As

Rudolph Bultmann sees it, in the OT the godly person was always directed to what God will do, so that his hope for the future consisted in a wholly general trust in God's protection and help. The time of salvation, he says, was the time of confidence. The attitude of waiting and trusting hope became more and more an expression of knowledge concerning the provisional nature of everything earthly and present, and a hope in the eschatological future (*Bible Key Words*, ed. G. Kittel, 5/1 [1963]; cf. P. S. Minear in *Scottish Journal of Theology* 6 [1953]: 340).

Bultmann's stress here on what God will do is doubtless justified; but his emphasis on the provisional character of our present, earthly situation in comparison with the eschatological future is open to question. One may grant that man by himself is ineffective and weak, that he is a sinner in need of God's redeeming grace, and that his days are numbered: like a flower of the field he flourishes, for the wind passes over it and it is gone, and its place knows it no more (Ps. 103:15–16; cf. 62:9; 144:4). All this refers to the limitations of human power, commitment to wrong values, the brevity of the present life, and dependence on God. It does not refer to the intellectual, moral, and spiritual structure of our being, nor to the life that we live when God's Spirit takes possession of us. As far as basic features go, the life hereafter that the Christian hopes for and his present earthly existence are of one piece. However much imagery and symbolism may be used elsewhere, Paul characterizes this life in sober, literal terms. He says, "And now these three remain: faith, hope, and love" (1 Cor. 13:13). From this it appears that Paul conceived of "the perfect" that is coming as something living, dynamic, and growing, like the present existence, not as something static or consummated in every way; nor as something totally different from what is known already. Hope is one of the characteristics of human life today. With faith and love it will also be a characteristic of human life on a higher plane hereafter.

It is noteworthy that Bultmann interprets hope in the NT in a way similar to his interpretation of it in the OT. Taking hope in that sense, he holds that it will persist. In virtue of its idea of God, he says, Christian being, also in perfection, cannot be conceived apart from hope, that is, from a trust in God that looks away from itself and the world and patiently waits for God's gift; and when God has granted his gift, he will assuredly maintain what he has given (*Bible Key Words*, 37; see also *TDNT*, 2:530–33). Bultmann's contention that hope will persist is doubtless right; but he fails to recognize that since the love of which Paul speaks is a love of other human beings (1 Cor. 13:4–7) as well as of God, the hope springing from it can hardly be simply the kind of trust he says it is. It is rather a hope both in God and in the future as man envisions it on the basis of the knowledge, faith, and love that will be his.

VI. Prominence of hope in the Bible. The main reason hope is prominent in the Bible is its high concept of God and its strongly prevailing faith in him. Such a God and such strong faith in him cannot but instill great hope in us. But a further reason is the freedom the Bible assumes we have. God is ultimately in full control of things, but not in a fatalistic way. His control is one of intelligent and loving purpose, not a matter of blind, unintelligent determination. Furthermore, God leaves us as free agents. He does not force us in our deliberate choices or against our will, but rather indirectly and directly controls those personal factors that go to form our will freely. Along with this, the Bible also affirms that God has ordained great principles of life for us to rely on, to give meaning and stability to life in a world of vast possibilities. With such a view of God, man, and the world, there is ample room for hope on the part of the believer.

(See further F. J. Denbeaux in *Int* 5 [1951]: 285–303; H. J. A. Bouman in *Concordia Theological Monthly* 26 [1955]: 241–55; H. C. Snape in *The Modern Churchman* 7 [1963]: 84–92; R. E. Osborne and D. D. Williams in *Encounter* 24 [1963]:, 61–73; C. F. D. Moule, *The Meaning of Hope* [1963]; D. Moody, *The Hope of Glory* [1964]; D. J. Harrington, *What Are We Hoping For?* [2006]; *NIDOTTE*, 3:892–96; *NIDNTT*, 2:238–46.)

P. H. Monsma

Hophni hof´ni (חָפְנִי *H2909*, possibly from Egyp. *hfn*, "tadpole"). Son of Eli, who was the high priest at Shiloh (1 Sam. 1:3; 2:34; 4:4, 11, 17). Hophni and his brother Phinehas were greedy and rapacious when ministering as priests before the altar of Yahweh (2:12–17), and they acted immorally with the women who served at the entrance to the TABERNACLE (2:22). According to the law of MOSES, the worshiper at the altar was required to present to the priest the fat of the sacrificed animal along with the breast and shoulder (Lev. 7:29–34). The fat was to be burned on the altar as an offering to Yahweh (3:3–5); the breast and shoulder became the portion of the priest. Hophni and Phinehas,

The plain N of Aphek where Hophni and Phinehas died in battle. (View to the N.)

not content with the share assigned to them, sent a servant to interrupt the preparation of the sacrificial meal and to seize a further portion. They also insisted on getting their share of the offering before the parts dedicated to God were burned on the altar, and they demanded the best part of the animal raw, not boiled, before the offering had been made. All this, together with their immorality, brought great discredit to their father Eli. He remonstrated with them, but not severely enough. In consequence God's judgment was pronounced against him and his house first by an unknown prophet and later through SAMUEL (1 Sam. 2:27–36; 3:11–14). Hophni and Phinehas died in the battle against the PHILISTINES at APHEK; and Eli fell down and died when he heard of their death. This rejection of the house of Eli provides the setting for the emergence of a rightful priest, Samuel. S. BARABAS

Hophra hof′ruh (חָפְרַע *H2922*, from Egyp. *ḥaʿaʿibreʿ*, meaning possibly "Re [the sun-god] is long-suffering [*or* of constant heart *or* happy-hearted]"). Fourth king of the 26th dynasty in EGYPT. Better known as Apries (through Gk. adaptation; his Egyp. birthname was Wahibrē), this PHARAOH reigned nineteen years, 589–570 B.C. When NEBUCHADNEZZAR II of Babylon besieged Jerusalem in 589, Hophra rashly marched against him at the appeal of ZEDEKIAH of Judah (sending a fleet to PHOENICIA; see Herodotus, *Hist.* 2.161). As soon as the Babylonians turned from Jerusalem to meet him, the pharaoh seems to have retreated homeward, thus affording the Hebrews no relief (Jer. 37; cf. Ezek. 17:15, 17). In his reign, and taken unwillingly to TAHPANHES in the NILE delta, JEREMIAH prophesied that Nebuchadnezzar would in turn invade Egypt (Jer. 43:9–13; 46:13–26), while in far distant Babylon, EZEKIEL in the tenth to twelfth years of his captivity (c. 587–585) uttered further judgments on the pharaoh and his land (Ezek. 29:1–16; 30:20–26; 31–32), and again in his twenty-seventh year, c. 570 (29:17—30:19) on the very eve of Hophra's final fall. Hophra's end was prophesied by Jeremiah (Jer. 44:30, sole biblical reference to Hophra by name) and resulted from a military defeat in LIBYA and a consequent revolt against him in Egypt; Nebuchadnezzar duly attacked Egypt in 568/567 (*ANET*, 308; see further *ABD*, 3:286–87).

K. A. KITCHEN

Hor hor (הֹר *H2216*, possibly equivalent to הַר *H2215*, "mountain"; the name always appears in the phrase הֹר הָהָר, "Hor, the mountain"). **(1)** A mountain on the border of the land of EDOM at the foot of which the Israelites encamped on their journey from KADESH to the Promised Land (Num. 20:22–23). It was here that God told MOSES and AARON that, because of their sin at MERIBAH, Aaron would die on Mount Hor in the sight of the people of Israel. The two men ascended the mount with ELEAZAR, Aaron's son, and there Moses removed Aaron's high priestly garments and put them on Eleazar; then Aaron died, 123 years old. This was in the fortieth year after Israel had come out of Egypt (Num 33:33–37; in Deut. 10:6 it is said that Aaron died at MOSERAH, possibly a neighboring area).

According to JOSEPHUS (*Ant.* 4.4.7), Mount Hor was one of the mountains surrounding

Petra, namely, Jebel Nebi Harun ("Mountain of the Prophet Aaron"), which rises 4,800 ft. and is approximately half-way between the S end of the Dead Sea and the N end of the Gulf of Aqabah. It is the highest of the mountains in Edom. On the top is a tomb said to belong to Aaron, but the upper part at least is a Muslim tomb. Islamic tradition has it that this is the Mount Hor where Aaron is buried. This identification is doubtful, however. For one thing, Jebel Nebi Harun is in the middle of Edom and not on its border as was Mount Hor; since Edom denied the request of the Israelites to pass through its territory, and came out against Israel with a strong force of men, it is not likely that Israel would encamp at a mountain in the middle of Edom. It is also too far E of Kadesh. Moreover, the mountain is too high for the people to have witnessed from below what went on above, and too rugged for the three men to ascend it.

Jebel Madurah (Madrah), a mountain c. 15 mi. NE of Kadesh, on the NW border of Edom, is a more likely site. Its topography is such that Israel could observe the ceremony on the top. It is on the direct route from Kadesh to Moab. Another possibility is Imaret el-Khureisheh, some 10 mi. NE of Kadesh (and 40 mi. SW of Beer Sheba).

(2) Another mountain peak with the same name was to mark the N boundary of Israel's promised inheritance (Num. 34:7–8). Its exact location is unknown, but it was undoubtedly a prominent peak in the Lebanon range between the Mediterranean and Lebo Hamath. Mount Hermon, Jebel Akkar (a NE spur of Lebanon), and Ras Shaqqa (on the coast, some 40 mi. NNE of Beirut) have been suggested.

S. Barabas

Horam hor′am (הֹרָם H2235, meaning unknown). King of Gezer; when Lachish was attacked by the Israelites, Horam came to its assistance, "but Joshua defeated him and his army—until no survivors were left" (Josh. 10:33; cf. 12:12).

Horeb hor′eb (חֹרֵב H2998, "dry, desolate"). See Sinai, Mount.

Horem hor′em (חֳרֵם H3054, possibly "consecrated" or "[small] rock crevice"). A fortified town in the hill country of Naphtali (Josh. 19:38). It was probably in N Galilee, but the precise site is unknown.

Horesh hor′esh (חֹרֶשׁ H3092, found only in its locative form, חֹרְשָׁה, and usually with the definite article, "the woodland"). A place in the Desert of Ziph where David took refuge from Saul; there David and Jonathan made a compact (1 Sam. 23:15–18). The "strongholds at Horesh" are further identified as being on the hill of Hakilah and S of Jeshimon (v. 19). Though the precise location is uncertain, it is often identified with Khirbet Khoreisa, about 6 mi. S of Hebron. A few scholars, however, have thought that the word should be understood as a common noun (thus "the thicket in the Desert of Ziph") rather than as a place name.

Hor Haggidgad hor′huh-gid′gad (חֹר הַגִּדְגָּד H2988, "cave of Gidgad"). KJV Hor-hagidgad. A station of the Israelites in the wilderness, located between Bene Jaakan and Jotbathah (Num. 33:31–33); apparently the same as Gudgodah (Deut. 10:7). The site is unknown, though one proposed identification is Wadi Ghadhaghedh.

Hori hor′i (חֹרִי H3036, derivation uncertain; see Horite and Hurrian). (1) Firstborn son of Lotan and grandson of Seir the Horite (Gen. 36:22; 1 Chr. 1:39). He was no doubt the ancestor of a tribal group in Edom. The form of his name is the same as that of the gentilic "Horite," but the connection between the personal and the ethnic name is unclear. Perhaps Hori was viewed as the Horite par excellence. It has also been suggested that his name reflects a tribal struggle for supremacy.

(2) Father of Shaphat, who was the leader from the tribe of Simeon included among the twelve spies sent by Moses to explore the land of Canaan (Num. 13:5).

Horite hor′it (חֹרִי H3037, perhaps "cave dweller" or "nobleman" or "son"). Phonetically, this name is the OT Hebrew equivalent of extrabiblical Hurrian, but the OT references to "Horites" do not fit what we know about the Hurrians, a non-Semitic people. The personal names of the "Horites" in Gen. 36:20–30 are inconsistent with Hurrian patterns and seem rather to be Semitic. It is moreover claimed that no archaeological evidence exists for Hurrian settlements in EDOM or TRANSJORDAN in general, whereas the OT reports "Horites" living there (Gen. 14:6; Deut. 2:12, 22 [KJV, "Horim"]). These people, whom we may refer to as E Horites, and who were driven out and destroyed by the Edomites, were apparently not Hurrians.

On the other hand, it is thought by some that the name Horite originally stood in two places where the Hebrew text has HIVITE (see LXX Gen. 34:2 and Josh. 9:7; cf. also Isa. 17:9). If so, these passages would refer to a group that we may call W Horites, because they are said to reside in the region to the W of the Jordan. They are to be kept distinct from the E Horites, the predecessors of the Edomites. The W Horites, it is claimed by some, are non-Semites related to the peoples called Hurrians in extrabiblical texts of the 2nd millennium B.C. The etymology of the name of the E Horites may be the Semitic noun for "cave" (*hōr H2986*), identifying the pre-Edomites of SEIR as "cave dwellers," whereas the etymology of the name of the W Horites is obscure, being involved with the uncertain origins and relationships of the poorly understood Hurrian language. (See E. Meyer, *Die Israeliten und deren Nachbarstämme* [1906]; E. A. Speiser in *AASOR* 13 [1933]: 26–31; I. J. Gelb, *Hurrians and Subarians* [1944]; E. A. Speiser in *JAOS* 68 [1948]: 1–13; H. G. Guterbock in *Journal of World History* 2 [1954]: 383–94; E. A. Speiser in *IDB*, 2:645; G. Wilhelm, *The Hurrians* [1989].)

H. A. HOFFNER, JR.

Hormah hor′muh (חָרְמָה *H3055*, possibly "consecration, destruction" or "rock crevice"). One of the southernmost cities of the tribe of JUDAH, located in the NEGEV, toward the boundary of EDOM (Josh. 15:30; cf. v. 21); it was subsequently allotted to the tribe of SIMEON (Josh. 19:4; 1 Chr. 4:30). According to some, it was officially a Simeonite town incorporated into Judah's tribal territory (note that it was regarded as Judahite in the time of DAVID, 1 Sam. 30:30; cf. v 26).

Hormah is first mentioned in Num. 14:45, which records that when the Israelites rashly invaded Canaan at KADESH against the will of God, the Amalekites and Canaanites defeated and pursued them as far as Hormah. Toward the end of the wilderness wanderings, the Canaanite king of ARAD fought against Israel and took some of them captives. The Israelites vowed to the Lord that if he would help them conquer the Canaanites, they would utterly destroy their cities (Num 21:1–2, using the verb *ḥāram H3049*, "to consecrate, devote [to destruction], place under the ban", see BAN). God answered their prayer, they conquered the Canaanite towns, and "the place" (referring either to a cluster of cities or only to the specific spot of the defeat) was named Hormah (Num. 21:3).

Some scholars believe that the biblical text reflects conflicting traditions, for JOSHUA is later said to have conquered the king of Hormah (Josh. 12:14). Moreover, the book of Judges relates that many years later "the men of Judah went with the Simeonites their brothers and attacked the Canaanites living in Zephath, and they totally destroyed the city. Therefore it was called Hormah" (Jdg. 1:17). A possible explanation is that at the time of Moses the Israelites were satisfied with the defeat of the Canaanites of Arad and deferred "the complete execution of their vow until the time when they had gained a firm footing in Canaan" (KD, *Pentateuch*, 3:137). According to this view, Num. 21:3 does not refer specifically to ZEPHATH, a town within the country of the king of Arad that was renamed Hormah only later (Jdg. 1:17, though referred to by this name proleptically in the book of Joshua).

The location of Hormah/Zephath is uncertain. It is mentioned between Geder and Arad (Josh. 12:14), between Kesil and Ziklag (15:30), and between Bethul and Ziklag (19:4). Proposed sites include Tell el-Milḥ (c. 7 mi. NE of BEERSHEBA, but see ARAD and cf. Y. Aharoni, *The Land of the Bible: A Historical Geography*, rev. ed. [1979], 201), Tell esh-Shariʿah (c. 12 mi. NW of Beersheba, but see ZIKLAG), Khirbet el-Meshash (= T. Masos, c. 8 mi. ESE of Beersheba; see esp. Y. Aharoni in *BA* 39 [1976]: 55–76, and cf. *NEAEHL*, 3:986–89), Khirbet Gharra (= T. ʿIra, c. 2 mi. NE of el-Meshash), and Tell Khuweilifeh (= T. Ḥalif, c. 9.5 mi. NNE of Beersheba, but see RIMMON (PLACE) #1).

horn. This term, usually the rendering of Hebrew *qeren H7967*, can refer literally to the bony structure projecting from the head of rams and other animals (e.g., Gen. 22:13), but it is also used as a symbol of power, victory, and salvation (e.g., Ps. 18:2; cf. Gk. *keras* G3043, Lk. 1:69). Musical instruments were made from rams' horns (see MUSIC, MUSICAL INSTRUMENTS IV.C). See also HORNS OF THE ALTAR.

hornet. This English term is used by some Bible versions to render Hebrew *ṣirʿâ* H7667, a word that occurs three times, possibly referring to a stinging wasp (*Vespa orientalis*). God told the Israelites that he would send his terror ahead of them to throw the pagan nations into confusion. Then he added, "I will send the hornet ahead of you to drive the Hivites, Canaanites and Hittites out of your way" (Exod. 23:28; similarly Deut. 7:20; Josh. 24:12; in all three passages the NRSV renders "pestilence," and others suggest it means "terror" or "discouragement").

In modern Hebrew, the name is given to a number of large and conspicuously banded hymenopterous insects that live in colonies of varying sizes. The largest of all is more specifically known as *hornet* in English; it is over one and a half inches long and its sting can be both unpleasant and dangerous because of the large volume of venom that can be injected. The word *wasp* refers generally to a large assortment of smaller, but generally similar, insects. In contrast to the BEE, both hornets and wasps are basically carnivorous, and in Palestine hornets often prey on honeybees.

The true hornet is found in many parts of Palestine and in all types of country, including the desert around the Dead Sea. Although wasps have a less painful sting, some common species live in large colonies, some of which make nests suspended from tree branches. Such a nest could easily be disturbed, with serious results, by soldiers and their mounts going through scrub and woodland. The widespread occurrence of these stinging insects, whose massive interference could have caused some panic and thus affected the outcome of a battle, makes it possible that the use in these three passages is purely literal. On the other hand, J. Garstang (*The Foundations of Bible History: Joshua-Judges* [1931], 112ff., 258ff.) identified the hornet with the sacred symbol of the pharaohs and saw the fulfillment of this promise in the Egyptian campaigns in Canaan prior to the exodus, but this view has not been generally accepted.
G. S. CANSDALE

horns of the altar. The four protrusions at the corners of a hewn stone ALTAR, a feature common to the ancient world (Exod. 27:2 et al.). It is clear that the horns of the altar conferred sanctuary to the accused (1 Ki. 1:50).

Horon. See BETH HORON.

Horonaim hor´uh-nay´im (חֹרֹנַיִם H2589, prob. "twin caves"). **(1)** According to the SEPTUAGINT (CODEX VATICANUS), a place near BAAL HAZOR, mentioned in connection with the killing of AMNON by the men of ABSALOM (2 Sam. 13:34; Baal Hazor is mentioned in v. 23). The KJV, following the MT, reads: "But Absalom fled. And the young man that kept the watch lifted up his eyes, and looked, and, behold, there came much people by the way of the hill side behind him." The Greek versions, however, add a sentence that takes the following form in Codex Vaticanus: "The watchman went and told the king, 'I see men in the direction of Horonaim [*ek tēs hodou tēs Ōrōnēn*], on the side of the hill'" (NIV rendering; the NRSV accepts the reference to Horonaim, but reconstructs the text differently). The omission in the MT can reasonably be explained as a result of haplography (the scribe's eye skipping from *miṣad hāhār*, "beside the hill," in the middle of the verse to its repetition at the end). If Horonaim is indeed original, the reference is probably to "the twin Horons," that is, Upper and Lower BETH HORON (c. 12 mi. SW of Baal Hazor). "The royal party must have fled Baal-hazor by way of Bethel and picked up the Horonaim road to Jerusalem near Gibeon" (P. K. McCarter, Jr., *II Samuel*, AB 9 [1984], 333).

(2) A city of MOAB, mentioned in two prophetic oracles (Isa. 15:5; Jer. 48:3, 5, 34). The name Horonaim (in the form *ḥwrnn*, Hauronen) also occurs in the MOABITE STONE, where King MESHA states that he fought against it and presumably conquered it (cf. *ANET*, 322). During the OT period, it appears that Israel was never in possession of Horonaim, but subsequently, according to JOSEPHUS, Alexander Jannaeus (see HASMONEAN II.C) took it from the Arabs (*Ant.* 13.15.4 §398; Hyrcanus later restored it to Aretas, 14.1.4 §18). The city was apparently near Luhith at the foot of a descent (Jer. 48:5), but its exact location is unknown. It probably lay on one of the roads leading from the Moabite plateau to the Arabah. Various identifications have been proposed (cf. *ABD*, 3:289), among them el-Iraq, some 9 mi. E of the S tip of the Dead Sea and 6 mi. N of the Zered river.

Horonite hor´uh-nit (חֹרֹנִי H3061). An epithet applied to Sanballat, who opposed Nehemiah in his attempt to restore Jerusalem (Neh. 2:10, 19; 13:28). The name may denote a citizen of Horonaim in Moab or, more probably, of Beth Horon.

horse. This term (Heb. *sûs* H6061, Gk. *hippos* G2691) is applied equally to a mounted horse or to a horse without rider. The male is called a *stallion*; the female, *mare* (Heb. *sûsâ* H6063, Cant. 1:9); the young (usually born singly), *colt* or *foal*.

I. Introduction. The horse was the latest and strongest transport animal to be developed; it spread rapidly, first over Eurasia and N Africa, later to the Americas and Australasia, escaping and becoming feral in suitable areas. Everywhere it has become the most important beast of burden and an intimate associate of man, next only to the dog. This factor may have helped to fix a prejudice against eating horsemeat in English-speaking lands. Horsemeat was forbidden to the Hebrews because, like its close relative the donkey (see ass, donkey), the horse is single-hoofed and does not ruminate; there is no obvious hygienic basis for this ban.

II. Origin. F. E. Zeuner (*A History of Domesticated Animals* [1963]) sets out in detail the archaeological and zoological evidence of the horse's early history, and the following owes much to his research. The equines once formed four groups, fairly distinct geographically: (1) the zebras in E and S Africa, where sporadic attempts to use them had only temporary success; (2) the true asses of N and NE Africa, from which the donkey is derived; (3) the half-asses (see wild ass) from the dry belt running from Palestine eastward to the Gobi Desert; (4) the horses of the grassy lowlands of Eurasia N of the great mountain ranges. All four groups were divided into local species or races. Of the true horses, only Przewalski's, the E race, survives precariously in Mongolia and some zoo parks. It stands about forty inches at the shoulder and is reddish brown, the hair becoming longer and paler in winter; the mane is dark brown. Like all equines it runs in herds. The W race was the tarpan, of which the last known specimen died in 1851 in the Ukraine. It was a small gray-brown horse with upright mane and the chief ancestor of the many breeds of domestic horses today, with the Plains of Turkestan a likely center of domestication, though not the only one.

III. Domestication. Undoubtedly horses were domesticated later than the sheep, goat, ox, and ass, but nothing is known of its early pattern. Oxen had long been used for pulling wheeled carts, and with the fertile patches of plains country becoming exhausted and dried out (as happened after a few centuries of primitive agriculture), the need for faster draught animals might have prompted the farmers to catch and tame these wild horses. The actual means remains a mystery; modern humans have achieved nothing like it, other than the catching and training of a few zebras. Regarding its original domestication, this must have been during the 3rd millennium B.C., but evidence prior to 2000 B.C. is not reliable. The Sumerians mention the horse in proverbs from c. 2100 but apparently did not use it. The horse first found regular mention about 1800, though it was not yet important (the Code of Hammurabi, c. 1750, does not list it). Within the next fifty years it spread rapidly to the SW, including Asia, Palestine, and Egypt, where it arrived in the Hyksos era not many decades before Joseph came to power. This spread, which took it as far as Troy, resulted from its use in war chariots. Whatever its purpose when first brought into service, the horse added a new dimension to invading armies.

IV. The horse in biblical narrative. The first biblical mention is Gen. 47:17, which states that the Egyptians "brought their livestock to Joseph, and he gave them food in exchange for their horses, their sheep and goats, their cattle and donkeys." At this time, and for some centuries, the horse was used mainly for draught purposes, mostly drawing

Assyrian soldiers on horse back. Reconstruction of the Balawat Gate of Shalmaneser III (858–824 B.C.) at Nineveh.

CHARIOTS, and the first clear evidence of one being ridden is a figurine of the 18th Egyptian dynasty (c. 1580 B.C.). An individual rider appears first in 1 Ki. 20:20 ("Ben-Hadad king of Aram escaped on horseback with some of his horsemen"), but Gen. 50:9 records that both horsemen and chariots accompanied the great cortege that took JACOB's body for burial in Canaan, and the Egyptian armies used both chariots and cavalry to pursue the escaping Hebrews. It is unlikely that the Israelites had owned horses in GOSHEN or taken any with them to the desert.

Later, when SOLOMON had control of the two main routes parallel to the coast along which animals could be brought safely, Egypt became an important source of horses for Israel (1 Ki. 10:28–29). The amassing of horses had been specifically forbidden by God (Deut. 17:16), and the context of this ban is notable: it follows the statement that the Hebrews would one day demand a king. When the people made this request some two centuries later (1 Sam. 8:11), SAMUEL warned them that the ban would be ignored to their detriment; however, it may have been observed through the reigns of SAUL and DAVID, when the main reference is to horses in the enemy armies. It appears from 2 Sam. 8:4 that David kept some for his own use; he killed most, but left enough for a hundred chariots. This turned out to be a tragic mistake, for they were available for two of his sons to use. ABSALOM, plotting against him, "provided himself with a chariot and horses" (2 Sam. 15:1). Some twelve years later, when David was on his death bed, a younger son, ADONIJAH, in an effort to take over the kingdom, "got chariots and horses ready" (1 Ki. 1:5).

Solomon made no attempt to obey God on this point, and within a year or so of becoming king he had built stables for 4,000 horses (2 Chr. 9:25; the figure of 40,000 in the corresponding passage in the MT of 1 Ki. 4:26 [cf KJV] must be a scribal error). He imported horses from Egypt, with which he had profitable connections through marrying the daughter of the pharaoh, paying 150 shekels of silver (60 ounces) per horse. Horses also formed part of the regular tribute paid him (1 Ki. 10:25). From then on both Judah and Israel regarded horses and chariots as essential for fighting the frequent wars with neighboring nations. Early in its history the horse sometimes had sacred connections. The only biblical instance is in 2 Ki. 23:11, where JOSIAH, in his sweeping reforms, removed horses that earlier kings had dedicated to the sun.

V. Biblical significance. There is nothing about the horse's biology or habits in the many biblical contexts, in contrast to other major animals. The psalmist associates it with the mule as animals that "have no understanding but must be controlled by bit and bridle or they will not come to you" (Ps. 32:9). Many carvings illustrate the early use of the BIT AND BRIDLE. Job's description (Job 39:19–25) is of a war horse and speaks merely of its strength and fearlessness in battle. Horses are also mentioned in connection with the famine foretold by ELIJAH (1 Ki. 18:5). Donkeys were much more numerous, but could manage on poorer forage and were used in ones and twos.

The horse's place in the Scriptures contrasts markedly with that of the donkey. Of over 140 references to horses, only about 50 are truly literal; the rest, with all the 15 NT references (except horsemen, Acts 23:23, 32), are figurative or prophetic. In a small minority of cases a single horse is mentioned (notably 1 Ki. 10:29; Esth. 6:8–11; and nine quasi-proverbial expressions in Job, Psalms, and Proverbs). There is no record of a horse being owned by the common people; throughout OT times the horse was a monopoly of kings and their nobles in both Palestine and nearby countries and thus, in effect, a symbol of human power. This confirms its metaphorical significance. Some of the prophetic passages of Zechariah and Revelation are highly symbolic and beyond the scope of comment here, but the tenor of all the many figurative passages may be summed up in two verses: Ps. 33:17, "A horse is a vain hope for deliverance"; and Hos. 1:7, "I will save them—not by bow, sword or battle, or by horse and horsemen." (See further G. S. Cansdale, *Animals and Man* [1952]; *FFB*, 43–45; *ABD*, 6:1136–37.)

G. S. CANSDALE

Horse Gate. A JERUSALEM gate on the E wall of the city (Jer. 31:40). Restored by NEHEMIAH (Neh. 3:28), it was apparently N of the WATER GATE and S of the EAST GATE (vv. 26, 29), therefore near the SE corner of the TEMPLE. Queen ATHALIAH was killed "at the entrance of the Horse Gate [*mĕbôʾ šaʿar-hassûsîm*] on the palace grounds" (2 Chr. 23:15; the parallel passage, 2 Ki. 11:16, has simply *mĕbôʾ hassûsîm*, lit., "the entrance of the horses"), and some argue that this was a different entrance, situated between the palace and the temple, and that it led to the stables in the Palace of the Forest of Lebanon (see M. Avi-Yonah in *IEJ* 4 [1954]: 240, 247; *ABD*, 3:290).

horseleach. See LEECH.

Hosah (person) hoh'suh (חֹסָה *H2880*, possibly "refuge"). A Levite descended from MERARI whom DAVID made a gatekeeper of the tent housing the ARK OF THE COVENANT when it was brought into Jerusalem (1 Chr. 16:38). He and his family were later part of the organization of the gatekeepers (26:10–11) and were made responsible for providing guards for the SHALLEKETH Gate on the W (26:16).

Hosah (place) hoh'suh (חֹסָה *H2881*, possibly "refuge"). A town on the N border of the tribal territory of ASHER, near TYRE on the Mediterranean coast (Josh. 19:29). Its precise location is uncertain, but many scholars identify it with ancient Usu (mentioned for example in Seti I's lists) and modern Tell Rashidiyeh, a coastal town c. 3 mi. SSE of Tyre (cf. Y. Aharoni, *The Land of the Bible: A Historical Geography*, rev. ed. [1979], 178, 258). Others question the connection with Usu and identify Hosah with modern Khirbet el-Hos, just E of Tell Rashidiyeh

(cf. the discussion in Z. Kallai, *Historical Geography of the Bible* [1986], 218–20).

hosanna hoh-zan'uh (ὡσαννά *G6057*, a transliteration of Heb. [or possibly Aram.] הוֹשַׁע נָא, "Save, please," though this precise form is not attested). This term was originally a Hebrew invocation addressed to God (found only in Ps. 118:25 [KJV, "Save now"], which uses the more common long form of the imperative, *hôšîʿâ nnāʾ*). Later it apparently came to be used as a joyous acclamation, an ascription of praise to God (cf. R. H. Gundry, *The Use of the Old Testament in St. Matthew's Gospel: With Special Reference to the Messianic Hope* [1967], 41–43). Already in Jeremiah's time the verb could almost be used as a shout of welcome, for God instructs Israel to give praise by saying, *hôšaʿ yhwh ʾet-ʿammĕkā*, "O LORD, save your people" (Jer. 31:7). In this sense it was used at the joyous Feast of Tabernacles, the seventh day of which came to be called the "Great Hosanna" or "Hosanna Day." (For further data, and for arguments that the term is Aram. and reflects pre-Christian usage, see J. A. Fitzmyer in *Tradition and Interpretation in the New Testament*, ed. G. F. Hawthorne and O. Betz [1987], 110–18.)

The English transliteration *hosanna* appears in Bible versions only in connection with Jesus' TRIUMPHAL ENTRY into Jerusalem on Palm Sunday. Three of the evangelists give accounts of this incident, containing both identical and supplementary phrases. Matthew records: "The crowds that went ahead of him and those that followed shouted, 'Hosanna to the Son of David!' 'Blessed is he who comes in the name of the Lord!' [= Ps. 118:26] 'Hosanna in the highest!'" (Matt. 21:9; cf. also v. 15). Mark adds the statement, "Blessed is the kingdom of our father David that is coming!" (Mk. 11:9–10), whereas John gives a briefer report (Jn. 12:13). Luke, in keeping with his tendency not to include Hebrew or Aramaic terms and expressions, which would be obscure to his Gentile audience, omits the word *hosanna* in his account of the people's acclamation (Lk. 19:37–38).

It may be noted that according to some scholars the use of the term as a shout of praise reflects an early Christian misunderstanding of the cries of the crowd, who really meant either "Please save the Son of David" (taking the underlying Semitic particle *l-* as a sign of the direct object) or "O Son of David, please save us!" (for the latter, cf. M. H. Pope in *ABD*, 3:290–91, who assumes that the crowds were using *l-* as a vocative, an obsolete function found in Ugaritic but not clearly attested in postbiblical Heb. or Aram.). This approach is problematic because it suggests that Matthew, who was either unaware of what the crowd meant or deliberately ignored it, mistranslated the statement with the Greek dative case (*tō huiō Dauid*), and that Mark and John as well failed to represent the incident accurately.

Hosea, Book of hoh-zay′uh (הוֹשֵׁעַ H2107, "salvation," or short form of הוֹשַׁעְיָה H2108, "Yahweh has saved" [see HOSHAIAH]; Ὡσηέ G6060). First book of the Minor Prophets. The name in Hebrew is identical with that of HOSHEA, the last king of Israel (2 Ki. 17:1); it is also the original form of the name of JOSHUA (Num. 13:16; Deut. 32:44).

    I. Historical background
    II. Unity and problems of integrity
   III. Authorship
   IV. Date
    V. Place of origin and destination
   VI. Occasion and purpose
  VII. Canonicity
 VIII. Textual considerations
   IX. Content
    X. Theology

I. Historical background. The activity of the prophet Hosea took place in the 8th cent. B.C. (Hos. 1:1), at a time when Israel and, to a lesser extent, Judah were experiencing an upsurge of material prosperity reminiscent of the golden age of the early monarchy. The principal reasons for this economic resurgence were political in nature, and resulted from the decline of Syria (ARAM), under BEN-HADAD III (c. 796–770), as a serious military threat to the northern kingdom. According to the Zakir stela (see *ANET*, 655–56), Ben-Hadad, who had previously brought considerable pressure to bear upon JEHOASH of Israel (798–782/81), formed a military alliance to attack Zakir of HAMATH, a political opportunist from Luʿath, who had seized control of the entire kingdom of Hamath-Luʿath. The stela, which was found in 1907 in Afis, 25 mi. SW of ALEPPO, commemorated the way in which Zakir and his allies defeated the coalition led by Ben-hadad at Ḥatarikka (HADRAK, Zech. 9:1).

This victory marked the effective end of the dominance in Syria of the Aramean dynasty of DAMASCUS, and it was not long after this reverse that Damascus was itself placed under the control of JEROBOAM II (2 Ki. 14:28). The territory of the N kingdom was thus in effect extended to Hamath, whereas to the S and E the limits of Israel and Judah came close to those obtained in the days of DAVID and SOLOMON. During this period, Assyria was also showing signs of becoming a political threat to Syria and Palestine, although its military prowess under TIGLATH-PILESER III (745–727 B.C.) was still a rather remote prospect when Jeroboam II succeeded to sole rule in Israel.

Once the necessity for maintaining a standing army in Israel had been removed, the nation was able to devote itself to more peaceful pursuits. As a result, there occurred a remarkable revival in the areas of trade, commerce, culture, and economic life in Israel, a situation that brought about similar benefits for Judah also. The acquisition of Damascus

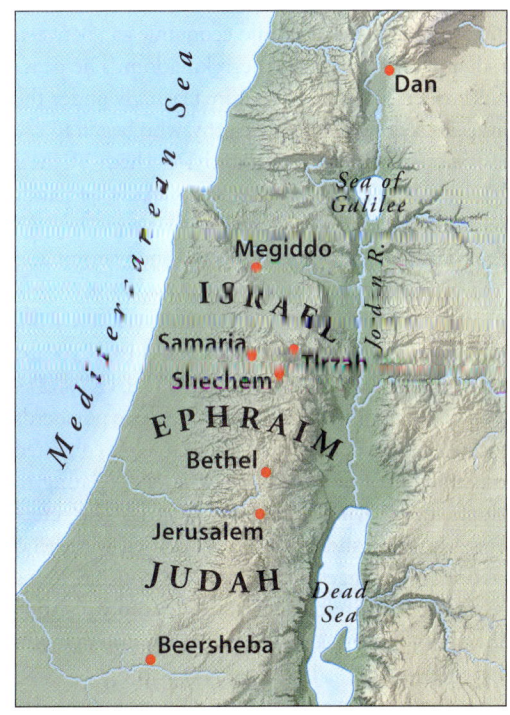

Hosea preached against abuses in Israel.

meant that Israel was once again able to control the ancient caravan trading routes, and this stimulated the growth of a mercantile class that quickly became prosperous and shared with the nobility the wealth of the kingdom.

This situation caused a marked change in the character of the Israelites, for the newly won degree of prosperity was accompanied by a demand for those luxury items that previously were restricted to the ruling classes. Wealthy merchants began to build houses similar to those occupied by the nobility, and they imported various commodities from Egypt and the Orient to decorate them. The skills of Phoenician workmen were in great demand in this connection, particularly where work in ivory was being executed. Numerous ivory inlays, the earliest of which went back to the time of AHAB (874/3–853 B.C.), have been found during excavations at the hill of SAMARIA (modern Sebastiyeh), occurring mostly in the form of small panels in relief. The remains of a bed decorated with ivory inlays (cf. Amos 6:4) have also been recovered, with such items as ivory lions, palmettes, lilies, and winged human figures executed in the typical Phoenician style.

The rise of the wealthy mercantile class accentuated the widening social and economic gap between rich and poor in the northern kingdom. The peasant farmers and artisans fell increasingly under the avaricious designs of the wealthy, who began to use every possible means of depriving them of their land holdings, and in other areas made demands on their skills and productivity that were beyond their abilities. Stark testimony to the wanton and luxurious desires of the upper classes has been furnished by the famous Samaritan OSTRACA from the reign of Jeroboam II, discovered in 1910 just W of the site of the royal palace (cf. *ANET*, 321). When the fragments of these sixty-three potsherds were deciphered, they were found to have consisted originally of administrative documents relating to shipments of wine and oil to Samaria. The references in these sherds to "pure clarified wine" and "refined oil" suggest the demand for luxury items by the social elite of Samaria, and amply justified the prophetic rebukes concerning wanton living in Israel (Amos 3:15; 1 Ki. 22:39; et al.).

Perhaps the most insidious influence of the day came from pagan religious sources. Since the time of Joshua, the life of the Israelites had been tainted by the corruptions of Canaanite worship. Archaeological discoveries in N Syria at Ras Shamra (UGARIT) have supplied much information about the religion of the Canaanites, who had occupied Palestine from an early period (Gen. 12:6). This seductive cult, which was by far the most degenerate morally in the entire ANE, gained a foothold in Israelite religious life prior to the period of the judges, being incorporated by processes of religious syncretism into the Hebrew cultus, and by the time of Amos and Hosea it had become the worship of the masses.

The principal deities venerated by the Canaanites and Phoenicians were the fertility god BAAL (a term meaning "lord," "master," or "husband"), who was the mythical offspring of the supreme deity EL and his consort Asherat, and the goddess ANATH, sometimes known to the Israelites as ASHTORETH or ASHERAH. Baal and Anath functioned as fertility deities in the cult, which was notorious for its emphasis upon fecundity. Both deities were often worshiped under the form of bulls and cows, so that when Jeroboam I set up two golden calves, one at BETHEL and the other at DAN (PLACE) (1 Ki. 12:28), he was actually encouraging the people to indulge in the FERTILITY CULTS of CANAAN (see CALF, GOLDEN). The cultic ceremonies were observed several times each year, marked by ritual PROSTITUTION, acts of violence, drunkenness, and indulgence in pagan forms of worship at the HIGH PLACES or shrines. The widespread prevalence of cultic prostitution is evident from the fact that in the time of JEREMIAH, a century after the mission of Hosea to Israel, prostitution flourished in the temple precincts of Jerusalem (2 Ki. 23:7).

II. Unity and problems of integrity. The unity of the prophecy is closely bound up with the nature of the sources dealing with the marriage of Hosea (see H. H. Rowley in *BJRL* 39 [1956]: 200–233). The first primary source (Hos. 1:1–11) contains a third-person account of the marriage of the prophet, whereas the second (3:1–5) comprises a short selection of material written in the first person along the same lines. The first source describes how Hosea was ordered to marry a harlot, GOMER, who later bore three children, whereas the second source narrates Hosea's declaration that God had commanded him to love a woman cherished by her paramour, and described the way in which he purchased and disciplined this adulteress.

These two sources comprise a single unit of biographical and autobiographical material, linked by a sermon to Israel in the second chapter. This organic unity of narrative is characterized by the fact that the first three chapters use the figure of the MARRIAGE relationship to describe the bond between God and Israel, as well as the behavior of the latter within this situation in terms of the adultery of the wife. Some scholars have held that the account of the marriage in Hos. 3 is a parallel though variant description of the way in which Gomer came to be the wife of Hosea, and that historically it antecedes what was described in the first chapter. If this is so, it becomes hard to account for the absence of the mention of Gomer's children, who played such a prominent part in the narrative. The period of isolation mentioned in 3:3, indicating that the prophet abstained from sexual relations with Gomer, would appear to contradict the facts of 1:3, which suggest that the first child was born within a year of the marriage. Consequently it seems more logical to integrate the contents of the third chapter with the events of the first two, the second of which could only have been written after the birth of the third child.

Some scholars have suggested that the third chapter refers to events that occurred before the marriage, whereas the first furnishes a record of the marriage and its outcome. Such a view endeavors to place Gomer in a better light by supposing that the infidelity from which Hosea ransomed his wife, was not actually misbehavior toward the prophet himself. In the unlikely event that Hos. 3 actually preceded ch. 1, the fact is that Gomer was unfaithful after her marriage to Hosea (2:2), something also implied by an absence of direct claim by Hosea to paternity in connection with the second and third children.

Varying somewhat from the foregoing are the views of other scholars that Gomer had become a temple prostitute by the time that she was reclaimed (Hos. 3:2), or that a distinction ought to be made between Gomer and the harlot of ch. 3, the latter presumably being a cultic prostitute. Such theories fail to satisfy a straightforward reading of the text, which shows clearly that Gomer was a prostitute both before and after her marriage to Hosea. It is hardly possible to maintain that chs. 1 and 3 refer to two different women because of the difficulties surrounding the idea that, after Israel had rejected her espoused deity, he went in search of another bride. If the prophetic analogy regarding Israel is to be truly valid, the wife of one chapter must be identified with the wife of the other.

Some scholars have explained the infidelity of Gomer by supposing that she was a temple prostitute before her marriage. Despite numerous OT references to ritual prostitution, little is known about the women who functioned as hierodules in the Baal fertility cults. There is insufficient evidence for the view that they were ever respected as a class in Israel, or that Gomer had been some kind of sacred or devoted person at a local shrine. By contrast, certain writers have reconstructed events to the point where they could refute the assertion of the text that Gomer was a harlot, and others, following medieval Jewish tradition, held that her bad reputation was due to her being an inhabitant of debauched Israel. Another view thought of "harlot" in Hos. 1:2 as used proleptically, so that Gomer was actually pure, or thought to be so, when Hosea married her. Whether this is true or not, the term "wife of whoredoms" (KJV) implies unchaste behavior before or after marriage, and the description of her as an adulteress in ch. 3 cannot possibly be proleptic. For those who have balked at the idea of a moral deity commanding his servant to marry a harlot, it should be noted that it was equally reprehensible among the Semites for a man to take back an adulterous wife.

Some older scholars, such as P. Volz and K. Marti, denied to Hosea certain sections of the book containing promises of blessing and salvation (Hos. 11:8–11; 14:2–9). Other secondary interpolations that have been entertained include some of the passages mentioning the southern kingdom. Yet A. Bentzen and O. Eissfeldt have shown that in the undoubtedly genuine portions of the book (chs. 1–3) there is mention of salvation following punishment, thereby modifying the effect of the foregoing views. There seems no adequate reason for denying to Hosea any portion of the prophecy, and the mention of Judah seems quite logical since the prophet regarded the northern kingdom as a usurpation (8:4; cf. 3:5). No doubt this standpoint led him to date his utterances in terms of the southern regime. (See further A. D. Tushingham in *JNES* 12 [1953]: 150–59; L. Ruppert in *BZ* 26 [1982]: 208–23.)

III. Authorship. Little is known of Hosea himself. He was the only northern prophet whose writings have survived, but his actual birthplace in Israel remains unknown, as does his occupation in life. It has been suggested that he worked as a baker (Hos. 7:4–8) or a farmer. Certainly his grasp of history and religion and the elegance of his language virtually preclude a peasant origin. Some clue as to his birthplace has been sought in the description of Gomer as the daughter of DIBLAIM (1:3), taking the latter as a reference to a location in GILEAD. This, however, is doubtful for lack of evidence.

Estimates of the length of Hosea's ministry vary. Since Hos. 1:4 was spoken before the fall of JEHU's dynasty, Hosea must have been preaching prior to the death of Jeroboam II in 753 B.C. Thus his marriage and the birth of his first child evidently anteceded this event also. Hosea was an ardent patriot and a warm humanitarian, whose love for his people shone through each of his prophetic oracles. Unlike AMOS, he never once referred to foreign nations except in terms of their relationship to Israel.

IV. Date. The work of Hosea occurred in the last generation of the history of the northern kingdom. According to the superscription in Hos. 1:1, the chronology was related to both the northern and southern kingdoms, in the reigns of JEROBOAM II (c. 782–753 B.C.) and UZZIAH (767–740), JOTHAM (740–732), AHAZ (732–716), and HEZEKIAH (716–687). It has been suggested that the verse in question may, in part or whole, comprise a Judahite editorial revision, since the mention of kings of Judah took precedence over that of Jeroboam II. This need not necessarily be the case, however, for such an arrangement could well imply that Hosea regarded the Davidic line as alone legitimate. If so, the superscription probably originated with the prophet himself.

The reference in Hos. 1:4 indicates a date prior to the death of Jeroboam II for the start of the ministry, as noted above, and if the allusion to Assyria (8:9) is to the tribute paid to TIGLATH-PILESER III by MENAHEM about 739 B.C., this would indicate that the ministry of Hosea was well established by 743. Its continuation beyond the death of Jeroboam II in 753 is assured if the reference in 5:8—6:6 is to the Syro-Ephraimite conflict of 735–734. Furthermore, the mention of relations with Egypt (7:11; 9:6; 12:2) would point to the political activity of HOSHEA, the last king of Israel, who ruled for a decade prior to the fall of Samaria in 722. The ministry of Hosea could thus be placed between 753 and c. 723. Just what happened to Hosea after this time is unknown, but from the Judean content of the superscription it is reasonable to assume that the oracles of this prophet were known in the southern kingdom. Possibly Hosea spent his declining days in Judah, though there is no real evidence for this view.

The development of Hosea's prophetic ministry seems closely related to the process by which his work arrived at its extant form. Accordingly it should be noted that the symbolic names given to the three children of Gomer over a period of some six years parallel the same themes of inescapable doom (Hos. 2:2–13) and the oracles in chs. 4–13. Any estimate of the date and compilatory processes of the prophecy should consider the view that chs. 4–14 may have circulated separately from chs. 1–3 for some time, and also the theory that the message of hope for Israel seems inconsistent with the tenets of Hosea, belonging more properly to the exilic period. Although it is true that the contents of chs. 4–14 concerned the depravity of cultic Baalism and the moral and spiritual failures of Israel, it is hard to see how the basic message of Hosea, with its powerful marital allegory as a foundation, could have been proclaimed in the absence of chs. 1–3.

By the time the contents of Hos. 4–14 were in writing, the material in the first three chapters would form a necessary prerequisite to the prophecy as a whole. Although it is just possible that chs. 4–14 circulated independently for a period of time, that would have taken place only within the lifetime of Hosea himself, since Hebrew tradition does not know of the prophecy as anything other than a unity. With regard to Hosea's hopeful outlook for the nation, it should be noted that a distinct element of hope formed a consistent part of 8th-cent. prophetic teaching, and there is no evidence for any assertion that would deny such aspirations to Hosea. Indeed, it could well be argued that the prophet's own experience of divine mercy, in which love triumphed over judgment, suggested a similar prospect for the nation.

The question of alleged Judahite editorial activity also affects the matter of dating. Whereas it is possible to suppose that Judean scribes modified the text of the prophecy, which undoubtedly contains many corruptions, it is hard to see how this could have been done in the lifetime of Hosea himself, particularly since no "school" was associated with him (so far as is known), nor would it even have been thought necessary to make alterations after 722 B.C., since the apostasy of the northern kingdom (and by contrast the implied fidelity of Judah) was no longer a current issue. Furthermore, only about four references to Judah are at all commendatory, and the rest are critical of the southern kingdom, and thus could hardly have been the work of Judean scribes anxious to glorify their own people at the expense of Israel (cf. Hos. 6:11; 8:14; 12:2). There is nothing in the material relating to Judah that would necessitate an exilic date for the prophecy, much less a final recension of postexilic provenance. The present state of the evidence gives firm support to the traditional view that the prophecy was the work of one individual who ministered to the house of Israel (3:5) in the 8th cent., and in whose lifetime the book was compiled and edited.

V. Place of origin and destination. The oracles clearly originated in the northern kingdom against the background of material prosperity and social and spiritual corruption characteristic of the time of Jeroboam II. Although their primary destination was the territory of the northern tribes, the concern of the prophet was with the nation as a whole. In this respect, the inclusion of Judean kings in the superscription made the scope of the utterances clear. No doubt the written prophecy was well-known in Judah at the time when Hosea died, and may even have been used in subsequent days of political and religious turmoil.

VI. Occasion and purpose. The apostasy of Israel and her enslavement to pagan Canaanite traditions—in open neglect of the provisions of the Sinai covenant—evoked from Hosea a strong plea for repentance and spiritual renewal. The social corruption and moral decay of the northern tribes had made them ripe for destruction, and the purpose of the prophet was to reveal the love of God for the chosen and apostate nation. Taking the appropriate symbol, namely the marriage relationship, he sought to show Israel how she had become a faithless wife by the standards of the covenant, committing spiritual adultery and repudiating her association with her divine spouse. Such behavior, if unaltered by acts of repentance, contrition, and renewal, could only issue in a period of seclusion and punishment for the nation, after which divine mercy would again be manifested. Whereas Amos had denounced the social inequalities of his day and the exploitation of the lower classes, Hosea was primarily concerned with the political, religious, and moral evils of the nation. The political vacillation toward Assyria that took place under Menahem, and the interest in Egypt shown by Hoshea, were a source of complaint on the part of the prophet (Hos. 5:13; 7:11; 12:1), who rebuked Israel for turning everywhere for help except to God.

Hosea's great affection for his people was an epitome of the divine love for Israel, and the marital experiences of the prophet furnished the immediate occasion for his fervent challenging prophecies, which were given force and urgency by the use of symbolic names for Gomer's children. The first of these, Jezreel (Hos. 1:4), implied that God would

These Assyrian iron swords (8th–7th cent. B.C.) are a reminder of Hosea's proclamation that God would judge the idolatry of the Israelites by bringing the Assyrian army against them.

Hosea prophesied that God would "break Israel's bow in the Valley of Jezreel" (Hos. 1:5). (View to ENE toward Mount Moreh.)

punish the dynasty of Jehu for the bloodshed of Jezreel (cf. 2 Ki. 10:12–28). The second, Lo-Ruhamah (Hos. 1:6), meant "unpitied," and signified a withholding of divine compassion from Israel, and the third, Lo-Ammi (1:9), meaning "no people of mine," brought the promise of divine rejection to an assured climax. For an ardent patriot such as Hosea, the situation demanded immediate action if the house of Israel was to be spared the horror of divine punishment by exile. (See H. G. May in *JBL* 55 [1936]: 285–91.)

VII. Canonicity. The book of Hosea stands first in the canonical list of the twelve Minor Prophets, an arrangement that had obtained as early as Ben-Sira (Sir. 49:10), if not earlier. Although a variant order of the first six books occurs in some SEPTUAGINT MSS, Hosea always claimed priority, perhaps because of its length. In *Baba Bathra* 14b, Rabbi Johanan was cited as placing Hosea chronologically before Amos, a position that most scholars would reject, although absolute certainty on the point is lacking. The book itself was named after its attributive author.

VIII. Textual considerations. The text of the prophecy presents the interpreter with great difficulties, since it is probably more corrupt than that of any other OT work. Why this should be the case is not clear, though it may possibly have arisen from the widespread usage of the prophecy in the southern kingdom during the late 8th and early 7th centuries B.C. Many textual problems, however, arise from such accidents of scribal activity as the transposition of consonants, the occasional confusion of similar consonants, and an incorrect division of the letters forming words. Others may have been occasioned by the peculiarities of N Israelite dialect as misunderstood and miscopied by Judean scribes. There are often marked variations in translation when scholars resort to textual emendation in an attempt to restore the Hebrew where the versions have proved inadequate for such purposes.

The SEPTUAGINT is often of great help in recovering the original, even though it was apparently made from a Hebrew text that had close ties with that preserved by the Masoretes; this was also true of the Syriac version. See TEXT AND MANUSCRIPTS (OT). From the differences in the vocalizing of the Hebrew it seems clear that the MSS used by the Greek translators did not contain certain consonants in the MT used as vowel letters (*matres lectionis*), particularly *waw* and *yod*. There appear to be places where the LXX has preserved superior readings (Hos. 2:20; 5:15; 8:10; 10:10), as well as some additional phrases (2:4; 8:13; 13:13). Noteworthy difficulties in the MT are, among others: Hos 4:18; 5:2; 7:16; 8:10; 9:13; 11:7; 12:9. The complexity of the textual problem in the prophecy may be one reason why scholars have differed so widely in their approach to passages such as ch. 11. In general, the style of the prophetic oracles of Hosea is brief and concise, and has marked emotional overtones evident in the sensitive, pleading quality of the utterances.

IX. Content. The prophecy may be summarized as follows:

A. Using his marriage as an illustration, Hosea depicts the relations of Israel with her God (Hos. 1:1—3:5).

B. Denunciation of Israelite pride, immorality, and idolatry (4:1—8:14).

C. The certainty of doom for the northern kingdom (9:1—10:15).

D. A parenthetical utterance relating to God's mercy and love (11:1–11).

E. The rebellion and apostasy of Israel will issue in destruction (11:12—13:16).

F. Future blessings will overtake a penitent nation (14:1–9).

X. Theology. There is little doubt that the Hebrew term *ḥesed* H2876 (Hos. 6:1 et al.) crystallizes the message of Hosea. This comprehensive word is difficult to render adequately by means of a single term, and renderings such as "zeal," "piety," "mercy," and "lovingkindness" hardly do justice to the meaning of the expression. It can be said to embody the idea of true love in the light of some specific relationship, and has special emotional and spiritual content. The distinctive contribution of Hosea to OT theology was his recognition that reciprocity on the part of Israel was an important feature of the relationship between God and his people. Whereas Amos had stressed that the sin of Israel lay in failure to meet God's demand for righteousness, Hosea proclaimed that the real iniquity of the nation commenced with the breaking of a COVENANT or agreement that by nature needed to be upheld by both parties involved.

For Hosea the essence of this covenant is *ḥesed*, which was characteristic of the relationship forged at SINAI between God and Israel. On that solemn occasion the nation had made a voluntary pact with God that involved her surrender, loyalty, and obedience to his will. The result was that Israel became God's son (Hos. 11:1; cf. Exod. 4:22) by adoption and divine grace. It was the primary duty of Hosea to recall the wayward and indifferent Israel to its obligations entered into at Sinai. Although the prophet was aware that divine love and grace had provided the initiative for the covenant, he also realized the importance of emphasizing the free cooperative acceptance of that spiritual relationship by the chosen people. For this reason he stressed that Israel was actually God's bride (Hos. 2:7, 16, 19) and used the marriage metaphor with telling effect to demonstrate the nature of the association between the bride and her divine Lover.

Hosea's own marital experience furnished dramatic illustration of the situation that had overtaken the nation of Israel. The prophet had been ordered by God to marry a harlot (who would later continue in her old ways), to have children by her, and to give them symbolic names typifying divine displeasure with Israel. After this woman had consorted with her paramours, he was told to ransom her and with patient love and tenderness to readmit her to his home, there to await in penitence and grief the time of restoration to full favor. For those who had eyes to see, this was a clear illustration of wanton, apostate Israel in its historic relationship with God, and showed the enduring fidelity of the Almighty.

Because of the way Israel had become tainted by the corruption of idolatry, immorality, and materialism, God was compelled to leave the nation to her own devices until she gave clear proof that she no longer coveted the old idolatrous ways of life. The discipline to be imposed as a means of producing REPENTANCE was actually an indication of divine love and concern, since it would help to awaken in the Israelites an awareness of true spiritual values. The stern, forbidding picture of retribution presented by Amos is absent from Hosea, being replaced by an image of God as a kindly, loving father who is concerned for the welfare of his family, or as a sympathetic farmer who attends continually to the welfare of his livestock (Hos. 11:3–4).

The expression of REPENTANCE (Hos. 6:1–4) has been treated by scholars either as a genuine emotional experience, reflecting the nation's desired forgiveness in the recognition that the people were sinful, or as a shallow declaration on the part of a people who felt that the covenant association automatically guaranteed them an assured future under divine protection without any particular reciprocity on their part. The prophet made it clear that true repentance was a hard-wrought experience involving the mind and will as well as the emotions (cf. 14:2). For him the chief difficulty encountered in the historic relationship between God and Israel was the fact that the nation had no real intellectual awareness of the moral and ethical qualities of its God, and the way in which the Sinai covenant made these binding on the chosen people.

To a large extent, the Israelites had been beguiled by the corrupt ethos of the Phoenician-Canaanite religious tradition, which by nature was entirely remote from the advanced ethical characteristics of the God of Sinai, and which saw no incongruity between religious observances and a morally corrupt way of life. Nonetheless, the fact that the spirituality of the Sinai agreement had been ignored for generations did not mean that it was no longer valid, and Hosea taught that the coming divine judgment upon sin would be the result of the disruption of the ancient covenant relationship, rather than constituting an arbitrary divine act. Out of this experience could still come hope for the nation, for divine grace would intervene to rescue Israel from bondage and open the way for a restoration of the covenant and an outpouring of blessing on the nation.

(Significant commentaries include W. R. Harper, *A Critical and Exegetical Commentary on Amos and Hosea*, ICC [1905]; G. A. F. Knight, *Hosea: Introduction and Commentary* [1960]; J. L. Mays, *Hosea*, OTL [1969]; H. W. Wolff, *Hosea*, Hermeneia [1974]; F. I. Andersen and D. N. Freedman, *Hosea*, AB 24 [1980]; D. K. Stuart, *Hosea-Jonah*, WBC 31 [1987]; D. A. Hubbard, *Hosea: An Introduction and Commentary*, TOTC [1989]; T. McComiskey in *The Minor Prophets: An Exegetical and Expository Commentary*, ed. T. McComiskey [1992–98], 1:1–237; D. A. Garrett, *Hosea, Joel*, NAC 19A [1997]; A. A. Macintosh, *A Critical and Exegetical Commentary on Hosea*, ICC [1997]; E. Ben Zvi, *Hosea*, FOTL 21A [2005].)

(Among many monographs, see H. S. Nyberg, *Studien zum Hoseabuch* [1935]; N. H. Snaith, *Mercy and Sacrifice: A Study of the Book of Hosea* [1953]; G. Östborn, *Yahweh and Baal: Studies in the Book of Hosea* [1956]; R. K. Harrison, *Introduction to the Old Testament* [1969], 859–73; D. Kinet, *Baʿal und Jahweh: Ein Beitrag zur Theologie des Hoseabuches* [1977]; G. I. Emmerson, *Hosea: An Israelite Prophet in Judean Perspective* [1984]; D. R. Daniels, *Hosea and Salvation History: The Early Traditions of Israel in the Prophecy of Hosea* [1990]; E. K. Holt, *Prophesying the Past: The Use of Israel's History in the Book of Hosea* [1995]; G. A. Yee, *Composition and Tradition in the Book of Hosea: A Redaction Critical Investigation* [1987]; J. M. Trotter, *Reading Hosea in Achaemenid Yehud* [2001]; B. E. Kelle, *Hosea 2: Metaphor and Rhetoric in Historical Perspective* [2005]; J. P. Kakkanattu, *God's Enduring Love in the Book of Hosea: A Synchronic and Diachronic Analysis of Hosea 11:1–11* [2006]; and the bibliography compiled by W. E. Mills, *Hosea-Joel* [2002].)   R. K. Harrison

hosen. This archaic English word (meaning "long trousers") is used by the KJV to render the noun *paṭṭîš* H10582 (Dan. 3:21). The meaning of this Aramaic term is uncertain; both the NIV and the NRSV render it "trousers," but rabbinic traditions also suggest "turbans" and "coats."

Hoshaiah hoh-shay′yuh (הוֹשַׁעְיָה H2108, "Yahweh has saved [*or* helped]"; cf. Hosea and Joshua). **(1)** A leader of Judah who took a prominent part in the ceremonial processions at the dedication of the walls of Jerusalem (Neh. 12:32).

(2) Father of Azariah; the latter was one of the army officers opposed to Jeremiah (Jer. 43:2 [LXX 50:2]). Elsewhere (42:1 [LXX 49:1]), the MT has "Jezaniah son of Hoshaiah" (see Jaazaniah), but the LXX reads "Azariah son of Maaseiah," and some scholars emend the MT to read "Azariah son of Hoshaiah" (cf. NRSV). If Jezaniah/Jaazaniah is the same person as Azariah, then his father Hoshaiah was a Maacathite (2 Ki. 25:23; Jer. 40:8).

Hoshama hosh′uh-muh (הוֹשָׁמָע H2106, prob. short form of the unattested name יְהוֹשָׁמָע, "Yahweh has heard"). Son of King Jeconiah (i.e., Jehoiachin), apparently born after the royal family was led away into exile in Babylon (1 Chr. 3:18).

Hoshea hoh-shee′uh (הוֹשֵׁעַ H2107, "salvation," or short form of הוֹשַׁעְיָה H2108, "Yahweh has saved" [see HOSHAIAH]). The name in Hebrew is identical with that of HOSEA the prophet.

(1) Original name of JOSHUA son of Nun before MOSES changed it (Num. 13:8, 16); apparently he was known by both names for a time (Deut. 32:44 MT).

(2) Son of Azaziah; he was an officer of DAVID set over the tribe of EPHRAIM (1 Chr. 27:20).

(3) One of the leaders of the people who set their seal to the covenant of NEHEMIAH (Neh. 10:23).

(4) Son of Elah and last king of Israel (2 Ki. 15:30; 17:1–6; 18:1, 9–10). Hoshea ruled for nine years (732–724 B.C.) during a time of social and moral upheaval when a total of six kings came to the throne of Israel in a period of only fourteen years (746–732). Hoshea became king by forming a conspiracy against and murdering his predecessor PEKAH son of Remaliah (2 Ki. 15:30), apparently due to the utter failure of Pekah's policy of resistance to ASSYRIA. This policy had ended in complete defeat.

When Hoshea came to the throne in 732, TIGLATH-PILESER had annexed virtually the whole kingdom of Israel to the Assyrian empire. In 733 he attacked the northern part of the Jordan Valley, making GILEAD and GALILEE into Assyrian provinces (2 Ki. 15:29; cf. Isa. 9:1). These actions meant the removal of all Israelite holdings in TRANSJORDAN and the extension of Assyrian power to S of MEGIDDO (administrative capital of GALILEE). In his own annals, Tiglath-Pileser records that he also added the coastal plain of SHARON as a third province with a capital at DOR, probably extending all the way to the PHILISTINE border near JOPPA (see Y. Aharoni, *The Land of the Bible: A Historical Geography*, rev. ed. [1979], 371–76, esp. map 31). This campaign left only the capital city of SAMARIA and the surrounding hill country of Ephraim as Israelite domain. It is likely that Samaria too would have been taken had not Hoshea murdered Pekah, apparently with Assyrian confirmation (at least Tiglath-Pileser could say in one of his annals that he "placed Hosea as king over them [i.e., the Israelites]"; see *ANET*, 284).

Over this truncated kingdom Hoshea reigned as the vassal king of Assyria, under heavy tribute (cf. 2 Ki. 17:3). Nothing is known of the details of his reign except the laconic evaluation of the editor of 2 Kings: "He did evil in the eyes of the LORD, but not like the kings of Israel who preceded him" (17:2). Tiglath-Pileser III died in 727 B.C. and SHALMANESER V succeeded him. This change probably led Hoshea, apparently seeking such an opportunity, to withhold tribute and so declare independence. At the same time he sought help from Egypt, sending messengers to So king of Egypt (17:4). The prophet HOSEA denounced the Israelites for their divided loyalty and machinations: "Ephraim is like a dove, / easily deceived and senseless— / now calling to Egypt, / now turning to Assyria" (Hos 7:11); "Ephraim feeds on the wind, / he pursues the east wind all day / and multiplies lies and violence. / He makes a treaty with Assyria / and sends olive oil to Egypt" (12:1). Shalmaneser marched against Israel in 724. Hoshea capitulated and paid tribute (2 Ki. 17:3), but he was too badly compromised to clear himself. Shalmaneser, doubting his loyalty, imprisoned him (2 Ki. 17:4).

Shalmaneser then surrounded Samaria, and after a siege of three years, the city fell. Whether it was captured before Shalmaneser died, or in the first few weeks of his successor, SARGON II, is still a matter of some doubt. Although the vast majority of scholars have accepted the latter view, some investigations have cast doubt on the credibility of the scribes of the Khorsabad inscriptions that mention Sargon's capture of Samaria (see E. R. Thiele, *The Mysterious Numbers of the Hebrew Kings*, 3rd ed. [1983], 163–68; H. Tadmor in *Journal of Cuneiform Studies* 12 [1958]: 33–39). This latter approach fits best with the natural understanding of 2 Ki. 17:6, where the "king of Assyria" is most simply taken as the "Shalmaneser" of v. 3 (so also 18:9–10). After Hoshea's imprisonment by Shalmaneser, nothing more is heard of him. It would appear that Samaria endured the three years of her siege without royal leadership. F. W. BUSH

hospitality. In the ANE, the generous treatment of guests played a distinctly important role in tribal and domestic life. Existence in the desert made hospitality a necessity, and among the nomads it became a highly esteemed virtue. By it the FOREIGNER or weary traveler found rest, food and shelter, and asylum. (Even today a nomad can remain under his host's roof for three days in safety and subsequently receive protection "until the salt he has eaten has left his stomach"; see R. de Vaux, *Ancient Israel* [1961], 10.) The custom was supported by the thought that the host himself might some day be a stranger, and by the possibility that the visitor was divinely sent.

Cella frieze depicting a Greek banquet scene, with participants sitting on cushions. Both in the OT and NT, hospitality was demonstrated by providing a meal for one's guests.

I. In OT Times. While no specific term meaning "hospitality" occurs in the Hebrew OT, many heart-warming stories reflect this practice. A definitive account of the custom is given in the story of ABRAHAM's entertainment of three strangers who turned out to be angels (see ANGEL). He hastened from his tent door to welcome them, washed their feet, provided a sumptuous meal—of veal, milk, curds, and fresh baked bread—in the shade of a tree, and stood attentively by while they ate (Gen. 18:1–8). That night in the city of SODOM, LOT entertained two of the same angelic guests (19:1–11). Of similar interest is the idyllic story of the courtship of REBEKAH. When Abraham's servant and attendants arrived at the home of BETHUEL in search of a wife for ISAAC, Rebekah and her brother LABAN cordially received them into their father's house. There they were entertained lavishly while they, in turn, adorned Rebekah with costly jewelry and raiment (24:11–61).

Nomadic hospitality was preserved by the settled Israelites in Canaan. DAVID made SAUL's grandson a permanent guest at his royal table (2 Sam. 9:7). Solomon's daily dinners were astounding, not to mention his banquets for royal guests like the QUEEN OF SHEBA (1 Ki. 4:22–23; 10:4–5). NEHEMIAH, governor of Jerusalem, fed daily at his table 150 Jews plus numerous aliens (Neh. 5:17–18). Excesses in hospitable asylum are seen in the instances of Lot (Gen. 19:1–8) and of the old man at GIBEAH (Jdg. 19:16–24).

II. In NT Times. Even though the NT makes reference to the availability of inns, as at BETHLEHEM and JERICHO (Lk. 2:7; 10:34), one looked to the private home for hospitality. Jesus practiced hospitality in feeding the multitudes (Mk. 6:30–44; 8:1–10) and his disciples (Lk. 22:7–13; Jn. 21:9–14). Similarly, he availed himself of hospitality from two prominent PHARISEES (Lk. 7:36–50; 14:1–14), the BETHANY family (Lk. 10:38–42; Matt. 26:6–13; cf. Mk. 14:3–9; Jn. 12:1–8), ZACCHAEUS (Lk. 19:5–10), and the EMMAUS hosts (Lk. 24:29–32).

The apostles availed themselves of Jewish and Gentile hospitality wherever they spread the gospel over the Roman empire. PETER was entertained by SIMON at JOPPA and by CORNELIUS at CAESAREA (Acts 9:43; 10:5, 23–48). PAUL and his companions received hospitality in numerous private homes. Among their hosts were LYDIA and the jailer at PHILIPPI (16:14–15, 25–34), AQUILA AND PRISCILLA as well as TITIUS JUSTUS at CORINTH (18:1–3, 7), PHILIP in Caesarea and MNASON at Jerusalem (21:8, 16), and PUBLIUS on MALTA (28:7). Christians were to "practice hospitality" (*philoxenia G5810*, Rom. 12:13; cf. the cognate adjective in 1 Pet. 4:9). Bishops and widows were to be hospitable (1 Tim. 3:2; 5:10; Tit. 1:8). Finally, like Abraham and Lot, "Do not neglect to show hospitality to strangers, for by doing that some have entertained angels without knowing it" (Heb. 13:2 NRSV). (See E. W. K. Mould, *Bible History* [1966], 103–7, 170–73; J. Koenig, *New Testament Hospitality: Partnership with Strangers as Promise and Mission* [1985].) G. B. FUNDERBURK

hostage. This English term is used to render the Hebrew phrase, *běnê haṭṭaʿărûbôt* (lit., "sons of the pledges," i.e., captives kept as surety against further political upheavals), which occurs only in the record of the victory of JEHOASH of Israel over AMAZIAH of Judah, when hostages were carried off to SAMARIA (2 Ki. 14:14=2 Chr. 25:24; the LXX mistranslates *tous huious tōn symmixeōn*, "the sons of intermixture"). Similar records from CUNEIFORM sources indicate that such hostages were treated as members of a special social class and often integrated into the conquering society. Although they were in jeopardy, they were not slaves or servants.

W. WHITE, JR.

hostility. See ENEMY.

hostility, dividing wall of. See WALL OF PARTITION.

host of heaven. This phrase is used by the KJV and other versions as a literal rendering of Hebrew *ṣĕbāʾ haššāmayim*, which occurs eighteen times in the OT (Deut. 4:19 et al., in addition to five places where "their host" is used with probable reference to the heavens). The NIV uses a variety of translations, such as "heavenly array" (Deut. 4:19) and "starry hosts" (2 Ki. 17:16). In some instances (e.g., 1 Ki. 22:19), the SEPTUAGINT renders the phrase with *hē stratia tou ouranou*, and this language is reflected in the Lukan writings (Lk. 2:13; Acts 7:42).

I. Basic meaning. Although the most frequent meaning of *ṣābāʾ* H7372 may have to do with warfare or an army, it does not seem that this sense is the most fundamental. At least some passages do not bear that meaning easily (Num. 4:3). It becomes a question then whether these passages should be explained as metaphorical extensions of the basic meaning "army" or taken as themselves illustrative of a broader basic meaning such as "group," of which the examples meaning "army" are a specialization. In this light, is the host of heaven to be thought of as an army of heaven, or a group of beings inhabiting heaven? Contrary to some of the standard lexical tools (e.g., BDB, 838), it would appear that comparative Semitic data does not support the meaning "army" as the basic force of the word. The *Chicago Assyrian Dictionary* gives the meaning of *ṣābu* as "group of people, contingent of workers, troop of soldiers."

II. Linguistic aspects of the phrase. In the phrase under consideration, the word for "host" is always used in the singular-collective form (contrast the pl. use in the common phrase *yhwh ṣĕbāʾôt*, LORD OF HOSTS). It is generally in the form "*all* the host of heaven." One must be careful to distinguish between "host of heaven," "host[s] of Yahweh" (both sing. and pl.), and "Yahweh of hosts" (always pl.). There is no necessary connection between these phrases (for the last one, which is not the main concern of this article, see M. Tsevat in *HUCA* 36 [1965]: 49–58, who interprets it to mean "Yahweh [is] armies," i.e., "God is protection"). In addition to using the term *stratia*, the SEPTUAGINT renders the word *ṣābāʾ* in many ways, including *kosmos*, "world" (Deut. 4:19), *dynamis*, "power" (2 Ki. 17:16), and *astron*, "star" (Isa. 34:4).

III. The host of heaven as heavenly bodies. In most of the passages, the phrase probably has reference to heavenly bodies, either in general or in reference to stars in particular. These are mentioned in several different connections. For example, the host of heaven is not to receive worship (Deut. 4:19; 17:3). On the other hand, various passages show that Israel did worship the host of heaven. It is mentioned in the summary of the sins of the northern kingdom (2 Ki. 17:16). In the southern kingdom, MANASSEH advanced this practice, probably under the syncretism at the height of Assyrian power (2 Ki. 21:3, 5; 2 Chr. 33:3, 5). Jeremiah alludes to the practice (Jer. 8:2) and states that such worship was performed on the roof tops (19:13; cf. Zeph. 1:5), an incidental proof that the host of heaven was indeed thought of as heavenly bodies. Josiah attempted to stamp out the idolatrous worship of his day, among which was the burning of incense to all the host of heaven (2 Ki. 23:4–5).

Alongside these direct references stand passages that refer to the same activity, but where the phrase "host of heaven" is not used. Among Josiah's reforms was the taking away from the temple the horses "dedicated to the sun" (2 Ki. 23:11). Men worshiping the SUN was an abomination to Ezekiel (Ezek. 8:16). It is possible that the references to the QUEEN OF HEAVEN (Jer. 7:18; 44:17–19, 25) have in mind the worship of some heavenly body, perhaps the sun (cf. M. Dahood in *Revista*

Biblica [1960]). An alternative would be to identify this deity with Ishtar, who was called Queen of heaven in Assyria and was identified with Venus. Another probable reference to Israelite worship of the host of heaven is found in Amos 5:26, where the words translated "tabernacle" and "Chiun" in KJV are probably names of the Assyrian astral deity Sakkuth or Kaiwan (i.e., Saturn; the Masoretes evidently have changed the vowels of these objectionable names to *sikkût* and *kiyyûn*, after the pattern of the word *šiqqûṣ H9199*, "abomination").

Very striking is the relationship expressed in the statement that the host of heaven was allotted (*ḥālaq H2745*) by God to all the peoples of the earth (Deut. 4:19) except Israel. That this must mean allotment not only for the regulation of time and life but also for worship is shown by Deut. 29:26, where Israel is accused of worshiping gods that were not "allotted" to them (see KD, *Pentateuch*, 3:312, and cf. Rom. 1:18–25).

Sometimes the host of heaven is seen as the object of God's creative activity, rendering obedience to the divine will. It may be that the "host" of Gen. 2:1 (KJV) is a broader conception: the host of heaven and earth, including the whole of creation. The host of heaven was made by divine breath (Ps. 33:6), named and controlled by God (Isa. 40:26; 45:12). The faithful working of the heavenly bodies is probably what is meant by "the host of heaven worships you" (Neh. 9:6 NRSV; NIV, "the multitudes of heaven"), and their seemingly endless number is used as an illustration of the number of the descendants of David (Jer. 33:22). Probably Jdg. 5:20 is to be included here: "from the heavens the stars fought … against Sisera"—a figure for God using nature to defeat his enemies.

At least once the phrase is used in the context of receiving God's judgment: "All the host of heaven shall rot away" (Isa. 34:4 NRSV) must be referring to heavenly bodies, since it is parallel to "the skies roll up like a scroll." It is uncertain whether this is also the meaning in Isa. 24:21, inasmuch as there "host of heaven" is parallel to "kings of the earth," although v. 23 mentions the involvement of the moon and sun.

IV. Worship of heavenly bodies in the ANE.

(1) *The sun.* In ancient times sun worship was widespread. In Egypt the sun was worshiped in its various aspects under different names, the chief of which were Re and Aton. In Assyro-Babylonia the sun appeared as a male deity called Shamash (Sumerian Utu). The same word used in Ugarit as Shepesh was thought of as female. In Canaan itself, old place names such as Beth Shemesh ("house of the sun") probably reveal the early practice of sun worship. At Ugarit this practice may have taken place on roof tops as is mentioned in the Bible. The fact that Shemesh was called a chariot-rider in Assyrian texts might explain the placement of horses and chariots at the entrance of the Jerusalem temple as idolatrous sun worship (2 Ki. 23:11).

(2) *The moon.* In Ur and Haran, both places of patriarchal contact, the moon was worshiped under the name Sin as a male deity. Earlier Sumerian names were Nanna and Ningal. This last name appears in the Ugaritic story of the marriage between Yerah, the Ugaritic moon god, and Nikkal, here a female deity. The probable purpose of this story was the desire for fertility. Again in Canaan a place name, Jericho (from *yārēaḥ H3734*, "moon"), testifies to the early moon worship under a Canaanite name. Ornaments in the shape of the crescent moon have been found in Palestine.

(3) *Venus.* In Mesopotamia the goddess Ishtar is connected with Venus, but it is thought that originally Ishtar was a male deity. This would explain why in the western lands (Ugarit) Venus was thought of as male. In this case, however, it is not one deity but two, one for the morning phase of Venus (Shahar, "Dawn"), the other for the evening phase (Shalem, "Dusk"). An important Ugaritic text (C. H. Gordon, *Ugaritic Literature* [1949], no. 52) describes the origin of these deities. In another text (no. 49) mention is made of Athtar, which is probably the same as Ishtar, only in Ugarit considered male. The fact that the feminine form Ashtoreth occurs frequently in Hebrew shows how much the Israelites must have been involved in worship of the host of heaven.

(4) *Saturn.* The names for Saturn have been given above in connection with Amos 5:26. (See further S. N. Kramer, ed., *Mythologies of the Ancient World* [1961].)

V. The host of heaven as angels.

Although "host of heaven" most frequently means heavenly

bodies, there are a few passages where it clearly means something else. According to 1 Ki. 22:19 (= 2 Chr. 18:18), the prophet MICAIAH saw the host of heaven standing beside God's throne conversing with the Lord, and in v. 21 they are called spirits. This conception of the host of heaven as angelic beings is also seen in Lk. 2:13, where the phrase must refer to angels. A transitional passage between this meaning and that of heavenly bodies is Job 38:7, where "morning stars" is parallel to "sons of God" (NIV, "angels"). Note that the phrase "host[s] of Yahweh" sometimes is used of angels (Pss. 103:21; 148:2; once it is used of Israel, Exod. 7:4, while the being who appeared to JOSHUA could be commander of God's heavenly host or of a human army, Josh. 5:14–15). The thought of angels as God's host is also expressed by another Hebrew word, *maḥăneh* H4722, "[military] camp, army" (Gen. 32:2 [MT, v. 3]).

VI. Daniel. One specific passage, Dan. 8:10–13, must receive special consideration. Although vv. 12–13 are quite difficult, four explanations of the phrase "host of heaven" can be given for vv. 10–11. One takes the host of heaven as the stars and explains the little horn's attack against the stars as figurative of his impiety (Isa. 14:13). A second understands the phrase as the deities represented by the heavenly bodies and revered by peoples of antiquity; these deities the horn attempted to desecrate, and it even carried the attempt to God himself (Dan. 8:11). A third interpretation views the host of heaven as the people of God who are opposed by the horn. Finally, the phrase may mean angelic beings. Perhaps it is unwise to make a judgment in such a potentially symbolic context, but the second alternative seems most plausible. (See further *ABD*, 3:301–4; *NIDOTTE*, 3:733–35.)

D. K. HUTTAR

hosts, Lord of. See LORD OF HOSTS.

Hotham hoh´thuhm (חוֹתָם H2598, "signet, seal"). (1) Son of Heber and great-grandson of ASHER (1 Chr. 7:32; apparently called HELEM in v. 35).

(2) A man from AROER who was the father of Shama and Jeiel, two of DAVID's mighty warriors (1 Chr. 11:44; KJV, "Hothan," following LXX).

F. W. BUSH

Hothan hoh´thuhn. See HOTHAM #2.

Hothir hoh´thuhr (הוֹתִיר H2110, possibly "abundance" or "[God/Yahweh] has left over"). Son of HEMAN, the king's seer (1 Chr. 25:4). The fourteen sons of Heman, along with the sons of ASAPH and JEDUTHUN, were set apart "for the ministry of prophesying, accompanied by harps, lyres and cymbals" (v. 1). The assignment of duty was done by lot, and the twenty-first lot fell to Hothir, his sons, and his relatives (25:28).

hough. An archaic English verb used by the KJV to render Hebrew *ʿāqar* H6828, which in the piel form means "to cripple, hamstring" (Josh. 11:6 et al.)

hour. The OT does not use a specific Hebrew term for "hour" (in the sense of a unit of time marking intervals during the day), for apparently the Israelites had no system of equal hours for dividing the day. In the earlier periods of OT history, the only divisions of the natural day were morning, noonday, and evening (Gen. 1:5; 43:16). The night appears under the threefold division of first, middle, and morning watches (Exod. 14:24; Jdg. 7:19; Lam. 2:19). The Babylonians must have been among the first to adopt the division of twelve equal parts for the day, for HERODOTUS (*Hist.* 2.109) testifies that the Greeks derived this custom from them. The sun DIAL of AHAZ (2 Ki. 20:11, Isa. 38:8) was undoubtedly introduced from Babylonia.

Although the Greek term *pēchys* G4388 ("forearm, cubit") should perhaps be rendered "hour" in one saying of Jesus (Matt. 6:27 = Lk. 12:25), the standard term is *hōra* G6052, which the NT uses in different ways. (1) It may signify a brief period of time of no definite length (Matt. 26:40). (2) It is used in connection with the broad divisions of time, that is, third, sixth, and ninth hour (corresponding roughly to our 9 a.m., noon, and 3 p.m.); the third and the ninth were the regular times of worship in the temple (Acts 2:15; 3:1), the times for the morning and evening sacrifice. (3) The Greek term may also refer to a definite period of time, that is, one twelfth of the day: although only one NT passage expressly mentions the twelve hours of the day (Jn. 11:9), there are references to "two hours" (Acts

19:34), the "seventh hour" (Jn. 4:52), the "tenth hour" (Jn. 1:39). (4) An "hour" may be simply the point of time at which an event occurs (Matt. 8:13; 9:22 [NIV, "moment"]; 15:28). (5) The term is used of the appointed time of God's intervention in history (Matt. 24:36, 44, 50; 25:13; Mk. 13:32; Lk. 12:12, 39, 46; 22:53; Rev. 3:3, 10; 9:15; 14:7, 15; 18:10); see ESCHATOLOGY. (6) Another theological use is with reference to God's appointed time for specific events in the life of Christ. Jesus again and again made clear that the Father had a fixed time for every event in his life. This is evident especially in the Gospel of John (Jn. 2:4; 12:23, 27; 13:1; 17:1), but the other Gospels also make it clear (Matt. 26:45; Mk. 14:35; Lk. 22:53); and the disciples of Jesus were aware of it, at least in retrospect (Jn. 7:30; 8:20). There was nothing accidental in the life of Jesus; everything he did was done according to the will of his Father. (For a discussion of the various Gk. terms for time, see *NIDNTT*, 3:826–50.) See ETERNITY. S. BARABAS

house. Words for "house" (mainly Heb. *bayit* H1074, Gk. *oikia* G3864 and *oikos* G3875) are very frequent throughout the Bible, denoting a dwelling place and including references to the rudest huts, the palace, and the temple of God. Earliest houses of the ANE found to date occur at Haçilar in Anatolia (ASIA MINOR) from the 7th millennium B.C. These already were rectangular in plan, indicating the early solution to roof framing, whereas in the area near the Persian Gulf and in Egypt, where reeds were plentiful, the natural shape was a round plan, having woven reed walls with the tops of tall reeds bent over dome-like to form the roof. A later variation was the row of center posts formed of bundled reeds with woven reed walls on either side, with the tops bent over to form the roof and fastened to a pole set atop the center posts (G. Contenau, *Everyday Life in Babylon and Assyria* [1954], 26). Only with the advent of the rectangular plan and the use of tree poles as roof beams could expansion of living space occur, for reeds grow only to limited height and have little inherent strength.

In EGYPT stone was plentiful, but the houses of the lower classes in all ages, after mud-brick was developed c. 3500 B.C., were always constructed of BRICK. In MESOPOTAMIA, the situation was reversed: there was no native stone and thus stone had to be imported, whereas mud was everywhere available and mud-brick was developed earlier here than in Egypt (cf. Gen. 11:3). In PALESTINE stone was available, but prior to the Greek period it was not used in constructing public buildings except by SOLOMON, OMRI, and AHAB. However, buildings were erected either of rubble stone set in mud (plastered or unplastered) or of mud-brick on stone base courses and plastered over with mud, and in some cases whitewashed (see ARCHITECTURE). In Mesopotamia, asphalt (see BITUMEN) was the mortar, whereas in Egypt it was fine CLAY, with the brick laid when three-quarters dry to form a tight bond between brick. JERICHO, however, provided the earliest usage of mud brick in the plano-convex shape; although these came later in Mesopotamia, it is not known whether Jericho builders influenced the Mesopotamians.

After the 4th millennium B.C., houses with rooms enclosing an inner court, frequently two stories high, were developed in Mesopotamia, providing for a self-contained unit to carry on family and craft occupations within the shelter of the home. A porter would have had charge of the gate from the street. Family quarters were on the second floor, and animals were housed on the first floor, where were also rooms for storage and the craft rooms. Second-floor rooms were served by a wood balcony with access gained by a wooden stair from the court. Two-story houses are found already in the 5th millennium B.C. at Haçilar, well before those of Ur III. Poorer houses usually consisted of one room, with people and animals sharing the space.

Roof structures were formed of tree poles or palm tree trunks, over which smaller branches, brush, reeds, or palm fronds were placed to form a base for a packed clay layer rolled into place with stone rollers, some of which have been found in house ruins. In some areas marly stone was pulverized and spread over the clay, and this method provided a much more impervious surface. The roof, accessible by outside stairs, became a favorite sitting area in the evening to enjoy cooling breezes (1 Sam. 9:25–26; 2 Sam. 11:2; Acts 10:9). Representations of awnings demonstrate attempts to protect the roof terrace during the heat of the day. It was also a place where flax was easily spread out to dry

(Josh. 2:6), and probably other field products were stored there. In cases where roofs were occupied, a parapet (KJV, "battlement") was to be supplied to prevent persons from falling off (Deut. 22:8). In Assyrian reliefs, some houses are pictured as having a cupola that served as a shelter (summer parlor, Jdg. 3:20). In NT times, roofs were gabled as well as flat; for the gabled type of the better houses, roof tiles formed the covering. In the case of the house where the paralytic was healed (Lk. 5:18–26), the type of roof, whether flat or pitched, is uncertain.

Floors for ground levels were of beaten clay and in some cases given a thin lime plaster coating. Second floors were framed and formed as for roofs with the addition in some cases of the lime plaster topping. Cooling effect was obtained in Mesopotamia by facing the houses toward the NE and providing for drafts of cooler air to work through the rooms. In Egypt, houses were oriented northward to cut off the southern heat. Frequently they had a device on the roof to deflect the breezes into the house.

Doors were generally made of wood panels from imported wood in Egypt and Mesopotamia, and the forests of Palestine adequately provided for local needs. In other cases, cloth or hide hangings were used. Enough houses have been excavated from the time of David lacking sockets at sill and lintel to indicate that the need of doors was not pressing, and revealing general social and political safety. It would appear that David had organized the military forces to act as a police force (J. P. Free, *Archaeology and Bible History* [1950], 62).

Windows in walls fronting inner courts were of larger size, while any occurring in street walls were most likely small, with a protective lattice to prevent ingress (2 Ki. 1:2). In the house of Rahab, a window looked out over the city wall, a convenient place to observe an attacker as well as to escape, hence the query addressed to her about the spies (cf. Josh. 2:15). At Damascus, the window was high enough above ground to dispense with the lattice, allowing Paul to be lowered to the ground (2 Cor. 11:33).

Sanitary systems were built sporadically. In many cases in Egypt, these systems discharged into the sand outside the houses. In preplanned towns and fortresses in Nubia, drains ran down the streets and emptied outside the gates (A. Badawy, *Architecture in Ancient Egypt and the Near East* [1966]). A house in Ugarit of c. 1400 B.C. had cesspools (ibid., 156). In poorer quarters, the gutter in the street was more frequent than the cesspool. In Mesopotamia, in other cases, an aperture in the floor received

Partial reconstruction of an Israelite four-room house.

wastes that were conducted off through clay pipes to cesspools (ibid., 160). Water was transported to the houses, and evidence indicates that, at least for the better homes, storage jars set in courtyards provided immediate storage facility.

Furniture varied with the economic status of the householder. Cooking was done over an open hearth, the smoke finding the best way out. A stone mill of base and quern was a certain item in any kitchen to provide flour. Ovens occurred in outer courts, the poor using a community oven in a public court. In Egypt, the living room was furnished in some cases with a bench on one wall. Better class homes contained (in different periods) chairs, stools, tables, and beds. In poorer homes, mats on the floor served for sleeping. Chests of various sizes, some highly decorated, provided closed storage for some household items. Pottery of various shapes and sizes served as dishes. Metal bowls and basins have been recovered from the better houses. Babylonians had short-legged tray-like tables as well as the usual types. Houses of Haçilar from the 6th millennium B.C. had plastered wall cupboards, in addition to fire boxes, which were safer than the open hearths.

If storage room was provided in the house, large storage jars with lids were sunk in the floor for storing oil, grain, and wine. Other rooms stored rough goods, that is, field produce. Where occasion demanded, rooms provided for crafts (e.g., weaving), as shown in tomb models from Egypt.

Typical interior of a 1st-cent. Judean home.

Lighting for the house was a clay dish with a wick, set either in a pinched rim or in its own spout, the latter being the LAMP of Matt. 25:1. Fuel was olive OIL, but in Mesopotamia, frequently a crude oil provided better light. Sesame oil was sometimes used. Methods to shield or cover the candle were suggested (Matt. 5:15). Torches were secured by the use of pitch on a stick. Heating for houses varied according to the climate. Egypt required little, furnished by simple means. In Mesopotamia, braziers were used for both cooking and heating in winter. In Anatolia, palace remains indicate a few cases of movable hearths (Badawy, *Architecture*, 133). Where the kitchen hearth was used, it furnished heat for one-room houses (See further A. Badawy, "Architectural Provision Against Heat in the Orient," *JNES* 17 [1958]: 123.)

Decoration varied from mere whitewashed walls to painted plaster in the better houses, often a painted wainscot, dark in color with a top stripe. Ceilings in some cases were finished with plaster or painted lath. In wealthy homes in Egypt, gold and electrum were used on a stucco base as a lining on low relief. In Mesopotamia, elaborately painted plaster was frequent. Door frames at times were painted red, and in other cases stone slabs as wainscots provided the only decorative elements.

(See further H. E. Winlock, *Models of Daily Life in Ancient Egypt* [1955]; National Geographic Society, *Everyday Life in Ancient Times* [1964]; J. S. Holladay, "House, Israelite," *ABD*, 3:308–18; P. M. M. Daviau, *Houses and Their Furnishings in Bronze Age Palestine* [1993]; P. J. King and L. E. Stager, *Life in Biblical Israel* [2001], 21–35.) H. G. STIGERS

household. See FAMILY.

household code. This term (also German *Haustafel*, "house table," pl. *Haustafeln*) refers to a set of behavioral standards for members of an extended family. The term is applied to lists of various kinds found in Greco-Roman literature and to several NT passages, especially Eph. 5:21—6:9 and Col. 3:18—4:1. See ETHICS OF PAUL III.C.

householder. This English term (as well as "goodman of the house") is used in the KJV to render Greek *oikodespotēs* G3867, "master [*or* owner] of the house." The word, which appears only in the Synoptic Gospels, is applied to differentiate between employer and employee in Jesus' parables (Matt. 13:27 et al.). It is used also to describe Christ himself in his overlordship of the KINGDOM OF GOD (Lk. 13:25). The rendering "householder" is used consistently by the RSV (in NRSV only at Matt. 13:27), but more recent translations prefer "master of the household," "landowner," etc.

W. WHITE, JR.

household gods. See IDOLATRY; TERAPHIM.

House of the Forest of Lebanon. See FOREST.

Hozai hoh'zi (חוֹזָי H2559 [not in NIV]). According to the MT (followed by NJPS), the apparent name of the author of a chronicle or history in which the prayer of MANASSEH, his sinfulness, and certain of his impious acts were recorded (2 Chr. 33:19 [KJV mg., "Hosai"]; cf. 32:32, which says that the events in the reign of Hezekiah were "written in the vision of the prophet Isaiah"). Most versions, however, follow the reading of one Hebrew MS, *ḥōzim* (pl. of *ḥōzeh* H2602), and of the SEPTUAGINT (*tōn horontōn*), and translate "the seers." Some scholars have suggested reading *ḥōzāyw*, "his [Manasseh's] seers." F. W. BUSH

Hubbah huh´buh (חֻבָּה H2405 [*Ketib* יַחְבָּה; cf. BHS], derivation uncertain). Son of Shomer (KJV, "Shamer"; NRSV, "Shemer") and descendant of ASHER (1 Chr. 7:34; KJV, "Jehubbah," following the *Ketib* consonants but the *Qere* vocalization).

Hukkok huh´kok (חֻקֹּק [some edd., חֻקֹק] H2982). A town on the W border of the tribal territory of NAPHTALI (Josh. 19:34; NJPS, "Hukok"). It has often been identified with Yaquq, some 3 mi. NW of GENNESARET. Others, objecting that Yaquq is much too far to the E, propose Khirbet el-Jemeijmeh, 15 mi. W of Gennesaret and 12 mi. ESE of Acco. See also HUKOK.

Hukok hyoo´kok (חוּקֹק H2577). A town within the tribal territory of ASHER assigned to the Levites descended from GERSHON (1 Chr. 6:75 [Heb. 6:60]). Some think it may be the same as HUKKOK, but the parallel passage (Josh. 21:31) leads most scholars to identify it with HELKATH.

Hul huhl (חוּל H2566, meaning uncertain). Son of ARAM and grandson of SHEM, included in the Table of NATIONS (Gen. 10:23). In the parallel list (1 Chr. 1:17), the phrase "the sons of Aram" is missing from the MT, making it appear that Hul was a son of Shem and thus a brother of Aram. It is possible that this passage intends to list the descendants of Shem without distinguishing generations (cf. NRSV), but many scholars believe that the phrase in question dropped out by scribal mistake at an early stage in the textual transmission of the book (cf. NIV).

Huldah huhl´duh (חֻלְדָּה H2701, "mole, weasel"). A prophetess who lived during the reign of King JOSIAH (2 Ki. 22:14-20; 2 Chr. 34:22-28). Identified as the wife of SHALLUM, who was the "keeper of the wardrobe," Huldah lived in the *mišneh* H5467, that is, the SECOND DISTRICT, of JERUSALEM (cf. Zeph. 1:10 and esp. J. Simons, *Jerusalem in the Old Testament* [1952], 290-93). HILKIAH the priest, SHAPHAN the scribe, and some others, having been commanded by Josiah to seek an oracle from the Lord concerning the lawbook found in the TEMPLE, came to her to fulfill the request. She then prophesied judgment and disaster upon Jerusalem and its people, but not for Josiah, since his reading of the lawbook had led to repentance. For him she relayed God's message, "I will gather you to your fathers, and you will be buried [*lit.*, be gathered to your grave] in peace. Your eyes will not see all the disaster I am going to bring on this place" (1 Ki. 22:20). Since Josiah actually died in battle (23:29-30), the words "you will be buried in peace" may mean that he would be gathered to his rest before the catastrophe befell the city. It is interesting to note that she was consulted on the matter even though both JEREMIAH and ZEPHANIAH were prophesying at the time. In this regard she had a precursor in DEBORAH (Jdg. 4) and a worthy follower in the prophetess ANNA (Lk. 2:36). F. W. BUSH

human nature. The psalmist, in asking "what is man?" (Ps. 8:5), voiced a question as old as mankind. One facet of human uniqueness is man's ability to transcend himself and to make himself his own object. The problem may be raised within many contexts, these being broadly divisible into two types, the theistic and the nontheistic.

Human nature is a complex phenomenon, so that definitions of it tend to lack comprehensiveness. While some appear more adequate than others, all tend to be partial. There is need for balance between discussion of the essential nature of human beings on the one hand, and their existential relationships on the other. Any discussion of human nature must take account of many thought-currents, including those flowing in the recent past. It is proposed here to approach the subject historically, beginning with views explicated in the OT and NT. Other views will be noted, particularly as they affect the course of the history of the doctrine since NT times. The interaction of biblical and classical views forms a proper part of this discussion and affords a basis for an assessment of more recent and contemporary modes of interpretation of the subject.

It is of the nature of Christian theology to articulate a credible view of human nature, which determines both a person's general orientation and one's total religious commitment. While anthropology does not ultimately condition theology, it is questionable whether any adequate view of redemption is possible until there has been made a reasoned and credible understanding of its subject, human beings.

    I. In the OT
   II. In the NT
  III. The classical period
  IV. The patristic period
   V. Medieval and Renaissance periods
  VI. The Reformation
 VII. The modern period

I. In the OT. The Genesis account of CREATION presents human origination as involving two stages, apparently occurring in close sequence. A body was formed "from the dust of the ground," and was then permeated with "breath of life," so that the resultant man, ADAM, was "a living being" (Gen. 2:7). While the OT does not labor to articulate a detailed anthropology, it implies that the human BODY was tenanted by a vital principle that made it alive and responsive to the outside world. The first man was "diversified" by the creation of a female counterpart, EVE; and from this point the human being was bisexual, both with respect to personality and in the matter of reproduction.

With respect to physical heritage, the OT sees the human race as having sprung from a common origin and as being the progeny of a single primal pair. The origins of the diverse races are shrouded in mystery, while the proliferation of human languages is described in one brief account, the incident of the Tower of BABEL (Gen. 11:1–9). Language considerations are seen as accounting, in part at least, for geographical dispersal.

There is indication in Genesis that profound changes took place, at certain stages, in the human biological structure. It is suggested that at the FALL the human reproductive cycle was accelerated and, as well, that the process of childbirth became painful and even dangerous. It is also indicated that the human lifespan was markedly, and rather suddenly, shortened soon after the flood (see FLOOD, GENESIS). This abbreviation came, by one apparent transitional stage, from about 900 years, to nearly its present length. During the transitional stage, following the diversification of language, longevity shrank from about 500 years to 200 years, after which the normal age-span lowered to about a century, and then to the level of "threescore years and ten" (Ps. 90:10 KJV). The factors entering into this development are not given, but one is left with the impression that it resulted from direct providential action.

The account of human origins as given in the book of Genesis is serious, orderly, and straightforward in its appeal to human REASON. Like the rest of the created universe, human beings are shown to have originated in a free act of God's will. Their appearance culminates an ascending series of divine acts; and in their creation, the originative activity of God came to rest. They are portrayed as being linked, in the physical side of their being, with organic nature, while at the same time transcending nature in their spiritual endowment. With respect to this latter quality, they are portrayed as being made in the IMAGE OF GOD. The *imago dei* will be described elsewhere in this work; for the present it must be said only that man's organic frame received the "breath of life" and a "living being" (lit., "living soul") upon which the print of likeness to God is stamped.

In man and woman, as originally formed, there existed a dignity, and as well a sovereignty over nature, that was analogous to God's own dignity and sovereignty. Answerable to this dignity and sovereignty, God placed the first human pair over nature that they might discipline, order, and enjoy it. Implied in this action is their original sinlessness, their possession of a primeval righteousness, and a consequent unclouded relation to their Maker. Human beings are personal, self-conscious, rational, social, and above all, accountable in a moral sense to God.

Evil was no part of their original donation, but the book of Genesis indicates that a primal disobedience, seemingly occurring early in their career, introduced a new and damaging element into the human predicament, which affected both their existential being and their relation to their Maker. The details of the fall are few, but basic are the following: the first pair was placed under one clear and simple prohibition; they were subject to the solicitation of a tempter; they heeded the voice of the serpent; they disobeyed; and certain consequences followed.

The impact of the fall upon human nature is sketched in bold strokes: the first pair came to possess new awarenesses (e.g., of being unclad and thus exposed), their relation to their Creator was disturbed, and interpersonal relationships (i.e., between Adam and his wife) were corrupted. The resultant changes within human nature are rather illustrated than spelled out in the OT. Between the human pair, now fallen, and God there arose alienation and tension. Aware of their guilty behavior, they sought to conceal themselves from the divine presence. God, in accordance with his original word, sent the first pair forth from their original environment and into a hostile nature.

Within man there appeared almost immediately character disturbances. Adam reproached his wife, in an attempted transfer of responsibility. Within the first growing primary group (the family), the malignancy with which mankind was henceforth to be afflicted began to appear. Murder invaded the sanctuary of the first family, revealing the emerging irresponsibility of CAIN (Gen. 4:9) and his consequent and growing alienation from self and kindred.

Outward from this familial pattern of tragedy there radiated social and cultural disorientation: "The LORD saw how great man's wickedness on the earth had become, and that every inclination of the thoughts of his heart was only evil all the time" (Gen. 6:5). Thus is portrayed the ruin of the divine image that was sustained by man. His moral resemblance to God became largely destroyed, his God consciousness became clouded, and even his natural virtues became a mere shadow of those with which he was originally endowed.

There remained the human personality (albeit in maimed and distorted form), the self-consciousness, and *some* measure of capacity to respond to the claims of the moral and spiritual realm. His propensities toward society and toward societal living are shown to be capable of gross distortion, as are also his capabilities for the erection of culture. A false sense of autonomy, and a narrowly based pride of achievement, corroded and corrupted the human enterprise (Gen. 4:23–24).

Moral aberration, leading to spiritual and moral degradation, multiplied; sins of both flesh and spirit became the major expressions of fallen human nature. Parallel, however, was a line of spiritually receptive persons who gave attention to God's mandates and who preserved in obedience the element of faith, this latter often leading to the maintenance of family expiatory rites. The behavior of such seems to be related to the continuing striving of the Spirit of the Lord with men (Gen. 6:3).

The major bearers of early cultural history are shown by the OT to have been arrogant and systematically evil, until the Lord determined to preserve providentially the family of NOAH and make a new beginning with the race. The postdiluvian history reveals human nature as expressing itself continuingly in terms of intoxication, pride, and greed. The patriarchal period, the period of the captivity in Egypt, the epoch of the exodus and the settlement in Canaan, and the period of the judges, all reveal essentially the same pattern of human behavior. The OT dramatizes this feature in the historical book of Judges, in which it is said that selfish human wants and desires ruled society. Like a refrain, it is said, "the Israelites once again did evil in the sight of the LORD" (Jdg. 4:1; 6:1; 10:6; 13:1; et al.). This pattern issued from the fact that "everyone did as he saw fit" (17:6; 21:25). Writing centuries later, Jeremiah summed up the OT estimate of the natural man thus: "The heart is deceitful above all things and beyond cure. / Who can understand it?" (Jer. 17:9).

From the foregoing it is clear that the OT views human nature in terms of the following: (1) Man was created morally undefiled, a special creation at God's hand. (2) He was placed under a clearly understood order of probation, with a specific prohibition at its heart. (3) The initial disobedience brought swift consequences of a radically negative sort, both upon the first pair and upon their progeny. (4) The original "image of God" became disfigured and distorted, while at the same time God left mankind capable of some measure of response and of hope. (5) Evil became a constant and malignant element in the whole of human experience. (6) Evil centered in an imbalance in the relation between God and man, so that man asserted a false claim of autonomy, and chronically pitted himself against the deliverances of conscience, of seer and prophet, and of the entire pattern of divine revelation. (7) Evil brought social and interpersonal strife, disorganizing human relationships and corrupting all human institutions. (8) Overt evildoing objectified a deep-seated disturbance within human beings, a disorientation that was hereditary in nature and malignant in its intricate pattern of manifestations.

It needs to be said, in summary, that the OT understanding of human nature finds a certain focal expression in the doctrine of the "evil impulse." This idea is rooted in the statements of Gen. 6:5 and 8:21 that the "inclination" (*yēṣer* H3671) of the human heart was found to be "only evil all the time" and "evil from childhood." Even at an early period in Israel's history, the teaching concerning the ingrained evil in human nature had taken root and was beginning to take shape.

This usage of the term *yēṣer* occurs elsewhere (Deut. 31:21; 1 Chr. 28:9; 29:18). The OT suggests with growing clarity that evil entrenches itself in the mind and that there is a resultant pervading sinfulness which is universal among mankind. Such an inclination to evil is inherent in human beings as a part of the nature they inherit (Ps. 51:5). This view was continued in the rabbinical literature, which draws a contrast between the *yēṣer hārāʿ* (the evil impulse) and *yēṣer haṭṭôb* (the good impulse).

II. In the NT. The estimate of human beings in the NT, and more especially in the teachings of our Lord, rests basically upon the Hebraic understanding of human nature and the OT interpretation of human racial history. The four Gospels do not undertake to articulate a "doctrine of man" as such; they do portray the activities of our Lord as he met men and women in concrete and often crucial situations; and out of these situations emerged rather definite teachings with respect to human nature.

People were regarded as sinners, and the lot of the human race was that which resulted from its sinfulness. Jesus addressed his disciples with the words, "If you then, though you are evil, know how to give good gifts ..." (Lk. 11:13), thus suggesting man's universal involvement in the sinful predicament. He recognized that the defilement of SIN reached the springs of human action and operated outward from a hidden sanctuary (Matt. 15:11; Mk. 7:15). He further stated that "out of the heart come evil thoughts, murder, adultery, sexual immorality, theft, false testimony, slander. These are what make a man 'unclean'" (Matt. 15:19–20a; cf. Mk. 7:21–23).

These and similar passages indicate the emphasis of our Lord upon the solidarity of the human race in the predicament of sinfulness. While he made reference to what may be called the "sins of the flesh," his emphasis was more frequently upon the "sins of the spirit," such as covetousness, pride, and self-sufficiency. Such forms of evil were most frequently seen as barriers to entry into the kingdom, as witness for example the dealing with the rich ruler (Lk. 18:18–24). Underlying these analytical statements of Jesus is the statement by John to the effect that Jesus needed no one to instruct him concerning human nature, "for he knew what was in man" (Jn. 2:25). This suggests a realistic view of human sinfulness upon the part of our Lord.

Jesus saw all people as needing "healing" (i.e., salvation), and referred in irony to those who felt no such need. Even those who outwardly "appear to people as righteous" were held to be inwardly "full of hypocrisy and wickedness" (Matt. 23:28). Mankind was likewise indicted for "hardness of heart," this being held to render necessary Yahweh's earlier permissions of such evils as divorce—and even here the suggestion is that this was not part of man's original order of conduct (i.e., before the fall) but the result of the sin-order (Matt. 19:8).

While our Lord gave full recognition to the evils and ills that are part of the experience of the race, he never regarded these as final, for he always viewed human beings from the standpoint of God's redemptive power and will toward humanity. While he saw that recompense, in the form of suffering here and hereafter, came as a result of sin, he saw the sin-order as modified by the order of GRACE. With this in mind, he sought out sinners without minimizing the gravity of the evil that was part of fallen man's endowment. He recognized that human beings, in the deepest layers of their being, harbored a pernicious mood of revolt against their Creator.

The four Gospels thus portray humanity— seen through the eyes of Jesus Christ—as having suffered an original catastrophe that cast its long and melancholy shadow across human experience and human history. The nature of man thus bore the disastrous effects of the fall; but as a foil to this, it was made clear that humanity possesses a residual capacity for sonship with God through grace.

Similar estimates are discoverable in the apostolic preaching, particularly as recorded in the book of Acts. PETER's sermon on the day of PENTECOST makes incidental mention of the wickedness that led to the CRUCIFIXION (Acts 2:23), while the conclusion of that address shows the hearers as convinced of their sins and openly penitent (2:37–38). Human ignorance is seen as a cause of some human wrongdoing (3:17), an ignorance that is now no longer excusable (3:19; 17:30).

The book of Acts presents, in contrast to the usual declarations of man's evil nature, the newness of life that believers come to enjoy. Thus "the multitude of them that believed" were no longer hostile to one another (Acts 4:32 KJV) but manifested a new spirit of amity and of generosity. Hypocrisy was shown to be both immediately uncovered and summarily punished in the early Christian community, particularly in the account of ANANIAS and SAPPHIRA (5:1–10).

Believers, now renewed in their inner natures, showed an uncommon boldness and a rare disregard for the opposition of the ungodly, extending to the most unusual capacity for the bearing of physical pain. The contrast between "man by nature" and "man by grace" recurs throughout the apostolic KERYGMA, both in the book of Acts and in the writings of PAUL, whose personal experience is adduced as a primary illustration (Acts 9:1–2, cf. 9:27–29; 22:3–6, 19–20; 26:9–11, cf. vv. 16–19).

The book of Acts reiterates the negative judgment pronounced upon the natural human heart for its covetousness (Acts 5:2–4), for its wrongheaded desire for power (8:18–23), for its narrow prejudice (10:10–16; cf. 10:34), its willingness to exploit others (16:16–20), its tenacious adherence to evil doing (24:25–27), and its obduracy against truth (28:25–27). Thus the early apostolic preaching took for granted the OT and rabbinical view of human nature as subject to the "evil inclination," a negative propensity that is universal in its distribution within mankind.

The Pauline understanding of human nature finds its most systematic presentation in the epistle to the ROMANS, although it is by no means absent from his other writings. It needs to be said that his major concern was not with the Christian estimation of humanity as such, but with the message of Christian redemption which was designed to meet each person's deepest needs. Salvation meant deliverance from the deep and entrenched forms of evil that oppress everyone.

Men and women are seen by nature to be "carnal, sold under sin" (Rom. 7:14), like slaves being bought by a cruel master and driven to a twisted course of action. This situation is declared to be universal (3:10–18), with every member of the race being involved in a situation in which the flesh was subject to sin. This does not mean that Paul subscribed to the Greco-Eastern view of the inherent evil of the human BODY, but that people are held to be under the sovereign sway of sin and death, with sin regarded as universal and death regarded as its inevitable penalty.

Paul's use of the term *sarx* G4922 is treated elsewhere (see FLESH), but it needs to be said here that Paul regards "flesh" as the weak and corrupted instrument of sin as a controlling principle. It is of great significance at this point to note that when Paul lists the "works of the flesh" (Gal. 5:19–21; NIV, "the acts of the sinful nature"), only five of the seventeen forms of evil are direct expression of the physical appetites. Sin is entrenched in the flesh, and from this as a base of operations, wages war against the higher impulses of human beings.

Parallel to the prevailing temper of the book of Acts, in which (as noted previously) there is a stress upon that which human beings may become by grace, Paul emphasizes that human nature can become the dwelling place of the HOLY SPIRIT of God (Rom. 8:11), whose role in human life is that of deliverer "from this body of death" (Rom. 7:24) and of imparter of the "fruit of the Spirit" (Gal. 5:22–23).

It needs to be noted that the NT, especially in the Epistles, recognizes not only that the human being is a composite creature (i.e., composed of body and soul and/or spirit), but also that the whole person is to be the subject of redemption. Paul makes it clear that in the RESURRECTION we will have a body that, while being the lineal descendant of and successor to our "natural" body, will nevertheless not consist of "flesh and blood" (1 Cor. 15:42–50).

The Johannine understanding of human nature does not differ markedly from that of the Pauline epistles. John proclaims the universal sinfulness of mankind (1 Jn. 1.8) and describes the natural man as being "in darkness" (2:9) and as being among "the children of the devil" (3:10). Reference is made to the primal murder (3:12) and the contrast between the works of the redeemed and the ways of the unregenerate. The Johannine picture of the generality of worldly people is not an optimistic one: "the whole world is under the control of the evil one" (5:19) and its citizens are subject to deception on a grand scale (2 Jn. 7).

The understanding of human nature in the Revelation of John follows the general lines laid down in the rest of the NT. The catalogues of the misdeeds of the unregenerate resemble those of the Gospels and the Pauline epistles, while the possibilities for the redemption of human nature in Christ form part of the NT's general message of hope for man in his fallen predicament.

The NT thus takes for granted, and builds upon, the major themes of Hebrew religion, and in the light of revealed redemption, brings the portrait of human nature to a new fullness. There is given a realistic view of the negative results of sin in human nature, by which the original "image of God" in the human creature is distorted and disfigured. At the same time, man bears the marks of a high ancestry. While evil has touched adversely every aspect and quality of his nature, there remain elements upon which the Spirit of grace may lay hold.

It follows that, though fallen, men and women are at the same time capable of bearing the restored image through grace. It is in redemption that their unfulfilled capacities begin to be realized, although they must live in relative incompleteness in this life. The NT suggests, further, that their spiritual part is imperishable and survives DEATH. While little is specifically stated concerning the INTERMEDIATE STATE, the NT makes clear that the disembodied existence is a temporary one, and that all await the resurrection of the body, some to everlasting righteousness, and others to final spiritual loss.

Seen within the context of grace, the NT view of man is neither fully pessimistic nor largely optimistic, but rather melioristic. Man is not what he may become; he is dependent and unfulfilled, and no genuine realization of his potentialities is possible apart from the restoration of his fractured relationship with his Creator through Jesus Christ. Human beings normally exist in society, in human community. Within this context, they are loved by an everlasting Heart that seeks to draw them into a higher community, through the transformation of their nature by the agency of the divine Spirit, for whose indwelling they have a basic capacity that survived the fall.

In the INCARNATION, the eternal LOGOS appeared in human form to show what redeemed man might become. In One who was "very God and very man," human beings behold the Image to which they are to be conformed through being transformed by him who shared our common life in the days of his flesh. In him we can glimpse human nature as it ought to be, and as it will be when he brings many sons to glory.

III. The classical period. The views of human nature that prevailed in the Greco-Roman world impinged upon Christian thinking at several points: first, during the intertestamental period, as Jewish thinkers confronted HELLENISM, especially at ALEXANDRIA; second, during the early Christian centuries; and third, in the later medieval and early Renaissance eras. Christian thinkers have from the time of the apostles been under necessity of understanding the major elements of the classical anthropology, particularly as this was articulated by Plato, Aristotle, the Stoics, and the Epicureans.

The anthropology of the Greco-Roman world was itself complex, being composed of several strands and embodying conceptions that reached back to the times of Homer and Hesiod, for the thinkers of Greece's Golden Age were indebted to those who preceded them. Classical thought in general regarded man as being distinguished from mere nature by his possession of a rational capacity. Even in Stoicism, in which the universe was invested with an immanent REASON, there was still the lingering contention that reason must somehow transcend the seemingly nonrational parts of nature. Thus when Aristotle defines man as "a rational animal," he speaks for the classical tradition as a whole. This marked a radical departure from, for example, the Ionian physicists or the atomists. Thus, classical anthropology possessed a deeply-rooted DUALISM (i.e., of reason versus matter) which distinguished between "man as body" and "man as mind."

Concerning moral endowment, the classical world had no doctrine of "original sin" as such; Plato suggested that human beings may possess a "fount of reason that is as yet uncurbed" (*Laws* 792.) but it is still assumed that they, as rational beings, would ultimately perceive and seek "the Good" in both individual and social behavior. This was, of course, a corollary of the dictum of Socrates to the effect that "Virtue is knowledge, and can be taught."

The further implication of classical thought for the understanding of human nature is that the rational creature that man is—imperfect yet capable of knowing and achieving the Good—must rely upon his own endowment(s) for the solution of his problems. There was little or no place within this system for a belief in any concept of moral and spiritual assistance from any Power outside and above man, for his relation to the gods was primarily one of etiquette.

In classical thought, and more especially in Plato, the ultimate aim and directing impulse in human beings is the imitation of the ideal. This finds its best expression in the operation of the human essence, which is their reason, and which Plato thought to be divine and immortal. It seems that Socrates may have been the mentor of his more famous pupil at this point; both shared a profound belief that the person with the enlightened reason would in the final analysis pursue "the Good." It was, of course, the more practical Aristotle who asked, at a point crucial to the discussion, "But what of the passions?"

It needs to be said that classical anthropology, from Socrates onward, recognized that the SOUL or spiritual part of human beings was subject to a multitude of inward strains, since there existed a multiplicity of factors within the soul. To bring these into harmonious pattern, it was regarded as essential that these factors be brought into an ordered hierarchy or household, with each element functioning in its proper place. Like the well-ordered state, in which there is a proper division of labor according to the several abilities of the citizens, the healthy soul is the one in which each capacity is directed toward its proper end, so that none works in interference with any other.

The chief competitors for moral supremacy, in this view, are reason and desire. The former speaks for the "good in man," the latter contests "the Good" in the name of supposed lesser goods. Desire is clamorous, and it has faculties of memory by which former situations can be recalled and be made a competitor for higher goods.

With respect to human freedom, classical anthropology regarded it to inhere in man's status as a rational being—a being who can act in accordance with "the Good" as it is freely apprehended. Human beings can thus be enslaved only by the irrational. The free person thus achieves freedom through the apprehension of the rational good.

Evil in people rests basically in ignorance, upon a lack of apprehension of the goals of their reason. This deficiency, in turn, is usually the product of the shortcomings of the social environment. Evil is not regarded in terms of the violation of any

Bronze statue of a Hellenistic Greek thinker (c. 300 B.C.), positioned in the reflective posture of a philosopher. Aristotle taught that reason was the highest faculty of mortals.

divinely constituted mandate, but of the irrational shortcomings or comings-short of the normally rational person. Concerning the ultimate origin of human evil, classical thought has no clearly articulated view. To Plato, it seems that the human "fall" consisted of a wrong choice upon the part of the soul in its antenatal state, by which it is incarcerated, through human generation, in a BODY, in which it, in turn, becomes involved in complications of the most grave sort. In the earthly career, each person is composite and becomes an arena for combat, the contestants being chiefly three: reason, the irrational elements of the being, and the goading drives of the body.

Aristotle's views had much in common with that of Socrates and Plato. He felt, with earlier classical thinkers, that reason was man's highest faculty. He disagreed especially with Plato, who held the view that reason was diffused in the "lower" faculties. He protested also the rigid compartmentalization of human beings into soul-and-body, feeling that these two elements were more closely interrelated. Aristotle made more of the power of both will and passions, and thus differentiated the moral qualities. His view of freedom was more analytical than that of his predecessors in that he distinguished more sharply between voluntary and nonvoluntary acts, and in that he gave a diminished place to the reflective reason, in favor of a more organic view of human beings.

Concerning the final end of man, classical thought was ambiguous at the point of personal IMMORTALITY. Earlier thinkers, especially Socrates and Plato, had a relatively clear understanding at the point of the survival of the soul after the dissolution of the body, as expressed in Plato's Myth of Er in book 10 of the *Republic*. Aristotle was less clear in his beliefs at this point, while STOIC thought, understanding Reason as a spark of the all-pervading divine fire, held more or less clearly to the imperishability of human reason. Epicurus and his followers ignored or denied the doctrine of immortality, as a corollary of their materialism (see EPICUREAN). Nowhere in classical anthropology does one find the human body to be the subject of immortality, nor is there any clear teaching at the point of qualitative differences between the destination of the good and the evil persons respectively, save possibly as such differences inhered in notions inherited from the preclassical past.

The anthropology of the Greco-Roman period oscillated between acceptance of happiness as the highest goal for man on the one hand, and the concept of discipline on the other. This dialectic centered largely in the differences between the Epicureans and the Stoics. Epicurus himself believed that happiness or pleasure was the proper goal of human striving, but sought to distinguish between grades of pleasure, as producing varying degrees of happiness. His followers failed to perpetuate this discriminating attitude, and tended to move in the direction of straightforward hedonism in which sensory pleasure became the highest good.

Stoicism, on the other hand, pursued happiness in terms of discipline. The good life was the life lived in terms of reason; in consequence, the Stoics distrusted sensory pleasure as tending to obscure reason and thus to undercut the deeper forms of happiness, notably tranquillity of soul. The CYNICS adopted the coarser features of Stoicism, making ASCETICISM and nature-harshness the highest goal.

In summary, the classical anthropology contained variety at a number of points. Chief among these were the following: (1) the structure of man—whether dualistic as in the Platonic tradition, or monistic as in either the pantheistic-Stoic or the materialistic-Epicurean form; (2) the precise role of reason; (3) the nature of freedom; (4) and the role of immortality. It did, however, possess unifying elements, especially (1) a general regard for man as a creature of reason; (2) a belief in the general goodness of human life; (3) a belief in man's capabilities for "salvation"; (4) the conviction that there was something "divine" in man; and (5) the belief that man's well-being was somehow bound up with inner harmony. It was this latter holistic tendency, which related the classical ethic to the classical ideal of beauty, that pervaded the esthetics of the classical and Hellenistic periods.

IV. The patristic period. It has been noted that the Christian view of human nature as developed in the NT is basically a continuation of that found in the Hebrew religion. Modifications within it were of a secondary character, consisting largely of elaborations; but with the period of the church fathers, more influences from the classical and Hellenistic eras were felt within the Christian thought stream, and certain changes in the understanding of man, particularly of his psychology, began to be discernible.

The analytic trend of classical anthropology found expression within the systematic writings of Irenaeus, Tertullian, and especially Origen. Irenaeus distinguished, for example, between the "higher" and "lower" elements in the soul, while Tertullian expressed belief in the essential corporeality of the soul. This latter feature, probably derived from Stoic dogma, found expression in the teaching of the Gregorys, while Origen propounded a view of the preexistence of the soul that has strong affinities with the view of Plato and was later condemned.

Origen expressed a negative value judgment upon the human body reflective of the Platonic dualism. His view of the "image of God" is fairly typical of the ante-Nicene period; it inhered in the endowment for the ultimate perfect realization of the "divine likeness" and thus has affinities with the Aristotelian ideal of man.

With respect to the *imago dei*, JUSTIN MARTYR makes it to inhere in good part in man's rational endowment, while Tertullian sees it in terms of man's imperishability, and the Alexandrian writers locate it in both reason and immortality. This represents an attempt to be analytic at the point of teachings that Hebrew thought tended to regard concretely and synthetically.

With respect to the doctrine of human sinfulness, patristic writers tended to polarize around two patterns: the eastern, which regarded Adam's fall as the first in a long line of sinful acts, leading to human frailty and ultimate mortality, and the western, which regarded Adam's fall as a corrupting influence that left man not only mortal, but also guilty and impotent with respect to good.

The post-Nicene fathers developed, in the main, the two branches of this dichotomy. Roughly representative of the former view is that of the British monk Pelagius, who held that man in his present state possesses the capability of going either toward righteousness or toward evil. God's grace meant, in this view, little more than a kind of superadded assistance to human capability. AUGUSTINE, on the other hand, formulated the view that is generally associated with his name, in which human beings were regarded as being, since Adam, incapable of choosing righteousness, being rather wholly corrupt.

With respect to human freedom, Pelagius maintained man's ability, in his present state, to elect either alternative in the conflict between good and evil. Augustine, on the other hand, held that man's present freedom consisted only in the ability to express his corrupted nature. In the former view, one may either commit evil or abstain from it; in the latter, only commission is possible.

The church of the patristic period struggled with the radically dualistic modes of thought with which its environment confronted it, notably the systems of the Gnostics (see GNOSTICISM) and the MANICHEANS. The fathers resisted both of these, probably chiefly because of the fact that the pairs of opposites tended to be rooted in nature rather than spirit.

It may be said that in Augustine the anthropology of the Western church found a synthesis that was dominant for several centuries of Christian history. Augustine looked deeply into human nature, and gave a formula for the understanding of the ills he found there. He set safeguards around the will of man, particularly at the point of the indeterminism that had been overstressed by some of the fathers. He emphasized the universality of sin, the racial nature of corruption, and the profundity of human need for divine grace. He saw that no element of human nature escaped the negative effects of the fall, and thus made a permanent place in Christian anthropology for the need for inward grace.

V. Medieval and Renaissance periods. The church of the medieval period was, in a large measure, concerned with practical matters such as the evangelization of the Germanic peoples, the relating of herself to the secular power, and the fusion of Latin and Teutonic cultures under her banner. There were, however, creative thinkers in the area of anthropology, insofar as this was requisite to the larger academic task of bringing the whole of knowledge into a synthetic unity.

Augustine patterned much of early medieval thought; the writings of Gregory the Great indicate a heavy dependence upon the Bishop of Hippo, although with modifications. These were largely in the direction of the substitution of weakness for inability, and (in some measure) the substitution of outer for inner grace. More place began to be made for human cooperation with grace, this element being a derivative of the thought of Pelagius. Abelard, with his emphasis upon freedom and upon the distinction between motive and act, seemed to be likewise akin to Pelagius, while Anselm was, on the surface at least, nearer to Augustine. The latter diverged from Augustine's view chiefly in his insistence that original sin was negative and privative, rather than aggressive and positive.

Thomas Aquinas marked a milestone in the medieval understanding of human nature. With him, there came a larger ascription of freedom to human beings, possibly as a corollary to the doctrines of penitence and of merit. Thomas understood the "image of God" to inhere in man's natural inclination toward the good, and in the original gift of grace that began to be bestowed at creation. Such was the emphasis upon the quantity of ability native to fallen man that Aquinas's position is frequently regarded to be Pelagian. While the practical drift of Scholasticism was in the direction of the glorification of the ascetic life, there was less emphasis upon concupiscence as the major expression of original sin than seems to have been placed by Augustine in his system. When this element did express itself, it was regarded by Aquinas to be the consequence of the absence of original righteousness. Man appears in Thomism thus to be innately evil, but with a capacity for some initiative toward God and against sin. He is likewise capable of receiving the operation of grace; and it was but a short step from this to the assertion of the capacity of cooperation, a belief that was consonant with the medieval conception of merit.

The Pelagianizing tendencies, seen to have been present in Abelard, and to a lesser extent in Anselm and Bonaventura, expressed themselves more forcibly in John Duns Scotus. The latter, with his emphasis upon the will, regarded human nature as being sinful only insofar as the will allows people to overstep the bounds set by a harmonious constitution, and good insofar as the will works with the offered grace of God. The crucial issue seems to be whether grace is a gift of God or whether it is acquired by meritorious conduct. The Council of Trent failed to resolve the differences between the Thomistic view on the one hand, and the Nominalistic views of Abelard and Duns Scotus on the other. It was proclaimed at Trent that original sin is removable only by Christ's grace as applied by baptism, and that this removal is total. It goes without saying that this last requires a radical readjustment of the evaluation placed upon the so-called "sins of the flesh."

The Renaissance represented, in part at least, a return to the classics, first for their literary value, but shortly also for their contents. It is not surprising that Renaissance anthropology expressed many features which appeared in the Greco-Roman era. Science, which was one of the major outgrowths of the Renaissance, early came to stress the operation of unvarying law throughout the realm of nature. Its spirit was nominalistic, and its thinkers were more hospitable to nature-oriented views of man than to the views which found expression in Scholastic realism. Throughout the Renaissance, the thought of Aristotle inspired the intellectual life of many of the theological schools of Europe. Perhaps the best exponent of the Renaissance doctrine of man was Giacomo Zabarella (1532–1589), who held that the soul was a function of the body, and that reason was the principle of natural life in the body. While man was finite, yet he was immortal in the sense that intellect does not perish.

Giovanni Pico, count of Mirandola (1463–1494), stressed the dignity of human beings, asserting that their true distinctiveness lay not in their origin as God's creation, but in their ability to share in the properties of all other beings as a result of their capacity for freedom. Pietro Pomponazzi of Mantua (1462–1525) developed a doctrine of immortality that restated Aristotle's view of the soul's immateriality and its consequent immortality. It follows that the Renaissance viewed man in terms of classical antiquity, giving a restatement, in the light of the advance of knowledge of the time, of that which was thought in antiquity. The mood of the period was humanistic, stressing the dignity and the competence of human beings.

VI. The Reformation. The Reformation begun by Luther retained much of Catholicism's formulations, but with specific emphases upon aspects of earlier views. Less attention was given to man's origin than to his present salvation and future destiny. As a result of original sin, men and women were regarded to be under condemnation, being weak and unable to find their own way of deliverance from present guilt and future judgment. They were held to be profoundly and directly dependent upon God. Their future hope was by means of the act of faith, and they were regarded to be delivered thus from the uncertainties and weaknesses of human action.

John Calvin continued Luther's stress upon "the will bound" and upon the purely divine origin of redemption. The malignancy of sin in human life was taken for granted, so that the Augustinian emphasis upon absolute original sin and the unconditional natural corruption of human powers was retained, and in some cases accentuated. The immortality of the soul was accepted as a matter of course. In general, also, classical views were implicitly rejected, particularly insofar as they stressed natural human dignity and human adequacy in the face of the human predicament of evil.

The Reformation in German-speaking Switzerland under the guidance of Ulrich Zwingli followed in general Lutheran lines. Zwingli's classical orientation did lead him to express some views concerning human nature divergent from those of the great Saxon. Zwingli recognized the common human inheritance of a corrupted nature, regarding this as analogous to the state of slavery, into which one may be born without any personal culpability. He is one with Luther in rejecting the Pelagianizing tendencies of the medieval scholastics.

The emphasis upon human incompetence in the face of man's sinful predicament that began with Luther and was continued in Calvin, with some further refinements, provoked a reaction both within Protestantism and in the Roman Catholic tradition. Within the latter came the Jansenist response (in the direction of Augustinianism), while within Protestantism came the Remonstrance (in the direction of Pelagianism) to which is attached the name of Jacobus Arminius.

The Remonstrance brought to the fore the question of human competence, so that the first of its Five Articles asserts that the divine purpose is to save those who believe on Jesus Christ "with the help of" grace. This emphasis led to the reply formulated by the Synod of Dort (1619), which reemphasized the major positions of the Reformed tradition in its strict limitation of the contribution of sinners in their response to the

Portrait of Martin Luther in a book containing seventy of his sermons. Through his preaching and writing, Luther taught that human incompetence is a product of the sinful nature found in all men and women.

call of grace. More specifically, Dort affirmed particular election, its unconditional quality, and the inalienability of Christ's grace, doctrines that also found expression in the *Westminster Confession of Faith* (1646).

It may be properly said that this stage marks the close of specific formulation of Reformation teaching concerning the nature of man. Significant also is the fact that this development occurred almost wholly within the specifically Reformation tradition, and largely severed from the influence of the Renaissance, which had pursued a course largely independent of the religious and spiritual revolution precipitated by Luther.

VII. The modern period. Modern science, which is one of the major aspects of the legacy of the Renaissance, brought massive forces to bear upon the more recent understanding of human nature. Parallel to theistic views of man's being, there developed nontheistic modes of understanding that had for a common denominator, as Reinhold Niebuhr observes, "primarily faith in man."

In the post-Reformation era, these newer views challenged earlier understandings of man, most or all of which, however, continued to command some adherence. Within the general orthodox tradition, certain modifications occurred, chiefly with respect to the dimensions of the retained image of God within a fallen race, and its corollary of the competence (or lack of it) on the part of sinners to respond to grace. Semi-Pelagian (or more properly, semi-Augustinian) positions developed with the repeated recurrences of mass evangelism, with its appeal to the element of human decision.

The "liberal" theologies that emerged in opposition to historic orthodoxy elaborated a wide range of anthropologies, most of which were deeply influenced by Kant's assertion of human autonomy, particularly in the ethical sphere. Historic understanding(s) of man were challenged as being pessimistic and as infringing upon human freedom. It came to be asserted that if human beings are to be "truly ethical," they must be autonomous in a sense incompatible with the teaching concerning original sin. The doctrines of the fall, of sin, of grace, and of salvation (applied) were held to be in need of reinterpretation in terms of a "new moral consciousness."

In some strands, for example, that of Friedrich Schleiermacher, sinfulness was seen in terms of finite defectiveness rather than as a distortion of the will inherited from our first parents. Ruled out are the motifs of man's solidarity in evil, the imputation of sin, and native inability. These denials rest upon a non-Christian metaphysic of evil, and ultimately upon a nonbiblical understanding of human origin.

The theological liberalism of the 19th and early 20th cent., with its refashioning of the Christian understanding of both sin and grace in relation to human nature was challenged by the Dialectical Theology, of which Karl Barth, H. Emil Brunner, and Reinhold Niebuhr were major exponents. These sought to establish, on grounds relatively independent of the Christian Scriptures, a form of "Christian realism" with respect to human nature. The Dialectical Theology tended to regard Adam as a nonhistorical paradigm of the fate of Everyman. Likewise it saw man's original endowment to consist in moral potentiality rather than in created righteousness.

Theological liberalism, confronted by the historical crises that have shown the earlier optimistic and idealistic faith in man to be untenable, has sought to recover some form of realism with respect to human nature, and in case of some of its exponents, has accepted the discipline imposed upon it by some forms of existentialist philosophy. Such motifs as alienation, despair, and meaninglessness have forced new explorations of the subject. The interpretations placed upon human nature by Schleiermacher, Ritschl, Harnack, and Troeltsch have come to be regarded as products of an age that has passed.

The resurgence of evangelicalism that paralleled in time the period of largest acceptance of the Dialectical Theology has brought a renewed concern for an articulation of a view of human nature that would at one and the same time be in harmony with the whole scriptural portrayal and, as well, come to grips with the challenges presented by newer researches. These have come, in particular, from naturalism and much of current psychological studies. It is in the light of the former of these, with its explanation of causality in terms of random selection during an almost infinite time scale, that evangelicals assert again the historic conviction that man is a special creation, composite in nature, and originally endowed with the qualities of pristine holiness, in which the *imago dei* centered and which was forfeited in a historical fall. With respect to contemporary psychologies, evangelicals have rejected, in the name of the Christian REVELATION, the extremes of determinism (which robs man of his essentially moral and accountable nature) and of voluntarism (which in some strands of Existentialism deprives man of any genuine "nature").

Against these forms of thought, it is asserted that human nature cannot be understood apart from a fearless application of the teachings of the Christian Scriptures. Evangelicals maintain that it is only in this light that our nature can be assessed with accuracy, so that the two elements of our "dark side" and of our high destiny are kept in balance.

(See further J. Laidlaw, *The Bible Doctrine of Man* [1905]; J. Orr, *God's Image in Man* [1905]; H. W. Robinson, *The Christian Doctrine of Man* [1911], J. G. Machen, *The Christian View of Man* [1937]; R. Niebuhr, *The Nature and Destiny of Man*

[1941]; S. Doniger, ed., *The Nature of Man* [1962]; C. F. H. Henry, ed., *Christian Faith and Modern Theology* [1964], 147–89; P. E. Hughes, *The True Image: The Origin and Destiny of Man* [1989]; W. Grudem, *Systematic Theology: An Introduction to Christian Doctrine* [1994], 439–525; P. K. Jewett, *Who We Are: Our Dignity as Human: A Neo-Evangelical Theology* [1996]; J. P. Moreland and S. B. Rae, *Body and Soul: Human Nature and the Crisis in Ethics* [2000]; I. G. Barbour, *Nature, Human Nature, and God* [2002]; K. Corcoran, *Rethinking Human Nature* [2006].) H. KUHN

humiliation of Christ. See EXALTATION OF CHRIST.

humility. Distinctive of biblical faith, humility is a virtue to which many other religions accord no honor and even fail to recognize. Philosophers, except those positively influenced by the Judeo-Christian tradition, likewise ignore or belittle it. Thus Aristotle, in his masterful systemization of pre-Christian wisdom, *Nichomachean Ethics*, praises a high-minded self-sufficiency that is the obverse of *tapeinophrosynē* G5425 ("lowliness, humility"). Centuries later Fredrich Nietzsche castigates humility as part and parcel of a perverted morality, a Christian transvaluation of values in which inferior individuals like PAUL resentfully metamorphose their baseness and weakness, exalting servility to the apex of excellence. Humility, therefore, is attacked by Nietzsche as a denial of that genuine humanity which will be embodied in the anti-Christian, aristocratic Superman.

Within the framework of revelational theism, however, humility is indeed a virtue, the proper attitude of the human creature toward his divine Creator. It is the spontaneous recognition of the creature's absolute dependence on God, an ungrudging, unhypocritical acknowledgment of the gulf that separates Self-subsistent Being from utterly contingent being, Kierkegaard's "infinite qualitative difference between God and man." It is the bent-knee stance of awed and grateful awareness that existence is a gift of grace, that inscrutable mercy which, having called a person out of nonbeing, sustains him moment by moment from lapsing back into nothingness. Humility, then, is explicated in Abraham's confession that he is "nothing but dust and ashes" (Gen. 18:27). It is explicated again in Paul's sharp reminder to the inflated Corinthians that each person's position before God is necessarily that of a recipient, a beggar whose hands are empty until divine benevolence fills them (1 Cor. 4:6–7).

Within the theistic framework, furthermore, humility is the altogether right reaction of a guilty creature in the presence of his holy Creator. It is the sinner's admission that his irreducible insufficiency as a finite creature has nevertheless been immeasurably diminished by rebellion against his Creator. In the OT it is the cry of the young prophet as he sees the Lord: "Woe to me! ... I am ruined! For I am a man of unclean lips" (Isa. 6:5). In the NT it is the apostle's honest self-deprecation as he reflects on his stubborn disobedience to the truth (1 Cor. 15:9; Eph. 3:8; 1 Tim. 1:15). Humility is the logical corollary of sin-consciousness. Despite his dignity, therefore, his inestimable worth as *imago dei*, man as a finite agent of rebellion is indeed "dust and ashes."

It follows, then, that humility is the essence of OT piety. A frequent theme in the book of Proverbs (Prov. 3:34; 11:2; 15:33; 16:19; 25:7), humility is exemplified by ABRAHAM (Gen. 32:10); preeminently MOSES ("a very humble man, more humble than anyone else on the face of the earth," Num. 12:3); SAUL at the outset of his career (1 Sam. 9:21); and SOLOMON, whose self-knowledge motivated a sincere self-abasement (1 Ki. 3:7). As a foundation of godliness, this virtue is classically expressed in Mic. 6:8, "And what does the LORD require of you? / To act justly and to love mercy / and to walk humbly with your God." So Rabbi Joshua ben Levi was simply epitomizing the OT when, discussing the comparative merit of various blessings, he insisted: "Humility is the greatest of them all, for it is said, 'The Spirit of the Lord God is upon me, to bring good tidings to the humble' (Isa. 61:1). It is not said 'to the saints,' but 'to the humble,' whence you learn that humility is the greatest of them all" (quoted by M. S. Enslin, *The Ethics of Paul* [1930], 249).

Humility is likewise the essence of NT piety. How could it be otherwise in view of Christ's own example? As Paul brings out in the greatest of all KENOSIS passages, the Savior "humbled himself," voluntarily abandoning his divine status, surrendering his beatitude and dignity in order to live as a human being on the lowest level of poverty and obscurity, eventually sinking to the bottommost depths of ignominy and agony (Phil. 2:5–8). In self-giving *agape* is the antithesis and contradiction of all self-seeking *eros*. Moreover, the character of Jesus exhibited nothing of pride or arrogance. Though unflinchingly courageous and at times scathingly outspoken, he was "gentle and humble in heart" (Matt. 11:29). So his teaching on poverty of spirit had no hypocritical ring to it (Matt. 5:3). Rather than accepting praise, he bore witness to total dependence on his Father as the source of his own wisdom and power; rather than grasping for glory, he ascribed all GLORY to his Father (Jn. 5:19; 6:38; 7:16; 8:28, 50; 14:10, 24). When he stooped to wash the feet of his disciples, Jesus was not indulging in a piece of ostentatious theatrics; instead, he was symbolizing with perfect integrity the whole meaning and message of his ministry. In that act the ground-motif of his person and work broke through, that motif which reached its crescendo on the CROSS.

Consequently, since *imitatio Christi* is the NT imperative, the life of the faithful disciple must be a life of humility. Concerned to exalt the Savior as the Savior was concerned to exalt his Father, the disciple declares with the Savior's baptizer, "He must become greater; I must become less" (Jn. 3:30). The disciple turns his back on status, security, and success, asking only an opportunity to serve, however inconspicuously (Matt. 23:8, 10; Mk. 10:35–45). Glorying in nothing but the cross (Gal. 6:14), he struggles to achieve a proper self-evaluation, neither unrealistically deflated or egotistically conceited (Rom. 12:3). He takes seriously the injunction to make the attitude of Jesus his all-controlling life principle whether in relationship to God or to his brother (Rom. 12:10; Jas. 4:10; 1 Pet. 5:5–6). In short, the faithful disciple fights a continual battle against that pride which is the root of sin, that egoism which breeds self-centeredness, self-exaltation, self-will, self-sufficiency, self-confidence, self-righteousness, self-glorying, and hence self-delusion with its ultimate fruit of self-frustration and self-despair (Rom. 10:2). As he keeps on winning the battle against pride and presumption, he matures in that HOLINESS which flourishes only in the soil of humility.

This virtue is susceptible of gross misunderstanding. Let it be said flatly, therefore, that biblical humility is not the inverted conceit which disguises itself as lowliness. It is that attitude which results from a fearlessly honest self-appraisal, a self-appraisal that neither minimizes one's achievements nor exaggerates one's failures. Humility is not the subtle masochism that enjoys its own debasement. It is not that cowardice which protects itself by a groveling Uriah Heep servility. It is not, moreover, a purely privatistic virtue. It is the child of that radical theocentricity which gratefully acknowledges God's sovereign bestowal of gifts and his sovereign enablement in service; thus it eliminates the arrogance that destroys community. Completely devoid of arrogance, humility nevertheless rejoices with Mary in saying, "the Mighty One has done great things for me—and holy is his name" (Lk. 1:49).

AUGUSTINE, therefore, was right. The secret of sanctity is, as he gave it triple emphasis, "Humility! Humility! Humility!" Or in the penetrating words of Kenneth Kirk: "Without humility there can be no service worth the name; patronizing service is self-destructive—it may be the greatest of all disservices. Hence to serve his fellows *at all*—to avoid *doing* them harm greater even than the good he proposed to confer on them—a man must find a place for worship in his life.... If we would attempt to do good with any sure hope that it will prove good and not evil, we must act from the spirit of humility; worship alone can make us humble" (*The Vision of God* [1931], 449).   V. C. GROUNDS

humor. Humor may be defined as constituting a facetious turn of mind that issues in jocularity. It involves a perception of the incongruous or comic elements of life, and an ability not merely to appreciate them but to communicate them so that others may perceive the amusing factors also. It is generally less subtle than wit, which is marked by the full expression of the intellect in terms of some minor issue to produce a result that can be incisive, caustic, or merely amusing. Humor is normally more genial, sympathetic, and pleasant than wit, for since the latter is primarily an intellectual exercise, it is frequently of a keen, cold, analytical character, and lacks the saving grace of being able to laugh at itself. See LAUGHTER. Humor and wit are alike, however, in being frequently associated with such moral values as truth and virtue. Humor is one of the principal antidotes to personal pride.

I. The English term. The origin of the word is in the Latin *umor* (also *humor*), which in a general sense meant "moisture" or "vapor." In medieval physiology, the word was used of the four cardinal fluids (blood, phlegm, yellow bile, and black bile), whose relative proportions in the body were thought to determine the physical and mental qualities, as well as the disposition, of the individual concerned. Black bile (black choler) produced melancholy, whereas yellow bile resulted in a brighter disposition. In the sense of caprice or whim, the term *humor* was commonly found in 16th-cent. writings, though from the next century the meaning was broadened to include both the quality of action, speech, or writing that excited amusement and the faculty of perceiving and conveying what was ludicrous or comical. In its most developed form, the word was applied to the jocular treatment of a topic, whether in oral or written form.

II. Eastern humor. As in so many other areas of life, the Eastern attitude toward a matter such as humor is quite different from that of Western countries. Judging from the literature, life in the ANE seems to have been a depressingly insecure affair, and if ever circumstances produced anything parallel to the modern occidental situation-comedy, it was not given prominence in written records. Yet such things are bound to have happened periodically, and to have produced a purely comic, if perhaps rather unintentional result. One of the oldest jokes known to man is thought to have originated in Mesopotamia before the prosperous third dynasty of Ur of the Chaldees (c. 2150–2050 B.C.), and perpetuated in something approaching the following conversation: "Who was that lady I saw you out with last night?" "That was no lady, that was my wife." In general, the conditions of ancient life seldom admitted of sheer gaiety, and much of the laughter doubtless occurred under the influence of alcohol, when indelicate subjects and allusions would provoke raucous amusement.

In his days of prosperity, Job may have been a buoyant, cheerful individual (Job 29:24), but aside from the joy of childbirth (Gen. 21:6) and the merry laughter of children at play, scorn and derision seem to have been widely conveyed in laughter (Job 22:19; Pss. 22:7; 52:6 et al.). Thus when God was spoken of as laughing, it invariably involved ridicule (Pss. 37:13; 59:8 et al.).

Because there was nothing of the Western self-consciousness evident in the Eastern male-female relationship, jokes about sex had little place in oriental humor, though indelicate comments on sexual functions would inevitably occur in conversation periodically. In general, the Hebrews had a curious modesty about sex, sometimes referring to the male genitalia by such euphemisms as "hands" or "feet." For people in the ANE, sex was meant to be indulged in, and precisely the same held true of religion. To the superstitious Mesopotamians, there could be no thought whatever of humor being associated with religion, and this stands in forcible contrast to the modern Western attitude as represented in a cartoon that showed two angels, one of which was saying to the other, "I don't mind being ignored so much; it's the awful stories they tell about us that I dislike." Because humor and wit have been linked in Western thought with certain absolute values, it is inevitable that such religious matters as God, the saints, heaven, and hell should be mentioned in a jocular context. For the orientals, however, and not least the Hebrews, religious beliefs, customs, duties, and the like simply did not admit of anything but the most sober of interpretations.

III. Humor in the OT and Apocrypha. Oriental humor seems to come most properly into the category of wit, since there is usually a degree of intellectual subtlety present in the situation. Probably the most common literary form conveying wit is *paronomasia*, or wordplay, which was a favored device of poets (see Hebrew poetry), though not exclusively so. According to one estimate there are more than 500 wordplays in the OT, and obviously only a few examples can be given.

The force of paronomasia lies in the seriousness with which ANE peoples normally treated words. Thus in Gen. 2:7, man (*ʾādām*) was formed from the ground (*ʾădāmâ*), a pun on his earthy nature, whereas in 2:23 the name "woman" (*ʾiššâ*) was given to the creature taken out of man (*ʾîš*). In 3:20 is a play on the name of Eve (*ḥawwâ*), the mother of all living (*ḥay*). The Tower of Babel (*bābel*) narrative related the name to the babble (*bālal*) occasioned by the confusion of tongues (11:9), and similar puns on names occurred in the patriarchal narratives. Thus Abram and Abraham were based on "father" (*ʾāb*); Esau suggests "hairy" (25:25); Edom is similar to the word "red" (25:30); Manasseh may indicate "forgetfulness" (41:51); and Ephraim may be a play on the verb "to be fruitful" (41:52).

The narratives of Sarah have comic aspects also, as, for example, in the embarrassment of her being caught eavesdropping (Gen. 18:10) and subsequently experiencing geriatric conception, which must have produced knowing grins, and perhaps even snide remarks about virility. The son of Sarah was given a name that would remind her of her premature laughter (18:12), and if Isaac ("laughter") could be dubbed by the modern slang name of "Joker," the laugh was clearly upon Sarah in the end. However, if Isaac was a delicate, hypertonic infant, as is often the case with children born to elderly parents, the experience of rearing him even to the point of weaning would be far from amusing.

The pun was most forcefully developed by the prophets, who used it with deadly effect to proclaim the destiny of a disobedient Israel. Thus Amos spoke of Gilgal going into exile (*gālâ*, Amos 5:5), and an eschatological note was struck in the play on "summer fruit" (*qayiṣ*) and "the end" (*qēṣ*), where the literary figure was sharpened even more by the thought of the fruit being overripe (8:2). Hosea also used paronomasia effectively to show that the "standing grain" (*qāmâ*) would actually yield no "fruit" (*qemaḥ*, Hos. 8:7). The highly literary style of Isaiah lent itself admirably to wordplay, as in Isa. 5:7, where we read that the Lord looked for judgment (*mišpaṭ*) but found bloodshed (*mišpāḥ*), and for righteousness (*ṣedāqâ*) but discovered only a cry (*ṣeʿaqâ*). Again, Isaiah (34:14) spoke of wild beasts (*ṣiyyim*) meeting hyenas (*ʾiyyim*), and of a wife bereft (*ʿăzûbâ*) and grieved (*ʿăṣûbat*, Isa. 54:6). A stern note was sounded by Jeremiah: "Be appalled [*šommû*], O heavens [*šāmayim*]" (Jer. 2:12), while pathos was the basis of the plea, "Return [*šûbû*], faithless [*šôbābîm*] sons, I will heal your infidelity [*mešûbōt*]" (3:22). Because of the similarity between some forms of the Hebrew verbs for "to see" and "to fear," a number of wordplays resulted, such as, "Ashkelon shall see [*tēreʾ*] and fear [*tîrāʾ*]" (Zech. 9:5).

From the foregoing it is evident that comparatively few of the puns in the OT accord with the modern understanding of humor, although all of them are undeniably witty. Satire, an applied form of humor that usually has a didactic or moralistic objective, can be seen in the remark in Job 12:2, "Doubtless you are the people, and wisdom will die with you!" which is timeless in its implications. Other OT passages that can be interpreted humorously include the bargaining of Abraham with God (Gen. 18:22–23), the stabbing by Ehud of the portly Eglon (Jdg. 3:15–27), the death of Abimelech at the hands of a woman (9:50–54), the sarcastic and satirical ridicule by Elijah of the Baal prophets on Mount Carmel (1 Ki. 18:26–29), the irony of Haman being unwittingly the cause of his enemy's promotion (Esth. 6:1–11), Haman's retribution in being hanged on his own gallows (5:14—7:10), the scolding wife (Prov. 21:9; 25:24), the mockery of Micah (Mic. 2:6–7, 11), and the taunts of Nahum over Nineveh (Nah. 3:1–19).

Paronomasia in the Apocrypha has been largely lost in translation, although in *Susanna and the Elders* two pungent wordplays related the fate of the lying elders to the names of the trees that they had supplied in giving evidence, as follows: "A mastic tree [Gk. *schinon*] … God will split [*schisei*] you" (vv. 54, 55), and "a live oak tree [*prinon*] … God is waiting to split [*kataprisē*] you in two" (vv. 58, 59). Other instances of humor are seen in the beguiling of Holofernes by feminine wiles (Jdt. 12–13), the discovery of priestly deception (Bel 19–22), and the bursting open of the great dragon (Bel 23–28).

IV. Humor in the NT. As can be expected, Semitic concepts of wit, as opposed to the more earthy and coarse characteristics of Greek humor, are found periodically in the NT, although as with the Apocrypha they have tended to suffer through being rendered in Greek form. Thus the Aramaic preserved a play on words not found in the Greek of the versions: "you are to give him the name Jesus [*yĕhôshûaʿ*], because he will save [*yāšaʿ*] his people from their sins" (Matt. 1:21). Certain witty forms, however, are reflected by the Greek, as with a humorous pun that can perhaps be rendered:

Greek comic actor depicted on a flask (c. 150 B.C.).

"They disguise [*aphanizousin*] their appearance so as to put on a pose [*phanōsin*] of fasting in public" (6:16). A more familiar wordplay (16:18) involved PETER (*Petros*) and rock (*petra*). The name Christ ("the Anointed") was reflected (2 Cor. 1:21) in the verb *chrisas* ("has commissioned"). What was obviously intended as a genuinely humorous remark, and one which is the only example in the NT of the "little woman" joke, was the mention by Christ of the man who had "married a wife" and therefore could not go to the feast when invited (Lk. 14:20). This comment, when accompanied by a smile, must have brought a touch of comic relief to an otherwise deeply serious situation.

Other examples of NT passages with humorous implications include the ridiculous contrast between the speck and the beam (Matt. 7:3–5), the way in which Christ outwitted the PHARISEES in the matter of paying taxes to CAESAR (Mk. 12:13–17), and the SADDUCEES on the question of a much-married woman and her husbands in the resurrection (12:18–27), the ludicrous procedure of straining out a small insect from wine and swallowing a camel (Matt. 23:24), and *double entendre* in Paul's remark that "it is better to marry than to burn" (1 Cor. 7:9 KJV), in which he may have been quoting a popular proverb. As opposed to modern custom, the mother-in-law was treated with respect and kindness (cf. Mk. 1:30–31), and was never the subject of humor in the Bible.

(See further D. Zuver, *Salvation by Laughter* [1933]; F. Rosenthal, *Humor in Early Islam* [1956]; W. F. Stinespring in *IDB*, 2:660–62; F. Landy in *Jewish Quarterly* 28/1 [Spring 1980]: 13–19; M. C. Hyers, *And God Created Laughter: The Bible as Divine Comedy* [1987]; D. A. Peters, *The Many Faces of Biblical Humor* [2007]; *ABD*, 3:325–33.)

R. K. HARRISON

Humtah huhm′tuh (חֻמְטָה *H2794*, "[place of] lizard"). A town in the hill country within the tribal territory of Judah (Josh. 15:54). It was apparently near HEBRON, but its precise location is unknown.

Hundred, Tower of the (מִגְדַּל הַמֵּאָה). The name of a tower on the N wall of the city of JERUSALEM, located between the Tower of HANANEL and the SHEEP GATE; it was restored by Eliashib the high priest and his fellow priests (Neh. 3:1; 12:39; KJV, "tower of Meah"). Both the Tower of the Hundred and the Tower of Hananel protected the NW approach to the TEMPLE area (see M. Avi-yonah in *IEJ* 4 [1954]: 241–42.)

F. W. BUSH

hunger. This word and the term FAMINE are both used by KJV and modern translations to represent the Hebrew word *rāʿāb H8280*, which may refer not only to an individual's hunger but also to acute and general lack of food (similarly Gk. *limos G3350*). It is not always clear in a given context which is meant. In a few passages individual hunger is meant (e.g. Deut. 28:48; Jer. 38:9), but the great majority of the uses of the word refer to famine. The cognate Hebrew verb *rāʿēb H8279*, "to be hungry," is more often used of the individual (Prov. 19:15; cf. Gk. *peinaō G4277*, Matt. 5:6 et al.), but it also can be used to mean "to experience famine" (Gen. 41:55).

F. W. BUSH

hunting. The quest for animals as a source of food or in order to check marauding, or for sport. There are few references to hunting in the OT, and no direct allusions in the NT. Hunting for food is most common among rural or nomadic peoples except for those who participate in it as a sport. The description "hunter" (Heb. *ṣayid H7473*) is applied to NIMROD, the founder of BABEL and other cities of the Mesopotamian valley (Gen. 10:9). Evidently the word implies his warlike qualities and his feats as a conqueror. ESAU, also called a hunter (25:27), was commissioned by his father ISAAC to find wild game for him (verb *ṣûd H7421*, Gen. 27:3); and ISHMAEL, who grew up in the wilderness, became an ARCHER (21:20), adept with the use of the bow and arrow.

Occasional allusions to the killing of wild animals occur in the OT, but they seem to refer mostly to the defense of sheep or cattle against predators, such as the episode of SAMSON and the lion (Jdg.

In this panel from a palace in Nineveh (c. 640 B.C.), Assyrian hunters deploy nets across the path of running deer.

14:56), or DAVID's adventures with a lion and bear (1 Sam. 17:34–36), or BENAIAH's encounter with a lion in a pit (2 Sam. 23:20). Wild animals as well as domesticated cattle are mentioned in the dietary laws, which implies that the Jewish people ate them, and must have been dependent on hunters to supply their needs (Lev. 17:13; Deut. 14:5; 1 Sam. 26:20).

Weapons for hunting included the bow and arrow (Gen. 27:3), nets for birds and fish (Prov. 1:17; Eccl. 9:12), traps (Amos 3:5), and pits into which animals would fall (Ps. 35:17; Ezek. 19:1–4). These terms are frequently used metaphorically. The Israelites were a settled pastoral people rather than nomads who lived by hunting and plundering; consequently the language that they used reflected only the occasional use of weapons. Allusions to the phenomena of hunting are largely figurative. Among other nations of the time, such as the Egyptians and Assyrians, hunting was regarded as a pastime, and was probably a favorite royal sport. The monuments bear ample witness to the practice of hunting in these countries. M. C. TENNEY

Hupham hyoo'luhm (חוּפָם H2573, derivation uncertain; gentilic חוּפָמִי H2574, "Huphamite"). Son of BENJAMIN, grandson of JACOB, and eponymous ancestor of the Huphamite clan; the name occurs only in a census list (Num. 26:39). He is probably to be identified with HUPPIM (Gen. 46:21; 1 Chr. 7:12). See also NOHAH.

Huppah hup'uh (חֻפָּה H2904, possibly "shelter"). The leader of a priestly family whom DAVID appointed by lot as the head of the thirteenth division for duties in the sanctuary (1 Chr. 24:13).

Huppim hup'im (חֻפִּים H2907, derivation uncertain). Son or descendant of BENJAMIN (Gen. 46:21), usually identified with HUPHAM (Num. 26:39). Elsewhere (1 Chr. 7:12) he is called a son or descendant of Ir (presumably the same as Iri, apparently a grandson of Benjamin, v. 7), but some understand this occurrence as a gentilic, "Huppites" (cf. NIV in vv. 12 and 15, though in the latter passage many scholars suspect textual corruption and delete lĕḥuppim ûlĕšuppim). See also MUPPIM and SHEPHUPHAM.

Huppite hup'it. See HUPPIM.

Hur huhr (חוּר H2581, possibly "son," but derivation disputed). (1) A prominent Israelite who aided AARON in holding aloft the hands of MOSES at REPHIDIM so that the Israelites could win over the Amalekites (Exod. 17:10–13). He also assisted in the ruling of the tribes during Moses' absence on Mount Sinai (24:14).

(2) Son of CALEB (the son of Hezron), but primarily identified as the grandfather of BEZALEL (one of the craftsmen who built the TABERNACLE, Exod. 31:2; 35:30; 38:22 1 Chr. 2:19–20, 50; 2 Chr. 1:5). He is also called a "son" (that is, descendant) of JUDAH and "father" (i.e., founder) of BETHLEHEM (1 Chr. 4:1, 4). Jewish tradition makes him the husband of MIRIAM (cf. Jos. Ant. 3.2.4 §54); additional rabbinic traditions make this man Miriam's son.

(3) A king of MIDIAN in alliance with SIHON the AMORITE; Hur and four other Midianite rulers, along with BALAAM, were defeated and put to death by the Israelites (Num. 31:1–8; Josh. 13:21). Some associate his name with the NABATEAN town of Ḥaura' (cf. ABD 3:334).

(4) According to the KJV, the father of one of the twelve district governors who supplied provi-

sions for Solomon and the royal household (1 Ki. 4:8). Modern versions, however, do not render the Hebrew as "the son of Hur," but rather understand the name of this officer to be Ben-Hur, who was perhaps a descendant of #2 above.

(5) Father of a certain Rephaiah who was "ruler of a half-district of Jerusalem" in the time of Nehemiah and who repaired a section of the wall (Neh. 3:9). It is possible that "son of Hur" identified Rephaiah as belonging to a clan descended from #2 above.   W. White, Jr.

Hurai hyoor´i (חוּרַי H2504). See Hiddai.

Huram hyoor´uhm (חוּרָם H2586, "my brother is lifted up"; see Hiram). (1) Son of Bela and grandson of Benjamin (1 Chr. 8:5).

(2) A king of Tyre, allied with David and Solomon. See Hiram #1.

(3) A skilled craftsman from Tyre employed by Solomon to build his palace and the temple. See Hiram #2.

Huram-Abi hyoor´uhm-ay´bi (חוּרָם אָבִי H2587). See Hiram #2.

Huri hyoor´i (חוּרִי H2585, possibly "son," but derivation disputed). Son of Jaroah and descendant of Gad (1 Chr. 5:14).

Hurrians hoor´ee-uhnz. A non-Semitic people group that figured prominently in the ANE during the 2nd millennium B.C. Although the name Horite is sometimes associated with them, the Hurrians are probably not referred to in the Bible.

I. Origin and geographic distribution. Groups either designating themselves as Hurrians (cuneiform *Hurri*) or writing a language linked elsewhere with them, have been identified all over the ANE from ancient Nuzi (E of the Tigris River) to Hattusha (Khattusha, in central Asia Minor), but also to Palestine and even Lower (i.e., northern) Egypt. In the Hittite texts from ancient Hattusha, the term for the people of Huri was *Hurlas*. The term for the language that they spoke and wrote, of which many samples were found at Hattusha, was *hurlili*. In Akkadian sources, whether from Nuzi, Mari, Hattusha, Alalakh, Ugarit, or Egypt (Tell el-Amarna), the people and their language were termed *Hurri*. At Ugarit, the native (W Semitic) term must also have been pronounced *hurrī* (although we have only the consonantal writing *hry*). The Egyptians called the land of Palestine *hurri/u*, but spelled it in consonants, *hr*. In the Mitanni Letter found at Tell el-Amarna, the native Hurrian term was *hurri* in *hur*-. In the OT, the corresponding term is *hōrī* H3037, "Horite" (LXX *Chorraioi*), but it is apparently applied to a different ethnic group.

The language of the Hurrians, which is still only partially understood, seems related to only one other known language—Urartian, in which the kings of Urartu around Lake Van composed inscriptions during the first half of the 1st millennium B.C. (c. 900–600 B.C.) It is believed by some that both Hurrian and Urartian belong to languages of the Caucasus (ancient Armenia). Although Hurrian shares some structural features with members of the Caucasic family's modern representatives, no convincing case for relationship between the two has been made.

II. History. Hurrians appeared in the ANE as early as the middle of the 3rd millennium B.C. They occupied the great half-circle of the Taurus Mountains from Urkish, N of Carchemish, to the country of Namar, around Lake Van, and perhaps as far as the Upper Zab River. Hurrian kings (at least kings whose names appear to be of a Hurrian type) reigned in Assyria c. 2200–2000 B.C. The so-called Assyrian King List found at Khorsabad includes the names Tudiya, Ushpia, Sulili, and Kikkia, which are neither Semitic nor Hurrian.

During the reign of the Hittite king Hattushili I (c. 1700 B.C.), Hurrians appeared along the Upper Euphrates to the E of the Hittite heartland and carried out occasional raids to the W to harass the Hittites. When Hattushili's successor, Murshili I (c. 1595), led his armies through Syria to sack Babylon, he recorded military encounters with Hurrians. But it was during the following few centuries (c. 1600–1400) that the great Hurrian buildup in Syria transpired. Hurrians dominated, if not actually ruled, the kingdom of Kizzuwatna (Cilicia), as well as the kingdom of Alalakh to the S. Indeed,

The Hurrians.

the new dynasty of the Hittites, of which Suppiluliuma I is the most illustrious representative, seems to have been of Hurrian extraction. It is from c. 1400 that the great influx of Hurrian deities and Hurrian myths in the Hittite corpus is dated.

The greatest political achievement of the Hurrians was the kingdom of Mitanni, whose capital was Washukkanni in the Middle Euphrates Valley. At its height (c. 1400 B.C.), Mitanni dominated Kizzuwatna and N Syria on the W, Assyria in the central region, and Nuzi in the E. During this period (c. 1500–1400), Mitanni was ruled by kings who bore Indo-Aryan (i.e., not Hurrian) names: Shuttarna, Parsashatar, Shaushshatar, Artatama, and Tushratta. They carried on royal correspondence and international trade with the pharaohs of the 18th dynasty of Egypt as equals. Several Mitannian princesses became wives of the pharaohs. It is through the royal correspondence between Tushratta of Mitanni and Amenophis III of Egypt that we possess in the El-Amarna archive the famous Mitanni Letter, still the primary source for the Hurrian language. King Suppiluliuma I of Hatti put an end to the kingdom of Mitanni c. 1380. But the principal contribution of the Hurrians was not in their organized political authority; it was the cultural infusion that they brought into Hittite, Babylonian, Ugaritic, and Hebrew societies that left its permanent mark.

III. Hurrians and Hurrian culture in the OT. The degree of Hurrian cultural influence on the peoples of southern and central Palestine was far less than that in Syria and northern Mesopotamia and Asia Minor. Since ABRAHAM emigrated into Palestine from the E via the HARAN region in Upper Mesopotamia, he brought with him many customs acquired while he lived in that city. Many hitherto obscure aspects of the patriarchal narratives, chiefly having to do with legal customs, have been remarkably clarified by the tablets from Nuzi, a Hurrian settlement in northern Iraq, E of the Tigris.

The presence in Palestine proper of Hurrians can be shown by Hurrian names. The El-Amarna tablets indicate that the Jebusite ruler of Jerusalem (see JEBUS) bore a name that means "servant of (the goddess) Hepa." Hepa is a shortened form of the name Hepat, or Hebat, the name of the leading goddess in the Hurrian pantheon, the consort of the god Teshub. A Jebusite successor to "Servant of Hepa" is the individual from whom DAVID purchased the site for the future temple of Yahweh (2 Sam. 24:18–25; cf. 1 Chr. 21:18–30). English versions call this king either ARAUNAH or Ornan. The Hebrew consonantal text renders it either *’rwnh* (with definite article, 2 Sam. 24:16; the Qere is *’rwnh*) or *’rnn* (1 Chr. 21:18). The correct form is the first one, for the name (or perhaps title) is Hurrian, and the meaning is supplied by a recently recovered dictionary tablet from Ugarit, which equates Hurrian *ewri* with Akkadian *bēlu* ("lord"), and *ewir-ne* with *šarru* ("king"). Hurrian *ewir-ne* is clearly the origin of the Jebusite (king) *’wrnh*.

Clay tablets found in TAANACH and SHECHEM in central Palestine also contain Hurrian personal names. In the OT, several groups that appear to be Hurrian bear the names Jebusite, Horite, and even HIVITE (note that in Gen. 34:2 and Josh. 9:7, the LXX has "Horite" for MT "Hivite," possibly reflecting scribal confusion between *r* and *w*). It is possible that HAMOR the Hivite, who is connected with the town of Shechem, was a Hurrian. Other Hivite centers were at GIBEON (Josh. 3–7; 11:19), and in the LEBANON (Jdg. 3:3) and HERMON (Josh. 11:3) mountains.

(See further E. Meyer, *Die Israeliten und deren Nachbarstämme* [1906]; E. A. Speiser in AASOR 13 [1933]: 26–31; A. Götze, *Hethiter, Churriter und Assyrer* [1936]; I. J. Gelb, *Hurrians and Subarians* [1944]; R. T. O'Callaghan, *Aram Naharaim* [1948]; E. A. Speiser in *JAOS* 68 [1948]: 1–13; H. G. Guterbock in *Journal of World History* 2 [1954]: 383–94; E. A. Speiser in *IDB*, 2:664–66; J.-R. Kupper in *CAH* 2/1, 3rd ed. [1973], ch. 1; G. Wilhelm, *The Hurrians* [1989].)

H. A. HOFFNER, JR.

husband. The MARRIAGE relation imposed upon the husband certain obligations and conferred upon him certain rights more generally described in the Scripture but rather minutely regulated in the rabbinical law. The modern Jews, in all the civilized countries of the world, are more mindful of and govern themselves much more, if not entirely, by the laws of the countries whose citizens they are.

I. The husband's duties. The OT and the Mosaic law in particular do not contain express provisions concerning marital rights and responsibilities, except the injunction not to deprive a wife of "her food, clothing and marital rights" (Exod. 21:10). It is upon this casual intimation that the elaborate regulations of the rabbinical code are based. The responsibilities of the husband can be included largely under the following headings: (1) He is to provide his wife with the necessities of life, such as food, clothing, and dwelling; the extent of this responsibility depended upon his fortune and situation in life, and also upon the local customs. (2) He is to have conjugal cohabitation with his wife; a continued refusal, on either side, regarding this duty was not excused by sickness and circumstances and offered sufficient grounds for divorce. (3) He is to provide proper medical care and nursing when the wife is sick. (4) He is to protect his wife and to ransom her in the eventuality of her falling into captivity; the frequent invasion of BEDOUINS in the Near Eastern countries and the continued wars in Europe during the Middle Ages made the provision for such an eventuality quite necessary. (5) He is to provide for her burial in case of her death; this duty included also that of providing for her a tombstone and the covering of expenses for funeral solemnities according to his and her station in society.

II. The husband's rights. The husband's rights according to the Jewish law were as follows: (1) He was entitled to whatever the wife earned by her labor and industry; his right to her earnings was based on the consideration of his obligation to support her. (2) He was entitled to whatever she gained by chance, inheritance, donation, legacy, or

Egyptian sculpture of Sobekhotep with his wife and maternal aunt. (From the Fayum, 18th cent. B.C.)

in any other way. (3) He was entitled to the usufruct of all the property she brought into marriage at the time of their marriage. (4) He was entitled to become her sole heir on her death. (Cf. L. A. Lambert, *Thesaurus biblicus* [1880], 386–89; M. Mielzinger, *The Jewish Law of Marriage and Divorce* [1901], 100–102. For additional bibliography see MARRIAGE.) P. TRUTZA

husbandman. This English word is used by the KJV to render several terms, including Hebrew *ʾikkār* H438, "plowman" (e.g., Jer. 51:23 [NIV, "farmer"]) and Greek *geōrgos* G1177, "agricultural worker" (e.g., Lk. 20:9 [NIV, "farmers"]; Jn. 15:1 [NIV, "gardener"]). See also AGRICULTURE; FARMER; TRADE.

Hushah hoosh´uh (חוּשָׁה H2592, perhaps "haste"; gentilic חֻשָׁתִי H3144, "Hushathite"). Son of Ezer and descendant of JUDAH (1 Chr. 4:4). However, the word "father" in that verse probably means "founder" or "ruler," in which case Hushah was a Judean town, perhaps the same as modern Ḥusan (c. 4.5 mi. W of BETHLEHEM). The term Hushathite (that is, an inhabitant of Hushah or someone belonging to a clan that bore that name) is applied to a warrior named SIBBECAI (2 Sam. 21:18; 1 Chr. 11:29; 20:4; 27:11; apparently the same as Mebunnai in 2 Sam. 23:27).

Hushai hoosh´i (חוּשַׁי H2593, possibly short form of חֲשַׁבְיָה H3116, "Yahweh has taken account" [see HASHABIAH]). (1) An ARKITE, from the territory W of BETHEL (Josh. 16:1–2), who was DAVID's adviser and "friend" (1 Chr. 27:33). When ABSALOM rebelled, Hushai came out to join the fleeing king, but David asked him to return to Jerusalem and to pretend to favor Absalom, in order that he might defeat the counsel of AHITHOPHEL, David's former counselor, who had gone over to Absalom (2 Sam. 15:32–37). Ahithophel and Hushai both advised Absalom how to defeat David (16:15—17:4), but Absalom adopted Hushai's advice. Hushai then sent word to David to escape across the Jordan (17:15–22). When Ahithophel found that his advice was not taken, he hanged himself (17:23).

(2) Father of BAANA; the latter was one of the twelve officers commissioned to supply provisions for King SOLOMON's court (1 Ki. 4:16). Some have thought that this Hushai is the same as #1 above, but it seems improbable that the son of an Arkite (i.e., someone with roots in the tribe of BENJAMIN) would have been placed in charge of a town in ASHER. E. RUSSELL

Husham hoosh´uhm (חוּשָׁם H2595 [in Gen. 36:34–35, חֻשָׁם], possibly "big-nosed"). A royal figure from TEMAN (some say TEMA) who succeeded Jobab as king of EDOM (Gen. 36:34–35; 1 Chr. 1:45–46). He lived "before any Israelite king reigned" (Gen. 36:31).

Hushathite hoosh´uh-thit. See HUSHAH.

Hushim hoosh´im (חֻשִׁים H3123 [Gen. 46:23], חֻשָׁם H3131 [1 Chr. 7:12], חוּשִׁים H2594 [1 Chr. 8:8, 11], derivation unknown). (1) Son (Heb., "sons") of DAN and grandson of JACOB (Gen. 46:23). He is elsewhere called SHUHAM (Num. 26:42), and the relationship between the two names is unclear.

(2) Son (Heb., "sons") of Aher and descendant of BENJAMIN (1 Chr. 7:12; NRSV). However, the NIV takes this name as a true plural and renders, "the Hushites." Some scholars emend the genealogy and propose that the reference here is to the same person(s) as in #1 above.

(3) One of the wives of SHAHARAIM, a Benjamite; she bore him two children (1 Chr. 8:8, 11).

Hushite hoosh´it. See HUSHIM #2.

husk. This English word is used by the KJV to render two Hebrew terms of uncertain meaning (*zāg* H2293, perhaps "skin [of grape]," Num. 6:4; *ṣiqlōnô*, perhaps "in his sack," 2 Ki. 4:42 NRSV [apparently untranslated in NIV]). It is also used by the KJV in the NT to render Greek *keration* G3044, referring to the food, usually fed to animals, which the prodigal son in his hunger would willingly have eaten (Lk. 15:16; see POD).

Huz huhz. KJV form of Uz.

Huzzab huh´zuhb. According to the KJV, Huzzab is the name of a city that was to be taken captive (Nah. 2:7 [Heb. 2:8]). The Hebrew word in question, however, is *huṣṣab*, which can be easily understood as a hophal perfect of the verb *naṣab* H5893, hiphil, "to set up, establish" (thus NIV and NRSV, "It is decreed"). Such a verb, however, fits the context with extreme difficulty and leaves the sentence without a subject (the verbs in v. 7 are fem. and there is no fem. noun in the context that can function as the subject, the words "gates" and "palace" in v. 6 are masc.). R. D. Patterson (*Nahum, Habakkuk, Zephaniah* [1991], 69–70) understands it as a verb meaning "dissolved" but links it with the end of the previous verse, "the palace collapses and crumbles."

If the word is taken as a noun, its meaning can only be guessed at. Various suggestions have been made, most of them connecting the word by various etymologies either with the Assyrian "queen" (cf. Targum) or the city of Nineveh (cf. RSV, "its [i.e., Nineveh] mistress"). Others have suggested an Assyrian proper name, perhaps that of the queen, but without evidence. The text may be corrupt.

F. W. BUSH

hyacinth. See JACINTH.

Hydaspes hi-das′peez (Ὑδάσπης). A river mentioned only in the book of JUDITH along with the EUPHRATES and the TIGRIS (Jdt. 1:6). The context mentions also the king of the Elimeans; see ELAM (COUNTRY). If a river Hydaspes did exist in that general area, it must have been located in a region of the Tigris and Euphrates near the Persian Gulf (one possibility is the Karkheh River, known as Choaspes in ancient times). However, the name Hydaspes is used by Greek writers with reference to a tributary of the Indus, and the author may simply be alluding to some vague and distant geographical area for dramatic purposes.

hyena. A scavenging carnivore larger than a wolf, common in Africa and Asia. The rendering "hyena" is used by the NIV and the NRSV for Hebrew *ʾî* H363 (Isa. 13:22; 34:14; Jer. 50:39), by the NRSV for *ṣābûaʿ* H7380 (only Jer. 12:9, but cf. the place name *ṣĕbōʿîm* H7391, ZEBOIM, 1 Sam. 13:18; Neh. 11:34), and by others for *ṣî* H7470 (Isa. 13:21 et al.; NIV, "desert creature").

Whether or not the hyena can be properly identified in the OT, this animal was in biblical times a common member of the Palestine FAUNA; it is still found in less populated areas, though much rarer than it once was. The striped hyena (*Hyaena striata*) ranges from India through SW Asia to N and E Africa; it is about forty inches long, with a very powerful head and forequarters and rather sloping back. It is largely a nocturnal scavenger, though where there is plenty of game it is now known to do more actual hunting than was thought possible. In some countries it was the custom to encourage hyenas to remove refuse from compounds and villages, and even human bodies were left exposed, with no trace being left in the morning. Hyenas must have been known to the Israelites to whom their habits would make them unspeakably unclean, but in a land peopled by a nation having a hygienic code far in advance of its times, hyenas would have found fewer pickings than in the countries around. (See E. P. Walker, *Mammals of the World*, 3 vols. [1964], 2:1263–67; *FFB*, 45–46.)

G. S. CANSDALE

Hyksos hik′sohs (Ὑκσώς or Ὑκουσσώς, from Egyptian *ḥḳ3w-ḫ3swt*, "rulers of foreign lands"). Term used by the Egyptian historian Manetho (3rd cent. B.C., quoted in Jos. *Ag. Ap.* 1.14 §82) for the foreign rulers of the 15th and 16th dynasties in EGYPT, but wrongly interpreted by him as "shepherd kings," confusing *shoshu* ("bedouin") with *shosu*, the late pronunciation of *khosu* ("foreign lands"). Corresponding to the six kings of Manetho's 15th dynasty, the Turin Canon of Kings

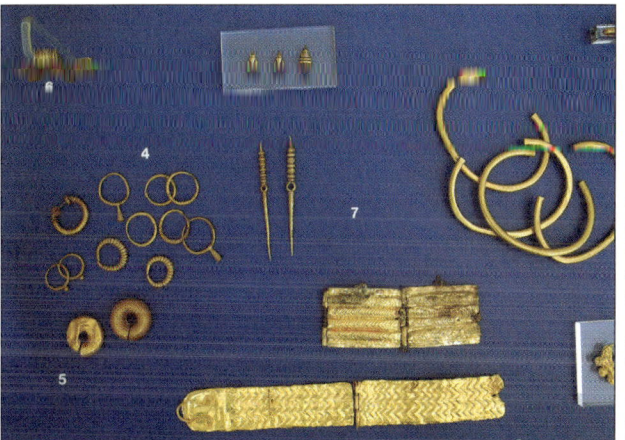

Hyksos gold jewelry from Tell el-ʿAjjul (prob. ancient Sharuhen) dating to the 17th cent. B.C.

(13th cent. B.C.) has a damaged total: "6 [Hyk]sos who reigned 10[8] years." The final expulsion of the Hyksos perhaps did not precede the eleventh year of Ahmose I (c. 1540; see C. F. Nims, *Thebes of the Pharaoh: Pattern for Every City* [1965], 199 n. 2), and Apophis was contemporary of Ahmose's predecessor Kamose. The 108 years of the main Hyksos 15th dynasty may be reckoned at c. 1648–1540; the "16th dynasty" consisted of petty local princelings subordinate to the main Hyksos rulers.

The origins and rise to power of the Hyksos are much discussed. The JOSEPHUS version of Manetho with its sweeping invasion may be less realistic than the picture of an internal coup d'état in the E NILE delta and MEMPHIS presented in the other views. Such a coup would have supplanted in Memphis (and Ithet-Tawy, its administrative suburb) the ruling 13th dynasty for the mastery of Egypt. The ousted dynasty found refuge in THEBES, perhaps as vassal of the Hyksos kings. Monuments of the latter are very few; only Khayan and Apophis have left statues and building fragments; other princes are known only from scarab amulets. (On Hyksos fortifications, see BETH EGLAIM.)

The career of JOSEPH may have fallen into the late 13th dynasty and early Hyksos period. Apparently, the Hyksos dynasty largely took over the existing Egyptian administrative machine. Its rulers adopted pharaonic style, including the title "Son of Re"; Hatshepsut's later remark that they ruled without RE reflects on their legitimacy in her eyes, not any hostility of theirs for Re. Scarabs indicate that foreigners duly attained to administrative posts, such as did the chancellor Hur (cf. Joseph). The surviving names of Hyksos rulers are usually W Semitic when not assimilated to Egyptian, such as Khayan, ʾAnat har, etc. (according to Manetho, the Hyksos came from Phoenicia). Hurrian and Indo-Aryan elements were unimportant, even if present at all. Before the Hyksos' takeover, Semitic kings had already occasionally ruled Egypt in the 13th dynasty.

(See further A. H. Gardiner, *The Royal Canon of Turin* [1959], 17, note on col. X, line 21, also plate III; J. von Beckerath, *Untersuchungen zur politischen Geschichte der zweiten Zwischenzeit Ägyptens* [1965]; J. van Seters, *The Hyksos: A New Investigation* [1966]; W. C. Hayes and T. G. H. James, *CAH*, 3rd ed., 2/1 [1973], chs. 2, 8; H. Goedicke in *Egyptological Studies in Honor of Richard A. Parker*, ed. L. H. Lesko [1986], 37–47; E. D. Oren, ed., *The Hyksos: New Historical and Archaeological Perspectives* [1997]; *SacBr*, 57, 59–60; *ABD*, 3:341–48, which includes a very full bibliography.)   K. A. KITCHEN

Hymenaeus hi´muh-nee´uhs (Ὑμέναιος, "pertaining to Hymen," the god of marriage [see *DDD*, 820–22]). A heretical teacher at EPHESUS who opposed PAUL, mentioned with ALEXANDER (1 Tim. 1:20) and with PHILETUS (2 Tim. 2:17). The same man is doubtless in view in both passages. That he is mentioned first in both places implies that he was the leader among these false teachers.

Hymenaeus and Alexander were among those who, rejecting conscience, had made shipwreck of their faith (1 Tim. 1:20). Paul's delivery of them to SATAN has been much discussed (cf. 1 Cor. 5:5). Some take the meaning to be simply EXCOMMUNICATION from the church, thereby placing them back into the world, the sphere of SATAN. Others think it rather signifies supernaturally inflicted bodily punishment. A combination of both views may be involved. That more than excommunication is meant seems clear (Job 2:6, 7; 1 Cor. 11:30; Rev. 2:22) when compared with cases of apostolic DISCIPLINE (Acts 5:1–11; 13:11). The discipline, whatever its precise nature, was remedial in its intention, "to be taught not to blaspheme," that is, that they may cease their railing against the true gospel.

The discipline had not produced the desired repentance in Hymenaeus when 2 Tim. 2:17–18 was written. The doctrinal error of Hymenaeus and Philetus, destructively spreading like gangrene, was their denial of an eschatological resurrection. They allegorized the RESURRECTION by insisting that it was a past spiritual experience, having occurred when they were raised from ignorance and sin as they came to know the true God. When they believed that the resurrection took place in the lives of believers is not indicated, perhaps at baptism. They probably based their teaching on a misinterpretation of Rom. 6:1–11 and Col. 3:1. It was motivated by incipient GNOSTICISM, which held that matter was evil and that consequently salvation consisted in liberation from the body. The teaching of a future bodily resurrection was deemed illogical and inconceivable (cf. 1 Cor. 15:12). That Hymenaeus taught that the resurrection takes place in one's children is unlikely (cf. *Acts of Paul and Thecla* 2.14; Sir. 30:4). The development of this heretical teaching in the Ephesian church was a fulfillment of the warning Paul had given the Ephesian elders (Acts 20:29–30).

(See further R. C. H. Lenski, *Interpretation of St. Paul's Epistles to the Colossians, to the Thessalonians, to Timothy* [1937], 545–46, 811–13; W. Hendriksen, *New Testament Commentary: The Pastoral Epistles* [1957], 86, 87, 264–66; I. H. Marshall and P. H. Towner, *A Critical and Exegetical Commentary on the Pastoral Epistles*, ICC [1999], 411–15, 750–54.)   D. E. HIEBERT

hymn. See MUSIC, MUSICAL INSTRUMENTS.

Hymn of the Pearl. See THOMAS, ACTS OF.

Hymn of the Three Young Men. See AZARIAH, PRAYER OF.

hypocrisy. In the NT, the Greek word *hypokrisis G5694* (with its cognates) is applied to human conduct that was externally religious but insincerely motivated, that is, the simulation of goodness.

I. Classical Greek. In the classical authors, the term had no evil connotation. The cognate verb (*hypokrinomai G5693*) could mean simply "to answer." The interpretation of dreams, the oratorical ability of a Demosthenes, the public recitation of poetry, and acting in a play could all be designated with this word. It was, however, especially the part of an actor in a Greek drama represented by this term that influenced its subsequent development. This background in Greek drama and theater was totally unparalleled in the thought and the culture of the Hebrew people. Because of this absence of correspondence of thought and situation, the RSV eliminated both "hypocrisy" and "hypocrite" from its translation of the OT (but cf. NRSV and NIV at Ps. 26:4) even though the KJV employed both.

II. Septuagint. By the time the OT was translated into Greek, the word had taken on negative connotations. Later, in Aquila's famous revision of the SEPTUAGINT, the term became equivalent to "impiety" or "lawlessness." The *Epistle of Barnabas* shows where the development revealed in the LXX eventually took this word. In the description of two ways of life it was noted, "you must not join yourself with those who walk in the way of death; you must hate everything not pleasing to God; you must hate all *hypokrisis*, and you must not abandon the commands of the Lord" (*Barn.* 19.2). In English, the word came to signify active evil. The Hebrew term frequently translated by the KJV with "hypocrite" is *ḥānēp H2868*, "godless" (Job 8:13 et al.).

III. The NT. No sin was so sternly denounced by Jesus as that of hypocrisy. The PHARISEES were guilty at this point, and Jesus both summed up the case against them and warned his disciples against such conduct by the use of this term: "Be on your guard against the yeast of the Pharisees, which is hypocrisy" (Lk. 12:1). Jesus did not charge all Pharisees with hypocrisy, nor did he mean that all hypocrites were Pharisees. He did indicate with these words that Pharisees were especially prone to hypocrisy; it was the natural consequence of their teaching. Some of them were play actors of the first order: they had sacrificed truth to appearance and were concerned more about reputation than they were about reality. They lost sight of reality in their deception of others to such a degree that they deceived themselves. God, however, was not deceived; he knew what was only pretense, which would be exposed in his judgment. Jesus consistently called for REPENTANCE from the Pharisees. Repentance requires facing the truth, the very thing hypocrites find difficult to do.

The most graphic representation of hypocrisy was Jesus' description of the Pharisees as "whitewashed tombs, which look beautiful on the outside but on the inside are full of dead men's bones and everything unclean. In the same way, on the outside you appear to people as righteous but on the inside you are full of hypocrisy and wickedness" (Matt. 23:27–28). Some Pharisees were intensely religious in their outward actions, but inside their hearts were full of sin and wickedness. Their true motives were concealed under a cloak of pretense.

The topic comes up also in the Epistles. Hypocrites are denounced because they seduce believers from the way of God in the name of religion. They persuade others to listen to them rather than to God (1 Tim. 4:2; 1 Pet. 2:1). PAUL in GALATIANS charges PETER, BARNABAS, and other Jewish Christians with dissimulation because they ate with Gentile Christians at ANTIOCH OF SYRIA, but only until the JUDAIZERS came; then they refused to do so under the pressure of those strict traditionalists (Gal. 2:11–21). In this context the term "hypocrisy" need not be taken as indicating evil motives; rather, it reflects the broader sense of "play-acting."

H. L. DRUMWRIGHT, JR.

Hypostasis of the Archons. A Jewish-Gnostic document preserved in the NAG HAMMADI LIBRARY (NHC II, 4). While the Coptic codex itself is dated to the 4th cent., the original Greek was likely composed in Egypt a century earlier. The work, which has affinities with various "Sethian" texts from Nag Hammadi, may be described as a mythological narrative based on Gen. 1–6, offering esoteric knowledge to Christians. (English trans. in *NHL*, 161–69.)

Hypsiphrone. The last tractate in the NAG HAMMADI LIBRARY (NHC XI, 4). It purports to record certain visions revealed to Hypsiphrone ("Highminded Woman"), and includes a first-person description of her descent into the world. Since only a few fragmentary paragraphs are preserved, it is difficult to form a good understanding of the document. (English trans. in *NHL*, 501–2.)

Hyrcanus hihr-kay′nuhs (Ὑρκανός). Son (or descendant) of TOBIAS (2 Macc. 3:11; according to JOSEPHUS [see *Ant.* 12.4.2 §160; 12.4.6 §186], Hyrcanus was the son of Joseph and the grandson of Tobias). Hyrcanus was a prominent Jewish man who had deposited a large sum of money in the temple. HELIODORUS, an official of the Syrian ruler SELEUCUS IV, came to Jerusalem to confiscate the money, but was overwhelmed as the result of seeing an apparition, and thus the treasure was saved for the temple (3:24–29). Hyrcanus is a name derived from Hyrcania, a region S of the Caspian Sea to which many Jews had been transported. For John Hyrcanus and Hyrcanus II, see HASMONEAN II.A and II.E.

C. H. PFEIFFER

New growth on a hyssop plant.

hyssop his′ahp. This English term is used to translate Hebrew ʾēzôb H257 (which occurs ten times in the OT) and Greek *hyssōpos* G5727 (only twice in the NT). The most striking reference is in Jn. 19:29, which records that our Lord was given VINEGAR in a sponge put on a stalk of hyssop. The Greek term, however, is also definitely connected with the blood used in sacrifices (Heb. 9:19). Directions are given by MOSES to take a bunch of hyssop and dip it into the blood of the lamb that was in the basin, in order to be able to apply it to the lintel and the two sideposts of the front door of the house; this was the beginning of the PASSOVER (Exod. 12:22; cf. also Lev. 14:4–6, 49–52; Num. 19:6, 18). The reference in Ps. 51:7, "Cleanse me with hyssop," obviously refers to the application of the blood of the lamb, for it is only, Scripture says, with the shedding of blood that there can be remission of sin (Heb. 9:22). In the description of SOLOMON's wisdom given by God, we read, "He described plant life, from the cedar of Lebanon to the hyssop that grows out of walls" (1 Ki. 4:33).

To discover the true name of the plant, one must examine carefully the references. (1) The plant should be bushy; (2) liquid should easily cling to its leaves; (3) it can grow between the stones of a wall; (4) it would be useful if it were aromatic; (5) it could be a "purifier"; (6) it should grow well in Egypt (where the Israelites first used it); in the desert (where again they used it at the Passover service, year by year, on the way to Israel); and in Palestine (where it would have to be used at the Passover service each year).

The hyssop grown today is *Hyssopus officinalis*, which produces blue flowers from June to September, plus aromatic leaves; when these, with the flowers, are infused in hot water, they are used as an expectorant. It does not grow in Palestine or Egypt, however, and so cannot be the plant mentioned in Scripture. As far as Egypt is concerned, there are indications that it was the sorghum grass. In the case of Solomon's reference, it could easily be the *Capparis sicula* (see CAPERBERRY). This plant is found in the SINAI desert and grows on the walls of JERUSALEM. It would have been possible to have used the end of a branch of this shrub to transfer the vinegar in the sponge to the Lord Jesus. Capparis is a straggling, deciduous shrub with white flowers, tinged red on the outside, that fade before mid-day.

Those who believe the plant was the marjoram argue (1) that it grows easily in walls; (2) that it has hairy stems and leaves, which would hold water or blood well; and (3) that it is pleasantly aromatic. The marjoram could be either *Origanum maru*, of Syrian origin (see *FFB*, 129–30), or *Origanum aegyptiacum*, from Egypt.

W. H. STITWELL-CASPER

Canaanite incense burner from Taanak (12th and 13th cent. B.C.).

I am (who I am). The name of God revealed to Moses when he asked for credentials that would convince the children of Israel that God had indeed authorized him to lead them out of Egypt (Exod. 3:13–14). The disclosure of the name was given at the BURNING BUSH, which had aroused Moses' curiosity because it was not consumed. Such a phenomenon suggests something eternal and constant. Moreover, the giving of this name was preceded by God's declaration to Moses, "I am the God of your father, the God of Abraham, the God of Isaac and the God of Jacob," the God who knew the sorrows of his people's bondage in Egypt and had come down to deliver them (3:6–8). Thus the name "I am" (Heb. ʾehyeh, impf. of hāyâ H2118, "to be") or "I am who I am" (ʾehyeh ʾăšer ʾehyeh) overarches the past and the future history of the children of Israel and suggests that what God is in the present, he was in the past, and will be in the future to this people.

God's identification with this people is forever, for he has willed to be known as the God who is the God of ABRAHAM, ISAAC, and JACOB, a name which is "my name forever, the name by which I am to be remembered from generation to generation" (Exod. 3:15 KJV). Thus Moses' credentials, and the faith of the children of Israel in God's action of deliverance in the future, are grounded in, and are an extension of, what God has done for their fathers in the past.

There is a difference of opinion whether the expression ʾehyeh ʾăšer ʾehyeh should be translated "I am who I am" or "I will be what I will be." It should be observed that nothing in the record of Exod. 3 attempts to demonstrate or urge that which God was in the past to Abraham, Isaac, and Jacob. This truth was a part of the faith of the children of Israel; even in Egypt, they held this faith. What was requested by Moses and needed by the children of Israel was not a name which disclosed that God was what he was, but that he is and will be in the future what he admittedly was in the past: the God of their fathers and, therefore, the God of their children, the children of Israel, who therefore should accept Moses' claim that God had called him to deliver them out of Egypt.

The most distinctive name by which God was known in Israel is Yahweh (*yhwh*; KJV, "Jehovah"), which comes from the same root as "I am," but in the third person rather than first, and whose significance throughout the OT is that God has made a covenant with the children of Israel to which he will ever remain faithful. It is within this content of the meaning of Yahweh—a name that appears repeatedly in Exod. 3—that the "I am" was given to Moses as a credential that would convince the children of Israel that God willed through Moses to lead the children of Israel out of Egypt into a better future. (Cf. *DDD*, 910–19, s.v. "Yawheh.")

The meaning of this "I am" reappears in the claim of Jesus in the NT. Throughout the Gospel of John, the corresponding Greek phrase *egō eimi* seems to allude to God's name (see esp. Jn. 4:26; 8:24, 28; 18:5–8; this usage possibly also reflects the Heb. ʾănî hûʾ, "I [am] he," Isa. 43:10 et al., LXX *egō eimi*). The Jews of the NT resisted the summons of Jesus to lead them out of the slavery of sin into a future of freedom by appealing to the past, asserting that they were the children of Abraham—an assertion which Jesus countered, in the interest of his present and future liberating achievements, by declaring, "before Abraham was, I am" (Jn. 8:58).

A more speculative and metaphysical theology sees in the "I am" of Exod. 3 an assertion of God's ontological Being, who is the only reality, and in the light of which the opposition of Pharaoh, the concern of Moses, and the doubts of Israel regarding the future to which Moses is commanded to lead them is, in comparison to the "I am," nothing. But whatever may be legitimately deduced about the metaphysical character of God—that is, of God-as-he-is-in-himself, in distinction from created reality which in itself is nothing except contingent being—the entire context of the passage is historically conditioned. It was given by God not to disclose what he-is-in-himself but to disclose what he is, was, and will be in that historical situation of Egypt's sin, Moses' need, and the doubts and fears that Moses contemplated as the reaction of the children of Israel to God's redemptive purpose for them. See GOD, BIBLICAL DOCTRINE OF; GOD, NAMES OF. J. DAANE

Iaoel. See ABRAHAM, APOCALYPSE OF.

ibex. A mountain goat of the genus *Capra* (esp. *C. ibex nubiana*), distinguished by its long and backward-curving horns. The English term is used in modern Bible versions to render Hebrew *dišōn* H1913, which occurs only once (Deut. 14:5; KJV, "pygarg," following LXX *pygargos*, "white-

An ibex at En Gedi in Israel.

rump [antelope]"); other possible translations are "antelope" and "bison." According to some scholars, "ibex" should be the rendering of a different Hebrew term, *yāʿēl* H3604, which almost all versions translate as "wild goat" (1 Sam. 24:2 [here a place name]; Job 39:1 ["mountain goat"]; Ps. 104:18; cf. *yaʿălâ* H3607, Prov. 5:19, which may be a reference to a female ibex or to a doe). See also ORYX; WILD GOAT.

The incident described in 1 Sam. 24 took place at EN GEDI (Spring of Young Goat), where there is today a wildlife sanctuary especially to preserve the Nubian ibex in the hills where they have always lived. All points seem to confirm the identification. This ibex is the same size as the better known alpine ibex (steinbock) of Switzerland and Italy, with more slender but clearly ridged, curved horns. The general color is gray, becoming browner in winter. Like most goats it both browses and grazes. It is confined to the mountains E of the Nile, in Sinai and S Arabia, with some outlying groups in Israel and perhaps Jordan. (See *FFB*, 2–3, 46–47; *ABD*, 6:27–29.) G. S. CANSDALE

Ibhar ib´hahr (יִבְחָר H3295, "[Yahweh] chooses [him]"). One of the sons of DAVID born at Jerusalem (2 Sam. 5:15; 1 Chr. 3:6; 14:5). All that is known of him is that his mother was a wife, not a concubine, of David.

ibis. A wading bird similar to the stork. The term is used once by the RSV (following LXX, *ibis*) to render *yanšûp* H3568 (Lev. 11:17), but this Hebrew word is more properly translated "(great) owl," as the RSV itself does elsewhere (Deut. 14:16; Isa. 34:11 [*yanšôp*]). The root may suggest a bird that comes out at dusk or one that hisses. Neither would fit the ibis, nor the fact that the setting of Isa. 34:11 is a desolate place. The "sacred ibis" would have been known to the Israelites while in Egypt, where it was a deity, but it did not carry over to Palestine. Another species, the "glossy ibis," is an uncommon passage migrant. See OWL. G. S. CANSDALE

Ibleam ib´lee-uhm (יִבְלְעָם H3300, meaning uncertain; cf. BALAAM). A Canaanite town allotted to the tribe of MANASSEH but apparently located within the territory of ISSACHAR and ASHER (Josh. 17:11).

This perplexing description may indicate that the city was in an area "reckoned at first to the other two tribes" (Y. Aharoni, *The Land of the Bible: A Historical Geography*, rev. ed. [1979], 235); however, Y. Kaufmann (*The Biblical Account of the Conquest of Palestine* [1953], 36–40) argues that the text should not be translated "(with)in" Issachar and Asher, but rather "beside (or "along" or "by") the lands of these other two tribes. Manasseh was unable to drive the Canaanites from this city (Jdg. 1:27). AHAZIAH, king of Judah, was slain by JEHU when he fled by chariot at the ascent of GUR, which was near Ibleam (2 Ki. 9:27; in 15:10, some would correct the awkward phrase "in front of the people" to "in Ibleam," on the basis of the Lucianic recension of the SEPTUAGINT, thus making Ibleam infamous again as the site of SHALLUM's assassination of the king of Israel, ZECHARIAH).

The name Ibleam is attested already in the 15th cent. B.C. by THUTMOSE III's list of 119 Canaanite towns (no. 43, *Ybrᶜm*; cf. Aharoni, *Land of the Bible*, 160). It was on the southern point of the JEZREEL Valley proper, guarding one of the four or five passes on the VIA MARIS from the SHARON Plain. Ibleam is identified with the Levitical city BILEAM (1 Chr. 6:70) and with modern Khirbet Belᶜameh, about 16 mi. N of SHECHEM and 12 mi. SE of MEGIDDO. W. C. KAISER, JR.

Ibneiah ib-nee′yah (יִבְנְיָה *H3307*, "Yahweh builds up"; cf. IBNIJAH and JABNEEL). Son of Jehoram and descendant of BENJAMIN; listed among those who returned from the Babylonian EXILE and resettled in Jerusalem (1 Chr. 9:8).

Ibnijah ib-ni′juh (יִבְנִיָּה *H3308*, "Yahweh builds up"; cf. IBNEIAH and JABNEEL). Descendant of BENJAMIN and ancestor of Meshullam, who is listed among those who returned from the Babylonian EXILE and resettled in Jerusalem (1 Chr. 9:8).

Ibri ib′ri (עִבְרִי *H6304*, "Hebrew"). Son of Jaaziah and descendant of LEVI through MERARI (1 Chr. 24:27); listed among "the rest" of the Levites in the time of DAVID (cf. vv. 20, 31).

Ibsam ib′sam (יִבְשָׂם *H3311*, "fragrant"; cf. BASEMATH, MIBSAM). KJV Jibsam. Son (or descendant) of Tola and grandson (or more distant descendant) of ISSACHAR; he is described as head of his family, which probably means he was a military officer (1 Chr. 7:2).

Ibzan ib′zan (אִבְצָן *H83*, prob. "swift"). One of the minor judges (Jdg. 12:8–10). See JUDGES, PERIOD OF. All that is known about him is that he came from BETHLEHEM, where he was also buried, that he led Israel for seven years, and that he had thirty sons and thirty daughters for whom he secured an equal number of husbands and wives from abroad. The large family and the special reference to these marriages indicates his wealth and social status. JOSEPHUS (*Ant.* 5.7.13) states that Ibzan's Bethlehem was the well-known town in Judah, but he is probably wrong because the latter is generally distinguished by adding the words "of Judah" or "Ephratah"; the reference is more likely to Bethlehem of Zebulun (Josh. 19:15, modern Beit Laḥm, 7 mi. NW of NAZARETH). Probably stemming from this same confusion, Jewish tradition identified Ibzan as the BOAZ of the RUTH story, making him an ancestor of DAVID (*b. Baba Batra* 91a).

C. F. Keil (KD, *Joshua, Judges, Ruth*, 276–92, 397–98) makes a good case for limiting the extent of the rule of Jephthah, Ibzan, Elon, and Abdon primarily to the Transjordanian situation with the Ammonite oppression. The author of Judges first gives a short summary of the subject matter for the

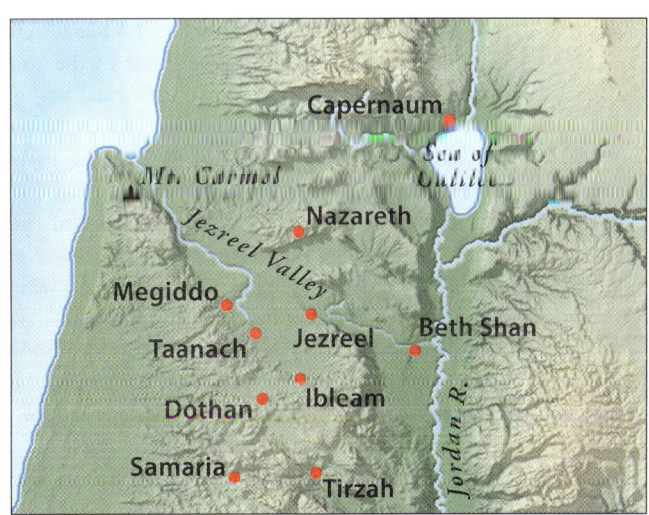

Ibleam.

whole section by introducing the Philistine and the Ammonite threat simultaneously (Jdg. 10:7–9). He next eliminates as quickly as possible that which falls outside the scope of his real theme in chs. 11–12, leaving him free to return to the Philistines as his main concern in ch. 13 and the theme that carries on the narrative to its real goal. Therefore, the forty years of the Philistine oppression cover the same time and go beyond the thirty-one years total for the four judges summoned by the Transjordanian people (Jdg. 12:6–13).

W. C. Kaiser, Jr.

ice. Because of the mildness of the climate, ice is almost never seen in Palestine and Syria except on the highest mountains. Hail is common in the winter and is sometimes very destructive. The pools at Jerusalem have sometimes been covered with ice, but this is rare. At heights of about 4,000 ft., a little ice sometimes forms during the night in winter, but it melts in the sun the next day. Ice (Heb. *qeraḥ* H7943, which can also refer to frost) is mentioned in the Bible three times in connection with the power of God (Job 37:10; 38:29; Ps. 147:17). The word is used once in a figurative sense to describe treacherous friends, who are like torrents of water "darkened by thawing ice" (Job 6:16).

S. Barabas

Ichabod ik´uh-bod (אִי־כָבוֹד H376, possibly "inglorious" or "where is the glory?" or "alas [for] the glory!"; cf. P. K. McCarter, Jr., *I Samuel*, AB 8 [1980], 115–16). The name given to the son of Phinehas (one of Eli's two evil sons) by his mother when she bore him on her deathbed. News arrived from the battle of Aphek that the Philistines had killed both Hophni and Phinehas and captured the ark of the covenant of the Lord. When their father heard this tragic news, he fell backward and broke his neck. Phinehas's wife, upon hearing that her husband and father-in-law had died and that the ark was gone, immediately went into labor. In her despondency she named the child Ichabod, saying, "The glory has departed [*lit.*, gone into exile] from Israel" (1 Sam. 4:21–22). Ichabod's nephew, Ahijah (i.e., Ahimelech), was the priest who stayed with Saul and his 600 men at Gibeah (14.3).

W. C. Kaiser, Jr.

Iconium i-koh´nee-uhm (Ἰκόνιον G2658). A city of Asia Minor, modern Konya. According to Xenophon (*Anab.* 1.2.19), Iconium was the last city of Phrygia for one traveling E. In Greek and Roman times, it was considered the chief town of Lycaonia. It is mentioned several times in the NT (Acts 13:51; 14:1, 19, 21, 16:2; 2 Tim. 3:11). Paul and Barnabas reached Iconium from Antioch of Pisidia, a journey of perhaps 80 mi. if they followed the route that took them up the Sultan Range, and across 50–60 mi. of the central plateau by the great eastern road from Ephesus to the Euphrates. The Galatian plateau is high and healthy, more like the great Asian steppes than any other portion of the peninsula.

The city's beginnings are lost in history. Iconium is probably a Phrygian word, but a myth was invented to give it a Greek meaning. According to the legend, King Nannakos (the Phrygian Methuselah) had a prophecy that said a deluge would come when he passed away. The king called his people to repentance and supplication, and certain it is, from the evidence of Herondas, the 3rd-cent. B.C. writer of comic pieces, that "the weeping of Nannakos' day" was a proverb. It was of no avail. The flood came as predicted, and with the subsiding of the waters Prometheus and Athena remade man by means of images of mud into which life was breathed. The Greek for "image" is *eikōn* G1635, hence Iconium. The story is a typical "etiological myth," a story invented to account for an existing fact. Another similar legend was attached to the name of Perseus and an "image" of the Gorgon presented to him. The flood story is not a sign of Jewish influence. The district was subject to flooding.

Section of an ancient city wall at Iconium.

Turning from myth to history, it may be said with certainty that an ancient Phrygian town was transformed into a Greek city by colonization. Rome chose LYSTRA and Antioch as its bastions, but Iconium, in spite of becoming a Roman colony under HADRIAN, remained predominantly Greek in tone and somewhat resistant toward Roman influence. Claudius, for example, gave some attention to the organization of the rich and fertile area, and granted Iconium the honor of incorporating his name. Claudiconium, however, like Londonderry, similarly prefixed, rapidly shed its honorific syllables. The compounded name was a curiosity of coinage, a sphere in which such formalities of nomenclature most commonly find place and perpetuation.

As a city of the Galatian "heartland" of Asia Minor, Iconium shared the fortunes of the area. In the 3rd cent. B.C. it fell within the domains of the SELEUCID monarchs of ANTIOCH OF SYRIA, and in the middle of the 2nd cent. was probably dominated by the intruding Gauls who were later confined to the northern uplands of the region. After approximately a generation under such subservience, Iconium was taken over by the kings of PONTUS, to be set free as a political gesture during the Mithridatic wars with Rome. In 39 B.C., Mark Antony handed the city to Polemon, king of CILICA Tracheia, and three years later to Amyntas, who became king of GALATIA at that time of flux and change. Upon Amyntas's death, with the organizing of the Roman PROVINCE of Galatia, Iconium became an independent unit once more within the provincial structure.

As a Greek city, Iconium was governed by its assembly of citizens. Greek was the language of its public documents. Even where the Roman name Claudiconium is used on coinage it appears in its Greek form. It was a beautiful place, a natural center of human activity, as its survival into modern times indicates. Two hundred square miles of fertile plain surrounded it, cool, well-watered, and tree-filled. W. M. Ramsay (*The Cities of St. Paul: Their Influence on His Life and Thought* [1907], 317–19) regards Iconium as the DAMASCUS of Asia Minor, blessed like the great Syrian city with water, genial climate, and the prosperity that goes with both.

The first impact of Christianity on Iconium provoked bitter opposition. The 2nd-cent. story of Paul and Thecla, fiction though it is, contains as its core of truth the tribulations of the apostle and his first converts (see PAUL, ACTS OF). Writing from Rome to TIMOTHY, during his last imprisonment twenty years later, Paul still remembered his ordeal in the Phrygian city. Paul's foundation,

Iconium.

however, stood firm, and the church in Iconium, whose continued presence and activity is signified by numerous Christian inscriptions from the 3rd cent. onward, appears to have triumphed over the attempts of its Judaistic wing to corrupt the simplicity of its doctrine, the assault that occasioned the epistle to the GALATIANS. (See also S. E. Johnson, *Paul the Apostle and His Cities* [1987], 62–65.)

E. M. BLAIKLOCK

Idalah id´uh-luh (יִדְאֲלָה *H3339*, possibly from a root meaning "jackal"). A town in the tribal territory of ZEBULUN, named with SHIMRON and BETHLEHEM (Josh. 19:15; not to be confused with Bethlehem of Judah). Its location is uncertain, but a possible identification is modern Khirbet el-Ḥuwarah, about 6.5 mi. W of NAZARETH.

Idbash id´bash (יִדְבָּשׁ *H3340*, "honey-sweet" or "honey-brown"). Son of Etam, included in the genealogy of JUDAH (1 Chr. 4:3, following LXX).

The MT appears to be textually corrupt; see discussion under EDOM.

Iddo id'oh (עִדּוֹ H6333, also עִדּוֹא and עִדּוֹ, possibly short form of עֲדָיָהוּ H6348, "Yahweh has adorned" or "pleasing to Yahweh" [see ADAIAH]; the additional forms אִדּוֹ H120 [Ezra 8:17], יַדַּי H3350 [Ezra 10:43 *Ketib*; *Qere* יַדּוֹ], יֶעְדּוֹ H3587 [2 Chr. 9:29 *Qere*; *Ketib* יַעְדִּי], and יִדּוֹ H3346 [1 Chr. 27:21] appear to derive from one or two different roots). **(1)** Father of Abinadab, who was one of SOLOMON's twelve district officers (1 Ki. 4:14).

(2) Son of Joah and descendant of LEVI through GERSHON (1 Chr. 6:21; apparently the same as ADAIAH, v. 41).

(3) Son of a certain Zechariah; he was an officer appointed by DAVID over the half-tribe of MANASSEH in GILEAD (1 Chr. 27:21).

(4) One of the descendants of Nooma (Nebo) who agreed to put away their foreign wives (1 Esd. 9:35 NRSV [cf. Codex B, *Ēdos*]; KJV, "Edes" [most Gk. MSS., *Ēdais*]; the parallel passage, Ezra 10:43, has JADDAI [Heb. *yadday*, but note that the *Ketib* is *yaddô*]).

(5) A seer (also called a prophet) who received visions concerning SOLOMON and JEROBOAM (2 Chr. 9:29), recorded genealogies associated with REHOBOAM (12:15), and composed "annotations" (*midrāš* H4535) respecting ABIJAH (13:22). His writings served as a source for the Chronicler's material. See CHRONICLES, BOOKS OF, V.

(6) The leader of a group of Levites at CASIPHIA who provided EZRA with attendants for the temple upon their return to Jerusalem after the EXILE (Ezra 8:17; 1 Esd. 8:45–46 [KJV, "Saddeus" and "Daddeus," due to variants in the Gk. MSS]).

(7) One of the priests and Levites who returned with ZERUBBABEL to Jerusalem (Neh. 12:4). Because his priestly family was headed by someone named Zechariah (v. 16), this Iddo is probably the grandfather of the prophet ZECHARIAH (Zech. 1:1, 7; Ezra 5:1; 6:14). W. C. KAISER

idleness. Various Hebrew terms can be rendered "idle(ness)" or laziness. For example, the niphal participle of the verb *rāpâ* H8332, "to relax, become slack," is used in PHARAOH's criticism of the Israelites because of their desire to go away to worship God (Exod. 5:8; 5:17). The noun *ʿaṣlût* H6701 is used in the description of the virtuous woman as one who "watches over the affairs of her household / and does not eat the bread of idleness" (Prov. 31:27; cf. 19:15). In the NT, "idle" renders the Greek words *argos* G734, "inactive, unproductive" (1 Tim. 5:13 et al.), and *ataktos* G864 (with cognates), "undisciplined, disorderly" (1 Thess. 5:14 et al.).

The Scriptures criticize the idle person when the situation demands effort and work, as well as the busy person who speaks "idle words" (KJV), that is, who uses meaningless and careless language (Matt. 12:36). Idleness can be both a failure to respond to a situation calling for action and a busy loquaciousness that speaks to no purpose. The Scriptures call for purposeful work and also for purposeful rest (Exod. 20:8–11). The biblically enjoined SABBATH rest is not to be confused with idleness: such rest comes after labor, and implies not laziness but an enjoyment of what has been accomplished. If the laborer is worthy of his hire, he is also free to enjoy his hire, and such enjoyment of the product of his labor is not idleness. In biblical thought, work as mere busyness is not virtuous. The opposite of idleness is not activity, but such purposeful activity as achieves its purpose and can thereupon be entered into and enjoyed. The "busybody" is, therefore, a person who is very active but to no good purpose, and the idle man is the unproductive man, who does nothing and comes to a time of need. See also SLUGGARD. J. DAANE

idolatry (Gk. εἰδωλολατρία G1630, from εἶδος G1626, "that which is seen, appearance," and λατρεία G3301, "service, worship"). The worship of idols or images; in a derived sense, the word can refer to blind or excessive devotion to something or someone.

I. Idolatry in ancient times. The ancients believed that the image was the dwelling place of a superhuman force or being, or was the deity itself. Idols were made of wood, stone, or clay, and sometimes of gold or silver. For the Hebrews, idolatry included the worship of anything other than Yahweh. Rabbinic writers considered idolaters as enemies of Israel. According to the TALMUD (*Yoma*

9b et al.), the three cardinal sins are idolatry, immorality, and bloodshed. Idolatry was given precedence because it implied a denial of REVELATION, thus shattering the entire basis of religion and ethics. In the NT, the term was extended to mean obsession with anything to the degree that it took the place of devotion to God.

Idolatry was the embodiment of human desire and thought. Idols, though made in many shapes and sizes, really represented the image of man, for they expressed his thoughts, desires, and purposes. Pride caused human beings to trust in themselves rather than in God, hence their idols were really expressions of self-worship (Isa. 2:8–22). The Bible repeatedly depicts people as debasing themselves when they worship that which they have made with their own hands.

Idolatry has been practiced from primitive times. The ANE was thoroughly polytheistic. Everything that occurred, whether good or bad, was attributed to the gods, because life was not separated into religious and secular categories. Nature and its unexplained forces were probably the earliest deities worshiped by primitive peoples. The sun, moon, stars, fire, and lightning were objects of worship; for man could not explain them, and they seemed more powerful than he.

The various gods of MESOPOTAMIA, EGYPT, and CANAAN were known to the Israelites. BABYLON exercised greater formative influence upon Hebrew religion than either Egypt or Canaan. Even the father of ABRAHAM worshiped other gods (Josh. 24:2). Abraham must have been acquainted with the cult of the moon-god Sin. His contemporaries built impressive TEMPLES and ZIGGURATS in honor of the moon-god. It is not inconceivable that Abraham himself was a worshiper of the Babylonian deities before God called him to leave his home and land. His willingness to sacrifice his son ISAAC gives evidence that human sacrifice to the gods was not unknown to the patriarch. The ancient Sumerians (see SUMER) believed that the universe was directed by a pantheon of gods, the chief ones being An, Ki, Enlil, and Enki, who controlled, respectively, heaven, earth, air, and water. The Mesopotamian pantheon was composed of more than 1,500 gods, some of the better known ones being ISHTAR, MARDUK, Shamash, and Sin. The fertility gods were especially honored. Ishtar, goddess of love, descended to the underworld to seek her husband TAMMUZ. Nabu (NEBO) was the patron of science and learning. NERGAL was the god of war and hunting.

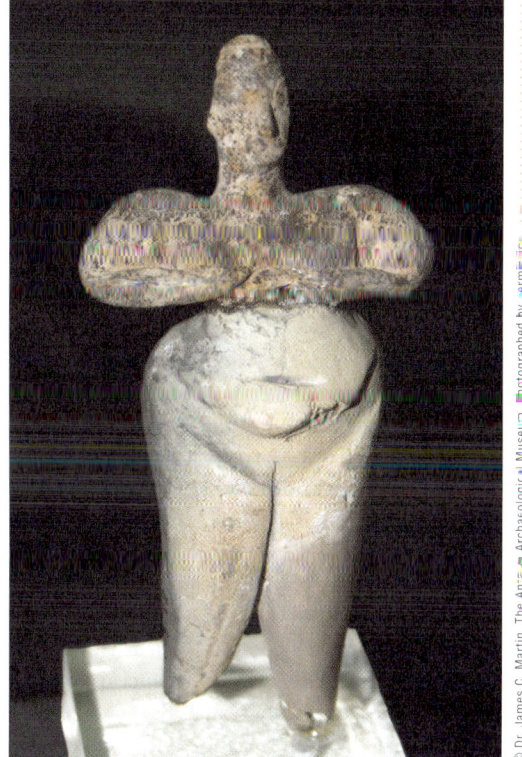

This very ancient idol (found in Atlaya, Turkey) is dated to c. 5200 B.C. or even earlier.

Ancient Egyptian religion was polytheistic and complex. Though the chief gods were represented in human form, most of the numerous deities were depicted in animal form, such as the crocodile god Sobek and Anubis with the head of a jackal. There were cosmic deities, such as RE, the sun-god. OSIRIS (the patron of agriculture) and his wife Isis (counterpart of Astarte) were associated with regeneration. There were triads of gods such as Osiris, Isis, and their son Horus. Hieroglyphic inscriptions on obelisks on the tombs give the impression that the Egyptians had thousands of deities. Every aspect of nature, animate and inanimate, was thought to be inhabited by a deity. There was even a merger of gods, such as Amun with Re (see AMON #4). The ruler himself was considered to be the incarnation of a god; each one while living assumed the name Horus, the deity who avenged the death of Osiris.

Of particular interest for biblical studies are the gods of Canaan because of the syncretism of Israelite religion with the Canaanite FERTILITY CULTS. Such cults were also common to Mesopotamia and Egypt, but they exerted their strongest influence on the Israelites in Canaan. The chief Canaanite deities were EL, the creator of the earth and controller of storms, and BAAL (both symbolized by the bull as indicative of their procreative powers), and the fertility goddess Astarte (biblical ASHTORETH). She was immensely popular at the temples, and PROSTITUTION was a legalized part of the cult. The consort of El was ASHERAH, the mother goddess (the symbol of fruitfulness). There were many other Canaanite deities, such as Melkart, Koshar (the Vulcan of the Canaanites), and Hauron, the shepherd god. Mot was the god of death and sterility.

The Canaanite religion was particularly dangerous for the Israelites because of its appeal to carnal human desires, especially sexual. Baal and Astarte were associated with fornication and drunkenness. Sacred prostitution and various orgiastic rites characterized the religion. Amos charged that Hebrew participation in these rites profaned the name of God (Amos 2:7). Canaanite religion was a debasing form of paganism. MOSES warned the Israelites against the dangers of Canaanite influence and instructed them to destroy all the inhabitants of the land so that the nation would not be tempted to follow their gods (Deut. 7:1–5; 20:18). They were also instructed to destroy the high places, the wooden asherim, pillars, and graven images (12:2–3), which were associated with the sexual aspects of Canaanite worship practices.

II. Idolatry in the OT. The worship of idols was an abomination to the protagonists of Hebrew monotheism. They condemned as "idolatry" the tendency of the people to adopt the local Canaanite cults. The OT emphasizes that the worst sin was to acknowledge other gods besides Yahweh and to make an image or likeness of the deity. The ban on images was a new concept in the ANE, even producing a great struggle among the people of Israel, who continually returned to image worship.

The horror and scorn of the biblical writers toward idolatry may be gauged by the variety of terms used for "idol" or "image": *ʾāwen* H224, "trouble, sorrow" (Isa. 66:3); *ʾêmâ* H399, "terror" (Jer. 50:38; cf. NRSV); *ʾĕlîl* H496, "worthlessness" (Lev. 19:4); *gillûlîm* H1658, "rolled about, [shapeless] blocks" (Ezek. 20:31); *mipleṣet* H5145, "horrible thing, a cause of trembling" (1 Ki. 15:13); *ʿāṣāb* H6773, "shape" or "distress" (1 Sam. 31:9). All these words express the lifelessness and absence of true deity in an idol or image.

A recurring theme in the OT is the ridicule heaped upon those who would make an idol with their hands and then bow down and worship it (Isa. 44:9–20; Jer. 10:2–10; Hos. 8:5; 13:2; Hab. 2:18). The OT also emphasizes the powerlessness of idols and the gods of the Canaanites. GIDEON destroyed the altar of Baal, and his father mocked the irate worshipers (Jdg. 6:25–32). The image of DAGON fell on the ground before the ARK OF THE COVENANT (1 Sam. 5). ELIJAH mocked the priests of Baal in the contest on Mount Carmel (1 Ki. 18:27).

The extent to which the Hebrews participated in the grosser religious practices in pre-Mosaic times can only be a matter of conjecture. It is a safe assumption that the influence of other religions upon them was great. The prohibition against idolatry found expression in the TEN COMMANDMENTS (Exod. 20:4), which forbade the representation of God in any form. The commandment was not an attack on artists and sculptors, but on idolaters. To worship idols was to go a-whoring after other gods; therefore idolatry was described as adultery (Hos. 1:2; 9:1, 10; Ezek. 16; 23).

There was no period in Hebrew history when the people were free from the attraction of idols. RACHEL took the TERAPHIM (household gods represented by clay figurines) with her when JACOB and his family fled from LABAN (Gen. 31:34). The Israelites worshiped the idols of Egypt during their sojourn there and did not give them up even when led by Moses out of bondage (Josh. 24:14; Ezek. 20:8–18; 23:3–8). They made a molten calf to worship when Moses tarried on the mountain receiving the law from God (Exod. 32, see CALF, GOLDEN). God would have destroyed them for their idolatries had not Moses interceded for them. Even

Figurine of the Canaanite god El, made of bronze with gold leaf (from Megiddo, 1400–1200 B.C.).

as they neared the end of the wilderness wanderings, they joined with the people of MOAB in the worship of Baal (Num. 25:1–3; 31:16). Just before they entered the Promised Land, Moses warned them not to make any images or to worship other gods (Deut. 4:15–19; 7:1–5), or they would perish (8:19). The one who would entice his fellow Hebrew to worship other gods was to be put to death by stoning (13:6–16; 17:2–5).

The Israelites did not obey the injunctions given by Moses to destroy the Canaanites completely, but instead settled down among them. They continued to worship the foreign gods they had brought from Egypt (Josh. 24:14–15, 23) and also were enticed by the gods of the Canaanites after they settled in the land (Jdg. 2:11–13; 6:25–32; see also chs. 17–18). The EPHOD made by GIDEON became an object of worship (8:24–27). The exact nature of the ephod in early Israel is not certain. It was apparently a garment (1 Sam. 2:18) worn or carried by the priest (14:3) and used in divination (30:7–18).

SAMUEL the prophet said the subjugation of the people to the PHILISTINES was due to their idolatry and promised that they would be delivered if they would put away their false gods (1 Sam. 7:3–4). The teraphim placed in DAVID's bed by MICHAL when he fled from SAUL (19:11–17) has been interpreted as a household idol. However, W. F. Albright, basing his argument on the texts from UGARIT, has identified it as a bundle of rags arranged to look like a sleeping man. The teraphim were used in divination (Ezek. 21:21; Zech. 10:2), though such use was condemned (1 Sam. 15:23). The OT says little about idolatry during the reign of David, but it must have flourished during the reign of SOLOMON, for he permitted his foreign wives to worship their gods and was, in his old age, enticed to worship them also, including the abominable CHEMOSH and MOLECH (1 Ki. 11:1–8). His sin prompted God to divide the kingdom upon his death (11:9–13).

JEROBOAM, who became ruler of the N tribes that seceded upon the death of Solomon, placed golden calves at DAN (PLACE) and BETHEL so that the people would not desire to return to Jerusalem to worship (1 Ki. 12:25–33). These calves were either images of the Canaanite deities or pedestals symbolizing their presence, as the ark of the covenant was the symbol of the presence of God. This act brought God's wrath upon the house of Jeroboam (14:7–11). Matters were no better in Judah at this time. Idolatrous practices flourished there also during the reign of REHOBOAM, Solomon's son (14:21–24). During the reign of Solomon's grandson ASA, an "abominable image" for Asherah was destroyed, which had been set up by the queen mother MAACAH (15:13 NRSV; NIV, "repulsive Asherah pole").

A hundred years later, following a succession of kings who "walked in the way of Jeroboam," AHAB came to the throne of Israel and established the cult of Baal of SIDON at SAMARIA under the influence of his Phoenician wife JEZEBEL (1 Ki. 16:32). ELIJAH denounced Ahab and challenged the power of Baal (ch. 18). The principal struggle in which Elijah and

Elisha were engaged was to see whether God or Baal would be acknowledged as God. Jehu, who succeeded the Omride dynasty, made an attempt to uproot Baalism by the wholesale destruction of the temple, priests, and worshipers of Baal (2 Ki. 10:18–28) but was not wholly successful in stamping out idolatry, for "he did not turn away from the sins of Jeroboam" (10:29–31).

Beginning with the prophets of the 8th cent. B.C., there was an emphatic rejection of any material representations of God. Amos protested against the Canaanite high places and the images of their gods (Amos 5:26). Hosea denounced the stubborn harlotry of Israel (Hos. 2:16, 17; 8:4–6; 13:2). Isaiah, looking upon the appalling apostasy of the age, grieved over the golden images, the work of men's own hands, and the sins of the new-moon festivals (Isa. 2:8; 40:18–20; 41:6–7; 44:9–20; 45:20; 46:1–2, 5–7). The Bible contains a stinging indictment against Israel as justification for God's destruction of the northern kingdom in 722 B.C. (1 Ki. 17:7–18). Among the charges made were that they built high places and pillars, served idols, burned their children as offerings, and refused to obey the commandments of God.

Conditions were not much better in Judah, as evidenced by the idolatrous practices when Hezekiah came to the throne. The people were worshiping the bronze serpent that Moses had made, so Hezekiah destroyed it (2 Ki. 18:4; see Nehushtan). All the great reforms of Hezekiah were undone, however, by his successor Manasseh, whose idolatries are among the most shocking in all the OT (21:1–18). He revived Baal worship and built altars to astrological gods within the very temple at Jerusalem. He offered his own son as a human sacrifice. An interesting reference to human sacrifice is found in Ps. 106, where the pagan influences upon Israel are denounced.

In the period before the end of the kingdom of Judah, the prophets struggled against the widespread idolatry that filled the land. Zephaniah warned against the worship of astral deities, against Milcom, and against pagan superstitions (Zeph. 1:2–9). Habakkuk pronounced woes upon those who would worship a god made with their own hands (Hab. 2:18–19). No prophet fought the apostasies of Judah more vehemently than Jeremiah. He inveighed against the sacrifices to Molech, the worship of the Baalim, the offering of cakes to the Queen of Heaven, and against the gods that were as many as their cities (Jer. 2:23–25; 8:1–2; 10:2–10; 11:13; 23:13–14). Even the sweeping reforms of Josiah, which included the destruction of a sanctuary of Chemosh and Milcom built by Solomon (1 Ki. 11:7; 2 Ki. 23:13), could not save the nation that was so polluted by her idolatries (23:4–20), for the people immediately returned to their old ways under his successors. Ezekiel revealed that worship of animals, of the vegetation god Tammuz, and of the sun were taking place within the temple area itself in the final years before the destruction of Jerusalem (Ezek. 8:7–16). He also denounced the sacrifice of children to the gods (16:20–21).

During the period of the Babylonian captivity, Nebuchadnezzar built a great image and demanded that the people worship it. The refusal of Daniel's three friends to worship the image would have cost them their lives except for divine intervention (Dan. 3). In the postexilic period, Malachi, Ezra, and Nehemiah violently opposed marriages with foreigners that were taking place. They undoubtedly remembered that such alliances had been denounced in the past and had contributed to the introduction of idolatrous practices that eventually caused God to destroy the nation.

In the 2nd cent. B.C., the Seleucid rulers of Palestine attempted to revive the worship of local fertility gods and the Hellenistic deities. Antiochus IV Epiphanes (175–164 B.C.) issued an edict establishing one religion for all his subjects. He erected an altar to Zeus over the altar of burnt offering in the temple at Jerusalem. He required the Jews to take part in the heathen festivals or be slain. His oppressive measures brought about the Maccabean revolt that resulted in a brief period of religious and political freedom for the Jews (see Maccabee).

III. Idolatry in the NT. Idolatry is not mentioned as frequently in the NT as in the OT. The Christian church arose in a world given to idolatry but also out of a Jewish background that maintained a stubborn protest against image worship. Paul gives a picture of the widespread idolatry of the pagan world (Rom. 1:18–25). He observed that idol worship was so multifarious that the Athenians had even erected an altar to an UNKNOWN GOD (Acts 17:23). He never intimated an interpretation widely held today that idolatry represents a primitive phase of religious development. Paul considered it a perversion, a turning away from the knowledge of the true God. Paul called idolatry a work of the flesh (Gal. 5:20) and warned Christians to shun the worship of idols (1 Cor. 10:14).

Church members who lived in heathen communities had to be careful not to compromise themselves with idolatry (Acts 15:29). One problem for early Christians was the eating of meat that had been offered to idols. Paul said that idols had no real existence, so eating meat offered to them would not be wrong, but he added that a Christian should do nothing that would cause a weaker brother to stumble (1 Cor. 8:1–13; 10:14–33; cf. W. L. Willis, *Idol Meat in Corinth* [1985]; A. T. Cheung, *Idol Food in Corinth: Jewish Background and Pauline Legacy* [1999]; J. Fotopoulos, *Food Offered to Idols in Roman Corinth: A Social-Rhetorical Reconsideration of 1 Cor. 8:1–11:1* [2003]; see also CORINTHIANS, FIRST EPISTLE TO THE). Paul warned that one may abhor idols but commit other sins (Rom. 2:22). He emphatically denied that idols have any real existence (1 Cor. 12:2; Gal. 4:8; 1 Thess. 1:9). His protest against idolatry was so effective in EPHESUS that it hurt the business of those engaged in making silver images of Diana (Acts 19:23–27; see ARTEMIS). Idolatry is used figuratively by Paul to include covetousness (Eph. 5:5; Col. 3:5; see COVET; GREED) and GLUTTONY (Phil. 3:19).

MYSTERY RELIGIONS, where the individual or the community sought to appropriate the experiences of dying or rising nature gods such as Osiris, were widespread in the Greco-Roman world of Paul's time. EMPEROR WORSHIP was an accepted practice. HEROD the Great established the cult of AUGUSTUS at Samaria. CALIGULA (A.D. 37–41) ordered his image to be set up in the temple at Jerusalem. Christians suffered severely at the hands of DOMITIAN (A.D. 81–96), who insisted that he be worshiped as "God" and "Lord." The book of Revelation appeared at such a time with its warning against the danger of idolatry (Rev. 2:14, 20). It affirms the powerlessness of idols (9:20), warns against worshiping an image of the beast (13:14–15; 14:9–11), and promises the exaltation of those who refuse to worship the beast or its image (20:4).

IV. Why idolatry is condemned in the Bible.

Idolatry is vigorously condemned both in the OT and NT because it degrades both God and human beings. It denies the existence of the true God who created the world and mankind, and whose GLORY cannot be adequately captured in any tangible form. It is absurd that a person could carve an idol with his own hands and then be afraid of what he has made.

Some religions claim that an image is an aid to worship, though not an object of worship. The danger of such reasoning is that two people may have a different idea of what the image signifies. One person may look upon it as a representation and void of value or power in itself, but another may regard it as the abode of the god and fraught with power, and therefore he will worship the image. A visible representation of the deity tends to restrict people's concept of God, for they will base that concept, consciously or unconsciously, upon the image or picture. Finally, human beings become like that which they worship (Hos. 9:10). If their god is lifeless and cold, it can bring them no real hope or comfort. Only the true and living God can fulfill the hope of eternal life.

(See further J. Robertson, *The Early Religion of Israel* [1892], 1:187–268; A. C. Knudson, *The Religious Teaching of the Old Testament* [1918], 108–14; W. R. Smith, *The Religion of the Semites* [1927]; E. Bevan, *Holy Images* [1940]; R. Otto, *The Idea of the Holy*, 2nd ed. [1950]; O. J. Baab, *The Theology of the Old Testament* [1959], 84–113; T. C. Vriezen, *The Religion of Ancient Israel* [1963], 22–78; T. W. Overholt in *JTS* 16 [1965]: 1–12; H. Ringgren, *Israelite Religion* [1966]; J. Faur in *JQR* 69 [1978–79]: 1–15; J. H. Tigay, *You Shall Have No Other Gods before Me: Israelite Religion in the Light of Hebrew Inscriptions* [1986]; W. Brueggemann, *Israel's Praise: Doxology against Idolatry and Ideology* [1988]; M. Halbertal and A. Margalit, *Idolatry* [1992]; S. C. Barton, ed., *Idolatry: False Worship in the Bible, Early Judaism and Christianity* [2007].)

F. B. HUEY, JR.

idol makers. Craftsmen made idols of various materials—wood, stone, metal, and pottery. Besides this, there were miniature idols or amulets and scarabs made by jewelers and workers in steatite and semiprecious stones. Because of the value of the metal, idols made of silver or gold might be cast hollow. Those made of bronze or lead might be overlaid with silver or gold. There is, however, a bronze alloy that looks much like gold, and this was probably not overlaid with a precious metal. Silver and gold were sometimes beaten into thin plates and then fashioned into shape over wooden, stone, or metal idols (Isa. 30:22). Occasionally idols were decorated with chains and other jewelry (Isa. 40:19).

Small household gods, usually of Astarte (see ASHTORETH), were often made of POTTERY, either in a press mold or fashioned by hand. Small figurines of BAAL were common in SYRIA, but they were usually cast of a base metal and overlaid with gold foil. Isaiah provides a good description of the making of a wooden idol: "The carpenter measures with a line and makes an outline with a marker; he roughs it out with chisels and marks it with compasses. He shapes it in the form of man ..." (Isa. 44:13). The following verse mentions some trees used for idol making—the cedar, the holm, and the oak. It is known that each god had his particular sacred tree.

The most famous animal idols in the history of Israel were AARON's golden calf of SINAI (Exod. 32:2–4) and JEROBOAM's golden calves at BETHEL and DAN (PLACE) (1 Ki. 12:28–29; see CALF, GOLDEN). The idols that Ezekiel in vision saw portrayed on a wall of the TEMPLE could hardly have been real; the scene is undoubtedly symbolical (Ezek. 8:10). The NT has nothing to say about idol making. See IDOLATRY.   J. L. KELSO

Iduel id´yoo-uhl (Ἰδουηλος). One of the leaders sent by EZRA to IDDO in CASIPHIA, with an order to bring attendants for the house of God (1 Esd. 8:43; called ARIEL in Ezra 8:16).

Idumea id´yoo-mee´uh (Ἰδουμαία *G2628*, from Heb. אֱדוֹם *H121*). Also Idumaea. One of the regions from which crowds came to follow Jesus (Mk. 3:8). A Greco-Roman province carved out of southern Palestine after the Alexandrian conquest, Idumea was larger than the ancient EDOM. The new boundaries included the deserts of the NEGEV and the SHEPHELAH as well as the sites of LACHISH and HEBRON. Because its inhabitants had aided NEBUCHADNEZZAR in his conquest of the Jewish state, they are the subjects of some of the bitterest prophetic invective in the OT (Lam. 4:21; Ezek. 25:12; 35:3; Obad. 1–21; et al.). Edom was overthrown by the NABATEAN Arabs about 300 B.C.

View of Idumea (looking NW from the northern Negev to the southern Shephelah).

who made the red rock-hewn city of PETRA their capital. HEROD's grandfather was appointed governor of Idumea by Alexander Jannaeus after it was conquered by the Jews first under Judas MACCABEE in 165 B.C. and finally by John Hyrcanus in 126 B.C. (see HASMONEAN). Because of this subjection of his country, Herod considered himself a Jew. (See further A. Kasher, *Jews, Idumaeans, and Ancient Arabs* [1988].) W. WHITE, JR.

Iezer *i*-ee´zuhr (אִיעֶזֶר H404, "help," apparently short form of ABIEZER; gentilic אִיעֶזְרִי H405, Iezerite). Son of Gilead, a descendant of MANASSEH, and ancestor of the Iezerite clan (Num. 26:30, KJV, "Jeezer"). He is probably the same as Abiezer, the son of Gilead's sister (1 Chr. 7:18); if so, Gilead was considered his male progenitor for genealogical purposes.

Igal *i*´gal (יִגְאָל H3319, "[Yahweh] redeems"). **(1)** Son of Joseph and descendant of ISSACHAR; one of the twelve spies sent by MOSES to Canaan (Num. 13:7).

(2) Son of Nathan from ZOBAH and one of DAVID's mighty warriors (2 Sam. 23:36). The parallel list, which appears to have suffered textual corruption, reads "Joel the brother of Nathan" (1 Chr. 11:38; this reading is followed by the Lucianic recension of the SEPTUAGINT in both passages).

(3) Son of Shemaiah and descendant of David in the line of ZERUBBABEL (1 Chr. 3:22; KJV, "Igeal"). According to some scholars, the phrase "and the sons of Shemaiah" (NIV has simply "and his sons") should be omitted, in which case both Shemaiah and Igal were sons of Shecaniah. See HATTUSH #1. S. BARABAS

Igdaliah ig´duh-li´uh (יִגְדַּלְיָהוּ H3323, "Yahweh is great"). Father of a certain HANAN who is described as "the man of God" (although this epithet perhaps applies to Igdaliah), and whose "sons" (possibly a reference to a prophetic guild) occupied a chamber in the temple into which JEREMIAH brought the family of the Recabites (Jer. 35:4; see RECAB).

Igeal *i*´gee-uhl. KJV alternate form of IGAL (1 Chr. 3:22).

Ignatius, Epistles of ig-nay´shuhs (Ἰγνάτιος). Letters to several churches written by a Syrian bishop early in the 2nd cent., included among the APOSTOLIC FATHERS.

I. Number and integrity. Ignatius, bishop of ANTIOCH OF SYRIA, was arrested by Roman authorities during the reign of Emperor Trajan (A.D. 98-117) and taken by a military guard toward ROME (Euseb. *Hist.* 3.36.3). His only writings to be preserved are seven letters written on this trip, from two places where he stopped. Four letters were written from Smyrna, three of which were sent to the churches at Tralles, Magnesia on the Maeander, and Ephesus, cities that lay on an alternate route that Ignatius and his guards had not followed (thus these letters were in lieu of a personal visit for which probably they had hoped). The fourth letter from Smyrna was written to go ahead of Ignatius to the church at Rome, his destination. A little later, from TROAS, Ignatius wrote three more letters: one was to PHILADELPHIA, which he had passed through on the way to Smyrna; one to the church at Smyrna where he had recently stopped; and one to POLYCARP, the bishop in Smyrna.

These are the only genuine writings of Ignatius that are extant. There exists, however, a "long recension" that includes ten spurious letters; the genuine letters were also expanded by interpolation in both

Idumea.

Greek and Latin texts. This material appeared by the 6th cent. and may have originated as early as the late 4th cent. There is, in addition, what has been called a "short recension," really a condensed Syriac version that includes only the letters to the Ephesians, to the Romans, and to Polycarp. This confused textual picture was finally clarified in the last third of the 19th cent. through the research of T. Zahn (*Ignatius von Antiochien* [1873]), J. B. Lightfoot (*The Apostolic Fathers, Part II: S. Ignatius, S. Polycarp*, 2nd ed., 3 vols. [1889]), F. X. Funk (*Kirchengeschichtliche Abhandlungen und Untersuchungen*, 3 vols. [1897–1907]), and others, who established the authenticity of the seven letters (the so-called "middle recension," though some scholars prefer to use the term "short recension" for this group).

II. Date. EUSEBIUS in his *Chronicle* placed the death of Ignatius in the tenth year of Trajan (A.D. 107–108), but Eusebius's dates are not dependable here. It is impossible to be dogmatic concerning the exact year when the letters were written. The one to the Romans is dated August 24, according to the present system of reckoning, but the year is not given. Ignatius was called the second bishop of Antioch by ORIGEN (*Hom. VI in Luc.* §1) and Eusebius (*Eccl. Hist.* 3.22), whatever that might mean. It tends to support the suggestion of Lightfoot that Ignatius died a few years on one side or the other of A.D. 110, that is, during the reign of Trajan, rather than somewhat later under HADRIAN, as suggested by Adolf von Harnack. Theodor Zahn also favored the reign of Trajan. The best suggestion for the date is c. A.D. 115. (Some recent scholars, however, have argued for a date two or three decades later.)

III. Occasion and purpose. The three letters to the churches that he could not visit (the Trallians, the Magnesians, and the Ephesians) were to encourage them to continue on their Christian way, to recognize the authority of their officers, and to keep themselves from heresy. The aim was to "attain unto God." Jesus' death is the way to God. Ignatius was thankful for the representatives from these churches (including local bishops) who had come to Smyrna to bring greetings and to assist him. The letter to the Romans, written also from Smyrna, was to prepare the Romans for his coming and to urge them to do nothing to hinder his approaching martyrdom, but rather to rejoice in it as an end devoutly to be desired by a Christian. A phrase in this letter seems to imply that Ignatius had once been a slave (*Rom.* 4.3), but it may be read otherwise.

From Smyrna Ignatius proceeded to Troas, over one hundred miles to the N, by land or sea. Here he wrote his second and, so far as is known, last group of letters. He wrote with the aid of Burrhus, the Ephesian deacon, who had helped at Smyrna and continued with him to Troas. Probably Burrhus was acting as a secretary. The letter to the Philadelphians from Smyrna was written to a church he had visited shortly before on his journey, though doubtless the visit was brief. Apparently the church at Philadelphia was having trouble with strange or divisive doctrine. Ignatius suggested that Philadelphia greet Antioch by sending a deacon to bring them congratulations. There is an odd reference to the fact that some at Philadelphia had not treated Ignatius's companions with respect (*Phld.* 11.1).

There were two more letters from Troas, one to the church at Smyrna, which he had just left, and a personal one to its bishop, Polycarp. Ignatius had a high opinion of the church at Smyrna. He urged them to accept the leadership of their bishop in everything. DOCETISM was a pressing danger. The suggestion made to Philadelphia that a representative be sent to the church at Antioch in Syria was repeated to the Smyrneans. His great love and admiration for Polycarp shines through his letter to him. Ignatius stressed the importance of the unity of the church and its patient endurance in the service of Christ. The care of the individual was highly important. It is better for slaves to accept their lot than to seek freedom with the cost charged to the church treasury. All Christians should be suffering in some way. Freedom might simply release them to opportunities for sinning. Ignatius placed a high value on sexual abstinence, though it was not required.

IV. General character. Ignatius wrote in a vivid, compressed style. He was enthusiastic and confident of God. He used metaphors frequently and liked balanced sentences with reciprocal parts. Warmth, love, and concern gleam through his words. Eduard Norden regarded these letters "as the most exquisite part of the literary remains of this time" (see J. A. Kleist, *The Epistles of St. Clement of Rome and St. Ignatius of Antioch* [1946], 118).

Ignatius was concerned strongly with the message that Jesus Christ is God, God who has become man. He referred to Jesus as God at least twelve times. Jesus was born of a virgin, was baptized, suffered, and rose again. He was the Son of David and the Son of God. The reason for his suffering was "that we might be saved" (*Smyrn.* 2.1). The result is the potentiality of UNION WITH CHRIST. The prophets of the OT looked forward to Christ. Now one may "attain to" Christ. Believers are members of him and form the body of his CHURCH (see BODY OF CHRIST). The church is like a bride, the bride of Christ. The members who have faith do not sin (*Eph.* 14.2). When this is not true, repentance is possible (*Phld.* 8.1).

Two errors that greatly concerned Ignatius were the Judaizing heresy and Docetism. He warned the Magnesians against living according to Judaism and said, "it is monstrous to talk of Jesus Christ and to practice Judaism" (*Magn.* 8.3). The Philadelphians were also cautioned about Judaism. The members at Tralles and at Smyrna were asked to consider the evil results of Docetism. Christ was truly in the flesh. He rose in the flesh. To reject this is to deny him absolutely (*Smyrn.* 5.2).

One of the strongest emphases in Ignatius is on CHURCH GOVERNMENT. He was the earliest writer to reflect the existence of the monarchical episcopate. He not only reflected it but insisted upon the importance of such an organization. The BISHOP is like God or like Christ, the elders were compared to the apostles. See ELDER (NT). The DEACONS are the servants of the church, deacons of the mysteries of Jesus Christ. The elders were attuned to the bishop as the strings to a harp. Ignatius spoke as though there were a single bishop in each church and advocated that this should be universal ecclesiastical procedure.

(See further C. C. Richardson, *The Christianity of Ignatius of Antioch* [1935]; V. Corwin, *St. Ignatius and Christianity in Antioch* [1960]; R. M. Grant, *The Apostolic Fathers, Vol. 4: Ignatius of Antioch* [1966]; R. Joly, *Le dossier d'Ignace d'Antioche* [1979]; H. Paulsen, *Die Briefe des Ignatius von Antiochia und der Brief des Polykarp von Smyrna*, HNT 18, 2nd ed. [1985]; W. R. Schoedel, *Ignatius of Antioch: A Commentary on the Letters of Ignatius of Antioch*, Hermeneia [1985]; C. Trevett, *A Study of Ignatius of Antioch in Syria and Asia* [1992]; C. T. Brown, *The Gospel and Ignatius of Antioch* [2000]; P. Trebilco, *The Early Christians in Ephesus from Paul to Ignatius* [2004]; A. Brent, *Ignatius of Antioch* [2007].)

P. WOOLLEY

ignorance. In some instances, ignorance in biblical usage denotes merely an innocent lack of information (Acts 23:5; 2 Cor. 1:8). In its distinctively biblical meaning, it is a specifically religious rather than an intellectual concept. Ignorance is a quality, not of the academically unschooled, but of the sinner. It is a result of SIN and refers to the lack of the KNOWLEDGE of God. Thus ignorance no more indicates an intellectual state of poverty than WISDOM is a state of intellectual fullness. Ignorance is the lack of that religious knowledge which, possessed and practiced, is what the Bible calls wisdom. To know religious TRUTH is knowledge; to practice religious truth is wisdom, to know truth and not to practice it is FOLLY, the mark of the fool. Not to know religious truth and, consequently, to live in untruth, is ignorance.

Ignorance is a consequence of sin, for sin darkens the mind, depriving it of true knowledge of God and the self. Ignorance is, therefore, also a matrix of sin. People sin in ignorance because of ignorance. Thus PAUL says about the "princes of this world" who crucified Christ that they know not the wisdom of God, "for had they known it, they would not have crucified the Lord of glory (1 Cor. 2:8 KJV). Christians, non-Christians, and even the church itself, sin because of ignorance. Yet, since ignorance is the consequence of human sin, sins done in ignorance are sinful, and those who commit such sins are culpable.

Nonetheless, sins done in ignorance incur less guilt than sins done in full knowledge of their sinful character and which, accordingly, incur greater guilt. Thus PILATE's guilt for the CRUCIFIXION of Christ is less than that of the Jews (Jn. 19:11); but even the Jews were not fully conscious of the nature of their act, and Jesus, therefore, invoked their forgiveness, "Father, forgive them, for they do not know what they are doing" (Lk. 23:34). The same lesser guilt and greater forgiveability of sins done in ignorance appears in Paul's admission that he was a blasphemer and a persecutor of the church, and indeed the worst of sinners (1 Tim. 1:15) but that he obtained mercy because he acted "in ignorance and unbelief" (1:13 KJV). Paul spoke in a similar vein on Mars' Hill when he declared that God "overlooked" ("winked at") the "times of ignorance" during which men likened God to an idol made of stone and worshiped the idol (Acts 17:30). God in his MERCY acts with forbearance on sins done in ignorance by pagans today and in all centuries past; there is a mercy of God greater than all human sins. Hence Paul's prayer for Israel—who had a zeal that was not according to knowledge, for "they did not know the righteousness that comes from God and sought to establish their own" (Rom. 10:3)—is that "they may be saved" (10:1).

There is, however, a willful ignorance of God's truth. There is a knowledge of God given in the things that are made that pagans sinfully suppressed (Rom. 1:18), exchanged for a lie (v. 25), and were therefore without excuse (v. 20) and were accordingly punished (vv. 24–32). Yet even such sins of willful ignorance of the truth given in general REVELATION incur less culpability than sins of willful ignorance against the economy of special revelation; the former shall perish without law but the latter shall be judged by the law. Sins done either in ignorance, or willfully against the knowledge of God given to all men in the general revelation "that enlightens every man" (Jn. 1:9), can be overlooked by God and can also be followed by REPENTANCE and FORGIVENESS (which is more than being overlooked). That willful ignorance which is the consequence of a conscious rejection of the knowledge of the truth revealed in Christ and made known in the Gospel proclamation, God will not overlook but subject to a divine judgment and fire that will devour the enemies of Christ (Heb. 10:26–27). In self-conscious and knowledgeable rejection of Christ in his disclosure in gospel proclamation, the sin of willful ignorance excludes a person from that mercy of God that can overlook all other sins of ignorance.　　　　　　　　　　　J. Daane

Iim i′im (עִיִּים H6517, "[place of] ruins"; cf. Ai).
(1) One of the southernmost cities of the tribe of Judah, located in the Negev, toward the boundary of Edom (Josh. 15:29). Although not included in the parallel passages (Josh. 19:3; 1 Chr. 4:29), Iim, like other towns in those lists, may have been allotted to Simeon. Its location is unknown.

(2) KJV and TNIV form of Iyim.

Ije-abarim i′-juh-ab′uh-rim. KJV form of Iye Abarim.

Ijon i′jon (עִיּוֹן H6510, possibly "heap"). A town in N Israel, apparently within the tribal territory of Naphtali in the Huleh Valley, mentioned as having been conquered by Ben-Hadad of Damascus (1 Ki. 15:20; 2 Chr. 16:4) and later by Tiglath-Pileser of Assyria (2 Ki. 15:29). The Huleh Valley is bounded on the W by the Litani River and on the E by Mount Hermon. Both Amen-hotep II and Ramses II took this route on their campaigns as they headed up to the Orontes River, while northern invaders used it to enter Palestine.

The name possibly appears on the 19th-cent. Execration Texts as one of the sixty-four place names given on small figurines (ʿynw, no. E. 18; so G. Posener, *Princes et pays d'Asie et de Nubie* [1940], 74, but see S. Aḥituv, *Canaanite Toponyms in Ancient Egyptian Documents* [1984], 120). Thutmose III includes the town in his roster of 119 Canaanite towns (ʿyn, no. 95). Tiglath-Pileser III does not list Ijon, but he does mention the city to the S in a broken passage of the Nimrud tablet. The site is probably to be identified with modern Tell ed-Dibbin in Lebanon (near Merj ʿAyyun, which seems to preserve the ancient name), 9 mi. N of Abel Beth Maacah. Others have doubted this identification because surface explorations have not yielded any Iron II (900–600 B.C.) pottery, as the narrative in Kings requires. (See further Y. Aharoni, *The Land of the Bible: A Historical Geography*, rev. ed. [1979], 32, 53, 114, 146, 163 et al.) See also Dan Jaan.　　W. C. Kaiser

Ikkesh ik′ish (עִקֵּשׁ H6837, "crooked" [perhaps referring to a physical defect]). A man from Tekoa; his son Ira was one of David's thirty mighty warriors and the commander of a division of 24,000 men (2 Sam. 23:26; 1 Chr. 11:28; 27:9).

Ilai i′li (עִילַי H6519). An AHOHITE, one of DAVID's thirty mighty warriors (1 Chr. 11:29; called ZALMON in 2 Sam. 23:28).

Iliadun i-li′uh-duhn (Ἰλιαδουν). Ancestor of some Levites who labored on the rebuilding of the TEMPLE (1 Esd. 5:58; KJV "Eliadun"). His name does not occur in the parallel passages (Ezra 3:9).

Illyricum i-lihr′i-kuhm (Ἰλλυρικόν G2665). A Roman PROVINCE in the western portion of the Balkan peninsula N of GREECE. Now principally occupied by Yugoslavia and Albania, it was bounded in antiquity by the Adriatic, the Eastern Alps, the Danube, the Shar-Dagh and the Ceraunian mountains. According to Strabo (*Geogr.* 7.317), the seacoast boasted of good harbors and the coastal plains were sunny and fertile, but the interior was mountainous and cold. The Greeks were first attracted to the region because of the mines, but the ferocious and piratical nature of the people prevented extensive colonization.

In the 2nd millennium B.C., it was occupied by Indo-European speaking people. The Greeks first colonized it in the 6th cent. B.C. The Macedonian kings warred against the tribes of Illyricum in the 4th cent., but it was not until the 3rd cent. that the kingdom of Scodra was established. Because of attacks on the Greek colonies and acts of piracy against Greek and Roman shipping, the Romans fought two wars (229–228 and 219 B.C.) against the Illyrians led by Queen Teuta. After the defeat of Genthius in 167 it was divided into three parts and connected alternately with the administration of Italy, Macedonia, and Cisalpine Gaul. CAESAR was proconsul there in 59. Octavian (see AUGUSTUS) subdued a number of the tribes in 35–33. In 27 he made it a senatorial province, Illyricum became an imperial province in 11 B.C. because of outbreaks of violence among the Pannonii. At that time the province was extended to the Danube. The last revolt was put down in three years of fighting by TIBERIUS in A.D. 9 and it became a settled part of the empire.

Two references are made to Illyricum in the NT. In a somewhat obscure statement PAUL remarked that "from Jerusalem all the way around to Illyricum, I have fully proclaimed the gospel of Christ" (Rom. 15:19). It is not clear whether Paul meant that Illyricum was the western boundary of the Eastern world and that he preached up to it, or that he actually preached and established churches there. The phrase "in these regions" (v. 23), describing to the extent of Paul's preaching, would suggest an area larger than MACEDONIA and probably refers also to Illyricum. Furthermore, the remark in his second letter to TIMOTHY (2 Tim. 4:10) intimates that the gospel was being preached there. It is well within the realm of possibility for Paul to have gone to Illyricum. The VIA EGNATIA, which ran from the Hellespont to Dyrrhachium, a seaport on the Adriatic, made the southern portion of Illyricum readily accessible to him on the third missionary journey. (See S. Casson, *Macedonia, Thrace and Illyria* [1926], passim; Pauly-Wissowa, *Real-Encyclopädie der classischen Altertumswissenschaft* IX/1 [1914], cols. 1085–88 s.v. "Illyricum," and supplement V [1931], cols. 311–45 s.v. "Illyrioi"; C. E. B. Cranfield, *A Critical and Exegetical Commentary on the Epistle to the Romans*, ICC, 2 vols. [1975–79], 2:761–62.) A. RUPPRECHT

image. See IDOLATRY.

image of God. A phrase used three times in Scripture (Gen. 1:27; 9:6; 2 Cor. 4:4), pointing to a basic theological concept.

I. OT background. Primary evidence for the "image of God" is found in Genesis with some

Illyricum.

poetic support in Ps. 8. The basic description of man's CREATION is as follows. "Then God said, 'Let us make man in our image, in our likeness, and let them rule. ...' So God created man in his own image, / in the image of God he created him; / male and female he created them" (Gen. 1:26–27). Other passages use "likeness" and "image" where the likeness of man to God and the image of ADAM in SETH are brought together in the same treatment (5:1–3); and the special value and dignity of human beings as the image of God are emphasized elsewhere (9:6). In poetic form, the psalmist writes: "You made him a little lower than the heavenly beings [or than God] / and crowned him with glory and honor. / You made him ruler over the works of your hands; / you put everything under his feet" (Ps. 8:5–6).

Linguistic studies bring out no sharp distinction between the two nouns, "image" (Heb. *ṣelem* H7512) and "likeness" (*dĕmût* H1952). Undoubtedly the writer wished to make some distinction, or increase the impact, or further define the first term by adding the second. The word *ṣelem* occurs seventeen times in the OT; in addition to the five occurrences in the Genesis passages, ten of the remaining usages are quite concrete and may be translated "statue," "model," or "picture" (in the remaining two passages, the sense "shadow" or "phantom" is more appropriate, Ps. 39:6; 73:20). The general use of the word, therefore, seems to demand the idea of "image" in some concrete sense, and prevalent scholarship always calls for this as the first interpretation.

The second term, *dĕmût*, "likeness," appears to be a more abstract notion. The author may be attempting to express a very difficult idea, wanting to make clear that human beings are in some way the concrete reflection of God, but at the same time seeking to spiritualize this idea toward abstraction. However, James Barr (in *BJRL* 51 [1968–69]: 14–15) has argued that the second term is simply "added in order to define and limit" the somewhat ambiguous meaning of the first: thus the meaning intended by *ṣelem* is that which overlaps with the notion of "similarity."

It must be borne in mind that the OT writers, being Semitic, leaned heavily on concrete terms and spoke about God in an anthropomorphic way to make themselves clear at all to a people unfamiliar with philosophic abstractions. The use of "likeness" in addition to "image" is a solution insofar as a Hebrew may deal in abstractions at all. It must be pointed out also that in Hebrew thought, the total personality is not treated as a BODY over against a SPIRIT, but as an "inspirited-by-the-breath-of-God" kind of a body. It is not a dichotomy of FLESH and spirit, but the total personality, which is treated in modern times as a gestalt. The representation that the man and the woman were made "in the image of God" might mean superficially that they look like God, but to the writer it meant much more. It meant likeness in the inner person as it is embodied in a physical manifestation—powers of thought, of communication, of transcendence, creativity, a sense of humor (which is a kind of transcendence), powers of abstraction, and what are generally put together in personality, that is, self-consciousness and self-determination. Just as art, architecture, poetry, and music may set forth the person of the artist, so the physical human body may set forth to some extent the nature of the Creator.

Interpretations of the image of God, therefore, may swing between two extremes: (a) the absolute, literal, physical resemblance, which seems to be supported in Gen. 5:1–3, where the image of God is clearly paralleled with SETH as the image of his father, Adam; (b) and over against this, the necessary spiritual interpretation supported by Jesus' classic definition of God, namely, that "God is spirit" (Jn. 4:24). In addition, the OT seems to support the idea that no one ever really looks on God. There is the necessity of a sacramental interpretation, where a sacrament is best defined as "the physical sign of a spiritual reality." (See further *NIDOTTE*, 4:643–48.)

II. The NT approach. The OT view of the image of God moves into the NT with similar vocabulary and with the same problems of interpretation, but also with what appears to be a very radical shift in emphasis. PAUL speaks of "the image and glory of God" (1 Cor. 11:7), and the word for image uniformly used is *eikōn* G1635 (the LXX rendering of *ṣelem*). The NT also speaks of "God's likeness" (e.g., Jas. 3:9), using the word *homoiōsis* G3932 (the LXX rendering of *dĕmût*).

There is no question that *eikōn* refers to perfect reflection. In the NT, however, the focus is no longer on human beings as the image of God but on Christ, who is that perfect reflection or perfect correspondence; Christ is the prototype of essential man perfectly reflecting God. "The Son is the radiance of God's glory and the exact representation of his being" (Heb. 1:3). To whatever extent "image" in the OT may be associated with the meaning "shadow," there is no question that reality has now come to take the place of shadow. In Christ there is the true man, and there is no longer the question of a fallen human being. "The Word became flesh and made his dwelling among us" (Jn. 1:14). To see Christ is to see the Father (12:45; 14:9), and what the NT emphasizes is that human beings, whatever their condition may have become after the FALL, may now be a "new creation in Christ," a new person. "We shall be like him" (1 Jn. 3:2).

The intercessory prayer of Jesus has in it the amazing possibility of UNION WITH CHRIST in such fashion that believers are caught up into the very life and nature of God. Jesus prays "that all of them may be one, Father, just as you are in me and I am in you" (Jn. 17:21). We are to be "conformed to the image of his [God's] son" (Rom. 8:29 NRSV, NIV, "likeness"). Followers of Christ are directed to "put on the new self, created to be like God" (Eph. 4:24). Paul seems to bypass the whole nest of problems growing out of creation in the image of God to emphasize Christ as the real "Image of the invisible God" (Col. 1:15). He thinks of the first Adam as physical. He was "a living being," but the last Adam [Christ] is "a life-giving spirit. The spiritual did not come first, but the natural, and after that the spiritual.... Just as we have borne the likeness [*eikōn*] of the earthly man, so shall we bear the likeness of the man from heaven" (1 Cor. 15:45–49).

III. Persistent questions. Continued study on the image of God keeps raising the same questions, which at least to date have no final answers. The first question is the nature of the image itself; the second question is some understanding of what was lost of the image of God in the fall; and the third question has to do with what is restored or recreated when a person is saved.

Both Roman Catholic and Protestant theologies, with some exceptions, hold that the idea of image in the first Adam has to do with spiritual qualities and powers. Roman Catholics hold that man had a *similitudo Dei* that was destroyed by original SIN and which can be restored only by BAPTISM. Other qualities were obscured but not lost in

Paul spoke of "the glory of Christ, who is the image of God" (2 Cor. 4:4). This representation of the risen Jesus speaking to the disciples (with the Latin text of Jn. 20:23a) is found at the Church of the Annunciation in Nazareth.

the fall. Protestants have traditionally been in general agreement with this understanding, although they express it somewhat differently. Adam was by nature endowed with original RIGHTEOUSNESS. He had a moral likeness to God; he possessed HOLINESS, although he was in no sense equal to God, nor need one argue that he had attained to the fullness of his own potential. At least the slant and direction of his life were toward God. What he lost in the fall was original righteousness, and thenceforth the slant of his life was affected by sin, that is, sin at the origin of every act. But there are elements that he did not lose—elements having to do with his image of God as a person or a personality—traits such as self-consciousness, self-determination, superiority over nature, creativity, and the like.

It must be pointed out, however, that after the fall these powers were impaired and could not be used together harmoniously. The restoration (a process) of these human powers plus original righteousness awaits the new creation, the new birth, the indwelling of Christ, so that a Christian may say with Paul, "I no longer live, but Christ lives in me" (Gal. 2:20). The hope of the Christian faith is the full attainment of that "new self ... in the image of its Creator" (Col. 3:10).

IV. Modern discussions. In Protestant theology, primarily in the Barthian tradition, the image of God has been a live issue. There is a clear recognition throughout of the terrible and radically disintegrating effect of the fall. Emil Brunner (*Natur und Gnade* [1934]) argues somewhat after the manner of Roman Catholic doctrine that there was a "formal" image, that which constituted man as man, which could not be destroyed without destroying mankind. The remains of this "formal" image are necessary for any point of contact for the grace of God. Only what Brunner calls the "material" image has been lost.

Karl Barth (*Nein!* [1934]) rejected the "formal" image, held that man was utterly corrupted by sin and thus quite incapable of discovering any kind of truth about God or his own condition. Barth constantly demanded the "break-in" of God himself in a new creative way. Both Barth and Brunner engaged in a running fight for many years over the possibilities of natural theology, natural REVELATION, and the salvability of man. In general, however, Protestants still hold to Calvin's view that there is a natural revelation, or natural theology, but also that apart from the effectual work of the HOLY SPIRIT through the special revelation of Scripture, we cannot see and grasp this knowledge in any saving way.

Another turn in the modern discussion on the image of God is generally related to the writings of Emil Brunner. In brief, it is a shift of emphasis in the use of the term by which one is not to think of the term "image of God" as a noun. It is not that a man *has* the "image" of God, but that a man "images" God. This particular approach is characteristically Christian, although it has no basis in the straightforward use of the nouns in the OT. It is more helpful as an interpretation or as an illustration than as an exegesis. Emphasis is laid at the outset on the perfect OBEDIENCE OF CHRIST. "My food ... is to do the will of him who sent me" (Jn. 4:34). Whereas the first Adam fell in disobedience, Jesus brought "Paradise Regained" when he, under the awful pressure of temptation, continued to obey absolutely. Followers of Christ are not so concerned therefore with the "image" of God as they are with "imaging" God, by obeying him. It is clear how this kind of thinking lends itself to an existential decision, with its emphasis on action rather than on being.

(See further F. Turretin, *Opera: De Hominus Creatione* [1847]; C. Hodge, *Systematic Theology*, 3 vols. [1871–73], 2:42–116; W. G. T. Shedd, *Dogmatic Theology*, 3 vols. in 4 [1889], 2:4–114; A. M. Fairbairn, *The Philosophy of the Christian Religion* [1902]; A. B. Davidson, *The Theology of the Old Testament* [1904]; A. H. Strong, *Systematic Theology* [1907], 514–32; H. Wheeler Robinson, *The Christian Doctrine of Man* [1911], 4–150; G. C. Berkouwer, *Man: The Image of God* [1962]; A. A. Hoekema, *Created in God's Image* [1986]; P. E. Hughes, *The True Image: The Origin and Destiny of Man in Christ* [1989]; W. Grudem, *Systematic Theology: An Introduction to Christian Doctrine* [1994], 442–50; T. Smail, *Like Father, Like Son: The Trinity Imaged in Our Humanity* [2006]; *ABD*, 3:389–91.) A. H. LEITCH

image of Nebuchadnezzar. See NEBUCHADNEZZAR, IMAGE OF.

imagery. This English word is used once by the KJV to render Hebrew *maśkît* H5381, "image" (Ezek. 8:12; NIV, "idol"). In a vision of the temple, EZEKIEL broke through a hole in the wall, entered a door, and saw pictures of all kinds of animals represented on the walls of the rooms to which he had gained entrance. The seventy elders of Israel were in front of these pictures, burning incense and worshiping the images. The meaning of the prophet's vision is to be found in the practices of the people of his day and the religious condition of Israel. The secret chamber into which he had gained entrance represented the secret IDOLATRY of the people. The seventy elders represented the whole of the nation, revealing how widespread the infection of idolatry was. The pictures on the walls represented some form of animal worship that revealed how very degraded the worship of Israel had become. The pictures are thought to have been of reptiles, suggesting either an Egyptian or Babylonian origin of the cult, although other interpreters have proposed that they represent the hanging on of animistic religion that was indigenous to the area—a totemistic religion that has somehow managed to survive through the centuries. In all likelihood it was a general reference to the lowest form of idolatrous worship, designed to reveal the very low level to which the people had sunk, without any specific reference to a particular cult.

H. L. DRUMWRIGHT, JR.

imagine. This English verb, in its earlier meaning "to think," is used with some frequency by the KJV (Gen. 11:6 et al.). In modern versions it is used occasionally to render, for example, Hebrew *ḥāšab* H3108 (Ps. 41:7) and Greek *noeō* G3783 (Eph. 3:20).

Imalkue i-mal´kyoo-ee (Ιμαλκουε, possibly corresponding to the Heb. name JAMLECH). KJV Simalcue. An "Arabian who brought up Antiochus, the son of Alexander" (Jos. *Ant.* 13.5.1 §131). See ALEXANDER #2. This wording seems to be taken from 1 Macc. 11:39 by JOSEPHUS, though Josephus calls him "Malchus" (but cf. the more usual transcription of the same name as *Iamblichos, Ant.* 14.8.1 §129). TRYPHO, one of the commanders of the SELEUCID army, went to Imalkue to tell him of the soldiers' ill will toward DEMETRIUS and urged him to allow Alexander's son to be proclaimed king as ANTIOCHUS VI. At first, Imalkue opposed this plot to overthrow Demetrius, but being convinced by Trypho's evidence, the young child Antiochus was crowned (1 Macc. 11:54). Antiochus gathered around him "all the men of war, whom Demetrius had put away and they fought against Demetrius, who turned his back and fled" (11:55 KJV). At the same time Antiochus confirmed the high priesthood of Jonathan and made him one of the king's friends (11:57). See MACCABEE.

W. C. KAISER, JR.

imitate. See ETHICS OF PAUL III.A.

Imla im´luh KJV alternate form of IMLAH.

Imlah im´luh (יִמְלָא H3550 [1 Ki.] and יִמְלָה H3551 [2 Chr.], possibly "[God] fills"). Father of the prophet MICAIAH, who predicted the death of King AHAB in battle (1 Ki. 22:8–9; 2 Chr. 18:7–8 [KJV, "Imla"]).

S. BARABAS

immaculate conception. In Roman Catholic doctrine, the belief that "the most Blessed Virgin Mary, in the first instant of her conception, by a singular grace and privilege granted by Almighty God, in view of the merits of Jesus Christ, the Savior of the human race, was preserved free from all stain of original sin" (Pius IX, *Ineffabilis Deus,* December 8, 1854). See MARY, MOTHER OF JESUS.

I. Meaning of the doctrine. Although a full explanation of the theology of the immaculate conception is not possible here, a brief discussion of the meaning of the doctrine is in order. Karl Rahner (*Theological Investigations,* 1 [1961], 201–13) typifies the newer Catholic tendency to put the doctrine in the broader context of God's grace in Christ: (a) The dogma of the immaculate conception demonstrates God's concern with the beginning of each person's life. (b) It manifests the love of God which surrounds all life ("Now if that is true for one, it is true for all"). (c) It is also a rich promise that God will be faithful after life's beginning. (d) It means that in a unique way Mary received sanctifying grace, that is, "the gift which is God himself," from the beginning of her life. (e) It shows that God calls individuals and not just mankind in general to perform special tasks and prepares them in advance to become what they are in Christ. Rahner sees the immaculate conception as one facet of Mary's unique predestination and as "the most radical and most blessed mode of redemption" (ibid., 211).

II. Common misunderstandings. Catholic theologians frequently mention that many laymen, even Catholics, have seriously distorted views of this doctrine. (a) It is not to be confused with the virginal conception of Jesus in Mary's womb (although admittedly most Mariology is strikingly parallel to most Christology); Catholic theologians point out that Mary was conceived in the usual way (unlike Jesus), but without contracting original sin. See VIRGIN BIRTH. (b) It does not imply that Mary's coming into existence was in any way different physically from that of other human beings; therefore the immaculate conception of Mary in

IMMACULATE CONCEPTION

The angel Gabriel announces that Mary would be the mother of the Messiah. Painting from the Church of the Annunciation in Nazareth.

no way suggests preservation from any supposed defilement through the marital relations of her parents. (c) It is not based on any future merits of Mary, but is solely based on the redemptive death of Jesus. (d) It is not based primarily on sanctifying grace but more on Mary's unique predestination to be the mother of the Savior.

III. Alleged biblical support. Catholic scholars readily admit that there is no direct reference anywhere in the NT to Mary's conception. T. O'Meara (*Mary in Protestant and Catholic Theology* [1966], 65) is even willing to say, "If the Scriptures contain explicitly all of revelation then the dogma of 1854 is an absurd innovation"; he also speaks of the doctrine as "the first of those Marian beliefs which seem so foreign to the gospel and seem to be lacking even in the Fathers" (ibid., 60). This does not mean, of course, that most Catholic scholars are now willing to conclude that the doctrine is an innovation or in any way contrary to the primitive kerygma. Following the lead of Pope Pius IX in *Ineffabilis Deus*, they see implicit and undeveloped references to the belief in at least three passages of Scripture.

(a) Genesis 3:15, the famous protevangelium, is seen as a reference to Mary's nothing, through the birth of her Son, the power of Satan over human nature since Adam's fall. As E. D. O'Connor admits, however, "this text by itself would hardly suffice to make the doctrine known" (*NCE*, 7:378). It is based on the Latin VULGATE translation, "She [*ipsa*] shall crush your head." Catholics therefore agree that the verse can no longer be quoted in support of the doctrine. (b) Luke 1:28 is used to argue that if Mary were truly "full of grace" she must have been born with it. Catholic exegetes admit, however, that the Greek *kecharitōmenē* (pf. pass. ptc. of *charitoō* G5923) indicates only that Mary was highly favored by God without indicating the extent of that favor. (c) Matthew 1 and Luke 1–2 emphasize Mary's exceptional holiness. "It is clear that only a flawless holiness would be in any way proportionate to the sacredness of her office" (ibid., 379). But even this deductive argument is the result of further centuries of development. Some theologians have therefore toyed with the idea that the doctrine may have belonged to the nonrecorded oral traditions of the apostles, but most Catholics today agree that historical evidence does not seem to support such a conclusion.

IV. Patristic materials. Explicit evidence from the early church fathers is lacking, and it is acknowledged that Mary's immaculate conception was not an explicit part of the faith until somewhere between the 7th and 12th centuries at the very earliest, although a precise date when the belief actually was held as a matter of faith is avowedly impossible to determine. Historically, the belief evolved out of "an obscure yet powerful impulse of Christian hearts to attribute to [Mary] the greatest holiness and glory compatible with her status as a creature" (ibid., 379). Among fathers cited in connection with the dogma are the following: (a) ORIGEN, who sharply attacks those who hold that Mary is sinless; in his Homily XVII on Luke, Origen says that Mary must have committed at least one sin for her to be redeemed by Christ. (b) Ambrose, who is cited as a supporter of the belief that Mary was free from the stain of sin. (c) AUGUSTINE, who in a famous but ambiguous passage in *De natura et gratia* says, "Concerning the Virgin I wish to raise no question when it touches the subject of sin, out of honor to the Lord, for from him we know what abundance of grace to overcome sin in every way was conferred upon her who undoubtedly had no sin" (quoted in O'Meara, *Mary*, 62). Other references suggest that Augustine was thinking only about actual sin, not original sin. Some have suggested that in a time when Pelagianism was denying the full reality of original sin, Augustine was reluctant to support their position even implicitly by affirming Mary's preservation from original sin. (d) Nestorius is held to imply that Mary was free from sin. (e) Andrew of Crete and John of Damascus in the 7th and early 8th centuries mention that Mary's perfect sinlessness is implied in her title "Theotokos" (God-bearer).

V. Some later developments. (a) A feast in honor of Mary's conception begins in the 7th century and spreads widely in the centuries following. (b) Anselm in 1099 says, "It was fitting that she be clothed with a purity so splendid that none greater under God could be conceived" (*De conceptu virginali* 18). (c) In the Eastern church, the belief actually disappears after a decline in emphasis, so that in 1854 the Orthodox charge the Roman Catholics with innovation in doctrine. (d) In England in the 12th cent., the monk Eadmer defends both the feast and Mary's sinless conception. (e) In the W it was opposed by some of the greatest theologians of the Middle Ages, including Bernard of Clairvaux, Albert the Great, Bonaventure, and Thomas Aquinas. (f) Franciscans supported the doctrine, and their position eventually grew in influence until its official definition in 1854. (g) Luther's view seems to have vacillated. Until 1527 he accepts Mary's complete sinlessness. In a sermon he preached in 1527, however, he first states that Mary's body had original sin like anyone else's, but that her soul was infused into her body without contracting original sin, and in the years following he explicitly affirms the belief that Mary had sinned. Yet in 1544 he seems to revert to his earlier position: "God has formed the soul and body of the Virgin Mary full of the Holy Spirit, so that she is without all sin" (cf. O'Meara, *Mary*, 117).

VI. Evaluation. Protestants do not in any way deny God's favor to Mary. Nor do they necessarily deny that God favored her in a unique way. But they do insist that the doctrine cannot be accepted as historical fact simply on the basis of centuries of pious reflection and in the absence of any historical data. All that can be legitimately affirmed is that Mary's "immaculate conception" expresses symbolically and kerygmatically the conviction that Mary's life was holy in an unusual way as a result of her closeness to Jesus Christ. From a purely historical perspective Protestants sense the importance of a healthy agnosticism as to the nature of Mary's conception. Some Catholics too say they do not have the slightest idea of what the dogma means (J. L. McKenzie, quoted by Calvin J. Eichhorst in *Dialog* 10 [Autumn, 1971], 273).

Certainly from a purely biblical perspective Protestants and Catholics are in accord on the conclusion that there are no explicit and only tangentially implicit references at best to the immaculate conception in the Bible. The doctrine, they agree, owes more to Christian piety than to Scripture or history. The Protestant Christian agrees most wholeheartedly that "Catholics and Protestants both must learn to listen to what the Bible says of Mary. If this is done, a greater similarity will be attained in their theologies of Mary and in their total theological approach" (O'Meara, *Mary*, 347; see further *SHERK*, 5:455–57; *ERE*, 7:165–67; W. H. C. Frend in *Modern Churchman* 44 [1954]: 107–19; D. Moody in *Review and Expositor* 51 [1954]: 495–507; E. D. O'Connor, ed., *The Dogma of the Immaculate Conception* [1958]; E. L. Mascall and H. S. Box, eds., *The Blessed Virgin Mary* [1963]; K. Rahner, *Mary, Mother of the Lord* [1963]; M. Lamy, *L'immaculée conception* [2000].) L. R. KEYLOCK

Immanuel (Heb. עִמָּנוּ אֵל *ʿimmānû ʾēl* H6672, "with us [is] God"; Ἐμμανουήλ *G1842*). Also Emmanuel (NT, KJV and other versions). The name given to the child born of the VIRGIN (Isa. 7:14; 8:8 [cf. v. 10]; Matt. 1:23).

I. The "Immanuel" passages. The ISAIAH passages are set in the context of God's sign to Israel of hope of deliverance at a time when enemies threatened to take Jerusalem. The seventh chapter of Isaiah states that in the days of King AHAZ, ARAM and EPHRAIM (northern Israel) were in league to capture JUDAH. Ahaz was frightened and God sent Isaiah to assure the wicked king of

God's deliverance. When God offered a sign, Ahaz refused to ask for one, thus refusing to glorify God. God gave a sign anyway, but not for Ahaz's benefit. The sign given was for Israel's benefit (Isa. 7:13). The sign was that a virgin would conceive and bear a child whom she would call Immanuel.

"For the Son of Man came … to save what was lost" (Lk. 19:10). From the Church of the Annunciation in Nazareth.

In Isa. 8 again the name occurs twice. In v. 8 it is used in connection with the warning that Immanuel's land will be overrun by Assyria. In v. 10 the words "God is with us" occur as a comfort to God's people assuring them that the forces of men cannot triumph. The name Immanuel, given to the son born of the virgin, is to be the watchword for God's people, the word of hope, no matter how desperate conditions become. He is the hope because his name means that God is with us. This would indicate that the one born of the virgin is more than man. He is also God. The following chapter would seem to support this inference, for there the child is called "Mighty God" (Isa. 9:6). See further Isaiah, Book of VI.A.

That this interpretation is correct from the biblical standpoint is made quite clear in the Matthean passage, which states that the birth of Jesus by the Virgin Mary fulfills this prophesy from Isaiah (Matt. 1:23). The meaning of Jesus' birth, we are told, is that now God is truly with us in the person of Jesus the Christ.

II. The beginning of the concept of "God with us." The prophecy in Isa. 7:14 is not the beginning but the climax to the concept of God's being with his covenant people. The development of this concept is a remarkable record of revelation from God. The Bible indicates a growing awareness on the part of his people of both the concept and its meaning.

One day, when Moses was about eighty years old, God confronted him in a burning bush as he wandered on the hills of the Sinai mountains. He gave to Moses a great commission, to lead the Israelite slaves out of Egypt into the land of Canaan. Canaan was then held by various peoples who would have to be driven out. Understandably Moses felt unequal to such a task and said so. God's answer was the beginning of God's revelation of his presence with his people.

First, God said in response to Moses' misgivings, "I will be [ʾehyeh] with you" (Exod. 3:12). Hence, the answer to all Moses' fears was simply this—"God is with you." Moses then asked what he should give as the name of the God who is with us (3:13). To this, God answered by the well-known words "I am who I am" (or "I will be what I will be," ʾehyeh ʾăšer ʾehyeh, 3:14; see the article I am). Nothing more is needed than this context to demonstrate the meaning of the words. The "I will be" is a reminder of the words of v. 12, where God had said, "I will be *with you.*" From this answer comes that special name for God which is found throughout Scripture, *yhwh*, Yahweh, the covenant name of God, known by his people as "the God who will be with us." See God, names of.

III. The relationship between the names Yahweh and Immanuel. The clear relationship between the personal name of God, Yahweh, and the concept of "God with his people," can be easily and clearly demonstrated. The Hebrew preposition ʿim H6640 ("with") occurs at least eighty-nine times in the OT in contexts which indicate God's presence with his people. Either the object of the preposition is named specifically or it is used in conjunction with some pronoun ("with me," "with you," etc.) In all but nine of these passages, the personal name Yahweh occurs as the one who is *with* his people.

In the remaining nine passages, the context usually makes clear why the name Yahweh does not occur. Sometimes the person speaking is not part of the people of God (Abimelech, Gen. 21:22; Jethro, Exod. 18:19; Pharaoh, 2 Chr. 35:21). The other passages chiefly concern JACOB (Gen. 28:20; 31:5; 35:3; 48:21); since the revelation to Moses had not yet been given, Jacob spoke quite often of God's being with him without using the personal name of God (cf. Exod. 6:3). In the overwhelming number of passages, then, where God's people individually or collectively are assured of his presence, the name Yahweh is used.

IV. The development of the concept in the OT. The concept does occur in certain passages in connection with the patriarchs. Yahweh occurs once in connection with the concept of "God with" in speaking of ABRAHAM (Gen. 24:27), twice with reference to ISAAC (26.3, 20), and three times in the case of Jacob (28:15; 31:3; 46:4). These occurrences may appear inconsistent with the four other references to Jacob, but one must remember that Moses is the author of these passages. We can see that since he knew God as Yahweh, he would understand that same Yahweh to be the One who dealt with Abraham, Isaac, and Jacob, though they did not actually know God by that name (again see Exod. 6:3).

Four times it is stated that Yahweh is with Moses (Exod. 4:12, 15; Josh. 1:5, 17), in addition to the occurrences in Exod. 3, which have been noted already. Four times it is said of JOSHUA (Deut. 31:23; Josh. 1:5, 9, 17; 3:7). Yahweh is also said to be with the house of Joseph (Jdg. 1:22), with the judges themselves (2:18), and specifically with GIDEON, one of the judges (6:12, 16); then after a considerable lapse of time, with SAMUEL (1 Sam. 3:19), with SAUL (10:7), and with DAVID (17.37, 18.12, 14, 28; 20:13; 2 Sam. 5:10; 7:3, 9; 14:17; 16:18; 1 Ki. 1:37; Ps. 89:3–4, 24). Cf. Ps. 23:4. Finally it is used in connection with SOLOMON (1 Chr. 17:13; 22:11, 16; 28:20; 2 Chr. 1:1). Then after another lapse of time Yahweh is said to be with ASA (2 Chr. 15:2, 9), with JEHOSHAPHAT (17:3), and with HEZEKIAH (2 Ki. 18:7), all good kings of Judah.

In a more general sense Yahweh is said to be with "the good" (2 Chr. 19:12), with the believer when he calls on God (Ps. 91:15), and with judges who judge righteously (2 Chr. 19:6). Yahweh frequently is mentioned as being with Israel (Exod. 24:8; 33:16; Num. 23:21; Deut. 2:7; 5:2; 20:1, 4; 29:14; 31:6, 8; 32:12; Jdg. 6:13; 1 Ki. 8:57; 1 Chr. 22:18; 2 Chr. 15:2; 20:17; 32:8; 36:23; Zech. 10:5). More particularly Yahweh is with Judah (2 Chr. 13:12; 32:7–8). However, Yahweh will not be with the Israelites when they fail to follow him (Exod. 24:8) and when they tolerate evil (Josh. 7:12).

From the above passages it is clear that Yahweh is with his people who trust in him, from the time of the establishing of the covenant with Abraham until the end of the OT. Those who walk closely with him in life are more frequently reminded of this fact.

V. The meaning of the concept to God's people. Clearly, the COVENANT God made with his people is involved in the concept of Immanuel (Exod. 24:8; Deut. 5:2). What does this presence of God mean then to the people themselves? First, it means that God will not leave, forsake, or fail them. That doctrine is taught frequently in Scripture (Deut. 31:6; Josh. 1:5, 7; 3:7; 1 Ki. 8:57; 1 Chr. 28:20). Related to this doctrine is the promise of God's truth and mercy ever present when Yahweh is with his people (Gen. 24:27; cf. Ps. 89:33; 1 Chr. 17:13). Second, it means that they need not fear evil or be dismayed (Deut. 31:8; 1 Chr. 28:20; 2 Chr. 20:17; Ps. 23:4; Isa. 41:10). They can therefore be strong and of good courage (Deut. 31:23). In the third place, they learn that if Yahweh is with them, they lack nothing (Deut. 2:7). God will purge their evil and perverseness (Num. 13:32; 14:36–37; 32:13), inclining their hearts to go in his way and to keep his commandments (1 Ki. 8:58). This truth then will bring to them peace (1 Sam. 20:42; 1 Chr. 22:18), both personal and as a nation. The concept of God with his people is the great distinguishing mark between Israel and the rest of mankind (Exod. 33:16).

There are other benefits related to the covenant of God with his people. He will protect them from their enemies (Gen. 28:15; 31:3; 46:4; Deut. 20:4; Josh. 1:5, 7; Jdg. 2:18; 1 Sam. 18:12, 28), bring victory in battle (Jdg. 1:22; 6:16; 1 Sam. 17:37; 2 Sam. 7:9; 1 Chr. 22:18; 2 Chr. 13:12; 32:7, 8; Zech. 10:5), and cause them to prosper in all that they do (1 Sam. 3:19; 7:3; 10:7; 18:28; 2 Ki. 18:7; 1 Chr. 22:11,

16; 2 Chr. 1:1). The OT then is replete with the concept of Yahweh with his people and with all the benefits that accrue to them by this great covenant. The Immanuel passages of Isa. 7–8 point to the ultimate fulfillment of these promises in the person of One born among men who truly will be "God with us" in the flesh.

VI. The concept of "God with us" in the NT. It is then quite proper to expect that in the NT the coming of Christ is seen as the fulfillment to the utmost of the promise of God to be with his people. At his birth, Jesus was shown to be Immanuel (Matt. 1:23). He is indeed "God with us" in the flesh. This meaning was fully developed in the NT.

A. In Jesus' earthly life. JOHN THE APOSTLE develops this concept more exhaustively than any other writer of the NT. NICODEMUS, he records, believed that God was with Jesus (Jn. 3:2), and later Jesus assured the disciples that the Father was with him (8:29; 16:32). From this comes the further assurance that Christ would be with the disciples for a little while in the flesh (7:33; 12:35; 13:33; 17:12). Then before his ascension, he assured them that he would never truly leave or forsake them, but be with them forever (Matt. 28:20).

B. The continuing presence of Christ with his church. Jesus, before his ascension, taught his disciples that his departure would make it possible for his Spirit to be with them forever (Jn. 14:16). In the book of Acts the disciples testified that the Father had been with Jesus (Acts 10:38). They also were assured that Christ was now still with them (18:10). Therefore, they were able to assure believers that Christ was and would continue to be with his church. They constantly spoke of the God of peace (Rom. 15:33; Phil. 4:9), and of the grace of the Lord being with the believers (Rom. 16:20; Gal. 6:18). Most emphatically they speak of Christ with believers (Phil. 4:23; 1 Thess. 5:28; 2 Thess. 3:16, 18; et al.).

C. Christ with us forever. When Jesus was on earth, he prayed that the believers should be with him forever (Jn. 17:24). In fulfillment of this prayer, the tabernacle of God in heaven will be with the faithful forever (Rev. 21:3). Those who have died in Christ will be with him when he returns to gather the remainder (1 Thess. 3:13).

In summary, the term "Immanuel" is directly related to the biblical doctrine of the presence of God with his people, so clearly promised in Exod. 3:12, so eloquently declared in Isa. 7:14, and so certainly applied to Jesus in Matt. 1:23. The closing wish expressed in Scripture is just this—"The grace of the Lord Jesus be with God's people. Amen" (Rev. 22:21; lit., "with the saints"). (See further W. DeBurgh, *The Messianic Prophecies of Isaiah* [1863], 41–78; W. Arnold in *JBL* 24 [1905]: 107–65; E. Kraeling in *JBL* 50 [1931]: 277–97; J. Hyatt in *VT* 5 [1955]: 130–36; J. Lindblom, *A Study on the Immanuel Section in Isaiah: Isa. vii, 1—ix, 6* [1958]; A. Laato, *Who Is Immanuel?* [1988]; A. H. Bartelt, *The Book around Immanuel* [1996].) J. B. SCOTT

Immer (person) im´uhr (אִמֵּר H612, "lamb"). **(1)** A descendant of AARON whose family in the time of DAVID made up the sixteenth division of priests (1 Chr. 24:14). He thus became the ancestral head of that division and gave his name to an extensive family of descendants; among the priestly clans that returned from the EXILE, his was the second largest (1 Chr. 9:12; Ezra 2:37; Neh. 7:40; 11:13; 1 Esd. 5:24 [KJV, "Meruth"]). Two members of his family at that time, Hanani and Zebadiah, were among those who agreed to put away their foreign wives (Ezra 10:20; 1 Esd. 9:21 [KJV, "Emmer"]).

(2) Father of PASHHUR; the latter was chief officer of the temple in the time of JEREMIAH (Jer. 20:1). It is likely, however, that "son of Immer" here is an indication of ancestry, in which case this Immer would be the same as #1 above; the phrase then distinguishes Pashhur from another priest identified as the "son [descendant] of Malkijah" (21:1; Malkijah was the head of the fifth division, 1 Chr. 24:9).

(3) Father (or ancestor) of ZADOK, who made repairs to the wall of Jerusalem opposite his house, near the HORSE GATE (Neh. 3:29). This Immer too may be the same as #1 above.

Immer (place) im´uhr (אִמֵּר H613, "lamb"). One of five Babylonian places from which certain

Jewish exiles returned who were unable to prove their Israelite ancestry (Ezra 2:59; Neh. 7:61). If Immer here is indeed a place name, its location is unknown. However, the parallel in the APOCRYPHA reads, "The following are those who came up from Tel-melah and Tel-harsha, under the leadership of Cherub, Addan [KJV, Aalar], and Immer" (1 Esd. 5:36 NRSV, following a generally accepted conjectural emendation), and some scholars argue that this reading is original.

immortality. In the Scriptures, immortality (*athanasia* G114; cf. *aphtharsia* G914, "incorruptibility"), which is attributed to God, and secondarily to human beings, means freedom from decay, dissolution, and DEATH.

I. The immortality of God. The apostle PAUL states the fundamental truth that God alone is intrinsically free from subjection to death; he does not cease to exist or to be active as God (1 Tim. 6:16). This same truth is enunciated by Christ: "the Father has life in himself" (Jn. 5:26). The immortality of God contrasts sharply with human mortality or corruptibility, which comes to expression vividly in the decay and dissolution of the body (Rom. 1:23). God's incorruptibility does not reside in the fact that he is SPIRIT without body, but in his essential immortality as the living and true God (1 Thess. 1:9). Since God alone is immortal, any immortality predicated of human beings can only be derivative, the gift of grace.

Scripture testifies repeatedly that God is eternally, characteristically, and uniquely the living God (Ps. 18:46; 90:2; 115:3–8; Jer. 10:11). This life is not a bare existing or being. God has created and upholds all things by his power (Gen. 1:1; Heb. 1:3). He knows what takes place in the earth; he punishes the wicked, but intercedes to save his people. See ETERNITY; GOD, BIBLICAL DOCTRINE OF.

II. The immortality of human beings

A. In the OT. God made man a living creature (Gen. 2:7) and placed him in the Garden of Eden. The loving obedience required of him was focused in the command not to eat of a particular tree, and the threat attached to disobedience was death (2:17). The implication is that humans were not created mortal. God's word to ADAM that he was dust and would return to dust (3:19) imposed physical dissolution as punishment, and does not, as commonly understood, describe merely the outworking of a natural process.

On the other hand, man as created was not truly and properly immortal. The probation carried with it the possibility of failure and subjection to death. Obedience would receive as a reward of grace (not of merit) confirmation in life corresponding to the immortality of the NT. When Adam sinned, he died spiritually, being alienated from the source of life. Physically, he was expelled from the original sphere of life in the garden and was denied access to the tree of life. Bodily death intervened at a later point, but not before Adam received the promise of life through the seed of the woman (Gen. 3:15, 20).

The basic principle established from the beginning is the inviolable correlation of SIN and DEATH on the one hand, and of RIGHTEOUSNESS and LIFE on the other (cf. Deut. 30:15–20; Ezek. 33:10–20; Rom. 2:7–8). Confirmation in righteousness carries with it confirmation in life, or immortality. God, who is uncreated and perfectly holy, is uniquely immortal. The unfolding of the principle of sin and death is evidenced in the repeated refrain of Gen. 5, "... and he died," but preeminently in the virtually total destruction of the race by the flood (Gen. 6:5–7). The correlation of righteousness and life is manifest in the statement that God took ENOCH away because he walked with God (5:24), and in the experience of the PATRIARCHS.

Length of life and sustained fellowship with the covenant God and community is the normal expectation of the righteous. ABRAHAM "died in a good old age, an old man and full of years." His passing was a transition to renewed fellowship with his people (Gen. 25:8). Similar circumstances are recorded of other great men of faith (e.g., Isaac, Jacob, Joseph, Moses, Joshua, David). The fact of death is not denied, but even the place of burial becomes a sign of hope (50:13). Death is a transition from life to life. The God of the fathers is the God of the living (Matt. 22:32), and death results in deepened fellowship with him (Ps. 16:11; 17:15; 73:24).

IMMORTALITY

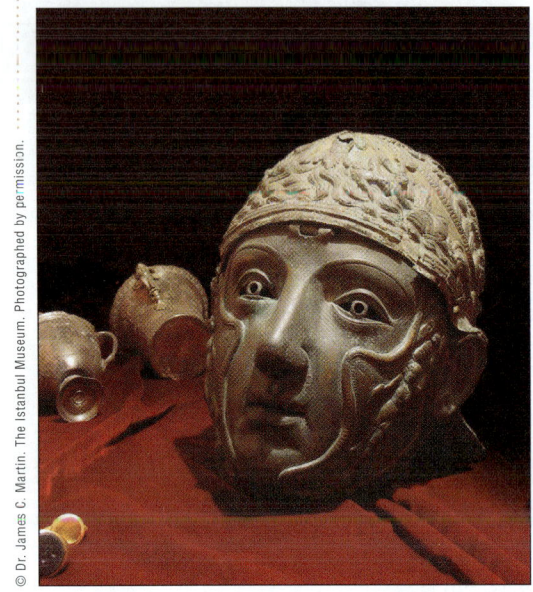

Artifacts discovered in the tumulus at Vize (NW Turkey, ancient Thracia). Objects were buried with the dead for their use in the afterlife.

The wicked, however, are prematurely cut off from the land of the living (Exod. 14:28; Ps. 52:5; Ezek. 32). The heathen who are without God naturally fall into this category, but also the disobedient from among the covenant people (Lev. 19:8; Num. 16:31–33). Death for the wicked is not annihilation but descent into SHEOL or the Pit. It is a conscious experience of separation from God, of destruction, and therefore of retribution (Ps. 49:11, 14, 19; 88:10–12; Isa. 14:9–11). The commonly accepted thesis that Sheol is the receptacle indifferently of the righteous as well as the wicked needs further clarification and refinement. The hypothetical descent of JOSEPH and JACOB into Sheol would result from an early and unnatural death (Gen. 37:35; 44:31). Premature death is experienced as judgment whether deserved or not (cf. Isa. 38:10, 17–18). JOB falsely imagines that the supposed rest and peace of Sheol is preferable to continued earthly life (Job 3.11–26). It is an expression of the same weakness of faith which causes him to curse the day of his birth. Ultimately Job dies in the full enjoyment of family, wealth, and old age (42:10–17).

The major problem for OT piety arises when the righteous die prematurely and the prosperity of the wicked is prolonged on the earth. The solution lies in the realization that the wicked ultimately will be destroyed (Ps. 37:10, 73:16–20), but, in mercy, God spares the righteous from the brink of total destruction (Ps. 30:3; 116; and frequently in the Psalms). The salvation of the righteous is grounded ultimately in the substitutionary death and resurrection of the Lord's Servant (Isa. 53:8, 10). The reality of a resurrection that includes the body comes to explicit expression in the OT (Job 19:25–27; Isa. 25:8; 26:19; Dan. 12:2).

B. In the NT. Throughout the intertestamental period there was a growing apprehension, more or less adequate, of the doctrine of the RESURRECTION, though it was denied in some quarters. PAUL is able to align himself with the teaching of the PHARISEES over against the SADDUCEES (Acts 23:6; 24:14). However, it is through the gospel of Jesus Christ, who abolished death, that life and immortality are brought to light (2 Tim. 1:10; the word here, lit. "incorruptibility," suggests that life through Jesus Christ is not to be dissociated from the resurrection of the body).

Jesus bore the sins of his people and therefore endured their full penalty. He was cut off from the land of the living in his youth, but his death made ATONEMENT for sin. When the penalty was exhausted, he was raised from the grave with a newness of life corresponding to the perfect divine righteousness which he embodies (Ps. 16:9–10; Isa. 53:8–12; Acts 2:27–28; 13:35). Therefore he is the living one who died but is alive forevermore (Rev. 1:18). By the preaching of the gospel, Christ's own are regenerated and through faith are united to their Savior. From him they receive eternal life. Immortality is, in the biblical pattern of thought, not a universal natural possession but the gift of redemptive GRACE.

Because the Savior gives life at every point where death has intervened, the body also participates in immortality (1 Cor. 15:54). The bodies of those alive at the consummation are transformed, while the bodies of deceased believers are transformed in the resurrection; all are made incorruptible (15:51–55). The necessary correlation of righteousness and life finds fulfillment in the IMPUTATION of Christ's righteousness to believers.

Even in the OT it is not human righteousness that is crowned with life. By faith Enoch was pleasing to God and did not see death (Heb. 11:5–6). The justifying FAITH of Abraham is in God who gives life to the dead (Rom. 4:17). The gospel of both Testaments is that the righteous by faith shall live (Hab. 2:4; Rom. 1:17).

The NT deepens the ancient truth that believers who experience the unnatural lingering consequences of sin in the death of the body before the resurrection are more than compensated by a continuing and fuller communion with God (2 Cor. 5:1–5; Phil. 1:23). Their bodies also are still united to Christ awaiting the resurrection (Rom. 8:23). The INTERMEDIATE STATE of both the righteous and the wicked is one of conscious experience rather than annihilation (see PUNISHMENT, ETERNAL). The wicked begin to endure the torments of destruction (Lk. 16:23), but only at the final judgment in the unity of body and spirit are they cast into HELL forever (Rev. 20:13–15). The resurrection of the unjust (Jn. 5:29; Acts 24:15) reveals that death as penalty does not come to expression exclusively or even primarily in the dissolution of the body.

III. In philosophy and recent theology. The biblical teaching on immortality must be radically distinguished from the notion found in Greek thought (cf. Acts 17:32), but also in later idealist philosophy, that the SOUL is naturally immortal, while the BODY being mortal is subject to death and decay. The Greek idea has been incorporated into Roman Catholic theology and is prevalent in some forms of Protestantism. This view presupposes a fundamental but unbiblical anthropological DUALISM of body and soul. While the Bible recognizes a duality, God deals with human beings in their created integrity. Immortality conceived of merely as a personal, conscious, disembodied existence that continues beyond the grave does not measure up to the richness of blessing comprehended by the term in the NT.

Immanuel Kant rejected all attempts to demonstrate the fact of immortality from the substantiality of the soul, but maintained it as a postulate of the practical reason. It is not the redemptive reality revealed and wrought finally and fully through Jesus Christ alone. The philosophy of the Cosmonomic Idea (D. H. T. Vollenhoven, H. Dooyeweerd) has exposed the unbiblical character of much philosophical speculation, but has been less successful in establishing a positive view of immortality.

Recent theology has vigorously opposed Christian accommodation to the Greek view by stressing the unity of man. There is a corresponding recognition that the biblical hope of life is in terms of the resurrection of the body (O. Cullmann). The biblical teaching is effectively dissipated, however, when the resurrection is conceived of as suprahistorical (*geschichtlich*) event (neoorthodoxy) or as myth pointing simultaneously to man's existence in, and transcendence of, the world (existentialist-oriented theologies).

(See further S. D. F. Salmond, *The Christian Doctrine of Immortality* [1907]; L. Boettner, *Immortality* [1956]; O. Cullmann, *Immortality of the Soul or Resurrection of the Dead?* [1958]; C. R. Smith, *The Bible Doctrine of the Hereafter* [1958]; E. Brunner, *Dogmatics*, 4/3 [1962], 339–444; G. C. Berkouwer, *Man: The Image of God* [1962], 234–78; K. Stendahl, ed., *Immortality and Resurrection* [1965]; M. J. Harris, *Raised Immortal: Resurrection and Immortality in the New Testament* [1983]; J. Barr, *The Garden of Eden and the Hope of Immortality* [1992].)

N. SHEPHERD

immutability. The quality of not being susceptible to change. In theology it signifies the attribute, or perfection, of God whereby he remains the same in his divine nature and purpose. See GOD, BIBLICAL DOCTRINE OF. The heavens and the earth, the work of God's hands, will perish, says the psalmist, but he will endure; they change, but he is the same and his years have no end. Therefore, believers and their children can dwell secure (Ps. 102:26–29; Heb. 1:10–12). He alone is God forever, with none before him and no god after him or beside him (Isa. 43:10; Deut. 32:39). He is the first and the last (Isa. 41:4; 48:2), who alone is immortal (Rom. 1:23; 1 Tim. 1:17; 6:16). Because the Lord does not change, the sons of Jacob are not consumed (Mal. 3:6). Jesus Christ, Son of God as well as Son of Man, is the same yesterday, today, and forever (Heb. 13:8).

God is immutable also in his saving purpose. He will fulfill his purpose for us because his steadfast love "endures forever" (Ps. 138:8). "He who is the Glory of Israel does not lie or change his mind; for he is not a man, that he should change his mind" (1 Sam. 15:29). "God's gifts and his call are irrevocable" (Gk. *ametamelētos G294*, lit. "not to be repented of," Rom. 11:29). He does not cast away his people (11:1); rather, he completes what he begins (Phil. 1:6).

There are passages that seem to contradict this doctrine. In anthropomorphic terms God is represented as changing his mind or repenting (Gen. 6:6; 1 Sam. 15:11; Jer. 18:8, 10; 26:3; Joel 2:13; Amos 7:3; Jon. 3:9; 4:2); as changing his purpose (Exod. 32:10–14); of becoming angry and then turning from his anger (Exod. 32:10–14; Num. 11:1, 10; Deut. 13:17; 2 Chr. 12:12; 30:8; Ps. 106:40; Zech. 10:3). See ANTHROPOMORPHISM. On one occasion Israel experiences the love of God, on another his wrath. God becomes man in the person of Jesus Christ and becomes subject to the vicissitudes of human experience. The ascended Christ can sympathize with our weaknesses (Heb. 4:15), and the Holy Spirit can be grieved (Eph. 4:30).

Nevertheless, Scripture remains firm in its insistence that in all these relationships with his people, in which God is set forth almost as one of them, he remains God and that his purposes do not fail. He accommodates himself to his people in his revelation and presence among them, but he ever remains the same. That is why he is referred to so often as the ROCK (Deut. 32:4, 15, 18, 30–31, 37; 1 Sam. 2:2; 2 Sam. 22:3, 32; Ps. 19:14; 31:2; 62:2, 6; et al.). He does not change in his nature or purpose. His people can trust in him. This does not mean, however, that God is inert or inactive. He is within, as well as outside, his creation and ever working (Jn. 5:17). Immutability is not immobility but God's sovereign constancy over against, as well as within, a universe of change.

(See further S. Charnock, *Discourses upon the Existence and Attributes of God* [1849], 195–230; L. Berkhof, *Reformed Dogmatics* [1941], 58–59; H. Bavinck, *The Doctrine of God* [1951], 145–52; W. Grudem, *Systematic Theology: An Introduction to Christian Doctrine* [1994], 163–68.)

M. E. OSTERHAVEN

Imna im´nuh (יִמְנָע *H3557*, "[God] holds back" or "strong"). Son of Helem, listed among the brave warriors who were heads of families of the tribe of ASHER (1 Chr. 7:35; cf. v. 40). Some scholars believe that Imna is a variant of IMNAH and (through textual corruption) of IMRAH, both of which appear in the same genealogy (vv. 30, 36; see D. V. Edelman in *ABD*, 3:396–97).

Imnah im´nuh (יִמְנָה *H3555*, "fortunate" or "[God] assigns"). **(1)** Son of ASHER, grandson of JACOB, and eponymous ancestor of the Imnite clan (Gen. 46:17 [KJV, "Jimnah"]; Num. 26:44 [KJV, "Jimna," "Jimnites"]; 1 Chr. 7:30). According to some scholars, IMRAH (1 Chr. 7:36) is a textual corruption of Imnah. See also IMNA.

(2) A Levite whose son KORE was in charge of the EAST GATE and of the free will offerings during the reign of HEZEKIAH (2 Chr. 31:14).

Imnite im´nite. See IMNAH.

impediment of speech. See DISEASE.

Imperial Regiment. See AUGUSTAN COHORT.

imprecatory psalms. In the book of PSALMS, the authors sometimes appeal in PRAYER to God requesting that he pour out his wrath upon their enemies (notable examples are Ps. 55; 59; 69; 79; 109; 137). Even JEREMIAH prayed for God's vengeance to be meted out to those who persecuted him (Jer. 11). Such prayers have raised a moral difficulty. This is especially true when these petitions are seen as prayers of revenge and therefore regarded as contrary to the teaching of Jesus (Matt. 5:43–48).

PAUL, in writing to the Romans, used the language of imprecatory prayers to indict those who in their sinfulness defiantly oppose God (Rom. 3:10–18). When viewed from the perspective of a holy God, the question does arise—as it did with ZEPHANIAH and HABAKKUK—concerning God's tolerance of sin. In the case of JEREMIAH, the circumstances and the context are partially given. Jeremiah's enemies were seeking the life of a man who had been commissioned to proclaim God's message to a generation awaiting judgment. If Jeremiah, however, made this request merely on the basis of a self-pitying motive, it must be recognized that possibly his prayer was not acceptable to God.

Basically significant in consideration of these imprecatory passages is the fact that such expressions represent prayers or appeals to God. Those who express them do not execute them but make their appeal to God to implement their request. Ultimately the appeal is subject to divine discretion. Jeremiah declared that God exercises kindness, judgment, and righteousness in the earth (Jer 9:23–24).

When ABRAHAM prayed for the salvation of the wicked cities of SODOM and GOMORRAH, the cities were not saved, but the righteous people were rescued. Abraham made his appeal on the basis that ultimately the judge of all the earth would do right (Gen. 18:25). When James and John (see JAMES I; JOHN THE APOSTLE) appealed to Jesus to destroy the SAMARITANS (Lk. 9:54–55), their prayer was not answered. Whatever the human motivation was in reference to these requests, they were given consideration only in terms of God's righteous judgment. This same principle undoubtedly prevailed concerning the imprecatory psalms, of which relatively little is known about the particular circumstances in which they were written. (Cf. J. Vos in *WTJ* 4 [1941–42]: 123–38; H. E. Guillebaud, *Some Moral Difficulties* [1949], 126–35; J. E. Adams, *War Psalms of the Prince of Peace: Lessons from the Imprecatory Psalms* [1991].) S. J. SCHULTZ

impurity. See CLEAN; PURITY; UNCLEANNESS.

imputation. The act of attributing something to a person. The Hebrew verb *ḥāšab* **H3108** ("to value, consider") and the Greek verb *logizomai* **G3357** ("to count, estimate, consider") can both be used in the sense of setting to one's account or reckoning something to a person. It is said in Gen. 15:6 that God reckoned righteousness to believing ABRAHAM; that is, God regarded him as righteous, attributing or crediting to him that which he did not have in himself. In Gal. 3:6 and Rom. 4:3 the apostle PAUL quotes this passage in arguing a person's JUSTIFICATION by God through GRACE alone.

If Abraham had been able to justify himself by works he might boast, but man is unable thus to save himself. If he should insist on trying it anyway, Paul reasons, "his wages are not credited to him as a gift, but as an obligation" (Rom. 4:4). If, however, he does not seek to achieve his own justification, "but trusts God who justifies the wicked, his faith is credited as righteousness" (4:5). The meaning is not that God accepted Abraham's FAITH instead of perfect righteousness as the meritorious ground for his justification. It is rather that God accepted Abraham because he trusted in God rather than in anything that he could do. The former meaning is excluded, first, by the apostle's argument that Abraham was justified with no merit whatsoever. Justification takes place "freely by his grace through the redemption that came by Christ Jesus" (Rom. 3:24); the fourth chapter uses Abraham and DAVID as examples of salvation by free, unmerited grace. Second, it is excluded by Paul's conception of faith, which is simple trust in the grace of God manifest in Christ, with no claim to merit.

After the mention of Abraham as an illustration of salvation by pure grace, the apostle refers to David, who pronounced a blessing on those to whom God reckons righteousness apart from works: "Blessed are they whose transgressions are forgiven, / whose sins are covered. / Blessed is the man whose sin the Lord will never count against him" (Rom. 4:7–8). The Scripture from which these lines are taken (Ps. 32:1–2), like the writings of Paul, emphasizes the sinner's hopelessness apart from God and the sovereignty of grace. In utter weakness the psalmist confesses his transgressions. He knows that only God can forgive sin. The person who is forgiven is not regarded as wicked, for the Lord does not impute to him his iniquity, but is reckoned as a child of God. His sin is covered; he is counted righteous.

In order to emphasize the relevance to his readers of this teaching about the gracious imputation of righteousness to Abraham, the apostle included all those of later generations who come to God as Abraham did and have faith reckoned to them. "The words 'it was credited to him' were written not for him alone, but also for us, to whom God will credit righteousness—for us who believe in him who raised Jesus our Lord from the dead" (Rom. 4:23–24; cf. v. 11b).

That this reckoning, or imputation, of righteousness to the believer lies at the heart of the biblical doctrine of SALVATION is corroborated by other Scripture. The apostle Paul uses the phrase "righteousness/justice of God" nine times (Rom. 1:17; 3:5, 21–26; 10:3; 2 Cor. 5:21), and in most of these instances it is mentioned in order to teach that God grants the sinner a new legal standing; that is, the person is counted righteous even while a sinner. A righteousness of God "apart from the law" has been manifested, says Paul, although both law and prophets bear witness to it. It is a righteousness of God "effective through faith in Christ for all who have such faith" (Rom. 3:22 NEB). This righteousness is seen in Christ who brought redemption. In him God proves that he is righteous when he justifies the sinful believer (3:25–26). Law is not overthrown but upheld in this redemption of lost man (v. 31).

Later in the same epistle the author affirms that the great error of his own nation was its ignorance of the righteousness of God and its attempt to establish its own righteousness: "they did not submit to God's righteousness" (Rom. 10:3). Men and women are not righteous in themselves: "all have sinned and fall short of the glory of God" (3:23). They need God's righteousness, which has been made manifest in Christ. Above all else Paul wants to be found in Christ. Concerning this and its relation to righteousness, he writes: "... not having a righteousness of my own that comes from the law, but that which is through faith in Christ — the righteousness that comes from God and is by faith" (Phil. 3:9). This righteousness is imputed, or reckoned, to him so that, while strictly speaking it is not his own, yet God reckons it to him; thus the believer is *simul justus ac peccator* (at the same time righteous and a sinner), to use Luther's phrase.

The imputation of the righteousness of Christ to the sinner lies at the heart of the doctrine of salvation. It is strange then to hear it denied, as, for example, by Vincent Taylor: "Imputation ... can never be anything else than an ethical fiction. ... Righteousness cannot be transferred from the account of one person to another. Righteousness can no more be imputed to a sinner than bravery to a coward or wisdom to a fool. If through faith a man is accounted righteous, it must be because, in a reputable sense of the term, he is righteous, and not because another is righteous in his stead" (*Forgiveness and Reconciliation* [1940], 57). With such denial of a cardinal teaching one is not surprised to read the following definition of justification later in the discussion: "It is the divine activity in which God gives effect to his redeeming work in Christ by making possible that righteous mind necessary to communion with himself" (ibid., 66). Taylor here denies clear biblical teaching and endangers the Christian doctrine of salvation. (More recently, some evangelical scholars here questioned, on different grounds, the traditional understanding of imputation. See the discussion by B. Vickers, *Jesus' Blood and Righteousness* [2006], which reaffirms this doctrine.)

A second sense in which the word *imputation* has been used in Christian doctrine is the reckoning of our sin to Jesus Christ. "God made him who had no sin to be sin for us, so that in him we might become the righteousness of God" (2 Cor. 5:21). In this classic text the apostle brings together the two truths of the doctrine of salvation: the burden of human sin became Christ's burden, and the righteousness of God, or of Christ, became ours. The meaning obviously is *not* that Christ actually became a sinner, for all of the gospel contradicts that position. It is rather that by virtue of his identification with the human race sin was *reckoned* to him. Although it is not explicitly said in Scripture that sin is reckoned, or imputed, to Christ, the meaning is clear. It is said that he "bore our sins in his body on the tree" (1 Pet. 2:24), that "the LORD has laid on him the iniquity of us all" (Isa. 53:6; cf. Acts 8:35), that he was made to "bear" or "take away" the iniquities of his people (Isa. 53:11; Heb. 9:28). Each of these passages of Scripture, the one from Hebrews especially, has in mind the OT institution of SACRIFICE in which guilt was symbolically and ceremoniously transferred to an animal with the laying on of hands on the head of the victim. Applied to Christ, to whom the sacrifices of the OT pointed, the teaching is that he "bore the punishment of our sin vicariously, its guilt having been imputed to Him. The thought of the prophecy is, as Delitzsch says, that of vicarious punishment, which implies the idea of the imputation of the guilt of our sins to Christ" (C. W. Hodge in *ISBE* [1929], 3:1464).

The same teaching is set forth graphically by Paul in Gal. 3:13, where Christ is said to have "become a curse for us." The meaning is that he bore the penalty for human sin, that, as Luther declared when commenting on this passage, God dealt with him as though he were the greatest of sinners. Sin was imputed, was reckoned, to him so that man might be forgiven. Imputation is thus bound together with the teaching of vicarious salvation.

Besides the two above doctrines of imputation, a third is the imputation of the sin of ADAM to the human race, based on the narrative of the FALL (Gen. 3; Rom. 5:12–21; 1 Cor. 15:21–22). According to one interpretation of this Scripture, Adam's sin was imputed to his posterity by virtue of his having been the federal representative of the human race. Among those who hold this view, there is a difference as to whether that sin was imputed "mediately" (J. La Place, 17th cent.) or "immediately" (also known as the "federalist" view; C. Hodge, *Systematic Theology*, 3 vols. [1871–73], 2:192–227). According to another interpretation of the fall, Adam's sin was not merely imputed to his descendants but, inasmuch as they were generically "in" him, his sin is truly theirs. This latter "realistic" theory of the imputation of Adam's sin was held by W. G. T. Shedd (*Dogmatic Theology*, 3 vols. in 4 [1889], 2:148–257) and A. H. Strong (*Systematic Theology* [1912], 597–637). (See further the summaries by B. B. Warfield in *SHERK*, 5:465–67, reprinted in his *Biblical and Theological Studies* [1952], 262–69.) M. E. OSTERHAVEN

Imrah im'ruh (יִמְרָה H3559, possibly "he rebels"). Son of Zophah and descendant of ASHER (1 Chr. 7:36). Some scholars emend the text to IMNAH.

Imri im'ri (אִמְרִי H617, prob. short form of אֲמַרְיָה H616 "Yahweh has said"). (1) Son of Bani and descendant of JUDAH through PEREZ (1 Chr. 9:4). Some have thought he may be the same as the AMARIAH mentioned in a partially parallel passage (Neh. 11:4).

(2) Father (or ancestor) of ZACCUR; the latter helped rebuild the wall of Jerusalem in NEHEMIAH's time (Neh. 3:2).

incarnation (Lat. *incarnatio*, from *caro* [gen. *carnis*], "flesh"). In Christian theology, this term refers to the event summed up in Jn. 1:14, "The Word became flesh and made his dwelling among us."

I. The term
  A. Derivation
  B. Signification
II. The origin of the doctrine
III. The NT presentation
  A. The Synoptic Gospels
  B. Johannine literature
  C. Acts
  D. Pauline epistles
  E. 1 and 2 Peter
  F. Hebrews
IV. The OT foreshadowing
V. Summary of doctrine
  A. Nature of the incarnation
  B. Mode
  C. Purpose
    1. Revelational
    2. Soteriological
    3. Consummation of creation
VI. Subsequent history of the doctrine

I. The term

A. Derivation. The term can be traced to the Latin version of Jn. 1:14 ("et Verbum caro factum est") and was used frequently by Latin writers from the 4th cent. There is no exact Greek equivalent in the NT, but the phrase *en sarki* ("in the flesh") is not uncommon (1 Jn. 4:2, "Jesus Christ has come in the flesh"; cf. Rom. 8:3; Eph. 2:15; Col. 1:22; 1 Tim. 3:16; 1 Pet. 3:18; 4:1; 2 Jn. 7).

B. Signification. This term refers, in the first instance, to the act wherein the eternal Son "became flesh," but it is intended to signify the whole experience of human life into which he entered, and also embraces within its reference the fact that Christ still bears his humanity and will do so forever.

II. The origin of the doctrine.
While, in the light of the NT, certain OT passages can be seen to point to the incarnation, the OT predictions were not such that the incarnation was anticipated. The idea of God becoming man would have been and still is a scandal to the Jew, and only the overwhelming evidence seen in the person and ministry of Christ could lead any to believe that he was none less than the incarnate Son of God. This belief was no ideal

that owed its origin to the fertile imagination of the early church (which allegedly "wrote back" into the Gospels myths of the miraculous birth and ministry of Jesus). The doctrine arose out of the observation of the actual life of Jesus and against all possible explanation of what had been observed.

The Latin inscription on this altar reads, "The Word became flesh" (Jn. 1:14). From the cave at the Church of the Annunciation in Nazareth.

Men found in their midst this Galilean, Jesus. By virtue of his manner of life and personal character they could not but ask who he was—Messiah? Prophet? Or more? There gradually dawned the almost incredible conviction that, human Messiah and prophet that he was, he was so much more; man that he was, he was also divine. The Son of God had "become flesh and made his dwelling among us."

III. The NT presentation

A. The Synoptic Gospels. Both Matthew and Luke open with accounts of the miraculous conception of Jesus. See VIRGIN BIRTH. Matthew interprets this unique birth to mean the special presence of God (Matt. 1:23, citing Isa. 7:14). In Luke the angelic messenger designates Jesus Son of the Most High, Son of God (Lk. 1:32, 35). This is not the primary viewpoint from which Jesus is presented in the synoptics. Rather, he is shown as a human child, of claimed descent from Adam, Abraham, and David (Matt. 1:1–17, Lk. 3:23–28). In Luke's genealogy, Adam is termed "son of God" (3:38), so that as a human Jesus shared in this sonship, the sonship common to all people as the "offspring of God" (Acts 17:29). He went through the normal stages of human development (Lk. 2:52, which speaks of his fourfold development: wisdom, stature, favor with God, favor with men), a full-orbed childhood-to-manhood experience. As a man he was subject to hunger, weariness, human emotions (Matt. 4:2; 8:24; Mk. 1:41; 3:5; Lk. 2:44).

This man came before the notice of men, and all three evangelists trace the impact of his ministry, and the way people were constrained to ask, "Who is he?" "What kind of man is this?" (Matt. 8:27; cf. 16:13–14). The evangelists' obvious intention is to enable the reader to see as people saw when they beheld his ministry (Matt. 16:16–17), so that, with them, it might be clearly perceived who he really was. The evangelists recorded Jesus' prayers and other words by which he assumed a relationship with his Father that in essence was different from that of all other human beings (Matt. 10:32–33; 11:27–28; 15:13; 16:17; 18:10–14, 35; Lk. 2:29; 23:34, 46; 24:49). Not only did he claim unique sonship, but he was owned as distinctively the SON OF GOD in the voice at his baptism (see JESUS CHRIST V.C) and at the TRANSFIGURATION (Matt. 3:17; 17:5). Even the demons recognized him (Matt. 8:28; Mk. 3:11).

The synoptics carefully balance Jesus' common humanity against this uniqueness. Constantly he uses his self-designation, SON OF MAN. The full significance of this term cannot be discussed here, but wherever the roots of this term may be traced and whatever else it may mean, it undoubtedly signified both the genuineness and the representative character of Christ's humanity. He was truly human, sharing with all men and women that which belongs essentially to humanity.

B. Johannine literature. The marked difference between the Gospel of John and the synoptics is due largely to the different viewpoints from which they are written. Here, the primary view is not of the Man whom men came to see as more than man, but of the eternal Son who came into the world to live as man. It is not that John stresses the DEITY OF CHRIST at the expense of his humanity; indeed, one reads more of the human experiences of joy, weariness, and the like in this gospel than in the others. But the primary standpoint, regulative of the whole gospel, is that in an unbroken continuity he who was "from the beginning" entered into human history as a human participant in this history.

The primary question then is not, Who is this man? but, What kind of life and to what purpose did the Word, as man, live in this world? The key, then, to the whole gospel (and much more the foundation to the entire Gospel of John than are the birth stories to the Gospels of Matthew and Luke) is the prologue, Jn. 1:1–18. The heart of this are vv. 1–3, 14, 18, particularly: *theos ēn ho logos ... kai ho logos sarx egeneto* ("the Word was God ... and the Word became flesh"). Even more directly than the Pauline "human form" (Phil. 2:8), the use of this term "flesh" (*sarx* G4922) indicates the full extent of the incarnation, and by his statement John expressly counters the docetic error (cf. 1 Jn. 4:2–3). See Logos.

The use of *egeneto* of Jn. 1:14 is to be compared with the *egeneto* (impf. of *ginomai* G1181) in v. 3. The significance is that all things "came into being"—what was not came to be. Similarly, what the Word previously was not, he came to be, that is, "flesh" (v. 14). We are not to conclude, however, that from being God alone he became man alone, for he continued to be the "only begotten" (v. 18), manifesting the Father's glory.

A certain temporality (see below) may perhaps be read into the verb *eskēnōsen* ("dwelt, pitched a tent, tabernacled"), but the primary reference is to the substantial reality and presence of the Word in this world. Just as the TABERNACLE was a real feature of the Israelite camp, and enshrined the manifestation of the glory and presence of God, so was Christ in "real presence" among men, and in and from him shone the divine glory—the glory primarily of love and moral grandeur (cf. Exod. 33:18–19; other aspects of his divine glory were hidden—see below).

In Jn. 1:18 one purpose of the incarnation is explicitly stated: that this was God's word to human beings, this was he who has "declared" (*exēgēsato*—the verb has no object), that is, opened to mortals the divine mysteries (v. 18). The clearly attested reading *monogenēs theos* (read in apposition, "only-begotten, God") emphatically asserts that he who was made flesh is the unique Son, none less than God. This makes his REVELATION an immediate and direct and therefore a truly authentic representation and manifestation of God.

John apparently had no adoptionist error immediately in mind, nor does he make any reference to the mode of incarnation set forth in Matthew and Luke. His account clearly shows that Jesus was not simply a man in whom the Logos took up residence.

Though in this prologue philosophical and metaphysical questions of vast import are touched upon, the evangelist's interest is intensely practical. The truths of the prologue lie at the base of the rest of the gospel; it is all that which gives validity and significance to the ministry of Jesus. As the Word, his life on earth is a revelation; as the only-begotten, God, incarnate, he can be the "lamb of God" able to "take away the sins of the world" (Jn. 1:29). It is because of who he is that his works become "signs" (2:11; 20:30), and his personal claims can be taken at fullest value.

That Christ was Son of God from all eternity follows from two of his recorded claims: his descent from heaven (Jn. 3:13) and his pre-Abrahamic existence (8:58; cf. the self-assertion in 17:5). In the first of these another truth is carefully presented. This preexistent Son, whom God gave (3:16), is just as truly Son of Man (3:13–14; cf. 6:27, 53, 62; 12:23; 13:31). This title occurs much less frequently in the fourth gospel than in the synoptics, but against the theme of the prologue its use is profoundly significant. So too are indications of human suffering in body and soul (Jn. 4:6; 11:35; 12:27; 19:28).

Throughout his earthly ministry he claimed immediate oneness with the Father. This oneness meant not simply a fullness of fellowship or unity of purpose, but a certain equality (Jn. 5:18–23; 10:30, 38; 14:9–11). From this last reference at least two significant conclusions follow. (1) In the fullest sense possible Jesus claimed to be the "image of God," a full and true revelation of God. (2) There is no "God beyond God," none beyond him who is made manifest in Christ. Not to say that all that God is, all that ever ultimately is to be known, was visible to men in the incarnate Christ. But all that is revealed in him is a revelation of the one and only true God. The incarnation is the incarnation of the one true God (1:1, 14), and thus a revelation which will never be found to have been in any way false. To question or deprecate the full value of this revelation in Christ is to dishonor God himself (cf. 5:23).

In theme, the opening verses of 1 John are not unlike those of the gospel, though the terms used ("heard," "seen," "touched," 1 Jn. 1:1) more graphically present Christ as not only in the flesh but present to men of flesh: the Word was open to the most direct observation possible. None can deny in any regard the reality of the incarnation without thereby being found to oppose Christ himself, and to be estranged from the Father (2:22–23; 4:1–3; 2 Jn. 7).

This artistic impression from the Church of the Annunciation in Nazareth reads, "Today a Savior has been born to you" (Lk. 2:11).

C. Acts. The early chapters of the book of Acts are especially significant as representing the earliest understanding of the church after the ASCENSION OF CHRIST. There is not, perhaps, the full apprehension of Christ's person that is found in the Epistles. It is not true, however, as some assert, that there is to be found here an adoptionist theology—that Christ, the man, in due time was made divine. The assigning of certain OT passages to Christ (Acts 2:25–28, 34), and titles given to Christ, such as "the Holy and Righteous One," "the Author of life" (3:14–15; 7:52), show that Christ is more than mere man. Paul, upon his conversion, almost immediately called Jesus "the Son of God" (9:20).

D. Pauline epistles. Paul sees the cross, by which Christ became the propitiation for our sins and reconciled us to God (Rom. 3:25; 8:3, 32; 2 Cor. 5:19; cf. Eph. 2:13–16), as the real purpose and goal of the incarnation. Moreover, it is that death, and not simply the incarnate life of Christ, that reveals to us the fact and measure of the love of God (Rom. 5:8).

While the earthly life of Christ, and especially his death and resurrection, is of great importance to Paul (see, for example, 1 Cor. 15:3–5, 12–20), the focus of his attention is on the present exalted Christ (2 Cor. 3:17; Col. 3:1–4), though at the same time Christ is to us what he is, not only because of who he is, but also because of what he accomplished in his earthly ministry (1 Cor. 1:23).

Paul constantly designates Jesus Christ as LORD, a term that appears unquestionably to recognize his deity. It is the risen, exalted Christ of whom he so speaks (Phil. 2:11), but there is no suggestion that while he was on earth he was any less the Son of God. It was the Son who came from God (Gal. 4:4), lived on earth, and is now exalted—the one person throughout. So important is it that Jesus is the risen Lord, that he must so be acknowledged if one is to know him as Savior (Rom. 10:9).

There is no doubt with Paul concerning the reality of Christ's humanity. Christ is the "second Adam" (Acts 5:17–18). However, in two passages claiming his physical descent from David (Rom. 1:2; 9:5) and his real humanity, there is the careful qualification, "according to the flesh." Christ is also of other Sonship.

Three passages call for special note: Gal. 4:4–5, already noted, recognizes the preexistence and deity of him who was born in Bethlehem, but also his essential humanity in the phrase, "born of woman." Further, the extent of his condescension in becoming man is seen in his becoming subject to the law designed for sinful men and women.

The second passage is Phil. 2:5–8. Several phrases in these verses have been given widely different interpretations. Full account of these cannot be taken here, but certain facts seem clear. The phrases "form of God" and "form of a servant" and "in the likeness of men" and "in human form" bring out the three essential aspects of the incarnation: he who came into the world was the eternally existing God the Son. He, with no discontinuity of person, became truly man. The now highly exalted Lord is this same Jesus.

The phrase occasioning most controversy is *heauton ekenōsen* (Phil. 2:7), variously rendered, "made himself of no reputation" (KJV), "emptied himself" (NRSV), "laid it aside" (Goodspeed), "stripped himself [of all privileges and rightful dignity]" (*Amplified Bible*). Though "emptied himself" is the most literal rendering, its adequacy may be open to question. In any case, the vital issue still is the need to determine what it was that he laid aside. Charles Wesley's "emptied himself of all but love" is purely poetical. It could not be that he renounced any essential elements of deity so that in the flesh he was no longer truly God. Too much elsewhere in Scripture makes this view impossible. Some suggest he laid aside at least the exercise of his divine attributes of omnipotence, omniscience, and omnipresence, if not the possession of them. Others argue that it was simply certain aspects of the divine glory that were set aside.

Two things seem necessary to say: (1) It is not possible to determine with absolute certainty what was laid aside; one can only say that there was such self-renunciation as was necessary for the assumption of authentic human experience, which involves geographical location, human development in mind and body, the requirement of food and sleep, a real dependence as man upon the heavenly Father, and so on. Truly, "though he was rich … he became poor" (2 Cor. 8:9). (2) It is wholly invalid, on the basis of this passage, to argue for the possible fallibility of the Lord in his earthly ministry. More important, there is solid reason to believe that the question "What did he set aside" may be an inappropriate one. The verb *kenoō* G3033 is most likely being used figuratively, "to make of no account" (cf. Rom. 4:14), and thus the phrase means "he made himself nothing" (NIV), being parallel to the later phrase, "he humbled himself" (Phil. 2:8).

In the third passage, Col. 1:15–20, Paul speaks of the one person who "*is* the image of the invisible God" by whom "all things *were* created," who "*is before* all things … firstborn from among the dead … For God *was* pleased to have all his fullness dwell in him." The apostle clearly sees him as the same one throughout his preincarnate existence, his incarnate earthly life, and his present glory. For the purposes of his epistle the emphasis is on the present Christ, he who as Creator, Sustainer, Redeemer, Reconciler, is the all-supreme, all-sufficient Savior and Lord—no other mediator is needed. The later statement that "in Christ all the fullness of the Deity lives [*or* dwells] in bodily form" (Col. 2:9) refers to Christ in the present.

Obviously, from the way Paul elsewhere strongly contrasts a this-worldly "natural body" with a "spiritual body" (1 Cor. 15:44), there is some great difference between the "body of Christ's humiliation" and his "body of glory." The specifically earthly body is his "body of flesh" (Col. 1:22 [NIV, "physical body"]; cf. Heb. 5:7). It might therefore be argued that strictly speaking Christ is not now *incarnate*. However, he is certainly still possessed of a body (Col. 2:9; cf. Phil. 3:21), and is still man.

Two passages in the PASTORAL EPISTLES are relevant: 1 Tim. 2:5–6 and 3:16. Important in the first is the reference to "the *man* Christ Jesus," and the present tense, "there *is* … one mediator." Clearly Jesus is still man and by reason of his ATONEMENT (1:6) is able to act as a sufficient mediator. In 3:16 Paul incorporates an early creedal hymn which refers directly to the incarnation in terms of "appearing" (cf. 2 Tim. 1:10).

E. 1 and 2 Peter. In the Petrine literature there is no direct reference to the incarnation, but there is considerable emphasis on the reality of the earthly ministry of Christ, his sufferings and resurrection (1 Pet. 1:3, 11, 19; 2:21–24; 3:18; 4:13; 2 Pet. 1:16), and the glory to which this led (1 Pet. 1:7, 11, 21; 4:13). There is no direct reference to his preincarnate existence, but there is to the predetermined purpose of God that he should appear and should suffer (1 Pet. 1:20; cf. 1:11).

F. Hebrews. The theme of this epistle is the perfection of Christ's ministry, past, present, and future. He is the perfect Mediator by whom sinful men are reconciled to God. To establish this, the writer points especially to Christ's deity and humanity, and from this, and by comparison and contrast with the whole OT sacrificial system, to the superiority of his priesthood and the all-sufficiency of his sacrifice.

Reminiscent of John and Colossians is the opening chapter. Reflecting God's glory and bearing "the exact representation [*charaktēr* G5917] of his being," the Son is the perfect Word, the one through whom supremely God has spoken. As the Son he is superior to angels (Heb. 1:3–4) and to all human prophets and leaders (4:3 et al.). Through him all things were created (1:2; cf. Jn. 1:3; Col. 1:16). All this demonstrates the depth of condescension of the Son in becoming man (Heb. 2:9, 14), in every respect like ourselves, including being subject to temptation (2:17; 4:15), even having to "learn obedience" (5:8), yet sinless (4:15).

There is in this book no reference to the mode of the incarnation, but by a quotation in Heb. 10:5–7 from Ps. 40 (following the LXX), there is specific reference to it as the work of God. The language used ("a body you prepared for me"; "I have come to do your will") is clearly intended to indicate the preincarnate existence of him who thereby came into the world (10:5; cf. 9:11) to be made an offering for sin (10:10).

Here, as elsewhere (cf. 1 Tim. 1:15), the title "Christ" is not limited strictly to the Son *after* his incarnation, though this might seem technically appropriate. The point is that though at the incarnation he *became man*, being made "like his brothers" (Heb. 2:17), there was no discontinuity of person. He who was on earth, who lives as High Priest now and forever, is he who lived before and from his exalted position became man ("a little lower than the angels," 2:9). In this respect, Hebrews is wholly consistent with other epistles.

IV. The OT foreshadowing.

NT writers frequently claim the fulfillment of OT prophecies in the life of Jesus, including prediction of the incarnation (see, for example, Matt. 1:23). In general, however, it is difficult to find clear, direct reference to the full truth of the incarnation: that the eternal Son would become flesh and dwell among men and women, and that it would be in this way that the promise of the Servant-Messiah would be fulfilled. In the light of the NT, certain passages take on fuller meaning: the protevangelium of Gen. 3:15 points to Jesus, "the seed of the woman"; Isa. 9:6 foretells the incarnation, speaking of the Son to be *given*, the child to be *born*, who is God, and even "Father"; Mic. 5:2–4 foretells at least certain aspects of the incarnation. So also the promise of the "seed of Abraham" (Gen. 12:7; 22:17–18; et al.) finely interpreted by Paul (Gal. 3:16); the promise to David (2 Sam. 7:12–16) which could find complete fulfillment only in Christ, a fact lying at the base of the dilemma Christ raised in reference to Ps. 110:1 (Matt. 22:41–45).

V. Summary of doctrine

A. Nature of the incarnation. From the foregoing examination certain essential truths can be established. (1) The church has spoken of the "preexistence" (more exactly the "preincarnate existence") of Christ, for he who was born of the Virgin Mary was the Son of God who had lived from all eternity. "In the fulness of time" (Gal. 4:4 KJV), he who was the Creator of all became himself possessor of that human nature which he had created.

(2) Christ became truly human. In saying "the Word became *flesh*" the evangelist asserts the completeness of the incarnation, that his was the full physico-psychical nature essential to true humanity.

(3) In the incarnation there was a certain *temporality* yet also *permanence*. Reference to "the days of his flesh" (Heb. 5:7 KJV) marks out his time as man on earth as a distinct and limited period during which his human nature was in every respect of that kind which God created for life within this physical environment. After this resurrection, Jesus appeared still in the flesh (Lk. 24:39). Yet, at least from and after the ascension, Jesus possesses, not a "lowly body" such as we have, but a body of glory fitted for the environment of the eternal Glory (and into that form we shall be changed, Phil. 3:21). There was thus a temporality in Christ's assumption of the present bodily form and of the limitations that

Gabriel announced the Incarnation to Mary at Nazareth.

belong essentially to this present world—but also a permanence, for he became man forever. Glorified, he is still "the *man* Christ Jesus" (1 Tim. 2:5).

(4) In becoming man, Christ did not cease to be God. It was an incarnation, not a metamorphosis. It is true that certain aspects of his preincarnate existence were not manifested for a time, such as his full divine glory (Jn. 17:5); he also apparently chose not to exercise his uniquely divine powers, at least *on his own behalf* (Matt. 3:3–4). He did, however, work miracles; and although these were not done without the Father, Christ made no disclaimers such as did Peter and Paul (Acts 3:12; 14:14–15).

(5) From before, and through the "days of his flesh" and forever, Christ is the one person. Furthermore, in the flesh he was a truly unified, or integrated, personality. Though he may properly be regarded as the "God-man," he was not, and did not act as, two persons, as though there was simply a coordination, albeit perfect, of the two natures. It was the one person, God incarnate, whose life and ministry is recorded in the Gospels.

(6) As IMMANUEL, "God with us," Christ can be said to represent the absolute immanence of God. He who was present *to* men and women prior to the incarnation—concerned with their needs, directing their history to achieve his providential purposes, drawing some into the privilege of more immediate fellowship with him—became immediately present *with* and *among* them. The incarnation thus demonstrates in fullest measure the immanence of God; such an event, however, was possible in the first place because God is not only transcendent, but also immanent. Then, through the consummation of the ministry of the incarnate Son, every believer experiences the immediate immanence of God in the presence of the indwelling HOLY SPIRIT (Jn. 7:37–39).

B. Mode. The only passages that set out to describe the mode by which the incarnation took place are Matt. 1:18–25; Lk. 1:26–38; 2:1–7. Many have argued against the factuality of these birth narratives, mainly on the basis of assumed improbabilities and highly subjective standards of judgment. However, if the accounts are not accepted, then either Jesus was born of Joseph and Mary through normal sexual intercourse, or Jesus was the illegitimate son of Mary and some other man. In either case, it would make nonsense of the accounts, and it would become impossible to explain the complete untrustworthiness of the evangelists, the contradictory character (in that event) of Mary, and the whole nature, character, and claims of our Lord.

The apparent silence of all other NT writers in this matter need not be explained by asserting that they must have been entirely ignorant of any such thing and that their ignorance must be taken as strong presumption against the credibility of the accounts. Where the incarnation is elsewhere referred to, the attention is not upon its mode but upon its fact and the consequences. Many events described in Scripture are universally accepted on much less documentation. (See VIRGIN BIRTH.)

C. Purpose. At least two purposes are indicated in Scripture, and by some a third is suggested.

1. Revelational. The incarnate Son is the supreme Word, that is, the revelation of God to human beings; this is the force of Jn. 1:1–3, 14, 18. He is the IMAGE OF GOD (2 Cor. 4:4; Col. 1:15). By him, as in no other way, God has spoken (Heb. 1:1–3) He who has seen Jesus has seen the Father (Jn. 14:9). God, as it were, placed himself in the immediate presence of human beings, accessible even to observation by the common senses (1 Jn. 1:1–3), not to be comprehended, however, except through the illumination of the Spirit (1 Cor. 2:7–16). It was the realization of who Christ was and of the nature of his relationship with the Father that gave people a new understanding of God and led them to see his triune nature.

In a double sense Jesus Christ was the image of God. As Son in an immediate and unique sense revealing the divine nature, Jesus was the image of God. As man he also was the perfect example of what was in the mind of God when he said, "Let us make man in our image" (Gen. 1:26). In him is revealed ideal man, man in true and perfect fellowship with God, man as the reflection of the grace and goodness of God, showing the inner graces of love, joy, goodness, and such like. By this, Christ becomes a revelation of what sinful human beings are; by contrast with Christ, they are obviously short of the glory of God (contrast Jn. 1:14 with Rom. 3:23). At the same time he reveals God's purpose for all who commit themselves to his saving purpose, for into this image God transforms them (Rom. 8:29; 2 Cor. 3:18; cf. 2 Cor. 5:17; Col. 3:10).

There is nevertheless a certain hiddenness in the very form of the self-revelation of God in the incarnation. God was, as it were, veiled in Christ so that sinners might look upon him. Certainly, in human flesh the Son of God was not easily recognized (1 Jn. 3:1; cf. 1 Cor. 2:8). For the unrepentant sinner, the full vision of God will occasion unspeakable terror (Rev. 6:15–17); for the believer, the final transformation (1 Jn. 3:2; cf. 2 Cor. 3:18).

2. Soteriological. The last point leads to the truth that the incarnation was essential in the plan of God to deliver men and women from sin and all its dire consequences. Through Christ becoming man, sinful human beings were able in an immediate and direct fashion to receive and acknowledge him as Lord or to repudiate and reject him. For the most part people rejected him; in their laying hands upon the incarnate Lord they were giving the fullest possible expression to sin, and in the act of CRUCIFIXION is exhibited as in no other way the real nature of sin: man's willful refusal to accept the sovereign right and rule of his Creator Lord. Allowing sinners so to act he was still Lord, for it was ordained that in and through his death on the cross he should bear their sins (Acts 2:23; 4:26–28; cf. Jn. 1:29, 36; Rev. 5:6; 13:8; 1 Pet. 2:24). In him God was reconciling the world to himself (2 Cor. 5:19). This was the basic purpose in the incarnation (Heb. 10:5, 10). Furthermore, by virtue of his incarnation, death, and resurrection, he became the new Adam and head of the new race of redeemed humanity (Rom. 5:12–19; Col. 1:18).

These two purposes, revelational and soteriological, are inseparably related. God's revealing activity in all its forms, and supremely in Christ, is soteriological in purpose. This is his answer to human ignorance through sin. Christ is the light of the world (Jn. 8:12), the one through whom God has shone into our hearts (2 Cor. 4:6). The Son came that people might see their sin, learn of God's grace, and so turn to God in true penitence and faith. God's revelatory activity always involves a certain giving of himself to men, and especially was this so in the incarnation. Then in self-giving, God is taking the initial act in restoring them to fellowship with himself. This restoration could not take place, however, without that to which the self-giving of the incarnation led, namely the CROSS (see ATONEMENT). The cross, in turn, is a revelation: in it is revealed as in no other way the inestimable LOVE of the Father and of the Son (Rom. 5:8; 1 Jn. 4:9–10).

3. Consummation of creation. It has been suggested that the incarnation was in the mind of God independently of his redemptive purpose for fallen sinners; that even had Adam not sinned, the Son would still have become incarnate. Indeed, when Adam was created in the image of God, the pattern was that incarnate form which God purposed in due time for his Son. Of this idea, however, Scripture seems to give no clear hint.

VI. Subsequent history of the doctrine. Even within the apostolic period, the reality of the incarnation was challenged. An early and persistent error, strongly denounced in 1 and 2 John (known as DOCETISM, from Greek *dokeō* G1506, "to seem"), was that Christ only appeared to be human, that his inner spirit was divine, not human, or even that his body was not a truly human body. Despite the emphatic scriptural condemnation of this error, many attempts to define the incarnation have tended to be docetic. Docetism includes any view which sees in Jesus less than a full humanity—less than a full experience of the limitations that essentially belong to human existence (though not the additional limitations inherent in *sinful* humanity). Jesus Christ was "made like his brothers in every way" (Heb. 2:17).

With the early rise of conflicting views and a natural continued interest in the nature of Jesus of Nazareth, the church had to give increasing and urgent attention to the doctrine of the incarnation. There were two main issues around which there was great controversy in the early centuries after the apostolic period. (1) One was the actual nature of Jesus Christ—to which the church gave answer: he was both human and divine. (2) If so, how were these two natures united in one person? In answer to this second question, the tendency was, and in modern theology still is, to commence from and emphasize either the deity or the humanity, to some diminution of the other.

An early attempt at solution, "Monarchianism," insisted on the unity of God, arguing either that Jesus was in the first place but man, though filled at baptism with divine power and after the resurrection existing as divine ("Dynamic Monarchianism"), or that the Father, Son, and Spirit were only temporary phases (*prosōpa*) of the one God ("Modalistic Monarchianism"). This latter denied an essential element in the incarnation: the Father *sent* the Son; it is the Son alone who became incarnate. And though the Son is truly divine ("What God was, the Word was," Jn. 1:1 NEB), one cannot say that in the Word is the totality of God.

The occasion of the great Arian controversy of the 4th cent. was the assertion that the Son is a creature, different in essence (*ousia*) from and not coeternal with the Father (see ARIUS). Furthermore, the Logos was said to have taken the place of a human soul (a denial, in effect, of his true humanity). The issues were at times clouded by problems of semantics, key words of high technical significance (such as *ousia*, *prosōpon*, *persona*) being used with subtly different meanings.

Prolonged controversy issued in the declaration of the full deity and full and perfect humanity of Christ, but left unresolved the question concerning how these two natures were united in one person, and this question gave rise to further division. Apollinarius (4th cent.) argued that two natures would mean two persons, and that therefore though the body and soul of Christ were purely human, the human mind or spirit was replaced by the Logos. This denied that Christ was truly man, for the mind is the distinctly human element in man's nature. Nestorius, on the other hand, held Jesus to be truly a man, but not in himself divine; rather that God was present in him as he was in the prophets, though in perfection. Any substantial union, he urged, would have meant an alteration in the Logos. This would have meant, not a true incarnation, but simply a unique conjunction, a concord of will and purpose, not the oneness of a single, personal life. Eutyches, strongly anti-Nestorian, asserted that in the incarnation either there was an *absorption* of the human nature into the divine, or a *fusion* of the two natures making one new nature ("monophysitism"). Christ then would not have been true man, nor could he be man's true representative, substitute or mediator.

At the Council of Chalcedon, A.D. 451, the last three views were condemned. The formula accepted had at heart the assertion of two natures in the one Christ "without confusion, without mutation, without division, without separation; the distinction of natures being by no means taken away by the union, but rather the property of each nature being preserved and concurring in one person and one hypostasis." The formula is open to certain serious criticisms: it is overly negative in form; it is static in form and impersonal in feeling, remote from the living Christ; its terms are too closely linked with the background philosophies of the day. Yet, it was a worthy attempt to preserve the essential scriptural truths.

This Chalcedonian formula has dominated Christian thinking ever since, though the last two centuries have seen much dissatisfaction with it and many new attempts to explain the nature of Christ. Schleiermacher, consistent with his approach to Christian doctrine through personal and subjective religious experience, saw in Christ the supremely God-conscious man, divine in experience rather than in essential nature. Ritschl, critical of much of the traditional formula as being purely speculative, insisted that the inner nature of Christ transcends inquiry. Jesus is known only to the believer, and then mainly as the bearer of perfect revelation.

Of another sort is the KENOSIS theory. There are many variations of this theory but they are alike in two respects. Their beginning point is the preexistent Son who became incarnate, rather than the man, Jesus; and they attempt, then, to define specifically the "self-emptying" (from the Greek verb *kenoō*, "to empty," Phil. 2:7) involved in his becoming man. There is much difference of opinion as to what this latter entailed. For most, it means at least the laying aside of the divine attributes of omnipotence, omniscience, and omnipresence. The major danger is that in strictly defining the "self-emptying," Christ is seen as less than truly divine. Thomasius was the first advocate of this theory.

More modern advocates are A. B. Bruce, Fairbairn, Gore, Forsyth, and Mackintosh.

A "back to the Jesus of history" movement rightly repudiated Docetism, but so emphasized Christ's humanity and generally denied any supernatural activity in his ministry, as to reduce him to the supreme religious hero. D. M. Baillie has likewise emphasized Jesus' humanity, and charges much traditional thinking with the error of Docetism. He insists on the human nature (and human limits) of Christ's knowledge, the human character of his miracles and of his moral and religious life. This insistence tends to question the reality of his deity, leaving the impression of Christ as the supremely inspired man.

Into the radical break with all traditional understanding of the historical Jesus made by Rudolf Bultmann, and his demythologizing of the Gospels, one cannot go here. With the denial of the historicity of the recorded life of Christ, including the resurrection and ascension, and the emphasis not on the historical, incarnate Son and his earthly ministry, but on the Christ of the kerygma, so much of the NT explanation of Christ is thrown aside.

From the metaphor of the CHURCH as the BODY OF CHRIST, one modern school of thought sees the church as the extension of the incarnation, the continuation upon earth of the incarnate Christ, his present visible body. However, the metaphor of the body is not used in this way in the NT, which simply stresses the relationship between members of the body of Christ with one another, and emphasizes the mutual dependence and harmony that should prevail. To develop the metaphor further as some have done is to lead to dangerous ideas regarding the authority of the church, and to the church becoming an object of worship and trust as the now incarnate Christ.

Conclusion. On the evidence of Scripture one is compelled, basically, to affirm the traditional formulation of the doctrine of the incarnation, though holding it as subject to, and not as regulative of, the NT presentation. Further, one must guard against the impulse to answer all possible questions in such a way that much more is dogmatically asserted than God has been pleased to reveal. One must unreservedly accept what is revealed in Scripture, and humbly acknowledge and accept the limitations of our understanding of this divine mystery. Sufficient is revealed to constrain adoring worship of, and the fullest faith in, the Lord of Glory, "who for us men, and for our salvation, came down from heaven, and was incarnate by the Holy Ghost of the Virgin Mary ... was crucified ... rose again ... ascended ... shall come again ... whose kingdom shall have no end." See also CHRISTOLOGY; JESUS CHRIST.

(Important works include A. B. Bruce, *The Humiliation of Christ* [1876]; E. H. Gifford, *The Incarnation* [1897]; C. Gore, *Dissertations on Subjects Connected with the Incarnation* [1895]; P. T. Forsyth, *The Person and Place of Jesus Christ* [1909]; H. R. Mackintosh, *The Doctrine of the Person of Christ* [1912]; S. Cave, *The Doctrine of the Person of Christ* [1925]; L. Hodgson, *And Was Made Man* [1928]; E. Brunner, *The Mediator* [1934]; L. Boettner, *The Person of Christ* [1943]; G. C. Berkouwer, *The Person of Christ* [1954]; K. Barth, *Church Dogmatics* [1964–82], 1/2:122–202; A. M. Stibbs, *God Became Man* [1957]; L. Morris, *The Lord From Heaven* [1958]; D. M. Baillie, *God Was in Christ* [1961]; J. D. G. Dunn, *Christology in the Making* [1980]; D. F. Wells, *The Person of Christ: A Biblical and Historical Analysis of the Incarnation* [1984]; M. de Jonge, *Christology in Context: The Earliest Response to Jesus* [1988]; M. Erickson, *The Word Became Flesh: A Contemporary Incarnational Christology* [1991]; W. Grudem, *Systematic Theology: An Introduction to Christian Doctrine* [1994], ch. 26; P. D. Molnar, *Incarnation and Resurrection* [2007].) V. W. JOHNSTON

incense. Material which is burned to make a fragrant smoke; the fragrant smoke thus produced.

I. Terminology. The most common Hebrew word for "incense," occurring almost sixty times, primarily in the PENTATEUCH, is *qĕṭōret* H7792 (Exod. 25:6 et al.). Note also its cognates with the same meaning, occurring only once each, *qiṭṭēr* H7789 (Jer. 44:21), *qĕṭôrâ* H7777 (Deut. 33:10), and *muqṭār* H5231 (Mal. 1:11). All of these are derived from the verb *qāṭar* H7787 (piel and hiphil, "to burn incense"). The term *lĕbōnâ* H4247, often rendered "frankincense," occurs over twenty times (Lev. 2:1–2 et al.; cf. Gk. *libanos* G3337, only Matt. 9:4). In the NT, the Greek word for "incense" is *thymiama* G2592 (only Lk. 1:10–11; Rev. 5:8; 8:3–4; 18:13; verb *thymiaō* G2594, "to burn incense," only Lk. 1:9).

II. Incense in the ANE. From the earliest times for which there are records about worship, incense was used by the Egyptians, Babylonians, Assyrians, Arabians, and Canaanites. The Canaanites, who were the nearest neighbors of the Hebrews, have left various incense stands, altars, censers, and spoons in city levels dated in the 2nd millennium B.C. Egyptian representations of sieges of Canaanite cities sometimes show a man on the wall holding a stand in which incense is smoking, doubtless to reinforce the prayers offered by men standing behind him with upraised arms.

III. Sources of incense. Incense came from S Arabia (FRANKINCENSE, MYRRH), Somaliland (frankincense), Palestine (SAFFRON, STACTE), Red Sea (ONYCHA), Persia (GALBANUM), India (SPIKENARD), and Ceylon (CINNAMON). Arabs controlled much of the incense trade (Gen. 37:25; 1 Ki. 10:10; Ezek. 27:22), and this trade brought wealth to SHEBA and other kingdoms of S ARABIA. (See also SPICE.)

IV. Kinds and preparation of incense. The incense most often mentioned in the Bible is frankincense, sometimes used alone and also as part of the holy incense. Equal parts of this and of stacte, onycha, and galbanum with a little salt (RSV) were mixed together to make the holy incense used on the incense altar (Exod. 30:34–35; cf. Sir. 24:15). This formula was not to be used for secular purposes (Exod. 30:38). Gifts provided incense for use in the sanctuary (Num. 7:14–86; Jer. 17:26; 41:5), and it was stored in the temple (Neh. 13:5, 9).

The writer of JUBILEES, reflecting the Jewish practice of the 2nd cent. B.C., attributed incense offerings to the patriarchs: to Adam, frankincense and galbanum (Jub. 3.27); to Abraham, frankincense, galbanum, stacte, nard, myrrh, spice, and costus (16.24); to Jacob, incense (32.6). JOSEPHUS says that in the temple of his day (1st cent. A.D.) thirteen elements were used in the holy incense (War 5.5.5). According to the TALMUD (Keritot 6a), the following ingredients were used in making the holy incense of the second temple: resin (corresponding to stacte in Exod. 30:34), onycha, galbanum, frankincense, each seventy manehs; myrrh, cassia, spikenard, saffron, each sixteen manehs; costus, twelve manehs; aromatic rind, three manehs; cinnamon, nine manehs; lye from leeks, six kabs; Cyprus wine, three seahs and three kabs; salt of Sodom, one quarter kab; smoke-raiser, a small quantity; and, according to Rabbi Nathan, also Jordan resin, a small quantity, a total of 368. According to PLUTARCH (Isis and Osiris, 80), the Egyptian incense called kyphi had sixteen elements, and several materials were combined in Babylonian and Assyrian incense offerings. The priestly family of Abtinas was in charge of pounding and mixing the holy incense, and only they knew the secret of making incense whose smoke rose straight up (b. Yoma 38a).

V. Incense in common life. Incense, like PERFUME, brings joy (Prov. 27:9). It might be burned at a revel (Ezek. 23:41) or was passed around in bowls after a banquet (m. Berakot 6:6). It perfumed the carriage of SOLOMON (Cant. 3:6) and was an element of the luxurious life at Rome (Rev. 18:13). Incense was used as fumigation to stop a plague (Num. 16:46–48). It was burned at the funerals of kings (2 Chr. 16:14; 21:19; Jer. 34:5), and perhaps the same custom was observed by the common people (Amos 6:9–10).

VI. Religious use of incense. The worship of BAAL, the QUEEN OF HEAVEN, and other foreign gods by means of incense often is condemned in the OT (e.g., 1 Ki. 11:8; in the Apocrypha, Ep. Jer. 43). Also condemned are the pagan "incense altars" (Lev. 26:30; 2 Chr. 30:14). The burning of incense at the shrines on HIGH PLACES also is often criticized (e.g., 1 Ki. 22:43), either because these high places were associated with IDOLATRY (14:23) or because they conflicted with the centralization of worship in Jerusalem (3.2). The prophetic criticism of incense offering in the worship of the Lord (Isa. 1:13; 66:3; Jer. 6:20) is not an absolute negation but only part of the prophets' condemnation of empty formalism. The NEHUSHTAN or bronze serpent (Num. 21:9) was worshiped with incense until HEZEKIAH removed this temptation to idolatry (2 King 18:4).

According to the law, only the priests descended from AARON could offer incense (Lev. 2:2). Those who tried to usurp this priestly function were punished by death (Num. 16:31–32) or disease

(2 Chr. 26:19), and even priests who offered incense improperly were killed (Lev. 10:1–2). In the special case of a plague, Aaron offered the incense with a censer, not in the sanctuary as usually, but in the camp (Num. 16:16–17).

Coptic priests using incense during a liturgical procession at the Church of the Holy Sepulchre in Jerusalem. © Dr. James C. Martin

Frankincense was added to various meal offerings on the altar of burnt offering (Lev. 2:1–2, 15–16; 6:15). It also was added to the bread of the Presence (Lev. 24:7) in two dishes (*m. Menaḥot* 11:5–8), which Josephus says were of gold (*Ant.* 3.10.7). After a week this frankincense accompanying the bread was burned on the altar of burnt offering (ibid.). The priest offered the compounded holy incense morning and evening on the gold-covered altar in front of the veil. According to Exod. 30:1–10, Aaron as the high priest did this; later priests were chosen by lot to perform this function (*m. Tamid* 2:5; 5:2, 4; 6:1–3; cf. Lk. 1:9). On the Day of Atonement, the high priest offered the compounded incense in a censer on the ark, or, in the second temple, on a stone in the holy of holies (Lev. 16:12–13; *m. Yoma* 1:2; 2:4; 3:3–4; 5:1–2; 7:4). According to the apocryphal book of TOBIT, incense was thought to help in the exorcism of demons (Tob. 6:7; 8:2–3).

VII. Figurative references to incense. In the book of ECCLESIASTICUS, the beauty of wisdom and the memory of Josiah are compared to incense (Sir. 24:15; 49:1). In the NT, the word *incense* is used as a symbol of the knowledge of Christ (2 Cor. 2:14), of the Philippians' offering to Paul (Phil. 4:18), and of the prayers of the saints (Rev. 5:8; 8:3–4). PHILO JUDAEUS (*Who Is the Heir of Divine Things?*, 41) and Josephus (*War* 5.5.5) interpret the varied materials of the holy incense allegorically as symbolic of God's proprietorship over the whole world.

VIII. The function of the incense offering. The basic purpose of incense, as of other offerings, was to honor God (Mal. 1:11). Incense symbolized and expressed prayer (Ps. 141:2; Jdt. 9:1; Lk. 1:10; Rev. 5:8; 8:3–4). The offering of incense made atonement for sin (Num. 16:46–47). The smoke of the incense on the Day of Atonement veiled the mercy seat from the eyes of the high priest so that he would not die from seeing God's glory (Lev. 16:13). Divine revelations were given to Hyrcanus (Jos. *Ant.* 13.10.3) and to Zechariah (Lk. 1:5–21) while they were offering incense. Maimonides, a physician, suggested that incense also may have had the practical value of counteracting the smell of the bloody sacrifices (*Guide of the Perplexed* 3.45). See CENSER; INCENSE, ALTAR OF; WORSHIP.

(See further E. G. C. F. Atchley, *A History of the Use of Incense in Divine Worship* [1909]; A. Schmidt, *Drogen und Drogenhandel im Altertum* [1924]; M. Löhr, *Das Räucheropfer im Alten Testament* [1927]; F. Blome, *Die Opfermaterie in Babylonien und Israel* [1934]; G. W. Van Beek in *BA* 23 [1960]: 70–95; M. Haran in *VT* 10 [1960]: 113–29; N. Groom, *Frankincense and Myrrh: A Study of the Arabian Incense Trade* [1981]; K. Nielsen, *Incense in Ancient Israel* [1986].) J. ALEXANDER THOMPSON

incense, altar of. One of the pieces of furniture prescribed in the orders God gave to MOSES for the construction of the TABERNACLE in the wilderness (Exod. 30:1–11). It was a cubit square and two cubits high (approximately 1.5 by 3 ft.), with horns on the corners, formed of ACACIA wood and plated with GOLD (Exod. 37:25–28). Rings were added through which poles could be inserted for the purpose of carrying it. The high priest was directed to burn incense on it every morning and evening, but to offer no sacrifice or pour no libation upon it. Presumably this is identical with the golden altar mentioned later (Exod. 39:38), and is distinguished from the large bronze altar that stood in the courtyard of the tabernacle.

The position of this altar in the tabernacle seems to have been within the inner sanctuary just in front of the ARK OF THE COVENANT (Exod. 40:5; Lev. 16:11–14), on which the high priest sprinkled the blood of atonement once a year (Exod. 30:10). The golden altar of Solomon's TEMPLE was placed in the inner sanctuary (1 Ki. 6:20, 22), but in Herod's temple it seems to have been outside the veil within the "Holy Place" (Lk. 1:10). Revelation speaks of an altar of incense that stood before the throne of God (Rev. 8:3). The reference to the golden altar in Hebrews agrees that it was within the inner sanctuary (Heb. 9:3).

The apparent conflict between those passages that locate the altar in front of the curtain (Exod. 30:6; 40:26) and those that place it in the inner sanctuary has been given different solutions. N. Snaith (*Leviticus and Numbers* [1967], 43) suggests that the original text was modified to suit the arrangement of the second and third temples, and that there was no altar of incense in the tabernacle. He follows J. Wellhausen's argument that two separate sources are responsible for the difference. In the light of the fact that small incense altars were used by the Canaanites from the earliest times in Palestine, it is hardly possible that such were unknown, or that an altar of incense could not have been part of the furniture of the tabernacle. The apparent discrepancy in the location of the golden altar may arise from differing usages between the tabernacle and the temple, or from the fact that it stood so close to the ark that it was classed with the Holy of Holies because it represented an intercessory ministry in the presence of God. One Jewish source suggests that Exod. 25:1—27:19 is the blueprint for the construction of the tabernacle, while Exod. 40:1–33 describes the actual assembling of the building, and consequently a modification of position. See also ALTAR. M. C. TENNEY

Incest. See CRIMES AND PUNISHMENTS.

in Christ. See UNION WITH CHRIST.

India. The great peninsula and subcontinent located S of the Himalaya Mountains, occupied in modern times by the nation of India and other countries. Although explicit references to India occur only twice in the Bible (Esth. 1:1; 8:9; Heb. *hōddû* H2064, prob. referring only to the area lying W of the Indus and forming the eastern part of the Persian empire), the evidence seems to indicate that Palestine had established commercial relations with the subcontinent much earlier. Some interpreters have contended that the river PISHON (Gen. 2:11) in the land of HAVILAH refers to India. The suggestion also has been made that the goods brought from OPHIR, such as sandalwood (almug trees, 1 Ki. 10:11; 2 Chr. 2:8), ivory, and apes, were Indian. The Tyrian merchandise mentioned in Ezek. 27:15 may also have been from India.

The NT makes no reference to India, but the apocryphal literature of both OT and NT do mention it. ANTIOCHUS Eupator employed elephants ridden by Indians against the Jewish armies (1 Macc. 6:37; Gk. *Indos*), and he eventually ceded India to the Romans, although, in fact, he had never owned it (1 Macc. 8:8; Gk. *Indikē*). The principal reference to India in the NT Apocrypha is to be found in the Gnostic *Acts of Thomas* which purports to tell of the apostle's missionary journey to the Indo-Scythian kingdom of Gundaphorus. There is, however, little indication that it offers any actual historical information. Some Christian missionary may have gone to India in the 1st or 2nd centuries, and this perhaps formed the foundation of the story concerning THOMAS. India has little significance in the biblical record. W. S. REID

inerrancy. See INSPIRATION.

infallibility. See INSPIRATION.

Infancy Gospels. See APOCRYPHAL NEW TESTAMENT I.C.

infidel (from Lat. *infidelis*, "unfaithful"). One who is not among the faithful; an unbeliever. Its earliest English reference was to the Saracens (Muslims) who embraced a religion opposed to Christianity. Muslims came to use an equivalent expression denoting all who are not part of Islam. In the ecclesiastical language of Rome, *infidelis* came to mean "unbelieving," and signified all those outside the church. Used particularly of missionary work in non-Christian lands, it was used synonymously with heathen. As used popularly, an infidel is a person who has knowledge of the Christian faith but avowedly rejects its claims to divine origin and authority. It is usually a term of opprobrium.

M. E. OSTERHAVEN

inflammation. See DISEASE.

Ingathering, Feast of. See FEASTS.

inheritance. Something received from an ancestor through a legal will or TESTAMENT. In the Bible, the term (Heb. *naḥălâ* H5709, Gk. *klēronomia* G3100) is often used figuratively in a theological sense.

I. In the OT. In the patriarchal narratives, the principles of inheritance are tied to the BIRTHRIGHT. The FIRSTBORN son—"my might, the first sign of my strength," as the aged JACOB described REUBEN (Gen. 49:3)—had special privileges, deference, and associated duties (44:33). It seems clear that he held by such right a double portion of his father's goods (Deut. 21:17). It is also apparent that, at the dictate of the father, this special position could be forfeited (Gen. 49:3–4; 1 Chr. 5:1). ESAU traded his birthright for food in contempt (Gen. 25:29–34), and ISAAC, in a moment of insight, realizing that action thrust upon him by forces beyond his control had caused him to transfer the firstborn's blessing to another, confirmed what he had unwittingly done (27:33; Heb. 12:16); hence the effort in the passage already quoted (Deut. 21:15–17) to insure protection for the legal firstborn in the case of parental caprice or inequity.

It follows that, if the ancient principles were observed in conservative households of Palestine in NT times, the portion demanded by the prodigal son (Lk. 15:12) was one-third only of the estate, and given by some custom that allowed the younger son to anticipate division and seek his fortune abroad. SARAH's anger over HAGAR's son ISHMAEL (Gen. 21:10) appears to show that the sons of wives not in full status could claim a share in the inheritance (Jdg. 11:2). It is a matter of conjecture how far this was carried out, and tension is evident over the rights of inheritance of sons of a secondary marriage.

Considerable illustration of the importance of ordered inheritance is to be found in the records of civilizations contemporary with patriarchal times. The suspicion lingers that the patriarchs, having emancipated themselves from urban society, had shed some of the legal obligations that went closely with membership of an ancient state. In the NUZI tablets, for example, inheritance is revealed as a matter of supreme legal importance. Property was theoretically inalienable, and complicated laws of adoption were necessary to secure any freedom of transfer and conveyance at all. J. A. Thompson quotes details and also an interesting document (*The Bible and Archaeology* [1962], 27–31). It is evident that Hebrew law, when Moses came to formulate its provisions, had much to order and to regularize.

It was done with brevity and clarity. If a man died without sons to follow him, the inheritance went to the daughters, if there were any; in default of daughters, to his brothers; in default of brothers, to his uncles on the father's side, or to their next of kin (Num. 27:8–11). There was one important provision. If the inheritance fell to a daughter, it was obligatory upon her that she marry within the tribe, a provision designed to keep tribal property stable and uneroded (36:6). (It has been plausibly suggested that in this social legislation lies the explanation for the variant genealogies in Matthew's and Luke's gospels. Matthew gives Joseph's line because he was legally regarded as Jesus' father, an important point in law. It was also necessary, in view of the legislation on inheritance in the closing chapters of Numbers, to establish and record the fact that Mary had fulfilled her obligations by marrying within the tribe. A reasonable hypothesis, therefore, suggests that Luke gives the genealogy of Mary. Joseph, not Mary, is set down as the immediate descendant of Eli, because Joseph authenticated Mary's inheritance by the legal provisions recorded in Num. 27:1–11 and 36:1–13. It is probable that fuller and more exact information would establish some procedure of adoption in such cases. (See GENEALOGY OF JESUS CHRIST.)

One notable aspect of the Hebrew law of inheritance was that the widow was not provided for; she was almost considered a part of the inheritance. In the case of a man dying childless, his brother could marry the widow and possibly provide the deceased with heirs (Gen. 38:8, 9; Deut. 25:5–10; Matt. 22:23–25). It was possible for this right or obligation to be transferred to the nearest kinsman. The story of RUTH is built round this theme. NAOMI was past the age of childbearing. Ruth took her place, and BOAZ went through the complicated process of acquiring the right to marry her (Ruth 2:20; 3:9–13; 4:1–12). See GOEL.

The inheritance of landed property was very carefully guarded. Land could not, for example, by Levitical law (Lev. 25:23, 24) be alienated forever. If it was sold it could be redeemed by the next of kin (25:25). AHAB's offer to buy NABOTH's vineyard was therefore a flagrant violation of the law (1 Ki. 21:3). The land of Canaan itself was regarded as the inheritance of the whole nation (Exod. 15:17; Josh. 21:19). The Abrahamic COVENANT (Gen. 12:7; 15:18–21) made mention of a land to possess, as well as offspring to possess it. Israel never wavered in this conviction that the land was theirs, that their title was a rightful one, and although they never possessed it to the full limits of its prescribed boundaries, they firmly held the thought that the intruder had no right to be there and could not be permanent.

The prophets who had caught the wider vision of Israel's mission to the world at large looked upon the land as a base from which all Israel's contribution could be made. The firm possession of the land was the essential condition, while its loss in exile or invasion was considered a loss of God's favor and the deprivation of a rightful inheritance. From this privilege the Levites alone were excluded: God was their inheritance (Deut. 18:1–2) (See PRIESTS AND LEVITES.) They were supported by dues and tribute levied on the remaining tribes (Deut. 18:3–5). This idea, like most ideas in the experience of the Hebrew people, acquired spiritual extension, and God was similarly regarded in the language of prayer and devotion as the inheritance of the whole nation (Ps. 16:5–6). There are other figurative elaborations, as for example, the use of the term for God's own "inheritance," his faithful people (Ps. 2:8). It should be noted that the two common Hebrew verbs that can be rendered "to inherit" (*yāraš* H3769 and *nāḥal* H5706) convey primarily the notion of rightful possession rather than succession. (See C. J. H. Wright, *God's People in God's Land: Family, Land and Property in the Old Testament* [1990]; M. Weinfeld, *The Promise of Land: The Inheritance of the Land of Canaan by the Israelites* [1993]; *NIDOTTE*, 2:547–49; 3:77–81.)

Such is the information that may be gleaned from the provisions of the law and from incidents relevant to the theme in the historical books, together with the extension semantically into figure and symbol. Wills were not made in Jewish society until Hellenistic times, when the custom was adopted from the Greeks. The rabbis studied the process with their usual meticulous care, and carefully regulated all details. The NT reflects current testamentary practice in two contexts (Gal. 3:15 and Heb. 9:16–17).

II. In the NT. The figurative meaning of inheritance is universal in the NT. Note, for example, the story of the wicked tenants (Matt. 21:33–41), in which the concept of inheritance, though literal in the context of events, is symbolic in its significance. The simplest method of dealing with the theme will be to list all occurrences of the subject under the heading of the words commonly employed.

The Greek verb *klēronomeō* G3099 originally meant to obtain by means of a lot (*klēros* G3102), and then to receive, in whole or in part, an estate, property, or possession (Matt. 5:5; 19:29; 25:34; Mk. 10:17; Lk. 10:25; 18:18; 1 Cor. 6:9–10; 15:50 [twice]; Gal. 5:21; Heb. 6:12; 12:17; 1 Pet. 3:9; Rev. 21:7). The cognate noun *klēronomia* G3100, from its use in a literal sense of an estate to be passed on, can refer to a divine possession bestowed in virtue of sonship or adoption. This meaning stems largely from the figurative use of the word in the OT for Israel's "inheritance." It reflects the development of the idea of a national Israel into a spiritual body, which is a major development of thought between the Testaments (Matt. 21:38; Mk. 12:7; Lk. 12:13; 20:14; Acts 7:5; 20:32; Gal. 3:18; Eph. 1:14, 18; 5:5; Col. 3:24; Heb. 9:15; 11:8; 1 Pet. 1:4; cf. also the verb *klēroō* G3103, Eph. 1:11, and the use of the noun *klēros* in Acts 26:28 and Col. 1:12).

The word *klēronomos* G3101, "heir," is used figuratively of Christ, who as the son of Adam inherits, or comes into possession of, universal dominion (Gen. 1:26, 27; Ps. 8:4–8; Heb. 2:6–8); as son of Abraham, he is heir to the land of the promise (Gen. 22:16–18; Heb. 2:16; Rom. 4:13); as son of David, heir to the royal throne (Matt. 1:1, 6; Lk. 1:30–33); as the Son of God, the heir of all things (Heb. 1:1–2; Acts 10:36). (See also Matt. 21:38; Mk. 12:7; Lk. 20:14; Rom. 4:13, 14; Gal. 3:29; 4:1, 7, 30; Eph. 3:6; Tit. 3:7; Heb. 1:2, 14; 6:17; Jas. 2:5.) All of these contexts show facets of the extension of the idea of the heirship of Christ to all those accepted in him. (See J. D. Hester, *Paul's Concept of Inheritance* [1968]; *NIDNTT*, 2:295–304.)

III. Greece and Rome. The law of inheritance in Greek and Roman society has no necessary place in this survey, but it is well to remember that the NT was written and read in a Greco-Roman world. Inheritance in the Greek world was automatic and formal, on the same model as the Hebrew with a scale of priorities, and rather less subject to modification by the will of the father than appears to have been the case in Hebrew society. A will need not be written. It was valid if made by declaration before appropriate witnesses. In Rome, on the other hand, the will or testamentary deposition was paramount, a legal order of succession coming into operation only in cases of intestacy. The will was a public document, guarded by law, and formalized in law with set forms of language (details are succinctly set out in the *OCD*, 757–58). As an illustration of a Roman will, note the following document (Pap. Tebt. 381, from Egypt, A.D. 123):

"The 8th year of the Emperor Caesar Trajanus Hadrianus Augustus, Choiak 22, at Tebtunis in the division of Polemon of the Arsinoite name. Thaesis daughter of Orsenouphis son of Onnophris, her mother being Thenobastis, of the aforesaid village of Tebtunis, aged about seventy-eight years, having a scar on the right forearm, acting with her guardian, her kinsman Cronion son of Ameis, aged about twenty-seven, having a scar between his eyebrows, acknowledges that she, the acknowledging party, Thaesis, has consented that after her death there shall belong to Thenpetesuchus, her daughter by her late departed husband Pansais, and also to Sansenus son of Tephersos, the son of her other daughter Taorseus, now dead, to the two of them, property as follows: to Thenpetesuchus alone, the house, yard and all effects belonging to Thaesis in the said village of Tebtunis by right of purchase from Thenpetesuchus daughter of Petesuchus, and the furniture, utensils, household stock and apparel left by Thaesis, and the sums due to her and other property of any kind whatsoever, while to Sansenus she has bequeathed eight drachmae of silver, which Sansenus shall receive from Thenpetesuchus after the death of Thaesis; on condition that the daughter Thenpetesuchus shall properly perform the obsequies and laying out of her mother, and shall discharge such private debts as Thaesis shall prove to owe, but as long as her mother Thaesis lives she shall have power to …" E. M. BLAIKLOCK

iniquity. See SIN.

ink. A writing fluid whose chief ingredient was soot or black carbon. It was mixed with gum or oil for use on parchment, or with a metallic substance for use on PAPYRUS. The early use of metallic ink in Israel is shown in the LACHISH letters (c. 586 B.C.). The DEAD SEA SCROLLS were written with

Copper inkpot discovered at Qumran.

ink made of carbon. The *Letter of Aristeas* says that the copy of the law sent to Ptolemy II was written in gold. The Egyptians must have used a good quality ink, as the bright colors in some papyri show. The ingredients for making ink were kept in a writing case. The word is used once in the OT (Heb. *děyô* H1902, Jer. 36:18) and three times in the NT (Gk. *melan* G3506 ["black"], 2 Cor. 3:3; 2 Jn. 12; 3 Jn. 13). S. Barabas

inkhorn. This English term (meaning a vessel made from a horn and used to hold ink) is used by the KJV to render *qeset* H7879, which occurs in only one passage (Ezek. 9:2–3, 11). This Hebrew word refers to a writing case for reed pens and some sort of container for ink near the upper end of the case. It was carried in the belt. Monuments of all periods show the Egyptian palette, a long narrow board with grooves for pens and circular hollows for ink.

inn. The Hebrew word *mālôn* H4869 (rendered "inn" by the KJV in Gen. 42:27; 43:21; Exod. 4:24) means "lodging place" or "camping ground." It may refer to the camping place of an individual (Jer. 9:2); of a family on a journey (Exod. 4:24); of a caravan (Gen. 42:27; 43:21); of an army (2 Ki. 19:23); or even of a nation (Josh. 4:3, 8). In none of these references is there any implication of a structure, with the possible exception of the one in Jeremiah. When travelers could not find lodging in private dwellings they stayed in the open (cf. Gen. 19:2; 28:11; Jdg. 19:15).

In the Targum of Josh. 2:1, Rahab is called an innkeeper (cf. Jos. *Ant.* 5.1.2). Perhaps she combined this occupation with her profession as harlot, a practice attested occasionally in Roman times. It is interesting to note that the Aramaic word used in this passage is of foreign origin (*pûndĕqîtāʾ*, from Gk. *pandocheion* G4106), possibly indicating that the organized inn was an importation into the ANE. It is common knowledge that inns existed in Greek times and throughout the period of the Roman empire. Generally they were considered bad, the traveler being subject not only to discomfort, but also robbery and even death. For this reason, wealthy people who traveled maintained their own *deversoria* (lodging houses) along the route, or stayed with friends on a reciprocal basis. Inns sometimes were managed independently, sometimes by the slaves or freedmen of the owner of a nearby villa. (See *OCD*, 759–60.)

When Mary and Joseph discovered that "there was no room for them in the inn" (Gk. *katalyma* G2906, Lk. 2:7), one should not think of anything resembling a hotel. More likely they found themselves in some sort of village guest house. Indeed, the same word is used to describe the upper room where Jesus ate the Passover with his disciples (Mk. 14:14; Lk. 22:11). It is in fact possible that Mary and Joseph had to stay in the lower level of a house (perhaps the home of a distant relative), where the animals were kept, because the normal living area was full.

In the story of the good Samaritan, the term used is *pandocheion* (Lk. 10:34). An innkeeper (*pandocheus* G4107, lit., "one who receives all") is mentioned who is paid to provide food and lodging for the man who was left in his care. Something resembling a modern inn seems to be in view in this passage. If one may judge from the Khan Hathrur, located today midway between Jerusalem and Jericho, the inn of Jesus' day perhaps consisted of a large building, with an arched doorway opening into a spacious courtyard with a well in the center. R. C. Stone

inner being. This phrase is used by the NIV and other translations to render Greek *esō anthrōpos*, (lit., "man inside," Rom. 7:22 [KJV, "inward man"; NRSV, "inmost self"]; Eph. 3:16). The concept of an inner being is reflected elsewhere in the Bible. It refers to the true ego, whereas the outer person may or may not be a genuine portrayal of the inner being. Jesus castigated the scribes and Pharisees for their religious hypocrisy, comparing them to "whitewashed tombs" because they appear righteous "on the outside," whereas "on the inside" they were full of sin (Matt. 23:27–28). He also warned his disciples against false prophets who come "in sheep's clothing, but inwardly they are ferocious wolves" (7:15).

In the period of the judges, when Israel was clamoring for a king, Samuel, under divine guidance, had to make a distinction between the inner and outer person. Seven of Jesse's sons were rejected, but David, the youngest, was selected for king. Samuel explained, "Man looks at the outward appearance, but the LORD looks at the heart" (1 Sam. 16:7). The inner person is the real and dominant self. PAUL was a living example of the distinction in the better way, and consequently prayed that God would strengthen the Ephesians "with power through his Spirit in your inner being" (Eph. 3:16).

G. B. FUNDERBURK

innocence. This English noun and the adjective *innocent* are used variously in Bible version to render several Hebrew and Greek terms. Especially common is the Hebrew adjective *nāqî H5929*, which occurs a number of times in legal passages (Exod. 23:7; Deut. 19:10; et al.), but in other contexts as well (Job 4:7; Ps. 10:8; et al.). The primary Greek term for "innocent" is *athōon G127* (in the NT only in Matt. 27:4, 24). In addition, a number of words that mean "clean," "good," or the like can properly be rendered "innocent" in some contexts (e.g., Heb. *ṣaddîq H7404*, "righteous," Gen. 20:4; Gk. *akeraios G193*, "unmixed, pure," Matt. 10:16).

It must be remembered that the OT terms are not freely and easily interchanged and that the underlying idea of neutral or nonjuridicial innocence is foreign to the OT world of thought. The modern concept of a state of noncommitment between two alternative moral choices simply does not exist. Therefore, all men and nations in the OT either are justified by the will of Yahweh or condemned. There is no middle ground. The same set of concepts carries over to the NT, which utilizes a large number of Greek terms to define precisely the notion of JUSTIFICATION by God's proclamation and upon an ATONEMENT accomplished by Christ.

W. WHITE, JR.

innocents, massacre of the. This is the conventional name given to the slaughter of children two years old and under in BETHLEHEM at the time of the birth of Christ (Matt. 2:16–18). The statement of the MAGI about a child to be born in Bethlehem who would become "king of the Jews" aroused in HEROD the Great the fear of a claimant to his petty royal power. In his rage when the Wise Men deceived him and did not return to Jerusalem, he ordered the killing, thinking to put an end to any possible rival. Estimates of the number of victims range from 20 to 30 to as high as 60 or 70 (the numbers 3,000 and 144,000 mentioned in some early Christian writings have no support). The objective and detached manner in which the narrative is presented indicates its historicity. It fits perfectly the character and deeds of Herod, especially in his later years; for JOSEPHUS mentions even worse atrocities committed by the king in his obsession for power.

Matthew sees in this incident a fulfillment of Jer. 31:15, though the connection between this verse and Bethlehem is not clear, for RAMAH, the traditional burial place of RACHEL, is about 10 mi. N of JERUSALEM. Many have thought that the citation is "of doubtful appositeness in a strict sense" (A. B. Bruce in *EGT*, 1:76). However, the passage in Jeremiah is an expression of hope that the tears of exile will come to an end when the people return from captivity. For Matthew, "the tears begun in Jeremiah's day are climaxed and ended by the tears of the mothers of Bethlehem. The heir to David's throne has come, the exile is over, the true Son of God has arrived, and he will introduce the new covenant ... promised by Jeremiah" (D. A. Carson in *EBC*, 8:95).

R. C. STONE

inquire. To seek information, especially to consult God with regard to his will. Various terms meaning "to ask," "to search," and the like may be used in this connection (such as Heb. *bāqaš H1335* piel, Exod. 33:7 et al.; *dāraš H2011*, Gen. 25:22; *šāʾal H8626* [with the preposition *bĕ-*], Jdg. 18:5 et al.). The people of Israel would come to MOSES to inquire of God in a dispute (Exod. 18:15 NRSV; cf. 33:7–11). The priestly EPHOD was a kind of pouch attached to the breastpiece of the high priest in which the sacred lots URIM AND THUMMIM were placed (Exod. 28:28–30). JOSHUA was to come to the priest to inquire of God and receive answer by the use of these lots to determine when Israel should move (Exod. 28:30). DAVID resorted to the ephod on occasion when he was fleeing from Saul (1 Sam. 23:9–12). SAUL used the same method to decide a vexed question (1 Sam. 14.41). (See further R. de Vaux, *Ancient Israel* [1961], 349–53.)

When denied divine guidance by this means, Saul resorted to an unlawful medium (1 Sam. 28:6–7). Mediums, wizards, and other such forms of DIVINATION were under God's ban (Isa. 8:19; cf. Deut. 18:10–12). Later on people would inquire of God by prophets, as King JEHOSHAPHAT did of ELISHA (2 Ki. 3:11–12; cf. Jer. 42:2–7). On JOSIAH's orders, even HILKIAH the priest went with other leaders to inquire of HULDAH the prophetess (2 Ki. 22:12–16). In the NT direct PRAYER is the prevailing form of inquiry, both by teaching (Jas. 1,5) and by practice, as in the case of Jesus in the Garden of GETHSEMANE (Matt. 26:39), and PAUL, when he inquired of God about his nagging thorn in the flesh (2 Cor. 12:7–9). N. B. BAKER

I.N.R.I. These letters constitute the abbreviation of the supposed Latin inscription on the cross of Jesus: *Iesus Nazarenus Rex Iudaeorum* — "Jesus of Nazareth, King of the Jews." All four Gospels mention the inscription but vary as to the contents. The traditional Latin wording of the title seems to be based on Jn. 19:19 rather than on the synoptic parallels. The abbreviation I.N.R.I. is ascribed by tradition to Helena, Emperor Constantine's mother,

An artistic conception of the board on which Pilate placed the charge against Jesus (in Hebrew, Latin, and Greek).

who claimed to have discovered it on a board (with the three crosses found in a cave identified as the holy sepulchre; cf. *Ecclesiastical History of Sozomen*, 2.1–2). It appears in paintings of the CRUCIFIXION by M. Munkacsy, F. Pesellino, Ed. Burne-Jones.

J. C. DEYOUNG

insanity. See MADNESS.

inscriptions. The discovery of many inscriptions from Bible times has revolutionized the knowledge of its background. Until the 19th cent., students of the Bible were primarily limited in their research to a small number of books in monasteries and libraries, such as the writings of JOSEPHUS and EUSEBIUS. Now from all over the Bible lands inscriptions are available containing laws, treaties, decrees, private letters, memorials, etc. Such inscriptions lead back directly to the ancient setting, bypassing the problems of MS transmission.

Ancient inscriptions were incised on clay, marble, stone, metal, and terra cotta. In the lands of the TIGRIS and EUPHRATES, clay was extensively used, but in EGYPT the hieroglyphs were carefully incised on stone (see WRITING). In GREECE the best inscribing was done in the 5th and 4th cent. B.C., in ATHENS. The direction of writing varies. The letters or symbols may be arranged vertically, read from top to bottom, or horizontally, read either from right to left or left to right; they also can be arranged in a pattern in which case their order may be indeterminate, or in a wandering curved line, or left to right and right to left alternately (*boustrophedon*, "as an ox ploughing"). Most Semitic inscriptions read from right to left; the earliest Greek followed the same direction. The direction left to right became regular in Greece after the 6th cent. B.C. and consequently was adopted by the Roman and European systems.

The place and position of the inscription varies with its use. Sometimes on Mesopotamian statues or reliefs the inscriptions were cut right across the figures without regard to artistic effect. In Egypt the inscriptions were often inscribed or painted upon the inner walls of tombs; these were intended for the benefit of the dead rather than a source of information for the living, but they now provide a wealth of information. On the other hand, inscriptions which were intended to be seen by the public and to perpetuate a record of events, or to supply useful information, were usually placed in locales of common resort, especially temples and sacred precincts. Sometimes they were cut on convenient rock faces, sometimes on walls of public buildings.

In some cases (as in MOAB) these inscriptions form the only source of information in the absence of literary records; in others (Greece and Rome) they offer a valuable supplement. These inscriptions were written in various languages, most of which have been deciphered, and originated in many different places.

    I. Inscriptions relating to Palestine before the settlement of the Israelites
      A. Egyptian
      B. Sumerian-Akkadian
      C. Ugaritic
      D. Alphabetic texts
    II. Inscriptions of the Israelite Period
      A. Egyptian
      B. Akkadian
      C. Hebrew
      D. Aramaic
      E. Greek

I. Inscriptions relating to Palestine before the settlement of the Israelites

A. Egyptian. The earliest references to Palestine occur in two collections of writings found in EGYPT called the EXECRATION TEXTS, which date from the 20th and 19th centuries B.C. The Egyptians wrote the names of enemy tribes, towns, and rulers on clay figurines or vessels and then broke them in a symbolic act intended to insure the PHARAOH's victory over the enemy named. Cities named in these lists include Ashkelon, Jerusalem, Aphek, Acre, Mash'al, Achshaph, Tyre, and many others. Such texts yield valuable information on the political conditions in Syria-Palestine.

Later Egyptian inscriptions left by the pharaohs describe their recurrent campaigns in Canaan to keep the city-states of that country under their domination. THUTMOSE III (c. 1490–1436 B.C.) listed in the temple of Amon at Karnak the names of 119 cities and towns which he captured in Canaan and Syria, thus recording the names of important cities of 15th-century Palestine. Together with his "annals," these lists serve to document the history of Palestine-Egypt relations. The names of places in Palestine contained in the later lists of RAMSES II (c. 1290–1223; found on the Ramesseum at Thebes) and of Ramses III (c. 1179–1147; at Medinet Habu) are mere copies of the list of Thutmose III. Other pharaohs also engaged in campaigns to maintain their sovereignty over Canaan, the corridor to their great rivals in the N, the HITTITES and HURRIANS.

A number of Egyptian inscriptions have turned up at various sites in Palestine. Three stelae, one of Ramses II and two of his predecessor Seti I (c. 1303–1290), came from BETH SHAN, which was occupied by an Egyptian garrison. The larger stela of Seti tells of the capture of Beth Shan by the ruler of HAMATH and its relief by Seti; his smaller one mentions the HABIRU. Many short hieroglyphic inscriptions on the scarabs of various Egyptian kings were also discovered in the mounds of Palestine.

B. Sumerian-Akkadian. Some of the texts from SUMER and Babylonia (see ASSYRIA AND BABYLONIA) were incised on stone, but most of them on clay that was then baked. There is a vast amount of material preserved in Akkadian (see LANGUAGES OF THE ANE II.A); several entire libraries have been found, containing many thousands of texts. Much of the material written in MESOPOTAMIA has great significance for biblical studies. The Sumerian King List records the reigns of the earliest rulers in Mesopotamia who are noted for their longevity: the eight antediluvian kings are given reigns totaling 241,200 years!

The earliest known legal codes were written in CUNEIFORM, and the information they contain greatly illuminates the legal background of the OT. The most famous, the Code of HAMMURABI (c. 1792–1750 B.C.) was beautifully inscribed on diorite and is known also from copies on clay tablets. Actually it was a compilation of laws already in existence, many of which were copied from Sumer. Similar collections of law date from the reign of Ur-Nammu of Ur (c. 2060), Bilalama of Eshnunna (c. 1930), and Lipit-Ishtar of Isin (c. 1865).

From MARI, on the middle of the Euphrates, some 20,000 tablets from the 19th and 18th centuries B.C. have been recovered. These texts supply much information on the background of the PATRIARCHS. Another large collection of Akkadian texts was found at NUZI, in NW Mesopotamia, an area inhabited largely by Hurrians. These texts illuminate many customs preserved in the OT, such as the selling of BIRTHRIGHT, and the fact that possession of household gods virtually gave title to an estate.

In Akkadian and Sumerian literature are found a creation story (ENUMA ELISH) and the flood story

(GILGAMESH Epic), which have been compared with the biblical account of the flood; the flood story is also preserved in Hittite and Hurrian versions. The TELL EL-AMARNA letters are clay tablets dating from c. 1400–1350 B.C., written in cuneiform, in a form of Akkadian heavily influenced by Canaanite. They were discovered in the palace of Pharaoh Akhenaten and were sent to him by his vassals in Phoenicia, Syria, and Canaan. These letters supplemented by the letters found at TAANACH, reflect the political and social systems of 15th-cent. Canaan. The personal names in these letters bear witness to the ethnic composition of the country's population at that time. Among others, the Hurrians who are known to have lived in Canaan (Gen. 36:20) are prominently mentioned. Similar tablets written in cuneiform have been discovered also in SHECHEM, GEZER, EGLON, JERICHO, and MEGIDDO.

C. Ugaritic. This is a Canaanite language written in an alphabetic cuneiform script. In addition to the many texts found at UGARIT (dating from the 14th cent. B.C.), other objects inscribed in this script and language have been unearthed in Palestine: a knife found near Mount TABOR in lower Galilee and a clay mold of an axe blade found in BETH SHEMESH. The Ugaritic texts have provided much information on the religion and the language of the Canaanites.

D. Alphabetic texts. At Serabit el-Khadim, in the Sinai desert, inscriptions in the Proto-Sinaitic script were found and dated in the 16th and 15th centuries B.C. These inscriptions are brief and their bearing on the OT is indirect but significant. About ten inscriptions in alphabetic writing dating from the 2nd millennium B.C. have been found in Palestine; these are also very brief but significant for the knowledge of the history of the alphabet. Their language is apparently Canaanite.

II. Inscriptions of the Israelite period. This section describes some inscriptions related to the conquest and settlement of Israel in Palestine, and also to the remainder of biblical history.

A. Egyptian. MERNEPTAH (c. 1224–1216 B.C.) commemorated his achievements by inscribing a series of victory hymns on a stela which he set up in his mortuary temple at Thebes (a duplicate is preserved on the temple of Amon at Karnak). Here is found a reference to Israel, which is described as having been defeated along with Ashkelon and Gezer.

The SEA PEOPLES, who had been repulsed by Merneptah, made a full scale attack on Egypt during the reign of Ramses III (c. 1179–1147). Included in the Sea Peoples were the PHILISTINES, who settled on the Palestinian coastal plain after they were driven back by Ramses. The records of these naval and land battles were inscribed on Ramses' mortuary temple at Medinet Habu.

SHISHAK (Shoshenk) campaigned in Israel in the fifth year of the reign of REHOBOAM king of Judah (1 Ki. 14:25–26; 2 Chr. 12:2–9). On the temple of Karnak, Shishak recorded the cities he conquered, confirming the account in 2 Chr. 12 (esp. vv. 4 and 7) that Jerusalem was not captured; the Egyptians were satisfied with the heavy tribute from the temple treasures, including SOLOMON's gold shields.

B. Akkadian. The royal annals of the Assyrian kings provided a valuable supplement to the historical books of the Bible. On the "monolith inscription" of SHALMANESER III (858–824 B.C.), AHAB king of Israel appears as one of the leaders of an anti-Assyrian coalition. In the mid-9th cent. the growing menace from Assyrian imperialism forced the kings of Aram and Palestine to join forces in an attempt to stem the tide. The king of Aram of DAMASCUS and Ahab king of Israel, who had hitherto been enemies, are described as leading the alliance that faced Shalmaneser III at the battle of Qarqar in 853.

Another inscription of Shalmaneser III (his "black obelisk") describes, and illustrates with a relief, the submission of JEHU of Israel (this event too is not mentioned in the Bible). TIGLATH-PILESER III (744–727) records how MENAHEM of Israel paid tribute (2 Ki. 15:19–20) and mentions the Syro-Ephraimite War, which involved AHAZ of Judah (cf. 2 Ki. 16:5–18).

SARGON II (721–705) described the destruction of SAMARIA and the deportation of the Israelite population (cf. 2 Ki. 18:9–12). SENNACHERIB

sons (cf. 2 Ki. 25:27–30). Other Akkadian records also shed light on Nabonidus, Cyrus, and other personalities who are related to the OT record.

C. Hebrew. A number of inscriptions written in "Hebrew" have been found in Palestine. At El-Khadr, near Bethlehem, were found three bronze javelin heads, each inscribed with the owner's name. On the basis of paleography these arrowheads are dated from about the 12th century B.C. In Byblos (see Gebal), metal blades bearing indecipherable inscriptions were found, and in the Lebanon valley another arrowhead (dated c. the 11th cent.) bearing the owner's name was found. In the Gezer excavations, a list of the various agricultural seasons was found inscribed in early Hebrew characters and dating from perhaps the 10th cent. (see agriculture V).

Phoenician inscriptions dating back to the 10th cent. are significant for the knowledge of the history of that period and place (see Phoenicia), and also provide information on the evolution of the alphabet. The longest Phoenician inscription comes from Karatepe in E Cilicia and is especially significant because the same text is found in hieroglyphic Hittite.

The Moabite Stone, erected by Mesha king of Moab, dates from the 9th cent. and is the only significant inscription in the Moabite dialect of Canaanite. This inscription mentions the Israelite ruler Omri and sheds additional light on OT history of that period.

About seventy ostraca with Hebrew inscriptions were found at Samaria in the storerooms of the king's palace. These date from about the 8th cent. and consist of invoices for the deliveries of oil and wine to the royal treasury. Another group of twenty-one ostraca was uncovered at Lachish; these date from the 6th cent., just before the capture of the town by Nebuchadnezzar, in the time of Jeremiah and Zedekiah.

The Siloam Inscription, found in an ancient tunnel in Jerusalem, dates from the reign of King Hezekiah and describes the construction of the tunnel, which was a remarkable engineering achievement. Two ostraca found at Tel Kasileh date from the 8th cent. and are certificates of the shipment of quantities of oil and gold sent through this port to

Scribal practice tablet written in cuneiform script (c. 700 B.C.).

© Dr. James C. Martin. Sola Scriptura. The Van Kampen Collection on display at the Holy Land Experience in Orlando, Florida. Photographed by permission.

(704–681) described his campaigns in Palestine and mentioned Sidon (in Phoenicia), Jaffa, Beth Dagon, Eltekeh, Timnah, and Ekron in addition to forty fortified towns in Judah. His inscription narrates how he locked Hezekiah in Jerusalem "like a bird in a cage," but it says nothing about the fate of Jerusalem, which withstood the Assyrian assault (2 Ki. 18:17–35). Sennacherib based his general staff in Lachish. This is confirmed in the Bible and also in the reliefs (unearthed in Nineveh) showing the capture of Lachish.

The annals of Esarhaddon (680–669) mention King Manasseh of Judah as a vassal, and those of Ashurbanipal (668–633) describe his invasion of Syria-Palestine and Egypt. Later Babylonian chronicles describe the fall of Nineveh and the collapse of the Assyrian Empire. These records fix the date of the fall of Nineveh and Jerusalem. About 300 tablets from Babylon, dated between 595 and 570, during the reign of Nebuchadnezzar II (605–562), describe rations for captives and skilled workmen around Babylon. Listed in these records are Jehoiachin, king of Judah, and his five

Phoenicia or Egypt. These ostraca are not written with ink, like the others mentioned above, but are incised.

Three funerary inscriptions found in the village of Siloam, E of Jerusalem, originate from a date close to Hezekiah, judging from their paleography. Also dating from about the time of Hezekiah are rock engravings found in a burial cave E of Lachish. The Yabneh-yam ostraca were found in 1960 during the excavation of an ancient fort named Matzad Hashabyahu (on the sea coast S of Yabneh-Yam). The most significant ostracon of these is a fourteen-line Hebrew letter that may date from the 7th cent.

Because the climate of most of Palestine does not share the extreme dryness of Egypt, organic writing materials like PARCHMENT or PAPYRUS have rotted away over the centuries. Recently, however, a papyrus dating from about the 8th cent. B.C. was found in a cave of Wadi Murabbaʿat near the Dead Sea. This papyrus is a palimpsest (i.e., later writing has been superimposed upon an earlier text); the two decipherable lines of the original text suggest that the piece of papyrus was part of a long letter. Hundreds of other Hebrew inscriptions, usually very brief, have been found on such miscellaneous objects as seals, weights, jar handles, ossuaries, coins, etc.

D. Aramaic. An ARAMAIC stela, found near ALEPPO, was erected in the 9th cent. by a certain Bir-Hadad king of Aram in honor of the god Melkart; many have thought that the reference is to BEN-HADAD (*ANET*, 655, confirming 1 Ki. 15:18), but recent research has cast doubt on that identification. A brief Aramaic inscription on an ivory from Arslan Tash mentions the name of HAZAEL (cf. 2 Ki. 8:15). This inscription, along with some Assyrian inscriptions, confirms and illuminates the biblical record.

Several significant Old Aramaic inscriptions from Sujin and Zenjirli provide important information for the history of the Aramaic kingdoms. Later Aramaic inscriptions from various sites like Nerab and Asshur provide additional light on history and the language. The most important discoveries from the Persian period are the group of papyri found in Yeb (ELEPHANTINE, in upper Egypt). These documents illustrate the history and manner of life of a Jewish military colony. They also yield information bearing on the history of the Israelites in Palestine under Persian rule.

Various other Aramaic inscriptions of a later period are brief and contain largely personal names. These, however, do shed some light on the evolution of the language.

E. Greek. Inscriptions on Jewish synagogues show that it was the custom in the Hellenistic period for Jews of the DIASPORA to honor the pagan king and his family by naming the synagogue for them.

An inscription found near Hefzi-bah, in northern Palestine, consists of thirty-eight lines dealing with the damage caused to villages in the northern part of the country by the forced stationing of soldiers there. The contents reflect the reign of ANTIOCHUS III (223–187 B.C.). Another inscription consists of eight lines engraved on marble and was discovered in the Acre excavations in 1959 (see ACCO). This inscription was a dedication to Zeus Soter, and it mentions Antiochus VII.

A number of Greek inscriptions were found in the family burial sites in Maresha (159–119 B.C.). In Samaria (Sebaste), a number of inscriptions from the period of the Ptolemies were found (see PTOLEMY). In Kefar Yasif, NE of Acre, a limestone tablet with a seven-line inscription was found. This inscription, dating from the middle of the 2nd cent. B.C., dedicated an altar to the eastern gods HADAD and ATARGATIS.

It should be added that the sands of Egypt have yielded a mass of Greek papyri that shed much light upon the life and language of the early centuries A.D. (see PAPYRUS). Also, a unique Latin inscription was discovered in the excavations of the CAESAREA theater (a building dedicated in honor of the Emperor TIBERIUS), placed there by the prefect Pontius PILATE.

(Translations of the most significant inscriptions for biblical studies are contained in such volumes as *ANET*; *COS*; D. W. Thomas, ed., *Documents from Old Testament Times* [1958]. Note also M. Lidzbarski, *Handbuch der nordsemitischen Epigraphik* [1898]; id., *Ephemeris für semitische Epigraphik* [1900–1915]; G. A. Cooke, *Text-Book of North-Semitic Inscriptions* [1903]; D. Diringer, *Le iscrizioni antico-ebraiche palestinesi* [1934]; F. M. Cross and D. N. Freedman, *Early Hebrew Orthography* [1952]; H. Donner and W. Röllig, *Kanaanäische und aramäische Inschriften*, 3 vols. [1966–69]; J. C. L. Gibson, *Textbook of Syrian Semitic Inscriptions*, 3 vols. [1971–82]; G. I. Davies et al., *Ancient Hebrew Inscriptions: Corpus and Concordance*, 2 vols. [1991–2004]; J. Renz and W. Röllig, *Handbuch der althebräischen Epigraphik*, 3 vols. in 4 [1995–2003]; D. Noy et al., *Inscriptiones Judaica Orientis*, 3 vols. [2004]. On the Safaitic inscriptions, written during the early centuries of our era by ancient bedouins in the Syro-Arabian desert, see M. C. A. Macdonald in *ABD*, 3:418–23.)   L. L. WALKER

insects. see FAUNA.

Inspection Gate. See MUSTER GATE.

inspiration. Inspiration is the supernatural work of the HOLY SPIRIT, who moves upon specially chosen individuals so that they may receive divine truth from him and communicate that truth in written form, the Bible. See also BIBLE; SCRIPTURE.

   I. Theological definitions
     A. Revelation
     B. Inspiration
     C. Authority
     D. Illumination
     E. Infallibility and inerrancy
   II. Biblical exegesis
     A. The testimony of Jesus
     B. The testimony of the apostle Paul
     C. The testimony of the apostle Peter
     D. Conclusion
   III. Historical summary
     A. The canon of Scripture
     B. Jesus and Josephus and the OT
     C. The early church fathers
     D. The Roman Catholic Church
     E. The Reformers
     F. Warfield and liberalism

I. Theological definitions. Inspiration does not stand alone. Along with it are such concepts as revelation, authority, illumination, infallibility, and inerrancy—all of which require precise definition to understand what is meant by the inspiration of the Scripture.

A. Revelation. Basic to the evangelical view of Scripture is the conviction that God has chosen to disclose himself. REVELATION is the term used to depict his self-disclosure. God has revealed himself in nature, his CREATION. He has chosen also to reveal himself supremely in the person of Jesus Christ, who is God incarnate (see INCARNATION). The revelation of Jesus Christ is known through the written Word of God, which is special revelation. The purpose of this written Word is to reveal the incarnate Word, Jesus Christ, and the purpose of the incarnate Word is to reveal the Father and bring salvation. Therefore, the Bible is the objective, propositionally revealed Word of God.

God's self-revelation was given through two media. Parts of that revelation came directly and immediately from God in the form of oracular words, signs, visions, and dreams. This kind of data is known only because God chose to communicate it directly to human beings. A great part of the biblical material, however, has come through God's operations in history via his saving acts. This historical material has been made available either through oral tradition or written records, both of which were used when the books of the Bible were indited. MOSES, in the PENTATEUCH, undoubtedly used oral tradition and extant written records in addition to recording what he had experienced personally and what was revealed to him directly by God. In the case of the historical books in the OT, much of the material used in them was taken from extant court records. The same procedure is true for the NT. LUKE, the physician, was also a historian. He searched out his material, using written records and verifying oral traditions. In contrast, JOHN THE APOSTLE penned the Revelation not from oral tradition or written records, but from direct revelation by God.

B. Inspiration. Technically, revelation preceded inspiration. The latter has to do with the divine method of inscripturating the revelation, whether what was written came to the writer by direct communication from God, from his own research, from his own experience, or from extant records. Inspiration includes the superintending work of the Holy Spirit, but the human writers of Scripture were not automatons. Each writer had his own style. Each one used the Hebrew, Aramaic, or Greek language according to his unique gifts and educational background. At the same time that God used human authors in harmony with their gifts he also indited holy Scripture.

Some have argued falsely that Scripture was dictated by God and that the writers were mere secretaries who took down for inscripturation what God spoke, and thus were passive rather than active agents in the process. However, evangelicals generally have held that the Scriptures are both the words of men and the words of God. This dynamic view allows for the use of human faculties and at the same time assures that God secured his predetermined ends so that in the fullest sense the Bible is the Word of God written. The purpose of inspiration was to render the writers infallible in their teaching. Inspiration extends to the whole corpus of Scripture so that in its thoughts and words it is plenarily, or fully, and verbally inspired.

C. Authority. Inspiration carries with it the divine AUTHORITY of God so that Scripture is binding upon the mind, heart, and conscience as the only rule of faith and practice for the believer. In its authority, Scripture stands above men, creeds, and the church itself. All of them are subject to Scripture, and any authority that any one of them may exert is valid insofar as it can be supported from Scripture. A CREED is to be accepted only when it concurs with Scripture, for Christian conscience cannot be bound by anything not taught explicitly in Scripture or logically derived from it. Nor can any CHURCH bind people to its teaching except as it reflects the truth of Scripture. Believers, like creeds and churches, are likewise bound to Scripture so that they can neither release others from what it teaches nor bind them to what it does not teach. *Sola Scriptura* (the Bible alone) is the enduring principle.

D. Illumination. This is the work of the Holy Spirit, who enlightens the minds of believers as they read the Scripture. Because of SIN and its effects, we are incapable of understanding aright the Scripture apart from the enlightenment that comes only from the Holy Spirit (1 Cor. 2:6–16). Illumination is not to be confused with inspiration. The latter refers to those who penned the Scripture. The former refers to those who read the Scripture. The writers of Scripture were inspired; the readers of Scripture are illuminated.

E. Infallibility and inerrancy. Although inspiration is different from infallibility or inerrancy, no discussion of inspiration can be continued without considering these terms. Infallibility and inerrancy are synonymous. The ordinary dictionary meaning of *infallible* is "inerrant" or "unerring." In bygone years, the term *infallible* was used extensively with respect to Scripture, but the word was watered down and began to lose some of its force. In the mid 20th cent., many evangelicals began to substitute the word *inerrancy*. At stake is the question whether inspiration includes infallibility/inerrancy, and whether the latter extends to all of Scripture or only to some of the teachings of Scripture.

Neither of the terms is found in the earliest creeds, yet both are there implicitly. That they are not mentioned specifically is no substantive reason to suppose that they were unimportant concepts. The creeds and confessions of the Reformation and post-Reformation period generally speak about inspiration and infallibility. The *Westminster*

Illustration of Luke writing under divine inspiration (from a 9th-cent. Greek MS of the Gospels).

Confession of Faith says the Scriptures "are given by inspiration of God." They are to be received as the Word of God and are to be believed and obeyed. It also speaks of the Bible's "incomparable excellencies, and the entire perfection thereof" as well as "our full persuasion and assurance of the infallible truth." The Baptist *New Hampshire Confession* states: "We believe that the Holy Bible was written by men divinely inspired, and is a perfect treasure of heavenly instruction; that it has God for its author, salvation for its end, and truth without mixture of error for its matter; that it reveals the principles by which God will judge us, and therefore is, and shall remain to the end of the world, the true center of Christian union, and the supreme standard by which all human conduct, creeds, and opinions should be tried."

Unquestionably, the evangelical creeds commonly stress inspiration and infallibility (or inerrancy). In recent decades, efforts have been made among those formally attached to evangelical theology to reexamine the concept of inerrancy and in some instances to qualify it. At the same time, they have sought to retain a doctrine of biblical authority. These efforts have not produced any really new formulations. Some have said that the purpose and intent of the writers is important and that in some parts of Scripture it was not their intention to write inerrantly. Others have alleged that the writers were men of their times in respect to history, cosmology, physics, and astronomy. They penned what people then believed but now is known to be untrue. Some say that the biblical writers were infallible teachers, but that errors exist in those portions of the Bible that were not written for teaching purposes.

The effort to maintain the inspiration of Scripture while allowing for error is self-defeating. To retain an errant inerrancy dilutes the doctrine of inspiration and radically undermines its meaning and its usefulness. Few theologians would hold that adherence to orthodox notions of inspiration or inerrancy is necessary to salvation, but this should in no way obscure the importance of these concepts.

Inspiration is inextricably linked to authority and inerrancy. Charles Hodge (*Systematic Theology*, 3 vols. [1871–73], 1:170–71) perceived this connection when he inquired whether the Bible contains historical and scientific untruths. He asserted that there is a vital difference between what the biblical writers thought and believed on the personal level and what they wrote in Scripture. They may have believed that the sun revolves around the earth, but they did not teach this in Scripture. The language of the Bible is everyday language and is based upon the apparent. Phenomenological language was used in that day as it is used today. Moreover, Hodge distinguished between fact and theory. Theories are man-made. Facts are of God. The Bible never contradicts facts but it does contradict human theories. When interpretation conflicts with established facts then interpretation must yield. The Bible has stood this test, and it will stand through all ages with its claims unshaken and its teaching unimpaired.

Those who reject inerrancy often argue that inspiration is a biblically based doctrine but inerrancy is not. It can only be inferred and therefore should not be binding or made a test of faith. This question, which belongs not so much to the realm of theological definitions as it does to biblical exegesis, leads logically to a discussion of the teaching of Scripture about itself, its inspiration, its infallibility, and its authority.

II. Biblical exegesis. The Bible claims for itself the unique distinction of being the Word of God. The phrase "Thus says the Lord," or its equivalent, occurs over 2,000 times in the OT. Isaiah asserted: "The Lord said to me ... The Lord spoke thus to me ..." (Isa. 8:1, 11). David exclaimed: "The Spirit of the Lord spoke through me; / his word was on my tongue. / The God of Israel spoke, / the Rock of Israel said to me ..." (2 Sam. 23:2–3). Similarly, Jeremiah said: "Then the Lord reached out his hand and touched my mouth and said to me, 'Now, I have put my words in your mouth'" (Jer. 1:9; cf. 5:14; 7:27; 13:12).

The NT writers do the same. They assert that the OT prophets spoke the Word of God. "In the past God spoke to our forefathers through the prophets at many times and in various ways" (Heb. 1:1). OT prophecies concerning Jesus Christ were "what the Lord had said through the prophet" (Matt. 1:22; 2:15). The Holy Spirit spoke "through the mouth of David" (Acts 1:16), and "through

INSPIRATION

Isaiah the prophet" (28:25). The Jews of Jesus' day believed the OT to be the infallible Word of God, accepting on every hand the testimony of the writers that what they said was what God said.

A. The testimony of Jesus. Jesus claimed that the Word of God is inspired and infallible. In Matt. 5:18 he said: "I tell you the truth, until heaven and earth disappear, not the smallest letter [Gk. *iota* G2740], not the least stroke of a pen [*keraia* G3037, "dot, tittle"], will by any means disappear from the Law until everything is accomplished." The use of "iota" and "dot," referring to the smallest character of the Hebrew alphabet and the tiniest part of any Hebrew letter (see DOT), makes clear how highly Jesus regarded the OT (see *IB*, 7:292). Even so radical a critic as Rudolf Bultmann says that "Jesus agreed with the scribes of his time in accepting without question the *authority of the* [OT] *Law*" (*Jesus and the Word* [1958], 61).

In many instances, Jesus reiterated his belief in the infallibility of OT Scripture (e.g., Mk. 7:13; Lk. 16:31; 24:27; Jn. 10:35). It was Jesus who "preauthenticated" the NT (Jn. 14:26; 16:12–13). So great was Jesus' view of the Scripture that in two instances (Matt. 22:43–45 and Jn. 10:34–35) his whole argument rested upon a single word. He viewed the Scripture as verbally inspired and wholly trustworthy. To deny his view is to deny his person and to accept his person is to accept his view of Scripture.

B. The testimony of the apostle Paul. Paul, in a key passage dealing with inspiration, said to Timothy, "All Scripture is God-breathed [*theopneustos* G2535; KJV, given by inspiration of God] and is useful for teaching, rebuking, correcting and training in righteousness, so that the man of God may be thoroughly equipped for every good work" (2 Tim. 3:16–17). The Greek word *theopneustos* is a compound of *theos* G2536 (God) and a derivative of the verb *pneō* G4463 (to breathe). The ending *-tos* makes the word passive in meaning, so it is properly translated "breathed of God" or "that which is breathed out by God." (Although some have argued that the verse should read, "Every scripture inspired of God is also useful …," the traditional rendering is certainly accurate.)

Thus Scripture has its origin in God, not in man. The creative breath of God himself gave us Scripture. Moreover, the phrase "all Scripture" (*pasa graphē*) refers to the written words, not simply to the divine meaning. The very words of Scripture are thus inspired, or breathed out, by God. Some conservative Bible scholars are not happy that *theopneustos* has been translated "inspired," as though to suggest that the Scriptures are human writings to which has been added the divine breath. Paul says that the Scriptures originated from God himself, not simply from men upon whom a divine influence came. Once it has been established that the Scriptures are "breathed out by God," it follows axiomatically that the books of the Bible are free from error and trustworthy in every regard.

Inspiration guarantees the truth-claim of Scripture, but this has to do with the originals (the autographs), not the copies, for few would deny that there are some copyists' errors. The human authors of Scripture accepted the common scientific and other notions of their day, but when they wrote about factual, historical, and scientific matters they were preserved from error by the Holy Spirit and never wrote or taught what is not true. Paul's claim is one that extends to *all* Scripture, not just parts of it (he does not say that all Scripture is of equal value, however).

Paul's teaching about biblical inspiration does not mean that everything in the Bible is true per se. Scripture assures us that what Satan said to

Medieval Hebrew scroll of the book of Isaiah in Hebrew (A.D. 1350). The lips of Isaiah were cleansed with a live coal so that he might be sent out to speak the words of God (Isa. 6:6–7).

Jesus in the wilderness temptation and what JOB's friends said to him in conversation are what they really said. Whether what they said is true or false is determined by the context. The biblical writers used figures of speech, and Jesus himself spoke in PARABLES and employed ALLEGORY. These are not to be taken literally. Rather, their meanings are to be ferreted out in accordance with the principles of hermeneutics (see INTERPRETATION).

Elsewhere Paul asserts clearly that what he has written is the revelation of God. In 1 Cor. 2:12–13 he says: "We have not received the spirit of the world but the Spirit who is from God, that we may understand what God has freely given us. This is what we speak, not in words taught us by human wisdom but in words taught by the Spirit, expressing spiritual truths in spiritual words." A. T. Robertson (*Word Pictures in the New Testament*, 6 vols. [1930–33], 4:88] comments: "So then Paul claims the help of the Holy Spirit in the utterance (*laloumen*) of the words ... Clearly Paul means that the help of the Holy Spirit in the utterance of the revelation extends to the words. No theory of inspiration is here stated, but it is not *mere* human wisdom. Paul's own Epistles bear eloquent witness to the lofty claim here made. They remain today after nearly nineteen centuries throbbing with the power of the Spirit of God, dynamic with life for the problems of today as when Paul wrote them for the needs of the believers in his time, the greatest epistles of all time, surcharged with the energy of God."

In 1 Cor. 14:37 Paul writes: "If anybody thinks he is a prophet or spiritually gifted, let him acknowledge that what I am writing to you is the Lord's command." Here he claims inspiration for his position. As if this were not enough, Paul tells the Thessalonians, "And we also thank God continually because, when you received the word of God, which you heard from us, you accepted it not as the word of men, but as it actually is, the word of God, which is at work in you who believe" (1 Thess. 2:13). Paul says that what he has written is really the word of God. It is not the words of men, although penned by men. It does not *contain* the word of God; it *is* the word of God. The Thessalonians accepted Paul's claim and received what he preached and wrote as that which came from God. Nothing could have been more plain. Paul asserts that his words are Spirit-taught and do not spring from human reason (cf. 1 Cor. 2:13).

C. The testimony of the apostle Peter. Peter writes: "Above all, you must understand that no prophecy of Scripture came about by the prophet's own interpretation. For prophecy never had its origin in the will of man, but men spoke from God as they were carried along by the Holy Spirit" (2 Pet. 1:20–21). He was seeking to persuade his readers of the divine origin of Scripture. In doing this he said negatively that it did not come from the human will. Rather, the authors of Scripture were holy men moved by the Holy Spirit, who "powerfully excited and effectually engaged them to speak (and write) what he had put in their mouths. He so wisely and carefully assisted and directed them in the delivery of what they had received from him that they were effectually secured from any mistake in expressing what they revealed; so that the very words of scripture are to be accounted the words of the Holy Ghost" (Matthew Henry, *A Commentary on the Holy Bible*, 6 vols. [repr. 1960], 6:1044).

D. Conclusion. The teaching of Christ, the prophets, and the apostles should settle the matter of biblical authority and inspiration once for all. But for those who desire further confirmation, in addition to the teaching of Scripture concerning itself, there are other evidences. Predictive prophecy testifies to biblical inspiration and trustworthiness (see PROPHETS AND PROPHECY). ARCHAEOLOGY continues to confirm the historical accuracy of the Bible. The pragmatic test of personal experience shows that when people taste and see, they discover that the Bible works in their lives (cf. Ps. 34:8; 119:103). The Holy Spirit bears witness to the spirits of men and women that the Bible is the very Word of God (cf. 1 Jn. 5:6).

Any view of inspiration produces problems, some of which yield easily to solutions and others do not. But this is true of other biblical doctrines as well. No one surrenders his belief in the love of God because of unresolved problems. The church has not dismissed the doctrine of the Trinity because the concept of one God eternally subsistent in three persons is most difficult to understand. So it is with inspiration. Many of the difficult problems have been resolved; some problems remain; but it is unnecessary to surrender the Bible's own teaching with respect to its inspiration because of some unresolved problems.

The Bible teaches that it is the Word of God and the only infallible rule of faith and practice. But this teaching of the Bible concerning itself would be relatively useless if no one accepted its claims and propagated them. Thus no discussion of inspiration is complete without a historical overview in which the attitude of the Christian church and its theologians toward the Scripture is delineated.

III. Historical summary.

The foundation of the church is Jesus Christ. Scripture reveals him, and therefore it has been regarded by the church as the written Word of God and held in highest esteem. The testimony of the church to Scripture is one in which its inspiration, authority, and infallibility have been taught, and its truth-claim accepted. In recent times, however, a sustained interest in comparative religion and biblical higher criticism has challenged the truth-claim of Scripture and called into question the normative orthodox view. Therefore, some word must be said about the CANON of Scripture and the attitude of the church toward it over the centuries.

A. The canon of Scripture. Historically, which books belonged in the OT and the NT was determined differently. In Jesus' day, the Greek SEPTUAGINT already existed and included not only the OT books that Protestants generally acknowledge to be canonical, but also the apocryphal books which they do not accept. The OT Scripture was divided into three categories: the Law, the Prophets, and the Writings. The books of the Law and the Prophets were firmly fixed by NT times. But there were differences of opinion about certain of the books included in the Writings. By A.D. 90, Josephus could write that the canon of the OT was fixed and unalterable and did not include the apocryphal books. It has even been asserted by some that the rabbis at the Council of Jamnia (c. A.D. 100) excluded the Apocrypha from the OT canon. The apocryphal books, which the Jews did not regard as canonical, were included by Jerome in his Latin translation (Vulgate), although he did so reluctantly. These were generally accepted by the church as part of Scripture until the 4th cent. The Reformers, however, refused to regard the Apocrypha as Scripture since they were not included in the Hebrew canon. The Roman Catholic Council of Trent (1545–1563) affirmed the inclusion of the Apocrypha as part of the canon of OT Scripture.

The canon of the NT was fixed after a long battle accompanied by much dissent. By the end of the 2nd cent., the four Gospels and the thirteen letters of Paul were universally regarded as Scripture, and by the end of the 4th century, the NT as now known was fixed, although doubts persisted about the books of Hebrews, Jude, 2 Peter, 2 and 3 John, and the Revelation.

B. Jesus and Josephus and the OT. It is certain that Jesus was familiar with the Hebrew OT canon and unequivocally affirmed that its books are inspired, infallible, and authoritative. Liberal and conservative scholars alike generally agree that Jesus believed as the Jews of his day did, that the OT was inerrant and everywhere binding. So did the apostles of Jesus. Moreover, nothing in the Gospels suggests that Jesus ever raised any questions about the truth-claims of the OT.

The Jewish historian Josephus, in his treatise *Contra Apionem*, insisted on the inviolability of the OT and did so in words that called for complete historical reliability and freedom from error. Eusebius, the church historian, quoted Josephus as believing that the OT books had unique authority and sanctity, that they were to be regarded as "oracles of God," and that they contain no discrepancies of fact.

C. The early church fathers. Once the question of the canon was settled, it was almost universally believed that the books of the Bible were the infallible Word of God written. It is true that inspiration and infallibility were not pivotal issues as the Christological controversies were. Some of the early churchmen held to a mechanical dictation view of the process of inscripturation, and all of them spoke of Scripture in the highest terms and agreed that it was the ultimate source of authority.

In a work known as the *Appeal to the Greeks* (8.38), the unknown author clearly accepted verbal inspiration, although he seemed to limit inspiration to that which had for its purpose the impartation of religious truths. JUSTIN MARTYR (*Dialogue with Trypho* 65) held to full inspiration and authority, declaring that there are no contradictions in Scripture. Athenagoras (*A Plea for the Christians* 9) believed that the writers were passive human instruments played upon by God as men play on harps. IRENAEUS (*Against Heresies* 1.10; 3.16; 4.20, 34) said God came upon the writers of Scripture so that they had perfect knowledge on every subject. He called the Scriptures "perfect." TERTULLIAN (*On Prescription Against Heretics* 22) averred that the Holy Spirit so aided the writers of Scripture "that there was nothing of which they were ignorant."

AUGUSTINE was undoubtedly the greatest of the church fathers. Of the Scriptures he wrote (*Letters of St. Augustine* 82.3): "For I confess to your Charity that I have learned to yield this respect and honour only to the canonical books of Scripture: of these alone do I most firmly believe that the authors were completely free from error. And if in these writings I am perplexed by anything which appears to me opposed to truth, I do not hesitate to suppose that either the MS is faulty, or the translator has not caught the meaning of what was said, or I myself have failed to understand it. As to all other writings, in reading them, however great the superiority of the authors to myself in sanctity and learning, I do not accept their teaching as true on the mere ground of the opinion being held by them; but only because they have succeeded in convincing my judgment of its truth either by means of these canonical writings themselves, or by arguments addressed to my reason. I believe, my brother, that this is your opinion as well as mine. I do not need to say that I do not suppose you to wish your books to be read like those of the prophets or of the apostles, concerning which it would be wrong to doubt that they are free from error."

D. The Roman Catholic Church. This church has consistently taught that the Bible is inspired and also that it is inerrant. *The Catholic Encyclopedia* (1910 ed., p. 48) says: "For the last three centuries there have been authors—theologians, exegetes, and especially apologists, such as Holden, Rohling, Lenormont, di Bartoli, and others—who maintained, with more or less confidence, that inspiration was limited to moral and dogmatic teaching, excluding everything in the Bible relating to history and the natural sciences. They think that, in this way, a whole mass of difficulties against the inerrancy of the Bible would be removed. But the Church has never ceased to protest against this attempt to restrict the inspiration of the sacred books. This is what took place when Mgr. d'Hulst, Rector of the Institut Catholique of Paris, gave a sympathetic account of this opinion in 'Le Correspondent' of 25 Jan. 1893. The reply was quickly forthcoming in the Encyclical 'Providentissimus Deus' of the same year. In that Encyclical Leo XIII said: 'It will never be lawful to restrict inspiration to certain parts of the Holy Scriptures, or to grant that the sacred writer could have made a mistake. Nor may the opinion of those be tolerated, who, in order to get out of these difficulties, do not hesitate to suppose that Divine inspiration extends only to what touches faith and morals, on the false plea that the true meaning is sought less in what God has said than in the motive for which he has said it.' In fact, a limited inspiration contradicts Christian tradition and theological teaching. … As for the inerrancy of the inspired text it is to the Inspirer that it must finally be attributed, and it matters little if God has insured the truth of his scripture by the grace of inspiration itself, as the adherents of verbal inspiration teach, rather than by a providential assistance."

The Roman Catholic Church did not stop with biblical infallibility. It added tradition as an additional source of revelation, and the *magisterium* (teaching authority) of the church was used to determine the meaning of Scripture. Thus the church built upon the doctrine of the church fathers and exceeded anything they could have imagined.

E. The Reformers. The Reformation represented a return to the teachings of the apostles and prophets. The Reformers vigorously opposed tradition as a source of revelation. They had no patience with the *magisterium* of the church. The *sola Scriptura* to the Reformers meant the Bible *alone*, minus tradition. It left no room whatever for the church as the final teaching authority. The universal priesthood of all believers brought interpretation of Scripture back to the individual under the guidance of the Holy Spirit. Churches, creeds, and people were all subject to the Scripture and nothing else.

F. Warfield and liberalism. At no time during the first nineteen centuries of the Christian era did the question of inspiration and authority rack the church as did the Christological and anthropological controversies of the early centuries, when the nature of Christ and the Augustinian-Pelagian differences were being decided. Only from the 19th cent. on, when German higher criticism and the study of comparative religion dominated the scene, did inspiration, infallibility, and authority become a watershed. Since that time, there have been radical departures both from Reformation and Roman Catholic views of Scripture.

At the turn of the 20th cent., the issue was highlighted by the struggle between the Princeton divines (the Hodges and B. B. Warfield) and their opponents, a key leader of whom was Charles Augustus Briggs of Union Theological Seminary in New York City. In the ensuing battle, the Presbyterian Church, U.S.A., affirmed the views of Warfield, and Briggs was defrocked. The 1920s became a battlefield over biblical inspiration for Presbyterians and many other denominations. Liberalism triumphed over orthodoxy by the 1930s in America even while Europe was embracing the neoorthodoxy of Karl Barth, whose work on Romans appeared in 1919. By the mid-1930s, liberalism's advance appeared to have been halted decisively by neoorthodoxy, and orthodoxy itself seemed to have gained a new lease on life. In the 1940s, neoevangelicalism became a live option, but its impetus was hampered quickly when, having been established as a counterbalance to fundamentalism on the right and neoorthodoxy and liberalism on the left, it was itself fractured by the inroads of higher criticism.

It appears that the inspiration of the Scripture will continue to be a pivotal problem for the church at large, and there is little doubt that any marked departure from the historic view of the church on this matter always leads to further heresies and finally to apostasy.

(See further F. Gaussen, *Theopneustia* [1852]; J. Orr, *Revelation and Inspiration* [1927]; T. Engelder, *Scripture Cannot Be Broken* [1944]; N. B. Stonehouse and P. Woolley, eds., *The Infallible Word* [1946]; B. B. Warfield, *The Inspiration and Authority of the Bible* [1948]; R. L. Harris, *Inspiration and Canonicity of the Bible* [1957]; J. E. Young, *Thy Word Is Truth* [1957]; C. F. H. Henry, ed., *Revelation and the Bible* [1958]; M. C. Tenney, ed., *The Bible—The Living Word of Revelation* [1968]; G. C. Berkouwer, *Holy Scripture* [1975]; H. Lindsell, *The Battle for the Bible* [1976]; J. B. Rogers and D. K. McKim, *The Authority and Interpretation of the Bible: An Historical Approach* [1979]; J. Woodbridge, *Biblical Authority: A Critique of the Rogers/McKim Proposal* 1982]; D. A. Carson and J. Woodbridge, eds., *Scripture and Truth* [1983]; K. R. Trembath, *Evangelical Theories of Biblical Inspiration: A Review and Proposal* [1987]; D. S. Dockery, *Christian Scripture: An Evangelical Perspective on Inspiration, Authority, and Interpretation* [1995]; P. J. Achtemeier, *Inspiration and Authority: Nature and Function of Christian Scripture* [1999].) H. LINDSELL

instruction. See LAW (OT); TEACHER.

instrument. See MUSIC, MUSICAL INSTRUMENTS.

integrity. Moral soundness; steadfast uprightness; incorruptibility. Although several Hebrew words can be translated "integrity," this English term usually renders the noun *tōm* H9448, "completeness, wholeness, perfection" (1 Ki. 9:4 et al.; less frequently, *tummâ* H9450, Job 2:3 et al.); the term occurs especially in the poetic WISDOM Literature (Prov. 19:1 et al.). The adjectives *tām* H9447 and *tāmîm* H9459, both meaning "complete, blameless," are often used to describe sacrificial animals that have no defects (Exod. 12:5 et al.), but also godly men such as NOAH, ABRAHAM, and DAVID (Gen. 6:8; 17:1; 2 Sam. 22:24). (See *NIDOTTE*, 4:306–8.)

In the NT, "integrity" is used by modern versions to render Greek *aphthoria* G917, "incorruption"

INTERCESSION

Copper statue of a Babylonian worshiper from approximately the time of Abraham. God challenged Abraham (Abram) to demonstrate integrity in all he did, including his worship (Gen. 17:1).

(Tit. 2:7). The concept is certainly reflected in other passages, however, and the NIV in one context uses the phrase "man of integrity" to translate *alēthēs* G239 (Matt. 22:16=Mk. 12:14; NRSV, "sincere"). See RIGHTEOUSNESS; SINCERE.

intercession. The act of pleading on behalf of someone else. See PRAYER.

intercession of Christ. The intercession of Christ refers to PRAYER offered by Christ on behalf of others. It is frequently understood as the activity he exercises in this respect in his exalted glory at the right hand of the Father (see EXALTATION OF CHRIST). This aspect of his heavenly ministry is all-important, and the passages of Scripture that speak expressly of Jesus' "intercession" refer to it. There are also the examples of Jesus' intercession while he was on earth, especially Jn. 17. This address to the Father is not exclusively intercession. It includes prayer on his own behalf (vv. 1, 5). But it is largely prayer on behalf of others and is an index to the content of Jesus' intercession in heaven. Not only do we have this example, but we have express reference to this ministry on his own part (Lk. 22:32) and also the record of intercessory utterance (23:34).

In Rom. 8:34 and Heb. 7:25 (cf. Isa. 53:12), the term for making intercession (*entynchanō* G1961) is used with reference to Christ. In both passages, it is the intercession offered in heaven. But to this same activity Jesus referred when he said to the disciples: "And I will ask the Father, and he will give you another Counselor to be with you forever—the Spirit of truth" (Jn. 14:16–17; cf. 16:26–27). There are two observations of particular relevance: (1) Intercession is directed to God the Father; this is corroborated by Jesus' great intercessory prayer in Jn. 17 (cf. vv. 1, 5, 11, 21, 24–25), and it is striking how frequently the name of the Father appears. (2) The prayer to the Father is closely related to the office of ADVOCATE that Jesus executes; the Holy Spirit as the *other* Counselor (Advocate) implies that Jesus himself performed this function. He is the advocate now with the Father (1 Jn. 2:1). It may well be, therefore, that intercession includes more than prayer; that it involves the pleading of the case of those who come within the scope of the intercession (cf. Acts 25:24; Rom. 11:2). See PARACLETE.

That Jesus pleads the case of God's people and prays on their behalf points to the economy of redemption and to the distinct functions performed by the persons of the Godhead in terms of that economy. The process of redemption is not yet consummated, and therefore the distinguishing operations of the three Persons are still in effect. If it was consonant with supreme love and wisdom for the Father to send his own Son into this world to redeem his people, it is consonant with the same love and wisdom for the Father to act now in the progressive realization of his saving counsel through a mediation that the Son exercises in intercession.

In those contexts where the heavenly intercession is mentioned, there is an index to the kind of intercession Jesus offers. In Rom. 8:34, the context is one in which believers are viewed as challenged by their adversaries, and the apostle provides the answer to any charge laid against them. The intercession is coordinated with the death, resurrection, and exalted glory of Christ as that which insures the security of the people of God. The active and abiding intercession of Christ is engaged with the bond that unites them to Christ. See UNION WITH CHRIST. The intercession is appealed to for the purpose of assuring believers that the exalted Lord is unceasingly concerned with the conflicts and trials that beset them, concerned by way of prayer on their behalf. As a result they will be more than conquerors in every engagement with their adversaries. It is intercession directed to every exigency of their warfare.

The intercession of Christ is mentioned as that which insures SALVATION to the uttermost (Heb. 7:25). Such salvation is inclusive; it is salvation complete and perfect. The intercession, therefore, brings within its scope all that is necessary to salvation in its consummated perfection; it is interposed to meet every need of the believer. No blessing enjoyed, no need supplied is outside the range of Christ's intercession, and it is the guarantee of all grace.

The intercession must be construed as based upon and proceeding from Jesus' atoning accomplishment. In the two passages mentioned above, this dependence is clearly implied. "Christ Jesus, who died—more than that, who was raised to life—is at the right hand of God and is also interceding for us" (Rom. 8:34). Both the preceding and succeeding contexts of Heb. 7:25 are replete with references to Christ's high priestly identity and sacrifice. The intercession is, therefore, to be viewed specifically as a phase of Jesus' high priestly function (cf. also 1 Jn. 2:1–2, which intimates the same relationship). As in the priestly propitiation, the notion that the Father is won over to clemency finds no place. The intercession is one aspect of that provision that God the Father in love has made to bring to perfection his redemptive design. (See further J. Calvin, *Institutes of the Christian Religion*, 3.20.17–20; W. Symington, *On the Atonement and Intercession of Jesus Christ* [1839], 239–81; J. Murray, *The Heavenly Priestly Activity of Christ* [1958]; J. G. S. S. Thomson, *The Praying Christ* [1959]; T. F. Torrance, *The Mediation of Christ*, 2nd ed. [1992].)

J. MURRAY

interest. The profit received by a lender as inducement for making a loan (KJV, "usury," but this term in modern usage connotes excessive, ruinous rates of interest). The primary Hebrew term for "interest" is *nešek* H5968 (Exod. 22:25 et al.), from the verb *nāšak* H5967, which can be rendered "to charge [interest]" (Deut. 23:20–21; cf. Hab. 2:7; the latter passage suggests that this meaning may be a metaphorical extension of the verb *nāšak* H5966, "to bite," as by a snake). The noun *tarbît* H9552 appears to imply "excessive interest" (Ezek. 18:8 et al.). Note also the use of the verb *nāšā'* H5957 ("to lend") with its cognate noun *maššā'* H5391, which apparently can mean "interest" (Neh. 5:7 [NIV, "exacting usury"]; cf. vv. 10–11; 10:31). In the NT the term is Greek *tokos* G5527 ("offspring, produce [of money]"), used in the parable of the talents/pounds (Matt. 25:27; Lk. 19:23).

It should be understood that, as a rule, ancient rates of interest were ruinously high; in BABYLON, for example, it was common to lend food or produce at about 33 percent interest, and money (i.e., silver bullion) at 20 percent. In NUZI some loans were made at a 50 percent rate. Modern rates of interest at less than 15 percent were quite unheard of. The PENTATEUCH absolutely forbade the lending of money or produce to a fellow Israelite at interest (Lev. 25:36–37; Deut. 23:19–20); the simple condition for lending was return of the principal (Exod. 22:25). In later times these sanctions were disregarded, with resulting hardship to the borrowers, even to the point of taking their children off into slavery (cf. 2 Ki. 4:1). Early in the 6th cent. B.C., EZEKIEL summoned his countrymen to return to the humane rule of the TORAH in this regard (Ezek. 18:8, 13, 17; 22:12), and after the RESTORATION,

NEHEMIAH found that the exaction of usurious rates of interest had resulted in the loss of the property and homes of the poor in Judah (Neh. 5:6–13). In his capacity as governor he compelled the lenders to give back all that they had taken at usury, and thus restore a brotherly relationship with their fellow believers. In the NT the practice of lending money at interest, at least through the agency of banks, seems to be accepted by Jesus as normal business procedure (Matt. 25:27; Lk. 19:23). See BORROW; CREDIT; DEBT.

G. L. ARCHER

intermediate state. This expression commonly designates that realm or condition in which the soul exists between the decease of the body and the RESURRECTION. Although the Bible says little about the state of the DEAD, it is clear even from the OT that the human personality survives DEATH, whereas the doctrine of IMMORTALITY is a firm tenet of NT faith. Differences of opinion regarding the intermediate state relate to its nature: whether or not it is purgatorial in function, whether or not the human spirit has a chance to repent, and whether or not the soul is conscious of its environment. Regarding the state of the dead, the Bible views bodily resurrection as the goal of individual ESCHATOLOGY. Man does not consist of separate units of BODY and SOUL (or SPIRIT), but is a dynamic integrated personality of which these are aspects. Immortality, therefore, does not mean endless existence so much as freedom from death (1 Cor. 15:53) and from corruption (Rom. 2:7). In Christ, believers will exchange their mortality for immortality at the resurrection (1 Cor. 15:53–54). See also DEAD, ABODE OF THE.

In OT belief, the human personality (*nepeš* H5883) went at death to SHEOL, a lowly region of darkness and silence (Ps. 86:13; Prov. 15:24; Ezek. 26:20; Job 10:22). The dead, who were gathered in tribes (Ezek. 32:17–32), received the dying (Isa 14:9–10). Although Sheol was not so much the realm as the style of the dead, it was not life, since that could only flourish in the divine presence (Ps. 16:10), to which God's people would ultimately be brought (16:9–11, 73.24, Job 19:25–26).

The Greek HADES (Matt. 11:23; Lk. 10:15; Acts 2:27; 1 Cor. 15:55; et al.) is the equivalent of Sheol, and takes its place with the other concepts of life after death, such as PARADISE. NT thought about the intermediate state was influenced in the intertestamental period by Pharisaic views on Sheol, the resurrection, and the judgment. In the pre-Christian period, Sheol was regarded not as the permanent home, but only the intermediate place, for the departed spirits. It was the intermediate abode of the righteous only, who would leave it later on at the resurrection (*Pss. Sol.* 14.6–7; 2 Macc. 7:9; 14:46). Although OT thought saw little connection between God and Sheol, 2 Macc. 12:43–45 records Judas MACCABEE as praying that his fallen soldiers would be released from their sins there to prepare them for the resurrection. According to *1 En.* 22, Sheol was divided into three separate places, one for the righteous, another for the wicked who died before divine retribution overtook them, and a third for the wicked who were punished adequately while still alive. In 2 Esd. 7:95 and *2 Bar.* 21.23–24, the souls of the wicked are said to go straight to Sheol, whereas the righteous ascend to heavenly chambers to enjoy rest and quietness under the protection of angels before being resurrected.

All intertestamental eschatology was founded upon a "three-storied universe," with HEAVEN (or a series of heavens) being the divine abode above the earth, and Sheol (the place of departed spirits) or GEHENNA (the place where the wicked were punished) as an underworld. Occasionally, Sheol was regarded as the place of punishment also. The soul of ADAM ascended at death to paradise, the third of seven heavens. The term *paradise* originally meant a "park" or "enclosed garden," and for pre-Christian Judaism it designated the original Garden of Eden as either the eternal abode of the righteous or their locale prior to the resurrection (see EDEN, GARDEN OF). In the NT, the parabolic reference to ABRAHAM'S BOSOM (Lk. 16:22–31) made use of such thought, but was probably not intended to teach anything about the state of the dead. If PAUL's experience was that of a visit to paradise where he received a revelation (2 Cor. 12:1–4), it appears that he thought of the righteous dead as already living in paradise with the Lord (cf. 2 Cor. 5:8; Phil. 1:23). On the cross, Christ promised the penitent thief an abode in paradise (Lk. 23:43), which indicates that the righteous entered paradise at death. The book of Revelation also teaches clearly that at least some righteous enter a celestial abode after death but before the final resurrection (Rev. 6:9–11; 7:9–17).

Intertestamental beliefs regarding the intermediate state were closely linked with the concept of physical resurrection, a doctrine espoused by the PHARISEES but denied by the SADDUCEES. The resurrection of the dead was anticipated in a few OT passages (Isa. 25.8, 26.19, Dan. 12.2), and was encouraged both by speculation on the nature of the intermediate state in Sheol and the joys of the coming messianic age. In the light of the latter in particular, it was only just that the righteous departed should share the joys of divine rule, and the wicked dead be punished correspondingly. The concept of the physical resurrection was a necessary accompaniment to such thought, and in most instances the soul was imagined as coming from Sheol or some other intermediate state to rejoin the body buried on earth previously. Under Pharisaic influence the doctrine of resurrection sometimes developed certain coarse, materialistic features.

People came to assume the existence of another intermediate state later known as *purgatory*, which was frequently confused with Sheol (2 Macc. 12.39–45). The Roman Catholic and Greek Orthodox churches proclaimed the existence of such a place of temporal punishment in the intermediate realm. According to this view, all who died in a state of ecclesiastical grace must undergo a period of purifying so as to make them perfect before God. Thus the bulk of baptized people dying in fellowship with the church would have to pass through purgatory before being translated to heaven. Cultic prescriptions for the duration of the experience vary in degree, as do the sufferings of those thought to be in this state. Monetary and other gifts to the church, prayers, and acts of devotion, are held to shorten or even eliminate the stay of the individual soul in purgatory. This view has no OT or NT support, runs counter to the biblical doctrine of a final judgment, and is flatly contradicted by a passage which the Roman Catholics regard as Scripture (Wisd. 3.1–4).

In the NT, other expressions than "paradise" refer to the existence of the righteous after death (Mk. 12:18–27; Lk. 16:9, 19–31; Rev. 6:9–11; et al.), and whereas much of the language concerning the state of the dead is symbolic, it does at least enlarge the OT revelation that death does not terminate individual existence. It is clear that the saints live on after death in glory in the divine presence realizing the goal of redemption in Christ (2 Cor. 5:8; Phil. 1:23; Rev. 14:13). Because the total person is saved, references to the "salvation of your souls" (1 Pet. 1:9; Jas. 1:21) do not contemplate the salvation of the "soul" apart from the "body." Describing the intermediate state as "rest" (cf. Heb. 4:10) does not mean that those present in it are indolent or inactive, but rather that they are satisfied by the joy of accomplishment.

Even for the righteous, the intermediate state would seem to be one of imperfection, partly because the spirit is without a bodily manifestation and partly because the joys of heaven are not forthcoming for the saints until after the SECOND COMING of Christ and the final judgment. Thus, the experience of the intermediate state presages future divine blessings. Life in the resurrection body in heaven marks the final stage of individual salvation.

(See further G. Vos, *The Pauline Eschatology* [1952]; G. R. Beasley-Murray, *Jesus and the Future* [1954]; E. Brunner, *Eternal Hope* [1954]; J. E. Fison, *The Christian Hope* [1954]; R. Summers, *The Life Beyond* [1959]; A. A. Hoekema, *The Bible and the Future*, rev. ed. [1982]; W. Grudem, *Systematic Theology: An Introduction to Christian Doctrine* [1994], ch. 41; J. W. Cooper, *Body, Soul, and Life Everlasting: Biblical Anthropology and the Monism-Dualism Debate*, updated ed. [2000].)

R. K. HARRISON

interpretation. The correct reproduction of the thoughts of another (either a writer or speaker), often from a different language. Especially when applied to the BIBLE, interpretation has been called *hermeneutics*, a term first occurring in a work by J. C. Dannhaur in the 17th cent. (from the Gk. verb *hermēneuō* G2257, "to express, explain, translate, interpret"). See also SCRIPTURE.

  I. Biblical interpretation
    A. Nature
    B. Method
    C. Means
 II. History of biblical interpretation
    A. Pre-Christian interpretation

B. Jesus as an interpreter
  C. Apostolic interpretation
  D. Patristic interpretation
  E. Medieval interpretation
  F. Reformation interpretation
  G. Modern interpretation
III. Principles of Biblical interpretation
  A. Words
  B. Syntax
  C. Context
  D. History
  E. Analogy of Scripture
  F. Correct procedure

I. Biblical interpretation. Interpretation has as its goal the discovery of the thought processes and the meanings of the writer, or writers, of the books of the Bible. The ultimate design is to convey that meaning to contemporary persons. The material of the Bible, written between 2,000 and 3,500 years ago, poses a special problem for the modern interpreter because it was formulated in environments and in languages considerably different from those that prevail in the modern world.

A. Nature. Biblical interpretation has a dual nature: (1) the problem of the language, and (2) the theological significance of the material. The discovery of the true meaning of all words and terms in any biblical passage is the place where interpretation begins. This is essentially an interpretation of language. It embraces such considerations as definition of words, contextual analysis, literary types and forms, historical analogy, and syntactical distinctives. In addition, biblical material is of such a nature as to demand special consideration. The doctrine of INSPIRATION holds the biblical interpreter to a proper regard for the fundamental character of Scripture. It demands a recognition of the theological significance of Scripture, resting upon the REVELATION of God that is not found in any other literature. The extraordinary character of Scripture transcends the usual and ordinary analysis of nonbiblical materials.

B. Method. The language of the Bible is human language and, as such, is subject to the same principles and laws that govern the interpretation of any book or writing other than the Bible. If the language of the Bible were other than a true human language subject to the usual rules of human communication, there would be no basis for human beings to interpret or come by any trustworthy knowledge of its meaning. Because the books of the Bible are records in human speech, they must be handled in view of literary structure, literary form, and literary relations as any other book or writing. In 1860, *Essays and Reviews* introduced the now famous axiom of Benjamin Jowett: "Interpret the Bible like any other book." Jowett had in mind the meaning of words, the correct reading of the text, etc., but unfortunately his remark has come to mean for many: "just like any other book for there is nothing special about the Bible."

There are legitimate presuppositions to be brought to Scripture that cannot be brought to other books. Because the Bible has God as its ultimate author, it must be expected that its contents will bear true and faithful relation to that fact. The Scripture itself offers the best insight into how it is to be interpreted—in light of its inspired character. To one who objects that it is illegitimate to bring a presupposition to the Bible as an interpreter, it is to be remarked that in the nature of things every interpreter comes with a presupposition. The question is: Which presupposition? Is the Bible the Word of God or the word of men? The theological problem of interpretation is in a large degree the result of modern studies related to the changing attitudes of scholars toward the doctrine of inspiration and revelation.

C. Means. The evangelical interpreter dares not neglect history in any of its relation to the problem of setting out the true meaning of a biblical text. Indeed, the knowledge of history strengthens the hand of the interpreter who accepts the ultimate authorship of the God of history. Every means of the historical-critical method of interpretation should claim his attention: textual criticism, literary criticism, comparative religion criticism, historical criticism, etc. Beyond all of this, however, the Holy Spirit is to be acknowledged as the only infallible interpreter of God's Word. The mind of the Lord, as given to the interpreter through the ministry of the Spirit, is an absolute necessity for the interpretation of Scripture. The Bible is not only a special book, but its faithful interpreter must be a special person.

II. History of biblical interpretation. Antecedent to any interpretation of the Bible that could be called Christian were nearly 400 years of Jewish interpretation of the OT. Perhaps EZRA (450 B.C.) made the earliest effort at a definite, systematic interpretation of the law. He was the founding father of that class within JUDAISM, known subsequently as the SCRIBES, who devoted themselves to the exposition of the meaning of the law.

A. Pre-Christian interpretation. Out of Ezra's emphasis on the observance of the law grew a formulation of the oral law, an interpretation of the law of MOSES that, legalistic and fanciful as it often was, created a hedge about the law, making it difficult for the scribes in NT times to interpret the OT correctly. See MISHNAH.

1. Jewish literalism. The OT was dissected by the scribes into its separate words and phrases, to which meanings were sometimes given that disregarded the history, spirit, or context of the material being interpreted. In the decades preceding the NT, three rabbinical leaders were preeminent. HILLEL, who was born in Babylon and came to Jerusalem as a youth, had the greatest influence on his own and succeeding generations. Hillel is said to have drawn up seven laws of interpretation that were influential for generations.

The first of Hillel's rules was known as the rule of "light and heavy" and was simply an application of the usual argument of "from the lesser to the greater." The second rule dealt with an inferred relation between two subjects from identical expressions of reference; for instance, it was written that both the SABBATH and the PASSOVER sacrifice must be "at the due season," and if this meant that the "daily" sacrifice must be offered on a Sabbath, then the Passover sacrifice may also be offered on a Sabbath. The third rule was the "extension from the special to the general"; for example, necessary work on a Sabbath became authorized work on any holy day. The fourth rule was the explanation of two passages by a third. The fifth rule allowed drawing from a general situation an inference that governed special situations. The sixth rule was the explanation of a passage from the analogy of other passages. Rule seven was an application of inferences from passages that were self-evident. In the hands of the scribes these simple rules became the basis for much unwarranted interpretation.

SHAMMAI was the second important rabbi, a rival of Hillel and a formalist in the extreme school of Jewish legalism. According to some, total disregard for the real spirit of the law brought him and his followers into blind slavery to its letter. It has been told that his formalism led him to starve his infant grandson nearly to death in an attempt to make him fast on the Great Day of Atonement. At the Feast of Tabernacles, he insisted that the booth required at the season be built over the bed of his daughter, who was in the agony of childbirth.

GAMALIEL, regarded as the grandson of Hillel, is of special interest because he was the teacher of PAUL. He seems to have been broadminded in his interpretation of the law, due to the fact that he studied and taught Greek literature and advocated the rights and privileges of the Gentiles.

Page from a MS of the Mishnah (tractate *Yebamot*), offering interpretation on the subject of levirate marriage.

Until later than NT times, the rabbis transmitted all their teachings orally, but in the oral tradition were several methods of interpretation that were preserved in the later written code (c. 3rd Christian cent.). The Mishnah was the earliest collection of the oral interpretation committed to writing. It consisted of an elaboration of the law of Moses, dealing with its application, called HALAKAH, and a hortatory and illustrative commentary called HAGGADAH. The Midrashim (plural of MIDRASH) were commentaries on selected portions of the biblical books. Halakah combined with Haggadah appeared in the TALMUD as GEMARA, which consisted of rabbinical comments on the Mishnah. (See the important work by A. Samely, *Rabbinic Interpretation of Scripture in the Mishnah* [2002].)

2. Jewish allegorism. ALEXANDRIA, Egypt, was the center of Jewish allegorical interpretation. Although some ALLEGORY was found in the Palestinian exegesis known as Haggadah, or midrashic interpretation, the philosophical environment of Alexandria was causative to its full development; it was there that Jewish rabbis were equipped to make a philosophical exposition of the OT. The earliest known Jewish exponent of the allegorical approach was Aristobulus, a famous teacher in the Judaism of Alexandria. He was the first to propose that the Greek philosophers and poets derived their ideas from a translation of the law of Moses into Greek, which he believed greatly antedated the SEPTUAGINT.

The most important representative of this school was PHILO JUDAEUS, who made the supreme effort to harmonize the institutions and ideas of Judaism with Hellenistic culture. He taught that all Scripture contained a twofold meaning—literal and allegorical, which corresponded to the body and soul of man. As the soul was judged to be more important than the body, so the allegorical meaning of Scripture was more important than its obvious meaning. By way of example, in his commentary on Gen. 2:10–14, Philo made the four rivers of Eden stand for virtues: prudence, temperance, courage, justice. Likewise, the main source from which the four rivers branched represented goodness, which was judged to be the basic virtue. Philo occupied himself almost exclusively with the Pentateuch.

B. Jesus as an interpreter. JESUS CHRIST never intimated any criticism of the OT as the record of divine revelation. He shared the high regard of his contemporaries for the sacred Scriptures. See TEACHINGS OF JESUS.

1. Relations to rabbis. Jesus was not a RABBI in the tradition of the Jews, especially regarding interpretation of the OT. His familiarity with the interpretation of the rabbis, both concerning method and content, is clearly evident in the NT, for he often protested against it. Although he never attended a rabbinical school, he knew accurately what the rabbis pronounced as the chief commandments (Matt. 22:37–39). Jesus was much more practically religious and ethical in his interpretations than were the rabbinical schools as they are known through Jewish literature. He saw a problem in the first verse of Ps. 110 that the rabbis were unable to explain (Matt. 22:41–45). On another occasion Jesus reminded his fellow townsmen that the OT revealed the great principle that God was no respecter of persons, citing the ministry of ELIJAH to the woman of SIDON and of ELISHA to the Syrian NAAMAN (Lk. 4:25–27). This was exasperating to the rabbis. When the complaint was lodged with him by the Pharisees that his disciples plucked and husked grain on the Sabbath, he cited the case of David who ate the "showbread." He described the

Statue of Jerome, an early translator and interpreter of the Bible. From the Church of the Nativity in Bethlehem.

Pharisees and their followers in the words, "Hear and hear, but do not understand; see and see, but do not perceive" (Isa. 6:9 RSV; cf. Matt. 13:14 et al.).

2. View of the OT. Jesus' teaching contained no formulated doctrine of inspiration, but he obviously held the OT to possess divine authority (Matt. 5:18; Lk. 16:17). At least in one direct statement he attributed David's words to the Holy Spirit (Mk. 12:36). The use Jesus made of the OT further substantiates his regard for the OT. He confirmed the historical validity of those Scriptures of the Jews by holding the OT documents to be dependable historical records. He nowhere raised a doubt about the historical reality of any OT event, but assumed the truth of every OT reference that he made. Jesus' entire and exclusive interest was in the spiritual values of the OT; he is not to be viewed as a biblical critic, but as one who saw in the Scriptures God's redemptive designs for the human race.

3. Knowledge of the OT. There are thirty-six direct quotations of the OT by Jesus recorded in the Gospels. In addition, he frequently weaved OT terminology into his own teaching. When he appealed to the OT, it was most often for the purpose of reinforcing his teaching by way of a practical illustration. Jesus' knowledge of the OT was both extensive and detailed, having begun no doubt as a child in Nazareth. From his devout parents and some half-dozen years in a synagogue school, he gained this knowledge. For eighteen additional years, while he worked as a carpenter in Nazareth, he studied the message of Israel's prophets and gave thought to his own relation to that message.

4. Interpretation of the OT. Jesus was in the main the authoritative origin of his own teaching. He appealed to no higher authority than himself: "he taught them as one who had authority, and not as the teachers of the law" (Mk. 1:22). Jesus gave a completely new solution to the fundamental question of the meaning of the OT. Luke wrote, "he explained to them what was said in all the Scriptures concerning himself" (Lk. 24:27). The originality of Jesus' interpretation was not some new intellectual insight, but the happening of an event. With the intervention of God into the human scene through himself, Jesus found the transition from the figure and image of the OT to the reality and actuality recorded in the NT. The fundamentally new principle introduced by the Christ-event was that the distinction was no longer to be made between a text and its true meaning, but instead a relationship was introduced between the meaning of a text and the historical facts of Jesus' life and ministry as he appropriated that text to himself.

C. Apostolic interpretation. The methods employed by the writers of NT in interpreting the OT have created much debate. Liberal scholarship has viewed the problems related to this subject in such a way as to discredit the doctrine of inspiration. Conservative scholarship, on the other hand, has either denied or ignored the difficulties raised by the use of the OT in the NT, in a supposed defense of that doctrine. There is an undeniable difference between Jesus' interpretation of the OT and that of the writers of the NT. As previously noticed, Jesus wonderfully transcended the methods of interpretation common in his day. He stood independent of the rabbinic approach to Scriptures in a most remarkable way. The writers of the NT revealed their Jewish heritage in interpreting the OT, but it must be insisted that, though their methods of interpretation were those common in their day, they did not miss the message of the OT. The writers of the NT always viewed the message of the OT through the prism of the Christ event. It was a reinterpretation of the OT by the methods commonly in use—but with a different import, because of the centrality of the facts of Jesus' life, death, and resurrection in their own experience.

1. Relation to the rabbis. Generally, the interpretation of NT writers was of the kind practiced by the rabbis, though it must be added that the extremes of rabbinism were not brought into the NT. Inspiration did not separate the writers of the NT from their background, but it did guard their message. Although Paul was probably the only contributor to the NT who had experienced formal rabbinical training, most likely all of them had been under the influence of the rabbinical method in the synagogue, with the possible exception of Luke, who may have been a Gentile.

Some would argue that the rabbinic disregard of context and historical background in interpretation also appears in the NT. In Rom. 9:25, for example, Paul appears to ignore the primary meaning of Hos. 2:23, but the apostle in no way abuses the essential spirit of the passage, for through Christ a new light had come upon the OT page. A prime example of the allegorical interpretation of the rabbis is thought to be found in Gal. 4:21–31. Again it must be remembered, however, that Paul never implied that the story of Hagar and Sarah was not literal history; he only found in it a parallel between himself and the Judaizers over the issue of Christian freedom as opposed to Jewish legalism. Paul's "allegory" attributed nothing that was false to the OT record. The modern interpreter cannot expect to find modern principles of interpretation in use by the writers of the NT; neither can he justify the uncritical use of the 1st-cent. rabbinical methods of interpretation in modern times.

2. Reverence for the OT. The writers of the NT accepted without question the inspiration and authority of the OT. Over and over again the proof of a matter for the writer of a NT passage was the simple statement of an OT proof text. For the modern reader nothing seems to have been proved, but for the NT writer it was enough simply that he had the word of the OT on the matter (Rom. 3:10–19; 9:14–18; Heb. 1:5–13; et al.). It was undoubtedly the view of NT writers that "not the smallest letter, not the least stroke of a pen, will by any means disappear from the Law until everything is accomplished" (Matt. 5:18).

The NT writers were especially involved with the messianic prophecies of the OT. They believed that of necessity all such prophecies were fulfilled in Jesus. As a result they seem to have regarded many incidents as having happened primarily for the fulfillment of some prophecy (Jn. 12:37–41). Those writers were eagerly alert to see in the OT any allusion to Christ. Undoubtedly they reflected their times, and most likely many other messianic passages in the OT were used by early Christians that never found their way into the NT. The fact that Matthew saw in Hos. 11.1 "Out of Egypt I called my son"—a reference to the sojourn of the infant Christ in Egypt (Matt. 2:15), is a prime example of such interpretation. Because of the Christ-event, for the NT writers there was a new light on the sacred page. For them, the essential and fundamental truth of the OT was messianic, which they found fulfilled in Christ.

D. Patristic interpretation. The patristic writers looked to the OT as inspired and authoritative in much the same fashion as did the writers of the NT. The new note in the church fathers was their view of the NT writings as revelation, constantly increasing in influence until they had been collected into an authoritative canon, taking a position of superiority over the OT. In the beginning, the patristic writers were preoccupied with the OT (Clement of Rome made 149 quotations from the OT, none from the NT; see CLEMENT, FIRST EPISTLE OF), but came at last to put the main emphasis upon the NT. (IGNATIUS made frequent use of the NT and only slight use of the OT.)

1. Testimony of 2 Peter. This work—although not to be classed with the patristic writings—dealt with the issue of biblical interpretation and was perhaps the earliest book to face the problem of interpreting the materials that were later canonized as the NT. The author of 2 Peter was aware of those who twisted the letters of Paul (2 Pet. 3:15–16), and he was confronted by certain critics who asked, "Where is this 'coming' he promised?" (3:4). One passage reads, "no prophecy of scripture is a matter of one's own interpretation" (1:20 NRSV). Those who have defended ecclesiastical authority have used this verse to teach that the church, not the individual, is the proper agent to interpret the Bible. Others have understood the verse to mean that no prophetic passage can be interpreted in isolation from other such passages. In all probability, the correct meaning has nothing to do with interpretation, but sees the verse only as an emphasis upon the divine origin of prophecy (cf. NIV).

The author clarified his meaning in the following statement (2 Pet. 1:21) when he emphatically indicated that the prophets were inspired by the Holy Spirit. Peter was clear in his indication that the doctrine of inspiration did not mean that Scripture was easily understood. In fact, Peter indicated that the prophets themselves were puzzled by what they wrote (1 Pet. 1:10–12) and that Paul wrote some things hard to interpret (2 Pet. 3:16). Second Peter seems to represent a time when the eschatological hope was under attack and Paul was regarded as an author of Scripture. The expression "the other Scriptures" (2 Pet. 3:16) would indicate that the Pauline letters had come to be regarded as Scripture.

2. Epistle of Barnabas. This letter includes 119 quotations from the OT and five from the APOCRYPHA (see BARNABAS, EPISTLE OF). There are twenty-one references to the NT (mostly from Paul and the Synoptic Gospels). The point made by the *Epistle of Barnabas* was that the OT had meaning only when it was understood in terms of the gospel. This author was given to an extreme TYPOLOGY. History was meaningless; God's covenant had always been made with Christians. In fact, his attitude toward the OT was not far from that of the Gnostics (see GNOSTICISM). In everything he had to find Christ, so that typology was his basic principle of interpretation.

The celebrated example of Abraham's 318 servants serves to illustrate his methodology. By combining two separate passages, he arrived at the number of Abraham's servants as 318, which was represented by the numerical value of the three Greek letters TIH. He said the first letter stood for the cross, and the combination IH for IHΣOYΣ, "Jesus." This was the mystery that Abraham meant to communicate by the number of his servants. *Barnabas* also contains the earliest Christian attempt to explain the Jewish food laws about the clean and unclean, including a reference to the hyena, which was forbidden as food because it changed its sex, and thus revealed that men must not be corrupters. He was also the earliest Christian writer to base the duration of the world (6,000 years) on the six days of creation combined with the Psalmist's statement that "a thousand years in your sight are like a day that has just gone by" (Ps. 90:4). In spite of its fantastic interpretation, this letter was highly regarded in the early church and contended for a place in the CANON.

3. Marcion the heretic. MARCION rejected the OT and most of the NT (except an edited version of Luke and ten expurgated Pauline epistles), and his negative views forced the church to decide on the canon of Scripture. Marcion's attitude toward the OT was thoroughly dualistic; he postulated two gods—the God of the OT, known for his justice and laws, and the God of the NT, known for his goodness and mercy. Marcion also insisted upon a literal interpretation of the OT to justify his rejection of it as Christian Scripture, pointing by literalism to its crudity and not allowing typology to erase that character. Jesus, he believed, destroyed the prophets and the law. As far as the NT was concerned, Marcion made it speak his language by scissoring out as "interpolations" those parts that did not suit him. To the material that remained from the NT he applied a literal interpretation. To his credit, Marcion emphasized the radical newness of Christianity at a time when many forgot that unique difference; on the other hand, he seriously failed as he sought to sever the continuity of the Christian message with its historical heritage in Judaism.

4. Irenaeus. No one of the patristic period did more to determine Christian thought for centuries to come than did IRENAEUS, Bishop of Lugdunum in Gaul (c. A.D. 177–197). He did not approach the Christian message along the line of philosophy, but gave himself exclusively to the exposition of the Bible. He was preeminently a biblical theologian, making a most extensive use of Scripture. He was the first to quote from almost the entire NT, and extensively from the OT as well. It has been said that, as far as biblical interpretation is concerned, he conserved the best that had gone before and anticipated at least in embryo form nearly all that was to follow in Origen and Augustine, and perhaps even in Luther and Calvin.

Irenaeus's principles of interpretation were governed above all else by his doctrine of inspiration. He spoke of the Scriptures as "perfect," "spoken by the Word of God and his Spirit," and as a "gift from God." For him the foundation of interpretation was the recognition that Christ was the heart of the Scripture. Scripture is about the Savior, and all Scripture must be considered in its redemptive nature. The only way to understand the OT is in the light of that Savior's coming. The unity between the two Testaments is the Savior. Both Testaments have God as their single author.

The harmony of Scripture and the recognition of the Scripture as its own interpreter were two related principles of interpretation that grew out of his conviction of the unity of the Bible. He believed that every part of Scripture had its proper place and that nothing was included by accident. The principle that Scripture was its own best interpreter likewise came from his belief in the unity of Scripture. He urged that obscure passages must be clarified by appeal to and comparison with passages that were understood. He did not, however, turn from the allegorical method altogether. He did apply mystical interpretations to Scripture and looked for deeper and hidden meanings in the Bible. Some have accused Irenaeus of letting tradition sit in judgment on Scripture, and beyond a doubt he did emphasize the rule of faith enshrined in the heritage of Christianity. It cannot, however, be demonstrated that he ever made tradition the last court of appeal in interpretation, setting tradition over against Scripture.

5. Origen. In a sense, ORIGEN was the first "systematic" theologian of Christianity, employing the entire Bible as the basis for his teaching; and he may also deserve to be designated the first Christian scholar to give serious attention to textual criticism. His interest in exegesis grew out of his concern with the text. It has been said that he did more exegetical work than any other scholar until the Reformation. Origen's problem was his proclivity for philosophy. His philosophical interest led him again and again to express in extreme allegorism what he regarded as orthodox Christian teaching. Origen was not dedicated to the rule of faith as it had come down from his predecessors, but he tended to rely on his individual scholarship and intelligence.

Origen was the student and successor to CLEMENT OF ALEXANDRIA in the catechetical school of that city, and from Clement he acquired his theory of the threefold meaning of Scripture. It was compared with the three aspects of human personality as Origen understood it: body, soul, and spirit. The literal meaning of Scripture corresponded to the body, the moral to the soul, and the spiritual to the spirit. In practicality, this reduced to only a twofold distinction, as the shade of difference between the moral and spiritual was almost impossible to maintain. As far as value was concerned, as the spirit of a person had value beyond the body, so the spiritual meaning of Scripture had value beyond the literal. Thus the purpose of Scripture was in terms of the revelation of intellectual truths rather than in terms of a divine intervention in history.

Origen was ambivalent regarding literal interpretation because he identified this with the limited understanding of uneducated and simple people who could not distinguish between parables, allegories, and metaphors in Scripture, and who further insisted that every syllable was literally true. Origen sought to set out the spiritual meaning of Scripture by the allegorical method of interpretation. His influence on subsequent interpretation was considerable, both negatively and positively. He was attacked by the important exegetical school at Antioch (see CHRYSOSTOM, JOHN) and others. His own pupils, however, continued his work; and in the Greek church, Origen's views were published by Basil the Great and Gregory of Nazianzus. Indirectly, he influenced the medieval allegorists who followed centuries later.

6. Augustine. For a millennium, AUGUSTINE dominated the theology of western Christianity. Whereas Origen had been specifically interested in the means and methods of interpretation, Augustine, his successor in influence, was primarily a theologian, and a biblical theologian comparable to Irenaeus. Augustine accepted the inspiration of Scripture without reservation and became famous for his dictum that the Bible was a "narrative of the past, a prophecy of the future, and a description of the present." Augustine's foremost contribution to interpretation was his emphasis upon faith as a necessity for understanding. He taught that understanding of the Scripture was the reward of faith and in direct proportion to the interpreter's faith. He did not eliminate human reason from interpretation, but reason was especially necessary for unbelievers if they were to understand and believe. For believers, it was another matter; understanding and insight into the Scripture came as the result of faith.

Augustine's teaching included a sort of twofold authority for interpretation: first of all Scripture must be believed, and secondly, the tradition of the church measured and assured the accuracy of such belief. To him, the tradition of the church was the final authority, and the principal function of Scripture was to provide a foundation for the creed of the church.

E. Medieval interpretation. During the medieval period (the period from Augustine to the Reformation), the study of the Bible was restricted almost entirely to the monasteries and consisted mostly of the recitation of texts and the copying of biblical MSS. Medieval interpretation cannot be understood apart from a recognition of the prevalence of illiteracy both among the clergy and the congregations, there being practically no public education. During this time the right of declaring the meaning of Scripture became fixed in Rome. The biblical interpretation that did develop had only one objective — to promulgate and support the dogmas of the Roman Church.

1. Dependence on the patristic writers. Tradition was the key to biblical interpretation in the medieval period. All interpretation had to conform to tradition, and tradition was the heritage of the patristic period. It was especially the teaching of the Latin tradition, in light of the Roman Church, that made this period one of religious despotism. The effort of the interpreter was in the direction of harmonizing the patristic writers, and that for the purpose of forming a foundation under Roman dogma. The commentaries of this period were primarily the collection of patristic comments, very much in the fashion of rabbinical practice of NT times. The literal meaning of the Bible faded into insignificance during this period.

2. Scholasticism. Toward the beginning of the second Christian millennium, c. A.D. 1000, an intellectual awakening that anticipated the later Renaissance occurred in religion. This movement was contained within the rigid boundaries of traditional dogmatism and produced a deductive religious philosophy with some dependence upon the principles of Greek philosophy — a movement that came to be known as Scholasticism. It was in reality largely a reshaping of tradition, and interpretation remained to reside in the conformity to the patristic teachings. Scholasticism depended almost exclusively upon the allegorical method of interpretation, but it further perverted the truth of Scripture by use of the dialectical methods of Greek philosophy. There was no recognition of the importance of the original languages of biblical texts, and the entire thought of the interpreter was to support the dogma of Rome. Anselm (Archbishop of Canterbury), Thomas Aquinas, and Guilbert of Nogent were the chief leaders in this movement.

3. Mysticism. Medieval mysticism was a reaction against the traditionalism of the times. It grew out of the instinctive human hunger for conscious fellowship with God, which could not be found in the rigid forms of established religion. Mysticism produced the extreme view that all the individual needed of God could be appropriated directly from communion with God apart from historical revelation. As for interpretation, emphasis was placed upon the devotional study of the Scriptures as might be expected, with allegory freely employed as its method. Hugo of St. Victor and Bernard of Clairvaux were distinguished leaders in this direction. (For a more positive evaluation of biblical hermeneutics in the ancient and medieval periods, see M. Silva, *Has the Church Misread the Bible?* reprinted in *FCI*, 17–90; cf. also B. Smalley, *The Study of the Bible in the Middle Ages*, 2nd ed. [1952].)

F. Reformation interpretation. This movement was primarily a rebellion against the traditionalism of the past, a movement that sought the enthronement of the Scriptures in the thought and life of Christianity. It was the beginning of a revolution that has continued to modern times. The work of three men delineates the issues of interpretation in this period: Luther, Melanchthon, Calvin.

1. Luther. Although Luther broke with the traditionalism of Rome, he nonetheless remained under the influence of the patristic period to a large degree, being especially indebted to Augustine. In his interpretation he was motivated by theological considerations, reflecting again and again his struggle with Rome that became determinative in his interpretation (i.e. the papal antichrist). Luther did not fully discover the significance of the historical setting of the text for interpretation, but he did make a step in that direction. This tendency is reflected in his reading of Christian teachings into the OT. The literal sense of Scripture was important to Luther, and he placed an emphasis upon contextual significance. To a large degree he escaped the ever-present threat to the interpreter—the allegory. (See further Jaroslav Pelikan, *Luther the Expositor: Introduction to the Reformer's Exegetical Writings* [1959].)

2. Melanchthon. This disciple of Luther reflected the theological interests of his mentor, his interpretation being entirely governed by such interests. He failed, as did Luther, to distinguish the doctrinal distinctions of the OT from the NT and freely used OT material as support for Christian doctrine. He was, however, able to arrive at the view that the NT was revelation in a complete and final sense, which transcended the OT. Because of his training in humanism, he elevated reason alongside revelation in his theological study.

3. Calvin. John Calvin influenced Protestantism more than any other Reformer. He broke completely with the allegorical method of the past and employed a strong literalism. He escaped almost completely the methods of the patristic writers in interpretation. He was more accomplished in his interpretation of the NT than he was in the OT. The importance he attached to history is obvious in all his writings. Although limited by the lack of historical resources, Calvin ever placed the emphasis upon the historical connection of the text. He was accomplished for his day in literary criticism, recognizing the distinction to be made between the Synoptic Gospels and the Gospel of John. Like most of his contemporaries, however, Calvin showed dogmatism and had scorn for interpretations other than his own. He also contended for the existence of a complete system of theology in apostolic Christianity and gave little place for the doctrine of progressive revelation, even from the OT to the NT. (See further T. H. L. Parker, *Calvin's New Testament Commentaries* [1971] and *Calvin's Old Testament Commentaries* [1986].)

G. Modern interpretation. Until modern times, Protestantism practiced a type of traditionalism of its own, based on the principle of the verbal inspiration of Scripture, and going back to the confessions of faith worked out by the Reformers. There developed however, an ever increasing emphasis on the historical-critical approach to the Bible.

1. Historical criticism. Historical criticism arose in an atmosphere that challenged the inspiration of the Bible, insisting that the only truly scientific approach to the Bible was the same approach applied to any other ancient document. It was a thoroughly human and rationalistic approach. The modern critical approach began in England with Deism and in Germany with the Aufklärung (Enlightenment) in the 18th cent. H. S. Reimarus, professor of oriental languages at Hamburg, insisted that the Gospels preserved only a faint trace of the real Jesus, a man whom his disciples had transformed into the Savior of the world. J. P. Gabler introduced the thought that Christianity like any other religion was to be understood in terms of its history, what men believed in ancient times, without regard to revelation. J. J. Wettstein followed with an emphasis on the parallels between Jewish and pagan literary sources with the NT.

John Calvin played an important role in the history of interpretation.

© Dr. James C. Martin. Sola Scriptura. The Van Kampen library at the Holy Land Experience in Orlando, Florida. Photographed by permission.

G. W. F. Hegel brought to the forefront the thought of the Christian religion as evolving from its spiritual antecedents, and interpreted history as the manifestation of an absolute spirit in the affairs of men. F. C. Baur fathered the Tübingen school in Germany and taught that Christianity evolved from the historical struggle between Pauline and Jewish influences in the early church, with 2nd-cent. Christianity forming the harmonization of those two contradictory influences. In all of this, the theology of the Scriptures was totally subjected to the history of religions. Albert Schweitzer, who in many ways eliminated the movement, believed that Jesus was an apocalyptic teacher of the 1st cent. and judged the historical Jesus to be irrelevant to modern man. (See E. G. Kraeling, *The Old Testament since the Reformation* [1955]; W. G. Kümmel, *The New Testament. The History of the Investigation of Its Problems* [1972]; S. Neill and T. Wright, *The Interpretation of the New Testament, 1861–1986* [1988]; W. Baird, *History of New Testament Research*, 2 vols. [1992–2003].)

2. Karl Barth. Barth rose to challenge historical criticism in its purely scientific approach to the Scriptures. In a sense, the preface to his commentary on Romans marked the beginning of modern interpretation. In this preface, Barth embraced the contribution of historical criticism but rejected the use that had been made of the historical-critical method to give the final explanation of Scripture. The purpose of historical criticism in his judgment was simply to establish the facts that were to be interpreted. He resorted to the Reformation principle that Scripture must interpret Scripture. The interpreter of Scripture must learn the spiritual language of Scripture if he is to discover its internal meaning. Above all, he insisted upon due recognition of the inexhaustible reality of divine revelation. In Barth's understanding, historical criticism had the first word for the interpreter, but revelation had the last.

3. Rudolph Bultmann. Although he praised Barth's work, in many respects Bultmann's significance arose out of his opposition to it. Bultmann combined the history of religions approach with existential philosophy. He rejected as a historian the worldview of the Bible that proclaimed a God who acted directly in history. There was no goal in history, and all ideas that proclaimed such a divine intervention in human affairs Bultmann called mythology (see MYTH). He occupied the same position of the rationalists as far as history was concerned; his difference was in his reinterpretation of that which he called mythology. God's acts were not to be found in history but in human existence. The meaning of the gospel was no longer in a historical Jesus of centuries gone, but in the human being of the present time. The supernatural was discarded, and by the use of existential philosophy he sought to find all meaning of Scripture in Christian experience without reference to history.

4. Oscar Cullmann. Cullmann may be considered representative of the "salvation history" approach to interpretation that Kümmel, Goppelt, and others encouraged as a recognition of the limitations of the historical-critical method. Cullmann believed that both revelation and redemption were in connection with historical events, of which Jesus Christ was supremely important. The acts of God were, however, always accompanied by interpretation, never standing alone. The interpretation of the redemptive acts of God was never to be separated from the acts themselves, but the interpretation became a part of history itself. The NT was the supreme interpretation of God in history, therefore the NT could be interpreted correctly only when it was interpreted theologically.

5. The New Hermeneutic. This school was created by Gerhard Ebeling and Ernst Fuchs, students of R. Bultmann and M. Heidegger, in the early 1960s. They sought to wed the centrality of human existence with the phenomenon of language by creating a method in which Jesus' words and deeds become "language events" when encountered through faith. Since all of existence is made available in language, man encounters ultimate being only through "word event," accomplished via the hermeneutical circle: as readers encounter the Word, they discover the Word is encountering them.

6. Hans-Georg Gadamer. Strongly influenced by the later Heidegger's concern for language as providing the framework for being, Gadamer in 1960 published his magisterial *Truth and Method*, widely considered the most important hermeneutical work of the 20th cent. He argued that interpretation is not so much a method-laden enterprise as it is an aesthetic experience akin to music and art. Therefore, the historian cannot simply go back to an ancient text and allow that text to speak without distortion from one's own tradition. So one must allow the effects of that history to become part of the process. Gadamer calls the process of coming-to-understanding the "fusion of horizons," that is, the coming together of the present horizon of the text with that of the interpreter. It is not unlocking the past meaning of the text but establishing a dialectic with it in the present (p. 353). The "temporal distance" between the text and the reader is bridged when the "preunderstanding" of the reader is made part of the process and provides a common ground with the world of the text. In this way past and present are fused in the act of communication between text and reader (p. 258). The autonomous text has a life of its own, transcending the original author and situation and thereby addressing the reader in the present. The circle occurs as the text addresses the readers and draws them into its world.

7. Structuralism. This movement began with the demise of French existentialism and had its heyday in the 1960s and early 70s. Its proponents believed meaning inheres not in an author's intentions or in the historical setting of a text but rather in the literary structure itself. Structuralists argue that diachronic or historical interests are a barrier to true meaning and that only synchronic or literary factors can guide one to actual understanding.

Two precursors led to this school. First, Ferdinand de Saussure (1915) distinguished *langue* (the language system) from *parole* (the individual speech-act), leading to a separation between signifier (term) and signified (the meaning it connotes). Second, Claude Lévi-Strauss, an anthropologist in the 1950s, said that meaning in primitive cultures inhered not in the conscious or surface level of communication but in the deep or unconscious level of mytho-poetic symbols. Structuralists took this approach and constructed a system whereby a text will be broken up into its "codes" or action units and studied to determine the underlying system of reality it represents. This narrative sequence of codes is then decoded, and the result, proponents claimed, is a timeless meaning, unlike the results of historical criticism. However, due to its preoccupation with linguistics and its failure to develop a strong philosophical foundation, it was largely superseded by poststructuralism by the late 70s.

8. Poststructuralism. Several biblical scholars in the late 1970s (Detweiler, Peterson, McKnight) tried to overcome the problems of a purely diachronic method (historical criticism) and a purely synchronic method (structuralism) by positing a phenomenological "bracketing" of conscious meaning in order to uncover the reality that lay behind it. Poststructuralists like J. Calloud or R. Barthes deny that there is any kind of underlying system that makes linguistic communication intelligible. All meaning is the result of interaction between the reader and the text, and the text is autonomous from all historical understandings, that of the original author as well as of all past interpreters. It is a wholly subjective act, for past understanding must be "bracketed" when one enters the thought world of the text. Susan Wittig in "A Theory of Multiple Meanings" (*Semeia* 9 [1977]: 75–103) calls for a "semiotic" (signs-oriented) approach with a "second-order" system in which the text has an "unstated" significance that compels the interpreter to complete it. This interplay between text and interpreter demands "polyvalence" or multiple-meaning possibilities. A text is incomplete without a reader who can actualize its meaning, and the process in a sense can be called "at play in the fields of the text." Any text is a playground in which each interpreter brings his or her own game with its own set of rules. All the games are equally valid, for the field itself is simply there to be played on.

9. Paul Ricoeur. He is the leading philosopher who has intersected biblical hermeneutics and, along with Gadamer, the towering giant in the field. He has wed phenomenology with semiotics and applied it to biblical interpretation. From phenomenology he believes that language forms the core of being and that reading the symbolic expression of a text is a moment of self-understanding. From semiotics he believes the text is a discourse-event divorced from the author and original historical context and therefore open only to a present coming-to-understanding. Yet the worlds of text and interpreter do come together and merge (in this he agrees with Gadamer). Ricoeur's desire has always been to enable biblical hermeneutics to be done in an atmosphere of philosophical inquiry. For him a text has its own structural integrity apart from its author and so shapes the reader's understanding by guiding the process of interpretation. It is a "written discourse" that establishes a dialectic with a reader, thus referring beyond itself into its world. The reader must have a "second naïveté" or postcritical attitude that remains open to the text's imaginative thought-world. Still, like Gadamer, it is the thought-world in the present text, not the referential intent of a past author. He emphasizes the intention of the text, not that of the author. The author is present as part of the action of the text but does not guide the interpretive process. For Ricoeur the author's intended meaning is possible but can never be more than a theoretical construct while the world-referential aspect grasps the reader in the present. For instance, a parable has a subversive effect upon a reader's experience of reality and establishes a semantic incongruence that grasps the reader and draws him or her into its textual world.

10. Deconstructionism. For the past two decades no school has been as influential as this brain-child of Jacques Derrida. The leading poststructuralist in the 60s, he published three master works in the same year, 1967—*On Grammatology*, *Writing and Difference*, and *Speech and Phenomenon*. He attacks the very foundation of Western philosophy, trying to free language from the constraints of epistemology and metaphysics as currently defined. He argues that logic pretends to be rational but is actually metaphorical, and so "truth" is radically relative. In this he follows Nietzsche, who said, "What, then, is truth? An army of metaphors ... a sum of human relations ... which after long use seem firm, canonical and obligatory to a people: truths are illusions about which one has forgotten that this is what they are: metaphors which are worn out and without sensuous power; coins which have lost their pictures and now matter only as metal, no longer as coins" (*The Portable Nietzsche*, 46–47).

Derrida defines deconstruction as a "decentering" process in which the meaning of a structure is disrupted via an infinite number of sign-substitutions, that is, of meaning possibilities. The concepts of sign (with constant interplay between signifier and signified) and play (which destroys the metaphysical via discourse) demand the absence of meaning at the core of the interpretive process. There is no "presence" of meaning in a text, because all attempts to encode the text, to define its horizon or locus of meaning, end up with an endless number of viable interpretations. Since all language is metaphorical at the core, and since all metaphors are open-ended, there is no such thing as *the* meaning of a text, only an infinite string of possibilities.

Derrida believes that writing has priority over speech and that thinking is simply writing on the mind. So since writing always results in an autonomous text, the speaker's so-called "presence" in speech becomes a myth, for the spoken word is autonomous the second it is uttered. The result is "difference" (the opposition between the signifier and the signified, resulting in "deferred" meanings) and "absence" (writing as a freeplay that displaces meaning). There is only one solution, to recognize that there is no true transfer of meaning in the interpretive process, for the signified is transformed via the act of reading, and meaning both differs and is deferred from its relationship to all other interpretations, including the original author's.

So deconstruction is not a formal school but a perspective on discourse and reading. The search for meaning is never ending in the same way that a sign is never complete in itself. A text is neither past nor present but is a repository of an ever-reconstituted process of discovery. So the interpreter must deconstruct meaning from the restraints of an artificial rational process and engage in freeplay with the infinite meaning possibilities of a text so as to construct their own understanding. In this way followers of deconstruction believe theirs is a positive rather than negative movement. They do not consider themselves hermeneutical anarchists but view themselves as liberators, freeing readers from the false Western constraint of searching for final meaning in a text.

11. Reader-response criticism. A sister movement to deconstruction locates all meaning not in author or text but in the reader. There are two types: the moderate movement of Wolfgang Iser (*The Act of Reading: A Theory of Aesthetic Response* [1978]), who believes the text guides the process, and the radical one of Stanley Fish (*Is There a Text in This Class? The Authority of Interpretive Communities* [1980]), who sees the text as an empty work waiting for a reader to give it meaning. Most biblical reader-response critics like Robert Fowler or Robert Culpepper would follow Iser and believe the text has multiple possible meanings but still controls the interpretive process.

For Fish there is an ontological union between text and reader, so that the text disappears and the reader "creates" meaning. However, anarchy does not reign. There is still a determinative force in reading, the interpretive community. All human beings are part of a community, and their understanding is shaped by that community. Therefore, the "reading strategy" is developed within the community, and both critical reflection and understanding come via that community. As Kevin Vanhoozer describes the movement, "Postmodernity does not mean the end of all authority, however, only of universal norms; local norms remain in force. Interpretation is always 'from below,' shaped by the reader's contextually conditioned context and regulated by the authority of community-based norms" (*Is There a Meaning in This Text? The Bible, the Reader, and the Morality of Literary Knowledge* [1998], 168). The reader/community is now the generating force in hermeneutics, and readers can exult in the present moment of creation, as "readers performing acts" find meaning.

12. The conservative response. It is clear that the last half of the 20th cent. moved inexorably away from author-centered meaning to text-centered (Gadamer, Ricoeur) and then to reader-centered (deconstruction, reader response) hermeneutics. There is much of value in the challenge from the postmodern critics. The importance of the community and the central place preunderstanding has in the interpretive process must be accounted for in hermeneutical theory. Each of us has become part of a faith community, and whether that is Reformed, Lutheran, Baptist, Pentecostal, or some other will determine how we look at Scripture and how we interpret texts. Fish is correct for most of us—community will *determine* how we interpret passages. Yet it must be asked whether it has to be this way. Can we as readers allow the author-text to guide us to its own meaning?

There is a twofold counter-movement back to the author and the text as the determining force. First, those who follow E. D. Hirsch (*Validity in Interpretation* [1967])—Walter Kaiser, Elliott Johnson—separate meaning (comprehending a text on the basis of its semantic core) from significance (inserting that meaning into individual modern contexts). Meaning then is grounded in authorial intention and original historical setting and is unchanging, while significance applies fixed meaning to differing situations. Hirsch believes that every text contains "intrinsic genres" that supply the rules which enable interpreters to understand its meaning.

Second, there are those—e.g., Anthony Thiselton, Kevin Vanhoozer, Grant Osborne—who follow Ludwig Wittgenstein (*Philosophical Investigations* [1953]) and his followers (in particular J. L. Austin, *How to Do Things with Words* [1962], and John Searle, *Speech Acts: An Essay in the Philosophy of Language* [1969]) and have developed a "speech act" approach. Wittgenstein took a "game" theory approach, in which the multifaceted character of language leads it to speak differently in various semantic situations or "games." This functional view of language was developed further by Austin, who argued language has a performative function as well as an assertive dimension. As such, speech acts have three aspects: the locutionary act (the prepositional level of assertion), the illocutionary act (what the utterance accomplishes, such as command, assertion, promise etc.), and the perlocutionary act (the intended effects, such as persuading, teaching, shocking). The latter two are actions and demand an author or agent who decides what the communication is intended to do. Searle says that language is both referential and performative, the sentence is an intentional device that brings the hearers into an arena in which they can apply rules of the language game and recognize its meaning. The context of this "illocutionary act" then provides the proper conditions that guide the listener to the referential meaning. While uncovering the intended meaning is difficult, it is not impossible.

(Historical surveys of biblical interpretation include F. W. Farrar, *History of Interpretation* [1886]; P. R. Ackroyd et al., eds., *The Cambridge History of the Bible*, 3 vols. [1963–70]; R. M. Grant and D. Tracy, *A Short History of the Interpretation of the Bible*, 2nd ed. [1984]; A. J. Hauser and D. F. Watson, *A History of Biblical Interpretation*, 4 vols. [2003–].)

III. Principles of biblical interpretation.

Exegesis is the term applied to the practice of interpretation.

A. Words. To interpret Scripture lexically, the interpreter should have some knowledge of the historical development of words in their meaning. At the same time, one should avoid the "etymological fallacy," that is, assuming that the meaning of a word can be found in its history (diachronic approach) rather than its conventional use in its current period (synchronic approach). An example of this is reading Hebrew meanings into Greek words used in the NT. It is more important to understand the usage of words by the particular writer being interpreted. Current usage rather than history alone must determine a word's meaning. An author can refer to a past use of a word, but the context must indicate he is doing so. A good lexicon is the best source of this information. The meaning of words should be considered in light of the different periods in the development of the biblical languages. Comparison should be made between different authors of the same period where such is possible.

B. Syntax. To interpret syntactically, the grammatical principles of the language in which the text was written must be understood. A grammar of that language is the source of such information. It must always be remembered that the function of grammar is not to determine the laws of language but to explain them. Language developed first, as a means of expressing thought; grammars were written later to explain the laws and principles of language as it functioned in expressing ideas. In the interpreter's native language, these meanings of grammatical constructions are more or less sensed at once subconsciously; but when work is being done in a foreign language, it is difficult to isolate and understand the ways of expressing thought peculiar to that language, or the idioms of the language. If the interpreter wishes to get the meaning from the text, it is necessary to have the viewpoint of the writer, and follow closely the idioms that the writer used.

Moreover, our understanding of how languages function is constantly developing, so it is important to keep in touch with the latest developments in grammar. For instance, in the past it was common to give the aorist tense in Greek a "once for all" force, and this led to certain theological conclusions, such as the view that Rom. 12:1 ("present [aorist imp.] your bodies a living sacrifice," KJV) teaches a crisis experience of a second work of grace. We now know the aorist tense did not have such a force, and so such conclusions are grammatical errors.

C. Context. To interpret contextually it is necessary to have regard for the entire composition being interpreted. The nature of the composition is of paramount importance to the interpreter, whether it is a unified discourse or some other type of writing. The subject under discussion immediately surrounding the passage colors the interpretation also. Often a shade of meaning is given to words by the nature of the discussion of which they are a part. The division of the biblical text into chapters and verses has created a considerable problem for interpretation from time to time because the impression is given that the context is insignificant, that each verse stands alone. Also, the sections fail to correspond to the correct divisions of thought. A good example is Col. 2:21, which has been used not infrequently as a text for a sermon on temperance, when actually in its context it is a condemnation of asceticism.

Failure to note context is one of the basic errors in interpretation. For instance, "Behold, I stand at the door, and knock" (Rev. 3:20 KJV) has always been understood as evangelistic, but in its context it refers to a church that needs to repent of sin. Scholars have also tended to interpret PARABLES in highly creative ways by ignoring the context in which a particular parable has been embedded. At the micro level, terms and sentences can only be understood properly when seen in light of their immediate context. At the macro level, episodes like parables or miracle stories can only be understood in light of the developing context of that particular Gospel.

D. History. It is important for interpreters to discover the circumstances that surrounded and called forth the document being interpreted. The source of such information is in the introductory notes to a biblical book in some good commentary, or a special volume of introduction to the OT or the NT. The manners, customs, and psychology of the people associated with the book being studied are of tremendous importance to a correct understanding of the text. The study of the people would include their methods of recording history, figures of speech, types of literature, and their concept of time or chronology. Both general and particular historical works can supply this need for the interpreter.

Every book of the Bible is historical, written to encounter God's people at a certain time and with certain problems. Failure to understand that dimension will cause us to misinterpret God's Word, as with the prophecy movement that treats the book of Revelation as a code-book addressing only current history. Background studies can make a text come alive by turning it virtually into a cinematic event. However, in so doing one must be certain that the proper background has been chosen. Allow the meaning of the text to guide the choice of background, so that the fit will be exact. For instance, the relationship between Jesus and his disciples was not based on wandering CYNIC philosophers (as some have alleged) but on Jewish rabbi-disciple models. When such background is applied to texts (e.g., the laws of inheritance and patriarch-son relationships to the parable of the lost son in Lk. 15), the story becomes quite exciting.

E. Analogy of Scripture. One of the most important safeguards for interpreters is to do their work with a regard for the analogy of Scripture. They must use Scripture itself as a guide to understanding Scripture. Any bizarre interpretation of a passage that conflicts with the whole trend of Scripture must be judged to be wrong. Scripture confirms itself. A thorough and accurate knowledge of the biblical viewpoint is a necessity. It is hoped that interpreters seek to divest themselves of their prejudices and seek to read the text through the eyes of its author.

This principle is also critical in developing a systematic theology. When studying an individual doctrine it is critical to collect all the biblical passages on the issue and then to allow Scripture to interpret Scripture. Most determine doctrine on the basis of tradition (the dogma of the particular church or movement one belongs to) more than Scripture. Each side has its own collection of proof texts (a "canon within a canon") on which they base their views; to that extent the "reader-response" critics are correct (see above). However, the principle of the analogy of Scripture demands that all texts (on both sides of the issue) be studied before a decision is reached. While our tradition is important, it must always be placed under the teaching of Scripture itself.

F. Correct procedure. The goal of interpretation is always the author's intended meaning, which includes all three aspects pointed out by Austin (see above): the assertion of the text, the act it produces, and the effect it attains. Moreover, it is attainable so long as we realize the goal is probable rather than certain knowledge; that is, what our research unlocks as the more likely reading. There will always be finiteness in all human enterprises.

A "field approach" to hermeneutics has five aspects (cf. G. R. Osborne, *The Hermeneutical Spiral: A Comprehensive Introduction to Biblical Interpretation* [1991], 412–15): (1) Be aware of your preunderstanding and seek critical interaction with other reading communities; they will force you to be honest with your prejudices. (2) Place yourself "in front of" the text rather than behind it (Ricoeur's metaphor), thereby allowing the text to have priority in the interpretive process. Let the text challenge, reshape, and change as necessary the presuppositions you bring to it. Until this happens, you can never discover the original meaning, for you will always look for the meaning you wish to find. (3) Seek controls that enable you to work with your preunderstanding rather than be dominated by it. Be open to new possibilities and welcome challenge; seek truth rather than dogma. (4) While polyvalent meanings are unnecessary, a polyvalent attitude is critical. Seek an "interpretive realism" that remains in dialogue with other faith communities, and be willing to change your mind if the data so demands. (5) Above all, allow good hermeneutical principles to guide your study and to draw you out of your narrow world and introduce you to the world of the text and the author behind it. Take the time to use the exegetical tools that alone will help you go back to the historical world of the Bible — good commentaries, dictionaries, encyclopedias, word study books, background books etc.

The hermeneutical process is not as complex as one might think. First, be aware of the genre or type of literature and utilize those rules of the language game that apply to each (for this see G. D. Fee and D. Stuart, *How to Read the Bible for All Its Worth*, 3rd ed. [2003]). Second, study the structural development of the passage and see how the various parts relate to the whole, thereby seeing how the context develops. Third, study the grammatical and lexical components of the sentence to determine the probable meaning of the developing text (see M. Silva, *Biblical Words and Their Meaning: An Introduction to Lexical Semantics*, rev. ed. [1994]). The goal is to discover what the author was saying to his original audience, to leap the gap between our world and his. Fourth, use background information to fill in the gaps between what the author expected his original readers to understand and our world today. Unlock the culture and the historical world implied in the text. Fifth, look for the theological threads that tie your passage to others in the book and in the Bible as a whole. Try to determine the theological message of your text and the way it fits into the larger theology of the book as a whole.

Finally, take a critical realist approach to testing your conclusions, searching for their adequacy, coherence, and comprehensiveness. Verify them by studying the conclusions of other scholars and of the community of faith as a whole, then comparing them with your own. Of course, this is done at every level of the process as you make decisions regarding the meaning of the parts within the whole. Still, the constant desire to learn from others and the humble openness to their perspectives is the determining factor in a mature scholar.

(In addition to the works mentioned in the body of this article, see M. S. Terry, *Biblical Hermeneutics: A Treatise on the Interpretation of the Old and New Testaments*, rev. ed. [1890]; S. Burnham, *The Elements of Hermeneutics* [1916]; A. B. Mickelsen, *Interpreting the Bible* [1963]; R. Marle, *Introduction to Hermeneutics* [1967]; A. S. Wood, *The Principles of Biblical Interpretation* [1967]; B. L. Ramm, *Protestant Biblical Interpretation: A Textbook of Hermeneutics*, 3rd ed. [1970]; A. C. Thiselton, *The Two Horizons: New Testament Hermeneutics and Philosophical Description with Special Reference to Heidegger, Bultmann, Gadamer, and Wittgenstein* [1980]; G. R. Osborne, *The Hermeneutical Spiral: A Comprehensive Introduction to Biblical Interpretation* [1991]; W. C. Kaiser and M. Silva, *An Introduction to Biblical Hermeneutics: The Search for Meaning* [1994, rev. ed. 2007]; G. Bray, *Biblical Interpretation: Past and Present* [1996]; K. J. Vanhoozer, *Is There a Meaning in This Text? The Bible, the Reader, and the Morality of Literary Knowledge* [1998]; H. Hayes, ed., *Dictionary of Biblical Interpretation*, 2 vols. [1999]; K. J. Vanhoozer et al., eds., *Dictionary for Theological Interpretation of the Bible* [2005].)

H. L. DRUMWRIGHT, JR.; rev. by G. R. OSBORNE

Interpretation of Knowledge. A Gnostic document preserved in the NAG HAMMADI LIBRARY (NHC XI, 1). Written in the form of a homily, the author addresses the problem of jealousy over spiritual gifts in a Christian community. The Coptic MS, which is badly damaged, dates to the middle of the 4th cent., but the work was probably composed about a century earlier. Its content and terminology suggest an origin in Valentinian circles (see GNOSTICISM; VALENTINUS). (English trans. in *NHL*, 472–80.)

interpreter. This English term, referring to a person who translates from one language to another or who otherwise explains the meaning of a message (as in a DREAM), may be used to render Hebrew *mēlîṣ* H4885 (Gen. 42:23; this word elsewhere means "mediator" or the like); note also the participle of the verb *pātar* H7354 (40:8 et al.). In the NT it renders Greek *diermēneutēs* G1449, referring to someone who explains the speech of those with the gift of glossolalia (1 Cor. 14:28). See TONGUES, GIFT OF.

Iob i′ohb (יוֹב H3410 [not in NIV]). Variant of JASHUB (Gen. 46:13 RSV and other versions, following MT).

iota i-oh′tuh (ἰῶτα G2740). KJV *jot*. Seventh letter of the Greek ALPHABET. In the Hebrew/Aramaic alphabet, the corresponding consonant (י, "yod") is the smallest letter, and Jesus alludes to it in his statement, "Till heaven and earth pass, one jot or one tittle shall in no wise pass from the law, till all be fulfilled" (Matt. 5:17 KJV). See discussion under DOT.

Iphdeiah if-dee′yah (יִפְדְיָה H3635, "Yahweh redeems"). KJV Iphedeiah. Son of Shashak and descendant of BENJAMIN; listed among the heads of families that lived in Jerusalem (1 Chr. 8:25; cf. v. 28).

Iphedeiah if′uh-dee′yah. KJV form of IPHDEIAH.

Iphtah if′tuh (יִפְתָּח H3652, prob. "[God] opens"; see IPHTAH EL). KJV Jiphtah. A town in the SHEPHELAH, within the tribal territory of JUDAH (Josh. 15:43). Because it was in the same district as KEILAH and MARESHAH, some tentatively identify Iphtah with modern Tarqumiyeh, about 6 mi. NW of HEBRON.

Iphtah El if′tuh-el′ (יִפְתַּח־אֵל H3654, "God opens"). KJV Jiphthah-el; NRSV Iphtah-el. A valley on the N border of the tribe of ZEBULUN and the SE border of ASHER (Josh. 19:14, 27). Its location is uncertain, but two possibilities are Wadi el-Malik and Wadi ʾAbbelin.

Ir ihr (עִיר H6553, possibly "stallion [of donkey]" or "city"). (1) Descendant of BENJAMIN and (according to NIV) ancestor of the Shupites and Huppites (1 Chr. 7:12; see HUPPIM); some scholars have suggested that he is the same as IRI (v. 7).

(2) According to some scholars, the name of an otherwise unknown city mentioned by BALAAM in one of his oracles (Num. 24:19; cf. NRSV, NJPS). Most versions understand the term here as the common noun for "city."

Ira i′ruh (עִירָא H6562, possibly "stallion [of donkey]" or "city"). (1) A Jairite identified as "David's priest" (2 Sam. 20:26). Since the Jairites were probably descendants of JAIR, from the tribe of MANASSEH (rather than LEVI), his position could not have been sacerdotal. Some have thought that, in DAVID's time, a few non-Levites were permitted to serve in some sort of priestly capacity; otherwise, the term "priest" here refers to some chief official in the service of the king (cf. the use of the same term in 2 Sam. 8:18, rendered "royal adviser" by NIV on the basis of 1 Chr. 18:17). Because of ambiguous versional evidence, some scholars emend "Jairite" to "Ithrite" and identify this Ira with #3 below.

(2) Son of Ikkesh of TEKOA; he was one of David's thirty mighty warriors and served as commander in charge of the division for the sixth month (2 Sam. 23:26; 1 Chr. 11:28; 27:9).

(3) An ITHRITE who was also one of David's thirty mighty warriors (2 Sam. 23:38; 1 Chr. 11:40).

S. BARABAS

Irad i′rad (עִירָד H6563, derivation uncertain). Son of ENOCH and grandson of CAIN (Gen. 4:18).

Iram i′ram (עִירָם H6566, possibly "stallion [of donkey]"). Descendant of ESAU, listed among the clan chiefs of EDOM (Gen. 36:43; 1 Chr. 1:54).

Irenaeus i′ruh-nee′uhs (Εἰρηναῖος, "peaceful"). Born c. A.D. 130–140 in ASIA MINOR (possibly SMYRNA, where in his youth he saw POLYCARP), Irenaeus was educated in Rome, then settled in Lyons, Gaul, where he eventually became bishop. He died, perhaps as a martyr, around the year 200. A firm opponent of GNOSTICISM and other unorthodox movements, Irenaeus is widely regarded as the first great theologian of the Christian church. His principal work was the *Adversus omnes haereses* (Against All Heresies); fragments are preserved in the original Greek, but all of it is extant in a faithful Latin translation (English trans. in vol. 1 of *ANF*).

This material provides invaluable information about early church history and theology. Among other contributions, Irenaeus was the first known Christian writer to articulate a clear understanding of the canon; see CANON (NT) V. Also, his many scriptural quotations constitute very early evidence for NT textual criticism; see TEXT AND MANUSCRIPTS (NT) III.C. (Cf. M. A. Donovan in *ABD*, 3:457–61; R. M. Grant, *Irenaeus of Lyons* [1997]; E. Osborn, *Irenaeus of Lyons* [2001].)

Ir-ha-heres. See DESTRUCTION, CITY OF; SUN, CITY OF.

Iri *i'ri* (עִירִי H6565, possibly "my stallion [of a donkey]" or "my city"). **(1)** Son of Bela, grandson of BENJAMIN, and family head (1 Chr. 7:7); some scholars identify him with IR (v. 12).

(2) KJV Apoc. variant form of URIAH (1 Esd. 8:62).

Irijah *i-ri'juh* (יִרְאִיָּיה H3713, "Yahweh sees"). Son of Shelemiah; he was an officer posted at the BENJAMIN GATE in Jerusalem who arrested JEREMIAH on the charge of planning to desert to the Babylonians (Jer. 37.13–14).

Ir-moab *ihr-moh'ab* (עִיר מוֹאָב, "city of Moab"). An otherwise unknown town on the ARNON River where BALAK went to meet BALAAM (Num. 22:36, NRSV, NJPS). Most versions, however, render the phrase, "a [*or* the] city of Moab."

Ir Nahash *ihr-nay'hash* (עִיר נָחָשׁ H6560, "city of the serpent"). Son of Tehinnah and descendant of JUDAH (1 Chr. 4:12). More likely, the text should be rendered "Tehinnah the founder [*or* leader] of Ir [*or* of the city of] Nahash," in which case the reference is to a Judahite town, perhaps to be identified with Deir Naḥas (c. 7 mi. W of KEILAH) or with Khirbet en-Naḥas in the ARABAH (for the latter, see Z. Kallai, *Historical Geography of the Bible* [1986], 117).

iron (metal). A metallic element much used in the manufacture of tools and other articles of everyday use (see METAL AND METALLURGY). Pure iron, which is difficult to make, is almost white and has a density of 7.9. It softens at red heat and may be readily welded at white heat, above which it becomes brittle; it melts at c. 1540°C. Native iron is rare as crustal material, being found as steel-gray to iron-black, strongly magnetic masses in some basaltic lava flows. However, evidence indicates that the core of the earth is made up of a nickel-iron alloy with a density of about 12, and native iron makes up the bulk of meteorites. Most meteorites consist of a nickel-iron alloy (average composition: iron 91%, nickel 8.5%, cobalt 0.5%), thought to be indicative of the composition of the earth's core. On an etched surface, these iron-meteorites show intergrowth of lamellae of a nickel-poor alloy in a nickel-rich base.

The presence of nickel in iron beads used for jewelry in predynastic EGYPT (before c. 3400 B.C.) suggests that at least part of man's early use of iron was of extraterrestrial material. This iron, with nickel, is subject to little or no rusting and survives through time, while most articles of iron, or steel, made from local terrestrial iron ores, rust away in a relatively short time. However, iron rust containing no nickel and associated with Egyptian copper implements of c. 2700–2500 B.C. is indicative of human use, from at least this early date, of iron obtained from local ores by primitive metallurgical processes. The earliest OT reference to iron is in connection with TUBAL-CAIN (Gen. 4:22, Heb. *barzel* H1366), but the term occurs frequently. It is used figuratively in both OT and NT as a symbol of

Iron sickle used for harvesting grain.

hardness and strength (e.g., Deut. 28:23; Rev. 2:27; Gk. *sidēreos* G4969, an adj. from *sidēros* G4970).

Iron is one of the most abundant metals in the earth's crust, making up just more than 5% of crustal material. Although iron-bearing minerals are very numerous, only four of them are important ores of the metal: magnetite (ferroso-ferric oxide), haematite (ferric oxide), limonite (hydrated ferric oxide) and siderite (ferrous carbonate). These ores readily yield the metal by smelting with carbon. A certain amount of free or combined carbon occurs in this metal and its proportion and condition regulate the properties and give rise to the three main varieties: wrought iron, steel, and cast iron.

Magnetite (from Magnesia in Asia Minor, where the mineral was known to the ancients), an iron-gray strongly magnetic mineral, occurs as a primary constituent of most igneous rocks, including those of the Aqabah granite complex which crops out on either side of the Red Sea. It occurs as magmatic segregations or at the contact of igneous masses and their host rocks, particularly limestone, as in parts of the ANE, including Armenia. The other iron ores occur as sedimentary beds or accumulations. Haematite (from Gk. *haima* G135, "blood") is steel-gray to black in color when massive, but in finely powdered or earthy varieties it is cherry-red and as red ocher has been used from earliest times as a pigment. This mineral was worked in ancient times, particularly during the reigns of David and Solomon, between the Dead Sea and Feinan and further S in Wadi Sabra, 5 mi. SSE of Petra. Limonite (from Gk. *leimōn*, "meadow") shows various shades of brown, with the earthy variety being yellow ocher. Much of it is derived from other iron minerals by alteration, although some limonite beds are true precipitates. The carbonate siderite (or chalybite, from Gk. *chalyps*, "steel," named from the Chalybes, an ancient tribe of Asiatic iron-workers) varies in color from buff-brown to brownish-black or brownish-red. Some deposits result from direct precipitation, either in lakes or in the sea.

The legendary home of iron is NE Asia Minor where, together with the central plateau of Anatolia, there are rich iron deposits, including magnetite, with a present-day estimated reserve of fifteen million tons of ore with 65% iron in the region of Divrige, E central Turkey. Remains of early iron manufacture are found in this region and also at sites in Syria and Iraq dating from no later than 2700 B.C. As early as 7000–6000 has been suggested for the initial discovery of iron in Egypt. Oxidized iron beads dated about 4000 were found at El Gerzeh, and an iron tool dating from the 4th dynasty (c. 3100) was found inside the great pyramid of Khufu at Giza. It has been argued that there must have been skilled steel workers in ancient Egypt to have built the pyramids and other great constructions of the time as well as to carve statues and hieroglyphics from hard rocks (cf. Job 19:24), including granite. However, the earliest iron objects in Egypt, and elsewhere, were mainly weapons and ornaments. The common manufacture of tools did not come until the beginning of the Iron Age proper (c. 1200 B.C.).

While it is possible that the first iron tools were made (forged) from meteoritic iron, it seems likely that native iron was first found in the ashes of a large fire adjacent to rocks containing haematite or limonite or smelted accidentally from red or yellow ocher pigments in furnaces used for pottery. With the association of red and yellow ocher with fire and iron, the next steps would have been to build fires against exposures of these colored rocks which were subjected to the prevailing winds, and then to fan, with bellows, fires in pits or primitive furnaces. These methods still survive today in the Catalan forge in which the iron ore is reduced to iron, the glowing ball of iron pulled out of the furnace (cf. Deut. 4:20; 1 Ki. 8:51; Jer. 11:4), and while still white hot, hammered vigorously, both to expel as much slag as possible and to weld the hot particles of metal into a coherent mass. The product was wrought iron, with the metal being worked hot enough to be shaped, but not melted. Accidentally steel, containing more carbon, was sometimes produced. With progressive incorporation of various improvements both in methods of producing the air blast and in furnace design, this method, used by the ancients, produced all the iron up to the 14th cent. of our era. Only from the early 14th cent. on, has liquid pig iron and the resultant cast iron been produced. (See further R. Partington, *A Textbook of Inorganic Chemistry*, 6th ed. [1950], 913–26; H. H. Read, *Rutley's Elements of Mineralogy*, 26th ed. [1970], 513–23.)

The history of the OT is very much influenced both by the distribution of iron deposits and by the ability to master the metallurgical processes related to the metal. The Israelites in Egypt would have been familiar with the smelting of iron (Deut. 4:20) and its many uses. Accordingly, the indication of an abundance of iron in the Promised Land (Deut. 8:9) would have been very significant. However, the secret of toughening the metal by repeated hammering when hot, and subsequent quenching with water, was guarded by the HITTITES, to the N in Asia Minor, from c. 1400–1200 B.C., but with trade in the metal carried on by the Phoenicians. Part of the reason for the success of Canaanite opposition to Israelite occupation, in the later part of the 13th cent., was the inferior state of Hebrew technology, especially as far as horse-drawn war chariots (Josh. 17:18) and other iron weapons were concerned.

With the decline and fall of the Hittite empire after 1200 B.C., it was the turn of the PHILISTINES to control both the manufacture and export of iron. These people, who had arrived in the Canaanite coastlands during the transition from the Bronze to the Iron Age (see SEA PEOPLES), had probably obtained the secrets of the metallurgical processes as part of the booty of their defeat of the Hittites in Asia Minor. This technological monopoly was guarded by the Philistines who lived on the plains, with the hill-dwelling Israelites too poor to be able to trade for iron. About this time iron was as valuable as gold and silver, with iron weapons and implements being highly prized commodities for the following century.

The possession of up-to-date weapons, as well as experience of military campaigns, assisted the Philistines to defeat the Israelites time after time (e.g. 1 Sam. 4:1–2, 10). To meet this situation, which threatened the work of two hundred years of colonization, the loosely federated tribes of Israel united as a monarchy, with SAUL as king. The Philistines attempted to stop the making of new weapons by prohibiting the trade of smiths (1 Sam. 13:19–20), but the Israelites successfully waged guerrilla war in the hill country using knowledge of the local terrain to more than offset deficiencies in weapons (e.g., 1 Sam. 14:1–16). Nevertheless, pitched battle on the plains, against an enemy with a vastly superior technology, proved to be disastrous (1 Sam. 31).

DAVID managed to keep the Israelites together and, with the decline of Egypt after the death of Ramses XI in 1085 B.C., was able to advance southwards into EDOM (2 Sam. 8:14) to gain control of his own iron (haematite) deposits as well as copper deposits, S of the Dead Sea. These deposits were among the largest in the ANE, and the taking and utilization of them was a turning point in the history of Israel, for with natural resources a more advanced technology could be developed (cf. 1 Chr. 22:3). These factors were harnessed for conquest (e.g., 1 Chr. 18:10), for industry (2 Sam. 12:31), and for subsequent prosperity under SOLOMON (1 Ki. 4–10).   D. R. BOWES

Iron (place) i'ron (יִרְאוֹן *yir'ôn*, meaning uncertain). RSV Yiron. A fortified town within the tribal territory of NAPHTALI (Josh. 19:39). It is possibly mentioned by TIGLATH-PILESER III in the list of towns he conquered in GALILEE (cf. Y. Aharoni, *The Land of the Bible: A Historical Geography*, rev. ed. [1979], 372). Iron is identified with modern Yarun, some 22 mi. NE of Acco.

Irpeel ihr'pee-uhl (יִרְפְּאֵל H3761, "God heals"). A town allotted to the tribe of BENJAMIN (Josh. 18:27). It was in the same general area as GIBEON (v. 25) and neighboring towns, but its precise location cannot be ascertained (one possibility is Khirbet Rafat, c. 7 mi. NNW of JERUSALEM).

irrigation. The most explicit reference to irrigation in the Bible is an assertion that the Egyptian practice is irrelevant to the Palestinian hills, where the "rain from heaven" would serve as a perpetual reminder of divine approval or disfavor (Deut. 11:10–17); but the contrast was relative, not absolute. See PALESTINE; RAIN. From Chalcolithic times, irrigation had become widespread in the FERTILE CRESCENT, and the exiles on the river or canal KEBAR were renewing contact with a system of perennial irrigation predating Abraham. Though Egypt's "basin system" of breaching mud walls to inundate adjacent plots was inappropriate in the hills, patches of the JORDAN Valley were explicitly reminiscent of Egypt (Gen. 13:10).

Many a WADI of the rift wall was channeled into flourishing fields along the escarpment base until disaster and malaria-breeding neglect supervened, while larger centers like BETH SHAN and JERICHO with its powerful springs long remained oases of irrigated productivity.

The role of irrigation in the hill country of ancient Israel is less clear. Canaanite settlement was notably concentrated near the spring lines that margined the hills, and it is no accident that over seventy historic sites of Palestine contain the word ʿayin H6524 ("spring," e.g., EN GEDI), and over sixty have bĕʾēr H931 ("well," e.g., BEERSHEBA). See FOUNTAIN. The land was arid, and the uplands that Israel colonized were largely porous limestone, droughty, yet stippled with springs and increasingly with artificial wells. With the adoption of slaked-lime sealing about 1300 B.C., pool and cistern construction increased, largely for domestic and city supply, but also for stock watering and the irrigation of gardens and orchards (2 Chr. 26:10; Eccl. 2:4–6); the practice increased per-acreage production tenfold.

Methods varied: spaced apertures funneled the water of SILOAM to terraced gardens, bucketfuls were splashed across riverbank and agricultural terrace (Num. 24:7), canals flanked some streams such as the KISHON, while *foggaras* (a system of vertical shafts and horizontal tunnels) tapped the underground seepages of SYRIA and TRANSJORDAN. Transient flash floods were trapped in soil, conserving and irrigating dams, such as the intricate engineering complex of Kurnub in the NEGEV, where dams, channels, and cisterns were later multiplied by NABATEANS and Byzantines. Herodian and Roman times witnessed the extension of reservoir and AQUEDUCT, but irrigation was singularly vulnerable to the vicissitudes of misgovernment and war: its subsequent decline and recent revival largely postdate the biblical era. (Cf. N. Glueck, *The River Jordan* [1946]; M. S. Drower in *A History of Technology*, ed. C. Singer et al., 1 [1954], 520–57; A. Reifenberg, *The Struggle Between the Desert and the Sown* [1955]; N. Glueck, *Rivers in the Desert* [1960]; R. O. Whyte in *A History of Land Use in Arid Regions*, ed. L. D. Stamp [1961], 57–118; P. Briant, ed., *Irrigation et drainage dans l'antiquité* [2001].) See also AGRICULTURE; WATER.

G. R. LEWTHWAITE

Ir Shemesh ihr-shem´ish (עִיר שֶׁמֶשׁ H6561, "city of the sun"). A town allotted to the tribe of DAN (Josh. 19.41). The Danites were unable to occupy the towns in this territory (v. 47), and Ir Shemesh apparently became part of JUDAH, where it was better known as BETH SHEMESH. (See Y. Aharoni, *The Land of the Bible: A Historical Geography*, rev. ed. [1979], 216, 311–13.)

Iru i´roo (עִירוּ H6564, possibly "stallion [of donkey]" or "city"). Eldest son of CALEB, listed in the genealogy of the tribe of JUDAH (1 Chr. 4:15). According to some scholars, the words ʿîrû ʾēlâ ("Iru, Elah") should be read ʿîr wĕʾēlâ ("Ir and Elah"; cf. LXX *Ēra Ala*, Vulg. *Hir et Hela*).

Isaac i´zik (יִצְחָק H3663, "he laughs"). Son of ABRAHAM and SARAH, half-brother of ISHMAEL, husband of REBEKAH.

I. Etymology. There is obviously a wordplay on the name Isaac (from ṣāḥaq H7464, "to laugh"). Different persons are said to have laughed: Abraham, when he was assured that in old age he would have a son (Gen. 17:17); Sarah, when after a long wait, she too heard that the promise would yet come to pass (18:12); also all persons who finally heard that the promise actually was fulfilled (21:6). Various shades of meaning are to be associated with these instances of laughter, the least acceptable being Sarah's amusement. These instances are then summed up in the name finally given to the child. This approach may still be maintained—especially if other cases of the use of the verb (like 26:8) are also taken into account—as long as only the obvious fact is kept in mind that the biblical writers hardly engage in scholarly etymological studies, but do allow themselves a sort of popular etymology, or a play on words.

Over against this approach, a new attempt to explain the name of Isaac has gained prominence. This is the one which looks at Ugaritic texts in which the god EL is said to laugh. If with this is coupled the fact that many biblical names are, or originally were, theophoric (i.e., verb-forms having some name of a god as subject), then Isaac could be a short form of the unattested name yiṣḥaqʾēl, "the god laughs" (cf. Ugar. *il yṣḥq*). However, to ignore all the historic instances of laughter in connection with the Isaac story and to have Israel, for all of its literary material, go borrowing from its neighbors, would appear to put the emphasis in the wrong place. In other words, to have "Isaac" mean "let God laugh," puts an emphasis into the story for which there is no textual warrant.

II. Origin of the Isaac tradition. Some thought may be given to the whole problem of how the Isaac tradition came into being and was transmitted to later generations. The so-called sources (J, E, and P), all of which are thought to have contributed their share to the narrative, have been accepted on the strength of insufficient evidence. It could have happened, as some suppose, that there was an old sanctuary at BEERSHEBA where Isaac in his day worshiped and where some basic tales regarding his life were perpetuated. The shrine continued to exist, and around the original tales clustered others that ultimately came to constitute the body of Isaac tradition now embodied in Genesis. The case hangs on slender evidence, but for want of a better approach, one may regard this as a reasonable possibility.

III. Early life. Though not listed in the catalog of the heroes of the faith in Heb. 11, Isaac still deserves to be classed among the great fathers of the OT and has a character distinctive by itself and not devoid of some elements of greatness. He is the child long waited for according to the OT record and may in some sense in this respect be regarded as a type of Christ. When Abraham first appears on the scene, he is already seventy-five years old and has a long futile wait for a son behind him. From Gen. 12 on the wait continues, reinforced by divine words of encouragement, until the patriarch, at the age of one hundred, finally sees the fulfillment of God's promise (21:21).

The other major incident in which Isaac figures during his father's lifetime is the memorable one of the incomplete sacrifice at MORIAH (Gen. 22; the story is often referred to as the Akedah or Aqedah, from the verb ʿāqad H6818, "to tie, bind," used in v. 9). There the son of promise, according to human insight, was all but lost. The providence of God interposed in a striking manner and the son was spared. That Isaac submitted as he did, when the father was making the preparations for the sacrifice, indicates one of the chief characteristics of Isaac: he was meek and submissive in all situations of life. Nor do we imply that his submission was of a merely weak and cowardly nature. He was by disposition quite unassertive. (For the history of interpretation of this passage, see E. Noort and

This painting from the wall of the Beni Hasan tomb, dating approximately to the period of Abraham, recalls the story of the patriarch and his son Isaac in Gen. 22.

E. Tigchelaar, eds., *The Sacrifice of Isaac (Genesis 22) and Its Interpretations* [2002]; E. Kessler, *Bound by the Bible: Jews, Christians and the Sacrifice of Isaac* [2004].)

This fact comes to light also in Isaac's acceptance of the wife that his father procures for him through the agency of the "old servant" of his household, presumably ELIEZER (Gen. 15:2). It apparently was customary in those days to a large extent for parents to arrange marriages for their children. Nor does the servant regard the assignment as a simple business transaction. He fulfills his task in the spirit of prayer. Isaac, no doubt entirely aware of the spirit that animated both his father and the servant, is totally in sympathy with the choice made in his behalf (24:67). It may properly be said that his attitude is one worthy of a good man and an obedient son. Under entirely different circumstances, Isaac's son JACOB acted on his own initiative and made his own matrimonial arrangements.

IV. Relation to those close to him. Though Isaac and Rebekah were a loving couple (Gen. 26:8), it still appears, especially at the point where Isaac arranges to bless his sons, that the wife is the dominating personality. In his contacts with Ishmael, Isaac, being somewhat younger, was at a disadvantage. The elder lad dominated him to an extent, and Hagar and Ishmael had to be cast out. Whatever difficulties there may have been at an earlier date, it is interesting to observe that apparently the differences were resolved and the two men cooperated in the matter of the burial of their father (25:9).

V. Relation to Jacob. Jacob is a unique child as Isaac was. Both were born, not after the flesh, but according to promise. Rebekah was barren for a long while as Sarah had been. The parents made it a matter of prayer and received a direct answer to their prayer, an answer which defined, from the divine point of view, the ultimate relation of the two sons to be born (Gen. 25:23). Over against Jacob, it appears that there was too wide a disparity of temperament for both to get along in the best of relationships. This led to Jacob's being preferred by Rebekah, but Esau was the favorite of Isaac. It almost appears as though Isaac could not quite understand the spiritual aggressiveness of Jacob. It made him uneasy, being himself of a passive disposition and utterly unaggressive. For that matter, father and son failed almost completely to understand one another. After the imparted blessing, Isaac would seem to have perceived the issues involved in sharper focus. All this goes on the assumption that when Jacob connived to obtain the blessing of the firstborn, one of the motivations involved was that he had some wholesome spiritual objectives, based in part at least on the promises of God. It seems somewhat remarkable that the stolid Esau should have been closer to Isaac and preferred by him.

VI. In his father's footsteps. When one of the periodic famines occurred in the land in the days of Isaac, he sought first of all to go to the land of Egypt. When God refused to let him take that journey and leave the land of promise, Isaac went to Gerar to the land later held by the Philistines. It is amazing that he resorted to the same stratagem as did his father when the problem arose as to how he was to safeguard his wife in a land of strangers. He represented Rebekah to be his sister, allowing for a broad usage of the term. Like his father, he then had to suffer the humiliation to be justly rebuked by the king of Gerar, a saint rebuked by a sinner.

In another respect, similarity to his father appears to good advantage on Isaac's part. The Lord appeared to him at least twice (Gen. 26:1–5, 24–25). To Abraham he appeared a number of times. For all his shortcomings, Isaac still carried on the line of Abraham, and the promises made originally to Abraham are specifically referred to Isaac also. The spiritual stature of a man cannot be measured in all its aspects by the number of times he is deemed worthy of a divine visitation. God never once appeared to Joseph. Isaac can be said to have been a man who also walked with God. If his gifts and capacities were less and fewer than those of his father, that is a matter of divine apportionment.

VII. His life in summary. Isaac was indeed blessed most abundantly by the Lord, reaping abundantly, even to the point of a "hundredfold" (Gen. 26:12). He was equally blessed in his cattle and, adding to the wealth of Abraham, he became "very wealthy." His household also increased proportionately, so much so that he became the object of envy in the land. Isaac, for the most part, lived on the fringes of the land, either close to Gerar or down by Beersheba. Abraham, on the contrary, moved freely up and down through the length and breadth of the land, seeking contacts rather than shunning them. Connected with Isaac's retiring nature is the fact that he cannot be described as an innovator. Typical is the incident of 26:18, where after a more or less systematic harassment by the shepherds in the area of Gerar, including the filling in of certain wells, it is reported that Isaac "reopened the wells that had been dug in the time of his father Abraham" (apparently he did dig one new well, v. 25).

VIII. The big mistake. So strongly did Isaac sympathize with his son Esau that finally, when he became ill and took to his bed and decided to give his final blessing to his sons, he singled out Esau for his blessing, and gave him directions accordingly, directions that were overheard by Rebekah. Esau was to be designated to be the major member of the family, carrying the rich tradition and promises for the future. All this was done in spite of the secondary role that had been divinely assigned to Esau ("the older will serve the younger," Gen. 25:23). Even though this important word was spoken to Rebekah, there is every ground for believing that Isaac was apprised of what the divine intention was. With a stubbornness that does him little credit, Isaac sought to circumvent this divine pronouncement. This can in no sense be condoned. It makes Isaac's guilt in the whole episode appear practically as heavy as that of Jacob, who resorted to crafty deceit rather than to silent evasion.

IX. Correction accepted. The plan to send Jacob into Mesopotamia, to be removed from the reach of the anger of Esau, apparently originated with Rebekah, but met with the total approval of Isaac, who seems to have recognized his mistake and was seeking to remedy it. One objective specified in the plan was that the trip to Mesopotamia was to be for the purpose of enabling Jacob to obtain a wife of his own relationship, one with whom the knowledge of the Lord still remained. The parting blessing on this occasion apparently originated with Isaac. He sought to confirm the blessing that had by trickery been diverted to Jacob. This was a tacit admission of his own mistake and a comfort to Jacob, who after all had been divinely designated as the heir of the line of the promise of Abraham.

X. "The Fear of Isaac." One feature that reaches into the theology of Genesis ought yet to be examined briefly, namely, the unusual designation of God that appears to date from the days of Isaac, the divine name FEAR OF ISAAC, which appears twice (Heb. *paḥad yiṣḥāq*, Gen. 31:42, 53). This seems to have been one of the names that catch a different aspect of the divine being than the other patriarchs perceived in their day. The name, rightly construed, seems to accord well with the unique temperament of Isaac, his docile, retiring, unassertive attitude. For "Fear" is to be construed as "the object of fear and reverence" as Isaac knew him. In other words, he was the God before whom Isaac bowed in deep reverence, trembling often as he worshiped him.

It was to have been expected that each patriarch would catch a partial glimpse of the fullness of the divine being, each experience of this being giving rise to its own designation.

XI. Death. Contrary to expectations, Isaac did not die soon after he had blessed his sons. If all the dates be sifted, it would appear that he lived another thirty or forty years and finally died at the age of 180, having lived the longest of the three great patriarchs.

XII. Typology. There remains the necessity of evaluating the typological aspects of the life and career of Isaac: to what extent may Isaac and his life be construed as having some Christological undertones? There is first of all the overall picture of a father giving his son into death. This element came to full realization in the fact that God "did not spare his own son" (Rom. 8:32). That the Son acquiesced to this demand is a second factor that stands out. It is also noteworthy that the Son bore the very wood on which he was to be sacrificed. All this is typological (see TYPOLOGY). One can well understand why in the early church the sacrifice of Isaac was highly regarded as foreshadowing the sacrificial death of our Lord. Isaac is repeatedly ranked together with Abraham and Jacob (Exod. 2:24–25; Matt. 8:11; 22:32, Acts 3:13, et al.). To this may be added one further aspect in which the Isaac image is used in Scripture (Gal. 4:28). "Now you, brothers, like Isaac, are children of promise." (See further J. Swetnam, *Jesus and Isaac* [1981]. For important commentaries, see GENESIS, BOOK OF.)

H. C. LEUPOLD

Isaac and Jacob, Testaments of. Two works that originally may have been written in Greek in the 2nd or 3rd cent. A.D. but that have survived only in Arabic, Coptic, and Ethiopic translations. Derived from the *Apocalypse of Abraham* (see ABRAHAM, TESTAMENT OF), they appear to be Christian compositions that commemorate the days set aside to honor these two patriarchs according to the Coptic church calendar. Some scholars, however, think that they are Christianized versions of earlier Jewish documents. Both works, in which the patriarchs are described as being taken to heaven, emphasize holy conduct, with the *Testament of Isaac* focusing on ASCETICISM. (English trans. in *OTP*, 1·903–18.)

Isaiah, Book of *i*-zay´yuh (יְשַׁעְיָהוּ H3833, "Yahweh is salvation [*or* victorious]"). KJV NT Esaias. The first and largest of the Major Prophets; probably the most widely cherished of the OT prophetical books. The prophet Isaiah is mentioned repeatedly in the book that bears his name and in 2 Ki. 19–20 (also 2 Chr. 26:22; 32:20, 32). The book is dated in the reigns of UZZIAH, JOTHAM, AHAZ, and HEZEKIAH, kings of Judah (Isa. 1:1). Late tradition asserts that the prophet was martyred in the reign of MANASSEH.

    I. Historical background
      A. General
      B. Fall of Samaria
      C. Sennacherib's invasions of Judah
      D. The Syro-Ephraimite war
      E. The situation in Egypt
      F. Babylon
      G. Dates of Hezekiah's reign
    II. The unity of Isaiah
      A. Traditional view
      B. Modern criticism
      C. Prophecies of the exile
      D. Unity of Isa. 1–39
    III. Authorship, date, and place of origin
    IV. Isaiah's canonicity
    V. The text of Isaiah
    VI. Special problems
      A. The book of Immanuel and the virgin birth
      B. The eschatological use of Edom
      C. The servant poems
      D. Other messianic passages
      E. Eschatological passages
    VII. Contents of the book
    VIII. Isaiah's theology

I. Historical background

A. General. These were troublous times in Israel's history. During this period the northern kingdom fell and was taken captive. The southern kingdom (Judah) was heavily attacked. Isaiah lived to see the menace of ASSYRIA wane, and his faith in God's promises to Jerusalem fully vindicated.

The period was the era of Assyria's expansion to the W. In a previous century, a coalition of kings that included AHAB had halted an Assyrian drive in the battle of Qarqar in 854 B.C., but the Assyrians were on the march again. TIGLATH-PILESER III (745–727 B.C.) invaded the W, conquered the Phoenician coast, and informed the world that he had taken the tribute of REZIN of DAMASCUS, MENAHEM of SAMARIA, and many other kings. These campaigns are mentioned in 2 Ki. 15:19–29, where Tiglath-Pileser III is also called Pul—his native name witnessed in Babylonian sources. Apparently, about the year 732 he conquered much of GALILEE and deported the two and a half tribes of that area. He had revived the old Assyrian practice of intermixing the peoples of his empire (2 Ki. 17:6, 24).

B. Fall of Samaria. SHALMANESER V (726–722 B.C.) followed his father, Tiglath-Pileser III, and continued his policies. In 731, PEKAH king of Israel had been murdered as a result of an internal conspiracy; HOSHEA then became king and served as a virtual puppet of Assyria. Shalmaneser came W and received tribute from Hoshea (2 Ki. 17:3), but the latter eventually rebelled. Then began the bitter three-year siege of Samaria that destroyed the northern kingdom forever, in 722/1. The impending doom is recorded in the books of AMOS and HOSEA, who were specifically commissioned as prophets to the northern kingdom, before it fell (Shalmaneser is prob. referred to in Hos. 10:14).

It has been debated whether Shalmaneser V actually conquered Samaria or whether it fell to his general and successor, SARGON II (721–705). The latter claims the conquest but may have exaggerated (see E. R. Thiele, *The Mysterious Numbers of the Hebrew Kings*, 3rd ed. [1983], pp. 163–68). At all events, the northern kingdom was no more, and Judah lay exposed to the Assyrian menace on both the northern and western flanks. Already Tiglath-Pileser III had taken ASHKELON. Sargon deported 27,290 people of Samaria and ravaged the Philistine plain. Later he defeated a rebellious coalition of allies, including Egyptian troops at the border of Egypt in 711. Due to Isaiah's urgent warnings (Isa. 20:1–6), Judah had not joined the coalition and was spared Sargon's wrath. Sargon ruled from 721 to 705. Much of his time was taken up with wars in Asia Minor and the Ararat area and against Babylon.

C. Sennacherib's invasions of Judah. Sargon's son, Sennacherib (705–681), invaded Judah, which had on several occasions before paid tribute to Assyria. Tiglath-Pileser III claimed having received tribute from "Azriau of Yaudi" (possibly Azariah of Judah; cf. *ANET*, 282b and see Uzziah) and "Jehoahaz (Ahaz) of Judah." The Bible mentions tribute paid by Ahaz to Tiglath-Pileser III (2 Ki. 16:8), and it is probable that Sargon also received tribute. Hezekiah gave to Sennacherib 300 talents of silver and thirty talents of gold (18:14). The Philistines had rebelled with Egyptian help; they bound Padi, the Assyrian puppet, at Ekron and sent him to Hezekiah. Sennacherib overcame the Egyptians and the coalition in the battle of Eltekeh about 701. He conquered forty-six cities of Judah, took 200,150 captives, resettled Padi in Ekron, and received Hezekiah's submission. Sennacherib claims that he received 30 talents of gold and 800 talents of silver (an amount that may be a more inclusive reckoning than 2 Ki. 18:14 or, more likely, a mere exaggeration), and much other plunder. Judah was brought low. Significantly, Sennacherib says he besieged Jerusalem and Hezekiah "like a caged bird shut up in Jerusalem his royal city," but does not claim that he conquered the city. The Bible makes clear that Jerusalem was spared.

Sennacherib was murdered and succeeded by his son Esarhaddon (Isa. 37:38), who reigned from 681 to 669. Possibly under his reign Manasseh was detained for a time in Babylon (2 Chr. 33:11). Assyria was the main power in the days of Isaiah, but as the above synopsis suggests, the interplay of world politics brought several other nations on the scene of Judah's history.

D. The Syro-Ephraimite war. When Tiglath-Pileser first struck W, the natural reaction of the border states was to form an alliance and halt his advance, as Ahab had done at Qarqar a hundred years earlier. In such an attempt, Rezin of Damascus and Pekah of Israel evidently tried to enlist the cooperation of Ahaz about 733 B.C. When Ahaz refused, they determined to overthrow him and seat their own puppet, the son of Tabeel, on the throne of Judah (Isa. 7:1–7). They were not fully successful (2 Ki. 16:5) but did much damage (16:6; 2 Chr. 28:5–15), and the W was thus further weakened by its internecine struggles.

Such local wars led Ahaz to seek help from Assyria in opening a second front to the N of Damascus. Assyria gladly responded to his plea and aided Judah in its struggle against Ephraim (i.e., Israel) and Syria (Aram). Ahaz thereby brought in the very foreign power that became the scourge of God to Judah's own near destruction. This Syro-Ephraimite war and Assyrian intrigue is the background of the so-called book of Immanuel (Isa. 7–12), where Isaiah bitterly denounces Ahaz's statecraft. A further consequence of the king's vassalage to Assyria was the implied requirement that Ahaz must adopt Assyria's state religion (J. Bright, *A History of Israel*, 4th ed. [2000], 276–77). Against all the foreign intrigues, Isaiah consistently demanded a policy of nonalignment and full reliance on Yahweh to protect the nation. Isaiah's counsel prevailed, and it is of some note that Judah was the only kingdom in the area that did not fall to the Assyrian might—not even excepting Egypt.

E. The situation in Egypt. Egypt during this period was weak. The native king of the Nile delta to the N was Tefnakhte (c. 726–716). He reigned at a city called Saias (spelled *Sa-a-a* in cuneiform). Apparently Hoshea sent to him for help (2 Ki. 17:4; see So). The Ethiopian kings to the S were on the point of conquering the delta, and Shabaka of the 25th dynasty succeeded in about 709, ruling over a unified Egypt until 695. Egypt at this time gave promise of helping to repulse the Assyrian power, and there was a powerful pro-Egyptian party at Jerusalem, against which Isaiah inveighed (Isa. 18–20, 30–31). Finally, in 690, Shabaka's nephew Taharko (Tirhakah, Isa. 37:9) came to the throne (he was born about 710) and furnished a diversion for the Assyrians in their attacks on Jerusalem.

F. Babylon. Babylon also was a prominent power of the day. The history of Babylon concerned not only the times of Isaiah, but also the predictions he made concerning the Babylonian captivity. Contrary to the usual picture, Babylon was an international

Cities and nations targeted for judgment in Isaiah.

force during Hezekiah's reign. During the reign of Tiglath-Pileser III, CHALDEAN forces had possessed Babylon for a few years, but the Assyrians had retaken it, and Tiglath-Pileser reigned there under the name of Pulu. Marduk-apal-iddina (MERODACH-BALADAN), also a Chaldean, usurped the throne of Babylon in 721 when Sargon was occupied in wars against Samaria, King Midas in Asia Minor (the king of the fabled golden touch), and the peoples of Ararat (Urartu).

Merodach-Baladan held the throne until 721 when Sargon, returning from his victory at ASHDOD, reconquered Babylon for Assyria. Merodach-Baladan professed subjection, but in 703 shortly after Sennacherib ascended the throne, he usurped Babylon again. This was the occasion of his envoys to Hezekiah (Isa. 39:1–8, though some have associated these messengers with events of the rebellion against Sargon in 711). Hezekiah, against the strong rebuke of Isaiah, entered into the alliance of Egypt (30:1–10), Babylon (39:1–4), and the Philistine area. According to 2 Ki. 18:8, Hezekiah conquered PHILISTIA, which agrees well with Sennacherib's statement that Padi king of Ekron, who was loyal to the Assyrians, lay bound in Jerusalem until Sennacherib put down the rebellion. Sennacherib's prism inscription names Ekron, Ashdod, Ashkelon, Egypt (the Ethiopian dynasty), Hezekiah, and others, in the conspiracy. He first disposed of Merodach-Baladan, then soundly defeated the alliance in the battle of Eltekeh, and thoroughly ravaged the country including Judah. Captives numbering 200,150 were taken, as recorded by Sennacherib. The Egyptian and Babylonian help had been in vain.

It has been questioned whether this campaign of 701 was Sennacherib's only invasion of Judah. It is the only one according to available Assyrian records, but information is scanty for the latter years of his reign. The Bible at first sight gives the impression that there was one campaign only, but it does mention both subjection with tribute, which clearly took place in 701 (2 Ki. 18:14), and a successful resistance when Sennacherib's army was miraculously decimated (18:17—19:37). In connection with this latter action it mentions Tirhakah (19:9) of the Ethiopian dynasty of Egypt, who was only nine years old in 701. It seems therefore better to assume that Sennacherib invaded again in about 688 after Tirhakah became king in Egypt (690), and at this time Hezekiah trusted in the Lord more than in alliances and was marvelously delivered. (See the excellent discussion in Bright, *History*, 284–88.)

The city of Babylon was destroyed by Sennacherib in 689, perhaps in connection with the assumed rebellion of Hezekiah in 688. Esarhaddon (681–699) rebuilt Babylon and placed his son Shamash-shamukin as crown prince over it. ASHURBANIPAL (668–626) left his brother Shamash-shamukin in control over Babylon until 647, when he had to subjugate the rebellious city again, and held the reins himself until just before his death. The Chaldeans under NABOPOLASSAR retook the city. Nabopolassar held it, expanded its influence, and finally joined with others in overthrowing NINEVEH, the Assyrian capital, in 612. From 605 to 562, his great son NEBUCHADNEZZAR ruled over all Mesopotamia and the W in a brief but brilliant revival of Babylonian power. He was followed in quick succession by Amel Marduk (EVIL-MERODACH, 562–560; cf. 2 Ki. 25:27), Neriglisar (560–550), Labashi-Marduk (556), and NABONIDUS (556–539). Nabonidus retired to TEMA, an oasis in ARABIA, and left his son BELSHAZZAR as coregent in Babylon. Belshazzar therefore bore the brunt of the Persian feeling and died when CYRUS conquered Babylon in the year 539. Through Cyrus was fulfilled Isaiah's great prophecy, "Leave Babylon, flee from the Babylonians.... The LORD has redeemed his servant Jacob" (Isa. 48:20).

In summary of the above history, Isaiah lived in the era of empire-building as Assyria conquered the whole ANE. He also saw the rising power of Babylon and predicted the Jews' unhappy captivity in that land and their deliverance under Cyrus of PERSIA. In these international movements and intrigues, Isaiah held strongly to his principle that Judah's hope was not in armies or alliances, but in the promised protection of Yahweh. Judah was different from all lands. As a theocracy, it was under the special electing love of God. "Say ye not, A confederacy.... Sanctify the LORD of hosts himself, and let him be your dread" (Isa. 8:12–13 KJV).

G. Dates of Hezekiah's reign. The dates of Isaiah have not been given in the above survey. He prophesied in the reigns of "Uzziah, Jotham, Ahaz, and Hezekiah, kings of Judah" (Isa. 1:1); but what dates do these cover? The problem is complicated by the fact that the reigns of these kings overlapped in ways that are hard to identify with precision. The date of Uzziah's death is given by Thiele (*Mysterious Numbers*, 118–20) as 740/39. Jotham and Ahaz reigned sixteen years each, and Hezekiah ruled six years before Samaria fell in 721. Obviously there were coregencies. This period has been treated successfully by H. G. Stigers (in *ETSB* 9 [1966]: 81–90). The details are not essential to the present subject. However, the reckoning of the date of Hezekiah is of significance to the interpretation of the book of Isaiah.

According to 1 Ki. 18:10, Hezekiah began to reign six years before Samaria fell, therefore in 728/7. On the other hand, the writer says (18:13) that Hezekiah began to reign fourteen years before Sennacherib's invasion, therefore in 715. This is by no means a contradiction. It merely indicates a coregency with his father Ahaz. The consequences, however, are important for the background of Isaiah. If Hezekiah reigned twenty-nine years after 715, he died in 686 instead of 699, which would be

This famous terra-cotta prism from Nineveh describes the campaigns of Sennacherib in Israel (701 B.C.). The same events are described in Isa. 36–37.

the case if the twenty-nine years are counted from 728. The later date for Hezekiah's death allows a later date for Isaiah's ministry. He may well have lived into Esarhaddon's reign and witnessed the beginning of the revival of Babylonian greatness. The last chapters of Isaiah may have a background either in the Babylonian struggles for power of the late 8th cent. or in the Babylonian renascence under Esarhaddon. This would give Isaiah a ministry of some sixty years, which is long but by no means impossible. Actually it is practically necessitated by the reference to Hezekiah's sickness (Isa. 38:1–5). His sickness was "in those days," apparently in the days of Sennacherib's early campaigns. He received ambassadors from Merodach-Baladan who, among other things, congratulated him on his recovery. This would be about 701, and it was predicted that he would live fifteen more years—to 686 as suggested above.

II. The unity of Isaiah

A. Traditional view. The unity of the book of Isaiah was not questioned until the rise of higher biblical criticism in the 18th cent. The book is ascribed to Isaiah in the title, and his name is mentioned in various other chapters (Isa. 2:1; 7:3; 13:1; 20:2–3; 37:2; et al.). The NT quotes from all sections of the book and repeatedly refers to it as the work of Isaiah.

There is no MS or traditional evidence to show that the book is not a unity. If more than one author was involved in the composition, this fact is totally lost to history, and tradition on the matter begins at about 180 B.C. (Sir. 48:22–25). The DEAD SEA SCROLLS include various copies of the book as well as documents that have numerous references ascribing it to Isaiah, as does the NT. The best preserved document of the Qumran treasures is the great Isaiah scroll (QIsa^a), which dates from around 125 B.C. and gives no hint of a division at Isa. 40, the primary spot at which critics allege a break.

B. Modern criticism. Nonetheless, the rationalistic criticism of Germany beginning with J. C. Döderlein (*Esaias* [1775]) has proclaimed with great assurance that Isaiah did not write the second major section of the book (Isa. 40–66). This section is often referred to as Deutero-Isaiah. The impression is abroad that everyone agrees that Isaiah wrote only the first thirty-nine chapters, and an unnamed author (but a man of genius) wrote the last twenty-seven chapters during the Babylonian EXILE.

This popular impression is hardly accurate. The unity of Isa. 40–66 has also been questioned, and many, beginning with B. Duhm, ascribe chs. 56–66 to still another hand—a Trito Isaiah about 400 B.C. Also the first Isaiah must be dissolved. Few scholars who deny that Isaiah wrote the last part believe that he wrote all the first thirty-nine chapters. Chapters 13–14 at least, and probably chs. 24–27 and 34–35, are also said to be the work of a later hand. Indeed, once the unity of the book is questioned, there seems to be no end of the possible fragmentation. The course of these fragmentizing tendencies can be followed in O. T. Allis (*The Unity of Isaiah* [1950], 43–50) and E. J. Young (*Who Wrote Isaiah?* [1958]), as well as in the various OT introductions of the critical school (e.g., O. Eissfeldt, R. H. Pfeiffer) and of conservative persuasion (e.g., E. J. Young, G. L. Archer).

The reasons for this pervasive literary criticism are alleged to be various. The two halves of the book are said to manifest quite distinct styles. This argument is hard for the ordinary reader to evaluate, not knowing Hebrew. It is still harder to establish, in view of the fact that those who fragment Isaiah excessively must deny that there are just two distinct

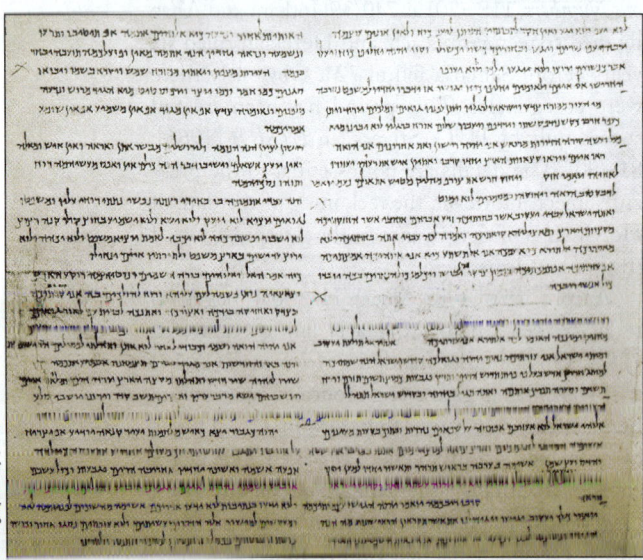

Facsimile of the Great Isaiah Scroll (1QIsa^a) discovered in Qumran (2nd cent. B.C.).

styles visible in the book. There is some talk that the writer (or school of writers) of Trito-Isaiah was immersed in the work of Deutero-Isaiah and copied him, but such a viewpoint is not so convincing when it is remembered that also Isa. 1–39 is allegedly composite. A later school emphasizing oral tradition would have it that all of Isaiah was preserved by word of mouth and all of it written down after the restoration—approximately 450 B.C. Was it all written by one school? If so, is it believable that there were two or three styles? Was it written by three circles of Isaianic disciples? Why were the pieces so cleverly interwoven into one composition without a trace in the MS or tradition?

Actually the Hebrew of the various parts of Isaiah is eloquent, beautiful, and forceful, and no more diverse than that of any other great author, such as Shakespeare. Parts of the book may have been written at a later stage of the author's life. Part may have been sermonic and orally delivered at first. Part of the book (Isa. 36–39) is obviously historical and quite parallel to 2 Ki. 18–20. Part may have been produced originally by Isaiah as a written composition. As many have pointed out in the past, there are significant signs of unity in style in the book (cf. G. L. Robinson in *ISBE* [1929], 3:1495–1508). And since the 1980s there has been growing appreciation for these features even among critical scholars who do not attribute the whole book to the 8th-cent. B.C. prophet (e.g., see the commentary by J. Blenkinsopp listed at the end of this article).

C. Prophecies of the exile. The most significant objection to the unity of Isaiah is found in the charge that the background of the author of Isa. 40–66 is different from that of Isaiah himself. The claim is made that these chapters reflect the times of the Babylonian captivity and therefore could not have been written in about 700 by Isaiah. Conservatives have answered this charge by pointing out that those chapters include passages that are prophetic. Cyrus, the Persian monarch who conquered Babylon in 539, is mentioned by name (44:28; 45:1). His name is mentioned as the climax of a great prediction of future things. Naturalists, who do not believe in predictive prophecy, must of course postdate such a section, but this is to beg the question. The claim of Isaiah and Christian expositors through the ages has been that such prophecies are true predictions.

O. T. Allis follows out this approach in some detail. He shows that the critical view of the unity of Isaiah rests largely on the preconceived rationalistic assumption. In a chapter entitled "Prophecy according to the Critics" (*The Unity of Isaiah*, 1–21), he quotes numerous sources to show that the basic reason for the critics' dating of OT prophetical material after the event concerned is that the critical school cannot believe that the OT prophet spoke directly the words of a God who knows whatsoever comes to pass.

Critical students sometimes object to this analysis. They argue that Isa. 40–55 does not even claim to predict the Babylonian captivity. True, it predicts the conquest of Babylon under Cyrus and a return from the exile. But, it is said, these chapters are written as if the exile had already begun; therefore, the exile is assumed, not predicted. The prophet is writing in the middle of the exile and predicts, perhaps by keen insight and devout hope, the return from Babylonian captivity. Therefore it is claimed that at least these chapters must be due to an anonymous prophet writing during the exile.

The critical view must therefore be examined a bit further. What is the background of Isa. 40–66? Anyone can read these chapters for himself to seek an answer to this question. This section of Isaiah is obviously a message to Zion, to Jerusalem (40:2; 41:27). God promised to bring back the captivity of Israel from the E, W, N, and S (43:5–6; cf. 11:11, doubtless written early), which does not seem to refer to the Babylonian exile specifically or exclusively. It is true that the downfall of Babylon is predicted (43:14; 47:1; 48:14), and the return of the Jews and the rebuilding of Jerusalem is predicted (44:26–28; 45:13; 48:20; 51:11). A return from the N, the W, and from Egypt is predicted (49:12, where "Sinim" in the DSS is spelled to indicate that it refers to SYENE or Aswan, then under the control of the Ethiopian king of Egypt).

But it is too much to say that the prophet speaks from the location of a Babylonian exile. James Smart summarizes, "The simple fact, which should be frankly acknowledged, is that the author of chs. 40 to 55 nowhere makes clear to us his geographical location" (J. D. Smart, *History and Theology in Second Isaiah* [1955], 22). It is, of course, true that the captivity in Babylon is predicted by Isaiah. Critics by their unwarranted division lose the force of Isa. 39:6–8, which is a specific prediction and clearly was written in connection with the well-known usurper king of Babylon, Merodach-Baladan, therefore no later than 701. There are also references to captivity (45:13; 47:6; 49:21; 51:3, 11, 19). The last four of these could as well refer to the awful desolations and captivities in the days of Sennacherib. In any case, they are not written from the standpoint of the Babylonian exile. Contrast them with Ps. 137, which is truly an exilic composition.

The view of J. Barton Payne (in *ETSB* 6 [1963]: 50–57) should be mentioned, which holds that Isa. 40–55 have their background in the 8th cent. B.C. and the conqueror from the E (41:2) is Sennacherib. This view may not be acceptable in some details, but it underscores the remark by Smart that the background of these chapters is not clearly marked. Either in geography or chronology, it cannot be said that Isa. 40–55 was written by a prophet of the exile, unless the critical assumption be made that truly predictive prophecy referring accurately to distant events is impossible. This idea conservatives refuse to allow.

As to the background of the larger section (Isa. 40–66), it is widely admitted that chs. 55–66 were written in Palestine. The mountain (57:7) does not look like Babylon. The walls of Jerusalem are established (62:6). The Lord appears from Edom (63:1, though this is doubtless eschatological). On the contrary, a complaint (64:10–11) describes the times after Nebuchadnezzar. This section is ascribed by many to Trito-Isaiah writing in Palestine about 400 B.C. This date seems impossible in view of the temple's restoration in 516. Smart (*History and Theology*, 47) objects to the division at ch. 55, for he claims it posits "two great prophets who were almost identical." Perhaps the simplest answer to the complex problems is to follow L. Koehler and J. Begrich and others, who are pictured by Smart as "treating the text of second Isaiah as a compendium of seventy independent oracles and applying to them the methods of form criticism in order to discover the original character and context of each" (ibid., 18).

Such is the logical outcome of the critical attack. What a genius the final editor must have been to assemble seventy different snippets of writing with varied background and messages, and weld them into a book of the beauty and power and lasting influence of Isa. 40–66! This dynamic genius lived sometime within those dark two centuries from 400 to 200, when Israel was impoverished and her history a blank. His name and fame, however, left no imprint upon his contemporaries or successors. It is perhaps easier to believe in predictive prophecy.

It should be noted that the author of Isa. 40–48 at least does not present his ideas as contemporary material, which anyone of keen political insight could deduce. His is not a late anonymous writing picked up and attached to the earlier book by accident. Nor is his work a pious fraud merely claiming the authority of the great old prophet Isaiah. He claims to predict the future because he gives the word of a God who differs from the idols of the heathen (Isa. 41:22; 42:9; 44:7–8; 45:4; 46:10; 48:3–6; and other less clear passages). Cyrus himself is pictured as coming in answer to a prediction, and the poem predicting his work is a climax and crescendo of prophecy (cf. Robinson in *ISBE* [1929], 3:1507a; Allis, *Unity of Isaiah*, 62–78). The alternatives left by such studies are that these chapters in Isaiah are truly predictive of a future captivity and return, or they were written after the event by a deliberate trickster and impersonator. That the wonderful words of this section in Isaiah are the words of a cheat and liar is too much to allow.

D. Unity of Isa. 1–39. Bearing upon these matters is the question of the unity of Isa. 1–39, or at least chs. 1–35. Chapters 13–14 are usually denied to first Isaiah, but the text ascribes this material to him. These chapters refer to Babylon's fall by the hand of the Medes, not exactly like the Persian conquest pictured in chs. 44–45. They are part of a larger whole of prophecies against surrounding nations and some of these other passages concern the time of Isaiah (14:25). The truth is best served by making these chapters fit an early date and regarding the mention of Babylon as a true prediction.

After the oracles against the nations comes a section (Isa. 24–27) widely denied to Isaiah. The reason is not history, but theology. The resurrection of the dead is mentioned (25:8; 26:19). The general attitude toward the doctrine is exhibited by James Smart, who on this basis argues against finding the doctrine of RESURRECTION in Isa. 53:10: "Those who see an individual in the servant have on their hands in this verse the resurrection of an individual from the dead, a somewhat embarrassing phenomenon if the chapter is to be retained as written by the prophet in the sixth century B.C." (*History and Theology*, 212). The error is that critics think they are able to reconstruct with assurance the history of Israel's religious thought, in spite of the documents, in accordance with their own theories. The psalms of David, the book of Job, Isa. 53, Dan. 12:2, and the section Isa. 24–27 must all be dated late because critics have concluded that the doctrine of the resurrection was derived from the Persians rather than revealed by God.

By the same token, Isa. 34 and 35 are denied to Isaiah because of their APOCALYPTIC cast. The word *apocalyptic* used of this section and chs. 24–27 needs elucidation. It is held that the prophetic interpretation of history was that repentance will bring God's favor. But after the exile this theory was seen to be deficient, and an apocalyptic view prevailed in which the pious must wait in resignation for God to bring universal vengeance and judgment (cf. S. B. Frost in *The Bible in Modern Scholarship*, ed. J. P. Hyatt [1965], 104–13). This theology of apocalyptic is denied to earlier times on subjective grounds, although the wording of Isa. 35:8–10 is much like that of the earlier section (11:15–16). It seems that a confusion has arisen between an apocalyptic theology and apocalyptic as a literary style. As the literary style, the apocalyptic typically includes bizarre images symbolizing world history and eschatological events. Examples of such literature are the books of Daniel, Enoch, and Revelation. No one really knows when such literature began. There is no positive evidence against an early date for Daniel, and certainly Isa. 24–27 and 34–35 do not exhibit such symbolic animals; the only exception is 27:1, where LEVIATHAN is described. Unfortunately for higher criticism, Isaiah's description of this evil power is given in terms almost identical with a passage found in the Ugaritic literature of 1400 B.C.

It is obvious that Isa. 36–39 are practically identical with 2 Ki. 18:19—20:19. The main difference is that Isaiah includes Hezekiah's psalm concerning his sickness (38:9–20, note the title). The question is, do these chapters break the unity of Isaiah or of Kings? The answer is, neither one. The chapters certainly belong in the historical record of the kings of Judah. They are said to be abstracted from the chronicles of these kings (2 Ki. 20:20), as are the histories of the previous and following kings. The material is abstracted in 2 Chronicles, which says, "The other events of Hezekiah's reign and his acts of devotion are written in the vision of the prophet Isaiah son of Amoz in the book of the kings of Judah and Israel" (2 Chr. 32:32). It cannot be pressed that this refers to the books of Isaiah and of 2 Kings. In other cases, a writing of a prophet is cited in Chronicles which appears to be a section of the current books of Samuel-Kings (1 Chr. 29:29; 2 Chr. 9:29; 20:34; et al.). Therefore 2 Chr. 32:32 could mean no more than that this portion of 2 Kings was written by Isaiah, something reasonable enough in view of the other writings of prophets cited as sources by Chronicles—which, of course, uses Samuel-Kings as its main source. However, the reference (2 Chr. 32:32) to both the vision of Isaiah and the book of the kings of Israel and Judah looks much like a declaration that both Isaiah and 2 Kings had these parallel portions in the days of the Chronicles, now widely admitted to be about 400 B.C. There is no problem here, for the chapters fit admirably into the book of Isaiah. The prophecy of Babylonian captivity (Isa. 39:6–7) forms almost a necessary background for the treatment of the Babylonian captivity (chs. 40–48). Quite clearly felt that these chapters helped to explain the material in the book of Isaiah. There is no solid reason why Isaiah himself could not have put them here.

III. Authorship, date, and place of origin. As has been argued above, the author of the whole book is Isaiah the son of Amoz (to be distinguished from the prophet Amos), writing from about 739 to 681 B.C. or slightly longer. Of this man nothing more is known. The prophetic office was not hereditary, and no genealogy is given of any of the prophets except those who also served in other connections (e.g., David). Isaiah was a highly educated man, as shown by the breadth of his vocabulary and the quality of his literature. He was also a prophet of the greatest faith and power. F. Delitzsch (*Biblical Commentary on the Prophecies of Isaiah* [1866]) calls him "the universal prophet of Israel." Robinson (*ISBE* [1929], 3:1496a) calls his style "the climax of Hebrew literary art." It is hard to overemphasize the influence of his book or the strength of attraction it has had over the centuries. Isaiah, Deuteronomy, and Psalms were the three books most used in the Qumran community. The NT alludes to it over 250 times and quotes it expressly at least 50 times.

Isaiah was a confidante of Hezekiah and moved easily in the royal circles of Jerusalem. Many of the religious reforms of Hezekiah can probably be traced to the influence of this godly court preacher. More uncertain is the question of his priestly office. His inaugural vision is set in the temple of the Lord, into which only priests could go. It was a vision, and the temple that he saw could have been the heavenly prototype. Nowhere is Isaiah specifically called a priest. The idea that he continued into the reign of Manasseh is indicated by Isa. 37:37–38 unless, as is unlikely, this passage is considered a later addition. Further tradition has it that, being persecuted by Manasseh, Isaiah took refuge in a hollow tree; the tree closed around him, but Manasseh had the tree, prophet and all, sawed in two. This legend is from the Ascension of Isaiah, a post-Christian work now lost. It is possible, but no means certain, that Heb. 11:37 refers to this incident. Other Hebrew tradition found in the Talmud (*b. Yebamot* 49b) relates that he suffered under Manasseh, which is probable.

Isaiah's influence was restricted to the southern kingdom (Judah). Samaria is mentioned only as an enemy power in one section (Isa. 7–12). Bethel and Gilgal, prominent sanctuaries of the N against which Hosea and Amos spoke, are not mentioned in Isaiah. It cannot be proved that the chapters are all chronological, but at least Sargon, the Assyrian king who immediately followed the fall of Samaria, is introduced in ch. 20. The fall of Samaria is hardly referred to (10:9–11). The location and outlook of the prophet is exclusively that of the kingdom of Judah. Zion is the center of his interest all through the book, and the policies of the court are his constant concern. They were turbulent days in Judah. Isaiah was God's man for the time of crisis.

IV. Isaiah's canonicity. Isaiah's place in the canon is sure. As the longest and in many ways the richest of the prophets, it was early accorded high esteem. The evidence of contemporary religious documents is lacking, but later documents honor Isaiah in terms still used today. Ecclesiasticus (c. 180 B.C.) speaks of "the prophet Isaiah, who was great and trustworthy in his visions. In Isaiah's days the sun went backward, and he prolonged the life of the king. By his dauntless spirit he saw the future, and comforted the mourners in Zion. He revealed what was to occur to the end of time, and the hidden things before they happened" (Sir. 48:22–25). These statements allude to all parts of the book and show the highest regard for it as the work of a prophet by the Spirit of God. There is no earlier postbiblical witness.

The DSS include the complete scroll of Isaiah dating from around 150 B.C. plus over twenty other copies more or less fragmentary. Beyond this there are several quotations from the book of Isaiah in the Dead Sea literature. The *Manual of Discipline*, coming from perhaps the late 2nd cent. B.C., quotes Isa. 40:3 as "Scripture" and interprets this verse as referring to "the study of the Law which God commanded through Moses … and with what the prophets also have revealed through God's Holy Spirit" (T. D. Gaster, *The Dead Sea Scriptures*, rev. ed. [1964], 64–65).

The *Zadokite Document* (see Zadokite Fragments) is also found in Qumran in fragmentary form, but there are later copies of it available from the Cairo Genizah. It also quotes Isaiah with the words, "as God has said through the prophet Isaiah the son of Amoz" (Gaster, 75). Again there is a reference to "what is described by the prophet Isaiah the son of Amoz" (ibid., 80). The book of Isaiah also is clearly utilized by the author of the *Thanksgiving Hymns* (ibid., 149, 180). It is clear that Isaiah was regarded as Scripture, as the Word of God and fully authoritative. The words of the prophets are regularly quoted in Qumran on a par with the law of Moses. And one who should "transgress a single word of the Law of Moses" was to be excommunicated (ibid., 65).

As noted above, the Qumran scribes called their sacred books the "law and the prophets." Qumran (and the similar NT) usage shows that this sacred canon included the Pentateuch, historical books like Joshua, prophetical books like Isaiah, Jeremiah, Ezekiel, Nahum, Habakkuk, Daniel, et al., and books of poetry and instruction, such as Psalms, Proverbs, and Job. All of these books and others are mentioned in such a way as to show that they were held sacred. In short, the canon of the OT held by the Qumran scribes was probably just like the present canon, although the evidence for every book is not considered. Isaiah evidently was especially beloved.

Some earlier information can be gained from comparing Jer. 48 with Isa. 15–16. Many verses are parallel so that it would seem likely that one writing borrowed from the other (cf., e.g., Isa. 15:5 with Jer. 48:34; Isa. 16:6 with Jer. 48:29). It is not at once apparent who borrowed from whom. Yet Jeremiah predicts the end of MOAB (Jer. 48:42, 46), whereas Isaiah speaks more generally (Isa. 16:14). Jeremiah in this section quotes from the book of Numbers (Jer. 48:45, citing Num. 21:28; 24:17). Jeremiah elsewhere quotes Mic. 3:12 (Jer. 26:18); Hos. 10:12; 3:5 (Jer. 4:3; 30:9); Deut. 24:1–4 (Jer. 3:1 and elsewhere); and Ps. 106:1 (Jer. 33:11). In view of Jeremiah's practice elsewhere, it is likely that Jer. 48 quoted from Isa. 15–16, and not vice versa. In short, such scanty evidence before 180 B.C. is from tradition and a few quotations, but there is no positive evidence against Isaiah's ancient position in the canon.

V. The text of Isaiah. The remarkable discovery of a MS of Isaiah (1QIsa^a) among the DSS in 1947 gave Bible students for the first time a pre-Christian copy of an OT book. It was most gratifying to find that the text of the scroll supported the basic authenticity of the MT, which in turn is reproduced in the current Hebrew Bibles. The agreement is not as extensive as is found among MSS of the MT, but is more like that among NT MSS. It appears that the scribes were careful, but did not work with the painstaking exactitude of the medieval scribes. For instance, in the famous passage Isa. 9:5–7, the only differences between the Qumran scroll and the MT are that "peace" has the Hebrew article attached and the words "to establish it, and to uphold it" have "it" in the masculine instead of the feminine. The differences are minimal. In ch. 53, there are several minor differences of spelling and endings that do not change the sense; the conjunction *waw*, "and," is added or subtracted about ten times (prob. a matter of style), while equivalent synonymous words are used in two places. The only meaningful difference is in v. 11, where the reading is "he shall see *light*," an addition also found in the SEPTUAGINT and accepted by some scholars. (See further O. Pulikottil, *Transmission of Biblical Texts in Qumran: The Case of the Large Isaiah Scroll 1QIsa^a* [2001]).

The conclusion is that the MT can now be traced back in this scroll to the 2nd cent. B.C. (and in other documents almost a century earlier). It is significant that the newly discovered document, though very ancient and valuable, is obviously a poorer witness to the original than the later more careful copies that are available. Therefore this early MS actually serves to authenticate the extant text. Another slightly later copy of Isaiah (1QIsa^b), which is rather fragmentary, is in even closer agreement with the later MT text.

The SEPTUAGINT text of Isaiah has been long known to reflect a Hebrew text very similar to the MT, though there are problems in detail. The famous commission to Isaiah (Isa. 6:9–10) is given in the imperative in the MT, but in the past tense in the LXX (quoted in Matt. 13:14–15 and Acts 28:26–27). Actually the difference is one of vocalization (vowel markings were not used until the early Middle Ages); the consonants are the same for both readings. In general it may be concluded that the text of the book has been well supported by recent study and discoveries. As previously noted, none of the new finds suggests a division of the book in accordance with the critical hypotheses. See TEXT AND MANUSCRIPTS (OT).

VI. Special problems

A. The book of Immanuel and the virgin birth. The section comprised by Isa. 7–12 often is called the book of IMMANUEL because of the great messianic prophecy in 7:14. It is probable, though not certain, that all of these chapters come from that early period in Isaiah's ministry when he opposed Ahaz's policies. It will be remembered that Tiglath Pileser was expanding westward about 733. Syria and Israel (northern kingdom) were building defensive alliances and wished Ahaz to join. Ahaz refused, and the coalition threatened to attack Jerusalem to replace Ahaz with a king who would be more cooperative. Isaiah counseled Ahaz not to fear but to rely upon the Lord. Ahaz, no orthodox believer, bypassed Isaiah and appealed to Tiglath-Pileser to help him by establishing a second front beyond Damascus. What happened then is not known in detail. It seems that the Assyrians did help Ahaz, but not in time, for he was defeated by Syria and Israel. The Assyrians also came, though perhaps too late, and carried captive much of Damascus and Galilee.

In such critical days, Isaiah with his son SHEAR-JASHUB accosted Ahaz, probably while he was inspecting the city's defenses and water resources. He first urged Ahaz not to fear the northern coalition. He declared that within sixty-five years Ephraim would be destroyed (Isa. 7:8). It is clear that this prophecy was fulfilled in due time. In about ten years Samaria became a province of the Assyrian empire. Ashurbanipal (668–633) interchanged the populations of Ephraim and Mesopotamia, in effect destroying Ephraim as a people (Ezra 4:10; 2 Ki. 17:24). It is a puzzle, however, why Isaiah speaks of this event as he does. Actually he repeats this prophecy (Isa. 8:1–4), for he predicts that before his second son MAHER-SHALAL-HASH-BAZ will be old enough to talk, Ahaz's two enemies will fall before the Assyrians, which would mean two or three years. The problem is solved summarily for some by cutting out the last half of Isa. 7:8. There is no evidence for this, however, in ancient texts or versions. Commentators have few suggestions of merit. If the writer be permitted any theory, it would be that it refers to the age of one of the kings concerned. It could then be understood to mean that before Rezin's sixty-fifth year these things would happen; but scholars know so little of the details that this must remain as theory.

At all events, the prophet bade Ahaz seek a sign that the promise would come to pass (Isa. 7:12). Ahaz answered with what seems clearly a quotation (Deut. 6:16), the same verse cited by Christ in answer to Satan (Matt. 4:7). Ahaz was not sincere. Isaiah probably knew his hypocrisy and that he had already relied on payment of tribute and an alliance with Assyria for help. Isaiah therefore turns on Ahaz with a sharp rebuke.

The famous Immanuel passage (Isa. 7:10–17) is usually thought of as a promised blessing for Ahaz, or at least for the house of David. This view comes from stopping the paragraph at the end of v. 16 (cf. KJV). Rather, the section should be continued through v. 17 (cf. NIV and other modern versions). The prophet in rebuke tells Ahaz that his real enemy is Assyria (v. 17). The petty kings of Israel and Syria are of little account. The real tragedy will be the invasion of Assyria whom Ahaz has hired.

Seen in this light, the VIRGIN BIRTH prophecy was not necessarily a current event full of blessed meaning for Ahaz. For him it was a threat. Before this occurs, the land will be desolated by Assyria. Isaiah did not set a date, for he did not know the date. Elsewhere he speaks of the coming wonderful king of David's line without giving the time. The coming of "the stump of Jesse" is prophesied (Isa. 11:1) in close succession to the downfall of the Assyrians (10:24–34). Isaiah was only to know that at an unspecified time the MESSIAH would come, and he warns Ahaz to mend his ways, because before the coming of the Messiah the Assyrians would invade and bring tragedy greater than the division of Ephraim from Judah. Actually there is no information that this invasion came before the days of Sennacherib in 701, thirty years after the prophecy was given. It could not in any case refer to a child of Ahaz or of Isaiah.

Isaiah refers to the birth of a child. In Isa. 9:6–7 he makes it plain that the longed-for king of David's line will come as a child, indeed a divine child. The names given then are not just names applicable to any human being. Note that the name "Mighty God" is applied to the Lord God (10:20–21). Isaiah was expecting a divine child of David's line. This child had nothing to do with Isaiah's second son Maher-Shalal-Hash-Baz (8:1–4), who was not of David's line. He was born in the normal course to Isaiah and his wife. He was given a rather ordinary symbolic name (meaning "hasten to the booty, hasten to the spoil"), as was Isaiah's first son Shear-Jashub ("a remnant shall return").

ISAIAH, BOOK OF

Olive tree with a new shoot extending from the base. Isaiah prophesied, "A shoot will come up from the stump of Jesse" (Isa. 11:1).

The prophesied child is named Immanuel (Isa. 7:14), which is apparently the name of God (8:8; the name is translated in 8:10). The child is to be born of a virgin (Heb. ʿalmâ H6625). Much controversy has revolved about this word. A Hebrew concordance will show that it occurs six other times (Gen. 24:43; Exod. 2:8; Ps. 68:25; Prov. 30:19; Cant. 1:3; 6:8). Never is it applied to a married woman. The word is used for REBEKAH about to be married (Gen. 24:43), and for MIRIAM, who was evidently just a young girl (Exod. 2:8). The cognate term ʿelem H6624, meaning "boy," is used of DAVID at the time when he slew GOLIATH and before (1 Sam. 17:56; cf. 20:22). That word also is not used in reference to a married person. The root ʿlm may be related to the verb "conceal" (ʿālam H6623), but this is not sure. It would be an attractive thought that the word refers to a girl still kept at home in her father's house. The emphasis is not so much on virginity (there is another specific word for that) as on being young and unmarried, which, of course, implies virginity. The translation "young woman" is not specific enough; "unmarried girl" is nearer to the meaning. The older use of English *maid* or German *magd* (used by Luther) captures the idea very well. The only further light on this word is from Ugaritic, where the cognate word *ǵalmat* is used in poetic parallel with a cognate of the word used of a virgin in the OT (*bětûlâ* H1435). It is also given as the name of a goddess.

The reference to butter and honey (Isa. 7:15) has been variously interpreted. Some think of it as heavenly food. Others regard it as food of luxury—which it is (7:22). The simplest idea is that in v. 15 it refers to a baby's first food after weaning. The passage thus declares that before the Messiah Immanuel is born of a virgin and is weaned, the Assyrians will come and depopulate the land.

That this passage predicts a virgin birth is further indicated by the ancient translations. The LXX version, which was made about two centuries before Christ, translates the word ʿalmâ by Greek *parthenos* G4221, the usual Greek word for "virgin" (though it too can mean "young [or unmarried] woman"). It is significant that in places where an OT quotation is found in Matthew alone, Matthew does not follow the LXX. Thus in Matt. 1:23 also, the quotation, though it is short and there is a problem in details, does not agree with the LXX in the best texts. It may be concluded that Matthew gives independent evidence for the rendering "virgin" (Isa. 7:14). The Syriac Peshitta of Isa. 7:14 uses the specific word *bětulâ*, "virgin." The force of the Peshitta, however, is diminished by the fact that there is no definite information on whether it was translated by Christians or Jews.

The usual critical view is that Isa. 7:14 refers to a contemporary birth of a child by the wife of Ahaz or Hezekiah. This view denies both the miraculous and the prophetic element. Some who hold a high view of Scripture speak of an immediate as well as a distant fulfillment. If the verse speaks of a truly virgin birth, there is no point in failing to apply it to Jesus. In any case, the prophecy was not fulfilled until after Sennacherib's campaign of 701, thirty years after Isaiah spoke. If it be remembered that Isaiah shared the ancient hope of the coming of a divine child, then this prediction finds its full raison d'être as a timeless threat to the rebellious Ahaz.

B. The eschatological use of Edom. Many will not have sensed a problem in Isaiah's mention of the overthrow of Edom in the last days, but the subject does raise some important questions. The prophecy of Isa. 34:4 presents a picture used by Christ to refer to his coming in judgment (Matt. 24:29; cf. Rev. 6:13–14). This seems therefore to be a prediction of Christ's return in judgment. The

Wadi and rocky escarpment in Edom, a country to which Isaiah refers symbolically as the eschatological enemy of God's people (Isa. 34).

next verses (Isa. 34:5–6) refer to a great slaughter in Edom. Of this the NT is silent. A suggested solution can be found by examining the mention of Moab in Isa. 25:7–10. There the promise is given that death will be conquered (v. 8, quoted in 1 Cor. 15:54). In Isaiah it is said that Moab shall be vanquished (Isa. 25:10). Moab is not mentioned in this way in the NT. Rather the NT pictures Babylon as the evil power of the end—indeed, not literal Babylon, but Babylon symbolizing Rome, the city that sits on seven hills (Rev. 17:5, 9). It may be held that these verses are eschatological, as is indicated by their context and the NT quotations, and that the various enemy nations were mentioned as symbolic of the last evil persecuting power. The fact that several different nations are so mentioned supports this idea.

C. The servant poems. Extensive literature has grown up around the problem of interpreting the servant passages (Isa. 41:8 through 53:12). The main sections are 42:1–9; 49:1–6; 50:4–10; and 52:13—53:12. Isaiah also contains brief references to a servant (41:8–9; 42:19; 43:10; 44:1–2, 21, 26; 45:4; 48:20). This usage is distinctive in the book of Isaiah.

The SERVANT OF THE LORD presents a problem, for several times he is clearly stated to be Israel or Jacob, that is, the Hebrew nation. At other times he seems to be an individual and is clearly referred to in the NT as Christ. This situation has given rise to various viewpoints. The interpretation of naturalistic criticism is that the writer was speaking of Israel, and the NT references by error or accommodation transfer the words to Christ. A more conservative view is that of F. Delitzsch, who argues that the prophet speaks of the nation whose spiritual activity culminates in Christ. The nation is pictured as a pyramid, with the Messiah as the top stone representing all the others. Another opinion is that the prophet refers first to the nation, then as the nation fails in its witness for God, he turns to speak of the Messiah who will not fail. There is a cultic view to be added—that the prophet speaks of the king as representing the nation in the cultic drama in which on the feast days the fortunes of the nation are portrayed and God's favor secured.

The present writer's view is that there has been too strenuous an effort to force the various passages into one mold. Other prophets speak of various individuals as God's servants. David is called the Lord's servant; Nebuchadnezzar, likewise (Jer. 27:6). Jeremiah also calls Jacob (the nation) God's servant (Jer. 46:27–28). Zerubbabel is called God's servant (Hag. 2:23). Zechariah called the Branch of David "my servant" (Zech. 3:8), and Ezekiel calls Jacob (the nation) and David God's servant (Ezek. 37:25). Why, then, should there not be some variety of usage in Isaiah?

This variety of usage is rather clearly shown in the second song (Isa. 49:3–6). The servant is clearly called Israel, the nation (v. 3). A complaint is made by Israel, "I said, I have labored to no purposes" (v. 4). The servant continues, however, "The LORD … formed me in the womb to be his servant / to bring Jacob back to him" (v. 5); and continues that the servant will raise up the tribes of Jacob and restore the preserved of Israel and be a light to the nations and God's salvation to the ends of the earth (v. 6). Evidently Israel fails as a servant, and God raises up another servant to accomplish salvation. This should be no more surprising than Ezek. 37:25, where both Israel and the messianic king are called God's servants.

According to this view, each passage should be scrutinized by itself to determine which servant is intended. Israel is named as the servant, the object of God's care (Isa. 41:8). The servant is anointed by God's Spirit for a great work of witness, of judgment, and of testimony (42:1–6). The verses do not fit Israel but apply accurately to Christ, which the NT quotes (Matt. 12:18–21).

Israel is the object of God's care and forgiving grace (Isa. 44:1–2, 21–22). God is the agent, the servant is the recipient. God calls Cyrus for the sake of Israel (45:4), but the situation later becomes more obscure (50:4–10). Christ's humiliation is noticeable (50:6, but the NT does not quote vv. 4–10). The context does not imply that the suffering is vicarious; it says that God will help his servant. These statements could apply to Christ, but it is not clear that they do.

The most famous segment of the book is Isa. 52:13—53:12. This central unit has been greatly used in Christian testimony. It is quoted about ten times in the NT, usually with explicit reference to Christ (Matt. 8:17; Lk. 22:37; Jn. 12:38; Acts 8:32–33; Rom. 10:16; 15:21; Heb. 9:28; 1 Pet. 2:22–25). The portion begins with a reference to the disfigurement of the servant beyond recognition (Isa. 52:14). His rejection is beyond belief, but his suffering is substitutionary. His affliction is more than severe; it is fatal. He is dead, buried, and without issue. His death is said to be a sin-offering (53:10). This remarkable verse unites the work of the Suffering Servant with the symbolism of the temple sacrifices. Emphatically it states that he bears the sin of transgressors and justifies many by his death. It is often overlooked that the next chapters, in sounding the joyful note of praise for the benefits of this sacrifice, go on to base this salvation on the everlasting covenant, based on God's sure love for David (55:3, cf. "David my servant," Ps. 89:20–24). In this great section, the promises of the Suffering Servant, the Son of David, and the Lamb of God are brought together.

Extensive efforts have been put forth to show that this portion refers to the nation, not to an individual. The statement "my servant shall prosper" (Isa. 52:13 NRSV; NIV, "will act wisely") includes the Hebrew word *yaśkîl* (hiphil impf. of *śākal* H8505). It has been suggested that this is a mistake for the word Israel (*yiśrā'ēl* H3776), and that the text should read, "my servant Israel." There is however no evidence for this view (note that the same verb is used of the righteous Branch, the expected Davidic king, in Jer. 23:5).

The expressions of the servant's suffering and death are so explicit that all attempts to refer the servant to Israel fail. When did Israel ever suffer for sins other than her own and without any deceit in her mouth? In the previous section (Isa. 52:1–12), the Lord promises to redeem Jerusalem and bring again Zion. Israel is as usual the object of Yahweh's salvation, not the instrument of redemption. The saving work of the Suffering Servant is a work for Israel, not a work by Israel. The Servant will die (53:9), but no weapon formed against Israel shall prosper (54:17). The two must not be confounded.

Effort also has been made to speak of Israel as the Servant and to liken the resurrection of the Servant (53:10) to the return of Israel from Babylonian captivity. Ezekiel likens the return from exile to a resurrection from the dead (Ezek. 37), but the exile is nowhere recorded in the OT as a sacrificial death. Rather, the exile was the judgment of God for obvious sin. Furthermore, Isaiah does not too patently speak of a resurrection (Isa. 53:10). James Smart has been quoted above in a different connection: "Those who see an individual in the Servant have on their hands in this verse (10) the resurrection of an individual from the dead, a somewhat embarrassing phenomenon if the chapter is to be retained as written by the prophet in the sixth century B.C." (*History and Theology*, 212). Notice that Smart's argument is based on purely theoretical reconstruction of Israel's early theology. Why should the mention of the resurrection of an individual in the 6th cent. be embarrassing? Only by postdating the resurrection psalms, the book of Job, Isa. 24–27, Dan. 12:2, and other passages can the early date of the resurrection doctrine be denied. Smart's argument is subjective.

Another denial of the messianic interpretation comes from the cultic ideas of the sacral kingship theory. S. Mowinckel (*He That Cometh* [1954]),

I. Engnell (in *BJRL* 31 [1948]: 54–93), A. R. Johnson (*Sacral Kingship in Ancient Israel* [1955]), and accept argue that an it in Israel, like Babylon and Egypt, deified its kings. The king was the head of the religion. On the great festival days, parallel to the Babylonian New Year festival, the king was first humiliated to bear the bad luck of the preceding year, then was enthroned again amid general rejoicing and acclaimed as deity. This school finds the humiliation of Israel's king expressed in Isa. 53, Ps. 22, and similar passages. His reenthronement is celebrated in Ps. 2; 110; 45; et al. H. Ringgren finds the metaphors of Isa. 53 derived principally from "two circles of motifs; the Tammuz literature and the kingship ideology" (*The Messiah in the Old Testament* [1956], 50). These views have been challenged not only because they assume that Israel's religion was parallel to that of Babylon, but also because it is a fallacious assumption that the Babylonian king was deified (H. Frankfort, *Kingship and the Gods* [1948], 224, 342). The whole idea is a curious application of the comparative religion approach. Critical scholars place this chapter usually at a late date. Where was any king in Judah then, let alone a king to lead the cult? Or did they think in exile that the Babylonian king was bruised for Israel's iniquities?

The plain traditional messianic interpretation of the chapter still fits the OT best, and surely is taught in the NT. The coming root of Jesse's line was also to suffer for sin. In him would be united the symbols of Israel's faith, the sacrificial death, the Davidic kingship, and the divine child. In him is found the mighty victory of God's grace. "For your Maker is your husband— / the LORD Almighty is his name— / the Holy one of Israel is your Redeemer" (Isa. 54:5). This chapter is not in intimate association with the Babylonian captivity nor the return therefrom; it is far deeper than that. The consequent triumph is far higher than a return from exile. This chapter opens the door on those heavenly passages in the latter part of Isaiah that tell of a time when Zion's walls shall be Salvation and her gates, Praise (60:18). Then "the LORD will be your everlasting light, / and your God will be your glory" (60:19). (See further B. Jankowski and P. Stuhlmacher, eds., *The Suffering Servant: Isaiah 53 in Jewish and Christian Sources* [2004].)

D. Other messianic passages. Isaiah is often called "the evangelical prophet" because of his predictions of Christ and his great salvation. In studying Isaiah's great predictions, it should be remembered that he was expressing the general hope of Israel that appears in other prophets as well. Isaiah's prophecies do not stand alone. The stream of messianic prophecy, which began with Gen. 3:15, expanded markedly with God's promises to David (2 Sam. 7). This Davidic covenant is reflected in several psalms and forms the basis of the teaching of the prophets. The Messiah was to be of David's line. Even Amos, a prophet to the northern kingdom, cites the tabernacle of David as Israel's hope (Amos 9:11). Other passages, such as Jer. 23:5 and, even after the fall of Jerusalem, Ezek. 37:24–25, are quite clear.

The PHARISEES, in answer to Christ's question, answered readily that the Messiah was to be David's Son (Matt. 22:42). Isaiah repeatedly advances this hope and expectation. Note that the divine child was to rule on David's throne (Isa. 9:6–7). To whom could this refer? Surely not to Ahaz with whom Isaiah was perpetually at odds. This prophecy is datable to the Syro-Ephraimite war (9:11) and therefore is not a prediction of Hezekiah's birth. He was born at least by 740 B.C. To speak in times like these of the young Hezekiah would surely be inappropriate even allowing for hyperbole, exaggeration, or symbolism of any kind. As argued earlier in connection with Isa. 7:14, the passage reflects rather a future hope for the Son of David who would not be just another king, but would be the messianic deliverer.

In line with this image, Isa. 11 promises the "stump of Jesse," the "Branch," the "Root of Jesse" (11:1, 10). He is pictured as a conqueror, but his is no ordinary conquest. His weapon is his sovereign Word. The results of victory are eternal peace, and a peace such as the world has not seen since paradise (11:6–9). There is a close parallel between 11:9 and 65:25, but there is one significant difference. The latter verse speaks of the removal of the curse from men and nature, but mentions that the curse on the serpent given in Gen. 3 will not be removed. The conclusion would be that the curses that are removed are the others mentioned in Genesis, and the Messiah will really come in his ultimate power to undo the curse that was put upon the first parents for sin. No mere earthly Son of David could accomplish this. The hope of Israel was not for a better monarch, but for an ultimate kingdom. It is for this reason that the work of the Suffering Servant (Isa. 53) opens the door not only to pardon from sin, but to those glorious vistas of peace and blessing found in the succeeding chapters. All this is involved in the One who fulfills the Davidic covenant (55:3).

The concluding chapters of Isaiah contain a few references to the coming of Christ, but their identification is not clear because they refer to God's activity for Israel. The application of these passages to Christ in the NT is a strong argument for his deity. In Isa. 59:15–21 we see the reaction of the Lord to Israel's sin. All had turned aside; therefore God himself would save, and the Redeemer would come at last to Zion. Verse 20 is quoted in Rom. 11:26 as referring to the salvation of Israel after the period of Gentile salvation.

A superficial reading might suggest that Isaiah was referring to himself as the anointed to preach good tidings (Isa. 61:1–3). The promises given to Israel in the succeeding verses outstrip any legitimate expectation from Isaiah's ministry or from an ordinary king's reign. The "year of the LORD's favor" was as truly future to Isaiah as was "the day of vengeance of our God." It often has been pointed out that when Christ quoted these verses in the synagogue at Nazareth (Lk. 4:16–21), he claimed they were fulfilled in himself, but he did not continue with reference to the "day of vengeance of our God." Evidently this judgment remains to be fulfilled.

Later verses give further details on this subject. Another passage, Isa. 63:1–6, threatens total judgment at that "day of vengeance" and likens it to the treading of a winepress in anger. The NT references to coming judgment at the SECOND COMING of Christ are unmistakable (Rev. 14:19–20; 19:15). The conclusion is that through the latter part of Isaiah, the predicted work of the expected One is portrayed on such a large canvas that it is not limited to the first coming of Christ, much less could it have been fulfilled by any ordinary king of David's line. God showed Isaiah final things, and the only Person suitable for their accomplishment is the coming child of David's line who is also the divine Lord and Savior.

E. Eschatological passages. Passages speaking of God's ultimate kingdom already have been referred to in connection with the messianic hope. These portions are claimed as eschatological: Isa. 2:1–5; 11:1–16; 25:6—26:21; 34; 35; 52:7–12; 54; 60; 65:17–25; 66:10–24. Some of these may be grouped together for treatment.

Perhaps the most striking passages are Isa. 11:1–16 and 65:17–25. Indeed, 11:9a is identical with 65:25b. The picture in ch. 11 concerns the coming of the Branch of David's line. His kingdom will be one of perfection and his rule will be in supernatural power. Verse 4 of this chapter has an echo in 2 Thess. 2:8, where it is used of Christ's conquest of the man of sin (see ANTICHRIST) at his return. There is another allusion to it in Rev. 19:15, where Christ returns in glory to destroy the beast and false prophet and to bind the dragon. The three verses help to interpret each other and seem to indicate a fulfillment at Christ's return. The often reprinted picture of the wolf and the lamb dwelling together would also fit that horizon. Surely it does not fit the present church age. As already noted, in the parallel section (Isa. 65:25) is a slight but significant variation. It is said that the curse on nature will be lifted, but there is the curious additional expression, "dust will be the serpent's food." This clause informs us that the curse upon the serpent (Gen. 3:14) is not to be lifted. The natural conclusion is that the other curses that are lifted are those stated in Gen. 3. In short, Isaiah predicts a day when God's curse on nature will be lifted, but the curse on Satan will remain. This obviously does not refer to the present situation, but speaks of the day of Christ's return (cf. Rom. 8:19–23). That day is pictured as a time of great longevity (Isa. 65:21–22). It is not clear whether Isa. 65:17 places the new heavens and earth at this time or not. Many would hold that this verse refers to the eternal state, as the reference in Rev. 21:1 would imply.

Another passage (Isa. 25:6—26:21) emphasizes not so much the glories of Christ's return as the fact of the eventual resurrection of the dead. The swallowing up of death really refers to resurrection, as is shown both by the expression, "the Sovereign LORD God will wipe away the tears" (Isa. 25:8), and the quotation in the NT (1 Cor. 15:54). The reference to Moab in Isa. 25:10 need not argue against the eschatological character of the passage. Probably Moab is taken as a type of evil just as Edom is in Isa. 34:5. In 26:19, the Hebrew word *nebelati* ("my dead body," KJV) should probably be read as a plural to fit the context, thus: "But your dead will live; their bodies [*niblōtām*] will rise. You who dwell in the dust, wake up and and shout for joy" (NIV). The statement is in contrast to vv. 14–15, where the wicked are said to perish, but God's own shall live. Most critical scholars hold that resurrection is a later doctrine, and they either date these verses late or deny that they could refer to resurrection. This is reasoning in a circle. There is no reason why Isaiah by God's revelation should not have spoken at an early time of the resurrection day.

As mentioned before, Isa. 34 refers to Edom symbolically as the eschatological enemy of God's people. Verse 4, which speaks of the signs in heaven, is quoted both by Christ of his coming (Matt. 24:29) and by John (Rev. 6:14) in connection with the day of the wrath of the Lamb. The glorious picture (Isa. 35) subsequent to this judgment in ch. 34 shows a world of beauty and blessing in which God's people return to Zion with everlasting joy. This figure of a highway back to Zion and a regathering of God's people is also proclaimed elsewhere (11:16; 60:8–9; and prob. 2:2–3).

The picture of Zion's glory given in Isa. 60 really has 59:20–21 for its backdrop. Israel will not be blessed without a Redeemer. The Hebrew (also LXX and the quotation in Rom. 11:26) can better be taken, "The Redeemer shall come for the sake of Zion." Paul quotes this verse with the comment that God's promises are inviolable. The Romans passage has been taken in two ways. One interpretation has it that Isa. 59:20 is fulfilled in the "church age." It is said that the church inherits the promises of Israel and "so" or "in this manner" all Israel shall be saved. The other and more natural view is defended by John Murray (*The Epistle to the Romans*, NICNT, 2 vols. [1959–65], 2:96–98). This view holds that the apostle distinguishes national Israel from the church and promises eventual salvation for Israel as a nation in the final time. This view prepares the way for the great sixtieth chapter of Isaiah with its exaltation of Zion and her sons, in a day when violence is heard no more and Jerusalem shall be inhabited by the Lord in his glory. The passage is similar to Isa. 54 and is the basis for the great description of the city foursquare in Rev. 21.

The prophecy of Isaiah ends with a solemn note (Isa. 66). The picture of the glory of Zion is counterbalanced by the punishment to be meted out to the enemies of God. The many slain by the Lord (66:16) and the punishments of the transgressors are described in terms used by Christ of eternal hell (Isa. 66:24; cf. Mk. 9:44, 46, 48).

VII. Contents of the book. The major divisions of Isaiah are clearly marked. Disregarding critical approaches, the book may be outlined as follows:

A. Introduction and condemnation of Judah (Isa. 1–5)
B. The prophet's call and commission (ch. 6)
C. The book of Immanuel (chs. 7–12)
   1. Warnings against alliance with Assyria and the sign of Immanuel's birth (ch. 7)
   2. More warnings against foreign alliances (ch. 8)
   3. The divine son of David, Israel's hope (9:1–7)
   4. The invasion of Assyria and its final defeat (9:8—10:34)
   5. The rod of Jesse and Israel's final blessing (ch. 11)
   6. A psalm of thanksgiving (ch. 12)
D. Prophecies against surrounding nations (chs. 13–23)
   1. Babylon's fall to the Medes (13:1—14:23)
   2. Failure of the Assyrian invasion (14:24–27)
   3. Philistia's temporary relief in 715 B.C. (14:28–32)
   4. Judgment on Moab (chs. 15–16)
   5. Overthrow of Damascus (ch. 17)
   6. Failure of the Ethiopian dynasty of Egypt (ch. 18)
   7. Failure of Egypt and her eventual blessing (ch. 19)
   8. Isaiah's warning against joining the coalition of Ashdod and Egypt against Assyria in 714 B.C. (ch. 20)
   9. The fall of Babylon to the Medes (21:1–10)
   10. Burden of Edom and Arabia (21:11–17)

11. Jerusalem's military preparation and lack of repentance (ch. 22)
  12. Tyre to fall to the Babylonians (ch. 23)
E. The resurrection and eschatology (chs. 24–27)
F. Woes upon God's rebellious people (chs. 28–31)
  1. The sins of the northern kingdom (28:1–13)
  2. Warnings to Judah (28:14—29:24)
  3. Trust in Egypt versus trust in the Lord (chs. 30–31)
G. Eventual blessing for Zion (chs. 32–35)
H. Historical material (chs. 36–39)
  1. Sennacherib's invasions of Judah (chs. 36–37)
  2. Hezekiah's sickness in 701 B.C. (ch. 38)
  3. Babylon's bid for an alliance (ch. 39)
I. The Babylonian exile and Babylon's fall (chs. 40–48)
  1. God's promises and his greatness (ch. 40)
  2. God's help for Judah by Cyrus (chs. 41–48)
J. Final deliverance through the suffering servant (chs. 49–53)
K. Blessings following such salvation (chs. 54–55)
L. Current sins of Judah rebuked (56:1—58:15)
M. God's Redeemer and redemption of Zion (58:16–62)
N. The Messiah's vengeance and Isaiah's prayer (63:7—64:12)
O. God's answer and promised kingdom (chs. 65–66)

The above outline shows a wealth of material in the book of Isaiah. There is condemnation of the people for their sin, warnings in a critical international situation, promises of a Redeemer, and visions of the kingdom of glory. In general, the book may be divided into five major parts, although the same themes often recur in the various divisions.

First, there are the introductory chapters (Isa. 1–6). Isaiah sets the tone of the book. He describes his vision, which was probably his prophetic call (ch. 6), and utters many condemnations of the sins of Judah. It may be that these chapters reflect an early period in his ministry. At the same time, this section includes the passage dealing with ultimate peace—when swords shall be beaten into plowshares and nations shall not learn war any more (2:1–4; cf. Mic. 4:1–4). This section is united with the next by a refrain common to both (Isa. 5:25; 9:12, 17, 21; 10:4).

The so-called book of Immanuel has been discussed above in connection with the virgin birth prophecy of Isa. 7:14. Its approximate period is 732 B.C., although in ch. 10 the Assyrian invasion of 701 is described. It is probable that this invasion is stated prophetically, but it is very vivid and pictures the Assyrian army coming right up to the gates of Jerusalem before its downfall is announced (10:34). This section declares in no uncertain terms the sovereignty of Israel's God, who directs the Assyrian invader as a carpenter uses his ax and saw (10:15). The Assyrians come of their own free will and pride, and will be punished accordingly (10:7–12). The coming of Jesse's rod is a promise that goes far beyond the deliverance from Assyria, as has been argued above. The concluding psalm of thanksgiving (ch. 12) has an interesting quotation from Miriam's song of deliverance of Exod. 15.

The third major section, which includes material of varied content, extends from Isa. 13 to ch. 35. It begins with the burdens on the surrounding Gentile nations. This sort of condemnation is repeated in Jer. 46–51 and Ezek. 25–32. It may have been influenced by Amos's rhetorical condemnation

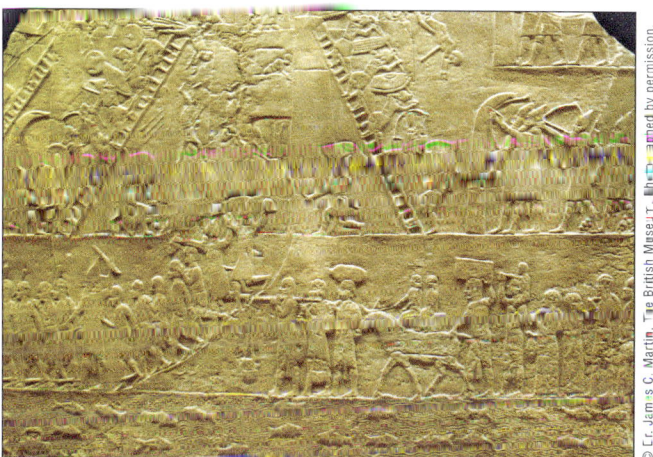

This panel from a palace in Nineveh (c. 640 B.C.) depicts the Assyrian capture of an Egyptian fortress. Isaiah warned God's people against making alliances with either Egypt or Assyria.

on surrounding peoples (Amos 1:3—2:6). Some of the burdens are rather general. Some, like Isa. 14:28 and 20:1, are given specific dates. The section seems to come from that time before Assyria actually invaded Judah in 701. The period was one of great international tension. Political opinions in Judah were many and fluid. Hope was sought in alliance with Egypt or submission to Assyria. Isaiah has strong warnings against an Egyptian or any other alliance. In scorn he calls their treaty with Assyria a covenant with death and SHEOL, with lies and falsehood. In contrast he calls the people to trust in the sure foundation, the precious cornerstone, whom the Lord will establish in Zion (cf. Isa. 8:12–14 and Rom. 9:33; 1 Pet. 2:4, 6). This section also looks beyond the present trials to the future glory (Isa. 35 et al.), as mentioned above.

The so-called Deutero-Isaiah comprises Isa. 40–66. It evidences a different background from the parts considered above, as is rightly noticed by critics. No longer is Assyria considered the great enemy, but Babylon. The background for this last section is given by the historical division (chs. 35–39) that tells of Hezekiah's alliance with the Babylonian usurper Merodach-Baladan, probably around 703–701. This ill-fated alliance brings forth Isaiah's revelations of Babylon's future enslavement of Israel and her eventual fall.

These chapters were doubtless written later in Isaiah's life. In those years Babylon was a power with which to reckon. When Isaiah denounced it, his contemporaries got the point and shuddered. Although Sennacherib eventually burned Babylon, the Chaldean power in ELAM remained strong, and later made a comeback, destroying Assyria and conquering Israel as Isaiah had promised.

Through these chapters run two threads of prophecy. The Babylonian exile and the deliverance by Cyrus have been mentioned. This motif ends in Isa. 48. Another thread, which begins in 42:1 and goes through ch. 53, is the mention of God's servant. God's servant is sometimes called Israel, but sometimes he cannot be identified as the nation. As shown above, the word *servant* is common and has many uses. In the crowning passage, ch. 53, the Servant refers to Christ's suffering, and has been so recognized in many NT passages and in the literature of the church. Significantly, after ch. 53 the word *servant* in the singular does not occur again. But this is the section where the vistas of the future open up before the prophet's inspired vision. The consequences of the servant's suffering are nothing less than the creation of a new heaven and a new earth. These chapters, perhaps written in Isaiah's retirement, are full of comfort and promise for the people of God.

VIII. Isaiah's theology. The book of Isaiah, as it stands, is acknowledged to be one of the richest in the OT. Only by dissecting it do critical students reach conclusions concerning a development of Israel's religion in the postexilic times. The great doctrines of God (his creation and providence), of man (his sin and need), and of redemption and the coming Redeemer are all given prominence. The book is not a collection of abstract dogmas. The lessons of God's greatness and love in respect to human need are stated in the concrete historical realities of one of Judah's most critical periods. Isaiah spoke to his own day. What he spoke to his contemporaries was the eternal Word of life.

A phrase characteristic of the whole book is the expression "the Holy One of Israel," used thirteen times in the first thirty-nine chapters and another thirteen times in the last part. This phrase, so expressive of the moral character of God, possibly derives from the triple ascription of HOLINESS to God in the prophet's vision (Isa. 6). No book speaks more earnestly of God's sovereign power and righteous character. In chs. 2 and 5 especially, the moral sins and the idolatry of Judah are rebuked, and the conclusion is, "Therefore the LORD's anger burns against his people" (5:25). The thought is matched later in the book by the statement, "your iniquities separated you from your God" (59:2).

Perhaps the most famous passage in the OT on God's work of CREATION is Isa. 40:12–31. In fine irony, the prophet distinguishes the dumb idol from the transcendent Lord. The same condemnation of IDOLATRY is given elsewhere in scattered verses (2:7–8, 18–21; 30:21, 22; 57:5–8; et al.). Likewise the PROVIDENCE of God is given emphasis. As already mentioned, ch. 10 describes Assyria as only God's tool. Similar expressions of God's control of the Assyrians are given (37:29). Isaiah's picture of the transcendence of the Lord (37:23–35) matches the lofty tenor of the better known ch. 40. Whereas 40:15 likens the nations to the dust of a balance, chs. 10 and 37 also show God in absolute control of the international scene.

Isaiah gives vivid descriptions of human SIN: sins are like scarlet (1:18); God's people "have removed their heart far from me" (29:13 KJV); "Their feet run to evil, and they are swift to shed innocent blood" (59:7). It may be added that Isaiah narrows the responsibility of sin down to the individual: the man that does righteousness as well as the son of the stranger and the eunuch who keep the SABBATH will all receive the promised blessing of God (56:2–5). God hears the cause of the fatherless and the widow (1:23). The faithful individual ELIAKIM will be preserved, though the proud SHEBNA would be carried captive (22:15–25).

The topic of REDEMPTION is so prominent that Isaiah is called the evangelical prophet. Not only is the Son of David frequently prophesied, but as already has been seen, the very sacrificial work of Christ is delineated in the great fifty-third chapter. It may be helpful, however, to note Isaiah's attitude toward the OT sacrificial system. It is perfectly clear that he did not regard the sacrifices as automatic in effect. In a famous passage (1:11–17) he denounces the altar, incense, and the feast days. Yet in 56:2, the Sabbath is enjoined as a thing of blessing. This is no contradiction. In the second passage, the context shows that an insincere fast day is an abomination. This is the key to Isaiah's attitude. He protested against hypocritical and idolatrous sacrifices, but upon his original call to service his own lips were cleansed by a coal from off the altar (6:7). The prophet protests that the beasts of the great mountain Lebanon are insufficient for a burnt offering (40:16), yet the sin offering is central in the interpretation of the suffering servant's work (53:10).

Of Isaiah's ESCHATOLOGY one need not speak further. He sees into the future with eagle eye because God has drawn aside the curtain just a little. Isaiah does not see in balanced perspective the relationship between the current international problems, the coming of the Servant in humility, the coming of the day of vengeance, and the future redemption of the earth from its curse. All of these facets of the future are portrayed upon Isaiah's canvas in wonderfully brilliant hues, so that the final book of the NT could borrow the wording of Isa. 60 to depict the time when Zion will have no need of the sun or moon, "for the glory of God gives it light, and the Lamb is its lamp" (Rev. 21:23).

(Significant commentaries include J. A. Alexander, *Commentary on the Prophecies of Isaiah* [1846]; F. Delitzsch, *Biblical Commentary on the Prophecies of Isaiah* [1866]; G. B. Gray, *A Critical and Exegetical Commentary on the Book of Isaiah 1–27*, ICC [1912]; E. J. Kissane, *The Book of Isaiah*, 2 vols. [1941–1943]; C. Westermann, *Isaiah 40–66*, OTL [1969]; E. J. Young, *The Book of Isaiah*, 3 vols., NICOT [1965–72]; O. Kaiser, *Isaiah 1–39*, OTL [1972]; C. R. North, *Isaiah 40–55* [1975]; J. Watts, *Isaiah*, 2 vols., WBC 24–25 [1985–87]; J. A. Motyer, *The Prophecy of Isaiah* [1993]; J. N. Oswalt, *The Book of Isaiah*, 2 vols., NICOT [1986–98]; W. Brueggemann, *Isaiah*, 2 vols. [1998]; J. L. Koole, *Isaiah: Part 3* [chs. 40–55, 1997–98]; W. A. M. Beuken, *Isaiah: Part 2* [chs. 28–39, 2000]; K. Baltzer, *Deutero-Isaiah: A Commentary on Isaiah 40–55* [2001]; B. S. Childs, *Isaiah*, OTL [2001]; J. Wildberger, *Isaiah: A Commentary* [chs. 1–39], 3 vols. [1991–2002]; J. Blenkinsopp, *Isaiah 1–39*, AB 19 [2000]; id., *Isaiah 40–55*, AB 19A [2002]; id., *Isaiah 55–66*, AB 19B [2003]; J. Goldingay and D. Payne, *A Critical and Exegetical Commentary on Isaiah 40–55*, ICC [2006].

(In addition, there are numerous monographs that include detailed expositions of selected passages; cf. the bibliographies in commentaries and in W. E. Mills, *Isaiah* [2002]. Among recent works, see A. Laato, *"About Zion I Will Not Be Silent": The Book of Isaiah as an Ideological Unity* [1998]; P. D. Quinn-Miscall, *Reading Isaiah: Poetry and Vision* [2001]; T. L. Leclerc, *Yahweh Is Exalted in Justice: Solidarity and Conflict in Isaiah* [2001]; B. S. Childs, *The Struggle to Understand Isaiah as Christian Scripture* [2004]; R. Heskett, *Messianism within the Scriptural Scroll of Isaiah* [2007].) R. L. HARRIS

Isaiah, Martyrdom and Ascension of. See ASCENSION OF ISAIAH.

Iscah is´kuh (יִסְכָּה H3576, derivation uncertain). TNIV Iskah. Daughter of HARAN and niece of ABRAHAM (Gen. 11:29).

Iscariot is-kair′ee-uht. See JUDAS ISCARIOT.

Isdael iz-dee′uhl (Ἰσδαήλ). Ancestor of a family of temple servants (NETHINIM) who returned after the EXILE (1 Esd. 5:33; RSV, "Giddel"; the reading *Geddēl* is preferred by R. Hanhart, *Esdrae liber I*, Septuaginta 8/1 [1974], ad loc.). Apparently the same as GIDDEL (Ezra 2:56; Neh. 7:58).

Ishbaal ish′bay-uhl. See ISH-BOSHETH.

Ishbah ish′buh (יִשְׁבָּח H3786, "[God] soothes" or "may [God's wrath] subside" or "[God] congratulates"). Son of MERED (apparently by his wife BITHIAH, Pharaoh's daughter) and father of ESHTEMOA; included in the genealogy of JUDAH (1 Chr. 4:17; note that NRSV, to clarify the sense, includes here part of v. 18).

Ishbak ish′bak (יִשְׁבָּק H3791, possibly from a root that in Arabic means "to anticipate, surpass"). Son of ABRAHAM and KETURAH (Gen. 25:2; 1 Chr. 1:32); no descendants are mentioned.

Ishbi-Benob ish′bi-bee′nob (יִשְׁבִּי בְּנֹב H3787, meaning unknown). A descendant of Rapha (see REPHAITES) of GATH whose bronze spearhead weighed more than seven pounds; fighting on the side of the PHILISTINES against the Israelites, he vowed to kill DAVID but was defeated by ABISHAI (2 Sam. 21:16–17, 22). As a result of this incident, the Israelite soldiers would not allow David to fight again. Many scholars, on the basis of the *Ketib* (*wyšbw* instead of *wyšby*), emend the text to *wayyēšbû bĕgōb*, "and they dwelt in Gob" (cf. vv. 18–19). (For a more substantial emendation, based on some Gk. MSS, see P. K. McCarter, Jr., *II Samuel*, AB 9 [1984], 448; and for the view that the term *yālîd* H3535 should be rendered "votary" rather than "descendant," see ibid., 449–50.)

Ish-Bosheth ish boh′shith (אִישׁ־בֹּשֶׁת H410, "man of shame"). Son of SAUL, he was made king over Israel by Abner in opposition to DAVID's claim to the throne (2 Sam. 2:8—4:12; NRSV, "Ishbaal"). He is also called ESH-BAAL (אֶשְׁבַּעַל H843), meaning "man of the Lord" or "the Lord exists," which was probably his original name (1 Chr. 8:33; 9:39; these two references suggest that he was Saul's youngest son, unless he is the same as ISHVI, listed second in 1 Sam. 14:49). The difference between Ish-Bosheth and Esh-Baal is generally attributed to an intentional alteration of the name of BAAL because of intense hatred for that pagan deity (this word, which means "lord," could apparently be applied to Yahweh early in Israelite history). It is also possible that the name was given him as a result of his shameful demise. (For a different view, see M. Tsevat in *HUCA* 46 [1975]: 71–87.)

The appointment of Ish-Bosheth brought forth the question of the means of royal succession. David's right was charismatic, Ish-Bosheth's was hereditary, and the former eventually prevailed. Ish-Bosheth was forty years of age when he was enthroned at MAHANAIM and reigned for only two years (2 Sam. 2:10). Abner transferred his loyalty to David as a result of an accusation by Ish-Bosheth (3:7–12; but Abner was murdered shortly thereafter, v. 27). Ish-Bosheth, lacking support, was finally assassinated (4:5–8). (See J. A. Soggin, *Old Testament and Oriental Studies* [1975], 31–49; J. C. VanderKam in *JBL* 99 [1980]: 521–39; D. V. Edelman, "Eshbaal," in *ABD*, 2:615–17.) T. E. MCCOMISKEY

Ish-hai ish′hi (אִישׁ־חַי, "man of life"). Father of Jehoiada and grandfather of BENAIAH (one of DAVID's mighty warriors), according to 2 Sam. 23:20 KJV, following the *Ketib*. The *Qere*, however, has *ben-ʾîš-ḥayil*, lit., "son of a man of power," an expression applied to Benaiah and probably meaning "valiant warrior" or the like; this reading (found in the parallel, 1 Chr. 11:22) is followed by most versions.

Ishhod ish′hod (אִישְׁהוֹד H412, "man of splendor [or vitality]"). KJV Ishod. Son of HAMMOLEKETH, who was apparently the sister of GILEAD; included in the genealogy of MANASSEH (1 Chr. 7:18). It is unclear why his father's name is not given. See discussion under ABIEZER #1.

Ishi (divine name) ish′i (אִישִׁי, from אִישׁ H408, "man, husband," plus first person sing. pronoun). This name appears in the KJV of Hos. 2:16, "And it shall be at that day, saith the LORD, *that* thou shalt call me Ishi; and shalt call me no more Baali"

(modern versions usually translate the first name with "my husband," and the second with either "my Baal" [NRSV] or "my master" [NIV]). The word for BAAL (*baʿal* H1251) means "owner" or "lord," but it too can mean "husband." Because of its associations with the idolatrous worship of the pagan Baal, the prophet declares that this name will not be used in the worship of the true God. Some have thought that this word, when it has the meaning "husband," implies a formal or legal arrangement, and that the change of name may thus indicate also a return to a closer spiritual relationship.

Ishi (person) ish'i (יִשְׁעִי H3801, prob. short form of יְשַׁעְיָה H3833 [ISAIAH], "Yahweh is salvation"). (1) Son of Appaim and descendant of JUDAH through the line of JERAHMEEL (1 Chr. 2:31).

(2) A descendant of JUDAH (1 Chr. 4:20); his genealogical connection is unclear.

(3) A member of the tribe of SIMEON whose sons led five hundred Simeonites in an invasion of the hill country of SEIR (1 Chr. 4:42).

(4) A head of family in the eastern part of the tribe of MANASSEH; he and several others are described as "brave warriors, famous men" (1 Chr. 5:24). The larger context of the passage (vv. 18-26) focuses on how the Reubenites, the Gadites, and the half-tribe of Manasseh were successful in enlarging their territories but fell into idolatry and were taken captive by the king of Assyria.

Ishiah i-shi'uh. TNIV form of ISSHIAH.

Ishijah i-shi'juh (יִשִּׁיָּה H3807, prob. "Yahweh forgets"; see ISSHIAH). NRSV Isshijah. One of the descendants of Harim who put away their foreign wives (Ezra 10:31; called *Aseas* in 1 Esd. 9:32 [KJV, "Aseas"]).

Ishma ish'muh (יִשְׁמָא H3816, "[God] hears"; short form of ISHMAEL). Son of Etam and descendant of JUDAH (1 Chr. 4:3, NIV and other versions, following LXX). The MT is unintelligible; see discussion under ETAM #1.

Ishmael ish'may-uhl (יִשְׁמָעֵאל H3817, "God hears"; gentilic יִשְׁמְעֵאלִי H3818, "Ishmaelite"). (1) Son of ABRAHAM and HAGAR, and eponymous ancestor of the Ishmaelites (Gen. 16:11-16; 17:18-27; 21:9-21; 25:12-18; et al.); see further below.

(2) Son of Azel and descendant of BENJAMIN through SAUL (1 Chr. 8:38; 9:44).

(3) Father of a certain Zebadiah who was head of the tribe of Judah during the reign of JEHOSHAPHAT (2 Chr. 19:11).

(4) Son of Jehohanan; he was one of the commanders under JEHOIADA who took part in the revolt against ATHALIAH (2 Chr. 23:1).

(5) Son of Nethaniah, known primarily as the royal officer who assassinated GEDALIAH, the governor appointed by the Babylonians over Judah (2 Ki. 25:25; Jer. 40:7—41:18). Ishmael himself belonged to the royal family (2 Ki. 25:25; Jer. 41:1). After the destruction of Jerusalem, he had joined Gedaliah in MIZPAH. Perhaps hoping to lay a claim to the throne, Ishmael with ten of his men killed not only Gedaliah, but also the Jews who were with him in Mizpah and the Babylonian soldiers. The following day he slaughtered a large group of men who were bringing offerings to the temple. He then took the rest of the people captive and set out to join the Ammonites. The army officers, led by Johanan son of Kareah, pursued Ishmael and were able to rescue the captives, although Ishmael himself escaped.

(6) One of the descendants of Pashhur who agreed to put away their foreign wives (Ezra 10:22).

The rest of this article is devoted to Ishmael son of Abraham.

I. Name. The name Ishmael is patterned on a common Semitic theophoric formation in which the deity is the subject of a sentence, in this case EL (*ʾēl* H440, "God"), and the other element the predicate, in this case the verb "to hear" (*šāmaʿ* H9048). The time and mode of the sentence are determined by the circumstances leading to the naming, particularly the circumstances surrounding the person's birth. Thus "Ishmael" may mean "God will hear," "God hears," "God heard," "May God hear." In this case the significance is that God had heard, or given heed to, the affliction of Hagar (Gen. 16:11; cf. also 17:20; 21:17). There is no reason to doubt this meaning, as the circumstance surrounding birth was a perfectly normal way to arrive at a name for a child (see R. de Vaux, *Ancient Israel* [1961], 43–46).

II. The birth of Ishmael. In some parts of the ANE it was obligatory for a wife who was barren to provide her husband with a slave woman who would bear children for her. The children were to be under the control of the wife, not the slave; a case from NUZI is discussed by E. A. Speiser (*Genesis*, AB 1 [1964], 120–21). Childless SARAH obtained a son by Hagar, and Ishmael was legally the child of Sarah. This does not explain Sarah's treatment of Hagar, in spite of the fact that some translations of the Nuzi document in question add the clause "Kelimninu may not send the offspring away" (cf. *ANET*, 220). This translation is based on a misreading of the tablet, which Speiser renders, "Kelimninu will obtain offspring (by the slave)." The closest parallel is still to be found in the Code of HAMMURABI, §146. Although this is a specialized case involving the rights of a priestess, the principle seems to be established that a productive slave woman may not assert herself against the unproductive wife. If she does so, she would be reduced to slave status. As Hagar violated this principle, Sarah was within her right to "deal harshly" with her (Gen. 16:6).

III. Life of Ishmael. Ishmael was born when Abraham was eighty-six years old (Gen. 16:16) while he was dwelling near HEBRON (13:18). His mother Hagar was an Egyptian, but she had been confronted by God in a time of her need (16:7–13). When Ishmael was thirteen (17:1), God made his COVENANT with Abraham, according to which all the members of Abraham's household were to be circumcised (see CIRCUMCISION). Ishmael was included. When it was announced to Abraham that Sarah would bear a son, his response, "Oh that Ishmael might live in thy sight" (17:18 NRSV), suggests that Ishmael fell short of Abraham's expectation.

Several years later, after ISAAC had been born and weaned, Ishmael and his mother were expelled from the family to wander in the desert around BEERSHEBA. At one point they were near death from thirst when God *heard* the boy crying and provided water (Gen. 21:17). With the help of God, Ishmael lived the rest of his life in the desert, especially in the wilderness of PARAN. It was here that he became proficient in the use of the bow; and the relative proximity to Egypt, as well as his mother's background, explains his marriage to an Egyptian. That he did not altogether break contact with the main patriarchal family is shown by his presence at the burial of Abraham (25:9) and by the fact that ESAU married Ishmael's daughter MAHALATH (28:9). Ishmael lived 137 years and "was gathered to his people" (25:17).

IV. Divine statements concerning Ishmael. (a) God selects his name and, whatever the significance, the similarity of wording to Isa. 7:14 is striking. (b) God describes his character as that of a wild donkey (Gen. 16:12) in the sense of his being a wandering nomad (cf. Job 39:5–8). As such, he will be in opposition to his more settled kinsmen. He shall camp "in defiance of them" rather than "to the east of them" (Speiser, *Genesis*, 118). (c) God destines him for greatness *outside* the covenant; Gen. 17:20–21 makes it clear that Ishmael was to be blessed by God as a great nation with the same twelvefold organizational structure as Israel was to have, but without direct experience of the covenant. This distinction between national greatness and covenant experience says implicitly a great deal about what the covenant really involved (G. von Rad, *Genesis* [1961], 203; note that national greatness is also promised in 21:13, 18). Moreover, 17:22, 27 shows that the covenant is not to be identified with circumcision no matter how much that identification may appear to be necessitated by 17:10. For Ishmael was circumcised as God had commanded (v. 23) and yet was not the covenant son.

V. Abraham and Sarah's treatment of Ishmael. Abraham treated Ishmael as the son whom God had promised. Even when God revealed that Sarah was to have a son, Abraham did not understand why that was necessary rather than having Ishmael as heir (Gen. 17:18). Even after Isaac's birth, Abraham acted kindly toward Ishmael and was grieved at Sarah's desire to repudiate him. On the other hand, Sarah saw Ishmael as a threat to Isaac's position in the family and found opportunity to have him expelled (ch. 21). This request to cast out the handmaid and her son seems to be

The Wilderness of Paran, where Ishmael spent much of his life.

against all principle of ancient law. The children of handmaids could be demoted if there was adequate reason, but hardly cast out. The fact that Abraham was against such a treatment and followed only on God's command suggests that the action taken was not in accordance with contemporary patterns.

The question also must be asked whether there was something that Ishmael did that was a threat to Isaac or whether it was his existence which constituted such a threat. This is bound up with the meaning of the term *ṣāḥaq* H7464 (piel ptc. *mĕṣaḥēq*) in Gen. 21:9, whether it represents Ishmael as "mocking" or "playing with" Isaac. It is questionable whether the word ever means in the OT "to mock, deride," and it is likely that Sarah objected to Ishmael as a competitor of Isaac, not for some specific action he had done. (See below, section VI.)

VI. Purpose of the Ishmael sequence in Genesis. The author of Genesis includes the Ishmael account primarily to bring about a contrast between Isaac and Ishmael, not so much as persons but as illustrations of God's working. The point is that God, in fulfilling his promises to Abraham, was in no way bound to the natural and the ordinary (the FLESH). He allowed the operation of these in the birth of Ishmael but he superseded them in the birth of Isaac. Although God's preference for Isaac, as son of the wife, was in accord with custom, the rejection of Hagar and Ishmael served to make the contrast bolder, and thus ultimately to remind Israel that all was of GRACE.

VII. Descendants. The descendants of Ishmael are given identically in two passages (Gen. 25:12–16; 1 Chr. 1:29–31). What is most striking is the fact that there were twelve sons listed as there were twelve sons counted to Jacob. With this is to be compared the twelve sons of Nahor (Gen. 22:21–24) and the twelve "sons" of Esau (36:10–14). Other parallels are possible (Keturah's "sons" [25:1–4] are thirteen) and suggest an organizational pattern common to these peoples. The Ishmaelites were ruled by tribal princes (*nāśîʾ* H5954, 25:16). These Ishmaelite tribes settled in the general area where their ancestor had grown up, that is, the wilderness of Paran. This area is described in 25:18 as "from Havilah to Shur, near the border of Egypt, as you go toward Asshur" (Assyria).

Some of the names of his descendants are attested in Assyrian records as tribes. More important of the twelve are NEBAIOTH (prob. on linguistic grounds not to be identified with the later NABATEANS) and JETUR, a name found later in the name ITUREA of NT times (Lk. 3:1). (For details see J. Montgomery, *Arabia and the Bible* [1934].) On occasion the Ishmaelites are pictured as hostile to the Israelites (1 Chr. 5:19) in accordance with the statement of God concerning Ishmael (Gen. 16:12). Finally, the Ishmaelites are coupled with the Midianites (some of the descendants of KETURAH) in some passages, thus suggesting an overlapping of the two terms (see MIDIAN). The term ISHMAELITE is applied to the Midianites (Jdg. 8:24), and the same group receives both names in connection with the story of JOSEPH (Gen. 37:25–28, 36; 39:1; there is no need to distinguish a Midianite from an Ishmaelite account of the sale of Joseph).

VIII. Paul's use of the Ishmael sequence. Although he does not mention Ishmael by name, PAUL is obviously developing his teaching in Gal. 4:21–31 on the basis of the Genesis passages. Ishmael was born "according to the flesh" (NIV, "in the ordinary way") and "persecuted him that was born according to the Spirit" (Gal. 4:29 RSV). The fact that the next verse is a quotation from Gen. 21:10 suggests that Paul has that context before his mind, and that it is from that context that he derives the remark about Ishmael persecuting Isaac. However, the Genesis context does not suggest any such persecution. J. B. Lightfoot (*Saint Paul's Epistle to the Galatians*, 10th ed. [1898], 184) presents two explanations: (1) Paul was influenced by, although without endorsing, rabbinical traditions of Ishmael's opposition to Isaac that were read into the Genesis account; (2) Paul read back into the individuals that enmity which characterized their descendants. From this, Paul concluded that the Galatians, who are free in Christ, should cast out the ones seeking to bring them into bondage. Of these facts drawn from the OT, Paul says that they are *allēgoroumena* (Gal. 4:24, from *allēgoreō* G251), an expression which is open to different interpretations. Does he mean that the passage in Genesis is to be understood as an ALLEGORY, or that it is to be applied allegorically?   D. K. HUTTAR

Ishmael, Rabbi. A prominent Jewish sage during the first decades of the second century A.D. He has traditionally been viewed as the founder of a school of interpretation that stressed the ordinary use of biblical language, in contrast to the emphasis on linguistic detail characterized by his contemporary, Rabbi AKIBA. Rabbi Ishmael is credited with the elaboration of thirteen rules of biblical exegesis (cf. H. L. Strack and G. Stemberger, *Introduction to the Talmud and Midrash* [1992], 23–25); he is also associated with some mystical movements. (See the extensive work by G. Porton, *The Traditions of Rabbi Ishmael*, 4 vols. [1976–82].)

Ishmaelite ish´may-uh-līt (יִשְׁמְעֵאלִי H3818). A descendant of ISHMAEL. The Bible refers to the Ishmaelites in connection with the story of JOSEPH (Gen. 37:25–28; 39:1), in the narrative of GIDEON and the Midianites (Jdg. 8:24), and in a list of enemies of Israel (Ps. 83:6). In addition, a certain JETHER the Ishmaelite is included in the genealogy of JUDAH (1 Chr. 2:17; called "Ithra the Israelite" in the MT of 2 Sam. 17:24), and the man in charge of DAVID's camels was an Ishmaelite named OBIL.

Twelve sons (or descendants) of Ishmael are listed in the Bible (Gen. 25:13–15; 1 Chr. 1:29–31), and most of these names correspond to Arabian tribes (or place names) attested in extrabiblical sources. For example, the second name, KEDAR, clearly corresponds to the Qedarites, a particularly powerful tribe mentioned in Assyrian inscriptions as early as the 8th cent. B.C. (cf. I. Eph‘al, *The Ancient Arabs: Nomads on the Borders of the Fertile Crescent 9th-5th Centuries B.C.* [1982], 223–27). Similarly, TEMA (Teima, Tayma) gave his name to a major trade center in N ARABIA.

It is clear that, no later than the 8th cent. B.C., the Ishmaelites formed a major tribal confederacy spread throughout most of N Arabia. Some scholars (e.g., Eph‘al, *Ancient Arabs*, 233–40) dispute that these tribes are to be linked with the biblical "sons of Ishmael," but the evidence seems to favor ethnic and political identity (see E. A. Knauf in *ABD*, 3:513–20, including map on p. 516). In addition, there is reason to believe that the name Ishmaelite functions in the Bible as a generic term for desert tribal peoples, since it can apparently include the Midianites (cf. Gen. 37:28, 36 [MT "Medanites"]; Jdg. 8:24 [cf. v. 22]; see E. A. Knauf, "Midianites and Ishmaelites," in *Midian, Moab and Edom*, ed. J. F. A. Sawyer and D. J. A. Clines [1983], 147–62; id., *Ismael*, 2nd ed. [1989]).

Ishmaiah ish-may´yuh (יִשְׁמַעְיָה H3819, "Yahweh hears"). (**1**) One of the band of warriors, kinsmen of

SAUL, who joined with DAVID when the latter took refuge at ZIKLAG (1 Chr. 12:4; KJV, "Ismaiah"). He was from GIBEON (as was Saul) and is described as "a mighty man among the Thirty, who was a leader of the Thirty" (his name does not appear in the list of 2 Sam. 23:24–39, presumably because the composition of the Thirty changed over time).

(2) Son of Obadiah; he was a ruler appointed by David over the tribe of ZEBULUN (1 Chr. 27:19). The appointments were part of an extensive effort to bring greater organization to the nation.

Ishmerai ish′muh-ri (יִשְׁמְרַי H3821, "[Yahweh] preserves"). Son of ELPAAL and descendant of BENJAMIN (1 Chr. 8:18); he is listed among the heads of families who lived in Jerusalem (cf. v. 28).

Ishod ish′od. KJV form of ISHHOD.

Ishpah ish′puh (יִשְׁפָּה H3834, possibly "smooth or bald"). KJV Ispah. Son of BERIAH and descendant of BENJAMIN (1 Chr. 8:16); he is listed among the heads of families who lived in Jerusalem (cf. v. 28). His father and uncle, however, are described as "heads of families of those living in Aijalon and who drove out the inhabitants of Gath" (v. 13).

Ishpan ish′pan (יִשְׁפָּן H3836, derivation uncertain). Son of Shashak and descendant of BENJAMIN (1 Chr. 8:22); he is listed among the heads of families who lived in Jerusalem (cf. v. 28).

Ish-sechel ish-see′kuhl (אִישׁ שֶׂכֶל, "man of understanding"). This transliteration is used by some in Ezra 8:18 (e.g., ASV mg.) on the grounds that the context calls for a proper name. Most versions, however, take the words as common nouns (e.g., NRSV, "a man of discretion"; NIV, "a capable man").

Ishtar ish′tahr. The Sumero-Semitic goddess of love and fertility and, mainly in ASSYRIA, goddess of war. In SUMER she was known as Inanna (or [I]nnini). Ishtar was worshiped widely throughout Babylonia and Assyria, where temples were dedicated to her in the main cities and chapels in many towns. In addition, at BABYLON alone there were 180 wayside open-air shrines, for hymns and prayers to her as goddess of fertility were frequent. As "Lady of the lands," she was revered throughout the ANE, though sometimes under other names. She was identified with Isis (in EGYPT; see OSIRIS), the male deity ʾAttar (S ARABIA), Astarte (GREECE) and Anath (Syria; see UGARIT).

In the OT, Ishtar is referred to as ASHTORETH. The women of Judah were upbraided for making sacrificial cakes of incense for her under her title as QUEEN OF HEAVEN (Jer. 7:18; 44:19). According to Babylonian tradition, this goddess descended to the underworld in search of her missing lover TAMMUZ, with the result that fertility ceased and women wept (cf. Ezek. 5:14). In her various capacities, Ishtar is represented as the evening and morning star (Venus). (See J. Nougayrol and J.-M. Aynard, *La Mésopotamie* [1965], 41–44; C. Wilcke and U. Seidl in *Reallexikon der Assyriologie* 5 [1976–80], 74–89; D. Wolkstein and S. N. Kramer, *Inanna, Queen of Heaven and Earth* [1984]; J. Black and A. Green, *Gods, Demons and Symbols of Ancient Mesopotamia: An Illustrated Dictionary* [1992], 108–9; B. R. M. Groneberg, *Lob der Ištar: Gebet und Ritual an die altbabylonische Venusgöttin Tanatti Ištar* [1997]; DDD, 452–56.) D. J. WISEMAN

Ish-tob ish′tob (אִישׁ טוֹב, "man of Tob"). The KJV transliteration of a phrase that is better rendered "the men of Tob" (2 Sam. 10:6, 8). See TOB.

Ishuah ish′yoo-uh. KJV alternate form of ISHVAH.

Ishuai, Ishui ish-yoo′i. KJV forms of ISHVI.

Ishvah ish′vuh (יִשְׁוָה H3796, perhaps "[God] rules"; see A. A. Wieder in *JBL* 84 [1965]: 161). Son of ASHER and grandson of JACOB (Gen. 46:17 [KJV, "Isuah"], 1 Chr. 7:30 [KJV, "Ishuah"]). Because he does not appear in the list of Asherite clans (Num. 26:44–45), some suspect that the name Ishvah is the result of textual corruption of ISHVI; others speculate that he may have died childless.

Ishvi ish′vi (יִשְׁוִי H3798, derivation disputed [see ISHVAH and ABD, 3.522], gentilic יִשְׁוִי H3799, "Ishvite" [KJV, "Jesuite"]). **(1)** Son of ASHER, grandson of JACOB, and ancestor of the Ishvite clan (Gen. 46:17 [KJV, "Isui"]; Num. 26:44 [KJV, "Jesui"]; 1 Chr. 7:30 [KJV, "Ishuai"]).

(2) Son of King SAUL (1 Sam. 14:49; KJV, "Ishui"). While this passage lists only three sons of Saul, 1 Chronicles includes four: Jonathan, Malki-Shua, Abinadab, and Esh-Baal (= ISH-BOSHETH; 1 Chr. 8:33; 9:39). Many believe Ishvi is the same as Esh-Baal/Ish-Bosheth; others speculate that 1 Samuel preserves an earlier list, prior to the birth of Abinadab and Esh-Baal, and that Ishvi died before these last two sons were born.

Isis i´sis. See OSIRIS.

Iskah is´kuh. TNIV form of ISCAH.

island, isle. The Hebrew term *ʾî* H362 can mean a true island (whether in general, Ezek. 26:18, or referring to a specific one, 27:6), dry land as distinct from wet (Isa. 42:15), and especially a coastland. Sometimes littoral regions are distinguished from interior (Esth. 10:1), and the nearby shores of PALESTINE (Isa. 20:6) and PHOENICIA (23:2, 6) are included. But more commonly distance is implied, especially where "the coastlands/islands of the nations," extending into the western Mediterranean, are in view (Gen. 10:5 [KJV, "isles of the Gentiles"; NIV, "maritime peoples"]; Zeph. 2:11).

Though references are scattered, a notable concentration appears in the Major Prophets, and a definite pattern of Israelite geographical knowledge (based partially on Phoenician and Philistine contacts) seems implied. Items of trade suggest E African or Indian contacts through AQABAH (1 Ki. 10:22; Ezek. 27:15), but neighboring Mediterranean areas, especially KITTIM (CYPRUS), CAPHTOR (CRETE?), and DEDAN (RHODES?) were in clearer view. ELISHAH (Ezek. 27:7) was perhaps the Peloponnesus or S Italy, and metal smelting TARSHISH may have been Cilician TARSUS, Sardinia, or, most likely, Tartessus in Spain. NT references, naturally more explicit, include MALTA and specific AEGEAN islands, while in Rev. 6:14 and 16:20 the broader idea reappears. G. R. LEWTHWAITE

Ismachiah is´muh-ki´uh. See ISMAKIAH.

Ismalah is-may´uh. KJV alternate form of ISMAIAH.

Ismakiah is´muh-ki´uh (יִסְמַכְיָהוּ H3577, "Yahweh sustains"; cf. SEMAKIAH). Also Ismachiah. One of the temple supervisors under CONANIAH, who was in charge of the contributions during the reign of HEZEKIAH (2 Chr. 31:13).

Ispah is´pah. KJV form of ISHPAH.

Israel iz´ray-uhl (יִשְׂרָאֵל H3776, by popular etymology, "he struggles with God"; gentilic יִשְׂרְאֵלִי H3778, "Israelite"). The new name given to JACOB by "a man" with whom he wrestled prior to meeting ESAU. The man wrenched Jacob's hip, but Jacob said, "I will not let you go unless you bless me" (Gen. 32:26). The blessing was this: "Your name will no longer be Jacob, but Israel, because you have struggled with God and with men and have overcome" (v. 28; cf. Hos. 12:3–4). The scientific etymology of the name is disputed. Most theophoric names have the deity as the subject of the verb; thus, "God struggles." Others argue that *yiśrāʾēl* is originally derived not from the verb *śārâ* H8575 ("to contend, strive"), but from a different root; alternate meanings suggested include "God rules," "God saves," and others (see *HALOT*, 2:442; J. D. Fowler, *Theophoric Personal Names in Ancient Hebrew* [1988], 108). Israel subsequently became the name of the nation formed by Jacob's descendants. See HEBREW PEOPLE; ISRAEL, HISTORY OF; ISRAEL, RELIGION OF; ISRAELITE.

Israel, history of. The origins of the HEBREW PEOPLE go back to the patriarch ABRAHAM, whereas the designation ISRAEL derives from the new name given to JACOB. Israel was constituted a nation at the time of the exodus and had become a kingdom by the year 1000 B.C. Though not always independent, it remained a political entity until A.D. 135.

 I. Sources
 II. The exodus
 III. Wandering in the wilderness
 IV. The conquest of Canaan
 V. The period of the judges
 VI. The united monarchy
  A. Saul
  B. David
  C. Solomon

ISRAEL, HISTORY OF

   VII. The separate kingdoms of Israel and Judah
  VIII. The fall of Samaria
    IX. The kingdom of Judah alone
     X. The fall of Jerusalem
    XI. The exile
   XII. The Persian period
  XIII. The Greek period
  XIV. The Hasmonean period
   XV. The Roman period

I. Sources. The primary source for the history of ancient Israel is, of course, the Bible. The Bible gives more relative space to history than any other sacred book. The biblical historians and biographers, however, were more concerned with the moral and theological implications of events than with the mere recital of facts. Archaeological excavations in the Near E have illuminated and supplemented biblical history, which is largely Israelite history. The records and inscriptions of the Egyptians, Assyrians, Babylonians, Persians, Greeks, and Romans give a background for, and sometimes deal directly with, the history of Israel. Some Greek and Roman historians record events involving the people of Israel. The histories of the Jewish general and writer JOSEPHUS (c. A.D. 37–103), *The Jewish War* and *The Jewish Antiquities*, are important sources, especially for the last two centuries of the history of ancient Israel. (The dates below usually follow G. E. Wright and F. V. Filson, *The Westminster Historical Atlas of the Bible*, rev. ed. [1956]. Unless otherwise indicated, the dates are B.C.)

II. The exodus (c. 1280, though some scholars place this event much earlier, c. 1450). The exodus, "the going out" (from Egypt) was regarded by the Israelites themselves as the beginning of their national history. The book of Genesis traces Israelite origins back to Abraham, and particularly to his grandson Jacob, also called Israel, and the latter's twelve sons, the progenitors of the twelve tribes of Israel. These accounts in Genesis, however, are not histories but biographies, dealing with persons and families, not with the nation. The book of Exodus opens with the Hebrews as unorganized slaves in EGYPT. With the exodus, the deliverance from slavery in Egypt, the Israelites became a nation and entered on the course of national development which is recorded in the historical books of the Bible. See EXODUS, THE.

Some of the data that are significant for fitting the exodus into the framework of history are as follows: (1) The name MOSES is probably Egyptian, meaning "son of" or the like, an element of royal names in the 18th dynasty (1570–1305, e.g., THUTMOSE) and in the 19th dynasty (1305–1208, e.g., RAMSES).

(2) A people group known as the *Apiru* are mentioned in Egyptian records as Asiatic slaves who worked as builders, as did the Hebrews, for pharaohs in the 18th dynasty (e.g., Amen-hotep II) and in the 19th dynasty (e.g., Ramses II). The word *Apiru* may be related to *ʿibri* וֹ֫ר֫בֹע, "Hebrew," and some of these Apiru may have been the Hebrews of the Bible.

(3) Some have equated the HABIRU of the TELL EL-AMARNA letters of the 14th cent. with the biblical Hebrews and therefore have argued for an exodus in the 15th cent. The name Habiru is probably related to Apiru and to Hebrew, and the three names may denote the same class of semi-nomads. The Habiru of the Amarna letters, however, were attacking different cities in Canaan from those which the Hebrews attacked, and elsewhere Habiru are mentioned in SYRIA and MESOPOTAMIA and therefore cannot be identified with the biblical Hebrews.

(4) The Bible (1 Ki. 6:1) places the building of the TEMPLE (c. 958) 480 years after the exodus, indicating a date for the exodus about 1438. Since forty years means a generation, however, many scholars think that 480 years means twelve generations, which is the actual number of high priests from Aaron to Zadok in Solomon's time. And because the number of years in a generation is often less than forty, the actual time was probably less than 480 years.

(5) Another date is given in Jdg. 11:26, which places the coming of the Israelites "three hundred years" before JEPHTHAH and seems to favor an exodus in the 15th cent. But this number may be simply the addition of the periods of the preceding judges and servitudes, some of which were probably contemporaneous, and so the actual time involved was doubtless less than 300 years. See JUDGES, PERIOD OF.

(6) A key passage for the historical setting of the exodus is Exod. 1:11, which states that the Israelites built PITHOM and RAMESES for Pharaoh. Since Ramses II (c. 1290–1224) built both these cities, many scholars put the exodus early in the 13th cent.

(7) The narratives of Moses' meetings with Pharaoh imply that the royal residence was in northern Egypt, probably in Rameses, also called Tanis, not far from the Hebrew settlement in GOSHEN. Tanis was the capital in the time of the 19th dynasty, which ruled during the 13th cent., whereas THEBES in southern Egypt, about 500 mi. up the NILE, was the capital during the 18th dynasty, which ruled during the 15th cent.

(8) Finally, the destruction of LACHISH, EGLON, BETHEL, DEBIR, and HAZOR (all of which the Israelites captured) is dated by archaeological evidence in the latter part of the 13th cent., and therefore the exodus would fall early in that period, about 1280. Some scholars have tried to account for the ambiguity of the evidence regarding the date of the exodus by proposing that some tribes never went to Egypt but rather entered Canaan before the tribes that sojourned in Egypt. But this theory contradicts the evidence that the twelve tribes acted together in the wilderness and in the conquest of Canaan.

Connected with the exodus were certain mighty acts of God. The plagues, showing Yahweh's control over the forces of nature, finally persuaded Pharaoh to let the Israelites leave Egypt. The opening of the RED SEA by a strong E wind to let the Israelites cross and the destruction of the pursuing Egyptians by the returning waters were further evidences of God's hand in the deliverance of Israel. The Red Sea which the Israelites crossed is literally the Sea of Reeds (*yam-sûp*), and the equivalent of this name was given by the Egyptians to one of the lakes or marshes on the NE border of Egypt. This lake, which has not yet been finally identified, was probably the site of the Israelites' crossing, rather than any portion of what is now called the Red Sea.

For the Israelites, the important thing about the exodus was not the date or the place, but the fact that God had delivered them from bondage and had called them to be his special people with a unique role in history. This great event was commemorated each spring in the PASSOVER festival.

Moses was the leader of the Israelites both in the exodus and in the wandering in the wilderness. As an Israelite of the tribe of LEVI, he was naturally able to sympathize with the sufferings of his own people. As the adopted son of Pharaoh's daughter, he was brought up in the royal court and was fitted to speak to the king on behalf of the Hebrews. Moses would know Egyptian art, literature, law, and methods of administration. He would also know the many gods of Egypt, and he must have heard of the Aten monotheism, which had been introduced a few generations before by AKHENATEN (but which disappeared with the latter's death because it had not reached the common people). Furthermore, Moses' years with the Midianites in Sinai gave him a knowledge of the topography of the wilderness and of the Arab tribes there, an experience that served him well as he later led the Israelites through that same wilderness.

III. Wandering in the wilderness (c. 1280–1240?). The route of the wandering is connected with the location of Mount SINAI, also called Horeb. Some have located Mount Sinai E of KADESH, but this conflicts with the tradition that the Israelites went to Sinai before Kadesh. Others have located Mount Sinai in NW ARABIA because Midianites lived there and because the phenomena at the giving of the law (fire, cloud, rumbling) are thought to

God brought Moses and the Israelites through the Sinai mountains following the exodus from Egypt.

indicate a volcanic eruption, which has taken place in that area. But the Midianites were nomadic, and the fire, cloud, and rumbling could betoken a thunderstorm. The above two locations of Mount Sinai would imply that the Israelites crossed the Peninsula of Sinai along a northern route.

The traditional identification of Mount Sinai with Jebel Musa in the *southern* part of the Peninsula of Sinai agrees with suggested identifications of MARAH, ELIM, DOPHKAH, and REPHIDIM on the way to Mount Sinai, and with a possible identification of HAZEROTH on the way N from Mount Sinai. Also the time recorded for the journey from Egypt to Mount Sinai and from Mount Sinai to Kadesh agrees with this location of the mount. If this traditional location of Mount Sinai is accepted, the Israelites made their way by stages southeastward near the shore of the Peninsula of Sinai and then turned inland to Dophkah, Rephidim, and Mount Sinai.

One problem with the wandering in the wilderness is the large number of Israelites thought to be involved. The usual translation of Exod. 12:37, "about six hundred thousand men on foot," implies a total population of two and a half million. In addition to "thousand," however, the Hebrew term *ʾelep* H547 can also mean "clan" or "family." The latter meaning would reduce the total to a reasonable and manageable number. Others consider the number a mere exaggeration or believe that it is the number of a much later census.

Several of the miraculous provisions for the food and water of the Israelites in the wilderness are related to actual conditions in the Peninsula of Sinai. The MANNA agrees in many respects with the sweet, white exudations of scale insects on the tamarisk bushes that abound in parts of Sinai. When migrating QUAIL reach land after crossing the Mediterranean in the fall, or the Red Sea in the spring, they often fall exhausted and are easily captured, as they were by the Israelites. Under the soil and rocks of the wilderness there is sometimes water waiting to be tapped (cf. Exod. 17:3–6; Num. 20:11).

The Israelites had hostile contacts with some of the nomadic inhabitants of the wilderness and friendly relations with others. At REPHIDIM they struggled successfully with Amalekites (see AMALEK) over the use of the spring there. On the other hand, JETHRO, the priest of MIDIAN and Moses' father-in-law, came to visit Moses and joined with him in worship of Yahweh. He also gave the good advice to appoint elders to adjudicate lesser cases, while Moses retained jurisdiction over the most serious cases. See ELDER (OT). Later HOBAB the Midianite agreed to guide the Israelites through the wilderness as they proceeded from Mount Sinai.

The first goal of the Israelites was Mount Sinai, the mountain of God, where Moses had received God's call to liberate the children of Israel. There Moses now received moral, civil, and religious laws, as well as directions for the TABERNACLE, a portable tent-shrine. The basic TEN COMMANDMENTS, written on stone tablets, were placed in the ARK OF THE COVENANT, a sacred box similar to the palladium carried by Arab tribes in ancient and modern times. At Mount Sinai also the Israelites made a COVENANT with Yahweh to worship him alone and to keep his laws.

The second focus of the wandering, Kadesh, was also a holy place, which is the meaning of its name. Near this site in northeastern Sinai there are three springs, and this area was Israel's center for many years. From Kadesh spies were sent N into Canaan, and then an expedition entered the land, but was defeated at HORMAH. At Kadesh, Moses and his brother AARON the priest had to deal with various revolts against their civil and religious authority. After most of the generation that left Egypt had died, and when the new generation had been united and hardened by the wandering life in the desert, the Israelites finally set out from Kadesh to enter the land which they believed God had promised to their ancestor Abraham and to them.

IV. The conquest of Canaan (c. 1240–1200). The Israelites approached Canaan from the SE and therefore conquered and settled territory E of the Jordan first. They did not attack EDOM or MOAB, because of ancestral relationship to these nations. SIHON, the AMORITE king whose capital was HESHBON, refused to let the Israelites pass and was defeated by them at JAHAZ near MEDEBA. As a result the Israelites occupied much of the land between the ARNON and JABBOK Rivers. They did not attack the the people of AMMON to the E who were related to them. As they pressed northward,

Og, the giant AMORITE king of BASHAN, opposed them at EDREI, but was defeated. Thereupon the Israelites occupied his kingdom from the Jabbok River northward to Mount HERMON. This conquered territory of TRANSJORDAN was settled (a) by the tribe of REUBEN in the southern part, E of the DEAD SEA and N of the Arnon River, (b) by GAD in the center, S and N of the Jabbok River, and (c) by a branch of MANASSEH in the northern part, E of the Sea of Galilee. The soldiers of these two and a half tribes agreed to help in conquering the land W of the Jordan.

Moses continued to be the leader of the Israelites during the conquest of Transjordan, but JOSHUA was the commander of the army in battle. Finally Moses died on Mount NEBO after viewing, but not entering, the land to the W of the Jordan. As liberator, leader, lawgiver, and prophet, he was the founder and former, under God, of the nation of Israel. The leadership of the people during the conquest and settlement of the W devolved upon Joshua, who had long been assistant to Moses. Joshua and CALEB were the only spies who encouraged the people to enter Canaan years before when they were at Kadesh. Now he and Caleb were the only ones who came out of Egypt as adults and who also entered the land.

In order to enter CANAAN proper, the people had to cross the river JORDAN. The waters of the river stopped at a town named Adam so that the people could walk across the river bed. See ADAM (PLACE). It is recorded that in the years A.D. 1215, 1906, and 1927 the high bank opposite Adam fell into the Jordan, temporarily damming the water. So some have suggested that, as in the crossing of the Red Sea, God used natural means with wonderful timing to help the Israelites to go forward.

West of the Jordan, the Israelites first attacked JERICHO, which guarded the valleys leading up into central Canaan. The city was defended by walls, but these fell as the Israelites marched around them. The Israelites spared only RAHAB and her family, because she had sheltered Israelite spies who had visited the city. The Israelites then made their way up a valley and on the central ridge attacked AI. They were repulsed in their first attempt, but in their second attack they lured the inhabitants out of the city and were victorious. By these initial victories in central Canaan, Joshua prevented the N Canaanites from joining those in the S.

Joshua then called the people to sacrifice to Yahweh on Mount EBAL in the center of Canaan. Since there is no reference to a capture of SHECHEM at the foot of Mount Ebal, some have deduced that Israelites were already living there before Joshua came, but there is no direct evidence for this. To the S, the Gibeonite confederacy, including the cities of GIBEON, KEPHIRAH, BEEROTH, and KIRIATH JEARIM, made a peace treaty with the invaders. The Gibeonite ambassadors pretended to come from afar and so not to be of the inhabitants of Canaan, whom the Israelites considered under the ban of destruction.

The kings of five cities in the S—JERUSALEM, HEBRON, JARMUTH, LACHISH, and EGLON—now joined to attack the Gibeonites because they had allied themselves with the invaders. Joshua drove the southern coalition from Gibeon and down the valley of AIJALON on the famous long day of battle. The Israelites were then able to capture many cities in the S one by one. Excavations at Lachish, Eglon, and Debir show that these cities were destroyed in the later 13th cent. Having taken cities in central and southern Canaan, Joshua was free for a campaign in GALILEE in the N. There he captured the city of HAZOR, which excavations have shown was destroyed in the 13th cent.

Then representatives of the tribes were gathered at the central city of Shechem, and portions of the land were assigned to the twelve tribes. Reuben, Gad, and part of the tribe of Manasseh had already been settled E of the Jordan. In western Canaan, Simeon was located in the extreme S, and then going northward were the portions of Judah, Dan, Benjamin, Ephraim, part of Manasseh, Issachar, Zebulun, Asher, and Naphtali. To the Levites (assistant priests) were assigned cities W and E of the Jordan, and to the priests (descendants of Aaron) were given cities in Simeon, Judah, and Benjamin. This assignment of territory illustrates the tribal organization of the Israelites.

By the latter part of the 13th cent., the Israelites were settled in many parts of Canaan. That Israel was in Canaan by this time is confirmed by Pharaoh MERNEPTAH's stela of about 1230 listing Israel among the nations he overcame in Canaan. This

A view of Mount Ebal, looking N from Mount Gerizim. Joshua gathered the Israelites in this valley to allot their tribal inheritances in the Promised Land.

boast of Merneptah's, which is not mentioned in the Bible, may be based on an Egyptian campaign which had no lasting effects. The lists of captured cities in Israelite hands show that important cities, especially in the plains and lowlands, were still under Canaanite control. West of the Jordan, Israel was largely limited to the central mountains.

V. The period of the judges (c. 1200–1020). The judges of Israel were not so much officials who decided judicial cases as special leaders who saved their people in times of danger from surrounding nations. The judges were of different tribes and were active in different areas, and some of them must have been contemporaneous with one or more of the others. Also some of the oppressions by other nations in different areas may have been contemporaneous. Therefore, if the years of the judgeships and of the oppressions are simply added, the sum would be much longer than the actual time involved between Joshua and Samuel.

The Canaanites in the N under JABIN of Hazor and his general SISERA tried to subdue the Israelites. A judge and prophetess, DEBORAH, summoned the Israelite tribes to send soldiers to throw off the Canaanite yoke. Six of the northern tribes responded, and the Israelite forces were led by BARAK. Sisera deployed his iron chariots, said to be 900 in number, on the plain of ESDRAELON near the river KISHON. A torrential rain caused the Kishon to overflow, and the Canaanite chariots were mired or swept away. The Israelites, who had no chariots, came down from Mount TABOR and defeated the Canaanites. This victory was celebrated in the Song of Deborah (Jdg. 5), which most scholars think was composed shortly after the event.

Another serious threat came from the Midianites, who made raids riding on camels from the eastern deserts, and seized the crops and the herds of the Israelites. This is the first known example of the use of the CAMEL in warfare. In response to God's call, GIDEON, who was known for his opposition to BAAL worship, summoned men from his own tribe of W Manasseh and other northern tribes. By the use of torches and trumpets at night, the Israelites terrified the Midianites and drove them eastward across the Jordan.

The most persistent danger to Israelite independence came from the PHILISTINES. Like the Israelites, they were recent invaders; soon after the Israelites came from the desert to the SE, the Philistines came by sea from the NW, particularly from CRETE. They belonged to a group of Aegeans, whom the Egyptians called the SEA PEOPLES, who attacked the shores of Egypt at the same time and are depicted on the walls of Ramses III's

(c. 1175–1144) temple at Madinat Habu in western Thebes. The Philistines established themselves in cities near the coast of Canaan, particularly in GAZA, ASHKELON, ASHDOD, EKRON, GATH, and also S of GERAR and in DOR. The Philistines brought with them the secret of smelting IRON, giving them a superiority over the Israelites, who had weapons and tools of COPPER and BRONZE. The Philistines forced the tribe of DAN to move from its original location between Judah and Ephraim northward into Galilee near one of the sources of the Jordan. The influence of the Philistines is indicated by the fact that after their coming Canaan was often called PALESTINE, that is, the land of the Philistines.

Several Israelite leaders tried to resist the Philistines. The exploits of SHAMGAR and the herculean feats of SAMSON in killing Philistines or burning their fields were on an individual basis and did not remove the Philistine dominance. Finally the Israelites attempted a pitched battle with the Philistines at EBENEZER. They summoned HOPHNI and PHINEHAS, the corrupt sons of ELI, the priest of the central Israelite sanctuary at SHILOH, to bring the sacred ark to insure an Israelite victory. Nevertheless, the Philistines were victorious, killed Hophni and Phinehas, seized the ark (which they later returned), and destroyed Shiloh, as evidenced by excavations there. The Philistines established garrisons to control the Israelites, who became their vassals. SAMUEL, a judge and priest who had been trained by Eli at Shiloh, called the people back to God and led them to a victory over the Philistines at MIZPAH, thus restoring a measure of independence to Israel.

The period of the judges was one of alternate IDOLATRY and return to the Lord, of periodic dominance by surrounding nations, and of tribal disunity as evidenced by the war between BENJAMIN and the rest of the tribes. There was need for a strong, centralized government if Israel and its faith were to survive. ABIMELECH, the son of Gideon, tried to establish a monarchy, but he lacked prophetic and popular support, and his attempt died with his death. See JUDGES, PERIOD OF.

VI. The united monarchy (c. 1090–922).

A. Saul (c. 1020–1000). When Samuel grew old, the elders of Israel asked him to appoint a king to give them political unity and military leadership against their enemies. Samuel saw the wish for a king as a rejection of his authority as well as God's, and warned that a king would curtail their liberties. Finally Samuel consented, and SAUL of the tribe of Benjamin was chosen by lot as king. Samuel drew up a constitution stating the rights and duties of the king.

Saul showed his military ability by victories over the Ammonites E of the Jordan, the Philistines in central Palestine, and the Amalekites who had invaded the S. Saul also built a fortified palace at GIBEAH, which has been excavated, the most impressive structure built by Israelites up to that date.

Saul's later years were embittered by disagreements with Samuel and other priests, and by his jealousy of the young officer DAVID. The latter gained fame by killing the Philistine giant, GOLIATH, and was a close friend of Saul's son, JONATHAN. Saul's attempts to kill David forced the latter to become a wandering outlaw with a band of followers in Judah and eventually to take temporary service in the army of the Philistine ruler of GATH.

The Philistines, whom Saul had driven from the highlands, extended their control along the Valley of JEZREEL as far as BETH SHAN, which oversees the route from the Jordan to the W. This movement of the Philistines cut off the northern tribes from contact with the rest of Israel. Saul led his army to Mount GILBOA, where the Philistines were victorious and killed Saul and Jonathan. The bodies of the Israelite king and his son were displayed by the Philistines on the wall of BETH SHAN, and Saul's armor was placed there in the temple of the goddess Ashtaroth, which has been excavated.

B. David (king of Judah c. 1000–994, king of all Israel c. 994–961). It was David who completed the work that Saul had begun in uniting the Israelites and in defeating their enemies, and David went on to found a little empire that controlled the surrounding nations. After the defeat and death of Saul, his son ISH-BOSHETH was made king in GILEAD E of the Jordan, and David was recognized as king in Judah, making his capital at HEBRON. After the assassination of Ish-Bosheth, the elders of northern Israel invited David to become the king of all the tribes, as Saul had been.

David's first move as king of all Israel was to capture JERUSALEM from the Jebusites (see JEBUS) and to make it his capital. This action helped to allay tribal and sectional jealousies, because Jerusalem had not belonged to any Israelite tribe and lay on the border between Judah and the N. Furthermore, David had the sacred ark transported to Jerusalem, a move that made that city the religious as well as the political center of the nation.

David's genius as a leader was illustrated in Israelite victories over the surrounding nations. In a reversal of fortune, the Philistines were forced back to their original cities and became vassals of Israel. MOAB and AMMON to the E, the Aramean kingdoms of ZOBAH and DAMASCUS to the N (see ARAM), and EDOM to the SE were also subdued and included in David's empire. With TYRE, David was on friendly terms. Within Israel, David had to cope with various rebellions, one of them led by one of his own sons, ABSALOM. The rebellion of SHEBA revealed a sectional jealousy between N and S that boded ill for the continuing unity of Israel.

David's cultural activities included building a palace in Jerusalem and gathering material for the temple to be built by his son. He composed many psalms and is said to have organized the Levitical liturgical singers and musicians for WORSHIP. Excavations show that in his time iron became plentiful in Israelite cities, since the Philistine monopoly on the use of this metal had been broken.

C. Solomon (c. 961–922). SOLOMON, born of BATHSHEBA, David's favorite wife, acceded to the throne, although he was a younger son. After his coronation Solomon killed his older brother ADONIJAH, who had aspired to the crown, and also killed or exiled Adonijah's supporters. In spite of this bloody beginning, Solomon's reign was noteworthy, not for military, but for cultural and economic developments.

Solomon's building enterprises were amazing in view of the limited resources of Israel. The most famous building by Solomon was, of course, the TEMPLE of Yahweh in Jerusalem. Solomon employed Phoenician craftsmen to build it and to make its furniture and utensils, the bronze pillars that stood before it, and the great bronze basin for water. The temple itself was built of great stones, and the interior walls were lined with cedar and covered with gold leaf. In the Holy of Holies was the ark, protected by gold-plated statues of cherubim, above which the invisible Yahweh was thought to be enthroned. The construction of the temple took seven years, and Solomon took thirteen years to construct his own palace.

Solomon also constructed administrative buildings and palaces for his many wives. By this building program he extended the city of Jerusalem northward. Outside of Jerusalem, Solomon's building activity is known from excavations in MEGIDDO, GEZER, EGLON, and EZION GEBER. At Megiddo new walls, gates, and forts were constructed. At Ezion Geber the Solomonic structures formerly thought to be smelters are now recognized as storehouses, doubtless connected with Solomon's commerce through that port.

The wealth to support Solomon's building enterprises came more from international commerce than from rocky Palestine. With the cooperation of HIRAM, king of TYRE, Solomon built a merchant fleet at Ezion Geber, which brought back gold, silver, ivory, apes, peacocks, almug wood, and precious stones from the E. Among the products sent out from this port was probably copper, which was mined and smelted in the Arabah Valley S of the Dead Sea. Solomon also traded in Egyptian and Cilician horses and Egyptian chariots. The purpose of the visit of the QUEEN OF SHEBA to Solomon was not only to hear his proverbial wisdom, but also to trade. Solomon imported cedar wood for his buildings from Tyre, and he repaid with olive oil, grain, and some cities in northern Israel. One reason that Solomon was able to control and profit from the commerce between E and W was that neither Egypt nor Assyria was trying to dominate Palestine at that time.

Solomon's building and luxury were also supported by tribute from the subject nations his father had conquered, from heavy taxes on the Israelites, and from levies of forced Israelite laborers. To secure these taxes and levies of workers and to organize the government Solomon divided the country into twelve districts, each of which had a governor. These districts did not coincide with the territory of the twelve tribes, a break with the tribal traditions.

ISRAEL, HISTORY OF

Ruin of the royal palace at Samaria, a city destroyed by the Assyrians in 722 B.C.

Solomon's activities brought magnificence to Jerusalem, but roused discontent in many quarters. Leaders in Edom and Syria revolted. Furthermore, many Israelites themselves, particularly in the N, resented the heavy taxes, the forced levies of workers, and the favored position of Judah. The prophets objected to the introduction of the worship of foreign gods that came to Jerusalem with Solomon's foreign wives. Solomon had a reputation for WISDOM and he composed many proverbs, but his later policies were not wise, for they harmed his people, his religion, and his dynasty.

VII. The separate kingdoms of Israel and Judah (922–722). REHOBOAM, Solomon's son and successor, by trying to carry on the oppressive policies of his father, precipitated the secession of northern Israel. JEROBOAM, the spokesman of the northern tribes, had earlier been superintendent of workers under Solomon, had been encouraged to lead a revolt of the northern tribes by the prophet Ahijah, and had fled to Egypt in fear of Solomon. When Rehoboam arrogantly refused to mitigate the taxes and forced labor, the northern Israelites seceded and chose Jeroboam as their king.

After this break (c. 922), the two kingdoms continued a separate but interrelated existence for 200 years till the fall of SAMARIA in 722. The northern kingdom—including the territories of Ephraim, W Manasseh, Asher, Zebulun, Issachar, Dan, and Naphtali, which were W of the Jordan, as well as the Transjordan territories of E Manasseh, Gad, and Reuben—was larger than the southern kingdom, which included only Judah, Simeon, and Benjamin. The northern kingdom was also richer both agriculturally, because of its plains, and commercially, because of the international trade routes running through it. The southern kingdom was more mountainous and more isolated.

For the same reasons, however, the northern kingdom was also more open to foreign cultural and religious influences as well as to foreign conquest. The southern kingdom was more provincial, more faithful in maintaining the religion of Yahweh, and it continued an independent existence for a century and a half after the fall of the northern kingdom. Stabilizing factors in the S were the one Davidic dynasty, the one capital, Jerusalem, and the temple, housing the ark, which symbolized Israel's original covenant with Yahweh. In the N there were nine dynasties, violently replacing each other, three different capitals, and two shrines at BETHEL and DAN (PLACE), which lacked symbolic connection with Israel's religious traditions.

Jeroboam I (c. 922–901) made his political capital at SHECHEM, which had been a national center in the time of Joshua. He felt the need of religious centers to keep his people from making pilgrimages to Jerusalem in the S. Therefore he set up golden calves in Bethel and Dan, perhaps under the influence of the animal gods he had seen in Egypt during his exile there in Solomon's time. See CALF, GOLDEN. Since Yahweh was worshiped at these shrines, some have suggested that the calves were considered as pedestals for the invisible God. The prophetic writers condemned these images. During the reign of Jeroboam in Israel, and of Rehoboam (c. 922–915) in Judah, Pharaoh SHISHAK invaded Palestine. The biblical account of his plundering of Jerusalem is illustrated and amplified by Shishak's own list on a wall of the temple at Karnak listing the towns he captured both in Judah and in Israel.

BAASHA (c. 900–877) founded a new dynasty in Israel and moved the capital to TIRZAH. He fought with ASA of Judah (c. 913–873) over the border between them. Asa's fortification of the border town of MIZPAH is illustrated by the thick walls discovered there. ZERAH the Ethiopian, who was repulsed by Asa, was probably a leader in the Egyptian army. OMRI (c. 876–869) does not receive much space in the book of Kings, perhaps because he was not regarded as religiously important, but his political importance is indicated by the fact that a century later the Assyrians were still calling Israel "the land of Omri." Omri moved the capital of Israel to a new site, SAMARIA, which soon vied with Jerusalem in the beauty of its buildings. Omri cemented an alliance with Tyre by marrying his son AHAB to JEZEBEL, daughter of ETHBAAL, king of Tyre and Sidon. To the SE, Omri conquered Moab, as recorded on the MOABITE STONE.

Ahab (c. 869–850) continued the beautification of Samaria, building there an "ivory house" (1 Ki. 22:39 NRSV). This means that his palace's walls and its furniture were embellished with carved ivory inlaid panels, such as have been found in excavations there. In MEGIDDO, Ahab built tremendous stables with stalls for about 450 horses. Jezebel, Ahab's Phoenician wife, brought with her and encouraged the worship of BAAL and of the goddess ASHERAH. Such idolatry as well as Ahab's seizure of a private citizen's vineyard (see NABOTH) were condemned by the prophet ELIJAH.

Ahab was one of the leaders of a Syrian (Aramean) coalition that checked the advance of SHALMANESER III of Assyria in the battle of Qarqar in 853. According to Assyrian records, Ahab brought to this battle 2,000 chariots (more than any other Syrian contingent) and 10,000 foot soldiers. When they were not menaced by a common foe, Ahab and the king of DAMASCUS fought over the control of GILEAD. Finally the Syrians defeated and killed Ahab at RAMOTH GILEAD, though he was supported by JEHOSHAPHAT of Judah.

JEHORAM (c. 849–842), Ahab's son, tried with Jehoshaphat's help to quell a rebellion of Moab led by MESHA. The combined forces of Israel and Judah failed to capture KIR HARESETH, the Moabite capital. Mesha later commemorated the independence of Moab on the Moabite Stone.

The Divided Kingdom.

In Judah, Jehoshaphat's reign (c. 873–849) was marked by cooperation with Israel, as indicated above, and by internal religious reforms. He appointed judges in the cities and arranged for appeals to a supreme court in Jerusalem. He destroyed idols and pagan sanctuaries and sent out teachers of the law of the Lord. By defeating a coalition of Moabites, Ammonites, and Edomites, he reestablished Judah's control over Edom.

An Israelite general, JEHU (c. 842–815), supported by prophets, led a revolt against Jehoram. Jehu killed not only Jehoram, but also the latter's nephew, AHAZIAH king of Judah (c. 842), who was a grandson of Ahab. In executing judgment on Ahab's house, Jehu ordered the death of Jezebel, Ahab's widow, and of the brothers of Jehoram and of Ahaziah. He also killed the worshipers of Baal. Shalmaneser III's Black Obelisk shows Jehu bowing down before Shalmaneser, and the inscription states that Jehu presented tribute. In Jehu's later years, HAZAEL of Damascus took away from Israel the control of Transjordan.

Meanwhile in Judah, a daughter of Ahab, ATHALIAH (c. 842–837), was trying to wipe out the Davidic dynasty and to encourage Baal worship. After hearing that Jehu had killed her son Ahaziah, she seized power herself and killed her own grandchildren, except for a baby boy, JOASH, who was hidden in the temple. After six years, the high priest JEHOIADA had Joash (c. 837–800) crowned as king. Athaliah and MATTAN the priest of Baal were killed, and the temple of Baal was destroyed. Jehoiada gave Joash wise guidance while he was young. In his later years Joash turned to idolatry. The prophets saw it as God's judgment when the Syrians attacked Judah and plundered Jerusalem.

Both JEHOAHAZ (c. 815–801) and Joash (c. 801–786) of Israel continued to resist Aramean raids, which reached as far as an unsuccessful siege of Samaria itself. In this resistance to Syria, the kings of Israel were encouraged by the prophet ELISHA.

Jeroboam II (c. 786–746), the son of Joash, brought the kingdom of Israel to its greatest extent and prosperity. He not only recovered Transjordan from Syria, but also conquered Damascus itself. The material prosperity of Israel is illustrated by large buildings that have been discovered in Samaria, Megiddo, and Tirzah. But beside the great buildings in Tirzah, for example, are the remains of hovels, evidencing the injustice to the poor which the prophet Amos condemned. In Samaria from Jeroboam's time there have been found many tax receipts written on potsherds. These receipts indicate prosperity, and the names on the receipts are compounded not only with Yahweh, like Jedaiah, but also with Baal, like Elibaal, evidences of the combination of Yahwism and idolatry denounced by Hosea and Amos. One reason for the prosperity and expansion of Israel under Jeroboam was the absence of aggression from the great powers of Egypt and Mesopotamia.

Judah also prospered at this time during the long reign of UZZIAH, also called AZARIAH (c. 783–742). He defeated the Philistines on the W and the Arabs on the E, and he carried on his father Amaziah's work of subjugating Edom by rebuilding the port city of ELATH on the Gulf of AQABAH. Some scholars think he is the "Azriau of Yaudi" who, according to Assyrian records, headed a Syrian coalition opposing Assyria (see *ANET*, 282b).

In the latter 8th cent., Judah came under Assyrian dominance, but was not wiped out. AHAZ of Judah (c. 735–715) refused to join PEKAH of Israel and REZIN of Damascus in an alliance against Assyria. When the latter two kings attacked Jerusalem, the prophet ISAIAH urged Ahaz to trust in God for deliverance. Ahaz sent gifts to TIGLATH-PILESER of Assyria and asked his help. The Assyrians subdued both Syria and Israel and exacted tribute from Ahaz also. Ahaz forsook the worship of Yahweh and adopted an Assyrian type of altar.

Since the Assyrians came from the N, Israel more keenly than Judah felt the force of their expansion under Tiglath-Pileser III (c. 745–727). This king forced MENAHEM (c. 745–738) of Israel to pay tribute in 738. Pekah (c. 737–732) of Israel and Rezin of Damascus made an alliance to resist Assyria. Nevertheless in 732 Tiglath-Pileser captured Damascus and took away from Israel the Mediterranean coast to the W, Galilee in the N, and Gilead to the E, carrying many Israelites into exile. When HOSHEA (c. 732–724), the king of the remnant of Israel, refused to pay tribute to Assyria and turned for help to Egypt, Shalmaneser V of Assyria began the siege of Samaria.

VIII. The fall of Samaria (722). Samaria withstood the Assyrian siege for three years, but the city finally fell in 722, shortly before the death of Shalmaneser. His son SARGON doubtless assisted in the siege and claims credit for the capture of the city. Sargon states that he carried away captive 27,290 Israelites, and the Bible indicates that they were taken to NW Mesopotamia and to MEDIA. Hebrew names have been found in records at NINEVEH and Nimrud (CALAH), and the later story of TOBIT deals with Israelites who were settled in Nineveh and Media. In place of the deported Israelites the Assyrians introduced settlers from Babylonia and Syria who brought their idols with them. In time these pagan settlers were assimilated to the remaining Israelites and to Yahwism. So the later SAMARITANS were a mixture of Israelite and foreign elements and were therefore despised by the Judeans.

IX. The kingdom of Judah alone (722–586). In Judah, Ahaz was followed by HEZEKIAH (c. 715–687), who tried to throw off Assyrian control and tribute. He probably took part in the revolt against Assyria led by the Philistine city of Ashdod c. 711, for Sargon in his account of the suppression of this revolt states that he subdued the land of Judah. Hezekiah welcomed ambassadors of MERODACH-BALADAN of Babylon, who was also scheming to rebel against Assyria. Hezekiah strengthened Jerusalem's walls and dug a tunnel 1,777 ft. through solid rock to carry water from the GIHON SPRING to the Pool of SILOAM within the city walls, to insure the water supply during a siege.

Then Hezekiah led other Palestinian states in another rebellion against Assyria. In 701 SENNACHERIB of Assyria crushed this revolt, destroying forty-six cities in Judah, including LACHISH, whose siege is depicted in reliefs from Sennacherib's palace in Nineveh. Sennacherib's records claim that he besieged (but not that he took) Jerusalem and imposed on Hezekiah tribute including the exact amount of gold mentioned in the parallel account in the Bible. Isaiah assured the pious Hezekiah that Jerusalem would not be captured, and the biblical record states that "the angel of the Lord" slew many of the besieging Assyrians in the night. An Egyptian story preserved by HERODOTUS (*Hist.* 2.141), telling that at this time the Assyrian army was infested with mice, may indicate that bubonic plague was the means used by God to remove the Assyrian army from Jerusalem. Because of the mention of TIRHAKAH (born 710) as leader of the Egyptian army that tried to repulse the Assyrians, some scholars suggest that there may have been a second invasion by Sennacherib in Palestine about 688, but this is not clearly stated in the Bible or in Assyrian records. Within Judah, Hezekiah was known for his religious reforms and his return to the law of the Lord.

The tribute paid by MANASSEH (c. 687–642) is mentioned in Assyrian records. He must have tried to revolt, because the Assyrians carried him a prisoner to Babylon, which they controlled. The Chronicler sees this as a punishment for Manasseh's idolatry. After Manasseh repented and returned to the Lord, the Assyrians allowed him to return to his throne in Jerusalem.

JOSIAH (c. 640–609) introduced religious reforms, like Jehoshaphat and Hezekiah before him, but he was more thorough than they in removing local shrines and idols. These reforms were based on a book of the law found in the temple. Since Josiah centralized public worship and the observance of Passover in Jerusalem, and since the book of Deuteronomy stresses the one central sanctuary for sacrifice, many scholars have deduced that the book which was found was some form of Deuteronomy. Because Assyrian power was waning, Josiah was able to extend his control and the elimination of idolatry northward as far as Naphtali.

In 609 Pharaoh NECO went through Palestine to aid the Assyrians, who were hard pressed by the Babylonians. Josiah saw this move as a danger to his kingdom, and he opposed Neco's army at the pass of Megiddo in northern Israel. Josiah was defeated and killed, and the prophet JEREMIAH composed a lamentation for him. Neco was delayed by this battle, and the last Assyrian effort to repulse the Babylonians was defeated. With the extinguishing of Assyrian power, Neco took over control of Syria-Palestine. JEHOAHAZ (609), who succeeded Josiah, probably tried to follow an independent policy; Neco deposed him and took him captive to Egypt. Neco put his brother Eliakim in his place and gave him the throne name JEHOIAKIM (609–598).

After NEBUCHADNEZZAR of Babylon defeated Neco at CARCHEMISH in northern Syria in 605, Jehoiakim became a vassal of Nebuchadnezzar, and some of the Judean nobility, including DANIEL, were taken to Babylon. After the Egyptian army repulsed the Babylonians in 601, Jehoiakim revolted against Babylon, contrary to the advice of JEREMIAH. The Babylonians besieged Jerusalem, and Jehoiakim was taken captive and died.

JEHOIACHIN (598–597) succeeded to the throne of Judah during the siege of Jerusalem. In 597 the Babylonians finally took the city and seized treasures from the palace and temple. Jehoiachin was carried captive to Babylon with thousands of Jewish leaders, soldiers, and artisans. Records discovered in Babylon show that Jehoiachin and his family received regular rations from the Babylonian government. Nebuchadnezzar placed Jehoiachin's uncle Mattaniah on the throne of Judah, giving him the throne name ZEDEKIAH (597–587). After some years Zedekiah, disregarding the warnings of Jeremiah, revolted against Babylonia, relying on possible Egyptian help.

X. The fall of Jerusalem (586). Again Nebuchadnezzar invaded rebellious Judah. Letters on potsherds sent to the Jewish commander at Lachish illustrate the advance of the Babylonians as they captured town after town. Lachish itself was taken and burned. Jerusalem withstood the Babylonian siege for eighteen months. An Egyptian expedition to relieve Jerusalem was turned back. Eventually the Babylonians broke through the walls. Zedekiah tried to escape, but he was captured, blinded, and taken to Babylon. In August the Babylonians burned the city, including the temple, and broke down the walls. Some of the Jewish leaders were executed, and 852 others were taken to Babylonia. Only the poor were left to till the soil.

The Babylonians appointed a Jew, GEDALIAH, to govern Judah. At the instigation of the king of Ammon, Gedaliah was murdered together with some Babylonian soldiers. Fearing a reprisal, a group of Jews fled to Egypt, taking Jeremiah with them, though he objected to the move. In 582 the Babylonian reprisal was forthcoming in taking 745 more Jews as exiles to Babylonia.

XI. The exile (586–538). Though the EXILE is usually thought of as beginning in 586 with the fall of Jerusalem, it must be remembered that thousands had gone into exile from Israel in 735 and in 722 and from Judah in 597 and in 582. Furthermore, though the main body of exiles from Judah was in Babylonia, there were also exiles from Israel in northern Mesopotamia and in Media, and exiles from Judah in Egypt. In Babylonia the prophet EZEKIEL and other Jewish exiles lived at TEL ABIB on the River Kebar, a canal near the city of Nippur. Other places in Babylonia where Jewish exiles lived were TEL HARSHA, TEL MELAH, and CASIPHIA.

The prophet Jeremiah wrote to the exiles in Babylonia urging them to build houses, plant gardens, and live normal lives. The exiles were allowed to maintain some community organization headed by their own elders. Some Jews went into business and prospered. Daniel is said to have risen to the position of counselor to the king. EVIL-MERODACH (562–560), Nebuchadnezzar's son and successor, removed the exiled Jewish king Jehoiachin from prison and gave him residence in the royal palace in Babylon.

Jeremiah in writing and Ezekiel in person taught the exiles that the destruction of Jerusalem and the exile were Yahweh's punishments for their sins. They urged the exiles to keep faith in Yahweh in the midst of idolatry and held out the hope of return to Judah. The prophecies of the second part of Isaiah comforted the exiles with the assurance that God, the controller of history, would lead them out of Babylonia in a new exodus back to Zion, from which the faith in the one true God would spread to all nations.

XII. The Persian period (538–333). CYRUS king of PERSIA (c. 559–530) was regarded in the second part of Isaiah as an instrument appointed by God to deliver the Israelite exiles. In 539 the army of Cyrus took Babylon, and Babylonia and its dependencies were incorporated into the Persian empire. Cyrus followed a more tolerant policy toward subject peoples and their religions than that of Assyria or Babylonia. Throughout his empire Cyrus favored local cultural autonomy and respected local gods and their temples. The Jews also benefited from this policy, for Cyrus decreed that the temple of Yahweh, God of heaven, should be rebuilt in Jerusalem and that Jews wishing to return to Judah could do so.

SHESHBAZZAR, a prince of Judah and perhaps a son of Jehoiachin, was appointed governor of Judah. He led the first group of returnees. With them they carried, with Cyrus's permission, vessels of gold and silver which Nebuchadnezzar had taken from the temple in Jerusalem. On their arrival in Jerusalem, the returnees set up an altar and began the foundations of a new temple. They were suspicious of the racial purity and religious orthodoxy of the Israelites who had not gone into exile and refused to let them help in rebuilding the temple. These "people of the land" retaliated by urging the Persian authorities to halt the construction of the temple and the walls.

Another much larger group of Jewish exiles returned with ZERUBBABEL, who was a nephew of Sheshbazzar, and followed him as governor of Judah. With Zerubbabel came many priests and Levites led by the high priest JESHUA (Joshua). In 520 work was begun again on the temple with the encouragement of the prophets Haggai and Zechariah, and the permission of King DARIUS I (522–486). Finally in 515 this second temple of Yahweh in Jerusalem was completed.

The book of ESTHER indicates that there were Jews in many parts of the Persian empire during the reign of Ahasuerus, usually identified with XERXES I (486–465). The assembling of his military commanders and satraps in his third year (Esth. 1:3) may have been in preparation for his expedition against GREECE. A Persian record mentions an official in Xerxes' court at Susa (Shushan) named Marduka, who may be MORDECAI, the cousin and guardian of Esther. The Jewish feast of PURIM celebrates the deliverance of the Jews from their enemies as described in this book.

The prosperity of some of the Jews who continued in exile is illustrated by the business records of the Jewish bankers and traders, Murashu and his sons. These records come from Nippur and cover the second half of the 5th cent. This family traded in many commodities and services with Persians, Medes, Babylonians, Arameans, and fellow-Jews.

EZRA, a priest and scribe and perhaps the adviser for Jewish affairs at the Persian court, led several hundred more exiles back to Judah in the seventh year of ARTAXERXES (Ezra 7:7). Ezra was armed with a royal decree permitting Jews to return with him, commissioning him to reform religious life in Judah according to the law of God, and granting him money and vessels for the sacrificial worship in the temple at Jerusalem.

According to the traditional view that Ezra returned under Artaxerxes I (465–424), the date of his return would be 458. Some suggest that the king was Artaxerxes II (404–358), in which case Ezra's return would be in 398, but this dating contradicts several passages that make Ezra and Nehemiah collaborators (e.g., Neh. 8:1–2, 5–6, 9; 12:36). Others conjecturally emend "seventh" in Ezra 7:7 to "twenty-seventh" or to "thirty-seventh," keeping the identification of the king as Artaxerxes I, which would yield 438 or 428 as dates for Ezra's return. One of the arguments for placing Nehemiah before Ezra is that the "wall" of Ezra 9:9 seems to imply that Nehemiah's rebuilding preceded Ezra's arrival. On the other hand, "wall" may refer to a structure that was pulled down shortly before Nehemiah arrived, or more probably to "protection" (RSV; cf. NJPS, "giving us a hold") by the Persians, since the Hebrew word here (gādēr, fence) is not the usual one for a physical wall, and the whole district of Judah is said to be protected. The difficulties of the traditional order, Ezra then Nehemiah, seem to be less than the problems arising from the assumption that Jews, writing a few generations after the events, confused the order of the two most outstanding figures of their recent history.

Nehemiah, cupbearer to the Persian king, first came to Jerusalem as governor in 445, the twentieth year of Artaxerxes I. He had a commission from Artaxerxes I to rebuild the walls of Jerusalem with help and supplies from the Persian officials in the province called Beyond the River (i.e., Syria-Palestine beyond the EUPHRATES). This move to strengthen Judah was opposed by the Samaritans, led by their governor SANBALLAT, by TOBIAH, the Israelite governor of Ammon, and by GESHEM, identified in inscriptions as the king of the Kedarite Arabs in NW Arabia. Because of this opposition the Jews had to work on the walls under pressure and with weapons near at hand. Thanks to Nehemiah's planning and encouragement the walls were completed in fifty-two days. At the celebration of the Feast of Trumpets (Lev. 23:24–25, first day of the seventh Jewish month), Ezra with assisting Levites read to the people from the Hebrew law and interpreted, probably in ARAMAIC, the lingua franca of the time, adopted by the Jews in exile. Nehemiah was the first signer of a national covenant with God to obey the law, to avoid marriage with Samaritans and heterodox Jews, to observe the Sabbath and the sabbatical year, and to give tithes for the temple and the priests.

Nehemiah returned to the Persian court in 433, but soon afterward he was sent back to Judah for a second term as governor. This time Nehemiah busied himself with religious reforms: providing for the Levites, enforcing the Sabbath, and condemning marriages with pagans. Ezra and Nehemiah, with their emphasis on racial exclusiveness and on the ceremonial law, strongly influenced later Judaism.

The clash between Nehemiah and Sanballat widened the political and religious breach between the Judeans and the Samaritans. Nehemiah chased out of the temple a son of the high priest who had married a daughter of Sanballat. Some think that this incident is the same as that described by JOSEPHUS (*Ant.* 11.7.2; 11.8.2) but placed by him, perhaps through an error, a century later in the time of ALEXANDER THE GREAT. Josephus says that the expelled priest's name was Manasseh and that he officiated in a rival temple that Sanballat constructed on Mount GERIZIM for the Samaritans.

Fifth-century Aramaic records from ELEPHANTINE, an island in the Nile near Aswan in southern Egypt, show many aspects of the life of a Jewish garrison there employed by the Persians. In 419 the Jews there received a decree from Darius I, communicated through Hananiah of Jerusalem (perhaps Nehemiah's brother) and Arsames the Persian satrap of Egypt, about the observance of Passover. Later they wrote to Johanan, high priest in Jerusalem, to the sons of Sanballat, the governor of Samaria, and to Bagoas, the Persian governor in Judah, about the rebuilding of their temple in Elephantine. They agreed not to sacrifice animals in their new temple, because of Persian and Egyptian opposition to such sacrifice and because of the Jewish law limiting sacrifice to the central national sanctuary, the temple in Jerusalem.

Artaxerxes III (358–338) had to face serious revolts in Egypt, Syria, and Palestine. In 345 his armies destroyed Sidon and took captives from Judah to Hyrcania, SE of the Caspian Sea.

XIII. The Greek period (333–167). In 333 Alexander the Great (336–323) defeated Darius III (336–331) of Persia at Issus, near the border between Asia Minor and Syria. Then he made his victorious way conquering and receiving submission through Syria and Palestine. While he was besieging Tyre, Alexander sent to Jaddua, the high priest in Jerusalem, according to Josephus, asking auxiliary troops and provisions. Jaddua refused, saying that he had promised loyalty to King Darius. After Alexander had taken Tyre and Gaza, he headed for Jerusalem. Warned in a dream to submit, Jaddua went out peacefully to meet Alexander, who entered Jerusalem and offered sacrifices in the Temple. Alexander granted the high priest's request that the Jews should be allowed to follow their own religious laws and that the Jews of Judea should be exempt from taxation on the seventh, or sabbatical, year when they took no harvests. Some have questioned Josephus's story of Alexander's visit to Jerusalem, but elsewhere also Alexander visited local sanctuaries and respected local religious customs.

In the division of Alexander's empire among his generals, Palestine was assigned to PTOLEMY I (323–283) of Egypt, though SELEUCUS also wanted it. To establish his control of Palestine, Ptolemy had to conduct several campaigns there. He first took control of Jerusalem in 320, entering the city on the Sabbath, when the Jews made no resistance. He took many Jewish captives and settled them, some in ALEXANDRIA, some in CYRENE, and some he made garrisons in various cities of Egypt. In the Hellenistic period that followed, Jews scattered to many places, especially in the eastern Mediterranean countries. These settlements of Jews often became the seed plots for the early Christian church. In the time of Ptolemy I, the high priest in Jerusalem was ONIAS I. That the high priest was the political as well as the religious leader in Judea is shown by the fact that Onias made a treaty of friendship with the king of Sparta.

Ptolemy II (285–246) rebuilt and hellenized cities in Palestine, including Rabbah (now Amman) in Transjordan, which he renamed Philadelphia, and Acre (biblical Acco) on the northern coast, which he renamed Ptolemais. The correspondence of Zeno (the steward of Ptolemy II's minister of finance, Apollonius) shows that the family of Tobiah, an enemy of Nehemiah, was in charge of collecting taxes for the Ptolemies in Transjordan as it had been for the Persians. In Egypt, Ptolemy II freed the Jewish slaves who had been taken captive in his father's time.

A letter falsely attributed to ARISTEAS, an officer in Ptolemy II's court, gives a legendary story that Ptolemy sent rich gifts to the temple in Jerusalem and invited the high priest, Eleazar, to send six men from each of the twelve tribes to Alexandria. These seventy-two men are said to have produced a translation of the OT into Greek, called the SEPTUAGINT (LXX) in their honor. It is probably true that Ptolemy sent gifts to the temple in Jerusalem and that at least the PENTATEUCH was translated into Greek in Alexandria in his time. But the translation was probably produced by Alexandrian rather than by Palestinian Jews for the use of the numerous Greek-speaking Jews.

After Ptolemy III (246–221) lost a battle with Seleucus II of Syria, the high priest in Jerusalem, ONIAS II, who favored the Seleucids, withheld the payment of tribute to Ptolemy. Ptolemy threatened to send soldiers to dispossess the Judeans of their lands. Joseph of the Tobiah family (see TOBIAS #2) arranged with Ptolemy to take over the collection of taxes and the payment of tribute for Judea. Ptolemy IV (221–203) was able to keep control of Palestine by defeating ANTIOCHUS III (223–187) of Syria at Raphia on the border of Egypt in 217. After the battle Ptolemy tried to enter the temple in Jerusalem, but the high priest, SIMON II, prevented him. This Simon is given fulsome praise in the book of ECCLESIASTICUS (Sir. 50:21).

Finally in 198, in the battle of Paneas in N Palestine, Antiochus III defeated the army of young Ptolemy V, and Palestine became a part of the Seleucid empire. The people of Jerusalem welcomed Antiochus, who promised the return of Jewish war refugees to their homes, reduction of taxes, the right to follow their religious laws, help in the repair of the temple, and regular contributions to the expenses of the temple worship. The successors

Ptolemy II coin from Acco.

of Antiochus did not follow his benevolent policy toward Judea, however. For example, Seleucus IV (187–175), under the pressure of paying heavy tribute to Rome, tried, though without success, to get money from the temple in Jerusalem. His emissary Heliodorus entered the temple, but was beaten and frightened away.

Antiochus IV (175–162), in addition to encouraging Greek culture and customs in Judea, also tried to force Greek religion on the Jews. The high priest, Onias III, was murdered, and Antiochus sold the high priesthood to JASON and then to MENELAUS. In need of money for his wars, Antiochus robbed the temple in Jerusalem. Because of ensuing riots he sent an army which killed, plundered, and destroyed in Jerusalem. Jewish sacrifices and feasts were halted, copies of the Law were destroyed, and circumcision was forbidden. Finally the worship of Zeus Olympios was introduced in the temple, perhaps with the assumption that the supreme Greek god could be identified with Yahweh. Jews who refused to comply with these measures were tortured and killed. The nation of Israel and the monotheistic religion of Israel were in danger of extinction.

XIV. The Hasmonean period (167–163). The standard of Jewish revolt was raised by MATTATHIAS, a priest who lived in Modein, near Lydda, with his five sons: John, Simon, Judas, Eleazar, and Jonathan. Mattathias was the descendant of a priest named Hashmon, and therefore the members of his family were sometimes called HASMONEANS. Mattathias refused to offer sacrifice to a pagan god and killed the Syrian (Seleucid) officer who ordered the sacrifice and also a Jew who was willing to participate. Then Mattathias and his sons fled to the hills and were joined by some of the HASIDEANS (Hasidim, pious Jews).

After the death of the aged Mattathias, his son Judas (166–160) took the leadership of the revolt. Because of his skill in leading guerrilla attacks he was called MACCABEE, probably meaning "the Hammerer." While Antiochus was away with the main Syrian army fighting the PARTHIANS, Judas defeated several Syrian detachments. Finally LYSIAS, the regent of Antiochus, rescinded the orders proscribing Jewish religious practices. In Jerusalem, Judas removed pagan elements from the temple, rebuilt the altar of Yahweh, and rededicated the temple in December, 164. This event is memorialized in the Jewish feast of Hanukkah (DEDICATION).

Antiochus died in 163, and his successor, DEMETRIUS I, appointed ALCIMUS high priest in Jerusalem. Perhaps in disappointment at not being chosen high priest or in fear, Onias, son of the murdered Onias III, fled to Egypt. There he established a Jewish temple at Leontopolis, 10 mi. N of Heliopolis. In Judea, since religious freedom had been attained, some Jews stopped fighting; but Judas carried on the war to achieve political independence from Syria also. To secure foreign support, he made a treaty of friendship with the Romans, who were interested in weakening the Seleucid power. After some victories over the Syrians, he was finally defeated and killed at Elasa in 160.

Judas's brother, Jonathan (160–142), carried on the fight for independence. Because of internal struggles for power in Syria, many Syrian garrisons were withdrawn from Judea. One of the claimants for the Seleucid throne, Alexander Balas, appointed Jonathan high priest and then civil governor in Judea. Jonathan took control of several cities on the coast: Joppa, Azotus (Ashdod), and Ekron. A Syrian general, Trypho, offered to parley with Jonathan, but instead imprisoned and killed him.

SIMON MACCABEE, the last surviving son of Mattathias, took over the rule and high priesthood of Judea (142–134). Demetrius II, in return for Simon's aid against Trypho, who had usurped the Syrian throne, granted to Judea freedom from taxation, which meant practical independence. Simon renewed treaties with Sparta and Rome, and Rome warned the Ptolemies and the Seleucids to respect the independence of Judea. Simon drove out the last Seleucid garrisons in Judea, those in Gazara (Gezer) as well as the Acra fortress beside the temple in Jerusalem. The Jewish people in 140 declared Simon their ethnarch, or national ruler, with the right of succession for his descendants. Antiochus VI sent an army into Judea, trying to reestablish some Syrian control. Simon's sons, Judas and John Hyrcanus, led a Jewish force that defeated the Syrians and forced them to retreat. Except for this incident, Simon's rule was marked by peace and prosperity.

Early in the rule of John Hyrcanus (134–104), Simon's son and successor, Jerusalem was besieged by a Syrian army of Antiochus VII. Finally John Hyrcanus had to surrender and pay tribute. After Antiochus was killed fighting the Parthians, John was able to reassert Judean independence. He proceeded to expand his rule beyond the borders of Judea. East of the Dead Sea he captured Medeba. Then he subjugated the Samaritans, taking both Shechem and Samaria and destroying the Samaritan temple on Mount Gerizim. His northward conquests went as far as Scythopolis (Beth Shan). To the S he subdued the IDUMEANS (Edomites), who had moved into the NEGEV S of Judea after the capture of Jerusalem by the Babylonians. John compelled the Idumeans to be circumcised and to observe the Jewish religious laws.

John Hyrcanus ceased to support the party of the PHARISEES, because they said he should relinquish the high priesthood. The Pharisees carried on the tradition of the pious Hasidim, who had originally supported the Maccabean revolt. The Pharisees emphasized personal piety, study of the law, and observance of the details of traditional ceremonial requirements. John came to favor the SADDUCEES, because they supported him in his priestly as well as in his civil office. The Sadducees were the aristocratic priests who were concerned about the temple, its ritual, and its income.

Some coins of John Hyrcanus have been found at QUMRAN, indicating that the ESSENE community was there in his time or soon thereafter (see DEAD SEA SCROLLS). This monastic group withdrew from the world to copy and study the Scriptures and to perform religious rituals, including frequent ablutions. They considered themselves as preparing for the soon coming of the messianic prophet, king, and priest.

Aristobulus I (104–103) is said by Josephus to have taken the title of king. He conquered Galilee and forced the Gentile inhabitants to become Jews. Under Alexander Jannaeus (103–76), the power of the Hasmoneans reached its greatest extent, but their original religious purpose for the national good was replaced by personal ambition and cruel oppression. Alexander won territory E of the Jordan and cities on the SW coast of Palestine, but he had to fight almost continually with the Egyptians, the Syrians, or the Nabateans. The Pharisee party rebelled against him because of his lax performance of his high priestly duties. Josephus says that Alexander's troops killed 6,000 rioting worshipers in Jerusalem and that Alexander crucified 800 of the Pharisees who had opposed him.

Alexandra (76–67), the widow of Alexander Jannaeus, succeeded him as civil ruler. She appointed her son Hyrcanus high priest; another son, Aristobulus, was made commander of the army. Alexandra was known for her piety, and she favored the Pharisees, who sought revenge on those who had wronged them in the time of Alexander Jannaeus.

On the death of Alexandra, the ambitious Aristobulus II, with the help of the Sadducees, seized the throne (67–63). Hyrcanus, a mild and retiring person, conceded the high priesthood also to his brother Aristobulus. Antipater, an Idumean, persuaded Hyrcanus to seek help from the Nabatean king, ARETAS III. Hyrcanus and Aretas besieged Aristobulus in Jerusalem. The Roman general Scaurus, a lieutenant of POMPEY, forced Aretas to withdraw from Jerusalem. Aristobulus, Hyrcanus, and a delegation of Pharisees all appealed to Pompey, who was in the process of making Syria a Roman province. Pompey came to Jerusalem and captured the temple after a siege of three months. Aristobulus was sent to Rome to appear in Pompey's triumph. Judea came under the control of the Roman proconsul of Syria. The independence which the Maccabees so bravely won lasted only eighty years.

XV. The Roman period (63 B.C. to A.D. 135). Pompey took away from Jewish control the Greek cities E of the Jordan and Scythopolis (which formed a league called DECAPOLIS, "Ten Cities"), the cities of the coastal plain, and Samaria. Hyrcanus II was confirmed as high priest and leader of the Jewish nation with administration over Judea, Idumea, Perea beyond the Jordan, and Galilee. The real direction in the administration of these Jewish areas came from Hyrcanus's adviser, Antipater the Idumean. All of Palestine was under the oversight of the Roman governor of Syria, and the Jewish administrators of Judea had to come to terms with whatever Roman happened to be in power. The confusion in Palestine in the mid-1st cent. B.C. was due partly to internal factions and partly to changes in Rome and on the international scene.

When Pompey was defeated and killed, Antipater and Hyrcanus gave their allegiance to the victorious Julius CAESAR, who named Antipater procurator and Hyrcanus ethnarch. Antipater gave the administration of Judea to his son Phasael, and of Galilee to another son, HEROD. Herod distinguished himself by the suppression of brigands in Galilee. Aristobulus II and his sons Alexander and Antigonus made various attempts to regain power in Judea. After Antipater was poisoned in 41, his sons Phasael and Herod were appointed joint tetrarchs of Judea by Antony, who at that time controlled the eastern Roman provinces. In 40 the Parthians aided Antigonus the son of Aristobulus II to seize power in Judea. He forced Hyrcanus out of the high priesthood and ruled as the last Maccabean king and high priest 40–37, facing the growing challenge of Herod.

The Romans did not want an ally of Parthia in control of Judea and appointed Herod king of Judea in 40. With Roman help Herod finally overcame Antigonus and took Jerusalem in 37. Octavian, when he had defeated Antony and Cleopatra, gave to Herod the cities on the coast, as well as Samaria,

Jericho, and cities E of the Jordan. When Octavian had become emperor with the title Augustus, he gave Herod other territories E and N of the Sea of Galilee. So Herod finally controlled all of Palestine, except for the independent cities of the Decapolis and Ascalon.

Herod's building accomplishments, like those of Solomon, were truly remarkable, especially when the small size of Palestine is considered. He rebuilt much of the city of JERUSALEM and its walls. He also rebuilt SAMARIA, giving it the name *Sebaste* (corresponding in meaning to Lat. *Augustus*), and Strato's Tower, calling it CAESAREA, also in honor of Caesar Augustus. In JERICHO he constructed a winter palace, which has recently been excavated. For defense he built fortresses such as the HERODIUM, MASADA, and MACHAERUS. He also donated money for buildings, including pagan temples, in Tyre, Sidon, and even in Rhodes and Athens. His most famous building project was the new TEMPLE, which he began in Jerusalem c. 20 B.C. He used tremendous stones for the wall of the court, which can still be seen, marble for the temple itself, and gold on the domes. This was the temple that was often visited by Jesus and which he warned would soon be destroyed.

Herod sponsored not only Hellenistic architecture but also Greek literature. His court chronicler, Nicolas of Damascus, wrote a *Universal History*, on which Josephus drew for his histories. In his relations to his family, Herod showed jealousy, fear, and cruelty. Out of ill-founded jealousy he killed his favorite wife, Mariamne (MARIAMME), the granddaughter of Aristobulus II. Out of fear he killed three of his own sons. These characteristics are also shown in Herod's attempt to kill Jesus after the latter was born in Bethlehem toward the end of Herod's reign. Herod's physical accomplishments were great, but he was not loved.

Herod left Judea, Samaria, and Idumea to his son Archelaus, who ruled 4 B.C. to A.D. 6 (see HEROD IV). During his rule Joseph and Mary brought the young Jesus back from Egypt to live in Nazareth. After Augustus deposed Archelaus, this area was ruled by Roman procurators A.D. 6–41. The procurator during Jesus' ministry was Pontius PILATE (A.D. 26–36), who was finally removed for his cruelty to the Jews and the Samaritans.

Another son, Herod Antipas (see HEROD V), was given GALILEE and PEREA, which he ruled as tetrarch from 4 B.C. to A.D. 39. His marriage to his brother's wife, HERODIAS, brought the rebuke of JOHN THE BAPTIST, whom Antipas executed in the fortress-palace of Machaerus, according to Josephus. To marry Herodias he cast off his former wife, and her father, the Nabatean King ARETAS IV, waged war against him and took some cities in Perea. It was this Herod who examined Jesus in Jerusalem before the crucifixion.

A third son of Herod, Philip (see HEROD VI), was tetrarch of the territory N and E of the Sea of Galilee from 4 B.C. to A.D. 34. He made BETHSAIDA, the home of some of Jesus' disciples, his capital and gave it the added name Julias in honor of the daughter of Augustus. He rebuilt Paneas at a source of the Jordan and called it CAESAREA PHILIPPI, in honor of the Emperor TIBERIUS Caesar and of himself. Here PETER confessed that Jesus was the Messiah, the Son of God.

At the CRUCIFIXION of Jesus near Jerusalem most of the elements of Israel's history are represented: the Romans in Pontius Pilate who sentenced him, the Sadducean priests who resented his interference with moneymaking in the temple, the Pharisees who resented his teaching, the Jews

Roman helmet from the Tenth Legion (Fretensis), stationed in Jerusalem. Rome gained control of Israel in the 1st cent. B.C.

of the Dispersion in Simon of Cyrene, the family of Herod in Herod Antipas who examined him—but also the promises of Moses and the prophets that Jesus claimed to fulfill.

The Emperor CALIGULA made Herod Agrippa I (A.D. 37–44; see HEROD VII) king over the territory that had been ruled by Philip and over Abilene W of Damascus. Agrippa was the grandson of Herod the Great and the Maccabean princess Mariamne. The fact that he had Maccabean blood made him popular with the Jews. Agrippa's visit to Alexandria, through no fault of his, touched off a violent anti-Jewish riot there. The Alexandrian Jewish philosopher PHILO JUDAEUS, who interpreted the Bible in the light of Plato, headed an Alexandrian Jewish delegation to complain to Caligula about this riot. While Agrippa was in Rome, he persuaded Caligula to withdraw an order to set up the emperor's statue in Jerusalem, an action that would have precipitated a revolution. In A.D. 39 after the deposition of Herod Antipas, Caligula gave Galilee and Perea to Agrippa also. Finally in 41 the Emperor CLAUDIUS added Judea and Samaria to Agrippa's kingdom. The book of Acts, calling him only Herod, indicates that he wanted to please the Jews and therefore executed the apostle James and imprisoned the apostle Peter. Josephus confirms the biblical account of Agrippa's sudden and painful death at a celebration in Caesarea.

During this time, in the mid-1st cent., JUDAISM was prospering in Mesopotamia. A Jew, Asinaeus, rose to be governor of Babylonia under the Parthians. In Seleucia (near modern Baghdad) the thousands of Jews gained such power that there was a violent riot against them. In the little kingdom of Adiabene in NE Mesopotamia the royal house was converted to Judaism. Queen Hellena of Adiabene sent supplies to Judea in time of famine as did the Christians of Antioch through Barnabas and Saul. Helena's tomb can be seen in Jerusalem near St. George's Cathedral.

In A.D. 48 the right to appoint the high priest in Jerusalem was given to Agrippa II (see HEROD VIII). The Romans made him king of Chalcis in Syria two years later, and in the year 53 they gave him in exchange the territory N and E of the Sea of Galilee which his father had ruled. In 56 the Emperor NERO added Galilee and Perea to his kingdom. This Agrippa took part in the examination of PAUL, who paid tribute to his concern for Jewish affairs. Agrippa tried to prevent the Jews from revolting, and when the revolt came, he remained loyal to Rome who had given him his kingdom. He ruled these northern and eastern sections of Palestine until c. 93.

After Herod Agrippa I's death, Judea was again ruled by Roman procurators (A.D. 44–66). Two of the procurators are mentioned in the book of Acts, FELIX (52–60), who tried Paul when the latter was arrested by Jewish leaders, and FESTUS (60–62) who sent Paul to Rome for trial before Nero. Some

New Testament Israel.

of the procurators had little understanding of the Jewish religion and roused opposition by dishonoring Jewish customs and sacred places. Others like Gessius Florus (65–66) openly plundered towns and released brigands in return for bribes. There were repeated demonstrations and rebellions led by such persons as an Egyptian Jew (Acts 21:38) who promised his followers that the walls of Jerusalem would fall before them. The Romans crushed such rebellions with severity.

Finally in A.D. 66, after the procurator Florus had seized money from the temple treasury, widespread revolt broke out. The rebels killed the Roman soldiers in Jerusalem and defeated the forces of the Roman legate of Syria at Beth Horon, where Joshua and Judas Maccabee had won victories. In 67 Nero sent one of his best generals, VESPASIAN, with three legions to quell the revolt. Vespasian first defeated the Jewish forces in Galilee. He spared the life of the Jewish commander there, Josephus, who joined the Romans and vainly urged his countrymen to surrender. It was this Josephus who later wrote histories of his people including this very war. In 69 Vespasian was declared emperor, and he departed for Rome, leaving his son TITUS to complete the subjugation of Judea. In April of the year 70, Titus began the siege of Jerusalem. Finally the temple was burned on August 27, according to Josephus, the anniversary of its burning by the Babylonians in 58 B.C. Thousands of Jews were killed or sold into slavery. Rather than surrender, the garrison of MASADA, the last Jewish fort to fall, committed mass suicide.

After a Jewish revolt in Cyrenaica in A.D. 115, a fresh revolt broke out in Judea in 132 over a decree forbidding circumcision. BAR KOKHBA, who was regarded as a messianic figure, was the leader of the Jews. This name, "son of the star," may have been an epithet, for some of his letters, recently discovered, give his name as Simon ben Kosiba. In the year 135 the Romans captured and destroyed Jerusalem, as they had in 70. This time the emperor HADRIAN rebuilt the city, naming it Aelia Capitolina, and decreed that no Jew should enter it. The political history of ancient Israel was at an end. The religious fruits of that history, during which monotheism was preserved, continue in scattered Jewish communities, including modern Israel and in the worldwide Christian church, which has sometimes called itself the new Israel. See WARS, JEWISH.

(Significant surveys include R. Kittel, *Geschichte des Volkes Israel*, 3 vols., 6th ed. [1923–29]; W. O. E. Oesterley and T. H. Robinson, *A History of Israel*, 2 vols [1932]; H. M. Orlinsky, *Ancient Israel* [1954]; G. Ricciotti, *The History of Israel*, 2 vols. [1955]; J. Bright, *Early Israel in Recent History Writing* [1956]; W. F. Albright, *From the Stone Age to Christianity*, 2nd ed. [1957]; M. Noth, *The History of Israel*, 2nd ed. [1960]; J. A. Thompson, *The Bible and Archaeology* [1962]; F. F. Bruce, *Israel and the Nations* [1963]; H. J. Flanders et al., *People of the Covenant* [1963]; R. K. Harrison, *Old Testament Times* [1970]; B. Halpern, *The Emergence of Israel in Canaan* [1983]; R. B. Coote and K. W. Whitelam, *The Emergence of Early Israel in Historical Perspective* [1987]; E. H. Merrill, *Kingdom of Priests: A History of Old Testament Israel* [1987]; N. P. Lemche, *Ancient Israel: A New History of Israelite Society* [1988]; J. A. Soggin, *An Introduction to the History of Israel and Judah*, 2nd ed. [1993]; W. C. Kaiser, *A History of Israel: From the Bronze Age through the Jewish Wars* [1998]; P. McNutt, *Reconstructing the Society of Ancient Israel* [1999]; J. Bright, *A History of Israel*, 4th ed. [2000]; M. Avi-Yonah, ed., *A History of Israel and the Holy Land*, rev. ed. [2001]; V. P. Long et al., eds., *Windows into Old Testament History: Evidence, Argument and the Crisis of "Biblical Israel"* [2002]; I. Provan et al., *A Biblical History of Israel* [2003]; J. M. Miller and J. H. Hayes, *A History of Ancient Israel and Judah*, 2nd ed. [2006].)

J. ALEXANDER THOMPSON

Israel, kingdom of. See ISRAEL, HISTORY OF.

Israel, religion of. Hebrew religion was unquestionably unique in character in the ANE. From geographical origins in MESOPOTAMIA it was gradually fostered through the patriarchal period until it assumed its normative covenantal character at SINAI. The subsequent history of Hebrew religion to the EXILE was one of periodic relapse from covenantal ideals, followed by prophetic exhortations and occasional revivals of religion. The IDOLATRY that was responsible for the deterioration of Israelite faith was purged by the exile, and in the postexilic period, a theocratic religious community in Judea gave rise to the JUDAISM of the immediate pre-Christian period. The religion of Israel is distinctly historical in nature, founded on the mighty acts and revelations of God in definite times and places. More than a series of events, however, this religion is a complex of beliefs about God and his relationships. Therefore the last part of this article summarizes Israel's central religious beliefs.

    I. Religious attitudes in ancient Mesopotamia
    II. Patriarchal religion
        A. Divine names
        B. Covenants
    III. Religion in the time of Moses
        A. Theological laws
        B. Ritual laws
        C. Ethical and civil laws
    IV. Religion during the conquest and settlement of Canaan
        A. Circumcision
        B. Holy war
        C. Renewals of the covenant
        D. Special leaders
        E. The conflict of Yahwism and idolatry
        F. The shrine at Shiloh and the ark
    V. Religion during the united monarchy
        A. Religion under Saul
        B. Religion under David
        C. Religion under Solomon
    VI. Religion in the northern kingdom
        A. Jeroboam's golden calves
        B. Elijah
        C. Elisha
        D. Micaiah
        E. The revolt of Jehu
        F. Amos
        G. Hosea
        H. Religious interpretation of the fall of Samaria
    VII. Religion in the southern kingdom
        A. Rehoboam
        B. Asa
        C. Jehoshaphat
        D. Athaliah
        E. Joash and Jehoiada
        F. Ahaz
        G. Isaiah
        H. Micah
        I. Hezekiah
        J. Manasseh
        K. Josiah
        L. Zephaniah
        M. Nahum
        N. Habakkuk
        O. Jeremiah
        P. Jehoiakim
        Q. Zedekiah
    VIII. Religion during the exile and the restoration
    IX. The rise of Judaism
    X. Israel's main religious beliefs
        A. God's revelation, acts, qualities, and nature
        B. God's relationships
        C. Israel's duty to God
        D. The future
        E. Conclusion: Permanent and temporary in the religion of Israel

I. Religious attitudes in ancient Mesopotamia. From the standpoint of method, any attempt to study the religion of the Hebrews must be grounded firmly in an awareness of the nature and functions of ANE religions generally. This is necessary because the ANE was coterminate with the world of the OT, and its religious concepts and ideals had a continuous bearing on those of the Hebrew people. It is also extremely important to see Hebrew religion in the wide geographical, historical, and cultural setting to obtain a correct perspective with regard to ideas of its growth. Scholars in the 19th cent. who studied the subject usually followed an evolutionary methodology popularized by J. Wellhausen. According to them, the mature Israelite faith grew from the animism and totemism that was attributed to patriarchal WORSHIP, and, under the influence of the literary prophets, developed slowly into ethical MONOTHEISM.

This approach, which leaned heavily on Hegelian philosophy and on the concept of biological evolution current in the mid-19th cent., stood in marked contrast to the OT view of Hebrew religion that attributed monotheism to the earliest of the Hebrews, placing the appearance of ethical concepts at an early rather than a late stage in Israelite religious history. On the basis of a vastly wider range of historical, archaeological, and religious information than was available during the first three decades of the 20th cent., it is now possible for the religion of the Hebrews to be correlated with its counterparts in the ANE at each phase of development for purposes of comparative study and proper methodology. Most important, it can now be asserted that the prehistory of Hebrew religion is to be sought, not in primitive or late BEDOUIN sources, but in the mature cultures of the ANE.

Archaeological excavations have made abundantly clear that the oriental world had left such practices as animism for centuries before the Hebrew patriarchs came on the historical scene, and that the animism or polydemonism in which they and their pagan contemporaries were thought by earlier scholars to have indulged were nothing more than the survivals of religious conservatism from the Neolithic period. Accredited temples dating from the end of the 5th or the beginning of the 4th millennium B.C. have been unearthed from the Ubaid period at Tepe Gawra, Eridu, Uruk and elsewhere, from which were recovered rough models of animals, along with human figurines, generally of the female, with exaggerated sexual characteristics. A similar shrine from the prepottery Neolithic at JERICHO was found to contain some plastic studies of groups of human beings, probably of a family. These artifacts suggest that an animistic phase had long since passed, and this conclusion is further strengthened by the highly developed polytheism that typified Mesopotamian and Egyptian religion in the 3rd millennium B.C.

By this time, the Mesopotamian nations had applied categories of personality to the great cosmic powers that comprised their pantheon, and were venerating them in temples that were thought of as their earthly residences. Furthermore, they had abstracted the concept of divinity from the divine beings of the pantheon, and were already associating it with all that they knew to be of positive value in social relationships. The desirability of positing a single head for any complex organization had led them to infer the existence of a single power behind the manifold operations of the universe. The high god in charge of the cosmos was known to the Egyptians as RE, the sun deity, whereas for the Sumerians of Erech it was An, the god of heaven, who was so worshiped. In Canaan, the supreme being was the god EL, whose offspring BAAL wielded executive power over gods and men alike.

As far as their votaries were concerned, each of these high gods embodied goodness and power in social relationships, making it evident that a comparatively sophisticated cultural and religious situation prevailed in the ANE long before the patriarchal period. Babylonian thought viewed happenings as individual events, with the result that the phenomena involved were given qualities of personality and will. Because natural occurrences were thought of in terms of human experience, the confrontation with the forces of nature or environment involved a mode of cognition far beyond that normally attributed to animism. In Babylonia, this attitude was most fully expressed in the yearly *akitu* festival, which was intended to secure an identification with the ruling powers of the cosmos and an assurance of blessing and fertility for the land. Even this procedure went far beyond the animism of the Neolithic period in its emphasis and intent.

The same is true regarding totemism, of which Egyptian religion used to be held up as a prime example, but which on examination has none of the characteristic features of totemism as found in Australian, African, or North American forms. If the existence of a genuine totemistic phase in Egyptian religion is suspect, there are even more reasons for denying it to Mesopotamian religion, where there is almost no association whatever of the names of deities with animals or plants. Certainly as far as the sophisticated culture of the late 3rd and early 2nd millennia B.C. was concerned, the original significance of any possible animistic survivals had been long obscured with the passing of time.

II. Patriarchal religion

A. Divine names. The evidence furnished by both biblical and extrabiblical texts of the 2nd millennium B.C. shows that patriarchal religion was of a distinctive variety, and different in character from the pagan forms of contemporary society. The deity of the PATRIARCHS was the personal God of the clan chief, as indicated by such archaic titles as "the God [shield?] of Abraham" (Gen. 31:53, cf. 15:1), "the Fear [kinsman] of Isaac" (31:42, 53), and "the Mighty One [champion] of Jacob" (49:24). The patriarchal deity was the unseen head of the clan whom the individual patriarch had undertaken to serve, and who was expected to bestow his blessings on the land. The deliberate choice of God by each successive generation of patriarchs represents an extremely ancient religious concept, which is thoroughly consistent with the OT tradition.

The patriarchs also worshiped God under the name EL, a general Semitic designation for deity, which appeared frequently in Hebrew personal names. This situation has been paralleled in Mesopotamia during the Old Akkadian period (c. 2360–2180 B.C.) and also in the AMORITE names occurring between 2100 and 1600 B.C., the latter dates embracing the period of ABRAHAM, ISAAC, JACOB, and JOSEPH. In Palestine the patriarchs worshiped God under such ancient pre-Israelite appellations as EL SHADDAI (Gen. 17:1), which may have meant "god of the mountains," EL ELYON ("God Most High," 14:18), and EL-ROI ("the God who sees me" [?], 16:13; cf. also El Olam or "Eternal God," 21:33 [see *DDD*, 288–91]). These were not intended primarily as place names, and the extent to which they became associated with the localities where the revelations took place is highly debatable. The patriarchs believed that their God was not confined to one specific area, but was instead the object of veneration of a family that stood in a special relationship of obedience and faith to him.

Although the Genesis narratives convey the general impression that the patriarchs followed a monotheistic religious tradition, it appears from other sources (e.g., Josh. 24:2) that they were still to some extent involved in Mesopotamian polytheism. There seems to be no warrant from the PENTATEUCH for the view that Abraham originated the concept of monotheism, or that he formulated a monotheistic cult within the framework of his own semisedentary society. However, Genesis makes it apparent that Abraham was the ancestor of a nation that was destined to become monotheistic. The patriarchs were consistently represented as objects of divine revelation (cf. Gen. 12:1, 7; 15:1), who were convinced of the need for a personal relationship with their God, characterized by faith and obedience. On such a basis, the patriarchs could confidently expect their God to protect them and meet their material and spiritual needs. When they had been given divine guidance on specific matters they had no choice but to obey the revealed will of God (cf. ch. 22). The closeness of this relationship with the deity led them to commemorate divine beneficence in the names of some of their children (16:11; 30:13; et al.), and in the designations of some areas where a revelation from God had been received (16:14; 32:30; 35:15; et al.). The forms of worship employed in the patriarchal period included SACRIFICE and the offering of PRAYER to God (12:8; 26:25; et al.).

B. Covenants. Contractual agreements of various kinds were a common feature of ANE life, ranging from international treaties to COVENANTS made between individuals for private purposes. In the case of Abraham (Gen. 12:1–3), God made an unconditional promise to bring him into a new land, increase his offspring, and make him a blessing to others. Indeed, pagan nations would have cause to bless themselves because of the influence of Abraham, a theme that was continued in Deut. 28:1–14. A subsequent covenant instituted by God was of a more particular and detailed nature (Gen. 17:2–14), and provided that God would make of Abraham a mighty nation, protecting him and his descendants in Canaan in return for their undivided allegiance and worship. On this occasion, the rite of CIRCUMCISION was adopted to mark out specifically those who were members of the covenant family. This act seems to have been of great significance in designating the ancestors of Israel as a distinctive unit, since it is known that, in contrast to the Egyptians, the peoples of Babylonia did not practice circumcision.

III. Religion in the time of Moses. In calling MOSES, God identified himself as "the God of your father, the God of Abraham, the God of Isaac and the God of Jacob" (Exod. 3:6). Thus the God of Moses is the same God who promised to bless Abraham's descendants (Gen. 12:1–3), to bring them out of Egypt, and to give them the land of Canaan (15:13–21).

Then, in response to Moses' request, God revealed his name, "I AM [WHO I AM]" (Exod. 3:14; see GOD, NAMES OF; I AM). Then the name is given as *yhwh* **H3378** (v. 15), in the third person form of the verb, probably originally vocalized *Yahweh*, "he is," or "he causes to be." The new name revealed to Moses became the name of God most used by the Israelites. In time, as fear of frivolous use of the sacred name increased, the title *ʾădōnāy* **H151**, "my Lord," was substituted by Jews in reading the Bible. This practice, at least as old as the Septuagint rendering (Gk. *kyrios* **G3261**, "Lord") is followed by most English versions, which render *yhwh* as "the Lord."

Several times in the call of Moses, God refers to Israel as "my people" (e.g. Exod. 3:7, 10). Israel's special relation to God is also expressed by the figure "firstborn son" (4:22). Among the blessings which Israel is chosen to receive are the knowledge of God (6:7), deliverance from slavery in Egypt (3:8), the privilege of worshiping God (3:12), and possession of the land of Canaan. God delivered the Israelites from slavery in Egypt—that was the pivotal event in the national and religious life of Israel. The exodus demonstrated God's election of Israel for a special historical and religious purpose. This act of deliverance showed that God cared about Israel (Exod. 3:7) and that he was able to control the forces of nature (7:14—12:30; 13:21—14:29) and the army of Pharaoh to accomplish his purpose. Thereafter Yahweh for Israel was the one who brought them out of the land of Egypt, out of the house of bondage (20:2).

The form of God's covenant with Israel at Sinai has been illustrated by the study of Hittite suzerainty treaties coming from about the time of Moses (see Treaty). In these treaties the Hittite king reminds his vassals of his benevolent acts toward them (cf. Exod. 20:2), the requirements the king imposes are stated (cf. 20:3–17 and the other laws of the Pentateuch), vassals are to appear before the king each year bringing tribute (cf. Deut. 26:5–10), a copy of the treaty is to be placed in the temple and periodically is to be read publicly (cf. 31:9–13), and blessings are pronounced for those who keep the treaty and curses for those who break it (cf. chs. 27–28). Finally, the covenant at Sinai was sealed by a sacrifice whose blood was sprinkled on the altar and on the people establishing a bond of relationship between God and Israel (Exod. 24:6–8). The laws that Israel must observe to maintain the covenant with God occupy much of the Pentateuch (from Exod. 20 through Deut. 30).

A. Theological laws. The commandments of the Decalogue (Exod. 20:1–17; Deut. 5:6–21; see Ten Commandments) teach that God is one (in contradistinction to the many gods of the other nations), that he only is to be worshiped, that he cannot be represented by an image made and manipulated by human beings, that God's name is not to be used lightly or profanely or for false swearing or magic, and that he is the Creator of all. The Decalogue also gives some of God's attributes: he is a jealous God who brooks no rival; he is a judge who punishes those who hate and disobey him; he is merciful to those who love him and keep his commandments. These laws certainly teach monolatry for Israel; monotheism (that there is only one real God) is implicit in the Mosaic laws. Some trace the origin of the Israelite belief in one God to Egyptian Atenism or to the Kenite religion (of which very little is known), but according to the Bible Moses received the knowledge of the one Yahweh by direct revelation.

B. Ritual laws. (1) *Sacrifices* might be called enacted prayers (Ps. 141:2). The placing of the offerer's hand on the head of the animal to be sacrificed (Lev. 1:4) seems to indicate that the offerer identified himself with the animal, which became his representative and substitute. The symbolism of the sacrifices included Atonement (sin and guilt offerings), communion and thanksgiving (peace offering), dedication (burnt offering). Incense later was interpreted as symbolizing prayer (Ps. 141:2; Rev. 8:3–4). Some, following Wellhausen, have considered this scheme of sacrifices too complex for the time of Moses, but the discovery of related names for various sacrifices among the people of Ugarit has given support to the antiquity of the Mosaic sacrificial laws. See Sacrifice and Offerings.

(2) *Purification.* Some things which the laws classified as ceremonially unclean or defiling were a dead body (Num. 19:11–22), skin diseases including leprosy (Lev. 13–14), secretions connected with reproduction and childbirth (Lev. 12; 15), and various animals, particularly animals of prey (Lev.

11; Deut. 14). Ceremonial UNCLEANNESS resulting from the above causes debarred a person from public sacrificial worship. Cleansing from uncleanness was effected by water (Lev. 15:5, 8, 10–11), sacrifice (Lev. 12:6–8; 14:10–32; 15:14–15), blood (Lev. 14:25), or fire (Num. 31:23). These laws helped to keep Israelites separate from idolaters. Ceremonial cleanness is connected with the HOLINESS of God and with the holiness which he demands from his people (Lev. 11:45). Later the language of ceremonial cleansing was applied to moral and spiritual PURITY (Ps. 51:7). See CLEAN.

(3) *The Tent of Meeting and its furniture.* At the heart of the Tent of Meeting was the ARK OF THE COVENANT, which contained the stone tablets of the Ten Commandments, the basic requirements of the covenant. The tent reminded the people of the covenant, it illustrated both the availability of God and his holiness, and it served as the center for public sacrificial worship in which the people met with God. Some have suggested that this tent was only an imaginary half-size retrojection of Solomon's TEMPLE, but the study of portable shrines in ancient Egypt and of tent shrines among the Carthaginians and Arabs has persuaded many scholars of the essential historicity of Israel's tent shrine in the wilderness. See TABERNACLE.

(4) *Priests.* The primary duty of the priests was to perform various rituals in the WORSHIP at the central shrine. For example, the priest placed on the altar the blood and parts of the sacrifice brought by individuals (Lev. 1:5, 8) and he also performed the daily morning and evening general sacrifice (Exod. 29:38–42). Only the priests could enter the holy place of the tent, where they presented the bread of the Presence (see SHOWBREAD), supplied oil for the lamps, and offered incense. Second, the priests were to teach the people all the statutes that the Lord had spoken to them through Moses (Lev. 11:10; Deut. 33:10). Finally, the priests acted as judges in difficult cases (Deut. 17:8–9, 12). In general the function of the priest was to serve as a mediator between the people and God.

The first high priest was AARON. The high priest was to manipulate the URIM AND THUMMIM, which were kept in a pouch of his breastpiece (Exod. 28:30). These were small objects used to discover the Lord's will, especially for the nation and its leader (Num. 27:21). Another distinctive duty of the high priest was to enter the holy of holies on the Day of Atonement to sprinkle on the cover of the ark the blood of the sin offering to make atonement for the people (Lev. 16:11–16). See ATONEMENT, DAY OF.

The Levites were men of the tribe of Levi but not priests of Aaron's line. They were to carry the tent and its furnishings as the people journeyed, to

Reconstruction of the tabernacle from the time of Moses.

set it up when the people encamped, and to guard it (Num. 1:47–53; 3:25–37). They were also to assist the priests in the rituals (Num. 3:6–9), and they might be called assistant priests. Some have thought that the distinction of different grades of priests did not arise till the time of Ezekiel, but in Egypt, Mesopotamia, and Ugarit there were hierarchies of high priest, priests, and assistants before the time of Moses. Therefore such a hierarchy in the Mosaic laws certainly is possible and even to be expected. See PRIESTS AND LEVITES.

(5) *Holy days.* The command to keep the SABBATH is included in the Decalogue, which links human work (six days) and rest (seventh day) to God's working in CREATION and then resting (Exod. 20:11); in addition, the social significance of rest for servants is emphasized by the reminder that the Israelites were servants in Egypt (Deut. 5:15). The feast of PASSOVER and Unleavened Bread was instituted at the time of the exodus (Exod. 12:1–28); the sacrifice of a lamb and the presentation of a sheaf of the FIRSTFRUITS of barley

acknowledged God as the giver of flocks and crops (Lev. 23.3-14). There are many reminiscences of the Israelites' escape from Egypt in the observance of this feast. The Feast of Weeks (PENTECOST) was primarily a celebration of the wheat HARVEST (Exod. 23:16; Lev. 23:15–21); Jews later connected it with the covenant (perhaps 2 Chr. 15:10–12) and the giving of the Law at Sinai (*b. Pesaḥim* 68b).

At the Feast of Booths, as at Passover and Weeks, all adult male Israelites were supposed to gather at the central sanctuary for celebration and worship; this was the final harvest thanksgiving festival (Exod. 23:16; (Lev. 23:33–43). The people lived in booths during the week of the feast in memory of the booths their ancestors had lived in after coming out of Egypt. On the basis of certain psalms (Ps. 47; 93; 95–99) some scholars have connected with this feast a celebration of the enthronement of Yahweh on a Babylonian model, but most students question such an observance in Israel. See FEASTS.

The Day of Atonement (Lev. 16:1–34; 23:26–32) was the only fast of the Mosaic law. On this day the high priest sprinkled the blood of a goat on the cover of the ark to make atonement for the sins of the people. Then he confessed over another goat the sins of the people and sent this goat into the wilderness to AZAZEL. Perhaps Azazel was a demon of the wilderness, and sending the goat to him may have symbolized removing sins to their evil source. Some followers of Wellhausen have proposed an exilic origin for the Day of Atonement, but now many scholars recognize ancient elements in this ritual which may well go back to Mosaic times.

So the holy days of Israel served to remind them of their history, their blessings, their sins, and above all of Yahweh, their covenant God, their Deliverer, their Provider, and their Forgiver.

C. Ethical and civil laws. The covenant required duties not only to God, but also to human beings (Exod. 20:12–27; Deut. 5:16–21). The Mosaic civil and ethical laws came from God and are constantly related to him, his righteousness, his judgment, and his mercy. These laws in the Decalogue include a positive command to respect one's parents as well as various prohibitions: murder (implying respect for the human person created in the image of God), adultery (respect for the unity of husband and wife as ordained by God, and sexual relations within marriage only), stealing (respect for the owner of objects he uses for his livelihood or for his enjoyment), false witness (respect for one's neighbor, whose name, property rights, and life should be maintained by true witness before the judge and God), and coveting. This last prohibition goes beyond ethical law to the psychological and theological source of sin—a person's desire for something that is not rightfully his. Most of the Mosaic civil laws can be classified under these commandments of the Decalogue. The Mosaic laws of the covenant may be summarized in LOVE for God (Deut. 6:5) and love for your neighbor as yourself (Lev. 19:18; cf. Matt. 22:34–40).

Though the Israelites at Sinai had pledged to obey these laws (Exod. 19:5–6; 24:7–8), they broke the covenant by making and worshiping the golden calf (ch. 32; see CALF, GOLDEN). Some have interpreted the calf as another god, such as Apis, the bull god of Egypt, and thus a breaking of the first commandment against other gods. Since the worship of the calf was part of a feast to Yahweh (32:5), others think that the calf was intended as a pedestal on which the invisible Yahweh stood, a breaking of the second commandment against worshiping images. When Moses came down from the mountain, he broke the tablets of the Decalogue as a sign that Israel had broken the commandments of the covenant. Levites killed many of the worshipers of the calf, and the Lord sent a plague on the people. After Moses' intercession (32:31–32) and the mourning of the people (33:4), a new copy of the Decalogue was provided, and God renewed the covenant with them (34:1–28). This story illustrates the waywardness of man, the sureness of God's punishment on those who break the covenant, and his grace in renewing the covenant. Some have regarded this story as a retrojection of JEROBOAM's golden calves (1 Ki. 12:28–29), but it is questionable whether Israelites would have invented a story that cast such a blot on their ancestors in the wilderness and on Aaron.

IV. Religion during the conquest and settlement of Canaan. This was not only a period of military conflict between Israel and the Canaanites but also of spiritual conflict between the imageless worship of the one Yahweh and the idolatrous worship of the many gods of Canaan.

A. Circumcision. As the Israelites entered Canaan, they renewed the covenant with God by observing the rite of circumcision (Josh. 5:2–9). This sign of the covenant went back to Abraham (Gen. 17:9–14). They had practiced it in Egypt, as did the Egyptians, but not in the wilderness (Josh. 5:4–7), though it is required in Exod. 12:48 and Lev. 12:3. From the time of their entrance into Canaan, circumcision was practiced by the Israelites and distinguished them from the uncircumcised PHILISTINES (Jdg. 14:3; 15:18). Circumcision was also a symbol of spiritual cleansing (Deut. 10:16).

B. Holy war. The conquest of Canaan and Israel's defensive wars under the judges were wars of Yahweh, holy wars. Those who fought in such wars were sanctified in a state of ritual purity (Josh. 3:5). Sacrifices were offered before battle (1 Sam. 7:9), and God was consulted (Jdg. 20:23, 27). Sometimes the ark was with the army as a sign of God's presence (Num. 10:35–36; Josh. 3:6; 6:6). In the battle Yahweh fought for Israel (Josh. 10:14, 42), sometimes using the forces of nature (10:11) and throwing the enemy into confusion (Jdg. 7:22). Everything captured was dedicated to God; for example, after the taking of JERICHO the captured people and animals were slaughtered, combustible objects were burned, and metals were put in the treasury of the sanctuary (Josh. 6:18–24). The reason behind such destruction was that pagans left alive might lead the Israelites into idolatry (Deut. 7:16; Num. 33:55). Sometimes unmarried women (Num. 31:14–18), cattle, and movable goods (Deut. 2:34–36) were divided among the victors.

C. Renewals of the covenant. At Mount EBAL, JOSHUA gathered the people for a renewal of the covenant including sacrifice, writing the law upon stones, reading the law, and the pronouncement of blessings for obedience and curses for disobedience—all in the presence of the ark of the covenant (Josh. 8:30–35). Similarly at SHECHEM, in Joshua's old age, the covenant was again renewed with a recital of God's past dealings with Israel, a call to serve the Lord, the people's promise to obey God, the recording of the covenant, and its memorialization by a stone (Josh. 24:1–27). Such covenant renewals gave religious unity to the confederacy of the twelve tribes of Israel. That there was at SHECHEM a temple of BAAL BERITH ("Lord of the Covenant," Jdg. 9.4) may indicate that there was a covenant-making tradition there.

D. Special leaders. (1) The judges were leaders called by God to rouse and defend the people. They were endowed by God's Spirit with courage, wisdom, and strength for military leadership against Israel's enemies (Jdg. 3:10, 6:34, 14:19). See JUDGES, PERIOD OF. In addition, some of them did judge legal cases, like DEBORAH and SAMUEL. Some of the judges were religious reformers, destroying idols (Jdg. 6:25–32) and calling people to repent and turn back to the Lord (1 Sam. 7:3–9). Two judges were also priests, ELI and Samuel.

(2) The NAZIRITES were people dedicated to God. For the period of their vow they were not to shave or to drink wine or to cut their hair (Num. 6:1–21). SAMSON (Jdg. 13:4, 5) and Samuel (1 Sam. 1:11, 28) were life-long Nazirites according to the vow of their parents.

(3) The PROPHETS began to give religious leadership during the period of the judges. Among them were Deborah (Jdg. 4:4), Samuel (1 Sam. 3:20), and some unnamed prophets (Jdg. 6:7–10; 1 Sam. 2:27–36). In the time of Samuel there were bands of prophets who used the playing of musical instruments to induce a state of ecstasy (1 Sam. 10:5–6, 10). In Samuel's day a prophet was called a seer (9:9), and as one gifted with clairvoyance Samuel could tell SAUL where the lost donkeys were (9:20). The prophet also was called a man of God (1 Sam. 2:27; 9:6). Of course, the basic work of the prophet was to give God's word of reproof or warning (Jdg. 6:7–10; 1 Sam. 2:27–36; 3:11–18) or of encouragement (1 Sam. 7:3).

F. The conflict of Yahwism and idolatry. Even before entering Canaan, at SHITTIM in TRANSJORDAN, some Israelites had been lured into the worship of BAAL PEOR. These Israelites also indulged in promiscuity with Moabite women, for sacred PROSTITUTION was part of Canaanite worship. This idolatry and adultery were punished by execution of the offending Israelites (Num. 25:1–9).

At OPHRAH the angel of the Lord appeared to GIDEON at a sacred tree and received Gideon's sacrifice (Jdg. 6:11–23). Then Gideon built an altar to the Lord which he called Yahweh Shalom, "the LORD is Peace" (v. 24). There too was Gideon's father's pagan altar to Baal and beside it the wooden

Asherah figures carved into a Canaanite altar.

symbol of Baal's consort, the goddess ASHERAH. According to the Lord's command, Gideon pulled down the altar of Baal and cut down the symbol of Asherah (6:25–32). Later however Gideon himself made a golden EPHOD and deposited it at the shrine in Ophrah (8:29). The ephod was perhaps a sacred garment holding the sacred lots that were used to discover God's will. This golden ephod itself was worshiped, an example of how objects can become idols.

The priests of the shrine at DAN (PLACE) were Levites, descendants of Moses himself (Jdg. 18:30). Presumably Yahweh was worshiped at this shrine, but in it was an image, an ephod, and TERAPHIM. Teraphim probably were small images of household gods (Gen. 31:19, 34) used in divination (Ezek. 21:21). Here Canaanite idolatry had contaminated Yahwism.

F. The shrine at Shiloh and the ark. At SHILOH the Tent of Meeting was set up (Josh. 18:1). Thereby Shiloh became the religious center for the Israelite tribal confederacy or amphictyony. There were, of course, other local shrines, for example, at Gilgal, Shechem, Ophrah, Dan, and Mizpah. At Shiloh an annual vintage festival was observed, perhaps the Feast of Booths or Ingathering (Jdg. 21:19). To the sanctuary at Shiloh the family of Samuel made an annual pilgrimage (1 Sam. 1:3). The boy Samuel served in the sanctuary there with Eli the high priest. To Samuel God gave the warning of coming judgment on the priestly house of Eli because of the sins of his two sons (1 Sam. 3:10–15). After defeating the Israelites in the battle of APHEK, the Philistines destroyed Shiloh and the shrine of Yahweh (1 Sam. 4:3, 4; Jer. 7:12).

Eli's sons carried the ark from the shrine at Shiloh with the Israelite army to the battle of Aphek. The Philistines defeated the Israelites, killed Eli's sons, and captured the ark. The ark was taken to various Philistine cities, in each of which plague broke out. Also in Ashdod the image of the grain god DAGON fell down and broke before the ark, a sign of Yahweh's superiority over the gods of the Philistines. Finally the Philistines in fear sent the ark back to the Israelites. It was kept at KIRIATH JEARIM till the time of David (1 Sam. 5; 6).

V. Religion during the united monarchy. At first Samuel opposed the people's request for a king like the surrounding nations. Taking a human king would be rejecting Samuel and the charismatic judgeship and ultimately rejecting God as King. Samuel warned the people that a king would reduce their liberties, take them as servants, and tax them to support his own luxury (1 Sam. 8:7–18; 10:18–19; 12:17). Finally Samuel helped in making SAUL king and drew up a constitution stating the rights and responsibilities of the king (10:25). Probably some of Samuel's regulations for the king were similar to the law of the king in Deut. 17:14–20. There it is stipulated that the king should be chosen by God, that he should not depend on horses or alliances for security, that he should avoid luxury, and that he should rule in the fear of God, remembering that his subjects are his brothers. On the basis of royal psalms (e.g., Ps. 2; 72; 110), some have thought that the king was considered divine in Israel as he was in Egypt. But divine kingship is contrary to Israelite conceptions of God as the Creator and Ruler, of human beings as the created subjects of God, and of the king as limited by a constitution and by prophetic criticism.

A. Religion under Saul. God's selection of SAUL was shown in the revelation to Samuel and in controlling the lots. Saul was anointed with oil, a symbol of spiritual empowerment, and shortly thereafter he joined some prophets in ecstatic prophesying (1 Sam. 10:9–13). Samuel's relations with Saul changed from initial support to rejection. Saul failed to wait for Samuel, according to appointment, to offer sacrifices at GILGAL. Samuel warned that because of this disregard for him as God's representative God would put another king in Saul's place (13:8–14). Later, Saul again did not completely carry out God's command through Samuel to destroy all the possessions and people of the Amalekites. Because of this disobedience Samuel declared that God had rejected Saul from being king (1 Sam. 15).

Saul's relations with the priests also deteriorated. At the battle of MICMASH the high priest was with Saul, and Saul sought the guidance of God through the sacred lots manipulated by the priest (1 Sam. 14:18–19, 37, 41). Later Saul killed the priests of NOB and their families because they had given hospitality and weapons to David, whom they regarded as still in Saul's employ (22:11–19). When Saul received no further guidance by dreams, by the sacred lots, or by prophets, he sought advice from a medium as a substitute for God (28:3–25). Saul himself had banned mediums and wizards following the law of Lev. 20:27 and Deut. 18:10–11 (see DIVINATION). His acceptance of the medium's report of the appearance of Samuel at least shows a belief in a personal, conscious future life.

B. Religion under David. By the time DAVID became king (c. 1000 B.C.), he himself had had a variety of religious experiences. He believed that God had chosen him to be king, that God had enabled him to overcome GOLIATH and other enemies of Israel, that God had delivered him from jealous Saul, and that God finally had made him king and given him a much larger kingdom than Saul's. Later, David also experienced prophetic condemnation when NATHAN convicted him of the double sin of adultery with BATHSHEBA and the murder of her husband URIAH. According to the heading of Ps. 51, David truly repented and experienced God's forgiveness. The psalms that are most surely David's (e.g., Ps. 3; 4; 7; 8; 11; 18) show strong confidence that God will help him, deliver him from his enemies, and guide him in the right way.

Through Nathan came the announcement of God's covenant with David (1 Sam. 7:4–17). God promised to give David rest from all his enemies, to establish the kingdom of David's son who would build the TEMPLE, and to make sure forever David's royal line and kingdom. This promise was the basis for the hope for the royal Messiah, the ideal king of the Davidic house. David made JERUSALEM the religious as well as the political capital of Israel. He brought the ark from Kiriath Jearim to Jerusalem (2 Sam. 6). Guided by God, he purchased a threshing floor just N of the city and designated it as the site for the future temple (2 Sam. 24:18–25; 1 Chr. 22:1). David also gathered materials for the temple (1 Chr. 22:2–19; 29:1–9), organized its functionaries and singers (23:2–4), and gave to Solomon a plan for its construction (28:11–19).

C. Religion under Solomon. At the beginning of his reign (c. 961 B.C.), SOLOMON deposed ABIATHAR as high priest and replaced him by ZADOK (1 Ki. 2:26–27). In the contest for the successor to David, Abiathar had backed ADONIJAH (1:25), while Zadok had supported Solomon (vv. 38–39). Thereafter the priests at Jerusalem were regularly descendants of Zadok (2 Chr. 31:10; Ezek. 40:46).

Solomon hired HIRAM from Tyre to supervise the construction of the temple in Jerusalem, and much of the fine work was done by Phoenician craftsmen (1 Ki. 5:10, 18; 7:13–14). It is therefore not surprising that some features have parallels in ancient temples in Syria like that at Tell Tainat. In general plan the temple resembled the Tent of Meeting, but in a grander and more permanent form. It was thought of as the dwelling place of God. At the dedication of the temple, the building was filled with a cloud symbolizing the presence of God (1 Ki. 8:10; cf. Exod. 33:9). His "name" or presence was there (Deut. 12:5, 11). At the same time Solomon in his dedicatory prayer recognized that heaven could not contain God, much less the house that he had built (1 Ki. 8.27). The temple was intended as a focus of prayer (8:28–53), not only for the Israelite but also for the believing foreigner (8:41–43).

Solomon was famous for his WISDOM and known for his many PROVERBS and songs (1 Ki. 4:29–34). Two collections of proverbs are attributed to him (Prov. 10:1—22:16; 25:1—29:27), and SONG OF SOLOMON and ECCLESIASTES are associated with him. Though many proverbs at first glance seem to be distilled and memorable common sense, Israelite wisdom had a religious basis, namely, the principle that the fear of the Lord is the beginning of wisdom (Prov. 9:10).

Unfortunately Solomon did not follow the law of the king (Deut. 17:14–20) that prohibited luxury and many wives, and his foreign wives led him into idolatry. He built shrines for his wives' gods, ASHTORETH of the Sidonians, MILCOM and MOLECH of the Ammonites, and CHEMOSH of the Moabites (1 Ki. 11:1–8). Such idolatry not only was a violation of the first commandment, but also had evil moral and social results. Sacred prostitution was part of the worship of Ashtoreth, and child sacrifice was offered to Molech and Chemosh.

VI. Religion in the northern kingdom. The prophet AHIJAH promised the ten northern tribes to JEROBOAM. These tribes were to be broken away from Solomon's house because Solomon had broken God's laws, specifically in worshiping other gods. To Jeroboam was promised a lasting dynasty in the northern kingdom, if he would obey God's commandments (1 Ki. 11:29–39).

A. Jeroboam's golden calves. Unfortunately for Yahwism in the northern kingdom, Jeroboam (c. 922–901) set up golden calves for worship in BETHEL and DAN (PLACE) (1 Ki. 12:26–33; see CALF, GOLDEN). Jeroboam did not intend to depart from Yahwism, for he stated that the calves represented the God who brought them out of Egypt. Probably Yahweh was thought of as present but invisible above the calf, just as in the temple in Jerusalem he was present over the cherubim. There was this difference, that the cherubim were thought of as servants of God and were never worshiped, while Jeroboam said that the calves represented God and were to be worshiped. Therefore the calves clashed with the commandment forbidding the worship of any image (Exod. 20:4–6). Furthermore the bull was associated with other gods by the Egyptians and the Canaanites so that the calves endangered the uniqueness of Yahweh and easily led to syncretism.

Jeroboam's purpose was that Bethel and Dan would replace Jerusalem as centers for corporate worship for northern Israelites. He expelled regular priests and Levites and installed priests who would carry out his religio-political program (2 Chr. 11:13–15). These moves broke the religious unity of Israel. For all these reasons the prophets (1 Ki. 13:1–5; Hos. 8:5–6; 13:2) and the prophetic historians (2 Ki. 17:16) condemned the calf-worship of northern Israel.

B. Elijah. In most of the incidents of ELIJAH's ministry he is the protagonist for Yahweh in the contest with the Tyrian Baal, whose worship was introduced by Queen JEZEBEL, wife of AHAB king of northern Israel (c. 869–850). In ZAREPHATH in Phoenicia, Elijah miraculously provided food for a widow and healed her son (1 Ki. 17:8–24). This demonstration of power in the territory of the Tyrian Baal for a Canaanite woman indicates Yahweh's universal rule and concern (cf. Lk. 4:26).

At Mount Carmel, Elijah represented Yahweh in the showdown with the priests of Baal and of his consort Asherah (1 Ki. 18). There was no answer to the prayers of the prophets of Baal, but in answer to Elijah's prayer, Yahweh sent fire down to burn the sacrifice. So the assembled people acknowledged that Yahweh was the real God, and the priests of Baal were killed. At the same time Yahweh showed his superiority over Baal (who the Canaanites thought controlled the weather) by sending rain after he had withheld it for three years.

At Mount Horeb, God gave to Elijah a demonstration of the ways of revelation (1 Ki. 19:9–18). God sent wind, earthquake, and fire, showing his control over natural forces. But God's message came to Elijah in a still small voice, indicating that God also reveals himself in quiet ways. The contents of God's message shows that God acts also

Looking W across the Valley of Jezreel toward Mount Carmel, where Elijah defeated the prophets of Baal.

in history, in this case by judgments on the house of Ahab through HAZAEL king of Syria (ARAM) and also through JEHU, who would take the crown in Israel. In addition, God shows concern with the perpetuation of the faith by raising up a new prophet (Elisha) and by preserving a sizable remnant of the people who are true to Yahweh.

Elijah also condemned King Ahab for seizing NABOTH's vineyard and arranging for the death of Naboth (1 Ki. 21). This courageous condemnation demonstrated that even the Israelite king was subject to God's law. The description of the death of Elijah as a departure in a fiery chariot certainly points to a belief in a personal future life where earthly service is rewarded (2 Ki. 2,11).

C. Elisha. While Elijah is a grand and lonely figure, his successor ELISHA worked in cooperation with other prophets. Elisha was anointed by Elijah and received the latter's mantle as signs of endowment with spiritual power (1 Ki. 19:16, 19–21; 2 Ki. 2:9–14). He served as Elijah's assistant during his mentor's later years. Elisha is associated closely with the prophetic groups called the sons of the prophets at Bethel (2 Ki. 2:3) and at Jericho (2:15), and he was acknowledged as "master" of the group of prophets in Gilgal, for whom he performed some miraculous services (4:42–44; 6:1–7). When prophesying, Elisha sometimes required music (3:15), as did other members of the prophetic guilds (cf. 1 Sam. 10:5).

Elisha took an active part in the affairs of state. He sent a young prophet to anoint Jehu as king of Israel to bring judgment on the house of Ahab and on Queen Jezebel (2 Ki. 9:1–11). Elisha often gave counsel and help to the kings of Israel in their wars against the invading Arameans (6:24—7:20; 13:14–19) and together with Judah against Moab (3:1–27). Elisha also demonstrated Yahweh's rule over the history and kings of other countries, for example in encouraging Hazael to take the throne of Aram (8:7–15). Elisha even directed the healing of the Aramean general NAAMAN who had invaded Israel (5:1–27). Many of Elisha's beneficent miracles manifested God's concern for the poor and the sick (4:1–37).

D. Micaiah. MICAIAH was one of the prophets consulted by King Ahab of Israel and King JEHOSHAPHAT of Judah before their battle with the Arameans (1 Ki. 22:5–28). ZEDEKIAH, leading four hundred prophets, used iron horns to symbolize the victory he promised over Aram. Only Micaiah warned of defeat and death for Ahab, though he knew this message would be unwelcome. Events showed that Zedekiah and his four hundred were

...... prophets and that Micaiah had brought the true word of the Lord.

E. The revolt of Jehu. As pointed out above, Jehu (c. 842–815 B.C.) was anointed by a prophet and commissioned to execute judgment on the house of Ahab (2 Ki. 9:1–11). Jehu first removed Jezebel and the descendants and even the friends of Ahab, a wholesale slaughter which Hosea later condemned (Hos. 1:4). By these acts Jehu won the support of the RECABITES, who tried to maintain the desert way of life in order to preserve pure and original Yahwism (2 Ki. 10:15, 16; cf. 1 Chr. 2:55; Jer. 35). Then in Samaria Jehu assembled the priests, prophets, and worshipers of Baal in Baal's temple and killed them all. Though Jehu wiped out Baalism, he maintained the worship of the golden calves (2 Ki. 10:28, 29).

F. Amos. Though he was a Judean, AMOS was called to preach God's message in Bethel, the chief shrine of northern Israel. Under Jeroboam II (c. 786–746) in Israel there was luxury for some, injustice for the poor, and a booming performance of feasts and sacrifices. Amos saw God as sovereign over nature (Amos 4:6–9; 5:8) and over history (2:9–10), and as the righteous Judge of the nations (1:3—2:8). God's primary requirement, according to Amos, is justice (5:24), which he often saw denied to the poor of Israel.

Amos criticized and reinterpreted some assumptions of Israelite popular religion. Many Israelites thought that God's election of Israel meant that God was not interested in other nations and that Israel's security was inviolable. Against such chauvinism Amos preached that God was concerned also with the movements of other peoples, like the enemy Philistines and Arameans (Amos 9:7). God's election of Israel to special religious privilege meant that the judgment of their iniquities would be heavier (3:1–2). Another assumption of popular Israelite religion was that the proper performance of ritual was God's principal requirement and that such sacrifices guaranteed God's favor. Amos, on the other hand, asserted that God hated offerings without righteousness in life (5:21–25). The cult centers, Bethel, Gilgal, and Dan, where the rich drank wine, indulged in prostitution, and oppressed the poor, would be destroyed, warned Amos (2:7; 8; 5:5–7).

Many Israelites thought that the DAY OF THE LORD meant victory over their enemies. On the contrary, said Amos, the day of God's judgment will bring darkness on Israel (Amos 5:18), and Israel will go into exile beyond Damascus (i.e., to Assyria) (5:27). According to 9:9–15, Amos, like most other prophets, looked forward to a restoration and prosperity. Some think that this passage is inconsistent with the dark judgment of the rest of the book. Elsewhere also there are gleams of light, such as the hope that God may be gracious to a remnant who will practice justice (5:15).

G. Hosea. HOSEA prophesied not only during the prosperity of Jeroboam II but also during the following internal confusion and increasing external pressure from Assyria. Hosea's wife was unfaithful to him and fell into prostitution and slavery, but Hosea bought her back in continuing love. He saw in his experience with his wayward wife an illustration of God's experience with unfaithful Israel, who had broken her covenant vows to God by engaging in idolatry and who would be punished and eventually restored to fellowship and favor with God. According to Hosea, God wants from his people faithfulness (Hos. 2:20; 4:1; 5:7; 14:4), steadfast love or kindness (2:19; 4:1; 6:6; 12:6), and knowledge of God (4:1; 5:4; 6:3). Love is a characteristic of the covenant-keeping God himself (11:1–4; 14:4).

Hosea condemns Baal worship (which he calls adultery) and also the empty formalism and syncretism of the supposed worship of Yahweh. He maintains that the calves, which the Israelites worship, are not God and are rejected by Yahweh (Hos. 8:5–6; 10:5; 13:2). The many altars of the Israelites have been places for sin, not true worship, and Yahweh is not pleased with their sacrifices and feasts (8:11, 13). Some Israelites observe the feast days of Baal and forget Yahweh (2:13). At the idolatrous shrines men consort with cult prostitutes, and women commit adultery also (4:13–14). Israel does not realize that food and wealth come from Yahweh, not from Baal (2:8).

Because of these religious and social sins, Hosea warns that the Israelites will go into captivity to

Egypt and to Assyria (Hos. 9:3, 6; 10:6; 11:5). Samaria's king will perish (10:7), and many of its people will be slaughtered (13:16). Much more than Amos, Hosea speaks of Israel's future return to God (14:1-2) and to their homes (11:10-11) and of God's spiritual and physical blessings on them (14:4-7).

H. Religious Interpretation of the fall of Samaria. The writer of 2 Ki. 17:7-23 lists religious sins as the ultimate reason for the fall of Samaria (722 B.C.) and the captivity of the Israelites in Assyria. The Israelites had despised God's statutes and his covenant and had refused to listen to the warnings of the prophets. They had worshiped other gods, even sacrificing their children. They had practiced magic and worshiped the golden calves. Therefore the Lord was angry and removed the northern Israelites.

VII. Religion in the southern kingdom. Judah was more stable and less open to foreign influences than Israel in religion as well as in politics. In Judah there were faithless and idolatrous kings, but there were more faithful and reforming kings than in Israel. There were true prophets of Yahweh in the N, but there were more such prophets in the S, and their messages have been more fully preserved.

A. Rehoboam. King REHOBOAM, son of Solomon, forsook the law of the Lord (2 Chr. 12:1), and under him the Judeans worshiped idols on the high places and at sacred trees (1 Ki. 14:23-24), even making use of male cult prostitutes. When SHISHAK of Egypt invaded Palestine and the prophet SHEMAIAH rebuked the idolatry of Judah, Rehoboam and the princes humbled themselves before God (2 Chr. 12:5-6).

B. Asa. King ASA removed idolatrous images and altars and halted the pagan practice of cultic prostitution (2 Ki. 15:12; 2 Chr. 14:3-5). He even deposed his mother from her position as queen mother because of her idolatry and burned the image of the goddess Asherah which she had made (1 Ki. 15:13). Encouraged by the prophet ODED (2 Chr. 15:1-7), he summoned the people to renew their covenant with God, and they promised to seek the Lord with all their heart (15:9-15). Asa, however, imprisoned the seer HANANI, who had upbraided him for relying on help from Aram instead of on God during a war against the northern kingdom (16:7-10).

C. Jehoshaphat. Good King JEHOSHAPHAT also removed pagan shrines and obeyed God's law (1 Ki. 22:46; 2 Chr. 17:6). He inaugurated a program of popular religious education by sending out princes, Levites, and priests with the Book of the Law to teach the people (2 Chr. 17:7-9). Furthermore Jehoshaphat reorganized the judicial system of Judah on the basis of judging honestly with the Lord's guidance. In addition to local judges, Jehoshaphat appointed Levites, priests, and heads of families as a supreme court in Jerusalem to judge cases of murder and conflict of laws (2 Chr. 19:4-11). Before a battle against the Moabites, Ammonites, and Edomites, Jehoshaphat prayed for God's help, and a Levite, Jehaziel, under the power of the Spirit promised victory (ch. 20). On the other hand, the prophets Jehu (19:1-3) and Eliezer (20:37) condemned Jehoshaphat for cooperating with the apostate kings of northern Israel.

D. Athaliah. Since Queen ATHALIAH was probably the daughter of Jezebel, it is not surprising that she followed Jezebel's example and tried to foster Baalism in Judah. She was the wife of King JEHORAM. After the latter's death, she counseled her

This site in Arad appears to be a "holy of holies," indicating that some of the Israelites of the southern kingdom worshiped in locations other than Jerusalem.

son King AHAZIAH to do wickedly like the house of Ahab (2 Chr. 22:3). After Jehu killed Ahaziah, she killed all Ahaziah's sons, except for JOASH, and took the royal power herself (2 Ki. 11:1–3). Under her patronage there was in Jerusalem a temple of Baal (2 Ki. 11:18). To Baal's temple Athaliah transported some of the treasures from Yahweh's temple (2 Chr. 24:7). Finally, Athaliah and her Baalism were swept away under the leadership of JEHOIADA the high priest of Yahweh (2 Ki. 11:13–20).

E. Joash and Jehoiada. After he had crowned the young Joash, Jehoiada the high priest made a covenant with the people that they would be the Lord's people (2 Ki. 11:17). They destroyed Baal's temple and killed his priest (11:18). Yahweh's temple was repaired, and its worship was reorganized (2 Chr. 24:12–14). After Jehoiada died, however, Joash fell into idolatry and killed Jehoiada's son ZEDEKIAH because of the latter's rebuke (24:17–22).

F. Ahaz. King AHAZ refused to trust in the Lord, as Isaiah urged him to do, when Jerusalem was besieged by the armies of Israel and Aram (Isa. 7:1–12). Instead he used some of the treasure of the Lord's temple to buy the help of the king of Assyria (2 Ki. 16:7–8). In Jerusalem he set up a new altar copied from an Assyrian model (16:10–13). Yahweh's brazen altar he used for divination, doubtless by inspecting the entrails of animals to predict the future as was done in Assyria (16:14–15). According to 2 Chr. 28:24, he closed the doors of the temple of Yahweh, halting the regular worship there. He also sacrificed his son, probably to Molech (2 Ki. 16:3), and made images of Baal (2 Chr. 28:2). In other words, Ahaz deserted Yahwism and adopted Assyrian and Canaanite polytheism.

G. Isaiah. In his inaugural vision in the temple, ISAIAH (late 8th cent. B.C.) heard the seraphim praising God, "Holy, holy, holy" (Isa. 6:3). One of Isaiah's characteristic titles for God is "the holy One of Israel" (1:4; 5:19, 24; 10:20; 12:6; 17:7; 29:19; 30:11–12, 15; 31:1; 37:23). That God is holy means that he is highly exalted above his creatures in power and wisdom and also in justice and righteousness (5:16). Yahweh alone is God of all the kingdoms of the earth (37:16), a clear statement of monotheism. God has chosen Israel for special privilege like a son (1:2) or a loved one (5:1–7), but he also rules and judges the other nations (10:5–9, 13–19).

The Holy God demands goodness and justice (Isa. 1:17). He will judge such social sins as murder (1:15, 21; 5:7), stealing (1:23), bribery (1:23; 5:23), oppression of the poor (3:14–15; 10:2), luxury (3:16–26; 5:9; 32:9–12), and drunkenness (5:11–12, 22; 28:7). God cannot endure sacrifices, feasts, or even prayers if they are combined with iniquity and murder (1:11–15). Idols are only the work of men's hands, and idolatry will incur God's judgment (2:8, 10). Because of Israel's rebelliousness toward God (1:2; 30:1) and injustice toward man, judgment will come upon them (2:6–21; 5:24; 9:8-10:4), and they will go into exile (5:13). Only a REMNANT will survive the judgment and will return to God (7:3; 10:20–23). To faithful believers Isaiah promised that God will protect them. The faithless Ahaz rejected this promise (7:1–11). Later Hezekiah believed Isaiah's word, and God did destroy the Assyrian army besieging Jerusalem (2 Ki. 19).

At the time of his call, Isaiah had a vision of God as the enthroned King whose glory filled the whole earth (Isa. 6:1, 3), and the prophet looked forward to the messianic kingdom when God's glory would be manifest everywhere. It will be a kingdom of peace centering in Jerusalem, and all nations will acknowledge God's law (2:1–4). The messianic king, of the line of David, will rule in peace and justice for ever (9:6–7). The MESSIAH, endowed with wisdom and power by God's Spirit, will punish the wicked and give justice to the poor. Everything harmful will be transformed into good, and the earth will be filled with the knowledge of God (11:1–9).

H. Micah. According to MICAH, a contemporary of Isaiah, the primary demands of God are not sacrifices, but justice, kindness, and humility before God (Mic. 6:6–8). The sins Micah condemns include the idolatry of Samaria (1:5–7), oppression of the poor and the weak by the rich (2:1–11), extortion by the rulers (3:1–4), false predictions of peace by the prophets to get food (3:5–8), perversion of justice by the judges to get bribes (3:9–10; 7:3), teaching for money by the priests (3:11), false measures used by merchants (6:10–11), and murder (7:2). Because of these sins, Micah predicts the destruction of Samaria (1.7) and of Jerusalem (3:12). The Judeans will go as exiles to Babylon (4:10).

Micah looks forward to the universal messianic kingdom of peace (Mic. 4:1–3 equals Isa. 2:2–4). But he pictures the Messiah from BETHLEHEM (David's town), not as a king (as Isaiah does), but as a SHEPHERD of his people (5:2–4). He also refers to God with the same shepherd imagery (7:4) and is confident that God will show steadfast love and compassion to the remnant of Israel (7:18, 19).

I. Hezekiah. A reforming king, HEZEKIAH destroyed idolatrous shrines and images and also the bronze serpent Moses had made in the wilderness (Num. 21:9), which had become an object of superstitious reverence (2 Ki. 18:4–6; see NEHUSHTAN). He opened the doors of the temple of Yahweh, which Ahaz had closed, and ordered that it be cleansed and reconsecrated (2 Chr. 29:3–36). The Passover was observed with great celebration, and many from northern Israel as well as from Judah came to Jerusalem to participate (30:1–22). Through the prophet Isaiah, God sent assurances to Hezekiah that the Assyrians would not capture Jerusalem (19:6–7, 20–36) and that he would recover from sickness (2 Ki. 20:1–11). Also Isaiah rebuked Hezekiah for boastfully showing his treasures to the Babylonian embassy and warned that these treasures would later be taken as booty to Babylon (20:12–19).

J. Manasseh. The many idolatries of King MANASSEH, even within the courts of Yahweh's temple, are listed in 2 Ki. 21:2–9 (cf. 23:26–27). After he was imprisoned by the Assyrians for revolting, he turned back to the God of his fathers. Manasseh then returned to his throne, removed the idols he had made, and served the Lord at the end of his life (2 Chr. 33:11–16).

K. Josiah. King JOSIAH ruled c. 640–609 B.C., and his destruction of idolatry was more thorough than any preceding reform (2 Ki. 23:4–14; 2 Chr. 34:3–7). His abolition of local altars, which were pagan or syncretistic, extended not only throughout Judah but also into northern Israel, including the altar of the golden calf in Bethel (2 Ki. 23:15–20; 2 Chr. 34:5–6). Also Josiah removed or killed the idolatrous priests (2 Ki. 23:5, 20).

When the temple was cleansed, the Book of the Law was found and brought to Josiah. Many scholars have thought that this book was some form of DEUTERONOMY because Josiah's reforms centralized public worship in Jerusalem. Josiah was much concerned when he heard the punishments threatened in this book (perhaps Deut. 28) if Israel disobeyed God's law (2 Ki. 22:9–13). The prophetess HULDAH explained that the threatened judgments would come, but not in Josiah's day because of his piety (22:14–20). Josiah then made a covenant before the Lord to keep God's commandments as found in the Book of the Law (2 Chr. 34:31–32). Like Hezekiah, Josiah celebrated a memorable Passover in Jerusalem, in which not only Judeans but also Israelites from the N participated (35:1–19).

L. Zephaniah. A prophet during the early reign of Josiah, ZEPHANIAH condemned the idolatries of Judah (Zeph. 1:4–5), the luxury of the officials (1:8), the accumulation of wealth by the merchants (1:11, 13), the rapaciousness of judges (3:3), the faithlessness of prophets (3:4), and the twisting of the law by the priests (3:4). Because of such sins, a day of wrath would come on Judah and on all nations (1:14–18; 2:4–15). For those who would escape this wrath God requires obedience, righteousness, and humility (2:3). Zephaniah also foresees a day of joy when the remnant of Israel would be cleansed from their sins and freed from their fears. All nations will join in worshiping the Lord (3:9–20).

M. Nahum. The main religious teaching of NAHUM is that, though God is slow to anger, he does eventually judge the nations through the events of history, in this case the destruction of NINEVEH in 612 B.C. Nineveh was the capital of the Assyrians, who had terrorized and plundered the ANE for two hundred years. The obverse message is that by the downfall of Assyria God was bringing peace and freedom to the countries Assyria had oppressed, particularly to Judah (Nah. 1:15).

N. Habakkuk. The book of HABAKKUK deals searchingly with the religious problem of THEODICY, the vindication of the justice of God. The prophet asks why God allows violence, flaunting of the law, and injustice in Judah. God's answer is that he is punishing Judah by means of the conquering Babylonians (Hab. 1:2–11). This leaves the prophet with the more difficult problem of why God allows the Babylonians' violence and sins, which are worse than those of Judah. God's answer is twofold. As for the righteous they will survive because of their faith in God and faithfulness to God (2:4; cf. Rom. 1:17; Gal. 3:11; Heb. 10:38-39). As for the Babylonians, their pride, their plundering, their killing, their destruction of cities and countryside, and their idolatry will lead to inevitable doom (2:5–19). On the basis of God's mighty acts in creation and in history (the exodus), the prophet rises to joyful faith in God whatever the immediate physical problems may be (3:2–19). He is confident that ultimately the earth will be filled with knowledge of the glory of God (2:14).

O. Jeremiah. More than any other prophet, JEREMIAH reveals his personal religious experience. At his call Jeremiah objects that he is too young to be a prophet, but God insists and promises to be with him in the ministry of uprooting and planting (Jer. 1:4–10). Later Jeremiah makes many complaints, such as that God has deceived him, that everyone mocks him, that he regrets his birth (11:18–23; 12:1–6; 15:10–12, 15–18; 17:12–18; 18:18–23; 20:17–18). In reply to such complaints, God promises to strengthen him like a brazen wall (15:19–21).

Jeremiah uses various figures to describe God, such as the fountain of living waters (Jer. 2:13), the potter with Israel the clay (18:1–12), the husband of Israel (2:2), and the father of the nation (3:19). Like other prophets, Jeremiah condemns the sins of idolatry (2:11, 13; 7:18; 32:29, 34–35) and of breaking the ethical laws of the covenant (7:9). More than any other prophet, Jeremiah traces sin back to its source in the wicked heart, the evil thoughts (3:17; 4:14; 5:23; 11:8; 13:10; 17:1, 9; 18:12; 23:17).

The cure for Israel's sin is REPENTANCE and a cleansed heart (Jer. 4:14). No prophet more insistently calls the people to return to God (3:12–14; 4:1–4; 18:11). Jeremiah seems to have supported the reforms of Josiah based on a return to God's law (22:15–16), but later Jeremiah became convinced that the people would not repent any more than a leopard would change its spots (13:23).

Because of Israel's sins and lack of repentance, God has sent and will send judgments upon them. In Jer. 14:1–6, 12, a drought and a famine in Judah are described as such a judgment. Jerusalem will be besieged by an enemy (1:13–16; 4:11–22), identified as NEBUCHADNEZZAR king of Babylon (cf. ch. 25), who is God's servant to chastise Judah. The whole land of Israel will become a ruin, and Judah and other nations will serve the king of Babylon for a period. In predicting capture and captivity for his people, Jeremiah came in conflict with the false prophets who promised peace when no peace was morally or politically possible (6:13–15; 8:10–12). Such prophets were prophesying lies that came from their own minds, not from God (14:14–18; 23:9–40; 27; 28). Events proved that Jeremiah was right and these prophets were wrong.

Jeremiah criticizes confidence in the outward forms of Israel's religion and gives to some of these forms a moral meaning. The people thought that God's temple was inviolable and that Jerusalem was safe because of it. But Jeremiah points out that a previous national shrine at Shiloh was destroyed because of the sins of the people (Jer. 7:4, 10, 12, 14; 26:6, 9, 12). The people thought that the performance of the sacrifices guaranteed God's favor. Jeremiah maintains that obedience rather than sacrifice is God's primary requirement (7:21–23) and that sacrifice with vile deeds will never save them from judgment (11:15; 14:12). Jeremiah interprets the covenant sign of circumcision as a symbol of cleansing from sin (4:4, 14; 9:26) and of obedience (6:10). When the ark (3:16) is gone (as in the exile), the spiritual reality of God's presence (3:17) will remain.

Jeremiah looks forward to Israel's return to Palestine after the exile (Jer. 30:17–22; 32:9–44; 33:9–12). This return will be not only geographical but also a spiritual return to the Lord in penitence (31:16–20). Moreover, Jeremiah foresees a new covenant between God and his people (31:31–34, see COVENANT, THE NEW). Then God's law will be inward, written on the heart. The knowledge of God will be universal. The forgiveness of sins will be complete. The rule of the Messiah of David's line will be characterized by justice, righteousness, salvation, and security (23:5–6; 30:9, 21; 33:15–16). One of his titles will be "The LORD Our Righteousness," indicating that God is the source of salvation (23:6). Not only Judah and Israel but also all nations will join in the worship of the Lord (3:17–18).

P. Jehoiakim. King JEHOIAKIM persecuted the true prophets and rejected their messages. He killed the prophet URIAH because the latter warned of coming judgment on Judah (Jer. 26:20–23). Jeremiah's scroll denouncing Judah's sins and calling for repentance was cut up and burned by Jehoiakim, who vainly tried to arrest the prophet (36:20–26).

Q. Zedekiah. The prophet EZEKIEL describes the idolatry and moral degeneracy of Jerusalem during ZEDEKIAH's reign (Ezek. 5–11). Zedekiah sought Jeremiah's advice, but because of popular pressure, he was not willing to follow the submission to Babylon that Jeremiah counseled (Jer. 26:12–15; 38:14–28). Jeremiah condemned Zedekiah for making a covenant to free Hebrew slaves (cf. Exod. 21:2; Deut. 15:12) and then failing to carry out this promise made before God (Jer. 34:8–22). Zedekiah is condemned also for revolting and so breaking the covenant in God's name to be a vassal of the king of Babylon (2 Chr. 36:13; Ezek. 17:13–19). According to 2 Chr. 36:13–16, Zedekiah's failure to turn to God, the idolatry of the people and even of the priests, and their rejection of the warnings of the prophets were the theological reasons for the destruction of Jerusalem and the captivity of Judah.

VIII. Religion during the exile and the restoration. Deprived of their historic rituals and unable to follow their usual religious patterns, the exiles were compelled to adopt new forms of worship. Those who had learned the spiritual lessons of the EXILE were ready to follow the teachings of EZEKIEL, who directed them to a rigid monotheism and encouraged a high standard of personal and social morality. It is a testimony to his diligence that pagan practices ceased among the faithful remnant in Babylonia for all intents and purposes. Because worship of the old semipagan type was impossible under the conditions of captivity, a degree of adaptation was a pressing necessity in the expression of Israel's historic faith.

The work of Ezekiel marked an important turning point in Hebrew religion, since it coincided with the breaking of the connection between the service of God and the outward form in which it had for many centuries found its embodiment. Under the new situation, it was necessary to improvise in worship and devise new means of expressing spiritual loyalty to God. Memorial celebrations replaced the preexilic feasts, and acts of special significance for the covenant relationship such as circumcision were stressed anew. Open-air meetings by the Kinnan canal replaced gatherings in the temple and its precincts, and a nonsacrificial type of worship stressed confession, fasting, prayer, and the reading of the law.

The book of DANIEL indicates that the Babylonians were quite tolerant toward the Jewish captives, and even permitted gifted individuals, such as Daniel, to exert authority in the kingdom. Consequently the Jews did not suffer religious persecution as such during the exile, despite the aim of the faithful community to differentiate itself as much as possible from its pagan neighbors. With the growth of house gatherings and the importance attached to the knowledge and observance of the Torah, the basis was laid for subsequent synagogue worship after the return. Of concern to Ezekiel in particular was the role of the Levites, for unlike Jeremiah, who entertained a covenant with the Levitical priests (Jer. 33:17–22), Ezekiel distinguished sharply between the Levitical priests and the Levites (Ezek. 40:46; 43:19). He described the former as the "sons of Zadok" who had remained faithful to God (40:46; 44:15; 48:11), distinguishing them from the Levites, whom he regarded as having gone astray after idols and therefore as unsuited for handling sacred things or approaching the altar (44:10–14). This concept seems to return to the careful distinction between priest and Levite found in Numbers, as a corrective to the rather more lax attitudes of the monarchy.

With the return from exile began the growth of JUDAISM proper. The returned community assumed the form of a theocracy, making it a church rather than a nation in the strictest sense. It felt itself to be the remnant of Israel, brought by divine grace from bondage in a new exodus and summoned to live once again by the precepts of divine law as the people of God. Cultic personnel were prominent in the lists of repatriates, with Levites, priestly families, and temple servants (NETHINIM) returning under JOSHUA and ZERUBBABEL (Ezra 2). The number of priests was considerably larger than that of Levites, perhaps because many of the latter adopted priestly status. The other Levites responsible for menial duties in the temple were apparently reluctant to return with their compatriots (Ezra 8:15–20).

At the laying of the foundation of the second temple, the Levites played a prominent part (Ezra 3:8–10) and were also conspicuous when the finished structure was dedicated (6:16–20). The books of HAGGAI and ZECHARIAH show that the initial enthusiasm of the repatriates had waned somewhat, requiring considerable stimulation before the new temple was built. The prophecy of MALACHI shows that, about 450 B.C., the Jerusalem priesthood was once again in decline (Mal. 2:1–9) and was beginning to exhibit some of those features that had found such fatal expression in the preexilic period. The work of EZRA and NEHEMIAH brought these tendencies to a halt, however, and gave characteristic expression to the concept that the divine will was to be proclaimed to the Jewish commonwealth through the priesthood. Ezra was particularly concerned to see that the latter was a suitable vehicle for the task, and accordingly some of his more urgent reforms were directed at the priests. After recruiting the Levites to his side (Ezra 8:15–20), he instituted a reform to ban marriage with non-Jewish women, a move that affected both priests and Levites (9:1–2; 10:5–44).

Under Nehemiah, the priests and Levites carried on with their full range of duties. Once a section of the wall had been repaired (Neh. 3:17), the Levites occupied themselves with instructing the people in the law (8:7–9), and in general participation in the religious life of the nation (11:3; 12:27). The need for strong central enforcement of the Levitical regulations became apparent after Nehemiah had left Jerusalem for a time and certain abuses crept back into the cultus. Thus TOBIAH the Ammonite was allowed to occupy the area in the temple that should have served as a storeroom for the Levitical tithes (13:4–5). Because they were deprived of the allotted revenue (10:37–39; 12:47), the Levites had forsaken the temple and had gone to work their lands so as to sustain themselves (13:10), a situation which Nehemiah rectified on his return to Jerusalem. In the theocracy, the high priesthood returned to the historic house of ELEAZAR, third son of AARON, in the person of Zadok, and his descendants retained the office continuously until 171 B.C., when it was transferred to MENELAUS by ANTIOCHUS IV.

IX. The rise of Judaism. The aspirations of Ezekiel in this direction for the new commonwealth died hard, and even after 171 B.C., a Zadokite priesthood controlled the Jewish temple at Leontopolis in Egypt until the building was closed by VESPASIAN soon after A.D. 70. The religious community at QUMRAN rejected the contemporary Jerusalem priesthood in favor of a Zadokite regime, and looked forward confidently to the time when the Zadokites would again be priests in Jerusalem (see DEAD SEA SCROLLS).

In the solemn covenant with Ezra, the nation saw as its spiritual ideal the realizing of the covenant concept of a "kingdom of priests and a holy nation" (Exod. 19:6). It was a community whose interests were governed by covenant and law, both of which were necessary if the life and witness of the theocracy was not to be threatened once more by pagan influences. The incursions of HELLENISM in the Greek period presented a serious challenge to the very existence of Judaism, but the emphasis that Ezra had placed upon the covenant, the Torah, and other distinctively Jewish institutions proved to be the salvation of the theocracy. As the Jews were in danger of being swallowed up by the pagan nations that surrounded them (cf. Neh. 13:15–31), it was necessary for Judaism to remain as distinctive as possible in its outlook. The emphasis that Ezekiel laid upon attention to ritual requirements in the worship of the temple was given prominence in the cultus, and served as an effective safeguard against further infiltrations of paganism.

None of the postexilic prophets, however, ever suggested that correctness of ritual would be acceptable to God as a substitute for proper moral and spiritual attitudes. The principles of Judaism were fostered by the weekly worship of the SYNAGOGUE, an institution that more than any other gave character to the Jewish faith and brought people in all parts of the land into contact with their religious leaders. The synagogue became the cradle of an entirely new kind of social and religious life, and established the foundation for a spiritual community of universal scope. The early Christian church was quick to capitalize on this situation, and the book of Acts shows the significant role played by the synagogue in the propagation of the new messianic faith.

Typical of developed Judaism was the stress on the keeping of the Torah. To clarify obscurities in the written law there arose a body of oral teaching that gradually acquired a status equivalent to that of the Mosaic enactments themselves. This tradition served to safeguard the provisions of the Torah lest they be broken through ignorance or inadvertence. For Judaism, the law exemplified the ideal concept of a people dedicated to the service of God. Although cultic rites were prominent in the postexilic period, the emphasis in spirituality shifted so that Judaism became a religion of the book, namely that of the law. A class of SCRIBES arose in the pre-Christian period who were experts in the study of the Torah and prominent in synagogue worship as a result. After A.D. 70, they became increasingly important for the way they preserved in written form the oral law and transmitted with great fidelity the Hebrew Scriptures. See MISHNAH; TALMUD.

One of the pre-Christian political parties, that of the SADDUCEES, was important because of its connection with the high priesthood in NT times. Both the name and origin of the party are disputed, but they seem to have been a priestly aristocracy of rather boorish disposition that came to prominence under the HASMONEAN rulers until the reign of Salome ALEXANDRA (76–67 B.C.), who preferred the PHARISEES. The Sadducees were highly conservative, attributing divine authority only to the Torah, and rejecting any form of doctrine that could not find support therein. Although a religious minority in NT times, they monopolized the office of high priest, and thus were involved in the condemnation of Christ.

The other chief political party in the pre-Christian era, the Pharisees, laid great emphasis upon the keeping of the Torah and its traditional exposition in the belief that the Babylonian exile had been caused by the failure of the nation to observe the Mosaic law at both individual and corporate levels. Whereas the Sadducees held that temple worship was the center and main purpose of the law, the Pharisees stressed the individual fulfillment of all aspects of the law, of which cultic worship was only one part, since for them inner attitudes were manifested in outward disposition.

The attempt to safeguard the faith from the inroads of Hellenism led to a growing particularism within Judaism that fostered the idea that Israel alone was the elect of God. Jews tended to draw apart from Gentiles out of self-defense, and even separated from those of their own number who succumbed to the blandishments of Greek culture. On the other hand, the universalism implicit in the ancient monotheistic faith found periodic expression. Proselytes were welcomed into Judaism (cf. Zech. 8:20–23) and were given equality before the law in accord with the ancient traditions of Moses (cf. Lev. 19:34; 24:22). By the time of the NT era, a great many converts to Judaism had been made in this manner, although the Jews of the theocracy followed their ancestors in refusing to become an active missionary force in contemporary society.

For orthodox Jews, postexilic doctrine was uniformly monotheistic in emphasis, with the sovereignty and power of God claiming special prominence. In the period between the Testaments there arose an increasing interest in the role of angelic beings. The Qumran sect saw the world as the focal point of conflict between good and evil forces, without, however, entertaining any DUALISM of a Persian character. Orthodox belief held unshakably to the conviction that the God of the Fathers was sovereign in all things and just in all his doings.

From this period emerged also a belief in the existence of PARADISE as an abode of the faithful after death. Although the term *paradise* occurred in the OT (Neh. 2:8; Eccl. 2:5; Cant. 4:13) it was not used there in any eschatological sense. The belief had its roots in the concept of primeval bliss, but was expanded to include speculations concerning a glorious messianic future. The coming age of grace and glory would have a great deal in common with the Garden of Eden of antiquity, but the Jews also held that paradise was present in their own time, although concealed. This location was the present abode of the ancient patriarchs, and would be the place where the chosen of the present and future would go at death. In the NT (Lk. 23:43), Christ used the term for the location of the soul immediately after death (cf. 16:19–31), thereby supporting earlier ideas of the survival of the human personality beyond physical decease. See INTERMEDIATE STATE.

The future hope of Judaism seems to have been a matter of some interest and concern throughout the intertestamental period. Apostate Jews had become involved in the political life of Judea to the point where, in the HASMONEAN period, they were supporting the persecution of their compatriots. For them the traditional faith was bereft of value, and all that lay ahead was an uncertain materialism. Those Jews who were faithful to the ancestral traditions valued the teachings of the synagogue equally with the elaborate cultic rituals of the second temple which, under the Herods, was extended as a political gesture of appeasement. Hope for the future also focused on the person of the Messiah.

From the time of the early monarchy (2 Sam. 7:12–16), a promise had been made by God to the nation that from the house of David would emerge a stable kingdom and throne. Although the Davidic dynasty faced many a crisis, the hope of a royal personage from the renowned house survived all the vicissitudes of history. The MESSIAH or "anointed one" was also depicted under such figures as the Servant (Isa. 42:1; 49:5; et al.), who was identified with the Davidic Messiah (55:3–4); the Anointed Conqueror, who would make Israel supreme over the Gentiles (60:1–22); the Branch (Jer. 23:5–6; Zech. 3:8; et al.), who was the Messiah in his kingly and priestly offices; and the Son of Man (Dan. 7:1–28), a messianic individual who, although man, originated with God. In the fullness of time, this figure was completely perfected in Jesus Christ. In him the aspirations of ancient Israel were fulfilled, and through him and his church, the Israel of the Spirit, the benefits of the new covenant were given to the world, in a manner that realized the missionary destiny so long neglected in ancient Israelite religious life.

X. Israel's main religious beliefs

A. God's revelation, acts, qualities, and nature. Israel's God was a dynamic and articulate Being who spoke to his creatures and manifested himself to them in many different ways. God shows his power and wisdom generally through nature, which is his CREATION, and through his deeds in history. In nature the heavens are telling the glory of God (Ps. 19:1). After describing the winds and the rain, the plants and the animals, the psalmist exclaims, "How many are your works, O LORD! In wisdom you made them all" (104:24). In history God shows his control over men and nations and events; for example, in the deliverance of Israel from Egypt, the saving of Jerusalem from the Assyrians in the time of Hezekiah, and the punitive destruction of Jerusalem by the Babylonians in the time of Zedekiah.

In special revelations God sometimes shows himself in visible manifestations or theophanies. For example, he appears to Abraham in human form, receives Abraham's hospitality, and talks with him (Gen. 18). Sometimes God appears as "the angel of the Lord" who identifies himself with God (e.g., Exod. 3:2, 6). A more vague manifestation of God is his "glory," which on Sinai resembled fire (24:16–17). God sometimes reveals his will or the future by dreams or visions. Dreamers are recognized in the law as recipients of messages from God (Deut. 13:1–5), and Solomon received God's promise of wisdom in a dream (1 Ki. 3:5). A vision is some supernatural seeing, as when Isaiah had the vision of the Lord in the temple (Isa. 6). Israelites also believed that God revealed his will through the URIM AND THUMMIM, small objects kept in the breastplate of the high priest's ephod (Exod. 28:30). These sacred lots were used to decide between alternatives (1 Sam. 14:41). With the rise of personal prophetism in Israel, the more mechanical Urim and Thummim were less used. Sometimes God's REVELATION was spoken in words like the Decalogue (Exod. 20:1); Moses is said to have written God's words (24:3–4).

Most noteworthy in Israel was INSPIRATION, that is, internal and personal revelation to and through prophets. The prophet was God's messenger, God's mouthpiece (Jer. 15:19). So the prophet could say, "This is what the LORD says" (e.g., Amos 1:3 and often). There were prophets, for example, in ancient Byblos and Mari; but their function was to offer advice in specific situations. The depth and breadth of the theological and ethical teaching of Israel's prophets are unmatched in the ANE.

Many of God's statements about himself (e.g., Josh. 24:2–13) and many of Israel's confessions of faith (e.g., Deut. 26:5–15) deal primarily with God's actions. (1) *Deliverer*. In the introduction to the Decalogue, God says, "I am the LORD your God who brought you out of the land of Egypt, out of the land of slavery" (Exod. 20:2). God is also the deliverer of the believer from enemies, as in the case of David (Ps. 18), and from sickness, as with Hezekiah (2 Ki. 20:1–11). (2) *Creator*. The Decalogue states that God created the heavens, the earth, the sea, and all that is in them (Exod. 20:11). God created by his word (Gen. 1:3 and often), by his Spirit (Ps. 104:30), and by wisdom (Prov. 8:22–31). New life depends on the continued creative activity of God (Ps. 104:30). (3) *Provider*. The Israelites in offering the firstfruits of the harvest acknowledged that God was the ultimate giver of crops (Deut. 26:10). God also provided for special needs as he gave water, manna, and quail to the Israelites in the wilderness. (4) *Lord and ruler*. God controls the forces of nature, as in the plagues of Egypt. He directs the lives of individuals, commissioning Moses to free the Israelites (Exod. 3–4). He manages the nations, bringing the Israelites from Egypt and the Philistines from Caphtor (Amos 9:7). God's kingdom rules over all (Ps. 103:19). (5) *Righteous judge*. The Decalogue mentions God's activity in punishing iniquity (Exod. 20:5). He punishes individuals like Saul and David. The prophets often picture God as a judge trying Israel (Isa. 1; Jer. 2; Mic. 6). Ultimately God will judge all nations (Ps. 96; Isa. 24:1, 6, 16–23).

God also reveals much about his qualities. (1) *Power*. The power of God over nature and human beings is shown in such acts as creation, the flood, the crossing of the Red Sea, and the provision of water and manna for the Israelites in the wilderness. The regular forces of nature, such as the wind and the rain, also are demonstrations of his power (Ps. 104). Thus his power is used morally, sometimes in the provision for human needs, sometimes in saving the righteous, sometimes in judgment on the wicked. (2) *Knowledge*. God knows the actions and even the thoughts of every individual (Ps. 139:1–6). Since God knows the future, he can declare to his prophets things to come (1 Sam. 10:2–6; 2 Ki. 19:7, 32–34). "His understanding has no limit" (Ps. 147:5). (3) *Omnipresence*. God is active everywhere through his Spirit (Ps. 139:7). He is a God at hand, filling heaven and earth (Jer. 23:23–24). Because God is everywhere, no image can adequately represent him or localize him. (4) *Eternity*. "From everlasting to everlasting you are God" (Ps. 90:2). "But you, O LORD, sit enthroned forever" (102:12). (5) *Moral attributes*. A list of God's moral attributes that reveal his "name" or personality is found in Exod. 34:6–7: merciful, gracious, slow to anger, abounding in steadfast love and faithfulness, forgiving, and punishing iniquity. It is noteworthy that this list stresses the goodness much more than the wrath of God. (6) *Holiness*. The holiness of God is his "otherness and perfection when compared with all created things" (W. Eichrodt, *Theology of the Old Testament*, 2 vols. [1961–67], 1:273). Holiness expresses the awesome superiority of God not only in power but also in goodness (Lev. 19:2; Isa. 5:16, 6:1–5).

Israelite religion is more concerned with the actions and character of God than with his essence, which remains a mystery. Two aspects of God's nature, however, are apparent in his revelations to Israel. (1) *God is personal*. He plans, he loves and hates, he acts. He speaks, hears, and sees. He is living (Deut. 5:26). Yahweh differs from the pagan gods, who often are only personifications of natural forces. Some have said that Israel's God was anthropomorphic, like man (see ANTHROPOMORPHISM). In Israelite terms this likeness is expressed by the reverse comparison: man is theomorphic, like God in personality. (2) *God is one*. Here also Israelite religion differed from the surrounding polytheisms. The oneness of Yahweh, taken in conjunction with his activities such as creator and ruler of all, certainly implies monotheism, which becomes explicit in Amos and Isaiah. If Yahweh is the only real God, he cannot but be jealous of the worship of idols, which are no gods. Finally, though God is one, some references in the OT to his Spirit, his word, and his wisdom, and to the angel of the Lord imply a complexity in the divine unity.

B. God's relationships. God created the heavens and the earth and everything in them (Gen. 1). He also controls the world and supports its creatures and ongoing processes (Gen. 8:12; Job 38–41; Ps. 74:16–17; 104). In the messianic kingdom peace will be established among animals as well as among human beings (Isa. 11:6–9).

God sends superhuman creatures called *angels* as his messengers to encourage and protect the righteous (Josh. 5:13–15; Ps. 34:7) or to destroy the wicked (2 Sam. 24:16; 2 Ki. 19:35). Angels also offer praise to God (Ps. 148:2). The ministers of God called *cherubim* (Gen. 3:24) and *seraphim* (Isa. 6:2, 3) were later classified as angels. See ANGEL; CHERUB; SERAPH.

In the prologue of the book of JOB (whose dates of origin and of composition are uncertain), SATAN, the accuser of Job and the cause of his troubles, acts only by permission of God. God finally turns Satan's evil to a good end for Job. Two preexilic figures were later identified with Satan: the tempting serpent in the Garden of Eden (Gen. 3) and the Day Star fallen from heaven (Isa. 14:12). The doctrine of Satan was more developed in postexilic times.

God made man, male and female, in his image. One aspect of man's likeness to God is the dominion God has given him over the earth and its creatures (Gen. 1:27–28). We are intended to obey, worship, and love God (Deut. 6:4–5). Man has rebelled against God (Gen. 3), but if a person confesses his sin and repents from the heart, God will forgive him (Ps. 32; 51).

One answer to the problem of suffering is that it is God's punishment of sin (Gen. 3:15–19). Often specific suffering is a punishment for specific sins (Deut. 28; Jdg. 2:11–15; 2 Sam. 12:14–18; Hos. 8:7). Some, like Job's three friends, made the false deduction that all suffering is punishment for specific sins (Job 4:7–9; 8:4–6; 22:21–29), but this deduction is rejected by God himself (42:8). Another explanation of suffering is given in the prologue of Job (Job 1–2): that God sometimes permits suffering as a means through which a believer can give a witness of disinterested faith before the world. Still another view of suffering is that God uses it to humble our pride and teach us our need of him. This disciplinary aspect of suffering is presented to Job by Elihu (chs. 32–37). Another attitude toward suffering is to admit that we cannot understand all the reasons for suffering and to have faith that the wise and good God is doing right (42:1–6).

God's election of Israel began with the call and promises of blessing to their ancestor Abraham. God gave to Israel special privileges in the exodus, the covenant at Sinai to be their God, the law, and in the conquest of Canaan. God's special concern for Israel also was shown in the warnings and instruction of the prophets. The prophets interpreted the exile as a punishment of Israel's sins, but also promised that a remnant would return.

But God also has an interest in the NATIONS. He created Adam, from whom all nations are descended. God promised that through Abraham's descendants all nations would receive blessing. God watches over the history of nations, moving the Philistines from Caphtor and the Arameans from Kir (Amos 9:7). God judges the nations for their sins (Amos 1:1—2:3; Isa. 13–19), but he also uses Assyria (Isa. 10:5) and Babylonia (Jer. 25:9) as instruments for disciplining other nations including Israel. Eventually all nations will have a part in the worship of the Lord and in the universal blessings of the messianic kingdom of peace (Isa. 2:2–4; Jer. 3:17; 16:19; Zeph. 3:9, 10).

C. Israel's duty to God. Israel is to pay obedience to the law and to wisdom, both of which come from God. While the law deals primarily with religious and civil matters, PROVERBS emphasizes personal affairs, like family relationships, friendship, honesty, industriousness, chastity, and sobriety. The fear and love of God and love and justice to one's neighbor are basic principles of both law and wisdom (Deut. 6:4; Lev. 19:18; Prov. 1:7).

Israel is also instructed to worship God. The rituals, place, and priestly personnel of sacrificial worship as found in Exodus and Leviticus are outlined above. Sacrifices had the value of teaching the need for confession, atonement, forgiveness, dedication, and fellowship with God. The prophets stressed obedience (1 Sam. 15:22) and steadfast love (Hos. 6:6) as more basic requirements than sacrifice. According to Ps. 51:17, the sacrifice God most desires from a sinner is a contrite heart. To understand the meaning of Israelite worship one must turn to the PSALMS, the hymnbook and prayerbook of Israel. The Hebrew name of this book means "praises," and in the Psalms God is praised for his greatness and his grace (Ps. 116–118; 146–150), for his works in nature (19; 104) and in history (105–106), for his word (19; 119), and for forgiveness (32). The psalmists pray for forgiveness (6; 25; 32; 38; 51; 130; 143), for deliverance from disease (88), and from enemies (35, 69, 109). Many of the psalms express joy in worship: "I rejoiced with those who said to me, 'Let us go to the house of the LORD'" (122:1).

D. The future. Certain indications point to Israel's belief in the personal conscious existence of a man's spirit after DEATH. The burial of a body was considered very important (Gen. 23; 2 Sam. 21:13–14). Death is sometimes described as being gathered to one's fathers (Gen. 25:8). The very forbidding of necromancy (Lev. 20:27) indicates that the spirits of the dead were considered to have a conscious existence. The place of the spirits of the dead was SHEOL, in the depths of the earth (Deut. 32:22), sometimes pictured as a gloomy place (Job 10:21–22). On the other hand, it is implied that the future life holds a reward for Enoch (Gen. 5:24) and Elijah (2 Ki. 2:11). Finally, some passages in the Psalms point to a joyous future life in the presence of God (Ps. 16:10–11; 49:15; 73:24).

The time of final judgment is called "the day of the Lord" or "the day." All nations will be included in this judgment, and all God's enemies will be destroyed (Isa. 13:9–16; 24:21–22; Zeph. 1:14–18; 3:8). The final kingdom of God will be characterized by peace (Isa. 2:4). All harmful things in nature will be transformed to good (11:6–9). Death and sorrow will be no more (25:8). The kingdom will be inaugurated with a great feast (25:6). Both Israel and the nations will join in the worship of the Lord and in obedience to his law (2:2–3). The king of the line of David will be endowed by the Spirit with wisdom and power. He will rule with justice and righteousness for ever (Isa. 9:5–6; 11:1–5). His name, his qualities, will be "Wonderful Counselor, Mighty God, Everlasting Father, Prince of Peace" (Isa. 9:6).

Ketef Hinnom tombs (Jerusalem, c. 600 B.C.). Within Israelite religion, burial of the body was considered very important.

E. Conclusion: Permanent and temporary in the religion of Israel. Some aspects of the religion of Israel are of permanent validity for the Christian. First is the OT teaching about God, that he is one, personal, good, and just, that he created and rules the world, guides human history, and answers prayer. Another is the Israelite belief about man, that he was created in the image of God, that he is a sinner, that he can be forgiven and transformed by the grace of God. The moral law is the best guide to satisfying individual and social life. The hope of the Israelite, like that of the Christian, is that God's kingdom will come. The above beliefs are assumed in the NT and are basic for understanding the NT.

From a Christian standpoint, some temporary aspects of Israelite religion have been abolished or fulfilled in the NT. The oft-repeated sacrifices of animals have been fulfilled in the one sacrifice of Christ. The sometimes narrow nationalism of Israel has given way to the conviction that Jew and Gentile can be united in Christ. The OT concern with ceremonial defilement is replaced in the NT by an emphasis on moral purity. The distinction between clean and unclean foods that separated

Israelites from Gentiles is no longer appropriate in the international fellowship of the CHURCH. The old covenant with its law written on stone has been replaced by a new covenant whose law of love is written on the heart. The dimness of the OT view of immortality has been illuminated by the RESURRECTION of Christ. The Israelite hope that the Messiah would come has become reality in Jesus, IMMANUEL, "God with us" (Matt. 1:23). The prophetic promise of the outpouring of God's Spirit (Joel 2:28–29) has been fulfilled in PENTECOST (Acts 2) and in the continuing experience of God's people in the church. See also BIBLICAL THEOLOGY; ISRAEL, HISTORY OF; OLD TESTAMENT THEOLOGY.

(Important studies include A. Alt, *Der Gott der Väter* [1921]; G. E. Wright, *The Old Testament against Its Environment* [1950]; id., *God Who Acts* [1952]; W. F. Albright, *Archaeology and the Religion of Israel*, 3rd ed. [1953]; H. H. Rowley, *The Faith of Israel* [1956]; E. Jacob, *Theology of the Old Testament* [1958]; T. C. Vriezen, *An Outline of Old Testament Theology* [1958]; Y. Kaufmann, *The Religion of Israel from Its Beginnings to the Babylonian Exile* [1960]; W. Eichrodt, *Theology of the Old Testament*, 2 vols. [1961–67]; R. de Vaux, *Ancient Israel: Its Life and Institutions* [1961]; G. von Rad, *Old Testament Theology*, 2 vols. [1962–65]; H. J. Kraus, *Worship in Israel* [1966]; H. Ringgren, *Israelite Religion* [1966]; H. H. Rowley, *Worship in Ancient Israel* [1967]; T. C. Vriezen, *The Religion of Ancient Israel* [1967]; W. F. Albright, *Yahweh and the Gods of Canaan* [1968]; J. N. Schofield, *Law, Prophets, and Writings: The Religion of the Books of the Old Testament* [1969]; G. E. Wright, *The Old Testament and Theology* [1969]; R. K. Harrison, *Introduction to the Old Testament* [1969], 351–414; N. K. Gottwald, *The Tribes of Yahweh: A Sociology of the Religion of Liberated Israel, 1250–1050 B.C.* [1979]; S. J. De Vries, *The Achievements of Biblical Religion: A Prolegomenon to Old Testament Theology* [1983]; J. A. Deaman, *Religion and Culture in Ancient Israel* [1992]; R. Albertz, *A History of Israelite Religion in the Old Testament Period*, 2 vols. [1994]; P. D. Miller, *The Religion of Ancient Israel* [2000]; B. M. Gitlen, ed., *Sacred Time, Sacred Place: Archaeology and the Religion of Israel* [2002]; R. Albertz and Bob Becking, eds., *Yahwism after the Exile: Perspectives on Israelite Religion in the Persian Era* [2003]; G. Beckman and T. J. Lewis, eds., *Text, Artifact, and Image: Revealing Ancient Israelite Religion* [2006].)

J. ALEXANDER THOMPSON
R. K. HARRISON

Israelite iz′ray-uh-lit. One who belongs to the nation of ISRAEL. The gentilic Hebrew form *yiśrĕʾēlî* H3778 occurs only four times (twice feminine and once masculine in Lev. 24:10–11 [KJV, "Israelitish"]; and masculine also in a textually uncertain passage, 2 Sam. 17:25 [NRSV "Ishmaelite," on the basis of 1 Chr. 2:17]). The corresponding Greek form, *Israēlitēs* G2703, occurs nine times in the NT (Jn. 1:47; Acts 2:22; et al.). The KJV uses "Israelites" in some passages to render the Hebrew *yiśrāʾēl* H3776 (particularly if it is the subject of a plural verb; e.g., Josh. 3:17), or the singular "Israelite" to render *ʾîš yiśrāʾēl*, "a man of Israel" (Num. 25:14). In addition, modern versions frequently use the term to render the phrase *bĕnê-yiśrāʾēl*, "sons/children of Israel" (Gen. 32:32 et al.).

Issachar is′uh-kahr′ (יִשָּׂשכָר H3779 [*Qere* יִשָּׂכָר], possibly "a man of [*or* there is] hire/reward"). **(1)** The ninth son of JACOB and the fifth of LEAH (Gen. 30:18; 35:23). **(2)** Seventh son of OBED-EDOM, included in the list of divisions of the Korahite doorkeepers in the reign of DAVID (1 Chr. 26:5). The rest of this article is devoted to Issachar son of Jacob.

Issachar had four sons and with them went down into Egypt with Jacob (Gen. 46:13; Exod. 1:3). Practically nothing is preserved of the personal history of the patriarch beyond his share in the common actions of the sons of Jacob. Issachar died in Egypt and was buried there; his descendants formed a tribe, consisting of five great tribal families (Num. 26:23–24). At Sinai the tribe of Issachar numbered 54,400 men of war over twenty years of age (1:29); at the end of the wanderings, the number had grown to 64,300 (26:25). The place of Issachar in the desert march was with the standard of the tribe of JUDAH (along with ZEBULUN) on the E side of the TABERNACLE (2:5); this group formed the vanguard of the host (10:14–17). Igal, son of Joseph, was Issachar's representative to spy out the land of Canaan (13:7).

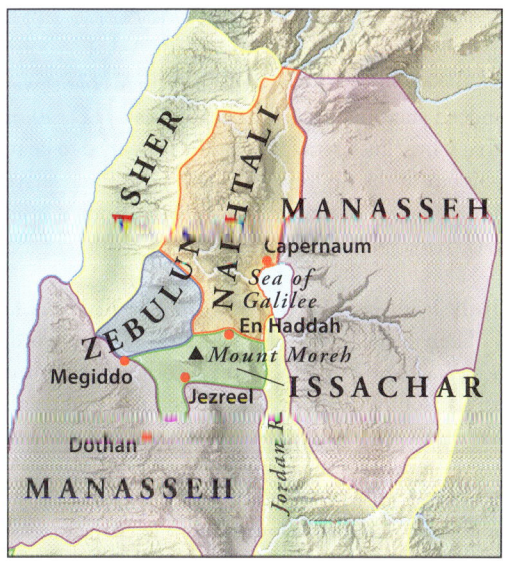

Issachar.

Although a dozen or more towns are listed in Josh. 19:17–23 as belonging to Issachar, the location of most of these is uncertain. In the ceremony described in Deut. 27–28, it was the tribe of Issachar, along with several other tribes, who stood upon Mount Gerizim "to bless the people" (27:11). The territory of Issachar lay S of Zebulun and NAPHTALI, and N of MANASSEH. On the E it was bounded by the Jordan. Whether it ever reached the sea is uncertain (Deut. 33:18–19); it probably remained an inland tribe. Its lot included the very fertile plain of ESDRAELON, but this area for the most part remained in the possession of the Canaanites. See TRIBES, LOCATION OF.

TOLA, one of the JUDGES, was from Issachar (Jdg. 10:1), as were two kings, BAASHA and his son ELAH (1 Ki. 15:27, 16:6). DEBORAH and BARAK belonged to Issachar; and in Deborah's song (Jdg. 5:15), the tribe is mentioned as having taken part in the battle against SISERA. The battle took place on the plain of Issachar, and the victory secured free passage between the Israelites in the hill country of Ephraim and those in Galilee.

In the time of DAVID, the tribe of Issachar numbered 87,000 (1 Chr. 7:5). Of the 200 "heads" of the men of Issachar who came to David at Hebron it is said that they were men "who understood the times and knew what Israel should do" (1 Chr. 12:32). In Solomon's arrangement of administrative districts, Issachar's territory formed an independent province (1 Ki. 4:17). In the arrangement of 1 Chr. 4–7, the extended genealogy of Issachar may be found in 7:1–5, whereas that of Zebulun is missing. A company from Issachar came to the celebration of the PASSOVER when it was restored by HEZEKIAH (2 Chr. 30:18). In the ideal division of the land according to the vision of Ezek. 48:25, the territory of Issachar lies between that of Simeon and of Zebulun; these three tribes have the three gates on the S side of the new Jerusalem named after them (Ezek. 48:33). The tribe of Issachar is also mentioned in Rev. 7:7, where it is said that 12,000 were sealed. L. L. WALKER

Isshiah i-shi´uh (יִשִּׁיָּה H3807, short form of יְשִׁיָּהוּ H3808 [used in 1 Chr. 12:6], probably "Yahweh forgets"; see ISHIJAH). TNIV Ishiah. (1) Son of Izrahiah and descendant of ISSACHAR; a military chief (1 Chr. 7:3 [KJV, "Ishiah"]).

(2) One of several Korahite warriors who joined DAVID at ZIKLAG (1 Chr. 12:6 [KJV, "Jesiah"]; cf. vv. 1–2). These soldiers may have been Levites from the family of KORAH, but some argue that the reference is to a different Korah or even to a locality in the tribe of BENJAMIN.

(3) Son of Uzziel and descendant of LEVI (1 Chr. 23:20 [KJV, "Jesiah"]; 24:25).

(4) Son of Rehabiah and descendant of Levi (1 Chr. 24:21). L. L. WALKER

Isshijah i-shi´juh. See ISHIJAH.

issue of blood. See DISEASE.

Istalcurus is´tuhl-kyoor´uhs (Ἰσταλκουρος). Descendant of Bigvai and father of Uthai, who was among those who returned from the EXILE (1 Esd. 8:40). It is possible, however, that "Uthai the son of Istalcurus" is a corruption of "Uthai and Zaccur" in the parallel passage (Ezra 8:14).

Itala version. See VERSIONS OF THE BIBLE, ANCIENT, II.A.

Italian Regiment (σπεῖρα Ἰταλική). Also Italian Band, Italian Cohort. A unit of the Roman army to which CORNELIUS, who was a CENTURION, belonged (Acts 10:1). Because there is no direct evidence for any such regiment at the time, some have doubted the story of Cornelius (cf. *HJP*, rev. ed. [1973–87], 1:365 and 366 n. 60). Several inscriptions, however, attest that a force called *cohors II Italica* was stationed in Syria from at least A.D. 69 and possibly earlier. It would have been composed, at least originally, of as many as 1000 troops mustered in Italy and holding Roman citizenship (however, see F. F. Bruce, *The Acts of the Apostles: The Greek Text with Introduction and Commentary*, 3rd ed. [1990], 252). Some have thought that an Italian cohort was indeed stationed in CAESAREA around A.D. 40 or that Cornelius (perhaps retired?) happened to be in this city at the time even though the unit may have been on duty elsewhere (see T. R. S. Broughton in *BC*, 5:441–43). See also AUGUSTAN COHORT.

Italy it′uh-lee (Ἰταλία *G2712*). The name *Italia* is likely a hellenized form of an old Italic word, *Vitelia*, "[land of] calves." It was originally applied to the southern tip or "toe" of the peninsula, and then extended gradually with the unification of the peninsula under Roman power (see ROME). Northern Italy (Cisalpine Gaul) was not incorporated and included under the name until the time of AUGUSTUS. It was only then that Italy first reached its Alpine frontiers. Italy is mentioned three times by Luke, once in connection with PRISCILLA AND AQUILA, who had to leave the country when CLAUDIUS expelled the Jews (Acts 18:2), and twice in connection with PAUL's voyage to Rome (27:1, 6); it is also mentioned once by the author of HEBREWS when conveying greetings from Italian friends to his readers (Heb. 13:24), an important detail for determining the historical context of the epistle.

The leg-shaped peninsula is less than 700 mi. long and in breadth never more than 150 mi., except in the northern plain. The Alps form a northern barrier, but not impassable, as Hannibal demonstrated. The northern plain, wide open to invasion, lies between the Alps and the Apennines. This chain branches from the Alps near Genoa, thus eastward to bound old Cisalpine Gaul, rises in height, and sweeps southeastward toward the Adriatic coast, and forms a spine for the peninsula. The mountains, and the plains which they enclose, form the Italian landscape, the former beautiful but infertile, the latter rich and productive, and well watered. Timber, in early days, was abundant, and Italy has always grown the olive and the vine, temperate fruits, and cereals in rich quantity.

Hence the attraction that the peninsula held for invaders, the Etruscans from Asia Minor, as well as the Latins, Oscans, and Umbrians (three branches of Indo-European stock), and other groups of migrants, including the founders of the chain of

Marble statue of Septimius Severus (emperor A.D. 193–211) in military dress. Cornelius, a member of the Roman army stationed in Judea, would have worn a similar uniform.

Greek cities around the southern coasts. The Latin stock, from their enclave around the Tiber, prevailed. Seven centuries of expansion resulted in Rome's political unification of the most strategically located of the Mediterranean peninsulas, the key, as demonstrated from the days of Carthage to the Second World War, to the possession of the central Mediterranean. (See E. T. Salmon, *The Making of Roman Italy* [1982]; T. W. Potter, *Roman Italy* [1987].)   E. M. BLAIKLOCK

itch. See DISEASE.

Ithai ith´i (אִיתַי H416, variant אִיתָי H1015, possibly "[God is] with me"; see ITHIEL). Son of Ribai, a Benjamite from GIBEAH; he was numbered among DAVID's mighty warriors (2 Sam. 23:29 [most versions, ITTAI]; 1 Chr. 11:31).

Ithamar ith´uh-mahr (אִיתָמָר H418, derivation uncertain; see *HALOT*, 1:44, *ABD*, 3:579). Youngest son of AARON and Elisheba (Exod. 6:23; Num. 3:2; 1 Chr. 6:3; 24:1). Together with his three brothers (ELEAZAR, NADAB, and ABIHU) and Aaron, Ithamar was consecrated to the priesthood (Exod. 28:1). His two elder brothers, Nadab and Abihu, were slain for offering strange fire (Lev. 10; cf. Num. 3:4; 26:61; 1 Chr. 24:2).

During the wilderness wanderings he was leader over all the Levites (Exod. 38:21), and more specifically over the Gershonites (Num. 4:28) and the Merarites (4:33; 7:8). He founded a priestly family, to which ELI and his descendants belonged (1 Chr. 24:4–6). Because of this connection, some scholars believe that a conflict developed between the descendants of Ithamar and those of Eleazar (the Zadokites; cf. *ABD*, 3:579–81). According to Ezra 8:2, the family of Ithamar continued after the captivity.   L. L. WALKER

Ithiel ith´ee-uhl (אִיתִיאֵל H417, "God is with me"). **(1)** Son of Jeshaiah, descendant of BENJAMIN, and ancestor of Sallu; the latter was one of the provincial leaders who settled in Jerusalem after the EXILE (Neh. 11:7).

(2) An otherwise unknown man to whom the words of AGUR were addressed (Prov. 30:1). Many argue, however, that instead of "to Ithiel, to Ithiel and Ucal" (לְאִיתִיאֵל לְאִיתִיאֵל וְאֻכָל), the text should be rendered, for example, "I am weary, O God; I am weary, O God, and I languish" (*laʾiti ʾel laʾiti ʾel waʾekel*; cf. NIV mg.). Other changes have been proposed (cf. NRSV), but none has received wide support (cf. B. K. Waltke, *The Book of Proverbs Chapters 15–31*, NICOT [2005], 455–56, 467–68). See also UCAL.

Ithlah ith´luh (יִתְלָה H3849, possibly from תָּלָה H9434, "to hang"). KJV Jethlah. A town within the territory allotted to the tribe of DAN (Josh. 19:42). It was apparently near AIJALON, but its precise location is unknown. The Danites were unable to take possession of this territory (v. 47).

Ithmah ith´muh (יִתְמָה H3850, perhaps "fatherless"). A Moabite, numbered among DAVID's mighty warriors known as the "Thirty" (1 Chr. 11:46).

Ithnan ith´nan (יִתְנָן H3854, derivation uncertain). A town in the NEGEV allotted to the tribe of JUDAH (Josh. 15:23). It was near the boundary of EDOM (v. 21), but its location is unknown.

Ithra ith´ruh (יִתְרָא H3859, "abundance"). Father of AMASA, who led ABSALOM's rebel army; Ithra was married to ABIGAIL, David's sister or half-sister. In 2 Sam. 17:25 MT (cf. KJV, RSV), he is called "Ithra the Israelite," but in 1 Chr. 2:17, where the variant form JETHER occurs (cf. also 1 Ki. 2:5, 32), he is described as "the Ishmaelite." Perhaps he was an ISHMAELITE by race who had joined the nation of Israel. In the former passage, some emend "Ithra" to "Jether" (cf. NIV), or "Israelite" to "Ishmaelite" (cf. NRSV), or both. It has been suggested that he should be identified with NAHASH (see J. D. Levenson and B. Halpern in *JBL* 99 [1980]: 511–12). Because the Hebrew text of 2 Sam. 17:25 says only that Ithra "went to Abigail," some argue that the two were not legally married (cf. P. K. McCarter, *II Samuel*, AB 9 [1984], 393).

Ithran ith´ran (יִתְרָן H3864, prob. "abundance" [יֶתֶר with a diminutive suffix; see *HALOT*, 2:442]; cf. ITHRA; JETHER). **(1)** Son of Dishon and descendant of SEIR the Horite (Gen. 36:26; 1 Chr. 1:41).

(2) Son of Zophah and descendant of ASHER (1 Chr. 7:37); apparently also called Jether (v. 38).

Ithream ith´ree-uhm (יִתְרְעָם H3865, "the Kinsman [*i.e.*, ancestral god] excels" or "remainder of the people"). The sixth and last of the sons of DAVID who were born in HEBRON; his mother was Eglah (2 Sam. 3:5; 1 Chr. 3:3).

Ithrite ith´rit (יִתְרִי H3863, gentilic of יֶתֶר H3858 [JETHER] or יִתְרוֹ H3861 [JETHRO]). A Judahite clan descended from CALEB through HUR and SHOBAL; the Ithrites made up one of several families associated with KIRIATH JEARIM (1 Chr. 2:53). Two of David's mighty warriors, Ira and Gareb, are described as Ithrites (2 Sam. 23:38; 1 Chr. 11:40); however, some argue that the Hebrew here should read *yattirî*, that is, a native of the city of JATTIR.

Ittah-kazin it´uh-kay´zin. KJV form of ETH KAZIN.

Ittai it´i (אִתַּי H915, variant אִיתַי H416, possibly "[God is] with me"; see ITHIEL). (1) Son of Ribai, a Benjamin from GIBEAH; he was numbered among David's mighty warriors (2 Sam. 23:29 [NIV, "Ithai"]; called ITHAI in 1 Chr. 11:31).

(2) A Gittite (i.e., from GATH) who joined himself to David and commanded six hundred men and families. When ABSALOM rebelled against David, Ittai fled with the king and refused to return to Jerusalem. David made him commander of a third part of his army, with JOAB and ABISHAI; he participated in the battle in the forest of Ephraim when Absalom was killed (2 Sam. 15:18–22; 18:2, 5, 12).

L. L. WALKER

Iturea it´yoor-ee´uh (ἡ Ἰτουραία χώρα, "the Iturean country," from Ἰτουραῖος G2714). Also Ituraea. A small principality in the northern section of Palestine that included the Lebanon and Antilebanon mountain ranges and the Lake country around Huleh with its watershed. The capital was at Chalcis. It is mentioned only in Lk. 3:1 as one of the sections of Palestine ruled over by the tetrarch Philip, son of HEROD the Great. The Greek term usually occurs in the masculine plural, *Itouraioi* (i.e., "the Iturean people"). It was thought, though not without disagreement, to be derived from the name of one of ISHMAEL's sons, JETUR (Heb. *yĕṭûr* H3515, LXX *Iettour*, Gen. 25:15; 1 Chr. 1:31; in 1 Chr. 5:19, LXX has *Itouraioi*).

With the decline of the power of the Seleucid empire (see SELEUCIA), which had come into being after the conquests of ALEXANDER THE GREAT, the native rulers and their vassals began to carve out of the decaying central administration little principalities of their own. Not the least of these was Iturea, established in the region known to the Seleucids as COELESYRIA. Stephanus of Byzantium, a geographer of the time of Constantine IV (emperor of Constantinople c. A.D. 685), records a chieftain of the Arabs, Maniko, who established a dynasty of indigenous princes at Chalcis in the 2nd cent. B.C. The tribespeople of Iturea, though probably of Arab ancestry, utilized the ARAMAIC LANGUAGE, which was then the *lingua franca* of large portions of the ANE. They also adopted much of the mixed Greek and Semitic culture that was then in vogue.

In 161 B.C. Judas MACCABEE defeated the army of Nicanor the commander of the Seleucid forces, which led to Jewish independence. During the era of the remaining Maccabees and their successors, the political fortunes of Israel expanded into the power vacuum that existed between Ptolemaic Egypt on the S and Seleucid Syria on the N. John Hyrcanus, the second HASMONEAN ruler, continued this policy in the N, and his son Aristobulus captured a large portion of the area of Iturea in 105–104 B.C. The inhabitants were circumcised and forced to become Jews (Jos. *Ant.* 13.9.3).

The Itureans are mentioned by Strabo (*Geogr.* 16.2.18), who locates them as follows, "All the mountainous areas are occupied by Itureans and Arabians, all of whom are brigands … [who] use strongholds as bases." An inscription of the time of P. Sulpicius Quirinius (c. A.D. 5) indicates that the Itureans had established themselves on the plain of Massyas, between Laodicea and their capital of Chalcis. Some coinage is known from the eras before and after the Jewish conquest. Aristobulus was a popular ruler among the Greek and Arab elements in his Jewish kingdom. The PHARISEES did not approve of this new pro-Greek aristocracy nor did they favor a kingship that was not of the Davidic family.

In 65 B.C. Rome began its eastward expansion under the consulship of G. POMPEY, who soon conquered the northern reaches of Syria and finally took Jerusalem. He enlarged the province of CILICIA and generally settled matters between the previously disputing royalty of the ANE. The ruler of Iturea at the time was a certain Ptolemy son of Menneus; he sent Pompey a payment of 1,000 talents to assure Rome's agreement to his tenure as Iturean king. He shielded the last of the Hasmoneans and was reasonably able to stay aloof from Roman interference; his son Lysanias, however, was murdered by the agents of CLEOPATRA with the compliance of Antony, c. 36 B.C. (Jos. *Ant.* 15.92.3). At this time the once sizable realm was greatly diminished, although the name was still retained for the area of Chalcis and its environs.

Another and more obscure LYSANIAS then inherited the throne of Iturea. He may have been a descendant of the king of the same name murdered by Cleopatra; in any case he held his kingdom by the authority of Rome. It is he who is mentioned in Lk. 3:1 as the tetrarch of ABILENE, one of the remnants into which the old Iturean state had been divided. Herod the Great had annexed segments of the old state to their holdings. When Herod died the Roman emperor, AUGUSTUS, then added the area to that ruled by the tetrarch Philip about 4 B.C. His lands consisted of Auranitis, Batanea, and Traconitis, all of which once had been sections of the Arab kingdom of Iturea, and it was this fact which Luke assumes in the statement, "Philip tetrarch of Iturea." When the Syria-Palestine political system was again overhauled after the invasion of TITUS, c. A.D. 70, Iturea disappeared from the map. (See the articles by G. Schmitt and W. Schottroff in *ZDPV* 90 [1902], 110–24 and 125–52, note also the discussion by E. A. Knauf in *ABD*, 3:583–84.)   W. WHITE, JR.

Ivah i'vuh. KJV form of IVVAH.

ivory. A hard substance that forms the tusks of ELEPHANTS. Ivory was indicative of wealth in ancient times. Ivory tusks were brought to TYRE, a trading nation, in exchange for her abundant goods (Ezek. 27:15; Heb. *šēn H9094*, the usual word for "tooth"). In Rev. 18:12–13, "articles of every kind made of ivory [*elephantinos G1804*]" are mentioned with other numerous products of great value in trade and commerce. The material was secured from a breed of Indian elephants in the upper EUPHRATES, where there were large herds in the 2nd millennium B.C. There are Assyrian accounts of elephant hunts with many slain in that period. They became extinct there about the 8th cent. B.C. Ivory was also obtained from INDIA by ocean-going ships, and from Africa-Rhodes (or Dedan, KJV), doubtless referring to that traffic passing through (Ezek. 27:15). In Solomon's time his "ships of Tarshish" brought in ivory with gold and silver (1 Ki. 10:22). The fact that they came every three years shows how far ranging they were, probably reaching India. Excavations at ALALAKH in Syria turned up large ivory tusks. Egyptian and Assyrian art shows tusks as trophies of war.

In the Bible we learn that there were ivory beds (Amos 6:4) and houses (1 Ki. 22:39; Ps. 45:8; Amos 3:15); and Solomon's throne was of ivory overlaid with gold (1 Ki. 10:18; 2 Chr. 9:17). The Phoenicians may have decorated their ships with it, for Tyre is said metaphorically to be a ship with ivory-inlaid decks (Ezek. 27:6). Qualities of the body are likened to ivory (Cant. 5:14; 7:4), the product being suitable to represent flesh.

We learn from extrabiblical sources that ivory was used in making figurines, spoons, flasks, gaming boards, combs, boxes, and articles of furniture such as chairs and beds in which there was doubtless much inlay work. There were guilds of ivory workers

Ivory backrest, possibly from a couch, discovered in Nimrud (8th cent. B.C.); it depicts warriors and the fruit of the lotus tree.

in Phoenicia who supplied products for export to middle eastern lands and probably beyond. Conquerors have listed objects of ivory in booty taken from Palestine, as did Sennacherib, who listed in the tribute paid him by Hezekiah in 701 B.C. "couches (inlaid) with ivory" (*ANET*, 288). Extraordinary stores of ivory have been found at Ras Shamra (see UGARIT) and MEGIDDO, a hoard of 383 pieces of carved work from the latter alone in 1932, ascribed to 1350–1150 B.C. Thus, whether as raw material or in the form of finished products, ivory was of considerable value in the commerce of the ancient world. (See J. W. and G. M. Crowfoot, *Early Ivories from Samaria* [1938]; G. Loud, *The Megiddo Ivories* [1939]; R. D. Barnett, "Phoenicia and the Ivory Trade," *Archaeology* 9 [1956]: 87–97; R. D. Barnett, *Ancient Ivories in the Middle East* [1982].)

N. B. BAKER

Ivvah iv´uh (עִוָּה H6394). KJV Ivah. One of several Syrian city-states vanquished by SENNACHERIB (2 Ki. 18:34; 2 Ki. 19:13; Isa. 37:13). The commander of the Assyrian forces, seeking to shake HEZEKIAH's confidence in the Lord, claimed that the gods and kings of those cities were powerless before Sennacherib. Because Ivvah is listed along with HAMATH and ARPAD (also SEPHARVAIM and HENA), it is thought to have been located in N Syria, but the location is unknown. It is probably the same as AVVAH (2 Ki. 17:24, 31). Some scholars, noticing that Hena and Ivvah are not mentioned in similar lists (2 Ki. 17:24; Isa. 36:19), and suspecting that they are not true geographical names, have suggested that they are pagan deities, or that the text is corrupt, or that the words should be rendered "he has taken away and overthrown" (see *ABD*, 3:137–38).

ivy. This term (Gk. *kissos*) occurs only once in the APOCRYPHA, which states that, on the birthday celebration of ANTIOCHUS IV, the Jews "were compelled to wear wreathes of ivy and to walk in the procession in honor of Dionysus" (2 Macc. 6:7; see MACCABEES). This plant is undoubtedly *Hedera helix*, a climbing plant. It is found on walls and rocks in the Holy Land, and is connected with Bacchus (DIONYSUS), the God of wine. In ancient Roman days, a spray of ivy hung outside the door of every tavern in which wine was sold. This sign was similar in effect to the colored, striped poles outside barbers' shops. The Greeks dedicated the ivy to Bacchus, and the Jews therefore hated entering the pagan temple to be made to worship, carrying his plant, the ivy.

W. E. SHEWELL-COOPER

Iyar ee´yahr. Also Iyyar. The second month of the Hebrew CALENDAR, corresponding to April-May. Its earliest occurrence is in the ELEPHANTINE PAPYRI (*ʾyr*), but the name is equivalent to Babylonian *Aiaru*. In the Bible, the second month is known by its Canaanite name, ZIV.

Iye Abarim i´yuh-ab´uh-rim (עִיֵּי הָעֲבָרִים H6516, "ruins of the regions beyond"). Also called IYIM. A stopping place of the Israelites in their wilderness wanderings, between Oboth and the Valley of ZERED or DIBON Gad (Num. 21:11–12; 33:44–45). It was either in MOAB (33:44; NIV, "on the border of Moab") or in its vicinity (21:11). Its location is uncertain, though one possible identification is modern el-Medeiyineh, c. 19 mi. ESE of the S tip of the DEAD SEA (on the N slope of the Zered Valley). Possibly the place was associated with the ABARIM mountain range.

Iyim i´yim (עִיִּים H6517, "ruins, stone heaps"). KJV and TNIV Iim. A shortened form of IYE-ABARIM (Num. 33:45). This place is not to be confused with IIM (Josh. 15:29), even though the form is identical in Hebrew.

Izehar, Izeharite iz´uh-hahr, iz´uh-hah-rit. KJV alternate forms of IZHAR and IZHARITE.

Izhar iz´hahr (יִצְהָר H3659, "[God] shines"; gentilic יִצְהָרִי H3660, "Izharite"). KJV also Izehar, Izeharite. (1) Son of KOHATH, grandson of LEVI, father of KORAH (and two other sons), uncle of MOSES, and eponymous ancestor of the Izrahite clan (Exod. 6:18, 21; Num. 3:19, 27; 16:1; 1 Chr. 6:2, 18, 38; 23:12, 18). Several of his descendants were prominent Levites (1 Chr. 23:18 [cf. v. 33]; 24:22; 26:23, 29).

(2) Son of Asshur (by his wife Helah) and descendant of JUDAH (1 Chr. 4:7; cf. v. 5). So the NRSV, following the *Ketib*; the NIV and NJPS follow the

Qere in reading ZOHAR (Heb. *ṣōḥar* H7468), while the KJV's "Jezoar" is a hybrid of the two forms.

Izliah iz-li′uh (יִזְלִיאָה H3468, "long-living" or "Yahweh delivers"). KJV Jezliah. Son of ELPAAL and descendant of BENJAMIN (1 Chr. 8:18); he is listed among the heads of families who lived in Jerusalem (cf. v. 28).

Izrahiah iz′ruh-hi′uh (יִזְרַחְיָה H3474, "Yahweh goes forth [*or* shines]"; see JEZRAHIAH). Son of Uzzi and great-grandson of ISSACHAR; a military chief (1 Chr. 7:3).

Izrahite iz′ruh-hit (יִזְרָח H3473). Although this term in Hebrew does not have the usual gentilic form (i.e., with the ending *-i*), it apparently refers to someone from Izrah, a place otherwise unknown. The term is applied to a certain SHAMHUTH, who was the commander of the fifth monthly division under DAVID (1 Chr. 27:8). Some emend the text to read *zarḥi* H2439, "Zerahite" (i.e., a descendant of ZERAH of Judah; cf. v. 11). The problem is further complicated by the likelihood that "Shamhuth the Izrahite" is the same as "Shammah the Harodite" (2 Sam. 23:25), also called "Shammoth the Harorite" (1 Chr. 11:27). Clearly scribal activity has created confusion, and we are no longer able to identify the original form(s) of the name.

Izri iz′ri (יִצְרִי H3673, possibly "[Yahweh] has formed"; see JEZER). A Levitical musican who, with his sons and relatives, received the fourth lot (1 Chr. 25:11); the name is probably a variant of ZERI (v. 3).

Izziah i-zi′uh (יִזִּיָּה H3466, "Yahweh sprinkles"). One of the descendants of Parosh who agreed to put away their foreign wives (Ezra 10:25 [KJV, "Jeziah"]; 1 Esd. 9:26 [KJV, "Eddias"]).

This capital from the 11th or 12th cent. A.D. depicts the beheading of James.

J

J (Jahwist) yah′wist. An abbreviation for Yahwist (German *Jahwist*); it is used (along with D, E, and P) to designate one of the supposed sources of the PENTATEUCH, according to the Documentary Hypothesis.

Jaakan jay′uh-kan (יַעֲקָן [not in NIV]), KJV Jakan. Son of EZER and grandson of SEIR the HORITE; he probably became the progenitor of a clan in EDOM (1 Chr. 1:42 NRSV, following MT). On the basis of some Hebrew MSS and the parallel passage (Gen. 36:37), many scholars emend *ya‘ăqān* to *wa‘ăqān* ("and Akan"; cf. NIV). See also BEEROTH-BENE-JAAKAN and BENE JAAKAN.

Jaakanite jay-a′kuh-nit. See BEEROTH-BENE-JAAKAN.

Jaakobah jay′uh-koh′buh (יַעֲקֹבָה H3621, "[God] protects"; see JACOB). A clan leader in the tribe of SIMEON (1 Chr. 4:36). He is listed among those whose families increased greatly during the days of King HEZEKIAH and who dispossessed the Hamites and Meunites near GEDOR (vv. 38–41).

Jaala jay′uh-luh (יַעְלָא H3605, variant יַעְלָה H3606, "mountain goat"). Also Jaalah. A servant of SOLOMON whose descendants returned from the EXILE (Ezra 2:56 [KJV, NRSV, "Jaalah"]; Neh. 7:58; 1 Esd. 5:33 [KJV, "Jeeli"; NRSV, "Jaalah"]).

Jaalah jay′uh-luh. See JAALA.

Jaalam jay′uh-lam. KJV form of JALAM.

Jaanai jay′uh-ni. KJV form of JANAI.

Jaar jay′uhr (יַעַר H3625, "forest"). The name of a place that, along with EPHRATHAH, was associated with the ARK OF THE COVENANT (Ps. 132:6; KJV, "the wood" [cf. LXX]). Jaar is generally regarded as a (poetic) short form of KIRIATH JEARIM (meaning "town of forests"), where the ark remained twenty years before DAVID brought it to Jerusalem. Some believe that the name was applied to a wooded area in the environs of Kiriath Jearim. It is possible that in this passage Ephrathah does not refer to BETHLEHEM specifically, but to a larger area that extended as far N as the border between the tribes of Judah and Benjamin.   E. RUSSELL

Jaare-Oregim jay′uh-ree-or′uh-gim (יַעֲרֵי אֹרְגִים H3629, "forests of weavers" [but scribal error suspected]). Father of Elhanan; the latter is described as the killer of GOLIATH the Gittite (2 Sam. 21:19). Jaare-Oregim is apparently called JAIR in the parallel passage (1 Chr. 20:5). For possible solutions to the discrepancies between these two verses, see ELHANAN.

Jaareshiah jay′uh-ree-shi′uh (יַעֲרֶשְׁיָה H3631, "Yahweh plants"), KJV Jaresiah. Son of Jeroham and descendant of BENJAMIN, he is listed among the heads of families who lived in Jerusalem (1 Chr. 8:27).

Jaasau jay′uh-saw. KJV form of JAASU.

Jaasiel jay-ay′see-uhl (יַעֲשִׂיאֵל H3634, "God makes [*or* carries out, *or* treats well]") KJV Jasiel. **(1)** Son of ABNER (SAUL's cousin); he was made an officer over the tribe of BENJAMIN during the reign of DAVID (1 Chr. 27:21).

435

(2) A Mezobaite, mentioned last among David's mighty warriors (1 Chr. 11:47). Some scholars emend "Mezobaite" to "from Zobah." It has also been suggested, but without good reason, that this Jaasiel is the same as #1 above.

Jaasu jay'uh-soo (יַעֲשׂוּ H3632 [*Qere* יַעֲשָׂי], possibly "[God] treats well"; see Jaasiel). KJV Jaasau. One of the descendants of Bani who agreed to put away their foreign wives (Ezra 10:37).

Jaazaniah jay-az'uh-ni'uh (יַאֲזַנְיָהוּ H3280, variants יַאֲזַנְיָה H3279 [Jer. 35:3; Ezek. 11:1] and יְזַנְיָה H3471 [Jer. 40:8], "Yahweh listens"; see Jezaniah). The name appears on a number of ancient archaeological remains, showing that it was common in OT times.

(1) A military commander identified as "the son of the Maacathite"; he was among the officers who went to Mizpah to join Gedaliah, the governor appointed by the Babylonians after the fall of Jerusalem (2 Ki. 25:23; Jer. 40:8 [KJV, NRSV, "Jezaniah"]). It is usually thought that Jaazaniah belonged to the family that descended from Maacah, Caleb's concubine (1 Chr. 2:48), but there are other possibilities. Some speculate that this is the Jaazaniah whose name is inscribed on a seal discovered in Mizpah (modern Tell en-Nasbeh; see M. Cogan and H. Tadmor, *II Kings*, AB 11 [1988], 326).

(2) Son of Jeremiah (not the prophet), a leader of the Recabites, whose loyalty to their ancestral precepts the prophet Jeremiah used as a lesson to his own countrymen (Jer. 35:3).

(3) Son of Shaphan and, apparently, a prominent elder in Jerusalem at the time of the exile; he is the only one mentioned by name among the seventy elders of Israel whom Ezekiel, in a vision, saw offering incense to idols (Ezek. 8:11).

(4) Son of Azzur; he and Pelatiah son of Benaiah were leaders of the people in Jerusalem at the time of the exile, and Ezekiel was commanded to prophesy against their sin (Ezek. 11:1).

Jaazer jay'uh-zuhr. KJV alternate form of Jazer (Num. 21:32; 32:35).

Jaaziah jay'uh-zi'uh (יַעֲזִיָּהוּ H3596, "Yahweh nourishes"; see Jaaziel). Son of Merari and grandson of Levi; he is not mentioned in most of the genealogies (e.g., Exod. 6:19), but only in a list of Levitical families that served during the time of David (1 Chr. 24:26–27). The Hebrew text is difficult, however, and some regard it as a later gloss (e.g., KD, *Chronicles*, 259 [on 23:23]).

Jaaziel jay-ay'zee-uhl (יַעֲזִיאֵל H3595, "God nourishes"; see Jaaziah). One of the Levites who played the lyre when the ark of the covenant was brought to Jerusalem (1 Chr. 15:18; called Aziel in v. 20; some also identify him with the first Jeiel listed in 16:5).

Jabal jay'buhl (יָבָל H3299, possibly "[God] leads" or "wanderer"). First son of Lamech by Adah; he was "the father of those who live in tents and raise livestock," meaning probably that he originated the profession of herding animals, which often required the nomadic lifestyle of constant travel in search of pasture (Gen. 4:20). The word for "livestock" (*miqneh* H5238), which more generally means "possessions," may be a wordplay on the name of his ancestor Cain (*qayin* H7803). Less likely is the suggestion that the name Jabal alludes to Abel, the first shepherd. See also Jubal.

Jabbok jab'uhk (יַבֹּק H3309, prob. "overflowing"). A river in Transjordan (Nahr ez-Zerka, "river of blue"), about 60 mi. in length and, next to the Yarmuk River, having the greatest drainage area in that region. It is a perennial stream, deriving from the 28–32 in. of rainfall annually. Its average fall is c. 80 ft. per mi., cutting a deep valley or gorge through the E Jordan Valley escarpment. The source lies in the vicinity of modern Amman (ancient Rabbah of Ammon, and Hellenistic Philadelphia), from whence it swings eastward and northward, forming a large loop before wending westward to the Jordan Valley. The lower gorge is under sea level to a point 7 mi. E of the rift, at an elevation of more than 2,000 ft. below the Gilead Plateau to the N and the Amman Plateau to the S. Colorful oleanders line most of its banks in the hill country. After emerging into the Jordan Valley near Tell Deir 'Alla (prob. ancient Succoth), it meanders across the Ghor before joining the Jordan River near ed-Damiyeh (biblical Adam).

JABESH GILEAD 437

The Jabbok River valley looking W.

The loop N of Amman formed the W boundary of the Ammonites at the time of the conquest (Num. 21:24), and the contained area was settled by the tribe of GAD, as far W as present es-Salt. The western part of the river formed a physical and political boundary between the two parts of GILEAD (Deut. 3:12, 16; Josh. 12:2–6), and also divided the kingdoms of SIHON and OG. Nelson Glueck found numerous occupation sites in the Wadi ez-Zerka in his surveys, and several biblical cities were located on, or near, its course. The specific ford referred to in Gen. 32:22 has not been identified, but the nearby site called Peniel (v. 31) is probably Tell edh-Dhahab esh-Sherqiyeh, about 8 mi. E of the Jordan; see PENUEL (PLACE). (See D. Baly, *The Geography of the Bible* [1957], 229; E. Orni and E. Efrat, *Geography of Israel* [1964], 91–94; Y. Aharoni, *The Land of the Bible: A Historical Geography*, rev. ed. [1979], 34, 38, 327.)

M. H. HEICKSEN

Jabesh jay´bish (יָבֵשׁ H3314, "dry"). Father of King SHALLUM of Israel, who murdered King ZECHARIAH and usurped the throne (2 Ki. 15:10, 13–14). However, since the name Jabesh (*yābēš* H3315) is also a short form of JABESH GILEAD, the expression "son of Jabesh" may mean "a native of Jabesh [Gilead]."

S. BARABAS

Jabesh Gilead jay´bish-gil´ee-uhd (יָבֵשׁ גִּלְעָד H3316, "dry place of Gilead"; also referred to simply as יָבֵשׁ H3315). A city in N TRANSJORDAN (see GILEAD). The first mention of Jabesh Gilead comes at the end of a long story beginning in Jdg. 19 and continuing to the end of ch. 21. Briefly told, a Levite and a concubine, after spending some time with her people in BETHLEHEM, made their way N. They stopped for the night in GIBEAH, where an old man entertained them. In the course of the night, the Levite yielded to the sadistic cravings of the men of Gibeah and gave to them his concubine. In the morning she was dead on the doorstep, so the

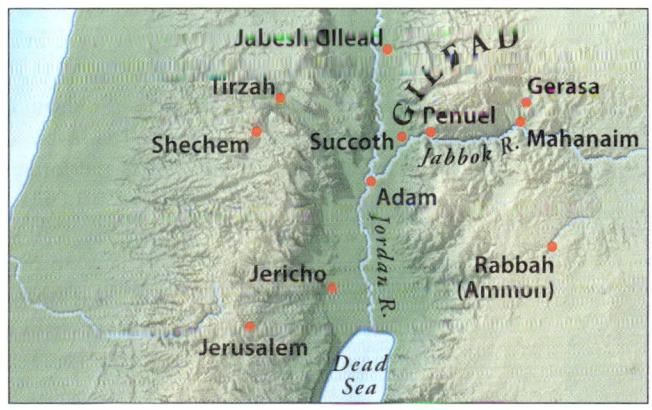

Jabbok River.

Levite dismembered her and sent the parts around the country. This incident started a war between BENJAMIN (of which Gibeah was a part) and the other Israelite tribes. The battle was indecisive for a while, but finally the Benjamites were defeated and almost completely annihilated. Because no one from Jabesh Gilead had fought against Benjamin, the Israelites went and slaughtered all but 400 eligible virgins in the city, and these were given to 400 surviving soldiers of Benjamin for wives. The 200 others were given permission to seize girls as they danced at the annual SHILOH festival (Jdg. 21:23). Apparently the town of Jabesh was repopulated by neighboring Gileadites.

The next episode centering on Jabesh is recorded in 1 Sam. 11, where the Ammonite NAHASH attacked the town. The only peace treaty acceptable to Nahash was that he gouge out one eye from each man of Jabesh. During the week of deliberations the citizens requested help from SAUL, the newly crowned king. He mustered the forces of Israel at BEZEK, marched all night, attacked Nahash early in the morning, and by noon had the enemy scattered. Because of this, Saul gained the allegiance of Jabesh Gilead and all Transjordan. Its inhabitants showed their devotion to Saul by giving him an honorable burial when, after his and JONATHAN's defeat and death on Mount GILBOA, their decapitated bodies were hung on the wall of BETH SHAN. The valorous gesture involved an all-night walk and a crossing of the Jordan by the men of Jabesh Gilead (1 Sam. 31:8–13; 1 Chr. 10:8–12).

When DAVID came to power, one of the first things he did was to commend, congratulate, and bless the brave men of Jabesh Gilead for what they had done for Saul (2 Sam. 2:4–6). Later, David had the bones of Saul and Jonathan removed from Jabesh Gilead and buried in the land of Benjamin with KISH, Saul's father (2 Sam. 21:10–14).

Modern Wadi Yabis, which enters the Jordan from the E about 25 mi. S of the Sea of Galilee, bears the same name as this ancient town. One might well expect to find Jabesh Gilead on this river. Since the often correct *Onomasticon* of EUSEBIUS locates it c. 6 mi. S of PELLA (Tabaqat Fahil), the double mounds of Tell el-Meqbereh and Tell Abu Kharaz are favored by some (N. Glueck, *The River Jordan* [1946], 159–69, and AASOR 25–28 [1951]: 211–23). Both of these have produced surface pottery of the period of Saul and stand near enough to the Jordan—in fact, on the edge of the valley itself—to fit well the story of the recovery of Saul and Jonathan's bodies. Most scholars, however, prefer Tell el-Maqlub, farther up the Wadi Yabis, about 7 mi. E of the Jordan (cf. Y. Aharoni, *The Land of the Bible: A Historical Geography*, rev. ed. [1979], 127–28). It has been objected that such a location is too far from Beth Shan (about 13 mi. SE of this city) to allow for the events described in 1 Sam. 31:11–13, but it is quite possible that the men of Jabesh Gilead on that occasion traveled a good part of the day as well as all night to retrieve the bodies (see *ABD*, 3:594). R. L. ALDEN

Jabez (person) jay'biz (יַעְבֵּץ H3584, derivation uncertain). A man in the line of JUDAH noted for his honorable character (1 Chr. 4:9–10). In this passage, the genealogy is interrupted with the following information: "Jabez was more honorable than his brothers. His mother had named him Jabez [*ya'bēṣ*], saying, 'I gave birth to him in pain [*bĕ'ōṣeb*].' Jabez cried out to the God of Israel, 'Oh, that you would bless me and enlarge my territory! Let your hand be with me, and keep me from harm so that I will be free from pain.' And God granted his request." (The wordplay on his name requires a transposition of the consonants *b* and *ṣ*; the meaning "pain" must be regarded as a popular etymology.) This abrupt introduction of Jabez, who had not previously been mentioned, is puzzling. Some speculate that he may have been a son (or brother) of Koz (v. 8; it has even been suggested that in this verse the name Hazzobebah [*haṣṣōbēbâ*] is a corruption of Jabez). A few scholars have further speculated that Jabez was the founder of the town by the same name. See JABEZ (PLACE).

Jabez (place) jay'biz (יַעְבֵּץ H3583, derivation uncertain). A city in JUDAH, perhaps near BETHLEHEM, occupied by clans of scribes that were descendants of CALEB through Hur and Salma (1 Chr. 2:55). However, these clans, which consisted of Tirathites, Shimeathites, and Sucathites, are also identified as "the Kenites who came from Hammath, the father of the house of Recab." C. F. Keil (KD, *Chronicles*, 77) seeks to "explain the incorporation of the Kenites in the Judaean family of the Calebite Salma, on the supposition that one of these Kenites of the family of Hobab, the brother-in-law of Moses, married an heiress of the race of Caleb. On this account the children and descendants sprung of this marriage would be incorporated in the family of Caleb, although they were on their father's side Kenites, and where they followed the manner of life of their fathers, might continue to be regarded as such, and to bear the name." See HOBAB; KENITES. (For further discussion of this verse, see esp. G. N. Knoppers, *I Chronicles 1–9*, AB 12 [2004], 315–16.)

Jabin jay'bin (יָבִין *H3296*, possibly "perceptive"). (1) King of HAZOR and head of a coalition of Canaanite kings who sought to withstand the Israelites (Josh. 11:1–12). The confederacy of Canaanite princes produced an army "as numerous as the sand on the seashore" (v. 4). Excavations at Hazor, conducted by Y. Yadin in 1955, indicate that the city was quite extensive, with a population of about 40,000. In view of the size of the coalition, an imposing force blocked further entry into Canaan. JOSHUA's advance, however, took the Canaanites by surprise and enabled the Israelites to defeat them. Hazor was then destroyed, and Jabin was put to death along with the other princes of the confederation (vv. 10–12).

(2) A Canaanite king who reigned in Hazor; probably a descendant of #1 above (Jdg. 4:2; some suggest that Jabin was a dynastic title). The idolatry of the Israelites led to their being oppressed by him for twenty years. His armament was extensive, being described as 900 chariots of iron (v. 3). The commander of his forces was SISERA, who seemed to be more prominent in the incident than Jabin the king. The oppression of the Canaanites was overthrown by DEBORAH's plan. BARAK effected the strategy that resulted in eventual victory (vv. 23–24). The victory was celebrated in song (Jdg. 5; cf. Ps. 83:9). T. E. MCCOMISKEY

Jabneel, Jabneh jab'nee-uhl, jab'neh (יַבְנְאֵל *H3305*, "God builds"; short form יַבְנֶה *H3306* [2 Chr. 26:6]; Ἰάμνεια [1 Macc. 4:15 et al.]; gentilic Ἰαμνίτης, "Jamnite," 2 Macc. 12:9], also Ιεμναων [Jdt. 2:28]). (1) A town on the S boundary of the tribal territory of NAPHTALI (Josh. 19:33). It is identified with Tell en-Naʿam, 3.5 mi. W of the S tip of the Sea of Galilee; the modern village of Yavneel is situated nearby (the Talmudic Jabneel is identified with Kh. Yamma).

(2) A town on the W boundary of the tribal territory of JUDAH, between JOPPA and GAZA, near the coast (Josh. 15:11). It was an important station on the VIA MARIS, and was later also known as Jamnia. The modern town of Yavne (Yebna), c. 13 mi S of Joppa, is located on the site.

The only biblical event associated with this city took place in the 8th cent. B.C., when King UZZIAH, campaigning against the PHILISTINES, "broke down the walls of Gath, Jabneh and Ashdod" (2 Chr. 26:6), thus gaining an access to the sea at the mouth of the Yarkon River. After the OT period, in 332 B.C., ALEXANDER THE GREAT moved down the Palestinian coast. After capturing Acco, he proceeded to Strato's Tower, then probably inland before returning to the coast at LOD, thence through Jabneh (Jamnia) and ASHKELON, to the siege of Gaza, which lasted two months, after which he wintered in Egypt.

In 163 B.C., there was an unsuccessful attack on Jamnia by the Maccabean Jewish army leaders, Joseph and Azarias (1 Macc. 5:55–62; see MACCABEE). Jamnia was an important SELEUCID military base (1 Macc. 4:15; cf. 10:69; 15:40), and in a subsequent campaign, Judas razed the port of Jamnia with fire (2 Macc. 12:8–9, 40). In 147 B.C., the Battle of Jamnia was fought. Jonathan was challenged by Demetrius II's general, Apollonius, and having 10,000 men, was joined by Simon with another battalion. Together they moved against Joppa, then S, and were ambushed between Jamnia and Azotus. Heavy fighting occurred, with a signal victory for the Jews (1 Macc. 10:69–87). The Seleucid forces continued to occupy Jamnia, and under the leadership of Cendebeus, built a fort at Kidron (near modern Gedera), from which they harassed the Judeans. John Hyrcanus attacked the fort and gained a solid victory (see HASMONEAN II.A). The town is also mentioned in JUDITH (Jdt. 2:28; KJV, "Jemnaan").

Along with several coastal and interior towns, Jamnia was liberated by POMPEY (63–55 B.C.) from Jewish rule and annexed to Syria. It is probable that AUGUSTUS (c. 30 B.C.) added the city to the kingdom of HEROD, for the latter left it in his will to his sister Salome (who in turn bequeathed it to the Empress Livia). Jamnia probably was visited by Philip on his preaching tour from Azotus (Ashdod) to Caesarea (Acts 8:40). In A.D. 67, during Vespasian's campaign, Jamnia and Azotus were captured by the Romans. The city became the headquarters of the exiled Sanhedrin from the time of the fall of Jerusalem (70) to the second revolt (132–135).

Jamnia is best known as the site of a gathering that supposedly made formal decisions about the canon c. A.D. 90. The primary basis for this "Council (or Synod) of Jamnia (Yavneh)" is a statement by Rabbi Simeon ben Azzai recorded in the Mishnah: "I have heard a tradition from the seventy-two elders on the day when they made R. Eleazar b. Azariah head of the college [of Sages], that the Song of Songs and Ecclesiastes both render the hands unclean" (the expression "render the hands unclean" indicates canonical status). There was then some debate on the matter, but in the end, "According to the words of Ben Azzai so did they dispute and so did they decide" (*m. Yadaim* 3:5; a number of other rabbinic references to "on that day" refer to the time when Eleazar was appointed head of the academy). Some modern scholars speculated that it was at this meeting that the OT canon was officially closed, the Hebrew text standardized, and the breach between Judaism and Christianity formalized. This hypothesis was widely accepted, and many works published in the 20th cent. treat such a council as proven fact.

While it is true that for a number of decades after A.D. 70 Jewish sages gathered in Jamnia from time to time to debate a variety of problems, and that these meetings often led to decisions (whether by formal vote or by consensus), the use of such terms as *council* or *synod* is misleading. These gatherings should not be compared with the Christian ecumenical councils that reached decisions binding on the church as a whole. Moreover, there is no evidence that questions about the canon were a major concern when the rabbis met (See R. C. Newman in *WTJ* 38 [1975–76], 319–49; S. J. D. Cohen in *HUCA* 55 [1986], 17–53; J. P. Lewis, "Jamnia," in *ABD*, 3:634–37; id., "Jamnia Revisited" in *The Canon Debate*, ed. L. M. McDonald and J. A. Sanders [2002], 146–62.)   M. H. Heicksen

Jabneh. See Jabneel.

Jacan jay′kuhn (יָעְכָּן H3602, meaning uncertain). KJV Jachan, TNIV Jakan. Son of Abihail; he was one of seven relatives from the tribe of Gad who occupied the region E of Gilead (1 Chr. 5:13; cf. v. 10, 14).

Jachan jay′kuhn. KJV form of Jacan.

Jachin jay′kin. See Jakin.

jacinth. A gem variety of the mineral zircon (zirconium silicate), now almost universally referred to as *hyacinth*. It is transparent and generally red in color; sometimes it is orange or brownish. Jacinth (hyacinth) is not a common mineral. It occurs, together with other zircons, in the gem gravels of Ceylon, but many gem stones called hyacinth are deep orange-brown garnets (cinnamon-stone or hessonite). The Hebrew term *lešem* H4385, of uncertain meaning, is rendered "jacinth" by the NIV and other versions (it is found only in Exod. 28:19; 39:12 [KJV, "ligure"]). The Greek term *hyakinthos* G5610 probably was used by ancient writers to refer to a blue mineral (cf. NIV "dark blue," Rev. 9:17; NRSV, "sapphire"; both versions render it "jacinth" in 21:20).   D. R. Bowes

jackal. The usual Hebrew term for "jackal" is *tan* H9478 (always pl. and used in figurative contexts), but *šû'āl* H8785, which most often refers to the fox, can be used with the same meaning (Lam. 5:18; Ezek. 13:4), as can perhaps other terms (cf. Isa. 13:21 NIV; *FFB*, 31–32). Jackals are related to foxes and even more closely to domestic dogs, for with them they belong to the genus *Canis*. The Palestine species is the oriental jackal (*Canis aureus*), with head and body 24–30 in. in length, and a tail of up to 12 in.; its color is a dirty yellow mixed with reds and blacks. Jackals usually go about in packs of up to a dozen, feeding mostly at night, and it is interesting that in all cases the Hebrew word is plural. The jackal is basically a scavenger, living rather as a hyena in game country, where it can clean up after the larger carnivores have killed. In contrast, the fox is more solitary, feeding on a wide range of vegetable matter and small animals, and

A jackal.

taking less refuse than the jackal. Several times it is prophesied that lands (e.g., Babylon, Jer. 51:37; Edom, Mal. 1:3) shall become the haunt of jackals, which are almost a symbol of desolation (more than half of the passages have this theme). To the casual observer foxes and jackals look very similar, and it is possible that they were often given the same name.

G. S. CANSDALE

Jackal Well. Also Jackal's Well (RSV). A well or spring in JERUSALEM, apparently between the VALLEY GATE and the DUNG GATE (Neh. 2:13 NIV). The rendering "Jackal," however, assumes that the Hebrew *tannîn* H9490, which means "serpent" or "sea monster," should be read as *tannîm* (pl. of *tan* H9478, JACKAL; cf. the *Ketib* at Lam. 4:3). Others take the word in its usual sense (thus KJV, "dragon well"; NRSV, "Dragon's Spring"). It is common to identify the Jackal (or Dragon) Well with EN ROGEL, a spring about 800 ft. S of the SE ridge of Jerusalem (thus just below the junction of the HINNOM and KIDRON Valleys). It has also been argued that the reference is to the GIHON SPRING, which follows a serpentine course. Some, however, suggest that the Hebrew term *ʿayin* H6524 here means "eye" rather than "spring" (if so, no one knows what Serpent's Eye might refer to). Finally, it should be noted that the SEPTUAGINT rendered the Hebrew phrase as *pēgēs tōn sykōn*, "fountain of the figs" (no doubt reading *tĕʾēnîm*, pl. of *tĕʾēnâ* H9300, "fig"). See also ZOHELETH, STONE OF.

Jacob jay´kuhb (יַעֲקֹב H3620; possibly "[God] protects," but by popular etymology, "he takes by the heel, supplants, deceives"; Ἰακώβ G2609, Ἰά-κωβος G2610 [see JAMES]). (1) Son of ISAAC and REBECCA, younger twin brother of ESAU, husband of LEAH and RACHEL. He later was called ISRAEL (Gen. 32:28; 49:2) and thus, through his twelve sons, became the eponymous ancestor of the Israelites. (2) Son of Matthan and father of JOSEPH, Mary's husband, listed in Matthew's GENEALOGY OF JESUS CHRIST (Matt. 1:15–16; see also HELI). The rest of this article is devoted to the Hebrew patriarch.

    I. Birth
    II. Jacob and Esau
    III. In Haran
    IV. Return from Haran
    V. Jacob the patriarch

I. Birth. At his birth he was holding his older brother's heel and thus was named Jacob (Gen. 25:26). The word for "heel" is the Hebrew noun *ʿāqēb* H6811, and its cognate verb, *ʿāqab* H6810, can mean both "to take by the heel" (Hos. 12:3) and "to supplant, deceive" (Jer. 9:3). When Jacob stole his older brother's blessing, Esau affirmed that Jacob was correctly named, "For he has supplanted me [*wayyaʿqĕbēnî*] these two times" (27:36 NRSV; NIV, "has deceived me"). Personal names containing this same Semitic root (but prob. with the meaning "protect") are also found in the extrabiblical documents contemporary with the patriarchs but are not found elsewhere in the OT. No individual in Israel, apart from the patriarch, bore the name Jacob until the Hellenistic period, when it usually occurs in the Greek form *Iakōbos*.

    The birth of Jacob is described in Gen. 25 and his death is recorded in Gen. 50, so that his life covers one-half of Genesis. Since Rebecca, like SARAH, was barren, the birth of Jacob was miraculous and an answer to prayer (25:21). This miraculous conception of Rebecca resulted in the birth of twins: Esau, the firstborn, was hairy and later became a hunter; but Jacob, who was born holding Esau's heel, became "a quiet man, staying among the tents" (25:25–27). Almost immediately, tension and strife existed in the home because Isaac favored Esau whereas Rebecca favored Jacob.

II. Jacob and Esau. One day when Esau the hunter came in from a futile chase, he bargained away his BIRTHRIGHT to Jacob for a batch of pottage (Gen. 25:30), and thus Jacob gained the rights which by birth were not his. This custom of selling a birthright is described in the NUZI tablets. (On this and other cultural parallels, see C. Gordon in *BA* 3 [1940]: 1–12; more cautious is M. J. Selman in *Essays on the Patriarchal Narratives*, ed. A. R. Millard and D. J. Wiseman [1980], 93–138; very skeptical is T. J. Thompson, *The Historicity of the Patriarchal Narratives* [1974].)

On another day when Esau was out hunting, Jacob listened to his mother and followed her strategy for deceiving his father, whereby he received the father's blessing that was intended for Esau, the FIRSTBORN (Gen. 27; see BLESS). Although Isaac was suspicious and doubtful, in his blindness he pronounced upon Jacob the death-bed benediction. Shortly thereafter Esau returned and Isaac realized how he had been deceived, but the oral blessing could not be revoked (another custom apparently confirmed and illuminated by the Nuzi tablets). Since Isaac's blessing was irrevocable, as the Bible emphasizes (27:33–37), Jacob became the bearer of God's promise and the inheritor of Canaan (cf. Rom. 9:10–13), and Esau received the less fertile area known as EDOM. Rebecca, the mother, obtained Isaac's permission for Jacob to flee from Esau's anger to her home in PADDAN ARAM (Gen. 27:41—28:5). Jacob was no longer a young man when he sought to escape from his brother's vengeance and to find a wife from his mother's kindred (note that Esau at the age of forty had married the HITTITE women, 26:34; 27:46).

III. In Haran. En route from BEERSHEBA to HARAN, Jacob camped one night near BETHEL, and as he slept he was granted a vision of a ladder between heaven and earth with ascending and descending angels upon it. The God of his fathers again revealed himself and confirmed to Jacob the promise previously given to Isaac and ABRAHAM. Jacob commemorated this dream by setting up the stone on which he had rested his head, pouring a libation of oil over it, and assigning the name Bethel ("House of God") to the site (Gen. 28:18–19).

The next scene reveals Jacob at a well in "the land of eastern peoples" (Gen. 29:1). The following verses reveal the great love Jacob had for Rachel, a love probably reflected in the great display of physical power at the wellside (29:10), as well as during the patient years of toil for Rachel, which "seemed like only a few days to him because of his love for her" (29:20). After this love-at-first-sight episode, LABAN came and took his nephew Jacob home and agreed to give him Rachel in exchange for seven years' service. Jacob fulfilled the bargain and brought his uncle great prosperity (30:27–30). Laban, however, deceived Jacob, making him take the elder and less attractive sister, Leah. A week later Jacob married Rachel after agreeing to serve Laban seven additional years. Jacob should not be primarily blamed for the polygamy that brought trouble into his home life. The rivalry between Leah and Rachel—Judah and Joseph—was not based on Jacob's choice but Laban's fraud. Laban "changed the wages" of Jacob ten times (31:7, 41).

Jacob's years of service for his wives were followed by six years of service rendered for a stipulated wage. Laban's cunning in limiting the amount of this wage in a variety of ways was matched by Jacob's cunning in devising means to overreach his uncle, so that the poor wanderer of twenty years before became the wealthy owner of countless cattle and of the hosts of slaves necessary for their care (Gen. 32:10). God gave to each his due reward: to Jacob, the rich returns of skillful, patient industry; to Laban, rebuke and warning.

Jacob's journey to Haran.

At least twelve children were born to Jacob during his stay in Mesopotamia (Gen. 29:31—30:24). The disdained Leah bore REUBEN, SIMEON, LEVI, JUDAH, ISSACHAR, ZEBULUN, and a daughter, DINAH. Leah's maid ZILPAH bore GAD and ASHER. Rachel, being barren (29:31; 30:1–2), gave her maid BILHAH to Jacob to obtain children by her (30.3-9). Bilhah bore Dan and Naphtali. Finally, Rachel herself bore a son, JOSEPH, a positive answer to her prayer (30:22–24). It is probable that other unnamed daughters were born during this time (cf. 37:35).

IV. Return from Haran. Eventually the Lord told Jacob (Gen. 31:3, 13) to leave the area of Haran, a region noted for trade as well as agriculture and pasturage, and return to "the land of your fathers and to your relatives." A two-day head start enabled Jacob and his flocks to travel as far as GILEAD in N TRANSJORDAN before he was overtaken by Laban after seven days' travel. Jacob reminded Laban of how well he had served him, complying with all the requirements of a good herdsman, and how ill he had been rewarded. A pact was made and Laban used his authoritative position to dictate the terms: his daughters would not be harmed, nor would Jacob take another wife. A pillar was then erected to commemorate this covenant, a sacrifice was made, and the two parties shared a meal as a sign of their good will. Throughout these episodes in Jacob's life, the hand of God was at work, protecting and prospering Jacob in the midst of family quarrels.

As Jacob approached the land that God had promised him, a band of angels met him (Gen. 32). Next he sent out scouts to discover Esau's attitude. Meanwhile, Jacob took care to safeguard half of his possessions and also sent a large gift to his brother. After he had asked for divine protection, and as he was about to ford the river JABBOK, he became engaged with a stranger who wrestled with him until daybreak. The man prevailed only by dislocating Jacob's thigh, but Jacob eventually won from the antagonist a blessing that entailed the change of Jacob's name to Israel, showing that he was able to contend with God (cf. Hos. 12:4).

As Esau came to meet him, Jacob feared that Esau's hostility had not subsided with the years, and therefore approached the dreaded meeting with his usual cleverness, seeking to pacify his wronged twin and also to protect himself and his family from any possible attack. To his strategy, however, Jacob added prayer (Gen. 32:9–12), for he realized that it was ultimately God with whom he dealt. Esau's friendly greeting did not overcome the fears of Jacob, who turned down to SUCCOTH instead of following his brother. Esau went to SEIR and there became the ancestor of a nation; Jacob remained in Palestine to assume his inheritance. These twins were not to meet again until their father's death (35:27–29).

From Succoth Jacob traveled to SHECHEM, where he built an altar (Gen. 33:20). Jacob's experiences at Shechem (ch. 34) in his relations with the Canaanites are reminiscent of Abraham's relations with these inhabitants of the land (14:23), or Isaac's (ch. 26). God then instructed Jacob to return to Bethel and make an altar "to God, who appeared to you when you were fleeing from your brother Esau" (35:1). In preparation for this, the people put away their foreign gods and purified themselves. At Bethel, the patriarchal promises were again given to Jacob, and again he was told that Israel would be his new name. At this, Jacob raised anew his monument of stone, and stamped forever by this public act upon ancient Luz (35:6) the name of Bethel, which he had privately given it before (28:19).

Losses and griefs characterized the life of Jacob during this period. The death of his mother's nurse at Bethel (Gen. 35:8; 24:59) was followed by the death of his beloved wife Rachel at EPHRATH (35:19; 48:7) in bringing forth the youngest of his

Agricultural area outside Bethel, where Jacob experienced a vision from God (Gen. 28:10–19).

twelve sons, BENJAMIN. At about the same time the eldest of the twelve, Reuben, forfeited the honor of his station in the family by becoming intimate with Bilhah, an act that showed all too clearly the effect of recent association with Canaanites (35:22–23). Finally, death claimed Jacob's aged father, whose latest years had been robbed of the companionship, not only of this son, but also of the son Esau. At Isaac's grave in HEBRON, the poorly matched twins met once more, thenceforth to go their separate ways, both in their personal careers and in their descendants' history (35:29).

Next, Jacob resided near Hebron (Gen. 37:14). Although the following material revolves around Joseph, Jacob remains the true center of the narrative until his death. The self-willed older sons come and go at his bidding (42:1–5), and Joseph's great concern is for his aged father (43:27; 44:19; 45:3, 9, 13, 23; 46:29).

Finally, when severe famine gripped Canaan, Jacob and his sons set out for Egypt. At Beersheba he received further assurance of God's favor (Gen. 46:1–4). In Egypt he dwelt in the land of GOSHEN until his death. At the end, Jacob bestowed a blessing upon Joseph's sons, EPHRAIM and MANASSEH (48:8–20), and then upon his own sons (ch. 49). God's promise to Jacob was beautifully fulfilled; at his death the Egyptians paid him great homage, and his sons buried him with Isaac and Abraham at the family grave in MACHPELAH.

V. Jacob the patriarch. The mighty patriarch Jacob inherited from his father Isaac an affectionate attachment to his family, which appears in his life from beginning to end. From his mother Rebecca he inherited shrewdness, initiative, and resourcefulness—qualities that she apparently shared with her brother Laban. Like both Isaac and Abraham, he sometimes lacked courage, and his life frequently revealed deceit and dishonesty. Yet through the entire narrative there is a persistent faith in the God of his fathers. Jacob's life is a story of conflict. He was constantly beset with dangers from every area of life, and upon many occasions his inheritance of the blessing was threatened.

Outside GENESIS, the OT has much to say about Jacob's life (Josh. 24:3–4, 32; Ps. 105:10–23; Hos. 12:2–4, 12; Mal. 1:2). If the book of Genesis were lost, the significance as well as the basic outline of his life could be reconstructed. The NT references recall events in his life or traits of his character (Jn. 4:5–6, 12; Acts 7:12, 14–16; Rom. 9:10–13; Heb. 11:9, 20–21). Jacob is considered the child of favor (Mal. 1:2; Rom. 9:10–13), an heir of the divine promise (Heb. 11:9), and a man of blessing (Heb. 11:20–21). As Israel's third great patriarch, he is often linked with Abraham and Isaac, especially in connection with their God (Deut. 29:13; 2 Ki. 13:23; Matt. 8:11; Mk. 12:26–27; Acts 3:13).

Jacob as a synonym for Israel and thus as a poetic name for the Israelites occurs especially in the prophets. Besides being called the house of Jacob (Exod. 19:3; Isa. 2:5–6.; 8:17; 27:9; Amos 3:13; 9:8; Mic. 2:7), or the sons of Jacob (1 Ki. 18:31; Mal. 3:6), or the seed of Jacob (Isa. 45:19; Jer. 33:26), or the assembly of Jacob (Deut. 33:4), the Israelites are also simply called Jacob (Isa. 9:8; Hos. 10:11); in Mic. 1:5 the name refers to the northern kingdom alone, and in Nah. 2:2 to Judah alone. Jacob is sometimes used also as a representative of the nation that bears his name. Israel is the "house of Jacob" (Lk. 1:33); its God is the "King of Jacob" (Isa. 41:21); and his temple is a "habitation for the God of Jacob" (Acts 7:46).

(In addition to the standard commentaries on Genesis, see J. M. Holt, *The Patriarchs of Israel* [1964]; I. Hunt, *The World of the Patriarchs* [1966]; R. S. Hendel, *The Epic of the Patriarch: The Jacob Cycle and the Narrative Traditions of Canaan and Israel* [1987]; S. D. Walters, "Jacob Narrative," in *ABD*, 3:599–608.)   L. L. WALKER

Jacob, Ladder of. Title given to a pseudepigraphic writing, dating possibly to c. A.D. 100, but preserved only, and with many editorial changes, in a medieval Slavonic work. It may be described as an apocalyptic expansion of the narrative about JACOB's vision of a ladder (Gen. 28:11–22). The work places great stress on monotheism and on the future glory of Jacob's descendants. (English trans. in *OTP*, 2:401–11.)

Jacob, Prayer of. A brief pseudepigraphic work, preserved in a 4th-cent. Greek ms, but composed probably two centuries earlier. Much of the prayer is a series of invocations (perhaps influenced by

GNOSTICISM), but near the end there is this request: "Fill me with wisdom; empower me, Lord; fill my heart with good things, Lord." (English trans. in *OTP*, 2:715–23.)

Jacob, Testament of. See ISAAC AND JACOB, TESTAMENTS OF.

Jacob's well. There is just one reference naming Jacob's well in the Bible (*pēgē tou Iakōb*). According to the Gospel of John, Jesus early in his ministry had to pass through SAMARIA and in so doing reached SYCHAR, "near the plot of ground that Jacob had given to his son Joseph. Jacob's well was there" (Jn. 4:5–6). The location of Sychar is problematic. The modern ʿAskar, which sounds most like it, though in the vicinity, is not near enough to the well. Furthermore, ʿAskar has its own spring. Perhaps Sychar is an evolution of the name SHECHEM. When JACOB came to Shechem, he bought the land on which he was camped (Gen. 33:18). There is no OT record of his digging a well there, but that he should do so is certainly reasonable and expected (cf. 48:22). Shechem is identified with modern Tell Balaṭah, and Bir Yaʿaqub (as the well is presently called) is about one mile E of this tell. It is also at the foot of Mount GERIZIM, to which the Samaritan woman alluded (Jn. 4:20).

According to the woman's comment, the well was deep (Jn. 4:11). Today it is c. 75 ft. deep, but it has probably been filled with much debris over the years since it was dug. There are hardly any sites that have less doubt as to their authenticity than the site of Jacob's well. All traditions agree on this as being the scene described in Jn. 4, and the biblical details fit perfectly. Through the centuries, churches have been built over the well, as various medieval pilgrims have recorded. Today the well is in a cave, or crypt, under the floor of a Greek Orthodox church that has never been finished above the exterior walls.

Jacob's well is known for its soft, or light, water that is supplied in two ways: through underground sources that make it a true well and by percolated surface water, which makes it a cistern (Gk. *phrear* G5853, Jn. 4:11). This detail may have prompted Jesus' remark about living water (v. 14). (See G. H. Dalman, *Sacred Sites and Ways* [1935], 212–215.)

R. L. ALDEN

Jacubus juh-kyoo'buhs. KJV Apoc. form of AKKUB (1 Esd. 9:48).

Jada jay'duh (יָדָע H3360, possibly "[God] has known [i.e., cared]" or "skillful, shrewd"). Son of Onam, grandson of JERAHMEEL, and descendant of JUDAH (1 Chr. 2:28, 32).

Jadah jay'duh (יַעְרָה H3586 [MT יַעְרָה], short form of יְהוֹעַדָּה H3389, possibly "Yahweh has adorned"). KJV, NRSV, Jarah. Son of Ahaz and descendant of King SAUL through JONATHAN (1 Chr. 9:42 NIV, following some Heb. MSS and LXX; MT, "Jarah"); called JEHOADDAH in the parallel passage (8:36).

Jadau jay'daw. KJV form of JADDAI.

Jaddai jad'i (יַדַּי H3350 [Qere יְדַּי]), derivation uncertain; see IDDO). KJV Jadau. One of the descendants of Nebo who agreed to put away their foreign wives (Ezra 10:43; called "Iddo" in 1 Esd. 9:35 [KJV, "Edes"]).

Jaddua jad'yoo-uh (יַדּוּעַ H3348, "known [by Yahweh]"; see JEDAIAH). (1) One of the Israelite leaders who sealed the covenant with NEHEMIAH after the return from the Babylonian captivity (Neh. 10:21). The covenant signified the willingness of the people to abide by the Law of God.

(2) Son of Jonathan (or Johanan) and descendant of JESHUA the high priest (Neh. 12:11, 22). He

Jacob's well.

is widely thought to be the Jaddua whom Josephus refers to as a high priest at the time that Alexander the Great was beginning his conquests (*Ant.* 11.8.2; however, see E. M. Yamauchi in *EBC*, 4:582–83; detailed discussion in J. C. VanderKam, *From Joshua to Caiaphas: High Priests after the Exile* [2004], 63–85). T. E. McComiskey

Jaddus jad′uhs (Ιαδδους, variant Ιαδδους). Husband of Agia and ancestor of some Israelites that could not prove their right to the priesthood because their genealogy was lost (1 Esd. 5:38; KJV, "Addus"). He is said to have taken his father-in-law's name, Barzillai, and that is the name found in the parallel passages (Ezra 2:61; Neh. 7:63). S. Barabas

jade. A general term used to include various mineral substances of tough compact texture, and nearly white to dark green color, used by early man for utensils and ornaments. It includes two mineral species: (1) nephrite, a variety of fibrous amphibole, either tremolite (whitish calcium-magnesium silicate) or actinolite (green calcium-magnesium-iron silicate), and (2) jadeite, a green sodium-aluminum silicate of the pyroxene group, and a dark green to nearly black kind of jadeite called chloromelanite. Much jade has come from Upper Burma, Central India, and southeastern Turkestan. The term is used by the NEB to render Hebrew *yāhălōm* H3402, a word of uncertain meaning (Exod. 28:18; 39:11; Ezek. 28:13; NIV, "emerald"; NRSV, "moonstone"). D. R. Bowes

Jadon jay′don (יָדוֹן H3347, possibly "[Yahweh] rules" or "frail one"). A man from Meronoth (see Meronothite) who, along with Melatiah of Gibeon, helped in rebuilding the walls of Jerusalem (Neh. 3:7). These two individuals are further described as "men from Gibeon and Mizpah," suggesting that Meronoth and Mizpah are somehow connected or even that they are two names for the same town. Gibeon and Mizpah (or Melatiah and Jadon personally—cf. NRSV) are described as being "under the authority of the governor of Trans-Euphrates." (Josephus [*Ant.* 8.8.5] gives the name Jadon to the man of God who went from Judah to Jeroboam to warn the king of his sin, 1 Ki. 13; later Jewish tradition identifies this prophet with Iddo the seer, 2 Chr. 9:29.) S. Barabas

Jael jay′uhl (יָעֵל H3605, "mountain goat"). The wife of Heber the Kenite and slayer of Sisera, a Canaanite commander (Jdg. 4:17–22; 5:6, 24). The Canaanite King Jabin of Hazor oppressed Israel for twenty years. The Canaanites had a formidable force of 900 chariots. The Kenites were their friends, and, because of the Kenite skill in metalworking, were doubtless useful to the Canaanites. Heber, however, lived apart from the other Kenites (4:11). Under the inspiration of Deborah, Barak formed a large force of Israelites at Mount Tabor to fight the Canaanite army, led by Sisera their general, along the River Kishon. The Israelite assault, probably aided by a storm (5:20–21), routed the Canaanites. Sisera ran away on foot and came to the tent of Jael, who extended him hospitality. She covered him with a rug, and in response to his request for water gave him milk. Then, as Sisera slept, Jael murdered him by hammering a tent peg through his temple into the ground. Jael's act is celebrated in the ancient Song of Deborah (ch. 5). N. B. Baker

Jagur jay′guhr (יָגוּר H3327, possibly "stone heap"). A town in the Negev, the extreme S of the tribal territory of Judah, near the border of Edom (Josh. 15:21). Its precise location is unknown, although one suggestion is Khirbet el-Gharrah, some 11 mi. E of Beersheba (J. Simons, *The Geographical and Topographical Texts of the Old Testament* [1959], 142).

Jah jah (יָהּ H3363, short form of יהוה). This name, an abbreviation of Yahweh (Jehovah), is used in the KJV only once (Ps. 68:4), but the corresponding Hebrew form occurs over forty times (Exod. 15:2; 17:16; Isa. 12:2; 26:4; 38:11; the rest of the occurrences are in Psalms). In all these other passages it is translated "the Lord." See God, names of.

Jahath jay′hath (יַחַת H3511, perhaps "[God] snatches up"). (1) Son of Reiah and descendant of Judah; Jahath's sons, Ahumai and Lahad, and possibly also other relatives, are identified as "the clans of the Zorathites" (1 Chr. 4:2). See Zorah.

(2) Son of Libni, grandson of Gershon, and great-grandson of Levi (1 Chr. 6:20 [NIV, "Jehath,"

apparently a misprint]). He is also described as the son (descendant?) of Gershon and as the father of Shimei in a list of Asaph's ancestors (v. 43), but this may be the result of a scribal error. See SHIMEI #1.

(3) Son of Shimei and descendant of Gershon (1 Chr. 23:10–11).

(4) Son of Shelomoth and descendant of Levi (1 Chr. 24:22).

(5) Descendant of Levi through MERARI and an overseer of the workmen who repaired the temple in the reign of King JOSIAH (2 Chr. 34:12).

S. BARABAS

Jahaz, Jahzah jay'haz, jah'zuh (יַהַץ H3403, variant יַהְצָה H3404 [1 Chr. 6:78; Jer. 48:21], derivation unknown). KJV also Jahaza (Josh. 13:18) and Jahazah (21:36). A city in TRANSJORDAN where SIHON, an AMORITE king, was defeated in a great battle by the Israelites when he refused to allow them to pass through his territory (Num. 21:23; Deut. 2:32; Jdg. 11:20). Moses assigned the city to the tribe of REUBEN (Josh. 13:18), and it was one of the cities given to the Levites descended from MERARI (21:36; 1 Chr. 6:78 ["Jahzah"]). According to the MOABITE STONE, the king of Israel lived in Jahaz while at war with MOAB, but he was driven out, and MESHA took the city and added it to Moabite territory (see also ATAROTH). The Bible also refers to Jahaz as a city of Moab (Isa. 15:4; Jer. 48:21 ["Jahzah"], 34). Its precise location is uncertain, although some tentatively identify it with Khirbet el-Medeiyineh, c. 11 mi. SE of MEDEBA (for other possibilities, see *ABD*, 3:612).

S. BARABAS

Jahaziah jay'hu-zi'uh. KJV form of JAHZEIAH.

Jahaziel juh-hay'zee-uhl (יַחֲזִיאֵל H3487, "God sees"; cf. JAHZEIAH). **(1)** One of the ambidextrous Benjamite warriors who joined DAVID while he was in exile from SAUL at the PHILISTINE city of ZIKLAG (1 Chr. 12:4; cf. v. 2).

(2) One of two priests appointed to blow trumpets before the ARK OF THE COVENANT when David brought it to Jerusalem (1 Chr. 16:6).

(3) Son of Hebron and descendant of LEVI in the line of KOHATH; contemporary of David (1 Chr. 23:19; 24:23).

(4) Son of Zechariah and descendant of Levi through ASAPH; moved by the Spirit, he encouraged King JEHOSHAPHAT of Judah and his army to fight against the Moabite, Ammonite, and Edomite invaders (2 Chr. 20:14–17).

(5) Descendant of Zattu and father of Shecaniah; the latter was among the family heads that returned to Jerusalem after the EXILE (Ezra 8:5, following some LXX MSS; 1 Esd. 8:32 [KJV, "Jezelus"]). However, the MT does not include the name Zattu and leaves the connection between Shecaniah and Jahaziel unclear (cf. KJV).

S. BARABAS

Jahdai jah'di (יַהְדָּי H3367, prob. "Yahweh leads"). Apparently a descendant of JUDAH, included in the genealogy of CALEB (1 Chr. 2:47). The genealogical connection is unclear, although the expression "The sons of Jahdai …" suggests that the reference is to a man, probably a descendant of Caleb. In the light of the context (cf. vv. 46, 48), some believe that Jahdai was one of Caleb's concubines, possibly Ephah. (See discussion in G. N. Knoppers, *I Chronicles 1–9*, AB 12 [2004], 313.)

Jahdiel jah'dee-uhl (יַחְדִּיאֵל H3484, "God rejoices" or "may God give joy"; cf. JEHDEIAH). A clan chief of the half-tribe of MANASSEH; he and others are described as "brave warriors, famous men, and heads of their families" (1 Chr. 5:24). Because of their unfaithfulness, however, they and their families were taken captive by the Assyrians (vv. 25–26).

Jahdo jah'doh (יַחְדּוֹ H3482 [see *BHK*[3] apparatus for the reading יַחְדִּי], possibly "[God] rejoices," otherwise related to a root meaning "to join, be together with"). Son of Buz, descendant of GAD, and ancestor of Abihail; the sons of Abihail and other Gadites occupied the region E. of GILEAD (1 Chr. 5:14; cf. v. 10).

Jahleel jah'lee-uhl (יַחְלְאֵל H3499, "wait for God" or "God shows himself friendly"; gentilic יַחְלְאֵלִי H3500, "Jahleelite"). Son of ZEBULUN and eponymous ancestor of the Jahleelite clan (Gen. 46:14; Num. 26:26).

Jahmai jah'mi (יַחְמַי H3503, "[God] protects"). Son (or descendant) of Tola and grandson (or more distant descendant) of Issachar; he is described as head of his family, which probably means he was a military officer (1 Chr. 7:2).

Jahoel. See Abraham, Apocalypse of.

Jahweh. Variant spelling of *Yahweh*. See God, names of; Jehovah.

Jahzah jah´zuh. Alternate form of Jahaz.

Jahzeel jah´zee-uhl (יַחְצְאֵל H3505, variant יַחְצִיאֵל H3507 [1 Chr. 7:13], "God apportions" or "God favors"; gentilic יַחְצְאֵלִי H3506, "Jahzeelite"). Firstborn son of Naphtali, grandson of Jacob, and eponymous ancestor of the Jahzeelite clan (Gen. 46:24 [NIV, "Jahziel"]; Num. 26:48; called "Jahziel" in 1 Chr. 7:13).

Jahzeiah jah-zee´yah (יַחְזְיָה H3488, "Yahweh sees"; cf. Jahaziel). KJV Jahaziah. Son of Tikvah. When Ezra told the Israelites that those who had married foreign women should divorce their wives, Jahzeiah was one of four men who opposed him (Ezra 10:15). The Hebrew text, however, can be understood to mean that these four men supported Ezra (cf. LXX as well as the parallel in 1 Esd. 9:14 [KJV, "Ezechias"]); thus the NJPS renders, "Only Jonathan son of Asahel and Jahzeiah son of Tikvah remained for this purpose, assisted by Meshullam and Shabbethai, the Levites." According to some scholars, the Hebrew expression (ʿomdû ʿal-zōʾt, lit., "stood upon this") does indicate opposition (cf. 2 Chr. 20:23 et al.), but what Jahzeiah and the others resisted was the delay proposed by the assembly (Ezra 10:12–14); in other words, the four men favored Ezra's decision and argued for swift punishment (cf. H. G. M. Williamson, *Ezra-Nehemiah*, WBC 16 [1985], 156–57).

Jahzerah jah´zuh-ruh (יַחְזֵרָה H3492, possibly "prudent" or "cunning"). Descendant of Immer and grandfather (or ancestor) of a certain Maasai, who was one of the priests to resettle in Jerusalem after the exile (1 Chr. 9:12), probably the same as Ahzai (Neh 11:13).

Jahziel jah´zee-uhl. Variant form of Jahzeel.

Jair jay´uhr (יָאִיר H3281, "[God] gives light"; עִיר H3600 [only 1 Chr. 20:5; *Ketib* עוּר], "[God] stirs"). (1) Descendant (lit., "son") of Manasseh who at the time of the conquest of Canaan occupied sixty villages on the border of Gilead and Bashan (see also Argob); these settlements came to be known as Havvoth Jair (Num. 32:41; Deut. 3:14; Josh. 13:30; 1 Ki. 4:13). According to 1 Chr. 2:21–23, Jair's father was Segub, who descended from Judah through Hezron, but whose mother is described as the daughter of Manasseh's son, Makir; thus Jair was apparently regarded as a Manassite through his mother's side.

(2) A Gileadite who judged or led Israel for twenty-two years (Jdg. 10:3–5). He is said to have had thirty sons, each of whom rode a donkey and ruled one of the towns of Havvoth Jair. The connection between this man and #1 above is unclear. It is possible that Jair of Gilead inherited the towns that had been previously under Jair of Segub.

(3) Son of Shimei, descendant of Benjamin, and father of Mordecai, who was the cousin and guardian of Esther (Esth. 2:5).

(4) Father of Elhanan, who killed the brother of Goliath (1 Chr. 20:5; on the apparent discrepancies between this verse and 2 Sam. 21:19, see Elhanan).

Jairite jay´uh-rit (יָאִרִי H3285, "of Jair"). A gentilic referring apparently to someone who descended from Jair #1. It is used to identify Ira, a priest (or royal adviser) of David (2 Sam. 20:26).

Jairus jay-i´ruhs (Ἰάϊρος G2608 [WH, Ἰάειρος], prob. from Heb. יָאִיר H3281 [see Jair]). (1) Ancestor of a family of temple servants (Nethinim) who returned from the exile (1 Esd. 5:31 [KJV, "Airus"]; possibly corresponding with Reaiah in the parallels, Ezra 2:47; Neh. 7:50).

(2) The name of a synagogue official whose dead daughter Jesus raised to life (Mk. 5:22; Lk. 8:41). The incident, which took place near Lake Galilee, is recorded in all three Synoptic Gospels (Mk. 5:21–24, 35–43; Lk. 8:40–42, 49–56; Matt. 9:18–19, 23–26), but the name Jairus is not given by Matthew. (Although the words "named Jairus" in Mk. 5:22 are omitted by Codex Beza and by the Old Latin, there is no reason to suspect,

as some have done, that the name was originally absent and added from Luke later.) Jairus is called an *archisynagōgos* G801, "synagogue ruler" (Mk. 5:22, 35; Lk. 8:41; but Matt. 9:18 and 23 simply say *archōn* G807, "ruler"), thus indicating he was a leader, whose duties included responsibility for the physical arrangements of the worship services (see RULER OF THE SYNAGOGUE).

Jairus came to Jesus and implored him to heal his daughter (Mk. 5:22–23), who was twelve years old (cf. v. 42). As they walked toward his house, a woman who had suffered bleeding for a period of twelve years touched Jesus' cloak and was immediately healed (vv. 25–29). At that point, some men arrived and reported that Jairus's daughter had died, but Jesus said to him, "Don't be afraid; just believe" (v. 36). When they reached the house, Jesus stated that the girl was not dead but asleep (prob. indicating that her death had no finality), then took the girl by the hand and said, "*Talitha koum*" (Aramaic for "Little girl, get up"), and at once she got up and began to walk around (vv. 39–42; see TALITHA CUMI).

It has been suggested that the name Jairus is symbolical, being derived from Hebrew *yāʿir* H3600, meaning "he stirs up, awakens," and that the narrative is therefore legendary. This name, however, occurs only once in the OT (1 Chr. 20:5), where the more common name is *yāʾir* G3281, which means "he gives light"; moreover, Jesus did not tell the girl to wake up, but to get up or arise (Gk. *egeirō* G1586). It is perhaps possible, though, that the early Aramaic-speaking Christians preserved the memory of the ruler's name because they saw such a connection (cf. R. H. Gundry, *Mark: A Commentary on His Apology for the Cross* [1993], 267).   W. H. MARE

Iakan jay'kuhn. KJV form of JAAKAN; TNIV form of JACAN.

Jakeh jay'kuh (יָקֶה H3681, possibly "prudent" or "[God] preserves"). Father of AGUR, who was the author of sayings recorded in the book of PROVERBS (Prov. 30:1).

Jakim jay'kim (יָקִים H3691, "[God] establishes" [or takes a stand]; see JEKAMIAH). **(1)** Son of Shimei and Benjamite family head who lived in Jerusalem in David's day (1 Chr. 8:19; cf. v. 28).

(2) A priest chosen during the time of David to head the twelfth of the twenty-four courses of priests who took turns serving in the sanctuary (1 Chr. 24:12).

Jakin (person) jay'kin (יָכִין H3520, "[God] establishes"; gentilic יָכִינִי H3522, "Jakinite"). Also Jachin. **(1)** Son of SIMEON and eponymous ancestor of the Jakinite clan (Gen. 46:10; Exod. 6:15; Num. 26:12; apparently called JARIB in 1 Chr. 4:24).

(2) A leader of the Levites, appointed by lot as the head of the twenty-first course of priests during DAVID's time (1 Chr. 24:17).

(3) One of the priests who lived in Jerusalem after the EXILE (1 Chr. 9:10; Neh. 11:10). It is possible, however, that the name may here be used as a family name denoting the priests in the twenty-first course, or the division of which Jakin was the head. In a list of six priests (1 Chr. 9:10–13), three of them have names that may be found in the list of divisions (24:17), and two of the remaining names (Adaiah and Maasai) are carefully traced back to ancestors who were the heads of courses.

T. E. MCCOMISKEY

Jakin (pillar) jay'kin (יָכִין H3521, "[God] establishes"). Also Jachin. The name of one of two bronze pillars SOLOMON placed in front of the TEMPLE; the one he placed on the N side was named Boaz, and the one on the S, Jakin (1 Ki. 7:21; 2 Chr. 3:17). See BOAZ (PILLAR); TEMPLE, JERUSALEM IV.B.5. Both pillars were beautifully adorned with capitals of lily-work, and their primary purpose appears to have been decorative and symbolic. As gateposts visible to the people (most of whom were not allowed inside), they probably indicated the entrance of the God of Israel into his earthly dwelling. (See S. Yeivin in *PEQ* 91 [1959]: 6–22; C. L. Meyers in *CBQ* 45 [1983]: 167–78.)   T. E. MCCOMISKEY

Jalam jay'luhm (יַעְלָם H3609, derivation uncertain). KJV Jaalam. Son of ESAU by OHOLIBAMAH; an Edomite chief (Gen. 36:5, 14, 18; 1 Chr. 1:35).

Jalon jay'lon (יָלוֹן H3534, derivation uncertain). Son of Ezrah and descendant of JUDAH (1 Chr. 4:17).

Jambres. See JANNES AND JAMBRES.

JAMBRI

Jambri jam′bri (Ιαμβρι). The name of a family or tribe that came out of MEDEBA (originally an AMORITE city, Num. 21:31) and took captive John, the brother of Jonathan MACCABEE, and seized everything that he possessed. This outrage was avenged by his brothers, Jonathan and Simon, who ambushed a wedding party of "the sons of Jambri," killing many, and taking their spoils (1 Macc. 9:36). See MACCABEES.   S. BARABAS

James jaymz (Ἰάκωβος G2610, hellenized form of Ἰακώβ G2609 [see JACOB]; English *James* derives from *Jacomus*, an alteration of Latin *Jacobus*). This name in the NT most frequently refers to James son of ZEBEDEE, one of the original twelve disciples and brother of the apostle John; his early martyrdom (c. A.D. 41) is recorded in Acts 12:1–2. Another James, the brother of Jesus, was not a believer until after the resurrection, but during the 40s he became the leader of the church in Jerusalem (cf. Acts 15:13–21); he was probably the author of the epistle of James. A third individual named James, the son of Alphaeus, was one of the twelve disciples. A certain "James the younger" (Mk. 15:40; KJV, "the less") is sometimes identified with the son of Zebedee and more often with the son of Alphaeus, but he may be a fourth person with the same name. Finally, the father of the disciple Judas (not Iscariot) was named James.

 I. James son of Zebedee
  A. Family
  B. Call
  C. Discipleship
  D. Death
  E. Apocryphal accounts
 II. James, "the Lord's brother"
  A. Family
  B. Conversion
  C. Prominence
  D. Character
  E. Writing
  F. Death
 III. James son of Alphaeus
 IV. James the younger
 V. James the father of Judas

I. James son of Zebedee. References to this James are found only in the Synoptic Gospels and Acts (Matt. 4:21; 10:2; 17:1; Mk. 1:19, 29; 3:17; 5:37; 9:2; 10:35, 41; 13:3; 14:33; Lk. 5:10; 6:14; 8:51; 9:28, 54; Acts 1:13; 12:2). Modestly, John in his gospel refrained from mentioning his brother by name, though he revealed his presence with the other apostles after Jesus' resurrection (Jn. 21:2). The only mention of James by name outside the first three Gospels is in the listing of the apostles (Acts 1:13) and the reference to his death (12:2).

A. Family. James was called the son of Zebedee and the brother of John (see JOHN THE APOSTLE). In the Gospels, the common use of James's name before that of John probably indicates that James was older (Matt. 10:2; 17:1; Mk. 3:17; 5:37). In each of these passages John is identified as the "brother of James." However, in Acts the identification is reversed. James is mentioned as the "brother of John" to those who were less familiar with the earlier unbroken circle of apostles (Acts 12:2).

 The father, Zebedee, was a fisherman who owned several boats on the Sea of Galilee and had hired servants (Mk. 1:20; Lk. 5:11). The establishment must have been considerable. Some infer additional evidence of affluence from the fact that John was "known to the high priest" (Jn. 18:15). Perhaps the family owned property in Jerusalem and spent some of their time there. Fishermen with large boats and sufficient manpower were able to catch more and larger fish in the deep waters. When the local market of BETHSAIDA Julias and even of CAPERNAUM had been satisfied, salted fish were delivered as far inland as Jerusalem. Not only

Old photo of men repairing their fishing nets on the shore of the Sea of Galilee. James son of Zebedee worked as a fisherman on these same shores.

James and John belonged to the firm (Matt. 4:21); Simon PETER was also a partner (Lk. 5:10), and possibly ANDREW (Mk. 1:16). The mother of James and John was probably SALOME, thought by some to be the sister of the mother of Jesus (cf. Matt. 27:56; Mk. 15:40; Jn. 19:25).

B. Call. James seems not to have been with Peter and Andrew in their pilgrimage to Judea, where they learned of the coming of the "Lamb of God" and received their first call to discipleship (Jn. 1:35–51). Perhaps John son of Zebedee was the other disciple of JOHN THE BAPTIST who was with Andrew (v. 40). If so, James probably stayed home to tend the business while three members of the company went to observe the great movement under the Baptist and even attached themselves to him as his disciples. When, upon their return to GALILEE, they recounted the events of Judea, James no doubt caught their faith and enthusiasm. At any rate, he was well prepared for the seemingly abrupt call later at the Sea of Galilee (Lk. 5:2–11).

C. Discipleship. Once James became a disciple, he soon occupied a prominent place. He was chosen among the twelve disciples. In each list he stands second or third among the names mentioned, always in company with Peter, John, and Andrew (Matt. 10:2; Mk. 3:17; Lk. 6:14; Acts 1:13). Along with Peter and John, he became a special confidant of Jesus. The three were together at the house of Peter's mother-in-law with Andrew (Mk. 1:29–31). At the house of JAIRUS, Jesus permitted only these three from the circle of the disciples to enter the room with him to the child (Mk. 5:37; Lk. 8:51). At the TRANSFIGURATION, Jesus chose these three to climb the mountain with him (Matt. 17:1; Mk. 9:2; Lk. 9:28). They were not even allowed to tell what they had seen until after Jesus arose from the dead (Mk. 9:9). Finally, at GETHSEMANE, they were again chosen to accompany Jesus (Matt. 26:37; Mk. 14:33).

James was involved in two less complimentary episodes. Soon after the transfiguration, when Jesus was passing through SAMARIA on his way to JERUSALEM (Lk. 9:51–52), James and John were deeply offended at the poor reception accorded Jesus by the populace (9:53). So recently having seen the transcendent glory of their Lord, they could not bear the humiliations to which he was subjected. They asked Jesus, "Lord, do you want us to call fire down from heaven to destroy them?" (v. 54). Jesus rebuked them (v. 55). Perhaps this tendency to impetuosity and even fanaticism was in the mind of Jesus when he called them BOANERGES, "Sons of Thunder" (Mk. 3:17).

The other outburst was more selfish. On the occasion of Jesus' last journey to Jerusalem (Mk. 10:32), presuming on their intimacy with Jesus and possibly on their kinship, the two brothers made the request, "Let one of us sit at your right and the other at your left in your glory" (10:37). The appeal was supported by their mother, a follower of Jesus and faithful supporter of the group (Matt. 20:20–28). Jesus rebuked the request (Mk. 10:40) and restored peace (vv. 42–45).

On two other occasions, James's presence is mentioned. He was one of the four on the MOUNT OF OLIVES who asked questions about the end times (Mk. 13:3–4). He was also present at the Sea of Galilee when the risen Lord appeared a third time to the disciples and when the miraculous draught of fishes was made (Jn. 21:1–14). Of course, the presence of James was also assumed among the disciples at other times when the names were not listed.

D. Death. James is the only one of the Twelve whose martyrdom is related in the NT. He was also the first martyr among the apostles. King Herod Agrippa I (see HEROD VII) made James the first target in his attack upon the church in a wider move

This carved capital from the Church of the Annunciation (Nazareth) depicts the beheading of James son of Zebedee (Acts 12:1–3).

of persecution that included the arrest of Peter (Acts 12:1–3). That James was prominent enough to be singled out for execution may indicate that Peter, James, and John still formed a special group among the leaders in the church at Jerusalem, as they had among the followers of Jesus, though the martyrdom is the only episode related of James in Acts. If James was not among the most prominent, he must certainly have been among the most feared and hated of the Christians. In his death James fulfilled the prophecy of Jesus that he too should drink of his Master's cup (Mk. 10:39).

E. Apocryphal accounts. Later legends expand the narrative of the NT. CLEMENT OF ALEXANDRIA (*Hypotyposis*) and EUSEBIUS (*Hist.* 3.25) refer to *The Acts of St. John*, a heretical work of the 2nd cent., which gives an account of the call of James and of his presence at the transfiguration. Fantastic details regarding the body of Jesus are given. Other accounts are recorded of missionary journeys of James to India, to the "Twelve Tribes" scattered abroad, and to Spain. Based on late legend (6th or 7th cent.), James was made the patron saint of Spain. Marvelous stories are told of his evangelizing and of the return of his body by angels after his martyrdom in Palestine. The angels are said to have guided a ship without sail or rudder to Spain with the holy cargo that was prepared by a series of miracles for veneration. The apostle's alleged bones were discovered in the 9th cent. near a town that was named Santiago de Compostela and that became a place of Roman Catholic pilgrimage (*Santiago* is Spanish for Saint James, from Latin Sanctus Iacobus, shortened to Sanct Iagus). Though the early death of James robs the legends of even a minimal historical base, the son of Zebedee is known in Christian tradition as James the Great to distinguish him from James the Less (possibly the son of Alphaeus).

II. James, "the Lord's brother." This James is listed first among the BROTHERS OF JESUS, indicating, no doubt, that he was the oldest (Matt. 13:55; Mk. 6:3). PAUL names him as one of the two leaders he met in Jerusalem three years after his own conversion (Gal. 1:19; some argue from this text that Paul regarded him as an apostle, but the Greek is ambiguous). In various passages he is simply called James (Acts 12:17; 15:13; 21:18; 1 Cor. 15:7; Gal. 2:9, 12; Jas. 1:1; Jude 1). In the Gospels he is mentioned by name only twice, and then only to reflect on Jesus' humble origin (Matt. 13:55; Mk. 6:3). However, he is almost certainly included in the brothers who sought to interview Jesus and to dissuade him from his strenuous ministry (Matt. 12:46; Mk. 3:20–21, 31–32). The brothers also accompanied him to Capernaum (Jn. 2:12). Later they attempted to persuade Jesus to leave Galilee and go to Judea at the time of the Feast of Tabernacles (7:3). At this time the brothers did not believe in Jesus (v. 5), but, as good Jews, they went to the feast (v. 10).

A. Family. The relationship between Jesus and his "brothers" has been much discussed. The most natural interpretation of the word "brother" at the time of the writing of the NT and of other early Christian literature is the literal one—that James and the others were children of Joseph and Mary after the birth of Jesus, Mary's "firstborn." This is called the Helvidian view (named for Helvidius, a 4th-cent. Latin theologian). On this view, it appears that James was of a fairly large family. Four brothers of Jesus are named—James, Joseph, Simon, and Judas. Reference is made also to "all his sisters" (Matt. 13:56), an expression that suggests there were at least three of them. It appears then that Jesus had at least seven siblings. The specific references to brothers and sisters for the sake of identification support the Helvidian position, for it would seem remarkable that the speaker or writer had only a general relationship in mind in the use of the terms. This impression is strengthened by the seemingly normal use of the words "son" and "mother" (Matt. 13:55, 56; Mk. 6:3).

An early alternate view, the Epiphanian (named for its chief advocate, EPIPHANIUS, c. 315–403, Bishop of Salamis), became popular in the context of reverence for Mary and belief in her perpetual virginity. This idea, supported by various church fathers, was that these "brothers" were children of Joseph by a previous marriage. Since the canonical Gospels furnished no evidence for this position, several apocryphal writings attempted to supply the lack (see APOCRYPHAL NEW TESTAMENT I). The tradition that Joseph was over eighty years old at the time of his second marriage lent plausibility to his acceptance of Mary's perpetual virginity and gave sufficient time for a family that was no real kin of Jesus or Mary. It did, of course, introduce other complications, not the least of which is putting the "brethren" in the wrong generation to match the data of the Gospels, Acts, and the Epistles.

The third major view, the Hieronymian, was suggested by the youthful JEROME to refute Helvidius. He argued that the word "brothers" is a broad and general term that could as well mean "kindred" or "cousins." Jerome claimed no traditional authority for his theory, but depended entirely upon critical and theological arguments. Though Jerome did not hold to his theory staunchly or consistently (cf. J. B. Lightfoot, *Saint Paul's Epistle to the Galatians*, 10th ed. [1898], 259–60), it has been widely held and is the officially recognized view of the Roman Catholic Church. Elaborate but uncertain identifications have been made of relatives, friends, and followers of Jesus to support the Epiphanian and Hieronymian views or at least to provide alternatives to the natural meaning of brother.

The vigorous objections that have been raised against the Helvidian view do not stem from the NT accounts themselves, but from an ASCETICISM that is foreign to both Jewish theology and the teaching of Jesus, and from the emerging doctrine of the perpetual virginity of Mary. On the basis of the gospel records themselves, some degree of departure from the ordinary meaning of words is required if one is to build a case against the view that Joseph's abstinence was only "until she [Mary] gave birth to a son" (Matt. 1:25; "her firstborn," Lk. 2:7) and that later several brothers and sisters were born. Judging not only from the place of leadership that James assumed in the church, but also from the fact that his name occurs first in the list of the brothers of the Lord, he must have been the oldest of these children of Joseph and Mary and but a little younger than Jesus himself.

B. Conversion. James and the other brothers were not in sympathy with the ministry and claims of Jesus. Though reared in a godly home and apparently responsive to the religion of the Jews, they did not believe in Jesus (Jn. 7:5). At times they chided him (vv. 2–4). Even the mother seems to have doubted his equilibrium on at least one occasion (Mk. 3:21, 31). When Jesus was rejected at NAZARETH, he implied that opposition was even "among his relatives and in his own house" (6:4). Perhaps this same loneliness and sadness of personal experience is reflected in the warnings of Jesus that his followers must be prepared for the opposition of those nearest and dearest to them (Matt. 10:34–37; Lk. 14:26). However, the tension between James and Jesus seems not to have reflected long-standing dislike. It is likely that a warm friendship had existed, based on a real admiration for Jesus. Otherwise, would James have so quickly reacted from hostility to faith at the time of the resurrection? There may have been some family resentment over the economic loss when Jesus left his employment to be a rabbi. Such claims as he made must have embarrassed and puzzled the brothers.

The conversion of James must have been a surprising and unexpected event to those who had known his attitude toward Jesus. However, as with Paul, the eruption of faith likely had antecedents that prepared for the crisis. The claims of Jesus may have caused earlier stirrings of conscience that James had ruthlessly suppressed. Even the hostility toward Jesus may have been a reflection of James's own confusion and frustration. In any case, the matter was resolved by a special appearance of the risen Christ (1 Cor. 15:7). Two results followed at once. James became a staunch believer, joined to the Jerusalem group. Secondly, having seen the risen Lord, he was recognized as a part of the select group of witnesses to the resurrection, a fact without which he would likely never have risen to so great prominence in the church (1 Cor. 9:1, Acts 1:22). The place and circumstances of the appearance to James are unknown. The account in the *Gospel of the Hebrews* is fanciful, late, and legendary (see HEBREWS, GOSPEL OF THE), but the crucial importance of the event is clear.

C. Prominence. Tradition makes James the BISHOP of Jerusalem (Euseb. *Hist.* 2.1). It is not likely that he was ever so elected. But the personal character and high spiritual gifts of James, together with his kinship to the Lord, most certainly exerted an influence that soon became a vigorous leadership. As the apostles became involved in broader ministries and missions, James, who stayed in Jerusalem, became the practical leader. At any rate, no one disputes his prominence and influence. Paul, three years after his conversion, met James in Jerusalem (Gal. 1:19). Peter, having escaped from prison, sent word to James and the other believers (Acts 12:17). At the COUNCIL OF JERUSALEM, James's opinion bore the most weight (15:12–21). On Paul's last return to Jerusalem, it was James and the elders who received him (21:18). It was "certain men … from James" who influenced Peter in Antioch (Gal. 2:12). The epistle of James makes evident the authority and wide influence of its writer. JUDE found "brother of James" sufficient identification for himself (Jude 1). This prominence, however, does not indicate office in a separate formal organization called the church. The believers still considered themselves loyal to their Jewish heritage and sought to win their countrymen to the faith. Neither James nor the others in Jerusalem had any thought that he was a "bishop" in the technical sense.

If James achieved leadership in Jerusalem, it is only natural that his influence would spread to the rest of Palestine, whose life centered in Jerusalem. Beyond Palestine, the prestige would be observed mostly among the Jewish Christians of the Gentile lands. Note ANTIOCH OF SYRIA, for instance, where a visit of emissaries from James sent Peter scurrying from the informal fellowship of the gospel to a strict Jewish ceremonialism (Gal. 2:11–14).

D. Character. Tradition supports the NT picture of James as a man of large influence, impressive character, and intense piety according to the finest Hebrew ideals. According to the 2nd-cent. writer Hegesippus (as recorded by Euseb. *Eccl. Hist.* 2.23), James was known as "the Just" and as "the bulwark of the people." He lived a life of such holiness and piety that he was respected even by nonbelieving Jews. He never ceased to keep the Jewish law with rigor and care. In Hegesippus's exaggerated account, James was both a NAZIRITE and an ascetic—"he was holy from his mother's womb, wine and strong drink he drank not, nor did he eat flesh; no razor touched his head; he never anointed himself with oil; and he used not the bath." His knees were said to be hard as a camel's because he was so constant in prayer and entreaty to God for pardon for the people.

Though the extreme statements must be discounted, the basic picture agrees with what is known of James. He may have been stern and austere, but he was not narrow and mean. Note his insight and consideration during the Council at Jerusalem (Acts 15:13–19). He may have been somewhat prosaic in temperament, but no one doubts his uprightness. The epithet "the Just" correctly reflects the consistency of his faithful conformity to the right way of life as he saw it. Along with his outstanding sincerity and zeal was also a costly fault. Though he admitted the legitimacy of Gentile Christianity, he was too steeped in tradition to follow the Spirit of God into the broad universal thrust of the gospel in an adequate way. The nationalistic faith of James was outstripped by Paul's more adequate grasp and proclamation. Worse than that, James found himself tied to a doomed and perishing sectionalism, though he had sniffed the air beyond.

E. Writing. One of the NT Epistles identifies the author as "James, a servant of God and of the Lord Jesus Christ" (Jas. 1:1). Although the authorship of this letter has been disputed, it seems most likely that it was written by James, the Lord's brother. If so, it may have been composed in the late 40s, making it the earliest NT writing, but some date it as late as the year 60. See further JAMES, EPISTLE OF.

F. Death. JOSEPHUS (*Ant.* 20.9.1) relates that between the death of FESTUS and the arrival of a new governor, the high priest ANANIAS seized the opportunity to call the judicial council together. He charged James and others with violating the law. Details are not known, but the charges probably involved Christian doctrine. Because of this, James was stoned to death. Josephus reports that the unjust act was protested by pious non-Christian Jews who respected James for his faithfulness to Jewish observances. The high priest was relieved of his office.

Hegesippus (Euseb. *Eccl. Hist.* 2.23) gives a much more elaborate account of the martyrdom, presumably with legendary embellishments. He reports that, misled by James's careful keeping of the law, the Jewish authorities supposedly did not realize all that James believed. Having caused him to stand on the wing of the temple to dissuade people from becoming Christians, the Jews were grieved and enraged to hear him give powerful testimony for Jesus. They responded by throwing him down and stoning him. A priest tried to stop the murder, but a fuller ran up and beat James to death with the club he used to beat clothes. This much is true: James died about A.D. 62 for his faith. (See B. Chilton and J. Neusner, eds., *The Brother of Jesus: James the Just and His Mission* [2001]; P. J. Hartin, *James of Jerusalem: Heir to Jesus of Nazareth* [2004]; J. Painter, *Just James: The Brother of Jesus in History and Tradition*, 2nd ed. [2004].)

III. James son of Alphaeus. The only references to James the son of ALPHAEUS in the NT are mere inclusions of his name in the lists of the twelve apostles (Matt. 10:3; Mk. 3:18; Lk. 6:15; Acts 1:13), unless, as many suppose, he is the same person as James the younger (discussed in section IV, below). He heads the third group of four disciples in each of the lists of the Twelve, being coupled with Thaddaeus in Matthew and Mark, and with Simon the Zealot in Luke and Acts. Since MATTHEW, or Levi, is also called the son of Alphaeus (cf. Matt. 9:9; Mk. 2:14), he may possibly be a brother of James. If this is true, however, it is remarkable that these brothers were not associated in any way in the Gospels, or were Simon and Andrew and the sons of Zebedee. Legend says that James was of the house of Gad, was stoned by the Jews for preaching Christ, and was buried near the sanctuary in Jerusalem (E. A. W. Budge, *The Contendings of the Apostles*, 2 vols. [1899–1901], 2:50, 264–66).

IV. James the younger. Many believe that James the son of Alphaeus is designated by various names, including "James the younger" (Mk. 15:40; Gk. *mikros* G3625, lit., "little"; KJV, "James the less"). The expression may refer to his small stature. Or, if he is being compared with the son of Zebedee, he might be both younger and less renowned. James the younger was the son of a certain Mary and the brother of JOSES. "Mary the mother of James" is mentioned as present at the crucifixion (Matt. 27:56; Mk. 15:40) and at the discovery of the empty tomb (Mk. 16:1; Lk. 24:10). She is often thought to be the same person as Mary of CLOPAS (Jn. 19:25). Most English versions translate the text "wife of," but the Arabic renders it "Mary the daughter of Clopas" (E. Bishop, "Mary [of] Clopas and Her Father," *EvT* 73 [1962]: 339). On this basis, the common identification of James the son of Alphaeus with the son of Mary becomes more natural, though it is entirely possible that the same man bore both names, Alphaeus and Clopas. Literature refers to a Simon son of Clopas (Budge, *Contendings of the Apostles*, 2:50) who has been identified with Simon the Zealot (see CANANAEAN). If this were admissible, it would account for pairing James with Simon in Luke and Acts (as other brothers are listed among the Twelve). Others argue that "Mary the mother of James" is the same as the mother of Jesus (cf. Mk. 6:3 and see R. H. Gundry, *Mark: A Commentary on His Apology for the Cross* [1993], 977). With so few explicit references in the NT, most of these identifications will likely continue to be conjectural, at best.

V. James the father of Judas. All that is known of this James is that he is the father of the apostle JUDAS (not Iscariot), as recorded in Lk. 6:16 and Acts 1:13 (KJV, "Judas *the brother* of James").

(See further A. Plummer, *The General Epistles of St. James and St. Jude* [1891], 25–41; G. Purves, *Christianity in the Apostolic Age* [1900], 130–50; J. B. Mayor, *The Epistle of St. James* [1913], i–lxv; F. Filson, *Pioneers of the Primitive Church* [1940], 155–83; A. Smith, *The Twelve Christ Chose* [1958], 33–48, 109–18; W. Barclay, *The Master's Men* [1959], 82–86, 100–104; D. A. Hagner in *ABD*, 3:616–18.)

W. T. DAYTON

James, Apocalypse of. Two documents under this title (to be distinguished from the *Apocryphon of James*) are contained in Codex V of the NAG HAMMADI LIBRARY. The *First Apocalypse* (NHC V, 3) takes the form of a dialogue between Jesus and JAMES, the brother of the Lord. The first part of this document falls before the PASSION and deals with questions raised by James, who is fearful of future sufferings; the second part, more fragmentary, falls after the resurrection. Most of the *Second Apocalypse* (NHC V, 4) is formally a speech delivered by

James prior to his martyrdom, including an account of an appearance of Jesus and the revelation given by him. Part of the interest of these texts lies in the link that they provide between GNOSTICISM and the Jewish Christianity that gave so high a place to James. (English trans. in *NHL*, 260–69; see also C. W. Hedrick *Nag Hammadi Codices V,2–5 and VI, with Papyrus Berolinensis 8502,1 and 4*, ed. D. Parrott [1979], 105–49.) — R. McL. WILSON

James, Apocryphon of. A "secret book" included in the NAG HAMMADI LIBRARY (NHC I, 2; cf. line 10). Composed in the form of a letter written by JAMES, the Lord's brother, it reports a postresurrection dialogue between Jesus and both James and PETER, though much of it may be regarded as a revelatory discourse. The work is preserved only in a 4th-cent. Coptic MS, but the original Greek was produced at least a century earlier and seems to reflect the teachings of Valentinian GNOSTICISM. (Text, English trans., and notes in *Nag Hammadi Codex I (The Jung Codex)*, ed. H. W. Attridge, 2 vols. [1985], 1:13–53, 2:7–37; trans. also in *NHL*, 29–37.)

James, Ascents of. A document mentioned in connection with the EBIONITES by EPIPHANIUS (*Pan.* 30.16), who says it presented JAMES, the Lord's brother, as speaking against the temple, sacrifice, and the altar fire. He also says that it was violently hostile to PAUL. Taking Acts 21:39 as a starting point, the Ebionites alleged that Paul was a Greek, born of Greek parents, who after a stay in Jerusalem wanted to marry the high priest's daughter, and so became a proselyte and submitted to circumcision. Later, enraged at the disappointment of his hopes, he wrote against circumcision, the Sabbath, and the law.

The presentation of James and the hostility to Paul recall the Jewish Christianity of the CLEMENTINE LITERATURE, especially the final chapters of the first book of the *Recognitions* (G. Strecker, *Das Judenchristentum in den Pseudoklementinen* [1958], 252–53, postulates a common archetype). There are also links with the account of the martyrdom of James from Hegesippus (quoted in Euseb. *Eccl. Hist.* 2.23.3–18), and J. B. Lightfoot suggests that the story to which Hegesippus was indebted "was the grand *finale* of these 'ascents,' of which the earlier portions are preserved in the *Recognitions*" (*Saint Paul's Epistle to the Galatians*, 10th ed. [1898], 367 n. 1). The book probably owes its title to the fact that it described the ascents of James up the temple stairs, from which he harangued the people (Lightfoot, *Galatians*, 330 n. 2). H. J. Schoeps (*Theologie und Geschichte des Judenchristentums* [1949], 381ff.) discusses possible connections with a lost Ebionite Book of Acts. — R. McL. WILSON

James, Epistle of. The first of the CATHOLIC EPISTLES of the NT.
  I. Background
  II. Unity
  III. Authorship
  IV. Date
  V. Place of origin
  VI. Destination
  VII. Occasion
  VIII. Purpose
  IX. Canonicity
  X. Text
  XI. Special problems
  XII. Contents
  XIII. Theology

I. Background. The epistle of James is the most Jewish book in the NT. Except for two or three explicit references to Christ, it would fit rather well in the OT. The life to which the epistle exhorts is that of a profoundly pious Jew who is fulfilling the law in every regard. Gospel, redemption, incarnation, and resurrection are not mentioned. The interest is in the fruits, not the roots. The author is indeed a Christian, writing to believers, but the focus is not on how to become believers. It is on the second stage—on how to advance along the way of HOLINESS and to translate the ethical implications of the new faith into practical realities (R. V. G. Tasker, *The General Epistle of James*, TNTC [1957], 11). The gospel fulfilled the law.

Though there are only five direct verbal quotations from the OT (Jas. 1:11; 2:8; 2:11; 2:23; 4:6), the atmosphere of the Hebrew Bible dominates the book. Allusion is made to passages from all three divisions of the OT CANON. Among specifically Jewish terms used are "Lord of hosts" (5:4 NRSV)

and GEHENNA ("hell," 3:6). W. E. Oesterley (in *EGT*, 4:393ff.) remarks that a still more cogent Jewish factor is the accumulation of many small points that indicate Hebrew methods of thought, expression, and phraseology. This Hebraic coloring is, he believes, one of the most pronounced characteristics of the epistle. Though the Greek is often compared with the best in the NT, the stylistic expression seems, occasionally at least, to be molded from a Hebrew pattern. A strong tendency to assonance and pleonasm as well as a terse and forceful way of putting things are Hebrew qualities.

A still more striking fact is the number of parallels between this epistle and the words of Jesus. As A. Ross says, "this Epistle contains more verbal reminiscences of the teaching of Jesus than all of the other apostolic writings" (*The Epistles of James and John*, NICNT [1954], 16). Instead of quoting specifically from the Gospels, it seems that the author is simply reflecting the words he heard from the lips of Jesus himself, perhaps as they worked together as youths in NAZARETH. He certainly knew and shared the insights and attitudes reflected in the SERMON ON THE MOUNT, in PARABLES, and in other teachings about life, poverty, and values (cf. Jas. 1:22 with Matt. 7:20, 24; Jas. 2:13 with Matt. 7:16; Jas. 2:5 with Matt. 5:3; Jas. 4:11–12 with Matt. 7:1; Jas. 5:2 with Matt. 6:19; and Jas. 5:12 with Matt. 5:34–37).

II. Unity. Opinions differ concerning the unity of this epistle. Some see no particular thematic connection in it (A. Jülicher, *An Introduction to the New Testament* [1904], 215). Various ideas of composite authorship have been suggested, often based on a core of materials coming from James in Jerusalem, perhaps in Aramaic, later rewritten in good Greek (e.g., F. C. Burkitt, *Christian Beginnings: Three Lectures* [1924], 65–70). A. T. Cadoux, at the other extreme, finds the epistle "probably the most completely patterned book in the Bible" (*The Thought of St. James* [1944], 6). He calls attention to its four divisions, each containing four subdivisions.

The truth may not be at either extreme. There is a tone of authority that hardly goes with a late and composite authorship. Fifty-four imperatives occur in one hundred eight verses. This seems to reflect the kind of certainty that belongs to a recognized leader and spokesman among the apostles. Likewise, the absence of the usual references to incarnation, atonement, and the death and resurrection of Jesus inclines toward unity of authorship. Late editors, overlooking the cause for the omissions, would almost certainly have supplied this lack. Furthermore, literary forms tend to have their own peculiar kind of unity. Wisdom literature, of which James is a part, is sometimes more like a string of beads — a series of loosely connected ideas. There may be some truth in Tasker's suggestion (*James*, 9) that the epistle is more of a "collection of sermon notes" than a polished sermon. Even so, there is a unity and pattern of thought centering around the exhortation to constancy and holy living that could hardly have been the work of any but the original writer. (Note below, under Contents, how the main body of the epistle is an elaboration of the three elements of Jas. 1:19.) The authority, freshness, directness, and intrinsic outline can hardly be explained other than by unity of authorship.

III. Authorship. The epistle, if not pseudepigraphic, must have been written by JAMES, the

Babylonian design of a horse with a bit and bridle. James compares the power of the tongue to the power of the bit placed into the mouth of a horse to guide it (Jas. 3:3).

brother of the Lord. EUSEBIUS and JEROME mention the opinion of some in the early church that it may have been published by another under James's name. This view has also appealed to those modern scholars who on general considerations assign it a late date and who regard it as a moral treatise instead of a letter. However, the absence of motive for a pseudonymous production is a strong argument against it. If it is merely a moralizing tract, why did it need James's authority, and why should he be chosen? Furthermore, the epistle bears none of the marks usually claimed as indications of PSEUDONYMITY. In the one verse that exhibits any strictly epistolary character (Jas. 1:1), there is no mention of apostleship. Nor is there any autobiographical reference in the body of the writing.

In view of these facts and of the total absence of proof that any canonical book was ever written under an assumed name, it is better to believe that the church's acceptance of the book involved a general agreement on its genuineness. Besides, would an unknown 2nd-cent. writer really have gained a hearing for such a discursive document merely by taking the common name of James? Does not the meaning of the name depend on the well-accepted authority of this president of the Jerusalem church? Once this identity is established, does it not carry with it a *Sitz im Leben* quite impossible to counterfeit?

Certainly the author was a Jew (see below, section V). Moreover, he calls himself simply "James, a servant of God and of the Lord Jesus Christ" (Jas. 1:1). If this had been the son of ZEBEDEE or the son of ALPHAEUS, he would likely have called himself an apostle or would have given some added identification, as did JUDE (Jude 1), and as is common with all but one who bore the name of James. At any rate, the son of Zebedee died too early (no later than A.D. 44), and there is no evidence that the early church assigned the epistle to the son of Alphaeus. The James at Jerusalem who needed no further identification was unquestionably the Lord's brother. He had the recognized authority that would permit him to speak so freely in the imperative mood. It was he who appeared in the unvarying role of leader in Jerusalem—when Peter escaped from prison (Acts 12:17), at the COUNCIL OF JERUSALEM (15:13–21), when Paul made his final visit to Palestine (21:18), and whenever his name appears in Scripture or tradition.

Other factors support the identification. There are coincidences of phraseology between the epistle and both the speech of James at the Council of Jerusalem and the letter from that council (cf. Acts 15:23 with Jas. 1:1; Acts 15:13 with Jas. 2:5; Acts 15:19 with Jas. 5:19–20; and Acts 15:17 with Jas. 2:7). The epistle therefore is the work of the type of mind reflected in all that is known of this James. He was strict, careful, and zealous, possibly to the point of ASCETICISM. Severe with himself, he commanded discipline on the part of others. Finally, there are the verbal reminiscences of the teaching of Jesus, to which attention has already been called. The abundance and naturalness of these do not indicate the work of a 2nd-cent. forger. These are not formal quotations from a hardened tradition. They drop freely as from a mind saturated with the thoughts of Jesus from long association with him.

Objections have been raised. W. Barclay, for example, marvels that such a book should have only two incidental references to Jesus, and none at all to the resurrection, or to Jesus as the MESSIAH (*The Letters of James and Peter* [1958], 38–39). The good Greek also seems strange to some as coming from a Jew. The answer to the first problem seems to be in the purpose of the book. James is not presenting the gospel. He is defending the practical and ethical demands of God upon his people. The point at issue is not God's provision, but human obligation. The epistle is a prophetic diatribe against unfaithfulness and lack of discipline. Why should it be complicated with theological questions that would only divert the pressure from their smarting consciences? As to the excellence of the Greek, estimates vary. Is there any reason that a bilingual Jew from Galilee of the Gentiles could not polish his Greek in thirty-two years of discussion and debate at a center like Jerusalem until he could handle it with skill, especially in its simple terse forms? It should be remembered that James avoided complex sentences. Short, pungent commands served his purpose better.

IV. Date. Those who accept James the Just, brother of the Lord, as author of the epistle are obliged to date it before A.D. 62, the year of the death of James, between the governorships of Festus and Albinus. Others tend to date it anywhere from late 1st cent. to late 2nd cent., with perhaps A.D. 125 a general favorite. W. E. Oesterley (in *EGT*, 4:405) avoids the difficult choice by suggesting the possibility that the core of the epistle was a work of James, but was elaborated as time went on by commentary—much after the manner that, on a much larger scale, the comments on the words of Scripture became the MISHNAH, the comments on these the GEMARA, and finally the TALMUD. For reasons already discussed (see above under Unity), this composite authorship should likely be rejected. If Lightfoot and others are correct in seeing James reflected in *1 Clement* (see CLEMENT, EPISTLES OF), the epistle must belong to the 1st cent. James gives the thought in a more terse and rugged form than Clement, and he must have written first (J. B. Mayor, *The Epistle of St. James* [1913], clxix). Once a 1st-cent. date has been conceded, little reason remains for rejecting James as author and for objecting to the early date. The writing comes too close to the lifetime of James for one to borrow his name successfully.

A choice still remains for those who accept James as the author. Was it before or after the COUNCIL OF JERUSALEM? The seemingly settled condition of affairs and the presence of wealth and perhaps intellectualism in the Christian communities tend to indicate as late a date as possible, therefore around A.D. 60. JOSEPHUS, at least, makes abundant mention of the oppressive rich in the period leading up to the rebellion against Rome (A.D. 67–70). However, none of these arguments are conclusive for the later period. Would not the foundations of the Jewish Christian church have already been well laid by the year 45 or 50? Were there not people of means among the followers of Jesus and even among the apostles (as, for example, the sons of Zebedee, Matthew, and the ladies who ministered of their means)? Did not Mary the mother of Mark have a large home with servants in the early days of the Jerusalem church? And might not the temptation to fawn on the rich be all the greater where their numbers were few?

It still seems possible to hold, with Mayor and others, to an early date, even the earliest of any NT book. Indeed, the epistle reflects no knowledge of the existence of Gentile Christians. There is no whisper of the controversy relating to the Council of Jerusalem. James came early to a position of authority (Acts 12:17). No man in the apostolic circle at this period had the ear of the Jewish Christians as did James. One does not have to wait many decades to find need for strong ethical preaching to those converted out of either heathen practices or the sins of the Jews. The extreme "Jewishness" of writer and reader in every way tends to confirm the probability of an early date—perhaps A.D. 45–48.

V. Place of origin. If the previous conclusions are accepted, there can be little doubt as to the place of origin of this epistle. There is no record of James's absence from Jerusalem after his assumption of the leadership of the Jewish church, nor would there need to be. The influence of the Jerusalem church provided a natural support for the leadership of its president in matters that affected Jewish Christians, wherever they were found. As the temple in Jerusalem had been the hub of the Jewish world to which worshipers traveled from afar, so the believing Jews gravitated to Jerusalem with their questions and problems. James was apparently a cosmopolitan figure without the necessity for travel. The thoroughly Jewish background of the writer has already been discussed (see above, section I). Though it must be admitted that he knew Greek well and constantly associated with Hellenistic as well as Palestinian Jews, there is nothing in the epistle incongruous with the view that it originated in Jerusalem under the pen of James the brother of the Lord.

VI. Destination. The epistle presupposes not only a Jewish author but also readers of the same background. The most natural understanding of "the twelve tribes in the Dispersion" (Jas. 1:1 NRSV) would be that the epistle is addressed to Jews scattered throughout the Roman empire. The fact that they are repeatedly called "brethren" and "beloved brethren" perhaps implies that they are Christian believers. The matter is practically settled by reference to their having faith "in our glorious Lord Jesus Christ" (2:1). Further confirmation, if needed, is found in the appeal to the near return of the Lord (5:8). If the epistle was written before the

Jerusalem council, the only generally recognized Christians would be Jewish Christians, meeting in synagogues and homes. Indeed, the word for "synagogue" is used in the Greek (2:2). The distinctly Jewish references throughout appear to communicate rather than obstruct. The primary addressees are Jews scattered abroad but bound together in a common faith in Jesus Christ. However, unconverted Jews would find much that is familiar in the ethical treatise that demands fulfillment of the law. And Gentile Christians, when they appear, would certainly find in it the way of Christian living. If the epistle was written much later than here suggested, it might then be necessary to apply it to the spiritual Israel, the Christian believers of whatever background who were scattered for their faith.

VII. Occasion. Some deny that the epistle is occasional; that is, they see no particular circumstance that specifically called for the book to be written. Several circumstances did, indeed, precede the writing. Some see an allusion to a period of persecution in the reference to trials (Jas. 1:2). However, the epistle reflects not a major peak of persecution but animosities aroused, losses endured, liability to insults, and interference with ways of life and religious services. Another circumstance, largely learned from other sources, is the strong position of leadership early achieved by James the Just. It is evident from the writing itself that sufficient time had elapsed for some of the original fervor of the converts to wane. This, of course, need not be many years. Possibly none of these circumstances was the occasion of the writing in any specific sense. All together, they perhaps constituted a situation in which the Spirit of God moved his messenger to rebuke the sins into which the readers were slipping and to call the believers into a disciplined life of holiness.

Alternative views have been held. Some see James engaged in an unlikely diatribe against PAUL's view of JUSTIFICATION by faith alone. Others see him attacking those who perverted Paul's teaching. Both of these ideas demand a late date of the epistle and tend to exaggerate the differences between Paul and James. Cadoux (*The Thought of St. James*, 26) offers a better suggestion: there was need to send something back with Jewish Christians who visited Jerusalem so that they could encourage and establish the believers scattered abroad. This concern may have been the occasion for the writing.

VIII. Purpose. The purpose of the epistle is clearly practical and ethical. Doctrine is assumed more than enunciated. The thrust is for action and obedience. The law is to be lived. The ethical implications of the new faith need to be translated into practical realities if the believers are to advance along the way of holiness. The mood is hortatory. The purpose is to correct faults, to instruct the wavering, to instill discipline, to rebuke backslidings, and to encourage genuine godliness throughout the redeemed fellowship, wherever believers could be found among the Jews who were scattered abroad.

IX. Canonicity. Direct external evidence for the acceptance of the epistle is relatively late and sometimes ambiguous. This is not strange if its original thrust was toward a Jewish Christianity that soon withered and was displaced by a more viable universal mission. Unlike the writings of Paul and the Gospels, this epistle had to work its way back into the general church as a secondary audience after its original audience had perished. Not written by one of the Twelve and not addressed to a single church that would preserve and defend it, the epistle's comeback was slow.

ORIGEN is the first to cite James, though he spoke as if some would demur to its authority. The Syriac version includes it, and F. J. A. Hort (*The Epistle of St. James* [1909], xxviii) thinks it likely that it did so from the first in the older Syriac translation. EUSEBIUS (*Hist.* 2.23) places James among the *antilegomena*, as practically accepted in most churches but not in all. He himself, however, quotes Jas. 4:11 as Scripture and 5:13 as spoken by the holy apostle. From Eusebius onward the book had a firm place in the Greek churches. It was used freely by Didymus and Cyril of Alexandria, Cyril of Jerusalem, Gregory Nazianzus, and Ephraem of Edessa. The Antiochene Fathers (like CHRYSOSTOM), who kept to the Syrian Canon, used James.

In the W the reception was not so rapid. Neglected largely until late in the 4th cent., it was then adopted through Jerome and AUGUSTINE. The Third Council of Carthage, in 397, finally clarified the status for the Western church, and from that date forward its canonicity was unquestioned until the time of the Reformation, when Erasmus and Cajetan revived old doubts. Luther, finding much straw in it in comparison with his favorites, Romans and Galatians, assigned it a secondary place. Luther's judgment, however, has not been sustained by Protestantism in general.

Thus far, only the more formal evidences for the canonicity of the epistle have been discussed. The more casual references, quotations, and allusions may be even more revealing of the faith of the early church. Formal literature often waits for doubts and questions to arise. Quotations and allusions follow normal use and acceptance from the first. It is remarkable that the earliest witnesses belong to the church at Rome, which was one of the latest to recognize the epistle formally. In the early days, the church at Rome had a large Jewish component (see ROME, CHURCH AT). Having lost this, it had to rediscover James.

At any rate, Clement of Rome, in the 1st cent., reflects knowledge of the epistle. In the 2nd cent., the same appears to be true of IGNATIUS, POLYCARP, JUSTIN MARTYR, the Epistle to DIOGNETUS, IRENAEUS, and HERMAS (see HERMAS, SHEPHERD OF). Since canonicity depends not on decrees of councils but on the INSPIRATION of the HOLY SPIRIT, recognized by believers, perhaps the evidence of an early wide use of the epistle of James speaks more loudly for canonicity than the temporary "official silence" could speak against it. See also CANON (NT).

X. Text. Aside from a papyrus of Jas. 2:19—3:9 (P^{20}=POxy 1171), the earliest Greek text of James is found in CODEX VATICANUS (B, 4th cent). Other uncials, in order of relative importance, are CODEX SINAITICUS (ℵ, 4th cent.), CODEX EPHRAEMI (C, 5th cent.), and CODEX ALEXANDRINUS (A, 5th cent.). Relatively brief portions are also found from the 4th cent. in P^{23} (POxy 1229), and from the 5th cent. in 048 (Codex Patriensis), 0166 (Heidelberg), and P^{54}. Several others are scattered through the 8th and 9th centuries, including minuscule 33, the "queen of the cursives." J. H. Ropes says that "in addition about 475 manuscripts dating from the tenth to eighteenth centuries are enumerated in the lists of Gregory and H. von Soden" (*A Critical and Exegetical Commentary on the Epistle of St. James*, ICC [1916], 75).

Since most of the important variants were in existence about as early as B, the value of the documents is not primarily based on date but on the soundness of the principles or tastes on which they are built. Careful testing shows that B is relatively free from emendation and thus, with due precaution, should generally be followed except when positive evidence from "transcriptional" or other internal probability outweighs the authority of B. The other witnesses serve two purposes: when they disagree with B, their readings may commend themselves by internal character as superior; when they agree with B, they guarantee that the reading was not due to an idiosyncrasy of B. The wider currency of the reading also increases confidence.

By following the above guidelines, Ropes believes (*Commentary*, 86), one will not have a perfect text of the epistle but will have fewer emended readings than by following any other document or group of documents. The versions prove that the oldest MSS as a whole are immensely superior to the later eclectic texts commonly used in the Greek-speaking churches from the middle of the 4th cent. The recensions are valuable for the fragments of older texts they contain and not for their continuous texts.

XI. Special problems. The most publicized problem of the epistle is its seeming contradiction to Paul's doctrine of justification by faith. Luther in particular was greatly disturbed by the position of James (*Colloquia*, 2:202; see *Table Talk* in *Luther's Works*, vol. 54, ed. H. T. Lehmann [1967], 424–35). Paul said, "For we hold that a person is justified by faith apart from works prescribed by the law" (Rom. 3:28 NRSV). James said, "You see that a person is justified by works and not by faith alone" (Jas. 2:24 NRSV). It is important to understand what each meant. FAITH, to Paul, was a trust that cannot exist without obedience. It must be a vital, working faith, a faith that works by love (Gal. 5:6). For this truth James also contended. Faith is not a magic formula. It must have works that demonstrate its genuineness and efficacy, otherwise it is dead. James and Paul were not fighting each other; they were opposing a common enemy.

Roman Catholics have also claimed the epistle as authority for the sacrament of extreme unction. Anointing with oil is not only reported but recommended in connection with prayer for physical and spiritual healing (Jas. 5:14–15; see ANOINT).

"But when he asks, he must believe and not doubt, because he who doubts is like a wave of the sea, blown and tossed by the wind" (Jas. 1:6).

This injunction has been followed and this promise claimed many times in the history of the church. Considerable shift occurred when this practice was divorced from the healing of the sick and made a sacrament for the dying. The problem is not in the text but in its distortion.

The word *elder* (Jas. 5:14) in an early epistle has puzzled some scholars. See ELDER (NT). Did the early Jerusalem church have that much organization? They did worship in "synagogues." Jewish synagogues had elders, older men of influence, who directed the affairs. What would be so strange about calling by the same name those who performed a similar function, regardless of the stage of organization (cf. Acts 15:6)?

XII. Contents. Some have likened WISDOM Literature in general and this epistle in particular to a string of beads. In this intensely hortatory situation, one might expect only a series of ideas instead of a logically developed structure. However, even beads may be strung in a pattern; James did outline his thoughts.

The governing idea is PATIENCE, in terms of steadfastness, constancy, or endurance. The frequent use of the word *patience* in the KJV emphasizes the pattern (Jas. 1:3–4; 5:7–8, 10–11), though synonyms in other versions may communicate better. James is exhorting the readers to endure, to overcome all opposition from within and without, and to remain with undeviating constancy on the course of the heavenly wisdom. Only thus can blessedness be experienced here or hereafter (1:2–3, 12). In view of the goodness of God and the source of life in him (1:16–18), three rules emerge that form the basic outline of the body of the book: be quick to hear, slow to speak, slow to anger (v. 19). Chapter 5 returns to the theme of patience or constancy, now in terms of the imminent coming of the Lord and of the efficacy of prayer.

- A. Exhortation to constancy (1:1–22)
    1. The use of trials (vv. 1–4)
    2. The use of faith (vv. 5–11)
    3. Triumph over temptation (vv. 12–15)
    4. Divine provision (vv. 16–18)
    5. Human response (vv. 19–22)
- B. Elements of constancy (1:23—4:17)
    1. Quick to hear (1:23—2:26)
        a. Hearing and doing (1:23–27)
        b. Hearing and impartiality (2:1–13)
        c. Faith and works (2:14–26)
    2. Slow to speak (3:1–12)
        a. Temptation of leaders (vv. 1–5)
        b. Threat of speech (vv. 6–12)
    3. Slow to anger (3:13—4:17)
        a. Pure and peaceable wisdom (3:13–18)
        b. Chaos of human passions (4:1–4)
        c. Provision for deliverance (4:5–10)
        d. Humble obedience (4:11–17)
- C. Confirmation of constancy (5:1–20)
    1. The certainty of justice (vv. 1–6)
    2. The imminence of the judge (vv. 7–12)
    3. The power of prayer (vv. 13–18)
    4. The value of righteousness (vv. 19–20)

XIII. Theology. The theology of the epistle is more implicit than explicit. The thrust is hortatory and ethical. It is addressed to people who already are familiar with the OT and who have been informed of the relevance of Jesus as the One who fulfilled the promises of redemption. They have already believed on him, found life in him, and suffered for their faith. It is not new doctrine that is needed. Rather, the necessary element is steadfastness in what they already know and experience. Theology is not discussed for its own sake in the epistle. It is introduced from time to time in support of practical exhortations.

Even so, James finds expression for his theology. Twice he uses the formula "Lord Jesus Christ" (Jas 1.1, 2.1), as if the person of the divine Christ were beyond debate. The holiness of God does not even admit of temptation (1:13). Spiritual life comes to us by direct divine bestowal (1:18). God demands ethical righteousness of his people (4:4–5). There is a personal devil who can and must be resisted (4:7). Nothing escapes the ears of the Judge, who is already at the door (5:9). The hope of the return of the Lord is sure (5:7–8). Prayer is real and effective (5:13–18). Nothing is too hard for God.

(Significant commentaries include E. Plumptre, *The General Epistle of St. James* [1886]; A. Plummer, *The General Epistles of St. James and St. Jude* [1891]; J. B. Mayor, *The Epistle of St. James* [1913]; J. H. Ropes, *A Critical and Exegetical Commentary on the Epistle of St. James*, ICC [1916]; C. Mitton, *The Epistle of James* [1966]; J. B. Adamson, *The Epistle of James*, NICNT [1976]; M. Dibelius, *James: A Commentary on the Epistle of James*, rev. H. Greeven, Hermeneia [1976]; S. Laws, *A Commentary on the Epistle of James*, HNTC [1980]; P. H. Davids, *The Epistle of James: A Commentary on the Greek Text*, NIGTC [1982]; S. Kistemaker, *Exposition of the Epistle of James and the Epistles of John* [1986]; R. P. Martin, *James*, WBC 48 [1988]; L. T. Johnson, *The Letter of James: A New Translation with Introduction and Commentary*, AB 37A [1995]; R. W. Wall, *Community of the Wise: The Letter of James* [1997]; D. J. Moo, *The Letter of James: An Introduction and Commentary* [2000]; P. J. Hartin, *James*, SP 14 [2003]; W. F. Brosend II, *James and Jude* [2004]. See also S. Paine, *Studies in the Book of James* [1955]; A. T. Robertson, *Studies in the Epistle of James*, rev. H. F. Peacock [1959]; P. L. Maier, *James, the Apostle of Faith: A Primary Christological Epistle for the Persecuted Church* [1983]; J. B. Adamson, *James: The Man and His Message* [1989]; T. B. Cargal, *Restoring the Diaspora: Discursive Structure and Purpose in the Epistle of James* [1993]; D. Hutchinson Edgar, *Has God Not Chosen the Poor? The Social Setting of the Epistle of James* [2001]; L. L. Cheung, *The Genre, Composition and Hermeneutics of the Epistle of James* [2003]; L. T. Johnson, *Brother of Jesus, Friend of God: Studies in the Letter of James* [2004]; R. L. Webb and J. S. Kloppenborg, eds., *Reading James with New Eyes* [2007].) W. T. DAYTON

James, Protevangelium of. The oldest and most famous of the infancy gospels, this document is significant (a) for its evidence of the extent to which devotion to MARY, MOTHER OF JESUS, had already developed by the time of its composition, and (b) for its influence on later developments in the history of Mariology. With the *Infancy Gospel of Thomas*, this work formed the basis on which the later infancy gospels were constructed (e.g., the Arabic and Armenian infancy gospels, the *Gospel of Pseudo-Matthew*, etc.); most of them incorporate considerable parts of its contents along with material drawn from other sources.

I. Content. The infancy narratives in Matthew and Luke carry the story of Jesus back to his birth and to the birth of his forerunner, JOHN THE BAPTIST. The *Protevangelium* begins with the birth of Mary. The story starts with a wealthy but childless couple, Joachim and Anna. Publicly reproached because he alone has not begotten children in Israel, Joachim goes off sadly to the wilderness, where he remains forty days and forty nights. Meanwhile his wife Anna mourns her childlessness. An angel appears to her (and also to Joachim), promising that her prayers will be granted. In due time the child is born and named Mary. At the age of three she is presented in the temple, and remains there, nurtured like a dove and receiving food from the hand of an angel.

When Mary reaches the age of twelve, the widowers of Israel are summoned together, and JOSEPH is chosen by a miraculous sign to take her under his charge. Leaving her in his home he goes off to his work of building. Mary is chosen with other virgins to weave a veil for the temple, and during this time, the ANNUNCIATION takes place, followed by the visit to ELIZABETH (cf. Lk. 1). On his return after some months' absence, Joseph finds Mary with child, but is reassured by an angel (cf. Matt. 1:18–21). The matter is reported to the high priest, and Mary and Joseph are subjected to trial by ordeal, from which they emerge unscathed. Following the edict of AUGUSTUS, they travel to

BETHLEHEM. Joseph finds a cave for Mary, leaves her in the care of his sons, and goes in search of a midwife. (Here there is a sudden switch to the first person, as Joseph describes the silence of all things at the nativity.) After episodes concerning the midwife and the unbelieving Salome, the story continues with the visit of the MAGI and the slaughter of the innocents. It is Mary's fear at the news that leads her to lay her child in a manger; John and Elizabeth are miraculously delivered, but Zacharias (ZECHARIAH) is murdered at the altar (he is thus identified with the Zechariah of Matt. 23:35). The final paragraph gives the writer's name as JAMES.

II. Character.

The document is marked by evident use of OT motifs, especially from the story of SAMUEL, and by equally clear use of the canonical Gospels. There are quotations from the infancy narratives of both Matthew and Luke, and several passages are written in imitation of the canticles in Luke. The book therefore presupposes the canonical Gospels, although it makes free use of the material drawn from them, and may at some points supplement this material from oral tradition (e.g., in placing the birth in a cave). There is a strong element of the miraculous in the description of Mary's childhood and upbringing, but the tone of the work is on the whole comparatively restrained.

The author was not familiar with Jewish customs and thus was probably neither a Jew nor a Jewish Christian. For example, Joachim's childlessness is made to debar him from presenting his offering; Mary is brought up within the temple; the altar seems to be thought of as indoors. On the other hand, there is nothing specifically heretical in the book, although it was later to be condemned in the Western church. It was clearly written for the glorification of Mary, the Jewish slanders relating to the VIRGIN BIRTH being refuted by implication, and testimony provided for Mary's subsequent virginity by outside witnesses.

III. Text.

The oldest MS is the Papyrus Bodmer V, published in 1958 and dated by its editor to the 3rd cent. (E. de Strycker, *La forme la plus ancienne du Protévangile de Jacques* [1961], 14 n. 3, corrects to the first half of the 4th). Most of the other Greek MSS are comparatively late, from the 10th cent. and after. No complete Latin MS has survived, but there are ancient Latin texts that incorporate portions, and there is evidence that a Latin version was once current (*Bib* 43 [1962]: 57ff.). In addition, there are versions in Syriac, Armenian, Ethiopic, Georgian, and other languages, not to mention the various paraphrases and adaptations based upon the work. The MS tradition has been exhaustively examined by de Strycker, who concludes that it shows a remarkable homogeneity and continuity (pp. 374–75). Even the Bodmer Papyrus, however, already shows numerous errors, although most of them are superficial and it remains by far the most faithful witness.

IV. Title.

The title *Protevangelium* owes its established position to Postel and Neander, who in the 16th cent. were the first to publish the text. The Bodmer Papyrus has the unusual double title "Birth of Mary, Revelation of James," of which the second part is almost certainly wrong (two *Apocalypses of James* and an *Apocryphon of James* in the NAG HAMMADI LIBRARY have no connection whatever with the present work). Later Greek MSS usually have "Story," "History," or "Account," and a statement of the contents, without mention of James; but as noted above the final paragraph affirms that the book was written by James. ORIGEN refers to a "Book of James" for the view that Jesus' "brothers" were Joseph's sons by a previous marriage. The James in question is commonly identified with the Lord's brother, not the son of Zebedee; but some authorities simply speak of James without further identification.

V. Date.

The Bodmer Papyrus is proof that the document by the early 4th cent. had been in existence long enough for errors to creep into the text. How much earlier it can be placed depends on our assessment of patristic evidence. Origen apparently knew it, although he gives a different account of the death of Zacharias. It is also possible that the work was known to CLEMENT OF ALEXANDRIA. On the other hand, while there are links with JUSTIN MARTYR in the reference to the cave and to the Davidic descent of Mary, these are not sufficient to justify the claim that Justin knew the book. The materials from which it is composed may have been current about A.D. 150, but this does not mean that the book itself was already in existence. The use of the canonical Gospels points to a period when these were already fairly well established, although oral tradition was still available. This suggests a date in the latter half of the 2nd cent., but there are also problems relating to the composition and integrity of the work.

VI. Integrity. Three points in particular have given rise to doubts concerning the unity of the work: (a) the first-person passage in 18.2, already mentioned (it is missing from the Bodmer papyrus); (b) Origen's use of a different story of the death of Zacharias, which suggests that this passage was not in the text he knew; and (c) certain variations in chs. 18–21 (the Bodmer text is shorter and omits some of the dialogue in the episode of Salome and the midwife).

Following earlier scholars, A. von Harnack distinguished three documents incorporated into the work as we have it; a "Nativity of Mary" (chs. 1–17), an "Apocryphon of Joseph" (chs. 18–20), and an "Apocryphon of Zacharias" (chs. 22–24). The Zacharias section is often considered a later addition in view of Origen's silence, but whether the other two sections were originally separate is more doubtful. The story seems to require the birth of Jesus for its completion, and this leads naturally to the story of the Magi. Possibly only chs. 23–24 are later interpolations, together with the passage in 18.2. De Strycker claims that the Bodmer text is not an original version later to be expanded but an abridgement that presupposes the longer version. He rejects Harnack's three-document theory and argues for the unity of the book, although admitting that there are certain redactional anomalies (English trans. in *NTAp*, 1:421–39, see also II. R. Smid, *Protevangelium Jacobi: A Commentary* [1965]; J. H. Charlesworth, *The New Testament Apocrypha and Pseudepigrapha: A Guide to Publications, with Excurses on Apocalypses* [1987], 218–28; W. S. Vorster in *ABD*, 3:629–32.)   R. McL. Wilson

Jamin jay′min (יָמִין *H3546*, "valued, fortunate"; gentilic יָמִינִי *H3547*, "Jaminite"). **(1)** Son of Simeon, grandson of Jacob, and eponymous ancestor of the Jaminite clan (Gen. 46:10; Exod. 6:15; Num. 26:12; 1 Chr. 4:24).

(2) Son of Ram, grandson of Jerahmeel, and descendant of Judah (1 Chr. 2:27).

(3) A Levite who helped Ezra instruct the people in the law (Neh. 8:7; 1 Esd. 9:48 RSV [KJV, "Adinus"; NRSV, "Jadinus"]).

Jamlech jam′lik (יַמְלֵךְ *H3553*, "[God] grants dominion"). A clan leader in the tribe of Simeon (1 Chr. 4:34). He is listed among those whose families increased greatly during the days of King Hezekiah and who dispossessed the Hamites and Meunites near Gedor (vv. 38–41).

Jamnia, Jamnite jam′nee-uh, jam′nit. See Jabneel #2.

Janai jay′ni (יַעְנַי *H3614*, "[God] answers"). KJV Jaanai. A leader in the tribe of Gad in Bashan, listed as third in importance (1 Chr. 5:12; some take the next name, "Shaphat," as a common noun, thus, "and Janai a judge in Bashan" [see Shaphat #4]). He may have been a son of Abihail (v. 14; more likely, this comment refers only to the seven individuals listed in v. 13).

Janim jay′nim (יָנִים *H3565* [*Qere* יָנוּם], derivation uncertain). KJV Janum. A town allotted to the tribe of Judah in the hill district of Hebron (Josh. 15:53); the location is unknown, although one proposed identification is modern Beni Naʿim, c. 4 mi. E of Hebron.

Janna jan′uh. KJV form of Jannai.

Jannaeus, Alexander. See Hasmonean II.C.

Jannai jan′i (Ἰανναί *G2613*). KJV Janna. Son of a certain Joseph, included in Luke's genealogy of Jesus Christ (Lk. 3:24).

Jannes and Jambres jan′iz, jam′briz (Ἰάννης *G2614* and Ἰαμβρῆς *G2612* [v.l. Μαμβρῆς]; in Heb./Aram. sources, יוחני and ממרא, but there are spelling variations). The traditional names of Egyptian sorcerers who opposed Moses before Pharaoh (2 Tim. 3:8, evidently a reference back to unnamed magicians mentioned in Exod. 7:11–12, 22). *Jannes and Jambres* is also the title of a pseudepigraphic work.

In the exodus narrative, Moses and Aaron delivered to Pharaoh the Lord's message that Israel be allowed to go into the wilderness to worship God, and the monarch refused (Exod. 5:1–4). Then Moses performed authenticating miracles, such as making his staff a serpent, which the sorcerers with their magic also did (7:10–12, 20–22; 8:5–7, 17–18). It is to this series of events that PAUL is referring in 2 Tim. 3:8.

The names Jannes and Jambres are mentioned in Scripture only in 2 Tim. 3:8, no doubt reflecting Jewish tradition (*Tg. Ps.-J.* on Exod. 1:15 et al.; *b. Menaḥ.* 85a; cf. CD V, 18–19); they also occur in pagan and early Christian literature. Both PLINY the Elder (*Nat.* 30.2 §11) and the 2nd-cent. writer Apuleius (*Apologia pro se de magia* 2.90) refer to Jannes, whereas the Neo-Platonist philosopher Numenius of Apamea (see Euseb. *Praeparatio evangelica* 9.8.1) was acquainted with both Jannes and Jambres, calling them holy scribes and magicians of Egypt. Various early Christian works refer to these names (e.g., *Evangelium Nicodemi* 5; *Apostolic Constitution* 8.1; Cyprian, *De unitate ecclesia* 16).

A book that had the title *Iannes et Mambres* is mentioned by ORIGEN (according to the Latin trans. of his commentary on Matthew, at 23:37 and 27:9) and in a few other sources (see *HJP*, rev. ed. [1973–87], 3/2:781–83). Fragments of this work are preserved in a few early Greek papyri and in a medieval Latin MS (for an English trans. and full introduction, see *OTP*, 2:427–42).

That the apostle Paul mentions Jannes and Jambres evidences his acquaintance with this current Jewish tradition (which possibly preserved historical information from OT times). By referring to them, Paul seemingly demonstrates his desire to make vivid the personal and forceful opposition of the Egyptian magician class against Moses. The Jewish tradition about Jannes and Jambres is confused, as shown by EUSEBIUS's statement (*Praeparatio evangelica* 9.8) that these two men were sons of Baalim but yet teachers of Moses and later his opponents, and that they died with the Egyptian army in the Red Sea. W. H. MARE

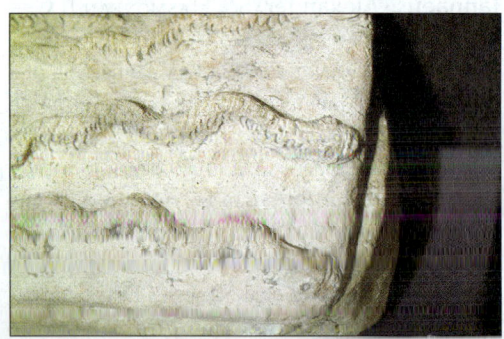

Sorcerers such as Jannes and Jambres may have used magical artifacts comparable to this terra cotta box with snakes carved into the lid (from Ur, early 2nd millennium B.C.).

Janoah juh-noh´uh (יָנוֹחַ H3562, "resting place"). **(1)** A town on the E border of the tribal territory of EPHRAIM (Jos. 16:6–7; KJV, "Janohah"; some believe that the form *yānôḥâ* here is the actual name, but most interpret the *-â* as a locative ending). EUSEBIUS (*Onomasticon* 108.20), who calls it *Ianō*, says it is 12 Roman mi. E of Neapolis (SHECHEM). Janoah is generally identified with Khirbet Yanun (c. 6.5 mi. SE of Shechem) or with the nearby town of Yanun.

(2) One of five cities in N Israel captured by TIGLATH-PILESER, king of Assyria (2 Ki. 15:29). Among several proposals, the most likely identifications are two places, both of which are now known as Yanuḥ. One of them is c. 6 mi. E of Tyre; the other, much farther S, is c. 11 mi. NE of ACCO (cf. *ABD*, 3:641).

Janum jay´nuhm. KJV form of JANIM.

Jaoel. See ABRAHAM, APOCALYPSE OF.

Japheth (person) jay´fith (יֶפֶת H3651, possibly "spacious" or "[God] enlarges"). Son of NOAH. In most of the passages referring to him (Gen. 5:32; 6:10; 7:13; 9:18; 10:1; 1 Chr. 1:4), Japheth is listed as the third of Noah's sons. However, one passage (Gen. 9:24; cf. v. 22) seems to indicate that HAM was the youngest. An additional statement (10:21) has also been construed to support the idea that Japheth was the second son rather than the third.

Sometime after the flood, Noah planted a vineyard and became drunk from the wine that he made. In a drunken stupor he lay uncovered in his tent. His son Ham broke the contemporary moral code by looking upon his father's nakedness (although the precise significance of the episode is disputed).

Ham seems to have immediately told his brothers what had happened (Gen. 9:20–22). SHEM and Japheth placed a garment on their shoulders and walking backward covered their father without looking upon him. Thus they were not guilty of committing the sin. When Noah awoke and learned of the matter, he pronounced a curse upon CANAAN the son of Ham (vv. 23–25). He then blessed Shem and Japheth: "May God extend the territory of Japheth; / may Japheth live in the tents of Shem, / and may Canaan be his slave" (9:27). Later generations considered this blessing as a prediction that the descendants of Shem and Japheth would live amicably together, and that the Canaanites would be their servants. The subjugation of the Canaanites in the time of JOSHUA is supposed to be fulfillment of Noah's curse.

The blessing pronounced upon Japheth by his father carried with it the idea that his descendants would be greatly multiplied (enlarged) in the future. The Table of NATIONS recorded in Gen. 10 indicates that Japheth became the father of a wide-ranging family of peoples, whose homes lay to the N of Palestine and then W. In fact, fourteen nations of Japhethites are listed in that chapter. The area of their occupation ranged all the way from the smelting plants of TARSHISH (prob. in Spain) on the W to the Caspian Sea on the E. This included what is now the steppes of southern Russia, much of ASIA MINOR, the islands of the Mediterranean, and the coasts of southern Europe. Japheth is said to be the father of Gomer, Magog, Madai, Javan, Tubal, Meshech, and Tiras (Gen. 10:2; 1 Chr. 1:4). These appear to be the progenitors of the Indo-European (Caucasian) family of nations.

Although all the descendants of Japheth are more or less important to biblical history, the writer of Gen. 10 appears to single out the sons of GOMER and JAVAN for special attention. The descendants of Gomer seem to be the Gimirrai (Gimirraya) of the Assyrian chronicles, but known to the Greeks as CIMMERIANS. The sons of Javan are the Greeks, that is, the Ionians of Homer, and especially the Ionians who lived along the coast of western Asia Minor and the islands of the AEGEAN Sea. (See C. H. Gordon, *Introduction to Old Testament Times* [1953], 25–28; M. F. Unger, *Archaeology and the Old Testament* [1954], 73–82.) C. P. GRAY

Japheth (place) jay'fith (Ιαφεθ). An unknown region "facing Arabia" mentioned in connection with the military advances of HOLOFERNES (Jdt. 2:25). Most scholars believe that this and other geographical references in the book of JUDITH are unreliable.

Japhia (person) juh-fi'uh (יָפִיעַ H3644, possibly "high, tall" or "[God] shines forth"). (1) A king of LACHISH who formed a league with four other AMORITE kings to punish GIBEON for submitting to the Israelites (Josh. 10:3–5). JOSHUA defeated them in battle at BETH HORON, killed the five kings, and cast their bodies into a cave (10:6–27).

(2) One of the sons of DAVID born at Jerusalem (2 Sam. 5:15; 1 Chr. 3:7; 14:6). All that is known of him is that his mother was a wife, not a concubine, of David.

Japhia (place) juh-fi'uh (יָפִיעַ H3643, possibly "high, tall" or "[God] shines forth"). A town on the S border of the tribal territory of ZEBULUN (Josh. 19:13). JOSEPHUS, who calls it Japha, fortified it during the Jewish war (*War* 2.20.6; cf. *Life* 45). It is usually identified with modern Yafa, c. 1.5 mi. SW of NAZARETH but without archaeological support (cf. *NEAEHL*, 2:659–60).

Japhlet jaf'lit (יַפְלֵט H3646, "[God] delivers"). Son of Heber and descendant of ASHER (1 Chr. 7:32–33). See also JAPHLETITE.

Japhleti jaf'luh-ti. KJV form of JAPHLETITE.

Japhletite jaf'luh-tit (יַפְלֵטִי H3647, gentilic of יַפְלֵט H3646). KJV Japhleti. A clan or larger people group whose territory, in a BETH HORON, served as much the S border of the tribe of EPHRAIM (Josh. 16:3). It is possible that they were descendants of JAPHLET, an Asherite, but nothing is known about them.

Japho jay'foh. KJV alternate form of JOPPA (Josh. 19:46).

Jarah jair'uh. See JADAH.

Jareb jair'ib (יָרֵב H3714, derivation disputed). According to the KJV, Jareb is the name of an Assyrian king (Hos. 5:13; 10:6). There is however no evidence, linguistically or historically, of an Assyrian king by that name (though it has been suggested that Jareb was the earlier name of SARGON, who destroyed SAMARIA in 722 B.C.). Because the Hebrew term can be understood as a form of the verb *rîb* H8189 (qal jussive impf., "let him contend"), some have thought that *melek yārēb* is a facetious epithet, "King Pick-Quarrel." Most scholars, however, believe that these words parallel the common Assyrian phrase, *šarru rabû*, "the great king" (cf. NIV and other modern versions). Such a meaning for the Hebrew requires either dividing the words differently (*malkî rāb*) or understanding *yārēb* as an Aramaism (see J. Barr, *Comparative Philology and the Text of the Old Testament* [1968], 123).

Jared jair´id (יֶרֶד H3719 [pausal form יָרֶד], derivation disputed; Ἰάρετ G2616). Son of Mahalalel and father of ENOCH (Gen. 5:15–20; 1 Chr. 1:2 [KJV, "Jered"]); his name is included in Luke's GENEALOGY OF JESUS CHRIST (Lk. 3:37).

Jaresiah jair´uh-si´uh. KJV form of JAARESHIAH.

Jarha jahr´huh (יַרְחָע H3739, meaning unknown). An Egyptian servant belonging to SHESHAN (1 Chr. 2:34–35). Jarha married Sheshan's daughter (prob. AHLAI, v. 31) and thus was included in the genealogy of JERAHMEEL. Some speculate that by this action Sheshan, who had no sons, made Jarha his heir (cf. ELIEZER, Gen. 15:2–3).

Jarib jair´ib (יָרִיב H3743, "[Yahweh] contends [for me]"; cf. JEHOIARIB, JERIBAI, JOIARIB). **(1)** Son of SIMEON (1 Chr. 4:24; apparently called JAKIN in Gen. 46:10; Exod. 6:15; Num. 26:12).

(2) One of a group of leaders sent by EZRA to IDDO to get attendants for the house of God (Ezra 8:16; 1 Esd. 8:44 [KJV, "Joribas"]).

(3) A descendant of JESHUA son of Jozadak, listed among the priests in Ezra's time who agreed to put away their foreign wives (Ezra 10:18; 1 Esd. 9:19 [KJV, "Joribus"]).

(4) KJV Apoc. alternate form of JOARIB (1 Macc. 14:29). G. DARABAS

Jarimoth jair´uh-moth. KJV Apoc. form of JEREMOTH (1 Esd. 9:28).

Jarkon jahr´kon. See ME JARKON.

Jarmuth jahr´muhth (יַרְמוּת H3754, "swelling [of the ground], height"). **(1)** A city in the SHEPHELAH whose king, PIRAM, entered into a conspiracy with four other AMORITE kings against the Gibeonites to revenge their submission to Joshua (Josh. 10:3–5). JOSHUA defeated the five kings at GIBEON and slew them at MAKKEDAH (vv. 9–26; cf. 12:11). After the conquest of Canaan, Jarmuth was assigned to the tribe of JUDAH (15:35). Some Jews returned there after the Babylonian exile (Neh. 11:29). According to EUSEBIUS (*Onomasticon* 106.24), Jarmuth was the same as Byzantine *Hiermochōs*, about 10 Roman mi. from Eleutheropolis, on the way toward Jerusalem. On this basis, the biblical site is tentatively identified with modern Khirbet el-Yarmuk (Tell Yarmut), c. 17 mi. WSW of Jerusalem, even though there is no archaeological confirmation (cf. *ABD*, 3:645).

(2) A city within the tribal territory of ISSACHAR allotted to the Levite clans descended from GERSHON (Josh. 21:29). In other lists Jarmuth is apparently called REMETH (19:21) and RAMOTH (1 Chr. 6:73). The site is tentatively identified with Kaukab el-Hawa (Hellenistic Agrippina, c. 6 mi. NNE of BETH SHAN); on this imposing location, 1,500 ft. above the Jordan Valley, the Crusaders built the Belvoir castle (Y. Aharoni, *The Land of the Bible: A Historical Geography*, rev. ed. [1979], 28; *NEAEHL*, 2:661–65).

Jaroah juh-roh´uh (יָרֹחַ H3726, "soft" or "pitied"; see JEROHAM). Son of Gilead, descendant of GAD, and ancestor of Abihail; the sons of Abihail and other Gadites occupied the region E of GILEAD (1 Chr. 5:14; cf. v. 10).

Jasael jay´say-uhl. KJV Apoc. form of SHEAL (1 Esd. 9:30).

Jashar, Book of jay´shuhr (שָׁר H3839, "upright"; LXX [only 2 Sam. 1:18], τοῦ εὐθοῦς, "of the upright one"). KJV Jasher. An ancient writing, no longer extant, mentioned twice in the OT (Josh. 10:13; 2 Sam. 1:18). Some scholars think that the phrase "in the book of the song" (preserved only in supplementary material by the LXX, 1 Ki. 8:53) may refer to

The Beth Horon ridge looking W into the Valley of Aijalon. Joshua chased the fleeing Amorite forces down this ridge, scoring a great victory for Israel (Josh. 10). The events of this memorable day, when "the sun stood still," were also summarized in the Book of Jashar.

the same writing if the Hebrew consonants *yšr* were read by mistake as *šyr*, "song"; conversely, it may be that Book of the Song was the original title.

On the basis of the material preserved in these passages, it has been inferred that the book was poetical in nature and that it contained songs of a national character. The references to the book imply that it was well known and respected, and consequently it may have been the source for other material found in the OT (perhaps, e.g., the songs of MIRIAM and DEBORAH in Exod. 15:21 and Jdg. 5). The origin of this document is a matter of speculation, but many scholars believe that it was the result of a gradual compilation begun in the early period of Israel's history. As time went on it was expanded, and at the time of the institution of the monarchy it probably became a part, and perhaps was the beginning, of the literary archives that formed the official records of the nation. (For a detailed study, see H. St. J. Thackeray in *JTS* 11 [1910]. 518–32; cf. E. Nielsen, *Oral Tradition: A Modern Problem in the Old Testament Introduction* [1954].) See also WARS OF THE LORD, BOOK OF THE.

The uncertain and mysterious character of the missing Book of Jashar has led to attempts to reproduce, imitate, or falsify it. An example is a late writing also entitled *Book of Jashar*, one of the last compositions of the haggadic literature of Judaism. It is written in good Hebrew and has to do with the era from Adam to the judges. The greater part of this work is concerned with pre-Mosaic material. Much of the material is invention, interpolated between biblical texts, in the author's desire to reconstruct the original Book of Jashar. Many legends are added to the biblical narrative. The account of Abraham is given in elaborate detail, including stories of his two journeys to see his son Ishmael, and of an apparition of a star. It contains a detailed explanation of the murder of Abel by Cain. It is believed by some scholars that this attempt to reconstruct the OT Book of Jashar originated in southern Italy. The author was familiar with Italian place names, and the Arabic names in the book are due to the strong influence of Islamic culture on that region. (See L. Goldschmidt, *The Book of Jashar* [1923].)

A. C. SCHULTZ

Jashen jay´shuhn (יָשֵׁן, H3826, possibly "sleepy"). The father of two or more unnamed warriors included among DAVID's Thirty (2 Sam. 23:32). It is widely thought, however, that the unusual MT reading here (*bĕnê yāšēn*, "the sons of Jashen," without naming them) has suffered textual corruption. The consonants *bny* are very likely an erroneous repetition (from the ending of the previous word *haššaʿalbōnî*, "the Shaalbonite"); moreover, the parallel passage (1 Chr. 11:34) reads, "the sons of Hashem the Gizonite." Many scholars argue that the original reading was "Jashen the Gizonite" (cf. P. K. McCarter, Jr., *II Samuel*, AB 9 [1984], 492–93). See GIZONITE; HASHEM. S. BARABAS

Jasher. KJV form of JASHAR.

Jashobeam juh-shoh´bee-uhm (יָשָׁבְעָם H3790, "the people [*or* the father's relative] has returned"). **(1)** A Hacmonite (lit., "son of HACMONI") and chief of DAVID's officers (*haššālišîm*) who killed 300 men in one battle (1 Chr. 17:11). The parallel passage (2 Sam. 23:8), which has very likely suffered textual corruption, speaks of "Josheb-Basshebeth, a Tahkemonite," chief of the Three (*haššālišî*), who slew 800 men in one battle. The Hebrew words for 300 and 800 begin with the same letter, making a copyist's error possible. It has been suggested (Kennicott) that "Basshebeth" is a dittography from the line above (last word of 2 Sam. 23:7) in place of the correct ending, "-am." Many scholars, following the SEPTUAGINT (2 Sam. *Iebosthe*, 1 Chr. *Iesebaal*), think that the original name was Ish-Baal (ISH-BOSHETH arising when the Heb. word for "shame" was substituted for the hated name BAAL) and that both Jashobeam and Josheb-Basshebeth are later scribal corruptions. (See further R. F. Youngblood in *EBC*, 3:1087–88; R. K. Duke in *ABD*, 3:647–48.)

(2) One of several Korahite warriors who joined David at ZIKLAG (1 Chr. 12:6; cf. vv. 1–2). Since apparently he was a Levite from the family of KORAH, he probably should not be identified with #1 above. Some argue, however, that the reference is to a different Korah or even to a locality in the tribe of BENJAMIN.

(3) Son of Zabdiel, descendant of PEREZ, and a commander in charge of the division for the first month during the reign of David (1 Chr. 27:2–3). Because most of the other commanders listed in this chapter are also mentioned in ch. 11, many believe this Jashobeam is the same as #1 above; if so, it is unclear why one passage describes him as "son of Hacmoni" and the other as "son of Zabdiel" (possibly the former designation refers to the larger clan or is used as some kind of title). J. OSWALT

Jashub jay´shuhb (יָשׁוּב H3793 [*Ketib* יָשִׁיב, 1 Chr. 7:1], possibly "[God] returns"; gentilic יָשׁוּבִי H3795, "Jashubite"; cf. SHEAR-JASHUB). **(1)** Son of ISSACHAR and eponymous ancestor of the Jashubite clan (Num. 26:24; 1 Chr. 7:1). In another passage (Gen. 46:13) the MT has *yôb*, and this reading is followed by the KJV ("Job"), the RSV ("Iob"), and other versions; on the basis of some Greek MSS, the SAMARITAN PENTATEUCH, and the biblical parallels, the NIV and NRSV read "Jashub" here as well.

(2) One of the descendants of Bani who agreed to put away their foreign wives (Ezra 10:29; 1 Esd. 9:30 [KJV, "Jasubus"]).

Jashubi Lehem juh-shoo´buh-lee´hem (יָשֻׁבִי לֶחֶם H3788). KJV Jashubi-lehem. An otherwise unknown place ruled by descendants of JUDAH (1 Chr. 4:22 NIV; the KJV interprets it as the name of a person). The Hebrew text is difficult, however, and the NRSV translates, "who married [Heb. *bāʿălû*] into Moab but returned to Lehem" (this rendering involves an emendation of *wěyāšubî* to *wayyāšubû*). But a place by the name of Lehem is also unknown, so others further emend the word to BETHLEHEM (cf. *BHS*) or, following the SEPTUAGINT, to the idiom *lāhem* (lit., "to them," yielding the simple meaning, "but they returned"; cf. Deut. 5:30).

Jasiel jay´see-uhl. KJV form of JAASIEL.

Jason jay´suhn (Ἰάσων G2619, "healing"; the name was sometimes substituted for Joshua/Jesus by Greek-speaking Jews [cf. Jos. *Ant.* 12.5.1]). **(1)** Son of Eleazar; he and Eupolemus were sent by Judas MACCABEE to solicit Roman aid against the Syrians, 161 B.C. (1 Macc. 8:17). Jason's son Antipater sought to renew the alliance in 144 B.C. (1 Macc. 12:16; 14:22; Jos. *Ant.* 12.10.6).

(2) Son of SIMON II and brother of the high priest ONIAS III; by bribery he secured the high priestly office for himself, and through his influence Greek customs became popularized (2 Macc. 4:7–26; see J. C. VanderKam, *From Joshua to Caiaphas: High Priests after the Exile* [2004], 197–203). He gave large gifts for the sacred games at TYRE honoring HERCULES (4:16–20). His tenure was only three years (174–171 B.C.), for he was supplanted by MENELAUS, who offered ANTIOCHUS IV Epiphanes a greater bribe. Jason fled to the Ammonites, but a false rumor of Antiochus's death in Egypt brought him back to Jerusalem with a large following to overthrow Menelaus. Antiochus returned to wreak vengeance on the Jews; and Jason again fled to Ammon, then to Egypt, and later to Sparta, where he died (5:1–10).

(3) A Cyrenian who wrote a history of the Jewish freedom-struggle against Antiochus Epiphanes and his successor Antiochus Eupator. The book of 2 Maccabees is a condensation of this history. Jason's name and residence indicate that he was Greek. His account ends with the year 160 B.C.; the book was probably written shortly after that date. The preface of the book tells what is known of Jason. See MACCABEES, BOOKS OF.

(4) A Jewish Christian of THESSALONICA who was probably host to the missionaries PAUL and SILAS. He and others were summoned to court on a charge of being hospitable to seditionists, but freedom was obtained by giving security for good conduct (Acts 17:5–9). See also #5, below.

(5) One of two or three "relatives" of Paul (the others being SOSIPATER and possibly LUCIUS) who sent greetings to the Christians in Rome (Rom. 16:21). According to many scholars, however, the Greek term *syngenēs* G5150 here means "kinsman" (cf. RSV) and should be understood in the sense of "fellow-Jew" (cf. 9:3). In either case, this Jason is possibly the same as #4 above. Some have speculated that he became a travel companion of Paul and thus was with him in CORINTH when the letter to the ROMANS was written. D. D. GRIDDLE

jasper. An impure, opaque variety of very fine grained silica (silicon dioxide), allied to CHALCEDONY and FLINT. It is usually red, brown, or yellow (more rarely green, blue, or black), and the brighter-colored varieties are used as gem stones (Heb. *yōšpēh* H3835, Exod. 28:20 et al.; Gk. *iaspis* G2618, Rev. 4:3 et al.). Even on the thinner edges it is opaque, so the reference to "a jasper, clear as crystal" in Rev. 21:11 may indicate that the ancient jaspis included CHRYSOPRASE as well as partially translucent chalcedony. Egyptian jasper is beautifully banded with different shades of brown. It occurs in nodules, like AGATE, both in the Nile Valley and the Libyan desert. Riband (or ribbon) jasper has the colors, generally brown, in broad stripes. Like other varieties of very fine grained silica, jasper is deposited from circulating water, either ground water or hydrothermal solutions of igneous origin. D. R. BOWES

Jasubus juh-soo'buhs. KJV Apoc. form of JASHUB.

Jathan jay'thuhn (Ιαθαν). Son of Shemaiah; apparently a relative of TOBIT (Tob. 5:13 RSV; KJV, "Jonathas"; NRSV [v. 14] reads "Nathan," following CODEX SINAITICUS).

Jathniel jath'nee-uhl (יַתְנִיאֵל H3853, derivation uncertain; see J. D. Fowler, *Theophoric Personal Names in Ancient Hebrew* [1988], 134). Fourth son of Meshelemiah and descendant of KORAH; like his father, he and his brothers were Levitical gatekeepers in the time of DAVID (1 Chr. 26:2).

Jattir jat'uhr (יַתִּיר H3848, possibly "extraordinary"). A town in the hill country within the tribal territory of JUDAH (Josh. 15:48); it was allotted to the Levites (21:14; 1 Chr. 6:57). David sent spoil from ZIKLAG to it after his victory over the Amalekites (1 Sam. 30:27). It is identified with modern Khirbet 'Attir, c. 13 mi. SW of HEBRON.

Javan jay'vuhn (יָוָן H3430, from Gk. Ἰωνες [earlier Ἰάωνες]). Son of JAPHETH, grandson of NOAH, and father of ELISHAH, TARSHISH, KITTIM, and RODANIM (Gen. 10:2, 4; 1 Chr. 1:5, 7). The name corresponds etymologically to Ionia. As such it is used in the prophets to denote the descendants of Javan in Ionia proper (W coast of ASIA MINOR) but also in GREECE and MACEDONIA; thus the NIV renders the name "Greece" or "Greeks" in these books.

In Isa. 66:19 Javan, in conjunction with Tarshish, Lud, Put, and Tubal, is spoken of as one of the far-off nations to whom messengers will be dispatched to tell of Yahweh's glory and the restoration of Jerusalem; the nations mentioned seem to represent the far western edge of the known world in the OT. In Ezek. 27:13 Javan is included as one of the contributors to the wealth of TYRE; it is grouped with TUBAL and MESHECH as traders of slaves and bronze. In the same vein, Tyre is condemned in Joel 3:6 because she sold citizens of Judah and Jerusalem to Javan as slaves.

The book of Daniel identifies Javan with Alexander's Greco-Macedonian empire. Thus Dan. 8:21 interprets the he-goat from the W as the king of Javan; 10:20 tells of the angel whose task was to fight the prince of Persia and afterward the prince of Javan; and 11:2 refers to the strong king of Persia who would stir up opposition to the kingdom of Javan. In Zech. 9:13, God asserts that he will triumph over the nations, brandishing the sons of Zion over the sons of Javan. Since the theme is God's superiority over warlike nations, Greece is probably singled out for attention here because of the fearsome reputation of Greek mercenary soldiers in the ANE, rather than because of any special enmity between Jews and Greeks at the time of the writing of Zechariah (c. 520 B.C.; see ZECHARIAH, BOOK OF).

Javan occurs in the Hebrew text of Ezek. 27:19 (cf. above on v. 13). However, the context seems to demand a location in ARABIA rather than in the W. The problem is further complicated by the SEPTUAGINT, which has "wine," apparently representing Hebrew *yayin* H3516. The LXX rendering may reflect an attempt to interpret the difficult statement, but some consider it a witness to the original Hebrew text. Those who adhere to the MT suggest that a Greek trading colony in Arabia is meant, while others propose GAZA. (See also B. Stade, *Das Volk Javan* [1880]; D. D. Luckenbill in *Zeitschrift für Assyriologie* 28 [1913]: 92–99; P.-R. Berger in *Die Welt des Orients* 13 [1982]: 50–78, esp. 68–69.)

J. OSWALT

javelin. See ARMOR, ARMS.

jaw. This English term is commonly the rendering of Hebrew *lĕḥî* H4305, used often of animals (e.g., the "jowls" of a bull or sheep, Deut. 18:3; a donkey's "jawbone," Jdg. 15:15–17), but also with reference to the "face" or "cheek" of people (e.g., 1 Ki. 22:24; Job 16:10). Several occurrences are figurative uses (e.g., Isa. 30:28; Ezek. 29:4). See also CHEEK.

Jazer jay´zuhr (יַעְזֵר H3597, "[God] helps"). KJV Jaazer. An AMORITE city in GILEAD. There are a dozen biblical references to it, usually as a "city" (e.g., Josh. 21:39), but once as a "land" (Num. 32:1) and once as a "territory" (Josh. 13:25). Jazer was taken by MOSES (Num. 21:32), then settled and fortified by the tribe of GAD. It bordered Ammonite territory (Num. 21:24) and was one of the four towns of Gad given to the Levites (Josh. 21:39). Some of DAVID's most able men came from Jazer (1 Chr. 26:31), and his census takers reached it (2 Sam. 24:5). Following the death of AHAB, it was captured by the Moabites (cf. Isa. 16:9; Jer. 48:32). During Hellenistic times Judas MACCABEE took it from the Ammonites (1 Macc. 5:8; possibly the same as "Gazara" in 2 Macc. 10:32 [see GEZER]). Jazer is mentioned by JOSEPHUS (*Ant.* 12.8.1) and EUSEBIUS (*Onomasticon* 12.1–4).

The identification of Jazer has been much disputed. Biblical description places it in S Gilead, WNW of RABBAH of the Ammonites (modern Amman, Josh. 13:25; 2 Sam. 24:5). The *Onomasticon* places it 8–10 Roman mi. W of Philadelphia (i.e., Rabbah) and 15 from HESHBON; it also states that a large river (prob. a perennial flowing stream) flowed from the town to the Jordan. Several proposals have been made, the most likely being

Jazer.

Khirbet es-Sar (c. 6 mi. W of Amman, overlooking the Wadi esh-Shita) and Khirbet Jazzir (c. 7 mi. WNW of es-Sar, at the head of Wadi Shuʿeib). J. L. Peterson (*ABD*, 3:651) claims there is "little doubt" that the latter is biblical Jazer. (See further S. Merrill, *East of the Jordan* [1883], 272–77, 404–6; N. Glueck, *Explorations in Eastern Palestine*, 4 vols., AASOR [1934–51], 3:153ff.)

M. H. HEICKSEN

Jaziz jay´ziz (יָעִיז *H3467*, possibly from a root that in Arabic means "to incite"). A HAGRITE who was in charge of King DAVID's flocks (1 Chr. 27:31; NRSV, v. 31).

jealousy. This English term is used in Bible versions to render several words, primarily Hebrew *qinʾâ H7863* (Num. 5:14 et al.) and Greek *zēlos G2419* (Acts 5:17 et al.). The concept is plainly present in several places where the precise term is not used. Both the Hebrew and Greek words refer to the intensity of emotion involved, with the Hebrew possibly alluding to the rising of color in the face (in Arabic the verb *qanaʾa* can mean "to become red"). In each case it seems to indicate an ardor or zeal for something believed to belong properly to one. The term may refer both to a favorable or appropriate variety of this ardor, and to an improper form of it.

I. Proper jealousy. When jealousy reflects concern for God's honor and glory, it is proper and good. Thus, God himself is several times described as jealous for his honor, his holy name. He desires fervently that his due status and honor be preserved, that the WORSHIP that belongs to him should be given to him. The analogy frequently used is a husband's concern for the love of his wife. This is an expression of the HOLINESS of God, which cannot endure any unfaithfulness. Just as a husband is not indulgent of adultery on the part of his wife, so no infidelity is permitted by God.

It was this exclusiveness of concern that underlay the strong emphasis upon monotheistic worship among the Jews. Because Yahweh is the only true God, he alone is deserving of human worship and devotion. It motivated the prohibition of intermarriage with the heathen nations around Israel, lest they should depart from the exclusive worship of the one true God. An OT example of God's jealousy is found in Exod. 32, where God was angered by the Israelites' worshiping the golden calf (see CALF, GOLDEN). Herod Agrippa (see HEROD VII)

Sculpture of a bull representing the Egyptian god Apis. Given the Israelites' experience with idols in Egypt, God jealously demanded the exclusive devotion of his people.

was struck dead because he did not disavow the attribution of deity to himself (Acts 12:21–23).

Similarly, this exclusiveness is reflected in the teachings of Jesus: "I am the way and the truth and the life. No one comes to the Father except through me" (Jn. 14:6). "Anyone who loves his father or mother more than me is not worthy of me" (Matt. 10:37). To determine that a potential follower really was giving to him his supremacy, Jesus would put such a person to a test, as when he asked the rich young man to sell all that he had, and come and follow him (Lk. 18:22). Because Jesus, like the Father, is the only true God, and because he is the only MEDIATOR, he could rightfully exercise this jealousy. God also is jealous for his people. He identifies with them and watches over them (Zech 2:8; Matt. 6:28–33).

The concern for God's due is also found among his people. ELIJAH spoke of his jealousy for the Lord of Hosts in connection with the contest with BAAL on Mount Carmel (1 Ki. 19:14). He had arranged a demonstration to prove that Yahweh alone was God. A similar motivation, but under different circumstances, was shown by PAUL and BARNABAS when the men of LYSTRA tried to worship them as gods (Acts 14:8–18).

II. Improper jealousy. Another meaning or application of the word and concept of jealousy is negative in its effect and is strongly condemned by God. It is excessive concern for one's own self, and what one fancies or desires. It may also involve resentment of the good fortune of another. It is an inordinate self-centeredness or possessiveness. It may mean an unreasonable demanding of another person, such as a mate, more than is one's rightful due—requiring total and sole attention, for example.

Biblical examples of this type of jealousy abound, although they are not always labeled as such. The brothers of JOSEPH resented the special favor shown by JACOB, symbolized by a conspicuous coat (Gen. 37:34). King SAUL, hearing the people chant "Saul has slain his thousands, / and David his tens of thousands" (1 Sam. 18:6–9), burned with jealousy. In the NT, the older brother complained of the injustice of the prodigal son being given a celebration, when he had never been extended a similar privilege (Lk. 15:25–30).

Jealousy that involves an improper inward feeling toward another person is sin in itself, because Jesus said that thoughts and attitudes constitute sin, even without overt acts (Matt. 5:21–31). Jealousy is often the motive for sinful actions. Joseph's brothers planned to murder him, and ultimately sold him into slavery. Saul tried to kill David by hurling his spear at him. The older son refused to participate in the celebration over the return of the younger.

It is not surprising that jealousy is so prevalent in human beings. Natural man is self-centered and resists anything that subtracts from his own pleasure or aggrandizement. Because of his finiteness, he is also insecure and is therefore threatened by anything competitive with him. The antidote to jealousy is perfect LOVE. Because love is not self-seeking (1 Cor. 13:5), it does not go beyond its rightful claims. This love, the Scripture teaches, is of divine origin and consequently must come from above. It is only the progressive remaking of the nature of the person that can overcome his tendency toward jealousy.

III. Distinction between the two. A problem arises when these two varieties of jealousy are compared. If jealousy of the second type is wrong for human beings, then is not jealousy of the first type also wrong for God? Is not God guilty of the very thing that he condemns in humans namely self-centered concern for his own rights?

Part of the solution lies in recognizing that the description of God as jealous is an ANTHROPOMORPHISM, and, consequently, jealousy in God is not identical with jealousy in human beings. God ought not to be pictured as seething with anger over injustices done to him. His jealousy does not originate in insecurity or anxiety. However, one distinction between the proper and improper varieties of this ardor also lies in the object of that zeal. Because the latter kind is concern for the welfare and status of a finite object of value, the human being, it is unjustified. Because God is the highest object, however, everything is rightfully his, and zeal that this be carried out is in order. Indeed, it would be wrong for God not to enforce his rights. Man's concern for his own possessions and honor would be right only if he were God, for then they would be rightfully his.   M. ERICKSON

jealousy, water of. By the so-called "law of jealousy", a husband who suspected his wife of ADULTERY brought her before the priest with a meal offering. The priest had her take an oath, then drink holy water mixed with dust from the tabernacle floor, as an appeal to God to decide the issue. If no ill effects followed, she was innocent; otherwise she was guilty (Num. 5:11–31).
E. RUSSELL

Jearim jee´uh-rim (יְעָרִים H3630, "woods"). The name of a mountain or mountain ridge on the N border of the tribe of JUDAH (Josh. 15:10). The text identifies or associates Mount Jearim with KESALON, which was apparently the name of a border town, today known as Kesla, c. 11 mi. W of Jerusalem. See also SEIR.

Jeaterai jee-at´uh-ri. KJV form of JEATHERAI.

Jeatherai jee-ath´uh-ri (יְאָתְרַי H3290). Son of Zerah and descendant of LEVI through GERSHON

(1 Chr. 6:21). Some believe the text has suffered textual corruption and emend the name to ETHNI (v. 41; note that the Heb. consonants of this name, ʾtny, are similar to those of Jeatherai, yʾtry); others simply point out that the genealogies are incomplete.

Jeberechiah ji-berʹuh-ki-uh. See JEBEREKIAH.

Jeberekiah ji-berʹuh-kiʹuh (יְבֶרֶכְיָהוּ *H3310*, "Yahweh blesses"). Also Jeberechiah. Father of a certain Zechariah who was called upon by ISAIAH as a witness of his prophecy against Damascus and Samaria (Isa. 8:2).

Jebus jeeʹbuhs (יְבוּס *H3293*, gentilic יְבוּסִי *H3294*, "Jebusite" [KJV, "Jebusi" in Josh. 18:16, 28]). Alternate early name for JERUSALEM. The name Jerusalem goes far back into the history of the land of Canaan, as is known from mention of it in connection with early biblical incidents and from the extrabiblical occurrence of the corresponding name Ur-salimmu (e.g., in the TELL EL-AMARNA letters). However, Jebus was apparently preferred in some circles (Jdg. 19:10–11; cf. 1 Chr. 11:4). During several centuries before the time of DAVID, the city was known as the home of the Jebusites, and some argue that Jebus received its name from this people group (rather than the place giving its name to its inhabitants). The Jebusites remained here until David conquered the city, made it his capital, and restored its name to Jerusalem.

Jebusites are first mentioned in the Bible in a list of Canaanite clans (Gen. 10:16–18). Essentially the same grouping is mentioned a number of times in other books of the Pentateuch as among the peoples whose land had been promised to Israel (Exod. 3:8; 13:5; 23:23; 33:2; 34:11; Num. 13:29; Deut. 7:1; 20:17; Josh. 3:10; 12:8; 24:11; Jdg. 3:5). Other references provide interesting details about the Jebusites. After Israel's smashing victories W of the Jordan, the Jebusites became intensely concerned about stopping JOSHUA and turning the people back (Josh. 9:1). They were among those to whom JABIN of HAZOR sent for help in an attempt to rally sufficient strength to withstand Joshua (11:3). They were known as a people who lived "in the hill country" (11:3). The border of the territory allotted to the tribe of JUDAH apparently ran along the Valley of Ben HINNOM, which as a natural, physical feature was also the terminus of the S slope of the Jebusite area, a locale also called Jerusalem (15:8). These Jebusites were the Canaanite inhabitants of Jerusalem/Jebus whom the Israelites "could not dislodge," and who dwelt with the people of Judah in

The ancient city of Jebus was located on the V-shaped ridge descending S into the valley in front of what is now known as the temple mount. (View to the NE up the Kidron Valley, with the Mount of Olives in view.)

Jerusalem from the time of occupation (15.63, cf. also Jdg. 1:21). They were therefore known as the residents of the city of Jebus well into the time of the judges (Jdg. 19:11).

David's rise to power as ruler over all Israel included the ousting of the Jebusites from this area. He devised a cunning strategy to wrest Jerusalem from its taunting, jeering inhabitants (see 2 Sam. 5:6–10; cf. 1 Chr. 11:4–7). The usual explanation of the Samuel passage is that David made use of an underground tunnel that, presumably, was part of a water system the Canaanites had built to bring water from a point outside the city to a reservoir located within the city. This system, as well as another one similar to it built by HEZEKIAH (see 2 Ki. 20:20), has been discovered and explored by archaeologists. Knowledge about the system provides a basis for understanding that David could have discovered the concealed source of water outside the city and then followed the tunnel bringing the water to the reservoir within the city. Thus, surely by surprise, he was able to get up "the water shaft" (Heb. *ṣinnôr* H7562) to attack and to defeat the Jebusites. William F. Albright, however, has offered the plausible explanation that the Hebrew word can just as well be rendered "scaling-hook" (see *Old Testament Commentary*, ed. H. C. Alleman and E. E. Flack [1948], 149). Thus he would understand that David successfully attacked the Jebusites by storming and scaling the wall, rather than by using the underground water system. See also JERUSALEM III.B.

After capturing the city, David purchased a rocky hilltop from ARAUNAH the Jebusite (2 Sam. 24:18, 25; 1 Chr. 21:15, 18–28), a place used as a threshing floor on which he envisioned a "house" for the ARK OF THE COVENANT. Successful in these endeavors, David made the conquered city his political and religious center. References to the Jebusites after the time of David are infrequent (in lists, Ezra 9:1; Neh. 9:8, and in a prophetic oracle that recalls their fate, Zech. 9:7). (See J. Simons, *Jerusalem in the Old Testament* [1952], 60–61, 246–47; M. F. Unger, *Archaeology and the Old Testament* [1954], 92–93, 206–9; G. E. Wright, *Biblical Archaeology* [1962], 127–29. For the view that Jebus and Jerusalem were distinct places, see J. M. Miller in *ZDPV* 90 [1974]: 115–27.)

H. E. FINLEY

Jecamiah jek´uh-mi´uh. KJV alternate form of JEKAMIAH (1 Chr. 3:18).

Jechiliah jek´uh-li´uh. See JECOLIAH.

Jecholiah jek´uh-li´uh. KJV alternate form of JECOLIAH (2 Ki. 15:2).

Jechoniah, Jechonias jek´uh-ni´uh(s). See JECONIAH.

Jecoliah jek´uh-li´uh יְכָלְיָהוּ H3525, יְכָלְיָה H3524 [2 Chr. 26:3, *Ketib* וִיכִילְיָה], "Yahweh is [or proves himself] able, powerful"; see JEHUCAL). TNIV Jekoliah. Mother of King Azariah (UZZIAH) of Judah (2 Ki. 15:2 [KJV, "Jecholiah"]; 2 Chr. 26:3 [ASV, "Jechiliah"]).

Jeconiah jek´uh-ni´uh (יְכָנְיָהוּ H3527 [only Jer. 24:1], יְכָנְיָה H3526, "Yahweh supports" or "may Yahweh establish"; Ἰεχονίας G2651). Also Jechoniah, Jechonias, Jeconias. **(1)** Alternate name of JEHOIACHIN, king of Judah (1 Chr. 3:16–17; Esth. 2:6; Jer. 24:1; 27:20; 28:4; 29:2; Add. Esth. 11:4; Bar. 1:3, 9; Matt. 1:11–12).

(2) A Levite who lived in the time of King JOSIAH and who gave sheep and calves for the PASSOVER (1 Esd. 1:9; called "Conaniah" in 2 Chr. 35:9).

(3) Alternate Apoc. name of JEHOAHAZ, King of Judah (1 Esd. 1:34; KJV, "Joachaz").

Jeconias jek´uh-ni´uhs. KJV Apoc. form of JECONIAH (1 Esd. 1:9).

Jedaiah ji-day´yuh (יְדָיָה H3355 [only #1 and #5 below], "Yahweh has favored"; יְדַעְיָה H3361, "Yahweh has known"). **(1)** Son of Shimri and descendant of SIMEON (1 Chr. 4:37); included in the genealogy of Ziza, a clan leader.

(2) Chief of the second division of priests as appointed by DAVID (1 Chr. 24:7). Possibly the ancestor of the 973 priests (of the family of JESHUA) who returned from the EXILE (Ezra 2:36; Neh. 7:39; 1 Esd. 5:24 [KJV, "Jeddu"]).

(3) One of the priests who returned from the exile (1 Chr. 9:10; Neh. 11:10 [possibly through textual corruption, the following person on the list,

Joiarib, seems to be regarded as Jedaiah's father]; 12:6); Uzzi became head of Jedaiah's priestly family (12:19). There may be a connection between this Jedaiah and #2 above.

(4) Evidently another (but less important) priest of the same name, since he is included in two of the same lists as #3 above (Neh. 12:7, 21).

(5) Son of Harumaph; he made repairs on the wall of JERUSALEM opposite his house (Neh. 3:10).

(6) One of a group of Jewish exiles who brought gold and silver from Babylon to help those who had returned under ZERUBBABEL; from these gifts a crown was to be made for Joshua (JESHUA) the high priest (Zech. 6:10).   J. OSWALT

Jeddu jed′oo. KJV Apoc. form of JEDAIAH (1 Esd. 5:24).

Jedeus jed′ee-uhs. KJV Apoc. form of ADAIAH (1 Esd. 9:30).

Jediael ji-di′ay-uhl (יְדִיעֲאֵל *H3356*, "known of God"). **(1)** Son (or descendant) of BENJAMIN (1 Chr. 7:6, 10–11). Since Jediael is not mentioned in the other genealogies of Benjamin (Gen. 46:21; Num. 26:38–40; 1 Chr. 8:1–2), and since the genealogy of ZEBULUN is not included in the context of 1 Chr. 7, some have thought that the passage is textually corrupt and that the family of Jediael was part of the tribe of Zebulun. It is more likely that 1 Chr. 7 preserves a late, independent list giving information about a small Benjamite clan.

(2) Son of Shimri; he and his brother Joha the Tizite were among DAVID's mighty warriors (1 Chr. 11:45).

(3) A military leader from the tribe of MANASSEH who defected from SAUL and joined David at ZIKLAG (1 Chr. 12:20); some have suggested that he may be the same as #2 above.

(4) Son of Meshelemiah and descendant of KORAH; like his father, he and his brothers were Levitical gatekeepers in the time of DAVID (1 Chr. 26:2).

Jedidah ji-di′duh (יְדִידָה *H3352*, "beloved [of God or Yahweh]"; see JEDIDIAH). Daughter of Adaiah and mother of JOSIAH, king of Judah (2 Ki. 22:1).

Jedidiah jed′uh-di′uh (יְדִידְיָה *H3354*, "beloved of Yahweh" [cf. Deut. 33:12, יְדִיד יהוה]). The name God gave, through the prophet NATHAN, to SOLOMON when he was born, because "the LORD loved him" (2 Sam. 12:25; lit., "for the sake of the LORD"). The giving of this second name—which appears to be related to that of DAVID and does not occur elsewhere in the Bible—has caused considerable debate. One proposal is that Jedidiah was his initial name and that Solomon (a name that, like JERUSALEM, is apparently built on Heb. *šālôm H8934*, "peace") was a throne name David gave to him in anticipation of the child's future rule in Jerusalem (cf. S. Talmon, *King, Cult, and Calendar in Ancient Israel: Collected Studies* [1986], 152 n. 19). Others argue that Jedidiah was the throne name (cf. P. K. McCarter, Jr., *II Samuel*, AB 9 [1984], 303–4).

Jeduthun ji-dyoo′thuhn (יְדוּתוּן *H3349*, possibly derived from יָדָה *H3344*, "to praise, thank"). **(1)** A Levitical musician in the time of DAVID who, with HEMAN, was "responsible for the sounding of the trumpets and cymbals and for the playing of the other instruments for sacred song" (1 Chr. 16:41–42). His sons, along with the sons of Heman and ASAPH, were set aside "for the ministry of prophesying, accompanied by harps, lyres and cymbals" (25:1–6). He is usually thought to be the same as Ethan, which may have been an earlier name of his (6:44); see ETHAN #4. Jeduthun is also called a royal seer (2 Chr. 35:15), though this description possibly means no more than that he gave good advice to David. The name appears repeatedly in connection with temple music at important occasions in the reigns of SOLOMON (2 Chr. 5:12), HEZEKIAH (29:14, with reference to his descendants Shemaiah and Uzziel), and JOSIAH (35:15, with reference to the descendants of Asaph; cf. 1 Esd. 1:15 [NRSV, "Eddinus"] and 1 Chr. 9:16). The family continued to officiate after the EXILE (Neh. 11:17). The phrase "for Jeduthun" (NRSV, "according to Jeduthun") is found in the titles of Pss. 39; 62; 77. What the connection may be with David's musician is unclear; some believe it refers to an instrument or to a tune.

(2) Father of OBED-EDOM, who was a gatekeeper (1 Chr. 16:38). It is often taken for granted that he is the same as #1 above, but some argue that insofar as the Obed-Edom mentioned here was descended from KORAH (26:1, 4) and not from MERARI, this Jeduthun must be different (see KD, *Chronicles*, 219; this argument assumes that Jeduthun the musician is the same as Ethan, who indeed was a Merarite). S. BARABAS

Jeeli jee'uh-li. KJV Apoc. form of JAALA (1 Esd. 5:33).

Jeelus ji-ee'luhs. KJV Apoc. alternate form of JEHIEL (1 Esd. 8:92).

Jeezer ji-ee'zuhr. KJV form of IEZER.

Jegar Sahadutha jee'guhr-say-huh-doo'thuh (יְגַר שָׂהֲדוּתָא H3337, "heap of witness"). The Aramaic name that LABAN gave to a heap of stones set up as sign of a covenant between him and JACOB; the latter called it by the equivalent Hebrew name, GALEED (Gen. 31:47). This passage provides the oldest evidence of the ARAMAIC LANGUAGE found in the Bible, and it is part of the evidence that ABRAHAM spoke Aramaic before adopting a Canaanite dialect (which eventually developed into the HEBREW LANGUAGE).

Jehaleleel, Jehalelel jee'-huh-lee'lee-uhl, ji-hal'uh-luhl. KJV forms of JEHALLELEL.

Jehallelel ji-hal'uh-luhl (יְהַלֶּלְאֵל H3401, possibly "God shines forth" or "may God praise [the child]"; see discussion in J. D. Fowler, *Theophoric Personal Names in Ancient Hebrew* [1988], 136). (**1**) A descendant of JUDAH (1 Chr. 4:16; KJV, "Jehaleleel"). His genealogical connection is unclear, but he may have been the eponymous ancestor of a clan related to CALEB son of Jephunneh (cf. v. 15).
(**2**) A descendant of LEVI through MERARI, and father of Azariah; the latter was one of the Levites assigned to consecrate the temple in the days of HEZEKIAH (2 Chr. 29:12; KJV, "Jehalelel").

Jehath. See JAHATH #2.

Jehdeiah ji-dee'yah (יֶחְדְּיָהוּ H3485, "Yahweh rejoices"). (**1**) Son or descendant of Shubael; he was a Levite who served in the time of King DAVID (1 Chr. 24:20).
(**2**) A MERONOTHITE who was in charge of David's donkeys (1 Chr. 27:30).

Jehezekel ji-hez'uh-kel. KJV form of JEHEZKEL.

Jehezkel ji-hez'kel (יְחֶזְקֵאל H3489, "God strengthens"; cf. EZEKIEL, HEZEKIAH, JEHIZKIAH). KJV Jehezekel. A priest who lived in the time of DAVID; he was head of the twentieth division (1 Chr. 24:16). The Hebrew form of this name is identical to that of Ezekiel.

Jehiah ji-hi'uh (יְחִיָּה H3496, "Yahweh lives"; cf. JEHIEL). A Levite who, with OBED-EDOM, was appointed as a doorkeeper for the ARK OF THE COVENANT when DAVID had it brought to Jerusalem (1 Chr. 15:24). He may be the same as JEIEL (v. 18).

Jehiel ji-hi'uhl (יְחִיאֵל H3493, "God lives" [cf. JEHIAH]; also יְחִיאֵלִי H3494 [gentilic in form, 1 Chr. 26:21–22]). (**1**) A Levite in the time of DAVID appointed among others to play the lyre (NRSV, harp) as a part of the ministrations before the ARK OF THE COVENANT (1 Chr. 15:18, 20; 16:5).
(**2**) Firstborn son of Ladan and descendant of LEVI through GERSHON; he was placed in charge of the temple treasury in the time of David (1 Chr. 23:8; 29:8; 26:21–22 ["Jehieli"; the Heb. text here is difficult]).
(**3**) Son of Hacmoni; he was an important official who took care of David's sons (1 Chr. 27:32).
(**4**) Son of JEHOSHAPHAT, king of Judah (1 Chr. 21:2). He and his brothers received a very generous inheritance (v. 3). Jehoshaphat's firstborn, JEHORAM, killed all his brothers when he became king (v. 4).
(**5**) Descendant of HEMAN the musician; he and his brother Shimei were among the Levites assigned to consecrate the temple in the days of HEZEKIAH (2 Chr. 29:14; NRSV, "Jehuel," following the *Ketib*, *yĕḥûʾēl*). He is probably the same Jehiel included in the list of supervisors of the temple storerooms (31:13).
(**6**) One of three temple administrators during the reign of JOSIAH (2 Chr. 35:8; 1 Esd. 1:8 [KJV, "Syellus"]); he is mentioned with Hilkiah and

Zechariah as providing numerous offerings for the celebration of the Passover.

(7) Descendant of Joab and father of Obadiah; the latter was head of a large family who returned to Jerusalem from Babylon with Ezra (Ezra 8:9; 1 Esd. 8:35 [KJV, "Jezelus"]).

(8) Descendant of Elam and father of Shecaniah; the latter led a public confession concerning mixed marriages forbidden by the law (Ezra 10:2; 1 Esd. 8:92 [KJV, "Jeelus"]). It is interesting to note that this Jehiel is possibly the same one listed among the descendants of Elam who agreed to put away their foreign wives (Ezra 10:26, called "Jezrielus" in 1 Esd. 9:27 [KJV, "Hierielus"]). If so, Shecaniah may have been the child of a mixed marriage, and thus he apparently supported the sending away of his own mother (but see H. G. M. Williamson, *Ezra-Nehemiah*, WBC 16 [1985], 149–50).

(9) One of the priestly descendants of Harim who agreed to put away their foreign wives (Ezra 10:21; 1 Esd. 9:21 [KJV, "Hiereel"]).

Jehieli ji-hi′uh-li. See Jehiel #2.

Jehizkiah jee′hiz-ki′uh (יְחִזְקִיָּהוּ H3491, "Yahweh strengthens [me]", cf. Ezekiel, Hezekiah, Jehezkel). Son of Shallum; he was one of the princes of Ephraim who supported Oded the prophet in warning the Israelites not to take captives from Judah (2 Chr. 28:12).

Jehoadah ji-hoh′uh-duh. KJV form of Jehoaddah.

Jehoaddah ji-hoh′uh-duh (יְהוֹעַדָּה H3389, possibly "Yahweh has adorned [me]" or "Yahweh is adornment" or "Yahweh reckons"). KJV Jehoadah. Son of Ahaz and descendant of King Saul through Jonathan (1 Chr. 8:36; called Jarah or Jadah in the parallel passage, 9:42).

Jehoaddan ji-hoh′uh-duhn. See Jehoaddin.

Jehoaddin ji-hoh′uh-din (יְהוֹעַדִּין H3390, variant יְהוֹעַדָּן H3301 [2 Chr. 25:1 and *Qere* of 2 Ki. 14:2], "Yahweh is delight"). The mother of Amaziah, king of Judah; she is identified as being a native of Jerusalem (2 Ki. 14:2 [KJV, "Jehoaddan"]; 2 Chr. 25:1 [KJV, NRSV, "Jehoaddan"]).

Jehoahaz ji-hoh′uh-haz (יְהוֹאָחָז H3370, "Yahweh has taken hold [for protection]" or "whom Yahweh sustains," short form יוֹאָחָז H3407 [2 Ki. 14:1; 2 Chr. 34:8; 36:2, 4]; cf. Ahaz, Ahaziah, Joahaz).

(1) Son of Jehu and king of Israel (2 Ki. 10:35; 13:1–9; in 14:1, the NRSV has "Joahaz") Jehoahaz became king in 814/3 B.C. (the twenty-third year of Joash of Judah) and reigned for seventeen years. His son Joash (Jehoash) of Israel succeeded in the thirty-seventh year of Joash of Judah (13:10), and some therefore emend "seventeen" to "fifteen" in 13:1 or "thirty-seventh" to "thirty-ninth" in 13:10. Thiele solves the discrepancy by assuming a shift in the reckoning system (E. R. Thiele, *The Mysterious Numbers of the Hebrew Kings*, 3rd ed. [1983], ch. 2); this theory avoids emendations, but the motive for change is obscure. Others suggest a three-year coregency of Jehu and Jehoahaz.

When Jehoahaz ascended the throne, Syria (Aram) controlled virtually the whole country, having penetrated down the coastal road, taken Gath, and extracted heavy tribute from Judah. Jehoahaz was only allowed to maintain ten chariots and fifty horsemen with 10,000 footmen (earlier, Ahab's army at Qarqar, with the same infantry, had included 2,000 chariots). Although Jehoahaz had no idea of abandoning the apostate cult of Bethel ("the sins of Jeroboam") or removing the Asherah from Samaria (2 Ki. 13:6, cf. 21:3), he did in desperation invoke the name of the Lord, and his prayer was answered in God's compassion for his people (13:4–5). The oblique reference to "a deliverer" may suggest Adadnirari III, the Assyrian king who began in 805 B.C. to resume the pressure on Syria, but several other identifications have been proposed.

(2) Son of Josiah and king of Judah (2 Ki. 23:30–34; 2 Chr. 36:1–4). Also known as Shallum (prob. his personal name as opposed to his throne name, 1 Chr. 3:15; Jer. 22:11), Jehoahaz succeeded Josiah in the summer of 609 B.C., but he was deposed by Pharaoh Neco three months later. According to the biblical narrative, it was "the people of the land" who made him king, and this information suggests that Jehoahaz was not the natural successor (subsequently, his older brother Eliakim, renamed Jehoiakim, was placed on the throne by the Egyptians, 2 Ki. 23:36).

The precise meaning of the term "people of the land" has been debated, but it clearly refers to the countryfolk as distinct from the population of Jerusalem, though not quite in the rabbinic sense of "provincials." They were not necessarily less royalist, but they retained a tribal view of the nature of the kingship. They must have invaded the city in considerable numbers at times of crisis or at festivals, besides coming in the ordinary course of commerce or under threat of invasion (cf. 2 Ki. 11:14; 21:24; 25:19; Jer. 26:2; 36:9; et al.; see AM HA-AREZ). Their action in 609 B.C. recalls the enthronement of Josiah thirty years earlier; but if they felt they had established their right to control the succession, the harsh realities of great power politics soon destroyed this hope. Returning that fall from his campaign in Assyria, and aiming to secure his passage for the future, Neco installed Eliakim/Jehoiakim as his vassal and deported Jehoahaz to Egypt. Comparison of 2 Chr. 36:3 (abbreviated and perhaps miscopied) with 2 Ki. 23:33 indicates that he directed the operation from Riblah (cf. Jer. 22:10–12).

(3) Son of JEHORAM and king of Judah. See AHAZIAH #2.

(4) Father of JOAH; the latter was one of three officials who were sent to repair the temple in the time of Josiah (2 Chr. 34:8; rendered "Joahaz" in English versions). J. LILLEY

Jehoash jee-hoh′ash. Alternate form of JOASH. (For the sake of clarity and consistency, the NIV uses "Jehoash" always when the reference is to the son of Jehoahaz, king of Israel, and "Joash" when referring to the son of Ahaziah, king of Judah.)

Jehohanan jee-hoh-hay′nuhn (יְהוֹחָנָן H3380, "Yahweh is [or has been] gracious"; cf. HANANIAH, JOHANAN, JOHN). (1) Sixth son of Meshelemiah and descendant of KORAH; like his father, he and his brothers were Levitical gatekeepers in the time of David (1 Chr. 26:3).

(2) A commander of units of one thousand in the army of Judah during the reign of JEHOSHAPHAT (2 Chr. 17:15).

(3) Father of Ishmael, who was one of the commanders of units of one hundred upon whom JEHOIADA relied in his planning to move against ATHALIAH (2 Chr. 23:1).

(4) Father of Azariah; the latter was a leader in the tribe of EPHRAIM during the reign of PEKAH king of Israel (2 Chr. 28:12; KJV and NRSV, "Johanan").

(5) Son of Eliashib; he provided a room for EZRA's mourning (Ezra 10:6 [KJV, "Johanan"]; 1 Esd. 9:1 [KJV, "Joanan"]). The identification of this Jehohanan is disputed because of disagreements regarding the date of Ezra's mission (cf. JOHANAN in Neh. 12:22–23).

(6) One of the descendants of Bebai who agreed to put away their foreign wives (Ezra 10:28).

(7) Son of TOBIAH, who was an opponent of NEHEMIAH; Jehohanan married the daughter of Meshullam son of Berekiah (Neh. 6:18; KJV, "Johanan").

(8) Head of the priestly family of Amariah during the time of JOIAKIM the high priest (Neh. 12:13).

(9) One of the singers who participated in the purification and dedication of the wall of Jerusalem (Neh. 12:42). H. E. FINLEY

Jehoiachin ji-hoi′uh-kin (יְהוֹיָכִין H3382, short form יוֹיָכִין H3422 [only Ezek. 1:2], "Yahweh establishes [or protects]"; see W. F. Albright in JBL 51 [1932]: 81, and in BASOR 99 [1945]: 11; cf. also M. Noth, IPN, 28, 62, 202 n. 1). Son of JEHOIAKIM and last king of Judah before the EXILE (597 B.C.). Also known as JECONIAH and CONIAH.

I. Chronology. Jehoiachin reigned three months and ten days (2 Chr. 36:9), from the death of his father till the capture of Jerusalem (March 16, 597 B.C., dated by the Babylonian Chronicle). This means that Jehoiakim died early in Dec. 598 (D. J. Wiseman in Documents from Old testament Times, ed. D. W. Thomas [1958], 81); some consider that Jehoiachin's reign ended on his departure for Babylon in April, but agree that he became king before the city was besieged (cf. E. Auerbach in VT 9 [1959]: 113–21, and 11 [1961]: 128–36). If the first year of his exile (spring reckoning) was 597/596, the thirty-seventh was 561/560, the first (full, regnal) of Amel-Marduk (EVIL-MERODACH, 2 Ki. 25:27; Jer. 52:31).

II. Names. Jehoiachin was probably his throne name, because (1) it parallels Jehoiakim, Jehoahaz, and Josiah; (2) it occurs in the Babylonian "ration tablets" and on the seal of Eliakim steward of Yaukin; (3) Jeconiah/Coniah, like Shallum (see JEHOAHAZ), is used by Jeremiah (cf. the personal comment in Jer. 22:28), whereas Kings and Chronicles use Jehoiachin (however, Jeconiah and Shallum occur in 1 Chr. 3).

III. Reign. Jehoiachin came to the throne at the age of eighteen (2 Ki. 24:8). The figure "eight" in the parallel passage (2 Chr. 36:9 KJV, following the MT) is certainly a scribal error; the "ration tablets" show that he had five sons at latest by 592 B.C. (if he was born in 615, Jehoiakim's early paternity would be consistent with that of all the last kings of Judah).

It may be assumed that Jehoiachin had virtually no chance of developing an independent policy, because it is recorded that he endorsed the religious and social attitudes of his father (2 Ki. 24:9). At his accession, Judah was already under pressure from Moabites and other Transjordanians, who had been encouraged by NEBUCHADNEZZAR. The Babylonian king now advanced S from Syria, where he had reestablished his authority after recovering from his repulse by Egypt in 601 B.C., and was able to invest Jerusalem, which offered surprisingly little resistance. In view of the sieges that the city withstood on other occasions (for instance, a few years later under ZEDEKIAH), it is obvious that the Jewish leaders thought it politic to make terms with Nebuchadnezzar (see Albright in *JBL* 51 [1932]: 84–92, who argues that NEHUSHTA the queen-mother, of a Jerusalem family, would have exercised no small influence).

Nebuchadnezzar aimed at rendering Judah powerless to hinder his operations against Egypt. Accordingly he deported the nobility, soldiers, and men of ability, leaving only a population sufficient to maintain agriculture; appointed a puppet king (Zedekiah), binding him by a special oath of loyalty; and stripped the capital of significant wealth, even from the temple, leaving only what was needed for the religious service. Thus there is no need to see, with J. Gray (*I and II Kings*, 2nd ed. [1970], 760), a contradiction in 2 Ki. 24:13 with Jer. 27:19–20; moreover, the Babylonian Chronicle mentions heavy tribute, and it appears that the prisoners and booty were not moved till late April or May (cf. 2 Chr. 36:9–10; D. J. Wiseman, *Chronicles of the Chaldaean Kings* [1956], 34; E. Kutsch in *ZAW* 71 [1959]: 270–74).

IV. Exile. Jehoiachin was not a hostage for the good behavior of those left in Jerusalem, else his story would have ended at Zedekiah's revolt. Taken with his people, he was treated as their chief representative, under duress and later in relaxation; for toward the end of the thirty-seventh year (spring 560 B.C.), King Amel-Marduk released him from prison and gave him a place at court. Tablets have been found in the ruins of a storehouse in Babylon, recording issues of oil rations to prisoners, among whom "Jehoiachin king of Judah" is named with his sons and their Jewish governor; the sons, five of the seven named in 1 Chr. 3:17, were therefore children. One of the Jehoiachin tablets published by E. Weidner (*Melanges syriens II* [1939], 146–48) is dated 592 B.C.; others in the find date from 595 to 569 (cf. 2 Ki. 25:27–30).

The discovery of two impressions at Tell Beit Mirsim, and one at Beth Shemesh, from a seal of Eliakim "steward of Joiachin," suggests that Jehoiachin's

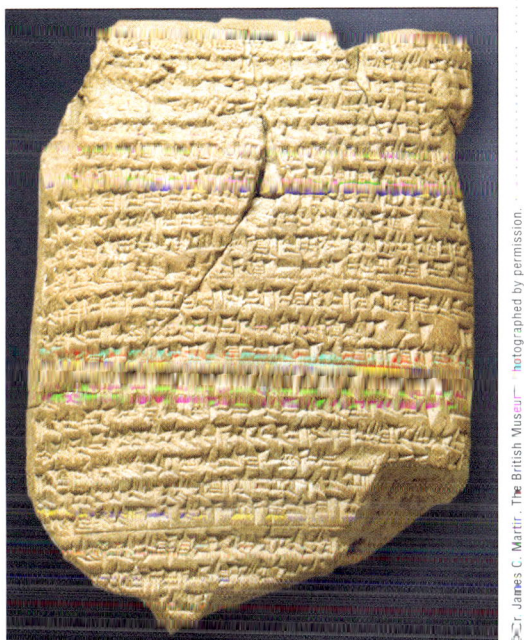

The Babylonian Chronicle recounts historical events during the years 605–595 B.C., including Nebuchadnezzar's capture of Jerusalem while Jehoiachin was king.

estates were not confiscated, and probably his needs were largely supplied from them. It seems that the Babylonians regarded him as the legitimate king, even in prison, whereas Zedekiah and Gedaliah were virtually regents. A party in Jerusalem yet hoped and schemed for his return; and it has been pointed out that dating by years of captivity (Ezekiel) was equivalent to dating by the reign of Jehoiachin (Albright in *JBL* 51 [1932]: 93ff.; cf. H. May in *AJSL* 56 [1939]: 146–48). JEREMIAH, however, although he saw the exiles as "good figs" and heirs of the promise, would have nothing to do with the idea of the king's return (Jer. 28–29), and had even denied that his posterity would reign (22:24–30). (See further *ABD*, 3:661–63.) See also CHRONOLOGY (OT); ISRAEL, HISTORY OF.

J. LILLEY

Jehoiada ji-hoi′uh-duh (יְהוֹיָדָע *H3381*, "Yahweh has known [*i.e.*, has been concerned]"; for a technical sense, see H. Huffmon in *BASOR* 181 [Feb. 1966]: 31ff.; cf. also JOIADA). **(1)** Father of BENAIAH, who was a commander of DAVID's bodyguard (2 Sam. 8:18; 20:23; 23:20–22; 1 Ki. 1:8; et al.); once he is referred to as a priest (1 Chr. 27:5). See also #2 below.

(2) An Aaronite leader who joined David at HEBRON (1 Chr. 12:27). He is probably the same as #1 above.

(3) Son of a certain Benaiah and successor of AHITHOPHEL as David's counselor (1 Chr. 27:34). It has been suggested that "Jehoiada son of Benaiah" here should be emended to "Benaiah son of Jehoiada" and that therefore this Jehoiada is the same as #1 above.

(4) A very influential high priest in Jerusalem who organized the coup that ousted ATHALIAH and set JOASH on the throne; he was for many years the young king's trusted adviser (2 Ki. 11–12; 2 Chr. 23–24). Jehoiada already had adult children when Athaliah massacred the royal family (2 Chr. 23:11), but his wife JEHOSHEBA, daughter of King JEHORAM, must have been relatively young.

Some six years after Jehosheba had rescued her infant nephew Joash from the massacre, Jehoiada ventured all when he appealed to popular loyalty to the House of David. First he secured the support of the mercenaries (CARITES), who were assigned as temple and palace guards (2 Ki. 11:4–8). The Chronicler adds that he enlisted the chiefs of the towns where the Levites resided; this tallies with references to "the people of the land" (vv. 14, 20; see AM HA-AREZ). W. Rudolph (in *Festschrift Alfred Bertholet*, ed. W. Baumgartner et al. [1950]: 473–78) thinks this is an interpolation, arguing that such an assembly could not have been secret; however, the queen's policy had evidently not restricted access to the temple, and the crowd present when the guard was changed that Sabbath appeared orderly and peaceable. Upon the king's coronation, their rejoicing drew the attention of Athaliah; but Jehoiada was ready, and her death ended all opposition. Jehoiada followed up the coronation with a covenant of religious restoration in which "the people" took part (vv. 16–17; not the country folk as such, but the congregation, as representing all Judah).

Jehoiada continued to guide Joash, though age doubtless weakened his administrative ability (2 Chr. 24:4–7). He was honored with a royal burial; but the nobility soon rebelled against his strict religious tradition (vv. 17–18).

(5) A priest during the time of JEREMIAH; Shemaiah the Nehelamite replaced him as chief officer of the temple with a certain Zephaniah so that the latter might arrest Jeremiah (Jer. 29:26). Some have argued, without good reason, that this Jehoiada is the same as #4 above.

(6) KJV alternate form of JOIADA (Neh. 3:6).

(7) NRSV alternate form of JOIADA (Neh. 13:28).

J. LILLEY

Jehoiakim ji-hoi′uh-kim (יְהוֹיָקִים *H3383*, "Yahweh raises up," i.e., "may Yahweh deliver"; cf. ELIAKIM, "God raises up," see also JOIAKIM). Throne name of Eliakim, son of JOSIAH, appointed king of Judah by Pharaoh NECO. The form *Yoqim* is found on a seal of unknown provenance (D. Diringer, *Le iscrizioni antico-ebraiche palestinesi* [1934], 197, perhaps 5th cent., G. A. Cooke, *A Text-Book of North-Semitic Inscriptions* [1903], no. 150/8, p. 361; the formation with the imperfect is rather unusual (Noth, *IPN*, 28; but cf. postexilic examples including "Joiakim," Neh. 12:10; note also "Jehoioakim" for "Eliakim," the son of Hilkiah, in Bar. 1:7).

I. Chronology. Whereas the dates of Jehoiakim's accession (autumn 609 B.C.) and death (winter

598/7) are now known to within a month, his regnal years are still debated for two reasons. (a) Authorities differ as to whether a fall or spring New Year was used, and whether a change in that system was made at this time. (b) The date of Josiah's death is not exactly known. Jehoiakim's eleventh year began in Tishri or in Nisan 598; his fourth (which saw the battle of CARCHEMISH, Jer. 46:2) began in Tishri 606 or Nisan 605. Josiah probably used a fall regnal year; Jehoiakim's first would then run from Tishri 609, with his accession a little earlier. On this basis, however, at the end of 598 he would have reigned twelve years by Hebrew reckoning. E. Auerbach (in *VT* 10 [1960]: 69–70) has therefore suggested that Jehoiakim was compelled, when he submitted to NEBUCHADNEZZAR, to use the Babylonian CALENDAR, which would have extended his fifth year by six months to Nisan 603. The winter "ninth month" of Jer. 36:9, 22 is not strictly relevant to this conclusion, for months were always numbered from the spring (cf. 1 Ki. 6:1; 12:33; 2 Chr. 35:1).

The correlation of Jehoiakim's fourth year with Nebuchadnezzar's first (Jer. 25:1) may be explained by taking "first" (Heb. *rēʾšōnî* H8038) as the Akkadian *rēš šarrūti*, that is, accession year (J. Finegan, *Handbook of Biblical Chronology*, rev. ed. [1998], 247), or by assuming that Jewish scribes regarded Nebuchadnezzar as already king (so D. Freedman in *BA* 19 [1956]: 50–60; cf. Jer. 52:12 with 52:29). Daniel may have interpreted the standard correlation by Babylonian information, thus dating Carchemish in Jehoiakim's third (Dan. 1:1), and making no distinction of the years immediately following.

II. Family. In 1 Chr. 3:15, Jehoiakim is named as Josiah's second son, ranking before JEHOAHAZ (Shallum). In 609 B.C., they were twenty-five and twenty-three respectively (2 Ki. 23:31, 36); but ZEDEKIAH, only ten (24:18), appears between them in the Chronicles passage. W. F. Albright (in *JBL* 51 [1932]: 92) would emend 2 Ki. 23:36 to avoid making Josiah a father at fourteen; but 2 Chr. 36:5 preserves the same reading, and in that year Jehoiakim's son was already seven (2 Ki. 24:8).

III. Egyptian overlordship. Neco, committed to support the failing power of Assyria against the Babylonians, needed to secure the flank of his line of march up the coast. He had no time to turn aside at MEGIDDO, but on his return that fall, taking Jehoahaz as hostage, he appointed Eliakim to govern in the Egyptian interest, symbolizing his dependence by giving him a new name, Jehoiakim. The fact that he only altered the divine prefix (from God to Yahweh) suggests that he was aiming to conciliate Judean feeling. The tribute (a talent of gold and a hundred of silver) was more of a warning than a penalty. Jehoiakim remained loyal to the Egyptian cause, if only from self-interest. The majority of the people also, or at any rate of the ruling class, preferred Egyptian overlordship to that of the Babylonians, if it came to a choice.

IV. Relations with Nebuchadnezzar. For nearly four years, Jehoiakim lived secure in Egypt's shadow; then the "pot" of Jeremiah's vision (Jer. 1:13) was upset. The Babylonian victory at Carchemish not only finished the Assyrians, but spelled the end of

Seal of Gemaryahu son of Shaphan (c. 600 B.C.), possibly a scribe who functioned in the court of King Jehoiakim. (The top image is an enlarged reproduction.)

Egyptian power in Asia, though for years the rulers of Judah could not believe this. Nebuchadnezzar's follow-through was interrupted by the death of his father, but in 604 B.C., according to the Babylonian Chronicle, he received tribute from "all the kings of Hatti-land"; it is probable that Judah was included. ASHKELON fell early in 603. Its king became Nebuchadnezzar's vassal for three years, but rebelled, evidently after the Egyptian repulse of the Babylonians (601).

In December of 599, Nebuchadnezzar returned to Syria, reestablishing his authority there as a preliminary to renewing the contest with Egypt. A year later he advanced S to recover Judah. Meanwhile, he induced the Ammonites and Moabites and the "Arameans" (2 Ki. 24:2; possibly, as Peshitta, "Edomites," cf. Jer. 35:11) to raid Judah. Their incursions are explained by H. Ginsberg (in *Alexander Marx Jubilee Volume*, ed. S. Lieberman [1950], 350ff.) as motivated by fear that Jehoiakim might repeat the recovery of Israelite territory E of the Jordan, which Ginsberg attributes to Josiah; he appears to underrate the age-old enmity of these peoples, who would more readily have seen Judah as a prey than "fellow-vassal" (cf. Ps. 137:7; Obad. 8–16).

V. Attitude to Jeremiah. The prophet JEREMIAH characterized Jehoiakim as competing in cedar (Jer. 22:15 NRSV), greedy and unprincipled. He ordered the death of URIAH of KIRIATH JEARIM, who prophesied as Jeremiah did (26:20–23) "against this city," but clearly it was the call to repent that was unacceptable to the people and leaders as well as to the king. In December 605 (or, less prob., a year later) Jehoiakim burned the first written edition of Jeremiah's prophecies, which had been confiscated after BARUCH had read from it in the temple; he would have arrested (and doubtless murdered) both Jeremiah and Baruch, "but the Lord had hidden them" (Jer. 36:26). His antagonism might indicate determination to resist the Babylonians, or resentment that the outcome of his diplomacy was being questioned.

VI. Death and burial. If the three-month reign of Jehoiakim's son, JEHOIACHIN, ended with his surrender on 2 Adar (March 16) 597, Jehoiakim must have died about 7 December 598, before Nebuchadnezzar reached Jerusalem, but while the district was subject to raids from across the Jordan (2 Ki. 24:2; Freedman in *BA* 19 [1956]: 53 n. 2). Some mystery surrounds Jehoiakim's burial (cf. A. R. Green in *AUSS* 20 [1982]: 103–9). The phrase "rested with his fathers" (2 Ki. 24:6) normally indicates a natural death, and as the same information was available to the Chronicler, he can hardly have meant that Jehoiakim ended his reign in captivity (2 Chr. 36:6). However, several authorities note the possibility that he was murdered, referring either to Jer. 22:19; 36:30, or to JOSEPHUS's account of a double siege in 598/7 B.C. (*Ant.* 10.6.3). The latter cannot be reconciled with the Babylonian Chronicle, but may have been constructed from Jeremiah's words; whereas these may well have been fulfilled in an undignified burial because of the raids. There is a dispute whether a proper burial would have been in the palace or outside the city; Manasseh and Amon were buried in the "garden of Uzza," which is named in 2 Chr. 36:8 (LXX). S. Yeivin (in *JNES* 7 [1948]: 34ff.) accepts this suggestion but locates the garden in the city. See also CHRONOLOGY (OT); ISRAEL, HISTORY OF. J. LILLEY

Jehoiarib ji-hoi'uh-rib (יְהוֹיָרִיב H3384, "Yahweh contends [for me]"; see JARIB, JOARIB, JOIARIB). **(1)** A priest who received the first lot of the twenty-four divisions in DAVID's time (1 Chr. 24:7). He was possibly the ancestor of #2 below. In the Maccabean period, MATTATHIAS traced his lineage to him (called JOARIB, 1 Macc. 2:1).

(2) One of six priests (prob. family heads) who resettled in Jerusalem after the EXILE (1 Chr. 9:10). He is usually identified with a JOIARIB mentioned three times in Nehemiah's lists (Neh. 11:10; 12:6, 19). S. BARABAS

Jehonadab ji-hoh'nuh-dab. See JONADAB.

Jehonathan ji-hon'uh-thuhn (יְהוֹנָתָן H3387, "Yahweh has given [a child]"; see JONATHAN). **(1)** Son of Uzziah, an official in the time of DAVID who was in charge of storehouses (1 Chr. 27:25 KJV; modern versions render the name "Jonathan").

(2) One of six Levites whom King JEHOSHAPHAT sent to teach the law in the cities of Judah

(2 Chr. 17:8). Appointed to the same mission were a number of princes and priests.

(3) The head of the priestly family of Shemaiah in the days when JOIAKIM son of Jeshua was high priest (Neh. 12:18).   S. BARABAS

Jehoram jĭ-hôr´rȧm (יְהוֹרָם *yĕhôrām* יוֹרָם *yôrām* H3456, "Yahweh is exalted"). (1) One of six Levites whom King JEHOSHAPHAT sent to teach the law in the cities of Judah (2 Chr. 17:8). Appointed to the same mission were a number of princes and priests.

(2) Son of AHAB and ninth king of the northern kingdom of Israel; mainly called Joram (2 Ki. 1:17; 3:1-13; 8:16; 9:15-24; 2 Chr. 22:5-7). The NIV consistently uses Joram to distinguish him from the son of Jehoshaphat (see #3 below), and that practice will be followed in this article. A number of stories in connection with the marvelous deeds of ELIJAH and ELISHA refer to "the king" of Israel without mentioning his name; inasmuch as the precise chronological connections of the Elijah-Elisha narratives are seldom clarified, it is hard to know for certain just how many of those in which "the king" figures in some way are related to King Joram of Israel.

Elijah must have survived at least until the sixth year of his reign (cf. 2 Chr. 21:12), while Elisha began his remarkable ministry during that reign. The seven years of famine foretold to the Shunammite woman (2 Ki. 8:1) must be the same as that referred to at 4:38 (note the "had said" of 8:1), and this period would have begun no later than the fifth or sixth year of Joram, who seems still to have been alive seven years later. Likely, then, the many exploits of Elisha detailed in 2 Ki. 3-9 took place during Joram's reign (c. 852-841 B.C.; see E. R. Thiele, *The Mysterious Numbers of the Hebrew Kings*, 3rd ed. [1983], 99). If ever a Jewish king was witness to miracles enough to encourage faith, Joram was he.

Throughout his reign the two Jewish kingdoms were allied. Upon his accession, almost at once he was joined by Judah (under Jehoshaphat) and EDOM (tributary to Judah) in a war against the Moabites in an effort to recover the submission of MOAB under its King MESHA. The combined expedition came to near disaster from want of water near the frontier of Edom and Moab. It was Jehoshaphat's truly pious reliance on genuine prophecy that saved them all, for Elisha was brought forward from the ranks, and through his function as prophet a life-saving miracle brought both water and military victory (2 Ki. 3:4-27). This alliance ended with the destruction of the house of Ahab by Joram's successor, JEHU. After that, enmity between the two Hebrew kingdoms was renewed.

Though a venal and weak man, he was not without some good, for he at least diminished BAAL worship early in his reign (2 Ki. 3:2), though he did not end the divisive and perverse worship of the calves' images at BETHEL and DAN (PLACE) (3:3; cf. 1 Ki. 12:25-33; see CALF, GOLDEN). Baal worship was thoroughly prosperous when Jehu destroyed it scarcely a decade later (2 Ki. 10:15-28). Though in a moment of desperation he once sought to kill Elisha (6:24—7:20, esp. vv. 31-32), Joram did on occasion give heed to Elisha's wise and frequently friendly advice (6:20-23; 3:13). Yet when the Syrian raids diminished he seems to have begun to resent Elisha's advice and admonition (6:23) and quickly relapsed to worse idolatry. Divine judgment in the form of siege and famine were not slow to follow (6:24-25). It was at this juncture that Joram (for he is surely "the king" here), in despair, sought to kill Elisha (6:31-32).

Joram was the last king of the line of OMRI. His mother JEZEBEL and he both were killed by the rampaging Jehu, who also exterminated all

Ruins of the royal palace at Samaria, from where Jehoram son of Ahab ruled the northern kingdom.

members of the family and all officials of the Baal cult (2 Ki. 9–10). The two long chapters devoted to the extermination of the house of Ahab indicate what a terrible peril they were to the ongoing of the messianic nation and thereby the divinely revealed Mosaic faith. Through ATHALIAH (daughter of Ahab and Jezebel), who married Jehoram son of Jehoshaphat, the line of Ahab may have passed into the ancestral line of the Lord Jesus Christ (Matt. 1:8). This wife of the Davidic Jehoram became a "second Jezebel," as she is sometimes called, being responsible not only for introducing vile paganism to the house of David, but also for the murder, in her old age, of all male members of the line of David save one (see JOASH #7).

(3) Son of JEHOSHAPHAT and fifth king of the southern kingdom of Judah; sometimes called Joram (c. 848–841 B.C., but previously regent, 853–848; see Thiele, *Mysterious Numbers*, 99–101). Scripture portions relating to this man are chiefly an entire chapter in Chronicles (2 Chr. 21), but only four verses in Kings (2 Ki. 8:16–19). The latter passage gives an important picture of the relations familial and diplomatic between the two Jehorams: "In the fifth year of Joram son of Ahab king of Israel, when Jehoshaphat was king of Judah, Jehoram son of Jehoshaphat began his reign as king of Judah. He was thirty-two years old when he became king, and he reigned in Jerusalem eight years. He walked in the ways of the kings of Israel, as the house of Ahab had done, for he married a daughter of Ahab. He did evil in the eyes of the LORD." Except for a few months when his son AHAZIAH reigned after him, his reign corresponds with the last eight years of the reign of the northern Joram. His life and reign make up one of the saddest and most to be regretted pages of the history of the Davidic dynasty.

Jehoram's personal and domestic life were tragically wrong. His wife, Athaliah, brought with her the corruption of the Baalism (fertility cult religion) of her mother's Phoenician ancestors. As a result, Jehoram "walked in the ways of the kings of Israel, as the house of Ahab had done, for he married a daughter of Ahab" (2 Chr. 21:6). Soon after ascending the throne, Jehoram assassinated his six brothers and other "princes of Israel" (21:4; in light of Athaliah's behavior after Jehoram's death, she may have engineered this murder). The motive may have been either to gain the wealth with which the prosperous father Jehoshaphat had richly endowed them; it is also possible that they opposed his ruinous political and religious policies. At any rate, the direct line of the reigning family was in consequence reduced during his reign to one male descendant (Ahaziah, 21:16–17), as it was again shortly after his death when the bloodthirsty Athaliah superintended the slaughter of all Jehoram's grandsons except Joash. Everything recorded of this man indicates complete religious and moral apostasy, even worse than that of the Baal-worshiping heathen of his time. Apostates usually find themselves in complete reaction against the holy faith and practice of the biblical religion.

The expected consequence of such apostasy would have been destruction of the dynasty and transfer of the regnal power to another leading family. This is how the house of JEROBOAM I had been punished for apostasy (1 Ki. 14:10–11), as likewise the house of BAASHA (16:1–4), of AHAB (21:20–26), and of SAUL (1 Sam. 13:13–14; 15:22–26). The promises of God, however, guaranteed that such would not be the case with the now ancient dynasty of David (2 Ki. 8:19). The terms of the David COVENANT were: "I will raise up your offspring to succeed you … and I will establish his kingdom. … When he does wrong, I will punish him. … But my love will never be taken away from him, as I took it away from Saul. … Your house and your kingdom will endure forever before me" (2 Sam. 7:12–16). This covenant is specifically related to Jehoram's case: "Nevertheless, for the sake of his servant David, the LORD was not willing to destroy Judah. He had promised to maintain a lamp for David and his descendants forever" (2 Ki. 8:19; cf. 16–18). This perpetual "light" is mentioned also elsewhere (1 Ki. 15:4; 2 Chr. 21:7). The figure is apparently a popular one drawn from the custom of reserving the home fire perpetually by a pilot light in an oil burning lamp (cf. Prov. 31:18). This "promise doctrine," so eminently illustrated in Jehoram's case, is the great theme of the Samuel-Kings narrative.

Nor was the chastening promised for apostasy withheld. There was first a revolt of Edom, which since David's time had been under tributary kings with only brief interruptions (2 Ki. 8:20; cf. 2 Sam. 8:14; 1 Ki. 11:14–16). From that point on throughout OT times the Edomites would have a "king over themselves" who owed neither fealty nor tribute to Judah (note Isaac's prophecy of this revolt, Gen. 27:40). Not only so, a southwestern area with a center at Libnah also successfully revolted (2 Ki. 8:22). Further chastening came through successful inroads by rampaging Philistines and Arabs (2 Chr. 21:16–17). Not for generations was there significant recovery of this lost ground.

The climax of these judgments to Jehoram himself was the particularly horrible manner in which he died (2 Chr. 21:15, "disease of your bowels, until your bowels come out," NRSV) after living to see God's judgment on all his sons save one, 1000 of his harem and all his goods. His sons had joined in destruction of the Lord's worship as "seed royal" in a manner lesser citizens would not have dared to do (24:7) and therefore were destroyed, according to the word of Elijah, sent by letter to the miserable apostate king (21:12–17; the report of this letter shows that Elijah's attention was not confined to the affairs of the northern kingdom only, and indicates that he was still alive after the death of Jehoshaphat). What horrible consequences from a bad marriage arranged by an otherwise wise and godly parent! See also CHRONOLOGY (OT); ISRAEL, HISTORY OF. R. D. CULVER

Jehoshabeath jee′hoh-shab′ee-ath. Alternate form of JEHOSHEBA.

Jehoshaphat ji-hosh′uh-fat (יְהוֹשָׁפָט H3398, "Yahweh has judged"; cf. JOSHAPHAT, ELISHAPHAT, SHEPHATIAH; Ἰωσαφάτ G2734). **(1)** Son of Ahilud and recorder in the time of DAVID and SOLOMON (2 Sam. 8:16; 20:24; 1 Ki. 4:3). **(2)** One of the priests appointed to blow the trumpet when David transferred the ARK OF THE COVENANT to Jerusalem (1 Chr. 15:24 KJV; modern versions render the name "Joshaphat"). **(3)** Son of Paruah; he was one of twelve district governors of Solomon commissioned to supply provisions for the royal household (1 Ki. 4:17). **(4)** Son of Asa and fourth king of the southern kingdom of Judah (1 Ki. 22; 2 Chr. 17–20; included in Matthew's GENEALOGY OF JESUS CHRIST, Matt. 1:8). **(5)** Father of King JEHU of Samaria (2 Ki. 9:2, 14). The rest of this article is devoted to Jehoshaphat king of Judah.

I. Introduction. Jehoshaphat reigned twenty-five years, 873–849 B.C., and was thus contemporary to the reigns (in whole or part) of the entire Omride dynasty—OMRI, AHAB, AHAZIAH, JEHORAM—and contemporary to the ministries of the prophets ELIJAH and ELISHA. One of the oddities of the biblical narrative is that his notable reign is almost passed over in the books of KINGS, except as it impinges on the affairs of the northern kingdom (1 Ki. 15:24; 22:1–49; 2 Ki. 1:17; 3:1, 7–27; 8:16, 24–25; 12:18), while in the CHRONICLES account four long chapters (2 Chr. 17–20) are devoted to his story, scarcely equalled in extent by any other king (there are also notices in 1 Chr. 3:10; 2 Chr. 22:9). The reason seems to be that important matters leading to the ultimate demise of the northern kingdom are the center of interest in the Kings account, the disobedience to the Mosaic covenant and the efforts of Elijah and Elisha to correct matters being more central to the author's interest. In Chronicles the famous piety of the great king and his succession, both reviving and preserving the institutions and standards of the Mosaic covenant, are cited at length to the postexilic RESTORATION community to produce both guidance and inspiration for that dispirited generation. The colorful career of Elijah is emphasized in the one, while the marvels of Jehoshaphat's faith and his revivals of religion are detailed in the other.

II. His military policy. The Hebrew text of 2 Chr. 17:1–2 indicates a policy of strong defense against expected inroads from the N. Omri, founder of the current dynasty at SAMARIA, had been a military commander-in-chief (1 Ki. 16:16); his son Ahab, Jehoshaphat's opposite number in Samaria, while not courageous, was strong. The reign of Asa, Jehoshaphat's father, had been one of uninterrupted warfare with the kings of Israel (2 Chr. 16:1–9; 1 Ki. 15:32). As a patriotic and foresighted head of state, Jehoshaphat placed armed men in all the fortified cities of Judah and garrisons of soldiers in lesser towns. The warfare of the time offered small protection to rural village folk. At the approach of enemy forces, they simply drove their livestock ahead of them to the fortified cities and moved in. Under such circumstances, conflict tended to be siege warfare unless there was professional military organization and soldiery to drive invading forces from the field. Jehoshaphat believed: "In time of peace prepare war."

III. His general religious policy. The Mosaic commonwealth of Israel was no democracy in matters of religion. Obedience to the law of Moses was not optional for anyone. It was the duty of magistrates and priests to practice the Mosaic faith and to see that all citizens at least outwardly and publicly did the same. Jehoshaphat was outstanding in the way in which as head of state he put the religious laws into effect. He heartily embraced the ancestral religion (2 Chr. 17:3–6), following the example of DAVID. Two striking expressions underscore this fact: "His heart was devoted to the ways of the LORD" (17:6) and the comment of Jehu the seer: "[you] have set your heart on seeking God" (19:3). The success of the public measures taken to restore the practice of Mosaic faith to the entire nation is summarized in these words: "Jehoshaphat lived in Jerusalem, and he went out again among the people from Beersheba to the hill country of Ephraim and turned them back to the LORD, the God of their fathers" (19:4).

IV. Special measures employed for restoring Mosaic religion. In his religious reforms, Jehoshaphat built upon the effective measures taken by Asa, his pious and energetic father. The backslidings of SOLOMON in his last years, the juvenile policies of REHOBOAM, and the religious carelessness of ABIJAH had brought matters, moral and religious, sadly downward. It was Asa's praiseworthy accomplishment that he rid the land of foreign altars and the cult objects of Canaanite Baalism (2 Chr. 14:3–5). He also reviewed the physical instruments of Yahweh worship, and compelled outward conformity to the Mosaic observances (15:8–11) even threatening death for apostates (as provided by the Law, Deut. 13). Yet the need for public instruction pointed out plainly by a certain prophet named Azariah (2 Chr. 15:1–7) evidently remained unmet. It was Jehoshaphat's goal to correct that omission, a matter he cared for early in the third year of his reign, by sending officials, Levites, and priests "to teach in the towns of Judah"; these men "taught throughout Judah, taking with them the Book of the Law of the LORD" (2 Chr. 17:7–9). Evidently the Pentateuchal provisions for acquainting the people with the content and meaning of the law had been long neglected (Deut. 31:9–13; cf. 4:10; 6:1–9).

V. Prosperity of his reign. Jehoshaphat's military and religious measures were successful: "The fear of the LORD fell on all the kingdoms of the lands surrounding Judah, so that they did not make war against Jehoshaphat" (2 Chr. 17:10). He brought the nation back, at least formally, to "the God of their fathers" (19:4).

VI. The new policy of conciliation with Israel. Whereas the policy of his three predecessors, beginning with Rehoboam, had been one of unremitting enmity, and frequently warfare, toward Israel (1 Ki. 14:30; 15:6), some time fairly early in his reign Jehoshaphat and Ahab of Samaria put an end to the old feud. After the custom of the time, the two reigning families were united by marriage—in this case ATHALIAH daughter of Ahab and Jezebel with Jehoram son of Jehoshaphat. The poisonous effect of that marriage is traced elsewhere (see esp. JEHORAM #3). The arrangement became expensive to Judah by reason of the treasure and manpower contributed to Ahab's wars (1 Ki. 22; 2 Chr. 18), and to the wars of Jehoram/Joram son of Ahab (2 Ki. 3), for Jehoshaphat assisted in at least two fruitless campaigns of the kings of Israel. This was not without personal physical peril to Jehoshaphat (2 Chr. 18:28–32; 1 Ki. 22:29–33) and spiritual loss to himself and his kingdom (2 Chr. 19:1–3). Nevertheless, the reduction in armament possible upon the cessation of the military feud with Israel produced material prosperity—"less guns; more butter"—though it scarcely lasted beyond the lifetime of the pious king. Since the conciliatory policy led in the three following reigns (Jehoram, Ahaziah, and Queen Grandmother Athaliah) to the near extinction of the dynasty, it was an ill conceived policy.

VII. His judicial reforms. Judicial laws and procedures prescribed by Pentateuchal laws provided mainly for courts of the local level. There was really no distinction between civil laws and courts on the one hand and religious on the other. To the present day in the Near East, including the new secular-religious state of Israel, the distinctions are frequently obscure. But with the institution of the monarchy, with its claims of taxes and services as well as manpower upon the population, there was need to expand the judicial system. Hence the "chief priest" was made head of the system of religious courts ("Amariah the chief priest will be over you in any matter concerning the LORD," 2 Chr. 19:11), while a separate non-Levite became head of a court dealing strictly with secular matters ("Zebadiah son of Ishmael, the leader of the tribe of Judah, will be over you in any matter concerning the king"). These national courts were not courts of appeal for plaintiffs dissatisfied with rulings of local courts, but they functioned rather as courts of referral for local judges who ruled themselves incompetent for some reason (Deut. 17:8). Equity was a matter, in the main, for courts of local elders and appears not to have been involved in Jehoshaphat's reforms. (See further W. F. Albright, "The Judicial Reform of Jehoshaphat," in *Alexander Marx Jubilee Volume*, ed. S. Lieberman [1950], 61–82.)

VIII. Foreign invasion and its miraculous repulse in the wilderness of Tekoa. There appears to be only one reference to this quite amazing incident in the book of Kings, and that a very oblique statement to the effect that Jehoshaphat successfully conducted certain undescribed wars (1 Ki. 22:43). On the other hand, 2 Chr. 20:11 represents the invaders (Moabites, Ammonites, and Meunites, 20:1; cf. 26:7) as seeking actually to dispossess the Jews of their land rather than mere conquest. Precisely because the invaders expected to stay and brought along families, flocks, and goods, the people of Judah reaped the large and valuable booty reported. The locale is the desert border area SE of BETHLEHEM and NE of HEBRON. The present road between these two cities skirts the western edge of the territory involved in this incident.

IX. Assessment of his reign. Although he attained a moderately advanced age (sixty years) and enjoyed twenty-five years of prosperous reign, and although personally loyal to the ancestral faith and pure of life and motive, Jehoshaphat's greatest failures lay in the precise areas of his greatest success—international relations and religious reformation (2 Chr. 20:31–37). He could not root out the unlawful (Deut. 12, esp. vv. 5–7) and probably clandestine high place worship, for "the people still had not set their hearts on the God of their fathers" (2 Chr. 20:33). His diplomacy by intermarriage of his own house with that of Ahab brought all his gains to ruin within a few years of his death. Already in his lifetime it was bearing unwanted and bitter fruit (1 Ki. 22:48–49; cf. 2 Chr. 20:35–37) in a futile joint naval venture with Ahaziah of Israel. His death and succession are recorded in a laconic statement (2 Chr. 21:1), to which JOSEPHUS adds: "he was buried in a magnificent manner in Jerusalem, for he had imitated the actions of David" (*Ant.* 9.3.2).

K. D. CULVER

Jehoshaphat, Valley of. A valley adjacent to the city of JERUSALEM and regarded as the place of the judging of the nations (Joel 3:2, 12); it is also referred to as the "valley of decision" (3:14; cf. Zech. 14:1–5).

Christian tradition has identified it as the Valley of the KIDRON (the portion just E of the city) at least as early as the 4th cent., perhaps beginning with the Bordeaux Pilgrim's account (A.D. 333): "Also as one goes from Jerusalem to the gate which is to the eastward, in order to ascend the Mount of Olives, is the valley called that of Josaphat" (P. Geyer, *Itinera Hierosolymitana saeculi IIII–VIII* [1898], 23; English trans. by A. Stewart, *Itinerary from Bordeaux to Jerusalem* [1887], 24). EUSEBIUS at one point (*Onomasticon* 118.18–19) describes the Valley of Jehoshaphat as being "between Jerusalem and the Mount of Olives," thus the Kidron Valley, but elsewhere (170.8–10) he appears to identify it with the Valley of HINNOM. The concept of it as a place of final judgment is shared by Jewish, Muslim, and Christian tradition, and is witnessed to by the extensive cemeteries of all three faiths on the slopes of the valley. The pseudepigraphical book of *1 Enoch* (53.1) places the judgment in a deep valley near Hinnom.

The valley probably was named after King JEHOSHAPHAT (a name meaning "Yahweh has judged") and also was known as the "King's Valley" (2 Sam. 18:18), where ABSALOM erected a pillar and apparently expected to be buried (the monument now called Absalom's Tomb is of a later period, as are the adjacent Tomb of St. James and Tomb of Zechariah). The GIHON SPRING and the Pool of

Looking N through the Kidron Valley, thought by many to be the same as the Valley of Jehoshaphat.

Siloam, with the exits of Hezekiah's (or Siloam) Tunnel, as well as the Spring of En Rogel, are to be seen, with some remnants of older water systems. The Garden of Gethsemane and the nearby Basilica of the Agony are located in the floor of the valley, and at the confluence of the Kidron with the Valley of Gehenna (OT Hinnom) there is the Potter's Field.

The theme of judgment is perpetuated in the names of the gates in the E wall of the city. Up to the 14th cent. the northern gate, now called the Damascus Gate, was designated as St. Stephen's Gate, and later the name was transferred to the gate opening on the Kidron Valley, previously known as the Gate of the Valley of Josaphat. The Vulgate identifies the Muster Gate (NIV, "Inspection Gate," Neh. 3:31) as *Porto judicialis*, "Gate of Judgment." A 6th-cent. Laura (i.e., monastic center) was located near the gate, and a 12th-cent. monastery nearby was called St. Mary of Josaphat, corresponding to the Arabic *Bab Sitt Mariam*. Muslim legends name the two closed portals of the Golden Gate the "door of mercy" and the "door of contrition," continuing the judgment theme, and the part of the Kidron Valley opposite this gate is called by them the *Jyahannum* (Gehenna). (See E. Robinson and E. Smith, *Biblical Researches in Palestine* 1 [1841]. 396–405; J. Simons, *Jerusalem in the Old Testament* [1952], 10, 14; E. Kraeling, *Rand McNally Bible Atlas* [1956], 342.)

M. H. Heicksen

Jehosheba ji-hosh′uh-buh (יְהוֹשֶׁבַע H3394, variant יְהוֹשַׁבְעַת H3395, "Yahweh is abundance [or prosperity, happiness]"). The daughter of King Jehoram (Joram) of Judah (2 Ki. 11:2) and wife of Jehoiada, the high priest (2 Chr. 22:11; KJV, NRSV, "Jehoshabeath"). When her brother Ahaziah and most of the rest of the royal family were about to be murdered, she took Ahaziah's son Joash, who was kept hidden for six years, until he could be made king.

Jehoshua ji-hosh′yoo-uh. KJV alternate form of Joshua (Num. 13:16; 1 Chr. 7:27 [some editions, "Jehoshuah"]).

Jehovah ji-hoh′vuh. Traditional English rendering of the Tetragrammaton or divine name, *Yahweh* (Heb. יהוה H3378; Exod. 6:3 et al., KJV). Because Jewish tradition does not allow the pronunciation of this name, in public reading it is regularly substituted with *Adonay*, "my Lord" (אֲדֹנָי from יהוה H123). To indicate such a reading, Hebrew copies of the Bible preserve the consonants of *Yahweh*, but insert the vowels of *Adonay* (thus, יְהֹוָה, the first vowel being a short sound pronounced ĕ, roughly equivalent to ă); according to some, the inserted vowels come from Aram. שְׁמָא, "the Name" (partly on the grounds that in some MSS the Tetragrammaton is pointed simply יְהוָֹה, that is, without the *o* vowel). This practice in the writing of the divine name misled translators (not only in English) to create the hybrid form *Jehovah*, which never existed in Hebrew. Most versions render the name with small caps as "the Lord." See God, names of.

Jehovah-jireh ji-hoh'vuh-ji'ruh (יְהוָֹה יִרְאֶה, the latter word being impf. of רָאָה H8011, "to see, consider, be concerned about"). The name Abraham gave the place on Mount Moriah where God substituted a ram for his son Isaac (Gen. 22:14 KJV; NIV, "The Lord Will Provide"). Evidently, by the time of the Mosaic record, the statement had become a current proverb. The designation "mount of the Lord" was the usual one for the temple mount in Jerusalem (Isa. 2:3, among many others). In view of the end of Gen. 22:14 (which has the verb *rāʾâ* in the niphal stem), some have suggested that a better vocalization of the Hebrew text would read: "Yahweh will be seen" (the passive force) or "Yahweh will reveal himself" (the reflexive force). Actually, a supposed inconsistency does not exist between the renderings "Yahweh will provide" and "Yahweh will be seen [*i.e.*, appear]," for there is an evident play on the Hebrew word that can convey both significations, depending on the stem in which it occurs. Interestingly, the Syriac and Latin versions render the two Hebrew forms as though they were in the same verbal stem. C. L. Feinberg

Jehovah-nissi ji-hoh'vuh-nis'i (יְהוָֹה נִסִּי, "Yahweh is my banner"). The name given the altar erected by Moses to commemorate the defeat of the Amalekites (see Amalek) in the wilderness at Rephidim at the hands of Israel under the leadership of Joshua (Exod. 17:15 KJV; NIV, "The Lord is my Banner"; the Gk. and Aram. versions read differently). The name revealed Israel's assurance that God was the One who gave them the victory and that he was the One around whom they in the future were to rally as a standard. C. L. Feinberg

Jehovah-shalom ji-hoh'vuh-shah'lohm (יְהוָֹה שָׁלוֹם, "Yahweh is peace"). The name Gideon gave the altar he constructed in Ophrah to commemorate the visit of the angel of the Lord, who assured Gideon that he would not die as a result of seeing an angel, and commissioned him to liberate Israel from the Midianites (Jdg. 6:23–24 KJV; NIV, "The Lord is Peace"). C. L. Feinberg

Jehovah-shammah ji-hoh'vuh-sham'muh (יְהוָֹה שָׁמָּה, "Yahweh is there"). The name to be given the restored and beautified Jerusalem of the Messiah's kingdom (Ezek. 48:35 KJV mg.). The Lord had departed from his temple and city (ch. 11); he is to return to Jerusalem (ch. 43) and remain in favor and glory among his redeemed people forever. This is God's goal for his elect people. God's name is inseparably linked with his chosen city, the place of his abode. Compare the parallel in Rev. 21.
C. L. Feinberg

Jehovah-tsidkenu ji-hoh'vuh-tsid-kee'nyoo (יְהוָֹה צִדְקֵנוּ, "Yahweh is our righteousness"). This name is employed, by Jeremiah alone, in a twofold way. It is the designation of the future Davidic king, who will rule over restored Israel (Jer. 23:6 KJV mg.). Righteousness is a divine attribute of the Messiah in providing salvation; the implication appears to be that his righteousness becomes ours (cf. the notion of imputed righteousness, 1 Cor. 1:30; 2 Cor. 5:21). In the second reference (Jer. 33:16 KJV mg.), the prophet is pointing to the capital of the king, which partakes of the nature of the righteous monarch. C. L. Feinberg

Jehozabad ji-hoh'zuh-bad (יְהוֹזָבָד H3379, "Yahweh has granted"; cf. Elzabad and Jozabad). **(1)** Son of Shomer; he was an official who, with Jozabad (NRSV, "Jozacar," following many Heb. MSS) son of Shimeath, murdered King Joash of Judah at Beth Millo (2 Ki. 12:21). The parallel passage identifies the officials as "Zabad, son of Shimeath an Ammonite woman, and Jehozabad, son of Shimrith a Moabite woman" (2 Chr. 24:26). Some consider Shimrith a variant form of Shomer (cf. NIV mg.); others speculate that Shomer was Shimrith's father.

(2) Son of Obed-Edom, included in the list of divisions of the Korahite doorkeepers in the reign of David (1 Chr. 26:4).

(3) A commander of units of one thousand in the army of Judah during the reign of Jehoshaphat (2 Chr. 17:18).   S. Barabas

Jehozadak ji-hoh´zuh-dak (יְהוֹצָדָק H3392, short form יוֹצָדָק H3449 "Yahweh has been righteous"). Son of Seraiah and descendant of Aaron through Eleazar; apparently the last high priest prior to the destruction of the temple, he was among those deported to Babylon by Nebuchadnezzar (1 Chr. 6:14–15). He is known primarily for being the father of Joshua (Jeshua) the high priest (Hag. 1:1, 12, 14; 2:2, 4; Zech. 6:11; KJV, "Josedech"). In Ezra–Nehemiah the name is shortened to Jozadak (Ezra 3:2, 8; 5:2; 10:18; Neh. 12:26); similarly in the Apocrypha (1 Esd. 5:5, 48, 56; 6:2; 9:19; Sir. 49:12; KJV, "Josedec").   S. Barabas

Jehu jee´hyoo, jay´hoo (יֵהוּא H3369, "Yahweh is he" [i.e., he is the true God; cf. Noth, *IPN*, 15ff., 143]; see Elihu). **(1)** Son of Obed and descendant of Jerahmeel, included in the genealogy of Judah (1 Chr. 2:38).

(2) Son of Joshibiah, listed among clan leaders in the tribe of Simeon whose families increased greatly during the days of King Hezekiah and who dispossessed the Hamites and Meunites near Gedor (1 Chr. 4:36; cf. vv. 38–41).

(3) A man from Anathoth, listed among the warriors, kinsmen of Saul, who joined with David when the latter took refuge at Ziklag (1 Chr. 12:3).

(4) Son of Hanani; he was a prophet who warned King Baasha (c. 909–886 B.C.) that he would be judged for following the heretical cult instituted by Jeroboam (1 Ki. 16:1–4, 7). Much later (c. 853), Jehu had to rebuke King Jehoshaphat for allying himself with Ahab in an attempt to recover Ramoth Gilead from the Arameans (2 Chr. 19:2, where he is called "the seer"). Jehu wrote annals on the reign of Jehoshaphat that were incorporated in "the book of the kings of Israel" (1 Chr. 20:34).

(5) Son of a certain Jehoshaphat (not the king of Judah), sometimes also identified as son of Nimshi (apparently his grandfather; cf. 1 Ki. 19:16 with 2 Ki. 9:2). Jehu was king of the northern kingdom of Israel, c. 841–814 B.C. Jehu had been a commander in the Israelite army who accepted the divine commission through Elisha to take over the royal office, avenge the persecution of Yahwists, and extirpate Phoenician Baal worship from Israel (1 Ki. 19:16–17; 2 Ki.9–10; brief references elsewhere). The rest of this article is devoted to King Jehu.

I. Chronology. According to 2 Ki. 3:1; 8:25, Jehoram (Joram) of Israel reigned twelve years; Ahaziah of Judah acceded in Jehoram's twelfth (or eleventh, by the accession-year reckoning that appears to have been used in 9:29) and reigned (part of) one year. This was the year of Jehu's coup, in which both kings were killed. A definite synchronism is available with Assyrian history, for Shalmaneser III records the battle of Qarqar (at which Ahab fought), in his sixth year, and the receipt of tribute from Jehu in his eighteenth (respectively 853/2 and 841/0 B.C.; there is a faint possibility that the dates should be one year higher; see E. R. Thiele, *The Mysterious Numbers of the Hebrew Kings*, 3rd ed. [1983], ch. 3). If Ahab was killed at Ramoth Gilead in the campaign season of 853, Ahaziah of Israel reigned in 853/2 and 852/1; Jehoram's first year was 852/1, and his twelfth, 841/0.

In 841, Shalmaneser attacked Damascus, devastating Syria (Aram) and Hauran, so Jehu's revolt can hardly have been later than the middle of the campaigning season of 841. This correlation with the years of a single Assyrian king affords the clearest proof that nonaccession-year reckoning ("antedating") was used in Israel, and that it was being adopted also in Judah, presumably as a result of the intermarriage between the royal houses (and, perhaps, of the close alignment of foreign policy). It may seem unlikely that the Arameans attacked Ramoth in the year of Shalmaneser's expedition; J. Miller (in *JBL* 76 [1967]: 285ff.) therefore adopts Lucian's recension of the synchronisms, implying a shorter reign for Jehoram, and allowing 844/2 for Jehu's revolt. Jehu reigned twenty-eight years (2 Ki. 10:36), dying in 814/3.

II. Revolution. In Jehoram's twelfth year the Israelites held a defensive position at Ramoth Gilead, a key point on the N-S trade route E of the Jordan, against the Arameans. Jehoram, wounded in an Aramean attack, had gone to Jezreel to recover, leaving his commanders (of whom Jehu may have been chief) to carry on the war in Gilead. Ahaziah, king of Judah, who was assisting Jehoram in the campaign, later went down to Jezreel to see how he was progressing; and the court was there, including JEZEBEL the queen mother.

At this juncture, a young emissary arrived from the community of prophets in the Jordan valley, of which ELISHA was head. As directed by Elisha, he requested a private interview with Jehu, and commissioned him in the name of the Lord to avenge the murder of Yahwist prophets on the Omride dynasty and to take over the kingdom. To confirm his message, he anointed Jehu on the spot. Jehu's fellow officers, on hearing this, rallied immediately and proclaimed him king (2 Ki. 9:1–13).

The subsequent passage (2 Ki. 9:14–37) begins by restating that Jehu rebelled against Jehoram while the latter was in Jezreel recovering from a war wound. Jehu requested his colleagues to prevent anyone else from leaving Ramoth while he went to Jezreel in his chariot (prob. with a small guard, as inferred by JOSEPHUS in *Ant*. 9.6.3). As Jehu approached Jezreel, he detained two scouts who were sent to question him, which probably gave Jehoram the impression that he wanted to confer privately. Puzzled by his commander's presence and behavior, and perhaps fearing that something extraordinary had happened at Ramoth, Jehoram went with Ahaziah to meet him.

Jehu was waiting by the royal garden that Ahab had obtained by the death of NABOTH. Having witnessed, as a young officer, ELIJAH's condemnation of this murder, Jehu may already have been thinking of the scandal (2 Ki. 9:25). He returned Jehoram's greeting with a challenge and shot him as he turned to escape; then he pursued Ahaziah and wounded him mortally as he took the hill road by Ibleam (v. 27). Ahaziah was evidently making for Samaria by the DOTHAN valley; if the text of Kings is sound, his charioteer then turned along the plain to MEGIDDO (cf. 2 Chr. 22:9). Jehu, in returning to Jezreel, came face to face with Jezebel, who tried to reassert her authority from the vantage point of an upper window; but her courtiers were not prepared to stand against the new master, and on his orders two or three of them seized Jezebel and hurled her down in front of his chariot.

In view of the family loyalty characteristic of Semitic people, Jehu could only secure his hold by extirpating Ahab's family; his problem was to do so and yet avoid the odium of sole responsibility for the blood bath. He wrote to the governors of the royal household at Samaria, offering them the choice of putting up a successor to the throne (and taking the consequences) or pledging their submission with the heads of Jehoram's children and young relatives. They took the latter course, enabling Jehu to point to the evidence and deny responsibility (2 Ki. 10). The number of victims is given as seventy, which may be conventional (G. A. Cooke, *A Text-Book of North-Semitic Inscriptions* [1903], no. 62, pp 171ff, cites a parallel example from Zenjirli in N Syria), but there were enough to make "two heaps" (10:8).

Jehu now moved to Samaria; on the way he met and liquidated a group of forty-two relatives of Ahaziah who, all unsuspecting, were on their way to visit the royal house in Jezreel. Clearly, Ahaziah's body had not yet reached Jerusalem when they left. The rest of the Judean royal family (except JOASH) were then killed by ATHALIAH; so when she died, the Phoenician contamination had been eradicated, whereas the Davidic succession hung by a slender thread.

In Samaria, Jehu completed his purge of the Omride family and partisans. The next objective, to break the grip of Phoenician culture and religion, was gained by stratagem. He announced that he would adopt Baalism with even more fervor than Ahab, proclaiming an assembly in the temple of Baal to celebrate his accession; when the ceremony was fairly under way, he sent in his guards to

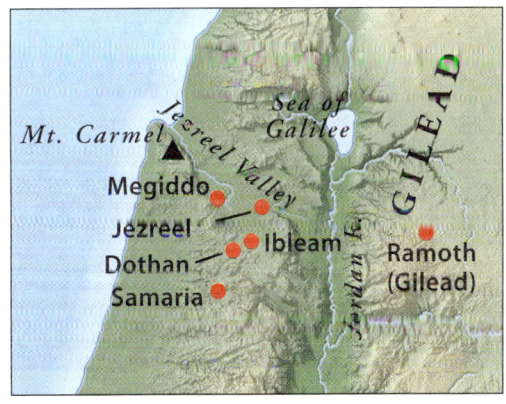

Jehu liberates Israel from Baal worship.

massacre the Baalists. Although some scholars can scarcely believe that Jehu was accepted as a Baalist, there is reason enough for his coup to be seen first as an army revolt or possibly as social in character (see below). Yahwism was thus reestablished as the official religion; but further reform stopped, not touching the cult of Bethel and Dan, nor were the older forms of Baalism abandoned.

III. Jehu's reign. Jehu ruled for twenty-eight years (2 Ki. 10:36) and died a natural death; but his reign was a period of decline. Having broken with the Phoenicians, he found himself paying tribute as they did to Shalmaneser III; this is recorded in the "black obelisk" from Nimrud (where he is called "Yaua son of Omri"). E. Kraeling (*Aram and Israel* [1918], 80) defines Jehu's policy as "continued political alignment" with PHOENICIA, but this appears to go beyond the evidence, and his citation of 2 Ki. 10:31 is hardly relevant.

As other authorities rightly point out, Jehu had administered the most insulting rebuffs to TYRE. Neither is it evident that the Phoenicians paid tribute for any reason but to secure their own safety. Jehu may have been seeking the protection of Assyria against the Arameans; but a discovered copy of Shalmaneser's annals supports the suggestion that the Assyrians reached the sea, not first at Nahr el-Kelb toward Byblos, but at Mount Carmel, after marching through Hauran and northern Israel (A. T. Olmstead, *History of Assyria* [1923], 139). The tribute apparently was not large; probably Shalmaneser was not seeking more than a satisfactory climax to his somewhat inconclusive campaign against HAZAEL.

The threat from the Assyrians faded out as their attention was engaged first by Urartu (see ARMENIA), then by civil war. Hazael, regaining his strength, went on to occupy the country E of Jordan (see 2 Ki. 10:33; there is no need to infer from this text that Jehu first retook the MEDEBA district and then lost it to Hazael). Isaiah and Jeremiah refer to many of the towns there as Moabite (Isa. 15:16; Jer. 48), so MESHA of MOAB had probably settled and held them, though at various times Aramean suzerainty was asserted.

IV. Evaluation. Jehu failed to keep his early promise, both in religious zeal and in leadership (cf. the negative judgment in Hos. 1:4). One can only guess whether he found the problems too big, or succumbed to the deeper temptations of the society that he had set out to purge. Certainly, he was gifted with courage, even audacity, and with a power of command. His name, and his father's, indicate a conservative background, which helps to explain his readiness to do Elisha's bidding. His association with Jehonadab (JONADAB) the RECABITE is unquestionably significant (2 Ki. 10:15, 23). J. Morgenstern (in *HUCA* 15 [1940]. 230–48), who finds the significance sinister, claims that Jehonadab brought Elisha's directions for the religious purge, which he sees as a follow-through from ASA's reforms (fifty-eight years earlier). It is more probable, as W. F. Albright suggests (*The Biblical Period* [1952], 36), that the support of the pastoral Recabite leader stemmed from hatred of civilized society, which had brought poverty to the country and also discontent to the militia, as well as frustration to at least some of the officers. Jezebel miscalculated when she compared Jehu to Zimri; this time, the army did not react.

Socially, the episode may be seen as a revolt against the abuses of wealth. It could not touch the roots of the problem; as prosperity returned, so did the abuse, as observed in the prophecy of Amos in the next century. In divine providence, Israel was saved on the brink of desperate peril and utter rejection of the Lord, and given yet another opportunity of repentance. The purge, as Morgenstern points

The famous Black Obelisk of Shalmaneser III (859–824 B.C.). This register shows King Jehu prostrate as he brings tribute to the Assyrian king.

out, seriously weakened the upper class and therefore the army. This, however, only partly explains the failure to withstand Hazael; the stories of Elisha record dramatic reversals of position in wars between BEN HADAD and Jehoram. The apparent lethargy of Jehu's reign is still an enigma. (See L. M. W. Deal, *The Deuteronomist's Prophetic Narrative: Control of Approval and Disapproval in the Story of Jehu (2 Kings 9 and 10)* [2007].) J. LILLEY

Jehubbah ji-hub´uh. KJV, RSV form of HUBBAH.

Jehucal ji-hyoo´kuhl (יְהוּכַל H3385, short form יוּכַל H3426, "Yahweh has been [or has proven himself] able, powerful"; cf. JECOLIAH). TNIV Jehukal. Son of Shelemiah; he and a priest were sent by King ZEDEKIAH to JEREMIAH to ask the prophet to pray for him and the people (Jer. 37:3). He was also one of four officials who told the king to kill Jeremiah for predicting the fall of Jerusalem (38:1; KJV and other versions, "Jucal").

Jehud jee´huhd (יְהֻד H3372; in Heb. inscriptions and in Aram., this form corresponds to יְהוּדָה H3373; see JUDAH). One of the towns originally allotted to the tribe of DAN (Josh. 19:45; the Danites were unable to occupy the territory, v. 47). Mentioned between BAALATH and BENE BERAK (19:45), Jehud is identified with modern el-Yahudiyeh, 8.5 mi. ESE of JOPPAH.

Jehudi ji-hyoo´di (יְהוּדִי H3375, "of Judah," "Jewish"). Son of Nethaniah; an officer, probably a scribe, of King JEHOIAKIM who was sent to BARUCH so that the latter might read the prophecies of Jeremiah to the princes of Judah, and who himself afterward read them to the king (Jer. 36:14, 21, 23). His great-grandfather's name is given as CUSHI. The tracing of Jehudi's lineage to the third generation suggests the importance of his family and thus the significance of his task. Some argue that the name Cushi indicates a Cushite (i.e., Ethiopian) origin and that therefore Jehudi was a naturalized Judean. Because an extended genealogy in this context is unusual, various scholars emend the text from "Jehudi son of Nethaniah, the son of Shelemiah, the son of Cushi" to "Jehudi son of Methaniah and Shelemiah son of Cushi."

Jehudijah jee´huh-di´juh. KJV rendering of *yěhudiyyâ* (fem. of *yěhudi* H3374, "Judean, Judahite") with reference to a wife of MERED (1 Chr. 4:18). Modern versions more accurately translate "his Judean wife" (cf. KJV mg., "the Jewess"); the word is probably used to distinguish the woman from BITHIAH, an Egyptian also mentioned in this verse.

Jehuel ji-hyoo´uhl. Alternate form of JEHIEL (2 Chr. 29:14 NRSV).

Jehukal ji-hyoo´kuhl. TNIV form of JEHUCAL.

Jehush. See JEUSH #3.

Jeiel ji-i´uhl (יְעִיאֵל H3599, variant יְעוּאֵל H3590, possibly "God is strong" or "God cures"; see also JEUEL). (1) A clan chief from the tribe of REUBEN (1 Chr. 5:7). His genealogical connection as well as the period in which he lived are unclear.

(2) Descendant of BENJAMIN, "father" (i.e., founder or leader) of GIBEON, and ancestor of King SAUL (1 Chr. 9:35 [*Ketib*, "Jeuel"]; the name is missing in 8:29 MT, but NIV and NRSV insert it on the basis of some Gk. MSS). Many identify Jeiel with ABIEL.

(3) A Levite in the time of DAVID appointed among others to play the lyre (NRSV, harp) as a part of the ministrations before the ARK OF THE COVENANT (1 Chr. 15:18, 21; 16:5; the latter passage mentions Jeiel twice, but the first occurrence should probably be emended to JAAZIEL).

(4) Son of Hotham the Aroerite (see AROER); he and his brother Shama are included among DAVID's mighty warriors (1 Chr. 11:44 [*Ketib*, "Jeuel"]).

(5) Son of Mattaniah, descendant of LEVI through ASAPH, and ancestor of a certain JAHAZIEL who prophesied in aid of King JEHOSHAPHAT just before the famous victory of BERACAH (2 Chr. 20:14).

(6) An official who held the office of secretary under King UZZIAH (2 Chr. 26:11 [*Ketib*, "Jeuel"]).

(7) A Levite, descendant of ELIZAPHAN, who served during the reign of HEZEKIAH (2 Chr. 29:13; NRSV, "Jeuel," following the *Ketib*).

(8) A leader of the Levites in the reign of JOSIAH who gave liberally toward the sacrifices (2 Chr. 35:9; called "Ochiel" in 1 Esd. 1:9).

(9) One of the descendants of Nebo who agreed to put away their foreign wives (Ezra 10:43).

(10) One of the descendants of Adonikam who returned with Ezra from Babylon (Ezra 8:13 KJV [most other versions have "Jeuel," following the Bomberg ed. of the Hebrew text]; the parallel in 1 Esd. 8:39 has "Jeuel" [KJV, "Jewel"]).

R. D. Culver

Jekabzeel ji-kab´zee-uhl. Alternate form of Kabzeel.

Jekameam jek´uh-mee´uhm (יָקְמְעָם H3694, possibly "the Kinsman [i.e., ancestral god] establishes [or takes a stand]"). Son of Hebron, grandson of Kohath, and great-grandson of Levi (1 Chr. 23:19; 24:23).

Jekamiah jek´uh-mi´uh (יְקַמְיָה H3693, "Yahweh establishes [or takes a stand]"; see Jakim). **(1)** Son of Shallum and descendant of Judah through Jerahmeel (1 Chr. 2:41).

(2) Son of Jehoiachin, last king of Judah (1 Chr. 3:18; KJV "Jecamiah"); he was apparently born after the royal family was led away into exile in Babylon.

Jekoliah jek´uh-li´uh. TNIV form of Jecoliah.

Jekuthiel ji-kyoo´thee-uhl (יְקוּתִיאֵל H3688, "God nourishes"). Son of Mered by his Judean wife; included in the genealogy of Judah (1 Chr. 4:18).

Jemima je-mi´muh. KJV form of Jemimah.

Jemimah je-mi´muh (יְמִימָה H3544, possibly "dove"). KJV Jemima. The first daughter of Job born to him after his fortunes were restored (Job 42:14).

Jemnaan jem´nay-uhn. KJV alternate Apoc. form of Jabneel (Jdt. 2:28).

Jemuel jem´yoo-uhl (יְמוּאֵל H3543, derivation uncertain). First son of Simeon and grandson of Jacob (Gen. 46:10; Exod 6:15); called Nemuel in the parallel passages (Num. 26:12; 1 Chr. 4:24).

Jephthae jef´thee. KJV NT form of Jephthah (Heb. 11:32).

Jephthah jef´thuh (יִפְתָּח H3653, "[God] opens [the womb?]" or "[God] frees" [see also Iphtah, Pethahiah]; Ἰεφθάε G2650). A Gileadite warrior who as a judge delivered Israel from the Ammonites (see Ammon), sacrificed his daughter to fulfill his vow to God, and defeated the Ephraimites (Jdg. 11:1—12:7).

I. The Ammonite oppression. The pattern of the episodes in the book of Judges is cyclical. The people of Israel lapsed into idolatry and disobedience of God's commands. God punished them by surrendering them to one of the surrounding nations who oppressed them. In their misery, the Israelites repented of their apostasy and cried out for forgiveness and deliverance. God sent a leader (called a "judge") through whom he gave victory over the enemy oppressor.

The background of the Jephthah story, therefore, is an Israelite lapse followed by oppression from Ammon (Jdg. 10:6–9). The duration of the Ammonite oppression was eighteen years (10:8). It consisted of two phases. First, the Ammonites exerted direct and sustained pressure on the Israelites settled in Gilead to the E of the Jordan, in the land formerly controlled by the two Amorite kings, Og king of Bashan and Sihon king of Heshbon (Deut. 2–3). Second, Ammonite raiding parties crossed over the Jordan to plunder and harass settlements in the territories of Ephraim, Benjamin, and Judah (Jdg. 10:9). This twofold campaign caused intense suffering and misery among the Israelites, who confessed they had forsaken Yahweh to serve the local Baals (10:10, 15) and removed the idols of foreign gods from their midst to show their sincere determination to return to the God of their fathers (10:16).

II. Jephthah the judge. Jephthah was the son of a man named Gilead. Some scholars have supposed that the real name of his father was unknown, so he was reputed to be the son of an eponymous hero who had given his name to the territory of Gilead. But since the term gil'ad occurs as the name of an ordinary citizen in the tablets from Ugarit (c. 1250 B.C., only a century before Jephthah), it seems unreasonable to refuse the possibility that a real man named Gilead was Jephthah's father, regardless of the

Looking W up the Jabbok River in the land of Gilead. When the Ammonites oppressed the Israelites living in Gilead, they requested the help of Jephthah.

relationship of that man with the place of the same name. Jephthah's mother was a prostitute (Heb. *zōnâ* H2390; some think she was a temple prostitute, but the word for this is the fem. of *qādēš* H7728). Because he was not born of Gilead's legitimate wife, Jephthah was excluded from his father's inheritance by his half-brothers (Jdg. 11:1–2). To make a living, Jephthah gathered a group of comrades in arms and formed a band of robbers who operated out of Tob, NE of Ramoth Gilead (v. 3).

When the Ammonite crisis arose, the leaders or elders of Gilead traveled to the land of Tob to secure the services of the robber baron against the Ammonites. The elders offered to make him their temporary commander against the Ammonites and, following the successful defeat of the enemy, their permanent chieftain (Heb. *rōʾš* H8031, "head"). The contract was solemnly entered at Mizpah, accompanied by the exchange of oaths (Jdg. 11:4–11). The term "judge" was employed by neither of the two parties. It was applied to him in retrospect by the inspired author-editor of Judges, who saw Jephthah as a member of the larger group of "judges" whose stories are told in this book. See JUDGES, PERIOD OF.

III. Jephthah defeats the Ammonites.

In Jdg. 11:12–28 is recorded an exchange of indictments between Jephthah and the Ammonite chief much in the spirit of the charges and countercharges exchanged before battle by later kings (ABIJAH and JEROBOAM in 2 Chr. 13:2–20; AMAZIAH and Jehoash [JOASH] in 2 Ki. 14:8–10 and 2 Chr. 25:17; cf. also the exchange of challenges before battle in 1 Sam. 17:41–47). Some scholars insist that this is unhistorical and the adornment of a Deuteronomic editor (see DEUTERONOMISTIC HISTORY), but such indictments were exchanged through envoys before most battles in the ANE (cf. many examples in the Annals of the HITTITE King Mursili II). Indeed, even in modern times a nation is not likely to go to war before first attempting to seek redress of wrongs through diplomatic channels.

Other scholars consider this section (Jdg. 11:12–28) irrelevant to the Jephthah story, since it deals with Israel's seizure of the land from the Amorites and the Moabites, not the Ammonites. They also point to Jephthah's identification of his enemy's god as CHEMOSH (11:24), who was the national god of MOAB, whereas Ammon's god was MILCOM. But Jephthah recounted the story of the Israelite conquest, singling out Moab and the Amorites, because the Ammonites had accused Israel of taking *their* land when they took the territory of Gilead. Jephthah's reply was to point out that Israel took it from the Amorites (Og and Sihon), and not from either Ammon or Moab. His second argument was that a people should keep what its god gives to it. The mention of Chemosh may be explicable in that Ammonites and Moabites venerated one another's gods, as was often the practice in polytheistic societies.

When negotiation failed (Jdg. 11:28), the case was submitted to a trial by battle. God would decide the case by granting victory to the party in the right (11:27). Jephthah apparently did not feel sufficiently secure in the knowledge of the justness of his people's cause. He made a vow that, if Yahweh would grant him victory over the Ammonites, he would make a human sacrifice to God of whoever came forth from the doors of his house to meet him (11:31). Because of Jephthah's consternation (11:35) when his daughter came forth to meet him, some have supposed that he anticipated an animal. But an ordinary sacrificial animal (ox, sheep, goat) would hardly come forth to meet him from his own house. A pet dog would hardly have been an acceptable sacrifice to any god. The entire context rather suggests that he contemplated human sacrifice from the beginning. The battle took place near Mizpah of Gilead and was a total victory for Jephthah (11:32–33).

IV. Jephthah sacrifices his daughter. The daughter who came to meet Jephthah on his return (cf. Miriam in Exod. 15:20–21 and the women in 1 Sam. 18:6–7) was his only child (Jdg. 11:34). Perhaps he had hoped that a slave would greet him. But despite his grief (11:35), he was determined to keep his promise to God, perhaps still hoping that God would spare the child at the last moment, as with Abraham (Gen. 22). The girl (like Isaac in Gen. 22) was calm and full of faith (Jdg. 11:36), only asking that she be permitted a final farewell to life with her friends (11:37). And thus was born the custom in Israel of an annual pilgrimage of Israelite girls to lament the daughter of Jephthah for four days (11:39–40; cf. 21:19–20 for another such annual convocation of virgins). Some scholars believe that the annual four-day lamentation for Jephthah's daughter masks a heathen rite in which women wept for the vegetation god Tammuz (cf. Ezek. 8:14) or his Canaanite counterpart Baal, fearing the perpetual "virginity" (i.e., barrenness) of "Mother Earth." Because the season of the year of this four-day ritual is not given here, this conjecture cannot be verified. (See B. Miller, *Tell It on the Mountain: The Daughter of Jephthah in Judges 11* [2005].)

V. Jephthah and the Ephraimites. The Ammonites during their period of harassment had raided the territory of Ephraim to the W of Jordan (Jdg. 10:9). Jephthah had not recruited here (12:1; cf. 11:29), apparently feeling more secure with troops from his own country, perhaps many of them members of his band. Indeed Jephthah says that he *did* call upon Ephraimites (12:2), although stressing at the same time that the feud with the Ammonites was his and his people's. The entire provocation may have grown out of a long-standing hostility felt by the Ephraimites W of Jordan and the Gileadites to the E, the former sarcastically labeling the latter as "renegades from Ephraim and Manasseh" (12:4). The fighting broke out to the E of Jordan and soon went badly for the Ephraimites. When many attempted to flee across the Jordan to safety they were put to a linguistic test by the Gileadite guards at the fording places. Since the two dialects of Hebrew treated the initial (sibilant) consonant in the word *šibbōlet* H0072 differently, it was a simple matter for the Gileadite guards to detect Ephraimites. Forty-two thousand of them failed the test and were slain (12:5–6; see J. A. Emerton in *Melanges*

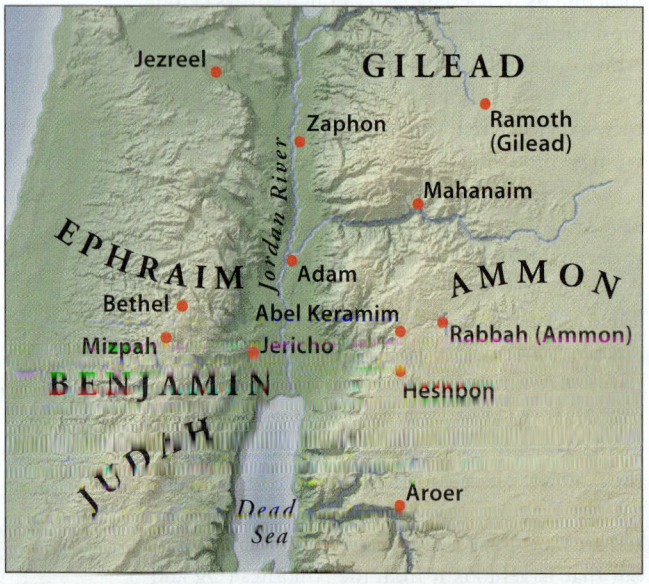

Locations in the story of Jephthah.

bibliques et orientaux en l'honneur de M. Mathias Delcore, ed. A. Caquot et al. [1985], 149–57).

Jephthah emerges from these chapters as a man of faith (Heb. 11:32) who overcame the disadvantages of his disreputable birth, was chosen by God and his people in their hour of need, led God's people to victory over the Ammonites (q.v.), and secured them against further threat from that quarter until the days of Saul. He was firm with himself, refusing to hold back his only child from God. As such he was long remembered in Israel (1 Sam. 12:11) and in the early Christian communities (Heb. 11:32). When judged by the standards of the Christian community today, Jephthah may appear crude, impulsive, and bloodthirsty. But the Spirit of God saw fit to use him (Jdg. 11:29), and the Word of God honors him. (See JUDGES, BOOK OF, and the commentaries listed there.) H. A. HOFFNER, JR.

Jephunneh ji-fuhn´uh (יְפֻנֶּה *H3648*, possibly "[God] turns [*i.e.*, becomes reconciled]"). **(1)** A Kenizzite (see KENAZ), descendant of JUDAH; always referred to as the father of CALEB (Num. 13:6; 32:12; et al.).

(2) Son of JETHER (1 Chr. 7:38), listed among the "heads of families, choice men, brave warriors and outstanding leaders" of the tribe of ASHER (v. 40).

Jerah jihr´uh (יֶרַח *H3733*, "month," possibly a reference to the S Arabian moon god, cf. J. A. Montgomery, *Arabia and the Bible* [1934], 40 n. 10). Son of JOKTAN, grandson of EBER, and descendant of SHEM (Gen. 10:26; 1 Chr. 1:20). Some believe the name Jerah is reflected in Arabic *Warāḫ*, the designation of a region in S ARABIA (cf. *ABD*, 3:683).

Jerahmeel ji-rah´mee-uhl (יְרַחְמְאֵל *H3737*, "God has compassion"; gentilic יְרַחְמְאֵלִי *H3738*, "Jerahmeelite"; see JEREMIEL). **(1)** Firstborn son of HEZRON, grandson of PEREZ, and great-grandson of JUDAH (1 Chr. 2:9). His brothers were RAM and CALEB, although the identity of the latter is disputed. Jerahmeel had two wives and six sons (2:25–26), and his many descendants are given prominence in this genealogy (2:27–41), suggesting that his clan played a significant role in the history of the tribe of Judah. Because the Jerahmeelites, who lived in the NEGEV, are mentioned in connection with the KENITES (1 Sam. 27:10; 30:29), some scholars argue that the clan had non-Israelite origins and that the Chronicler's genealogy is a means of legitimating the status of its families during the postexilic period (cf. *ABD*, 3:683).

(2) Son of Kish (not the father of King SAUL) and descendant of LEVI through MERARI; he was among the first Levites to serve in the permanent sanctuary established under DAVID (1 Chr. 24:29). He apparently married a daughter of Kish's brother ELEAZAR, who had no sons (cf. 23:21–22). A central sanctuary, successor to David's, was being fitted and staffed when 1 Chronicles was written, which explains the emphasis on Levite genealogies.

(3) A royal official (the apparent meaning of the designation "a son of the king") who, with two others, was deputized by King JEHOIAKIM to arrest JEREMIAH and his assistant, BARUCH; the effort ended in failure because "the LORD had hidden them" (Jer. 36:26; the KJV understands the Heb. word for "the king" as a proper name and translates "the son of Hammelech"; cf. also 38:6 and see HAMMELECH). The same individual is apparently referred to in a 7th-cent. seal that bears the inscription, "Belonging to Jerahmeel, the king's son" (see N. Avigad in *BA* 42 [1979]: 114–18).

R. D. CULVER

Jerechus jer´uh-kuhs (Ιερεχους). Ancestor (or place of origin) of a family that returned from the EXILE (1 Esd. 5:22 [RSV, "Jericho"]; the parallel passage has JERICHO, Ezra 2:34).

Jered jihr´id (יֶרֶד *H3719*, derivation disputed; cf. JARED) **(1)** Son of MERED (by the latter's Judahite wife), "father" (i.e., founder) of GEDOR, and descendant of JUDAH, although his precise genealogical connection is unclear (1 Chr. 4:18). Apparently, the town of Gedor was founded by both Jered and PENUEL (v. 4).

(2) KJV alternate form of JARED (1 Chr. 1:2).

Jeremai jer´uh-mi (יְרֵמַי *H3757*, possibly short form of JEREMIAH or JEREMOTH). One of the descendants of Hashum who agreed to put away their foreign wives (Ezra 10:33; 1 Esd. 9:34 [KJV, "Jeremias"]).

JEREMIAH

Jeremiah jer´uh-mi´uh יִרְמְיָהוּ H3759, short form יִרְמְיָה H3758, derivation uncertain, possibly "Yahweh loosens [the womb?]" or "Yahweh raises up"; Ἰερεμίας G2635). KJV NT Jeremias (Matt. 16:14) and Jeremy (2:17; 27:9). **(1)** Son of Hilkiah; a prophet in the southern kingdom (Judah) during the last forty years of its existence (627–586 B.C.). He lived through the period of the disintegration of the kingdom, witnessed the destruction of Jerusalem and the temple, and spent the remaining years of his life in Egypt. See JEREMIAH, BOOK OF.

(2) One of the ambidextrous Benjamite warriors who joined DAVID while he was in exile from SAUL at the Philistine city of ZIKLAG (1 Chr. 12:4; cf. v. 2).

(3–4) Two Gadite warriors who joined David at Ziklag (1 Chr. 10, 13); these Gadites are described as "brave warriors, ready for battle and able to handle the shield and spear. Their faces were the faces of lions, and they were as swift as gazelles in the mountains" (v. 8).

(5) A clan chief of the half-tribe of MANASSEH; he and others are described as "brave warriors, famous men, and heads of their families" (1 Chr. 5:24). Because of their unfaithfulness, however, they and their families were taken captive by the Assyrians (vv. 25–26).

(6) Father of Hamutal, who was the mother of Kings JEHOAHAZ and ZEDEKIAH (2 Ki. 23:31; 24:18; Jer. 52:1) and thus the wife of King JOSIAH. This Jeremiah is identified as being from LIBNAH.

(7) Son of Habazziniah and father of Jaazaniah; the latter was a leader of the RECABITES, whose loyalty to their ancestral precepts the prophet Jeremiah used as a lesson to his own countrymen (Jer. 35:3).

(8) A priest who returned from the EXILE (Neh. 12:1, 12). He is probably the same who signed the covenant with NEHEMIAH (10:2), while the Jeremiah who took part in one of the choirs at the dedication of the wall may be a different individual (12:34).

Jeremiah, Additions to. See BARUCH, BOOK OF; JEREMIAH, EPISTLE OF.

Jeremiah, Book of. The second book among the Major Prophets.

  I. Jeremian times
    A. Chronology
    B. Political and religious conditions
 II. Biography of Jeremiah
    A. During Josiah's reign
    B. Under Jehoiakim's rule
    C. During Zedekiah's reign
    D. Last days in Egypt
III. Authorship and text
IV. Archaeological light on Jeremiah
 V. Outline of contents
VI. The message and ministry of Jeremiah
    A. The prophet and his people
    B. The prophet and the leaders
    C. Restoration prospects
    D. Disintegration of the kingdom
    E. Jeremiah's post-Jerusalem activity
    F. Foreign nations and cities in prophecy
    G. Appendix

I. Jeremian times

A. Chronology

686	Manasseh assumes sole kingship
648	Birth of Josiah
642	Amon succeeds Manasseh as king
640	Josiah succeeds Amon
633	Josiah seeks after God (2 Chr. 34:3)
	Ashurbanipal king of Assyria dies
	Cyaxares becomes king of Media
628	Josiah begins reforms
627	Jeremiah called to be a prophet
626	Nabopolassar becomes king of Babylonia
621	book of the law found in the temple
612	Nineveh destroyed
609	Josiah slain at Megiddo
	Jehoahaz rules three months
	Jehoiakim enthroned in Jerusalem
605	Babylonia defeats Egypt at Carchemish
	Hostages and vessels taken to Babylon
	Nebuchadnezzar becomes king of Babylon
604	Nebuchadnezzar returns to Palestine to receive tribute

> 601—Nebuchadnezzar defeated near Egypt
> 598—Jehoiakim's reign ends
> > Jehoiachin rules 9 Dec 598 to 16 March 597
> 597—Jehoiachin deported 22 April
> > Zedekiah becomes king in Judah
> 588—Siege of Jerusalem begins 15 January
> 587—Jeremiah imprisoned (Jer. 32:1–2)
> 586—July 18, Zedekiah flees (Jer. 39:4)
> > Aug. 14, destruction begins (2 Ki. 25:8–10)
> > Oct. 7, Gedaliah slain, Jews migrate to Egypt

B. Political and religious conditions. About the mid-7th cent., when Jeremiah was born, the kingdom of Judah was at a very low point religiously as well as politically. Following the era of HEZEKIAH's extensive religious reformation and successful resistance of Assyrian aggression, Judah was plunged into ominous reverses when MANASSEH became sole ruler after Hezekiah's death in 686 B.C.

Religiously, Manasseh plunged Judah into gross idolatry similar to that which had prevailed in the northern kingdom under AHAB and JEZEBEL. Altars to BAAL were erected, and Asherim were built (see ASHERAH). MOLECH, the Ammonite deity, was acknowledged by the sacrificing of children in the Valley of HINNOM near Jerusalem. Worship of stars and planets was instituted. Official approval was given to ASTROLOGY, DIVINATION, and occultism. The TEMPLE itself was desecrated with graven images of Asherah, the wife of Baal. God was openly defied at altars in the court of the temple, where the host of heaven was worshiped (cf. Jer. 19:13).

Innocent blood was shed under the rule of Manasseh. It is likely many prophets and pious leaders who raised their voices in protest were silenced by death (2 Ki. 21:16). The tradition that charges Manasseh with the martyrdom of ISAIAH may be correct, since this prophet is mentioned no more after the death of Hezekiah. If the report of SENNACHERIB's death is acknowledged in Isa. 37:38, then Isaiah lived at least until 681/80 B.C. With the martyrdom of the righteous God-fearing people, it is quite likely that the copies of the law were neglected and possibly destroyed. The religious feasts and seasons must have been curtailed, and it is doubtful that the law was ever publicly read to the people during the reign of Manasseh.

Politically, ASSYRIA extended its domination of the FERTILE CRESCENT and reached its pinnacle of wealth and prestige under ESARHADDON (681–668 B.C.) and ASHURBANIPAL (668–633). Esarhaddon rebuilt the city of BABYLON (which his father had destroyed in 689), resubjugated TYRE in 678, occupied MEMPHIS in 673, and captured TIRHAKAH. Among the twenty-two kings he brought from the HITTITE country on a compulsory visit to NINEVEH in 678, Esarhaddon lists Manasseh. By the year 663 the city of THEBES was sacked by the Assyrians, but the little kingdom of Judah continued without destruction under the shadows of the Assyrian advance. It may have been that Manasseh subsequently involved Judah in the rebellion of the Moabites and Edomites against Assyria. Afterwards he was taken as a prisoner to Babylon (2 Chr. 33:10–13) and then released after his repentance. During the last half of the 7th cent., Assyria was weakened by rebellions throughout the kingdom, especially in Babylon. After the death of Ashurbanipal in 633, the kingdom declined rapidly and terminated with the destruction of Nineveh by the coalition of the Medes under Cyaxares and the Babylonians under Nabopolassar in 612.

In the course of these developments throughout the Fertile Crescent, the little kingdom of Judah had three decades of relative freedom, c. 640–610 B.C. When Manasseh died in 642, he was succeeded by AMON, who was slain by his servants after a two-year reign. This left the throne to eight-year-old JOSIAH. As the young king grew to manhood and assumed leadership, he had the opportunity to develop religious and political policies without interference from the surrounding nations, especially Assyria, which had exerted a continual influence upon Judah for over a century.

Josiah reacted against the apostate conditions that had prevailed under his predecessors. At the age of sixteen, or about 632 B.C., he began to seek after God, turning away from the idolatry that surrounded him. In 621, while the temple was being repaired, the "Book of the Law" was found. Greatly concerned, Josiah sponsored an observance of the PASSOVER that was unsurpassed in the history of Judah. Drastic measures were taken to rid the land of idolatry. Pagan practices were abolished, Asherim were demolished, chambers of cult PROSTITUTION were renovated, horses dedicated to the sun and chariots in the temple entrance were destroyed by fire. Manasseh's altars were destroyed and high places remaining from the Solomonic times were demolished and desecrated with dead men's bones. Priests appointed by former kings but committed to idolatry were removed from office. This terminated the burning of incense to Baal, the sun, moon, and stars. Josiah, however, made material provision for the support of these men who could no longer serve as priests.

The political leaders associated with Josiah may have had aspirations of gaining control of the area that formerly constituted the northern kingdom to re-establish the Solomonic kingdom boundaries. How far these hopes were realized is not delineated in the scriptural accounts, but the religious reformation did extend into the northern tribes. People from numerous cities responded to invitations extended by Josiah and joined in the festivities in Jerusalem as well as the reformation program throughout the land.

The era of religious and political optimism was suddenly terminated in 609 B.C. when Josiah was fatally wounded in his attempt to stop NECO of Egypt at MEGIDDO. After three months, Neco returned from his military expedition to the EUPHRATES, where he temporarily stopped the Babylonians and took JEHOAHAZ captive, enthroning JEHOIAKIM in Jerusalem as king of Judah. Since Josiah as king had prompted the religious reformation, it is likely that many leaders in Judah supported him primarily for the sake of expediency. Under Jehoiakim, the God-fearing people and prophets such as Jeremiah faced opposition repeatedly and even martyrdom.

Politically, the fortunes of Judah waned rapidly. In 605 B.C. the Babylonians defeated the Egyptians at CARCHEMISH so that they withdrew to the borders of Egypt. Babylonian domination of Palestine included Judah so that in 605 Jehoiakim yielded tribute and royal hostages (among whom was DANIEL) to NEBUCHADNEZZAR. In 601 the Babylonian advance was temporarily stopped on the borders of Egypt, which may have encouraged Jehoiakim to resist the Babylonians in 598. Before the latter came to Jerusalem, Jehoiakim likely was killed and was succeeded on the throne by his son JEHOIACHIN, who ruled only three months. The Babylonian armies arrived in Jerusalem by the spring of 597, taking the king with at least 10,000 captives to Babylonian exile. ZEDEKIAH, another son of Josiah, was left to rule in Jerusalem, but his rebellion ultimately resulted in the destruction of Jerusalem and the temple in 586. This event represented the most extensive and severe judgment upon the nation of Israel in OT times. With the people in exile, the Israelites were regarded as a byword among the nations from the human perspective.

II. Biography of Jeremiah. Jeremiah was born into the priestly family of HILKIAH, from ANATHOTH (this Hilkiah is not to be confused with the high priest in Jerusalem associated with the discovery of the law in the temple, 2 Ki. 22:4–11). The city of Anathoth, though near Jerusalem, was within the borders of the tribe of BENJAMIN and assigned to the Levites (Josh. 21:18). ABIATHAR, who served as priest under DAVID, resided in Anathoth (1 Ki. 2:26). It is quite reasonable to conclude that Jeremiah was from the Abiathar lineage of priests and not from the Zadokite line that had been instituted under Solomon in Jerusalem (see ZADOK). The birth of Jeremiah (c. 650 B.C.) would have been overshadowed by the birth of Josiah in the royal family. Living only about 2.5 mi. from Jerusalem, Jeremiah may have followed with keen interest the coronation and reign of Josiah, who grew to young manhood about the same time.

A. During Josiah's reign. Jeremiah was called to the prophetic ministry in 627 B.C. (Jer. 1:1–2) when he was probably in his early twenties. Although the account of his call is brief, Jeremiah was divinely informed that he had been created, sanctified, and ordained to be a prophet (1:4–10). His ministry was not to be limited to his own people, but he was commissioned to be a prophet to the nations. Explicit was God's message to Jeremiah

JEREMIAH, BOOK OF

The modern village of Anathoth marks the site of Jeremiah's hometown. (View to the S.)

that he was to be a spokesman who would convey God's message. In addition to being specifically created and equipped as God's messenger, Jeremiah was also assured of divine deliverance.

As a representative of God, Jeremiah was assured that he would not lose face. The fulfillment of his message was as certain as the annual budding of the almond tree that was the harbinger of spring in Palestine. That this message contained divine judgment upon Jerusalem and that the invader of Judah would come from the N was also explicitly made plain to Jeremiah in his call (Jer. 1:11–19). During the first eighteen years of Jeremiah's ministry, when Josiah was providing leadership in religious reformation, it may not have seemed reasonable to Jeremiah that Jerusalem and the temple would actually be destroyed. Furthermore, the Assyrian power, which for over a century had dominated the Fertile Crescent, had been declining since 633 B.C. and capitulated with the fall of Nineveh in 612.

In his call to service Jeremiah was also prepared for the fact that he would need to withstand much opposition. He was warned that the kings of Judah, the princes, the priests, and the common people would be against him as the Lord's messenger. Not only was he promised divine protection, but he was assured that God would make him like a fortified city to stand successfully against them. This divine assurance must have taken on realistic significance during the period from 609 to 586 B.C., when he was subjected to persecution and suffering as others were martyred or exiled.

The relationship between Jeremiah and King Josiah is almost passed over in silence in the scriptural accounts. The only mention of Jeremiah in the accounts of the books of Kings and Chronicles is the fact that Jeremiah lamented the death of Josiah (2 Chr. 35:25). In the book of Jeremiah, the only direct references to Josiah are in Jer. 1:2, where Jeremiah dates his call in Josiah's thirteenth year; in 3:6, where he indicates that he was speaking in the days of Josiah; and in 25:1–3, where he points out that in the fourth year of Jehoiakim he had been active for twenty-three years having begun his ministry in the days of Josiah.

Since Jeremiah and Josiah were both God-fearing men and genuinely concerned with the reformation of idolatrous Judah, it is generally recognized that these two leaders must have worked in close harmony. The major part of Jer. 1–18 is usually regarded as representing the preaching of Jeremiah during the reign of Josiah. Having the favor of the king, it was possible for Jeremiah to delineate the sins and the apostasy of the people without being molested. Illustrative of this probability is the "temple speech" (ch. 7). Although there are many similarities between chs. 7 and 26, the former likely was given during Josiah's reign when no one dared to oppose the prophet openly. The latter is definitely dated during Jehoiakim's reign when the people and religious leaders were keenly aware of the fact that the king supported them in their opposition to Jeremiah.

Jeremiah's preaching undoubtedly aided Josiah in his reform program. Under the leadership of this young king, optimism may have prevailed politically as well as religiously. Nationally and internationally, conditions seemed to be favorable, so that both Josiah and Jeremiah may have enjoyed popular support with a minimum of opposition to their efforts. The fall of Nineveh in 612 B.C. may have intensified the hopes for the kingdom of Judah.

B. Under Jehoiakim's rule. For Jeremiah, the sudden and unexpected death of Josiah in 609 B.C. must have been one of the crucial periods in his entire ministry. Jeremiah lamented the king's death. The tenuous three months' reign of Jehoahaz ended with his captivity in Egypt. Jehoiakim, enthroned by King Neco of Egypt, was not favorably disposed toward Jeremiah nor his message. After this crisis, the disintegration of the kingdom of Judah took its course as the political and religious optimism faded away, leading to the termination of the kingdom of Judah and the destruction of Jerusalem in 586.

Not too long after Josiah's death, Jeremiah may have delivered his message against the wicked leadership exhibited by the kings of Judah (Jer. 22–23). He specifically admonished the people not to weep for the "dead one," which may be a reference to Josiah. He also predicted that Jehoahaz would not return from Egyptian exile but would die in Egypt. Boldly he denounced the wickedness and injustice prevailing under Jehoiakim. The latter would be given the burial of a donkey and the people would not lament his death. Jehoiachin, heir to the Davidic throne, would be taken into Babylonian exile without royal succession in the kingdom of Judah.

Numerous experiences of Jeremiah that occurred are identified in his book. In the beginning of his reign when he delivered the "temple speech," the public opposition led by the priests and prophets developed to the point of threatening Jeremiah's life. Through the influence of Ahikam and some of the elders, Jeremiah's life was saved. Their defense brief for the prophet was the historic precedent in the days of Hezekiah, when Micah also had announced the destruction of Jerusalem but was not executed by the king. The attitude of Jehoiakim and the military leaders was apparent in the execution of the prophet Uriah, who proclaimed the same message of judgment that was given by Jeremiah. Under the godless rule of Jehoiakim it became increasingly difficult for Jeremiah to continue an effective ministry. In all likelihood, many of the religious leaders who had before cooperated with Josiah for the sake of expediency openly took issue with Jeremiah and influenced the populace to ignore God's message of warning and reverted to idolatry.

The fourth year of Jehoiakim was a crucial and eventful year in the ministry of Jeremiah. This was the year in which Nebuchadnezzar defeated the Egyptians in the Battle of Carchemish in June of 605. By September, Nebuchadnezzar was enthroned as the king of Babylonia. During these crucial months the Babylonians exacted royal hostages from Jerusalem as a token of Jehoiakim's subservience to Nebuchadnezzar. During this fourth year of Jehoiakim, Jeremiah reminded the citizens and leaders of Israel that he had warned them for twenty-three years. Since they had not responded to God's message, the kingdom of Judah as well as the surrounding nations would be devastated by the Babylonians (Jer. 25:1–38). The enemy from the N (1:14) was now identified as Nebuchadnezzar, who was God's servant to bring judgment upon God's chosen people in Jerusalem. This cup of God's fury was for Judah and all the nations mentioned in Jeremiah's message. The fourth year marked the beginning of the end for the kingdom of Judah. The captivity, according to Jeremiah's prediction, would last seventy years. This warning and prediction, given during the year that the Judeans took into Babylonian exile began, offered little hope for the immediate future, but with it came the assurance that there would be a restoration after seventy years.

During this crucial year Jeremiah was also instructed to provide a written record of his messages.

The purpose was to make available a copy for the people to read, with the hope that the citizens of Judah would be informed about God's plan and given the opportunity to repent. BARUCH served as Jeremiah's secretary (Jer. 36:1–8), and then was instructed to read these messages to the people who were assembled in the temple for the annual day of fasting.

During the fifth year of Jehoiakim, when Baruch was reading publicly from Jeremiah's scroll, some of the political leaders who heard Jeremiah's message advised Baruch and Jeremiah to hide while they made known to the king the content of the message (Jer. 36:9–19). King Jehoiakim called for the scroll, listened to the contents, and then supervised the burning of the scroll, page after page in spite of the pleas of some of his associates and servants. Jehoiakim not only ignored the solemn message of warning by the prophet but ordered the arrest of Jeremiah and Baruch, who fortunately could not be located at that particular time (36:20–26).

Once more Jeremiah was divinely commissioned to replace the scroll that the king had destroyed. Among the additional messages of Jeremiah was the specific prediction that Babylonian occupation was certain and that Jehoiakim's body would be exposed to the heat by day and the frost by night (Jer. 36:27–32). The reference to frost indicated the time of year when the king's death would occur. War conditions would be such that this king, who had defied God's message by burning the prophet's scroll, would not be given a royal burial. Little seems to be known about the remaining years of Jeremiah's ministry under Jehoiakim.

C. During Zedekiah's reign.

Jeremiah apparently was less restricted in his ministry after the second Babylonian captivity, 597 B.C. Jehoiakim's policy and the Babylonian advance had resulted in Jehoiakim's death in 598. When Jehoiachin (after a three month reign) and 10,000 Jews were exiled, Jeremiah remained in Jerusalem and continued his ministry to the poorer class of people, who were left under the rule of Zedekiah.

Soon after this deportation, Jeremiah proclaimed a message concerning good and bad figs (Jer. 24:1–10). The interpretation was plain. The good figs depicted the people in exile and the bad figs represented those who remained in Jerusalem. Consequently they would also be taken into exile in due time. Jeremiah's prophecy against ELAM is also dated at this time. To the exiles in Babylon, Jeremiah wrote letters advising them to be submissive, and warned them not to listen to the false prophets who

The cracked wall of a cistern. God said through Jeremiah, "My people have committed two sins: They have forsaken me, the spring of living water, and have dug their own cisterns, broken cisterns that cannot hold water" (Jer. 2:13).

predicted a speedy return to Jerusalem (29:1–23). After Shemaiah in Babylon sent instructions back to Jerusalem to have Jeremiah placed in stocks for writing to the exiles, Jeremiah announced God's judgment upon Shemaiah (29:24–32).

In the year 593 Jeremiah addressed a group of ambassadors from surrounding nations who were gathered in Jerusalem. He urged them to be submissive to Babylon, illustrating the power of this nation by placing a wooden yoke about his own neck (Jer. 27:1–22). When HANANIAH, a prophet from Gibeon, publicly broke Jeremiah's yoke and announced that within two years the exiles would return, Jeremiah predicted Hananiah's death within one year (28:1–17). Hananiah died before the year ended.

In spite of Jeremiah's continual advice of submission to Babylon, Zedekiah concurred with the pro-Egyptian leaders in rebelling against the Babylonians (Jer. 34:1–7). By 15 January 588, the latter began a siege of the city of Jerusalem. As Nebuchadnezzar was advancing toward Jerusalem, Zedekiah sent to Jeremiah for advice, hoping a miraculous deliverance might be in the offing (21:1–14). Jeremiah once more pointedly predicted defeat and death, with unconditional surrender as the only way of escape.

During the serious conditions of the siege, Zedekiah secured the cooperation of the people to make a covenant to emancipate the slaves (Jer. 34:8–11). When the siege was temporarily lifted, this covenant was revoked and the servants were enslaved again (34:12–22). While the siege was temporarily lifted, Jeremiah was arrested, beaten, and imprisoned (37:11–21). Zedekiah, however, called for Jeremiah and secretly inquired about God's message. In response to Jeremiah's warning and appeal, Zedekiah did not return the prophet to the prison but assigned him to the court of the guard, with an allowance of bread as long as the supply in Jerusalem lasted. While held in the court of the guard, Jeremiah received an option on the purchase of Hanameel's field in Anathoth. Divinely instructed, Jeremiah secured this piece of property, and with this transaction proclaimed the message that after the Babylonian EXILE the Israelites would be gathered to their own land (32:1–44).

As conditions became more severe, some of the leaders accused Jeremiah of treason and secured the consent of Zedekiah to put Jeremiah into the cistern in the court of the guard. Abandoned and sinking in the mire, Jeremiah was rescued by EBED-MELECH, an Ethiopian EUNUCH (Jer. 38:1–13), and returned to the court of the guard. For this Ebed-Melech was promised safety through the period of Jerusalem's siege and destruction (39:15–18). Zedekiah had one final consultation with Jeremiah (38:14–28). On 18 July 586, Zedekiah escaped as far as Jericho, but there was overtaken by the Babylonians and exiled as Jeremiah had predicted (39:1–10).

D. Last days in Egypt. Jeremiah lived through the destruction of Jerusalem, which began on 14 August 586 B.C. (2 Ki. 25:8; Jer. 52:12). Jeremiah was courteously treated by the Babylonians and entrusted for safety to GEDALIAH, who was appointed as ruler over those who were not taken into exile (39:11–14). About two months later Gedaliah was killed. Shortly after that, Jeremiah was taken by the remnant down to Egypt, even though he patiently advised them to remain in Palestine (42.1–43.7). At TAHPANHES, Jeremiah warned his people in a symbolic message that God would send Nebuchadnezzar into Egypt to execute judgment (43:8–13). In ch. 44, Jeremiah reminded the people that Jerusalem was in ruins and that God's judgment had come upon them because they had ignored the messages of warning delivered through the prophets.

Judah had become a curse and a taunt among the nations because she had provoked God to anger. The people however were not moved by Jeremiah's message and warning even in Egypt after they had seen all these developments take place. They claimed that this evil had come upon them because they ceased to worship the QUEEN OF HEAVEN. Very likely Jeremiah died in Egypt among a people who still were not willing to repent.

III. Authorship and text. Although more is known about Jeremiah and the circumstances concerning the writing of the book bearing his name than about the other books of the OT, numerous questions about its composition remain. It was in the fourth year of Jehoiakim, 605 B.C., that Jeremiah was specifically instructed to commit his messages to writing (Jer. 36:1–8). Baruch was engaged as the prophet's scribe to record that which pertained to Jeremiah's ministry, which had begun in 627. This scroll was burned by King Jehoiakim the next year.

Once more Jeremiah was instructed to write down what had been consumed in the fire. Again it was Baruch who served as scribe. How much was included in the "many similar words" that were added (Jer. 36:32) is difficult to ascertain. Significant also is the fact that in the year 605 Baruch was assured by Jeremiah that his life would be preserved through the perilous years that awaited Judah and Jerusalem as predicted in the prophet's message, which was committed to writing (45:1–5).

The MT and the SEPTUAGINT texts of the book of Jeremiah vary in length and arrangement. The latter is about one-eighth, or approximately 2,700 words, shorter than the MT. Among the DEAD SEA SCROLLS there are some fragments that attest a shorter Hebrew text; some such form may lie behind the Greek version (cf. K. H. Jobes and M. Silva, *Invitation to the Septuagint* [2000], 173–77). Some other fragments among these scrolls, however, reflect the longer Hebrew text.

The order of the material in the SEPTUAGINT differs from the Hebrew (and English), as follows:

LXX	MT
1:1 to 25:12	1:1 to 25:12
25:14–20	49:34–39
26:1–28	ch. 46
ch. 27	ch. 50
ch. 28	ch. 51
ch. 29	ch. 47
ch. 30	ch. 49
ch. 31	ch. 48
chs. 32–51	25:13 to 45:5

Two variations are apparent in this rearrangement. The prophecies concerning foreign nations given in Jer. 46–51 are inserted in the Greek text beginning with 25:14. The order within this series of messages has also been changed. In addition to the differences noted above is the fact that in the Greek text some verses in whole or part are omitted, as well as some longer passages (e.g., 33:14–26; 39:4–13; 51:44b–49a; 52:27b–30. Although some of these minor omissions can be explained as errors in transmission, it is apparent that the LXX reflects a variant edition from the MT.

That Baruch was primarily responsible for writing (recording) Jeremiah's messages is clearly evident in the book itself. After the burning of the first scroll by Jehoiakim in 604, a second edition was again prepared by Baruch. During the next two decades or more that remained of Jeremiah's ministry, Baruch undoubtedly added more messages and recorded the events associated with his master in Jerusalem as well as later in Egypt. One possible explanation of the variance in the two texts is that the MT represents the final edition of this book by Baruch after Jeremiah's death. In this would be reflected Baruch's arrangement and additions. The shorter text—which was subsequently preserved in the Greek version—may have been an earlier form that Baruch later rearranged and edited (cf. Archer, Eissfeldt, and Young).

A number of rationalistic scholars deny considerable portions of the book of Jeremiah both to the prophet himself and to Baruch. Beyond that, some consider the present text to reflect numerous editorial additions subsequent to Jeremian times. The ascription of Jer. 10:1–16 to "Deutero-Isaiah," warning the exilic Jews against idolatry, is based on the theory that denies the unity of the book of ISAIAH. The viewpoint that Jer. 17:19–27 is dependent upon the Sabbath-keeping passages in EZEKIEL, or the priestly code, is based on the theory that document P (see PENTATEUCH) is postexilic. Moreover, chs. 30–31 are assigned to the postexilic era on the assumption of an evolutionary hypothesis concerning the development of the messianic hope, in contrast to the view that such messages were given to the prophets through divine revelation.

Since positive evidence is lacking to the contrary, it is reasonable to ascribe to Baruch the entire book in its written form. Intimately associated with Jeremiah, he faithfully recorded the messages and the events as long as the prophet lived, and then may have completed and arranged the final edition subsequent to Jeremiah's death.

IV. Archaeological light on Jeremiah. The LACHISH letters provided interesting aspects concerning the book of Jeremiah from historical and linguistic perspectives. At the 22-acre site of the ancient city of Lachish (Tell ed-Duweir), located in a strategic valley 25 mi. SW of Jerusalem, an excavation was conducted by J. K. Starkey (1932–38). In a guard room of the outer western gate were found twenty-one letters written on broken pieces of pottery. These OSTRACA date from the year 588 B.C. (cf. *ANET*, 321–22).

Historically, the Lachish letters reflect the wartime conditions that prevailed during these years. Lachish and AZEKAH were the last two cities to be conquered by the Babylonians before the fall of Jerusalem (Jer. 34:7). These letters were written by a military captain named Hoshaiah to his superior, Joash, at Lachish. Although a reference in these letters to "the prophet" may be ambiguous, and other matters may be difficult to interpret, it

JEREMIAH, BOOK OF

Excavated ruins at Elephantine, Egypt, from the time when the Israelites were present. Jeremiah was forced to travel to Egypt shortly after Gedaliah was killed.

is quite apparent that they were written during the siege of Lachish, which fell to the Babylonians in 587. Linguistically, these ostraca, written with carbon ink in the ancient Hebrew script, are even more important. A marked similarity between them and the book of Jeremiah in the area of grammar and style seems to confirm the dating of these letters in the beginning of the 6th cent.

The Babylonian Chronicle provides more extensive information concerning numerous references in Jeremiah's book. In the year 606, Nebuchadnezzar as crown prince commanded the Babylonian army in Assyria, and the following year he defeated Neco II of Egypt at Carchemish and Hamath (cf. Jer. 46:2; 2 Ki. 23:29; 2 Chr. 35:20). He advanced to take the whole land of Hatti, namely Syria and Palestine, and exacted hostages from Jehoiakim, king of Judah. When news reached him about his father's death, Nebuchadnezzar rushed across the desert to be enthroned as king of Babylon on 6 September 605. For three years Jehoiakim remained a vassal of Nebuchadnezzar (Jer. 25:1), but in 601, when the Egyptians defeated the Babylonians, he transferred his loyalty to the former despite the warnings of Jeremiah (27:9–11). In 599/98, Nebuchadnezzar defeated the Arab tribes of KEDAR and the region E of Jordan as Jeremiah had predicted (49:28–33).

When he reached Jerusalem, Jehoiakim had already been killed and was succeeded by Jehoiachin. Jerusalem yielded to the Babylonians not only her king but also 10,000 captives. In 596, Nebuchadnezzar fought against Elam (49:34).

In 587, the Babylonians used RIBLAH as their base of operation to direct another campaign against Jerusalem when Zedekiah rebelled. The siege of Jerusalem was temporarily interrupted when Apries, who succeeded Neco II as king of Egypt, invaded Gaza and Phoenicia (Jer. 47:1). Subsequent to the fall of Jerusalem, Nebuchadnezzar ordered another deportation of Jews to Babylon (52:30) in 582, which was the twenty-third year of his reign.

V. Outline of contents.
  A. Jeremiah's mission and message (Jer. 1:1—18:23)
    1. His divine commission (1:1–19)
    2. The sinfulness of Israel (2:1—3:5)
    3. Impending judgment (3:6—6:30)
    4. The threat of exile (7:1—10:25)
    5. Consequences of the broken covenant (11:1—13:27)
    6. Uselessness of intercessory prayer (14:1—15:21)

    7. Celibacy of Jeremiah (16:1–21)
    8. Faith in man denounced (17:1–27)
    9. Judah must be remolded (18:1–23)
  B. The prophet confronts the leaders (19:1—29:32)
    1. Elders and priests—Jeremiah imprisoned (19:1—20:18)
    2. Advice for Zedekiah (21:1–14)
    3. Kings and false prophets (22:1—24:10)
    4. Cup of wrath for all nations (25:1–38)
    5. Jeremiah spared execution (26:1–24)
    6. Opposition in Jerusalem and Babylon (27:1—29:32)
  C. Restoration prospects (30:1—33:26)
    1. A new covenant (30:1—31:40)
    2. Sign of restoration (32:1–44)
    3. The Davidic covenant (33:1–26)
  D. Disintegration of the kingdom (34:1—39:18)
    1. Example of the Recabites (34:1–22)
    2. Warnings to the people (35:1—36:32)
    3. The fall of Jerusalem (37:1—39:18)
  E. Jeremiah's post-Jerusalem ministry (40:1—45:5)
    1. To the remnant in Palestine (40:1—41:18)
    2. En route to Egypt (42:1—43:7)
    3. To the fugitives in Egypt (43:8—44:30)
    4. The personal promise to Baruch (45:1–5)
  F. Foreign nations and cities in prophecy (46:1—51:64)
    1. Egypt (46:1–28)
    2. Philistia (47:1–7)
    3. Moab (48:1–47)
    4. Ammon (49:1–6)
    5. Edom (49:7–22)
    6. Damascus, Kedar, and Hazor (49:23–33)
    7. Elam (49:34–39)
    8. Babylon (50:1—51:64)
  G. Appendix—conquest and deportation (52:1–34)

VI. The message and ministry of Jeremiah

A. The prophet and his people (Jer 1:1—18:23). To read the messages and experiences of Jeremiah is to get acquainted with this great prophet. He revealed more of his inner feelings and personal reactions toward God and people than did any other prophet in OT times. His deep involvement with his own nation was intensified by the imminence of the terrible judgment of God that was awaiting Jerusalem within his own lifetime. His theology and character emerged in his preaching.

The messages of Jeremiah reflect the response and reaction that the people had toward him and his message. Although he seldom recorded what the people said to him, his message can often be regarded as his part in the dialogue, leaving the reader to fill in the counterpart by the participants. Jeremiah's messages were timely and directly related to the prevailing conditions in the political, social, and religious life of the people. Since the reproof, warnings, and admonitions of Jeremiah were so pointed and incisive, the response often was very intense—at times reaching the stage of violence as conditions permitted.

The content of Jer. 1–18 may well be the summary of his messages and activities during the reign of Josiah. When the book is considered as a whole, it is apparent that the events and messages are not in chronological order (esp. evident beginning with ch. 20). Consequently there may be some passages even in the first eighteen chapters that should possibly be dated later. Since there is no indication of violent opposition erupting in these chapters, it seems probable that they represent the period during Josiah's reign when Jeremiah likely enjoyed the favor of the ruling king. Although there were threats made to Jeremiah's life by the men of Anathoth, it is quite apparent that there was no open or public interference with the prophet's ministry as long as Josiah lived.

Portraying the sinful conditions existing in Judah, Jeremiah pointed out the basic problem—their love and devotion toward God was lacking (Jer. 2:1—3:5). Positively, they had forsaken God, who had redeemed them from Egyptian bondage and entrusted them with the blessings of Canaan. They had ignored the instructions, given them by Moses in Deuteronomy, of exemplifying in their daily lives a wholehearted love for God. Negatively they had turned to idolatry and consequently they were guilty of harlotry. Fear, reverence, respect, and love for God were missing.

Pointing to history, Jeremiah warned his people that the northern kingdom had been taken into captivity because the people had turned to idolatry and were guilty of religious harlotry. God's judgment upon Judah was near at hand. Because they had forsaken God, they would be abandoned by God to exilic conditions to serve strangers in a foreign land. Priests and prophets had practiced deceit and the people had followed their examples. Because of their evil actions calamity would befall them. Like refuse silver, God had rejected them, and time for judgment had come (3:6—6:30).

Jeremiah became explicit in pointing out the social evils and injustice that prevailed, as well as the fact that the temple would be destroyed. The people oppressed the widows, orphans, and strangers, and simultaneously assumed that God's presence was continuing among them in the temple. They evidently reasoned from the correct theological basis that God is powerful enough to save the temple, but were wrong in their assumption that God's presence was limited to the building in Jerusalem. By their sins of murder, adultery, burning incense to Baal, and other idolatrous practices, they had made the temple into a den of robbers. Consequently Jerusalem and the temple would be razed to the ground. Jeremiah warned them that the ruins of SHILOH served as an example of what would happen to Jerusalem (7:1–15).

Jeremiah was warned not to pray for his people who worshiped other gods on the streets of Jerusalem and throughout the cities of Judah. Repeatedly they ignored the prophets. The people assumed that they were wise but at the same time disregarded God's written revelation as given in the law. Prophets and priests alike misinterpreted God's message. Consequently, God's judgment was coming upon them like serpents from whose sting they would not be able to escape (7:16—8:17).

This message so gripped Jeremiah that he was moved to deep compassion for his people (8:18—9:26). Conscious of the fact that it was too late to avert this terrible judgment upon them, Jeremiah was moved to tears. He pondered the rationale for God's judgment. Jeremiah recognized that punishment was due because they had forsaken the law of God and had been disobedient. The time was coming when they would lament greatly because of the devastation, destruction, death, and exile that was imminent. Consequently his ultimate perspective was that man's confidence in his own wisdom, might, and riches were all futile. Ultimate value rests in the knowledge that God is the one who exercises loving-kindness, justice, and righteousness in the earth. Israel was uncircumcised in heart—therefore divine judgment overtook them.

When Jeremiah warned his people not to conform to the pattern of behavior of the heathen nations (Jer. 10:1–5), he pondered the question of who God is. He pointed out that God is the everlasting King who created all things in nature. This God who is the Lord of hosts is the God of Israel. Since Israel had not sought after God, they were to be scattered. Even though Jeremiah knew this, he still appealed to God to save them (10:6–25). Once more God's message comes through explicitly clear. Israel is God's covenant people, but they have broken the COVENANT (11:1–13). Jeremiah was commanded not to pray for them. They had no right to be in God's house because of their wickedness (11:14–17).

When suffering and threats came to Jeremiah personally, his concern for himself emerged in self-pity. The men of Anathoth, his home town, plotted to kill him if he did not stop prophesying in the name of God. Learning of this plot, Jeremiah's reaction was expressed in his imprecatory prayer in which he requested divine vengeance upon his enemies (Jer. 11:18—12:4). Although he was assured that these enemies would be subjected to the exile without a remnant of them remaining, he was troubled by the apparent prosperity of the wicked. For this, however, God's servant was rebuked. Even though he was mistreated by his relatives, he was not to be enticed by them. God had forsaken his people and was abandoning them to the exile. In the near future the entire land would be desolate, but ultimately God would have compassion on them (12:5–17).

Dramatically Jeremiah portrayed the reality of the exile (Jer. 13:1–27). In obedience to a divine command, Jeremiah purchased a linen waistcloth and deposited it in the cleft of a rock near the Euphrates (NIV, "Perath"). Later he recovered it, but in the meantime it was ruined. The application was cogently plain: what had happened to the garment would also occur concerning the pride of Judah in Babylonian captivity, because of their stubborn attitude and their refusal to obey God. Likewise, the leaders of Judah—kings, priests, and prophets—were filled with drunkenness and could end up like jars filled with wine that break when dashed one against another. The pride of Judah resulted in the downfall of the nation. Because of this haughty attitude, God allotted to them the humiliation of destruction and exile.

When a drought brought suffering to the people because of their erring ways, Jeremiah once more was commanded not to pray or intercede for his fellow citizens (Jer. 14:1–22). Moved with compassion for them, Jeremiah appealed to God again, pointing out that the false prophets and priests had misled the people. At this point Jeremiah raised the question as to whether or not God had utterly rejected his people. In his prayer the prophet reasoned that God should do something for the sake of God's name and glory.

God's answer was sobering indeed (Jer. 15:1–21). Even if Moses and Samuel would intercede, God would not avert the fourfold judgment awaiting them. The sword and exile were divinely fixed upon them because of their sin, but with it came the assurance of restoration for some. Once more Jeremiah reflected on the fact that he as God's messenger, proclaiming such an unpopular message, was cursed and persecuted by his people. Faithful in his service, he did not participate in the festivities of his people but suffered reproach for God's sake. In this state of despondency Jeremiah was divinely assured that God would sustain him successfully against the opposition of the people. He would be delivered out of the hands of the wicked and the grip of the tyrants.

The nearness of the national doom of Judah was also realistically conveyed through word and deed in Jeremiah's ministry. As God's representative at that particular time, he was forbidden to marry, nor was he to participate in any normal festivities or pleasure. His celibacy was to signify to the people that Jerusalem would be destroyed during his lifetime. Consequently, if he married and in the course of time had a family, Jeremiah's children would be taken into captivity (Jer. 16:1–21).

The gravity of Israel's sin is vividly projected in Jer. 17:1–18:17. The nation's sins were engraved on the horns of the altar where the people came to bring their sacrifices to God. These sins were inscribed with the point of a diamond so that they could not be erased. It was their sinfulness that precipitated God's judgment. God's curse rested upon them because they had put their trust in man rather than God. By contrast, however, was the promise of God's blessing upon the one who placed his trust and confidence in God. Such a person would prosper. Externally, the observance of the SABBATH was a sign of acknowledging God, whereas those who broke the Sabbath reflected their disregard for God. In the potter's house, Jeremiah learned the lesson that when the clay was not pliable it had to be remolded. In a similar manner the people of Judah would have to go through the remolding process in captivity.

Keenly conscious of the sneering attitude his people had toward him because of this message of God's judgment upon them, Jeremiah reminded God again of the fact that their enemies had dug a pit for his life. He prayed that God would not forgive their sin but subject them to his wrath (Jer. 18:18–23). It is significant, however, that Jeremiah did not assume responsibility for bringing judgment upon his enemies, but appealed to God to deal with them.

B. The prophet and the leaders (Jer. 19:1–29:32). Repeatedly Jeremiah came face to face with the religious and political leaders of Judah. For better or for worse, Jeremiah faithfully confronted them with the message God had given to him. Some heeded his warning whereas others responded with persecution and hatred.

Leading some of the elders southward out of Jerusalem into the Valley of Ben Hinnom, Jeremiah broke the potter's vessel before them. This signified the destruction of Jerusalem that was precipitated by their gross idolatry (Jer. 19:1–15). Returning to the temple to proclaim this same message, Jeremiah was subjected to a whipping by PASHHUR and then confined to the prison for one night. Released the next morning, Jeremiah pointedly rebuked Pashhur. In the wake of this experience, Jeremiah sank into another slough of despondency and cursed the day he was born. He was keenly sensitive to the fact that God had called him, and that God's word within him was like a burning fire that he could not contain without sharing it with others (20:1–18).

Zedekiah's interest in the prophet's advice at the time Nebuchadnezzar besieged Jerusalem (c. 588 B.C.), is significantly reported in Jer. 21. This must have been years or even decades after the personal experience of Jeremiah recorded in the previous chapter. It has been suggested that the sequence in the text is to assure the reader that Jeremiah did not despair when he cursed the day of his birth, but was still active when Jerusalem was about to fall to the Babylonians. Zedekiah probably hoped for a word of encouragement, but Jeremiah warned the king that Jewish resistance was futile. God was about to deliver the king as well as the people into the hands of Nebuchadnezzar.

Jeremiah's denunciation of the kings succeeding Josiah is explicit and direct (Jer. 22:1–30). Speaking during Jehoiakim's reign (c. 609–598 B.C.), he admonished the king that it was his responsibility as ruler on the throne of David to execute justice and to rule righteously. Jehoiakim was warned, however, that since he had forsaken the Lord in his responsibilities, he would die, and would not be accorded the honor of a decent burial. Shallum, also known as Jehoahaz, would not be restored to the throne but would die in Egypt. Coniah, also known as Jehoiachin, would be exiled to Babylon and not be succeeded by a son as ruler.

Jeremiah's denunciation of the false shepherds (Jer. 23) is not dated, but may have been given during the reign of Zedekiah. The people had been deceived and misled by the prophets who were not true representatives of God. The prophets of Samaria prophesied in the name of Baal, and the prophets in Jerusalem were guilty of adultery and evil devices. Consequently, God was against these prophets; they therefore would be driven out of Jerusalem. In contrast to this denunciation, Jeremiah offers a message of hope. The Lord, the God of Israel, will gather the remnant of his people from all lands. These people shall be secure and safe under a ruler seated on the throne of David who will be identified as "The Lord Our Righteousness" (23:6).

After Jehoiachin was exiled to Babylon in 597 B.C., Jeremiah had a vision of two baskets of figs, which provided the basis for a very timely message (Jer. 24:1–10). The good figs represented the exiled people from whom a remnant would return according to the divine promise. The bad figs symbolized the people who were still left in Jerusalem. Zedekiah and his people would be subjected to the curse of the sword, famine, and pestilence until they would be completely dispersed from the promised land.

Among the messages of Jeremiah that were given in the crucial fourth year of Jehoiakim (605 B.C.) was the explicit word that the Babylonian captivity would last seventy years (Jer. 25:1–38). The prophet's warning was not only to Judah but also to all the surrounding nations and city-states. Babylon was compared to God's "cup filled with the wine of my wrath" (v. 15). All the nations Jeremiah listed—Judah, Egypt, Philistine cities, Moab, Edom, Tyre, and others—were to be subjected to Babylon. The seventy years allotted to the Jews has received two basic interpretations. Since this message was given in the year 605, when the Babylonians initially invaded Judah, some have regarded the return of ZERUBBABEL and Joshua (JESHUA) in 538–536 as the termination of this seventy-year period. Others consider 586 as the *terminus a quo*, and the dedication of the rebuilt temple in 516 as the *terminus ad quem*. Support for the latter is based on Zech. 1:12, which is dated in 519. If this verse is correctly interpreted as saying that the seventy-year period is still unexpired, then it would seem logical that the resumption of sacrifice in the rebuilt temple would be considered the terminal point.

The drastic political and religious changes in Jerusalem after Jehoiakim became king are realistically apparent in Jeremiah's experience (Jer. 26). Publicly preaching that the temple would be destroyed, Jeremiah no longer had the protection or favor of the king that he had formerly enjoyed under Josiah (cf. ch. 7). The priests and prophets led the people in seeking the execution of Jeremiah. Fortunately some of the elders supported by Ahikam saved Jeremiah's life, appealing to the historic precedent set by Hezekiah, who did not execute Micah for preaching a similar message of judgment concerning Jerusalem.

After the second captivity of the Jews in 597 B.C., Jeremiah vividly portrayed the reality of

Babylonian servitude by publicly wearing a yoke around his neck (Jer. 27:1—28:17). Jeremiah warned his people not to listen to the false prophets who predicted that the temple vessels the Babylonians had taken would soon be returned. One of these prophets, named Hananiah, took the yoke of Jeremiah and broke it in pieces, predicting that in a similar manner the Jews would break the yoke of Babylonian bondage within two years. Although Jeremiah withdrew and "went on his way" at that time (28:11), he returned, subsequently predicting that Hananiah would die that year. Hananiah died that same year, but there is no indication in this account that the people were any more favorably inclined to believe Jeremiah after this public confirmation of his prophetic ministry.

Jeremiah continued to maintain contact with his people even after they were taken to Babylon. By letters he advised the exiles that they should plant vineyards, build houses, and adjust to the situation since their captivity would last for seventy years. Jeremiah warned that the false prophets, named Ahab and Zedekiah, would be executed by Nebuchadnezzar. He also had a message of rebuke for Shemaiah, who negated God's word as Jeremiah proclaimed it (Jer. 29:1–32). In this manner Jeremiah tried to counter the false prophets who were active in exile as well as those in Jerusalem. In accordance with the warning in ch. 1, Jeremiah frequently had kings, prophets, priests, and the people against him as he proclaimed the message that God had given him.

C. Restoration prospects (Jer. 30:1—33:26). Jeremiah was so involved in his message of warning that he seldom delineated the prospects of restoration. Ministering on the eve of Israel's greatest judgment in OT times, Jeremiah dogmatically asserted that the Israelites would again be brought back from exile. His messages in these chapters are more specific concerning the future kingdom of Israel than those of any other prophet in the OT.

God's purpose in sending this judgment upon Israel was to discipline them through servitude in exile. The day was coming, however, when they would no more serve other nations, but their service would be wholly devoted to God. Divine compassion and love would be manifest in Israel's restoration. The city of Zion would be rebuilt and the people would rejoice in the fact that Israel had been redeemed. Both Judah and Israel (the latter often identified as Ephraim) would be gathered from the distant parts of the earth where they had been scattered. God who had caused his people to be dispersed would also regather them.

Jeremiah did not minimize the severity of God's discipline upon Judah and Israel. In this process of uprooting and destroying his people, God watched over them as they were sown with the seed of man and the seed of beasts. God, however, would also watch over them in like manner in building and planting them again. A new covenant was to be made between God and his people (see COVENANT, THE NEW). Unlike the old covenant that they had broken, the new covenant would be written upon their hearts. Teaching about God would be unnecessary since every one would be fully acquainted with God. All their sins would be forgiven. The assurance that Israel would be restored is stated in the strongest language possible. God, who ordained the sun, moon, and stars in their courses and controls the seas and the armies— this God asserts that if the ordinances cease, if the heavens can be measured and the foundations of the earth can be explored, then God will also cast off his people.

During the siege of Jerusalem (586 B.C.), when Jeremiah had been confined to the court of the guard by King Zedekiah, the divine message was again made known that Israel would be restored after the destruction of the city. Jeremiah was given option on a field in Anathoth by the right of inheritance and redemption. Purchasing this real estate, Jeremiah meticulously sealed the purchase deeds so that they would be preserved for a long time. The divine message with this transaction was that in the future, houses, fields, and vineyards would again be bought in the land of Judah. When Jeremiah realized what this prediction involved he was almost overwhelmed. With the Chaldeans besieging Jerusalem and the fall of the kingdom inevitable, due to the persistent disobedience of the people, Jeremiah prayed expressing his doubt about the prospects of restoration but recognized that he had acted and spoken according to divine instructions by purchasing this real estate.

Once more God's message came to the prophet confirming that God was working out his purpose. The Chaldeans would burn the city of Jerusalem because the Jews had aroused God's wrath and anger through their gross idolatry and had even used the temple for their foreign gods. Consequently God abandoned Jerusalem and Judah to the invading Babylonians. However, it was God who also would gather the Israelites out of all the countries where he had scattered them. God would establish an everlasting covenant with them so that they would revere and honor him and not turn again to idolatry. In this land that was occupied by the Babylonians, the real estate business would thrive once more. The fortunes of Israel would be restored.

Jeremiah was still confined to the court of the guard. Another divine message came delineating to Jeremiah the hopes of restoration even more explicitly (Jer. 33:1–26). Because of its wickedness, Jerusalem would be destroyed but God would subsequently cleanse her from her iniquity and pardon her sin. The goodness of God manifested in Israel's restoration was to be an amazement and wonder among all the nations. Desolation and ruin would be replaced by prosperity, so that the Israelites would once more be jubilant and thankful in making their sacrifices to God.

At that time a Branch of Righteousness would be ruling on the Davidic throne executing justice and equity for all. Peace and prosperity was to be so extensive in Jerusalem and Judah that the kingdom would be known as "The LORD Our Righteousness." The fulfillment of this promise of the new covenant was as certain as God's established order of maintaining the ordinances of day and night with regularity. Israel's national fortunes would be restored with an innumerable multitude enjoying the blessings of the Davidic covenant and the ministry of the Levites.

D. Disintegration of the Kingdom

(Jer. 34:1—39:18) Jeremiah lived through one of the most difficult experiences that any prophet faced in his ministry. Having been active for over eighteen years during the favorable circumstances of the rule of Josiah, Jeremiah endured the discouraging developments under the reigns of Jehoiakim and Zedekiah as the kingdom gradually disintegrated. Although these events are not in chronological order, they provide insight into the conditions that precipitated the terminal judgment upon the kingdom of Judah.

When the Babylonians began the final siege of Jerusalem in 588 B.C., Jeremiah significantly informed Zedekiah that the city would capitulate and that he would be taken into captivity. During this time of pressure Zedekiah made a covenant with the people to release the slaves. Subsequently the siege of Jerusalem was temporarily lifted while the Babylonians pursued the Egyptians. When this dramatic act of releasing the slaves was revoked as soon as the siege was lifted and the famine ended, Jeremiah announced God's judgment upon the covenant breakers. The city of Jerusalem was doomed for burning by the Chaldeans (Jer. 34:1–22).

The godless attitude of the leaders had already been apparent in the reign of Jehoiakim (Jer. 35:1—36:32). On one occasion Jeremiah led the Recabites into the temple and offered them wine to drink. They, however, refused to accept this wine to be faithful to an oath that their forefathers had made over two centuries earlier. Jeremiah used this loyalty of the Recabites as an example to warn the Jews. If the Recabites were faithful to a promise made by their ancestors, how much more should the Israelites be to their covenant with God. In spite of the fact that prophet after prophet had been sent to them, they had disobeyed and ignored God and turned to idols. Consequently God's blessing awaited the Recabites, whereas the citizens of Judah would be subjected to the exile.

Jehoiakim's attitude toward Jeremiah was pointedly expressed in his burning of the scroll (Jer. 36:1–32). As king of Judah sitting on the Davidic throne, Jehoiakim failed to recognize that he had stewardship responsibility to obey the law and the messages given by the prophets. Since he was not a God-fearing man, he was alarmed at the divine judgment announced concerning Jerusalem. Demanding that Jeremiah's scroll be read to him, Jehoiakim listened to three or four columns at a time, cut them in pieces and threw them into the brazier fire before him. Subsequent to this, Jeremiah announced that Jehoiakim would not have a successor upon his throne, and that circumstances at the time of his death would be such that his body would be exposed to the frost by night and the heat by day.

The conditions during the siege and fall of Jerusalem did not facilitate the ministry of Jeremiah (Jer. 37:1—39:19). Neither the people nor the king were genuinely interested in listening to Jeremiah's message from God. Zedekiah, however, sent to Jeremiah to request prayer. While the siege was temporarily lifted, Jeremiah warned Zedekiah not to be deceived by this relief. The Chaldeans would soon return to burn the city of Jerusalem.

During this brief period of freedom Jeremiah was arrested, beaten, and imprisoned by the princes. Hearing this, Zedekiah sent for Jeremiah to inquire once more about God's word concerning the siege. Again Jeremiah emphasized that Jerusalem would be conquered. In addition, Jeremiah reminded the king that the false prophets had predicted that the Babylonians would not even come to Jerusalem. Subsequently Zedekiah assured Jeremiah a supply of bread as long as the royal supply lasted and confined him to the court of the guard.

When Jeremiah announced safety for those who surrendered to the Babylonians, and sword, famine, and pestilence for those who resisted, some of the princes exerted pressure on Zedekiah so that they were able to cast Jeremiah into a cistern. Left to sink in the mire, Jeremiah was rescued by an Ethiopian eunuch named Ebed-Melech. After this, Zedekiah requested further counsel from Jeremiah. With the verbal assurance from the king to spare his life, Jeremiah once more spoke to Zedekiah. The alternative was plainly set before him. Surrendering to the Babylonians would preserve his life, whereas rebellion would precipitate the burning of Jerusalem and the capture of the king. Zedekiah, however, was not willing to comply with Jeremiah's advice. Jeremiah remained in the court of the guard until Jerusalem was conquered by the Chaldeans.

When Jerusalem was on the verge of capitulation, Zedekiah and his associates fled as far as Jericho, where they were overtaken by the Babylonians. Taken to Riblah, Zedekiah was sentenced by Nebuchadnezzar. The sons of Zedekiah were killed, after which he was blinded and then taken in chains to Babylon. Jeremiah, in accordance with Nebuchadnezzar's orders, was treated with favor.

Ebed-Melech likewise lived through these difficult days, having been previously assured that his life would be spared.

E. Jeremiah's post-Jerusalem activity (Jer. 40:1—45:5). Even though Jeremiah was taken in chains from Jerusalem, he was freed at Ramah. Given the option of joining the exiles in Babylon or remaining in Palestine, he chose the latter.

The remnant of Jews remaining in Palestine settled at MIZPAH, which was identified by EUSEBIUS with Nabi Samwil, located about 5 mi. NW of Jerusalem. Contemporary biblical scholarship is more inclined to identify Mizpah with Tell en-Nasbeh, located about 8 mi. N of Jerusalem. Gedaliah was appointed as governor of this remnant by Nebuchadnezzar. In a plot designed by Baalis (the chieftain of the bedouin Ammonites

Nebuchadnezzar's invasion and defeat of Judah.

E of Jordan) and executed by Ishmael, this newly appointed governor was killed. Ishmael brutally killed many of the pilgrims en route to Jerusalem and then forced the citizens of Mizpah to march southward, hoping to take them to Ammon across the Jordan.

At GIBEON, Johanan rescued this group and put Ishmael to flight. Going southward this remnant settled temporarily at KIMHAM, a caravansary near BETHLEHEM. On their way they must have passed by the ruins of Jerusalem and the temple, which had been burned to the ground. Seeing the desolate remains of the city where Jeremiah spent forty years of his ministry may have provided the occasion for writing the book of LAMENTATIONS.

Uprooted from Mizpah, these Jews were determined to migrate to Egypt. They prevailed upon Jeremiah, however, to pray for divine guidance. After a ten-day period Jeremiah had an answer instructing them to remain in Palestine (Jer. 42:10) and warning them that war, famine, and death awaited them if they migrated to Egypt. In spite of their being definitely informed what God's will was, they went down to Egypt under the leadership of Johanan (43:1–7). Jeremiah and Baruch apparently had no choice but to go with them.

In Egypt, Jeremiah continued as God's messenger as he reflected interpretively on the developments of his life and ministry. He predicted that Nebuchadnezzar would come down into Egypt to execute divine judgment. Jerusalem was in ruins because the Israelites abandoned God and failed to heed the warnings of the prophets. Divine wrath had come because of their disobedience, so that God's people had become a taunt and a proverb among the nations. Jeremiah's audience, however, did not repent. They had a different interpretation. Defiantly they asserted that they would not obey, and claimed that this evil had come upon them because they ceased to worship the queen of heaven. Once more Jeremiah announced God's wrath upon them. He warned them that when they experienced the consequences they would realize that God was fulfilling his word (Jer. 43:8—44:30).

Significantly, after being informed about all these developments, we learn in Jer. 45 that Baruch some twenty years earlier had been assured that his life would be spared. Intimately associated with Jeremiah, Baruch also was exposed to danger but was assured of divine protection. This promise was fulfilled in his continued ministry even after he migrated to Egypt.

F. Foreign nations and cities in prophecy (Jer. 46:1—51:64). It was in the crucial fourth year of Jehoiakim that Jeremiah delivered these messages against foreign nations. The decisive defeat of the Egyptians at Carchemish advanced the Babylonians into Palestine, signaling the Jews that this was the beginning of the end for the kingdom of Judah. Isaiah had predicted nearly a century earlier that Jerusalem would be conquered by the Babylonians (Isa. 39).

Jeremiah predicted that Nebuchadnezzar, who began to rule that year, would ultimately conquer Amon of Thebes, 500 mi. up the Nile River. Philistia would be invaded and Moab's national life would be destroyed because of her pride. The Ammonites would be scattered without any promise of restoration, and even Edom would be demoted from her haughty position. Judgment likewise awaited Damascus, Hazor, Kedar, and Elam.

The most powerful nation of all—Babylon—would likewise be severely judged. Babylon with her idols faced destruction. This was dramatically portrayed by sending Seraiah, a brother of Baruch, to Babylon. There he read this message, tied the scroll to a rock, and then threw it into the Euphrates River. In a similar manner, Babylon was doomed, never to rise again.

G. Appendix (Jer. 52:1–34). The last chapter of the book seems to provide an appropriate conclusion to the ministry of Jeremiah. The predictions he had given as warnings for over forty years had actually been fulfilled. In spite of his compassionate pleas and prayers, the people had been disobedient and consequently had to face the realities of the exile. This conclusion likely was added by Baruch.

(Significant commentaries include T. Laetsch, *Jeremiah* [1952]; J. A. Thompson, *The Book of Jeremiah*, NICOT [1979]; R. P. Carroll, *Jeremiah: A Commentary*, OTL [1986]; W. L. Holladay, *Jeremiah: A Commentary on the Book of the Prophet Jeremiah*, Hermeneia, 2 vols. [1986–89]; P. C. Craigie et al., *Jeremiah 1–25*, WBC 26 [1991]; W. McKane,

A Critical and Exegetical Commentary on Jeremiah, ICC, 2 vols. [1986–96]; W. Brueggemann, *A Commentary on Jeremiah: Exile and Homecoming* [1998]; J. R. Lundbom, *Jeremiah*, 3 vols., AB 21A-C [1999–2004]; T. E. Fretheim, *Jeremiah* [2002]; L. Stulman, *Jeremiah* [2005]. Note also A. R. Diamond, *The Confessions of Jeremiah in Context: Scenes of Prophetic Drama* [1987]; L. Stulman, *Order amid Chaos: Jeremiah as Symbolic Tapestry* [1998]; H. Lalleman-de Winkel, *Jeremiah in Prophetic Tradition: An Examination of the Book of Jeremiah in the Light of Israel's Prophetic Traditions* [2000]; M. Kessler, ed., *Reading the Book of Jeremiah: A Search for Coherence* [2004]; W. Brueggemann, *The Theology of the Book of Jeremiah* [2007]; and see the extensive bibliography compiled by W. E. Mills, *Jeremiah-Lamentations* [2002].)   S. J. SCHULTZ

Jeremiah, Epistle of (Ἐπιστολὴ Ἰερεμίου). A short pseudonymous writing, known also as the Letter of Jeremy, included in the APOCRYPHA as an addendum to Baruch (see BARUCH, BOOK OF). In the SEPTUAGINT, the book of LAMENTATIONS is usually inserted between Baruch and the Epistle of Jeremiah, the three works together being appended to the book of Jeremiah. In the VULGATE (and KJV), the letter is reckoned as Bar. 6 (some English versions follow this numbering, but title it separately).

I. Content. Despite the introductory assertion that it is a copy of the letter sent by Jeremiah to give instruction to those about to be deported to BABYLON, this document is not by Jeremiah, nor is it really a letter. It is, in fact, a powerful exhortation against IDOLATRY. The author's argument, which is quite repetitious, focuses on the powerlessness of idols and the consequent futility of idol worship. Two main threads of mockery run through the course of the book. First is the utter inability of these gods to do anything for themselves. They cannot speak; they cannot hear; they cannot see; they cannot move. They cannot defend themselves against the robbery of unscrupulous priests. They cannot keep themselves clean from dust and tarnish; their garments rot upon their backs. They cannot protect themselves against termites and worms, nor from the defilement of all manner of birds and the prowling of cats. Finally, they are made only as men choose to make them. The second thread of mockery runs: If they are unable to help themselves, neither are they able to help others. They can in no way bless or curse a man. Therefore it is of no use to worship or fear them, and only humiliation awaits those who put their trust in them.

There is no logical development in the structure of the book, but the contents are punctuated by the repeated refrain, "Since you know by these things that they are not gods, do not fear them" (which occurs five times with slight variations, and an additional five times in the form of a rhetorical question).

II. Origin. This polemic against idolatry was easily set forth as a product of Jeremiah. Not only is Jeremiah known to have written at least one letter to the exiles (Jer. 29), but he was also the author of a similar diatribe against idolatry (10:1–10). See JEREMIAH, BOOK OF. The unknown author of the Epistle of Jeremiah seems indeed to have borrowed from this very passage (cf. Jer. 10:5 with Ep. Jer. 70), and was possibly also influenced by other OT traditions on the same subject (cf. Isa. 44:9–20; Pss. 115:4–8; 135:15–18). Either the author himself or a later editor added the opening sentence, which identifies the treatise as a letter of Jeremiah.

Whereas the "letter" ostensibly attacks the idolatry of Babylonia, referring to sacred processions (Ep. Jer. 4, 26), cultic prostitution (v. 43), the god BEL (v. 41), and the mourning for a dying god (prob. TAMMUZ, v. 32), occasional lapses into pagan idolatry are known to have occurred among the Jews in Palestine during the 3rd and 2nd centuries B.C., and thus a Babylonian provenance for the polemic is by no means assured. If this is true, the addressees of the "letter" also remain unknown. Was it originally written for a particular community of the DIASPORA, or for the Diaspora generally, or perhaps for Jews living in Palestine?

With regard to the dating of this writing, there is considerable uncertainty. A fragment dated to the 1st cent. B.C. has been discovered among the DEAD SEA SCROLLS, and since the Greek text seems to be a translation of a Hebrew (or Aramaic) document, the Semitic original was probably produced no later than the 2nd cent. B.C. A further clue is perhaps found in Ep. Jer. 3, which states that the exiles are to remain in Babylon "for a long time, up to seven generations." Reckoned from 586 B.C., seven generations leads to about 300 B.C., and some scholars infer that the writing must have been composed late in the 4th cent. B.C. (cf. C. A. Moore, "Jeremiah, Additions to," in *ABD*, 3:698–706). Others date it in the 3rd or even 2nd cent B.C.

III. Canonicity and text. As one of the writings not contained in the Hebrew Bible, the Epistle of Jeremiah has never been accepted as canonical by the Protestant church. It is, however, accepted as fully canonical by the Roman Catholic Church (since the Council of Trent) where, following the Vulgate, it is reckoned not as a separate book, but as the concluding chapter of Baruch. The Greek text of the epistle (which survives in the main MSS, except CODEX SINAITICUS) is obtainable in the standard printed editions of the LXX (but regularly following Lamentations, and not Baruch). English translations are ready at hand in the various editions of the Apocrypha. (See further C. J. Ball in *APOT*, 1:596–611; R. H. Pfeiffer, *History of New Testament Times with an Introduction to the Apocrypha* [1949], 426–432; D. J. Harrington, *Invitation to the Apocrypha* [1999], ch. 8; D. A. deSilva, *Introducing the Apocrypha: Message, Context, and Significance* [2002], ch. 9.) On the *Paraleipomena Jeremiou*, see BARUCH, FOURTH.   D. A. HAGNER

Jeremiah, Paraleipomena of. See BARUCH, FOURTH.

Jeremias jer´uh-mi´uhs. KJV Apoc. and alternate NT form of JEREMIAH (Sir. 49:6 et al.; Matt. 16:14).

Jeremiel ji-rem´ee-uhl (Lat. *Hieremihel*, possibly corresponding to JERAHMEEL). An archangel who answers the questions asked by the righteous dead (2 Esd. 4:36; KJV, "Uriel"). He is perhaps to be identified with Ramiel/Remiel (2 Bar. 55:3; 1 En. 20:8). See URIEL #3.

Jeremoth jer´uh-moth (יְרֵמוֹת H3756, variant יְרִימוֹת H3748 [JERIMOTH], possibly "stout" or "exalted"). **(1)** Son of BEKER and grandson of BENJAMIN (1 Chr. 7:8; KJV, "Jerimoth").

(2) Son of BERIAH (or of ELPAAL; cf. NRSV) and descendant of Benjamin, listed among the heads of families living in Jerusalem (1 Chr. 8:14; cf. v. 28). He is usually identified with JEROHAM (v. 27; see the discussion in KD, *Chronicles*, 147–48). See also AHIO.

(3) Son (or descendant) of Mushi; he was one of the descendants of LEVI through MERARI appointed by DAVID to work in the temple (1 Chr. 23:23 KJV, NRSV; the NIV has "Jerimoth" on the basis of 24:30).

(4) Son of HEMAN, David's seer (1 Chr. 25:4, 22; in the former verse he is called "Jerimoth," and on that basis the NIV has "Jerimoth" in v. 22 as well). He and his thirteen brothers were set apart "for the ministry of prophesying, accompanied by harps, lyres and cymbal" (v. 1). When lots were cast to determine the duties of the Levitical singers, he, along with his sons and relatives, received the fifteenth lot (v. 22).

(5) One of the descendants of Elam who agreed to put away their foreign wives (Ezra 10:26; 1 Esd. 9:27 [KJV, "Hieremoth"]).

(6) One of the descendants of Zattu who agreed to put away their foreign wives (Ezra 10:27; 1 Esd. 9:28 [KJV, "Jarimoth"]).

(7) One of the descendants of Bani who agreed to put away their foreign wives (Ezra 10:29 [KJV, "Ramoth," following the *Qere*]; 1 Esd. 9:30 [KJV, "Hieremoth"]).

Jeremy jer´uh-mee. KJV alternate NT form of JEREMIAH (Matt. 2:17; 27:9).

Jeriah ji-ri´uh (יְרִיָּהוּ H3746, short form יְרִיָּה H3745 "Yahweh sees [me]"; cf. JERIEL). Firstborn son (or most important descendant) of Hebron; he was one of the descendants of LEVI through KOHATH appointed by DAVID to work in the temple (1 Chr. 23:19; 24:23). He is also described as chief of the Hebronites; his twenty-seven hundred relatives were heads of families whom David put in charge of the tribes E of the Jordan (1 Chr. 26:31–32; KJV and other versions, "Jerijah"). See HEBRON (PERSON) #1.

Jeribai jer´uh-b*i* (יְרִיבַי H3744, "[Yahweh] contends [for me]"; see JARIB, JEHOIARIB, JOIARIB.

Son of Elnaam; he and his brother Joshaviah are included in the Chronicler's list of DAVID's mighty warriors (1 Chr. 11:46), which adds sixteen names (vv. 41b–47) beyond the military elite known as the Thirty (vv. 10–41=2 Sam. 23:8–39).

Jericho jer′uh-koh (יְרִיחוֹ *H3735* [with variant spellings], possibly "[city of] the moon [god]"; Ἰεριχώ *G2637*). The OT city of Jericho is today represented by a much eroded ovoid-shaped mound identified as Tell es-Sultan on the NW outskirts of the modern town. This tell is about 10 mi. NW of the mouth of the DEAD SEA and about 17 mi. ENE of Jerusalem. Because the occupation of the site lasted many centuries, there has been built up a mound which rises some 50 ft. above bedrock. A modern road cuts into the E side of the tell. Across the road from the tell is the spring of ʿAin es-Sultan, which explains the attraction of the site from the earliest times. It is this copious spring which waters the modern oasis. Tell es-Sultan is about 400 yards long from N to S and covers about ten acres. NT or Herodian Jericho is located one mile W of the modern city in the ruins on both banks of the Wadi Qelt. This site is known as Tulul Abu el-ʿAlayiq. The hills of JUDEA rise abruptly W of the two sites.

I. Ancient Jericho. The history of Jericho goes back far beyond the time of JOSHUA. A Neolithic community settled by the perennial spring around the 8th millennium B.C. The inhabitants had not yet begun to manufacture pottery. It is possible that these food-gathering hunters may have constructed a shrine at the site. Early in the 7th millennium a town was built with a revetment wall, at least one tower, round houses, and many of the attributes of civilization except that of a written language. This first urban phase of Jericho gave way to a later Neolithic phase that marked the beginning of pottery. The inhabitants were probably seminomadic and did not build houses. They seem to have camped on the ruins in flimsy huts. In every way these occupants represent a retrogression from the life of the first occupants except that they began to make pottery.

In the Early Bronze Age (c. 3000 B.C.), Jericho again was occupied by a people who built up a settlement with defense walls and towers around the edge of the mound. This occupation did not have a long history. In fact, from that time on there was much building and rebuilding because of a variety of catastrophes that hit the community. Earthquake and fire ended some occupations and required from the new settlers major rebuilding activity. Sometimes existing foundations were used. On occasion a new foundation was constructed on the smoothed-over debris of the earlier occupations or the trench for the foundation was dug out of earlier occupation levels. Some of the building or repair work was required because wind and rain erosion had weakened or collapsed the existing wall or structure. In early archaeological excavations these Early Bronze Age walls were incorrectly dated to the time of JOSHUA (an error often repeated in subsequent literature).

Because of Jericho's location, it was a point at which nomadic tribes entered the land W of the JORDAN. Joshua's instruction to the spies to "Go, look over the land … especially Jericho" (Josh. 2:1) was ancient practice. The site was W of the main ford on the lower Jordan River. From Jericho ascend several main valleys going up to the central ridge of the country. At Jericho the occupants controlled also a vital fresh water supply. In addition, the citizens could and did become greatly involved in commerce as well as in agriculture. The proximity to the Dead Sea made the citizens dealers in salt, bitumen, and sulphur. These settlers also continued to display their nomadic training and frequently moved on W toward the Mediterranean

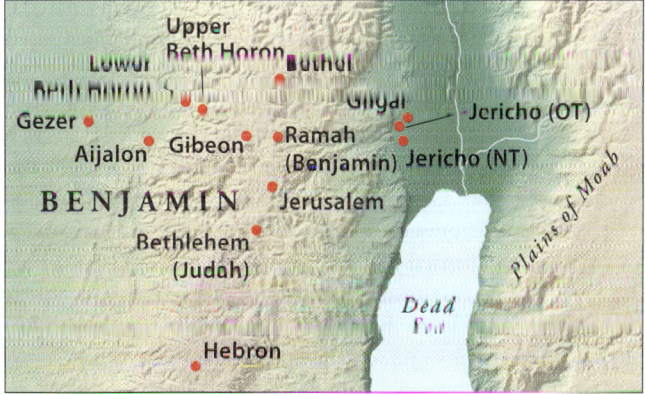

Jericho.

mingling and merging with the people already there.

The Early Bronze Age occupation of Jericho was destroyed by nomadic invaders about 2300 B.C. These invaders were identified by Kathleen M. Kenyon as AMORITES (*Digging Up Jericho* [1957]; cf. K. M. Kenyon et al., *Excavations at Jericho*, 5 vols. [1960–83]). Jericho was not the only city destroyed in the Amorite invasion of Palestine and Syria. Excavations of Jericho tombs provide much of the information that gives an understanding of the wave of nomadic newcomers. In turn, a new inundation of immigrants hit Jericho and the Jordan area in the Middle Bronze Age, about 1900 B.C. These invaders were the Canaanites (cf. Num. 13:29, "the Hittites, Jebusites and Amorites live in the hill country; and the Canaanites live near the sea and along the Jordan"). Their culture has been found extending the full length of the Palestinian-Syrian coast in the 2nd millennium. The excavated artifacts at Jericho show that this Middle Bronze Age culture lasted until at least 1200 B.C.

The rule of foreigners such as the HYKSOS did not change the pattern greatly. The Hyksos did introduce the sloping bank defensive wall in place of the independent free-standing wall but they had very little additional cultural impact. The tombs of Jericho make it possible to reconstruct town life in the time of the PATRIARCHS. Excellent pottery, wooden three-legged and four-legged tables, stools and beds, basketry, trinket-boxes of bone inlay, metal daggers, circlets, platters of fruit, and joints of meat have all been preserved due to the presence of methane gas in some of the tombs. This material made available to the dead was the equipment used by the living.

About 1550 B.C. Jericho was violently destroyed. This was probably the work of EGYPT's 18th dynasty as it expelled the Hyksos from the area. One of the benefits of a violent destruction is the preservation of archaeological evidence under collapsed walls. Fire also hardens walls and preserves organic material in carbon form, which then can be analyzed. Middle Bronze Age Jericho has been so preserved. The cobbled streets have been uncovered. The one-room shops opening out to the street have been preserved. A two-story house with living quarters on the first floor and a grain-milling complex and storage facility were found. In both the tombs and the houses, the evidence indicates that the people of Jericho were not wealthy. This town was not a major trade center, but rather a typical urban complex similar to many towns of that period.

After the destruction of Jericho in 1550, the only Late Bronze Age occupation verified by archaeological evidence dates mainly between 1400 and 1350. There was a definite abandonment of the town between 1550 and 1400. Wash-layers cover the burned town, and the burned material was gradually spread down the slope of the mound. Much of the material from the Middle Bronze Age city did not survive at all, but was scattered and destroyed by the power of the wind and the rains. The material that is preserved under the wash layers provides a distinct contrast with the Late Bronze Age material from the 1400–1350 occupation. There is also evidence in the form of tomb material.

II. OT Jericho. From the 13th cent. B.C., the frequently accepted date of the Israelite conquest of Palestine, virtually nothing is known about Jericho from either John Garstang's reports of his six seasons of archaeological work on the site (*Jericho: City and Necropolis* [1932–36]), or from Kenyon's seven seasons. Unfortunately, when the highest site on the mound was excavated by the Austro-German archaeologists in 1907–09, there was a greater interest in architecture than in ceramic materials. The plans of those excavations show no house walls from the Late Bronze period, 1300–1200. Noted French scholar L.-H. Vincent, however, reported in his writings that sufficient pottery sherds were recovered from the period to demonstrate conclusively that there was a city on the site at that time.

The excavations carried out by John Garstang at Jericho from 1930 to 1936 bear upon the 13th cent. B.C. in the clearing of five tombs. These burial spots were constructed originally in the Middle Bronze Age but were reused for burial in that century. Nothing survived on the tell from the city defenses of the period. No wall structure left for study relates to that which figures prominently in the OT record in the conquest of Palestine by

Looking SE across the site of OT Jericho.

Joshua and the Israelites. Archaeology can offer little evidence of the conquest of Jericho in the 13th cent. because that period of the city's history has been eroded by winter storms and modern surface structures that have cut into the level.

The OT narrative of Josh. 3–8 tells of the fall of Jericho. The Israelites crossed the Jordan River without a problem because the water ceased to flow. Earth slides and the shutting off of the water of the Jordan for an extended period of time have been reported periodically. In A.D. 1267 such an event was recorded. In 1906 and again in 1927 the phenomenon was observed and reported. Older students of the conquest assumed that the capture of Jericho was the most important factor in the conquest. Actually it was the crossing of the Jordan River at high flood that was of the greatest significance. All the evidence that can be gathered to date seems to imply that the Jericho of Joshua's conquest was only a small city guarding the crossing of the Jordan.

The key city in Joshua's conquest of Palestine is HAZOR, which was the largest urban center in all of Palestine and a major city in the ANE as a whole. Comparing the size of Hazor and Jericho, Jericho would be simply a small oasis town. Hazor, internationally known, grew to a great size because it was located strategically as an international trade center. The key emphasis on the conquest of Jericho in Scripture is that it was the firstfruits of the conquest and completely dedicated to Yahweh.

The book of JUDGES demonstrates the chaotic nature of the Early Iron Age in Palestine. This condition is reflected in the lack of substantial remains of the period at Jericho. While ʿAin es-Sultan is an ideal source of irrigation, the volume of the WATER demands a strong stable government for its efficient use. Jericho flourished when irrigation systems were developed and maintained.

A curse was placed on Jericho by Joshua (Josh. 6:26). The oasis was occupied by EGLON, king of MOAB (Jdg. 3:14), for a short time. Some representatives of DAVID spent time at Jericho after being mistreated by HANUN of AMMON (2 Sam. 10:4; 2 Chr. 20:22–23). In the time of AHAB (9th cent. B.C.), HIEL of BETHEL attempted to build a city at Jericho. The archaeological evidence for this occupation is meager. The loss of Hiel's two sons is interpreted as a fulfillment of a curse placed on the site by Joshua (1 Ki. 16:34). This was the Jericho of ELIJAH and ELISHA (2 Ki. 2:4–5, 18–22). It was the locale of a school of the prophets. The purifying of the spring by Elisha is described as an act which had permanent results. Several times in the OT, Jericho is referred to as the City of Palms (Deut. 34:3; Jdg. 1:16; 3:13; 2 Chr. 28:15; cf. Jos. *War* 1.7.6 §138).

There is a little archaeological evidence indicating that there was an occupation of Jericho in the 7th cent. B.C. This town came to an end at the time of the Babylonian capture of ZEDEKIAH, the last king of Judah, in the Plains of Jericho (2 Ki. 25:5; 2 Chr. 28:15; Jer. 39:5; 52:8). From that time Tell es-Sultan was not occupied as far as archaeological evidence is concerned. Both EZRA and NEHEMIAH refer to a Persian period occupation at Jericho (Ezra 2:34; Neh. 7:36). The population is numbered at 345. These people are credited with aiding the rebuilding of the walls of Jerusalem (Neh. 3:2). When the Arabs, Crusaders, and Turks moved into Palestine, they utilized the waters of ʿAin es-Sultan but they built the town of Jericho about 2 mi. SE of the ancient tell. The present city of Jericho has expanded to the place where it surrounds the old mound.

III. NT Jericho. HEROD the Great and his successors built a winter capital S of OT Jericho on both banks of the Wadi Qelt. The ruins of this site are known today as Tulul Abu el-ʿAlayiq. Usually the winter climate at this site is warm and pleasant compared to the frequent damp and chilly winter days and nights in Jerusalem. The site for Herodian Jericho was determined by the constant ample supply of water in the Wadi Qelt at a point where the stream opens out onto the plain of the Jordan River. A small fortress had been erected on the site as a control point over a road from the Jordan Valley to Jerusalem. In the Maccabean Period, BACCHIDES fortified Jericho (1 Macc. 9:50). Simon MACCABEE was killed by his son-in-law Ptolemy at Jericho (16:14–16). In 63 B.C. POMPEY captured two forts at Jericho, Threx and Taurus. These are probably the Maccabean fortresses built on the N and S banks of the Qelt.

Herod the Great apparently carried out a two-phased building program at Jericho. In the first phase, the construction was of cut-stone similar to that used in other cities. In the second phase, a peculiar use of small uniform rectangular stones set in mortar characterized the construction. This *opus reticulatum* architectural feature noted by the archaeologists in many walls is peculiar to Jericho in the whole of the Middle East. This feature has been discovered on the Tiber and dated to the time of AUGUSTUS. It has also been uncovered at Pompeii. Apparently Herod was attracted to this unique form of construction on a visit to Rome.

Herodian Jericho was oriented toward the Qelt. This stream provided water for elaborate reflecting

Portion of Herod's northern palace with the remains of NT Jericho in the background. (View to the N.)

pools lined by fifty statuary niches which were in a sunken garden. At each end of the garden were several buildings. At the E end a grand stairway 150 ft. long rose to a prominent building looking down upon the garden and the stream. In the account of JOSEPHUS, reference is made to the burning of the palace and some other buildings at Jericho at the time of the death of Herod the Great. His son Archelaus restored the town. (See *Excavations at New Testament Jericho and Khirbet en-Nitla*, ed. W. F. Albright and V. Winnett, AASOR 29–30 [1955].)

ZACCHAEUS had a lucrative position as TAX COLLECTOR in Jericho (Lk. 19:1–10). Jericho was the winter capital of the kingdom. In addition, rich balsam groves were nearby and the tax on the product was considerable. When Jesus of Nazareth was entertained by the tax collector in Jericho, it would likely be in a home in keeping with Herod's grand building program. The finest villas in Pompeii would be similar. One of the Hellenistic forts had sycamore timbers in it indicating that this wood was common in the area. The gospel accounts make reference to the presence of blind beggars in the vicinity of Jericho (Matt. 20:29–34; Mk. 10:46–52; Lk. 18:35–43). Wherever wealth exists in the Middle East, a multiplicity of beggars can be noted.

NT Jericho was captured by VESPASIAN's troops. There is no archaeological evidence of a destruction of the city. From Jericho, Vespasian sent his army 7 mi. S to Khirbet QUMRAN and destroyed that sectarian site on the W shore of the Dead Sea. The fact that the sect abandoned the site while Herod was at Jericho raises unanswered questions about the relationship between Jericho and Qumran during that time. Upon Herod's death Qumran was reoccupied by the followers of the Teacher of Righteousness. See DEAD SEA SCROLLS.

After TITUS destroyed Jerusalem in A.D. 70, sending the Tenth Legion from Jericho for the final assault, the town declined. There was a brief revival at the time of BAR KOKHBA's defiance of Rome in A.D. 132–135. The Bordeaux Pilgrim reported the location of Jericho in A.D. 333 to be where Herod built. A Byzantine Jericho was built a mile or more E of Herodian Jericho. The present city is built on the Byzantine site. (See further T. A. Holland and E. Netzer in *ABD*, 3:723–40.) H. JAMIESON

Jeriel jihr′i·uhl (יְרִיאֵל *H3711*, "God sees [me]"; cf. JERIAH). Son of TOLA and grandson of ISSACHAR, described as head of family (1 Chr. 7:2).

Jerijah ji-ri′jah. See JERIAH.

Jerimoth jer′i-moth (יְרִימוֹת *H3740*, variant יְרֵמוֹת *H3756* [JEREMOTH], possibly "stout" or "exalted"). (1) Son of BELA and grandson of BENJAMIN (1 Chr. 7:7).

(2) One of the ambidextrous Benjamite warriors who joined DAVID while he was in exile from SAUL at the Philistine city of ZIKLAG (1 Chr. 12:5; cf. v. 2).

(3) Son (or descendant) of Mushi; he was one of the descendants of LEVI through MERARI appointed by DAVID to work in the temple (1 Chr. 23:23 [KJV, NRSV, "Jeremoth"]; 24:30).

(4) Son of HEMAN, David's seer (1 Chr. 25:4). He and his thirteen brothers were set apart "for the ministry of prophesying, accompanied by harps, lyres and cymbal" (v. 1). When lots were cast to determine the duties of the Levitical singers, he, along with his sons and relatives, received the fifteenth lot (v. 22 [KJV and other versions, "Jeremoth"]).

(5) Son of Azriel; an officer over the tribe of NAPHTALI during the reign of David (1 Chr. 27:19 [RSV, "Jeremoth"]).

(6) Son of David and father of MAHALATH; the latter married REHOBOAM (2 Chr. 11:18). The name of Jerimoth does not appear in any of the lists of David's sons, and some scholars argue that the text is not reliable.

(7) A Levite included in the list of supervisors of the temple storerooms during the reign of HEZEKIAH (2 Chr. 31:13).

Jerioth jer′ee-oth (יְרִיעוֹת *H3750*, possibly "fearful" or "tents"). Wife of CALEB son of Hezron (1 Chr. 2:18). The MT is difficult, however, and can be interpreted in different ways: (a) Jerioth may be another name for Caleb's wife AZUBAH; (b) Azubah had been previously the wife of a man called Jerioth; (c) Jerioth was the daughter of Caleb and Azubah. Other suggestions have been made (cf. R. Braun, *1 Chronicles*, WBC 14 [1986], 37; G. N. Knoppers, *I Chronicles 1–9*, AB 12 [2004], 298–99).

Jeroboam Jer′uh-boh′uhm (יָרָבְעָם H3716, "the people are great" or "my kinsman [=deity?] is great"; some believe that this form is a scribal alteration of an original ירבעל, "Baal is great," but a beautiful jasper seal from biblical times, picturing a roaring lion, bears the inscription לשמע עבד ירבעם, "belonging to Shema, the minister of Jeroboam"). The name of two kings of the northern kingdom of Israel.

I. Jeroboam I. As the first king of the secessionist kingdom of Israel, he reigned twenty-two years (1 Ki. 14:20; 930–909 B.C. according to E. R. Thiele, *The Mysterious Numbers of the Hebrew Kings*, 3rd ed. [1983], 81; according to an alternate chronology, 922–901) and established a short-lived dynasty: his son NADAB was assassinated by BAASHA after a reign of less than two years (1 Ki. 15:25–30). Jeroboam's career is described in 1 Ki. 11:26—14:20 and 2 Chr. 10:1—13:20.

A. His rise to power

1. Three different accounts. There are three different accounts of Jeroboam's life prior to his becoming king, two in the SEPTUAGINT and a third in the MT; the latter forms the basis of most English translations. (a) The Greek version of 1 Ki. 11:26—12:24 agrees in substance with the MT, with the following variations. It omits 12:2–3a, but in place of that material it reads as follows at 11:43: "And Solomon slept with his fathers, and they buried him in the city of David his father. And when Jeroboam son of Nebat—now he was yet in Egypt, as he had fled from before Solomon and dwelled in Egypt—heard, he went directly and came to his city, to Sarira in the hill country of Ephraim. King Solomon slept with his fathers, and Rehoboam his son reigned in his stead." In addition, the SEPTUAGINT omits the reference to Jeroboam at 12:12, reading, "And all Israel came to King Rehoboam on the third day."

(b) A second account is found in the LXX as a lengthy addition to 1 Ki. 12:24 (marked "a–z" in Rahlfs's ed.). This account differs markedly from the previous one and often contradicts it. Some believe that there is "a genuine historical source behind" it (J. Gray, *I and II Kings* [1963], 268), but the material is suspect (see D. W. Gooding in *VT* 17 [1967]: 173–89, esp. 188). Among the midrashic elements added to put Jeroboam in the worst possible light are the following: his mother Sarira was a harlot, so his father is unnamed; he attempted a siege of Jerusalem during SOLOMON's reign; having fled to Egypt, he married Shishak's eldest and most prominent daughter Ano, who bore him a son, Abia; Shemaiah (not Ahijah; cf. 1 Ki. 11:29–39) the prophet was told by the Lord to go to Jeroboam at SHECHEM, to tear a new garment into twelve pieces, and to tell Jeroboam, "Take for yourself ten shreds *for you to wear*" (a rather sarcastic purpose clause!). Each of these details seeks to discredit Jeroboam and should probably be ignored when reconstructing his rise to power.

(c) The MT of 1 Ki. 11:26—12:24 raises several questions when compared with the LXX. When did Jeroboam return from his exile in Egypt? Immediately upon hearing of the death of Solomon (LXX 11:43) or after Israel had assembled in Shechem to make Rehoboam king (MT 12:1–3a)? What part did Jeroboam play in the negotiations with Rehoboam? Did he stay in the background until after the revolt, or did he take a prominent role, perhaps even lead, in the grievances against the king (MT vv. 3a and 12a)? Furthermore, many scholars have argued that the MT is inconsistent and that the LXX is to be preferred.

2. Evaluation of the accounts. The reason for the scholarly skepticism of the MT account and preference for the LXX of 1 Ki. 11:26—12:24 (but not LXX additions to 12:24) is a supposed contradiction in the MT account. It is thought, the argument runs, that the MT at two points (12:1–3a and v. 12a) places the return of Jeroboam in the context of the Shechem conference, but that elsewhere (v. 20) it places his return to prominence after the revolt. By omitting any reference to Jeroboam in these same verses, LXX^BL (i.e., CODEX VATICANUS and the Lucianic recension) represents a better Hebrew *Vorlage* than that preserved in MT; the latter is said to have borrowed 2 Chr. 10:2–3a, placed it in its present location as MT 1 Ki. 12:2–3a, and changed v. 12 to include Jeroboam.

On the contrary, the evidence presently available argues that the MT represents the original text.

The following reasons can be cited: (a) It is not true that LXX[BL] has omitted the material in MT 1 Ki. 12:2–3a. Rather, the Greek version has placed its account at 11:43, modified it for a purpose, and, in the process, left a clue that this is, in fact, what has occurred. In fitting in the account, the LXX has interrupted the stock formula: (i) X slept with his fathers, (ii) was buried in Y, and (iii) Z reigned in his stead. The unparalleled result of the insertion, as quoted above, is: (i) X slept with his fathers, (ii) was buried in Y, (iii) inserted account of Jeroboam, (iv) X slept with his fathers, and (v) Z reigned in his stead.

(b) It is far more probable that the LXX felt the same difficulty with its Hebrew *Vorlage* as modern scholars do with the MT and excised or repositioned the offending texts than that MT added vv. 2–3a from 2 Chronicles and the name "Rehoboam" to v. 12, which in fact would create a difficulty.

(c) The grammatical difficulty in the Hebrew text of vv. 2–3a can be solved simply by ending the parenthesis, not at the end of v. 2 (as KJV does), but rather at the words, "… and they sent and called him" (e.g., ASV; for the alternate solution found in NIV and NRSV, see below).

(d) It is more likely that the Chronicler quoted 1 Ki. 12 extensively with slight changes to suit his purposes than that a later recension of Kings added vv. 2–3a from the parallel in Chronicles. First, as the texts now stand, 2 Chr. 10:2 has *šĕlōmōh hammelek* ("Solomon the King"), whereas 1 Ki. 12:2 has the reverse order, *hammelek šĕlōmōh* ("King Solomon"). The former order is more typical of later Hebrew (BDB, 573a), so if the recension of Kings had borrowed from 2 Chronicles, one could expect to find the normal late order of these words preserved in Kings. Second, the preposition *b* in *bĕmiṣrayim* at the end of v. 2 probably has the older meaning "from" rather than the more common meaning "in," so by repointing the verb *wayēšeb* as *wayāšāb*, the resulting translation is "and Jeroboam returned from Egypt" (rather than "and Jeroboam lived in Egypt"; cf. 2 Chr. 10:2 and N. M. Sarna in *JBL* 78 [1959]: 310–16; so also NIV and NRSV). Third, there is no sufficiently good reason to suppose that the reference to "the whole assembly [*qāhāl* H7736] of Israel" (1 Ki. 12:3a) and to "the congregation [*ʿēdâ* H6337]" (v. 20) indicates two different sources, with the earlier reference and its context supposed to be an insertion from Chronicles (2 Chr. 10:3 does not even have the word *qāhāl*). It is more likely that there were in fact two assemblies. If so, 1 Ki. 12:3a would refer to the assembled group that had come to meet with Rehoboam, and the more specific term *ʿēdâ* would refer to the national assembly convened at Shechem for the express purpose of making Jeroboam king (v. 20).

For these reasons, the MT is to be preferred to the LXX in its account of Jeroboam's rise to power.

3. Resultant picture. Jeroboam the son of Nebat and Zeruah (a widow) became a recognized leader during the reign of SOLOMON, who put him in charge of the forced labor crew from the house of Joseph (Ephraim and Manasseh). Meeting Jeroboam alone in the country, the prophet AHIJAH from SHILOH tore his own new garment into twelve pieces and had Jeroboam take ten to symbolize the fact that God was about to tear ten of the tribes away from Solomon and his son. Only one tribe, JUDAH, would remain to perpetuate the Davidic line (BENJAMIN, which never seems to have recovered from the slaughter and near extinction mentioned in Jdg. 20–21, was counted with Judah; cf. 1 Ki. 11:32, 36; 12:20–21). When Solomon heard of the prophecy, or perhaps of a plot by Jeroboam to bring Ahijah's prophecy to an early fulfillment, he sought to kill Jeroboam, who fled to safety in Egypt (the full account is in 1 Ki. 11:26–40).

When Solomon died, his son Rehoboam went to SHECHEM to be made king over the twelve tribes. "When Jeroboam son of Nebat heard this (he was still in Egypt, where he had fled from King Solomon), he returned from Egypt. So they sent for Jeroboam, and he and the whole assembly of Israel went to Rehoboam" (1 Ki. 12:2–3 NIV; for the basis of this translation see above). With Jeroboam leading a delegation, the twelve tribes demanded that Rehoboam lighten the demands of the monarchy. Instead, three days later, he announced burdensome increases. At that, the northern tribes revolted.

Soon afterward, Rehoboam foolishly sent the worst possible man he could have chosen, Adoram (ADONIRAM), who headed the hated corvée, to try to pacify the northern ten tribes. They stoned

Aerial view of Dan (looking NE), with the spring in the foreground and Mount Hermon and Caesarea Philippi in the background. Jeroboam I established a golden calf worship site at Dan.

Adoram to death and forced Rehoboam to flee back to Jerusalem. By now it was widely known that Jeroboam had returned from exile in Egypt, that he had played a prominent part in the futile negotiations with King Rehoboam and was sympathetic to their cause, and most importantly, that one of their own prophets, Ahijah from Shiloh, had prophesied that Jeroboam would be king after the death of Solomon. So northern Israel called Jeroboam to the coronation convocation to make him their king (1 Ki. 12:4–20; cf. the reaction later to the prophetic word that JEHU was to be king, 2 Ki. 9:1–13).

B. His reign. The first threat to newly crowned Jeroboam came from Rehoboam, who massed an army for an invasion of Israel. SHEMAIAH intervened with a word from the Lord not to begin intertribal warfare, so the troops returned home. Meanwhile, Jeroboam fortified Shechem and Penuel, both in strategic passes and both connected with the patriarchs.

1. The sins of Jeroboam. Contrary to the message of Ahijah that had brought him to power (1 Ki. 11:38–39), Jeroboam perverted the worship of the Lord by reviving the Mesopotamian bull worship of pre-Abrahamic days as AARON had done (12:27–30; Exod. 32:1–5; Josh. 24:14–15; on comparisons between Jeroboam and Aaron, see *JBL* 76 [1967]: 129–40, and U. Cassuto, *A Commentary on the Book of Exodus* [1967], 407–10), to keep the people from making religious pilgrimages to Jerusalem. Golden bulls (prob. not just bull-pedestals; see R. K. Harrison, *Old Testament Times* [1970], 210–11) became the objects of worship at BETHEL and at DAN (PLACE), contrary to the law (Exod. 20:4; see CALF, GOLDEN). This was the great sin of Jeroboam. Further, he promoted worship at the HIGH PLACES, appointed non-Levites as priests, and changed the date of the Feast of Tabernacles (perhaps by changing the calendar; see *JBL* 83 [1964]: 109–18). An unnamed prophet from Judah prophesied at Bethel against the altar there: JOSIAH would profane it by burning dead men's bones upon it and tear it down (fulfilled about 300 years later, 2 Ki. 23:15–16). Jeroboam continued his policies and became the prime biblical example of an idolatrous king. (See E. T. Mullen, Jr., "The Sins of Jeroboam: A Redactional Assessment," *CBQ* 49 [1987]: 212–32.)

2. The wars of Jeroboam. After the initial peace resulting from Shemaiah's prophecy (1 Ki. 12:22–24), Jeroboam's kingdom was at war first with Rehoboam and then with Abijam of Judah (14:30; 15:6; 2 Chr. 12:15). In the fifth year of his reign, Shishak of Egypt invaded Judah and Israel in an attempt to gain control of Palestine during the civil war that had weakened both parties (1 Ki. 14:25-28; Egypt's invasion of Israel is not mentioned in the Bible, but Shishak's victory inscription at Karnak lists Taanach, Shunem, Rehob, Mahanaim, and Megiddo—all Israelite cities— among the conquered places).

C. His ruin. Finally, in a decisive battle with Abijam, described in 2 Chr. 13:1-22, Jeroboam's forces were decisively defeated with the loss of Bethel and other border cities. Jeroboam never regained his power, and his son Nadab lasted only two years before Baasha's coup d'état. Ahijah's second recorded prophecy had been fulfilled (1 Ki. 14:2-18; 15:27-30). The dynasty of Jeroboam I was finished.

II. Jeroboam II. As the thirteenth (fourteenth, if Tibni is counted) king of Israel (coregent 793-782 B.C.; king, 782-753 according to Thiele; others, c. 786-746), Jeroboam II extended the Israelite empire into Transjordan from the Arabah to the borders of Hamath, in accordance with Jonah's lesser-known prophecy of national expansion (2 Ki. 14:25). The biblical account is very short (14:23-29; he is mentioned in 1 Chr. 5:17 in a genealogy), but his territorial expansion occurred in a power vacuum in the ANE and can be pieced together from archaeological sources (for the most thorough discussion, see Menahem Haran in *VT* 17 [1967]: 266-97). Briefly, the Assyrians weakened the kingdom of Ben-Hadad, Jeroboam recovered Transjordania from Ben-Hadad, and then the Assyrians were too busy with more important local and national problems to worry about Jeroboam's increasing power until after his death.

During this period, Israel enjoyed a peace, political prestige, and economic prosperity unparalleled since the days of Solomon, but its moral and religious life was bankrupt. Hosea and Amos reflect the religious and social decay (e.g., Hos. 6:4-10; 10:1-15; Amos 2:6-8; 3:13-4:5) of this period. The prosperity was only temporary. When Jeroboam II died, his son Zechariah ruled only six months before he was murdered, ending the Jehu dynasty in the fourth generation (2 Ki. 15:8-12). Thirty years later, Israel was no longer a nation. See also Israel, history of. — J. F. Babcock

Jeroham ji-roh'ham (ירֹחָם, H3739, derivation debated, possibly "soft" or "[God] is compassionate"; see Jaroah). **(1)** Son (or descendant) of Elihu, father of Elkanah, and grandfather of Samuel (1 Sam. 1:1). In the Levitical genealogies of Korah, his immediate ancestor is given as Eliab or Eliel (1 Chr. 6:27, 34). He may have been a nonpracticing Levite domiciled in the tribe of Ephraim (there were grave anomalies in the period of the judges that affected the Levites; cf. Jdg. 17:7-18:31).

(2) A descendant of Benjamin whose sons are listed among the heads of families living in Jerusalem (1 Chr. 8:27; cf. v. 28). He is usually identified with Jeremoth (v. 14; see the discussion in KD, *Chronicles*, 147-48).

(3) Descendant of Benjamin and father of Ibneiah; the latter was an early settler in Jerusalem following the exile (1 Chr. 9:8; cf. vv. 2-3).

(4) Son (or descendant) of Passhur and father of Adaiah; the latter is included in a list of priests who were heads of families and who are described as "able men, responsible for ministering in the house of God" in postexilic Jerusalem (1 Chr. 9:12-13; in Neh. 11:12 his immediate ancestor listed is Pelaliah, with Passhur given as a more distant ancestor).

(5) A Benjamite living in Gedor whose two sons, Joelah and Zebadiah, were among the ambidextrous warriors who joined David at Ziklag (1 Chr. 12:7).

(6) Father of Azarel; the latter was an officer over the tribe of Dan during David's reign (1 Chr. 27:22).

(7) Father of Azariah; the latter was a military commander who assisted the high priest Jehoiada in the successful overthrow of the apostate queen Athaliah (2 Chr. 23:1). — A. E. Cundall

Jerome juh-rohm'. Eusebius Sophronius Hieronymus was born of Christian parents about A.D. 345 (according to some, 330) in Strido, a town in Dalmatia, near the border with Italy and not far from the N coast of the Adriatic Sea. He studied literature and rhetoric in Rome, traveled in Gaul, and settled for a time in the Italian city of Aquileia, which was a short distance from Strido. Then, with some friends, he traveled to Palestine around 374 and spent a few years as a hermit in the Syrian desert, after which he was ordained as priest in ANTIOCH OF SYRIA. In 382 he was called to Rome by Pope Damasus, whom he served as secretary, but four years later he returned to the E and settled in BETHLEHEM, devoting the rest of his life to biblical and theological scholarship.

Jerome was a vigorous proponent of ASCETICISM, became involved in various theological controversies, and was at times unrestrained in his polemics. But as one of the few church fathers who knew the Hebrew language and who had firsthand familiarity with the Holy Land, Jerome made a singular contribution to the study of Scripture through voluminous writings, especially his commentaries and his translation of the Bible into Latin (see VULGATE). He died in the year 420. (See further J. Steinmann, *Saint Jérôme* [1958]; H. F. D. Sparks in *The Cambridge History of the Bible*, ed. P. R. Ackroyd et al., 3 vols. [1963–70], 1:510–41; J. N. D. Kelley, *Jerome: His Life, Writings, and Controversies* [1975]; D. Brown, *Vir Trilinguis: A Study in the Biblical Exegesis of Saint Jerome* [1992]; A. Bernet, *Saint Jérôme* [2002]; S. Rebenich, *Jerome* [2002]; M. H. Williams, *The Monk and the Book: Jerome and the Making of Christian Scholarship* [2006].)

Jerub-Baal ji´ruhb-bay´uhl (יְרֻבַּעַל *H3715*, "Baal contends [for me]"; cf. JARIB; alternately, "Baal is [*or* shows himself] great"). Also Jerubbaal. The name given to GIDEON when he destroyed his father's BAAL altar at OPHRAH. The text says, "So that day they called Gideon 'Jerub-Baal,' saying, 'Let Baal contend with him,' because he broke down Baal's altar" (Jdg. 6:32; the name is also used in 7:1; 8:29, 35 [the last occurrence of the name Gideon]; ch. 9 [which according to some scholars is the product of literary confusion and refers to someone other than Gideon]; and 1 Sam. 12:11). Some suggest that prior to this incident Jerub-Baal had been his name, reflecting the syncretism which then prevailed among the Israelites, but that his act of iconoclasm gave it a new significance. It should be noted that the Hebrew word *baʿal H1251* means "lord, owner," and in the early history of Israel was sometimes applied to the true God. Later, when the term came to be regarded as disgraceful, the name Jerub-Baal was altered to Jerub-Besheth (from *bōšet H1425*, "shame," 2 Sam. 11:21); cf. ISH-BOSHETH and MEPHIBOSHETH. (See J. A. Emerton in *JTS* 27 [1976]: 289–312.)   S. BARABAS

Jerub-Besheth ji-rub´uh-sheth (יְרֻבֶּשֶׁת *H3717*, deformation of יְרֻבַּעַל *H3715*). Also Jerubbesheth. See JERUB-BAAL.

Jeruel ji-roo´uhl (יְרוּאֵל *H3725*, "foundation of God"). An area in the Judean wilderness where King JEHOSHAPHAT defeated a Transjordanian coalition (2 Chr. 20:16). The exact location is not known, but it was apparently between the Pass of ZIZ (just N or NW of EN GEDI, cf. v. 2) and the Desert of TEKOA (cf. v. 20; see Y. Aharoni et al., *The Carta Bible Atlas*, 4th ed. [2002], map 129).   S. BARABAS

Jerusalem ji-roo´suh-luhm (יְרוּשָׁלֵם *H3731* [*Ketib* apparently יְרוּשָׁלֵם, while the fully written *Qere perpetuum*, יְרוּשָׁלַיִם in Jer. 26:18 et al., seems to be a late form, perhaps after the analogy of מִצְרַיִם *H5213*, see EGYPT], meaning "foundation of peace" or "foundation of the god Shalem"; Aram. יְרוּשְׁלֵם *H10332*; Gk. Ἰερουσαλήμ *G2647*, variant Ἱεροσόλυμα [cf. BDF §56.1], gentilic Ἱεροσολυμίτης *G2643*). Capital of the Hebrew nation and of modern Israel, widely regarded as the world's most significant city (cf. Ps. 87:2–5). Beginning with the time of DAVID, it served as God's dwelling place (1 Ki. 8:13). Jerusalem was the scene of Christ's passion, death, and resurrection (cf. Lk. 9:51), and it will be the venue of the events of the end time (Zech. 14).

  I. Geography
    A. Location
    B. Topography
    C. Characteristics
  II. History
    A. Canaanite
    B. United kingdom
    C. Divided kingdom
    D. Restoration
    E. Roman
    F. Postbiblical

III. Installations
   A. Borders
   B. Interior
IV. Symbolism
   A. Significations
   B. Personification
   C. Universalization

I. Geography

A. Location. Jerusalem is situated 33 mi. E of the Mediterranean Sea and 14 mi. W of the Dead Sea, at an elevation of c. 2,500 ft., at a major road junction on the crest of W Palestine's central ridge. This ridge rises slowly from the promontory of Mount GILBOA in the N (1,700 ft.) to a point near HEBRON, c. 20 mi. S of Jerusalem (3,370 ft.). Although Jerusalem's highest point (under 2,600 ft.) cannot rival Hebron to its S, DAVID properly described its location, for most of his subjects, as a place "where the tribes go up" (Ps. 122:4).

From the W, the rail line approaches Jerusalem through SAMSON's rugged valley of SOREK (Jdg. 16:4), and ending in the valley of REPHAIM (2 Sam. 5:22) just S of the city. For most of the city's modern history, the only alternative route consisted of the Jaffa highway, which branched off from the valley of AIJALON to the N and snaked its way along the canyons through Abu Ghosh. But the burned out bodies of modern Israeli armored cars that have lined its shoulders bear mute testimony to the difficulty of going up to ZION (cf. Isa. 7:6).

From the E, one leaves the JORDAN, by JERICHO, at over 1,200 ft. below sea level and must then ascend through the barren Senonian chalk wilderness of Judah by the gorge ADUMMIM (Josh. 15:7), today called "the ascent of blood," probably because of its red ochre deposits. Rainfall is practically nonexistent here, the winds from the western sea having been drained of their life-giving moisture by the intervening ridge. The highest point is reached just E of the city, on the 2,650 ft. crest of the MOUNT OF OLIVES.

Though difficult of access, Jerusalem enjoys a correspondingly protected location. Furthermore, whereas lacking significant natural resources, it does lie astride the major N-S trade route, which renders its location both commercially and politically strategic. It was its control of this ridge route that probably dictated its settlement in the first place. Because of the mountains that "surround Jerusalem" (Ps. 125:2), the city's plateau remains hidden until the traveler suddenly tops one of the higher ridges that surround it. From the E, for example, as one crosses Olivet — as is still done every Palm Sunday, following the course of Christ's triumphal entry — the whole city of Jerusalem suddenly appears, spread out in a great panorama.

B. Topography. Jerusalem consists of a complex of five hills, once sharply distinguished, carved out of hard Cenomanian limestone, roughly one half mile square. On the W and S sides lies the "L" shaped Valley of HINNOM (Josh. 15:8); eastward is the gorge of the brook KIDRON, perhaps Joel's Valley of Jehoshaphat (Joel 3:2; see JEHOSHAPHAT, VALLEY OF).

Aerial view of Jerusalem looking N.

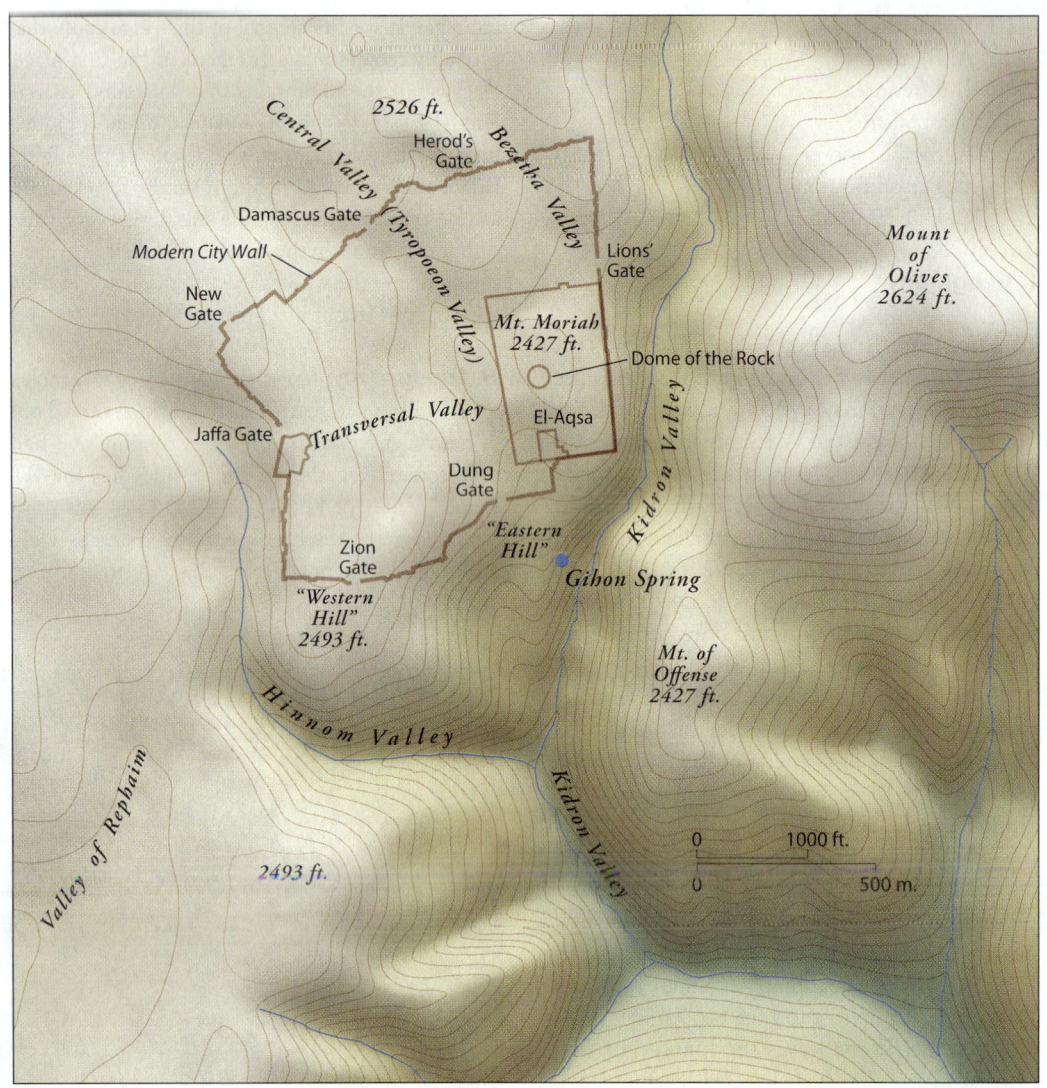

The topography of modern Jerusalem.

The interior of the square was once bisected by a ravine running from N to S and finally curving into the Kidron just N of its junction with the Hinnom. In NT times it was called the Tyropoeon Valley (Jos. *War* 5.4.1, *ton tyropoion*, "of the cheesemakers," possibly a corruption of some Heb. or Aram. term), and it may be (partially) equivalent to the OT "Mortar" (Zeph. 1:11 NRSV). Though still discernible in the N, in the form of a depression W of the Damascus Gate, successive destructions of the city have now obliterated most of its course. Jerusalem's present day profile, with its apparently uninterrupted rise from the Kidron escarpment westward to "Mount Zion" (see below) and then with an abrupt drop into the Hinnom Valley, fails to indicate the up to 100 ft. of debris with which the central ravine is now choked.

East of the Tyropoeon lie three hills. The southernmost is the smallest, its crest having an elevation of only c. 2,250 ft.; but its sharp declivities and narrow ridge-like character, slightly pinched off in the N (cf. K. M. Kenyon, *Jerusalem: Excavating 3000 Years of History* [1967], 27), made it the most easily defensible part of the whole. Archaeological investigation has confirmed that this was the original ZION, or CITY OF DAVID (2 Sam. 5:7).

Northward (Ps. 48:2) lies the broader summit of MORIAH, originally a threshing floor, but designated by David as a place of sacrifice and the temple mount (2 Chr. 3:1), which it has remained to this day. Its rocky peak, over which the altar of sacrifice was erected, may be identified with the spot on which ABRAHAM was willing to offer up his son ISAAC, "on one of the mountains" of "the region of Moriah" (Gen. 22:2). For nearly thirteen centuries it has been covered by the Muslim shrine known as the Dome of the Rock. The surrounding area is now artificially leveled off to form a roughly rectangular court (1,000 by 1,500 ft.; 2,450 ft. in elevation) called the Ḥaram esh-Sharîf, or "Noble Sanctuary."

A fairly flat saddle once separated Moriah from the third or NE hill, Mount Bezetha, the peak of which still lies outside the NE city wall. The natural lines of demarcation are somewhat obscured, for when HEROD expanded the Ḥaram area northward, he obliterated a ravine that had formerly cut across the NE corner of the temple area. It should also be noted that between Moriah and the City of David lies a promontory, usually referred to as the OPHEL ("swelling"; see below), which in the past was a distinct hill at almost 2,400 ft. in elevation, but no longer visible because of quarrying and construction.

Jerusalem's western half was subdivided by a larger ravine that branched off midway in the course of the Tyropoeon: the "cross valley" (Transversal Valley) cutting westward to the present Jaffa Gate. To its S lay what the OT may have designated as Mount GAREB (Jer. 31:39; cf. J. Simons, *Jerusalem in the Old Testament* [1952], 231–33, and *IDB*, 2:853, though see below, II.C.3), but to which subsequent history, after the abandonment of the original City of David in A.D. 70, has assigned the old name of Zion (Jos. *War* 5.4.1), probably because of the dominant position of its 2,550 ft. elevation peak. Though Gareb was once again embraced within expanded Byzantine Jerusalem, in A.D. 985 the Muslim Caliph of Cairo, so as to shorten the city's line of defense, once more redirected the southern wall roughly 1,000 ft. farther N, with the result that the southern part of Gareb, together with the whole of ancient Zion, have henceforward remained outside the walls of Jerusalem and have become partially unoccupied.

To the NW, the land stretches off in an incline, broken only by what was once a hill or spur, on which now rests the Church of the Holy Sepulchre.

C. Characteristics. The annual rainfall at Jerusalem amounts to about 25 in., but this is concentrated in the winter months (see RAIN). Temperature, moderated by the elevation, shows seasonal averages ranging from 40° to 85°F. Snow is rare; but the stone buildings of old Jerusalem can, upon occasion, become dank and cold. Yet from May until October, the grass turns brown, and the *hamsin* wind that blows from off the eastern deserts may produce a period of serious heat and drought. Generally, however, the western sea breeze keeps the days mild and the evenings cool.

Two springs provide the water that was so essential for occupation, especially prior to the coming of the Israelites, with whom appeared also the development of cisterns with linings of waterproof lime. The GIHON SPRING (1 Ki. 1:33; 2 Chr. 32:30), or Virgin's Spring, issues from a grotto on the Kidron Valley side of the City of David and produces an intermittent stream. EN ROGEL (Josh. 15:7; 2 Sam. 17:17), or Job's Well, perhaps the JACKAL WELL of Neh. 2:13, lies farther S, below the junction of the Kidron and the Hinnom. It is a true well, which in winter bubbles up in artesian fashion (November to March, after the seasonal rain has raised the surrounding water table).

II. History. The scientific study of Jerusalem's history begins with the coming of Edward Robinson, an American pastor, to the city in 1838. It was taken up in earnest by the Palestinian Exploration Fund in 1865, who sponsored the extensive tunneling projects of Captain (later Sir) Charles Warren (1867–1869), around the temple area. Muslim opposition then brought such work generally to an end, though F. J. Bliss and E. C. Dickie were able to sink similar shafts and tunnels around parts of the perimeter of the former city (1894–97). Scientifically controlled excavation, checked by an accurate system of pottery chronology, began yet another generation later; and even then, religious controls, plus the urban construction that covers most of the land, prevented thorough archaeological investigation. A noteworthy exception was the series of campaigns conducted by Kathleen Kenyon in various parts of the city (1961–67). With the reunification of the city under Israeli control in 1967, opportunities reopened; and the Hebrew University excavations, commenced by B. Mazar in 1968 outside the western and southern walls of the temple area, have helped to clear up a number of remaining historical uncertainties (see further N. Avigad, *Discovering Jerusalem* [1983], 13–22). The Bible constitutes the primary source for reconstructing the history of Jerusalem, unequaled for any other ANE city. Its words are supplemented by an increasing flow of archaeological data and also, especially in its later periods, by contemporaneous, secular literary sources.

A. Canaanite. The earliest remains from Jerusalem consist of Early Paleolithic hand-axes (but no skeletons), systematically excavated in 1933 from the SOREK plain, or Valley of Rephaim (see REPHAIM, VALLEY OF), just SW of the present city. Urban culture, however, arose with the coming of the Canaanites in 3000 B.C.

1. Pre-Israelite, to 1406 B.C. The Early Bronze Age (3000–2000 B.C.) Canaanitish settlement developed on the SE ridge, the old city of Zion. Its first historical mention is found at the close of this period, in Scripture, when the patriarch ABRAHAM honored its priest-king MELCHIZEDEK, minister of EL ELYON ("God Most High," Gen. 14:19) as a true servant of Yahweh (v. 22; he serves indeed in his double office as a type of Jesus Christ, Ps. 110:4; Heb. 7). It was to the adjoining hill of Moriah (2 Chr. 3:1) that Abraham later returned, c. 2015, to offer up his son ISAAC as a sacrifice to God (Gen. 22:2).

The city is first named in Middle Bronze Age times (2000–1600) in Egyptian 12th-dynasty EXECRATION TEXTS, c. 1900–1800, which employ the form *(U)rušalimum*, "foundation [?] of Shalem"; compare its initial biblical designation, in Moses' writing of Genesis, as SALEM (Gen. 14:18; cf. Ps. 76:2). The Hebrew adjective *šālēm* H8969 signifies "complete, prosperous, safe, peaceful" (cf. Heb. 7:2), though it may also have been the name of a "pros-

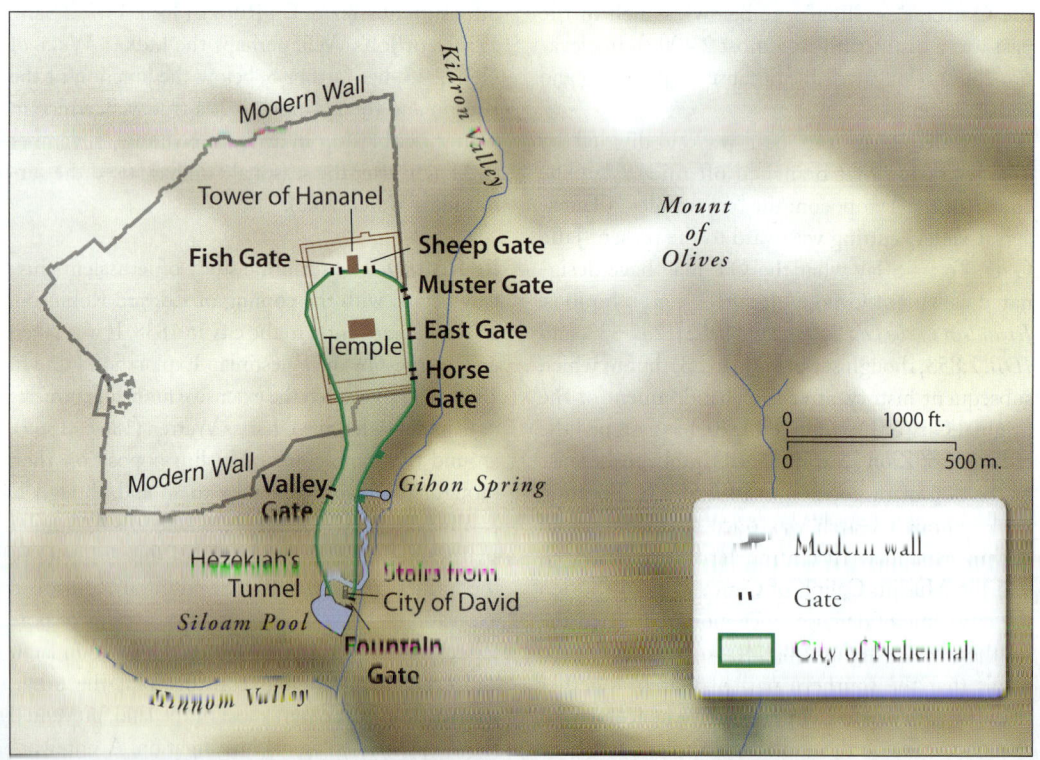

Jerusalem in the time of Nehemiah.

This excavation in the City of David (Area G) reveals a 9th-cent. B.C. stepped-stone structure, an 8th/7th-cent. B.C. four-room house, and a Persian period tower.

pering" Canaanite deity, Shalem. The name was not originally Hebrew in any event.

The choice of Jerusalem's location seems to have been dictated by factors of defense and of WATER. The latter was supplied from the Gihon Spring in the Kidron Valley below and to the E (2 Chr. 32:30, and see below). Correspondingly, the E walls, which were once thought to have run along the eastern edge of the crest, and hence to have restricted the city to a width of about 100 yards, are now known to have lain, at least from 1800 B.C. onward, some 50 yards farther E, two thirds of the way down the slope, which was crowded with houses. The area of the wide northern wall, over 20 ft. in thickness, has been closely pinpointed by K. Kenyon's excavations. They demonstrate that occupation prior to the 10th cent. B.C. began at a point 100 yards S of the present S wall of Jerusalem (Kenyon, *Jerusalem*, 26). The city then extended about one-quarter mile southward. Its western wall lay on the summit of the ridge, along its W side. Its total area, once thought to have been less than 8 acres (not uncharacteristic of Canaan's towns), is now known to have been at least 12 acres. Finally, its elevation, while less than Moriah or Gareb, was not such as to impair its security, fire power being limited as it was in those days. To sustain its population, the surrounding cultivated areas must have covered some 10,000 acres (M. Ben-Dov, *Historical Atlas of Jerusalem* [2002], 15).

2. Jebusite, to 1003 B.C. Midway in the Late Bronze Age (1600–1200), the records of JOSHUA's wars at the time of the conquest (1406–1400) identify a certain ADONI-ZEDEK as "king of Jerusalem" (Josh. 10:1). This Amorite, indeed, headed up the confederacy of southern Canaanitish kings that opposed Joshua; and he lost his life, following their defeat at BETH HORON (10:23, 26; 12:10). But Jerusalem itself seems to have escaped unscathed.

A decade or so later, after the death of Joshua, Jerusalem was captured by the tribe of JUDAH (Jdg. 1:1, 8), only to be reoccupied by the Canaanitish Jebusites (1:21; see JEBUS). The TELL EL-AMARNA tablets, from the Egyptian 18th dynasty, include letters from an ʿAbdi-Kheba (a HURRIAN, or HORITE, name), king of *Urusalim* or *Bethšalem*, to the pharaoh AKHENATEN (prob. 1379–1361; see

This recent discovery in Jerusalem is thought to have been part of David's palace.

CAH 2/2, 3rd ed. [1975], 105). They speak of the former's need for Egyptian mercenary troops in view of the threatening presence of the Habiru, possibly the Hebrews. At the time of the Benjamite outrage early in the 14th cent. (cf. 20:28: Aaron's grandson was still high priest), Jerusalem is thus disparagingly described as "the city of foreigners" (19:12 NRSV), "this city of the Jebusites" (v. 11), though actually its moral standards could not have been worse than those of the Hebrew Benjamites to its N (vv. 18, 22, 25). It remained Jebusite until David's final victory and conquest in 1003 (Josh. 15:63; 1 Chr. 11:5).

During the period of the judges, the city carried the corresponding name of Jebus (Jdg. 19:10–11; 1 Chr. 11:4). It was at this point, in the 14th cent., that the Jebusites constructed a series of stone-filled platforms down the hill slope to the wall on the E side of the city (cf. Josh. 15:8; 18:16, though technically the city did not then reach to the Hinnom Valley). These stone "shoulders" enabled a more efficient use of the slope for building; but unhappily the eventual collapse of the hillside platforms, combined with quarryings on the crest, have removed all traces of Canaanite buildings.

B. United kingdom

1. David, to 970 B.C. Immediately after his consecration in Hebron in 1003 as king over the united tribes of Israel (2 Sam. 5:3) and his repulse of the Philistines' attempt to check him at Baal Perazim in the Valley of Rephaim (vv. 18–20), David advanced against the still Canaanitish city of Jerusalem, which was separating his own tribe of Judah from that of Benjamin and from the other tribes farther N. Rather than risk a direct assault against the well-nigh impregnable walls of the Jebusites (cf. v. 6), David ordered a surprise attack through the "water shaft" (v. 8; but see below, III.B). Both to reward the individual who would lead this dangerous ascent through the water tunnel, and possibly at the same time to accomplish the replacement of his uncontrollable half-nephew Joab as commander of the armed forces (cf. 3:23–27, 39), David offered this supreme post to whoever should "lead the attack against the Jebusites"; but Joab himself "went up first, and so he received the command" (1 Chr. 11:6). The term Zion (Heb. *ṣiyyôn* H7482, possibly meaning "fortress") described the citadel that David then succeeded in taking (v. 7), though it came to signify the SE hill as a whole (2 Ki. 19:31) and eventually the entire, expanded city of Jerusalem (cf. Ps. 133:3).

David forthwith transferred his residence to Zion, the fortified city of Jerusalem, and named it after himself, "the City of David" (2 Sam. 5:9). He also engaged in considerable building. This included his palace, by means of cedar timbers and skilled craftsmen provided by Hiram king of Tyre (v. 11), and the Millo (v. 9), "a filling," which may refer to a reinforcing of the system of platforms and terraces already established by the Canaanites on the eastern slope of Zion (cf. NIV and see K. Kenyon in *BA* 27 [1964]: 43; note also the similar activity by Solomon, 1 Ki. 9:15, 24, and Hezekiah, 2 Chr. 32:1–5).

The strategic importance of David's move cannot be overestimated. Although the "City of David" was no larger than 15 acres (at the SE corner of modern Jerusalem), it gave him a military location of exceptional strength as well as a political position in a city that was essentially his "personal property," not subject to any of the Israelitish tribes. It was "neutral" as well, being situated on a tribal border and associated with neither N Israel nor S Judah. David then proceeded to the most significant act of all—making it the religious capital of his nation, by bringing up within its walls the Ark of the

COVENANT (2 Sam. 6:12), which made Jerusalem the dwelling place of God himself. For Yahweh had graciously condescended to come to his people in the form of the SHEKINAH or glory cloud (Exod. 40:34–35), which rested between the two cherubim on the golden plate or "mercy seat" that covered the ark (25:21–22; cf. Num. 7:89). He could thus be described as "the LORD Almighty, who is enthroned [*lit.*, dwells] between the cherubim" (1 Sam. 4:4; 2 Sam. 6:2).

Ever since its capture by the Philistines at the battle of EBENEZER, c. 1080 (1 Sam. 4:11, 22), the ark had remained apart from the public worship of Israel (1 Chr. 13:3; but cf. 1 Sam. 14:18). Even after its return to Israel, however, because of the disaster it had produced at BETH SHEMESH (1 Sam. 6:19–20), it had been left at KIRIATH JEARIM (7:1–2), farther inland on the road to Jerusalem. But soon after his occupation of Zion in 1003, David assembled 30,000 of the leading men of Israel formally to conduct it into his new capital (2 Sam. 6:1–2). After a three-months' delay at the house of OBED-EDOM, occasioned by the death of UZZAH for having profaned the sacred object (vv. 7, 11), the king finally achieved his goal, conducting the ark within the walls of the City of David and placing it in a tent sanctuary (vv. 12, 17). He instituted regular offerings and a musical service in conjunction with it (1 Chr. 16); henceforward Zion was to be "the city of God" (Ps. 46:4; cf. 48:2). See below under IV.

David reigned in Jerusalem for thirty-three years, 1003–970 (2 Sam. 5:5). He "took more concubines and wives in Jerusalem" (v. 13), and there were born to him eleven additional sons, including both NATHAN and SOLOMON (vv. 14–16), who appear respectively in the lineal and the official genealogies of Christ as recorded in the Gospels (Lk. 3; Matt. 1; see GENEALOGY OF JESUS CHRIST). The city came increasingly to be settled by Israelites, especially of the neighboring tribe of Benjamin (1 Chr. 8:28, 32), but also the tribes of Judah, Ephraim, and Manasseh (9:3), and of course the Levites (v. 34). Within his new palace, David cared for MEPHIBOSHETH, the crippled son of his former friend JONATHAN, and his family (2 Sam. 9:12–13); he received officials (10:15; 11:8, 13, 22; 20:22; 24:8); but he also committed his basest crimes, adultery with BATHSHEBA and the murder of her husband (11:1–4, 14–15). Solomon was eventually born of this union (12:24), c. 990. David's own high-handedness seems to have contributed to the subsequent deeds of lawlessness committed by his own sons; cf. the insinuation of immunity for AMNON as "the king's son" (13:4) and yet his murder two years later by his half brother ABSALOM (vv. 23, 28–29).

After three years of flight and exile from Jerusalem (2 Sam. 13:38), Absalom was enabled to return (14:23; cf. 15:8); but in about 980, after additional years of plotting, this oldest surviving son succeeded in driving his father out of Zion (15:16, 37) and even occupied the palace, on the roof of which he publicly cohabited with his father's concubines (16:22; on its retributive character, cf. 11:2; 12:8, 11–12). Scripture traces David's flight in detail. Whereas certain points, such as his initial tarrying "at a place some distance away" (Heb. *bêt hammerḥāq*, 15:17; ASV mg., "at the Far House") remain uncertain, much of his route is identified by yet recognizable geographical features.

When David's party had moved eastward, across the brook Kidron (2 Sam. 15:23), he was overtaken by the high priest ZADOK and all the Levites bearing the ark of the covenant from its tent on Mount Zion; but David had them return to Jerusalem. The group moved E and "continued up the Mount of Olives" (v. 30). David was met by HUSHAI at "the summit, where people used to worship God" (v. 32), indicating the existence of a shrine, perhaps near the present Dome of the Ascension close to the summit of Olivet. David had taken the shorter, and harder, route over the crest of the ridge rather than going around the S end of Olivet, as does the modern highway to Jericho. Then, "a short distance beyond the summit" (16:1), he was met by ZIBA with provisions, from which point he proceeded past BAHURIM (v. 5), perhaps the modern Ras et-Temim, E of Mount Scopus (N of Olivet; cf. G. Wright and F. Filson, *The Westminster Historical Atlas to the Bible*, rev. ed. [1956], 108) and on toward the Jordan. Meanwhile the sons of the priests Zadok and Abiathar were waiting at En Rogel, just S of Jerusalem, to carry intelligence from Hushai to David (17:16–17); they were almost apprehended at Bahurim (v. 18), but managed to hide and then get the necessary word to David for a prompt crossing of the Jordan River (v. 22). After the defeat and death of Absalom, David was again installed in his capital of Jerusalem (19:15, 40; 20:3).

Near the end of his reign, David, in a moment of faithlessness (cf. Ps. 30:5–6), ordered a military census of Israel (2 Sam. 24:1–3), with the result that a divinely sent plague decimated the land (v. 15). When the angel of Yahweh had reached the threshing floor of ARAUNAH the Jebusite on Mount Moriah, he "stretched out his hand to destroy Jerusalem" (v. 16), but God stayed his hand. The king therefore erected an altar on the spot and offered up propitiating sacrifices (v. 25). He then consecrated the site as "the house of the LORD [Yahweh] God," where would be "the altar of burnt offering for Israel" (1 Chr. 22:1; cf. 2 Chr. 3:1); and he proceeded to make elaborate preparations for the construction there of the temple of Yahweh (1 Chr. 22:2–19; 28:1—29:19), to replace the tent sanctuary on Mount Zion (cf. 2 Sam. 1:1–7; 1 Chr. 6:32).

In 970, at the close of David's reign, his son ADONIJAH, who stood next to Absalom in point of age, proposed to usurp the throne of Israel from Solomon, the heir designate. While in the very act of being crowned at En Rogel (1 Ki. 1:9), Adonijah heard sounds from the Gihon Spring, 700 yards farther up the Kidron (which seems incredible but is still possible today), indicating that Nathan and Zadok had persuaded David to have Solomon anointed there, immediately, as his successor (vv. 38–45). Thus Adonijah's attempt was frustrated. Shortly thereafter, David died and was buried in the City of David (2:10; see below, III.B).

2. Solomon, to 930 B.C. Along with his positive admonitions of faithfulness to God and to the Mosaic law (1 Ki. 2:2–4), David had given his son Solomon certain more negative, deathbed instructions about the removal or liquidation of those who had at various times opposed the king (vv. 5–9). Some were soon slain by Solomon (vv. 25, 34) or banished from Jerusalem (vv. 26–27); but the Benjamite SHIMEI, who had cursed David during his flight through Bahurim (2 Sam. 16:5–13; cf. 19:16–23), was ordered to build a house in Jerusalem, with the understanding that this asylum should last only so long as he stayed within the city. He was to make no attempt to cross even the Kidron, eastward toward his home (1 Ki. 2:36–38; cf. J. A. Montgomery, *A Critical and Exegetical Commentary on the Books of Kings*, ed. H. S. Gehman, ICC [1951], 96). Three years later, in 967, Shimei broke his parole by a sudden pursuit westward to Gath to recover two runaway slaves. Upon his return Solomon was informed and Shimei was executed (vv. 39–49).

Like most of his royal successors in Judah, Solomon was born, lived, reigned, died, and was buried at Jerusalem (2 Sam. 12:24; 1 Ki. 11:42–43; 2 Chr. 1:13; 9:30; cf. Cant. 3:3). He considered Jerusalem as a standard of perfection (Cant. 6:4). Solomon conducted his Egyptian bride into this Davidic city, until he had built her a palace of her own (1 Ki. 3:1). He sacrificed before God's ark in Jerusalem (v. 15), and he left the city for his initial act of dedication to Yahweh (and his resultant acquisition of divine wisdom) only because the Mosaic TABERNACLE had not yet been moved down from GIBEON, 6 mi. to the N (1 Ki. 3:4; 2 Chr. 1:3–6).

Solomon proceeded to perform the actual construction of the Jerusalem TEMPLE that his father David had wished to build. It took from April/May of 966 (1 Ki. 6:1) to October/November of 959 (v. 38). Israel provided the labor force (5:13–17), but once again it was Hiram and the Phoenicians of Tyre who furnished both the timber and the skilled workers (5:6–12; cf. 2 Chr. 2:7). The great cedar logs were floated as rafts to the port of JOPPA, from which they were then transported overland to Jerusalem (2 Chr. 2:16). The basic plans for the temple called for an arrangement twice the size of the older tabernacle but also corresponded to the double chamber, porch, and court of known Egyptian and Phoenician temples of this period. They had been given their written formulation by David and, more fundamentally, by the very Spirit of God (1 Chr. 28:11–12, 19): it was the dwelling of God and, as the tabernacle before it, symbolized and typified the way of salvation, by which sinners may come to the presence of God (cf. Heb. 8:1–5; 9:23–24). The building itself faced E and was relatively small: 60 cubits (c. 90 ft.) long, 20 cubits (30 ft.) wide, and 30 cubits (45 ft.) high. Importance lay not only in the building but also in the sacred enclosure, with presumably the outdoor altar rather than the most holy place (the "oracle") of the building resting over the Moriah threshing floor (1 Chr. 22:1). This in turn would have required certain leveling and construction of retaining walls (see below, III.B).

The city walls of Jerusalem were necessarily extended northward to include the Moriah area (1 Ki. 3:1); and Kenyon discovered that occupation N of the original Canaanite northern wall (see above, A.1) did in fact begin in Solomonic times (*Jerusalem*, 56). On the W, the new walls simply continued along the western edge of the summit of the Zion-Moriah ridge; on the E, however, Zion's walls stood two-thirds of the way down the slope. These Solomon did not seek to extend, but built his northern prolongation along the eastern edge of the crest only (Kenyon, *Jerusalem*, 200 n. 20a), thus pinching off the width of the city to a little more than 50 yards, at least at the point where Solomon's addition joined the former northern wall. As a result of this expansion, the city grew from about 12–15 acres (and a population of perhaps 2,000–3,000) to about 35 acres (with a doubling or tripling of the population).

Solomon brought the ark up to Mount Moriah from Mount Zion during the Feast of Tabernacles the following year, 958 (2 Chr. 5:2–10). He also reunited it with the remaining elements of the Mosaic sanctuary by bodily transporting the tabernacle to Jerusalem from Gibeon and laying it up within the new temple (5:5). The climax of the dedication occurred when the theophanic cloud of God's glory entered and filled the temple (1 Ki. 8:10–11), so that it became in very truth the "house of the LORD." Jerusalem was thus confirmed as the chosen city of God, as the place in which his Name condescended to dwell (2 Chr. 6:6).

Solomon also constructed an acropolis complex, with casemate walls and presumably extensive stable facilities (cf. 1 Ki. 9:19; 10:26), at the N end of the crest of Zion (K. Kenyon, *BA* 27 [1964]: 41; cf. *Jerusalem*, 56). Among his other public buildings were the following: the "House of the Forest of Lebanon," a 180-ft. hall resting on 45 columns of cedar in three rows; the throne room, which was distinguished as "the porch of judgment"; and a large palace, adequate for the king's HAREM of 1,000 women (1 Ki. 7:2–8). This last edifice, in fact, required thirteen years for its construction, as opposed to the seven for the temple (v. 1), though the latter did have the benefit of David's advance preparations. These structures are described as built "of blocks of high-grade stone cut to size and trimmed with a saw on their inner and outer faces of costly stones" (v. 9), topped by courses of cedar beams (v. 12). Kenyon's discovery, by the N wall of the old city of Zion, of a proto-Aeolic pilaster capital and of carefully polished facing stones similar to those found in Ahab's (Phoenician) palace at Samaria suggest the remnants of at least one of the Solomonic buildings at this point (*Jerusalem*, 59). Others were presumably erected to the S of the temple (where the Aksa Mosque now stands), at the SE end of Moriah, and in nearby areas.

The palace of the daughter of PHARAOH lay outside the City of David (1 Ki. 9:24), perhaps between Moriah and Zion, but not *on* either because of the presence of the holy ark, with which her own residence was felt to be incompatible (2 Chr. 8:11). It may have been associated with Ophel, possibly to the NE of the old Zion, where the ridge swings eastward; for the same term (*ʿōpel* H6755) may designate a similar "hill" or "projection" at Samaria (2 Ki. 5:24).

Scripture states also that Solomon made pools to water his trees (Eccl. 2:6), which may well refer to an "upper pool" near Gihon (cf. Isa. 7:3; 36:2; the old pool of 8:11?) and to the construction of the Shiloah water conduit (Isa. 8:6) for the water of the spring along the eastern side of Zion to the "Lower Pool" (22:9). This latter may be identified with the "King's Pool" (Neh. 2:14), or the Pool of Shelah (3:15), at the southern end of the city by the king's garden (2 Ki. 25:4), below the later Pool of SILOAM.

Evidence concerning the higher, western hill of Jerusalem used to be sparse. Kathleen Kenyon discovered no occupation on its SE slopes prior to the first Christian century, so she and others inferred that its S portion must not have been included within the city walls until HASMONEAN times. Excavations during the 1970s, however, have changed the picture dramatically (see below, II.C.3), and it is possible that some expansion to the W may have taken place as early as Solomon, who is said to have labored on the wall of Jerusalem (1 Ki. 9:15).

View looking SE across the Kidron Valley to the village of Silwan. The forested area above is called the Mount of Offense or Hill of Corruption because Solomon built residences and worship sites here for his foreign wives.

In the absence of clear evidence, we may envision a city shaped like a great inverted "L," extending W and S from Mount Moriah. The large wall at the extreme S that moves across the central Tyropoeon Valley and along the rim of the Hinnom Valley was first identified by F. J. Bliss and E. C. Dickie in 1898 as the original Solomonic wall, but Kenyon dated it only to the time of Herod Agrippa I, A.D. 41–44 (*Jerusalem*, 155–161), and must be abandoned in favor of something more closely approximating the present SW wall of Jerusalem. The N wall of the W arm would have followed the natural defense line along the S edge of the "cross valley" (see above, I.B), moving directly W from the temple area (Jos. *War* 5.4.1).

Some time after the completion of Solomon's various building projects, c. 945, he was visited in Jerusalem by the Arabian QUEEN OF SHEBA (1 Ki. 10.2), who was amazed by his civic accomplishments (vv. 4–5) as well as by his wisdom and spiritual blessings. The king had "made silver as common in Jerusalem as stones, and cedar as plentiful as sycamore-fig trees in the foothills" (v. 27). Yet in his latter years, Solomon's faith suffered eclipse as he became ensnared in the idolatrous practices of his numerous foreign (pagan) wives (11:4–8). He built, for example, "a high place for Chemosh the detestable god of Moab" on a hill E of the city (v. 7). Tradition locates its site on "the Mount of Offense," across the Kidron from the Pool of Siloam and the southern end of the SE hill that is Zion. See CORRUPTION, HILL (MOUNT) OF. As a result, Yahweh threatened the forfeiture of his kingdom (v. 11); indeed, it was at one of the very exits from Jerusalem that he awarded the whole of N and E Israel to JEROBOAM, subsequently the first ruler of the northern kingdom of Ephraim (v. 29). (For evidence that Jerusalem was a major city in the time of David and Solomon, see J. Cahill in *BAR* 30/6 [Nov.–Dec. 2004]: 20–31, 62–63.)

C. Divided kingdom. Even in his condemnation of Solomon's latter-day apostasy (cf. Eccl. 1:16–17; 2:9–11), Yahweh had promised a continuation for at least one tribe under the Davidic dynasty, "for the sake of David my servant and for the sake of

Jerusalem, which I have chosen" (1 Ki. 11:13; cf. vv. 32, 36). Actually, to the one group related to David, the tribe of Judah (12:20), there was added the tribe of Benjamin also (12:20–21), due doubtless to the location of Benjamin, "on the border of which Jerusalem was situated" (KD, *Kings*, 179). The prophet Ahijah thus symbolically awarded JEROBOAM ten of the tribes, reserving two for Solomon's son REHOBOAM (11:31; on Benjamin's association with Judah, cf. 2 Chr. 11:3, 23; the tribe of Simeon, though in the S, was associated with the northern kingdom of Israel, 15:9; 34:6).

1. Judah, to Jehu's revolt, 841 B.C. Upon Solomon's death in 930, and the refusal at SHECHEM of northern Israel (often referred to as EPHRAIM) to accept the kingship of Rehoboam, the latter fled to Jerusalem and sought to raise troops to subdue Ephraim (1 Ki. 12:18, 21). But God forbade it, and Rehoboam was forced to content himself with defensive measures (2 Chr. 11:5–12). Immediately after his own accession in the N, Jeroboam prohibited further pilgrimages to Jerusalem by members of the ten tribes (1 Ki. 12:27–28), though as a result many of the Levites emigrated S, strengthening the religious position of Jerusalem. Northern secular support for Rehoboam came to an end in three years (2 Chr. 11:14–17).

The division left Judah seriously weakened from a military standpoint, so that in 926, SHISHAK (Sheshonk I), first pharaoh of Egypt's 22nd dynasty, was able to raid, almost at will, throughout Israel (2 Chr. 12:2–4). Jerusalem escaped actual plundering, but only by the payment of a heavy indemnity in treasure (v. 9) arranged between Shishak and Rehoboam, presumably at Gibeon (Y. Aharoni, *The Land of the Bible. A Historical Geography*, rev. ed. [1979], 327). This is confirmed by the omission of Jerusalem from the list of plundered cities, as inscribed on the wall of Shishak's Karnak temple. The years that followed witnessed a further comparative impoverishment of Judah as opposed to the wealth of Israel and its successive capitals. ABIJAM (913–910) acted in faith and gained a striking victory against Israel, but only when almost overcome (2 Chr. 13).

All of the Judean kings of this period are stated to have been buried "in the City of David" (2 Chr. 12:16; 14:1; 21:1, 20), just as had David and Solomon before them (1 Ki. 2:10; 11:43). In the case of Asa son of Abijam in 869, Scripture states, "They buried him in the tomb that he had cut out for himself in the City of David" (2 Chr. 16:14). This statement might suggest that he was not buried "in the general tomb of the kings" (KD, *Chronicles*, 370), but elsewhere he is said to have been "buried with his fathers" (1 Ki. 15:24 KJV), a feature that had not appeared in the summaries of previous reigns but that is found henceforth for every monarch up to Hezekiah. Some infer from it that Asa may have been responsible for the construction of Jerusalem's royal necropolis (see below, III.B, and cf. Simons, *Jerusalem*, chart of biblical citations on pp. 201–4).

JEHOSHAPHAT (872–848) succeeded in strengthening the garrisons in Jerusalem (2 Chr. 17:2, 13, 19); and he regularly employed the city as a center for judicial reform (19:8), for assembly in times of crisis (20:4–5, 18), and for the celebration of triumphs (vv. 27–28). Under his son JEHORAM, Jerusalem suffered attack by Philistines and Arabs, who succeeded in breaking into the city and even looting the royal palace (21:16–17). It is significant that Jehoram is singled out for having led Jerusalem into apostasy (vv. 11, 13), due in large measure to his wife ATHALIAH, daughter of AHAB and JEZEBEL in the N (v. 6). He died early in 841, after a reign of only eight years, of an incurable disease of the bowels (vv. 18–19). This, plus the fact of his whole unworthy administration, may account for his burial outside the tomb of the kings, though still in the City of David (v. 20) and "with his fathers" (2 Ki. 8:24, i.e., others of the royal family). His son AHAZIAH reigned during only part of one year and then lost his life to JEHU, in the latter's northern revolt against the dynasty of Ahab. Ahaziah was brought to Jerusalem and buried in the royal tomb (9:28).

2. To the fall of Samaria, 722 B.C. Jehu's revolt of 841 disrupted the course of both Hebrew kingdoms. In the S it led to a six-year usurpation by Athaliah, queen mother of Ahaziah. The boy king JOASH was restored to the throne at the age of seven by the high priest JEHOIADA. The latter had commissioned faithful leaders out of all Judah (2 Chr. 23:2) and had Athaliah executed at the horse gate of the palace (v. 15, prob. not to be confused with the HORSE

GATE that was one of the main entrances to the city; see below, III.A). In both N and S, it made possible a period of Aramean domination. See ARAM (COUNTRY). HAZAEL of Damascus advanced as far as Gath in the SW, and only a tribute gained by stripping Jerusalem's temple and royal palace of their gold and treasures was able to save the city itself (2 Ki. 12:18–19). This was particularly discouraging, for Joash had been distinguished by his concern for the repair of the now deteriorating temple (v. 5). Finally in 813, his twenty-third year, he and his high priestly adviser, Jehoiada, had overcome priestly inertia and inefficiency by means of a special campaign and offering chest, so that considerable improvement was achieved (vv. 11–14). It was Joash's own later faithlessness, including even the execution of Jehoiada's son Zechariah, who had rebuked him, that led Yahweh to deliver up Jerusalem to a markedly inferior Aramean army (2 Chr. 24:23–24). The merit of Joash's regent Jehoiada is indicated by the latter's receiving burial in the City of David among the kings (v. 16); but, as in the case of his grandfather Jehoram, Joash died in disgrace and was buried outside the tomb of the kings, but within the City of David (v. 25).

His son AMAZIAH, who acceded to the throne in 796, suffered such a defeat before the armies of N Israel that Jerusalem was plundered; in this attack, much of the northern wall, from the EPHRAIM GATE to the (NW) CORNER GATE, was demolished (2 Ki. 14:13–14). This event can be dated precisely to 790 B.C., the time of UZZIAH's elevation to coregency (E. R. Thiele, *The Mysterious Numbers of the Hebrew Kings*, 1st ed. [1951], 70–72; contrast his less likely, earlier date in the 2nd ed. [1965], 83; cf. the 3rd ed. [1983], 118–119).

Uzziah, the son, accomplished major reconstruction, including the wrecked Corner Gate and the VALLEY GATE (see below, III.A; 2 Chr. 26:9). He erected catapults and other military engines for the defense of Jerusalem's ramparts. "His fame spread far and wide, for he was greatly helped until he became powerful" (v. 15). Kenyon's excavations have indicated a fairly complete rebuilding of the old Jebusite walls of 1800 B.C. at this time, after some 1,000 years of use, and a bit farther down the E slope of Zion (*Jerusalem*, 67; cf. Manasseh's "outer" wall, 2 Chr. 33:14). Uzziah may also have been responsible for a fortress and palace 3 mi. to the S of Zion, modern Ramat Rahel (M. Avi-Yonah, *Jerusalem* [1960], 38).

Uzziah and his son and coregent JOTHAM (751–736) seem to have been responsible for leveling out the "pinched off" area of the Solomonic extension of Jerusalem between Zion and Moriah (2 Chr. 27:3; cf. above, II.B.2, and see OPHEL), by running a wall so as to include much of the slope of this eastern part of the ridge, just as was already included along Mount Zion to the S (cf. ANGLE, THE). Because of Uzziah's eventual death by leprosy in 739, his interment, although in the City of David (2 Ki. 15:7), is specified as "in a field for burial that belonged to the kings" (2 Chr. 26:23); that is, he "was not buried in the graves of the kings, but only in the neighbourhood of them ... that his body might not defile the royal graves" (KD, *Chronicles*, 430). That he was buried "with his fathers" (2 Ki. 15:7) might then indicate the less honorable tomb of his grandfather Joash, and perhaps of Jehoram as well (see above). Simons, however, suggests: "not in one of the monumental rock tombs underneath, but in the 'field' above" (*Jerusalem*, 205). This might account in turn for the subsequent removal of his remains to another location. In 1931, E. L. Sukenik discovered in a museum on the Mount of Olives a marble tablet, a little over one foot square, dating to the late 1st cent. B.C., and reading in four lines of Aramaic, "Hither were brought the bones of Uzziah, king of Judah. Not to be opened." (See photo under UZZIAH.)

The works of Uzziah and Jotham proved sufficient for the latter's son, AHAZ, to withstand a siege by PEKAH of Samaria and REZIN of Damascus in 734 (2 Ki. 16:5; Isa. 7:1–2). Both Ephraimites and Arameans were able to carry off thousands of Judean captives (2 Chr. 28:5, 8; cf. vv. 9–15 on the return of 200,000 from Samaria). The Philistines and Edomites did the same on their respective borders (vv. 17–18), which may account for the prophecies of Obadiah and Joel at this time (cf. Obad. 11, 19–20; Joel 3:4, 19; cf. E. J. Young, *An Introduction to the Old Testament*, rev. ed. [1960], 255, 260) and Joel's proclamation of a fast and solemn assembly in Jerusalem (2:15). Contrary to the admonitions of Isaiah (Isa. 7:4–9), Ahaz forsook faith in God, submitted to the rising power of the Assyrians, and appealed to them for deliverance (2 Ki. 16:7–9; 2 Chr. 28:16), though this led to the fall of the northern kingdom, twelve years later in 722, and to the great Assyrian oppressions of Judah in the decades following.

Ahaz (743–728) was one of Judah's most undesirable monarchs. He "cut in pieces the utensils of the house of God. He shut up the doors of the house of the LORD and made himself altars in every corner of Jerusalem" (2 Chr. 28:24 NRSV). He is the first to be mentioned as practicing idolatry in the Hinnom Valley (v. 3), going as far as child sacrifice. Among the 8th-cent. prophets, Isaiah and Micah were particularly outspoken in their condemnation of the sins of contemporary Jerusalem (cf. Isa. 3:8; 10:10–11; Mic. 1:5; 3:10; cf. also Amos 2:4–5 regarding the northern kingdom). Ahaz lost his throne in 728 after a sixteen-year reign (2 Ki. 16:2; cf. 17:1; 18:1) and died two years later (Isa. 14:28; cf. v. 29 and see J. B. Payne in *BSac* 126 [1969]: 41–42). For his weakness and iniquity he was excluded from the tombs of the kings, though he was interred in Jerusalem (2 Chr. 28:27) in the City of David (2 Ki. 16:20).

In 725, which seems to have constituted the first official year of his son HEZEKIAH, the latter instituted a series of reforms in Jerusalem: reopening the temple (2 Chr. 29:3); burning the pagan articles that were found in its courts, over the ledge in the Kidron Valley to its E (v. 16; cf. 30:14); and sending from Dan to Beersheba, including the northern tribes, proclamations to keep the Passover (30:1, 5–9). Some of the Ephraimites mocked, but others did come (vv. 10–11, 26); for the Assyrians had already begun their final assault on Samaria and perhaps even encouraged such departures from the authority of N Israel (cf. ibid., 44).

3. To the fall of Jerusalem, 586 B.C. Hezekiah strengthened the walls of Jerusalem in the face of the Assyrian danger (2 Chr. 32:5; cf. Isa. 22:10). He stopped up the local water sources (2 Chr. 32:3–4) and constructed his famous tunnel (see below, III.B). He seems also to have advanced Jerusalem's line of fortifications southward by "another wall" (v. 5), so as to include the KING'S GARDEN and the Pool of SHELAH (Neh. 3:15 NRSV; NIV, SILOAM; cf. the "reservoir between the two walls," Isa. 22:11). An impressive wall (about 210 ft. long and 23 ft. thick) has been discovered in what is now the Jewish Quarter, and many scholars are confident that it should be identified with Hezekiah's new wall and with Nehemiah's BROAD WALL (Neh. 3:8; 12:38; see the account of this dramatic find in Avigad, *Discovering Jerusalem*, 46–54; according to Ben-Dov, *Historical Atlas*, 64 [illustration on p. 65], this wall was part of an internal system of fortifications, possibly protecting a palace). The evidence now makes clear that, by this time, the city had expanded to cover 120 acres or more, and that therefore the population had grown to at least 15,000 and perhaps as many as 25,000 (possibly in part because of the influx of refugees from the N after the Assyrian conquests; see Avigad, *Discovering Jerusalem*, 55).

The entire ministry of the greatest of the prophets, ISAIAH, centered in Zion (cf. Isa. 2:1; 40:2; 62:1), though it is chs. 13–66 of his book that date to the reign of Hezekiah (14:28; 20:1; 36:1; cf. 1:1). He preached justice and holiness (e.g., 28:14, 15; 29:13; ch. 57) and condemned Hezekiah's dependence upon an Egyptian alliance or upon his own building projects, in the king's vain hope of defying Assyria (20:5–6; 22:11–12; 30:1–5). In the days of Ahaz, shortly after 734, Isaiah had predicted an Assyrian attack, advancing against Jerusalem from Bethel and Ai (Aiath) in the N down to Nob, from which the Assyrians could "shake their fist at the mount of the Daughter of Zion, at the hill of Jerusalem" (10:28–32; cf. Mic. 1:9). NOB probably identifies the ridge with that which was later called Mount Scopus, NE of the city, a N extension of Olivet.

SARGON II of Assyria campaigned in the W in 720, when he defeated the Egyptians at RAPHIA on their border, and again in 711, when he destroyed ASHDOD on the Philistine plain. Because in his annals of the latter event Sargon spoke of "punishing Judah," the Isa. 8 passage may be descriptive of the route of the 711 attack (G. A. Barton, *Archaeology and the Bible* [1937], 469). Yet it may refer to the year 701, when although the main army of Sargon's successor SENNACHERIB moved against Jerusalem from LACHISH in the SW (cf. Mic. 1:10–15), another Assyrian unit may have marched against it via Samaria (cf. Aharoni, *The Land of the Bible*, 393).

Although Hezekiah had been forced to make peace with Sennacherib soon after the latter's advance into the outlying areas of Judah, and although he had surrendered a rich tribute by stripping the Jerusalem temple and palace of their treasures (2 Ki. 18:13–16), the Assyrians had treacherously broken faith with Hezekiah (cf. Isa. 33:7–8; 36:2), perhaps in the hope of further plunder from Jerusalem itself. Having laid the city under siege, the Assyrian commander or RABSHAKEH stood by the old Solomonic conduit and upper pool in the Kidron and ridiculed and blasphemed the God whose agent Assyria had, up to this point, unwittingly been (Isa. 10:5–7; 36:17, 20; cf. 37:10, 12). Rabshakeh's speech bears indirect testimony to the effectiveness of Hezekiah's earlier reforms toward a purified, centralized sanctuary, for he accused the king of opposing Yahweh, "whose high places and altars Hezekiah removed, saying to Judah and Jerusalem, 'You must worship before this altar in Jerusalem'" (2 Ki. 18:22; cf. Isa. 36:7).

In sincere repentance for his militarism, Hezekiah then turned to Yahweh and to his servant Isaiah (Isa. 37:2–7). As a result, the prophet fearlessly proclaimed the inviolability of Zion, that "the Virgin [inviolate] Daughter of Zion" would laugh the Assyrian to scorn (v. 22), and that God would defend Jerusalem, saving it "for my sake and for the sake of David my servant" (v. 35; cf. v. 33, or 31:4–5, 8–9). Soon thereafter, the Assyrian armies withdrew from the capital because of word of an Egyptian advance from the SW (37:8–9); and though Sennacherib's messengers continued to bring threatening letters against the city (vv. 10–14), the Lord did miraculously deliver Judah, striking down 185,000 of the enemy in one night, so that Sennacherib withdrew, never to return (vv. 36–38; 31:8; cf. 2 Chr. 32:23).

It is significant, however, that Isaiah's contemporary, Micah, proclaimed an opposite destructibility for Zion because of sin (Mic. 3:10–12). Punishment had been merely alleviated through the king's repentance (Jer. 26:19), and Isaiah too could speak of a postponed but still inevitable destruction (Isa. 39:5–8). Even at that time it was but a "remnant" that escaped the depredations and deportations of Sennacherib (37:32; cf. 36:1), and much of the next period of Isaiah's ministry was devoted to comforting Jerusalem, which had received of Yahweh's hand (through Sennacherib) double for all her sins (40:2; 51:17; cf. J. B. Payne in *WTJ* 29 [1966–67]: 179–90, and 30 [1967–68]: 50–59, 185–203).

Hezekiah's burial is located "on the ascent to the tombs of the descendants of David" (2 Chr. 32:33 NRSV). The language does not necessarily imply a burial place outside the royal sepulchres, but possibly the higher part of the graves, perhaps "due to the lack of room in the hereditary burying place of the kings" (E. L. Curtis, *A Critical and Exegetical Commentary on the Books of Chronicles*, ICC [1910], 493–94; see below, III.B). During the preceding 8th cent., Hezekiah's grandfather Jotham (2 Ki. 15:38) and great-great-grandfather Amaziah (14:20; 2 Chr. 25:28) had been buried in the royal necropolis, and Hezekiah was apparently the last monarch to be so interred.

Hezekiah's weaker successor, MANASSEH, resubmitted to Assyria and forfeited the independence that his father had gained at such cost (cf. 2 Chr. 33:11), though he did later rebuild the walls of old Zion (v. 14). K. Kenyon (*Jerusalem*, 66–68) describes, in fact, no less than six rebuildings of the SE wall during the last century and a half of the southern kingdom (Judah). None were built on the bedrock, as had been the previous Jebusite wall, which may account for some of the collapses even apart from hostile attack.

The ruins of a few small 7th-cent. houses have also been recovered from the top of the E slope of Zion, the earliest actual floorplans known from Jerusalem (ibid., 82–84). Their contributions to cultural knowledge, however, are disappointing. The homes there must have belonged to the lower classes: irregular in shape, with poorly built walls of rough stone covered with mud plaster. Pottery fragments were abundant, including a number of figurines of the fertility goddess and of animals, perhaps also used in apostate worship. Most significant were forty-one disk shaped stone weights of assorted sizes up to twenty-four shekels (c. 10 ounces), carefully polished and marked with their values.

The reign of Manasseh marked, indeed, the lowest point of religious practice in Jerusalem since the time of the Jebusites; and from a theological viewpoint the sins of this king rendered the destruction of Jerusalem inescapable (2 Ki. 21:13; cf. 23:26; 24:3). Both he and his short-lived son and successor AMON (642–640) maintained the idolatrous Solomonic shrines that still existed on the Hill of Corruption (23:13). "In both courts of the temple of the LORD" (2 Ki. 21:5) he practiced astral worship, which had been a temptation even from Mosaic times (Deut. 4:19; 17:3) but which now revived, perhaps as an adjunct to Assyrian overlordship. He rebuilt the high places that his father Hezekiah had overthrown (2 Ki. 21:3), "shed so much innocent blood that he filled Jerusalem from end to end" (v. 16), and even returned to the practices of the Canaanites, whom the Lord had cast out from before the children of Israel (2 Chr. 33:2), including child sacrifice in the Valley of Hinnom (v. 6). "Manasseh led Judah and the people of Jerusalem astray, so that they did more evil than the nations the LORD had destroyed before the Israelites" (v. 9).

Late in his reign, Manasseh was summoned to Babylon by the Assyrian monarch ASHURBANIPAL, perhaps in 648 after a major revolt in that city had been brought to an end. In fear for his life, Manasseh turned to Yahweh and was delivered (2 Chr. 33:12–13). Although he removed "all the altars he had built on the temple hill and in Jerusalem," throwing them out of the city (v. 15), he was unable at that late date to undo a lifetime of corruption or to stop the people from a continuing resort to the high places (v. 17).

At some point during his long, fifty-five year reign, the original tombs of the kings seem to have been sealed off or at least abandoned, perhaps because of being filled. As a result, royal burials from the time of Manasseh onward to the end of the southern kingdom were performed in "the garden of Uzza" (2 Ki. 21:18, 26; cf. 23:30 with 2 Chr. 35:24). The location is undefinable, except that it formed a part of the gardens of Manasseh's palace.

Upon the murder of Amon in 640, JOSIAH acceded to the throne of Judah at the age of eight years. Twelve years later, in 628, Assyria was overrun by the SCYTHIANS; and Josiah assumed adult

Evidence of the Babylonian siege and destruction of Jerusalem was discovered along these foundation walls (Area G, Bullae House).

control in Jerusalem, expanding his nation politically as far as Naphtali in N Galilee (2 Chr. 34:6) and purifying it religiously, especially its capital, of all forms of idolatry (vv. 3–4). Still, the prophets Zephaniah and Jeremiah paint a gloomy picture of the complacency and yet continuing superstitions of the Jerusalem of this period (cf. Zeph. 1:4, 12; Jer. 1:15–16; 4:14; 7:17–18).

With the discovery of the Mosaic lawbook in 622 came Josiah's great reformation. "He did away with the pagan priests ... around Jerusalem" (2 Ki. 23:5; cf. v. 13) and eliminated the high places and local sanctuaries, even when conducted in the name of Yahweh, that he might bring the priests to the one authorized, central temple (v. 8; cf. Deut. 12:4–14). The Passover on Zion in 622 proved thus to be the greatest one observed in Israel since the days of the judges (2 Ki. 23:22–23; cf. 2 Chr. 35:18). Many of the local priests, however, refused to transfer to the service of the Jerusalem altar (2 Ki. 23:9).

Three specific areas of Jerusalem are first mentioned at this time. A place named TOPHETH lay in the Valley of Hinnom near the Potsherd Gate (Jer. 19:2, 6, 14). The name means "hearth, fireplace" (cf. Isa. 30:33), for it was here on HIGH PLACES in the valley that in previous reigns children had been burned as sacrifices (Jer. 7:31). But Josiah defiled Topheth by converting it into the city refuse dump (2 Ki. 23:10) so that the Valley of Hinnom (NT GEHENNA) and its constant fires became a designation for HELL itself (Mk. 9:47–48). Within the city, Scripture speaks of Josiah's SECOND DISTRICT or "New Quarter" (*mišneh* H5467, 2 Ki. 22:14; Zeph. 1:10), presumably indicating the N and W portion of the city (Montgomery, *Kings*, 526); cf. Nehemiah's later division of the city's administration into half-districts (Neh. 3:9, 12). On Moriah, at the NW corner of the temple, was built the Tower of HANANEL (Jer. 31:38; Neh. 3:1; Zech. 14:10).

After Josiah's death in 609, Jerusalem suffered under its four last, incompetent Davidic kings. JEHOIAKIM (608–598), for example, practiced injustice and the enslavement of his people to erect an extravagant palace (Jer. 22:13–15; cf. 2 Ki. 24:4) that was doomed to destruction within a score of years and not a stone of which can yet be identified in Jerusalem. In 605, Jehoiakim was forced to submit to NEBUCHADNEZZAR II of Babylon, who proceeded to plunder the temple treasure and take captive certain prominent hostages (2 Chr. 36:7; Dan. 1:1–4), a fact validated by the appearing of the king's own contemporaneous chronicles of his western campaigns (D. J. Wiseman, *Chronicles of Chaldean Kings* [1956]). A subsequent revolt resulted in a brief Babylonian siege of Jerusalem in 597. The city capitulated on March 16, with more plundering as a result, as well as the deportation of the newly installed Jewish king with over 10,000 captives (2 Ki. 24:10–16).

Shortly after this event (cf. Jer. 29:2), the prophet JEREMIAH attempted to encourage his people with a prediction of future restoration, in the course of which he defined a rough outline of the city of Jerusalem: "this city will be rebuilt for me from the Tower of Hananel to the Corner Gate. The measuring line will stretch from there straight to the hill of Gareb and then turn to Goah. The whole valley where dead bodies and ashes are thrown, and all the terraces out to the Kidron Valley on the east as far as the corner of the Horse Gate, will be holy to the LORD. The city will never again be uprooted or demolished" (31:38–41).

Because the Tower of Hananel stood at the NW corner of the temple and the Horse Gate at its SE (see below, III.A), the prophet must have been making a counterclockwise circuit of what would some day be a dedicated community, omitting the temple area on the city's NE as already holy ground. The geographical question involved is whether Jeremiah was envisioning a future expansion or simply describing the preexilic city as it existed in 597, that is, whether Mount Gareb (if it really is the SW hill of Jerusalem; see above, I.B) did or did not as yet lie within the existing walls. It probably did, especially since the Corner Gate had existed since at least 800 B.C. (2 Ki. 14:13; 2 Chr. 26:9; cf. Simons, *Jerusalem*, 231, and see above, B.2).

A final desperate revolt under Judah's last king, ZEDEKIAH, ended in a two and one-half year siege of Jerusalem, from January 588 to July 586 (2 Ki 25:1–3). One month later, the Babylonian commander burned the temple, the palaces, and the houses of Jerusalem and broke down its surrounding walls (vv. 8–11).

D. Restoration. As indicated above, the same prophets who had foretold the fall of Jerusalem were often the very ones who went on to anticipate its restoration (cf. Isa. 39:7 with 52:2, 11–12; and Mic. 3:12 with 7:11). In 587, just one year before the final catastrophe, Jeremiah was even directed of God to purchase property in nearby Anathoth as a concrete testimony to Jerusalem's forthcoming reoccupation (Jer. 32:1, 9, 43–44).

1. Exile, to 538 B.C. From the burning of the temple, which began on 14 August 586 (2 Ki. 25:8–9; Thiele, *Mysterious Numbers*, 3rd ed., 190), Jerusalem lay desolate. Jeremiah, who had elected to stay in Judah (Jer. 40:4–6), remained in Mizpah with the Jewish governor GEDALIAH; and he had no more apparent contacts with the ex-capital, except by way of allusion to its former sins and to God's punitive wrath (42:18; 44:9, 13). It was presumably he who at this time composed the moving LAMENTATIONS, with their description of Jerusalem's burning, deaths, and incurable overthrow (e.g., Lam. 2:3–5, 13), due however to her sins (1:8; 4:13). The city is personified as one who, during a time of affliction, "remembers all the treasures that were hers in days of old" (1:7) and exclaims, "Is it nothing to you, all you who pass by?" (v. 12).

At the Feast of Tabernacles in September/October of 586 (cf. Jer. 41:1), groups of pilgrims came from N Israel, having "shaved off their beards, torn their clothes and cut themselves," yet "bringing grain offerings and incense with them to the house of the Lord" (41:5), for the site of the temple "still retained its sanctity even after it was destroyed" (J. Bright, *Jeremiah*, AB 21 [1965], 254). It was at this time that Gedaliah was murdered (41:2–3), and the last hope of Judah was extinguished (cf. 52:30 on a final, fourth deportation of 745 persons, in 582, that may have been the result of this action). Jeremiah, in Egypt, spoke of Jerusalem and the cities of Judah as "deserted and in ruins" (44:2; cf. v. 6). Although it is possible that the disorganized remnant that was scattered over the countryside (cf. 2 Ki. 25:12, 22) may have continued some sort of ritual on Mount Moriah, the actual city lay in ruins. The critical theories of C. C. Torrey, who denied any real exile, have been discredited by convincing archaeological testimony to the thoroughgoing depopulation of Judah and the transfer of the center of Jewish life to Babylonia (cf. W. Albright, *From the Stone Age to Christianity: Monotheism and the Historical Process*, 2nd ed. [1957], 322–23).

Among the exiles of all four deportations (years 605, 597, 586, and 582), Jerusalem remained the focus of their devotion, first in sorrow (Ps. 137:1) but then in hope of restoration (e.g., Ezek. 34:13; 36:38). They were determined not to forget Jerusalem (Ps. 137:5). The custom of making prayer when facing toward the holy city (1 Ki. 8:30, 35) was maintained at three regular times in the day (Dan. 6:10), and at all events Jeremiah had limited the time of captivity and of Jerusalem's desolations to seventy years (Jer. 25:11–12; 29:10; cf. Dan. 9:2), presumably from the date of 605 (Jer. 25:1). As this time approached, EZEKIEL in particular gave detailed instructions and patterns for a reconstruction of the Jerusalem temple by his exilic contemporaries (cf. Ezek. 43:10–11).

When Babylon finally fell to the armies of Medo-Persia in October of 539, DANIEL fervently interceded, "turn away your anger and your wrath from Jerusalem, your city, your holy hill" (Dan. 9:16); and he was assured of a decree "to restore and rebuild Jerusalem" (v. 25). In point of fact, the Persian decrees for the *reconstruction of the city* were not issued until the following century, under ARTAXERXES I. But in 538, the first official year of CYRUS as king in Babylon, permission was granted for the Jews to return and *rebuild the house* (temple) of God which was in Jerusalem (2 Chr. 36:23; Ezra 1:2; cf. Isaiah's Cyrus prophecy, which had spoken of Jerusalem's rebuilding, but with emphasis upon the temple, Isa. 44:28).

2. Persian, to 332 B.C. Cyrus's decree of 538, which authorized the Jews to go up to Jerusalem out of their Babylonian exile and to reestablish the services of the temple (Ezra 1:2–4; cf. 6:2–5), came because of Yahweh's having touched the heart of the Persian king (v. 1). Even in its religious wording it is not without parallel among other contemporaneous grants of freedom that he bestowed to win over former Babylonian subjects to his own administration (cf. J. Finegan, *Light from the Ancient Past*, 2nd ed. [1959], 229–30). Cyrus even ordered the return to

Jerusalem of the temple vessels that had been plundered by Nebuchadnezzar (Ezra 1:7, 11; 5:14–15; 6:5). This was followed in 637 by the return of the Jews under SHESHBAZZAR (1:8, 11; 5:14; he was presumably the Shenazzar of 1 Chr. 3:18, and hence a Jewish prince, one of the seven sons of Jehoiachin; cf. IDB, 4:325–326) and by the rededication of the altar under his nephew ZERUBBABEL, who had become associated with him as governor (Ezra 2:2; 3:1–2). Then in the spring of 536 the people reassembled in Jerusalem (3:8; cf. v. 1) and began the rebuilding of the temple, under both Sheshbazzar and Zerubbabel (3:8; 5:16), by an official relaying of the foundation accompanied by trumpets, singing, and thanksgiving (3:8–11; cf. 2:69). See CHRONOLOGY (OT) XII.

SAMARITAN opposition, however, prevented further progress in the construction of the second temple until 520, sixteen years later (Ezra 4:4, 5, 24). The ex-captives were not lacking in potential, since they numbered c. 50,000 (2:64–67); but most of them settled down in their respective towns and villages rather than in Jerusalem (vv. 1, 70; cf. vv. 21–28), becoming increasingly concerned with their own individual welfare, whereas the Lord's house lay waste (Hag. 1:2–4). God then sent a series of natural catastrophes that resulted in impoverishment for the entire community (Hag. 1:6, 9–11; 2:16–17; Zech. 8:10).

In the summer of 520, by the preaching of the prophets HAGGAI and ZECHARIAH, God shook the Jewish leaders and people out of their lethargy (Ezra 5:1; cf. Hag. 1:7–8; Zech. 1:16; 4:7–9); he reiterated his own undying concern for Jerusalem (Zech. 1:17; 2:4, 12; 3:2; 8:3, 15), and building was resumed. The Persian satrap TATTENAI was initially suspicious; but an inquiry sent to the new king DARIUS I not only confirmed Cyrus's original decree (Ezra 6:2) but also granted imperial support for the Jerusalem temple, where God "has caused his Name to dwell" (v. 12). It was finally completed early in 515 and dedicated with joy, and the regular Mosaic service was reestablished (vv. 14–18).

No remains of Zerubbabel's temple have survived; not even a description is extant. Only negative data is available, namely, that it failed badly of attaining the specifications that Ezekiel had laid down for the postexilic sanctuary, as stated above (cf. the disappointment expressed by certain of its contemporaries when comparing it with the first temple, Ezra 3:12). Jerusalem lay undefended and largely uninhabited except for the leaders of the community (Ezra 6:9; Neh. 11:1; cf. Zech. 7:3). There were factors involved in Jerusalem and its new shrine, however, that were greater than mere population or silver and gold; for the postexilic prophets spoke of Messiah's coming to this second temple (Zech. 9:9; 11:12–13; Mal. 3:1). Thus the city's name, Jerusalem, "foundation of peace," took on a new and deeper meaning as the place in which God would effectuate his peace (Hag. 2:9; Heb. 7:2; cf. Matt. 11:28; Jn. 14:27).

Conditions in late-6th and early-5th-cent. Jerusalem can be only surmised from Scripture. In 518, the prophet Zechariah recorded the coming of a delegation from Bethel to inquire of the priests and prophets at the temple about a matter of ceremony, which indicates the capital's status as a center for religious guidance (Zech. 7:1–3). Their particular inquiry concerned the need for a continual observance of fasting, commemorative of the tragic events of 586—the fall of Jerusalem on July 18 (fourth month), its burning on August 14 (fifth month, vv. 3, 5), and the murder of Gedaliah in October (seventh month, 8:18), as well as the inception of the siege on 15 January 588 (tenth month, 8:18; cf. Thiele, *Mysterious Numbers*, 3rd ed., 190)—now that seventy years had passed and the temple was well on its way to restoration (7:5). God's reply through Zechariah laid down ethical standards of truth, justice, and mercy (7:8–10; 8:16–17), by the observance of which the fasts should be converted into "happy festivals" (8:19; cf. the beautiful picture of vv. 4–5). That the actual continuation of the *fasts* suggests a generally unreformed society in Jerusalem received confirmation from later, 5th-cent. writers (cf. Neh. 5:5–8; Mal. 2:7, 11; 3:15).

At the close of his ministry, probably after the Greco-Persian war of 480–479 (cf. Zech. 9:13), Zechariah predicted that the city would be "raised up and remain in its place, from the Benjamin Gate [on the E, probably the MUSTER GATE] to the site of the First Gate [perhaps the EPHRAIM GATE or the OLD GATE], to the Corner Gate [on the W], and from the Tower of Hananel [on the N] to the royal winepresses [perhaps at the KING'S GARDEN on the S]" (14:10). These details indicate a set of traditional extremities for the city (see below, under "Nehemiah's walls," and in III.A). The nature of Samaritan complaints against the inhabitants of Judah and Jerusalem during the reign of XERXES, 485–465 (Ezra 4:6), remains unknown; but they were probably due to a continuing policy of exclusion by the Jews (cf. v. 3).

A major, second return of Israel to Jerusalem was accomplished in the 5th cent., in the summer of 458, under the leadership of EZRA (Ezra 7:7), with authorization and support by the Persian monarch ARTAXERXES I (vv. 12–26). The numbers were smaller, about 1,500; but the wealth that was brought to beautify God's house was greater (7:27; 8:25–30, 33–36). Ezra then assembled the men of Judah and Benjamin in Jerusalem, early in January of 457 (10:7–10), this time to enforce the regulations of the Mosaic law, to which he had committed himself (cf. 7:10, 25–26), especially in reference to mixed marriages.

At some point during the reign of Artaxerxes (465–424), the Samaritans are known to have frustrated an attempt to reconstruct the walls of Jerusalem (Ezra 4:16, 23), presumably by Ezra, at his return in 458 (cf. 9:9 with 7:19, 25). Their accusations of intended rebellion were false (4:12–13, 16), though they provide a significant commentary on both the power and the faithless rebelliousness of preexilic Jerusalem (v. 15; cf. vv. 19–20).

A decade later, NEHEMIAH, a high-ranking Jew and cupbearer to King Artaxerxes, upon learning of the overthrow of Ezra's attempt at refortification (Neh. 1:3), gained royal permission to return and reconstruct the walls of Jerusalem (2:8). Three days after his arrival, Nehemiah made a nighttime reconnaissance of the S part of the city (vv. 11–15), then formulated his plans, and upon their presentation was able to persuade the Jewish rulers to undertake the task (vv. 17–18). Like Zerubbabel before him (Ezra 4:3), Nehemiah made it clear that only God's redeemed people of Israel had portion or right in respect to Jerusalem (Neh. 2:20). The result was bitter opposition on the part of the Samaritans (4:7–8; 6:2, 5–7, 12, 19; cf. 2:19). During the summer of 444, by an energetic campaign of only fifty two days, during which assigned segments of the wall were rebuilt by specific groups of volunteers, Nehemiah was able to achieve his goal (4:6, 6:15).

The third chapter of Nehemiah's book describes the course of the walls, beginning at the NE of Jerusalem and moving in a counterclockwise direction (by this time the size of the city had been reduced to about 30 acres). The features he listed are these:

1. the SHEEP GATE (Neh. 3:1)
2. the Tower of the HUNDRED (3:1; KJV, "Meah")
3. the Tower of HANANEL (3:1)
4. the FISH GATE (3:3)
5. the OLD GATE (3:6; NIV, "Jeshanah")
6. the BROAD WALL (3:8)
7. the Tower of the OVENS (3:11; KJV, "furnaces")
8. the VALLEY GATE (3:13)
9. the DUNG GATE (3:14)
10. the wall of the Pool of SHELAH (NIV, SILOAM) by the KING'S GARDEN (3:15)
11. the FOUNTAIN GATE (3:15)
12. a place "opposite the tombs of David" (3:16)
13. a place "facing the ascent to the armory as far as the angle" (3:19; cf. vv. 20, 24–25; see ANGLE, THE)
14. "the tower projecting from the upper palace near the court of the guard" (3:25)
15. the WATER GATE on the E (3:26)
16. the wall of OPHEL (3:27)
17. the HORSE GATE (3:28);
18. the EAST GATE (3:29)
19. the MUSTER GATE (3:31; KJV, "Miphkad"; NIV, "Inspection")
20. "the corner" (3:31–32; see CORNER, UPPER ROOM OF THE)
21. the SHEEP GATE (3:32, repeated).

Apparently Nehemiah did not intend this list to be exhaustive of distinguishable points on the perimeter of Jerusalem, but simply to mark off the building segments. Elsewhere he mentions other landmarks: the CORNER GATE (Zech. 14:10); the JACKAL WELL (Neh. 2:13; see above, I.C); and the Gate of the Guard (12:39; see GUARD, GATE OF THE), though this last may have been only an inner gate of the temple. No distances for the segments are given, except for 1,000 cubits (c. 1,500 ft.) between the Valley Gate and the Dung Gate

(3:13), one of the two unusually long assignments on the SW side of the city.

A general agreement now exists over the location of items no. 1–3 and 9–20 (cf. Simons, *Jerusalem*, ch. 7); but that of nos. 4–8 depends upon whether Nehemiah's city embraced all of Jerusalem's SW hill (L.-H. Vincent, J. Simons, M. Ben-Dov), only part of it, or none (K. Kenyon, Y. Aharoni, and M. Avi-Yonah; see maps with alternate views in Ben-Dov, *Historical Atlas*, 86–87). The total length of the walls in Nehemiah's time may thus have been as little as c. 2,500 meters (8,200 ft.) or as much as 4,000 meters (13,000 ft.). (Correspondingly, the population may have been as small as several hundred or as large as a few thousand.) The longer distance is supported by the large number of gates mentioned; small cities usually had only one or two gates for security reasons. In any event, large elements of earlier walls must have been reused for their completion in the fifty-two days indicated.

In its S portion, however, the work of 444 enclosed only the crest of the City of David. These are the solid but rough walls, 9 ft. thick, reported by J. W. Crowfoot and R. A. S. Macalister, which the latter from his digging in 1923–26 erroneously identified as David's eastern wall. Nehemiah's reduced circuit would seem to have been dictated by the availability of water from Hezekiah's tunnel, which obviated the need for fortifications that would extend down to the lower slopes on the E side of Zion for access to the Gihon Spring, and by the now irreparable collapse of the old Jebusite terraces above it, following 586 (note Nehemiah's inability even to pick a way through while on his initial reconnaissance, Neh. 2:14). Thus, whereas the W part of his reconstruction may have consisted in the repair of former gates and walls still largely in existence (e.g., nos. 8, 9, 11; 3:1–15), his really new and hardest work lay along the E crest of Zion (note how nos. 12, 13, 14, 16 are all interior designations; vv. 16–27). It was an ascent (12:37), and a resumed notation of former gates comes only with the N part of the eastern walls (e.g., nos. 17–19, 28–32), which would have again followed the line of Solomonic fortifications.

To the W lay no. 8, the Valley Gate, whichever be its location among the above-cited proposals.

Tower structure and wall line dating to the time of Nehemiah.

From it Nehemiah set out, and to it he returned, on his preliminary tour of inspection (Neh. 2:13–15). From it also set out the two great companies of national leaders, priests, and Levitical singers, to march along the walls at their dedication (12:27–43). The one group, under Ezra, turned right, moving S, E, and N to the temple area, where they were met by the other, under Nehemiah, which had turned left and moved N, E, and S to Moriah (see below, III.A, on modern locations that correspond to the points listed on the perimeter of restored Jerusalem).

Almost immediately, Nehemiah set up regular daily watches on the walls of the capital (Neh. 7:3), for "the city was large and spacious, but there were few people in it, and the houses had not yet been rebuilt" (v. 4). In the fall of 444, he assembled all Israel to Zion to hear the law read by Ezra and his fellow Levites at "the square before the Water Gate" (8:1–3) and to keep a Feast of Tabernacles in Jerusalem that proved to be the greatest since the days of Joshua (vv. 14–18). Then, by a casting of lots, Nehemiah set about repopulating the "holy city" (11:1, 18) with ten percent of the Judean community (vv. 1–2). Figures follow that list 1,400 valiant men of Judah and Benjamin (vv. 4–9) and 1,650 men in the various Levitical ranks (vv. 10–19), though the totals may not be complete.

Nehemiah's first governorship, of twelve years, expired in 432; and he returned to the court of Artaxerxes (Neh. 13:6). After a time, however, he was granted leave to reassume oversight of the affairs of Jerusalem. He executed a number of reforms in both temple and city (v. 7), which correspond to the problems described by the (presumably contemporaneous) prophet Malachi. Nehemiah specifically utilized the rebuilt gates to keep certain Tyrian merchants out of the city, who were attempting to conduct business on the Sabbath (vv. 19–22). The expiration date of his second governorship is unknown, except that it seems to have extended into the reign of Darius II, 423–404 B.C. (12:22), at which point the OT and its information about Jerusalem comes to a close.

Letters from the Jewish colony of ELEPHANTINE in S Egypt refer in 410 B.C. to Johanan (Neh. 12:22) as high priest in Jerusalem and in 407 to a Persian governor Bagoas over Judah (*ANET*, 491–92). During the reign of Artaxerxes II, 404–359 (cf. T. H. Robinson and W. O. E. Oesterley, *A History of Israel*, 2 vols. [1932], 2:170n.), a brief allusion is made by JOSEPHUS (*Ant.* 11.7.1) to an attempt of Bagoas to replace Johanan with his brother Jeshua, to Jeshua's murder within the temple by Johanan, and to subsequent reprisals by Bagoas. Otherwise, the only known facts of the remaining Persian period that relate to Jerusalem concern Artaxerxes III, who carried many Jews captive in 344, following an unsuccessful revolt incited by Pharaoh Nekhtenebef II of Egypt's thirtieth dynasty.

3. Hellenistic, to 165 B.C. In 332, during his advance into Egypt (prob. between the capture of Tyre in July and that of Gaza in November), ALEXANDER THE GREAT assumed control over Jerusalem from the Persians, thus inaugurating its Greek period. Josephus (*Ant.* 11.8.3–5) has preserved legends of an armed advance by Alexander against the capital and of the city's miraculous preservation, following which the conqueror is said to have made sacrifices to God under the direction of the Jewish high priest. But behind these unreliable tales, it does appear that the Greeks treated Jerusalem with tolerance and that a number of Jews actually enlisted in his armies (cf. Robinson and Oesterley, *History of Israel*, 2:189–90).

Upon Alexander's death in 323, Antigonus, one of his senior generals, gained control over Palestine, only to lose it to PTOLEMY, the Greek monarch in Egypt, after the Battle of Ipsus in 301. The Ptolemies continued to hold it for over a century. Ptolemy IV probably visited Jerusalem after his victory over ANTIOCHUS III, Greek monarch of Syria, in 217, though the story (in 3 Macc. 1:9—2:24) about Yahweh's thwarting his attempt to enter the most holy place of the temple is legendary. Subsequent fighting led to considerable destruction within Jerusalem by Ptolemy V's general Scopas in the year 200, but in 198 Antiochus did permanently conquer Palestine and was welcomed into the capital city (Jos. *Ant.* 12.3.3). An official of his son SELEUCUS IV (187–175), in accordance with Daniel's prophecy of over three centuries before (Dan. 11:20), attempted to rob the temple but was in some way prevented (cf. 2 Macc. 3:7–40).

Archaeological information on Jerusalem is lacking for most of the Greek period, except for certain tomb construction in the Kidron Valley (see below, III.B). During Hellenistic times, the ARAMAIC LANGUAGE came increasingly to replace Hebrew as the commonly spoken language, and the city's Aramaic name, *yĕrûšlem* (Ezra 4:8 et al.; cf. *šālēm* H8970 in Ps. 76:2), was rendered into Greek as *Ierousalēm*. This is the form used in the biblical books of the SEPTUAGINT and later adopted by the NT. An alternate NT form, *Hierosolyma*, is first documented by the Greek historian Polybius (c. 140 B.C.; see *Hist.* 16.39.4), and is frequent in the APOCRYPHA (1 Esd. 2:11 et al.). The two names appear to be interchangeable, but the latter, with its declensional ending, is the more Hellenistic form, and it may have been designed to suggest *hieros Salēm*, "sacred Salem."

Antiochus IV (175–164), called Epiphanes, reduced Jerusalem to the lowest point in its religious history. In his attempt to spread Hellenistic culture, he and his supporters among the Jewish aristocracy introduced a cultural center (1 Macc. 1:14; see GYMNASIUM), which may have included a stadium, probably in the Tyropoeon Valley. In 170, after a victory in Egypt, he broke into the sanctuary, plundered it of its golden vessels, and killed a number of the Jews (vv. 19–24; cf. the prediction of Dan. 11:28). Finally in December of 168, following a repulse by the Romans, Antiochus resolved to put an end to the distinctive practices of Judaism, including the worship of Yahweh in Jerusalem; and he set up the ABOMINATION OF DESOLATION, an altar to ZEUS upon the brazen altar of the temple (1 Macc. 1:54, 59; cf. Dan. 11:30–31). As a part of his general oppression, Antiochus is said to have burned houses and to have destroyed city walls (1 Macc. 1:31).

In 167, a Greco-Syrian garrison erected and then continued to maintain the *akra* ("citadel") on a site near the Jerusalem temple, so as to maintain full control over the area (cf. 1 Macc. 9.15). "They fortified the city of David with a great strong wall and strong towers, and it became their citadel" (1:33). "They stored up arms and food, and collecting the spoils of Jerusalem they stored them there, and became a great menace, for the citadel became an ambush against the sanctuary, an evil adversary of Israel at all times" (1:35–36).

The location of this acra has been one of the major problems in the topographical history of Jerusalem. Its association with the City of David (1 Macc. 1:33; 14:36) suggests Ophel or Zion to the S of the temple (see below, on the possible artificial lowering of this hill under Simon). On the other hand, presently known altitudes would suggest the E slope of Gareb as preferable for dominating the temple (although Ben-Dov argues that the acra was at the foot of the temple mount, which could be supervised from the top of the fortress towers; see *Historical Atlas*, 93–94, with map and illustrations on 92–97). It appears significant, however, that in contrast with the strongly Hellenistic type pottery found at Samaria, with its Greek colonies, that jar fragments from 2nd-cent. Jerusalem exhibit only slight Grecian influence: Zion was not about to capitulate to the sons of Greece (Zech. 9:13; cf. Kenyon, *Jerusalem*, 136–37).

4. Hasmonean, to 63 B.C. At this point, in 167, a priest named MATTATHIAS raised the standard of revolt in MODEIN, E of LYDDA (1 Macc. 2:1–28); and when Mattathias died later that same year, his son Judas MACCABEE, or "Hammerer," proceeded to win a series of brilliant victories against four successively larger armies of the Greeks (3:10-4:35; cf. Dan. 8:25; Zech. 9:13–17). The climax came in December of 165 when Judas was able to reoccupy Jerusalem and cleanse the temple and its courts of the abomination of Antiochus. Despite the continuing presence of the Greek garrison in the acra (1 Macc. 4:41), he rebuilt the altar (v. 47) and celebrated an eight-day feast of dedication (v. 56), which has continued to be observed as Hanukkah, or the Feast of the DEDICATION (Jn. 10:22). Judas went on to subdue various Gentile territories that surrounded Judah and in 163 gained an edict of religious toleration from young Antiochus V (1 Macc. 6:57–61).

Meanwhile, Judas had rebuilt the fortifications of Jerusalem (1 Macc. 4:60), but Antiochus took advantage of the edict to enter the city and then to destroy the protecting walls that Judas had raised (6:62). The following year Judas defeated another

Greek army under NICANOR, who fled to Jerusalem and threatened to burn the temple (7:32–35). The priests prayed for divine intervention; in March of 161 Judas proceeded to rout the Greeks, and Nicanor's head and right hand were subsequently exhibited outside Jerusalem (v. 47).

In 160, after the death of Judas, the corrupt high priest, ALCIMUS, attempted further to dismantle Jerusalem's inner temple walls, but he was prevented by a fatal attack of palsy (1 Macc. 9:54–56). Starting in 153, Judas's brothers Jonathan and Simon were able progressively to refortify the city "with squared stones, for better fortification" (10:11; cf. 12:36–37; 13:10; 14:37); but it was not until Jonathan's death in 143 that SIMON MACCABEE was granted full political liberty from Demetrius II (13:36–42).

Simon finally starved out the acra in 142 (1 Macc. 13:49–51; 14:36). Josephus (*Ant.* 13.6.7) elaborates: "He also … cast it down to the ground, that it might not be any more a place of refuge to their enemies, when they took it, to do them a mischief, as it had been till now. And when he had done this, he thought it their best way, and most for their advantage, to level the very mountain itself upon which the citadel happened to stand, that so the temple might be higher than it. And, indeed, when he had called the multitude to an assembly, he persuaded them to have it so demolished. … so they all set themselves to the work, and levelled the mountain, and in that work spent both day and night without any intermission, which cost them three whole years before it was removed, and brought to an entire level with the plain of the rest of the city. After which the temple was the highest of all the buildings, now [that] the citadel, as well as the mountain whereon it stood, were demolished." If the site of the acra was indeed the old City of David, this would account for much of the disappearance of earlier relics from this part of Jerusalem (though it suffered post-NT quarrying as well). The whole tale, however, remains suspect because Simon seems actually to have cleansed and continued to use the acra (1 Macc. 13:50; 14:37).

The later HASMONEANS constructed a palace across the central valley and connected it with the temple area by a bridge. Over the ruins of the 7th-cent. houses along the eastern edge of the summit of Zion, they constructed a series of bulwarks; and archaeological remains become more plentiful with this period. At the top of Kenyon's 1961 digging above the Gihon Spring stands a large tower with corners of squared stones; formerly credited to David and Solomon, the tower now is usually assigned to the second half of the 2nd cent. B.C. (Kenyon, *Jerusalem*, 114–16) as the work of Simon (143–135) or of his son John Hyrcanus (135–105). The so-called Jebusite ramp to its N must therefore have been a slightly later, subterranean stone buttress to support a weakness in the wall above it. The statement in 1 Macc. 13:52 that Simon "strengthened the fortifications of the temple hill alongside the citadel, and he and his men dwelt there" probably refers to the NW corner of Moriah, where the preexilic Tower of Hananel had stood. This fortress came to be called Baris (and later the Tower of Antonia; see below, E.1).

The history of Hasmonean Jerusalem is one of repeated devastations. Antiochus VII (139–129) besieged the city and, when a submission was arranged, broke down the walls. John Hyrcanus rebuilt them (1 Macc. 16:23). His son Alexander Jannaeus (104–78) maintained constant warfare with his Greek neighbors but alienated his own Jewish people by an increasing secularism, which led after his reign to a final loss of independence for the restored Jewish state in 63 B.C. and to the downfall of the Hasmoneans.

E. Roman. Alexander's son Hyrcanus II, the last legitimate Hasmonean priest-king, was displaced from Jerusalem by his brother Aristobulus II (69–63 B.C.). Both appealed to the Roman general POMPEY in Damascus, but when the latter arrived at Jerusalem, Aristobulus resisted. Hyrcanus surrendered the W part of the city, on Gareb; but Aristobulus cut the Tyropoeon bridge and held out in Baris and the temple area to the E. After a three months' siege, the citadel fell; Pompey killed 12,000 Jews and carried many more off as slaves. He dismantled the walls of Jerusalem but allowed Hyrcanus to continue as high priest and as an ETHNARCH under Rome, though with the actual power slipping more and more into the hands of Antipater, an Idumean (Edomite) administrator. The Romans entered Jerusalem again in 54 but allowed its walls to be rebuilt. In 40 B.C.,

552 JERUSALEM

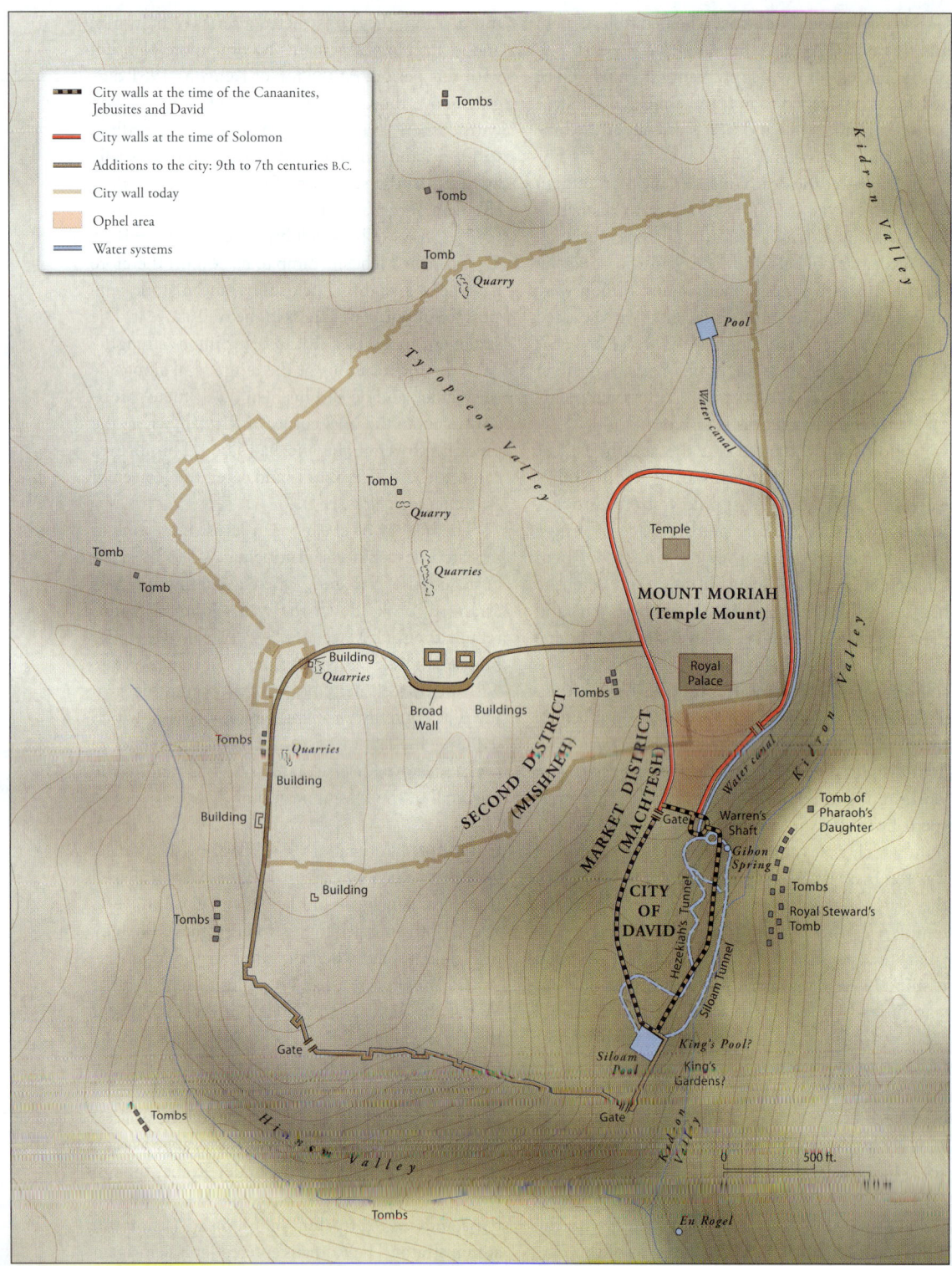

Old Testament Jerusalem.

JERUSALEM 553

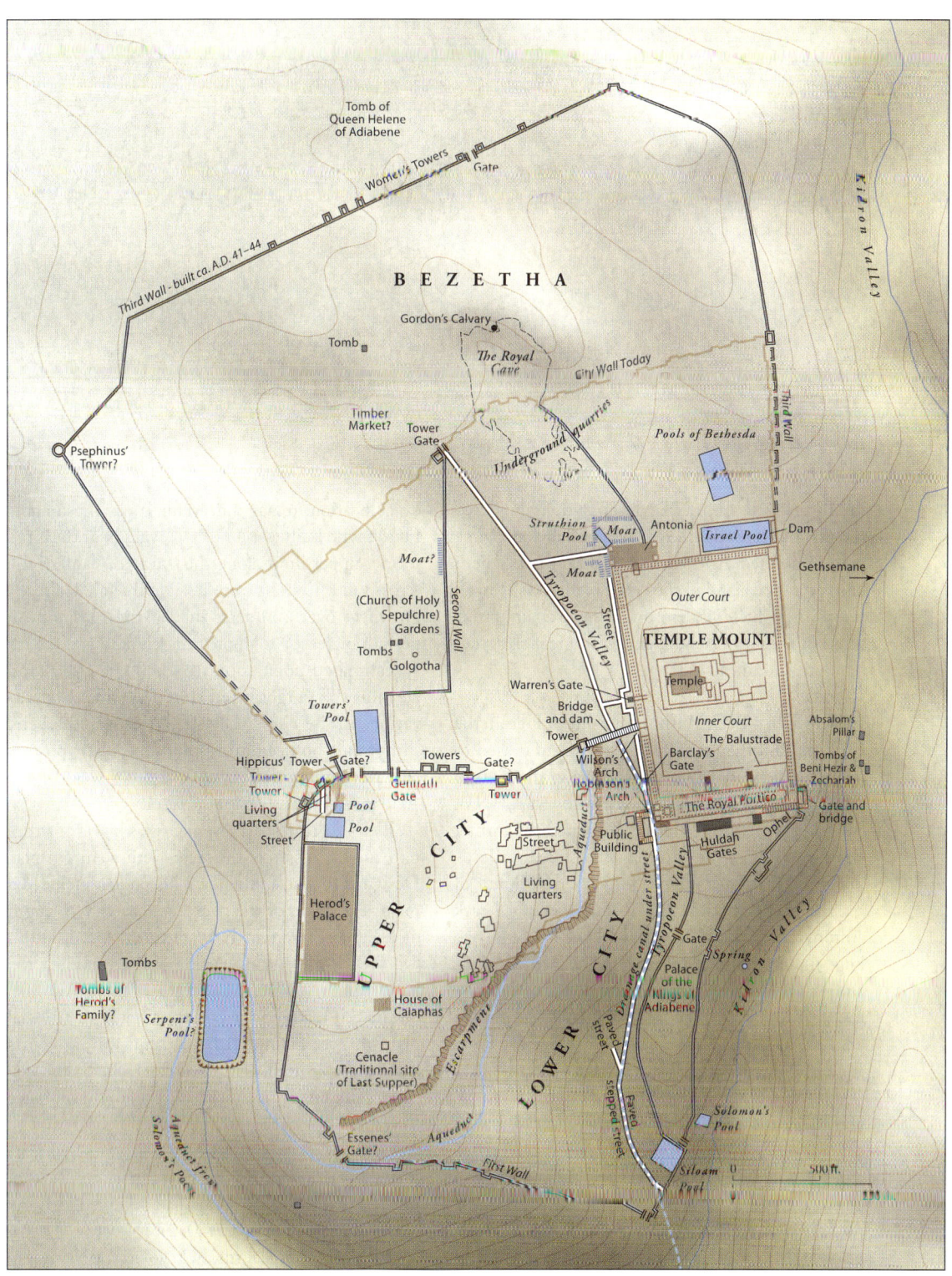

New Testament Jerusalem.

Pavement stones from the Antonia Fortress.

the PARTHIANS from NE Mesopotamia plundered the city and carried off Hyrcanus to Babylon. Rome then appointed Antipater's son HEROD as client king over Israel; and in the year 37, Herod's Roman troops brought Jerusalem under siege again, broke through the city's N wall, and with great slaughter set up this Idumean as king.

1. Herod, to 4 B.C. With the advent of Herod, the Romans, and their aqueducts, Jerusalem ceased to remain dependent upon the springs in the Kidron and expanded rapidly northwestward. At the NW corner of the temple, Herod developed the former Baris into one of his two major fortresses in Jerusalem: his Tower of ANTONIA, named in honor of his friend and patron, the Roman general Mark Antony. Beneath the paving stones of its court, two huge underground cisterns were cut into the rock, and at each of its four corners stood an interior tower: the tallest, to the SE, dominated the temple area (cf. its use in Acts 21:34 as a refuge for PAUL from the Jewish mob).

Herod's other major fortress guarded the W (Jaffa) gate of the city, with three great towers named for his friend Hippicus, his brother Phasael, and his wife Mariamne. To its S lay his extensive personal palace, which he connected with the temple area by a great bridge over the Tyropoeon (see below, III.B). Farther S in the valley were his theater, amphitheater, and hippodrome, though their exact locations remain uncertain. It was presumably Herod who built a second NW wall, N of the city's former upper limit along the southern bank of the "cross valley." The size of the city, which had already grown to over 160 acres during the Hasmonean period, increased to approximately 230 acres, with an estimated population of 40,000–50,000 (and considerably larger after Herod Agrippa). Excavations in the Upper City have uncovered several sumptuous homes during this time; their pottery and furnishings reflect considerable wealth (see Avidgad, *Discovering Jerusalem*, ch. 3).

Herod's greatest achievement was his reconstruction and expansion of the sacred Jerusalem TEMPLE. Designed to placate the Jews, his project included a major extension of the court area, to a N-S length of c. 2,500 ft. and an E-W breadth of c. 1,000 ft. On the N, this meant cutting off and leveling the base rock, up to the very foundations of Antonia; on the S it required the construction of an artificial platform (see below, III.B). Within various courts lay the temple itself, of approximately the Solomonic surface dimensions, but with the roof of the entrance tower 165 ft. in height. Begun in 20 B.C., the work was not completed until A.D. 64, six years before its total destruction (cf. the statement made to Christ in Jn. 2:20 that the construction had occupied forty-six years up to that point, c. A.D. 27).

The biblical records, whose narrative references to Jerusalem had closed with Nehemiah shortly after 423 B.C., resume with the last years of Herod's reign. The opening chapters of the Gospels describe the annunciation of the birth of JOHN THE BAPTIST to his father ZECHARIAH while performing his Levitical function within the temple (Lk. 1:8–23). John was probably born early in 5 B.C.; six months later (cf. v. 36), at Jesus' birth, "Magi from the east came to Jerusalem and asked, 'Where is the one who has been born king of the Jews?'" (Matt. 2:1–2). They were informed from the prophecy of Micah that Christ should be born in David's city of BETHLEHEM, 5 mi. to the S (vv. 5–6). While the climax of history, the saving INCARNATION of the divine Son IMMANUEL ("God with us") occurred outside the city of the great King (Ps. 48:2), Zion was the first place to which Joseph and Mary took the baby Jesus after his birth for presentation in the temple. There he received prophetic blessings from Simeon and also from Anna, who "spoke about the child to all who were looking forward to the redemption of Jerusalem" (Lk. 2:38). Almost immediately, however, the holy family was compelled to flee to Egypt to escape the jealous wrath of Herod (Matt. 2:13–18). The latter's slaying of the Bethlehem innocents, although not recorded outside of Scripture, corresponds to Herod's other, numerous, known political murders, which culminated just before he died in 4 B.C.

2. Jesus and Jerusalem, to A.D. 30. Advised by an angel of Herod's death, Joseph brought his family back to NAZARETH, avoiding Judah and Jerusalem for fear of Herod's son Archelaus, who ruled in the city as ethnarch of Judah until A.D. 6 (Matt. 2:19–23). Jesus, when of the age of twelve, traveled again to Jerusalem for a Passover feast, where he amazed the teachers with his understanding and answers (Lk. 2:41–50). His youth was spent in Nazareth, his baptism occurred at the Jordan, and his inaugural temptations were located in the neighboring wilderness (prob. of Judah). At this time, Satan took him "to the holy city and had him stand on the highest point of the temple," vainly tempting Christ to cast himself down and thus question Yahweh's care (Matt. 4:5–7). But it was some time after his ministry had begun, in Galilee, before he revisited his "Father's house" (cf. Lk. 2:49).

Archelaus was replaced by Roman PROCURATORS who ruled Jerusalem successively from A.D. 6 to 41 and then from 44 to 66, but who preferred coastal CAESAREA for actual residence. Although they were generally unscrupulous and wasteful, the fifth in the series, Pontius PILATE (26–36), succeeded in constructing a major aqueduct from Bethlehem to Jerusalem, sections of which remain to this day. It was under Pilate's administration that all of Jesus' adult contacts with Jerusalem transpired. Up until the Passion Week, the Synoptic Gospels generally limit themselves to noting the presence of Jerusalemites among Jesus' hearers (e.g., Mk. 3:8, 22; 7:1); but John records three Jerusalem Passovers (Jn. 2:13; 6:4; and 12:1 in Passion Week), with the "feast" of 5:1 probably constituting a fourth (A. T. Robertson, *A Harmony of the Gospels for Students of the Life of Christ* [1922], 269–70). On the first, probably A.D. 27 (according to some, A.D. 30), Jesus cleansed the temple of its commerce (Jn. 2:14–16), gained many believers among the pilgrims (v. 23), and spoke of salvation to NICODEMUS, who came to him by night at an unspecified location (3:2; cf. 4:1–3 on his departure). On the second, in the year 28 (or 31), he healed a lame man by the Pool of Bethesda (5:8; see below, III.B); but he left again, following a controversy over his having performed this miracle on the Sabbath (5:9; 6:1).

Jesus deliberately avoided Jerusalem on the third Passover (Jn. 6:4; 7:1) because the Jewish leaders were now threatening his life. But he did appear in the midst of the fall Feast of Tabernacles and taught in the temple (7:14–39), so effectively indeed that the officers of the priests refused to apprehend him (vv. 45–46). This was followed by further teaching in the temple (8:12–58, until he was almost stoned, v. 59), and by his healing of a blind man whom he sent to wash in the Pool of Siloam (ch. 9; cf. 10:1–21). In December, at Hanukkah, he spoke in SOLOMON'S COLONNADE, asserting his Messiahship and deity (10:22–38) and yet escaping beyond Jordan "from their hands" (v. 39). His return to Judea for the raising of LAZARUS (11:7) brought him to the village of BETHANY just over the Olivet ridge from Jerusalem (vv. 17–18), but apparently not to the city itself until his final Passover (vv. 55–57) in the year 30 (or 33).

Jesus had forewarned the disciples that his death would occur in Jerusalem (Matt. 16:21; 20:17–18; cf. Lk. 9:31; 13:33). On Palm Sunday, his triumphal entry started from Bethany (Jn. 12:1) and passed through BETHPHAGE (Matt. 21:1), down the slope of Olivet (where he wept over Jerusalem's blindness toward himself and its resultant destruction, Lk. 19:41–44), across the Kidron, and on into the city, into the temple area, before his return to Bethany (Mk. 11:11). On Monday he cleansed the temple a second time (vv. 15–18), and on Tuesday debated in its courts with the Jewish leaders (11:27—12:35, 41). He concluded with his lament over the city, "O Jerusalem, Jerusalem, you who kill the prophets and stone those sent to you, how often I have longed to gather your children together, as a hen gathers her chicks under her wings, but you were not willing. Look, your house is left to you desolate. For I tell you, you will not see me again until you say, 'Blessed is he who comes in the name of the Lord'" (Matt. 23:37–39). These words indicated his triumph that was yet to be, in Jerusalem. Later that day, as he and the disciples rested on Olivet, he again predicted the city's fall of A.D. 70 (e.g., Lk. 21:5–24) but also the coming of false Christs, final tribulation, heavenly wrath, and his own second advent in glory (vv. 25–36; cf. Matt. 24:23—25:13).

On Wednesday he probably remained at Bethany (Mk. 14:1–9; Jn. 12:2–8); but on Thursday came the Paschal last supper at an unlocated "large upper room" in Jerusalem (Mk. 14:15; Lk. 22:12), where Jesus confirmed the testament in his blood (Matt. 26:28). This was followed by his night arrest in GETHSEMANE on the slopes of Olivet (Mk. 14:26–52). Before dawn Jesus was tried, first before the senior priest, ANNAS (Jn. 18:12–13), then at the house of the current high priest, CAIAPHAS (18:24; Matt. 26:57), and then before Pilate in the praetorium (Jn. 18:28), before Herod's son Antipas (Lk. 23:7), perhaps in the old Hasmonean palace (IDB, 2:862), and again before Pilate (v. 11). He was condemned and led outside the city to GOLGOTHA (Jn. 19:20), wherever this may have been (see SEPULCHRE, CHURCH OF THE HOLY). On the afternoon when others were preparing Passover lambs, the Son of God offered himself on the CROSS as the ultimate sacrifice for our sins (Isa. 53:10; 1 Cor. 5:7). His burial was by "the place where he was crucified" (Jn. 19:41 NRSV).

Good Friday was followed by Easter Sunday. Through his victorious resurrection from the tomb, Christ assured his people's triumph over condemnation and death (Rom. 4:25; 2 Tim. 1:10). After forty days of postresurrection appearances, both in Jerusalem and in Galilee, he ascended bodily into heaven from the Mount of Olives on the E of Jerusalem (Acts 1:12; cf. Lk. 24:50), whence he shall return to judge the world in righteousness.

3. To the fall of Jerusalem, A.D. 70. Jesus had commanded his disciples to preach "repentance and forgiveness of sins ... to all nations, beginning at Jerusalem," but they were to "stay in the city, until ... clothed with power from on high" (Lk. 24:47–49; cf. v. 52). Ten days later, in a Jerusalem "upper room" or some other unknown "place" (Acts 1:13; 2:1), they did in fact experience the Pentecostal outpouring of God's Spirit, which empowered them to carry the gospel world-wide (2:1–3; cf. 1:8; 2:41–42).

The history of the early church, recorded in Acts, continued to center in Jerusalem. The early Christians engaged in worship and evangelization, both at the temple and in private homes (Acts 2:46; 3:1; 5:12, 21, 42; 21:26; 24:11); note the references to PETER's activities at the temple's BEAUTIFUL GATE (3:2, its main interior entrance on the E) and Solomon's Colonnade (KJV, "porch"; NRSV, "Portico"; 3:11; 5:12) and the church's gathering for prayer at the house of MARY the mother of John Mark (12:12). The apostles regularly reported to Jerusalem the progress of their missions (11:2; 21:17) and here sought for important decisions (11:18; 15:2; cf. 8:14). On several occasions PAUL carried relief offerings to the city's impoverished believers (11:29–30; 24:17; cf. Rom. 15:25–27; 1 Cor. 16:1–6; 2 Cor. 8:1–4; 9:1–11). Peter, Paul, and others suffered from Jerusalem trials and imprisonments, sometimes with miraculous releases (Acts 4:3, 7; 5:18–19, 27; 12:3–4, 7–10; 22:24, 30), perhaps at the house of Caiaphas and later at the barracks of Antonia (21:34; 22:24); and STEPHEN and JAMES the apostle suffered martyrdom, within or near the city (7:58; 12:2). Though increasingly

Debris at the SW corner of the temple platform from the destruction of the temple by the Romans in A.D. 70.

scattered by persecution (8:1, 4), the Jerusalem church in the mid-50s was composed of thousands of believing Jews (21:20).

Earlier, in A.D. 41, all Palestine had been united for a three year period under the rule of Herod's grandson, Herod Agrippa I (cf. Acts 12:1, 19–23; see HEROD VII). This energetic monarch commenced a third N wall, approximately coextensive with the present N fortifications of the "Old City." His Tower of Psephinus (Jos. *War* 5.4.2) would thus have stood at about the NW corner of the modern walls; and the main N gateway (or at least its small side arch, for pedestrians) was uncovered by J. B. Hennessy (1966), directly beneath the present Damascus Gate. There does, confessedly, exist a ruin, the "Castle of Goliath," farther to the N, as well as certain wall fragments found in 1925–27 by E. Sukenik and L. Mayer (*The Third Wall of Jerusalem: An Account of Excavations* [1930]). The latter were once identified with Agrippa's third N wall but are now known to be of a later date and may represent Titus's siege works of A.D. 70. Josephus had indeed located the third wall over the "royal caverns" (*War* 5.4.2; cf. also *Ant*. 20.4.3), which are near today's Damascus Gate. According to Kenyon, it was also Herod Agrippa who first enclosed the S part of Gareb, joining it to Zion on the E by the massive walls and gates discovered by Bliss and Dickie in 1894–97. (See maps and diagrams in Ben-Dov, *Historical Atlas*, 111–22.)

The later Roman procurators faced an increasing breakdown of law and order in Jerusalem. JAMES the brother of the Lord (Acts 15:13; 21:18) suffered martyrdom by stoning in 62 (Jos. *Ant*. 20.9.1); and before the city's demise, its Christian community fled to safety across the Jordan, in obedience to Christ's word in Matt. 24:15–22. The fatal Jewish revolt began in 66 and lasted three and one-half years (cf. Lk. 19:43; 21:20). The Roman general Titus finally forced his way into the city, breaking successively through the three N walls; and on August 6 of the year 70 his army burned the temple, eventually leveling it, just as Jesus had predicted (Mk. 13:2). Except for Herod's three W towers, the city and its fortifications were totally destroyed.

F. Postbiblical. The history of Jerusalem by no means terminated with Titus. Rebuilt in 135 as the Roman colony Aelia Capitolina, the city has since experienced nine major periods: Roman, which continued to 330; Byzantine, to 638; Arab, to 1099; Crusader, to 1187 (plus 1229–44); Arab again, to 1516; Turkish, to 1917; British, to 1948; Jordanian, to 1967; and Israeli, to the present. But Jesus made it clear that until his eschatological kingdom should appear (Lk. 19:11; Acts 1:6), Jerusalem was to have no preeminence in matters relating to God and his worship (Jn. 4:20–24).

Yet with the visible SECOND COMING of Christ, the biblical history of Jerusalem will resume. Christ and his saints will descend to Olivet on its E (Isa. 35:10; Zech. 14:4–5; Acts 1:11); and, though unbelievers will ravage Jerusalem (Zech. 12:2; 14:2), Christ shall rescue its repentant and purified Jewish remnant (Isa. 4:3–4; Zech. 12:10, 13:1, 14:5; Mal. 3:2, 5) and, at Zion, join them to his church (Zech. 12:5; Rom. 11:26). Prophecy, if interpreted literally, describes Jerusalem as the Messiah's millennial capital (Jer. 31:40; 33:16; Zech. 8:4–5; 14:20–21). His peace-making law will go forth from its "house of God" (Mic. 4:1–4), causing submission (Isa. 23:18;

45:14) and worship (60:3; Zech. 14:16–17). This temple will involve sacrifices, not of atonement (Heb. 9:12–28; note that Ezek. 43:20–21 seems to concern postexilic times only, cf. vv. 10–11), but of praise and thanksgiving (Isa. 60:6–7; Jer. 17:26; 33:18). At Zion, even nature will be affected (Isa. 65:25; Ezek. 47:1–12; Zech. 14:10). If interpreted nonliterally (amillennialism), these verses symbolize the church (cf. below, IV.C).

An attack by GOG and MAGOG (Ezek. 38–39) will bring in God's final judgment; but Jerusalem will continue eternally (Isa. 33:20; Mic. 4:7; cf. Heb. 12:27), though without a temple (Rev. 21:22) because of the perfect holiness (v. 27) of the new earth (Isa. 65:17–18; Rev. 21:2). In language drawn from both Eden and Zion (cf. Isa. 54:11; Rev. 21:19), the final state of the church is identified as "the Holy City, the new Jerusalem" (Rev. 21:2, 10–27; see NEW JERUSALEM).

III. Installations. From a literary viewpoint, Jerusalem is blessed with an abundance of citations both canonical and otherwise, far more than for any other ancient capital. Josephus in particular describes the city just prior to its fall to Rome in A.D. 70 (*War* 5.4.1–4). Yet with but few exceptions, these references concern its outer boundaries and fortifications, not its inner structure. From an archaeological viewpoint, Jerusalem remains largely inaccessible. It has not been systematically excavated, like other sites, due in part to religious taboos. Particularly in the Ḥaram area, these cut off any major investigation, from the time of C. Warren and his primitive shafts of 1867 up until the start of excavation by B. Mazar and the Hebrew University at the Southern temple wall, which commenced in 1968. Even more, the lack of archaeological work is due to the continuous occupation of the city; it is primarily the fringes of Jerusalem that have been touched, where certain walls and tower fragments can be dated as far back as the pre-Davidic Jebusites.

A. Borders. The present "Old City" walls and gates stem from A.D. 1542 and the Turkish sultan Suleiman II. Admittedly, this city does not extend all the way southward to the Hinnom Valley: its perimeter excludes part of modern "Zion" (the ancient SW hill of Gareb) and almost the whole of the City of David (SE hill). This receives compensation from its bulged out Christian Quarters to the NW and its large Muslim Quarter E of Bezetha, resulting in a somewhat disproportionate 4,200 ft. for Suleiman's N wall. As a result, the Old City walls as visited by today's traveler do not differ too greatly in total length from those known by Jesus. Especially on the E and W sides of the temple area, the huge lower stones, with their characteristically Herodian grooved edges, indicate rebuilding on top of the actual NT foundations. The extent of these fortifications far outstrips that of the other towns of Palestine (contrast the one gate of the northern capital of Samaria [1 Ki. 22:10] with Jerusalem's seven).

On the N, over the central Tyropoeon Valley, lies the commercially important Damascus Gate, equivalent to Nehemiah's more southerly located Ephraim, Old, and Fish Gates (Neh. 3:6; 12:39; 2 Ki. 14:13; 2 Chr. 33:14; the last named may be the Middle Gate mentioned in Jer. 39:3). Farther E is Herod's Gate, S of which, probably opening into the temple area itself (which constituted at the time the NE corner of the city), lay the biblical Sheep Gate (Neh. 3:1; 12:39; Jn. 5:2). West of the Sheep Gate were the Tower of the Hundred—so called perhaps because of its height, in steps or cubits, or its capacity for troops—and the Tower of Hananel (Neh. 3:1). Around the NE corner and facing the Kidron Valley stood the Benjamin or Muster Gate (Jer. 37:13; 38:7; Zech. 14:10), now called St. Stephen's Gate. (See above, II.D.2, for a list of landmarks in Nehemiah's days.)

On the E, opposite Olivet and opening directly into the Ḥaram esh-Sharif, is the Golden Gate (possibly corresponding in the OT to the East Gate, Neh. 3:29), with its double Byzantine arch. It probably corresponds to the location of Christ's triumphal entry, or exit, on Palm Sunday (Mk. 11:11); and farther inside the temple area is the site of the Beautiful Gate (Gk. *Hōraia*, mistranslated in Latin as *aurea*, thus "Golden" Gate), scene of Peter's great healing miracle (Acts 3:1–10). With the expulsion of the crusaders from Jerusalem in A.D. 1187, the Golden Gate was mortared in, as have been four other gates on the E and S Ḥaram walls (cf. the Horse Gate, 2 Ki. 11:16; Jer. 31:40; Neh. 3:28), probably for security reasons. According to Arabic legend, it will not be reopened until the resurrection and the final judgment in the Valley of Jehoshaphat (Kidron), the slopes of which around the Golden Gate are crowded with Muslim graves. The OT's Water Gate should correspond to the Gihon Spring, midway in the E wall of Zion (Neh. 3:26; 12:37). S of the "angle" wall (3:19, 24), near the SE extremity of Zion, lay the Fountain Gate (v. 15), corresponding to the Pool of Siloam, the "gate between the two walls" (Jer. 39:4; cf. Isa. 22:11; see above, II.C.3).

On the S, over the old central valley, lies the Gate of the Moors, or Dung Gate — but the OT Dung Gate (perhaps the Potsherd Gate of Jer. 19:2) was farther S, on Hinnom's edge (Neh. 2:13; 3:13), at the southern limit of the OT walls. Westward, up on the crest of Gareb, is the Zion (or David) Gate, considerably W of the OT Valley Gate (2 Chr. 26:9; Neh. 2:13), which would seem to correspond more closely to the Gate of the Moors (contrast Simons, *Jerusalem*, 443).

On the W, where the "cross valley" used to drop into the Hinnom, stands the Jaffa Gate (OT Corner Gate, 2 Ki. 14:13; 2 Chr. 26:9), once again, since the reunification of Jerusalem in 1967, the main artery for commerce to the coast or to Hebron. To its N stood Nehemiah's Tower of the Ovens (Neh. 2:11); and built into the foundations of the present "Tower of David," just S of the Gate, are the typically grooved stones of Herod's Tower of Phasael. Similar stones appear in the basement of the nearby School of the Brethren. In 1890, the Turkish government opened up the New Gate just past the NW corner of the city, thus restoring the number of gates to seven. From 1948 to 1967, when no-man's-land extended along the W part of the wall, the New Gate, Jaffa Gate, and Zion Gate were barricaded and unapproachable.

B. Interior. Until recently, most scholars have thought that water was supplied to the city through a rock-cut feature known as Warren's Shaft, a vertical well 6 ft. in diameter and extending upward over 40 ft. from the water level (other sloping passages extend westward into the rock for an additional 100 ft.; cf. the existence of similar tunnels to reach water at MEGIDDO, GIBEON, and GEZER). It now appears, however, that the ancient water system bypassed this opening and that a short tunnel led water from the Gihon Spring to a large basin (see P. J. King and L. E. Stager, *Life in Biblical Israel* [2001], 213–15). Although the entrance to Warren's Shaft lies over 30 yards outside and below Macalister's wall on the crest of the slope, it is still located 20 yards inside the Jebusite wall discovered by Kenyon in 1961. Many have thought that it was by this tunnel that David encouraged Joab and his men to advance at the capture of Jerusalem in 1003 B.C. (2 Sam. 5:8; see above, II.B.1), but recent archaeologists have argued that Warren's Shaft must be dated later than that. Its ascent would have been difficult and dangerous under any circumstances.

The site of David's palace can no longer be identified, though it seems to have been in the SE of Zion, the City of David (Neh. 12:37). Although most tombs that are claimed for kings or prophets of Israel are spurious, David's sepulchre is known to have been at the S end of the E side of Zion, near the surviving "steps going down from the City of David" (3:15–16); the same site is presumably confirmed by Peter's words that David's tomb "is with us to this day" (Acts 2:29 NRSV). It may possibly be equated with two "barrel vaults" at that point.

First excavated by R. Weill in 1913–14, these tunnel-like structures were reached at their S ends by vertical shafts and arched doorways, 3.5 ft. high and 2 ft. wide. The tunnels themselves are about 6 ft. wide and 50 ft. long. Both have lost much of their upper portions through Roman quarrying in post-NT times; but half of the more western tunnel's vaulted ceiling is preserved, over 12 ft. from the floor. Yet the floor in the back 20 ft. (N) is higher, only 6 ft. from the ceiling, and a deep groove midway up the stone walls of the front portion (S) still shows remains of a masonry flooring and indicates a division into two stories. Features of the construction indicate that the lower was the later addition. A trough across the rear of the upper level, 3.5 ft. wide and 1 ft. deep, might possibly have served as a sarcophagus for David or Asa (2 Chr. 16:14; see above, II.C.1); or the added level, as Hezekiah's added part (32.33, see above, II.C.3). Certain notches and lines do correspond to features of Hezekiah's undeniably authentic water tunnel, and Simons finds it "difficult to resist the impression that with these tombs we have indeed come into possession of some remains of the royal sepulchres" (*Jerusalem*, 220–21). Josephus (*War* 5.4.1; cf.

The site of Araunah's threshing floor purchased by David was probably located near the present Dome of the Rock. (View to the NW across the Kidron Valley.)

Ant. 7:15.3; 13.8.4; 16.7.1) seems to have located falsely the tomb of David on Gareb, where a Jewish shrine is marked to this day, next to the Church of the Dormition, S of the present Old City walls.

North of Zion, the threshing floor of Araunah the Jebusite probably stood on the highest point of Moriah, which is clearly distinguished by a crag that is now surmounted by the Muslim Dome of the Rock (Qubbet es-Sakhra). In addition, Solomon built the house of Yahweh "on Mount Moriah, where the LORD had appeared to his father David. It was on the threshing floor of Araunah the Jebusite, the place provided by David" (2 Chr. 3:1); this description may suggest that it was the most holy place of the temple that rested on the rock (cf. R. de Vaux, *Ancient Israel* [1961], 318–19; cf. L. Ritmeyer's more recent investigation in *Secrets of Jerusalem's Temple Mount* [1998], ch. 5). Such a resting place would indeed provide a level foundation for the temple; but it would considerably crowd the holy place, the porch, and the courts, all of which then would have had to lie to the E, before the sharp drop-off of the Kidron. (For the view that the temple was located some 300 ft. NW of the Dome of the Rock, see A. S. Kaufman in *BAR* 9/2 [March–April 1983]. 40–59.)

It should be noted that (a) a channel runs N from the rock, presumably to carry off the blood and the other liquids that were employed in libations; (b) a cave exists under the rock, which would serve well for ashes and other refuse; and (c) 1 Chr. 22:1 specifically designates the rock for the altar. In light of these facts, it seems more likely that the rock supported the foundation of the altar and that the temple would originally have stood to its W, probably on supporting walls that were built up. Whether or not any such still remain within and beneath the sacred enclosure of the Ḥaram it has been impossible to investigate.

From Gihon, the Solomonic aqueduct that once flowed southward and irrigated the E slopes of Zion (2 Chr. 32:4; Eccl. 2:6) and terminated in the "old pool" (Isa. 22:11) may find some correspondence in the modern garden of Birket el-Hamra. Under threat of the Assyrian attack that materialized in 701 B.C., Hezekiah sent a large force of men who "blocked all the springs and the stream [Solomon's aqueduct?] that flowed through the land" (2 Chr. 32:4); he also "made the pool and the tunnel by which he brought water into the city" (2 Ki. 20:20) and "built a reservoir between the two walls for the water of the Old Pool" (Isa. 22:11). Specifically, he constructed a 1,750-ft. gravity tunnel out of solid rock and channeled Gihon's water southward, under the walls, into a new pool of SILOAM (Jn. 9:7; cf. its celebration into intertestamental times, Sir. 48:17). The present pool of Birket Silwan, deeply sunk below the surface, is built over a later Roman installation; but the authenticity of the tunnel is demonstrated by the dedicatory

Siloam Inscription, discovered on the tunnel wall in 1880 (see further Ben-Dov, *Historical Atlas*, 59–64).

The so-called tombs of Absalom and Zechariah, on the E side of the Kidron Valley, are actually examples of what is called the *nepeš* H5883 ("soul") or monument placed above a tomb, the latter for the priestly family of Bene Hezir. Their pyramid, or conical, tops with supporting Ionic columns and cornices cut out of the solid rock of the hillside indicate a Greco-Egyptian style of the 3rd cent. B.C. Many more Hebrew graves followed in this general Olivet area, probably because of Zechariah's prophecy that the Messiah's advent in victory would occur upon this ridge (Zech. 14:5); and it is then that the resurrection of the saints will take place (1 Thess. 4:16).

In the Hellenistic period, oven-like horizontal shafts began to replace the bench-like shelves or alcoves cut into tomb walls for the reception of bodies. The so-called Tomb of Joseph of Arimathaea, inside the Church of the Holy Sepulchre, exhibits this structure. Examples that contain dozens of such shafts appear in the "Tombs of the Kings" (actually, of the family of Queen Helen of Adiabene, mid-1st Christian cent.), N of the city, beyond the present St. George Cathedral, and in the "Tombs of the Judges" (or, Sanhedrin), with their Greek façades and even with a great forecourt and benches cut from the living rock for funerary meals, to the NW. At the former, and at a Herodian family tomb W of the Hinnom, SE of the King David Hotel, may still be found in place the 6-ft. disks of stone that were rolled in a carved trench to seal the tomb doorways. The trench, though not the stone, appears likewise at the Garden Tomb, just N of the Damascus Gate. Ordinarily, tombs were located outside the walls of the city.

Of King Herod's mighty building projects, only some significant fragments survive. His temple has vanished, but much of the Herodian terracing for its surrounding courts (see above, II.E.1) remains intact. This is especially the case for the southern platform, with its supporting arches—the so-called "Stables of Solomon," dating to the Crusader period, but with the lower parts of the pillars being genuinely Herodian—and for its surrounding wall. On the W are the massive stones of the "Wailing Wall"; and at the SE corner, where the platform rises 150 ft. above the natural ground level, what some have identified with the "pinnacle" of the temple (Matt. 4:5, Lk. 4:9). At this point, the Herodian construction still rises 130 ft., or to within 20 ft. of its original height (cf. Mk. 13:1). Indeed, one of the top "railing" stones was recovered in the 1968 excavations of the Hebrew University, at the very spot where it fell outside the S wall in A.D. 70.

Two stone bridges connected the temple area with, respectively, valley stairs and Herod's palace to the W. Only the spring of ROBINSON's ARCH, projecting from the SW temple wall, remains of what was once a great span. About 150 yards farther N is "Wilson's Arch," which yet stands practically intact, though beneath more modern structures. Smaller arches carry the causeway westward from what was once the Tyropoeon Valley to his citadel between the SW and the NW hills. There the footings of his three huge towers of Hippicus, Phasael (incorporated into the present "Tower of David"), and Mariamne still determine the pattern of the Turkish fort at the Jaffa Gate.

Finally, Herod's Tower of Antonia (Acts 21:34–37) underlies today's convent of the Dames of Zion. They may be similar to GABBATHA, "the Stone Pavement" (Jn. 19:13), where Jesus appeared before Pilate. The location of the PRAETORIUM (Mk. 15:16) cannot be conclusively verified. Though some might identify it with Herod's palace, to the W, the factor of the pavement at Antonia would indicate that the present "Via Dolorosa" does commence at the proper point, namely, at this Tower.

Except for such general locations as the Garden of GETHSEMANE, somewhere on the W side of Olivet (Matt. 26:30, 36; cf. Acts 1:12), little can be said for authentic sites associated with the Jerusalem ministries of Jesus. The Pool of BETHESDA, near the Sheep Gate (Jn. 5:2), just may be identifiable with a reservoir, far below the present land surface, by the Abbey of St. Anne in the Bezetha area; and a case can be made for the equation of the ruins at St. Peter's of Gallicantu "cockcrowing" on Gareb with the house of Caiaphas and hence of the trial of Christ and the prison of the apostles (Matt. 26:57; Acts 5:18; however, see J. Wilkinson, *Jerusalem as Jesus Knew It* [1978], 133–36). A 1st-cent. flight of steps that here descends into the Tyropoeon Valley may have felt the feet of the Master. The present western site of the "House of the Last Supper" has little to commend it; and Calvary-Golgotha, "the place of a skull" (Jn.

19:17), despite popular identification with a "hill," is not even known to have been an elevation.

The hill of "Gordon's Calvary," with its accompanying "Garden Tomb," now resembles a skull, but probably did not do so in A.D. 30. Its location cannot be said to be impossible. The same is the case for the traditional Church of the Holy Sepulchre, on a spur of Jerusalem's NW hill. The one known fact of Calvary is that it lay outside the city (Jn. 19:17, 20; Heb. 13:12). On the one hand, wherever it was above the "cross valley" that Herod built his second N wall, it might seem unlikely that this commanding spur would not have been included within his defenses. On the other hand, excavations have found fragments of ancient walls S and E of the church and have failed to establish settled occupation of this area until after the time of Pontius Pilate. The presence within the church of the so-called "Tomb of Joseph" might favor its location outside the city of A.D. 30. K. Kenyon's excavation just S of the church uncovered an old quarry that lay outside the 7th-cent. B.C. town and that remained vacant until the Roman rebuilding of A.D. 135. She therefore insists that the church site must have lain outside also (*Jerusalem*, 154). Because this area clearly lay within Agrippa's third N wall, it seems possible that it might have lain within the second wall as well.

Two inscriptions from ancient Jerusalem have been plausibly associated with incidents in the early apostolic church. At the southern end of old Zion has appeared the floor plan of a building complex and the "Inscription of Theodotus," identifying it as a synagogue, hospice, and bathing establishment for pilgrims "from abroad" (see photos in "Freedmen, Synagogue of" and "ruler of the synagogue"); it may correspond to the Synagogue of the FREEDMEN that opposed Stephen (Acts 6:9). From the temple area have come two separate inscriptions (out of a whole regularly spaced series) that warned Gentiles to approach no closer into the inner courts: "Whosoever may be caught attempting to do so will have only himself to blame if his death should ensue in consequence," a prohibition that Paul was accused of violating (21:28). (See inscription photo under COUNCIL OF JERUSALEM.)

IV. Symbolism. Because of the city's role in the history of the people of God, the name *Jerusalem* inevitably acquired broad metaphorical usage within Scripture, especially among the OT prophets and poets (cf. Pss. 48; 87; 122).

A. Significations. A capital city typically represents its nation. "What is Jacob's transgression? / Is it not Samaria? / What is Judah's high place? / Is it

"Pray for the peace of Jerusalem" (Ps. 122:6). (In this aerial view looking NW, the temple mount is left of center, with the Kidron Valley below it and the slope of the Mount of Olives to the far right.)

not Jerusalem?" (Mic. 1:5). Frequently, therefore, Jerusalem simply designates the southern kingdom (Judah), whether in commendation (Jer. 2:2; Obad. 20) or in censure (Mic. 3:10; Zeph. 1:12).

More significantly, however, God's approval upon David at his bringing up the ark to Zion (2 Sam. 6:12) meant in effect that he had chosen Jerusalem for his habitation (Ps. 132:13). It had come to fulfill the Pentateuchal anticipations of the place the Lord would choose "to put his Name there for his dwelling" (Deut. 12:5); it became "the city of the Great King" (Ps. 48:2; Matt. 5:35). As the "holy mountain" of his presence (Ps. 48:1), Jerusalem received the highest of praises: "It is beautiful in its loftiness / the joy of the whole earth" (v. 2). Men were to pray for "the peace of Jerusalem" (Ps. 122:6–9; cf. 137:5–6), enshrining the House of God. The city came thus to signify the confidence of those who trusted in Yahweh (Pss. 48:3; 128:5); hence, "God is within her, she will not fall; / God will help her at break of day" (46:5). To be "born in Zion" means neither more nor less than to participate in the salvation of those who know God (Ps. 87:4–5; cf. 9:10), in "moral and religious adoption by Yahweh" (C. A. and E. G. Briggs, *A Critical and Exegetical Commentary on the Book of Psalms*, ICC, 2 vols. [1906–07], 2:240). The person who is "recorded among the living in Jerusalem" (Isa. 4:3; cf. Ps. 87:6) is thereby a justified saint of God; he is "spiritually a citizen of Zion" (*IB*, 4:470).

Though Jerusalem was "the city of God" (Pss. 46:4; 48:1, 8), it became also the city of God's anger. Isaiah thus took what may have been a name of one of the parts of Jerusalem, Ariel ("lion [or hearth] of God"), and used it as a symbolical name for the doomed city: "Woe to you, Ariel, Ariel, / the city where David settled! / Add year to year / and let your cycle of festivals go on. / Yet I will besiege Ariel; / she will mourn and lament, / she will be to me like an altar hearth [NRSV, like an Ariel]" (Isa. 29:1–2). Jerusalem's character as a "mountain of holiness" comes also to symbolize Israel's reformation and restoration, whether postexilic (Jer. 31:23) or yet future (Joel 3:17).

D. Personification. On more than one occasion Christ addressed the city as though it were a person: "O Jerusalem, Jerusalem, you who kill the prophets and stone those sent to you, how often I have longed to gather your children together, as a hen gathers her chicks under her wings, but you were not willing!"(Lk. 13:34; cf. v. 35 and 19:42–44). The city's women, or possibly all of its inhabitants, are spoken of as her "daughters" (Lam. 3:51 KJV; cf. Zech. 9:9; Lk. 23:28; Cant. 3:5, 11); or sometimes the "daughter of Jerusalem" is simply the city herself (Lam. 2:13, 15). If the poet could exclaim, "Let the daughters of Judah rejoice," it required but a step to the parallelistic expression, "Let Mount Zion be glad" (Ps. 48:11 NRSV); Jerusalem became the entire nation personified. She also personified the privileges of the people of God; the psalmist could therefore picture the water of life and address the city, saying, "All my fountains are in you" (Ps. 87:7).

The person addressed might exhibit changing connotations. Referring to the national return from exile, Isaiah exclaims: "Awake, awake, O Zion, / clothe yourself with strength. / Put on your garments of splendor, / O Jerusalem, the holy city. … Shake off your dust; / rise up, sit enthroned, O Jerusalem. / Free yourself from the chains on your neck, / O captive Daughter of Zion" (Isa. 52:1–2). But after the Servant Song of ch. 53 and Jerusalem's justification Isaiah continues "Sing, O barren woman, / you who never bore a child; / burst into song, shout for joy, / you who were never in labor; / because more are the children of the desolate woman / than of her who has a husband" (54:1, cf. 53:10). The prophet thus symbolically predicts the church as the bride of Christ (54:5), persecuted, but gaining gentile converts (v. 3) more numerous than Israel had before (Gal. 4:26–28). This suggests a final symbolism:

C. Universalization. If the phrase "born in Zion" represents the salvation of those who know God, it is significant that the psalmist also lists Rahab (or "Egypt," Ps. 87:5, ASV mg.; cf. Isa. 30:7; Pss. 74:13; 89:10), Babylon, Philistia, Tyre, and Ethiopia as "among those who acknowledge me"; and, after describing the assurance of those native to Jerusalem, he adds, "The LORD will write in the register of the peoples [note the pl.], 'This one was born in Zion'" (Ps. 87:6). As Briggs summarizes it, "Other nations are enrolled with Israel as the people of Yahweh, cf. Is. 19[18–25]" (*Psalms*, 2:240). From this comes the NT usage with its references to the church militant and the newer testament, when it asserts, "But the Jerusalem that is above is free, and she is our mother" (Gal. 4:26), or to the church triumphant, when it explains, "But you have come to Mount Zion, to the heavenly Jerusalem, the city of the living God. You have come to thousands upon thousands of angels in joyful assembly, to the church of the firstborn, whose names are written in heaven" (Heb. 12:22–23).

(In addition to the works mentioned in the body of the article, see G. A. Smith, *Jerusalem: The Topography, Economics and History from the Earliest Times to A.D. 70*, 2 vols. [1907–08]; L.-H. Vincent, *Jérusalem antique* [1912]; L.-H. Vincent and F. Abel, *Jérusalem nouvelle* [1914–26]; F. Hollis, *The Archaeology of Herod's Temple* [1934]; L.-H. Vincent and A. Steve, *Jérusalem de l'Ancien Testament* [1954–56]; Marie Aline de Sion, *La forteresse Antonia à Jérusalem et la question du Prétoire* [1956]; id., *Le Lithostrotos et le problème du Prétoire à Jérusalem* [1957]; M. Join-Lambert, *Jerusalem* [1958]; M. Avi-Yonah, *Jerusalem* [1960]; J. B. Payne, *Theology of the Older Testament* [1962], 492–504; J. Jeremias, *Jerusalem in the Time of Jesus* [1969]; Y. Yadin, ed., *Jerusalem Revealed: Archaeology in the Holy City, 1968–1974* [1975]; J. Wilkinson, *Jerusalem as Jesus Knew It* [1978]; N. Avigad, *Discovering Jerusalem* [1983]; Y. Shiloh, *Excavations at the City of David 1978–1982*, Qedem 19 [1984, with subsequent volumes by D. T. Ariel]; F. E. Peters, *Jerusalem: The Holy City in the Eyes of Chroniclers, Visitors, Pilgrims, and Prophets from the Days of Abraham to the Beginnings of Modern Times* [1985]; W. H. Mare, *The Archaeology of the Jerusalem Area* [1987]; J. D. Purvis, *Jerusalem the Holy City: A Bibliography*, 2 vols. [1988–91]; *NEAEHL*, 2:698–804; H. Shanks, *Jerusalem: An Archaeological Biography* [1995]; D. Bahat and C. T. Rubinstein, *The Illustrated Atlas of Jerusalem* [1996]; G. Auld and M. Steiner, *Jerusalem I: From the Bronze Age to the Maccabees* [2000]; L. J. Hoppe, *The Holy City: Jerusalem in the Theology of the Old Testament* [2000]; M. Ben-Dov, *Historical Atlas of Jerusalem* [2002]; L. I. Levine, *Jerusalem: Portrait of the City in the Second Temple Period (538 B.C.E.–70 C.E.)* [2003]; T. L. Thompson, ed., *Jerusalem in Ancient History and Tradition* [2003]; A. G. Vaughn and A. E. Killebrew, eds., *Jerusalem in Bible and Archaeology: The First Temple Period* [2003]; R. Reich, *Jerusalem as Jesus Knew It* [2004]; L. and K. Ritmeyer, *Jerusalem in the Year 30 A.D.* [2004]; id., *Jerusalem in the Time of Nehemiah* [2005]; M. Küchler, *Jerusalem: Ein Handbuch und Studienreiseführer zur Heiligen Stadt* [2006]. The Jerusalem Archaeological Park website [www.archpark.org.il] includes interactive map tours as well as a virtual reconstruction model of the temple displayed in 360-degree panoramas.) J. B. PAYNE

Jerusalem, Council of. See COUNCIL OF JERUSALEM.

Jerusalem, new. See NEW JERUSALEM.

Jerusha ji-roo´shah (יְרוּשָׁא H3729, variant יְרוּשָׁה H3730, "possession" or "inherited one"). Daughter of a certain Zadok, wife of King UZZIAH, and mother of King JOTHAM (2 Ki. 15:33; 2 Chr. 27:1 [KJV and other versions, "Jerushah"]).

Jerushah ji-roo´shah. See JERUSHA.

Jesaiah ji-say´yuh. KJV alternate form of JESHAIAH (1 Chr. 3:21; Neh. 11:7).

Jesarelah jes´uh-ree´luh (יְשַׂרְאֵלָה H3777). KJV Jesharelah. See ASARELAH.

Jeshaiah ji-shay´yuh (יְשַׁעְיָה H3832, short form of יְשַׁעְיָהוּ H3833, "Yahweh is salvation [or victorious]"; see ISAIAH). **(1)** Son of Hananiah, grandson of ZERUBBABEL, and descendant of DAVID (1 Chr. 3:21 [KJV, "Jesaiah"]).

(2) Son of JEDUTHUN; he and his brothers "prophesied, using the harp in thanking and praising the LORD" (1 Chr. 25:3). He was also the head of the eighth company of temple musicians appointed by lot under David (v. 15).

(3) Son of Rehabiah; his descendant SHELOMITH was a Levite who shared the supervision of David's treasury (1 Chr. 26:25).

(4) Son of Athaliah and descendant of Elam; he was head of a family that returned with EZRA to Jerusalem (Ezra 8:7; 1 Esd. 8:33 [KJV, "Josias"]).

(5) Descendant of MERARI; he was head of a Levitical family that returned with EZRA to Jerusalem (Ezra 8:19; 1 Esd. 8:48 [KJV, "Osaias"]).

(6) Descendant of BENJAMIN and ancestor of Sallu; the latter is mentioned in a list of Israelites living in Jerusalem after the EXILE (Neh. 11:7 [KJV, "Jesaiah"]).　　　　　　　　　　S. BARABAS

Jeshanah jesh´uh-nuh (יְשָׁנָה H3827, "old [city]"). A town taken by ABIJAH king of Judah from JEROBOAM king of Israel (2 Chr. 13:19). It is mentioned with BETHEL and EPHRON, and was probably located on the border of Judah and Israel. Jeshanah is thought to be the same as Isanas, where HEROD the Great achieved a great military victory over the Syrian king Antigonus (Jos. *Ant.* 14.15.12). The generally accepted identification is modern Burj el-Isaneh, some 16 mi. N of Jerusalem, and about 5 mi. N of Bethel. (Some believe that Jeshana in 1 Sam. 7:12 is a variant of Jeshanah; cf. NRSV.)　　　S. BARABAS

Jeshanah Gate. See OLD GATE.

Jesharelah jesh´uh-ree´luh. KJV form of Jesarelah; see ASARELAH.

Jeshebeab ji-sheb´ee-ab (יְשֶׁבְאָב H3784, possibly "[my] father lives" or "may [my] father stay alive"). A descendant of AARON whose family in the time of DAVID made up the fourteenth division of priests (1 Chr. 24:13).

Jesher jesh´uhr (יֵשֶׁר H3840, "uprightness"). Son of CALEB (apparently by AZUBAH); included in the genealogy of JUDAH (1 Chr. 2:18).

Jeshimon ji-shi´mon (יְשִׁימוֹן H3810, "wasteland"). Name given to a desolate area in the Judean wilderness, apparently S of the Desert of ZIPH and N of the Desert of MAON. This region, described as facing the hill of HAKILAH (to the N), is mentioned to help locate DAVID's whereabouts when he fled from SAUL and hid in the strongholds of HORESH (1 Sam. 23:19, 24; 26:1, 3). The name Jeshimon also occurs in the KJV with reference to the region of PISGAH in MOAB (Num. 21:20; 23:28), but in these passages the Hebrew word is probably used as a common noun (cf. NIV and NRSV, "the wasteland").

Jeshimoth. See BETH JESHIMOTH.

Jeshishai ji-shish´i (יְשִׁישַׁי H3814, "aged"). Son of Jahdo, descendant of GAD, and ancestor of Abihail; the sons of Abihail and other Gadites occupied the region E of GILEAD (1 Chr. 5:14; cf. v. 10).

Jeshohaiah jesh´uh-hay´yah (יְשׁוֹחָיָה H3797, meaning uncertain). A clan leader in the tribe of SIMEON (1 Chr. 4:36). He is listed among those whose families increased greatly during the days of King HEZEKIAH and who dispossessed the Hamites and Meunites near GEDOR (vv. 38–41).

Jeshua (person) jesh´yoo-uh (יֵשׁוּעַ H3800, short form of יְהוֹשֻׁעַ H3397, "Yahweh is salvation [or help]";

The wilderness area of Jeshimon.

see JOSHUA, JESUS). **(1)** Son of JEHOZADAK and high priest at the time of the return from Babylon and the rebuilding of the TEMPLE (Ezra 3:2). In EZRA and NEHEMIAH he is mentioned because of his official position; the only personal statement is that one or more of his sons were among those who had married foreign wives (10:18). In HAGGAI and ZECHARIAH he is called Joshua. He and ZERUBBABEL were exhorted to further the work of rebuilding the temple (Hag. 1:14; 2:2, 4). He figures in the great prophecies regarding the "Branch": one of them describes in vision the replacing of the filthy garments of the high priest by clean ones (Zech. 3), and the other refers to the crowns to be placed upon his head as the type of the man whose name is "the Branch" and who "will be a priest on his throne" (6:11–13). (See J. C. VanderKam, *From Joshua to Caiaphas: High Priests after the Exile* [2004], 18–42.)

(2) A descendant of AARON whose family in the time of DAVID made up the ninth division of priests (1 Chr. 24:11 [some KJV editions, "Jeshuah"]). He was probably the ancestor of a large priestly family that returned to Jerusalem under Zerubbabel (Ezra 2:36; Neh. 7:39; 1 Esd. 5:24 [KJV, "Jesus"]).

(3) A Levite who faithfully assisted KORE in distributing the contributions made to the temple (2 Chr. 31:15).

(4) Ancestor of a group (connected with the families of Pahath-Moab and Joab) that returned to Jerusalem under Zerubbabel (Ezra 2:6; Neh. 7:11; 1 Esd. 5:11 [KJV omits]).

(5) A Levite who, with others, "joined together in supervising those working on the house of God" (Ezra 3:9; 1 Esd. 5:58 [KJV, "Jesus"]). He is probably the same Jeshua listed among returnees (Ezra 2:40; Neh. 7:43; 1 Esd. 5:26 [KJV, "Jessue"]) and named first among thirteen Levites who explained the law to the people in the days of Nehemiah (Neh. 11:26; 1 Esd. 9:48 [KJV, "Jesus"]). There are several other passages that likely refer to him: he was a leader in worship (Neh. 9:4–5; 12:8) and was among those who sealed the covenant (10:9, where he is identified as "son of Azaniah"; in 12:24 he is called "son of Kadmiel," but many scholars suspect textual corruption and emend "son of" [*ben*] to "Bani"). It is often thought that this Jeshua was also the father of EZER, ruler of MIZPAH, listed among those who helped to repair the wall (3:19), as well as the father of JOZABAD, a Levite who assisted in taking inventory of the silver, gold, and sacred articles (Ezra 8:33).

(6) Alternate name for JOSHUA son of Nun (Neh. 8:17 KJV and other versions).

Jeshua (place) jesh´yoo-uh (יֵשׁוּעַ H3801, possibly "prosperous [town]" or short form of יְהוֹשֻׁעַ H3397, "Yahweh is salvation [*or* help]"; see JOSHUA). A town in the S of Judah, listed among the settlements occupied by those who returned from the EXILE (Neh. 11:26). Its location is uncertain, but some identify it with modern Tell Jeshua, about 9 mi. ENE of BEERSHEBA.

Jeshuah jesh´yoo-uh. KJV alternate form of JESHUA (1 Chr. 24:11, some editions).

Jeshurun jesh´uh-ruhn (יְשֻׁרוּן H3843, "upright" [cf. JASHAR]; according to some, a diminutive, affectionate form). A poetic designation for Israel as the ideal "righteous" nation. It occurs three times in Deuteronomy, both in negative and positive contexts (Deut. 32:15; 33:5, 26), and once in Isaiah: "Do not be afraid, O Jacob, my servant, / Jeshurun, whom I have chosen" (Isa. 44:2). Some have speculated that the name may be linguistically connected with *yiśrāʾēl* H3776 (Israel) and that it originally designated a non-Israelite people group (see *ABD*, 3:771–72).

Jesiah ji-si´uh. KJV alternate form of ISSHIAH (1 Chr. 12:6).

Jesimiel ji-sim´ee-uhl (יְשִׂימִאֵל H3774, "God sets down, establishes"). A clan leader in the tribe of SIMEON (1 Chr. 4:36). He is listed among those whose families increased greatly during the days of King HEZEKIAH and who dispossessed the Hamites and Meunites near GEDOR (vv. 38–41).

Jesse jes´ee (יִשַׁי H3005 [variant אִישַׁי H414, 1 Chr. 2:13], possibly short form of יִשִׁיָּהוּ H3808 [see ISSHIAH], Ἰεσσαί G2649). Son of Obed, grandson of BOAZ and RUTH, father of King DAVID (Ruth 4:17, 22; 1 Chr. 2:12); included in the GENEALOGY OF JESUS CHRIST (Matt. 1:5–6; Lk. 3:32). A member of the tribe of Judah, Jesse was a wealthy landholder in BETHLEHEM. He was the father of seven or eight sons and two daughters (1 Sam. 16:1–2; 17:12; the name of Elihu is omitted in 1 Chr. 2:13–17). The two daughters were mothers of famous warriors in David's army: ZERUIAH's sons were JOAB, ABISHAI, and ASAHEL; ABIGAIL's son was AMASA. (The difficult statement in 2 Sam. 17:25 that Abigail [Abigal] was the daughter of NAHASH has been interpreted by some to mean that David's mother had been married to Nahash before she married Jesse, making Zeruiah and Abigail stepdaughters of Jesse and stepsisters of David. Other explanations have been offered, but the matter cannot be settled with certainty.)

Jesse is formally introduced to the reader of the OT at the point where SAMUEL is instructed to anoint the future king of Israel (1 Sam. 16:1–13). At the command of Yahweh, the prophet journeyed to Bethlehem for a sacrificial meal to which Jesse and his family were invited. In the course of events, seven of Jesse's sons passed in review before Samuel, but none was chosen of God. Upon inquiry, the prophet found that the eighth and youngest son was in the field tending sheep. David was summoned, reviewed, given the divine sanction, and anointed. The indications are that neither Jesse nor David understood all the implications of Samuel's actions on this occasion.

Jesse is next mentioned in connection with SAUL, who sent a messenger requesting him to allow David to come to court and play his harp to cure the king's melancholia (1 Sam. 16:14–15). Jesse agreed to the king's request, and not only sent his son, but also a present of meat, bread, and wine for the king. This indicates that Jesse was a prosperous and generous farmer, and also one who knew the courtly protocol of his day. He was also magnanimous enough to leave David at Saul's court when the latter made further request of his services (16:22–23).

Jesse, on another occasion, unwittingly initiated David into his military career by sending him to the battle front at the appropriate moment. Laden with fresh provisions for his three older brothers who were serving in Saul's army, David stumbled into camp just as the Israelites were confronted by a huge PHILISTINE force whose champion was GOLIATH of GATH. The stripling David gained immortal renown by slaying the Philistine giant (1 Sam. 17).

Jesse's safety and welfare became the concern of David during the years he lived as a fugitive from Saul. Fearing that Saul, in one of his periodic fits of depression, might harm his aged parents, David sent them away to the land of MOAB until the danger was past. They apparently survived the sojourn in MOAB without mishap (1 Sam. 22:2–4).

David is often called "the son of Jesse" in the OT. It was a derisive and hateful term in the mouth of Saul and other enemies of David (1 Sam. 20:27, 30–31; 22:7–9, 13; 25:10; 2 Sam. 20:1; 1 Ki. 12:16; 2 Chr. 10:16). In time, however, it became a term of honor and renown, and greatly beloved by the people of Israel (2 Sam. 23:1; 1 Chr. 10:14; 29:26; Ps. 72:20; Acts 13:22).

Jesse is mentioned in the prophecies of Isaiah as an ancestor of the future messianic king. Here the shoot that "will come up from the stump of Jesse" (Isa. 11:1; cf. v. 10, "the Root of Jesse") is symbolic for that messianic personage who was to bring in the long-awaited end-times. Paul used the expression "the Root of Jesse" (Rom. 15:12) to identify Jesus with the messianic prophecies of the OT. The same could be said for Matthew's and Luke's inclusion of Jesse in the genealogies of Jesus (Matt. 1:5–6; Lk. 3:32; cf. Acts 13:22).   C. P. GRAY

Jesui jes´yoo-i. KJV alternate form of ISHVI (Num. 26:44).

Jesus jee´zuhs (Ἰησοῦς G2652, from יֵשׁוּעַ H3800, short form of יְהוֹשֻׁעַ H3397, "Yahweh is salvation [or help]"; see JOSHUA). (1) Jesus Christ. See separate article.

(2) Son of Sirach (named after his grandfather) and author of ECCLESIASTICUS.

(3) KJV Apoc. alternate form of JESHUA (1 Esd. 5:5 et al.).

(4) Son of Eliezer, included in Luke's GENEALOGY OF JESUS CHRIST (Lk. 3:29 NJB and other versions; KJV, "Jose"; most versions, "Joshua").

(5) Possibly the personal name of BARABBAS (Matt. 27:16–17 v.l.).

(6) A Jewish fellow worker of PAUL (Col. 4:11). See JUSTUS #3.

(7) KJV NT form of JOSHUA (Acts 7:45; Heb. 4:8).   D. E. HIEBERT

Jesus Christ jee´zuhs krīst (Ἰησοῦς G2653, from יֵשׁוּעַ H3800, short form of יְהוֹשֻׁעַ H3397, "Yahweh is salvation [or help]" [see JOSHUA]; Χριστός G5986, "anointed"). The double title occurs only five times in the Gospels, usually in the initial material of these books (see Matt. 1:1, 18; Mk. 1:1; Jn. 1:17; 17:3), whereas it is very frequent in Acts and the Epistles. This article will consider various aspects of the life, teaching, and death of Jesus according to the following outline.

  I. The significance of the name
 II. The background to the life of Jesus
     A. The political situation
     B. The social situation
     C. The cultural situation
     D. The religious situation
III. Various approaches to the life of Christ
     A. The traditional approach
     B. The rationalistic approach
     C. The mythological approach
     D. The sentimental approach
     E. The liberal lives of Jesus
     F. Nineteenth-century British approaches
     G. Twentieth-century viewpoints
 IV. Literary sources for the life of Christ
     A. The Synoptic Gospels
     B. The fourth gospel
     C. The fourfold presentation of Jesus
     D. Other NT evidence for the life of Jesus
     E. Extracanonical material for the life of Jesus
  V. The early life and ministry of Jesus Christ
     A. Summary of methods
     B. The thirty years in Nazareth
     C. The period of preparation
     D. The Judean ministry of Jesus
     E. The Galilean ministry
     F. The closing period of the ministry
     G. The passion and resurrection of Jesus
 VI. The teaching of Jesus
     A. His teaching method
     B. The content of the teaching of Jesus
VII. The miracles of Jesus
     A. The validity of miracles
     B. The purpose of the miracles
VIII. Jesus Christ in early Christian thought
     A. Primitive thought
     B. Pauline thought
     C. Johannine thought
     D. Other aspects of Christ
     E. Conclusion

I. The significance of the name. The separate names warrant careful examination. *Jesus* represents the Greek form of Hebrew *Joshua* (*yĕhôšuaʿ*, short form *yēšûaʿ*, meaning "Yahweh is salvation" or "Yahweh saves"), a name borne by several OT characters. It was a common name among the Jews in the time of Jesus. Jesus Christ is generally distinguished from other bearers of the same name by the addition of the description "of Nazareth," at least when first introduced in the gospel narrative. Mark, after using the title Jesus Christ in the introductory statement, refers to Jesus as having come from NAZARETH of GALILEE (Mk. 1:9). A similar procedure is followed by Matthew, who nevertheless also uses the description several times in the body of his work. In all the Gospels, the name Jesus is used alone in the great majority of cases, while in Acts we find a mixture of uses. In Matt. 1:21, the Christian significance of the name is explained. It is seen as a divinely appointed name and its meaning is derived from the root idea of salvation—"because he will save his people from their sins." It was not until later in the postresurrection period that the significance of the name was recognized.

The other name, *Christ*, is of essential importance, because it at once makes an assertion about the human Jesus that differentiates him from all other men. There had been false Christs, but only one true Christ. The word corresponds to the Hebrew MESSIAH (*māšiaḥ* H5431), which means "anointed one," but had come to be used specifically of *the* Anointed of God, who was to come in fulfillment of ancient prophecies. At this point it is the intent of this article not to discuss the variety of concepts current among the Jews regarding this messianic hope, but rather to denote its meaning in the Christian sense. There can be no doubt that the identification of the historical Jesus with the expected Messiah was the key to the early Jewish Christian understanding of the mission of Jesus. The name Jesus Christ carries with it therefore deep theological significance. One must consider not only the bare historical facts about Jesus of Nazareth, but also the interpretation of those facts.

II. The background to the life of Jesus. A vast store of literature describes the historical background of the period of the life of Jesus. A true

The Church of the Annunciation lies in the midst of the modern city of Nazareth, Jesus' hometown. (View to the SW.)

historical perspective cannot afford to neglect this information, which has been valuably reinforced by the DEAD SEA SCROLLS and related discoveries. Since only the briefest sketch can be given of the historical background, the developments within JUDAISM from a religious point of view and the political position leading to the time of the INCARNATION of Jesus will have to be largely by-passed. Our concern will be the conditions that obtained during the brief span of the life of Jesus, and to this end some account will be given of the political, social, cultural, and religious situation.

A. The political situation. The Roman occupation of Palestine had brought with it many benefits, but it had also incurred the implacable hatred of the Jewish people. The occupying forces were in their eyes a threat to their national heritage and aspirations. They accordingly objected most violently to the taxation system that had been introduced and that was the cause of constant irritation. Any Jew who stooped low enough to assist in the collection of any of these taxes was the object of contempt and was socially ostracized. Under the system, a chief TAX COLLECTOR was responsible for a whole district and then farmed out the task of collecting the taxes to subcollectors, a process that lent itself to considerable abuse and extortion.

One feature of the political situation was the considerable measure of self-government allowed to the Jews. Much of the government of Palestine was in the hands of the ruling religious party and was conducted in accordance with OT principles. There was a central council (SANHEDRIN) in Jerusalem and local councils in various other centers. Punishment, where possible, was administered as the Jewish law decreed, the main method being flogging, of which there are several instances in the NT (note esp. the case of Jesus himself). The fact that the Jewish accusers of Jesus required PILATE's sanction for the execution of the death sentence suggests that this was the usual procedure, although in the case of STEPHEN it was not followed. No doubt there were many occurrences of the operation of a kind of mob law. The central Jewish council consisted of elders, chief priests, and scribes, a grouping often mentioned in the Gospels and Acts. Although there was officially only one high priest who presided over the ecclesiastical-political administration, those who had previously held office could be included under the same term, as were also others who held high temple offices (cf. J. Jeremias, *Jerusalem in the Time of Jesus* [1969], ch. 8).

Within the Roman empire as a whole, a fair degree of political stability had been achieved under the rule of AUGUSTUS. It was a period of

Bronze statuette of a Roman auxiliary soldier (2nd cent. A.D.). During the time of Jesus, Rome controlled the politics in the Promised Land.

great consolidation in the realm of administration and jurisdiction. The Romans found that the Jews were, however, among the most turbulent of their subjects, mainly because of their religious peculiarities and their strongly isolationist and nationalistic aspirations.

It was the policy of the occupying power to attempt to achieve some degree of adhesion among the various peoples of the provinces by absorbing their local deities into the Roman pantheon, but this policy was impossible in the case of the Jews, who possessed no image for their God. No doubt the Romans had little real understanding of the Jewish people, which was reflected in their series of procurators sent to Palestine. Pilate may be cited as an example, although he was worse than most, as is seen from the fact that the Roman authorities recalled him because of his mishandling of the situation. He committed many atrocities against the Jews that bitterly antagonized them. He took no steps to avoid offending their religious scruples. It is no wonder that at the trial of Jesus they threatened to regard Pilate as ill-disposed toward Caesar if he let Jesus go, a threat that had considerable thrust in view of the mounting tension between the procurator and the people, and in view of the former's fear of incurring the emperor's displeasure. On a previous occasion the Jews had appealed to Caesar, who overrode Pilate's action. Such was the uneasy political situation into which Jesus Christ came and under which he died.

B. The social situation. The main points to be noted here are the structure of society generally and of the home in particular. The Jewish nation was still governed by the patriarchal concept of society. Moreover, there was considerable veneration for age, which placed the older men in a position of influence. Women and children were not favorably placed in the Jewish society. In this respect the Romans had advanced further toward their emancipation. There are incidents in the Gospels, such as the story regarding the Samaritan woman, that illustrate the inferior position of women. As far as the law was concerned, women were not obliged to be taught the law. Jewish education, which centered in the learning and interpretation of the law, was provided for boys but not for girls. It is one of the more surprising features of the ministry of Jesus, although it took place in an essentially Jewish setting, that women were numbered among his followers.

In the realm of marriage there were two divergent schools of thought among Jewish teachers regarding the permissibility of divorce. The school of HILLEL was less stringent than that of Shammai, the former allowing divorce for a number of reasons in which the wife displeased the husband, while the latter allowed it only in the case of infidelity. This illustrates the fluidity of social ethics even among the PHARISEES. Generally speaking, the home was an important unit in the Jewish social structure. It was a matter of social honor for a man to marry (see FAMILY; MARRIAGE). Moreover, among the Jews there was no sanction for the widespread heathen practice of exposing unwanted babies to the elements to die.

In the time of Jesus the Jewish society was roughly divided into two groups. The religious parties—especially the SADDUCEES and Pharisees—considered themselves apart from the ordinary people. There was considerable contempt for the "people of the land" (AM HA-AREZ), particularly among the Pharisees, a factor that will be commented on when the religious situation is outlined below. From a social point of view it is important to recognize this distinct division, because it explains many of the sayings of Jesus about his contemporaries.

C. The cultural situation. In the northern district of Palestine there were many Hellenistic cities in which Greek ideas and practices flourished. Not only was this true of the cities known as the DECAPOLIS, but also of many other cities on the borders of Palestine. Something of the impact of Hellenistic culture could not fail to affect those sections of Jewish society that were most open to outside influence. See HELLENISM. Previous to the discovery of the Dead Sea Scrolls, it seemed most unlikely that Hellenistic ideas would have permeated into Jewish circles, but the Qumran community, although Jewish, was not impervious to Greek and even Oriental influences. Whereas the major currents of Jewish thought, particularly that of the Pharisees, were still resistant to the inroads of Greek culture, yet in the time of Jesus the narrower exclusiveness was beginning to break down.

An interesting question arises regarding the possibility that Jesus may have used the GREEK LANGUAGE in Galilee, in addition to ARAMAIC. No certain answer can be given, but there is little doubt that many in Galilee used Greek. In all probability the area was bilingual, and it is very likely that Jesus was acquainted with Greek. Most of his teaching was certainly in Aramaic, for not only have a few of the Aramaic expressions been preserved in the Greek Gospels, but Aramaic was the language of the common people, to whom Jesus mainly addressed himself. It is not impossible, however, that Jesus was acquainted with Greek modes of thought, and it need not be considered incredible that at times he expressed his teaching in forms that would have affinity with those modes (as appears at times to happen in the fourth gospel).

D. The religious situation

1. Worship among the Jews. In the Jewish religious outlook of the 1st cent. there were two major foci, the law and the temple. The Jewish people may well be described as the people of the Torah, for the teaching of the law was normative for Jewish life. It was not just the written code of law (the TORAH), but also a great body of oral tradition (see MISHNAH), which for them possessed equal validity. All Jewish boys were grounded in the teaching of the PENTATEUCH from their earliest schooling. The book of LEVITICUS was, in fact, their first textbook. It was the parents' responsibility to instruct their children in the minutiae of the ceremonial law as the various festivals came around. The SYNAGOGUE services would serve the same purpose. These services comprised confession of faith, prayer, Scripture reading, address, and benediction.

The Scripture reading was in accordance with a lectionary, based on a three-year cycle, in which a passage from the books of the law was linked with a passage from the prophets. It is possible, however, that no fixed passages were set for the prophetical books in the time of Jesus, although such an arrangement is known to have been followed at a later date. The choice of reader and preacher was left to the RULER OF THE SYNAGOGUE, who could invite anyone capable of doing it. This accounts for the number of occasions when Jesus addressed synagogue audiences. The ruler of the synagogue exercised a great deal of influence and was regarded with respect by the people. The local communities were essentially religious communities.

Although the synagogue was the center of community life, the TEMPLE cultus exerted a powerful influence over the pious Jew for a number of reasons. The Jews of Palestine and those of the DIASPORA (in regions outside Palestine) were still considered a single unit, and one important unifying factor was a common allegiance to the temple cultus. Every year pilgrims came to Jerusalem from other parts of Palestine, and from Jewish settlements throughout the empire, to attend the various festivals and particularly at Passover time. The temple worship was highly organized, with twenty-four divisions of priests who worked on a rotation system to insure continuity and efficiency.

The sacrifices of burnt offerings were offered twice daily in the temple, but there were many other kinds of offerings in addition. The burnt offering was significant for the people of Israel as a whole, but there were other types of offerings for individuals, whether offerings for unintentional sins, or votive offerings before some hazardous undertaking, or thank offerings for some deliverance. The temple cultus had great relevance to the everyday life of the people. But it was at festival times that special focus was upon the temple. Since the festivals play some part in the gospel events, it is fitting for some description to be given, as John makes a feature of them in his account of the activity of Jesus.

There was a festival for the New Year, but this is not referred to in the Gospels, nor in fact is the Day of Atonement, observed shortly afterward, in which the high priest alone was permitted to enter the Holy of Holies (see ATONEMENT, DAY OF). There are several references to the PASSOVER, which assumes particular importance for the life of Jesus, for this festival was in progress at the time of the crucifixion. It was not long before the historical connection led to the recognition of a theological link. This was indeed implicit in the institution of the Last Supper. It was customary for the family group, in fact, to remain together over the Passover night. This throws light upon the group of disciples whom Jesus had with him for the final Passover meal, and explains why he did not leave Jerusalem that night for Bethany. In close connection with the Passover was the feast of Unleavened Bread, also mentioned in the Gospels. This was held as a festival of remembrance of the exodus, although it originally commemorated the commencement of harvest.

The most joyful festival was Tabernacles (see FEASTS), which was popular because it involved the worshipers in dwelling in booths constructed from foliage. In the temple courts were special illuminations and a daily ritual involving the pouring out of water. Both of these features furnished Jesus with a teaching point when he was in Jerusalem at the time of the feast (Jn. 7). In John's gospel the feast of DEDICATION is also mentioned, but no particular significance is attached to it. The feast of PENTECOST, which was a thanksgiving festival for the grain harvest, is not mentioned in the Gospels, but is prominent in Acts.

It is a fair deduction that since Jesus was a Jew the temple cultus must have had great importance for him, a fact that is borne out by two particular occasions: the first when he questioned the doctors of the law in the temple at the age of twelve and regarded this incident as his Father's business, and the second when he cleansed the temple of unworthy elements by appealing to what Scripture said about his Father's house.

There was one more feature that was shared by all Jews regardless of the party to which they belonged, namely, their sense of exclusiveness. In some ways this was a beneficial feature, but in other ways not. Those tenets which the Jewish people held to tenaciously were better preserved through an exclusive policy than would have been the case had they allowed themselves to become mixed up with Gentile ideas and practices. The Maccabean wars had been sparked off by an attempt to do this (see MACCABEE), and in the time of Jesus the Jewish people could not forget the heroism that had preserved for them the uniqueness of their faith. There were two main areas in which the Jews were superior to their heathen neighbors — in their theology and in their ethics. Their concept of God was infinitely more exalted than the idolatry of the contemporary Gentile world and caused many of the finer minds among the Gentiles to seek satisfaction as Jewish proselytes. The same may be said of the ethical ideals of Judaism, which were in marked superiority to the debased morals of the heathen religions. This sense of superiority and the desire to hedge themselves around contributed in no small measure to the intense dislike for Jews noticeable among many Gentile peoples.

2. The Jewish parties. For a right evaluation of the religious atmosphere in the time of Jesus it is necessary to survey the four major groups — Pharisees, Sadducees, Essenes, and Zealots. Of these the first is the most important for one's purpose because of its more dominant religious influence and because of the frequent interchange Jesus had with them. The Sadducees were more politically powerful, but Jesus did not find himself so often taking up issues with them on religious matters. The Essenes are not mentioned in the Gospels at all, but should not for that reason be ignored, for their very existence was a protest against the other parties, a protest with some aspects of which Jesus would find himself in sympathy. The Zealots come into the gospel story only incidentally.

(a) *A comparison between Sadducees and Pharisees.* It will be valuable to make such a comparison before giving more detailed attention to the Pharisees. The Pharisaic party had its rise in the movement of the Hasidim (see Hasideans), who were opposed to the militarism of the Hasmoneans and were devoted to a campaign to bring about repentance and spiritual renewal. Among the Pharisees this concern sometimes developed into a legalistic approach, which is amply illustrated by many incidents recorded in the Gospels. They spared nothing in their devotion to the law. They were committed to carry out what the scribes prescribed. It is not surprising, therefore, that at the time of Jesus the majority of scribes belonged to the Pharisees. The party was characterized by a deep religious zeal that extended not only toward the Torah, but also to the oral law. This was the same position that rabbinic Judaism maintained toward the Halakah, or traditional law. Pharisaism can be rightly assessed only against this sense of devotion to a tradition that was as binding as the written code. Some of the reasons for this legalistic approach will be discussed below, but for the present it is the purpose to compare Pharisaism in these features with Sadducean ideas.

The Sadducees adhered only to the teaching of the Pentateuch and strongly rejected the Pharisaic

This modern reconstruction of Jerusalem in Jesus' day shows the Nicanor Gate with the temple behind. The Sadducees exerted their control from the temple.

overloading of the law with tradition. The Sadducees thus appeared to be nearer to a strictly biblical approach, although it must be remembered that the Pharisees sincerely believed that oral tradition provided an adequate, indeed the most adequate, interpretation of the Mosaic law. They were basically agreed therefore on the importance of the Pentateuch as a foundation for Jewish society.

The difference in attitude toward the oral law led to some fundamental disagreements. The most notable controversies were over the resurrection, which Pharisees maintained, but which Sadducees denied. The latter disputed supernaturalism generally, as is seen from their rejection of belief in angels. They were, in fact, hard-headed, with a tendency toward materialism.

In Palestine in the time of Jesus, the Sadducees were the land-owning class, whose main interests were political rather than religious. They regarded the Roman subjugation as rather less obnoxious than their Pharisaic brethren. In matters of jurisdiction, the Sadducees were inclined to greater severity of action than the Pharisees, who erred on the side of leniency for fear of unwittingly opposing truth. GAMALIEL's advice of caution (Acts 5:38–39) is typical of this approach. When the Sadducean CAIAPHAS was considering the threat of Jesus to the Jewish hierarchy, he displayed a devotion to political expediency which no Pharisee would have expressed so unequivocally (Jn. 11:48). Compared with the Pharisees, the Sadducees had a lesser concept of God and a greater confidence in man, although still related to the Jewish law.

(b) *The Pharisees and their doctrines.* Mention has already been made of the schools of Hillel and Shammai, but it is important to have a clear understanding of the difference between them when considering the attitude of Jesus toward Pharisaism as a whole. Hillel, who originally came from Babylon, maintained a liberal approach toward the law, whereas Shammai was more rigorous. The former was probably a city man and the latter more in touch with agriculture, and this difference appears to have had some bearing on their general religious attitudes. It should be remembered that these two schools of thought virtually constituted the national bar for local jurisdiction under the Roman constitution. Their decisions were more than niceties of Jewish casuistry, but affected the everyday running of the country.

Some examples of the differences in their rulings may be given to illustrate the fact that judgments on some issues could differ considerably. It has already been pointed out that Shammai allowed divorce only for unchastity or gross immodesty, whereas Hillel admitted it for any cause that displeased the husband. The same tendency is seen in relation to debts outstanding in the Sabbatical year. Since the law specified that all debts must be forgiven during that year, it became impossible for poor people to obtain loans during the previous period, but Hillel found a way around this by inventing the device known as *Prosbul*, which circumvented the requirement for all debts to be forgiven. This is an example of the liberalizing treatment of the law which went to such an extent that it virtually nullified the Mosaic requirement.

The Pharisees, particularly Hillel's party, were making serious attempts to face new problems realistically. The Sadducees tended to take the view that where no law existed on any issue, none could be made. But the Pharisees, convinced that the law must be normative in all situations, were prepared to see how the law could be adapted to new issues. Some of the criticism of Jesus directed against this party were against the casuistry with which they were attempting to apply their chosen policies. It may assist in appreciating the tendency of Pharisaism to impose minute directions in all spheres of ethical conduct if it is realized that the restrictions themselves were regarded as safeguards. The common people, it was supposed, would too easily transgress the law if sufficient barriers were not erected to hedge it around. Their casuistry was thought to possess social implications, and whereas they despised the common people as an inferior breed, they prided themselves with having their welfare at heart.

Of the Pharisees and Sadducees, the former were the most popular with the people. They shared with them a common hatred of the Romans, as against the more compromising tendencies of the Sadducees. Moreover, their doctrines and practices were respected even when they were not acted upon. They had a studied policy to court popularity, as for instance, by street corner prayers, which were condemned by Jesus for ostentation. In the light of this popularity, it may seem strange that Jesus was so strongly critical of them, but reasons will later be given why his denunciations were so strong.

The tenets of Pharisaism formed the background for some of the teaching of Jesus. The Pharisees had a high concept of God. He was powerfully active in human history, particularly in the history of Israel. This exalted concept had been pushed so far that he had become transcendental. While there was still divine activity, it was through intermediaries. The Torah had indeed become the major agency of God in his dealings with his people. It was against such a view of God that the teaching of Jesus about the FATHERHOOD OF GOD must be placed.

It was because the law was the expression of the eternal will of God that it became for the Pharisee the norm in all matters of behavior. Any action that contravened the law, as the Pharisees understood it, was an act of impiety and must be condemned. It was not easy for a Pharisee to accept such authoritative pronouncements as those which fell from the lips of Jesus, which went beyond the precepts of the law. The national existence was so bound up with observation of and loyalty to the law that the Pharisees could not accept that any personal authority could abrogate or even modify the official understanding of the law.

It is not surprising to find that some Pharisees were addicted to pride. Their theology centered not only in the superiority of Israel over other nations as special objects of God's favor, but also in the additional favor shown to those whose piety was proved by exceptional devotion to legal observance. It is the very nature of legalism, with its emphasis on human achievement, to engender pride.

Another feature of Pharisaic belief was acceptance of the immortality of the soul, the resurrection of the body, and future retribution. Those eligible for resurrection, according to JOSEPHUS, seem to have been restricted to the righteous. Since the Sadducees denied the resurrection altogether, it is evident that in the realm of ESCHATOLOGY Jesus stood nearer to the Pharisees. For the latter the future world judgment was regarded as the consummation toward which all human history was moving. This accounts for the absence, among the Pharisees, of the materialistic and political considerations that were so dominant with the Sadducees. The idea of the end (*eschaton*) played no inconsiderable part in the teaching of Jesus.

When the messianic beliefs of the Pharisees are examined, it is not easy to form a consistent picture. There was frequent use of both the titles, Messiah and Son of David. These show the expectancy that one would come to occupy the throne as King in Israel. This Messiah was to be anointed by God, raised up to lead the people in righteousness. It was as much a spiritual as a political leadership, it had inevitable political overtones, since Israel was itself a theocratic nation. Various opinions existed concerning the nature of the Messiah to come. Some thought in terms of a heavenly being, others in terms of a warrior king. None ever supposed that the Messiah would be rejected by his people. It was for this reason that the notion of a suffering Messiah was a great stumbling block to the Jewish people. The bare idea of a suffering Messiah was not completely unknown, but where it existed it was in the sense of chastisements encountered through fidelity to the law, and in any case it did not belong to Jewish beliefs in the time of Jesus.

Many of the rigid ceremonial requirements imposed on the Pharisees were aimed at preserving ritual purity. The detailed requirements had obscured the original purpose of the law, which merited and received the severest condemnation of Jesus. Yet, it is important to note that at no time did he condemn their sincere desire to fulfill the law. He made it clear that he himself had not come to destroy the law but to fulfill it. It will be seen that whereas there is much in the actions and teaching of Jesus that would not have conflicted with the Pharisaic ideals, the unique approach of Jesus would lead to a direct confrontation with cherished traditions, and the many controversies recorded in the Gospels are therefore not surprising.

(C) *The Essenes.* Until the discovery of the DSS, knowledge of this group came mainly from PHILO JUDAEUS, JOSEPHUS, and PLINY the Elder. Most scholars are convinced that there is a close relationship between the Essenes and the community of Qumran, although there are some who seriously dispute this. The Qumran community may well have been a special sect within the Essene movement, which would account for the similarities and differences between the evidence from the scrolls and that from Josephus. The main divergences concern the regulations for admittance.

The Essenes were a separatist group who regarded the Jerusalem temple worship as corrupt. Their monasticism was therefore essentially a protest. They were as devoted to the law as the Pharisees, but in a different way. They were, in fact, more

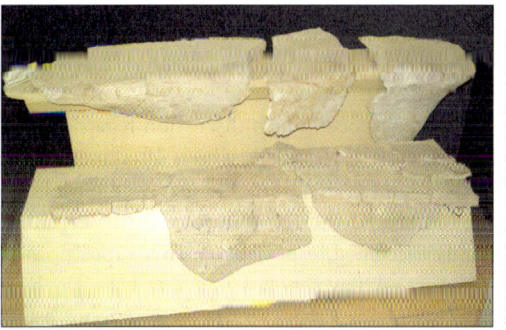

Writing benches discovered at Qumran. The documents attributed to the Essenes may have been completed on a table like this.

stringent. There were rigorous rules for the government of the group, as the *Rule of the Community* or *Manual of Discipline* shows. There were severe penalties for any offense against the community. The organization was equally rigid, but the details need not be repeated. The purpose is to show what possible contribution the Qumran evidence can make to the understanding of the mission of Jesus, and the following considerations may be noted.

The absence from the gospel records of any reference to contact between Jesus and the people of Qumran is not surprising. Qumran was essentially a monastic order to which men withdrew to escape involvement in the contemporary Jewish world. The ministry of Jesus, therefore, passed it by. Yet the movement points to a real dissatisfaction within Judaism with current religious life and enables a better understanding to be made of the protests of Jesus himself against the Pharisees and Sadducees. Moreover, the teaching of Jesus in some aspects possessed greater affinity with Essenism than with the other groups. As far as the Essenic doctrine is concerned, an interesting factor was the belief in two Messiahs, a Messiah of Aaron and a Messiah of Israel. Since the Messiah of Aaron takes precedence, it no doubt arose from the conception of Qumran as a priestly community. In itself the messianism of this community contributes little to the understanding of the messianic claims of Jesus.

Of more importance is the place of the COVENANT in the community. The members were people of the "new covenant," and each person had to signify annually his allegiance to it. It was really a reaffirmation of the old covenant, which contrasts with the new covenant inaugurated by Jesus (see COVENANT, THE NEW). His presentation of the covenant was in line with the prediction of Jeremiah (Jer. 31).

There has been much discussion regarding the Teacher of Righteousness, who is often mentioned in the Qumran literature. He may well have been the founder of the community. He was certainly highly esteemed, especially for his exposition of Scripture. A few scholars (such as J. L. Teicher) have maintained that the title is describing Jesus, but this view is generally discounted. Unlike Jesus, the Teacher of Righteousness was not regarded as the subject of OT prophecies, nor was he regarded as the Messiah. Although no connection can be established, the striking parallel between this Teacher and Jesus the Teacher, who came to impart righteousness, cannot pass unnoticed. It shows that there were elements in Judaism that were reaching out toward greater purity.

The men of Qumran were deeply conscious of forces opposing the truth, as is seen particularly in the references to the Wicked Priest. It is also apparent in the strong antitheses that are found in the modes of thought. The community members are sons of light engaging in battle with the sons of darkness. Truth is in conflict with error. This is of special importance as a background against which to place the Johannine portrait of Jesus. No longer can the antitheses that are so characteristic of John's gospel be ascribed to Hellenism, without taking fully into account the syncretism which before the time of Jesus had already taken place within the Essene branch of Judaism (see JOHN, GOSPEL OF).

(d) *The Zealots.* These belonged to a religious political movement that opposed payment of tribute to a heathen emperor on the grounds that allegiance was due only to God. The movement began as a revolt in A.D. 6 under Judas the Galilean and continued its activities until after the siege of Jerusalem. It played an important part in resistance against the Roman occupation. Its last stronghold, MASADA, fell in A.D. 73. One of the twelve apostles is named Simon the Zealot; whether the adjective was added simply to describe his zeal or as an indication of his association with the political party is not known. The theory that Jesus himself was associated with the Zealots (so S. G. F. Brandon, *Jesus and the Zealots: A Study of the Political Factor in Primitive Christianity* [1967]) may be discounted, not only because it lacks evidence, but also because it is impossible to interpret the words of Jesus as the words of a political enthusiast. Jesus left Rome severely alone. His mission was spiritual, not national.

III. Various approaches to the life of Christ

A. The traditional approach. Although the available sources are insufficient to construct a biography of Jesus in the modern sense of the term, the traditional approach to the sources has always maintained that the historical reports in the Gospels are essentially trustworthy. It had always been assumed, until the rise of 18th-cent. rationalism challenged it. The large amount of space devoted to the passion and resurrection narratives was no problem for those who saw no discrepancy between the historical Jesus and the Christ of faith. Primitive Christian belief fastened on the importance of Christ's death and resurrection, abundantly proved by Acts and the Epistles within the NT. The apparently lopsided arrangement of material in both the Synoptic Gospels and in John bears witness to the major content of the early Christian faith. It was not unreasonable to suppose that if so important an element of faith was accurately reflected in the evangelist's arrangement, the rest of the material should be regarded as equally historical.

Certain difficulties were nonetheless recognized. Some explanation had to be given of the instances where apparent disagreements occurred within the Synoptic Gospels or between them and John. The traditional approach to such problems was harmonistic. Since it was maintained that there could be no discrepancy within the inspired records, it must be possible to reconcile apparent contradictions. Many of these harmonistic attempts were more ingenious than convincing. When, for instance, it was maintained (e.g., by the 16th-cent. theologian Andreas Osiander) that JAIRUS's daughter must have been resurrected more than once because the incident is placed in a different sequence within the Synoptic Gospels, the improbability of such a solution becomes at once apparent. It was the weakness of much of the traditional approach to the Gospels that it tended to overstress some feature, such as the order of events, without sufficient examination of the validity of the basic assumptions. Dogmatic considerations were more important than historical, with the consequence that the older traditionalists exposed themselves to rationalistic attacks. Until that time there had been no question about the validity of the miraculous. The Christ of faith was so deeply entrenched in the religious concepts that it was perfectly reasonable to suppose that he had power over the natural world to such a degree that in his hands the abnormal became normal.

The advantage of such an approach is obvious. All the Gospels may without question be treated as historical sources, and the main preoccupation of any scholar producing an outline of the life of Jesus is to discover the best method of harmonizing the accounts. Since John's account presupposes a longer period of ministry than the synoptics, it has been the usual procedure of traditionalists to fit the synoptic outlines as far as possible into the Johannine structure. This traditional approach to the sources has been attacked on several fronts during the last two centuries of BIBLICAL CRITICISM. It is essential to have some insight into the grounds for these attacks to appreciate the position of modern criticism in its approach to the historical Jesus.

B. The rationalistic approach. Rationalism showed its attack upon the gospel material in the deistic renunciation of MIRACLES as support for Jesus' claims to messiahship. This antipathy toward the miraculous has been characteristic of rationalism ever since and has affected many schools of thought that have otherwise had little in common with the basic tenets of deism. It was an attack on the supernatural element, and once the miraculous was pronounced either impossible or suspect, it was essential to view with suspicion other elements in any sources which treated the miraculous as normal. This was the starting point for German critical appraisals of the historical Jesus. Whatever in the Gospels did not square with the assumption that the supernatural interpretation of the life of Jesus was impossible must be excised from the records as later interpolations. Such was the rationalistic impact on the sources of the life of Jesus. It was not surprising, therefore, that the 19th cent. was to see a whole crop of unhistorical "histories" of Jesus, many of them almost wholly fictitious.

Before the dawn of the 19th cent., H. Reimarus had produced a book in which he regarded the resurrection of Jesus as an invention of the apostles, who themselves inaugurated a community to await the return of Christ. To avoid possible exposure they stole the body of Jesus. See RESURRECTION OF JESUS CHRIST V. This kind of approach won no support in Reimarus's own time, but was a precursor of the eschatological theory of A. Schweitzer more than a century later. Reimarus made no attempt to come to grips with the Johannine problem. He preferred the Synoptic Gospels and imposed his fraud theory on them. During the 19th cent., many others were either to reject or to ignore the Johannine account.

Attempts were next made to write historical accounts of Jesus from the standpoint of the contemporary climate of opinion. There was no hesitation in making Jesus speak as nearly as possible in rationalistic forms. Modifications of both sayings and events were unrestrained. Representatives of this tendency were J. J. Hess and F. V. Reinhard. Another who illustrates the awakening of the critical faculties in relation to the sources of the life of Jesus is J. G. Herder, who considered it to be impossible to harmonize the Synoptic Gospels with John, and who treated the latter as something of a protest against the former.

It was H. E. G. Paulus who presented the most thoroughgoing rationalistic approach to the Gospels, for he regarded the miracles as due to the eyewitnesses' ignorance of the laws of nature. This left him free to explain away the miraculous. Such incidents as the raisings of the dead were described as "deliverances from primitive burial." This is even alleged of the resurrection of Jesus. His basic skepticism has often since been reflected in other theories.

A rather modified view of the gospel miracles is seen in the life of Jesus written by K. Hase, who had a higher regard for the Johannine miracles than for those of the synoptics. Again the impossibility of accepting both accounts is assumed. A similar position was taken by F. E. D. Schleiermacher. Although less avowedly rationalistic than Paulus, he nevertheless shows the influence of the latter in his explanation of the resurrection as recovery from a state of suspended animation. None of the Synoptic Gospels, in his opinion, presents historical facts. There is no doubt that his view of these Gospels was governed by his preconceived idea of Christ.

C. The mythological approach. It was the radical criticism of David Strauss which marked a turning point in German approaches to the life of Jesus. He followed Hegel's philosophy and this governed his attitude to the sources. He was not hesitant to interpret the events mythologically. Anything inexplicable to Strauss was treated as MYTH. It is not surprising that the result was radical. Many of the mythical elements he traced to OT motives. John's gospel he regarded as apologetic and therefore inferior to the others. But the latter contained much composite material due to the influence of the church upon the tradition. Although his opinions were too radical for his own age, they set the pattern for later developments, both in the views of liberal critics and in the ideas of the later form critics.

Strauss's skepticism bore some fruit in the radical opinions of Bruno Bauer, who treated John's gospel as an artistic product, and then transferred similar principles of criticism to the synoptics. His conclusion was that the records were the conceptions of evangelists woven around the historical personality of Jesus. After an interval Bauer reached the logical conclusion of denying the historicity of Jesus.

D. The sentimental approach. Ernest Renan's life of Jesus may be described as imaginative rather than skeptical. It was certainly not historical, for Renan appealed to aesthetic taste rather than to fact. He treated the whole story as a dramatist would a play. The Jesus he produced was a Jesus of his own creation.

E. The liberal lives of Jesus. The heyday of liberal criticism produced its crop of interpretations, the purpose of which was to discover and present the historical Jesus apart from the dogmatic presentations of Christ. A typical example of this point of view may be found in H. Holtzmann's book on the Synoptic Gospels. In this he propounded a theory for the life of Jesus based on Mark in which he drew a distinction between the earlier period of success and the later period of decline. This idea exercised a strong influence on the liberal lives of Jesus during this period. Holtzmann was not adverse to drawing from both the synoptic and the Johannine traditions.

Adolf Harnack's interpretation of Christianity was governed by his acceptance of the so-called historical figure of Jesus of Nazareth, whose main function was to found the kingdom of God on earth, and whose death did no more than set the seal on this mission. The result was that the portrait of Jesus was conformed to the contemporary pattern of 19th-cent. life. In spite of the attempt to arrive at a historical presentation, the principles of criticism which these liberal scholars followed did not enable them to produce an objective account. It must be recognized that these principles were affected by the earlier rationalism, which attempted to pass all the gospel material through the sieve of what is intelligible to reason. Yet, there can be no doubt that these liberal interpreters of Jesus were convinced of the historicity of their account. Christianity became a matter of conformity to the ethics of Jesus, and by that fact it had ceased to be a gospel.

F. Nineteenth-century British approaches. Some British scholars followed closely in the wake of German criticism, of whom the most notable was perhaps F. W. Farrar, *The Life of Christ* (1886). There was no tendency to discriminate between the synoptics and John, as among the Germans, although the emphasis was essentially upon the Jesus of history. Among the more conservative works may be mentioned the valuable study by A. Edersheim, *Life and Times of Jesus the Messiah* (1883), which provided many insights into the Jewish background and was the ablest attempt to integrate the synoptic and Johannine traditions. He made no attempt to differentiate between the Christ of faith and the Jesus of history. In much the same vein may be mentioned W. Sanday's article on Jesus Christ in Hasting's *Dictionary of the Bible*. These British representatives at the close of the 19th cent. show how little the German movements had affected the mainstream of opinion relating to the historical Jesus, but the 20th cent. tells a rather different story.

G. Twentieth-century viewpoints

1. The eschatological movement. The book *Von Reimarus zu Wrede* (1906), by Albert Schweitzer, translated into English under the title of *The Quest of the Historical Jesus* (1910), created a sensation. It gave a penetrating analysis of the inadequacies of the rationalistic and liberal approaches and then presented the theory that only from an eschatological point of view could a true history of Jesus be written. Schweitzer's eschatology was of his own making. He conceived that the dominating factor in the history of Jesus was his firm belief in the imminent establishment of the kingdom. He rejected Wilhelm Wrede's idea of the messianic secret (*Das Messiasgeheimnis in den Evangelien* [1901]), and maintained that Jesus' hopes were frustrated. The cross was the failure of the mission of Jesus. All that remained of the Jesus of history was the example of his noble purpose, which never came to anything. Even the ETHICS OF JESUS was only an interim measure and therefore possessed no abiding validity.

Schweitzer's counterblast to the liberal Jesus was no less unhistorical. His strange eschatological blunderer was not the Jesus who lived and taught in Palestine. The difference between Schweitzer and the liberals was that whereas the latter sought to dress Jesus in modern garb, the former sought to put him back into a 1st-cent. wholly APOCALYPTIC milieu. Neither viewpoint came to grips with the real problem of how their interpretation of Jesus contributed to an understanding of what came to be the place of Jesus in the historic Christian faith. There is no doubt that Schweitzer's hypothesis gained more support than it would have done because of the aridity of the previous liberal theories. As Hugh Anderson has said, "By his tremendous stress on the non-advent of the Parousia, for the inauguration of which and for nothing else Jesus died in vain, Schweitzer helped to pave the way for recent versions of the primitive Church's Christology which left no place therein for faith in the historical Jesus as the decisive revelation of God for the past as well as for the present" (*Jesus and Christian Origins* [1964], 21–22).

2. The dialectical approach. Another major 20th-cent. trend is seen in Karl Barth's dialectical theology. This movement was contemporary with that of Rudolf Bultmann in its origin. Both men were reared in the same theological climate, both being taught by the same liberal teachers. They both belonged to the *Religionsgeschichte* (history of religions) school, which believed in the broadest basis for the study of the life of Jesus in the context of an examination of comparative religions. Those who exercised most influence upon both Barth and Bultmann were determined to eliminate from the sources of the life of Jesus whatever belonged to the dogmatic theology of the Christian Church. These liberal scholars concentrated on the immanence of God in Jesus in a way which saw in Jesus only the exaltation to the highest possible degree of what is potential in every man. There was an absence of all thought of the divine transcendence of Jesus, and it was this that challenged Barth.

In one sense, Barth did not enter into the literary problems surrounding the sources of the life of Jesus, but he strongly reacted against the liberal idea of the historical Jesus. By concentrating on the NT texts and rejecting the possibility of going behind them, Barth went some way toward counteracting the approach to the texts which characterized the earlier critics. Barth's doctrine of the Word within Scripture allowed him freedom in his treatment of the biblical text. What he insists upon is a theological rather than a historical exegesis. Any attempt to reconstitute the historical Jesus as the liberals had done is no part of the Christian faith as Barth understands it. Yet he does not dispute that the object of the church's faith must be related to the past. Jesus was distinctive as compared with other men "in his inescapability, in his critical function, in his unforgettable lordliness, in his irrevocability which bursts and transcends all the limits of his life and time" (*Church Dogmatics* [1964–81] 4/2:156ff.). This is not the place to expand on the theology of Barth. It suffices to show that Barth differs from his contemporary Bultmann in by-passing the problems of literary origins, with which the latter has been so closely concerned in his reaction to the same liberalism in which both were reared. Bultmann has retained more of the essential spirit of liberalism than Barth.

3. The form-critical approach. Bultmann's position must be considered within the context of an examination of the whole form-critical movement, of which he is representative of that section which attaches least historical validity to the sources. Form criticism is a movement which derived its main impulse from the failure of a rigid application of source criticism to solve the problems of the Gospels. It was a method which had previously been developed to get behind the sources proposed for OT criticism.

H. Gunkel's attempt to reduce the preliterary oral material to some sort of classification by means of different forms in which the material was preserved provided a method that appeared serviceable for NT criticism. The most that source criticism could do was to posit sources which were no earlier than thirty years after the events related, and it was naturally considered important to attempt to fill in the gap. The main objectives were still within the field of scientific historical inquiry. Form criticism as a literary discipline belongs essentially to the period of liberal approaches to the life of Jesus, although in some of its developments, most notably in the hands of Bultmann, it became a tool to be used against the concept of the historical Jesus. This was possible because Bultmann went beyond the purely literary idea of form criticism and developed from it the form-historical method. To make clear this important distinction, the two main schools of form criticism will be considered, irrespective of the chronological development, classification being dependent on whether it is used to support historical evaluation or not.

The real focus of attention was upon Mark's gospel. It had been assumed by the Jesus-of-history school that Mark's account was basically historical and that whatever material could be fitted in from the other synoptics was acceptable. The liberal representation of Jesus was therefore very much tied up with Mark's gospel. When Wrede challenged the historicity of Mark by his theory of the messianic secret, the whole hypothesis of the historical Jesus was also challenged. Wrede maintained that Mark had preserved no chronological sequence and that the material of the gospel had originally existed as unconnected units. Whatever unity there was in the record had been imposed upon it by Mark, who had

A 15th-cent. illuminated manuscript from the monastery of Iveron on Mount Athos, Greece, depicting Christ's entry into Jerusalem.

made it appear that Jesus claimed to be the Messiah and was recognized as such by the disciples, although in Wrede's view this did not happen until after the resurrection of Jesus. The stage was therefore set for a more radical reinterpretation of the gospel narratives in the light of editorial processes that were conditioned by the Easter event. This particular trend was to play an important part in Bultmann's theory of form criticism.

The unitary view of the Markan material was further stressed by such scholars as J. Wellhausen (*Einleitung in die drei ersten Evangelien* [1905]) and K. L. Schmidt (*Der Rahmen der Geschichte Jesu* [1919]). The former contended that Mark's gospel was overlaid by editorial additions, which it was necessary to excise if the historical material was to be laid bare. The latter maintained the unreliability of Mark's chronological and geographical data and consequently challenged the possibility of producing a connected account of the life of Jesus.

In 1919 Martin Dibelius published a book entitled *Die Formgeschichte des Evangeliums*, in which he analyzed various forms of gospel material according to the use to which it had been put in the period of oral transmission. Since these forms developed in what was essentially a missionary period, Dibelius found their *Sitz im Leben* (the situation in the life of the church) in the needs faced by the different types of church workers—preachers, teachers, and narrators. Such forms as *paradigms*—short narratives concluding with an important saying—would be valuable for preachers, while teachers concerned with the catechizing of new converts would use sayings that were unattached to narratives and varied in subject matter, which would be matched to the practical needs of the communities. Narrators would relate tales, often of a supernatural character, which were either created by or at least embellished by the narrators. Other categories of forms proposed by Dibelius were legends and myths, the first being material about holy people paralleled in secular writings; and the second, material in which some mythological interchange took place (e.g., the TEMPTATION OF CHRIST and the TRANSFIGURATION). It will at once be seen that the sources for the life of Jesus have therefore been subjected to influences which have introduced many nonhistorical elements. Nevertheless, Dibelius did not, as Bultmann did, deny the possibility of a historical account of Jesus. At the same time, his postulation of different classes of people using different forms of material is highly unlikely and accordingly weakens his theory. Moreover, it is clear that he has done more than classify the forms; he has evaluated them and in so doing has used his own criteria. The miraculous element is not attributed to the supernatural but to the composition of the storytellers, who wished to heighten the appeal of the tales they were telling.

A more moderate approach may be seen in the work of M. Albertz, B. S. Easton, and Vincent Taylor. Albertz (*Die synoptischen Streitgespräche: Ein Beitrag zur Formengeschichte des Urchristentums* [1921]) admitted that the church had adapted the original traditions, but nevertheless strongly maintained the possibility of arriving at a concept of the historical Jesus. It is important to note that German criticism had other voices contemporary with Bultmann that did not agree with his approach toward history in the Gospels.

B. S. Easton (*The Gospel before the Gospels* [1928]) treated form criticism essentially as a literary discipline. Although he admitted that the traditions had been influenced by ecclesiastical and apologetic motives, he declined to use the classification of forms in the assessment of the historicity of the material.

Vincent Taylor (*The Formation of the Gospel Tradition* [1935]) is a representative of that school of form criticism which sees a limited value in the discipline, but is strongly opposed to the skepticism so characteristic of Bultmann's theories. He rightly calls attention to the existence of eyewitnesses, which must have exerted a powerful restraining influence upon the creation of nonhistorical elements in the tradition and provided some guarantee of the historicity of the material that has been preserved. It is significant that Vincent Taylor declines to accept the right of form critics, on the basis of their method of criticism, to deny the miraculous. The determination of the validity or otherwise of the miracle stories belongs not to the literary but to the historical critic. Compared with the exponents of radical form criticism, Vincent Taylor is moderate, for he believes in the actuality of the historical Jesus. In fact, his trilogy on Christ (*The Names of Jesus* [1953], *The Life and Ministry of Jesus* [1954], and *The Person of Christ in New Testament Teachings* [1958]) shows an approach that seeks to combine the Jesus of history with the Christ of faith. Such moderate use of form criticism clearly puts him in a different camp from Dibelius and Bultmann.

The same may be said of some other British scholars who have partially used form-critical methods, while at the same time rejecting some of its assumptions. C. H. Dodd (*New Testament Studies* [1953]), for instance, staunchly maintains the reliability of the chronological structure of Mark on the grounds of the evidence of Acts, which counteracts the notion of Mark as a collection of disconnected units. When using form criticism, his main interest is to discover how far the different forms can be employed in verifying the historicity of the material. Although he does not conclude for the historicity of all the material, he sees beneath the interpretive elements a substantial basis of historical fact. He seems to stand midway between the older liberalism and the newer Christ-of-faith school.

Another in the same tradition, but even more insistent on the historicity of the Markan account, was T. W. Manson (*Studies in the Gospels and Epistles* [1962]). He not only maintained the reliability of the Markan outline, but vigorously resisted the skepticism of the radical form critics. He correctly pointed out that there was less credibility in the form-critical suppositions than in the gospel accounts. He believed that it was possible to arrive at the facts of the life of Jesus from the gospel sources and to make some kind of chronological reconstruction. He did not, however, cling to a purely historical quest, for he recognized that a historical reconstruction would be meaningless apart from the early Christian belief in Jesus as the object of faith. He was reluctant to create an antithesis between history and faith.

4. The existential approach. It was quite different with Rudolf Bultmann, whose dissatisfaction with the liberal attempts to produce a history of Jesus turned his attention toward the Christ of faith. It will be necessary to consider his point of view in more detail, since it has had a profound influence over European thought regarding Jesus Christ and has not lacked support in British and American circles. Bultmann's approach to the records is via the KERYGMA, that is, the proclamation of the resurrected Christ. It would not be true to say that Bultmann denies the historicity of Jesus, although he comes nearer to this at times than he himself is prepared specifically to admit. He considers that all that can be asserted without question is the "thatness," the bare fact, of the cross of Christ. It is difficult to think intelligently of a bare "thatness" which is unrelated to a historical personality of whom at least something can be historically known. In any case, this is a different kind of *kerygma* from what the early Christians proclaimed.

Nevertheless, Bultmann has performed a valuable service in drawing attention to the problem of the connection between the historical Jesus and the Christ of faith, even if his own solution proves to be totally unacceptable. The Jesus of history can become a living factor in each era of the Christian church only if it is possible to establish the connection between him and the faith of each era. Bultmann's probing goes deeper than that, for he maintains that since no connection is possible, there is no point in pursuing the historical Jesus at all. (For Bultmann's views, see his *Jesus and the Word* [1926] and *Form Criticism* [1934].)

(a) *Influences upon Bultmann.* To understand Bultmann's methods it is necessary to be aware of influences that have had a share in the molding of them. The liberal background to which he belonged was dominated by R. Reitzenstein's theory that primitive Christianity drew much from the MYSTERY RELIGIONS (*Die hellenistischen Mysterienreligionen* [1927]), and by W. Bousset (*Kyrios Christos*, 3rd. ed. [1926]), who maintained that Jesus was Lord, not Messiah, to Gentile Christians. While these theories had more effect on Bultmann's approach to PAULINE THEOLOGY, they are not unimportant for his theory of gospel origins, since, if true, they must find a place in his idea of the *kerygma* among Gentile Christians.

Acceptance of the view that mystery religions and Gnostic myths were a molding factor in early Christian doctrine disposes the exegete to search for pagan parallels to account for the form, if not the content, of some of the gospel materials. Careful examination, however, shows that most of the parallels are tenuous. Can it be accepted as a legitimate method of exegesis to attribute anything remotely resembling a pagan parallel to such a source? Reitzenstein's evidence is drawn from a much later period, which makes it difficult to place any reliance upon it. As far as GNOSTICISM is concerned, when this became a powerful 2nd-cent. movement, it met with strong resistance from the Christian church. Had there been a close kinship between it and Christianity, it is impossible to see why this kinship was unrecognized.

Any presupposition of a distinction so radical between Palestinian and Hellenistic Christianity must inevitably affect assessment of historical data. The presupposition is unsupported by adequate evidence. The most damaging objection is the failure to recognize the uniqueness, not only of Christ himself, but also of the church, whose faith was based in him. This was the ineradicable weakness of the whole *religionsgeschichtliche Schule*.

Another important influence upon Bultmann affecting his approach to the history of Jesus was the philosophy of Martin Heidegger. It was Bultmann's conviction that an existential encounter with Christ is of paramount importance in Christian faith, and this led him to play down the historical Jesus. Even though little of the true history of Jesus is available, this existential encounter can take place. Such a presupposition naturally conditioned Bultmann in his estimation of the gospel material. There is no doubt that his purpose was to make that material relevant to his contemporaries, and this led him to exclude anything that to his mind belonged to the 1st cent., but was irrelevant or unacceptable to modern culture.

(b) *Some basic assumptions.* Bultmann, in the treatment of his sources, proceeded on the assumption that there are definite laws governing popular narrative and tradition. He first supposed that narratives in the course of oral transmission tend to become more explicit and to acquire details lacking in the most primitive form. For example, Luke's comment, "And one of them struck the servant of the high priest, cutting off his right ear" (Lk. 22:50), is said to show a development from Mark's account, which does not say it was the *right* ear (Mk. 14:47). Moreover, he appeals to apocryphal tradition for the tendency to attach names to people who were unnamed in earlier tradition. Hence Bultmann begins by being skeptical about the names used in the records (cf. Lk. 22:8, where the disciples referred to in Mk. 14:13 are named as Peter and John). Furthermore, there is said to be a tendency for indirect discourse to become direct discourse (cf. Mk. 8:32; Matt. 16:22). That in some cases the material is preserved in both forms cannot be denied, but to deduce from this a general law of tradition may be considerably wide of the mark. An alternative explanation might be that the more direct form was nevertheless from an authentic source.

(c) *Classification of materials for the life of Jesus.* A brief reference to Bultmann's classifications will not be amiss (for full details see his foundational work, *The History of the Synoptic Tradition* [1963], first published in German in 1921). The miracle stories are at once suspect. Sufficient parallels can be cited from pagan sources to show, in Bultmann's opinion, that the gospel miracles conform to a similar pattern. Parallels of forms do not prove similarity of origin. The uniqueness of the gospel stories rests not in their form but in the uniqueness of the miracle worker. Another of Bultmann's forms are *apothegms*, important sayings of Jesus for which short scenes serve as a framework. He takes the view that the saying may be authentic, while the setting is the creation of the community, although in some cases both are nonauthentic.

His criterion of differentiation seems to be that what can be conceived as a community product must have been a community product. Clearly,

A 15th-cent. illuminated manuscript from the monastery of Iveron on Mount Athos depicting Jesus washing the feet of his disciples.

this does not follow. The probability of communities creating narratives and sayings is open to most serious challenge. The assumption appears to be that Christian groups would wish to attribute sayings to Jesus that had no basis in fact, because they were the kind of words the Christ of faith might be expected to say. Of the biographical apothegms (e.g., the calling of the disciples in Mk. 1:16–20), Bultmann maintains that they give expression to what Christians had experienced of their Master or what he had experienced at the hands of his people. They become therefore symbols instead of historical events (*History of the Synoptic Tradition*, 56).

It is difficult to believe that any Christian author would have written what purports to be a historical narrative if his intentions were purely symbolical. Nor is it much easier to conceive that the evangelists genuinely thought that the materials used were historical, even if much of it was the symbolic creation of some community or other. Where can parallels be found for such a procedure? The apocryphal literature, which abounds in narratives regarding Jesus and the apostles that are manifestly the creations of the apocryphal authors, cannot furnish an adequate parallel, for these are stamped so evidently with fantasy that no contemporary ever placed them on the same footing as the canonical Gospels. Moreover, the majority of these productions were written in the interests of some aberration from Christian doctrine. They are too late to provide any guide to the probable procedure of the primitive church. See APOCRYPHAL NEW TESTAMENT.

When Bultmann deals with the sayings of Jesus, he assumes, to begin with, that some are authentic and some are not. This leads him to seek some method of distinguishing between them. He first maintains that different evangelists have placed the same saying in different contexts, which means that one cannot know what the original context was. Since the context affects the interpretation, he concludes that one cannot now know the meaning as it was originally intended. For example, the sayings about salt and light (Matt. 5:13–15; Mk. 4:21; 9:50; Lk. 11:33; 14:34–35) are compared, and the conclusion is reached that each evangelist is experimenting with his interpretations. This principle is then applied generally even to sayings that occur in only one gospel, for example, many of the parables. In the case of the parables, Bultmann also appeals to rabbinic parallels. An example of his method in reconstructing the words of Jesus is seen in his treatment of the SON OF MAN saying in Matt. 10:32–33; Mk. 8:38; Lk. 12:8–9. Since he considers that it was axiomatic for the Christian community that Jesus was the Son of Man, he maintains that this belief has affected the original saying, which allegedly drew a distinction between the two individuals. Bultmann does not explain how it became axiomatic for the church if it was not derived from Jesus himself.

Bultmann is not content to suggest modification of Jesus' words. He considers that frequently words spoken by other Jewish teachers or words first used in the Christian community were put into the mouth of Christ. As examples he cites some of the wisdom words of Jesus that can be paralleled from Jewish sources (cf. Lk. 12:16–20 and Sir. 11:18–19). His basic assumption is that parallels point to nonauthenticity. When dealing with the prophetic apocalyptic sayings, he is rather more inclined to find some authentic sayings, since the eschatological enthusiasm of the early Christians was probably derived from the prophetic appearance of Jesus.

Another of Bultmann's categories is law sayings. Of these he says, "Even though many of the sayings may have originated in the community, the spirit that lives in them goes back to the work of Jesus" (*Form Criticism* [1934], 58). The reason for this greater willingness to accept these law sayings is their fundamental disagreement with contemporary Judaism. Sayings supported by OT citations and those containing rules of discipline are suspect as community products. Sometimes Bultmann expresses his views as possibilities, but more often he makes statements dogmatically, as when he maintains that the passion predictions in Mark (Mk. 8:31; 9:31; 10:33–34) "were first created by the Christian community" (ibid., 59).

From the above it might be supposed that Bultmann is skeptical about all the sayings of Jesus, but he does attach historical credence to some, as the following extract shows: "Though one may admit the fact that for no single word of Jesus is it possible to produce positive evidence of its authenticity, still one may point to a whole series of words found in the oldest stratum of tradition which do give a consistent representation of the historical message of Jesus" (ibid., 61). Included here would be sayings that echo the prophetic calls to repentance, that announce salvation, or that express the consciousness of the prophet. Bultmann lays great stress on the prophetic role of Jesus.

Another category to which he appeals is legend, which, in his view, became attached to the narratives through cultic influences. Such legends would serve the needs of the worshiping community. This applies to the passion narrative (e.g., the death of Judas and the watch at the tomb), the resurrection narratives ("composed in the interests of faith and under the influence of devout imagination"), the Last Supper (which was referred back to the last meal of Jesus and was transformed into a cult legend), the baptismal narrative, the transfiguration, the temptation, the entry into Jerusalem, and many other narratives. When all the overgrowth of legend which Bultmann finds in the sources is removed, it will be seen that there is little life that can be considered historical. This is why he disputes the possibility of knowledge of the historical Jesus. All he will allow is some knowledge of his message, which he sums up as twofold: eschatological and ethical, both understood existentially.

From this survey of Bultmann's position it will be apparent that his view of the sources of the life of Jesus is radically different from the traditional view of the Christian church. Although it may be a matter of indifference to Bultmann whether or not the historical Jesus can be traced and known, such indifference is not characteristic of NT scholars generally, and even among Bultmann's closest disciples it was questioned to some extent. The emergence of a reaction within the Bultmann school was significant because it reflected dissatisfaction with his outright skepticism.

5. The new quest. The reaction has become known as "The New Quest of the Historical Jesus." This description must be understood against the background of the older liberal quest, although its advocates vigorously reject the liberal Jesus. What they are concerned to do is in some measure to fill the gap between the Jesus of history and the Christ of faith. E. Käsemann (cf. his *Essays on New Testament Themes* [1960]) has done this by fastening attention on the preaching of Jesus. By this means he hoped to avoid the risk of DOCETISM (which drew a distinction between the human Jesus and the divine Christ and which concentrated on the latter at the expense of the former) and to bridge the gap between the earthly Jesus and the church's proclamation of faith. Käsemann recognized, as Bultmann did not, the authority of Jesus as a preacher and as an exorciser of demons.

G. Bornkamm (*Jesus of Nazareth* [1960]) went further by including aspects of Jesus' attitude toward people (as, for instance, his readiness to forgive sins). In this case, the records have preserved certain aspects of the historical Jesus. E. Fuchs (*Studies of the Historical Jesus* [1960]) focused on Jesus' determination to minister to social outcasts, like tax collectors and sinners. This was his mission and by it he revealed God's will. His attitude to his death was influenced by the death of John the Baptist. E. Fuchs departs from the Bultmann position by asserting some continuity between the proclamation of Jesus and the *kerygma*, and by focusing on some psychological aspects which Bultmann neglected.

J. M. Robinson (*The Problem of History in Mark* [1957]) maintained a closer relationship between the historical Jesus in the Gospels and the kerygmatic Christ, to such an extent that he was charged with reversion to the liberal quest, but he defended his position by claiming that his quest is centered on the existential selfhood and not the personality of Jesus (*A New Quest of the Historical Jesus* [1959]). The difference in terminology may be noted, but Robinson's critics were not convinced that he meant anything different. Throughout the debate that developed among his own supporters, Bultmann consistently denied any essential relationship between the historic Jesus and the kerygmatic Christ. His point was not so much the impossibility as the irrelevance of such a connection.

Before any effective use can be made of the gospel records in a presentation of the events in the life of Jesus, the interpreter must make clear his own position in regard to the influence of the *kerygma*. It cannot be assumed that the apostolic kerygma bore no relation to the proclamation of Jesus himself. There is no proof for this, and in the absence of proof the interpreter has every right to assume that the evan-

Mosaic of Jesus Christ from the Byzantine Church Chora in Istanbul (15th cent.).

gelists have presented material which they believe to be historical. Since the church accepted the records without question, Christians must have believed in the historicity of the events recorded. In the presence of a considerable number of eyewitnesses, it is inconceivable that material which had no foundation in fact would have been created by communities. The Christ of faith becomes unintelligible apart from continuity with the historical Jesus.

6. Redaction criticism. The *redaktionsgeschichtliche* movement has arisen out of form criticism and concentrates on the edited forms of the material: it treats the whole of each gospel book rather than the units, although the units are presupposed. The evangelists are viewed as theologians who have imparted something of their own ideas to the material. In some respects this movement is derived from Wrede's approach to Mark's gospel. The difference is that whereas Wrede began with presuppositions regarding the messianic secret, modern interpreters are more inclined to begin with the gospel material and work back to the writer's theology. There is no doubt that concentration upon the importance of the evangelists is all to the good, for during the period of form criticism this had been largely overlooked. The question arises whether accounts written by authors with a specific theological approach could be considered valid sources for the life of Jesus. None of the evangelists was free from theological influences. They were all personally involved with the Christian faith. They were conscious that the Jesus they were describing in their gospels was more to them at the time of writing than he was to his contemporaries at the time of the events recorded. But it is not true to say that Mark has theologized the history. His record gives the impression of a deep interest in the facts (cf. C. F. D. Moule, "The Intention of the Evangelists," in *New Testament Essays*, ed. A. J. B. Higgins [1959]).

It is Bornkamm who has especially drawn attention to Matthew's theological interests. He deals with Matthew's Christology, ecclesiology, and eschatology (in *Tradition and Interpretation in Matthew* [1963]). Under the first, Jesus is presented as Israel's humiliated king and then, after the resurrection, as a world-wide teacher; under the second, the focus is upon the application of the Mosaic law to the new community; and under the third, upon the period of the mission of the community. A similar position is taken by G. Barth and H. Held (in the same volume). It is assumed that tradition and interpretation have been interwoven.

The Gospel of Luke presents a different phenomenon. Hans Conzelmann (*The Theology of Luke* [1960], translation of *Die Mitte der Zeit* [1954]) attributes a great deal to Luke's theological interests and correspondingly discounts him as an historian. He approaches the gospel from the standpoint of Luke's threefold time scheme—the time of Israel, the time of Jesus, and the time of the church. The gospel is concerned, therefore, with "the middle of time." In addition to geasing his interpretation to this point of view, Conzelmann sees much more importance in Luke's geographical references than had previously been the case, attaching to them a symbolic significance, particularly Jerusalem Clearly the challenge of these various theories must be faced. If the evangelists were primarily theologians, could they have produced history? There seems to be no reason why not, although their purpose was at no time a bare recital of facts, but an endeavor to present the object of their faith in an enduring light.

7. Heilsgeschichte. This term, meaning "salvation history," characterizes a trend that places emphasis upon the acts of God in history. The historical Jesus becomes a vital part of the REVELATION of God. Some who follow this movement are nearer to a conservative position than others. The nearest is perhaps Oscar Cullmann, who insists that no true Christian faith can exist apart from a belief that Jesus conceived himself to be the Messiah (*Christology of the New Testament*, 2nd. ed. [1963]). To Cullmann, revelation resides not only in the interpretation but in the event itself. Because of this he attaches importance to eyewitnesses. In these aspects he is diametrically opposed to the views of the more radical form critics. He has done much to redress the balance in showing the importance of history in the *kerygma*.

8. The third quest. The last decades of the 20th cent. saw the emergence of various approaches and perspectives. Interest in historical questions led, for example, to the development of the Jesus Seminar, a research project seeking to determine the authenticity of the gospel material. Its publications take a rather skeptical approach (see esp. R. W. Funk et al., *The Five Gospels: The Search for the Authentic Words of Jesus* [1993]). One of the more radical members of this seminar, J. D. Crossan (*The Historical Jesus: The Life of a Mediterranean Jewish Peasant* [1991]), argues that Jesus was not concerned with eschatological issues but rather proclaimed the need for an egalitarian society.

On the other hand, many scholars take a more positive approach, and their work is often characterized as a "third quest" for the historical Jesus. This movement highlights, among other things, the significance of Jewish eschatology for understanding Jesus' teaching. Particularly influential has been J. P. Meier (*A Marginal Jew: Rethinking the Historical Jesus*, 3 vols. [1991–2001]), who seeks to provide a moderately critical synthesis and goes so far as to propose a likely chronology of Jesus' life. (For a valuable review of the literature, including sharp criticisms of the Jesus Seminar, see N T Wright, *Jesus and the Victory of God* [1996], chs. 2–3.)

IV. Literary sources for the life of Christ.

In any historical reconstruction, sources of information are indispensable, and these have never been more important than in the account of the historical Jesus. All the available sources will now be collated.

A. The Synoptic Gospels

1. The synoptic problem. The reason Matthew, Mark, and Luke are known as *synoptic* is that they follow a common pattern in describing the ministry of Jesus. What is known as the synoptic problem arises when these three Gospels are compared with one another. Both the similarities and the differences are significant. Sometimes there are three witnesses to the same incident, sometimes two, and not infrequently only one. In many cases the witnesses agree verbally, in other cases they do not. Two major questions arise: in what order did the Gospels originate, and what is their precise relationship to each other?

It will not be necessary here to go into detail over the various solutions of this problem, but some indication must be given, since the approach to the literary sources will inevitably influence the approach to the historical Jesus. The traditional view of gospel origins was that Matthew was the prior gospel and that Mark was no more than an extract from Matthew. This was AUGUSTINE's view and held sway until well into the 19th cent. Of the three Gospels, Matthew was the most used. This view tended to cause Mark to fall into neglect as a source of data for the historical Jesus. In modern times, it has still been maintained by some Roman Catholic scholars (e.g., C. Butler, L. Vaganay, and L. Cerfaux) that Matthew is prior, but with considerable modifications of the older traditional form of the theory.

2. The priority of Mark. Both the other Synoptic Gospels have been regarded as prior by various scholars. Whereas few have supported the priority of Luke, most modern scholars have concluded for the priority of Mark as offering the best solution to this difficult problem. It cannot even now be considered as an unchallengeable hypothesis, nor must its hypothetical character be forgotten. Acceptance of the Markan hypothesis draws attention to one important aspect of the historical data. It was strongly attested in the ancient tradition that Mark was Peter's interpreter, and if the tradition is true it has obvious bearing on the relation of Mark's gospel to the events recorded. If an eyewitness is behind a writing, it is at once invested with greater importance as a historical source. This would be particularly true of Mark's gospel, as Peter could have been present at most of the events which Mark describes.

Such traditional ascription has been severely challenged by form-critical schools of thought, which deny eyewitness control of the transmitted material. The strength of the external evidence for this tradition cannot be denied and full weight must be given to it. The most important witness is PAPIAS, who claimed that Mark wrote down what he learned from Peter's preaching and that he aimed for accuracy, but was not concerned about order. This means that Papias, while unprepared to attach too much importance to Mark's chronology, did not dispute the historical veracity of his account. Since later patristic writers accept this opinion of Papias regarding Mark's relation to Peter, it must have been considered reliable tradition.

3. The sayings source (Q). If this theory of Markan priority is accepted as a beginning point in surveying the materials for a life of Christ, it leads to the problem of the source of the non-Markan material in Matthew and Luke. Mark has a limited scope, consisting mainly of events, and including little teaching material. What then is the main source for the teaching material in Matthew and Luke? The answer generally given is that they were indebted to a common source called "Q" (apparently from the German word for "source," *Quelle*). For the present purpose, "Q," whether it be treated as a written source or as a symbol for common teaching material, will be restricted to that material which is shared by Matthew and Luke but is not found in Mark. Since this consists almost wholly of sayings of Jesus, it is clearly a most valuable additional source of information about the Jesus of history.

Had Mark been the sole source, there would have been little idea of the wide range and variety of the teaching of Jesus, with a consequent lessening of the concept of him as a teacher. Many source critics therefore place the sayings source on a level with Mark as an important witness to the life of Jesus, but there is an important difference. The existence of Mark as a source is beyond doubt, but the same cannot be said for Q. There is no external evidence, as there is for Mark, concerning the one who produced it, nor is there any indication of the source of the material contained in it. Did it have apostolic sanction? Was it based on witnesses? Can it be assumed that care was taken to preserve the sayings of Jesus without corruption? Since Q is generally considered to be the major source for this teaching material, answers to these questions are clearly of basic importance.

Some have supposed that Matthew was its author, on the strength of what Papias said about Matthew writing the "oracles" (of Jesus). If this is a true deduction from Papias, it would supply apostolic authority for the sayings collection. Matthew must have heard Jesus teach many times and may well have been present on most of the occasions when discourses or connected sayings are attributed to him. But this interpretation of Papias's words was probably not shared by IRENAEUS, for he repeated similar wording but made Matthew the author of an Aramaic gospel. This was the common conviction of the ancients. If Matthew was not the author of Q, who was? There is no satisfactory answer. If such a source existed, all that can be asserted is that it was clearly highly regarded by both Matthew and Luke for them both to incorporate it in their gospels.

While the possibility of a sayings collection cannot be denied, its hypothetical character has caused some scholars to look elsewhere for a solution. The view that Matthew used Luke, although not without difficulties, would at once dispense with Q (as A. M. Farrer pointed out in *Studies in the Gospels*, ed. D. E. Nineham [1955]). This would enhance the value of Matthew as a source, for it would mean that the sayings material incorporated by him was the result of his own collection, if the apostolic authorship is maintained. Whoever is the author of the first gospel, the strong patristic connection of it with Matthew's name shows the high esteem in which all the material, including the teaching portion, was held. To maintain a close contact between Matthew and the sayings material is, therefore, not only more in harmony with the external evidence, but is also more satisfactory than attributing Q to an anonymous author.

4. Material peculiar to Matthew and Luke. Following up the Q hypothesis, attention must be drawn to the material peculiar to Matthew and Luke. These two authors record considerably more material separately than is recorded by Mark alone. There has been a tendency among many scholars to prefer what appears in two or three witnesses as superior to what is testified to by only one. A single witness cannot for that reason alone be considered suspect. Such a principle of criticism would at once put Matthew's and Luke's special material at a discount, but this is not historically sound. The reliability of a witness depends on the reliability of his character and not on the existence or otherwise of other witnesses to corroborate what he says. Nonetheless, some of Matthew's special material has been regarded as less authentic because it raises difficult apologetic problems. Such details as John the Baptist's hesitation to baptize Jesus, the coin found in the fish's mouth, and the opening of the graves during the crucifixion are considered secondary tradition because of the difficulties they raise.

That there is need for explanation is undeniable, but that the material must be considered secondary through ecclesiastical influence upon the tradition is not self-evident. The heightening of the miraculous is of such a character that it is difficult to imagine that it would have remained unchallenged had it been wholly fictitious. In any case, the proportion of material in this category is so small a part of the whole of Matthew's special material that it would be unjustifiable if it were allowed to dominate any evaluation of the whole.

Both Matthew and Luke include special sections dealing with the sayings of Jesus. Matthew generally combines his with the material assigned to Q, whereas Luke is more inclined to keep his separate. Both include parables of Jesus, but their differences are significant. Matthew's are generally kingdom parables whereas Luke's are not so specified. Moreover, Luke's parables tend to concentrate on a more personal interest than Matthew's. This difference reveals the individual approach of the two evangelists, and also points to the wide variety of the teaching material of Jesus. Comparison of the matter peculiar to each with that common to both reveals the additional insights which their individual choice of sayings provides.

For instance, the SERMON ON THE MOUNT in Matthew contains considerably more sayings than Luke's Sermon on the Plain, particularly about Jesus' attitude toward the law. Similarly, our knowledge of many incidents and sayings from the latter part of the Lord's ministry is wholly dependent upon Luke (e.g., Zacchaeus, the parables of the lost things). Some comment will be made later on the particular contribution of each evangelist toward a reconstruction of the historical Jesus, but now the purpose is to draw attention to the value of sources of information that are peculiar to any of them. Unless there is some adequate reason for regarding such sources as inferior, it is reasonable to receive them as data for a historical reconstruction.

5. The birth narratives. One special aspect of both Matthew and Luke is their inclusion of birth narratives that are without doubt drawn from entirely different sources. It has rightly been pointed out that Matthew shows more clearly Joseph's position, whereas Luke's narratives are more concerned with Mary's. Some scholars have contended that in both

According to tradition, the Sermon on the Mount took place on the hillsides above Capernaum. (View to the WNW, with the "Mount of Beatitudes" at top right and Capernaum in the foreground.)

accounts the narratives have been influenced by OT motives, but there is a difference between narratives created from OT patterns and those influenced by OT thought. Matthew includes many instances in his birth narratives of fulfillments of OT prophecy, but any suggestion that he has created the narratives to fit in with the prediction is unworthy of the high spiritual tone of these narratives as a whole.

Some have seen in Luke's narratives something in the nature of a poetic idyll that was never intended to be regarded as historical, but if this is so, it is strange that Luke takes such pains to stress that his gospel was based on careful historical inquiry (Lk. 1:1–4). It is reasonable to suppose that Luke received the material for his birth narratives from a reliable source. There is, in fact, no reason why he should not have had communication with Mary, although this cannot be proved. Some prefer to maintain that Luke has incorporated into his gospel an earlier source that dealt with the birth story.

Some mention must be made of the theory that Matthew used a book of OT testimonies to Jesus, if only to point out the great importance of the idea of fulfillment in the gospel accounts. Matthew includes twelve citations introduced by a special formula apparently drawn from the Hebrew rather than the SEPTUAGINT, and this has given rise to the theory that he used a testimony book (see TESTIMONIA) containing OT citations which had a bearing on the events in the life of Jesus the Messiah. A modification of this theory is that the early church was more interested in passages that contained messianic predictions than in isolated OT texts bearing on the life of the Messiah (cf. C. H. Dodd, *According to the Scriptures* [1952]). Whether either of these theories, or alternatively the further suggestion that the collection is the work of the evangelist is true, is immaterial for the present purpose. What is important is that none of the Synoptic Gospels, or for that matter the fourth gospel either, treats the events and teaching of Jesus in isolation from the OT. His incarnation, ministry, death, and resurrection were all viewed by the early Christians as fulfillments of OT predictions. No approach to the life of Jesus is valid which does not give considerable weight to the OT background.

B. The fourth gospel

1. The problems of historicity. The use of this gospel as a source of data for the life of Jesus has been variously regarded throughout the period of NT criticism. Sometimes the synoptics have been considered superior, and sometimes John has held first place. Throughout the first half of the 20th cent., John's gospel was discounted as a historical source, but subsequently there was a greater readiness to reinstate it. This has been due in no small measure to the discovery of the DSS. It would be a mistake to maintain that the connection between these scrolls and John's gospel was close, but what parallels there are support the view that both may belong to a similar milieu of thought. This means that the gospel cannot be considered a wholly Hellenistic production in which the author attempts to present a Hellenistic portrait of Jesus, as earlier scholars had frequently maintained, but must be viewed against the background of a Jewish syncretistic milieu. If the men of Qumran could talk in abstract terms (e.g., the symbolic use of light and darkness), there is no reason why Jesus should not have done the same. It is against such a "new look" on the fourth gospel (to use Bishop J. A. T. Robinson's phrase; see his *Twelve New Testament Studies* [1962]) that the Johannine problem must be considered in its bearing on the historical Jesus.

The first consideration is to decide what relation the gospel has to the events it relates. Did the writer intend to write facts, or interpretation, or both? In what sense can the details of the narratives be considered historically valid? No answer to these questions can begin in a better place than with John's purpose, according to his own statement (Jn. 20:30–31). Whereas he makes clear his evangelistic purpose—to lead to faith in Jesus as the Christ and as Son of God—yet the faith is based on "signs" that have been performed in the presence of the disciples. The basic facts of the gospel were therefore verifiable by responsible witnesses. It cannot be denied that what John purports to write has a close connection with events that happened, although his own purpose is concerned with the Christ of faith. In view of John's stated purpose, the theological aspect of his gospel must be borne in mind throughout. He was not concerned to write bare history, but history with a specific aim in view.

The validity of the history will naturally depend on the trustworthiness of the author, and this raises the whole problem of authorship. It is not my intention to discuss the problem here, but rather to consider the effects of various suggestions on the problem of historicity. If the traditional view that the apostle John is the author be maintained, the validity of the data must be highly ranked, for the whole gospel would then be basically an eyewitness account. Much more importance would attach to the farewell discourses (Jn. 13–17) if the author was personally present. In spite of the external evidence, corroborated by several internal hints of an eyewitness, many have found difficulty with this view and have postulated another author—either a John the Elder or else some entirely unknown person. Many who dispute apostolic authorship, however, do concede some apostolic connection. Some regard the apostle John as the witness behind the gospel, if he is not the author.

The problem of authorship is less crucial than that of history. A few illustrations will show the force of this. In the realm of chronology John places a cleansing of the temple near the beginning of the ministry of Jesus, whereas the synoptists place it at the end. If John's narrative is taken symbolically of the cleansing of Judaism by Jesus, the chronological problem ceases to exist. But the record does not read like a symbolic account. Another problem is the form of teaching. The absence of parables and the presence of much discourse material, including rabbinic type dialogue, marks John off from the Synoptic Gospels. The problem is not insuperable, for some parabolic forms are included in John in addition to the allegories of the vine and shepherd, while some extended discourse material is found in the other Gospels, particularly Matthew. Moreover, it must be remembered that John's material almost wholly centers in Jerusalem, whereas the synoptists concentrate on Galilee. In spite of the historical difficulties, it is not impossible to integrate John as a historical source with the synoptics.

2. Relationship to the Synoptic Gospels. A comparison of John with the synoptics shows how much he has left out and also how much new material he has included. The question naturally arises whether John is independent of the synoptics or whether he used them as a source. In view of the small amount of material common to all the Gospels, there is much to be said for the theory that John did not use the others as literary sources. The largest amount of common material is in the passion narrative. It seems indisputable that John assumed the synoptic tradition even if he did not use them as sources. He speaks, for instance, of the Twelve without further definition. His omission of the institution of the LORD's SUPPER would be unintelligible if he did not assume that details of this were already widely known. It is a reasonable hypothesis that John intended his gospel to be complementary to the synoptics. There was no question in his mind that his gospel would be used alongside the others. Patristic testimony shows that at a fairly early period this happened. John and the synoptics were the only Gospels found acceptable. It must not be overlooked that whatever incongruities modern scholars find between John and the synoptics, the ancients were not conscious of them (with the sole exception of a group known as the Alogi, who were opposed to John's doctrine).

The major problem facing the historian of the life of Jesus is to find some satisfactory way of dovetailing the separate accounts. The cleansing of the temple is an example. Some decision must be made about this issue, either the postulation of a double cleansing or else a choice between the Johannine and synoptic chronology. Most choose the synoptic dating, but the former suggestion is not impossible. The dating of the Last Supper is another well-known crux, since John appears to set it on the 13th of Nisan, while the synoptics prefer the 14th. Another problem is to fit into the Galilean account of the ministry in the synoptics the events recorded by John as happening at Jerusalem. Moreover, the length of the public ministry of Jesus poses a problem, for John suggests that the period must be at least two if not three years, whereas the synoptics give the impression of one year. The matter is not irresoluble, since a reference to a harvest in the midst of the synoptic ministry shows that more than one year must have been involved, although the events appear on the surface to have happened all within two Passovers. Clearly the synoptists were not as interested in the festival days as John, who for this very reason must be regarded as a better guide in such matters of chronology.

Attempts at harmonizing must at best be regarded as tentative and in some cases as purely arbitrary. In dealing with such sources, one must conclude that the chronological data in the Gospels is so sparse that it is impossible to reconstruct the order of events with any certainty (for a recent and valuable attempt, see D. L. Bock, *Jesus according to Scripture: Restoring the Portrait from the Gospels* [2002]). Unless the purpose is to trace some psychological development in the mind of Jesus, the order of events is of little importance. Of the major events there can be no question. The absence of chronological data makes a biography impossible, but the material is sufficient to show the reality of the Jesus of history. In the outline that follows some order had to be selected. In many points of detail the order chosen is admittedly arbitrary.

C. The fourfold presentation of Jesus. It is significant that in spite of an early attempt at producing a harmony of the Gospels (see DIATESSARON), it was always preferred to keep the Gospels separate. Each presents its own portrait and each is needed for the total picture. It will be valuable, therefore, to give some indication of the characteristic features of each evangelist's presentation of Jesus, for this approach is more valid than any attempt to reconstruct a continuous account from material in all four gospels.

1. Matthew's portrait. This gospel has many distinctive features, portraying Jesus as a royal figure. The line of descent in the genealogy is through David, who is named at the head of the second main section in Matthew's list. The expression "Son of David" occurs on various occasions in the gospel, to a greater extent than in the other synoptics. Matthew's birth narrative concentrates on homage fit for a king (Matt. 2), as compared with Luke's account of the worship of the lowly shepherds. In the narrative of the triumphal entry into Jerusalem, both Matthew and Luke refer to the kingly scene, but only Matthew cites the OT passage, "See, your king comes to you" (21:5). While all the synoptics mention Jesus' teaching about the kingdom of God, it is Matthew in particular who concentrates upon it. His parables are kingdom parables. The message of Jesus is concerned with the proclamation of the kingdom.

Another characteristic of Matthew's gospel is the authoritative nature of Jesus as a teacher. In the great discourses that Matthew has sandwiched between blocks of narrative, he specially emphasizes the teaching ministry of Jesus. Yet, he does not portray Jesus as a Jewish rabbi. In fact, Jesus claims authority to supersede the law, which the rabbis considered their highest duty to uphold. In view of this fundamental difference, it is no wonder that Jesus so often was at variance with the religious leaders of his day. Matthew comments that "he taught as one who had authority, and not as their teachers of the law" (Matt. 7:29; cf. Mk. 1:22; Lk. 4:32, where similar comment is made about Jesus' visit to the synagogue). Matthew's gospel is dominated by his five great discourse sections—Matt. 5–7; 10; 13; 18; 23–25—which illustrate various aspects of the teaching of Jesus about the kingdom.

Matthew shares with the other Gospels the picture of Jesus as Son of Man, a title that Jesus uses both redemptively and eschatologically. He also shares with them the belief in the messianic claims of Jesus. He alone records the words of Jesus about the coming church and gives some indication of its nature (cf. Matt. 16:18–19; 18:15–20). In this respect Matthew's work leads into the early church

Model of the temple looking S over the Court of Women toward the two-story colonnades of the Royal Stoa where the money changers did business.

period, for it is Matthew who gives the Great Commission of Jesus to his disciples before his ascension and ends with the assurance of Jesus' continuing presence with them (see COMMISSION, GREAT). One cannot put aside this gospel without awareness of the future of the people of God because of the resurrection of Jesus Christ.

2. Mark's portrait. Mark's distinctive contribution is one of emphasis rather than unique material. The first feature is the constant activity of Jesus. The relative absence of teaching material contributes to this impression. Mark often says that the actions of Jesus were performed immediately. One saying may fittingly be chosen as summing up Mark's portrait of Jesus (Mk. 10:45; cf. Matt. 20:28), namely, that the Son of Man came not to be served but to serve. His is essentially the gospel of Christ the servant, a gospel full of bustling activity that would make a great appeal to men of action. Jesus was no religious recluse, but a man deeply aware of the needs of those around him.

This gospel is also remarkable for the large proportion of space devoted to the passion and resurrection narratives. There is little specific teaching about the meaning of Christ's death (except Mk. 10:45), but the arrangement of the whole book gives the impression that for Mark the real focus was upon the concluding events, and that the opening two-thirds of the gospel was only a preparation for this. Mark obviously did not attempt to write a biography. Indeed, it is he alone of all the evangelists who describes his book as "the gospel of Jesus Christ" (Mk. 1:1). Undoubtedly for him the major part of that gospel was the redemptive work accomplished by Jesus on the cross.

It should be noted that Mark begins by identifying Jesus as Son of God (according to the most probable textual reading) and yet proceeds to include, more than any of the other gospels, a presentation of Jesus as a human being. Since Mark seems more drawn by actions than by words, it is most natural to see the evidence for the deity and humanity of Jesus in what he did rather than what he said. The humanity of Jesus may be seen in his acts of compassion, and his divine power in the fact that so many of these acts of compassion are portrayed as miracles.

Mention has already been made of those who have claimed that Mark has imposed his own theory of a messianic secret upon his material, but since the theory is not demanded by the evidence, it may be said that Mark's portrait of Jesus implies the awareness of his own messianic mission. The earthly life of Jesus was not the appointed time for this to be made known. The Messiah must first be recognized in the risen Christ.

3. Luke's portrait. There is a warm human touch in Luke's account. The birth stories are more intimate. The contacts of Jesus with the people of his day are more varied, with special emphasis upon his concern for women and children. The parables more frequently have a human touch about them, as is specially illustrated in the parables of Lk. 15. Luke records more of the theme of joy in Jesus' teaching than the other evangelists. The ministry of Jesus was not intended to give a somber impression. Even in his passion references, Luke dwells less on the tragic aspects, although no description of the crucifixion scene can avoid such an aspect. In Luke's account of the transfiguration, the conversation concerned the "exodus" or departure of Jesus rather than his death (Lk. 9:31). When he describes the crucifixion scene, he does not include Jesus' cry of separation, "Why have you forsaken me?" (found in Matt. 27:46; Mk. 15:34). In Luke the last words of Jesus are a prayer of committal to the Father (Lk. 23:46). Nevertheless, if the starkness of the cross is somewhat toned down, its centrality is as clear in Luke as in the others. It is in Luke that the risen Christ is recorded as expounding from the Scriptures the necessity for his sufferings (24:26–27). He ends his gospel on a note of great joy, which was now no longer dependent upon the earthly presence of Jesus. In no other way could Luke have indicated the continuity of the historical Jesus with the Christ of faith.

4. John's portrait. The Johannine portrait is different, although many common features with the other Gospels enable the depiction to be identified as the same person. He is introduced in a different way, in the concept of a divine intermediary, the divine Word who nevertheless became flesh (see LOGOS). There is nothing comparable in the synoptics. Had John proceeded in the same vein throughout his gospel, the difference in approach would have been insuperable. As soon as John has spoken of the incarnation, his narrative proceeds to illustrate in human terms what it meant for the Word to become flesh.

The most marked characteristic of his portrait is the filial relationship between Jesus and the Father. This is essentially the gospel of Jesus the Son. Its purpose was that men might believe that Jesus is the Son of God, and the author took care that much of the gospel testifies to this fact. Scattered throughout the book are statements that show the consciousness of Jesus and of his dependence on the Father. He is the Sent One. It is the Father's will that he has done. He calls men and women to the Father's purpose for them. The climax of this aspect of Jesus is seen in the prayer in Jn. 17, which has not inappropriately been called the high priestly prayer, but which is really a filial supplication on behalf of his disciples.

Another feature of John's portrait is the miraculous signs included as an attestation of Jesus. These signs are intended to be authenticating and are said to redound to God's glory. The signs are themselves in agreement with the portrait of the divine Son. They are the deeds the Son might be expected to perform. They were further intended to be aids to faith, for Jesus himself appealed to his works if men would not believe him for his own sake.

Linked with these characteristics is the remarkable fact that John records more evidence of the perfect humanity of Jesus than any of the other evangelists. Jesus is described as thirsty and tired. At the tomb of LAZARUS he is moved with indignation. He does the most menial service in the upper room. There is no doubt about the fact that the Word had become flesh. This Johannine portrait was wholly different from the Docetic representation of Jesus, according to which his humanity was more apparent than real.

There is a certain unhurried atmosphere about this gospel, in strong contrast to Mark's. Jesus has time to discuss and converse. The action is slow-moving and sometimes nonexistent. There is more sense of inevitability about this portrait than about the others. The idea of the "hour" of destiny runs through the whole gospel. At first it is said that it has not yet come, and this prepares the reader to look for its dawning and draws the narrative to a

Opening into a subterranean area known traditionally as the Tomb of Lazarus (Bethany).

climax, when eventually it does come in the passion narrative. There is nothing accidental about the cross; it is seen as part of the purpose of God.

When these four portraits are compared, they present four different aspects of Jesus, none of which can be dispensed with without loss. Any attempt at recognizing the historical Jesus cannot proceed without recognizing the many-sided character of the person of Jesus as the four evangelists saw him.

D. Other NT evidence for the life of Jesus.

An important question arises over the relation of Acts and the Epistles to the testimony of the Gospels to the historical Jesus. The letters of PAUL are of particular interest. One needs to inquire what knowledge these writings reveal of the apostle's acquaintance with the events and the teaching of Jesus. First impressions might suggest that Paul was either ignorant of or else uninterested in the historical Jesus. Such impressions would not be entirely justified, for there are passing allusions in his epistles that bear testimony to his knowledge of certain historical facts.

When Paul is contending with the JUDAIZERS at GALATIA, he asserts that "God sent his Son, born of a woman, born under law" (Gal. 4:4), by which it is clear that he regarded him as a true man who lived in an environment of Jewish law. According to human reckoning he was of the seed of David (Rom. 1:3). Whether this latter reference is regarded as part of the primitive *kerygma* (as C. H. Dodd believes, *The Apostolic Preaching and its Developments*, 2nd ed. [1944]), or as Paul's own thought, is of small consequence. It shows, however, Paul's acquaintance with the lineage of Jesus through the Davidic line.

Some glimpses of his knowledge of the character of Jesus are seen from the references to the meekness and gentleness of Christ (2 Cor. 10:1), to his compassion (Phil. 1:8), and to his willingness to bear reproaches (Rom. 15:3). Some background knowledge of the historical Jesus would appear to be indispensable if these expressions are to have intelligible meaning for Paul and his readers. The apostle is certainly aware of the external circumstances of the life of Jesus, for he refers to the poverty of Christ in 2 Cor. 8:9. Moreover, there are references to him as an example, and this must presuppose some detailed knowledge of his actions.

It is concerning the passion and resurrection of Jesus that there is the greatest clarity in the testimony of Paul. He knows about the betrayal (1 Cor. 11:23). Those who crucified him are said to be "the rulers of this age" (2:8), although he includes the Jews as partners in the offense (1 Thess. 2:14–15). His knowledge of Jesus' resurrection is detailed (1 Cor. 15:3–8). This passage merits careful attention, for it supplies information additional to the gospel accounts. The death and burial of Jesus are mentioned before the resurrection appearances to show the connection of these appearances with the historical events. Since Paul states explicitly that he had "received" this information, it is evident that no small importance was attached in the primitive period to the fact of the burial. Of special interest is the mention of the appearances. To begin with, some of the gospel appearances are omitted, such as the appearance to the women and to the two on the EMMAUS road. Whether the 500 are the same people Luke refers to on the occasion when Jesus ascended (Lk. 24:50) is not clear, but only Paul mentions the number. Moreover, it is he alone who refers to an appearance to JAMES. It is not easy to fit in Paul's data with those mentioned in the Gospels, but for that reason the evidence must be regarded as independent. The primitive *kerygma* clearly emphasized the need for historical verification of the central factor of the Christian faith. The resurrection was certainly more than a subjective experience.

Paul is specific about the details of the institution of the Last Supper, but his account supplements the gospel records by preserving the Lord's words, "do this, whenever you drink it, in remembrance of me" (1 Cor. 11:25). This section is of particular interest, as Paul maintains that he received the tradition from the Lord, by which he must mean that the tradition carried with it the divine sanction.

There are various occasions when Paul appears to be referring to the teaching of Jesus in a way that shows his acquaintance with it. It is possible that his reference to love as a fulfillment of the law (Rom. 13:10; Gal. 5:14) is an echo of the teaching of Jesus. More specific is the occasion when Paul, on the issue of marriage, distinguishes between his own opinion and the express teaching of Jesus, although he clearly believed that his opinion was in harmony with that teaching (1 Cor. 7:10–12, 25). In the PASTORAL EPISTLES two references may be noted. Timothy is advised that true teachers must conform their teaching to "the sound instruction of our Lord Jesus Christ" (1 Tim. 6:3), which could be a reference to words taught by him. The other reference is linked with a scriptural citation that is clearly a saying of Jesus, and possibly a quotation, to the effect that the laborer deserves his wages (1 Tim. 5:18; Lk. 10:7).

Some have found difficulty in the fact that Paul does not show more acquaintance with the historic facts of the life of Jesus. This is not altogether unexpected. The apostle's letters are incidental correspondence dealing with practical and theological problems that arose in the church. The fact is that there are few occasions within these epistles where recording of events and sayings of Jesus would have been appropriate. But it may be said that the epistles are written against such a basic understanding of the historical Jesus that they would not have been intelligible without it. (Cf. R. J. Knowling, *The Witness of the Epistles: A Study in Modern Criticism* [1892], and *The Testimony of St. Paul to Christ Viewed in some of Its Aspects* [1905].)

The witness of the book of Acts shows everywhere an emphasis on the death and resurrection of Jesus as the major content of the early preaching. What information does it supply about the life of Jesus? The most obvious is the brief résumé in PETER's address to CORNELIUS and his household (Acts 10:36–43). Peter speaks of Jesus of Nazareth as one anointed by God with the Holy Spirit. His deeds are referred to as doing good and healing (esp. exorcisms). Death by hanging on a tree is also mentioned. This testifies to the place of historical details about Jesus in the earlier proclamations. In the earlier speeches there is recognition that the responsibility for the crucifixion must rest upon the Jews (cf. 2:23, 36; 7:52) and of the choice of a murderer in place of Jesus (3:14). Both Peter (3:14) and Stephen (7:52) describe Jesus as the Righteous One, thus bearing witness to their knowledge of his holy character.

In the other epistles the data is sparse. In the epistle to the HEBREWS there is a knowledge of Jesus' temptation (Heb. 2:18; 4:15). The powerful intercessions of Jesus with strong crying and tears in the days of his flesh are mentioned in 5:7, and this seems to be a specific reference to the agony in GETHSEMANE. There is also a passing allusion to the hostility that Jesus endured (12:3), which is regarded as an example for the readers. It is clear, therefore, that the writer is conscious of much of the background of the historical Jesus.

In the epistle of James the main feature of interest is the manner in which the author so frequently reflects knowledge of the sayings of Jesus, particularly from the Sermon on the Mount (cf. Jas. 1:2 and Matt. 5:10–12; Jas. 1:22 and Matt. 7:24–27; Jas. 5:2–3 and Matt. 6:19, to cite only a few examples). This is of particular importance because James reflects more of the sayings of Jesus than any other NT author. But his epistle is the most practical of any, and the ethical teaching of Jesus was for him of greatest relevance.

The Petrine letters provide a few allusions to the historical Jesus. The suffering of Christ is referred to as an example (1 Pet. 2:21) and his sufferings are described (cf. Isa. 53). The statement in 1 Pet. 2:12 about men seeing one's good deeds seems to be an echo of the saying of Jesus in Matt. 5:16. This epistle also preserves the enigmatic statement about Christ preaching to the spirits in prison (1 Pet. 3:19), which is nowhere hinted at in the Gospels. There is a reference to the transfiguration of Jesus and to the fact that there were eyewitnesses of this event (2 Pet. 1:17–18). John speaks of what eyes have seen and hands handled (1 Jn. 1:1), but gives no historical details. The book of Revelation is centered so much on the heavenly Christ that no reference is made to events in the life of Jesus, but the Lamb is referred to as slain. One saying that recurs—he who has an ear, let him hear—may well be an echo of the words of Jesus.

To sum up, it will be seen that specific data regarding the historic Jesus outside the Gospels in the NT is frugal, but that everywhere they are assumed. It is no wonder that the early church placed such store on its gospel sources.

E. Extracanonical material for the life of Jesus.

There is little information about the history of Jesus from outside the NT, and most of what has survived is unlikely to be authentic; yet every avenue must be explored.

The Execution of John the Baptist (Renaissance painting by Bernardino Luini).

1. Non-Christian evidences. Under this, two subdivisions will be considered, pagan and Jewish. The pagan evidence may be dealt with quickly, since it is practically nonexistent. TACITUS reports about the Christians in the time of NERO's persecutions (A.D. 64) and mentions that Christ was executed in the reign of TIBERIUS by the procurator Pontius Pilate. PLINY the Younger, in his letter to the Emperor TRAJAN concerning the superstition of Christianity, refers to Christ, but only as an object of reviling by those persuaded to apostatize. Another historian, SUETONIUS, mentions the expulsion from Rome of the Jews who had caused a great tumult under the influence of "Chrestus" (who may well be identified with Christ), but he gives no further evidence about this person. These are the major pagan witnesses to the historical Jesus. In spite of the rapid spread of the Christian church, the pagan world approached no nearer to it than to call the whole movement a superstition which was accompanied by vile practices. Against such a background the progress of the Christian church is remarkable.

When one turns to Jewish evidences the situation is not too different. Three passages in JOSEPHUS's *Antiquities* may be noted. One gives an account of Herod's action in killing JOHN THE BAPTIST, which is of value in support of the validity of the gospel records, although there are different motives stated. Another passage makes specific statements about Jesus, although many have disputed the authenticity of the passage because no writer before EUSEBIUS (4th cent.) mentions it. It may be genuine, and will accordingly be cited in full: "Now about this time arose Jesus, a wise man, if indeed he should be called a man. For he was a doer of marvellous deeds, a teacher of men who receive the truth with pleasure; and he won over to himself many Jews and many also of the Greek (nation). He was the Christ. And when on the indictment of the principal men among us Pilate had sentenced him to the cross, those who had loved him at the first did not cease; for he appeared to them on the third day alive again, the divine prophets having foretold these and ten thousand other wonderful things concerning him. And even now the tribe of Christians named after him is not extinct."

This statement certainly seems rather too sympathetic toward Christianity for Josephus, particularly the reference to the resurrection. If it be considered authentic, it shows the extent to which knowledge of the historical Jesus had penetrated into the circle in which this Jewish historian moved. What details are given are in full agreement with the gospel narratives. The third passage in the *Antiquities* mentions Jesus but only insofar as referring to his connection with James, the brother of Jesus, whose murder by the Sanhedrin Josephus describes (*Ant.* 20.9.1 §200). Space will not allow discussion of the passages in the Slavonic version of Josephus's *Jewish War*, for there is considerable doubt about their genuineness as a 1st-cent. testimony. If any historical value may be attached to them, they witness to the view that Jesus was concerned about armed political agitation.

In addition to the witness of Josephus, Jewish testimony must include references in the TALMUD. These are not numerous and may be restricted to eight that can be considered of any value. One refers to the hanging of Jeshu of Nazareth and mentions his practice of sorcery. This appears to be a Jewish attempt to explain away the responsibility of the Jews for the crucifixion. The second refers to five disciples of Jesus by name, but none of the names coincide with those mentioned in the Gospels. The third describes a proselyte calling up the spirit of Jesus by spells; while the fourth refers to a man "born of a woman" who was to arise and "make himself God," against whom people are warned. There is also a reference to him departing and coming again. Another feature is the recognition that this man will lead the whole world astray, showing the universal appeal of Christianity. In two sayings there is a description of Jesus (under a pseudonym) reflecting Jewish ridicule of the VIRGIN BIRTH. The seventh reference is a saying attributed to Jesus concerning the hire of a harlot, which is almost certainly spurious; the eighth contains a story involving a Christian philosopher in which reference is made to the gospel, but the first supposed citation, "Son and daughter shall inherit together," does not occur in the NT, neither does the second citation, although it looks like a modified version of Matt. 5:17. (For a concise account of these sayings, cf. R. Dunkerly, *Beyond the Gospels* [1957].) What value is to be placed on these Jewish comments on Jesus must remain doubtful, but the references demonstrate some knowledge of Jesus as a historical figure and give some indication of the scorn with which the rabbis regarded him.

2. Christian evidences. During the earliest period of church history extracanonical evidence is sparse. The present concern will be with two lines of evidence, archaeological and patristic. In the archaeological field almost the only evidence comes from the catacomb inscriptions. These supply information concerning what the early Christians thought about Jesus rather than information of a historical character. There is an early painting of him as a youthful and beardless person, but there is no knowing whether it was based on anyone other than in the imagination of the artist.

There might be some slight contribution from the *SATOR-ROTAS*, a word square that was widely used in early Christian circles. There is considerable dispute over its significance, but it has been suggested that the center word *TENET* in both directions forms the symbol of a cross, thus reminding the Christians of the basic belief in their faith. Others have seen the square as an indirect reference to the Lord's Prayer in Latin, since the letters in the square make up *PATER-NOSTER* twice with two *A*'s and two *O*'s surplus, representing Christ as Alpha and Omega. Such evidence is so tenuous that it can contribute nothing to the understanding of the history of Jesus. (The square is prob. pre-Christian, and some argue that it has its origins in MITHRAISM.) The famous fish symbol more clearly testifies to early Christian faith in Christ as Savior (see FISH IV), but it too fails to contribute to the historical knowledge of Jesus.

Among the APOSTOLIC FATHERS there are various sayings attributed to Jesus, though the majority of these are variants of canonical sayings, which may well be accounted for by loose reminiscences of the teaching. Clement of Rome (see CLEMENT, EPISTLES OF) has passages of this kind, but it seems best to regard these as evidence of his knowledge of the canonical sources, rather than as independent evidence. In the DIDACHE there are a number of statements that echo the teaching of Jesus in the Sermon on the Mount, without attributing the words to Jesus. Some think that a genuine saying is recorded by the *Epistle of Barnabas* (see BARNABAS, EPISTLE OF) in the following words, "So he says, Those who wish to see me and lay hold of my kingdom must receive me through tribulation and suffering." While this might be conceived as a genuine saying, it might equally well be no more than a general summary of the gist of Jesus' teaching about those who seek the kingdom. Many canonical sayings mention the tribulation which followers of Jesus must endure.

In the epistles of IGNATIUS there occurs a resurrection account which differs from the canonical accounts. The *Shepherd of Hermas* (see HERMAS, SHEPHERD OF) is interesting because it includes authoritative parables that are quite different from the canonical Gospels, but these are not directly attributed to Jesus. It is extraordinary how little material from the Apostolic Fathers preserves what might conceivably be regarded as genuine noncanonical sayings. It must be noted that not a great many canonical sayings were cited either, but if a large number of AGRAPHA (unwritten sayings) were circulating in the oral tradition, it might have been supposed that far more would have been preserved by the earliest writers had they considered them genuine. This kind of argument has obvious limitations, since the purpose of these patristic writers was not focused on showing their acquaintance with the sayings of Jesus.

There is little evidence in the writings of the apologists, although two testimonies may be mentioned. The *Apology of Aristides* (see ARISTIDES, APOLOGY OF) contains passages that show affinity with the Gospels, although introducing variations. It is clear that the author is echoing their language without making direct reference to the sayings of Jesus. There is certainly no evidence here of noncanonical sayings of Jesus. The other witness is JUSTIN MARTYR, who mentions the birth of Jesus as having taken place in a "cave" rather than in a "stable." Both terms might in this case be correct since stables in caves were not unknown in the ANE. There are sundry sayings of Jesus that are reminiscent of the gospel sayings. Bearing in mind that Justin often does not quote accurately, it may reasonably be supposed that he himself is responsible for the variations and is not citing some independent traditions. For instance, when Justin records the saying, "I came not to call the righteous to repentance but sinners, for the Heavenly Father desires the sinner's repentance rather than his punishment" (*Apology* 15), this looks like a Justinian enlargement of Lk. 5:32. One of the best attested *agrapha* in Justin is, "In whatsoever things I apprehend you, in these I shall judge you" (*Dialogue with Trypho* 47), which is reminiscent of various statements of Jesus on judgment in the gospels, but it may be an independent saying.

3. Apocryphal gospels. A large number of these appeared from the 2nd cent. onward, and in them are included many incidents that relate either to the birth and childhood of Jesus or to his passion. None of the material has any claim to be genuine. The additional data—such as the story of Jesus making clay birds that flew away—are generally fantastic. Moreover, these gospels were generally, if not always, heretical in purpose. The *Gospel of Peter*, for instance, is known to have been published in the interests of the Docetic heresy, for Serapion testified to this fact. It was not difficult for those gripped by a dogmatic purpose of a heretical kind to give vent to imagination in an attempt to strengthen their unorthodox position. The evidence from this source therefore lacks historical validity, but it does, by way of contrast, bring out vividly the remarkably restrained nature of the canonical testimony to Christ.

Some fragmentary evidence has been preserved of a "Hebrew Gospel" (see HEBREWS, GOSPEL OF THE), which cannot be classed as heretical and which may preserve some genuine material not found in the canonical Gospels. An examination of the most likely passages (see Dunkerly, *Beyond the Gospels*, 102ff.) shows some interesting deviations. For instance, Jesus' mother and brethren urge him to be baptized with them by John the Baptist, but Jesus hesitates because of his sinlessness. Some dogmatic consideration seems to have entered. Most of the other sayings possess a secondary-looking character which suggests the need for caution in accepting them as genuine.

4. Gnostic works. Little need be said about Gnostic sources as a possible quarry for authentic sayings of Jesus. The most notable books which preserve sayings of a similar kind to those in the canonical Gospels are the *Gospel of Thomas* and the *Gospel of Philip*. The parallels in the former alone warrant serious attention. There are many which echo the thought of the Synoptic Gospels, and in these cases it is almost certain that the author has used them, although there have been various other theories to account for the parallels (cf. the discussion of R. M. Wilson, *Studies in the Gospel of Thomas* [1960]). The possibility of some independently authentic material being preserved in Gnostic circles cannot be entirely ruled out. But probability is strongly against it, for in this work some of the known sayings of Jesus have been adapted for Gnostic purposes and this tendency may well have led to the creation of other sayings. Gnostics are not a safe source for authentic teaching. The early church fathers constantly charged them with distorting the Scriptures. Would any genuine oral tradition have escaped? See PHILIP, GOSPEL OF; THOMAS, GOSPEL OF.

V. The early life and ministry of Jesus Christ

A. Summary of method. It is impossible to produce a biography of Jesus as understood by the modern use of that term. Since Christianity is a historic religion, however, it is essential to provide at least an outline of the main events which went to make up his earthly life. It will be valuable by way of introduction to give a summary of the main stages of the story as it can be reconstructed from the Gospels.

The thirty years in Nazareth. In spite of the length of this period, the material preserved is confined to the birth stories and one brief incident when Jesus was twelve.

The period of preparation. This covers the ministry of John the Baptist in heralding the coming of Christ.

The Judean ministry. This includes the earliest period of the Lord's work until the commencement of the Galilean ministry.

The Galilean ministry. This ministry may be divided for convenience into three periods. The first ends with the choosing of the Twelve, the second with the withdrawal of Jesus from northern Galilee, and the third with his departure for Jerusalem on his last journey.

The closing period of the ministry. This is a convenient heading for the material fitted into the journey to the time when Jesus enters Jerusalem mainly centered beyond Jordan.

The passion and resurrection narratives. Under this caption are included all the events from the entry into Jerusalem until the resurrection and the various postresurrection appearances of Jesus to his disciples, culminating with the ascension.

The following outline of events and teaching will fill out in considerable detail these main stages to bring into focus the major purpose of Jesus. It is important to recognize that the theology of Jesus is seen both in his acts and in his teaching. An overconcentration on one or the other would be a mistake. They are inextricably linked. The many deeds of compassion, the demonstrations of power, the human interest, are all part of the total picture and form the background of the teaching. At the same time the teaching throws light upon the true nature and interpretation of the acts. Nevertheless, in the outline itself the emphasis will be on the events, since a separate section will deal with the teaching, both in method and content.

B. The thirty years in Nazareth. The most important part of this preliminary section of the life of Jesus is his advent into human life. It is for this reason that Matthew and Luke begin with narratives relating to the birth of Jesus, while John goes back and reflects upon his eternal preexistence. One would not expect the story of Jesus to begin where John begins, for he sets the scene beyond the realm of history. Nevertheless, by reason of what the evangelists believed Jesus to be, his is the most logical beginning.

1. John's prologue (Jn. 1:1–18). At first glance it seems strange that John should introduce his book with statements about the *Word*, especially as he does not identify the Word as Jesus Christ until toward the end of the prologue. Evidently the first readers of the gospel must have known what John was describing, otherwise his opening would have been more mystifying than elucidating. One cannot now be certain of its source for John. PHILO JUDAEUS of Alexandria has much to say about the Logos, which in his system was an intermediary principle between God and man, but he denied the possibility of the Logos becoming flesh. When John says that the Logos did become flesh he is clearly presenting a different kind of Logos from Philo. For all his great erudition, Philo could not present a Logos capable of dwelling among human beings, who could move them into action and give them power to become sons of God. This was a new element in the contemporary Greek world. Jewish thought had also prepared for the coming of Jesus, not only with the messianic hope, but by its concept of the intermediary *Memra*, God's agent in the world of creation.

Far more important than the origin of the idea of the Word are the statements concerning him which John makes in his prologue. Not only does he stress his preexistence, but also his divine nature. His power is evidence of his creative energy and of his re-creative activity. The Word is identified as Light shining in an atmosphere of darkness, which describes the moral environment into which Jesus came. The Word becoming flesh is pivotal to John's introduction to his gospel. The whole account is basically a human and historic story, because the becoming flesh had taken place among men and the glory of the incarnate Word had been seen. There is an unquestionable connection between the prologue and the events that follow. The same Jesus Christ whose actions and words are recorded is the means whereby grace and truth come to human beings, and through whom God makes known his revelation. Unless the records of all the Gospels are seen in the light of this mission, there can be no proper evaluation of the life of Jesus.

One significant feature about John's introduction is the mention of John (the Baptist) by name, the witness to the Light, before the Light had himself been identified. This shows, in agreement with the Synoptic Gospels, the importance of the ministry of John the Baptist.

2. The birth narratives (Matt. 1:1—2:23; Lk. 1:1—2:38). John's statement that the Word became flesh at once raises the question in what circumstances it happened. Matthew and Luke supply the answer. The narratives, although brief, are nevertheless sufficient to establish the historical reality of the incarnation. There is a restraint about them that immediately impresses. Matthew approaches the subject from a different point of view than Luke, and yet their narratives are complementary to each other. Both stress the supernatural character of the advent of Jesus. In Matthew this is brought out by the narration of several dreams that reveal various stages of development, from the announcement of Joseph's

JESUS CHRIST

View from Mount Tabor looking NW over the Nazareth Ridge and the modern city of Nazareth. Despite Jesus' extended stay in Nazareth during his early years, the Gospels say very little about this time in his earthly life.

reaction when he learns of Mary's pregnancy until the return from Egypt. In Luke's account a similar impression is created by the angel's announcement to Mary. It is at once clear that this is no ordinary birth. It is not surprising therefore that Matthew records a citation that a virgin would conceive (Matt. 1:23). It is true that Isaiah's statement need not refer to a virgin, but to a young woman, but it is equally evident that Matthew intended the readers to understand that the advent of Jesus was effected in a miraculous way by conception taking place in a virgin. Luke's account supports this in the promise to Mary that the Holy Spirit should come upon her (Lk. 1:35).

It is never suggested in these narratives or anywhere else in the Gospels that people generally regarded Jesus as any other than the son of Joseph (cf. Jn. 6:41; Matt. 13:55; Lk. 2:27, 41, 48). Popular opinion is no sure guide to truth, and both Matthew and Luke have set out to stress the uniqueness of the birth of Jesus as a necessary prelude to their accounts of his life and ministry. Whatever modern attempts may be made to approach the life of Jesus from a purely human point of view, it is beyond dispute that the evangelists made no such attempt.

In Matthew's gospel the ANNUNCIATION is made to Joseph, and the most characteristic feature of the revelation made to him is the clear statement of the purpose of the advent. Jesus was coming to save his people from their sins (Matt. 1:21). At the beginning of the gospel a theological note is introduced. The subsequent doings of Jesus are all geared to this purpose, which provides their motive force.

In Luke's gospel the annunciation is to Mary and is accompanied by an account of the promise of the birth of John the Baptist and its fulfillment. The most significant feature of this account is the inclusion of the hymns known as the MAGNIFICAT and BENEDICTUS, both of which are formed on the pattern of the OT Psalms. They create an atmosphere of rejoicing over the coming of Jesus that is frequently reflected in the subsequent narrative, for Luke's account has more references to joy than any of the others.

The story of the angel's announcement to the shepherds draws attention to the same feature. The day of the advent of Jesus was a day of good tidings of great joy. At the same time, the announcement was made of peace on earth to all men of (God's) good will, which gives a distinctly universal aspect to the purpose of Jesus. The mission of Jesus could never be understood against a background of narrow nationalistic aspirations. It needed a broader canvas. The homage of humble shepherds signifies something of the receptivity of the common people, a feature which was to be abundantly illustrated in the subsequent ministry of Jesus.

Matthew's account of the homage of the Magi presents a rather different aspect. These were Gentile inquirers for the coming Christ. They believed themselves to have been divinely led, and indeed through being supernaturally warned of Herod's devices were able to frustrate his intention to take adverse action against the child Jesus. This homage of Gentiles is specially noteworthy at the beginning of a gospel that is primarily written with Jewish interests in mind. The Messiah was not so Jewish that Gentiles had no desire to worship him, and in harmony with this is the conclusion of this same gospel, in which the commission of Jesus to his disciples is worldwide.

It is not possible to be certain when the wise men arrived at the place where Jesus was. Some think it was a considerable time after his birth, a view based mainly on the evidence that Herod sought to kill all the children under two years old. Herod did not know how long ago the child had been born. He knew only when the star appeared. The flight into Egypt, recorded only in Matt. 2:13–14, is seen as a direct fulfillment of prophecy. This therefore plays an important part in Matthew's purpose, that is, to show that the course of the life of Jesus was no accidental happening, but a designed fulfillment of what God had foretold.

In the meantime, Jesus was present at the temple for the ritual of consecration, according to Jewish custom (Lk. 2:22–24). On this occasion SIMEON and ANNA both bore witness to Jesus. Simeon's song (the NUNC DIMITTIS) again conveys a universal viewpoint, for Jesus was to become a light for Gentile illumination (2:32) as well as Israel's glory. At the same time, Simeon foresaw hostility toward Jesus, for some would speak evil against him (2:34). Both Simeon and Anna typify the realization of the fulfillment in Jesus of long-awaited messianic hopes. The story of the ministry of Jesus is intended to be read against such a background.

Both Matthew and Luke include genealogies. Matthew uses one to introduce his gospel, tracing the list from Abraham to Jesus. Luke, who does not refer to the genealogy until after recording the ministry of John the Baptist (Lk. 3), begins with Jesus and traces his ancestry back to Adam. Although some of the names in these two genealogical lists are the same, most of them are not. A partial explanation may be found in the schematic arrangement adopted by Matthew, having three groups of fourteen names (Matt. 1:17). This is made possible only by various omissions. It has been suggested that whereas Matthew follows the lineage of Joseph, Luke follows Mary's, but this supposition seems to run counter to what Luke himself states, since he does not even mention Mary. It is impossible to tell either the sources of these genealogies or the extent to which either author depended upon his own investigations. The major contribution of both lists for the life of Jesus is clear enough—both trace the ancestry through David and Abraham. He came of a royal line which gave rise to the title Son of David, which was used by various people in the course of the narrative. See GENEALOGY OF JESUS CHRIST.

Of all the evangelists it is only Luke who makes any attempt to set the record of Jesus on the stage of secular history. Even he concentrates on the timing of the appearance of John the Baptist rather than on the appearance of Jesus, although he shows the two events to be inseparable. The dating is sixfold (Lk. 3:1–2) and points to the major political figures in the Jewish world. This note by Luke is of great importance in establishing the historical setting of Christianity.

One other contact with secular history mentioned by Luke is the CENSUS of QUIRINIUS, governor of SYRIA (Lk. 2:2), which is said to be the occasion for Mary and Joseph to travel to Bethlehem just prior to the birth of Jesus. There is known to have been a census held under this official in A.D. 6, but this would be too late for the birth of Jesus. There is some reason to think that an earlier census was held in Syria more approximate to Luke's chronology, but the difficulty of Quirinius still remains, unless, as Sir William Ramsay supposed, this official held an extraordinary command at the same time as the governorship of Varus. See CHRONOLOGY (NT) I.B.

3. Home life at Nazareth (Lk. 2:39–52). Contrary to the modern idea of biographical studies that seeks traces from the early years of influences that may have contributed to the later development of a character, none of the evangelists shows the slightest interest in early environmental factors. Luke alone mentions an incident during the thirty years that Jesus spent in Nazareth. The visit to the temple when Jesus was twelve was no doubt included to draw attention to the fact that in the home of Jesus the usual Jewish practices were observed. Twelve was the age at which Jewish boys attended the Passover feast. For Luke it had more significance than this because of the opportunity it afforded to illustrate Jesus' first contact with the temple teachers.

The incident not only reveals their amazement at the wisdom of Jesus, but also his own consciousness of a divine mission, which his family did not understand. They evidently were incapable of appreciating his fullness of wisdom and his possession of special divine grace (Lk. 2:40). Mary appears to have understood most, but she kept her reflections to herself (2:51). She must have wondered often at the grace with which he was subject to her. The restraint of the canonical account of the childhood of Jesus contrasts vividly with the spate of childish stories that were later current in the apocryphal gospels. The processes of thought by which Jesus arrived at his messianic consciousness may claim the interest of some modern theologians, but were never considered important by the evangelists.

In the body of the Gospels there are a few hints given of the attitude of the inhabitants of Nazareth toward Jesus. He was known as the carpenter or the carpenter's son (Mk. 6:3; Matt. 13:55). Moreover, there were other children in the family—James, Joses, Simon, Judas, and some sisters (Matt. 13:55–56). None of the Nazareth inhabitants apparently expected Jesus to show much wisdom or to do mighty works, for they were astonished when his ministry was in progress. The mystery of the hidden years is deepened by the obvious hardness of the people who knew him best.

C. The period of preparation. Before the actual commencement of the ministry of Jesus, there were several significant events—the preaching of John the Baptist, Jesus' baptism, and the temptation. All three of these events are of basic importance for the records of the public ministry of Jesus in the Synoptic Gospels, although Mark makes only a passing reference to the temptation.

1. John the Baptist (Matt. 3:1–12; Mk. 1:1–8; Lk. 3:1–17). The ministry of JOHN THE BAPTIST must be considered in the light of contemporary Judaism. There were certainly messianic hopes and the expectation of the dawning of a new age. There was belief in the approach of the KINGDOM OF GOD, although popular ideas were mostly materialistic, but John did not follow the normal pattern. In his methods and teaching he was like one of the ancient PROPHETS. In many respects he was the last of an era. He was this only because he was able to point to the Inaugurator of another era and the dawn of a new kingdom. All three synoptic writers mention the testimony of Isaiah to the coming of John the Baptist. The link with the past is thus established and a divine authority is given to the work of the herald of Jesus. All the writers record the preparatory ministry of the Baptist, but it is LUKE in particular who carries on the quotation from Isaiah to include the promise that all flesh should see God's salvation. The records clearly bring out John the Baptist's call to repent, and his prediction of the Coming One who would be greater than he, and would baptize with the HOLY SPIRIT (see BAPTISM OF THE HOLY SPIRIT). Both Matthew and Luke further call attention to the judgment that would follow the arrival of the One to come.

When John preached a baptism of REPENTANCE, there was immediate criticism of the Pharisees and Sadducees, who were described as a generation of vipers, a particularly strong expression of adverse opinion that was intended to bring them to a state of true repentance. There is a forthrightness and sternness about John's message that showed the serious character of his preparatory work. With such a herald as he, whose clothing of camel's hair drew attention to the sternness of his character, the coming of Jesus was set against a morally challenging situation. Men were being prepared by the serious call to repentance. Moreover, the challenge to moral reformation was made specific by the Baptist, as Luke brings out clearly by samples of the advice given to tax collectors and soldiers.

The rite of baptism was not new with John. The Jews practiced proselyte baptism, and some groups, such as the Essenes, appear to have practiced ritual cleansing, which was closely akin to initiatory baptism. The group at Qumran placed some importance on the rite, and it is interesting to conjecture whether John had had personal contact with the community. If he did, he had certainly departed from their pattern, for they were essentially inward-looking and their rites were exclusively for initiates; John was essentially outward-looking, directing his call for repentance to the multitudes. According to Matthew's account, he announced the imminence of the kingdom of heaven in the same terms that Jesus began to preach. This is clearly intended to show the continuity between the preaching of both, although the fundamental difference between them is that Jesus is himself the Inaugurator of the kingdom, whereas John was only the herald.

2. The baptism of Jesus (Matt. 3:13–17; Mk. 1:9–11; Lk. 3:21–22). The baptism of Jesus is the climax of John's work. When the king arrived, the herald's work was done. John was expecting to announce Jesus, but he never expected that Jesus would present himself for baptism. The one he was expecting was surely beyond the need for repentance. His greatness was such that John felt himself unworthy to unloose his sandals. Why did he request a baptism of repentance? Matthew alone records John's hesitation, and for this reason some scholars have regarded the detail as a later addition, prompted by motives of reverence, but in view of John's overwhelming conviction that Jesus was infinitely greater than he, it would have been much more surprising if no hesitation had been recorded. At the same time the reason for Jesus' action must be considered. According to Matthew, it was to fulfill all righteousness (Matt. 3:15), by which Jesus made clear to John that it was the right and proper thing for him to be baptized.

The problem arises concerning Jesus' submission to a rite that was specifically described as a baptism of repentance for the remission of sins. None of the synoptic evangelists gives the explanation, but all record the attestation of the heavenly voice bearing witness to the beloved Son in whom the Father is well pleased. The identification of Jesus with those needing repentance was clearly part of the divine plan. For the multitudes the baptismal rite symbolized their desire to forsake their sins, but for Jesus it meant a call to identify himself with a sinful people. Neither John nor any of the witnesses could recognize the theological implications of this symbolic act. It was part of the process in which Christ, as Paul later recognized, was made sin for mankind (2 Cor. 5:21).

Undoubtedly all the evangelists see the baptism as the commencement of the public ministry of Jesus. This is marked especially by the descent of the Spirit upon him (in the form of a dove) and by the heavenly attestation. This differentiated Jesus from all others who attended John's baptism. It is improbable that these supernatural signs were seen by any apart from John and Jesus, but for the evangelists their importance lay in their revelation of the nature of the mission of Jesus. John's gospel is most specific of all in recording the remarkable pronouncement of John the Baptist that Jesus was the Lamb of God who takes away the world's sin (Jn. 1:29). The writer of the gospel gives no indication of the extent of the Baptist's own understanding of his statement, although he clearly sees its importance in distinguishing the Baptist's work from that of Jesus. The fact that later doubts gripped the mind of the Baptist regarding the claims of Jesus does not vitiate his confident prediction at the commencement of the ministry.

3. The temptation of Jesus (Matt. 4:1–11; Mk. 1:12–13; Lk. 4:1–13). This was perhaps the most revealing event in the preparatory period. The fact that it followed immediately from the baptism is regarded as significant by all the synoptic evangelists. As Jesus had identified himself with sinners in John's baptism, so he exposed himself to the temptings of SATAN. It would be better to speak of testings rather than temptations, since the latter word has too often become associated with an element of

The Judean Desert, which was the setting of Jesus' temptation. (View to the N.)

yielding that was certainly not present in the case of Jesus. Details of the characteristics of the testings that came to him are given only by Matthew and Luke, although Mark mentions some important features, such as the presence of wild beasts and the ministration of angels.

In all the accounts the idea of a supernatural conflict is inescapable and clearly forms a basic introduction to the later passion narratives, in which the climax of the conflict is enacted. The three temptations mentioned by Matthew and Luke are to be regarded not as exhaustive but as exemplary. They are typical of the avenues along which testings continually come. They are, moreover, not to be restricted to the period of forty days, as Luke makes clear when he mentions that the devil's withdrawal was until a convenient season. The course of the ministry frequently presented occasions in which the testings would be repeated.

To understand the temptations, account must be taken of the messianic consciousness of Jesus. He was deeply aware of his mission and his power to accomplish it. The testings concerned the methods he would use to accomplish it. The use of miraculous power for his own preservation (to turn stone to bread) was rejected as totally unworthy of his mission. It would amount to a failure to maintain true priorities. Moreover, the urge to use the same miraculous powers to impress upon the world at large his messianic claims was equally alien to his true purpose. It would appeal to the spectacular, but would be diametrically opposed to the divine methods.

The other recorded testing concerned the character of the kingdom that Jesus had come to inaugurate. Was it to be comparable to the kingdoms of this world? Was it to share its glory with theirs? Such a possibility was unthinkable, and would amount to conceding allegiance to the devil, in whose hands, as Jesus acknowledged, were the imperial ambitions of the present age. His kingdom was of a totally different order. In all three of the temptations recorded, the Lord overcomes the tempting of the devil by means of the Scriptures, as the most appropriate medium for establishing the principles of divine action.

The difference in the order of the temptations in Matthew and Luke is more significant for the respective purpose of each than for the consciousness of Jesus himself. Matthew places the temptation to an earthly imperial status last, probably because of his design to show the true kingly status of Jesus, while Luke places last the urge to self-display because of his desire to show Jesus as essentially a man among men. Whether either knew the precise order or whether either attached any special importance to it is impossible to say.

The record of these temptations is generally appealed to as evidence that Jesus was in all respects tempted as we are (cf. Heb. 4:15), but this is true in only a limited respect. Since Jesus alone possessed messianic consciousness and power, the testings that came to him were unique. But it cannot be denied that they are allied to those which afflict all human beings. It must be recognized that Jesus was exposed to many more temptations than those recorded. Clearly, the public ministry of Jesus opened against

The Judean ministry of Jesus.

a background of tremendous struggle and a resolute rejection of all methods of achieving his mission that were opposed to the real purpose for which he came. See TEMPTATION OF JESUS.

D. The Judean ministry of Jesus. It is in John's gospel alone that any information is given about the early Judean ministry, a fact that raises some problems but need not lead to historical skepticism regarding this period. It may, in fact, be stated that the accounts in the other Gospels would be unintelligible apart from John's account of the initial introduction of the disciples to Jesus. This event followed immediately upon the impact that the statements of John the Baptist had upon them (beginning at Jn. 1:19). They may not have understood the full importance of the pronouncement about the Lamb of God, if they had any insight at all, which is certainly questionable. They were drawn as by a magnet to the Person about whom the words were spoken.

It is significant that John does not record a mass following, but rather the response of individuals. Discipleship was at this stage loose and needed confirmation by a further specific call later on, as the synoptics record. There is no doubt about the deep impression made by Jesus. He was acclaimed as Messiah by his first two followers. He was acknowledged as Son of God and King of Israel by NATHANAEL. He was winning men by means utterly different from those suggested by Satan at the time of the temptation.

During this period of personal contact with future apostles, Jesus made a visit to GALILEE, and while there he was involved in a wedding at CANA, which is noted by the evangelist as being the place of the first of Jesus' signs (Jn. 2:1–11). The purpose of the signs was to reveal the glory of Christ, and it is not without meaning that the first sample should be in a purely domestic setting. It throws light upon the humanity of Jesus.

Two other incidents in Jerusalem preceded the opening of the public ministry in Galilee. The first was a public act, the second a private conversation. The cleansing of the temple by the expulsion of money changers (Jn. 2:13–17) was a daring commencement to public work, and for this reason many prefer to regard this incident as misplaced by John, especially in view of the similar incident recorded by the synoptics at the end of the ministry. A double cleansing cannot be dismissed as impossible, although many regard it as improbable. Some consider it to be symbolic of the purifying purpose of Jesus in the citadel of contemporary Judaism. John clearly regarded the historical details as important, for he mentions the Passover feast. The incident itself reveals the great authority that the presence of Jesus must have conveyed. It also illuminates one aspect of the mission of Jesus, for he alludes to his coming resurrection (as Jn. 2:18–22 shows).

The conversation with NICODEMUS (Jn. 3) is of a different order, although akin insofar as Nicodemus was himself associated with official Judaism. His quest was typical of those who were dissatisfied with their religion, and yet who were mystified by the spiritual emphasis of Jesus. The dialogue John relates is important as showing the place of REGENERATION in the thought of Jesus and the inability of Nicodemus to grasp its true meaning. This was symbolic of the reaction of people generally to the spiritual message of Jesus.

John's account brings out clearly the connection between the work of Jesus and John the Baptist. Both practiced baptism in the Jordan. This similarity caused difficulties among John's disciples (Jn.

Sunshine lights up the Church of Jacob's Well at Sychar. When Jesus left Judea for Galilee early in his ministry, he traveled through Samaria and ministered to the woman at the well (Jn. 4), a site now covered by this church. (View to the NE.)

3:25), who were unable to grasp the preparatory character of John's work, and necessitated a repetition of John's denial that he was the Messiah. He was only a witness, and his testimony agreed with the self-testimony of Jesus himself.

When Jesus left Judea for Galilee to commence his ministry there, he passed through SAMARIA, and his experiences, recorded only by John, are a significant introduction to the synoptic account of the ministry (Jn. 4:1–45). Samaria had little in common with Jerusalem except for possessing its own central worship and maintaining some kind of messianic hope. The Jews and Samaritans had no personal dealings with each other, as John makes clear. All the more remarkable, therefore, was the Lord's interview with a Samaritan woman. It proves beyond doubt that he had no intention of being restricted by narrow Jewish nationalism. It shows furthermore that his approach to women differed from that of his Jewish contemporaries. His conversation with this woman revealed his extraordinary insight into human nature, and it has since become a pattern for personal evangelism.

The most striking feature about the whole incident is the self-revelation of Jesus. He acknowledged himself to be the Messiah (Jn. 4:26), in spite of the fact that he later showed a consistent refusal to permit his disciples to make this known. It appears that he took a different line with the Samaritans because their messianic hope differed from that of the Jews. It was not so closely tied to nationalistic aspirations and was therefore less open to serious misapprehensions. Moreover, the sequel to the conversation shows the spiritual character of the Lord's mission in the manifest joy that he had when people believed on him. The dialogue itself supports this view, since Jesus soon turns the conversation away from material to spiritual concerns, especially the spiritual nature of God.

E. The Galilean ministry. After the events in Samaria, Jesus returns to the place where water was turned into wine and, while there, performs another miracle, the healing of a royal official's son, who was in a different city, CAPERNAUM (Jn. 4:46–53). Although a similar incident is recorded in the synoptics later on in the ministry, several differences in detail suggest that the miracle related by John is distinct. Moreover, John points out specifically that this was the second of Jesus' signs in Galilee, as if he were attaching some importance to this fact. The healing of the official's son serves as a fitting prelude to the whole Galilean ministry, for Jesus had not yet become well known in Galilee for his miraculous works, and this fact heightens all the more the father's faith, which is specifically mentioned as a factor in the healing.

It has already been noted that the Galilean ministry may be divided into three periods, and these will be separately described. It should be observed, however, that although the general heading relates to Galilee, there must have been some activity in Jerusalem, if John's record is to be taken into account. Most of the time, however, Jesus worked and taught in Galilee.

1. The period up to the choosing of the Twelve. (a) *The initial call of disciples.* The choosing of the Twelve began in the specific calling of four men from their fishing, PETER and ANDREW, JAMES and JOHN (Matt. 4:18–22; Mk. 1:16–20; Lk. 5:1–11). From John's account one can see that these men had

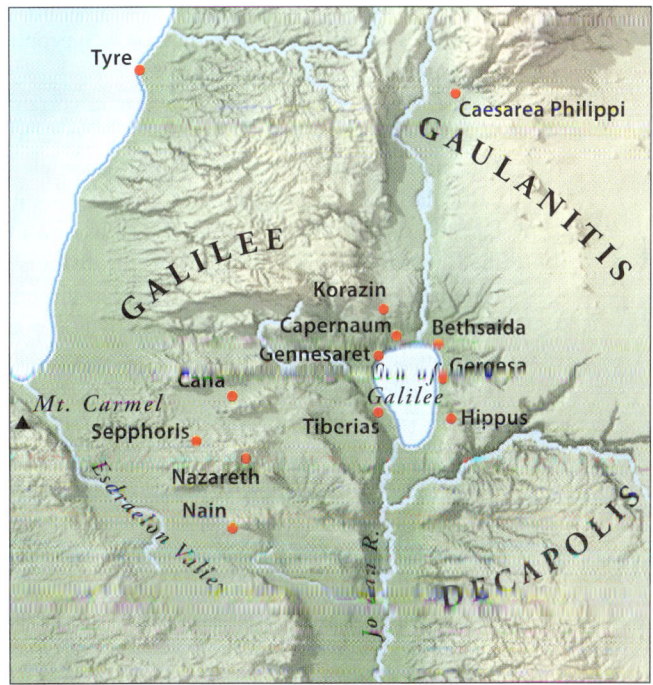

Jesus' ministry in Galilee.

earlier contact with Jesus, but now they are called to devote themselves more wholeheartedly to his work. In the process of time others were added, but it was not until the number had reached twelve that Jesus appointed them as an officially constituted body of apostles, which did not occur until the end of this period. Connected with the call of the first disciples is the incident of the miraculous catch of fish (Lk. 5:1–11), which is intended to emphasize the superior achievement of catching men. The spiritual is more excellent than the material.

It is impossible to be certain about the exact order of events in this period, and it is consequently better to group the main incidents into similar categories. With this in mind, the call of Levi will be mentioned first, although not occurring until later on in the period (Matt. 9:9–13; Mk. 2:13–17; Lk. 5:27–32). Levi, who became known as MATTHEW, is representative of a class of people greatly despised in the contemporary Jewish world. He was a TAX COLLECTOR, and since taxes were a sore point with the Jews, those who collected them became the targets for social contempt. No information is given about the grounds on which Jesus based his choice of men, but many of them seem to have been unlikely characters. It is one of the most illuminating studies to consider how he molded such people for his purpose.

b. *The Sermon on the Mount.* Another important aspect of the early ministry of Jesus was his preaching, and it is mainly Matthew who gives samples, particularly in the long discourse known as the SERMON ON THE MOUNT (Matt. 5–7). In view of the fact that Luke records much of this discourse material in isolated passages, many scholars dispute whether Matthew's material was delivered on one occasion. It is possible that Matthew is responsible for the collection of the material into a discourse, but this is by no means certain. He undoubtedly leads his readers to assume that one particular occasion was in mind. Moreover, it is reasonable to maintain that the Lord frequently repeated the same teaching, as was customary among Jewish rabbis, and in this case there is no basis for disputing the unity of the Sermon on the Mount. The content is more important, however, than this historical question. Since a separate section is devoted to a general summary of the teaching of Jesus, it will be necessary only to indicate the special characteristics of this important discourse.

The main emphasis is ethical. Jesus had in mind the establishment of his kingdom and the consequent need of new patterns of behavior. His own teaching is set forth as an advance on the teaching of MOSES. A wide variety of themes is covered, mostly of a social character, such as murder, divorce, retaliation, and attitudes toward one's enemies. There are, however, many sayings that deal with personal religious motives, such as prayer and fasting, self-deception, and varying reactions to the hearing of the Word. The BEATITUDES at the beginning of the discourse similarly encourage spiritual and moral values. Matthew records what the hearers thought of the sermon. They were astonished, and this may be regarded as typical during the early ministry. It was the authoritative nature of the teaching that so deeply impressed the hearers.

(c) *Healings and other miracles.* There were during this period many acts of healing, of which various samples are recorded. Matthew, particularly, groups the healing miracles (Matt. 8:1—9:8; cf. Mk. 1:40—2:12; Lk. 5:12–26). He places the following incidents in a sequence: the healing of the leper (Matt. 8:1–4), the centurion's servant (8:5–13), Peter's mother-in-law (8:14–15), the sick in the evening (8:16–17), the Gadarene demoniac (8:28–34), the palsied man (9:1–8), Jairus's daughter and the woman with a hemorrhage (9:18–26), two blind men (9:27–31), and the demoniac who was mute (9:32–34). Most of these healings appear also in Mark and Luke, but in a different order. Matthew's arrangement vividly emphasizes the nature of the healing ministry. Although not mentioned in every case, there is frequent reference to the FAITH of the people healed. In the case of the paralytic, the power of Jesus to forgive sins is linked with his power to heal (Matt. 9:2). This is a reminder that the spiritual ministry was of more concern to Jesus than the healing work. None of the Gospels presents him as a wonder-worker. The miracles of healing are related to bring out the element of compassion. The attention is focused on the human aspects and not on the extraordinary nature of the cure. There is no suggestion of magic, nor are there any incantations or formulas. Jesus is always master of the situation (see below the section on the miracles of Jesus).

Of special importance is the power of Jesus over evil spirits, for this is a marked feature of all stages of the ministry. The work of Jesus was set in an atmosphere of spiritual conflict. The examples quoted showing his power over demoniacs are to be regarded as illustrations of spiritual victories. See EXORCISM.

During this earlier period of the ministry, one miracle is recorded that affected the world of nature, namely, the stilling of the storm (Matt. 8:23–27; cf. Mk. 4:35–41; Lk. 8:22–25). It is placed earlier in Matthew than in the other synoptics. The focus of attention is once again not so much on the marvelous power of Jesus as on the lack of faith on the part of the disciples. Nonetheless, the element of marvel is not absent, as the miracle caused the disciples to discuss what kind of man he was that the wind and sea obeyed him (Matt. 8:27; Mk. 4:41; Lk. 8:25). Throughout the gospel story there is an element of mystery about the person of Jesus.

(d) *Popularity and criticism.* The evangelists are deeply interested in the impact Jesus made on various types of people. This is most marked in their comments on the early popularity of Jesus. The summary in Matt. 4:23–25 makes this clear—his fame spread throughout all Syria (cf. Mk. 1:28). This enthusiasm over his healing work was undoubtedly superficial. The real meaning of his message and the self-effacing spiritual character of his mission had not yet dawned upon the multitudes, nor were they capable of comprehending it. By way of contrast with this superficial popularity, the criticism of the Pharisees is brought out in equally clear fashion. Mark, in fact, preserves a sequence of incidents designed to show the increasing hostility of the scribes and Pharisees (Mk. 2:1–3:6). The culmination of this sequence shows the intensity of the hostility since the Pharisees joined forces with the Herodians, an association that rarely formed.

At a later stage of the ministry, Jesus makes some pointed criticisms of the Pharisees, mainly on the grounds of their hypocrisy (cf. Matt. 23). At this early stage, however, he presents them with a reasoned approach to provide them with the opportunity to respond. The stumbling-stone for them was the unorthodoxy of Jesus. In their eyes he was a lawbreaker in his attitude toward the SABBATH, while his social fellowship with tax collectors and sinners could only invite Pharisaic contempt. No doubt the Pharisees soon reacted to the popular opinion that Jesus taught and acted with authority, in contrast to the scribes (Matt. 7:29). They could not fail to see a very dangerous threat to their own grip upon the common people.

(e) *The choosing of the Twelve.* The naming of twelve specially chosen disciples and the description of their first mission is of such importance that all the Synoptic Gospels mention it. In both Matthew and Mark the commissioning is linked with authority over unclean spirits (Matt. 10:1; Mk. 3:13–19). In addition, Matthew mentions the power to heal, and Mark the command to preach. Luke separates the story of the choosing of the Twelve from the special purpose of the office of apostle (cf. Lk. 6:12–16; 9:1–2). The men whom Jesus chose were a representative group. They were not all drawn from the poorer classes, for the father of James and John possessed his own boat and employed servants (Mk. 1:20). Matthew as a tax collector would be well-to-do, although hated by his compatriots. Simon may have been an erstwhile revolutionary.

Such importance did Jesus attach to the mission of the Twelve that he gave them specific instructions that served not only for their immediate benefit on their first preaching tour, but also as a pattern for the subsequent missions of the Christian church. The charge to the Twelve is more fully recorded in Matthew than in the other Gospels (Matt. 10:5–42; cf. Lk. 9:1–6; and Mk. 6:7–13). Special emphasis is placed on material provisions, for Jesus advises that nothing unnecessary should be taken. The disciples are instructed how to proceed if any town or village receives them, and what to do if it does not. The advice is essentially practical. The message they are to proclaim is confined to an announcement of the nearness of the kingdom. They were not to imagine that all would warm to this message, for much hostility and persecution would await them.

The advice is obviously to prepare Jesus' disciples for future rather than immediate opposition and is well illustrated from the story of the early church. To fortify them they are reminded of the certainty of their heavenly Father's care over them.

The most startling prediction given to the Twelve was the certainty that the message of Jesus would result in serious division within households. He who had himself experienced the hostility of the Pharisees, even during this initial period, was in no doubt concerning the difficulties that would confront his disciples. Victory would not come except through enduring much for Christ's sake.

Some comment has already been made on the relationship between Jesus and John the Baptist, but Matthew and Luke include further sayings of Jesus on the subject, and these deserve notice. It has been seen that Jesus began by preaching what John had preached, but he soon went on to proclaim his unique message. John had already recognized and publicly announced Jesus to be greater than he, but it is not surprising that he became perplexed by later developments. When doubts arose, he sent messengers from his prison, where he had been incarcerated by Herod, to ascertain whether Jesus was prepared to confirm his messiahship (Matt. 11:2–6). Jesus not only sent an encouraging word back to John, but also commended him for his greatness in the hearing of the crowds.

2. The period up to the withdrawal of Jesus from northern Galilee. (a) *Sabbath controversies and healings.* It is convenient at this point to include the incident recorded only by John, when an impotent man was healed at the pool of BETHESDA. It is impossible to identify the feast during which the healing occurred (Jn. 5:1, though many assume it was the Passover) and equally impossible to know precisely where to place this incident within the synoptic framework. Its main significance is in the fact that the man's own attitude of faith is not specifically stated, although it is clearly implied by his ready response to the command from Jesus to take up his bed and walk. Since the miracle was performed on the Sabbath, the action again aroused the antagonism of the Jews, although in this case was added the further charge that Jesus made himself equal with God.

Another Sabbath controversy occurred when the disciples plucked ears of grain from a grainfield on the Sabbath (Matt. 12:1–8; Mk. 2:23–28; Lk. 6:1–5), an action which Pharisaic casuistry regarded as work and was therefore forbidden. This led to a specific claim by Jesus to be "Lord of the Sabbath" (Matt. 12:8), which placed him in a superior position to the scribes in the interpretation of the Law. Again the plot of the Pharisees to destroy Jesus is mentioned (12:14), after another healing on the Sabbath day.

During the course of his accounts of healing miracles, Matthew refers to the fulfillment of prophecy, citing a passage from the SERVANT OF THE LORD songs of ISAIAH (Matt. 12:15–21). This is an important aspect of his record of Jesus' ministry, but it is also seen to a lesser extent in all the Gospels. Luke records two outstanding miracles that occurred during this period, the healing of the centurion's servant at Capernaum (Lk. 7:1–10) and the raising of the widow's son at Nain (7:11–17). The first is remarkable for the faith of a non-Jew who was prepared to believe the authoritative word of Jesus, and the second for the effect it had upon the crowds, who glorified God (7:16).

An incident that shows the deep human understanding of Jesus is the anointing of his feet by a woman, well-known for her sinful character, in the house of a Pharisee (Lk. 7:36–50). Luke vividly tells the story of the woman's devotion and of the Pharisee's carping criticisms. By means of a parable Jesus shows Simon the Pharisee that the woman, in spite of her known character, had nevertheless outshone him in devotion. Such an incident is an acted parable of the effect of Jesus on the two representative groups, the religious and the nonreligious. Those who should have set an example in devotion dismally failed, while the underprivileged responded.

(b) *Division and attack.* Controversies were never far away in the ministry of Jesus, but one of the most pointed of these followed the exorcism of a devil (Matt. 12:22–29; Mk. 3:20–27; Lk. 11:14–22). The Pharisees attributed it to BEELZEBUB, prince of the devils, but Jesus points out how ludicrous it is to think of Satan casting out Satan. The power to cast out demons is by the Spirit of God. Never more vividly than this did the spiritual character of the conflict come to the fore. The tragedy was that the Pharisees with all their religious scrupulosity were near to committing the UNPARDONABLE SIN. Some of the scribes and Pharisees then pursued a different line against Jesus—the demand for a sign,

A path on the slopes just above the shore of the Sea of Galilee, illustrative of the setting for Jesus' parable of the sower.

which he emphatically rejected. He was so essentially different from the messianic concept of the Jews that it is not surprising that they required a sign to resolve their perplexity. But they were too blind to take notice of earlier signs, such as Jonah and Solomon. It was necessary now for Jesus to make clear his true relationship to his family, and he shows the development of a relationship which far transcends family ties (Matt. 12:46–50).

(c) *Samples of the teaching of Jesus.* The teaching of Jesus remained much the same as in the earlier period. Luke records many sayings parallel to those in the Sermon on the Mount, although in a different context. There is no doubt that Jesus frequently repeated the same sayings, and there is no need therefore to identify Luke's sermon with Matthew's. The common people who gladly listened to Jesus needed constant repetition of the teaching. Luke records some material common with Matthew, but his sermon is brief, and even in the common material shows a fair amount of variation in the wording. Acknowledgment of the fact that much of the teaching material was given on a number of occasions supports the contention that in some respects the teaching methods of the rabbis influenced the method of Jesus (cf. B. Gerhardsson, *Memory and Manuscript* [1961]). The uniqueness of Jesus' teaching material and method must, nevertheless, be fully acknowledged. He understood better than the rabbis the psychology of teaching.

Luke gives an interesting insight into one aspect of Jesus' life at this period. Not only was he accompanied by the Twelve, but also by a group of women, some of whom were wealthy enough to supply means of support for the company (Lk. 8:1–3).

Several parables of the kingdom were taught by Jesus in the course of his preaching tours. It is Matthew who shows a special interest in these and collects them into a group (Matt. 13). Since a discussion of the parabolic teaching of Jesus will be included below, it will be sufficient here to point out the significance of this method of teaching in this particular period of the ministry. Crowds were still flocking to hear Jesus, but the basic receptivity was varied. The parable of the sower (or more accurately the parable of the soils) was intended to show Jesus' recognition of this fact in his own ministry, and also illustrates what the disciples might expect. The choice of the parabolic method was itself intended to show that Jesus had a selective purpose in his teaching. Vivid stories would be most readily stored in the mind, but their significance would become plain only to those with a serious intention to discover their meaning. No doubt the disciples who received an interpretation of both the parable of the sower and the parable of the tares were puzzled by the thought that the teaching of Jesus would neither appeal to nor persuade all who heard it. There were many adverse influences to combat it. At the conclusion of the special parable section, Matthew includes a saying of Jesus that well illustrates his own approach to his hearers. A scribe "instructed about the kingdom of heaven is like the owner of a house who brings out of his storeroom new treasures as well as old" (13:52). Although there is much that is not new in the teaching of Jesus, there is much that is unique and this takes precedence over the old.

(d) *Unbelief at Nazareth.* Another incident in his own town of Nazareth occurred at this time. Although the synagogue congregation was astonished at the wisdom with which he taught, especially in view of his humble family connections, yet they were offended because of him and they disbelieved in him (Matt. 13:53–58; Mk. 6:1–6; cf. Lk. 4:16–30). Matthew records that because of this he could not perform many miracles, while Mark mentions that he healed only a "few sick people" (Mk. 6:5). Jesus' own comment on this sad state of affairs was to cite a proverb about a prophet never having honor in his own country. He was clearly not surprised at the limitations imposed on his activity through human unbelief.

(e) *The death of John the Baptist.* So far there has been little indication of the attitude of the civil authorities toward Jesus, but all the synoptics mention that Jesus' fame reached the ears of Herod Antipas (see HEROD V). It troubled Herod because rumors were spreading that John the Baptist, whom he had beheaded, was risen from the dead. It was for this reason that he desired to see Jesus. Both Matthew and Mark relate the circumstances of the beheading (Matt. 14:3–12; Mk. 6:17–29). It happened in response to a malicious request by Herod's wife (and former sister-in-law) named HERODIAS, at a drunken festival at which Herodias's own daughter danced. Both evangelists refer to Herod's dismay at the request for John the Baptist's head on a platter, but he had made his rash promise under oath and would not break the oath for fear of losing face with the courtiers. The whole sordid incident throws into stark relief the ignominious end of the noble forerunner of Jesus.

(f) *The feeding of the multitude.* When the apostles returned from their preaching mission, Jesus invited them to come apart from the crowds for a time. No doubt they had much to report and some solitary place would be more conducive for this than the midst of a bustling multitude. On this occasion solitude eluded Jesus and his disciples, who were seen crossing the Sea of Galilee by boat. As a result, a multitude gathered to welcome Jesus when his boat arrived at the shore, and this provided an opportunity for further extensive teaching and for a miraculous feeding of the multitude. This latter event was so remarkable that all four evangelists record it (Matt. 14:13–21; Mk. 6:30–44; Lk. 9:10–17; Jn. 6:1–15). Two of the evangelists (Matthew and Mark) mention the compassion of Jesus, which must be considered the prime motive for the miracle. Another feature of the incident is the way in which the disciples were challenged to provide food for all to eat, which they were clearly incapable of doing. All the evangelists draw attention to the smallness of the food supply available (five small loaves and two fishes) and all refer to the twelve basketsful that were left over. Mark's account is the most vivid, for he not only mentions the greenness of the grass, but also the size and arrangement of the companies into which the multitude was divided (Mk. 6:39–40). It is John, however, who brings out the significance of the event. The people who saw the miracle wanted to make Jesus king (Jn. 6:15), but their motives were wholly materialistic and political. So alien was this to

View from a boat traveling toward the eastern shore of the Sea of Galilee. Jesus showed his power over nature while calming a storm on this portion of the lake.

the purpose of Jesus that he was obliged to withdraw from the crowds.

A more important aspect of the incident, which John alone reveals, is the discourse of Jesus on the theme of the true bread from heaven (Jn. 6:26–58). The first part of the discourse probably was given immediately after the incident of Jesus walking on the water (see next section), in the open air, but the second part clearly was delivered in the synagogue (6:59). The dividing line may be the point at which John introduces the murmuring Jews into his narrative (6:41).

The type of discussion that John relates must have been typical of many dialogues. It shows Jesus always taking the initiative in turning attention to spiritual issues. The Jews wanted to satisfy their curiosity as to when Jesus had arrived on the far side of the sea, then they wanted to know what work they must do to accomplish God's work; and they requested a sign as a basis of belief, citing God's gift of manna in the wilderness. To each question Jesus gives a spiritual answer: to the first, an exhortation to seek food that endures; to the second, an exhortation to believe in God's messenger, Jesus; to the third, a reminder that the bread of God is sent from heaven, not by Moses but by God himself. This bread is then identified with Jesus himself. This latter theme is developed in the second part of the discourse, which shows the spiritual importance of the work Jesus came to do — to give his flesh for the life of the world (Jn. 6:51). Many of the disciples who followed Jesus found this type of teaching so perplexing and unpalatable that they withdrew from the company of Jesus. This prompted him to challenge the Twelve. He elicited an enthusiastic expression of faith from Peter and made a prediction of Judas's betrayal (6:66–71).

(g) *The walking on the water.* Reference must be made to the incident of Jesus' walking on the sea of Galilee, which is recorded by all the evangelists except Luke, immediately after the feeding of the multitudes (Matt. 14:22–33; Mk. 6:45–52; Jn. 6:16–21). Conditions at sea were adverse, but Jesus took command of the situation. The linking of these two miracles is not accidental, for both demonstrate power over the natural creation. In the midst of the storm Jesus brought a message of peace. The attempt of Peter to emulate Jesus by walking on the sea is related only by Matthew. It is wholly in character, as far as Peter was concerned. His impulsive action and inadequate faith are seen against the background of the Lord's mild rebuke of him. This was part of the training of the man who was to be so greatly used in the early history of the church.

(h) *The tradition of the elders.* The encounter between Jesus and some Jerusalem scribes and Pharisees (Matt. 15:1) shows the sharp dispute that arose between them over matters of TRADITION. The tradition of the elders was of paramount importance to the Jews. Since it ranked equal or even superior to the written law, it was invested with great authority. Over a long period of time its demands had increased in quantity and burdensomeness, so as to become oppressive for the serious adherents of Judaism. The system was open to abuse, and Matthew later records some severe criticism of it on the part of Jesus. It should be recognized that the intention of these traditions was to safeguard the law for the benefit of the populace. In the present case the Pharisees were bothered about the disciples' neglect of the ritual handwashing before meals, but Jesus points out their own failure to comply with a far more fundamental demand — the Mosaic commandment to honor parents, which was nullified by Pharisaic casuistry (Matt. 15:5). He tells the people in the presence of the Pharisees that defilement is a matter of thought and not of ritual.

3. The period up to the departure of Jesus for Jerusalem on his last journey. (a) *In a Gentile district.* After this criticism of current traditions, Jesus proceeded to the predominantly Gentile district around TYRE and SIDON. This visit is notable because of his treatment of the SYROPHOENICIAN woman, who came to him on behalf of her demon-possessed daughter (Matt. 15:21–28; Mk. 7:24–30). The disciples believed that a non-Jew had no right to make any demands upon Jesus, and the statement of Jesus himself that he was sent only to "the lost sheep of Israel" (Matt. 15:24) seemed to support this view. The saying is important for it shows the limits of the main field of his mission and the reason he did not go further afield. His response to the remarkable faith of this Gentile woman, who was prepared to beg for a dog's share if she did not qualify among the children, shows that the limits of the mission could be liberally interpreted where the need existed.

Matthew reports in summary form other healings after Jesus' return from Tyre and Sidon (Matt. 15:29–31), and records that the crowd glorified God. Mark tells of Jesus healing a man who was deaf and mute, and says that the people were astonished beyond measure (Mk. 7:31–37). His account includes a specific charge to silence for those who had witnessed the miracle, although the charge went unheeded (7:36). The question arises why Jesus issued such a command. Some have seen here evidence of the messianic secret theory that has already been noted, but there is no need to embrace that theory to find an explanation of the present charge. It was never the intention of Jesus to set himself up as a wonder-worker, and it was therefore essential that it should be known that he did not accept such a role.

(b) *The second feeding of a multitude.* It is at this point that Matthew and Mark relate the feeding of the 4,000 (Matt. 15:32–38; Mk. 8:1–9). There are many similarities with the former incident, and these have led some scholars to treat the passages as duplicate accounts of the same event. Yet there are significant differences that were obviously regarded by the evangelists as sufficient to demonstrate that there were two accounts, not one. There was a different number of people and a different supply of available food. There were also fewer baskets of fragments left over.

If it be maintained that the details became enhanced in process of transmission, it would be necessary to regard this account as more primitive than the account of the feeding of the 5,000. It is difficult to see why another 1,000 people were added and why two fewer loaves and less fish were introduced, and yet five more baskets of fragments were added. Moreover, both evangelists used a different word for "basket" in the present account as compared with the former story. Nevertheless, if two such events actually took place, some reason must be found for the inclusion of both of them in Matthew and Mark. They both must have considered the repetition of similar incidents of some importance. Both record the specific reference

This mosaic, on the floor of the Church of Loaves and Fishes, in Tabgha, Galilee, alludes to Jesus' feeding of the 5,000.

by Jesus to the two events (Matt. 16:9–10; Mk. 8:19–20). Even with the repetition the disciples had not learned their lesson, while the Pharisees were still seeking a sign from heaven. The two recorded incidents therefore emphasize not only the constantly remarkable power of Jesus, but also the obduracy of the observers who failed to interpret its message. As for the Pharisees' request for a heavenly sign, it is no wonder that this brought from Jesus a deep sigh (Mk. 8:12) and a flat rejection of any other sign than that of Jonah (Matt. 16:4). It was no doubt this incident which caused Jesus to warn the disciples about the leaven of the Pharisees and Sadducees, by which he meant their teaching (Matt. 16:5–12; Mk. 8:14–21).

(c) *Caesarea Philippi.* One may pass by the healing of the blind man at BETHSAIDA, which is notable mainly because it was performed in two stages (Mk. 8:22–26), and come to the highly important discussions at CAESAREA PHILIPPI (Matt. 16:13–28; Mk. 8:27–38; Lk. 9:18–27). Jesus posed the question, "Who do people say that I am?" Four general replies were given: John the Baptist, Elijah, Jeremiah, or one of the prophets. Peter's own conception, however, went much further. Matthew gives his testimony in its fullest form: "You are the Christ, the Son of the living God" (Matt. 16:16). Since it was from this point onward that Jesus began to concentrate on the training of the Twelve, this confession must have possessed special significance for him. All the synoptists say that Jesus charged his disciples to tell no one about this, which reveals his awareness of the difficulties people would have in recognizing his true character.

No reasons are given why Peter and, presumably, others were led to identify Jesus so confidently with the long-awaited Messiah. They had seen evidences of his power, but many others had witnessed the miracles and yet had not believed. Jesus himself reminded Peter that he had not come to this conclusion through any human agency, but by revelation from God the Father.

It is impossible to ascertain what content was conveyed by the title "Son of the living God," but Peter was clearly recognizing some claims to deity. What such a confession meant to Jesus may be inferred from the blessing that he immediately pronounced on Peter, and from his prediction about him. When Jesus said to Peter, "on this rock I will build my church" (Matt. 16:18), it was one of the only two recorded occasions when he used the word CHURCH (*ekklēsia* G1711; cf. 18:17).

It is impossible to discuss here the problems that have been raised concerning this statement, but the crux of the matter is the interpretation of the word *rock*. Is Peter himself intended, or is it his confession? In favor of the former is the play on Peter's name, and in favor of the latter is the teaching of other Scriptures that speak of Christ as the church's foundation. If the former is correct, it could only draw attention to the important place Peter would occupy in the coming church, and one may recall that it was through his preaching that both the first Jews and the first Gentiles became Christians (Acts 2 and 10). Nevertheless, a church that was to withstand the gates of hell, as Jesus predicted, would need a surer foundation than the unstable Peter. He was further given the promise of the keys of the kingdom, which carried with it the power to bind and loose. This statement must be understood in conjunction with the similar injunction in Matt. 18:18, which is addressed to all the disciples. It is fitting that when Jesus turned to the training of the Twelve he first concentrated on Peter, for it was this man who immediately afterward tried to rebuke him for predicting his death.

That Caesarea Philippi marks a turning point in the ministry of Jesus is clear from the fact that he at once began to share with his disciples something of the dreaded events which he knew lay ahead. It is significant that this first prediction of the passion was inseparably linked to the resurrection, as were the subsequent predictions. It was not easy for the disciples to grasp the need for Jesus to suffer, and it was still harder for them to understand the place of suffering in their own lives. Self-denial is no easy lesson to learn, and it was necessary for Jesus to begin the conditioning process at this stage of the ministry to allow opportunities for much more teaching in the same vein.

(d) *The Transfiguration*. The immediate sequence of events at this period is not in doubt, for all three synoptists agree on the order of events. The TRANSFIGURATION of Jesus follows the Caesarea confession, and this is followed by the healing of the epileptic boy, the second prediction of the passion, and the dispute about greatness (cf. Matt 17; Mk 9; Lk 9:28–48). In any account of the life of Jesus the transfiguration must assume an important place because of its revelation of the glory of Jesus in a unique manner. The fact that even this revelation was seen by only three of the disciples is also significant, for it shows the existence of an inner group within the Twelve. It is not at once apparent why Jesus did not invite others to accompany him, but the failure of the three to appreciate the meaning of the event is a significant indication of what would probably have been the reaction of the rest. In any case, Jesus was not to be transfigured before people as a public spectacle. Only enough witnesses were to be present to vouch for the reality of the experience.

The vision itself consisted of three stages. First, Jesus was changed so that not only his face but also his clothes radiated an extraordinary light, and there appeared with him MOSES and ELIJAH. Second, Peter makes his perfectly understandable, but thoroughly inappropriate, suggestion that some kind of dwelling booths should be constructed for the transfigured Christ and his two heavenly companions. Third, a voice from the cloud urged them to concentrate on hearing Jesus because he is the beloved Son in whom God delights. The reaction of awe on the part of the disciples marks the climax of the occasion, after which Jesus resumes his normal appearance.

In assessing the place of this event in the mission of Jesus various factors must be borne in mind. It showed the true nature of Jesus, and by way of contrast helps mankind to understand more fully the meaning of his humiliation through the incarnation and subsequent passion. This was no ordinary man. He was truly the Son of the living God, as Peter had just previously confessed. The confession, if but dimly understood when made, assumed a glorious realization for Peter as he gazed at the transfigured Christ. Neither for Peter nor for the other two did that transient glimpse of the glories of Jesus allay the appalling doubts, and, in the case of Peter, prevent the emphatic denials that were to mark their reactions to the passion of Jesus. Their abiding grasp of the glories of Jesus was not to come this way, but by the hard experiences of his suffering leading to his resurrection.

Another factor of this event to bear in mind is the part played in it by Moses and Elijah. It is generally supposed that they represent the Law and the Prophets, to which Jesus is seen to be superior. Luke tells that they talked about the coming death of Jesus at Jerusalem, and this must have been designed to add supernatural sanction to the prediction of his death that Jesus had made to his disciples just prior to the transfiguration. It was not intended to be generally understood until after the resurrection, for Jesus forbids the three disciples to tell any others until then (Matt. 17:9).

The sight of Elijah in the vision raised a problem in their minds. They recalled the scribal teaching about Elijah as the forerunner of the Messiah. Perhaps they wondered why they had not seen him before, since it had now dawned upon them that Jesus was the Messiah. This opened the way for Jesus to make clear to them that John the Baptist had fulfilled the role of Elijah.

(e) *More miracles.* At the foot of the mountain another problem confronted the rest of the disciples (Matt. 17:14–20; Mk. 9:14–29; Lk. 9:37–43). In the absence of the Master they were clearly impotent to deal with an abnormality such as an epileptic demoniac. Jesus was deeply affected by their lack of faith. The incident showed something of the caliber of the men whom Jesus was training for the future ministry of the church. They had yet to learn how to deal with the impossible (Matt. 17:21; cf. Mk. 9:23). This was a lesson that had to be repeated on other occasions (cf. Matt. 21:21; Mk. 11:22; Lk. 17:6). The present incident gives an example of a direct confrontation between the power of Jesus and the power of the devil, an illustration of Christ's constant struggle, which had earlier found its classic expression in the temptation in the wilderness.

The second prediction by Jesus of his passion and resurrection is a natural sequel to his transfiguration (Matt. 17:22–23; Mk. 9:30–32; Lk. 9:43–45). All the synoptic writers mention the disciples' reactions. Matthew says they were distressed (Matt. 17:23), while Mark and Luke mention their lack of understanding and their hesitancy to ask Jesus for an explanation (Mk. 9:32; Lk. 9:45). He found no support for his coming trials, even from his closest disciples. This was the temper of mind that caused them all finally to forsake him during the passion.

There are two more events that throw light on the approach of Jesus during this period. Matthew records the occasion when Peter was asked whether his master paid the temple tax, and he answered in the affirmative. The incident led Jesus to point out to him that only subjects of kings, not sons, are obliged to pay taxes (Matt. 17:24–27). Even in the matter of the temple tax Jesus desired that no offense should be given, and he instructed Peter to pay the tax for himself and for Jesus from a shekel to be found in the mouth of a fish. Many have found difficulties about this story on the grounds of the strange character of the miracle and the fact that it was performed for Jesus' own needs. Some seek a solution by attributing the story to less reliable tradition and claim it as an example of embel-

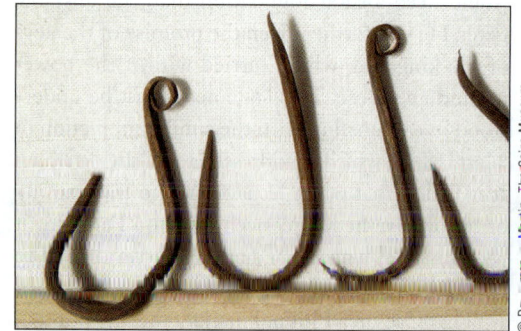

Collection of ancient fish hooks. When questioned about the temple tax, Jesus directed Peter to go fishing, and Peter paid the tax with a coin taken from the mouth of a fish.

lishment of the miraculous that took place in the tradition. The evidence does not require such a theory. The miracle is essentially of supernatural knowledge rather than a suspension of the laws of nature. It is certainly strange and indeed unexpected, but these are not sufficient factors to disprove its authenticity.

(t) *More sayings of Jesus.* Of the sayings of this period the most notable is Jesus' answer to the disciples when they were disputing about who is the greatest in the kingdom of heaven. He used a small child as an object lesson and taught by this means that HUMILITY is of the greatest importance in his kingdom (Matt. 18:1–4). In the process of training the Twelve, Jesus imparted to them a totally new code of values. They needed to learn that greatness lies along the path of service. The incident provided an occasion for Jesus to warn the disciples about causing offense to others and to give some drastic advice for dealing with the source of the offense (Matt. 18:6–9; Mk. 9:42–48).

Matthew includes a striking parable to illustrate the need for FORGIVENESS (Matt. 18:23–35). It concerned two servants of a king. One owed him a very large sum that he was unable to pay. He received full remission of the debt because of the king's mercy. The same servant was himself a creditor to the other servant who owed him a paltry sum compared with his own debt, but he treated him without mercy. The king's wrath was turned against the servant whom he had forgiven. From this story Jesus brings out the need for all to exercise forgiveness. It was told in answer to Peter's query concerning how many times a brother should be forgiven. In the kingdom of heaven there is no limit either to the number of times or to the size of the offense involved. Such forgiveness demands largesse of heart.

F. The closing period of the ministry. This is the most difficult period in which to arrange the narrative in any certain sequence either chronologically or geographically. Matthew and Mark are very brief, while Luke collects into a journey narrative a great deal of material which appears to be loosely linked.

1. Moving toward Jerusalem. For Luke there is a sense of an inevitable movement of Jesus toward Jerusalem, subsequent to the two specific predictions of the passion. Nevertheless, it cannot be denied that the impression of movement is slight. In one section (Lk. 9:51—18:31), the references to Jerusalem are perplexing: 9:51 indicates that Jesus set his face toward Jerusalem; 10:38 shows him in the village of Mary and Martha (Bethany); 17:11 shows him passing along between Samaria and Galilee on his way to Jerusalem; 18:31 records his declared intention to go up to Jerusalem; 18:35 and 19:1 shows him in the region of Jericho; finally, 19:28 tells of his final movement toward Jerusalem and leads to the record of his entry into the city.

It is difficult to fit all these references to Jerusalem into the same visit. Indeed, it is simpler to find suitable occasions for the Johannine material (Jn. 7–10) if at least two distinct visits to Jerusalem are postulated. Even then no satisfactory chronological arrangement can be made. It may be questioned whether any advantage would accrue from such an arrangement. It is better to retain as far as possible the impressions given by Luke and to deal separately with the additional material belonging to the Jerusalem ministry related by John. For convenience, therefore, the travel narrative of Luke will be divided at the end of Lk. 13 (the lament over Jerusalem) in order to record the events and discourses of Jn. 7–10. It should be noted that whereas the greater part of the material in this section of Luke is peculiar to him, there is much that is paralleled in other contexts in Matthew and there are a few sections that are shared by all three synoptists. In the following brief survey emphasis will fall on Luke's special contribution.

(a) *From Galilee to Bethany.* In none of the other Gospels is Jesus' own dramatic awareness of the nearness of the climax brought out as vividly as it is in Luke's brief comment on the commencement of the final journey (Lk. 9:51). The resoluteness with which Jesus faces Jerusalem is specifically marked. The first event on the journey occurred when he was about to pass through a Samaritan village (9:51–56). The direction of his travel roused the opposition of the inhabitants. The desire of James and John to wreak vengeance by means of heavenly fire is remarkable for its naive incongruity. It was not in their power to do what they suggested, and it was utterly alien to the spirit of Jesus. His path to Jerusalem was not to be strewn with burned villages as emblems of anger, but with many instances of patient forbearance toward those who had little understanding of the burden of his mission. His rebuke of the suggestion could hardly have been otherwise.

Some mission activity must nonetheless be organized. First, the disciples needed instruction about what type of people were suitable to be followers of Christ, and Luke records Jesus' dealing with three typical examples (Lk. 9:57–62). The main characteristics are a willingness to bear hardship and a persistence that would never look back. Even the apostles forsook him during the passion and would certainly not have been fit for the kingdom apart from the restoring grace of God. These rigorous demands form the prelude to the sending out of the SEVENTY DISCIPLES (10:1–16 KJV; NIV, "seventy-two"). There are strong similarities between the mission charge to the Seventy and the one given to the Twelve. Luke makes clear that the main purpose of the mission of the Seventy was to prepare the way in the places where Jesus was intending to visit. They were to proclaim the nearness of the kingdom (10:9). They were in fact ambassadors for Jesus himself (cf. 10:16). In his commission Jesus adds a special denunciation of Korazin, Bethsaida, and Capernaum, in all of which towns the spiritual significance of his mighty works had been utterly lost. No doubt this reflection of his own experience was intended to prepare the disciples for similar negative responses to their ministry.

The mission of the Seventy was presumably of short duration, for Luke tells of their return with joy soon afterward. It was their power over demons that especially elated them, but Jesus has to warn them to get their priorities right: God's estimate of them is of greater moment than their authority over demons (Lk. 10:17–20). The immaturity and yet the genuineness of these men must have particularly struck Jesus at this time, for he offered a prayer of thanksgiving that revelation comes not through a person's own understanding, but by the sovereign act of God (10:21–22). As compared with others, the disciples were in a particularly privileged position (10:23–24).

Unlike the Matthean parables, the Lukan parables are not generally collected into groups, but they have as their setting some incident that gives them their immediate purpose. The parable of the good Samaritan is an admirable illustration of this feature (Lk. 10:25–37). A Jewish lawyer's dialogue with Jesus concerning eternal life draws out the parable that is intended to show the practical application of what the lawyer already knew theoretically. It was one thing to pronounce love to one's neighbor as part of the divine requirement for the inheriting of eternal life; it was quite another to recognize that the term *neighbor* was so extensive that it even included Samaritans. In view of the constant animosity that existed between the Jews and Samaritans, the lawyer's astonishment at Jesus' interpretation of what being a good neighbor is can well be imagined. Moreover, the parable itself conveys more than an example. It illustrates vividly the basic principle of compassion, which was one of the most characteristic features in the life of Jesus.

By this time Jesus had arrived at Bethany, near Jerusalem (Lk. 10:38–42). There is no way of knowing whether this was the first time that Jesus had visited the home of MARY and MARTHA. Luke's interest in the story is to show the quite different reactions of the two sisters, one revealing her devotion to Jesus by practical domestic chores, the other listening to his teaching. His commendation of the latter emphasizes the aspect of his mission that was uppermost in his mind at the time.

(b) *Some teaching on prayer*. The disciples must often have watched Jesus praying, and on one occasion they asked him to teach them to pray. He gave them a pattern prayer similar to the one in the Sermon on the Mount, only more brief (Lk. 11:2–4). To give them further guidance he told a parable about a persistent man who begged food from his friend at midnight and who, because of his persistence, received what he needed (11:5–8). This story led to Jesus' comprehensive assurances regarding PRAYER. The heavenly Father may be relied upon to be infinitely more considerate than human fathers, who with all their limitations would not mock their own children's earnest requests. Again, Jesus was himself the finest example of his own teaching, for he lived in constant dependence on his Father.

(c) *More teaching by parables*. In the remaining section of Luke, where much of the material is peculiar to him, the sequence appears to be governed by alternating passages dealing with the disciples and the Pharisees. It is evidently Luke's purpose to illustrate by this means the different approach of Jesus to the two groups. It will be convenient to split Luke's material at Lk. 13:35.

In response to a question about inheritance from one of the crowd surrounding Jesus at the time, he told the parable of the rich fool (Lk. 12:13–21). The inheritance this rich man had stored up so laboriously was never enjoyed because of his death. This led Jesus to add a general application of the parable to warn all who have a wrong concept of riches. Following this, Luke includes a collection of sayings reminiscent of the teaching in the Sermon on the Mount. Next he relates the incident in which Pilate killed some Galileans and mixed their blood with sacrifices, and after that the calamity of the people killed by the fall of the tower of Siloam upon them (13:1–5). Such disasters obviously raise problems, but it is significant that Jesus does not give a theological or philosophical discussion of the problems involved. He used the incidents as a challenge to his hearers to repent. This challenge is strengthened by means of a parable about a fig tree that was producing no fruit and for which the vinedresser pleads that it be given one more chance with adequate watering and fertilizing (13:6–9). The parable is not applied by Jesus, but its application is clear enough. A real change of life should be evident by the fruit produced, but without such fruit the tree itself is useless.

(d) *Encounters with Pharisees.* In the next section Pharisees are mainly involved, although not exclusively. It was the ruler of a synagogue who took exception to Jesus' action when, on the Sabbath day, he healed an infirm woman whose illness was of long standing (Lk. 13:10–17). Jesus' answer was strongly worded. He condemned the hypocrisy of his opponents, who would not hesitate to care for their domestic animals on the Sabbath. It is with some relish that Luke records that his adversaries were put to shame, while the people generally rejoiced.

While Jesus was again on his way toward Jerusalem, he was accosted by some Pharisees who advised him to flee from Herod Antipas (Lk. 13:31–33). These Pharisees had reckoned without taking into account the fixed purpose of Jesus, which was not to be thwarted by a man like Herod, whom Jesus described as "that fox." His destiny was, in fact, in the hands of God, not Herod. It is directly subsequent to this that Luke includes the lament over Jerusalem which Matthew gives later (cf. Matt. 23:37–39). Jesus reveals both tenderness and rebuke in this lament, as he uses the vivid imagery of a hen gathering her chickens under her wings. Since he said, "How often would I have gathered your children," it seems to point to more visits to Jerusalem than the synoptists record.

(e) *Jesus at two Jewish feasts.* Luke's story will be left at this point to consider John's account of the events that took place at the Feasts of Tabernacles and Dedication, both held at Jerusalem. John recounts that Jesus was in Galilee just before the Feast of Tabernacles (Jn. 7:2). His family urged him to go to the feast for its prestige value, but they did not believe in him and clearly misunderstood the real nature of his mission. Jesus made clear that his time had not yet come and any open demonstration to the world would have been contrary to God's timing. Throughout, Jesus was deeply conscious of working according to a divine timetable. Although he specifically avoided any public demonstration, he nevertheless went to the feast privately after his brothers had gone on ahead.

Many were looking for him at the feast. People were privately expressing diverse opinions about him. When he finally did show himself, it was without ostentation, in the role of a teacher. Indeed, his skill in that role caused the Jews to marvel. This led Jesus to make some comments about the theme of authority (Jn. 7:14–29). His own authority was from the One who sent him, in contrast to Moses whose teaching they did not keep. The Jews raised the question of origins and dismissed any possibility of Jesus being the Messiah on the grounds that his parentage and origin were known. Jesus repeated that he came from the One who sent him.

Teaching of this sort among the people prompted the Pharisees to take action to arrest Jesus. Officers were commissioned to do this (Jn. 7:32). They overheard Jesus having a discussion with the Jews over his future destiny, which completely baffled his audience (7:33–36). They thought he might be referring to the dispersion. Still the officers took no action when on the last day of the feast Jesus made a public announcement about the gift of the Spirit which he would give to his disciples (7:37–39). He took advantage of the water ceremonial performed at the feast to illustrate a spiritual truth. John records more specific teaching about the HOLY SPIRIT than any of the other evangelists. The statement in the present context is important because it makes clear that the gift of the Spirit depends on and consequently follows the glorifying of Jesus.

Such teaching as this only further baffled the hearers and caused a dispute as to whether or not Jesus could possibly be the Christ. His Galilean connections caused difficulties (Jn. 7:41). The same problem was raised again, when the Pharisees discussed the matter at the highest level following the return of their officers without arresting Jesus. They had been deeply impressed by his teaching (7:46). At the council the attitude of Nicodemus is interesting in the light of his earlier interview with Jesus. He issues a mild rebuke to those who wish to condemn him without a hearing. In this incident the attitude of the Pharisees fully agrees with that recorded in the synoptics.

There followed further discussions with the Jews, mainly about the testimony of Jesus to himself (Jn. 8:12–18). When he claimed to be the light of the world, the Pharisees asserted that self-testimony of this kind cannot be true. The whole dispute focuses attention on the difficulties that confronted Jesus in expressing concepts which were foreign to the way of thinking of the religious leaders of his day. It was unintelligible to them when Jesus claimed the testimony of the Father in support of him. To them the Father was known only through the law, not through Jesus. He had to remind them that the nature of his authority would be understood only when the Son of Man had been lifted up (8:28).

The conversation next turns to ABRAHAM and the relation of the Pharisees to him (Jn. 8:39–40). When Jesus spoke of freedom, even the Jews who had believed in him protested. The promise of freedom implies the absence of it and no son of Abraham could ever conceive of himself as a slave. It is not surprising that the discussion became rather bitter, with the Jews actually maintaining that Jesus was demon-possessed (8:48). This incident shows Jesus confronted with the national pride of the Jewish people in their connection with Abraham, but he points out that racial connections need to be supported by deeds worthy of Abraham. The inconsistency of the position of his accusers led Jesus to the astonishing charge that they were of their father the devil (8:44).

The strength of the conflict in which Jesus was engaged is vividly seen. The accusers still cannot get away from the Abraham theme, for they challenge Jesus to say whether he is greater than Abraham (Jn. 8:53), and again he appeals to the testimony of the Father. He even maintains that Abraham rejoiced to see his day (8:56), and that he was in existence before Abraham. The immediate reaction of the Jews is not left to imagination. John concisely reports that they took up stones to stone him, but that Jesus hid himself from them.

John's account of the healing by Jesus of a man born blind and the subsequent encounter of the man with the Pharisees is dramatically told (Jn. 9). There are several features in this incident that call for special comment. The disciples were bothered about the explanation of the blind man's calamity, but Jesus does not offer any assistance in answering the theological problem. He is concerned about what will bring most glory to God. Moreover, he makes clear that his proposed action is inextricably bound up with his mission as the light of the world. The application of the mission is twofold, for not only was the man's physical sight restored by Jesus, but through this event his spiritual perception was also sharpened.

John traces the growth of the man's faith as he disputes with the Pharisees. Every conceivable reason was advanced for disbelieving the reality of the miracle, but the man himself asserted his own personal experience, which could not be disputed. As a result of his bold testimony, he was cast out of the synagogue. Knowledge of his expulsion having come to Jesus, he sought out the man in order to challenge him regarding his faith. The confession this drew from the man forms the climax of the story. With restored physical sight and awakened spiritual insight, he contrasts strongly with the Pharisees who constantly demonstrated their blindness, although they were not aware of it.

Following this incident, John records further teaching of Jesus concerning himself, this time under the imagery of a shepherd (Jn. 10). The illustration from the sheepfold would have been

Shepherd walking up a hill in Palestine, leading a flock of sheep grazing on the hillside. Jesus describes the relationship between himself and his followers by using the metaphor of the shepherd and his sheep.

familiar to his hearers. The shepherd's care to protect the sheep, the sharp distinction between the real shepherd and the man hired to do the job who had no interest in the welfare of the sheep, the intimate relationship between the shepherd and each individual sheep, and the picture of the shepherd leading out his flock to pasture would all have been well-known features of the contemporary pastoral scene. But they did not understand the implications of what Jesus was illustrating (10:6). Because of this, Jesus adds some further comments, the most important of which is that the good Shepherd lays down his life for the sheep (10:11, 15). The voluntary character of this act is particularly stressed (10:18). Another important factor is that Jesus distinguishes between folds and flocks. Not all belong to the same fold or sheep pen, but all belong to the same flock (10:16). This seems to be a pointed reminder that the Jews were not the only group of people with a claim upon the good Shepherd's care. Once again the teaching of Jesus evoked the charge of demon possession from some of the Jews, but others were not convinced of this in view of the character of the sayings and the miraculous healing of the blind man.

Similar teaching was given by Jesus at the Feast of Dedication held in winter time. Some of the Jews wanted Jesus to state plainly whether or not he was the Messiah, and Jesus rebuked them for not believing. The reason for their unbelief, he said, was that they were not part of his sheep (Jn. 10:26). The security of Christ's sheep is nothing less than the security of the good Shepherd's hand. On this occasion the opposition to him was more violent. They took up stones to kill him. In spite of the ugliness of the situation, Jesus shows himself in command by attempting to reason with the Jews. His appeal to them was based on Scripture, which, he says, cannot be broken (10:35). Significantly, Jesus urges them to believe his works if they cannot believe his words. Once again they tried without success to arrest him (10:39).

At this point Jesus goes again to TRANSJORDAN (Jn. 10:40); this will be a convenient place to return to Luke's travel narrative, which is also much concerned with Jesus' clash with Pharisees.

(f) *Jesus dines with Pharisees.* It must often have happened that Jesus was offered hospitality in a home, though no doubt infrequently at the home of a Pharisee. We may be grateful to Luke for recording a sequence of events and discussions that occurred during one such meal (Lk. 14:1–24). Lawyers and Pharisees were on the watch to see what Jesus would do, since it was the Sabbath. They were anticipating that he might contravene the Jewish law. He knew what was in their minds, for before healing a man with dropsy he addressed his observers with a question about the lawfulness of healing on the Sabbath day. No answer was given—a silent testimony to their embarrassment.

Luke next records a parable especially designed for the guests of the dinner (Lk. 14:7–14). Jesus had noted their eagerness to choose the chief seats and reminded them that it was humble people who would be exalted. This led to an exhortation urging hospitality for poor and unfortunate people, which reflects the social attitude of Jesus. His deep compassion was in marked contrast to the Pharisaic quibbles over Sabbath procedure, to the detriment of individual welfare.

One of the Pharisees ventured to draw attention to the blessedness of eating bread in the kingdom (Lk. 14:15), but again Jesus detected a misunderstanding. He told another parable, one about some people who made excuses when invited to a banquet. The excuses appeared legitimate enough, but they showed a discourteous attitude to the hosts. The point of the story is seen in the sequel. The social outcasts were to be invited instead, a fact that adds further emphasis to the social consciousness of Jesus. In this he differed strongly from most of the Pharisees.

(g) *Address to the multitudes.* Jesus was once more followed by great multitudes and turned to address them on the subject of the cost of discipleship (Lk. 14:25–35). This in itself was not a new theme, for it had been mentioned before, just after the confession at Caesarea Philippi (cf. 9:23). Here, however, it is elaborated. Discipleship involves some testing of priorities. Jesus speaks of the need for hating one's own family connections, but the idea of hating in this context must be regarded as relative. It is a question of wholehearted committal to the cause of Christ. Jesus illustrates his meaning by saying that no one puts in a foundation without estimating the cost of the whole house, or goes to war against a well-organized and powerful enemy without weighing the possibilities of carrying the campaign through to success. That is simple human prudence.

The same principle of forethought should apply to Christian discipleship. It demands wholehearted renunciation, and those not willing for so great a cost would be well advised to make no start. Disciples who begin and then lose their effectiveness are like salt that has lost its taste and hence becomes good for nothing. In this simile Jesus was using a Jewish proverb.

(h) *Further parables for the Pharisees.* Pharisaism had no message for sinners and little sympathy for those who were concerned about them. In their eyes sinners and tax collectors were outcasts of society. No wonder, therefore, that they regarded with contempt anyone who actually sat down to a meal with them. It was common knowledge that Jesus shared their hospitality, and when the Pharisees and scribes saw that Jesus had so large a following among these outcasts, they murmured against him in his hearing.

This response brought from Jesus a sequence of three parables to illustrate God's attitude toward those who were being officially treated as lost and for whom Pharisaism held out no hope (Lk. 15). These parables are essentially parables of restoration. A shepherd restores his lost sheep to the fold, a woman restores a lost coin to her treasure store, and a father restores a wayward son to the family circle. In all of the parables the element of JOY is emphasized; in the first two, there is joy in heaven over restored sinners; in the third, joy is an expression of the father's feelings when his son returns.

The application of the parables to the Pharisees is clear enough. They did not even desire the restoration of sinners, let alone show any inclination to rejoice over the possibility. There is no doubt that their murmuring formed the setting for the parables and that it finds a distinctive echo in the attitude of the elder brother in the third parable, who objected to the father's rejoicing because his brother had lived so utterly irresponsibly. In a way reminiscent of some Pharisees, this elder brother was more concerned about his own loyal achievements than about the miserable state of his brother, and more anxious to condemn than to forgive.

The vividness of the parables in their portrayal of human sentiments throws further light on the human insight and sympathy of Jesus. He was ever more concerned with the uplifting of human lives than with those who considered themselves superior.

(i) *Teaching for the disciples.* The next brief section (Lk. 16:1–13) is addressed to the disciples (understood in the widest sense of a group of generally interested people), and takes the form of a parable with comments upon it. It was a story about an unjust steward who had wasted his master's pos sessions and had been informed that as a consequence he would lose his job. He makes provision for the emergency by giving considerable discounts to those who owed money to his master; his purpose was to win their friendship, which would stand him in good stead for the future. The action itself appears dishonest, but the master recognized the man's prudence. Presumably the steward, until actually dismissed, had powers to remit portions of debts, and the master did not condemn him on this account. The parable, therefore, illustrates prudence for selfish ends, without regard for moral principles.

Jesus recommends the disciples to make friends by means of unrighteous MAMMON. Does this mean that Jesus is condoning an unprincipled approach? It may at first sight appear so, but it must be kept in mind that the details of the parable should not be pressed. The major purpose is to urge greater wisdom on the part of disciples than was evident among unprincipled men. On purely materialistic principles, unrighteous mammon is a person's only means of security.

Jesus proceeded to contrast true riches with this unrighteous mammon. Faithfulness in using the one is the test for the using of the other. Unrighteous mammon is therefore to be regarded as no more than a means to an end. No one can serve both mammon and God. This section of the teaching of Jesus illuminates his own attitude toward materialistic things. He did not ignore their usefulness, but demanded their subservience to God.

(j) *Another clash with the Pharisees.* The preceding parable fell on some Pharisaic ears and caused scoffing at Jesus' attitude to money (Lk. 16:14). Jesus not only insisted that God's judgments are based on knowledge of the heart, and not on outward appearances, but also told a parable to show how unreliable a guide material wealth can be (16:19–31). A contrast is made between a poor man who was afflicted with disease and a rich man at whose gate the poor man had sat and begged (see LAZARUS AND DIVES). The rich man went to HADES, and the poor man to ABRAHAM'S BOSOM, with a fixed chasm between them. There follows a dialogue between the rich man and Abraham, with whom he pleads in vain for some relief. Abraham says that even if it were possible for Lazarus to return to earth to warn the rich man's relatives, he would not be believed any more than Moses, whose teaching they already possessed but did not heed. The Pharisees, with their love of money (v. 14), would see the point of the challenge. The rich man's plight was not because he was rich, but because of his failure to use his riches to alleviate the needs of others, while indulging in luxuries for himself.

(k) *The apostles receive teaching about service.* Jesus now appeals to common procedure in the employment of servants (Lk. 17:5–11). If a servant's job is to do both agricultural and domestic work, he would not expect to be thanked if his master called him in from the field and asked him to serve him at table. He would only be performing his duty. In the same way, no one can ever say that he has done more than his duty to God, for even after doing all that is commanded of him, he has done only what is his duty. If this teaching was overheard by the Pharisees, they must have been astonished at such a statement. The idea of reward loomed large in their system and they believed that merit could be stored up in heaven. Jesus' teaching was diametrically opposed to theirs.

(l) *The healing of the lepers.* Luke again draws attention to the fact that Jesus was approaching Jerusalem and then introduces an event that happened in the vicinity of Samaria (Lk. 17:11–19). Ten lepers begging for mercy met Jesus, who com-

The Chamber of the Lepers is on the lower right of this model of the 1st-cent. temple (view to the S). After healing the ten lepers in Samaria, Jesus directed them to show themselves to the priests.

manded them to show themselves to the priests; and as they went they were healed. They must have acted in faith that healing would be given. This was not the main feature of the incident, for when they discovered that they were healed, only one returned to give thanks to Jesus, and he was a Samaritan. Jesus particularly pointed out the fact that only a foreigner had returned (17:18). The whole incident shows not only the compassion of Jesus but also the universal scope of his mission. The story is probably intended to illustrate the ingratitude that was characteristic of the Jewish nation in response to the merciful acts of God.

(m) *Sayings about the kingdom and about the future.* A question put by the Pharisees about the kingdom drew from Jesus a statement that the kingdom was in their midst or was within them (17:20–21). This would directly counteract any materialistic concept of the kingdom as it was currently held among the Jews. Luke then records some teaching of Jesus addressed to the disciples (17:22–37) on the subject of the days of the Son of Man. There would be false claims that these days were near, and of these they must beware. To give them indication of the timing of those days would be as impossible as tracking lightning across the sky. Before they can come, however, the Son of Man must first be rejected. The consciousness of the nearness of that event must have been strong in the mind of Jesus. There are, moreover, certain OT events from the times of NOAH and LOT that serve as a pattern of the times preceding the coming of the Messiah. In both cases the masses of people were totally unprepared for the divine judgment that came to them. In view of this, Jesus warns about the sharp division among men which the coming of the Son of Man will create.

(n) *Two parables about prayer.* Luke includes two parables, presumably addressed to the disciples, which possess certain features in common and which deal with different aspects of prayer (Lk. 18:1–18). The first, the parable of the unjust judge, commends constancy in prayer, and the second, the parable of the Pharisee and the tax collector, commends humility. The first provides an example of unrighteousness, the second of self-righteousness. In the first parable the judge is portrayed in the worst possible light, as a man who had no thought of God and no respect for man. The impression is at once created that justice is impossible from such a man, and this impression is deepened by the description of the plaintiff as a poor widow who had no one to protect her against an adversary. The judge gave in, not because he cared for justice, but because of the continual requests of the widow: to have refused would have caused him more embarrassment than to yield. The focus of the parable is on the power of constant petition, not on the character of the judge. When Jesus applies the parable he argues from the lesser to the greater. What a rascally unrighteous man will do is nothing compared with what may be expected from a righteous God. Jesus leads up to an exhortation to his hearers that such constancy of faith, as was exemplified by the persistent widow, might be found when he returns.

The other parable presents in strong contrast the attitude of a self-righteous Pharisee and the attitude of a man whom the Pharisees despised—a tax collector. Both are represented as praying in the temple, but the Pharisee is more conscious of himself and of his own superiority over others than he is of God. Consequently, his prayer is regarded as ineffective. The tax collector, overwhelmed with a deep sense of his own need, can do no more than cry to God for mercy. The egotism of the Pharisee may have been heightened to emphasize the contrast between these two men, but there is evidence to prove that a sense of self-achievement was an accepted characteristic among some Pharisees. No Pharisee would readily have admitted that his achievements were useless in his approach to God, for his whole religious life centered around what he himself could do in the pursuit of piety. How very distasteful such attitudes must have been to Jesus is suggested by his warm commendation of the opposite quality, humility.

At this point Luke returns to material that is shared by the other Synoptic Gospels, and these two parables may be said to terminate his special travel narrative. Before considering the final journey to Jerusalem, it will be necessary to include the account of the raising of LAZARUS and to consider the consequences.

(o) *The raising of Lazarus.* This is unquestionably the most astonishing of all the miracles performed by Jesus. It is the climax of John's "book of signs" and sets out the humanity as well as the deity of Jesus (Jn. 11). The bare details may be stated in few words. Lazarus dies in Bethany. Jesus is in Transjordan, but although he knows about the illness of Lazarus, he delays his visit to Bethany until it is too late to find him alive. His sisters, Mary and Martha, who have already been introduced earlier through Luke's account, are convinced that had Jesus arrived soon enough he would have prevented their brother's death, but they do not show faith enough to believe that he could or would raise Lazarus from the dead. Jesus was deeply moved at the scene and wept, but he coupled with this human emotion the tremendous power of divine authority as he commanded Lazarus to come out of the grave.

What distinguishes this story from a narrative of sheer wonder-working power are the deep personal reactions that are faithfully reported. These are: the fear of the disciples to go to Judea, followed by their rash resolve to die with Jesus; the different reactions of Martha and Mary, the former more outspoken than the latter; the comment of the Jews when they saw Jesus weeping; and the reaction of the Pharisees and the chief priests in renewing their plans to kill Jesus.

When John records this stupendous miracle, he does so with a spiritual objective. It is part of his testimony to lead people to believe that Jesus is the Christ, the Son of God. If this incident is true, then Jesus immediately is seen to have unique power. However conceivable it might be to explain away some of the other miracles, it is impossible in this case. It is a foreshadowing of the far greater event of the resurrection of Christ.

Throughout the incident Jesus took advantage of the opportunity to impart teaching so that the significance of the miracle might be understood. He told the disciples that Lazarus' illness was for God's glory (Jn. 11:4). When he made known to them that Lazarus was dead, he explained that the delay in his coming to Bethany was to assist them to believe (11:5). When Martha discussed the resurrection with Jesus, he declared, "I am the resurrection and the life" (11:25), connecting the whole matter of life and death with his person. This led to a definite affirmation of faith on her part, expressed in the same terms as John stated the purpose of his entire gospel (11:27). Just prior to the miracle, Martha was assured that she was about to see the glory of God if she believed.

John pays special attention to the Pharisees' reaction. They were worried about the probable impact of the signs upon the common people, particularly if it led to any action by the occupying Roman forces. It was Caiaphas the Sadducee who gave the official opinion of the hierarchy (Jn. 11:49). John states that he was the high priest during that fateful year, in commenting on Caiaphas's statement that it was more fitting for one person to die for the nation than that the whole nation should perish. The statement was more prophetic than Caiaphas realized, as John points out. Moreover, its application was also more universal than he realized, for Jesus was to die to gather many people into one family of God. Because of the decision of the Sanhedrin to seek his death, Jesus withdrew for a time to Ephraim (11:54) and remained there until the approach of the Passover season, at which point the synoptic and Johannine narratives coalesce.

2. The journey into Jerusalem. Jesus was now in the region of PEREA, from where he proceeded toward Jerusalem by way of Jericho and Bethany. Various incidents took place, and discourses were given before he arrived in Jericho.

(a) *Conclusion of the ministry in Perea.* The Pharisees were still pursuing Jesus, trying to trap him with difficult questions. This must have happened frequently during this period, but both Matthew and Mark record a particular question that Jesus was asked about DIVORCE (Matt. 19:1–12; Mk. 10:1–12). The subject had already been touched upon in the Sermon on the Mount. Here it was a question based on the teaching of the law. Jesus shows that Moses allowed divorce only because of the hardness of people's hearts, although the creation ordinances presupposed a permanent union between husband and wife. By appealing to the basic principles of the law, Jesus silenced his critics. The whole question of divorce was currently a disputed issue within the Pharisaic party itself. (See above, section II.) One school under Hillel took a much more liberal attitude toward it than the other under Shammai. It is clear that the approach of Jesus is nearer the latter than the former. Some of the disciples objected to the stringency of the teaching of Jesus, but he reminded them that not all could receive such teaching.

Next comes a charming interlude that shows Jesus in another role (Matt. 19:13–15; Mk. 10:13–16; Lk. 18:15–17). Little children were brought to him for his blessing, but the disciples rebuked those who brought them. Jesus, in turn, rebuked the disciples, telling them that children were not to be hindered from coming to him, and he used them as an example of true discipleship. The kingdom of God, he said, must be received as a little child, a principle that would not have been readily appreciated in the 1st-cent. world. Humility was not a virtue admired by either Jews or Greeks, the latter, in fact, despising it.

A rich young ruler now comes to Jesus and asks him about eternal life (Matt. 19:16–30; Mk. 10:17–31; Lk. 18:18–30). The questioner is a pious man, for he claims to have kept the commandments from his youth. There is no necessity to question his sincerity, for Jesus does not challenge him on this account. Jesus recognized that riches were his stumbling block, which led to the suggestion that he should sell his possessions to give to the poor. The young man refused and went away sorrowful. Since riches could be such an obstacle, Jesus makes some general comments on the danger of riches and goes on to tell a parable that had a bearing on this theme. He acknowledges that the wealthy would find it more difficult than the poor to enter the kingdom, but he makes it clear that it was not impossible for them to do so with the help of God. One of the requirements of the kingdom is to put the interests of Christ before everything else, even before one's closest family connections.

The parable of the workers in the vineyard, which is related only in Matthew (Matt. 20:1–16), is intended to illustrate the justice of God. Those who worked for only a small part of the day received the same pay as those who had done a full day's work. When the latter complained, they were reminded that the terms of their contract had been fulfilled. It was not that they had received less, but that the others had received proportionately more. The parable is not a pattern for industrial relationships, but an illustration of the right of the owner of the vineyard to do what he chooses. So Jesus taught the sovereignty of God.

At this point, as they drew nearer to Jerusalem, Jesus addressed himself to the Twelve. He reminded them for the third time that he was going up to Jerusalem to be killed, even to be crucified (Matt. 20:17–19; Mk. 10:32–34; Lk. 18:31–34). This brief mention of his death highlights the severe loneliness of Jesus in his mission, for Luke comments that the disciples had no understanding of what he said (Lk. 18:34). His mind must have been disturbed by the knowledge that there was rivalry among the disciples over who was to be the greatest in the coming kingdom, and especially over the request of James and John for preferential treatment. When Jesus challenged the two about their ability to drink his cup, he alone knew the bitter experiences that were involved. The other ten were just as bad, for they could not refrain from anger at the audacity of the two. In spite of what Jesus had already said about humility, they had not learned the lesson that the greatest in the kingdom is he who serves most. Matthew attributes the ambition of James and John to their mother, who makes the request, but Mark shows that the responsibility rested equally upon them (cf. Matt. 20:20; Mk. 10:35).

The most significant feature of this incident is the statement of Jesus' own purpose in terms of service—to give his life a ransom for many (Matt. 20:28; Mk. 10:45). During this period his thoughts must often have been on the essential meaning of his mission. Among those whose thoughts were so dominated by ambition to lord it over others, his own principle of sacrificial service stood out in strong contrast.

(b) *In Jericho*. It is not without some point that all the synoptists relate a healing of blind eyes at this stage in the ministry (Matt. 20:29–34; Mk. 10:46–52; Lk. 18:35–43). The result of this miracle brought rejoicing to the multitudes. It was a welcome contrast to the quibbling of the disciples. Matthew refers to two blind men, while Mark and Luke to one; moreover, Matthew and Luke differ in their placing of the incident. It seems clear that there were two men healed, of whom Mark and Luke select only one, and it seems equally clear that the incident happened on the outskirts of JERICHO, somewhere between the old and the new Jericho.

Luke alone recounts the meeting of Jesus with ZACCHAEUS in Jericho (Lk. 19:1–10). This inci-

Zacchaeus, the tax collector, was sitting in the branches of a sycamore tree when Jesus called out to him.

dent again throws into bold relief the purpose of Jesus—to seek out and to save the lost (19:10). The Savior's consciousness of his immediate task thus finds opportunity to bring a challenge to a despised class of men, tax collectors. The social effects of the gospel are vividly seen in the immediate restitution Zacchaeus made to those whom he had wronged. Something of the tremendous achievements of the mission of Jesus is therefore visible in token form immediately prior to the final entry into Jerusalem.

A parable recorded in Luke's gospel is especially fitting as a prelude to the entry into Jerusalem (Lk. 19:11–27). It was told to correct the mistaken impression that the establishing of the kingdom was imminent. A nobleman about to go away to receive a kingdom commits money to his servants with the command that they trade with it. While he is away the citizens reject the nobleman as king, and when he returns he requires each servant to give account of his trading. Responsibility is apportioned according to the results obtained. The parable ends with a statement that the nobleman's enemies were to be destroyed. It must have been in the mind of Jesus as he approached Jerusalem that its people would reject him as king, and he knew that this would be a shock to the disciples. The recognition of faithful service during this period of rejection was essential for them to realize at this time, although they did not then fully appreciate its significance. The destruction of the enemies (if Jerusalem was in mind) took place some forty years later under the Roman siege.

(c) *Jesus at Bethany*. It was six days before the Passover. The mind of Jesus was more than ever on his approaching passion, and he sought retreat at Bethany with Mary, Martha, and Lazarus. While seated at supper, Jesus was anointed by Mary with precious ointment (Jn. 12:1–8). The act was viewed differently by different people. The attitude of Jesus is strongly contrasted with that of Judas, to whom it was sheer waste. To Jesus it was an act that showed some understanding of his spiritual mission and its involvement. Mary had seized what Jesus knew was to be her last opportunity to show her identification with him. In Jesus' mind she had prepared for his burial, and no cost was too great for that. The sense of inevitability of the coming events cannot be erased from the record. Both Matthew and Mark preserve the promise of Jesus that the woman's act would be remembered wherever the gospel was preached.

As if to prepare still further for the doom awaiting Jesus in Jerusalem, John mentions that the Jews now proceeded to add the further intention of killing Lazarus to the earlier decision to kill Jesus (Jn. 12:10). Nothing could bring out more vividly the appalling spiritual blindness of the Jewish national leaders.

3. The ministry in Jerusalem. The preceding events have all prepared for the concluding week in Jerusalem. The hour of the Messiah has come. He had arrived only to be rejected by the leaders of his people. The point of entry is therefore the beginning of the end. But the real significance of it came to the disciples only later when they were more able to see these closing events as a whole.

(a) *The entry into Jerusalem and the cleansing of the temple*. The fact that all four Gospels relate the TRIUMPHAL ENTRY of Jesus into Jerusalem shows the importance that must be attached to it (Matt. 21:1–9; Mk. 11:1–10; Lk. 19:28–38; Jn. 12:12–16). In view of the forebodings Jesus had revealed from time to time, the manner of his entry is unexpected. From the acclamation of the multitude it would not have appeared evident that Jesus was riding into the city to be crucified within a few days. All the Gospels have prepared the reader to consider more fully the attitude of Jesus than the attitude of the multitude. Matthew and John mention the fulfillment of a prophecy as if to account for the strange paradox (Matt. 21:5; Jn. 12:15). In this way both draw attention to an important element in the consciousness of Jesus at this time—the testimony of Scripture. The royal nature of the entry is stressed in all the accounts and is clearly meant to provide a backdrop against which the somber events of the passion might be described. As in the preceding parable (Lk. 19:11–27), Jesus had come to take up his kingdom, but not in the manner of earthly kings. The impression of triumph created by the entry is introduced only to be quickly dispelled. As Jesus drew near, he wept over the city and predicted its doom (19:41).

According to Matthew, the first action of Jesus in Jerusalem was to cleanse the temple (Matt. 21:12–13), but Mark's more detailed narrative requires the prior cursing of the fig tree (Mk. 11:12–18). The two events are not unrelated in their significance; both have a symbolic meaning for the Jewish nation. The fig tree was impressive because of its leaves, which that year must have appeared earlier than usual. It caught the eyes of Jesus, who supposed that the first figs, which normally appear before the leaves, should have been on the tree. On finding none, Jesus cursed the tree. According to Mark, it was not until the next day that the disciples noticed that the tree had suddenly withered (11:20–21). They drew the attention of Jesus to this fact, revealing in doing so that to them it was no more than a marvel, although he, no doubt, intended it to be symbolic of Israel. The nation had all the external appearance of flourishing religiously, but had not produced the fruits of righteousness. The destruction of the tree was an illustration of God's judgment on Israel. Jesus knew, as the disciples did not, that that judgment was not far distant, as far as Jerusalem was concerned.

The drastic action of Jesus in casting out the moneychangers from the temple is also symbolic. It was the practice for these people to exchange other currencies for the temple currency, in which money alone the temple tax could be paid. This enabled the unscrupulous to charge more than was due, and the same applied to the sellers of pigeons. It was no wonder that Jesus' wrath was kindled against them. His act of righteous indignation was representative of the revulsion of perfect goodness at the sight of all injustice, especially in the name of, and in the central place of, the worship of God. All the synoptics record the quotation from the Scriptures made by Jesus in justification of his action. What was intended as a house of prayer had become a den of thieves. It was a symbol of what had happened to Israel as a whole. Judgment would come to it as surely as it had come to the temple. The evangelists report various reactions to what Jesus had done. Children cried out in the temple, "Hosanna to the Son of David" (Matt. 21:15); the multitude was astonished; at the same time the chief priests and scribes intensified their determination to kill Jesus. Such a cross section of reactions was also representative of the nation as a whole.

(b) *Days of controversy.* During the closing days in Jerusalem, one of the marked features was the number of conflicts Jesus had with religious leaders and others. The priests, scribes, and elders debated with him the question of authority, but he countered with a challenge on the problem of the authority of John the Baptist (Matt. 21:23–27; Mk. 11:27–33; Lk. 20:1–8). This led to the relating of the parable about the wicked husbandmen (Matt. 21:33–46; Mk. 12:1–12; Lk. 20:9–19), which again focuses upon divine judgment on those who have wrongly used their office in the vineyard of Israel, particularly in the killing of the heir. Nevertheless, Jesus assures his hearers that the stone the builders rejected (i.e., himself) would become the cornerstone of God's building.

The next controversy concerned tribute money to Caesar (Matt. 22:15–22; Mk. 12:13–17; Lk. 20:20–26). In this case the Pharisees joined with the Herodians, whom they usually avoided through dislike of their politics, to attempt to ensnare Jesus. By using a simple coin with the image of Caesar on it, he appealed to the testimony of the currency that the Jews were a subservient people, which was intensely unpalatable to the Pharisees, but nevertheless true. All the synoptists note that the opponents marveled at the answer of Jesus. Were they truly challenged to render to God what belonged to him?

Following this, the Sadducees asked a question about the resurrection, but they fared no better (Matt. 22:23–33; Mk. 12:18–27; Lk. 20:27–40). Jesus showed that their problem about marriage in heaven displayed a misunderstanding of the spiritual nature of the resurrection. Matthew reports astonishment from the multitude; and Luke commendation from certain scribes. The masterly wisdom of Jesus made the "catch" questions put to him look foolish, but the various hostile parties came back for more exposure from him. A Pharisaic lawyer tried out the problem of the greatest commandment (Matt. 22:34–40; Mk. 12:28–34). This was a stock question that Jesus had earlier illustrated by the parable of the good Samaritan.

Jesus himself now put a question to the Pharisees about the lineage of the Messiah and the interpretation of Ps. 110:1. He confounded them on a matter of exegesis, over which they especially prided themselves (Matt. 22:41–46; Mk. 12:35–37; Lk. 20:41–44). If the Messiah was the Son of David, how could David also call him Lord? Although all the synoptists record the question, it is Matthew alone who comments that no one was able to answer him. This is not surprising, for the hearers had no concept of the two natures of the Messiah, that is, human and divine.

All the quibbling of the Jewish religious leaders led Jesus to denounce in strong terms the abuses of the scribes and Pharisees (Matt. 23). He does not condemn their allegiance to the law, but rather their abuse of their position as teachers. Some have thought that his criticisms of these religious leaders was undeserved. It must be said, however, that although there was undoubtedly much good in Judaism, the burdens imposed on the common people had become intolerable, and much supposed piety was marred by inconsistency and HYPOCRISY.

The language of denunciation as reported in Matt. 23 is strongly expressed. Jesus first points out the love of ostentation among the Pharisees. Their good deeds are done in public to be seen of men. They love places of honor. They delight in receiving titles of respect from others. This kind of attitude is foreign to that of Jesus, who maintains again that those who humble themselves will be exalted and

Jesus said to the teachers of the law and the Pharisees, "You blind guides! You strain out a gnat but swallow a camel" (Matt. 23:24).

those who exalt themselves will be humbled. There was need for a reversal of current Pharisaic values. Several times in the course of the denunciation Jesus calls them hypocrites, which is a word having the force of play-acting. They were not what they appeared to be. Even their great proselytizing activity did no more than add others who were no better than themselves. Moreover, they are described as blind guides, incapable of discernment. Their petty rules about oaths illustrate the point. They cannot differentiate between important and unimportant matters: they strain out gnats and swallow camels (Matt. 23:24).

Other features that came in for heavy criticism from Jesus were their burdensome ritual requirements and their opposition to God's true messengers. In connection with the first, an example is cited from their interpretation of ritual cleansing. The outside of the cup is to be cleansed at all costs, but the inside is neglected, said Jesus, by which he meant that external adherence to cleansing regulations was useless unless it was accompanied by spiritual renewal. Another illustration Jesus turned against them was their practice of whitewashing sepulchres so that people might see them and avoid defiling themselves by walking over them. He likened the sepulchres to their hearts, and the whitewashing to their outward show of piety. He further criticized them for outwardly honoring the prophets and yet inwardly being of the same spiritual outlook as their fathers who murdered the prophets. All through the comments of Jesus upon the scribes and Pharisees runs the same theme—they professed one thing and did another. It is not to be supposed that every Pharisee was guilty of all the abuses that Jesus mentioned, nor may it even be supposed that these abuses were generally typical. Jesus saw the logical results of the tendencies which a legalistic system must produce, and by exposing these results he aimed to warn people against them.

It is fitting that after such denunciation of the scribes and Pharisees Jesus should once again lament over Jerusalem. Moreover, an incident he observed at the temple treasury served by way of contrast to illustrate his own concept of true piety. It was not the many rich men giving their large sums, but a poor widow giving a humble gift who was commended by him (Mk. 12:41–44; Lk. 21:1–14).

There were, however, some sincere inquirers who came to him, for John records the quest of some Greeks who sought him (Jn. 12:20–22), which led Jesus to speak to them about his hour of glorification. Once again attention is drawn to the thoughts uppermost in the mind of Jesus on the eve of his passion. He thinks of himself as a grain of wheat that must die to reproduce itself, and prays that God's name may be glorified through him. To mark the critical character of this occasion, the Father's voice is heard from heaven, saying that he had glorified it and would glorify it again, but the crowd did not understand. John, indeed, mentions that those who had seen many signs did not believe in him (Jn. 12:37). At the same time Jesus states that their disbelief is not merely in him but in the Father.

(c) *Words about the future.* As his own hour draws near, Jesus instructs his disciples about future happenings. All the synoptists record parts of this eschatological teaching (Matt. 24–25; Mk. 13; Lk. 21:5–38). The discourse was occasioned by the disciples' admiration for the temple buildings, causing Jesus to predict its destruction. When this raised curiosity among them, Jesus unfolded some of the events that must happen in the future—false Christs, wars among the nations, and natural calamities. Then he predicted persecutions in store for the disciples, desolations in Judea, the rise of false teachers, celestial signs, and the coming of the Son of Man. No one could know the date of this coming, but a description of it is included, couched in APOCALYPTIC terms. Of more importance than the details of the coming is the present attitude of the disciples. The exhortation to watch and pray is essentially practical. A definite moral challenge is provided by the thought that life must be lived in the light of that coming. In the teaching of Jesus eschatology is never removed from ethical implications.

More will be said about the future aspects of the kingdom when the teaching of Jesus is separately considered, but it is worth noting here that he did not hesitate to use apocalyptic language to express his meaning. This does not require us to think that he shared much in common with the apocalyptists. Their approach was largely pessimistic. They were visionaries whose hopes were based on insecure foundations. They testify, however, to earnest aspirations which the Christian gospel was able to fulfill in an infinitely better way than they were able to conceive. The eschatological teaching of Jesus centers upon the coming triumph of the Son of Man.

In Matthew's account of the discourse, three parables are included—the ten virgins, the talents, and the sheep and the goats—all of which also contain practical implications. The wise virgins who took oil in their lamps while they waited for the bridegroom to come are commended for their preparedness, but the sorry outcome for those who did not take oil and who were not ready for the bridegroom is intended as a solemn warning. In the parable of the talents, the men who used their resources to gain other talents for their master are commended for their faithfulness, whether their gains were large or small. It was the man who did nothing, and was therefore unfaithful, who was condemned. In the third parable, it is the need of others which is the focus of attention. The sheep are those who cared for others, the goats those who did not. The former are commended, but the latter are condemned. All three parables bring out the sharp distinctions that arise in connection with the kingdom.

G. The passion and resurrection of Jesus

1. From the plot to the arrest. The amount of space devoted by all four evangelists to the account of the passion of Jesus is strong testimony to its paramount importance. The previous outline of events and teaching gains its significance only in the light of the climax. If Jesus was an enigma to the religious leaders and to the common people of his day, it was because he had come to fulfill a unique mission that found its fulfillment in an act of crucifixion. The sense of coming doom is unmistakable in the progressive stages of the story. At various times previously the intentions of the leaders to kill Jesus have been mentioned, but a definite plan is decided on with the treacherous cooperation of JUDAS ISCARIOT (Matt. 26:1–16; Mk. 14:1–16; Lk. 22:1–22:6). This betrayal was already arranged before the last meeting of Jesus with the Twelve.

Even the details of the closing events have an air of destiny about them (Matt. 26:17–19; Mk. 14:12–16; Lk. 22:7–13). Someone with an upper room offers its use to Jesus for the purpose of the feast. It was arranged for a man with a pitcher to guide the disciples to it, where the meal could be prepared. Before sitting down to the meal, Jesus washed his disciples' feet as an example in humility (Jn. 13:1–20). Peter's objection that the Master should not perform for him so humble a task is overruled. As Jesus performed this service, his mind was centered on the tragedy of the betrayer for almost immediately after resuming his seat he quoted Scripture alluding to the coming treachery (13:18). With deep disturbance of spirit he announced that the betrayer was in the room with them. Jesus shows his feelings by offering to Judas the portion of honor. At length Judas withdrew, but it is not certain at what stage in the proceedings this happened, except that it took place before the farewell discourses.

The institution of the LORD'S SUPPER is described in all the synoptics, but not in John. Its purpose was to provide a memorial feast to draw attention to the main mission of Jesus, namely, to shed his blood for the remission of sins. In this way he was insuring that the memory of his work should not cease, but more than that, he was providing an interpretation of it that was to become central in the Christian church. Bread symbolized his broken body, and wine his poured-out blood, though none but he knew the significance of the feast that night. His was a lonely path to Calvary, in spite of the fact that Peter had offered to lay down his life for him (Jn. 13:37). Peter was reminded that he would deny Jesus three times before cockcrow next morning (Matt. 26:30–35; Mk. 14:26–31; Lk. 22:31–34; Jn. 13:36–38).

It is not possible in an outline of this nature to detail the contents of the farewell discourses. Part took place in the upper room (Jn. 14), but the following parts (chs. 15–16) form an essential unity with it. The most characteristic feature throughout is the atmosphere of calm assurance that the words of Jesus convey. There is no sense of distress on his part. Instead, he talks of his joy and peace, which the disciples will later share. There is a confidence in the perfect planning of the Father which would make anxiety incongruous. A main feature is the repeated

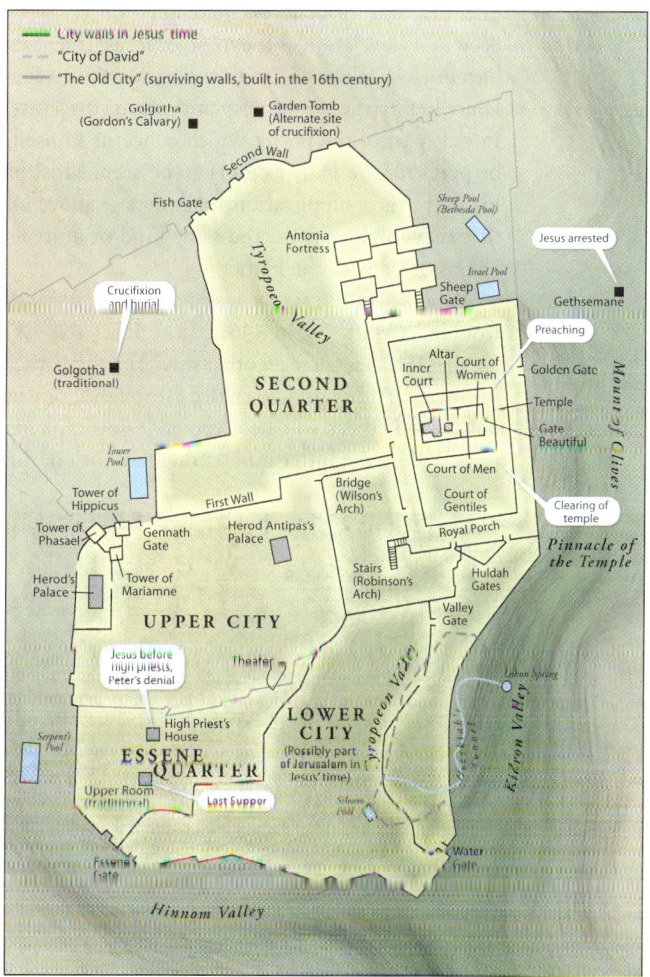

The passion of Jesus in Jerusalem.

promises regarding the Holy Spirit, who would continue the work of Jesus after he had departed.

It was possibly immediately after leaving the upper room that Jesus gave the allegory of the vine and the branches to show how important it was for the disciples to abide in him. Their future life was to be inextricably bound up with him. Apart from this inseparable connection, they would not be able to accomplish anything. Throughout the discourses there is much that was calculated to encourage the disciples, especially when they were to pass through tribulation. It is characteristic of the whole approach of Jesus that he shows greater concern about the disciples than about himself in the hour of his crisis.

John records a prayer of Jesus for himself, for the disciples, and for believers generally (Jn. 17). It is deep in its revelation of the mind of Jesus. It reveals him in close fellowship with the Father only a few hours before the cry of desolation from the cross. In that part of the prayer which concerns himself, he prays for the Father's glory to be seen. Most of his prayer is a supplication for others—above all that they might possess the same kind of unity as he possessed with the Father.

When GETHSEMANE was reached, Jesus was troubled (Matt. 26:36–46; Mk. 14:32–42; Lk. 22:40–46). Was there no other way? Yet, the Father knew best. Although Jesus passed through agony in doing the Father's will, he accepted it uncomplainingly. While the bitter inner struggle went on, the three disciples specially chosen to share his sorrow fell asleep, while another was leading a band of soldiers and officers to arrest him. It was greater sadness for Jesus to see the indifference of the three than to receive a kiss from the betrayer. Peter at least had protested his loyalty.

The arrest of Jesus set him in noble contrast to his captors (Matt. 26:47–56; Mk. 14:43–52; Lk. 22:47–53; Jn. 18:1–12). John says that some of them fell back in amazement. Peter cut off the ear of the high priest's servant. Jesus rebuked Peter and chided the multitude for bringing their swords and clubs. He offered no resistance. This was the Father's will; his hour had come, but all the disciples fled.

2. The passion. There were several stages in the process that took Jesus to the cross. He was first examined in the house of the (former) high priest, ANNAS, during which time Peter denied him three times before cockcrow (Jn. 18:12–17). It was therefore early morning. No specific charge was brought at this stage, but mockery was heaped upon him.

It was later that Jesus was brought before the SANHEDRIN (Matt. 26:57–68; Mk. 14:53–65; Lk. 22:54), but previously there had been much activity on the part of the officials to find false witnesses to testify against him. It was finally agreed to proceed on the charge of threatened destruction of the temple, linked with the charge of blasphemy. Throughout this trial the dignity of Jesus remained unimpaired in the face of degrading mockery, which would have been a disgrace at any trial.

Next, Jesus was sent to PILATE because the Sanhedrin had no power to execute its own decision to have him put to death without the governor's consent. (At this stage in Matthew's account the remorse and death of Judas is narrated to form a tragic background to the callous attitude of the religious leaders [Matt. 27:3–10].) Pilate's examination convinced him that Jesus was innocent of the charges brought against him. In view of this, Pilate tried to avoid having to make a decision by sending him to Herod Antipas when he learned that Jesus was a Galilean.

Herod could do nothing but mock Jesus, and Pilate was again faced with the necessity of deciding on some course of action. He decided to offer the multitude a choice between Jesus and BARAB-

Mosaic from the Church of All Nations depicting Jesus' struggles in the Garden of Gethsemane.

The Church of All Nations is built on the traditional site of the Garden of Gethsemane. (View to the E.)

bas as the one to be released according to custom at the feast, but the multitude cried for Barabbas. In spite of a warning from his wife and his own conviction of the innocence of Jesus, Pilate at length capitulated. No more sorry figure than this Roman governor has ever disgraced the name of justice. Yet Jesus had known beforehand that he had come to Jerusalem to be scourged and crucified. After the governor's decision to hand Jesus over to be crucified, further mockery took place with the arraying of Jesus by the soldiers in a scarlet robe and a crown of thorns (Matt. 27:27–30; Mk. 15:16–19).

Two noteworthy events occurred on the route to CALVARY, where Jesus was crucified. Simon from Cyrene was forced to carry his cross (Lk. 23:26) and a group of women lamented over Jesus (23:27–31). All the evangelists describe in detail the various stages of the CRUCIFIXION, the most cruel form of death, but none includes all the data (Matt. 27:33–56; Mk. 15:33–47; Lk. 23:33–49; Jn. 19:17–37). The focal points are the dispute of Pilate with the Jews about the superscription on the cross, the reaction of the two political insurrectionists who were crucified with Jesus, the attitude of the soldiers, the jibes of the passers by and of the chief priests and scribes, the physical signs accompanying the crucifixion, including the unnatural darkness, the sudden rending of the veil, but most of all the seven sayings of Jesus from the cross. Apart from the momentary cry of dereliction, the suffering Jesus dies triumphantly, his work fully accomplished.

The mass of detail which the evangelists have preserved about the crucifixion reflects the great importance of the event in the minds of the early Christians. There was no attempt to gloss over the shame of it. The glory of the cross was real beyond the appalling physical sufferings that the Messiah endured. The actuality of the sufferings was indispensable to the glory. When Jesus said, "It is finished," he was not thinking of his mortal life, but of his mission of redemption.

When the body of Jesus was removed from the cross, it was placed in a rich man's tomb (Matt. 27:57–60; Mk. 15:42–46; Lk. 23:50–54; Jn. 19:38–42). Joseph of Arimathaea was bold enough to make special application to the governor. Matthew relates the request of the chief priests and Pharisees for the sealing of the tomb and the appointment of a guard to insure that the body was not stolen. That the fact of the burial had some importance for the early Christians is seen from a special mention of it by Paul (1 Cor. 15:4).

3. The resurrection. The Gospels relate the fact of the RESURRECTION OF JESUS CHRIST on the third day. That the tomb was empty is established by all the witnesses. There were a number of appearances of Jesus during the period between the resurrection and the ascension.

The appearances may be given as follows: (1) the appearance to Mary Magdalene (Jn. 20:11–18); (2) to the other women (Matt. 28:9–10); (3) to Peter (Lk. 24:33–35; 1 Cor. 15:5); (4) to two people on the way to Emmaus (Lk. 24:13–32); (5) to the ten apostles and others (Lk. 24:36–43; Jn. 20:19–25). All these occurred on one day, Easter Sunday.

The other five occurred on different days: (6) to the eleven (Jn. 20:26–31; 1 Cor. 15:5); (7) to seven disciples in Galilee (Jn. 21:1–25); (8) to the apostles and over 500 disciples in Galilee (Matt. 28:16–20; 1 Cor. 15:6); (9) to James, the Lord's brother (1 Cor. 15:7); (10) the concluding appearance to the apostles (Lk. 24:44–53; Acts 1:1–12). In the book of Acts, Luke states in his introduction that Jesus presented himself alive to his apostles: "After his suffering, he showed himself to these men and gave many convincing proofs that he was alive. He appeared to them over a period of forty days and spoke about the kingdom of God" (1:3). These appearances therefore were regarded by the early church as sufficient proofs of the reality of the resurrection.

Several observations are necessary concerning the character of the evidence. Paul's list (1 Cor. 15) is clearly selective, but the principle of selection is not at once evident. It has been suggested, not improbably, that this list is confined to those whose evidence had been used in preaching. This may account for the omission of specific reference to women witnesses or to the two on the Emmaus road. Whatever the reason for the selection, the evidence is invaluable, for Paul's testimony is in all probability prior to the writing of the Gospels. The evidence he cites is based on traditions he had received.

The remaining evidence is spread throughout the Gospels, although that from Mark is somewhat uncertain due to doubts about the original ending of his book. Nevertheless the existing ending (Mk. 16:9–20) can certainly lay claim to antiquity and may well preserve an authentic tradition distinct from the rest of Mark. It appears to support the evidence for four of the appearances mentioned above (nos. 1, 4, 8, 10), all of which also occur in either Luke or John. The difficulty of unraveling the sequence of the appearances is in itself a testimony to the authenticity of the various streams of tradition. There was no collusion between the evangelists to insure an account without difficulties, nor was there the use of a common source.

One of the major problems is the difference in location of the various appearances. Those of Mark and Matthew are set in Galilee, those of Luke in Jerusalem, and those of John in Jerusalem and Galilee. Paul gives no hint of location, which suggests that in the early tradition it was not regarded as important. It should be noted, however, that Luke shows a special interest in Jerusalem in his gospel, which may account for his exclusive selection of Jerusalem-based appearances. Those who see two conflicting traditions are driven to choose one and reject the other. There is no insuperable obstacle to both being correct, as is suggested by John's account. The journey to Galilee and back would naturally take time, but is not impossible. It is undeniable that the fact of the resurrection of Jesus is one of the best attested facts of history.

A change of attitude toward the resurrection has occurred in the realm of criticism. Earlier critics attempted to explain away the fact of the resurrection on the basis of a swoon theory, a vision theory, or a hallucination theory, but these attempts failed to square with the evidence. Since that time, there has been a tendency (e.g., in the Bultmannian position) not so much to explain away the resurrection

Painting of the ascension of Jesus (from the dome of the Church of the Ascension on the Mount of Olives).

but to reinterpret it. According to this view, the fact of a raised body ceases to have relevance because its crucial importance is as a factor in faith rather than history. Such an emphasis tends to nullify the objective reality of the resurrection and makes it difficult to see how any common experience could be shared in the faith of all believers. The NT witnesses are not only varied in type, but also in the number who experienced the visitations at the same time.

Accepting therefore the fact of the resurrection as a historical event, it is next necessary to inquire what details the narratives supply about the risen Lord. (a) He was in human form and yet his resurrection body possessed properties beyond those of normal bodies. He could pass into rooms without visible entry and could appear and disappear at will. (b) He had features that were not readily identifiable with the Jesus they had known. More than one of the stories of the appearances refer to the fact that he was not recognized. The nail prints and the familiar voice were the marks of identification. (c) There was a definite continuity with the historical Jesus, as when he conversed with and challenged Peter in a threefold way (Jn. 21). (d) The realization of the risen Lord on the part of the disciples was the occasion of remarkable joy and transformation. That Jesus was not dead but risen changed the despair of the disciples into incredible hope. (e) The resurrection appearances were occasions for specific instruction. Acts 1:3 mentions the kingdom and Lk. 24:44–45 refers to the Scriptures and relates his present to his past teaching. It is reasonable to suppose that Jesus explained the significance of his own death and resurrection during these appearances.

The major significance of the resurrection for Christian faith was left to the early Christians to think through under the guidance of the Holy Spirit. Two factors may be mentioned. It became the firstfruits for the believer's own experience. As Christ was raised from the dead, so shall the believer be. The resurrection is, therefore, the surety for the ultimate triumph of faith over the grave. Second, it is by the resurrection that the divine approval is shown for the work of Christ upon the cross. The resurrection is the coping stone of the whole ministry of Jesus.

4. The ascension. It is only Luke among the evangelists who records this event. It took place at Bethany when, after lifting up his hands to bless the disciples, Jesus vanished from sight (Lk. 24:50–51). Acts 1:1–11 fills in the picture with more details, the most noteworthy of which are the discussion between Jesus and the disciples regarding the restoration of the kingdom to Israel—an evidence of the disciples' current immature understanding—and the announcement of his future return by two men in white. The disciples were not left with mere memories, but with a deep conviction that the same Lord who had companied with them in a historical sense had returned to his former glory, exalted by God and ever living to perform a high priestly function on their behalf (Acts 2:36; Phil. 2.9–10, Heb. 2:17; 4:14–15 passim).

VI. The teaching of Jesus. So large a proportion of the Gospels is taken up with the teaching of Jesus that the importance of what he said is at once seen to be as great as what he did. He was regarded by many as a RABBI and was pleased to accept this title for himself. Yet, the question immediately arises to what extent his teaching methods and content can be considered typical of Jewish teachers of the 1st cent. The populace at least were discerning enough to note one important distinction: contrasted with the SCRIBES, Jesus taught with authority. He did not, as they continually did, appeal to older Jewish authority. Even when he cited the law, he claimed authority to go beyond it. Approaching his teaching, therefore, one is conscious of his uniqueness as well as his indebtedness to contemporary thought. These two aspects will be brought out in the following survey of his teaching.

A. His teaching methods. It will be valuable to note the major characteristics of the teaching methods of Jesus as a prelude to the study of the content, because this will help to place the teaching in its life-situation (*Sitz im Leben*).

1. Its adaptability. In the Gospels the first feature that strikes the reader is the way in which Jesus adapted his teaching to the type of hearer with whom he was dealing. There are many kinds of audiences mentioned. The common people gathered in crowds to hear him and to them he spoke in parables, drawing from a wide range of everyday illustrations. He did not generally address discourses to multitudes, although a notable exception is the SERMON ON THE MOUNT, if this is to be regarded as a continuous discourse. There is a marked difference in the style of his teaching to the Galilean crowds and to the intelligentsia in Jerusalem. Further, the Synoptic Gospels draw a distinction between his teaching to the multitudes and his teaching to the Twelve, for the latter portion of the ministry of Jesus is devoted to the disciples.

There is no doubt that for Jesus the teaching ministry was a means to an end. As far as the Twelve were concerned, it was part of the process of training, although without question Jesus also had in mind the future ministry of the church and the incomparable value that his teaching was then to have. This factor of adaptability is particularly seen in his readiness to use every opportunity to impart some spiritual truth, whether it was an ordinary incident such as a rich young ruler's request to him, or some festival occasion as the Feast of Tabernacles. It is not surprising that the high priests' officers sent to arrest Jesus returned without him, but with a deep impression of his incomparable teaching. A further illustration of his adaptability was the readiness of Jesus to impart teaching to an audience of one if occasion demanded.

2. Use of rhetoric. Jesus is never portrayed in the role of an orator, although he used certain rhetorical devices (but always in a natural way). This may be illustrated with examples. He used the dialogue method, sometimes posing questions himself and sometimes responding to the questions of others. The collection of controversies recorded as taking place in the temple area, prior to the passion, is a marked illustration. The attempts of PHARISEES and SADDUCEES to trick him with difficult questions were simply regarded by him as opportunities to express principles, a process that invariably silenced his questioners. When Jesus was asked about his own authority, he posed a counterquestion about the authority of John the Baptist and put his questioners on the horns of a dilemma, which effectively made them withdraw their challenge.

In John's gospel are preserved, moreover, instances where Jesus engaged in extended dialogue with various Jewish groups (e.g., Jn. 6), in which cases he not infrequently used rabbinical methods of argument, which would have been appreciated by his contemporaries, although their force may not always be apparent in modern times. An example from the synoptics is the statement regarding the resurrection (Matt. 22:32). It must be recognized that even when Jesus used rabbinical methods, he was doing so to express a deeper spiritual truth than appears on the surface. The truth does not depend on the form in which it is expressed, but on the validity it possesses.

3. Logical devices. On occasions Jesus used various logical devices that are worth noting. An example of *a fortiori* type of argument (corresponding to the rabbinic hermeneutical rule of *qal wāḥômer*, "light and heavy") may be seen in the Sermon on the Mount, where Jesus proceeds from the lesser example of the heavenly Father's care for the birds to the greater example of his care for men: "Are you not much more valuable they?" (Matt. 6:26). Another method is *reductio ad absurdum*, a classic example of which is the controversy with the Pharisees over BEELZEBUB: their charge that Jesus was casting out devils by the prince of the devils would make the devil war against himself, which is unthinkable. The type of argument known as *ad hominem* (in its valid form, i.e., when based on an opponent's premises) was often used when Jesus appealed to the teaching of the law (e.g., Jn. 10:34). Many times Jesus left his hearers to apply his illustrations on the strength of an analogy between the physical and spiritual worlds; thus to demonstrate the Father's willingness to give, he appeals to what might be expected from earthly fathers (Matt. 7:9).

4. The use of repetition. One important aspect of the teaching method of Jesus was his practice of repeating his sayings. Many source theories have been based on the assumption that this did not happen, and consequently similar sayings were regarded as variant duplicates in the tradition. This method of dealing with the teaching of Jesus is open to criticism on the ground that it does not sufficiently take account of the usual practice of repetition among Jewish teachers (see B. Gerhardsson's *Memory and*

Manuscript [1961], which cites evidence for this prevalent procedure) Moreover, this is a basic educational method. It cannot be expected that profound truths will be grasped at one hearing, and it must be accepted that this principle was recognized by Jesus. This may well account for a considerable amount of the variation in the synoptics when they report the sayings of Jesus.

Examples of repetition may be found both in content and in verbal form. Some themes, such as the kingdom or the law, frequently recur. The repetition is always purposive. In the Sermon on the Mount, there is a sequence of instances introduced by the formula, "You have heard that it was said ... But I tell you" (Matt. 5:21–22 et al.), which heightens the effect of the distinctive teaching given. There were other techniques Jesus used to aid the memory of his hearers. Of special interest is similarity of form, as, for instance, the BEATITUDES, which would be easier to retain in the mind than a collection of dissimilar sayings.

5. Illustrations. No one can read the Gospels without being impressed by the colorful character of Jesus' teaching. He made frequent use of metaphors, often of the most striking kind. His self-description as light, door, vine, shepherd, are drawn from common illustrations that were all the more effective because of their simplicity. He promised that his disciples would be "fishers of men" and "the salt of the earth." The contemporary Jewish teachers were "a brood of vipers." Other examples abound in the Gospels. It is sufficient, however, to note that the teaching of Jesus was never dull. It was intended to be recalled. Similarly, he made constant use of similes, of which the best examples are in the parables, but by no means exclusively so. For instance, the disciples are as "sheep among wolves," and they are to be "as shrewd as snakes and as innocent as doves" (Matt. 10:16).

There can be no doubt that as a teacher Jesus possessed a sense of humor, as is seen by the extraordinary exaggerations he sometimes mentioned. The reference to "the plank in your own eye" (Matt. 7:3–5) was intended to heighten the contrast with the speck, but would be wholly inappropriate as a possible obstruction in the eye. Similarly, a camel in a needle's eye (Mk. 10:25) was surely not to be taken literally. With the same purpose of arresting attention is the use of paradoxical sayings (e.g., those who would be great must become slaves, Matt. 20:27), or of apparently contradictory sayings, which speak of the purpose of Jesus to divide households (Lk. 12:51–53).

6. Poetic forms. Some of the sayings of Jesus were expressed in poetic form, no doubt to help the hearer in retaining them. C. F. Burney, in his book *The Poetry of our Lord* (1925), has given detailed attention to the formal poetic elements in the discourses of Jesus. He draws special attention to the methods of parallelism and rhythm, which were characteristic of HEBREW POETRY, and he is convinced that the teaching of Jesus could provide many instances of these features. Only a few examples will be given to illustrate the poetic skill of Jesus.

Parallelism had two main forms: synonymous and antithetic (a third, synthetic, is not parallelism in the strict sense). In synonymous parallelism a statement is made in two successive lines, the second of which rewords (and usually enhances) the first. Take, for example, Mk. 4:30, where Jesus asks, "What shall we say the kingdom of God is like, or what parable shall we use to describe it?" This method effectively emphasizes the thought and often moves it forward as well. The second type, antithetic parallelism, is a statement in which the second line denies the

Mosaic on the altar of the church Dominus Flevit ("The Lord Wept"). It includes the Latin text of Jesus' words to Jerusalem: "how often I have longed to gather your children together, as a hen gathers her chicks under her wings, but you were not willing" (Matt. 23:37). Jesus often used metaphors in his teaching.

opposite of the first, or merely states the opposite of the first by way of contrast. An example is the well known saying, "So the last will be first, and the first will be last" (Matt. 20:16; cf. also Mk. 4:25 and Jn. 3:6). Throughout the teaching of Jesus antithesis was powerfully used, especially in John's gospel, not only in the themes used, such as light and darkness, truth and falseness, "my disciples" and "the world," but also in the actual forms of the sayings. Note, for instance 5:29, where doers of good are contrasted with doers of evil; 11:9–10, walking in the day contrasted with walking in the night; and 15:2, bearing fruit with not bearing fruit. (In so-called synthetic parallelism the thought is actually developed through a sequence of sayings, as in Matt. 23:5–7.)

Some comment needs to be made on the subject of rhythm, since this element would focus even greater attention on the artistic methods Jesus employed. The form of the statement, "Do not give dogs what is sacred; do not throw your pearls to pigs" (Matt. 7:6), has an unmistakable rhythmic quality, which could be illustrated in many other sayings (see esp. J. Jeremias, *New Testament Theology. Part One: The Proclamation of Jesus* [1971], 20–27). This demonstrates again that Jesus was not unmindful of the form of his teaching. In addition, when an attempt is made to translate the sayings of Jesus back to their probable Aramaic form, they reflect the use of assonance of various kinds (see M. Black, *An Aramaic Approach to the Gospels and Acts*, 3rd ed. [1967], 160–85).

7. The influence of the OT. The teaching of Jesus was without doubt influenced by the OT. He was constantly making use of allusions to OT incidents in such a way as to appeal to the knowledge of the hearers. The reference to Lot's wife, for instance, is not enlarged upon, but knowledge of the details of the story is assumed (Lk. 17:29). Similarly, the allusions to Solomon's magnificence (Matt. 6:29) or to the Queen of the South's persistence (12:42) are remarkably concise and incidental. This emphasizes an important feature about the teaching of Jesus. It was addressed to people who were versed in OT ideas and who were able to understand the allusions. Any attempt therefore to interpret the teaching of Jesus apart from its OT background would be to wrench it out of its proper context.

This factor is further borne out by the fact that Jesus' work of teaching was a direct continuation of the preaching of John the Baptist, who is portrayed in terms which suggest that he is the last of the OT type prophets. It is not without significance that Jesus began proclaiming the same message as John about the need for REPENTANCE owing to the imminence of the kingdom (cf. Mk. 1:4, 14). At the same time, the teaching of Jesus soon went beyond that of John, whose task was essentially preparatory.

8. Parabolic forms. The most characteristic form in the teaching of Jesus is the PARABLE, which was particularly used in the latter part of his ministry. The purpose of the parabolic form often has been debated, especially in view of the reason Jesus gives for using this form: "Though seeing, they do not see; though hearing, they do not hear or understand" (Matt. 13:13; cf. Mk. 4:11–12; Lk. 8:9–10). The point is not that Jesus used parables to obscure the message. Parables are simple and relatively easy to remember, and for that reason they caused people to think. Those spurred on by no more than idle curiosity or by a rebellious heart would gain nothing, and in this sense would be unable to see or understand.

Many problems have surrounded the interpretation of the parables, which cannot be discussed here. It must be noted, however, that it is this form of the teaching of Jesus that has led to many misunderstandings. Some schools of interpretation have considered that spiritual importance must attach to every detail of the story (e.g., the allegorical school). Others have gone to the opposite extreme and restricted the point of the parable to one generally applicable principle of a moral kind (moralizing school). Still others have considered the eschatological relevance to be uppermost (eschatological school). No interpretation that does not relate the parable to the historical situation of Jesus is likely to be correct. Joachim Jeremias (*The Parables of Jesus* [1962]) has attempted to read the parables against the historical background, but he excises many supposed influences which he considers to have obscured their original form. The interpreter may make good sense of the life situation of these parables without resorting to editorial methods.

One or two of the parables recorded (the sower, the tares) are more in the nature of an ALLEGORY.

PARABLES OF JESUS IN THE GOSPELS

Recorded only in Matthew

The tares	Matt. 13:24–30
The hidden treasure	Matt. 13:44
The pearl of great price	Matt. 13:45–46
The fishing net	Matt. 13:47–48
The unmerciful servant	Matt. 18:23–34
Laborers in the vineyard	Matt. 20:1–16
The man with two sons	Matt. 21:28–32
The marriage feast (given by the King's son)	Matt. 22:1–14
The ten virgins	Matt. 25:1–13
The talents	Matt. 25:14–30
The sheep and the goats	Matt. 25:31–46

Recorded only in Mark

The blade, the ear, the full grain	Mk. 4:26–29
Watch for His coming!	Mk. 13:34–36

Recorded only in Luke

The two debtors	Lk. 7:36–50
The good Samaritan	Lk. 10:25–37
The friend at midnight	Lk. 11:5–8
The rich fool	Lk. 12:16–21
The watchful servants	Lk. 12:35–40
The wise steward	Lk. 12:42–48
The barren fig tree	Lk. 13:6–9
The great banquet	Lk. 14:16–24
The tower and counting its cost	Lk. 14:28–33
The lost sheep	Lk. 15:3–7
The lost coin	Lk. 15:8–10
The prodigal son	Lk. 15:11–32
The unjust steward	Lk. 16:1–13
The rich man and Lazarus	Lk. 16:19–31
The master and servant	Lk. 17:7–10
The importunate widow	Lk. 18:1–8
The Pharisee and the publican	Lk. 18:9–14
The pounds	Lk. 19:12–27

Recorded in Matthew and Luke

House built on the rock	Matt. 7:24–27; Lk. 6:48–49
The leaven	Matt. 13:33; Lk. 13:20–21
The lost sheep	Matt. 18:12–14; Lk. 15:3–7

Recorded in Matthew, Mark, and Luke

The candle under a bushel	Matt. 5:14–16; Mk. 4:21–22; Lk. 8:16–17
The new cloth on old garment	Matt. 9:16; Mk. 2:21; Lk. 5:36
New wine and old bottles	Matt. 9:17; Mk. 2:22; Lk. 5:37–38
The sower	Matt. 13:3–9, 18–23; Mk. 4:3–20; Lk. 8:4–15
The mustard seed	Matt. 13:31–32; Mk. 4:31–32; Lk. 13:18–19
The vineyard and husbandmen	Matt. 21:33–41; Mk. 12:1–9; Lk. 20:9–16
Young leaves of the fig tree	Matt. 24:32–35; Mk. 13:28–31; Lk. 21:29

These come nearest to the allegorical forms found in the fourth gospel (cf. the shepherd and vine) There are also many sayings in John that are parabolic in style although not in form; but too rigid a distinction must not be drawn between the Synoptic Gospels and the Johannine tradition in this field (cf. C. H. Dodd, *Historical Tradition in the Fourth Gospel* [1963]).

B. The content of the teaching of Jesus. When an attempt is made to produce a summary of the teaching of Jesus, the difficulties of classifying it in a concise manner are at once apparent, for different scholars select different aspects as being of most importance. Nevertheless, a useful summary may be produced, provided it is borne in mind throughout that Jesus was not a dogmatic theologian. What he taught had an essentially practical value, and it is necessary to examine the teaching as a whole to obtain a satisfactory concept of it. Some effort has therefore been made to classify the teaching under major themes.

1. Teaching about God. There are three main aspects in the teaching of Jesus about God—as Creator, Father, and King. (See GOD, BIBLICAL DOCTRINE OF.) It will be noted that these aspects are expressed in terms of activities rather than as attributes, but the latter are not excluded. The creatorship of God is seen especially in teaching on his providential care for his creatures. That God was Creator of the world is assumed rather than explicitly stated. The clearest statement is in Mk. 13:19 (NRSV), "the creation that God created." That Jesus taught a special providential care is seen particularly in his statements regarding the heavenly Father's care for and knowledge of such creatures as sparrows (Matt. 10:31). It was basic to the teaching of Jesus that God watched over the whole creation.

It is in the realm of God's fatherhood that the uniqueness of Jesus' teaching becomes most evident. Israel had learned to conceive of God as Father, because Israel as a corporate whole was viewed as God's son. (See FATHERHOOD OF GOD.) Sonship in this sense, however, was primarily national rather than individual. It was not until Jesus taught it that the possibility of a truly filial relationship with God came to the fore. Certainly his Jewish contemporaries, with their transcendental view of God, did not typically think of God in terms of intimate fellowship. As a mode of address in Jewish prayers, "Our Father" is not unknown (cf. G. F. Moore, *Judaism in the First Centuries of the Christian Era: The Age of the Tannaim*, 3 vols. [1927–30], 2:202ff.). The use by Jesus of such expressions as "Your heavenly Father knows," however, or the whole approach to God seen in the Lord's Prayer strikes a new note. People accustomed to approach God with holy fear would find strange the insistence on the father-son relationship in the teaching of Jesus. This was the unique feature in his approach.

It should be remembered that the idea of human beings as sons of God is based on the fact that God is the Father of Jesus. At the same time Jesus drew a distinction between our sonship and his own sonship. The most striking illustration of this distinction is found in Jn. 20:17, when Jesus said to Mary that she was to report to the disciples, "I am returning to my Father and your Father, to my God and to your God." Our sonship cannot, of course, be considered apart from the divine Son, but the distinction must be maintained.

At the baptism of Jesus a heavenly voice attested his divine sonship, and this concept may be regarded as normative for his whole ministry. He was not called as the prophets were to a specific task, but was attested as possessing a specific status. It was in the consciousness of this status that he executed his ministry in obedience to the Father's will. Nowhere is this brought out more forcefully than in John's gospel, where Father and Son are seen in such close relationship. It is on the strength of his consciousness of his own special relationship with God that Jesus brings to human beings the concept of God as their own Father. Even though they had had the word on their lips previous to his teaching, they had never entered into the spirit of it. God had never before become such a living reality as the heavenly Father. This was no mere accepted formula, but adoption into a new family relationship.

It was maintained by T. W. Manson (*The Teachings of Jesus* [1945], 113ff.) that the LORD's PRAYER contains a concise summary of the main aspects of Jesus' teaching on the fatherhood of God. He sees two main divisions, the Father as sovereign arbiter of world history and the Father who cares for and ministers to each child. Under the first division the focus is upon God as a person to be glorified (cf. Matt. 5:16). The prayer for the coming of the kingdom is in accordance with the Father's pleasure (Lk. 12:32). It is the Father's appointment that his people should possess a kingdom (Lk. 22:29). The necessity for God's will to be done is an integral part of Jesus' own relation to the Father, as is seen in the prayer at Gethsemane (Mk. 14:36).

Under the second main division there are three requests in the Lord's Prayer that draw attention to different facets of the Father's care for his children. Daily bread is indispensable, and Jesus therefore assured his disciples, "Your Father knows that you have need of these things" (i.e., food and clothing, Matt. 6:32; Lk. 12:30). Next, forgiveness of sins is requested, and again the request may be echoed from the sayings of Jesus elsewhere (cf. Matt. 6:14–15; Mk. 11:25). The third request is for protection and deliverance, and this draws further attention to that providential care that was noted under the creatorship of God.

No one can consider these aspects of the teaching of Jesus about God without being impressed by the closeness of the relationship between him and the Father and between the Father and his earthly children. Whatever parallels in terminology may be found in the rabbinical writings, there is nothing in them to compare with the sense of filial obedience and affection toward God inculcated by Jesus, of which he himself was the best example.

The third aspect of God—as King—will be more fully dealt with under the heading of the kingdom. But no true approach can be made to the kingdom without recognizing that its basis is the character of God as King. This involves not only the concept of majesty, but also of SOVEREIGNTY. It is assumed that what God has purposed he is competent to bring to fruition. It is, therefore, taken for granted throughout that his designs cannot ultimately be thwarted. The teaching of Jesus regarding the kingdom, which will be considered in the next section, is supported by the absolute certainty of the final triumph of God in his world.

2. Teaching about the kingdom. (a) *Various schools of thought.* Undoubtedly, the teaching of Jesus regarding the KINGDOM OF GOD must be ranked among the most important themes. Much debate has been occasioned by it, and it will, therefore, be necessary to give a careful definition of the concept to avoid confusion. The notion of a kingdom in the sense of a community over which a king reigns is not the dominant concept. It is, rather, the rule of God which is uppermost. This, however, needs further definition in the light of the various uses of the term by Jesus. These uses may conveniently be grouped under two categories: those statements announcing a future kingdom and those announcing a present kingdom. The existence of these two aspects has created a real problem in interpretation. Many have considered them to be mutually exclusive and have, therefore, rejected one or the other of them.

The view that for Jesus the concept of the kingdom was wholly eschatological was strongly maintained by Johannes Weiss (*Die Predigt Jesu vom Reiche Gottes*, 2nd. ed. [1900]) and Albert Schweitzer (*The Quest of the Historical Jesus* [1910]), whose approach has come to be known as "consistent [i.e., thoroughgoing] eschatology." (See ESCHATOLOGY.) According to this view, the APOCALYPTIC elements in the teaching of Jesus are the most important elements, and his mission is to be understood as wholly eschatological. Moreover, it is said that Jesus expected this eschatological event to take place in his lifetime. There have been many modifications of this eschatological view since Schweitzer's interpretation, but there is still support for the basic presuppositions behind it. Thus for Rudolf Bultmann, Jesus is seen as an apocalyptic prophet who expected the imminent arrival of the kingdom (*Theology of the New Testament*, 2 vols. [1952], 1:22). A similar position is adopted by M. Werner (*Formation of Christian Dogma* [1957], 9–27) and R. H. Fuller (*The Mission and Achievement of Jesus* [1954], 25ff.), who both maintain that Jesus' teaching on the kingdom was eschatological.

A strong movement in reaction to this school of thought may be termed the noneschatological interpretation of the kingdom. This was the view taken by T. W. Manson (*The Teachings of Jesus* [1915]), who regarded the kingdom as coming in the experience of individuals. The kingdom is not eschatological, but present. It is God's will being done here and now, supremely in the obedience of Jesus. The mission of Jesus was to lead others into a similar experience, and the mission of the church is to win the world for Christ. Since, when this is done, there will be no need for an eschatological consummation, the eschatological interpretation can be dispensed with.

Many others have taken up a similar view, such as F. C. Grant (*The Gospel of the Kingdom* [1946]) and J. W. Bowman (*Prophetic Realism and the Gospel* [1955]). The former of these considers that Jesus' kingdom teaching was a social gospel, while the latter propounds a theory of prophetic realism that conceives of the kingdom in terms of present personal relationships between God and human beings. But it is C. H. Dodd who has suggested the most thoroughgoing noneschatological view by his theory of "realized eschatology," by which he means that in Jesus' original teaching the kingdom had already arrived (cf. *The Apostolic Preaching and Its Developments*, 2nd ed. [1944]). He finds his support for his theory in Paul's eschatology and in that of the fourth gospel. The apocalyptic language of Jesus is regarded as symbolic. Another advocate of noneschatological kingdom teaching was William Manson (*Jesus the Messiah* [1946]), who confined the kingdom to an inner consciousness in men and women.

Since both of these opposing views were obliged to explain away the alternative elements, they were equally unsatisfactory, and it is not surprising that various attempts have been made to find a synthesis between the present and future aspects of the kingdom. Such a synthesis has gained considerable support and would seem to be the most reasonable deduction from the evidence. The disparity between different interpreters is due to different ideas of how the kingdom is a present reality: (i) some maintain that the kingdom is present only in the person and acts of Jesus; (ii) others, that it is timeless and can therefore be present and future at the same time; (iii) still others, that the kingdom is essentially the powerful activity of God and is immediate, although the fullest consummation is future; (iv) still others, that the kingdom is essentially future, but is so near that its effects have spilled over into the present; (v) and yet others, that the kingdom must be understood existentially, in which case time ceases to have relevance for it.

It is impossible here to discuss these various views, but enough has been said to demonstrate the complexity of understanding precisely what Jesus meant when he spoke of the kingdom. At the same time, we shall not be amiss if we recognize that the teaching of Jesus cannot be understood unless room is made for both present and future aspects. Some attempt will now be made to summarize the main facets of this kingdom teaching.

(b) *The kingdom as present.* The more important sayings that set forth the present reality of the kingdom will first be enumerated. Luke records the saying, "the kingdom of God is in the midst of you" (Lk. 17:21 RSV; cf. NRSV, "among you"), which might alternatively be rendered "within [Gk. *entos* G1955] you" (cf. KJV, NIV). This statement appears to demand some present realization, whichever interpretation is followed. Another saying is one found in both Matt. 12:28 and Lk. 11:20, where Jesus refers to the EXORCISM of demons and adds, "If I drive out demons by the Spirit [Luke has 'finger'] of God, then the kingdom of God has come upon you." Here the present reality of the kingdom is again unmistakable.

The nature of the present realization is seen as a triumph over evil agencies. When Jesus referred to violent or forceful people entering the kingdom (Matt. 11:11–12; Lk. 7:28), he was relating his statement to John the Baptist, and the words seem to mean that those who are now in the kingdom are greater than John, because he was before the kingdom. The enigmatic reference to people of violence taking the kingdom by force also draws attention to a present activity. Much discussion has surrounded the meaning of this verse. Some take

Jesus said that the kingdom of God was like a dragnet.

the verb passively as meaning "to suffer violence," while others regard it as middle voice and as meaning "to act violently." The latter of these renderings is more probably correct and gives a more dynamic force to the statement. A fourth important passage testifying to the present reality of the kingdom is Matt. 21:31 (cf. Lk. 11:52), where Jesus states that tax collectors and prostitutes enter the kingdom before the chief priests and scribes.

(c) *Aspects of the kingdom.* Sufficient has been said to show that Jesus himself taught a present experience of the kingdom. But it is necessary to outline briefly in what that experience consists. G. E. Ladd (*Jesus and the Kingdom* [1964]) has focused attention on three aspects of this question, which will serve admirably as a summary of the teaching. The first is the kingdom as dynamic power. The concept here is of a spiritual conquest over spiritual forces. The many instances of exorcism in the Gospels are evidence of the dynamic power of Jesus over the spiritual adversaries. The binding of the strong man armed, in one of the parables of Jesus (Lk. 11:21–22), is symbolic of his ministry and of the present realization of the kingdom. In this connection the remark of Jesus when the Seventy returned from their mission of announcing the kingdom is significant, "I saw Satan fall like lightning from heaven" (Lk. 10:18). The whole concept of the ministry is dynamic, consisting not only in words but also in healing deeds. The authority of Jesus in his teaching bears the mark of the present reality of his kingdom and differentiates it from the hopes of the scribes.

Second, it is important to note that in all his teaching Jesus made it clear that the kingdom is God's, not man's. The mission of Jesus was the mission of God in redemptive activity. Ladd brings into his considerations here the fact that God is a seeking, inviting, fatherly, and judging God. In other words, he deduces the nature of the kingdom from the nature of God. But as it is God's kingdom, it differs from all other kingdom concepts. It is supernatural in character.

Third, the whole concept of salvation must be related to the present character of the kingdom. Ladd speaks here of the aspect of salvation which is present and links with this the gift God now gives to the members of the kingdom, namely, SALVATION and RIGHTEOUSNESS. This is an attempt to integrate the salvation teaching of Jesus with the kingdom concept. If the kingdom is central in Jesus' teaching, then all other aspects of his teaching must be related to it.

Membership in the kingdom is, therefore, for those who receive God's gift of salvation. This feature distinguishes it at once from any notions of a materialistic or nationalistic kingdom. It makes clear, moreover, that the kingdom will not be established by the converting of the world to the Christian faith. Jesus never foresaw a universal acceptance of the gospel, as the parable of the sower and the seeds shows. It is nevertheless a kingdom that could be the subject of prayer for its establishment, as is seen by the petition, "Your kingdom come," in the Lord's Prayer. The offering of such a prayer expresses a desire for a fuller realization of what is already taking place. The constant emphasis on repentance and faith as prerequisites for approach to God demonstrates the essentially spiritual nature of the kingdom. More will be said later about the ethics of the kingdom.

(d) *The eschatological event.* This aspect of the kingdom is equally important and must be given full weight. It is undeniable that, in addition to viewing the kingdom as present, Jesus also looked toward a future event. These two aspects are complementary. In the eschatological discourse (Matt. 24; Mk. 13; Lk. 21), Jesus used apocalyptic imagery in such a way that some kind of catastrophic event in the future, in the *eschaton*, must be understood. The best way to incorporate both present and future aspects of the kingdom is by maintaining that the same kingdom, which at present exists in a dynamic form in the activity of God among men, will receive its consummation in an event at the end of history. These two aspects are brought into close proximity in the kingdom parables, which must next be considered.

(e) *The parables of the kingdom.* First, they illustrate the growth of the kingdom. It will not be established by irresistible power, but by action akin to the growth of seed. The most evident feature here is the fact that only one of the four types of soil mentioned in the parable of the sower is productive. There is a considerable element of mystery about the kingdom, a mystery given only to some to understand. The unexpected character of the kingdom is illustrated by the parable of the tares, where the distinction between the true and the false was not at once apparent. Indeed, separation will not take place until the *eschaton*. The kingdom in its present state cannot, therefore, be considered as an identifiable entity.

The same quality of unexpectedness is seen in the parable of the mustard seed. Smallness is difficult to reconcile with the divine kingdom, but there is a marked contrast between its beginnings and its end state. This is the main point of the parable. The present is related to the future as the mustard seed to the tree. Jesus' contemporaries could see only the seed, but he looked beyond to the further demonstration of the kingdom.

A similar truth is taught in the parable of the leaven, where the imperceptibility of the operation of the kingdom is in mind. Some problem exists over the fact that the whole lump of dough is leavened, which has sometimes been regarded as illustrating the permeation of evil within the church and sometimes of the permeation of good in the world through the church. But neither interpretation is as probable as that which sees the ultimate triumph of the kingdom at the consummation of the existing world order.

Two parables, the treasure and the pearl, draw attention to the value of the kingdom. It does not appear worthwhile to all, but those who are discerning will recognize its inestimable worth, exceeding all other values. On the other hand, the parable of the net reminds the hearer that, for the time being, some who are not fit for it will share in the benefits of the kingdom until its final establishment.

That the kingdom of God is not to be restricted to Jews is clear from the parable of the vineyard, which was addressed to the Jewish leaders and which concluded with the statement, "the kingdom of God will be taken away from you and given to a people that will produce its fruit" (Matt. 21:43). This aspect of universality of the kingdom is also found elsewhere (Matt 8:11–12). In both these passages the Jews receive the offer of the kingdom before the Gentiles. The kingdom applies not only to all nationalities, but to all classes within nations (cf. Matt. 12:31). This latter thought comes in the application of the parable of the two sons, which stresses the need for repentance and faith. The parable of the marriage feast in Matt. 22 shows the fate of those who scorn or ignore the summons of the kingdom. This passage once again seems to point to the rejection of the kingdom by the Jewish people and differentiates the kingdom of God from their nationalistic concepts.

It remains to note the relationship of the kingdom to the CHURCH. Many exegetes have identified the two, but this is difficult for several reasons. Nowhere does Jesus describe his disciples exclusively as members of the kingdom. Moreover, the church appears to have arisen out of the kingdom. It is the church's task to witness to the kingdom, and the church is the instrument and custodian of the kingdom. Ladd maintains that they are separate concepts, one taking its point of departure from God, the other from his people (*Jesus and the Kingdom*, 258–73).

(f) *The ethics of the kingdom.* The problem of the ETHICS OF JESUS is important in this context. No survey of the teaching of Jesus can in fact ignore the predominant place that ethical injunctions have in the total sayings of Jesus. Yet it is the ethical teaching that has been most paralleled in Jewish ethical sayings and instructions, and this raises the problem of the extent to which the ethics of Jesus can be considered unique. Even though many of the individual sayings of Jesus may be paralleled, the overall impression of the Jewish ethical teaching is "legalistic," whereas the teaching of Jesus breathes a different atmosphere. It is no longer conformity to law, whether written or oral, but the pursuance of the will of God understood as the norm for the kingdom of God.

Our purpose is only to draw attention to the salient features of the ethics of Jesus in relation to the kingdom teaching. The first characteristic is that the authority for the ethics rests in the authority of Jesus who rejected several scribal interpretations of the law and modified the whole approach to ceremonial observances. The basis of Jesus' own authority for ethics was his claim to fulfill perfectly the will of God. Second, it is noted that the ethical teaching is an essential feature of both the present and future aspects of the kingdom. Where God's rule is active, that rule must find expression in behavior that befits the character of God. This is essentially the religious sanction in Christian ethics. It is not the sole sanction, for the eschatological aspect is equally important. There is no support for excluding either, and such a one-sided view as

Schweitzer's *Interimsethik* (the ethic of Jesus was intended to be only temporary) must be rejected.

What Jesus taught was of more than passing significance. It possessed eternal validity and is as relevant to the present age as to the future. This does not mean that there are no difficulties in fulfilling the ethical demands. To love one's neighbor as oneself and, even more, to love one's enemies makes absolute demands upon any person. There can be no denying that these demands are an expression of divine love.

One special facet of the ethics of Jesus is the emphasis on inner motives. Such things as anger, hatred, restraint, humility, cannot be judged by external law. They belong not to adherence to a code of rules, but to the manifestation of character (cf. Lk. 6:45). The demands of Jesus are exacting—even careless words will have to be accounted for (Matt. 12:36). Moreover, the claims of the kingdom are such that they must at times take precedence over family ties (cf. Matt. 10:34–39; Lk. 9:60–61). Indeed the ethic of Jesus involves self-denial (Matt. 16:24), which means that the claims of the kingdom must take precedence even over the claims of self. There is no other ethical system that demands the negation of the existing order to such an extent as to require the hating of one's own life (Lk. 14:26). Self ceases to matter. The affairs of the kingdom are of paramount importance.

It is extraordinary how much is said about rewards in the teaching of Jesus (cf. Matt. 5:12, 46; 6:4, 18; 18:1–4). The idea of return for merit was conspicuous in the theology of the Jews, but Jesus' teaching goes beyond it. The parable about the laborers in the vineyard admirably illustrates this point (20:1–10). The first group of laborers worked a whole day for a day's pay; that was just. The last group worked only an hour for a day's pay; that was an act of grace. The basis of rewards in the ethics of Jesus is wholly different from normal human reckoning. The citizens of his kingdom must be prepared for new standards.

3. Jesus' testimony concerning himself. The evidence from the teaching of Jesus regarding his own person may be conveniently summarized under two main classifications: the names he applied to himself and the specific references to his person. Under the first heading it is important to distinguish those names he applied to himself from those applied to him by others. See also CHRISTOLOGY.

(a) *The names that Jesus used of himself.* The most widely used was SON OF MAN and it will be well to begin with this title, especially as in the Gospels it is found only on the lips of Jesus. A considerable amount of literature has gathered around his use of the term in an endeavor to discover what he meant by it, but it will be possible here to give only a brief survey of the major considerations. The different interpreters may be classified in two groups, those who hold that Jesus himself used the title and those who reject such a view. Clearly if the latter group is correct, the Son of Man passages do not belong to the teaching of Jesus and should not be further considered for our immediate purpose. It is necessary, therefore, to comment on this point of view before proceeding to outline the self-testimony of Jesus.

On what grounds are the Son of Man sayings regarded either as inauthentic or else interpreted of someone other than Jesus himself? First, to take the view that most of the sayings are not authentic, mention may be made of P. Vielhauer, who rejects those sayings about the Son of Man's earthly work and those about his sufferings, and deals only with those referring to his glory. But even these he denies to Jesus because of the lack of connection between the kingdom of God and the Son of Man sayings. His deduction is that since one of these (the kingdom) is authentic, the other cannot be, but apart from the fact that this appears to be a non sequitur, the preservation of both lines of tradition in the Gospels, without any apparent incongruity, militates against his view (H. E. Todt fully discusses it in *Der Menschensohn in der synoptischen Überlieferung* [1959], 298–316). Bultmann (*Theology of the New Testament*, 1:29) considered the Son of Man passion sayings as *vaticinia ex eventu* (i.e., prophecies fabricated by the church based on past events) but without adequate basis. A comparison of the three passion predictions (cf. Matt. 16:21; 17:22–23; 20:18–19) shows that the evangelists had no doubt that Jesus intended the Son of Man to be understood as himself. It will not do to regard these sayings as community creations, for in that case the use of the title becomes doubly unintelligible.

There are many advocates for the view that

Jesus used the term Son of Man, but that it was the church which identified him with the title (cf Todt, *Der Menschensohn*, and A. J. B. Higgins, *Jesus and the Son of Man* [1964]). It is impossible for our present purpose to discuss the detailed evidence on the grounds of which it is maintained that Jesus did not use the title of himself, but the following survey will proceed on the assumption that Jesus meant to call himself Son of Man (cf. O. Cullmann, *The Christology of the New Testament* [1959]).

It will be convenient to group the sayings according to the classification already mentioned. First to be considered are the sayings connected with the earthly work of Jesus. Mark records two such sayings (Mk. 2:10 on the authority to forgive sins; 2:27 on the lordship of the Sabbath). Matthew and Luke share four such sayings (Matt. 5:11; 8:20; 11:19; 12:32; Lk. 6:22; 7:34; 9:58; 12:10). Luke alone has one (Lk. 19:10) and Matthew alone has two (Matt. 13:37; 16:13). On the most straightforward understanding of these passages it is inescapable that Jesus intends himself to be understood as the Son of Man. Two of them (Mk. 2:10, 27) attribute to him special authority. It is God who is generally spoken of as forgiving sins and it is God who ordained the Sabbath. It is difficult to avoid the conclusion that Jesus was making a high claim for himself, unless these passages are regarded as not originating in Jesus (Higgins, for instance, sees them as community products).

In the four shared by Matthew and Luke it appears equally clear that Jesus is referring to himself. Men will hate the disciples on account of Jesus. The Son of Man is contrasted with John the Baptist in such a way that the title must be understood of Jesus himself. Moreover, the Son of Man is described as having nowhere to lay his head, which fact relates to Jesus' own itinerant ministry. And while blasphemy against the Holy Spirit cannot be forgiven, blasphemy against the Son of Man can be. All of these instances are intelligible if Jesus is describing himself, although it still needs to be examined why he chose to use this title rather than the simple "I." A comparison of Matt. 16:13 with Mk. 8:27 shows how both forms have been preserved for the same question. Matthew has, "Who do people say the Son of Man is?" whereas Mark has, "Who do people say that I am?" Since in both narratives Peter confesses Christ in the same form of words, "You are the Christ," the conclusion is inescapable that the disciples understood Jesus to mean himself.

Of the sayings connected with the sufferings of Jesus most are in Mark and are shared by the other synoptists (cf. Mk. 8:31; 9:12, 31; 10:33–34, 45; 14:21, 41; cf. also Lk. 17:25; 22:48; 24:7; and Matt. 26:2). These statements show that as Jesus anticipated his passion, he made increasing use of the title. Its meaning for him was inextricably bound up with his work of redemption.

The third group of sayings all have an eschatological emphasis and in this case there are more in Matthew than in Mark (cf. Mk. 8:38; 9:9; 13:26; 14:62; in Luke, with parallels in Matthew, Lk. 1:30; 12:8, 40; 17:24, 26; in Luke alone, 17:22, 30; 18:8b; 21:36; in Matthew alone, Matt. 10:23; 13:41; 16:27, 28; 19:28; 24:30, 39b; 25:31). There is clearly a strong tradition behind these sayings and some are inclined to accept an authenticity for them which they deny for the other groups. But it is difficult to maintain that Jesus reserved the title for his part in eschatological events and for no other purpose. This would have meaning only if the title had an accepted eschatological significance. But the sayings themselves gain in meaning if Jesus used the title in connection with his earthly work as well as for his future heavenly functions.

The two main aspects in the use of the title are therefore suffering and glory, and there is much to be said for the view that the title is a synthesis of the suffering servant of Isaiah and of the "son of man" in Dan. 7:13–14. This view led T. W. Manson (*The Teaching of Jesus* [1931], 211ff., and *The Servant Messiah* [1953], 72–74) to regard the title as corporate, supposing that Jesus was including his disciples in it. But it is difficult to believe that the disciples or any others would have understood it in this sense. It makes little difference what the antecedents of the title were unless they were recognized by Jesus' contemporaries. A distinction must, however, be made between what Jesus himself meant by it and what the disciples and others understood by it. It may be regarded as an Aramaic expression meaning either man in general or man in particular. The latter seems the only reasonable proposition of the two. It may be that at least to the disciples Jesus was The Man par excellence. But for himself the title no doubt carried far deeper significance. He probably avoided it as the most suitable alternative to the title "Messiah," which he avoided for political reasons.

The titles Son of David, Son of God, and Messiah, although used of him by others, were not used specifically by Jesus himself. They do not therefore enter into the present discussion. Yet attention must be drawn to the fact that Jesus did implicitly accept them. In the case of his Sonship, his teaching in John's gospel is full of references to his filial relationship with God. The title Son of God is therefore seen to be highly applicable to express that relationship.

(b) *Other indications.* What other evidence is there in the Gospels regarding Jesus' view of himself? There is more to assist here in John's gospel than in the synoptics. Jesus frequently speaks of himself as being sent. He is deeply conscious of his mission to do the Father's will (e.g., Jn. 5:17). He knows that he is sent for a specific purpose that no one else can fulfill. His testimony to himself comes out vividly in the great "I am" statements in this gospel. "I am the way and the truth and the life" (14:6) is a unique claim. The same may be said of "I am the resurrection and the life" (11:25). No less far-reaching is his claim to be the light of the world (8:12), which could hardly be more comprehensive and universal.

It is difficult to escape the conclusion that in the mind of Jesus there was a connection with the great I AM as the name of Yahweh in the OT (see GOD, NAMES OF), particularly in view of the statement of Jn. 8:58, "Before Abraham was born, I am!" In the Synoptic Gospels, the saying of Jesus nearest to the Johannine evidence is found in Matt. 11:27, which is a clear claim to uniqueness of filial relationship (but see also the accounts of Jesus' baptism). Yet there are also hints in all the Gospels, but especially in John, that Jesus was conscious of human limitations. He knew hunger and thirst and the need for sleep and rest. He could express human anger and show compassion. He needed prayer to sustain him. But the human side, as we should expect, comes out more clearly in his actions than in his teaching.

4. The teaching about the work of Christ. The mission of Jesus was many-sided, but his special work was concerned with the significance of the passion. This forms the focal point of the gospel narratives, and all that precedes it must be interpreted in the light of it. The kingdom teaching, for instance, is seen in its true perspective only in the light of the cross.

Before examining the statements of Jesus relating to his own work, there are some preliminary observations that must be made. There is no doubt, to begin with, that Jesus regarded his mission as a direct fulfillment of Scripture. He stated his purpose to be the fulfillment of the law (Matt. 5:17). In the upper room, after the reference to the betrayal, Jesus added, "The Son of Man will go just as it is written of him" (Matt. 26:24), a clear allusion to the coming passion. After the transfiguration, Mark records a question of Jesus, "Why then is it written that the Son of Man must suffer much and be rejected?" (Mk. 9:12). Other references add support to the view that Jesus was deeply aware that his own experience was the subject of prophecy (cf. Matt. 26:56; Lk. 18:31; 24:25–27, 44–45).

It has sometimes been supposed that in John's gospel a different account of the work of Jesus is found as compared with the synoptics. One such view is that it is the incarnation rather than the passion which is the basis of redemption. This interpretation is supported from Jn. 6:53, where Jesus says, "unless you eat the flesh of the Son of Man and drink his blood, you have no life in you" (cf. also 6:56). But if this text is intended to relate to the incarnation it would need to be understood in a quasi-physical way. It is more in harmony with the general tenor of the teaching in the passage to understand it in a spiritual manner. Another view is that redemption is by illumination, and for this an appeal is made to such passages as 8:12 ("I am the light of the world"), 17:17 ("Sanctify them by the truth; your word is truth"), 14:9 ("Anyone who has seen me has seen the Father"). It is undeniable that there has been an effective illumination of the mind as a result of the coming of Jesus, but it would rob the mission of Jesus of its primary purpose if it were restricted to an educative process. As an examination of the evidence will show, the death of Christ is plainly presented in the fourth gospel as the object of the incarnation.

(a) *His death as a sacrificial offering.* There is much evidence for this aspect of the passion of Christ. In addition to the statement in Jn. 6 cited above, which makes it clear that Jesus conceived of his flesh and blood as having been given for the life of the world, the most important evidence comes from the words used in the institution of the LORD's SUPPER. The institution must be seen against an OT background. Jesus describes his blood as connected with the new covenant and as being "poured out for many for the forgiveness of sins" (Matt. 26:28; see COVENANT, THE NEW). There can be no doubt that Jesus intended his disciples to understand that his death would result in remission of sins. The connection of this act with the sacrificial system of the old covenant seems impossible to deny. Some have treated this evidence with reserve, because the words "for the forgiveness of sins" occur only in Matthew, but they are so fully in harmony with the whole teaching of Jesus that they cannot reasonably be disputed on those grounds. Two of the sayings of Jesus in John's gospel emphasize the finality of his work (Jn. 17:4; 19:30). The latter of these statements, coming as it does direct from the cross, shows that the death itself was viewed as an accomplishment.

(b) *His death was voluntary.* Jesus not only states that the good shepherd gives his life for his sheep (Jn. 10:11), but that he himself lays down his life of his own accord (10:18). He maintained that Pilate had no power over him except as it was granted from above (19:10–11). He made clear that no love is greater than that which sacrifices life for the sake of friends (15:13). In his gospel, John seems to be particularly concerned to show this aspect of the voluntary self-giving of Jesus.

(c) *His death was a divine necessity.* In the fourth gospel there is a developing sense of the inevitable character of the passion, described as the "hour" (NIV, "time"). Several times John mentions that his hour is not yet, until Jesus himself says, "Father, the time has come" (Jn. 17:1). This sense of divine necessity is seen in the first prediction of the passion in Matt. 16:21, "From that time on Jesus began to explain to his disciples that he must [*dei* G1256] go to Jerusalem ... be killed and on the third day be raised to life." Compare also the angel's reminder of Jesus' words to the women at the tomb (Lk. 24:7). The same idea is found in Jn. 3:14, "the Son of Man must be lifted up." In all the Gospels the death of Christ is seen as the climax to the mission of Jesus. There is no indication that it happened by accident. It was all part of a divine plan.

(d) *His death was substitutionary.* When Jesus identified himself with those who attended the baptism of John and when John hesitated at the thought of baptizing Jesus (according to Matt. 3:14), Jesus said that he requested baptism because it was fitting for him to fulfill all righteousness. Although he needed no repentance, he became one with those who did. In Lk. 22:37 ("he was numbered with the transgressors"), Jesus appeals to Isa. 53:12 as fulfilled in himself, which suggests that he regarded himself in the role of the suffering servant.

There is one statement of Jesus that suggests the idea of substitution, for it uses the Greek word *anti* G505, which can often be rendered "in the place of." It occurs in Mk. 10:45 (cf. Matt. 20:28), where Jesus says that the Son of Man came "to give his life as a ransom for [*anti*] many." The word *ransom* (*lytron* G3389) means "an equivalent exchange price," and while the imagery used cannot be pressed, the idea that the Son of Man did something in the stead of others is inescapable. There are, in addition, passages where a different preposition is used, but where the context suggests substitution. For instance, in the words of institution of the Lord's Supper (Matt. 26:28, "poured out for many"), the preposition is *peri* G4309, while in the statement by Jesus that the good shepherd lays down his life for the sheep (Jn. 10:15), *hyper* G5642 is used. Some scholars (e.g., Vincent Taylor) interpret these prepositions as expressing representation rather than substitution, but neither of these ideas does full justice to the meaning.

(e) *His death was a triumph over the devil.* When the conflict of the passion became imminent and Judas had already betrayed his Master with a kiss, Jesus conceded to those who arrested him, "this is your hour—when darkness reigns" (Lk. 22:53). Moreover, when Jesus referred to his death in the figure of a grain of wheat falling to the ground (Jn. 12:23), he went on to announce, "Now is the time for judgment on this world; now the prince of this world will be driven out" (12:31). He must have had something of this intense spiritual conflict in mind in his parable of the strong man who needed first to be bound before his goods could be seized (Matt. 12:29). In a strong denunciation of Herod, Jesus told the Pharisees, "Go tell that fox, 'I will drive out demons and heal people today and tomorrow, and on the third day I will reach my goal'" (Lk. 13:32).

(f) *His death is applicable only through repentance and faith.* At the commencement of his ministry, Jesus preached the imminence of the kingdom and exhorted his hearers to repent and believe the gospel (Mk. 1:14, 15). That gospel involved the whole of his mission, which centered on his death. His mission was never designed for righteous people, but for sinners willing to repent (Matt. 9:12–13; Mk. 2:17; Lk. 5:31–32). There are many allusions to faith in the teaching of Jesus, and it is clear that he conceived of no other means by which the benefits of his work might be appropriated (cf. Jn. 3:16; 5:24; 6:29). One of the immediate results for those who come to Jesus in response to his invitation and join themselves to his mission is that they find spiritual rest (Matt. 11:28). There can be no doubt that Jesus desired a radical change to be effected in the lives of those who followed him on the basis of his mission.

5. The teaching about the Holy Spirit. The Synoptic Gospels have considerably less teaching about the HOLY SPIRIT than John's gospel, but there are nevertheless some significant statements. Jesus makes clear his own consciousness of the Spirit's part in his mission. In Matt. 12:28 he says, "But if I drive out demons by the Spirit of God, then the kingdom of God has come upon you." It is true that in the parallel passage in Luke, "the Spirit of God" is replaced by "the finger of God," but there can be no doubt that this alternative must be interpreted in the light of Matthew's text. Particularly is this necessary since the statement comes within the context of the Beelzebub controversy (see below). Here then is the claim that Jesus' activity in the spiritual realm is by the Spirit of God. When at the commencement of his ministry Jesus applied the prophecy of Isa. 61:1–2 to himself (Lk. 4:17–21), it was evidence of his own specific claim to the Spirit's power. This was no doubt closely linked in the mind of Jesus with the descent of the Spirit on the occasion of his baptism and also his consciousness of being led by the Spirit to the place of temptation.

The blasphemy saying, which occurs in all three Synoptic Gospels, is an important evidence of Jesus' teaching about the Holy Spirit. The occasion was the charge that Jesus cast out demons by Beelzebub, the prince of the demons. Jesus in reply not only shows the impossibility of Satan casting out Satan, but also shows the true nature of the charge as a blasphemy against the Holy Spirit. This is unforgivable, although blasphemy against Jesus himself as Son of Man (according to Matthew and Luke) may be forgiven. In no more striking way could he have brought out the sovereign character of the Spirit's work. Jesus recognized that the kind of obduracy that could attribute such beneficial results of the Spirit's work to evil agencies was beyond forgiveness. See UNPARDONABLE SIN.

Another aspect of the teaching of Jesus regarding the Spirit is the promise of the Spirit's guidance when the disciples have to answer for their faith (Matt. 10:19–20; Mk. 13:11). In Mark's account it occurs in the eschatological discourse, whereas in Matthew's it is in the instruction given prior to the mission of the Twelve, but it is the kind of assurance that may well have been repeated several times. Luke has a similar statement placed in yet a different context (Lk. 12:11–12). In Lk. 11:13 the Spirit is promised to those who ask the heavenly Father, and it is significant that Matthew records a parallel statement in which the promise is for "good things." Luke's account may be interpretive, but Jesus' meaning may certainly have included this aspect of the gift of the Spirit. It seems a fair interpretation that by the gift of the Spirit is to be

This column from the 1st cent. was reused by the Crusaders during the construction of the Church of St. Mary's, which pilgrims now use to recall the events that occurred in the upper room, such as Jesus' explicit teaching on the Holy Spirit.

understood the source of all "good things" which the Father is willing to bestow. Yet another comment of Jesus that illuminates the work of the Spirit is found in Mk. 12:36, where Jesus attributes to the INSPIRATION of the Spirit the statement of David in Ps. 110:1. In this Jesus shows himself to be in line with contemporary Jewish views of inspiration.

The evidence from the fourth gospel falls naturally into two parts, the sayings before the passion narratives and the sayings within these narratives. In the discourse with Nicodemus the Spirit is shown as the agent of REGENERATION (Jn. 3:5–6). Without his activity there can be no rebirth. Whether or not there is in this chapter a reference to Christian baptism is a matter of debate, but it does not affect the essential work of the Spirit in spiritual renewal. In the same discourse in Jn. 3, Jesus makes it clear that God does not give the Spirit by measure (v. 34), which suggests an unlimited gift. In the conversation with the Samaritan woman, Jesus speaks of the spiritual nature of God and the need for his worshipers to worship in spirit and in truth (4:24), and there must be seen here an allusion to the work of the Holy Spirit.

At the Feast of Tabernacles Jesus promised that rivers of living waters should flow from those who come to him, and John adds the comment that Jesus was referring to the Spirit. Although this is an editorial note, it is valuable as an interpretation of the imagery that Jesus used (cf. Jn. 7:37–39).

It is in the farewell discourses in the upper room that the teaching about the Spirit becomes more explicit. There are several sayings in which the Spirit is described as the PARACLETE, which is better rendered Counselor, since the latter involves the functions of both advocate and helper (though the intercessory function, which might be suggested by "advocate," is lacking). The passages are Jn. 14:16–17, 25–26; 15:26; 16:7–11, 13–15. In three of these passages (14:16; 15:26; 16:13) the Spirit is named as the Spirit of truth; in the first two of them, in conjunction with the word Paraclete. A summary of the function of the Holy Spirit must include the following: (a) in relation to the church, he calls to remembrance and acts as guide into the truth; (b) in relation to the world, he convicts of sin and brings recognition of the rightness of judgment. From these functions it may be deduced that the Paraclete was to continue the work of Jesus on earth. He was to be the alter ego of Christ. The witness of the Spirit was to be essentially the same as the witness of Christ, with the obvious further development that the Spirit would testify to the risen Christ.

The other mention of the Spirit in the teaching of Jesus occurs when he breathes upon the disciples and says, "Receive the Holy Spirit" (Jn. 20:22). Here it is the risen Christ who speaks and shows again the close connection between the Spirit's work and his own. The gift of the Spirit was to be given at PENTECOST, but here Jesus gives his own sanction to what may be regarded as a foretaste of that event. The power to forgive and to retain sins is granted at the same time (20:23) and cannot be divorced from the activity of the Spirit. It is not incongruous with the fact that God alone forgives sins, for Jesus himself did not hesitate to pronounce forgiveness, and the same sovereign power is vested in the Spirit and then mediately through those possessing the Spirit.

VII. The miracles of Jesus. Separate consideration is here given to the MIRACLES of Jesus because of their importance for a right understanding of his mission. The approach of many toward the gospel narratives is governed by their prior approach to the miracles. It is essential therefore to discuss something of their validity and character before examining their purpose.

A. The validity of miracles

1. Various approaches to Jesus' miracles. No one looking at the life of Jesus Christ can proceed far without being required to come to terms with his miracles. There are philosophical and scientific problems that at once arise, as a result of which many conclude for the impossibility of miracles. It is not in place here to debate this issue, but no serious investigation of the life of Jesus can pass it by. It naturally follows that those who adopt the position that miracles do not happen are obliged to explain away the miraculous elements in the gospel narratives. During the period of 19th-cent. criticism, as pointed out earlier, either the miracles were rationalized and retained in the narrative or else they were discounted and consequently ignored. There is no denying that the presence of these miraculous elements was a considerable embarrassment.

MIRACLES OF JESUS IN THE GOSPELS

Recorded only in Matthew
Two blind men cured	Matt. 9:27–31
Dumb spirit cast out	Matt. 9:32–33
Tax money in the fish's mouth	Matt. 17:24–27

Recorded only in Mark
Deaf and dumb man cured	Mk. 7:31–37
Blind man cured	Mk. 8:22–26

Recorded only in Luke
Draught of fishes	Lk. 5:1–11
Widow's son raised from the dead at Nain	Lk. 7:11–17
Woman's infirmity cured	Lk. 13:11–17
Dropsy cured	Lk. 14:1–6
Ten lepers cleansed	Lk. 17:11–19
Malchus' ear healed	Lk. 22:50–51

Recorded only in John
Water made wine at Cana	Jn. 2:1–11
Nobleman's son cured of fever	Jn. 4:46–54
Impotent man cured at Jerusalem	Jn. 5:1–9
Man born blind cured at Jerusalem	Jn. 9:1–7
Lazarus raised from the dead	Jn. 11:38–44
Catch of 153 fish	Jn. 21:1–14

Recorded in Matthew and Mark
Syrophoenician's daughter cured	Matt. 15:28; Mk. 7:24
The 4,000 fed	Matt. 15:32; Mk. 8:1
Fig-tree cursed	Matt. 21:19; Mk. 11:13–14

Recorded in Matthew and Luke
Centurion's palsied servant cured	Matt. 8:5; Lk. 7:1
Blind and dumb demoniac cured	Matt. 12:22; Lk. 11:14

Recorded in Mark and Luke
Demoniac in synagogue cured	Mk. 1:23; Lk. 4:33

Recorded in Matthew, Mark, Luke
Leper cured	Matt. 8:2; Mk. 1:40; Lk. 5:12
Peter's mother-in-law cured	Matt. 8:14; Mk. 1:30; Lk. 4:38
Tempest stilled	Matt. 8:23; Mk. 4:37; Lk. 8:22
Demoniacs cured	Matt. 8:28; Mk. 5:1; Lk. 8:26
Paralytic cured	Matt. 9:2; Mk. 2:3; Lk. 5:18
Jairus' daughter raised	Matt. 9:23; Mk. 5:23; Lk. 8:41
Woman's issue of blood cured	Matt. 9:20; Mk. 5:25; Lk. 8:43
Man's withered hand cured	Matt. 12:10; Mk. 3:1; Lk. 6:6
Devil cast out of boy	Matt. 17:14; Mk. 9:17; Lk. 9:37
Blind man cured	Matt. 20:30; Mk. 10:46; Lk. 18:35

Recorded in Matthew, Mark, and John
Christ walks on the sea	Matt. 14:25; Mk. 6:48; Jn. 6:19

Recorded in all the Gospels
The 5,000 fed	Matt. 14:15; Mk. 6:34; Lk. 9:10; Jn. 6:1–14

During the 20th cent. however, there was much recession of scientific skepticism regarding the possibility of miracles, although the discounting of the miracles as data for a reconstruction of the historical Jesus is still a powerful movement. Those of the Bultmann school of thought who challenge the Jesus of history find no difficulty over the miracles, for the miracle stories are considered to be creations of the primitive communities. But it should be noted that the dispensing with the miraculous in this case is part of the essentially a priori position of this school and does not follow from a detailed consideration of the evidence. Some who have passionately believed in the historical Jesus, as the classical liberal schools did (late 1800s and early 1900s), have attempted to produce lives of Jesus that lack the miraculous element, but these have more the appearance of what their authors wanted to see as the historical Jesus rather than what corresponds to historical facts. The miracles of Jesus are too baffling for those who wish to reduce everything to the level of their own experience.

The fact is that miracles are deeply imprinted on the records of the Gospels, and it seems reasonable to consider them as an essential part of the overall presentation of Jesus. The problem whether they may be regarded as actual happenings or whether they have been modified or even created in course of the transmission of the traditions is a relevant one and will be considered in the course of the general comments below.

2. The classification of miracles. The various miracles that are attributed to Jesus may be placed into one of two categories, healing miracles and nature miracles. The distinction is important because less difficulty is thought to attach to many of the healing miracles than to the nature miracles, mainly because they are more open to medical explanation.

Among the healing miracles a further classification has been suggested between cases of nervous disorders and other cases, because for the former modern science has methods of bringing relief that were unknown to the time of Jesus. Some conditions related in the Gospels may certainly be cases where mind has dominated over matter and where the greater mind of Jesus brought physical relief. Such an explanation may be the right one in some instances, but Jesus in his miracles was infinitely more than a great psychologist or psychiatrist. Those cases in which he concerned himself with the sin of those who were healed shows that his main concern was spiritual. At the same time, what power the modern psychologist has is but a pale reflection of the competence Jesus showed when dealing with nervous disorders.

Moreover, Jesus certainly performed some healing miracles that cannot be regarded as cases with which modern medical science could deal to bring about a similar result. A withered hand cannot be restored, nor can dead people be brought back to life after an interval of time. There is a considerable element of the inexplicable in the miracles attributed to Jesus, which in the end must either be accepted or rejected. The issue really rests on the question, "Was Jesus the kind of person who might reasonably be expected to do the inexplicable?" An attempt will be made below to give adequate reasons for an affirmative answer to this question, but before doing so some comments are necessary on the nature miracles.

Among these miracles the most notable are the draught of fishes (Lk. 5:1–11; cf. Jn. 21:1–11), the stilling of the storm (Matt. 8:26; Mk. 4:37–39; Lk. 8:22–24), and the feeding of the 5,000 (Matt. 14:15–21; Mk. 6:35–44; Lk. 9:12–17; Jn. 6:5–13). The last miracle is the only one that appears in all four Gospels, a fact which fixes special attention upon it. This miracle appears to involve the operation of forces that are quite different from natural processes, while the other two are instances of control over such processes. Leaving aside for the moment the question of the purpose of these miracles in the mind of Jesus, the impact of them on the observers is beyond doubt. As a result of the draught of fishes Peter becomes overwhelmed with a sense of sinfulness, while all were afraid after the storm had abated at Jesus' command.

3. The characteristics of the gospel miracles. Form critics have pointed out that the healing miracle stories conform to a pattern, since they contain a description of the condition, followed generally by some indication that the person desired to be healed, with some evidence of faith on the part of the healed, and this is then followed by an account of the healing, usually with some comment on the result. It is not surprising that most healing stories follow a similar pattern. But it is significant that the part played by faith is often stressed in the synoptics, although it is not mentioned in every case. The ten lepers' cry for mercy was evidently regarded as evidence of a sufficient faith-relationship (Lk 17:11–19), for Jesus at once proceeded to heal them. The faith element marks out Jesus as distinct from a mere wonder-worker whose actions are directed toward drawing attention to himself. That the healing miracles depended on a relationship of trust is evident from the Gospels, and in this respect the miracles themselves are valuable evidence that Jesus was the kind of person who elicited trust from others.

The faith-element is not brought to the fore to the same extent in the fourth gospel, but it is by no means absent. The characteristic feature in this gospel is the use of the word SIGN, which draws attention to the spiritual significance behind the event. More will be said on this when the purpose of the miracles is discussed, but it is again clear that none of these miracles was performed for its own sake. Throughout the accounts there is a marked restraint, and indeed on many occasions, silence regarding a healing is specifically enjoined.

4. Principles of verification. Due to the various source theories that have been propounded, there has been a tendency to differentiate between the miracle stories on the basis of the number of witnesses attesting to any individual incident. Thus those in three or four of the Gospels are regarded as superior to those which appear in only one or two. In this way such miracles as the coin in the fish's mouth (Matt. 17:24–25) or the mass raisings from the tombs (27:52–53) are regarded as inferior. But the criterion used is not a good one, for a single witness may be as reliable as two or three. If the testimony of one witness becomes suspect in comparison with others this is a different matter, but in the instances cited this is not proved. Matthew does not heighten the miraculous when relating events also mentioned by others, and in view of this there is no reason to expect that he will do so when recording unique material.

It must be assumed that all the miracles that have been preserved in the gospel tradition were evidently regarded as equally authentic. All that the modern scholar can do is to examine each individually with a view to ascertaining its probability, but this quest may be futile, since probability will depend on a prior concept of the power of Jesus. Thus this whole question of probability deserves further examination.

5. The probability of the miracles. As mentioned at the commencement of this section on miracles, probability may be decided on philosophical or scientific grounds. If this results in a negative conclusion, no specific discussion of the miracles of Jesus will be valid. But another and more satisfactory method, which does not in itself exclude philosophical and scientific considerations, is to view the whole matter historically and theologically. The first stage is the gospel accounts, for these testify to the strong belief on the part of the evangelists, and presumably also on the part of the early church as a whole, that Jesus performed such miracles. This fact raises the question of the origin of such a firm faith. If Jesus had performed no works of this character, it is difficult to believe that in such a comparatively short period so many remarkable works would have been attributed to him. Some argue that the early Christians created stories out of the impetus of their new-found faith in Jesus Christ, but it is incredible that they would have created them ex nihilo. The fact that they found nothing incongruous between the gospel account of the miracles and their view of Jesus suggests that their high regard for him had some basis in historical fact. The church's Easter

Burial shroud with a round opening that was placed over the eyes of the deceased. After the resurrection of Jesus, his burial garments were found on the tomb bench.

faith presupposed that the historical Jesus was capable of performing miracles.

This leads to what is probably the most important consideration in any approach to miracles: the relevance of the RESURRECTION OF JESUS CHRIST for the inquiry. Christianity itself rests on a stupendous miracle—the raising of Christ from the dead—and it may reasonably be maintained that, if God raised Christ from the dead, the other miracles present no difficulty. The force of this position is naturally lost on those who regard the resurrection not as historical but as having taken place in the experience of believers (as Bultmann). If the remarkable emergence of the Christian faith in the form of a personal faith in the risen Christ is to be explained at all, it demands some explanation that adequately accounts for the totally unexpected transformation in the first Christian disciples. The actual resurrection of Christ as an objective and verifiable reality, testified to by innumerable eyewitnesses, is alone sufficient. Moreover, the evidences for the appearances of the risen Christ are so well attested that they cannot be explained away without doing injustice to the witnesses' testimony.

Granted, therefore, that the resurrection of Jesus must be regarded as an integral part of the Christian faith, it is difficult to see how lesser miracles could be treated as incongruous, unless they were out of keeping with what the Gospels record about the risen Christ. But this is not true. It may be safely claimed that there is not one of the miracles which could not be conceived of as the work of Jesus. There is a complete absence of the tendency, seen all too vividly in the later church, to embellish miracle stories with fantastic details.

A further consideration is the evidence from the temptation of Jesus, which shows his general approach to the miraculous. It is clear that self interest was at once rejected as an unworthy motive for the performing of miracles. This is clear from the refusal to provide bread from stones, although there is an implicit assumption that Jesus had power to do so; otherwise the temptation would have been entirely unreal. Moreover, the suggestion that Jesus should throw himself from the pinnacle of the temple was equally refused because he did not accept the principle that miraculous power should be used for self-display. If the miracle stories are approached through the temptation narrative, the motives behind them will not be misconstrued.

Following this reference to the temptation, some mention must be made of the various instances of exorcisms in the Gospels, for they show the close connection between many of the healing miracles and the spirit world. Some of the conditions described in the Gospels may now be described in psychiatric terminology, but this does not explain away the spiritual conflict involved. Exorcism forms an important aspect of the ministry of the church, and it is inconceivable that Jesus regarded his own exorcisms as anything other than evidence of his power over the enemy. It should be noted, however, that the cases of demon possession which are recorded are not cases of excessive wickedness in the individual possessed.

The characteristic features of the condition of those possessed must have presented Jesus with a constant challenge. A primitive church, which believed that Jesus in his death and resurrection had vanquished the power of evil, would find no difficulty in the cases of exorcisms in the Gospels. It would have been more surprising if such cases had been lacking.

B. The purpose of the miracles. It is to the Gospel of John that we must turn for a statement of the evangelist's purpose in including the "signs" of Jesus. He says it is that his readers might "believe that Jesus is the Messiah, the Son of God" (Jn. 20:30–31), but it is relevant to inquire whether Jesus himself had a similar view. It is at once noticeable that he does not describe his own works as signs, but he does, according to John, urge his hearers to believe his works if they cannot believe his words (10.38). Did he then regard his miracles as didactic, as designed to impart some spiritual truth? Some scholars have argued this point to such an extent as to suggest that some of the stories were first parables, which in course of transmission have been transformed into miracles. The withering of the fig tree has been cited as an example. But even if a miracle performs the function of a parable, one need not infer that this function accounts for its origin. In many of the events recorded some spiritual lessons are discernible, and it seems reasonable to suppose that this was part of the purpose of Jesus. The stilling of the storm, for instance, drew attention to the poverty of the disciples' faith.

Do the miracles have any bearing upon the messianic claims of Jesus? Whatever the general expectancy that the coming Messiah would perform signs, the Gospels do not give the impression that Jesus intended observers to deduce from his miracles evidence of his messianic office. Indeed, the temptation narrative would seem to be against any display. Miracles may be regarded as corroborating evidence for Christians who had already come to identify the risen Christ with the long-awaited Jewish Messiah, but this factor does not appear to be a main motive for the miracles. One motive that is much stressed in the synoptics is compassion. The healing miracles were often performed when a person's need awoke compassion in the Healer, and this element draws attention to the intensely human aspect of many of the miracles. That Jesus was frequently most concerned with this aspect is seen from the fact that silence was sometimes immediately enjoined. A few acts of compassion could otherwise easily have grown into a mass ministry of healing, which Jesus clearly avoided, because it would deflect him from his main redemptive purpose.

The most important thing about the miracles is what one learns from them about Jesus himself. The element of restraint is self-evident. The miracles are samples of a power that belonged to the nature of Jesus, and his refraining from using that power is on occasions more eloquent than its use. He could have commanded more than twelve legions of angels to come to his aid (Matt. 26:53), but this exercise of power would have run counter to the purpose of his mission. Indeed, it is here that the key to an understanding of the miracles is to be found, for Jesus had one dominating purpose—to fulfill the Father's will. This is brought out more clearly in John's gospel than elsewhere, but it is of utmost importance. He did not regard any of his works as his own. They were the Father's works. They are evidences, therefore, of the Father's pleasure in the Son, and are accordingly a witness to his divine claims.

The miracles may be incredible as works of a man, however perfect, but new possibilities are opened up when the man concerned not only claimed to be Son of God, but was acknowledged to be so by the early Christians.

VIII. Jesus Christ in early Christian thought. It does not lie within the scope of this book to give a full discussion of Christological problems, but no account of Jesus Christ would be complete that failed to consider the place he gained in the theology of the developing church. For this reason a brief survey will be given of the different though complementary lines of approach found in the various NT books.

A. Primitive thought. First to be considered must be the view of Jesus found in the primitive *kerygma* (the content of preaching), the sources for which are the early speeches in Acts and some earlier traditional material taken over by Paul. To this must be added any data that can be deduced from the manner in which the evangelists commented on their materials. That Jesus Christ immediately became the center of the church's proclamation is not only an undeniable fact, but in the nature of the case could not have been otherwise. It was his resurrection which transformed the tragedy of the cross into a triumph. The church was founded on the fact that Jesus was not dead, but alive.

Various titles used of Jesus in the speeches in Acts reveal what the early Christians understood of the nature of his mission. He is certainly identified as the Messiah (Christ), as is clear from Peter's first sermon (Acts 2:36), where the messiahship is linked with lordship. This shows a remarkable penetration into the real nature of Jesus of Nazareth, which was basic to all primitive Christian theology. The human Jesus is now the exalted Lord. For a further clear identification of Jesus as the Christ, see Acts 3:20; 4:10; 5:42; 8:5.

More distinctive of the Acts speeches is the description "servant," which connects Jesus with the SERVANT OF THE LORD passages of Isaiah. It seems reasonable to suggest that the early Christians made this identification on the strength of the marked similarity between Isa. 53 and the death of Jesus. Some have disputed this identification as an element in primitive theology (e.g., M. D. Hooker, *Jesus and the Servant* [1959]), but it cannot be excised from all the streams of early Christian thought where it appears. It occurs in Acts 3:13, 26; 4:27. In the first two occurrences it is God who takes the part of the Servant and exalts him. This Servant concept played an important part in the primitive interpretation of the death of Christ, and also supplied a powerful example for Christians under trial (cf. 1 Pet. 2:21–25).

Another designation distinctive of the book of Acts is "author of life" (Acts 3:15; KJV, "Prince of life"), indicating that Jesus is for the Christians the dispenser of life, but life understood in a new way, namely, life dominated by the power of the risen Christ. Stephen, in his defense before the Sanhedrin, introduces Jesus under the name of the "Righteous One" (7:52), which must be understood as a confession of the sinless character of Jesus. It is noteworthy that in neither of the mission speeches of Paul recorded in Acts does the apostle use any specific title for Jesus other than "Savior" (13:23).

Although interest in the historical life of Jesus is overshadowed by the dominant focus upon his resurrection, such references are not entirely lacking. Peter's speech to Cornelius is of the greatest importance (Acts 10:34–43). This passage shows interest in Jesus' preaching ministry in Galilee and Judea, in his endowment with the Spirit (understood as a divine anointing—evidently at his baptism by John), in his works of healing and exorcism, and in his death and resurrection. The exalted Lord was none other than Jesus of Nazareth, whose doings and words could be recalled by those who saw and heard them.

From the speeches in Acts may be deduced not only the exalted concept of Jesus Christ that was held by the early believers, but also the fact that on the basis of his death and resurrection, salvation could now be offered to all who would repent and believe in him (cf. Acts 2:38–39; 3:19, 25–26; 4:12; 5:14). Jesus Christ had become the key to the divine offer of forgiveness. Moreover, the Holy Spirit's activity is inseparably connected with the continuing activity of Jesus in his church (cf. 2:33; 5:32).

In the editorial sections of the Gospels, a similar exalted concept of Jesus is seen. Matthew and Luke, for instance, in their different ways include supernatural elements in the birth story. Mark begins his gospel with a description of Jesus as Son of God (Mk. 1:1). In Matthew and to a lesser extent in Mark and Luke the coming of Jesus is set against the background of OT prophecy. The evangelists never thought of Jesus except as the One foreshadowed by the prophets. Both Matthew and Mark made it clear that the dynamic works of Jesus were restricted through unbelief (Matt. 13:58; Mk. 6:5), showing how the incarnation was in some ways conditioned by human response.

The *kerygma* is seen in the works of Paul in those sections where he is indebted to others for the tradition. The most notable passage is 1 Cor. 15:3–9, in which certain facts about Christ are said to have been received. These include the fact of his death and its interpretation as "for our sins," the fact of his burial, the fact of his resurrection on the third day, and the fact of his appearances to various people, many of them named witnesses. It is clear, therefore, that while Paul is not unmindful of the importance of the facts, he is more interested in their significance, and this becomes most evident in his own distinctive Christology.

Before considering this aspect, reference must be made to two other Scripture sections singled out by Dodd as belonging to the primitive *kerygma*. Paul in Rom. 10:9 presents a primitive confession

Artistic relief of the baptism of Jesus by John the Baptist. From the door of the Church of the Annunciation in Nazareth.

of faith, "Jesus is Lord," which is said to be sufficient for salvation. Dodd also sees Rom. 1:1–4 as a possible early Christian creedal statement; if this is true, it shows the recognition of his Davidic descent, of his Sonship, of the powerful effects of the Lordship. All these features are fully developed by the apostle in his doctrinal teaching.

B. Pauline thought

1. Preliminary observations. The history of criticism shows that Paul has often been accused of imposing upon the primitive gospel his own concepts of Jesus Christ. For this reason it is essential to recognize the unity of Paul's view of Jesus Christ with that of the primitive community and, indeed, with that taught by Jesus concerning himself. Some of the earlier critics, such as F. C. Baur, maintained that Paul's concept of Christ was due directly to his logical processes of mind. This theory failed because it did not take into account sufficiently the objective reality of Paul's Damascus road experience.

Later interpreters of Paul have regarded his Christology as representing Hellenistic Christianity, a process also claimed for Johannine Christology. Again, the thoroughly Jewish character of some of Paul's fundamental concepts (e.g., his concept of righteousness) cannot be so explained. The same goes for supposed pagan influences upon Paul's mind (as in Bultmann's theory of the redeemer myth and the heavenly man). Quite apart from the fact that supporting evidence is much too late to be valid for the period of Paul's ministry, the claim that Christianity was mixed in Paul's mind with such pagan myths would require indubitable evidence to substantiate it (see GNOSTICISM). Probability is heavily weighted against it. It is more credible to see Paul's view of Christ as a development of what was inherently present in the primitive ideas.

Attention has already been drawn to the apostle's knowledge of the earthly life of Jesus. This must presuppose that he accepted some connection between the historic Jesus and the Jesus who met him on the Damascus road. His experience at that time confirmed the activity of the risen Lord in the experience of his people. It was essentially Christ, not the Christians, who was the object of Paul's persecuting zeal, a realization that may well have caused him to ponder the indwelling of Christ in his people through the Spirit, which became a cardinal feature of his Christology. There can be no doubt that in Paul's case he did not begin with detailed knowledge of the historical Jesus and then work up toward an exalted Christology. It was the risen Christ who arrested him in his religious quest and it was the risen Christ who dominated his theology. There is no evidence in his epistles that it was immaterial to him whether the Jesus of the Damascus road was the same Jesus who lived in Palestine and died on a cross. His Christology makes sense only if such an identification is assumed.

2. Summary of Paul's Christology. A brief summary of the main elements in Paul's own special understanding of Christ is needed to set the historical Jesus firmly in the faith of the Christian church.

(a) *The new Adam.* Paul is deeply conscious of the human need, summarized in the failure of the first ADAM with its consequent disastrous effects on the whole race (Rom. 5:12–19). He sees, however, in Christ the head of a new race as Adam was of the old. The contrast is striking, for whereas Adam is believed to be "natural" and "earthly," Christ is seen as "spiritual" and "of heaven" (1 Cor. 15:45–48), and whereas Adam could only bring death, Christ brings life. There is no need to look to non-Jewish ideas of a heavenly man, although some parallels may exist. It is sufficient to see in this concept of the apostle a development from the comparison of the old order with the new.

(b) *The preexistent Christ.* There are certain indications that Paul accepted the preexistence of Christ. It was in the fullness of time that God sent forth his Son (Gal. 4:4). It is possible that when Paul identified the rock which followed the children of Israel as being Christ (1 Cor. 10:4), he was thinking of the existence of Christ in the period of the wilderness wanderings. When the apostle refers in 2 Cor. 8:9 to the fact that though Christ was rich yet he became poor for our sakes, there may be the suggestion of a voluntary act. There is no denying this element in the great Christological passage of Phil. 2:5–11, where the concept of Christ's humbling himself to the death of the cross, rather than grasping at equality with God, shows the profound understanding the apostle had of the incarnation.

Even if it be maintained that Paul is using an existing hymn to Christ, his use of it shows his own endorsement of this conception of Christ. The idea of Christ's preexistence does not, however, depend on a few passages, but is basic to Paul's Christology. It is directly connected with his idea of the cosmic significance of Christ.

(c) *Cosmic significance.* The major statement concerning this concept is found in Col. 1:15–20, where Paul shows Christ as (i) instrument in creation, (ii) sustainer of all, and (iii) goal of all. These ideas show that Paul's understanding of the death and resurrection of Christ in the spiritual and moral realm extend also to the cosmic realm. His superiority in the one implies his superiority in the other. He who is head of the church is head of the created order. It is important to note that the creatorship of Christ is not dwelt upon for its own sake, but for its essential part in the whole scheme of redemption. The one in whom men and women have forgiveness of sins is the same one in whom the fullness of God dwells. Such a Christology seems far removed from the historical Jesus, but there is nothing in the developed Christology of Paul that could not have come from the essential character of Jesus as seen in the Gospels. An earlier passage adumbrates something of the same thought (1 Cor. 8:6). While there are certain parallels of language between Paul's cosmic view of Christ and Greek speculative thought, his concept is unique, for Christ as agent in creation is also redeemer and head of his people. Again, the idea of WISDOM personified in Jewish wisdom literature (e.g., Prov. 8:22–23, 29–30; Wisd. 9:2) supplies certain parallels, but Paul's concept is not a personification but a person. In viewing the created world he sees all things summed up in one person, Christ as the perfect expression of the mind of God (Eph. 1:10).

(d) *Relationship with the Father.* Some passages in Paul's epistles suggest the subordination of Christ to the Father, but these must be understood by a direct comparison with the statements of Jesus. The Son is sent by God (Gal. 4:4). It is God who highly exalted him (Phil. 2:9). He will deliver up the kingdom to the Father (1 Cor. 15:28). The idea that God spared not his own Son (Rom. 8:32) may also suggest the same idea. There is much that is akin to the teaching of Jesus about himself in the fourth gospel, especially the constantly reiterated theme of his being sent to do the will of the Father. Jesus was speaking in a historical context, and it is equally clear that Paul is thinking of him in such a context rather than stating an absolute truth.

(e) *Relationship with the Spirit.* According to Paul, there is an indissoluble union between Christ and the Spirit, as there is between Christ and the Father. So close is it that some, on the strength of 2 Cor. 3:17, have suggested the idea of identity, but when Paul speaks of the Spirit of the Lord, a distinction is in mind. There is a close affinity between his concept here and that found in Acts, where the work of the Spirit and the continuing work of Jesus in his church are essentially related.

It will be seen that Paul's view of Christ is inseparably linked with the historical Jesus, who is everywhere assumed, and reaches out toward a full-orbed concept of him in harmony with the revelation of the Easter event. The resurrection of Jesus did not make him what he was not before in his essence, but it did reveal his true nature and released divine power for salvation.

C. Johannine thought. The teaching of Jesus about himself in the fourth gospel has already been mentioned, but there are features in the presentation of Jesus by John in this gospel that throw light on early Christology. The most significant is the LOGOS doctrine in the prologue (Jn. 1:1–18). The choice of such an opening is illuminating by way of comparison with the synoptics. It at once draws attention to the preexistence of Christ, to his creatorship, and to his Godhead. What the origin is of the term Logos, used in this sense, is not of vital importance for our present purpose, for it is the characteristic, rather than the origin, of the Logos that reveals John's concept of Christ. Unlike Philo's Logos, John's Logos reaches his fulfillment in incarnation (1:14). Since, after mentioning it here, John does not again refer to the Logos, it cannot be regarded as the key for the understanding of his gospel. Nevertheless, in his account of the historical Jesus, he does not intend the reader to be unaware that this Jesus possessed a divine nature. He never thought of his narrative as the record of a man, however perfect, but as the record of the eternal Son of God in human form.

Jesus on his throne flanked by John and Mary. From the Church of Hagia Sophia in Istanbul.

The stated purpose of the Gospel in Jn. 20:30–31 must be noted, for it shows not only John's evangelical purpose, but also his essential view of Christ. "That you may believe that Jesus is the Messiah, the Son of God" reveals a double aspect of his person. His messiahship and his divine Sonship are reckoned to shine through his words and works. To John, Jesus is nothing less than "God the One and Only, who is at the Father's side" (1:18). That John's account is primarily theological in purpose rather than historical cannot be denied, but this does not mean that the history was unimportant. John's whole purpose is, in fact, to show the entry of the divine into history. It has earlier been mentioned that John records more specific examples of the real humanity of Jesus than the synoptics do. He is wearied with travel, suffers thirst (ch. 4), expresses strong indignation (cf. 11:33, 38), and weeps (11:35).

The Johannine epistles share the same exalted view of Christ as does the fourth gospel. His Sonship is frequently stressed. He is called our ADVOCATE (1 Jn. 2:1 NRSV; NIV, "one who speaks ... in our defense") and is named as Jesus the righteous. His messiahship is insisted upon (2:22; 4:2; 5:1) in such a way as to exclude any Docetic notion of drawing a distinction between Jesus and the Christ. He is moreover named as Savior of the world (4:14). Indeed, there is much in 1 John that echoes the language and ideas of John's gospel and shows that both books share the same Christological viewpoint. Second John reflects the same position (cf. 2 Jn. 7, 9).

In the Apocalypse, a further aspect of Christology is seen. The central figure is the Lamb, who is a slain yet triumphant figure. The link with the historical Jesus is unmistakable, but the Lamb's exaltation shows his commanding position in the cosmic drama. Although many setbacks come to God's people, there is never any doubt about the ultimate result. The most dominant factor is that the Lamb has become the Judge to execute judgment upon those opposed to the divine will. This aspect is seen in the writer's vision of the one like the Son of Man in the midst of the candlesticks (Rev. 1:12–16). From his mouth there issued a sword, in his hand were securely held the stars that represented his people. It is important to note that the name he bears at the moment of judgment is "the Word of God" (19:13), which provides a direct link with the prologue of John's gospel. He is, moreover, King of kings and Lord of lords, the ALPHA AND OMEGA, all titles that suggest the sovereignty of the Lamb.

D. Other aspects of Christ. In the epistle to the Hebrews, the most characteristic concept of Jesus is that of High Priest, which controls the development of the argument of the whole epistle. The new revelation that has come in Christ marks him out as superior to the prophets (Heb. 1:1), to Moses (3:1–6), and to Aaron (5:1–6). He belongs to a new order, that of MELCHIZEDEK, which nevertheless is essentially a priestly order. The writer sets the tone for his letter in 1:2–3, where he reveals his exalted concept of Christ as heir and creator of all things, and bearing the very stamp of God's nature. He could not have expressed more vividly the absolute sovereignty of Christ, and yet he links with this the fact that he has purged our sins. The inseparable connection between the historical act of redemption and the present exalted position of Christ is inescapable. This is borne out by the references in the epistle to aspects of the earthly experience of Jesus: his temporarily inferior position to the angels, his condescension to suffering and death (2:9), his subjection to temptation (2:18), his faithfulness (3:6), his agonizing prayers (5:7), the specific reference to "the days of his flesh" (5:7 NRSV), and his determination to do God's will (10:5–7).

The mission of Jesus historically is viewed in sacrificial terms. The difference between the offering of Jesus and the offerings of the Aaronic order rested in the character of both offering and offerer. The perfection of Christ insured the complete adequacy of his offering. This interpretation of the work of Christ shows the exalted concept of his character which the writer held. His exposition is also valuable because it draws attention to the present mission of Jesus in his exalted position. It is a ministry of intercession (Heb. 4:15; 7:25). There is a constant representative of man at the right hand of God, who, in spite of the fact that he is a consuming fire (12:29), is nevertheless a God of mercy (4:16).

Another view of Christ brought to the fore in Hebrews is that of ratifier of the new covenant (Heb. 8:6—9:28). Because of the inadequacy of the old covenant, the inauguration of the new was of vital concern to mankind. What Jesus himself foreshadowed at the institution of the Lord's Supper, the writer to the Hebrews develops. Here is seen the fulfillment of Jeremiah's prophecy (Jer. 31:31–34, cf. Heb. 8:8), which emphasizes the essential inwardness of the new as contrasted with the old. In this is shown once again the superiority of Christ over Moses, and, ipso facto, the superiority of Christianity over Judaism.

In 1 Peter the Christology conforms to a pattern similar to the other streams of thought already mentioned. There is awareness, on the one hand, of the human aspect of the character of Jesus Christ, for he is said to have left us an example to follow in his steps. This must mean a concentration on the historical Jesus, whose sufferings in order to form an example for believers must be of the same kind as theirs. The uniqueness of his sufferings lies in the fact that he bore our sins (1 Pet. 2:24; 4:18). He is called "Shepherd and Overseer" (2:25; cf. 5:4), both of which titles stress his special care for his people. The Lordship of Christ is assumed (cf. 1 Pet. 1:3; 3:15, 21–22). His role as Redeemer of his people is particularly brought out by means of the Servant passage in 2:21–24, by the allusions to the exodus in 1:15–16, and by the frequent reference to his sufferings.

There are undoubtedly affinities between the Christology of 1 Peter and that of Paul. It is quite unnecessary to suppose that in all these relationships Peter is dependent on Paul, for most are basic to the primitive *kerygma*. Both Peter and Paul develop these basic concepts in their own way. It is possible that the affinities between 1 Peter and Romans and Ephesians may be due to literary influences. But it is certain, whatever the decision on that matter may be, that both apostles held the same exalted view of Christ and the same conviction about the continuity between this concept and the historic Jesus. The most individualistic feature in Peter's Christology is his reference to the descent of Christ into HADES, presumably in the interval between his death and resurrection (1 Pet. 3:18–19). Whatever the precise explanation of this difficult statement, it is evident that Peter conceived of an extension of the preaching ministry of Jesus even after his death.

In 2 Peter Jesus Christ is named as Savior (2 Pet. 1:1) and as Lord (1:2; cf. also 1:8, 11; 2:20; 3:2, 18). His majesty is specially mentioned and leads to a specific reference to the transfiguration (1:16–17). Another allusion is to the Master who bought them (2:1), a clear reference to the redemptive activity of Christ as in 1 Pet. 1. Although far less developed in its Christology as compared with 1 Peter, this epistle is nonetheless in line with the general primitive position.

James is remarkably sparse in its references to Christ, the only specific instances being in Jas. 1:1 and 2:1. In both of these he is called the Lord Jesus Christ, and in the latter also the Lord of glory. Yet this is not the extent of the witness of this epistle to Christ. There are more echoes of the sayings of Jesus in this epistle than in any other NT book, particularly from the Sermon on the Mount. It may be inferred that James knew much of the historical Jesus, but he nonetheless conceived him to be the Lord of glory. If his interests are mainly ethical in this epistle, this is no criterion for supposing that the two references to Christ are the total extent of his Christological understanding.

The brief epistle of Jude shares a Christology similar to 2 Peter. Christ is Master and Lord (Jude 4), and the same title Lord Jesus Christ is used three times (vv. 17, 21, 25).

E. Conclusion. However many-sided the views of the early Christians regarding Jesus, there is a basic oneness throughout. Jesus is more than a figure of history, although he is that. He is the exalted Lord whose power ranges over the whole created order, but he holds a special relationship to his church.

(In addition to the works mentioned in the body of the article, important studies in the areas of background and sources include the following: C. G. Montefiore, *Rabbinic Literature and Gospel*

Teachings [1930]; J. Bonsirven, *Le judaisme palestinien au temps de Jésus-Christ* [1935]; J. Jocz, *The Jewish People and Jesus Christ* [1949]; W. L. Bundy, *Jesus and the First Three Gospels* [1955]; J. Jeremias, *Unknown Sayings of Jesus* [1957]; R. Bultmann, *Jesus Christ and Mythology* [1958]; P. Althaus, *The So-called Kerygma and the Historical Jesus* [1959]; R. M. Grant and D. N. Freedman, *The Secret Sayings of Jesus* [1960]; F. W. Beare, *The Earliest Records of Jesus* [1962]; C. E. Braaten and R. A. Harrisville, *The Historical Jesus and the Kerygmatic Christ* [1964]; G. Vermes, *Jesus and the World of Judaism* [1983]; E. P. Sanders, *Jesus and Judaism* [1985].

(Influential works on the life of Christ include C. Geikie, *The Life and Words of Christ* [1891]; B. Weiss, *The Life of Christ* [1894]; W. Bousset, *Jesus* [1906]; D. Smith, *The Days of His Flesh*, 5th ed. [1906]; W. Sanday, *The Life of Christ in Recent Research* [1907]; J. Seeley, *Ecce Homo* [1908]; T. R. Glover, *The Jesus of History* [1920]; A. C. Headlam, *The Life and Teaching of Jesus* [1923]; W. Sanday, *Outlines of the Life of Christ* [1925]; J. Klausner, *Jesus of Nazareth*, 2nd ed. [1929]; M. Goguel, *Life of Jesus* [1933]; H. J. Cadbury, *The Peril of Modernizing Jesus* [1937]; M. Dibelius, *Jesus* [1949]; A. M. Hunter, *The Work and Words of Jesus* [1950]; E. J. Goodspeed, *A Life of Jesus* [1950]; V. Taylor, *The Life and Ministry of Jesus* [1955]; M. J. Borg, *Jesus: A New Vision* [1987]; G. Theissen, *The Shadow of the Galilean* [1987]; B. Witherington, *The Jesus Quest: The Third Search for the Jew of Nazareth* [1995]; M. J. Borg and N. T. Wright, *The Meaning of Jesus: Two Visions* [1999]; J. D. G. Dunn and S. McKnight, eds., *The Historical Jesus in Recent Research* [2005]; P. R. Eddy and G. A. Boyd, *The Jesus Legend: A Case for the Historical Reliability of the Synoptic Jesus Tradition* [2007].

(On the teaching, miracles, and theological significance of Jesus, see G. B. Stevens, *The Teaching of Jesus* [1901]; J. Denney, *Jesus and the Gospel* [1909]; H. R. Mackintosh, *The Doctrine of the Person of Jesus Christ*, 3rd ed. [1914]; B. S. Easton, *Christ in the Gospels* [1930]; R. Bultmann, *Jesus and the Word* [1935]; C. H. Dodd, *The Parables of the Kingdom* [1935]; R. Otto, *The Kingdom of God and the Son of Man* [1938]; A. N. Wilder, *Eschatology and Ethics in the Teaching of Jesus* [1939]; A. Richardson, *Miracle Stories of the Gospels* [1941]; V. Taylor, *Jesus and His Sacrifice* [1943]; E. C. Colwell, *An Approach to the Teaching of Jesus* [1947]; F. V. Filson, *Jesus Christ the Risen Lord* [1956]; W. G. Kümmel, *Promise and Fulfillment* [1956]; J. Knox, *Jesus Lord and Christ* [1958]; J. S. Stewart, *The Life and Teaching of Jesus Christ*, 2nd ed. [1958]; G. E. Ladd, *The Gospel of the Kingdom* [1959]; A. M. Hunter, *Interpreting the Parables* [1960]; H. Ridderbos, *The Coming of the Kingdom* [1962]; R. H. Fuller, *Interpreting the Miracles* [1963]; I. H. Marshall, *Eschatology and the Parables* [1963]; W. D. Davies, *The Setting of the Sermon on the Mount* [1964]; E. Best, *The Temptation and the Passion* [1965]; C. H. F. Henry, ed., *Jesus of Nazareth, Saviour and Lord* [1966]; B. F. Meyer, *The Aims of Jesus* [1979]; E. Schillebeeckx, *Jesus: An Experiment in Christology* [1979]; J. Macquarrie, *Jesus Christ in Modern Thought* [1990]; G. R. Beasley-Murray, *Jesus and the Last Days: The Interpretation of the Olivet Discourse* [1993]; N. T. Wright, *Jesus and the Victory of God* [1996]; J. D. G. Dunn, *Jesus Remembered* [2003]; L. W. Hurtado, *Lord Jesus Christ: Devotion to Jesus in Earliest Christianity* [2003]. For many substantial essays with extensive bibliographies, see J. B. Green et al., eds., *Dictionary of Jesus and the Gospels* [1992].)

D. GUTHRIE

AN OUTLINE OF THE LIFE OF CHRIST

Facts before his birth: The angel Gabriel appears to Mary (Lk. 1:26–38); Mary visits Elisabeth (1:39–56); Mary's Magnificat (1:46–55); an angel appears to Joseph concerning Mary (Matt. 1:18–25).

Birth (Lk. 2:1–7).

Angels appear to the shepherds (Lk. 2:8–20).

Magi visit (Matt. 2:1–12).

Circumcision (Lk. 2:21); presented in the temple (2:21–38).

Flight into, and return from, Egypt (Matt. 2:13–23).

Disputes with the doctors in the temple (Lk. 2:41–52).

Is baptized by John (Matt. 3:13–17; Mk. 1:9–11; Lk. 3:21–23).

Temptation (Matt. 4:1–11; Mk. 1:12–13; Lk. 4:1–13).
John's testimony concerning him (Jn. 1:1–18).
Testimony of John the Baptist concerning him (Jn. 1:19–34).
Disciples adhere to him (Jn. 1:35–51).
Miracle at Cana of Galilee (Jn. 2:1–12).
Drives the money changers from the temple (Jn. 2:13–25); Nicodemus (3:1–21).
Baptizes (Jn. 3:22, with 4:2).
Returns to Galilee (Matt. 4:12; Mk. 1:14; Lk. 4:14; Jn. 4:1–3).
Visits Sychar and teaches the Samaritan woman (Jn. 4:4–42).
Teaches in Galilee (Matt. 4:17; Mk. 1:14–15; Lk. 4:14–15; Jn 4:43–45).
Heals a nobleman's son of Capernaum (Jn. 4:46–54).
Is rejected by the people of Nazareth, dwells at Capernaum (Matt. 4:13–16; Lk. 4:16–31).
Chooses Peter, Andrew, James, and John as disciples, miracle of the draught of fishes (Matt. 4:18–22; Mk. 1:16–20; Lk. 5:1–11).
Preaches throughout Galilee (Matt. 4:23–25; Mk. 1:35–39; Lk. 4:42–44).
Heals a demoniac (Mk. 1:21–28; Lk. 4:31–37).
Heals Peter's mother-in-law (Matt. 8:14–17; Mk. 1:29–34; Lk. 4:38–41).
Heals a leper in Galilee (Matt. 8:2–4; Mk. 1:40–45; Lk. 5:12–16).
Heals a paralytic (Matt. 9:2–8; Mk. 2:1–12; Lk. 5:17–26).
Calls Matthew (Matt. 9:9; Mk. 2:13–14; Lk. 5:27–28).
Heals an impotent man at the pool of Bethesda on the Sabbath day, is persecuted, and makes his defense (Jn. 5).
Defines the law of the Sabbath on the occasion of his disciples plucking the ears of corn (Matt. 12:9–14; Mk. 3:1–6; Lk. 6:6–11).
Withdraws from Capernaum to the Sea of Galilee, where he heals many (Matt. 12:15–21; Mk 3:7–12).
Goes up into a mountain, and calls and ordains twelve disciples (Matt. 10:2–4; Mk. 3:13–19; Lk. 6:12–19).
Delivers the Sermon on the Mount (Matt. 5—7; Lk. 6:20–49).
Heals the servant of the centurion (Matt. 8:5–13; Lk. 7:1–10).
Raises from the dead the son of the widow of Nain (Lk. 7:11–17).
Receives the message from John the Baptist (Matt. 11:2–19; Lk. 7:18–35).
Upbraids the unbelieving cities around Capernaum (Matt. 11:20–30).
Anointed by a sinful woman (Lk. 7:36–50).
Preaches in the cities of Galilee (Lk. 8:1–3).
Heals a demoniac and denounces the scribes and Pharisees (Matt. 12:22–37; Mk. 3:19–30; Lk. 11:14–20).
Replies to the scribes and Pharisees who seek a sign from him (Matt. 12:38–45; Lk. 11:16–36).
Denounces the Pharisees and other hypocrites (Lk. 11:37–54).
Discourses to his disciples (Lk. 12:1–59).
Parable of the barren fig tree (Lk. 13:6–9).
Parable of the sower (Matt. 13:1–23; Mk. 4:1–25; Lk. 8:4–18).
Parable of the tares and other teachings (Matt. 13:24–53; Mk. 4:26–34).
Crosses the Sea of Galilee, and stills the tempest (Matt. 8:18–27; Mk. 4:35–41; Lk. 8:22–25).
Miracle of the swine (Matt. 8:28–33; Mk. 5:1–21; Lk. 8:26–40).
Returns to Capernaum (Matt. 9.1; Mk. 5:21; Lk. 8:40).
Eats with publicans and sinners, and discourses on fasting (Matt. 9:10–17; Mk. 2:15–22; Lk. 5:29–39).
Raises to life the daughter of Jairus, and heals the woman who has the issue of blood (Matt. 9:18–26; Mk. 5:22–43; Lk. 8:41–56).
Heals two blind men, and casts out a dumb spirit (Matt. 9:27–34).
Returns to Nazareth (Matt. 13:53–58; Mk. 6:1–6).
Teaches in various cities in Galilee (Matt. 9:35–38).
Instructs his disciples and empowers them to heal diseases and cast out unclean spirits (Matt. 10; Mk. 6:6–13; Lk. 9:1–6).
Herod falsely supposes him to be John, whom he had beheaded (Matt. 14:1–2, 6–12; Mk. 6:14–16, 21–29; Lk. 9:7–9).
The twelve return, he goes to the desert, multitudes follow him, and he feeds 5,000

(Matt. 14:13–21; Mk. 6:30–44; Lk. 9:10–17; Jn. 6:1–14).

Walks on the sea (Matt. 14:22–36; Mk. 6:45–56; Jn. 6:15–21).

Teaches in the synagogue in Capernaum (Jn. 6:22–65).

Disciples forsake him (Jn. 6:66–71).

He justifies his disciples in eating without washing their hands (Matt. 15:1–20; Mk. 7:1–23).

Heals the daughter of the Syrophoenician woman (Matt. 15:21–28; Mk. 7:24–30).

Heals a dumb man (Matt. 15:29–31; Mk. 7:31–37).

Feeds 4,000 (Matt. 15:32–39; Mk. 8:1–9).

Refuses to give a sign to the Pharisees (Matt. 16:1–4; Mk. 8:10–12).

Cautions his disciples against the leaven of hypocrisy (Matt. 16:4–12; Mk. 8:13–21).

Heals a blind man (Mk. 8:22–26).

Foretells his death and resurrection (Matt. 16:21–28; Mk. 8:31–38; 9:1; Lk. 9:21–27).

Is transfigured (Matt. 17:1–13; Mk. 9:2–13; Lk. 9:28–36).

Heals a demoniac (Matt. 17:14–21; Mk. 9:14–29; Lk. 9:37–43).

Foretells his death and resurrection (Matt. 17:22, 23; Mk. 9:30–32; Lk. 9:43–45).

Miracle of tribute money in the fish's mouth (Matt. 17:24–27).

Reproves the ambition of his disciples (Matt. 18:1–35; Mk. 9:33–50; Lk. 9:46–50).

Reproves the intolerance of his disciples (Mk. 9:38–39; Lk. 9:49–50).

Journeys to Jerusalem to attend the Feast of Tabernacles, passing through Samaria (Lk. 9:51–62; Jn. 7:2–11).

Commissions the Seventy (Lk. 10:1–16).

Heals ten lepers (Lk. 17:11–19).

Teaches in Jerusalem at the Feast of Tabernacles (Jn. 7:14–53; 8).

Answers a lawyer, who tests his wisdom with the question, "What shall I do to inherit eternal life?" by the parable of the good Samaritan (Lk. 10:25–37).

Hears the report of the Seventy (Lk. 10:17–24).

Teaches in the house of Mary, Martha, and Lazarus, in Bethany (Lk. 10:38–42).

Teaches his disciples to pray (Lk. 11:1–13).

Heals a blind man, who, because of his faith in Jesus, was excommunicated (Jn. 9).

Teaches in Jerusalem (Jn. 9:39–41; 10:1–21).

Teaches in the temple at Jerusalem, at the Feast of Dedication (Jn. 10:22–39).

Goes to Bethabara to escape violence from the rulers (Jn. 10:40–42; 11:3–16).

Returns to Bethany and raises Lazarus from the dead (Jn. 11:1–46).

Escapes to the city of Ephraim from the conspiracy led by Caiaphas, the high priest (Jn. 11:47–54).

Journeys toward Jerusalem to attend the Passover, heals many who are diseased, and teaches the people (Matt. 19:1, 2; Mk. 10:1; Lk. 13:10–35).

Dines with a Pharisee on the Sabbath (Lk. 14:1–24).

Teaches the multitude the conditions of discipleship (Lk. 14:25–35).

Tells the parables of the lost sheep, the lost piece of silver, prodigal son, unjust steward (Lk. 15:1–32; 16:1–13).

Reproves the hypocrisy of the Pharisees (Lk. 16).

Tells the parable of the rich man and Lazarus (Lk. 16:19–31).

Teaches his disciples concerning offenses, meekness, and humility (Lk. 17:1–10).

Teaches the Pharisees concerning the coming of his kingdom (Lk. 17:20–37).

Tells the parables of the unjust judge and of the Pharisee and publican praying in the temple (Lk. 18:1–14).

Interprets the law concerning marriage and divorce (Matt. 19:3–12; Mk. 10:2–12).

Blesses little children (Matt. 19:13–15; Mk. 10:13–16; Lk. 18:15–17).

Receives the rich young ruler, who asks what he shall do to inherit eternal life (Matt. 19:16–22; Mk. 10:17–22; Lk. 18:18–24).

Tells the parable of the vineyard (Matt. 20:1–16).

Foretells his death and resurrection (Matt. 20:17–19; Mk. 10:32–34; Lk. 18:31–34).

Listens to the mother of James and John in behalf of her sons (Matt. 20:20–28; Mk. 10:35–45).

Heals two blind men at Jericho (Matt. 20:29–34; Mk. 10:46–50; Lk. 18:35–43).

Visits Zacchaeus (Lk. 19:1–10).

Tells the parable of the pounds (Lk. 19:11–28).
Goes to Bethany six days before the passover (Jn. 12:1–9).
Triumphal entry into Jerusalem, while the people throw palm branches in the way (Matt. 21:1–11; Mk. 11:1–11; Lk. 19:29–44; Jn. 12:12–19).
Enters the temple (Matt. 21:12; Mk. 11:11; Lk. 19:45).
Drives the money changers out of the temple (Matt. 21:12–13; Lk. 19:45–46).
Heals the infirm in the temple (Matt. 21:14).
Teaches daily in the temple (Lk. 19:47–48).
Performs the miracle of causing the barren fig tree to wither (Matt. 21:17–22; Mk. 11:12–14, 20–22).
Tells the parable of the two sons (Matt. 21:28–31); the parable of the wicked husbandmen (Matt. 21:33–46; Mk. 12:1–12; Lk. 20:9–19); of the marriage (Matt. 22:1–14; Lk. 14:16–24).
Tested by the Pharisees and Herodians, and enunciates the duty of the citizen to his government (Matt. 22:15–22; Mk. 12:13–17; Lk. 20:20–26).
Tried by the Sadducees concerning the resurrection of the dead (Matt. 22:23–33; Mk. 12:18–27; Lk. 20:27–40); and by a lawyer (Matt. 22:34–40; Mk. 12:28–34).
Exposes the hypocrisies of the scribes and Pharisees (Matt. 23; Mk. 12:38–40; Lk. 20:45–47).
Extols the widow who casts two mites into the treasury (Mk. 12:41–44; Lk. 21:1–4).
Verifies the prophecy of Isaiah concerning the unbelieving Jews (Jn. 12:37–50).
Foretells the destruction of the temple and of Jerusalem (Matt. 24; Mk. 13; Lk. 21:5–36).
Laments over Jerusalem (Matt. 23:37; Lk. 19:41–44).
Tells the parables of the ten virgins and of the talents (Matt. 25:1–30).
Foretells the scenes of the day of judgment (Matt. 25:31–46).
Anointed with the box of precious ointment (Matt. 26:6–13; Mk. 14:3–9; Jn. 12:1–8).
Last Passover, and institution of the sacrament of the holy eucharist (Matt. 26:17–30; Mk. 14:12–25; Lk. 22:7–20).
Washes the disciples' feet (Jn. 13:1–17).
Foretells his betrayal (Matt. 26:23; Mk. 14:18–21; Lk. 22:21; Jn. 13:18).
Accuses Judas of his betrayal (Matt. 26:21–25; Mk. 14:18–21; Lk. 22:21–23; Jn. 13:21–30).
Teaches his disciples, comforts them, and promises the gift of the Holy Spirit (Jn. 14–16).
Last prayer (Jn. 17).
Retreats to Gethsemane (Matt. 26:30, 36–46; Mk. 14:26, 32–42; Lk. 22:39–46; Jn. 18:1).
Is betrayed and apprehended (Matt. 26:47–56; Mk. 14:43–54, 66–72; Lk. 22:47–53; Jn. 18:2–12).
Trial before Caiaphas (Matt. 26:57–58, 69–75; Mk. 14:53–54, 66–72; Lk. 22:54–62; Jn. 18:13–18, 25–27).
Led by the council to Pilate (Matt. 27:1–2, 11–14; Mk. 15:1–5; Lk. 23:1–5; Jn. 18:28–38).
Arraigned before Herod (Lk. 23:6–12).
Tried before Pilate (Matt. 27:15–26; Mk. 15:6–15; Lk. 23:13–25; Jn. 18:39–40; 19:1–16).
Mocked by the soldiers (Matt. 27:27–31; Mk. 15:16–20).
Is led away to be crucified (Matt. 27:31–34; Mk. 15:20–23; Lk. 23:26–32; Jn. 19:16–17).
Crucified (Matt. 27:35–56; Mk. 15:24–41; Lk. 23:33–49; Jn. 19:18–30).
Taken from the cross and buried (Matt. 27:57–66; Mk. 15:42–47; Lk. 23:50–56; Jn. 19:31–42).
Arises from the dead (Matt. 28:2–15; Mk. 16:1–11; Lk. 24:1–12; Jn. 20:1–18).
Is seen by Mary Magdalene (Matt. 28:1–10; Mk. 16:9; Jn. 20:11–17); by Peter (Lk. 24:34; 1 Cor. 15:5).
Appears to two disciples who journey to Emmaus (Mk. 16:12, 13; Lk. 24:13–35).
Appears in the midst of the disciples, when Thomas is absent (Mk. 16:14–18; Lk. 24:36–49; Jn. 20:19–23); when Thomas is present (Jn. 20:26–29); at the Sea of Galilee (Matt. 28:16; Jn. 21:1–14); to the apostles and upwards of 500 brethren on a mountain in Galilee (Matt. 28:16–20, with Acts 10:40–42; see also Acts 13:31; 1 Cor. 15:6–7).
Appears to James and also to all the apostles (Acts 1:3–8; 1 Cor 15:7).
Ascends to heaven (Mk. 16:19–20; Lk. 24:50–53; Acts 1:9–12).

Jesus Justus. See JUSTUS.

Jether jee´thuhr (יֶתֶר *H3508*, "abundance"; cf. ITHRA, ITHRAN, JETHRO). (1) Eldest son of GIDEON. Because of his youth, he was afraid to slay the prisoners ZEBAH AND ZALMUNNA, kings of MIDIAN, and so Gideon killed them himself (Jdg. 8:20–21).

(2) Father of AMASA, an Israelite commander who was killed by JOAB (1 Ki. 2:5, 32). Jether is identified as an Ishmaelite in 1 Chr. 2:17, but he is called "Ithra the Israelite" in 2 Sam. 17:25 MT. See ITHRA for a discussion of this problem.

(3) Son of Jada, great-grandson of JERAHMEEL, and descendant of JUDAH; he is said to have died without children (1 Chr. 2:32; cf. vv. 27–28).

(4) Son of Ezrah and descendant of Judah (1 Chr. 4:17). His precise place in the genealogy is unclear, and the verse contains some textual problems (see discussion in G. N. Knoppers, *I Chronicles 1–9*, AB 12 [2004], 341, 352–56).

(5) Descendant of ASHER (1 Chr. 7:38); apparently the same as ITHRAN son of Zophah (v. 37).

S. BARABAS

Jetheth jee´theth (יְתֵת *H3867*, derivation uncertain). Descendant of ESAU, listed among the clan chiefs of EDOM (Gen. 36:40; 1 Chr. 1:51). The name was probably applied to a territory as well.

Jethlah jeth´luh. KJV form of ITHLAH.

Jethro jeth´roh (יִתְרוֹ *H3861*, "abundance"; cf. JETHER). Priest of MIDIAN and father-in-law of MOSES (Exod. 3:1; 4:18; 18:1–12, 27). Jethro is called REUEL in two places (Exod. 2:18; Num. 10:29). In addition, Moses' father-in-law appears to be called HOBAB in Jdg. 4:11 (NRSV), but Hobab was the son of Jethro/Reuel (Num. 10:29), and it is possible that the Hebrew term *ḥōtēn H3162* in the Judges passage should be rendered "brother-in-law" (so NIV).

When Moses fled from Egypt (Exod. 2:15), he came to the land of Midian. Stopping at a watering place, he had occasion to champion the cause of seven shepherdesses, and thus gain the favor and protection of their father Jethro, a priest. Moses was content to dwell with Jethro and tend his sheep. In time he married ZIPPORAH, one of Jethro's daughters. We are not told in what religion Jethro served as priest, nor the name of its deity. We are told, however, that Moses received God's call while tending Jethro's sheep (3:1; see BURNING BUSH). In this divine-human encounter he was commissioned to deliver the enslaved Israelites. In due time Moses took his wife and children and set out for Egypt (4:20), but he must have sent them back to Midian soon after that, for they joined the camp of Israel, apparently for the first time, when Jethro made his visit there (18:1–6).

In addition to reuniting Moses and his family, the visit of Jethro was important for at least two reasons: (1) at this time he acknowledged—or perhaps reaffirmed—his faith in the supremacy of Israel's God; and (2) he assisted Moses in setting up an administrative and judicial system for Israel. On Jethro's arrival in camp, Moses seemed eager to tell his father-in-law of God's marvelous deliverance of Israel at the Red Sea, and of God's continued protection and guidance in the wilderness. When he had finished, Jethro was so deeply impressed that he began to bless the God of Israel, saying, "Now I know that the LORD [Yahweh] is greater than all other gods" (Exod. 18:11). He then witnessed his faith in Israel's God by conducting a sacrificial meal to which, along with Moses, AARON and the elders of Israel were invited. Had Jethro been previously acquainted with the God of the Hebrews? Some scholars think he was.

Jethro's next contribution came when he observed Moses trying to serve as judge and moderator for the vast multitude of ex-slaves (Exod. 18:13). He immediately saw that it was too much for one man. He advised Moses to set up a system that would organize the Israelites into a respectable nation of people, and at the same time relieve their leader of an unmanageable amount of responsibility. He outlined his method of organization (18:17–23): the multitude should be separated into units, with a leader over each unit to whom authority for settling minor problems is delegated. In this way only the more difficult problems would come to Moses. Moses quickly saw that his father-in-law was correct in his evaluation of the situation, and accepted his advice.

In the past some scholars have sought to credit Jethro for originating Mosaic religion. Involved in the problem is the name for God used in the OT.

See GOD, NAMES OF. Basing their views on Exod. 6:3, these scholars claim that God was not known to Israel as Yahweh (the LORD) until the time of Moses. They insist that Moses learned all he knew about Yahweh from Jethro, who was allegedly a Yahwistic priest among the Midianites. Moses, in turn, introduced this tribal god of the KENITES to Israel, perhaps changing things a bit to suit his needs.

Although much at this point is hidden from our view, it is evident from the Scriptures that God was known by his name Yahweh in the Palestinian area long before the time of Moses (see Gen. 4:26; 6:3, 5; 12:1, 4; et al.). To say that Moses and the children of Israel had never heard of Yahweh before meeting Jethro is inaccurate. He was none other than "the God of your fathers" (Exod. 3:13). On the other hand, it is true that Moses took an old and familiar name and deepened and enriched its meaning from his own experience with God at the burning bush, at the Red Sea, and on Mount Sinai—and in doing so he became the founder of Hebrew religion.

Because the divine name Yahweh was evidently known among the tribes of the ANE, it is altogether possible that Jethro knew and worshiped God as Yahweh before visiting Moses' camp. When one remembers that the Midianites were descendants of ABRAHAM by KETURAH (Gen. 25:2, 4; 1 Chr. 1:32–33), it is not unlikely that at least some of the Midianite tribes, such as the Kenites (Jdg. 1:16; 4:11), may have continued to worship God as Yahweh until the time of Moses. (See F. James, *Personalities of the Old Testament* [1939], 24–25; N. Glueck, *Rivers in the Desert* [1959], 132–34; W. Harrelson, *Interpreting the Old Testament* [1964], 77–80; G. L. Archer, *Survey of Old Testament Introduction*, rev. ed. [1994], 127–31.)　　C. P. GRAY

Jetur jee′tuhr (יְטוּר H3515, possibly related to צוּר H7446, "rock" [see *ABD*, 3:822]). Son of ISHMAEL and eponymous ancestor of an ISHMAELITE tribe (Gen. 25:15; 1 Chr. 1:31). The two and a half Israelite tribes in Transjordan warred with the tribe of Jetur (1 Chr. 5:19). It is possible that the inhabitants of ITUREA in NT times were descended from it (see F. V. Winnett, "The Arabian Genealogies in Genesis," in *Translating and Understanding the Old Testament*, ed. H. T. Frank and W. L. Reed [1970], 171–96, esp. 193–96).

Jeuel ji-yoo′uhl (יְעוּאֵל H3590, possibly "God is strong" or "God cures"; see also JEIEL). (1) Head of the Zerahite clan and one of the descendants of JUDAH listed among those who settled in Jerusalem after the EXILE (1 Chr. 9:6).

(2) A Levite, descendant of ELIZAPHAN, who served during the reign of HEZEKIAH (2 Chr. 29:13 NRSV; the NIV has "Jeiel," following the *Qere* and the LXX).

(3) Descendant of Adonikam and a family head who returned with EZRA from Babylon (Ezra 8:13 [KJV, "Jeiel"]; 1 Esd. 8:39 [KJV, "Jewel"]).

Jeush jee′ush (יְעוּשׁ H3593, "[God] helps"; the name *yʿš* occurs in the Samaria OSTRACA, see R. Lawton in *Bib* 65 [1984]: 330–46, esp. 340). (1) Son of ESAU by OHOLIBAMAH; an Edomite chief (Gen. 36:5, 14, 18; 1 Chr. 1:35).

(2) Son of Bilhan and descendant of BENJAMIN (1 Chr. 7:10); he was a head of family in the clan of JEDIAEL (v. 11).

(3) Son of Eshek and descendant of King SAUL (1 Chr. 8:39; KJV, "Jehus").

(4) Son of Shimei and descendant of LEVI through GERSHON (1 Chr. 23:10); because Jeush and his brother Beriah had few sons, their two families were reckoned as one (v. 11).

(5) Son of King REHOBOAM by Mahalath (2 Chr. 11:19).　　S. BARABAS

Jeuz jee′uhz (יְעוּץ H3591, possibly "he counsels"). Son of SHAHARAIM and descendant of BENJAMIN; a family head (1 Chr. 8:10). Jeuz was one of seven children that were born to Shaharaim in MOAB by his wife HODESH after he had divorced Hushim and Baara (vv. 8–9).

Jew joo (יְהוּדִי H3374, "of Judah, Judahite, Judean"; Aram. יְהוּדִי H10316; Gk. Ἰουδαῖος G2681 [the English form comes from Old French *giu*, an alteration of Lat. *Iudaeus*]). A descendant of the tribe of JUDAH and more specifically an inhabitant of the land of JUDEA; hence the OT distinction between Judeans and other nations (2 Ki. 25:25; Jer. 38:19, Neh. 5:8). Following the disruption of the Solomonic kingdom (cf. 1 Ki. 12:16), those in the S became separated from the northern tribes. After 722 B.C., Judah (which included at least parts of

SIMEON, LEVI, and BENJAMIN) became the only claimant to the COVENANT (cf. Rom. 9:4–5). The prophet ZECHARIAH looked forward to the time when "ten men from all languages and nations will take firm hold of one Jew by the hem of his robe and say, 'Let us go with you, because we have heard that God is with you'" (Zech. 8:23).

Because Hebrew remained the language of all Israelites, it was natural to identify the terms *yĕhûdî* H3374, "Judahite," and *'ibrî* H6303, "Hebrew" (Jer. 34:9; see HEBREW PEOPLE). Similarly, the term *yĕhûdît* H3376, "the language of Judah/Judea," came to mean the HEBREW LANGUAGE (cf. 2 Ki. 18:26; Neh. 13:24; Isa. 36:11, 13). The name *yĕhûdî* acquires special prominence in postexilic literature, especially in Ezra, Nehemiah, and Esther.

In the Greek and Roman world, *Ioudaioi* was the accepted name for the Hebrews. Judas MACCABEE, in a letter to Rome described his people as *to ethnos tōn Ioudaiōn*, "the nation of the Jews/Judeans" (1 Macc. 8:23–27). JOSEPHUS, who seems to reserve the name Hebrews for Israel's more ancient history, uses Jews/Judeans throughout, and the same applies to the NT. The DIASPORA made it possible to give to the name Jew a purely religious sense detached from geography. PAUL was a Jew born in TARSUS (Acts 21:39). According to Josephus (*Ant.* 14.10.1–2), the large Jewish community of ALEXANDRIA enjoyed full citizenship granted by Julius Caesar. They were Jews because they professed JUDAISM (cf. Gal. 1:13–14; 2:14). In the Gospel of John, the term *Ioudaioi*, though translated "Jews" consistently in most versions, often refers not to Jews in general but to prominent religious leaders from Judea (Jerusalem), particularly those who belonged to the Pharisaic party (for further discussion, see *Anti-Judaism and the Fourth Gospel*, ed. R. Bieringer et al. [2001]).

Paul pressed for a redefinition of the meaning of this term. Physical descent was not enough to define a Jew. CIRCUMCISION of the heart (Rom. 2:29, cf. Phil. 3:3; Col. 3:11–12; Deut. 10:16; Jer. 4:4) is what makes a person a true Jew. For this reason, the apostle claimed that not all who are descended from Israel belong to Israel (Rom. 9:6, cf. Rev. 2:9). To live "Jewishly" (*Ioudaïkōs*) was the Jew's special obligation (Gal. 2:14), and for this reason there was an advantage in being a Jew (Rom. 3:1–2; cf. Gal. 1:15). This was not a matter of privilege but responsibility. It is on this basis that those who believe in Christ, though originally non-Jews, become Abraham's offspring and heirs according to promise (Gal. 3:29).

Since the creation of the modern State of Israel, the question who is a Jew has assumed new significance. In the past, Judaism was the characteristic mark of the Jew. In secularized society, religion is only a matter of private preference. Even Reformed Judaism, which initially denied Jewish nationhood, is now tending toward a more particularistic interpretation of Jewish existence. Peoplehood in terms of Jewish ethnicity and culture is the present trend in Jewry. "Reconstructionism" that puts the emphasis upon Jewish culture rather than religion is increasingly gaining ground. (See further M. M. Kaplan, *Judaism as a Civilization* [1934]; R. Gordis, *Judaism for the Modern Age* [1955]; S. Zeitlin, "Who is a Jew?" *JQR* 49 [1959]: 241–70; J. Jocz, "The 'Advantage' of the Jew," in *Jews and Christians*, ed. G. A. F. Knight [1965], 78–93; B. Chilton, "Jews in the NT," in *ABD*, 3:845–48.) J. Jocz

jewels and precious stones. Jewels are objects worn for adornment, a practice as old as the history of mankind. Much jewelry consists largely of precious or semiprecious stones (gemstones). However, various METALS, particularly GOLD and SILVER, are commonly used, and some jewelry consists of elaborately designed metalwork as a setting for gemstones, which are mostly naturally occurring inorganic compounds called MINERALS. Organic materials such as amber, shell, and coral also have been used, not solely because of their inherent beauty, but also because they could be engraved to produce objects of beauty. In the upper Palaeolithic era (25,000 to 16,000 B.C.), organic materials such as teeth, claws, and bones were the main objects fashioned as jewelry.

The use of gems for adornment has commonly gone side by side with their use for symbolic purposes, for most gems have had supernatural characteristics and virtues associated with them. AMULETS or charms were used to keep away evil spirits or disease, or to bring good luck, with particular gems having particular significance attached to them. The wearing of AMETHYST was considered

JEWELS AND PRECIOUS STONES

Gold broaches and figurines representing hawks. From the sanctuary dedicated to Artemis at Ephesus (650–600 B.C.).

to prevent drunkenness, while the DIAMOND was considered to give its wearer strength in battle. The traditional symbol of heavenly bliss has been SAPPHIRE and its wearing considered to be a protection against betrayal and poverty. In the same way, the RUBY was associated with love and happiness. These and many other beliefs concerning the significance of the various precious stones used as gems would have been known to those responsible for ecclesiastical vestments and regalia (e.g., Exod. 28) as well as to the author of Revelation, in which gemstones figure prominently in the portrayal of things to be (e.g., Rev. 21:18–20).

Because of their value, gemstones have been used as a medium of exchange and trade (cf. Job 28:15–19) and as gifts, particularly by monarchs on important occasions (1 Ki. 10:2). Abundance of jewelry and precious stones has been taken as indicative of personal prosperity and of national prosperity in the case of a monarch (1 Ki. 10:14–23). It has also gone hand in hand with many established religions (1 Chr. 29:2), although the existence of things of more value than jewels has often been pointed out (Prov. 3:15 NRSV, NIV, "rubies"). Because of their small size, and thus ease of transport in the event of catastrophic happenings, gems and jewelry have been a much favored form of wealth. Their value, however, has made them objects of plunder (Exod. 3:22; 12:35–36; 2 Chr. 20:25). With their virtual indestructibility and the consistent human desire to possess them, many gems of ancient times have been bought and sold by generation after generation and some preserved to the present day.

Gems have certain characters that set them apart from the common varieties of minerals. Of these, beauty is the most important; among the qualities of color, brilliance, and luster, which give beauty to gems, color is the most important. The only mineral that is of great value when colorless is diamond. This is because of its outstanding brilliance, luster, and hardness, but even in the case of diamond, colored varieties are generally more valuable.

Because many of the precious stones of ancient times came from INDIA—with Burma a source of rubies, and Ceylon a source of sapphire, rubies, and other gemstones for at least 2,500 years—it was thought at one time that beautifully colored gemstones were produced only by tropical climates. However, it is now known that the production of the characteristic color of most gemstones is the result of the presence of a small proportion of impurities. For example, ruby and sapphire are both varieties of corundum (aluminum oxide), their red and blue colors respectively being thought to be due to the presence of traces of chromium in the former and titanium in the latter. Other gem varieties of the same mineral (corundum) include oriental emerald (green), oriental amethyst (purple), and oriental topaz (yellow), in each case small impurities producing the colors (respectively, beryllium aluminum silicate, silicon dioxide, and aluminum fluosilicate).

The making of fine jewelry in the ANE began in the 4th millennium B.C., particularly in Iraq and northern Syria, with the engraving of relatively hard stones, which required a wheel technique. By the 3rd millennium the amount of jewelry being made was considerable, with the work of the Sumerian smiths centered at UR on the lower EUPHRATES River being outstanding (see SUMER). Much of their jewelry was manufactured for the adornment of those taking part in the elaborate religious ceremonies of the time and region (cf. Gen. 11:2–11). Around the year 2000, jewelry was manufactured in considerable amounts in Anatolia (ASIA MINOR) and on the coast of PHOENICIA, with the Phoenicians traveling as far as Scandinavia to obtain amber for making engraved jewelry.

MATERIALS USED AS PRECIOUS STONES AND IN THE MANUFACTURE OF JEWELRY

Alloys	**Oxides of silicon**
BRONZE (2 Chr. 24:12; see also BRASS)	AGATE (Exod. 28:19)
Carbonates	AMETHYST (Rev. 21:20)
MALACHITE (Est. 1:6 NEB)	CARNELIAN (Rev. 4:3)
Native elements	CHALCEDONY (Rev. 21:19)
COPPER (2 Tim. 4:14 NRSV)	CHRYSOPRASE (Rev. 21:20; see also BERYL)
DIAMOND OR FLINT (Jer. 17:1; see ADAMANT)	CRYSTAL (Rev. 21:11)
GOLD (Ps. 21:3)	JASPER (Exod. 28:20)
IRON (2 Chr. 18:10)	ONYX (Ezek. 28:13; see also MARBLE)
SILVER (Exod. 3:22)	SARDONYX (Rev. 21:20)
Organic material	**Silicates**
AMBER (Ezek. 1:4 NRSV)	BERYL (Rev. 21:20; see also EMERALD)
CORAL (Job 28:18)	CARBUNCLE (Isa. 54:12 KJV; see also GARNET)
PEARL (Matt. 13:45)	CHRYSOLITE (Exod. 28:17 NRSV; Rev. 21:20)
Oxides of aluminum	EMERALD (Rev. 21:19; see also BERYL)
ADAMANT (Ezek. 3:9 KJV)	GARNET (Ezek. 27:16 NEB; see also CARBUNCLE)
RUBY (Lam. 4:7; see also CORAL)	JACINTH (Exod. 39:12)
SAPPHIRE (Exod. 24:10)	JADE (Ezek. 28:13 NEB)
	LIGURE (Exod. 28:19 KJV)
	TOPAZ (Rev. 21:20)
	TURQUOISE (Exod. 28:18)

In EGYPT some of the jewelry made was of fragile, glazed material, and this was used to decorate the mummy of a dead person. The jewelry made for adorning the living was mainly of semiprecious stones set in gold; varieties of chalcedonic silica, including CARNELIAN and JASPER, available locally, were used. Also used was TURQUOISE, a blue-colored mineral that was considered to prevent accidents, particularly falls from horses. From before 3000 this mineral was mined on the Sinai Peninsula, and it probably was the first gemstone to be mined extensively (see MINES, MINING), although the ancient Egyptians also sank hundreds of shafts in the search for emeralds on the coast of the RED SEA. LAPIS LAZULI, which is soft and could be carved, was used by the Egyptians, particularly for amulets but also with other semiprecious stones set in elaborate designs. In the case of amethyst, it was generally used by itself, as its color did not blend with the other semiprecious stones also being used at the time.

(See further E. S. Dana, *A Textbook of Mineralogy*, 4th ed. [1932]; M. Manutchehr-Danai, *Dictionary of Gems and Gemology* [2000]; O. Johnson, *Minerals of the World* [2002]; H.-R. Wenk and A. Bulakh, *Minerals: Their Constitution and Origin* [2004].)

D. R. BOWES

Jewish Christianity. See COUNCIL OF JERUSALEM; EBIONITES; GALATIANS, EPISTLE TO THE.

Jewish wars. See WARS, JEWISH.

Jewry joo'ree. This English term is used by the KJV on three occasions where it stands for JUDAH or JUDEA (Dan. 5:13; Lk. 23:5; Jn. 7:1). In the course of time the name changed from a geographical to an ethnic description. It now connotes: (1) the

Jewish quarters in a town or city (e.g., Old Jewry in London); (2) the religion of the Jewish people, i.e., Judaism (this however is not common); (3) the Jewish people in the ethnic and cultural sense as a distinct community. See also JEW. J. Jocz

Jezaniah jez´uh-ni´uh (יְזַנְיָה H3470, "Yahweh listens"). **(1)** Variant of JAAZANIAH (Jer. 40:8).

(2) Son of HOSHAIAH; he was an army officer who, with JOHANAN son of Kareah and the survivors from an attack at MIZPAH, asked JEREMIAH to pray for them (Jer. 42:1). Some scholars, on the basis of 43:2 and the SEPTUAGINT, emend the text to "Azariah" (cf. NRSV).

Jezebel jez´uh-bel (אִיזֶבֶל H374, possibly from Phoen. אִי + זְבֻל, "where is the prince?" [i.e., Baal; cf. *ANET*, 141a], perhaps understood by the Hebrews as אִי H364 + זְבֻל H2292, "not exalted" [with later modification of the second element; cf. postbiblical זֶבֶל, "manure," and 2 Ki. 9:37, where however דֹּמֶן H1961 is used]; Gk. Ἰεζάβελ G2630). Daughter of ETHBAAL king of SIDON (in PHOENICIA), wife of AHAB king of Israel, and mother of ATHALIAH queen of Judah (1 Ki. 16:31; 18:4, 13; 19:1–2; 21:5–25; 2 Ki. 9:7–37; Rev. 2:20).

This remarkable evil woman was derived from a Phoenician clan which she truly represented. Her family happens to constitute one of the earliest confluences of biblical history with the written classical history of Greece—if one may suppose that such were the sources of JOSEPHUS. Though called "king of the Sidonians," Ethbaal (1 Ki. 16:31) her father was king of all Phoenicia. By assassination of his predecessor he had established his reign at the age of thirty-six. His reign lasted thirty-two years. His dynasty included a great-grandson, Pygmalion, who, at the time of his death ninety-four years after Ethbaal's accession, brought the reign of the dynasty to an end.

Although marriage of Hebrews with the Canaanite peoples of the Levant was strictly forbidden by the Mosaic law, it was precisely her unlawful conjugal union with Ahab (1 Ki. 16:31) that rescued her name from the oblivion of most other ancients and secured for her a perpetual infamy wherever the Holy Scriptures are known. The Bible traces her husband's apostasy to her influence (16:30–34). His evils, said to be more than those of any of his predecessors in office, are laid at her door. These were chiefly giving himself to BAAL worship, with all its vile accompaniments, establishing a Baal cult center at SAMARIA, the national capital, and thereby leading the whole nation into apostasy. At her instigation (Ahab consenting), a systematic program aimed at extermination of all leadership of Yahweh worship in Israel was begun. Evidently the Lord's prophets were slaughtered by the hundreds (18:1–4). At the same time Baal prophets were given national prominence, a number even being housed and fed in precincts of the royal palace (18:17–19).

It was in this climate of national tension that the prophet ELIJAH appeared as single public advocate of the ancestral faith. The striking events of Elijah's career recorded in 2 Ki. 17–19—the prophesied drought, his period of hiding and divine sustenance, the contest with the 850 prophets of Baal, the breaking of the drought, the flight to Horeb—are all features of Elijah's personal contest with Jezebel. The murder of NABOTH (1 Ki. 21:5–15; cf. 2 Ki. 9:26), an incident that displays the worst side of Ahab's weak character, shows his wife as a true daughter of a pagan court—involved in intrigue, treason, and deception, with public displays of legality and virtue to cover unrighteousness. The scrupulosity of apparent observance of legal details (in Mosaic law, for it was still the official constitution), while perpetrating murder and theft, is a lesson in betrayal of public trust by official persons. Because of this act, Elijah was sent to prophesy the destruction of Ahab's family (1 Ki. 21:17–24), with specific reference to his wife: "Dogs will devour Jezebel by the wall of Jezreel" (v. 23; cf. the fulfillment of this horrible prophecy in 2 Ki. 9).

Scripture says that Ahab "sold himself to do evil in the eyes of the LORD, urged on by Jezebel his wife" (1 Ki. 21:25). Through him, Jezebel corrupted the kingdom of Israel. And through her offspring, Athaliah (who was married to JEHORAM, the leading scion of the house of DAVID), Jezebel came near to bringing the Davidic dynasty to extinction (see 2 Ki. 8:25–27; 11:1–3; 2 Chr. 21:5–7; 22:10—23:21). Jezebel's name became symbolic of APOSTASY and is used in the book of Revelation with reference to a false prophetess (prob. representing a larger group) in THYATIRA: "By her teaching she misleads my servants into sexual immorality and the eating of food sacrificed to idols. I have given her time to repent of her immorality, but she is unwilling. So I will cast her on a bed of suffering, and I will make those who commit adultery with her suffer intensely, unless they repent of her ways" (Rev. 2:20–22). (See P. R. Ackroyd, "Goddesses, Women and Jezebel," in *Images of Women in Antiquity*, ed. A. Cameron and A. Kuhrt [1983], 245–59; P. Dutcher-Walls, *Jezebel: Portraits of a Queen* [2004]; D. Pruin, *Geschichten und Geschichte: Isebel als literarische und historische Gestalt* [2006].)   R. D. CULVER

Jezelus jez´uh-luhs. KJV Apoc. form of JAHAZIEL (1 Esd. 8:32) and JEHIEL (8:35).

Jezer jee´zuhr (יֵ֫צֶר H3672, possibly "[Yahweh] has formed"; gentilic יִצְרִי H3673, "Jezerite"; see IZRI). Son of NAPHTALI, grandson of JACOB, and eponymous ancestor of the Jezerite clan (Gen. 46:24; Num. 26:49; 1 Chr. 7:13).

Jeziah ji-zi´uh. KJV form of IZZIAH.

Jeziel jee´zee-uhl (יְזִיאֵל H3465, possibly "sprinkled by God"; cf. IZZIAH and see J. D. Fowler, *Theophoric Personal Names in Ancient Hebrew* [1988], 137). Son of Azmaveth; he and his brother Pelet are listed among the warriors, kinsmen of SAUL, who joined with DAVID when the latter took refuge at ZIKLAG (1 Chr. 12:3).

Jezliah jez-li´uh. KJV form of IZLIAH.

Jezoar ji-zoh´ahr. KJV form of IZHAR #2.

Jezrahiah jez'ruh-hi´uh (יִזְרַחְיָה H3474, "Yahweh goes forth [*or* shines]"; see IZRAHIAH). Director of the choirs who took part in the dedication of the walls of Jerusalem (Neh. 12:42).

Jezreel (person) jez´ree-uhl (יִזְרְעֶאל H3475, "God sows"). (1) Son of Etam and descendant of JUDAH (1 Chr. 4:3; MT and some mss, Athar ing LXX). The MT is unintelligible; see discussion under ETAM.

(2) A symbolic name of one of the sons of HOSEA. God commanded the prophet to give his first child this name and then promptly interpreted the significance of it. "Call him Jezreel, because I will soon punish the house of Jehu for the massacre at Jezreel, and I will put an end to the kingdom of Israel. In that day I will break Israel's bow in the Valley of Jezreel" (Hos. 1:4–5). There is first an allusion to JEHU's slaughter of the house of AHAB—a slaughter that went far beyond God's intention (2 Ki. 10:11). Second, there is a play on words between Jezreel (*yizrĕ'e'l*) and Israel (*yiśrā'ēl*). The reference to Jezreel in Hos. 1:11 and 2:22 has a significance opposite to that in 1:5. The scene of the breaking of the bow of Israel will become the scene of mending and reunification. The place of through disruption and scattering will become the place that God makes fertile (as implied by the meaning of the name). See JEZREEL (PLACE).   R. L. ALDEN

Jezreel (place) jez´ree-uhl (יִזְרְעֶאל H3476, "God sows"). (1) A town in the hill country of the tribe of JUDAH (Josh. 15:56). Jezreel is listed as part of

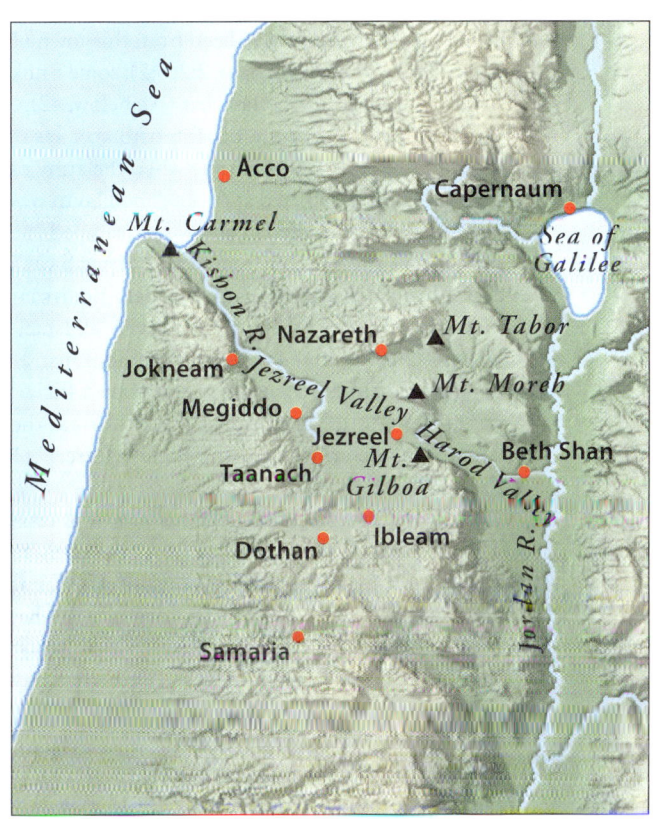

Jezreel.

Aerial view of Tel Yizreʿel (biblical Jezreel in Issachar) looking N across the Jezreel (Esdraelon) Valley.

a group of towns 4–10 mi. S and SE of HEBRON, but its precise location is unknown. AHINOAM, one of DAVID's wives, may have been from this town (1 Sam. 25:43; 27:3; 30:5; 2 Sam. 2:2; 3:2); some think she came from Jezreel of Issachar (see below, #2).

(2) A town within the tribal territory of ISSACHAR (Josh. 19:18). At the time when the army of the PHILISTINES gathered at APHEK and DAVID was dismissed by them, the Israelites were camped "by the spring in Jezreel" (1 Sam. 29:1). After SAUL's death, his general set up Saul's son ISH-BOSHETH as king over Jezreel, other cities, and even "all Israel" (2 Sam. 2:8–9; cf. 4:4). During the administration of SOLOMON, one of the twelve court officials was at TAANACH, MEGIDDO, and BETH SHAN, the latter being described as being "below Jezreel" (1 Ki. 4:12).

Apparently Jezreel had been made a royal residence by King AHAB of Israel, for it was there that ELIJAH met him after the episode at Mount Carmel and the ending of the drought (1 Ki. 10:15–46; see CARMEL, MOUNT). Elijah must have been given superhuman strength that day to run ahead of Ahab's chariot for those 20 mi. between Carmel and Jezreel. Ahab, whose capital was SAMARIA, had a palace at Jezreel (21:1), adjacent to NABOTH's vineyard. The ruthless scheming Queen JEZEBEL, through false accusation and subsequent murder of Naboth, got the land for a garden for Ahab. For this wicked deed, Elijah pronounced doom on both Ahab and Jezebel (21:17–24). The king, who had been more passive in the matter, repented (21:27), but Jezebel was eventually eaten by dogs within the bounds of Jezreel (1 Ki. 21:23; 2 Ki. 9:10, 30–37).

Ahab's son Joram (JEHORAM), who reigned in Israel after his father's death, went to war against SYRIA (ARAM) in coalition with AHAZIAH king of Judah (2 Ki. 8:28). There is no account of victory for the Hebrews, only that King Joram returned to Jezreel to recuperate from wounds that the Syrians had inflicted (2 Ki. 8:29; 2 Chr. 22:6). According to 2 Ki. 9, Elijah anointed JEHU as king over Israel when Joram was still alive. This event occurred in TRANSJORDAN at RAMOTH GILEAD. The city of Jezreel must have been situated so as to afford a view of the Valley of Jezreel and the Jordan Valley. The watchmen saw Jehu come near, driving "like a madman," and take away the messengers with him (2 Ki. 9:20).

Then Joram and Ahaziah, who had been visiting his wounded neighbor, met Jehu in the garden that had been the vineyard of Naboth (2 Ki. 9:21). Jehu shot Joram with his bow and arrow, and Ahaziah, wounded at the hands of Jehu's men, died after fleeing to Megiddo (9:27). Jehu entered the city of Jezreel and ordered the attendants to throw the painted and adorned Jezebel out the window (9:30–33). And so she died without burial, covered with disgrace as Elijah the prophet had said (1 Ki. 21:23). Jehu ordered the heads of Ahab's surviving sons to be sent to him at Jezreel from Samaria. When this was done, Jehu also "killed everyone in Jezreel who remained of the house of Ahab, as well as all his chief men, his close friends and his priests, leaving him no survivor" (2 Ki. 10:11).

Jezreel is identified with the modern village of Zerʿin at the foot of Mount GILBOA, approximately halfway between Megiddo and Beth Shan.

(3) A wadi that divides Galilee on the N from SAMARIA on the S. See ESDRAELON.

R. L. ALDEN

Jezrielus jez-ri-ee'luhs. See JEHIEL #8.

Jibsam jib'sam. KJV form of IBSAM.

Jidlaph jid'laph (יִדְלָף H3358, possibly "he weeps" or "he is sleepless"). Son of NAHOR by his wife MILCAH; nephew of ABRAHAM (Gen. 22:22).

Jimna, Jimnah jim'nuh. KJV forms of IMNAH.

Jiphtah jif'tuh. KJV form of IPHTAH.

Jiphthah-el jif'thuh-el. KJV form of IPHTAH EL.

Joab joh'ab (יוֹאָב H3405, "Yahweh is [my] father"). (1) Son of Seraiah, nephew of OTHNIEL, descendant of JUDAH through the line of KENAZ, and father (founder) of GE HARASHIM, a town inhabited by craftsmen (1 Chr. 4:14).

(2) Ancestor of a group (connected with the families of Pahath-Moab and Jeshua) that returned to Jerusalem under ZERUBBABEL (Ezra 2:6; Neh. 7:11; 1 Esd. 5:11 [KJV omits]); apparently, some of his descendants returned later with EZRA (Ezra 8:9; 1 Esd. 8:35).

(3) Son of ZERUIAH (King DAVID's sister), brother of valiant warriors ABISHAI and ASAHEL, and commander in chief under David (2 Sam. 2:13–32 et al.). His father's name is unknown. The rest of this article deals with Joab son of Zeruiah. (For the phrase "the house of Joab" in 1 Chr. 2:54 KJV, see ATROTH BETH JOAB.)

I. Early military career. Although Joab was a nephew of David, the two men were probably near the same age, for Zeruiah appears to have been one of the older children of JESSE, whereas David was his youngest son. (It is interesting to note that AMASA, who replaced Joab as commander of the Israelite armies on two occasions, was a cousin of Joab and also a nephew of David; see 2 Sam. 17:25; 19:13; 1 Chr. 2:17.) Joab presumably joined David's guerrilla band in the wilderness, but he is first mentioned in the Bible in connection with a battle at the pool of GIBEON (2 Sam. 2:13–32). David had sent him with an army against ABNER and the followers of the house of SAUL. When the two armies met, Abner suggested that twelve young warriors from each side should settle the matter by a test of skill. Joab readily agreed.

The young warriors arose and took their positions, but the contest was so evenly matched that all twenty-four men fell together with each man's sword in the heart of his opponent. This precipitated a battle between the two armies, with Joab's men routing the soldiers of the house of Saul. As Abner and his men fled, Asahel, brother of Joab, fleet of foot and impetuous, sought to overtake Abner and engage that seasoned veteran in combat. Twice Abner pled with the youth to turn aside. Each time Asahel refused, whereupon Abner, with a backward thrust, drove the butt of his spear through the overconfident warrior so that he died (2 Sam. 2:23).

With the law of blood revenge operating in ancient Israel (Num. 35:19; see AVENGER OF BLOOD), it was inevitable that Joab would seek to avenge his brother's death, and the opportunity arose a short time later. Abner, as commander-in-chief of Saul's armies, had enabled ISH-BOSHETH to retain the throne of his father (2 Sam. 2:8–9). His task was not an easy one, for the house of Saul was growing constantly weaker. The turning point came when the miserable Ish-Bosheth accused him of illicit relations with one of the concubines of his dead father (3:6–7). Angered deeply, Abner opened negotiations with David for the purpose of uniting all Israel under David's leadership (vv. 12–13). David responded favorably. Abner and a diplomatic corps visited David in HEBRON, where final arrangements were carefully worked out. After sealing the bargain with a feast, Abner and his men left for home.

Shortly after their departure, Joab returned from a frontier skirmish and was informed of what had happened (2 Sam. 3:22–23). Joab's anger blazed hot and strong. He saw all too clearly that the man who had slain his brother might well become his commanding officer. He moved quickly. Messengers were sent in the name of David to overtake Abner and bring him back to Hebron (3:26–27). The king was not aware of Joab's sinister plot. The unsuspecting Abner returned and foolishly agreed to speak privately with Joab, who drawing him aside, slew him in the gate of the city. When David heard the sad news, his grief was spontaneous and profuse. He immediately declared himself and his kingdom free of the guilt of so dastardly a deed. Furthermore, he pronounced a curse upon the house of Joab, and became the chief mourner at the funeral of Abner (3:28, 31).

II. Field marshal. With all his ruthlessness, Joab was a brave and ingenious military leader and was completely loyal to David and the emerging Israelite kingdom. No better example of his military prowess can be found than the part he played in the capture of the city of JERUSALEM (2 Sam. 5:6–10; 1 Chr. 11:4–9). David wanted this excellently fortified city for his capital, and sought to dislodge the Jebusites who had long occupied the fortress (see JEBUS). The Jebusites were so overconfident and insulting in their resistance, that David promised the job of field commander to the man who would lead a successful attack against the city. The redoubtable Joab met the king's challenge. His clever mind devised a scheme that involved the city's water supply. His ruse was imminently successful and the city was taken. Joab was made field marshal and remained in that position for many years (cf. 2 Sam. 8:16; 20:23; 1 Chr. 18:15; 27:34).

David often led his own armies to battle, but Joab was his strong right arm. It was Joab who executed David's plan to destroy the Edomites, cutting off every male in the population (2 Sam. 8:13–14; 1 Ki. 11:15–16). It was Joab who masterminded the defeat of the Syro-Ammonite coalition (2 Sam. 10:6–14; 1 Chr. 19:6–15). A shrewd tactician, he threw the Syrians (Arameans) into hopeless confusion, while Abishai routed the Ammonites. On a later occasion, Joab directed the armies of Israel against the rebellious sons of AMMON. He ravaged their country and laid siege to RABBAH, their capital (2 Sam. 11:1; 1 Chr. 20:1). During the siege of Rabbah, Joab was drawn into David's nefarious scheme to kill URIAH the Hittite. Joab seems to have had no compunction of conscience in putting Uriah at the front of the battle and then withdrawing his support (2 Sam. 11:14–25). Later on, when Joab knew that the city was ready to capitulate, he magnanimously asked David to come and take the credit for its surrender (12:26–31). Without doubt, Joab must have also played an outstanding part in the success of the wars that David fought against the PHILISTINES (5:17–18; 8:1), MOAB (8:2), ZOBAH (2 Sam. 8:3–4; 1 Chr. 18:3–4), and the Arameans (2 Sam. 8:5–6). There is no record where Joab ever lost a battle.

III. The irrepressible strategist. Joab was a tough realist. His mind was not only quick and incisive, but also calculating and logical. This is evident in his military accomplishments and in his involvement in the problems of the king's household.

By clever strategy, Joab secured the return of ABSALOM from the land of GESHUR, where the king's son had fled after slaying AMNON for the rape of his sister TAMAR (2 Sam. 14:1). He convinced David through the use of the wise woman of TEKOA of the inconsistency of his attitude toward Absalom. As a result David permitted Absalom to return to Jerusalem, but he was not allowed to return to the king's court. After two years of living in Jerusalem without seeing his father's face, Absalom decided to do something about the situation (14:28–29). He sent for Joab, but the latter, apparently suspecting the purpose of the summons, delayed his response. Absalom sent for Joab a second time, and still he did not come. Finally, Absalom commanded his servants to set fire to Joab's barley fields, which lay next to his own. This time his efforts proved successful. The matter ended with Joab intervening with David for Absalom. A reconciliation was effected between the king and his son.

In the insurrection of Absalom (2 Sam. 15:7), Joab seems to have been caught off guard. Absalom was able to carry a large segment of the king's standing army with him, but since he did not trust Joab, he made AMASA commander-in-chief in

Looking down into Warren's Shaft (Jerusalem). According to some, this shaft was the way Joab used to enter the city of Jebus.

his place (17:25). The next mention of Joab is in David's camp, but he is not in full command (1 Sam. 18:2-3). In deploying his forces against Absalom, David divided them into three groups and placed Joab at the head of only one section, with Abishai and Ittai over the other two. As his men marched away to fight, David gave explicit instruction to his three lieutenants in the hearing of all the people to spare the life of Absalom.

In the heat of the battle, however, Joab took over and directed the outcome of the encounter. Although knowing David's orders, the hardheaded old realist knew that the quickest way to victory was to destroy the treacherous Absalom. The times were harsh, and he did not hesitate to use harsh methods. When the fortunes of war delivered Absalom into his hand, he thrust him through with three darts as he hung by his hair in an oak tree (2 Sam. 18:9-10). With Absalom dead, the insurrection ended. Later in the day when David, due to his grief at the death of Absalom, did not so much as thank his splendid fighting men for the victory they had given that day, the unrelenting Joab withstood the king to his face (19:1-8). Fortunately, the king gave heed to the words of Joab and the situation was saved.

Although Joab brought the insurrection of Absalom to a quick, and perhaps merciful, end, he was not restored to his command. David appointed Amasa as field marshal in his place (2 Sam. 19:13). The move was apparently designed to ease political tensions and heal the wounds of a divided nation. It also served to punish Joab for his insubordination in the recent battle. The irrepressible old strategist seemed to accept his demotion without a word, but subsequent events amply indicate that Joab was soon scheming to regain his former position.

His opportunity was not long in coming. David was no sooner restored to the throne when a certain SHEBA from the tribe of Ephraim raised the cry of revolt against him (2 Sam. 20.1-2). The unity of the kingdom was again threatened. David promptly commanded Amasa to organize and equip an army to pursue Sheba. For some reason Amasa delayed beyond the appointed time. David, knowing that time was of the essence, placed some of his battle-tested warriors under Abishai and sent them on after the rebel leader. Joab was among the soldiers who went with Abishai. At Gibeon, Amasa sought to rejoin his troops. The crafty Joab, feigning friendship by taking hold of his beard as though to kiss him, disemboweled the unsuspecting Amasa with one stroke of his sword (20:8-9). Joab then assumed command of the expedition and finally overtook Sheba and destroyed him. Joab thus regained his former position as commander-in-chief of David's troops (20:23).

At least on one occasion Joab seems to have had a keen sense of what was religiously appropriate. He objected strenuously to David's plan to take a national census (2 Sam. 24:1-2; 1 Chr. 21:3). At this point he seems to have had more religious insight than David. In spite of his protests, the king insisted on carrying out his plan, and Joab was commissioned to supervise the project. He spent more than nine months in completing the task. Subsequent events proved him right in his original objections.

IV. Decline and death. In the end, Joab was fatally caught up in the intrigue that swirled around the household of David. When it became evident to all that the day of David's death could not be far away, ADONIJAH, one of his older sons, sought to claim his father's throne (1 Ki. 1:5-6). Convinced that he was worthy of being king, Joab and ABIATHAR the high priest threw the weight of their influence behind him. With the support of the commander-in-chief of the king's troops, and the head of the nation's religious order, the young prince seemed to have excellent prospects for achieving his objective. All their hopes, however, were doomed to failure. At the supposed coronation of Adonijah, the news came that David had already placed SOLOMON on the throne of Israel (1:38–39), and his kingship had been confirmed by the people. Adonijah's attempt had failed, and his followers were marked for destruction by the new king. Joab's subsequent flight to the horns of the altar of the Tent of Meeting was of no avail (2:28–29). Solomon dispatched BENAIAH to execute the old warrior, whose deeds of violence, according to the law of blood revenge (Num. 35:33), must be visited on his own head before the kingdom could have peace.

This period of history was harsh and primitive, and Joab was a product of his age. He was a decisive, fearless, and intrepid fighter, and a brilliant military strategist. He served his king and his country devotedly. He was generous and loyal to his friends, but utterly ruthless and vindictive toward his foes. He was not completely devoid of religious sentiment, but it played no decisive part in his conduct. He died as he had lived—by the sword. (See D. G. Schley, "Joab and David: Ties of Blood and Power," in *History and Interpretation: Essays in Honour of John H. Hayes*, ed. M. P. Graham et al. [1993], 90–105; S. K. Bietenhard, *Des Königs General: Die Heerführertraditionen in der vorstaatlichen und frühen staatlichen Zeit und die Joabgestalt in 2 Sam 2–20; 1 Kön 1–2* [1998]; M. A. Eschelbach, *Has Joab Failed David? A Literary Study of the Importance of Joab's Character in Relation to David* [2005].)

C. P. GRAY

Joachaz joh´uh-kaz. KJV Apoc. form of JEHOAHAZ (1 Esd. 1:34 [LXX v. 32], where NRSV, following Codex B, reads JECONIAH).

Joachim joh´uh-kim. KJV Apoc. form of JEHOIAKIM (Bar. 1:3, 7).

Joacim joh´uh-kim. KJV Apoc. form of JOAKIM (Jdt. 4:6 et al.).

Joadanus joh-ad´uh-nuhs. KJV Apoc. form of JODAN (1 Esd. 9:19).

Joah joh´uh (יוֹאָח *H3406*, "Yahweh is [my] brother"). **(1)** Son of a certain Asaph; he was "recorder" (*mazkîr H4654*, possibly the royal spokesperson) under HEZEKIAH, and member of a delegation sent by the king to deal with the Assyrian envoys during the siege of Jerusalem (2 Ki. 18:18, 26; Isa. 36:3, 11, 22).

(2) Son of Zimnah and descendant of LEVI through the line of GERSHON (1 Chr. 6:21; 2 Chr. 29:12).

(3) Third son of OBED-EDOM, included in the list of divisions of the Korahite doorkeepers in the reign of DAVID (1 Chr. 26:4).

(4) Son of a certain Joahaz (see JEHOAHAZ #4); he was recorder (cf. #1 above) under JOSIAH, and part of a group sent to repair the temple (2 Chr. 34:8).

S. BARABAS

Joahaz joh´uh-haz. Alternate form of JEHOAHAZ (2 Chr. 34:8; cf. also the MT at 2 Ki. 14:1 [here followed by NRSV and other versions]; 2 Chr. 36:2, 4).

Joakim joh´uh-kim (Ιωακιμ). KJV Joacim. **(1)** Son of ZERUBBABEL (1 Esd. 5:5; no son by that name is mentioned in 1 Chr. 3:19–20).

(2) A high priest in Jerusalem who exercised considerable authority in the days of JUDITH (Jdt. 4:6–8, 14; 15:8). Attempts to identify this figure have not been successful (see C. A. Moore, *Judith*, AB 40 [1985], 53–54); many scholars doubt the historicity of such a priest.

(3) The husband of SUSANNA (Sus. 1–6, 28–29, 63).

S. BARABAS

Joanan joh-ay´nuhn (Ἰωανάν *G2720*, from Heb. יוֹחָנָן *H3419*, "Yahweh has been gracious" [cf. HANANIAH, JOHANAN, JOHN]; the form occurs in the LXX [2 Chr. 17:15 et al.; see also BDF §53.2]). KJV Joanna. Son of Rhesa and grandson of ZERUBBABEL, included in Luke's GENEALOGY OF JESUS CHRIST (Lk. 3:27; v.l. *Iōannas*). Some scholars speculate that Joanan is the same as Hananiah (with the components of the name transposed) son of Zerubbabel (1 Chr. 3:19, 21) and that Rhesa is not a proper name but a transliteration of Aramaic *rēš*, "head, prince," thus a description of Zerubbabel (but see D. L. Bock, *Luke*, BECNT [1994–96], 1:354).

Joanna joh-an´uh (Ἰωάννα *G2721* [on the doubling of the consonant, see BDF §40], probably from Heb. יוֹחָנָה, "Yahweh has been gracious"; cf. HANNAH and see G. DALMAN, *Grammatik des jüdisch-palästinischen Aramäisch*, 2nd ed. [1905], 179 n. 5). The wife of CUZA, who managed the household of Herod Antipas (see HEROD V); she was one of several women who had been healed by Jesus and who helped to support him and his disciples in their travels (Lk. 8:3). She was probably among those who witnessed the crucifixion and then returned to the city to prepare spices and ointment for the anointing of the body (23:55–56). Joanna is specifically mentioned with Mary Magdalene and Mary the mother of James (see MARY ##4–5) as one of the women who returned to the tomb, found it empty, and brought the news to the apostles (24:10). (See B. Witherington, *Women in the Ministry of Jesus* [1984], 116–18; for the view that Lk. 8:1–3 is an unhistorical redaction of Mk. 15:40–41, see K. E. Corley, *Women and the Historical Jesus: Feminist Myths of Christian Origins* [2002], 29–31.) C. J. BARBER

Joarib joh'uh-rib (Ιωαριβ, from Heb. יוֹיָרִיב H3424, "Yahweh contends [for me]"; see JOIARIB). MATTATHIAS the priest, who instigated the Maccabean Revolt (see MACCABEE), is described as belonging to "the sons of Joarib" (1 Macc. 2:1; 14:29 [KJV, "Jarib"]). The reference is no doubt to JEHOIARIB, who received the first lot of the twenty-four priestly divisions in the time of DAVID (1 Chr. 24:7).

Joash, Jehoash joh'ash, ji-hoh'ash (יוֹאָשׁ H3409, short form of יְהוֹאָשׁ H3371, prob. "Yahweh has granted"). The short Hebrew form of this name is used for all eight individuals listed below. The longer form, which occurs only in 2 Kings (seventeen times), is used sometimes for both the son of AHAZIAH, king of Judah, and the son of JEHOAHAZ, king of Israel (note esp. 2 Ki. 14:13), but the NIV, in the interests of clarity, uses it only when referring to the king of Israel. M. Noth (*IPN*, 106, 171) points out that both forms are found on seal inscriptions, and that the longer form was usual at ELEPHANTINE.

(1) Father of GIDEON and descendant of MANASSEH through ABIEZER (Jdg. 6:11, 29–31; 7:14; 8:13, 29, 32). Joash lived in OPHRAH, where both he and Gideon were buried. The angel of the Lord appeared to Gideon by an oak tree that belonged to Joash. Later, when the men of the town wanted to kill Gideon for breaking down the altar of BAAL and the ASHERAH pole, his father came to his defense.

(2) Son of SHELA and grandson of JUDAH; he and one (or more) of his brothers are said to have "ruled in" (or "married into") MOAB and JASHUBI LEHEM (1 Chr. 4:22; the Heb. verb is *bāʿal* H1249, which means either "to rule over" or, more frequently, "to marry"). Some scholars believe that the words "and Jashubi Lehem" should be emended to either "but returned to Lehem" (so NRSV) or "and they resided in Bethlehem" (cf. G. N. Knoppers, *I Chronicles 1–9*, AB 12 [2004], 342–43).

(3) Son of BEKER and grandson of BENJAMIN (2 Chr. 7:8).

(4) Son of Shemaah of GIBEAH; he and his brother AHIEZER are listed among the warriors, kinsmen of SAUL, who joined with DAVID when the latter took refuge at ZIKLAG (1 Chr. 12:3; cf. v. 1).

(5) An official under David who was in charge of the supplies of olive oil (1 Chr. 27:28).

(6) Son of AHAB king of Israel; he and the governor of SAMARIA were charged with the custody of the prophet MICAIAH (1 Ki. 22:26; 2 Chr. 18:25); it is however likely that the phrase "the king's son" refers to a minor royal official with police duties (see R. de Vaux, *Ancient Israel* [1961], 119–20).

(7) Son of AHAZIAH and ninth king of Judah (2 Ki. 11:1—12:21; 2 Chr. 22:10—24:27) As an infant, Joash was saved from the massacre of the royal family, which ATHALIAH perpetrated on the death of her son Ahaziah. He owed his life to the courage and devotion of his aunt JEHOSHEBA, the wife of the priest JEHOIADA, who conveyed him away, concealed him, and brought him up in their own home (2 Ki. 11:1–3). When Joash was seven years old, Jehoiada took him to the temple court and crowned him before a congregation of Levites, temple guards, and elders and people from the country towns. As he was acclaimed king, his grandmother Athaliah appeared in the court and was swiftly removed to her death. With due ceremony Jehoiada inaugurated a fresh covenant of loyalty, acknowledging the Lord's dominion; and the temple of BAAL was destroyed by the crowd (11:4–20). (See P. Dutcher-Walls, *Narrative Art, Political Rhetoric: The Case of Athaliah and Joash* [1996].)

The definition of the "people of the land" (2 Ki. 4:18) as a political force is not so clear in this context as in the closing years of the monarchy (see JEHOAHAZ). The view that they were "tempering for the remainder of the history of Judah the power of the monarchy" (J. A. Montgomery, *A Critical and Exegetical Commentary on the Book of Kings*, ICC [1951], 417) may be an overstatement, for whereas the people elevated UZZIAH to the kingship, they seem to have had relatively little to do with making policy in the ensuing hundred years. Neither is it clear how "the people" could have maintained control from the accession of their chosen king until his majority. The "conservative circles of country nobility" postulated by G. von Rad appear largely hypothetical, and it is doubtful whether they can be equated with the "princes of Judah" who seem to have gravitated to Jerusalem. See AM HA-AREZ.

The concept of "the people," however, comes to the fore at the coronation of Joash, and von Rad is undoubtedly right in drawing attention to the related phrases "people of the land" and "people of the Lord." They were a free people who had almost been enslaved, and a covenant people who had neglected the covenant; for conservatism had not kept them from petty idolatry. This situation sufficiently explains the twin covenants made by Jehoiada, to the first of which (the one related in Chronicles) the king and the people stood as one party (2 Chr. 23:16; cf. Gen. 17:7). In the second covenant, there was a return to the traditional concept of the kingship; it is probable that the testimony (perhaps an inscribed stone or tablet; see *JBL* 67 [1938]: 181) was related to this notion. So Joash was enthroned, with Jehoiada as his tutor and regent.

The reign of Joash lasted forty years from 835 to 796 B.C. (so E. R. Thiele, *The Mysterious Numbers of the Hebrew Kings*, 3rd ed. [1983], 104; others puts the death of Joash in the year 800). See CHRONOLOGY (OT). The reign was not very distinguished, and it ended miserably; for after Jehoiada's death, Joash was persuaded to allow the revival of pagan worship, which led to much opposition from the prophets. In the end, he was responsible for the martyrdom of ZECHARIAH son of Jehoiada; and at the end of the year, after a disastrous raid by HAZAEL of ARAM in which Joash was badly wounded and lost many of his leading men, he was assassinated by two of his servants—JOZACAR (or Zabad) and JEHOZABAD, sons of an Ammonite woman and a Moabite woman respectively (2 Ki. 12:20–21; 2 Chr. 24:17–27).

The circumstances of Joash's death are not altogether clear. The text of 2 Ki. 12:21 (lit., the officials "smote Joash [in] the house of Millo going down to Silla") is obscure and some scholars emend it. The Chronicler, working evidently from another source, connects the assassination directly with the raid and may be taken to mean that he was deserted by his guards on the field of battle, or in his palace afterward. In this case the words "going down" (Kings) would hardly be appropriate unless Joash was being carried. "The house of Millo" is also obscure; the phrase is elsewhere used only of what was apparently an enclosed quarter of SHECHEM (Jdg. 9). The MILLO of Jerusalem (always with the article) is well known as a made-up part of the fortified city (the NIV renders BETH MILLO). According to Chronicles, Joash was not buried in the existing royal tombs; the phrase in Kings "with his fathers" is capable of a wider meaning than "in their tombs"; and Chronicles agrees on his burial in the city, as befitted a king (see S. Yeivin in *JNES* 7 [1948]: 32, 36).

The Aramean attack (2 Ki. 12:17–18) appears to have taken place some fifteen years before the death of Joash, at the beginning of Hazael's domination of the coastal plain; his interest at that time was in the trade route to Egypt. This was probably before the rebuilding of the temple, which was the main achievement of Joash, and which began in the twenty-third year of his reign. After years of neglect, and of spoliation by the Baalists, the temple—well past its century when Joash came to the throne—was in need of structural repairs. It was first arranged that these should be financed, as particular defects were observed, from the taxes that the priests were to collect and from the general fund of freewill offerings, but by 813 B.C. it was evident that nothing effective had been done, and it may be inferred from 2 Ki. 12:13 that any available money had been spent on furniture and utensils.

The fault lay in the system in the first place, though it might be regretted that the temple fabric was always left as the last call on the priests'

Looking NW from Aphek across the plateau of Bashan and toward the Plain of Bethsaida (on the NE shore of the Sea of Galilee). King Joash/Jehoash of Israel won a key victory over the Arameans near Aphek.

income, so that in practice nothing was ever begun. Perhaps it seemed too big a problem for ad hoc treatment, and so was always put off. The king imposed a reform by which the priests were relieved of responsibility for maintenance, and in return gave up their right to collect and dispose of the taxes, retaining only the dues or contributions directly relating to the service of the sanctuary. A special fund was launched, controlled jointly by the king and high priest, and the people responded with enthusiasm; indeed, when work on the building had been completed, there was a surplus available for equipment.

(In 2003 an inscription was discovered in which "[the son of] Ahaziah" claims to have acquired materials for the restoration of the temple. The inscription ends with the words: "and this day will be for a statute because the work prospered. May YHWH ordain blessing for his people." The Examining Committees of the Israeli Antiquities Authority concluded that this so-called Yehoash Inscription is a forgery, but some scholars dispute these findings. See the discussion by S. Norin in *VT* 55 [2005]: 61–74.)

(8) Son of JEHOAHAZ and twelfth (thirteenth, if TIBNI is counted) king of Israel (2 Ki. 13:10–25; 14:8–16; 2 Chr. 25:17–24). To distinguish him from Joash son of Ahaziah, king of Judah, this king of Israel is often referred to by his alternate name, Jehoash (cf. NIV); that practice will be followed in this article. Jehoash was the third king in the line of JEHU; he reigned sixteen years, from the thirty-seventh of Joash of Judah to the fifteenth of AMAZIAH (2 Ki. 13:10; 14:23). The cross references (particularly 14:1; Amaziah's reign began in the second year of Joash) corroborate Thiele's hypothesis of a return to postdating by this time in the source chronicles of both kingdoms (*Mysterious Numbers*, 111–12). The second year of Jehoash of Israel was the thirty-ninth and last of Joash of Judah, conformably with the statement (12:1) that he reigned forty years (by the traditional method of inclusive reckoning). The sixteen years of Jehoash, the first reign in the northern kingdom to be postdated, are reckoned exclusive of the accession year and run from 798 to 782 (for an earlier dating, see J. H. Hayes and P. K. Hooker, *A New Chronology for the Kings of Israel and Judah* [1988], 47–48). Thiele (*Mysterious Numbers*, 108–11) further argues that JEROBOAM II was coregent from 793/792, for when Amaziah died, fifteen years after Jehoash, his son Azariah (UZZIAH) succeeded him in the twenty-seventh year of Jeroboam (2 Ki. 15:1).

For the situation at the beginning of the reign of Jehoash, see JEHOAHAZ. Adadnirari III of Assyria (810–782) had already forced the Arameans to submit and pay heavy tribute (*ANET*, 281–82). Hazael died, and his son Ben-Hadad III was not in the same class as a military leader. Jehoash inflicted three defeats on him that marked the beginning of Israel's political revival. The story is preserved of how this event was prophesied by Elisha as he lay dying (2 Ki. 13:14–25). Jehoash obviously had a great regard for Elisha, although he retained allegiance to the cult of Bethel; he showed more concern at losing Elisha than faith in Elisha's God. Consequently, his response to the prophet's demand for symbolic action was halfhearted. With Elisha's hands on his, in token of the power of God in a human instrument, he shot an arrow; and Elisha assured him of victory. Then the prophet told him to take arrows and pitch them into the ground. Jehoash was not entering into the spirit of the thing; he pitched three and waited. Very disappointed, Elisha foresaw that the answer to prayer would be limited by the king's uncertainty, which betrayed his lack of earnestness and faith (cf. Jas. 1:7–8).

It is interesting that at least one battle was fought in Aphek, almost certainly in the valley running eastward from Lake Kinnereth toward Bashan (the other sites of this name, SE of Samaria and N of Carmel, are unlikely). This detail shows that Syria (Aram) was still very much concerned with the Transjordan trade route, and that Israel had not abandoned the Gilead area either. Defeat of the Arameans relieved pressure on Galilee.

In 2 Ki. 14:8–14 is recorded the defeat of Amaziah by Jehoash at Beth Shemesh, which may well have occasioned the start of Uzziah's coregency (791/790 B.C.). Some background to this affair is given in 2 Chr. 25; Amaziah had hired men from Israel to join him against Edom and had sent them home before the campaign, at the behest of a prophet. They got their pay, but no booty; and they vented their resentment on the border towns. It may have been for this reason that Amaziah, confident in the flush of victory, challenged Jehoash to defend his border at the western end; but the Israelites won the battle and sacked Jerusalem. Jehoash took hostages; it is not clear whether these were in addition to, or in exchange for, Amaziah himself. C. F. Keil (KD, *Kings*, 382–83) is probably right that Jehoash was more concerned with political security than with plunder—hence also his destruction of a length of wall not adjoining the temple, so that the breach was not defensible from the flank.

These events may be dated to 791 or perhaps a little earlier; but it is not at all certain that Jehoash made his son coregent as a precaution against his own death in the battle, as C. Schedl suggests (in *VT* 12 [1962]: 97); the regency began not later than 792, and it does not appear that the campaign was planned far ahead. The immediate reason for making Jeroboam coregent so early in the reign is thus obscure, though the general aim of securing the dynasty is not in doubt.

(See further H. Tadmor, *IEJ* 12 [1962]: 114–22; V. Pavlovský and E. Vogt, *Bib* 45 [1964], 321–47; W. H. Shea in *JCS* 30 [1978]: 101–13; Y. Aharoni, *The Land of the Bible: A Historical Geography*, rev. ed. [1979], 340–45.)

J. Lilley

Joatham joh´uh-thuhm. KJV NT form of Jotham.

Joazabdus joh´uh-zab´duhs. KJV Apoc. form of Jozabad (1 Esd. 9:48).

Job, Book of johb (אִיּוֹב *H373*, traditionally related to אֹיֵב *H367*, "enemy" [perhaps with passive meaning, "object of ill-will, persecuted"], but more probably the same name as Akk. *Ayyabum*, "where is [my] father?"). One of the poetic books of the Bible, named after its main character. (On the reading "Job" in Gen. 46:13, see Jashub.)

    I. Archaeological and linguistic background
   II. Authorship and literary unity
  III. Date and canonicity
  IV. Place of origin
    V. Text
  VI. Purpose and teaching
 VII. Outline and content
VIII. A special problem

I. Archaeological and linguistic background. The uniqueness of the book of Job derives from the depth and thoroughness with which it treats the subjects of human suffering and theodicy. Numerous documents from the ancient biblical world touch upon these matters but none so eloquently and so fully as Job. There was "The First

Job" (S. N. Kramer, *History Begins at Sumer* [1956], 114–18), a man who in his affliction complained to his "personal" god in the course of his wailing for mercy: "My companion says not a true word to me, / My friend gives the lie to my righteous word... / My God... how long will you neglect me, leave me unprotected?" This "Job," like his biblical counterpart, was restored: "His god harkened to his bitter tears and weeping," which "soothed the heart of his god."

Another poetic monologue also written in the 2nd millennium B.C. is commonly called, "I Will Praise the Lord of Wisdom" (*ANET*, 434–37). This Babylonian "Job" is not unlike the Sumerian, for as a righteous sufferer he reckons with the thought that MARDUK his god rules the world and allows him to suffer, but that by means of ritual piety he will obtain mercy. He had his doubts: "Oh that I only knew that these things are well pleasing to a god" (2.33). But he too is restored and ends with a thanksgiving hymn and offerings which "make happy the mood" of the gods and "gladden their hearts" (4.40).

These documents deal with suffering, but in a very simple way. Others more remote touch on some aspects of the book of Job but are hardly to be compared. For example, in "A Dispute over Suicide" (*ANET*, 405–7), a man of Egypt debates with his "KA" (soul?) over suicide because times are so bad (between the Old and Middle Kingdoms) and there is no justice or love anymore. He finally decides death is better because men then become like gods in the nether world. As Job longed for an advocate (Job 9:33; 16:19, 21; 19:25–27), so this man pleads for the advocacy of the gods and feels he is presenting his case before a divine tribunal (*ANET*, 405 n. 2). A somewhat superficial but striking likeness to the book of Job is the A-B-A literary format in this document, which begins, as does Job, with a short prose prologue, then follows a long poetic section and finally an epilogue in prose. This pattern finds expression in other ANE documents.

The only document dealing with the subject of theodicy is "A Dialogue about Human Misery" (*ANET*, 438). This is more like Job, being a dialogue involving a friend who accuses the sufferer of imbecility and evil thoughts and suggests he put aside such thoughts and seek the gracious favor of a god. The sufferer complains that animals do not have to make offerings, and even men who get rich quickly do so without paying attention to the gods while he who has done all this from his youth suffers. The friend warns him that "The mind of the god, like the center of the heavens, is remote; his knowledge is difficult, men cannot understand it" (lines 256–57). The friend's view seems to be that the gods have made men perverse and there is nothing that can be done about it. "Falsehood and untruth, they (the gods) conferred upon them forever" (line 280). The sufferer finally appeals to the gods for mercy and here the dialogue ends on a humble note. The document is from not earlier than about 1000 B.C.

Hence, we see that while the literary genre and overall format of the Job literature comes from the world of which it was a part, there is really nothing extant that compares with the biblical book in its philosophical and theological profundity. Moreover, the book of Job cannot be forced into any single classification as to its literary form. It is generally called WISDOM Literature, which was common in the biblical world, but it has other elements, such as drama and epic. Because the book is largely HEBREW POETRY (the dialogues) and poetry is the most difficult and the most archaic form of a language, Job abounds in *hapax legomena* (see HAPAX LEGOMENON). The syntax and orthography tend to represent a dialect other than the substratum of Judaic Hebrew found in most other parts of the OT (see HEBREW LANGUAGE). One must therefore turn to cognate languages that have an extensive literature, such as Arabic and ARAMAIC, for help in vocabulary and elements of grammar (see LANGUAGES OF THE ANE II).

Job has a strong Aramaic flavor, leading some to the view that the book was originally written in that language and later translated into Hebrew (cf. N. H. Tur Sinai, *The Book of Job A New Commentary* [1957]), but few agree. The mythological texts from UGARIT, a large corpus being poetry, have shed a great amount of light on both the language and text of Job. There are those who feel the book is possibly some form of Edomite (see EDOM), Job being regarded as one of "the people of the East" (Job 1:3), but there are no Edomite literary documents to test this view.

II. Authorship and literary unity. Is the book of single or composite authorship? The typical higher-critical approach would make it a gradual aggregation of materials on an original base. Among the dialogues, the Wisdom Poem of Job 28, the Elihu speeches in chs. 32–37, and the divine discourses in chs. 38–41 are said to be additions. Much has been made of the supposed incongruities between the prologue, epilogue, and dialogues of the book. In the prologue Job is presented as a saint of God who will not curse God and die, but in the discourses his complaints are bitter to the point of being shocking, while his friends seem to be saying all the right things. Then comes the unexpected rebuke of the friends and the commendation of Job in the epilogue.

These features are said to destroy the unity of the book, and when added to the different literary form (prose vs. poetry) and such things as Job's ritual piety in the prologue-epilogue, some have concluded the latter came from a different source. Ordinarily the claim is made that the prologue-epilogue represents an old epic tale that was used as a framework by the author of the dialogues. This tale about a legendary figure whose name was Job (cf. Ezek. 14:14, 20) was used to give more advanced concepts about theodicy a proper feel of antiquity. Heinrich Ewald, who advances this view (*Commentary on the Book of Job* [1882], 17–21), says that it is not fully legitimate to ask "whether the work of the poet as we possess it contains history or fiction, as if a third thing were not possible" (p. 20). The idea here is that the book is an artistic masterpiece put together skillfully by a great poet who used materials available to him. While it is true that the book does not claim to be written by Job (the prologue-epilogue is *about* him), nevertheless the discourses do claim to be from the lips of the same sufferer, and the integrity of the book is impaired if this is not so.

Returning to the problem of the apparent incongruities mentioned above, the Israeli scholar Y. Kaufmann (*The Religion of Israel* [1960], 335) explains God's rebuking the friends and not Job by suggesting that they were guilty of conventional clichés and empty phrases, while Job had challenged God out of a moral duty to speak only the truth before him. This is much more satisfactory than assuming, as some do, that the book has lost a large portion in which the friends, like his wife, told Job to curse God and die. Job himself accused his friends of saying things they did not believe to curry favor with God (Job 13:7–8). Without assuming there are no deletions or interpolations at all in Job, a fair mind must see the singular organic unity of this sizable piece of literature from OT times. The brevity of Bildad's speech and the omission of Zophar in chs. 24–27, added to Job's suddenly taking up his friend's argument, may indicate such a deletion and interpolation; but the complaints of some scholars against the first divine speech (ch. 38), on the basis that God seems indifferent to man's predicament, is simply a modern rejection of one of the book's most profound teachings regarding the sovereignty of God.

III. Date and canonicity. It is possible that the book of Job existed outside Israel for some time in oral form or even that it was partially written until an unknown Israelite author under divine inspiration put it into its present literary form. This would account for the non-Israelite flavor of the book, but also for its unquestioned place in the Hebrew CANON. It seems likely that Job himself lived in the 2nd millennium B.C. (2000–1000) and shared a tradition not far removed from the patriarchs. Job's longevity of 140 years, his position as a man whose wealth was measured in cattle possessions, and the picture of roving Sabean and Chaldean tribesmen fit the 2nd millennium better than a later period. The book, however, may not have reached its final form until the 1st millennium, perhaps in the Solomonic Age or somewhat later, when Hebrew Wisdom Literature was at its height. Attempts to put the authorship of Job in postexilic times, or even down to as late as the 2nd cent. B.C., have been dealt a decisive blow by the discovery of fragments of Job written in paleo-Hebrew script among the DEAD SEA SCROLLS.

It is most amazing that a book with nothing distinctively Israelite about it should find a place as part of the Hebrew canon and never be seriously challenged. This proves that the Hebrews recognized the superior spiritual message of this book from the earliest times. Since INSPIRATION was the test for canonicity, and a major test for inspiration was the acceptance of the book by the community of God's people, the Hebrews included Job in their canon of holy inspired books, placing it in the third section, called KETUBIM, "Writings" (also known as the HAGIOGRAPHA). The place of the book with relationship to PSALMS and PROVERBS has varied. Our English Bible follows the tradition reflected in the SEPTUAGINT, while printed editions of the Hebrew Bible follow the order Psalms, Proverbs, Job.

IV. Place of origin. Although Job is called "the greatest man among all the people of the east" (Job 1:3), the exact place of origin cannot be determined, just as the exact date is uncertain. The strong Aramaic flavor may mean that Job and his friends lived near the centers of Aramaic influence. During the 2nd millennium, that would have been ARAM NAHARAIM (Aram of the Two Rivers) or northern MESOPOTAMIA. At the end of the millennium Aramean tribes moved S, settling on the borders of Babylonia and Palestine, but continued to control the caravan route through the Khabur area, and at this time ALEPPO and DAMASCUS became Aramean centers. This was also the time when the Chaldean tribes invaded Babylonia (*CAH* 3 [1925], 4). If Job 1:17 means that Chaldean tribes were still roving, the event could reflect a time before they settled at about 1000 B.C. See ARAM (COUNTRY); CHALDEA.

According to Gen. 36:15, a certain ELIPHAZ was the firstborn of ESAU, and TEMAN was one of the chiefs. Esau was considered the progenitor of Edom, and geographically Teman was an Edomite city. Edom was apparently noted for its centers of wisdom (Jer. 49:7). Job, therefore, may have called on his counselors because of their fame for wisdom. Job himself lived in the land of Uz (Job 1:1), an area associated with the Arameans (Gen. 10:23; 22:20–22). The latter passage (22:22) also ties in Kesed (the Chaldeans) with the Arameans and the Uzites but does not make them identical. These passages refer to nations or tribes that were related sometimes only by their proximity. The land of Uz was E of Palestine but its precise location cannot be determined. Job had great influence in some town (Job 29:7) the name of which is not given. Edom was closely associated with the land of Uz (Lam. 4:21). It seems then that Uz might have been the name of a wide region encompassing many tribes E. of Palestine from Edom to Aram.

V. Text. Studies in the SEPTUAGINT of Job have shown that the oldest Greek text is shorter than the MT. This ancient Greek version omitted difficult lines, and subsequently ORIGEN filled in the missing material from Theodotion's translation. The Greek text is also somewhat of a paraphrase showing according to some a theological bias in places (M. H. Pope, *Job*, AB 15, 3rd ed. [1973], xlv).

Among other versions, the most helpful is the Syriac, through which the meaning of rare Hebrew words can sometimes be detected. A Latin translation comes directly from the Hebrew by JEROME in the 4th cent. A.D. Jerome was strongly influenced by the rabbis who taught him Hebrew but also by Origen's recension of the SEPTUAGINT. See VERSIONS OF THE BIBLE, ANCIENT. The MT is still the best source for the text of Job. Several pieces of a lost Targum of Job were found among the DSS (see JOB, TARGUM OF).

VI. Purpose and teaching. The author of the book of Job purposes to show how the theological position of Job's friends represents a shallow and only partial observation of life, namely, that human suffering is always proportionate to a person's sins. There is no studied attempt to justify God with regard to the innocent suffering, but the author does show God has higher purposes, and far from

Bedouin man with his animals. Job's wealth was measured by the livestock he owned.

abandoning the sufferer communicates with him at the proper time. A subsidiary purpose is to show that though people are often sinful, weak, and ignorant, they can, like Job, be relatively pure and upright even when in the midst of emotional turmoil and spiritual testing. SATAN was permitted to test Job sorely through the instrumentality of would-be helpers who used the language of traditional piety.

Job's problem was the vexing question of theodicy, that is, the justice of God in relation to the suffering of the innocent. The book pursues a middle way between fatalism—where divine power originates evil, as in the Babylonian Theodicy—and a view of human freedom that would ignore the SOVEREIGNTY OF GOD. There is no attempt to give a rational or philosophical solution to the problem of evil. The picture is the same as that given in Genesis, where the accuser (Satan), as a creature of God, subject to his will yet in rebellion, bears the responsibility for Job's trouble, although, indeed, he is permitted to do so by God. The problem of theodicy is left on the note that God is a sovereign Deity who made and sustains all that is, who in his OMNIPOTENCE and OMNISCIENCE can and does use secondary means to bring about his higher and perfect purposes. One of these higher purposes in Job's suffering is to prove to Satan that Job did not live righteously only that he might prosper. Satan challenges God to prove that Job's devotion is pure not only by removing his wealth but also by destroying his health.

Initially Job stands the test even when his wife says, "Curse God and die!" (Job 2:9). But as his troubles multiply, Job has second thoughts and in his dialogues with his counselors he wrestles with God, challenges God, sinks into depths of despair, and rises to peaks of trust and confidence in God. Throughout the book, Job defends his own essential innocence (not sinlessness) in rejecting the view of his friends, which rarely moves from the single theme that suffering is the immediate corollary of sin, and that because Job has grievously sinned God has become his enemy. Their view Job emphatically rejects, but his own view seems to be in a state of flux, for he says many unfortunate things. Yet, in it all, he does not do what Satan said he would; he does not curse God to his face (2:5).

While the counselors make no progress in their arguments, Job grows more and more serene as he approaches his eventual confrontation with God for which he has been asking. Job wants to argue his case before almighty God and also calls for an advocate to plead his cause at the divine tribunal. He is confident he will be vindicated, if not in this life, then later; but he is certain it will be in the flesh (Job 19:26). The counselors said many good things, but they could not seem to move from the fallacious idea that the righteous always prosper and sinners always suffer, and conversely, that suffering always implies sin and prosperity always implies righteousness. Their view was not always put so crassly. Eliphaz implies that since all have sinned, suffering is to some extent due to all and therefore the righteous might suffer a little and the unrighteous prosper a little, but that the righteous never come to an untimely end (4:7; 18:16–19); and the wicked when they prosper are in dread of the calamity ahead that they deserve (15:20–35).

Another feature of their monotonous arguments is that even if an unrighteous person prospers all his life his children will eventually pay the penalty (Job 5:4; 20:10). Their idea that suffering is chastisement to purify the character (5:17–27) is quite in keeping with the rest of Scripture. Much of their argument is thus orthodox expression, true in the abstract, but it did not necessarily apply to Job. It is not so much what they say that offends Job, but what they leave out, which makes what they say only a part of the truth. They finally reach the conclusion that since Job seems so obstinate and refuses even the idea of the disciplinary purpose of his suffering, he must have committed sins of great enormity. The position of the friends was normative Mesopotamian thought, but the OT also has in it the stories of such innocent sufferers as ABEL, URIAH, and NABOTH. Jesus, of course, taught his disciples that individual retribution in this life simply does not follow. "Neither this man nor his parents sinned ... but this happened so that the work of God might be displayed in his life" (Jn. 9:3).

Some have suggested the OT sometimes shares in this erroneous view. For example, Ps. 1:3 says of the righteous, "Whatever he does prospers," and Ps. 37:25 says, "I was young and now I am old, yet I have never seen the righteous forsaken or their children begging bread." This discrepancy is superficial because the Psalms are not making specific applications, as were the counselors of Job, but are expressing general principles. Perhaps the point where Job was agonizing the most was how to integrate those valid parts of what the friends said with his own experience. Job had no answer because God has not seen fit to give mortals a reason for everything he does. So Job blows hot and cold. Sometimes he blames the Lord for tormenting him and wishes God would leave him alone (Job 7:17–21; 10:20; 19:22). At other times he yearns for God to communicate with him (14:15) and wishes that he might see God. This emotional instability of Job in all likelihood arose from an internal conflict based on his intellectual acceptance of this false view of suffering (so much for so much sin), which conflicted with his experience.

The question arises as to whether the purpose of the book is to formulate an exact rational answer to the problem of theodicy, the justice of God in innocent suffering. In all Job's dialogues he nowhere calls for such, nor does the Lord give such an answer when he appears to speak to Job and his friends. What Job does call for is a vindication of the fact that he has not committed heinous sins for which he is being punished. When God does rebuke Job, it is for his ignorance (Job 38:2, 13) and presumption (42:2), not for a profligate life. God is apparently telling Job in chs. 38–41 that neither he nor his friends know enough about his ways to make judgments concerning the rightness of his dealings with men. This impugns especially the strictness of the friends and their whole theory of suffering, which implicitly laid claim to complete knowledge of God's ways.

Even though in his appearance God does not deal with the problem of theodicy and gives no rational explanation or excuse for Job's suffering, nevertheless Job is not crushed, only rebuked, and even that not as severely as his friends (Job 42:7). Job now realizes God does not need human advice to control the world and that no extremes of suffering gives one the right to question God's wisdom or justice, and for this failure he repents (42:2–6). On seeing the power and glory of God, Job's rebellious attitude dissolves and his resentment disappears. Job now gets at least part of what he sought for. His friends do not see him pronounced guilty and therefore the idea that suffering is proof of sin is refuted.

Nowhere does God impugn the basic integrity of Job's character; hence Satan has failed and Job's testing has come to an end. He has not demanded restoration, only vindication of his character; but God, having achieved his higher purpose through Job, now restores him who in his suffering, despite moments of weakness, surpassed in righteousness those who had not suffered as he had. After all his doubts and bitterness, Job arrived at that point of spiritual maturity where he could pray for those who abused him (Job 42:10; cf. Lk 6:28). The issues raised in this book are indeed among the most profound and difficult of human existence. The answer was already on Job's lips in the prologue when he said, "The LORD gave and the LORD has taken away; may the name of the LORD be praised" (1:21b); and later, "Shall we accept good from God, and not trouble?" (2:10). The truth Job knew was that God must be God, and that of all values and all existence only God and his glory must ultimately prevail.

VII. Outline and content

A. The prologue (Job 1:1—2:13)
  1. Job's felicity (1:1–5)
  2. Job tested (1:6—2:13)
     a. Satan accuses Job (1:6–12)
     b. Job's integrity in loss of family and property (1:13–22)
     c. Satan's second accusation (2:1–6)
     d. Job's integrity in personal suffering (2:7–10)
     e. The coming of the counselors (2:11–13)
B. The dialogues (3:1—42:6)
  1. Job curses the day of his birth (3:1–26)
  2. The first cycle of speeches (4:1—14:22)
     a. Eliphaz (4:1—5:27)
     b. Job's reply (6:1—7:21)
     c. Bildad (8:1–22)
     d. Job's reply (9:1—10:22)
     e. Zophar (11:1–20)
     f. Job's reply (12:1—14:22)
  3. The second cycle of speeches (15:1—21:34)

       a. Eliphaz (15:1–35)
       b. Job's reply (16:1—17:16)
       c. Bildad (18:1–21)
       d. Job's reply (19:1–29)
       e. Zophar (20:1–29)
       f. Job's reply (21:1–34)
   4. The third cycle of speeches (22:1—31:40)
       a. Eliphaz (22:1–30)
       b. Job's reply (23:1—24:25)
       c. Bildad (25:1–6)
       d. Job's reply (26:1—27:23)
       e. Job's poem on wisdom (28:1–28)
       f. Job's closing soliloquy and oath (29:1—31:40)
   5. Elihu's speeches (32:1—37:24)
       a. First speech (32:1—33:33)
       b. Second speech (34:1–37)
       c. Third speech (35:1–16)
       d. Fourth speech (36:1—37:24)
   6. The theophany (38:1—42:6)
       a. God's first discourse (38:1—40:2)
       b. Job humbled (40:3–5)
       c. God's second discourse (40:6—41:34)
       d. Job repents (42:1–6)
C. The epilogue (42:7–17)
   1. Job vindicated (42:7–9)
   2. Job restored (42:10–17)

The following summary of contents builds on the outline above.

A. The prologue (1:1—2:13). The prologue presents Job as a man of singular character and very prosperous. For reasons about which the reader is informed but which Job does not know, Job's wealth and health are taken from him while his character remains intact. The writer uses great restraint in the choice of details, giving no extraneous information; but in typical Semitic style he uses repetition skillfully for emphasis and effect (1:1, 8; 2:3 and 1:22; 2:10 and 1:14–19).

1. Job's felicity (1:1–5). Job was a man from the land of Uz, located somewhere E of Palestine on the edge of the desert (1:19). Here farming was carried on (1:14), and there was a town nearby (29:7). Job's wealth is given in terms similar to those used of the patriarchs, that is, animal possessions, sons and servants. Job is said to be "blameless and upright" (1:1; *tām wĕyāšār*, lit., "complete and straight" in character).

2. Job tested (1:6—2:13). There are two scenes in heaven (1:6–11 and 2:1–5), each followed by a series of happenings that result from these encounters between the Lord and Satan. In the first scene, Satan questions Job's motives in his religious devotion. "Does Job fear God for nothing?" (1:9). If God were to remove the hedge about Job and his house and let Satan smite him, Job would curse God to his face. After Job's children and wealth are taken away under the permissive will of God, still Job maintains his integrity toward God. Satan then calls on the Almighty to permit him to smite Job's body, for "a man will give all he has for his own life" (2:4). Satan then proceeds to afflict Job with a horrible disease. At this point even Job's wife advises, "Curse God and die!" (2:9); yet in spite of all these troubles, "Job did not sin in what he said" (v. 10).

It is at this point that Job's would-be comforters arrive. They sit with him seven days and nights mourning his affliction, and finally Job breaks the silence with the opening words of the so-called dialogues.

B. The dialogues (3:1—42:6).
1. Job curses the day of his birth (3:1–26). Job, now in a state of despondency, damns his own life. The theme continues throughout the chapter. He wishes that the day of his birth had never dawned (vv. 4, 9) or that there might have been an eclipse of the sun (v. 5) or that it never would have been numbered among the days of the year (v. 6). He yearns that the diviners might have put a curse on it so that the rays of that dawn never would have come up. Would that he had been a stillbirth, for then Job imagines he might now be at rest or even in the company of the illustrious dead (v. 14) rather than a blighted man lying in squalor.

Job questions the wisdom of God in prolonging life for those who are in misery (v. 20) and who long for death (v. 21). He ends his sad soliloquy on the mournful thought that the thing he feared most has happened to him; that is, he is in a state of complete torment physically and emotionally and there is no deliverance, no end in sight. The state of mind Job displays in this chapter marks his lowest ebb, the nearest he ever came to fulfilling Satan's prediction that he would curse God to his face. This attitude resulted from the repeated question, why? (3:11, 20).

Although not cursing God, he is certainly questioning God's sovereignty and wisdom, and for this he eventually repented (40:1-2; 42:1-6).

2. The first cycle of speeches (4:1—14:22)

(a) *Eliphaz* (4:1—5:27). ELIPHAZ the Temanite (see TEMAN), the oldest of the counselors, is the first to speak. He expresses both in words and in spirit the viewpoint that the friends will repeat over and over to Job. He begins modestly (4:2) and even a bit complimentary toward Job, but before his second statement is finished he is rebuking the sufferer (4:5) and telling Job that his only hope lies in a life of purity and fear of God (4:6). He gives expression to the traditional view of suffering in all its simplicity, the thought that the innocent do not perish but the plowers of iniquity reap the same (4:7-9). As an ultimate principle this idea is not invalid, but Eliphaz obviously is implicating Job and therefore applying the ultimate principle to a specific time and person which he did not know enough to do. The following verses (4:10-11) might be taken as a warning to Job, described as the old lion who does not die but just wastes away.

Eliphaz employs an age-old means for impressing others with one's religious authority. He tells of an eerie experience, a vision in the night so frightening that his hair stood up (4:15): he heard a spirit announce in a hushed voice the otherness of God as One so far removed from his creatures of clay that they are like fragile moths whose lives meaninglessly pass away forever (4:17-21).

Eliphaz continues in ch. 5 to describe the lot of foolish sinners who never prosper and who always have trouble (vv. 1-7), but he presents himself as one who commits his way to God (vv. 8-16). By implication Eliphaz admonishes Job not to "despise the discipline of the Almighty" (vv. 17-27). If Job will only heed this discipline, he will soon find that he is prospering again (vv. 19, 24-26, et al.). Eliphaz finishes with the admonition that his great wisdom has come from his own research and therefore deserves close attention (v. 27).

(b) *Job's reply* (6:1—7:21). Job does not bother to answer Eliphaz specifically but continues to give vent to his anguish. How great his distress is! If weighed against his words, his vexation would be heavier than the sand of the sea. That is why he complains so vehemently, for he has ample unsalted food; worse, it is putrid. Job pleads again for death (6:8-13). He complains that his flesh is not made of stone or bronze; it would be a comfort for him to die. Job chides his friends for their lack of pity. A sick man should have the pity of his friends even if he renounced the fear of God, but his friends have betrayed him. They have seen him in this awful condition and have panicked even when he asked for nothing but honest words. This, he says, is exactly what they have failed to speak (v. 25). Job challenges them to prove their contention that he has grievously sinned. They are callous enough to cast lots over an orphan or barter over a friend (v. 27). He pleads that they soften up and see that what he says is right.

Job's reply continues in ch. 7. Addressing God, Job laments man's plight and hardship on earth (7:1-2). He describes in detail his own sad condition. "My flesh is clothed with worms and scabs, my skin is broken and festering" (v. 5). He laments the human predicament in death, when people seem simply to evaporate and vanish: "he who goes down to the grave does not return" (v. 9). At this Job says he will not restrain his tongue any longer (v. 11) but will complain with all the bitterness of his soul. He then begins to accuse God of tormenting him with dreams and nightmares, of being like a watchman over his soul, inspecting him every morning and testing him every moment. He asks God to leave him alone, forgive him, and let him lie down and die (vv. 12-21).

(c) *Bildad* (8:1-22). BILDAD the Shuhite (see SHUAH) now speaks. He charges Job with producing nothing but a big wind. If Job's children have sinned they have been punished for it and Job himself could be delivered if only he were pure and upright. Surely Job should study what the ancients have said and find out what happens to people who forget God. The wicked wither as plants do when they are deprived of water (vv. 11-13), and their confidence is like a spider's web (v. 14) that can be brushed away in a second (v. 18), but Job should realize God never rejects the upright (v. 20).

(d) *Job's reply* (9:1—10:22). Perhaps with sarcasm, Job agrees with what Bildad has said, but he does not see how one ever can be justified before God. He goes on to tell what he means by this statement: in argumentation God always wins,

A 1905 photograph of individuals in Palestine disfigured by a skin disease. The Bible says that some terrible skin disease afflicted Job.

because he is too wise and powerful for us, no matter how clever or mighty we may be. Beginning in 9:5, Job describes God as the great controller of all the universe. "How then can I dispute with him? / How can I find words to argue with him?" (v. 14). Here Job seems to accuse God of being callous, as one who destroys both the guiltless and wicked (v. 22), and who laughs at the calamity of the innocent. Job continues to complain that God allows the earth to be controlled by the wicked: there is no justice on earth, and God is to blame (v. 24). Job's days are fleeing by and he has no hope because he feels God holds him guilty (v. 28). Even if he were clean (v. 30), God would plunge him in the muck so that his own clothes would abhor him. Moreover, the sufferer cannot even challenge God because the latter is so great. Job wishes for an arbiter who could equalize the situation (v. 33). He calls on God to put aside his club so that Job can speak to him without fear (v. 35).

But now Job says he is sick of life (10:1) and he is going to continue to give vent to his bitterness. He addresses God by asking if it is right that he should oppress and despise the creatures of his own hands while he favors the wicked (10:3). Job questions whether God can really sympathize with man's predicament (10:4–7). God will not let him alone even though he made man out of clay. Now he seeks to destroy him (10:8–9). Even though God fashioned his flesh and bones in the womb and granted him a time of happiness (10:10–12), yet God did it while planning to let him come to this horrible situation. Job sees himself as a victim whom God is oppressing as a lion stalks its prey (10:10). Why then did God allow him to be born? It would be better if God would let him alone for the few days he has left before he goes down to the land of darkness and gloom (10:20–22).

Despite Job's feeling of abandonment and his failure to see the love of God, it is obvious he is still wrestling spiritually and is by no means ready to curse God to his face.

(e) *Zophar* (11:1–20). Zophar the Naamathite (see Naamah (place)) takes up the challenge of Job lest it go unanswered. He will not allow Job's babbling to silence him. If God were to speak he would tell Job how guilty he is. God is greater than all; he sees and knows all the evil of humanity. If only Job will reach out a hand toward God and put away his evildoing, God would lift him up and he would be restored and soon forget all his troubles (vv. 13–19). Let Job keep in mind that the wicked have no refuge and no hope (v. 20).

(f) *Job* (12:1—14:22). Job addresses to his friends the first half of this reply (12:1—13:19); the second half he addresses to God (13:20—14:22). He starts by making sarcastic reference to the wisdom of his friends (vv. 1–2). Everything they have said he already knows (v. 3) but they understand very little of Job's troubles (vv. 4–5). They understand his problem about as well as do the beasts and creeping things (vv. 7–9). True, God is sovereign, controlling all things, but he seems to be capricious in the way he does it (vv. 20–25). Job claims he understands that God is almighty in wisdom and power (12:1–2), but he still wants to argue his case with God (v. 3). He accuses his "friends" of being dishonest, whitewashers, and worthless healers, because they overlook the real problem, namely, God's use of his might. They speak deceitfully in God's behalf (v. 7), piously contending for God in hope of currying favor with him (vv. 8–9). When God searches them out, they are going to be rebuked (vv. 9–12).

Job requests they keep quiet while he boldly speaks. Taking his life in his hand, he bravely declares that even if God slays him he has the confidence that he will yet (after death) maintain the basic integrity of his ways before God (vv. 13–16). He pleads with God to let him set out his case and is confident he will be justified (vv. 17–19). Two things Job requests of God: to withdraw his hand and cease terrifying him and to communicate with him (vv. 20–22). Then Job confesses his sins and pleads that God hide not his face nor become his enemy (vv. 23–28).

In ch. 14 Job laments the human predicament, "few days and full of trouble" (14:1). God knows how pathetically short Job's days are. Why will he not forbear and let man enjoy his day (vv. 1–6)? Job compares man to a tree which though cut down can be revived by "the scent of water" (v. 9). Poor creature, who dies and does not rise for ages on end. Again Job yearns for death, but this time he suggests that he may live again. In a moment of supreme tranquility, Job confesses he will gladly suffer "all the days of [his] hard service" and wait patiently for his release to come when he will hear God call and have a happy relationship with him again (vv. 14–15). But Job sinks back again into despondency. He feels at the end of this discourse that God will not forgive him (v. 16), that he has no hope (v. 19) and must look for more pain (v. 22) and final death (v. 20).

3. The second cycle of speeches (15:1—21:34)

(a) *Eliphaz* (15:1–35). This time Eliphaz is not courteous toward Job. He frankly labels Job's speech as hot air and charges him as guilty of the worst kind of impiety because he talks as if he were the first man who ever lived, who has a monopoly on wisdom, especially the counsels of God. Does Job not know that his counselors are older than Job's father? Does he not know how unrighteous man is? For even the angels and heaven itself are impure in God's sight (vv. 11–16). In vv. 17–35 Eliphaz gives a lengthy harangue about the troubles that come on the wicked (meaning Job, of course), who stretch out their hands against God (v. 25).

(b) *Job's reply* (16:1—17:16). Job is sick of their prattle. If the tables were turned and they were suffering he could harangue them with words and shake his head at them (16:1–5). At this Job begins to use figures of speech to describe what he thinks are God's actions against him. God is as one gnashing upon him with his teeth. God has set him up like a target for the archers, and warriors breach him like the wall of a city is breached (vv. 9–14). His miserable condition is such that his face is red with weeping and his eyelids are covered with darkness (v. 16). There is no justification for this because there has been no violence in his hands and his prayers have not been hypocritical. Moreover, Job claims to have an advocate in heaven, one who pleads his cause before God, as a man pleads for his friend. This is the umpire of 9:33 and the vindicator of 19:25.

These advocate passages in the book of Job are an amazing insight into our deep need of a mediator between us and God. Job, with all his complaining, reached an understanding of the mystery of godliness which the counselors did not even approach. Theirs was an ad nauseam repetition of a defective view of suffering. When Job called for an advocate who could put his hand on God and on the creature, he was touching in a prophetic way on the need for a reconciler who would be both human and divine. The forensic aspect of the mediatorial work of Christ (Rom. 5:1–5) fulfilled the great need of the sinner, who stands in the presence of the Almighty overwhelmed and condemned. As a believer Job felt this need. How much he understood is open to question.

After this moment of hope Job sinks back into despair. His spirit is broken, his days are spent, he looks only for the grave (17:1–3). He has no plans, no desires, no hope (17:11–16).

(c) *Bildad* (18:1–21). Bildad has no patience with Job's speeches, and he cannot understand why Job thinks his friends are stupid as beasts. Does Job expect the world to stop for him (v. 4)? From v. 5 on he dwells on the horrible fate of the wicked people, obviously meaning Job. Such people may expect to have terrors on every side and to be afflicted with fatal disease and plucked from their home to face the king of terrors, death itself. Nor may they expect to have any posterity or remembrance in the earth.

(d) *Job's reply* (19:1–29). How long are Job's friends going to vex his soul with their accusing words? Cannot they see how violently God has dealt with him (vv. 6–7)? Certainly it is not right that he should be treated as an adversary of God (v. 11), an enemy that needs to be destroyed. God has caused his family and acquaintances to reject him (vv. 13–20). Will the friends join God in persecuting him, will they not have pity on him (vv. 21–22)? Job wishes that his protestation of integrity might be eternally recorded (vv. 23–24); perhaps implying that someday, then, they would see he is right. For

Job knows that his Vindicator (Kinsman Redeemer; see GOEL; REDEMPTION) lives and will someday stand upon the earth and witness in his behalf (vv. 25–26). Job longs for that day when he himself will behold God (v. 27), on that day his friends will be judged for their false accusations.

(e) *Zophar* (20:1–29). Job's foolish words have made Zophar angry. Does Job not know one of the oldest facts of history (v. 4), that the wicked prosper only for a moment and then always perish forever like dung never to be seen again (vv. 7–9)? Even their children are reduced to poverty (v. 10) and the evil that seemed sweet becomes venom within the wicked (vv. 11–16). They never get to enjoy the riches gained by oppression and robbery (vv. 12–22) because God always punishes the wicked with his wrath (vv. 23–26). Even the heavens and the earth testify against the wicked, and the loss of everything is their portion from God (vv. 27–29).

(f) *Job's reply* (21:1–34). They have it all wrong, says Job, for the wicked often live to old age enjoying all kinds of prosperity (v. 7). Why is it that far from punishing them God appears to bless them even when they openly defy him (vv. 8–15)? Occasionally calamity comes to them, but how often (v. 17)? True, sometimes the children of the wicked suffer for their fathers' sins, but the wicked themselves escape (vv. 18–21). Those who enjoy prosperity and those who never taste the good things of life both end up in the dust (vv. 22–26). Job accuses his friends of being hostile toward him, even plotting against him (v. 27). But their ideas are no comfort at all and are sheer falsehood (v. 34). Any traveler can tell them how many wicked people prosper (vv. 29–30). The logic that says, "all the wicked suffer, Job suffers, and therefore Job is wicked," is simply not true to the facts.

4. The third cycle of speeches (22:1—31:40)

(a) *Eliphaz* (22:1–30). Man cannot benefit God by being righteous. On the other hand, does Job think God is reproving him for his righteousness? Indeed not; it is because his wickedness is great (vv. 1–5). Eliphaz now gives a detailed catalogue of the kinds of sin Job has probably committed. He accuses Job of oppressing the poor, the widow, and the orphan (vv. 5–9). God may be far away in heaven, but he sees and he will surely punish (vv. 12–20). So why does not Job yield to him and repent and take delight in the Almighty, who will surely hear and restore Job and even enable him to intercede for others (vv. 21–30)?

(b) *Job's reply* (23:1—24:25). God's hand is heavy on Job but still he cannot find God so that he might lay his case before him (23:1–7). Yes, God eludes him (vv. 8–9) perhaps because God knows Job's cause is just (v. 10) and that he is an upright man who has not neglected the Lord's commandments (vv. 11–12); and yet God continues to terrify him (vv. 13–17). Job then questions why God has not set times to judge the ungodly (24:1–2) when there is so much violence and oppression in the earth (vv. 3–17).

Some believe that beginning at 24:18 Job takes up the argument of his counselors, that is, that the wicked do not prosper. The RSV, for example, adds the words, "You say" (not found in the Heb. text), so that vv. 18–20 appear as a quotation of their argument. Others think this is a misplaced portion and belongs to one of the counselors (Pope, *Job*, xviii).

(c) *Bildad* (25:1–6). Bildad now gives a short speech in which he dwells on the majesty of God, who rules with awesome power (vv. 2–3) and before whom man, a mere maggot or worm, cannot possibly be pure (vv. 4–6). Some believe that Bildad's argument is brief because the dialogue has broken down, the arguments are exhausted. Others (cf. Pope, *Job*, xviii) maintain that something has happened to the text in chs. 24–27 and that 26:5–14, where Job deals with God's power, should be appended to 25:1–6. Also suggested is the insertion of the words "Zophar the Naamathite answered" before 27:8, since Zophar's third speech, which completes the cycle, is otherwise missing (the subject matter of 27:8–23 is said to be the counselors' argument about God's punishment of the wicked). That Zophar had a third speech is questionable. In 27:11–12, Job seems to be rebuking his friends. It is entirely possible that Job, finally realizing he was overstating the case about the wicked's prosperity, now balances his argument with a firm statement of God's punishment of the wicked.

(d) *Job's reply* (26:1—27:23). Once again Job with irony rebukes his friends for giving no help (26:2–4). In contrast to their powerlessness and lack of wisdom, Job extols the power and wisdom of God in a magnificent soliloquy (vv. 5–14). It is God who hung the earth on nothing (v. 7), who binds up the waters in thick clouds (v. 8), who set the limit to the circle of the horizon (v. 10), who makes the pillars of the heavens (the mountains) tremble (v. 11), who by his strength can stir up or make calm the elements, whether in the boisterous sea or in the heavens (vv. 12–13). All this is but a small whisper of the thunder of his power (v. 14). Although Job uses terms common in Canaanite mythology—Yam (the SEA), RAHAB (MONSTER), and the fleeing serpent (cf. Isa. 27:1)—his reference is to natural phenomena with which these names were identified.

Those who claim Zophar had a third speech usually begin it at about 27:8 and assume that an introductory line was lost or taken out by an overzealous scribe who wanted to tone down Job's argument. But it is just as likely that Job awaited Zophar's reply and, when none came, he then took up again the discourse (27:1); here for the first time he uses a solemn oath (v. 2) to declare his integrity and their deceit in accusing him (v. 5).

(e) *Job's poem on wisdom* (28:1–28). It is said that either Job himself or the Israelite writer who composed the book at this point inserted a poem on the immutable wisdom of God. If this is Job speaking, how do his words fit into the rest of his argument? And how could a man having such a disturbed state of mind give a poem so full of meditative tranquility? On the latter point it is well known that people who are disturbed sometimes produce poems or hymns in unexplained moments of extreme serenity. Nor dare one ignore the influence of the Spirit of God on Job. Many of the things he has said were his own fallible reasoning. Now, near the end of his rope, and still without a satisfactory answer to the conflict raging within him of how to reconcile his sufferings with his own integrity of life, he turns his mind to the wisdom of God. The human ability to find and extract precious metals and gems from the earth is amazing, but people cannot find wisdom so easily (v. 12). After a grand comparison of these human achievements (vv. 1–11) with the wisdom of the Almighty (vv. 12–27) Job asserts that true wisdom is to fear the Lord and obey him.

(f) *Job's closing soliloquy and oath* (29:1—31:40). Job begins his final remarks by recalling his for-

Chalcolithic shaft mine at Timnah with tool marks on the walls. "Man's hand assaults the flinty rock and lays bare the roots of the mountains" (Job 28:9).

mer happy and prosperous condition, when everyone poor and rich, young and old respected him (29:1–10). Those were the days when he was a champion of the poor, the orphan, and the widow. He was "eyes to the blind and feet to the lame," and he resisted the wicked (29:11–17). Surely, he thought, he would continue a strong man into ripe old age (29:18–20). Instead boys whose fathers were beneath him are now deriding him (30:1–7), and even worse he has become a gibe to vile hoodlums (30:13–23). Job laments that he who once wept for the needy and the poor now finds himself forsaken, lonesome, diseased, and dying (30:24–31).

In ch. 31 Job employs a form associated with ANE oaths of COVENANT allegiance to emphasize his final protestation of innocence. A vassal would use a formulation in which he called down curses on himself as proof that he was free from violating any of the stipulations laid down by his Sovereign. Such an oath was believed to have great efficacy and therefore was the ultimate test of honesty (cf. Exod. 22:10–11, Num. 5:20–22, Deut. 27:11–26; 28:18, 31, 35; 1 Ki. 8:31–32; note also the Hittite Soldiers' Oath, *ANET*, 353–54). Job's protestation of innocence is likened also to the negative confession in the Egyptian Book of the Dead, where the deceased at the final judgment lists the sins he has not done (*ANET*, 34). It is difficult for modern Westerners to realize the importance of the steps Job is taking: in his culture these were more meaningful than swearing before a judge and jury, where perjury has far less terrifying sanctions. By taking such oaths and affixing his signature (*ANET*, 35), Job closed the argument; there was nothing more the counselors could say, for Job must either suffer the sanctions or be acquitted.

The list of sins Job denies are largely social sins; he has not committed adultery (31:9–12) nor mistreated slaves, recognizing the unity of the human race as creatures of God (vv. 13–15). Nor has he ever oppressed the poor, the widowed, or the orphan; on the contrary, he has raised orphans from infancy (vv. 16–20). He has never trusted in gold or gloated over his wealth (vv. 24–25), nor has he ever worshiped, even secretly, the heavenly bodies (vv. 26–27), an act that would be a betrayal of God (v. 28). He has never rejoiced at the misfortune of his enemy nor even cursed his foe (vv. 29–30), nor even abused the tenants on his land (vv. 38–40). Job has kept his household pure and his door always has been open to the traveler (vv. 31–32). Therefore, far from hiding from God as did Adam, Job challenges God to write an indictment against him; rather than run from God he wants to confront God like a prince (vv. 35–37). While most of what Job says about himself may be true, one detects the smell of self-righteousness. The next speaker, Elihu, evidently was appointed by God to rebuke Job for this.

5. Elihu's speeches (32:1—37:24)

(a) *First speech* (32:1—33:33). The first six verses, written in prose, introduce a new character, Elihu son of Barakel the Buzite (see Buz), who was standing on the side listening to the debate. When the three failed to answer Job's oaths, an arrogant spirit of self-righteousness made the anger of this young man flare up. He injects himself into the discourse apologizing for his presumption while pointing out that wisdom is a gift of God and does not come automatically with age (32:7–9). He will speak without flattery nor be partial to any (vv. 21–22).

Elihu then assures Job, who has complained that God is too much for man (cf. 9:34), that he can dispute with Job on equal terms, for he is a fellow creature of clay (33:1–7). He then reminds Job of his own words (vv. 9–11) as spoken in 13:24b and 13:27a, where the patriarch in protesting his own innocence accuses God of making himself Job's enemy. He flatly tells Job he is wrong in this (33:12) and challenges Job's accusation that God ignores him (v. 13, cf. 19.7, 30.20).

On the contrary, God reveals himself in various ways to human beings. Sometimes by dream he seeks to deter them from evil, to spare them of sin's consequences (33:15–18); or it may be at the last minute on the bed of mortal illness, when an angel intervenes and pleads the cause of the sufferer, that God in grace accepts a ransom for his life and restores the sinner (vv. 23–26). Sinners should sing hymns in praise of God's grace. The words of such a hymn Elihu includes in the text (vv. 27–28). This evidence of grace God displays not once but often twice and thrice with a sinner (v. 29). Elihu has shown the chastening aspect of suffering and how it is a work of God's grace. Job has no reply (vv. 31–33).

(b) *Second speech* (34:1–37). Elihu's second speech follows the same pattern as the first. He calls for a hearing (vv. 2–4), quotes Job's words (vv. 5–9), then attempts to answer Job (vv. 10–28), ending with a challenge to Job to give an answer if he can (v. 33). The young man attacks Job at a vulnerable spot, Job's denial of divine justice (v. 9). He defends God as one who does only goodness and justice (vv. 10–12, 21–28). Indeed it is only because of the goodness of God that people continue their lives on earth (vv. 13–15). How could God govern the universe if he were not just? Job blasphemes the almighty Sovereign, so he is guilty of rebellion and has spoken without wisdom (v. 35). Job ought to be tried for his rebellion (vv. 36–37).

(c) *Third speech* (35:1–16). The exact meaning of Elihu is somewhat elusive at the beginning of this chapter, but it becomes clear from v. 3 that he opposes Job in his idea that righteousness does not pay. This would mean that God is not just. Elihu uses an argument already used by Eliphaz (22:2–4), that man cannot add or detract from God by his righteousness or evil (35:5–7), and therefore God's administration of justice is always fair. If it appears to sinners that God is indifferent to human virtue or wickedness, it is only because of the pride of their heart, because they do not seek God aright, to praise him as God (vv. 9–13). Job should not be so impatient, for in God's own time he will administer justice (vv. 14–16).

(d) *Fourth speech* (36:1—37:24). Elihu expresses his complete dedication to upholding the righteousness of the Creator (36:2–3), but it is difficult to tell whether he is ascribing perfect knowledge to himself or God (36:4b). God is also all powerful and he does punish the wicked and reward the righteous (vv. 5–9). One of his major purposes in sending affliction is discipline (vv. 10–12). When sinners learn their lessons God delivers them (v. 11). The godless in heart react in rage to God's warnings (vv. 13–14), but to the godly affliction becomes the means by which they are delivered (vv. 15–16). Job must be careful that he receive God's chastening in the right spirit (vv. 17–21). Rather, Job should magnify God for his great works (v. 22) and never blame God (v. 23), but join those who sing his doxologies (v. 24).

From here on Elihu extols the Lord in hymnic stanzas as the Maker and Controller of all earth's meteorological forces: the rain and evaporation cycle (vv. 26–28), the thunderstorm (36:29—37:4), the snow (37:6), the tornado (v. 9), the winter's cold blast (v. 9b), the ice (v. 10), and the lightning (vv. 11–13). Job is challenged to tell how the lightning is caused (v. 15), how the clouds form (v. 16), how the hot south wind comes (v. 17), etc. Can Job understand—much less do—any of this? If Job cannot understand God's power over the physical creation why does he think he knows so much about God's moral rule? This God of great power is also the God who will never violate his own righteous character (v. 23). Job should therefore be humbled and fear him (v. 24).

Elihu's ministry, far from being an interpolation, forms a unique transition between the speeches and the THEOPHANY of chs. 38–42. Since there is no rebuke of Elihu by God in ch. 42, one may safely assume that his words do not partake of the hypocritical spirit common to the three counselors. He has concentrated on the disciplinary nature of suffering and has checked Job where he sometimes lost sight of divine majesty and fell into accusing God of acts contrary to his nature. Elihu has prepared the way for the appearance of the Lord in the whirlwind, especially by his lengthy description of God's creation and control over the forces of nature.

6. The theophany (38:1—41:34)

(a) *God's first discourse* (38:1—40:2). The Lord speaks to Job out of a whirlwind, rebuking him for words spoken without knowledge and challenging the patriarch to brace himself like a man because God is now about to deliver a final blow in this struggle of a creature with his Maker (38:1–3). The final word is designed to convince Job that he lacks both the strength and wisdom to tell God how to rule the world. Where was Job when God founded the earth (vv. 4–7) and subdued the sea (vv. 8–11)? Can Job control the coming of dawn (vv. 12–15)? Does he know anything about the depths beneath the earth or the expanse above it (vv. 16–18)? Where do light and darkness come from (vv. 19–21)? What does Job know about storehouses of snow and hail, which God uses to accomplish his purposes on earth (vv. 22–24) or the production of rain and ice (vv. 28–30)? Can Job do anything about the movement of the constellations (vv. 31–33)?

Can Job command the clouds to give water or the lightning to strike (38:34–38)? Can he even control the wild animals of the plain, provide food for the lion or raven (vv. 39–41), watch the calving of the hinds (39:1–4) or domesticate the wild ox

Powerful Greek chariot horse depicted in marble (c. 350 B.C.). "Do you give the horse his strength or clothe his neck with a flowing mane?" (Job 39:19).

(vv. 9–12)? Even animals scorn human might, whether the dumb ostrich (vv. 13–18) or the snorting war horse (vv. 19–25). The animate creation's scorning of sophisticated man is a theme repeated throughout this chapter (vv. 7, 18, 22). As a final note of man's humiliation, God pictures the hawk and eagle triumphing over human beings when their young ones suck up the blood of those slain in battle (vv. 26–30). The Lord concludes this first discourse by calling on Job to give up his contention with the Almighty (40:2) and let God be God.

(b) *Job humbled* (40:3–5). Job had uttered some proud words, he had desired to approach God like a prince (31:37), but now he sees how far from wisdom his attitude was. "I am unworthy—how can I reply to you? / I put my hand over my mouth" (40:4). He will be silent and listen to his Creator (40:5).

(c) *God's second discourse* (40:6—41:34). Applying the figure of the ancient belt-wrestler (2 Sam. 2:14–16), God calls on Job to gird his loins like a hero and prepare again to grapple with the words of the Lord. Can Job deck himself with majesty and glory and put to nought his proud adversaries? If so, God will not fail to acknowledge his superiority (40:6–14). But rather let Job consider BEHEMOTH, the great bovine (?) monster whose bones are like tubes of bronze and limbs like bars of iron (vv. 15–18). As one of God's primeval works, his habitat and prowess are described. The surging river cannot overcome him nor can man capture him (vv. 19–24).

As for the sea monster, LEVIATHAN, man cannot snare nor tame him either, nor even lay his hands on him. The very sight of him instills fear. If this is true of God's creatures, who then can stand before God himself who made and owns all that is (41:1–11)? There might be an unannounced transition in the middle of this chapter, where due to a strong resemblance between two subjects there is movement toward the cosmological symbolism of LEVIATHAN, a creature who belches forth flame and smoke from his mouth and nostrils. He makes the sea boil, leaving behind him a great shining wake. He is a dragon who is king over all the sons of pride (vv. 12–34). If the passage is not so taken, then at least vv. 19–21 are pure hyperbole. In Ps. 104:26 Leviathan refers to a real monster of the sea, possibly the whale. But Job 3:8 is most clearly a reference to the well-known mythological serpent Lotan, known from extrabiblical literature, who has seven heads (C. H. Gordon, *Ugaritic Literature* [1949], 38). Similarly, Ps. 74:13–14 makes use of mythological terminology to describe the evil power of the Egyptian army that pursued Moses and the children of Israel. Isaiah applies the name symbolically to the evil dragon in the last day (Isa. 27:1; cf. the dragon symbol of Revelation).

With this background, it is easy to see in Job 41, if not a transition, then a double meaning where the dragon-like crocodile is in view. But God also intends to remind Job of the super-terrestrial forces that Leviathan also symbolizes. God says he made this creature (or creatures) as he had made Job (40:15b). If Job cannot vanquish the creatures of God, how can he win the contest with God himself (41:10b)? In his verbal wrestling with the Almighty, Job is made to realize that God is God, not only in his omnipotence, but in all aspects of his deity. Dare Job attribute injustice to him? Dare he condemn the One who has all knowledge and all power in order to justify himself (40:8)?

(d) *Job repents* (42:1–6). Earlier Job was humbled and silenced (40:3–5), now he has reached the place of REPENTANCE as a direct result of the convicting power of the Word of God. Job quotes God's words (38:2–3; 40:7) and abhors his own false words. No purpose of God can be thwarted, and Job has spoken as if it were within his power to do that very thing. He has talked glibly about things too wonderful for his finite mind to comprehend. He had heard about God, but now after a direct confrontation with him Job despises himself and repents in dust and ashes. His questions have not been answered, but he is assured God cares and does only right.

C. The epilogue (42:7–17)

1. Job vindicated (42:7–9). The Lord calls Job "my servant" whose prayer "I will accept." No dearer words could have reached the patriarch's ears, for this is full proof of his vindication and of Satan's defeat (1:8; 2:3). The friends, on the other hand, are clearly rebuked. "You have not spoken of me what is right" (42:7). God refers here to the gradual growth in understanding seen in Job's discourses—as contrasted to the clod-hopping repetition of the friends—and especially the final repentant words of the sufferer. The friends, in inventing charges against Job, had told lies to uphold their false view of God's relationship to human suffering. Job had spoken right, that is truthfully, even though he had been an impatient protester.

Job who had grown spiritually was asked to prove his newly found strength by praying for his adversaries (cf. Matt. 5:44), and they who needed to repent are warned to do so and to solemnize it with the proper blood offerings. They brought the sacrifices to Job, and the ceremony taught the truth of God's redemptive provision for sin.

2. Job restored (42:10–17). Some critics have questioned whether Job's restoration does not prove Satan's point when he asked, "Does Job fear God for nothing?" (1:9), or the friends' point when they maintained that the righteous only suffer briefly and must ultimately prosper (cf. S. R. Driver and G. B. Gray, *A Critical and Exegetical Commentary on the Book of Job*, ICC [1921], lxii). Job had not demanded nor even asked for restoration, only vindication of his character. Restoration came after the test was over and Job had received his vindication. His repentance was for an attitude acquired during his suffering, not for sins that caused his suffering. It would have been meaningless for Job to continue suffering after God's purpose had been accomplished.

Despite the friends' misinterpretations and misapplications, there is a righteousness-prosperity and sin-suffering relationship under the sovereign purposes of God. The righteous shall ultimately inherit the earth; the claim "I have never seen the righteous forsaken" (Ps. 37:25) is not contrary to the teaching of the book of Job. When Job had demonstrated faithful obedience in praying for those who abused him, the Lord restored Job's property double for all he had lost, and he begot a new family with three very beautiful daughters whose names mean, in the order given, Turtledove, Cinnamon, and Jar of Eyepaint. Their unique treatment in receiving inheritance along with their brothers reflects the high status of women in this patriarchal society (cf. C. H. Gordon in *HUCA* 26 [1955], 76–82). Job's 140 years reflect patriarchal longevity, and if he was 70 when afflicted this would fit the pattern of double restitution of his fortunes. So Job died full of days, having experienced "the purpose of the Lord, how the Lord is compassionate and merciful" (Jas. 5:11 NRSV).

VIII. A special problem: mythology and the Book of Job. How do the mythological allusions in Job fit with an evangelical view of the origin of the book as the Word of God? (See MYTH.) There is a rather limited number of categories or subjects where mythological terminology is employed. The most frequent usage is when the speaker deals with the forces of nature, the storm, fire, the sea, etc. A second category has to do with creatures, cosmic or otherwise; a third with cosmography; and a fourth with heathen cultic practices. Only one passage has the latter, which may be dealt with summarily.

In his initial monologue, Job calls for the enchanters who rouse Leviathan to curse the day of his birth (Job 3:8). This is usually taken as the rousing of the sea monster, who according to primitive notions was supposed to swallow the sun or moon and bring about an eclipse. Such a notion would fit the context, for Job has wished the day of his birth were indeed blotted out or made dark. He also seems to make a reference to the eclipse (v. 5b). This presents no special problem, since Job's whole mood here is erroneous: he is using a common forceful expression as he yields to his anguish of soul, even though he undoubtedly knew that the use of enchanters was forbidden by the Lord. His real sin, for which he can scarcely be excused, was in damning the day of his birth, questioning the sovereign purpose of God.

Job and his friends were theologically confused, especially in the matter of theodicy. In some places, therefore, they could be mouthing contemporaneous notions. However, one would not expect such a use in the words of God, as in the theophany of chs. 38–41. We thus need to ask whether there are any clear-cut mythological assumptions here.

The tendency of the naturalistic critic to see mythology everywhere results in more misinterpretation than is the case with the well-meant but misdirected attempt to rule out all mythological expression. Reading primitive meaning into a piece of monotheistic literature where the idiom can be viewed as a result of simple observation or the use of quaint expressions is poor methodology. On the other hand, one must be cautioned against the rejection of all mythological usage in a strained attempt to remove the writers of Scripture from such contamination.

There are references where the language of mythology appears as borrowed metaphors, use of names, etc. This is like the NT use of the heathen deity name BEELZEBUB for Satan. In a time of religious vitality and verbal fluency, such an idiom was used without necessarily a thought given to polytheistic usage. The Canaanite linguistic substratum was a readily available vehicle through which the prophets and poets could communicate the truth.

Job 26 is said to present a primitive cosmography, as in vv. 9–10: "He covers the face of the full moon, / and spreads over it his cloud. / He has described a circle on the face of the waters, / at the boundary between light and darkness" (NRSV). The statement in v. 10, however, may mean that when one is on the water out of the sight of land, everywhere he turns one sees only horizon (cf. NIV). Some argue that v. 9 pictures God seated on a throne (MT, *kisseʾ* H4058) above a solid firmament, conceived as a dome sitting on the pillars of heaven (cf. v. 11). The word, however, should probably be vocalized *keseʾ* H4057, "the full moon" (as in NIV and NRSV; cf. Ps. 81:3; Prov. 7:20).

No one has ever satisfactorily explained how the statement in Job 26:3 that God "hangs the earth upon nothing" (NRSV) fits into any primitive cosmography. M. Buttenwieser (*The Book of Job* [1922], 281) has commented that it is not surprising to meet with such a view in the book of Job in the light of advanced ideas of ASTRONOMY in Babylonia, Egypt, and Greece; such a notion cannot be summarily dismissed when those who do so make no attempt to interpret this verse. Nor does Job 38:4–6 necessarily contradict this conclusion. God may be questioning Job as to whether the earth was indeed built like a house with foundations.

Buttenwieser also contends that in 26:7a "the north" (RSV; Heb. *ṣāpôn* H7600) is the celestial pole formed by the seven stars of Ursa Minor, from which the movement of the universe was believed to proceed. One cannot ignore that Mount ZAPHON (actually Mons Casius, Jebel el-ʿAqra) is treated in Ugaritic literature as a kind of Canaanite Olympus, where it was thought BAAL built his marvelous palace. This concept explains why Zaphon means "north" in Hebrew. It is to be understood here as the celestial place where God dwells, using the available Canaanite expression just as Isaiah does (Isa. 14:13–14). Furthermore, the verb *nāṭâ* H5742 in Job 26:7a can be used for the stretching out or arching of the heavens (Ps. 104:2), and this concept parallels antithetically the other side of the bicolon. Thus the NIV renders, "He spreads out the northern skies over empty space; / he suspends the earth over nothing."

In Job 26:12–13 the terms used are again mythological, but the meaning is of God's powerful control over the raging force of the sea. N. H. Tur-Sinai (*The Book of Job: A New Commentary*, rev. ed. [1967], 382) translates as follows: "He drove back the sea with his power, / and by his cunning smote Rahab. / By his wind he put the sea into a net; / his hand slew the stretching dragon." Note that the first line parallels the third, and the second line parallels the fourth. Job says such dominion over the sea is only a bit of God's power, only a whisper (v. 14). Who can understand the real thunder of his mighty acts? Similarly, in 9:13 the cohorts of Rahab are mentioned as those who grovel beneath the Almighty, who shakes the earth and removes mountains. See RAHAB (MONSTER). God stretched out the heavens alone and made the constellations and treads on the back of Yam (the SEA). The Ugaritic phrase "treading on the back" is a well-known ANE symbol of overcoming one's foes (Isa. 63:6). The metaphor pictures God's complete control of the sea.

Likewise in Job 7:12, Job complains of imagined harassment by God when he says "Am I the sea [*yām* H3542], or the monster of the deep [*tannîn* H9490], / that you put me under guard?" According to Hebrew monotheism, God created and controls the *tannînim* (Gen. 1:21; Ps. 148:7), while in NW Semitic mythology the uncreated monsters of chaos were slain by hero gods, and only then creation begins as the land and sea are made from pieces of the slain monster. There is none of this when one might expect to see it in Job 38, where the sea is again personified and its birth pictured (vv. 8–11). Shutting the sea within doors is what the Babylonian god MARDUK did after slaying TIAMAT and creating the sea from her. Both here and there it merely refers to the limitations of the seas' boundaries. There appears also the use of "swaddling band" (v. 9), as in the birth of the Ugaritic bovine monsters called Eaters and Devourers (Pope, *Job*, 293), but both figures are borrowed from events of human birth, and the biblical account is tied closely to natural phenomena: "I made the clouds its garment and wrapped it in thick darkness" (NIV).

In Job 38:12b "morning" and "dawn" are personified, just as Dawn and Dusk were a divine pair in Ugaritic literature; but in v. 13 "earth" is personified, with coming of day likened to the snatching off of her skirts and shaking the wicked out of it. Apart from personification no other mythological distinctive is employed in these verses.

Just as Zaphon was a word originally meaning the abode of the gods, but in Hebrew it was used for the habitation of the only true God, so the terms Yam and Rahab are derived from the Canaanite Sea God and his monstrous cohort and is used for the sea as part of God's creation. It cannot be demonstrated that in a strong monotheistic context like the book of Job these personifications were more than rich linguistic expressions of the powers of nature. Even when viewed as Canaanite gods, part of their function was to describe and explain natural phenomena. Even if Job and his friends did know the mythology, this in itself would not prove they believed the myth anymore than my reference to Greek deities proves I believe them. This view is strengthened by Job 31:26–27, where the patriarch by oath with sanctions denies ever being tempted to participate in heathen worship of sun or moon.

Turning to Job 5:7, one reads: "Yet man is born to trouble / as surely as sparks fly upward." Pope (*Job*, 40) renders: "Man, indeed, is born for trouble / And Resheph's sons wing high." Here is another clear case where the name of a NW Semitic deity is used to refer to forces in nature with which the particular deity was identified in mythology. In the Ugaritic pantheon, RESHEPH is equated with NERGAL, the Mesopotamian god of pestilence and the netherworld. In the OT the word *rešep* H8404 is used of pestilence (Deut. 32:25; Hab. 3:5); the plural can be used of lightning (Ps. 78:48). In Ps. 76:3, however, it refers to "flashing arrows," where the context also speaks of shields and swords. In Ugaritic, the god Resheph is called "Lord of the arrow." Just as in Job 18:13 death is said to have a firstborn who devours wicked men's bodies, so here in 5:7 the "sons of Resheph" may be various forms of trouble or pestilence or flames which soar aloft.

What of BEHEMOTH and LEVIATHAN in Job 40 and 41? There is something to be said for simply taking them as a great bovine creature (or hippopotamus) and crocodile respectively. Both are used in other OT contexts without mythological or symbolic implication (Pss. 8:8; 50:10; 74:14; 104:26; Joel 1:20; 2:22; Hab. 2:17). The word *behemôt* H990 seems to be an intensive plural of *běhēmâ* H989, "beast, cattle," hence the beast par excellence. Behemoth is called in Job 40:19a "first among the ways of God." Pope (*Job*, 317) translates this "a primordial production of God," but M. Dahood (quoted by Pope on p. 324) says "he is the finest manifestation of God's power." In Ugaritic the goddess Anat conquered the seven-headed Leviathan along with a bovine creature called "the monstrous, ferocious bullock" (ibid., 321).

OT passages do speak of great evil powers, whether cosmic or political, in terms of monstrous creatures. In the day the Lord punishes the inhabitants of the earth for their iniquity he also will slay Leviathan, the swift, crooked serpent (Isa. 27:1; cf. 51:9–10). Rahab is Egypt, and in Ps. 74:12–13 the many-headed Leviathan is again Egypt. But in Job 40 and 41 the description of Leviathan becomes highly symbolic. One must assume a considerable amount of hyperbole to make of this description simply a crocodile. It is likely that after a reference to the crocodile an unannounced transition occurs because God intends to remind Job of those cosmic forces which Leviathan symbolizes, and against which no human strength can prevail.

I suggest the following translation of 41:9–12: "Behold his expectation is false, / (Though) the angels are hurled down at his appearance / (And) he is fierce when one arouses him. / (Yet) who can stand before me (God)? / Who can confront me and survive? / For everything under the heavens is mine. / Will not I silence his boastings / his proud (high) talk and his fair array of words?" And vv. 18–21: "His sneezings flash forth light, / his eyes are like the glow (eyelids) of dawn / Out of his mouth go torches / And sparks of fire leap forth. / His nostrils smoke, / Out of a seething pot and burning brushwood, / His breath kindles coals / And a flame pours out of his mouth." And vv. 33–34: "Upon earth there is not his like, / A creature without fear. / He beholds everything that is high; / he is king over all the sons of pride." The studied conclusion is that this is not a mere crocodile, but is to be understood in the light of Isa. 27:1 et al. (cf. the dragon symbol of Rev. 12).

The prologue of Job pictures the heavenly council before God, and in Job 5:1 Eliphaz says to Job, "Call if you will, but who will answer you? / To which of the holy ones will you turn?" Eliphaz is taunting Job that it is hopeless for him to appeal to the "holy ones." Critics take them to be the lesser divine beings who according to Mesopotamian concept were available as personal intercessors in the divine assembly. It should be noted that whether here or in the prologue or in Ps. 89:5, "the assembly of the holy ones" is most assuredly made up of created beings. Even in Mesopotamian concepts, the lesser divine beings were created. Whether in the progress of revelation Eliphaz had made the clear-cut monotheistic distinction we cannot tell, but one can be certain that neither the author of the book of Job nor the Psalms attribute to these "holy ones" any of the pagan concepts of deity.

In Job 15:8 Eliphaz, condemning Job for self-exaltation, questions his ability to sit in and eavesdrop on the divine council. And in 33:23–24 Elihu speaks of mediation by an angel. The Mesopotamian belief in a personal god who looked after the interest of his mortal client in the divine assembly may be a related concept, but it could represent a retrogression rather than a stage in the development of Hebrew religion. These "holy ones" among whom a man might find a defender should be tied to Job's appeal for an arbiter to argue his case (9:33) or a witness to testify of his integrity (16:19–21) or a vindicator or redeemer to stand in his behalf (19:25–27). In a most prophetic way, Job is touching on that mystery of godliness which says there must be one who can stand between God and man who must share in the nature of each. As Job says in 9:33, someone "to lay his hand upon us both." This concept finds further expression in the OT teaching regarding the suffering vicarious expiator.

Job 38:31a provides an example of how the KJV was influenced by the earlier Jewish interpretation taken over by Christian exegetes. The Jewish scholar Nachmanides and others understood the verse in an astrological sense, the "sweet influences" of Pleiades being the astrological forces that produce pleasure, flowers, and fruits in the spring. It is likely that the key word should be rendered "fetters," in parallel with the "bands" of Orion following (cf. 1 Sam. 15:32; see ASTROLOGY and ASTRONOMY).

Nor should Job 38:33 ("Do you know the laws of the heavens? / Can you set up God's dominion over the earth?) be taken astrologically. Some take these words to be pre-Newtonian allusions to the forces of gravity. The word for "laws" is parallel with *miṣṭār* H5428, usually rendered "rule, dominion," but related to a Semitic verb meaning "to write." The stars in Akkadian are called *šiṭir samê*, "heavenly writing." Tur-Sinai (in *Archiv orientální* 17 [1949]: 11) has come closest to understanding the verse by connecting it with Ps. 19, where the heavens write a message of God's glory.

An example of a forced attempt to read mythology into the text is found in this rendering of Job 38:36: "Who put wisdom in Thoth / Who gave Sekwi understanding?" (Pope, *Job*, 290, 302, following Dhorme). The RSV, with some philological support, takes the word *ṭuḥôt* H3219 as "clouds" and *śekwî* H8498 as "mist." The verses before and after are dealing with clouds, rain, and lightning, so the renderings by Thoth and Sekwi are completely out of context, since they are gods of wisdom and writing. More recent translations understand the terms as references to the heart and the mind.

On this general subject, W. F. Albright has said some cogent things in his *History, Archaeology and Christian Humanism* (1964). Remarking how the OT is a masterpiece of empirical logic not expressed in formal categories, Albright claims the OT has demythologized the poems on which some Hebrew literature is based. I would prefer to say that the OT writers demythologized not the literature but only the language. "Old words are kept but with new meanings, divested of all clear mythological connotations" (ibid., 94). Albright notes how the Puritan John Milton drew heavily on Greek mythology to enrich his poetic imagery even in his picture of creation.

For example, the use of plural terms for God, namely Elohim (see ELOAH) and Adonai, may have come from polytheistic usage, but in Hebrew came to mean the totality of all the manifestations and attributes of deity, which polytheism broke down into single elements. In some documents a high god is referred to with the plural ending, the so-called plural of majesty. Nothing sounds more polytheistic to some ears than the words used by the Chronicler, "our God is greater than all other gods" (2 Chr. 2:5). Albright observes that "much of the onslaught on early Israelite monotheism comes from scholars who represent certain theological points of view with reference to monotheism; i.e., who deny that orthodox trinitarian Christianity ... or orthodox Judaism or orthodox Islam are monotheistic. I do not need to stress the fact that neither of the last two religions can be called monotheistic by a theologian who insists that this term applies only to Unitarian Christianity or liberal Judaism. But no dictionary definition of monotheism was ever intended to exclude orthodox Christianity" (ibid., 155).

In conclusion, the distinguishing mark of a mythology is not reference to gods or the use of ANTHROPOMORPHISM and various descriptive metaphors that describe deity in concrete terminology, but rather the narration of the actions of numerous gods who have the same limitations and sins common to human beings, including especially sexual relations. Neither the book of Job nor any of the OT has the slightest hint of belief in any such mythology. (See further E. Smick in *WTJ* 40 [1977–78]: 213–28.)

(Important commentaries include F. Delitzsch, *The Book of Job* [1876]; A. B. Davidson, *The Book of Job* [1886]; S. R. Driver and G. B. Gray, *A Critical and Exegetical Commentary on the Book of Job*, ICC, [1921]; M. Buttenwieser, *The Book of Job* [1922]; E. Dhorme, *A Commentary on the Book of Job* [1926, Eng. trans. 1967]; V. E. Reichert, *Job: With Hebrew Text and English Translation* [1946]; E. J. Kissane, *The Book of Job* [1946]; W. B. Stevenson, *The Poem of Job* [1947]; id., *Critical Notes on the Hebrew Text of the Poem of Job* [1951]; N. H. Tur-Sinai, *The Book of Job: A New Commentary* [1957]; M. H. Pope, *Job*, AB 15, 3rd ed. [1973]; R. Gordis, *The Book of Job: Commentary, New Translation, and Special Studies* [1978]; N. C. Habel, *The Book of Job: A Commentary* [1985]; J. E. Hartley, *The Book of Job*, NICOT [1988]; D. J. A. Clines, *Job 1–20*, WBC 17 [1989]; C. D. Rabinowitz, *Commentary to the Book of Iyov* [2001]; S. E. Balentine, *Job* [2006]; D. J. A. Clines, *Job 21–37*, WBC 18A [2006].

(See also A. R. King, *The Problem of Evil: Christian Concepts and the Book of Job* [1952]; T. H. Robinson, *Job and his Friends* [1954]; A. R. Ceresko, *Job in the Light of Northwest Semitic* [1980]; W. E. Aufrecht, ed., *Studies in the Book of Job* [1985]; W. L. Michel, *Job in the Light of Northwest Semitic*, vol. 1 [1987]; W. A. M. Beuken, ed., *The Book of Job* [1994]; P. van der Lugt, *Rhetorical Criticism and the Poetry of the Book of Job* [1995]; A. Lo, *Job 28 as Rhetoric: An Analysis of Job 28 in the Context of Job 22–31* [2003]; C. A. Newsom, *The Book of Job: A Contest of Moral Imaginations* [2003]; F. R. Magdalene, *On the Scales of Righteousness: Neo-Babylonian Trial Law and the Book of Job* [2007].)   E. SMICK

Job, Targum of. In addition to the ARAMAIC version of JOB found in the standard rabbinical TARGUM, an earlier translation was found among the DEAD SEA SCROLLS (11QtgJob). This fragmentary document, which preserves approximately one fifth of the book (beginning with the middle of ch. 17), is of major significance for both Targumic and Aramaic studies. The translation from the Hebrew is quite literal, in contrast with the Palestinian Targumic tradition generally. The language provides an important link between the so-called Official Aramaic of Daniel and Ezra and the later Jewish Palestinian form. Two other small fragments of an Aramaic version of Job were found in a different cave (4QtgJob), but it is not clear whether these contain the same or a different translation. (See M. Sokoloff, *The Targum to Job from Qumran Cave XI* [1974]; D. M. Stec, *The Text of the Targum of Job: An Introduction and Critical Edition* [1994]; D. Shepherd, *Targum and Translation: A Reconsideration of the Qumran Aramaic Version of Job* [2004].)

Job, Testament of. A Jewish pseudepigraphic work, probably written in Greek in Egypt, maybe as early as the 1st cent. B.C. Following the pattern of the TESTAMENTS OF THE TWELVE PATRIARCHS and similar works, it purports to give Job's own account of his sickness and events related to it. The primary purpose of the work is clearly to commend the virtue of patience or endurance, but various other motifs (such as angels, women, and eschatological concerns) add interest to it. The *Testament of Job* has been preserved primarily in four medieval MSS, which appear to have undergone some Christian editing. (English trans., with introduction and notes, in *OTP*, 1:829–68. See also R. A. Kraft et al., *The Testament of Job according to the SV Text* [1974].)

Jobab joh′bab (יוֹבָב H3412 [H3411 for #1 below], derivation uncertain). **(1)** Son of JOKTAN and grandson of EBER, listed in the Table of NATIONS (Gen. 10:29; 1 Chr. 1:23). It may be the name of an ancient South Arabian tribe, and some scholars have noted the similarity between Jobab and Yuhaybab, a tribe in central Yemen (see *ABD*, 3:871).

(2) Son of Zerah and second king of EDOM; he came from BOZRAH (Gen. 36:33–34; 1 Chr. 1:44–45).

(3) King of MADON who joined the unsuccessful coalition formed by JABIN king of HAZOR against the Israelites (Josh. 11:1); the city of Madon is listed among those conquered by JOSHUA (12:19).

(4) Son of SHAHARAIM and descendant of BENJAMIN; a family head (1 Chr. 8:9). Jobab was one of seven children that were born to Shaharaim in MOAB by his wife HODESH after he had divorced Hushim and Baara (v. 8).

(5) Son of ELPAAL, grandson of Shaharaim (see above, #4), and descendant of Benjamin (1 Chr. 8:18); he is listed among the heads of families who lived in Jerusalem (cf. v. 28).

Jochebed jok′uh-bed (יוֹכֶבֶד H3425, "Yahweh is weighty [*or* honorable, glorious]"). Descendant of LEVI, wife (and aunt) of AMRAM, and mother of AARON, MOSES, and MIRIAM (Exod. 6:20; Num. 26:59). If the expression "daughter of Levi" (Num. 26:59) is understood literally, then she was the sister of KOHATH (Amram's father), and only a distant ancestor of Aaron, Moses, and Miriam. The expression "father's sister" (Exod. 6:20) renders Hebrew *dôdâ* H1860, which in its other two occurrences means "wife of father's brother" (cf. Lev. 18:14; 20:20). In either case, the marriage between Amram and Jochebed involved a union prohibited by the laws of Lev. 18; probably for that reason, the SEPTUAGINT renders Exod. 6:20 with "the daughter of his father's brother," which makes Jochebed the cousin of Amram.

Jod johd. See YOD.

Joda joh′duh (Ἰωδά G2726). **(1)** Son of Iliadun and head of a family of Levites who helped repair the wall of Jerusalem after the EXILE (1 Esd. 5:58; apparently called HODAVIAH in Ezra 2:40; 3:9 [MT, "Judah"]; Neh. 7:43 [MT, "Hodevah"], cf. also "Sudias" in 1 Esd. 5:26).

(2) Son of Joanan, included in Luke's GENEALOGY of JESUS CHRIST (Lk. 3:26). He is apparently not mentioned in the OT, although some have identified him with a postexilic descendant of SOLOMON named Hodaviah (1 Chr. 3:24).

Jodan joh′duhn (Ἰωδανος). A descendant of JESHUA son of Jozadak, listed among the priests in Ezra's time who agreed to put away their foreign wives (1 Esd. 9:19 [KJV, "Joadanus"]; called "Gedaliah" in Ezra 10:18).

Joed joh′ed (יוֹעֵד H3444, "Yahweh is witness"). Son of Pedaiah, descendant of BENJAMIN, and grandfather of Sallu; the latter is listed among those who resettled in Jerusalem under NEHEMIAH (Neh. 11:7; the name is not found in the parallel list, 1 Chr. 9:7).

Joel joh′uhl (יוֹאֵל H3408, "Yahweh is God"; Ἰωήλ G2727). A common name widely distributed among the Hebrew tribes; its meaning attests to the fact that faith in Yahweh as the only God was alive throughout the nation.

(1) Joel the prophet. See JOEL, BOOK OF.

(2) Firstborn son of SAMUEL and father of the musician HEMAN (1 Sam. 8:2; 1 Chr. 6:28 [NIV and other versions, following some Gk. MSS and Syr.; see VASHNI], 33; 15:17). Joel and his brother ABIJAH served as judges in BEERSHEBA, but they were found guilty of misconduct in office (1 Sam. 8:3–5).

(3) Son of Azariah, descendant of LEVI through KOHATH, and ancestor of Samuel and the musician Heman (1 Chr. 6:36).

(4) A clan leader in the tribe of SIMEON (1 Chr. 4:35). He is listed among those whose families increased greatly during the days of King HEZEKIAH and who dispossessed the Hamites and Meunites near GEDOR (vv. 38–41).

(5) A clan chief of the tribe of REUBEN whose descendant Beerah was taken captive by TIGLATH-PILESER (1 Chr. 5:4). He may be the same Joel listed later as father of Shema and ancestor of Jeiel (vv. 7–8). His genealogical connection as well as the period in which he lived are unclear.

(6) A leader of the Gadites (see GAD, TRIBE OF) in BASHAN, listed as first in importance (1 Chr. 5:12).

(7) Son of Izrahiah and descendant of ISSACHAR; a military chief (1 Chr. 7:3).

(8) One of David's mighty warriors, identified as the brother of a certain Nathan (1 Chr. 11:38). This passage appears to have suffered textual corruption, for the parallel list has IGAL son of Nathan (2 Sam. 23:36).

(9) Head of a Levitical family descended from GERSHON, listed among those who helped to bring the ARK OF THE COVENANT to Jerusalem in the reign of David (1 Chr. 15:7, 11). He may be the same as #10 below.

(10) Son of Jehieli (see JEHIEL) and descendant of Gershon; he and his brother Zetham were temple treasurers (1 Chr. 26:22). The Hebrew text is difficult, and elsewhere Jehiel, Zetham, and Joel are identified as sons (descendants?) of Ladan (23:8). This Joel may be the same as #9 above.

(11) Son of Pedaiah and a chief officer over the half-tribe of MANASSEH during David's reign (1 Chr. 27:20).

(12) Son of Azariah and descendant of LEVI through KOHATH; listed among the Levites who purified the temple in the reform under HEZEKIAH (2 Chr. 29:12).

(13) One of the descendants of Bani who agreed to put away their foreign wives (1 Esd. 9:34; this name does not occur in the parallel passage, Ezra 10:38).

(14) One of the descendants of Nebo who agreed to put away their foreign wives (Ezra 10:43; 1 Esd. 9:35).

(15) Son of Zicri and chief officer over the postexilic community in Jerusalem (Neh. 11:9). He held an office perhaps similar to that of mayor, and was assisted by Judah son of Hassenuah (the latter was either second in command [NRSV] or in charge of the "Second District" [NIV]). It is not clear whether these two men were Benjamites (v. 7) or Judahites (v. 4).   R. E. HAYDEN

Joel, Book of joh'uhl (יוֹאֵל H3408, "Yahweh is God"; Ἰωήλ G2727). Second book of the Minor Prophets (in the LXX it takes fourth place). In the MT the book consists of four chapters, but the English versions (following the LXX and Vulg.) combine Joel 2–3 MT into one chapter; thus ch. 4 MT corresponds to ch. 3 in the English Bible.

- I. Historical background
- II. Unity and special problems
- III. Authorship and compilation
- IV. Date
- V. Place of origin and destination
- VI. Occasion and purpose
- VII. Textual considerations
- VIII. Contents
- IX. Theology

I. Historical background. There can be no doubt as to the factual nature of the successive insect plagues that formed one of the principal themes of Joel, although the absence of the customary dating formula in the superscription, as well as the timeless nature of the contents of the book, makes the question of the date of composition, and therefore the whole matter of the historical background, one of great difficulty. Critical estimates of the date of Joel have ranged all the way from the 9th cent. B.C. to the Maccabean period (2nd cent. B.C.), and it must be admitted from the start that there are strong arguments in favor of both a preexilic and a postexilic date for the work. Certain verses of the prophecy can be taken as implying that the enemies of the nation were preexilic peoples such as EGYPT, EDOM (Joel 3:19), the PHILISTINES, and PHOENICIA (3:4), whereas other passages seem to indicate that the divided kingdom had ceased to exist, with the names of Judah and Israel being used synonymously (2:27; 3:2, 16, 20).

From a theological point of view, as the prophet used the familiar 8th-cent. eschatological term DAY OF THE LORD, he did so in a manner that differed significantly from its usage in the book of AMOS, and this fact might suggest an era other than that of the 8th or 7th centuries. Any description of the historical background of Joel is therefore dependent to a larger extent than in most other OT prophecies upon the date of composition that the individual scholar is prepared to assign to the work. Locust plagues, like many other natural phenomena, have been frequent occurrences in the Near E for millennia, and almost any visitation of that kind could provide at any time a proper and immediate background for the composition.

II. Unity and special problems. The main critical issue regarding the prophecy of Joel concerns its integrity as a literary composition. In particular, questions have been raised why a work from a single hand should have historical and APOCALYPTIC sections placed side by side. The chief objection to this procedure has been that, if the narrative material is to be understood literally, which seems most reasonable under the circumstances, it is not easy to see why an author should then intermingle such a different theme as an apocalyptic section of prophecy and still furnish what has all appearances of being a unified work.

Arguments for the unity of authorship of Joel have in some cases regarded the locusts as symbolic and in others as real, without apparently impairing the validity of the conclusions. Some conservative scholars have seen in the prophetic description of the plagues an accurate picture of a historical event, with the behavior of the insects indicating nothing more than an idealized description of the ruin and havoc wrought by a marauding enemy. Following the pattern of apocalyptic thought in EZEKIEL, DANIEL, or REVELATION, this disaster would suggest to the prophet something of the nature of the coming judgment. If these concepts were actually associated in this manner in the mind of the prophet, it would be easy to account for the eschatological references in the historical section of the prophecy (see ESCHATOLOGY).

Scholars who have postulated duality of authorship have generally argued that the apocalyptic passages, as well as the eschatological allusions in Joel 2:1–11, were added to the original oracle concerning the devastating plagues by a later, unknown editor. If this hypothesis is adduced for chs. 3–4 of Joel in the belief that this material was a later apocalypse supplementing the story of a locust plague, it also would seem reasonable to regard as interpolations by a later hand all eschatological applications of this event to the day of the Lord that are found in the first two chapters of the prophecy. Unfortunately for such a view, these sections give no indication whatever of being later insertions, since they fit with obvious smoothness into the work as a whole from the standpoint of both style and subject matter, thus pointing further to the unity of the prophecy. The view that the narrative portion of Joel was the work of a prophet and the eschatological section that of an apocalyptist, who used the prophetic oracle to substantiate his teachings about the coming day of the Lord, seems unnecessarily complicated and forced in view of the fact that a great many prophetic passages intermingled the contemporary with the eschatological without undue difficulty.

III. Authorship and compilation. Apart from the name Joel ben Pethuel, found in the title of the prophecy, nothing is known of the life or circumstances of the attributive author. In the SEPTUAGINT, his cognomen is rendered *Bathouēl*, "Bethuel," the name of ABRAHAM's nephew, who was also REBEKAH's father (Gen. 22:22–23 et al.; it is also close in form to the Canaanite personal name *Battiilu*, found in the TELL EL-AMARNA tablets). It may, however, simply constitute a variant that arose following a transcriptional error in the Hebrew. The name JOEL was in common usage in Israel over a number of centuries, and over a dozen persons were designated in this fashion in the canonical writings. As observed above, nothing is known about the background of the author, although he himself made it abundantly clear that he was not to be regarded as a member of the priesthood, a fact evident from the objective manner in which he referred to it (Joel 1:13; 2:17). In consequence of this attitude, certain European scholars (notably A. S. Kapelrud, *Joel Studies* [1948]) have thought of him as being a "temple prophet," although an assertion of this kind presents numerous difficulties.

As observed previously, the prophecy can be divided into two distinct units comprising (a) Joel 1:1—2:27, a section that contained a description of a calamitous plague of locusts and the urging of public repentance to bring about deliverance from the infestation and relief from the ensuing famine; and (b) Joel 2:28—3:21 (MT 3:1—4:21), which spoke of the future day of the Lord, the outpouring of the divine Spirit upon the nations, the judgment of the heathen, and the coming of a blessed age.

Questions of authorship and compilation are closely related to those of the interpretation and integrity of the work. The first section (Joel 1:1—2:27) seems to deal with a historical event of recent incidence, namely, a locust plague. These insects were described as a "northern army" (2:20), and although locust infestations in Palestine do not usually come from the N, invasions of these insects from that direction are by no means unknown. The devastation caused by these marauders was so severe that the prophet took the incident to be an indication of divine displeasure, and accordingly called the people to repentance. Evidently, the view of the prophet was also held by the populace generally, for they responded quickly to the call, and as a result Joel was able to foretell the destruction of the locusts and the renewal of agricultural prosperity for the land.

From the vividness and accuracy of the description, there is every reason to suppose that the locust plague was an actual historical fact. For purposes of interpretation, it is important to notice that the locust plague is described in terms of a human army. The insects are said to be *like* soldiers (Joel 2:7) and *like* horses and chariots (2:4–5). Once the figures of speech are understood for what they are, the description of a locust invasion and consequent devastation is of an extremely vivid nature, and is entirely in keeping with the normal usage of OT figurative language.

Whereas the first section was recognized by many scholars as having a predominantly historical basis, the second portion (Joel 2:28—3:21 [MT 3:1—4:21) seemed to be mainly eschatological in character, dealing with a future period in which a supernatural visitation of the divine Spirit would confer gifts of prophecy upon Israel (2:28). Equally important was the description in apocalyptic terms of the final battle between the forces of Yahweh and those of the pagan armies, a conflict that would conclude with the annihilation of the latter and the exaltation of Israel.

It is misleading to regard the prophecy as rigidly divisible into predominantly historical and apocalyptic sections of a rather independent nature. For one thing, the eschatological concept of the day of the Lord occurs in both suggested divisions (cf. Joel 1:15; 2:1–2; 2:31; 3:14), indicating a certain continuity of thought. For another, there are aspects of the narratives dealing with the marauding locusts which seem to have elements in common with the supernatural character of the incidents contained in the second portion of the prophecy (e.g., Joel 1:15; 2:10).

Some scholars have held that whenever the calamity described by the phrase "the day of the Lord" occurs, the meaning is uniformly of an eschatological nature, having reference either to the future disturbances that would preface the coming of the messianic day or to the actual day itself. On this interpretation, the locust plague described by Joel would depict the day of the Lord quite accurately. Other scholars have pointed out that, whereas the phrase is generally eschatological in usage, there is no ground for supposing that it must always be so. In this instance, therefore, it might possibly be that Joel was referring to the locust visitation as being a particular example of divine judgment and destruction. If such a devastating insect invasion that had reduced the land to a desert within a very short period of time was "a day of the Lord," it would be easy for the prophet to indicate how much more dreadful would be the situation when God punished a sinful world in the final day of the Lord.

Again, the interpretation of the locusts presents important considerations in the matter of compilation and integrity. If the locusts are to be regarded as symbolic of those heathen forces whose judgment is narrated in Joel 3:1–17, they could either represent specific onslaughts by pagan nations at particular times in Israelite history, or they could

Looking E across the Arabah into Edom. Joel prophesied that Edom would become "a desert waste because of the violence done to the people of Judah" (Joel 3:19).

be wholly apocalyptic in character, as with the "children of darkness" in the Qumran community writings (see DEAD SEA SCROLLS), or the locusts in Rev. 9:1–11. A major objection to the locusts in Joel being interpreted in terms of armed warriors is that they simply cannot be said to be like themselves (cf. Joel 2:4–7), and it seems clear that the locust plague was an actual historical incident and not symbolic of something else.

Consequently it would not be difficult for one prophet to use such a happening as the basis for an utterance dealing with the nature of future judgment and produce a unified composition in which the association of the locust plague with a larger disaster would account for the juxtaposition of historical and eschatological material in one prophetic work. The presence of apocalyptic elements in the first two chapters is surely a sufficient warrant for the apocalyptic expositions of the remaining portion of the prophecy, which is seen to constitute an expanded form of the futuristic theme implied in the first section. It is a commonplace observation that a great many of the Hebrew prophets interwove the contemporary with the eschatological in their utterances, and in view of this fact the arguments for divisive authorship of the book lose much of their force. That the prophecy was deliberately composed as one entity may be indicated by the elaborate correspondences between the section dealing with the locust visitation and that concerning the pagan enemies of the Israelites, which serve to knit the book together as a symmetrical unit.

Other features that support the integrity of the composition are to be found in the literary style of the author, and not least in the way he repeated important phrases and used expressions borrowed from other prophets. A final testimony to the unity of authorship is found in the uniform historical background that is clearly apparent throughout the work. From the foregoing arguments, therefore, it is difficult to find a valid reason for assuming that the whole prophecy was not written at one time by the attributive author Joel. As noted earlier, however, some scholars have suggested that the original prophecy comprised only Joel 1:1–2:27, with the remainder coming from the hand of a later apocalyptist. This attempt to disprove the integrity of the work and its unity of authorship has to face the serious problem of the references to the day of the Lord in the "original prophecy." Such passages (Joel 1:15; 2:1–2, 10–11), however, give no indication of being late apocalyptic insertions, for if they are removed from the text arbitrarily, the sense and smoothness of the narrative suffer seriously, thus indicating that the material as a whole was a unity from the beginning.

Perhaps more worthy of serious consideration is the theory that Joel 1:1–2:27 contains portions of liturgical poems that were used in conjunction with a supposed New Year festival ritual in Israel, to which certain apocalyptic fragments were added later. Unfortunately for this view, it yet remains to be shown satisfactorily that the Israelites ever engaged in a New Year fertility worship of the kind commonly found in ANE cultic rituals. If there are, in fact, isolated elements of "prophetic liturgies" in the first chapter of the book, it is more probable that they are citations of earlier prophetic teaching and not material formulated with a view to use in cultic worship. Furthermore, on the view outlined above, the presence of apocalyptic additions would disrupt the cultic nature of the original, and in effect would transform it from a popular vehicle of joyful celebration into one of private prophetic foreboding and doom, a procedure for which there is not the slightest evidence. Furthermore, if the apocalyptic elements were really as fragmentary as the theory supposes, it would be difficult to demonstrate their unity of theme, to say nothing of the way in which the latter is elaborated upon in the remainder of the prophecy. No studies in the history of the form of Joel have yet shown conclusively that the two principal sections come from different dates, and there is no firm evidence to demonstrate that the book was anything other than a unity and the product of its attributive author.

IV. Date. Although a great many scholars have viewed Joel as the work of one author, there has been much argument with regard to the date of composition of the prophecy, the divergent views expressed ranging over half a millennium. Since any specific historical references that would enable a firm assessment of the date of composition to be made are notably lacking, the period of authorship has to be considered on the basis of internal evidence alone. Particularly important in this connection are the implied political, social, and religious conditions existing in the nation, parallels in the matter of the distinctive ideas of the prophet to those that can be dated with reasonable assurance, the literary relationships between the book and other similar compositions, and questions of diction and style.

Political and social allusions present certain difficulties, for whereas there are clear references to peoples and places, such as Tyre, Sidon, Philistia, and the Greeks, they are too vague to furnish a reliable date for the composition of the prophecy. Although the monarchy had disappeared and many of the people were scattered in exile (Joel 3:2–3), the temple was still standing and was in full operation (1:13–14; 2:15–17), and the walls of Jerusalem were intact (2:9)—a situation that might indicate a date between 597 and 587 B.C. for the prophecy. Although it would appear that Israel and Judah had ceased to exist as separate entities, with the names being used synonymously (2:27; 3:2), the enemies of Judah that were mentioned were not those of the exilic age, such as the Babylonians, but rather the Philistines, Egyptians, and Phoenicians, most of whom came into conflict with Judah in some manner in preexilic days.

TYRE was denounced by Amos (Amos 1:9–10) in the 8th cent. B.C., apparently for slave trading, and it was also castigated by Ezekiel (Ezek. 27:13) for much the same reason, a situation which, however, is inconclusive for dating. The reference to the "captivity" that God would "bring again" had a futuristic situation in view, and again can hardly be used decisively for dating. The threat of desolation in Egypt and Edom (Joel 3:19) might possibly suggest an exilic date, but the mention of allusion to the Greeks (3:16) need not necessarily demand a postexilic date, since Ionians are referred to in Assyrian literary records as early as the 8th cent. B.C.

The idea that God would gather all nations to Jerusalem to battle and destruction occurs also in other prophets (Isa. 66:16; Ezek. 38:1—39:29; Zech. 12:1; 14:1), and in two of them is found the motif of a fountain proceeding from the temple and nourishing the locality (Ezek. 47:1; Zech. 14:8). A further question arises whether these concepts originated in the time of, say, Ezekiel or Zechariah, or whether they went much further back to a common prophetical eschatological motif, arising possibly in the 8th cent. If Joel was not actually living when Amos spoke about the day of the Lord (Amos 5:16), he was certainly familiar with such teaching, which might suggest that he was propagating 8th-cent. eschatology.

The parallels in phraseology with other prophetic writings are numerous, and indicate either that Joel was early and influenced subsequent writers greatly by his prophecy, or that, being later, he cited earlier prophets frequently or at least quoted from a common prophetic theology reaching back to the preexilic period. Although the majority of scholars have concluded that Joel is postexilic and that he quoted from earlier sources, it is still true that no single element of his thought is incompatible with a preexilic date for the prophecy. The difficulties of dating are not simplified by the literary style of the author, which is marked by striking rhythms, acutely descriptive figures of speech, the use of repetition to heighten expressions of contrast or succession, and the drawing of parallels between similar situations. Some writers have seen evidences of postexilic terminology in the work, including some Aramaic forms, but others have contested these assertions, making the whole matter inconclusive. In view of the prolonged history of the ARAMAIC LANGUAGE and its usage in preexilic Israel, the mere presence of Aramaisms in any canonical writing cannot be used as incontrovertible evidence for a late date of composition. The dating of Joel is a matter of great difficulty, and the prophecy has been assigned in consequence to dates that vary between the 9th cent. B.C. and the Maccabean period. From internal evidence it would appear that an earlier rather than a later date of composition is preferable. The most reasonable estimate appears to place the book during the childhood of King JOASH, about 830 B.C., at a time when JEHOIADA the high priest was regent in Judah.

V. Place of origin and destination. Just as nothing is known about the author, so there is no certain information about the place where the prophecy arose. The references to the temple and the official priesthood would suggest some area of Judah, perhaps even Jerusalem, which may also have been the recipient of the utterances, since their essential message involved the active participation of the priesthood. It is unlikely that the prophetic oracles originated in the northern kingdom, particularly if a comparatively late date of authorship is upheld.

VI. Occasion and purpose. The immediate occasion of the oracles was the incidence of a severe locust plague, and this natural calamity was used by Joel as the means of illustrating the nature and scope of an even more significant occurrence of an eschatological nature, the day of the Lord. It was the purpose of the author to call his people to repentance in order that divine punishment might be averted and the Spirit of God poured out upon Israel in blessing.

VII. Textual considerations. The Hebrew text has been transmitted very well, aside from a few minor corruptions. Some small additions occur in the SEPTUAGINT, but they do not seem to represent a better Hebrew text form. Similarly, the Syriac Peshitta and Vulgate diverge only slightly from the MT and from each other (see VERSIONS OF THE BIBLE, ANCIENT, II.B and III.C).

VIII. Contents
  A. The locust plague and its removal (Joel 1:1—2:27)
    1. The plague (1:1–20)
    2. A call to repentance (2:1–17)
    3. Divine pity and promised relief (2:18–27)
  B. The future day of the Lord (2:28—3:21)
    1. Outpouring of the divine Spirit (2:28–32)
    2. Judgment of the nations (3:1–17)
    3. Blessings upon Israel (3:18–21)

IX. Theology. The book reflects that attitude of religious particularism that deemed the Israelites to be the sole recipients of divine favor, a view that had both prophetic and priestly advocates. Joel, however, pointed out the responsibility that such an elevated position carried, and demanded to see in Israel those moral and spiritual qualities that merited divine blessing. He particularly stressed that only the remnant that was faithful to God would be saved, not the entire house of Israel (Joel 2:32). Pagan nations would be punished in the day of the Lord, not because of their non-Israelite character, but because of their inhuman acts toward their fellowmen.

In the final conflict, when divine judgment would be manifested, the heathen would be cut down like vegetation by a cataclysm, whereas the elect of God would be kept safe until the restoration of Jerusalem. Joel had a remarkable vision of the relationship of divine purpose to human history, even though a single messianic figure is lacking in his book. His abiding contribution to Christian thought is in his teaching about the outpouring of the divine Spirit on "all flesh" (Joel 2:28 NRSV), a prophecy quoted by Peter in his PENTECOST sermon (Acts 2:14–21). From that time on the personal possession of the HOLY SPIRIT was to be normative in Christian spiritual experience. Although in OT days the Holy Spirit came upon God's people and enabled them to serve God acceptably (Jdg. 6:34; 1 Sam. 16:13), the new age of grace begun at Pentecost was to be one of the Spirit (Isa. 32:15; Zech. 12:10; Jn. 7:39). Henceforth all God's people would be priests and prophets, thus fulfilling the ideal implicit in the Torah but never actually achieved.

(Important commentaries include J. A. Bewer, *A Critical and Exegetical Commentary on Obadiah and Joel*, ICC [1911, bound with other books]; E. Sellin, *Das Zwölfprophetenbuch*, KAT, 2 vols. [1929–30]; S. R. Driver, *The Books of Joel and Amos*, CBSC [1934]; L. C. Allen, *Joel, Obadiah, Jonah, and Micah*, NICOT [1976]; H. W. Wolff, *Joel and Amos*, Hermeneia [1977]; D. Stuart, *Hosea-Jonah*, WBC 31 [1987]; S. Romerowski, *Les livres de Joël et d'Abdias* [1989]; T. J. Finley, *Joel, Amos, Obadiah* [1990]; R. B. Dillard in *The Minor Prophets: An Exegetical and Expository Commentary*, ed. T. McComiskey [1992–98], 1:239–313; J. L. Crenshaw, *Joel*, AB 24C [1995]; D. A. Garrett, *Hosea, Joel*, NAC 19a [1997]; J. Barton, *Joel and Obadiah*, OTL [2001]; D. W. Baker, *Joel, Obadiah, Malachi*, NIVAC [2006]. See also A. S. Kapelrud, *Joel Studies* [1948]; W. S. Prinsloo, *The Theology of the Book of Joel* [1985]; S. Bergler, *Joel als Schriftinterpret* [1988]; R. Simkins, *Yahweh's Activity in History and Nature in the Book of Joel* [1991]; L. R. McQueen, *Joel and the Spirit: The Cry of a Prophetic Hermeneutic* [1995];

J. Strazicich, *Joel's Use of Scripture and Scripture's Use of Joel* [2007]; and the bibliography compiled by W. E. Mills, *Hosea-Joel* [2002].). R. K. HARRISON

Joelah joh-ee′luh (יוֹעֵאלָה *H3443*, perhaps "may [God] avail, help" [cf. BDB, 418b]). Son of Jeroham from GEDOR; he and his brother Zebadiah were among the ambidextrous warriors who joined DAVID at ZIKLAG (1 Chr. 12:7).

Joezer joh-ee′zuhr (יוֹעֶזֶר *H3445*, "Yahweh is help"). One of several Korahite warriors who joined DAVID at ZIKLAG (1 Chr. 12:6; cf. vv. 1–2). These soldiers may have been Levites from the family of KORAH, but some argue that the reference is to a different Korah or even to a locality in the tribe of BENJAMIN.

Jogbehah jog′buh-hah (יָגְבְּהָה *H3322*, "height"). A city in GILEAD fortified by the Gadites near the tribe's eastern border (Num. 32:35). See GAD, TRIBE OF. GIDEON made a circuit around Jogbehah in order to attack the Midianites from the rear (Jdg. 8:11). The town is generally identified with el-Jubeihat (about 7 mi. NW of RABBAH, modern Amman), where an Ammonite military tower has been found; another possibility is nearby Tell Ṣafuṭ (cf. the discussion in Z. Kallai, *Historical Geography of the Bible* [1986], 296–97, esp. n. 34; see also NOBAH).

Jogli jog′li (יָגְלִי *H3332*, possibly "Yahweh reveals"). Father of Bukki; the latter was a leader from the tribe of DAN chosen to help in the distribution of Canaan W of the Jordan among the Israelites (Num. 34:22).

Joha joh′hah (יוֹחָא *H3118*, short form of יְהוֹחָנָן *H3380*, "Yahweh is [or has been] gracious"; cf. JEHOHANAN, JOHANAN, JOHN). **(1)** Son of Beriah and descendant of BENJAMIN, listed among the heads of families living in postexilic Jerusalem (1 Chr. 8:16; cf. v. 28). His father and uncle, however, are described as "heads of families of those living in Aijalon" and as having driven out the inhabitants of GATH (v. 13).

(2) Son of Shimri; described as "the TIZITE," he and his brother Jediael are listed among DAVID's mighty warriors (1 Chr. 11:45).

Johanan joh-hay′nuhn (יוֹחָנָן *H3119*, short form of יְהוֹחָנָן *H3380*, "Yahweh is [or has been] gracious", cf. JEHOHANAN, JOHA, JOHN). **(1)** Son of Kareah; he was one of the captains of Jewish forces in the open country during the conquest of Judah by NEBUCHADNEZZAR (2 Ki. 25:23). After the appointment of GEDALIAH as governor of the land, Johanan came with other captains to Gedaliah at MIZPAH (Jer. 40:8, 13). He warned Gedaliah of ISHMAEL's plan to assassinate him (40:14) and asked permission to slay Ishmael (40:15). Permission was refused (40:16).

After Gedaliah's murder, Johanan led the forces against Ishmael (Jer. 41:11), overtook him at the great pool of GIBEON (41:12), and rescued everyone whom Ishmael had taken away by force (41:14). Ishmael and eight men escaped (41:15), but the rest of the people were brought back to Geruth Kimham, a place near BETHLEHEM (41:16–17), from where they intended to go to Egypt because they feared a Babylonian reprisal (41:17–18). Johanan and others approached JEREMIAH to ask his advice (42:1–6), promising they would listen to the voice of God. When he admonished them to stay in the land and not go to Egypt, they claimed he lied (43:2–3). Johanan took all the people, including Jeremiah and BARUCH, to Egypt (43:5–7). According to the MT at Jer. 40:8, Johanan had a brother named Jonathan, but this information is missing in the SEPTUAGINT (as well as in the parallel, 2 Ki. 25:23).

(2) Firstborn son of King JOSIAH (1 Chr. 3:15). Nothing else is known about him. Because he did not succeed his father on the throne, some speculate that he died at an early age.

(3) Son of Elioenai and postexilic descendant of DAVID through SOLOMON (1 Chr. 3:24).

(4) Son of Azariah, included in a genealogy of high priests (1 Chr. 6:9–10). See AZARIAH #7.

(5) One of David's ambidextrous warriors from the tribe of BENJAMIN who joined him at ZIKLAG (1 Chr. 12:4; cf. vv. 1–2).

(6) A Gadite warrior (see GAD, TRIBE OF) who joined David in the wilderness, listed eighth in rank among the officers (1 Chr. 12:12). These Gadites are described as "brave warriors, ready for battle and able to handle the shield and spear. Their faces were the faces of lions, and they were as swift as gazelles in the mountains" (v. 8).

Ancient Mizpah should probably be identified with this hill (Tell en-Naṣbeh). Johanan son of Kareah came to Mizpah and warned Gedaliah of an assassination attempt being plotted against him (Jer. 40:13–16).

(7) Son of Hakkatan; he was family head of the descendants of Azgad who returned to Jerusalem with EZRA (Ezra 8:12; 1 Esd. 8:38). According to some, the phrase *yôḥānān ben-haqqāṭān* should be rendered "Johanan the younger."

(8) "Son" (i.e., grandson) of ELIASHIB the high priest, and high priest himself during the reign of DARIUS II (Neh. 12:22–23, cf. vv. 10–11, where "Jonathan" perhaps should be read as "Johanan"). The identification of this individual has a bearing on the dispute regarding the date of Ezra's mission. Some argue that he is the same individual mentioned in a letter from ELEPHANTINE (see *ANET*, 492a) and/or in JOSEPHUS (*Ant.* 11.7.1 §§297–301; but see E. M. Yamauchi in *EBC*, 4:581–82, and H. G. M. Williamson, *Ezra-Nehemiah*, WBC 16 [1985], 151–54; detailed discussion in J. C. VanderKam, *From Joshua to Caiaphas: High Priests after the Exile* [2004], 54–63).

(9) Alternate form of JEHOHANAN (2 Chr. 28:12 [KJV, NRSV]; Neh. 6:18 [KJV]). R. E. HAYDEN

Johannine Comma. See COMMA JOHANNEUM.

Johannine theology joh-han'in. The teaching of JOHN THE APOSTLE as given in the NT books attributed to him. See JOHN, GOSPEL OF; JOHN, EPISTLES OF; REVELATION.

It is generally supposed that Johannine theology has its own distinctive features sufficient to mark it out from other streams of theological thought current in the APOSTOLIC AGE. Because of the usual dating of the Johannine literature at a time nearing the end of the 1st cent., the Johannine theology is seen usually as the latest development in the NT. Yet a strong warning is necessary against the too ready assumption that this theology has no roots in the earliest Christian traditions. It is wrong to suppose that John is a development from PAULINE THEOLOGY, for instance, without giving full consideration to the possibility that both preserve an early stream of thought that developed collaterally and not dependently.

The following survey will consider the contribution of the Johannine literature to the major aspects of Christian doctrine. In doing so, most attention will be paid to the Gospel of John, although some relevant data may be drawn from the epistles attributed to him. The Apocalypse, which may or may not have been written by the same author, will be included where applicable because it shares certain common theological features with the other literature.

  I. Doctrine of God
    A. The Hebrew basis for the doctrine
    B. Aspects of God

II. Jesus Christ
   A. The Logos
   B. The "I am" sayings
   C. The filial sayings
   D. Indications of the true humanity of Jesus
   E. Messianic considerations
III. Teaching about the Spirit
   A. At the baptism of Jesus
   B. The Nicodemus incident
   C. At the Feast of Tabernacles
   D. The Paraclete sayings
   E. Summary of Johannine teaching about the Spirit
IV. Facets of salvation
   A. Sin and judgment
   B. Atonement
   C. Faith
   D. Eternal life
V. Eschatology
   A. Relation to the OT
   B. The use of the title "Son of Man"
   C. References to resurrection and to the last day
   D. Time references in the gospel
   E. The approaching judgment
   F. References to the parousia
   G. Use of the term "eternal life"
   H. Summary of eschatology
VI. The church
   A. The Christian community
   B. The Christian ministry
   C. The ordinances

I. Doctrine of God. Basic to any approach to early Christian theology is the doctrine of God, for all other aspects of doctrine are affected by it. It was a marked feature of all the various streams of Christian thought that they shared a strong view of God. This is particularly evident in the Johannine literature. In the fourth gospel, both the recorded teaching of Jesus and the evangelist's own comments bear testimony to this.

A. The Hebrew basis for the doctrine. It is almost an axiom of primitive Christian theology that the doctrine of God was basically taken from JUDAISM. The OT had presented a high ethical concept that was superior to the inadequate and often capricious deities of the Gentile world. Judaism, by the time of Jesus, had exalted God to such high transcendence that intermediaries were necessary for him to maintain contact with men. This exalted notion of God made unique the revelation in Christ of a God who is at once unapproachably holy, yet condescendingly merciful. In the Johannine theology the more intimate aspect of God's relationship with human beings is brought vividly to the forefront. The various ways in which this feature compares and contrasts with the Hebrew background of thought will be brought out in the course of the following discussion.

B. Aspects of God

1. God as Creator. Although John does not use the term *create* in the prologue to his gospel, he definitely assumes the creative activity of God. His purpose in drawing attention to the part played by the LOGOS in CREATION is to show that creation is a divine activity. For this there is ample support from the OT, not only from the creation account in Genesis, but also in many other books. At the same time there is no suggestion that the creative activity of God has ceased. The statement of Jesus in Jn. 5:17 that the Father still works is basic to his whole teaching that God is active, especially in his own mission. This concept of the continuing work of God is more dynamic than the rabbinic understanding of the SABBATH rest of God; according to the rabbis, God's work related to judgment, not creation, for the latter was regarded by them as completed. The distinction, therefore, is made between the physical and the ethical activity of God. Whereas in the teaching of Jesus the ethical is decidedly dominant, the physical activity of God is not absent.

In connection with the activity of God, John's gospel draws attention to the works of Jesus as being works of God. So NICODEMUS is recorded as saying, "Rabbi, we know you are a teacher who has come from God. For no one could perform the miraculous signs you are doing if God were not with him" (Jn. 3:2). It is taken for granted that supernatural signs are directly attributable to the action of God. A man who does what is true shows that his works are wrought in God (3:21). Similar stress on the works of God is found in the answer Jesus gives to the disciples' query about the blind man (9:3). The unfortunate man was to be the means for the manifestation of the works of God, and the later deduction of the man himself that no one could do what Jesus did unless God were with him (9:33) shows how clearly he had come to appreciate the continuous activity of God. To this may be added the challenge of Jesus when his Jewish opponents took up stones to stone him, "I have shown you many great miracles [*lit.*, good works] from the Father. For which of these do you stone me?" (10:32). Good works are the direct result of the Father's activity.

2. God as Father. No other book of the NT lays such emphasis on the FATHERHOOD OF GOD as John's gospel, and special attention needs to be given to its contribution to this aspect of the doctrine. The idea of fatherhood was not new. There was some appreciation of the personal fatherhood of God in Hebrew thought, although the more dominant idea was corporate. God was father to his people Israel. There is certainly nothing to compare with the depth of personal relationship that is seen so clearly in the filial status of Jesus, which was divine fatherhood on a new plane.

It is in John's account of the cleansing of the temple that Jesus refers to the temple as "my Father's house" (Jn. 2:16). One reason the Jews sought to kill him was that he called God "Father," which in their eyes was tantamount to claiming equality with God (5:18). Therefore, they construed the Lord's references to the Father in a different way from traditional Hebrew thought. This comment by John on Jewish opposition leads into an extended discourse about the Lord's relationship with the Father. Since the Son is seen to be not only dependent upon but also wholly in harmony with the Father, the Jewish claim that he was making himself equal with God is seen to be justified. What the Jews regarded as blasphemy, the Christians recognized as revelation. The Father's life-giving work and judging activity are closely reflected in the Son (5:21). The Son, in fact, is endowed with all the authority of the Father in judgment (5:27).

Another extensive Johannine passage reveals the fatherhood of God prominently (Jn. 8:18–59), when a comment by Jesus prompted the question, "Where is your father?" (8:19). The dullness of understanding in the hearers is vividly brought out. In spite of Jesus' specific reference to the Father, John records, "They did not understand that he was telling them about his [*lit.*, the] Father" (8:27). Such teaching was unprecedented; nevertheless, the Jews themselves claimed to regard God as Father (8:41), although Jesus proceeded to disillusion them (cf. 8:44).

Another passage also reveals the fatherhood of God (Jn. 10:31–32). Again, there was a clash with Jews, whose intention to give vent to violence was challenged by Jesus with comments about the Father. Most significant about this incident is that it was prompted by the claim of Jesus to be one with the Father (10:30), and was followed by the equally astonishing statement that "the Father is in me, and I in the Father" (10:38). There is no denying that John desired to bring to the fore in his gospel the predominant part played by the filial consciousness of Jesus in the pursuance of his mission. After describing the incident in the upper room when Jesus arose to wash the disciples' feet, John comments that Jesus knew that the Father had given all things into his hands (13:3). In the subsequent discourse, PHILIP made the request, "Lord, show us the Father" (14:8), to which Jesus answered with a further question that presupposed that anyone who had seen him had seen the Father. The Father desired to communicate knowledge of himself in the person of Jesus. The whole farewell discourse contains constant references to the Father. Most illuminating in this respect is Jn. 17, which records the prayer of Jesus to the Father. In this section alone Jesus used descriptive adjectives with the title. God is addressed as both "Holy Father" (17:11) and "Righteous Father" (17:25). Nowhere else is the close relationship between Jesus and the Father seen as in these petitions, offered mainly on the behalf of others.

The major difference between the gospel and 1 John in references to God is that the idea of fatherhood is much more prominent in the gospel (119 times) than in the epistle (12 times), although God is mentioned 64 times in the epistle. The difference is due to the difference of purpose, but the fundamental concept of the divine fatherhood is common to both. There are few references to this theme in the Apocalypse, although those that do occur (all but one in the letters to the churches) are consonant with the usage in the gospel and epistles.

3. God as Spirit. The spiritual nature of God is specifically asserted in Jesus' discussion with the Samaritan woman (Jn. 4:24). It is not introduced as a new revelation; it is rather the deduction from it that appears to be new. WORSHIP must take place in accordance with the nature of the object of worship, which entails spiritual worship in view of the nature of God. It is important to note, as W. F. Howard points out, that "the initiative is with God, who *seeks* such worshipers, and himself bestows the Spirit of truth" (*Christianity according to St. John* [1943], 61). The teaching of Jesus on the subject of man's approach to God assumes this spiritual nature of God.

4. God as Light. In the prologue to the gospel the metaphorical use of LIGHT is introduced and is also used as a self-description of Jesus later in the gospel (cf. Jn. 1:4–9; 8:12–13). It is more specifically applied to God in 1 Jn. 1:5, and a similar idea is found in Rev. 21:23 (cf. 22:5). The idea is not unique to Christian thought. C. H. Dodd claims parallels with the HERMETIC WRITINGS and PHILO JUDAEUS (see *BJRL* 21 [1937]: 149; cf. also Dodd's important monograph, *The Interpretation of the Fourth Gospel* [1953], 201–2). If the imagery used may be paralleled, there is not the same depth of insight in the *Hermetica* and Philo as is found in 1 John, where the whole concept is brought into the sphere of human relationships as the readers are exhorted to walk in the light. Fellowship is possible only if some agreement exists between the natures of those communing.

5. God as Love. There is much on this theme in both the gospel and the epistle, but it is in the latter that the definitive assertion is made that "God is love" (1 Jn. 4:16). A marked distinction must be drawn between this Christian concept of LOVE and the contemporary Greek concept, which often failed to distinguish between love and lust (cf. A. Nygren, *Agape and Eros* [1953], 1.118ff., E. Stauffer in *TDNT*, 1:35–38; C. Spicq, *Agape in the New Testament I* [1963]). Moreover, in view of the inferior character of their notion of love, the pagans could not conceive of God loving human beings, for as E. K. Lee points out, "Such love would imply a downward movement, from the level of divine perfection to a lower level" (*The Religious Thought of St. John* [1950], 54). The statement in Jn. 3:16 that "God so loved the world that he gave his one and only Son" concisely sums up the uniqueness of the Christian approach. The spring of divine action in salvation was love. Such love is poured out toward us (cf. 1 Jn. 4:7–12).

6. Other aspects of God. In the prologue, the invisible nature of God is brought into focus (Jn. 1:18) to be modified by the knowledge that he has become revealed in Christ. This God who is so revealed is true (3:33), which means both true or real in contrast to no gods, and true in contrast with false. The former is nearer to the Hebrew idea of truth, the latter to the Greek idea. God is not only faithful but is eternally real. In the concluding statement of the epistle (1 Jn. 5:20), this characteristic of being true is applied to God who has been revealed in Christ.

God is seen not only in his redemptive activities, but also in his work of judgment. John does not hesitate to speak of the wrath of God abiding on those who disobey the Son (Jn. 3:36). His work in judgment already has been mentioned. The Johannine presentation of God may be summed up as exalted and yet loving, as holy and yet merciful, as Father and yet Judge. The other aspects of doctrine must be considered against this background.

II. Jesus Christ. In examining the CHRISTOLOGY of John, the obvious point of departure must be the prologue, although some discussion will be necessary concerning the extent to which this section can be regarded as normative for the whole gospel. It may be regarded as detached from the main body of the gospel, as it is by those who see it, essentially, as a Hellenistically orientated introduction. If, as others maintain, its basis is Semitic, it may more readily be treated as an integral part of the gospel (cf. the discussion in W. F. Howard's *The Fourth Gospel in Recent Criticism*, 2nd ed. [1955], 57). Others regard the major part of the prologue as originally a hymn on the Logos that has been adapted for the purpose. Whatever the origin of the Logos material, this prologue bears witness to an early Christology and is of great importance in any estimate of Johannine theology.

A. The Logos. There are various theories regarding the LOGOS that can only be touched upon here. The STOICS spoke of the *logos spermatikos*, which was the divine Reason that made nature function. It was what Howard called "theoretical pantheism" (*Christianity according to St. John*, 35). The term is used some 1,300 times in Philo, and the suggestion that there are points of contact between him and John is natural enough, but the distinctive features of the Johannine use of the term are lacking in Philo. There can be no denial that John implies the distinct personality of the Logos, as is clear from his identification of the Logos with Christ. In this respect he differed radically from Philo, who, although he used various terms to describe the part played by Logos in creation, never rises to the concept of a personal agent. Moreover, Philo never suggests what John asserts regarding the preexistence of the Logos. The most far-reaching contrast is in the absence from Philo of any idea of the INCARNATION of the Logos, whereas this is the key thought in John's presentation. It is as if John were saying that all this theorizing about the Logos is finished now that the Logos himself has come to dwell among men. It would be a fitting introduction to Christ for those accustomed to these Hellenistic modes of thought.

Other strands of Greek thinking can be seen in the *Hermetica*, where the term is also used; but in this case communion with God is attained through nature rather than through Christ. The parallel in usage is only superficial. In addition, some have seen a correspondence with the Jewish concept of the intermediary *Memra* (Aram. *mêmar* or *mêmrāʾ*, "word, command") that spanned the gap between the transcendental God and the created order. Although the notion undoubtedly throws light on what might have been the Jewish understanding of John's Logos—an important consideration if John's gospel comes from a Jewish source—yet this would not exhaust the meaning.

B. The "I am" sayings. Throughout this gospel are sayings of Jesus beginning with "I am," which

Typical Middle Eastern flat bread. Jesus asserted, "I am the bread of life" (Jn. 6:35).

present a wide variety of facets of his character and mission. "I am the bread of life," which forms the main theme of the discourse in Jn. 6, shows that the true spiritual nourishment that Jesus brings is nothing less than himself. The key statement in the whole interpretation is in 6:51—"the bread … is my flesh." Jesus declared himself to be the light of the world, as the source of all true illumination (Jn. 8:12; cf. 9:5). The shepherd discourse (ch. 10) contains two such statements—"I am the door" (10:7) and "I am the good shepherd" (10:11). Both draw attention to the uniqueness of Jesus in relation to his sheep. In the incident of the raising of LAZARUS, Jesus said to MARTHA, "I am the resurrection and the life" (11:25), which is tantamount to claiming that all life finds its basis in Jesus Christ, a thought supported by the further statement, "I am the way and the truth and the life" (14:6). The concluding saying is, "I am the true vine" (15:1).

In all these sayings, Jesus made claims for himself that would sound presumptuous if made by any other. It requires the exalted viewpoint of the prologue to make them intelligible. Some interpreters have further appealed to the OT name for Yahweh, I AM (WHO I AM) (Exod. 3:14), as a basis for the fullest understanding of Jesus' sayings. When used in the absolute, "I am" (Gk. *egō eimi*) would carry a weightier connotation than when used with a predicate. Nonetheless, there may well have been a significant connection in the mind of Jesus. The most extraordinary statement of Jesus involving an unqualified "I am" is Jn. 8:58, "Before Abraham was, I am" (NRSV), which cannot be otherwise interpreted than as a claim to preexistence. It is highly probable, therefore, that this usage bears relation to the exalted name for Yahweh. See GOD, NAMES OF.

C. The filial sayings. It has been pointed out already how frequently in the discourses in John's gospel Jesus speaks of God as Father and of himself as Son. This filial relationship is based on human analogy, but goes far beyond it, for the sonship of Jesus is unique. It is for this reason that the adjective *monogenēs* G3666 ("only" or "only-begotten") is applied to Jesus in John's gospel four times (Jn. 1:14, 18; 3:16, 18) and once in the first epistle (1 Jn. 4:9). The word focuses attention upon uniqueness. Jesus is Son in such a sense that he alone is the means whereby the Father reveals himself. Throughout the gospel, the awareness of Jesus of his unique relation with the Father is self-evident. He frequently refers to himself as one sent from God. He makes clear that he speaks on the basis of the Father's authority and conceives all his actions as conforming to the divine will. The charge brought by his enemies (Jn. 5:18) that he made himself equal with God may be understood in the rabbinic sense of acting independently of God, a charge that Jesus refutes (so H. Odeberg, *The Fourth Gospel* [1929], 203.)

This frequent use of the title "Son" in John's gospel compares and contrasts in some respects with the synoptic title of SON OF MAN. The latter title is not absent from John, but is infrequent when compared with the widespread and unqualified use of Son. Nevertheless, there are nearly as many occurrences of it in John as in Mark. In all of these there is an eschatological emphasis (see A. Corell, *Consummatum Est* [1958], 103–4). This draws attention to a change of emphasis in John from the identification of Jesus with man to his filial relationship with God. The two emphases are not mutually exclusive but are complementary. It should be noted that John's purpose was to lead the readers to faith in Jesus as the Christ and as Son of God (Jn. 20:30–31). An echo of this is found in Martha's confession (11:27). To John, nothing was more important than that the readers should recognize the divine nature of Jesus. He had no intention of portraying him as anyone less than Son of God.

D. Indications of the true humanity of Jesus. Although so much stress in John falls on Jesus' divine aspect, it is significant that nowhere else is the true humanity of Jesus more clearly brought out. At the scene by the well at SYCHAR, Jesus was both weary and thirsty. At the grave of Lazarus he was deeply moved with indignation and wept. In the account of the crucifixion John records the saying "I thirst" (Jn. 19:28). In addition, he notes his essentially human condescension in washing the disciples' feet (13:1–2).

The Jesus portrayed in John's gospel is not remote; he is interested in people. He takes time to talk with the two disciples of JOHN THE BAPTIST (Jn. 1:35–42). He concerns himself with the domestic arrangements at a village wedding (2:1–2). He accepts an intrusion from NICODEMUS at night time (3:1–2). He does the unconventional by talking with a Samaritan woman at midday (4:7). He seeks out the impotent man who had been healed to give him some moral instruction (5:14). A similar action follows the healing of the blind man (cf. 9:35). Such incidents bring out clearly the essential character of Jesus in his warm concern for people. Whereas this is not John's major interest, it is indispensable to his total picture of Jesus Christ.

E. Messianic considerations. In John's gospel the recognition of the messianic status of Jesus occurs much earlier than in the Synoptic Gospels, and this has given rise to problems regarding the veracity of John's references. The first of these comes when ANDREW tells his brother PETER that he has found the MESSIAH (Jn. 1:41). The second evidence comes in Jesus' conversation with the Samaritan woman when he acknowledges the title Messiah (4:25). In the synoptics, however, and particularly in Mark, there is reticence in allowing observers to publish any recognition of the messianic signs. This led Wilhelm Wrede to propose his theory of a "messianic secret," by which he meant that Mark has imposed these messianic hints upon his narrative (see MARK, GOSPEL OF). Such a theory has been resuscitated with modifications by T. A. Burkill. It requires, however, considerable reinterpretation of the evidence to excise from the Gospels the messianic consciousness of Jesus.

Certainly John presents a distinctive account of messianic claims, as is stated in his purpose statement (Jn. 20:31). There is no need to suppose that his account shows any fundamental difference from the synoptists. There were many stages in the development of the disciples' full understanding of Jesus as Messiah, and John does not imply that this had already happened in the earliest part of the ministry of Jesus. He shows occasions in his subsequent narrative when the disciples did not understand (cf. 2:22; 12:16; 13:36; 20:25). What John implies is that two of the disciples at least had an early flash of insight. The admission by Jesus of his messianic office to the Samaritan woman is in marked contrast to the synoptic restraint, but for Samaritans the messianic concept was not, as with the Jews, inextricably bound up with nationalistic aspirations.

Since John sets out his gospel in such a way that his readers might be led to believe in Jesus as Messiah, it is relevant to inquire how he achieved this purpose. The nationalistic motive is specifically rejected in Jn. 6:15. In this case Jesus himself takes the initiative in avoiding the crowds. On more than one occasion he avoids mere popular acclaim. The messianism seen in John's gospel is, on the contrary, essentially spiritual. Jesus is conscious of being the Sent One—that is, sent to do the will of God—and it is in this sense that the title Messiah must be understood. This explains why the Jewish nationalists found events unintelligible that for Jesus were fulfillment of a mission. The cross would be more than an enigma—a positive stumbling block—if the messianism of Jesus was understood in any other sense than spiritual.

The total Johannine Christology has many distinctive features, but there is a common basis with other streams of early thought about Jesus Christ. There are no grounds for the view that John's Christology is a special and independent development of his own.

III. Teaching about the Spirit.

It is in the sphere of teaching about the HOLY SPIRIT that John's contribution is especially noteworthy, for there is more about the activity of the Spirit in this gospel than in any other. It will be best to consider the references to the Spirit in order of mention and then to construct some summary of the whole teaching.

A. At the baptism of Jesus. The descent of the Spirit upon Jesus when he was baptized by John the Baptist closely follows the pattern of the synoptic accounts. John the Baptist's testimony that he saw the Spirit descend as a dove from heaven and that it rested on Jesus (Jn. 1:32) was strengthened by his (John the Baptist's) inner God-given conviction that whoever received the Spirit in this way would baptize with the Spirit (1:33). All the synoptics mention the dove-like appearance of the Spirit, but John alone records the prior message given to the Baptist concerning its significance.

The BAPTISM OF THE HOLY SPIRIT is clearly a major characteristic of the mission of Jesus, but the question arises as to when this activity happened. Does this refer to the baptism of the Spirit seen at PENTECOST and thereafter, or is there any evidence of such baptism during the earthly ministry of Jesus? There can be no doubt that in the fullest sense the baptism of the Spirit did not take place until after the glorification of Jesus. This is specifically supported by the statement in Jn. 7:39 (see discussion below). The close connection between the mission of Jesus and the work of the Spirit is basic to all the records. It suggests that the mission of Jesus could not be adequately applied apart from the activity of the Spirit, a conviction that is amply supported from the evidence in Acts.

B. The Nicodemus incident. The next allusion to the Spirit is in Jn. 3:5, where Jesus in conversing with NICODEMUS links the Spirit with water in emphasizing the necessity for new birth. Whereas there is dispute over the interpretation of "water," whether or not it refers to baptism, there can be no dispute about the essential role of the Spirit in the process of REGENERATION. The fact that Jesus proceeded to contrast natural and spiritual birth (3:6) shows that the work of the Spirit cannot be conceived in any other than spiritual terms. A human analogy is in mind. Whatever comes from human parents shares the nature of the parents, and John uses this basic principle to maintain the spiritual nature of those born of God. It is as if Jesus knew how likely people would be to desire to track with precision the activity of the Spirit, for he shows how impossible this is by using the analogy of the wind (3:8). The statement emphasizes the

JOHANNINE THEOLOGY

absolute sovereignty of the Spirit in the processes of regeneration. There is no set pattern, no much anization. The whole process is on an essentially personal basis.

In the same chapter, John records another significant statement about the Spirit. "For the one whom God has sent speaks the words of God, for God gives the Spirit without limit" (Jn. 3:34). Although there are other ways in which the sentence can be construed—e.g., with the Spirit as the subject rather than the object of the giving—the above rendering is the most probable. The words of God need the Spirit of God to interpret them, and the assurance is given that there will be no stinting in the supply of the Spirit. Again, the close connection between the mission of Jesus and the work of the Spirit is brought to the fore.

A parallel contrast between the Spirit and flesh is recorded later (Jn. 6:63), where once again Jesus connects his words with the Spirit, if *pneuma* G4460 is here understood as the Holy Spirit. Even if it be regarded as the human spirit set in contrast to the flesh, it may still be treated as evidence of the essentially spiritual character of the teaching of Jesus.

C. At the Feast of Tabernacles.

The important declaration of Jesus made at the Feast of Tabernacles concerned anyone who believed in him—"streams of living water will flow from within him," followed by the comment, "By this he meant the Spirit, whom those who believed in him were later to receive. Up to that time the Spirit had not been given, since Jesus had not yet been glorified" (Jn. 7:38–39). The interpretation comes from the evangelist and shows his own understanding, and presumably that of the early church, regarding the connection between the glorification of Jesus and the gift of the Spirit. The analogy of running water as a symbol of the Spirit is suggestive, for it represents both what is essential to life and what possesses cleansing power, which are prominent aspects of the Spirit's work. One important feature of the present statement is that the Spirit is in some way communicated through the agency of believers. The book of Acts contains instances of the gift of the Spirit coming by means of the apostles, which serves as an illustration of this aspect.

Worshipers at the Western Wall with citron and palm fronds in hand, celebrating the Feast of Tabernacles. Jesus used this feast to announce that streams of living water would flow from him (Jn. 7).

D. The Paraclete sayings.

The major passages about the Spirit in John's gospel are all found in the discourses in the upper room. There are five sayings in which the Spirit is referred to as the PARACLETE (a transliteration of the Greek *paraklētos* G4156). The passages are Jn. 14:15–17; 14:25–26; 15:26–27; 16:5–11, 12–15. Hans Windisch (*The Spirit-Paraclete in the Fourth Gospel* [1968, orig. 1927], 2–3) treated these passages as separate from the rest of the discourses, but it is valuable to regard them as forming a group that supplies much information regarding the Spirit. First the meaning of the Greek word should be noted. It is a legal term, but not exclusively so. Where it bears this significance it may be rendered "advocate," but it should not be confined to one who pleads another's cause in a legal sense, for the help to be given is more general. The rendering "counselor" conveys this more general sense. The sayings in John are sufficiently explicit to show in what ways the Spirit counsels.

The first passage (Jn. 14:15–17) identifies the Counselor as the Spirit of truth (cf. 15:26; 16:13). The idea of truth here is probably twofold—reality and veracity. Since God himself is truth, it is to be expected that truth will be a characteristic of his Spirit. The main activity of the Spirit is his continual presence with his people: "he lives with you and will be in you" (14:17). This statement focuses upon the Spirit's function to continue the presence of Jesus among his people. It is in this sense that he is another Counselor. The second passage (14:25–26) draws attention to his teaching ministry. When the Spirit comes, sent by the Father in the Son's name, he "will teach you all things and will remind you of everything I have said to you" (14:26). The close connection between the Spirit and the teaching of Jesus is to be observed, and the most significant feature is the Spirit's part in restoring that teaching to the disciples' mind. Jesus did not leave the transmission of his teaching to the faulty memories of men. The Spirit's activity had fundamental importance in the establishment of true Christian traditions.

The third passage (Jn. 15:26–27) lends support to the view that the major objective of the Spirit is the glorification of Christ. He who is said to proceed from the Father "will testify about me" (15:26). Because the disciples were called to do the same, their possession of the Spirit is at once seen to be indispensable. There was never any question of the disciples witnessing in their own strength. The fourth passage (16:5–11) is introduced as an assurance to the disciples in view of the coming departure of Jesus. It shows again that the coming of the Spirit depends upon the cessation of the earthly ministry of Jesus. The Spirit's ministry will follow the ministry of Jesus. It would consist in bringing conviction to the world. It concerns sin, righteousness, and judgment—the two former on the ground of Christ's position, the latter on the ground of the already pronounced judgment upon the prince of this world. Placed as they were in a hostile world, the disciples discovered later the reality of this promise.

The final passage (Jn. 16:12–15) is the promise that the revelation of truth given thus far would be developed through the agency of the Spirit. The Spirit's function in this was to glorify Christ. His authority was not his own. He was to declare not only things yet to come, but all that belongs to Christ. This ministry of the Spirit was therefore entirely Christ-centered. One remaining reference, "Receive the Holy Spirit" (20:22), contains the words of Jesus as he breathed on the disciples in the upper room after the resurrection. This seems to be a foreshadowing of Pentecost. It is accompanied by a promise regarding forgiving or retaining of sins, which is clearly connected with the authority of the Spirit.

E. Summary of Johannine teaching about the Spirit. To sum up the Johannine evidence concerning the Holy Spirit, it may be said that the essential ministry of the Spirit is assumed throughout. His activity is an integral part of the Johannine presentation of Christianity. Indeed, the writer must have been conscious of the fact that his own knowledge of the teaching of Jesus was derived from the Spirit's leading. Christianity was a dynamic faith and the power was that of the Spirit. At the outset of Christian experience, the Spirit's activity is dominant in the process of regeneration; so it is in the realm of faith. The believer is assured of the indwelling presence of the Spirit. The work of conviction cannot be achieved without his aid.

There is sufficient evidence in this gospel to show an exalted view of the Spirit. He proceeds from God, and he is sent by God. He is the gift accompanying the glorification of Jesus. His whole work depends upon what is essentially a continuation of the work of Jesus Christ. In a sense he is the other self of Jesus and called another Counselor. The personality of the Spirit in this gospel cannot be denied, for although some passages can be understood in a nonpersonal sense, others cannot, and these latter must be determinative. The basic idea of the Paraclete is personal. As a teacher he cannot be an impersonal influence or principle. If the Spirit is a fitting example of witnessing, his personality must be assumed. Indeed he cannot take the place of Christ unless he is a person. Moreover, the masculine personal pronoun is used in spite of the neuter gender of the word *pneuma* (cf. Jn. 14:26; 15:26; 16:7–8, 14). There is no doubt that the evangelist intentionally brought out the personal characteristics of the Spirit.

The question arises whether John presents any doctrine of the TRINITY. If by doctrine one understands a formal dogma, the answer must be in the negative. There is enough evidence, however, to show that the doctrine is here in embryo. The respective emphases on the different persons of the Trinity by John supply some of the data on which the Trinity came to be assumed.

In 1 John, the references to the Spirit of God are few, but what there are conform to the usage in the gospel. Knowledge of the indwelling Christ comes through the Spirit (1 Jn. 3:24). It is the Spirit of God who enables people to confess that Jesus Christ has come in the flesh, as contrasted with false spirits who deny this truth (4:2–3). The Spirit is a gift (4:13) and a witness (5:7–8). In the Apocalypse, John writes of being in the Spirit (Rev. 1:10; 4:2; 17:3; 21.10). There are various references to the seven spirits (1:4; 4:5; 5:6), probably referring to seven aspects of the Spirit or to his perfection. A heavenly voice (14:13) is identified as the Spirit, while the Spirit is linked with the Bride in the closing exhortation (22:17).

IV. Facets of salvation. The Johannine literature presents a picture of a world in need and then shows the means used to meet that need. It will be helpful therefore to discuss the Johannine doctrine of SALVATION under four sections: sin and judgment, atonement, faith, and eternal life.

A. Sin and judgment. Both in the specific teaching of Jesus and in the evangelist's own comments is a distinctive presentation of the WORLD, which is described as in direct contrast to the divine order. In John's writings, the term *kosmos* G3180 refers not to the world of the created order, but rather to the world of men and women in rebellion against God; it carries a moral connotation. For this reason Jesus spoke of the hatred of the world (Jn. 15:18). There is a dualism in this approach; yet it is not a theoretical or speculative dualism, but an essentially practical dualism. It arises from the indisputable clash between truth and error, and between God and the world. Into such a world Jesus came, a world already alienated from God. Indeed, John makes this clear in the prologue, which presents a fundamental antithesis between light and darkness (1:5). The world is opposed to the Word (1:9–10). It is in fact under the dominion of the devil (12:31; 16:11; cf. 1 Jn. 5:19). In 1 John the world is the domain of false prophets (4:1), is full of lust and pride (2:16), and is the object of the Christian's warfare in overcoming it (5:4–5).

This basically evil background sets in right perspective the Johannine teaching on sin. It is important to observe how sin is to be understood. Some of the evidence suggests that it is to be confined to the rejection of Jesus. He himself states, "If I had not come and spoken to them, they would not be guilty of sin," and, "If I had not done among them what no one else did, they would not be guilty of sin" (Jn. 15:22, 24). The work of the Spirit is to convince the world of sin "because men do not believe in me" (16:9). This is not the only view of sin found in the Johannine literature. The concept of sin is applicable to believers, but provision is made for forgiveness of recurring sin (1 Jn. 1:9). Moreover, sin is specifically defined as lawlessness (3:4).

Are there then two irreconcilable concepts? Clearly the people addressed will affect the definition of the term. In the passages cited from the gospel, Jesus is dealing not with the basic concept of sin, but with unbelief, and to make clear the serious character of the latter he includes it in the category of sin. But, to make sin equivalent to unbelief would restrict too strongly the category of sin. The Johannine view of the "world" demands a view of sin as distinctive, that is, as a rebellion against God. Closely linked with this is the view of JUDGMENT. Salvation is contrasted with condemnation (Jn. 3:17). In fact, it can be rightly understood only against the background of its antithesis. Sin had incurred condemnation, and because sinners could do nothing of themselves to alter the position, the plan of redemption was necessary. The same antithesis is seen in the contrast between eternal life and judgment (5:24). Rejection of Christ will incur judgment (12:48). To this must be linked the reference to the wrath of God (3:36), which is directed against those who disobey the Son.

B. Atonement. Like all the evangelists, John sees the major mission of Jesus as dealing with human need. There are, however, many distinctive features in John's presentation of that mission. Only the more important of these can be mentioned.

(1) John the Baptist announced Jesus as the Lamb of God who takes away the sin of the world (Jn. 1:29), which at once linked the mission of

Baby lamb flanked by two sheep. John the Baptist declared regarding Jesus, "Look, the Lamb of God, who takes away the sins of the world!" (Jn. 1:29).

Jesus with the removal of sin. But, in what sense? The figure of the lamb is suggestive of a sacrificial interpretation, and the imagery used is reminiscent of Isa. 53. The Greek word for lamb used by John differs from the SEPTUAGINT of Isa. 53, but this does not materially affect the sacrificial significance. The universal character of this sacrificial mission is clearly brought out. The lamb imagery is continued in the Apocalypse, where the whole sequence of visions is dominated by the figure of the lamb slain before the foundation of the world, but now exalted in heaven. It need not be supposed that John the Baptist understood the significance of his own statement, for it is only in the light of the cross that its relevance to the mission of Jesus is fully appreciated.

(2) An important statement was made by Jesus following the cleansing of the temple: "Destroy this temple, and I will raise it again in three days" (Jn. 2:19). John comments that the temple was his body (2:21). The statement reveals the consciousness of Jesus that his mission would end in death at the hands of men, but that it would be crowned with the resurrection.

(3) The promise that the Son of man must be lifted up as Moses raised the serpent (Jn. 3:14–15) is suggestive of the mode of his death. Faith is in some way related to this uplifted person, and eternal life depends on such faith.

(4) The statement regarding God's love (Jn. 3:16) is important because it grounds the divine giving in the divine love. There is more emphasis on love in the mission of Jesus in John's gospel than in the synoptics. To this may be linked the saying of Jesus, "Greater love has no one than this, that he lay down his life for his friends" (15:13). The connection between love and sacrifice is a key concept in the Johannine presentation of the passion.

(5) In the discourse on the bread of life, Jesus spoke of people as eating his flesh and drinking his blood (Jn. 6:51, 53). Some see a direct reference to the sacraments and suppose that this was John's attempt to counteract an excessive sacramentalism. Regarded as a statement of Jesus well before the institution of the Last Supper, the words may be understood in a preparatory sense. They provide the basic teaching that is essential for a right understanding of the words of institution. The giving of flesh and blood must again bear a sacrificial significance.

(6) The voluntary character of the death of Jesus is seen in the statement regarding the good shepherd who lays down his life for the sheep (Jn. 10:11). This principle is more specifically stated by Jesus in relation to himself—"No one takes it from me, but I lay it down of my own accord" (10:18). In the same context Jesus revealed the necessity for his mission when referring to the other sheep that he must bring into the flock (10:16). This idea of necessity may be supported also from the serpent passage (3:14).

(7) When CAIAPHAS commented that it was more fitting for one to die rather than that the whole people perish (Jn. 11:50), referring to the need to plot against Jesus, John recognized a prophetic voice, but understood it in an entirely different sense from Caiaphas's own meaning. To him it possessed significance that the words were uttered by the high priest; but the most important aspect was the spiritual expediency of the death of Jesus for many. The idea of substitution is unmistakable. The purpose was to gather into one the scattered children of God (11:52).

(8) In answer to a quest from some Greeks, Jesus spoke of the necessity for a grain of wheat to fall into the ground and die if it is to produce fruit (Jn. 12:24). He was clearly referring to his own death, and once again the major emphasis is upon the necessity for that death. The future success of the entire mission of Jesus depended upon it.

(9) Throughout the Gospel of John, the approach of the hour in which Jesus was to be glorified is

specially marked. Its delay is noted earlier (as in Jn. 2.4), but in 12.23 this hour has come, and since this was the commencement of the passion week there can be no doubt that the hour was the hour of the passion. There is a sense of inevitability; the death of Jesus fitted into a divine program. Nowhere is this so vividly revealed as in John's gospel. This idea is echoed in the prayer of Jesus, "I have brought you glory on earth by completing the work you gave me to do" (17:4). The whole prayer in this chapter shows that the mission of Jesus was directed toward the welfare of his people.

(10) The insistence by Jesus that even Pilate would have no power over him unless that power were granted by God (Jn. 19:11) again shows the divine pattern in the events of the passion.

(11) The completeness of the work of Christ is strikingly brought out by his declaration on the cross, "It is finished" (Jn. 19:30). This was more than the end of his earthly life; this was the completion of his redemptive mission.

Although no systematic doctrine of the ATONEMENT may be found, John's gospel provides much data toward the formulation of such a doctrine. The first epistle also provides useful data. The cleansing of sins is specifically attributed to the blood of Christ (1 Jn. 1:7). Christ is said to be an EXPIATION (or more accurately PROPITIATION) for our sins (2:2). The purpose of the incarnation was to destroy the works of the devil (3:8). The divine initiative in sending Jesus Christ for his work of expiation is made clear in 4:9–10 (cf. also 4:14). In the Apocalypse, doctrine is not prominent, but where reference is made to the cleansing of sin (Rev. 1:5; 7:14), this is through the blood of the Lamb. The anthem of adoration chanted by the twenty-four elders (5:9–10) centers upon the redeeming activities of the Lamb. It is important to note these features in a book so largely devoted to the theme of judgment and retribution. The new people of God are a redeemed people who stand out in vivid contrast to the agencies of evil that are finally to be overcome.

C. Faith. The provision of atonement is not enough without some knowledge of how its benefits may be appropriated, and the Johannine literature is specially rich in drawing attention to the function of FAITH. It is the verb rather than the noun that constantly recurs, vividly emphasizing the active aspect. The gospel is written to inculcate faith. First John was written to bring knowledge to that faith. The teaching of Jesus is full of exhortations to believe and full of promises to believers. It is by faith that men enter into a living relationship with Jesus Christ. Faith leads to life, and unbelief issues in condemnation (cf. Jn. 3:16–18). Of special significance is the often recurring preposition *eis* G1650 (lit., "into") after the verb "believe" when Jesus is the object of faith; for this introduces the idea of personal trust that goes beyond the simple idea of belief (cf. J. H. Moulton, *Grammar of New Testament Greek. Vol. I: Prolegomena*, 3rd ed. [1908], 68).

The close connection between knowing and believing is important in view of the Gnostic overemphasis on the former at the expense of the latter (see GNOSTICISM). Although the teaching of Jesus and the comments of John never propose that faith can exist without understanding, it is basic to Johannine Christianity that Jesus Christ came to do something more than merely to reveal truth.

D. Eternal life. The concept of ETERNAL life is not unique to the Johannine literature, but it is specially characteristic of it. It is seen as the end result of the process of redemption. In some respects it takes the place of the synoptic emphasis upon the KINGDOM OF GOD, but the two ideas are complementary. R. H. Charles (*Eschatology* [1899], 315), regarded eternal life in relation to the individual and the kingdom in relation to the community. Eternal life is essentially a present possession (Jn. 3:16; 5:24; 6:47; 1 Jn. 3:14; 5:11–12). This corresponds with the present aspect of the kingdom in the synoptics. It also involves fullness of life in the future. Eternal life is inseparable from the person of Jesus Christ, who declared himself to be the true LIFE.

V. Eschatology. Much debate has surrounded the problem of eschatology in this gospel. Many scholars have set its teaching in antithesis to the apocalyptic type of eschatology found in the synoptics. This has been mainly due to the belief that John is indebted to Hellenistic modes of thought, whereas the synoptics have been more influenced by Jewish concepts. (See HELLENISM.) The stress on the Hellenistic background for this gospel has somewhat lessened following the discovery of the DEAD SEA SCROLLS because of their testimony to the existence of similar concepts in nonconformist Judaism. Clearly a right assessment of background is essential for a true appreciation of Johannine eschatology. It is certain that no true appraisal can come along the way of strong antithesis. There is enough evidence to demonstrate that teaching akin to the synoptic eschatology is not absent from John, as the following survey will show.

Before considering the evidence, it would be well to indicate the various schools of interpretation. Some concentrate on "realized eschatology" and dismiss the futurist elements entirely, either by resorting to a thesis of editorial additions (e.g., R. Bultmann) or by explaining away the futuristic texts (e.g., C. H. Dodd). Although interpreting rather differently what they mean by realized eschatology, both agree that eschatology has to do with the present rather than the future. The reverse position has been adopted by others who insist that present eschatology has no meaning unless it is inseparably linked with a future emphasis (so W. Stählin, A. Corell). There can be no doubt that the latter approach takes more account of all the data in the gospel. Within this general position there is, of course, room for much difference of opinion regarding the relationship between John and the synoptics over eschatology.

A. Relation to the OT. The firm belief of the early church that the life and teaching of Jesus are a fulfillment of OT prediction gives an eschatological emphasis. In a sense the hopes and promises of the past are now "realized." They have ceased to be future. That this is implicit in John's approach is seen in the prologue, where the benefits received through Christ, that is, grace and truth, are compared with the law given through Moses (Jn. 1:17). There is considerable emphasis in the teaching of Jesus on ABRAHAM, and the superiority of Jesus to Abraham is specifically implied (8:53–54). A similar superiority to JACOB is evident (4:5, 12; cf. 1:50–51). As far as the OT patterns are concerned, the advent of Jesus was the *eschaton* (neut. of *eschatos* G2274, "end"); however, since he himself gave further predictions regarding his *parousia* G4242 ("return"), the final consummation is still in the future.

B. The use of the title "Son of Man." The main feature of the occurrence of SON OF MAN in John is the context in which it occurs. It is almost as frequent as in the synoptics; in the latter it is used sometimes generally, sometimes in relation to the passion of Jesus, and sometimes eschatologically, whereas in John it is uniformly used in the eschatological sense. It concerns the "lifting up" of Jesus, which refers in the first place to the event of the PASSION, but goes beyond that in conveying the idea of EXALTATION (Jn. 3:14; 8:28; 12:34; cf. 12:23; 13:31). The Son of Man was to be glorified. This is the climax of his mission. In this is a rather different emphasis from that found in the synoptic usage, where apocalyptic imagery is used; but the difference is not a contradiction. John concentrates more on the state than the event. For him eschatology has a spiritual importance.

C. References to resurrection and to the last day. Statements of Jesus are recorded that have a future reference (Jn. 5:25–29). The dead are to hear the voice of the Son of God. The Son has received from the Father authority to execute judgment. The time will come for a RESURRECTION to life for some and a resurrection to judgment for others. These references are in the style of Jewish apocalyptic literature (see J. H. Bernard, *A Critical and Exegetical Commentary on the Gospel according to St. John*, ICC, 2 vols. [1928], 1:clvi) and cannot be explained in terms of realized eschatology. There is a finality about these concepts that is wholly out of keeping with the present. Similarly, the theme of the last day is essentially futuristic (ch. 6). In the discourse in which these references occur Jesus clearly assumed that his hearers would have some understanding of the "last day."

D. Time references in the gospel. The terms "hour," "now," "not yet," "yet a little while," and similar expressions are frequent in John's gospel and must be regarded as characteristic. One deduction from them is that the eschatological event is not entirely future. There is a strong present element.

In Christ, and particularly in his death, the hour "has now come." This sense of completeness is present where Jesus announced that his hour had come (Jn. 12:23), and where he related the dawning of the hour to the accomplishment of the mission received from the Father (17:1). The major feature of these references, however, is not chronological but theological. The "hour" of Jesus was decisive for world history. Any future consummation must in some way be related to it.

E. The approaching judgment. Mention has already been made of the future judgment (Jn. 5:25–28). Other references have given rise to a different idea. Some passages (3:19; 12:31) seem to refer to a judgment that has already taken place; the ruler of this world has been deposed through Jesus. According to C. H. Dodd, this concept shows a conclusive reinterpretation of the eschatological idea of judgment. Although the action of Jesus in his passion shows the effectiveness of the overthrow of the evil agencies, this element does not exhaust the Johannine teaching about judgment. The gospel is not primarily concerned with this theme. Jesus makes clear that he came to save, not to judge, the world (12:47). Although the major emphasis is on the present, judgment is an indispensable part of the consummation of the present age.

F. References to the parousia. In the farewell discourse, Jesus refers to his SECOND COMING in such terms that a future PAROUSIA must be meant (Jn. 14:18, "I will come to you"; 16:16, "after a little while you will see me"). These statements are not understood in the sense of a future eschatology by advocates of the realized eschatology school, who regard them as "realized" in the coming of the Paraclete (so Dodd). This is not the most obvious meaning of passages like 14:2–3, where a closer connection between the going and coming again seems required (however, see R. H. Gundry in *ZNW* 58 [1967]: 68–72). It may be said, therefore, that whereas it is possible to interpret the words in the sense of a spiritual coming it is more natural to interpret them as referring to a future personal return.

G. Use of the term "eternal life." Mention already has been made of this concept when dealing with the effects of the work of Christ, but it is necessary to note its special eschatological significance. As noted, it may be considered as roughly equivalent to the concept of the kingdom of God, for it implies both a present and a future experience and is appropriated by faith. According to Howard (*Christianity according to St. John*, 181) "eternal life" is life in the age to come as contrasted with life in the present age and thus has a qualitative connotation. It is therefore essentially future, but Dodd regards it as realized in the present experience of believers. It is important to recognize its present appropriation (cf. Jn. 3:16), but the term cannot be emptied of its abiding significance.

H. Summary of eschatology. Taking the evidence as a whole, it is impossible to deny that a double aspect is involved. The outlook is both present and future. Salvation includes a present experience and in this sense it is realized, or, more accurately, is a continuous process of realization. Such specific future events as the parousia, resurrection, and judgment point to a coming consummation that will introduce features beyond present experience.

So far nothing has been said about the eschatology of the Johannine epistles or of the Apocalypse. One notable feature of this literature is the occurrences of the ANTICHRIST theme. The epistles have but little data apart from the name (cf. 1 Jn. 2:18, 22; 4:3; 2 Jn. 7). In one passage the plural *antichrists* is used (1 Jn. 2:18), which suggests that no particular individual is in mind. Other references are more specific (cf. 2 Jn. 7). Nothing in John's epistles is as informative as Paul's statement on this theme (2 Thess. 2). It should also be noted that the apocalyptic element is absent in the Johannine epistles.

In the Apocalypse are various descriptions of evil powers, and the reader is made vividly aware that the burden of the book is the spiritual conflict and the final overthrow of the evil powers. Such figures as the beast, the great red dragon, another beast, and similar descriptions are intended to convey the impression of highly organized hostility. One may dismiss the theory that some of these could be references to Nero, for the concept of spiritual conflict is characteristic of Johannine literature and the theory is totally unnecessary. Since the whole world lies in the lap of the wicked one, an intense clash between the deliverer and the usurper is to be expected, but the Lamb will obtain the final victory. The vision of the NEW JERUSALEM is intended to illustrate the age of blessing that will result from the final overthrow of evil. In contrast to the gospel and epistles, Revelation does not directly speak about "eternal life."

VI. The church. No direct reference is made in John's gospel to the church, and yet there are a number of indirect indications that Jesus conceived of a community of people who would continue his work. It is the cumulative effect that is important rather than any specific statements. The evidence will be divided into three main divisions: the concept of the Christian community; the ministry; and the ordinances.

A. The Christian community. That the mission of Jesus was outward-looking goes without saying, but in John's presentation of his teaching, this feature is brought into sharp focus. One of the key sayings is, "But I, when I am lifted up from the earth, will draw all men to myself" (Jn. 12:32). This at once links the idea of an emerging community with the passion. There can be no CHURCH that is not based on the death and resurrection of Jesus.

1. The shepherd allegory. The use of the SHEPHERD image to express the relationship between God and his people is not original. Many traces of it occur in the OT (e.g., Ps. 23; Isa. 40:11; Jer. 23:1; Ezek. 34:11). Jesus developed the idea to illustrate the special relationship between himself and the church. The word *flock* is used (Jn. 10:16) to describe the community of those who are said to be possessed by Jesus Christ. The distinction between the flock and different folds within the flock is important in the context of the Jewish and Gentile controversy that developed within the early church. The major significance of the shepherd allegory is the centrality of Christ. He laid down his life for his sheep. He knows his sheep and is known by them. He possesses his sheep and has a deep sense of urgency in bringing all his sheep into the flock. This accords well with the commission of Jesus as recorded in the synoptics (Matt. 28:18–20).

2. The vine allegory. The essential oneness of the VINE with its branches serves as an admirable illustration of the corporate nature of the church. The basis of the unity of the branches rests in the common dependence of each upon the vine, that is, Christ. The figure of speech draws attention to the church as an organism rather than as an organization. In the teaching of Jesus the relationship of each member to the vine is of more importance than their relationship to one another. The idea of abiding in the vine is the essential qualification for membership in the Christian community.

3. Mission teaching. The prayer of Jesus in Jn. 17 (often known as the high priestly prayer) is significant for several reasons, but for none more important than the close identification of the mission of the disciples with the mission of Jesus ("As you sent me into the world, I have sent them into the world," 17:18). The implications are far-reaching, for the disciples' work is described as a continuation of the mission of Jesus. Frequently John makes reference to the fact that God sent Jesus, and if the disciples are to be commissioned with the same burning sense of purpose, they are linked together in a corporate aim (see APOSTLE). The mission of both Jesus and the disciples is aimed to gather into one the children of God that are scattered abroad (Jn. 11:51–52). This emphasis on oneness is brought to focus in 17:20. Such oneness can exist only in an integrated community devoted to a common purpose.

Several features of the evidence from Jn. 17 may be noted. The disciples are to be a means for the glorification of Christ (vv. 6, 10). They have kept his word and they believe in him (vv. 6, 8). They will be kept from the evil in the world, although their mission is in the world (vv. 11, 14–15). They are to make known the word that they have received (vv. 20–21). Their consecration to their mission is consequent upon Christ's consecration of himself to his mission (v. 19). The entire prayer of Jesus shows his deep concern for his people.

4. The Paraclete sayings in relation to the church. A clear distinction exists between the world and the church in the fact that the latter (represented by the disciples addressed) alone possesses the Spirit (cf. Jn. 14:16–17; 15:26–27). What the Spirit teaches will be taught only to those in whom the Spirit abides. There is therefore to be a community consisting of people of the Spirit. This marks out the Christian church from all other communities.

B. The Christian ministry. Several passages in John bear upon the MINISTRY. It is seen as an integral part of the concept of the church. The teaching does not make reference to any church offices; it is rather a matter of functions.

1. The allegory of the door and shepherd. Although the primary reference is to Christ as the door and shepherd of his sheep, there is a derived sense in which the true shepherd, contrasted with the hireling, is an illustration of the pastoral office. The Christian ministry is concerned with a tender caring for the sheep.

2. The commission to Peter. The threefold commission to Peter also presents loving care for the sheep (Jn. 21). The metaphor of sheep is continued with Peter exhorted to feed both lambs and sheep. The pastoral office is directly concerned with those belonging to Jesus (my sheep, my lambs). The different terms used show the variety of functions of the true pastor.

3. The footwashing. Because Jesus specifically stated that his action in washing the disciples' feet was intended to be an example (Jn. 13:5, 14–15), the incident throws light on the attitude required in the servants of the church (see FOOTWASHING). The major demand is for HUMILITY; the emphasis is on service, however lowly. The sent one is essentially a SERVANT. It was on this occasion that Jesus made clear that those who receive his servants receive him (13:20), so demonstrating the inseparable character of Christ and his ministers.

4. The insufflation. Some difficulty has been found over the interpretation of Jn. 20:21–23, particularly the prediction regarding forgiving and retaining of sins as a future function of the disciples. The context shows that the words can be understood only in the light of the commission addressed to the disciples (v. 21). Moreover, they are applicable only through the agency of the Holy Spirit, for it is after the breathing of the Spirit upon them that the statement is made. The church consists essentially of those who possess the Spirit. Was the statement intended for all who possess the Spirit or restricted to those only who were the original recipients? In the latter case it would be restricted to apostles. Since the Holy

Grapevine with green branches supported by a rock. According to John, Jesus used the grapevine to illustrate the united nature of his church (Jn. 15:1–5).

Spirit descended on the whole church at Pentecost, a wider interpretation seems implied. It is the Spirit's task to bring FORGIVENESS into human experience, and those addressed possess that power only by virtue of the Holy Spirit. There can be no doubt that the ministry in John is an activity of the Spirit.

C. The ordinances. There is no specific mention of the institution of either BAPTISM or the LORD'S SUPPER in John's gospel, and this has given rise to various theories in an attempt to explain it. If there was a tendency to overstress the external features of the ordinances, this might supply a sufficient reason for John's intention not to mention them directly. If, as many hold, Jn. 3 and 6 allude to the ordinances indirectly, John may be bringing out their true spiritual significance. It must not be overlooked that when John wrote, the ordinances were well established in the churches, and it may well be that he omits reference to the institution because of the prior existence of the synoptic records.

1. Baptism. O. Cullmann (*Baptism in the New Testament* [1950], 15n.) finds references to baptism in many parts of this gospel, but most would restrict the mention of baptism to Jn. 3:3–5. This reference to baptism is not certain, for the expression "born of water" could be otherwise interpreted as being synonymous with physical birth. More likely, the phrase should be understood in the light of Ezek. 36:25–27, which speaks of spiritual cleansing in connection with spiritual renewal. If the reference is to baptism, its close connection with spiritual rebirth is the essential teaching. It has no value apart from the regenerating activity of the Spirit in the individual. This spiritual interpretation of an ordinance like baptism shows the Lord's perspective in regard to ritual requirements.

2. The Lord's Supper. The bread discourse in Jn. 6 shows such close connections with the institution of the Lord's Supper in the Synoptic Gospels that many scholars regard it as a substitution, or rather reinterpretation, of the ordinance. In this case it is claimed to have sacramental significance. Another view, however, is possible and much more probable. It cannot be supposed that Jesus gave no preparation for the ordinance that was to play so important a part in the worship of the church. The bread discourse furnished such an opportunity to bring out the spiritual principles. Yet, it may be objected that the setting of the discourse shows it to have been delivered to a Jewish audience who revealed no understanding of it (cf. 6:60). This has led some scholars (e.g., W. F. Howard) to regard the setting as unhistorical. But if the Jewish audience was baffled by the statements of Jesus, as the passage clearly indicates, this is no reason to suppose it to be unhistorical. Even the disciples who were present at the first supper understood the spiritual meaning only after the death and resurrection of Jesus. There was however nothing secret about the teaching. It was simply unintelligible to the unspiritually minded.

Christ identified the living bread from heaven as "my flesh" (Jn. 6:51). The spiritual MANNA, which is infinitely superior to the manna provided for the Israelites in the wilderness, is therefore meaningful only in the context of Jesus' self-giving for the "world." The further statement about eating the flesh and drinking the blood of the Son of Man (6:53) is even more obviously linked with the ideas that found expression in the Last Supper. One feature is particularly worth noting, namely, the reference in this context to the last day (v. 54). In the synoptics the Last Supper has a forward look; so have these adumbrations of it in John. (For additional discussion and bibliography, see JOHN, GOSPEL OF; NEW TESTAMENT THEOLOGY.) D. GUTHRIE

John jon (Ἰωάννης G2722, from Heb. יוֹחָנָן H3419, short form of יְהוֹחָנָן H3380, "Yahweh is [or has been] gracious"; see JEHOHANAN, JOHA, JOHANAN).

(1) JOHN THE APOSTLE. See separate article.

(2) JOHN THE BAPTIST. See separate article.

(3) John Mark. See MARK, JOHN.

(4) Father of ANDREW and PETER (Jn. 1:42; 21:15–17; the KJV has "Jona" and "Jonas" respectively, following TR *Iōnas* G2731 [gen. *Iōna*]); also called JONAS (Matt. 16:17, where the Gk. text reads *Bariōna* G980, from Aram. *bar yônâ*, "son of Jonas"). Most scholars believe, on the basis of the earliest MSS, that the original text of the fourth gospel had "John," and that later scribes, influenced by the Matthean text, changed it to "Jonas." Some speculate that these were alternate forms of his name; others posit divergent traditions in the early church.

(5) A relative of the high priests ANNAS and CAIAPHAS who participated in the cross-examination of the apostles Peter and John following the healing of the lame beggar at the temple (Acts 4:6). He is otherwise unknown.

In addition, several men mentioned in the APOCRYPHA bore the name John, as follows:

(6) Son of Simeon and father of MATTATHIAS, members of a priestly line; the latter led the Maccabean revolt in the 2nd. cent. B.C. (1 Macc. 2:1).

(7) Son of Mattathias; surnamed GADDI (1 Macc. 2:2; KJV, "Joannan, called Caddis"). With his brothers, John Gaddi took part in the Maccabean revolt, but was later captured by the family of Jambri from Medeba and executed (9:35–38).

(8) Son of SIMON MACCABEE and grandson of Mattathias; he was made a captain by his father, was victorious against a superior force W of Jerusalem, and eventually succeeded his father as high priest and leader of the nation (1 Macc. 16:1–11, 19–24). JOSEPHUS reports that John's surname was Hyrcanus (*Ant.* 13.7.4 §228) and gives us much detailed information about his rule. See HASMONEAN II.A.

(9) Son of Accos and father of Eupolemus; the latter and Jason son of Eleazar were sent by Judas Maccabee to solicit Roman aid against the Syrians, 161 B.C. (1 Macc. 8:17).

(10) A certain John and an individual named Absalom (both otherwise unknown) were sent by Judas Maccabee to the Syrian commander Lysias in 164 B.C. to arrange a treaty of peace (2 Macc. 11:17). G. A. Turner

John, Acts of. Two different apocryphal works bear this title. The earlier one, first attested before the end of the 3rd cent. as part of a Manichean collection, is preserved in fragmentary fashion in various languages. It purports to give an account of the travels, missionary work, and death of the apostle John. Two sections of gnostic character (see Gnosticism), the "Hymn of Christ" (§§94–96) and the "Mystery of the Cross" (§§97–102), appear to be separate compositions incorporated into the narrative. This *Acts of John*, along with other similar works, was attributed to a certain Leucius by later Christian writers. (Introduction and English trans. in *NTAp*, 2:152–209.) A second *Acts of John*, which claims to have been written by Prochorus (Procorus, Acts 6:5), is a 5th-cent. Greek novelistic account, with emphasis on supernatural events that allegedly took place on the island of Patmos. (See description in *NTAp*, 2:429–35; no English trans. has been published.)

John, Apocryphon of. A Gnostic treatise, also known as the *Secret Book of John*, that purports to preserve a revelation from the risen Christ to the apostle John. Originally written in Greek (prob. in the 2nd cent. A.D.), it has survived in four Coptic MSS. One of them (BG 8502, 2) was discovered in 1896; the other three are part of the Nag Hammadi Library (NHC II, 1; III, 1; IV, 1; tractates II, 1 and IV, 1 represent a longer recension). This work is generally regarded as the most important source for our understanding of the mythology adopted by Christian Gnosticism. (English trans. in *NHL*, 104–23. See also K. L. King, *The Secret Revelation of John* [2006].)

John, Epistles of. Three anonymous books from among the Catholic Epistles in the NT that traditionally have been ascribed to John the Apostle.

   I. Nature of the epistles
      A. Historical setting
      B. Literary characteristics
      C. Relation to John's gospel
   II. Authorship
      A. Arguments for John the apostle
      B. Arguments against John the apostle
   III. Locale
      A. Origin
      B. Destination
   IV. Date
   V. Contents
      A. 1 John
      B. 2 John
      C. 3 John

I. Nature of the epistles. Many distinctives set these three epistles apart from the other letters of the NT, and at the same time draw them together.

A. Historical setting

1. Earliest Gnostic tendencies. Many writers have concluded that incipient Gnosticism (which developed into a well-defined movement in the 2nd cent. A.D.) was in the background of several NT books, such as Colossians, Ephesians, and the Pastoral Epistles, but especially 1 John. Gnosticism, a popular form of Greco-Roman philosophy, had no doubt pervaded the thought world of the Roman empire and, confronting Christianity in the latter decades of the 1st cent., had produced serious conflict and confusion within the churches.

Gnosticism was the philosophical result of the blending of the cosmogony of Greek thought with the theology of oriental religions, especially Judaism (see Greek religion and philosophy, mystery religions, Roman religion). The first epistle of John reveals rather sharply three characteristics of Gnosticism that had serious implications for Christianity. (1) Dualism. Gnosticism held that matter was essentially evil and spirit was essentially good. Thus the human body and spirit had no effective contact with each other. Gnostics held that a redeemed soul in a sinful body was therefore not responsible for the deeds of that body. Such dualism led either to ANTINOMIANISM—the breakdown of morals and spiritual compromise on the part of some who professed Christ—or to ASCETICISM ("harsh treatment of the body," Col. 3:20–23). (2) Illumination. The name *Gnostic* came from the Greek word for "knowledge." Salvation according to the Gnostics came from knowing secrets rather than from faith in a Savior. Only the initiated who knew the Gnostic mysteries were in the light. (3) Rejection of the INCARNATION. Christ's earthly life posed a major problem for the Gnostics. God's spirit and human flesh could not have had any essential unity of personality in Jesus. A separation was made between Christ's deity and Jesus' humanity in one of two ways. Docetic Gnosticism taught that Christ was not really a divine person in human flesh; he was only a phantom playing the human role (see DOCETISM). Christ's humanity only appeared to be real. Cerinthian Gnosticism (CERINTHUS of Alexandria was linked by ancient tradition with John at Ephesus) taught that the human Jesus was an ordinary man upon whom the LOGOS of God came at his baptism, departing from him before the crucifixion. Only the human Jesus died upon the cross. The LOGOS was a kind of cape that the human Jesus wore during the period of the public ministry. John wrote against all of these heresies in his first epistle.

2. The pastoral scene. The homiletical tone of 1 John is probably due to the author's consciousness that his message was to be read to an assembled congregation (or congregations). It seems obvious from all three of these documents that the writer was a Christian leader of wide and prominent influence. An unmistakable air of authority and a noticeable desire to build up the readers in their faith are at the heart of the writer's effort. The danger of false teachers and teaching provoked the distinctive emphases on faith and love in 1 John (the clearest combination of those two virtues in the NT). The conduct of the readers had become a concern of the writer, who urged them not to love the world (his language suggests that there was a condition of worldliness among them).

First John may have been intended for a circle of churches. The term *elder* used in the other two letters has been thought to indicate the author's pastoral relationship to a community of faith. Because 2 John seems to be a miniature of 1 John, having scarcely a single phrase that had not already been employed in the longer letter, it has been thought that the elder mentioned in 2 John was a venerable church leader (perhaps bishop) who had previously written 1 John as a pastoral letter to deal with the danger of a spreading, false doctrine. B. H. Streeter advanced the idea that this elder was in fact a BISHOP with a responsibility for a circle of smaller churches, making him almost an archbishop. All three letters deal with real life and not with abstractions. The intense personal feelings of the author are everywhere evident. He was bound to his readers as they were to him. He made an appeal to them that reveals an acquaintance with both their needs and history.

3. The Johannine community. During the last decades of the 20th cent., much attention has been devoted to the Christian community that presumably was associated with the work of John the apostle in ASIA MINOR. According to some scholars, it was this community that was responsible for producing the writings attributed to the apostle. One theory suggests that the fourth gospel was written at a time when this group of believers (perhaps comprising several churches) formed a united front, but that subsequently a smaller group (perhaps one specific church) within that community developed views about Christ and Christian conduct that created a schism. The larger community (perhaps

Painting from within the Greek Orthodox portion of the Church of the Holy Sepulchre in Jerusalem. Docetic Gnosticism taught that Jesus was not fully human and thus that he only seemed to have died on the cross.

the parent church) produced 1 John to counteract what they perceived to be a heretical movement. Other speculative proposals along similar lines have been set forth by various scholars.

B. Literary characteristics. First John does not conform to the general characteristics of contemporary personal letters. It has no introduction, identification of author, thanksgiving, or author's greetings. Neither does it have a concluding salutation. There is a complete absence of any personal name. On the other hand, this may show the distinctive form of an encyclical that was intended for more than one congregation, being sent by messengers from church to church and being read in the general assembly by a leading elder.

The two shorter Johannine letters (the shortest books in the NT) were written in the more typical epistolary character of 1st-cent. correspondence. They are so brief (each has fewer than 1,200 Gk. letters) that they probably were written on one sheet of PAPYRUS each. They were written for local and personal situations.

1. Unity. Rudolf Bultmann has attacked the unity of 1 John (*The Johannine Epistles*, Hermeneia [1973], 2). He believes that the original letter ended at 1 Jn. 5:13 and that vv. 14–21 of that chapter were added by a later ecclesiastical editor. He suggests also that the author of 1 John worked over a previously existing document. He contends that 1:6–10 is stylistically different from 2:1–2. The latter section was believed to have been the author's own commentary upon the former passage. Generally, however, modern scholarship has insisted upon the unity of 1 John, because the style and ideas of the suspected sections have been found to be those of the letter as a whole.

2. Structure. Many scholars have felt that 1 John was plan-less. The author does not present his themes one by one, developing his message and then drawing his conclusions; as a result, it is almost impossible to outline the letter. Perhaps the best internal evidence as to any organization of thoughts in the mind of the author is found in connection with the ideas about God that he advanced: (1) God is light (1 Jn. 1:5); (2) God is life (2.25), (3) God is love (4:8). The subject discussed in connection with each idea is hortatory in nature: (1) walk in the light, (2) live God's life, (3) dwell in love.

Without doubt there is justification for the frequent observation that 1 John is spiral in form. The ideas introduced return for additional treatment and application. For example, "light" and "darkness" are introduced and then reintroduced and applied. The forgiveness of sins is treated in the same fashion, returning several times to the discussion. "Liar" is a recurring theme, as also "commandment." Perhaps the most important word of all is "love," which is also treated in this fashion. The foundation of the developing thoughts is laid in 1 Jn. 1:1–4—and from this foundation the message begins, ever broadening and expanding, each thought growing out of the other and ever circling to encompass and apply the previously introduced material.

3. Style. First John often has been compared to the WISDOM material in the NT, especially James (see JAMES, EPISTLE OF). The message is given in little pearls of wisdom. Simple words are used, and statements are brief and pithy. John did not argue as PAUL did; therefore his style was intuitional rather than logical. He was primarily a witness, depending not so much on logical deduction as upon spiritual insight. Another stylistic characteristic is the use of contrast, making opposites set against each other to underscore the teaching. Light is contrasted with darkness, truth with error, God with devil, righteousness with sin, love with hate, and life with death.

Repetition also was important to John. His ideas are relatively few, but they are repeated over and over again. Twice in 1 John it is said that "God is love," and several times love is offered as the evidence that a person has been born of God. Parallelism is another device used by this author. For example, 1 Jn. 1:8–10 contains three repetitions in parallel statements: "We deceive ourselves and the truth is not in us" (v. 8); "he is faithful and just and will forgive us our sins and purify us from all unrighteousness" (v. 9), "we make him out to be a liar and his word has no place in our lives" (v. 10). The letter is characterized by a vocabulary that is nontechnical, having nothing of instruction about churches, their offerings, ordinances, or activities. It has been judged a simple, nontechnical document, generally lacking in literary polish but strangely powerful for perhaps those very reasons. The rhythmic quality of this work has been thought to have been due both to the catechetical method of teaching converts to Christianity and to the method of teaching commonly employed in Judaism, which made much use of such repetitions and antithetical parallels.

C. Relation to John's gospel. Until the end of the 19th cent., almost all scholars held to a common authorship for the fourth gospel and the epistles of John. Tradition, moreover, has connected the name of John the son of Zebedee with all of these documents from the earliest times. The acceptance of a common authorship was furthered by the obvious similarity of idioms and phrases, common themes, and a shared theological viewpoint that was distinctive in the NT. In the 20th cent., a challenge to this commonly held view was raised by H. J. Holtzmann, and later by C. H. Dodd. Dodd (*The Johannine Epistles*, MNTC [1946]) concluded that a distinct theological divergence pointed in the direction of a disciple of John as the probable author of the epistle. He expressed the view that the theological distinctives are three principally: (1) the eschatology is more primitive in the gospel; (2) so also is the interpretation of the death of Christ; and (3) the doctrine of the Spirit is not as elevated in the epistles as it is in the gospel.

1. The question of priority. The chronological order of the epistles of John and the fourth gospel is so complicated that it has not been possible to determine their relationship with any degree of certainty. Some have believed that the epistles were written in the reverse order from their occurrence in the NT (i.e., 3 John first and 1 John last). In this scheme of writing the gospel has been put between 2 John and 1 John. It also has been conjectured that 1 John was written as a postscript to the gospel, the latter having been written to explain how we might have eternal life (Jn. 20:31), and the epistle to give assurance that they had it (1 Jn. 5:13). Still other commentators have believed that the epistles were written probably a year or two after the gospel, because it has been thought that such a passage as 1 Jn. 2:3–8 assumes that the readers were familiar with the fuller exposition of the themes of the gospel. This epistle has, therefore, been termed the first commentary on the Gospel of John. For example, 1 Jn. 1:3, 5, which deals with the theme that "God is light," has been considered a development of the same subject in the gospel. Furthermore, some scholars interpret the thrice-repeated phrase "I write [*egrapsa*, aor.] to you" (1 Jn. 2:13c–14) not as epistolary aorists but as historical aorists (thus, "I have written to you"), referring to the former communication contained in the gospel.

2. Similarities to John's gospel. The scholarly consensus is that 1 John and the gospel share the same theological approach and, generally speaking, treat the same subjects. Although narration is missing from the epistle, it does include subjects prominent in the gospel: eternal life, believers as God's children, love for God and brethren, and the indwelling of God in believers. Beyond that, there are interests shared by the two documents that relate them. "Witness" is a common emphasis in both (the term is used nine times in the epistle). The importance of the incarnation overshadows every other consideration in both of them. Structurally it seems that there must have been a connection between the prologues of the epistle and gospel that caused them to unfold in a similar fashion. B. F. Westcott (*The Epistles of John: The Greek Text with Notes*, 3rd ed. [1892], xli–xliii) set out the following list of notable parallels in the texts:

1 John 1:2–3	with	John 3:11
1 John 1:4	with	John 16:24
1 John 2:11	with	John 12:35
1 John 2:14	with	John 5:38
1 John 3:5	with	John 8:46
1 John 3:8	with	John 8:14
1 John 3:13	with	John 15:18
1 John 3:14	with	John 5:24
1 John 3:16	with	John 10:15
1 John 3:22	with	John 8:29
1 John 3:23	with	John 13:34
1 John 4:6	with	John 8:47
1 John 4:16	with	John 6:69
1 John 5:9	with	John 5:32
1 John 5:20	with	John 17:3

3. Differences from John's gospel. In spite of the striking similarities between 1 John and the fourth gospel, some differences are apparent. The doctrine of the incarnation, though important to both, is centered in the epistle in the true humanity of Jesus, whereas in the gospel it centers in the divine glory of Jesus. C. H. Dodd professed to find an eschatological difference, in that the ESCHATOLOGY of the epistle was judged more primitive than that of the gospel, because of an absence of the reinterpretation of that doctrine, which Dodd called "realized eschatology." The interpretation of the death of Christ in the epistle's use of "expiation" (1 Jn. 2:2; 4:10) and the absence of specific reference to the Spirit in the new birth discussion (as the gospel makes much of the Spirit in the same context) are examples of other acknowledged differences.

Linguistically there are differences also. Rhetorical questions characterize the epistle but are entirely neglected in the gospel. There is a tendency toward conditional sentences in the epistle that is not a trait of the gospel. The vocabulary of the gospel is naturally larger than that of the epistle, yet there are nearly forty words used by the writer of the epistle not found in the gospel, and there are also common words in the gospel that failed to make the epistle at all. In addition, the gospel makes much use of the OT, but the epistles contain no quotation from the OT, and perhaps only one reference. There is in the gospel an interest in Judaism as a living religion that is absent from the epistle and that suggests an earlier date.

II. Authorship. Traditionally, John the son of Zebedee was considered the author of the epistles. When tradition is combined with reasonable possibilities, it seems that he went to EPHESUS in the province of ASIA about A.D. 65–70. He remained there laboring among the churches until about 95, when he was exiled to the island of PATMOS during the persecution under DOMITIAN. Having returned to Ephesus about the year 97, this last of the apostles died there around the turn of the century.

A. Arguments for John the apostle. IRENAEUS, Bishop of Lyons in the latter part of the 2nd cent., quoted from both 1 John and 2 John, attributing both writings to John, the disciple of the Lord, to whom he also attributed the fourth gospel. His contemporary CLEMENT OF ALEXANDRIA, head of the catechetical school in that city, frequently quoted 1 John and attributed it to the apostle John. The MURATORIAN CANON, the first known ecclesiastical list of NT books, acknowledged two epistles of John, one of which was identified by quotation as 1 John. After the time of EUSEBIUS (c. A.D. 305), general consent was attained regarding the apostolic authorship of these epistles.

B. Arguments against John the apostle. IGNATIUS wrote to the church at Ephesus within twenty years of the time that John was supposed to have been there. He mentioned Paul's ministry, but was silent regarding John. Some have thought that an early martyrdom of John was prophesied by Jesus (Mk. 10:39; Matt. 20:23). George Hamartolos, a 9th-cent. writer, said that PAPIAS wrote that John was murdered by the Jews along with his brother. The calendar of the Syriac church, which dates from the 4th cent., observed the martyrdom of James and John in Jerusalem on December 27.

The possible confusion of John the apostle with an alleged "John the elder" has been cited against apostolic authorship. The latter has been suggested as the author of the epistles, both from the reference to "the elder" in 2 and 3 John, and from a reference by Papias to a John the elder who perhaps was a different person from the apostle John. The elder may have been a disciple of the apostle according to most of those who distinguish between the two. (See further JOHN THE APOSTLE.)

III. Locale

A. Origin. Traditionally, the epistles of John have been associated with EPHESUS and the Roman province of Asia. It has been supposed that 1 John was written only for congregations in that province, but in 1 Peter the address includes all those in PONTUS, GALATIA, CAPPADOCIA, ASIA, and BITHYNIA. If 1 John was written twenty-five or thirty years later than 1 Peter, it might well be that an even larger territory than Asia was addressed. Because tradition has pointed toward Ephesus as the residence of John, it is likely that all three epistles were written there. Unless 1 Jn. 5:21, which admonishes abstinence from

Roman forum and theater at Ephesus (view to the NE). Tradition says that the apostle John wrote his epistles from this city.

idol worship, is taken literally, there is no indication of whether these Christians were Jews or Gentiles.

B. Destination. About the 4th cent., it was thought by some that 1 John, and perhaps the other Johannine epistles, were addressed to PARTHIANS, and the title "To the Parthians" actually occurs in a few MSS. AUGUSTINE later supported this theory. An explanation has been found in a statement in the *Adumbriationes* (a work attributed to Clement of Alexandria) that 2 John was addressed to a Babylonian lady. Since Babylon was in the Parthian empire, the entire theory may have come from this single statement.

The question as to whether 2 John was addressed to an individual or a congregation awaits the discussion of the text, but 3 John undoubtedly was addressed to a trusted friend of "the elder." This trusted friend seems to have been a prosperous layman in a church within the radius of Ephesian influence.

IV. Date. The situation of the churches in the background of 1 John, especially with reference to the anti-Gnostic material, would suggest a later date than Colossians or the Pastoral Epistles, where the same tendencies seem to have been met in a less developed form. In all likelihood, the epistles of John were written toward the close of the 1st cent. The absence of any reference to persecution probably indicates a date before the time of the emperor TRAJAN (A.D. 98–117), and possibly even prior to the last years of DOMITIAN, who reigned until 96.

The relationship of the epistles to the gospel also includes the establishing of a date. The Gospel of John may have been written as late as 95–100. Many scholars are now inclined to date it about 85. If the epistles were written after the gospel and at least 1 John and 2 John at about the same time, a likely date would then be about 87 for the epistles. The apostle John would at that time have been a man in his late seventies, able still to travel and work (as suggested in 3 John). Christianity at that time was in difficulty in Asia but had not come under the intense persecution as occurred under Domitian. The Gnostic situation had the time to develop into a movement of some considerable importance and to spread over a wide area. In all likelihood, the epistles of John were written about the end of the 80s or the beginning of the 90s in the 1st cent.

V. Contents of the epistles of John

A. 1 John

1. The prologue (1 Jn. 1:1–4). Dionysius of Alexandria may have been the first to note the parallel structure between the prologue of the epistle and that of the gospel: (1) the main subject is described first; (2) then the historical manifestation of that subject; (3) last, the personal apprehension of it. The prologue of the epistle (also of the gospel) serves as the foundation upon which the remainder of the letter rests.

The main subject is declared to be the eternal Word, or better still "the living Logos." In Greek *logos* G3364 did not mean mere speech or utterance; it meant rational and articulate utterance of thought. It was the author's declared intention to speak of Christ as the eternal Logos who is in himself life, who is in union with God the Father before all time, and who became incarnate in time as the object of sensible experience among men and women. In a court of law in ancient times, the testimonies of two senses were required to make a witness authentic. Perhaps this is in the background of John's emphasis that the proof of the humanity of Jesus had been attested by three senses: hearing, seeing, and touching. The neuter reference "that which" may be explained as a reference to the gospel, but in light of the declaration, "That which was from the beginning," it is more likely that the author was thinking of Christ as a life—a fact of history. This stressed the truth that Jesus was not an optical illusion, as the Docetic Gnostics had claimed, but that he had an actual human body that was seen and heard.

The long and somewhat tangled sentence that makes up the prologue is also an emphasis upon the personal and collective apprehension of the eternal, divine life in Christ. There had been a shared experience of the historical Jesus by his people. The repeated "we" indicates not only the apostolic witness and testimony but also the collective witness of the people of Christ, the "salvation" people who had come to find life in Jesus. Fellowship was the common tie of such a community; their fellowship was a fellowship of witness that rested upon the fellowship of a shared experience (see Dodd, *The Johannine Epistles*, 13–16; B. F. Westcott, *The Epistles of St. John* [1883], 174–75). The textual problem in 1 Jn. 1:4 as to whether "our joy" or "your joy" should be read is incapable of a hard and fast decision, but most likely it was "our joy" in the apostolic sense.

2. Fellowship with God (1 Jn. 1:5—2:2). The first expansion of thought based upon the basic statement of 1:1–4 is in terms of "fellowship with God." The real meaning of all religious experience is caught up in this phrase for the writer. There were heretics in John's day who claimed to have a vital experience with God, but they denied that Jesus was truly the Son of God—God in human flesh. John insisted in this opening statement that no one has fellowship with God who does not acknowledge Jesus, for it is his blood alone that places sinners into fellowship with God and maintains them in such fellowship. John stated the facts of Christian experience that were related to the establishment and maintenance of such fellowship with the intended purpose that his readers might know that they truly possessed this fellowship and that they might readily recognize those who did not.

The statement "God is light" has nothing to do with a mysterious or esoteric nature of God. John was merely emphasizing that, in spite of what the Gnostics taught, God had no secret knowledge that was withheld from the entire body of believers, hidden just to give to a select few. The source of this information was Jesus himself. It did not come from rabbinic instruction in the synagogue nor from the dialectical reasonings of Greek philosophy. It was the message of REVELATION received directly through the historical Jesus. Beyond this fact LIGHT represents the perfect holiness of the unveiled nature of God as seen in Jesus Christ. DARKNESS is not simply a symbol of ignorance; it is also a symbol of moral evil. Anyone who rightly claims a personal knowledge of God in fellowship must measure his life against the character of God. It was B. F. Westcott who pointed out the trilogy: (1) God is light so those who fellowship with him must walk in the light; (2) God is spirit so those who fellowship with him must worship in the spirit; (3) God is love so those who fellowship with him must manifest love.

The repeated statement, "if we say," would indicate that the apostle was not tilting against men of straw but was combating the errors of his day. He had heard people say these things again and again. Entrance into fellowship with God did not come by denying sin, but by confessing it and being cleansed of it. The cross stands at the heart of any vital experience of a sinful person with the holy God. The blood of Jesus (real blood and not a phantom) is absolutely necessary to the establishment of fellowship between sinners and God. In the NT, the word FELLOWSHIP is used only in a good and sacred sense. It is never used to describe those who walked in darkness and did not do the truth.

According to some scholars, it is important in this passage to recognize the relation between the Greek present tense and aorist tense. To understand properly 1 Jn. 1:8 and relate it to 2:1 and 3:6, it is necessary to translate the present tense in these verses as "continue to sin," that is, "live a sinful life." The aorist tense should be translated "to commit a sin," that is, "do a sin." If so, in 1:8–10 John is saying that when people say that they have not committed a sin, they make God a liar. In the present tense John is speaking of living a life of sin, so that he can say that whoever abides in God does not continue living a sinful life. In the view of other scholars, however, tense distinctions (or more properly, distinctions in verbal aspect) are rather subtle and cannot bear so much theological weight (see further below on 3:9).

In any case, two erroneous conclusions might have been drawn from 1 Jn. 1:8–10 against which the author guarded in 2:1–2. The acknowledgement of the persistent malady of sin might lead a Christian to accept sin as inevitable in life, causing him to ease his struggle against sin. Also, the readily available forgiveness of sin might lead a Christian to presume on God as the God of forgiveness. The author hastened to assure his readers that everything that he was writing was written that they might not sin. His readers were encouraged to remember the facts that are inseparable from fellowship with God.

3. Keep the commandments (1 Jn. 2:3–11). The author begins this section by a reference to KNOWLEDGE, or ASSURANCE, of a personal relation to God. The word "know" (*ginōskō* G1182) is derived from the same root from which the Gnostics took their name. They claimed a monopoly on religious knowledge, which John denied with his bold assertion "we know him." The basis of this assurance is the keeping of his commandments.

The author uses the term *commandment(s)* six times in these verses. In fact, as is characteristic of 1 John (the repetition of previously introduced ideas), this term is used in the following sections also (1 Jn. 3:23–24; 4:21; 5:2–3). It is evidently a key thought in the author's expanding discussion. The relationship of this new term *commandment* to the previously dominant term *fellowship* is that the Christian's fellowship with God depends upon, and is assured by, keeping the commandments.

The phrase "his word" in 1 Jn. 2:5 is a synonym for "commandment." The idea of keeping the commandments is previously suggested in 1:6 by the emphasis upon the truth as something that the Christian lives. John probably took this term from Jesus himself (see Jn. 14:15, 21, 23–24; 15:10). It was Jesus himself who identified these commandments with his word. There is an objective basis behind all Christian experience that made it impossible for people to brand it a sham or an illusion. That objective basis is keeping the commandments.

The importance and meaning of keeping the commandments is developed by two illustrations: (1) love for the believing brother (1 Jn. 2:9–11), and (2) avoiding love for the world (vv. 12–17). It is probably better to treat the second of these as a separate subject because vv. 12–17 are most difficult to connect to the context. Some have judged it a parenthesis in which the writer definitely turned aside for a word of personal appeal. The commandment of LOVE is as old as God's revelation. In the Christian context, the readers may have heard it preached by Paul and John. Perhaps they read it in John's gospel also. Some who had professed the light had given the lie to that profession by the darkness of their hatred for their brethren. John was saying that the new commandment is to put the old commandment into practice; in that sense it is not a new commandment at all but the old one applied.

4. Don't love the world (1 Jn. 2:12–17). As previously noted, this passage is a personal appeal in the first instance. These tender words of personal exhortation are in sharp contrast with the rather severe words that follow. Here is primarily a warning against that which would destroy the believer's fellowship with God, and also his fellowship with his brethren—the love of the world. The basis upon which John wrote to them was that their sins had been forgiven them. Since this was true, he was able to write these things to them because they were in the fellowship.

John divides his readers into the young and the old, for apparently his common way of referring to all of his readers is with the word "children." In all probability, these words refer to natural age and are not spiritualizations of mature and immature Christians. The Gnostics claimed an exclusive knowledge of God and condemned John's readers as having no knowledge of God. He reassured his readers of their real knowledge of the Father. Their abiding knowledge of God was attested by their fellowship with him.

In John's writings, "to love the world" always means to replace love for God in one's life with love for wrong objects. The WORLD here means the realm of evil that excludes God. The word John chose for love (*agapaō* G26) denotes direction of the will and purposeful choice. There are two reasons that arise from the essential nature of the world that labels love of the world as unspiritual: (1) such love is fixed upon that which is in essential opposition to God; (2) such love is fixed upon that which is unable to stand the test of time.

5. Beware the antichrist (1 Jn. 2:18–28). In early Christianity the belief that an ANTICHRIST would come who would be the direct opponent of Christ was widespread and significant. Usually the thought centered on one antichrist, but here John considers anyone as an antichrist who taught the false doctrines that he had thus far considered. They have withdrawn from the fellowship, and this itself branded them as those who had never shared in the real life and fellowship of the brethren. They had not loved the brethren because they had not loved God. In a sense, their departure from the fellowship provided a key word to John at this point, the term *remain*. Seven times in these verses John uses some form of this verb (*menō* G3531), just as he previously emphasized *commandments*. Their withdrawal was beneficial. The cause of Christ had been in much greater danger before these false teachers were revealed for what they really were, that is, unbelievers.

The special heresy against which John warned his readers was related to the person of Christ. To deny that Jesus was at one and the same time the perfect man and the true God, was the supreme lie. Such a liar was antichrist. A denial such as this is also a denial of the Father, for it is only through the Son that the Father had been manifested in the flesh. Whereas previously it was affirmed that love of the world was proof that one did not love God, in this passage it is affirmed that the denial of the truth concerning Christ is evidence that there is no fellowship with God. Faith in Christ tests fellowship with God.

Loyalty to the truth of God in Christ is declared to have its rewards. The two advantages that result from such loyalty conclude the section. They are an eternal relationship with God through Christ and a secure knowledge of spiritual realities. It is the Holy Spirit's function to bring both of these to the knowledge of the believer. The Holy Spirit was John's answer to the Gnostic. It was not the proud human "knower" who brought secret, mystic knowledge that men needed, but the Holy Spirit's guidance.

6. Do right (1 Jn. 2:29—3:10). The Gnostics taught that restraint of sin was unnecessary. John confidently asserted that the real proof that someone has been born of God is right conduct in God's sight. John especially considered two matters in connection with the new faith: the privileges and the character of God's children. Though years of Christian experience had accumulated for John, he was still amazed that sinners should be accorded the privilege of being called God's children (1 Jn. 3:1); but perhaps fearing that someone might misunderstand the word *called*, he added more amazingly, "And that is what we are!" The reason the world did not recognize these Christians as children of God was that that world did not know God. Beyond all this, there awaits these believers a wonderful destiny more marvelous than anything yet experienced. This glorious destiny is not known in detail, but in essence it is that the Lord's people will be like him. John declared that to be like Christ is the Christian's destiny.

In 1 Jn. 3:4–8, John places the Christian's life of righteousness against a life of sin, by way of contrast. These two lives come from two personal sources—Christ and the devil. A new life principle has been imparted to the Christian, a life principle that could not possibly be the seed of sin because it comes from God. The children of God may be expected to resemble their Father, God, in righteousness. Conversely, the same thing is true of the devil's offspring, for he was from the beginning a sinner. The expression "from the beginning" as here related to the devil has been subject to three interpretations: (1) that it refers to eternity, thus the devil is associated with sin from all eternity; (2) that it has in view the beginning of the human race, thus in all of human experience the devil is the source of sin; (3) that it means "from the beginning of sin," thus the devil is the original sinner.

The most difficult verse in the epistle is 1 Jn. 3:9, where the author uses absolute and unqualified terms: "No one born of God commits sin; for God's nature abides in him, and he cannot sin because he is born of God" (RSV). A common interpretation focuses on the present tense (or aspect) of the verbs as indicating progressive action; thus the NIV renders, "No one who is born of God will continue to sin, because God's seed remains in him; he cannot go on sinning, because he has been born of God." Other scholars argue that if John wanted to express the idea in present (rather than past or future) time, he had no option but to use this tense, and that in any case Greek writers would probably not depend heavily on subtle aspectual distinctions to make important points. Even without stressing the grammatical detail, however, it may still be possible to understand John's statement as indicating characteristic behavior. A second interpretation views these absolute statements as moral imperatives (e.g., "teenagers cannot drink alcohol" really means "are not allowed to" or "must not"). Still others argue that John has a specific sin in mind, such as the ultimate act of APOSTASY (cf. 1 Jn. 2:19; 5:16–17).

7. Love the brethren (1 Jn. 3:11–18). A family member in the divine circle, one of God's children, is expected to love the other family members of the divine circle. Proud Gnosticism, boasting its intellectual superiority, produced a spirit of arrogance and self-assertiveness on the part of its followers. There was no place in it for the uninitiated who did not accept the Gnostic interpretation. Jealousy, contempt, and hatred characterized this heretical movement. John declared that love is fundamental to the Christian message, being "from the beginning." In contrast with CAIN, the first murderer and embodiment of hatred, stands Christ, the very revelation of love. Christ's death was offered as the supreme proof of his love and the ultimate requirement of love from his people. Love is thus declared to be the manifestation of this new life from God in human beings. It is not enough to profess this love; it is required that Christ's people practice this transforming love in their daily lives.

8. Be confident (1 Jn. 3:19–24). When Christians judge themselves by the high standard of Christian love, it is easy to become discouraged. The first verses of this paragraph are difficult to interpret (for the difficulties of the Greek constructions see Westcott, *The Epistles of St. John*, ad loc.). John apparently meant by HEART the entire conscious, moral nature of man. The declaration is that the refuge from a guilty CONSCIENCE is the greatness of God's forgiveness. God's greatness is not to be found in his justice that brings condemnation upon sinners, but in his mercy that brings salvation from sin. Prayer would have no foundation if it were not for the greatness of God. By keeping God's commandments, prayer becomes effective, which means that because his people are one with God's purpose, they can expect his help. The keeping of God's commandments is summarized by John as a true belief in Jesus and a real love for the brethren. This keeping of God's commandments is both the condition and result of true fellowship with God. The Spirit's presence in the Christian's life is adduced as the proof of such vital fellowship with God.

9. Test the spirits (1 Jn. 4:1–6). At the end of the previous paragraph (3:24), John had written that Christians can know that God is abiding in them because of the Holy Spirit's presence in their heart. Before he continued with his message, the author paused to warn his readers about the false doctrine of SPIRIT as held by the Gnostics. The Gnostics talked much about spirit. Matter, they said, was evil, but the spirit was the divine part of man because it was nonmaterial. They claimed that their knowledge of God was a spiritual knowledge. John urged his readers to be rigidly discriminating concerning the "spirit" that moved a follower in the church. The fundamental test to apply to a teacher was his attitude toward Christ. If such a teacher denied the reality of the incarnation, he then based his message upon the wisdom of human reason rather than on revelation from God.

10. Abide in God (1 Jn. 4:7–12). Twice already John has affirmed that LOVE is the test of the Christian life. In this passage, the letter reaches its climax, for it is intended not only to give tests by which the readers could measure their lives, but more importantly, to secure for them a deeper experience with God. Love is the supreme test both of the new life and the abiding fellowship of God. Love is the natural fruit of the saved life. John related this love to the reality of the incarnation of Jesus Christ in the flesh. If Jesus was not truly the Son of God, then the love of God for a lost world was a figment of the imagination. A true incarnation was necessary for God's love to be revealed in the world. When love is associated with faith and devotion toward Jesus Christ, it then becomes a valid evidence of life everlasting. God, because he is love, is the one source of love. This means that people have no love for God until they discover God's love for them. Love that is genuine, according to John, has to have its source in God.

11. Have faith (1 Jn. 5:1–12). Throughout 1 John we find a constant interplay of love, righteousness, and belief. The author insists upon the relation of belief and love. The readers must remember to identify love with keeping the commandments. Because they are children of God, it should not be burdensome for them. Also, those born of God will gain the victory over the world through FAITH. John commonly uses the verb "believe," and 5:4 is the only place where he uses the noun "faith." Faith is the victory. This was not the Gnostic victory of spirit over matter, but the Christian victory of righteousness over evil. Faith brings victory. Faith comes from love. Love results from being born again. These are the familiar Johannine themes brought again into combination and new emphasis.

The statement in 1 Jn. 5:6 may have been a direct thrust at the Gnostic leader CERINTHUS, who taught that the DEITY OF CHRIST came upon the human Jesus at his baptism in the form of the dove that descended from heaven, but left him in GETHSEMANE. The author acknowledges that the messianic ministry of Jesus began at his baptism, but the fulfillment of that ministry was in the sacrifice of the cross "in the blood." In the Jewish legal system a testimony was regarded as conclusive when supported by two or three witnesses. It was, therefore, important to John that he discerned three witnesses to the real incarnation of God in the historical Jesus: "the Spirit, the water and the blood" (v. 8). These witnesses combined to support the declaration that it was Jesus, God's Son, who died on the cross and thereby worked redemption for humanity. There is the record of Jesus' earthly ministry, the fact of his atoning death, and the subsequent witness of the Spirit in the life of the believer (as well as the witness of the Spirit to Jesus in the days of his flesh). So intense is the rejection of the Gnostic heresies, which taught that salvation was secured through a speculative *gnosis*, that John made the strong declaration that those who taught such heresy made God a liar. The true witness of Christian experience, given through the Spirit, is that salvation is accepted by faith in Jesus as the Son of God.

12. Ask God (1 Jn. 5:13–17). The word *ask* is interrelated with the word *know* throughout this passage. Knowledge not only brought the certainty of salvation but also boldness and confidence in PRAYER. There are, however, three important qualifications introduced in connection with effective prayer: (1) the Christian must ask in accordance with God's will (v. 14), (2) the Christian must ask with faith (v. 15), (3) the Christian must consign some things to the wisdom of God alone (vv. 16–17). The reference to mortal sin, and the fact that John did not encourage prayer for such, has created much bewilderment for Christian interpreters through the centuries. It must be remembered that confidence is expressed in the effectiveness of prayer for "a brother." The point of contrast is that the "mortal sin" raises the crucial question of salvation. A Christian cannot pray with complete confidence where the genuine experience of grace is questionable. No doubt, in John's mind, the Gnostic heresy of denying the redemptive work of God's Son was such a situation, perhaps the primary indication of it to him. He could not encourage hopeful prayer that such a one would be dealt with by God as he deals with his children. Rather, such teachers as the Gnostics who professed God but were infidels with reference to Jesus had put themselves beyond the pale of prayer that intercedes for a brother or sister. They were not brethren. See UNPARDONABLE SIN.

13. Know these (1 Jn. 5:18-21). As the previous section reveals an interplay of *know* and *ask*, here the word *know* dominates the scene. It becomes more than a declaration from the author; it is also an outreach to establish his readers. Including the larger section (beginning in v. 13), the word *know* occurs seven times. In the first six occurrences, the Greek verb used is *oida* G3857, which possibly refers to knowledge that comes from Christian instruction. In the last occurrence (v. 20b), the verb is *ginōskō* G1182, and some argue that this term signifies knowledge that is based upon experience. The entire sum of Christian teaching is imparted to the end that people may know in their own experience the reality of the gospel. The Gnostics made great use of what they called "knowledge"; but the Christian has real knowledge. Christians know security in the provision of God; they know the reality of an escape from the bondage of sin; they know the truth and not error; they know the reality of eternal life.

B. 2 John. This briefest of books may be analyzed as follows:

1. Greeting (2 Jn. 1-3). The concept of salvation in 2 John is similar to that of 3 John. The term *elder* may have referred to the office the author held in the Christian community, or it may have referred to his advanced age. See ELDER (NT). In all probability, it referred to his office (though for John at this time it would have been equally true as a reference to his age). This title had wide use in the Asiatic churches, and apparently the author felt it was sufficient identification of himself.

The ELECT LADY may have been a woman with a family, and her sister (2 Jn. 13) may have been the elder's hostess at the time of writing. Some have even thought that the word for "lady" (*kyria* G3257) should be translated "Cyria," the personal name of a woman (even as Gaius's name appears in 3 John). It is more likely that the reference is a figure of speech referring to the church to which the letter was addressed, and the closing reference to "sister" would be understood as a sister congregation.

The familiar Johannine theme of "love in the truth" is quickly introduced. The author assured those to whom he wrote that he loved them in the truth. His love was not sweet sentimentality. It was a love that was rationally and morally conditioned by the gospel. It was the spiritual knowledge of God in Christ that produced this love in his heart. The society of the faithful was established by, and has its very existence from, its relationship to this truth. The typical blessing, as Westcott has noted, begins with the activity of God in behalf of men and women, and continues to the final human satisfaction: "Grace, mercy, and peace."

2. Follow the truth (2 Jn. 4-6). The opening words of this passage have been held to indicate that only some of the people involved were following the truth; others among the "children" were not. This may have been true, but it seems better to understand the words simply as a positive comment. He has had contact with some of the children, and he found those to be following the truth. The phrase "walking in the truth" means that the gospel of Christ was manifested in their living.

John practiced love in his dealing with the recipients of the letter, as indicated by his tender appeal that they love one another. John appears to have reasoned in a circle. Love, he said, is to follow the truth, and to keep the commandments. On the other hand, he said the command is that they should love one another. It may be important to note that in v. 6 he shifts from the plural "commands" to the singular "command." The life of love seeks to obey God in all that he commanded; at the same time, all the commandments can be summarized in one—love!

3. Watch for deceivers (2 Jn. 7-11). The love of which John wrote never goes contrary to the interest of truth. It is not to be extended indiscriminately. Those who were perverters of the truth and enemies of Christ could not in the very nature of things be

Traditional House of Mary at Ephesus. John wrote, "If anyone comes to you and does not bring this teaching, do not take him into your house or welcome him" (2 Jn. 10).

made the object of brotherly love. Of compassion and care they should be objects, but of Christian fellowship and service they could not be in the nature of the situation. There were roving teachers of Gnosticism that propagated heresy in denying the reality of the incarnation of God in Christ. These antichrists did not abide in "the doctrine of Christ," which probably meant the teaching of the apostles about Christ. They felt they knew God but took a small view of Jesus. The readers were warned against such men. To such teachers they were not to give aid or offer Christian hospitality.

4. Future plans (2 Jn. 12–13). John found writing to his readers in this instance to be less than satisfactory for the communication of his message. He anxiously awaited an opportunity when he could visit them and speak to them "face to face." he anticipated such a meeting with joy. The reference to children of the sister may have been to nieces and nephews, or more likely was a greeting from the members of a sister church.

C. 3 John

1. Greeting (3 Jn. 1). This letter was addressed by "the elder" to Gaius. The name Gaius was very common in the 1st cent., and the individual in this instance cannot be positively identified. Three men of this name have been suggested from the NT. Gaius of Corinth (Rom. 16:23) was noted for his hospitality. Gaius of Macedonia (Acts 19:29) was a missionary companion of Paul. Gaius of Derbe (20:4) accompanied Paul on a missionary journey (possibly the same as the Gaius of Acts 19:29). The tie that bound the author to this man, whoever he was, was the love of a Christian brother in the context of the Gospel.

2. Follow the truth (3 Jn. 2–4). The author prayed that Gaius would prosper physically and materially in the same way that he had prospered spiritually. This interest in Gaius's prosperity was related in the first instance to the generosity that he had shown to the visiting missionaries with whom he had shared his material possessions. These missionaries had reported his devotion to the truth, his faithful stewardship that was manifested in his works. "Walking in the truth" is peculiarly Johannine terminology. It means that the man lived the life of the gospel, was shaped in character by it, and was dominated and controlled by his instruction in Christ.

3. Render service (3 Jn. 5–8). The act that particularly drew the author's praise had been Gaius's hospitality to the itinerant missionaries who ministered to the church of which he was a member. Apparently Gaius's kindness subjected him to criticism from his fellow members. Gaius was commended by the elder for doing wisely that which the "elect lady" was warned against doing unwisely (2 John). The expression "send them on their way," as found in the NT, means to provide expenses for a missionary undertaking (Acts 15:3; 21:5; et al.). These missionaries deserved such help because they were representatives of Christ, for this is the meaning of the statement that they went out "for the sake of the Name" (3 Jn. 7). These missionaries also refrained from accepting help from the heathen to whom they ministered so as not to open up their work to suspicion of unworthy motives. Gaius was reminded that as he supported these workers for Christ, he shared in their labor.

4. Warning against Diotrephes (3 Jn. 9–10). Here is found the explanation of John's writing to Gaius individually. He had tried the approach of writing to the church, but with no results. This letter to the church had possibly been sent by a faithful Christian missionary named DEMETRIUS (see below), but among the elders of the church was an arrogant, domineering, and conceited man named DIOTREPHES, who had assumed the leadership of the church. Diotrephes had barred from the church some brothers (perhaps including Demetrius) and had suppressed the elder's letter. Apparently this selfish man was fearful that the church would acknowledge an authority other than his own, so he forbade the reading of the elder's letter or the entertaining of any messenger from him. The elder promised to confront this man shortly if he was able to come himself.

5. Commendation of Demetrius (3 Jn. 11–12). Demetrius was likely the bearer of 3 John. Gaius not only was warned against being like Diotrephes, but he also was encouraged to be like Demetrius. Demetrius was given a threefold commendation: (1) he was widely known in the church as a man of good character; (2) his life revealed his Christianity through his loyalty to the truth; (3) John himself testified to the kind of man he was.

6. Conclusion (3 Jn. 13–15). This conclusion is strikingly similar to that of 2 John, which may suggest that the two letters were written close to the same time. The elder stated his definite plan to visit Gaius shortly. The closing greeting, typically Christian, reveals the writer's extensive personal acquaintance in the church of which Gaius was a part.

(Important commentaries include R. S. Candlish, *The First Epistle of John* [1869]; B. F. Westcott, *The Epistles of St. John* [1883]; A. E. Brooke, *A Critical and Exegetical Commentary on the Johannine Epistles*, ICC [1912]; C. H. Dodd, *The Johannine Epistles*, MNTC [1946]; W. T. Conner, *The Epistles of John* [1957]; R. Bultmann, *The Johannine Epistles*, Hermeneia [1973]; I. H. Marshall, *The Epistles of John*, NICNT [1978]; R. E. Brown, *The Epistles of John*, AB 30 [1982]; S. S. Smalley, *1, 2, 3 John*, WBC 51 [1984]; J. R. W. Stott, *The Letters of John*, TNTC, rev. ed. [1988]; J. L. Houlden, *A Commentary on the Johannine Epistles*, BNTC, rev. ed. [1994]; G. Strecker, *The Johannine Letters*, Hermeneia [1996]; C. G. Kruse, *The Letters of John* [2000]; D. L. Akin, *1, 2, 3 John*, NAC, 38 [2001]; J. Painter, *1, 2, and 3 John*, SP 18 [2002]; M. M. Culy, *1, 2, 3 John: A Handbook on the Greek Text* [2004].

(See also R. E. Brown, *The Community of the Beloved Disciple* [1979]; J. Lieu, *The Second and Third Epistles of John: History and Background* [1986]; G. M. Burge, *The Anointed Community: The Holy Spirit in the Johannine Tradition* [1987]; J. Lieu, *The Theology of the Johannine Epistles* [1991]; and the bibliography compiled by W. E. Mills, *The Letters of John* [2002].)   H. L. DRUMWRIGHT, JR.

John, Gospel of. The "fourth gospel," as it is often called, probably influenced Christian thought during the first centuries of the church more decisively than any other book of the NT. It was accorded a place of apostolic authority from the first, as witnessed by several patristic writers. After AUGUSTINE, however, Pauline writings made the major contribution to Christian theology. In recent times it often has been the center of controversy, occasioned more often by dogmatic considerations than historical or literary data. A major factor in the discussion is the relationship of this gospel to the other three. In this article consideration is given first to the data on which conclusions must be based, reserving for later consideration matters of interpretation. In this procedure a greater objectivity is sought.

   I. Structure
  II. Content
     A. Text
     B. Vocabulary
     C. Major events
     D. Major ideas
 III. Distinctive features
     A. Data peculiar to John
     B. Comparison with the synoptics and Acts
     C. Comparison with the Epistles
 IV. Background
     A. OT
     B. Jewish literature
     C. Pagan literature
  V. Purpose, date, and author
     A. Purpose
     B. Date
     C. Author
     D. John's gospel as history

I. Structure. No two students of John's gospel will agree as to the best way to exhibit the train of thought conveyed therein. The following detailed outline is presented as the result of careful study, but not necessarily as the original author himself would have displayed it.

I. Introduction (Jn. 1:1–51)
   A. Prologue (1:1–18)
      1. The relation of the Son to God (1:1–2)
      2. The relation of the Son to the cosmos (1:3–5)
      3. The relation of the Son to John the Baptist (1:6–8)
      4. The relation of the Son to the world (1:9–16)
      5. The relation of the Son to Moses (1:17–18)
   B. Jesus presented (1:19–51)
      1. By John the Baptist as the Lamb of God (1:19–36)
      2. To the disciples as the Messiah (1:37–51)

II. Public ministry: the book of signs (2:1—12:50)
   A. Initial encounters (2:1—4:54)
      1. The first sign (2:1–12)
         a. The occasion (2:1–5)
         b. The sign accomplished (2:6–8)
         c. The result—belief (2:9–11)
         d. In Capernaum (2:12)
      2. First Passover—the new temple (2:13–25)
         a. The temple cleansed (2:13–17)
         b. Reactions to the cleansing (2:18–25)
            (1) The Jews challenge it (2:18–20)
            (2) The disciples believe (2:21–22)
            (3) Many believe in Jesus (2:23–25)
      3. The new birth (3:1–17)
         a. Demanded (3:1–3)
         b. Explained (3:4–8)
         c. The condition of its reception (3:9–12)
         d. The ascent of the Son of Man (3:13–15)
         e. The descent of the Son of God (3:16–17)
      4. Responsible response to the light (3:18–21)
      5. The new Master (3:22–36)
         a. John and Jesus make disciples (3:22–26)
         b. The subordination of John (3:27–30)
         c. The supremacy of Jesus (3:31–36)
      6. Water of life for the Samaritans (4:1–42)
         a. Jesus tired and hungry (4:1–6)
         b. The Samaritan woman's awakening (4:7–15)
         c. The woman's conversion (4:16–26)
         d. The woman's witness (4:27–30)
         e. The disciples challenged (4:31–38)
         f. The Samaritans believe (4:39–42)
      7. The second sign: a son healed (4:43–54)
         a. Galileans believe (4:43–45)
         b. A king's officer believes (4:46–54)
            (1) The petition for healing (4:46–47)
            (2) Faith tested (4:48–50)
            (3) Faith confirmed (4:51–54)
   B. Mounting hostility (5:1—12:50)
      1. The third sign (5:1–47)
         a. The cripple healed (5:1–9)
         b. Jesus accused (5:10–18)
            (1) Of Sabbath desecration (5:10–16)
            (2) Of blasphemy (5:17–18)
         c. Jesus' defense (5:19–47)
            (1) Father and Son are coworkers (5:19–30)
            (2) Witnesses summoned (5:31–47)
      2. The fourth sign: the second Passover (6:1–71)
         a. Five thousand fed (6:1–15)
         b. Jesus, master of the storm (6:16–21)
         c. Works or faith? (6:22–29)
         d. Bread of Life (6:30–59)
         e. Words of Life (6:60–71)
      3. Feast of Tabernacles (7:1–71)
         a. Jesus' brothers skeptical (7:1–5)
         b. Jesus' delay in departure (7:6–9)
         c. Jesus' whereabouts questioned (7:10–13)

d. Jesus' teaching in the temple (7:14–24)
e. Jesus' origin and destination disputed (7:25–36)
f. The advent of the Spirit (7:37–43)
g. Nicodemus calls for justice (7:44–52)
4. Woman taken in adultery (7:53—8:11)
   a. The test question (7:53—8:6)
   b. Jesus' answer (8:7–11)
5. The fifth sign: the Light of the World (8:12—9:41)
   a. Its source in the Father (8:12–20)
   b. Its judgment (8:21–30)
   c. Its mission: freedom through truth (8:31–38)
   d. Its lineage (8:39–59)
   e. Its remedy for physical blindness (9:1–34)
   f. Its exposure of spiritual blindness (9:35–41)
6. True and false shepherds (10:1–39)
   a. The parable of the good shepherd (10:1–6)
   b. The parable explained (10:7–18)
   c. True and false sheep (10:19–30)
   d. Jesus nearly stoned (10:31–39)
7. Retirement to Judea and Bethany (10:40—12:11)
   a. Beyond Jordan: many believe (10:40–42)
   b. The sixth sign: resurrection (11:1–53)
      (1) Recalled to Bethany (11:1–16)
      (2) Lazarus lives again (11:17–53)
   c. Retirement near Ephraim (11:54–57)
   d. Anointing at Bethany (12:1–11)
8. Jesus' last public appearance (12:12–50)
   a. His triumphal entry (12:12–19)
   b. Request of the Greeks (12:20–26)
   c. Rationale of Jesus' death (12:27–36)
   d. Unbelief explained (12:37–43)
   e. Jesus' last public statement (12:44–50)

III. Private conference with disciples (13:1—17:26)
   A. The third Passover: Last Supper (13:1–38)
      1. The footwashing (13:1–11)
      2. The washing explained (13:12–20)
      3. Betrayal predicted (13:21–30)
      4. The new commandment (13:31–35)
      5. Denial predicted (13:36–38)
   B. Preparation for Jesus' departure (14:1—17:26)
      1. The true way (14:1–7)
      2. Father and Son together (14:7–11)
      3. Discipleship means obedience (14:12–17)
      4. Christian unity (14:18—15:11)
         a. Of Father, Son, believer (14:18–24)
         b. Of Son, Spirit, believer (14:25–31)
         c. Of vine and branches (15:1–8)
      5. Christian love (15:9–17)
      6. World's hatred (15:18–25)
      7. The Paraclete (15:26—16:15)
      8. Jesus' departure and return (16:16–33)
      9. Jesus' pastoral prayer (17:1–26)
         a. Petition for himself (17:1–5)
         b. Petition for disciples (17:6–11)
         c. Petition for future disciples (17:12–26)
IV. Jesus is glorified (18:1—21:25)
   A. In suffering and death (18:1—19:42)
      1. The arrest (18:1–14)
      2. Peter's denial (18:15–18, 25–27)
      3. The trial by the Jews (18:19–28)
      4. The trial before Pilate (18:29—19:16)
      5. The crucifixion scene (19:17–30)
      6. Jesus' death (19:31–37)
      7. Jesus' burial (19:38–42)
   B. In resurrection and life (20:1—21:25)
      1. The appearances in Jerusalem (20:1–31)
         a. To Mary (20:1–18)
         b. To ten disciples (20:19–23)
         c. To Thomas (20:24–31)
      2. Appearance in Galilee (21:1–23)
         a. Futile fishing (21:1–8)

b. Jesus at breakfast (21:9–14)
   c. Jesus interviews Peter (21:15–23)
3. Final attestation of authorship (21:24–25)

In structure, the fourth gospel differs from the other three in several respects: (1) there is no mention of Jesus' birth and youth; (2) relatively little is said about Jesus' early Galilean ministry, the stress being on his Jerusalem ministry; (3) in this account Jesus visits Jerusalem for the Passover three times, in the synoptics once; (4) in this gospel much more attention is given to Jesus' last words with his disciples; and (5) the book is introduced by what is often called a prologue (Jn. 1:1–18) and closes with an epilogue (ch. 21).

II. Content

A. Text. The earliest extant portion of the NT comes from the Gospel of John: Rylands Papyrus 457 (P^{52}) on Jn. 18:31–33, 37–38, dated c. A.D. 130. In addition, BODMER PAPYRI II (P^{66}, a nearly complete copy of the fourth gospel) and XV (P^{75}, which preserves most of the first 15 chapters) date from the first part of the 3rd cent. or earlier. Scholars have noted the high degree of correlation between these Bodmer texts (esp. P^{75}) and CODEX VATICANUS; in them, several passages of dubious authenticity are missing, including Jn. 5:4 and 7:59–8:11. In addition, they confirm the reading "only God" rather than "only Son" in 1:18. These findings tend to justify the labors of NT textual criticism, since they lend support to the general reliability of the Alexandrian text-type. See TEXT AND MANUSCRIPTS (NT) V. Many scholars consider 20:31 the original terminus of the gospel and ch. 21 an appendix added later. The stylistic differences, however, are slight, and all extant MSS include this chapter (the concluding postscript, 21:24–25, prob. is an attestation of apostolic authorship by the final editor).

B. Vocabulary. The characteristic Johannine vocabulary is an important clue to the meaning of the fourth gospel. Even the casual reader will be impressed by the remarkable paradox of simple diction and profound thought. The most characteristic terms in the Johannine vocabulary are common. Many of them, to the English reader, are monosyllabic. These include *word*, *son*, *light*, *life*, *know*, *love*, *hate*, and *truth*. Also prominent are *glory*, *darkness*, *belief*, and *evil*. Although the words are very commonplace, they carry an enormous weight of theology. Who can fathom the depth and breadth of such concepts in this gospel as life, light, glory, love, and truth? It is characteristic also of this author to use bold contrasts, such as between God and the devil, the believer and the world, light and darkness, truth and error, life and death. Probably the most important single term in this gospel is the word *life*. This is the central theme of the book. Although love is prominent here also, before there is love there must be life. However, in light of the Johannine prologue and its antecedents in the Genesis account of creation, it may well be that in a cosmological sense light comes before life. The basic theme of this gospel is that in Christ is life and "that life was the light of men" (Jn. 1:4) The purpose of the gospel is also summed up in terms of life. The end in view is eternal life and the means to that end is belief in the Son of God (20:31).

C. Major events

1. Events included. Most of the events reported in the Gospel of John are found nowhere else. Only one miracle, the feeding of the 5,000, is common to all four Gospels. John alone records the initial encounter between Jesus and the disciples of John in Judea. This is followed by the wedding in CANA, which John calls the first miracle, or SIGN. The cleansing of the temple in Jerusalem is reported in connection with the first PASSOVER visit, creating the problem of whether there were two cleansings or one; if the latter, then John's account places the event at the beginning of Jesus' public ministry, whereas the synoptics state that it comes at the close. The interview with Nicodemus in Jerusalem is reported at length, followed by a discourse concerning John and the followers of Jesus.

The scene then shifts to Samaria with a lengthy report of Jesus' interview with the woman of SYCHAR. In Jn. 5 Jesus is again in Jerusalem, where the third of his major signs, or miracles, occurred—the healing at the pool of BETHESDA. This event leads to a lengthy dialogue with hostile Jewish leaders about keeping the SABBATH and Jesus' relation to the Father.

At the second Passover, Jesus is in Galilee, and the discourse on the bread of life follows the feeding of 5,000, who are pilgrims (Jn. 6). The next chapter reports his presence again in Jerusalem for the Feast of Tabernacles, where he delivered a major speech on the coming of the Holy Spirit. Extensive discourses follow concerning his relation with God the Father. The theme of light is introduced again in ch. 8 and continued in ch. 9. Here Jesus cures a blind man at the pool of SILOAM and states that the people who are most truly blind are those whose blindness is spiritual and self-imposed, whereas those afflicted with physical blindness, through no fault of their own, are led to the light (9:39–41). Thus the miracle, like many others in this gospel, is also a parable. Still in Jerusalem, the discourse concerning the good shepherd is at the same time a condemnation of false shepherds and ends with added hostility so keen that Jesus retires from public view (10:40). The sickness and death of LAZARUS brings Jesus again from retirement into Bethany, where Lazarus is brought back to life. This, in turn, leads to a greater determination on the part of the Jewish leaders to do away with him (11:53–57).

The third Passover brought Jesus again to Jerusalem, or rather to his Bethany headquarters at the home of Mary, Martha, and Lazarus (see MARY #3). At a supper honoring Lazarus, Mary anointed Jesus with costly ointment, much to the disgust of JUDAS ISCARIOT. The Passover feast, meanwhile, had brought many hundreds of people to the Holy City, and it was then that the triumphal entry occurred with three groups of people centering on Jesus: a group who had witnessed the resurrection of Lazarus, another group of pilgrims from the N, and a third group residing in Jerusalem (Jn. 12:12–18). An inquiry by several Greeks led Jesus to make an important prediction concerning the significance of his death, using the analogy of grain that must be buried in the earth before it can bring forth new life, an obvious prediction of his own immediate future.

John devotes more attention to the last days of Jesus' ministry in Jerusalem than any of the other writers. Following the triumphal entry was the feast with the disciples and the announcement of the betrayal by Judas, the departure of Judas for this purpose, the washing of the feet of the Twelve by the Master. and the extended discourse concerning the future, followed by the high priestly intercessory prayer of Christ (Jn. 17).

In the events that follow, John's account parallels closely that of the synoptists. This includes the arrest in the garden, the trial before the Jewish authorities, then the trial before Pilate, the sentence to death, the crucifixion, and burial. In reporting the resurrection, John's account supplements that of the others and presents events otherwise unknown. These include the appearance to Mary Magdalene (see MARY #5), to THOMAS, and to seven disciples in Galilee, ending with Jesus' dialogue with Peter.

2. Events omitted. One of the problems of the fourth gospel is the large number of important events mentioned in the synoptics but ignored in John. These include the nativity stories and the parables. There is no mention in this gospel of the EXORCISM of devils, even though Jesus is thrice accused of being demon possessed. In this gospel no attention is paid to publicans, lepers, or children, as is characteristic of the other three. No mention is made of the naming of the twelve apostles. There is no SERMON ON THE MOUNT or on the Plain, such as Matthew and Luke report. The calling of sinners to repentance is notably absent in this account. The APOCALYPTIC features of the synoptists, including

Greek Orthodox priest standing beside the traditional well of Jacob (Church of Jacob's Well at Sychar). Jesus spoke with a Samaritan woman at this well (Jn. 4).

eschatological themes and the warnings against the judgment of hell, are not specified in this gospel. Many of Jesus' characteristic apothegms and proverbs, such as "you are the salt of the earth," are not included in this account. No mention is made of the institution of the EUCHARIST, although it is implied in Jn. 6. John also omits Jesus' prayer in Gethsemane. There is no description of the trial before Caiaphas, though it is alluded to in the account. Jesus' ascension on Mount Olivet is omitted, although the theme of ascent/descent is rather characteristic of the gospel. The major aspect of the Johannine problem is that of explaining the points at which this gospel differs so radically from the first three, and why.

D. Major ideas

1. Life. As noted previously, John's major concern is with divine LIFE, the life that is in God and which under certain conditions can be shared by men and women. The basic condition to this sharing is belief in Jesus as the Son of God. This overarching concern dominates the gospel from beginning to end. Unlike Luke, this author is not primarily concerned to set down an orderly account of the actual events. Instead, he is very selective, his choice being dictated by a didactic purpose; for John is interested not only in the events, but also in their significance.

2. Witness. One of the most distinctive features of the fourth gospel is the emphasis upon witness. The term *witness* occurs thirty-four times as a verb form and thirteen times as a noun, a total of forty-seven occurrences as compared with sixteen in all of the synoptics. The author classifies himself primarily as a witness (Jn. 1:14, 16; 19:35; 21:24; cf. 5:30–47). His method is not only that of marshaling evidence to convince the readers, but of making a personal declaration of what he has experienced. The point is that faith is based on evidence, either firsthand or secondhand, and whereas belief based on evidence is good, belief that is not dependent on sensory evidence is better (20:29).

3. Belief. Witnessing is designed to induce belief, that is, FAITH in Jesus' claim to be the Son of God and the only source of spiritual life. The noun *pistis* G4411 does not occur, but the verb *pisteuō* G4409 is used more than eighty times. Belief, or faith, is for John not primarily confidence in the final outcome, as in Hebrews, but rather committal to the person of Jesus Christ (Jn. 6:29; cf. 10:32; 17:3). It goes beyond the acceptance of testimony concerning the validity of the proposition; it is an existential decision between light and darkness, God and the world, truth and error. Hindrances to faith are not lack of evidence, but the subjective factors of pride, self-esteem, a desire for worldly honor, and stubbornness (5:44; 8:43; 9:22; 12:39).

4. Glory. Unlike the first epistle of Peter and the letters of Paul, GLORY (*doxa* G1518) is not that which follows humiliation in time; it is linked with humiliation and transforms it. Glory is basically a revelation of God's presence. This glory is resident in Jesus, and its radiance is in contrast to that of the OT (Jn. 1:14–18). Instead of the SHEKINAH glory dwelling in the Jerusalem temple, it dwells in Jesus, who is the true temple (2:19). The distinctive feature in this gospel is that glory emerges from the ignominy of death (11:4; 12:33; 21:19). Jesus' suffering, death, resurrection, and ascension are seen as one event (7:39; 12:28–33). John was convinced that the glory is essentially akin to that witnessed by Isaiah (Jn. 12:41).

5. Regeneration. A metaphor that John develops with an emphasis not found in the other Gospels is that of the "new birth," that is, REGENERATION. This underlying current surfaces at Jn. 1:12, 13; 3:1–10; 8:39–45. Whereas Paul speaks of the new life in Christ under the caption of JUSTIFICATION and employs legal terms, John uses the biological concept of birth. Thus the entrance into the Christian life is envisioned as being "born of God" in addition to being born in the natural manner (1:12). In the interview with Nicodemus, Jesus stated emphatically that the condition of participating in the KINGDOM OF GOD is being "born of water and the Spirit" (3:5). Here the contrast is made between physical life and spiritual life, a theme that is characteristic of this gospel. Just as physical life comes from one's human parents, so spiritual life comes from God through the Son and Holy Spirit. This matter of spiritual generation is explained at some length in ch. 8, where Jesus accused the Jews of having as their father the devil and asserted that a true Jew is not one who can trace his ancestry to Abraham, but rather one who is in the spiritual lineage of Abraham (8:39–58). This lineage can be identified by obedience to divine revelation. In this case, God's revelation is through his Son. The idea is not new, but the way John expresses it is unique. The concept of spiritual birth is found elsewhere in the NT (note esp. 1 Pet. 1:3, 23; 2:2). The concept has had a powerful influence on consequent Christian theology.

6. The world. This gospel contains strong emphasis upon a moral dualism—between light and darkness, good and evil, God and the evil one, the believer and the WORLD. This theme runs throughout the gospel but is especially prominent in the prologue (Jn. 1:5, 10–12). It occurs again in one of the key verses of the gospel: "This is the verdict: Light has come into the world, but men loved darkness instead of light because their deeds were evil" (3:19). It appears again in Jesus' discourse with his brothers, where the basic hostility between the redeemer and the world is stated: "The world cannot hate you, but it hates me because I testify that what it does is evil" (7:7). This hostility between light and darkness is again expressed after the healing of the blind man (9:38–41). The theme is especially prominent in the extended discourse with the disciples prior to Jesus' arrest. The hatred of the world is a basic fact of life that they must face (15:18—16:33). In the ensuing confrontation they are assured of the help of the Holy Spirit as their advocate (16:7–11; cf. Lk. 12:12).

7. Love. Although the theme of LOVE is prominent in all Christian writing, it is especially conspicuous in the Johannine writings. The relation of God to the hostile world is basically that of love (Jn. 3:16). Also, the quality that distinguishes Jesus' disciples from all others is love (13:34–35). The climax of Jesus' intercessory prayer is the request for the love that unites the Father, the Son, and the believers (17:26). In Jesus' dialogue with Peter, the quality prized in the relationship is love (21:15–19). This theme is emphasized even more in the companion volume to the gospel, the first epistle of John (see JOHN, EPISTLES OF).

8. Truth. The appeal of this gospel to the world dominated by Greek culture is perhaps reflected by the emphasis on TRUTH. God's revelation is equated with truth. The prologue points out that whereas the law was mediated through MOSES, Jesus Christ mediated a twofold blessing—the Hebraic benefit of grace and the Greek benefit of truth (though John prob. means "truth" primarily in the OT sense of "reliability" rather than in a philosophical sense). Both the Hebraic and Hellenistic spiritual blessings converge in Jesus, the Son of God. Later, Jesus assured his disciples that obedience to his word would assure them of the truth that emancipates (Jn. 8:31–32). Jesus is the embodiment of truth (14:6). This truth is projected into a skeptical and perplexed world represented by PILATE's unanswered query, "What is truth?" (18:38). The world itself is divided into those who are of the truth and those who are in sin and error (18:37). Finally, the gospel itself claims to be the expression of truth. The written record is that which conforms to the facts; such is the solemn affirmation that closes the volume (21:24).

These are some of the main ideas that constitute the fabric of this gospel. John is not content simply to record historical events; he is selective in the events he chooses to illustrate some of these themes. The themes are like the themes of great symphonies, many of them introduced in the prologue, or prelude, and woven throughout the fabric, one coming to prominence now, another later. John's thought is often described as cyclic. It is something like a circular staircase or a spiral, in which a theme will appear and then recede to appear later at a higher level. John does not treat one topic in one place and then go on to another topic, but keeps them in suspension through his narrative. The author, for example, takes care to point out hindrances to belief, such as an attitude of undue appreciation for the esteem of one's fellow men (Jn. 5:44) or the fear of community pressure to conform, for example, that which inhibited the parents of the man born blind (9:22). See further JOHANNINE THEOLOGY.

III. Distinctive features

A. Data peculiar to John. The relationship between John and the Synoptic Gospels is seen not only in what John omits, but also in what he includes and the others omit. The prologue is found nowhere else in the Scriptures, and the distinctive contribution is John's use of the term LOGOS and its application to Christ. The great affirmation is that the eternal word became flesh in time. This is John's way of referring to the INCARNATION, which parallels Paul's description of the KENOSIS (Phil. 2:5–11). Only John mentions the calling of the disciples of JOHN THE BAPTIST in the Jordan valley, specifically Peter, Andrew, Philip, Nathanael, and presumably, the author himself. The synoptic accounts place the formal enlisting of these men in the apostolic circle at the shores of the Sea of Galilee. To harmonize the two accounts, it is necessary to assume that the latter was the confirmation of an earlier acquaintance reported by John. Also peculiar to John is the reference to Jesus as the Lamb of God, from the lips of John the Baptist (Jn. 1:29, 36). The emphasis upon the SON OF MAN in this context is also quite distinctive, including the allusion to Jacob's ladder (1:51).

Only John reports the episode at CANA, the significance of which is that it strengthened the disciples' belief in the adequacy of their master (Jn. 2:11). The important interview with NICODEMUS, which is one expression of the heart of the gospel, is reported only in John, together with the allusion to the serpent in the wilderness (3:14). A portrayal of John the Baptist as friend of the bridegroom (3:29) is found nowhere else in the NT, although in Ephesians and in Revelation Christ is mentioned as the husband of the church (Eph. 5:25; Rev. 21:2). The interview with the woman at Samaria is the occasion of the introduction of Jesus as the giver of the water of life, a theme that reappears in Jesus' statement at the Feast of Tabernacles (Jn. 7:37).

In addition to the healing of the man at the pool of BETHESDA, John alone reports the dialogue between Jesus and his critics on the issue of belief and the witnesses (Jn. 5:32–47). Here, as elsewhere in the gospel, the author stresses the intimate relationship between Jesus Christ and God the Father. The problem is to state the closest conceivable relationship and yet maintain a distinction. It is compressed in a statement, "I and the Father are one" (10:30). The discourse on the bread of life following the feeding of the multitude is found only in John (ch. 6). This is the closest John comes to a teaching concerning the Eucharist. The visit to Jerusalem referred to in John (chs. 7–9) has no parallel in the synoptic accounts. This visit was characterized by an acrimonious dialogue between Jesus and his friends who registered an increasing degree of skepticism (7:5). The people speculate concerning Jesus' identity. The growing conviction on the part of the populace that he is what he claims to be is matched by a contrasting degree of hostility to the claim that he is the expected MESSIAH. This conflict is dramatically portrayed following the healing of the blind man at the Pool of SILOAM. The reader is enabled to see the issues laid bare. Effective use of contrast is made as the author delineates the reactions of the man himself, his parents, the Pharisees, and Jesus.

John is the only evangelist who employs the analogy of sheepfold and shepherd, although the image of "lost sheep" is found elsewhere (Lk. 15:3–7). The concept of SHEPHERD was a familiar one to users of the OT (Ps. 23; 80; Ezek. 34). It proved to be the church's favorite portrayal of its Lord and Savior (1 Pet. 2:25; 5:1–5). The miracles, or signs, that John singles out for special treatment

John alone records the healing of an invalid by the pool of Bethesda and the subsequent words of Jesus regarding belief and witness (Jn. 5). This model of 1st-cent. Jerusalem (looking SW) shows the twin pools that are probably referred to in this passage.

include the wedding feast at Cana, the nobleman's son, the lame man at Bethesda, the blind man at Siloam, the walking on the sea (ch. 6), and the culminating sign, that of bringing LAZARUS back to life.

The raising of Lazarus is presented as a historical event, but the account leaves the reader wondering why it was not mentioned in the synoptics. Whereas the latter view the cleansing of the temple as the immediate cause of the steps to kill Jesus, in John's account it is the raising of Lazarus that brings events to a head (Jn. 12:10–11). Only John reports the interpretation voiced by CAIAPHAS concerning the necessity of putting Jesus to death (11:49–51). Only John reports Jesus' interview with the Greeks and the ensuing theme of life out of death after the analogy of the sowing of the seed and the resulting harvest (12:20–26). Only John reports the washing of the disciples' feet and the lesson in humble service that it teaches (13:1–20).

Especially prized by readers of the gospel are chs. 14–17, which reflect the intimate conversation between Jesus and the worried disciples. The role of the PARACLETE—Comforter, Counselor, or Advocate—is found nowhere else in the Scriptures except in the first epistle of John (1 Jn. 2:1). The HOLY SPIRIT is equated with the Advocate and the Spirit of truth (Jn. 14:16, 17; 15:26; an interesting parallel to the latter designation is seen in the Qumran literature, where the spirit of truth is in contrast to the spirit of error and of darkness, 1QS, III, 13—IV, 26). This is climaxed by the Lord's intercessory prayer, which only John records.

Altogether, John reports fourteen dialogues that are characterized by (1) a question from the hearers, (2) the Master's answer in enigmatic form, (3) the misunderstanding of his answer, and (4) Jesus' clarification of the issue. The conversation with Nicodemus well illustrates this sequence. Nicodemus asks, "How can a man be born when he is old?" (Jn. 3:4). Jesus replied, "Flesh gives birth to flesh, but the Spirit gives birth to spirit" (3:6). The response was, "How can this be?" (3:9), leading to further explanation.

In this gospel, NATHANAEL and THOMAS are given special attention. The relation of the BELOVED DISCIPLE and Peter is given prominence, with the beloved disciple being, on at least three occasions, the first to perceive the spiritual significance of words and events, and then sharing it with Peter (Jn. 13:24–26; 2:8; 21:7). John alone reports the committal of Jesus' mother to the beloved disciple and the emergence of blood from the side of Jesus (19:25–27, 34–37). In John's account of the burial and resurrection, Mary Magdalene receives special prominence, as does Nicodemus. Nicodemus is mentioned three times in John and nowhere else in the NT. He appears first as a seeker, then as a defender of justice and of Jesus, and finally as one of the last to place him in the tomb (3:1; 7:50; 19:39).

These indicate that the fourth gospel presents an independent report from that of the other three. Although some scholars view this as a protest or a correction to the synoptics, others argue that it is designed to supplement rather than to alter the report of the other Gospels. Luke and John appear to have the most in common, but both show independence in presentation. All four evangelists drew on a common oral tradition.

B. Comparison with the synoptics and Acts. The fourth gospel is designed for the world at large, to convince the uncommitted (Jn. 20:31). The others are written with a somewhat different purpose. Luke, for example, writes to believers to confirm their faith (Lk. 1:1–4). It has been suggested that Matthew had in mind people of the Jewish nation because of his emphasis on fulfillment of prophecy. It has been suggested that Mark was concerned primarily with the Roman world, hence his emphasis upon action rather than upon discussion.

The eschatological element is not stressed in John. In the synoptics, John the Baptist predicts a coming judgment with the Messiah serving as judge, gathering the wheat and burning the chaff. This eschatological motif of judgment is lacking in the fourth gospel. In the synoptics, many of the parables deal with the last judgment, such as the parables of the tares and of the fish; John has nothing comparable. The warning against hell fire, where the worm dies not and the fire is not quenched, prominent in the synoptics, is completely lacking in John. The synoptists, especially Luke, have parables that stress repentance (Lk. 15) and God's willingness to accept the sinner, whereas in John's gospel, stress is placed on the obstacles the sinner encounters in his quest for saving faith. In this gospel, therefore, the stress is upon evidence, witness to the evidence, belief and hindrances thereto. Demonology, so prominent in the synoptics, has no parallel in John, although three times Jesus is accused of being demon possessed (Jn. 7:20; 8:48; 10:20; cf. Mk. 3:21).

The other evangelists stress that the HOLY SPIRIT will come to the defense of the disciples when they are persecuted for their faith (Matt. 10:20). A similar role is mentioned in the fourth gospel, where the Holy Spirit is the Paraclete, or the Advocate, who will defend persecuted disciples (Jn. 15:18—16:15). The same idea is common to all four evangelists, namely, that the Spirit will serve the believer as defense attorney. Formidable problems present themselves in an attempt to closely correlate the fourth gospel and the Acts with reference to the Holy Spirit. In Jn. 7:37, it is said that the Spirit is not to be given until after the glorification of Jesus. After his resurrection and before his ascension, Jesus breathed on the disciples and they received the Holy Spirit (20:22). Many scholars think of this inbreathing of the Spirit by the Master as prophetic of the fuller outpouring of the Holy Spirit at PENTECOST. According to E. F. Scott, C. H. Dodd, and others, however, the emphasis in this gospel is not upon the gift of the Spirit at Pentecost, nor on the second physical advent of the Lord, but rather upon the Spirit fulfilling the numerous predictions of Jesus' return, as set forth in Jn. 20. This hardly seems valid, inasmuch as Jesus was still with them when the inbreathing occurred. There seems to be, therefore, no essential contradiction between the doctrine of the Spirit in John and that in Luke–Acts.

There is, however, a difference of emphasis. In John, the ministry of the Spirit is to reveal Christ, to illuminate, to teach, and to console, whereas in Acts, the function of the Spirit is more activistic and dynamic. In Acts, it is the Spirit who inspired the witnesses and thrusted them out to the world at large; the Spirit bestowed the gift of tongues and other charismata (see SPIRITUAL GIFTS), and even transported a person bodily, as in the case of Philip (Acts 8:39). In John, however, the primary function of the Spirit is to provide guidance "into all truth" (Jn. 16:13). In Acts it is to empower, and in Paul's writings it is to cleanse (Gal. 5:15–16; cf. Acts 15:9). As E. F. Scott has noted, the doctrine of the Spirit in John is one of the most distinctive and important contributions this gospel makes to NT theology.

In John is no specific mention of the ascension into heaven as is true of the synoptics and Acts. The nearest approach to this is Jesus' statement to Mary that he had not yet ascended to his Father (Jn. 20:17). The theme of ascension, however, does appear in the gospel (chs. 3, 8, and 20). This has led some scholars, with C. H. Dodd, to see in John a "realized eschatology." In substance, this is the belief that when the gospel was written, the church had given up the expectation of the Lord's early bodily return and instead substituted a renewed emphasis upon the ministry of the Holy Spirit in whom Jesus actually returned. Thus John "demythologized" Jewish apocalyptic ESCHATOLOGY according to this viewpoint. (Others use the term "realized eschatology" as a notion complementary, not antithetical, to future eschatology.)

C. Comparison with the Epistles

1. Pauline. Paul shows concern with the sins that especially characterized the Gentiles (Rom. 1:18–32; 3:1–20; Gal. 5:15–21). When Paul speaks of the sins of the Jews, it is in the areas of unbelief, hypocrisy, and legalism (Rom. 2; 10). John is concerned less with the catalogue of the various types of sins that characterized the pagans of the day from whom Paul's converts came. John, rather, is concerned with the sinner's chronic preference for darkness rather than light (Jn. 3:19). He is concerned chiefly with the problem of unbelief and the things that hinder a person's coming to faith, hence to life (5:44). He does not catalogue the vices of Jesus' enemies, as is seen in Matthew (e.g., Matt. 23:2–39), but deals rather with the underlying principle that leads to rejection of the light and the light bearer (Jn. 3:19).

The concept of righteousness is less prominent in John than in Paul. Whereas Paul speaks of the righteousness of God as the dominant factor with which we must reckon, John stresses such attributes of God as LOVE and LIGHT. Both stress God's love to us (Jn. 3:16; cf. Rom. 5:6–11). Paul is more concerned with Mount Sinai and its application to the Christian gospel (Gal. 4); John dwells more in the wilderness with its symbolism of water and manna (Jn. 3:5; 6:31–35). Whereas Paul stresses Jesus' death and resurrection, John emphasizes Jesus' incarnation and ascension. By the ascension, John includes his death upon the cross that in itself is an ascension (3:14; 8:37; 12:25).

Because Paul thought in terms of law, his nomenclature is that of a court of law; hence his terms are adoption, justification, propitiation, and reconciliation. John preferred the biological analogy of birth (Jn. 1:12; 3:6; cf. 8:41, 44). Both, however, are in agreement with reference to the basic tenets of the Christian faith: upon the substitutionary nature of Christ's death, his vicarious atonement, bodily resurrection, appearances, and ascension. In eschatology, Paul gives much greater prominence to the return of Christ, the last judgment, and the restoration of all things to the jurisdiction of Christ. John seems less influenced by Jewish APOCALYPTIC thought.

2. Petrine. Both the Gospel of John and the first epistle of Peter stress the concept of persecution and suffering for the sake of the gospel. According to 1 Peter, the suffering is caused by external pressures, reflecting a period of persecution, presumably by the leaders of the Roman world. In the fourth gospel, however, the persecution is anticipated in the future, and its similarity to the persecution of Jesus by the Jews is pointed out. In John, the chief antagonists of the gospel light are the Jewish leaders, whereas in Peter, the opposition is not pinpointed, but presumably it is the pagan world. In John, the hostility is portrayed more in general principles, as the conflict between light and darkness, the two being mutually antagonistic. This is especially prominent in Jn. 8, though it is anticipated in the prologue.

Common to 1 Peter and the fourth gospel is the concept of the new birth. In John, the birth is by water and spirit (Jn. 3:5); in 1 Peter we read, "For you have been born again, not of perishable seed, but of imperishable, through the living and enduring word of God" (1 Pet. 1:23). In both, the contrast between the physically born and the spiritually born is striking. In John, the two genealogies, or family trees, are conspicuous, especially in Jn. 8, where the children of the devil are in contrast to the children of light. The same parallel is seen in the Qumran writings, especially the *Manual of Discipline* and the *War Rule*. In Peter, the birth is through the word of God. It is the word that brings to birth and the word that nourishes the newborn (1 Pet. 1:3, 23; 2:2).

Another concept common to both John and Peter is that of SHEPHERD. In John, the good shepherd gives his life for the sheep; likewise in Peter, "the Shepherd and Overseer of your souls" is he who "bore our sins in his body on the tree" (1 Pet. 2:24–25). The concept of feeding the sheep is found only in the fourth gospel and 1 Peter. As Peter was urged to feed the sheep (Jn. 21:17), so Peter urges the elders to be "shepherds of God's flock" so that they can render a good account to the "Chief Shepherd," who will bestow "the crown of glory that will never fade away" (1 Pet. 5:2–4).

In John, the prime virtue is spiritual insight that leads to belief and hence to life and witnessing. In Peter, the virtues most urgently needed are those of constancy, of patience under test, of submission to authority, and of quiet continuing witness in a hostile world (Jn. 3:16–19; cf. 1 Pet. 4:1–19).

The eschatological emphasis in 2 Peter is not paralleled in the fourth gospel, nor does the gospel give a great deal of attention to the matter of growth in grace of the believer as is true of 2 Peter (cf. 2 Pet. 1:3–11). This epistle is a stirring summons to holy living in view of the imminent return of the Lord. In John, the emphasis is more upon embracing Christ as Lord and Savior and walking henceforth in his way of love.

3. Johannine. Although C. H. Dodd and others doubt whether the same person wrote both the Gospel of John and 1 John, the preponderance of evidence favors a common authorship of both. Even a superficial examination indicates the prominence in both of such elemental concepts as *witness, light, love, truth*. Common to both is the simplicity of diction linked with profundity of thought. Common also to both is the concept of the believer's relation to God in biological terms. Thus in the epistle, the children of the devil and the children of God are in marked contrast not only with reference to their source of life, but in their relation to sin (Jn. 8:44; 1 Jn. 3:8–10). He that is born of God does not commit sin, whereas he that does sin is of the devil (1 Jn. 3:8–10). In both, the hostility of the world is stressed.

The central theme of both is spiritual life: it is not merely something temporal, or a continuation of the present life; it is rather a life that is different in nature. Because it is essentially spiritual rather than mental or physical, eternal life begins in the believer when he receives Christ (Jn. 1:12). It is a qualitatively superior type of life that begins with belief and lasts into eternity. Brotherly love is stressed in both, especially in ch. 13, and is found throughout the first epistle. Love is equated with God, and the "sons of God" possess this love as a bestowal of grace, not something inherited. The epistle is more concerned than is the gospel with expressing love in deeds, thus the epistle is the more practical of the two (1 Jn. 3:14–18). Both these writings contain the term Paraclete, which is found nowhere else in the NT (Jn. 14–16; 1 Jn. 2:1).

Among the differences is the fact that in the epistle there is no expressed concern for the apostasy of the nation of Israel. The CHRISTOLOGY is different as well. In the gospel, the stress is on Jesus' deity; in the epistle, the stress is on his humanity—to refute the heresy of DOCETISM, the doctrine that Jesus' humanity was not real.

4. Hebrews. Although the form and nomenclature is strikingly different, the basic theology of both the epistle to the HEBREWS and the fourth gospel is the same. In both there is stress upon Jesus as the Son of God; in both there is stress upon his condescension in taking human nature. The incarnation is spelled out more in detail in Hebrews, noting that incarnation involves sharing death with the rest of mankind (Heb. 2:5–18).

Both John and Hebrews lay stress upon the experience of the Israelites in the wilderness. This appears in Hebrews, where the readers are urged to follow their Joshua into the Promised Land lest they meet with the tragedy resulting from unbelief, as did their ancestors in Sinai (Heb. 3–4). In John's treatment, the book of Exodus appears in the background (esp. Jn. 3 and 6) as offering a precedent for faith.

However, whereas John stresses belief as that which leads to life—a belief centering in Jesus as the Son of God—in Hebrews faith is paradoxical in nature in that it is a conviction of realities visible only to spiritual eyes. It is this that enabled

The Desert of Zin (view to the S from Avdat, with monastery in center of image). Both John and the epistle to the Hebrews stress the importance of Israel's experience in the wilderness.

the heroes and heroines of old to survive obstacles and inherit life. Thus the readers of this epistle are taught that faith involves confidence in God's availability and in his capability of seeing things through to a successful conclusion.

The humanity of Jesus is stressed perhaps more in Hebrews than in John. In Hebrews, the stress is upon his work as mediator, thus stressing the incarnation and Jesus' experience as a real person, "he learned obedience from what he suffered" (Heb. 5:8; cf. vv. 1–7; 2:5–18). In Hebrews, the OT priesthood is held up as God's provision for sins, which had a temporary effectiveness. In John, there is little concern for the priesthood as such, either past or present. The purposes of the two books are in contrast, as is easily apparent. John was written primarily to win the adherence of the masses to Jesus as Savior and Lord, whereas in Hebrews, the problem is to help the believers to be stabilized and not to abandon their faith in Jesus as their Lord. The danger confronting the recipients of Hebrews was a relapse into Judaism or indifference to the claims of the gospel. The danger in John was conformity to the spirit of the age that had a basic hostility to divine revelation because it cherished its own ways, its pride, and its prejudices, and did not wish to be disturbed.

The thought of the writers is quite distinct. In John, several ideas are kept in abeyance and wait to urge themselves upon the readers' attention; in the epistle to the Hebrews, however, the author has his argument well organized and moves from one thought to the other in steady sequence, rather than in a spiral, or cyclic, fashion. In Hebrews, there is greater concern with the subjective effects of the atonement in cleansing the conscience from dead works to serve the living and true God. In John, relatively less concern is placed upon personal sanctity of the believer and more upon calling his attention to Christ. In Hebrews, Jesus is the leader, the author, and perfecter of faith; in the fourth gospel, he is the Lamb of God who takes away the sins of the world and the One who is worthy of being king, but who deliberately rejected this role.

5. James and Jude. Parallels between the fourth gospel and the epistle of James are rare. Whereas John speaks of being born of the Spirit, James speaks of being brought forth by the word of truth—a different metaphor, but the same idea (Jas. 1:18). In James, relatively little attention is placed on the person and teachings of Christ and much upon the believers' conduct and attitude. To John, the crucial issue is entering by faith into the Christian fellowship, whereas in James there is an attempt to get Christians to be more than nominal adherents, to become sincere exemplars of the pure faith and of the wisdom that comes from above (Jas. 3:13–18).

Jude, like 2 Peter, is preoccupied with heresy and the SECOND COMING. The need for sound doctrine is stressed more prominently than in the Gospel of John.

IV. Background. The fourth gospel contains phrases and ideas that make an understanding of its background very important for adequate appreciation of its message.

A. OT. In the first half of the 20th cent., the prevailing view among critical scholars was that Greek thought was the dominant influence on the Gospel of John. Since then, however, there has been a growing recognition that the prevailing influence was Hebraic. This position has been vastly strengthened by the discovery of literature from the QUMRAN area that has many words and ideas paralleling that of John and that provides evidence that many of the assumed Hellenistic phrases and ideas were already in Palestine during the 1st cent. (see DEAD SEA SCROLLS).

The influence of the OT is very pronounced from the opening words of this gospel. The prologue is evocative of the Genesis account of CREATION with its description of the origin of light and life. Both Genesis and this gospel speak of all things originating with God through his word. The link between Genesis and John is doubtless Ps. 33, which states, "By the word of the LORD were the heavens made, / their starry host by the breath of his mouth" (v. 6). The psalmist continues, "For he spoke, and it came to be; / he commanded, and it stood firm" (v. 9). In John's prologue, likewise, the word is the agent in creation. Also included in the first chapter of this gospel is the contrast between law and grace, Moses and Christ (Jn. 1:17–18).

Elijah and Isaiah are alluded to in John the Baptist's conversation with the priests and Levites (Jn. 1:19–23). The LAMB OF GOD to which Jesus is compared by the Baptist (*amnos* G303, 1:29) probably refers to the sacrificial lamb of the PASSOVER, although C. H. Dodd thinks it has greater affinity to the warlike lamb of the Apocalypse (*arnion* G768, Rev. 5:6 et al.). The key to the answer is that the lamb is described as taking away the sins of the world. Doubtless, it is an allusion to the Suffering Servant of Isaiah (Isa. 53:7–12; cf. 1 Pet. 2:21–25 and see SERVANT OF THE LORD).

The influence of Jacob's vision of the ladder reaching to heaven is reflected in Jesus' prediction of a similar vision by his followers (Gen. 28:12; cf. Jn. 1:51). In this one chapter, Jesus is said to be greater than Moses, greater than Elijah, greater than the patriarch Jacob, and believed by Nathanael to be the Son of God and king of Israel (Jn. 1:49). He also is believed to be greater than the temple. The same idea is found in the synoptics but in a completely different context (Matt. 12:6; cf. Jn. 2:19).

Reminders of the Passover occur frequently in John, where it is explicitly stated that he attended this feast thrice during his public ministry. The discourse in Jn. 6, with its insistence that believers must eat the flesh of the son of God to have life, is based upon eating the paschal lamb on this occasion. The background of Genesis and Exodus is especially conspicuous in Jn. 3–6. Nicodemus is reminded of the serpent in the wilderness (3:14). The episode at the well near Sychar evokes memories of the patriarch Jacob and his purchase of the land near Shechem. The reference to the living water is a poignant reminder of their ancestors' desperate need of water during their Sinai sojourn when water was sometimes miraculously provided, thus sustaining life. Chapter 5 introduces the Sabbath controversy and its background of the institution of the Sabbath in the Pentateuch. Even greater emphasis is placed upon the MANNA of the wilderness sojourn and its vastly superior counterpart in Jesus Christ (ch. 6). Thus Jesus tells his hearers that they are witnesses to a greater miracle than even were their fathers who ate the manna.

Water from the rock is recalled on the occasion of the Feast of Tabernacles (Jn. 7:38–39; cf. Lev. 23:34–36; Num. 20:10–13). The reference to the Spirit here and in Jn. 3:8 has striking affinity with Ezek. 36:25–27, where the outpouring of the Spirit and the bestowal of a "new heart" are predicted. The striking analogy of Jesus as the good shepherd recalls several OT passages (Ps. 23; Isa. 40:11; Jer. 23:1–4; Ezek. 34). The analogy of the vine and branches, descriptive of the relation between Jesus and his followers, is meaningful because of extensive use of this analogy in the OT (Ps. 80:8–13; Isa. 5:1–7; Ezek. 15).

The influence of Isaiah is perhaps slightly less in this gospel as compared with the synoptics, especially Mark, though John does allude to Isaiah's vision in summing up the nation's response to Jesus (Jn. 12:38–41). One misses, however, the connection between Isaiah's role of the Messiah and its fulfillment in Jesus' ministry (cf. Isa. 61:1–6; Lk. 4:18–20). There is less overt attention to prophecy and its fulfillment in this gospel as compared with Matthew. This author is not so much concerned with direct quotations as with allusions. OT influence is more implicit than explicit, but its influence is deep and pervasive. It is remarkable, however, that this author stresses Jesus' career, not so much as an explicit fulfillment of certain OT predictions, but as an event in which the OT is overshadowed by the glory incarnate in Jesus through whom came grace and truth, light and life. In Jesus, the glory of God is seen in human form in a manner that transforms all of life that responds to him.

In the epistle to the Hebrews, the "Christ-event" excels the OT by its greater amplitude and efficacy. In Paul, the gospel replaces the Torah both in time and in splendor. In John, the OT themes of glory, light, water, and manna are simply eclipsed by the splendor of the incarnate Son. Whereas Matthew goes from the OT to its fulfillment in Christ, John goes from the incarnation back to its antecedents in the old covenant.

B. Jewish literature

1. Rabbinic influence. The difficulty in ascertaining the extent of rabbinic influence on the fourth gospel arises from the fact that the teachings of the rabbis were not put in written form until the codification of the Mishnah about A.D. 200. There is reason to believe, however, that the oral tradition behind this document extended, essentially in its extant form, back to the time of Jesus. The evidences that indicate a knowledge of Jewish exegesis on the part of the author of this gospel are quite impressive. His sentence structure is at times reminiscent of Jewish literature. This may be explained as due to the influence of the Aramaic language or to the influence of the OT. In any case, the Semitic influence can be seen clearly in the style of this gospel. In this respect, the evangelist stands closer to rabbinic usage than does either Paul or James. For example, in the use of the term *law*, John treats it much the same as *tôrâ* H9368 is treated in rabbinic writings of the rabbis. The evangelist, however, states that the incarnate Logos fulfills the functions of the Torah, but does it more effectively (Jn. 1:14, 17). Also, whereas the rabbis likened the Torah to water, wine, bread, and light, the evangelist links these concepts with Jesus.

The author's acquaintance with rabbinic exegesis is reflected also, for example, when Jesus was criticized for healing on the Sabbath (Jn. 5:16). A similar defense of circumcising a child on the Sabbath was used by Rabbi Eliezer ben Azariah. The rabbis maintained that if one of the 248 members of the body was healed on the Sabbath following circumcision, how much more is the healing of the whole body commendable. In the light of this, Jesus wondered why they were indignant at him for giving help on the Sabbath to the whole man (7:23). Moreover, the rabbis agreed that in his capacity as judge, God did not rest on the Sabbath day; God maintains his judicial activities continuously. In a similar fashion, Jesus said, "My Father is always at work to this very day, and I, too, am working," indicating that it was in his role as judge that he worked on the Sabbath (5:17, 30).

The rabbis taught that at the coming of the Messiah he would be hidden during his childhood and suddenly appear as a mature man ready to take control. Some thought he would be hidden in Rome, others, the N, or Paradise, or in the sea. Familiarity with this doctrine is reflected in the rabbinic statement, "When the Christ comes, no one will know where he is from" (Jn. 7:27). The necessity for two witnesses and the accused's right to be heard in his own defense also reflect a knowledge of Jewish law (7:51; 8:17). The author of this gospel must have heard these themes discussed in the synagogues.

2. Philo. Scholars have been particularly intrigued by numerous parallels of thought and word between Philo Judaeus and the fourth gospel, especially the use of the term *logos* (word). Philo of Alexandria, who flourished during the time of Paul, reflects an intimate knowledge of Hellenistic literature and also of the OT. His concern was to combine the two by means of allegorization of the OT. The factors that have led many to conclude that the fourth gospel derived many of its ideas from Philo includes several considerations.

Both the evangelist and Philo emphasize light as symbolic of God. In Philo, the light of God is said to be the archetype of every other light (*Dreams* 1.75) reminiscent of the *logos* as the true light (Jn. 1:9). The conflict between light and darkness is also common to both. Philo observes that the Creator was aware of the essential conflict between light and darkness and parted them one from another by a wall of separation, evening and dawn being the boundary lines (*Creation* 9.33–34). Although both could have received the emphasis upon light from the OT, the conflict between light and darkness is less prominent in the OT than it is in either John or Philo. Both John and Philo spoke of water as symbolic of life. Both emphasized the role of God as Shepherd and King, perhaps because both were influenced by the OT. Many of the parallels can best be explained as both authors drawing from a common source, rather than the evangelist borrowing from Philo.

The differences are far more extensive than the similarities. The *logos* in Philo is impersonal; in John, personal. There is nothing in Philo comparable to the concept of the *logos* becoming flesh. Whereas John is interested in symbolism, he did not allegorize as did the Alexandrian philosopher. After weighing the evidence, it seems clear that the significance of Philo is not that of a source for the thought of the fourth gospel, but rather as an evidence of an audience to which the fourth gospel sought to appeal. John, therefore, was a witness not *of* Greek ideas but *to* Greek ideas.

3. Qumran literature. The discovery of the DEAD SEA SCROLLS bears particularly upon the background of the fourth gospel, as they are contemporary. Particularly significant is the fact that the Qumran literature was written prior to A.D. 70, when the community was destroyed, presumably by the Romans. The numerous similarities between these people and their literature with that of the ESSENES, described by JOSEPHUS and others, has led a majority to conclude that the producers of the scrolls were in reality Essenes, the third of three sects mentioned by Josephus.

The Essenes at Qumran believed themselves to be children of light and members of the new covenant who were preparing in the desert for the coming of the Lord as urged by Isaiah (Isa. 40:1–5). The scrolls speak of the spirit of truth, as does the fourth gospel, and also stress in common with John the eternal conflict between light and darkness, truth and error. Like John, their dualism was a modified moral dualism, a conflict between the good and evil rather than a metaphysical dualism between matter and spirit. In both, the spirit is truth and is the vehicle of divine revelation (1QH XIV, 27; cf. Jn. 14:26; 16:13–15). The verbal similarities between the fourth gospel and the Qumran literature is greater by far than the parallels between John and the other books of the NT. This fact virtually compels one to conclude that the dominant influence on the fourth gospel is Hebraic rather than Hellenistic.

C. Pagan literature

1. Gnosticism. It has been the contention of Rudolph Bultmann that the chief external factor in the fourth gospel is GNOSTICISM of the early 2nd cent. Gnosticism was a complex eclectic system of religious thought. It was widespread throughout the ANE, especially during the 2nd cent. A.D. Previously, our knowledge of Gnosticism was dependent almost entirely upon the Christian apologists who looked upon it very negatively. Recent discoveries in Egypt, especially near NAG HAMMADI, have yielded Coptic papyri written by the Gnostics themselves. There are many verbal similarities, but few ideological similarities, between the *Gospel of Truth*, discovered in 1945, and the Gospel of John.

One similarity is in the concept of the *logos* who, in John, enables the believer to know the Father and who is called the Savior because his work is that of redemption. The *logos* of the Gnostic writings, however, redeems not from sin but from error. The *Secret Book of John* (see JOHN, APOCRYPHON OF) states that foreknowledge gazed intensely into the pure light and gave birth to the spark of light, the only-begotten who revealed himself to the Father, the self-born. This work may have been produced before the end of the 1st cent. and provides additional evidence that the fourth gospel could easily have been produced within that century. In both cases, creation by way of the *logos* is affirmed.

Common to both John and the Gnostics is the emphasis upon KNOWLEDGE. Synonyms for knowledge appear frequently both in the first epistle of John and in the gospel. Divine life is said to come through the knowledge of God (Jn. 17:3). The Gnostics also stressed that knowledge is that which gives life. Like the classical Greeks, the Gnostics named knowledge as the supreme virtue, placing it above obedience or love. SALVATION was deliverance from ignorance rather than deliverance from sin. Those who were saved were those who professed knowledge or divine illumination. Salvation was not by faith but by insight. In John, however, the emphasis is upon belief, and knowledge was not regarded as an end in itself. Moreover, knowledge in the fourth gospel, like wisdom of the OT, is the knowledge of God, and it is something to which everyone may come by faith. It is not limited to a few.

There are, of course, interesting parallels between Gnosticism and modern Christian Science: in both, the emphasis is upon salvation from matter rather than salvation from sin—the main interest in religion centering in the realm of knowledge rather than in grace and faith. The same may be said for many facets of contemporary philosophical theology with its emphasis upon sophist action rather than on faith, love, and hope. In John, the emphasis is upon life—divine life clothed in humanity yet transcending it; not contaminated by proximity to the world and the flesh but transforming and redeeming it. It is a qualitatively different type of life, which may begin now by acceptance of the light and extends in unbroken sequence into eternity, into the life of God.

2. The Mandeans. This obscure Mesopotamian sect came to the attention of German scholars about 1920. The MANDEANS professed to be disciples of John the Baptist. Walter Bauer and Rudolph Bultmann compared statements in the three extant books attributed to them—the *Book of John*, the *Ginza*, and the *Qulasta*—with the fourth gospel, and concluded that John had borrowed from the Mandeans the concept of a Redeemer who descends and ascends for the salvation of mankind. Other parallels include that of the unity of Father and Son, the concept of the divine Shepherd, and the role of Son in bringing light. The parallels are rather impressive until one considers the contexts. Bultmann assumes that the Mandeans came from Palestine and that their writings antedate Christianity. F. C. Burkitt, C. H. Dodd, and others, however, have shown that neither of these assumptions is true. The evidence demonstrates that this literature came into existence after the rise of Islam (the spelling of John the Baptist follows the Koran rather than the NT). It is best viewed as an eclectic Gnosticism that borrowed elements from both Christianity and Islam, and therefore could not have influenced John's gospel.

V. Purpose, date, and author

A. Purpose. In modern discussion of the Johannine problem, interest has shifted from authorship to purpose. The ostensible purpose is clearly stated: it is to provide evidence upon which to base faith in Jesus Christ the Son of God with the view of obtaining life eternal (Jn. 20:31, although some interpret the statement to mean John wanted to strengthen the faith of believers). It is similar to the purpose announced in the first epistle of John, that of welcoming believers into the fellowship of the divine-human relationship (1 Jn. 1:3). John wrote his gospel with unbelievers in mind, in contrast with the author of Luke's gospel who wrote to instruct the believers (Lk. 1:4). It often has been observed that whereas Matthew had a Jewish audience in mind as he labored to show how OT prophecies were fulfilled in Jesus, and whereas Luke and Mark may have had the Gentile church especially in mind, the author of this gospel envisions a more universal audience, as seen in his emphasis upon such universals as light and life, bread and water, truth and error.

Beyond this explicitly stated purpose of the fourth gospel, modern scholarship has pressed further into the underlying purpose. Oscar Cullmann, for example, believes that the gospel was designed primarily for Palestinian Jews who were influenced by Greek culture. This argument is based upon the consideration that both the Hellenists and John's gospel had little enthusiasm for the temple and its worship (Acts 7:48; Jn. 2:13–22; 4:20–24). The visible evidence of God's presence in the temple, the SHEKINAH, becomes in John the glory resident in Jesus Christ (Jn. 1:14; 17:1, 24). In Cullmann's view, the synoptics reflect ideas held by Hebrew Christians, whereas the fourth gospel reflects those ideas prized by the Greek Christians. The fourth gospel, he believes, is designed to rehabilitate the latter. This intriguing hypothesis, however, rests upon rather scant evidence. W. C. Van Unnik, on the other hand, argues that the gospel is designed primarily for the Jews of the dispersion—a missionary book designed to convince Jews outside of Palestine that Jesus is the Messiah. He notes that the Johannine use of the term Messiah agrees with that of Paul, Apollos, and other evangelists as they labored among the DIASPORA (Acts 13:26; 17:2; 18:5, 25).

In the last decades of the 20th cent., scholars have focused attention on the historical context of the presumed Christian community associated with the apostle John at the end of the 1st cent. Some have argued, for example, that certain rabbinic decisions at the time excommunicated Jewish Christians from the synagogue, and that this event provides the real background to the story of the blind man in Jn. 9 (cf. J. L. Martyn, *History and Theology in the Fourth gospel* [1968]). Others have proposed even more detailed reconstructions of the Johannine Christians and the groups with whom they supposedly were interacting, such as adherents of John the Baptist, Jewish Christians who would not break with the synagogue (cf. Nicodemus), and so on (cf. R. E. Brown, *The Community of the Beloved Disciple* [1979]).

However fascinating these theories may be, a sounder perspective is likely to be similar to that of Alan Richardson, who sees the author's purpose as that of supplementing the work of the synoptics rather than providing an alternative. The fourth gospel is a product of long reflection upon the synoptic tradition. John's purpose is not so much to present new evidence as it is to clarify the issues upon which the evidence will be either accepted or rejected. He writes not so much to inform the reader as to confront him with the necessity for a decision. He is concerned with the moral and spiritual relevance of gospel history to the issues of life for the reader and the world in general. John points up the issues on a "take it or leave it" basis, employing all his ardor and skill in the hope that the reader will accept the incarnate Son who lived among us and who now provides life for those who accept it.

B. Date. Christian tradition usually considered the gospel to have been written during the last decade of the 1st cent. This is based both upon internal evidence and patristic writings. The tradition (preserved, for example, by IRENAEUS) is that John the elder lived in EPHESUS until a very old age. The internal evidence is that the author had pondered for some time upon the mission and message of Jesus and then wrote an interpretive history based upon careful selection of Jesus' deeds and words.

Critical scholarship at the end of the 19th cent. for the most part came to favor a later date for the gospel. This was a result of a new understanding of contemporary literature from the early centuries. Some scholars, after noting words and ideas that seem more congenial to Hellenistic ideas of the early 2nd cent., believed that the gospel was written by an unknown religious mystic and thinker who endeavored to present a hellenized version of early Christian tradition. The high percentage of theological material in this gospel, in contrast to the relative paucity of this in the Gospel of Mark, was explained as the result of the growth of tradition away from its historical source. Thus, in the words of F. C. Grant, the author "determined to make Jesus an un-Jewish, even as anti-Jewish, as possible" (*The Gospel of John*, 2 vols., Harper's Annotated Bible 13–14 [1956], 1:7). A similar view is the basis for a revised edition of the gospel by D. D. Runes (*The Gospel according to St. John* [1967])

A reaction to this extreme led to another extreme in which some scholars as early as 1922 thought of John as among the earliest of the Gospels because of its alleged Aramaic influence. Before the recent DSS discoveries, scholars like W. F. Howard (*Christianity according to St. John* [1946]) were pointing out the relative prominence of OT influence on this gospel. The Qumran literature proves that there is nothing in the fourth gospel that could not have been written in Palestine before A.D. 70 (R. M. Grant, *Earliest Lives of Jesus* [1961]). The independence of the fourth gospel is also indicated.

Another factor that argues strongly for an early date is the reflection in the gospel of the intense rivalry between church and synagogue. The hostility of the world that is luminous in every page is not the pagan world as such, nor is it the synagogue exclusively, but it is a basic hostility to the gospel which is seen first to stem from among the Jewish religious authorities, and which can be equally true of the Gentile world. It seems unlikely that the issues that are so prominent in this gospel, namely, the Jewish hierarchy and the temple, could be so prominent had the gospel been written after the fall of Jerusalem and the termination of temple worship. Prior to A.D. 70, these were the prime issues upon which the author of this gospel focused attention — in such a manner as to stress basic issues that have universal and perennial relevance.

Old photograph of men fishing on the Sea of Galilee by holding a net between the two boats. The author of the Gospel of John worked as a fisherman before Jesus called him to be his disciple.

C. Author. Among the authors that have been suggested from time to time are: Lazarus, whom Jesus raised from the dead; Nicodemus; the young man whom Mark reported as having fled naked from the scene of Jesus' arrest (Mk. 14:52); an unknown mystic of the 2nd cent.; JOHN THE APOSTLE; and John the presbyter of Ephesus. Evidence from early writers, specifically Papias and Irenaeus, favors the elder of Ephesus, who may well have been the apostle himself.

When both internal and external evidence is weighed, there seems no compelling reason to deny to John the son of Zebedee the honor of being its author. From internal evidence it is apparent that the author was intimately acquainted with the Palestine of the 1st cent., probably prior to the Jewish War of A.D. 66–70. This is confirmed by the Qumran literature. That the author was an eyewitness to the events reported is indicated by the inclusion of details that are not strictly relevant to the story. Psychologically, they can best be explained as reminiscences rather than the result of historical imagination. If he was an eyewitness, a process of elimination leaves the son of Zebedee as the most probable candidate. Another plausible theory is that a companion of the apostle wrote down his master's thought. This would help explain the writer's intimate acquaintance with Hellenistic thought forms. In any case, whether it represents the apostle's actual words, or the apostle's witness as recorded by a disciple, the fourth gospel does bear the evidences of apostolic authenticity.

However, its acceptance by the early church and its claim to credence rests on the "sheer power and attractiveness of its testimony to Christ" (Alan Richardson). In competition with it were many apocryphal gospels (see APOCRYPHAL NT I). In other words, it has won its way, not so much on the basis of its alleged apostolicity as upon its intrinsic worth.

D. John's gospel as history. To what extent is the portrait in the fourth gospel historically reliable? The older critics widely assumed that since John has more narrative, with less emphasis on activity, than the synoptics, especially Mark, it was more subjective and proportionately less valuable as history. More recently, existential hermeneutics has said that historicity is less important than the KERYGMA, or proclamation of faith. John, like other writers of the NT, demanded a faith based upon fact, upon observable and verifiable data (Jn. 20:27; 1 Jn. 1:3). Recent critical scholarship has swung to a less skeptical position with regard to the historical veracity of this account. At the same time it is apparent that this author was highly selective in his use of available material (Jn. 21:25). Whereas the synoptic writers were interested primarily in reporting the facts of Jesus' words and deeds, John's emphasis is upon interpretation of the events. He not only reports events, but also develops their significance. The author shows remarkable insight into the factors that help and hinder those who seek life eternal. The items selected for elaboration show the central importance of response in faith to Christ. The evidences of authenticity and apostolicity are so deeply ingrained in the gospel that the church generally agrees with the judgment of CLEMENT OF ALEXANDRIA that this is preeminently the "spiritual gospel."

Scholars often have stressed the contrast between the Jesus of history and the Christ of faith. See JESUS CHRIST III. As a reaction against existential hermeneutics, there was a renewed demand to ascertain the historical facts surrounding Jesus. Some currently argue that the important factor is the life of Jesus, bypassing the passion and resurrection; others emphasize that the "Easter faith" is not dependent upon the actual events of Jesus' life, death, and resurrection. The Gospel according to John is careful to stress both the historical Jesus and the Christ-centered faith that emerges. This gospel is even more Christological than the other three. Whereas the synoptic accounts all agree as focusing upon Jesus' actual deeds and words, this one demands that the reader recognize the personality behind the deeds and words. For this reason attention is called not only to the idea of resurrection but to the fact that Jesus Christ is the resurrection and the life. Christianity is not only "the Way" (as in Acts) but here Jesus Christ is "the way and the truth and the life."

(For a valuable summary of the history of research, see the introductory chapter in J. Ashton, *The Interpretation of John*, 2nd ed. [1997], which also reprints some influential essays. Important commentaries include B. F. Westcott, *The Gospel according to St. John: The Authorised Version with Introduction and Notes* [1902, reprinted from *The Speaker's Commentary*]; id., *The Gospel according to St. John: The Greek Text with Introduction and Notes*, 2 vols. [1908]; M. J. Lagrange, *Evangile selon saint Jean*, 7th ed. [1948]; J. H. Bernard, *A Critical and Exegetical Commentary on the Gospel according to St. John*, ICC, 2 vols. [1928]; E. C. Hoskyns, *The Fourth Gospel*, 2nd ed. [1947]; R. H. Lightfoot, *St. John's Gospel: A Commentary* [1956]; G. A. Turner and J. R. Mantey, *The Gospel according to John*, Evangelical Commentary on the Bible 4 [1964]; R. E. Brown, *The Gospel according to John*, 2 vols., AB 29–29A [1966–70]; R. Bultmann, *The Gospel of John: A Commentary* [1971, orig. in KEK, 1941]; C. K. Barrett, *The Gospel according to St. John: An Introduction with Commentary and Notes on the Greek Text*, 2nd ed. [1978]; R. Schnackenburg, *The Gospel according to St. John*, 3 vols. [1968–82; vol. 4 in German, 1984]; D. A. Carson, *The Gospel according to John* [1991]; L. Morris, *The Gospel according to John*, NICNT, rev. ed. [1995]; F. J. Moloney, *The Gospel of John*, SP 4 [1998]; G. R. Beasley-Murray, *John*, WBC 36, 2nd ed. [1999]; G. L. Borchert, *John*, NAC 25, 2 vols. [1996–2002]; C. S. Keener, *The Gospel of John: A Commentary*, 2 vols. [2003]; A. Köstenberger, *John*, BECNT [2004]; A. T. Lincoln, *Commentary on the Gospel according to St. John*, BNTC 4 [2005]; H. Thyen, *Das Johannesevangelium*, HNT 6 [2005].

(Among many significant monographs, see E. F. Scott, *The Fourth Gospel: Its Purpose and Theology*, 2nd ed. [1908]; C. F. Burney, *The Aramaic Origin of the Fourth Gospel* [1922]; H. Odeberg, *The Fourth Gospel Interpreted in Its Relation to Contemporaneous Religious Currents in Palestine and the Hellenistic-Oriental World* [1929]; P. Gardner-Smith, *St. John and the Synoptic Gospels* [1938]; W. F. Howard, *Christianity according to St. John* [1946]; C. H. Dodd, *The Interpretation of the Fourth Gospel* [1953]; W. F. Howard, *The Fourth Gospel in Recent Criticism and Interpretation* [1955]; A. Guilding, *The Fourth Gospel and Jewish Worship* [1960]; C. H. Dodd, *Historical Tradition in the Fourth Gospel* [1963]; T. F. Glasson, *Moses in the Fourth Gospel* [1963]; R. Kysar, *The Fourth Evangelist and His Gospel* [1976]; R. A. Culpepper, *The Anatomy of the Fourth Gospel* [1983]; J. A. T. Robinson, *The Priority of John* [1985]; G. R. O'Day, *Revelation in the Fourth Gospel* [1987]; C. L. Blomberg, *The Historical Reliability of John's Gospel: Issues and Commentary* [2001]; D. M. Smith, *John among the Gospels*, 2nd ed. [2001]; S. P. Kealy, *John's Gospel and the History of Biblical Interpretation*, 2 vols. [2002]; C. E. Hill, *The Johannine Corpus in the Early Church* [2004]; F. J. Moloney, *The Gospel of John: Text and Context* [2005]; J. Ashton, *Understanding the Fourth Gospel*, 2nd ed. [2007]; and the bibliography compiled by W. E. Mills, *The Gospel of John* [2002].)

G. A. Turner

John Mark. See Mark, John.

John the apostle. Son of Zebedee; after Simon Peter, second most prominent member of Jesus' twelve disciples. The amount of literature relating to John and his writings is very large in NT studies. More has been written about him and attributed to him than any of the other twelve apostles.

I. Sources. Most of the information about John the son of Zebedee comes from the NT itself. There is no mention of him in Josephus, but Christian literature of the 2nd cent. provides some additional and valuable data.

A. Sources that refer to John the apostle. The record of the first three Gospels states that John had a brother whose name was James; his father Zebedee was a fisherman residing near Capernaum on the Sea of Galilee (Matt. 4:21–22; Mk. 1:19–20; Lk. 5:10). The mother of John is thought to be Salome, for the third woman accompanying the two women to the tomb is called Salome in Mk. 16:1, while Matt. 27:56 describes her as "the mother of the sons of Zebedee." In Jn. 19:25, the third woman at the cross is said to be the sister of Jesus' mother, hence Jesus and John would be first cousins.

The name of John appears on each of the lists of the names of the apostles in the Synoptic Gospels (Matt. 10:2; Mk. 3:17; Lk. 6:14). John and his brother James were termed Sons of Thunder by the Master (Mk. 3:17). John was among the three of the inner circle who were with Jesus at the raising of Jairus's daughter (Mk. 5:37; Lk. 8:51), at the TRANSFIGURATION (Matt. 17:1; Mk. 9:2; Lk. 9:28), and with Jesus in a portion of the Garden of GETHSEMANE (Matt. 26:37; Mk. 14:33). He was among the four who asked Jesus about the coming events (Mk. 13:3–4). The synoptic records present Peter as the leader of the apostles, with John and James as the next two influential ones. Only once is John mentioned alone in these sources, namely, when he asked whether they should forbid one who was casting out demons in the name of Jesus (Mk. 9:38; Lk. 9:49).

In Acts, James is in the background and John is ranked along with Peter as one of the two leaders in the apostolic circle. Peter was spokesman for the group (Acts 1–2). John was with Peter at the healing of the lame man (3:1–10), and was arrested and placed on trial with Peter (4:3–21); together they investigated the reception by the Samaritans of the word of God (8:14–25). The only reference to John in the epistles is in Gal. 2:9, where he, together with Peter and James (the Lord's brother), are referred to as "pillars" in the early church. The fact that John was alive during this period refutes a late tradition that he was martyred at the same time as his brother James (Acts 12:1–2).

Earliest patristic records make little mention of John, but he is very prominent in the records from the latter part of the 2nd cent. through the 4th. One of the earliest extracanonical sources was a Gnostic document titled the *Acts of John* (see JOHN, ACTS OF). This work contains a report of miracles and discourses attributed to the apostle John near EPHESUS. It tells of his return from PATMOS, a shipwreck, the healing of a certain Cleopatra and the raising of her husband to life, the destruction of the temple of Artemis, and many other tales. In it John tells of his early association with Jesus. It closes with an account of John's death, at which time he was thankful for his celibate life. The book is strongly Docetic in nature, quite at variance with the emphasis of the first epistle of John. No confidence can be placed in this document as a historical source for the apostle.

The earliest known exegesis of John's gospel is that of Ptolemaus, of the school of Valentinus. Dated at approximately A.D. 150, it speaks of the fourth gospel as having been written by John, the Lord's disciple (Iren. *Haer*. 1.8.5). Another early commentator was a Gnostic named Heracleon who flourished in the latter half of the 2nd cent. In his commentary on Jn. 1:18, he implies that the author of this verse was a disciple of the Lord, namely, the apostle John. There is an indirect reference to John the apostle as the author of the fourth gospel in Tatian's DIATESSARON (c. 160). A writing sometimes referred to as the *Secret Book of John* is found in the Berlin Gnostic papyrus and in the recently discovered Gnostic library at NAG HAMMADI in Egypt (see JOHN, APOCRYPHON OF). It contains this interesting passage: "One day when John, the brother of James (these are the sons of Zebedee), went up to the temple, there a Pharisee … said to him 'This Nazarene deceived you'" (R. M. Grant, *Gnosticism* [1961], 69). Other Gnostic works, such as the *Gospel of Philip*, quote extensively from the fourth gospel but do not mention the author, the implication being that they believed John the apostle to be the author.

By far the most impressive of the early witnesses to John the apostle comes from IRENAEUS, who flourished in the last quarter of the 2nd cent. He testifies to a personal acquaintance with POLYCARP, bishop of SMYRNA, who had learned the gospel message directly from John and others who had seen the Lord. Irenaeus adds that after the three Synoptic Gospels had been written, "John, the disciple of the Lord who also had leaned upon his breast, did himself write a gospel during his residence at Ephesus in Asia" (*Her*. 3.1.1). He also states that, as reported by Polycarp, John saw CERINTHUS in the public bath and fled saying, "Let us flee, for Cerinthus, the enemy of the truth, is within." Irenaeus states that the church at Ephesus, founded by Paul, and the place where John remained until the time of TRAJAN (A.D. 98–117), is a true witness of the tradition of the church (*Her*. 3.3.4). Another witness is Polycrates, bishop of Ephesus (189–198), who states that "John, who also leaned on the Lord's breast, who was a priest wearing a mitre, and witness and teacher; he sleeps at Ephesus" (cited in Euseb. *Eccl. Hist*. 3.31.3). EUSEBIUS (c. 325) accepted and quoted this evidence as indicating John as author of the "undoubted writings of this apostle." He presents him as having lived to a very old age contemporary with the emperors Domitian, Nerva, and Trajan, and bishops Clement, Ignatius, and Simeon. This John, he concludes, wrote the fourth gospel, "read in all the churches under heaven," as an undoubted writing of the apostle. He adds that whereas the fourth gospel and the first epistle are undoubtedly the works of the apostle, the second and third epistles and the Apocalypse perhaps may be the works of others by the name of John (*Eccl. Hist.* 3.34.13).

B. Canonical books attributed to John the apostle. The date to be gleaned from the fourth gospel is dependent on whether or not references to the BELOVED DISCIPLE designate the apostle John. The identity of this individual has been widely debated, especially in recent times. Some say the Beloved Disciple was NICODEMUS; others that it was LAZARUS; while some believe it to be the MATTHIAS who was chosen by lot (Acts 1). Because the author of the gospel was evidently familiar with the inner circles of the apostolic twelve, the process of elimination reduces the possible candidates to only one, John the son of Zebedee.

This John is not mentioned by name in the fourth gospel, a phenomenon interpreted by many as another evidence that he is the author. He is named as one of the first two recruited by Jesus in the Jordan Valley where John the Baptist was ministering (Jn. 1:40). He is singled out at the Last Supper as the one reclining close to Jesus (13:23). The Beloved Disciple is mentioned at the Last Supper (13:23–26), at the cross where he was commanded to take Jesus' mother to his own home (19:26–27), at the empty tomb (20:2–10), and at the Sea of Tiberias, where he was the first to recognize the risen Jesus (21:7). The term again appears in connection with anxiety about the statement concerning his future (21:20–23). He is specifically stated to be the author of this gospel in the postscript (21:24).

The author of the first epistle likewise appears to have been an eyewitness (1 Jn. 1:1–3). If the apostle wrote the fourth gospel, it seems certain that he also wrote the first epistle. This is the easiest way to account for the high degree of similarity in language and ideas between the two documents. Common to both is the vocabulary of simple words, which include *knowledge, world, witness, life,* and *truth.* See JOHN, EPISTLES OF; JOHN, GOSPEL OF.

The author of the second and third epistles is said to be "the elder." The evidence that this is written by the author of the gospel and the first epistle is somewhat less weighty than that for a common authorship of the gospel and the first epistle. On the basis of PAPIAS, quoted by Eusebius (*Eccl. Hist.* 3.34.13), the author of these two short letters as well as the Apocalypse could well have been another John.

The author of the Apocalypse describes himself simply as a fellow servant named John (see REVELATION, BOOK OF). He does not address his readers from the viewpoint of an apostle or even that of an elder, but rather that of a brother, a companion in tribulation. The style, likewise, is different from that of the epistle or gospel, as many from the time of CLEMENT OF ALEXANDRIA on down have noticed. Those who reject the apostolic authorship of the gospel are more ready to admit it in reference to the Apocalypse, for the author of the Apocalypse seems to fit better the synoptic description of John as the "Son of Thunder" and as one who would like to command fire to come down to consume the noncommitted. Many think the same person could not have written books as diverse as the fourth gospel and the Apocalypse. But one cannot be sure that the difference of circumstances would in itself be sufficient reason for the change of style and imagery encountered in the Apocalypse. There are many other instances in history when widely diverse literary styles come from the same source, but under different circumstances. This may be seen, for example, in the works of Shakespeare, Milton, Luther, Kipling.

II. Life history. After sifting the sources and evaluating them, the life of John the son of Zebedee may be summarized in the following sequence. He was a convert of John the Baptist and spent some time with the proclaimer of the new covenant in the Jordan Valley. It was here that he met Jesus and transferred his allegiance from John to Jesus (Jn. 1:19–42). Some time after this, when John and his brother James had resumed fishing, they again encountered Jesus by the Sea of Galilee and at once decided to follow him (Matt. 4:21; Mk. 1:19–20; Lk. 5:10). The four partners, all fishermen, joined Jesus at the same time. They continued with Jesus through his Galilean ministry, witnessing the events reported chiefly in the Synoptic Gospels. He

The Monastery of St. John the Divine on the island of Patmos, built in the 11th cent. with a fortified exterior because of the threats of piracy.

was chosen along with eleven others as one of the Twelve (Matt. 10:2; Mk. 3:17; Lk. 6:14). As indicated earlier, he was an eyewitness of the raising of Jairus's daughter along with James and Peter (Mk. 5:37; Lk. 8:51). He was one of the three with Jesus on the mountain when the transfiguration occurred (Matt. 17:1; Mk. 9:2; Lk. 9:28).

When enroute to Jerusalem, John became incensed at the hostility of a Samaritan village (Lk. 9:54). His mistaken zeal is indicated by his rebuke of the man who was casting out demons without Jesus' authorization (Mk. 9:38; Lk. 9:49). The two Sons of Thunder threatened their relationship with the other ten by seeking a favored position in the future kingdom (Matt. 20:20; Mk. 10:35; cf. Lk. 22:24). Just before the Passover, John and Peter were commissioned by Jesus to prepare a place for partaking of the Passover (Lk. 22:8). At the Last Supper, according to the Johannine account, it was the Beloved Disciple who, reclining close to Jesus, first learned the identity of the betrayer. However, he seems not to have passed this information on to Peter, who had requested the information (Jn. 13:21–26).

Later in Gethsemane, John, with Peter and James, went a little farther during the time of Jesus' agony (Matt. 26:37; Mk. 14:33). It is widely believed that the unnamed disciple who entered the court of the high priest with Peter was John the apostle (Jn. 18:15–18), because this disciple was known to the high priest. The Beloved Disciple again is seen as the only disciple who witnessed the crucifixion. In response to Jesus' request, this disciple took Jesus' mother into his own home (19:25–27).

This disciple is also mentioned as the first to recognize the significance of the empty tomb (Jn. 20:1–8). At the Sea of Tiberias he was the one who first identified Jesus on the shore and reported to Peter, "It is the Lord!" (21:4–7). The two are linked again in the episode following Jesus' remarks, "If I want him to remain alive until I return, what is that to you?"—which evoked much speculation as to its meaning (21:20–23). He is linked with Peter in several important episodes reported in Acts. He was a prominent member of the Jerusalem church when Paul visited it later. Nothing further is known about him until, according to church tradition (related chiefly through Irenaeus but with many corroborating witnesses), he was bishop at Ephesus. This literary evidence is supported by the remains of churches bearing his name at Ephesus. There he was remembered as a vigorous champion of orthodoxy, which fits the description of the first epistle. He is reported to have brought back to Christ an errant convert at the risk of his own life. His exile in

Patmos during the last decade of the 1st cent. coincides with the persecution of Domitian. A conflict between church and state reflected in the book of Revelation also seems consistent with this picture of John's latter days.

The apostle John, as seen in these sources, is one who maintained a high CHRISTOLOGY in stressing Jesus as the Son of God. He was thoroughly familiar with the OT and with Jewish culture in general, as seen in the Synoptic Gospels and Acts. His spiritual insight and maturity led to his inclusion in the inner circle on several occasions. This is consistent with the picture in the fourth gospel as one for whom Jesus had a special affection. On the negative side, John had an apparent ambition for preferential treatment. His reaction to the inhospitality of the Samaritans indicates a certain volatile nature, which could easily pass from righteous indignation to vindictiveness. As reflected in the fourth gospel, he is seen to be one who quickly acquired an acute understanding of the Hellenistic mind; his vocabulary demonstrates an ability to communicate to the sophisticated as well as to the simple. He tended to see things in simple terms of black and white, good and evil; there were few median shades of gray in his perspective. To him everyone was either for or against the Lord; either a child of God or a child of the devil; either a child of light or a child of darkness. Christian maturity brought a measure of gentility to his natural sanguine temperament so that he became preeminently the "apostle of love," as his first epistle bears witness.

These two elements in his nature continued apparently to the end. In the first epistle, perhaps the last thing he wrote, there is the emphasis upon love and life and a corresponding warning against heresy and sin. As reflected in the Apocalypse, he is the "Son of Thunder" living between two worlds, the world of the righteous who were overcome by their testimony, and the world of the wicked who persist in unbelief even under affliction. There is the same insistence on walking in the light and living according to the law of love. Thus he is seen to be a person with many facets; a Hebrew of the Hebrews, who was able to communicate his ideas in the medium of Hellenistic idiom to the intellectually elite of his day, yet who could speak to the simplest in such elemental terms as light, life, darkness, water, and bread (For bibliography, see JOHN, GOSPEL OF.)

G. A. TURNER

John the Baptist (Βαπτιστής *G969*, called the "baptizer" [ptc. of βαπτίζω *G966*] in Mk. 6:14 and possibly in 1:4). Son of the priest ZECHARIAH and ELIZABETH; the latter was also of Aaronic descent and a relative of MARY, MOTHER OF JESUS (Lk. 1:5, 36). John was born approximately six months before the birth of Jesus (cf. v. 26). His youth was spent in obscurity until he received a divine call to the prophetic vocation (3:2) and entered upon a public ministry. After John placed his seal of approval upon Jesus (Jn. 1:24-36), their ministries overlapped for a short time. Soon after, John was arrested and put to death by Herod Antipas (Mk. 6:27; see HEROD V), leaving some disciples who had not joined Jesus' movement.

I. Importance. The NT places a very high estimate on John and his ministry. Jesus himself said of him, "I tell you, among those born of women there is no one greater than John" (Lk. 7:28). John was the forerunner of Christ (Mk. 1:2). His rite of BAPTISM became a central Christian ordinance (Acts 2:38). His imprisonment and death had a great effect upon Jesus (Mk. 1:14-15). The Master regarded him as the second ELIJAH sent by God in accord with ancient prophecy (Mal. 4:5; Mk. 9:13). He was the greatest figure yet produced under the old covenant (Matt. 11:11). He epitomized all the OT saints who stood at the threshold of the new order without entering in (Heb. 11:39b). He does not deserve the neglect the church often accords him.

His great importance lies in the fact that he bridged the old era and the new and was the link between the two. Neither Jesus nor John came preaching something absolutely new. Theirs was a word of fulfillment: "Repent, for the kingdom of heaven is near" (Matt. 3:2; 4:17). The long-awaited messianic day was about to dawn. The records of the birth of John make his role very clear (Lk. 1:5-25, 57-66, 67-80). He was to prepare a people for the Lord's coming, and for that end would be filled with the HOLY SPIRIT. The whole narrative has a strong OT flavoring: the aged and childless couple, the angelic visits, the announcement of a child, the revealing of his name.

John was born into a pious Jewish home, grounded in the messianic promises of the Scriptures and looking for the hope of Israel. The parents were delighted with the baby John because he represented the rebirth of prophecy and the fulfillment of the eschatological hope. Psalms were sung to herald his birth. The theory that the BENEDICTUS (Lk. 1:67–79) was a hymn originally written to glorify Jesus but later applied to John is without foundation. Obviously, the first half of the hymn was directed to Jesus, of whose birth Zechariah was well aware (1:40), and the remainder of it exalted the preparatory role of John himself. The parents of John recognized from the outset the relative greatness of Jesus over John (1:41–45). And because Mary was related to Elizabeth, Jesus had not only a tie with the house of DAVID through Joseph (1:27; 2:4; possibly through Mary too — see GENEALOGY OF JESUS CHRIST), but also with the line of Aaron through both Zechariah and Elizabeth (1:5).

Radical criticism has sought to discredit the historical value of the birth narrative in Luke. The theory is widely held that the section was at first a document of the Baptist movement, embellished with legends, and exalting his position. The section is thought to have been interpolated by one or two Christian stories, but left largely intact. There is, however, a complete lack of any evidence for the hypothesis. The creation of a Baptist sect to which these hypothetical sources are credited is poor criticism. There is no indication in any but the latest MANDEAN sources, themselves valueless as history, that John regarded Jesus with hostility or envied his rising fame and honor. All the data suggests that both John and his followers welcomed the advent of Christ and readily gave way to his leadership. The argument is wholly circular, insofar as it discovers in the sect the alleged sources that are then attributed to it. This kind of criticism does not discredit Luke, but only the critics. The narrative in Luke bears all the marks of an authentic piece of historical tradition culled by the author in his research, which is generally credited with substantial accuracy. There was no motive in making John the son of an obscure priest if he was not. It is most unlikely that legends crept into the work of Luke, a first-rate historical source. Pessimism over his integrity is unwarranted and reflects an anti-supernaturalistic bias.

II. Ministry. Jesus held the ministry of John to be of the highest importance, because John was a part of the messianic complex of events that form the grand object of prophecy. He was called to be the great eschatological pioneer, the forerunner of the MESSIAH himself (see ESCHATOLOGY). Although he exercised his ministry just before Jesus did, and belonged to the time of promise, yet in another sense he belonged also to the time of fulfillment. John was the line of demarcation in the history of salvation. In him the future predictions of the OT began to find fulfillment (Matt. 11:10–15). Jesus strongly endorsed John's ministry, indicating the close solidarity he felt with John's calling. Although Jesus stated, "he who is least in the kingdom of heaven is greater than [John]" (11:11), he did not intend to depreciate the greatness of John, who was foremost among the revered OT worthies, but rather to exalt the superb opportunities open to one who will partake of the messianic promises in Christ himself (cf. Matt. 13:17).

John entered dramatically onto the stage of history probably in A.D. 28 (possibly earlier; see CHRONOLOGY [NT]). Clothed in a cloak of camel's hair and eating locusts and wild honey, he proclaimed to all who would hear the need for repentance and rectitude of life. He located in southern TRANSJORDAN, not far from JUDEA, in the uninhabited country bordering on PEREA, the realm of Herod Antipas. Everything about him recalled the prophet Elijah — his mantle, his living in the wilderness, his message — and people flocked to hear him. His food and clothing indicated his rejection of official Israel of the time and his conviction of a prophetic calling. Like the ESSENE community, John withdrew from society; but unlike them he sought to reform it by his preaching.

The wilderness represented more than a solitary place to John. It was the place to which Elijah had fled (1 Ki. 19:4), and the place where God led his people to the promised land. The wilderness was a place where the Lord revealed himself, and where some believed the Messiah would appear (Matt. 24:26). The setting only added to the excitement that John's ministry stimulated among the expectant

Village of En Kerem ('Ain Karim, just W of Jerusalem), the traditional home of Zechariah, Elizabeth, and John the Baptist. (View to the S.)

people of Judea. He did not go to the desert to hide from people. In fact he attracted large crowds (Lk. 3:10). The fourth gospel reveals that John's ministry extended into Samaritan territory (Jn. 3:23). AENON near SALIM where John baptized people was probably near ancient SHECHEM (modern Nablus). Later, when Jesus spoke of entering into the labors of others (4:38), he was no doubt referring to the work of John. Both men were contemptuous of the "sons of Abraham" who rested so complacently upon their inherited election, and both made mission trips into foreign areas.

It is not easy to fit John into the pattern of Jewish sects and parties current at the time. With the discovery of the Qumran documents (see DEAD SEA SCROLLS), a hypothesis has become popular that ties John in with the Essene community. Perhaps John, the son of aged parents, was left an orphan and adopted by the Essene community. The community was situated not far from John's home or from the place where he began to minister. By the time of his ministry, however, John clearly had broken any connection he might have had with them. Although it is true that similarities exist between John and the community, differences also exist, and the theory is entirely speculative. It would seem somewhat closer to reality to think that John made an attempt at following the profession of his father, being under a solemn obligation to do so as a son, but was so disgusted by the political machinations and corruption he encountered in the priesthood that he concluded Israel deserved the divine wrath. Whereupon he separated himself from official religion and called upon the Israelites to form a righteous remnant. John and Qumran practiced baptism, both saw their ministry in terms of the "voice" prophecy (Isa. 40:3), and both were ascetic, but the resemblance is superficial. On the other hand, the Qumran sect was a closed system in retreat from the world, and would have frowned upon John's efforts to convert sinners. The degree of anticipation was different. Qumran still waited for the Messiah to come; John knew he was already here. (See H. Stegemann, *The Library of Qumran: On the Essenes, Qumran, John the Baptist, and Jesus* [1998].)

The Jewish historian JOSEPHUS gives an interesting account of John the Baptist in his *Antiquities* (18.5.2):

> But some of the Jews believed that Herod's army was destroyed by God, God punishing him very justly for John called the Baptist, whom Herod had put to death. For John was a pious man, and he was bidding the Jews

who practiced virtue and exercised righteousness toward each other and piety toward God, to come together for baptism. For thus, it seemed to him, would baptismal ablution be acceptable, if it were not used to beg off from sins committed, but for the purification of the body when the soul had previously been cleansed by righteous conduct. And when everybody turned to John—for they were profoundly stirred by what he said—Herod feared that John's so extensive influence over the people might lead to an uprising (for the people seemed likely to do everything he might counsel). He thought it much better, under the circumstances, to get John out of the way in advance, before any insurrection might develop, than for himself to get into trouble and be sorry not to have acted, once an insurrection had begun. So because of Herod's suspicion, John was sent as a prisoner to Machaerus, the fortress already mentioned, and there put to death. But the Jews believed that the destruction which overtook the army came as a punishment for Herod, God wishing to do him harm.

There is no reason to doubt the authenticity of this passage in Josephus. It shows no mark of Christian invention or interpolation. Josephus presents John as a humanistic philosopher advocating virtue, but suppresses the messianic overtones to his ministry, just as one would expect from Josephus writing for Roman and Greek readers. Josephus merely supplements what is known already from the Gospels. His account brings out the political side to John's ministry as Herod saw it, whereas the Gospels emphasize the moral and religious side. Undoubtedly Herod feared the political consequences of John's popularity. His moral charges only added fuel to the flames. The testimony of Josephus reminds us that the memory of John lasted a long time after his death. (Another passage in the Slavonic version of Josephus is clearly a later Christian interpolation. See further E. Nodet, "Jésus et Jean-Baptiste selon Josèphe," in *RB* 92 [1985]: 321–48; 497–524.)

III. Message. John was a preacher who stood in the tradition of the PROPHETS, and he proclaimed the message God laid upon his heart. All of his preaching rings of OT imagery, content, and vividness. There is the winnowing fan, the threshing floor, the ax at the root of the trees, the brood of vipers, and a baptism with the Spirit. Prophecy was reborn in John's message, and people flocked to hear him. His message included ethical instruction, prophetic denunciation, and eschatological teaching. All of his recorded thought roots back to OT teaching. The novel aspect about his ministry was the urgency with which he announced the relevance of his theme. The KINGDOM OF GOD had drawn nigh (Matt. 3:2). The OT saints had longed for the advent of God's kingly rule over their nation for centuries; now its blessedness was about to be realized. The messianic claim is implicit in this announcement. John's prediction of a mightier one to come after him is repeated no less than seven times in one form or other in the NT (Matt. 3:11; Mk. 1:7; Lk. 3:16; Jn. 1:25, 27, 30; Acts 13:25). He was content to be the voice of one crying in the wilderness (Jn. 1:23). He pointed not to himself but to the One who would bear away sins and baptize with the Spirit (1:29, 33).

Byzantine mosaic of John the Baptist, from the Church of Hagia Sophia (Istanbul).

The good news was accompanied with severe denunciations of the status quo in Israel. Physical descent from ABRAHAM did not guarantee the favor of God. Spiritual kinship with God must be evidenced in daily life. Even as a Gentile needed to be baptized to become a proselyte to Judaism, so the Jews needed to be baptized to become a part of God's purified remnant of the latter days (Matt. 3:10; 21:31). It was the hour of universal judgment, beginning with the house of Israel and extending throughout the world. The imminence of judgment in John's preaching is plain. The work of judgment would belong to the ministry of the Messiah, whose purpose it was to destroy the wicked and purge the remnant of sin. When Jesus came preaching "the year of the Lord's favor" (Lk. 4:19), choosing to neglect the judgmental side of the prophecy in Isaiah (61:2), it gave John reason for pause. He hesitated for a time in his wholehearted support of Jesus' claims for himself because Jesus did not appear to be exactly the kind of Messiah he had expected. The explanation lies in Jesus' own understanding of his twofold coming. The kingdom was present in its mystery form (Matt. 13:11; Eph. 3:5) in advance of its APOCALYPTIC manifestation, which was still future. John shared the OT time perspective of prophecy, wherein the two comings of the Messiah were combined as one.

John followed his prophetic warnings about wrath with the appeal for REPENTANCE. A radical change of attitude resulting in a substantial alteration of life was demanded. His ethical instructions were exceedingly radical. When the multitude asked him what they ought to do to show their willingness to change, John gave some very harsh, practical steps to take. They ought to share their possessions with those who had none (Lk. 3:11). The tax collectors ought to keep their demands within just limits (v. 13)—a severe requirement because the job was not a pleasant one, and this policy could guarantee only the most meager earnings. The soldiers he asked to be content with their rations and to avoid all extortion and violence in the carrying out of their duties. He did not imply it was sinful to be a soldier. Forbidding pillaging of the local population could be a significant restriction at a time when the soldiers were extremely hard up and in need of money or food. John made no effort to make his ethical demands palatable. Clearly exhortation (*parenesis*) goes along with proclamation (*kerygma*). Repentance and FAITH is to be accompanied with a serious attempt to reform one's life. "Produce fruit in keeping with repentance" (Matt. 3:8). A genuine experience of grace must reveal itself in spiritual fruit.

IV. Baptism. The rite that John performed on penitent sinners was the outstanding feature of his whole ministry; yet he was by no means its originator. Its distinctiveness lay in the meaning John put into the act. Basically this had two facets: a messianic or eschatological orientation, and personal renewal in the life of the person baptized. John saw himself as a figure of the end times sent in accord with divine prophecy to set in motion the complex of events in which the Messiah would be revealed to Israel and the world. John's water baptism was a sign of a greater BAPTISM OF THE HOLY SPIRIT that the Messiah would administer. At the same time, John was conscious of the unworthiness of Israel to receive her messianic King. He was no universalist—God would deal with his people, not some other—yet John rejected the notion that simply being a Jew was enough to insure divine favor. Repentance and reform of life were prerequisites to entering the Messiah's kingdom. Baptism was the first evidence of the sincere desire to alter one's way of behavior.

From what source did John derive inspiration for his practice and theology of baptism? Scholars such as M. Lidzbarski (*Das Johannesbuch der Mandäer* [1915]) have sought to relate John's baptism with that of the Mandeans, but there is a serious problem of chronology. The Mandean sect arose centuries after the time of John and borrowed their rite from Nestorian Christians. Their esteem for John came in during the Islamic period. It is utterly impossible to detect any influence on John from such a source. Something of the same is true of Jewish PROSELYTE baptism. It is questionable whether the practice existed in the time of John. It may have had an influence upon later Christian practices, but cannot be used as a sure source for John's baptism. Differences also exist in essence. Proselyte baptism was politically and ritualistically oriented, whereas John's was eschatological and ethical. One needs to be very cautious in assuming that proselyte baptism gives a model for John's. The fact that it is not mentioned in the NT limits its usefulness. (See further D. Smith, "Jewish Proselyte Baptism and the Baptism of John," *Restoration Quarterly* 25 [1982]: 13–32.)

The most natural place to look for an antecedent is the OT itself. Ceremonial lustrations to effect PURITY are common in the ancient world and in the Bible. In Lev. 15, bathing in water is prescribed to cope with uncleanness. All forms of Jewish baptism sprang from such a source. It is unlikely that any real distinction was made between outward bodily cleanness and inward spiritual purity. The outer lustrations had deep spiritual significance. The believer ought to have "clean hands and a pure heart," an inner purging with hyssop as well as outward ablutions (Pss. 24:4; 51:7). Ultimately, all baptism looks forward to the opening of a fountain that can cleanse from sin and uncleanness (Zech. 13:1).

The Qumran sect carried on their activities very near the place where John began his, which is often pointed out as the source of John's rite and theology. The Qumran community practiced a kind of baptism or washing ritual for repentance. According to the *Manual of Discipline* (or *Community Rule*), such a ritual could have no effect unless accompanied with sincere repentance (1QS V, 13–14). There may be no distinction between inner and outer, but there is also no separation of the two. The practices at Qumran go a long way in providing a possible source for John's baptism. The coincidence is striking, and a positive relationship may indeed have existed between them.

There are, however, important differences to note before assuming any substantial identity. John's baptism was a once-and-for-all, final act of repentance, not to be repeated. There is no indication that the first baptism at Qumran was thought of as an initiatory rite. The whole tenor of John's preaching was more urgent and eschatological than theirs. His message was offered to the whole nation, not to exclusive members of the sect. If he did borrow some of the ideas of Qumran, he altered them before use. More likely John saw his rite in terms of prophetic symbolism. The word of the Lord could be performed as well as preached. Adapting the practice of Jewish lustration to his purposes gave John the ideal instrument for putting his message before men. His baptism was a plenary cleansing from all sin and uncleanness, an eschatological act that united the penitent with the remnant Israel of the latter days.

V. John and Jesus. The earliest part of Jesus' public ministry was spent in the circle of the Baptist. The fourth gospel makes this fact apparent. Theirs was one joint ministry. It is not simply that their work overlapped or that they worked in the same area, but rather that they shared a common outlook and concern. The cleansing of the temple (Jn. 2:13–22) shows Jesus putting into effect the terms of John's prediction of purging and judgment. The first chapter in the ministry of Jesus is one of the closing chapters in the ministry of John, so closely related were they at this point. After his baptism, Jesus retired to the wilderness for fasting and prayer. Soon afterward, Jesus surrounded himself with a band of disciples and practiced baptism in Judea (1:35–51; 3:22). They carried on parallel ministries, both of them penetrating even into SAMARITAN territory. As Jesus' fame grew, John's diminished (3:30). While in association with John, however, Jesus remained in the background, concealing his identity from all but a few (2:24). At CANA only his mother knew the secret (2:3–4), but after Cana his disciples knew it also (2:11). Both Jesus and John claimed authority from heaven for themselves and for one another (Matt. 21:23–27). Soon after John was arrested and imprisoned in the fortress of MACHAERUS, Jesus began an open ministry in GALILEE (Mk. 1:14). John was able even in prison to keep in touch with the activities of Jesus through his followers (Matt. 11:2). He was concerned about the progress of the eschatological event he himself had announced.

A question arises as to the identity of John. When John was approached by the party from Jerusalem, and asked if he was the Christ or Elijah, he replied emphatically in the negative (Jn. 1:20–21). When Jesus ventured to reveal his evaluation of John, he affirmed unmistakably that John was Elijah (Matt. 11:14). Is it possible that Jesus regarded him as Elijah, whereas John did not? John certainly played the part of Elijah, both the historical and the eschatological figure. Could he have done so without modeling himself upon the pattern set entirely? He knew himself to be the forerunner of the Messiah (Jn. 3:28). The answer must lie in the sense of the question posed to John. Although John lived in the spirit and power of Elijah (Lk. 1:17) and was called Elijah by Christ himself, he was not Elijah *redivivus* in a literal sense. Figuratively he was Elijah, and he carried out the functions of the forerunner, but he did not want to accept the Jewish interpretation of this figure. He preferred to designate himself simply as the "voice" (Jn. 1:23), because this title was not loaded with traditional misinterpretations.

VI. Death. The account of John's death is the only major story in the Gospel of Mark that is not about Jesus (Mk. 6:17–29). It must have reached its place in the narrative after being preserved and told by the disciples of John who claimed his dead body (6:29). Many radical critics regard the story as legendary, containing merely a historical kernel. It is clear from both Mark and Josephus that Herod Antipas regarded John as a prime instigator in the messianic ferment that gripped Judea. When he heard about Jesus' miracles, he thought John must have been raised from the dead (6:14). John constituted a political threat to Herod's reign, and when John also criticized the morals of HERODIAS, his bride, Herod locked John in prison. There is nothing intrinsically unlikely in the story and nothing historically impossible. The death had an effect on Jesus himself. When he first heard of the arrest, he withdrew into Galilee, sensing danger to himself (Matt. 4:12); when he learned of John's execution he went into a lonely place (14:13), doubtless to contemplate the dreadful meaning of this for his own future.

VII. Followers. As the prophets of old, John and Jesus both gathered a band of disciples (Isa. 8:14). Some of John's disciples came to Jesus and joined his group (Jn. 1:35–42). In a short ministry of six months, John had gained great popularity. "The whole Judean countryside and all the people of Jerusalem went out to him" (Mk. 1:5). Loyalty to John's memory was still strong several years later when Jesus played upon it to avoid answering a loaded question (Matt. 21:26). John trained his men in prayer (Lk. 11:1) and in fasting (Matt. 9:14). Although Jesus himself did not recommend fasting, he predicted that when he was taken away, his disciples would again fast (9:15). The Christian practice of fasting is found again in the DIDACHE (8.1).

Long after the death of Jesus, PRISCILLA AND AQUILA met a Jew named APOLLOS who was a disciple of John the Baptist and came from ALEXANDRIA (Acts 18:24–28), and soon after PAUL encountered a band of twelve of John's disciples at EPHESUS (19:1–7). This indicates that John's followers were fairly numerous and widespread long after his death. The two messianic communities were hardly in competition, because as soon as John's disciples heard the gospel of Christ, they gladly accepted the message. The Gospels are plain in the conviction that Jesus had been under John's ministry in the beginning and that he identified Jesus to be the One whose way he was called to prepare. Competition and rivalry are not the words to use in this context. The problem was one of complete correlation between the wide sections of support each man received separately.

There is no evidence of conflict between the two groups until much later, when the *Clementine Recognitions* were written (see CLEMENTINE LITERATURE). But it is not known whether this group could actually trace their roots back to John; it is possible that they simply adopt him as their patron saint because of their practice of baptism and their desire to outdo the Christian groups. Years later, Josephus could still write that many people in his day held to the theory that Herod suffered defeat because of his treatment of John, and this proves how deep a loyalty and impression John created in the minds of his contemporaries. Even today there exists a sect called the Mandeans that claims to perpetuate the movement begun by John the Baptist. Without doubt, John the Baptist was a profound influence upon the people of his day and upon the birth and growth of the church. His prophetic passion and burning zeal set the stage for the emergence of Jesus Christ.

(See further A. T. Robertson, *John the Loyal* [1911]; A. Blakiston, *John the Baptist and his Relation to Jesus* [1912]; C. H. Kraeling, *John the Baptist* [1951]; J. Steinmann, *Saint John the Baptist and the Desert Tradition* [1957]; J. A. T. Robinson, *Twelve*

New Testament Studies [1962], chs. 1–2; W. Wink, *John the Baptist in the Gospel Tradition* [1968]; G. Lindeskog, "Johannes der Täufer: Einige Randbemerkungen zum heutigen Stand der Forschung," *ASTI* 12 [1983]: 55–83; J. E. Taylor, *The Immerser: John the Baptist within Second Temple Judaism* [1997]; G. Yamasaki, *John the Baptist in Life and Death: Audience-oriented Criticism of Matthew's Narrative* [1998]; C. K. Rothschild, *Baptist Traditions and Q* [2005].) C. H. PINNOCK

Joiada joi´uh-duh (יוֹיָדָע *H3421*, short form of יְהוֹיָדָע *H3381*, "Yahweh has known [*i.e.*, has been concerned]"; see JEHOIADA). (1) Son of Paseah; he and Meshullam repaired the Jeshanah Gate (see OLD GATE) under NEHEMIAH (Neh. 3:6; KJV, "Jehoiada"). They are said to have "laid its beams and put its doors and bolts and bars in place."

(2) Son of ELIASHIB and descendant of JESHUA the high priest (Neh. 12:10–11, 22). A son of his married the daughter of SANBALLAT the Horonite (Neh. 13:28; NRSV, "Jehoiada"). (See J. C. VanderKam, *From Joshua to Caiaphas: High Priests after the Exile* [2004], 53–54.)

Joiakim joi´uh-kim (יוֹיָקִים *H3423*, short form of יְהוֹיָקִים *H3383*, "Yahweh raises up"; see JEHOIAKIM, JOKIM). Son of JESHUA and father of ELIASHIB; all three held the office of high priest after the EXILE (Neh. 12:10, 12, 26). (See J. C. VanderKam, *From Joshua to Caiaphas: High Priests after the Exile* [2004], 45–49.)

Joiarib joi´uh-rib (יוֹיָרִיב *H3424*, short form of יְהוֹיָרִיב *H3384*, "Yahweh contends [for me]"; see JEHOIARIB and JOARIB). (1) One of two "men of learning" who, with others, were sent by EZRA to search for Levites (Ezra 8:16). See discussion under ELNATHAN #3.

(2) Son of Zechariah and ancestor of Maaseiah; the latter was a prominent member of the tribe of JUDAH who lived in Jerusalem after the EXILE (Neh. 11:5).

(3) A man included among the "leaders of the priests and their associates in the days of Jeshua" (Neh. 12:6; cf. v. 7). He may be the same individual who is apparently described as the father of JEDAIAH (11:10 NRSV; the text may have suffered textual corruption, and the NIV dissociates the names of Jedaiah and Joiarib). Later, in the days of the high priest JOIAKIM, the head of Joiarib's family was Mattenai (12:19; cf. v. 12). This Joiarib is probably the same as JEHOIARIB (1 Chr. 9:10). (See the discussion in *ABD*, 3:932.)

Jokdeam jok´dee-uhm (יָקְדְעָם *H3680*, derivation uncertain). A town in the hill country of the tribe of JUDAH (Josh. 15:56); it is usually identified with JORKEAM (1 Chr. 2:44). The precise location of Jokdeam is unknown, but it is listed with towns that lie approximately 4–10 mi. S and SE of HEBRON, so a few scholars have tentatively identified it with modern Khirbet er-Raq‘ah, about one mile N of JUTTAH.

Jokim joh´kim (יוֹקִים *H3451*, short form of יְהוֹיָקִים *H3383*, "Yahweh raises up," i.e., "may Yahweh deliver"; see JEHOIAKIM, JOIAKIM). Son of SHELA and grandson of JUDAH; he and one (or more) of his brothers are said to have "ruled in" (or "married into") MOAB and JASHUBI LEHEM (1 Chr. 4:22; the Heb. verb is *bāʿal H1249*, which means either "to rule over" or, more frequently, "to marry"). Some scholars believe that the words "and Jashubi Lehem" should be emended to either "but returned to Lehem" (so NRSV) or "and they resided in Bethlehem" (cf. G. N. Knoppers, *I Chronicles 1–9*, AB 12 [2004], 342–43).

Jokmeam jok´mee-uhm (יָקְמְעָם *H3695* [also יָקְמָעָם], perhaps "the Kinsman [*i.e.*, ancestral god] takes a stand [*or* establishes]"; see JEKAMEAM). A Levitical city within the tribal territory of EPHRAIM, allotted to the clan of KOHATH (1 Chr. 6:68; called KIBZAIM in the parallel list, Josh. 21:22); it is mentioned between GEZER and BETH HORON, which were in SW Ephraim, but its precise location is unknown. In addition, a town by the name of Jokmeam marked the border of SOLOMON's fifth administrative district (1 Ki. 4:12; KJV, "Jokneam"); because it is listed after BETH SHAN and ABEL MEHOLAH, this town was probably in the JORDAN Valley, in E Ephraim, and it may be identified with modern Tell es-Samadi (some 12 mi. ESE of SHECHEM) or nearby Tell el Mazar (but see Z. Kallai, *Historical Geography of the Bible* [1986],

101, who thinks it possible that Tall al-Manar is Abarim, in which case Jokneam should perhaps be identified with Tell Sheikh edh-Dhiab).

Some scholars argue that both 1 Chronicles and 1 Kings refer to the eastern town (cf. Y. Aharoni, *The Land of the Bible: A Historical Geography*, rev. ed. [1979], 313); others believe that two distinct towns bore the name Jokmeam. Still others think that 1 Ki. 4:12 (which may have suffered transpositions) refers to a completely different town, JOKNEAM; if so, the spelling "Jokmeam" may be an alternate form or the result of scribal corruption (M. Cogan, *1 Kings*, AB 10 [2001], 208, defends the textual integrity of the passage).

Jokneam jok′nee-uhm (יָקְנְעָם, *H3696*, derivation uncertain). **(1)** A town in the tribal territory of ZEBULUN that served to mark its SW boundary (Josh. 19:11); it was assigned to the descendants of MERARI as a Levitical city (21:34; 1 Chr. 6:77). The king of this royal Canaanite city, said to be located in CARMEL, is included in the list of kings defeated by JOSHUA on the W of the Jordan (Josh. 12:22). This list probably includes the major cities that participated in the war as allies of HAZOR against Israel (see Y. Aharoni, *The Land of the Bible: A Historical Geography*, rev. ed. [1979], 223, 230–32). Jokneam is identified with Tell Qeimun, a mound located at the NW end of the plain of ESDRAELON, 7 mi. NW of MEGIDDO.

Jokneam was one of the fortresses that guarded the routes across Carmel. Although Jokneam was not on the main N-S trade route (VIA MARIS), it was on the branch of it that ran from Megiddo to the plain of Acco (Aharoni, *The Land of the Bible*, 52). It secured the only pass across Carmel which had access to the port of DOR, and it had the advantage of being the lowest of the passes in elevation. Jokneam appears as number 113 in a list of 119 towns captured by THUTMOSE III (written ʿn qnʿm). The route was considered by the officers of Thutmose as a possible alternate to the Megiddo route (Napoleon used the Jokneam route for his march against Acre/Acco). Intensive archaeological excavations, which began in 1977, have revealed destructions of the city both in the Late Bronze Age (late 13th cent. B.C.) and in the Iron Age (late 11th cent.), resulting from either military or natural disasters. Jokneam was subsequently resettled, and by the 9th cent. it was a well-fortified Israelite city. There is also evidence that it participated in international trade during the Persian period. (See A. Ben-Tor in *ABD*, 3:933–35; id. in *NEAEHL*, 3:805–11.) R. E. HAYDEN

(2) KJV form of JOKMEAM (only 1 Ki. 4.12).

Jokshan jok′shan (יָקְשָׁן, *H3705*, derivation uncertain). Son of ABRAHAM and KETURAH, and father of SHEBA and DEDAN (Gen. 25:2–3; 1 Chr. 1:32). Abraham sent the sons of Keturah to the E (Gen. 25:6), where they became the ancestors of Arabian tribes. Because the names Sheba and Dedan appear in the Table of NATIONS (10:7, 28), some identify Jokshan with JOKTAN (10:25–29), but etymological considerations speak against it (see F. V. Winnett, "The Arabian Genealogies in Genesis," in *Translating and Understanding the Old Testament*, ed. H. T. Frank and W. L. Reed [1970], 171–96, esp. 189).

Joktan jok′tan (יָקְטָן, *H3690*, possibly from a root meaning "vigilant"). Son of EBER and descendant of SHEM, included in the Table of NATIONS (Gen. 10:25–29; 1 Chr. 1:19–23). His thirteen children are said to have lived from MESHA to SEPHAR (Gen. 10:30), probably referring to locations in SW ARABIA. Some see a connection between Joktan and Qahtan, the latter reputed to be the ancestor of the S Arabian tribes (cf. J. Simons, *The Geographical and Topographical Texts of the Old Testament* [1959], 48–49). See also JOKSHAN.

Joktheel jok′thee-uhl (יָקְתְאֵל, *H3706*, possibly "God nourishes"; cf. JEKUTHIEL). **(1)** A town within the tribal territory of JUDAH (Josh. 15:38). Included in the S SHEPHELAH district, it was presumably near MIZPEH and LACHISH, but its precise location is unknown.

(2) Name given to the Edomite city of SELA by AMAZIAH, king of Judah, after he captured it (2 Ki. 14:7).

Jona joh′nuh. According to the KJV, the father of Simon PETER (Jn. 1:42). See JOHN #4.

Jonadab, Jehonadab joh′nuh-dab, ji-hoh′nuh-dab (יוֹנָדָב, *H3432*, short form of יְהוֹנָדָב *H3386*

[2 Sam. 13:5; 1 Ki. 10:15, 23; Jer. 35:8, 14, 16, 18], "Yahweh is [or shows himself] willing [or noble or generous]"; cf. NEDABIAH). **(1)** Son of SHIMEAH (or SHAMMAH) and nephew of King DAVID (2 Sam. 13:3–5, 32–35). Scripture calls him "a very shrewd man," and he used his craftiness to promote the incestuous lust of AMNON. The result was Amnon's rape of TAMAR, then ABSALOM's murder of Amnon, and ultimately civil war. The same Jonadab, however, at least for a time, evidently remained intimate with the royal household, for upon the death of Amnon, he reassured David that his other sons had not been killed. Some scholars identify Jonadab with Shimeah's son JONATHAN, who is credited with killing a giant (2 Sam. 21:21; 1 Chr. 20:7); others believe Jonadab and Jonathan were brothers.

(2) Son (or descendant) of Recab; he encouraged JEHU in the abolition of BAAL worship in SAMARIA (1 Ki. 10:15, 23 ["Jehonadab"]) and was the founder of a nomadic community (Jer. 35:6–19). For full discussion, see RECABITE.

Jonah joh'nuh (יוֹנָה *H3434*, "dove"; Ἰωνᾶς *G2731*). **(1)** Son of Amittai; Israelite prophet. See JONAH, BOOK OF.

(2) One of the Levites who agreed to put away their foreign wives (1 Esd. 9:23; the parallel account has "Eliezer," Ezra 10:23).

(3) Father of Simon PETER (Matt. 16:17). See JOHN #4.

Jonah, Book of. Fifth book of the Minor Prophets, attributed to Jonah son of Amittai, an 8th-cent. prophet of Israel. This little book of four chapters has been the subject of intense disagreement concerning its historicity and interpretation. The debate is occasioned primarily by the narrative's supernatural elements: the great fish, the repentance of NINEVEH, and the gourd and worm.

I. Background. Other than the mention of Nineveh and of Jonah, the contents offer little help in relating the book to its background. The events recorded in the book must have taken place prior to 612 B.C., when Nineveh was destroyed. Some evidence seems to support a date in the 8th cent., the period mentioned in 2 Ki. 14:25 in which Jonah the prophet lived. If this dating (to be discussed later) is accepted, then the historical situation would be that of the domination of the Assyrian empire over the ANE (see ASSYRIA AND BABYLONIA) and the resurgence of the northern kingdom (Israel) during its golden age under JEROBOAM II. The supposed motif of the book—its implicit rebuke of narrow nationalism and its implicit appeal for the universality of God's love—would fit well into the historical era when the Assyrians were a feared and despised

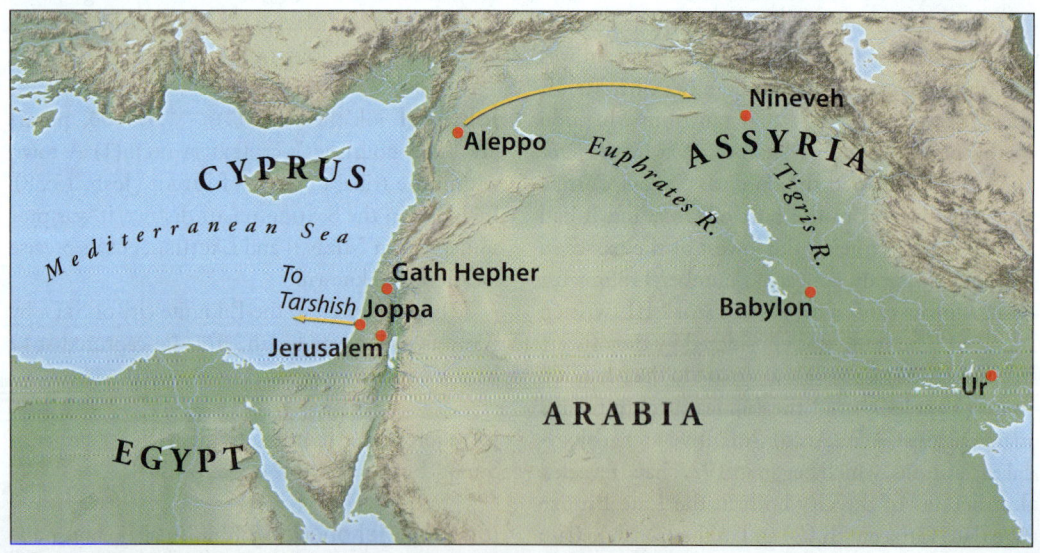

Jonah's ministry in Nineveh.

always. After Assyria had been vanquished, the book would not have carried as much weight to its own generation. In attempting to interpret its message, one can understand it perfectly by positing an 8th-cent. real life situation as the background.

II. Unity. Most modern scholars agree that the book is a unit, although some would prefer to think the psalm (Jon. 2:2–9) was written by someone other than the author of the narrative portions, and perhaps later as well. Since the psalm makes extensive use of the canonical psalms, some regard it as a "scissors and paste pot" composition. E. J. Young (*Introduction to the Old Testament* [1960], 281) points out that the chapter is essential to the book and that chs. 1–2 are balanced by chs. 3–4 (1:1–3a and 2:2 are paralleled respectively by 3:1–3a and 4:2). Some have objected that 2:1 is inconsistent with the content of the psalm, namely, thanksgiving. However, Ps. 86 is labelled "a prayer," though it too contains thanksgiving. Others have objected to the thanksgiving psalm on the basis that being in the monster's belly would be no deliverance. However, the content of the psalm indicates that it gives thanks for deliverance from drowning, not for ultimate deposition on dry land. Otto Eissfeldt (*The Old Testament: An Introduction* [1965], 405) viewed Jonah as being composed of two legends: the first (Jon. 1–3) tells of Jonah's disobedience, while the second (ch. 4) tells of Jonah's controversy with God. More radical critics see three or more sources used in the composition of the book. This is a minority opinion not generally shared, even by those who reject the book's historicity.

III. Authorship. Traditionally, the book has been ascribed to Jonah son of Amittai, who lived during the 8th cent. B.C. He was born at GATH-HEPHER (cf. Josh. 19:13), in the territory of ZEBULUN, about 3 mi. NE of NAZARETH (cf. 2 Ki. 14:25). According to legend, he was the son of the widow of ZAREPHATH, and was the youth whom ELISHA sent to anoint JEHU to be the king of Israel.

Most modern scholars, other than conservative ones, reject the traditional belief that Jonah wrote the book. Among the arguments advanced against the thesis are the following: (1) The book itself does not claim he is the author. In rebuttal, one notes that the introductory formula (Jon. 1:1) is parallel to that used in Hosea, Joel, Micah, and Zephaniah, and close to that used in other prophetic books of whose authorship there is little or no debate. (2) The book refers to the prophet Jonah in the third person. Again, the introductory formula shows this to be common practice that can be seen in works attributed to Moses, Xenophon, and Julius Caesar. (3) The book is later than the 8th cent., therefore it cannot be by Jonah ben Amittai. The date of the book is discussed below. If objections to an early date are overcome, then there seems little reason to deny the authorship of the book to the prophet whose name it bears.

IV. Date. Acceptance of the book's authorship by Jonah would necessitate a date in the first half of the 8th cent. B.C. Events in Assyrian history, such as the trend toward monotheism in the reign of Adad-Nirari III (c. 810–783), or the great plague of the reign of Assurdan III (c. 771–754), would help explain the mass repentance. Gleason L. Archer (*A Survey of Old Testament Introduction*, rev. ed. [1994], 342) would date the book near the end of Jonah's career, c. 760.

A *terminus ad quem* for the book's composition would be 200 B.C., because Sir. 49:10 refers to "twelve minor prophets" and Tob. 14:4, 8 specifically refers to Jonah. Most critical scholars would date the book between 500 and 300 B.C. J. A. Bewer suggests a date in the Hellenistic period (300–200 B.C.), perhaps because he posits Joppa as the locale of the Perseus-Andromeda legend and sees reflections of that legend in Jonah (*A Critical and Exegetical Commentary on Haggai, Zechariah, Malachi and Jonah*, ICC [1912], 403). The most frequently accepted late date is c. 450 B.C. (cf. S. R. Driver, *Introduction to the Literature of the Old testament* [1897], 322) although others opt for a date c. 350 B.C. (cf. W. O. E. Oesterley and T. H. Robinson, *Introduction to the Books of the Old Testament* [1958], 374).

Many arguments are advanced to support a late date. Among them should be mentioned the following: (1) Nineveh is spoken of as a city no longer in existence (Jon. 3:3). However, note the similar language in Lk. 24:13, though no one doubts that EMMAUS existed in the 1st cent. A.D. (2) The use of the phrase "king of Nineveh" would not be normal in the 8th cent., when "king of Assyria" would be the title employed. The OT, however, amply illustrates the former usage (cf. 1 Ki. 21:1 with 20:43; 2 Ki. 3:9, 12; 2 Chr. 24:23). (3) The general thought and ideas of Jonah presuppose that the author knew the great prophets. Examples cited include Jon. 3:10 (cf. Jer. 18:7–8); Jon. 3:5 (cf. Joel 1:13–14); Jon. 3:9 (cf. Joel 2:14); and Jon. 4:2 (cf. Joel 2:13). The evidence is far from overwhelming that Jonah borrowed from Jeremiah, and the comparison with Joel begs the question of whether or not Joel is late. (4) It is further argued that the ideas found in the book are late, designed to rebuke the exclusivism shown by such writers as Haggai, Zechariah, Malachi, Ezra, and Nehemiah. The concept of missionary universalism (cf. Isa. 40–66) is said to be postexilic. Aside from the *petitio principi* error of the reference to Isaiah, this argument ignores the fact that universalism is found in the prophets prior to the EXILE (cf. Amos 9:7). (5) Since the psalm of thanksgiving of Jon. 2 reflects the canonical Psalms, it is inferred that this passage is not original and must be dated late. Modern linguistic discoveries, however, show how the canonical Psalms reflect earlier Canaanite literature, which contradicts any such late dating of Psalms as was popular in the first half of the 20th cent. (6) The use of Aramaisms in Jonah is said to prove its late date because ARAMAIC vocabulary and usage infiltrated the HEBREW LANGUAGE in the exilic and postexilic periods. Archer (*Survey*, 345, 348) has carefully refuted specific examples of Aramaisms sometimes given to support the late date.

The tendency to date the book late appears to be based on the theological bias that the book is a rebuke of postexilic exclusivism and hypernationalism. These traits are seldom completely missing in any nation in any period. The late date seems predicated upon a *religionsgeschichtliche* approach to the content of Jonah. It leaves the student with the haunting question, "If Jonah was not written by the 8th-century prophet, why was it admitted to the canon?"

V. Occasion and purpose. It would seem evident that the book was called forth by God's concern for the spiritual welfare of the great city of Nineveh. Some would also see another factor at work, namely, God's concern for his chosen people who needed teaching and admonition which the prophet accomplished through the events recorded in the book rather than by direct oracles or prophetic utterances.

Various scholars have seen different purposes for the book of Jonah. One suggestion (advocated by Eduard Riehm) has been that it was written as an apologetic: it explains that prophecy of doom is conditional (cf. Jer. 18:7–8). Some think the book is didactic: it was written to teach that God's forgiveness is available to all upon the basis of individual fear of Yahweh and repentance; God's mercy is not limited to Israel. Others view the book as a parable whose purpose is to drive home to Israel her sin in her national failure to fulfill God's mission among the nations. Related to this view is the idea that the book is basically a missionary tractate, designed to break down Hebrew particularism and exclusiveness (cf. Jon. 3:10; 4:11), of which Jonah himself is an example; his spirit is akin to that of Nahum, who expects God to destroy Nineveh in the 7th cent. A serious objection to this view is that it leaves unexplained Jonah's message of judgment. One brief clause ("Forty more days and Nineveh will be overturned," Jon. 3:4) calls for unrelieved doom, not the offering of God's grace to the Ninevites. Young (*Introduction*, 280) denies this universalistic purpose and stresses instead the element of predictive history in the book, but such a view deprives the book of meaning for its first readers. As in many literary works, so in Jonah, the purpose may be manifold, not limited to a single idea.

VI. Canonicity and text. Since the book is mentioned during the intertestamental period as one of the twelve prophets, there seems to have been an early acceptance of it as canonical. The Hebrew text of Jonah is well preserved. The language is clear, classical Hebrew, with a few Aramaisms that some consider late, but Aramaic influences are found in preexilic times. The SEPTUAGINT adds little to our understanding of the text. Some scholars think Jon. 4:5 is misplaced and belongs after 3:4.

VII. Literary form. Various students have placed Jonah in widely different literary genres. Traditionally, it has been listed as history (except Jon. 2). In the 19th cent. the tendency arose to view the book as allegory, parable, or pure legend. It is evident that the book does not follow the pattern of the other prophetic books that are collections of oracles. Rather, it is a story about a prophet, similar to the ELIJAH cycles in 1 Kings. There are partial parallels to personal history being embedded in prophecy in the experiences recorded by the prophets Hosea, Isaiah, and Ezekiel.

Those who view the book as ALLEGORY frequently identify the following elements: Jonah is disobedient Israel; the sea is the Gentile world (the dispersion); the great fish is Babylon (cf. Jer. 51:34, 44); the three days is the captivity; the gourd is Zerubbabel (cf. A. Bentzen, *Introduction to the Old Testament*, 2nd ed., 2 vols. [1952], 2:146). Archer (*Survey*, 343) criticizes this approach: "If the whale represented Babylon, what did Nineveh represent? As for the ship ... it is hard to see what this would correspond to in the allegory; nor is it clear why three days should be selected to represent seventy years of captivity." Allegory, by definition, is supposed to be worked out in all details. It seems evident that Jonah does not fit the definition.

The view that the book is legend or myth was advocated by T. K. Cheyne. Oesterley refuted the mythological interpretation that the great fish was Tehom (the deep, i.e., the salt sea), pointing out that in Jonah the sea is not looked upon as evil. Others have viewed the monster as a reference to NEBUCHADNEZZAR. While there are supernatural elements in the Jonah story as there are in MYTH, these supernatural elements may be interpreted historically rather than mythically.

Those who look upon Jonah as a parable appeal to passages such as 2 Sam. 12:1–4; Isa. 5; Lk. 10:25–37. This approach interprets the book as parabolic of how God will yet act in history (cf. Matt. 24:32–33). Another view is that the book is part of a sermon in which certain events, either actual or fictitious, are narrated to impart a spiritual truth much as a modern minister may use anecdotes of actual or imaginary events to drive home his points. Thus Jonah would be an early example of a midrashic homily.

Finally, the view most commonly espoused by conservatives is that the book is history. Except for Jon. 2, the book is concerned exclusively with events that happened in the life of Jonah. Although there is some indication of the general tenor of the theology of the writer in the book, the only point of the story driven home is that suggested in 4:10–11. Since the historicity of the book has been the subject of extensive debate it deserves separate treatment.

VIII. Historicity. Many critics deny the historicity of Jonah. Usually this is done because of the supernatural elements in the story. These include the great fish that swallowed Jonah, the conversion of the whole city of Nineveh, the gourd prepared to shelter Jonah, and the worm that destroyed the gourd. For all these objections to the supernatural the response must be to ask whether God is limited by his creation or is free to supervene in the operation of so-called "natural laws."

The arguments for the late date of the book also are used to support the thesis that the book is not historical. These arguments include the use of the phrase "king of Nineveh" (Jon. 3:6), and the use of the past tense, "Nineveh was a great city" (3:2; Archer [*Survey*, 344] would translate the verb, "had become"). Other arguments against the historicity of Jonah have included the following:

(1) The enormous size of Nineveh. However, the text simply says Jonah took three days preaching on street corners, not that the city required three days walking to traverse it. The city, including its suburbs, may have had a population of about 600,000; the administrative district covered a much greater area. It has also been argued, however, that the text speaks of Nineveh's importance and that therefore the "three days" refers to the time needed for a proper diplomatic visit (cf. NIV).

(2) The sudden repentance of the people. As indicated above, there were at least two incidents in the 8th cent. that would provide a suitable background for wholesale repentance. Modern missionaries to Muslim peoples have experienced similar phenomena. Nor should any limit be put upon the working of God's Spirit. According to a different view (D. Stuart, *Hosea–Jonah*, WBC 31 [1987], 494), the repentance of the Ninevites did not involve spiritual conversion to Yahweh, but a mass movement of mourning and reform such as is otherwise attested among pagan nations generally.

(3) The great fish. This element has been the prime target of arguments against the historicity of the book. Accepting the supernatural—"the Lord provided a great fish" (Jon. 1:17)—removes this difficulty. Some have attempted to make the story more credible by references to modern seamen who have been rescued after spending hours in the stomachs of denizens of the oceans (e.g., cf. A. J. Wilson in *PTR* 25 [1927]: 630–42).

The historicity of the book has been upheld by some outstanding scholars in the 19th cent. as well as almost all conservative scholars of the 20th cent. In addition to refuting the arguments for the non-historical character of the book, most advocates of its historicity point out that from early times the Jews regarded it as historical (cf. 3 Macc. 6:8; Tob. 14:4, 8; Jos. *Ant.* 9.10.2 §§208ff.). These scholars also point out that Christ regarded the book as historical (cf. Matt. 12:39–40; 16:4; Lk. 11:29). In the first passage from Matthew, there is no MS evidence of interpolation in the text as some have claimed. A careful comparison of Jn. 3:14 and 1 Cor. 10:1–11 would indicate that the formula Christ used in referring to Jonah ("as ... so") was used in referring to historical events.

IX. Content and outline. The chapter divisions of the English versions of Jonah follow the natural thought of the book. The first chapter tells of Jonah's call to go to Nineveh and declare the city's doom, but Jonah disobeyed and boarded a ship bound for TARSHISH (or "a refinery ship"). A violent storm arose at sea, and it abated only after the sailors threw Jonah overboard, having cast lots to determine the culprit. Jonah was then swallowed by a great fish and remained in its belly three days and three nights. The second chapter gives a psalm of deliverance uttered by the prophet within the belly of the fish, and concludes with his being deposited once more on dry land. The following section tells how Jonah was recommissioned to proclaim Nineveh's doom, went to the city, and preached in it for three days. The result was a wholesale repentance of the city, king and commoner alike, so that even the beasts were clad in garments signifying repentance. The last chapter tells how Jonah was angry because God had "changed his mind" (cf. Jon. 3:10 NRSV) about destroying Nineveh because it

Metal relief on the door of the Church of the Annunciation (Nazareth) depicting Jonah being spewed out on dry land.

had repented, how a GOURD (prob. a *ricinus*, castor bean plant) was prepared to shelter Jonah from the intense near eastern sun, and how the worm was sent to destroy the plant so that Jonah might be taught the lesson of God's love for a city—even as Jonah mourned over the withering of the gourd.

Some have seen in the book of Jonah a detailed TYPOLOGY of Christ. In some items this typology has been positive, in some details it has been a typology of contrast. (1) Both Jonah and Christ have a special commission (cf. Jn. 3:17). (2) Jonah was disobedient, Christ was perfectly obedient. (3) Both are involved in a storm at sea. (4) Jonah sacrificed himself, so did Christ (but Jonah was not blameless). (5) The great fish was a figure of death: Christ suffered a literal death and burial. (6) The cry from the fish's belly is parallel to Christ's "My God, my God, why ... ?" (7) The deliverance from the fish's belly is paralleled by Christ's resurrection on the third day. (8) Jonah's mission to Nineveh after his metaphoric death and resurrection is typical of Christ's successful postresurrection preaching.

Jonah also has been taken by most premillennialists to be typical of Israel. (1) He was called to witness to Gentiles. (2) Jonah suffered a disaster in a great storm as Israel suffered disaster in rejecting Christ. (3) Jonah, like Israel, did not deny his people or his God. (4) Jonah's grave was the belly of a fish, while Israel's grave is among the nations.

(5) Jonah cried out to God as Israel will do at the end of time. (6) As Jonah was delivered from the fish, so Israel will be given a national resurrection (7) Jonah preached to Nineveh, so Israel will be God's witness (Rom. 11:12, 15).

The book of Jonah may be called biographic typology. Some view the book as predictive history. It is predictive of Christ, who was sent by the Father, suffered entombment, was resurrected, and preached salvation for "all the world." It is predictive of Israel, who was a trouble to the Gentiles (as Jonah was to the sailors), was a witness to them, but was cast out by Gentiles and miraculously preserved for twenty centuries to be God's missionaries at the end of time (Zech. 8:7–23).

The book may be outlined as follows:
A. God's commission: Jonah's disobedience (Jon. 1)
B. God's care: Jonah's deliverance (Jon. 2)
C. God's renewed commission: Jonah's obedience (Jon. 3)
D. God's concern: Jonah's petulance rebuked (Jon. 4)

X. Theology. The book of Jonah offers some insights into the theology of the writer. He viewed God as having universal rule (vs. the henotheism so prevalent in the ANE). God is in all places—the land of Zebulun, the sea, Nineveh. He is also among all nations—the Israelites, the sailors (Phoenicians?), the Assyrians. He offers mercy and forgiveness to all. The terms of forgiveness for Nineveh are the same as for Israel—repentance. One notes, too, that the book freely depicts the openness of GENTILES to the message of Yahweh. The sailors hearken to his command to cast Jonah overboard. The Ninevites (as the Samaritans in the Gospels) are open to God's message. A third major topic of the book's theology is the inference that Israel (and the church) is responsible for proclaiming God's message, and must leave the results to God. Some have inferred that Jonah's reluctance to go to Nineveh was rooted in his belief that the message would bring repentance (which as an ardent nationalist he did not want to see happen).

(Important commentaries include J. A. Bewer et al., *A Critical and Exegetical Commentary on Haggai, Zechariah, Malachi and Jonah*, ICC [1912]; L. C. Allen, *Joel, Obadiah, Jonah, and Micah*, NICOT [1976]; H. W. Wolff, *Obadiah and Jonah: A Commentary* [1986]; D. Stuart, *Hosea-Jonah*, WBC 31 [1987]; J. Limburg, *Jonah: A Commentary*, OTL [1993]; B. K. Smith and F. S. Page, *Amos, Obadiah, Jonah*, NAC 19B [1995]; J. Baldwin in *The Minor Prophets: An Exegetical and Expository Commentary*, ed. T. McComiskey [1992–98], 2:543–90; J. K. Bruckner, *Jonah, Nahum, Habakkuk, Zephaniah*, NIVAC [2004]; R. R. Lessing, *Jonah* [2007].

(See also G. H. Aalders, *The Problem of Jonah* [1948]; J. D. Magonet, *Form and Meaning: Studies in Literary Techniques in the Book of Jonah*, 2nd ed. [1983]; K. M. Craig, Jr., *A Poetics of Jonah: Art in the Service of Ideology*, 2nd. ed. [1999]; J. H. Gaines, *Forgiveness in a Wounded World: Jonah's Dilemma* [2003]; A. Kamp, *Inner Worlds: A Cognitive-Linguistic Approach to the Book of Jonah* [2004]; T. A. Perry, *The Honeymoon Is Over: Jonah's Argument with God* [2006]; and the bibliography compiled by W. E. Mills, *Jonah-Micah* [2002].)   A. HELMBOLD

Jonam joh′nuhm (Ἰωνάμ *G2729*). KJV Jonan. Son of Elikaim, included in Luke's GENEALOGY OF JESUS CHRIST (Lk. 3:30).

Jonan joh′nuhn. KJV form of JONAM.

Jonas joh′nuhs. (1) KJV Apoc. and NT form of JONAH.

(2) According to the KJV, the father of Simon PETER (Jn. 21:15–17). See JOHN #4.

Jonathan jon′uh-thun (יוֹנָתָן *H3440*, short form of יְהוֹנָתָן *H3387*, "Yahweh has given [a child]"; the longer form is almost twice as common, but is almost always rendered "Jonathan" in English Bibles; see also JEHONATHAN). A very common name among the Israelites in all periods.

(1) Firstborn son of King SAUL and heir apparent to the throne of Israel (however, cf. J. Morgenstern in *JBL* 78 [1959], 322–25, who argues that Jonathan regarded David as the legitimate successor because the latter was both a hero and Saul's son-in-law). Jonathan is first mentioned as the commander of one-third of the forces of Israel (1 Sam. 13:2), so it may be assumed that he had earlier proved himself in his father's service (perhaps

against the Ammonites at JABESH GILEAD, 11:1–11). His contingent of 1,000 troops was at GIBEAH of BENJAMIN, while Saul himself commanded a larger detachment of 2,000 troops in MICMASH (13:5). Jonathan had initiated action by striking the PHILISTINES at GEBA (13:3). He either killed the "prefect," the officer of the Philistines, or destroyed a Philistine "garrison" by means of a surprise attack. Either event would have been sufficient to bring down wrath from the Philistines, who viewed the act as a revolt by the Israelites and thus mustered their forces to put down the uprising (13:5). Saul called for the mobilization of the militia (13:4), but most of the people either hid in caves, holes, cisterns, and tombs, or fled across the JORDAN to the E (13:6–7). Saul was forced to fall back from Micmash.

All the forces of Israel were at Geba when Jonathan and his armor-bearer decided to probe the Philistine defenses (1 Sam. 14:1). How much time had elapsed during the period of inactivity is indefinite, but Saul had waited at least seven days for the appearance of SAMUEL. The Philistines had sent out three raiding parties to the N, W, and E. This was probably intended to harass the tribes of Israel and to scatter Saul's forces before he was in a position for a decisive encounter. Jonathan crossed over the deep and precipitous Wadi es-Suweinit, which separates Geba from Micmash. Through a predetermined sign—the response of the Philistine sentries—Jonathan ascertained the will of God and fell upon the Philistine camp, killing about twenty men (14:8–14).

The confusion in the camp alerted Saul and his remaining force of 600 men, and they, together with some of the Israelites who had been pressed into service by the Philistines (1 Sam. 14:21), and with others who came out of hiding (14:22), pursued the Philistines who fled via the BETH HORON pass. During the engagement, Saul laid an oath on the people that none should eat anything until evening, and until he was avenged on his enemies (14:24). Jonathan, ignorant of the oath, ate some honey he found along the way (14:27). His act prevented the function of the oracle, and his sin was discovered (14:27, 42). Saul would have killed his own son, but the people ransomed him (14:45).

Although Saul was engaged in constant warfare with MOAB, AMMON, EDOM, the kings of ZOBAH, and the Philistines, nothing more is said concerning the military exploits of Jonathan until he met death with his father and brothers (ABINADAB and MALKI-SHUA), on Mount GILBOA. His sterling character is manifest, however, in another warfare—the warfare for prestige and popularity between his father and DAVID. Jonathan met David soon after the latter's successful encounter with GOLIATH, and he "became one in spirit with David, and he loved him as himself" (1 Sam. 18:1). No other friendship has surpassed that of his for David. He had nothing to gain by his unceasing devotion, but everything to lose.

At least three covenants between Jonathan and David are recorded. (a) At the first meeting, Jonathan made a covenant with David and sealed it by presenting his clothing and armor to David (1 Sam. 18:3–4). Later, when open hostility broke out between Saul and David because of David's continued military success and his growing popularity, Jonathan intervened and brought about a temporary reconciliation (19:1–6).

(b) Eventually, however, Saul again decided to rid himself of his rival by direct means. Jonathan, apparently unaware of Saul's intentions, was approached by David in an attempt to ascertain the reasoning behind Saul's action. Jonathan's guilelessness and naïveté are clearly evident when he confidently asserts, "Look, my father doesn't do anything, great or small, without confiding in

Jonathan son of Saul distinguished himself in battle against the Philistines at Micmash, a site identified with the modern village of Mukhmas in the foreground. (The canyon in the background is Wadi es-Suweinit.)

life." (1 Sam. 20:2). By means of a plan devised by David, Jonathan learned the real intent of his father and relayed this information to David. A second covenant arose out of this meeting that stressed David's attitude toward Jonathan and his descendants. Jonathan acknowledged that David would be the next king, and he wished David to swear that he would have mercy on his house (20:14–17). David kept this covenant and proved himself true to his friend.

(c) The third covenant is mentioned only briefly (1 Sam. 23:18). David was an exile hiding in the wilderness of ZIPH at HORESH. Despite his father's known enmity toward David, Jonathan visited him there. He stated clearly that David would be the next king and claimed that his father Saul also realized this fact. The covenant was renewed and the friendship sealed again.

Though in a very difficult position, Jonathan remained true to David until that fateful day when he also proved his undying devotion to his father on Mount Gilboa. David summarized it well when he wrote, "In life and in death they were not divided" (2 Sam. 1:23 NRSV). The men of Jabesh Gilead rescued the bodies of Saul and his sons from the walls of BETH SHAN and gave them a burial worthy of heroes (1 Sam. 31:11–13). Later, David removed the bones of Saul and Jonathan from Jabesh Gilead and buried them in the tomb of KISH, in ZELA of Benjamin (2 Sam. 21:12–14). Jonathan was survived by only one son, MEPHIBOSHETH (4:4; originally, Meribbaal, 1 Chr. 8:34); two sisters, Merab and Michal (1 Sam. 14:49); and a brother, ISH-BOSHETH (2 Sam. 2:8; originally, Ishvi, 1 Sam. 14:49, or Eshbaal, 1 Chr. 8:33).

(2) Son of GERSHOM and grandson of MOSES (Jdg. 18:30; the MT inserts the letter *n* into the name *mōšeh*, "Moses," and vocalizes it *měnaššeh*, "Manasseh," clearly an attempt to distance the descendants of Moses from idolatry). He is apparently to be identified with the Levite from BETHLEHEM of Judah who traveled to the hill country of Ephraim and was installed by MICAH as his household priest (17:7–9). Jonathan was discovered by five spies from the tribe of DAN who recognized him and made use of his divinatory ability (18:2–6). Later, when some of the Danites migrated to the N, they stopped again at the house of Micah, stole the cultic equipment accumulated by Micah (including an EPHOD, TERAPHIM, and "an idol of cast metal" [NRSV; NIV, "a carved image and a cast idol"]), and talked the willing Jonathan into becoming priest for the entire tribe of Dan (18:14–20). A sanctuary was established at Dan, a site formerly called Laish; see DAN (PLACE). There Jonathan and his descendants served as priests until the fall of Israel to the Assyrians in the 8th cent. B.C. (18:29–31). Perhaps the intention of the author is to indicate how far removed this worship was from the established religion of the ancestor Moses.

(3) Son of ABIATHAR the priest (2 Sam. 15:27). With AHIMAAZ the son of ZADOK, he acted as a courier for DAVID during the revolt by ABSALOM. The young men waited at EN ROGEL (17:17) for word brought by a maidservant concerning events in Jerusalem, and this word they carried to David at the fords of the Jordan. Later, when ADONIJAH proclaimed himself successor to his father David, Jonathan carried word to the celebrants at En Rogel that King David had ordered SOLOMON anointed king at GIHON (1 Ki. 1:42–45).

(4) Son of Shimei (2 Sam. 21:21 NRSV; Shimea in 1 Chr. 20:7), David's brother. This Jonathan killed a giant from GATH who had six fingers on each hand and six toes on each foot. Some identify him with JONADAB son of Shimeah, but it is more likely that they were brothers. This Jonathan should not be confused with the son of Shammah (#5, below), since this latter was not a Bethlehemite, but perhaps he may be equated with the "uncle" of David (#8).

(5) Son of Shammah the HARARITE, included among the Thirty, David's elite force (2 Sam. 23:33 [the MT lacks the words "son of"]; identified as son of Shagee in 1 Chr. 11:34).

(6) Son of Jada and descendant of JERAHMEEL, included in the genealogy of JUDAH (1 Chr. 2:32–33).

(7) Son of Uzziah and overseer of the provincial storehouses (treasuries) in the country, towns, villages, and watchtowers during the reign of David (1 Chr. 27:25).

(8) Uncle of David, described as "a counselor, a man of insight and a scribe" (1 Chr. 27:32). According to the RSV and other translations, both he and

Jehiel son of Hacmoni were in charge of the king's sons, but it is likely that the Hebrew attributes that responsibility only to Jehiel. Because the word for "uncle" (*dôd* H1856) can be used less specifically of kinship on the father's side, some have proposed that here it means "brother's son" and that therefore this Jonathan should be identified with #4 above, the son Shimei.

(9) Father of Ebed; the latter was head of the family of Adin and returned to Jerusalem from the EXILE with fifty of his clan and EZRA the scribe (Ezra 8:6; 1 Esd. 8:32).

(10) Son of Asahel; he and "Jahzeiah son of Tikvah, supported by Meshullam and Shabbethai the Levite," apparently challenged Ezra's instruction that those who had married foreign women should divorce them (Ezra 10:15; cf. 1 Esd. 9:14). The Hebrew text, however, can be understood differently. See discussion under JAHZEIAH.

(11) Son of Joiada, descendant of JESHUA, and father of JADDUA, all of them postexilic high priests (Neh. 12:11). Some believe that the text should read "Johanan" rather than "Jonathan" (cf. v. 22). See JOHANAN #8.

(12) Head of the priestly family of Malluch (KJV, "Melicu"; NRSV, "Malluchi") during the high priesthood of Joiakim (Neh. 12:14).

(13) Son of Shemaiah, descendant of ASAPH, and father of Zechariah; the latter was one of the Levitical musicians who took part in the procession celebrating the rebuilding of the wall (Neh. 12:35).

(14) A secretary during the reign of King ZEDEKIAH of Judah; Jonathan's house was used as a prison in which JEREMIAH was confined for a time (Jer. 37:15, 20; 38:26).

(15) Son of Kareah; he and his brother JOHANAN were among those who joined GEDALIAH at MIZPAH (Jer. 40:8). The NRSV, following the SEPTUAGINT (as well as the parallel passage, 2 Ki. 25:23), omits the name of Jonathan.

(16) Son of MATTATHIAS and Maccabean leader. Surnamed Apphus (1 Macc. 2:5), Jonathan succeeded his brother Judas as head of the Judeans in 160 B.C. (9:28–31), became high priest in 152 (10:18–21), and was killed in 143 (12:48). According to one interpretation, Jonathan is the "Wicked Priest" mentioned in the DEAD SEA SCROLLS. Full discussion under MACCABEE II.D. (See J. C. VanderKam, *From Joshua to Caiaphas: High Priests after the Exile* [2004], 251–70.)

(17) Son of Absalom; he was sent by SIMON MACCABEE to occupy the city of JOPPA (1 Macc. 13:11).

(18) A priest who led in prayer at a sacrifice organized by NEHEMIAH (2 Macc. 1:23).

R. E. HAYDEN

Jonathan, Pseudo-. See TARGUM.

Jonathas jon'uh-thus. KJV Apoc. variant of "Jathan" (Tob. 5:13; NRSV, v. 14).

Jonath-elem-rechokim joh'nuth-ee'luhm-ri-koh'kim (יוֹנַת אֵלֶם רְחֹקִים). KJV transliteration of a Hebrew phrase that probably refers to a musical tune (Ps. 56 title; NIV, "To the tune of 'A Dove on Distant Oaks'"). See MUSIC VI.

Joppa jop'uh (יָפוֹ H3639, יָפוֹא [Ezra 3:7], "beautiful [city]"; Ἰόππη G2673). KJV also Japho (Josh. 19:46). A coastal city c. 35 mi. NW of JERUSALEM; it served as the seaport for the Israelite capital. Joppa was the only natural harbor on the Mediterranean between Egypt and Acco (NT Ptolemais). A rocky cape projected into the sea and, since its elevation was about 125 ft. above the sea, it made an ideal military and commercial site. Reefs formed a rough semicircle c. 300 ft. to 400 ft. off the shore but boats could enter from the N. Nearby were sandy beaches where shallow craft could come ashore. Two good springs supplied the city with water. The land around the city was very fertile. The site today is known as Jaffa and is a suburb of Tel Aviv.

The first historic reference to Joppa is in the list of Palestinian cities captured by THUTMOSE III, 1472 B.C. Joppa remained one of the key Egyptian administrative cities in Palestine from that time until the Israelite invasion. It is mentioned twice in the TELL EL-AMARNA letters. It was then allied with Jerusalem. In the Papyrus Anastasi I of the 13th cent. B.C., Joppa was described as surrounded by beautiful gardens, and her craftsmen were specialists in working metals, wood, and leather. At the time of JOSHUA's conquest, the city was assigned to the suburb of Dan (Josh. 19:46). The Danites were soon displaced by the invading PHILISTINES, who made Joppa their N seaport, but it was not one of their major political centers. After DAVID's conquest of the Philistines, Joppa was restored to Israel. SOLOMON made it the port of reception for the cedar log rafts brought down from the LEBANON mountains for use in the new temple-palace complex he was building at Jerusalem (2 Chr. 2:16).

The next reference to Joppa is Jon. 1:3. The prophet JONAH was commanded to preach to NINEVEH, but he refused to obey. Instead, he went to Joppa and boarded a ship sailing to TARSHISH (prob. a city on the Atlantic coast of Spain near the mouth of the Guadalquivir River). This historic episode is best dated about the time of SHALMANESER III. In 743 B.C., TIGLATH-PILESER III invaded PHILISTIA, capturing GAZA and its major fortress. Joppa must have fallen to him in this campaign. In 701 SENNACHERIB came to S Palestine to put down a revolt against his Assyrian empire. HEZEKIAH of Judah was one of these rebels. According to Sennacherib's record of this campaign, Joppa is one of the cities he destroyed. It is not known when the city was rebuilt, but by the time of EZRA this commercial port was again in service, and the cedar logs from Lebanon needed for the new temple at Jerusalem were rafted to Joppa (Ezra 3:7). About the 4th cent. B.C., the Persian king gave Joppa and the adjacent farmland to Eshmunazar, king of SIDON. Later, Sidon revolted and was destroyed by Artaxerxes III; Joppa probably became a free city at that time.

ALEXANDER THE GREAT favored the city, for he changed its name from Hebrew *Yapho* to Greek *Ioppē*, a new name that honored the daughter of the Greek god of the Winds. Alexander also established a mint in Joppa. After his death, the city was fought over by his successors on several occasions. In 301 B.C., PTOLEMY took the city. Joppa remained Egyptian until 197, when it became a part of the Seleucid empire (see SELEUCUS). Joppa had a brief but complex military history in the Maccabean period. At Joppa, ANTIOCHUS IV Epiphanes landed his army with plans to enforce the hellenization of Jerusalem, where later he plundered the temple. Judas MACCABEE later burned the harbor, but the city was too strong to be captured. Jonathan, however, did capture it, although he soon lost it. Simon finally made it an all-Jewish city. After POMPEY captured Palestine in 63 B.C., he declared Joppa a free city. Julius CAESAR returned it to the Jews in 47, but ten years later HEROD the Great captured the city when he established his reign. Because of the city's continued hatred of him, Herod built a magnificent new port at CAESAREA, c. 40 mi. N of Joppa.

Old photograph (1905) of the coastal town of Joppa. (View to the S.)

Joppa was one of the earliest cities to have a Christian congregation. Its most famous member was Tabitha (DORCAS). She was the church's best social worker, and was raised from the dead by PETER (Acts 9:36–42). Later, Peter was again at Joppa visiting at the home of Simon the tanner where he was called to preach to the centurion CORNELIUS at the rival seaport of Caesarea (10:1–48).

Joppa was one of the centers of the first Jewish revolt, and it was destroyed in the early days of the war by the Syrian proconsul, Cestius Gallus. The citizens refortified the site, but it was again destroyed. It was then replaced by a Roman army camp in A.D. 68. Some of the Roman coins struck in honor of the Romans' victory over the Jews portray the destruction of the Jewish fleet at Joppa. (See S. Tolkowsky, *The Gateway of Palestine: A History of Jaffa* [1925]; Y. Aharoni, *The Land of the Bible: A Historical Geography*, rev. ed. [1979], 25 and index; *ABD*, 3:946–49; *NEAEHL*, s.v. "Jaffa," 2:655–59.)

J. L. KELSO

Jorah jo′hri (יוֹרָה H3454, "[born during] autumn rains"). Ancestor of a family of 112 members that returned from exile with ZERUBBABEL (Ezra 2:18; called HARIPH in Neh. 7:24 and Arsiphurith in 1 Esd. 5:16).

Jorai jo′hri (יוֹרַי H3455, perhaps "[whom] Yahweh teaches" [cf. BDB, 436]). Son of Abihail; he was one of seven relatives from the tribe of GAD who occupied the region E of GILEAD (1 Chr. 5:13; cf. vv. 10, 14).

Joram jor′uhm (יוֹרָם H3456, short form of יְהוֹרָם H3393, "Yahweh is exalted"; see JEHORAM). KJV also Jehoram (1 Ki. 22:50; 2 Ki. 3:1). **(1)** Son of TOU (Toi) king of HAMATH; he was sent by his father with presents to DAVID "to greet him and congratulate him on his victory in battle over Hadadezer, who had been at war with Tou" (2 Sam. 8:10). The name here is thought by some to be a corruption of HADORAM (found in the parallel passage, 1 Chr. 18:10), but Joram may be its Israelite equivalent (that is, using an abbreviated form of Yahweh rather than the pagan name HADAD; cf. A. Malamat in *JNES* 22 [1963]: 1–17, esp. 6–7).

(2) Son of AHAB and ninth king of the northern kingdom of Israel (2 Ki. 1:17 et al.). See JEHORAM #2.

(3) Son of JEHOSHAPHAT and fifth king of the southern kingdom of Judah (2 Ki. 8:16–19; 2 Chr. 21). See JEHORAM #3.

(4) Son of Jeshaiah; his descendant Shelomith was a Levite who shared the supervision of DAVID's treasury (1 Chr. 26:25).

(5) According to the SEPTUAGINT, a brother of TIBNI (1 Ki. 16:22); this information is missing in the MT, but some scholars consider the Greek text to reflect the original.

(6) A captain over thousands in the time of King JOSIAH (1 Esd. 1:9; called "Jozabad" and described as a Levite leader in 2 Chr. 35:9). S. BARABAS

Jordan jor′duhn (יַרְדֵּן H3720, derivation uncertain; Ἰορδάνης G2674). The major river of PALESTINE, which begins at Mount HERMON in the N, flows through the Sea of GALILEE and ends at the DEAD SEA in the S. The most popular etymology for the name is from the Hebrew verb *yārad* H3718 ("to go down"), thus, "The Descender." Other suggestions include: the HURRIAN word for "water" (*iar*); the Hebrew verb for "judge, bring justice" (*din* H1906, thus, "the river is the judge," reflecting an ancient practice of throwing a suspected criminal into the river—survival meant that the "judge" acquitted him); the city of Dan, which is near one of the river's sources (chronological considerations militate against this). See DAN (PLACE). In Arabic it is called esh-Sheriʿa, "the watering place."

   I. The river itself
      A. The sources
      B. The upper Jordan
      C. Galilee
      D. Tributaries of the Jordan
      E. The Dead Sea
   II. The river valley
      A. The Great Rift Valley and the structure of the Jordan Valley
      B. Cities in the Jordan Valley
      C. Fords and bridges
   III. History
      A. Prebiblical times
      B. In the OT
      C. In the NT
      D. In modern times

I. The river itself. The Jordan loses altitude rapidly. From the confluence of its major tributaries to Lake Huleh is a distance of 7 mi. and a drop of 140 ft.; from Huleh to Galilee is 10.5 mi. and a drop of 689 ft.; and from Galilee to the Dead Sea, 60 mi. to the S, it drops another 610 ft. to nearly 1,300 ft. below sea level.

A. The sources. There are four sources for the Jordan, all of which are near Mount Hermon. The easternmost of these is Nahr Banias. Banias is named after the pagan god Pan who was worshiped near where the water issues forth to form the river c. 1,200 ft. above sea level. It is the CAESAREA PHILIPPI of the Gospels (Matt. 16:13; Mk. 8:27). To this day, niches for the statues of the ancient pagan deity can be seen. This stream flows some 5 mi. before joining the waters of the Nahr el-Leddan. The Leddan begins at a spring called ʿAin Leddan, near the ancient city of Dan (both names having the same element in them), known today as

Tell el Qadi. Dan and Mount Hermon were the northernmost points of the Promised Land (Jdg 20:1; Deut. 4:48; et al.). The third source is the Nahr Hasbani. It begins 1,700 ft. above sea level from a spring in the western slopes of Mount Hermon and flows 24 mi. before joining the others about a half mile below their confluence. The fourth and westernmost source is the Nahr Bareighit, which joins the Hasbani just before it merges with the others. The Bareighit contains a spectacular waterfall, although it is not as large a river as the others.

B. The upper Jordan. The Jordan River enters what has been called Lake Huleh, a large swampy area c. 4 mi. long. It is never more than 15 ft. deep. JOSEPHUS (*War* 3.10.7; 4.1.1) calls it Lake Semechonitis. In modern times the government of the State of Israel drained and reclaimed this malaria-infested area and made it a wildlife sanctuary. Some have associated this lake with the Waters of MEROM (Josh. 11:5), but that is probably erroneous.

The Jordan exits the Huleh basin from the S and flows rather quietly for 2 mi. At this point the Bridge of Jacob's Daughters, on the old highway to DAMASCUS, crosses the Jordan. Then the river enters a gorge that is steep and rugged and has many rapids. About one mile above the Sea of Galilee the river levels into the plain. Finally it empties into the lake, which is 690 ft. below sea level and a mere 10 mi. or so from Huleh. The Jordan carries with it a certain amount of silt, but it is a very fresh stream compared with what it becomes by the time it empties into the Sea of Salt, another 600 ft. below the Mediterranean.

C. Galilee. Kinnereth, to use its OT name, is an amazing and beautiful lake (see GALILEE, SEA OF). The Jordan enters it as a small stream and leaves it a considerably more formidable river. There are no other major streams entering the lake; the additional water comes from underground springs. Swimmers in the lake learn this quickly as they discover hot and cold currents warming and then chilling them.

The lake is beautiful, first because it is so blue—a fact that can be explained by its great depth, which in one place is 150 ft. It is also beautiful because of its setting—a framework of brown hills dotted with green, especially on the W. It is amazing because of its altitude, 690 ft. below sea level; because of the storms that can quickly enrage it; and because of the variety and uniqueness of the fish that swim and are caught in it. The Sea of Galilee is c. 12.5 mi. long and 8 mi. wide at its widest point.

D. Tributaries of the Jordan. After leaving Galilee, the Jordan encounters no more lakes until its absorption into the Dead Sea, 65 mi. to the S as the crow flies. There are, however, several notable tributaries or WADIS (from the Arab. term; in Heb., *naḥal* H5707). The northernmost of these and the largest is the YARMUK. This mighty river nearly doubles the volume of the Jordan when it joins it just 5 mi. S of Galilee. It was called by the Greeks Hieroumax, and it drains much of GILEAD and

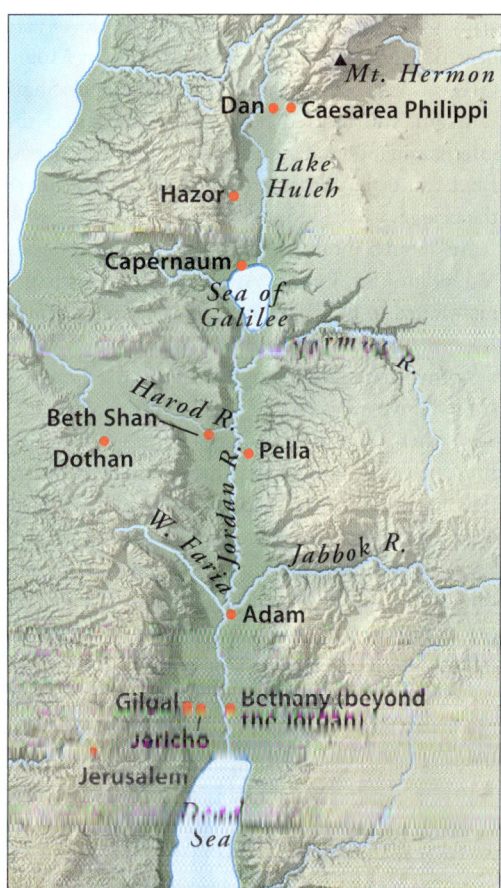

The Jordan River.

Bashan, modern Syria, and N Transjordan. The Jordanians have diverted much of the water into a hydro-electric plant and thence into an irrigation canal that parallels the Jordan. High above the S bank of the Yarmuk is the village of Umm Qeis, which contains the remains of the biblical Gadara, one of the Decapolis cities.

About 4 mi. below the Yarmuk, the Wadi Bira (Naḥal Tavor) contributes its water to the Jordan. Waters running off Mount Tabor to the W and from the Nazareth region make up this stream. At nearly the same latitude the Wadi Arab joins the Jordan from the E. It is the second of eleven perennial streams which flow into the Jordan from Transjordan. The Wadi Tayibeh is the next one down from the E, and the Naḥal Harod (Jalud) next from the W. The latter was made famous by Gideon, who had his men drink from the stream to determine which men to dismiss from the army (Jdg. 7:5–8). The Naḥal Harod flows very near Beth Shan and drains the N side of Mount Gilboa. Just below Harod is the Bridge of Sheik Hussein, still unused because the Jordan is the international boundary. The Wadi Jurm flows past Pella into the Jordan from the E c. 5 mi. below the bridge.

In about 5 more mi. the Wadi Yabis empties its waters into the Jordan. Although the river is not mentioned in the Bible, it bears the same name as Jabesh Gilead, which one might expect to find near this stream. It drains the northern "dome" of Gilead. Five miles farther on, the Jordan welcomes the rather insignificant water of the Wadi Malih, flowing from the W. Two more smaller streams flow from the E, the Wadi Kufrinji and the Wadi Rajib; their mouths are c. 5 mi. apart.

About 40 mi. from the Sea of Galilee is the biblical Jabbok, called Wadi Zerqa in Arabic. It actually has its beginning near Amman, makes a huge bend N and then W to the Jordan, and thus it provided the E border for ancient Ammon. It flows through the valley that separates N and S Gilead. Near its mouth is the biblical Adam, modern Damiya (Josh. 3:16), where the waters stopped for Joshua. See Adam (place).

Near the biblical Tirzah (1 Ki. 15:21 et al.) is an ʿAin Farʿah, which is the beginning of Wadi Farʿah, the next stream to contribute to the Jordan. It flows in from the W c. 7 mi. S of the Jabbok. The Jordan twists and turns for many miles before the waters of Wadi Mallaha join it from the W. Below that stream c. 5 mi. is the Wadi Nimrin, which is just above the Allenby Bridge. Neither the Nuʿeima nor the Qelt, which run above and below Jericho, can be called rivers; but when they contain water they release it into the Jordan near that ancient and modern city. Then from the E comes the southernmost tributary, the Wadi Abu Gharaba, which flows into "The Descender" just 3 mi. before it finally levels and loses itself in the Sea of Salt.

E. The Dead Sea. The Jordan River ends its 250 mi. journey in the depths of the Dead Sea (120 mi. in a straight line). By then it has reached the lowest level of any river on earth — c. 1,290 ft. below the "face of the sea," as the expression is in Hebrew. This makes the Salt Sea the lowest body of water in the world. It is c. 1,300 ft. deep in places, thus making those points c. 2,600 ft. below sea level (by no means the deepest hole in the earth). In addition to the Jordan, two other rivers enter from the E — the Arnon (Wadi Mojib), about halfway down its 60-mi. length, and the Zered at the S end. From the W are the little streams coming from En Gedi and ʿAin Feshkah, the latter being the water supply for the Qumran community (see Dead Sea Scrolls).

The Dead Sea has no outlet except by evaporation. Over the millennia, the mineral and organic content have risen to more than twenty percent. Nothing lives in the "Sea of Lot," as the Arabs call it. In Josephus's day the salts, tars, and other solids dissolved in the water gave it the name of Lake Asphalt.

II. The river valley. In several respects the Jordan River has no peers. It is the lowest river on this planet. It had some of civilization's earliest settlers on its banks. It is the central river in a land hallowed by three major world religions. For its size, it is one of the most overplayed, famous, and sentimental rivers in the world.

A. The Great Rift Valley and the structure of the Jordan Valley. Beginning in Lebanon to the N, a natural N-S cleft in the earth first separates

The Upper Jordan River, N of the Sea of Galilee. (View to the N, with the river cutting through Rosh Pina.)

the Lebanon from the Antilebanon mountains. Farther S, that cleft is filled by the Jordan River and the Dead Sea for c. 150 mi. It continues southward through the Wadi ARABAH, the Gulf of AQABAH of the RED SEA, and even into Africa as far S as Tanganyika. The Jordan Valley is the most spectacular section of the Great Rift Valley.

The mountain range in Palestine reaches a height of 3,000 ft. at HEBRON. On the Transjordanian side the plateau exceeds 4,000 ft. in several places. Separating these heights are the Jordan Valley and the Dead Sea, sinking to 1,290 ft. below sea level. The distance from the spine of Palestine to the heights of GILEAD or MOAB averages 25 mi. Within this greater rift is the Jordan Valley, called the GHOR by the Arabs. The Jordan Valley varies in width from nearly 15 mi. at its mouth to c. 5 mi. near Galilee. The upper Jordan flows through some even narrower canyon-like passages. Within the Ghor is the Zor, or flood plain. This half-mile wide inner valley is flooded at harvest time (Josh. 3:15) and is always luxuriant with heavy bushes. It was in these thickets, particularly in the southern part, that lions roamed in olden times (Jer. 49:19). Within the Zor, the river winds in a serpentine fashion. Air photographs clearly show the courses of abandoned channels and the many oxbow loops of the river.

The soil of the valley is generally inhospitable to growth. It seldom rains in the valley, which is dotted with shallow, chalky-gray marl hills. Remains of ancient aqueducts and other irrigation systems are visible up and down the valley. Today there is no extensive AGRICULTURE except in the N just below the Sea of Galilee.

The temperature of the southern Jordan Valley is torrid in the summer. It may not go below 100°F many nights. This same weather makes Jericho a resort town in the winter. Students of botany and biology find much of the plant and animal life of the valley related to African species.

B. Cities in the Jordan Valley. The names of most of the abandoned cities in the Jordan Valley are not known. There are native names for some of the *tells*, but these usually are based on some obvious feature of the site or some relatively modern happening or personage. The events of the Bible, ordinarily a major source of such information, took place when habitation of the valley was thin and inconsequential.

The oldest and best known valley cities are JERICHO in the S and BETH SHAN in the N. Both of these sites date to the Chalcolithic Period and older, and both played important roles in the OT. Jericho also was inhabited in NT times and is still a prominent city today. It is almost due E of Jerusalem and due W of Amman, and its location near the southernmost ford of the Jordan has contributed to its importance over the years. Beth Shan (Herodian Scythopolis and modern Beisan) is more removed from the river but lies in the basin of the Naḥal Jalud toward the SE end of the valley of JEZREEL (see ESDRAELON).

A major excavation at Beth Yerah, near where the Jordan leaves the Sea of Galilee, produced Bronze Age artifacts. This town is not mentioned in the Bible. Two biblical towns of the Jordan Valley appear in Egyptian execration texts. They are REHOB just S of Beth Shan (Num. 13:21 et al.), and ZARETHAN (Josh. 3:16) N of Adam at the Jabbok's mouth. Pehel, or PELLA, is mentioned in the same Egyptian texts. Although Pella is not in the Bible, it played an important role in NT times and later, as a city of the Decapolis.

SUCCOTH receives early mention in the Bible. Genesis refers to this Jordan Valley town in connection with Jacob (Gen. 33:17). It was here that Solomon cast in clay the brass temple furnishings (1 Ki. 7:46; 2 Chr. 4:17). It is identified with the modern Tell Deir ʿAlla. The ZAPHON of Josh. 13:27 also is mentioned in the TELL EL-AMARNA Letters. It is N of Zarethan.

The city of GILGAL, which served Joshua and the Israelites as a base of operations during the conquest of Canaan, is certainly to be considered as being in the Jordan Valley, since it is a suburb of Jericho (Josh. 4:19 et al.). JABESH GILEAD (2 Sam. 2:4 et al.) can possibly be identified with Tel el-Meqbereh near the mouth of the Wadi Yabis, or with Tell el-Maqlub, farther up the wadi. The BETH ARABAH of Joshua is probably the ʿAin el-Gharabeh near Jericho (Josh. 15:6, 61; 18:22). MEPHIBOSHETH, the surviving crippled son of JONATHAN, lived with MAKIR the Ammonite in the Jordan Valley city of LO DEBAR. The latter has been tentatively identified with Umm ed-Dabar, S of Umm Qeis, on the E bank (2 Sam. 9:3–6).

Two or three cities in the Jordan Valley are mentioned in the NT. Two of these relate to John's baptizing activity: BETHANY (Jn. 1:28; KJV, "Bethabara") on the E of the Jordan, and AENON near SALIM (3:23). BETHSAIDA could also be considered in the Jordan Valley even though it is on the N shore of the Sea of Galilee; it is near the exit of the Jordan into that Sea.

C. Fords and bridges. Until Roman times there were no bridges across the Jordan; but it can be forded in dozens of places where it is only waist deep. For this reason the river itself did not create a definitive border. Abraham, for example, surely crossed the river above or below the Sea of Galilee, but there is no mention of it. Fords are mentioned several times in the Bible. The Jericho police searched for the Israelite spies all the way to the fords of the Jordan (Josh. 2:7), and the Ephraimites under EHUD defeated the Moabites at the fords of the Jordan (Jdg. 3:28). The best fords were near the mouths of the major tributaries. The silt from the tributary would create something like a sandbar and thus facilitate crossing. The Jordan River is not ordinarily navigable and there are no records of anyone shipping or sailing on it. It is very shallow in places and there are many rapids, even in the lower part.

The Romans built several bridges, remains of which can be seen at Damiya, at the mouth of the Yarmuk, and where the Jordan leaves the Sea of Galilee. In modern times the major bridges have been the Allenby Bridge, E of Jericho; the Damiya Bridge, below the Jabbok's mouth; the Sheik Hussein Bridge, E of Beth Shan; and the Bridge of Jacob's Daughters, N of the Sea of Galilee.

III. History. The Jordan serves as a natural N–S boundary dividing Palestine (Cisjordan) on the W from Transjordan on the E. Not only the water itself, which is not too formidable, but also the whole valley provides a difficult-to-cross barrier between the two halves of the Holy Land. As it was in ancient times, so it is today.

A. Prebiblical times. Anthropologists and archaeologists believe that the Jordan Valley was occupied in prehistoric times. As early as the Middle Stone Age, civilizations existed on the plains and in the valley of the river. The number of sites varies through the Early and Middle Bronze Periods, but the sites were generally on the decline when the Israelites appeared on the scene.

That this valley should have hosted some of humankind's earliest settlements is understand-

Aerial photograph looking N up the Jordan Valley toward the Sea of Galilee.

able. The valley itself is nearly tropical; the water is abundant, and with some coaxing the land will produce food. Furthermore, the thick growth paralleling the river shelters many wild animals. In fact, skeletal remains of elephants and rhinoceroses were found near the Jordan S of Lake Huleh. At the S end, the excavations of Kathleen Kenyon at Jericho have shown that city to be one of the oldest in the world. A prepottery Neolithic city appeared at the bottom of the dig into Tell es-Sultan, which is the OT Jericho. Teleilat Ghassul, across the river from Jericho, has given its name to the Ghassulian Period within the Chalcolithic Age. In the N, at Shaar Ha-Golan in the Yarmuk valley, somewhat older artifacts have been discovered.

B. In the OT. The first mention of the Jordan in the Bible is in connection with LOT, who chose "the whole plain of the Jordan" because it was well watered (Gen. 13:10). The word for "plain" is *kikkār* H3971, used of round thin objects, such as loaf (Jdg. 8:5) or "talent" (Exod. 25:39). In regard to the Jordan, opinion varies as to whether the word refers to the broadening out of the plain just N of the Dead Sea or to all the valley in which the Dead Sea lies. This is particularly crucial in the matter of locating the CITIES OF THE PLAIN in Gen. 13 and 19. In any event, Lot went somewhere to the E and S of his uncle ABRAHAM. The same word also describes the Jericho valley in Deut. 34:3 (cf. the use of the term in Neh. 3:22; 12:28). Another passage (1 Ki. 7:46=2 Chr. 4:17) locates Succoth, the site where Solomon had the temple vessels cast in clay, in the plain of the Jordan.

JACOB in his prayer for deliverance from ESAU mentioned that he passed over the Jordan with only his staff (Gen. 32:10). He probably crossed at one of the many fords, as had his grandfather Abraham, either above or below the Sea of Galilee. After the Israelites' forty years of wandering and before the conquest of the Promised Land, the Jordan River was a focus of attention. The Israelites camped in the plains of MOAB by the Jordan (Num. 22:1 et al.). As the tribal allotments were delimited, the Jordan formed a mutual boundary between several of the tribes. MANASSEH had the longest border on the Jordan with half its tribe on the W and half on the E, reaching almost from Galilee to Jericho. NAPHTALI's territory on the W of the river went from N of the Sea of Galilee northward to include the Jordan's sources. To a lesser extent, BENJAMIN and JUDAH bordered the river on the W, and REUBEN until GAD on the E (Num. 32 and 34, and Josh. 13–19, outline the borders in great detail).

The most momentous event involving the Jordan River was when the Israelite nation crossed it dry shod. The book of Joshua relates that as soon as the feet of the priests who bore the ARK OF THE COVENANT touched the river, "the water from upstream stopped flowing. It piled up in a heap a great distance away, at a town called Adam in the vicinity of Zarethan, while the water flowing down to the Sea of the Arabah (the Salt Sea) was completely cut off" (Josh. 3:16). A landslide probably occurred at Adam, as has happened as recently as 1927, and stopped the river. The miraculous element was in the timing of such a natural dam (Ps. 114:3 and 5 say that the Jordan "turned back").

Because Transjordan was part of the nation, the Jordan was crossed and recrossed many times in the business and exploits of the centuries that followed. Crossing to the E side of the river provided something of a refuge from the mainstream of activity. Hence, the Gileadites guarded the fords of Jordan against the pursuing enemy (Jdg. 12:5–6). ABSALOM sought refuge across the Jordan (2 Sam. 17:24), and thence ELIJAH fled from AHAB (1 Ki. 17:3, 5). It was a baptism in the muddy waters of the Jordan that ELISHA prescribed for the leprosy of NAAMAN, the Aramean general (2 Ki. 5:10). On these same waters floated the lost axe head at the behest of Elisha (6:1–7).

There are a few literary allusions to the Jordan and to the jungle that parallels it. Describing the strength of BEHEMOTH, Job says, "he is secure, though the Jordan should surge against his mouth" (Job 40:23). Jeremiah and Zechariah allude to the lions of the Jordan jungle (Jer. 49:19; 50:44; Zech. 11:3). None has been seen since the 19th cent.

C. In the NT. One might say that Jesus' public ministry began at the Jordan River, where JOHN THE BAPTIST baptized him and where the HOLY SPIRIT descended in the form of a dove (Matt. 3:13–17; Mk. 1:9–11; Lk. 3:21–22). There is some question as to where the baptism took place. The Matthean account indicates somewhere toward the S end of the Jordan (Matt. 3:5; 4:1), whereas Mark suggests a place in the N near Galilee (Mk. 1:9). There are no less than seven shrines along the Jordan outside of Jericho to mark the exact spot of the baptism. If the alleged connection of John the Baptist with the Qumran community is correct, then the theory of a southern site is more likely. Later, John baptized at Aenon near Salim, which may be a few miles S of Beth Shan (Jn. 3:23).

If residents of Nazareth and Galilee regularly avoided passing through Samaria, then it is most likely that Jesus crossed the Jordan many times on his way from Nazareth to the festivals in Jerusalem. He may have crossed into PEREA near Beth Shan and then back onto the W bank near Jericho. This would account for his being in Jericho to heal the blind man (Matt. 20:29–34; Mk. 10:46–52; Lk. 18:35–43). He was "passing through" Jericho when he met ZACCHAEUS (Lk. 19:1–2). Jesus and his disciples were near the source of the Jordan when, at Caesarea Philippi, Peter confessed Christ's deity (Matt. 16:13–16; Mk. 8:27–29). Beyond these references and inferences, the Jordan plays no role in the NT.

D. In modern times. The Jordan receives little mention in the pages of history books. Perhaps the reason for this is that it did not again serve as a political boundary until modern times. From the Romans to the Ottomans both sides of the Jordan were one political entity. Pilgrims of the Middle Ages had almost nothing to report of this fabled river.

At the conclusion of World War I, however, the Jordan once more served as a political frontier. The Hashemite kingdom of Transjordan was then on the E and the British Mandate of Palestine on the W. As a result of Great Britain's and the United Nation's decisions in 1947 and 1948, the Israeli War of Independence made at least part of the Jordan the international frontier between Israel and the present Hashemite kingdom of Jordan. With the six-day war of June, 1967, the Jordan almost in its entirety from Galilee to the Dead Sea came to be the cease-fire line between these two hostile states. Thus the Jordan River, insignificant in size though it be, with more than its share of the headlines both ancient and modern, continues to play a major role in international intrigue.

The Jordan River also has strong symbolic associations. Being the border of the ancient promised land, it illustrates the barrier between this life and the next. Songs such as "I Won't Have to Cross Jordan Alone," or "On Jordan's Stormy Banks," illustrate the death of the saint. (See further G. A. Smith, *The Historical Geography of the Holy Land*, 25th ed. [1931], chs. 21–23; N. Glueck, *The River Jordan* [1946]; D.

Valley*, The Geography of the Bible, rev. ed. [1974], ch. 17; R. G. Khouri, *The Jordan Valley: Life and Society below Sea Level* [1981]; B. Ball and L. Kessel, eds., *The River Jordan: An Illustrated Guide from Bible Days to the Present* [1998]; A. Horowitz et al., *The Jordan Rift Valley* [2001].) R. L. ALDEN

Joribas, Joribus juh-ri′buhs. KJV Apoc. forms of JARIB (1 Esd. 8:44; 9:19).

Jorim jor′im (Ἰωρίμ G2733). Son of Matthat, included in Luke's GENEALOGY OF JESUS CHRIST (Lk. 3:29).

Jorkeam jor′kee-uhm (יָרְקֳעָם H3767, derivation uncertain). KJV Jorkoam. Son of Raham, included in the genealogy of CALEB (1 Chr. 2:44). It is likely, however, that "Jorkeam" is a place name and that the text should be rendered, "Raham the founder of Jorkeam"; the town referred to may be the same as JOKDEAM (Josh. 15:56).

Josabad joh′suh-bad. KJV alternate form of JOZABAD (1 Chr. 12:4; 1 Esd. 8:63; 9:29).

Josaphat jos′uh-fat. KJV NT form of JEHOSHAPHAT.

Josaphias joh′suh-fi′uhs. KJV Apoc. form of JOSIPHIAH (1 Esd. 8:36).

Jose joh′see. KJV NT form of JOSHUA (only Lk. 3:29).

Josech joh′sik (Ἰωσήχ G2738). TNIV Josek. Son of Joda, included in Luke's GENEALOGY OF JESUS CHRIST (Lk. 3:26; KJV, "Joseph").

Josedec joh′suh-dek. KJV Apoc. form of JEHOZADAK (1 Esd. 5:5 et al.).

Josedech joh′suh-dek. KJV OT alternate form of JEHOZADAK (Hag. 1:1 et al.; Zech. 6:11).

Josek joh′sik. TNIV form of JOSECH.

Joseph joh′sif (יוֹסֵף H3441, "may [God] add" [cf. JOSIPHIAH]; Ἰωσήφ G2737). **(1)** Son of JACOB and

JOSEPH 787

Rachel (see HEAD). While in PADDAN ARAM, Jacob saw and loved Rachel, and arranged to work seven years for her (29:17–18). LABAN, her father, gave his oldest daughter LEAH to Jacob, insisting that custom demanded that the oldest daughter be married first. Jacob worked seven more years for Rachel. Leah bore several children, but Rachel was barren for an extended period before giving birth to Joseph. Because Joseph was the first son of the favorite wife, Jacob was partial to him. Evidence of this is seen in the coat he gave to Joseph, alone, of all his sons (37:3).

The antagonism of Joseph's brothers grew when Joseph told them of the dreams he had, suggesting that they, along with his father and mother, would one day bow before him (Gen. 37:5–11). When Joseph was seventeen years old, his father sent him to SHECHEM to inquire about the welfare of his brothers. They had gone on to DOTHAN, where Joseph found them. The brothers saw him approaching and determined to kill him, but REUBEN, the oldest son of Jacob, persuaded his brothers to spare the life of Joseph and instead to cast him into a pit. Reuben hoped to rescue Joseph from the pit, but before he could do so a company of ISHMAELITE merchants passed. While Reuben was away, the other brothers sold Joseph as a slave to the Ishmaelites, who took him to Egypt. The brothers then dipped Joseph's coat in the blood of a goat, and told their father that they had found

This canal, known as the River of Joseph, is said to have been dug during the time of Joseph to provide irrigation to agricultural fields during the Egyptian drought he predicted. (View to the NW.)

his blood-soaked coat. Jacob concluded that a wild animal had killed Joseph (37:12–36).

In Egypt, Joseph was sold to the captain of Pharaoh's guard, Potiphar. As a trustworthy worker, Joseph was given a responsible position. Potiphar's wife was attracted to Joseph and attempted to seduce him. When Joseph spurned her advances, she accused him of being the aggressor, with the result that he was imprisoned for several years (Gen. 39).

In prison, Joseph again proved himself worthy of a position of trust. He interpreted the dreams of the chief butler and the chief baker; the former was restored to Pharaoh's confidence, and the second, beheaded (Gen. 40). After two years Pharaoh had a dream, and the chief butler remembered how Joseph had correctly interpreted the dreams. Joseph was sent for, and he explained that the Pharaoh's dreams foretold seven years of plenty, to be followed by seven years of famine. Pharaoh was so impressed with Joseph that he appointed him superintendent of the royal granaries. Joseph was now second in rank to Pharaoh himself. He married Asenath, daughter of a priestly family at On (Heliopolis). Before the famine began, Joseph had two sons: Manasseh and Ephraim (Gen. 41).

When the famine came, the entire world of the eastern Mediterranean lands suffered, but Joseph's advice saved Egypt. Joseph's brothers came from Canaan to buy food, but they did not recognize him. He recognized them, however, and questioned them closely concerning their family. The welfare of Jacob, his father, and Benjamin, his full brother who had remained at home, was his prime concern. Keeping Simeon as a hostage, Joseph permitted his brothers to return home (Gen. 42).

On their second visit they brought along Benjamin, and Joseph plotted to find an excuse to keep Benjamin with him. Joseph ordered that a silver cup be placed in Benjamin's bag. This was done and Joseph then sent his men after the caravan to search for the supposed thief. When the cup was found in Benjamin's bag, all returned. Judah, however, insisted that Benjamin must return home. Jacob had lost his favorite son already, and the loss of the second child of the beloved Rachel would be too much for him. Judah offered to remain himself if Benjamin were permitted to go with his brothers home to Jacob (Gen. 43–44). Years before the brothers had been jealous of Joseph to the point that they were prepared to kill him. Now, however, they were willing to indulge their father in his special love for Benjamin.

Joseph was so moved at Judah's words that he could contain his emotions no longer. He ordered his courtiers out of the room, and revealed himself to his brothers. They were frightened, feeling that he would seek revenge for their treatment of him, but he assured them that he saw the hand of God in all that had happened. Joseph urged them to bring their father and settle in the eastern delta region of Egypt—in the land of Goshen. Jacob, who had difficulty believing that Joseph was really alive, joined his sons in moving down to Egypt. They were settled near Joseph's palace and enjoyed a favored position (Gen. 45–46). Jacob thus died a happy man. Joseph lived to the age of 110 (50:26), the ideal life span in Egyptian thought. At the exodus, the mummified remains of Joseph were taken from Egypt and, following the conquest, they were buried at Shechem (Exod. 13:19; Josh. 24:32). For a discussion of the tribes descended from Joseph, see Ephraim (person and tribe); Manasseh (tribe).

Many scholars suggest that Joseph rose to prominence during the Second Intermediate, or Hyksos, period of Egyptian history (c. 1780–1570 B.C.; see Egypt V.D). Since the Pharaoh is not named, certainty is impossible. The Hyksos were Semites, and it is thought likely that Joseph would have been given a position of trust by fellow Semites. A further bit of evidence is the fact that the capital was located in the Nile delta, near Goshen, "in the region of Zoan" (Ps. 78:12, 43). The king "who did not know Joseph" (Exod. 1:8) was evidently of a new dynasty, and was certainly a ruler of the new kingdom, or empire period (after 1570 B.C.). Egyptian records document the presence of many Semites in Egypt during the time of Joseph. Forty-five Semites are named in a prison register from c. 1740 B.C. The list, known as Papyrus Brooklyn 35.1446, contains NW Semitic names similar to the biblical Jacob, Issachar, Asher, Job, and Menahem (cf. W. F. Albright in *JAOS* 74 [1954]: 222–33). For dress during the time of Joseph, the Beni Hasan tomb painting, showing Semitic traders entering Egypt, may be studied (see Benjamin Mazar et al., *Views of the Biblical World* [1959], 1·114–15).

Egyptian literature is thought by some to provide parallels to the Joseph narrative. The so-called Story of Two Brothers tells of a young man who rejected the advances of his elder brother's wife, after which she accused him of attempting to seduce her (see *ANET*, 23–25). Another story concerns a man named Sinuhe, who left Egypt for political reasons and spent many years in Canaan and Syria. Sinuhe married the daughter of a bedouin chief and prospered in his adopted country. In old age, however, he had the opportunity to return to his native land, and did so. He was properly embalmed and buried in a pyramid (*ANET*, 18–22). Joseph, on the other hand, gave orders that his remains should be returned to his native land. In accord with Egyptian custom, Joseph, too, was embalmed. Subsequently his body was taken from Egypt to the Shechem area for burial.

(See further G. W. Coats, *From Canaan to Egypt: Structural and Theological Context for the Joseph Story* [1975]; R. E. Longacre, *Joseph: A Story of Divine Providence. A Text Theoretical and Text-linguistic Analysis of Genesis 37 and 39–48* [1989]; T. L. Hettema, *Reading for Good: Narrative Theology and Ethics in the Joseph Story from the Perspective of Ricoeur's Hermeneutics* [1996]; L. Wilson, *Joseph, Wise and Otherwise: The Intersection of Wisdom and Covenant in Genesis 37–50* [2004].)

(2) Descendant of ISSACHAR and father of Igal; the latter was one of the twelve spies sent by MOSES to Canaan (Num. 13:7).

(3) One of the sons of ASAPH who assisted their father in the prophetic ministry of MUSIC; he was the head of the first company of temple musicians appointed by lot under DAVID (1 Chr. 25:2, 9).

(4) One of the descendants of Binnui who agreed to put away their foreign wives (Ezra 10:42; in 1 Esd. 9:34 [KJV, "Josephus"], Joseph is listed as a descendant of Ezora).

(5) Head of the priestly family of Shecaniah during the high priesthood of Joiakim (Neh. 12:14, which reads, MT text read "Shebaniah").

(6) Son of Oziel and ancestor of JUDITH (Jdt. 8:1).

(7) Son of Zechariah and commander in the Maccabean army; he and another commander, Azariah, launched an unsuccessful attack against Jamnia (1 Macc. 5:18, 55–60).

(8) Son of MATTATHIAS (leader of the Maccabean Revolt); he was appointed by his brother Judas MACCABEE to command a military division (2 Macc. 8:22; 10:19). The name "Joseph" here is probably a variant of "John" (1 Macc. 2:2), but some have argued that it refers to a different person, perhaps a half-brother of Judas who should be identified with #7 above.

(9–10) The name of two individuals included in Luke's GENEALOGY OF JESUS CHRIST: the son of Mattathias (not the leader of the Maccabean Revolt) and the son of Jonam (Lk. 3:25, 30).

(11) Son of Jacob and husband of MARY, MOTHER OF JESUS (Matt. 1:16; according to Lk. 3:23, he was the son [grandson?] of HELI; see GENEALOGY OF JESUS CHRIST). The Gospels of Matthew and Luke assert that Jesus was born to Mary at a time when she was betrothed to Joseph, before their marriage was consummated (Matt. 1:18; Lk. 1:27, 35). Joseph was a carpenter (Matt. 13:55) and was known as "a righteous man" (1:19). When he learned that Mary was bearing a child, he was understandably disturbed. After he was told by an angel that she was to become the mother of Israel's MESSIAH through the instrumentality of the Holy Spirit, he proceeded with his plans, which brought him and Mary to BETHLEHEM, where the child Jesus was born.

A tradition embodied in the 4th-cent. *History of Joseph the Carpenter* states that Joseph was a widower with children at the time he espoused Mary, a girl of twelve. The Scriptures make one reference to Joseph following the Passover journey when Jesus was twelve years old (Lk. 2:41–48). Later references mention Mary and the BROTHERS OF JESUS (Mk. 3:31; 6:3), but not Joseph. Jesus asked John to treat Mary as his own mother (Jn. 19:26–27), implying that she had need of someone to care for her. References to the brothers of Jesus (Mk. 6:3) imply that Mary and Joseph had other children after the virgin birth of Jesus. Some scholars have maintained that these "brothers" were sons of Joseph by a previous marriage, or cousins of Jesus. The natural meaning of the words, however, implies that Mary and Joseph came together subsequent to the birth of Jesus (Matt. 1:25), and that they had children who grew up with Jesus and were known in the community as his "brothers."

(12) Son of Mary and thus probably a half-brother of Jesus; listed with other brothers, James, Simon, and Judas (Matt. 13:55; instead of "Joseph," some MSS have "Joses" and others have "John"). A parallel list includes James, Joses, Judas, and Simon (Mk. 6:3 NRSV; here the NIV understands JOSES as an alternate form of Joseph. See BROTHERS OF JESUS; JAMES II.

(13) Son of a certain Mary, possibly the wife of CLOPAS (Matt. 27:56 NRSV; NIV reads "Joses," the reading found in a majority of MSS, though probably not original). This Joseph is no doubt to be identified with Joses, the brother of James the younger (Mk. 15:40). See JAMES III.

(14) A rich man from the town of ARIMATHEA who became a disciple of Jesus. After the crucifixion, he asked PILATE for the body of Jesus; the request being granted, he wrapped the body "in a linen cloth, and placed it in his own new tomb that he had cut out of the rock" (Matt. 27:57–60). Both Mark and Luke add the information that Joseph was a member of the Council, a term that probably refers to the SANHEDRIN, and that he "was waiting for the kingdom of God" (Mk. 15:43–46; Lk. 23:50–53). Luke also states that Joseph was "a good and upright man, who had not consented to their decision and action." John points out that Joseph was a secret disciple of Jesus "because he feared the Jews," and that NICODEMUS helped him bury the body (Jn. 19:38–40). (For further details on the BURIAL of Jesus, see R. E. Brown in *CBQ* 50 [1988]: 233–45.)

(15) A disciple of Jesus who also bore the surnames BARSABBAS and JUSTUS; he was one of the two men nominated to succeed JUDAS ISCARIOT in the apostolic band (Acts 1:23).

(16) An early Christian leader better known as BARNABAS (Acts 4:36).   C. F. PFEIFFER

Joseph, History of. Title given to a document very fragmentarily preserved in a few pieces of Greek papyri that may be dated to c. A.D. 600 (the work itself was prob. composed several centuries earlier). Very little can be inferred from the small amount of text that has survived, but it appears to be a retelling of the story of the patriarch JOSEPH, particularly his illustrious career in Egypt. At one point Joseph is referred to as "king of the people." The phrase "Joseph remembering Jacob" apparently occurs several times in the surviving text, and this concept is thought to be an important theme in the document. (Introduction and trans. in *OTP*, 2:467–75.)

Joseph, Prayer of. An OT pseudepigraphal work no longer extant. The knowledge of this work is based largely upon the many quotations in Greek from it in the writings of ORIGEN. In the so-called *Stichometry of Necephorus* is a list of OT apocryphal works, as well as the canonical books of the Bible, together with the number of verses in each book. The *Prayer of Joseph* is third in this list, and the number of verses given is 1,100. The passages quoted by Origen have to do mainly with Jacob, who describes, among other things, a meeting with URIEL, whom he met on a journey from Mesopotamia. Uriel wrestled with him claiming that he was the greatest of the angels. Although Abraham and Isaac were great, Jacob is "the firstborn of all living beings," in fact, the head of all the angels. This comment has been interpreted by some scholars to be a reflection of an anti-Christian bias, appearing to revere the patriarchs above Christ. Origen, however, held the book in high regard, making this view improbable. Origen also says it was used by the Jews, which indicates it was of Jewish origin. Nothing is known about is authorship.   A. C. SCHULTZ

Joseph and Asenath. Also *Joseph and Aseneth*. A lengthy apocryphal Jewish story, probably written in Greek in the 1st cent. B.C. or a little later. Expanding on the brief OT material (Gen. 41:45, 50–52; 46:20), this document recounts how ASENATH, the very beautiful daughter of an Egyptian priest, refused to marry JOSEPH. For his part, Joseph, who would not kiss an idolatrous woman, prayed for her conversion. Asenath repented, was visited by an angelic being, and married Joseph. Subsequently, the son of Pharaoh kidnapped Asenath, but she was rescued by Joseph's brothers. The work was doubtlessly written to warn Jewish readers from IDOLATRY and to discourage them from marrying pagans. It has also been argued that the author wished to enhance the status of converts to Judaism. (Full introduction and English trans. by C. Burchard in *OTP*, 2:177–247; on the state of modern research, C. Burchard in *New*

Perspectives on Ancient Judaism, ed. J. Neusner et al., vol. 2 [1987], 31–52; on the document's relevance for NT studies, id., in *NTS* 33 [1987]: 102–34. See also R. D. Chesnutt, "The Social Setting and Purpose of Joseph and Aseneth," *JSP* 2 [1988]: 21–48; E. M. Humphrey, *Joseph and Aseneth* [2000].)

Joseph the Carpenter, History of. Also known as the *Arabic History of Joseph the Carpenter*. An account of the life and more particularly the death of Joseph, the foster-father of Jesus, allegedly given by the Lord himself to his disciples. In it Joseph is described as a carpenter, a widower with six children (four boys and two girls), and quite old when he married the virgin, a girl of twelve years. The latter part of the book describes Joseph's sickness, death, and burial, and contains a eulogy spoken over him by Jesus. His death at 111 years of age is given as a model of holy dying. His burial is according to the burial rites of the Egyptian cult of OSIRIS.

This document, the oldest one extant intended to exalt Joseph and foster his cult, was written in Egypt no earlier than the 4th cent. and shows strong influences of Egyptian religions and GNOSTICISM upon it. Its original language may have been Greek (S. Morenz, *Die Geschichte von Joseph dem Zimmermann* [1951]), but it is extant now only in Arabic and Coptic (on which the Arabic depends). A 14th-cent. Latin translation based on the Coptic also exists. Materials from earlier apocryphal gospels, such as *Protevangelium of James*, are found in it. (English trans. in *ANF*, 8:388–94; summary in *NTAp*, 1:483–85.) G. F. HAWTHORNE

Josephus, Flavius joh-see´fuhs, flay´vee-uhs. First-century Jewish writer; our main source of information for Jewish history during the intertestamental and NT periods. (The name Josephus occurs once in the KJV Apoc. as a form of JOSEPH, referring to a postexilic Israelite [1 Esd. 9:34].)

I. Life. Josephus was born in Jerusalem, A.D. 37 or 38. His father Matthias was a priest, and his mother a descendant of the royal house of the Hasmoneans. When he grew up he joined the PHARISEES, a group that he likened to the STOICS among the Greeks. In the year 64, at age twenty-six, he went to Rome and secured the release of certain priests who were being held there on rather nebulous charges. Upon his return he found the people smarting under the high-handed administration of the procurator Florus and ready for revolt. From this he attempted to dissuade them, having seen at firsthand something of Roman power.

Because of his attitude, he was sent to GALILEE to keep the peace there. The accounts of his activity in this region are conflicting and confused. The *Jewish War* seems to indicate that he was sent up as a general to take command of the situation; while in the *Life* he claims that he went up as a priest to pacify the disaffected. At any rate, because he was afraid that his pacification efforts would bring him under suspicion of favoring Rome, he finally pretended to concur with the views of the war party, going so far as to get them paid as mercenaries, but at the same time trying to persuade them to act on the defensive: not to attack the Romans, but let them make the first move. Thus he played a kind of double game, waiting to see the direction in which events would develop, accused by some of pro-Roman sentiment, by others of aiming at tyranny.

Finally the extremists forced him to a decision; either he would lose his post, or take over the active leadership of the war party. At this juncture the Roman general VESPASIAN arrived on the scene (A.D. 67), and Josephus was captured, after almost being killed by his companions. When Vespasian was summoned to Rome in 69, and his son TITUS was left to conduct the siege of Jerusalem, Josephus was used by the Roman commander as a mediator, going around the walls counseling the Jews to submit, but hated by the ZEALOTS and suspected by the Romans. See WARS, JEWISH. After the capture of Jerusalem he went to Rome with Titus and was shown great favor by Vespasian (now the emperor), by Titus, and later by DOMITIAN. He received Roman citizenship and took the name Flavius in deference to his patrons. He was married three times; one wife deserted him, and a second marriage ended in divorce. He died at about the beginning of the second century.

II. Works. Three major works have come from the pen of Josephus. (a) The *Jewish War*, written between 75 and 79, in seven books. This account of the struggle between the Jews and Romans was written under Roman auspices, Titus having urged

Josephus to undertake the work. King HEROD Agrippa vouched for its accuracy. It was produced first in an Aramaic version, now lost, and this was followed by the Greek edition. One purpose for the writing of the book was certainly to deter others from revolting against the Romans as the Jews had done. The work is in the main a trustworthy account, for Josephus had firsthand materials: his own experience and the commentaries of Vespasian and Titus, the commanders involved in the struggle.

The camel-shaped hill of Gamala (looking W). Josephus reports on various battles between the Jews and Romans, including one that occurred here. (An excavated synagogue is visible in the lower left, right of it is a wall line and the remains of an ancient tower.)
© Dr. James C. Martin

(b) The *Antiquities of the Jews*, written in 93 or 94. This is a long work of twenty books, beginning with creation and extending to the outbreak of the war with the Romans. Nothing like it was ever attempted before; it represents a new departure in literary form. The first part of the work, to the end of the exile, follows closely the biblical narrative; the second part, dealing with the postexilic period, is compiled from miscellaneous sources. To the *Antiquities* is appended a biographical sketch (*Life*) written by Josephus as a defense against the accusations of a rival historian named Justus.

(c) *Against Apion*, a defense of the Jewish religion.

III. Importance of Josephus.
He is the principal source for Jewish history between 100 B.C. and A.D. 100, and is invaluable for a knowledge of the geography of Bible lands. Recent archaeological discoveries at QUMRAN (see DEAD SEA SCROLLS) and MASADA have indicated that the account of Josephus is remarkably accurate and ranks him high as a topographer. The student of the NT has in Josephus a wealth of material on agriculture, industry, religion, politics, and the outstanding personalities of gospel history: Herod, Pilate, the two Agrippas, Felix, and others.

As a historian many have distrusted him, mostly because they disapprove of him as a traitor. He is no more affected by human error (of memory, faulty sources, bias, and the like) than others of his time. The passage concerning Jesus (*Ant.* 18.3.3 §§63–64) is usually regarded as a Christian interpolation, though some argue that the bulk of evidence, both external and internal, marks it as genuine. Josephus must have known the main facts about the life and death of Jesus, and his historian's curiosity certainly would lead him to investigate the movement that was gaining adherents even in high circles. Arnold Toynbee rates him among the five greatest Hellenic historians, along with Herodotus, Thucydides, Xenophon, and Polybius.

Josephus was doubtless an egoist, motivated by self-interest, and a flatterer of the Romans. He was hated by his countrymen as a turncoat. Yet he possessed a high degree of patriotism, for instead of disowning his nation he wrote an elaborate history of it, and composed a brilliant apology for his native religion.

(See further R. Laqueur, *Der jüdische Historiker Flavius Josephus* [1920], a foundational work; H. St. John Thackeray, *Josephus: The Man and the Historian* [1929], a reliable and influential survey; S. J. D. Cohen, *Josephus in Galilee and Rome* [1979], skeptical of Josephus's reliability; S. Schwartz, *Josephus and Judean Politics* [1990], building on Laqueur; S. Mason, *Josephus and the New Testament* [1992], a useful synthesis; T. Rajak, *Josephus: The Historian and His Society*, 2nd ed. [2002], a positive interpretation; see also the new series edited by S. Mason, *Flavius Josephus: Translation and Commentary* [2000–].) R. C. STONE

Joses joh′siz (Ἰωσῆς *G2736*, hellenized form of Ἰωσήφ *G2737*; see JOSEPH). **(1)** Son of MARY, MOTHER OF JESUS, and thus apparently a half-brother of Jesus (Mk. 6:3 NRSV); the NIV, on the basis of the parallel passage (Matt. 13.55), renders the name as "Joseph" (a reading attested in some MSS). See JOSEPH #12; see also BROTHERS OF JESUS; JAMES II.

(2) Brother of James the younger, whose mother Mary stood by the cross of Jesus and watched his burial (Matt. 27:56 [NRSV, "Joseph," following the earliest MSS]; Mk. 15:40, 47). See JAMES III; JOSEPH #13; MARY #4.

(3) The original name of BARNABAS (Acts 4:36 KJV, following the TR; most modern versions read "Joseph"). D. E. HIEBERT

Joshah josh'uh (יוֹשָׁה H3459, derivation uncertain). A clan leader in the tribe of SIMEON (1 Chr. 4:34). He is listed among those whose families increased greatly during the days of King HEZEKIAH and who dispossessed the Hamites and Meunites near GEDOR (vv. 38–41).

Joshaphat josh'uh-fat (יוֹשָׁפָט H3461, short form of יְהוֹשָׁפָט H3398, "Yahweh has judged"; see JEHOSHAPHAT). (1) A Mithnite who was one of David's mighty warriors (1 Chr. 11:43; this list adds sixteen names beyond the military elite known as the Thirty, listed in vv. 10–41 = 2 Sam. 23:8–39). The description "Mithnite" may point to his hometown, perhaps in TRANSJORDAN.

(2) One of the priests appointed to blow the trumpet when David transferred the ARK OF THE COVENANT to Jerusalem (1 Chr. 15:24).

Joshaviah josh'uh-vi'uh (יוֹשַׁוְיָה H3460, possibly alternate form of יוֹשִׁבְיָה H3458, "Yahweh makes [me] dwell"; see JOSHIBIAH). Son of Elnaam; he and his brother Jeribai are included in the Chronicler's list of David's mighty warriors (1 Chr. 11:46), which adds sixteen names (vv. 41b–47) beyond the military elite known as the Thirty (vv. 10–41 = 2 Sam. 23:8–39).

Joshbekashah josh'bi-kay'shuh (יָשְׁבְקָשָׁה H3792, possibly "sitting in prayer [or in misfortune]"). Son of HEMAN, David's seer (1 Chr. 25:4). He and his thirteen brothers were set apart "for the ministry of prophesying, accompanied by harps, lyres and cymbal" (v. 1). When lots were cast to determine the duties of the Levitical singers, he, along with his sons and relatives, received the seventeenth lot (v. 26).

Josheb-Basshebeth josh'ib-buh-shee'bith' (יֹשֵׁב בַּשֶּׁבֶת H3783, "one sitting in the seat"). A Tahkemonite listed as chief of DAVID's three main officers (2 Sam. 23:8). See JASHOBEAM.

Joshibiah josh'uh-bi'uh (יוֹשִׁבְיָה H3458, "Yahweh makes [me] dwell"). KJV Josibiah. Son of Seraiah and father of Jehu; the latter is listed among the clan leaders in the tribe of SIMEON whose families increased greatly during the days of King HEZEKIAH and who dispossessed the Hamites and Meunites near GEDOR (1 Chr. 4:35; cf. vv. 38–41).

Joshua josh'yoo-uh (יְהוֹשֻׁעַ H3397, short form in postexilic writings יֵשׁוּעַ H3800 [see JESHUA], "Yahweh is salvation [or help]"; Ἰησοῦς G2652 [see JESUS]). (1) Son of Nun and commander of the Israelites during the conquest of Canaan. Although his name appears first as Joshua (Exod. 17:9–14), one reads subsequently (Num. 13:16; cf. v. 8 and Deut. 32:44 MT) that MOSES changed his name from HOSHEA (KJV, "Oshea"), meaning "Save," to Joshua (more accurately transliterated as Jehoshua), "Yahweh is salvation," making the name theophorous. This change may throw light upon the fact that names compounded with Yahweh were relatively rare in the period of the exodus. Moses (whose mother's name was JOCHEBED, "Yahweh is glorious," Exod. 6:20; Num. 26:59) may have wished to popularize such a custom by changing the name of his "minister" to Jehoshua. In the exilic period, the shorter form of the name (Jeshua) came into use (the son of Nun is called Jeshua in Neh. 8:17; the name of the postexilic priest is spelled "Jeshua" in Ezra and Nehemiah, but "Jehoshua" [Joshua] in Haggai and Zechariah).

Joshua son of Nun belonged to the tribe of EPHRAIM (Num. 13:8). After the conquest of Canaan, he settled in TIMNATH SERAH (Josh. 19:50 [Timnath Heres, Jdg. 2:9]) in the hill country of Ephraim, and was buried there (Josh. 24:30). As BEZALEL and OHOLIAB (Exod. 31:1–6) undoubtedly had received training in the arts and crafts of Egypt, and as JOSEPHUS (*Ant.* 2.10.1–2) imagines that Moses led an Egyptian army against the Ethiopians, it is likely that Joshua had served in Pharaoh's army before the exodus. Foreigners were common in the army of Egypt. Moses considered him sufficiently battle-tested to appoint him leader of the Israelite defense against the attack of the Amalekites at REPHIDIM (Exod. 17:8–16). Since Joshua was apparently known to Moses, he may already have been in charge of organizing the undisciplined crowd of slaves who had escaped from Egypt into orderly marching columns. Joshua served as personal minister to Moses when the latter was on Mount SINAI receiving the law (Exod. 24:13; 32:17). He was also in attendance whenever the Lord would speak to Moses in the Tent of Meeting outside the camp (33:11). On one occasion, when he wanted to forbid certain elders to prophesy, he learned from Moses the value of the anointing of God's Spirit (Num. 11:27–29).

His selection as one of the twelve spies gave Joshua the opportunity to learn the nature of the Canaanites and the topography of the land at first hand. This information became invaluable when his time came to plan the campaigns to conquer Canaan. Furthermore, he grew in strength of character as he and CALEB, with their report of the reconnaissance, stood against the majority (Num. 14:6–9). They called upon the community of Israel to rise up in faith and expect Yahweh to give them the excellent land to the N. Caleb and Joshua were spared when the ten who had incited the Israelites to grumble against Yahweh by disparaging the land were struck dead (14:30, 36–38). Of the generation numbered at the beginning of the wilderness journey, only Joshua and Caleb followed the Lord faithfully and remained alive to be registered at the end of the forty year period (26:65; 32:12; Deut. 1:34–40).

When Moses was told that he must die instead of being allowed to lead the Israelites into Canaan, the lawgiver asked God to give the community of Yahweh a new shepherd (Num. 27:12–17). Telling Moses to select Joshua, a man indwelt by the Spirit, the Lord replied: "Give him some of your authority so the whole Israelite community will obey him" (27:20). Moses formally ordained Joshua in the presence of ELEAZAR the priest and the whole community (27:21–23; Deut. 3:21–28), and imparted to him the spirit of wisdom by the laying on of hands (Deut. 34:9). Later, Moses commanded Joshua before the entire nation to be strong and to lead Israel across the JORDAN in order to possess the land promised to the patriarchs (Deut. 31:3, 7–8). Then the two presented themselves at the door of the TABERNACLE. There Joshua received the divine commission or charge from God (31:14–15, 23). After Moses' death the Lord graciously repeated this commission to Joshua privately and enlarged upon it, to prepare him for the overwhelming task lying ahead (Josh. 1:1–9).

Several outstanding characteristics enabled Joshua to perform the responsibilities committed to him. (a) First, he was humble enough to recognize that he was *not* the gifted and educated man that Moses was. Joshua accepted himself and thus leaned all the more heavily upon the Lord in his comparative ordinariness. He was not too big for God to use; hence God could exalt him (Josh. 3:7; 4:14).

(b) He was a man of strong faith and faithful to his calling. When the divine Commander-in-chief appeared in THEOPHANY to him as he scouted the JERICHO defenses, Joshua was quick to bow in worship (5:13–15) and to receive orders how to capture the enemy bastion (6:2–5). Even though the daily encirclement with trumpets blowing might seem militarily stupid, and be subjected to the ridicule of the defenders, Joshua obeyed implicitly. He cried to God in repentance for his nation after the Ai debacle (7:2–5). At the foot of Mount EBAL he put worship and covenant before further war and conquest (8:30–35). At GIBEON he prayed for supernatural assistance, and God answered with a terrifying hailstorm (10:10–14).

(c) Third, he saturated his mind and heart with the word of God, meditating therein day and night. Thus the people had confidence to execute his decisions (1:13–18; 8:30–35; 11:12, 15; 14:1–5), and he could appeal to them at his life's end to continue adhering to the law of Moses (23:6).

(d) Fourth, he displayed sound military strategy. He established his base of operations at GILGAL with its easy access to the TRANSJORDAN tribes as a source of supplies and in its position guarding two trade routes up into the central highlands. By capturing Ai and silencing BETHEL (Josh. 8:17; 12:16), he took the heart of Canaan first, and cut the land in two. He was able to campaign separately against the southern and the northern kings. His military policy was a combination of surprise and speed, of catching his enemies in the open and destroying their troops, since his own desert army was untrained in siege operations.

(e) Last, Joshua was an able administrator in peace as well as in war. His keen geographic judgment enabled him to draw up boundaries for the tribal allotments that were sensible and not provocative of intertribal wars. He did make mistakes, as W. S. La Sor points out (*Great Personalities of the Old Testament: Their Lives and Times* [1959], 75–76), by allowing the crafty Gibeonites to keep their territory (see GIBEON), by not capturing Jerusalem from the Jebusites (see JEBUS), and by failing to dispossess the small but growing enclaves of early PHILISTINES. These factions divided the country across the middle, so that after Solomon's death the nation split apart forming two kingdoms. Some would criticize Joshua for failing to pick and train a successor; on the other hand, after the partitioning of the land, God meant that each tribe should consolidate its own territory as Caleb did at HEBRON.

As seen in the similarity of their names, Joshua is a type of Christ as our conquering commander. Joshua was an agent both of grace (e.g., in the case of RAHAB) and of damnation in the holy war of Yahweh against the seven wicked nations in the Promised Land, just as Jesus is both the Savior and the Judge of all men, who metes out death as well as life. "Everything in Canaan was put into the hands of Joshua as trustee for the people. It was his responsibility to divide and assign the land as each tribe came to claim its portion from him" (A. Redpath, *Victorious Christian Living: Studies in the Book of Joshua* [1955], 22). Even so each believer who desires to walk in the realm of victory and full salvation must claim the spiritual blessings and authority and power that are his rightful inheritance in Christ. We may rest from personal struggle because every spiritual foe that we face already has been defeated by our Joshua (Heb. 3:12—4:8) (See F. B. Meyer, *Joshua and the Land of Promise* [n.d.]; C. Armerding, *The Fight for Palestine in the Days of Joshua* [1949]; J. L. Kelso, *Archaeology and Our Old Testament Contemporaries* [1966], 47–48. For a summary of the modern debate regarding the historicity of the Joshua traditions, see G. W. Ramsey in *ABD*, 3:999–1000.) See also JOSHUA, BOOK OF.

J. REA

(2) The owner of a field in the town of BETH SHEMESH (1 Sam. 6:14, 18). When the PHILISTINES returned the ARK OF THE COVENANT to the Israelites, the two cows pulling the cart "went straight up toward Beth Shemesh" and stopped near a large rock in Joshua's field (v. 12). Using the cart for wood and the cows as sacrifice, the people offered a burnt offering to the Lord that very day. The Levites placed the ark on the rock, which became a witness to these events.

(3) A city governor in the days of King JOSIAH (2 Ki. 23:8). As part of the religious reform during his reign, Josiah "desecrated the high places, from Geba to Beersheba, where the priests had burned incense. He broke down the shrines at the gates—at the Gate of Joshua, the city governor, which is to the left of the city gate" (the pl. "gates" can be construed in more than one way; cf. M. Cogan and H. Tadmor, *II Kings*, AB 11 [1988], 286–87). It is usually assumed that the city in question is JERUSALEM, but an alternate view sees here a reference to BEERSHEBA (Y. Yadin in *BASOR* 222 [Aug. 1976]: 5–17; but see Z. Herzog et al. in *BASOR* 225 [Feb. 1977]: 49–58).

(4) Son of Jehozadak and high priest at the time of the return from Babylon and the rebuilding of the TEMPLE (Hag. 1:1 et al.). See JESHUA #1.

(5) Son of Eliezer, included in Luke's GENEALOGY OF JESUS CHRIST (Lk. 3:29; KJV, "Jose").

Joshua, Book of. The sixth book of the OT. It is commonly regarded as the first of the historical books; in the Hebrew Bible, Joshua is the first of the Former Prophets. The book is named after JOSHUA, the leader of the Israelites during their invasion and settlement by tribes in the Promised Land.

    I. Background
   II. Authorship and date
  III. Destination and purpose
  IV. Canonicity
   V. Text and versions
  VI. Special problems
      A. Theological
      B. Archaeological
      C. Exegetical
 VII. Content and outline
VIII. Theology

I. Background. The events set forth in the book of Joshua follow immediately after the death of MOSES. The cultural and historical setting for the conquest of Palestine is similar to that of the exodus and the wilderness journey. The data for determining this background are supplied by the biblical records and archaeological research. The patriarchs sojourned in Canaan during what archaeologists call the Middle Bronze Age (2100–1550 B.C.). This was a time of change with the influx of new peoples such as the AMORITES. In the 19th and following centuries strongly fortified HYKSOS cities began to dot the land. ABRAHAM arrived at SHECHEM and BETHEL (Gen. 12) probably c. 2000 B.C. during the two centuries when settlements existed in the NEGEV (2100–1900) to sustain the caravan routes to Egypt (Gen. 12:9; 13:1–3; 20:1; 24:62). The narrative in Gen. 14 suggests a time after the collapse of the Sumerian Ur III dynasty (2113–1991) but before the strong first dynasty of Babylon under HAMMURABI (1792–1750), when several kings in MESOPOTAMIA might well have formed a coalition for mutual assistance to raid the asphalt pits and copper mines S of the DEAD SEA.

JOSEPH probably rose to power as vizier of Egypt during that country's illustrious 12th dynasty (1991–1786 B.C.). It is known that Pharaoh Sesostris III (1878–1843) broke the power of the landed nobility, "reducing the monarchs to the status of servants of the crown and doing away with their feudal states" (W. C. Hayes, *The Sceptre of Egypt*, 2 vols. [1953], 1:196). The explanation of how he accomplished this may possibly be found in Gen. 47:13–26, the account of Joseph's buying up the fields of Egypt for Pharaoh. The cultural milieu of the Joseph narratives is thoroughly Egyptian, and the international political situation seems peaceful enough throughout the land, unbroken by the later strife caused by the foreign Hyksos rule in the NILE delta (1730–1570). The seat of government remained in the MEMPHIS area (just S of modern Cairo) throughout the 12th and 13th dynasties. The region of GOSHEN would have been a comfortable distance from the palace (Gen. 46:28–34).

The new king who arose over (or against) Egypt and "who did not know Joseph" (Exod. 1:8 NRSV), that is, who refused to recognize Joseph's contribution to Egypt's history, was likely a Hyksos ruler in the Nile delta region. If the Hyksos afflicted instead of favoring the Israelites, and forced them to build PITHOM and RAAMSES (the Hyksos capital also known as Avaris or Tanis, most likely to be identified with the site of Qantir in the NE delta), this would explain why Israel did not flee Egypt when native Egyptians thrust out the Hyksos before 1550 B.C.

The Pharaohs of the 18th dynasty (1567–1320) evidently continued to enslave the Israelites until Moses finally led them into Sinai. According to one view, this event took place c. 1445, that is, 480 years before SOLOMON began to build the temple (1 Ki. 6:1). The exodus would have occurred during the reign of Amenhotep II (1450–1425), following the long reign of the mighty THUTMOSE III (1483–1450), the oppressor of Israel from whom Moses fled after killing the Egyptian taskmaster

The Israelite campaigns in the Promised Land.

(Exod. 2:15). While the capital of these kings was at THEBES in Upper Egypt, they had subsidiary palaces at Memphis, HELIOPOLIS (near Cairo), and probably Bubastis (see PI BESETH), where Pharaoh could have been in residence during the time of the plagues. The exodus occurred 430 years after Israel had come to dwell in Egypt (Exod. 12:40; or as the SEPTUAGINT and the SAMARITAN PENTATEUCH indicate, after he had come to dwell both in Canaan and in Egypt), returning with his family and flocks from PADAN ARAM. According to the 18th-dynasty date for the exodus, Joshua would have led Israel across the Jordan c. 1405, at the close of the Late Bronze I Age (1550–1400). After making the tribal allotments, Joshua lived on until 1390–1380, or even later. The period of the judges then would have lasted over 300 years until SAUL was anointed king c. 1040. This is known as the "early date" view of the exodus and conquest.

An alternate view dates Joseph's career to the Hyksos period and the exodus during the reign of Pharaoh RAMSES II (1304–1237) or even of his successor MERNEPTAH (a stela of the latter mentioning Israel as being in Canaan makes any later date for the exodus highly improbable). Proponents of this view base their interpretation on the appearance of the name Raamses in Exod. 1:11, on the settled Edomite and Moabite towns and line of fortresses which archaeologists claim were not built until the 13th cent, and on the widespread destruction of Canaanite cities c. 1250–1200. Those who hold this "late date" view take the 480 years of 1 Ki. 6:1 to be a conventional number for twelve generations, supposedly lasting forty years each, but in actuality only about twenty-five years each. The exodus would be only 300 years before Solomon began his temple, or c. 1270. JEPHTHAH's figure of 300 years from Moses' capture of HESHBON to his own day (Jdg. 11:26) cannot be taken literally, and the periods of rest (and perhaps of oppression as well) in the era of the judges must be foreshortened and/or drastically overlapped. (For an extensive defense of an early date, see J. J. Bimson, *Redating the Exodus and the Conquest* [1978]; cf. also B. K. Waltke in *WTJ* 52 [1990]: 181–200.) See also CHRONOLOGY (OT) IV; EXODUS, THE II.

Even more serious to the careful interpretation of Scripture, the adherents of the late date view find it necessary to reject the biblical picture of a unified movement of all twelve tribes from Egypt to Canaan under Moses and Joshua. They believe they must account for certain extrabiblical evidence, such as a seeming 14th-cent. date for the destruction of JERICHO and the occurrence in inscriptions of Seti I and Ramses II of the name Asher as a territory in southern Phoenicia. Some scholars admit that the term HABIRU, mentioned in the TELL EL-AMARNA Letters (c. 1390–1360), refers to bands of Hebrew Israelites. By suggesting that the supposed late documents that make up the sources of the Pentateuch and Joshua (the so-called JEDP theory) contain conflicting data, such scholars believe they are able to reevaluate the biblical statements and to see some of the Israelite tribes entering Palestine c. 1400 and others c. 1250. Some tribes supposedly may have infiltrated from the N, some from KADESH BARNEA into the NEGEV, and some crossed the Jordan to attack Jericho. Some tribal groups may never have left Canaan to sojourn in Egypt. (For an extreme fragmentation of the settlement of Canaan by the various clans or tribes, which later amalgamated under the name of Israel, see N. K. Gottwald, *A Light to the Nations* [1959], 152–65, and his later work, *The Tribes of Yahweh: A Sociology of the Religion of Liberated Israel, 1250–1050 B.C.E.* [1979, reprinted with new preface, 1999].)

This picture of the conquest and settlement differs greatly from that presented in the books of Moses and of Joshua. The Bible indicates that all twelve sons of Jacob were with him in Egypt, all twelve tribes were at Mount Sinai when God gave them the covenant and the laws and were numbered there, all were present at Kadesh Barnea, and all encamped at ABEL SHITTIM where another census was taken. All twelve tribes crossed the Jordan together with Joshua and erected two monuments of twelve stones each, all assembled at Mount Ebal, and all the tribes *received* their territorial allotments from either Moses or Joshua before they began to settle. To argue for two or three successive waves of conquest or infiltration is to invalidate the biblical record.

According to the early date view, by the time of the Israelite invasion of Canaan, Pharaoh Amenhotep III (1417–1379) was losing interest in his Asiatic territories. The campaigns of Thutmose III and his successors into Palestine and the oppressive administration of their oft-corrupt commissioners had seriously weakened the feudal system and towns established by the Hyksos. Most of the petty kings of Canaan and Syria soon revolted from Egypt or stopped paying annual tribute. CUNEIFORM tablets found at Tell el-Amarna in Egypt, the site of the capital of Amenhotep's son AKHENATEN (1379–1362), are part of the royal archives of these two pharaohs. The majority were letters from vassal princes in Palestine and Syria pleading for aid from the Pharaoh against neighboring city-states or against the Habiru (cuneiform ideogram SA.GAZ). Apparently most of these pleas went unanswered. The silence in the books of Joshua and Judges concerning Egypt thus may be explained by the fact that Egypt had a weak foreign policy from Amenhotep III until Seti I (1318–1304), the next pharaoh to march into Palestine. Even then the Egyptian armies did not always attempt to invade the mountains but stuck to the coastal route when going to campaign against the HITTITES in Syria.

The Amarna tablets show that the book of Joshua accurately portrays the political situation in Canaan—a country divided into numerous small feudal city-states prone to war with one another. It is perhaps significant that none of the extant Amarna letters come from or mention Jericho, Ai, Bethel, or Gibeon, cities destroyed or controlled by Joshua and the Israelites. Cities not captured or not permanently occupied by Israel are those from which letters were sent to Egypt requesting help—Jerusalem, Gezer, Lachish, Jarmuth, and Eglon. The Amarna correspondence seems to reflect the situation in Palestine early in the period of the judges, although probably not during the time of the conquest itself under Joshua. (See Gleason L. Archer, *A Survey of Old Testament Introduction*, 3rd ed. [1994], 288–95.)

By the period of Joshua and the Judges, Canaanite religion had become exceedingly degraded. The chief emphasis was upon fertility and sex. The Ras Shamra tablets (see UGARIT) reveal the licentious and brutal characteristics of Baal, Anath, Ashtoreth, Asherah, and other deities. The extant relics of fertility cult practices and serpent worship unearthed at Beth Shan, Megiddo, Hazor, Gezer, etc., and evidence of child sacrifice as in a foundation at Dothan, bear mute testimony to the need for strong measures on the part of the invading Israel-

Joshua divided the land among the twelve tribes of Israel.

ites. Since sacred PROSTITUTION and other religious practices were spiritually contaminating, one can understand why God commanded Israel to exterminate the seven nations in Canaan. In holy war they and their cities were to be devoted to destruction lest the religious life of God's people be endangered through contact with such idolatrous peoples (W. F. Albright, *From the Stone Age to Christianity* [1957], 230–35, 281; Archer, *Survey*, 296–99).

II. Authorship and date. The book of Joshua in its present form appears to be a literary unit, composed by an anonymous author. Critical scholars have insisted that the book is a composite work of several source documents, later compiled, revised, and supplemented by various Deuteronomic editors (see DEUTERONOMISTIC HISTORY). When one recognizes the different types of literary materials found in the book of Joshua—narrative, topographic description, exhortation—there remain no strong arguments against its internal unity.

Artur Weiser (*The Old Testament: Its Formation and Development*, 4th ed. [1961], 143–47) and Gerhard von Rad (*Old Testament Theology*, 2 vols. [1962], 1:296–305) are typical of modern critics in their views of the sources used in Joshua. They say that the book belongs to the PENTATEUCH in that it continues the story of those books, but the method of using the various strands or sources is different. The basis of Josh. 1–12 is mainly the "E" (Elohist) strand, though later revised by the Deuteronomic school. In chs. 2–9 "E" has transformed old Benjamite traditions, presumably nurtured at the tribal sanctuary of Gilgal, into a narrative of the conquest of central Canaan by all of Israel under Joshua. In ch. 10 "E" uses a piece of an old Ephraimite heroic saga, in which the figure of Joshua was original, and combines it with a song about Joshua out of the Book of JASHAR (10:12–14), and in ch. 11 employs an equally isolated Galilean tradition. A few traces of the Yahwist or "J" (Jehovistic) writer still may be seen in 5:13, 14; 9:6–7; 17:14–18. These "E" and "J" strands were not shaped until early in the monarchy. A major Deuteronomistic revision that agreed with the E tradition of the conquest of Canaan took place around the time of King JOSIAH, perhaps to reflect the northward expansion of the kingdom of Judah during his reign. The "D" (Deuteronomistic) additions were chiefly ch. 1; 10:16–43 and 11:10—12:24 (lists of captured towns and kings); 21:43—22:16; and ch. 23; ch. 24 is substantially "E" with "D" editing. Later, in the time of EZRA, the "P" (Priestly) writer(s) added most of the contents of chs. 13—21 and 22:7–34.

Other scholars, especially Martin Noth (*Das Buch Joshua* [1938]) and John Bright (in *IB*, 2:541–48), reject this analysis, claiming that it is impossible to trace out Pentateuchal documents in Joshua. The only literary contact on which a majority of scholars are agreed is with the book DEUTERONOMY itself, so the book of Joshua is described as "thoroughly Deuteronomic" in its present form.

It is true that the author of the book of Joshua did make use of sources. He specifically refers to the Book of Jashar (Josh. 10:13) and indicates that Joshua ordered a description of the land to be written (18:9). Joshua himself wrote the words of the covenant renewal and various statutes and ordinances for the people in the book of the law of God at Shechem (24:25–26). Furthermore, a comparison of Josh. 6:26 with 1 Ki. 16:34 suggests that Joshua also wrote down the oath he made regarding Jericho and the curse upon any future rebuilding; the passage in 1 Kings says literally that HIEL restored Jericho at the cost of his two sons,

Aerial view of OT Jericho (looking SE). The Lord gave Joshua and the Israelites a memorable victory over this city.

according to the word of the Lord which he spoke "by Joshua the son of Nun" (16:34).

Joshua cannot have been the final author of the book bearing his name, since it records his death (Josh. 24:29–30). While the TALMUD attributes the book to Joshua, it explains that this death notice was written by ELEAZAR the priest, and that his son PHINEHAS appended the last verse (24:33) to finish the book (*b. Baba Batra*, 14b–15b). Several events are mentioned that did not occur until after Joshua's death: Caleb's conquest of HEBRON (15:13–14; cf. Jdg. 1:1, 10, 20), OTHNIEL's capture of DEBIR (Josh. 15:15–19; cf. Jdg. 1:1, 11–15), and the migration of the Danites to Leshem/LAISH (Josh. 19:47; cf. Jdg. 17–18) at a time after idolatry was tolerated in Israel (idolatry was apparently held in check during Joshua's lifetime, Josh. 24:31). The author evidently employs the name HORMAH (12:14; 15:30; 19:4) for the town earlier known as ZEPHATH, and the name was not changed until the days of the Judges (Jdg. 1:16–17). The phrase "all the Hittite country" (Josh. 1:4) in referring to Syria SW of the EUPHRATES would not have been historically accurate until the takeover of that territory by King Suppiluliuma c. 1350 B.C. The phrase is not in Deut. 11:24.

On the other hand, the author was an eyewitness of some of the events he described. He speaks of the Lord's blocking Jordan "until *we* had crossed over" (Josh. 5:1 [following the *Ketib*], italics added).

Excavation Area A of OT Jericho (looking N from the southern base of the tell). Defensive walls like these, built before the time of Joshua, may have continued to function until the time of his attack against this city.

© Dr. James C. Martin

He identifies Israel's previous generation by saying, "For the LORD had sworn to them that they would not see the land that he had solemnly promised their fathers to give *us*" (5:6, italics added). RAHAB was still living at the time of writing (6:25). After outlining their boundaries the author himself addresses Judah directly: "This shall be your south boundary" (15:4 NRSV). Consider also his detailed narratives (2:3–22; 3:14–17; 4:8–18; 7:16–26) and the repeated use of preconquest place names (15:9, 49, 54).

The book must be pre-Solomonic, since Canaanites still held GEZER (Josh. 16:10; cf. 1 Ki. 9:16), and pre-Davidic, because JERUSALEM was still inhabited by the Jebusites (Josh. 15:8, 63; cf. 1 Sam. 5:5–9 and see JEBUS). It must have been written before the reign of King SAUL, who massacred many Gibeonites and planned to destroy them all (2 Sam. 21:1–9), because the Gibeonites were still servants around the tabernacle at the time of writing (Josh. 9:27). One can also argue that the book is earlier than the 12th cent., because SIDON rather than TYRE is considered to be the leading city of PHOENICIA (11:8; 19:28), and the people of that region are called Sidonians (13:4–6), whereas Tyre gained the ascendancy over Sidon c. 1200. At the time of writing, moreover, the PHILISTINES were not yet considered to be a menace, occupying at that time only a part of the "south" (Negev), along with the Geshurites and the Avvim; and the territory as a whole was reckoned as Canaanite (13:2b–4a; the Philistines are mentioned only here in Joshua). Not until after 1200, according to the Egyptian records of Ramses III, did the Philistines come in force to the Palestinian coastal plain (for corroborating archaeological evidence see K. M. Kenyon, *Archaeology in the Holy Land* [1960], 221–32).

Since the author follows the style that Moses employed in writing the book of Deuteronomy, and since he seemingly had access to Joshua himself in order to learn of the leader's private confrontation with the Lord near Jericho (Josh. 5:13–15), a proposed author has been PHINEHAS, the last person named in the book (24:33). Phinehas, the son and successor of Eleazar the high priest, stood firmly for the Lord at PEOR (Num. 25:7–13) and fought the Midianites, killing BALAAM (31:6–8). He, rather than Joshua, is the prominent figure in settling the dispute over the altar erected by the two and one-half eastern tribes in the Jordan valley (Josh. 22:10–34). He would have been about forty years old at the time of the invasion of Canaan, apparently having been born in Egypt before the exodus (Exod. 6:25). Joshua may have lived until c. 1380, Eleazar a few more years, and Phinehas until perhaps 1360–1350, living to be eighty or ninety years old. Thus Phinehas could have written during the judgeship of Othniel (Jdg. 3:8–11; cf. Josh. 15:17). He was given a town in the hill country of Ephraim (Josh. 24:33).

On the other hand, there are indications that the writer may have been an unnamed priest closely associated with Phinehas, but who resided within Judah, perhaps even in Hebron, one of the cities of refuge (Josh. 20:7; 21:13). Special interest is shown in Hebron in describing its being assigned to Caleb before any other allotments were made (14:6–15), in relating its recapture by Caleb (15:13–14; cf. 10:36–37), and in naming it not only first but with special notation among the forty-eight cities for the Levites (21:11–13). The far greater familiarity with the territory finally occupied by the tribe of Judah (cf. the detailed account of the southern campaign, 10:1–43) and the lengthy list of the borders and towns of Judah (15:1–63) may indicate that this became the author's homeland. He only sketchily traces the borders of the important Joseph tribes to the N, even though within them lay both Shiloh and Shechem (chs. 16–17).

If he lived in Judah, it is understandable that he might list the geographical areas of that territory first without specifying that the hill country near the Negev belonged to Judah (Josh. 11:16). Since there is repeated mention of the fact that no territorial inheritance was allotted to the tribe of Levi (13:14, 33; 14:3–4; 18:7), perhaps he was a Levite if not a priest (see J. J. Lias, *Joshua*, in *Pulpit Commentary* 3 [1881], xi-xii). Whoever the author, his book evidences thorough knowledge of and dependence on the fourth and fifth books of Moses (e.g., cf. the description of Aroer in Josh. 13:9 with that in Deut. 2:36).

III. Destination and purpose. Just as Moses wrote down the words and works of God and had the scroll(s) placed beside the ARK OF THE COVENANT in the sanctuary to remain there as a witness to the nation (Deut. 31:9, 24–27), so also later prophets such as SAMUEL wrote additional material "in the book" (MT, *basseper*, 1 Sam. 10:25) and laid it up before the Lord. Evidently true prophets of the Lord were enrolled in the register of the house of Israel (Ezek. 13:9), implying that they and their writings were accepted during their own lifetimes as having divine authority. The book of Joshua would likewise have been added to the sacred Scriptures of Moses soon after writing, and kept along with them in the tabernacle for the benefit of God's chosen people and their anointed leaders. The Scriptures were to be read periodically at the time of the annual feasts and on special occasions of covenant renewal, as in the time of EZRA and NEHEMIAH (Neh. 8–9).

The book of Joshua was written to continue the sacred history of Israel begun in the Pentateuch. Deuteronomy set forth the historical basis of God's election of Israel and fully stated the COVENANT (or theocratic constitution), which was revised and mediated to Israel afresh by Moses before his death. The book of Joshua proceeds to show how this chosen people under the covenant became established in its Promised Land. Herein is found the record of Yahweh's faithfulness to his covenants with the patriarchs and with the nation (first given to it at Sinai). This Scripture is to inspire and guide God's people to corresponding covenant loyalty and unity and high morale in future generations.

The fundamental purpose of all of the prophetic books of the Hebrew canon is to exhort and warn Israel to return and adhere to the Mosaic covenant (Neh. 9:30; Zech. 7:8–12). This book teaches that God is fully able to perform all of his good promises to his people (Josh. 21:45), that he is ever guiding them and overruling in the dangers that beset them. By comparing, for instance, the lengthy record of ACHAN's sin and punishment (ch. 7) with the brief report of the whole northern campaign (11:1–15), it becomes apparent that there is a selection of materials in the account of the conquest—much interesting factual data is obviously omitted. The clear aim is to set forth moral and religious lessons and to demonstrate that Israel is God's chosen agent for the carrying forward of his purposes on earth.

IV. Canonicity. In the Hebrew Bible, Joshua heads the division known as the Former Prophets, which covers Israelite history from the conquest to the Babylonian exile; it includes the books of Joshua, Judges, 1–2 Samuel, and 1–2 Kings. See CANON (OT).

As already noted, Martin Noth and others claim that this theological history of Israel in Palestine began with the book of Deuteronomy as its introduction. It is clear, however, that in Jewish history Deuteronomy always has been considered as part of the TORAH, as one of the five books of the law. In 2 Ki. 14:6 the statement that King AMAZIAH followed what was written in the Book of the Law of Moses is accompanied by a quotation in full of Deut. 24:16. The postbiblical book of ECCLESIASTICUS, both in the translator's foreword and in the text, distinguishes between the Law and the Prophets (Sir. 45:21; 48:22—49:12). When asked which is the great commandment in the law, Jesus Christ replied by quoting Deut. 6:5 (Matt. 22:36–38). Likewise he attributed the provision for divorce in the law (found in Deut. 24:1–4) to Moses (Matt. 19:8), not to some later writer. The apostles continued to recognize statements in Deuteronomy as belonging to Moses (Acts 3:22, citing Deut. 18:15) or as written in the law of Moses (1 Cor. 9:9, citing Deut. 25:4; Heb. 10:28–30, referring to Deut. 17:6; 19:15; 32:35–36). JOSEPHUS (*Ag. Ap.* 1.7–8) clearly states that the Jews of his day had five books belonging to Moses, and thirteen by prophets who wrote down what was done in their times from the death of Moses till the reign of ARTAXERXES.

Further difficulties for the theory of a Deuteronomistic History of Israel occur in the lack of any recognizable Deuteronomic framework (the covenant renewal pattern of Deuteronomy and Joshua) for the books of Judges through 2 Kings. The Deuteronomic style that purportedly characterizes Joshua is not evident in Judges, as the critics S. R. Driver and C. F. Burney admit.

The older theory that Joshua was the sixth book of a late Jewish collection dubbed the HEXATEUCH is also unrealistic. This view seems first to have been suggested by Alexander Geddes in 1792. It was developed in line with the documentary (JEDP) theory of the Pentateuch by such critical scholars as Bleek, Knobel, and Nöldeke in the 19th cent. The classic presentation in English of the Hexateuchal analysis and its defense is by J. E. Carpenter and G. Harford-Battersby (*The Hexateuch*, 2 vols. [1900]). It was argued that there must be a suitable conclusion to the story of Israel's beginnings described in the first five books of the OT. The theme of the Promised Land permeates the Pentateuch from Abraham to the Israelites' wilderness wanderings;

View NW from Mount Gerizim across Nablus to Mount Ebal. Joshua built an altar to the Lord on Mount Ebal shortly after the conquest of the Promised Land had begun (Josh. 8:30–31).

© Dr. James C. Martin

it is said that without Joshua the narrative would be incomplete. Furthermore, source analysis spotted the familiar Pentateuchal documents in the sixth book. Especially the P source was thought to be present in Joshua but not in the subsequent books of Judges–2 Kings.

The term Hexateuch has no basis, however, in Jewish tradition. There is no evidence that Joshua was ever considered as forming a unit with the five books of Moses. Evidence already has been given that the Law always was distinguished from the other books. Joshua was not included in the annual and triennial systems of reading the Law, whereas selections from Joshua were included in the Haphtaroth (selected readings from the Prophets).

As E. J. Young (*Introduction to the Old Testament* [1949], 158) points out, there are linguistic peculiarities in the Pentateuch that do not appear in Joshua. In the former, the masculine singular personal pronoun (*hû* H2085) is commonly used for both genders, but not in Joshua. The name Jericho is spelled *yĕrēḥô* in the Pentateuch (e.g., Num. 22:1; Deut. 32:49) but *yĕrîḥô* in Joshua (Josh. 2:1 et al.). The phrase "Yahweh, the God of Israel" occurs fourteen times in Joshua but is very rare in the Pentateuch.

Even from the standpoint of documentary analysis, the idea of a Hexateuch is inconsistent. In Genesis–Numbers, the Priestly source supposedly provides the framework, but in Joshua, P is said to appear only in the section about the land allotments (Josh. 13–22). If the alleged sources of the Pentateuch are continuous and run through Joshua, why is P completely absent from Deuteronomy and from Josh. 1–12; 23–24?

The strongest argument against a Hexateuch is that the SAMARITANS considered only the Pentateuch to be canonical. For them, Joshua was not considered part of the canon even though it contains various elements that would have commended it to Samaritan sectarianism. It features Shechem (their city of Nablus is next to Shechem) as a city of refuge and the center where all the tribes of Israel were gathered for the covenant renewal ceremony (Josh. 24:1) and where Joseph's bones were finally buried (24:32). No intimation of Jerusalem's future importance as Israel's center of worship is to be found. It even describes the formal reading of the law by the entire nation at the foot of Mount GERIZIM (8:33), where the Samaritans later worshiped (cf. Jn. 4:20). As G. L. Archer concludes, "the only possible explanation for the failure of the Samaritans to include *Joshua* in their authoritative canon was that it was not actually a part of the Mosaic Torah. The Torah must, therefore, have existed as a separate Pentateuch at the time of the Samaritan schism" (*Survey*, 288).

Actually, the connection of Joshua with Deuteronomy is no closer than its connection with Judges. Both the books of Joshua and Judges begin with an identical formula, *wayhî ʾaḥărê môt*, lit., "And after the death of …" The most logical explanation is that the Scriptures are *one* record, since by divine INSPIRATION they have one ultimate Author. Thus each human writer, performing the function of a prophet, added to the existing Word that already had been recorded and recognized as canonical. On the other hand, the various higher-critical theories have proved to be destructive of one another, without proposing an explanation in line with Jewish tradition and the Bible's own testimony concerning itself.

That the book of Joshua was accepted by the early church as the Word of God may be seen in the quotation from Josh. 1:5 to be found in Heb. 13:5, "for he has said, 'I will never fail you or forsake you'" (NRSV). Numerous other references may be found in the NT to persons and events mentioned in Joshua, showing that there was no doubt as to the authenticity of its record.

V. Text and versions. The Hebrew text of Joshua contains relatively few corruptions. B. J. Roberts lists five or six minor scribal errors that have crept into the MT of this book (*The Old Testament Text and Versions* [1951], 96–98). The Hebrew MSS from the Qumran caves, especially the fragments from Cave IV, indicate that there was existent in Palestine a Hebrew text of Joshua somewhat different from the MT and closer to the text that lies behind the SEPTUAGINT. The DSS "establish once for all that in the historical books the Septuagint translators faithfully and with extreme literalness reproduced their Hebrew *Vorlage*" (F. M. Cross, Jr., *The Ancient Library of Qumran and Modern Biblical Studies* [1958], 134). Whether the LXX-type text is superior to the MT must be decided in the case of each individual reading.

In general, however, it would seem that no important corrections are suggested by the LXX. Its rendering of geographical names is unreliable. A. S. Geden (*ISBE* [1929], 3:1751) lists a number of slight variations from the MT in the last six chapters of Joshua. There remains some question as to which LXX recension, the Lucianic or the shorter form, preserves the more original Greek text. (A comprehensive critical edition of the LXX was produced by M. L. Margolis, *The Book of Joshua in Greek*, 5 vols. [vols. 1–4, 1931–38; vol. 5, 1992]; see also L. J. Greenspoon, *Textual Studies in the Book of Joshua* [1983]; M. N. van der Meer, *Formation and Reformulation: The Redaction of the Book of Joshua in the Light of the Oldest Textual Witnesses* [2004].) The value of the other ancient versions for the restoration of the Hebrew text is minimal; most of them are secondary, rendered from the Greek LXX.

VI. Special problems. These may be designated as theological, archaeological, and exegetical.

A. Theological. Many preachers and writers have sensed a contradiction between the goodness and love of God and his command to exterminate the Canaanites (Deut. 7:1–5; 20:16–18; Josh. 11:20). Typical is the view that "the God of Joshua is infinitely remote from the God of Jesus," that he is "a purely nationalistic deity, a God of Battles whose power is chiefly manifested in the prosecution of Holy War" (*The Oxford Annotated Bible*, ed. H. G. May and B. M. Metzger [1962], 263).

In answering such a charge, we must recognize that God is one, that he does not change, that he is the same both in the OT and the NT. He shows love and mercy both to the heathen (e.g., to Nineveh, Jon. 4:11) and to Israel in the OT; and he shows wrath and takes vengeance on the wicked and idolaters in the NT (e.g., on the money-changers, Jn. 2:14–16; cf. Rom. 2:1–9; Eph. 4:17–24; 5:3–11; 2 Thess. 1:5–9; Rev. 21:8). God is no respecter of persons. Equally severe judgment was inflicted upon false prophets and idolaters among the ranks of Israel (Exod. 32:25–29, 35; Deut. 13:1–18). God warned his own chosen people of the consequences of disobedience, and later executed punishment upon them by the sword of cruel nations. He will do so again in the end time when Jerusalem will be besieged and trodden down yet once more (Lk. 21:24; Rev. 11:2; 13:5).

But why exterminate the Canaanites? Were they actually more wicked in Joshua's day than other idolatrous peoples on earth? The Aztecs and Mayas of Central America, for instance, practiced human sacrifice. But in his inscrutable wisdom God selected Canaan, not another region, as the land he promised to Abraham. He considered it to be at the center (lit., "navel") of the earth (Ezek. 38:12; cf. 5:5); hence it would exert an influence on the rest of the world throughout history out of all proportion to its size.

Did the Canaanites bear a greater responsibility? In Joshua's time Canaan benefited from civilizations on either side that were already illustrious and old. Furthermore, the Canaanites were sinning against spiritual light. In the days of MELCHIZEDEK and ABRAHAM, they had a witness from the one true God, they saw divine judgment fall upon SODOM and its sister cities, and before the conquest they quaked to hear about him (Josh. 2:8–11). God delayed judging Canaan because in Abraham's time "the sin of the Amorites has not yet reached its full measure" (Gen. 15:16). Baalism had not yet developed. BAAL is never mentioned in the patriarchal narratives, and EL was still the high god of the Canaanites according to the Ugaritic epics. By 1400 B.C. the Canaanite civilization and religion had become one of the weakest, most decadent, and most immoral cultures of the civilized world. Many of its repulsive practices were prohibited to Israel in Lev. 18. In view of the sexual perversions listed, it is more than likely that venereal diseases ravaged a large part of the population. Hence stern measures were required to prevent decimation of the Israelites by the spread of these and other diseases such as malaria and smallpox. Contagion would be possible by sudden fraternization before immunity could develop (R. E. D. Clark, *The Christian Stake in Science* [1967], 55, 150). Yet in his control of history God grants freedom of will and motive to his agents. He is not therefore responsible for their greed and atrocities.

Finally, it should be noted that in the midst of wrath Yahweh remembered mercy. Rahab and her family were spared, delivered from death "by grace through faith." For the significance of people and things cursed and devoted to destruction (Josh. 6:17–21; 8:21–29), see DEVOTED (THINGS); for the concept of holy war (5:13–15), see WAR.

B. Archaeological. The proper interpretation and dating of mute archaeological findings taxes the skill of the most experienced excavator. With regard to JERICHO, Kathleen M. Kenyon believes her excavations have shown that the strong Middle Bronze Age Hyksos city lay abandoned from c. 1550 to c. 1400 B.C. Most of the evidence for a town during the Late Bronze Age had been removed by previous expeditions or had disappeared through erosion. But burials in tombs and stratification on the town site (a portion of a house floor with an oven and juglet) testify to occupation in the Late Bronze Age II. Kenyon dated this to the 14th cent. B.C., but not the 13th. Her dating, based on meager evidence, is within fifty years of the early date of the conquest, but clearly does not aid the late date theory ("Jericho," in *Archaeology and Old Testament Study*, ed. D. W. Thomas [1967], 271–75).

The identification of AI with any known archaeological site cannot yet be established. The imposing ruins of Khirbet et-Tell, 2 mi. ESE of BETHEL and covering an area of c. 25 acres, well fits the biblical geographical description (Josh. 7:2; 8:9, 12). French (1933–35) and American (1964, 1966) expeditions have discovered, however, that there was no Middle or Late Bronze occupation of the mound. While it was one of the best fortified cities in the Early Bronze Age (c. 2900–2500 B.C.) and villagers settled there from 1200 to 1000, "nothing in the present evidence warrants an identification of the village with the city of Ai captured by Joshua as described in Josh. 8:1–29" (J. A. Callaway in *BASOR* 178 [April 1965]: 27–28). Soundings in the vicinity at Khirbet Haiyan, in a yard of a resident of the modern village of Deir Dibwan, and at Khirbet Khudriya have produced no remains of a settlement as early as the OT period. Perhaps Ai was ENE of Bethel, at or near Rimmon (Jdg. 20:45). This puzzle has spawned such attempted explanations as the view that Ai was simply a military outpost of Bethel, leaving no occupational debris; or that Josh. 7–8 really refers to the destruction of Bethel (cf. Jdg. 1:22–25), the story being changed etiologically to explain the ruins of et-Tell.

C. Exegetical. The proper understanding of the so-called "long-day" passage (Josh. 10:12–14) remains a *crux interpretum* for the biblical scholar. Did God miraculously prolong the daylight about a whole day? A number of modern commentators have suggested that instead of asking for a lengthened day, Joshua prayed that the sun and moon would, literally, be dumb or keep silent, that is, cease their normal "speech" of shining. The reason for this request is that following their all-night forced march from Gilgal, Joshua's troops would become exhausted quickly by having to pursue the Amorites in the hot sunlight. God answered miraculously by sending an unseasonal storm with destructive hailstones (Archer, *Survey*).

J. S. Holladay (in *JBL* 87 [1968]: 166–78) presents an alternate view in keeping with the ancient practice of observing the astral bodies. If the full moon first appears opposite the rising sun on the fourteenth day of the lunar month (i.e., at midmonth), things are in balance and normal, suggesting that prosperity and victory will ensue (cf. "The Creation Epic," 5.18, in *ANET*, 68). Hence Joshua asked for the sun and moon to stand in opposition at dawn as a sign or good omen of victory, that this day might be auspicious, even as Gideon asked for signs with respect to his fleece. See also DAY, JOSHUA'S LONG.

VII. Content and outline. The book of Joshua divides easily into two equal parts: conquest (Josh. 1–12) and settlement (chs. 13–24). The first division recounts how Joshua must both lead Israel across the Jordan and break the fighting potential of the Canaanites. The Lord enabled him to face several problems: his own doubts (1:1–9); the two and one-half eastern tribes (1:12–18); the defenders of Jericho who would perhaps be patrolling the W bank of the Jordan (but the spies reported that the terrified inhabitants had barricaded themselves in Jericho, ch. 2); fording the flooded Jordan (chs. 3–4); and dealing with "the reproach of Egypt" by circumcising the men of Israel at Gilgal (5:2–9).

By means of the sound military strategy of "divide and conquer," and by brilliant field tactics,

Joshua was enabled to capture the key fortresses guarding the trade routes to the highlands. In times of crisis divine power was manifested to reduce strong cities (Josh. 6) or to wipe out superior armies (10:10–11); but usually Joshua employed tactics known to Hittite commanders of that day, such as surprise attacks, night marches, rapid marches by a "flying column," and destruction of enemies in the open and burning their cities rather than long sieges and stationing garrisons in every captured town (see *JNES* 25 [1966]: 162–91). Since it was a holy war, sin in his own camp could not go unpunished (ch. 7), and worship and covenant ceremony must have priority over further conquest (8:30–35). Failure to seek the mind of the Lord as to the identity of the Gibeonites led Joshua to make an unholy alliance that generations later erupted in much bitterness and grief (ch. 9; cf. 2 Sam. 21:1–14).

In the second division of the book, Israel's settlement lists embrace Joshua's territorial allotments made at Gilgal (Josh. 13–17) and at Shiloh (chs. 18–21), including the CITIES OF REFUGE and Levitical towns, before the tribes had begun to colonize their portions. The method of delineating borders by naming towns and topographical landmarks was also used at that time by the Hittites in Syria. The partitioning of the land was no simple task, but a complex one that demanded wisdom, careful direction, and considerable time.

Joshua's final acts sought to prepare the nation to love and continue on with their faithful God after his own decease. Peace was restored between eastern and western tribes (Josh. 22); he urged the officials to cleave to the Lord (ch. 23); and he gathered all the people to Shechem to lead them formally and solemnly to pledge anew their covenant allegiance to God (ch. 24). The book may be outlined as follows.

A. The conquest of Canaan (Josh. 1–12)
  1. Preparation for the conquest (1:1—5:12)
    a. Divine charge to Joshua (1:1–9)
    b. Joshua's orders for the invasion (1:10–18)
    c. Mission of the two spies (2:1–24)
    d. Crossing the Jordan (3:1—5:1)
    e. Ceremonies at Gilgal (5:2–12)
  2. Conduct of the campaigns (5:13—11:15)
    a. Central campaign (5:13—8:29)
    b. Covenant ceremony at Ebal (8:30–35)
    c. Southern campaign (9:1—10:43)
    d. Northern campaign (11:1–15)
  3. Summary of Israel's wars (11:16—12:24)
    a. Territorial conquests of Joshua (11:16–23)
    b. Kings conquered by Moses (12:1–6)
    c. Catalog of kings defeated by Joshua (12:7–24)
B. The settlement in Canaan (chs. 13–24)
  1. Allotment of the Promised Land (13:1—21:45)
    a. Divine command to divide the land (13:1–7)
    b. Territories of the eastern tribes (13:8–33)
    c. Beginning of the distribution of Canaan (14:1–15)
    d. Territory of the tribe of Judah (15:1–63)
    e. Territories of the Joseph tribes (16:1—17:18)
    f. Partition for the seven remaining tribes (18:1—19:51)
    g. City-inheritances of Levi (20:1—21:42)
    h. Summary of the settlement (21:43–45)
  2. Consecration of the chosen people (22:1—24:28)
    a. Peace restored with the eastern tribes (22:1–34)
    b. Joshua's final charge to the elders (23:1–16)
    c. National covenant renewal at Shechem (24:1–28)
  3. Epilogue: death of Joshua and subsequent conduct of Israel (24:29–33).

VIII. Theology. Meaning is found in Israel's history as one understands the theology of Yahweh's covenants with the nation. The Promised Land is given by God to his people as their conditional inheritance, contingent upon obedient loyalty to the Mosaic covenant. In each generation the tribes must renew the vows taken by their ancestors at Sinai. This step of recommitment they took upon

Joshua's exhortation (Josh. 24:14–24) God is shown to be utterly faithful to his covenants with the patriarchs and the theocratic nation by fighting for them, winning their battles, and settling the tribes in their promised homeland (4:23–24; 10:14; 11:6–8; 21:43–45; 23:3, 9–10; 24:2–13, 18). The triumph of faith is stressed in Joshua as it portrays an entire nation marching unitedly to victory in total dependence upon the Lord.

The spiritual victory God provides in Christ is beautifully pictured in this book. The very name "Joshua," the Greek form of which is "Jesus," means "Yahweh is salvation." The redemptive history of Israel's crossing the Jordan, battling the Canaanites, and possessing her inheritance illustrates the Christian's spiritual experience of conflict, triumph, and blessing in the "heavenly realms" (Eph. 1:3; 2:6; 6:12) through the mighty power of God (1:19, 20; 6:10).

According to Isa. 49:8, the predicted MESSIAH will be a second Joshua whom God gives as a covenant to the people to establish the land and apportion the desolate heritages (cf. Josh. 1:6). PAUL teaches that the events of the exodus and the conquest have typological significance (1 Cor. 10:1–11; see TYPOLOGY). Therefore Joshua serves as a type, prefiguring Jesus as the "captain" of our salvation (Heb. 2:10 KJV). As Joshua led the people of God into the Promised Land and allotted their territories, so Jesus brings believers today into Promised Rest (Heb. 4:8–9; Acts 20:32; 26:18). As Joshua interceded for Israel when the nation sinned and was defeated (Josh. 7:6–15), so Jesus is our Advocate who intercedes continually for his own (Rom. 8:34; Heb. 7:25; 1 Jn. 2:1). As Joshua led the Israelites to victory over the enemies of God, so Christ makes possible victory over sin (Rom. 8:37; 2 Cor. 1:10; 2:14) and over Satan (Heb. 2:14–15; 1 Jn. 3:8).

(Important commentaries include C. F. Keil in KD [1869]; F. R. Fay in *Lange's Commentary on the Holy Scriptures* [1870]; M. Noth, *Das Buch Josua*, HAT 1/7 [1938]; J. Soggin, *Joshua*, OTL [1972]; M. Woudstra, *The Book of Joshua*, NICOT [1981]; R. G. Boling and G. E. Wright, *Joshua*, AB 6 [1982]; T. C. Butler, *Joshua*, WBC 7 [1983]; R. D. Nelson, *Joshua*, OTL [1997]; D. M. Howard, *Joshua*, NAC 5 [1998]; L. D. Hawk, *Joshua* [2000]; A. G. Auld, *Joshua: Jesus, Son of Nauē, in Codex Vaticanus*, Septuagint Commentary Series [2005]. See also J. Garstang, *Joshua–Judges: The Foundation of Bible History* [1931]; Y. Kaufmann, *The Biblical Account of the Conquest of Palestine* [1953]; A. G. Auld, *Joshua, Moses and the Land: Tetrateuch-Pentateuch-Hexateuch in a Generation since 1938* [1980]; G. Mitchell, *Together in the Land: A Reading of the Book of Joshua* [1993]; and the bibliography compiled by W. E. Mills, *Joshua* [2001].) J. REA

Josiah joh-si´uh (יֹאשִׁיָהוּ H3288, derivation uncertain, possibly "Yahweh heals"; Ἰωσίας G2739). **(1)** Son of AMON and sixteenth king of the southern kingdom of Judah (2 Ki. 22—23; 2 Chr. 34—35; Matt. 1:10–11). **(2)** Son of a certain Zephaniah; the prophet ZECHARIAH was told to go to Josiah's house and crown the high priest Joshua (JESHUA, Zech. 6:10). The rest of this article is devoted to King Josiah.

I. Chronology. Josiah's reign of thirty-one years (2 Ki. 22:1) ended with his death in battle at MEGIDDO, now firmly dated in June/July of 609 B.C. (cf. J. Finegan, *Handbook of Biblical Chronology*, rev. ed. [1998], §430). The date 608 has been argued from the synchronism of JEHOIAKIM's fourth year with NEBUCHADNEZZAR's "first" (Jer. 25:1); but CARCHEMISH in 605 was also in Jehoiakim's fourth (46:1), and it can be shown that Jewish sources (2 Ki. 24:12; 25:8; Jer. 52:12, 28–30) reckoned an extra year to Nebuchadnezzar as compared with Babylonian sources (see D. N. Freedman in *BA* 19 [1956]: 50–60). The Babylonian Chronicle makes no reference to a major Egyptian expedition in 608. If Josiah died in 610/9 (fall reckoning), his reign began in 640/39.

II. Early years. After MANASSEH's reign of terror, his son AMON (at twenty-two) showed similar tendencies. His assassins may have wanted a dynastic change or rebellion against Assyria (so A. Malamat in *JNES* 9 [1950]: 218–27); but the country party rejected them (2 Ki. 21:24), installing Josiah at the age of eight (there is slight textual support for "eighteen," but Amon's youth precludes this). There must have been a regency, controlled by supporters of the dynasty who welcomed relief from its misgovernment. As J. M. Myers suggests (*II Chronicles*,

Looking SW across the Jezreel Valley toward Megiddo, near which King Josiah died in a battle with Pharaoh Neco (2 Chr. 35:20–23).

AB 13 [1965], 205), Zephaniah may well have had some influence. Josiah's active pursuit of a godly policy is dated from 631 B.C. (2 Chr. 34:3).

III. Contemporary events and foreign policy.

Early in Josiah's reign, the Assyrian grip on Palestine was already relaxing, and Psamtik (Psammetichus) I was gradually reestablishing Egyptian authority on the coast of PHILISTIA. NABOPOLASSAR's enthronement in BABYLON (Nov. 626 B.C.) heralded the extinction of the Assyrian empire; by 616, the situation was serious enough for Egypt to align herself with Assyria. NINEVEH fell in 612; Assyrian forces kept the field in upper Mesopotamia, with Egyptian support, until their final defeat at Carchemish.

Josiah, starting as Assyria's vassal at least in name, found increasing scope for acting independently. The covenant (622 B.C.), amounting to formal defiance of the Assyrian deity, brought no political repercussions; and it is possible, though perhaps irrelevant, that his assumption of authority in the provinces of Samaria (2 Ki. 23:19–20) and Megiddo could have been represented as in the Assyrian interest. Josiah may have hoped to restore the kingdom of DAVID; it should be noted, however, that the description of the land (23:8) is still "from Geba to Beersheba"; whereas, so far, none of the stamped jar handles associated with this reign have been found N of Tell en-Naṣbeh (see MIZPAH). It is going beyond the evidence to ascribe Josiah's PASSOVER feast to an expansionist policy (J. Segal, *The Hebrew Passover* [1963], 216ff.).

Westward expansion may be attested by traces of settlement at Meṣad Ḥashavyahu (Y. Aharoni, *The Land of the Bible. A Historical Geography*, rev. ed. [1979], 403; for the theory that the boundary lists in Joshua relate to Josiah's kingdom, see the discussion on pp. 347–49). Josiah married Hamutal of Libnah, perhaps for diplomatic reasons (2 Ki. 23:31; cf. 8:22), and Zebidah of Rumah (23:36; some emend to "Dumah").

IV. Josiah's reformation.

In 2 Ki. 22:3–7, it is related that Josiah gave orders for major repairs to the TEMPLE in 622/1 B.C., during which the high priest found the Book of the Law (v. 8). The king was greatly shocked by what he read; when the prophetess HULDAH confirmed its message of doom, he held a national assembly to renew the COVENANT that it contained. This was followed by a purge of IDOLATRY, extended to Bethel and the Samaritan cities (23:4–20), and the Passover celebration (23:21–23). The narrative includes an appreciation of Josiah's work (23:25) and records his death (23:28–30).

The Chronicler traces Josiah's devotion from boyhood through his first reforms in 628/7 B.C. (2 Chr. 34–35). Having mentioned Josiah's activity in Israel, the Chronicler describes how the book was found and the covenant made after "he had purged the land and the house" (34:8 NRSV). The effect in Israel is again noted (v. 33). The Passover is described, and characterized as surpassing all previous celebrations under the monarchy (35:18). In Kings, Josiah's recall to the covenant is the most important event of the reign; Huldah's prophecy holds the key—the curse must be fulfilled, but Josiah's faith was accepted. To this, all else is incidental. The Chronicler is concerned mainly with the record of Israel's last God-fearing king, and with the witness to God's ordinances even in the shadow of disaster. The presentation in Kings is not incompatible with the earlier reforms recorded in Chronicles, which are implied in 2 Ki. 22:2 and indeed by the temple repair fund.

The covenant was established in the terms of the Book of the Law, which Josiah read at the ceremony. Many scholars (esp. those who reject the Chronicler's account) have concluded that the reforms followed more or less specifically the directions of the book. This may be debated (see below); moreover, the book was found during the restoration of the temple, which would hardly have been undertaken without religious reform. Recognizing this, some scholars see Josiah as following HEZEKIAH's lead toward making the temple the one and only sanctuary of the Lord, where the Passover would be kept. On this view, the book supported but did not inspire Josiah's moves (see KD on 2 Chr. 35:19); and the Passover was not new in principle but in the number of participants and the ordering of the service (both 2 Ki. 23:22 and 2 Chr. 35:18 can be understood thus). Some authorities, however (e.g., J. Gray, A. Alt) see this Passover as instituting a "pilgrimage" in place of a family festival.

It is not clear whether the Passover was unique or a pattern for the rest of the reign. G. Widengren (in *JSS* 1 [1949]; 1–20) connects Passover and the covenant with the New Year as an annual ceremony (similarly, S. Mowinckel, *Psalmstudien*, 2 vols. [1961], 2:204–6). This means a fall Passover and a celebration at the beginning of Josiah's eighteenth year, both very improbable—so much had already happened in that (regnal) year. The restoration of the temple may well have started in October (2 Ki. 22:3 LXX, though Keil [KD on 2 Chr. 35:19], reckons this detail "a worthless gloss").

As with the Passover, the reformation does not seem to have originated with the book, though the covenant terms clearly denounced pagan worship to the point of allowing only one national place of sacrifice. It was the severity of the penalties in the covenant that alarmed Josiah. These penalties, the directions for the Passover, and the prohibition of idolatry, are all that we know directly of the book. On the reasonable assumption that it formed part of the PENTATEUCH, it was most probably DEUTERONOMY; of the principal alternatives, the EXODUS covenant does not specify penalties, whereas the "Holiness Code" (Lev. 17–26) barely mentions the Passover (23:5).

The explicit command in Deut. 12 to "centralize" worship has received so much attention that many scholars have inferred a direct connection and correspondence between the book and the reforms. H. H. Rowley (*The Growth of the Old Testament*, 3rd ed. [1967], 30) claims that only as regards country priests "did the reform not implement the provisions of Deuteronomy." This is an exaggeration (J. Gray, *I and II Kings: A Commentary*, 2nd ed. [1970], 715n.); most of Deuteronomy relates to other things (A. Alt, *Kleine Schriften zur Geschichte des Volkes Israel*, 3 vols. [1953], 2:252ff., finds wide variations from the reform).

V. Death of Josiah. In the summer of 609 B.C., Josiah opposed the Egyptian army as it approached the MEGIDDO pass en route to support the Assyrian attempt to recapture HARAN. Despite assurance by NECO that he had no aggressive designs on Judah, Josiah persisted, and was defeated and mortally wounded. The account in 2 Ki. 23:29 is brief, and various reconstructions have been proposed. A. C. Welch (in *ZAW* 2 [1925], 255–60) and others think that Neco summoned Josiah, but the details given in 2 Chr. 35:20–22 tell against this. English versions at v. 21 (e.g., NRSV, "against … against") conceal a change in the Hebrew preposition: the phrase *'el bêt milḥamtî* probably means "to my (forward) base" (cf. A. Malamat in *JNES* 9 [1950]: 218–27). Neco had no time to exploit his victory until the fall (see JEHOAHAZ). It is difficult to understand Josiah's rash initiative. He may just have been opposing Egypt and Assyria on principle, or deliberately working with the Babylonians (D. N. Freedman in *BA* 19 [1956]: 52 n. 10; but this is highly inferential). Nevertheless, these events fulfilled the promise of 2 Ki. 22:20. See ISRAEL, HISTORY OF.

(See further E. Junge, *Wiederaufbau des Heerwesens* [1937]; D. Diringer in *BA* 12 [1949]: 74–86; F. M. Cross and D. N. Freedman in *JNES* 12 [1953]: 56–58; G. von Rad, *Deuteronomy* [1953], 60ff.; F. M. Cross and G. E. Wright in *JBL* 75 [1956]: 203–19; H. H. Rowley, *Men of God* [1963], 159–67; J. Amusin et al. in *IEJ* 14 [1964], 148–59; H. Cazelles in *RB* 74 [1967]: 24–44; W. E. Claburn in *JBL* 92 [1973]: 11–22; H. G. M. Williamson in *VT* 32 [1982]: 242–48; C. T. Begg in *VT* 37 [1987]: 1–8 [reply by Williamson on pp. 9–15]; E. Eynikel, *The Reform of King Josiah and the Composition of the Deuteronomistic History* [1996]; M. A. Sweeney, *King Josiah of Judah: The Lost Messiah of Israel* [2001]; W. B. Barrick, *The King and the Cemeteries: Toward a New Understanding of Josiah's Reform* [2002]; M. Leuchter, *Josiah's Reform and Jeremiah's Scroll* [2006].)   J. LILLEY

Josias joh-si´uhs. KJV Apoc. form of JOSIAH (1 Esd. 8:33) and JOSIAH (1:1 et al.).

Josibiah jos-i-bi´uh. KJV form of JOSHIBIAH.

Josiphiah jos-i-fi´uh (יוֹסִפְיָה H3442, "may Yahweh add"; cf. JOSEPH). Descendant of BANI (so LXX; MT omits name) and father of Shelomith; the latter, head of a family of 160 men, is listed among those who returned to Palestine with EZRA (Ezra 8:10; 1 Esd. 8:36 [KJV, "Josaphias"]).

Josippon. A Medieval Hebrew work based primarily on the *Antiquities* of JOSEPHUS. It has usually been regarded as a pseudepigraphon (i.e., a writing falsely ascribed to Josephus), but recent research has made clear that the author, whose name has not survived, sought to produce a reliable account that made use of, and gave credit to, the 1st-cent. Jewish historian. (See D. Flusser in *ABD*, 3:1018–20.)

jot jot. KJV transliteration of Greek *iōta* G2740 (Matt. 5:18; NIV, "smallest letter"). See DOT; IOTA; YOD.

Jotbah jot´buh (יָטְבָה H3513, "pleasant"). Hometown of MESHULLEMETH, wife of King MANASSEH (2 Ki. 21:19). The town is possibly mentioned by TIGLATH-PILESER III in the account of his conquest of GALILEE (Y. Aharoni, *The Land of the Bible: A Historical Geography*, rev. ed. [1979], 372); and it is almost certainly the Jotapata that JOSEPHUS fortified and defended (*War* 2.20.6 §573). Jotbah is usually thought to be the same as modern Khirbet Jefat (Shifat), some 9 mi. NNW of NAZARETH (Aharoni, *Land of the Bible*, 403), but this identification has not been confirmed by archaeological finds. Alternate proposals are Kerem el-Ras, c. 4 mi. NNE of Nazareth (see *ABD*, 3:1020), and JOTBATHAH, to the far S, near the Gulf of AQABAH (see J. A. Montgomery, *A Critical and Exegetical Commentary on the Book of Kings*, ICC [1951], 521).

Jotbath jot´bath. KJV alternate form of JOTBATHAH (Deut. 10:7).

Jotbathah jot´buh-thuh (יָטְבָתָה H3514, "pleasant"). A stopping place of the Israelites in their forty years of wilderness wanderings (Num. 33:33–34). They found it to be "a land with streams of water" (Deut. 10:7; KJV, "Jotbath"). Some scholars identify it with modern Ṭabeh, c. 6.5 mi. SW of ELATH (see Y. Aharoni, *The Land of the Bible: A Historical Geography*, rev. ed. [1979], 199–200).

Jotham joh´thuhm (יוֹתָם H3462, "Yahweh is perfect" or "may Yahweh complete"). **(1)** Youngest son of GIDEON (Jerub-Baal). Jotham escaped the massacre of his family by the citizens of SHECHEM, who had been incited by his half-brother ABIMELECH (Jdg. 9:5). Upon hearing that Abimelech had been proclaimed king, Jotham went up to the top of Mount GERIZIM and spoke his famous fable of the trees, depicting Abimelech as a worthless bramble incapable of offering the men of Shechem security or profit. He then predicted their mutual destruction and fled to BEER (vv. 6–21). Three years later (v. 22), when Abimelech besieged THEBEZ, the curse was fulfilled (vv. 50–57).

View looking W at Mount Gerizim, from where Jotham told his famous fable of the trees.

(2) Son of JAHDAI and, apparently, a descendant of JUDAH somehow related to CALEB (1 Chr. 2:47).

(3) Son of UZZIAH (Azariah) and king of the southern kingdom of Judah (2 Ki. 15:32–38; 2 Chr. 26:21—27:9). The rest of this article is devoted to King Jotham.

I. Chronology. Jotham was made regent when his father Uzziah became ill (2 Ki. 15:5); Uzziah died about 740 B.C. and Jotham became king (v. 7). According to the narrative, Jotham began to reign in the second year of PEKAH of Israel (v. 30), and he was still on the throne when the Aramean REZIN began trying to force Judah into alliance against ASSYRIA. However, it was Jotham's son, AHAZ, who bore the brunt of this pressure (cf. Isa. 7) and who invoked help from Assyria, leading to the fall of DAMASCUS in 732. Ahaz was followed by HEZEKIAH, in whose fourteenth year (prob. 701) SENNACHERIB invaded Judah (2 Ki. 18:13). This implies that Ahaz began his sixteen-year reign about 730; it could be inferred that Jotham had surrendered the reins of government a few years earlier.

The dating of HOSHEA's accession (731) in the twentieth year of Jotham (2 Ki. 15:30), and the allotting of only sixteen years for Jotham's reign (v. 33), may point to the same conclusion. Jotham's "twentieth year" may well be reckoned from his coregency; his "sixteen" could be taken in the same way (E. R. Thiele, *The Mysterious Numbers of the Hebrew Kings*, 3rd ed. [1983], 132), or emended to "six" (J. Gray, *I and II Kings: A Commentary*, 2nd ed. [1970], 57, 70). It is clear that the chronological data in 2 Ki. 15–18 is not based on a single system of reckoning. C. Schedl (*VT* 12 [1962]: 90–98) has propounded the theory that some of the original figures were increased by ten as a result of referring Jotham's sixteen years to the death of Uzziah, whereas Thiele shows that the synchronisms (in 17:1; 18:1, 9–10), which do not match with the remaining data, could arise from taking PEKAH's years as following those of MENAHEM and PEKAHIAH, instead of running concurrently. Jotham on this basis became sole ruler in 740/39, and his reign ended effectively in 736/5 B.C. See also CHRONOLOGY (OT).

II. Regency. Jotham's position during his father's illness is described as being "over the house" (2 Ki. 15:5, NIV, "had charge of the palace"). As J. A. Montgomery (*A Critical and Exegetical Commentary on the Book of Kings*, ICC [1951], 117) and H. Katzenstein (*IEJ* 10 [1960]: 149ff.) have shown, this office developed in importance during the monarchy; it is low on the list in 1 Ki. 4:6, whereas in 2 Ki. 19:2 the holder is principal deputy for the king. There is no hint elsewhere of this "chamberlain" having judicial functions, which properly belonged to the king; because Uzziah was not actually deposed, Jotham may have held the office purely for status, whereas he was in effect carrying out the royal functions.

It is interesting to compare this recorded coregency with those inferred by Thiele to solve chronological problems of the divided monarchy. JEHOSHAPHAT, probably coregent because of ASA's incapacitation, provides the clearest precedent. The lack of an explicit statement about Jehoshaphat's coregency may reflect the difference in circumstances; though Asa's disease is noted in a context of spiritual failing, there was no dramatic event of direct interest to the biblical historians that would have led them to mention a coregency, nor was Asa necessarily deprived of all his royal functions.

A seal bearing Jotham's name was found at ELATH and published by N. Glueck (*BASOR* 79 [Oct. 1940]: 13–15). W. F. Albright (*BASOR* 100 [Dec. 1945]: 18–21) argued from the absence of any patronymic or official designation that the owner was a very important person indeed; but that, being mounted in copper, the seal was probably used by a local officer for royal business. Subsequent discussion suggests that Jotham himself might have had charge of the fort before his regency (N. Avigad in *BASOR* 163 [Oct. 1961]: 18–22). There is little evidence either way; Elath was in Judean hands for most of Jotham's lifetime.

III. Achievement. Jotham followed the steps of his father both in religious faith and in other state policy; both Kings and Chronicles credit him with a steadfast loyalty to the Lord, but observe that local sacrifices were still permitted in Judah.

It is recorded in Kings that Jotham built the UPPER GATE of the TEMPLE (2 Ki. 15:35); the Chronicler adds that he built extensively on the OPHEL wall and set up other defense works in the country (2 Chr. 27:3). J. Simons (*Jerusalem in the Old Testament* [1952], 330) sees the building in Jerusalem as part of a long-range plan to extend the city walls around the outlying quarters, because later Hezekiah built a new N wall and Manasseh completed the circuit. It might be inaccurate, however, to think of a "plan" in any more formal sense than the evolution of a response to a continuously growing need. In the country, Jotham seemed to have strengthened and guarded the places of habitation rather than the frontiers; the "wooded areas" (2 Chr. 27:4) indicate the western and particularly the northwestern areas.

The Ammonites, who had brought tribute to Uzziah, were defeated in battle by Jotham, and appear to have paid heavy tribute for three years running (2 Chr. 27:5; the text is not clear and may be defective, but there is no doubt of the general sense). The limitation at the third year may be due to the turn of the tide as REZIN of ARAM began to press southward (2 Ki. 15:37). (Note further S. Horn in *AUSS* 2 [1964]: 40–52; V. Pavlovský and E. Vogt, *Bib* 45 [1964]: 321–30.) See also ISRAEL, HISTORY OF. J. LILLEY

joy. The feeling or expression of intense happiness; in the Bible, it is viewed especially as the result of a right relationship with God.

I. In the OT. There is a general usage of the term *joy* in the OT (most commonly Heb. *śimḥâ H8525*) that applies to the state of mind in any pleasurable experience. A more particular usage, however, refers to religious emotion. This is most notable in the PSALMS, where it appears as a natural consequence of the individual's fellowship with God, who is the source of joy (Pss. 16:11; 51:12). Various attributes and works of God evoke this joy, such as his judgments (Ps. 48:11), and his governance over the earth (Ps. 97).

Joy was prominent in the total national and religious life of Israel. The inward emotion found expression in outward shouting, singing, leaping, and dancing. The most complete occasion or motivation for this religious joy was the experience of SALVATION, which came to particular intensity in the contemplation of the future state (Isa. 49:13; 61:10–11). Nor is joy solely a human quality. God is pictured as rejoicing in his works (Ps. 104:31), and delighting in prospering his people (Deut. 30:9). (See J. B. Payne, *The Theology of the Older Testament* [1962], 417–19; *NIDOTTE*, 3:1251–54.)

II. In the NT. The NT is richer yet in its description of joy (primarily Gk. *chara G5915*). The mighty redemptive works of God, especially the coming of his Son (Lk. 2:10), and the resurrection of Christ (24:41), were causes of joy. Joy in the NT is not merely an emotion, but a *characteristic of the Christian*. It is a fruit produced by the inner working of the HOLY SPIRIT (Gal. 5:22), being dynamic rather than static. It is not affected by circumstances, however adverse and painful; in fact, joy may be the outcome of suffering for Christ's sake (Col. 1:24).

Jesus was characterized by joy in the task and goal set before him (Heb. 12:2). The Father is pictured as rejoicing over the salvation of one lost sinner in the three parables of the lost sheep, the lost coin, and the lost son (Lk. 15:3–24). Paul also found joy in the spiritual development and steadfastness of fellow believers (Phil. 4:1). (See further E. G. Gulin, *Die Freude im Neuen Testament*, 2 vols. [1932–36]; W. Morrice, *Joy in the New Testament* [1984]; *NIDNTT*, 2:352–61.)   M. ERICKSON

Jozabad joh'zuh-bad (יוֹזָבָד H3416, short form of יְהוֹזָבָד H3379, "Yahweh has granted"; cf. ELZABAD, JEHOZABAD). **(1)** Son of SHIMEATH; an official who, with JEHOZABAD son of SHOMER, murdered King JOASH of Judah at BETH MILLO (2 Ki. 12:21; NRSV has JOZACAR, following many Heb. MSS). The parallel passage identifies him as "Zabad, son of Shimeath an Ammonite woman" (2 Chr. 24:26).

(2) A man from GEDERAH who joined DAVID at ZIKLAG (1 Chr. 12:4); he was among the ambidextrous warriors from the tribe of BENJAMIN who were kinsmen of SAUL (v. 2).

(3–4) Two warriors from the tribe of MANASSEH who joined David at Ziklag; they are described as "leaders of units of a thousand" (1 Chr. 12:20). Some believe that there was only one Manassite warrior named Jozabad and that the second name is a scribal mistake of dittography.

(5) A Levite included in the list of supervisors of the temple storerooms during the reign of HEZEKIAH (2 Chr. 31:13).

(6) A leader of the Levites in the reign of JOSIAH who gave liberally toward the sacrifices (2 Chr. 35:9; called "Joram" in 1 Esd. 1:9).

(7) Son of Jeshua, a Levite, who is mentioned as one serving in Jerusalem at the time of EZRA's return (Ezra 8:33). This is probably the same man mentioned as agreeing to put away a foreign wife (10:23), as helping the people to understand the law (Neh. 8:7; 1 Esd. 9:48 [KJV, "Joazabdus"]), and as one who had charge over the outside work of the house of God (Neh. 11:16).

(8) One of the descendants of PASSHUR who agreed to put away their foreign wives (Ezra 10:22; the parallel passage at this point has "Gedaliah," 1 Esd. 9:22 [KJV, "Ocidelus"]).   W. B. COKER

Jozacar joh'zuh-kahr (יוֹזָכָר [not in NIV], "Yahweh has remembered"). According to many Hebrew MSS, Jozacar was the son of Shimeath; he and JEHOZABAD son of Shomer murdered King JOASH of Judah (2 Ki. 12:21 [cf. KJV, NRSV]; called "Zabad" in 2 Chr. 24:26). The NIV, following other Hebrew MSS, including Codex Leningradensis (the basis of *BHS*), has JOZABAD.

Jozadak joh'zuh-dak. See JEHOZADAK.

Jubal joo'buhl (יוּבָל H3415, meaning uncertain). Son of LAMECH and ADAH; described as "the father of all who play the harp and flute," apparently indicating that he invented musical instruments (Gen. 4:21). The form of his name can be interpreted as a passive (pual) participle from the verb *yābal* H3297, which in another verbal stem (hophal) means "to be brought, led" (cf. Isa. 55:12, and note the name of Jubal's brother, JABAL). Moreover, the consonants in the name are identical to those of the Hebrew word for the musical instrument known as "ram's horn" (*yōbēl* H3413, Exod. 19:13 [here written defectively]; cf. Josh. 6:4–8), which in turn became the term for JUBILEE YEAR (inaugurated by the blowing of the trumpet, Lev. 25:8–13). Thus some speculate that the name Jubal may mean "led in procession" or the like (cf. R. North, "The Cain Music," *JBL* 83 [1964]: 373–89, esp. 380).

Jubilees, Book of (τὰ Ἰωβηλαῖα or οἱ Ἰωβηλαῖοι). A pseudepigraphic work, claiming to be a revelation given to MOSES on Mount SINAI, and consisting of a midrashic expansion of the biblical narrative from Gen. 1 to Exod. 12. It is also known as the Little Genesis and as the Apocalypse (or Testament) of Moses; in the DEAD SEA SCROLLS it is referred to as the Book of the Divisions of the Times into Their Jubilees and Weeks (CD XVI, 3–4).

JUBILEES, BOOK OF

The common designation *Jubilees* refers to the fact that the book divides the history of the world—from the time of CREATION to the giving of the law on Mount Sinai—into jubilee periods of forty-nine years each (cf. Lev. 25 and see JUBILEE YEAR). Israel entered Canaan, according to the author, at the close of the fiftieth jubilee, that is, 2,450 years after creation. Much that is characteristic of the book is due to the use of other PSEUDEPIGRAPHA and ancient traditions of a haggadic and halakic character (see HAGGADAH; HALAKAH). *Jubilees* appears to be the work of one author, who based his narrative on much older material. He interpreted earlier history in the light of the ideals of his own time, especially the emphasis on legalism.

The book can be compared with the rewriting of 1–2 Samuel and 1–2 Kings in the work of the Chronicler. The author tried to do with the traditions concerning the patriarchs and Moses what the author of Chronicles had done for the stories about Samuel and the kings of Israel and Judah. The PATRIARCHS are presented in *Jubilees* as having been rigorous observers of the law, as it was understood during the time when the author lived. The work is closely related in spirit to writings like *1 Enoch* (see ENOCH, BOOKS OF) and the older portions of the TESTAMENTS OF THE TWELVE PATRIARCHS, but also to writings of the QUMRAN community. There is strong evidence to support the assumption that the author of *Jubilees* also belonged to this group. He may have been a priest, because he exalted Levi over Judah (cf. *Jub.* 30 with Gen. 49:5–12). The writer seems to have been a supporter of the HASMONEAN princes, since he applied to Levi's successors the title first assumed by the Hasmoneans, "priests of the Most High God" (*Jub.* 32.1). The book must have been composed prior to 100 B.C. (the apparent date of Hebrew fragments found in Qumran), but probably no earlier than 170.

The book was written originally in Hebrew, but only fragments of several MSS in this language are preserved. An Ethiopic translation, dating back probably to the 6th cent. A.D., was found and published in the middle of the 19th cent., and fragments of a Latin version (prob. 5th cent.) came to light in 1861, covering about one fourth of the whole. Both the Ethiopic and the Latin translations go back to a Greek version of the original Hebrew. The fragments of the book found at Qumran correspond closely to the Ethiopic and Latin translations. It therefore can be assumed that these provide relatively good versions of the original text.

The author claims that an angel spoke to Moses upon God's order and dictated the complete history of creation and that of early mankind until Moses' own time. He was bidden to write down everything he heard. The angel is supposed to have used the heavenly chronological tablets for this dictation, namely "the tables of the divisions of years—from the time of creation—of the law, and of the testimony of the weeks of jubilees, according to the individual years, according to the number of the jubilees …" (*Jub.* 1.29). Through these traditions the Israelites were supposed to get information about "the laws of the seasons, and the seasons according to the division of their days" (50.13). The laws were to be observed upon the threat of divine punishment.

The theology expressed in *Jubilees* differs in many respects from that of the OT. The author expected a MESSIAH sprung from Judah, without however attaching much significance to this figure. A messianic kingdom was to be brought about gradually, resulting in one thousand years of peace and happiness. A final judgment was expected at the end of this messianic age. No hope for the RESURRECTION of the body is expressed, but the book expects an IMMORTALITY OF THE SOULS of the righteous after death. There are parallels in the belief in angels and demons between *Jubilees* and the NT, views that were shared also by the PHARISEES, but not by the SADDUCEES (cf. Acts 23:7). In many other respects, however, there are marked differences from the NT. The laws concerning Sabbath observances, tithes, marriage, circumcision, Passover, firstfruits, and others, are stricter in *Jubilees* than in the Talmudic literature. The author expresses the view that there is no longer any prophet, because the law has made the free exercise of such an office an offense against itself and God.

A matter of much scholarly debate is the calendar for the festive seasons suggested in *Jubilees*. It seems quite likely that the Qumran community used the calendar claimed to be the law of God in this book, which was radically different from the system used by other Jewish groups. This evidence in particular is what makes it likely that the author was not a Pharisee, but a Qumran covenanter. It is certain, in any case, that *Jubilees* influenced that community more than any other group in Judaism.

Jubilees expresses the view that there is no hope whatsoever for the GENTILES. Complete separation from them is the best course of action. This view certainly was in the most radical way practiced at Qumran; but it was the opposite of what the early Christians learned to do (cf. Acts 11:18 et al.). (Introduction and English trans. by R. H. Charles in *APOT*, 2:1–82; and by O. S. Wintermute in *OTP*, 2:35–142. See also J. VanderKam, *A Critical Text and English Translation of the Ethiopic Book of Jubilees* [1989]; M. Albani et al., *Studies in the Book of Jubilees* [1997]; J. T. van Ruiten, *Primaeval History Interpreted: The Rewriting of Genesis I–II in the Book of Jubilees* [2000]; J. VanderKam, *The Book of Jubilees* [2001]; M. Segal, *The Book of Jubilees* [2007].)   G. STROTHOTTE

Jubilee Year. KJV Jubile. The Hebrew term (found both with and without the word for "year") is *yôbēl* H3413, used of a "ram's horn" as a musical instrument (Exod. 19:13; in Josh. 6:4–13 it is always constructed with "horn" or "trumpet"). The connection may be that the Year of Jubilee began with the sounding of a trumpet on the Day of Atonement (Lev. 25:9, though here the usual term for "trumpet," *šôpār* H8795, is used). Other etymologies are possible, however. Some, for example, think it derives from the verb *yābal* H3297 (hiphil, "to bring [as gift or sacrifice]") and that it has agricultural origins (cf. R. North, *Sociology of the Biblical Jubilee* [1954], 96–108; H. Cazelles in *VT* 5 [1955]: 321–24). When *yôbēl* refers to the Year of Release, the SEPTUAGINT renders it with Greek *aphesis* G912 ("release, forgiveness"), but subsequently the Hebrew word itself was borrowed in the form *iōbēl* and further hellenized as *iobelaios*, thence Latin *iobeleus* (later, under the influence of the unrelated Lat. term *iubilare*, "to rejoice," the word became *iubilaeus*, thence English *jubilee*).

I. Provisions. The law of the Jubilee is laid out in Lev. 25:8–55 (cf. also 27:16–25) and affects the dedication of property. The law was operative in

The beginning of the Jubilee Year was marked by the sounding of the shofar.

the case of the daughters of ZELOPHEHAD: it was ruled that an heiress in possession could not marry outside her tribe, because her property would then not revert to her family even at the Jubilee (Num. 36:4). The Jubilee (unlike the SABBATICAL YEAR; see below) is not mentioned elsewhere in the canonical or apocryphal writings.

The first part of the law (Lev. 25:8–17) includes the following provisions: (a) the Jubilee is to be announced on the Day of Atonement in the "fiftieth year"; (b) it consists in the return to alienated land of its original owners, including any who were in bondservice; (c) it includes the prohibition of sowing, vintage, and harvest; (d) land valuation is to take into account the years to run before the Jubilee (note that the guarantee of provision to cover the sabbath year, vv. 18–24, appears to be conditional on the observance of these laws; cf. also vv. 1–7).

The provisions of the second part (Lev. 25:25–38) are that (a) the land may be redeemed within the Jubilee period; (b) the redemption option on city dwellings is limited to one year, and if not so exercised, such property is exempt from next release (Levitical property not subject to these provisions); (c) the poor are to be a charge on the community, in the last resort.

Part three (Lev. 25:39–55) includes two items: (a) Israelite bondmen are to be discharged at the Jubilee and not subjected to the full rigors of slavery; (2) Israelites bound to foreigners may redeem themselves or be redeemed by kinsmen, at a proportion of their original price depending on the years remaining to the Jubilee, or else be released at the Jubilee.

II. Aims. The primary aim was to reunite owners (or their heirs) with their property, so far as practicable, thus (a) restricting the estates from growing to the detriment of small holders, and (b) maintaining the basic security of a property-owning, agricultural community. It is assumed that owners would sell only in extreme necessity, which would usually entail going into hired service; the intention was to give such servants a fair opportunity to become self-supporting again. In practice, usury and profiteering made recovery almost impossible (Neh. 5 illustrates this aspect).

The law would be frustrated unless bondservants were freed to claim their property. Further, as a buyer was virtually taking leasehold, there had to be a fair valuation of the lease in relation to expected yield, and definition of redemption rights. The Mosaic law sought to forestall a tendency toward aggregation, which throughout history has been a cause of political revolution.

III. Relation to the sabbatical year. The laws of the seventh or SABBATICAL YEAR are found in Lev. 25:1–7 (cf. Exod. 23:10–11) and in Deut. 15:1–11 (release, with attached provisions for individual release of slaves after six years' service, 15:12–19; cf. Exod. 21:2–6). The phrase "seven years" occurs as a time-unit as early as Gen. 29:8–30, but the term "weeks [sabbaths] of years," used freely in Daniel, is explained in Lev. 25:8 as if it were unfamiliar.

The Deuteronomic release or discharge from indebtedness (šĕmiṭṭâ *H9024*, Deut. 15:1–2) is not concerned with land; neither did a servant, released on expiry of his six years, necessarily recover any land (hence 15:13–14). The Jubilee property law, on the other hand, did not assume any outstanding debt, whereas the general release was merely to facilitate the restoration (North's emphasis on "mortgage" is misplaced; cf. Cazelles).

IV. Observance of Sabbath and release laws. The prophet JEREMIAH could appeal to the law limiting bondservice (Jer. 34:14, although v. 8 does not refer directly to the law or to the SABBATH [see *IDB*, 4:142]; the nonobservance of it had made release overdue). One of the provisions of Nehemiah's covenant (Neh. 10:31) also implies past neglect of a known law. The saying that the land would "enjoy its sabbaths years" during the exile (Lev. 26:34–35, 43; Deut. 31:10; 2 Chr. 36:21), although connoting rest rather than a time interval, presumes the latter, since the point is that crops would not be raised. In 163 B.C., warfare during the "sabbath for the land" (1 Macc. 6:49; or "seventh year," v. 53) found cities unable to stand a siege because reserves of food were soon exhausted. JOSEPHUS (*Ant.* 14.16.2; 15.1.2) refers to the sabbath year as a fallow-year and asserts that both ALEXANDER THE GREAT and Julius CAESAR recognized this practice and granted remission of tribute (11.8.5–6; 14.10.6; it involved abstaining from offensive war, 13.8.2; *War* 1.2.4). He mentions the Jubilee in his account of the law (*Ant.* 3.12.3), apparently taking the "fiftieth" as the seventh sabbath, and discussing value adjustment as at release (based on profits) rather than as at sale (based on expected yield). The book of *Jubilees* regards the forty-ninth year purely as a calendar event. The official Mishnaic view is that the Jubilee was abolished after the EXILE (*m. Šebiʿit* 10:3); expedients for avoiding release of debt relate, presumably, to the šĕmiṭṭâ (indebtedness).

V. The problem of the fallow. Despite Josephus's testimony and the more convincing (because it is incidental) evidence of 1 Macc. 6:49, authorities have doubted whether a national fallow would be practicable; some have tried to relate sabbatical year and Jubilee to intercalary periods, despite the explicit mention of sowing and harvest. North (*Sociology*, 120) sees the fallow as applied to individual fields on a staggered basis, arguing that a general fallow would not help the poor. It is difficult, however, to imagine such restraint being introduced otherwise than generally. The law was directed primarily at stewardship of the land, and was only one of many measures aimed at the relief of poverty.

The apparent implication of a two-year fallow in Lev. 25:20–22 is difficult. J. Morgenstern (*HUCA* 10 [1935]: 83ff.) infers a spring new year: the crop sown at the end of the sixth, unharvested, would provide food; and with no sowing in the next year, there would be no proper harvest in the eighth. Admittedly, 25:8–11 suggests a fall new year; Morgenstern concludes that vv. 20–22 are editorial. The passage can hardly refer to a Jubilee fallow after the seventh sabbath, for despite its position, it refers to "seventh," etc., not "forty ninth, fiftieth"; 25:15–16 may show that "fiftieth" was used for a seventh sabbath, as Josephus and *Jubilees* understood it. (R. S. Kawashima, in *VT* 53 [2003]: 117–19, argues that there was no distinctive Hebrew counting system and that therefore the Jubilee was supposed to take place every fifty years. For NT implications, see S. H. Ringe, *Jesus, Liberation, and the Biblical Jubilee: Images for Ethics and Christology* [1985]. See also C. J. H. Wright in *ABD*, 3:1025–36.) J. LILLEY

Jucal joo´kuhl. See JEHUCAL.

Juda joo´duh. KJV NT form of JUDAH.

Judaea. See JUDEA.

Judah joo´duh (יְהוּדָה H3373, "[God/Yahweh] be praised," by popular etymology and possibly actual derivation, Gen. 29:35; 49:8; see J. D. Fowler, *Theophoric Personal Names in Ancient Hebrew* [1988], 165; gentilic יְהוּדִי H3374 [see JEW] Ἰούδας G2683; see also JUDAS). KJV NT Juda, Judas. **(1)** Fourth son of JACOB by LEAH (Gen. 29:35). Early in his life, Judah apparently rose to prominence in the family. It was he who said, "What will we gain if we kill our brother [JOSEPH] and cover up his blood? Come, let's sell him to the Ishmaelites and not lay our hands on him; after all, he is our brother, our own flesh and blood" (37:26).

Significantly, the narrative concerning Joseph is interrupted to relate some negative incidents in Judah's life. Judah withdrew from his brothers and married a Canaanite woman (Gen. 38:1–2). His firstborn ER was a wicked man, and the Lord took his life (38:6–7). His second son, ONAN, was told to have intercourse with Er's widow, TAMAR, to preserve his brother's line, but Onan "spilled his semen on the ground to keep from producing offspring for his brother," and so the Lord "put him to death also" (38:10). At that point Judah promised Tamar that he would give her to his next son, SHELAH, but he failed to do so. Many years later Tamar, disguised as a shrine prostitute, had intercourse with Judah himself and eventually gave birth to twins, PEREZ and ZERAH (38:13–30). The material in ch. 38 is inserted at this point in the narrative no doubt for the purpose of highlighting the moral contrast between Judah and Joseph. It is remarkable that Matthew's GENEALOGY OF JESUS CHRIST not only includes Judah, but also mentions Tamar, Perez, and Zerah (Matt. 1:3; cf. Lk. 3:33).

Subsequently, Judah played a positive role both in persuading Jacob to let BENJAMIN accompany the brothers to Egypt (Gen. 43:1–10) and in interceding for Benjamin before Joseph (44:14–34). His leadership role is reflected even in an incidental comment, when we are told that Jacob, as he himself prepared to leave for Egypt, sent Judah ahead to lead the way (46:28). Moreover, Jacob's deathbed blessing upon Judah (49:8–12) takes on special significance: Judah would be victorious over his enemies, and the scepter would not depart from him until the coming of a promised one (for a discussion of this prophecy see SHILOH). The genealogies of Judah's offspring occur in 1 Chr. 2–4. See further JUDAH, KINGDOM OF; JUDAH, TRIBE OF.

(2) Ancestor of a family of Levites who returned from the EXILE (Ezra 3:9 KJV; see HODAVIAH #3).

(3) One of the Levites who agreed to put away their foreign wives (Ezra 10:23; 1 Esd. 9:23 [KJV, "Judas"]).

(4) Son of Hassenuah; a postexilic leader who had charge "over the Second District" of Jerusalem (Neh. 11:9; according to NRSV, he was "second in charge" after Joel son of Zicri).

(5) A Levite who returned from the exile and served as worship leader (Neh. 12:8).

(6) A leader who took part in the procession at the dedication of the wall (Neh. 12:34).

(7) A priest who played a musical instrument at the dedication of the wall (Neh. 12:36).

(8) Son of a certain Joseph, included in Luke's GENEALOGY OF JESUS CHRIST (Lk. 3:30).

Judah, kingdom of. One of the two kingdoms of the Hebrews into which Israel was divided after the death of Solomon. The twelve tribes of Israel had previously constituted a united kingdom. The dynasty established by DAVID continued to rule in JERUSALEM until the destruction of the southern kingdom in 586 B.C. by NEBUCHADNEZZAR, but the power and influence of the dynasty were seriously limited after the division of the kingdom upon the death of Solomon in 936. The tensions between the northern and southern sections of the country polarized around Rehoboam of Judah, the son of Solomon, and Jeroboam son of Nebat, of the tribe of Ephraim in the N. Jeroboam's secession movement was successful, and he became the first king of the northern kingdom, whereas Rehoboam retained the crown of David as king of the kingdom of Judah in the S.

    I. The nature of Judah's territory
   II. The history of the kingdom of Judah
      A. Judah and Israel
      B. Judah and Assyria
      C. Judah and Babylon

I. The nature of Judah's territory. The kingdom of Judah comprised, besides the tribe of Judah (see Judah, tribe of), most of Benjamin, and apparently the tribe of Simeon, which was isolated in the southernmost area of Israel. As the tribe of Judah grew in power, it practically absorbed Benjamin and Simeon. The physical characteristics of Judah's territory had important effects upon the life, culture, and history of the people. The W boundary of Judah was the Mediterranean Sea, and the E was bounded by the Jordan River and the Dead Sea. On the S was the desert, incapable of sustaining life without a system of irrigation. On the N there was no natural division between the territory of Judah and that of the rest of Israel. The boundary seems to have shifted somewhat but was usually thought to run a little to the N or S of Bethel (modern Beitin). The line extended approximately from a point a little N of Joppa to the Jordan River at a point about 13 mi. N of the Dead Sea. It was along this line that the frontier fortresses of Micmash, Ramah, Gibeon, Bethel, and others were built. The territory of the kingdom of Judah roughly resembled a square, covering approximately 45 square miles.

This area includes a variety of physical features, climate, and resources, which may be divided into three main sections; the coastal plain, the Shephelah, and the hill country. The coastal plain was never completely dominated by the Hebrews due to the power of the Philistines, who gave the name to the whole country in the word Palestine. Because of their dominance, the coastal plain came to be known as the "land of the Philistines" (2 Ki. 8:2). In modern times, the success of the citrus groves has demonstrated the fertility of the area, but the ancient Israelites were not able to develop it. The unbroken coast line of the plain did not provide suitable harbor facilities for the development of commerce as did the rugged coast of the Phoenicians to the N.

East of the coastal plain was the Shephelah, or lowlands (Josh. 11:2, 16), a district formed by the broken foothills of the Judean highlands. Situated between the coastal plain and the hill country, the Shephelah was the scene of many battles between the Philistines and the Israelites. The strongholds of Azekah, Beth Shemesh, Debir, Lachish, and Libnah were located here. The region was extremely important to Judah for defensive reasons, but also for the olive orchards of its hills and the grain of its valleys. The Shephelah is separated from the central mountain range by a system of valleys, the most famous of which is the valley of Aijalon.

The hill country is an area about 35 mi. long and 15 mi. wide. Approaching Jerusalem from Samaria, the range descends to c. 2,500 ft. above sea level, and then as they go S they rise to the highest

The kingdom of Judah.

point of 3,370 ft. just N of HEBRON. This area did more to form the character and influence the life of the Jews than any other geographical feature of the country. The mountains form an adequate watershed on the W slope; clouds that come in from the Mediterranean Sea deposit rainfall that sustains the life of the country. The eastern slope is the wilderness of Judah (Jdg. 1:16), a wasteland deeply cut by valleys, leading to the Jordan River and the Dead Sea. The descent to the Dead Sea, 1,291 ft. below sea level, is so sharp that there is little possibility for agricultural development. In this eastern area of the country were located Jericho, En Gedi, Qumran, and Masada.

II. The history of the kingdom of Judah.

The dynasty of David occupied the throne during its entire history, with the capital at JERUSALEM. This gave the country a stability that was lacking in the northern kingdom, and contributed to the life of the people until the disintegration of the southern kingdom set in. Its history is recorded in 1 Ki. 12–25; 2 Chr. 10–36, and in the writings of the contemporary prophets. The kings of Judah, with their approximate dates (all B.C.), are as follows:

1. Rehoboam (936–919)
2. Abijah (919–916)
3. Asa (916–875)
4. Jehoshaphat (875–851)
5. Joram (850–842)
6. Ahaziah (842–841)
7. Athaliah (841–835)
8. Joash (835–795)
9. Amaziah (795–768)
10. Uzziah (768–740)
11. Jotham (740–731)
12. Ahaz (731–725)
13. Hezekiah (725–696)
14. Manasseh (696–641)
15. Amon (641–639)
16. Josiah (639–608)
17. Jehoahaz (608)
18. Jehoiakim (608–597)
19. Jehoiachin (597)
20. Zedekiah (597–586)

The history of the kingdom of Judah may be conveniently divided with respect to the relations it had with other nations (Israel, Assyria, and Babylon). The first period extends from Rehoboam to Jotham (936–741); the second from Ahaz to Josiah (731–608); the third from Jehoiakim to Zedekiah (608–586).

A. Judah and Israel. The first period was characterized by Judah's relations with Israel. The inevitable strife between the two Hebrew kingdoms began immediately upon their separation, as REHOBOAM mustered an army to force Israel back under the domination of the house of David. Because of the intervention of the prophet Shemaiah, however, he did not complete his plan.

Rehoboam fortified the country by building fortresses in at least fifteen cities throughout the land; but this did not prevent SHISHAK (Sheshonk) of Egypt, who had supported JEROBOAM in his rebellion, from invading Judah and plundering the treasures of the temple and palace. Rehoboam's numerous wives had a corrupting effect on him, drawing him under the influence of foreign gods. The defeat at the hands of Shishak was interpreted to be divine judgment, and the king and people confessed their sin. Rehoboam's son and successor, ABIJAH, gained a great military victory over Jeroboam. As a result, Judah recovered some border cities from Israel. Religiously, there was widespread apostasy to the worship of strange gods and images, with sacred groves as worship centers. Abijah had sought an alliance with SYRIA (ARAM) against Israel as did his successor ASA against BAASHA of the northern kingdom. Before the end of his reign in 875 B.C., Asa was able to establish friendship with Israel, which endured until the Assyrians destroyed the northern kingdom in 722. According to the records, Asa was the first of the kings to combat actively the pagan cult of ASHERAH, even deposing his mother "from her position as queen mother, because she had made a repulsive Asherah pole" (2 Chr. 15:16). In the later years of his reign, however, Asa became a victim of the BAAL cult.

Asa's son JEHOSHAPHAT continued to fight against Baalism. He also reformed the courts of justice, but in his attempt to revive the maritime commerce of Solomon, he was not very successful. In the extended wars waged by the Arameans and MESHA of MOAB against the northern kingdom, Judah took no direct action beyond sending

Looking E through the wide U-shaped valleys of the Shephelah toward the Judean hill country.

aid to the sister kingdom. In the battle of RAMOTH GILEAD against the Syrians, Jehoshaphat himself fought side by side with AHAB of Israel with almost disastrous results (2 Chr. 18:31–32). Judah's alliance with Israel was strengthened by the marriage of Jehoshaphat's son JEHORAM to ATHALIAH, the daughter of Ahab and the Phoenician JEZEBEL. One evil result of this marriage was the introduction of the degrading FERTILITY CULT of the Tyrian Baal to Jerusalem. When JEHU rebelled against Joram of Israel and killed him, King AHAZIAH, the son of Jehoram and Jezebel, who was visiting his uncle Joram, also was slain by Jehu. Ahaziah had reigned only a year. Athaliah seized the throne of Judah and proceeded to exterminate the Davidic line by murdering the children of Ahaziah. Of Ahaziah's sons, only the infant JOASH was rescued by the quick action of the priest JEHOIADA and his wife JEHOSHEBA, the daughter of King Jehoram (2 Chr. 22:10–12).

Athaliah, the only woman to rule over the Israelites, was able to maintain herself in power for six years. She was executed in a rebellion led by the priest Jehoiada, who then placed on the throne the legitimate heir—seven-year-old Joash, the son of Ahaziah (2 Chr. 23:1—24:1). Jehoiada also led the move to suppress Baalism, and governed the state until Joash became of age. Joash proved to be weak and inept and was assassinated after a long reign because he paid tribute to the Aramean HAZAEL with the temple treasure as a price for withdrawing from Jerusalem. From this time on, the priesthood grew in influence in the affairs of the state.

Under AMAZIAH, the son and successor of Joash, Judah began a period of prosperity and progress that eventually made it one of the leading kingdoms of the western ANE. An important factor in this success was the recapture of EDOM and its capital SELA (later Petra), which Judah had lost under Jehoram. This victory gained the control of overland traffic of W ARABIA as well as that of the RED SEA from the Gulf of AQABAH and ELATH. Amaziah's success led to overconfidence, which led to war with Israel. He was defeated and taken prisoner, but he was released upon paying a ransom with the treasures of the temple and the royal palace, together with submission to the destruction of the walls of Jerusalem and the surrender of hostages.

UZZIAH (Azariah), Amaziah's son, was unusually capable and brought Judah to its greatest power. He strengthened the country internally as well as the army, built fortresses in the NEGEV, and extended his kingdom to control some of the Philistine and Ammonite territory. He developed the natural resources of Judah by promoting agriculture, constructing cisterns, and making use of the harbor at Elath (EZION GEBER). Near the close of his life, Uzziah was stricken with leprosy and was succeeded by his son JOTHAM, who acted as regent until the death of his father. "The year that King Uzziah died" (Isa. 6:1) was 740 B.C. Jotham's reign in many respects resembled his father's. The success of Judah in the period of Uzziah was contemporaneous with the same development of Israel under Jeroboam II. The surrounding nations, weak at the time, were in no position to interfere in the affairs of Judah and Israel.

B. Judah and Assyria. The second period of Judah's history began with the reign of AHAZ son of Jotham, and was characterized by the surge of Assyrian might with its threat to Israel and Judah. It was TIGLATH-PILESER III (the Pul of 2 Ki. 15:19; 1 Chr. 5:26) who initiated this period of ASSYRIA's expansion, much to the concern of the small nations of the ANE. In expectation of an Assyrian advance, PEKAH king of Israel and REZIN of Aram tried to coerce first Jotham and then Ahaz into an alliance against Tiglath-Pileser III. To frustrate an invasion of Judah by Pekah and Rezin, Ahaz, against the admonitions of ISAIAH, called upon Assyria for help, which Tiglath-Pileser III was happy to grant on the basis of a treaty for which Judah paid heavy tribute. Ahaz thus introduced into Judah a policy of treaty-making that was proving to be fatal to the northern kingdom.

Tiglath-Pileser III destroyed Aram and divided Israel, the northern half of which was annexed by Assyria. Isaiah's advice proved to be correct, for Ahaz had to pay tribute to Tiglath-Pileser III as a vassal, and he witnessed Assyrian paganism introduced into the temple in Jerusalem. The incident of Pekah and Rezin forms the historical background of Isaiah's IMMANUEL prophecy (Isa. 7). It was largely due to the influence of Isaiah that Judah did not become involved in the machinations of the small states of the ANE that eventuated in the final destruction of Israel by the Assyrians in 722 B.C.

HEZEKIAH followed Ahaz to the throne and in the early successful years of his reign accepted the advice of Isaiah, which led to a religious reform and the repudiation of the Assyrian gods imported during the reign of Ahaz. The repudiation of the gods of Assyria was a part of the attempt to throw off Assyrian domination. Against the prophets' advice, he became involved in a coalition with MERODACH-BALADAN of Babylonia, with Egypt, and with other countries, which was directed against Assyria. Isaiah reflects his feeling of disappointment in Hezekiah's involvement in international power politics (Isa. 28). The Assyrians (now under King SENNACHERIB) moved against the coalition; Judah was soon overrun and Jerusalem besieged. According to Sennacherib's inscriptions, he captured forty-six cities in Judah and noted that he considered their inhabitants numbering 200,150 as his subjects.

Isaiah had consistently prophesied that Jerusalem itself would be spared. Hezekiah, anticipating the Assyrian invasion, had strengthened the defenses of the city and, to insure the water supply of the city, had excavated the SILOAM tunnel. As Sennacherib invested Jerusalem (c. 701 B.C.), Isaiah encouraged Hezekiah to hold out. Isaiah as usual was right, for Sennacherib suddenly was forced to raise the siege because "the angel of the LORD went out and put to death a hundred and eighty-five thousand men in the Assyrian camp" (Isa. 37:36). In his inscriptions describing his campaign into Judah and his siege of Jerusalem, Sennacherib boasts of his victories and investment of the city but says nothing about the catastrophe that overwhelmed his army. Of Hezekiah he says, "Himself I made a prisoner in Jerusalem, his royal residence, like a bird in a cage" (*ANET*, 288a). It was not the custom of the ancient monarchs to record their defeats.

The defeat of the major objective of Sennacherib vindicated the preaching of Isaiah and led the people to cooperate in expurgating the temple of paganism. They broke in pieces the brazen serpent of the wilderness wanderings that had come to be worshiped, and they returned to the ethical monotheism of Yahwism (2 Ki. 18.4). On the other hand, there developed a formality in religion and a superstitious veneration of the temple that prompted the prophet MICAH to warn, "Therefore because of you, Zion will be plowed like a field" (Mic. 3:12).

Hezekiah died in comparative youth and was followed by his son MANASSEH, who reversed the policy of his father, and the prophets saw in his reign the deathblow to the kingdom of Judah. He submitted to Assyria as a vassal, and the land was practically under their control. Both ESARHADDON (681–669) and ASHURBANIPAL (669–630) list Manasseh with Edom, Gaza, Ammon, Tyre, and others, as tributaries. Cuneiform tablets discovered at GEZER indicate that the Assyrians had a garrison there. The situation was such that the infiltration of foreign ideas and customs into the life of Judah was inevitable. Religion and politics were inseparable, resulting in unlimited religious syncretism that included Baal, Asherah, the host of heaven, and even the sacrifice of children upon the pagan altars in the Valley of HINNOM. The reign of Manasseh was characterized by degeneracy in worship, faith, and morals (2 Chr. 33:1–20). In the later years of Manasseh's fifty-five year reign, he was taken a prisoner to Babylon by the Assyrian Esarhaddon, perhaps for an attempted insurrection, and then permitted to return to Jerusalem. The chronicler indicates that the incident of the king's arrest was divine punishment, and upon his repentance he was released to return to Jerusalem to begin a religious reform, which apparently did not succeed very well (33:1–2, 11–17).

During the reign of Manasseh, Assyrian power reached its zenith, but before the end of that reign, there were evidences of Assyrian disintegration. Manasseh's son AMON succeeded and continued his father's evil practices (2 Chr. 33:22–25). He was assassinated after he had reigned two years and was followed on the throne by his eight-year-old son JOSIAH, who was proclaimed king by "the people of the land" (v. 25).

The decay of Assyria is reflected in the inscriptions of Ashurbanipal, which state that the provinces of his empire were inflamed by the revolt of his brother Shamash-shum-ukin. The situation encouraged throughout the Assyrian empire the expression of national feelings of independence, and Josiah's reign was an example. The preceding regime had been one of corruption and oppression, when worshipers of Yahweh dared not confide in their closest relatives and friends (Mic. 7:5–6). In a new political situation, Josiah, king by popular choice, was upon the throne. Under him the reforming party gained the upper hand.

A principal event of Josiah's reign was the discovery in 621 B.C. of "the Book of the Law of the LORD that had been given through Moses" (2 Chr. 34:14–15). The scroll discovered at this time is said by some scholars to have been the newly written book of DEUTERONOMY, or at least the core, which was promulgated as the law of Moses. This is contrary to the plain statement of the reference and other scriptural evidence. The book terrified the king and the priests, and with the support of the prophet JEREMIAH a widespread reformation was initiated. Abominations in religion and morals were eradicated, but though the reform of Josiah was more thoroughgoing than that of Hezekiah, it was not permanent (Jer. 25:3–7; 36:1–32). An indication of the weakness of Assyria is the fact that Josiah extended his reformation into northern Israel, especially the areas of Galilee, Ephraim, and Manasseh (2 Ki. 23:19; 2 Chr. 34:6–7). He destroyed the pagan shrine at Bethel, which was a special abomination to Jerusalem. The effect of Josiah's reformation in northern Israel indicates that Judah also experienced a political renaissance, partly due to the weakness of Assyria hard pressed by Media and Babylonia. The political influence of Josiah in the N does not represent a defiance of Assyria as much as his position as a vassal of Assyria who ruled not only his own country but also controlled the Assyrian provinces of Megiddo and Samaria.

The hegemony of Assyria in the fertile crescent now was being challenged by Babylonia. Nineveh fell in 612 B.C. under an onslaught of a coalition of Medes, Persians, Scythians, and Babylonians led by the Babylonian NABOPOLASSAR. Sinshariskun, the last king of the great Assyrian dynasty, died in the battle; but his army, under the leadership of Ashur-uballit, prepared itself for the final battle, which took place at CARCHEMISH in 605.

As Assyria decayed, EGYPT recovered from the attacks of Ashurbanipal to which NAHUM refers (Nah. 3:7–10). Pharaoh NECO, fearful of the growing power of Babylonia, allied himself with the Assyrians and in 608 marched through Judah. Josiah, against the advice of Jeremiah, tried to stop the Egyptians and was slain at MEGIDDO (2 Chr. 35:20–27). Pharaoh Neco now controlled both Judah and Syria. JEHOAHAZ (Shallum) was made king of Judah by the people, but after three months was deposed by Neco and exiled to Egypt, where he died (36:1–4; Jer. 22:11). He was replaced by Josiah's oldest son, Eliakim, whose name was changed by Neco to JEHOIAKIM to demonstrate his change of allegiance. Neco joined Ashur-uballit and the Assyrians to fight the battle of Carchemish against the coalition led by the Babylonians under NEBUCHADNEZZAR the son of Nabopolassar. This battle was a turning point of history; the Babylonian victory ended Assyrian hegemony in ANE.

C. Judah and Babylon. The third period of Judah's history began with the Babylonian defeat of the Assyrians. Jehoiakim, who was placed upon the throne of Judah as a vassal by Neco in 608 B.C., was friendly to Egypt, but he was a Babylonian subject after the battle of Carchemish and paid tribute to Babylon. His policies encouraged Baalism in Judah, and he disregarded Jeremiah's advice not to disturb existing relations with Nebuchadnezzar. He renounced allegiance to Babylonia (2 Ki. 24:1), which brought Nebuchadnezzar to Jerusalem to besiege the city, in the course of which Jehoiakim died or was assassinated. Jerusalem fell in March of the year 597.

JEHOIACHIN, who followed his father on the throne, after a reign of only three months was taken into EXILE, along with his mother, many of the leaders of Judah, and the treasures of the royal palace and the temple. Among the exiles was EZEKIEL, who dates the chronology of his prophecy from the date of his captivity. Archaeological discoveries in BABYLON in the form of cuneiform tablets, which list among the people receiving rations of grain "Yaukin [i.e., Jehoiachin], King of Judah," five of his sons, and other Hebrews, provide a valuable addition to the biblical narrative. Jehoiachin was released from prison by EVIL-MERODACH in 560, the thirty-seventh year of his exile. His remaining years were spent in captivity, but in royal comfort (2 Ki. 25:27–30).

Nebuchadnezzar placed Mattaniah, another son of Josiah, upon the throne of Judah to replace Jehoiachin, and changed his name to ZEDEKIAH. This last king of Judah took an oath of loyalty to Nebuchadnezzar (Ezek. 17:13), but soon wavered in his allegiance by conspiring with the Egyptians against the Babylonians. Jeremiah again remonstrated strongly against Judah's involvement in international intrigue but without success. Zedekiah's disloyalty to his oath brought Nebuchadnezzar back to Jerusalem. The siege began on 10 January 587 and lasted until 9 July 586. Nebuchadnezzar was encamped at RIBLAH on the ORONTES, from where he directed the siege. The help that Zedekiah expected from Egypt did not come, and Nebuchadnezzar ravished the country. The OSTRACA discovered at LACHISH reflect the progress of the Babylonian campaign and the confusion and panic in Judah and Jerusalem. These are dispatches from a Judean military officer leading a party of scouts near Lachish. The messages, sent to his commander in the city, report the advance of the Babylonians and also allude to the tensions, intrigues, and suspicions that gripped the people of Jerusalem. Disloyalty, famine, and pestilence contributed to the horror of the siege until the Chaldeans breached the city wall built by Hezekiah (2 Chr. 32:5).

Zedekiah and his entourage fled toward the Jordan Valley but were intercepted and taken to Nebuchadnezzar at Riblah. He was forced to witness the execution of his sons, and then was blinded and taken in chains to Babylon after a reign of eleven years. The chief priest Seraiah and other leaders were taken to Riblah and executed upon the orders of Nebuchadnezzar. On 7 August 586 B.C. NEBUZARADAN, the captain of Nebuchadnezzar's bodyguard, ordered Jerusalem destroyed. The temple and palace were burned, the walls of the city broken down, and many people carried off into captivity (2 Ki. 24:20—25:21; Jer. 39:1–10). This disaster was the fulfillment of Jeremiah's warning.

The Babylonian policy toward her defeated enemies was not as destructive as that of the Assyrians. GEDALIAH, the former mayor of Zedekiah's palace, was appointed governor of Judea by Nebuchadnezzar. He exercised his office in MIZPAH, about 5 mi. NW of Jerusalem. Gedaliah issued an appeal for loyalty to Babylon and tried to restore the country to normal life. He was treacherously assassinated by ISHMAEL, a member of the royal family, who also killed many members of Gedaliah's court and Babylonians stationed at Mizpah. This new rebellion brought the Chaldeans back to Jerusalem, and in 581 another deportation of Hebrews to Babylonia took place. Some of the Hebrews of anti-Babylonian sentiment fled to Egypt, and forced Jeremiah, who had been given special consideration by Nebuchadnezzar, to accompany them (2 Ki. 25:22–26; Jer. 40–44).

The kingdom of Judah was now completely crushed. It had been in existence as an independent kingdom for 350 years, calculating from the year of the disruption in 936 B.C. This was 214 years longer than the existence of the northern kingdom, the longer survival of the kingdom of Judah being due primarily to the loyalty of the people to Yahweh. (For further details and bibliography, see ISRAEL, HISTORY OF.)

A. C. SCHULTZ

Judah, tribe of. Judah belonged to the major group of Israelite tribes descended from LEAH. The tribe played no special part in either the exodus or the wilderness wanderings apart from leading the vanguard (Num. 2:9). The defeat at Ai was occasioned by ACHAN, a member of the tribe (Josh. 7), and this may have been why Judah was required to mount an independent attack on the Canaanites (Jdg. 1:1–2).

The territory given to Judah was not allocated by lot in SHILOH before being conquered (Josh. 18:1–10; Jdg. 1:3). The tribe occupied the Palestinian uplands, being bounded on the N by parts of Dan and Benjamin, and on the E and W by the Dead and Mediterranean Seas (although the tribe never had full control of the coastal plain, Jdg 1:19). To the S it stretched as far as cultivation permitted. Part of the land, however, was given to the tribe of SIMEON, "because Judah's portion was more than they needed" (Josh. 19:9).

The hill country of Judah is characterized by a semidissected plateau, trending N–S, primarily a pastoral land, but supporting some agriculture on its small fields and terraced hillsides. Its natural boundaries provided defenses on three sides, only the N being militarily vulnerable. In the W the hills rise abruptly from the SHEPHELAH, traversed by a series of steep valleys leading upward to the central high land. The desert of the NEGEV lay across the S, and on the E was the formidable wilderness of Judea, with its rugged terrain rising sharply from the Dead Sea and Jordan Valley.

The biblical narrative gives a detailed treatment of the settlements within this territory. Of special importance were the frontiers, with their towns (Josh. 15:1–12). This is followed by a listing of the places in the NEGEV (vv. 21–32), the lowlands (vv. 33–47), the hill country (vv. 48–60), and the wilderness (vv. 61–62). The adjacent portions of Benjamin (18:11–28) and Dan (19:40–48) also played a large part in the continuing history of Judah. The rugged barrenness of this environment greatly influenced the life and literature of its inhabitants.

The possession of Jerusalem by the Jebusites (see JEBUS) made for a degree of separation between Judah and the centrally located tribes, and this situation may account for the lack of appeal to the other tribes when Judah became tributary to the Philistines. The isolation of Judah seems to have been recognized as a fact in the time of SAUL, when the men from Judah were enumerated separately (1 Sam. 11:8; 15:4; et al.). Because the confederation of tribes still remained loosely associated in the time of Saul, the economic and military dangers of Philistine aggression presented further problems for Judah, although the anointing of David over the twelve tribes (2 Sam. 5:1–5) prevented the separation from becoming more acute. (Certain details, such as the absence of any reference to Judah in the ancient Song of Deborah [Jdg. 5], have led some scholars to deny its existence as a distinct tribe prior to David. Cf. *ABD*, 3:1033–36.) See also JUDAH, KINGDOM OF; JUDEA; TRIBES, LOCATION OF.

M. H. HEICKSEN

Judaism. The Greek word *Ioudaismos* (ΙΟΥΔΑΙΣΜΟΣ) occurs in only one biblical passage (Gal. 1:13–14, KJV, "the Jews' religion"; cf. also 2:14). Although the term *Judaism* can be used broadly of the Hebrew culture as a whole, it often refers to the religion of the Jews subsequent to the OT period. As such, Judaism is typically contrasted to the OT, but one cannot forget that the postbiblical developments were firmly rooted in the religious attitudes and practices of the Hebrew Scriptures.

I. The rise of Judaism
   A. Exile
   B. Haggai, Zechariah, and Malachi
   C. Ezra
   D. The Greek period
   E. The Roman period
II. Doctrines of Judaism
   A. Theocracy and covenant
   B. The Torah
   C. Paradise and resurrection
   D. Messianic hope

I. The rise of Judaism

A. Exile. Properly speaking, Judaism ought to be regarded as beginning with the Babylonian EXILE. This experience proved to be a watershed in the history of Hebrew religion, for it marked a break with the type of pagan cultic observance that had occupied the attention of both Israel and Judah to varying degrees previously, and set the scene for a different type of religious observance based more firmly upon the ancient covenantal ideals. See ISRAEL, HISTORY OF; ISRAEL, RELIGION OF.

Life in Palestine had been totally disrupted when the Babylonians ravaged Jerusalem in 586 B.C., and though a few survivors of the catastrophe continued to live around Jerusalem, the most important elements of the nation had been carried in captivity to BABYLON. Deprived of all their former religious and cultic associations, the exiles were forced by circumstances to consider the adoption of a type of nonsacrificial religion contemplated by Jeremiah. The full formulation of this concept did not occur until a later period, and as far as the exiles were concerned, the most pressing need was for a fresh outlook on life that was completely divorced from the earlier sanctuary worship.

In this situation of emotional crisis, a firm lead was given by EZEKIEL, who shared the spiritual ideals of JEREMIAH and brought them to fuller development. His ministry to the exiles had as its aim the inculcation of a sense of repentance for the past transgressions of the nation, and a firm resolve to exemplify under the conditions of a restored community life in Palestine the ideals and spirituality of the Sinai covenant. He saw that the only way to preserve the spirit of nationality among the exiles was by a careful attention to those religious customs that could be observed with impunity on alien soil. Thus memorial celebrations were substituted for the preexilic FEASTS, and special fasts were instituted on anniversaries connected with the fall of Jerusalem. CIRCUMCISION was stressed as a distinguishing mark of the exiles, and the ancient laws of PURITY in the Pentateuch were more closely observed. The SABBATH came into particular prominence as the weekly day of WORSHIP, and marked the time when people gathered in houses to hear the law read and to pray. Open-air services also were held by the KEBAR irrigation canal, at which confession and the recitation of parts of the TORAH were consistent features.

The house meetings instituted by Ezekiel laid the basis of subsequent SYNAGOGUE worship, and were of great significance in focusing the attention of the exiles on the divine word rather than on ritual or cultic performances. Other distinctive exercises of piety by the exiles were designed to stimulate a greater sense of national sin and the consequent need for ATONEMENT. By the time that liberty was proclaimed to the captives through the decree of CYRUS in 538 B.C., there had arisen among the exiles a consciousness of being different from and superior to other peoples in view of the higher religious character that participation in the covenant relationship offered them.

B. Haggai, Zechariah, and Malachi. The pattern that life in the returned community of Judea followed was that of a THEOCRACY or religious commonwealth in which the will of God was mediated to the people through the priesthood. The Persian authorities encouraged the repatriates to follow this form of government, and between 520 and 515 B.C., under the prophetic leadership of HAGGAI and ZECHARIAH, the TEMPLE was rebuilt and worship renewed in Jerusalem. From the writings of these two men, it is apparent that the zeal

Jewish worshipers at the Western Wall in Jerusalem. Following the return from the Babylonian exile, the celebration of the Sabbath became more prominent within Judaism.

with which the repatriates returned to Palestine was soon dissipated, and only after considerable exhortation were the Jews inspired to reconstruct the temple. The prophecy of MALACHI, dated about 450, shows that certain abuses had crept into the temple worship and the religious life of the theocracy, and there was a real danger that a lax priesthood would once again bring the people to the brink of spiritual ruin.

C. Ezra. These tendencies were brought to an abrupt halt by the work of EZRA the SCRIBE, who was appointed by ARTAXERXES I as minister for Jewish affairs to regulate life in Judea. He instituted various reforms that purified the priesthood and established the covenantal ideal of the theocracy more firmly than ever. He placed great emphasis upon the primacy of the Torah, which he interpreted less as a law code than a set of principles that could be applied to every aspect of life, and that were particularly binding upon the Jews. Ezra has been described quite accurately as the "father of Judaism," for in coming to Judea he was not introducing a new law so much as demonstrating a new way of keeping the old one.

D. The Greek period. The centuries that followed saw determined opposition to the policies of Ezra both from the richer priestly classes and the SAMARITANS, the latter having benefited from the reforms in Judea to the extent of having gained a high priest from Jerusalem who had been unwilling to surrender his foreign wife. The dramatic rise of HELLENISM throughout the empire of ALEXANDER THE GREAT brought about important changes in ANE culture that by nature were more pervasive and threatening than anything the Jews had experienced previously in their varied history.

The Judeans struggled hard against these influences, being determined to maintain their historic religious distinctiveness. The upper classes of Jews found Greek traditions fairly attractive, and to counteract this tendency, the theocratic ideal was widened and strengthened. The high priesthood played an important role in this process, since it represented the most advanced and influential levels of administration in the religious community. The high priest was the spiritual head and representative of the state, controlling a hierarchy of priests, Levites, and temple officers.

The most characteristic emphasis of Judaism was upon keeping the law, and when many of the priests succumbed to Hellenism, the priestly interpreters of the law, who were known as scribes, succeeded them as guardians of the Torah. Their interpretations gradually acquired an authority of their own, and during the Greek period the scribes became accepted as the real instructors of the faithful Jews, using the synagogues as their principal sphere of influence. In the 2nd cent. B.C., another group of zealous teachers arose who came to be known as PHARISEES, or "separatists," because of their sanctity and moral strictness in such matters as food and religious ceremonies. They accepted the oral tradition of the law as having equal authority with the Torah itself, and maintained that if a person carried out all the injunctions of the law and the tradition, he or she could obtain justification with God. The Pharisees claimed support from the general mass of the people, and became so influential in the 2nd cent. B.C. that they challenged the authority of the priestly scribes by training their own instructors in the traditional law. They brought a degree of stability to bear upon normative Judaism, which enabled it to survive the catastrophe of A.D. 70.

Another religious group that arose in the 2nd cent. B.C. was that of the SADDUCEES. The origin of the term has been disputed, but the influence of this party was unquestionably great. It was composed of priestly aristocratic families who kept aloof from the general populace, preferring instead to exercise control over national life at an intellectual, political, and cultic level. Although the Sadducees were in contact with Hellenism sooner than the Pharisees, they were better equipped intellectually to resist its attractions. The Sadducees claimed authority for the Pentateuch alone, and rejected any doctrine that could not be proved from the Torah. Though a decided minority, they secured control of the high priesthood, an office they monopolized until Jerusalem was destroyed in A.D. 70.

The Samaritans comprised one of the chief schismatic elements in early Judaism, and when they broke with the postexilic theocracy as a result of the reforms of Ezra and Nehemiah, they established their own temple on Mount GERIZIM and formed a flourishing community in nearby SHECHEM In the 4th cent. B.C. During the conquests of Alexander they revolted, but were crushed and expelled from Samaria. Alexander placed the province of Samaria under Jewish control, so that when the Samaritans ultimately returned to Shechem they found themselves once again in the power of their religious opponents. Like the Sadducees, the Samaritans accepted the Torah as canonical, and they furnish independent testimony to the antiquity of this section of the Hebrew CANON.

The upheaval that followed the death of Alexander in 323 B.C. had repercussions in Judea as elsewhere. PTOLEMY I, who succeeded to power in EGYPT, annexed SYRIA shortly after 320, and marching into Jerusalem he occupied the city and deported a number of its inhabitants to Egypt. After he had gained control of Judea by this show of force, he pursued the liberal policies of Alexander—ultimately winning the confidence of the Jews to the extent that many of them emigrated to Egypt. Friendship with the Jews characterized the early SELEUCID regime also, and Nicator I was as successful as Ptolemy in encouraging Jews to migrate to more distant parts of his realm. The influence of the Jerusalem priesthood was greatly enhanced in the time of Ptolemy I by the wise administration of SIMON I (c. 300–287), but political intrigue began with his successor, ONIAS II. Under Ptolemy II (285–246), the task of translating the Hebrew Scriptures into Greek was begun; the end result was the SEPTUAGINT version. This proved to be the principal means by which Hebrew thought was conveyed to the Jews living outside Palestine. About 225 B.C., a reactionary group in Judea agitated for allegiance to the Syrian regime of ANTIOCHUS III instead of to Egypt, but the ambitions of the latter were thwarted by Ptolemy, who marched into Judea and quelled the dissident elements. In 198, however, Antiochus defeated Egyptian forces in battle near Sidon and incorporated Judea into Syria.

E. The Roman period. When the Romans invaded ASIA MINOR c. 197 B.C., Seleucid influence over Palestine was menaced. Intrigue in Judea increased under SELEUCUS IV (187–175), heightening the tension between orthodox Jews and those who had succumbed to the hellenizing policies of the Seleucids. Matters came to a head under Antiochus IV Epiphanes (175–164), whose avowed intent was to eradicate Judaism in his territories. A HASMONEAN priest led a revolt at Modein in 167, and with this commenced the Maccabean conflict. See MACCABEE.

A protracted struggle saw military successes on both sides, and in 141 B.C. the Syrians issued a decree that recognized the independence of Judea. A period of prosperity ensued, during which the traditional customs and beliefs of the Jews were enforced and the supremacy of the law was asserted. This brief respite ended in 129, when Antiochus VII made Judea tributary, but independence was restored under John Hyrcanus (135–104), a Hasmonean leader. After 104, civil strife broke out in Judea, during which the Pharisees came to the fore as a political influence. Syrian control over Palestine came to an end when POMPEY marched into Syria in 64 B.C. and made it a Roman province. Jerusalem was subjugated and placed under the control of the Herodian dynasty in the person of Antipater, father of HEROD the Great. Although the latter did not impose hellenizing policies upon the Jews, his acts of brutality during his reign (37–4 B.C.) gained him the hatred of his subjects and more than offset his generosity in enlarging the temple. Throughout the period of the Gospels, an uneasy peace was maintained in Judea marked by periodic revolts against the occupying Roman power. The destruction of Jerusalem in A.D. 70 marked the

The traditional tomb of King David, who holds an exalted place in Judaism.

end of Judea as a state, but the complete liquidation of popular resistance was not accomplished until the ill-fated Second Jewish Revolt against Rome (A.D. 132–135). See WARS, JEWISH.

II. Doctrines of Judaism

A. Theocracy and covenant. The form of the returned community was that of a religious commonwealth rather than a nation. The remnant had been redeemed to attempt again the task of exemplifying the ideals of the Sinai covenant in communal life. The Jews had been called by divine grace to be witnesses to the ransoming and renewing power of God, and the theocracy was to be the vehicle for such a testimony to contemporary society. As Ezekiel had foreseen, the priesthood occupied an important place in the community, for it was by this means that the will of God was revealed to the people after the voice of prophecy ceased with Malachi (c. 450 B.C.).

The destiny of the nation was to realize within itself the COVENANT concept of a kingdom of priests, which would reflect the HOLINESS inherent in the divine nature (cf. Exod. 19:6). Strict observance of the divine will would prevent any further disastrous lapses into idolatry or apostasy, and would preserve the ancestral faith intact. As a result of this, pagan nations round about could expect to receive the blessings of God, for the nation had the responsibility as the servant of the Lord of bringing the light of divine rule to the heathen (Isa. 42:1–9; 49:1–6). The theocratic ideal assumed the form of covenant obligations with the work of Ezra, who made covenant and law the normative elements of community life. Because the Jews were surrounded by pagans, the danger of cultural and ideological assimilation was real. Consequently it was necessary then as during the exile for the Jews to maintain a distinctive character. This particularistic attitude, unfortunately, had the side effect of provoking a conflict with the universalism inherent in OT prophecy, a tension that remained unresolved in Judaism throughout the NT period. Nevertheless, the basic commission of the theocracy was that of absolute fidelity to the provisions of the covenant and the exemplification of divine holiness in society as a means of blessing for the world.

D. The Torah. The keeping of the law was the most characteristic emphasis of Judaism, and in this area the Pharisees exercised a dominant influence. So exalted did the role and value of the Torah become that the keeping of the precepts associated with it, both written and oral, became the explanation and justification for the existence of Judaism. The obligations of covenant law had always been a dominant feature of Hebrew religion, but in Judaism they were developed to the fullest extent. Because the prophets had insisted that the punishment of the exile was the result of a breach of covenant law, the repatriates were encouraged to take its observance far more seriously in the future. Its permanence and stability could not be questioned, since it alone had survived when cult and nation alike had been destroyed in the exile.

Because the theocracy was based upon observance of covenant law, the Torah came into its greatest prominence as the regulative norm for individual and corporate behavior. If the observance of the Torah, or written law, was of such importance, it was necessary to formulate agreed principles for its study and exegesis. Such principles and their application to daily living became the oral Torah or "tradition," of the priestly and later the Pharisaic scribes. The tradition protected the enactments in the written Torah by the formulation of new rules that when observed would guarantee the keeping of the basic commandments. This procedure became known as "making a hedge about the Torah," and found its fullest development in the TALMUD. The Talmud consisted of the MISHNAH, the oral law in existence by the end of the 2nd cent. A.D. as collected by Rabbi Judah ha-Nasi (c. A.D. 200), and the GEMARA, or rabbinical comments on the Mishnah, between 200 and 500. In addition, the Midrashim (see MIDRASH) were the official expositions of the OT books and consisted of homiletical and expository material.

For the pious Jew, keeping the law was virtually the whole of his religious obligation. Although the cult of the Jerusalem temple continued to carry out the rites and ceremonies prescribed by the law, it became less important with the growth of the synagogues. The ancient Levitical function of instruction was given prominence in the theocracy, and even the smallest village had its synagogue where the law was read and explained. The Torah thus superseded priestly functions, and with the end of prophecy it became the prime source of the divine will for Judaism.

C. Paradise and resurrection. The word PARADISE (originally Old Persian) occurs only in a few OT Scriptures (Neh. 2:8; Eccl. 2:5; Cant. 4:13). In Hebrew thought, it originally expressed primeval bliss, an idea that was subsequently applied to the glories of the future messianic kingdom. About c. 200 B.C., as a belief in the RESURRECTION of the dead emerged in Judaism (cf. Isa. 26:19; Dan. 12:2–3), there arose the conviction that the righteous would live, after their resurrection, in the Garden, or "paradise," of Eden (see EDEN, GARDEN OF). The Jews also held that paradise was a reality in their own day, but was concealed from view. It was the location to which the souls of the patriarchs and the righteous had been taken at death, and constituted their eternal home.

The idea of paradise among pre-Christian Jews was thus rather fluid and gives the impression that the concept fulfilled varying roles in different periods of thought. The TREE OF LIFE (Gen. 2:9) naturally acquired prominence in descriptions of paradise as the abode of the righteous dead (cf. *1 En.* 25.4–5; *4 Ezra* 8.52; et al.). Whereas the Sadducees denied the resurrection altogether (Acts 23.8, Jos. *Ant.* 18.1.4), since it could not be proved from the Torah, the Pharisees accepted the doctrine warmly, and only excluded from the privilege of resurrection certain classes of apostates. Their tenets became normative in Judaism and found expression in their liturgies. Pharisaic concepts of resurrection, however, were sometimes both gross and materialistic, for they conveyed the impression that in the next world men would live in opulent luxury—eating, drinking, and having carnal relations with their wives.

D. Messianic hope. As a teleological figure, the MESSIAH had been long present in Israelite thought. The specific attachment of this hope to a future royal figure went back to the early monarchy (2 Sam. 7:12–16) and the promise of a stable dynasty of DAVID. Isaiah prophesied gifts of wisdom for this great ruler who would usher in the glorious kingdom (Isa. 9:6–7), and Ezekiel spoke of him as the shepherd of Israel (Ezek. 34:23–24). This anointed one from God also appeared in prophecy as the Servant (Isa. 41:8; 42:1; et al.), the anointed Redeemer (59:20), the Branch (Jer. 23:5; Zech. 3:8; 6:12), and the Son of Man (Dan. 7:1–28). Under Roman occupation, the Jews looked for a leader who would restore national greatness (cf. Acts 1:6), and by the time that Christ entered upon his ministry, popular expectation was at its peak. Consequently Christ, to avoid misunderstanding, rarely employed the term "Messiah."

(See further G. F. Moore, *Judaism in the First Three Centuries of the Christian Era: The Age of the Tannaim*, 3 vols. [1927–30]; A. Cohen, *Everyman's Talmud* [1932]; H. Danby, *The Mishnah* [1933]; J. Jocz, *The Jewish People and Jesus Christ* [1949]; I. Epstein, *Judaism* [1959]; M. Hengel, *Judaism and Hellenism*, 2 vols. [1974]; R. A. Kraft and G. W. E. Nickelsburg, *Early Judaism and Its Modern Interpreters* [1986]; E. P. Sanders, *Judaism: Practice and Belief, 63 BCE—66 CE* [1992]; W. D. Davies and L. Finkelstein, eds., *The Cambridge History of Judaism*, 3 vols. [1984–99]; G. Boccaccini, *Roots of Rabbinic Judaism: An Intellectual History, from Ezekiel to Daniel* [2002]; M. Goodman et al., eds., *The Oxford Handbook of Jewish Studies* [2002; this work includes essays on the medieval and modern periods]; F. J. Murphy, *Early Judaism: The Exile to the Time of Jesus* [2002]; G. W. E. Nickelsburg, *Ancient Judaism and Christian Origins: Diversity, Continuity, and Transformation* [2003]; C. E. Hayes, *The Emergence of Judaism* [2007].)   R. K. HARRISON

Judaizer. The Greek verb *ioudaizō* G2678, used only once in the NT (Gal. 2:14, but found already in the LXX of Esth. 8:17; cf. also Jos. *War* 2.17.10 §454; 2.18.2 §463; Plutarch, *Cicero* 864 [7.6]), has an intransitive meaning, "live as a Jew, become a Jew, adopt the traditions of Judaism." PAUL, however, uses it in combination with the verb *anankazō* G337, "to compel," and that has led to the modern use of *Judaize* in the transitive sense "to force/coerce Gentiles to become Jews." In biblical scholarship, therefore, the noun *Judaizers* is most frequently applied to early Christian Jews who opposed Paul's message of freedom from the law and insisted that GENTILE Christians should become circumcised and follow the Mosaic regulations (cf. Acts 15:1–2;

Gal. 2:3–5). See COUNCIL OF JERUSALEM; GALATIANS, EPISTLE TO THE.

Judas joo′duhs (Ἰούδας *G2683*, from Heb. יְהוּדָה *H3373*, "praise"). Greek form of Hebrew JUDAH, which originally was the name of one of the sons of JACOB. After the EXILE, it became one of the names most frequently used by the Jews, and it is not surprising that in the APOCRYPHA and NT it designates a considerable number of different men.

(1) Son of MATTATHIAS and leader of the Maccabean Revolt (1 Macc. 2:4 et al.). See MACCABEE.

(2) Son of Chalphi and commander of the Maccabean forces (1 Macc. 11:70). Only this Judas and another commander, Mattathias son of Absalom, stood with Jonathan Maccabee when others fled at Hazor after walking into an ambush. Jonathan was able to rally the forces and routed the enemy, killing 3,000 men.

(3) Son of SIMON MACCABEE (1 Macc. 16:2, 9, 14). This Judas and his brother John were sent to fight the Seleucids in Kedron; the Jewish forces were victorious, though Judas was wounded. Some time later, Judas was killed in the same ambush that took the life of his father and of his brother Mattathias.

(4) Judas the Galilean, described by GAMALIEL as a man who "appeared in the days of the census and led a band of people in revolt. He too was killed, and all his followers were scattered" (Acts 5:37). The enrollment or assessment for tax purposes here in view was that under QUIRINIUS during his governorship of SYRIA in A.D. 6–7. JOSEPHUS too in a number of places (e.g., *Ant.* 18.1.6) calls this Judas a Galilean, but elsewhere, evidently referring to his place of birth, calls him a Gaulanite from the city of Gamala (18.1.1). Josephus regards Judas of Galilee as a founder of a fourth sect or school of philosophy among the Jews (18.1.6; *War* 2.8.1). Those in this party agreed with the position of the Pharisees in all matters, he reports, except that they acknowledged God alone to be their governor and lord and were passionately devoted to liberty.

With the support of a Pharisee named Saddok, Judas vigorously opposed the enrollment under Quirinius and engendered strife, violence, and bloodshed (*Ant.* 18.1.1). From Judas's incendiary activity and teaching, the ZEALOTS and the Sicarii (see ASSASSINS) would seem to have sprung. Josephus mentions the violent deaths which a number of Judas's descendants suffered. Two of his sons, James and Simon, were sentenced by Tiberius Alexander to be crucified (20.5.2). Another son, Menahem, prominent and influential shortly before the fall of Jerusalem, was tortured and put to death (*War* 2.17.8–9). A descendant (perhaps grandson) of Judas named Eleazar was a leader of the Zealots or Sicarii who urged death at their own hands on his followers rather than capture by the Romans at MASADA. Practically all of them accepted his counsel in the matter (*War* 7.8–9). (Josephus also mentions a Judas who was the son of a notorious bandit in the days of King HEROD [*Ant.* 17.10.5; *War* 2.4.1]; there is some question as to whether this man is to be identified with Judas of Galilee.)

(5) Judas son of MARY, MOTHER OF JESUS, and thus probably a half-brother of the Lord; he is listed with other brothers, James, Joseph (Joses), and Simon (Matt. 13:55; Mk. 6:3). He is to be distinguished from the apostle Judas, one of the Twelve (see below, #6), because the BROTHERS OF JESUS did not believe in him during his ministry (Jn. 7:5). After the resurrection, however, they are represented as believers (Acts 1:14, where, it is to be noted, they are distinguished from the apostles). They appear to have gone about in the interests of the gospel, some at least accompanied by their wives (1 Cor. 9:5).

The author of the epistle of JUDE was in all probability this Judas. He does not designate himself as one of the apostles, and seems to distinguish himself from them (see Jude 17–18 and cf. v. 3). He identifies himself as "Jude [Gk. Judas], a servant of Jesus Christ and a brother of James" (v. 1), no doubt meaning James the Lord's brother (see JAMES II). EUSEBIUS (*Eccl. Hist.* 3.19–20) quotes Hegesippus to the effect that two grandsons of Jude (Judas) were required to appear before DOMITIAN, but on their explaining that the kingdom which they were awaiting was not of this world, but heavenly, and would come with Christ's return, they were released. (See further R. J. Bauckham, *Jude and the Relatives of Jesus in the Early Church* [1990].)

(6) Judas son of James, included among the twelve apostles (Lk. 6:16; Acts 1:13). The KJV interprets the ambiguous Greek to mean "Judas *the brother* of James," but it appears that when Luke means "brother" rather than "son," he makes the designation explicit (Lk. 3:1; 6:14; Acts 12:2; the same construction is used in designating this Judas as is used in the case of James *the son of* Alphaeus, Lk. 6:15; Acts 1:13). In the other lists of the Twelve, THADDAEUS occurs instead of Judas of James (Matt. 10:3 [KJV, "Lebbaeus, whose surname was Thaddaeus," following the TR]; Mk. 3:18); the same apostle may well have been called by both these names, but not all scholars adopt this solution. In Jn. 14:22 he is sharply distinguished from Judas Iscariot and is reported to have asked a question of Jesus: "Then Judas (not Judas Iscariot) said, 'But, Lord, why do you intend to show yourself to us and not to the world?'" In the Syriac tradition, this Judas is identified with THOMAS. (See the discussion in R. E. Brown, *The Gospel according to John (xiii–xxi)*, AB 29A [1966], 641.)

(7) JUDAS ISCARIOT (see separate article).

(8) Judas of Damascus. After the Lord had appeared to Saul (PAUL) on the road to DAMASCUS, Saul was led into the city and stayed in the house of a man named Judas, presumably a believer himself (Acts 9:11). The Lord directed ANANIAS to go to the street called STRAIGHT and inquire for Saul in Judas's house.

(9) Judas surnamed BARSABBAS. At the COUNCIL OF JERUSALEM, the apostles and the elders selected out of their company Judas Barsabbas and SILAS, "two men who were leaders among the brothers," to go to ANTIOCH OF SYRIA with Paul and BARNABAS (Acts 15:22) to confirm by word of mouth the contents of the letter containing the decree of the council (15:27). The epistle from the council was delivered to the church in Antioch, and Judas and Silas, "who themselves were prophets, said much to encourage and strengthen the brothers" (15:32). After they had been some time in Antioch, "they were sent off by the brothers with the blessing of peace to return to those who had sent them" (15:33). Possibly this Judas was a brother of the Joseph called Barsabbas, surnamed JUSTUS, who was chosen with MATTHIAS as a candidate for the place from which Judas Iscariot fell away (1:25).

J. H. CHURCH

Judas, Gospel of. Writing late in the 2nd cent., IRENAEUS makes reference to a certain sect whose members claimed that JUDAS ISCARIOT "knowing the truth as no others did, accomplished the mystery of the betrayal by him all things, both earthly and heavenly, were thus thrown into confusion. They produce a fictitious history of this kind, which they style the Gospel of Judas" (*Haer.* 1.31.1). Nothing more was known about this document until the beginning of the 21st cent., when a team under the direction of R. Kasser was able to reassemble and analyze the fragments of a codex that had been discovered in the 1970s near El Minya, Egypt (c. 150 mi. S of Cairo). This MS contains several writings, including a Coptic version of the *Gospel of Judas*, which was probably composed in Greek about the middle of the 2nd cent.

The book purports to record a revelation that Jesus gave to Judas some days before the crucifixion. Much of the account is consonant with material found in other Gnostic writings (see APOCRYPHAL NEW TESTAMENT; NAG HAMMADI LIBRARY). Near the end of the document, however, Jesus says to Judas, "Look, you have been told everything. Lift up your eyes and look at the cloud and the light within it and the stars surrounding it. The star that leads the way is your star." We are then told that "Judas lifted up his eyes and saw the luminous cloud, and he entered it." The account concludes with a brief description of the betrayal. The natural implication seems to be that Judas was following Jesus' instructions when he handed the Lord over to the authorities. (See R. Kasser et al., eds., *The Gospel of Judas: From Codex Tchacos* [2006]; H. Krosney, *The Lost Gospel: The Quest for the Gospel of Judas Iscariot* [2006]; S. E. Porter and G. L. Heath, *The Lost Gospel of Judas: Separating Fact from Fiction* [2007].)

Judas Iscariot joo'duhs is-kair'ee-uht (Ἰούδας Ἰσκαριώτης *G2683* + *G2697*). One of the Twelve, known primarily as the disciple who betrayed Jesus to the authorities. The Gospel of John further identifies him as "the son of Simon" (Jn. 6:71; 13:2, 26). The meaning of the epithet *Iscariot* is uncertain; some scholars relate it to the word *sicarii*, "dagger-men" (see ASSASSINS), and speculate that he may have belonged to the party of the ZEALOTS; others to Hebrew *ʾîš qeriyyôt*, "false [one]"; or to Aramaic *ʾasharyāʾ*, "choking (alluding to his death; see Origen, *Comm. Matt.* 35); and so on. A widely accepted interpretation is that the term is a hellenized form of *ʾiš qĕriyyôt*, "man of KERIOTH," and thus serves to indicate his origin.

Nothing is known for certain of the early life of Judas. If he came from Kerioth he may have been the only Judean among the disciples. He is first mentioned in the choosing of the Twelve (Matt. 10:4; Mk. 3:19; Lk. 6:16), at which point all the synoptics add the clause, "who betrayed him." His relation to Jesus is not mentioned until the episode at BETHANY when MARY anointed Jesus with a vial of expensive ointment. John notes that Judas initiated the protest of the gift as a waste, and adds the footnote that Judas's interest was prompted by his avarice. Had the ointment been sold, the cash proceeds would have become available to Judas, who was the treasurer of the Twelve (Matt. 26:6–13; Mk. 14:3–10; Jn. 12:1–8). The synoptics leave the impression that Jesus' rebuke evoked the displeasure of Judas, and that he immediately went to the chief priests to bargain for the betrayal (see also Lk. 22:3). According to Jn. 13:26–30, Judas withdrew from the meal in the upper room in order to complete his arrangement. The two accounts are not irreconcilable. He may have begun negotiations early, subsequently informing the priests of the proper occasion for arrest. John implies this definitely by saying that Judas had already been motivated to betray Jesus (13:2), but that the decisive act came during the LAST SUPPER (13:26–30).

The motive for Judas's treachery is not stated categorically in the Gospels. Probably he joined Jesus' company because, like the rest of the disciples (cf. Matt. 16:16; Jn. 1:41, 45, 49; 11:27), he believed that Jesus was the promised MESSIAH, and that he would recover the independence of Israel from Gentile domination (Matt. 19:27; 20:20–23; Lk. 24:21; Acts 1:6). Jesus' consistent refusal to make his mission political, and his open declaration at the feast of Bethany that his death was imminent, may have spurred Judas to action. If he could not be assured of a prominent place in the coming messianic kingdom, he could at least profit by disposing of Jesus to his enemies. Disillusionment, the frustration of his expectations, and greed as John indicates, plus a definite Satanic influence (Jn. 13:2, 27), prompted his treachery.

Not only did he arrange for the capture of Jesus, but he also identified him in the garden of GETHSEMANE, where the arrest took place (Matt. 26:47; Mk. 14:43; Lk. 22:47; Jn. 18:3–5). When Jesus was officially condemned to death, Judas was overwhelmed with remorse and attempted to undo his evil deed by returning the money, only to be contemptuously rejected (Matt. 27:3–8). Matthew states that he hanged himself; Luke adds a footnote in Acts to the effect that he was killed by a fall (Acts 1:18–19). The money was used by the priests to buy the potter's field, later called AKELDAMA, the Field of Blood, as a burial place for strangers.

(See further J. G. Tasker in *DCG*, 1:907–13; K. Lake in *BC*, 5:22–30; R. B. Halas, *Judas Iscariot: A Scriptural and Theological Study of His Person, His Deeds, and His Eternal Lot* [1946]; E. F. Harrison in *BSac* 417 [1948]: 170–81; G. Schwarz, *Jesus und Judas: Aramaistische Untersuchungen zur Jesus-Judas-Überlieferung der Evangelien und der Apostelgeschichte* [1988]; W. Klassen, *Judas: Betrayer or Friend of Jesus?* [1996]; A. W. Zwiep, *Judas and the Choice of Matthias* [2004].)   M. C. TENNEY

Judas Maccabeus. See MACCABEE.

Judas tree. Name given to *Cercis siliquastrum*, which according to legend is the tree from which JUDAS ISCARIOT hanged himself (the biblical accounts of Judas's death do not expressly mention a tree; see Matt. 27:5; Acts 1:18). The tree is a native of Palestine. It grows about 30 ft. tall, and could provide branches on which a person might

Above this rocky escarpment lies the traditional Field of Blood, where Judas was buried after he hanged himself. (View to the SE into the Hinnom Valley.)

hang. Reddish flowers like drops of blood appear before the foliage, not only on the young wood, but straight out of the trunk itself. Tradition has it that the tree weeps blood each spring in memory of Judas. The leaves, shaped like a heart, are said to refer to the hard heart of Judas.

W. E. SHEWELL-COOPER

Jude, Epistle of jood. The last of the CATHOLIC EPISTLES.

I. Background. This letter is one of the shortest books in the Bible, containing only twenty-five verses and considerably fewer than 1,000 words in the original Greek text. As is true of the other NT epistles, it originated as a personal letter from one of the leaders of the early church to one or more of the congregations dispersed throughout the ROMAN EMPIRE. As the church developed and grew, its historical situation changed, and the officers had to meet new challenges, opportunities, and draw out further applications of the gospel message. The alterations in the church's relationship to the pagan world about it is reflected in the epistolary tradition of the NT. The epistle of Jude was written during a phase of the church's growth when it was represented among all levels of Hellenistic society and extended to every corner of the known world.

The dangers facing the church at this time were not those of outright persecution and extinction. Some areas of the Roman empire were still to suffer extensive repression, but the threat of internal subversion and accommodation to the resurgent paganism of the times was considerably more dangerous. As the Christian gospel, with its theme of creation-fall-redemption-restoration, came into conflict with the form-matter notions of Greek thought, popular among both Hellenists and Romans, the danger of synthesis arose. The latter epistles of the NT deal with this new problem, which threatened both the purity of the gospel message and the expansion of the church.

II. Authorship. The first verse of the epistle follows the form of Jewish and Aramaic correspondence of the Hellenistic age by indicating the names of both the sender and recipient of the letter. The author-sender is introduced simply as: "Jude [Gk. JUDAS=JUDAH], a servant of Jesus Christ and brother of James [Jacob]." Since the most widely known JAMES in the early church was the head of the congregation in Jerusalem, the brother of Jesus Christ, and the author of the epistle of James, Jude must have been his younger brother. Indeed such a brother of Jesus, a son of Mary and Joseph, is mentioned in Matt. 13:55 and Mk. 6:3. See BROTHERS OF JESUS.

The humble self-designation of the author, who denotes himself only as "the brother of James," is of great significance in understanding his belief in the Messiah, Jesus. He is to the messianic figure not a brother but a servant. According to an ancient patristic tradition, the grandsons of Jude were brought before Emperor DOMITIAN (A.D. 81–96) as descendants of King David and subjects of Christ the King. When it was discovered they were only poor farmers and that they did not plan any political revolution but were subjects of a heavenly domain, the emperor dismissed them with disdain (Euseb. *Eccl. Hist.* 3.19–20). Whether or not the epistle actually was written by the hand of Jude or by one of his helpers in preaching the gospel cannot now be determined. It is also possible that the epistle is the compendium of his teachings over many years.

III. Date. The dating of this epistle is an extremely difficult problem, as there is no direct evidence within the book or in the rest of the NT regarding the time of composition. The book is not mentioned elsewhere in the NT, and rarely by the historians of the apostolic age. However, since the main thrust of the argument follows that of GALATIANS and other warnings against subversive heresies, it must be placed after the initial period of missionary expansion. All the NT writings contain specific references to false teachers and their evil notions. Jude mentions them as perverting the Christian gospel for personal gain (Jude 4). Such heresies probably made their appearance at the end of the age of the apostolic church. Such a date would fall about A.D. 80–90 during the reign of Domitian, a period of incitement by paid schismatics seeking to bring the latent power of the church closer to the political leadership of the senate and people of Rome.

IV. Origin and destination. The epistle of Jude contains no geographical references from which its place of origin may be known. Since it appears to have been written well after the fall of Jerusalem and the age of the Roman conquest under TITUS, it was probably penned outside of Palestine. Some authorities insist on an Alexandrian origin for the work (see ALEXANDRIA). The recipients are addressed simply as "those who have been called, who are loved by God the Father and kept by Jesus Christ" (Jude 1). This designation denotes two divine activities of which the readers were recipients. First, they were beloved of God, a phrase entirely applicable to the Jew (Rom. 11), and applied to these readers also. Second, they were kept by (or for) Jesus Christ, as though they once were partakers of the old covenant and had later accepted the Messiah.

It seems reasonable to infer that the readers were Jews of the DIASPORA who had joined the church. This assumption is further strengthened by the numerous references in the epistle to obscure persons and events in the OT and several allusions to the APOCRYPHA and PSEUDEPIGRAPHA. Such readers, already separated from Judaism and aware of the nonrabbinical writings of the time, would be open to the heretical appeals they had received. By properly interpreting the OT on these points, the author was no doubt attempting to turn them again to the truth.

V. Occasion and purpose. In the NT it is clear that the message of the apostles is based on the messianic blessing promised in the OT. Jude applies the OT imprecations to those who pervert the new covenant. In this negative sense the author connects the old and the new revelations. The purpose of the epistle is threefold: (1) It identifies the false doctrine and its adherents as one with the infidels of all ages. (2) It demonstrates the full extremity of their perversion and the degradation to which they have sunk in their twisting of the truth. (3) The faith of the true believer is pointed toward the longsuffering of God and the maintenance of his promises. Each of these three aspects is presented as centered in the apostolic teachings and demonstrable from the OT text. The purpose of the epistle is to warn and to commend, and it succeeds admirably.

VI. Canonicity. The inclusion of the epistle within the CANON appears to have been based largely upon the assumption that it was, in fact, written by the brother of James, the author of the epistle attributed to him, and the younger brother of Jesus. Its final acceptance, however, was quite probably based upon its reliance on OT quotations and points of doctrine identical to many in 2 Peter. Its inclusion of apocryphal material caused some concern about its proper place. Of special interest is the possibility that Jude had actually intended to write a more theological or pastoral treatise entitled, *peri tēs koinēs hēmōn sōtērias*, "concerning the common salvation" (Jude 3). Instead, however, events forced the author to produce this strong condemnation of certain heretics. The fact that the offenders are nameless in the book has added to the mystery about its writing and purpose.

In detailed evidence the canonicity of Jude is better attested in the early church than that of 2 Peter and James. The one point of rejection was that by the Syrian church, which also rejected 2 Peter and 2–3 John. Among the patristic writers who mention the book, EUSEBIUS, writing in the year 337–338, includes both James and Jude among "those [books] that are disputed, yet familiar to most" (*Eccl. Hist.* 3.25). TERTULLIAN, CLEMENT OF ALEXANDRIA, ORIGEN, JEROME, and the MURATORIAN CANON all receive the book as authoritative. Certainly by the time of the Nicene council A.D. 325, Jude was accepted as Scripture by the preponderant majority of congregations of Christendom.

VII. Sources and style. Of the twenty-five verses of Jude, nineteen are to some degree reduplicated by 2 Peter. The question of literary dependence has been raised many times but is not clearly answerable. It is highly probable that both made use of a common body of apostolic preaching and teaching about the heresies of the time. So far all arguments for or against the originality of the text of Jude are specious.

After the initial address and greeting, the epistle leaves the traditional epistolary style and does not resort to it until the doxology at the close (Jude 24–25). Whether or not the book as we have it is derived from a Hebrew or Aramaic original is impossible to determine from the text. The Greek of the epistle is reasonably polished and flows swiftly in its short compass from one OT citation to another. These quotations and allusions are based upon the SEPTUAGINT. There are a number of phrases peculiar to the NT. These may be stylistic variants of the author (or of the translator). Jude also has a marked favor for triplets of all kinds, both semantic and stylistic, which may be a hint at an original Hebrew text, since such a usage is known from Semitic sources of the Hellenistic age (vv. 2, 7, 8, et al.).

VIII. Use of Apocryphal and Pseudepigraphic books. One point of concern about both the canonicity and authority of Jude throughout the history of exegesis has been the inclusion of the story of the dispute between MICHAEL and the devil over the body of MOSES (Jude 9) and a speech of ENOCH (v. 14). In v. 6 there is a reference to the legend of the judgment of the fallen angels. Clement of Alexandria and others assumed that these references in an otherwise canonical book confirmed the authority of the noncanonical writings. This extreme view has been repudiated in more recent study.

The events of Jude 9 are derived from the apocryphal *Assumption of Moses*, which has survived in a badly damaged Greek version only (see MOSES, ASSUMPTION OF). In this text the passage containing the dispute is lacking. Undoubtedly, the ultimate origin of the story was a now long lost Aramaic commentary on Genesis. In the Slavonic translation of some of these commentaries and in some Greek fragments, the passage is preserved. In the passage it is against MOSES, as slayer of the Egyptian (Exod. 2:11–15), that the devil brings his accusation, but the archangel MICHAEL makes no reply of the same sort. The allusions in Jude 6, 14–15 are taken from the pseudepigraphic *1 Enoch*, fragments of which in the original Hebrew were discovered at Qumran (see ENOCH, BOOKS OF). The quotations are to be explained as necessary to the author's argument against the false teachers. It is well known that the sectarian Jewish texts were disseminated among the Diaspora. The author demonstrates that even these texts were misused by the heretics, and he seeks to demonstrate that even the legends, when rightly interpreted, support the orthodox view of the OT.

IX. Content
 A. The greeting and occasion (Jude 1–3)
 B. Warnings against heretics (vv. 4–16)
  1. False teachers pervert God's grace (v. 4)
  2. Biblical and other examples (vv. 5–7)
  3. The defamation of authorities (vv. 8–10)
  4. The cases of Cain, Balaam, and Korah, who rebelled (vv. 11–13)
  5. The prophecy of Enoch (vv. 14–16)
 C. Perseverance in the apostolic faith (vv. 17–25)
  1. Apostolic warnings against the mockers (vv. 17–19)
  2. The life of Christian love (vv. 20–23)
  3. Doxology (vv. 24–25)

X. Theology. The theological teaching of the epistle seems to follow closely that of the Pauline and Petrine epistles. The fate of the wicked is described as vividly as in Revelation, and in that sense it seems fitting that it should come between these two sections of the NT. It calls down upon the unbeliever and the seducer no other judgment than that meted out by God. The book contains several liturgical phrases from the earliest period of Christian worship and smoothly weaves these into the fabric of the argument. The resignation to the mercy and faithfulness of God is as clearly encouraged as anywhere in Scripture. Of special interest is the inclusion of many doctrinal assumptions. They are perseverance (Jude 3), predestination (v. 4), redemption (v. 5 et al.), judgment (v. 11), sacraments (v. 12), and glorification (v. 24). It is in its essence a book of warning and an assurance of hope.

(Important commentaries include F. Spitta, *Das zweite Brief des Petrus und der Brief des Judas* [1885]; J. E. Huther, *Critical and Exegetical Handbook to the General Epistles of James, Peter, John and Jude* [1887]; J. B. Mayor, *The Epistle of St. Jude and the Second Epistle of St. Peter* [1907]; C. Bigg, *A Critical and Exegetical Commentary on the Epistles of St. Peter and St. Jude*, ICC, 2nd ed. [1902]; J. W. C. Wand, *The General Epistles of St. Peter and St. Jude* [1934]; B. Reicke, *The Epistles of James, Peter and Jude*, AB 37 [1964]; M. Green, *The Second Epistle General of Peter, and the General Epistle of Jude*, TNTC [1968]; R. Bauckham, *Jude, 2 Peter*, WBC 50 [1983];

J. H. Neyrey, *2 Peter, Jude*, AB 37 [1993]; J. D. Turner et al., *Jude: A Structural Commentary* [1996]; T. R. Schreiner, *1, 2 Peter, Jude*, NAC 37 [2003]; P. H. Davids, *The Letters of 2 Peter and Jude* [2006]. See also R. J. Bauckham, "The Letter of Jude: An Account of Research," *ANRW* 2/25/5 [1988], 3791–3826; J. D. Charles, *Literary Strategy in the Epistle of Jude* [1993]; R. A. Reese, *Writing Jude: The Reader, the Text, and the Author in Constructs of Power and Desire* [2000]; P. R. Jones, *The Epistle of Jude as Expounded by the Fathers* [2001]; T. Wasserman, *The Epistle of Jude: Its Text and Transmission* [2006]; and the bibliography compiled by W. E. Mills, *2 Peter and Jude* [2000].)   W. WHITE, JR.

Judea joo-dee′uh (Ἰουδαία *G2677*, from Heb. יְהוּדָה *H3373*; see JUDAH). Also Judaea. Name used for the southern part of PALESTINE, especially after the end of the kingdom of Judah (see JUDAH, KINGDOM OF).

I. The name. Judea is the Greco-Roman designation of an area earlier included in the former kingdom of Judah, and to which the Hebrews of the Babylonian captivity returned. Added to this is the fact that most of the returnees from the EXILE were of the tribe of Judah (see JUDAH, TRIBE OF). The name is used first in Tob. 1:18, where it refers to the Davidic kingdom of Judah. The term is sometimes used freely to designate western Palestine (Lk. 23:5; Acts 10:37). Used strictly, it specified the southernmost of the three traditional divisions of ancient Palestine. The other two were SAMARIA (in the center) and GALILEE (in the N).

II. The nature of Judea's territory. The geographical area of Judea seems to have varied somewhat in different periods. There was no clearly marked boundary to divide Judea from Samaria. The line separating the two regions customarily was thought to run a little to the N or S of BETHEL (modern Beitin). There is no valley or any sharp break in the terrain to separate the two areas, since the hill country of southern Samaria levels to a plateau. The line of this northern boundary of Judea extended approximately from a little N of JOPPA to the JORDAN River at a point about 13 mi. N of the DEAD SEA.

The S boundary of Judea was even more nebulous than the N boundary. BEERSHEBA was considered to be at the southern limit of Judea, as it was the traditional boundary of Israel as a people (Jdg. 20:1). Farther S beyond that point was the dry NEGEV wilderness that without irrigation could support little life. The W boundary of Judea was the Mediterranean Sea from a little below GAZA northward to Joppa. The E boundary was the Dead Sea from about MASADA northward to the southern reaches of the Jordan River and a little N of JERUSALEM. Thus Judea resembled a square of about 45 mi. on each side.

The heart of Judea was the upper hill country, a plateau extending from Bethel to Beersheba and including such well-known cities as JERUSALEM, BETHLEHEM, and HEBRON. Near Jerusalem the plateau rises to an altitude of 2,693 ft. and at Hebron to 3,346 ft. This was the center of the life of the people of this area from the earliest times. The plateau gently slopes downward to the W through the SHEPHELAH to the maritime plane and finally the Mediterranean. Clouds moving eastward in from the sea supplied rainfall sufficient to sustain the farming and pastoral life of the people. It is estimated that in Roman times c. 200,000 Jews lived in Judea, a large proportion of them in Jerusalem.

Eastward from the plateau, the terrain slopes rapidly down toward the Dead Sea and the Jordan River. This eastern area is known as the Wilderness

Judea.

St. George's Monastery in the Judean Desert near Jericho.

of Judea (or Judean Desert) because the rain clouds empty their moisture on the plateau and its W slope, leaving little for the E section of the country. It was in the Wilderness of Judea that JOHN THE BAPTIST appeared as the forerunner of Christ (Matt. 3:1; cf. Mk. 1:4; Lk. 3:2). The most important city in this eastern area was JERICHO. There was also MASADA, the site of HEROD the Great's fortress, where the Jews made a heroic last defense in A.D. 73 against the Romans who had destroyed Jerusalem three years before. There is also EN GEDI, an oasis of fresh-water springs, and QUMRAN, the center of the discoveries of the DEAD SEA SCROLLS.

Judea depended upon the natural resources of her territory for some of her wealth. Grain was grown in the valleys, and grapes, figs, olives, and citrus fruits were an important part of the annual crop. The importance of the pastoral life in Judea is reflected everywhere in the Bible. From the Dead Sea came salt, potash, and other minerals. Perhaps the most important source of income for Judea was the TEMPLE in Jerusalem. The annual half-shekel tax paid by all adult male Jews, even those of the DIASPORA, brought large regular sums to Jerusalem. Added to this were the pilgrims who contributed to the income of the government. Contributing also to the influence of Judea was the SANHEDRIN, which sat in Jerusalem. It ruled over all Judea, but its influence was also felt in other areas of Palestine.

It should be noted that along the Mediterranean coast, and within Judea's territory, was PHILISTIA with its powerful cities. Among these were ASHKELON, GAZA, EKRON, ASHDOD, and GATH, a group of towns sometimes referred to as the Philistine pentapolis. These cities were a constant source of difficulty for the Jews, and even during the Roman domination of Judea, much of the maritime plane was governed separately from Judea proper by the Romans. In this area also was JABNEEL, later called Jamnia, the center of important rabbinical activity after the fall of Jerusalem in A.D. 70.

III. History of Judea. The history of Judea may be said to begin when CYRUS, the first Persian emperor, gave the captive Hebrews permission to return to their native land to rebuild Jerusalem and the temple. Later, after the fragmentation of the empire of ALEXANDER THE GREAT, Palestine was eventually ruled by the SELEUCIDS. The attempt of the Seleucids to destroy the religion of the Jews was thwarted by the courage of the HASMONEANS, which initiated events leading to a short period of Jewish independence.

Palestine came under Roman control in 63 B.C., and Antipater, called Procurator of Judea, was its nominal ruler under Julius CAESAR in 47–43 B.C. Herod the Great, who rebuilt the TEMPLE, was king of all Palestine from 40 to 4 B.C. His son Herod Archelaus (see HEROD IV) ruled Palestine from 4 B.C. to A.D. 6. He was deposed by the Romans, who then appointed a series of governors that ruled Judea, Samaria, and Idumea from A.D. 6 to 41. The most familiar of these is Pontius PILATE (A.D. 26–36), under whom Jesus was crucified. Herod Agrippa I (see HEROD V), grandson of Herod the Great, was king of all Palestine from A.D. 41 to 44, after which Roman governors again ruled Judea and the surrounding areas until the Jewish rebellion of 66–73. The Romans destroyed Jerusalem in the year 70, and in 135 crushed another Jewish revolt. Jerusalem was soon rebuilt, under the Roman emperor HADRIAN, and called Aelia Capitolina, but Jews were forbidden to live there. See WARS, JEWISH.

It is notable that in the following period in Judea, many Christian churches were built, not only in Jerusalem and Bethlehem but also in various Christian settlements, for example, at Eleutheropolis (Beit Jibrin) and at Messana ('Auja el-Hafir). Constantine the Great reorganized the area and called Judea and Samaria by the name of Palestina Prima. The Muslims took Judea in 637 and held it (except for the Crusader kingdom from 1099 to 1187) until it was made part of the British mandate of Palestine after World War I. Judea was partitioned between Israel and the Hashemite kingdom of the Jordan by the United Nations, after the 1947–48 war between the Jews and the Arabs. As a result of the Six-Day War of June, 1967, the Jews regained control of Judea. (See further G. A. Smith, *Historical Geography of the Holy Land* [1931], 237–315; H. Daniel-Rops, *Israel and the Ancient World* [1964], 279–358; R. Y. T. Lee, *Romanization in Palestine: A Study of Urban Development from Herod the Great to AD 70* [2003].) A. C. SCHULTZ

Judea, ridge of. According to the book of JUDITH, HOLOFERNES brought an enormous army from NINEVEH to Palestine. "Then he came toward Esdraelon, near Dothan, facing the great ridge of Judea [*tou prionos tou megalou tēs Ioudaias*]," and there he camped for a month as he waited for supplies (Jdt. 3:9; the Gk. word *priōn* means "saw" or "jagged row"). Because DOTHAN is near the hills of SAMARIA, far from the Judean range, a textual error is suspected. S. BARABAS

judge. One who governs, dispenses justice, judgment, and protection, and as such is the representative of God. See also JUDGMENT.

I. In the OT. Significantly, the first mention of a judge in the first book of the OT applies the title to Yahweh. In his intercession for SODOM, ABRAHAM prays: "Will not the Judge [ptc. of *šāpaṭ* H9149] of all the earth do right?" (Gen. 18:25). The thought underlying Genesis and all that follows is that God is the righteous judge of both peoples and individuals (3:14–19; 6:3–7; 11:5–9; 15:14; 16:5; 20:3; 31:53).

Under the PATRIARCHS, judicial authority is exercised by the head of the household (Gen. 21; 22; 27). Disputes between families are settled by force or mutual agreement (chs. 21; 31). Although judges were not unknown outside the chosen people (19:9; Exod. 2:14), they were first instituted in Israel at the suggestion of MOSES' father-in-law, JETHRO, to assist Moses in acting on behalf of God in settling disputes (Exod. 18:13–27; Deut. 1:9–18). The Deuteronomic code provided for the appointment of "judges and officials" in every town (Deut. 16:18). More important cases were to be tried by a judge with priests as assessors (17:8–13).

During the conquest of Canaan, judges took part in the solemn assemblies of the nation (Josh. 8:33; 24:1). After the death of JOSHUA, Israel's fortunes depended upon judges whom Yahweh "raised up" to save "them out of the hands of … raiders" (Jdg. 2:16). Their task was not merely to try cases, but to keep the nation from idolatry and lead it in battle (vv. 17–19). They were sometimes called "saviors" or "deliverers" (3:9, 15). The book of Judges records their exploits from OTHNIEL (3:9) to SAMSON (chs. 13–16). Among them was the prophetess DEBORAH (4:4–5). See JUDGES, BOOK OF; JUDGES, PERIOD OF. The last of the line was the priest and prophet SAMUEL (1 Sam. 1–19; cf. Acts 13:20; 3:24), who "continued as judge over Israel all the days of his life," visiting key centers annually (1 Sam. 7:15–16). In his old age the people wanted a thing to "judge" them (Heb. *šāpaṭ*, 1 Sam. 8:5 [NIV, "lead"]; cf. Deut. 17:14–20).

Under the monarchy the king was the supreme — and at times apparently the sole — judge (2 Sam. 15:2–3). JEHOSHAPHAT (whose name means "Yahweh has judged") appointed judges in all the fortified cities of Judah (2 Chr. 19:5–7). With the EXILE the monarchy lapsed, but on the return EZRA was authorized to "appoint magistrates and judges to administer justice" according to the laws of God and of the king of PERSIA (Ezra 7:25–26).

Judges are even occasionally called "gods" (*ʾĕlōhîm* H166) in view of their divinely authorized function (Ps. 82:1, 6; cf. Jn. 10:34–35; and possibly Exod. 21:6; 22:7–8). (See further R. de Vaux, *Ancient Israel* [1961], 143–63; *NIDOTTE*, 4:213–20.)

II. In the NT. It was Roman policy to preserve as far as possible the culture and self-government of subject peoples. In Palestine justice was administered by the SANHEDRIN, which could inflict flogging and expulsion (Lk. 6:22; Jn. 9:22; 12:42; 16:2; Acts 5:40; 2 Cor. 11:24), but not the death penalty (cf. Matt. 27:1–2). At the same time individual judges (*kritēs* G3216) were familiar enough figures to provide vivid illustrations in the teaching of Jesus (Matt. 5:25; Lk. 12:14, 58; 18:2, 6).

As in the OT, judges have God's authority, even though they may be pagan (Rom. 13:1–7; 1 Tim. 2:2; 1 Pet. 2:13–14; cf. Matt. 22:15–22). As such they must be respected. Individuals are never to set themselves up as judges (Matt. 7:1–5; Lk. 6:37–38; Rom. 2:1; 12:19–21; 14:10). JUDGMENT will be passed on all people by God, the supreme Judge (Rom. 3:6; Heb. 10:30; 12:23; Jas. 4:12; 5:9; cf. Matt. 5:21–26; Deut. 32:35–36). It is an indirect testimony to his divinity that the Judge will be one who as a man was himself judged by men, Jesus Christ (Matt. 25:31–46; Jn. 8:16; Acts 10:42; 17:31; 2 Tim. 4:1; 1 Pet. 4:5; cf. 1 Cor. 15:24–28). All human beings will appear before his JUDGMENT SEAT. As in the OT THEOCRACY, so in the kingdom the saints will receive delegated authority to judge (Lk. 22:30; 1 Cor. 6:2–3; Rev. 20:4; cf. Dan. 7:9, 22, 27). (See further O. Cullmann, *The State in the New Testament* [1957]; L. Morris, *The Biblical Doctrine of Judgment* [1960]; *NIDNTT*, 2:361–71.)

C. BROWN

Judges, Book of. The seventh book of the OT. In the Hebrew Bible, Judges is included among the Former Prophets.

I. Archaeological background
II. Purpose
III. Composition, unity, and date
  A. Composition
  B. Unity
  C. Date
IV. Place in canon
V. Text
VI. The moral problem of Israel's judges
VII. Permanent value
VIII. Contents
  A. The partial conquest of Canaan
  B. Israel's judges
  C. Appendices

I. Archaeological background. It is apparent that the Israelites settled down immediately in the land, for archaeological excavation at several of the cities destroyed at this time show no subsequent break in occupation. The absence of any transitional period is a witness to the fact that the Israelites were not typical nomads. There is, however, a clear distinction between the well-built Canaanite structures and the simpler, almost primitive type of Israelite occupation that succeeded it. This decline in architectural standards is illustrative of a lower cultural standard among the incoming Israelites.

The evidence of continuing Canaanite occupation of the low-lying areas (e.g., at MEGIDDO and BETH SHAN), where their extensive chariot forces gave them a tactical advantage, confirms the biblical admission that these areas were not occupied in the earlier part of the judges' period (e.g., Josh. 11:13; 13:1–7; 17:16; Jdg. 1:19, 27; et al.). Before the Israelite invasion, because of the uncertain water supply, there was limited Canaanite occupation of the central hill country. Coincident with the entry of Israel was the widespread employment of underground cisterns to store water during the prolonged summer drought, facilitated by the use of a waterproof lime plaster that made them leak proof. This discovery made possible the extensive Israelite settlement in areas that previously were sparsely populated. The fact that no Israelite sanctuary of the judges' period has yet been discovered may be

A dry cistern at Beersheba, with the rock lined and plastered in places. Israel's arrival in the Promised Land is marked by an increased use of cisterns to capture water for everyday use.

attributable to their inferior building techniques. However, it may also be an indication of the divine prohibition against an indiscriminate erection of sanctuaries (Exod. 20:24–26; Deut. 12:1–7).

Many clay figurines representing a naked female about to give birth have been found. The lack of any insignia of a goddess calls into question an identification with the fertility goddesses of Canaan; they may simply have been good-luck charms associated with childbirth. It is not impossible, however, that this may be an incidental witness to the fundamental prohibition against idol worship (Exod. 20:4–6 et al.). No representation of a male deity has been found at any known Israelite site of this period.

The decisive victory of Deborah and Barak took place "at Taanach by the waters of Megiddo" (Jdg. 5:19). This cryptic allusion to Megiddo has been illumined by archaeological research, which suggests that this town and Taanach, about 5 mi. apart, were not occupied simultaneously. The inference is that Taanach was settled at the time of this battle, whereas Megiddo was in ruins. For many scholars, the convergence of historical, archaeological, and literary evidence has made a date c. 1125 B.C. virtually certain.

Archaeological research in Transjordan has illumined the state of the small kingdoms, which were as thorns in Israel's side during the period (esp. Moab and Ammon). Westward, our knowledge of the culture and organization of the Philistines has been enriched by discoveries in the Negev, the Shephelah, and even as far away as Cyprus. It is clear that the Philistines formed a ruling class over a subject population whose religion and culture they assimilated. The god of the Philistines was Dagon, an old Amorite deity (1 Sam. 5:2–5). The extent of the Philistine penetration of the hinterland may be estimated by the degree of distribution of a distinctive type of pottery known generally as "Philistine ware." This accords with the literary evidence of Judges and 1 Samuel.

The destruction of the shrine at Shiloh is not mentioned in Judges, but its place in Israelite tradition is witnessed by Ps. 78:60 and Jer. 7:12; 26:6. Archaeological research shows that it was, in fact, destroyed by fire c. 1050 B.C. It is clear that this followed the double defeat inflicted upon the Israelite army at Aphek (1 Sam. 4). Other Israelite cities were destroyed at this time, doubtless by the same agency, which reflects the Philistines' dominance in the immediate premonarchic period. (See also JUDGES, PERIOD OF.)

II. Purpose. The purpose of the editor of the book of Judges determined his selection and use of material. The book covers the period from the death of Joshua (Jdg. 1:1; 2:8) to the point when the Philistine menace had become acute, c. 1060 B.C. His concern was to account for, as well as to describe, the political, moral, and religious decline during the period, and to demonstrate its effect upon the life of the community. This general observation will throw light upon the consideration of such things as structure and date.

III. Composition, unity, and date

A. Composition. The book of Judges divides naturally into three distinct sections: (1) Jdg. 1:1—2:5

Mold for making idols dated to the Late Bronze Age. The attraction of Canaanite worship was a nagging problem throughout the period of the judges.

sets forth the settlement in Canaan. The major portion (1:1–36) deals with the attempt by the tribes to occupy their territory. The general movement is from S to N, beginning with the tribe of Judah, whose exploits are dealt with in far greater detail (see JUDAH, TRIBE OF). This may indicate that this section originated in Judah. A certain deterioration is discernible as the chapter progresses; Judah (1:1–19) and the JOSEPH tribes (vv. 22–27) are relatively successful, but the remainder of the tribes had scant success (vv. 21, 27–36 give a catalogue of unoccupied territory). The close connections with the book of Joshua (cf Josh. 15:13–19 with Jdg. 1:10–15; Josh. 15:63 with Jdg. 1:21; Josh. 17:11–13 with Jdg. 1:27–28; Josh. 16:10 with Jdg. 1:29) show that this is an account, or extracts from an account, of the conquest. It is, therefore, a valuable complement to the account in Joshua. The opening words, "After the death of Joshua," cannot therefore apply to this section but are rather a general introduction and title to the whole book. The reason for the inclusion of this historical survey is to set the scene for the period of the judges. This was a disordered situation, with only a minority of the tribes occupying their territory, whereas the remainder dwelt in varying degrees of tension with the Canaanites. Judges 2:1–5 completes this bleak picture by bringing into prominence the fact of the broken covenant.

(2) Judges 2:6—16:31 presents the judges of Israel. In this, the main portion of the book, are recorded the exploits of Othniel (3:7–11), Ehud (3:12–30), Deborah and Barak (4:1—5:31), Gideon (6:1—8:35), Jephthah (10:6—12:7), and Samson (13:1—16:31). These are usually classified as the major judges, in contradistinction to the minor judges, of whom little is recorded. This second group comprises Shamgar (3:31), Tola and Jair (10:1–5), and Ibzan, Elon, and Abdon (12:8–15).

The individual passages undoubtedly had a history of their own before they were gathered together. Possibly they were preserved in both oral and written forms in the areas in which the exploits were performed (Jdg. 8:14 is an important attestation to an early, widespread diffusion of the art of writing). Some of the difficulties of the stories, and the alleged duplications, are readily explicable on this assumption. The author of this selection may have used more than one account of the same event, for example, the prose and poetical accounts of deliverance from the Canaanites (chs. 4–5). Or there may be an incidental witness to the art of the storyteller with his use of reiteration to preserve the vital thread of the narrative.

Recent literary conventions should not be imposed upon the literature of the ANE. One of the fallacies of the Graf-Wellhausen documentary hypothesis was its examination of the text of the OT without reference to literature from Israel's contemporaries. The criteria used for dissecting the early books of the Bible — including double names of individuals, groups, places, common nouns, the deity, and even changes of style — consist of features that are in fact paralleled in contemporary documents from Israel's neighbors. For this and many other reasons, the classic documentary hypothesis has been widely abandoned or modified. In particular, it is not now generally held that the so called Elohist or Yahwist sources can be traced in Judges.

The individual stories have been brought together in an orderly manner, in which their chronological sequence has been maintained (see JUDGES, PERIOD OF III), and set in a framework of editorial comment. A standard form of introduction is discernible in the stories of Othniel (3:7–9), Ehud (3:12–15), Deborah (4:1–3), Gideon (6:1–6), Jephthah (10:6–10), and Samson (13:1). A standardized conclusion is discernible in 3:10–11, 30; 8:28; in the case of Deborah it is divided between 4:23 and 5:31. In the case of the minor judges, excepting Shamgar (3:31), the standard details include the length of judgeship and the place of burial (10:2–3, 5; 12:7, 9–15). The same details are given in the case of Samson (15:20; 16:31). An extended general introduction to the period is given in 2:6—3:6. This notes the general trends in the period after Joshua's death, with its pattern of apostasy, judgment, repentance, and deliverance, a cycle of events that is traced in the remainder of the period of the judges. The composition of this major section, therefore, reflects a certain artistry and a clear point of view. It may be described as interpretative history (cf. V. P. Long, *The Art of Biblical History* [1994], reprinted in *FCI*, 281–429).

(3) Judges 17:1—21:25, the final section of the book, contains two apparently unrelated events: (a) the shrine of MICAH and the Danite migration (17:1—18:31); (b) the outrage at GIBEAH and its aftermath (19:1—21:25). There is no evidence of the religiously motivated comment that characterizes 2:6—16:31. Instead, the reason for the disorders is found in the absence of the centralized authority of a monarchy (cf. 17:6; 18:1; 19:1; 21:25). It is unlikely that these narratives were preserved in the traditions of the two tribes principally involved (Dan and Benjamin), since they were shown in an uncomplimentary light. The link that connects these two incidents may be the ineffectiveness of the tribal organization. In the first story, Micah has no court of appeal against the heartless rapaciousness of the Danites. In the second narrative, the so-called AMPHICTYONY intervened to punish the men of Gibeah, but their judgment was so mismanaged that the complete extinction of the whole tribe of Benjamin was averted only by resorting to two desperate expedients. The historical setting of the editor of this section is, almost certainly, the reigns of DAVID and SOLOMON, when the kingdom was firmly but justly administered. These two incidents are of great importance in revealing the conditions operating in certain areas at definite points in the period of the judges. But allowance must be made for the selection of this kind of incident and the final judgment balanced by the completely different picture of the book of RUTH.

B. Unity. Attention has been drawn to the diversity of the contents of the book of Judges. However, there is an inward unity in that all the contents witness in one way or another to the political, social, moral, and religious decline in the period between the death of Joshua and the institution of the monarchy. The first section traces the incompleteness of the conquest, with at least a hint of deterioration within the dismal record of the first chapter. Judah and Simeon enjoy a measure of success, and Benjamin, Manasseh, Ephraim, and Naphtali seem to have dominated over local Canaanite populations, but in the case of Asher and the Danites, the reverse is true.

The second section traces the recurring cycle of apostasy and deliverance through the exploits of the judges. Once more there is a general deterioration with the passage of time, and from Abimelech onward there is no mention of peace. Gideon was able to avoid civil war with Ephraim (Jdg. 8:1–3), but Jephthah failed (12:1–6). The story of Abimelech demonstrates the clash between Israelite and Canaanite elements in the neighborhood of Shechem (9:1–57), and illustrates the effects of an incomplete conquest. Samson effected no real deliverance from the Philistines, and the material concerned with his exploits (chs. 13–16) shows a decline in the religious comment of the editor, perhaps even suggesting that the stories speak for themselves.

The final section is a graphic picture of the disorders of the period and is devoid of specifically religious comment, the implication being that the nonexistence of the monarchy was the cause of the national malaise. Thus there is an inherent unity in the whole book, and an unmistakable impression is created that this was the "Dark Ages" of Israel's history.

C. Date. The period of the early monarchy is the most likely date for the composition of Judges in what was basically its present form. The collection of the material in the main section (Jdg. 2:6—16:31), that is, the exploits of the individual judges, could hardly have taken place before the restoration of national unity. The time of David and Solomon was such a period, and the awakening of national pride would lead to an interest in recording past traditions (the literary activities of Samuel, Nathan, and Gad are noted in 1 Chr. 29:29, 2 Chr. 9:29.)

Moreover, there was a human motive underlying the promulgation of the book of Judges. The monarchy in the early period faced opposition from the champions of the old traditions. There was an active concern to show that the monarchy had achieved what the amphictyony had singularly failed to win—namely, a complete conquest and the establishment of law and stability, which indicates an early date rather than one after the disruption (922 B.C.). The favorable attitude to the monarchy thus implied makes the Talmudic tradition that Samuel himself was the author of Judges appear unlikely (his attitude to the monarchy is clearly revealed in 1 Sam. 8). To the main corpus of the book was added a prologue, itself a selection from an otherwise unknown source, showing the incompleteness of the conquest (Jdg. 1:1—2:5). Similarly, an epilogue was appended (17:1—21:25), underlining the low standards of the period now replaced by the monarchy.

It is impossible to determine precisely the date of the book of Judges, or whether more than one hand was involved in its production. The difference in attitude between the second and third sections points to two editors. One fact may be of significance, namely, that BETHLEHEM (in Judah) figures in both of the incidents narrated in the third section (Jdg. 17:7–9; 19:1–2) as well as in the events of the book of Ruth (Ruth 1:1–2, 19, 22). This lends slight support to a date in the reign of David, himself a native of Bethlehem. Although admitting the absence of definite proof, it seems most probable that the book of Judges was compiled during the reign of David, and that its human motive was to demonstrate the advantages of the monarchy in contrast to the ineffective system operating since the death of Joshua.

Brief mention may be made of two critical theories concerning the composition of Judges. One view proposes that certain sections (Jdg. 9; 16; 17—21) that are devoid of the religious comment found elsewhere are secondary, having been interpolated into the text at a later date. A second view asserts there were two editings. In the first, dated to the 7th cent. B.C., these sections were excluded, the remainder being subjected to editorial treatment from the so-called Deuteronomic school. In a second revision, in the following century, the omitted chapters were reincorporated as they stood, thus escaping the editorial comment that was characteristic of the first edition. The possibility of minor revisions and reshaping when the book of Judges was incorporated into the so-called Former Prophets, the official history of Israel from the conquest to the Babylonian Captivity, must not be excluded. The finalizing of this section was accomplished probably in the early years of the exile. But the most acceptable view of the origin of the book of Judges itself, is, as indicated, during the reign of David.

IV. Place in canon. In the Hebrew Bible, Judges is the second book of the Former Prophets (Joshua, Judges, Samuel, and Kings). The designation

The judges in Israel.

"prophet" is a witness to the belief that the will and purpose of God was mediated through the facts of history as well as by the mouths of the prophets. This section of the Hebrew Bible frequently is described as DEUTERONOMISTIC HISTORY, since it illustrates, both by example and editorial comment, the principles enunciated in the book of DEUTERONOMY. So long as no critical undertones concerning the date of Deuteronomy attach to this expression, no objection need be taken to its use. The book of Ruth was originally in the third section of the Hebrew CANON, the Writings (HAGIOGRAPHA). In the SEPTUAGINT it was placed immediately after Judges, presumably because it related to the same period. This order was followed in the VULGATE and most modern versions. The canonicity of Judges never has been seriously questioned.

V. Text. The Hebrew text of Judges has been remarkably well preserved. One exception to this, the Song of Deborah (Jdg. 5), is generally reckoned to be contemporary with the events it describes. The poetical form and its archaic features present considerable problems to the translator and probably have resulted in slight damage to the text in its transmission.

A unique problem relates to the SEPTUAGINT text, which witnesses to two apparently independent versions of Judges. The first is represented principally by CODEX ALEXANDRINUS or A (5th cent. A.D.), supported by most of the uncial and cursive MSS of the Greek texts. The second finds its main witness in CODEX VATICANUS or B (4th cent. A.D.), which has the support of texts emanating from Upper Egypt. There is no unity among scholars about the interrelationship of these recensions, or which approximates most closely to the original LXX text; each textual variant must be considered on its own merits. In Rahlfs's *Septuaginta*, the unusual expedient has been adopted of printing the two principal versions side by side.

VI. The moral problem of Israel's judges. The reader of Judges soon becomes aware of a difference in its leading characters when compared with Israel's leaders of other periods. The blemishes of Abraham, Jacob, Moses, and David, for example, are depicted honestly, without affecting the general estimate of the high quality of their lives. In Judges, on the other hand, the characters are of lesser stature; their shortcomings are more obvious; and there is a certain popular delight in their less reputable exploits. EHUD appeared as an assassin; JAEL was praised for a treacherous act (Jdg. 4:17–21; 5:24–27); GIDEON settled his family feud in the course of his victory over the Midianites (8:18–21); whereas JEPHTHAH is a brigand chief with a vindictive streak and a scant concept of the requirements of the Lord. The situation becomes most acute in connection with SAMSON, who, in spite of his NAZIRITE state, shows a regrettable lack of genuine consecration and indulges his own sensual appetite in an irresponsible manner. These men were anointed with the Spirit of the Lord, that is, they were charismatic individuals. How is this divine endowment to be equated with the low moral and spiritual tone of their lives? The following points must be considered:

First, one must differentiate between the popular verdict of the Israelites who lived through those times and the viewpoint of the editor who collected the stories. No doubt those who had firsthand experience of the various oppressions exulted in every savage detail of the overthrow of their overlords. But the editor who selected these incidents may well have been aware of these moral and religious blemishes. Indeed, part of his concern may have been to illustrate the low standard of leadership of the period (cf. his condemnation of Gideon in Jdg. 8:27). The judges lived in an age of low standards, and this fact is reflected in the narratives, giving a graphic representation of conditions in a period of apostasy, when the Mosaic covenant, with its high standards, was in partial abeyance.

Second, special attention must be given to the stories of Samson. It has been observed that in this section (Jdg. 13–16) there is an absence of the religiously motivated comment characteristic of the earlier section. A frequent explanation of this phenomenon is that the stories had become so fixed in tradition that the editor could not adapt them, although surely the same would apply equally to the other traditions. It seems more reasonable to suppose that these narratives were self-explanatory. Here was a leader, but of what character! Unable to effect a deliverance from the Philistines, his exploits were resented by his own countrymen (13.11). Similarly, the material in the appendix (chs. 17–21) could speak for itself, without adding to the politically motivated comments of 17:6; 18:1; 19:1; 20:25. One can be grateful for the overruling of the Holy Spirit in the selection and presentation of this history. It serves as a perpetual reminder of what happens to a nation, and the individuals comprising it, when the Lord is forsaken and his commandments broken. Some parts of Scripture are for inspiration and edification, but the book of Judges sounds a solemn note of warning.

In the third place, the OT events frequently are related directly to God himself. He hardened Pharaoh's heart (Exod. 4:21; 7:3, 13; et al.); he sent an evil spirit between Abimelech and the men of Shechem (Jdg. 9:23); an evil spirit from the Lord troubled Saul (1 Sam. 16:14; 18:10; 19:9); he put a lying spirit in the mouths of the false prophets (1 Ki. 22:23). It is the effect upon the object rather than the quality of the spirit itself that is prominent in the latter references. The significance of this in common life was that unusual power or qualities of any kind, such as strength or wisdom, were conceived to be a unique endowment from the Spirit of the Lord. But the vital connection is with the sovereignty of God, who influences and controls men and nations in accordance with his own will. This is reflected in Jdg. 14:4, where the parents of Samson, having understandably opposed their son's marriage outside of the covenant people, are shown to be unaware of the divine overruling. Samson himself was devoid of higher motives, but God used him to "begin to deliver Israel from the hand of the Philistines" (13:5).

Therefore, the charismatic anointing of the judges' period was for a limited but definite purpose. It must not be understood as parallel to the NT doctrine of the Spirit, which invariably is associated with holiness of life. The Lord made the judges a channel of his power or the means of his revelation, without any necessarily direct influence upon their moral character. Elsewhere in the OT God employed unlikely agents, such as Balaam, a professional prophet (Num. 22–24); Nebuchadnezzar, the Babylonian king who was called his servant (Jer. 25:9; 27:6; 43:10); and the Persian Cyrus, described as "my shepherd" and "his [God's] anointed" (Isa. 44:28; 45:1; cf. 45:4). The wisdom of God's choice is not always observable to human beings, and there must always remain an inscrutable element. He could use a man like Samson, whose short career centered upon his illicit relationships with Philistine women, some of whom were of dubious character. It must be stressed, however, that Samson and others should have lived up to the standards already revealed in the Mosaic law.

VII. Permanent value. The book of Judges sheds light on the political, social, and religious condition of Israel during the vital period between the conquest and the institution of the monarchy. The manner in which this is done allows the reader to capture the atmosphere of the period in a way that would be impossible in a formal history.

It provides a dramatic illustration of the effect of APOSTASY upon every aspect of life. The root cause of Israel's decline was that the COVENANT relationship with the Lord, with its requirement of absolute and loyal obedience to his commands, was broken. This led to disintegration in the political, religious, social, and family spheres and to a sharp increase in immorality. The book of Judges serves as a reminder that a nation cannot live on its past glories. The author of Judges was, of course, a preacher to his own generation, but his message has a permanent and universal application, and may be summed up in the words of Prov. 14:34, "Righteousness exalts a nation, / but sin is a disgrace to any people." Israel's chronic inability to profit by its own bitter history is a solemn exhortation to profit from the lessons of the past, whether observed or experienced.

Against this somber background, the enduring character of God stands out more clearly. He remained faithful to his COVENANT, not making a final end of his people in spite of their repeated infidelity. His RIGHTEOUSNESS is seen in his JUDGMENT, for sin is an affront to him that he cannot pass over lightly. The SOVEREIGNTY OF GOD is revealed in his use of the surrounding nations as the rod of his anger against Israel. He is able to save by few as well as by many (cf. Jdg. 7:2–7). The forces of nature are at his disposal (5:20–21). When his Spirit comes upon a human being, such an anointing makes that person invincible (3:10; 6:34; 11:29; 14:6; et al.). God's longsuffering evidences itself in his willingness to hear the cry of his distressed people, and to give them a new chance, however short-lived their REPENTANCE might be. While the solemn note of judgment may appear to predominate, it does not silence the undertones of GRACE.

The points made in the preceding paragraph reflect, in measure, the point of view of the later editor. He wrote from the standpoint of a living FAITH in God, for the spiritual edification of his contemporaries. This quality of faith also characterized the principal characters in Judges. They were not free of moral blemishes, nor did they always conform to the requirements of God's law; but there can be no question of their vital apprehension of their God. Since the Song of Deborah is agreed to be contemporaneous with the events it narrates, it is a telling example of this fact. It speaks of his effective past intervention on Israel's behalf (Jdg. 5:4), of his control of nature (5:4–5, 20–21), and of his present participation in Israel's fight against the Canaanites (5:23). The enemies of Israel are his enemies also (5:31). The intolerance that characterizes this poem cannot hide the incredibly vivid faith that it reveals. In an apostate age, people who knew their God in this way wrought great exploits for him (cf. Dan. 11:32), and four of them—Gideon, Barak, Samson, and Jephthah—are catalogued among the great heroes of faith (Heb. 11:32).

VIII. Contents

A. Partial conquest of Canaan (Jdg. 1:1—2:5)
  1. Relative success of the tribes of Judah and Simeon (1:1–21)
  2. Destruction of Bethel (1:22–26)
  3. Listing of unoccupied territory (1:27–36)
  4. Disobedience of Israel (2:1–5)
B. Israel's judges (2:6—16:31)
  1. Introduction (2:6—3:6)
  2. Othniel (3:7–11)
  3. Ehud (3:12–30)
  4. Shamgar (3:31)
  5. Deborah and Barak (4:1—5:31)
  6. Gideon (6:1—8:33)
  7. Supplement: Abimelech's kingship (9:1–56)
  8. Tola and Jair (10:1–5)
  9. Jephthah (10:6—12:7)
  10. Ibzan, Elon, and Abdon (12:8–15)
  11. Samson (13:1—16:31)
C. Appendices (17:1—21:25)
  1. Danites' move to the north (17:1—18:31)
  2. Civil war against the Benjamites (19:1—21:25)

A. The partial conquest of Canaan (Jdg. 1:1—2:5)

1. Relative success of the tribes of Judah and Simeon (Jdg. 1:1–21). Soon after an initial success, the tribe of SIMEON lost its identity and was absorbed into the more powerful tribe of JUDAH. This account is complementary to Josh. 10:1–43, which highlights the activities of the individual tribes recorded in Jdg. 1 within the overall strategy of JOSHUA's leadership. The fact that the general movement is from N to S, beginning at Jerusalem, is evidence against the view that this section witnesses to an independent invasion from the S by the Judah tribes. Jerusalem was defeated but not occupied (1:8). Subsequently reoccupied by the Jebusites (1:21), it resisted capture until David's reign (2 Sam. 5:6–11). The initial victory against the lowland cities, recorded in Jdg. 1:18, is qualified by the admission of 1:19.

2. Destruction of Bethel (Jdg. 1:22–26). Although the destruction of BETHEL is attested by archaeology, the event is not recorded in Joshua. The inhabitants of the city assisted in the defense of AI (Josh. 8:17), which was adjacent to Bethel. Some connection between the two accounts must be assumed, but the question is complicated by archaeological evidence from the site of Ai, which appears to have been unoccupied from c. 2200 B.C. Since Ai is described as a small town (Josh. 7:3), whereas the identified site of Ai shows a relatively large and well-defended city, the most likely explanation is that the survivors of the earlier city resettled at another adjacent site. The HITTITES (Jdg. 1:26) were a major power c. 1800–1200 B.C. Their empire spread over modern ASIA MINOR and SYRIA (cf. Josh. 1:4).

3. Listing of unoccupied territory (Jdg. 1:27–36). In certain cases the Israelites were strong enough to reduce the Canaanites to bondage (1:30, 33, 35), although this was not always achieved quickly (1:28). The Asherites appear to have been the weaker group (1:32), and the Danites were quite displaced (1:34). The Canaanites retained control of the low-lying areas, where their chariots could be effectively deployed, until the time of Deborah and Barak (chs. 4–5). The result was that many of the tribes failed to occupy their allotted portion, and the lists in Josh. 14:1 were consequently idealistic.

4. Disobedience of Israel (Jdg. 2:1–5). The Israelites' great sin of disobedience was, in effect, a breaking of their covenant with Yahweh. The idea of COVENANT, which was fundamental in the early history of Israel, has been illumined by archaeological evidence of covenant TREATY forms (mainly Hittite) of the 2nd millennium B.C. This provides further attestation of the reliability of the early OT records. The movement of the angel of the Lord from GILGAL to BOKIM probably is to be associated with the transference of the central sanctuary from Gilgal. The LXX connects Bokim (i.e., "Weepers") with Bethel, where the sanctuary was subsequently located (20:18–28; 21:1–4). Confronted with this challenge, and with the manifestation of the deity, the people wept, but their subsequent conduct shows that there was no permanent reformation.

B. Israel's Judges (Jdg. 2:6–16:31)

1. Introduction (Jdg. 2:6—3:6). The material in Jdg. 2:6–10 is paralleled in Josh. 24:28–31, a reminder that the death of a great man both begins and ends an era. It is a tribute to Joshua that the people remained faithful to the Lord in his generation, although they all had firsthand experience of the great works of the Lord (TIMNATH HERES in Jdg. 2:9 should be read as Timnath Serah, as in Josh. 19:50; 24:30; a scribe reversed the consonants).

The general tendency of the whole of the judges' period is summarized (Jdg. 2:11–15). It was a period of apostasy in which the nature-gods of Canaan were worshiped. BAAL, the god of the thunderstorm and the rain, was the great, active figure in the Canaanite pantheon. Astarte (see ASHTORETH) was one of the goddesses of war and fertility. The plural forms (vv. 11, 13) may hint at the many local variants and name derivatives (e.g., Num. 25:3, Josh. 11:17; Jdg. 9:4; 2 Ki. 1:2), but more likely it refers to the totality of the Canaanite gods who were worshiped in the FERTILITY CULTS. These gods were thought responsible for fertility in human beings, beasts, and agriculture, and possibly a semipagan generation of Israelites considered it wise to pay them due respect. They ignored the absolute sovereignty of the Lord, who chastised them for their infidelity.

The cycle of apostasy, servitude, and deliverance through a divinely empowered judge is outlined (Jdg. 2:16—3:6), along with the general deterioration characteristic of the period. For this reason they were unable to drive out the original inhabitants of the land. But the historian, conscious of an overruling sovereignty, saw other good reasons why these nations were allowed to remain (2:22; 3:1–2, 4). The PHILISTINES were a people of AEGEAN stock who inhabited their pentapolis of GAZA, ASHKELON, ASHDOD, EKRON, and GATH. Canaanites may designate all the inhabitants of the land, but sometimes the name is restricted to those settled in the low-lying areas. The Sidonians and Jebusites were the Canaanite inhabitants of SIDON and Jerusalem (see JEBUS) respectively. The HIVITES usually are associated with the HORITES, who established a strong kingdom in upper Mesopotamia some centuries before the judges' period. The AMORITES are ethnically indistinguishable from the Canaanites. They are often associated with the hill country, in contradistinction to the specialized use of the name Canaanite (Num. 13:29). Little is known of the PERIZZITES, who may have been an aboriginal group. One of the prime causes of Israel's apostasy was the intermarriage with this pagan population (Jdg. 3:6), in which the relationship of the individual deities would be a major problem. This is referred to as spiritual adultery (2:17; cf. Jer. 3:1–3).

2. Othniel (Jdg. 3:7–11). The first oppression came from ARAM NAHARAIM ("Aram of the two rivers"). The equivalent term Mesopotamia ("between the rivers") is a Greek form that usually describes the area drained by the rivers TIGRIS and EUPHRATES. The reference could be to the Euphrates and one of its tributaries. The name of the oppressor is disguised in the text: CUSHAN-RISHATHAIM possibly means "Cushan of double-wickedness." The Israelites were sufficiently united at this early period to be led by OTHNIEL, CALEB's nephew, who was associated with the southern tribe of Judah (cf. Josh. 14:13–15; Jdg. 1:10–15), against an invader from the N.

3. Ehud (Jdg. 3:12–30). The second oppression came from MOAB, which was located E of the DEAD SEA between the ARNON and the ZERED Rivers, her NE neighbor, AMMON, and the Amalekites (see AMALEK), who came from the area S of Judah. The Moabite penetration probably was limited to the territory of BENJAMIN and EPHRAIM. JERICHO (the City of Palms, v. 13) had been under a curse by Joshua (Josh. 6:26) and was not rebuilt until the time of AHAB (1 Ki. 16:34). The reference is probably to an adjacent site, which would utilize the natural resources of the region.

EHUD, a left-handed man (cf. Jdg. 20:16; 1 Chr. 12:2), was the deliverer on this occasion. His assassination of EGLON was cunningly planned and boldly executed. Disarming the Moabite king by the offering of tribute, he secured a private audience in the secluded roof chamber and used his left-handedness to devastating effect. The natural reticence of Eglon's servants gave him time to escape. The "sculptured stones" near Gilgal (Jdg. 3:19, 26 NRSV) were possibly the commemorative stones set up by Joshua (Josh. 4:19–24). The number of the Moabites slain ("ten thousand," v. 29) indicates an unusually large force W of the Jordan. Though the figure is not impossible, it may be that the word for "thousand" (*ʾelep* H547) refers to an army unit of indeterminate size.

4. Shamgar (Jdg. 3:31). Here is no mention of Israel's apostasy or cry for deliverance, or of an actual oppression, nor any reference to divine enablement. Moreover, Jdg. 4:1 takes up the story from the death of Ehud, not SHAMGAR. Since his name is non-Israelite (possibly Hittite or Hurrian), it has been conjectured that he was a foreigner whose exploits benefited Israel. ANATH was another of the Canaanite goddesses of war, etc., and the expression "the son of Anath" may refer to his warlike propensities. An oxgoad was a metal-pointed implement about 9 ft. long. Such a weapon may indicate that the Philistine policy of depriving the native population of weapons was already in force (1 Sam. 13:19–22). Certain Greek texts place Shamgar after the Samson stories (i.e., after Jdg. 16:31), but 5:6 confirms the chronology of the Hebrew text.

5. Deborah and Barak (Jdg. 4:1—5:31). Two accounts have been preserved of the deliverance from the Canaanites, a prose account (4:1–23) and a poem of victory (5:1–31), the latter being generally attributed to DEBORAH herself. There are difficulties in the interrelationships of the accounts. In ch. 4, JABIN appears as the nominal leader of the Canaanites, although SISERA, the commander of the chariot force, has the active part. Two tribes, Naphtali and Zebulun, are mentioned, and the engagement takes place between Mount TABOR and the River KISHON. In ch. 5 Jabin is not mentioned, although the coalition of the Canaanite city-states is implied (5:19); four more tribes—Ephraim, Benjamin, Makir (prob. W Manasseh), and Issachar—participate and the action moves westward to "Taanach by the waters of Megiddo" (5:19). There is also the question of another Jabin, king of HAZOR, who led an earlier Canaanite coalition against Joshua's Israelites (Josh. 11:1–15).

It is not necessary to assume that Jdg. 4 and 5 are contradictory accounts. Archaeology confirms the destruction of HAZOR by fire (cf. Josh. 11:11–13) about the time of the Israelite invasion. Thereafter, only the upper city (c. 25 acres) was occupied, the lower city (c. 150 acres) remaining unoccupied. Hazor, however, had a strategic position dominating a major trade route, and its emergence as the leader of a coalition of Canaanite city-states a century later is not surprising. It was probably more convenient to maintain the chariot force at HAROSHETH HAGGOYIM (Jdg. 4:2) under the control of the local king, Sisera, where they could deal more effectively with any Israelite uprising.

The biblical historians were concerned to give God the glory for the victory rather than to give a detailed account, but the following reconstruction is reasonable. Deborah, who was a civil judge (Jdg. 4:5) before she became a military judge, encouraged BARAK to break the Canaanite yoke, the initial movement being confined to the tribes principally affected, Naphtali and Zebulun. A considerable success was gained between Tabor and Kishon, which was followed by a general summons to the tribes, with the exception of Judah and Simeon, who were isolated because of geographical and political factors. The rout of Sisera's army was completed by this reinforced Israelite army in the vicinity of Taanach (5:19), which resulted in the precipitant westward flight of the Canaanites. Sisera's attempted escape was foiled by the treachery of JAEL, who efficiently dispatched the man whom she had lulled into a false sense of security. Hazor itself, and Jabin, survived the events of this campaign (4:23–24), but the Canaanite power was shattered.

Among the incidental details of these chapters are the following: (1) The picture of a God who controls the forces of nature (Jdg. 5:4–5, 20–21); probably an unseasonable thunderstorm immobilized the Canaanite chariotry and nullified Sisera's advantage. (2) The condition of Israel under the crippling bondage of the Canaanites (5:6–8). (3) The evidence of partial unity among the Israelites; six tribes participated in the deliverance, whereas four (Reuben, Gilead [prob. Gad and E Manasseh], Dan, and Asher, 5:15–17) were upbraided for their nonparticipation. The inference is that they ought to have been present, which confirms the existence of the tribal league. (4) The song of Deborah witnesses to a genuine faith in God.

6. Gideon (Jdg. 6:1—8:33). There is greater detail concerning the oppression by the people of MIDIAN and their allies, and GIDEON's liberation of his people, than about any other of the similar episodes narrated in Judges. Possibly the author combined two or more of the popular accounts of this great deliverance, including all that he considered significant. Or the apparent repetitions may be due to the technique of the ancient storyteller, who needed an occasional recapitulation—not unrelated to the natural element of repetition that appears in the parallelism of poetry, and which probably influenced prose composition.

The seasonal invasions of the Midianites and their allies had disastrous effects upon the economy of the land and the morale of the Israelites (Jdg. 6:1–6). In the patriarchal period there was a similar seasonal movement between the Negev and the central hill country that occasionally resulted in friction even though the land was sparsely populated (cf. Gen. 34). The Midianites came into areas that had a settled population, and their annual predatory raids reduced Israel to poverty. The full-scale use of the CAMEL in this passage is the first historically documented employment of this beast in warfare. It struck terror into the hearts of the Israelites. Gideon's action in beating out wheat in a wine press (Jdg. 6:11) shows both his fear and the smallness of his crop. His reply to the angelic visitor (6:13) illustrates the popular explanation of their plight; the Lord had forsaken them. But Gideon seemed unaware of the reason for this rejection (cf. 6:1, 7–10).

Gideon's hesitation to accept the divine commission is paralleled in the case of Moses (Exod. 4:13), Barak (Jdg. 4:8), and Jeremiah (Jer. 1:6; cf. 2 Cor. 3:5, 6). Before he could deliver Israel, work was to be done nearer at hand, for the syncretistic tendencies of the age were illustrated in the shrine of Baal, of which his father JOASH was custodian. Gideon broke down the shrine and also cut down the Asherah, a Canaanite cult-symbol (with undoubted sexual connections) made of wood, probably a formal substitute for a sacred tree. Joash was a man of good sense who saw that if Baal was a real god he could deal personally with this affront.

The seasonal invasion of the Midianites was the occasion of Gideon's charismatic anointing (Jdg. 6:34). Initial support came from his own town (showing the absence of resentment for the destruction of its Baal shrine), his fellow tribesmen of Manasseh, and the tribes of Asher, Zebulun, and Naphtali. Issachar is surprisingly omitted from this list, but its territory must have been affected. The faith of Gideon was strengthened by three signs from the Lord, who graciously accommodated himself to the timidity of his anointed (6:36–40; 7:9–14). From this point on, Gideon's faith did not waver. The first stage in the reduction of his army (7:2–3) followed the provisions of Deut. 20:8; the second stage (Jdg. 7:4–7) probably marked out those who remained on their guard, scooping up the water and lapping from their cupped hands without relaxing vigilance. Against the immense hordes of Midianites (6:5; 7:12), such a reduction of numbers must have appeared incredible, but it emphasized that this was the Lord's act of salvation, not man's.

The audacious plan of attack was implemented with careful attention to detail (Jdg. 7:19–25). The aim was to make as much noise as possible from

The battle between Gideon and the Midianites occurred here, in the Harod Valley. (View SE toward Mount Gilboa.)

all sides, the lights giving the impression of a great host. As the watch had just changed, more men than usual would be moving about in the darkness, thus increasing the confusion. The effect of the clamor upon the camels would be disastrous. A full-scale panic ensued, in which every man's sword was against his neighbor, followed by a desperate flight for the fords of Jordan. Gideon's men hardly seem to have been engaged in this phase, and they suffered few, if any casualties (8:4).

This initial overwhelming success led to the summoning of the tribal contingents, which doubtless included those who had no heart for battle at an earlier phase (Jdg. 7:23–24). An ugly crisis with the Ephraimites, which could have facilitated the Midianite escape, was averted by the diplomacy of Gideon (8:1–3). The refusal of the rulers of Succoth and Penuel to supply their brethren with provisions was an act of treachery motivated by self-interest; they were nearer to the haunts of the Midianites and were afraid of reprisals. They paid dearly for their unbrotherliness when Gideon returned (8:13–17; note the incidental witness to the widespread early use of writing in v. 14), after his successful pursuit of the remnant of the Midianite host that had escaped before the Ephraimites sealed the Jordan fords (7:24). The end of Gideon's campaign came at KARKOR (8:10), well to the E of the Dead Sea, where the Midianites must have felt secure. But Gideon, by forced marches along the caravan routes (8:11), took them by surprise a second time and completely routed them. Then, wisely, he returned home, exacting a personal revenge upon the two captured kings for their slaughter of his brothers (8:18–21).

Such was the sense of gratitude of the Israelites that they offered Gideon the kingship (Jdg. 8:22). Some scholars believe that his refusal was in fact an acceptance, but couched in ambiguous terms, hinting that such an honor would be within the kingly rule of the Lord. Support for this is seen in the fact that Gideon subsequently exercised the functions of a king, and it was assumed that his sons would rule after his death (9:2; cf. 8:35). However, v. 29 does not indicate any great accession of power, and in any case his influence would be limited to a small area and probably was not significantly greater than that of the other judges. His construction of an EPHOD, for oracular purposes, probably was innocent enough in its intention, but its very preciousness (8:26–27) meant that it became itself an object of worship, indicating that IDOLATRY was not far removed from the average Israelite at that time. Gideon's indulgence (8:31) involved his family in near extinction subsequently (9:1–5), and his example in his declining years made a sad contrast to his earlier devoted leadership.

7. Abimelech (Jdg. 9:1–56). Gideon's son ABIMELECH was not one of Israel's judges. His mother lived in SHECHEM, a city that retained many Canaanite characteristics; possibly it was incorporated into Israel by treaty. Since Abimelech's mother was a concubine, his own citizenship was attached to Shechem rather than to his father's family in OPHRAH. Abimelech himself appears as a vindictive and utterly unscrupulous individual, and the story witnesses to the tensions that existed between the Israelites and the original inhabitants of the land. His three-year rule in Shechem and its district was hardly an antecedent of the monarchy in Israel; rather it was a reversal to the localized rule of the king of a Canaanite city-state.

Abimelech's first act was to arrange the massacre of the legitimate sons of Gideon, securing the help of the citizens of Shechem by appealing to their self interest. The scheme was financed by funds from the heathen sanctuary (Jdg. 9:4). The one survivor, JOTHAM, fled after delivering his famous fable (vv. 7–21) from the top of Mount GERIZIM. The point of the fable was that the Shechemites had made the wrong choice of a king: the useless bramble created a fire hazard and was incapable of giving shade. The doom of the Shechemites already was sealed by their treacherous ingratitude to the house of Gideon.

The remainder of the chapter documents the fulfillment of this prophecy. The Shechemites soon tired of their new loyalty, and when open rebellion was advocated, Abimelech acted ruthlessly to crush it. The "tower of Shechem" (Jdg. 9:46), unlike that at THEBEZ (v. 50) and most ancient cities, was apparently outside the city. It was reduced by a stratagem that Abimelech sought to reapply at Thebez, with disastrous results. His request to his armor-bearer (v. 54) reflects the sense of dishonor at dying at the hands of a woman. His reputation, however, was not saved (2 Sam. 11:21). No reason is given for the campaign against Thebez, but the attitude of rebellion against Abimelech probably was widespread.

8. Tola and Jair (Jdg. 10:1–5). The lack of detail in this section means that the minor judges, in contrast to the rest, do not appear as dynamic characters. In the case of JAIR, the reference to his numerous sons, donkeys, and towns (v. 4) is an indication of prestige and prosperity.

9. Jephthah (Jdg. 10:6—12:7). An editorial section (10:6–16; cf. 2:6—3:6) introduces the oppressions of the Ammonites and the Philistines, which probably were contemporary (10:7). It outlines again the main characteristic of the period: Israel's apostasy, with the people oblivious to the Lord's past deliverances; Israel's weakness under the pressure of her neighbors; Israel's repentance and reformation; and the renewal of the Lord's mercy. The Ammonite raids had extended beyond the Jordan to include Judah, Benjamin, and Ephraim (v. 9), although the attack that brought JEPHTHAH to leadership apparently was confined to GILEAD. The Gileadites, in despair, turned to Jephthah, the leader of a band of brigands (10:17—11:1). Jephthah was the son of a prostitute, but unlike Abimelech, his lineage attached to his father's family, and thus his expulsion was clearly illegal. Nevertheless, he was opportunist enough to pocket his pride when he was offered the leadership of his people.

Judges 11:12–28 is surely one of the earliest diplomatic wrangles in recorded history. Jephthah met the Ammonite claim by reminding them of Israel's care not to offend Edom and Moab during the wilderness journeyings. SIHON, the Amorite king, had attacked Israel and consequently lost his kingdom. The disputed territory, therefore, had been Amorite, not Ammonite, and in any case, any Ammonite claim had lapsed with the passage of time (v. 26). As in many subsequent diplomatic exchanges, the Ammonites remained unconvinced. Two factual errors may be noted in Jephthah's message: CHEMOSH (v. 24) was the god of the Moabites, not the Ammonites; the 300 years (v. 26) can hardly be taken literally. Possibly it was unwise to expect absolute accuracy in the statement of a robber chief.

Jephthah's sweeping victory, under the influence of the Spirit of the Lord, is dealt with briefly (Jdg. 11:32–33). The main interest of the historian concerns Jephthah's rash vow and its tragic fulfillment. The vow, which was intended to secure the Lord's favor, was both unnecessary and undesirable. The practice of child sacrifice in the ancient world was usually reserved, as here, for an emergency (cf. 2 Ki. 3:27). It was alien to true Israelite worship and was not widely practiced until the latter period of the monarchy (2 Ki. 16:3; 21:6). Jephthah evidently intended a human sacrifice (Jdg. 11:31), but the emergence of his only daughter at his victorious return (v. 34) was unanticipated. The text will not allow any other interpretation than that Jephthah literally fulfilled this vow. There is something magnificent, if pathetic, about the acquiescence of Jephthah's daughter in her fate (vv. 36–40).

Although on an earlier occasion (Jdg. 8:1–2) Gideon had pacified the jealous Ephraimites with conciliatory words, Jephthah was not a man of peace, and he resented the nonintervention of the Ephraimites in Gilead's crisis. Recalling his recently dispersed army, he smote the Ephraimites and seized the fords of Jordan to prevent their escape. The Ephraimites apparently did not use the sound *sh* in their dialect. Any word with this sound included would have revealed their identity, and it was the word SHIBBOLETH (lit., "ear of corn") that was employed. This word has become proverbial as a catchword for certain groups.

10. Ibzan, Elon, and Abdon (Jdg. 12:8–15). The BETHLEHEM where IBZAN was from (v. 8) was not the well-known city of Judah, but a small town about 10 mi. N of MEGIDDO, within the tribal territory of Zebulun. The "hill country of the Amalekites" (v. 15) may indicate an Amalekite enclave, although this is inconsistent with the geographic and biblical evidence (Exod. 17:8–13; Deut. 25:17–19; 1 Sam. 15:2–3); or it may have some connection with the raids of Jdg. 3:13; 6:3; 7:12; 10:12.

11. Samson (Jdg. 13:1–16:31). The Philistine menace (13:1) was the greatest threat to Israel's existence during the period of the judges and the early monarchy. This was, in measure, due to the nature of Philistine control: a Philistine overlordship was superimposed upon an alien population, backed up by a military efficiency unknown in Israel. The men of Judah, who did not find this kind of rule particularly onerous, resented the activities of SAMSON (15:11). This apathetic acceptance of the situation was dangerous, and the value of Samson's exploits was in bringing the conflict out into the open. Samson waged a one-man war on the Philistines, who had penetrated into the territory of Dan and Judah. Later, during the time of Samuel and Saul, Israel would be engaged in a life-and-death struggle with the Philistines, whose power finally was broken by David (2 Sam. 5:17–25).

Samson's birth was announced by the angel of the Lord (Jdg. 13:2–20; cf. Gen. 18:10; Lk. 1:13), and special instructions were given concerning both mother and child. Two forms of the NAZIRITE vow are found in the OT. The regular vow was for a limited period and contained three stipulations: (1) abstinence from all products of the vine; (2) the hair was to be left unshorn; (3) all contact with the dead was to be avoided (Num. 6:1–21). A second type was a life vow taken by the parents of the one consecrated. Of the three stipulations, only the second was taken seriously by Samson, and his actual consecration to the Lord was nominal. The concern of the parents for the upbringing of their child was most laudable (Jdg. 13:12). They were unaware of the identity of their divine visitor until his ascent in the sacrificial flame, after which MANOAH's wife showed a great deal more common sense than her husband (vv. 22–23). It was widely believed that such an encounter was inevitably fatal (cf. Gen. 32:30; Exod. 33:20; Jdg. 6:22–23).

There is an interconnection between all the events recorded in Jdg. 14:1–15:20, which made Samson the principal public enemy of the Philistines. TIMNAH was 4 mi. SW of ZORAH, on the opposite side of the fruitful Valley of SOREK. The short distance between the two places may explain the ambiguity in the movements recorded in ch. 14; for example, the return journey of Samson's parents (cf. vv. 5, 9) is not noted. The editor of Judges accounts for the apostasy of the period by the prevalence of mixed marriages (3:6; cf. Exod. 34:16; Deut. 7:3); so it is more revealing when one of Israel's judges was involved in at least two relationships with foreign women (Jdg. 14:1–2; 16:1).

When Samson chose to marry a Philistine woman, his parents grieved (Jdg. 14:3)—an understandable reaction, particularly in the light of the supernatural nature of his birth, although they were unaware of the divine overruling (14:4). The marriage normally was consummated at the end of the wedding feast, but the enraged Samson left precipitately when the solution of his riddle was revealed (14:10–18). Such an event brought great shame upon the bride's family, so she was immediately given in marriage to the "best man." Samson evidently had made it clear that he knew who was responsible for the revealing of his secret (14:18b; 15:2). Several acts of revenge followed in quick succession. First, Samson destroyed the standing crops of the Philistines (15:3–5), a devastating blow in an agricultural community (cf. 2 Sam. 14:29–33). The Philistines, guessing correctly the identity of the incendiary, took a summary judgment upon the family responsible (15:6). Finally, Samson slaughtered an unspecified number of Philistines (15:7–8).

A fourth act of revenge was thwarted by Samson's incredible strength. A large force of Philistines sought to capture Samson in his hideout at the "rock of Etam," which has been tentatively identified about 2.5 mi. ESE of Zorah (see Etam #4). The apathetic acceptance of Philistine rule is shown by the concern of 3,000 men of Judah not to alienate their overlords. Even after Samson's exploit, they made no effort to secure their freedom. It is equally obvious that the Philistines did not regard the actions of Samson as representative of Israel generally. The "fresh jawbone of a donkey" (Jdg. 15:15) would be a formidable weapon in the hands of a determined man. The name of the place, Lehi ("jawbone," 15:14; also Ramath Lehi, "the hill of the jawbone," v. 17), was given as a result of this episode. Another etiological feature is the name En Hakkore ("the well, or spring, of him who called," v. 19; 1 Ki. 19:4–8 provides a parallel to God's gracious care for his overwrought servant). Some have thought that Jdg. 15:20, which records the length of Samson's judgeship, marked the end of an earlier version of the book of Judges.

Gaza was the southernmost of the five Philistine cities, and here Samson (Jdg. 16:1–3), a man of unbridled passions, sought the company of a prostitute. A plot to seize him when morning broke was foiled by Samson's incredible feat of uprooting gates, posts, and securing-bar. City gates were strong, for this was an obvious danger point in time of siege, but Samson transported this heavy load to the top of a prominent hill on the way to Hebron, 38 mi. distant. Small wonder that the Philistines were subsequently unwilling to approach him until they were sure he was rendered helpless.

Samson's passions were to prove his undoing (Jdg. 16:4–31). The movements of this chapter involve at least six visits to Delilah and indicate more than a passing infatuation. The large bribe that was offered (v. 5), as well as Delilah's use of the term "the Philistines" (vv. 9, 12, 14, 20), may indicate that she was an Israelite, although the bribe would be commensurate with the risk involved. Samson's playfulness in suggesting various explanations of his strength was countered by the heartless persistence of Delilah. In their second attempt (vv. 10–12), Delilah and the Philistines overlooked, or were unaware of, the earlier failure of this method (15:13–14). The third attempt, involving the weaving of Samson's hair, came perilously close to the truth.

Eventually, Delilah's desire for gain, perhaps aided by her unwillingness to concede defeat, wore down Samson's resistance. His capitulation led swiftly to his capture, degradation, and imprisonment. Samson's unshorn hair was, in one sense, only the symbol of his Nazirite consecration, but the surrender of this led to the withdrawal of the Lord's power. The sentence, "But he did not know that the Lord had left him" (Jdg. 16:20), is surely one of the saddest in the OT. Yet one final triumph was in store. It appears incredible that the Philistines, knowing the secret of Samson's strength, should have allowed his hair to grow again. Probably they thought they had nothing to fear from this blind shambles of a man who could be led about by a lad (v. 26).

Dagon (Jdg. 16:23) was an Amorite grain or vegetation god, and his worship by the Philistines shows their propensity to accept the culture and even the religion of the people they dominated. Samson's one act of true devotion is noted in v. 28, and even this contains a grim jest in the reference to "one of my two eyes" (RSV, a literal rendering of the Heb.). The house (v. 26 et al.) was supported by wooden pillars set on stone bases. The whole structure was rendered unstable because of the large number of spectators on the roof, pressing forward to see this Samson who had taken cover between the pillars. Samson's last feat of strength displaced two of the pillars from their bases and the whole building crashed in ruins. More Philistines died in this catastrophe than the total previously killed by Samson in his lifetime (16:30, cf. 14:19, 15:8, 15).

The final estimate of Samson is one of an unrealized potential, because his massive strength was not matched by discipline and genuine devotion.

C. Appendices (Jdg. 17:1—21:25)

1. Danites move to the north (Jdg. 17:1—18:31). The setting of the account of Micah and the Danites is the later period of the judges, when the intertribal organization had decayed and when the Danites, reduced by the Philistine pressure (chs. 13–16) to a small area around Zorah and Eshtaol (18:2), were compelled to migrate northward. Thus the events of the first appendix followed soon after those of the Samson narratives.

The low standards and the religious irregularities of the time are clearly evidenced (Jdg. 17:1–13). Micah's mother may have suspected her son, hence the uttering of a curse in his hearing (17:2). In the ancient world, a curse was considered to have effective power of fulfillment, but it could be countermanded by a blessing. Only part of the restored fortune was used to make an image, although this whole amount had been dedicated (17:3). Micah bypassed the Levitical priesthood by consecrating his own son, but when a true Levite appeared, he was immediately engaged in preference. His genealogy (18:30) confirms that the Levitical priesthood was operative at this period, and the reference in 17:7 must be construed accordingly. He was not of the tribe of Judah, but was a Levite attached to that tribe. However, some disorder is evident, for he had no secure place of service. The idolatrous nature of Micah's shrine is evident by the presence of an EPHOD, TERAPHIM, and a molten image. The teraphim probably were household gods and, like the ephod, were used to ascertain the divine will.

Events are sometimes determined by apparently insignificant details (Jdg. 18:1–31). The chance hearing of a Levite's voice secured a propitious oracle for the mission of the five spies, which seemed to be confirmed by the evidence of their own eyes (v. 7). LAISH, the modern Tell el-Qadi, was a large city in a fertile valley, with an assured water supply. See DAN (PLACE). Its secluded nature, shielded as it was by the LEBANON range and Mount HERMON, had lulled its inhabitants into a false state of security. The spies recognized a situation that offered rich rewards at minimum cost, and so the remnant of the tribe of Dan moved northward (v. 11). The recollection of the earlier oracle led to the theft of all the equipment of Micah's shrine and to the abduction of the Levite, who was willing to sell himself to a higher bidder. Micah's protestations (v. 24) were met with a thinly veiled threat, and being outnumbered by the Danites, Micah retreated. The mission was completed, and the Levite was duly installed in what was to become one of Israel's national shrines during the reign of JEROBOAM I (1 Ki. 12:26–30). The "time of the captivity of the land" (Jdg. 18:30) often is taken to refer to the Assyrian deportation under TIGLATH-PILESER or SARGON in the 8th cent. B.C. But the parallel time reference, "all the time the house of God was in Shiloh" (v. 31), suggests a reference to the Philistine control after the events of 1 Sam. 4.

2. Civil war against the Benjamites (Jdg. 19:1—21:25). The affair of the Levite's concubine and the subsequent war between Israel and Benjamin probably took place in the earlier part of the judges' period. There is no hint of Philistine oppression, and the tribal unity was still evident; the tribal league moved swiftly to deal with the outrage. PHINEHAS (20:28; cf. Josh. 24:33) was still alive, and the central sanctuary appears to be at Bethel, not Shiloh.

This sordid and tragic story began simply enough (Jdg. 19:1–15) with a Levite seeking to win back his estranged concubine. The joy of the father is understandable, since his daughter's return would bring shame to his house. This joy as well as leisureliness, characteristic of the E, are reflected in the prolonged festivities. The Levite and his party cannot have left much before 3 P.M. on the fifth day, when there was no possibility of reaching their destination before nightfall. Jerusalem, 5–6 mi. to the N and still a Jebusite city (cf. 2 Sam. 5:6–9), was avoided because it was non-Israelite—a fact that has added significance in the light of the sequel. GIBEAH and RAMAH were respectively 4 and 6 mi. N of Jerusalem. Sunset made a continuation of the journey impossible, so Gibeah was, of necessity, their stopping place; but they were met with an ominous lack of the traditional Eastern hospitality.

This omission of the Benjamites was made good by a generous sojourner (Jdg. 19:16–30), another detail that highlights the boorish conduct of the men of Gibeah. Faced by an intimidatory, homosexual demand, the Levite's host placed the claims of hospitality above those of family relationship and was willing to sacrifice his own daughter and the Levite's concubine (cf. Gen. 19:1–11). The Levite, confronted with acute personal danger, saved his own skin by thrusting out his concubine to endure a night of shame and terror. His reaction the next morning was no more creditable, for there was no indication of any intent to ascertain the fate of his concubine before setting off. His subsequent action is paralleled in 1 Sam. 11:1–8 and was clearly an urgent and solemn challenge to the tribes. There may have been a sacramental significance in that the nation was involved in the life that had been taken, or a magical connection invoking a curse of the blood of the life taken upon those who failed to

Aerial view looking NE across the ancient city of Laish, renamed Dan by the Danites after they migrated N to this area.

respond. The inference is that the tribe of Benjamin was included in this summons.

The reaction of the eleven tribes was immediate (Jdg. 20:1–11,) but the Benjamites stood by Gibeah, rejecting the subsequent appeal of the allied tribes (vv. 12–13). The allies assembled at Mizpah, a few miles nearer to Gibeah than the central sanctuary of Bethel. Careful plans were laid for an extended campaign, and Judah, whose tribal portion was similar to that of Benjamin, was chosen to lead the attack against a tribe renowned for the prowess of its fighting men (cf. Gen. 49:27; 1 Chr. 8:40; 12:2). The minor discrepancies in the numbers of the Benjamites (Jdg. 20:15, 35, 46–47) may be due to the fact that no casualties are recorded for the first two days. The 700 men of Gibeah (v. 15) probably are to be identified with the select group who were expert with the sling, a formidable weapon that could project a stone weighing a pound at great speed. In contested territory, these men wrought havoc on two successive days, causing the Israelites to seek the Lord's help with a greater sense of urgency.

A certain recapitulation, characteristic of the storyteller anxious not to omit any details, makes it difficult to understand the events of the third day (Jdg. 20:29–48). Further complication is the proximity of Gibeah, Gibeon, and Gebah, which frequently are confused. But the general movement is clear. A small ambush was set W of Gebah, which was NE of Gibeah (v. 33). The main attack came from the same direction as previously, that is, the NW, toward Gibeon (which should be read in v. 31, since two roads are indicated: the Gibeah-Bethel and the Gibeah-Gibeon highways). The main army, feigning flight, drew the Benjamites away from Gibeah (v. 32), which was then taken and burned by the force in ambush (v. 37). The smoke of the doomed city was the signal to the Israelite main force to turn (v. 38), and the Benjamites, fleeing eastward, probably between Gebah and Gibeah, were trapped in a pincers movement (v. 42) and decimated. The survivors turned northwards to the rock of Rimmon (v. 47), and the victorious Israelites put all that remained of Benjamin to the ban, which involved a dedication of total destruction to the Lord in fulfillment of a vow.

The attitude of the allied tribes, so roughly handled by Benjamin in the early stages of the battle, reflects creditably upon them (Jdg. 21:1–35). There was no sense of exultation, but rather, deep sorrow at the prospect of the elimination of one tribe, which reveals their sense of unity. It is evident that, in the heat of the crisis, ill-considered and hasty vows had been made. The Israelites extricated themselves from their dilemma by a somewhat casuistic weighing of one vow against another, and by their condoning of mass abduction. Their motives were good, but their methods were questionable and the editor regarded the proceedings as irregular (v. 25). The nonparticipation of the men from JABESH GILEAD (v. 9) may be due to their closer kinship with Benjamin; both were descendants of RACHEL. Subsequently there was an understandably close link between the Benjamites and Jabesh Gilead (cf. 1 Sam. 11:1–11; 31:11–13). The detailed description of Shiloh (Jdg. 21:19) shows that it had not yet become prominent as the central sanctuary; it may have been a Canaanite enclave (v. 12), since clearly it had no representative in the discussion of vv. 19–22. The "annual festival of the LORD" (v. 19) was possibly a Canaanized version of the Feast of Tabernacles.

(Important commentaries include G. F. Moore, *A Critical and Exegetical Commentary on Judges* [1895]; C. F. Burney, *The Book of Judges*, 2nd ed. [1930]; A. E. Cundall and L. Morris, *Judges and Ruth*, TOTC [1967]; R. G. Boling, *Judges*, AB 6A [1975]; J. A. Soggin, *Judges: A Commentary*, OTL [1981]; B. Lindars, *Judges 1–5: A New Translation and Commentary*, ed. A. D. H. Mayes [1995]; D. I. Block, *Judges, Ruth*, NAC [1999]; J. G. Harris, *Joshua, Judges, Ruth* [2000]; T. Schneider, *Judges* [2000]; V. H. Matthews, *Judges and Ruth* [2004]; D. M. Gunn, *Judges* [2005].

(See also J. Garstang, *The Foundations of Bible History: Joshua-Judges* [1931]; C. A. Simpson, *Composition of the Book of Judges* [1957]; R. H. O'Connell, *The Rhetoric of the Book of Judges* [1996]; Y. Amit, *The Book of Judges: The Art of Editing* [1999]; E. Assis, *Self-interest or Communal Interest: An Ideology of Leadership in the Gideon, Abimelech, and Jephthah Narratives (Judg. 6–12)* [2005]; G. Wong, *Compositional Strategy of the Book of Judges* [2006]; and the bibliography compiled by W. E. Watson, *Judges* [2001].)

A. E. CUNDALL

judges, period of. The time from the death of JOSHUA to the accession of SAUL as king. Apart from the evidence of ARCHAEOLOGY, the chief sources of information are the book of Judges and 1 Sam. 1–8. See JUDGES, BOOK OF; SAMUEL, BOOKS OF. It is evident that this is not a homogeneous account, although a unity of outlook can be discerned. It is likely that the Israelites entered the Promised Land c. 1230 B.C., though an earlier date in the 15th cent. cannot be ruled out. See CHRONOLOGY (OT). Making allowance for the latter years of Joshua and the elders who outlived him (Josh. 24:31; Jdg. 2:7), an approximate date for the commencement of the period of the judges may be set at 1200 B.C. There is considerable uncertainty concerning the length of Saul's reign, but a tentative date of 1020 may be nominated for his accession. The period of the judges, therefore, was c. 1200–1020, that is, approximately 180 years.

I. Internal chronology. The conclusion reached in the previous paragraph raises the problem of relating the chronological data supplied in Judges to a period of under two centuries. The following table provides the relevant facts:

Oppression of Cushan-Rishathaim	8 years
Period of rest following Othniel's deliverance	40 years
Moabite oppression	18 years
Period of rest following Ehud's deliverance	80 years
Canaanite oppression	20 years
Period of rest following Deborah's deliverance	40 years
Midianite oppression	7 years
Period of rest following Gideon's deliverance	40 years
Abimelech	3 years
Tola	23 years
Jair	22 years
Ammonite oppression	18 years
Jephthah	6 years
Ibzan	7 years
Elon	10 years
Abdon	8 years
Philistine oppression	40 years
Samson	20 years

To these 410 years there must also be added approximately twenty years for SAMUEL, making a total of 430 years. This figure could be reduced, since SAMSON's judgeship was probably within the period of PHILISTINE oppression, and the oppressions by AMMON and the Philistines were, in part, contemporaneous (Jdg. 10:7). No separate allowance has been made for the forty years of ELI's judgeship (1 Sam. 4:18). Among attempts to reduce the overall total are the exclusion of the years of foreign domination, or the exclusion of the minor judges and of the usurper ABIMELECH. All such attempts are conjectural, and a simpler explanation is that the chronology is relative rather than absolute.

An examination of the territories involved shows that only a small area was affected by each invasion. Sometimes the struggle against an aggressor was confined to one or two tribes, and only in the case of the Canaanite attack (Jdg. 4:5) and the later phase of the Philistine aggression (1 Sam. 4:7) was a majority of the tribes involved. It is likely, therefore, that the periods of foreign oppression and of the individual judges overlapped. This allows serious consideration of the chronological data within the book of Judges, but care is required in interpreting the figures. The recurrence of the figure forty and its multiples suggests that it may be a round figure to indicate a generation.

II. The structure of Israel. Many have thought that the structure of Israel during the period was an AMPHICTYONY, a form that had its parallels in Greece and elsewhere in the Mediterranean region (although recent scholars have found the analogy inadequate). The number of the tribes, the religious nature of the bond that united them, and the centralization of their religious and administrative organization at a sanctuary are features of this pattern and are consistent with Israel's traditions. The nation's structure originated with the COVENANT event at SINAI and is witnessed to in the wilderness period by the centrality in the twelve-tribe arrangement of the Tent of Meeting and the TABERNACLE; by the fact that the region where the Israelites spent the greater part of the period was named KADESH BARNEA (the Heb. word *qādēš* H7729 meaning "holy" or "sanctuary"); and by the fact that after the settlement the central sanctuary was to continue as the focal place of the national worship (Deut. 12:3-7, 16:1-2), where difficult cases were to be tried (17:8-13).

The events of Josh. 22:9-34, which occurred soon after the conquest, have been regarded as proof of the existence of the amphictyony, for it shows the nine and one half tribes W of the Jordan acting decisively against what was believed to be the setting up of a rival altar and sanctuary by the Transjordanian tribes. This was construed as an act of rebellion against Yahweh (22:12, 16-20). Following the settlement, the amphictyonic shrine was located successively at SHECHEM near Mount EBAL (Josh. 8:30-35); SHILOH (Josh. 18:1; 22:12); BETHEL (Jdg. 20:18, 26-28; 21:2); and again at Shiloh (Jdg. 18:31; 1 Sam. 1:3, 9; et al.). Shiloh was destroyed by the Philistines, almost certainly after the events of 1 Sam. 4. During the period of Philistine supremacy, it was not possible to rebuild the central sanctuary, and some of the functions of the amphictyony in this turbulent period appear to have attached themselves to Samuel (cf. 1 Sam. 7:15-17; 9:13; 13:8-14; 16:1). Later on, NOB (1 Sam. 21:1; 22:11, 19) and GIBEON (1 Ki. 3:4; cf. 1 Chr. 16:39; 21:29; 2 Chr. 1:3, 6, 13) appear prominently.

III. Historical background. Toward the end of the 13th cent. B.C., Egyptian influence in Canaan, apart from a brief foray by MERNEPTAH (c. 1220), was nominal. It continued so for the major part of the judges' period, except during the reign of the vigorous RAMSES III (c. 1176-1144). This allowed Israel a considerable degree of freedom to consolidate her position. The kingdoms of EDOM and MOAB were established about fifty years before the entry of Israel into Canaan, this latter event coinciding roughly with the settlement of AMMON. Moab, and Ammon in particular, with the predatory nomads from the desert (the people of the E, Jdg. 6:3 et al.), frequently sought to increase their territory at the expense of Israel. The Israelite failure to complete the conquest, particularly in ESDRAELON, led to a resurgence of Canaanite power that temporarily threatened Israel's independence (chs. 4-5).

The major threat came from the PHILISTINES, a people of AEGEAN stock who settled in large numbers on the eastern littoral of the Mediterranean during the first decades of the 12th cent. B.C., leaving a wake of destruction from UGARIT in the N to the Egyptian border. See SEA PEOPLES. Egypt, hard pressed to keep them at bay, allowed them to settle in their pentapolis (Gaza, Gath, Ashkelon, Ashdod, and Ekron). The decline of Egyptian power encouraged them to extend their territory at the expense of Israel; initially this was confined to the tribes of Dan and Judah (Jdg. 13–16), the former being completely displaced (ch. 18). By the time of Eli, the Philistine threat had assumed the proportions of a major national crisis.

Courtyard of a reconstructed Philistine house at the harbor city of Tel Qasile. The Philistine presence threatened the Israelites throughout the period of the judges.

IV. Israel's judges. The main feature of this period was the emergence of individuals who delivered their fellow countrymen from these oppressors. The rendering "judge" (for the ptc. of the Heb. verb *šāpaṭ* H9149, "decide, administer justice, rule") suggests a preoccupation with legal affairs and is thus misleading, for besides judicial functions they exercised a saving, liberating activity that was conceived to be the result of a direct endowment from Yahweh. Many prefer to describe this company as "charismatic" individuals, that is, they were the recipients of the divine grace. Othniel, Ehud, Shamgar, Deborah, Gideon, Jephthah, and Samson are rightly accounted judges because of their spectacular exploits against Israel's oppressors. Some of these appear to have ruled subsequently over the people almost like local kings.

The anointing of the Spirit was also revealed in the display of exceptional wisdom (as in the case of Solomon, 1 Ki. 3:4–15). This may have been the reason why the so-called minor, or pacific, judges—Tola, Jair, Ibzan, Elon, and Abdon—were regarded as judges, although the brevity of the records may account for the absence of any warlike exploits. Indeed there is a hint of unrecorded exploits in the case of Tola, who "rose to save Israel" (Jdg. 10:1). Deborah herself judged Israel before leading Israel against the Canaanites (4:4). The high priest would also be regarded as a judge (cf. 1 Sam. 4:18), as the central sanctuary was, traditionally, the place of arbitration. High priest, wise man, and warrior—from these three classes came Israel's judges. Their conduct frequently fell far below that of the great characters of the OT period, but they were people of faith (cf. Heb. 11:32–33) who fulfilled a vital role in a time of crisis.

V. The importance of the period

A. Division and disunity in Israel. The ideal picture of the twelve tribes of Israel, each settled in its own tribal portion, with an amphictyonic shrine that acted as the focal point of all aspects of the national life, was hardly ever realized. Political and geographic conditions combined to destroy effective unity. This was due largely to the failure to complete the conquest, particularly in such strategic areas as the ESDRAELON Valley (Jdg. 1:27–28), GEZER, the AIJALON Valley, JERUSALEM (1:21, 29, 35), and the northern coastal plain (1:31). Israelite control was limited to three separate areas—Judah, the central highlands, and a portion of Galilee. Only Ephraim appears to have completed the occupation of its designated area, which accounts for its preeminence during the period (8:1–3; 12:1). The remainder of the tribes were hard pressed to maintain their positions and often were involved in conflict with neighboring countries. In the case of Dan, the pressure was so great that the survivors had to migrate northward to win new territory (1:34; ch. 18). The tribe of Judah, effectively isolated for the major part of the period, never again achieved a full unity with the northern tribes. Even during the reigns of David and Solomon, the division between N and S was pronounced (2 Sam. 19:11, 41–43; 20:1–2, et al.).

APPROXIMATE CHRONOLOGY OF THE JUDGES' PERIOD

(Where relevant, Scripture references and the area of Israel involved in each incident are noted. All dates are B.C.)

Date	Event
1230	Israelite conquest of Canaan
1220	Philistine settlement commences
1205	The incident of the Levite's concubine and its aftermath (Jdg. 19:1—21:25)
1200	Commencement of the judges' period with the death of the elders who outlived Joshua (2:7)
1190	Othniel's defeat of Chushan-Rishathaim of Mesopotamia (3:7–11 South)
1170	Ehud's victory over the Moabites (3:12–30 Southeast)
1150	Shamgar's exploit against the Philistines (3:31 Southwest)
1125	Deborah and Barak triumph over Jabin and Sisera of Canaan (4:1—5:31 Central and North)
1110	Gideon defeats the Midianites and Amalekites (6:1—8:35 Central, North, and East)
1085	Abimelech the usurper becomes king over the Shechem District (9:1–56 Central)
1070	Jephthah defeats the Ammonites (10:9—12:7 South, Central, and East)
1070	Samson's exploits against the Philistines (13:1—16:31 Southwest)
1060	The Danite migration to Laish (18:1–31)
1050	The Philistine's twice defeat Israel and capture the ark. The death of Eli and the destruction of Shiloh (1 Sam. 4:1–22; Ps. 78:59–64; Jer. 7:14 South, West, and Central)
1040	Samuel becomes judge over Israel
1020	Saul anointed king over Israel (1 Sam. 10:1, 24; 11:15)

B. The rise of the monarchy. The breakdown in the amphictyonic structure is evident from the small number of tribes involved in each of the successive crises. Frequently a tribe was cast back on its own resources, and the maximum number of the tribes found cooperating at any one point is six (Jdg. 5:14–15, 18). Leadership became an acute problem; note the desperate expedient of the elders of Gilead in electing the brigand Jephthah to be their ruler (11:4–11). This situation led to the rise of the monarchy. Inevitably, the Israelites compared their own organization with that of the surrounding nations, whose kings appeared to organize their subjects into effective military units. This led to a desire for an Israelite king, and Gideon, following his success against the Midianites, was offered the kingly office (8:22). The events of ch. 9 also show the inclination toward the monarchy. However, it was not until the Philistine crisis threatened the very existence of Israel, coupled with the renewed Ammonite threat (1 Sam. 11; 12:12), that the traditional reluctance to replace amphictyonic government by a monarchy was overcome (8:4–22; 12:13).

C. Religious and moral decline. Canaanite religion was a polytheistic nature cult in which the observable powers of nature were personalized and worshiped. See CANAAN IX. This religion, as revealed in its cultus and mythology, was linked with the recurring seasons and was designed to promote fertility in agriculture, livestock, and human beings. Whereas it was not totally devoid of praiseworthy features, the moral level was relatively low; cultic prostitution of both sexes was a prominent feature. Human sacrifice was also practiced, but not as frequently as is commonly supposed.

Into this situation came Israel, with a religious faith that was expressed in forms superficially resembling Canaanite customs, but on an entirely different basis. Instead of a gross polytheism, there was a belief in Yahweh, whose sovereignty in nature and history was such that other gods paled into insignificance. It was accompanied by a highly moral approach to the whole of life, the result of a unique COVENANT relationship with Yahweh, following his mighty deeds in delivering them from Egypt. The final victory of Yahwism over the Canaanite religion has transformed history, but in the initial phases of the conflict was a pronounced religious and moral decline in Israel for the following reasons:

(1) Because of the failure to complete the conquest, Israel was surrounded by the Canaanite religion, which, by nature of its appeal to man's sensual nature, had a fatal fascination. Moreover, there would be a temptation to defer to the nature gods of the land, who were conceived to be responsible for its fertility because they controlled the rain and the springs. The problem of the relationship between Yahweh and the Canaanite gods would become acute as the number of mixed marriages multiplied. Syncretism was inevitable in such a situation, with the gods of one nation being absorbed into the pantheon of the other, a process in which the functions and even the names of the deities became confused. The prophets attacked this Canaanization of Yahweh worship (Hos. 2; Jer. 2; et al.), but not until the EXILE did the nation, as a whole, break free from this influence.

(2) Linked closely with this was the ineffective leadership exercised by the Israelite amphictyony. A strong central authority could have averted major religious deviations; its absence made possible a gradual decline from Mosaic standards. The later editor accounted for this moral decline by the absence of the firm centralized authority exercised by the king (Jdg. 17:6; 18:1; 19:1; 21:25).

(3) There was also a decline in the standard of individual leadership following the death of Joshua (Josh. 24:31; Jdg. 2:7). The stories of Deborah and Barak, Gideon, Jephthah, and Samson make thrilling reading, but their blemishes of character are for the most part sadly apparent. Not until Samuel arose, late in the period, was the leadership comparable to that of Moses and Joshua.

(4) Admittedly, the standards of the average Israelite usually fell below that of their leaders. This is hardly surprising when the background of bondage in Egypt and the fact that they were a "mixed multitude" (Exod. 12:38 KJV) are considered. The frequent murmuring and lapses of faith in the wilderness were ominous portents of future events. Even after two generations had witnessed Yahweh's power to deliver and provide, polytheism was still widely diffused (Josh. 24:15).

The moral and religious decline is carefully noted by the biblical historian. It appears (a) in the editorial comments of Jdg. 2:12, 17, 19; 3:6, 7; et al.; (b) in the lament of 17:6; 21:25; (c) in the clear evidence of syncretism in the Gideon narratives (6:25, 32; 8:27); (d) in Jephthah's tacit recognition of Chemosh as the god of the Ammonites and his sacrifice of his daughter (11:24, 30–31); (e) in Micah's construction of a graven image and a molten image, an ephod, and teraphim (ch. 17); (f) in the abysmally low standards shown in chs. 19–21; (g) in Eli's depraved sons, Hophni and Phinehas (1 Sam. 2:12–17, 22), and in the conduct of even Samuel's sons, Joel and Abijah (8:1–4).

It is apparent that the historian regards this period as the "Dark Age" of Israel's history, but the picture must not be overdrawn. Judges 19–21 also reveals a national conscience; and a sense of intertribal unity and the revival of Yahwism in the time of Samuel and the early monarchy show that there were those loyal to the old traditions. The book of RUTH provides another counterbalance to the conditions portrayed in Judges. (Cf. R. K. Harrison, *A History of Old Testament Times* [1957], 121–40; M. Noth, *The History of Israel*, 2nd ed. [1960], 141–68; W. F. Albright, *Archaeology of Palestine* [1960], 87–120; J. Bright, *A History of Israel*, 4th ed. [2000], 162–82.) See also ISRAEL, HISTORY OF; JUDGES, BOOK OF. A. E. CUNDALL

judgment. This English term and its cognate verb *to judge* have a variety of meanings. In logic, for example, *to judge* is no more than to establish a mental relation between two or more terms, and a *judgment* is simply a proposition that affirms or denies a connection between concepts. In psychology the noun is but another name for perspicacity or sagacity, a quality ascribed to one who has the gift of discernment and a capacity for sound appraisal (cf. Ps. 119:66; Phil. 1:9). In the OT, the usual word rendered "judgment" (*mišpāṭ* H5477, generally in the pl.) is sometimes used to designate the TORAH, "instruction, law," that is, the sum of God's testimonies and ORDINANCES (Deut. 4:1; Neh. 1–7; Ps. 119). The central context of the term is in jurisprudence, where *to judge* means "to test or try," and where a *judgment* is a "judicial decision." This is the context—the context of justice—in which the words are chiefly employed in the Bible.

Back of this, however, and providing the ultimate context of the words, is, on the one hand, the RIGHTEOUSNESS of God (a blend of justice and love), and, on the other, the moral and spiritual posture and behavior of people and societies residing in a fallen world. In this ethico-judicial context, the framework of judging and judgment is the divinely established moral order; the central concepts are those of good and evil, right and wrong; and the operative principle is, "whatsoever a man soweth, that shall he also reap" (Gal. 6:7 KJV). The standard of judgment, however, is not the bare law, but the LAW and the GOSPEL. What ultimately decides a person's eternal destiny is his attitude to the Savior Jesus Christ (Rom. 8:1). By faith in him, men and women are justified and acquitted (Rom. 3:24–26); by disbelief in or rejection of him, they remain under law and are by that law found guilty and condemned (Rom. 2:12; Gal. 2:16).

I. The Judge. In the Scriptures, God and Christ are presented as judges who, in terms of gospel and law, pass a verdict on human beings, their sentiments, and their actions, and who in history and at the end of it either vindicate or condemn them.

A. God. God is the Judge of all the earth (Gen. 18:25; Ps. 96:10; Isa. 33:22; Heb. 12:23; Jas. 4:12; 1 Pet. 1:17). He is fitted to be the Judge because with him is ultimate authority, unlimited knowledge, supreme righteousness, ineffable love, and unrestricted power.

1. Authority. God, as the Scriptures witness (Gen. 1:1), is the creator of heaven and earth (see CREATION). He is thus LORD of the universe. His jurisdiction knows no bounds, and his authority is absolute. Because he is God, he is the very standard of justice and equity; to his judgments all people are obliged to conform, and from his decisions there is no appeal (1 Sam. 2:10; Pss. 9:8; 58:11; 99:4; Prov. 8:15).

2. Knowledge. God is the great discerner. Being the ultimate determiner of good and evil, he perceives with unerring accuracy the distinction between them (Gen. 2:17; 3:4, 22; cf. 1 Ki. 3:9). He is also the great discriminator. With absolute nicety he sifts the elements in human behavior, and like an expert winnower, separates and weighs the good and evil ingredients in the human moral complex (1 Sam. 2:3; Prov. 8:14; 20:8). And he is omniscient (see OMNISCIENCE). Nothing is hid from his sight. Piercing beyond the superficial and external, he sees into the depths and perceives the intents and purposes of the heart (Job 22:13; Jer. 11:20; Rom. 2:16; 1 Cor. 4:5).

3. Righteousness. God is always found on the side of the good. To evil he addresses no word but No, and to every good his word is Yes. Indeed, it may be said that his affirmations and negations are what constitute good and evil, for he is the final determiner. In any case all his judgments are just and righteous (Gen. 18:25; Deut. 32:4; Pss. 33:5; 37:28; 89:14; Prov. 8:8; Jer. 11:20; Ezek. 33:20; Rom. 3:5; 1 Pet. 2:23; Rev. 16:7; 19:2). Because he judges rightly, the oppressed and aggrieved find in him their advocate and support. In this sense his judgments are often saving, and are as such a token of his love (Deut. 32:36; 1 Sam. 24:12, 15; Pss. 10:18; 76:9; 135:14; Isa. 30:18; 2 Thess. 1:5–6).

4. Love. God's justice most clearly coalesces with his LOVE in the act by which he delivered his only begotten Son into condemnation and death in order that through his sacrifice and merits believers may have pardon and life (Rom. 8:32; Gal. 1:4). The OT saint knew that God saved by his righteousness (Ps. 31:1), but in Christ it is made unmistakably clear that mercy and forgiveness flow to sinners through the judicial sentence passed by God on the Son of his love (Jn. 11:51, 52; Rom. 5:8; 1 Cor. 15:3; 1 Thess. 5:10).

5. Power. The POWER of God to execute the sentences he imposes and to protect those whom he vindicates is limitless. Those whom he judges are veritably judged, being gripped or upborne by his OMNIPOTENCE. No one is strong enough to snatch the lambs from his bosom or to withstand the vigor of his wrath and the force of his sentence (1 Sam. 2:10; Pss. 54:1; 110:5–6; Rev. 18:8).

B. Christ. Christ came in the flesh to inaugurate and establish the KINGDOM OF GOD, which had been promised beforehand and is to be consummated at the end of the age. He came, therefore, not in judgment, but in GRACE (Jn. 3:17; 8:15; 12:47). Yet, since in his person, message, and deeds he is the touchstone of destiny for all, his very presence in the world was a judgment. By his redeeming presence, the world was judged (9:39; 12:31); also its prince (16:11) and all who disbelieved (3:18; 5:24). Moreover, although he refused during his earthly ministry to be a judge in mundane matters (Lk. 12:14), he will reappear in glory at the last day to preside at the great and final assize in which all will appear before his JUDGMENT SEAT to receive from him the divine and irrevocable verdict upon their lives (Isa. 11:3–5; Jn. 5:22–30; 8:16; Acts 10:42; 17:31; Rom. 2:16; 1 Cor. 4:5; 2 Cor. 5:10; 2 Tim. 4:1, 8).

C. Others. Although the people of NINEVEH will arise at the judgment and condemn the evil generation that sought a sign from Jesus (Matt. 12:41), and although Christ gives his CHURCH the keys of the kingdom (16:19) and declares that his enthroned disciples will judge the twelve tribes of Israel (19:26), and although PAUL says that the saints will judge the world and angels (1 Cor. 6:2–3), God in Christ will not therefore vacate the judgment seat. Repentant Gentiles will no doubt shame the unbelieving Jews on the Day of the Lord, and the lives and testimonies of the redeemed will be to those who are not in Christ like the accusations of their conscience; but, with the saints concurring in his verdicts, Christ alone will be the Judge.

II. The judgments. Although the great day of judgment is still in the offing, divine judgments have long been upon the earth, and judgment is being passed daily. In the past, it was by the judgment of God that the antediluvian civilization was washed away by the flood (Gen. 6:5–7; see FLOOD, GENESIS), that Israel was sent into EXILE (Jer. 20:4), and that the several nations mentioned in the prophecies of Amos were scourged or destroyed. Chief and most fateful of all such judgments, was, of course, that which brought condemnation and death to all mankind on account of ADAM's trespass (Gal. 5:15–16).

In the present, because God maintains the moral order, his judgments still fall upon individuals and nations. More importantly, just as during his life on earth, so yet today Christ is set for the rise and fall of many, and the judgment that is implicit in his person is even now separating people into two camps. It is by virtue of this fact that believers can in the present, before the final judgment, know and rejoice that for them there is and will be no condemnation (Rom. 8:1, 38).

But a day is coming—which no man knows (Matt. 24:36)—when the Lord will come in majesty, put an end to history, gather before him all those who ever lived, and seal their destiny with a decisive and unalterable verdict of life or death (1 Chr. 16:33; Ps. 96:13; Eccl. 3:17; Joel 2:30–32; Matt. 12:36; 25:31–46; Jn. 12:48; Acts 17:31; Rom. 14:10; 2 Cor. 5:10; 2 Thess. 1:6–7; Heb. 9:27; 10:31; 2 Pet. 3:7; 4:5; Rev. 6:10; 11:18; 14:9; 20:12–15). See DAY OF THE LORD; ESCHATOLOGY.

III. Christian judging. Not only are judges in human courts of law authorized to make judgments in civil and criminal cases, but all people everywhere are permitted and even obliged to assess human claims upon truth, beauty, or goodness, and to appraise the character, conduct, and teaching both of themselves and of their fellows. This is a fortiori true of Christians (Lev. 19:15; Matt. 7:15–19; Lk. 12:57; Jn. 7:24; 1 Cor. 2:15; 1 Thess. 5:21).

But judgment that is uninformed, impulsive, superficial, premature, or biased is strictly forbidden in the Bible. Bigotry and censoriousness are emphatically denounced. Christians are urged, when they judge, to do it in a constructive spirit and in accordance with authentic norms. All other judging is contraband, particularly the sort that preempts Christ's prerogative to determine a person's eternal destiny (Matt. 7:1–2; Lk. 6:37; Rom. 2:1; 14:3–4; 1 Cor. 4:5; Col. 2:16; Jas. 2:4; 4:11).

H. STOB

judgment hall. This term is the doubtful KJV rendering of the Greek noun *praitōrion* G4550 (Jn. 18:28, 33; 19:9; Acts 23:35; the KJV renders at AMMAH Hill" in Matt. 27:27, "Praetorium" in Mk. 15:16; and "imperial guard" in Phil. 1:13). The Greek term is a Latin loanword that contains no reference to judgment. It was originally the tent of the Roman commander or PRAETOR. By extension it came to denote the army headquarters, residence of a provincial governor, palace, barracks (cf. Matt. 27:27; Mk. 15:16; Acts 23:35), and also the PRAETORIAN guard. These would all normally be housed in the same complex of buildings; Phil. 1:13 could refer either to the guard or to the buildings. The Roman GOVERNOR of JUDEA normally resided in the PRAETORIUM at CAESAREA (Acts 23:35), but there was also one in JERUSALEM. It was here that PILATE interrogated Jesus (Jn. 18:28–38; 19:9–11). But it was outside "at a place known as the Stone Pavement" that Pilate sat on "the judge's seat" (Jn. 19:13; see JUDGMENT SEAT) and handed Jesus over to the Jews. Jesus then was brought back into the praetorium for the soldiers to prepare his execution (Matt. 27:27; Mk. 15:16). (See C. Kopp, *The Holy Places of the Gospels* [1963], 354, 366–73.). On SOLOMON's "Hall of Judgment" (1 Ki. 7:7 RSV), see HALL. C. BROWN

judgment seat. The Greek word *bēma* G1037 (aside from Acts 7:5, where it means "step" or "height") usually refers to a "tribunal," "judicial bench," "judgment seat," or "throne," traditionally erected in public, and from which JUDGMENT and other official business was conducted. Herod Agrippa I (see HEROD VII) thus addressed the people of TYRE and SIDON (Acts 12:21). Jesus was brought before PILATE's judgment seat (Matt. 27:19; Jn. 19:13; NIV, "judge's seat"). Jews at CORINTH accused PAUL before the tribunal of the Proconsul GALLIO, who drove them out but ignored the beating of SOSTHENES there (Acts 18:12, 16–17). The remains of a public rostrum—probably the one before which Paul was brought—still stand among the ruins at Corinth (see photo under CORINTHIANS, FIRST). Later Paul was brought before the judgment seat of FESTUS at CAESAREA (25:6, 10, 17). (See O. Broneer, "Corinth: Center of St. Paul's Missionary Work in Greece," *BA* 14 [1951]: 91–92; A. N. Sherwin-White, *Roman Society and Roman Law in the New Testament*, 2nd ed. [1963].)

Ironically the roles will one day be reversed, and Jesus who was unjustly judged by men will sit in righteous judgment over them. "For we must all appear before the judgment seat of Christ, that each one may receive what is due him for the things done while in the body, whether good or bad" (2 Cor. 5:10; cf. Rom. 14:10). This includes even those

Aerial view looking NE into the theater at Caesarea Maritima. Herod Agrippa I met representatives of Tyre and Sidon at this theater to settle his quarrels with them.

who are reconciled. While they have the righteousness of Christ, their work will be tested (2 Cor. 5:18–21; cf. 1 Cor. 3:13–15). See ESCHATOLOGY.

C. BROWN

Judith joo´dith (יְהוּדִית H3377, fem. of יְהוּדִי H3374, "of Judah, Judean, Jewish"; Ιουδιθ). Daughter of Beeri the HITTITE and one of the wives of ESAU (Gen. 26:34). Since the name is Semitic, she and her family are not thought of as belonging to the Indo-European Hittites from ANATOLIA, but rather as Canaanites (cf. 36:2).

(2) The heroine of the book of Judith in the OT APOCRYPHA. She killed HOLOFERNES, the general of NEBUCHADNEZZAR, and thus saved Jerusalem and her countrymen (Jdt. 8:1 et al). See JUDITH, BOOK OF.

Judith, Book of. One of the books of the APOCRYPHA, bearing the name of its principal character.

I. Text and versions. Most scholars agree that the original text of Judith was written in Hebrew. Evidence for this is found in the many Hebraisms in language and ideas and from apparent errors in translation (see the material given by T. W. Davies in *ISBE* [1929], 3:1780). JEROME states that the Jews included Judith among their Apocrypha, but ORIGEN claims that the Jews did not use the book at all (*Letter to Africanus* 13). The older rabbinical literature fails to make any reference to Judith. In spite of these negative arguments, the evidence for a Hebrew original seems conclusive. The story exists in several forms in Hebrew from later sources. An ostracon found in Cairo in 1946 and dated to the 3rd cent. A.D. contains Jdt. 15:1–7.

Which of the versions most closely resembles the original is a matter of dispute. The Greek text appears in several recensions: (1) the most reliable one is represented in the major uncials—Alexandrinus, Vaticanus, and Sinaiticus—as well as most late minuscules; (2) the Antiochene or Lucianic recension, found in MSS 19 and 108; (3) an edition attested in MS 58 and a few other minuscules. The Old Latin and two Syriac versions appear to be based on the recension represented by MS 58.

Jerome asserts that he included in his VULGATE translation (actually a revision of the Old Latin) only what could be adequately supported by the "Chaldee" (Aramaic) text. The Vulgate omits some geographical details and concrete incidents found both in the SEPTUAGINT and the Old Latin. F. C. Porter (in *HDB*, 2:822) argues that the deviations of the Vulgate from the SEPTUAGINT are due mainly to the Aramaic version. He believes this is made even more probable by the additional concrete details found in the Vulgate but not in the other texts (see specifically Jdt. 7:6, 7; 11:11; 14:1–12; 16:31). Porter cites a Hebrew MIDRASH that summarizes chs. 1–5 briefly, but in chs. 7–14 it follows the Vulgate so closely that it is certain there is a relationship between them. Both in omissions and additions, as well as in a number of lesser details, the Vulgate and Midrash agree.

II. Date. The consensus of scholars is that the book of Judith was written in the 2nd cent. B.C., probably as a result of the Maccabean conflict (see MACCABEE). The persecution of ANTIOCHUS Epiphanes would provide a favorable background for this type of literature. Those who argue for this view point out several details: the book emphasizes zeal for orthodox Judaism (a characteristic of the Maccabean period); the high priest is head of the state; ONIAS (prob. Onias III) is named as high priest; the war in which they were engaged is regarded as a holy war. It is impossible to date the book from internal historical references. NEBUCHADNEZZAR is erroneously said to be the king of the Assyrians in NINEVEH, but Nineveh was destroyed in 612 B.C. A period of several years elapsed before Nebuchadnezzar was king in Babylon, and almost twenty years until the twelfth year of his reign. The Jews are described as having already returned from exile, an event that took place even later, in Persian times.

Porter argues that the author lived in the 1st cent. B.C., but wrote of an event that took place three centuries earlier. Thus he could speak of a period of peace and of a recent return from the EXILE, and make no mention of a king in Judah. Nebuchadnezzar would be a reflection of Artaxerxes Ochus, who made an expedition against Phoenicia and Egypt in 350 B.C. This king had generals by the name of HOLOFERNES and BAGOAS. C. C. Torrey (*The Apocryphal Literature* [1945], 88–93) suggests a post-Maccabean date in the first decades of the 1st cent. B.C. He argues that the glorification of SHECHEM (BETHULIA is identified as Shechem) is more likely after John Hyrcanus had destroyed the temple on Mount GERIZIM (c. 120) and had razed the city of SAMARIA (c. 109).

III. Historicity. There are differences of opinion concerning the author's historical reliability. Was he wholly ignorant of history so that he confused many outstanding events, or was he merely using his characters as symbols in a historical novel? Luther claimed the author was interested only in showing that Judah is preserved from any danger when it keeps the law. Others contend that present or recent history is disguised by the use of the names. Nebuchadnezzar has been identified with Antiochus IV Epiphanes or with Artaxerxes Ochus. R. Pfeiffer (*History of New Testament Times, with an Introduction to the Apocrypha* [1949], 285–303) has reproduced a list of seventeen kings (first published by Brunengo) with whom Nebuchadnezzar has been identified. These range from Adadnirari III (810–783 B.C.) to Hadrian (A.D. 117–138). The book has too many chronological, historical, and geographical errors to be taken literally.

IV. Setting. Identification of the geographical names is difficult. Torrey forcefully argues for an identification of Bethulia with Shechem and Betomasthaim with Samaria. Davies suggests that Bethulia is a disguised form of *Beth Eloah* (or *Elohim*) and simply means, "the place where God is with his people." He rejects Torrey's identification. In the Aramaic version used by Jerome, Bethulia may have been intended as Jerusalem, but the LXX account describes it as a place in N Samaria near DOTHAN. The descriptions in the book favor the position that the author was a resident of Palestine.

V. Purpose. Almost all scholars agree that the author was not trying to teach history. "It is evidently designed to entertain as well as to instruct," says Torrey, "and it is well fitted to accomplish both purposes. The author's chief interest, indeed, seems to have been in the story itself, rather than in any teaching to be gained from it." A similar view is expressed by L. H. Brockington (*A Critical Introduction to the Apocrypha* [1961], 40–48), but he places more emphasis on the purpose, which is to "encourage adherence to faith in God even in the direst circumstances." A more moderate view, and the one this writer supports, is that of B. M. Metzger (*An Introduction to the Apocrypha* [1957], 43–53), who states that the author "wished both to encourage his people in resisting their enemies and to inculcate a strict observance of the Law of God."

E. J. Goodspeed (*The Story of the Apocrypha* [1939], 45–51) is of the opinion that the author was more concerned for the early Pharisaic ideals (see PHARISEES) than for the history of the postexilic period. The religious views are certainly Pharisaic. These include the attitude toward the temple, tithes, food laws, prayer, fasting, and ceremonial washing. In the religious sphere, Judith resembles very much the book of TOBIT. In its concern for summoning the Jews to resistance at a time of national crisis, it compares favorably with DANIEL, ESTHER, and the books of the MACCABEES.

VI. Content. According to the book, Nebuchadnezzar made war on Arphaxad, who ruled over the Medes in Ecbatana. Nebuchadnezzar appealed to all his western subjects, those living in the area corresponding to modern Syria, Lebanon, Palestine, and Egypt, but they refused to join him in the war. Angered by this rebuff, he vowed to avenge himself on this whole territory. In his seventeenth year he defeated Arphaxad, then returned to Nineveh and feasted for 120 days. The next year he put into effect his plan to destroy all those who had not obeyed his command. Holofernes, his chief general and second in command, was dispatched with 120,000 infantry and 12,000 cavalry to carry out the king's wish.

Holofernes led his army westward, covering a distance of about 300 mi. in three days. The territory of Asia Minor and Syria was devastated. At DAMASCUS he burned the fields, destroyed the flocks, and executed all the young men. When news of this reached the seacoast cities of Sidon, Tyre, Jamnia, Azotus, and Ascalon, the people surrendered unconditionally. Their religious shrines were demolished, and they were instructed to worship only Nebuchadnezzar as god. Holofernes then moved to the edge of ESDRAELON and spent a month gathering supplies for this vast army, which now had been increased by troops from the neighboring countries.

The people of Israel began extensive preparations to defend themselves. Joakim, the high priest in Jerusalem, sent word to the people of Bethulia and Betomasthaim, two cities that faced Esdraelon, to hold the passes against the Assyrians so Judah would not be invaded. Reports of Israel's military activity reached Holofernes and angered him greatly. He summoned all the leaders of Moab, Ammon, and the coastal areas, to question them concerning this people who had defiantly refused to surrender. Achior, the Ammonite leader, related the history of the Jewish people to Holofernes. He concluded with the statement that if the Israelites sin against their God then they can be defeated easily, but if there is no transgression in the nation, then Holofernes might just as well go on by, because God will defend and protect them against all odds. This speech aroused the other leaders who had been listening and they suggested that Achior be put to death. When the clamor died down, Holofernes boasted that his forces would destroy Israel from the face of the earth. Achior was taken to the foot of the hill on which Bethulia was located. He was left bound, for Holofernes wanted him to die with the people of Israel. The men of Israel found Achior and brought him into the city.

The next day Holofernes ordered his troops into position against Bethulia. The force now numbered 170,000 infantry and 12,000 cavalry. On the third day, Holofernes took his cavalry out to survey the situation. They seized the springs of water, but made no further move against the city. Then the leaders of Edom, Moab, and the coastlands advised Holofernes not to make a direct attack on the city because that would cause unnecessary loss of life. Rather, they suggested, he should seize the spring of water at the foot of the mountain and destroy the people by thirst and famine. Guards placed on the nearby hills would see to it that not a man got out of the city.

The plight of the Israelites worsened. After thirty-four days most of the water in the city was gone and a strict ration was in effect. The people assembled and pleaded with Uzziah and the other rulers to surrender to the Assyrians, for they concluded that there was no one to help them; God had sold them into the hands of their enemies. Uzziah appealed for a delay of five days. If God did not deliver them within that time, then they would surrender.

At this point the heroine Judith is introduced: a beautiful widow, rich, and the model of piety. For over three years, since her husband died of sunstroke, she had lived at home, dressed in sackcloth and garments of her widowhood. She fasted every day except on days when it was forbidden to fast. She sent for the elders of the city and criticized them for the stand they had taken. She was particularly distressed that they "put God to the test." Such an act was unthinkable. Man cannot understand his own mind or heart, so how can he expect to search out God? She urged the people to look upon this experience as a test of them by God—to educate them, not punish them. Uzziah and the other rulers asked Judith to pray for them that God would send rain within the five days and fill their cisterns. Judith, however, had a plan of her own which she refused to reveal to the people or the rulers.

At the time when the evening incense was being offered in the temple at Jerusalem, Judith prayed to God. She asked strength for herself that she might do what she had planned, and that by the deceit of her lips she might bring about the defeat of the Assyrians. Her prayer ended, she removed her sackcloth and widow's garments, bathed with water, anointed herself with precious ointment, combed her hair, and put on her gayest clothes. She finished it off with jewelry—anklets, rings, earrings, bracelets, and ornaments—to be as appealing as possible to the eyes of all men. She prepared food for herself and gave this to her maid to carry, then she went to the city gate. All those gathered there were struck by her beauty. She ordered that the gate be opened that she might go out and accomplish her task.

Judith and her maid went straight to the Assyrian lines. When she was taken into custody by an Assyrian patrol, she said she was fleeing from the Hebrews, because they were about to be handed over to the Assyrians. She had come to Holofernes to "show him a way" he could capture the whole hill country without the loss of one of his men. The soldiers were completely captivated by her words and physical beauty. They chose a hundred men to escort her to the tent of Holofernes. A huge crowd gathered around her as she waited outside the tent. The reaction to her beauty was a general consensus that all the Israelites should be killed to a man, for if they had women like this, they would be able to ensnare the whole world.

Judith was graciously received by Holofernes, who assured her she had nothing to fear from him. Judith told him that the words of Achior were true. Now a sin had been committed by the people and they would soon provoke God to anger. When this happened, the people would be handed over to the Assyrians to be destroyed. She claimed that God had revealed this to her and sent her to Holofernes to accomplish through him something that would astonish the whole world. Every night she would go out into the valley to pray. God would tell her when the people had committed their sin and she in turn would inform Holofernes.

Holofernes fell for her ruse. He invited her to dine with him. She refused to eat any of his food, but ate only of that which she had brought with her. Judith slept until midnight. Then she arose and requested permission from Holofernes to be allowed to go out to pray. This procedure she followed for three days. On the fourth day, Holofernes held a private banquet to which he invited Judith, who seemed pleased with the invitation. Holofernes, overcome by the beauty of Judith and with his desire for her, drank much more wine than he had ever drunk before. When his slaves withdrew, Holofernes lay on his bed intoxicated. Alone with him, Judith seized the opportunity. She first prayed, then took his sword, took hold of his hair, prayed for strength, and hacked off his head with two blows of the sword. She pushed the body off the bed, pulled down the canopy from the bed, and calmly walked out and handed the head of Holofernes to her maid who placed it in her food bag.

Judith and her maid went out as they had done on previous nights, but this time they went to the city. When the elders had assembled, she showed them the head of Holofernes and indicated that her beauty had tricked him to destruction, but carefully noted that she had not committed any sinful act with him to accomplish her purpose. Judith gave orders that the head should be hung upon the wall, and at sunrise every man should go out of the city armed for battle. She predicted that the reaction of the Assyrians would be one of fear when they discovered the death of their general. She also requested that Achior be brought to see the head. At the first sight of the head he fainted, but when he recovered, he believed in God, was circumcised, and became a Jew.

At sunrise the events transpired as Judith predicted. The Assyrians were routed and their camp was plundered for thirty days. Joakim, the senate, and the people from Jerusalem came to see what God had done and to bless Judith. She was given the tent of Holofernes and all his furnishings. The women gathered to Judith and she led them in a dance. All the men of Israel followed, bearing their weapons, wearing garlands, and singing. Judith (as a personification of all Israel) sang a thanksgiving psalm.

All the people went to Jerusalem to celebrate. Judith dedicated to God all the vessels of Holofernes that the people had given to her and the canopy she had taken from his bed. The feasting in Jerusalem lasted for three months. Judith returned to Bethulia. She had many suitors, but she remained a widow until her death at 105 years of age. She freed her maid and divided her property among her husband's relatives and her own.

(See further T. Crave, *Artistry and Faith in the Book of Judith* [1983]; C. A. Moore, *Judith*, AB 40 [1985]; J. C. VanderKam, ed., *"No One Spoke Ill of Her": Essays on Judith* [1992]; M. Stocker, *Judith, Sexual Warrior: Women and Power in Western Culture* [1998]; D. J. Harrington, *Invitation to the Apocrypha* [1999], ch. 3; B. Otzen, *Tobit and Judith* [2002]; D. A. deSilva, *Introducing the Apocrypha: Message, Context, and Significance* [2002], ch. 4; H. Efthimiadis-Keith, *The Enemy is Within: A Jungian Psychoanalytic Approach to the Book of Judith* [2004].)

R. F. HAYDEN

Juel joo'uhl. KJV Apoc. form of JOEL (1 Esd. 9.34–35).

jug. See POTTERY.

Julia joo′lee-uh (Ἰουλία G2684, from Lat. *Iulia*, fem. of *Iulius*; see JULIUS). A Christian woman greeted by PAUL (Rom. 16:15). Because she appears to be linked with Philologus (by the use of Gk. *kai*, "and"), some have speculated that the two may have been related, possibly as husband and wife. Julia was a common Roman name, especially among freed slaves. (For a discussion of the names in Rom. 16, see P. Lampe in *The Romans Debate*, ed. K. P. Donfried, rev. ed. [1991], 216–30.)

Julius joo′lee-uhs (Ἰούλιος G2685, from Lat. *Iulius*). A Roman CENTURION of the Imperial Regiment stationed at CAESAREA; he was charged with the custody of PAUL for his trip to Rome and his hearing by the emperor (Acts 27:1). Why a centurion would have been given this responsibility has been a matter of some discussion (cf. *ABD*, 3:1125–26; on this and related questions, see AUGUSTAN COHORT). Although Julius did not listen to Paul's advice at one point (v. 11), the narrative suggests that there was a significant measure of mutual respect between them (cf. vv. 3, 31–32, 42–43).

Julius Caesar. See CAESAR.

Jung Codex. Alternate name given sometimes to Codex I in the NAG HAMMADI LIBRARY. Because the well-known Swiss psychologist Carl G. Jung had an interest in GNOSTICISM, this MS was initially acquired by the Jung Institute, though it was subsequently returned to Egypt.

Junia joo′nee-uh. KJV form of JUNIAS.

Junias joo′nee-uhs (Ἰουνιᾶς G2687, perhaps short form of Lat. *Iunianus*; because the form is elsewhere unattested, many understand it as the common fem. name Ἰουνία, thus KJV, "Junia"). A Christian at Rome whom Paul greets in Rom. 16:7. Both Junias and ANDRONICUS are described as "my relatives" (KJV, "my kinsmen") and as *epismoi en tois apostolois*; the latter phrase probably means "outstanding among the apostles," though some argue it should be rendered "well known to the apostles" (so ESV). There is debate also on whether the name should be understood as masculine (J. Piper and W. Grudem, eds., *Recovering Biblical Manhood and Womanhood: A Response to Evangelical Feminists* [1991], 79–81) or feminine (most recent commentators; cf. C. E. B. Cranfield, *A Critical and Exegetical Commentary on the Epistle to the Romans*, ICC, 2 vols. [1975–79], 2:788). If the reference is to a woman, she was probably the husband of Andronicus. (See now the extensive treatment by E. J. Epp, *Junia: The First Woman Apostle* [2005].)

juniper. An evergreen tree (or shrub) with leaves like needles or scales; their seed-bearing cones are aromatic. The KJV uses "juniper" to render Hebrew *rōtem* H8413 (1 Ki. 19:4–5; Job 30:4; Ps. 120:4), but this word appears to refer to the BROOM tree. According to some scholars, another Hebrew term, *bĕrôš* H1360, designates the *Juniperus phoenicia* (e.g., 1 Ki. 5:8; NIV, "pine logs"). The rare word ʿarʿār H6899 (Jer. 17:6) is identified by some with *J. phoenicia* or *J. oxycedrus*. (Cf. *FFB*, 131–32, 162–64.) See also FLORA (under *Leguminosae*).

Jupiter joo′puh-tuhr. The Roman name for the supreme deity, corresponding to Greek ZEUS (Acts 14:12–13; 19:35 KJV).

Bust of Jupiter (late 1st cent. A.D.).

Iushab Hesed joo´shab hee´sid (יוֹשַׁב חֶסֶד H3160, "mercy will be returned"). Son of ZERUBBABEL and descendant of DAVID through SOLOMON (1 Chr. 3:20), possibly born in Palestine (see HASHUBAH).

just, justice. See JUSTIFICATION; RIGHTEOUSNESS

justification. In Christian theology, justification is that act of God by which sinners, who are responsible for their guilt and are under condemnation but believe in Christ, are pronounced just and righteous, or acquitted, by God the JUDGE (Rom. 3:28; 4:25; 5:16, 18; 8:28–34). According to the Scriptures, God justifies by GRACE, for Christ's sake, through FAITH.

  I. Terminology
  II. Justification according to the apostle Paul
  III. Justification by works
  IV. Justification and the righteousness of God
  V. Justification and the atonement of Christ
  VI. Objective and subjective justification
  VII. Justification and forgiveness
  VIII. Justification as imputation of righteousness
  IX. Justification by faith
  X. Justification by faith as central doctrine of Christianity
  XI. Justification and the OT
  XII. Jesus and justification
  XIII. The relevance of justification today
  XIV. Summary of doctrine of justification

I. Terminology. The Greek noun that most closely approximates the meaning "justification," *dikaiōsis* G1470, occurs only twice in the NT (Rom. 4:25; 5:18). The infrequent occurrence of the term does not imply that the doctrine of justification is not important in biblical theology, only that the biblical writers, and Paul in particular, are prone to speak of justification in dynamic terms with the cognate verb, *dikaioō* G1467, "to justify," which is found also in the Septuagint translation of the OT. Moreover, the meaning "justification" is often represented by the word for "righteousness," *dikaiosynē* G1466 (cf. Heb. *ṣedāqâ* H6666), a pregnant dynamic term that may indicate God's act of "pronouncing righteous," "making righteous," or even "doing what is righteous." Certainly the concepts of justification and RIGHTEOUSNESS are very closely related.

The English term *justification* is derived from Latin *iustificare*, itself composed of two words, the adjective *iustus* ("righteous") and the verb *facio* ("to do, make"), thus "to make righteous" or "to do righteousness." In the Scriptures, however, the terms *justification* and *to justify* are typically used in a special forensic or judicial sense, "to declare or pronounce righteous," not "to make righteous." F. Godet says, "As to *dikaioun* (to justify), there is not an example in the whole of classic literature where it signifies: *to make just*" (*Commentary on St. Paul's Epistle to the Romans*, 2 vols. [1880–81], 1:157). It is thus a declarative act of the God of grace by which he declares sinners free from the guilt and consequences of their sin through faith in the ATONEMENT of Christ.

One should not be misled by the familiar use of these terms today. In present-day usage the "justified person" often refers to someone who is innocent. The terms are also used to excuse action or to prove one is right, to vindicate oneself either in the eyes of other people or before the law. A person may say, "The man accused of murder did not commit murder. He was 'justified' in killing the intruder because he acted in self-defense." A reliable dictionary today will define *justification* as "a reason, a fact, circumstance, or explanation that justifies or defends, for example, 'the insult was sufficient justification for her to leave the party.'" (In the art of printing, *justification* means the spacing of words and letters in a line so that all lines in a column have even margins.) Used in these ways, the term has little in common with the prevalent meaning in Scripture.

II. Justification according to the apostle Paul. When the apostle PAUL preached the doctrine of justification in the ancient Roman world, it appears that the term was readily understood by both Jew and Greek (Rom. 1:14). The apostle does not take great pains to define the term, although the word usually may be understood from the context in which it is used. To the Corinthians he simply wrote, "But you were washed, you were sanctified, you were justified in the name of the Lord Jesus Christ and by the Spirit of our God" (1 Cor. 6:11), and let it go at that.

Even in the epistle to the ROMANS, the longest and most detailed presentation of justification in the Bible, the apostle does not pause to explain these terms but assumes that his readers understand them. Although in his inspired written record of God's revelation of salvation to sinners the apostle uses other picture words to describe God's action, such as "redemption" (Rom. 3:24) and "reconciliation" (5:11), his favorite terms are *dikaiosynē* and its cognates. Whether Paul speaks of justification by faith or its opposite (justification by works), the meaning of the word by itself is basically declarative or forensic (the word *forensic* is used in connection with law, courtroom procedure, judgment, or public discussion and debate). A person justified by works would be pronounced righteous because he or she did the necessary works and a judge confirmed it; God pronounces sinners righteous because of Christ's work for them. In both cases the act of judging or justifying is forensic.

A study of Paul's letter to the Romans reveals that the idea of JUDGMENT or rendering a decision is the leitmotif of his entire presentation on justification. When he says that "God gave them over" (Rom. 1:24–28) in speaking of the sins of men and women, this act involved a judgment on the part of God. Another section in his treatise (2:6–11) especially exemplifies this meaning of justification. Since God's justice is righteous and perfect, he will pronounce judgment upon all human beings according to their works. Paul says that a judgment, a "justification," will be rendered for all—eternal life to those who have done well, wrath and damnation to those who have disobeyed. The verdict will be as it should be, for there is no partiality with God.

The forensic situation is the same as that of which MOSES writes: "When men have a dispute, they are to take it to court and the judges will decide the case, acquitting [hiphil of *ṣādaq* H7405; LXX, *dikaioō*] the innocent and condemning the guilty. If the guilty man deserves to be beaten, the judge shall make him lie down and have him flogged in his presence with the number of lashes his crime deserves" (Deut. 25:1–2). The apostle states that it is the "doers of the law who will be justified" (Rom. 2:13 NRSV). Using the term in a context of law and judgment, the apostle does not say the doers of law become righteous, or make themselves righteous, but that they are *pronounced or judged righteous* before God. Paul is not teaching salvation or justification by works but maintains the basic meaning of the term *justify*. No one can fulfill the law of God perfectly and cannot receive a judgment or justification by work. Nevertheless, even if sinners could fulfill its demands, they would not thereby *make* themselves righteous, but would have to be *pronounced* righteous or innocent by the judge.

In the phrase "justified by faith" (Rom. 3:28), the term means to judge or declare a sinner *not guilty*, that is, to acquit a guilty person (not an innocent one). Justification is a reversal of God's attitude toward the sinner because of his justification by faith in Christ. The sinner is *declared* free from guilt and the punishment of sin (cf. 2 Cor. 5:19–21; Acts 13:38–39). This is Paul's unique use of the term *justification*: God's acquittal of the sinner. A just person is not pronounced just because he is just; rather, a sinful person is pronounced just because his sins have been atoned for by the righteousness of Christ. In another illustration on this point, in Rom. 2:26, Paul says that a man's uncircumcision is regarded or counted as CIRCUMCISION. In other words, one thing is simply counted for another, or a person is regarded as something he really is not. This is the basic, scriptural concept of the idea of "to justify" or "justification."

Accordingly, the early Lutheran theologian Martin Chemnitz writes of Paul's teaching on justification: "Paul everywhere describes the article of justification as *a judicial process* wherein the conscience of the sinner, accused before the tribunal of God by the divine law, convicted, and subject to the sentence of eternal damnation, flees to the throne of grace and is restored, absolved, and freed from the sentence of condemnation and received to eternal life for the sake of the obedience and intercession of the Son of God, our Mediator, which is laid hold of and made one's own through faith" (*Justification: The Chief Article of Christian Doctrine as Expounded in Loci Theologici*, trans. J. A. O. Preus [1985], 69, emphasis added). According to this description, justification signifies "to be pronounced righteous" or "to be acquitted."

III. Justification by works.

In Rom. 3, Paul answers the vital question, How is a person justified? How does one obtain a favorable judgment or acquittal? He writes: "Then what becomes of boasting? It is excluded. By what law? By that of works? No, but by the law of faith. For we hold that a person is justified by faith apart from works prescribed by the law" (3:27–28 NRSV). The verdict may be "not guilty" or "guilty," whether rendered by God or by a human being, but in God's spiritual courtroom, we are always guilty under sin; therefore we cannot justify or render ourselves innocent (4:13–15). Considering all possible circumstances among all peoples, Paul is forced to conclude that no one can gain acquittal by his works or by himself. If the Jew with all of his advantages could not achieve justification by works, certainly no one else could (4:1–5). The verdict pronounced on every one from God's universal courtroom is that "every mouth ... be silenced [that is, if anyone protests God's decision] and the whole world held accountable to God. Therefore no one will be declared righteous in his sight by observing the law" (3:19–20). A triple truth thus emerges regarding justification by works: sinners cannot do sufficient good works to gain acquittal; they cannot render judgment on themselves because they are always guilty; a just God cannot render them just by their works, for they are sinners by nature (7:21–25).

IV. Justification and the righteousness of God.

In the broader concept of justification in both OT and NT, the idea of the righteousness of God (*dikaiosynē theou*) is closely related to God's judicial act of salvation. At times the terms "justification by faith" and "righteousness of God" can be used almost interchangeably: "But now a righteousness from God, apart from law, has been made known, to which the Law and the Prophets testify. This righteousness from God comes through faith in Jesus Christ to all who believe" (Rom. 3:21). The revelation of God's wrath in the first part of Romans (1:18) is answered by the revelation of God's saving righteousness (3:21–26).

The well-known phrase "righteousness of God" as Paul uses it in Rom. 1:17, however, is not an attribute of God but his activity in saving sinners. The concept of divine righteousness is found again and again in the OT, where God's salvation in Christ is witnessed by the Law and the Prophets (3:21). Especially in the Psalms and in Isaiah the term pictures God's grace in rescuing and delivering his people from sin and the oppressor. "The LORD has made his salvation known / and revealed his righteousness to the nations" (Ps. 98:2). "Maintain justice / and do what is right, / for my salvation is close at hand / and my righteousness will soon be revealed" (Isa. 56:1). Paul teaches that this righteous activity of God, this saving act of God, is fulfilled in Jesus Christ. God saves believers through the atonement of Christ, and his merit earned on the cross is appropriated by faith. To have this righteousness is to be justified.

The teaching is clear in Rom. 3:22–26, especially in these statements: "This righteousness from God comes through faith in Jesus Christ to all who believe" (v. 22); "God presented him as a sacrifice of atonement, through faith in his blood" (v. 25). All human righteousness and justification are excluded. God's righteousness revealed in the gospel is that act of grace by which he cancels the condemnation of his WRATH upon sinners. It is not the attribute of God's divine justice or HOLINESS, but that righteousness which is the justification of sinners in Christ, and by which he bestows salvation, for Christ's sake, through faith. Therefore, it is also faith-righteousness since it is God's righteousness. Faith receives the righteous saving act of God and renounces and looks away from self to find its all in all in Christ.

V. Justification and the atonement of Christ.

If God's righteousness is the saving act of God in Christ for our SALVATION, then justification is closely related to the Lord's ATONEMENT. In fact, Christ's atonement is the grounds for justification. Christ's person and activity is the justification or reconciliation with God and the basis of all individual justification. It is the only basis upon which God can and does justify the sinner (Rom. 3:24; 8:1; 2 Cor. 5:19–21). The atonement of Christ answers the question, "How can a just God acquit a sinner — yes, one who remains sinful even after being justified?" Justification does not mean God overlooks sin or pretends that we are not sinners. The sentimental view that conceives of God as a gracious old "grandfather," who winks at the sins of little children, denies the integrity of the true God and destroys any concept of justification. God's justice and holiness demand payment for sin, and this penalty Christ paid in the atonement on the cross. Thus in justification God devised a plan whereby both his attributes of justice and his love manifested in grace for salvation of sinners are given full meaning.

By making Christ a substitute for the sinner, God preserves his own justice and at the same time achieves salvation for us (Rom. 3:26). It is unbiblical, therefore, to speculate whether God could or does forgive without Christ. Sinners "are justified freely by his grace through the redemption that came by Christ Jesus," whom God presented "as a sacrifice of atonement, through faith in his blood" (vv. 24–25).

God is involved in the justification-atonement syndrome in three ways: (1) He is the initiator, who first loved the sinner. (2) He is the instrument or means, who gave himself in the incarnate Christ as the once-for-all sacrifice for our sin. (3) He is also the object of his saving work, who satisfied his wrath and justice over sin through Christ's all-atoning sacrifice. At one and the same time God satisfies himself and forgives the sinner. Therefore, only in Christ does God justify the sinner by imputing Christ's perfect righteousness to the sinner who has none of his own (2 Cor. 5:21). The Scriptures teach plainly that the wrath of God comes upon sinners or else the Son of God must die for them. Either the sinner dies or Christ dies. But God "shows his love for us in that while we were yet sinners Christ died for us" (Rom. 5:8).

VI. Objective and subjective justification.

The universal language used in some biblical passages has led to different interpretations. The position taken by the present writer is as follows: Christ's atonement covered the sins of all people—past, present, and future—and therefore justification may be described as objective or universal. By raising his Son from the dead, God pronounced absolution on the entire human race (1 Jn. 2:2). Those yet unborn were all included in Christ's sacrifice and God's universal declaration of justification or absolution: "For he chose us in him [Christ] before the creation of the world to be holy and blameless in his sight" (Eph. 1:4, though most scholars would argue that passages such as this one apply only to believers).

Objective justification, according to this view, does not mean universal salvation, but rather universal grace and forgiveness. God pronounced all people righteous in Christ, but many will not accept this forgiveness and many may not hear of it (Rom. 10:14–17). It does mean, however, that our sins were declared forgiven even though we were not personally involved. The apostle teaches that as sin came upon all through the death of ADAM, so Christ's act of righteousness leads to their acquittal (4:12, 18). This is what prompted Paul's statements that Christ "died for the ungodly" (5:6; cf. v. 8). This is why the church can and does proclaim the GOSPEL to the whole world (Jn. 3:16; Rom. 1:14–17).

Objective or universal justification is important for what may be called personal or subjective justification. It is clear that if God did not justify the ungodly, then one would be justified by works and there could be no justification by faith. Also, if God had not justified all mankind, the individual sinner might doubt that he was included. (For alternate approaches to this subject, see the articles on ATONEMENT; ELECTION; SALVATION.) Subjective or personal justification is simply this: when sinners hear the gospel and the Holy Ghost thereby works faith in Christ in their heart, then Christ's atonement becomes theirs and they personally possess God's forgiveness and belong to the family of God.

But it should be understood that universal or objective justification and subjective justification are really not two separate acts of God. The latter is only the application of the former. Missionaries through the centuries have declared that universal and personal justification should give the church great incentive to preach the gospel to all people. All of God's love and Christ's great atonement on the cross mean nothing to anyone if a person does not hear the gospel. In such a case, the gospel is just as meaningless as if Christ had not risen (1 Cor. 15:17). It should be kept in mind that terms like "objective justification," "subjective justification," and "forensic act," are not formulas the Bible uses, but were created by the church to illustrate, emphasize, and protect the great truths of God's salvation for sinners.

JUSTIFICATION

VII. Justification and forgiveness. Justification is really legal picture language for FORGIVENESS of sins. Christian theologians have considered justification above all else as forgiveness of sins and have used the two expressions interchangeably. Jesus' parable of the prodigal son illustrates this concept dramatically (Lk. 15:11–32). Paul affirms that it is taught in the OT: "David says the same thing when he speaks of the blessedness of the man to whom God credits righteousness apart from works: / 'Blessed are they / whose transgressions are forgiven, / whose sins are covered'" (Rom. 4:6–7). God says to the sinner, "I do not count your transgressions against you. My Son has paid the punishment of your sin. I pronounce you righteous in my sight. I forgive you your sin." This is what Christians do when they forgive each other their trespasses: "I do not hold your sin against you. I release you from obligation. I forgive you your sin. God has forgiven my sins, too." In like manner Jesus taught Christians to pray, "Father, forgive us our trespasses as we forgive those who trespass against us." Justification, then, is not only a judicial declarative act but it is at the same time a *remissive* act in which God actually forgives the sin of individuals. The demands of the law and condemnation to punishment also are satisfied in Christ and forgiven. Justification as forgiveness is more than a pardon from sin, but an actual forgiving of the sinner, who, though guilty, has his guilt and sin remitted in Christ.

VIII. Justification as imputation of righteousness. Justification as forgiveness of sin involves God's act of IMPUTATION. This act is both negative and positive: in justification there is *non-imputation* of sin but also imputation of Christ's righteousness. The merits of Christ are imputed to sinners. They are given a righteousness alien to themselves, namely, Christ's righteousness, just as their sins are not imputed or counted to them (2 Cor. 5:19). Through faith the sinner receives the righteousness Christ worked on the cross (Rom. 3:25–26). The Lutheran confessional statements, for example, teach imputation very clearly: "The second matter in a mediator is, that Christ's merits have been presented as those which make satisfaction for others, which are bestowed by divine imputation on others, in order that through these, just as by their own merits, they may be accounted righteous. As when my friend pays a debt for a friend, the debtor is freed by the merit of another, as though it were by his own. Thus the merits of Christ are bestowed upon us" (*The Apology of the Augsburg Confession* 21.19).

IX. Justification by faith. Because of the emphasis given to FAITH in the Bible, Christians speak of justification especially as justification by faith. The phrase *by faith* is just as vital as the term *justify* in understanding the nature of justification as taught in the Scriptures. Paul, for instance, states the theme of the book of Romans thus: "For in the gospel a righteousness of God is revealed, a righteousness that is by faith from first to last" (Rom. 1:17). The OT text Paul proceeds to quote (Hab. 2:4) also emphasizes the nature and function of faith: "The righteous will live by faith." Faith and justification go hand in hand. Neither is meaningful or even possible without the other. We read in the OT that "Abraham believed the LORD," but his faith is immediately linked to the words, "he [God] credited it to him as righteousness" (Gen. 15:6). Elsewhere Paul also says, "For it is by grace you have been saved, through faith—and this not from

Roman bronze relief of a boar being led to sacrifice by an attendant (c. A.D. 100). Jesus used the parable of the lost son, who was welcomed back by his father even though he had eaten with pigs, to illustrate the depth of forgiveness available to sinners.

yourselves, it is the gift of God—not by works, so that no one can boast" (Eph. 2:8–9).

In justification, what exactly is the significance of the phrase *by faith*? Christians have always been aware of pitfalls at this point. Justifying faith is not faith in one's works or merit; neither is it faith in a church, faith in an organization, faith in a certain system of theology, or knowing a certain set of facts. While saving faith is an act of the human intellect and will, it is much more than an intellectual accepting of the fact *that* God exists, *that* Christ died on the cross, and so on; saving faith is *believing in* the gospel, *relying on* Christ's merit, and *receiving* God's declared righteousness.

For Paul, *by faith* essentially meant three things (1) Salvation is without works. Faith and works in justification itself are mutually exclusive. Works never influence God in justifying a person; justification is "by grace." Works always *follow* faith. No one can add to the atonement of Christ because Christ has done all (Gal. 3:18, 23–29). (2) Faith in justification is the God-given instrument or means by which the sinner accepts God's justification of forgiveness in Christ (Rom. 1:17; 3:25; Eph. 2:8). (3) Faith is always *faith in Christ*. It appropriates Christ's work on the cross, which is the basis of justification or forgiveness. If faith justifies, it does so only because it receives Christ's merit. The righteousness of Christ is always intended for those who believe, and all who believe receive this righteousness. (This traditional understanding of Paul's teaching has been challenged by some recent scholars. See GALATIANS, EPISTLE TO THE, VII.)

Faith is essentially trust or confidence of the individual Christian that full forgiveness is bestowed for Christ's sake and that he or she is now a child of God possessing the Holy Spirit for a new life. Faith believes the gospel. Faith is always personal; each person believes for oneself and relies on the promises of the gospel. Thus faith is in no sense a moral achievement or ethical principle originating in a human being. If people call faith a good work, they do not mean that it merits favor or adds to Christ's work or influences God in justifying a sinner, but that it receives Christ. The person believes, but faith is really God's work in that person, for "no one can say, 'Jesus is Lord,' except by the Holy Spirit" (1 Cor. 12:3).

This is what the Reformation leaders meant when they stressed *sola fide* (by faith alone) and *sola gratia* (by grace alone). If justification is without works, and if God justifies sinners before they come to faith (as he did Abraham before he was circumcised), then faith's role in justification is to receive the forgiveness offered in the gospel as one's own. The apostle never says a person is justified *on account of* faith, or *because of* faith, but *by* or *through* faith. To speak in terms of the courtroom, as Paul does: when a guilty person is acquitted by faith all he can do is take the judge's word for it, and walk out of the courtroom a free person, exceedingly grateful and humble.

The reality of this teaching staggers the human mind. People have balked at the doctrine that God declares guilty sinners innocent, that he pronounces the unrighteous to be "not guilty as charged." People protest when they hear the teaching that God declares sinners to be what they are not and does so in strictest justice. They say, "In secular courts every effort is made to pronounce guilty people guilty and innocent people innocent. Every person must be responsible for his own sin. How can God do otherwise?" They label justification by faith as "a shocking doctrine," "unjust," "unworthy of God," "unethical and immoral," and "a license to sin." Justification by faith is not "rational" (proceeding from human reason), but theological. This is what it means to be justified by faith. It takes faith, which is the gift of God, to receive God's forgiveness in this matter. Human protests and criticisms only document the fact that it is justification by faith.

Justification by faith is always total and complete. There are no degrees of justification as in SANCTIFICATION. When God justifies, a person is forgiven completely, and that not in a long drawn-out process but in an instant. Also, all people are justified in the same way. Justification by faith is not REGENERATION, if this term is used to describe the entire life of a Christian; nor is it some psychosomatic or physical act that magically transforms an evil person into a righteous person. Justification by faith is complete and once-for-all; it involves nothing of injustice, since it is God who justifies (Rom. 3:26). If the judge himself has paid the debt, he has a perfect right to free the guilty person (8:31–34).

This free forgiveness he gives in the gospel and the sacraments by faith. These means of grace are God's dynamic power to convey, present, and seal to us his forgiveness through faith (Gal. 3:27; 1 Cor. 6:11). The Lutheran *Augsburg Confession* presents this concise definition of what it means to be justified by faith: "also they teach that men be justified before God by their own strength, merit, or works, but are freely justified for Christ's sake, through faith, when they believe that they are received into favor, and that their sins are forgiven for Christ's sake, who, by his death, has made satisfaction for our sins. This faith God imputes for righteousness in his sight." In summary, then, justification by faith should include these seven items:

1. God
2. Justifies
3. Sinners
4. By grace
5. For Christ's sake
6. Through faith alone
7. For a new life here on earth and in heaven.

X. Justification by faith as central doctrine of Christianity.
Justification by faith has been called the apex of all Christian teaching, the central and cardinal truth of Christianity. Paul declares: "For I resolved to know nothing while I was with you except Jesus Christ and him crucified" (1 Cor. 2:2). It is not only the central teaching of Paul, but also of Jesus and the apostles and of the prophets of the OT. In both the OT and NT, it is the heart of all of God's mighty salvation acts. It is like the hub of a wheel from which extend all other doctrines of Scripture. Properly understood, all doctrines of the Scriptures serve the doctrine of justification by faith. It involves all the fundamental teachings of the law and gospel and relates all truths of the Scriptures in one harmonious whole. If Christ is not God, how could he rise again? If he is not man, how could he die for man? If Christ were not man's substitute, how could God justify a sinner, for then God could justify only the righteous. If one denies that human beings are sinful, why bother with the gospel of forgiveness? If one asks, "What is the church?" the answer must be "all those who believe in Christ for forgiveness and reconciliation."

This is why Martin Luther and the other reformers of the 16th cent. called justification "the doctrine of the standing or the falling of the church." "This article is the head and cornerstone of the church, which alone begets, nourishes, builds, preserves, and protects the church; without it the church of God cannot subsist one hour. Neither can anyone teach correctly in the church or successfully resist any adversary if he does not maintain this article" (*Luther's Works*, 14:168).

XI. Justification and the OT.
It has been said that justification by faith is only a NT doctrine or only "Pauline theology." In reality, however, justification by faith is derived from the OT and simply spelled out in greater detail in the NT under various pictures. The SEPTUAGINT uses the same Greek terms as the NT. Paul did not invent either the words or their contents. From his epistles, we know that Paul was well acquainted with both the Hebrew OT and the Greek LXX.

Paul often quotes the OT for support of his doctrine of justification. An example is Ps. 51:4, which Paul quotes in Rom. 3:4, "So that you may be justified in thy words" (NRSV). Here the term "justified" (NIV, "proved right") is used of God in the declaratory or forensic sense, since one can scarcely say that the perfect God is in any way made righteous. Another outstanding example is Paul's appeal to David in Ps. 32:1–2, showing that justification by faith is embedded in the Scriptures of the OT: "Blessed are they / whose transgressions are forgiven, / whose sins are covered. / Blessed is the man / whose sin the Lord will never count against him" (Rom. 4:7–8). Here David speaks of nonimputation of sin as parallel to forgiveness of sin. The statement is also in opposition to salvation by works. Nothing could be more illustrative of Paul's thesis. The blessed are not those who have good works, but those whose sins are not laid to his account. Even without Paul's use of the terms in the context of his teaching on justification, the words in the Psalm by themselves clearly teach justification by faith as a declaratory act of God's forgiveness.

Perhaps the crowning example of the teaching of justification by faith in the OT is the believing patriarch ABRAHAM. It is stated in Genesis that he "believed the LORD, and he credited it to him as righteousness" (Gen. 15:6). Even without Paul's use of this passage to support his teachings in Rom. 4:3, the statement is as clear as that of David. The outstanding aspect of Abraham and justification by faith is that the great hero of the Jewish people, whom all called "Father Abraham," with all of his blessings and good works, still is recorded as believing and having it counted to him for righteousness. The example is somewhat the opposite of King David, who fell into sin and threw himself upon God's mercy. Yet both men were justified by faith.

Several important items may be pointed out concerning Abraham as an example of justification by faith: (1) Justification is reckoning or imputing to a person something he did not possess before, namely, righteousness before God. (2) God reckoned righteousness to Abraham entirely without merit on Abraham's part, as seen by the fact that it took place long before Abraham was circumcised or before the Jewish law was given. (3) It was, therefore, justification *by faith*, because he received righteousness through simple trust in God's precious promise of the Messiah through his people. (4) This led to his obedience to God so that by faith Abraham left the land of his fathers and went to a strange country (Heb. 11:8).

The essential features of justification by faith are to be found in embryo in simple short OT texts like this, particularly in Isaiah, the prophets, and the numerous messianic promises. Paul selected the examples of David and Abraham from among many others he could have used. After a thorough study of the concept of justification and related words in the LXX, Leon Morris (*The Apostolic Preaching of the Cross* [1955], 234) concludes: "When we turn to those passages where the term 'to justify' occurs, there can be no doubt that the meaning is to declare rather than to make righteous."

XII. Jesus and justification. Did Jesus teach justification by faith? This is an important question, for if Jesus and Paul taught a different doctrine on salvation, then there is such a thing as a special Pauline theology. The answer to the question is clearly in the affirmative, when seen in the light of our Lord's dealings with certain PHARISEES "who were confident of their own righteousness and looked down on everybody else" (Lk. 18:9), and to whom he said, "You are the ones who justify yourselves in the eyes of men, but God knows your hearts" (16:15). These words of Jesus to the Pharisees are also to the point: "It is not the healthy who need a doctor, but the sick. I have not come to call the righteous, but sinners to repentance" (5:31–32).

Several outstanding examples from the Lord's teaching might also be cited. In the parable of the Pharisee and the tax collector (Lk. 18:9–14), Jesus depicts the tax collector as someone who had nothing to offer God and who said, "God, have mercy on me [*lit.*, be propitiated for me], a sinner" (v. 13). On this worst of sinners in the Jewish world, Jesus' judgment is that "this man, rather than the other, went home justified before God" (v. 14). Another example is the story of the prodigal son (15:11–32). The picture or figure here is that of the family and not of the courtroom. The father (who represents God the forgiving Father in heaven) acquits a wayward and guilty son, forgives him, and reinstates him in the family without making any demands. Certainly the son had nothing to offer except to say "I'm sorry," but even his sorrow was not what caused the father to justify him: his father's love had forgiven him long before he came home. The "elder brother" in the story did not understand the father's verdict because he was thinking in terms of works, worthiness, and tradition.

Human reason (like that of the older brother) does not comprehend this situation. That Jesus' view of works, merit, grace, and forgiveness was something radically different from the traditions of the Jews is apparent in his parable of the workers in the vineyard (Matt. 20:1–16). The rational mind questions the employer's justice in giving the same pay for unequal number of hours of work, but this is the very nature of justification by grace through faith. The Lord will offer salvation as he will since he is the Lord. He has chosen to do so by grace and faith, and one's works will not influence his love. All of the grumbling in the world will not alter the situation these words describe: "'These men who were hired last worked only one hour,' they said, 'and you have made them equal to us who have borne the burden of the work and the heat of the day.' But he answered one of them, 'Friend, I am not being unfair to you. Didn't you agree to work for a denarius? Take your pay and go. I want to give the man who was hired last the same as I gave you. Don't I have the right to do what I want with my own money? Or are you envious because I am generous?'" (20:12–15).

Thus the Lord teaches the same amazing grace of God in Christ which Paul articulates and expands so well in his epistles. One may well infer that Paul and Jesus teach the same doctrine through different literary form and picture. Both Jesus and Paul preach this gospel to both Gentiles and Jews because grace breaks down all barriers and makes all people equal before God, both in sin and in grace (Eph. 2:1–22).

XIII. The relevance of justification today.

Many have, with good reason, criticized the doctrine of justification by faith, or *forensic justification*, when it remains only "forensic" in the lives of Christians. Some have said that Paul, for instance, took the simple gospel of the FATHERHOOD OF GOD and changed it into a drama of redemption through blood and antinomian justice. The point is made that Paul never heard of Darwin, Freud, or Dewey. What can a doctrine of forensic justification, through process of mind and intangible faith, say to modern man who has walked on the moon? "Who feels guilty?" they ask, "and who wants to be saved by works?" Involved is the fact of human sin and shortcomings, as well as people's inhumanity to others, which cannot easily be written off as ignorance or something that can be cured by education and better socioeconomic arrangements. Since the doctrine of justification by faith is central to the Christian religion, the important question must be asked, "Is this biblical diagnosis of sin and a cure through justification relevant and meaningful for modern human beings?"

The modern predicament—which society uses vast resources to remedy—is really of man's own making, whether he traces evil back to Adam, or looks around at his own existence. After centuries of conflict and many ineffective solutions from the greatest minds, the common person today knows that his world is not a delusion. More and more people have come to realize that the problem of the world is a theological one. The modern human predicament, found in various forms throughout the centuries, is the old predicament of sin of which the Scripture speaks. Justification by faith says that sinners are not hopeless and helpless in their situation, but that God has heard their cry and offers deliverance.

Three important areas immediately suggest themselves: (1) For the meaninglessness and emptiness of many today, the doctrine of justification by faith should mean "by the gospel alone." The heart of biblical revelation should teach mankind that God has not abandoned his creatures or his world. They are not cut off. He has adopted the children of this world as his own, freely and fully out of a compassion he would give them to live by. He has reconciled not only human beings but also the cosmos to himself (Rom. 8:12–37; Eph. 1:10). The importance of acceptance and "belonging" in psychotherapy, of "being" and "meaning"—answers to all these prominent current concerns may be found in God's justification and reconciliation of the world. God has redeemed sinners from the slavery of self. He himself has paid the supreme sacrifice. Men and women can now give up worship of themselves and material possessions and turn to the loving God who gives meaning to all things. We no longer need to create our own purpose or our right to exist. God has done this for us in Jesus Christ. In the language of the day, "We may stop trying to *justify* ourselves."

(2) Just when modern men and women need it most, justification by faith in Christ is a source of limitless spiritual and moral power for them in their world (Rom. 1:16–17). What often is called the doctrine's greatest weakness is actually its greatest strength. Faith in God does not cast off Christian works, but is the source and power of the greatest work of all, namely, LOVE. Luther said, "Good works do not make a good man but a good man does good works." When opponents suggested to Paul that a doctrine of salvation by faith and not by works implied "Let us do evil that good may result" (Rom. 3:8), his firm answer was: "By no means! We died to sin; how can we live in it any longer? Or don't you know that all of us who were baptized into Christ Jesus were baptized into his death? We were therefore buried with him through baptism into death in order that, just as Christ was raised from the dead through the glory of the Father, we

too may live a new life" (6:1–4). Justification by faith means not only forgiveness of sins but also the gift of the HOLY SPIRIT (15:13). To be justified is to experience the power of God in one's heart. Paul said: "I can do everything through him who gives me strength" (Phil. 4:13). Justification by faith is the act of God which connects us to the dynamo of all power for all good in the world.

Justification by faith should lead to all the Christian virtues. If the teaching is empty and meaningless today, it is because it has not been completely seen and taught in all its dimensions, or because it has been accepted as a mere creedal statement—only a legal fiction so that people remain as before. Not only the *act* of justification but also the *results* must be emphasized: peace, freedom, responsibility, compassion, the Spirit life, love, meekness, patience, strength to do well—the whole life of the Spirit of God. Luther once referred to the doctrine of justification as the *periculosissima doctrina*, the "most dangerous teaching," because it has been used to allow license to sin and be irresponsible. He pleaded that the teaching be proclaimed so as to inspire gratitude to God, daily repentance, and resolve to serve God and neighbor in a life of newness and obedience. Sinners have been accounted righteous not in some distant world, but here and now in the church, and in and for our world.

(3) Justification by faith assures all people of God's love and eternal life with him after death. We can face the future with confidence. Final judgment does not appall us, for we have already met our Judge and are forgiven. All systems of religion and philosophy that use or imply works for salvation result inevitably in wretchedness and tension of doubt. Those who trust in the doctrine of justification by faith, therefore, need no longer be the "devil's martyrs." In his commentary on Galatians, Luther used this pungent expression to describe those who worked harder trying to get to heaven by works than the wicked did in going to hell without them, only to arrive in the same place.

When God says he justifies the ungodly, all sinners know they are included. When God says to all, "the promise comes by faith, so that it may be by grace and may be guaranteed to all Abraham's offspring" (Rom. 4:16), all sinners know his grace is sufficient. When God takes human beings from eternity to eternity in justification (8:30), they receive the comfort that no words can convey. Beset by difficulties of every kind, this hope remains: "No, in all these things we are more than conquerors through him who loved us. For I am convinced that neither death nor life, neither angels nor demons, neither the present nor the future, nor any powers, neither height nor depth, nor anything else in all creation, will be able to separate us from the love of God that is in Christ Jesus our Lord" (8:37–39). Moderns are not dissimilar to their ancient counterparts in their needs of this truth, power, and certainty of life as offered by God through justification by faith.

XIV. Summary of doctrine of justification.

The following items or aspects may be considered a summary of the doctrine of justification as taught in the Holy Scriptures. (1) Justification is an *act* of God. In both the OT and NT, God is the initiator and actor in the COVENANT and our SALVATION. It is a once-for-all act that is already accomplished in Christ (Rom. 5:16–18).

(2) Justification is a *forensic act* of God. God declares the sinner or the ungodly righteous in his sight (Rom. 5:8).

(3) Justification is based upon the atonement of Christ. God justifies a sinner for Christ's sake. Without the substitutionary atonement of Christ, God could not forgive the sinner all his sins without being unjust (Rom. 3:24).

(4) Justification is objective or universal. In the gospel God offers the forgiveness of sins gained by Christ to the whole world (Jn. 3:16). Personal or subjective justification is impossible without universal justification.

(5) Justification is remission or forgiveness of sins. Justification is the same as forgiveness of sins. God does not count our sins against us but forgives them and sets us free (Rom. 4:7–8).

(6) Justification is remission of punishment. The justified believer is declared free from the demands of the law and all condemnation resulting from sin against the law (Rom. 3:25; 6:7). It is more than pardon of sin, but a declaration by God. The sinner, though guilty, is relieved of the consequences of his guilt and sin.

(7) Justification is RECONCILIATION of the sinner to God. Justification by faith restores the sinner to personal relationship with God as Father. Mere acquittal or remission of sin would be tantamount to discharging a criminal from the court room in alienation. Justification implies that God looks upon sinners as if they had not sinned since they are again his own (Lk. 15:11–32; Gal. 3:6; 2 Cor. 5:19–20).

(8) Justification is imputation of God's righteousness. Since sinners have no righteousness of their own by which to be justified in God's spiritual court, the salvation Christ wrought through his life and works is imputed to believers as their own righteousness (Rom. 3:25–26; 2 Cor. 5:19–20).

(9) Justification excludes salvation by works. Scripture not only teaches that we are justified without works, but also denounces any introduction of works into God's justification (Rom. 10:2–3; Gal. 3:10–14; 5:4).

(10) Justification presupposes God's universal grace. By grace God justified sinners, and not because of their influence on God (Eph. 1:1–4). God loves and therefore justifies all alike (Jn. 3:16).

(11) Justification is by faith. The fact that justification is "by faith alone" does not exclude God's grace, Christ's work, or the means of grace (word and sacrament). Being justified by grace, for Christ's sake, through the gospel, is being justified by faith alone to the exclusion of works. Faith alone is the instrument of receiving justification so that works are excluded (Rom. 3:28; Eph. 2:8–10).

(12) Justification is bestowed through the means of grace. Although God justifies us, he offers his justification through the word of the gospel and the sacraments. Justification is pronounced in the word of the gospel (Rom. 10:5–12).

(13) Justification is followed by good works and a life of faith. Although the presence of good works is not the condition to receive justification, justification through the gospel by faith offers the power of the Holy Spirit in people's lives so that they lead a life of good works (Jn. 2:14–15; Rom. 6:1–6).

(14) Justification is central to all Christian teaching. The teachings of God; the person and work of Christ, sin, anthropology, word and sacrament, law and gospel, are all involved in the doctrine of justification. In this broad sense, "justification by faith" is theological shorthand for the various terms and concepts of Scripture to describe the entire action of God for our salvation.

(See further L. Petersen, *The Doctrine of Justification by Faith the Leitmotif of the Apology of the Augsburg Confession* [thesis 1940]; J. Fritz, *Justification and Sanctification In the Daily Life of the Christian* [1948]; F. Kramer, *Through Justification to Sanctification* [1952]; G. C. Berkouwer, *Faith and Justification* [1954]; J. Murray, *Redemption: Accomplished and Applied* [1955]; H. Hammann, *Justification by Faith in Modern Theology* [1957]; H. Schmid, *Doctrinal Theology of The Evangelical Lutheran Church* [1961]; Lutheran World Federation Assembly, *A Study Document on Justification* [1963]; H. Stob et al., *A Reexamination of Lutheran and Reformed Traditions III: Justification and Sanctification* [1965]; H. Huxold, *Is Justification For Moderns?* [1965]; J. F. Crosby, *From Religion To Grace: The Doctrine of Justification* [1967]; W. Dantine, *Justification of the Ungodly* [1968]; R. Preus, *Lutheran Trends in Regard to Justification* [1968]; M. Barth, *Justification* [1971]; J. Reumann et al., *Righteousness in the New Testament* [1982]; A. E. McGrath, *Iustitia Dei: A History of the Christian Doctrine of Justification*, 2 vols. [1986]; id., *Justification by Faith: An Introduction* [1988]; D. A. Carson, ed., *Right with God: Justification in the Bible and the World* [1992]; M. A. Seifrid, *Justification by Faith: The Origin and Development of a Central Pauline Theme* [1992]; W. Grudem, *Systematic Theology: An Introduction to Christian Doctrine* [1994], ch. 36., R. K. Moore, *Rectification ("Justification") in Paul, in Historical Perspective, and in the English Bible: God's Gift of Right Relationship*, 3 vols. [2002]; D. A. Carson et al., eds., *Justification and Variegated Nomism*, 2 vols. [2001–2004]; P. A. Rainbow, *The Way of Salvation: The Role of Christian Obedience in Justification* [2006].)

L. M. PETERSEN

Justin Martyr juhs'tin-mahr'tuhr ('Ιουστίνος). Born of pagan parents in SAMARIA probably at the beginning of the 2nd cent. Justin was a student of philosophy who became a Christian sometime before A.D. 135. He taught Christianity for a period in EPHESUS, where he was opposed by a Jewish scholar named Trypho. Subsequently he

View from Mt. Gerizim into the modern city of Nablus, ancient Neapolis, with Mount Ebal in the background. Justin Martyr was born in Neapolis within the region of Samaria.

opened a school for Christians in ROME and taught there until his martyrdom in 165.

Widely regarded as the most important Christian apologist of his time, Justin wrote perhaps a dozen books (cf. Euseb. *Eccl. Hist.* 4.18). Two of his works have survived. The *Apology* (usually regarded as consisting of two distinct treatises, the *First Apology* and the *Second Apology*) refutes slanders against Christianity, delineates true Christian teaching (with emphasis on the fulfillment of the OT by Christ), and provides the earliest full description of baptism and the Eucharist. The *Dialogue with Trypho the Jew* seeks to demonstrate the transitory character of the old covenant, arguing that believing Gentiles take the place of Israel.

Justin, who includes numerous biblical quotations in his writings, is a primary source of information for establishing the texts of the SEPTUAGINT and the NT. Scholars are also dependent on him for an understanding of early church faith and practice. In addition, his theology (with its strong emphasis on the notion of the LOGOS) sheds much light on the development of Christian thought.

(English trans. of Justin's works in *ANF*, vol. 1. See also E. R. Goodenough, *The Theology of Justin Martyr* [1923]; P. Prigent, *Justin et l'Ancien Testament* [1964]; L. W. Barnard, *Justin Martyr: His Life and Thought* [1967]; E. F. Osborn, *Justin Martyr* [1973]; O. Skarsaune, *The Proof from Prophecy: A Study in Justin Martyr's Proof-Text Tradition* [1987]; R. M. Grant, *Greek Apologists of the Second Century* [1988]; T. J. Horner, *Listening to Trypho: Justin Martyr's Dialogue Reconsidered* [2001]; C. D. Allert, *Revelation, Truth, Canon, and Interpretation: Studies in Justin Martyr's Dialogue with Trypho* [2002].)

Justus juhs´tuhs (Ἰοῦστος G2688, from Lat. *Iustus*, "just, righteous"). The use of a double name was common among Jews and proselytes (cf. A. Deissmann, *Bible Studies* [1901], 315–16) and probably the appellation Justus denoted obedience and devotion to the law.

(1) Surname of Joseph BARSABBAS, one of the two men put forward to take the place of Judas in the apostolic band (Acts 1:23). PAPIAS relates that he survived a heathen plot by drinking deadly poison without injury (Euseb. *Eccl. Hist.* 3.39).

(2) Titius Justus, described as "a worshiper of God" at CORINTH who, after the closing of the Jewish synagogue, opened his home next door so that PAUL might continue preaching (Acts 18:7). The form of his name varies in the MSS: "Titius Justus," though found in very few witnesses (including CODEX VATICANUS), is probably original; "Titus Justus" (in CODEX SINAITICUS and a dozen or so other witnesses) is very likely a scribal

adjustment to the more familiar name of Titus; "Justus" by itself (attested in Codex Alexandrinus and the majority of mss, thus KJV) could easily have been the result of an accidental omission (cf. B. M. Metzger, *Textual Commentary on the Greek New Testament*, 2nd ed. [1994], 410). That he was the Titus of Paul's epistles is an ancient but unfounded guess. Some would identify him with Gaius of Corinth (Rom. 16:23); see Gaius #3.

(3) "Jesus, who is called Justus," Paul's appreciated Jewish coworker who sent greetings to the church in Colosse (Col. 4:11). The apostle describes him and two others—Aristarchus and Mark (see Mark, John)—as "the only Jews among my fellow workers for the kingdom of God, and they have proved a comfort to me." The remark indicates that during Paul's first Roman imprisonment almost all of the Jewish Christians at Rome failed to cooperate with Paul in the work of the gospel. These three Jewish believers, however, had been an encouragement to him.

Juttah jut′uh (יוּטָה *H3420*, possibly "level place" or "settlement"). A town in the hill country of the tribe of Judah (Josh. 15:55), later allotted to the Levites (21:16; the name is omitted in the MT of 1 Chr. 6:59, but see NIV and note). It is identified with modern Yaṭṭa, c. 5.5 mi. SSW of Hebron.

The Kadesh Treaty, dated c. 1258 B.C., is the earliest known international peace agreement.

K

kab. See WEIGHTS AND MEASURES III.B.

Kabbon kab′uhn. TNIV form of CABBON.

Kabul kay′buhl. TNIV form of CABUL.

Kabzeel kab′zee-uhl (קַבְצְאֵל H7696, "God has gathered"; alternate form יְקַבְצְאֵל H3677, "God will gather"). A town in the NEGEV, the extreme S of the tribal territory of JUDAH, near the border of EDOM (Josh. 15:21). Kabzeel was the native town of BENAIAH son of Jehoiada, a valiant warrior who was in charge of DAVID's bodyguard (2 Sam. 23:20; 1 Chr. 11:22). Also called Jekabzeel, it was reinhabited by the Judeans after the EXILE (Neh. 11:25). The town was at one point tentatively identified with Khirbet Gharreh (Tel ʿIra, c. 8 mi. E of BEERSHEBA), but this proposal has been abandoned; its precise location is unknown.   S. BARABAS

Kadesh Barnea kay′dish-bahr′nee-uh (קָדֵשׁ H7729, "holy [city]," and קָדֵשׁ בַּרְנֵעַ H7732, perhaps "sanctuary [at the place] of contention"). Also Kadesh-barnea. A site in the N of SINAI, often referred to simply as Kadesh.

I. Geography. The name Kadesh Barnea was applied to an oasis area made by the presence of four springs: ʿAin Qedeis, ʿAin el-Qudeirat, el-Qoseimeh, and el-Muweilih (moving E to W). This multiple spring area was the largest in the NEGEV district and was located approximately 50 mi. SW of BEERSHEBA and also about 50 mi. from the Mediterranean coast to the W. Earlier scholars usually applied the name Kadesh Barnea to only one of these springs. Since the name ʿAin Qedeis preserves the original name of Kadesh, some scholars accepted this site, but it was only a small spring. It might have been sufficient for the TABERNACLE and its staff, but no more. Kadesh Barnea is now generally identified with ʿAin el-Qudeirat, the largest of the springs between Suez and Beersheba. The ruins of a Judean fortress have been discovered at that site.

The name Kadesh, "Holy," is a natural designation for a site with so much water in a desert area. Only the gods could have done this! The meaning of Barnea is uncertain. Kadesh Barnea was the junction point on the Negev-Sinai border where the road from Beersheba forked into three tracks. The W road followed the Wadi el-ʿArish to the Mediterranean. The central road continued S to Egypt and the E track soon turned S to the Gulf of AQABAH.

II. History. The first biblical reference to the site (Gen. 14:7) uses the alternate name EN MISHPAT, "the spring of judgment": since it was a holy place, legal problems would be settled there. This was the W terminus of the armies of KEDORLAOMER and his allies, who invaded EDOM and Sinai for valuable COPPER supplies. During the wilderness wanderings, MOSES referred to Kadesh Barnea as being on the edge of the territory belonging to the king of Edom (Num. 20:16). Archaeological evidence, however, shows that the site was occupied as early as Late Chalcolithic times and the Early Bronze Age. ABRAHAM used Kadesh Barnea as a major supply depot on his trade road between GERAR, his Palestinian business base, and his Egyptian market (Gen. 20:1). His donkey caravans found both the water and the fodder they needed. The area's largest population in OT times was in the period of Middle Bronze I, which is the date for Abraham.

883

Kadesh Barnea.

Hagar's experience at Beer Lahai Roi was near here on the road to Egypt (16:7–14).

Kadesh Barnea shared with Mount Sinai the key historic events of the wilderness wanderings, although scholars differ concerning the exact amount of time Israel spent at Kadesh. In Deut. 1:19, the eleven-day journey from Mount Horeb to Kadesh Barnea is summarized: "Then, as the Lord our God commanded us, we set out from Horeb and went toward the hill country of the Amorites through all that vast and dreadful desert that you have seen, and so we reached Kadesh Barnea." (The same eleven-day schedule has been used on that trade route in modern times.) Kadesh Barnea became the key locale in the exodus story. The spies were sent from Kadesh Barnea (Deut. 1:22–24). The report of the returning spies (Num. 13:25—14:45), Israel's consequent revolt against Moses, and God's rejection of that rebellious generation took place here. The passage includes a brief résumé of Israel's defeat when the nation disobeyed God and attacked the hill country N of Kadesh Barnea.

The springs at Kadesh Barnea are also called "the waters of Meribah [contention] Kadesh" (Num. 27:14; Ezek. 47:19). It was here that the Israelites complained to Moses that there was no water for the people; and it was here that Moses forgot to give God the glory for the miracle of water (Num. 20:1–13). Miriam died at Kadesh (20:1), and nearby, in Mount Hor, Aaron was buried (20:22–29).

Moses sent messengers from Kadesh to the king of Edom asking permission to cross his territory, but the request was denied (Num. 20:14–21). As already mentioned, Kadesh was on the edge of Edomite territory, which at that time extended much farther W than many Bible readers realize. The S boundaries of the Promised Land are given in Num. 34:1–5. Kadesh Barnea is the first site mentioned after the ascent of Akrabbim. Then follows Hazar Addar, which is sometimes identified with ʿAin Qedeis, and Azmon, which is possibly ʿAin Muweilih. These are all at the headwaters of the Wadi of Egypt (el-ʿArish; see Egypt, Brook of). The same boundary is given in Josh. 15:3.

Joshua conquered Kadesh Barnea (Josh. 10:41). At Gilgal, Caleb refers to the earlier Kadesh Barnea spy episode and requests as his inheritance the hill country that had defeated Israel's abortive entry shortly after the exodus. Some time later, Jephthah too reviewed the story of Moses' request from Kadesh to pass through Edom (Jdg. 11:16–17).

III. Archaeological material. The Abraham period has archaeological material that illuminates the Genesis story (see B. Rothenberg, *God's Wilderness: Discoveries in Sinai* [1961], 35–56). Archaeologists have found no permanent buildings from the period of the exodus at any of the four Kadesh springs. The OT is specific, however, that the Israelites were nomads in Sinai; even their tabernacle was a mobile building; consequently, there is little for the archaeologist to discover. It is hoped, however, that further research may throw some light on this period.

The archaeologist resumes the story at Kadesh Barnea by the discovery of the fort that M. Dothan has excavated (see *IEJ* 15 [1965]: 134–51). Earlier work on it had been done by C. L. Woolley and T. E. Lawrence (*The Wilderness of Zin*, new ed. [1936]). The earliest phases belong to slightly earlier. The main fort dates from the 8th cent. B.C. or slightly earlier, and was used through the 6th cent. B.C. It was destroyed by Edomites. The fort was not on high ground, but in the valley alongside the stream that flows from ʿAin en-Qudeirat. It is a typical casemate-fortress measuring 60 x 41 meters. Each of its casemate walls is about a meter thick with four or five meters of open space between them. There were eight towers, one on each corner and one near the center of each side. The upper story of the fort was brick. This site became militarily important under JEHOSHAPHAT when he entered the Red Sea trade.

Some sherds from the Persian period show a postexilic occupation around the spring, but the next major occupation in the whole Kadesh Barnea area was NABATEAN. The last masters in the general area were the Byzantines. (See R. Cohen, *Kadesh-Barnea: A Fortress from the Time of the Judaean Kingdom* [1983]; *NEAEHL*, 3:841–47.)   J. L. KELSO

Kadesh on the Orontes. Also Kedesh and Qadesh (in TELL EL AMARNA texts, Qidša; see Y. Aharoni, *The Land of the Bible: A Historical Geography*, rev. ed. [1979], 159). A town on the ORONTES River in SYRIA, just S of the Lake of Humus (Homs). The familiar battle between RAMSES II and the HITTITES took place here in 1288 B.C. It is the modern Tell Nebi Mend, about 45 mi. S of HAMATH and 75 mi. N of DAMASCUS. Some believe that the term "Desert of Kadesh" (Ps. 29:8) is a reference to this area. Moreover, it has been

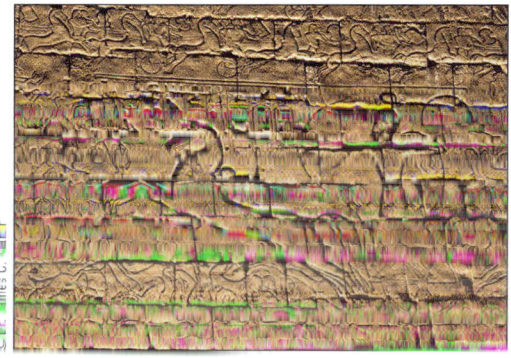

Relief of the military campaign of Ramses II against the Hittites at Kadesh on the Orontes in c. 1288 B.C.

argued that the words *ʾereṣ taḥtîm ḥodšî* (2 Sam. 24:6, NJV, "the region of Tahtim Hodshi") should be emended to read, *ʾereṣ haḥittîm qadēš*, "the land of the Hittites, namely, Kadesh" (cf. NRSV), perhaps a reference to Kadesh on the Orontes (or to KEDESH in Naphtali; for further discussion see TAHTIM HODSHI).   J. B. SCOTT

Kadmiel kad′mee-uhl (קַדְמִיאֵל H7718, possibly "God is the ancient one" [BDB, 870b] or "God is in front [*i.e.*, leads]"). The head of a Levitical family that returned from the EXILE with ZERUBBABEL (Ezra 2:40; 3:9; Neh. 7:43; 12:8, 24; 1 Esd. 5:26 [KJV, "Cadmiel"]). He is presumably the same Kadmiel who supervised the workmen that rebuilt the temple (Ezra 3:9; 1 Esd. 5:58 [KJV, "Cadmiel"]), sealed the covenant of NEHEMIAH (Neh. 10:9), and assisted in leading worship (9:4–5; 12:24).

S. BARABAS

Kadmonite kad′muh-nit (קַדְמֹנִי H7720, "easterner"). A people group whose land was promised to ABRAHAM's descendants (Gen. 15:19). They are mentioned with other groups as a people whose land was somewhere within the region stretching between "the river of Egypt" on the S (see EGYPT, RIVER OF) and the EUPHRATES on the N (v. 18). The name Kadmonite derives from *qedem* H7710, which means "front" or "before." The Hebrews and other peoples designated directions by facing toward the rising sun: "before" or "front" was the direction EAST, to the right was SOUTH, etc. Accordingly, the land eastward was the "land of Qedem" (25:6; NIV, "land of the east"), and the Kadmonites were people of the "east country."

The people who inhabited eastern lands also are called "sons of Qedem," that is, "eastern people"; they include JOB (Job 1:3), the camel-riding kings from MIDIAN (Jdg. 8:10–12), and certain wise men of SOLOMON's time (1 Ki. 4:30–31). See EAST, CHILDREN OF THE. Within the stretch between the river of Egypt and the Euphrates, the Syrian desert E of Byblos (see GEBAL) is perhaps more specifically the region of the Kadmonites. Some scholars, however, are hesitant to identify the Kadmonites with the people of Qedem and suggest that the list in Gen. 15:9 moves from S to N; if so, the Kadmonites, along with the KENITES and KENIZZITES, were Canaanites that lived in the S of Palestine and were later absorbed into the tribe of JUDAH (see T. Ishida in *Bib* 60 [1979]: 461–90, esp. 484).

H. E. FINLEY

Kain kayn (קַיִן *H7805*, possibly "[place of] metal workers"; cf. CAIN). A city of the hill country in conquered territory assigned to the tribe of JUDAH (Josh. 15:57; KJV, "Cain"). It is tentatively identified with en-Nabi Yaqin (Khirbet Bani Dar), 3.5 mi. SE of HEBRON. However, since the SEPTUAGINT omits the name and reduces the summarized number of cities from ten to nine, some scholars have proposed to read "Zanoah of Kain," that is, "of the Kenites" (the latter having been added by scribes to distinguish this ZANOAH from the one mentioned in v. 34). The same Hebrew word refers to the KENITES in two other passages (Num. 24:22 [cf. v. 21]; Jdg. 4:11).

Kaiwan kī'wuhn. Also Chiun, Kiyyun. Both this name and SAKKUTH (Amos 5:26 NRSV, NIV mg.), possibly referring to one or more pagan deities associated with stars, involve a revocalization of the MT, which has *kiyyûn H3962* (apparently "pedestal") and *sikkût* (perhaps a form of *sukkâ H6109*, "tent, tabernacle"; cf. NIV, "shrine"). The basis for the reading *Kaiwan* is Akkadian *kayamānu*, "the steady one," a term applied to Saturn (prob. because, being the farthest of the planets that are visible to the naked eye, it moves most slowly against the background of the stars). Later Aramaic texts definitely use the term *kywn* as a title for Saturn. The SEPTUAGINT renders the Hebrew term with Greek *Rhaiphan G4818* (cf. the quotation in Acts 7:43), an otherwise unknown word that, if not a textual corruption (see REPHAN), possibly reflects the Late Egyptian (Coptic) form Repa, equivalent to Seb, a god also associated with Saturn. The rendering Kaiwan remains uncertain, however (see R. Borger in *ZAW* 100 [1988]: 70–81; *DDD*, 478). C. de Moor translates, "But you carry around the stele of your king / and the pedestal of your statues" (in *UF* 27 [1995]: 1–20, esp. 9–12).

Kalkol kal'kol. TNIV form of CALCOL.

Kallai kal'i (קַלָּי *H7834*, derivation uncertain). Head of the priestly family of Sallu during the days of the high priest JOIAKIM (Neh. 12:20).

Kalneh, Kalno kal'neh, kal'noh. TNIV forms of CALNEH, CALNO.

Kamai. See LEB KAMAI.

Kamon kay'muhn (קָמוֹן *H7852*, derivation uncertain). KJV Camon. The town where JAIR, one of the "minor judges," was buried (Jdg. 10:3–5). Kamon was probably in GILEAD, but its location is uncertain; one possibility is modern Qamm, about 11.5 mi. SE of the Sea of Galilee. (See further *ABD*, 4:5.)

Kanah kay'nuh (קָנָה *H7867*, "reed"). (1) A brook or ravine mentioned in the delineation of the territories of EPHRAIM and MANASSEH (Josh. 16:8; 17:9). It is generally identified with the Wadi Qana, which runs to the W, joining other wadis and then the Yarkon River (see ME JARKON) before flowing into the Mediterranean Sea, just N of JOPPA.

(2) A town marking the boundary of the tribal territory of ASHER toward the N (Josh. 19:28). The village of Qanah still lives on and is about 7.5 mi. SE of TYRE.

J. B. SCOTT

Kandake kan'duh-kee. TNIV form of Candace.

Kanneh kan'uh. TNIV form of CANNEH.

kaph kaf (from כַּף *H4090*, "palm [of hand], hand"). The eleventh letter of the Hebrew ALPHABET (כ) with a numerical value of twenty. It is named for the shape of the letter, which in its original form resembled a three-fingered hand. Later it developed

The Hebrew word *kaph* is the name of the consonant *k* and means "palm of a hand."

KATYDID 887

an elongated diagonal stroke, and in this form was borrowed into the Greek alphabet as *kappa*, from which the *k* in the Roman (and English) alphabet was derived. — G. L. ARCHER

Kareah kuh-ree'uh (קָרֵחַ H7945, "bald head"). Father of Johanan and Jonathan, who were among those who joined GEDALIAH at Mizpah (2 Ki. 25:23 [KJV, "Careah"]; Jer. 40:8, 13, et al.). See JOHANAN #1.

Karka kahr'kuh (קַרְקַע H7978, "floor, ground"). KJV Karkaa. A settlement that served to mark the SW border of the tribe of JUDAH (Josh. 15:3; the name is missing in the parallel, Num. 34:4). It is listed between ADDAR and AZMON, and possibly should be identified with modern ʿAin el-Qeseimeh, c. 50 mi. SW of BEERSHEBA, not far from KADESH BARNEA.

Karkas kahr'kuhs. TNIV form of CARCAS.

Karkor kahr'kor (קַרְקֹר H7980, possibly "fountain"). A site in TRANSJORDAN where GIDEON defeated ZEBAH AND ZALMUNNA, kings of MIDIAN (Jdg. 8:10). Its location is uncertain. According to the text, Gideon reached the Midianites by taking "the route of the nomads east of Nobah and Jogbehah" (v. 11). Some scholars identify Karkor with modern Qarqar (on Wadi Sirhan; see Y. Aharoni et al., *Carta Bible Atlas*, 4th ed. [2002], map 9), but others consider this location too far (more than 100 mi. E of JOGBEHAH; see H. A. Thompson in *ABD*, 4:6).

Karmi, Karmite kahr'mi, kahr'mit. TNIV forms of CARMI, CARMITE.

Karnaim kahr-nay'im (קַרְנַיִם H7969, "[two] horns"). Also Carnaim. A city in N TRANSJORDAN that was captured by the Israelites (Amos 6:13, KJV, "horns"). It is identified with modern Sheikh Saʿd, c. 23 mi. E of the Sea of Galilee. Karnaim eventually replaced nearby ASHTAROTH (see also ASHTEROTH KARNAIM) in the center of the region and became the capital of the Persian fifth satrapy (see SATRAP). The city had a temple dedicated to ATARGATIS that was the scene of a great and bloody slaughter by the Jews under Judas MACCABEE in 165 B.C. (1 Macc. 5:26, 11–15; cf. 2 Macc. 12:21–26 [KJV, "Carnion"]).

Karshena kahr-shee'nuh. TNIV form of CARSHENA.

Kartah kahr'tuh (קַרְתָּה H7985, "city"). A Levitical town within the tribal territory of ZEBULUN, allotted to the descendants of MERARI (Josh. 21:34). The location of Kartah is unknown, and the name is missing in the parallel passage (1 Chr. 6:62 MT, but see LXX, followed by NIV); many scholars think it is an inadvertent scribal repetition of "Kartan" (Josh. 21:32).

Kartan kahr'tan (קַרְתָּן H7986, possibly "city"). A Levitical town within the tribal territory of NAPHTALI, allotted to the descendants of GERSHON (Josh. 21:32). The parallel passage has KIRIATHAIM (1 Chr. 6:76), probably an alternate form. Some identify Kartan/Kiriathaim with modern Khirbet el-Qureiyeh in Upper GALILEE, some 12 mi. SE of Tyre (cf. R. Boling in *Biblical and Related Studies Presented to Samuel Iwry*, ed. A. Kort and S. Morschauser [1985], 23–32, esp. 25); others believe it may be the same as RAKKATH, on the W shore of the Sea of Galilee (cf. Y. Aharoni, *The Land of the Bible: A Historical Geography*, rev. ed. [1979], 438 and map 22; for further details, see ABD, 4:7).

Kasiphia kuh-sif'ee-uh. TNIV form of CASIPHIA.

Kasluhites kas'luh-him, kas'luh-hits. TNIV form of CASLUHIM, CASLUHITES.

Kattath kat'ath (קַטָּת H7793, meaning unknown). A town allotted to the tribe of ZEBULUN (Josh. 19:15; NASB, "Kattah," apparently by mistake). It is mentioned next to NAHALAL, leading many scholars to think that Kattath is the same as KITRON (Jdg. 1:30), though the difference in form is difficult to explain. The town was probably in the N part of the Jezreel Valley (see ESDRAELON), but the precise location is unknown.

katydid. An insect related to the grasshopper. See LOCUST.

Kebar kee´bahr (כְּבָר H3894, perhaps "large, great"). A watercourse in Babylonia. In the OT, the name occurs eight times in the expression *nĕhal-kĕbār*, lit., "the river Kebar" (Ezek. 1:1, 3; 3:15, 23; 10:15, 20, 22; 43:3). The Babylonian equivalent, *nāru kabari*, appears on two contract tablets (from 443 and 423 B.C.) unearthed at NIPPUR. The *nāru kabari* was indeed a "great canal" that branched off from the EUPHRATES above BABYLON, flowed 60 mi. SE, through Nippur, and finally emptied back into the Euphrates near ERECH. Today, after centuries of neglect, this artificial watercourse is dry; the Arabs refer to it as Shaṭṭ en-Nil ("the river Nile"). Most scholars identify the "Kebar River" with this canal. NEBUCHADNEZZAR settled a colony of Jewish exiles on the banks of the Kebar; and EZEKIEL saw his earlier visions as he ministered here. Whether Kebar was dug with the forced labor of Jewish captives is unknown. R. C. RIDALL

Kedar kee´duhr (קֵדָר H7723, perhaps "mighty"; cf. E. A. Knauf, *Ismael*, 2nd ed. [1989], 66). Son of ISHMAEL and ancestor of a tribe in North ARABIA.

I. Importance in OT. Kedar is named second in each of the two lists of Ishmael's sons (Gen. 25:13; 1 Chr. 1:29), but the OT contains no further information about him. The name occurs ten other times as a designation of an Arabian tribe that does not enter directly into the OT history at any point, but must have been well known to the Israelites. It is used figuratively, along with the name of MESHECH (a different ethnic group that lived in an entirely different area), to describe the situation of one dwelling among barbarous strangers, either in a place distant from one's own home, or in a homeland in which the people have turned against truth (Ps. 120:5). In Isa. 42:11 and 60:7 it indicates the future wide extension of God's kingdom. In Jer. 2:10 it is used to point to the distant E, in parallel with KITTIM for the distant W.

Isaiah also refers to the many skillful archers and mighty warriors of Kedar (Isa. 21:17). The great multitude of its flocks, camels, and tents is mentioned elsewhere (Isa. 60:7; Jer. 49:28-29; Ezek. 27:21). In Ezek. 27:21 trade with the princes of Kedar is listed as one of the marks of the greatness of TYRE. The tents of Kedar are used along with the curtains of SOLOMON as a figure to depict the dark beauty of Solomon's beloved one (Cant. 1:5). All these comparisons show how well known distant Kedar must have been to the Israelites in the years between 1000 and 500 B.C. Isaiah predicts that God will soon remove the glory of Kedar and destroy its powerful forces (Isa. 21:16), and Jeremiah predicts a later destruction, this time at the hands of NEBUCHADNEZZAR (Jer. 49:28-29).

II. Extrabiblical references to Kedar. In view of the many biblical references to the N Arabian tribe of Kedar, it might seem strange that early Arabic literature contains no reference to it. Pre-Islamic N Arabic material, however, is extremely limited in quantity. Almost 1,200 years intervened between the time of Nebuchadnezzar and the rise of Islam. In the 19th cent., new light came from the discovery of the annals of ASHURBANIPAL, the last great king of ASSYRIA (669 to c. 632 B.C.). The account of Ashurbanipal's ninth campaign includes the record of an expedition against the people of Kedar (Qedar), which was evidently a powerful factor in N Arabia, both in his reign and in that of his predecessor. An Aramaic inscription from the 5th cent. B.C., found in Egypt, indicates that Geshem the Arabian (perhaps the same GESHEM as is mentioned in Neh. 2:19 and 6:1-6) was a king of Kedar, and that there were at that time Kedarites on the eastern border of Egypt, probably stationed there as guards by the Persians (see I. Rabinowitz in *JNES* 15 [1956]: 1-9). Thus the importance of Kedar in biblical statements is attested by archaeological discoveries.

After the blows inflicted by Ashurbanipal and Nebuchadnezzar, the tribe probably dwindled rapidly and in the course of a few centuries disappeared or was assimilated into other Arabian tribes. In constructing a genealogy of Muhammad, the Islamic hagiographers traced his descent from Abraham and Ishmael through Kedar. (See further F. V. Winnett, "The Arabian Genealogies in Genesis," in *Translating and Understanding the Old Testament*, ed. H. T. Frank and W. L. Reed [1970], 171-96, esp. 193-96; I. Eph'al, *The Ancient Arabs: Nomads on the Borders of the Fertile Crescent, 9th-5th Centuries B.C.* [1982], 223-27 et passim; E. A. Knauf in *ABD*, 4:9-10.) A. A. MACRAE

Kedemah ked´uh-muh (קֵדְמָה *H7716*, possibly "easterner"). Son of ISHMAEL and ancestor of a tribe in N ARABIA (Gen. 25:15; 1 Chr. 1:31). In contrast to the other tribes that descended from Ishmael, Kedemah is not attested in extrabiblical literature. See also NODAB.

Kedemoth ked´uh-moth (קְדֵמוֹת *H7717*, "eastern [place]"). A city, probably on the upper course of the ARNON River, from which MOSES sent messengers to SIHON, king of the AMORITES, requesting a passage through his country (Deut. 2:26; Josh. 13:18). Kedemoth was assigned to the tribe of REUBEN and became a Levitical city allotted to the descendants of MERAR (Josh. 21:37; 1 Chr. 6:79). Its location is uncertain; one of several possibilities is ʿAleiyan, c. 20 mi. E of the DEAD SEA and 6 mi. N of the Arnon (for other proposals, see Z. Kallai, *Historical Geography of the Bible* [1986], 441).

S. BARABAS

Kedesh kee´dish (קֶדֶשׁ *H7730*, "holy place"). Name of several places in Palestine (see also KADESH ON THE ORONTES); some of the identifications are debated. The name Kedesh (like KADESH, with which it is sometimes confused) generally indicated a place where some kind of shrine had stood. Since such shrines were probably common, the term may have been used at various locations, in some of which it was retained, eventually becoming simply a name with no continuing recollection of the cause of its origin.

(1) The most prominent city in Scripture that bore this name was conquered by JOSHUA from a Canaanite king (Josh. 12:22; however, some scholars believe this text refers to #3 below); it later became one of the "fortified cities" in the tribal territory of NAPHTALI (19:37). Described as "Kedesh in Galilee in the hill country of Naphtali," it is listed as one of the three cities of REFUGE W of the Jordan (20:7). It was also one of the Levitical cities allotted to the descendants of GERSHON (21:32; 1 Chr. 6:76). Kedesh is listed among the cities that TIGLATH-PILESER conquered, deporting its inhabitants to ASSYRIA in the reign of PEKAH (2 Ki. 15:29). Generally identified with modern Tell Qades (c. 17 mi. NNW of the Sea of Galilee), Kedesh had a strategic location, being in a fertile plain that overlooks the Jordan Valley (see NEMESIS, 3.855–59.)

(2) BARAK is said to have come from "Kedesh in Naphtali" (Jdg. 4:6), and it was to this city that he called the representatives of ZEBULUN and Naphtali to plan the gathering of troops at Mount TABOR (vv. 9–10). We are also told that HEBER the Kenite lived near it, by a great tree in ZAANANNIM (v. 11). Some scholars have argued that this Kedesh is the same as #1 above, but the text suggests strongly that Barak's hometown must have been relatively close to Mount Tabor and Zaanannim, not in Upper Galilee. A possible identification is modern Khirbet Qedish, about a mile W of the S tip of the Sea of Galilee (see Y. Aharoni, *The Land of the Bible: A Historical Geography*, rev. ed. [1979], 223–24; the same general area is suggested by Z. Kallai, *Historical Geography of the Bible* [1986], 231–35, but he acknowledges that there is no reliable identification). Still other scholars point to Jdg. 5:19, which places the battle "at Taanach by the waters of Megiddo," and argue that the Kedesh in question should be identified with #3 below (but see Aharoni, *Land of the Bible*, 208 n. 109).

(3) A Levitical city within the tribal territory of ISSACHAR, allotted to the Gershonites (1 Chr. 6:72; contrast Kedesh of Naphtali, v. 76). In the parallel list (Josh. 21:28), the place occupied by Kedesh is taken by the name KISHION (one wonders whether this could be another name for the same place based upon its nearness to the historic river KISHON). Because the reference to Kedesh in Josh. 12:22 seems to point to a city in the vicinity of TAANACH, MEGIDDO, and JOKNEAM (i.e., in or near the plain of ESDRAELON), some have argued that this Kedesh is the one in Issachar, not Kedesh in Upper Galilee (see #1 above), and that it should be identified with Tell Abu Qudeis, a small mound between Taanach and Megiddo. Others argue that this site is too far W to have been included in the territory of Issachar (see TRIBES, LOCATION OF). It has also been suggested that Kedesh in Issachar was Barak's hometown (Jdg. 4:6) and/or the place where Heber the Kenite lived (4:11; see #2 above).

(4) A town in the NEGEV, the extreme S of the tribal territory of JUDAH, near the border of EDOM (Josh. 15:23). Since there is no other mention

of such a place in the Scripture, it may be a city otherwise unknown or, as some have suggested, another name for KADESH BARNEA (but see Aharoni, *Land of the Bible*, 353).　　　A. A. MACRAE

Kedorlaomer ked′or-lay′oh-muhr (כְּדָרְלָעֹמֶר H3906, prob. from Elamite *kutir* [Akk. *kudur*] and *Lagamaru*, "servant of [the goddess] Lagamar"). Also Chedorlaomer. The king of ELAM defeated by ABRAHAM (Gen. 14:1–17). The goddess Lagamar (or Lakamal) is referred to in Akkadian texts of the Agade and Old Babylonian period (MARI) and is common in Middle Iranian. The name is therefore appropriate to the period c. 2000–1700 B.C.

Kedorlaomer is named as king of Elam and leader of a coalition (Gen. 14:4) with AMRAPHEL of SHINAR (Babylonia), ARIOCH of ELLASAR, and TIDAL king of GOIIM, which sacked SODOM and GOMORRAH when these cities revolted after a submission of twelve years. On their return near DAMASCUS, Abraham and his band of retainers defeated them in a surprise night attack. Archaeological evidence of an advanced civilization (Middle Bronze I) in TRANSJORDAN, the NEGEV, and SINAI that collapsed suddenly authenticates the background of this event.

The view that this text represents an authentic historical document is in no way belittled by present uncertainty in the identification of Kedorlaomer or his associates. Powerful coalitions of kings marching long distances in the 2nd millennium B.C. are known from CUNEIFORM texts. The commonest view is that which identifies Kedorlaomer with Kutir-naḫḫunti I of Elam c. 1625 B.C. (?) but this requires an unsupported equation of *naḫḫundi* with *laʿomar*, which is unlikely in view of the divine name given above. A more complex view, based on the so-called "Kedorlaomer" tablets in the British Museum (7th cent. B.C.), identifies him with a king of Elam named there KU.KU.KU.MAL. It has been suggested that the four kings represent different periods and the four "world-regions"—Babylonia (S), Elam (E), Ellasar (N = Assyria), and Goiim (W = Hatti). On this view, Gen. 14 would be an early MIDRASH. (See M. C. Astour in *Biblical Motifs: Origins and Transformations*, ed. A. Altmann [1966], 65–112, and in *ABD*, 1:893–95, s.v. "Chedorlaomer".)　　　D. J. WISEMAN

Kedron kee′druhn (Κεδρών). KJV Cedron. A town near Jamnia (see JABNEEL #2), fortified by the SELEUCID commander Cendebeus at the orders of ANTIOCHUS VII as preparation for an invasion of JUDEA during the time of SIMON MACCABEE (1 Macc. 15:39–41; 16:9). It provided strategic control of several roads into Judea. It is generally identified with modern Qatra, about 8 mi. SE of Jamnia and 25 mi. W of Jerusalem.　　　F. B. HUEY, JR.

keeper. This term is used over forty times in the KJV (but fewer than ten times in the NIV) to render various terms, especially the participle of Hebrew *šāmar* H9068, "to keep, guard" (e.g., Gen. 4:9; 1 Sam. 17:20 [NIV, "shepherd"]; Ps. 121:5 [NIV, "watches"]) and Greek *phylax* G5874, "guard" (e.g., Acts 5:23). The expression "keeper of the wardrobe" refers to a civil servant who was apparently in charge not only of the king's personal clothing, but also of robes used by others in the royal court (2 Ki. 10:22, where "wardrobe" translates the HAPAX LEGOMENON *meltāḥâ* H4921; in 22:14 and 2 Chr. 34:22 the term is *beged* H955, a very common word meaning "clothing, garment").

Kehelathah kee′huh-lay′thuh (קְהֵלָתָה H7739, "assembly"). A stopping place of the Israelites between Rissah and Mount Shepher on their wilderness journey (Num. 33:22–23; LXX *Makellath* [cf. vv. 25–26]). The site is unknown.

Keilah kee-i′luh (קְעִילָה H7881, derivation uncertain). (**1**) A town in the SHEPHELAH allotted to the tribe of JUDAH (Josh. 15:44). It is identified with modern Khirbet Qila, c. 17 mi. SW of JERUSALEM and 8 mi. NW of HEBRON. DAVID led a daring expedition to Keilah to deliver it from attacks by the PHILISTINES who were robbing the threshing floors. Hearing of it, SAUL sent troops there to capture him and his men. David was forced to retreat again into the wilderness of ZIPH, when it became apparent after consulting the ephod that the men of Keilah might turn him over to Saul (1 Sam. 23:1–13). Keilah is mentioned in the TELL EL-AMARNA letters as Qilti, an Egyptian base. Letters to AKHENATEN, pharaoh of Egypt, from the princes of Jerusalem and Hebron complained of each other's occupation of Keilah at various times.

The town was inhabited by Jews returning from the EXILE and was included in the roster of those who participated in rebuilding the walls of Jerusalem under NEHEMIAH (Neh. 3:17–18). There is a tradition that the prophet HABAKKUK was buried in Keilah.

(2) A GARMITE included in the genealogy of Judah (1 Chr. 4:19). The passage as a whole (vv. 16–20) lists a number of persons whose connection with the descendants of Judah is not given. Keilah probably gave his name to the town (above, #1). See also ESHTEMOA; HODIAH.   F. B. HUEY, JR.

Kelaiah ki-lay′yuh (כְּלָיָה H7835, meaning uncertain; see J. D. Fowler, *Theophoric Personal Names in Ancient Hebrew* [1988], 148). A Levite who agreed to put away his foreign wife (Ezra 10:23; 1 Esd. 9:23 [KJV, "Colius"]). The text further identifies him as KELITA.

Kelal kee′lal (כְּלָל H4006, possibly "completeness, perfection"). One of the descendants of PAHATH-MOAB who agreed to put away their foreign wives (Ezra 10:30).

Kelita ki-li′tuh (קְלִיטָא H7836, possibly "midget" or "cripple"). Also called KELAIAH (Kelita may be a nickname). A Levite who agreed to put away his foreign wife (Ezra 10:23; 1 Esd. 9:23 [KJV, "Calitas"]). He is probably the same Levite listed among those who instructed the people (Neh. 8:7) and who signed the covenant of NEHEMIAH (10:10; 1 Esd. 9:48 [KJV, "Calitas"]).

Kelub kee′luhb (כְּלוּב H3991, apparently from a word meaning "basket"). (1) A man identified as brother of Shuhah and father of Mehir (1 Chr. 4:11; the LXX has CALEB). These persons and others are referred to as "the men of Recah" (v. 12). They were apparently descendants of JUDAH, but their precise genealogical connection is not given.

(2) Father of Ezri; the latter was an official of DAVID charged with supervising "the field workers who farmed the land" (1 Chr. 27:26).
          K. L. BARKER

Kelubai. See CALEB #2.

Keluhi kel′yoo-hi (כְּלוּהִי H3988 [thus *Ketib*, but perhaps to be vocalized differently, *Qere* כְּלוּהוּ], possibly from a root meaning "complete"). KJV Chelluh; NRSV Cheluhi. One of the descendants of BANI who agreed to put away their foreign wives (Ezra 10:35 [LXX, *Chelia*]; the name is missing in the parallel passage, 1 Esd. 9:35).

Kemuel kem′yoo-uhl (קְמוּאֵל H7851, possibly "God has arisen" or "Qam is God"). (1) Son of NAHOR, nephew of ABRAHAM, and father of ARAM (Gen. 22:21).

(2) Son of Shiphtan; he was a leader from the tribe of EPHRAIM, chosen to assist in the distribution of the land (Num. 34:24).

(3) Father of Hashabiah; the latter was an officer over the tribe of LEVI in the days of King DAVID (1 Chr. 27:17).   S. BARABAS

Kenaanah ki-nay′uh-nuh (כְּנַעֲנָה H4049 [in form, fem. of כְּנַעַן H4046; see CANAAN]). Also Chenaanah. (1) Son of Bilhan and descendant of BENJAMIN (1 Chr. 7:10); he and his brothers were warriors and heads of families (v. 11).

(2) Father of ZEDEKIAH; the latter was a false prophet who predicted victory for AHAB at the battle of RAMOTH GILEAD (1 Ki. 22:11, 24; 2 Chr. 18:10, 23); 1 Ki. 22:24; 2 Chr. 18:23).
          F. W. BUSH

Kenan kee′nuhn (קֵינָן H7809, apparently derived from קַיִן H7803, CAIN; Καϊνάμ G2783). Son of ENOSH and grandson of SETH (Gen. 5:9–14 [KJV, "Cainan"]; 1 Chr. 1:2); included in Luke's GENEALOGY of Jesus Christ (Lk. 3:37 [KJV and NRSV, "Cainan"]; in v. 36, the same Gk. form is rendered CAINAN by the NIV).

Kenani ki-nay′ni (כְּנָנִי H4039, short form of כְּנַנְיָהוּ H4041, "Yahweh has strengthened"; see KENANIAH). Also Chenani. One of the Levites who led the people in confession and worship after EZRA read from the Book of the Law (Neh. 9:4).

Kenaniah ken′uh-ni′uh (כְּנַנְיָהוּ H4041 and כְּנַנְיָה H4040, "Yahweh has strengthened [or is firm]"; see KENANI). Also Chenaniah. (1) The head Levite who was "in charge of the singing" when the ARK OF THE

COVENANT was transported to Jerusalem (1 Chr. 15:22, 27). The term for "singing" is *maśśāʾ H5362*, "lifting, burden," usually interpreted to mean "the lifting [of song]," but some argue that it refers to "the lifting [of the ark]," indicating that Kenaniah supervised the proper handling of the ark of the covenant. Still others suggest that the word used here is the homonym *maśśāʾ H5363*, "pronouncement, oracle," and that Kenaniah was a leader of prophecy (cf. JB, "versed in divine oracles," v. 22).

(2) A Levite descended from IZHAR; in the time of DAVID, Kenaniah and his sons were "assigned duties away from the temple, as officials and judges over Israel" (1 Chr. 26:29; cf. Neh. 11:16).

M. R. WILSON

Kenath kee´nath (קְנָת *H7875*, derivation unknown). A city in BASHAN, taken from the AMORITES by a Manassite leader called NOBAH, who gave it his own name (Num. 32:42; cf. Jdg. 8:11). It was later lost to the Geshurites and Arameans (1 Chr. 2:23; the KJV rendering is incorrect). Kenath is mentioned in Egyptian and other extrabiblical texts. In Hellenistic times it became one of the cities of the DECAPOLIS under the name Kanatha; the Arabians defeated HEROD the Great there (Jos. *War* 1.19.2). It is usually identified with modern Qanawat in Syria (about 57 mi. E of the Sea of Galilee), where there are many impressive ruins from Greco-Roman times.

S. BARABAS

Kenaz, Kenizzite kee´naz, ken´uh-zit (קְנַז *H7869*, meaning uncertain; gentilic קְנִזִּי *H7870*, "Kenizzite" [KJV also "Kenezite"]). **(1)** Son of Eliphaz and grandson of ESAU; an Edomite chief (Gen. 36:11, 15, 42; 1 Chr. 1:36, 53).

(2) Younger brother of CALEB (son of Jephunneh the Kenizzite); father of Othniel and Seraiah (Josh. 15:17; Jdg. 1:13; 3:9, 11; 1 Chr. 4:13). For the view that Othniel was Caleb's younger brother and that therefore Kenaz was Caleb's father, see discussion under OTHNIEL.

(3) Son of Elah and grandson of Caleb (1 Chr. 4:15).

(4) Clan or family name. The Kenizzites are one of the S Palestinian tribes (listed between KENITES and KADMONITES) whose land God promised to Abraham's descendants (Gen. 15:19). Unless predictive prophecy is involved here, these Kenizzites must be a different family from that connected with Kenaz son of Eliphaz (#1 above). Caleb is said to be the son of Jephunneh the Kenizzite (Num. 32:12; Josh. 14:6, 14), but the exact meaning of the clan name here is not clear. On the one hand, the Kenizzites are described as an alien people (Gen. 15:19), and Caleb apparently is promised a portion of the land because of faithfulness rather than birthright (Josh. 14:6–14). On the other hand, the genealogy of 1 Chr. 2 (see vv. 9, 18) speaks of Caleb son of HEZRON (the latter being a grandson of JUDAH). Many scholars believe that Caleb belonged to the Edomite clan known as the Kenizzites (which along with other non-Israelite groups living in S Palestine was absorbed into the tribe of Judah) and that the Chronicles genealogy is an attempt to give the descendants of Caleb legal status in postexilic Judaism. It is possible that the apparent discrepancy may be accounted for by duplicate names. (See further H. L. Ginsberg and B. Maisler, "Semitized Hurrians in Syria and Palestine," *JPOS* 14 [1934]: 243–67; N. Glueck, "Kenites and Kenizzites," *PEQ* no vol. [1940]: 22–24; J. M. Miller and J. H. Hayes, *A History of Ancient Israel and Judah* [1986], 103.)

J. OSWALT

Kenezite ken´uh-zit. KJV alternate form of Kenizzite. See KENAZ.

Kenite ken´it (קֵינִי *H7808*, gentilic of קַיִן *H7803*, "metal worker"; see CAIN). Clan or tribal name of seminomadic peoples of S Palestine and Sinai. Its probable etymology suggests that the Kenites were METAL workers, especially since Sinai and the Wadi el-ʿArabah were rich in high-grade COPPER ore. W. F. Albright (in *CBQ* 25 [1963]: 1–11) has pointed to the Beni Hasan mural in Egypt (19th cent. B.C.) as an illustration of such a wandering group of smiths. This mural depicts thirty-six men, women, and children in characteristic Semitic dress leading, along with other animals, donkeys laden with musical instruments, weapons, and an item that Albright has identified as a bellows. He has further noted that LAMECH's three children (Gen. 4:19–22) were responsible for herds (JABAL), musical instruments (JUBAL), and metal work (TUBAL-CAIN, meaning possibly "Tubal the smith"), the three occupations which seem most evident in the mural.

I. General references. It is clear that references to the Kenites are not to a tightly knit group living in a narrowly defined area. The name rather applies to a number of loosely related groups possessing common skills or perhaps claiming a common ancestor. At times the term is used quite narrowly in the Bible and at other times more widely, but at no time must it be applied to *all* Kenites. The land of the Kenites is promised to ABRAHAM's descendants (Gen. 15:19). This would be the territory of a certain Kenite clan, probably S of HEBRON. Similarly, it is a particular group of Kenites that is condemned in BAALAM's oracle (Num. 24:21–22), while another group is praised for having been kind to the Hebrews in the wilderness (1 Sam. 15:6). The exact cause for Baalam's condemnation is not given, but in the context it appears that these Kenites had allied themselves with AMALEK against MOSES.

II. Relations with Moses. The exact identity of Moses' father-in-law is very complex. He seems to carry three personal names: JETHRO, REUEL, and HOBAB. In Exodus and Numbers he is called a Midianite (Exod. 2:16–21; 18:1; Num. 10:29), but in Jdg. 1:16 and 4:11 a Kenite. Albright has proposed the following solution: Jethro, a Kenite of the Reuel clan, was living in Midian (well-known for its rich copper lodes) when Moses first met him. Later, during the exodus, Moses' *son-in-law* (ḥātān H3163 rather than ḥōtēn H3162) named Hobab, also of the Reuel clan, was asked to act as guide for the Israelites. Whether this reconstruction of the relationship of the names is correct or not, it does appear that Kenite was the actual tribal affiliation, while the name Midianite refers to location only. It may be that the skill of Moses and Aaron in smelting and casting (cf. the golden calf and the brazen serpent) was gained through Moses' association with the Kenites. It has been proposed that the essentials of Yahwism were learned from the Kenites. Julian Morgenstern (in *HUCA* 4 [1927]: 1–138) claimed that the earliest document of the Pentateuch was the K, or Kenite, document. Although many scholars have espoused such a position at one time or another, no evidence within Scripture or without can be adduced to show that the Kenites were Yahwists before Moses.

III. During the period of the judges. According to Jdg. 1:16, the descendants of Moses' Kenite father-in-law (Jethro in LXX Codex B) allied themselves with the Israelites and settled with them in the Negev near ARAD (S of HEBRON and E of

Region S of Hebron where the Kenites lived. (View to the NW.)

Beersheba at the S edge of the Judean wilderness). The Hebrew text says that these Kenites "lived among the people [*hāʿām*]," but some scholars emend it to read "lived among the Amalekites [*hāʿămālēqi*]" (cf. NRSV). This emendation was occasioned by the reading of some Greek MSS, but perhaps more by 1 Sam. 15:6, which states that Saul, before attacking Amalek, told the Kenites to depart from Amalek lest they be destroyed as well. This may simply mean, however, that a nomadic group of Kenites was living among the Amalekites at that time rather than having been settled for many years.

The nomadic character of the Kenites is clearly seen in the detail that one family (not a whole tribe), that of Heber, had migrated northward to Galilee (Jdg. 4:11). The fact that the Canaanite general Sisera took refuge in Heber's tent because Jabin and Heber's clan were in good terms (4:17) shows that Kenites were expected to live among a people (in this case, the Hebrews) without having partisan loyalties. In this situation, unfortunately for Sisera, Heber's wife Jael did possess such loyalties (5:24–26). Since the Philistines had a monopoly on iron workers (1 Sam. 13:19–20), the Kenites probably worked only with copper and bronze.

IV. The early monarchy. During this period a significant concentration of Kenites was located in the southern Judean territory. This is clear from 1 Sam. 15:6, cited above, and also from David's relations with them. While David was a Philistine vassal, he attacked the enemies of Judah in the S while telling his superiors that he was attacking Judah, the Jerahmeelites, and the Kenites (27:10). Not only was he not attacking Judah and her friends, he was sending them gifts from his spoils (30:29).

The fact that the villages of Jezreel and Carmel, from which came two of David's wives (25:42–43), are listed in the same group with Kain (Josh. 15:55) has caused some scholars to say that David's wives were Kenites. However, there is no certainty that all the villages in that group were inhabited by these clans. R. North (*JBL* 83 [1964]: 373–89) has attempted to link David with the Kenites in another way. He argues that the Kenites were the musicians of the day, and that it was because David was a Kenite that he introduced music into the temple worship. While the Kenites may well have been musicians (note that Jabal, Jubal, and Tubal are all based on the root *ybl*, "to lead in [festival] procession"), the relationship with David is most tenuous. Much of the argument rests on the fact that David sent gifts to his "kinsmen" (Heb. *rēaʿ* H8276), the elders of Judah, and, among many others, the Kenites (1 Sam. 30:26–31), but the usual translation "friends" (i.e., "brothers" in a common cause) is the most likely interpretation.

V. Postexilic references. In 1 Chr. 2:55 the families of scribes living at Jabez are said to be Kenites. Apparently, during the kingdom and exile periods, certain Kenites had given up nomadic smithing and had taken on the more sedentary, but equally honorable, profession of scribe. The same text indicates some connection between them and the house of Recab; perhaps the Recabites were a clan within the Kenite lineage. (See further H. Schmökel, "Yahwe und die Keniter," *JBL* 52 [1933]: 212–29; B. Halpern in *ABD*, 4:17–22.)   J. Oswalt

Kenizzite. See Kenaz.

kenosis ki-noh´sis (κενώσις, "emptying, depletion"). This term, which occurs first in the patristic literature, was used in Christian theology from very early times, usually as a synonym for the Incarnation. It refers to a view that emphasizes Christ's humiliation or condescension. Support for the doctrine rests primarily on Phil. 2:6–8, with parallels having to do with his humiliation (2 Cor. 8:9) and exaltation (Jn. 17:5; see Exaltation of Christ). The cognate verb *kenoō* G3033 (with the reflexive pronoun) occurs in Phil. 2:7, which is often translated, "[Christ] emptied himself" (NIV, "made himself nothing"). Whereas the Philippian passage gives support to Christ's humiliation, the problem of interpretation is raised by those passages that clearly portray his divine powers, especially in the Gospel of John (cf. Jn. 1:14, 48; 5:19–24; 10:30; 11:41; 13:1–3).

The basic question, therefore, is how and to what extent Jesus' full humanity forced him to "empty" himself of the divine, and how and to what extent his divine powers remained. The theological issue is profoundly difficult, for it takes one into the nature of the TRINITY: when divine powers are allowed in the man Christ Jesus, what, if anything has happened to the person of God himself? Problems of interpretation are further aggravated by the fact that the other uses of the verb (Rom. 4:14; 1 Cor. 1:17; 9:15; 2 Cor. 9:3) are uniformly figurative in their context and will not bear the weight of literal usage that the Kenoticists demand of the same word in Phil. 2:7.

Solutions to the problem have moved across the spectrum of five possible interpretations. (1) In the incarnation, Christ gave up all divine attributes and thus was deprived of all cosmic functions and divine consciousness (Gess, Beecher, et al.). (2) A distinction is made between essential and relative attributes in God, so that Christ in his incarnation gave up not his essential attributes but only his relative attributes (Thomasius, Delitzsch, et al.). (3) In his obedience to his Father, Christ gave up no divine powers but gave up their independent exercise. (4) His humanity was such that he did not exercise his divine powers at all (Martensen and Gore). (5) The divine nature united itself with his humanity only gradually, and his full deity was consummated finally at the resurrection; the incarnation was process rather than act (Dorner).

Exegetes vary in their point of emphasis. The best interpretation of Phil. 2:6–8 seems to center not on *morphē theou*, "the form of God," but on *einai isa theō*, "being on an equality with God." In other words, he did not give up his powers but gave up his position. He no longer acted as sovereign but as servant. J. B. Lightfoot states the position by noting that Christ divested himself not of the divine nature, which was impossible, but "of the glories, the prerogatives, of Deity. This He did by taking upon Him the form of a servant" (*St. Paul's Epistle to the Philippians* [1869], 112). Modern interpreters tend to evade the theological and even the exegetical questions in terms of the general thrust of the passage, which simply states in vivid language Christ's willingness to leave his glory for the cross. He emptied himself so utterly that only the vision of his rights in glory as against the shame of the cross can give mankind the "mind of Christ."

(See further A. B. Bruce, *The Humiliation of Christ in Its Physical, Ethical, and Official Aspects*, 4th ed. [1895], Lectures 3–5; H. C. Sheldon, *History of Christian Doctrine*, 2nd ed., 2 vols. [1895], 2:134–37, 348–53; H. R. Mackintosh, *The Doctrine of the Person of Jesus Christ* [1912], 141–284; E. Brunner, *The Mediator: A Study of the Central Doctrine of the Christian Faith* [1934], passim, esp. ch. 12; L. Berkhof, *Systematic Theology* [1946], 327–30; W. Grudem, *Systematic Theology: An Introduction to Christian Doctrine* [1994], 549–52. For additional bibliography, see INCARNATION.)

A. H. LEITCH

Kephar Ammoni kee′fuhr-am′oh-ni כְּפַר הָעַמֹּנִי *H4112*, "village of the Ammonites"). KJV Chepharhaammonai; NRSV Chephar-ammoni. A town allotted to the tribe of BENJAMIN (Josh. 18:24). The name suggests that it was inhabited by (or perhaps captured from) Ammonites (see AMMON). The site is unknown, but like some of the other towns in the list (e.g., BETHEL, OPHRAH), it may have been N of Benjamin's boundary, within the territory of EPHRAIM. F. W. BUSH

Kephirah ki-fi′ruh (כְּפִירָה *H4098*, "[open] village"). Also Chephirah. A city of the Gibeonites (see GIBEON) included in the treaty they obtained from Israel by stealth (Josh. 9:17). They were apparently HIVITES (9:7). The town was later included in the tribal territory of BENJAMIN (18:26). Inhabitants of Kephirah were among those who returned from the EXILE with ZERUBBABEL (Ezra 2:25; Neh. 7:29; 1 Esd. 5:19 [KJV, "Caphira," with the additional clause, "they of Pira, seven hundred," for which there is very weak textual support]). The site is modern Khirbet el-Kefireh, about 8.5 mi. WNW of JERUSALEM (on the road to Jaffa), 5 mi. WSW of Gibeon (el-Jib), and less than 2 mi. N of KIRIATH JEARIM. F. W. BUSH

Kerak kuhr′ahk (Arab. name derived from Aram. כְּרַךְ, "fortified place"). (1) The modern name of a Transjordanian site probably to be identified with the Moabite city of KIR HARESET.

(2) Khirbet Kerak (not mentioned in the Bible) is a large and important archaeological site on the SW shore of the Sea of Galilee, just N of the present mouth of the Jordan River. It was strategically located at the crossroads of two important caravan routes. The site covers over 54 acres, and

is 1,200 by 350 meters in size. Excavations from 1941 to c. 1955 were carried out by B. Mazar, M. Stekelis, M. Avi-Yonah, P. Guy, and Mr. Bar-Adon (see *IEJ* 2 [1952]: 165–73, 218–29). Occupations during Late Chalcolithic through Middle Bronze II periods were reported, with a gap until Hellenistic times. The TALMUD identifies the site with Beth Yerah ("House of the Moon"), which L. Sukenik showed identical with Philoteria, named in honor of PTOLEMY Philadelphus's sister (*JPOS* 2 [1922]: 101–8).

The famous Khirbet Kerak pottery ware was first identified at this site, although it evidently originated in northern Anatolia and the Caucasus region. Its sudden appearance speaks of conquest from that direction. Khirbet Kerak was one of the region's major cities in its early history, but there was also an occupational gap between the end of the Early Bronze and beginning of the Middle Bronze Ages. Fortifications included Early Bronze walls of 30 ft. in thickness (fully demonstrating the city-state in urban structure), and strong Hellenistic structures. (See G. Smith, *The Historical Geography of the Holy Land*, 25th ed. [1932], 451–55; Y. Aharoni, *The Land of the Bible: A Historical Geography*, rev. ed. [1979], 134–35.) M. H. HEICKSEN

Keran kee′ruhn (כְּרָן *H4154*). Also Cheran. Son of DISHON and grandson of SEIR the HORITE (Gen. 36:26; 1 Chr. 1:41).

kerchief. This term is used by the KJV to render Hebrew *mispāḥâ H5029* (only Ezek. 13:18, 21). It is found in a passage dealing with DIVINATION, which required the head to be covered. It is not known what kerchiefs looked like or how they were used, but apparently they were veils varying in length with the height of the wearer and were worn by those who consulted the seers. S. BARABAS

Keren-Happuch ker′uhn-hap′uhk (קֶרֶן הַפּוּךְ *H7968*, "horn of ANTIMONY," i.e., "container of [black] eye-paint"). The youngest of JOB's daughters, born to him after his restoration from affliction (Job 42:14). The name alludes to her beauty (cf. v. 15).

Kerethite ker′uh-thit (כְּרֵתִי *H4165*, possibly "Cretan"). Also Cherethite (in Ezek. 25:16, KJV has the superfluous pl., "Cherethims"). The Kerethites were a people group that apparently came from the AEGEAN area; DAVID chose his personal guard from the Kerethites and the PELETHITES (1 Sam. 30:14; 2 Sam. 8:18; 15:18; 20:7, 23 [*Qere*, CARITES]; 1 Ki. 1:38, 44; 1 Chr. 18:17; Ezek. 25:16; Zeph. 2:5 [cf. also v. 6 NIV]).

Although some ancient versions (Targum, Syriac) and modern commentators (KD, *1–2 Samuel*, 367) have understood the words as common nouns ("executioners" and "runners"), the ending is denominative and frequently employed in proper names as a gentilic. It is virtually certain that the words refer to people groups. The Kerethites are generally said to have been Cretans on the basis of the similarity of the two names (the name CRETE for the Mediterranean island is already attested in Homeric times) and the connection between the Kerethites and the PHILISTINES (Aegeans who invaded Palestine). On the other hand, J. Prignaud (in *RB* 71 [1964]: 215–29) points out that the Kerethites are never directly associated with Crete; he believes that they may have had another origin and were subsequently assimilated by the Philistines. (See further M. Delcor in *VT* 28 [1978]: 409–22.) As for the Pelethites, they are generally held to be Philistines.

Whatever their identification, the Kerethites and Pelethites appear in the Bible as parts of David's army. They seem to have been especially active in times of crisis for David, remaining loyal to him in all three revolts against the king. They went with him when he had to flee from ABSALOM (2 Sam. 15:18); they pursued SHEBA after his rebellion (20:7); when ADONIJAH tried to succeed David as king, it was the Kerethites and Pelethites who formed the bodyguard for Solomon's anointing (1 Ki. 1:38). Their leader was BENAIAH son of Jehoiada (2 Sam. 8:18), who is also called the leader of David's bodyguard (23:23). It is probable that the Kerethites and Pelethites were this bodyguard. D. HUTTAR

Kerioth ker′ee-oth (קְרִיּוֹת *H7954*, pl. of קִרְיָה *H7953*, "town, city"). **(1)** A city in MOAB declared to be under God's judgment (Jer. 48:24, 41 [NRSV, "towns"]; Amos 2:2). Kerioth is probably to be identified with el-Qereiyat, about 8 mi. E of the DEAD SEA and 7 mi. NW of DIBON.

(2) According to the KJV, a city in the extreme S of the territory of JUDAH (Josh. 15:25). See KERI-OTH HEZRON.　　　　　　　　　　J. B. SCOTT

Kerioth Hezron ker′ee oth-hez′ruhn (קְרִיּוֹת חֶצְרוֹן H7955, "towns of HEZRON"). A town in the NEGEV, the extreme S of the tribal territory of JUDAH, near the border of EDOM; it was also known as HAZOR, a common name (Josh. 15:25; KJV, "Kerioth *and* Hezron"). Its location is uncertain, but it has been tentatively identified with modern Khirbet el-Qaryatein, about 13 mi. SSE of HEBRON and 4 mi. S of MAON.

Kerith kihr′ith (כְּרִית H4134, possibly "ditch" or "cutting"). Also Cherith. A brook or valley E of the JORDAN where ELIJAH fled after he had announced the coming drought to King AHAB of Israel (1 Ki. 17:3, 5; NIV, "Kerith Ravine"; NRSV, "Wadi Cherith"). The expression "before Jordan" (KJV) is not clear as to which side of that river was meant. Since Elijah's home was in GILEAD, the E side seems more likely, although there is a tradition that it is the Wadi Qelt near JERICHO on the W side. Any number of WADIS with their numerous caves could be the brook Kerith; one possibility is Wadi Yabis (Naḥal Yavesh) in Gilead, which empties into the Jordan about 22 mi. S of the Sea of Galilee.
　　　　　　　　　　　　R. L. ALDEN

Keros kihr′os (קֵרֹס H7820, perhaps "crooked"). Ancestor of a family of temple servants (NETH-INIM) who returned from the EXILE with ZERUB-BABEL (Ezra 2:44; Neh. 7:47; 1 Esd. 5:29 [KJV, "Ceras"]).

Kerub kihr′uhb (כְּרוּב H4132). Also Cherub. One of five Babylonian places from which certain Jew-ish exiles returned who were unable to prove their Israelite ancestry (Ezra 2:59; Neh. 7:61). If Kerub here is a place name, its location is unknown. How-ever, the parallel in the APOCRYPHA reads, "The following are those who came up from Tel-melah and Tel-harsha, under the leadership of Cherub [Gk. *Charaathalar*], Addan, and Immer" (1 Esd. 5:36 NRSV, following a generally accepted conjectural emendation), and some scholars argue that this reading is original.

kerygma ki-rig′muh (κήρυγμα G3060, "procla-mation"). This term is used in biblical scholarship to refer to the apostolic PREACHING of the GOSPEL, especially its original proclamation (e.g., the ser-mons in the book of Acts). It is often contrasted with the *didache* G1439, its "teaching" aspects. See DOCTRINE.

Kesalon kes′uh-luhn (כְּסָלוֹן H4076, possibly "[on the] flank, loin"; cf. KESIL and KESULLOTH). Also Chesalon. A town on the N boundary of the tribe of Judah (Josh. 15:10). Located between Mount SEIR and BETH SHEMESH, Kesalon is given in the text as another name for the "northern slope of Mount Jearim." The modern site is a ruin known as Kesla, about 11 mi. W of JERUSALEM, at an elevation of more than 1,900 ft. Although the region as a whole is characterized by oak forests (JEARIM means "woods"), Kesla itself is a summit on bare rock.

Kesed kee′sid (כֶּשֶׂד H4168, apparently related to כַּשְׂדִּים H4169, "Chaldeans, Babylonians"). Also Chesed. Son of NAHOR by his wife MILCAH; nephew of ABRAHAM (Gen. 22:22). The passage as a whole seems to indicate the origins of various tribes, and possibly Kesed is presented as the ances-tor of the Babylonians.

Kesil kee′sil (כְּסִיל H4069, "flank, side"; cf. KESA-LON and KESULLOTH). Also Chesil. A town in the NEGEV, the extreme S of the tribal territory of JUDAH, near the border of EDOM (Josh. 15:30). Much of this section of the city-list (beginning with Moladah) is presented elsewhere as an enclave of the tribe of SIMEON, but in those parallel passages the name Kesil seems to be replaced by Bethul (Josh. 19:4) and Bethuel (1 Chr. 4:30). For further discussion, see BETHUEL #2.　　　　F. W. BUSH

Kesulloth ki-suhl′oth (כְּסֻלּוֹת H4063, possibly "[on the] loins"; cf. KESALON and KESIL). Also Chesulloth. A town allotted to the tribe of ISSA-CHAR (Josh. 19:18). It is probably the same as KISLOTH TABOR, a town mentioned in the descrip-tion of the SE border of ZEBULUN (v. 12). It has been identified with Iksal, in the foothills about 2 mi. SE of NAZARETH and 3 mi. W of Mount TABOR (but see J. Simons, *The Geographical and*

Topographical Texts of the Old Testament [1959], 330). F. W. Bush

Ketab kee′tab (Κηταβ). Ancestor of a family of temple servants (Nethinim) who returned from the exile with Zerubbabel (1 Esd. 5:30; KJV, "Cetab"). The name is omitted in the parallel lists (Ezra 2:46; Neh. 7:48).

Kethibh kuh-theev′. See Ketib.

Kethubim ki-thoo′vim. See Ketubim.

Ketib kuh-teev′ (כְּתִיב, "written," pass. ptc. of Aram. כְּתַב H10374, "to write"). Also *Kethib, Ketiv*. The written, consonantal form of the Masoretic text of the Hebrew Bible (see Masorah). This term is used primarily in contrast to Qere, the latter indicating "what is to be read," that is, an alternate form or a textual variant preferred by the Masoretes. See text and manuscripts (OT) VI.

kettle. This English term is used by various Bible versions to render Hebrew *dûd* H1857 ("pot, basket") in one passage, referring to a deep cooking pot in which a sacrifice might be boiled (1 Sam. 2:14); in addition, the NRSV uses it once to translate *sîr* H6105 (Mic. 3:3; NIV, "pan"). In the NT, it occurs as the rendering of Greek *chalkion* G5000, "[copper] cauldron" (Mk. 7:4, KJV, "brasen vessel").

Ketubim ki-too′bim (כְּתוּבִים, "written things," from כְּתַב H4180, "to write"). Also *Kethubim, Ketuvim*. The "Writings" (also known as the Hagiographa, "Sacred Writings"), a term applied to the third division of the OT Hebrew canon, and consisting of the poetic books (Psalms, Job, Proverbs, Song of Solomon, Ecclesiastes, Lamentations) as well as Ruth, Esther, Daniel, Ezra, Nehemiah, and Chronicles. See canon (OT).

Keturah ki-tyoo′ruh (קְטוּרָה H7778, "one covered in incense [*i.e.*, perfumed]"). Wife of Abraham (Gen. 25:1, 4; 1 Chr. 1:32–33; in the latter passage, she is referred to as a concubine). Keturah is mentioned by name only, and nothing is known of her background. Although her name appears in the Genesis record only after the death of Sarah, it is possible that she bore sons to Abraham while Sarah was still living. On the other hand, Abraham's apparent rejuvenation at the age of 100 by becoming the father of Isaac may have been prolonged, so that after Sarah died and Abraham had reached the age of 137, he had sons born to him by Keturah. Scripture does not give enough data to determine these details.

To Keturah and Abraham were born six sons: Zimran, Jokshan, Medan, Midian, Ishbak, and Shuah (Gen. 25:1–4). Seven grandsons are also listed. Through these descendants a number of the N Arabian tribes trace their lineage back to Abraham and Keturah. Some Arabic writers mention an Arabian tribe near Mecca by the name of Keturah. Bildad the Shuhite, one of the friends of Job (Job 2:11), may have been a descendant of Shuah. Of the three tribes that were distinctly Arabian—Midian, Sheba, and Dedan—the Midianites are the best known. They located on the upper stretch of the Red Sea littoral and are mentioned in the biblical record as caravan merchants (Gen. 37), as related to Moses by marriage (Exod. 2:16; 3:1; 18:1), and as invaders of Israel (Jdg. 6–8). (Cf. J. A. Montgomery, *Arabia and the Bible* [1934], 37–53; H. C. Leupold, *Genesis* [1942], 688–93; I. Eph‘al, *The Ancient Arabs: Nomads on the Borders of the Fertile Crescent 9th-5th Centuries B.C.* [1982], 231–33). See Arabia. S. J. Schultz

Keveh kee′vuh. See Kue.

key. An instrument, usually of wood but sometimes of metal, for moving the bolt of a lock. Keys often were large. In OT times the key (Heb. *maptēaḥ* H5158) was worn on the shoulder as a symbol of authority (Isa. 22:22). Normally in the Bible, and always in the NT (Gk. *kleis* G3090), the term is used in a figurative sense to refer to the means of entry into the realms of spiritual destiny, thus keys symbolize spiritual authority.

I. Keys in the ancient world. Many ancient peoples thought of the realms of spiritual destiny as entered by doors, and of the gods and angelic beings or the demons as having the keys to those realms. Among the holders of such keys were Shamash (Babylonia), Dike (Greece), Janus (Rome), Aion-Kronos (Mithraism), and Helios (Neo-Platonic period). The underworld, too, had key-keepers:

Nedu (Babylonia), Pluto, Aiacos, Persephone and Selena-Hecate (Greece), Anubis (magic literature) and Isis (mystery religions). (Cf. J. Jeremias in *TDNT*, 3:744–45.)

II. Keys in the OT and Judaism. The only non-figurative use of the term is in Jdg. 3:25, which mentions the key to the doors of King ELGON's private quarters (cf. also 1 Chr. 9:27, where the Heb. word may mean simply "opening"). In Isa. 22:22, the reference is to the investing of ELIAKIM son of Hilkiah with authority as comptroller of DAVID's household: "I [Yahweh] will place on his shoulder the key to the house of David; what he opens no one can shut, and what he shuts no one can open." Of this crucial verse, J. Bright (in *Peake's Commentary on the Bible*, ed. M. Black and H. H. Rowley [1962], 505) comments most significantly for an understanding of NT usage: "The key, carried slung from the shoulder, was the symbol of the major-domo's authority to admit or deny access to the king." Consistent with Isaianic usage, later Jewish writings refer to the granting of authority with similar language. For example, the angel Michael is described as "the holder of the keys of the kingdom of heaven" (*3 Bar.* 11.2).

III. Keys in the NT. In Lk. 4:25 Jesus speaks of the time in the days of ELIJAH when the doors of heaven (the sky) did not open to let the rain come down; and Rev. 11:6 says the two witnesses "have power to shut up the sky so that it will not rain." Although the term *key* is not used in these passages, this language may reflect the rabbinic notion that God "keeps the key of rain and that He gave it only temporarily to Elijah" (*TDNT*, 3:745).

References to spiritual authority include several in the book of Revelation. One of them is in Rev. 3:7 (a clear allusion to Isa. 22:22), where Christ says to the church in Philadelphia: "These are the words of him who is holy and true, who holds the key of David. What he opens no one can shut, and what he shuts no one can open." In the next verse he adds, "See, I have placed before you an open door that no one can shut," that is, he has provided access to God and to David's city, the new Jerusalem, in the last age.

At the beginning of the book, the one "like a son of man" asserts, "I am the Living One; I was dead, and behold I am alive for ever and ever! And I hold the keys of death and Hades" (Rev. 1:18; cf. the saying attributed to Rabbi AKIBA to the effect that God will give Michael and Gabriel the keys to open the 40,000 gates of GEHENNA [*TDNT*, 3:746 n. 26]). W. Bousset (*Kyrios Christos* [1970], 65) suggests that to get these keys from the ruler of the underworld God must have won them in a victorious battle; O. Cullmann (*Peter: Disciple, Apostle, Martyr*, 2nd ed. [1962], 209) adds that God intends to open the doors of Death's domain for those imprisoned inside.

Finally, Rev. 9:1 and 20:1 refer to "the key to [the shaft of] the Abyss" (NRSV, "bottomless pit"; see ABYSS). Jeremias (*TDNT*, 3:746) sees this as a well-like shaft where evil spirits are imprisoned. It is to be opened in the end-time so that demonic locusts can blight the earth, and once again at the beginning of the MILLENNIUM so that SATAN can be incarcerated in it. Jeremias also argues that this abyss must be distinguished from death's domain. Death, hell, and the "bottomless pit" all reflect a view of the grave as a prison in which human beings are bound and held captive.

Moving to the teaching of Jesus, we note first Lk. 11:52, where he criticizes the Jewish experts in the law for taking away "the key of knowledge." Scholars have debated the meaning of this passage.

Keys dated to the 1st or 2nd cent. A.D.

On the lips of Jesus (*Sitz im Leben Jesu*), Jeremias suggests, the phrase *tēs gnōseōs* ("of knowledge") was probably a genitive of apposition: "You have taken away the key to God's kingdom, namely knowledge of him." But in its present Lukan context it would be more natural as an objective genitive: "You have taken away the key to knowledge" (cf. NIV), that is, the knowledge of God contained in the OT Scriptures, which the scribes were supposed to unlock for God's people (*TDNT*, 3:747–48). Jesus expresses a similar idea (though not using the term *key*) in Matt. 23:13, "You shut [*kleiō G3091*] the kingdom of heaven in men's faces." In the light of Bright's comment (above) and the Jewish tendency to use "heaven" as a substitute for "God," the Jewish leaders are accused of preventing the access of men to God's royal presence.

The best-known reference, however, is Matt. 16:19, where Jesus tells PETER, "I will give you the keys of the kingdom of heaven." The plural here may reflect a Jewish belief that God held four keys in his hand—to rain, conception, resuscitation of the dead, and crops. This passage (including vv. 17–19) assumed in the course of church history a significance far out of proportion to the role it plays in the Gospel of Matthew. Particularly as the doctrine of penance was elaborated in the Western church and at the time of the Protestant Reformation, it became a *crux interpretum*. Within the Roman Catholic tradition, the doctrine of the "privilege of Peter" developed into a doctrine of church unity centering in the bishop of Rome, the "pope." Peter is said to have delegated to those bishops and priests in communion with him the power to forgive sins through a system of penance and absolution.

Protestants traditionally have emphasized Peter's FAITH as the foundation "rock" of the CHURCH, and have rejected the idea that Peter's privilege was transmitted to Peter's successors. Although the keys are not specifically mentioned in Matt. 18:18, most contemporary biblical exegetes view the BINDING AND LOOSING mentioned there as corresponding to the giving of the keys to Peter. They therefore agree that the same authority given to Peter is given to the other apostles, and in fact to the whole Christian congregation (but for a different view, see *TDNT*, 3:752). Typical is the view of the Catholic biblical scholar T. Worden: "The actual power to forgive sins is not given directly to Peter and the apostles in Mt 16:19 and 18:18. These verses are better interpreted as referring to the full authority given to the Church in matters of doctrine and morals" (as summarized in *New Testament Abstracts* 2 [1958]: 262). There is a tendency to see the exercise of the keys in the threefold process of discipline by reprimand, public rebuke, and full excommunication (Matt. 18:15–17; Tit. 3:10). Agreement has not been reached on the extent of the correspondence between Peter's authority to bind and loose and the current Catholic practice of penance. L. R. KEYLOCK

Keziah ki-zi'uh (קְצִיעָה *H7905*, "cassia"). KJV Kczia. The second daughter born to JOB after his fortunes were restored (Job 42:14). The name, possibly referring to the sweet smell of CINNAMON (see CASSIA), alludes to her charm (cf. v. 15).

Kezib kee'zib (כְּזִיב *H3945*, "deceit"). Also Chezib. A town in the SHEPHELAH, near ADULLAM, where Shelah son of JUDAH was born (Gen. 38:5). Kezib is usually identified with ACZIB (#2) and COZEBA.
E. RUSSELL

Keziz. See EMEK KEZIZ.

khirbet kihr'bet. An Arabic term meaning "ruin" and often used in geographical names, such as Khirbet KERAK and Khirbet QUMRAN. The corresponding term in Hebrew is *ḥorbat* (construct of *ḥorbâ H2999*).

Kibroth Hattaavah kib'roth-huh-tay'uh-vuh (קִבְרוֹת הַתַּאֲוָה *H7701*, "graves of craving"). Also Kibroth-hattaavah. One of the stops of the Israelites in the wilderness (Num. 11:34–35; 33:16–17). It was probably 10–20 mi. NE of Mount SINAI (the next stop was HAZEROTH), but the exact location is unknown. Here the people, craving the foods they had left behind in Egypt, complained about the MANNA (11:4–6). In response, God sent QUAIL into the camp in such numbers that the people became satiated. As they ate, God smote the people with a severe plague (11:33). Because large numbers of Israelites died and were buried there, the place was called Kibroth Hattaavah ("graves of desire"). Later, MOSES reminded the people that here they had provoked God to wrath (Deut. 9:22). J. B. Scott

Kibzaim kib-zay′im (קִבְצַיִם H7608, possibly "[twin] heaps"). A Levitical city within the tribal territory of Ephraim, allotted to the clan of Kohath (Josh. 21:22). See Jokmeam.

kid. See goat.

kidnapping. See crimes and punishments I.B.6.

kidneys. Paired organs, approximately 4 x 2 x 1 inches in size, located in the loin directly in back of the abdominal cavity on either side of the vertebral spine. They are well protected from behind by the thick muscles of the back. Their function is primarily that of excretion of waste products from the blood. To accomplish this, blood flows through the capillaries of the glomerulus, of which there are approximately 1,000,000 in each kidney, each one being surrounded by a so-called Bowman's capsule. In the process, filtration from the blood which courses through these capillaries takes place. From each Bowman's capsule this filtrate fluid is carried off into a corresponding tubule from which the lining cells selectively reabsorb some of the substances the body needs to conserve, including water, and selectively excrete other substances of which the body needs to be relieved. The end product that is emptied out of these tubules is urine, which is collected into the funnel-shaped pelvis of the kidney, whence it passes down the ureter to the bladder for elimination from the body. Literal references to kidneys in the Bible occur primarily in descriptions of animal sacrifices (Exod. 29:13 et al.).

The ancients often attributed to the kidneys many of the functions that we now know are performed by the brain, including thinking and emotional reactions. When the kidneys become severely diseased, uremia (the accumulation of toxins in the blood) often precipitously puts in its appearance because of inadequate elimination. While symptoms of uremia are exceedingly variable, one of the most startling is sudden lapse into coma or unconsciousness. This state is not necessarily irreversible, and the return of consciousness was easily associated with the return of kidney function, as manifested by reappearance of urine excretion. Thus the ancients had some justification in attributing thinking and emotional reactions to the kidneys. This notion is possibly reflected in conventional language in the Bible, as when Hebrew *kilyâ* H4000, "kidney," is linked with *leb* H4213, "heart"; for example, Ps. 7:9 says literally that God "tests kidneys [KJV, reins] and hearts" (NIV, "searches minds and hearts"; see also Ps. 26:2 and Rev. 2:23 [Gk. *nephros* G3752], and cf. Ps. 16:7). P. E. Adolph

Kidon ki′duhn (כִּידֹן H3961, "javelin" or "[short] sword"). Also Chidon. The owner of a threshing floor (or possibly the name of the place itself) where Uzzah died because he touched the ark of the covenant while it was being transported toward Jerusalem (1 Chr. 13:9). The place is called Nacon in the parallel passage (2 Sam. 6:6 MT; LXX *Nōdab*), and P. K. McCarter (*II Samuel*, AB 9 [1984], 164) argues that both Kidon and Nacon (*kydn*, *nkwn*) are corruptions from an original Nodan (*nwdn*, which is the reading of 4QSam^a). Because of God's judgment here, David named the field Perez Uzzah ("outbreak [of wrath] against Uzzah").

The location of the threshing floor is unknown, but if the procession took a direct route from Kiriath Jearim, the site must have been W of Jerusalem. (Some suggest that David took the longer route through Gibeah of Benjamin—thus announcing to Saul's clan who was in charge—and that the threshing floor was on higher ground N of Jerusalem. See *ABD*, 1:904, s.v. "Chidon.") According to M. Ben-Dov (*Historical Atlas of Jerusalem* [2002], 41–42, maps on pp. 31 and 43), both the threshing floor of Kidon (Nacon) and the one belonging to Araunah were cultic sites outside the City of David, the former being on the western hill and the latter just N of the city walls. He further claims that David had intended to use the former as a permanent place for the ark but changed his mind because of what happened to Uzzah. Eventually David purchased Araunah's field, where the future home of the ark, Solomon's temple, would be built.

Kidron kid′ruhn (קִדְרוֹן H7724, "turbid [stream]"; Κεδρών G3022). KJV NT Cedron. A valley E of Jerusalem c. 3 mi. in length which lies between

KIDRON 901

the walls of the city and the Mount of Olives, and takes its name from the brook running through it. It is now known as the Wadi Sitti Maryam ("Valley of St. Mary"). Opposite St. Stephen's gate its depth is at least 100 ft. The lower part of the valley is today called Wadi en-Nar. After leaving Jerusalem the brook bears to the SE, winds through the wilderness of Judah, and eventually drains into the Dead Sea.

Jerusalem itself is located on the central limestone ridge of Palestine c. 2,500 ft. above sea level at a place where the ridge has become a small plateau. Extending S from this plateau are two promontories, separated by a valley called in Roman times the Tyropoeon Valley (now called El-Wad) but which today is largely filled with debris. The western side later became known as Zion and the eastern side was Ophel (City of David). East of Ophel, separating it from the Mount of Olives, is the Kidron Valley, through which the intermittent Gihon Spring courses. It was once the source of Jerusalem's main water supply. It is now called 'Ain Sitti Maryam ("Spring of St. Mary"). Water flows through it only during the season of heavy rains in the winter. To the S, where the Kidron and Hinnom Valleys meet, is a second spring, En Rogel.

Charles Warren (c. 1870) discovered a shaft cut through the rock from the city to the spring, similar to the one at Gezer, which enabled the inhabitants to secure water without going outside the city. The waters of the Gihon Spring were diverted through a tunnel to a cave that served as a reservoir. Going up from this point was a vertical shaft about 40 ft. high, at the top of which was a platform where the women could stand to lower and raise their water vessels. This water system was possibly in use when the Jebusites occupied Jerusalem through the period of the judges to the time of David, though some archaeologists argue that "Warren's Shaft" must have been constructed some time later (see Jerusalem III.B). The water was subsequently diverted by a rock tunnel to the pool of Siloam (prob. during the reign of Hezekiah).

The Davidic kings owned property in the Kidron, and thus it came to be known as the King's Valley. As David fled from Absalom, he crossed over the Kidron (2 Sam. 15:23). Shimei was warned by Solomon that if he left Jerusalem and crossed beyond the limits of the Kidron, he would be put to death (1 Ki. 2:37).

The portion of the valley on the E side has been used as a common burial ground from ancient times even until today. Perhaps for this reason one finds that idols, altars, images, and the Asherah were taken from the temple and burned here as a part of the reform of various kings (Asa, 1 Ki. 15:16; Josiah, 2 Ki. 23:4–12; Hezekiah, 2 Chr. 29:16;

Northern segment of the Kidron Valley with the Mount of Olives rising above it. (View to the SE.)

40:14). Josephus says Athaliah was taken to the Kidron for execution so that the temple would not be defiled by her blood (*Ant.* 9.7.3). There are four tower-like burial monuments in the Kidron Valley surrounded by a modern Jewish cemetery; tradition identifies them as the tombs of Jehoshaphat, Absalom, James the Less, and Zechariah, but they probably date from the Herodian period. Square letters (see ALPHABET IV) on stone inscriptions have been found at the so-called grave of Jacob in the Kidron Valley. The poorer people were interred outside the city in simple graves, one of these places being in the Kidron Valley (2 Ki. 23:6; cf. Jer. 26:23).

HEROD the Great restored the temple during his reign and greatly enlarged the surrounding area by erecting new foundation walls. At its outermost pinnacle (cf. Matt. 4:5) the temple enclosure was 170 ft. above the valley of the Kidron, prompting Josephus to comment, "One who looked down grew dizzy" (*Ant.* 15.11.5, LCL). GETHSEMANE was just across the brook Kidron, on the western slope of the Mount of Olives. From the western descent of the mount one has a view directly across the Kidron Valley to Jerusalem. Jesus crossed the valley with his disciples after leaving the upper room to spend the night in the Garden of Gethsemane (Jn. 18:1). JUDAS ISCARIOT undoubtedly led the soldiers across the Kidron to the place where Jesus was praying, for he "knew the place" well (18:2).

JEREMIAH looked forward from his time to the day when the city of Jerusalem would be rebuilt and the places of burial, including the fields as far as the Kidron Valley, would be sacred to God (Jer. 31:40). (See J. Finegan, *Light From the Ancient Past*, 2nd ed. [1959], 315 et passim; G. E. Wright, *Biblical Archaeology* [1957], 126, 221; M. Noth, *The Old Testament World* [1966], 155, 169, 171, 221; M. Ben-Dov, *Historical Atlas of Jerusalem* [2002], 11–19 et passim.) F. D. HIPPY, JR.

Kilan kī'lan (H????). Ancestor of a family that returned from exile with ZERUBBABEL (1 Esd. 5:15; KJV, "Ceilan").

Kileab kil'ee-ab (כִּלְאָב H3976, derivation uncertain). Also Chileab. DAVID's second son born at HEBRON, his first by ABIGAIL (2 Sam. 3:3). The SEPTUAGINT has *Dalouia* (a reading possibly reflected also in 4QSam[a]), and he is called Daniel in the parallel passage (1 Chr. 3:1). The last three Hebrew consonants of Kileab (לאב) are the same as the first three of the following word, so the text of Samuel may be corrupt. Some believe Daniel may be original; others follow the SEPTUAGINT and emend the Hebrew to *dlwyh*, "Daluiah" (P. K. McCarter, Jr., *II Samuel*, AB 9 [1984], 101). Nothing more is known about this son of David; presumably he died young.

Kilion kil'ee-uhn (כִּלְיוֹן H4002, possibly "frailty" or "destruction"). Also Chilion. Son of ELIMELECH and NAOMI (Ruth 1:2, 5; 4:9). When the family moved to MOAB, Kilion married a woman named ORPAH, and his brother MAHLON married RUTH. Both Kilion and his brother died some years later while they were still in Moab.

Kilmad kil'mad (כִּלְמַד H4008, derivation unknown). One of several places that were trading partners with TYRE (Ezek. 27:23). Its location is unknown, and various locations have been proposed (cf. *ABD*, 1:908, s.v. "Chilmad"). Since it is mentioned after ASSHUR, Kilmad was probably in N MESOPOTAMIA. The TARGUM, however, understands the name as a reference to MEDIA, and on that basis some scholars read the Hebrew text as *kol-māday*, "all Media."

kiln (oven). This term is used by the NRSV to render Hebrew *kibšān* H3901 in two passages (Exod. 9:8–10; 19:18; the only other occurrence of the Hebrew term is in Gen. 19:28). See FURNACE; OVEN.

Remains of a pottery kiln from Tarsus.

Kimham kim′ham (כִּמְהָם *H4016* [כִּמְהָן in 2 Sam. 19:40; in Heb., v. 41], possibly "pale face"). Also **Chimham**. Apparently a son of BARZILLAI the Gileadite (2 Sam. 19:37–38, 40; some MSS of the LXX, as well as the Syriac version, expressly identify Kimham as Barzillai's son; cf. also Jos. *Ant.* 7.11.4). While DAVID was in exile at MAHANAIM, Barzillai had provided him with food. After ABSALOM's rebellion had been quelled, David invited Barzillai to be his guest at Jerusalem. Barzillai declined but sent Kimham instead. Apparently David granted Kimham a royal pension (1 Ki. 2:7)—maybe even a piece of land near BETHLEHEM, as some have inferred from the comment that JOHANAN ben Kareah and his band, four centuries later, encamped at GERUTH KIMHAM, a name that means, "lodging place of Kimham" (Jer. 41:17). R. C. RIDALL

Kinah ki′nuh (קִינָה *H7807*, possibly "lament" or else related to the gentilic KENITE [cf. 1 Sam. 27:10]). A town in the NEGEV, the extreme S of the tribal territory of JUDAH, near the border of EDOM (Josh. 15:22). Its location is unknown, but because Wadi el-Qeni may preserve the name, some have identified Kinah with nearby Khirbet Ṭaiyib (c. 3 mi. NNE of ARAD [Tell ʿArad]) and others with Khirbet Ghazzeh (on a spur of the wadi, c. 4 mi. SE of Arad; cf. *NEAEHL*, 4:1495, s.v. "Uza, Ḥorvat"; but see RAMAH #4).

kindness. The state or quality of being kind: generosity, humaneness, tenderness. The word can also refer to a particular instance of kind behavior: a token of friendliness, good will, affection. This English term is used variously in Bible translations to render a number of words. In the OT, it occurs primarily as the rendering of Hebrew *ḥesed H2876*, which conveys various senses, such as "loyalty," "mercy," "grace," and "love" (Gen. 19:19 and frequently). In the NT, it translates Greek *philanthrōpia G5792*, "love or concern for humanity, benevolence" (Acts 28:2; Tit. 3:4), *chrēstotēs G5983*, "goodness, uprightness, generosity" (Rom. 2:4; 11:22; et al.), and other expressions. (See *NIDOTTE*, 2:203–6, 211–18; *NIDNTT*, 2:105–7.)

Kindness is both an attribute of God (Tit. 3:4) and a characteristic of true LOVE (1 Cor. 13:4, where the verb *chrēsteuomai G5980* is used). God's kindness is great (Joel 2:13; Jon. 4:2) and everlasting (Isa. 54:8, 10). God is kind to the ignorant and wayward (Heb. 5:2), to the ungrateful and evil (Lk. 6:35). Believers are exhorted to possess this trait (Col. 3:12; 2 Pet. 1:7). It is sinful to refuse kindness to one's neighbor, whereas those who are kind to the poor receive a blessing (Prov. 14:21, where the verb *ḥānan H2858*, "to be gracious," is used). The ideal woman speaks kind words (31:26 NRSV).

God's people should be kind to fellow-believers (Deut. 22:1; Zech. 7:9, 10; Rom. 15:5; Eph. 4:32; 1 Pet. 3:8; 4:8), neighbors (Rom. 15:2), foreigners (Lev. 19:34), widows (1 Tim. 5:9, 10), orphans (Zech. 7:10), the needy (Matt. 5:7; 1 Jn. 3:17–18), the weak (Acts 20:35; Rom. 15:1), the sorrowing (12:15), the weary (Gal. 6:2), the fallen (6:1), all men (6:10), even enemies (Lk. 6:34–35). At the final judgment, Christ will reward those who have been kind to his people (Matt. 25:34–36).

Biblical examples of kindness include the following: Pharaoh to Jacob (Gen. 45:16–20; 47:5–6), Pharaoh's daughter to Moses (Exod. 2:6–10), Rahab to the spies (Josh. 2:1–3; 6:17–25), David to Mephibosheth (2 Sam. 9:1–13), Joab to Absalom (14:1–24), Ahab to Ben-Hadad (1 Ki. 20:32–34), Elisha to the Shunammite (2 Ki. 8:1), Evil-Merodach to Jehoiachin (25:27–30), Jehoshabeath to Joash (2 Chr. 22:11), Jews to less fortunate brethren (Neh. 5:8–19), Mordecai to Esther (Esth. 2:7), Nebuchadnezzar to Jeremiah (Jer. 39:11–12), Joseph to Mary (Matt. 1:19), a centurion to his servant (Lk. 7:2–6), Jews to Mary and Martha (Jn. 11:19, 33), John to Mary (19:27), Felix to Paul (Acts 24:23), Julius to Paul (27:3, 43), Onesiphorus to Paul (2 Tim. 1:16–18), and Paul to Onesimus (Phlm. 17–19). See also GOOD; GRACE; MERCY. R. E. PERRY

kine. KJV plural form of COW.

king, kingship. The Hebrew word for "king," *melek H4889*, appears over 2,000 times in the OT. The SEPTUAGINT translates this term with the Greek equivalent, *basileus G995*, which occurs some fifty times in the NT.

  I. Kingship and the gods
  II. Kingship in Israel
  III. Kingship in the OT

IV. The royal establishment in Israel and the OT
V. The later history of the Jewish kingdom
VI. Kingship in the DSS
VII. The messianic kingship of Christ

I. Kingship and the gods. In the system of the ancient religious state, patriotism and religious piety were synonymous. To oust or overthrow the legitimate king was to commit treason against the state cult. Unless a new administration could gain the ritual approval of the hierarchy of the cult and the necessary legitimization of the city gods, it would be the victim of a counterrevolution that often degenerated into fratricidal feuds and harem intrigues.

Throughout the long centuries of Egypt's history, and sporadically in Mesopotamia, the gods were considered royalty and the rulers as divine. In Syria-Palestine and other border areas of the great river valley civilizations, the kings served as the high priests of the cult. Even in imperial Rome, the grandest of the Caesar's honorific titles was *pontifex maximus*. The approval of the town deities was of such importance that conquerors, with mock reverence, often listed the gods of captive regions in the place of geographic names. In fact it was the obeisance of the conqueror to these deities that could establish his right to the local authority even though the gods along with their towns had been captured. The supercilious prayers of these rulers contain their imprecations against their enemies and their implorations for victory addressed to a veritable menagerie of deities.

Undoubtedly this common kingly practice furthered the collection of elaborate pantheons containing deities of diverse origins. Such pantheons, like the king's courts they served, consisted of regular ordered hierarchies of superhuman beings; in effect they were divine prisoners of war. On the other hand, the PHARAOH of Egypt was the mundane and fleshly embodiment of the deity Horus, and every pharaoh possessed a long title or throne name including some mention of the deity. Just as an earthly monarch would have his circle and entourage of courtiers and servants, so the myths and epics picture the gods as bound to a feudal if not manorial scale of importance. In this divine state each is waited on by his heavenly vassals and company of retainers.

The epithets of many of the Mesopotamian deities are synonymous with those of human sovereigns. Some gods are characterized by a great feat of arms, while the names of others indicate their vocation in the supernal palaces. Some are addressed as "shepherds," others as "cup or throne bearers," others as "gardeners," "porters," and even "canal inspectors." From such myths and the popular folktales, many insights can be gained concerning the inner workings of an ancient oriental palace and its inhabitants.

The life of the kingly gods was viewed monistically as a rectilinear extension of endless time. The life unending sought by both Akkadian and Egyptian alike was a quantitative continuation of the life known on earth. In the Ugaritic *Legend of Aqhat*, the goddess Anath promises immortality to Aqhat and says, "Ask for life and I'll give it thee, / For deathlessness, and I'll bestow't on thee. / I'll make thee count years with Baal, / With the sons of El shalt thou count months" (A, vi; see *ANET*, 151b). It was probably this end to which the pharaoh built his PYRAMID, or to which the Lugal of Ur constructed the great "death pit."

However, although the people of Egypt may have considered the pharaoh divine, worshiping and reverencing him, his contemporaries who ruled the neighboring kingdoms certainly did not. They were addressed by their vassals in anything but reverential terms. As Egypt's Asiatic empire began to dissolve, the rulers of the petty states beyond its control treated the divine pharaoh with common contempt. Perhaps it was the aloofness of the pharaohs or the insularity of Egyptian culture and the enigma of their script, but the pharaonic institutions seem to have little influenced the development of the idea of kingship outside of Egypt and its vassals.

In some cultures of the ANE, annual agricultural festivals were held that were intended to insure the continuation of the system and the bounty of the harvest for the ensuing year. See AGRICULTURE. The best evidence for such celebrations comes from BABYLON, and it is possible that a similar ritual was enacted in UGARIT. Both traditions can be traced back to the old *zag-mukku* festivals of early SUMER.

This cuneiform tablet from the 2nd cent. B.C., discovered in Babylon, contains a Hellenistic king list.

and answered to the divine titles during and after the ceremony, and so gained legitimacy to continue his reign.

Some scholars, such as the Scandinavians I. Engnell and S. Mowinckel, have attempted to interpret certain passages in the OT as evidence that an annual "Enthronement Festival of Yahweh" was held and that in time it became the motive for OT ESCHATOLOGY. This type of construction of the biblical data is highly speculative and many necessary components of it are simply undemonstrable from the text. At heart there is the fact that no Jewish monarch at any time ever received the titles or reverence which belonged to Yahweh. Nor did any Jewish ruler act as lawgiver or legislator. All, whether good or bad, were subject to the Mosaic law and claimed to be nothing more than men. There is the added difficulty that the divine pronouncements of the OT come neither through the king nor the priests but through a special non-ritualistic office, the prophet. It is this spokesman of Yahweh who introduces and explains the OT eschatology and draws the prefiguration of the MESSIAH. The Scandinavian hypothesis of the enthronement ritual character of much of the OT is based on assumptions concerning the composition of the text and speculations on its humanistic development, all of which are suspect.

Part of the action consisted of a symbolic humiliation and reenthronement of the king as well as the presentation of offerings and sacrifices. In Babylon this involved also a long procession of the idols, their priests and devotees up from the festive boats on the river and into the temple of MARDUK, the magnificent Esagila.

The layout and architecture of the city was arranged in accord with the needs of the cultic calendar. The high holiday was the *rēsh shatti*, New Year's Festival, and had as its center activity the *akitu(m)* ceremony. In the ritual of the *akitu(m)* the epic of ENUMA ELISH was chanted as an accompaniment to an elaborate ritual of sympathetic magic. A ritual combat with chaos was produced, followed by a sacred marriage ceremony, in which the parts of the god and his consort were taken by the king and a temple prostitute. However, there were great divergencies in the style, actions, and interpretation of the ritual drama over the centuries. The sum and substance of the festival in all ages was the recoronation of the king for another year. It is not clear whether the king actually was considered a deity during the rites or whether he only took the part of the god. He must have taken

II. Kingship in Israel. The historic establishment of kingship in Israel appears to be a contradiction of the principle that the nation was peculiarly under Yahweh's providence. The judge SAMUEL, acting in the prophetic office, clearly declared the extent of the liability that such an earthly monarch would prove to be. After listing the avaricious requirements of a royal establishment, Samuel adds, "When that day comes, you will cry out for relief from the king you have chosen, and the LORD will not answer you in that day" (1 Sam. 8:18). The kingship of Yahweh had been expressly stated in Moses' first discourse from Sinai: "Now if you obey me fully and keep my covenant, then out of all nations you will be my treasured possession. Although the whole earth is mine, you will be for me a kingdom of priests and a holy nation" (Exod. 19:5–6). It was this aspect of God's sovereignty over Israel that the nation rejected when they asked for a king. As God said to Samuel, "Listen to all that the people are saying to you; it is not you they have rejected, but they have rejected me as their king" (1 Sam. 8:7). This statement has in view the revealed precepts of God in regard to the Mosaic law and its authority, it does not denote the decrees of God's sovereign providence in and over history. For this reason even the perverse desire for kingship in Israel was constructed in terms of the law of God, although it manifested itself as a rejection of his law.

The period of the judges was one of conflict between the migrant and tribal people of Israel and the loose knit confederacy of Canaanite city-states. See JUDGES, PERIOD OF. During the time preceding the exodus from Egypt, the Israelites had confronted the monolithic façade of the Egyptian religious state. As Egypt lost its Asiatic provinces, the Philistines pushed southward and Israel settled the land. In time the small states and trading villages of Syria-Palestine coalesced into petty monarchies and ultimately into dynasties. The achievement of Saul, David, and Solomon was not a novelty nor did it take place in vacuo, but was paralleled by centralization of authority elsewhere at that time and in that area of the ANE. The problem of synthesizing the archaeological material from the period of the conquest of Canaan is difficult and tedious, but it is clear that the first king, SAUL, came to the newly established throne at about 1030–1020 B.C.

III. Kingship in the OT. Kings and kingship are first mentioned in the OT in the narrative of the battle fought by Abram (ABRAHAM) with a number of rulers (Gen. 14). Even the pharaohs of Egypt during the time of Israel's sojourn are called "kings." After the conquest, settlement, and solidification of the tribal organization of Israel in Canaan, the judges became the legal and executive authorities of the twelve tribes. Even though a number of judges were also prophets, the judgeship was not an anointed office (1 Sam. 15:10) and thus it served no direct messianic function in the Israelite theocracy.

Samuel acted as a prophet in selecting and anointing Saul as the first king of Israel (1 Sam. 11:15). It is basic to the OT concept of kingship to recognize the necessity of the prophetic office. The prophet as spokesman for Yahweh assented to the people's request for a king, determined who should be king, and then marked him as a person of messianic character by anointing him. Therefore no king could claim legitimacy without the prophetic approval and its divine investiture. The impossibility of the royal line being infiltrated by foreigners or compromised from outside the community of Israel was assured. The later history of the Hebrew monarchy demonstrates the frequency with which the prophets rejected the iniquitous infatuation of the kings with Gentile and pagan royalty. For this reason both Persia and Greece found it necessary to unseat the monarchy totally, and to replace it with an authority based on their own culture, whereas in other civilizations they conquered they were able to gain the legitimization of the ancient cult.

In most of the nations thriving in the 1st millennium B.C., the rulers were chosen from a large group of pretenders, either by the officials of the state cult or by some settlement among the aristocratic families. In Israel it was the choice and direction of Yahweh which determined the successor to the throne, though a process of drawing by lots may have been involved (1 Sam. 10:21). In this text the verb translated "was chosen" literally means "to draw by lot" (cf. NRSV, "was taken by lot"), and this accords with the suggestion of several other texts. The prophetic anointing of the king not only indicated the messianic character of the Hebrew ruler, but imparted to him divine authority demanding the obedience of the people (11:7).

The king, like the prophet and the priest, was sacrosanct but never sacerdotal (1 Sam. 24:6). Even the members of the royal house and potential future kings were accorded reverence, as in the case of the boy JOASH (2 Ki. 11:2–3). The families of former and subsequently rejected rulers were shown certain honor (cf. the benefits King DAVID bestowed upon MEPHIBOSHETH, the grandson of Saul, 2 Sam. 9:6–10). This respect reached even to the pagan relations of a slain ruler, as in the case of the murdered JEZEBEL, concerning whose body JEHU commanded, "Take care of that cursed woman ... and bury her, for she was a king's daughter (2 Ki. 9:34). On the other hand, the divine approval of either king or royalty could be removed, and this decision too would be indicated to the king by the prophet (1 Sam. 16:14).

Unlike other monarchs of antiquity, the Jewish king was not an absolute autocrat. Like the humblest commoner, he was subject to the Mosaic legislation (Deut. 17:18–20). Kingship in Israel was not instituted by divine innovation, as were prophetism and the priesthood, so that from the beginning it was a reconstituted instrument, and its character and prerogatives were determined by nonrevelatory, nonbiblical and non-Jewish influences. Ideally the kingship and commonwealth of Israel were to have been a theocracy. For this reason the kingdom of God and the monarchy of Israel are neither parallel nor congruent at all points in the narrative of the OT. Often they were cojoined at the point that the redemptive sovereignty of God was worked through the historical events of the mundane monarchy of Israel. The Israelite kingship was in fact a paradigm or example of Yahweh's government of all human history. And in the same fashion that the nation of Israel was chosen to be the vehicle of divine revelation and the commissioners of the oracles of God, so the kingly office in the monarchy was to be the messianic prefigurement.

The kingdom of God is seen in the OT as operating in two separate domains. The first is the sovereignty of Yahweh over creation by virtue of his creative acts (Pss. 93; 103:19). The second is God's kingship by virtue of his redemption, the ransom of his covenant people. The messianic character of all three anointed offices—prophet, priest, and king—is directed toward the completion of this redemption and the fulfillment of the promise given to Abraham (Gen. 17:7–8). The three aspects of this blessing were the preservation of the children of Israel as Abraham's seed, the inheritance of the land of Canaan, and the appearance of the Messiah from the people and in the land. All these were bound up in the Israelite kingship. In a sense all were brought about and accomplished by means of the royal house of David and his heirs. The history of Israel cannot be understood apart from a realization that the monarchy was not only historical, but also supernatural. Although the kings did upon rare occasions prophesy (1 Sam. 10:10), they were forbidden to take the place of the priests in the ceremonies of the temple. The combination of the three sacrosanct offices in one historic personage was to await Messiah's coming.

Hebraic poetry as found in such books as Job and Psalms is so constructed that the rhythm and euphony is carried not by rhyme but by the duplication, replication, and contrast of ideas. Similar, complementary, and contrasting concepts are set in parallel pairs of phrases. These pairs of terms not only yield synonyms between parallel lines, but also indicate the subtle nuances of words. The word "king" and its extensions "kingship" and "dominion" appear frequently in OT poetic passages. By far the major number of citations, the term *melek* is in the initial half of the pair or the first line and may be considered the "A" term. The corresponding term in the second phrase, which may be called the "B" word, frequently adds depth of meaning to the structure of the whole. The following words are paired with *king* in parallel in OT poetry: chief (Job 29:25); nobles (34:18); rulers (Ps. 2:2); judges (2:10); mighty men (33:16); king's son (72:1); princes (Prov. 8:15); preeminent one (Ps. 105:20); anointed (18:50); David (144:10).

In the few number of citations when the order is reversed, there is some clear semantic indication of why it was done. In one set it indicates a rising gradation of social importance: princes/kings (Ps. 76:12), and in another the contrast is between the collective and one of its representative parts in a stylistic synecdoche: nations/kings (102:15; 135:10). Of primary importance is the point that whenever the divine kingdom or the godly reign is mentioned, the order is strictly such that the divine name appears as A, while "king," which is normally initial, serves as the B term (e.g., Yahweh/king,

Mosaic of a king banqueting among his friends. (Standard of Ur, c. 2600 B.C.)

47:2 (lord/king, 47:6). In all such synthetical relationships the name of Yahweh or his titles precedes all other parallels and ascriptions.

The view that these poetic passages were hymns for the rituals of the annual enthronement of Yahweh must deal with the basic semantics of such passages. It is necessary to relate the usage of such terms with the careful preservation of the transcendent quality of the divine name. The OT declares the present and eternal kingship of Yahweh unequivocally, and conforms to the A/B word sequence. The present and future temporal aspect of the divine kingship is stated definitively and uniquely in such biblical expressions as Ps. 10:16, which says literally, "Yahweh is King forever." The overt transcendence of God is so strictly maintained that he is declared to be superior over even all deities (95:3). Such expressions suppose the real existence of hierarchies of deities; they are used in the text for literary projection only. In light of the usage quoted above, it is not accidental that Ps. 149:2 declares the joy of Israel before Yahweh as both creator and king in a precise and beautiful parallelism, "Let Israel rejoice in their Maker, / let the people of Zion be glad in their King."

IV. The royal establishment in Israel and the OT.

Since the character of Israelite kingship was defined largely by the customs of the nations round about Canaan, in the same manner the duties and privileges of the Jewish rulers followed the ancient traditions. The customary ANE monarch possessed a palace, was installed upon a throne, and had access to a harem of wives and concubines. In time all these aspects became a part of the Jewish monarchical establishment. Interestingly enough, even the terms for some of these fixtures were assumed with the practices. The ancient Sumerian term for "large house" or "palace," *e-gal* (Akk. *ēkallu*, Ugaritic *hkl*), appears in the Hebrew Bible (apart from 1 Sam. 1:9) only after the founding of the monarchy. In its Hebrew form the word is *hêkāl* H2121, and it indicates the magnificence and luxury of the royal apartments (cf. Ps. 144:12).

Another term commonly used for "palace" is the Hebrew *bîrâ* H1072, as used in David's declaration concerning the building of Solomon's temple: "The task is great, because this palatial structure is not for man but for the LORD God" (1 Chr. 29:1). The word is never used of the abode of any Jewish king. It occurs mostly in the later books of the OT, especially Esther, Nehemiah, Ezra, and Daniel, and its frequent use with Persian geographical names has suggested a possible Indo-Iranian origin. However, it is more probable that it is to be connected with Akkadian *birtu*, meaning "citadel, castle." The OT word for "throne" (*kissēʾ* H4058) is also derived ultimately from the earliest monarchical foundation in the ANE. In the Sumerian orthography it is preceded by the determinative sign that designates an object made of wood. In later times the *kussu* was probably still made of wood, but overlaid with beaten gold and silver filigree.

Although the ultimate symbol among most of the ancients was the scepter, no such instrument is ever described or associated with a Jewish king. In an age when livery was considered of great importance, the royal garments of Israel are described as an outer robe or vestment befitting rank (1 Ki. 22:10, 30), and the usual cloak or under mantle (1 Sam. 24:4, 11) of the highest quality (1 Chr. 15:27; 2 Sam. 13:18). Two types of metallic ornaments are mentioned, the chaplets or fillets (2 Sam. 1:10) and the crown or diadem, which in Zechariah's time was made of silver and gold, possibly electrum (Zech. 6:11).

The maintenance of more than one wife must have been a feature of the monarchy, and in the later times the oriental HAREM appeared in Israel. In time the custom of political marriage, whereby a king would certify a treaty by marriage into the allied nation's royal family, became common in Israel. SOLOMON and his followers adhered to this tradition, and it was this contradiction of the divine commandment that led to the situation of AHAB and JEZEBEL, where a pagan princess, their daughter ATHALIAH, became queen.

The kings were accompanied by groups of retainers who acted as a bodyguard. Chief among these were the family detachments known as the Kerethites, Pelethites, and Gittites (2 Sam. 15:18). In the eighth chapter of 2 Samuel are listed the officers of David's court: Joab the general of the army, JEHOSHAPHAT the remembrancer, a sort of chief adviser; ZADOK and AHIMELECH the priests; SERAIAH the scribe; BENAIAH the chief of the bodyguard; and the princes of the palace who served as David's ministers. It is safe to assume that this list gives only the names of the king's cabinet and that there were armor-bearers (1 Sam. 16:21) and other military officials as well as a large group of cooks, wine stewards, butlers, tailors, and other such official craftsmen.

The relationship of the various classes one to another is not clear, and the evidence is further complicated by the recurrent changes of rulers and outside penetrations of the last one hundred years of the monarchy. An extrabiblical source yields some data on social classes among the W Semitic people. In the royal inscription of Azitawadda from Karatepe, there is a prohibition to all classes of mankind, and these are described as "a king among kings and a prince among princes or a man who is (just) a man" (*ANET*, 654a). This list follows the Mesopotamian system of kings, lords, and freemen. All the terms that appear in the Karatepe text also appear in the histories of the Israelite monarchy, so the social structure was undoubtedly similar.

Like other regents, the kings of Israel had the authority to levy taxes and collect tribute from their subjects (1 Ki. 4:6–21). Subject kingdoms and peoples under Israel's sovereignty paid their annual tribute in the same way as when Israel itself was a suzerain of ASSYRIA under HEZEKIAH (2 Ki. 18:15–16). Wealth was counted in material stores of gems, garments, precious metals, and livestock (2 Chr. 32:27–29). Opulence and magnificence were determined by the number of servants and retainers a king could command and support, as well as the style of dress, food, and appointments in which he kept them (2 Chr. 31:16–19). Taxation was mostly in kind, and the royal flocks, herds, and vineyards were tended by work corvées made up of the citizenry. The international trade was also in terms of goods and produce, most of which came from the royal forests and mines (1 Ki. 5:10–11). However, because of the Mosaic law, which bound even the kings of Israel, the right of commandeering except for military necessity was forbidden. The royal establishment had to pay its debts. The case of Ahab is quite clear (21:1–16). The same was true of the women of the land, who were not to be taken by the king and placed at his whim in the royal harem. The story of David and BATHSHEBA (2 Sam. 11) bears out the king's responsibility to the moral commandments.

V. The later history of the Jewish kingdom.

In the full perspective of the thousands of years of Jewish history, the monarchy actually involved a brief duration. Under the early rulers, Saul, David, and Solomon, the spirit of conquest was still lively enough to advance the kingdom territorially and materially to its greatest extent. Even this period of ascendancy above the neighboring petty states of the E Mediterranean coast lasted a scant century. After the division of the kingdom under REHOBOAM and JEROBOAM, the political power of the Jewish monarchy declined until in about 200 years' time Israel, the northern regency, had not the resources to forestall its destruction before Assyria (722 B.C.). Judah, the more stable principality, lingered on until 586 B.C., when Jerusalem fell to Babylon. Without ever being freed, the Jewish people passed under the domination of PERSIA and finally into the kingdom of SELEUCUS in the Age of Hellenism.

At last a respite came during the revolution of the Maccabees and the leadership of Judah MACCABEE and his brothers, 165–142 B.C. The dynasty of rulers they established ruled as the HASMONEANS until the last of their number was made a puppet of POMPEY. The Idumean chieftain Antipater was now actually ruling the country in the name of his Roman masters. His dynasty, the Herodian, brought about some of the blackest moments in the history of the Jewish people. The final collapse came after generations of alien puppet rule, when a series of abortive revolutions brought the invasion of TITUS and the destruction of Jerusalem in A.D. 70. The last remnants of the free and sovereign dominion of David fled to the fortress of MASADA in the Dead Sea region, where they died after a long siege by the Tenth Legion under Flavius Silva in the year 73. The immediate results of this final and irremediable disaster was the dispersion of the Jewish people throughout the Mediterranean world. This process of dispossession, which had been started by the Assyrian empire, was now complete.

VI. Kingship in the DSS.

Many of the Hebraic documents written by the Jews of the DIASPORA have apocalyptic subjects and indeed these points of view are found in both the APOCRYPHA and the PSEUDEPIGRAPHA. In the DEAD SEA SCROLLS, the image of a restored kingship to Judaism is a recurrent theme. In the *War Scroll* (1QM) the deeds of the past hero kings of Israel are quite prominent, but there is little said about the restoration of the monarchy.

VII. The messianic kingship of Christ. In the light of the prophecies of the coming of the King-Messiah of the OT, it is clear what is meant by the ascription of this fulfillment to the life of Christ. The kingship of Christ over his spiritual people of Israel was initiated with his accomplishment of ATONEMENT. By the one great act of redemption, the death on the cross and the resurrection, the theocratic kingdom was forever established, and the centuries of OT prefigurement were fulfilled and completed. However, in the NT one further as yet unforeseen aspect is still maintained, the final culmination of history and the establishment of the kingdom of heaven, wherein Yahweh will be absolutely and ideally represented before his subjects by the messianic King Jesus Christ. See KINGDOM OF GOD.

(See further I. Engnell, *Studies in Divine Kingship in the Ancient Near East* [1943]; H. Frankfort, *Kingship and the Gods* [1948]; G. Vos, *Biblical Theology* [1954]; W. Hallo, *Early Mesopotamian Royal Titles* [1957]; G. E. Wright, *The Bible and the Ancient Near East* [1961]; B. Halpern, *The Constitution of the Monarchy in Israel* [1981]; G. W. Ahlström, *Royal Administration and National Religion in Ancient Palestine* [1982]; M. W. Hamilton, *The Body Royal: The Social Poetics of Kingship in Ancient Israel* [2005].) W. WHITE, JR.

kingdom of God (of heaven). The sovereign activity of God as KING in saving sinners and overcoming evil, and the new order which is thus established.

  I. The kingship of God in OT teaching
    A. God as King of the universe
    B. God as King of Israel
    C. The future reign of God
  II. The kingship of God in Jewish thought
    A. The eternal sovereignty of God
    B. The establishment of God's future reign
    C. Kingdom of God and kingdom of heaven
  III. The kingship of God in the teaching of Jesus
    A. The centrality of the theme
    B. The nature of God's kingship
    C. The human response
  IV. The kingship of God in the early church
    A. The Acts of the Apostles
    B. The epistles of Paul
    C. Other writers

I. The kingship of God in OT teaching. Although the idea of the kingdom of God finds its main expression in the teaching of Jesus, it is a theme found throughout the Bible, and the teaching of Jesus can be understood only against the background of earlier thought. In the OT the actual word *kingdom* is infrequent; the basic notion is of the active rule of Yahweh as King over the whole world. This concept is developed in three ways.

A. God as King of the universe. God is regarded as sitting upon a THRONE (Ps. 103:19a; Ezek. 1:26–28) where he is surrounded by the heavenly host who serve him (1 Ki. 22:19) and from where he watches over the whole earth (Ps. 33:13–14). In the praise offered to him by Israel he was regarded as the King of the whole world (1 Chr. 29:11; Ps. 103:19b) and of all the kingdoms of the earth (2 Ki. 19:15; Ps. 47:2, 7). He is the eternal King (Ps. 145:13; Dan. 4:3–4), both from everlasting (Pss. 74:12; 93:2) and to everlasting (Exod. 15:18). His right to be king rests upon the fact that he is the Creator of the heaven and the earth (Ps. 95:3–5). His kingly rule is displayed in his present jurisdiction over the nations of the world (cf. Ps. 22:28; Jer. 46:18; 48:15; 51:57) and in his appointment of their rulers (Dan. 2:37; 4:17; 5:21; et al.). He overcomes the forces of chaos and disorder symbolized by the mighty floods and the sea (Pss. 29:10; 93:1–4), and his reign is characterized not only by power and glory (145:11–12) but also by truth and righteousness (96:13; 99:4), so that it is right and just that he should be the Judge of the world (96:10). He is worthy of praise (97:1; 98:6) and of fear from all peoples (99:1–3; Isa. 6:5; Jer. 10:7–10; Mal. 1:14).

B. God as King of Israel. Although the whole world is the sphere of God's rule, he is preeminently the King of Israel, the people whom he had created and chosen to be his special possession. Although

his throne was regarded as being in HEAVEN, there was also a sense in which it could be said to be above the cherubim in the TEMPLE (2 Ki. 19:15; Isa. 6:1), and he was described as ruling from Mount ZION or JERUSALEM (Pss. 48:2; 99:1-2; Jer. 8:19). A number of the psalms have been the subject of much discussion in recent years as to whether they imply that the kingship of God was celebrated annually in the temple at the new year festival (Pss. 47; 93; 96; 97; 99; cf. 68:24). Whatever be the truth in this theory, the kingship of God was certainly associated especially with his rule over Israel as his people. He was the true King of Israel (Deut. 33:5; 1 Sam. 12:12; cf. Jdg. 8:23), and Israel was the kingdom of Yahweh (1 Chr. 17:14; 28:5; 2 Chr. 13:8; cf. Exod. 19:6). He had created Israel (Isa. 41:20; 43:15) and brought the people out of Egypt to serve him (Ps. 74:12). He had given them their land and had overcome its inhabitants (Ps. 10:16; 44:4; 47:3-4).

When the people wished that they might have an earthly king like the other nations, they were in a sense rejecting the direct rule of Yahweh over them; nevertheless, he responded to their request by himself appointing their kings, SAUL (1 Sam. 15:11, 35), DAVID (1 Sam. 16:1), and SOLOMON (1 Ki. 3:7; 2 Chr. 1:8-11; Neh. 13:26), who were to rule not for themselves and their own ends but on behalf of God (2 Chr. 9:8). The human king occupied a most important place as the representative of God to the people, and of the people to God. He was the object of God's special concern, and stood to him in the relationship of a son to his father (2 Sam. 7:14). He could address Yahweh as "My God and king," but the use of this phrase in the psalms should not be regarded as restricted to the lips of the king; it expressed the close relationship which any pious Israelite could have with God (Pss. 5:2; 44:4; 68:24; 74:12; 84:3; 145:1).

C. The future reign of God. In the OT God is thought of as exercising his kingly rule from everlasting to everlasting. Alongside this belief in his eternal kingship, there is also the hope that he would exercise his kingly power in a special way as the king of Israel. Conscious of the fact that this present world and their own situation in it fell far short of God's purpose as a result of sin and evil, the prophets of Israel looked forward to a time in the future when God would give his people salvation. He would manifest his kingly power in saving his people from their enemies (Isa. 34:12; 44:6; Zeph. 3:15) and in bringing back those who were exiles held in foreign captivity to their own land (Isa. 52:7; Ezek. 20:33-38; Mic. 2:12-13). Then he would reign in Zion, setting up an everlasting kingdom and ruling over the nations of the world who would pay him their homage (Isa. 24:23; Obad. 21; Mic. 4:6-7; Zech. 14:9-17). In this way the promise of his eternal rule would be fulfilled (Ps. 146:10; Dan. 2:44; 7:27).

As "the saints of the Most High," the people of Israel looked forward to the privilege of rule in this kingdom (Dan. 7:18, 27). They frequently associated their hopes with the reign of an anointed king belonging to the line of David (Isa. 9:6-7; 11:1-5; Jer. 23:5-6; Ezek. 34:23-24; 37:23-24; Zech. 9:9-10). This coming king is customarily called the MESSIAH (i.e., the anointed one), although this title for such a future king is not used in the OT itself (but see Dan. 9:25-26). The hope of his coming grew up especially during the later period of Israel's history; disillusioned by their human kings and crushed by the tribulations of the EXILE, the people began to look forward to Yahweh, or his agent, the Davidic king, acting in power to establish a new era of peace and righteousness, and the prophets declared that their hopes would not be disappointed.

II. The kingship of God in Jewish thought. During the period between the composition of the bulk of the OT and the coming of Jesus, Jewish thought about the character of God's rule did not stand still, and it continued to develop for a long period afterward. One may trace its growth in the APOCALYPTIC LITERATURE, some of it produced prior to NT times, and in the rabbinic writings, which are of a much later date but contain the teaching ascribed to rabbis of the same period (see MISHNAH). Many different influences affected Jewish thought at this time, and there were several different schools of thought, often with highly individual points of view, so that it is impossible to present a system of beliefs generally held by all Jews or even to give a fully coherent account of the various shades of opinion that were held and of their historical development. The sources available are scanty and often imperfectly preserved; they present such problems of dating and interpretation that scholars are by no means unanimous in the conclusions they draw from the evidence.

A. The eternal sovereignty of God. As in the OT, the concept of the eternal kingship of God over the world, established at creation, forms the background of Jewish theology. It is found in the apocalyptic writings (e.g., *1 En.* 9.4; 84.2–3; *Pss. Sol.* 2.33–36; 17.4; 1QSb [1Q28b] IV, 25–26), but is especially prominent in the rabbinic literature (Str-B, 1:172–78). God's kingly power was regarded as being exercised primarily over Israel, the nation that recognized him as its king in contrast to the pagan peoples of the world (*Pss. Sol.* 5.21–22; 17.51). Consequently it was the duty of individual Jews to accept God's rule over them, as ABRAHAM had done (*Jub.* 12.19). The phrase frequently used for this act is "to take upon oneself the yoke of God's rule." For all practical purposes this meant acceptance of his will as revealed in detail in the law of Moses or TORAH. Since this law was expressed succinctly in the Shema (Deut. 6:4–5), it could be said that to recite the Shema was to take the yoke upon oneself. The saying of Jesus, "Take my yoke upon you" (Matt. 11:28–30), bears such a close relationship to this manner of speaking that he must have been echoing Jewish teaching.

B. The establishment of God's future reign. The center of Jewish theological interest, however, lay not so much in the idea that God was now king as in the expectation of his future activity, in setting up his rule visibly and powerfully among men. Within the Gospels there is ample proof of the mood of expectancy that filled the people quite apart from any stimulus to their enthusiasm supplied by Jesus himself. The raison d'être of the apocalyptic writings was their claim to supply information on precisely this topic by reinterpreting the OT prophecies and assuring the people that they were about to be fulfilled (e.g., *Pss. Sol.* 17–18; *Ass. Mos.* 10; *Sib. Or.* 3.46–50, 767–71). The QUMRAN community is the most notable example of a group of Jews who based their behavior on the hope that God would soon come in kingly power to lead them to victory over their oppressors (1QM [1Q33] VI,

The *War Scroll* from Qumran Cave 1. The Essenes taught that at the end of days the Children of Light would defeat the Children of Darkness and the kingdom of God would be established.

6; XII, 7; the interpretation of 1QSb III, 5 is uncertain). A number of Jewish prayers, dating in whole or in part from the NT period, contain the same hope. The *Qaddish* prayer is the best known. "May he set up his sovereignty in your lifetime, and in your days, and in the lifetime of the whole house of Israel, speedily and in a time that is near."

The form and content of this hope are greatly varied. In the earlier apocalyptic writings, the expectation was of an earthly rule of God, centered on Jerusalem with a rebuilt temple, and involving the defeat and destruction of Israel's enemies and judgment upon the ungodly. The righteous dead would be raised up to share in the bliss of the new age, and the people would live in peace and righteousness. They would be under the rule and protection of God. Sometimes he is thought of as himself ruling directly over the people (*1 En.* 6–36; 81–104; *Ass. Mos.* 10; *Jub.* passim), at other times the Messiah is his agent (*1 En.* 90; *T. 12 Patr.* passim, *Sib. Or.* 3.652–784; *Pss. Sol.* 17–18; *4 Ezra* 7.28–39; *2 Bar.* 39; *Tg. Onk.* on Gen. 49:10–11). Modern writers tend to call this era the messianic kingdom, whether or not the ancient writers explicitly refer to the Messiah. In some sources, however, the idea of the kingdom took on a more heavenly and transcendent character; there would be a renewal of the creation and the establishment of communication between heaven and earth (*Ass. Mos.* 10; *1 En.* 104). In *1 En.* 37–71 the SON OF MAN, a heavenly figure, takes over the place and functions of the earthly, Davidic Messiah.

The practice arose of referring to the messianic era as "the age to come" in contrast with the preceding "present age." Probably many Jews were unconscious of any incompatibility between a this-worldly, strongly nationalistic hope of the messianic kingdom and the more transcendent, cosmic hopes that were beginning to arise, although some thinkers began to separate the two concepts. The messianic age was regarded as a temporary, earthly prelude to the heavenly kingdom of God, from which it was separated by the RESURRECTION of the dead and the final judgment. The term "the age to come" was reserved for this eternal, heavenly kingdom of God. That this development goes back to the 1st cent. A.D. is shown by its occurrence in *4 Ezra* 7:27ff. and *2 Bar.* 40, possibly also in *1 En.* 104. (The date of *2 Enoch* is too uncertain for its evidence to be used with any confidence.) As far as the rabbinic material is concerned, most of it is of later date, but there is evidence that during the 1st cent. A.D. the rabbis accepted a scheme similar to that in *4 Ezra* with a temporary messianic kingdom preceding the final, eternal state of heavenly bliss (the age to come). Later developments of rabbinic terminology and thought may here be ignored. (For the interpretation given above see esp. Str-B, 1:178–80; 4/2:799–976.)

C. Kingdom of God and kingdom of heaven.
In the Aramaic TARGUMS (translations of the OT text that are often paraphrastic), the phrase "the kingdom of God" was used to translate OT expressions about God reigning. The way in which the phrase is used shows clearly that it expresses God's *activity* in ruling rather than the *area* or realm over which he rules, although of course the latter meaning is not excluded. In the rabbinic literature outside the Targums, the phrase used was "the kingdom of heaven." The two phrases are undoubtedly synonymous. The adoption of the latter was due to that same Jewish reverence for the name of God and consequent avoidance of uttering it which led to the substitution of "Lord" (Adonai) for the name "Yahweh" at the same time (see GOD, NAMES OF).

It is difficult to be certain which form of the phrase Jesus used. Mark, Luke, and John use "the kingdom of God" in every case, but Matthew has the form "the kingdom of heaven" thirty-two times and "the kingdom of God" only four times (Matt. 12:28; 19:24; 21:31, 43). Either Matthew has corrected the phrase used by Jesus in accordance with Jewish use, or the other Gospels have substituted the phrase that would be more intelligible to Gentiles. In any case, there is no difference in meaning between the two phrases; the distinctions drawn between them in *The Scofield Reference Bible* (note on Matt. 6:33) are unfounded.

The phrase "the age to come" (*1 En.* 71:15; *ʾAbot* 2:7; *4 Ezra* and *2 Baruch* passim) is rare in the Gospels (Matt. 12:32; Mk. 10:30; Lk. 18:30; 20:35). Whereas the rabbis used the phrase "the kingdom of heaven" only sparingly to refer to the new era and preferred to describe the awaited blessings of God's rule by the phrase "the age to come," Jesus preferred to use the term "the kingdom of God" to express the content of his message about God's future promise of salvation for his people.

III. The kingship of God in the teaching of Jesus.
(In what follows, questions regarding the authenticity of sayings attributed to Jesus in the Gospels have not been discussed because an adequate treatment would have seriously exceeded the limits of the article. See BIBLICAL CRITICISM; JESUS CHRIST VI.)

A. The centrality of the theme.
The Greek word for "kingdom" (*basileia* G993) is found fifty-five times in Matthew, twenty times in Mark, forty-six times in Luke, and five times in John. When allowance is made for the use of the word to refer to secular kingdoms and for parallel versions of the same sayings of Jesus, the phrase "the kingdom of God" and equivalent expressions (e.g., "the kingdom of heaven," "his kingdom") occurs about eighty times. The word "king" is used also of Jesus with considerable frequency but only rarely with reference to God (Matt. 5:35; cf. 18:23; 22:2). The verb "to rule" is rare (Lk. 1:33; cf. 19:14, 27).

These statistics show the great importance of the concept in the teaching of Jesus. According to Matthew, JOHN THE BAPTIST also spoke of the kingdom of heaven in words that anticipated those of Jesus (Matt. 3:2). Mark's introductory summary of Jesus' message makes it plain that the kingdom of God was his central theme (Mk. 1:15; cf. Matt. 4:17). Jesus stated that his task was to preach the gospel of the kingdom (Lk. 4:43), and the evangelists echo his words (Matt. 4:23; 9:35; Lk. 8:1; 9:11; cf. 16:16; Acts 1:3). He appointed his disciples to proclaim the same message (Matt. 10:7; 24:14; Lk. 9:2; 10:9). There can be little doubt, therefore, that the phrase "the kingdom of God" expresses the main theme of his teaching.

B. The nature of God's kingship

1. Its imminence. In making the kingdom or kingship of God the theme of his preaching, Jesus did not have to arouse interest in his message or to explain to the people what he meant. Although their ideas were often misguided, especially as a result of their narrowly nationalistic hopes, the people had some idea of what the kingship of God meant (Matt. 18:1; 20:21; Mk. 11:10; 15:43; Lk. 14:15; 17:20; 19:11; 23:42, 51; cf. Acts 1:6). At first sight, therefore, the new element in the teaching of Jesus was concerned not with the character of the kingdom but with the time of its coming. The time was fully accomplished and the kingdom of God was at hand (Mk. 1:15). What God had planned from the beginning (Matt. 25:34) and what his people had hoped for down the centuries was near.

This way of putting the matter indicates that by "the kingdom of God" Jesus meant the kingly action of God at the end of the age rather than the present, eternal rule of God in heaven, for it would be strange to say that the latter was at hand. Certainly Jesus did speak of the eternal kingship of God (Matt. 25:34–35), for it is upon the fact of his present rule that the hope of his future action depends.

What did Jesus mean by saying, "the kingdom of God has come near" (Matt. 11:5; Lk. 10:9, 11; Matt. 12:28 (?))? Was he indicating that at the time when he spoke the kingly action of God was about to take place or that it was already taking place? On purely linguistic grounds a decision is difficult, though the balance of probability favors the former interpretation. The problem must be solved by considering the whole teaching of Jesus.

At the beginning of the present century, such scholars as J. Weiss and A. Schweitzer advocated an interpretation now known as "thoroughgoing eschatology" (*konsequente Eschatologie*). In their view, Jesus preached that the kingdom of God was very near, and that by this phrase he meant exclusively the final, visible act of God in setting up his kingdom. Jesus expected the end of the age almost immediately; the inauguration of the new age would take place through a glorious cataclysmic event. Support for this view can be found in texts that speak of this transcendent era and its coming (Matt. 6:10 = Lk. 11:2; Matt. 8:11 = Lk. 13:29; Matt. 16:28 = Mk. 9:1 = Lk. 9:27; Matt. 22:1–14 = Lk. 14:16–24; Matt. 26:29 = Mk. 14:25 = Lk. 22:16, 18 [cf. 21:31]) or of the imminent coming of the SON OF MAN (Mk. 13:26–30; 14:62) and of future entry to the kingdom (Matt. 5:20; 7:21; 8:11–12 = Lk. 13:28–29; Matt. 18:3 = Mk. 10:15 = Lk. 18:17; Matt. 25:34; Mk. 9:47).

About thirty years later a different interpretation of the teaching of Jesus was put forward, principally by C. H. Dodd. He adopted the view that, according to Mk. 1:15, the kingdom had already come at the time when Jesus was speaking, and he showed that a number of other sayings indicated that the kingdom was already present during his ministry (Matt. 10:7 = Lk. 10:9, 11; Matt. 11:12 = Lk. 16:16; Matt. 12:28 = Lk. 11:20; 17:20–21). Jesus' own appearance and ministry were the final act of God for the salvation of sinners, and the kingship of God did not mean some mighty apocalyptic act at the end of history, but God's sovereign and gracious act in bringing redemption in Jesus. This theory earned the name of "realized eschatology," since it held that the eschatological events had already happened (the German phrase *sich realisierende Eschatologie* also is used to describe it).

The result of subsequent intense discussion has been to show that neither theory can stand on its own. Each can be defended only at the cost of explaining away, often by very dubious methods, the evidence for the other. The Weiss-Schweitzer theory paid a one-sided attention to the sayings about the future coming of the kingdom and ignored the sayings to which Dodd later drew attention. Dodd for his part was quite unconvincing in his attempts to interpret the future sayings in line with his view that the kingdom had already come. The most careful study of the evidence, that by W. G. Kümmel (*Promise and Fulfillment* [1957]), showed that Jesus spoke both of the presence and of the future coming of the kingdom.

Once this polarity or dualism has been recognized, the problem is to explain it. (a) R. Bultmann and his followers stressed the primacy of the future elements in the teaching of Jesus, but then reinterpreted his sayings in existential categories in such a manner that the concept of a real future coming of the kingdom has been effectively denied. (b) Kümmel's own solution was to restrict the presence of the kingdom to its presence in Jesus; in his own person the future consummation already had come, but apart from his presence the kingdom is not present and its coming lies in the future. (c) Others, taking their cue from Mk. 9:1, have distinguished between the coming of the kingdom in Jesus' ministry and its future coming in power (e.g., A. M. Hunter), or between the veiled revelation of the kingdom in the ministry of Jesus and its open manifestation at the end of time (e.g., C. E. B. Cranfield), or between the partial and provisional manner of its manifestation in the ministry of Jesus and its future full manifestation (e.g., H. Ridderbos).

There are elements of truth in all these various attempts at elucidation, and they may be combined with each other (as several scholars do combine them). (d) Perhaps the most satisfactory statement of the matter is that suggested independently by R. Schnackenburg and G. E. Ladd, who distinguish between the fulfillment and the consummation of the OT promise of the kingdom. "For Jesus, the kingdom of God was the dynamic rule of God which had invaded history in his own person and mission to bring men in the present age the blessings of the messianic age, and which would manifest itself yet again at the end of the age to bring this messianic salvation to its consummation" (G. E. Ladd, *Jesus and the Kingdom* [1966], 303). By this terminology the reality of the coming of the kingdom in the ministry of Jesus is safeguarded.

It is probably wasted labor to attempt to show that one aspect or the other of the coming of the kingdom had the greater significance for Jesus. Although the actual number of sayings referring explicitly to the future coming is greater, it remains true that the teaching about the presence of the kingdom was especially distinctive of Jesus and contained new ideas about its nature. The truth is that the two aspects were not rigidly separated by him. The future coming was near because God had begun to act; the present time was full of significance because God already was bringing his final gift of salvation to men.

2. The presence of the kingdom. It is necessary to examine more closely both aspects of Jesus' message about the kingdom. The evidence in the Gospels is fully consonant with the usage of the rabbinic literature in that the phrase "the kingdom of God" refers primarily to the action of God who follows out his sovereign will toward mankind. This means that the kingdom of God never refers to an action undertaken by human beings or a realm which they set up. However noble may be the idea of laboring to establish the kingdom of God, the biblical terminology is completely inconsistent with the language of modern liberal theology. The kingdom is a divine act, not a human accomplishment, nor even the accomplishment of dedicated Christians.

At the same time, however, although the idea of action is primary, the word *kingdom* also refers to the realm set up by God and the benefits associated with it. People may enter the kingdom (Lk. 16:16 = Matt. 11:12) or receive it as a gift (Lk. 12:32). Consequently, the message of the kingdom comes as a piece of good news (cf. above, section III.A). The present world is under the rule of SATAN (Matt. 4:9 = Lk. 4:6; Matt. 12:26 = Lk. 11:18; Lk. 13:16; cf. Jn. 12:31; 14:30), but the action of God in Jesus means that Satan is being attacked, his rule is being brought to an end, and his captives are being set free. If, therefore, the coming of the kingdom already means the hour of judgment upon wicked men (cf. Matt. 3:10 = Lk. 3:9), it is also the hour of deliverance in which sinners are set free from the demonic powers (Matt. 12:28 = Lk. 11:20).

The deeds of Jesus are, therefore, to be seen as signs of the coming and the presence of the kingdom. They are part of the message (cf. Matt. 4:23). They do not simply show the *power* of God—

KINGDOM OF GOD (OF HEAVEN)

hence there is no hard-and-fast division to be made between the miraculous and nonmiraculous deeds of Jesus—but rather the kind of power that he displays. The kingdom of God is characterized by grace (Matt. 20:1–16) and a compassion that is mighty to help the unfortunate and the outcast.

The teaching of Jesus is equally a sign of the presence of the kingdom. By proclaiming the kingship of God, Jesus made it possible for people to turn from their sin, own his kingship, and receive the blessings of his rule. This is seen particularly in the PARABLES. They present the rule of God as being like a hidden treasure or a costly pearl that people should make every effort to acquire (Matt. 13:44–46). They paint its joys as being like those of a marriage feast to which all are invited (22:2–14). They show how it has come quietly and secretly in the ministry of Jesus, like seed newly planted in the ground, but will one day come to a glorious and visible consummation, like an abundant harvest (Matt. 13:31–32 = Mk. 4:30–32 = Lk. 13:18–19; Matt. 13:33 = Lk. 13:20–21; Mk. 4:26–29). They indicate that the hour of decision has come: people must listen with care (Matt. 13:19), so that at the end when the harvest is gathered they may be numbered among the righteous (13:24–30, 36–43, 47–50).

In these various ways the MYSTERY or secret of the kingdom is revealed (Matt. 13:10–17; cf. Mk. 4:10–12 and Lk. 8:9–10). The content of the mystery is that God is at work in the ministry of Jesus for the salvation of human beings before the time comes for judgment and the opportunity for repentance is past. Although the mysterious working of God in this completely unexpected manner was no secret to the disciples (yet even they did not completely comprehend it), it remained hidden from many, who remained willfully blind to what God was doing in Jesus and refused to seek out the message concealed in the parables. They could not believe that God was working in Jesus, and so the secret remained hidden from them.

From what has been said, it will be apparent that the message of the kingdom is a message of salvation rather than a message about God in himself. Jesus said very little about God's reigning or acting as king, and he associated the term *kingdom* much more with the blessings that it brought to men and women. He preferred to think of God not so much in terms of kingship as of FATHERHOOD, and part of his message was the new filial relationship with God that God's children could enjoy in the kingdom (Matt. 6:9–10 = Lk. 11:2, Lk. 12:32, 22:29; cf. Matt. 18:3).

3. The coming of the kingdom. Although the kingdom was truly present in the ministry of Jesus, he also spoke of it as a future entity and told his disciples to pray for its coming (Matt. 6:10 = Lk. 11:2) and to be ready for its coming (Matt. 25:1–13). More than once he indicated that it would come soon (Matt. 16:28 = Mk. 9:1 = Lk. 9:27; Lk. 17:20–21; 21:31). By this manner of speaking Jesus was referring to the age to come (Mk. 10:30 = Lk. 18:30), which was associated with the coming of the Son of Man, the resurrection of the dead, and the setting up of an eternal realm of bliss, often described in the imagery of a banquet or marriage feast (Matt. 8:11–12 = Lk. 13:28–29; Matt. 22:1–10 = Lk. 14:16–24; Matt. 25:1–13; Lk. 22:28–30).

The closest connection exists between the presence of the kingdom in the ministry of Jesus and its future consummation. If the presence of the kingdom is closely associated with the person of Jesus (see above, III.B.4), its future coming is associated with the coming of the Son of Man. It is true that the connection is not explicitly made in the texts, but it is impossible not to believe that the two events formed part of one single eschatological hope.

The question of the imminence of the future kingdom has been the subject of much discussion. Against the contention of many scholars that Jesus expected its arrival immediately after his death, W. G. Kümmel has shown that he certainly envisaged an interval between his death and its arrival. During this time the disciples were to preach the gospel to all the nations (Matt. 24:14). Jesus spoke of founding his CHURCH, to which he entrusted the keys of the kingdom (16:18–19). The problem of whether the interval expected by Jesus was as long as it is turning out to be is part of the general question of ESCHATOLOGY in the Gospels, and is discussed elsewhere.

4. Jesus and the kingdom. How was Jesus himself related to the kingdom? Was he simply the herald of its coming like JOHN THE BAPTIST, or was it more closely linked to his person?

Earlier discussion has shown that Jesus brought the kingdom of God to human beings by his teaching and his mighty deeds. The point to be emphasized now is that they were *his* words and deeds or those of men sent out by *him*. It was through *him* that God had chosen to work. He was conscious that a new era had begun: the kingdom was pushing its way forward among men and being proclaimed as good news (Matt. 11:12 = Lk. 16:16).

Furthermore, although Jesus was extremely reticent on the matter in his public teaching, he knew himself to be the One who perfectly fulfilled the roles of the Messiah and the Son of Man. In other words, he was conscious of being the key figure associated with the coming of the kingdom (for the Son of Man exercising kingly functions, see Dan. 7:13–14; *1 En.* 69.26–29).

Jesus required of people to make a personal response to him if they wished to enter the kingdom. He called them to faith and discipleship, and, although the texts that directly link discipleship to the kingdom are few, the impression is inescapable that response to him is the condition for receiving the benefits of the kingdom both now and hereafter (Matt. 7:21; 13:52; Lk. 12:32; 22:29–30; 23:42). He declared authoritatively who was near to or who was excluded from the kingdom (Matt. 21:31, 43; 23:13; Mk. 12:34).

Jesus did not directly link the coming of the kingdom with his death upon the cross. Already before his death, the kingdom of God was present. Nevertheless, the connection is there, and the cross is to be regarded as one of the key stages in the coming of the kingdom. It is probable that the coming of the kingdom "with power" (Mk. 9:1) is to be connected with the events made possible by the death and resurrection of Jesus. The discussion of places of honor in the kingdom (10:35–45) is closely linked with the thought of the sacrificial death of Jesus; it is only by the way of suffering that the Son of Man may enter into his glory. The same thought recurs in Mk. 14:25 (cf. Lk. 22:16, 18), where Jesus stated that he would not drink of the fruit of the vine until the kingdom of God had come. These sayings show that Jesus was aware that the kingdom could not fully come except by his death, but they do not fully express the nature of a relationship that could become evident to his disciples only after his death and resurrection.

A number of passages speak of Jesus as ruling. The title of Messiah means an anointed king, and it was because he was thought to be claiming an earthly kingship that Jesus was crucified as "the king of the Jews" (Mk. 15: 2, 9, 12, 18, 26, 32, and parallels). This was in fact the status claimed for him at his birth (Matt. 2:2; Lk. 1:33), and by himself when he entered Jerusalem as the promised king (Matt. 21:5; Lk. 19:38). He also looked forward to his future role as king, although the relationship of this messianic kingdom to the kingdom of God is not clearly explained in the Gospels (Matt. 13:41; 16:28; cf. 20:21; Lk. 22:29–30; cf. 23:42).

All this evidence shows that the kingdom is inextricably linked with Jesus himself. One may well agree with MARCION, who said, "In the Gospel the kingdom of God is Christ himself," and with ORIGEN, who described Jesus as being "himself the kingdom" (*autobasileia*). It must be carefully observed that, since the kingdom of God is primarily God's action, it is not the person of Jesus in separation from his deeds which constitutes the presence of the kingdom but rather the activity of Jesus in coming into the world from God and in exercising God's power in bringing salvation and judgment to sinners.

C. The human response

1. Entry into the kingdom. The preaching of Jesus about the kingdom demanded a response from his hearers. They were to repent and believe the good news (Mk. 1:15). They were to make the seeking of the kingdom their foremost concern in life (Matt. 6:33; cf. Lk. 12:31). Those who took these steps were promised that here and now in this life they might receive the kingdom and its blessings (Lk. 12:32).

Jesus also spoke of entering the kingdom in the future tense, in the same way as that in which he spoke of receiving eternal life or being saved or having a share in the age to come (Mk. 10:17, 25–26, 30). These various phrases all signified entry into the everlasting, heavenly kingdom of God. The "conditions" for entry included willingness to become humble and receptive like little children (Matt. 18:3–4), and readiness to endure persecution and sacrifice (Matt. 5:10; 19:12; Lk. 9:60, 62). It would, however, be wrong to think of these as "conditions" in the normal sense, as standards of fitness that people must attain to enable them to qualify for entrance. The ministry of Jesus affords ample proof that entry into the kingdom depends solely upon the grace of God and that this grace comes to the undeserving and sinful. As stated above (III.B.4), the primary response that Jesus sought from his hearers was discipleship, the willingness to trust him and commit their life to him. We should, therefore, regard these "conditions" as the characteristics of those who are humbly receptive to the grace of God and prepared to make any effort to receive it.

In laying down this way of entry into the kingdom, Jesus was denying entry to any Jews who thought that the kingdom rightfully belonged to them and failed to show the evidence of true discipleship and humble trust in God (Matt. 8:11–12; cf. Lk. 13:28–29; Matt. 21:31, 43; cf. 23:13). The kingdom was no longer to be the exclusive property of the Jews, but was now open to the Gentiles. However, although the Jews as a nation had largely misused their opportunities (Matt. 23:13), the revelation of God in the OT was still a true means of knowing his will. A Jew who correctly understood the spiritual message of the OT was told by Jesus that he was not far from the kingdom (Mk. 12:34); the one thing necessary was that he should accept the Messiah promised in the OT and become a disciple (cf. 10:21).

2. The ethics of the kingdom. To acknowledge the kingship of God implies the acceptance of the kind of behavior he prescribes. It means submission to the concrete demands of the king (Matt. 5:19) and the production of a character more righteous than that of such men as the Pharisees and scribes (5:20; cf. 13:43). There must be a resolute determination to overcome temptation (Mk. 9:47) and a willingness to extend to others the FORGIVENESS God gives to his people (Matt. 18:23–35). The scribe who recognized the primacy of heart love for God and for his neighbor over external sacrifices was declared to be not far from the kingdom (Mk. 12:34).

Weiss and Schweitzer erred in thinking that this ethic of Jesus was teaching conditioned purely by the imminent approach of the end of the world, a set of stringent rules to be observed in a time of crisis but unsuitable for ordinary, everyday life. But it is not the nearness of a crisis that determines the content of Jesus' ethic but rather the nearness of God; and what is demanded is not something that can be fulfilled only by people who are keyed up by the expectation of imminent crisis, but is rather the unchanging requirement of God from his people. The ethic comes with new force in the context of the preaching of the kingdom, and it is expressed more radically than was possible in the legal code of the Pentateuch, but it remains the same ethic as that which is found in the OT.

Once again one must beware of thinking that the ethic is a "condition" of entry to the kingdom, as if God were laying down certain qualities of character as the entrance requirements. Jesus' message was the gospel of grace, and the ethic expresses the

Jesus said that one must "receive the kingdom of God like a little child" (Mk. 10:15).

response that sinners should make to the gospel. It is the way of life for those who have already accepted the rule of God and experienced its blessings and who now look forward to the consummation of his rule. See also ETHICS OF JESUS.

3. The kingdom and the church. Although the word CHURCH occurs only twice in the Gospels (Matt. 16:18–19; 18:17–18), the idea was certainly present in Jesus' teaching. The church is simply the company of those who accept the kingly rule of God and find themselves bound together by their common allegiance to God and his Son. During his ministry Jesus placed before men and women the need to commit themselves to him in discipleship, and this group of disciples must be regarded as the church in embryo. Within this larger company the Twelve occupied a special place. To them, and in particular to PETER, Jesus entrusted the keys of the kingdom, that is, the authority to preach the gospel of the kingdom and to admit people to it. This was their mission during his lifetime, and he commanded them to carry it on after his death.

The church, therefore, is not to be identified with the kingdom. It is rather part of the manifestation of the kingdom in the world, for it is the company of those who accept the message of the kingdom, own Jesus as their Lord and Master, and act as his agents in continuing to proclaim the gospel of the kingdom.

4. The kingdom and the world. Although the old translation of Lk. 17:21, "the kingdom of God is within you" (KJV, ASV, NIV), is rejected by many, it remains true that the kingship of God is fundamentally a spiritual matter. His kingdom is not to be put on a level with earthly kingdoms (Jn. 18:36), and entrance to it is possible only as a result of spiritual rebirth (3:3, 5). Nevertheless, the stage on which it is manifested is this world, and one day the forces of evil that control this world will finally yield to it. Although it is a spiritual realm and the natural man may be blind to its presence, those who accept God's rule enjoy an earnest of heavenly blessing here and now in this world, and find themselves required to take up a definite attitude to the "powers that be" that may be arrayed in opposition to it. The kingdom may be said to spread in the world as people accept the rule of God personally, and even as the people of the world are moved to higher principles and more ethical behavior as a result of its working. There is, however, nothing in the teaching of Jesus to suggest that the world is necessarily going to become better or that eventually all will accept the kingship of God. On the contrary, the establishment of the kingdom at the advent of the Son of Man takes place only after the persecution of the disciples and amid human indifference.

IV. The kingship of God in the early church

A. The Acts of the Apostles. One of the most striking things about the preaching of the early church is the way in which the message of the kingdom of God fell into the background, and its place as the theme of preaching was taken by the person of Jesus himself. The preaching of the kingdom did not entirely lapse (Acts 8:12; 14:22; 19:8; 20:25; 28:23, 31), and there was a genuine continuity between the message of Jesus and that of the apostles. It is now the King rather than the kingdom who comes to the fore (17:7), and when the kingdom was preached it was in conjunction with the name of Jesus (8:12; 28:31). The idea of the kingdom as a future realm appears in Acts 14:22.

B. The epistles of Paul. In a number of passages PAUL retains the concept of the kingdom of God as a description of the future age (1 Thess. 2:12; 2 Tim. 4:1, 18). It will be inherited only by those who have turned aside from sin (1 Cor. 6:9–10; Gal. 5:21; Eph. 5:5; 2 Thess. 1:5). Only in Rom. 14:17 and in 1 Cor. 4:20 is the kingdom of God clearly spoken of in the present tense. In the former passage its blessings are stated to be the spiritual qualities of righteousness, peace, and joy in the HOLY SPIRIT, and in the latter it is emphasized that it is a real dynamic force in the world.

Elsewhere when Paul speaks of the kingdom in the present tense, he refers specifically to the kingdom of Christ, who now reigns in heaven (1 Cor. 15:25) and admits sinners into his kingdom (Col. 1:13). He is the King of kings and Lord of lords (1 Tim. 6:15) alongside his Father (1:17), to whom he is ultimately subordinate and to whom he hands over his kingship so that the Father may be supreme

(1 Cor. 15:24). Although there is probably no reference to a millennial reign in this last quotation, the future kingship of Jesus is mentioned in 2 Tim. 4:1, 18. Believers will share in this reign (2:12; cf. 1 Cor. 4:8, which is expressed ironically), but even now they can be said to share in the privileges of reign (Rom. 5:17). Paul thinks of an active rule of God through Jesus Christ, both now in the period since the resurrection and also in the future dating from the PAROUSIA, but it cannot be said that the theme of the kingdom of God occupies a central position in his thought. For him, as for the other NT writers, the King has become more important than the kingdom, and in the context of the Hellenistic Roman world, the title of Lord gained much wider currency than the Jewish title of king.

C. Other writers. The rest of the NT does not contribute much to the development of the theme. The epistle to the Hebrews shares the common NT belief that Jesus now reigns as king, employing the language of Ps. 45:6 to express its confession of his divine kingship (Heb. 1:8). It also exhorts and encourages its readers with the thought that they possess a kingdom that cannot be shaken; with God as their king, it is implied, nothing should worry them, for the kingdom to which they belong will survive the fate of the perishable world (12:28).

In the epistle of James there is mention of the future blessings associated with the kingdom of God that are promised to the poor (Jas. 2:5). The thought of James is close to that of the gospel BEATITUDES, and elsewhere James speaks of the royal law that is promulgated by the king in the command to love one's neighbor as oneself (2:8). The first epistle of Peter speaks once of believers as a royal priesthood, thus combining the thoughts of their privilege of reigning and their duty of service (1 Pet. 2:9), and the second epistle stresses that people must live in such a way that they will gain entry to the eternal kingdom of their Lord and Savior Jesus Christ (2 Pet. 1:11).

Finally, the book of Revelation looks forward to the era of the kingship of God and of Christ when the kingdoms of the earth come under their rightful lord (Rev. 1:8; 4:8; 11:17; 15:3; 17:14; 19:6, 15) instead of being under the sway of evil demonic forces (9:11; 17:18; 18:7). Under the rule of God believers themselves already form a kingdom (1:6, 9), and they will share in the future reign of Christ both in the millennium and afterward (5:10; 20:4, 6; 22:5).

In the early church the concept of the kingdom of God was used, as in the teaching of Jesus, for the future triumphal reign of God. The church expressed the present era of salvation in other ways, but it did not altogether give up Jesus' manner of speaking about the presence of the kingdom, for it taught that he is now the exalted Lord and King to whom men and women must submit. At his SECOND COMING he will be displayed openly as king, and in the end God the Father will be seen to be all in all when the Son hands over sovereignty to him. In this life believers share in the blessings of his reign, just as the disciples did during the earthly ministry of Jesus, and they look forward to the consummation of their hopes in the coming kingdom of God and of his Son. See HEAVEN.

(Most works on NT theology pay close attention to the theme of the kingdom of God. See further J. Weiss, *Jesus' Proclamation of the Kingdom of God* [1892; Eng. trans. 1971]; G. Dalman, *The Words of Jesus* [1909]; W. Bousset and H. Gressmann, *Die Religion des Judentums im spätehellenistischen Zeitalter* [1926, 4th ed. 1966]; T. W. Manson, *The Teaching of Jesus*, 2nd ed. [1935]; C. H. Dodd, *The Parables of the Kingdom* [1935, 2nd ed. 1961]; A. M. Hunter, *The Work and Words of Jesus* [1950]; W. G. Kümmel, *Promise and Fulfillment* [1957]; C. E. B. Cranfield, *The Gospel according to St Mark*, CGT, 2nd ed. [1963]; H. Ridderbos, *The Coming of the Kingdom* [1962]; G. Lundstrom, *The Kingdom of God in the Teaching of Jesus* [1963]; N. Perrin, *The Kingdom of God in the Teaching of Jesus* [1963]; *Rediscovering the Teaching of Jesus* [1967]; R. Schnackenburg, *God's Rule and Kingdom* [Eng. trans. 1963]; D. S. Russell, *The Method and Message of Jewish Apocalyptic* [1964]; K. L. Schmidt and others in *TDNT*, 1 [1964]: 564–93; G. E. Ladd, *Jesus and the Kingdom* [1966]; S. E. Johnson, *The Theology of the Gospels* [1966]; R. H. Hiers, *The Kingdom of God in the Synoptic Tradition* [1970]; J. A. Baird, *Rediscovering the Power of the Gospel: Jesus' Theology of the Kingdom* [1982]; G. R. Beasley-Murray, *Jesus and the Kingdom of God* [1986]; B. Chiton and J. I. H. McDonald, *Jesus and the Ethics of the Kingdom*

[1987]; W. Willis, ed., *The Kingdom of God in 20th-Century Interpretation* [1987]; R. I. Vasholz, *Pillars of the Kingdom: Five Features of the Kingdom of God Progressively Revealed in the Old Testament* [1997]; J. Liebenberg, *The Language of the Kingdom and Jesus: Parable, Aphorism, and Metaphor in the Sayings Material Common to the Synoptic Tradition and the Gospel of Thomas* [2001]; R. A. Horsley, *Jesus and Empire: The Kingdom of God and the New World Disorder* [2003]; L. D. Chrupcała, *The Kingdom of God: A Bibliography of 20th Century Research* [2007].)

I. H. MARSHALL

kingdom of Israel. See ISRAEL, HISTORY OF.

kingdom of Judah. See JUDAH, KINGDOM OF.

Kingdoms, Books of. In the SEPTUAGINT, the books of 1–2 Samuel and 1–2 Kings bear the title 1–4 Kingdoms (or Reigns; Gk. *Basileiōn*). See KINGS, BOOKS OF; SAMUEL, BOOKS OF.

King James Version. See VERSIONS OF THE BIBLE, ENGLISH, V.

Kings, Books of. Two historical books of the OT that cover the period from the death of King DAVID to the end of the monarchy. The title derives from the Hebrew Bible (*mĕlākîm*), where they are the last two books in the section known as the Former Prophets (Joshua, Judges, 1–2 Samuel, 1–2 Kings). Originally, the narrative formed only one book. The division between 1 and 2 Kings first appears in the SEPTUAGINT (where 1–2 Samuel and 1–2 Kings are entitled 1–4 Kingdoms or Reigns). A few medieval Hebrew MSS also separate the two books, and the division became standard in the Hebrew Bible after it was introduced in the Bomberg printed edition (published in Venice, A.D. 1516–17). This segmentation of the narrative, however, is quite arbitrary and consequently does not reflect any significance as far as the original volume is concerned. The account of the Hebrew monarchy in 1–2 Kings will therefore be referred to in the singular in this article.

  I. Background
 II. Authorship, unity, and date
III. Place of origin
 IV. Occasion, purpose, and destination
  V. Canonicity
 VI. Text
VII. Chronology
VIII. Content and outline
 IX. Theology

I. Background. Spanning a period of more than four centuries (c. 971–562 B.C.), the historical survey in Kings portrays the Israelite kingdom in its most affluent era of political, economic, and religious achievements under SOLOMON. Due to Solomon's apostasy, the nation was divided, and ultimately both resulting kingdoms were terminated in exile.

International relations are frequently delineated. With Palestine as the geographical link between the Mesopotamian and Egyptian cultures, there were frequent political and economic pressures on the divided Israelite nation. Whereas the northern kingdom capitulated under the Assyrian advance in 722 B.C., the southern kingdom survived but ultimately succumbed to the Babylonian empire in 586. Numerous historical contacts with foreign nations have been noted in archaeological findings and related to the account in the book of Kings.

II. Authorship, unity, and date. The history in the book of Kings was distinctly religious history. The religious evaluation of each king throughout this long period of Israelite history is characteristic of the entire account. Every king in each kingdom is carefully noted, although some of the monarchs receive only a brief account in the record. Neither from the literary nor from the religious perspective is there any reason to suggest a diversity of authorship.

Although no one single author could have been associated with the events spanning over four centuries, it is quite apparent that the recurrent phrases throughout are characteristic of the prophetic school identified by many scholars as "Deuteronomic" (cf. C. F. Burney, *Notes on the Hebrew Text of the Book of Kings* [1903], xiii and 131). See DEUTERONOMISTIC HISTORY. E. R. Thiele (*The Mysterious Numbers of the Hebrew Kings,* rev. ed. [1965], 177) concurs that this "unusual type of religious history in Kings is certainly peculiar to Hebrew prophetic ways of thought and action." The language used by Isaiah, Jeremiah, and other prophets, as well as the language of Deuteronomy, is similar to that of Kings, since the spirit of admonition, exhortation, reproof, and encouragement is common throughout.

A basic framework also appears throughout the book of Kings concerning each individual ruler. This usually occurs in connection with the introduction and/or conclusion of each king's reign. Normally for each of the kings of Judah and Israel the length of his reign is reported. For the kings of Judah the author usually gives the name of the queen mother and the age of the king at the time of his accession. For kings who were violently deposed, the formula is often incomplete. Such was the case with Joram king of Israel (see JEHORAM #2) and AHAZIAH king of Judah, who were both murdered by JEHU. Likewise for Jehu the formula is missing, since he was a rebel and took the throne by killing the king under whom he served as captain of the Israelite army.

As a religious history, the account gives an appraisal of each king concerning his reign and his relationship to God. The kings of the northern kingdom were all committed to IDOLATRY, breaking the first commandment, which dealt with wholehearted devotion to God. JEROBOAM began this idolatrous trend, and his successors followed in the promotion of idolatry. In the southern kingdom there were periodic revivals under God-fearing kings. Outstanding for their piety were JEHOSHAPHAT, HEZEKIAH, and JOSIAH. ASA and UZZIAH were also concerned about the religious welfare of their people. Among the most idolatrous and defiant were JEHORAM, AHAZ, and MANASSEH.

Since this was a religious history covering so many centuries of time, it is quite reasonable to conclude that these records were kept by the PROPHETS. MOSES, through whom Israel was established as a nation, provided a written account of Israel's history and the divine revelation given through him. This written record by the prophet Moses was given so that future generations would have knowledge of God's requirements. Subsequent to Moses' time the history of Israel is recorded by authors who were sensitive to Israel's obedience in relationship to the covenant established at Sinai. In all likelihood these authors were prophets or spokesmen for God.

According to Deut. 17, the kings of Israel were to be obedient to the law. For this purpose they were to be provided with a personal copy of the law. In the anointing of both Saul and David, the prophet SAMUEL was personally involved (1 Sam. 10:1; 16:12–13). NATHAN the prophet and ZADOK the priest anointed SOLOMON, whose line continued throughout the history of Judah down to 586 B.C., interrupted only by the reign of terror under ATHALIAH. AHIJAH the prophet informed JEROBOAM about his prospects of ruling over the seceding tribes in the N (1 Ki. 11:29–38). The prophet JEHU announced God's judgment upon the dynasty of BAASHA (16:1–4). A different Jehu, an Israelite army captain, was anointed as king by ELISHA's servant, who actually implemented the divine commission given to ELIJAH at Mount Horeb (1 Ki. 19:6–7; 2 Ki. 9:9–12). Elijah and Elisha continually carried on a ministry that made Israelite and foreign kings conscious that they were representatives for God. Boldly they warned and denounced

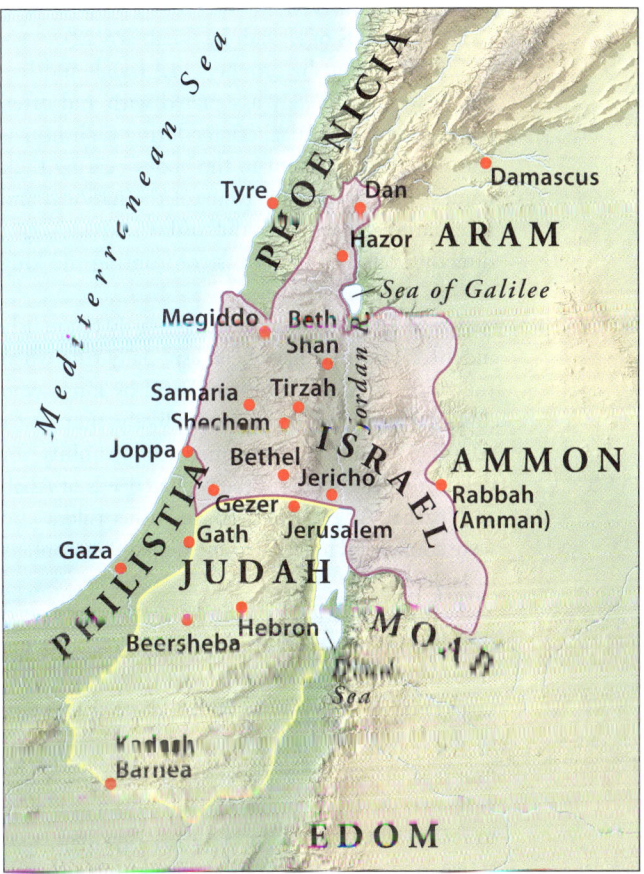

The Divided Kingdom.

kings, offered their aid in time of need, and made the people conscious of the solemn obligation that they ought to serve God instead of idols.

Since prophets apparently were active in every generation in the history of Israel, it seems that the concern was that the king should conform to the written revelation given to Moses, which would have been expressed in the written records. Consequently it is possible that many more prophets were engaged in keeping records than is indicated in the OT writings that have been preserved. Among those that are identified as providing written sources are the following: the book of Samuel the seer (1 Chr. 29:29); the book of Nathan the prophet (29:29; 2 Chr. 9:29); the book of Gad the seer (1 Chr. 29:29); the book of Nathan the prophet; the prophecy of Ahijah the Shilonite (2 Chr. 9:29); the visions of Iddo the seer (9:29); the book of Shemaiah the prophet (12:15); the book of Iddo the seer (12:15); the story of the prophet Iddo (13:22); the acts of Uzziah by Isaiah (26:22).

That some of the prophets like Isaiah and Jeremiah were intimately associated with and often involved in the political affairs during their ministries is readily apparent in the books bearing their names. They were fully aware of the national and international problems and often had messages directly related to the issues confronting the king and his people.

Court recorders were not necessarily religiously inclined. This may have been especially true when they were appointed and employed by kings who did not fear God. It seems unlikely that court recorders would have assumed responsibility for delineating the details of the wicked deeds of Ahab and Jezebel, Ahaz, Manasseh, and other rulers who were committed to idolatry and defied the prophets of Israel's God.

Prophets, on the other hand, were not employed by the king or any court officials. They were accountable to God and responsible to convey God's messages that were in harmony with and supplementary to the Mosaic revelation and the messages of the prophets that preceded them. By this standard they evaluated the kings and would have been at liberty to record these crucial facts only if they had been active in some neutral point removed from either of the capitals of the Hebrew kings.

The synchronism between the two kingdoms throughout the book of Kings seems to favor the idea that these records were kept by the prophets. It is unlikely that court recorders would have consistently made reference to the kings of the other kingdom, especially so when the two kingdoms were at war with each other. To the prophets, however, this approach would have been of significant interest, since the citizens of both kingdoms were Hebrews and descendants of Abraham.

On the basis of the above considerations, it seems reasonable and likely that the prophets kept the records throughout the generations of the Hebrew kingdoms. One or more of these prophets living between 600 and 550 B.C. probably was responsible for the final edition of the book of Kings in its present form. From earliest times it (along with Joshua, Judges, and 1–2 Samuel) seemingly has been associated with the writing of the prophets and classified with the books of Isaiah, Jeremiah, Ezekiel, and the Twelve.

III. Place of origin. If the conclusion is correct that the prophets were responsible for keeping these records, it seems reasonable to concur with Thiele (*Mysterious Numbers*, 174–91) that these prophetic centers were located in some of the cities in the border area between the N and the S. Here the prophets could have been engaged in such literary activities as are reflected in the book of Kings. Cities like Bethel, Gilgal, and Mizpah were teaching centers in the days of Samuel (1 Sam. 7:16). During the times of Elijah and Elisha the cities of Bethel, Gilgal, and Jericho had prophetic schools where groups of prophets were educated. These cultural, educational, and religious centers consequently were not under the direct control of the state.

Since the capital cities of Samaria and Jerusalem were 40 mi. apart, the towns in the border area were far enough from the political centers to allow them considerable freedom from direct interference. At the same time they were close enough so that the prophets who resided in the border area had access to the news as it happened in either kingdom. Furthermore, in time of war they were not the main object of attack as the capital cities were. In time of peace they undoubtedly had vital contact with both capitals.

It is doubtful that the records kept by the prophets were widely circulated during the period in which they were written. Consequently there was not much opportunity for the kings who were in power to react to the writings or the authors in question. Normally these accounts may not have reached the royal courts unless the king was particularly friendly to the prophets. The kings who cared neither for God nor the prophets and their messages may have generally ignored the activity of the prophets in keeping the records of their nation's history.

It is also probable that some of the prophets were primarily interested in their own kingdom and limited their literary activity to either the N or the S, reflecting the customs and interests peculiar to their native state. The developments in the other kingdom were only brought into their account when both kingdoms were involved in contemporary affairs. Representative of this approach are the books of CHRONICLES, in which the account is primarily limited to the southern kingdom. There may have existed a number of such historical records that are now lost, but they may have been used by the author who was responsible for the edition of the book of Kings as it is preserved in the OT.

After the northern kingdom capitulated to the Assyrians in 722 B.C., the border became less important. During Josian days, as the Assyrian domination diminished, the distinction between the N and the S may have been completely erased. It is during this era, by about 600, that this account in the book of Kings may have been completed and the subsequent events down to 586 added as they occurred. Nothing is reported beyond that concerning the Hebrew people except that Jehoiachin remained in Babylonian captivity until 561, when he was released.

IV. Occasion, purpose, and destination.

The minute details given in Kings seem to indicate that records were kept of the events as they happened throughout the centuries from the time of Solomon to Jehoiachin's release. Of primary issue are with the record concerning every king in both Hebrew kingdoms. What happened during each reign is reported briefly in some instances and again extensively concerning others. Frequently other leaders who were associated with the kings

This proto-Aeolic limestone capital, discovered in Jerusalem (Area G) may date to the time of King Solomon.

are mentioned, but special attention seems to be given to the religious leaders who were influential at various times. Prophets seem to be mentioned more frequently than priests.

Since the Hebrews were God's chosen people and as such had a covenant relationship with God, it was crucially important for them what the attitude of their king was toward God. A king in Israel, unlike kings of other nations, had a stewardship responsibility to God. When Samuel anointed Saul, it was explicitly stated that the king in Israel was captain of God's inheritance (1 Sam. 10:1). In his place of authority and power he was to be conscious of the fact that he was ruling over God's people. The basic requirement of each individual Israelite was that of exclusive devotion to God (Deut. 6:5). Consequently it was of vital significance whether or not the king exemplified this pattern of living in his place of leadership as head of the nation. The written copy of the revelation given through Moses was to provide guidance for the nation as well as the king. Moses had instructed the priests that a special copy was to be provided for the king's personal use as leader of God's people (17:18–20). Consequently, as the records are kept concerning the kings of the Hebrew people, the recorders or writers reflect a sensitivity to the responsibility a king had who was entrusted with the opportunity of ruling over God's chosen people. If the king exemplified a wholehearted devotion to God, the writers frequently gave a detailed account of their activities in leading their people to conform to God's requirements. If a king, however, led the people into idolatry, this was also noted.

Prophets are also frequently noted in this book of Kings. The prophets did not come into their ministries as spokesmen for God by virtue of being anointed or by inheritance, nor specifically take the position of another prophet when his term expired. Although priests continued in successive official positions, the book of Kings does not provide such a list. Some of the priests are occasionally mentioned. Prophets, however, are so frequently mentioned in this record that hardly a generation seems to be without the ministry of a man who claimed to deliver God's message.

Prophets also were crucially important in their ministry to the Hebrew people. Moses had assured the Israelites that they could expect prophets after his decease. Any prophet who did not conform to the basic requirement of worshiping God exclusively was to be regarded as a false prophet (Deut. 13:1–3). Throughout this record in the book of Kings, it was usually indicated concerning each prophet whether or not he was a God-fearing individual in his pattern of behavior. True prophets were directly accountable to God and some suffered martyrdom. Idolatry and its promotion provided specific evidence that a king or prophet was an apostate as far as the law of Moses was concerned.

The book of Kings is not addressed to anyone in particular. It is reasonable to assume that those who were responsible for keeping these records were primarily concerned about providing an account of Israel's history for future generations. The religious evaluation concerning the kings, prophets, and the people likely was intended to serve as a warning to the readers that they should be concerned about living as God's covenant people ought to live in expressing their love and devotion to God. As a whole the constructive periods, when real concern was expressed to serve God, are delineated in much greater detail than the accomplishments of godless kings like Omri and Jeroboam, even though they were the most powerful kings in the Northern Kingdom. The ministries of Elijah and Elisha are given much more coverage in this record.

The concluding paragraphs concerning the northern kingdom (2 Ki. 17:1–41) may be indicative of the purpose of the author or authors of the book of Kings. The Israelites had had a long succession of kings who had led the people into idolatry instead of influencing their people to serve God as outlined by Moses. Not only had the king and his people disobeyed the terms of God's covenant with them, but they had also ignored the prophets God had sent to them. The division of the kingdom had occurred because Solomon himself had turned to idolatry. This division came as a divine judgment upon his dynasty. The northern kingdom was terminated with the Assyrian captivity because the kings as well as the people had not responded positively to the warnings of the prophets who came as God's messengers. This indictment against Israel for their disobedience to the Mosaic law and the prophets may indicate the purpose of the author or authors in warning coming generations to learn from history.

V. Canonicity. The book of Kings, which constituted one large scroll in the collection of the sacred literature of the Hebrews, has never been questioned concerning its inclusion in the CANON. Due to its contents it always has been recognized as providing the continuing account of the Israelites subsequent to the books of Samuel. In the Greek and Latin versions, the books of Samuel and Kings were regarded as one continuous account in four volumes.

According to JOSEPHUS, the canon of the Jews was completed by about 400 B.C., composed of twenty-two books (representing thirty-nine books in the English versions). Although the arrangement or order of these twenty-two volumes may not have been fixed until several centuries after the beginning of the Christian era, the book of Kings usually was listed with the grouping identified as Prophets.

The fact that Joshua, Judges, Samuel, Kings, Isaiah, Jeremiah, Ezekiel, and the Twelve are included within the canonical division of Prophets may indicate that all of these books were regarded as being written by prophets and on that basis had the recognition of being canonical on a par with the books of Moses. For the prophets and their messages the book of Kings provided the essential background. Current scholarship seems to have no knowledge of any questions propounded concerning the proper place of Kings in the canon of the OT.

VI. Text. The Hebrew text of the book of Kings has been subject to intensive study and analysis. Some of the early 20th-cent. scholars had tentatively come to the conclusion that the biblical chronologies of the Hebrew kings—which are extensively delineated in the books of Kings and Chronicles—were notable for their undependability. Problems of chronology were already puzzling to the devout Jews who translated the Hebrew scriptures into the Greek language. Apparently they altered some of the numbers in the text, possibly attempting to eliminate some of the statements they considered as inconsistent. Josephus likewise reflects difficulties with the numbers in the Hebrew text.

Although other systems such as the absolute chronology of the Assyrians, were accepted as reliable by modern scholars, the Hebrew chronologies were often not recognized as trustworthy and accurate. Consequently, the text of these records in the Hebrew Bible usually was approached with excessive reserve as to its dependability. The chronological features often excited severe criticism and derision in the study of the book of Kings as well as the records in Chronicles.

The intensive scholarly analysis of the numbers of the Hebrew kings by Thiele (*Mysterious Numbers*) brought about a change in attitude as far as the reliability of the Hebrew text is concerned. In precisely the matters that were considered to be so inaccurate—the numbers in the text—Thiele provided evidence that they were recorded and transmitted accurately by the scribes throughout the centuries. Few were the errors that occurred in the process of transmission. When the data in the book of Kings are interpreted and understood in terms of the methods of dating systems used during the kingdom period of the Israelites, most of the difficulties in the text disappear. In the light of this approach the text may be regarded as remarkably accurate and reliable. (It should be noted, however, that not all scholars are persuaded by Thiele's method. For a recent defense of the LXX text, see A. Schenker, *Älteste Textgeschichte der Königsbücher: Die hebräische Vorlage der ursprünglichen Septuaginta als älteste Textform der Königsbücher* [2004].)

VII. Chronology. Since the systems of keeping historical records in ancient times were not understood correctly, it was impossible to develop a consistent chronology for the Hebrew kings who reigned during the divided kingdom era. Modern scholarship is indebted to Thiele for his intensive study in this area of OT scholarship. The fundamental principles he developed are essential for a correct interpretation of the data given concerning the Hebrew kings. These basic principles are noted briefly in the paragraphs following.

The system of counting years varied in the two Hebrew kingdoms. Whereas the accession-year system—also known as "postdating" since a king counted the first *full* year of his reign as his first year—was used in Assyria, Babylonia, and Persia, the system varied in the Hebrew kingdoms. Under Solomon the accession-year system of numbering a king's reign was used and continued in use in the southern kingdom until the middle of the 9th cent., when possibly Jehoram or Athaliah changed to the nonaccession-year system of numbering. This system of dating—also known as "antedating" because the king counted the part of the calendar year in which he began his reign as the first year regardless of its brevity—was used in the northern kingdom beginning with Jeroboam I in 931 B.C. Shortly after 800, both kingdoms—Judah under Amaziah and Israel under Jehoash—reverted to the accession-year method of numbering the reigns of their kings.

The calendar year used by the Hebrews is also usually important when interpreting these records. The religious calendar began with Nisan in spring, while the civil year began with Tishri in the fall. On the basis of the biblical text, Thiele ascertained the principle that in Judah the regnal years were dated from Tishri to Tishri under Solomon and

KINGS, BOOKS OF   927

continued in the historical records of the Hebrews down to the time of Nehemiah. Since specific evidence is lacking concerning the practice in the northern kingdom, Thiele has demonstrated that a harmonious chronological pattern can be established when a Nisan-to-Nisan year is used for the N and a Tishri-to-Tishri year for the S. Thiele suggests that Jeroboam may have been influenced in this practice by Egyptian customs, where the year at that time happened to begin in April. In this way Jeroboam conformed to Egypt and Mesopotamia in his regnal year rather than to the rival kingdom of Judah, which continued under the Davidic rule against which he had rebelled.

Another factor in interpreting the chronological data in the Hebrew records is the question of scribal usage in referring to the kings of another kingdom. This was particularly significant when one kingdom used the accession-year system and the other used the nonaccession-year system in keeping their records. Did the scribe use his own system for noting the year of a foreign ruler or that of the foreign nation involved?

The question of coregencies or interregna also is vitally important in analyzing chronological data. At times sons were made joint rulers, which then would duplicate the years during which both were living. It is only on the assumption of this practice that the references in 2 Ki. 1:17 and 8:16 can be understood properly. During times of revolt and dynastic changes, contending rulers might be in power in various districts at the same time. This also would account for a duplication of years in the history of the kingdom involved. Such was the case when Tibni and Ahab were both contending for the Israelite throne.

Within a kingdom there occurred changes from one chronological method to another. Although this change in method was not indicated by the scribes or authors in the book of Kings, it has become apparent to Thiele. This principle of change must be recognized in developing an accurate chronology for the Hebrew kingdoms and applied as necessary.

Another important factor for an absolute chronology is the correlation of dates that can be fixed with certainty in the records. Using the data in the book of Kings and the dating of Assyrian events also stated in the biblical records, Thiele has established the basis for an absolute Hebrew chronology. Although there were frequent contacts with Egypt, Syria, and lesser states, the contacts with Assyria and later with Babylon basically provided the basis for this correlation. The Assyrians used the solar year and kept records known as the Eponym Canon during the several centuries of the divided kingdom era.

The biblical data that are crucially important for establishing this absolute chronology are secured from the reigns of AHAB and JEHU in Israel and SHALMANESER III in Assyria. Ahab participated in the battle of Qarqar in 853 B.C. and Jehu paid tribute to Assyria in 841, which were respectively identified as the sixth and eighteenth years of Shalmaneser III according to his records. Within this twelve-year period occurred the end of Ahab's reign, the reigns of Ahaziah and Joram, and the enthronement of Jehu in the northern kingdom. During the same period in the southern kingdom occurred the end of Jehoshaphat's reign, the reigns of Jehoram and Ahaziah, and the beginning of Athaliah's rule. Furthermore, the fact that Jehu in his enthronement killed both kings—Joram king of Israel and Ahaziah the ruler in Judah—at the same time provided a fixed date within the same year when both kingdoms changed rulers.

Using these fixed dates of 853 and 841 B.C., Thiele has been able to develop an accurate chronology by correlating the data given concerning the

A metal frame outlines the shape of the altar at the location of the cult site in Dan. King Jeroboam I set up a golden calf here for worship.

CHRONOLOGY OF THE DIVIDED KINGDOM

Date	Northern Kings	Prophets	Southern Kings	Assyria	Aram (Syria)
931	Jeroboam Nadab	Ahijah Shemaiah Iddo	Rehoboam Abijah Asa		Rezon
909	Baasha Elah (Zimri)	Azariah Hanani Jehu			
885	Omri (Tibni) Ahab Ahaziah Joram	Elijah Micaiah Eliezer Elisha Jehoiada	Jehoshaphat Jehoram Ahaziah	Ashurnasirpal Shalmaneser III	Ben-Hadad
841	Jehu Jehoahaz Jehoash Jeroboam II Zechariah	Zechariah Jonah Hosea Amos	Athaliah Joash Amaziah Azariah		Hazael Ben-Hadad
752	Shallum Menahem Pekahiah Pekah Hoshea	Isaiah Oded	Jotham Ahaz	Tiglath-Pileser III Shalmaneser V Sargon II	Rezin
722	Fall of Samaria	Micah	Hezekiah Manasseh Amon	Sennacherib Esarhaddon Ashurbanipal	
640		Jeremiah Huldah (Ezekiel) (Daniel)	Josiah Jehoahaz Jehoiakim Jehoiachin Zedekiah	Babylon Nabopolassar Nebuchadnezzar	
586			Fall of Jerusalem		

The date of the division of the kingdom is variously placed between 983 and 931 B.C. There are difficulties in the chronology of the period; apparent discrepancies may, in part, be accounted for by "overlapping reigns," "associated sovereignty," "intervals of anarchy," and "parts of years as years." These dates are only approximate.

Jar handle from Lachish (Iron Age II) with a seal inscription that reads, "belonging to the king." Such jar handles are associated with King Hezekiah (8th cent. B.C.).

While some are briefly noted, others like Elijah and Elisha are given extensive consideration (1 Ki. 17 to 2 Ki. 9). Some of the writing prophets like Amos and Hosea are not mentioned in the record.

The content of this book may be outlined in numerous ways. For a brief analysis the following division may be used:

A. The reign of Solomon (1 Ki. 1–11)
B. Two Hebrew kingdoms (1 Ki. 12–22 and 2 Ki. 1–17)
C. The southern kingdom (2 Ki. 18–25)

If the content is to be studied with emphasis upon the developments in the southern kingdom the outline below may be helpful:

A. Solomon (1 Ki. 1–11)
B. Rehoboam to Jehoshaphat (1 Ki. 12–22)
C. Jehoram to Ahaz (2 Ki. 8–16)
D. Hezekiah to Amon (2 Ki. 18–21)
E. Josiah to Zedekiah (2 Ki. 22–25)

In the northern kingdom the ruling dynasties changed frequently. During the period of its existence as an independent kingdom—931–722 B.C.—its nineteen kings represented nine dynasties. Eight of these kings either were murdered or committed suicide. The complete list of dynasties is as follows: Jeroboam, Baasha, Zimri, Omri, Jehu, Shallum, Menahem, Pekah, and Hoshea. Some of these men, however, were in power for such a brief period of time—Zimri ruled seven days—and others had no dynastic successors or were so weak that they hardly deserve listing among the ruling families. The dynasty of Jehu had the longest rule, 841–753. In considering a concentrated study of the northern kingdom the content in this book may be outlined as follows:

A. Jeroboam's dynasty (1 Ki. 12–15)
B. Dynasty of Baasha (1 Ki. 15–16)
C. Dynasty of Omri (1 Ki. 16–22 and 2 Ki. 1–9)
D. Jehu's dynasty (2 Ki. 10–15)
E. The last kings (2 Ki. 16–17)

An analysis of the content of the book of Kings offers an interesting study. Approximately one-fourth of this volume (1 Ki. 1–11) is devoted to the forty-year reign of Solomon. The remainder accounts for nineteen kings in the southern kingdom who ruled for 345 years and for nineteen kings who ruled for 210 years in the northern kingdom. Solomon's reign,

Hebrew kings. Going backward and accounting for all the years allotted to the kings in both kingdoms in this period, the date for the division of Solomon's kingdom is given as 931. The terminal date for the northern kingdom is 723, and the destruction of Jerusalem that ended the southern kingdom occurred in 586. Since the Assyrian system provided modern scholarship with an absolute chronology fixed by modern astronomic calculations, the chronology for the Hebrew kings can now be regarded as a sound and accurate system for dating that period of OT times. (Although this chronology of the Hebrew kings is well established as a whole, some problems still remain. In particular, the notations concerning the Ahaz-Hezekiah era are still subject to intensive study by various scholars.) See CHRONOLOGY (OT).

VIII. Content and outline. The content of Kings is vitally important for the history of the Israelites in OT times. It narrates the developments from the establishment of the Davidic kingdom down to the exile in Babylon. Although Chronicles offers a survey of the history of the Davidic dynasty, only the book of Kings provides a continuous integrated account of the developments in both kingdoms—the northern kingdom known as Israel, and the southern, frequently identified as Judah. Crucially important is the emphasis given to the ministry of the prophets.

THE AGE OF THE MONARCHY		
\multicolumn{3}{c|}{Over 500 Years (1095–586 B.C.)}		
UNITED KINGDOM	**DIVIDED KINGDOM**	**SINGLE KINGDOM**
Saul to Solomon	Rehoboam to Hoshea	Hezekiah (6th) to Zedekiah
120 Years (1095–975)	253 Years (975–722)	136 Years (722–586)
1 Samuel 8–1 Kings 11 1 Chronicles 10–2 Chronicles 9	1 Kings 12–2 Kings 18:12 2 Chronicles 10–28	2 Kings 18:13–25:21 2 Chronicles 29–36:21

which significantly provides the introduction to this volume, may be outlined as follows:

   A. Solomon the king (1 Ki. 1:1—4:34)
      1. His enthronement (1:1—2:46)
      2. His prayer for wisdom (3:1–15)
      3. His wisdom in practice (3:16—4:34)
   B. Royal construction program (5:1—9:25)
      1. Temple and palace (5:1—7:51)
      2. Dedication of the temple (8:1—9:9)
      3. Cities built and fortified (9:10–25)
   C. International relations (9:26—10:29)
      1. Naval expeditions at Elath (9:26–28)
      2. The Queen of Sheba (10:1–13)
      3. Trade and revenue (10:14–29)
   D. Apostasy and its results (11:1–43)
      1. Intermarriage and idolatry (11:1–8)
      2. God's judgment (11:9–43)

Solomon inherited the kingdom established by David through a successful policy of military expansion. Under David, Israel emerged as the strongest nation in the Fertile Crescent, being respected by surrounding nations and unchallenged by any powers in either Egypt or Mesopotamia. Although David designated Solomon as his heir, Solomon's enthronement was challenged by Adonijah. With the blessing of Nathan the prophet and Zadok the priest, Solomon emerged as the sole ruler. In an attitude of humility and wholehearted devotion he prayed for divine wisdom to be granted to him in his responsibility as king of Israel. His administration is portrayed as reflecting the use of extraordinary wisdom.

Solomon built the temple that David had hoped to construct in Jerusalem. In seven years this was completed in all its beauty through the arrangements that had been made with Hiram the king of Tyre. Divine benediction on Solomon in this effort was apparent as the glory of God filled the temple. Solomon not only delivered the dedicatory sermon but also offered the dedicatory prayer. In this manner Solomon was divinely confirmed and recognized before his own nation as the ruler of God's people Israel, which enjoyed the acclaim as the strongest nation in the Fertile Crescent.

Brief is the information concerning the building of Solomon's palace, which was thirteen years in the process of building (1 Ki. 7:1–8). The fame of Solomon gained international attention. From the political, economic, and religious perspective, it appeared as though Israel had reached its zenith.

The conclusion to Solomon's reign is clearly delineated in 1 Ki. 11. Religiously Solomon was guilty of apostasy, having succumbed to idolatry. The foreign wives Solomon brought to Jerusalem erected shrines to their gods in the environs of the Holy City. Tolerant of their idolatry, Solomon broke the first commandment—the covenant relationship of wholehearted love toward God. Because of this, God permitted adversaries to rise in power in various parts of Solomon's kingdom. When Solomon died these rulers asserted themselves so that the Davidic throne was acknowledged only by the little area known as the southern kingdom or the kingdom of Judah. Besides the rebellion of the ten tribes under Jeroboam, there emerged strong rulers in Syria, Egypt, and other areas.

The first two centuries of the divided kingdom era are portrayed in 1 Ki. 12 through 2 Ki. 17. Due to the extensive accounts of the ministries of Elijah and Elisha, it seems that the author of this book allots more consideration to the northern kingdom than he does to the Davidic dynasty in the S. For an analysis of this part of the book of Kings as it relates to each of the kings, note the following:

Rehoboam (1 Ki. 12:1–24) Abijam (Abijah) (1 Ki. 15:1–8) Asa (1 Ki. 15:9–24)	Jeroboam (1 Ki. 12:25—14:20) Nadab (1 Ki. 15:25–31) Baasha (1 Ki. 15:32—16:7) Elah (1 Ki. 16:8–14) Zimri (1 Ki. 16:15–20) Omri (1 Ki. 16:21–28)
Jehoshaphat (1 Ki. 22:41–50)	Ahab (1 Ki. 16:29—22:40) Ahaziah (1 Ki. 22:51–53) (2 Ki. 1:1–18)
Jehoram (Joram) (2 Ki. 8:16–24)	Joram (Jehoram) (2 Ki. 1:19—8:15) (2 Ki. 9:1–37)
Ahaziah (2 Ki. 8:25–29)	
Athaliah (2 Ki. 11:1–21)	Jehu (2 Ki. 10:1–36)
Joash (Jehoash) (2 Ki. 12:1–21)	Jehoahaz (2 Ki. 13:1–9)
Amaziah (2 Ki. 14:1–22)	Jehoash (Joash) (2 Ki. 13:10–24)
Uzziah (Azariah) (2 Ki. 15:1–7)	Jeroboam II (2 Ki. 14:23–29) Zechariah (2 Ki. 15:8–12) Shallum (2 Ki. 15:13–15) Menahem (2 Ki. 15:16–22) Pekahiah (2 Ki. 15:23–26) Pekah (2 Ki. 15:27–31)
Jotham (2 Ki. 15:32–38)	
Ahaz (2 Ki. 16:1–20)	Hoshea (2 Ki. 17:1–41)

Among the kings listed above, there seem to be no God-fearing kings in the northern kingdom, which succumbed to the Assyrian advance in 722 B.C. The southern kingdom survived the era of Assyrian supremacy and continued to be ruled by the Davidic dynasty down to Babylonian times.

Jeroboam established the northern kingdom after the death of Solomon. Although Nadab succeeded his father on the throne for one year, this dynasty was exterminated after a twenty-three-year rule (931–909). The dynasty of Baasha was in power for approximately the same number of years and also was abruptly terminated when his son Elah was killed in 885.

While these two dynasties were ruling Israel, there was continual tension and warfare in their relations with Judah. Religiously both dynasties were committed to idolatry and ignored the warnings of the prophets who spoke of impending judgment. Militarily the northern kingdom was weak. When a religious revival in Jerusalem attracted people from the N, Baasha began to fortify Ramah, which was located 5 mi. N of Jerusalem, in order to keep his people from moving S. King Asa countered this aggressive military act by bribing Ben-Hadad, the Aramean king who captured numerous cities from the Israelites in the far N.

With the accession of Omri to the throne of Israel in 885 B.C. there came a reversal in international relations. Omri established policies of friendship with the surrounding nations. Often these were sealed by intermarriages of the royal families. Such was the case when his son Ahab married Jezebel, the daughter of Ethbaal the king of Tyre. Trade between Israel and Phoenicia, which had commercial contacts throughout the Mediterranean world, was mutually advantageous for both. Friendly relations with Judah were sealed in the marriage of Ahab's daughter Athaliah to Jehoram the son of Jehoshaphat.

Although Omri's reign was relatively short, he established Israel as a powerful kingdom. Economically his policies brought prosperity. It was under his leadership that the city of Samaria was built and fortified as the capital city of Israel. Religiously, however, the leadership of the Omride dynasty left much to be desired. Not only had Israel departed from serving God, but under Ahab

and Jezebel idolatry was promoted in Israel in an unprecedented manner by the erection of a Baal temple in Samaria. It was this nationalistic devotion to Baalism supported by hundreds of priests that the prophet Elijah was commissioned to challenge. As God's representative, Elijah confronted Ahab and made Israel conscious of the fact that they should serve God. The ministry of Elijah through his messages and miracles countered the royal family in their idolatry and gave the God-fearing people an opportunity to respond to God's concern for them. In spite of Elijah's warnings the Omride family continued in their God-defiant ways and were divinely judged in accordance with the prophet's predictions. Elijah was joined by Elisha, who continued as an effective prophet under the Jehu dynasty down to the turn of the century.

Jehu, who served as an army captain in Israel, usurped the throne and exterminated the Omride dynasty, killing Joram king of Israel, Ahaziah king of Judah, and Jezebel in 841. Jehu's dynasty continued in power for nearly a century down to 753. Because of such a drastic revolution, the policies of Israel were affected radically. The suppression of Baalism, which had been introduced from Phoenicia, must have abruptly affected Israel economically. With Athaliah seizing the throne in Judah, it is unlikely that friendship prevailed southward after Jehu shed so much royal blood in Samaria. About this time Hazael was enthroned in Damascus and he extended his military aggression southward, taking Israelite territory and at times threatening the city of Jerusalem. In addition Jehu faced the threat of an Assyrian invasion. To avoid this, Jehu sent tribute to Shalmaneser III, which the Assyrian king noted on the famous Black Obelisk. Although Jehu, who ruled down to 814, was unable to establish a strong kingdom, he maintained Israel's independent status.

After 800 B.C., Israel emerged gradually under Jeroboam II as the strongest nation in Palestine. He regained the territory previously lost to the Arameans, recovered international trade, and fortified the city of Samaria. Israel's political and economic prosperity was exceeded in history only by that of the Solomonic era.

Religiously the reign of Jeroboam was marked by idolatry and by indifference to the fact that the Israelites were God's chosen people who were to maintain a covenant relationship with him. The economic success and the religious lethargy of the Israelites during this time of prosperity are vividly portrayed in the messages of Hosea and Amos. Both of these prophets warned their people of God's judgment awaiting them, but apparently there was little response.

After the death of Jeroboam in 753, the kingdom disintegrated rapidly, weakened by internal strife and threatened by an Assyrian advance into Palestine. Under a pro-Assyrian policy, Menahem paid tribute to Tiglath-Pileser III, who ascended the Assyrian throne in 745, but in 736 Pekah adopted an anti-Assyrian policy when he formed an alliance with Rezin in Damascus for the purpose of resisting the Assyrian advance. In 732 Rezin was killed as the Assyrians occupied Damascus, and Pekah was replaced by Hoshea, who became a tributary vassal of Tiglath-Pileser. Hoshea's rebellion in 725 precipitated the conquest of Samaria in 722, whereby the northern kingdom was terminated and reduced to a provincial status in the great Assyrian kingdom.

Explicitly the account in 2 Ki. 18 delineates the reasons for the termination of the northern kingdom. When Jeroboam I established the Israelite throne in 931, he was assured by the prophet Ahijah that his kingdom would be established and endure if he would exemplify a wholehearted devotion to God. Neither he nor any of his successors did so. Prophet after prophet was ignored. Divine judgment came because they had disregarded the law of Moses under whom the covenant was established and the prophets whom God had sent to warn and admonish them.

The southern kingdom by contrast had occasional periods of revival as they continued to be ruled by the dynasty of David. When Rehoboam began his reign in 931, limited to a small fraction of the Solomonic kingdom, he was also faced by an invasion by Shishak the king of Egypt. Tension with the northern kingdom and idolatry characterized the reigns of Rehoboam and Abijam.

Asa and Jehoshaphat led in one of the great revival movements in Judah by enlisting the support of priests and prophets. Both kings, however, were severely rebuked for their alliances with ungodly kings. The marriage of Jehoram, Jehoshaphat's son, to Athaliah, the daughter of Ahab and Jezebel, brought well-nigh disastrous results. Jehoshaphat narrowly escaped with his life when he joined Ahab in battle against Syria. Jehoram and Athaliah promoted bloodshed and idolatry, and after Ahaziah their son was killed in the Jehu revolution, Athaliah promoted a bloody purge in Jerusalem that almost exterminated the Davidic dynasty as she began her reign of terror.

Under the leadership of the priest Jehoiada, Queen Athaliah was executed. Weakened by internal problems and foreign pressure in the following decades, Judah did not emerge as a strong power in Palestine until the reign of Uzziah. During the time of Jeroboam's reign in the N, Uzziah developed policies that strengthened Judah internally. After Jeroboam's death Uzziah headed Palestinian coalitions attempting to stop the advance of Tiglath-Pileser III southward in 742.

When Uzziah died in 740, Jotham attempted to maintain an anti-Assyrian policy. Internal pressure brought Ahaz to the Davidic throne while Jotham was still living, reversing this policy. Ignoring Isaiah's advice, Ahaz made an alliance with Tiglath-Pileser and introduced Assyrian cult worship into Jerusalem in the environs of the temple. Judah, however, warded off occupation by Assyria while the northern kingdom capitulated to the Assyrians.

The rest of the book of Kings continues to narrate the developments in the kingdom of Judah. The content of 2 Ki. 18–25 as related to each of the kings may be divided as follows:

Hezekiah (2 Ki. 18:1—20:21)
Manasseh (21:1–18)
Amon (21:19–26)
Josiah (22:1—23:30)
Johoahaz (Shallum) (23:31–34)
Jehoiakim (Eliakim) (23:35—24:7)
Jehoiachin (Jeconiah) (24:8–17)
Zedekiah (Mattaniah) (24:18—25:7)
Exile (25:8–30)

Hezekiah led in a very effective reform movement countering the idolatrous trends introduced by his father Ahaz. Anticipating the renewal of Assyrian aggression, Hezekiah fortified Jerusalem and prepared for enduring a siege of Jerusalem by building the Siloam tunnel. Assured by Isaiah during this crucial period, Hezekiah survived the Assyrian threats made by Sennacherib. During this period Hezekiah was also personally restored to health and his life was miraculously extended. Isaiah, the great prophet who had announced God's impending judgment upon Jerusalem, assured him that this judgment would be postponed and that ultimately the Babylonians—not the Assyrians—would take the Jews into captivity.

Under Manasseh the people of Judah reverted to gross idolatry. Even though Manasseh was temporarily taken captive, he was restored to his throne so that the dynastic rule of the Davidic line continued. Amon his son ruled only two years before he was murdered.

When Josiah at the age of eight came to the throne in 640 B.C., the Assyrian power, which had in the meantime extended down to Thebes in Egypt, began to diminish. Under his reign Judah not only was relatively free from Assyrian pressure, but Josiah also had the opportunity to lead effectively in an extensive religious reform. Politically and religiously, optimism prevailed under the leadership of this youthful aggressive king in Judah.

Sudden changes took place in 609. When Josiah suddenly rushed his army to Megiddo to stop the Egyptians from marching N to aid the Assyrians, he was killed. Subsequently the Egyptians enthroned Jehoiakim in Jerusalem as a tributary vassal. By 605 the Babylonians, who had previously routed the Assyrians, defeated the Egyptians and exacted royal hostages from Jerusalem as a token of Jehoiakim's subservience. In 597 the Babylonians took thousands of Jews into exile, including their king, Jehoiachin. Following Zedekiah's rebellion, the city of Jerusalem was destroyed and the temple was reduced to ruins by the Babylonians as the kingdom of Judah was terminated. Although the Israelites were in exile, the final notation in this book indicates that Jehoiachin was released from prison by Evil-Merodach, the king of Babylon.

IX. Theology. The book of Kings does not merely narrate the history of the Hebrew kingdoms. Throughout this account there is apparent a definite theological viewpoint that is in harmony with the Mosaic revelation and the prophets who followed Moses from generation to generation.

The religious achievement of each of the kings seems to be more important than their political success. Omri and Jeroboam II, the two kings who achieved the greatest measure of success in bringing political and economic prosperity to the northern kingdom, are allotted a very brief account in this record. Ahab and his sons were given extended coverage, but this is primarily related to the ministry of Elijah, Elisha, and other prophets who represented Israel's true religion in contrast to the idolatrous religion promoted by the kings. Other kings, such as Jehoshaphat, Hezekiah, and Josiah, are given much prominence since they led in reform movements guiding their people back into a right relationship with God. Although the account in the book of Kings offers a continuous history of the Hebrew kings, the reader always is conscious of the fact that this is a religious history with a definite theological perspective.

The theological viewpoint throughout is in harmony with the book of Deuteronomy. It may be identified as Deuteronomistic without adopting the reconstructed view of Israel's history based on the theory of the documents. Taken in its historical setting, the book of Deuteronomy summarizes the essence of God's revelation to Israel through Moses. God had chosen and redeemed Israel and entered into a relationship with the people in which mutual love should prevail. Exclusive devotion to God was the duty of the Israelites, and idolatry was a certain sign that this relationship did not prevail. All the evils within the nations were signs that this relationship had been broken. Throughout the account in the book of Kings, this criterion is applied to the leaders of the Hebrew people.

When David commissioned Solomon as king of Israel, the law of Moses was set before the new ruler and the elders as the standard to which they should adhere if they desired success and prosperity (1 Ki. 2:3). Extensive is the account of the building and dedication of the temple in which God was to be worshiped. When Solomon himself became tolerant of idolatry brought into the environs of Jerusalem by his foreign wives, the author explicitly narrates Solomon's failure. The disruption of the great Davidic and Solomonic kingdom came by divine permission because of the apostasy of Solomon. Kings in succeeding generations are repeatedly judged because of their failure to serve God in accordance with the law. In the northern kingdom dynasty after dynasty was exterminated because of their gross idolatry. Although the Davidic dynasty continued in power throughout the centuries of the existence of the southern kingdom because of David's devotion to God, the kings who were idolatrous are judged by the Deuteronomic standard.

The prophets and their messages were crucially important. They were spokesmen for God and were identified as true prophets if they were in harmony with the law of Moses. Any prophet who advocated or tolerated idolatry was a false prophet. Prophets who endorsed the law of Moses and were confirmed by signs and miracles were to be accorded the same recognition as the Deuteronomic revelation. The author of Kings distinctly points out that both Hebrew kingdoms as well as individual kings were judged and subjected to captivity because they failed to conform to the divine instructions given through Moses and the prophets.

Israel's history, according to the author of the book of Kings, is under the control of God who directs the affairs of the Hebrew people throughout. When the kings and their people failed to heed the warnings of the prophets, judgment followed. When they listened to the prophets and turned to God in an attitude of repentance and obedience, then the impending judgment was postponed. Ultimately, however, national judgment came in accordance with the principles delineated by Moses in his final messages to the new generation of Israelites, who were about to occupy the land of Palestine.

Theologically the book of Kings complements and continues the history of Israel, which begins with the Mosaic revelation and its background in the Pentateuch. The books of Joshua, Judges, and Samuel with the book of Kings provide a continuous record of the Israelites as God's chosen people from Moses to the Babylonian exile.

(Important commentaries include C. F. Burney, *Notes on the Hebrew Text of the Book of Kings* [1903]; J. A. Montgomery, *A Critical and Exegetical Commentary on the Book of Kings*, ICC [1951]; J. Gray, *I and II Kings*, OTL, 3rd ed. [1977]; M. Cogan and H. Tadmor, *II Kings*, AB 11 [1988]; D. J. Wiseman, *1 and 2 Kings*, TOTC [1993]; J. T. Walsh, *1 Kings* [1996]; M. J. Mulder, *1 Kings*, 3 vols. [1998–]; M. Cogan, *1 Kings*, AB 10 [2001]; S. DeVries, *1 Kings*, WBC

12, 2nd ed. [2003]; V. Fritz, *1 & 2 Kings: A Continental Commentary* [2003]; A. H. Konkel, *1 & 2 Kings*, NIVAC [2006]; M. A. Sweeney, *First and Second Kings*, OTL [2007]. See also I. W. Provan, *Hezekiah and the Book of Kings: A Contribution to the Debate about the Composition of the Deuteronomistic History* [1988]; C. Grottanelli, *Kings & Prophets: Monarchic Power, Inspired Leadership, & Sacred Text in Biblical Narrative* [1999]; J. Rogerson, *Chronicle of the Old Testament Kings: The Reign-by-Reign Record of the Rulers of Ancient Israel* [1999]; B. Becking, *From David to Gedaliah: The Book of Kings as Story and History* [2007]; and the bibliography compiled by W. E. Mills, *2 Samuel–2 Kings* [2002].) S. J. SCHULTZ

king's dale. See KING'S VALLEY.

king's garden. When the Babylonians laid siege to JERUSALEM and broke through the city wall, King ZEDEKIAH and his army fled, leaving "the city at night by way of the king's garden, through the gate between the two walls" (Jer. 39:4; cf. 52:7 and 2 Ki. 25:4). This garden may have been watered by the overflow from the Pool of SILOAM, near which it was located (Neh. 3:15). JOSEPHUS (*Ant.* 9.10.4 §225) speaks of "the royal gardens" as being near Eroge (EN ROGEL).

King's Gate. The name of a gate on the eastern side of the TEMPLE where a certain Shallum, chief of a group of postexilic gatekeepers, was stationed (1 Chr. 9:17–18; prob. the whole group was stationed there). See SHALLUM #8. Nothing else is known about this gate.

king's highway. (Often capitalized.) An important road running N and S from DAMASCUS to the Gulf of AQABAH, E of the DEAD SEA and the JORDAN Valley. Direct reference is made to the king's highway (*derek hammelek*) in the book of Numbers. MOSES requested permission to use this route for passing through the territory of EDOM (Num. 20:17; called simply *měsillâ* H5019, "highway, main road," in v. 19) and of the AMORITE king SIHON (21:22; cf. Deut. 2:27), promising to keep strictly to the highway. It was one of the essential caravan routes in international commerce. It ran through BASHAN (cf. Num. 21:33), GILEAD, AMMON, MOAB, and Edom, and connected with roads across the NEGEV leading into Egypt.

This route of travel is known to have existed well before 2000 B.C., for a number of Bronze Age fortresses have been discovered along its line. The invasion of KEDORLAOMER and his allies apparently followed it (Gen. 14:5–6); control of this road probably lay behind the invasion. Fortifications at strategic points guarded the road when the Edomites and Ammonites objected to Israel's use of the highway. During SOLOMON's reign it was an important trade link between EZION GEBER, Judah,

A modern road in the Kingdom of Jordan follows the same route taken by the king's highway through Wadi Wala. (View to the S.)

and Damascus. In the 2nd cent. A.D. the Romans under Trajan incorporated it in their important highway across Transjordan. The modern auto road follows the old track. (See N. Glueck, *The Other Side of the Jordan*, rev. ed. [1970], ch. 1; J. A. Thompson, *Archaeology and the Old Testament* [1957], 57–58; Y. Aharoni, *The Land of the Bible: A Historical Geography*, rev. ed. [1979], 54–57.)

D. E. Hiebert

King's Pool. A reservoir in Jerusalem located near the Fountain Gate (Neh. 2:14). It is thought to be an alternate designation for the Pool of Siloam, built by King Hezekiah.

King's Valley. KJV "king's dale." A broad valley in which the king of Sodom met Abraham (Gen. 14:17). Identical with the Valley of Shaveh, it was evidently near Salem, the city of which Melchizedek was king. Here too Absalom set up a pillar or monument (2 Sam. 18:18). The location is uncertain. A monument known as Absalom's Tomb (no earlier than the Hellenistic period) stands just E of Jerusalem, but the site can hardly be called a valley. Some scholars place the King's Valley to the S of the city, at the juncture of the Hinnom and Kidron Valleys (M. C. Astour ["Shaveh, Valley of," in *ABD*, 5:168] argues that it can be "definitely" located here, but not all would agree).

Kinnereth kin'uh-reth (כִּנֶּרֶת H4055, perhaps "lyre"; sometimes in the pl. forms כִּנְרוֹת H4054 [Josh. 11:2] and כִּנֲרוֹת H4054 [12:3; 1 Ki. 15:20]). Also Chinnereth. (1) A fortified town within the tribal territory of Naphtali (Josh. 19:35), identified with modern Khirbet el-ʿOreimeh, on the NW shore of the Sea of Galilee. The name is included among the cities listed by Thutmose III (Y. Aharoni, *The Land of the Bible: A Historical Geography*, rev. ed. [1979], 160). When Ben-Hadad invaded Israel, "all Kinnereth" was one of the places he conquered (1 Ki. 15:20; KJV, "Cinneroth"; NRSV, "Chinneroth"). The small plain in that area is referred to as Gennesaret in the NT (Matt. 14:34; Mk. 6:53). (See *ABD*, 1:909–200; *NEAEHL*, 3:872–73.)

(2) The Sea of Kinnereth is an old name applied to the Sea of Galilee (Num. 34:11; Josh. 12:3 [KJV, NRSV, "Chinneroth"]; 13:27). In two passages (Deut. 3:17; Josh. 11:2 [KJV, NRSV, "Chinneroth"]), the name Kinnereth may be an abbreviation for Sea of Kinnereth; otherwise, it refers to the town that gave the lake its name (see above, #1) or to the general area. Some have speculated that the name (if it is related to *kinnôr* H4036, "lyre, harp") may be derived from the shape of the lake itself or from the likelihood that shepherds played lyres in that area. See also Galilee, Sea of.   R. L. Alden

kinship. See family.

kinsman-redeemer. See avenger of blood; goel; redemption.

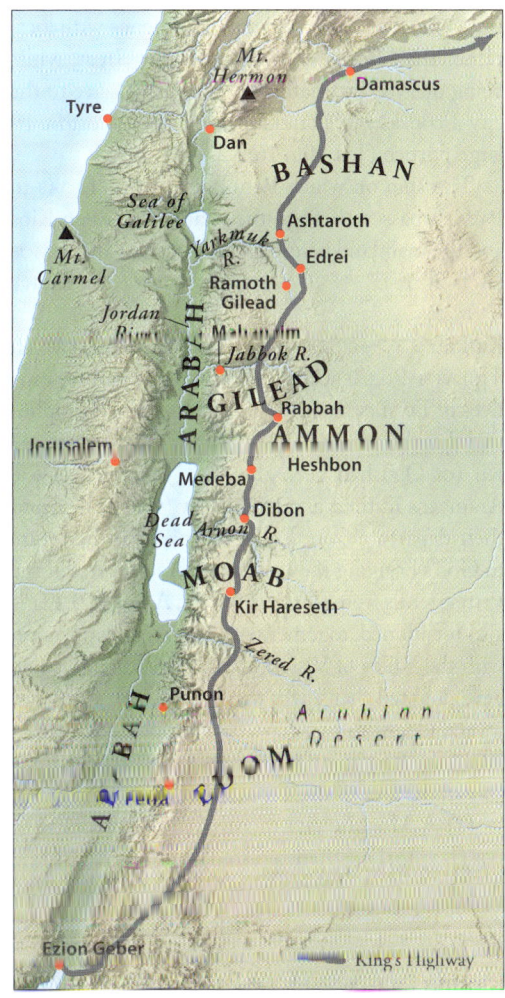

The king's highway.

Kios ki′os (Χίος *G5944*). Also Chios, Khios. A large island in the Aegean Sea, about 30 mi. long N to S and varying in width from 8 to 10 mi. It is separated from the coast of Asia Minor by a narrow channel. At its narrowest the channel is 5 mi. wide and contains a number of small islands. The island is generally rocky and unproductive, but its wines and gum mastic have been a source of trade in ancient and modern times.

Kios was the reputed home of the poet Homer and had a distinguished literary and artistic tradition. Its inhabitants were called the richest of the Greeks in the 5th cent. B.C. Later it became nominally a part of the Roman province of Asia, but Kios, the chief city of the island on the E coast, was a free port (until Vespasian suspended its rights). Thus it was generally administered in accordance with local rather than Roman law. Herod the Great, while being delayed by weather on the island, gave to the city a considerable amount of money to restore its large portico (Jos. *Ant.* 16.2.2 §§18–19).

The ship on which Paul sailed from Troas to Patara passed through the channel between Kios and the mainland before turning SE toward Samos (Acts 20:15). A. Rupprecht

Kir kihr′ (קִיר *H7817*, "wall"). (1) The place to which Tiglath Pileser, king of Assyria, carried the captives of Damascus (2 Ki. 16:9). Amos had prophesied that this would happen (Amos 1:5). Apparently Kir (or Qir) had been the place of origin of the Arameans in their ancient history (see Aram), and their departure from Kir is compared in Scripture to God's bringing the Israelites from Egypt and the Philistines from Caphtor (Crete; Amos 9:7). Kir is also mentioned, together with Elam, in connection with the Valley of Vision in Isa. 22:6 (though some have doubted that this is the same place). Although several identifications have been proposed (cf. *ABD*, 4:83), the location of Kir is not known; it was probably in the area of the Tigris River in S Babylonia.

(2) A Moabite city mentioned in parallel with Ar (Isa. 15:1). Often referred to as Kir of Moab, this city is probably the same as Kir Hareseth.

J. B. Scott

Kirama kuh-ray′muh (Κιραμας). Apoc. form of Ramah #3 (1 Esd. 5:20; KJV, "Cirama").

Kir-haraseth. KJV form of Kir Hareseth.

Kir Hareseth kihr-hair′uh-seth (קִיר חֲרֶשֶׂת *H7819* [2 Ki. 3:25; Isa. 16:11], קִיר־חֶרֶשׂ *H7818* [Isa. 16:7; Jer. 48:31, 36], "wall of pottery"). Also Kir-haraseth, Kir-haresh, Kir-heres. An important city in Moab, apparently its capital at the time of King Mesha. When Mesha rebelled against King Joram of Israel (see Jehoram #2), Jehoshaphat king of Judah and the king of Edom joined Israel in attacking the Moabites (2 Ki. 3:4–9). The allied forces ran out of water and were in danger of being defeated, but after the prophet Elisha performed a miracle, they successfully invaded Moab and destroyed its towns. "Only Kir Hareseth was left with its stones in place, but men armed with slings surrounded it and attacked it as well" (v. 25). Unable to take the city, the Israelites retreated (v. 27, though the meaning of this verse is debated), and Mesha boasted of having conquered the king of Israel (in the Moabite Stone; see *ANET*, 320–21).

Years later Isaiah, in his oracles against Moab, prophesied that Kir (prob. a reference to Kir Hareseth) would again be ruined (Isa. 15:1) and that the Moabites would grieve for the raisin cakes of the city (16:7), possibly referring to the destruction of the vineyards or perhaps using a wordplay on the similar-sounding word for "men" (cf. NIV and note the parallel in Jer. 48:31, 36). Isaiah himself lamented deeply for Kir Haseseth (Isa. 16:11; KJV, "Kir-haresh"; NRSV, "Kir-heres").

Kir Hareseth is to be identified with el-Kerak, some 10 mi. E of the S part of the Dead Sea. From ancient times it was a place of great importance in that area. It was a strategic site, easily defendable, being on a high place, with the sides of the mountain sloping steeply all around it. The city, located on the famous king's highway from Syria to Egypt, dominated the ancient caravan routes and was recognized by the Crusaders as a significant site. It towers about 3,690 ft. above sea level and was walled on all sides. The only problem with this location was water, for the springs were all outside the city. (See D. Baly, *The Geography of the Bible* [1957], 31, 87, 92, 118, 238; J. Simons, *The Geographical and Topographical Text of the Old Testament* [1959], 64–65, 265, 361, 435.) J. B. Scott

Kir-haresh, Kir-heres. See Kir Hareseth.

KIRIATH JEARIM   939

Kiriath kihr´ee-ath (קִרְיַת H7956, "city"), KJV Kirjath. A town within the tribal territory of BENJAMIN (Josh. 18:28). See KIRIATH JEARIM.

Kiriathaim kihr-ee-uh-thay´im (קִרְיָתַיִם H7964, "[twin] cities"). KJV also Kirjathaim. **(1)** A city built by the tribe of REUBEN in their territory (Num. 32:37; Josh. 13:19). Later it fell into the hands of MOAB, who rebuilt it (as recorded in the MOABITE STONE; see ANET, 320, "Qaryaten"), and was condemned to judgment by God (Jer. 48:1, 23; Ezek. 25:9). It is possibly to be identified with Qaryat el-Mekhaiyet, about 9 mi. E of the Dead Sea and the same distance N of the ARNON River.

(2) A town within the tribal territory of NAPHTALI, assigned to the Levites descended from GERSHON (1 Chr. 6:76). See KARTAN.   J. B. SCOTT

Kiriath Arba kihr´ee-ath-ahr´buh (קִרְיַת אַרְבַּע H7957, also קִרְיַת הָאַרְבַּע H7959 [Gen. 35:27; Neh. 11:25], "city of Arba" or "fourfold city"). KJV also Kirjath-arba. Ancient name of HEBRON, used again after the EXILE. It first appears in the patriarchal narratives as the place where ABRAHAM and ISAAC stayed and where SARAH died (Gen. 23:2; 35:27). It also occurs several times in Joshua, as well as in Jdg. 1:10 and Neh. 11:25. In all these references except the last, Kiriath Arba is expressly identified as Hebron. Because the name appears to mean "city of four," some have speculated that the city originally was a tetrapolis (a league of four towns), or was divided into quarters, or was identified either with four giants (Anakites) or with four clans descended from CALEB (cf. Josh. 14:13 with 1 Chr. 2:18–19, see HALOT, 3:1142). In several passages, however, the name is associated with a certain ARBA, said to be the ancestor of the Anakites (Josh. 14:15; 15:13; 21:11; see ANAK). One cannot rule out the possibility that the name refers to a pagan deity (cf. C. F. Burney, *The Book of Judges, with Introduction and Notes* [1903], 43–44) or that there is a play on words.

Kiriatharim kihr´ee-ath-air´im. NRSV form of KIRIATH JEARIM (Ezra 2:25 [KJV, "Kirjath-arim"]; 1 Esd. 5:19 [KJV, "Kiriathiarius"]).

Kiriath Baal kihr´ee-ath-bay´uhl (קִרְיַת־בַּעַל H7958, "city of the lord"). KJV Kirjath-baal. Older name of KIRIATH JEARIM (Josh. 15:50; 18:14).

Kiriath Huzoth kihr´ee-ath-hyoo´zoth (קִרְיַת חֻצוֹת H7960, "city of streets" or "city of open spaces"). KJV, Kirjath-huzoth. A Moabite city where BALAK and BALAAM went on their way to DAMOTH BAAL (Num. 22:39; LXX, *poleis epauleōn*, "cities of courtyards"). Its location is unknown, but it was probably not far from DIBON #2.

Kiriathiarius kihr´ee-ath-ee-air´ee-uhs. KJV Apoc. form of KIRIATH JEARIM (1 Esd. 5:19).

Kiriath Jearim kihr´ee-ath-jee´uh-rim (קִרְיַת יְעָרִים H7961, קִרְיַת עָרִים in Ezra 2:25, prob. by scribal mistake; cf. Neh. 7:29], "city of forests"). KJV Kirjath jearim (in Ezra 2:25, Kirjatharim). A city of the Gibeonites (see GIBEON) that was later on the border between the tribes of JUDAH and BENJAMIN. It was evidently the site of a pre-Israelite shrine to BAAL, as indicated by its alternate names in the Bible: KIRIATH BAAL (Josh. 15:60; 18:14), BAALAH (Josh. 15:9), and BAALE OF JUDAH (2 Sam. 6:2; cf. 1 Chr. 13:6; the LXX rejected this reading in both passages).

I. Identification. E. Robinson (*Biblical Researches in Palestine*, 2nd ed. [1856], 2:11–12) observed that the ancient name probably was preserved in Qaryat el-ʿInab (Arabic, "city of the grapes"), a town about 8.5 mi. WNW of Jerusalem. The identification with Kiriath Jearim is confirmed by Eutychius, Patriarch of Alexandria (A.D. 877–940), who says in his *Annals* that from BETH SHEMESH, the ARK OF THE COVENANT was taken by "the inhabitants of a village known as *Qaryet el-Inab*" (ed. L. Cheikho, *Corpus scriptorum christianorum orientalium, Scriptores arabici*, Ser. III, 6:43). The local Arab villagers used to call it simply Qaryeh, but the town is widely known as Abu Ghosh, being so named after famous sheiks of the 18th and 19th centuries who maintained hegemony over the highway between Jerusalem and the coast.

Though remains of the Roman and Crusader periods have been found in the village, the true site of the biblical period is the imposing mound upon which stands the Church of the Ark of the Covenant. This "tell" is known as Deir el-ʿAzar; some would see in this name an allusion to ELEAZAR son of ABINADAB, who was consecrated by the men of Kiriath Jearim to keep the ark (1 Sam. 7:1).

Abundant sherds of the Late Bronze and Iron Ages are found on the slopes of the mound. (Archaeological investigation of the Abu Ghosh area has usually concentrated on the Roman-Byzantine and Crusader structures on the one hand, or on prehistoric settlements on the other.)

The commanding position of this site satisfies all the requirements of the ancient sources for Kiriath Jearim. EUSEBIUS said that *Kariathiareim* was about 10 Roman mi. from Jerusalem on the road to Lod (Lydda); later he corrected the distance to 9 mi. It stands between NEPHTOAH (Lifta) and KESALON (Kesla), which suits its position on the N border of Judah (Josh. 15:9; 18:15). It is almost directly S of KEPHIRAH (Tell Kefireh), which conforms to the boundary between Benjamin and Dan (Josh. 18:14). Critics of Robinson's identification (e.g., C. R. Conder, *HDB*, 3:3; E. W. G. Masterman, *ISBE* [1929], 3:1812) made too much of JOSEPHUS's statement (*Ant.* 6.1.4 §17) that Kiriath Jearim was a "neighboring" town to Beth Shemesh, in combination with the allusion to MAHANEH DAN on the W of it (Jdg. 18:12), since they assumed the latter to be restricted to an area between ZORAH (modern Ṣarʿah) and ESHTAOL (Ishwaʿ) in accordance with Jdg. 13:25.

II. History. Kiriath Jearim was one of the four Gibeonite cities that made a covenant with the invading Israelites by deceiving them (Josh. 9:17). It served as a boundary marker between Judah and Benjamin (15:9; 18:14–15). One of the nearby heights apparently was known as Gibeah of Kiriath Jearim (1 Sam. 7:1; 2 Sam. 6:3, 4; ASV mg.), which probably is intended in Josh. 18:28 to mean that it belonged to Benjamin. The town of Kiriath Jearim was occupied by men of Judah (Jdg. 18:12). The "father" (prob. meaning "founder") of Kiriath Jearim was SHOBAL, a descendant of CALEB (1 Chr. 2:50b, 52). Shobal's descendants were the leading families of the town, namely, the Ithrites, the Puthites, the Shumathites, and the Mishraites, and some of their number moved down to settle in Zorah and Eshtaol (1 Chr. 2:53). In the administrative division of Judah, Kiriath Jearim and RABBAH comprised one small district (Josh. 15:60).

After the ark of the covenant had been returned by the Philistines to Beth Shemesh, it was transferred to Kiriath Jearim (1 Sam. 6:19—7:2); later it was brought by King DAVID to JERUSALEM (1 Sam. 6:1–15; 1 Chr. 13:5–14; 15:2–28; 2 Chr. 1:4). The BAALATH fortified by SOLOMON (1 Ki. 9:18; 2 Chr. 8:6; cf. Jos. *Ant.* 8.6.1 §152) was possibly Kiriath Jearim, which would provide an important link between GEZER and BETH HORON on the one hand and Jerusalem on the other. During the invasion by Pharaoh SHISHAK (1 Ki. 14:25–26; 2 Chr. 12:1–9), the Egyptian army apparently began its attack by taking Gezer, after which it advanced inland toward Jerusalem, taking Beth Horon and Rabbah on the way. Kiriath Jearim may have fallen before them (if the reading *qdtm* of no. 25 in Shishak's list can be understood as an error for *qrtm*; *r* and *d* are quite similar in the Egyptian hieratic script from which the hieroglyphs were probably copied).

During the reign of JEHOIAKIM, a prophet named URIAH son of Shemaliah from Kiriath Jearim spoke out against the regime and was forced to flee to Egypt for fear of the authorities. From thence he was extradited and put to death (Jer. 26:20–23). Some of the citizens from Kiriath Jearim returned from the Babylonian captivity with ZERUBBABEL (Ezra 2:25 [KJV, "Kirjath-arim"; NRSV, "Kiriatharim"]; Neh. 7:29; 1 Esd. 5:19 [KJV, "Kiriathiarius"; NRSV, "Kiriatharim"]). The supposed reference to this town in Ps. 132:6 (*śĕdê-yāʿar*, "the fields of JAAR") is doubtful. (See further C. R. Conder and H. H. Kitchener, *The Survey of Western Palestine: Memoirs* [1881–83], 3:43–52; F. D. Cooke in *AASOR* 5 [for 1923–24]: 105–120; Y. Aharoni, *The Land of the Bible: A Historical Geography*, rev. ed. [1979], 253–56, 326, 348–51; Z. Kallai, *Historical Geography of the Bible* [1986], 133–34, 347–48, 394–95.)

A. F. RAINEY

Kiriath Jearim

Kiriath Sannah kihr´ee-ath-san´uh (קִרְיַת־סַנָּה H7068, "city of Sannah"). Alternate name of Debir (Josh. 15:49). Possibly a textual corruption for *qiryat-sōpēr* ("city of the scribe[s]"; cf. LXX, *polis grammatōn*). See DEBIR (PLACE) #1; KIRIATH SEPHER.

Kiriath Sepher kihr´ee-ath-see´fuhr (קִרְיַת־סֵפֶר H7963, "city of book[s]"). Earlier name of Debir (Josh. 15:15–16; Jdg. 1:11–12). The SEPTUAGINT renders with *polis grammatōn* (or *polis tōn grammatōn*, "city of [the] scribes"), apparently reading *qiryat-sōpēr*. See DEBIR (PLACE) #1; KIRIATH SANNAH.

Kirjath kihr´jath. KJV form of KIRIATH. See also KIRIATHAIM; KIRIATH ARBA; etc.

Kish kish (קִישׁ H7821, possibly "gift"). (1) Son (or grandson) of ABIEL, descendant of BENJAMIN, and father of SAUL, who was the first king of Israel. In 1 Sam. 9:1, Kish is identified as the son of Abiel, but in 1 Chr. 8:33 and 9:39, Kish is listed as the son of NER. Since ABNER (commander of Saul's army) also is listed as the son of Ner in 1 Sam. 14:50, Abner and Kish would be brothers and, consequently, Abner would be the uncle of Saul. In the Hebrew of 14:50, however, the referent of "Saul's uncle" is ambiguous, and v. 51 can be understood to mean that both Ner and Kish were sons of Abiel (cf. NIV). In that case, Ner would be the uncle of Saul (cf. v. 50 NIV), and Saul and Abner would be cousins. This view necessitates either the altering of the text of 1 Chr. 8:33 and 9:39 or understanding Ner in those verses as a different individual, namely, a more remote ancestor of Kish.

At any rate, Kish was a wealthy man (1 Sam. 9:1). One day his donkeys went astray, and Saul was sent to find them (9:3); it was through this incident that Saul met SAMUEL and was anointed by him the first king of Israel (10:1). Kish was buried in Zela in the land of Benjamin (2 Sam. 21:14). He is mentioned once in the NT (Acts 13:21) in Paul's sermon at ANTIOCH OF PISIDIA.

(2) Son of Jeiel, of Gibeon, and descendant of Benjamin (1 Chr. 8:30; 9:36). Many believe that Jeiel is to be identified with ABIEL; if so, this Kish is the same as #1 above.

(3) Son of Mahli and descendant of LEVI through MERARI (1 Chr. 23:21–22). His sons married his brother's daughters. One of his sons was named Jerahmeel (24:29).

(4) Son of Abdi and descendant of LEVI through MERARI; he lived in the days of King HEZEKIAH and, as one of the priests, was chosen to cleanse the house of the Lord (2 Chr. 29:12).

(5) Ancestor of MORDECAI, the cousin of ESTHER, and descendant of Benjamin (Esth. 2:5). He was among those exiled from Jerusalem by NEBUCHADNEZZAR (v. 6). J. B. SCOTT

Kishi kish´i (קִישִׁי H7823, perhaps "gift"). Son of Abdi, descendant of LEVI through MERARI, and father of the musician ETHAN (1 Chr. 6:44; called KUSHAIAH in 15:17).

Kishion kish´ee-uhn (קִשְׁיוֹן H8002, meaning uncertain). A town within the tribal territory of ISSACHAR (Josh. 19:20), assigned to the Levites descended from GERSHON (21:28; KJV, "Kishon"). Proposed identifications include Tell el-Muqarqash, about 4 mi. SE of Mount TABOR, and El-Khirba (Khirbet Qasyun, Tel Qishyon), near the S slope of the same mountain (*ABD*, 4:88–89; cf. *NEAEHL*, 3:873–74). See also KEDESH #3.

Kishon River ki´shon (קִישׁוֹן H7822, meaning unknown). A WADI that drains the ESDRAELON Valley E to NW; it is mentioned in connection with DEBORAH (Jdg. 4:7, 13; 5:21; Ps. 83:9) and ELIJAH (1 Ki. 18:40). (Note also that the KJV uses "Kishon" once as an alternate form of KISHION [Josh. 21:28].)

I. Physical description. The total length of the Kishon River (Nahr el-Muqattaʿ) is only about 25 mi. Its source is S and E of modern Jenin, in the northern hills of SAMARIA, though it does not succeed in draining the Plain of DOTHAN. From Jenin to the narrow gap at Tell el-Qassis ("The Mound of the Priest," below the traditional location of the contest between Elijah and the priests of Baal) the stream fall amounts to c. 250 ft. Along its course, which roughly parallels the trend of the Carmel ridge (see CARMEL, MOUNT), several tributaries join the main stream. Drainage from one of them reaches it just N of Jenin, and another one a mile or so W of ʿAffuleh.

Springs along the Carmel front form a trellis-type drainage pattern, and a number of small tributaries from the Galilean hills to the N are to be noted, as well as several reaching it along its course across the Plain of Acco to the sea. The Wadi el-Melek drains much of SW Galilee, including the Plain of Asochis, and the heavier precipitation in this area makes the Kishon a perennial stream in this coastal portion. Crocodiles were reported there in ancient times. The heavy run-off in connection with the spring rains, combined with a flat marshy topography in the Esdraelon (Jezreel) Valley, made this river a substantial geographical barrier to travel and military activity for a part of the year, though it shrinks to a mere brook, sometimes dry, in the later seasons. Intensive recent land reclamation in this area has changed the drainage pattern considerably.

II. Historical events. The Kishon River is probably alluded to in connection with the important towns near its course, such as JOKNEAM (Josh. 19:11), TAANACH, and MEGIDDO (Jdg. 5:19). The river was crossed by the principal caravan routes, and became witness to numerous military movements and engagements, including war with the Midianites and with the Philistines; the slaying of King JOSIAH (2 Ki. 23:29); as well as campaigns during Hasmonean, Roman, Crusader, and later times.

A principal OT event is the battle between the Canaanites, under the leadership of SISERA, and the Israelites, under the direction of BARAK and DEBORAH, with the defeat of the former, in spite of their greatly superior chariot-equipped forces. There are conflicting opinions as to where along the Kishon the battle was fought. Sisera's army was encamped at HAROSHETH HAGGOYIM (Jdg. 4:7, 13), and Barak's men were rallied at Mount TABOR. The usual view has been that the principal fighting occurred toward the western part of the Esdraelon, and it is stated that Sisera's army, panicking when their chariots bogged down as the result of heavy rains and flooding of the marshes, fled in the direction of Harosheth Haggoyim and their camp. The river is referred to in the Song of Deborah as the "waters of Megiddo, at Taanach" (Jdg. 5:19), and a psalmist cites it as an exemplary victory over the enemies of God's people (Ps. 83:9).

William F. Albright (*The Archaeology of Palestine* [1960], 117–18) considered these references, with their general omission of Megiddo, to support an archaeological gap in the occupation of this city and the alternate vitality of Taanach. Yohanan Aharoni (*The Land of the Bible: A Historical Geography*, rev. ed. [1979], 221–25) places the battle near Mount Tabor, which lies between the Kishon River and his designation of Harosheth Haggoyim as a general

The Kishon River meanders down the Jezreel Valley towards Mount Carmel. (View to the W.)

term describing the highlands of Galilee to the N and E of Mount Tabor. He regards the reference to the "kings of Canaan" (Jdg. 5:19) as descriptive of the participants involved in JOSHUA's defeat of the HAZOR confederacy at nearby MEROM.

Another exciting drama was concluded at the Brook Kishon in connection with the contest between the prophets of BAAL and ELIJAH (1 Ki. 18:40). The defeated priests of Baal were taken to the Kishon, and there massacred. The reason for choosing this river location may have been the ritual cleansing provided by the water.

M. H. HEICKSEN

Kislev kis′lev (כִּסְלֵו H4075, from Akk. *kislimu* [*kisliwu*]). Also Chislev; KJV Chisleu. The ninth month (before the winter solstice) in the Hebrew CALENDAR, corresponding to November-December (Neh. 1:1; Zech. 7:1; Gk. *Chaseleu*, 1 Macc. 1:54 et al. [KJV, "Casleu"]).

J. LILLEY

Kislon kis′lon (כִּסְלוֹן H4077, possibly "sluggish"). Father of ELDAD; the latter was a Benjamite leader appointed to divide the land of Canaan among the tribes (Num. 34:21).

Kisloth Tabor kis′loth-tay′buhr (כִּסְלֹת תָּבוֹר H4079, meaning uncertain). Also Chisloth-tabor. A town mentioned in the description of the SE border of the tribe of ZEBULUN (Josh. 19:12); probably the same as KESULLOTH in ISSACHAR (v. 18).

kiss. A caress or touch of the lips (to another person's lips, cheek, beard, hands, or feet) in token of affection, greeting, or reverence. In Hebrew, the verb is *nāšaq* H5975 (Gen. 27:26 and frequently); the cognate noun *nĕšîqâ* H5965 occurs only twice (Prov. 27:6; Cant. 1:2). In the NT, the Greek verb *phileō* G5797, which usually means "to love, have special affection for," can also mean "to kiss" (Matt. 26:48 = Mk. 14:44 = Lk. 22:47), but the latter sense is normally conveyed by the compound *kataphileō* G2968 (Matt. 26:49 et al.), which the inspired writers employ with reference to several individuals: the sinful woman who kissed the feet of Jesus (Lk. 7:38, 45; cf. 1 Ki. 19:18); the prodigal son's father (Lk. 15:20); and JUDAS ISCARIOT, who betrayed Christ by kissing him (Matt. 26:49; Mk. 14:45; cf. 2 Sam. 20:9). The cognate noun is *philēma* G5799 (Lk. 7:45a et al.). (See further *NIDOTTE*, 3:196–97; *NIDNTT*, 2:549.)

The kiss has been common in the E since patriarchal times as a gesture of practical affection or homage. It was implanted upon the cheek but rarely upon the lips. The romantic kiss of lovers (Cant. 1:2; 8:1) and the seductive kiss of harlots (Prov. 7:13) are rare in Scripture. Usually one member of a family kissed another: (1) a son his father (Gen. 27:26, 27; 50:1), or parents (1 Ki. 19:20), or father-in-law (Exod. 18:7); (2) a father his son (2 Sam. 14:33), his children (Gen. 31:28, 55), or grandsons (48:10); (3) a man his brother (Gen. 33:4; 45:15; Exod. 4:27), cousin (Gen. 29:11), nephew (29:13),

The Kishon River.

or friend (1 Sam. 20:41); (4) a woman her daughters-in-law (Ruth 1:9). Among the Arabs even today, women and children kiss their husbands and fathers upon the beard; and it is returned upon the forehead.

Kissing is also often a common salutation and is practiced between individuals of the same sex (Gen. 29:13; 33:4; 45:15; Exod. 4:27; 18:7), and sometimes between those of opposite sex (Gen. 29:11)

It was also a farewell token both in life (Gen. 31:28, 55; Ruth 1:14; 1 Ki. 19:20; Acts 20:37) and at the approach of death (Gen. 50:1). Sometimes a kiss was the prelude to a solemn blessing (Gen. 27:26–27; 31:55; 2 Sam. 19:39). In addition, there was the ceremonial kiss; for example, SAMUEL kissed SAUL as he anointed him (1 Sam. 10:1). Kissing was used to show respect for idols (1 Ki. 19:18; Job 31:26, 27; Hos. 13:2); and even the ground was kissed to indicate total submission to the king (1 Sam. 24:8).

One dare not assume amorous overtones in the accounts of DAVID kissing JONATHAN (1 Sam. 20:41) or BARZILLAI (2 Sam. 19:39). ABSALOM kissed people hypocritically (15:5; cf. Prov. 27:6); JOAB kissed AMASA treacherously (2 Sam. 20:9); NAOMI kissed ORPHAH and RUTH sincerely (Ruth 1:9). One poetic thought surviving from the rabbinic period is that MOSES died with the kiss of God upon his lips (*Deut. Rab.* 11). Raguel wept as he kissed TOBIT (Tob. 7:7); later he and his wife both kissed their daughter farewell (10:12). In Sir. 29:5, kissing the hand might be a beggar's gesture of cowering submission.

Early Christians adopted the holy kiss (or kiss of love) as a friendly salutation (Rom. 16:16; 1 Cor. 16:20; 2 Cor. 13:12; 1 Thess. 5:26; 1 Pet. 5:14; cf. Lk. 7:45). It was a sacred bond that united the body of Christ and was undoubtedly exchanged by members of both the same (cf. *Apostolic Constitutions* 2.57.12) and opposite sex (St. Ambrose, *Hexaemeron* 6.9.68; Tertullian, *Ad uxor* 2.4).

It is difficult to establish the link between the kiss of love and the liturgical kiss of peace. The latter had an established place in public worship after the middle of the 2nd cent.: (1) neophytes were kissed after baptism; (2) penitents, when they were reconciled (cf. Lk. 15:20); (3) candidates for ordination; and even (4) the deceased. It was practiced most widely during the celebration of the EUCHARIST. Kissing the dead was prohibited by the Council of Auxerre (A.D. 578), perhaps on account of the prevalent abuse of either placing the Host in the mouth of the corpse, or burying it with him. The kiss of peace was observed in the W until the end of the Middle Ages. Apparently it was discontinued earlier in the E. In both E and W this custom was replaced by kissing the altar, etc. The practice of kissing relics in the W dates from perhaps the time of Bishop Walter of York (A.D. 1250). (See further *ABD*, 4:89–92; J. Ellington in *BT* 41 [1990]: 409–16; W. Klassen in *NTS* 39 [1993]: 122–35.)

R. E. PERRY

Cooking area in a reconstructed 1st-cent. home near the Sea of Galilee.

kitchen. This English term is used by modern Bible versions to render the Hebrew phrase *bêt hamĕbaššĕlîm*, lit., "house[s] of the ones who boil" (Ezek. 46:24). It refers to four subcourts at the corners of the outer court of EZEKIEL's ideal TEMPLE where the common people could have their sacrifices boiled at the hearths provided for the purpose. The priests protected themselves from defilement through contact with unconsecrated persons by cooking their offerings in their own kitchens (vv. 19–20).

S. BARABAS

kite. A predatory bird of the HAWK family. Kites are distinguished from other birds of prey by their long forked tails. In feeding habits they fall between VULTURES and hawks, taking a wide range of prey and also being content with carrion. Like all big raptors, they are masters of flight. The term is used by the KJV and other versions to render Hebrew *ʾayyâ H370* twice (Lev. 11:14; Deut. 14:13; NIV, "black kite"). The use of the word *kite* in the KJV is not surprising, for this was the most familiar bird of prey in English towns and cities of the 15th and 16th centuries, when they were important scavengers. Two species were found in Palestine. The red kite—once common in England—is partly resident, but numbers also come from N for the winter. The slightly smaller and darker black kite is mainly a migrant seen frequently when passing N after wintering in Africa. The NIV uses "red kite" as the rendering of *dāʾâ* H1798 and *rāʾâ* H8012 respectively in the same two passages (NRSV, "buzzard"; cf. *FFB*, 40–41). See also BUZZARD; FALCON.

G. S. CANSDALE

Kithlish kith′lish. KJV form of KITLISH.

Kitlish kit′lish (כִּתְלִישׁ H4186, derivation unknown). Also Chitlish, Chithlish, Kithlish. A town in the SHEPHELAH within the tribal territory of JUDAH (Josh. 15:40). Kitlish was in the same district as LACHISH (v. 39), but the precise site is unknown.

Kitron kit′ron (קִטְרוֹן H7790, possibly "smoke, incense"). A Canaanite town within the tribal territory of ZEBULUN from which the Israelites could not drive out the inhabitants (Jdg. 1:30). Some believe Kitron is the same as KATTATH, but the site is unknown.

Kittim kit′im (כִּתִּים H4183, gentilic of כת [a place name attested in Phoenician]). KJV also Chittim. (1) Third son of JAVAN, grandson of JAPHETH, brother of ELISHAH (associated with AEGEAN peoples), TARSHISH (Spain or N Africa?), and RODANIM (Rhodes?) (Gen. 10:4; 1 Chr. 1:7, LXX *Kitioi*). Many interpret the name as referring to a people group descended from Javan (cf. TNIV, "the Kittites," and see below, ##2–4).

(2) The island CYPRUS. Since the Hebrew form is a gentilic plural, "Kittim" originally would have referred to a people group. Indeed, JOSEPHUS (*Ant* 1.6.1 §128) relates the name to the city *Kition* on the SE coast of the island. Phoenician inscriptions referring to this city call it *kt* and *kty*. Apparently the city name was extended to the whole island, or perhaps the city was named after an older island name. HERODOTUS (*Hist.* 7.90) relates that the island was first colonized by Phoenicians, Ethiopians, and Greeks (respectively descendants of SHEM, HAM and JAPHETH). This situation would be similar to the one on the island of CRETE, where a Semitic people who lived apparently descended by way of Egypt (Minoans) were eventually displaced by Indo-Europeans from Greece (Mycenaeans). Probably a similar situation prevailed on Cyprus, although being nearer the Phoenician home-

KITTIM 945

land, the Greek influence took longer to become dominant. (In ANE literature, such as the *Tale of Wenamon*, Cyprus is sometimes called Alishiya [Elishah?].)

For those interested in controlling coastal trade, Cyprus was a necessary prize. Records of the Akkadian empire in lower Mesopotamia (c. 2400 B.C.) indicate that Sargon, the founder, stretched his power as far up the Euphrates as the Mediterranean. Recovery of a seal cylinder of Naram-Sin, Sargon's son, on Cyprus confirms that claim. Later, Cyprus became a tributary of THUTMOSE III. (This was by no means Egypt's first contact with Cyprus, since high-quality Cypriot pottery was found in the 1st-dynasty tombs at Abydos [c. 3000 B.C.].) Later still, SARGON II, conqueror of Samaria, erected a stela on Cyprus, commemorating the island's vassalage to himself (708 B.C.). This vassalage was renewed by both ESARHADDON and ASHURBANIPAL, the two final noteworthy Assyrian kings.

During the Neo-Babylonian period, the Egyptian Amosis, exercising pretensions toward empire, laid Cyprus under tribute. The Persians dashed such pretensions in turn, relinquishing their hold to the Greeks about 410 B.C. During most of the 1st millennium B.C., despite nominal political affiliations, the dominant cultural and mercantile influence upon Cyprus was Phoenician. Thus Ezekiel, in his dirge over TYRE, tells that Cyprus (Heb. *kittiyyim*, LXX *chettiin*) supplied decking for Phoenician ships from its pine forests (Ezek. 27:6). Similarly, Isa. 23:1 and 12 (LXX *Kitiaioi* and *Kitieoi*) report that Cyprus will be intimately related to the downfall of Tyre. Tyre will flee to Cyprus, and from Cyprus will come news of its final downfall. This corresponds with the boast of SENNACHERIB (cf. *ANET*, 288) that Luli, king of SIDON, fled from Sennacherib to Cyprus, but was killed there.

(3) On occasion the name Kittim, like Javan, is extended to include the W in general, but especially the seafaring western ones. Jeremiah, speaking of the whole world (Jer. 2:10), uses the isles of Kittim to symbolize the far W and KEDAR the far E. BAALAM, forecasting the coming dominance of the W over the ANE (Num. 24:24), tells that the ships of Kittim will afflict Asshur (Mesopotamia) and Eber (the Levant). Daniel apparently uses "ships of Kittim"

(Dan. 11:30; NIV, "Ships of the western coastlands") to represent the Romans, who thwarted ANTIOCHUS IV (Epiphanes) in Egypt in 169 B.C. The SEPTUAGINT makes this reference explicit by reading "Romans" at this point (*Rōmaioi*; Theod., *Kitioi*). It has been suggested that Daniel interprets that event as the fulfillment of Num. 24:24 (esp. since the *Targum of Onkelos* reads "Romans" and the Vulg. "Italy"). The Apoc. and Pseudep. contain several references to the Kittim, all of which seem to relate to the Greek empire. ALEXANDER THE GREAT of Macedon is said to have come from the land of Kittim (1 Macc. 1:1, LXX *Chettiim*); similarly, Perseus of Macedon is called "king of Kittim" (8:5, LXX *Kitieōn*).

(4) The occurrence of numerous references to the Kittim in the DEAD SEA SCROLLS has created considerable scholarly controversy over the correct interpretation. These references—occurring predominantly in the commentary on Habakkuk (1QpHab), where the "Chaldeans" of the text are called Kittim, and in the *War of the Sons of Light against the Sons of Darkness* (1QM)—have provoked suggestions that the Kittim were understood to be the Seleucid Greeks, the Romans, the Byzantines, the Crusaders, the Turks, or the unspecified eschatological foes of righteousness. In response to the last, it may be pointed out that apocalyptic terms, while they appear to be vague, have specific meaning for the initiate. Lack of specificity would be most unusual. Those who propose peoples after the time of Christ have generally done so because of a conviction that the DSS were a medieval production (cf. A. N. Poliak in *JQR* 49 [1958]: 89–107). This point of view seems to have been refuted adequately.

The majority of scholars have divided over an identification with the Greeks or with the Romans. H. H. Rowley (*The Zadokite Fragments and the Dead Sea Scrolls* [1952], passim; also in *PEQ* 88 [1956]: 92–109) has been the leading advocate for the Greeks, while F. M. Cross (*The Ancient Library of Qumran*, rev. ed. [1961], 82n, 123–24) has spoken out for the Romans. Implicit in the controversy has been the problem of dating 1QpHab and 1QM. A Maccabean or earlier date automatically precludes the Romans. The following references have been significant in the debate: the rulers of the Kittim fell one after another (1QpHab. IV, 11–12; decline of the Seleucid house or Roman civil war?); the Kittim sacrifice to their "signs" (1QpHab VI, 3–5; the deified standards of the Roman legions?); the Kittim of Egypt and Assyria (1QM I, 2–6; the Ptolemies and Seleucids?); the kings of Kittim will arise after the kings of Greece (4QpNah I, 3; a clear reference to Rome?). Perhaps Kittim meant for the Dead Sea Community, as #3 above, simply "Westerners" and could be applied to any particular western people as need arose. J. OSWALT

Kittites kit´tits. TNIV alternate form of KITTIM (Gen. 10:4; 1 Chr. 1:7).

Kiyyun ki´yuhn. See KAIWAN.

knead, kneading bowl, kneading trough. See BREAD.

knee, kneel. The ANE custom for public PRAYER was to stand, and so kneeling was confined to acts of obedience and obeisance. The official presentation of children on the father's knee was a sign legitimizing the child's legal claim in Israel (Gen. 30:3; 50:23; Job 3:12). Kneeling was a symbol of submission to royalty, and every letter in the vast CUNEIFORM collections mentions the bowing down at the feet of the superior personage. Such acts of humility are pictured on Babylonian, Egyptian, and Canaanite art works. The position of kneeling comes after that of total prostration, and indicates that certain rituals were observed if not performed in a kneeling posture (Ps. 95:6).

The Hebrew term for "knee" is *berek* H1386 (Gen. 30:3 and often; cf. Aram. ʾ*arkubbâ* H10072, Dan. 5:6), and the cognate verb *bārak* H1384 means "to kneel" (only Gen. 24:11; 2 Chr. 6:13; Ps. 95:6). Scholars in the past, assuming an etymological connection between these terms and *bārak* H1385 ("to bless" in piel stem), inferred a semantic link as well (e.g., persons knelt when they received a blessing), but most specialists today believe that two different roots are involved. Of course, one must leave open the possibility that speakers of the language, through popular etymologizing, associated the two.

In the NT, the common Greek term *gony* G1205 (Heb. 12:12 et al.) is used without exception as the noun, and the verb *gonypeteō* G1206 means specifically, "to kneel down before someone" (Matt. 17:14; 17:29; Mk. 1:40, 10:17). The verbal idea is often conveyed by the use of the noun in combination with such verbs as *prospiptō* G4700, "fall on" (Lk. 5:8); *kamptō* G2828, "bend" (Rom. 11:4; 14:11; Eph. 3:14; Phil. 2:10), and especially *tithēmi* G5502, "place, lay down" (Mk. 15:19; Lk. 5:8; 22:41; Acts 7:60; 9:40; 20:36; 21:5; this latter phrase probably influenced by Latin usage, *ponere genua*, "to genuflect"). In addition, the NIV and other versions use "kneel" as the rendering of the Greek verb *proskyneō* G4686 in a half dozen places in Matthew (Matt. 8:2; 9:18; 15:25; 17:14; 20:20; 27:29). This verb occurs in another seven places in this gospel with the usual meaning "to do obeisance, worship" (e.g., 2:2), and this sense is probably at least implicit in every instance.

This usage of bowing down became the traditional posture of prayer in the Christian church. It also appears as the posture of dying in the case of Stephen's martyrdom (Acts 7:20). Paul and his converts prayed and said farewell on their knees (20:36), and kneeling is mentioned in Paul's epistles. The apostle uses the conception of kneeling in the figurative sense of submission to the Almighty (Eph. 3:14), where it is his own confession that is foremost, and in the magnificent prophecy of Christ's ultimate triumph when all knees shall bow before the Messiah (Phil. 2:10). (See further *NIDOTTE*, 1:755–57; *NIDNTT*, 2:859–60, 875–79.) W. White, Jr.

knife. A small single-edged or double-edged cutting instrument of stone or metal. In form the knife generally resembled the dagger or short stabbing sword, but was smaller and usually without ornamentation. The usual Hebrew word for "knife" is *maʾăkelet* H4408 (Gen. 22:6 et al.), but the word for "sword" (*ḥereb* H2995) is rendered "knife" in Josh. 5:2–3 (cf. also KJV 1 Ki. 18:28; Ezek. 5:1–2). The knife generally had a straight blade 6 to 10 in. long, although knives with curved blades were known. The handles were made of one piece with the blade, or a wooden handle was fastened to the blade by a tang or by rivets.

Like other orientals, the Jews made little use of knives in their meals. Meat was cut into small pieces before being served, while bread was

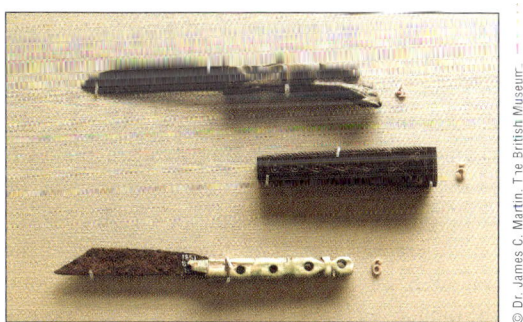

A collection of Roman knives (1st–3rd cent. A.D.).

broken by hand. The sharp edge of knives stands metaphorically for rapaciousness (Prov. 30:14; Heb. *śakkîn* H8501). A knife at table is used in a figure for restraint upon one's appetite (23:2).

Knives were used for various purposes. Joshua was commanded to use flint knives to circumcise the Israelites (Josh. 5:2–3; cf. Exod. 4:25). The use of flint knives when they were no longer in common domestic use implies an ancient ritual in which their use was still appropriate. Knives or small swords were used by the frenzied priests of Baal for self-mutilation (1 Ki. 18:28). Animals were killed and skinned with food-cutters. Abraham took one along to sacrifice Isaac (Gen. 22:6), and the Levite used one to dismember his concubine (Jdg. 19:29). The "scribe's knife" of Jer. 36:23 (Heb. *taʿar hassōpēr* H9509 + H6221; NRSV, "penknife") was used for trimming and splitting the reed employed in writing; the word *taʿar* was also used with reference to a razor (Num. 6:5; Ezek. 5:1).

The "pruning hooks" (Joel 3:10; Heb. *mazmērâ* H4661) were probably curved knives (cf. Isa. 18:5 NIV). In Ezra 1:9, the KJV includes some "knives" (Heb. *maḥălāp* H4709, a hapax legomenon) among the temple furniture returned under Ezra, but the RSV renders "censers," and the NIV, "pans." The Septuagint rendering, "of a different sort" (*parēllagmena*), does not give help on the real meaning. If they were knives, they doubtless were used to kill and cut up the sacrificial animals.

Herod the Great used a knife for paring an apple and attempted to use it as an instrument of suicide (Jos. *Ant.* 17,7,1; *War* 1.33.7). (See W. F. Petrie, *Tools and Weapons* [1917], W. 7A, C. Corswant, *A Dictionary of Life in Bible Times* [1956], 164.) D. E. Hiebert

knop. A small ornamental knob. This word is used by the KJV to render Hebrew *kaptôr H4117* in Exod. 25:31–36 and 37:17–22, referring to the decorations (knobby fruits or flower buds) of the golden CANDLESTICK or lampstand in the TABERNACLE. The KJV uses it also to render *pĕqāʿîm H7225*, "gourd-shaped ornaments," which describes the decorations carved on the cedar lining of the walls of Solomon's TEMPLE (1 Ki. 6:18) and around the molten sea (7:24). S. BARABAS

knowledge. This term may be defined simply as the sum of what has been perceived or learned, that is, truth or information acquired through experience and education. However, the problems that an analysis of knowledge entails are enormous.

   I. Biblical usage
  II. Faith and knowledge
 III. Epistemology
     A. Philosophical
     B. Biblical
 IV. Modern theology
  V. Knowledge of God

I. Biblical usage. The primary biblical terms used are Hebrew *yādaʿ H3359*, "to know, observe, recognize," and *daʿat H1981*, "knowledge, ability, insight"; Greek *ginōskō G1182*, "to know, learn, perceive," *gnōsis G1194*, "knowledge," and *oida G3857*, "to know." (See *NIDOTTE*, 2:409–14; *NIDNTT*, 2:390–409.)

The Bible frequently commends knowledge and WISDOM: "The LORD is a God of knowledge" (1 Sam. 2:3 NRSV); "Have they no knowledge, all the evil doers who … do not call upon the LORD?" (Ps. 14:4 NRSV); "Teach me knowledge and good judgment" (Ps. 119:66); "Choose my instruction instead of silver, / knowledge rather than choice gold" (Prov. 8:10); "by his knowledge my righteous servant will justify many" (Isa. 53:11); "you will know the truth, and the truth will set you free" (Jn. 8:32); "Now I know in part; then I shall know fully, even as I am fully known" (1 Cor. 13:12); "… asking God to fill you with the knowledge of his will through all spiritual wisdom and understanding." (Col. 1:9); "We know also that the Son of God has come and has given us understanding, so that we may know him who is true" (1 Jn. 5:20). One may note relative to this last verse that the so-called epistle of love uses the word "know" thirty times in its five chapters, not counting words like "understand," "teach," "see," "hear," "believe," and "truth," all of which have to do with knowledge.

In view of the misapprehensions of some, what the Bible does not say also should be pointed out. Nowhere does Scripture modify the high value it places on knowledge by deprecating "mere" human REASON. Reason and knowledge are integral parts of the IMAGE OF GOD in which human beings were created. In the OT the Hebrew terms for "heart" (*lēb H4213* and *lēbāb H4222*) designate the mind, intellect, or reason in about three-fourths of its 850 occurrences. Examples are: "The LORD … said in his heart" (Gen. 8:21; obviously he did not say in his emotions); "I will raise up for myself a faithful priest, who will do according to what is in my heart [*lēbāb*] and mind [*nepeš H5883*]" (1 Sam. 2:35); "Make the heart of this people calloused. … Otherwise they might … understand with their hearts" (Isa. 6:10); "their minds [*lēb*] closed so they cannot understand. No one stops to think [*lit.* turns to his heart]" (Isa. 44:18b–19a). The human mind or heart can be and is sinful, as some of these verses plainly indicate, but the antithesis between the heart and the head, along with the suggestion that the intellect is evil but the emotions are free from sin, is a distortion of the scriptural view of HUMAN NATURE.

Although the Hebrew and Greek verbs for knowing usually bear the most ordinary meaning (e.g., "I don't know who has done this," Gen. 21:26), they can also be used in other senses, some of which are sources of confusion in theology and philosophy. The sense in which the words are used to designate sexual intercourse (e.g., as in Gen. 4:1 RSV, "Now Adam knew his wife Eve, and she conceived and bore Cain") causes no difficulty; we simply note the usage and pass on. Confusion, however, may arise from another meaning that also has no place in epistemology, namely, "to choose, select, [and therefore] approve." When Ps. 1:6 RSV says that "the Lord knows the way of the righteous, but the way of the wicked will perish," it is not reflecting on divine OMNISCIENCE. In the ordinary sense, God knows the way of the wicked as well as he knows everything else. Here the word is used in the sense of approval (cf. NIV, "watches over"). Similarly, when Amos 3:2 RSV says, "You only have I known of all the families of the earth," the prophet is not denying that God knew the Egyptians and Canaanites. This verse is no denial of omniscience; here the verb means "to choose or elect" (cf. NIV).

This usage, so clear in the OT, causes some theological confusion when NT material is discussed. Those who reject the doctrines of predestination or unconditional ELECTION try to base salvation on foreseen FAITH and election on foreknowledge (see FOREKNOW). Such a view is inconsistent with the meaning of the words. In 1 Pet. 1:2, where the RSV gives the correct sense, "chosen and destined by God," the KJV has the more literal translation, "elect according to the foreknowledge of God." In v. 20 the KJV renders the same word "foreordained." Similarly Rom. 8:29 does not speak of a mere knowing ahead of time, as English usage would lead one to expect, as if God looked ahead into an independent and undetermined future and discovered (if anything undetermined could be discovered) what was going to happen; rather, foreknowledge means foreordination.

In addition to the above source of theological confusion, there is an alleged usage that causes philosophical confusion. Or perhaps it may be said that a certain philosophical confusion tries to construe knowledge in a still different sense. Some devout and fairly orthodox theologians, and in general the neoorthodox thinkers, insist that there is a radical difference between knowing a proposition and knowing a person, or between knowledge "about" and knowledge "by acquaintance."

According to the neoorthodox position, God does not reveal truths that can be intellectually apprehended, but he reveals himself in a direct encounter or confrontation. Now insofar as support for this view is sought in the different compounds of *ginōskō* or in other verbs, the attempt is a failure. R. Bultmann states that this knowledge "is achieved in all the acts in which a man can attain knowledge, in seeing and hearing, in investigating and reflecting. … [It] can also mean personal acquaintance and friendship with persons. … Whatever can be the object of enquiry can be an object of *ginōskein*" (*TDNT*, 1:691–92). And in the SEPTUAGINT *ginōskō* and *oida* both translate the one Hebrew verb *yādaʿ*. The *TDNT* is replete with all the lexicographical details, none of which are of any help in epistemology.

II. Faith and knowledge. Noting the usage of the word *knowledge* in its ordinary meaning offers little aid in solving problems of theology and philosophy. One such problem is the distinction between knowledge and FAITH. The statement "Knowledge puffs up, but love builds up" (1 Cor. 8:1) does not at first sight agree with the praises of knowledge quoted earlier; yet the following verse indicates that the knowledge referred to is either mistaken opinion or a true proposition so misapplied and conjoined with error that the combination is false. Some commentators explain v. 1 as ironical.

A similar explanation is required to understand the Christian opposition to GNOSTICISM. This religion in the early centuries, using Christian terminology, made SALVATION depend on knowledge

Statue of Sophia (wisdom) before the library of Celsus in Ephesus (2nd cent. A.D.).

and, by implication, not on faith. The great objection to Gnosticism, however, is not a repugnance to knowledge as such. The real objection was twofold. First, the Gnostic tenets amounted to a texture of superstitious mythology. Second, even if the Gnostics had propounded a true science of astronomy, such knowledge could not save. Salvation depends on faith in Christ.

What then is the relation between faith and knowledge? Protestants have traditionally analyzed faith into knowledge, assent, and trust. This analysis is not as simple as it seems. Knowledge in this context apparently refers only to understanding (not believing) the meaning of a proposition. Of course one can understand the meaning of false propositions, such as "David was king of Tyre"; but in the traditional analysis undoubtedly true propositions are intended, because assent to or belief in a false proposition would be error, not knowledge.

Note that in this last instance of the word, *knowledge* does not bear the same meaning it bears in the analysis. In the analysis knowledge occurs as distinct from assent, as a separate element in faith; but if knowledge is defined as the mind's possession of truth, there can be no knowledge apart from assent. This is one difficulty. Furthermore, worse, the element of trust, which Protestants emphasize, defies all explanation and remains in utter confusion. Illustrations, such as actually depositing money in a bank rather than merely believing that the bank is sound, depend on a physical action, in addition to the mental act of believing. Such additional external action is inappropriate to represent the thoroughly inner mental act of faith. Knowledge is an integral part of faith, and not its antithesis.

III. Epistemology

A. Philosophical. The main problem of knowledge, which is the crucial question in all the history of philosophy, concerns knowledge in its most ordinary sense. We say we know that two and two are four, that the earth revolves around the sun, or at least that a bright disk appears in the sky, and perhaps that God exists and stealing is immoral. Epistemology is a theory of how one can know anything. This question is not explicitly discussed in the Bible; but answers to it, however obtained, have a profound influence on theological formulations. Since the matter is extremely technical and difficult, some simplification is necessary.

Systems of philosophy generally can be divided into two groups: empirical philosophies are exemplified by Aristotle, Aquinas, Hume, and the modern schools of Pragmatism and Logical Positivism — the second group comprises the rationalistic or idealistic philosophies, exemplified by Plato, Augustine, Anselm, Spinoza, Kant, and Hegel. The first group exhibits serious divergencies, for Aristotle and Logical Positivism are rather far apart; but differences within the second group are perhaps even greater.

Empiricism is the view that all knowledge is based on experience alone. Experience has not always been restricted to the five senses, though this is a common form of the principle; but the Epicureans stressed the experience of pain, the Sophists acknowledged the experience of dreams and hallucinations (a fact Descartes and other rationalists use in opposition), others admit aesthetic experience (coining the word *aesthetics* from the Greek word for sensation), and finally Schleiermacher, the founder of modernism, and contemporary liberalism develop religion and theology out of religious experience. Sensation, however, remains basic in all forms of empiricism.

Rationalism (idealism is not a good name, for Berkeleyan idealism is completely empirical) holds that all or at least some knowledge is a priori, innate, rational, nonsensuous. Plato taught that the soul before birth is in contact with the ideal objects of knowledge, and that here on earth we *remember* what we previously knew. Spinoza taught that without the aid of sensation — doubtful aid because it is the source of error — all knowledge can be deduced from definitions by logic alone. Even the existence of God, as Anselm taught earlier, can be demonstrated from the definition that God is the all-perfect Being: if he did not exist, he would not be all-perfect. Kant said that the mind at birth is furnished with the a priori (independent of experience) intuitions of space and time, and a set of twelve a priori categories. Neither these by themselves, and much less sensations by themselves, are knowledge, but when sensory material is arranged and ordered by these a priori forms, the combination is knowledge. Finally, the dialectic of concepts of the last philosopher listed, Hegel, is just too complicated to characterize in any short space.

Two lines of procedure are now necessary: one should evaluate the merit of each of these main divisions of philosophy, and one should attempt to determine which, if either, the Bible favors. The first is a task for the professional philosopher. Some considerations, however, may be mentioned, which must be taken into account.

All philosophy, all theology, and all common conversation must make use of so-called abstract concepts. In philosophy the concepts of substance, cause, quality, relation find a necessary place; in theology there is sin and righteousness, atonement and justification, and so on; in common speech too one talks about causes and relations as well as about truth and falsity, times and places, cats and dogs.

Rationalism specifically asserts the reality of such concepts. These are the objects of knowledge that constitute Plato's World of Ideas. PHILO JUDAEUS and AUGUSTINE make them the content of the Divine Mind. Thus far rationalism makes philosophy, theology, and conversation possible.

Although nominalists such as Roscellinus and Occam assert that concepts refer to no reality whatever, that they are mere sounds in the air without meaning, and thus make philosophy and ordinary conversation both impossible, still the major empiricists try to explain the genesis of concepts. Aristotle attempted to abstract them from sensory experience. The concepts were somehow in the visible objects and could be detached, or abstracted by imagination and intellect. The British empiricists build up concepts by adding and subtracting particular sensations. Thus they claim to make knowledge possible.

The question, of course, is whether or not concepts can in fact be abstracted from sensations. Plato denied it. Further, even the abstraction of such "empirical" concepts as cat and dog depends on a theory of visual imagery that introspective psychology cannot sustain. It is all the more difficult to see how normative concepts, such as justice, can be derived from purely factual material.

Kant forcefully extended this argument in opposition to Hume. Knowledge, Kant insisted, contains necessary and universal judgments, such as two and two are (always are and must be) four and all pendulums always must swing in a certain way. Note definitely that when the law of the pendulum was formulated, the scientists thought that all pendulums in the past have swung and all future pendulums will swing just as described. But experience does not extend to all past pendulums, and with even greater clarity it does not extend to any future pendulums. Experience gives neither universality nor necessity. Similarly, normative moral principles can never be derived from experience. We see acts of honesty and instances of theft. The two are equally in experience. Experience can never determine that theft is wrong or that honesty is right.

Perhaps the simplest example of an a priori category is that of unity. The concept of the number one is essential, not only to mathematics, but also to all learning; for learning could never proceed unless we could distinguish one thing from another. Berkeley, the British empiricist, attempted to base the idea of unity in sensation. The unit, he said, is just any one thing you choose. You can count chairs or grains of sand. Thus we find our unit in experience. Kant demolished Berkeley's argument. First, the empiricist misstated the problem, which is not the selection of a unit from among other unities; the problem is the origin of the idea of unity. Second, the idea of one must be present before we can identify a chair or a grain of sand as one. The idea is not derived from the experienced object. And, finally, no experienced object is strictly a unity, since everything in space has parts. Therefore the concept of one must precede experience. These sample arguments must suffice to show the philosophic advantages of rationalism, or a priorism, over empiricism.

B. Biblical. Does Scripture take sides in the dispute between empiricism and rationalism? Obviously the Bible has no such technical arguments as those found in Kant. Nevertheless the prophets and apostles tell us something about HUMAN NATURE.

In the first place, God created man in his own image. The animals were not so created. The difference is that human beings are rational and animals are not. In Prov. 7:22–23 and Isa. 56:10, the natural ignorance of animals is used as a similitude to castigate the sinful ignorance of men and women. That knowledge is part of the image of God, and therefore that at least some knowledge is nonempirical, is broadly hinted in Col. 3:10, where the effect of REGENERATION is said to be the renewal of the knowledge original in the divine image.

Further, Rom. 1:32 and 2:14 show that even sin does not eradicate certain innate moral knowledge. And with respect to sin, all the historical churches acknowledge that a depravity of nature is inherited from ADAM. This is inconsistent with the view that the mind at birth is a blank sheet of paper (Locke), or morally neutral (Aristotle), and requires the admission of some sort of a priori. If therefore the more complex matters of morality are innate, how can one deny that simpler principles antecede experience? Scripture therefore seems to be on the side of a priorism.

IV. Modern theology. The discussion so far has maintained the position that knowledge is commendable and is essential to faith. Therefore religion, or at any rate Christianity, must hold theology in high esteem. At various times, however, protests are made against "cold" intellectualism or the pride of "mere" human reason. Mystics have commended trances; others make religion essentially emotional; and neoorthodoxy has enthroned paradox and contradiction.

These modern theologians have arrived at their position more by emotional reaction than by logic. They had been educated under a combination of Schleiermacher and Hegel. This liberalism looked on sin as a fast disappearing remnant of man's animal ancestors. The KINGDOM OF GOD was equated with socialism, and optimism flourished. Then World War I revealed human depravity to Europeans, and World War II to Americans. Machine guns and concentration camps liquidated the utopian doctrine of man's essential goodness and society's inevitable progress.

Furthermore, Hegel's rationalistic solution of all philosophic problems was too neat, and therefore unreal. The great dialectic came to appear as hollow wordplay. Yet these theologians were equally unable to solve the problems. They braved Socrates' sad scorn of misologists (haters of reason) and declared that the problems of life are rationally insoluble. Life is deeper than logic. The universe and God himself are self-contradictory. We must make our decisions in the freedom of blind faith. Besides, religion is not an intellectual matter anyhow: it is an experiential encounter with God.

Emil Brunner states this position clearly. Rejecting the idea that REVELATION is a communication of truth, Brunner asserts that "All words have only an instrumental value. Neither the spoken words nor their conceptual content are the Word itself, but only its frame" (*The Divine-Human Encounter* [1943], 110). He then adds that "God can, when he wills, speak his Word to a man even through false doctrine" (ibid., 117).

Karl Barth earlier, in his *Romans* (2nd German ed., 1922), had given great importance to contradictions and insoluble paradoxes. Though later he lost some of his exuberance, he still rejected logical consistency. In a section refuting a defense of logical consistency, he argues, "The very minimum postulate of freedom from contradiction is acceptable by theology only upon the very limited interpretation, by the scientific theorist upon the scarcely tolerable one, that theology will not assert an irremovability in principle of the 'contradictions' which it is bound to make good" (*Church Dogmatics* 1/1 [1956], 8). This sentence is obscure: it neither asserts nor denies that contradictions are removable; it merely says that theology should not assert their irremovability. What follows in the passage seems to let the contradictions stand, for he says, "But the propositions in which it asserts their removal will be propositions about the free action of God, and so not propositions that 'remove' the contradictions from the world." Continuing to talk of coherence and systematization, Barth insists that "The theologian ... should know what he is doing when he transgresses them, and that as a theologian he cannot escape the necessity of transgressing them." Or, in very plain words, a theologian must be incoherent.

Nevertheless the neoorthodox school writes theology, and Barth and Brunner have been especially voluminous. But if they do not recognize the necessity of being consistent, of what value can their theology be? In principle every one of their sentences is both true and false. If we discard logic, then, when

we believe that David was king of Israel, nothing prevents us from believing at the same time that David was not king of Israel. This would be simply the necessary incoherence of theology.

In particular, the neoorthodox theologians, and some modernists as well, believe that God reveals himself through contradictory systems in the Bible. Brunner concocts a remarkable conclusion that we could believe in the resurrection of Christ, even if there were no reports, because the witness to the resurrection is not that of eyewitnesses but of faith-witnesses. He further makes Christ sinless but fallible. Then, again, when Paul speaks of a time before Esau's birth, he means the Edomites in the days of Malachi. And, finally, "God and the medium of conceptuality exclude each other" (cf. Paul King Jewett, *Emil Brunner's Concept of Revelation* [1954], 184 and passim).

If, however, all our theological talk is self-contradictory, if faith must curb logic, and if God and thought are mutually exclusive, then no knowledge of God is possible, and religion must be emotional and experiential. But it will not be Christianity.

V. Knowledge of God. In opposition to this neoorthodoxy and to all other forms of thought that deny God can be known, we here conclude with what was strongly hinted at the beginning of this article in its commendation of knowledge in general. We shall simply add a few references to knowledge of God in particular.

In the first place, all Scripture is inspired of God and is profitable for doctrine. See INSPIRATION. The following verses are some of those that are most explicitly profitable for the doctrine of God. "In the beginning God created the heavens and the earth" introduces the concept of CREATION and of God as creator. That this creation was decreed from all eternity and is always controlled by providence is taught in Eph. 1:11, "predestined according to the plan of him who works out everything in conformity with the purpose of his will," and in Dan. 4:35, "he does according to his will in the host of heaven and among the inhabitants of the earth, and none can stay his hand" (KJV), and in many other passages. The Bible also tells us that God exists in three persons; that God is eternal, omniscient, and immutable. See GOD, BIBLICAL DOCTRINE OF; TRINITY.

That God can be known, that humans can entertain truth, that theology is possible, has been an unbroken tradition among all Christians. To depreciate knowledge in favor of some emotional upheaval, to repudiate logic and enthrone contradiction and incoherence, to reduce the biblical material to the status of a symbolism that points uncertainly to an unknowable Something or other, is to abandon Christianity and commit intellectual suicide. (See further S. Charnock, *Discourses on the Existence and Attributes of God* [1680]; I. Kant, *Critique of Pure Reason* [1780]; B. B. Warfield, "Augustine's Doctrine of Knowledge and Authority," in *Studies in Tertullian and Augustine* [1921], and "Calvin's Doctrine of the Knowledge of God," in *Calvin and Calvinism* [1930]; G. H. Clark, *Karl Barth's Theological Method* [1963]; J. Frame, *The Doctrine of the Knowledge of God* [1987].) G. H. CLARK

Knowledge, Interpretation of. See INTERPRETATION OF KNOWLEDGE.

knowledge, tree of. See TREE OF KNOWLEDGE.

Koa koh'uh (קוֹעַ H7760). An otherwise unknown place (or people) that, along with the Babylonians, Chaldeans, Pekod, Shoa, and the Assyrians, is named as being among the enemies of Jerusalem (Ezek. 23:23). Some scholars suggest that the name may refer to the Quti (Gutians), who lived E of the Tigris River. If so, the form *Koa* may be a deliberate distortion (cf. W. Eichrodt, *Ezekiel*, OTL [1970], 328). See PEKOD; SHOA.

Kohath koh'hath (קְהָת H7740 [also קֳהָת], meaning unknown; gentilic קְהָתִי H7741 [also קֳהָתִי], "Kohathite"). Second son of LEVI (Gen. 46:11; Exod. 6:16); he is said to have lived 133 years (Exod. 6:18). He was the father of AMRAM, IZHAR, HEBRON, and UZZIEL (Exod. 6:18; Num. 3:19, 27; 1 Chr. 6:2), who became Kohathite branches of the Levitical families (Num. 3:27). He was the grandfather, through Amram and his wife JOCHEBED (sister of Kohath), of AARON, MIRIAM, and MOSES (Exod. 6:20; Num. 26:59; 1 Chr. 6:3). The Kohathites were, therefore, the most prominent of the Levitical families.

After the construction of the TABERNACLE, the Kohathites, the Gershonites, and the Merarites were given charge over its care and transit (see GERSHON; MERARI). The Kohathites were to encamp on the S side of the tabernacle (Num. 3:29) and were to be responsible for "the ark, the table, the lampstand, the altars, the articles of the sanctuary used in ministering, the curtain, and everything related to their use" (3:31). Though these various items were the responsibility of the Kohathites, they were not to handle the holy things. Aaron and his sons were instructed to put a covering of goatskin upon these things before they were handled by the others (4:5–15). The manner of transportation was not to be in wagons, but upon the shoulders of the Kohathites. According to the census, there were 8,600 males above one month old (3:28) or 2,750 between the ages of thirty and fifty who attended to these duties (4:1–4, 34–37).

After the conquest of Palestine, the Kohathites were cared for in the same manner as the other Levitical families. Those who were descendants of Aaron received by lot thirteen cities and their pasture lands. The tribes of Judah and Simeon gave nine cities (Hebron [a refuge city for slayers], Libnah, Jattir, Eshtemoa, Holon, Debir, Ain, Juttah, and Beth Shemesh), while four cities were given by Benjamin (Gibeon, Geba, Anathoth, and Almon [Josh. 21:9–19]; the parallel passage [1 Chr. 6:57–60] lists only eleven of the thirteen, including the name Ashan with the former group). The rest of the Kohathites were provided ten cities (Josh. 21:20–26): four from the tribe of Ephraim (Shechem [a city of refuge], Gezer, Kibzaim [1 Chr. 6:68 has Jokmeam], and Beth Horon), four from Dan (Elteke, Gibbethon, Aijalon, and Gath Rimmon), and two from the half tribe of Manasseh (Taanach and Gath Rimmon [1 Chr. 6:70 has Aner and Bileam]).

During the reign of DAVID, the Levites were organized into three divisions according to the sons of Levi (1 Chr. 23:6). HEMAN represented the Kohathites in "the service of song in the house of the LORD" (6:31 NRSV), some had charge of the preparation of the showbread every Sabbath (9:32), and Uriel was appointed by David as chief of the 120 Kohathites chosen to assist in the return of the ARK OF THE COVENANT to Jerusalem (15:3–5).

When the Moabites and Ammonites came against Judah, JEHOSHAPHAT presented the situation before the Lord, bowing in worship together with all the people of Judah and Jerusalem. The Kohathites were ministering in the temple and "stood up and praised the LORD, the God of Israel, with very loud voice" (2 Chr. 20:19).

In two different reform movements the Kohathites were active participants. During the reign of HEZEKIAH (715–687/6 B.C.), Mahath son of Amasai and Joel son of Azariah were among those who purified the temple (29:12–16). In JOSIAH's reform and repair of the temple in 621, two Kohathites, Zechariah and Meshullam, were among the Levites whom the king set over the work on the temple (34:12). See also KORAH; PRIESTS AND LEVITES. W. B. COKER

Koheleth koh-hel′ith. See ECCLESIASTES.

Kola koh′luh (Κωλα, v.l. Χωλα). An otherwise unknown locality mentioned in the book of JUDITH (Jdt. 15:4; KJV, "Cola"). If the name is not fictitious, the town was probably not far from BETHULIA. On the basis of partial sound similarity, some identify it with KONA (Jdt. 4:4) or with HOLON (Josh. 15:51).

Kolaiah koh-lay′yuh (קוֹלָיָה H7755, possibly "Yahweh has spoken"). (1) Son of Maaseiah, descendant of BENJAMIN, and ancestor of Sallu; the latter was among those who settled in Jerusalem after the EXILE (Neh. 11:7).

(2) Father of a false prophet named AHAB (Jer. 29:21).

Kol-Hozeh kol-hoh′zuh. TNIV form of COL-HOZEH.

Kona koh′nuh (Κωνα). An otherwise unknown locality mentioned in the book of JUDITH (Jdt. 4:4; the KJV, following a different reading, has "the villages"). See also KOLA.

Konaniah kon′uh-ni′uh. TNIV form of CONANIAH.

koph kohf. See QOPH.

kor. Also cor. See WEIGHTS AND MEASURES III.B.2.

Korah kor′uh (קֹרַח H7946, "bald [head]," possibly diminutive form; gentilic קָרְחִי H7947, "Korahite" [KJV also "Korhite" and "Korathite"]; Κορέ G3160). (1) Son of Esau by Oholibamah (Gen. 36:5, 14, 18; 1 Chr. 1:35).

(2) Son of Eliphaz and grandson of Esau (Gen. 36:16; the name Korah is missing in the Samaritan Pentateuch here). The parallel passages (Gen. 36:11; 1 Chr. 1:35) omit the name.

(3) Son of Izhar, grandson of Kohath, and great-grandson of Levi (Exod. 6:21, 24). Korah, with 250 leaders of the congregation, rose up against Moses and Aaron, charging them with exalting themselves above the assembly of the Lord. "You have gone too far! The whole community is holy, every one of them, and the Lord is with them" (Num. 16:1-3). At the same time, Dathan and Abiram of the tribe of Reuben rebelled against Moses' leadership, charging him with failure to bring them into the Promised Land and making himself a prince over the people (16:1, 12-14).

Disconcerted by these indictments, Moses charged Korah and the Levites with seeking the priesthood as well as the ministry of service before the Lord (Num. 16:8-10). Therefore, he challenged the rebels to meet with him at the Tent of Meeting, each man taking a censer and offering incense before the Lord, that the Lord might show who was holy (vv. 4-9, 16-19). However, Dathan and Abiram refused to meet with Moses (vv. 12-14). Judgment fell against those who rebelled. The earth opened and swallowed up Korah, Dathan, Abiram, and their families, and fire from heaven consumed the 250 leaders offering their incense (vv. 23-35). In the brief account of Num. 26:9-11, it is pointed out that the line of Korah did not come to an end. The bronze censers were then collected and "hammered out to overlay the altar" (16:36-38). Still the people murmured against Moses and Aaron so that God sent a plague upon them that was checked only by Aaron's atonement for the people, but not before 14,700 people had died (vv. 41-49).

Some scholars regard this passage as a combination of several narratives. A. Kuenen and J. Wellhausen, working on the basis of the documentary hypothesis, indicate three narratives woven together. From the so-called JE document, the earliest source, comes the story of Dathan and Abiram, who were laymen revolting against the civil authority claimed by Moses (Num. 16:13); assigned to this source are vv. 1b-2a, 12, 15, 25, 26, and 27b-34. The remaining verses come from two different strata of P. The first stratum (vv. 1a, 2b-7a, 18-24, 27a, 32b, 35) concerns the revolt of Korah and the 250 leaders against the Levites as the only ones to discharge the religious offices. In this instance, Korah and the leaders are not regarded as Levites, but as laymen controverting Levitical preeminence: "The whole community is holy" (v. 3). When Moses and Aaron met with their adversaries before the Lord, each man with censer in hand, fire from the Lord destroyed the 250 leaders, vindicating Moses and Aaron. The second stratum (vv. 7b-11, 16, 17, 35, 36-40) regards Korah as a Levite and indicates a struggle within the Levitical tribe against an Aaronide priesthood: "This was to remind the Israelites that no one except a descendant of Aaron should come to burn incense before the Lord, or he would become like Korah and his followers" (v. 40). According to the documentary theorists, this concern would relate to the period of the Second Commonwealth, when these distinctions were first made. However, there is no satisfactory explanation for the fusion of the stories of Korah and of Dathan and Abiram.

J. Liver (in *Studies in the Bible*, ed. C. Rabin [1961], 189-217) argues that Deut. 11:6 and Ps. 106:16-18 mention only the revolt of Dathan and Abiram, indicative of its earlier existence. During the time of Solomon, when the priestly service was organized and consolidated for the large Temple, tensions arose over positions in the service. The Korahite Levites, one of the leading families, opposed the Jerusalem priesthood. To establish their position by tradition, this story was produced for authoritative support. It could not, however, achieve independent status and was thus appended to the tradition of the revolt of Dathan and Abiram against the authority and leadership of Moses.

There is no insuperable difficulty in viewing the passage as a harmonious unit. The proposed solutions to the various inferred problems are not only hypothetical, but often are equally problematic.

With regard to the miraculous judgments against Korah, Dathan, Abiram, and the 250 leaders, some have pointed to flash floods in the desert area accompanied by lightning, or to the mudflats in the region of the ARABAH, which under certain circumstances could well have swallowed up whatever was upon them (cf. G. Hort in *ABR* 7 [1959]: 2–26). While it may not be necessary to demonstrate natural phenomena that appear to corroborate the miracles in the Bible, it is always possible that God used such occurrences for his purposes. Korah's rebellion is mentioned in the NT (Jude 11; "Core").

Later, the Korahites were given responsibility "for guarding the thresholds of the Tent just as their fathers had been responsible for guarding the entrance to the dwelling of the LORD" (1 Chr. 9:19). One of these gatekeepers was SHALLUM, while his son, MATTITHIAH, "was entrusted with the responsibility for baking the offering bread" (9:31). A dozen psalms are given the superscription as "of the sons of Korah" (Pss. 42–49, 84–85, 87–88). It is probable that they originated among this guild of singers and were perhaps sung by them in the worship of the temple. Both the Korahites and the Kohathites led the worship when JEHOSHAPHAT gathered the people to seek the Lord (2 Chr. 20:19). See also PRIESTS AND LEVITES.

(4) Son of HEBRON, grandson of CALEB, and descendant of JUDAH (1 Chr. 2:43). Some argue that Korah here is the name of a town.

(5) Five of the men from the tribe of BENJAMIN who joined DAVID at ZIKLAG were called Korahites (1 Chr. 12:6). While it is possible that these were Levites descended from #3 above, some scholars believe that they descended from a different (and otherwise unknown) Korah or that the reference is to a locality in the tribe of Benjamin.

W. B. COKER

Korathite kor´uh-thit. KJV alternate form of Korahite. See KORAH.

Korazin kor-ay´zin (Χοραζίν *G5960*, variants Χοραζειν, Χωραζιν). Also Chorazin. A town situated near the Sea of Galilee, denounced by Jesus, and mentioned in the Bible in only one context (Matt. 11:21 = Lk. 10:13). Little is known of Korazin. The site is probably that of Khirbet Kerazeh, 2 mi. N of CAPERNAUM. This agrees with evidence provided by EUSEBIUS (*Onomasticon* 174.23) and JEROME (*The Sites and Names of Hebrew Places*, 194; but cf. *Commentary on Isaiah*, 3). Khirbet Kerazeh is high above Capernaum on the basalt hills, and evidence from the ruins indicates that it was inhabited as early as the later Stone Age. The TALMUD (*b. Menaḥot* 85a) mentions the town under the name Kerazim as being famous for its quality of wheat. A synagogue built of the black volcanic rock of the area forms part of the ruins. It was not as impressive as the synagogue in Capernaum, however. Also

Aerial view of the excavation at Korazin (looking NW).

among the ruins was a carved stone seat with an Aramaic inscription in honor of the donor. This may well be an example of "Moses' seat" (see Matt. 23:2). Eusebius indicates that the city had died out by his times. (See F.-M. Abel, *Géographie de la Palestine* [1938], 2:154, 299, 300; C. Kopp, *The Holy Places of the Gospels* [1963], 187–89; Z. Yeivin in *BAR* 13/5 [Sept.-Oct. 1987]: 22–36; *NEAEHL*, 1:301–4; *SacBr*, 356.) H. G. ANDERSEN

Korban. See CORBAN.

Kore kor´ee (קֹרֵא H7927, "one who calls out, partridge"). (1) Son of Ebiasaph (see ABIASAPH) and descendant of LEVI through KORAH (1 Chr. 9:19; 26:1 [here called son of Asaph]). Two of Kore's sons or descendants, SHALLUM and MESHELEMIAH (perhaps also OBED-EDOM, 26:4), were among the gatekeepers of the sanctuary.

(2) Son of Imnah; a Levite in the time of HEZEKIAH, he was keeper of the EAST GATE and "in charge of the freewill offerings given to God, distributing the contributions made to the LORD and also the consecrated gifts" (2 Chr. 31:14).

Korhite kor´hit. KJV alternate form of Korahite. See KORAH.

koum. See TALITHA CUM(I).

Koz koz (קוֹץ H7700, "thorn"). Also Coz. A man listed among the descendants of JUDAH (1 Chr. 4:8). His place in the genealogy is unclear, but the NIV links this verse with the previous one, making Koz a son of ASHHUR by Helah (see vv. 5, 7).

Kozbi koz´bi. TNIV form of COZBI.

Kozeba koh-zee´buh. TNIV form of COZEBA.

Kub kuhb. See CUB.

Kue kyoo´ee (קְוֵה H7750, meaning unknown). Also Keveh. A HITTITE kingdom occupying SE ASIA

MINOR, corresponding to E CILICIA. A document of NEBUCHADNEZZAR II, dated between 595 and 570 B.C., mentions the land of *Hu-m-e* (pronounced *Khuwe* or *Khwe*). It also occurs in the Istanbul Stela of NABONIDUS. The Annals of the Assyrian King SHALMANESER III (858–824) refer to Kue, and its king as an enemy. TIGLATH-PILESER III (744–727) received tribute from a ruler of Kue. HERODOTUS mentions Cilicia several times, hence it must be concluded that it was a country of some importance on the western Babylonian frontier.

An important trade route crossed this coastal plain, from the Syrian Gates in the Amanus Mountains to the Cilician Gates in the Taurus Range. IRON evidently was imported into SYRIA and BABYLON through Cilicia, but there is no evidence of its actually being mined there. The country was famous in ancient times as a source of the finest horses, many of which were imported by SOLOMON (1 Ki. 10:28; 2 Chr. 1:16; KJV, "linen yarn," following a Jewish interpretation). (See J. A. Montgomery, *A Critical and Exegetical Commentary on the Book of Kings*, ICC [1951], 227; Y. Ikeda in *Studies in the Period of David and Solomon and Other Essays*, ed. T. Ishida [1982], 215–38; D. D. Schley in *JBL* 106 [1987]: 595–601.)

Cilicia was made a Roman PROVINCE (Cilicia Pedias) in 103 B.C., and was governed by Cicero in 51 B.C. Later the administration was combined with that of Syria by VESPASIAN in A.D. 72. Both Luke and Paul were proper in combining Cilicia (Pedias) with Syria (Acts 15:23, 41; Gal. 1:21).
M. H. HEICKSEN

kum. See TALITHA CUM(I).

Kun kuhn. TNIV form of CUN.

Kushaiah koo-shay´yuh (קוּשָׁיָהוּ H7773, derivation uncertain). Descendant of LEVI through MERARI, and father of the musician ETHAN (1 Chr. 15:17); also called KISHI (6:44).

Kuthah kooth´uh. TNIV form of CUTHAH.

View of the Valley of Lebonah looking NW.

L. The symbol used to designate material peculiar to the Gospel of Luke; for some scholars, the symbol represents an independent literary source used by LUKE. If the infancy narratives are included, it comprises about half of the book. Some suppose that it originated c. A.D. 60, probably in CAESAREA, in either oral or written form. B. H. Streeter, in his Proto-Luke theory, held that Luke first wrote a gospel that consisted of Q (a sayings source from ANTIOCH OF SYRIA) and L, and that later on, when he became familiar with Mark's gospel, he alternated blocks of Proto-Luke with Markan material to form the canonical Gospel of Luke (*The Four Gospels: A Study of Origins* [1924], ch. 8). See GOSPELS; LUKE, GOSPEL OF. S. BARABAS

Laadah lay′uh-dah (לַעְדָּה H4355, possibly "plump neck"). Son of SHELAH and grandson of JUDAH (1 Chr. 4:21). He is described as the father of MARESHAH (possibly meaning the founder of the town by that name) and of "the clans of the linen workers at Beth Ashbea."

Laadan lay′uh-dan. KJV form of LADAN.

Laban (person) lay′buhn (לָבָן H4238, "white" or "Moon God" [see also LEBANAH]). Son of BETHUEL, grandson of NAHOR (ABRAHAM's brother), brother of REBEKAH (Gen. 24:29, cf. v. 15). The family is described as Arameans from PADAN ARAM (25:20). See ARAM (COUNTRY). It also is to be noted that Laban and his father were worshipers of the Lord (24:50).

Laban is first mentioned in connection with the arrival of Abraham's servant at the home of Nahor to find a wife for ISAAC. Although Bethuel was still living at the time of the servant's arrival, Laban was apparently the spokesman for the household (Gen. 24:29–33). In his meeting with Abraham's servant, Laban shows the oriental politeness of that day, as well as a certain shrewdness (v. 30) that is more apparent later in dealing with his sister's son, JACOB (29:13–26).

When Jacob was forced to leave his home, he was sent to his uncle Laban's home to escape the wrath of his brother ESAU (Gen. 27:42–46). Here Laban is described as a resident of HARAN (27:43), where TERAH had lived and died (11:32). Haran was the chief city of the region of PADDAN ARAM. Laban was undoubtedly well-known there, as is evidenced by his large holdings and the immediate recognition of his name by the strangers whom Jacob met at the shepherd's well (29:5). Jacob soon discovered that Laban had a beautiful daughter, RACHEL, and he immediately fell in love with her (29:6, 9–11, 16–18). Oriental politeness was once again shown by Laban toward Jacob as it had been earlier toward Abraham's servant.

After a month had passed, Laban offered to hire Jacob to work for him. Jacob willingly agreed to work for the privilege of marrying Rachel. After seven years' labor, Jacob asked for his wife. Laban's shrewdness became evident as he substituted LEAH, who was older and less attractive, for Rachel (Gen. 29:23). He pleaded the custom of the country in his duplicity (29:26), but agreed that Jacob could have Rachel also after a week, if Jacob would work for him seven more years.

Not able to outwit Laban, and still poor after fourteen years of labor, Jacob now put his trust in God to avenge the wrong. A second bargain was made with Laban by which Jacob would receive those sheep and goats in Laban's flock which were not of solid color (Gen. 30:20–34). It is not clear

959

whether Jacob believed his trick—having the sheep conceive where he had peeled the rods—would work or not (30:37–43). He later testified that God had promised him Laban's flocks and that all was of God's doing (31:7–9).

Nevertheless, Laban's flock did decrease and Jacob's increased, apparently not by any dishonesty on Jacob's part. Laban's sons, heretofore not mentioned, murmured and Laban himself no longer trusted Jacob (Gen. 31:1–2). Jacob accused Laban of cheating him in wages, and from Laban's past performance this is not hard to believe (31:6–7). Evidently Laban's daughters did not doubt the truth of Jacob's accusation (31:16). Jacob took his possessions and fled while Laban was away from home (31:20). Laban, on learning of Jacob's flight, angrily pursued. After seven days he overtook Jacob at GILEAD in the hill country SE of GALILEE.

In this last encounter between the two branches of Terah's family, the severe side of Laban is shown. He accused Jacob of cheating him by taking his daughters away without a farewell (Gen. 31:26–28). In addition he accused Jacob of stealing his household gods, something Jacob denied, not knowing that Rachel had indeed stolen them (31:19). Laban was unable to find the gods and Jacob soundly scolded him in return. He accused Laban of cheating him for twenty years though Jacob had faithfully served him (31:36–42). Laban never conceded a point in this argument, but yielded to Jacob anyway (31:43). Still distrusting one another, the two made a covenant whereby God was called to be a watcher over the two to prevent either from wronging the other. This has sometimes erroneously been called a "Benediction." After that, Laban departed and never appears again in the history of God's people.

A study of the NUZI tablets gives much insight into the biblical record concerning Laban and Jacob. Clarification is seen in the reason for Rachel's theft of her father's TERAPHIM, for by the teraphim she could claim inheritance in Laban's house. (See further A. Edersheim, *Bible History* [1890], 1:108–9, 125–31; D. Thomas, *Documents From Old Testament Times* [1958], 62, 122; J. Bright, *A History of Israel*, 4th ed. [2000], 86–90, 98–103; M. A. Morrison in *BA* 46 [1983]: 155–64; K. H. Zetterholm, *Portrait of a Villain: Laban the Aramean in Rabbinic Literature* [2003].)

Laban (place) lay′buhn ⟨לָבָן⟩ H4239, "white" or "Moon God"). A city in the area of encampment of Israel, across the JORDAN in the ARABAH (Deut. 1:1). In this area, MOSES spoke to Israel the words contained in Deuteronomy, just before his death. It is perhaps the same as LIBNAH, but the location is unknown.   J. B. SCOTT

Labana luh-bay′nuh. KJV Apoc. form of LEBANA (1 Esd. 5:29).

labor, work. The English term *labor* (as noun or verb) is used variously by Bible versions to render a number of terms, especially such nouns as Hebrew *yĕgîaʿ* H3330 and *ʿăbōdâ* H6275, and Greek *ergon* G2240 and *kopos* G3160 (as well as their cognate verbs). These can refer to work in the physical (originally agricultural) sphere, but also to moral action. (See *NIDOTTE*, 2:400–2; 3:304–9; *NIDNTT*, 1:262–63; 3:1147–59.) In general, the idea of labor or work in the Bible usage seems to embody four major concepts: the productive, the disciplinary, the socioeconomic, and the redemptive.

I. The productive concept. God's original purpose for human beings is expressed in the Bible in a twofold manner as stewardship of "production" and "preservation" in the Garden of Eden under the divine commission to "work it and take care of it" (Gen. 2:15; see EDEN, GARDEN OF). That this was God's purpose, in part at least, is evidenced by his prior statement, "there was no man to work the ground"

Laban's flock produced multicolored goats that became the property of Jacob (Gen. 30:30–43).

(2:5). However, this exalted divine purpose in the dignity of human labor finds its highest expression in God's commission involving the responsibility to "subdue" and "rule" the created natural order (1:28). Thus Adam and Eve were challenged to employ, under God's guidance and blessing, all phases of their personality (physical, 2:15; intellectual, 2:19–20; social, 2:18–24; and procreative, 1:28).

II. The disciplinary concept. This aspect of labor was added with a view to aiding human beings in their recovery from the divine-human alienation wrought by the fall. While human effort (labor) then, as always in the Bible, could never be a substitute for divine ATONEMENT in salvation, it did, nevertheless, as in PAUL's concept of the purpose of the LAW, direct and aid fallen sinners toward God's saving mercy (cf. Gal. 3:24–25).

Thus the "curse" or "judgment" pronounced by God upon humanity (Gen. 3:16–24), because of alienating sin, turned out to be God's most merciful blessing, designed to bring out of human beings, under the duress of difficult labor directed toward worthy objectives, the best and highest of their innate potential, and consequently to prevent them from yielding in slothfulness to the gravity of the fallen nature and degenerating to the lowest possible human denominator. Perhaps nothing short of the saving mercy of God in Christ is of greater benefit to human beings than honest, productive labor. If property is the extension of personality, then honest labor that produces or procures property contributes eminently to the realization of personal worth. Thus labor imposed upon humanity as a discipline because of SIN (3:17–19) turned out to be one of God's greatest corrective blessings.

III. The socioeconomic concept. The *one day of rest* derives its total significance from the *six days of labor* (Exod. 20:8–9; cf. Heb. 4:9–10). The success of the entire socioeconomic structure of all societies rests upon the various divisions of labor (men and women, skilled and unskilled, mental and manual, etc.), and the readiness of each person to perform his respective duties conscientiously and efficiently. It is as ethically obligatory upon the employed to thus serve his employer as it is for the employer to reward the employed equitably (Lk. 10:7; 1 Tim. 5:19). James pronounces strong condemnation upon the employer who withholds earned wages upon which the laborer is dependent for his livelihood (C. L. Mitton, *The Epistle of James* [1966], 179–80, on Jas. 5:4; cf. Lev. 19:13; Deut. 24:15; Matt. 20:1–15).

Such injustices gave rise to guilds, organized labor, and trade unions to protect the workers' interests from unprincipled employers. Since labor is exacted of the SLAVE who is deprived of personal earning power, slavery or forced labor, whether under a primitive totalitarianism or a contemporary sophisticated socialistic system, can never be justified ethically. "The entire problem of work and rest, labor and relaxation, diligence and laziness, capital and labor, production and consumption, inventory and distribution, receive light from the fourth commandment" (J. B. Coffman, *The Ten Commandments Yesterday and Today* [1961], 55).

Wisely did Paul admonish his converts, some of whom were "living in idleness, mere busybodies," evidently equating religion with exemption from labor: "If a man will not work, he shall not eat" (2 Thess. 3:10–11). The DIDACHE (*Teaching of the Twelve* 11) disqualifies a professed prophet if he remains with his host for more than three days, but especially if he asks for money. It has been well said that "Our highest happiness depends upon work and none should envy the poor parasite who manages to get along without it" (Coffman, *Ten Commandments*, 56).

IV. The redemptive concept. The ideas of labor for production and discipline merge with the biblical concept of labor in redemption. Thus

In this wall painting from the Beni Hasan tombs in Egypt (early 2nd millennium B.C.), workers are shown in various agricultural tasks including threshing, sifting, rope-making, and harvesting.

considered, labor has a distinctive eschatological significance in the NT. From the outset, man began the redemption of the earth from the curse caused by human sin by laboriously tilling the soil from which he produced his livelihood (Gen. 3:17–18). But the idea of redemption is also implicit in the divinely given commission to subdue and rule the natural order (1:28). Thus the efforts (labor) of scientists throughout human history have been both redemptive and productive. The biblical redemptive concept of labor becomes more explicit in the NT. Christ labored to accomplish human salvation (Lk. 22:44; Jn. 4:34; 5:17; 9:4; 17:4), and believers are exhorted to labor to enter into the salvation-rest provided for them by Christ (Matt. 11:28–30; Jn. 6:27; Heb. 4:11). Thus considered, Christ's eschatological provision offers deliverance from the wearisome burdens of the law. Labor for the reconciliation of unbelievers by believers is explicit and obligatory in the NT (Matt. 28:18–20; 2 Cor. 5:20; cf. 1 Thess. 1:3; Rev. 2:2). Accordingly, the last and distinctive NT use of labor for the believer on earth is in the interest of the Christian community (cf. 1 Cor. 9:16–25; Phil. 2:16; Col. 1:29; 1 Thess. 2:9). Finally, the redemptive labors of believers will be rewarded in eternal salvation by God himself (1 Cor. 15:58; Rev. 14:13).   C. W. Carter

Laccunus luh-koo'nuhs (Λακκουνος). One of the descendants of Addi who put away their foreign wives in the time of Ezra (1 Esd. 9:31; KJV, "Lacunus"); this name does not appear in the parallel list (Ezra 10).

lace. This English term is used by the KJV in the old sense of "band, cord" (Exod. 28:28, 37; 39:21, 31; Sir. 6:30).

Lacedaemonian las'uh-di-moh'nee-uhn (Λακεδαιμόνιος). KJV Lacedemonian. An inhabitant of Lacedaemon, more commonly called Sparta, in southern Greece. The term occurs once in the Apocrypha (2 Macc. 5:9; in the KJV, however, this English term is used regularly for Gk. *Spartiatai*, "Spartans," 1 Macc. 12:2 et al.). Friendly relations between Sparta and the Jews began early in the 3rd cent. B.C. when Arius (309–265) was king and Onias I was high priest (320–290) in Jerusalem. In 168 B.C. Jason, the high priest, after his unsuccessful attempt to seize Jerusalem, was forced to flee, and went to Sparta "in hope of finding protection because of their kinship."

This incident implies the existence of a Jewish colony in Sparta during the 2nd cent. In about 146 B.C., Jonathan wrote to the Spartans requesting renewal of the ancient friendship (1 Macc. 12:6–18) and reminding them of the earlier relations between Arius and Onias, even suggesting that the Spartans and Jews were both of the stock of Abraham and hence kinsmen (see Maccabee). After the death of Jonathan, his brother and successor, Simon, received a reply to this letter (1 Macc. 14:20–22). In 1 Macc. 15:16–22 there is a declaration of friendship between Rome and the Jews, written by the consul Lucius to Ptolemy, king of Egypt, requesting that kings and nations refrain from fighting against the Jews. The same letter was also sent to many other neighboring countries, including Sparta (v. 23). While some have doubted the authenticity of these letters in 1 Maccabees, there are many scholars who regard them as genuine. There is no doubt that during the 2nd cent. B.C. such declarations of friendship with the Jews were made by both Rome and Sparta.   R. C. Stone

Lachish lay'kish (לָכִישׁ H4337, meaning unknown). A town within the tribal territory of Judah in the foothills of the Shephelah, midway between Jerusalem and Gaza, some 30 mi. SW of Jerusalem.

  I. Name and identification
 II. Biblical history
III. Extrabiblical historical references
 IV. Excavation
  V. The Fosse temple
 VI. Inscriptions
VII. The Lachish letters

I. Name and identification. The town is mentioned over twenty times in the OT, several times in the Tell el-Amarna correspondence, and in a few other extrabiblical sources (as early as the commercial texts from Ebla, and also on a hieratic papyrus from the days of Thutmose III [in the form *Rakiša*], a pottery bowl found in Egypt [form *Latiša*], and a wall relief from Sennacherib's palace at Nineveh).

Lachish is identified with Tell ed-Duweir, a large mound some 18 acres in size, 15 mi. W of HEBRON and 5 mi. to the SW of Beit Jibrin, the ancient Eleutheropolis. This identification is based on the following considerations. It is the most impressive site in the region and was occupied during the Bronze and Iron Ages as required by historical facts. It also suits the description of EUSEBIUS that "Lachish.... is still a village today, seven miles from Eleutheropolis, towards the west as one goes to Daroma." Excavation has revealed a striking resemblance between the Iron Age ruins at Tell ed-Duweir and the city shown on a relief from Nineveh depicting the attack of Sennacherib on *Lakisu*; the history of the site as revealed from excavation is parallel to what is known from both biblical and nonbiblical sources.

II. Biblical history. Lachish first features in biblical history in the story of the conquest (see ISRAEL, HISTORY OF, IV). It was ruled by an AMORITE king named JAPHIA who formed a coalition with four other Amorite kings under the leadership of ADONI-ZEDEK of Jerusalem (Josh. 10:1–27; 12:11). JOSHUA overthrew the city despite the help of the king of GEZER (10:31–33). Lachish was numbered among cities allotted to the tribe of Judah (15:39). After SOLOMON's death it was fortified by REHOBOAM (2 Chr. 11:9). AMAZIAH, king of Judah, sought refuge here when conspirators sought his life, but he was pursued and slain in the city (2 Ki. 14:19; 2 Chr. 25:27). In the days of HEZEKIAH, Lachish was taken by Sennacherib the Assyrian. From here he sent a message to Hezekiah in Jerusalem demanding surrender (2 Ki. 18:14, 17; 19:8; 2 Chr. 32:9; Isa. 36:2; 37:8). A century and a quarter later, Lachish and AZEKAH were the last provincial centers to withstand NEBUCHADNEZZAR's attack (Jer. 34:7). After the EXILE, Lachish was resettled by the returning Jews (Neh. 11:30). An obscure description of Lachish as "the beginning of sin to the Daughter of Zion" (Mic. 1:13) may be a condemnation of Rehoboam's reliance on military defense rather than on God, or it may refer to the inauguration of an idolatrous cult there which later spread to other cities of Judah.

III. Extrabiblical historical references. Some meager but important references come from Syria, Egypt, and Assyria. As mentioned above, Lachish is mentioned in commercial documents discovered in Ebla (c. 2400 B.C.). An Egyptian papyrus of the time of Thutmose III (c. 1490–1435) points to Egyptian contact with the town. The Amarna correspondence of c. 1400–1360 mentions Lachish five times in contexts which show that Lachish was an important Egyptian strongpoint in Canaan. The city was involved in intrigue with the HABIRU, and other cities loyal to Egypt wrote appealing for help. In one letter from Jerusalem, the cities of Lachish, ASHKELON, and GEZER are blamed for supplying the Habiru with food and oil. Another letter refers to treachery in Lachish in which a certain Zimreda or Zimridi was slain. A bowl from Lachish dated c. 1200 or later and inscribed in hieratic refers to the "king of La ti ša(?)."

The Assyrian information, though limited, is important. The attack by Sennacherib on Lachish in 701 B.C. is depicted on alabaster bas-reliefs from Nineveh. The town of Lakisu is shown under siege. Some scenes depict Jewish prisoners being marched out, others being flayed, and some begging for mercy before Sennacherib seated on a throne. The inscription near the throne reads: "Sennacherib, king of the world, king of Assyria, sat upon a *nimedu*-throne and passed in review the booty (taken) from Lachish (*La-ki-su*)" (ANET, 288b).

IV. Excavation. The history of Lachish becomes much clearer when the biblical and nonbiblical records are supplemented by information revealed by the excavation of the town. Tell ed-Duweir and selected areas on the neighboring slopes were

Lachish.

excavated by the Wellcome-Marston Archaeological Research Expedition during the years 1932 to 1938. The director, James L. Starkey, was tragically murdered in 1938 by bandits, and the work was brought to completion by Charles H. Inge and Lankester Harding.

It is now clear that the region of Lachish was occupied very early. In Chalcolithic times (before c. 3000 B.C.) and in the first stages of the Early Bronze Age, there was a settlement in the Lachish area. Pottery, stone mortars and querns, stone maceheads and implements of flint and bone were found in natural caves over a considerable area. About 2800 in the Early Bronze II age, the settlement became confined to the present mound. The old cave dwellings then were used as tombs.

There is some disagreement about the actual dates of some of the levels, but in broad outline the following gives a general picture (all dates are B.C.):

Level I: 450–150
Gap: mound deserted
Level II: 700–586
Levels III and IV: 900–700
Level V: City of David and Rehoboam 1000–900
Gap: mound deserted
Level VI: 1300–1225 Late Bronze
Level VII: 1450–1350
Level VIII: 1567–1450

(Subsequent work has revealed the need to revise this scheme, such as renumbering the strata beneath Level VI. For an updated report, see D. Ussishkin et al., *The Renewed Archaeological Excavations at Lachish (1973–1994)*, 5 vols. [2004].)

Further excavation is needed to complete the story of the Early Bronze and the Middle Bronze Age. It is evident that during the HYKSOS period (c. 1720–1550) Lachish was a fortified site defended by a deep ditch or fosse and a plaster-covered glacis rising to about 100 ft. above the valley on top of which was a brick wall. These defenses fell into disuse early in the Late Bronze Age c. 1550, possibly as a result of Egyptian campaigns that drove the Hyksos conquerors out of Egypt and initiated the great period of Egyptian expansion into W Asia. A small temple was built over the debris that accumulated in the fosse, the so-called Fosse Temple (see below).

Egyptian influence in Lachish from the 12th dynasty (c. 1991–1786) onward is attested by Egyptian scarabs. The waning of Egyptian power may be marked by the destruction of the Fosse Temple c. 1220–1200, perhaps by Israelite tribesmen who followed up their earlier successes under Joshua (Josh. 10:3, 31–32). The inscribed bowl written in "year four" and mentioning the "king of Latish(?)" has been interpreted as a tax collector's memorandum from the fourth year of MERNEPTAH (c. 1224–1216). A variety of important inscriptions was discovered in the Late Bronze Age city.

After a period of desertion during the 12th and 11th centuries, the Israelite Iron Age city was built around the year 1000. A fine palace for the provincial governor rose over the ruins of old Canaanite buildings in the center of the mound. It was built on an earth-filled platform about 105 ft. square and 23 ft. high. This structure is reminiscent of the MILLO (lit., "filling") built by DAVID (2 Sam. 5:9) and SOLOMON (1 Ki. 9:15) in Jerusalem. Practically nothing of the original palace remains, but the ruins of a thick-walled brick building with long parallel rooms and high floors have been discovered, probably originally a granary or storehouse. Similar buildings are known from MEGIDDO and HAZOR during Solomon's reign, but their presence at Lachish and BETH SHEMESH only 15 mi. to the N suggests that David may have had a provincial administration in Judah before Solomon's organization of the N (1 Ki. 4:7–19). This platform was twice enlarged during the period 900–750. First it was lengthened to 256 ft. (Palace B), and then a strip 10 ft. wide was added on the E side (Palace C). On the stairway leading up to the citadel platform, the first five letters of the Hebrew ALPHABET in traditional order were scratched (dated c. 800 according to W. F. Albright).

During the late 10th cent. and at various times in the 9th, the kings of Judah improved the defenses of Lachish. The OT references to the work of REHOBOAM (2 Chr. 11:9) and possibly of ASA (14:7) before 900, then to JEHOSHAPHAT who set garrisons in the cities of Judah (17:12, 13), seem to point to occasions when the defense system of S Judah was strengthened against Philistines, Arabs, Egyptians, etc. (11:5–12). Excavation shows that during the 9th cent. Lachish was strongly protected with a double line of defense. The summit

Aerial view of Lachish looking E.

was surrounded by a ring wall some 19 ft. thick, with alternating salients and recesses and a series of defense towers. A farther 50 ft. down the slope was a second wall or revetment of stone and brick some 13 ft. thick, with alternate projecting and recessed sections and towers located at strategic points. The walls enclosed an area approximately rectangular in plan. On the W of the city, a roadway led up the hillside, and at the point where it entered the city gate a large square bastion was erected. This was later incorporated into the line of the outer wall. The masonry in the walls was mostly crudely squared boulders with more carefully prepared cornerstones. Inside the city, a street lined with shops led to the palace and the storerooms on the platform at the top of the mound. Numerous stamped jar handles dating to the 8th and 7th centuries come from what must represent Levels IV, III, II (see the discussion of inscriptions below).

There is some difference of interpretation about the destruction of Level III. Most archaeologists attribute it to the attack of Sennacherib in 701, but a few (e.g., Olga Tufnell) attribute it to NEBUCHADREZZAR in 590 B.C. The bas relief of Sennacherib and his written record suggest a severe attack on Lachish. In the debris outside the walls, scattered arrowheads, pieces of scale armor, sling stones, and an Assyrian-type helmet were found, and large earth ramps also were found built against the gateway area just as Sennacherib's relief depicts, so that the assignment of the destruction of Level III to the Assyrian assault is quite plausible. (See further D. Ussishkin, *The Conquest of Lachish by Sennacherib* [1982].)

On the NW slope of the mound was a huge communal grave containing the bones of 1,500 bodies in a heap. Many had been burned. On top of the human bones were animal bones, mostly of pigs. Large quantities of domestic pottery were scattered through the whole. It is suggested that the confused mass represents a gathering up of debris after the siege of Sennacherib. The pig bones may represent the food of the Assyrian soldiers. Three of the human skulls showed evidence of trepanning, a remarkable testimony to the standard of surgical skill in Judea in the days of Isaiah. Another feature of the Iron Age city was a great unfinished shaft on the SE side of the mound. It was a roughly hollow cube some 74 by 84 by 85 ft. in size and about half a million cubic ft. in capacity, probably intended for water storage.

After the fall of Lachish III the city probably was governed by an Assyrian governor and became a rallying point for levies from Philistines. Some reconstruction went on, and part of the ruined citadel was cleared for the building of a smaller gateway, but the rebuilding of city II was a slow process. Some claim that traces of SCYTHIAN warriors have been found in the city in the 7th cent., which may account for the slowness in rebuilding. However, the defenses were eventually restored, perhaps by MANASSEH (2 Chr. 33:11–14). A new stone wall replaced the inner wall, the former outworks were incorporated into the lower revetment as a bastion, and the entrance was by way of two gates, the outer one in the bastion facing S, and the inner one on the line of the upper wall facing W. This device exposed the invader on his right side as he approached the first gate. If he succeeded here, he turned right uphill across an enclosed court before he reached the second gate.

By the time of JEHOIAKIM, Lachish was once more a formidable city. There is evidence of two destructions early in the 6th cent. The first was no doubt due to the attack by the Babylonian army in 597, when the city gate and the citadel were partially destroyed. The brick superstructure of the palace collapsed and spread over the courtyard. The inner wall was rebuilt and some restoration undertaken, although the palace was not restored. In Nebuchadnezzar's second attack in 586 the full force of the Babylonian army was brought against the cities of Judah, which fell one by one until only Jerusalem, Azekah, and Lachish remained (Jer 34:7). Of these, Azekah was the first to fall. Evidence of a huge conflagration at Lachish is found all over the city. It was evidently reoccupied soon after. A fine seal impression was found above the debris reading "Gedaliah who is over the House" (Isa. 22:15; 36:3; see below, VI.2).

Lachish was abandoned between 586 and 450 B.C. The postexilic city, Level I, had two phases, one Persian and one Hellenistic. During the Persian phase a fine palace was built in the N Syrian style for a governor under GESHEM (Gashmu) the Arab (Neh. 6:1). A small structure that was probably a temple contained a small limestone altar bearing an inscription carrying the name "Yah(weh)" (see below, VI.9). The second phase is attested by a "solar shrine" of the SELEUCID period. Lachish was abandoned c. 150 B.C. and was not occupied again.

V. The Fosse temple. This structure lay outside the Late Bronze Age city walls in the Middle Bronze Age fosse. It was in use from c. 1600 to c. 1200 B.C. and was enlarged on at least two occasions. Essentially it was a large room with an offering table, a hearth in front of the table, and in its final form a mud-brick altar in front of the offering table with three steps (cf. Exod. 20:26). Votive gifts of ornaments, beads, etc., in ivory, glass, alabaster, etc., lay on the table. Many small dipper flasks lay on the ground at one end of the offering table. Bones of birds, animals, and fish were found in the floor debris. The animals were all young, mostly sheep, goats, oxen, gazelles; and the bones discovered were mostly the right foreleg corresponding to the priests' portion in Israelite sacrifices (Lev. 7:32). No statue was found inside the temple, but a bronze statuette of a male deity seated was found outside, and an ivory hand was recovered from a pit. Two inscribed pottery vessels, a ewer, and a bowl were found outside the temple (see below, VI.2). The exact nature of the Canaanite worship practiced is not clear, but evidently young animals were sacrificed, the right foreleg was reserved, gifts were placed on a cult table, fire burned in the hearth, and libation offerings were poured out. An altar with steps, an offering table, and a hearth were features of the temple furniture.

VI. Inscriptions. A variety of INSCRIPTIONS, many from the Late Bronze Age, have come from the excavation of Lachish. The following list is in chronological order (all dates are B.C.):

1. Four signs on a bronze dagger c. 1600. One sign, a human head, is possibly the ancient letter *r* (see RESH).

2. Five fragments with alphabetic signs of the Sinaitic type c. 1350–1200. These include a censer lid with three signs in red; a bowl with eleven signs of which five seem to be *lšlš*, "for three"; a ewer decorated around the neck with wavy lines and squares and with stylized animals; an inscription of eleven letters very similar to those used at Serabit el-Khadim in the Sinai peninsula. The words *mtn*, "gift," and *ʾlt*, "goddess," have been read.

3. A four-sided seal with the name of Amenhotep II (c. 1450–1425) on one side and a representation of Ptah and eight signs on another.

4. A fragment of a clay coffin c. 1200 or later, with unreadable hieroglyphic signs and two small hieratic inscribed sherds.

5. A pottery bowl with a hieratic text thought to be concerned with taxation including the words "King (of) Latish (?)," c. 1200 or later.

6. An inscription (c. 800) carrying the first five letters of the Hebrew alphabet in their traditional order (ʾ b g d h).

7. A jar fragment bearing the letters *btlmyk*, "the *bath* of the king" (a measure of capacity; see WEIGHTS AND MEASURES III.A).

8. Several seals or seal impressions with names in the old Hebrew script (8th to 6th cent.). One of them reads, "belonging to Gedaliah who is over the household"; it was possibly an official seal of GEDALIAH son of Ahikam, appointed governor of Judah by Nebuchadnezzar after the fall of Jerusalem in 586 (2 Ki. 25:22).

9. A great number of stamped jar handles (8th to early 6th cent.), some three hundred stamped *lmlk*, "belonging to the king," followed by the name of a town like Hebron, Ziph, Sochoh, or *mmšt*, and carrying a symbol such as a winged scroll.

10. A stone altar inscribed with three lines in Aramaic script of c. 5th to 4th cent. It begins with *lbntʾ*, "incense." The third line contains the words *lyh mrʾ*, "to Yah(weh) Lord (of heaven)."

11. A variety of stone weights of the 7th to 6th cent. inscribed *nsp, pym, bqʿ*. One had the letter *b*, others had numbers inscribed.

12. Twenty-one ostraca from the early 6th cent. written in black ink—the so-called "Lachish letters" (see next section).

VII. The Lachish letters. In 1935 eighteen ostraca inscribed in a cursive Hebrew of Jeremiah's time were recovered from the debris in a small guard room in one of the towers of the outer city gate. Subsequently, in 1938, three more ostraca were found, bringing the total to twenty one. These ostraca represent written documents in the classical Hebrew style from the last decade of the Judean kingdom. They are important historically because of the light they throw on the unsettled conditions in Judah during the Babylonian campaign of 586. The texts are not always clear, and scholars disagree about details of translation. (See the translations by W. F. Albright in *ANET*, 321–22, and by D. Winton Thomas, with extensive notes, in *DOTT*, 212–17.)

The Lachish letters. A portion of the 21 ostraca (potsherds inscribed in black ink) found in the gate area of Lachish destroyed by the Babylonians in 586 B.C. These letters comment on Nebuchadnezzar's invasion, which put Jerusalem under siege.

Three of the letters are of special interest. *Letter 3* gives the name of the writer, Hoshayahu, a subordinate officer in charge of an outpost of Lachish, within sight of Azekah, and of the recipient, Yaosh, the governor of Lachish. It is partly a complaint about some rebuke the writer had received, and partly a report of military movements, including reference to a journey to Egypt by a captain, Koniah son of Elnathan, and a warning message sent in by Tobyahu to Shallum, son of Yaddua, by the hand of an unidentified prophet. *Letter 4* reports about commands that had been carried out and indicates that certain people had been detained. It concludes, "Let my lord know that we are watching for the fire signals of Lachish according to the signs my lord has given, because we do not see Azekah" (cf. Jer. 34:7). *Letter 6* refers to disturbing letters from the king and the princes in Jerusalem: "The words of the pr(inces) are not good (but serve) to weaken our hands, (and to slac)ken the hands of the m(en) who are informed about them" (cf. Jer. 38:4). *Letter 16* refers to a prophet whose name ends in *-iah*, variously identified with Uriah (Jer. 26:20) or Jeremiah, or perhaps some other who is unknown.

(See further H. Torczyner et al., *Lachish I: The Lachish Letters* [1938]; O. Tufnell et al., *Lachish II:*

The Fosse Temple [1940]; O. Tufnell, *Lachish III: The Iron Age* [1953]; O. Tufnell et al., *Lachish IV: The Bronze Age* [1958]; Y. Aharoni et al., *Investigations at Lachish: The Sanctuary and the Residency (Lachish V)* [1975]; D. Ussishkin et al., *The Renewed Archaeological Excavations at Lachish (1973–1994)*, 5 vols. [2004]; *ABD*, 4:114–28; *NEAEHL*, 3:897–911.)

J. ARTHUR THOMPSON

Lacunus luh-koo′nuhs. KJV form of LACCUNUS.

Ladan lay′duhn (לַעְדָּן H4356, possibly "plump neck, double chin"). KJV Laadan. **(1)** Son of Tahan, descendant of EPHRAIM, and ancestor of JOSHUA (1 Chr. 7:26).

(2) Descendant of LEVI through GERSHON and ancestor of several Levitical families in charge of the temple treasuries (1 Chr. 23:7–9; 26:21). Because he is paired with SHIMEI (23:7), Ladan is usually identified with LIBNI son of Gershon (6:17), but some argue that both Ladan and the Shimei of 23:7 are more distant descendants of Gershon (KD, *Chronicles*, 256).

(3) KJV Apoc. form of DELAIAH (1 Esd. 5:37).

ladder. This English word is used by the KJV and other versions to render Hebrew *sullām* H6150, which occurs only in the account of JACOB's dream (Gen. 28:12; NIV, "stairway"). This image, it has been thought, was suggested by a flight of stone steps in the rock strata in the area where Jacob fell asleep. In ancient times ladders were used often in the siege of cities, and many are shown on Egyptian and Assyrian monuments. Scaling ladders are also mentioned in the APOCRYPHA (1 Macc. 5:30; Gk. *klimax*). See also LADDER OF TYRE. S. BARABAS

Ladder of Tyre (κλίμαξ Τύρου). A narrow strip of coastal alluvial plain about 5 mi. wide and a few hundred feet above the Mediterranean Sea, located between TYRE and the coastal town of ACZIB where the GALILEE hills come down almost to the sea. This strip of coast, near the present Israeli-Lebanese border, is marked by a series of intermittent low hills of Pleistocene limestone. No doubt, this narrow ledge made it difficult for any invader (or caravan) to pass from N to S, or vice versa.

The name Ladder of Tyre is not found in the canonical OT and NT, but it occurs in 1 Macc. 11:59, where ANTIOCHUS VI is said to have confirmed Jonathan MACCABEE, the Jew, as high priest, and his brother Simon as captain over the area from the Ladder of Tyre in the N to the borders of Egypt in the S. JOSEPHUS (*War* 2.11.2 §188) also refers to the Ladder and locates it at 11–12 mi. N of Roman Ptolemais (Acco), which would place it at about the present day Ras en-Naqura. (See D. Baly, *The Geography of the Bible* [1957], 8, 39, 128; Y. Aharoni, *The Land of the Bible: A Historical Geography*, rev. ed. [1979], 22, 182.) W. H. MARE

lady, chosen (elect). See ELECT LADY.

Lael lay′uhl (לָאֵל H4210, "belonging to God"). Father of ELIASAPH; during the wilderness period, the latter was a leader of the Levites descended from GERSHON (Num. 3:24).

Lagash lay′gash. An important city-state in SUMER during the first half of the 3rd millennium B.C. Lagash is identified with modern Tell al-Hiba in S Iraq, but it included the urban centers of Girsu and Nina-Sirara (modern Tello and Zurghul). Large temple complexes have been excavated. The *Lagash Kinglist* (early 2nd millennium), purportedly a record of the city's ancient rulers, includes a flood

This artistic depiction of an Assyrian attack on an enemy town features a scaling ladder. (From Nimrud, c. 860 B.C.)

narrative. (See K. I. Matthews, "Girsu and Lagash," in *The Oxford Encyclopedia of Archaeology in the Near East*, ed. E. M. Meyers [1997], 2:406–9; *CANE*, 2:2341–47.)

Lahad lay´had (לַהַד H4262, possibly "slow, lazy"). Son of Jahath, descendant of JUDAH, and ancestor of a Zorathite clan (1 Chr. 4:2; see ZORAH).

Lahai-roi. See BEER LAHAI ROI.

Lahmam lah´mam. See LAHMAS.

Lahmas lah´mahs (לַחְמָס H4314 [many mss לַחְמָם], meaning uncertain). Also Lahmam (if one follows the reading of many Heb. mss and of the TARGUM). A town of JUDAH in the SHEPHELAH district of LACHISH (Josh. 15:40). The location is unknown, although some have suggested modern Khirbet el-Laḥm, about 3 mi. E of Lachish.

Lahmi lah´mi (לַחְמִי H4313, in form a gentilic from the word meaning "bread" [cf. BETHLEHEM]). A PHILISTINE who is described as the brother of GOLIATH the Gittite and who was killed by Elhanan son of Jair (1 Chr. 20:5). The parallel passage (2 Sam. 21:19) reads differently. For a discussion of this problem, see ELHANAN #1.

Laish lay´ish (לַיִשׁ H4332, "lion"). **(1)** A Canaanite city in N Palestine captured by the Danites and renamed by them Dan (Jdg. 18:7, 14, 27, 29); earlier called LESHEM (in Josh. 19:47). See DAN (PERSON AND TRIBE); DAN (PLACE).

(2) Father of PALTIEL, to whom SAUL gave MICHAL, DAVID's wife (1 Sam. 25:44; 2 Sam. 3:15).

(3) KJV form of LAISHAH (Isa. 10:30).

S. BARABAS

Laishah lay´i-shah (לַיְשָׁה H4333, "lion"). KJV Laish. A village probably in BENJAMIN, named with GALLIM and ANATHOTH as lying along the usual invasion route of armies coming from the N (Isa. 10:30). The location is unknown, but it must have been a relatively short distance NNE of JERUSALEM.

lake. The Greek word for "lake," *limnē* G3349, is used only by Luke with reference to the Lake of GENNESARET—that is, the Sea of Galilee—and by the book of Revelation with reference to the LAKE OF FIRE (Lk. 5:1–2; 8:22–23, 33; Rev. 19:20; 20:10, 14–15; 21:8). To prevent misunderstanding, the NIV also employs "lake" frequently to render Greek *thalassa* G2498, "sea," whenever this term (in imitation of Heb. *yām* H3542 and Aram. *yam* H10322) is used by itself with reference to the Sea of Galilee (Matt. 4:18 et al.). There are not many lakes in Syria and Palestine. Among the most important are the following: the DEAD SEA; the Waters of MEROM (Josh. 11:5, 7); Yammuneh (in the LEBANON, W of BAALBEK); and some small lakes E of DAMASCUS into which the rivers of Damascus flow and are evaporated. See also GALILEE, SEA OF.

S. BARABAS

lake of fire. This phrase translates Greek *limnē tou pyros*, which occurs several times in the book of Revelation (Rev. 19:20; 20:10, 14–15; cf. 21:8). All the enemies of God—the beast and the false prophet (19:20), the devil (20:10), death and HADES (20:14), all whose names are not found written in the BOOK OF LIFE (20:15), the cowardly, the faithless, the murderers, etc. (21:8)—are to be consigned at the end of this age (in the case of the beast and the false prophet), or after the 1,000 years, to the lake of fire. This is said to be the second death (20:14)—the first being presumably physical death—and consists in eternal exclusion from the new heaven and the new earth, and the new Jerusalem (21:2). See DEATH, SECOND. For the devil, the beast, and the false prophet at least, it also will include being tormented for ever and ever (20:10). Orthodox theology, linking this text with what is said elsewhere in the NT on the destiny of unbelievers, has normally understood it to apply also to unsaved human beings. On the other hand, there have been, and still are, those who feel that consignment to the lake of fire will result in the complete destruction and annihilation of unbelievers. Discussion under PUNISHMENT, ETERNAL. (See further H. B. Swete, *The Apocalypse of St. John* [1911], 258, 270–74, 282–83; A. B. Mickelson, *Interpreting the Bible* [1963], 319–22.)

R. E. DAVIES

Lake of Gennesaret. See GALILEE, SEA OF.

Lakkum lak′uhm (לַקּוּם H4373, derivation uncertain). KJV Lakum. A town on the SE border of the tribal territory of NAPHTALI, named between JABNEEL and the JORDAN River (Josh. 19:33). Its precise location is uncertain, but some scholars identify it with modern Khirbet el-Mansurah, less than 2 mi. SW of the S tip of the Sea of Galilee, at the head of Wadi Fejjas.

lamb, Lamb of God. The principal words in Hebrew for "lamb," that is, the young of SHEEP, are *keśeb* H4166 (Gen. 30:33 et al.) and *śeh* H8445 (Gen. 22:7-8 et al.). The common term in Greek is *amnos* G303, but *arnion* G768 is used almost thirty times in Revelation (Rev. 5:6-13 et al.; elsewhere only in Jn. 21:15).

The lamb was the principal animal of SACRIFICE among the Jews, being the offering each morning and each evening in the Mosaic system (Exod. 29:38-42), and especially on the SABBATH. Also the lamb was sacrificed on special days of religious significance: the first day of the new month (Num. 28:11), each day of the Feast of PASSOVER (28:16-19), at the Feast of PENTECOST (28:26-27), the Feast of Trumpets (29:1-2), the Great Day of Atonement (29:7-8), and the Feast of Tabernacles (29:12-16). See ATONEMENT, DAY OF; FEASTS. Specific sacrifices of a personal nature also used the lamb (e.g., a woman after giving birth, Lev. 12:6; a leper after healing, 14:10-18).

To the Jews the lamb represented innocence and gentleness. The prophets portrayed the tender compassion of God for his people under the figure of the SHEPHERD and the lamb (Isa. 40:11), and the lamb was an important symbol of the ultimate intention of God for his people (11:6). The psalmist carried the imagery of the shepherd and the lamb to its most beautiful expression in Ps. 23. Likewise the lamb was the climax of prophetic symbolism of the suffering of God's people, the servant nation, which the NT found to be a prefiguring of Jesus (Isa. 53:7; Acts 8:32).

In the NT the term is used only symbolically. Of special importance is the designation of Jesus as "the Lamb of God" by JOHN THE BAPTIST (Jn. 1:29). Some have regarded that pronouncement by the Baptist to be a thematic statement of the contents of the fourth gospel, Jesus being presented throughout the document as the lamb of sacrifice to take away the sins of the world. Much speculation has centered on the OT reference believed to have been in the mind of John when he thus spoke of Jesus. The Mosaic lamb of the Passover has been suggested frequently because Jesus is thus identified by PAUL (1 Cor. 5:7). Naturally many have found the suffering lamb (Isa. 53) to have been foremost in his mind. Still others have sought to avoid any particular reference and have considered the lamb simply as the principal animal of sacrifice in the worship of God.

Two things about this designation as applied to Jesus were most notable: he was declared to be the lamb of God and his sacrifice was for the world. All other lambs in the sacrificial system had been offered by human beings under the commandment of God; but just as God had substituted his own provision of a lamb instead of ISAAC who was under ABRAHAM's hand, so God in Jesus provided his own Lamb. All other sacrifices of a lamb had been limited to the nation or to the individual; but the sacrifice of Jesus was worldwide, embracing all humanity in its scope. He was to take away the sins of the world. The lamb was a worthy symbol of Jesus, who in innocence patiently endured suffering as a substitute (Acts 8:32; 1 Pet. 1:19).

In the NT the term *lamb* was applied also to disciples of Jesus. Seventy disciples were sent forth "like lambs among wolves" (Lk. 10:3). Likewise the risen Christ charged the apostle PETER to feed his lambs (Jn. 21:15-17), which probably marked out Peter's special responsibility to nurture and advance the people the ascended Lord would leave behind.

Of special interest is the use of the term in Revelation, where it occurs twenty-eight times in symbolic reference to Christ and once as a comparative statement identifying some aspect of the beast (Rev. 13:11). The beast was, no doubt, represented as having the horns of a lamb to point to its religious significance. The introductory reference in Rev. 5:1-14 is to the Lamb triumphant. This description of the Lamb and the works attributed to him clearly identify him as the Christ. The characteristics of the Lamb are significant. He stood as "one slain," as if his throat had been cut in sacrifice. He had been slain, but was alive forevermore. He had seven horns, which probably were symbolic of his great power. He had seven eyes that represented his ceaseless vigilance for the people of God; thus the eyes were reinterpreted as the seven spirits of God, the fullness of God's Spirit working in behalf of his people. His attributes were those of God—OMNIPOTENCE and OMNISCIENCE. (See L. Johns, *The Lamb Christology of the Apocalypse of John* [2004].)

The significance of the difference between the terms *arnion* (used in Revelation) and *amnos* (elsewhere in the NT) has been much debated. It is most likely that the two words have the same essential meaning in the NT—a symbolic representation of the redemptive work of Christ, although in Revelation that redemptive work is viewed in connection with its triumphant victory over all things. (See *ABD*, 4:132–34.) H. L. DRUMWRIGHT, JR.

lame. This adjective (Heb. *pissēaḥ* H7177; Gk. *chōlos* G6000) is applied to a person who walks with difficulty or is entirely unable to do so. If lameness is present at birth it is called *congenital*, but if it develops subsequently it is known as *acquired*. One form of lameness recognizable from antiquity is *cyllosis*, or clubfoot, which appears in variant forms but always involves permanent disability of the extremities. Another was represented on an Egyptian stela of the 18th dynasty (1570–1310 B.C.), depicting a man with an atrophied right leg, evidently the result of infantile paralysis.

Imperfectly formed or proportioned lower limbs were not unknown in early Israel (Lev. 21:18); such deformities disqualified a man from serving in the priesthood. During the early monarchy there were numerous lame people among the Jebusite population of Jerusalem (see JEBUS), though precise information is lacking (2 Sam. 5:6, 8). Allusions to lameness were incorporated into the lore of the Hebrew sages, who formulated a saying to the effect that a proverb in the mouth of a fool was similar to the legs of a lame man (Prov. 26:7). By this they implied that only the wise could use a proverb properly, and thus when employed by a fool it was as useless as the legs of a cripple. Quite apart from congenital conditions, in any people doubtless became lame through accidents. Such was the case with MEPHIBOSHETH, the son of JONATHAN (2 Sam. 4:4; cf. 19:24).

Christ healed many lame persons (Matt. 15:30; 21:14), though the precise nature of the various conditions cannot be determined. More carefully described was the healing involved when PETER and JOHN were confronted by a congenital cripple at the BEAUTIFUL GATE (Acts 3:2–8). Luke used the medical terms *basis* G1000, "foot," and *sphydron* G5383, "ankles," in describing a weakness of the bones of the foot. While the exact nature of the pathology is unknown, it may have been a form of cyllosis or it could have resulted from a lesion of the spinal cord. Luke recorded the healing of another congenital cripple at LYSTRA by PAUL (Acts 14:8). Although this man had never walked, it is uncertain as to whether there was either malformation or atrophy present, since he was able to stand upright and walk when instructed to do so. See also DISEASE. R. K. HARRISON

Lamech lay'mik (לֶמֶךְ H4347, possibly "strong man"; Λάμεχ G3285). (**1**) Son of METHUSHAEL and descendant of CAIN; the first polygamist (Gen. 4:18–24). Lamech was married to ADAH and ZILLAH. By Adah he produced JABAL, the first tent dweller and herder, and JUBAL, who invented the harp and flute, indicative of leisure time. By Zillah he begat TUBAL-CAIN, the first artificer in metals, and a daughter, NAAMAH. Lamech's poem in Gen. 4:23–24 is an example of early HEBREW POETRY, with perfect parallelism. There are at least two interpretations of the poem: (a) one is historical, that is, Lamech had committed murder, and in remorse and self-justification he excused his crime as self-defense; (b) the other views the statements as anticipatory, that is, a threat of what Lamech could do, since his son, Tubal-Cain, had invented the sword. Cain could be avenged sevenfold, but with the sword Lamech could exact seventy-seven times (going beyond the LEX TALIONIS that limited vengeance to exact equivalents). In either case Lamech, drunk with self-confidence and self sufficiency, was not willing to wait for God's justice to operate. He did not trust in God, but rather his weapons became his gods—a phenomenon paralleled in Mesopotamian religion. The poem has been called an expression of titanic arrogance (KD, *Genesis*, 119). In Lamech, Cain's trend toward obstinate estrangement from God reached its climax.

(**2**) Son of METHUSELAH, descendant of SETH, and father of NOAH (Gen. 5:25–31; 1 Chr. 1:3; Lk. 3:36). This Lamech, weary because of the toil spent on the unfruitful land, expected the birth of his son (Noah) to remove the curse of ADAM (Gen. 5:29; cf. 3:17–19). As the son of Methuselah, he was in the godly line of Seth. The Qumran GENESIS APOCRYPHON also points this out. Since the number ten represented completion or conclusion, Lamech hoped that the tenth generation from Adam would bring fulfillment of the Edenic promise. He had lived 182 years when Noah was born, and died at the age of 777. (See G. Vos, *Biblical Theology: Old and New Testament* [1959], 57–59.)

According to some critics, the Cainite Lamech of Gen. 4 and the Sethite Lamech of ch. 5 were originally identical, with the two genealogies coming from one common legend or source. The alleged J document (ch. 4) preserved one variant list, and the P document (ch. 5) preserved another. However, the differences of spelling and order of names are as striking as the similarities (note the objections to this theory in J. P. Lange, *Genesis* [1882], 261). A. K. HELMBOLD

lamed lah´mid (לָמֶד, traditionally "ox-goad"). Also *lamedh*. The twelfth letter of the Hebrew alphabet (ל), with a numerical value of thirty. It is possibly named for the shape of the letter, which in its older form resembled a pointed stick. Its pronunciation corresponds approximately to that of English *l*.

lamentation. See MOURNING.

Lamentations, Book of. The third book among the five MEGILLOTH (Scrolls) in the Hebrew Bible; found after Jeremiah in English Bibles. (JOSEPHUS, in *Contra Apionem* 1.8, gives evidence of a twenty-two rather than twenty-four book CANON, apparently including Ruth with Judges, and Lamentations with Jeremiah.) Its title in Hebrew is taken from the first word in the book, *ʾêkâ H377* ("How!") and may express a deep sense of lament over the tragic reversal of events. In the SEPTUAGINT, the title is *Thrēnoi*, "funeral songs, dirges, laments," reflecting the Hebrew term *qînôt* (pl. of *qînâ H7806*), which is also used as a title for this book in the rabbinic writings. This Hebrew word designates a formal composition of grief that could be taught (Jer. 9:20), or written (2 Chr. 35:25), and that arose from tragic misfortune (2 Sam. 1:17–27; Amos 5:1). Later versions enlarged the title to "The Lamentations of Jeremiah."

   I. Background
  II. Unity
 III. Author and date
 IV. Style
  V. Form
 VI. Purpose and theology
VII. Content

I. Background. The destruction of JERUSALEM by NEBUCHADNEZZAR in 586 B.C. is the historical background for all five poems in the book. Although Lamentations offers no direct historical references—the only proper name is EDOM, Lam. 4:22—N. K. Gottwald (in *IDB*, 3:62) observed the following substantial and convincing correlations between Lamentations and the accounts of the last days of Judah found in Kings and Jeremiah: siege (2 Ki. 25:1–2; Lam. 2:22; 3:5, 7), famine (2 Ki. 25:3; Jer. 37:21; Lam. 1:11, 19; 2:11–12, 19–20; 4:4–5, 9–10), flight of the king (2 Ki. 25:4–7; Lam. 1:3, 6; 2:2; 4:19–20), looting of the temple (2 Ki. 25:13–15; Lam. 1:10; 2:6–7), burning of the temple, palace, and important buildings (2 Ki. 25:8, 9; Lam. 2:3–5; 4:11; 5:18), demolition of the city walls (2 Ki. 25:10; Lam. 2:7–9), slaughter of the leaders (2 Ki. 25:18–21; Jer. 39:6; Lam. 1:15, 2:2, 20, 4:16), exile of the inhabitants (2 Ki. 25:11–12; Lam. 1:1, 4–5, 18; 2:9, 14; 3:2, 19; 4:22; 5:2), expectation and collapse of foreign help (Jer. 27:1–11; 37:5–10; Lam. 4:17; 5:6), Judah's fickle political allies (2 Ki. 24:2; Jer. 40:14; Lam. 1:2, 8, 17, 19), and the provincial status of Judah (2 Ki. 25:22–25; Lam. 1:1; 5:8–9).

II. Unity. The usual critical view is that three or more authors over a period of perhaps two centuries produced these elegies (cf. R. H. Pfeiffer, *Introduction of the Old Testament* [1948], 723). But Gottwald argued for the book's unity thus: "… the affinities, linguistic and ideological, are considerable. Diversities within the same poem as great as those between poems can be singled out, and yet few would ignore the acrostic unity of each of the poems and argue for composite authorship for any one chapter. Several literary types and images have been freely appropriated but not wholly assimilated, yet a single mood pervades the collection. All the poems are rooted in the same historical era — i.e., the period of the Palestinian 'exile' (586–538 B.C.). Probably the first four poems, and possibly all five, come from the same poet" (*IDB*, 3:62).

III. Author and date. Most scholars argue that the dramatic descriptions of the horrors of the siege were written by an eyewitness of those dreadful events, but someone who did not see the rebuilding of the second temple (538 B.C.). Now if the book is a unity, it follows that its author wrote these poems between 586 and 538. The traditional author is JEREMIAH. The LXX begins with the following introductory words: "And it came to pass, after Israel was led into captivity and Jerusalem laid waste, that Jeremiah sat weeping and lamented with this lamentation over Jerusalem and said …"; subsequently the VULGATE added the qualifications, "with a bitter spirit sighing and wailing." This tradition was followed also by the TALMUD, the TARGUM (at Jer. 1:1), the Old Latin, and the Syriac version (see VERSIONS OF THE BIBLE, ANCIENT).

Against this tradition, N. K. Gottwald offered these objections: "One wonders if so adamant a prophet could have closely and sympathetically identified himself with the city's reliance on foreign help and facile trust in the king [Lam. 4:16, 19]. It is difficult to imagine the prophet, who remained in Palestine only a few weeks after Jerusalem's capture, writing the fifth poem, with its ennui and lassitude induced by years of foreign occupation. It is unlikely that Jeremiah, who in the whole of his identified writings never resorts to extensive poetic formalities, should have undertaken the construction of acrostic poems. And finally, if the poems are by the prophet, it is difficult to know why they were not included in the Book of Jeremiah, especially when we consider how many oracles of much later origin have been collected under his name" (*IDB*, 3:62).

Yet according to 2 Chr. 35:25, Jeremiah uttered laments for JOSIAH's death, demonstrating that the prophet did compose this type of literature. Moreover, Gottwald acknowledged that in addition to figures common to both books, appeal can be made to the large amount of Jeremianic diction (cf. M. Löhr, "Der Sprachgebrauch des Buches der Klagelieder," *ZAW* 14 [1894]: 36–37). Finally, many scholars recognize that the "I" in Lam. 3 represents Jeremiah; for example, Gottwald himself said: "The speaker in vv. 48–51 is none other than Jeremiah (cf. Jer. 7:16; 11:14; 14:11, 17; 15:11)" (*Studies in the Book of Lamentations* [1954], 38). J. Köberle maintained that the third poem represents the appropriation of Jeremianic religious individualism by a later age. The poet desired, in Köberle's opinion, to speak *e persona Jeremiae* (Gottwald, *Studies*, 39–40). The objections against Jeremianic authorship do not seem sufficient to lead to Gottwald's conclusion that an anonymous author chose Jeremiah to deliver a kind of penitential sermon in the first person. If the "I" of Lam. 3 is Jeremiah and the book is a unity, it seems more desirable to conclude that the unanimous traditional view probably is founded in fact. Finally, as S. R. Driver has remarked, the same sensitive temper, profoundly sympathetic in national sorrow and ready to pour forth its emotions unrestrainedly, manifests itself both in Lamentations and Jeremiah (*An Introduction to the Literature of the Old Testament* [1912], 462; see further W. W. Cannon, "The Authorship of Lamentations," *BSac* 81 [1924]: 42–58).

IV. Style. The first four poems are ACROSTIC; that is, the stanzas begin with the twenty-two letters of the Hebrew ALPHABET in succession. The first three poems have three lines to a stanza (except for four lines in Lam. 1:7; 2:19), whereas the fourth

In this artistic depiction (from Nimrud, c. 728 B.C.), captives deported by Tiglath-Pileser III are sitting in a cart drawn by an ox. The later Babylonian deportation of Jerusalem's residents, deplored in the book of Lamentations, would have had a similar appearance.

poem has but two lines to a stanza. In ch. 3, the central poem, each line begins with the appropriate letter (thus there are three *aleph* lines, three *beth* lines, etc.). The final poem is not acrostic, but it too contains twenty-two lines. Concerning the exceptions to this arrangement (e.g., the transposition of ʿ*ayin* and *peh* in chs. 2–4), Gottwald observed: "Like a great cathedral, its unity is broken in innumerable pleasing ways, never distracting but always contributing to the total impression" (*Studies*, 23).

The apparent contradiction between this artificial literary form and spontaneity of emotion can be harmonized by understanding the purpose of the acrostic construction. De Wette, Keil, and others suggested that it furnished a form for exhaustive completeness to the lamentation. Gottwald quoted A. Jeremias thus: "When a person says the alphabet, he has thereby embraced all possibilities of words" (cf. *Studies*, 29). By proceeding from *aleph* to *taw*, the author achieved an emotional catharsis, a complete statement of grief and a complete cleansing of conscience through a total confession of sin. Second, it obviously aided the memory. Finally, the acrostic enforced the most judicious economy upon the poet. The poet's self-imposed restraint led to the obvious compactness and concentration of emotion.

The acrostic is combined with the clipped *Qinah* metre 3 + 2 (with ample exceptions 2 + 2, 2 + 3, and 3 + 3). The two together leave the impression of deep feeling that is disciplined and restrained. The fifth poem is chiefly 3 + 3.

V. Form. As to literary form, the poems are composite. The setting in life is that of communal lament. Moreover, these poems exhibit common motifs with communal lament psalms: (1) direct address to Yahweh, (2) assigning Yahweh responsibility for the national calamity and the resulting humiliation, (3) a motivation, appealing to Yahweh to act, and (4) a supplication, addressing Yahweh in the imperative. To achieve his purpose, the author draws upon motifs from other types of literature as well, particularly the funeral song and the individual lament.

According to an article by H. Jahnow, "The Scheme of Reversal is the dominant element in the funeral song." Gottwald summarized this article thus: "Jahnow observes that in the funeral song there are two basic themes. One is praise and the other is lament. Encomiums of the dead consistently emphasize certain features of the *past* glory of the deceased: his bodily excellence (Lam. 4.7, cf. Isa. 52.14; 53.2), his splendorous garments, the number of his wives and children, his riches and luxuries (Lam. 4.5; Ezek. 27.3ff.). ... Laments, on the other hand, bewail the sad state of the present: ... the abandonment and defenselessness of the survivors (Lam. 1.1), the manner of death especially if unnatural (Jer. 38.22; II Sam 3.33f; Lam. 1.19f.; 2.11, 21; 4.5), the infamy of such a death (II Sam 3.33f.), and the malicious joy of the enemy (II Sam 1.20 [Lam. 2.15, 16]). Far from being unrelated elements, the motifs of praise and lament were frequently placed in a definite scheme which Jahnow calls, 'das Schema "Einst und Jetzt,"' i.e., *the then* and *the now*. By this means the starkest instances of past glory are deliberately contrasted with the most glaring examples of present misery and degradation. The effectiveness of both is doubled by their incongruity" (*Studies*, 53–54).

The motif as it appears in Lamentations is very complex. There is the primary and fundamental contrast between the former glory of Zion and her present ignominy, but there are variations of the theme. First, the central subject of the lament is not dead. Second, the contrast is between the expected future of Israel and the expected future of the nations. Gottwald referred to this latter variation as "the tragic reversal in reverse" (ibid., 55, 60). He concluded: "it is not overestimating the centrality of the category of tragic reversal to assert that nearly all of the other motifs are only related to it in one way or another, but that they actually find their mode of expression in its framework" (ibid., 61–62).

M. Löhr pointed out that two individual laments are found in Lam. 3:1–24 and 3:52–66 and are interrupted by a long passage in which Jeremiah is presented as the counselor of submissions and hope. In the lament psalms Jeremiah functions as the archetypal sufferer (M. Löhr, "Threni III. und die jeremianische Autorschaft des Buches der Klagelieder," *ZAW* 24 [1904]: 1–6). According to Gottwald, the author is not thinking in terms of an individual at all but is simply giving expression to the corporate personality. He said: "Jeremiah is the individual sufferer without equal, but by virtue of his representative position as the great prophet. ... He is Israel" (*Studies*, 40). C. Westermann (*Praise of God in the Psalms* [1965], 52–60) classified the fifth poem as a lament of the people manifesting the typical introductory address, lament, confession of trust, and petition.

VI. Purpose and theology. For H. Wiesmann, the chief task of the poem is to effect a development and improvement in human conduct in the face of suffering. Wiesmann sees various types of suffering: expiatory suffering, conversion suffering, purifying suffering, humbling suffering, and serviceable suffering ("Das Leid im Buche der Klagelieder," *Zeitschrift für Aszese und Mystik* 4 [1929]: 109). For Gottwald the situational key to the theology of lamentations is the tension between Deuteronomic faith and historic adversity. The Deuteronomist doctrine of retribution and reward is clear and simple: if the people of Israel obey the law of God and do his will, they will enjoy peace and blessing; if, on the other hand, they fail to keep God's commandments and laws, they will be visited by curses and misfortunes. But, according to Gottwald, the historical reality is that Judah suffered defeat after the Josianic reformation.

Yet Gottwald's thesis should be rejected, because this tension cannot be sustained in the book itself. On the contrary, the poet insists that it is precisely *because of* the people's sins that they have been struck by God's judgment (Lam. 1:5, 8–9, et passim). In reality he is in complete harmony with the theology of the Deuteronomist.

For B. Albrektson (*Studies in the Text and Theology of the Book of Lamentations* [1963]) the source of tension lies in the Zion traditions concerning the inviolability of Zion (Pss. 46:6–8; 48:2–9; 76:2–7), a doctrine familiar to the author (Lam. 2:15; 4:12; cf. also Lam. 5:19 with Ps. 48:2; and the reference to Elyon in Ps. 66:5 and Lam. 3:35, and the prophetic threats in Deut. 28). In fact, Albrektson convincingly demonstrated that the author consciously alluded to these visitations depicted in Deut. 28 as the wages of sin (cf. Lam. 1:3 with Deut. 28:58; Lam. 1:6 with Deut. 28:14, 44; Lam. 1:6 with Deut. 28:41; Lam. 1:9 with Deut. 28:43; Lam. 2:20 and 4:10 with Deut. 28:53; Lam. 3:14 and 45 with Deut. 28:37; Lam. 4:16 and 5:12 with Deut. 28:50).

(Significantly, he argues here that Deut. 28 is older than Lamentations and cannot have been written as *vaticinia ex eventu*.) But the same objection must be raised against his thesis as against Gottwald's: the text does not exhibit this fabricated tension.

In addition to providing the people with an emotional catharsis through an exhaustive expression of grief and confession, the author was also determined to inculcate an attitude of submission and a prospect of hope. Gottwald said: "By intimately binding together the themes of sin, suffering, submission and hope, he intended to implant the conviction of trust and confidence in the goodness and imminent intervention of Yahweh. That this is the case is evident in the third poem where the acrostic form is intensified at precisely the point where hope becomes the strongest" (*Studies*, 30). Christian interpretation has rightly seen in these poems an apt expression of Christ's lament when God vented his wrath on him as he was made the sin of the world.

VII. Content. The primary points of the poems are these: Jerusalem's lamentable state (Lam. 1); God's wrath against the city (ch. 2); God's faithfulness acknowledged (ch. 3); God's faithfulness seen in discipline (ch. 4); God's faithfulness trusted (ch. 5).

(Important commentaries include H.-J. Kraus, *Klagelieder (Threni)*, BKAT 20, 3rd ed. [1968]; N. Habel, *Jeremiah, Lamentations* [1968]; R. Gordis, *The Song of Songs and Lamentations: A Study, Modern Translation and Commentary*, rev. ed. [1974]; D. R. Hillers, *Lamentations*, AB 7A, 2nd ed. [1992]; F. B. Huey, Jr., *Jeremiah, Lamentations*, NAC 16 [1993]; U. Berges, *Klagelieder*, HTKAT [2002]; A. Berlin, *Lamentations: A Commentary*, OTL [2002]; D. Bergant, *Lamentations* [2003]; D. A. Garrett and P. R. House, *Song of Songs, Lamentations*, WBC 23B [2004]. See also C. Westermann, *Lamentations: Issues and Interpretation* [1994]; J. Hunter, *Faces of a Lamenting City: The Development and Coherence of the Book of Lamentations* [1996]; T. Linafelt, *Surviving Lamentations: Catastrophe, Lament, and Protest in the Afterlife of a Biblical Book* [2000]; E. Boase, *The Fulfillment of Doom?* [2006]; and the bibliography compiled by W. E. Mills, *Jeremiah–Lamentations* [2002].)

B. K. WALTKE

LAMP

lamp. The common household lamp is never described in the Bible, although the twisted flax wick is mentioned (Isa. 42:3), and so is olive OIL as fuel (Exod. 25:6; 27:20; Matt. 25:3–4). Palestinian tombs and excavations of towns, however, have provided innumerable lamps from the time of ABRAHAM onward, so that the archaeologist can carefully trace the development of lamp forms. While Scripture alludes to their common daily use (e.g., Prov. 31:18; Jer. 25:10), lamps also are mentioned with rich symbolical meaning.

Lamps found in Palestine from the OT period were made almost entirely of POTTERY. In some cases certain features indicate that metal prototypes were copied. In the Late Chalcolithic and Early Bronze Ages (3300–2100 B.C.) shallow round-based bowls for holding the oil seem—judging from marks of wicks burning on the rims—to have been used as lamps. Probably the incoming AMORITE tribesmen c. 2000 (Middle Bronze I) introduced the first true lamps; these are invariably fourspouted (i.e., the rim is pinched in four places to form wide lips for holding wicks). From c. 1850 onward, the ordinary lamp had a single lip. This became increasingly pinched together.

When the Israelites entered the Promised Land, they simply copied the Canaanite lamp shapes for many centuries. In the time of the prophets, potters in Judah added a base to make the lamp more stable. While the lip became more elongated, through the Persian period the lamp remained an open vessel, always with the danger of the oil slopping over when carried.

Imported Greek lamps were so practical, however, that in the Hellenistic age local potters soon switched from the open saucer lamp to the wheel-made lamp, with a central filling hole in the top of the round, enclosed body, to which a long projecting nozzle was attached. In the Roman period, the so-called Herodian lamp became popular in Jerusalem and the hill country, simple and small with round body and a short, flaring nozzle. Undoubtedly Jesus had this style in mind in his parable of the woman who lighted a lamp (Lk. 15:8; Gk. *lychnos G3394*) to search for her lost coin, and in the parable of the ten virgins who were awakened at midnight and arose to trim their lamps (Matt. 25:7; Gk. *lampas G3286*), that is, adjust the wicks.

Herodian oil lamps discovered at Masada.

The form of the individual lamps (Exod. 25:37; Heb. *nēr H5944*) on the golden lampstand (*měnôrâ H4963*, see CANDLESTICK) in the TABERNACLE is suggested by a correct understanding of Zech. 4:2. The envisioned gold lampstand consists of a large bowl, elevated on a stand, with seven lamps, each having seven spouts or channels (NRSV, "lips"; Heb. *mûṣāqâ H4609*), arranged around its broad rim. Such seven-lipped lamps have been found in tombs and house ruins at many Iron I and Iron II sites in Palestine, so that the style was enjoyed by commoners as well as in the sanctuary. Lamps of this type seem to have originated around Ras Shamra in Syria (see UGARIT), where they have been excavated from the Middle Bronze level. It can no longer be held that the concept of a seven-fold light source was a priestly invention of the 5th cent. B.C.

In practice, the ordinary lamp in OT times held enough oil to burn through the night, but the wick had to be adjusted every few hours as it burned down. Hence, the virtuous housewife (Prov. 31:18) needed to arise once or twice during the night to trim her lamp lest it go out and there be no pilot flame to light her fire in the morning. Lamps probably were placed in concave niches in the walls of houses, as they were in walls of tombs and of water tunnels. If lampstands were used (cf. Matt. 5:15; Lk. 8:16; 11:33; KJV, "candlestick"), they were probably made of wood, for ceramic and metal stands have been found only in ruins of shrines. (Candles were unknown in Bible times; hence every KJV use of "candle" or "candlestick" refers to a lamp or lampstand.)

In 2 Ki. 4:10, the *mûṣāqâ H4609* probably refers to a pottery lamp of a different style from the common *nēr*. It may have been the "cup-and-saucer" lamp, a high cup in the center of a small bowl, all made in one piece by the potter (see R. H. Smith in *BA* 27 [1964]: 14–17). More likely it was a pedestal lamp, a seven-spouted lamp on a terracotta pedestal in the form of a stylized tree, having religious significance and thus suitable for a "holy man of God" (ibid., 23–24).

Lamps in OT times were not adapted for night travel. Therefore the TORCH was used whenever light was needed, as in GIDEON's attack on the Midianite camp (Jdg. 7:16, 20; Heb. *lappid* H4365). The well-known verse "Your word is a lamp to my feet / and a light for my path" (Ps. 119:105) may depict two images, a lamplight for one's walk in his home, and a torchlight for his journey out-of-doors. By NT times actual lanterns (*phanos* G5749) as well as torches were available for the temple police going to arrest Jesus (Jn. 18:3; see R. H. Smith in *BA* 29 [1966]: 6–7).

Since ANE peoples feared darkness, the presence of a burning lamp with its light symbolized abundant life, joy, and peace (Ps. 18:28); whereas the extinguishing of the lamp suggested dying and utter gloom and desolation (2 Sam. 21:17; Job 18:5–6; 21:17; Prov. 13:9; 20:20; 24:20). The lamp of the wicked will go out because it lacks the true life-giving illumination of God (Smith in *BA* 27:21). Because the ancient considered his life to be continued through his offspring, his "light" was not put out if he had a son. The lamp also symbolized posterity (1 Ki. 11:36; 15:4; 2 Ki. 8:19). Placing lighted lamps in tombs was a symbolic act signifying belief in, and hope for, life after death.   J. REA

lampstand. See CANDLESTICK.

lance. See ARMOR, ARMS.

Land, Holy. See PALESTINE.

land, redemption of. See REDEMPTION.

land, theology of. The pervasive biblical concept of land is rooted in both CREATION and REDEMPTION. Because God is the creator of the world the whole belongs to him (Gen 14:24; Pss. 24:1; 89:11; et al.). The word *land* and related terms refer not only to the world, to countries, to regions, and to "turf," but in many instances to much more than the physical world.

Of primary concern is the fact that *land* is where God placed his creatures to live. "The LORD God took the man and put him in the Garden of Eden to work it and take care of it" (Gen. 2:15). See EDEN, GARDEN OF. This passage is generally interpreted to mean that "work" was part of the intended creative order of God, and that humans are to be good—ecologically aware—stewards of God's creation. While these ideas may be true, some have argued persuasively that a correct reading of this verse should be, "the LORD God took man and put him in the Garden of Eden to worship and obey" (J. Sailhamer in *EBC*, 1:44–48, following U. Cassuto). Humans were "placed" in the place that he had prepared for them, namely "Eden," for rest and safety, and as a sacrifice is placed by God's altar, to live their lives in God's presence. This verse also answers the question as to why humans were created: to live their lives in the presence of their Creator "worshiping and obeying" him.

When ADAM and EVE sinned, they were removed from the presence of the Holy Creator, from the idyllic "restful" environment of Eden. Genesis 3–11 describes in vivid detail the results of the FALL and life outside of "the land of Eden" (Cain and Abel, Lamech, the sons of God and the daughters of men, the flood, and the Tower of Babel incident). The words spoken to ABRAHAM, ISAAC, and JACOB form the foundational promise of God to humanity as to how Edenic conditions will be restored (see W. C. Kaiser, Jr., *Toward an Old Testament Theology* [1978], 88). The new people of God will descend from Abraham, and they will be empowered (= "blessed") to live their lives in God's presence in the land (Canaan; Gen. 12:7; 13:15, 17; 15:7–8; 17:8; et al.) that God will give them. This received community will be administered by God's regent (king; 17:6, 16; 35:11), and ultimately, selected people from all nations will join this community (12:3; 18:18; 22:17–18; et al).

After living in Egypt for over 400 years, God delivered the descendants of Abraham, Isaac, and Jacob from bondage in fulfillment of his promises. The goal of this deliverance was to establish them as a worshiping obedient community in the Land of Canaan (Exod. 6:1–9). Note especially that God was leading them to his holy habitation, to plant them in the mountain of his inheritance, the place of his dwelling, his sanctuary (15:13, 17). In other words, they were being led back to "Eden" where they could live their lives in worshipful obedience to God (Gen. 2:15). Thus life in the Land of Canaan is much more than mere human socio-economic relationships—it has to do with God's intended destiny for his people.

As the exodus progresses, God's presence fills the TABERNACLE (Exod. 40) in fulfillment of his promise to dwell in the tents of SHEM (Gen. 9:27), and then he leads his people in procession to the place where he will "put" them (i.e., cause them to "rest," a possible rendering of the hiphil of *nûaḥ* H5663 Gen. 2:15) and where he will dwell in their midst (Deut. 12). Viewed in this light, the legislation given at Mount SINAI provided the framework as to how God's people are to live obedient worshipful lives in his presence (in fulfillment of the true destiny of humanity). The biblical writers call this intended idyllic state "rest," and this was the goal of the conquest and settlement of Canaan as described in the books of Joshua and Judges (e.g., Josh. 1:13, 15; 22:4; 23:1; et al.).

Throughout the history of God's people, the foundational intention (Gen. 2:15) and the redemptive promise were always available for fulfillment as they lived in the land. Notice one of the progressive climaxes as God comes to "dwell" in the TEMPLE SOLOMON had built (1 Ki. 8). However, God's people failed to live their lives in grateful obedience, and the prophets were continually calling the people back to avoid punishment (Deut. 28) and to fulfill their destiny by truly obeying and worshiping God (e.g., Isa. 1 and Jer. 7). Because of continuing disobedience, God removed himself from their presence (Ezek. 9–11); then the covenant curses fell as the Babylonians devastated the land, destroyed Jerusalem, and carried many people into exile.

Prophets before, during, and after the physical exile wrote about a glorious day ahead when God and his people would return to the land to live in the idyllic conditions that would be established at that time (Ezek. 43; Isa. 40). They even prophesied that the Gentiles would experience blessing (empowerment) to worship and obey the true and living God (e.g., Isa. 2:1–5; 56). N. T. Wright has shown that during the time between the Testaments many Jews, even though physically living in the land, still thought of themselves as being in exile—for the glorious future described by the prophets had not developed (*Christian Origins and the Question of God. Vol. 1: The New Testament and the People of God* [1992], 268–69). Indeed, even though they were living in "the land," they were under foreign domination.

With the coming of Jesus as God incarnate, and thus the inauguration of the new age, it is evident that the promises with regard to the land, Jerusalem, the temple, and Israel find their fulfillment in him. Jesus is the "seed" that had been promised to the patriarchs and to David (Rom. 4, Gal. 3:16). In addition, those called by him and living in covenantal faithfulness are in another sense the "numerous seed" (descendants) promised to Abraham and are the true people of God who are called to bring blessings to the Gentiles (Rom. 4; Gal 3:7–9, 14, 29).

Not only was Jesus "God in the flesh," but his church (1 Cor. 3:16) and his followers (6:19) now exhibit his presence here on earth. Thus living "in Christ" now replaces the idea of living "in the land." This is no "mere" spiritualization of any of the promises, but is in fact a heightened fulfillment of them. For God's people, the call is the same as that to Adam and Eve in the garden (Gen. 2:15), and to Israel in Canaan—that is, to fulfill their God-appointed destiny by living their lives in his presence with true heartfelt worship and obedience.

Thus, just as the "seed" and "blessing" have been universalized, so too has "life in the land" been transposed to a higher and more intensive level. The believer's calling is thus to enjoy "life in the land," the "rest," and the city ("Jerusalem") that our spiritual ancestors were seeking on their earthly pilgrimage (Heb. 11:8–16; 12:22). The climax to the biblical idea of *land* is for God's people to ultimately return to "Edenic land conditions," but in a city—the new Jerusalem where God's people will dwell with him in blissful worship and obedience (Rev. 21–22).

(See further N. C. Habel, *The Land is Mine: Six Biblical Land Ideologies* [1995]; P. S. Johnston and P. W. L. Walker, eds., *The Land of Promise: Biblical, Theological and Contemporary Perspectives* [2000];

W. Brueggemann, *The Land: Place as Gift, Promise, and Challenge in Biblical Faith* [2002]; K. J. Wenell, *Jesus and Land: Sacred and Social Space in Second Temple Judaism* [2007].) C. G. RASMUSSEN

land crocodile. See LIZARD.

land laws. See LAW (OT) VI.

landmark. This English term is used by the KJV and other versions to render Hebrew *gĕbûl* H1473 ("boundary") when this term refers to an inscribed stone on which the boundaries of fields, districts, and nations were defined (cf. the heap and pillar set up by LABAN, Gen. 31:51–52). To remove a landmark was a serious offense. In Babylonia it was a crime, and it was forbidden in Egypt, Greece, and Rome. The law of Moses warns against the removal of landmarks (Deut. 19:14; 27:17; NIV, "boundary stone"). The removal of landmarks also is used in Scripture symbolically of overturning ancient customs or laws (Prov. 22:28; 23:10; cf. Job 24:2 [*gĕbûlâ* H1474]). S. BARABAS

languages of the Ancient Near East. Those languages of the Ancient Near East that have left behind many documents on clay, stone, PAPYRUS, or even PARCHMENT are fairly few in number and are for the most part well known. There were dozens of other languages and dialects spoken by the various nationalities and tribes of this region that left virtually no INSCRIPTIONS which have survived to our times, and whose existence is known either from references to them in extant literature or from archaeological recovery of their artifacts. In many cases all that have survived are a few of their personal names or the names of their gods, from which some elements of their language may be deduced. (For a general survey with useful bibliography, see J. Kaltner and S. L. McKenzie, eds., *Beyond Babel: A Handbook for Biblical Hebrew and Related Languages* [2002].)

I. The most ancient literary languages

A. Sumerian. The earliest pictographic inscriptions of Sumerian were found in clay tablets from about 3200 B.C. (see SUMER). It was characterized by a fairly rigid word order, in which the adjective always followed its noun rather than preceding it, and the verb tended to come at the end of its clause just as consistently as in classical Latin. Nouns were "inflected" by means of postpositions (equivalent to prepositions), and verbs were modified as to tense, aspect, pronoun subjects, and objects by prefixed or postfixed consonants or monosyllabic elements.

The pictographs, which later developed into CUNEIFORM equivalents, served not only as ideograms (i.e., a single sign conveying the entire word), but also as phonetic syllables available for sounding out other words having no relation in sense to the original pictograph (see WRITING). Thus the sign for a human mouth not only signified *KA* as the word for "mouth" itself, but also to spell out the cluster *Urimaka* (i.e., *Urim.ak.a*, "of Ur," followed by the *a* pointing to the subject of the verb). Other signs were used as determinatives (i.e., indicators of the class to which the noun belonged, whether a country, a city, a god, a man, or an animal) without having any phonetic value at all. This system of writing was adaptable to other languages besides Sumerian, since it provided a syllabary capable of sounding out the words of, for example, Akkadian, Hittite, or Hurrian (see below).

The younger nations that fell under the cultural influence of Sumerian tended to adopt its entire syllabic system, although adding new sound values to the characters in accord with the same rebus principle that Sumerian itself had followed. Furthermore, a great many of the Sumerian words written in one or two signs were preserved in these other languages unchanged, even though they were read aloud in the equivalent words from those languages. For example, the Sumerian sign for "king" was pronounced *lugal* (literally "great man"); but if used in an Akkadian inscription, it was pronounced *šarrum*. Likewise in Hittite the Sumerian sign for "man" (*lu*) was copied out to express the idea of "man," but it was undoubtedly pronounced *antuḫšaš*, the actual Hittite word for "man."

Sumerian was for the most part written in the *Eme-ku* dialect, but there was also a later dialect known as *Eme-sal*, which apparently was spoken particularly by women; it is not found in documents earlier than the 18th cent. B.C. (See further A. Falkenstein, *Das Sumerische* [1959]; M.-L. Thomsen,

This cuneiform tablet lists numerous foreign names with their Akkadian equivalents.

The Sumerian Language: An Introduction to Its History and Grammatical Structure, 2nd ed. [1987]; J. L. Hayes, *A Manual of Sumerian Grammar and Texts*, 2nd ed. [2000]; D. O. Edzard, *Sumerian Grammar* [2003].)

B. Egyptian. Traditionally, Egyptian has been considered an ancient representative of the so-called Hamitic languages. The connection between the Hamitic and the Semitic languages, however, has become more clearly understood in recent decades, and modern linguists prefer to use the term Afroasiatic (rather than Hamito-Semitic) and to view that large family as consisting of at least five branches: Egyptian, Semitic, Berber (spoken in N Africa), Cushitic (E Africa), and Chadic (sub-Saharan Africa); possibly also Omotic (SW Ethiopia). (See R. Hetzron, "Afroasiatic Languages," in *The World's Major Languages*, ed. B. Comrie [1990], 645–53; A. Loprieno, "Ancient Egyptian and Other Afroasiatic Languages," in *CANE*, 4:2135–50.)

Documents in Egyptian, the literary language of the ancient Nile Valley, were written in pictographs quite different in appearance from those of lower Mesopotamia, and they operated upon a somewhat different phonetic principle. That is to say, the vowels of the spoken language were virtually omitted from its written form, which uses consonantal units only. Some characters were used acrostically, that is, they were indicated by the initial consonant of the object portrayed by the sign (e.g., from the sign "hand," Egyptian $dr.t$ became the alphabetic value d when this sign was used to spell other words). Others were biconsonantal (thus, the sign for "house," pr, could be used to spell other words that contained the consonants p–r) or even tri-consonantal (like the scarab-beetle, $ḫpr$, which furnished the consonants $ḫ$–p–r to the common verb "become").

Egyptian used many ideograms, as did Sumerian especially in the earliest stage of the language, but, in addition, the use of the determinatives became so extensive that nearly every noun and verb was equipped with at least one of these nonphonetic sense indicators (fortunately for the modern scholars who first deciphered the language). Unlike Sumerian and Akkadian, which used most of their determinatives at the beginning of the word, Egyptian invariably placed them at the end. In morphology and syntax the Egyptian language basically resembled the Semitic languages, in that it retained a tense (the Old Perfective) with sufformatives similar to the perfect tense of NW Semitic and S Semitic and to the so-called permansive of Akkadian. Furthermore, the subject followed the verb, rather than preceding it, except for the pseudoverbal construction (where the subject preceded either a preposition-governed infinitive, or else an Old Perfective).

Egyptian developed a large number of compound verbal "tenses" by the use of various auxiliaries and qualifying particles, some of which indicated past tense or future tense, others of which indicated the action as of central importance, or as consequent upon the action of the preceding clause. Eventually this Middle Kingdom Egyptian gave way to a New Egyptian, which made far greater use of the pseudoverbal construction and employed more signs to spell many of their words. It also made full use of the definite article as early as the 18th dynasty (although this was rather frowned upon in official literary style until the 19th dynasty). By the 1st millennium a still later form of the language, called Demotic, came into use, and this led to Coptic, that form of Egyptian which was spoken in the Greco-Roman period, and written no longer in hieroglyphics or any of its cursive forms (as Hieratic and Demotic were), but in pure alphabetic Greek letters, supplemented by a few

Demotic signs to compensate for Egyptian sounds not present in the Greek alphabet.

Coptic appeared in several different dialects, of which the most important (considered also the most classical form) was Sahidic or Sa'idic, the language of S Egypt, in which the earliest literature and translations of the Bible were composed. From the standpoint of literary remains, the next most important dialect was Bohairic, spoken in N Egypt, the Delta. It eventually became the official language for the ritual of the Coptic Church, and has so remained to this day. In Middle Egypt the prevalent dialects were Akhmimic and Fayumic (called Bashmuric in older scholarship), of which far fewer specimens have survived to our day.

(See further A. H. Gardiner, *Egyptian Grammar*, 3rd ed. [1957]; J. Vergote, *Grammaire copte*, 2 vols. [1973–83]; J. Černý and S. I. Groll, *A Late Egyptian Grammar*, 3rd ed. [1984]; A. Loprieno, *Ancient Egyptian: A Linguistic Introduction* [1995]; J. P. Allen, *Middle Egyptian: An Introduction to the Language and Culture of Hieroglyphs* [1999]; B. Layton, *A Coptic Grammar with Chrestomathy and Glossary: Sahidic Dialect* [2000]; F. Junge, *Late Egyptian Grammar: An Introduction* [2001]; M. A. Murray, *The Ancient Egyptian Language: A Simplified Grammar with Hieroglyphs* [2003].)

II. The Semitic languages. This group of languages, now understood to be a branch of the larger Afroasiatic family (see I.B above), has traditionally been divided into (1) *East Semitic*, consisting of Akkadian, that is, Babylonian and Assyrian (possibly Eblaite as well); (2) *South Semitic*, consisting of Arabic, Ethiopic, and S Arabian; and (3) *Northwest Semitic*, which is further subdivided into Aramaic and Canaanite (the latter comprising Hebrew, Moabite, Phoenician, et al.; many scholars include Ugaritic here as well). Recent specialists, however, tend to view Arabic (N Arabian) as closely related to the NW Semitic family and prefer a classification along the following lines (cf. J. Huehnergard, "Semitic

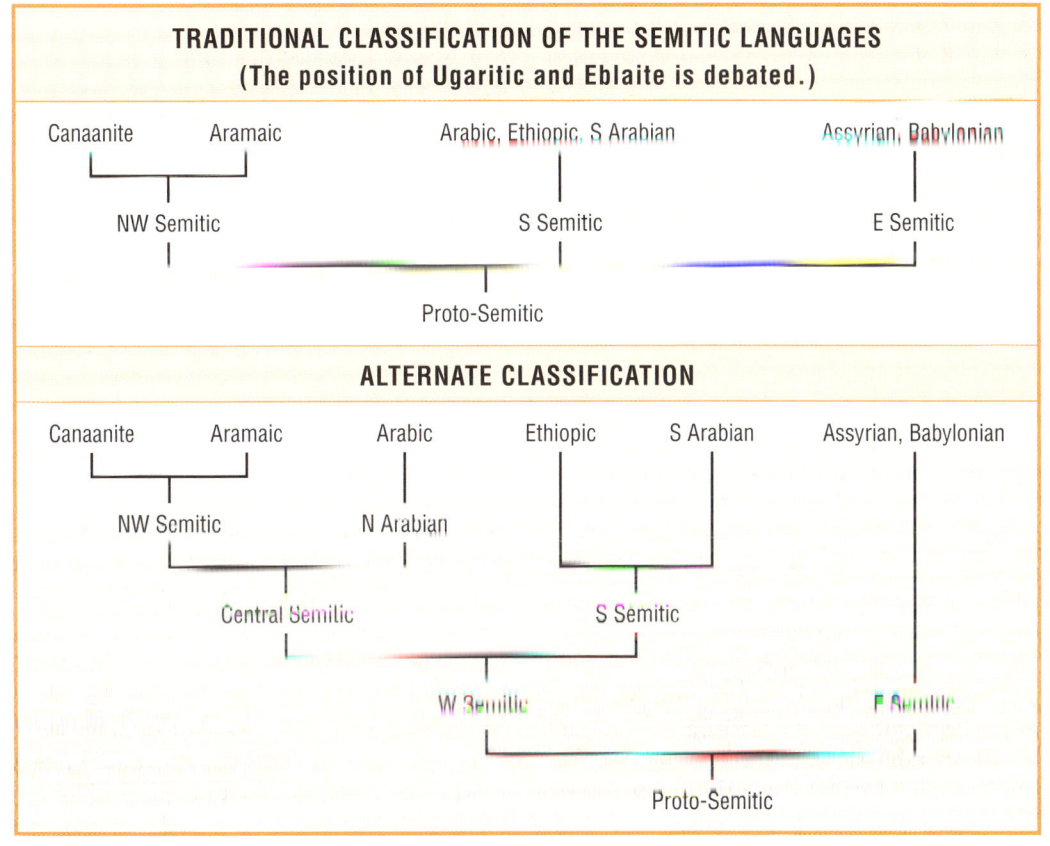

Languages," in *CANE*, 4:2117–34, who however prefers the term Levantine for NW Semitic):

    East Semitic (Akkadian)
    West Semitic
        South Semitic (S Arabian and Ethiopic)
        Central Semitic (N Arabian and NW Semitic)

It should also be noted that R. Hetzron ("Semitic Languages," in *The World's Major Languages*, 654–63) subdivides Central Semitic into S Central and Aramaic, then further subdivides S Central into Arabic and Canaanite. The suggestion that Hebrew may be genetically closer to Arabic than to Aramaic has not been widely accepted, but it does reflect a general dissatisfaction with the traditional analysis, even though no alternate classification has firmly taken hold in modern scholarship. It should also be noted that Eblaite (or Eblaic, the language of EBLA) is considered by some scholars to be an early form of NW Semitic, but a growing number of specialists regard it as E Semitic. (See further J. H. Hospers, *A Basic Bibliography for the Study of the Semitic Languages*, 2 vols. [1973]; J. Huehnergard, ed., *New Directions in the Study of Semitic Languages* [1996]; R. Hetzron, ed., *The Semitic Languages* [1997]; S. Izreʾel, ed., *Semitic Linguistics: The State of the Art at the Turn of the Twenty-first Century* [= *Israel Oriental Studies* 20, 2002].)

A. Akkadian. The earliest stage of this language, known as Old Akkadian, was spoken from about 2500 to 1950 B.C. and is represented by a modest number of documents from Sargon of Agade and various later royal inscriptions. From this stage ensued various Babylonian and Assyrian dialects (see ASSYRIA AND BABYLONIA).

Old Babylonian was spoken between 1950 and 1530 B.C. (cf. W. von Soden, *Grundriss der akkadischen Grammatik*, 2nd ed. [1969], 2) and found its best-known literary expression in the Code of HAMMURABI; but there are several religious texts, many letters, court dockets, contracts, receipt tablets, and other documents in the same dialect. Middle Babylonian was used from 1530 to 1000 in letters, records, royal inscriptions (in Assyria as well as Babylonia, since it was regarded as standard for literary expression), in the TELL EL-AMARNA letters, and at NUZI (in slightly Hurrian cast). New Babylonian included the 1st millennium (von Soden regards the period after 625 as Late Babylonian), and comprised a rather sparse selection of letters and documents until its final florescence under the Chaldean or Neobabylonian Empire (when a simplified form of the script and a loss of inflectional vocalic endings characterized those inscriptions not dominated by the scholarly archaizing style favored in official circles in the Chaldean court).

Old Assyrian (1950–1750 B.C.) is preserved largely in the mercantile letters and records of the Assyrian merchants who did business in CAPPADOCIA. Middle Assyrian (1500–1000) was represented largely by various legal codes and royal inscriptions and a few letters, but much of the official writing was couched in literary Babylonian, as indicated above. New Assyrian or Imperial Assyrian marked the period from 1000 to 600, when the Assyrians by fluctuating stages achieved complete dominance in the ANE and adorned their palaces with bas-reliefs inscribed with their glorious conquests. The inscriptions from this era contain the references to Israel that are of greatest interest to the student of Bible history.

It should be added that even after the fall of the Assyrian and Chaldean empires, the Akkadian language found employment in the Persian and even in the Seleucid period as a scholarly literary medium, usually in such bilingual or polylingual monuments as the BEHISTUN INSCRIPTION (c. 490 B.C.), but with occasional monolingual dedicatory inscriptions as late as the reign of ANTIOCHUS I (281–260 B.C.). (See further E. Reiner, *A Linguistic Analysis of Akkadian* [1966]; R. Caplice, *Introduction to Akkadian* [1988]; A. Ungnad and L. Matouš, *Akkadian Grammar*, trans. H. A. Hoffner, Jr. [1992]; J. Huehnergard, *A Grammar of Akkadian*, 3rd printing [2000].)

B. Arabic. Monuments of the Arabic (N Arabian) dialects begin around the 5th cent. B.C. and continue into the 4th cent. A.D. They are usually divided into Thamudic, Lihyanic, and Safaitic, and are preserved largely in funerary or dedicatory inscriptions. Classical literary Arabic was a northern dialect spoken at Mecca and Medina, and owed its supremacy to its use in the Koran (composed c. A.D. 620–630), which set the standard for the Islamic world from that day until this. It may represent, though only in some respects, the closest approximation to the parent Semitic language from which all the rest were derived. In its vocalized form, Arabic preserves the full inflectional system, complete with all the short-vowel endings for both nouns and verbs, and the full use of the dual number (which remains obligatory for literary Arabic even to this day when two individuals are involved, rather than three or more). Its remarkably rich vocabulary has rendered it the single most important source of information concerning the meaning of rare or disputed words in Hebrew and the other ancient Semitic languages. (See further W. Wright et al., *A Grammar of the Arabic Language*, 2 vols., 3rd ed. [1896]; C. Rabin, *Ancient West-Arabian* [1951]; F. W. Winnett and W. L. Reed, *Ancient Records from North Arabia* [1970]; W. Fischer, *A Grammar of Classical Arabic*, 3rd ed. [2002].)

C. South Arabian. The earliest inscribed monuments in S Arabian date from the 8th cent. B.C. and are found as late as the 6th cent. A.D. They consist of inscriptions on stone stelae, mostly of a dedicatory nature or records of the inauguration of buildings, with an assortment of conveyances of real estate, various laws, and occasional decrees. There were at least four dialects, one of which, the Sabean, used causatives and third person pronouns beginning with *h*- (whereas the rest begin these with *s*-). The other three were the Qatabanian (which preserved the earliest form of the language), Minean, and Ḥaḍramautian. The knowledge of these languages is hampered by their stylistic formalism, and also by their failure to include any verb forms or pronouns in the first or second person; all is couched in the third person singular or plural. It is noteworthy that in contradistinction to N Arabic, the S Arabian dialects preserved both kinds of *s* (cf. Heb. *samek* and *śin*) from Primitive Semitic. (See further W. Leslau, "Ethiopic and South Arabian," in *Linguistics in South West Asia and North Africa, Current Trends in Linguistics* 6, ed. T. A. Sebeok [1970], 467–527; A. F. L. Beeston, *Sabaic Grammar* [1984].)

D. Ethiopic. This language shows some affinity to the Old S Arabian dialects, adopting from them its alphabet. The original speakers of Geʿez, as the classical form of Ethiopic is known, migrated from S Arabia to Cush (now located in the Republic of Sudan) and pushed into northern Ethiopia, founding ultimately the powerful Kingdom of Axum (4th to 7th cent. A.D.) subsequent to smaller kingdoms and principalities such as that referred to in Acts 8:27 ("Candace, queen of the Ethiopians"). The earliest surviving inscriptions date from shortly before the rise of Axum, but the 4th cent. A.D. monuments from that kingdom furnish the first significant body of material in this language. Its phonology adheres quite closely to that of Arabic, except that it seems to have lost the aspirate quality of the *šin* quite early, and it developed two extra *p*'s (*pait* and *pesā*). In the morphology of the verb it lacks several of the stems found in Arabic, but it possesses an additional five stems (causative intensive, causative frequentative, reflexive ground-stem, causative reflexive intensive, and causative reflexive frequentative). It also used a gerundive to which pronoun suffixes were attached, resembling the Akkadian permansive. From ancient Ethiopic or Geʿez (which is still the cultic language of the Ethiopian Coptic Church) were derived Amharic, the official state language of modern Ethiopia, as well as Trigrinya, Tigré, and others. (See further W. Leslau, *Ethiopians Speak: Studies in Cultural Background*, 5 vols. [1965–83]; R. Hetzron, *Ethiopian Semitic: Studies in Classification* [1972]; T. Lambdin, *Introduction to Classical Ethiopic* [1978]; E. Ullendorff, *Ethiopia and the Bible*, rev. ed. [1988]).

E. Aramaic. Old Aramaic inscriptions date from the 9th cent. B.C. (the Zakir or Zakkur Stela from Hamath), although a quotation in Aramaic dates back to patriarchal times (Gen. 31:47). Two 8th-cent. inscriptions from Samʾal (modern Zenjirli) are classed by some as Yaʾudic (cf. S. Moscati: *Comparative Grammar of the Semitic Languages* [1964], 11) because of certain distinctive traits. Imperial Aramaic (in German *Reichsaramäisch*) was used as an official international language as early as the 7th cent. B.C. in the Assyrian Empire, and so continued under the Chaldeans and the Persians. It is basically the form of Aramaic used in portions of Daniel and Ezra, and also by the Jewish colony at Elephantine in the 5th and 4th centuries B.C.

In the last half of the 1st millennium, Aramaic began to divide into W and E branches. In the W branch, Jewish Palestinian Aramaic is represented by the GENESIS APOCRYPHON of the 1st cent. B.C. (found in Qumran Cave One), and by several versions of the TARGUM, some of the Midrashim (see MIDRASH), and the Palestinian TALMUD. Christian Palestinian Aramaic is preserved in an old version of the Gospels. In addition, the Samaritan sect developed some distinctive traits, as shown by its own Targum of the Pentateuch (4th cent. A.D.). In spoken form, W Aramaic survives today in a few villages near DAMASCUS, notably Maʾlula. The NABATEAN Arabs also adopted this dialect and left inscriptions from the 1st cent. B.C. to the 3rd cent. A.D.

Eastern Aramaic developed in EDESSA as the literary medium of Syrian Christians, who produced the Peshitta during the 3rd cent. A.D. and the Syriac Hexaplar and NT versions (Sinaitic and Harklean) as well. See VERSIONS OF THE BIBLE, ANCIENT, III. Outstanding authors in Syriac Christianity included EPHRAEM SYRUS and Bar Hebraeus. Jewish Babylonian Aramaic, as represented in the "Babylonian" Talmud, belongs to this eastern branch as well (5th and 6th cent. A.D.). The same is true of the Gnostic sect of the MANDEANS, who flourished in Mesopotamia from the 3rd to 8th cent. A.D. (For further discussion and bibliography, see ARAMAIC LANGUAGE.)

F. Canaanite. This branch of NW Semitic included several dialects. (1) *North Canaanite* or Ugaritic was used at Ras Shamra in N Syria during the 15th and 14th centuries (see UGARIT). It was written in a cuneiform alphabet of thirty characters, and preserved many more of the original Semitic phonemes than the later dialects did. Its verbal system included not only the seven stems found in Hebrew, but two additional ones as well (its causative was *shaphel* rather than *hiphil*). Many scholars believe that Ugaritic, in spite of its obvious affinities with Hebrew, should be treated not as Canaanite but as a separate NW Semitic language, possibly earlier than the split of this family into Aramaic and Canaanite. (See further C. H. Gordon, *Ugaritic Textbook* [1965]; S. Segert, *A Basic Grammar of the Ugaritic Language* [1984]; W. G. E. Watson and N. Wyatt, eds., *Handbook of Ugaritic Studies* [1999]; J. Tropper, *Ugaritische Grammatik* [2000]; D. Sivan, *A Grammar of the Ugaritic Language*, 2nd impression [2001]; G. del Olmo Lete and J. Sanmartín, *A Dictionary of the Ugaritic Language in the Alphabetic Tradition* [2003].)

(2) *Sinaitic* was used by the miners at Serabit el-Khadim and recorded in wall inscriptions dating between the 18th and 15th centuries B.C. and consisting of at least twenty-seven letters (cf. W. F. Albright, *Proto-Sinaitic Inscriptions and Their Decipherment* [1966], 13). According to Albright, it represents a very early stage of NW Semitic, when it stood much closer to Arabic (ibid., 3), but the matter is controversial. Related to this find are other pseudo-hieroglyphic inscriptions found at GEZER, SHECHEM, and LACHISH (dated 1800 to 1300). Unhappily these are of such brevity as to preclude accurate linguistic analysis.

(3) *Middle Canaanite* comprises the Phoenician branch of the Canaanite family, the earliest example of which is the Ahiram epitaph at Byblos (see GEBAL #2), dating from the 11th cent. B.C. or earlier. See PHOENICIA. It was spoken all the way down the coast, at Tripolis, Berytus, SIDON, and TYRE, at which a goodly number of inscriptions (mostly 5th–2nd cent. B.C.) have been discovered. The extensive colonies of Phoenician settlers in Cyprus, Sicily, Sardinia, and Malta have also yielded inscriptional material in this language, and even in Athens and Marseilles examples have been found. Particularly significant is the large body of documents and stelae of various sorts found in the Carthaginian Empire, from N Africa to Spain (and in Sicily as well), which exhibit a subdialect known as Punic. These date from the 3rd cent. B.C. to the 3rd cent. A.D., and increasingly make use of vowel letters ("weak" consonants employed to indicate vowel sounds) as time goes on—unlike the Phoenician of the homeland, which eschewed vowel letters almost to the very end. The information as to vocalization comes exclusively from transcriptions into Greek and Latin (notably a passage or two in Plautus's *Poenulus*). (Sea further Z. S. Harris, *A Grammar of the Phoenician Language* [1936]; S. Segert, *A Grammar of Phoenician and Punic* [1976]; C. R. Krahmalkov, *A Phoenician-Punic Grammar* [2001].)

(4) *Moabite* is known largely from the MOABITE STONE erected by King MESHA (c. 840 B.C.). It is distinguished from Hebrew by its retention of

the -*t* ending for feminine absolute nouns (a trait it shared with Phoenician). (Cf. A. Dearman, ed., *Studies in the Mesha Inscription and Moab* [1989].)

(5) Hebrew, the language of the OT, has been preserved largely in the Judean or Jerusalem dialect, although much of Hosea shows the influence of N Israelite traits, and Ecclesiastes shows strong Phoenician influence. Extrabiblical Hebrew inscriptions are quite few, prior to the MS material from the Qumran caves. They include the GEZER calendar (c. 925), the SILOAM inscription (c. 705), the Samaritan OSTRACA (c. 770), the LACHISH letters (c. 588), and the name lists at ARAD from about the same period. (For further discussion and bibliography, see HEBREW LANGUAGE.)

No doubt Edomite (see EDOM) and Ammonite (see AMMON) should be included among the Canaanite dialects, although inscriptional evidence on these is very meager. (See further Z. S. Harris, *The Development of the Canaanite Dialects* [1939]; J. C. L. Gibson, *Textbook of Syrian Semitic Inscriptions*, 3 vols. [1971–82]; K. P. Jackson, *The Ammonite Language of the Iron Age* [1983]; W. R. Garr, *Dialect Geography of Syria-Palestine, 1000–586 B.C.E.* [1985]; W. E. Aufrecht, *A Corpus of Ammonite Inscriptions* [1989].)

III. The Indo-European languages. This family comprises a very large number of languages that are widely distributed, including the so-called classical languages (Greek, Latin, Sanskrit), most modern European languages (English, French, Russian, etc.), and many languages spoken in eastern countries (Farsi in Iran [see PERSIA IV]; Hindustani and others in India; etc.). Earliest in appearance was the HITTITE language, or more accurately Nesite (to distinguish it from the non-Indo-European Proto-Khatti spoken by the original population in ASIA MINOR who were conquered by the Nesians in the 1st half of the 2nd millennium). Little is known about hieroglyphic Hittite as yet, although conjectural translations have been attempted; it may have been the literary medium of the Cilician kingdom of Kizzuwatna. Related dialects to Indo-European Hittite were Luwian and Palaic, Anatolian tongues of which very little remains. (See H. C. Melchert, "Indo-European Languages of Anatolia," in *CANE*, 4:2151–59.)

Phrygian was spoken in E Asia Minor, and was in the 7th to 6th centuries B.C. written in an alphabet related to W Greek. Neo-Phrygian was written in conventional Greek characters during the Greco-Roman period. Phrygian traditionally has been classified as a *satem*-language, like the Indo-Iranian language group. That is to say, the palatal *k* softened to *ç* or *s* before original *e* or *i*. (Nesian Hittite, in contrast, was a *centum* language. Sanskrit for "hundred" is *çata*, whereas the Latin is *centum* — hence the designation. The value of the *centum-satem* distinction is questioned by some recent scholars, however.)

The language recorded in the syllabary known as Cretan Linear A remains unidentified (it is thought by some to be a form of Phoenician), but there is no doubt that Cretan Linear B was Indo-European, specifically, a dialect of Greek called Achaean or Mycenaean, and used from the 15th cent. B.C. to the collapse of Minoan-Mycenaean civilization under the impact of the Dorian invasions, around the year 1000. These Linear B inscriptions are found at Pylos on the mainland of Greece, and in other Mycenaean centers. (Cf. J. Chadwick, *The Decipherment of Linear B* [1958]; J. T. Hooker, *Linear B: An Introduction* [1980].) On CYPRUS, the syllabary used was very similar and represented in all probability a closely related dialect of Greek.

Among the ANE languages one must include classical Greek as well, especially from the time of ALEXANDER THE GREAT's conquest c. 330 B.C., when Greek became the language of government in Asia all the way from the Bosphorus to the Indus. It was at this time that Attic, a derivative from Ionic Greek, became adapted to the needs of the entire Hellenistic world, and soon developed into the *Koine*, which furnished the linguistic medium for the SEPTUAGINT and the NT. See GREEK LANGUAGE. LATIN was introduced at the time of the Roman conquest in 63 B.C. (when POMPEY annexed JUDEA to the empire), but it was largely confined to the Romans themselves, since even the Italian conquerors of the ANE were content to use Greek in communicating with their subjects. Latin inscriptions are largely confined to dedicatory monuments in such romanized centers as CAESAREA (which was founded by HEROD the Great).

Greek inscription from an area in Alexandria thought to have housed its famous library.

Moving farther to the E we come to the Iranian branch of Indo-European, notably Old Persian, which was written in a sort of semisyllabic alphabet of thirty-six cuneiform signs, plus six others that were ideograms. Linguistically it was related to Sanskrit; it possessed a seven-case declension and a verbal system employing four tenses, three voices, five moods, four participles, a dual number, and a single infinitive. The earliest inscriptions date from the 6th cent. B.C. (CYRUS the Great), and they continue until after the Greek conquest. See PERSIA.

In the 2nd cent. B.C., the PARTHIANS became dominant E. of the TIGRIS; they spoke Arsacid PAHLAVI, derived from the Median form of Iranian (of Old Median we now possess only some names and a few glosses). The rise of the Sassanian Persians in the 3rd cent. A.D. led to the prevalence of Sassanian Pahlavi throughout their domains; closely related to this is Avestan, the language of the Zoroastrian or Parsee scriptures (see ZOROASTRIANISM). Apparently the SCYTHIAN peoples also spoke a type of Iranian, especially the Ossetians in the Caucasus. Virtually none of this has survived in written form. (See further R. G. Kent, *Old Persian: Grammar, Texts, Lexicon*, 2nd ed. [1953]; R. Schmitt, ed., *Compendium linguarum Iranicarum* [1989].)

IV. Miscellaneous languages. The HURRIANS spoke an agglutinative language unrelated to any other known to philology, except possibly Urartian. Although the original Mitannians must have been Indo-Iranian, judging from the names of their gods, the language of the Mitannian Empire (which flourished in the middle of the 2nd millennium) was Hurrian. Some inscriptions at MARI (18th to 17th cent.) were in Hurrian; Hurrian influences account for most of the peculiarities of the Akkadian used at NUZI. One long letter from King Tushratta in the Amarna collection was couched in Hurrian (early 14th cent.); so were some texts at the Hittite capital of Boğazköy. Like Hittite, Hurrian used the Akkadian syllabary and many of its ideograms to write their language.

Urartian was spoken by a non-Semitic, non-Indo-European people living near Lake Van (it is also called by some either Vannic or Kaldi). These people later were conquered by a race speaking a language related to Phrygian, and which developed into the later Armenian. See ARMENIA. Cuneiform inscriptions in Urartian come from about 840 to 640 B.C.

Elamite first appeared in a pictographic form as yet undeciphered; they have been found largely at SUSA, and are known as Proto-Elamite (see ELAM). About 2300 B.C. cuneiform inscriptions in Old Susian began to make their appearance. Neo-Susian inscriptions date from the 16th to the 8th cent.; and the latest form was Neo-Susian, in use during Achaemenid times (6th cent.). It was an agglutinative language unrelated to any other, except possibly Kassite. The language of the Kassite conquerors of Babylon is known only from personal names and a few glosses. For international correspondence (as in the Amarna letters), the Kassite rulers were content to use Babylonian.

In Asia Minor perhaps the most important language after Hittite was Lydian, the language of the empire of Croesus (6th to 4th cent.). As yet the inscriptions in this tongue are imperfectly understood, although a bilingual (with Aramaic) found at Sardis furnishes a helpful key. Carian has been found in three 7th-cent. bilingual inscriptions from Egypt; there are also some graffiti and glosses. Lycian is preserved in a strange alphabetic script as well as in a Greek script and in a few bilingual (Greek-Lycian) texts from the 1st cent. B.C. Little or nothing is known about Cilician, Pisidian, Mysian, Isaurian, or Lycaonian from this polyglot area of Anatolia. After the Alexandrian conquest this entire region became linguistically unified by the Greek language, and so remained until the Muslim conquest.

(See further G. R. Gragg, "Less Understood Languages of Ancient Western Asia," in *CANE*, 4:1161–79. For a more detailed survey of all the languages discussed in this article, see *ABD*, 4:155–229; note also R. D. Woodard, ed., *The Cambridge Encyclopedia of the World's Ancient Languages* [2004]; N. Postgate, ed., *Languages of Iraq, Ancient and Modern* [2007].) G. L. ARCHER

languages of the Bible. The OT was given originally in Hebrew (one of the Semitic languages), except for parts of Ezra and Daniel, which were written in the closely related language of Aramaic. The NT was composed in Greek, although some have argued that one or more of the NT books were originally written in Aramaic and then subsequently cast into Greek, possibly by the authors themselves. See ARAMAIC LANGUAGE; GREEK LANGUAGE; HEBREW LANGUAGE; LANGUAGES OF THE ANE.

lantern. This English term is used in Bible versions once to render Greek *phanos* G5749, which occurs only in Jn. 18:3. In that passage we are told that the soldiers and officials who went to arrest Jesus were carrying lanterns and torches (*lampas* G3286, usually LAMP). In contrast to other versions, the NIV seems to regard *phanos* as meaning "torch" (which in fact was the earlier meaning of the term) and *lampas* as "lantern." It is possible that either (or both) of these terms refers to some kind of TORCH, although Romans in the time of Christ did have lanterns of cylindrical shape with translucent sides.

Laodicea lay-od´i-see´uh (Λαοδίκεια G3293 [according to some eds., Λαοδικία]; gentilic Λαοδικεύς G3294, "Laodicean"). A city located on the southern bank of the Lycus River (a tributary of the Maeander River) in the SW region of ancient PHRYGIA, the so-called Cibyratic conventus, in central Turkey. It was known in antiquity as *Laodikeia he pros tō Lykō* (Lat. *Laodicea ad Lycum*), "Laodicea on the Lycus." The ancient town stood on a plateau nearly 100 ft. above the river. To the N and W of the town lay the open broadlands of the Maeander, to the SE was the high country of the Babadağ-Akdağ Ranges.

Although Laodicea was undoubtedly a station on the caravan route from EPHESUS to N SYRIA in Neolithic times, its historic foundation was begun by the Hellenistic ruler ANTIOCHUS II (261–246 B.C.), who named the town for his wife, Laodice. The Greek geographers Polybius (202–120 B.C.) and Strabo (64 B.C. TO A.D. 19) list it as a Phrygian town, while the Alexandrian scholar Ptolemy (2nd cent. A.D.) says it was part of CARIA. The town grew to wealth and prominence during the period of Roman supremacy, when it was a way station for the extensive shipments by which Rome exploited Syria-Palestine. The Romans continued the city's character as both a military outpost and a trade center after 133 B.C.

TACITUS (*Annals* 14.27) records that a serious earthquake struck Laodicea in A.D. 60, but that the city was rebuilt by the private wealth of her citizens ("propriis opibus revaluit"). An additional source of its wealth came from the wool of its famous black sheep, which was carded and woven in the locality, and its production of a poultice widely sought for treatment of eye ailments (see EYESALVE). In the environs were also the temples of the ancient deities, chiefly at Attuda, where the shrine of Men-of-the-Carians was located.

According to JOSEPHUS (*Ant.* 12.3.4 §§147–49), Antiochus III the Great settled 2,000 Jewish families in Phrygia and LYDIA after deporting them from Babylon. No doubt the rising economic position and business endeavors of the region caused the Jews to thrive. Two references to the Jews of Laodicea during the 1st cent. B.C. have survived.

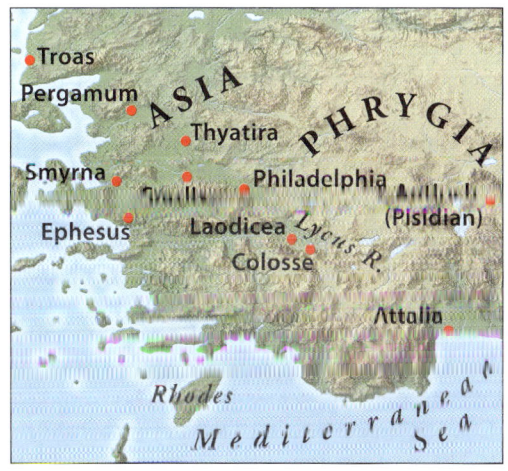

Laodicea.

Remains of a Roman stadium at Laodicea. (View to the W.)

In his defense of Flaccus, Cicero mentions that the Jews of Asia Minor were forbidden to send money to Jerusalem (*Pro Flacco* 28), and Josephus records that the Jews were guaranteed freedom of worship by the city magistrates (*Ant.* 14.10.20 §241). It was this wealth and independence which is the background of the remark recorded in Rev. 3:17–18. Laodicea was widely known as a banking center, and the business of money changing prospered. Laodicea minted its own coins several centuries before the Christian era, expressing on them the attributions and inscriptions of the ancient gods.

From its inception, Christianity in Laodicea was bound up with the other missionary churches of the Lycus Valley. It was to these churches that the encyclical epistle of Ephesians was most probably written. It is also mentioned in a similar context with the church of Colosse (Col. 2:1; 4:13, 15–16). A spurious Latin pseudepigraphic work by the title of the *Epistle to the Laodiceans* was circulated for a goodly part of the medieval and Renaissance eras. However, the citation to an "epistle from Laodicea" (Col. 4:16) probably refers to the text of Ephesians (see Laodiceans, Epistle to the). A certain Epaphras apparently ministered in the Lycus area and represented Paul and his coworkers (Col. 1:7, "on our behalf"; TR, "on your behalf").

The most extensive reference to the city and its inhabitants is found in the address to it in the Revelation of John. In the course of centuries, many theories of the proper hermeneutics for the interpretation of this passage (Rev. 3:14–22) have been advanced. In the historical prophetic views of the text, this church and its spiritual destitution has been seen as the final state of apostasy before the parousia. On the basis of the reiterative explanations, it has been viewed as a classic warning against shortsighted and superficial faith. Of the seven churches addressed, Laodicea, being farthest inland, is the last mentioned. Unfortunately the remains and explanations of the postapostolic period, along with the archaeological remnants, shed no light upon the state of the church that is assumed in the address in Revelation.

The profundity of the challenge declared to this congregation (Rev. 3:20–21) is rarely equaled in drama or finality elsewhere in Scripture. There is no doubt that John was well acquainted with the location. He enjoins them to recognize that they are poor, blind, naked. With all their wealth, they must come to Christ to acquire gold refined in fire (cf. 1 Pet. 1:7); with their surplus of fine woolen garments, to obtain white garments; and with their medical academies and eye ointments, to receive spiritual salve for their blindness (Rev. 3:17–18). It is an incredible and accurate description of the city and its citizens in the light of the biblical judgment. Traditions abounded in later ages about Epaphras,

Archippus, Nymphas (Col. 4.15), and Diotrephes (3 Jn. 9), but they are purely legendary. The city was the central episcopal seat of Phrygia by the 4th cent. A.D., but it was destroyed and abandoned during the internecine wars between the Muslims of the Middle Ages. The ruins known as Eski Hissar are all that remain.

(See further W. M. Ramsay, *The Cities and Bishoprics of Phrygia* [1895] 1:32–83; id., *The Letters to the Seven Churches* [1904], 413–31; W. M. Calder et al., *Monumenta Asiae Minoris Antiqua* 6 [1939], x–xi, 1–14; M. Rostovtzeff, *The Social and Economic History of the Hellenistic World* [1941], 479, 487, 822, 945, 1645; D. Magie, *Roman Rule in Asia Minor* [1950], 1:127; G. E. Bean, *Turkey Beyond the Maeander*, 2nd ed. [1980], ch. 21; E. Yamauchi, *The Archaeology of New Testament Cities in Western Asia Minor* [1980], ch. 10; C. J. Hemer, *The Letters to the Seven Churches of Asia in Their Local Setting* [1986], ch. 9; F. F. Bruce in *ABD*, 4:229–31.)

W. WHITE, JR.

Laodiceans, Epistle to the lay-od´i-see´uhns. Writing to the COLOSSIANS, PAUL mentions "the letter from Laodicea," which he instructs them to have read in their church (Col. 4:16). This phrase has been much discussed (see the excursus by J. B. Lightfoot in *Saint Paul's Epistles to the Colossians and to Philemon* [1875], 340ff.; the pagination differs in later editions). Three main suggestions have been advanced, each with several subordinate alternatives attached: (a) that it was a letter written *by the Laodiceans*; (b) that it was written *by Paul* from Laodicea; and (c) that it was addressed *to the* Laodiceans. The first two, on any of the alternatives suggested, present considerable difficulties, and the third is beyond question the most natural explanation; but it immediately raises the further question of identification. If written by Paul, the letter was presumably a companion to Colossians, but was it one of the extant letters (and if so, which?) or a letter now lost? According to TERTULLIAN (*Adv. Marc.* 5.11), the Marcionites identified it as EPHESIANS, but other suggestions also have been made. The MURATORIAN CANON mentions a letter to the Laodiceans "forged in Paul's name for the sect of Marcion."

A Latin *Epistle to the Laodiceans* is found in many MSS, the oldest being the Codex Fuldensis, written for Victor of Capua in the 6th cent. Its existence even earlier is proved by the warnings of the church fathers, especially JEROME (*Vir. ill.* 5), but despite these warnings it was widely disseminated in the W. This was due at least in part to the influence of Gregory the Great, who, although he limited the canonical epistles to fourteen, states nevertheless that Paul wrote fifteen, and was thus understood to affirm its authenticity. That it was read in the E in the 8th cent. is shown by the warning issued by the Second Council of Nicaea (A.D. 787).

Despite the arguments of A. von Harnack (*Die apokryphen Briefe des Paulus an die Laodicener und Korinther*, 2nd ed. [1931]), the Marcionite origin of this document remains uncertain (see MARCION). In fact, it contains nothing specifically Marcionite or calculated to promote the interests of the sect. Nor can one be sure of its identity with the letter mentioned in the Muratorian Canon. Its date can therefore be placed only approximately, between the 2nd and 4th centuries. In ancient MSS the letter is extant only in Latin, although it was to be translated into western vernaculars, notably English, but its use in the E and the evidence of the Greek fathers suggest that a Greek version was once current.

Lightfoot notes that this brief apocryphal document, largely a cento of passages from Paul, "has not the run of a Latin original," but contains frequent Grecisms, and differs widely both from the Old Latin and from the VULGATE of the Pauline letters. Accordingly he argues for a Greek original, and offers his own retranslation into Greek. Another Greek version is given in Elias Hutter's *Polyglot New Testament* (1599), while a MS in St. Andrews dated 1679 presents the epistle in Latin, Greek, and Hebrew (see R. Y. Ebied, *Bib* 47 [1966]: 243–54). Survival of an authentic Greek text to so late a date, when all the older MS tradition is in Latin, would be highly unlikely, and, in fact, this is Hutter's Greek version, with some transcriptional errors (he writes that, having found the letter only in a volume of apocrypha, "operae pretium esse indicavi ut eandem et in reliquas linguas converterem").

The letter is in fact no more than a patchwork of Pauline phrases, beginning with the opening words of Galatians but heavily dependent on Philippians. M. S. Enslin (in *IDB*, 3:72) aptly quotes the comment of Erasmus that there is "no argument which will more effectively convince that this is not by Paul than the epistle itself." The forgery was quite obviously occasioned by the desire to make good a gap in the Pauline Corpus by supplying the letter mentioned in Col. 4:16. (English trans. with introduction in *NTAp*, 2:42–46.) R. McL. Wilson

Lapidoth lap′i-doth. KJV form of Lappidoth.

lapis lazuli. An azure-blue or Berlin-blue colored mineral that has been valued as an ornamental stone since ancient times and may have been referred to as sapphire by some early writers (cf. Heb. *sappîr* H6209 in Exod. 28:18 et al.; Gk. *sapphiros* G4913 in Rev. 21:19). Lapis lazuli is possibly referred to also by the Hebrew word *šōham* H8732 (cf. the NJPS at Gen. 2:12 et al.; see onyx). It is a sodium aluminum silicate cut and polished for ornamental purposes (possibly explaining the reference in Lam. 4:7), and used in the manufacture of mosaics. While too soft to be much used in jewelry, ancient Egyptian amulets carved out of it are common. It occurs in limestones adjacent to granitic intrusions in Iran, Turkestan, Afghanistan, and Mongolia. D. R. Bowes

Lappidoth lap′i-doth (לַפִּידוֹת H4366, possibly "flames, lightning strikes"). KJV Lapidoth. Husband of Deborah, the prophetess and leader of Israel (Jdg. 4:4). Some have speculated that there may be a connection between Lappidoth and Deborah's military associate, Barak (v. 6; the latter's name means "lightning"); in any case, the text clearly distinguishes between the two.

lapwing. Also known as the green plover, the lapwing is a well-known British bird, and it is a winter visitor to Palestine. Some thirty other shore birds either winter there or pass through on migration, and only one member of this very wandering family is a resident—the spurwing plover. The term "lapwing" is used by the KJV in two passages where a better rendering is hoopoe (Lev. 11:19; Deut. 14:18). G. S. Cansdale

lasciviousness. This English term (derived from the Latin *lasciviosus*, earlier *lascivia*), meaning "lust, overt sexual desire," is used by the KJV to render Greek *aselgeia* G816 in a number of passages (e.g., 2 Cor. 12:21; NIV, "debauchery"; NRSV, "licentiousness"). The Greek noun occurs only twice in the Septuagint (Wisd. 14:26; 3 Macc. 2:26) and eight times in the NT. Plato and some Attic authors used the term to denote licentiousness or wanton violence, although the adjectival form generally meant "outrageous." Josephus used it occasionally of lewd women (cf. *War* 1.22.3).

The history of the Greek form is uncertain at best, and its etymological origins have been sought in the verb *thelgō*, which was used by both early and late writers with reference to enchanting, spellbinding, cheating, and entrapping. Significantly enough, in one passage (Gal. 5:19–20) *aselgeia* is followed by *pharmakeia* G5758, "witchcraft," although elsewhere (Mk. 7:22; Rom. 13:13; 2 Cor. 12:21; Eph. 4:19; 1 Pet. 4:3; 2 Pet. 2:2, 7, 18; Jude 4) the reference is clearly to sensuality, particularly that which outraged public decency. There could be no place for such behavior in the Christian life, as the NT references made clear. (The term also could imply insolence or violence toward another in NT times, and an A.D. 4th-cent. papyrus complained of a man using *aselgēmata*, "many abusive terms.")

R. K. Harrison

Lasea luh-see′uh (Λασαία G3297; also Λασέα and other variant forms). A city of Crete near Fair Havens, the bay that the ship on which Paul was being taken to Italy had reached with difficulty (Acts 27:8). Quite possibly ruins about 5 mi. E of Fair Havens are those of Lasea. Not much is known about this city, which has received little notice in surviving literature; but it has been thought that it is the same as the Lasos which Pliny the Elder mentions among the one hundred renowned cities of Crete (*Nat. Hist.* 4.12.58–59). J. H. Skilton

Lasha lay′shuh (לֶשַׁע H4388, meaning unknown). A place marking one of the boundary points of the land of the Canaanites, mentioned after Sodom, Gomorrah, Admah, and Zeboiim (Gen. 10:19). Its location is unknown, although a number of identifications have been suggested, among them Laish (surely too far N) and Callirrhoe (or Kallirhoe, a ravine E of the Dead Sea to which Herod the Great went for his health during his last illness; see Zereth Shahar).

Lasharon luh-shair′uhn (לַשָּׁרוֹן *H4000*, "belonging to Sharon [the plain]"). A Canaanite royal city whose king was defeated by JOSHUA (Josh. 12:18). However, the SEPTUAGINT variant accepted in Rahlfs's *Septuaginta* is *basilea Aphek tēs Sarōn*, "the king of Aphek of Sharon," and many scholars believe this reading is earlier than the MT (possibly an old gloss) or even original. If so, *laššārôn* is not the name of a city, but part of a phrase, distinguishing this APHEK from other cities of the same name. See SHARON.

lashes. See CRIMES AND PUNISHMENTS III.C.

last days, last times. See ESCHATOLOGY.

Lasthenes las′thuh-neez (Λασθενής). A prominent official under DEMETRIUS II Nicator in the 1st cent. B.C.; perhaps governor of COELESYRIA. JOSEPHUS (*Ant.* 13.4.3 §86) refers to him as a Cretan and says that he had provided many mercenaries for Demetrius at the very important time c. 147 B.C., when the latter sailed from CRETE for CILICIA. Demetrius, in writing to Jonathan the high priest of the Jews (see MACCABEE) and to the Jewish nation, enclosed a copy of a letter he had written to his "kinsman" Lasthenes. In that letter to Lasthenes, Demetrius addresses him as his "father" (*Ant.* 13.4.9 §§125–29; 1 Macc. 11:30–37). The terms "kinsman" and "father" do not necessarily indicate any family relationship, but they do point to the high standing of Lasthenes and the regard which the king had for him. The contents of the letter are of considerable interest, touching as they do, among other things, on the subject of the boundaries of Judea and the privileges granted to the Jews.   J. H. SKILTON

Last Supper. See LORD'S SUPPER.

latchet. This term and "shoelatchet" are used by the KJV with reference to SANDAL thongs (Gen. 14:23; Isa. 5:27; Mk. 1:7; Lk. 3:16; Jn. 1:27).

Latin. One of the Indo-European languages (see LANGUAGES OF THE ANE III), Latin was the official medium of communication in the Roman empire, and it was used in the provinces, such as JUDEA, in official acts and at the Roman courts. Greek was the language of commerce (see GREEK LANGUAGE). In Palestine itself, ARAMAIC was the language spoken in the rural districts and more remote towns, while in the cities both Aramaic and Greek were used. That is why the inscription on the cross of Christ was written in three languages (Matt. 27:37). The Greek word for "Latin" (*Rhōmaisti G4872*) is found in the NT once: "the sign was written in Aramaic, Latin and Greek" (Jn. 19:20; a similar phrase is also found as a variant in Lk. 23:38). Hellenistic Greek borrowed a number of words from Latin (e.g., *dēnarion G1324*, "denarius") and was otherwise influenced by this language, especially in the area of government (see the list in BDAG, xx). Many Latin names, such as PAUL (*Paulus*), are found in the NT. See also ROME.   S. BARABAS

Latin versions. See VERSIONS OF THE BIBLE, ANCIENT, II.

latter days. See ESCHATOLOGY.

latter rain. See RAIN.

lattice. A window covering made of crossed strips or bars of wood, metal, etc., and used as a screen (for Heb. *ḥărakkîm H3048*, Jdg. 5:28; 2 Ki. 1:2; Prov. 7:6; Cant. 2:9).

laughter. The term does not signify amusement in the Bible. As ABRAHAM considered his and SARAH's age, he laughed with gentle incredulity at the promise of an heir (Gen. 17:17; Heb. *ṣāḥaq H7464*). Most often, however, laughter denotes derision, mockery, and scorn in the Bible. The psalmist speaks of God's laughing derisively at the efforts of earthly rulers to declare their independence of him (Ps. 2:4; Heb. *śāḥaq H8471*). When HEZEKIAH sent couriers calling the people to return to the Lord and to celebrate the Passover, they were laughed to scorn (2 Chr. 30:10; cf. Isa. 37:22). Job expressed his sense of being unjustly afflicted by pointing out that he, a just and blameless man, was a laughingstock (Job 12:4; Heb. *śĕḥōq H8492*). The crowd of mourners laughed (Gk. *katagelaō G2860*) at Jesus when he said JAIRUS's daughter was sleeping, not dead (Matt. 9:24; Mk. 5:40; Lk. 8:53). The jaded cynic of ECCLESIASTES speaks of laughter as madness (Eccl. 2:2), and of mourning as better than laughter (7:3). Laughter, thus, occupied a different place in the ancient, oriental world than in the modern occidental world.

But laughter also is associated with joy at Zion's restoration (Ps. 126:2); bread is said to be made for laughter (Eccl. 10:19) and our Lord promised, "Blessed are you who weep now, for you will laugh" (Lk. 6:21; Gk. *gelaō* G1151). The Bible also contains hundreds of references to JOY. It is clear, therefore, that the common use of laughter for mockery and scorn does not suggest that a premium was placed on dourness nor that solemnity was a mark of sanctity.

The different references to laughter in the several passages cited can be subsumed under the categories of wit and humor. Wit is the aggressive use of humor. In wit, laughter is tinged with the sardonic. It contains elements of scorn, mockery, and disparagement, for it seeks to deflate or shrivel, to make a person feel small, foolish, and unworthy. True HUMOR springs from a sense of strength, security, and joy. It stems from the ability to take a healthy perspective on self, others, and the vicissitudes of life. True humor has a healing effect upon moods and upon relationships. It has been defined as a person's ability to laugh at the things he loves, including himself, while continuing to love them. This is the cheerful heart that "is good medicine" (Prov. 17:22). Its laughter is a healing force, and results from imagination, zestfulness, and delight.

L. I. GRANBERG

laver. This English term is the traditional rendering of Hebrew *kiyyôr* H3963, which the NIV and other modern versions translate as BASIN (it can also mean "pan" [1 Sam. 2:14], "pot" [Zech. 12:6], and "platform" [2 Chr. 6:13]).

The laver or basin for the TABERNACLE, with its base, was made of bronze (Exod. 30:18 et al.). It contained water so that AARON and his sons could bathe their hands and feet when they entered the Tent of Meeting or approached the altar to minister (30:18–19). The basin was made by BEZALEL of the tribe of Judah and OHOLIAB of the tribe of Dan (31:1–9), along with other able men among the people (35:10–16). We read that it was made "from the [bronze] mirrors of the women who served at the entrance to the Tent of Meeting" (38:8; P. Fairbairn, *The Typology of Scripture* [1900], 2:258, quotes Aben-Ezra's comment that "these were women in Israel that served the Lord, who abandoned this worldly delight [of beholding themselves in a mirror to dress their hair] and gave away their glasses as a free-will offering, for they had no more use of them"). After anointment with the prescribed oil (Exod. 30:22–29; Lev. 8:11) and acceptance by MOSES (Exod. 39:39), it was the last article set in place before the erection of the court (Exod. 40:7, 17). The Bible does not state its shape, size, ornamentation, or transport.

In the TEMPLE built by SOLOMON, a great "molten sea" (see SEA, MOLTEN) took the place of the laver in the tabernacle for the priests' ablutions (2 Chr. 4:6; NIV, "the Sea of cast metal"). This "sea" was five cubits in height, ten cubits in diameter from brim to brim, and thirty cubits in circumference (1 Ki. 7:23). Some regard the last two figures as a mathematical impossibility. The circumference, however, may not include the outward flare of its lily shape at the brim (7:26), whereas the diameter may refer to the brim at its widest section. Gourds ran under its brim, ten to the cubit, surrounding the sea in two rows and cast at the same time as the vessel itself (7:24). It rested upon four groups of three bronze oxen oriented to the four compass points (7:25). This selection represented the priestly service of the twelve tribes even as the lions on Solomon's throne represented the royal service. A basalt laver supported by two bulls from the early 1st millennium B.C. was found at CARCHEMISH (*NBD* [1962], 718, fig. 132). The thickness of the bronze metal was a hand's breadth and the vessel

Reconstruction of the bronze laver that stood in the tabernacle courtyard.

held 2,000 baths (1 Ki. 7:26; according to KD [*Chronicles*, 320], the MT the likeness of oxen and the "3,000 baths" in the synoptic account of 2 Chr. 4:3, 5 are the result of scribal error).

Besides the great molten sea located on the SE corner of the temple, Hiram (Huram) of Tyre (1 Ki. 7:13–14, 40–44) also made ten bronze lavers, distributed evenly between the N and S sides of the temple (7:39). These lavers, four cubits in diameter and containing forty baths (7:38), were used for washing the animals to be offered as burnt offerings (2 Chr. 4:6), and were set upon mobile bronze stands (1 Ki. 7:27–37). A similar construction from Cyprus, c. 1150 B.C., clarifies the painstaking study of these stands found in *A Dictionary of the Bible* (1863), edited by William Smith (2:66–67; cf. *NBD* [1962], 1244, fig. 205).

In connection with his apostasy, Ahaz cut off the panels of the stands, removed the lavers from them, and replaced the sea on a pediment of stone (2 Ki. 16:17). The Babylonians broke up what remained of the sea and stands and carried the bronze to Babylon (25:13). No mention is made in Scripture of the laver(s) in the second temple, nor by Josephus in his account of Herod's restoration.

B. K. Waltke

law (OT).

I. Meaning of the word Torah
II. Other terms for "law"
III. Two forms of Israel's law
IV. Contents of the law
V. Codes of the law
VI. Land laws in the OT
VII. Attitude to law in the OT

I. Meaning of the word Torah. The legal terminology of Semitic is very different from that of the familiar Indo-European languages. This in itself raises problems of interpretation and communication; but more serious is the fact that this difference in terminology corresponds to a basic difference in concept. Even Latin *lex* is not the same as Greek *nomos* G3795 (though perhaps Lat. *mos* or *jus* would come closer), and both words are totally different from Hebrew *tôrâ* H9368. There are several other words used for "law" in the OT, some of which will be discussed; but whether used of part or of the whole, Torah is the most frequent and the most characteristic.

Etymology is always a dangerous guide to the meaning of a word, especially if used as the only method (cf. James Barr, *The Semantics of Biblical Language* [1962]). Ultimately the meaning of a word is not determined by its etymology (of which most of its users are unaware) nor by the meaning in cognate languages, but by contemporary usage. Nevertheless, most scholars are now agreed that *tôrâ* (prob. from *yārâ* H3723, hiphil "instruct, teach," Exod. 24:12 et al.) originally meant "direction" or "guidance." (Cf. also the cognate noun *môreh* H4621, "teacher," Isa. 30:20 et al. Some have argued that *tôrâ* is derived from a different root, the homonym *yārâ* H3721, "to throw, shoot"; whether this once had reference to shooting of arrows, or "shaking" them out of a quiver, or the "casting" of lots as methods of obtaining divine guidance, is quite uncertain.)

There are cognate Semitic roots meaning "to guide, show the way," but older ideas of direct borrowing of the word from Babylonian *tērtu*, "oracle," are now generally rejected, although the rhythmic form of many of Israel's laws does suggest a priestly oracle. The etymological meaning at least seems clear in broad outline as "teaching, guidance instruction." (See further A. Bentzen, *Introduction to the Old Testament*, 5th ed. [1959], 213–14.) Next, this meaning must be tested from actual usage in the OT.

Here Ludwig Koehler's divisions (in *HAL*) seem sound. (1) He sees *tôrâ* as initially being direction or advice in a given situation, asked from God and mediated through the priests or perhaps also "prophets" (Hag. 2:10–13 is an example of this custom). It does not appear that in historical days the priest necessarily gave such direction by the sacred lot, Urim and Thummin, or by the ephod, although such methods were certainly used at times (1 Sam. 28:6; 30:7). Rather the priest seems to have acted as a prophet did later, in giving a spoken utterance (Hag. 2:12). (2) Second, *tôrâ* may be advice or instruction given by one human to another (e.g., Prov. 1:8, a mother to a son). This is a useful corrective, for it shows that the noun was by no means restricted to the religious or legal sphere; indeed, such specialization of reference is foreign

Torah scroll.

to the thought world of the OT. (3) The term may mean a single law or instruction (not apparently an enactment or a legal decision, however). An example of this use is Lev. 6:8, where *tôrâ* clearly means "instructions about" a particular offering. In this sense the word approaches the meaning of "regulation." (4) Finally, it is used (esp. with the definite article, or with the addition of a proper name to make it definite) to mean the totality of all such "instruction" in Israel. It may be in the singular or in the plural (the latter is also true of many synonyms); in either case, it has a collective sense. The plural noun may possibly denote a greater stress on separate laws, or separate codes of law.

The proper name qualifying *tôrâ*, and thus making it both definite and collective, is either Yahweh/God (Exod. 13:9; Josh. 24:26) or else MOSES (Josh. 8:31). In this last case, Moses is regarded as mediator, not source, of the law. At first, to judge from these contexts, the word is used as referring to the injunctions and commands in the law; then it is extended to cover narrative and all other parts of the PENTATEUCH. This is part of a general broadening of concept; by NT days, either "the Law and the Prophets" or just "the Law" is a general term embracing the whole OT (Matt. 22:40; Jn. 12:34). See also the article on TORAH.

II. Other terms for "law." There are several other words used in the OT to describe individual laws, rather than a complete corpus; nevertheless, when such a word is used in the plural (often with a second word also in the pl. as parallel), it does approach the collective meaning of *tôrôt*, "laws," meaning the totality of God's revelation in this field. Unfortunately there is no agreement among scholars as to the exact correspondence of these other terms to English words. This may be simply because of the different Semitic understanding of the nature of the law; or, as many have suggested, particularly in view of the frequent use of different terms in close parallelism in the Psalter, it may be that old distinctions of meaning had been blurred, and that the varied terms are really synonyms in many cases.

Nevertheless, there is at least one which is both clear and theologically important, in that the TEN COMMANDMENTS are called by the Jews the "Ten Words" (*'ăseret haddĕbārîm*, Deut. 4:13). This certainly corresponds to a basic difference in attitude: the English term "commandment" concentrates on the authoritarian nature, while the Hebrew "word" (*dābār* H1821) concentrates on the revelational nature. Authority is in the Ten Words, but it is not the primary thought, and the "words" only gain this authenticity because they are the revelation of Yahweh's will and purpose for the Israel whom he has redeemed by a revelation of his power. A. Weiser (*The Old Testament: Its Foundation and Development* [1961], 88) well points out that this combination of law and saving acts, exodus and Sinai, both equally regarded as the revelation of God, is typically Israelite.

This attitude to the Ten Commandments, as shown by the use of *dābār*, "word," is thus not an isolated phenomenon. Indeed it also corresponds to the way in which all legal matter is seen as *tôrâ*, "instruction," as much as any of Israel's history of salvation. The term *dābār* is not the name for a particular type of law; it is an expression of an attitude to law as a whole, a part of an Israelite philosophy of revelation. Some scholars have tried to distinguish between a sacred "word" and a secular "judgment" (*mišpāṭ* H5477). Even if our writings had corresponded, this would have been an impossible distinction for Israel to make, seeing that all process of judgment was to them a sacred task (Deut. 1:17). For this meaning of *dābār*, compare the common OT phrase "word of Yahweh" to describe an oracle or a revelation (Jdg. 3:20). Such revelation came with authority and could not be ignored.

The term *ḥōq* H2976, traditionally translated "statute," is another word of a general nature. By etymology it would seem to mean something "engraved" (or perhaps "fixed," from the root *ḥāqaq* H2980). This could perhaps refer to something "engraved" on tablets, like the Ten Words (Exod. 32:16), but Ps. 2:7 shows a much wider use of this noun in the sense of "decree" or "divine oracle," so that Koehler considers it as a mere parallel to *tôrâ*. Others, however, have regarded the word as referring to Israel's fixed annual festivals, perhaps once marked by notches on a stick, but this seems far-fetched. Yet others have seen it as referring to the "categoric" sections of Israel's law: the absolute commands of God (as in the Ten Words or the Twelve Curses) rather than the case-law, arising from judicial decisions. This is possible but cannot be proved. In any case, in later days such linguistic distinctions were blurred, if they had ever existed, especially when the word was used in the plural.

The noun *mišpāṭ* is quite clearly, from its linguistic form, a "judicial decision" or "act of judgment" or "precedent," which itself becomes law. It has been suggested, with some plausibility, that the *mišpāṭîm* in Israel's law are the sections of case-law, beginning "If ..." or "When. ..." No doubt in the lifetime of Moses himself there was much need for this sort of law, especially if the tradition of a forty-year stay in or around KADESH BARNEA is taken seriously (Deut. 1:46). In Gen. 14:7, the old name of Kadesh is in fact given as EN MISHPAT, "the well of judicial decision"; and in Num. 15:35 there is an example of Moses himself being compelled to seek a decision, in this sort of case-law, also called casuistic law, from Yahweh. Further, the story of the appointment of the seventy elders to share the burden of Moses shows that Moses was compelled to give many such decisions (Num. 11:16–25). The activity of DEBORAH (Jdg. 4,5) or SAMUEL (1 Sam. 7.15) or his sons, bad though they were (8:1–3), shows the continuance of this responsibility in Israel. Indeed it was through failure to fulfill it that DAVID nearly lost his throne to ABSALOM (2 Sam. 15:3).

The term *miṣwâ* H5184, "command," may, like *ḥōq*, correspond to the categoric framework of Israel's law, rather than its largely "casuistic" content. To put it another way, *miṣwâ* would be a definite order issued by Yahweh, rather than a case-law or application of divine principles. The etymology of the word would support this interpretation. It corresponds in association most to the English "command," though not, perhaps, to "law." However, like all the other terms, it frequently is used in the plural in a collective sense to describe Yahweh's law as a whole; in such cases, all distinctiveness of meaning has long since disappeared. In modern Hebrew usage, *bar-miṣwâ*, "son of law," means "under obligation to keep the law," and is used of the Jewish boy when, at puberty, he accepts the "yoke of the law" as his own responsibility. Here the term has become, even in the singular, a full equivalent of *tôrâ*.

III. Two forms of Israel's law. Whatever the reason, there are two distinct forms clearly discernible in Israel's law, even when broken into the smallest possible units. The two are not always as clearly marked now as they may have been initially, partly because of explanatory editorial additions, which blur the original clarity of the outline, and partly owing to the existence of "mixed forms" that combine, in one whole, features drawn from both forms.

The first form is that usually called categoric or apodictic, and is best illustrated in the format of the first part of each of the Ten Commandments. It is characterized by its terseness and abruptness, and is an absolute command, apparently admitting no exceptions, usually making use of the second person singular future (either in the positive or negative form). Sometimes the second person plural is used, and sometimes the imperative is substituted for the future. The style is heavy and impressive, the structure is rhythmic, assonant, parallel, and poetic. Presumably this was for ease of memory (cf. the NT

BEATITUDES) and perhaps for ease of recitation, if laws, or collections of laws, were indeed liturgical texts, read at the great religious folk-meetings of Israel, as many modern scholars believe, and as the law itself enjoins ("when all Israel comes to appear before the LORD your God at the place he will choose, you shall read this law before them in their hearing," Deut. 31:11).

Another early form, using the participial form instead of the second person singular, is the pattern "Anyone who strikes a man [*lit.*, One striking a man] ... shall surely be put to death" (Exod. 21:12 and following verses). In this type there is deliberate rhythm and assonance (Gen. 9:6 is an instance from a very early period). Bentzen reckons this type of law as belonging to the second or casuistic form, but it contains so many early features that it is best treated with the categoric commands of the type found in the Ten Words. Both of these, from their rhythmic nature, have been associated by some scholars with the concept of the divine oracle or Torah given originally by a prophet or priest of Yahweh. Whether this is so or not, it is quite clear that in Israel they are regarded, like all law, as a divine revelation. Moses by tradition was prophet and priest as well as law-giver.

This apodictic law used to be described as "desert law"—somber and authoritarian, with no concessions to the complexities of urban or even agrarian life in highly developed Canaan. Its austerity was therefore held to be typically Israelite, and it was considered to be the only original law of Israel. By contrast, all law belonging to the second or "casuistic" type was held to be a borrowing from the Canaanites after the Israelite entry into the land. Neither of these theses can now be sustained at least as far as the argument is based on the format of the laws.

As far as the "casuistic" law is concerned, direct borrowing from Canaan is not now held to be nearly as likely as inheritance from the "common law" of W Semitic folk, in which Israel shared as much as did the Canaanites, and which Moses must have known. Regarding the uniqueness of the apodictic form, R de Vaux (*Ancient Israel* [1961], 147) has shown that, while it is not characteristic of Semitic law as known largely from heavily settled Mesopotamia (naturally, no written laws from the desert survive), this form is characteristic of some HITTITE treaties (see TREATY). In view of the known fact that the Israelite theory and practice of COVENANT has many similarities with Hittite "suzerainty treaties" made by an imperial overlord with subject peoples, this is interesting as perhaps showing further Hittite links. It can, therefore, no longer be claimed that this form is either "desert" or "pure Israelite"; thus, any judgments as to the originality of the material, if based only on the form, would be erroneous. A safer position to take is to regard all Israel's laws, whether categoric or apodictic, as permeated with the light of the new revelation of Yahweh.

The second type of law to be found in the Torah is casuistic, or case-law. This normally introduces an instance, ending with a "then ...," as in the Mesopotamian case-law codes. Such laws should not be regarded as hypothetical instances, but as actual precedents or case judgments, whether earlier (Sinaitic) or later. It is in these areas that Israel's case-law approaches most closely that of her immediate Semitic neighbors. This is natural enough, since, given roughly similar levels of civilization and circumstances of life, similar problems were liable to arise, and broadly similar solutions to be found (although Israel's law is always more humane). Semitic law is most familiar to modern scholars in its later codifications, like that of HAMMURABI of Babylon, or the Middle Assyrian law code, or the neo-Babylonian laws. None of these were in any sense innovations. They were merely codifications and systematizations of far earlier laws, as can be seen from comparison with the Lipit-Ishtar Code and the Eshnunna Code.

How many of these precedents rested ultimately on early Semitic "common law" and how many on Sumerian codes, it would be hard to say; perhaps it would be wrong to consider these as ultimately distinct. In view of the proven widespread knowledge of these later codifications among the W Semitic peoples (annotated copies of Hammurabi's laws have been found in Egypt), one may safely assume a widespread knowledge of the earlier "customary law" that underlay them. There is no need to assume any direct or conscious borrowing by Israel of Canaanite case law at a comparatively late date (the conquest), the more so as there is no reason to

...... that Canaanite law was any different from the general Semitic pattern.

Naturally, where it is a matter of the content, Israel's laws throughout are dominated by the revelation of God received at Mount Sinai. There is a humaneness, an avoidance of mutilations and other savage punishments, and an awareness of the value of human personality and the individual, for which we would search in vain in other codes. This, and not any outward form, is the distinctiveness of Israel's law. One example will suffice: the small space given in Israel's code to property laws, and the large space to personal relations. Even in the case of the land laws, the motivation for every law is strongly personal and religious.

IV. Contents of the law. It comes as a surprise that, in the so-called law of Moses, strictly legal matter takes quite a minor place. Even if the area is enlarged to cover all matter of religious or ceremonial interest, it is still not dominant. If the basic meaning of Torah as "instruction" is kept in mind, this will no longer surprise. Israel's ancestral traditions—the salvation story of exodus, with the bittersweet experiences of the desert wandering—teach about God and his ways as surely as the Ten Commandments, or as the distinctions between "clean" and "unclean" which occupy especially Lev. 11–15. HISTORY is not law, but history seen through God's eyes is indeed *Torah* ("instruction")—just as later Israelite history was reckoned as "prophecy," and included the books of the Prophets in the CANON of the OT. This also explains another aspect—the evident love of Israel for the Torah, expressed, for instance, in Ps. 119. Few men except lawyers could love a legal system (although the PHARISEES of NT days seem to have done so); but all people could love the Torah, with its combination of poem and history, law and exhortation, for this was the very lifeblood of early Israel, cast in a literary form.

For the analysis of the material contained within the Torah, R. H. Pfeiffer (*Introduction to the Old Testament* [1941], 130–33) may be followed in the main, with minor modifications. (1) The origin of the world and of the nations of mankind (Gen. 1–11). (2) The patriarchs (chs. 12–50). (3) Moses and the exodus from Egypt (Exod. 1–18). (4) The divine revelation at Sinai (chs. 19–40). (5) The Levitical legislation at Sinai (Lev. 1–27). (6) The last events and laws of Sinai (Num. 1–10). (7) The journey to the plains of Moab (chs. 11–21). (8) Events in the plains of Moab (chs. 22–36). (9) The last discourses of Moses (Deut. 1–34).

At first sight, this looks like a coherent whole; and it is, in point of fact, a cogent historical arrangement of much diverse material. Even a cursory glance at the analysis above will show that of "law" in the narrower sense, only half of Exodus and all of Leviticus are constituted. Both Numbers and Deuteronomy contain sections of laws, but in the first, legal matter is subordinate to narrative, and in the second, to exhortation. Therefore the Torah has at least as good a claim to be called a history book as a lawbook; and considered from either angle, it is still uniquely God's "instruction."

V. Codes of the law. FORM CRITICISM has brought a new freshness to biblical studies by its isolation and study of the different "forms" within the books of the Bible instead of the endless documentary analysis. Where form criticism restricts itself to descriptive study, it can be a valuable analysis of biblical matter along entirely new lines; when some of its advocates push it further and base unwarranted value judgments on its conclusions, there is no need to follow them. Therefore, in isolating various "codes of law" within the Pentateuch for study, there is no necessity for postulating different sources or different dates. Indeed, all might well have originated in the Mosaic age, for all we know. Many of the codes cannot in any case have had an independent existence at any time in Israel's history. With this proviso, some seven or more separate codes may be cataloged as follows. They are mainly taken from Exodus, Leviticus, and Deuteronomy, with small sections from other books.

A. The Ten Commandments. These "Ten Words" stand at the very heart of the law and are fundamental to the whole. They appear twice, with minor differences in the explanatory additions (which may well themselves be early) in the second half of each verse: Exod. 20:1–17 and Deut. 5:6–21. It is these laws, probably in the shorter form consisting of the first half of each verse, without the explanation, which according to the Bible were engraved on the tablets in the ARK OF THE COVENANT (Exod. 24:12).

Violent controversy has raged over the date of the Ten Commandments (see H. H. Rowley, *Men of God* [1963]). Scholars like R. H. Pfeiffer reject any possibility of Mosaic mention of Sabbath or noniconic worship, and are even doubtful as to the forbidding of the worship of other gods as early as Mosaic times. Scholars of the Albright school, on the other hand, point to the literary form of the commandments, as well as their contents, as indicating "an original date of the Decalogue no later than the thirteenth century B.C." (W. F. Albright, *Yahweh and the Gods of Canaan* [1968]). With this, the basically aniconic nature of Israel's worship (as witnessed archaeologically for the days of the judges) agrees; there is no valid reason to doubt a Mosaic origin. It often has been argued that what is taught in the Ten Words is properly monolatry, not monotheism—the exclusive worship of one God, rather than the denial of the existence of all others, as presented in the second half of Isaiah. But this view usually assigns such passages as Gen. 1 to the postexilic period and fails to reckon with statements like Exod. 12:12, or misinterprets Exod. 15:11 and other such passages.

The Ten Commandments can be seen only, like the rest of the law, against the background of the COVENANT; this in turn rests on the salvation history of the exodus. Other codes within the law are basically an expansion and application of these principles to various facets of life, rather as the NT epistles apply the truth of the gospel. Thus the Ten Commandments became the root of all subsequent Israelite morality as well as of religion.

B. The Covenant Code. Immediately following the Ten Words (Exod. 20:22—23:33) is the Covenant Code, often called the Book of the Covenant. It seems to be regarded in Scripture not only as having been promulgated at the time of the covenant made between God and Israel at Sinai, but also as being the actual terms of this covenant. Whatever the underlying reason, it certainly is a coherent whole, and may be studied in isolation from the rest of the law without doing violence to its context.

Some scholars today, following the Albright school, would see it as a typical piece of Bronze Age legislation, and therefore of Mosaic date, although others would claim that it was borrowed at that date from Canaanite or other sources. Much depends upon whether the historian accepts the biblical tradition of a generation of semisettled life around the oasis of Kadesh before the conquest of Canaan (Deut. 1:46). Clearly the Covenant Code contemplates settled agricultural life of a simple nature such as could well be practiced there. Sheep and oxen and slaves are the usual forms of wealth; the old generic name "Hebrew" is still used, probably with a wider meaning than "Israelite" (Exod. 21:2); altars are of earth (20:24); crops are sown (22:5; 23:10); three agricultural festivals are kept (23:14–17). None of this goes beyond what was possible in that semisettled generation.

It is possible that much of this code (as no doubt parts of the Ten Commandments, cf. Gen. 26:12) antedates Moses. Whatever the duration of the Israelite stay in Egypt, they were certainly settled, not nomadic, in GOSHEN. Even in the earliest days of the migration, Israel's ancestors had been ass-nomads, not camel-nomads, which implies certain contacts with settled life. The branch of the clan settled at HARAN seems to have progressed in this direction even more rapidly than Abraham's group. It is therefore inconceivable that Moses should have been ignorant of all these legal traditions of his people. If it contains many of the customary laws of Israel's forefathers (no doubt now transformed by the fuller revelation given to Moses at Sinai), it is not surprising that the Covenant Code bears many similarities to other codes preserved by Israel's Semitic neighbors (likewise no doubt crystallizations of Semitic traditional law). Nor is it surprising that in part Deuteronomy repeats the provisions of the Covenant Code, in part supplements them, presumably by including other areas of the same ancestral law, purified by the clear light of "Yahwism."

Whether or not Moses' stay in MIDIAN had any influence on the law as a whole and the Covenant Code in particular is a question that cannot be answered with present limited knowledge. The biblical tradition is clear that Moses spent a generation in MIDIAN, that he married a Midianite girl, and that her father was a priest of Midian (Exod. 2:17–21). Midian was at least half settled at the time, Jethro was associated with Moses in judicial activity (18:13–22). It is thus unthinkable that Moses should have been ignorant of Midianite law and custom; it is highly likely that this was only another form of ancestral Semitic law.

C. The Deuteronomic Code. Found in Deut. 12–26, this code is another coherent group of laws about whose separate existence there can be no doubt. Even the most extreme critics usually recognize the book of DEUTERONOMY as an independent literary unit. While in some ways it is a summing up of the whole of the law and history of early Israel (a sort of *multum in parvo*), in other ways it is only a "supplement" of earlier codes, especially the Covenant Code, by covering areas initially omitted, as well as reinterpreting the old. That is why its position may be compared to that of John's gospel in the NT. Much of it is cast in discourse style, a sort of "reminiscences of Moses," with which the speeches in Acts may be compared. A recognition of the historicity of the material of John (cf. C. H. Dodd, *Historical Tradition in the Fourth Gospel* [1963]) is not without significance in such a parallel. Deuteronomy is infused throughout with a warmth of love that continually introduces new motives for keeping the law (Deut. 25:3) and humanitarian application of the law, even extending to wild animals (22:6). "Covenant love" so dominates the code that it has a right to be called a "Covenant Code" (Exod. 20–23), which it so closely resembles.

Many scholars have considered Deuteronomy a postprophetic production, both from its style and language (where it closely resembles Jeremiah) and also from its theology. But it does not in theology differ essentially from the Ten Words or the Book of the Covenant; indeed, it is precisely because of this similarity that some critical scholars "late-date" these two latter codes. In addition, many undoubtedly early features appear in the Deuteronomic Code (cf. the valuable study on Deuteronomy by M. Kline, *The Treaty of the Great King* [1963]). The old terminology "Hebrew" is still used (Deut. 15:12). Life is still basically simple and rural, though houses (22:8) and towns (13:12) are known. If, as suggested, Deuteronomy draws heavily on ancestral Semitic law (like the Covenant Code), then all is explicable. Similarities to Hammurabi's Code are likewise explicable if the latter is only a codification of common Semitic law; in any case, Moses would have known Hammurabi's Code, since it was widely studied in Egypt.

If Deuteronomy was the law book found in Josiah's day in the temple (2 Ki. 22:11), it would certainly have existed in 621 B.C. That does not necessarily prove that it was produced only then, the more so as, when read, it was immediately recognized as being the well-known substance of the "Law of Moses." Some scholars like E. Robertson (*The Old Testament Problem* [1950]) have considered that it was the formulation of Mosaic law made in Samuel's day; others have considered that it was a N Israelite law book, based on Mosaic tradition and preserved at some northern sanctuary. Samuel wrote out some constitution for the kingdom (1 Sam. 10:25) which must surely have had some relation to the material of Deut. 17:14–20. Perhaps all that can be said is that Deuteronomy, like the Book of the Covenant, is an instance of formulation of part of one and the same early Hebrew legal tradition apparently adopted and purified by Moses for the use of his people.

The two vexed questions of Deuteronomy are the so-called "Law of the Kingdom" (Deut. 17:14–20) and the "Law of the Single Sanctuary" (12:5). These are both reckoned as showing late dates, the first because of the nonexistence of kingship in Israel till two centuries after Moses; the second, because it seems to contradict Exod. 20:24, which appears to allow worship wherever Israel has received any divine revelation or theophany. As this included the patriarchal age, obviously there could be many such sites; and the OT does show that there was worship at Bethel, Beersheba, Gilgal, Jericho, etc. Neither of these passages is decisive, in itself alone, as proving a late date for the material of Deuteronomy. Israel might not have had kings, but all her sister peoples had kingship long before the time of Moses (Edom, Moab, Ammon, as well as the Canaanites) and from earliest days, while perhaps worship of Yahweh was tolerated elsewhere, there had been only one "amphictyonic sanctuary" where the annual religious folkmoots were held (cf. Josh. 22:10–12).

D. The Code of Holiness. This code is contained in Lev. 17–26, which again seems a cohesive "whole within a whole." It is dominated by the same lofty thought of the HOLINESS and transcendence of God as is found in Ezekiel. The code is full of elaborate instructions as to how to maintain, even in the physical realm, this holiness that comes from being the people of God. Leviticus, as a whole, makes less appeal to moderns than, say, Deuteronomy—partly because all of Leviticus is virtually a "priest's handbook" on technical matters of religion, and partly because such rules of cleanliness and worship have ceased to be directly applicable or practical in modern life. With no temple, no sacrifice, no distinction between clean and unclean food (Mk. 7.19), much of the direct relevance has gone for the Christian today. If Deut. 6:5 contained the first part of the Lord's summary of the law ("Love the LORD your God ... "), Lev. 19:18 contained the second ("love your neighbor as yourself"). No code that contains such a statement can be considered barren, and this verse is by no means an isolated instance of what might be called a "Deuteronomic attitude."

Further, the Code of Holiness contains the same sort of motivation as the Ten Commandments, by which ethics are deduced directly from theology (in the proper sense of that word, as being the known and revealed nature and will of God). A keynote of the Holiness Code is Lev. 19:2, "Be holy because I, the LORD [Yahweh] your God, am holy." Put more succinctly, the keynote becomes the simple phrase, "I am Yahweh" (19:4 and many other passages), placed at the end of a verse as the reason for the command that has gone before. No code can be called barren that contains such motivation, and the sonorous rhythm of the phrase sounds early.

The Code of Holiness usually is associated closely with the teaching of the prophet EZEKIEL; as he was a priest himself, this is not surprising. The minor differences between Ezekiel and the code may perhaps be explained by the possibility that Ezekiel recognized in the captivity the judgment of God, and was concerned to recall his people to the ancient law. Minor differences need not disturb, for in time some laws become inapplicable and disused. Ezekiel quotes from the Code of Holiness (Ezek. 20:11, 13, 21). The literary style may not be due only to a late date. Certain aspects may be typical of the clipped conservatism of religious and liturgical language.

E. The Priestly Code. This may be a useful name to apply to the material of the rest of Leviticus (which has no such one compelling motive as the Code of Holiness) and perhaps to certain other parts of the Pentateuch. To describe it as a code, as though it had existed in isolation, seems a misnomer; it is only a convenient term for the vast body of traditional material that every sacrificing priest in Israel must know. As he was not only priest, but also doctor and health inspector, as well as custodian of public and private morals, the Priestly Code covers a wide area of life.

The archaeological discoveries at Ras Shamra (see UGARIT) and elsewhere in the Middle E have shown, by the existence of parallels, the probable age of the material contained therein, whatever the date of the transcription. Perhaps therefore in the ritual area, too, Moses adopted and purified many of the sacrificial practices of Israel's ancestors. Although there appears to have been no specialized priesthood in Israel until Mosaic days (Exod. 32:29), it is hard to believe that the patriarchs had no customary rules governing their offerings and sacrifices.

F. The Ritual Decalogue. So far, the codes isolated have had at least some claim to individual identity. Whether the so-called Ritual Decalogue (Exod. 34:10–26) ever existed independently of its context, or whether it is a creation of biblical scholars, is most uncertain. It is undoubted that various ritual prescriptions existed; it is even possible that they were combined into lists or catalogs and read at festival times at one or other of the great early meeting places (Gilgal, Shechem, or Shiloh). There is no reason to isolate ten or twelve arbitrarily to make either a Decalogue (corresponding to the Ten Commandments) or a Dodecalogue (corresponding to the Twelve Tribes). Indeed, the first of these names is probably influenced by the false idea that there must be a set of "ritual" rules corresponding to the "ethical" rules of the Ten Words.

This view, however, ignores the fact that no such distinction was felt in early days; even the Ten Words contain two provisions that might be described as ritual (the prescribing of aniconic worship, and the enjoining of observance of every seventh day). With this proviso, it may be admitted freely that there is a concentration of "ritual laws" governing Israel's worship found in Exod. 34:10–26. R. H. Pfeiffer finds traces in various other parts of the Covenant Code and the Deuteronomic Code. Certainly this Exodus passage is couched in typically abrupt early Israelite style, with the use of the second person singular ("you shall … you shall not …"). The chief items are the destruction of Canaanite altars and images, and the observance of the SABBATH and the three great annual FEASTS of Yahweh.

In the biblical account, these laws are prefixed by a revelation of Yahweh's name and nature, accompanied by the recarving of the tablets of the law, and introduced by the words, "Behold, I make a covenant" (Exod. 34:10 KJV). Perhaps therefore "Second Book of the Covenant" would be a better name for this material; v. 27 is particularly clear, "for in accordance with these words I have made a covenant with you and with Israel."

G. Blessings and curses. The modern fashion is to see the blessings and curses (cf. the NT "Beatitudes" and "Woes") as liturgical forms, pronounced solemnly and in public at great religious ceremonies, and believed to be effective in themselves as producing the result described. While many will dissent from the latter part of such a definition, there is evidence in Scripture that the first part is true, at least on certain historic occasions, if not as part of the regular worship of Israel. A good example is Deut. 27:15–26, where twelve solemn curses are to be pronounced by the Levites at an assembly on the hills above SHECHEM (cf. Josh. 8:34).

Two things, however, should be noted: the liturgical curses pronounced are not on a set of new offenses, but on offenses condemned elsewhere in other Israelite "codes." The list of curses is only a summary of the negative aspect of Israel's law, and their direction and rhythm is that of the early Israelite Torah. Second, the curses are not pronounced in isolation. This is no magical ceremony, but a proclamation of the consequences of either obeying or disregarding the revealed mind of God.

Six tribes were to stand on Mount GERIZIM to bless, while the other six tribes stood on Mount EBAL to curse. Presumably the "blessings" are substantially those contained in Deut. 28, perhaps originally expressed in a more succinct form, corresponding to the form of the curses in the previous chapter. For examples of similar blessings see the poetic blessings of Jacob in Gen. 49 (which also contain curses in the case of Reuben, Simeon, and Levi; see vv. 3–7) and the blessing of Moses (Deut. 33), with the other smaller fragments. In addition Num. 23–24 contain some very oracular poems (the Oracles of BALAAM), which combine blessings with curses; nevertheless, it is hard to think that such found any regular place in public worship.

H. Moses and the law codes. Apart from these seven codes, others have been isolated from time to time with varying degrees of plausibility by different scholars, but none has commanded general acceptance. Even these seven are mainly of interest as showing the possible raw material that underlay the law of Moses.

Surely the background, training, and education of Moses was God's preparation for the writing of his great lifework. He was by birth an Israelite, and also a member of the wider Hebrew group, and thus an inheritor of the common law of all Semitic people; by training an Egyptian noble, and thus familiar with Hammurabi's law and Egyptian juristic comment on it; by force of circumstance, a great man in Midian, and both a spectator and participant in the legal processes of the semidesert. Who was better trained and equipped than he to become under God the great lawgiver of Israel, and codifier of his people's law? No doubt in the Torah of Moses' day, there was much that was new, in the shape of the fresh and deeper revelation of Yahweh. No doubt, since Yahweh was also expressly the "God of the Fathers," even if his name was not known to them (Exod. 6:3), there was also much that was old and familiar, although now purified and transformed by the new revelation. Both parts alike are God's self-revelation and the Torah.

VI. Land laws in the OT. As Israel was basically an agricultural people from the time of the conquest of Canaan until the Babylonian captivity (with a brief essay to the world of commerce and manufacturing, under Solomon), a study of their land laws may be of some interest. First, it is well to notice that no complete system of land laws can be built up from the Pentateuch alone; and yet no other codification of early Israelite laws is known, except for the MISHNAH, which seems to preserve additional laws in force at the time of the destruction of Herod's temple. Obviously, Israel had more land laws than these two works contain; therefore it is only reasonable to assume that in this area (as doubtless in that of commerce and elsewhere) she simply used the common Semitic law, supplementing it by specifically Israelite regulations where such were necessitated by Israel's revelation of Yahweh. Only some such practice can account for the otherwise inexplicable "gaps" in the Torah, here and elsewhere.

Second, Israel must have had some "land laws," even if only customary law, long before Moses. Nomads need no such laws, but ABRAHAM seems to buy the sepulchre for SARAH by good Hittite law (Gen. 23) which would illustrate both the need for land laws and the "law borrowing" mentioned above. As soon as ISAAC began to sow crops in the coastal plain (26:12), there must have been need to observe the local land laws, insofar as such laws were neutral religiously (vv. 17–22 suggest considerable litigation over water rights). In Egypt, whatever the exact duration of the stay of the Israelites, they seem to have been market gardeners as well as herdsmen, otherwise they would scarcely have longed for cucumbers, melons, onions, leeks, and garlic, when wandering in the Sinai desert (Num. 11:5). Complicated land laws would have been necessary for those whose garden plots were annually flooded by the NILE, obliterating all divisions.

If Israel was semisettled at Kadesh for a generation (Deut. 1:46), she surely grew crops around the oasis, as well as sending her flocks and herds to graze in the desert; at least primitive land law would have been necessary. JACOB bought land legally from the sons of HAMOR (Gen. 33:19), though the sons held the SHECHEM area by right of conquest (34:25–29), as Israel under Joshua held her Canaanite acres. Once the sacred lot had apportioned conquered land to tribe and family it must be held legally or not at all, and since the land was Yahweh's gift, such land law was religious law.

This last attitude can be seen clearly as late as the reign of AHAB in the N, where NABOTH asserts it (1 Ki. 21:3). For the same reason, the removal of a neighbor's land mark was a serious religious offense in Israel (Deut. 19:14), as well as stealing land from a neighbor. Jacob, as he lay dying, bequeathed his plot to JOSEPH (Gen. 48:22) by legal act of INHERITANCE. Once land was owned and assigned, the aim of the law was to keep it in perpetuity in the same family or clan. The principle had been established already by the Mosaic judgment (Num. 27:1–11), whereby a brotherless heiress could inherit her father's estate. In such cases, the husband who married her must belong to her own clan, lest the land should leave their possession. (See 26:33; 27:7; 36:11; Josh. 17:4 for the "test case" of the daughters of ZELOPHEHAD.) Numbers 27 and 36 are important passages for understanding this fundamental principle of Israelite land tenure, and also for seeing the importance gradually assumed by the "next

This cuneiform tablet from Alalakh (c. 1720 B.C.) is a legal document dealing with the legacy of certain houses in the region of Aleppo. (The tablet is still in its clay envelope, which includes the seal impressions of 10 witnesses.)

of kin" to whom the land fell in default of direct heirs.

In pursuance of the same principle, land might not be permanently alienated by its owner. Important here is the peculiarly Israelite custom of the JUBILEE YEAR, when all lands reverted to their original owners (Num. 36:4). While it appears that this law actually became a dead letter in Israel, in principle it corresponded to the modern practice of "leasing" land for a period of years, after which the land would revert to the state or the original landlord. Seven sevens of years was a doubly sacred number, and for the Israelite it corresponded to the "ninety nine years" or "nine hundred and ninety-nine years" of British leases. There is nothing inherently improbable in such a regulation, the more so as it is linked with the agrarian system by which fields were to be left fallow every seventh year—a wise provision in a marginal country with inadequate use of fertilizers.

The book of Leviticus deals in detail with both sabbatical and Jubilee years (Lev. 25:1–12). The great principle upon which all is based is clearly enunciated: "The land must not be sold permanently, because the land is mine and you are but aliens and my tenants" (v. 23). Naturally this custom, if observed, would govern the buying and selling prices of land. The duty to buy back temporarily alienated land, and thus keep it in the clan, rested with the "redeemer kinsman" (v. 25; see REDEMPTION). Another passage (27:16–25) shows that such "reversion" in the Jubilee Year was even intended to be true of land dedicated to God, so strongly was this legal principle felt. This provision prevented the accumulation of large landed estates to the detriment of the poor.

The custom of LEVIRATE LAW by which a husband's brother (or failing that, a husband's nearest male relative) was bound to marry his brother's childless widow, was doubtless connected with this desire to keep land in the family. There is detailed evidence of the persistence of this custom in the book of RUTH (where land inheritance rights were also involved, Ruth 4:5; the legal basis is in Deut. 25:5–10). By the date of Ruth, apparently the transference of the loosened sandal had lost its original meaning and corresponded to the transference of the land. The presence of ten wit-

Egyptian leather sandals stitched with papyrus twine (late 2nd millennium B.C.). By the time of Ruth, the transfer of land was confirmed with the loosened sandal (Ruth 4:7–8).

nesses (Ruth 4:2) is an interesting legal point; witnesses also appear essential in the land transference recorded in Abraham's day (Gen. 23:10) and Jeremiah's time (Jer. 32:10), where there is a full deed of purchase.

It seems certain that this simple agrarian system broke down under the twin impacts of industrial development and rapid urbanization from the time of Solomon onward. The increased importance of trade and consequent high rates of interest bore hard on the farmers. To judge from Amos and Hosea, many became landless laborers, and were even enslaved for debt, with their lands first mortgaged and then permanently alienated. But the example of Naboth in the northern kingdom of Ahab's day (1 Ki. 21:3) shows the persistence with which some Israelites still clung to the old ideas long after Solomon.

From Jeremiah's day there is full and detailed record of a land transaction (Jer. 32:6–15, apparently a "redemption," though with no marriage involved) mentioning witnesses and documents, both sealed deeds and open deeds, containing terms and conditions of purchase. Such deeds were stored, like the DEAD SEA SCROLLS, in earthenware jars (32:14). The probable nature of the documents can be seen from much of the ELEPHANTINE papyri as deal with property transfers. Jeremiah's action presupposes that the Jews would return to their ancestral properties after the EXILE (32:15) and, to judge from Ezra and Nehemiah, many did. No doubt the old legal forms of land tenure were resumed. This was possible because, unlike northern Israel,

Judah had not been "settled" by foreign farmers, but had apparently remained fallow during the exile. However, Judah seems to have learned little from the punishment of the exile; for the same agrarian troubles appear almost at once (high interest, mortgages, slavery for debt, and alienation of land, Neh. 5:1–13).

VII. Attitude to law in the OT

A. In early days. It is hard to avoid the conclusion that not only did observances like the sabbatical year or the Year of Jubilee quickly become a dead letter, but that most of the law was treated in the same way. True, archaeology shows that images appeared very slowly and late in early Israelite settlements in Canaan (presumably under Canaanite influence), so that the basic aniconic principle lasted for a time; in fact, images of Israel's God have never been discovered by archaeologists.

Even that principle began to crumble as the very national fabric of Israel seemed to break up in the days of the judges. See JUDGES, PERIOD OF. Some such declension was known by the authors of Josh. 24:31 and Jdg. 2:10–13. GIDEON's family openly worshiped symbols of BAAL and ASHERAH (6:25); he himself made a golden "ephod" (prob. an idol) in Ophrah with the spoils of victory (8:27). The book of Judges contains also the remarkable story of how an image was stolen from EPHRAIM and carried off by the men of DAN to their new northern sanctuary (chs. 17—18).

But this declension does not prove that the law was not known, still less that it did not exist; for Gideon knows that Yahweh alone is King in Israel (Jdg. 8:23). JEPHTHAH will not take Yahweh's name in vain (11:35); and SAMSON is a NAZIRITE (13:5). Even the darkest pages of Judges (the "holy war" against BENJAMIN in ch. 20) corresponded to an article of the old law, as recorded in Deut. 13:12–16. At least one of the yearly feasts of Yahweh was still being kept at SHILOH (Jdg. 21:19), and pious farmers like ELKANAH went up regularly to worship there (1 Sam. 1:3). Indeed, the whole story of SAMUEL shows how the daily life of the simple Israelite was bound in a nexus of religious custom that stemmed from Israel's law, however little he might know of its detailed prescriptions.

The same could be said for the idyllic picture of the country life in the book of Ruth.

B. The prophetic period. A generation ago most OT scholars considered that Israel's PROPHETS were from the beginning sharply opposed to her PRIESTS. The prophets were held to be great moral and ethical innovators, and thus foes of the entire sacrificial system of the law. Such scholars usually considered that the law did not contain any moral teaching, except perhaps general principles. Passages like Hos. 6:6 and Amos 5:21–24 were adduced to show the prophetic opposition to sacrifice (and indeed to all outward forms of religion), while Amos 5:25, like Jer. 7:22, was sometimes used to deny that even Israel's sacrificial system was truly Mosaic in date.

But Amos 2:4 distinctly says that God's punishment will come on Judah "because they have rejected the law of the LORD and have not kept his decrees," and 5:21–22 mentions by name several ritual ordinances of the law. Hosea gives the reason for God's rejection as "you have ignored the law of your God" (Hos. 4:6). The true prophetic attitude seems thus to be that expressed by SAMUEL to SAUL in 1 Sam. 15:22, "To obey is better than sacrifice." No man could say that this statement came from an enemy of the law; Samuel was a sacrificing priest, whose initial rift with Saul took place on a question of the propriety of a "layman" sacrificing (ch. 13:12–13).

The prophetic attitude is not a rejection of the law, but an emphasis on the moral basis that had always underlain it. Amos and Hosea, the first of the "writing prophets," certainly show knowledge of the Torah, the former perhaps mostly of the "history of salvation" (Amos 2:9–10) and the sacrificial system (5:21–25); the latter is well aware of the ethical law (Hos. 4:1–2, apparently referring to the Ten Commandments; cf. 12:9; 13:4) and the covenant (8:1). Hosea seems to know some written law (8:12), a tradition which, as seen above, goes back through Samuel (1 Sam. 10:25) and Joshua (Josh. 8:32) to Moses himself (Exod. 24:4).

The pendulum has swung completely to the other extreme. With the view that prophets in Israel were "cultic prophets," usually organized in bands at Israelite sanctuaries, and possibly identified with the Levites, and that they had a definite place in the liturgical life and worship of Israel, such opposition to the priesthood as that postulated above becomes muted. While this is certainly not overemphasized, it is a useful corrective to the older view. It is true that Jeremiah and Ezekiel were priests, and that Isaiah received his call in the temple (Isa. 6:1); but all three reserved their prophetic freedom to criticize sharply any leaning on outward observances to the exclusion of the spirit of the law. This was thoroughly Mosaic.

C. In later days. The great change in Israel's attitude to the Torah is marked not so much by a date as by an event, the Babylonian EXILE. In a foreign land, the law took on a new importance, by which Israel was distinguished from the countless other small racial groups of a polyglot empire. The exile was realized as the final result of failure to keep and obey the law, a lesson brought home by all the preexilic prophets. The law was certainly read in the returned community at Jerusalem (Neh. 8). As far as could be, it had become the state law of this tiny group; religious leaders like Ezra and political leaders like Nehemiah enforced it wherever they could. This was possible not only because of the preference of the imperial Persian government to rule subject peoples according to their own laws; it corresponded to a new will and purpose in Israel herself.

The number of references to "law" in Ezra and Nehemiah is remarkable, and it is undoubtedly no accident. Not since the old wilderness days had Torah held such a central place in Israel's life; its prestige was enhanced by the dying of the voice of prophecy (Zech. 13:3–4), and the fact that priests could apparently no longer give guidance by the use of Urim and Thummim (Neh. 7:65). Even such prophetic voice as still existed was raised in defense of the law; for Mal. 4:4 closes the OT with the words, "Remember the law of my servant Moses, the decrees and laws I gave him at Horeb for all Israel," followed by the promise of the "second Elijah."

It must have seemed to many as if the great promise of the new covenant (Jer. 31:33) had been fulfilled already, as though God had already written his law on human hearts (see COVENANT, THE NEW). The bitter experiences of the returned community give the lie to this; both Ezra and Nehemiah found, as Moses no doubt had, that the human heart is still the same (Ezra 9:3, Neh. 9:6). The returned exiles paid service to the law, but it was only lip service. For the fulfillment of the promise through Jeremiah, one must wait until PENTECOST and NT times. The hand of the law was not only an iron hand on Israel; it soon became a dead hand, stifling with its legalism the inner spiritual life. What it became for the PHARISEES can be seen from the NT; but even then PAUL insists that it is not the Torah that is at fault, but only fallen sinners (Rom. 7:7–12). See also CRIMES AND PUNISHMENTS; ETHICS IN THE OT.

(In addition to the works mentioned in the body of this article, see J. L'Hour, *Die Ethik der Bundestradition im Alten Testament* [1967]; H. J. Boecker, *Law and the Administration of Justice in the Old Testament and Ancient East* [1980]; R. Sonsino, *Motive Clauses in Hebrew Law: Biblical Forms and Near Eastern Parallels* [1980]; R. Westbrook, *Studies in Biblical and Cuneiform Law* [1988]; Z. W. Falk, *Hebrew Law in Biblical Times*, 2nd ed. [2001]; C. Wilcke, *Early Ancient Near Eastern Law: A History of Its Beginnings* [2007]; *ABD*, 4:242–54; *NIDOTTE*, 4:893–900; *DOTP*, 497–515.)   R. A. COLE

law (NT).
  I. Synoptic Gospels
  II. Early Christian community
  III. Paul's writings
  IV. Hebrews
  V. James
  VI. John's gospel

I. Synoptic Gospels. The word *nomos* G3795 occurs only eight times in Matthew (Matt. 5:17–18; 7:12; 11:13; 12:5; 22:36, 40; 23:23), nine times in Luke (Lk. 2:22–23, 24, 27, 39; 10:26; 16:16–17; 24:44), and not at all in Mark. In every passage except Lk. 2:23, it is used with the definite article. Generally *nomos* refers to the PENTATEUCH; however, when combined with *hoi prophētai* ("the prophets"), it broadens so as to give the phrase the meaning of the whole OT. More specifically *nomos* signifies both the law (Torah) and the Pentateuch. As law in terms of commandments it denotes both what we should do and not do (Matt. 5:19). With the possible exception of Matt. 12:5, it is never used in the synoptics for the whole OT.

Stone cups from the 1st cent. Jesus rebuked certain teachers and Pharisees who misused the law. He said, "First clean the inside of the cup and dish, and then the outside also will be clean" (Matt. 23:26).

Throughout his public ministry, Jesus severely criticized the scribal misuse of the law. He utterly denounced those who would interpret it mediatorially, setting it forth as a means whereby a person could gain acceptance with God (cf. the parables of Lk. 15). He further opposed the Pharisaical externalization of the law, by which one would have supposed that a person's relationship to God was determined simply by an outward conformity to its stipulations. In contrast to these errors, Jesus insisted that people's relationship to his own words and deeds determined their relationship to God. Not the law but Jesus himself was the mediator between God and sinners.

Jesus also criticized that use of the law whereby it served to protect disobedience to God. Keeping individual commandments is no necessary evidence of a readiness to give oneself completely to Jesus Christ. Again, Jesus warned against those who would obey the law in order to gain recognition from others (Matt. 23:5–12). To those whose obedience was motivated by a desire for the approval of men he declared, "they have received their reward in full" (6:2).

Jesus not only condemned the wrong use of the law, he also confirmed its validity and pointed the way to its right use. Although he negated it mediatorially he affirmed it ethically. Those who have become the recipients of his forgiving mercy find in the law a pattern for right conduct. The SERMON ON THE MOUNT, for example, has been appropriately called "A Pattern for Life," the life of the disciple. Jesus cannot accept as good any motive or action not governed by the will of God revealed in the law. There is no other acceptable standard of goodness.

Jesus' way of dealing with the sinner shows his recognition of the law's validity. He forgives sins and rejects those who as his professed followers practice lawlessness (*anomia G490*, Matt. 7:23). To be lawless is to be loveless (24:12 NASB). Concretely, the law demands love for God and neighbor (Mk. 12:28–31; Matt. 22:40). True discipleship to Jesus is evidenced in loving acts of obedience to the law.

II. Early Christian community. When the early Christians first began the move out to a largely GENTILE world, conflict arose concerning the law. The first clear record of this controversy is that found in Acts 15 and Gal. 2 (although some scholars believe that these two passages deal with different historical circumstances; see COUNCIL OF JERUSALEM).

The following information concerning this issue may be set forth from Gal. 2. First, there was essential agreement between PAUL's message and that proclaimed by the early Christian community (2:2, 6). Second, despite essential agreement, there were some practical questions about which there would yet be controversy (2:11–14). One concrete question was how far Jewish Christians could go in respect to living together in fellowship with Gentile Christians who did not keep the law. In particular, this matter might also have raised the question as to whether they could have fellowship in the LORD'S SUPPER.

According to Acts 15, the Apostolic Council concluded three things: (1) that the law is not to be kept as a means of acceptance before God, (2) that *only* faith in Jesus brings salvation to both Jews and Gentiles, (3) that the law is still applicable to Jews within this new theological perspective. It is important to understand here that the obedience rendered to the law by Jewish Christians was rendered out of love to God for his redeeming grace. Fulfillment of the law was not regarded as a presupposition for belonging to the KINGDOM OF GOD.

In the further unfolding of beliefs in the early church, conflicting views persisted despite the council's pronouncement. The radical party (JUDAIZERS) insisted that the Gentile Christians must keep the law, including circumcision, if they expected to belong to the redeemed community. From Paul's writings, especially his epistle to the GALATIANS, we learn that these Judaizers attempted to promote their view with great zeal among Pauline churches. Among the means employed to support their teaching were efforts to discredit Paul's apostleship (Gal. 1) and to expose his view of the law as leading to antinomianism (Rom. 5:20—6:1).

The orthodox party (represented by JAMES, PETER, and those of the community who followed them) seems to have followed the decisions laid down by the Jerusalem Council. Those of this position believed that the law was to be obeyed by Jewish Christians and that such obedience would enable them to have an effective witness to the Jewish world. They did not believe that obedience made them righteous before God, and they were prepared to accept believing Gentiles into their fellowship without requiring them to keep the law. In mixed congregations, Gentile Christians were advised to observe such points of the law as would make the fellowship of Jewish Christians defensible before the eyes of the Jewish world (Acts 15:19–21).

III. Paul's writings. Though Paul's use of *nomos* is not uniform, his starting point is to employ it predominantly for the Mosaic law (Rom. 7:22, 25; 8:7; 1 Cor. 9:9; et al.). Paul does not seem to make a significant distinction between the Decalogue and the rest of the legal material in the OT. The second use of *nomos* refers to the Pentateuch (Gal. 4:21). The two words "Law and Prophets" are taken together to refer to the whole OT (Rom. 3:21), and "Law" can refer to the OT generally (cf. 1 Cor. 14:21, a quotation from Isaiah). Paul combines verses from all parts of Scripture (Rom. 3:10–18) under the rubric of the law (v. 19).

Paul also saw law as the living will of God, not expressed exclusively in the Mosaic law (Rom. 2:14). In the context of this passage the apostle argues that there are no people who do not have a law of some kind. Sometimes Paul uses *nomos* in a figurative sense, generally with a word of explanation, such as in 3:27, where he distinguishes "the law of works" from "the law of faith." Here the word *nomos* means "principle" (cf. NIV, NRSV). Paul's point is that the "principle" of faith, not works, describes the basis on which human boasting is excluded. Likewise, it would seem best to take *nomos* figuratively in 7:21. Sometimes Paul uses *nomos* to denote some governing principle of conduct which comes from some source (the latter indicated by the genitive). This usage is found in such passages as Rom. 7:25; 8:2; Gal. 6:2. In the latter two passages "the law of the Spirit of life" and "the law of Christ" are in sharp contrast to the OT law.

It is most important to note that the demanding will of God is ultimately a matter of personal communication, not abstract formulation. In Rom. 3:19 the law is referred to as if it were personal, "whatever the law says, it says to those who are under the law"; one might substitute the word "God" here for the word "law." (Cf. Rom. 4:15; 7:1; 1 Cor. 9:8.)

Paul's concept of the law is decisively determined by the CROSS of Christ. From this perspective he both negates and affirms the law. The negation of the law as a consequence of the cross is stated clearly in Gal. 2:21, "I do not set aside the grace of God, for if righteousness could be gained through the law, Christ died for nothing!" In this and similar statements in other of his writings, the apostle repudiates the law as the basis for JUSTIFICATION. The law is the mediation of God's will for fallen human beings, but precisely because of their fallenness they are totally unable to keep it.

The apostle also affirms the law by teaching that it prohibits that which is sinful (Rom. 6:15). He strongly emphasizes the negative character of the law, stressing that it is God's word directed against sin, though all the negatives may be summed up in the one positive of love (3:19). Through the law the sinfulness of SIN is exposed. The law shows it to be rebellion against God. Though sin is always there, it comes to life through the law (7:8–9). It is the law which first makes sin real rebellion (5:20). Law drives sinners to Christ by revealing the enormity of their sin; it completely unmasks them before a Holy God. They are shut up by the law under sin (Gal. 3:22–23). Properly understood, then, the law prevents us from attempting to secure a righteous standing before God in any other way than by faith in the redeeming work of Jesus Christ.

God's eternally abiding standard of acceptance before him is that of obedience to his will. The story of God's GRACE centers just in this, that that obedience which sinners are unable to render has been rendered by another in their place. Paul states, "For just as through the disobedience of the one man the many were made sinners, so also through the obedience of the one man the many will be made righteous" (Rom. 5:19). Through faith in Christ, his obedience is accounted as ours.

The second affirmation of Paul regarding the law is found in such a passage as Rom. 8:4, where he states that Christ fulfilled the law in our place precisely "in order that the righteous requirement of the law might be fully met in us" through the dynamic of a new power, even that of the HOLY SPIRIT. Though the Christian is not under the law as a means of acceptance with God, he nevertheless seeks to obey the will of God in conformity to the pattern provided in the law. The *gift* of justification leads to a recognition of the *task* of obedience. (For further discussion of Paul's view of the law, including recent debate, see PAULINE THEOLOGY IV.)

IV. Hebrews. In this epistle *nomos* is used almost without exception to refer to the OT law, and more specifically to those laws that pertain to the priestly ministry and the priesthood. The law is viewed from a different perspective in this epistle from that found in the thought of either Jesus or Paul. While in the teaching of Jesus and Paul the law is primarily expressive of the will of God as regulatory of human conduct, in Hebrews it expresses that upon which the OT priesthood is based. The theme of this epistle is not the relation of law and gospel, but the relation of the priestly ministry of the OT to that of Christ's.

The author of Hebrews argues that though the OT priesthood finds its strength and authority in the law, it cannot bring perfection (Heb. 7:18–19). This can be achieved only by the distinguished High Priest, even Christ. For Paul the law is weak because people do not do it, for the author of Hebrews it is weak because people do it. Paul and the author of Hebrews agree, however, that the true purpose of the law is to point the sinner to Christ in order that through him he may find access to God. It is only through the high-priestly ministry of Jesus that we may approach the Holy God.

V. James. This author employs *nomos* in only three passages. In Jas. 1:25, *nomos* would seem to be best understood as pointing to that total evangelical message as it makes claims upon the conduct of the believer. In contrast to the OT law, it is a perfect law of liberty.

In Jas. 2:8–11, *nomos* means "commandment" in the strict sense. The crucial question here is whether it is used for the whole of the OT law with all its commandments or only for the summary of this law in the law of love. The statement in v. 10 ("whoever keeps the whole law and yet stumbles at just one point is guilty of breaking all of it") might suggest that the whole of the OT law is intended, but the context would seem to argue against this interpretation. The writer states (v. 8) that if one really fulfills the law of love he does well (note the summary of individual commands, vv. 9–11).

The last passage is Jas. 4:11–12. The "law of freedom" is the will of God conceived of in terms of its validity for the individual. From the Christian standpoint the law of liberty is that which binds the individual not to specific commandments but to the obedience of love. This conception of law does not force the freedom of obedience into a schema after the matter of law. It should be clearly understood that James agrees with the teaching of both Jesus and Paul that law is to be interpreted in terms of the obedience of faith.

VI. John's gospel. John uses *nomos* fourteen times. The meaning is the usual one, the Pentateuch, though it is also used more generally for the whole of the OT. Sometimes it is used to denote a specific commandment (Jn. 7:19, 23) or a legal ordinance (7:51). John does not use *nomos* to suggest principally that which is regulatory of human or Christian action; rather he views it as meaning revelation (1:17), set in comparison or contrast to Jesus. John's point is that it is only in Jesus that God is most adequately revealed. Only in him is there a full manifestation of God's grace and truth. Throughout this gospel the Torah is contrasted as word of revelation with the Son who is the perfect revelation. This is the distinctive contribution of John as respects the meaning of the law, though he does in a few instances view it as also regulative of human action (13:34–35).

See also ETHICS OF JESUS; ETHICS OF PAUL; JESUS CHRIST VI; NEW TESTAMENT THEOLOGY III.C.

(The recent literature on this topic is voluminous. For summary treatments see *TDNT*, 4:1059–85; *NIDNTT*, 2:436–56; *ABD*, 4:254–65; *DJG*, 450–61; *DPL*, 529–42. Substantial works include E. P. Sanders, *Paul, The Law and the Jewish People* [1983]; J. D. G. Dunn, *Jesus, Paul and the Law: Studies in Mark and Galatians* [1990]; N. T. Wright, *The Climax of the Covenant: Christ and the Law in Pauline Theology* [1991]; T. R. Schreiner, *The Law and Its Fulfillment: A Pauline Theology of Law* [1993]; G. L. Bahnsen et al., *Five Views on Law and Gospel* [1996]; F. Thielman, *The Law and the New Testament: The Question of Continuity* [1999]; S. Westerholm, *Perspectives Old and New on Paul: The "Lutheran" Paul and His Critics* [2003]; D. A. Carson et al., eds., *Justification and Variegated Nomism*, 2 vols. [2002–2004]; O. Behrends, ed., *Der biblische Gesetzbegriff* [2006].) C. M. HORNE

law, oral. See MISHNAH.

law, Roman. See ROMAN LAW.

lawgiver. This English term is used sometimes (e.g., Isa. 33:22 NIV) to render a Hebrew word for "leader, ruler," *měḥōqēq* (poal ptc. from *ḥāqaq* H2980, "to hew out" or "to decree"). The KJV uses it also in several places where the Hebrew term appears to mean "scepter," which is a symbol of a ruler's authority (Gen. 49:10 et al.). In the NT, it is the rendering of Greek *nomothetēs* G3794, which James applies to God (Jas. 4:12). The concept is expressed also in other ways. For example, the fourth gospel describes MOSES as the one through whom the law was given, thus as God's instrument and agent (Jn. 1:17; 7:19). The same function of delivering the law of God to the people was ascribed by STEPHEN and by PAUL to the intermediary agency of angels (Acts 7:53; Gal. 3:19; cf. Heb. 2:2). See ANGEL; LAW (OT).

lawyer. The common Greek term for "lawyer" is *nomikos* G3788 (see Tit. 3:13). In the NT it occurs primarily with reference to those learned in the law of Moses, both written and oral, of which they were the official interpreters (Matt. 22:35; in these instances the NIV translates "expert in the law"). The term is used synonymously with *nomodidaskalos* G3791 ("teacher of the law") and with *grammateus* G1208 (see SCRIBE), as a comparison of the following passages shows: Matt. 22:35; Mk. 12:28, Lk. 5:17, 21; 10:25; 11:44–46. In this sense, the word is found once in Matthew (Matt. 22:35) and six times in Luke (Lk. 7:30; 10:25; 11:45–46, 52; 14:3).

Since every detail of Jewish life was expected to be regulated by the law, and since it was impossible for an ordinary Jew to become familiar with the multitude of legal requirements and to apply them in the new situations of daily life, it was absolutely necessary for some men to devote themselves to a study of the law. Those who did were the lawyers. Among the leading duties of the lawyers were the following: to study, interpret, and expound the law; to teach the law in the schools and in the synagogues; to decide questions of law; to act as judges in the courts.

As depicted in the Gospels, the lawyers regularly showed themselves to be unsympathetic to Jesus, and they joined the PHARISEES in opposing him. They rejected the teaching of JOHN THE BAPTIST (Lk. 7:30). Jesus denounced them in severe language for putting unbearable burdens upon men, refusing to help them in their need, and for actually hindering those who sought the truth (11:45–52). They opposed Jesus for healing on the SABBATH day (14:3). During Passion Week one tried to embarrass Jesus by means of a difficult question (Matt. 22:35). J. L. KELSO

laying on of hands. See HANDS, LAYING ON OF.

Lazarus. laz'uh-ruhs (Λάζαρος G3276, from Heb. לְעָזָר, abbreviated form of אֶלְעָזָר H540, "God has helped"). Friend of Jesus, whom he raised from death; brother of MARTHA and MARY. Although the name was common among the Jews, he is the only historical personage in the NT bearing the name (however, see LAZARUS AND DIVES). He is mentioned only in Jn. 11 and 12.

The home of Lazarus was in BETHANY, near Jerusalem (Jn. 11:1, 30; 12:1), located SE of the MOUNT OF OLIVES. Jesus was a close friend of the Bethany household. He was entertained in their home more than once, probably often (Matt. 21:17; Lk. 10:38–41; Jn. 11). His love for all three was well known (Jn. 11:5, 36); to that love the sisters appealed in informing Jesus of Lazarus's sickness (11:3). Jesus called Lazarus "our friend" (11:11), indicating his friendship with the twelve disciples.

Illustration of Jesus before the tomb of Lazarus.

While the characters of Martha and Mary are distinctly drawn, nothing is known of the character and temper of Lazarus. Not a word from him is recorded. He appears in the gospel story, not for any shining qualities of character, but solely because of Christ's miracle restoring him to life and the impact that the restoration produced. His resuscitation after being dead four days caused many Jews to believe in Jesus (Jn. 11:45), but caused the SANHEDRIN to agree to put Jesus to death (11:47–53).

When Jesus returned to Bethany before the final PASSOVER, his friends there gave him a banquet; Lazarus was among those at table with him (Jn. 12:1–8; Mk. 14:3). The enthusiastic testimony of eyewitnesses of Lazarus's resurrection caused many from Jerusalem to flock to Bethany to see Lazarus as well as Jesus (Jn. 12:9). Their witness also caused the ovation Jesus received at the triumphal entry (12:17–18). The fact that Lazarus was a living witness to the power of Christ led the priests also to plot his death (12:10).

The narrative of the resurrection of Lazarus — longest gospel account of a miracle (Jn. 11) — is vivid, restrained, and perfectly coherent. It is the climax of the signs in John's gospel. This miracle has been vigorously assailed. Varied rationalistic attempts have been made to break the obvious meaning of the Johannine record. It has been claimed that Lazarus was in a trance, that it was a deliberate fraud arranged by Martha and Mary, with the connivance of Jesus; that it was an embellishment as professed history of Jesus' parable in Lk. 16:19–31. Such proposals are unconvincing and illustrate the credulity of unbelief.

Its historicity has been questioned because of the silence of the synoptics. This is an admitted difficulty. But the synoptics do not pretend to give all the deeds of Jesus; except for the final Passover, their story is Galilean. The enthusiasm at the triumphal entry in the synoptics is without explanation without some such event as the resurrection of Lazarus. The synoptics may have omitted the story to shield the members of the Bethany household.

Others admit that an actual event lies behind the account, but deny a literal resurrection. They see it as a symbolical portrayal of Christ's power to raise people from spiritual death in a life of sin. But the simple scriptural account gives no hint that the story was intended as an allegory. From the reactions of Christ's contemporaries, whether friend or foe, it is clear that they did not so demythologize the event. The miracle was intended by Christ to strengthen the faith of his disciples, challenge the nation to accept or reject him, and to foreshadow his own impending death and RESURRECTION.

(See further A. M. Fairbairn, *Studies in the Life of Christ* [1881], 201–18, who discusses the attacks of Paulus, Strauss, Bauer, Renan; J. D. Jones, *The Lord of Life and Death* [1919]; H. Daniel-Rops, *Jesus and his Times* [1954], 379–85; J. N. Sanders in *NTS* 1 [1954]: 29–41; W. Barclay, *And He Had Compassion on Them* [1955], 211–29, allegorizes the resurrection; D. A. Redding, *The Miracles of Christ* [1964], 169–76; J. Kremer, *Lazarus, die Geschichte einer Auferstehung* [1985]; F. S. Baltz, *Lazarus and the Fourth Gospel Community* [1996]; W. E. S. North, *The Lazarus Story within the Johannine Tradition* [2001]; A. J. Burke, *The Raising of Lazarus and the Passion of Jesus in John 11 and 12* [2003].)

D. E. HIEBERT

Lazarus and Dives laz′uh-ruhs, di′veez. Traditional title of Jesus' parable of "Lazarus and the rich man" (Lk. 16:19–31). The name Dives comes from the Latin word for "rich" (the first words of the parable, "There was a rich man," are translated in the Latin VULGATE as "Homo quidam erat dives"). In the narrative, however, the rich man remains indefinite and unnamed. The use of the name Dives is found early in English literature, probably due to the use of it in cathedral dramas enacting the story (e.g., "Lazar and Dives liveden diversly, and diverse guerdon hadden they thereby," in Chaucer, *The Summoner's Tale* 11.759–60). Other names for this anonymous rich man were current among the Syrian and Coptic rite churches, but they were not adopted in the W.

The central issue concerning the story has been the use of a name for the poor man—the only such ascription in all of our Lord's parables. This is especially important as the story takes place on two levels and in two universes of discourse, the life on this earth and the life of the world to come. The traditional orthodox position has been to assume that Jesus' narrative about the condition of the two men after death was based upon his divine OMNISCIENCE. However, some commentators judge that if this is so, it is out of character with the normative nature of Jesus' parabolic discourse. In the history of Lukan exegesis some have thought that here is a veiled allusion to characters living and well known in the apostolic age (e.g., TERTULLIAN thought that HEROD and JOHN THE BAPTIST were meant).

The major theme of the story is its condemnation of the self-righteous rich and its assurance that God's revelation is effective in calling men to repentance. The decisions of this life are thus eternally binding. It is probable that this is a singular usage of the omniscient power of Christ as it logically connects a group of typical parables to a definite prophetic statement in Lk. 17. The proposal of various writers that the evangelist here adopted the name of the more familiar Lazarus whom Jesus raised from the dead (Jn. 11) has no grounds to support it. (See E. W. Bullinger, *The Rich Man and Lazarus: The Intermediate State* [reprint 1997]; H. J. Cadbury in *JBL* 81 [1962]: 399–402; K. Grobel in *NTS* 10 [1963–64]: 373–82; *ABD*, 4:266–67.)

W. WHITE, JR.

laziness. See IDLENESS; SLUGGARD.

lead (metal). A very soft METAL, more than eleven times as dense as water (cf. Exod. 15:10; Heb. *ōperet* H6769), fusible with a melting point of 327°C; it forms alloys with SILVER (cf. Ezek. 22:18, 20) and TIN (solder). It can be inlaid to form letters (cf. Job 19:24) or patterns, particularly when heated, since above 300°C it is plastic. If perfectly pure, lead is silvery white in color. However, the metal is usually gray to bluish gray. Native lead is of rare occurrence. The main ore is galena (lead sulphide), which usually is found associated with minerals of zinc and generally contains up to 0.1 percent silver. Most workable lead deposits occur as veins or lodes cutting across or replacing sedimentary rocks, particularly limestone and dolomite.

The discovery of lead antedates recorded history. It is produced from lead ore simply by roasting in an oxidizing atmosphere, and it is possible that this was the first metallurgical process practiced by man. Lead coins were used in ancient Egyptian times as was lead in the glazing of pottery and the making of solder. The Hanging Gardens of Babylon are said to have been floored by lead sheets soldered together to retain moisture. The Phoenicians worked the lead deposits of Rio Tinto, Spain, and traded in the metal (Ezek. 27:12), possibly from Cornwall as well as from Spain. In Greek times lead was mined and smelted at Laurion, Greece, and by the time of the Roman civilization, the use of lead was widespread. (See J. R. Partington, *A Textbook of Inorganic Chemistry*, 6th ed. [1950], 833–34; *Collier's Encyclopedia* [1964], 14:401–4; *Encyclopedia Britannica*, 15th ed. [2002], 21:467–70.)

D. R. BOWES

Leah lee'uh (לֵאָה H4207, possibly "wild cow" [but not in a pejorative sense; cf. RACHEL, "ewe," and see *DDD*, 505–6]). The eldest daughter of LABAN, granddaughter of BETHUEL, and wife of JACOB (Gen. 29:16). ABRAHAM's brother NAHOR, who had remained in the homeland in HARAN, had eight children, of whom one was Bethuel (22:22). Bethuel, in turn, had two children who are named in the Bible: REBEKAH (24:15) and Laban (24:29). Rebekah married ISAAC and bore Jacob, while Laban begat two daughters, Leah and Rachel. Therefore, Leah and Jacob were first cousins.

Leah is described as "tender eyed" (Gen. 29:17 KJV), which may mean that her eyes were weak (cf. NIV). She was contrasted in appearance with her sister Rachel, who was beautiful to behold. Laban craftily gave his eldest daughter first in marriage to Jacob, although Jacob had bargained for Rachel (29:23). Jacob, resenting the deception, evidently made Leah feel unloved (29:30). To compensate for this, the Lord favored her by giving to her four sons, while her sister remained barren. Her sons were REUBEN, SIMEON, LEVI, and JUDAH. Leah hoped to gain Jacob's favor over her sister by these sons (29:32). Later Leah claimed two other sons, GAD and ASHER, by her handmaid ZILPAH (30:10, 12). The evidence of Leah's craving for Jacob's love and of her feeling spurned by him is seen in her bargain with Rachel for the privilege of lying with her own husband (30:14–18). In this period, ISSACHAR and ZEBULUN were born. In all, she bore him six sons and one daughter named DINAH.

When faced with a decision between staying with her father or going to Canaan with her husband, Leah showed her willingness to leave her homeland and go with Jacob (Gen. 31:14). Still Jacob favored Rachel, putting Leah ahead of her in the caravan to keep Rachel as far as possible from ESAU, whom he feared (33:1–2). Possibly the burial of the two wives of Jacob is more significant than anything else. Rachel, whom he had seemingly favored throughout his life, was buried in a tomb near BETHLEHEM. The place is still marked today. But Leah was buried in the family burial site at MACHPELAH, where Jacob himself chose to be buried (49:31). Thus perhaps Leah won out in the end over her sister.

Leah certainly was favored as far as God is concerned. Judah, the fourth son, was ultimately the one through whom Israel's greatness came. Both David and the Christ were of the line of Judah. (See A. Edersheim, *Bible History* [1890], 1:125–28, 143; G. von Rad, *Genesis* [1961], 284ff.; C. Pfeiffer, *Patriarchal Age* [1961], 55, 72, 78, 81, 83, 110; J. Bright, *A History of Israel*, 4th ed. [2000], 79.)

J. B. SCOTT

leannoth. See MAHALATH LEANNOTH.

leather. The SKIN or hide of an animal; an article of clothing made of tanned hide. Leather from the

Wineskins like this one were made of leather.

skins of animals is one of the most ancient materials used for clothing, shoes, and other purposes, and it is strange that the specific term "leather" is not found more often in the Bible. Most of the time, particularly in the OT, the term "skin" (ʿôr H6425) is used to speak of the articles made from animal hides. Once in the OT the term is used figuratively: "I have escaped by the skin of my teeth" (Job 19:20 NRSV)—a phrase which to this day describes a narrow escape from danger or a predicament.

The first clothes worn by humans were made of skins with the animal hair left on (Gen. 3:21). Later leather was widely used throughout the ANE and also by the early Hebrews. This is apparent from the test used to determine leprosy in humans or their clothing: "When there is a leprous disease in a garment … or in a skin or in anything made of skin, if the disease shows greenish or reddish in the garment … it is a leprous disease and shall be shown to the priest" (Lev. 13:47–49 NRSV). Some scholars believe that "leprosy in garments" was the result of green or badly tanned skin that was infected with decay (cf. NIV, "mildew"). Such garments, both of wool and of skin, were to be burned. People who either killed others or touched anyone who had been killed were to purify "every garment as well as everything made of leather, goat hair or wood" (Num. 31:19–20).

Even when textiles largely replaced leather as clothing, it was still used for some articles. The most common items were caps, hats, capes, skirts, aprons, and girdles. ELIJAH is said to have worn "a garment of hair and with a leather belt around his waist" (2 Ki. 1:8). JOHN THE BAPTIST also wore a garment of camel's hair and a leather belt around his waist (Matt. 3:4; Gk. adj. *dermatinos* G1294). In describing the sufferings of the saints, the writer of Hebrews says that they "went about in sheepskins [*mēlōtē* G3603] and goatskins [*aigeios derma* G128 + G1293], persecuted and mistreated" (Heb. 11:37).

Besides being used for clothing, leather was used to cover the TABERNACLE in the wilderness (Exod. 26:14; Num. 4:6). Complete hides of goats, properly tanned, with the holes sewn up, served as water and wine containers profusely in the ANE. Fermenting WINE could not be placed into old skins but into new and more flexible containers (Matt. 9:17; Jdg. 4:19). Early writing materials were of carefully tanned fine leather, particularly of kids or lambs. It became known as vellum and PARCHMENT. Paul asks Timothy to bring some type of parchment or articles made of parchment (*membrana* G3521) to him in prison (2 Tim. 4:13). Parchment, however, should not be confused with PAPYRUS, the most common writing material of ancient times.

It was the ARMY, especially in ASSYRIA, that truly appreciated leather. It used the corselet with or without mail. Some soldiers wore leather kilts. Many helmets were of leather, although the best were of coarse metal with a leather undercap. Frequently the soldier's boot made of leather came halfway up the leg. The dagger and the sword were carried in a sheath made of leather. The common foot soldier carried a leather shield, the archer a leather quiver and the slinger a leather sling. See ARMOR, ARMS. Tents and the cordage used on the march were often of leather. Individual soldiers crossed rivers on inflated skins, and baggage went on rafts supported in the same way. Riding saddles and pack saddles were of leather. CHARIOTS used much leather, including the tires as well as the harness and whips.

Leather was a fine upholstery used on chairs, thrones, and beds. The ancients had few materials for containers to hold dry materials such as grain, and fewer still for liquids. Pottery and leather were their only ordinary containers. Goatskins were the containers for water in dry areas and also for carrying large quantities of water in the cities. The rich women of the city suffered through having no vanity cases with toilet articles. The desert shepherd carried his food in a leather pouch. Ropes and thongs of many kinds were made of leather. Most percussion instruments used a high grade of leather.

Leather came from various kinds of animals: oxen, donkeys, sheep, goats, kids, and rams (Gen. 27:16; Exod. 25:5). Skins of lizards, badgers, leopards, and crocodiles also were used in OT times. Some scholars believe that a tough-lasting SANDAL was made from a special kind of skin, perhaps from a porpoise (Ezek. 16:10).

In the early nomadic life, each family tanned its own hides. In later times certain men took up the business of tanning (e.g., SIMON in JOPPA, Acts 10:6). Generally the TANNER cured leather by soaking it in large vats, scraping off all of the fat, blood, and hair with sharp knives or stones, and then laying it out to dry. Afterward it was oiled and rubbed until it became tough and pliable. The tanner used lime or juices of plants and fruits, sometimes bark from trees, animal and vegetable oils, to tan and preserve the hide as well as dye it in various colors. The ancients were very capable tanners, and it is surprising how durable and long-lasting their products were. No doubt the most expert tanners were employed to manufacture the sturdy shields for the army (2 Sam. 1:21; Isa. 22:6).

(See further A. Edersheim, *Sketches of Jewish Social Life* [1927], 182–83; A. E. Bailey, *Daily Life In Bible Times* [1943], 143, 167; A. Klinck, *Home Life in Bible Times* [1959], 96–97; A. Van Deursen, *Illustrated Dictionary of Bible Manners and Customs* [1967], 46–48, 60–76, 112, 124; P. J. King and L. E. Stager, *Life in Biblical Israel* [2001], 162–64, 230, 272–73.) L. M. PETERSEN; H. JAMIESON

leaven. A general term for agents that produce fermentation and cause dough to rise. It usually refers to yeast (the term used consistently by the NIV), which is a specific fungus of the genus *Saccharomyces*. The Hebrew term for "leaven" or "yeast" is *śeʾōr* H8419, which occurs five times (Exod. 12:15, 19, 13:7; Lev. 2:11; Deut. 16:4), while *ḥāmēṣ* H2809 (from a root meaning "bitter, sour"), occurring eleven times, refers to leavened bread or anything that has yeast in it; on the other hand, *maṣṣâ* H5174, used over forty times (almost always in the plural *maṣṣôt*, even today usually called *matzoth*) refers to unleavened bread, that is, bread made without yeast (note the use of all three terms in Exod. 12:15). In the NT, the Greek noun *zymē* G2434 occurs eleven times (cf. 1 Cor. 5:6 and Gal. 5:9, which also use the cognate verb *zymoō* G2435, "to leaven"); *azymos* G109, always in the plural, and almost always with reference to the Feast of Unleavened Bread, occurs nine times (Matt. 26:17 et al.).

I. Literal. BREAD was made to rise by putting a piece of sour dough (from a previous batch of dough) in the flour, bringing on fermentation of the whole. Leavened bread was a regular part of the diet of ancient Israel (Hos. 7:4). Bread made in haste without allowing it to rise is the unleavened bread often mentioned in Scripture (Gen. 19:3; Exod. 12:15; Jdg. 6:19; 1 Sam. 28:24; et al.). The haste to depart from Egypt left no time for bread to rise, therefore the people carried with them dough and kneading troughs (Exod. 12:34, 39).

In memorial of the exodus and its hurried flight (Exod. 12:11, 39; Deut. 16:3), Israel was commanded to cast out leaven from the house annually, on the fourteenth day of the first month (ABIB), and to eat unleavened bread ("the bread of affliction," Deut. 16:3) for seven days—the fourteenth to the twenty-first day—as the Feast of Unleavened Bread (Exod. 12:14–20; 13:4–7; 23:15; 34:18; Num. 28:17; 2 Chr. 35:17; cf. Matt. 26:17; Mk. 14:1, 12; Lk. 22:1; Acts 12:3; 20:6; see FEASTS). The penalty for the native or sojourner who ate that which was leavened in this period was to be cut off from the congregation (Exod. 12:15–30; 13:7).

This prohibition of leaven was interpreted to prohibit that which is fermented from grain rather than that from the grape (*m. Pesaḥim* 3:1). There is no mention in the MISHNAH of wine lees as leaven. The prohibition of leaven did not prohibit the drinking of wine at PASSOVER. The rabbis ruled that the poorest man in Israel was entitled to four cups even if it had to be supplied by charity (*m. Pesaḥim* 10:1).

The use of leaven and HONEY were prohibited in cereal offerings and blood offerings made by fire (Lev. 2:11; 6:17; 7:12; 8:2, 26; 10:12; Exod. 23:18; 29:2, 23; 34:25; cf. Amos 4:5); but the use of leaven was permitted in peace offerings (which the people consumed, Lev. 7:13) and in the wave loaves of the FIRSTFRUIT offering (23:17). Leviticus is not explicit that the SHOWBREAD should be unleavened, but we are informed by JOSEPHUS that it was (*Ant.* 3.6.6 §142).

II. Figurative. The significant thing about leaven is its power, which may become a symbol of either good or evil. Jesus, in the parable of the leaven (Matt. 13:33; Lk. 13:21), used the working of yeast to teach the pervasiveness of the KINGDOM OF GOD, which eventually transforms the world. The small bit of leaven—the Word—has power to accomplish this great result. The final point of the comparison is the whole lump permeated by the leaven. This parable is one of a pair with the parable of the grain of mustard seed. PHILO JUDAEUS (*Spec. Leg.* 2.184–85) seems also to use leaven as a symbol of something good. On the other hand, some (e.g., Scofield Bible), insisting that leaven in Scripture is always a symbol of evil, attempt to make the parable a picture of the true teaching being mingled with corrupt and corrupting false doctrine, resulting in the final apostasy of the professing church. One's approach to this issue is ordinarily determined by a prior decision on the question of whether the NT outlook for the kingdom is optimistic or pessimistic.

Jesus used leaven as a symbol of undesirable teaching when he warned against "the yeast of the Pharisees and Sadducees" (Matt. 16:6, 11–12). The parallel in Lk. 12:1 reads: "Be on your guard against the yeast of the Pharisees, which is hypocrisy." This interpretation turns aside any possible misunderstanding that Jesus is warning against the bread of the Pharisees as the rabbis warned against the "leaven or meat" of the Samaritans, which is interpreted by some rabbis to be a warning against mixed marriages (Str-B, 1:541–42). Another passage in the Gospels has a warning against "the yeast of the Pharisees and that of Herod" (Mk. 8:15; some MSS, "Herodians"). Leaven as a symbol of the undesirable is paralleled in the rabbis, who called the evil desire (*yēṣer hārāʿ*) "the yeast in the dough" (*b. Ber.* 17a; cf. *Gen. Rab.* 34:10).

Paul uses leaven as a symbol of the pervasiveness of evil (1 Cor. 5:6) and makes an allegory on the casting out of leaven at Passover. Here malice and evil are the leaven that need to be replaced by sincerity and truth so that the festival may be celebrated (vv. 7–8). Paul also uses leaven as a symbol of evil that has power to influence the whole, as he cites the proverb, "a little leaven leavens the whole lump" (1 Cor. 5:6; Gal. 5:9 RSV). (See H. Windisch in *TWNT*, 2:904–8; J. Jeremias, *The Parables of Jesus* [1955], 89–90.) J. P. Lewis

Lebana. See Lebanah.

Lebanah li-bay'nuh (לְבָנָה H4245 [the Bomberg ed. has לִבְנָא in Neh. 7:38], "white" or "full moon"). Ancestor of a family of temple servants (Nethinim) who returned from Babylon (Ezra 2:45; Neh. 7:48 [most versions "Lebana"]; 1 Esd. 5:29 [KJV, "Labana"]).

Lebanon leb'uh-nuhn (לְבָנוֹן H4248, "white [mountain]"). The name of a mountainous region in Phoenicia just inland from the coast (called simply *har hallĕbānôn*, "Mount Lebanon," in Jdg. 3:3; NIV, "the Lebanon mountains"). Its area corresponds roughly to that of the modern state of Lebanon, but the latter includes also the strip of land on the coast as well as the Beqaʿ Valley and the western slopes of the Antilebanon range.

I. Lebanon in history and in the Bible. The history of Lebanon is inseparable from that of Phoenicia. Here will be noted only the role of the cedars of Lebanon as an object both of military plunder and of peaceful trade. Both Mesopotamia and Egypt imported cedar wood from Lebanon. The Egyptian tale of Wenamon tells of an envoy sent to barter for cedar wood for Egypt.

In the Bible, Lebanon has meaning both for nationalistic ideology and in literature. Nationalistic ideology in Deuteronomy and Joshua from the beginning made Lebanon part of the Promised Land (Deut. 1:7; Josh. 1:4; cf. also Jdg. 3:3). Moses prayed to see the "good land beyond the Jordan—that fine hill country and Lebanon" (Deut. 3:25); moreover, the Phoenician coast as far as Byblos (i.e., "the area of the Gebalites; and all Lebanon to the east," Josh. 13:5; see Gebal) were included among the promised, but unconquered, territories. In their historical context, Solomon's building activities in the Lebanon (1 Ki. 9:19; 2 Chr. 8:6) probably refer to the eastern slopes of the Lebanon adjacent to the Beqaʿ into which the empire of David and Solomon extended. It is unlikely that the Hebrew empire ever extended into Phoenicia proper or far into the Lebanon range.

Lebanon's place in literary allusion is far more significant. There are literary motifs based upon the greatness of Lebanon and its cedars, motifs utilizing Lebanon as a romantic symbol, and motifs of prosperity and stability. A single trip into one of the high, rugged valleys of the Lebanon should be sufficient to demonstrate that the Lebanon range is a fitting symbol of rugged grandeur and greatness. Thus God's greatness is expressed poetically when the Lebanon "skips" at God's voice (Ps. 29:6) or by the fact that it is God who planted Lebanon's mighty cedars (104:16). God's destructive powers can destroy these same cedars (Isa. 10:34), which fittingly symbolize arrogant people (Ezek. 31:3).

The inaccessibility of the mountains may have been aided by the luxurious wealth of Phoenicia in making the Lebanon a symbol of the romantic, the

Lebanon.

Looking NE through the Beqaʿ Valley with the lower ridges of the Antilebanon mountains in the background.

exotic, and the mysterious. Solomon's carriage was of "wood from Lebanon" (Cant. 3:9). The bride's romantic beauty was extolled by summoning her as if from the Lebanon (and from the Antilebanon and Mount HERMON also; 4:8). Her garments were the scent of Lebanon (4:11; possibly a pun on "Lebanon" and *lĕbōnâ* H4247, "frankincense"). The Palace of the Forest of Lebanon was named to exploit the romantic connotation of the term (1 Ki. 7:2).

Prosperity and stability are symbolized by the statement that the righteous will "grow like a cedar in Lebanon" (Ps. 92:12; cf. 72:16). Hosea describes the restored Israel as rooted and fragrant like the Lebanon (Hos. 14:5–7).

II. Description. The Lebanon range extends from the Litani Gorge northward to the valley of the Nahr el-Kebir (the classical Eleutheros River), although the modern state extends some 15 mi. farther to the S. In general, the mountains are separated from the sea by a coastal plain seldom more than a mile wide. Ridges jutting to the sea and rugged stream beds interrupt the coastal plain, which is well-watered and quite productive. The plain of SIDON in the S and the valley of the Nahr el-Kebir provide more spacious agricultural areas.

Turning to the Lebanon range proper, its western face consists of a complicated system of ridges, highland plateaus, deep valleys, and foothills leading from the peaks to the coastal plain. Seasonal rains are adequate to make the highland plateaus and terraced hillsides quite productive. There are many villages on these western slopes. By contrast the eastern face tilts rather directly to the Beqaʿ, and sparse rainfall limits their usage for grazing of sheep and goats. Some of the major peaks of the Lebanon are Jebel Akkar in the N, Jebel Makhmal (with the summit, Qurnet es-Sauda, c. 11,000 ft.), Jebel Mneitreh (from which the Dog River flows), Jebel Sunnin (which is visible from Beirut), Jebel Kneisseh, Jebel Baruk, Jebel Niha, and Jebel Rihan.

The Beqaʿ, classical COELESYRIA, is the valley between the Lebanon and the Antilebanon. Its rainfall is limited so that it depends largely on streams and springs flowing from the mountains for agriculture. It is very fertile, particularly in the vicinity of Zahleh, Shtoura, and BAALBEK. Its rivers are the Nahr el-ʿAsi (classical ORONTES) flowing N and the Litani (classical Leontes) flowing S. The latter has been harnessed for Lebanon's major electrical power and irrigation work. The slopes of the Antilebanon are similar in appearance and usage to the eastern slopes of the Lebanon.

Lebanon produces a wide variety of crops. The plains and some of the plateaus and valleys are good for growing grain. The coastal plain and mountain terraces produce a wide variety of garden vegetables, nuts, and fruits. Among these, the olive and the vine still retain their age-old importance. In regions too high or too steep for agriculture, the forests flourish. Original growth included pines, myrtles, and the famous cedars of which only a few hundred remain until the present. In past decades, much reseeding of barren slopes with pine trees has been carried out. (See further P. K. Hitti, *Lebanon in History from the Earliest Times to the Present* [1962]; R. Fedden, *The Phoenix Land* [1965]; K. S. Salibi, *The Modern History of Lebanon* [1965]; M. K. Khayat and M. C. Keatinge, *Lebanon: Land of the Cedars* [1967]; M. J. Strazzulla, *Ancient Lebanon: Monuments Past and Present* [2004].)   A. BOWLING

Lebanon, House (Palace) of the Forest of. See FOREST.

Lebaoth li-bay´oth (לְבָאוֹת H4219, "lionesses"). One of the "southernmost towns of the tribe of Judah in the Negev toward the boundary of Edom" (Josh. 15:32; cf. v. 21). The site is unknown. Lebaoth is thought to be the same as BETH LEBAOTH (19:6), apparently later known as BETH BIRI (1 Chr. 4:31).

Lebbaeus li-bee´uhs (Λεββαῖος G3304 [not in NIV], corresponding to the Heb. or Aram. name לִבַּי, "heart"). According to the KJV (following the majority of Greek MSS and some ancient versional evidence), one of the twelve disciples was "Lebbaeus, whose surname was Thaddaeus" (Matt. 10:3; both in this passage and in Mk. 3:18, CODEX BEZAE and some Latin witnesses read Lebbaeus only instead of Thaddaeus). See THADDAEUS.

Leb Kamai leb´kuh-mi´ (לֵב קָמָי H4214, "heart of my adversaries"). NRSV Leb-qamai. In an oracle against BABYLON, God announces that he will stir up a destroying spirit (or wind) against "the people of Leb Kamai" (Jer. 51:1, KJV, "them that dwell in the midst of them that rise up against me"). It is generally thought, however, that the term is a code for CHALDEA. See ATBASH.

Lebo Hamath lee´boh-hay´muhth (לְבוֹא חֲמָת H4217, "entrance of Hamath"). Also Lebo-hamath. A place on the S border of the territory controlled by HAMATH, regarded in the OT as the ideal N border of the Promised Land of Israel. However, it was only under DAVID and SOLOMON, and later under JEROBOAM II, that the territory of Israel extended so far (Num. 13:21; 34:8; Josh. 13:5; Jdg. 3:3; 1 Ki. 8:65; 2 Ki. 14:25; 1 Chr. 13:5; 2 Chr. 7:8; Amos 6:14). EZEKIEL prophesied that some day it would be the boundary of the ideally restored Israel (Ezek. 47:16–17, 20). The KJV and other versions, taking the term as a general description, render it "the entrance of Hamath" or the like, but it is now generally thought to be the actual name of a particular region or city.

The precise location of Lebo Hamath has been debated. It was somewhere between the LEBANON and ANTILEBANON Mountains, in the BEQAʿ Valley, through which the road to Hamath lay. Among places that have been suggested for its location are the ORONTES Valley between ANTIOCH and SELEUCIA, a part of the valley of COELESYRIA, and the territory of RIBLAH. It is now generally identified with modern Lebweh, a town about 45 mi. N of DAMASCUS.   S. BARABAS

Lebonah li-boh´nah (לְבוֹנָה H4228, "frankincense"). A town in the hill country of EPHRAIM, mentioned only once when the writer of Judges gives the location of SHILOH, which is said to be "east of the road that goes from Bethel to Shechem, and to the south of Lebonah" (Jdg. 21:19). Lebonah is probably to be identified with modern el-Lubban, about 3 mi. WNW of Shiloh, 10 mi. SSW of SHECHEM, and 10.5 mi. N of BETHEL.

Lecah lee´kuh (לֵכָה H4336, meaning unknown). TNIV Lekah. Son of Er and great grandson of JUDAH (1 Chr. 4:21). Many believe, however, that Lecah is the name of an otherwise unknown town founded by Er (according to the view that "father" here and in some other genealogical passages means "founder" or "chief citizen").

lectionary. A book of biblical lections (i.e., lessons, readings) used for worship services. The term is used especially of Greek MSS in which Scripture portions are written, not in the order in which they appear in the Bible, but according to the schedule set for the church calendar. They are of great value in NT textual studies. See TEXT AND MANUSCRIPTS (NT).

ledge. This English term is used to render several Hebrew words, such as *karkōb H4136*, referring to a rim half way between the base and the top of the ALTAR in the TABERNACLE (Exod. 27:5; 38:4), and *ʿăzārâ H6478*, used of two ledges forming part of the altar described in Ezekiel's vision of a future temple (Ezek. 43:14, 17, 20; 45:19).

leech. The probable rendering of Hebrew *ʿălûqâ H6598*, a word of uncertain meaning that occurs only once (Prov. 30:15; KJV, "horseleach"). Leeches (*Hirudinea*) are found in many places. In the wet tropics they live on land, sometimes in great numbers, but in most regions they are confined to water. They feed mostly on blood, which is sucked until the leech's body is grossly distended. Leeches normally fasten on the skin, but some can invade the throat and nasal passages after being imbibed with water, possibly with fatal results. Both men and animals are attacked. Since early times physicians have used leeches to "let blood," and until about the mid-19th cent. great numbers still were being used, especially to remove blood from swellings. Today they are approved as medical devices for removing pooled blood, thus helping heal skin grafts and restore blood circulation in blocked veins. (Some commentators have identified the Heb. term with an Aram. word referring to a blood-sucking, vampire-like demon, but the only bats known to feed on blood are found in Central and South America. See further *FFB*, 47–48.)   G. S. CANSDALE

leek. A vegetable (*Allium porrum*) related to the ONION, mentioned only once as one of the foods that the Israelites missed on their trek to the Promised Land (Num. 11:5; it is uncertain whether the Hebrew term here, *ḥāṣîr H2946*, derives from the same root as the common term for GRASS, *ḥāṣîr H2945*). Leeks always have been considered important vegetables. In Saxon times in England, a vegetable garden was called a "leac tun." Leeks have a slight medicinal value. (See *FFB*, 159–60.)

Both the leek and the fenugreek (*Trigonella foenumgraecum*, a kind of green clover) were grown

Leeks.

in Egypt, and both were eaten. Can it be that the vegetable or salad that was missed so much was really fenugreek, which was sold in Egyptian markets in bundles? In Cairo today, this salad plant is bought as "Halbeh." See also FLORA (under *Leguminosae* and *Liliaceae*); GARLIC.

W. E. SHEWELL-COOPER

lees. A term used by the KJV and other versions for the dregs that settle at the bottom of wine jars and wine skins. It renders Hebrew *šĕmārîm* (pl. of *šemer H9069*), which occurs in four passages (Ps. 75:8 [here the KJV has "dregs"]; Isa. 25:6 [NIV, "aged wine"]; Jer. 48:11; Zeph. 1:12). WINE gained strength and flavor by being allowed to remain on the lees, and such wine was regarded as superior to the newly fermented product. The word is used in the OT only in a figurative sense.

left-handed. This description is used only regarding warriors from the tribe of BENJAMIN. They include EHUD, one of the judges (Jdg. 3:15); seven hundred soldiers who "could sling a stone at a hair and not miss" (20:16); and a group of ambidextrous relatives of SAUL who joined DAVID in ZIKLAG (1 Chr. 12:2).

leg. Several Hebrew terms may be rendered "leg," such as *keraʿ H4157*, found in OT passages dealing with sacrificial rituals and referring to the shank or splint-bone (Exod. 12:9; Lev. 1:9, 13; et al.); it is also used of the bending hind legs of locusts that were permitted for food (Lev. 11:21), and it formed the basis for an illustration of divine judgment (Amos 3:12). The word *mĕgal H8070*, which normally means "foot," refers once to the legs of GOLIATH (1 Sam. 17:6; the bronze greaves the giant wore normally protected the leg between the knee and the ankle rather than the foot). A term used to describe the upper leg of men (Deut. 28:35 et al.) as well as sacrificial animals (Exod. 29:22 et al.) is *šôq H8797*, which strictly means "thigh."

The narrow part of the THIGH was considered one of the choicest pieces of the sacrificial animal, and was reserved for the use of the priests. Animal bones from the upper portion of the right foreleg have been recovered from the debris of a Canaanite temple at LACHISH, destroyed c. 1220 B.C. by the invading Hebrews when apparently in use as a sanctuary. These bones evidently comprised the remains of the priestly perquisites, suggesting that the rest of the sacrifice had been eaten by the worshipers outside the sanctuary or in some adjoining room. There was little to indicate that the bones had been burned, and presumably the meat had been cooked by boiling (cf. 1 Sam. 2:15). This evidence provides an authentic historical background for the ritual prescriptions (Lev. 7:32 et al.).

In the NT the word *skelos G5003* occurs only in Jn. 19:31–33, and denotes the entire limb from the hip downward. In Rev. 10:1, *pous G4546*, which normally means "foot," clearly refers to the leg.

R. K. HARRISON

legion. The major unit in the Roman army, consisting of several thousand soldiers. Both the English term and the Greek (*legiōn G3305*) are borrowings from the Latin *legiō* (genitive *legiōnis*). In the NT the word is used only in the Gospels and with reference to angels and demons (Matt. 26:53; Mk. 5:9, 15; Lk. 8:30; see M. W. Newheart, *"My Name Is Legion": The Story and Soul of the Gerasene Demoniac* [2004]).

The word was thought by Roman tradition to be traceable to the age of the patrician army under the legendary founder, Romulus. Supposedly the whole of the Roman forces was collectively called *legiō* and consisted of 300 *equites*, "knights," and 3,000 *pedes*, "infantry." When the army expanded under the Tarquinian rulers, the army was divided in troop this same ratio of men in each regiment, which was then called a *legiō*. The battle array of the *legiō* was similar to that of the Greek phalanx, which had been developed by Epaminondas of Thebes c. 370 B.C. However, the phalanx was abolished by M. F. Camillus sometime during his dictatorship in the 4th cent. B.C.

The basic organization was maintained until the time of G. Marius (157–86 B.C.), who reorganized the Roman legions by abolishing the old citizen recruited militia, which had been associated with the propertied classes. In its place he instituted the mercenary system with its paid professionals volunteering regardless of social class. With this new force, Marius won several spectacular campaigns including the bloody Jugurthine War. At this time the legion consisted of about 300 knights and about 4,200 infantry. In the last century of the republic, the army was divided among the CONSULS, each of whom was assigned two legions of about 5,000 men. In the empire, the army was a standing body of mercenaries drawn from all parts of the Roman world. They were bound to the particular emperor by the oath (*sacramentum*) and were at his every command.

By the end of the 1st cent. A.D., the legion contained about 6,000 men when up to full strength. More often than not, they were under this figure by as much as 33 percent, so that ideally the statement of Christ in Matt. 26:53 would involve in excess of 144,000 of the heavenly beings. If the notion of double legions is accepted, it seems that such speculations are unwarranted by the context. The legion was subdivided into ten COHORTS, and these were divided into six centuries or "hundreds" each, the officer in charge of this last division being the CENTURION, mentioned often in the NT (Matt. 8:5 et al.). Over the whole legion there was the *tribūnī mīlitum*, "military tribune," with his subordinate the *lēgātus*, "lieutenant-general."

The feeding and clothing of such a force was accomplished by quartering the troops on the citizenry in foreign regions or by foraging, and in time of conflict by booty. The pay for an infantryman was 120 denarii per year, which was raised by Julius CAESAR to about 225 denarii, and the hope of booty including the sale of slaves heightened morale. The number of legions varied throughout the centuries, but under AUGUSTUS (27 B.C.–A.D. 14) it was set at twenty-five, each with a definite base usually on the border of the empire. (See further J. Pfitzner, *Geschichte der römische Kaiserlegion* [1881];

H. M. D. Parker, *The Roman Legions*, 2nd ed. [1958]; O. Hiltbrunner, "Militar," *Kleines Lexikon der Antike* [1961], 317–20; L. Keppie, *The Making of the Roman Army* [1984]; G. Webster, *The Roman Imperial Army of the First and Second Centuries A.D.*, 3rd ed. [1985], 102–40; *OCD*, 839–42.)   W. WHITE, JR.

Lehabim li-hay´bim. See LEHABITES.

Lehabites li-hay´bīts (לְהָבִים *H4260*). Also Lehabim. One of the people groups descended from MIZRAIM (Egypt), son of HAM (Gen. 10:13; 1 Chr. 1:11). Nothing is known about them, but many scholars suggest that the word is either a textual corruption or an alternate form of *lūbim*, "Libyans" (cf. LXX *Labiim* in Gen. 10:13). See LIBYA; NATIONS.

Lehem. See JASHUBI LEHEM.

Lehi lee´hi (לְחִי *H4306*, "cheek, jawbone," possibly in the fig. sense of "border"). An unknown site in JUDAH where SAMSON slew a thousand PHILISTINES with the jawbone of a donkey (Jdg. 15:9, 14, 19; cf. v. 17). Samson had been bound and delivered to the Philistines by his fellow tribesmen, who hoped thereby to avoid retaliation for his raids. The Spirit came upon him, however, so he broke the bonds, seized a jawbone, and struck down the Philistines.

There has been much debate regarding the identification of Lehi. One popular proposal (partly based on a slight sound similarity with *siagōn*, the Gk. word for "jawbone" [cf. LXX in Jdg. 15:14, 19]) is Khirbet eṣ-Ṣiyyaj, which lies some 4 mi. E of TIMNAH (cf. 14:1–2). The evidence for this and other identifications, however, is very ambiguous. M. Lubetski (in *ABD*, 4:274–75) argues, on the basis of Akkadian *lītu* (a term used to indicate real estate limits), that Lehi is a general term denoting the entire borderline between Judah and Philistia.   A. K. HELMBOLD

Lekah lee´kuh. TNIV form of LECAH.

Lemuel lem´yoo-uhl (לְמוּאֵל *H4345*, "belonging to God"). The reputed author of Prov. 31, who repeats his mother's teachings about good government, the dangers of sex and wine, and (if his sayings include vv. 9–29) the virtues of a noble wife. Rabbinic tradition equates Lemuel with SOLOMON, but modern scholars reject this view. Some translations, such as RSV and NJPS, understand the Hebrew term *maśśāʾ H5363* ("oracle," v. 1) as a proper name, making Lemuel king of MASSA.
   A. K. HELMBOLD

lend. See BORROW, LEND.

lentil. A leguminous plant (*Lens esculenta*), one of the earliest crops grown. It is first mentioned (Heb. *ʿădāšîm H6378*) when JACOB made a red lentil stew for his brother ESAU (Gen. 25:34). Lentils were brought to DAVID and his men when they were hungry (2 Sam. 17:28). A field of lentils was the scene of a battle between the Israelites and the Philistines (23:11). EZEKIEL was instructed to use "wheat and barley, beans and lentils, millet and spelt" for making bread (Ezek. 4:9).

Lentils are annuals, bearing small white and violet flowers, shaped like a sweet pea. These are followed by small flat pods, inside which are found the lentils, the size of small peas (the name *Lens* was given because they are like miniature convex lenses). These, when boiled, turn to a brownish-yellow or chocolate-red shade. Both these colors are often called "red" in the Middle East. Even today, lentils are made into red-colored stews and soups; they are often flavored with garlic. (See *FFB*, 134, fig. on 133.) See also FLORA (under *Leguminosae*); FOOD.   W. E. SHEWELL-COOPER

Lentulus, Epistle of len´chuh-luhs. A short document of uncertain date but hardly earlier than the 13th cent. and probably written in Italy. It is especially known because of its description of Jesus: "A man in stature middling tall, and comely, having a reverend countenance, which they that look upon may love and fear." The description follows closely the traditional portraits: hair parted in the middle, waving over his shoulders, brow smooth and calm, face without blemish or wrinkle, beard full and forked. The theme was popular from an early period (cf. Euseb. *Eccl. Hist.* 7.18.4). In the earliest MSS the document professes to quote Roman annals, but in later forms it appears as a letter addressed to the Senate by Lentulus, a Roman official in Judea in the time of Tiberius (See M. R. James, *The Apocryphal New Testament* [1924], 477–78.)

R. McL. Wilson

leopard. A large spotted carnivore of the lion family (*Felix pardus*). Leopards grow to a head and body length of about five feet, with a tail of two to three feet. The background color varies from deep chrome to pale gray or sandy, with rosettes of almost black spots. It was once widely distributed in Africa and warm parts of Asia, including most of Palestine and neighboring countries. The larger, darker specimens usually live in forest regions, while the smaller, paler ones inhabit open steppe or near-desert. The leopard takes a variety of prey, from antelopes and deer down to small birds. It has now been exterminated from many parts of its former range, both to protect stock and to obtain its skin, and it is generally rare. (See *FFB*, 48–49.)

That the Hebrew term *nāmēr* H5807 means "leopard" is confirmed by the proverb still current in English, "Can … the leopard [change] its spots?" (Jer. 13:23). Several passages refer to their preying nature (Jer. 5:6; Hos. 13:7) or to their speed (Hab. 1:8), "Their horses are swifter than leopards." The leopard is very fast for a short dash, but this passage could refer to the cheetah, or hunting leopard, which is rather similar and was known in Palestine (it was once tamed and trained there, as it still is in India). The prophetic passage in Isa. 11:6 is hard to comment on biologically, especially since it includes the statement that "the lion will eat straw like the ox" (v. 7). In the book of Revelation, John says he saw a beast that "resembled a leopard [*pardalis* G4203]" (Rev. 13:2).

G. S. Cansdale

Close-up photo of a leopard.

leper, leprosy. See DISEASE.

Leshem lee´chem (לֶשֶׁם H1386, possibly to be pointed לְשֶׁם, from לַיִשׁ H4332, "lion," plus afformative *mem* [cf. GKC §85*t*; *HALOT*, 2:537]). An alternate form of LAISH (only in Josh. 19:47); see DAN (PLACE).

lethech, lethek lee´thik. See WEIGHTS AND MEASURES III.B.

letter. This English word is used in various senses to translate several different terms in both Testaments. The Hebrew ʾ*iggeret* H115 (2 Chr. 30:1, 6; Neh. 2:7–9; 6:5, 17, 19; Esth. 9:26, 29), meaning an official or commercial communication, refers to a tablet of a specific small size with a clay envelope upon which the addresser and addressee were noted and on occasion some of the contents were indicated. The term is derived from Akkadian *egertu*, and its use in postexilic writings may reflect the influence of Neo-Assyrian and Neo-Babylonian culture.

The most common Hebrew term for written materials of all types is *sēper* H6219, which can refer to annals (Gen. 5:1; Num. 21:14; 1 Ki. 11:41; et al.), law codes (2 Chr. 17:9), prophecies (Nah. 1:1), as well as letters (Isa. 37:14 et al.). The specific rendering "letter" is largely a matter of context, and for this reason there are wide variations in the versions (in Jer. 36:2, 4 the term appears with the noun *mĕgillâ* H4479, "scroll, roll," as a secondary indication of the meaning). Cognates of this term, which could be applied to inscribed texts as well as to those written with ink, are found throughout the ANE languages. Two Aramaic terms that can be translated "letter" are *ništĕwān* H10496 (a Persian loanword referring to an official document or decree, Ezra 4:7, 18, 23; 5:5; 7:11) and *pitgām* H10601 ("word, reply, decree," also from Persian, Ezra 4:17; 5:7, 11; 6:11; Dan. 3:16; 4:17; cf. Heb. *pitgām* H7192 in Eccl. 8:11 and Esth. 1:20).

In considering the matter of written communication among the peoples and rulers of antiquity, it must be remembered that although by all the evidence now known literacy was low, yet those with position and wealth could avail themselves of the service of a SCRIBE, either slave or free, and so letters

This small clay tablet is one of the famous Tell el-Amarna letters (c. 1350 B.C.). In it, Burna-Buriash II writes to Amenhotep III of Egypt, requesting more gold with the next exchange of presents.

were commonplace. The vast royal correspondences from Mari, ancient center of Babylonian trade c. 1700 B.C., and Tell el-Amarna, the capital city of the pharaoh Akhenaten c. 14th cent. B.C., demonstrate the importance of such correspondence. In the past, great doubt was cast upon the historical reliability of the Hebrew text by various European and American schools of biblical criticism. However the discoveries of ancient letters of the type often alluded to and occasionally quoted in the OT has forced a major reconsideration of the more radical critical views.

In antiquity letters—messages set down on some material and sent by carrier from one location to another—consisted of three types. These were clay tablets (used with CUNEIFORM signs), sherds and fragments of pottery inscribed with inked letters (see OSTRACA), and sheets of PARCHMENT that had been scraped and dried and then been inked. Apparently all three of these were known in biblical times and are mentioned in the OT. Engraving cuneiform wedges (or in some areas hieroglyphic signs) was the common method in Sumer, Akkad, Babylon, Persia, and Egypt, and such a practice is mentioned in Job 19:24.

After the introduction of the Phoenician ALPHABET, the system of inscribed potsherds or ostraca became widespread, and even in Egypt memoranda and messages were dispatched in this fashion. The excavation of such ancient Hebrew letters at LACHISH concerning the siege of the city, written in the time of JEREMIAH, proved that such were also known to the Jews. Undoubtedly ostraca are involved in the stories of NABOTH (1 Ki. 21:8) and HEZEKIAH (2 Ki. 19:14), as well as in the other references in the annals of the First Commonwealth. The parchment type of letter is not expressly distinguished in the OT, but the discovery of the ARAMAIC papyri from the Jewish colony at ELEPHANTINE (c. 5th cent. B.C.) and the BAR KOKHBA letters (A.D. 132–135) written on parchment support the assumption that such letters were known at least after the Persian era.

In the NT, two Greek terms are translated "letter." One of them is *gramma* G1207 (from which the word *grammateus* G1208, "scribe," is derived). It can mean "letter" in the sense of a written communication (Acts 28:21) or "note" (Lk. 16:6–7), but more common is the meaning "letter [of the alphabet], written character" (cf. 2 Cor. 3:6–7; Gal. 6:11). Paul uses it in the sense of "written code," contrasted with *pneuma* G4460, "Spirit/spirit" (Rom. 2:27, 29; 7:6). The plural can mean "letters" in the sense of "education, learning" (Jn. 7:15; Acts 26:24), and it can also be applied to the Scriptures (2 Tim. 3:15).

The other term translated "letter" in the NT is the familiar *epistolē* G2186, which occurs more than twenty times. In all occurrences the term refers to a written message, an EPISTLE. It is used of Christian documents written in Greek (e.g., Rom. 16:22; 2 Cor. 7:8; 2 Pet. 3:1), as well as Jewish documents probably in Aramaic (Acts 9:2). Of special interest is PAUL's figurative use when he tells the Corinthians that he does not need letters of recommendation because the Corinthian believers themselves are "a letter from Christ," "known and read by everybody," "written not with ink but with the Spirit of the living God, not on tablets of stone but on tablets of human hearts" (2 Cor.

3:1–3) (See further D. Pardee, *Handbook of Ancient Hebrew Letters* [1982]; S. K. Stowers, *Letter Writing in Greco-Roman Antiquity* [1986]; J. M. Lindenberger, *Ancient Aramaic and Hebrew Letters*, 2nd ed. [2003]; H. J. Klauck, *Ancient Letters and the New Testament* [2006]; *ABD*, 4:282–93.)

W. WHITE, JR.

Letushim li-too´shim. See LETUSHITES.

Letushites li-too´shits (לְטוּשִׁים H4322, possibly "sharpened ones"). Also Letushim. A people group descended from DEDAN, grandson of ABRAHAM and KETURAH (Gen. 25:3). Neither this tribe nor the related ASSHURITES and LEUMMITES have been identified, but they probably inhabited parts of N ARABIA.

Leummim lee-uh´mim. See LEUMMITES.

Leummites lee-uh´mits (לְאֻמִּים H4212, possibly "hordes" or "tribesmen"). Also Leummim. A people group descended from DEDAN, grandson of ABRAHAM and KETURAH (Gen. 25:3). See LETUSHITES.

Levant luh-vant´. A modern name applied to the countries that border the E end of the Mediterranean Sea: Turkey, Syria, Lebanon, Israel, and Egypt.

Levi lee´vi (לֵוִי H4290, by popular etymology related to לָוָה H4277, "to join, attach" [Gen. 29:34], but actual derivation disputed [suggestions include S Arabian *lw'*, meaning "priest" or "one pledged for a debt," and Arab. *lawa*, "to give oracles"]; gentilic לֵוִי H4291, "Levite"). **(1)** Third son of JACOB and LEAH, and ancestor of the tribe bearing his name (Gen. 29:34; 35:23; Exod. 1:2; 1 Chr. 2:1). When SHECHEM the HIVITE assaulted DINAH, her brothers Levi and SIMEON led in executing vengeance by killing all the males and pillaging the city of Shechem (Gen. 34:25–31). In his final "testament," Jacob strongly disapproved of Levi's and Simeon's cruelty on that occasion (Gen. 49:5–7). Some scholars see a connection between this violent act and the role of Levi's descendants in killing 3,000 rebellious Hebrews under order of MOSES at the episode of the golden calf (Exod. 32:26–28; see CALF, GOLDEN), but God's blessing was invoked upon them for their obedience (v. 29).

Levi's three sons, GERSHON, KOHATH, and MERARI, were born before the exodus from Egypt (when Num. 26:59 mentions that JOCHEBED was born to Levi, the reference must be to the tribe, not to the son of Jacob). The descendants of Levi are called *Levites*, but because they were especially chosen to assist the priests (3:6–10; cf. also vv. 45–51), this term took on the sense of a religious office, almost meaning "ministers." Although AARON was a descendant of Levi (through Kohath), he and his progeny were granted the office of the priesthood and thus were distinguished from the Levites. The tribe of Levi did not receive a share of the territory in Canaan, for the Lord himself was their inheritance (18:20). See LEVITICAL CITIES; PRIESTS AND LEVITES.

(2) One of the men who assisted in the matter of the Israelites who had married foreign women (1 Esd. 9:14; KJV, "Levis"); the parallel passage (Ezra 10:15) has "Shabbethai the Levite" for "Levi and Shabbethai." See JAHZEIAH.

(3) Son of Melki, included in the GENEALOGY OF JESUS CHRIST (Lk. 3:24).

(4) Son of Simeon, included in the GENEALOGY OF JESUS CHRIST (Lk. 3:29).

(5) Son of Alphaeus; he was a TAX COLLECTOR (publican) who later became one of the twelve apostles (Mk. 2:14–17; Lk. 5:27–32). In the Gospel of Matthew he is always called MATTHEW instead of Levi (Matt. 9:9–13; Lk. 5:27–32). The name does not appear in any of the formal lists as a variant of Matthew.

A. K. HELMBOLD

Leviathan li-vi´uh-thuhn (לִוְיָתָן H4293, possibly "twisting one"). There can be no doubt that this name is basically the same as that found in Ugaritic documents for Lotan (Litan), the sea monster killed by BAAL (*ANET*, 137–38); it is there called "the crooked serpent" (cf. Isa. 27:1), and possibly "the seven-headed" (cf. Ps. 74:14). All five occurrences of the term in the OT (Job 3:8; 41:1; Pss. 74:14, 104:26; Isa. 27:1) are in poetic passages and belong to "dead mythology," that is, old mythic concepts employed without suggestion that they are still believed. For Canaanite mythology, Lotan belonged to the forces of chaos personified by the sea and its monsters, which were conquered by the gods of order. See MYTH.

Because Leviathan is merely poetic imagery, there is no absolute consistency in the OT use of the term. Yahweh is the defeater of chaos in Ps. 74:14, a passage uniting God's power at the creation and in the exodus. Chaos and its forces are God's creation, amenable to his will (Ps. 104:26). The use in Isa. 27:1 is part of the eschatological chs. 24–27; it refers to the future forces of lawlessness in terms of past chaos. In Job 3:8 there is a reference to black magic, which can threaten the settled world order, while in 41:1 Leviathan seems to be the CROCODILE (cf. the use of RAHAB (MONSTER), another mythological figure, 26:12). In Isa. 30:7, it is so depicted that some traits of the chaos monster are seen in it: if man finds it hard to deal with earth's monsters, how much more with those of God's primeval creation? (See J. Day, *God's Conflict with the Dragon and the Sea: Echoes of a Canaanite Myth in the Old Testament* [1985]; *ABD*, 4:295–96; *DDD*, 956–64.) H. L. ELLISON

levirate law. A law of MOSES which states that if two brothers live together, and one of them dies without leaving a male heir, his brother shall marry his widow, and the first son of the union shall take the name of the brother who died (the term derives from Latin *lēvir*, "husband's brother"). If the brother refuses to marry the widow, she shall bring him before the elders of the city, and in their presence remove a sandal from his foot and spit in his face. The purpose of the law obviously was to provide an heir for the dead brother (Deut. 25:5–10; cf. also Gen. 38:1–11; Ruth 4:1–12). (See M. Burrows in *JBL* 59 [1940]: 23–33; D. W. Manor in *Near East Archaeological Society Bulletin* 20 [Fall 1982]: 33–52; R. Ahroni in *Jewish Law and Current Legal Problems*, ed. N. Rakover [1984], 67–76.) See also MARRIAGE III.F. S. BARABAS

Levis lee´vis. KJV Apoc. form of LEVI (1 Esd. 9:14).

Levite lee´vit (לֵוִי H4291). A descendant of LEVI (Exod. 6:25 et al.); see PRIESTS AND LEVITES.

Levitical cities. Forty-eight cities were allotted to the Levites by MOSES and JOSHUA (Num. 35:1–8; Josh. 21; see PRIESTS AND LEVITES). A parallel passage (1 Chr. 6:54–81 [Heb. 6:39–66]) also gives a list of the Levitical cities, but it is smaller than the one in Joshua and it presents considerable differences in the names (cf. the chart in *ISBE* rev. [1979–88], 110). Some of the discrepancies simply reflect spelling or textual variations (it is usually thought that the Chronicler depended on Joshua's list, but that the latter was in a textual form different from that preserved in the MT). In other cases there may have been change to a new city due to the unsuitability of the original one, and a few of the older ones were perhaps no longer in use.

The tribe of LEVI did not receive any part of the land of CANAAN as an inheritance (Num. 18:20–24; 26:62; Deut. 10:9; 18:1–2; Josh. 18:7). As compensation, they received the tithes of Israelites for their support (Num. 18:21), and forty-eight cities were allotted to them out of the inheritance of the other tribes. Of these cities, the priests received thirteen, all of which were within the tribe of JUDAH (Josh. 21:4); and six were CITIES OF REFUGE, to which a person who had accidentally killed someone could go for protection (Num. 35:9–34; Deut. 4:41–43).

The Levitical cities were made up by taking four cities from each of the twelve tribes. The apparent purpose of thus dispersing the Levites throughout the land was to enable them, as the official representatives of the Hebrew faith, to instruct the people throughout the land in the law and in the worship of Yahweh. The description of the measurements of the cities and the pasture lands connected with them as given in Num. 35:4–5 is difficult to understand and has given rise to many different interpretations.

The Levites were not the sole possessors or occupiers of these cities. They were simply allowed to live in them and have fields for the pasture of their herds. These cities did not cease to belong to the tribes within which they were located. The Levites could sell their homes, but could redeem them at any time, and if they failed to do so the homes automatically returned to them in the JUBILEE YEAR. Their fields, however, could not be sold (Lev. 25:32–34).

THE LEVITICAL CITIES (acc. to Josh. 21)

Abdon (Asher)	Helkath (Asher)
Aijalon (Dan)	Heshbon (Gad)
Ain (Judah)	Holon (Judah)
Almon (Ben.)	Jahaz (Reuben)
Anathoth (Ben.)	Jarmuth (Man.)
Be Eshtarah (Man.)	Jattir (Judah)
Beth Horon (Ephraim)	Jazer (Gad)
Beth Shemesh (Judah)	Jokneam (Zeb.)
Bezer (Reuben)	Juttah (Judah)
Daberath (Iss.)	Kartah (Zeb.)
Debir (Judah)	Kartan (Naph.)
Dimnah (Zeb.)	Kedemoth (Reuben)
Eltekeh (Dan)	Kedesh (Naph.)
En Gannim (Iss.)	Kibzaim (Ephraim)
Eshtemoa (Judah)	Kishion (Iss.)
Gath Rimmon (Dan)	Libnah (Judah)
Gath Rimmon (Man.)	Mahanaim (Gad)
Geba (Ben.)	Mephaath (Reuben)
Gezer (Ephraim)	Mishal (Asher)
Gibbethon (Dan)	Nahalal (Zeb.)
Gibeon (Ben.)	Ramoth Gilead (Gad)
Golan (Man.)	Rehob (Asher)
Hammoth Dor (Naph.)	Shechem (Ephraim)
Hebron (Judah)	Taanach (Man.)

The Levites did not live only in Levitical cities. They appear to have been regarded, in some respects at least, as belonging to the tribe within which they resided, even if it did not happen to be a Levitical city; hence the statement in Jdg. 17:7, "Now there was a young man of Bethlehem in Judah, of the family of Judah, who was a Levite; and he sojourned there" (RSV). Thus also ELKANAH, the father of SAMUEL, who undoubtedly was a Levite, is called an Ephraimite (1 Sam. 1:1). The Levites are never regarded as a thirteenth tribe.

These cities were allocated to the Levites by anticipation, to be occupied by them only to the extent that they required them and the Israelites possessed them. It is unlikely that the Levites ever dwelt in all of them, or even most of them, for some of the cities did not belong to Israel until long after the time of Moses and Joshua. Levitical cities mentioned in Jewish history after the time of Joshua are Beth Shemesh (1 Sam 6:13-15), Jattir (1 Sam. 30:27), Anathoth (1 Ki. 2:26; Jer. 1:1; 32).

(See further W. F. Albright in *Louis Ginzberg Jubilee Volume* [1945], 49–73; M. F. Unger, *Archaeology and the Old Testament* [1954], 210–11; R. de Vaux, *Ancient Israel* [1961], 366–67; A. G. Auld in *ZAW* 91 [1979]: 194–206; R. G. Boling in *Biblical and Related Studies Presented to Samuel Iwry*, ed. A. Kort and S. Morschauser [1985], 23–32; R. D. Nelson, *Joshua*, OTL [1997], 236–43; G. N. Knoppers, *I Chronicles 1–9*, AB 12 [2004], 430–50; *ABD*, 4:310–11.) H. A. HANKE

Leviticus, Book of li-vit´i-kuhs. The third book of the Bible and traditionally one of the five books of MOSES (the PENTATEUCH or TORAH). Its Hebrew title is the first word, *wayyiqrāʾ*, "and he called." The English title is derived from the VULGATE's *Leviticus* (an adjective meaning "the Levitical"), which in turn is derived from the title prefixed to the SEPTUAGINT, *Leuitikon* (an adjective qualifying *biblion*, "book"), despite the fact that the book nowhere refers to the special functions of the Levites (see PRIESTS AND LEVITES). The designations given to it in the MISHNAH—"priests' law," "priests' book," "law of offerings"—better indicate its scope. But a study of the material shows that many of its regulations are addressed to the congregation of Israel as well as to MOSES and AARON.

    I. The unity of the book
    II. Authorship and date
    III. Purpose
    IV. Outline
    V. Selected studies
    VI. Text
    VII. Relationship to the NT

I. The unity of the book. Many scholars—literary critics, who regard the book as essentially the product of the so-called "priestly" writer, as well as form and tradition critics, both of whom see numerous sources behind it—view Lev. 17–26 as a separate body of material designated the Holiness Code (H) by A. Klostermann in 1877 (cf. his later work, *Der Pentateuch: Beiträge zu seinem Verständnis und seiner Entstehungsgeschichte* [1893], 368ff.).

A. Arguments for recognition of H. Several arguments have been advanced for the existence of an independent Holiness Code. First, critics allege that Lev. 17–26 is marked as a separate law code both by its beginning (17:1–2) and by its ending (26:46). Second, various writers have given lists of words and phrases that are peculiar to this section, and which show the author is nearer to EZEKIEL than to any other book in the OT. Because of this connection between H and Ezekiel, some claim Ezekiel is the author of H; many others conclude that the two are roughly contemporary and that possibly H originated among the exiles in Babylon. Third, their analysis reveals that the code contains much exhortatory material akin to DEUTERONOMY. Fourth, they claim the laws of this code are derived from another collection because they are much wider in scope than those in the preceding chapters. Finally, they note that reference is made in these chapters to matters that have already been dealt with (cf., e.g., 19:6–8 with 7:15–18; 20:25 with ch. 11; and 23:26–32 with ch. 16).

B. Arguments against the recognition of H. These arguments are readily refuted, and others can be advanced demonstrating that Lev. 17–26 is part and parcel with the rest of the legislation attributed to Moses in this book. First, the introductory formula in 17:1 is similar to others found in the book (passim) and appears to be a stereotyped way of introducing a fresh element in the revelation. In fact, this argument is so weak that C. A. Simpson ignored the issue when he suggested for reasons of his own that ch. 17 may have come from another source than chs. 18–26 (*HDB* rev., 581).

Second, the concluding statement in Lev. 26:46 might be referred better to the whole book than arbitrarily limited to these chapters. This suggestion is confirmed by noting that the curses and blessings formulae in ch. 26 more properly belong to the entire COVENANT enacted on SINAI. Korošec and Mendenhall demonstrated that the Sinaitic covenant is similar in its form to the HITTITE international treaties (see TREATY). In this connection they noted that such covenants typically include the curses and blessings formulae (G. E. Mendenhall in *BA* 17 [1954]: 50–76). By viewing Exod. 19—Lev. 26 as a unity, all six elements typically found in these Hittite treaties are present in the Sinaitic covenant. By denying this unity one is left with the anomaly that some of these elements are present in one code and others are present in later codes. Thus Mendenhall conceded that the last three out of the six elements are lacking in the Decalogue (see TEN COMMANDMENTS). Moreover, by separating Lev. 17–26 the critic produces the anomaly that the blessings and curses are now found in a code that is much later and lacks the other unifying elements. By accepting the biblical claim, on the other hand, one possesses an integer similar in structure to these Hittite covenants.

Third, there is no valid reason why the scope of legislation should not be expanded from laws governing the cult to other rules regulating the social, moral, and religious life of the people in whose midst Yahweh reigned.

Fourth, the change to sermonic style in Lev. 18–20 is appropriate to the subject matter. In these chapters Yahweh prohibits the Israelites from conforming to the corrupting practices of their pagan neighbors. Because of the temptation to conform to their degraded practices, Moses is not content simply to explain what the laws of God are, but he earnestly enjoins them upon the conscience of the people, and urges them to take with utmost seriousness God's call to a holy life. In a word, the change in subject matter readily accounts for the change in style and vocabulary.

Fifth, regarding the connection with Ezekiel, G. Henton Davies admitted that "it cannot be shown with certainty that H preceded Ezekiel or vice versa" (*IDB*, 3:119–20). Assuming that Lev. 17–26 preceded Ezekiel, why should it be surprising that Ezekiel reflects this material, which is foundational for the theocratic state?

Sixth, the connection of material found throughout the book argues for its homogeneity; for example, the ban on blood (Lev. 3:17; 7:26–27; 17:11), regulations regarding impurity (7:21; chs. 11–15), and the distinction between clean and unclean (10:10; ch. 11; note that 20:25 clearly alludes to the law concerning the clean and unclean animals in ch. 11 and clearly integrates the commandments of chs. 18–20 with chs. 11–15). Moreover, there are doublets within H itself (e.g., 17:12 = 19:26a; 19:27–28 = 21:5; 19:30 = 26:2; 19:31 = 20:6; 19:34 = 24:22). The dis-

elevant amplitude on Israel's holiness because her use of Yahweh's holiness found in 21:1—22:16 is stated earlier in 11:44–45; 19:2; 20:7.

II. Authorship and date. The question of the author and date of Leviticus is bound up with two prior considerations: the attitude of the scholar to the nature of Holy Scriptures, and the method employed in deciding these issues. Because of these factors, four distinct views can be presented. (For further discussion, see PENTATEUCH.)

A. The view of the literary critic. The dominating view is that Leviticus is part of P (the Priestly Code). This opinion on the date and origin of P since the days of Julius Wellhausen was well expressed by R. H. Pfeiffer: "The Priestly Code is a fifth century midrash, or historical commentary, on the embryonic Pentateuch (JED), including a series of narratives often illustrating legal precedents, and a codification of ritual laws based on earlier codes" (*Introduction to the Old Testament* [1948], 88).

The conclusion that P was later than the other strands is ultimately based on a wish to view the history of OT religion and literature in terms of the evolutionary philosophies of the age. For example, Wellhausen laid down the principle that the sense of sin in Israelite sacrifice was a decidedly late development (*Prolegomena to the History of Ancient Israel* [1957, orig. 1883], 81), but this understanding was refuted by R. J. Thompson (*Penitence and Sacrifice in Early Israel Outside Levitical Law*

In this view of the worship area at Arad (looking E), a broad room, the "holy of holies," and an altar are visible. The book of Leviticus carefully defined the worship life of God's people, including the sacrifices they were to make.

[1963]). Moreover, according to Wellhausen legal codes must be regarded as a late phenomenon in Israel's history of religion. This view has been discredited by the discovery of several ancient collections of laws since the recovery of HAMMURABI's stela in 1901–1902. (For Ur-Nammu laws, cf. S. N. Kramer and A. Falkenstein, *Orientalia* 23 [1954]: 40–48; for those of Lipit-Ishtar, Eshnunna, Hammurabi, and the Middle Assyrian and Hittite laws, see the translations with bibliographies in *ANET*, 159–198.) Significantly, the most striking parallels between the so-called P laws and these laws are found in the so-called H (cf. G. L. Archer, *Survey of Old Testament Introduction*, rev. ed. [1994], 261).

B. The view of the form critic. According to FORM CRITICISM, the book of Leviticus has come into existence in successive stages. For Martin Noth only Lev. 8–10 can be judged as primary and belonging to P. The remaining content of the book for him did not belong to the original or expanded P narrative. He said: "There are such striking departures in numerous details from P's account, especially with regard to the cultic personnel, and such notable differences in language, that one is led to this conclusion: the non-narrative parts of the book have been fitted into the narrative framework as a later addition and have their own independent history" (*Leviticus* [1965], 13). According to these critics the cultic and ritual regulations must ultimately be traced back to an oral stage. To quote Noth: "At the back of such compositions there lies most probably a form that was oral, handing on the relevant rules from one generation to another; and in the course of this oral 'tradition' new material must certainly have been added to the old" (ibid., 15). Even when fixed in writing, there was always the possibility of expansion and fresh additions. For form critics, dates must be approximate, and the final form contains both ancient and more ancient material. It is as important for them to fix the place of origin as it is to fix the date.

Having settled upon the history of these units of laws, these critics then seek to identify the combinations of laws of like character or similar theme into larger collections. This method is highly subjective and undisciplined. Significantly, after attempting to trace the history of the collections in Leviticus, G. Henton Davies admitted: "But the arguments which prompt such divisions may be countered by other considerations, and this suggests that the precise analysis of these laws into intermediary sections is unwise" (*IDB*, 3:117). Moreover, the theory of oral tradition is contradictory to observed scribal practices in the ANE. The religious rituals and incantations from the 3rd millennium B.C. texts in the pyramids of Unis, Teti, and Pepi (5th–6th dynasties) at Saqqara, as well as the Sumerian religious texts, divine hymns, and mythological texts from Ur, Nippur, and elsewhere, point to a custom of preserving at an early stage those sources of information or procedure that were of importance to a particular profession (cf. R. K. Harrison, *Introduction to the Old Testament* [1969], 592).

C. The view of the tradition critic. Ivan Engnell in his introduction to the OT (*Gamla Testamentet*, 1 [1945]), and in articles in *Svenskt Bibliskt Uppslagsverk*, did not regard P as the youngest of the "sources" of the Pentateuch, but as a complete work consisting of Genesis, Exodus, Leviticus, and Numbers. This work is the product of the "P-circle." In spite of the ancient traditions contained in P, Engnell found it necessary to date the work of the P-circle rather late, in the exilic or postexilic period, possibly even in the time of Ezra and Nehemiah.

But A. Kapelrud, who also recognized only a P-circle and a D-circle, contradicted Engnell by concluding that the work of the P-circle must have been completed before 550 B.C. He reasoned that so-called Second Isaiah used the work (particularly Gen. 1–2) in such a way that the prophet not only knew these chapters as we have them in MT, but he also supposed that his audience knew the passages. He concluded: "That must mean that P had got its final form not later than 550 B.C." ("The Date of the Priestly Code," *Annual of the Swedish Theological Institute* 3 [1964], 58–64). The only reason he advanced for dating it not earlier than 550 B.C. was that it could not be demonstrated to his satisfaction that Jeremiah and Ezekiel explicitly quote the P work, but surely this negative evidence does not lead necessarily to the conclusion that it was nonexistent in their times.

D. The view of the faithful. The Holy Spirit has convinced the faithful that Jesus of Nazareth is Lord and Christ and that the Scriptures he revered are the Word of God. His faith rests on the Spirit's convincing work; he rejoices in all truth; and he recognizes error by its inconsistency with Scripture.

Although the author of Leviticus is not named, a comparison of Exod. 40:1, 17 with Num. 1:1 suggests that these laws belong to the first month of the second year after the exodus. Moreover, the context for these laws is clearly the revelation given by Yahweh to Moses at Sinai. Thirty-eight times it is stated that Yahweh spoke to Moses at Sinai. However, the statement in Lev. 16:1 that the law for the Day of Atonement was given after the death of NADAB and ABIHU recounted in ch. 10 shows that the material is not arranged chronologically but logically (cf. J. S. Wright in *EvQ* 25 [1953]: 14). Although a later writer may have set this Mosaic material into its present order, there is no reason for thinking that Moses himself did not arrange the laws. If this historical setting for all the laws and narratives is the creation of a later writer's imagination, as the critics imply, one cannot escape the implication that he was immoral, using deceitful means to accomplish a righteous end. The work is morally tarnished according to their views and should be renounced as such.

The evidence suggests that their implied allegation is false. To this writer's knowledge there is no hard evidence dictating either that the book is late or that these laws did not come to Moses, the founder of the theocratic state. On the contrary, much evidence supports the claim of Scripture.

It will do little good to point out isolated details in these laws that show their early origin because the form critic and the tradition critic can fit these details into their theories. But if one examines the book as a whole against a Late Bronze environment, one finds that almost every major section of the book has analogues in the ANE literature from this time and earlier.

Thus the sacrifices mentioned in Lev. 1–7 have their analogies in UGARIT. For example, an offering analogous to the *minḥâ* H4966, "the cereal gift" (Lev. 2:1), is mentioned in a sacrificial tariff from Ugarit (*CIS*, 1:145); a propitiatory peace offering appears to have been known there also (D. M. L. Urie in *PEQ* no vol [1949]: 75ff). Votive and tributary offerings were familiar throughout the ANE (cf. T. H. Gaster in *IDB*, 4:148ff.). On the other hand, one should caution that the sacrificial system found in the Ugaritic texts lacks convincing correspondence with the Mosaic system (cf. A. DeGuglielmo in *CBQ* 17 [1955]: 196).

Even more compelling is the priestly nature of the material. In antiquity all forms of education were under the supervision of the priesthood, a tradition that was established by the Sumerians (J. Kaster in *IDB*, 2:27ff.). In this connection it is important to recall that this professional literature was put into writing at an early date. In addition, highly organized medical material of various kinds are known both in Babylonia and Egypt from at least the 2nd millennium B.C. onward. On this basis Harrison concluded regarding Lev. 11–15: "There is no *a priori* reason why the hygienic code of Leviticus cannot be confidently credited to its attributive author. ... there is no specific element in the prescriptions that requires a date later than the end of the Amarna period" (*Introduction*, 594).

Also, it is important to recall that the legal codes with striking parallels to material in so-called H are found in writing from a time before Moses. Furthermore, with regard to the FIRSTFRUITS in Lev. 23:9–14, note that similar offerings have been attested from Mesopotamian, Hittite, S Arabic, and Aegean sources (Harrison, *Introduction*, 601). Finally, recall that the curses and blessings formulae of Lev. 26 find their parallel in ancient Hittite treaties.

Taking all this material into account, one gains the impression that the content of Leviticus is very old. In short, in contrast to the speculative theories of the critics, the hard facts support the scriptural claim for the book from its beginning to its end, throughout each of its major divisions.

III. Purpose. Leviticus is a collection of enactments enabling the holy Yahweh to live in communion amid his unholy subjects. Cautioning the people to keep this covenant, Yahweh concludes that if they keep it: "I will put my dwelling place among you, and I will not abhor you. I will walk among you and be your God, and you will be my people" (Lev. 26:11–12). For this reason Yahweh legislates the cultic, civil, social, moral, and economic life of his redeemed people. Exodus concluded with the account of the completion of the TABERNACLE. From the tabernacle, rendered glorious by the divine Presence, issues the legislation contained in Leviticus.

As Yahweh draws near to the people in the tabernacle, so the people draw near to Yahweh in the prescribed offerings (Lev. 1–7), and through the prescribed priesthood (chs. 8–10). Moreover, Yahweh demands cleanness (chs. 11–15), and provides for their pollution through the Day of Atonement (ch. 16). To enjoy his fellowship, his people and priests must be holy in all particulars in contrast to their pagan neighbors (chs. 17–25). Blessings and curses will be determined by their response to the law (ch. 26). The laws concerning devoted property (ch. 27) stand apart from the prerequisite standards for Yahweh's residence among the people.

IV. Outline
 I. The laws concerning sacrifices (Lev. 1–7)
   A. The laws addressed to Israelite worshipers through Moses (1:1—6:7)
    1. The laws for the sweet savor offerings (chs. 1–3)
      a. The law of burnt offering (ch. 1)
       (1) Introduction (1:1–2a)
       (2) Of the herd (1:2b–9)
       (3) Of the flock (1:10–13)
       (4) Of fowls (1:14–17)
      b. The law of cereal offering (ch. 2)
       (1) In its uncooked form of fine flour with oil and frankincense (2:1–3)
       (2) In its cooked form (2:4–10)
       (3) The prohibition of leaven, and the direction to use salt in all cereal offerings (2:11–13)
       (4) The oblation of firstfruits (2:14–16)
      c. The law of peace offering (ch. 3)
       (1) Of the herd (3:1–5)
       (2) Of the flock: sheep (3:6–11), goats (3:12–16), perpetual statute concerning blood and

suet (3:17). [Apart from this last verse, these laws of the sweet savor offerings consist of a decalogue of instructions.]
2. The laws for the nonsweet savor offerings (4:1—6:7)
   a. The law of sin offering (ch. 4)
      (1) Introduction (4:1–2)
      (2) For the anointed priest (4:3–12)
      (3) For the whole congregation (4:13–21)
      (4) For a ruler (4:22–26)
      (5) For one of the common people: a goat (4:27–31), a lamb (4:32–35)
   b. The law of the guilt offering (5:1—6:7)
      (1) For three kinds of offenses (5:1–13)
         (a) For any person [lamb or goat] (5:1–6)
         (b) For poorer people [fowls] (5:7–10)
         (c) For the poorest [cereal] (5:11–13)
      (2) For deceit in holy things (5:14–16)
      (3) For unknown sins (5:17–19)
      (4) For crimes against a neighbor (6:1–7) [Again, this section may be analyzed as a decalogue.]
B. The laws addressed mainly to the priests (6:8—7:38)
   1. The law of the burnt offering (6:8–13)
   2. The law of the cereal offering (6:14–18)
   3. The offering of the priests (6:19–23)
   4. The law of the sin offering (6:24–30)
   5. The law of the guilt offering (7:1–10)
   6. The law of the peace offering (7:11–21)
   7. Exposition of 3:17: law prohibiting eating fat or blood (7:22–27)
   8. Selected portions for the priests: wave breast and heave thigh (7:28–34)
   9. The priest's portion for the anointing (7:35–36)
   10. Conclusion (7:37–38)
II. Historical interlude: the institution of the priesthood (chs. 8–10)
   A. The account of the consecration of Aaron (ch. 8)
   B. Aaron's first offering for himself and the people (ch. 9)
   C. Legislative narrative concerning the priests (ch. 10)
III. The laws concerning purity and impurity (chs. 11–15)
   A. The law of food and clean and unclean animals (ch. 11)
      1. Land animals (11:1–8)
      2. Water animals (11:9–12)
      3. Birds (11:13–19)
      4. Winged creeping things (11:20–23)
      5. The carcass of land animals making unclean (11:24–28)
      6. Specific unclean creeping things on earth (11:29–31)
      7. Things unclean by contact (11:32–38)
      8. Dead clean beasts (11:39–40)
      9. General unclean creeping things on earth (11:41–43)
      10. Concluding summaries (11:44–47)
   B. Purification following childbirth (ch. 12)
   C. Diagnosis and treatment of leprosy (chs. 13–14)
      1. Infection of various parts of the body (ch. 13)
      2. The law of the leper in the day of his cleansing (14:1–32). [The priest is mentioned in ten verses, each of which begins one of the ten sections of this law (vv. 3, 4, 5, 11, 12, 14, 15, 16, 19, 20).]
      3. The law for leprosy in a house (14:33–57)
   D. Ritual for bodily excretions (ch. 15)
IV. The law for the Day of Atonement (ch. 16)
   A. The occasion (16:1)
   B. The ceremony (16:2–28)
      1. The law for Aaron (16:2–25). [Dividing the text according to the

mention of Aaron there are eight divisions: vv. 2, 3–5, 6–7, 8, 9–10, 11–19, 20–22, 23–25.]
  2. The law for the man who lets the goat go to Azazel (16:26)
  3. The law for the man who burns the sin offering without the camp (16:27–28). [If this analysis is correct, once again there is a decalogue.]
  C. Instruction for annual repetition of the ceremony (16:29–34)
V. The law for sacrifice (ch. 17)
  A. The place for sacrifice (17:1–9)
  B. Eating with blood prohibited (17:10–14)
  C. Eating of carcasses forbidden (17:15–16)
VI. Laws commanding holiness and nonconformity with pagan practices (chs. 18–20)
  A. Sexual laws (ch. 18)
    1. Introduction (18:1–5)
    2. Twenty enactments (vv. 17 and 23 contain two) against consanguineous and illicit marriages and unnatural lusts (18:6–23)
    3. Concluding exhortations (18:24–30)
  B. Mixed moral and ceremonial laws (ch. 19)
  C. Miscellaneous laws (ch. 20)
VII. Laws for the priesthood (chs. 21–22)
  A. Laws for the personal purity of the priests (ch. 21)
  B. Laws for the eating and offering of sacrifices (ch. 22)
VIII. Cultic laws for the people (chs. 23–25)
  A. Laws of the sacred calendar (ch. 23)
  B. Law for the tabernacle and camp (ch. 24)
  C. Laws for the land (ch. 25)
    1. The sabbatical year (25:1–7)
    2. Year of Jubilee (25:8–23)
    3. Redemption of land (25:24–34)
    4. No usury for the landless (25:35–38)
    5. Slavery and the landless (25:39–55)
IX. Blessing for obedience and curses for disobedience to the code (ch. 26)
X. Appendix: Laws of vows and gifts (ch. 27)

V. Subject similes

A. The laws governing the sacrifices in chs. 1–7. For what follows see also the article on SACRIFICE AND OFFERINGS.

1. **The burnt offering** (Lev. 1). The motive behind the "[whole] burnt offering" (Lev. 1:3) is exhibited in the clause, "When any of you brings an offering [or gift, cf. v. 10] to the LORD …" (v. 2). The gift consisted of an animal and served to secure to the offerer the good pleasure of Yahweh (v. 3). The expression "that he may be accepted" (RSV) is never used in connection with the sin offering, whose peculiar function was to obtain the pardon, rather than the gracious favor of Yahweh. Accordingly, like the other two "sweet savor" offerings, it was voluntary. An example of its use is seen when the king offers up a burnt offering before going to battle (1 Sam. 7:9; 13:9; Ps. 20).

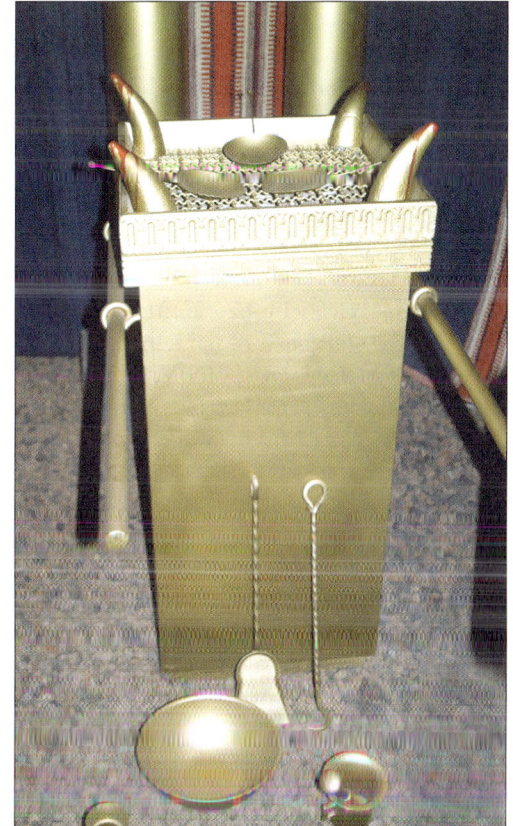

Reconstruction of the altar of incense.

2. The cereal offering (Lev. 2). The motive behind this sacrifice is identical with the first as seen in the clause: "When someone brings a grain offering …" (Lev. 2:1). The wording is almost identical with 1:2, except the gift is qualified by *minḥâ* H4966, "cereal, grain gift." Elsewhere this word is used for both bloody and nonbloody offerings (cf. Gen. 4:3–4), but under the law it is restricted to the bloodless offering. Again, the motive is not prompted through a divine demand but through an instinctive desire to commune with God. W. Eichrodt said: "Just as an inferior brings a present to his superior, or a client to his patron, or a vassal to his lord, as the normal expression of his subjection and fealty, so the pious worshiper makes an offering to God. Naturally, only something valuable, the surrender of which involves an act of renunciation on the part of the giver, is suitable for such an offering. Hence food—and that only at its best—accords admirably with this idea of a gift, because it is essential to life" (*Theology of the Old Testament* [1961], 1:144).

3. The peace offering (Lev. 3). The first verse of this chapter should be rendered: "If his gift is a sacrifice of well-being …"; the word translated "sacrifice" (*zebaḥ* H2285) denotes the concept of sacral communion. The peace offering is the only sacrifice eaten by the lay worshiper (Lev. 3:17; 7:20, 17:1–7) and the only animal sacrifice that does not make atonement (cf. 1:14; 4:20, 26, 31, 35; 5:16, 18, 26; 16:24). According to 7:12 and 7:16, the sacrifice was offered for "thanksgiving" (NIV, "as an expression of thankfulness") or as "a votive offering" (NIV, "the result of a vow") or "a freewill offering."

The word translated "thanksgiving" (*tôdâ* H9343) would be rendered better by "acknowledgement" (cf. C. Westermann, *The Praise of God in the Psalms* [1965], 25–30). Eichrodt concluded: "The *toda* springs spontaneously from man's need to give public and material expression to his gratitude for some deliverance or marvelous benefit" (*Theology*, 147). The vow (*nēder* H5624) springs from the spontaneous conviction that it is right to give a gift only to one's benefactor. "A real element in the vow," said Eichrodt, "is the spontaneous conviction that God's gifts require from men not merely words, but deeds of gratitude, and that for a person praying to make his readiness for such an act explicit is to express a right attitude of mind and to show a real awareness of God's graciousness in answering his prayer" (ibid., 145). Finally, the "freewill offering" (*nědābâ* H5607) expresses one's homage. Eichrodt commented: "The *nedaba* is an example of a free act of homage, which views man's humble recognition of and submission to his divine Lord, and was a common practice on the occasion of the regular visits to the sanctuary at the time of the great annual festivals (Exod. 23:15; 34:20)" (ibid., 145). Thus the basic motive prompting this sacrifice is that of appreciation.

4. The sin offering (Lev. 4). The term "sin offering" (*ḥaṭṭāʾt* H2633), presented in connection with the inadvertent transgression of some commandment (Lev. 4:2; Num. 15:22–29 [contrast vv. 30–31]; cf. Ezek. 45:20), designates the sacrifice that made ATONEMENT, that is, paid the price to appease the wrath of God (see below). Throughout the ritual, the ransom price demanded was blood.

5. The guilt offering (Lev. 5). The guilt offering made compensation for the damage done through sin. Eichrodt said: "A breach of trust between human beings involved the payment of compensation. The same obligation toward God was expressed in *the guilt offering or the sacrifice of reparation* (*ʾāsām*). Moreover, the proper legal compensation had to be made either directly to the injured fellowcitizen, or to the sanctuary at the same time as the sacrifice …" (*Theology*, 161).

B. The laws of purification (chs. 11–15)

1. The clean and unclean animals (Lev. 11). The categorizing of animal species into CLEAN and unclean is unique in the annals of ANE literature in its avoidance of magical considerations (see also UNCLEANNESS). R. K. Harrison wrote: "The system of therapeutics and preventive medicine … was grounded upon an empirical basis, in marked contrast to the contemporary peoples, who were dominated by *a priori* magical considerations and as a result tended invariably to spiritualize pathological phenomena in terms of the activity of demons" (*Introduction*, 603). The foods classified as clean are known to be beneficial in contrast to the unclean known to be noxious. These dietary regulations issue from Yahweh's design for his people. The word šeqeṣ H9211, "abomination, something detestable" (v. 10 et al.), is a technical term designating that which is cultically unacceptable (cf. Dan. 9:27) in contrast to the much more frequent term for "abomination," tôʿēbâ H9359, which can designate that which is repugnant to one's sensibilities (e.g., Gen. 43:32).

2. The laws governing leprosy (Lev. 13–14). Several scholars have argued convincingly that the affliction diagnosed in Lev. 13–14 is not exactly the same as Hansen's disease (as modern medical practitioners prefer to designate leprosy; see DISEASE). Regarding the description of diagnostic techniques and quarantine regulations derived from clinical procedure recorded in Leviticus, Harrison said: "The Hebrew of chapter 13 is technical, suited to a professional textbook for the priest-physician. The language is like that of the Egyptian medical texts, and it is obscure to the modern Biblical student as most advanced texts are to beginners in other fields of knowledge" (*Introduction*, 608).

C. The Day of Atonement (Lev. 16). A crucial word in Leviticus as a whole and foremost in Lev. 16 is *kippēr* (piel of *kāpar* H4105), "to make atonement." Some scholars define its original meaning as "to wipe away, expiate" on the basis of the Babylonian and Assyrian parallels (J. Milgrom in *JBL* 90 [1971]: 151). Others define its meaning as "to cover" on the basis of its Arabic parallel (BDB, 497). L. Morris has demonstrated on the basis of usage that it means "to pay a ransom price." In its noncultic use he concluded that the verb means "to avert a ransom. ... Thus extra-cultic *kipper* denotes a substitutionary process. ... In each case the essence of the transaction is the provision of an acceptable substitute" (*The Apostolic Preaching of the Cross* [1965], 166). He found the same nuance in its cultic use: "... the verb *kipper* carries with it the implication of a turning away of the divine wrath by an appropriate offering. This meaning accords well with the general usage of *exilaskomai*, and it seems clear that the verb is used so often to translate *kipper* precisely for this reason" (ibid., 170). He also noted that the atonement paid is always out of proportion to the price paid. "There is always an element of grace" (ibid., 167). See ATONEMENT, DAY OF.

D. The law governing blood (Lev. 17). The significance of BLOOD (*dām* H1947) in the scriptural sacrifices has been understood in two ways. Some argue that by "the blood" is meant LIFE rather than death so that the essential element in sacrifice is the presenting of life. Accepting this understanding, G. Henton Davies said: "The blood is the life, and sacrifice is surrendered life, and so involves surrendered time, surrendered property, and surrendered self (laying on of hands)" (*IDB*, 3:120). This interpretation is based on the narrow base of Lev. 17:11. But L. Morris demonstrated through an exhaustive word study that "blood" in Scripture denotes death. He properly rejected the above interpretation and concluded: "*dam* [blood] in the Old Testament signifies life violently taken rather than the continual presence of life available for some new function, in short, death rather than life, and that this is supported by the references to atonement" (*Apostolic Preaching*, 121). He argued that *nepeš* H5883, "life" (17:11), more probably means "life yielded up in death."

VI. Text. The book of Leviticus presents relatively few and minor textual problems. One of the significant discoveries among the DEAD SEA SCROLLS is a fragment of Leviticus in paleo-Hebrew script, dated by S. Birnbaum to the 5th cent. B.C., and to the Maccabean era by F. M. Cross, Jr. (*The Ancient Library of Qumran* [1961], 34). This document demonstrated the fidelity of the MT in Leviticus by its agreement with the traditional text (note also D. N. Freedman and K. A. Matthews, *The Paleo-Hebrew Leviticus Scroll (11 QpaleoLev)* [1985]). See TEXT AND MANUSCRIPTS (OT).

VII. Relationship to the NT. The Lord Jesus Christ said in Matt. 22:40 that the entire Law and Prophets depend on Deut. 6:5 and Lev. 19:18. The second injunction, "Love your neighbor as yourself," is repeated elsewhere (Matt. 19:19; Mk. 12:31; Lk. 10:27; Rom. 13:9, Gal. 5:14). When he cured the leper he instructed him to carry out the law regarding leprosy (cf. Lev. 14). In the SERMON on the Mount to his disciples he demanded the righteousness obtained by these laws (cf. Matt. 5:18–20, 44–45).

The apostles saw much in Leviticus as a type, a divinely inspired picture, of their doctrines (see TYPOLOGY). For example the priests and sacrifices connected with the tabernacle shadowed the work of Christ in connection with heaven (cf. Heb. 3:1; 4:14–16; chs. 9–10); the presence of God in Israel (Lev. 26:12) prefigured the templehood of Christian believers (2 Cor. 6:16). The apostles also insisted that these enactments were not binding on the church but had been superseded in Christ and through the indwelling Holy Spirit (cf. Acts 9:9–16; 15:1–21; Gal. 2:11–3.5, 1 Tim. 4.1–5; Heb. 9:10).

(Significant commentaries include M. Noth, *Leviticus: A Commentary*, OTL, rev. ed. [1977]; G. J. Wenham, *The Book of Leviticus*, NICOT [1979]; B. A. Levine, *Leviticus*, JPS Torah Commentary [1989]; J. E. Hartley, *Leviticus*, WBC 4 [1992]; P. J. Budd, *Leviticus*, NCBC [1996]; E. Gerstenberger, *Leviticus: A Commentary*, OTL [1996]; J. Milgrom, *Leviticus*, AB 3, 3A, 3B [1991–2001]; A. P. Ross, *Holiness to the Lord: A Guide to the Exposition of the Book of Leviticus* [2002]; J. W. Kleinig, *Leviticus* [2003]; L. R. Bailey, *Leviticus–Numbers* [2005]; N. Kiuchi, *Leviticus* [2007]. See also W. Kornfeld, *Studien zum Heiligkeitsgesetz* [1952]; J. Joosten, *People and Land in the Holiness Code: An Exegetical Study of the Ideational Framework of the Law in Leviticus 17–26* [1996]; W. Warning, *Literary Artistry in Leviticus* [1999]; M. Douglas, *Leviticus as Literature* [1999]; R. Rendtorff and R. A. Kugler, eds., *The Book of Leviticus: Composition and Reception* [2003]; W. J. Berge, *Reading Ritual: Leviticus in Postmodern Culture* [2005]; C. Nihan, *From Priestly Torah to Pentateuch: A Study in the Composition of the Book of Leviticus* [2007]; and the bibliography compiled by W. E. Mills, *Exodus-Leviticus* [2002].)

B. K. WALTKE

lex talionis leks´tal-ee-oh´nis. Also *ius talionis*. This Latin phrase (meaning literally "the law of that [same] kind") refers to a principle of retaliation whereby a person suffers the same harm that he or she has inflicted on someone else. The concept is expressed in the Bible as early as Gen. 9:6, "Whoever sheds the blood of man, by man shall his blood be shed," but especially in Exod. 21:23–25, "But if there is serious injury, you are to take life for life, eye for eye, tooth for tooth, hand for hand, foot for foot, burn for burn, wound for wound, bruise for bruise" (cf. Matt. 5:38). The principle expresses not only the validity of legal retaliation but also, and perhaps primarily, the requirement of equity and proportionality in the administration of punishment. The *lex talionis* therefore does not justify personal VENGEANCE or excessive retaliation. (See B. S. Jackson in *VT* 23 [1973]: 273–304; S. E. Loewenstamm in *VT* 27 [1977]: 352–60; C. Carmichael in *Hebrew Annual Review* 9 [1985]: 107–26; R. Westbrook in *RB* 93 [1986]: 52–69; J. F. Davis, *Lex Talionis in Early Judaism and the Exhortation of Jesus in Matthew 5:38–42* [2005].)

libation. The pouring of a liquid offering as a religious ritual. See SACRIFICE AND OFFERINGS.

liberalism. In a religious sense, this term (or better, Classical Liberalism, also known as Modernism) refers to a movement that arose in Protestant circles in the middle of the 19th cent. and was prominent through the first decades of the 20th. It was characterized by an emphasis on free intellectual inquiry, suspicion (or rejection) of orthodox theology, and confidence in the natural goodness of human beings. The label *liberalism* is often used more broadly to describe any departure from historical Christian thought, especially with regard to the INSPIRATION and authority of the Bible. In a less careful sense, the term *liberal* is sometimes applied loosely to scholars who use the methods of "higher criticism" or who otherwise do not appear to follow traditional views. See BIBLICAL CRITICISM.

libertine. A person who emphasizes liberty in moral questions and acts without ethical restraints; also, a freethinker who rejects religious authority. The term is used by the KJV with reference to freedmen who composed a synagogue in NT times (Acts 6:9). See FREEDMEN, SYNAGOGUE OF THE.

liberty. The condition of being free from slavery or forced subjection, whether physically, materially, or spiritually. In the OT the concept of liberty is used basically to refer to the physical freedom of slaves. Thus the Hebrew noun *dĕrôr H2002* is used in Lev. 25:10 for proclaiming liberty for Hebrew slaves in the JUBILEE YEAR (cf. Jer. 34:8–9, 14–17; Ezek. 46:17). In an important prophetic passage it describes a part of the Messiah's spiritual ministry of salvation as he will "proclaim freedom for the captives" (Isa. 61:1; cf. Lk. 4:16–21).

A different term, the adjective *ḥopšî H2930*, "free," is used also to indicate liberty granted to Hebrew bondslaves in the seventh year (Exod. 21:2, 5; Deut. 15:12–13, 18) and liberty to a male or female slave because of an injury inflicted by a master (Exod. 21:26–27). Job 3:19 speaks of a slave's freedom from his master after death, and in a more general sense the oppressed are spoken of as being set free (Isa. 58:6). In the area of material liberty, this adjective speaks of freedom from taxes and other types of obligations (1 Sam. 17:25). In one instance, the adjective *rāḥāb H8146* ("broad") is used as a noun ("wide or open place") figuratively of the psalmist's freedom in living a godly life since he has sought the Lord's precepts (Ps. 119:45). (See *NIDOTTE*, 1:986–89; 2:238042.)

In the NT there is reference to the physically free (Gk. *eleutheros G1801*), as opposed to the slave (1 Cor. 7:21–22), where the Christian who has his political and social freedom is enslaved to Christ and the Christian slave is free in Christ (cf. Gal. 3:28). The NT lays greater stress on spiritual liberty, with the one through whom spiritual freedom is obtained being clearly set forth. Christ's interpretation of Isa. 61:1 makes clear that he as the promised Messiah will bring to sinners deliverance from sin (the Greek is *aphesis G912* in Lk. 4:20); this notion is amplified by PAUL (e.g., Rom. 6:18; Gal. 5:1). In Jn. 8:32, 36, Christ and his word of truth are set forth as the means by which the sinner is really made free. Paul teaches that the authority of the life-giving HOLY SPIRIT has made the sinner free from the authority of sin (Rom. 8:2), and it is this same Spirit who frees us so that we may know the Lord and his Word (2 Cor. 3:1–17).

Having been liberated by Christ from the penalty of sin, believers are challenged to employ this liberty properly in Christian living. They are not to use it as an excuse to satisfy unchristian sinful desires; rather, they are to serve others by LOVE (Gal. 5:13; cf. vv. 19–21 and 2 Pet. 2:19). The works brought by God through the believer's freedom in Christ does not result in sin but issues in good works (1 Pet. 2:15–16). The Christian is to consider the conscience of another in his use of Christian liberty (1 Cor. 10:29). A divine means by which the believer's life is influenced to godly living is the perfect law of liberty, the Word of God (Jas. 1:25; 2:12). Finally, at the SECOND COMING of Christ the Christians will be given a glorious freedom from the effects of sin (Rom. 8:21). (See J. E. Frame in *JBL* 49 [1930]: 1–12; H. D. Betz, *Paul's Concept of Freedom in the Context of Hellenistic Discussions about the Possibilities of Human Freedom* [1977]; *NIDNTT*, 1:715–21; *ABD*, s.v. "Freedom," 2:855–59.)

W. H. MARE

Libnah lib'nuh (לִבְנָה *H4243*, possibly "white[ness]" or "poplar" or "storax tree"). **(1)** A stopping place of the Israelites between Rimmon Perez and Rissah on their wilderness journey (Num. 33:20–21; it is thought by some to be identical with LABAN, Deut. 1:1). The site is unknown.

(2) A Canaanite city located in the SHEPHELAH, conquered by the Israelites under JOSHUA (Josh. 10:29–32). The conquest of Libnah was an important factor in solidifying the territorial holdings of the Israelites in the campaign in S Palestine. Libnah is cited in the list of conquered Canaanite cities (12:15) and was one of the cities included in the territory allotted to the tribe of JUDAH (15:42). It later became one of the LEVITICAL CITIES, towns assigned exclusively to the priests and Levites for their places of residency in Palestine (21:13; 1 Chr. 6:57).

Libnah successfully revolted against Judah in the reign of JEHORAM, indicating the weakening hold of Judah on her outlying cities (2 Ki. 8:22; 2 Chr. 21:10). Judah apparently regained control of Libnah, however, for it appears as one of the fortified cities attacked by SENNACHERIB in his campaign against Judah during the reign of HEZEKIAH (2 Ki. 19:8; Isa. 37:8). It was during this siege that the Assyrian forces were decimated by a plague (2 Ki. 19:35–36). Libnah was the home of Hamutal, the mother of ZEDEKIAH (2 Ki. 23:31; 24:18; Jer. 52:1).

The identification of ancient Libnah is debated. The town was evidently not far from LACHISH (Josh.

10:31) and in the same district as ETHER, KEILAH, and MARESHAH (15:42–43). One early proposal was modern Tell eṣ-Ṣafi, about 10 mi. due N of Lachish (cf. *NEAEHL*, 4:4:1522–24, s.v. "Ẓafit, Tel"). The white limestone cliffs that dominate the site (leading the Crusaders to give to it the name Blanchegarde) may explain the origin of the name Libnah, and archaeological excavations have yielded evidence of the Assyrian presence there. This identification, however, would seem to place the town outside the district of Ether (cf. Y. Aharoni, *The Land of the Bible: A Historical Geography*, rev. ed. [1979], 86). A more widely accepted suggestion is Tell Bornaṭ, about 5 mi. NE of Lachish. Other proposals include Tell Judeideh, less than 2 mi. E of Tell Bornaṭ (Z. Kallai, *Historical Geography of the Bible* [1986], 379–81, but see MORESHETH-GATH) and Khirbet Tell el-Beida (an additional 2.5 mi. E, but see ACZIB #2). T. E. MCCOMISKEY

Libnath. See SHIHOR LIBNATH.

Libni lib´ni לִבְנִי *H4249*, "white"; gentilic לִבְנִי *H4250*, "Libnite"). **(1)** Son of GERSHON, grandson of LEVI, and ancestor of the Libnite clan (Exod. 6:17; Num. 3:18, 21; 26:58; 1 Chr. 6:17, 20). Some believe that the name Libnite is derived from the town of LIBNAH (see *ABD*, 4:322–23). See also LADAN #2.

(2) Son of MAHLI, grandson of MERARI, and great-grandson of Levi (1 Chr. 6:29).

T. E. MCCOMISKEY

library. A library is a collection of books, large or small, purposely brought together by, and in the possession of, an individual or an institution (as contrasted with an accumulation of books for commercial purposes). Often a library possessed by an individual ultimately becomes part of an institution more or less public, such as the J. Pierpont Morgan Library of New York. While BOOKS frequently are mentioned in the Bible, nowhere is there a reference to a *library* of books existing in Israel. SOLOMON, however, did complain, "Of making many books there is no end" (Eccl. 12:12), indicating that he was well acquainted with an existing body of literature.

There are numerous individual allusions in the Bible to the writing of books and to the places where they were deposited. The books of MOSES are mentioned more frequently than any others. As early as Israel's victory over AMALEK, Moses was commanded, "Write this on a scroll as something to be remembered" (Exod. 17:14). Though nothing is said as to where it should be deposited, it is interesting to note that the next verse reads, "Moses built an altar." This incident antedated the building of the TABERNACLE. Soon after the giving of the Decalogue, "Moses wrote down everything the LORD had said" (Exod. 24:4); then, apparently on the next day, "he took the Book of the Covenant, and read it to the people" (v. 7; the NT adds the comment that Moses "sprinkled the scroll and all the people," Heb. 9:19). Again, it is here recorded that Moses built an altar.

In the great code of DEUTERONOMY there is a famous passage that Israel's future king should "write for himself on a scroll a copy of this law, taken from that of the priests" (Deut. 17:18). The PRIESTS AND LEVITES were definitely acknowledged as the keepers of these sacred volumes. There is a similar statement toward the end of the Pentateuch: "After Moses finished writing in a book the words of this law from beginning to end, he gave this command to the Levites who carried the ark of the covenant of the LORD: 'Take this Book of the Law and place it beside the ark of the covenant of the LORD your God'" (31:24–26). See BOOKS II.

JOSHUA referred to these Mosaic writings (Josh. 8:31, 34; 23:6), as did EZRA centuries later (Ezra 6:18). Much of the Pentateuch came to be called "the Book of the Covenant," and was the volume lost for an undefined length of time and discovered by HILKIAH in the temple (2 Ki. 22:8–10; 23:2, 21; 2 Chr. 34:14–15). Permission must have been granted to borrow these volumes or to copy them, for JEHOSHAPHAT (870–848 B.C.) had earlier sent certain Levites to teach "throughout Judah, taking with them the Book of the Law of the LORD" (2 Chr. 17:9).

In an even earlier period, when the Israelites had enthusiastically received SAUL as their anointed king, SAMUEL "explained to the people the regulations of the kingship. He wrote them down on a scroll and deposited it before the LORD" (1 Sam. 10:25). Both JEREMIAH and ISAIAH were admonished frequently to write in books certain warnings sent of God (Isa. 30:9; Jer. 25:15; 30:2; 36; 51:60).

From these allusions one might finally assume these writings commanded by God were in some way identified with the ARK OF THE COVENANT, and later with the tabernacle, and generally were under the care of the priests and Levites. This would seem naturally to imply that there was a library in the TEMPLE in Jerusalem, but of this the Scriptures say nothing. The famous German scholar E. Sellin supposed that there were temple archives also at Ophra, Dan, Shiloh, Shechem, and Gibeon.

For many generations there was no record of the book of Moses or of any other biblical books. After the destruction of Jerusalem, DANIEL, far away in Babylon, "perceived in the books the number of years that, according to the word of the LORD to the prophet Jeremiah, must be fulfilled" (Dan. 9:2 NRSV). Perhaps Daniel had memorized these passages, but it is more likely that he had a copy of Jeremiah with him or accessible to him.

In the middle of the 5th cent. B.C., when some of the Jews returned from captivity, the people asked Ezra to read to them from "the Book of the Law of Moses" (Neh. 8:1–3; cf. 13:1). This passage indicates not only that Ezra possessed a copy of the law of Moses, but also that the people knew that he had it.

In spite of all these references to the writing of the books and sometimes of the assignment of them to the care of the Levites, there is no specific reference to a library, nor even a hint that there must have been extensive collections of books in Israel. Not only were there copies of the literature which is now included in the OT, but these Scriptures refer also to other books not included in the CANON, such as the Book of the Wars of the LORD (Num. 21:14), the Book of Jashar (Josh. 10:12–13); the records of Samuel the seer, Nathan the prophet, and Gad the seer (1 Chr. 29:29); and the records of the seers (2 Chr. 33:19). Besides all these, there must have been collections of treaties, genealogies, business transactions, etc. The first eleven chapters of 1 Chronicles demand an extensive collection of genealogical records.

There is, however, a remarkable reference in the OT to a library in PERSIA. When the enemies of Israel complained to DARIUS about the Jews, they asked that a search be made in the king's treasure house in BABYLON concerning the decree of CYRUS preceding the building of the second temple (Ezra 5:17). Then "King Darius issued an order, and they searched in the archives [*lit.*, the house of the books] stored in the treasury at Babylon" (6:1; see also 4:15). Jerome translated "the house of the books" by *bibliotheca*, a clear reference to an official library. The book of Esther states that the story of Mordecai "was recorded in the book of the annals in the presence of the king" (Esth. 2:23; cf. 1 Esd. 6:21, 23). When the king was not able to sleep, "he ordered the book of the chronicles, the records of his reign, to be brought in and read to him" (Esth. 6:1). There is a final reference to what is probably a more extensive record of "the book of the annals of the kings of Media and Persia" (10:2).

The NT gives no hint of actual collections of books, but from our Lord's experience in the synagogue at NAZARETH (Lk. 4:17) it is clear that the synagogues then, as today, had copies of the OT writings.

The fact that no libraries or archives of Israel have thus far been found is more amazing in consideration of the fact that vast collections of records, narratives, and other texts were amassed by Israel's neighbors. Few have been found that could be called Israelite. In the 1930s eighteen OSTRACA in a Hebrew script from about 588 B.C., relating to the siege of LACHISH, were discovered. They related to the siege of the city, but were really emergency correspondence, not a library. North of Lachish, on the southern edge of the Valley of JEZREEL, twelve CUNEIFORM tablets were discovered at TAANACH

Subterranean passage leading to a portion of the ancient library at Alexandria (Egypt). The scrolls were kept in niches.

that could be dated about 1450 B.C. before the arrival of Israel. Farther N, at Ras Shamra, 40 mi. SW of ANTIOCH, was found a large collection of texts and letters, mostly religious, from the middle of the 2nd millennium B.C. (see UGARIT). In MARI (SE Syria) 20,000 tablets of the 18th cent. B.C. came to light, and 370 clay tablets of the 14th cent. were found at TELL EL-AMARNA in Egypt. More recently, a very extensive collection of tablets, dating to the 24th cent., was discovered in EBLA.

Probably the greatest collection of tablets yet found—c. 25,000 in number—is the library of SARGON (722–705 B.C.), now in the British Museum. In the Royal Library of ASHURBANIPAL (662–626), some 20,000 tablets representing 10,000 different texts also rest there. It was called by Sir Frederic Kenyon "the first great private collection of books known to history" (*The Bible and Archaeology* [1940], 4). More than 3,500 tablets, inscribed during the first half of the 2nd millennium, were unearthed at NUZI. In the temple area at NIPPUR (50 mi. SE of Babylon), some 50,000 tablets dating from the 4th and 5th centuries B.C. were found. E. C. Richardson (*Biblical Libraries: A Sketch of Library History from 3400 BC to AD 150* [1914], 1) wrote, "The fact is that there were thousands or even tens of thousands of collections, containing millions of written books or documents in Biblical places in Biblical times."

The large libraries of the Greek and Roman world were gathered after the close of the OT period. Most of the SEPTUAGINT probably was produced at the great library of ALEXANDRIA in the middle of the 3rd cent. B.C. The libraries of the early church, such as the one used by ORIGEN at CAESAREA in the 3rd cent. A.D., do not belong within the biblical period, and are consequently outside the scope of this article.

In the year 1947 occurred what has been designated as "the greatest manuscript discovery of all times." For the most part, the thousands of tablets found in different libraries of the ANE do not relate directly to Israel or to the OT records. From the caves in the hills at the NW end of the Dead Sea, however, were recovered a large number of complete and fragmentary scrolls dealing with the literature of the intertestamental period, and containing specimens from every book of the OT except Esther. This body of MSS was gathered or produced by the pious men of the QUMRAN community between 200 B.C. and A.D. 50. Some of these documents had never been seen before, or at least not in entirety: the *Manual of Discipline*, the *Damascus Document*, the *War of the Sons of Light against the Sons of Darkness*, etc. The greatest treasure was the great *Isaiah Scroll*, which is remarkably close to the Hebrew text of ISAIAH that has been used by Jews and Christians alike for centuries. See DEAD SEA SCROLLS. W. M. SMITH

Libya lib´ee-uh (לוּב *H4275*, occurring only in the pl. לוּבִים, "Libyans" [לְבִים in Dan. 11:43]; Λιβύη *G3340* [in LXX, Λίβυες, "Libyans"]). A country in N Africa, the immediate western neighbor of EGYPT. Greek writers often identified Libya with Cyrenaica (see CYRENE); sometimes the name was used more broadly of the whole N African coastal zone.

Many believe that the LEHABITES listed in the Table of NATIONS (Gen. 10:13; 1 Chr. 1:11) are to be identified with the Libyans. The usual Hebrew term, *lûbîm*, like Greek *Libyē*, derives from the name of a particular people, the Libu (*Rbw*) in Egyptian records from RAMSES II (13th cent. B.C.) onward. The oldest Egyptian terms for Libyan peoples are Tjehenu and Tjemehu (from the 3rd millennium); fresh tribal names including the Libu appear in the New Kingdom. The Libu predominated in an invasion of Egypt that was vigorously repelled by MERNEPTAH, as reported on the "Israel Stela" and other texts (J. H. Breasted, *Ancient Records of Egypt*, 5 vols. [1906], 3:§§569–617). Under Ramses III (c. 1190) and later, the Libu were less prominent, but

Relief in Hatshepsut's temple at Karnak reflecting her conquest of Libya.

their name persisted in titles like "Great Chief of the Libu" in the 22nd–23rd dynasties, c. 945–715 (cf. J. Yoyotte in *Mélanges Maspero*, 1.4 [1961], 112–51).

In the OT, the Lubim appropriately feature in the forces of the pharaoh SHISHAK (himself of Libyan extraction) when he invaded Palestine (2 Chr. 12:3), and also in those of ZERAH defeated by ASA (cf. 16:8). Along with Put (see below), the Lubim were reckoned as part of the strength of THEBES by Nahum (Nah. 3:9). Libya and CUSH are also subordinate to Egypt (Dan. 11:43), as happened so often in their history. The MT reading *kûb* (see CUB) in Ezek. 30:5 is often emended to *lûb* on the basis of the SEPTUAGINT and the Syriac (cf. NIV and NRSV, "Libya"; some also would read *lûbîm* for *lûdîm* in Jer. 46:9, but see LUD). In the NT, we read that visitors from "the parts of Libya near Cyrene" were present in Jerusalem at Pentecost (Acts 2:10).

It should be noted that PUT (Heb. *pûṭ* H7033), which occurs separately in the Table of Nations (Gen. 10:6; 1 Chr. 1:8), reappears in the 7th and 6th cent. prophets, associated with Lubim in Nah. 3:9 and possibly in Jer. 46:9 (but see previous paragraph). Ezekiel has Put alongside Persia, Cush, and Lud, in prophecies against Tyre and Egypt, as a source of warriors (Ezek. 27:10; 30:5; 38:5) — a common role of Libyans in the 1st millennium B.C. It is conceivable that *pûṭ* in Isa. 66:19 may be a scribal error for *pûṭ* (cf. LXX *Phoud*, thus NRSV, "Put," and NIV, "Libyans").

The name Put occurs in Egyptian as *Pywd* (in a text of Osorkon II, c. 860 B.C.) and *Pwd* (in amuletic papyri) for Libyans alongside Syrians, Nubians, and Egyptians (see Jacquet-Gordon, *JEA* 46 [1960]: 16–17, 20 on line 16; cf. I. E. S. Edwards, *Hieratic Papyri in the British Museum, 4th Series*, 1 [1960], 10 and n. 23; 122 s.v.). In Egypt under the Persians, the names *Putiya* (Old Persian) and *Puṭa* (Akkadian) are equivalent to Egyptian *Tȝ-Ṯjemeḥu*, "Libya," as well as to Hebrew *Put* (see G. Posener, *La première domination perse en Égypte* [1936], 186–87). The origin of the term remains uncertain; with Posener (ibid., 186 n. 1), it may derive from Egyptian *Pedj-tiu* > *Pidate* (TELL EL-AMARNA tablets), originally "bowmen, foreigners," and then applied specifically to Libyans. (See further O. Bates, *The Eastern Libyans* [1914]; W. Hölscher, *Libyer und Ägypter* [1937]; A. H. Gardiner, *Ancient Egyptian Onomastica* [1947], 1:114*–125*, nos. 238–242 [valuable surveys of the Egyptian data]; F. Colin, *Les peuples libyens de la Cyrénaïque à l'Égypte* [2000].)

K. A. KITCHEN

Libya.

lice. Plural form of *louse*, a term applied to various wingless insects that live exclusively by sucking blood. Lice have been closely associated with humans since antiquity, and their preserved bodies have been found in Egyptian mummies. They are still abundant in parts of the Middle E and flourish in dirt and over-crowded conditions. Lice are vectors of serious diseases, including typhus fever, and have been responsible for many deaths as well as general ill health and discomfort. Each species of louse lives on a different host, sometimes on just one part of a host; few groups of animals are preyed upon, but these include cattle.

JOSEPHUS (*Ant.* 2.14.3 §300) describes the third plague in Egypt as consisting of lice (Gk. *phtheir*), an identification followed by the KJV and some modern scholars. However, the Hebrew word in the biblical text (*kēn* H4031, Exod. 8:16–18; Ps. 105:31; LXX *sknips*) probably refers to GNATS. Lice breed only on the host and would not spread in the pattern given in the narrative. Also, the priests had worked out a system of personal hygiene — including shaving hairy parts of the body and frequent washing of clothes — that probably made them immune to lice. See PLAGUES OF EGYPT.

G. S. CANSDALE

licentiousness. Disregard of accepted moral rules and standards; lack of moral restraint, especially in sexual conduct. The term is used by the NRSV and other versions to render Greek *aselgeia G816* (e.g., Rom. 13:13, where NIV has "debauchery"). See LASCIVIOUSNESS.

Lidbir, Lidebir lid′bihr, lid′uh-bihr. See DEBIR (PLACE) #3; LO DEBAR.

lie. A false statement presented as TRUTH; the sin of speaking or acting in such a way as to leave a false or misleading impression, especially with the intent to deceive. Various biblical terms are used in this sense, such as Hebrew *šeqer H9214* and *kāzāb H3942*, both of which occur in Prov. 6:19 (lit., "A witness of falsehoods breathes out lies"); other terms include *kaḥaš H3951* (Hos. 11:12 et al.) and *šāwʾ H8736* (Isa. 59:4 et al.). In the NT the noun *pseudos G6022* and its cognates are common (e.g., Rom. 9:1; 1 Tim. 4:2; 1 Jn. 2:21), but terms related to this concept include several verbs that can mean "to deceive" (e.g., *apataō G572*, Eph. 5:6; *dolioō G1514*, Rom. 3:13; *planaō G4414*, Matt. 24:5; *paralogizomai G4165*, Col. 2:4). (See *NIDOTTE*, 2:619–21; *NIDNTT*, 2:457–61, 470–74.)

Lying is everywhere condemned in the Scripture. SATAN is designated as the source of lies: The devil does not hold "to the truth, for there is no truth in him. When he lies, he speaks his native language, for he is a liar and the father of lies" (Jn. 8:44). The emissaries of Satan are denoted as using lies delivered through human agents (1 Tim. 4:2). On the other hand, it is impossible for God to lie (Heb. 6:18). In the final analysis, it is SIN against God (Acts 5:4).

In the OT lying is condemned in the TEN COMMANDMENTS (Exod. 20:16; Lev. 19:11–12). Later, OT references apply lying to IDOLATRY (Isa. 44:20; Jer. 10:14) and heathen worship (see Rom. 1:25). This is the greatest lie confronted in the course of the old covenant. The messages of false prophets and diviners are as deceitful lies (Isa. 9:15; Jer. 14:14; Ezek. 13:6–7). The paramount lie in the NT is the denial that Jesus is the Christ (1 Jn. 2:22). Simple honesty is a cardinal virtue of the follower of Christ, and lying is the basic sin denoting the opposite (Col. 3:9).

No doubt can be entertained that the Scriptures bear uniform testimony to the wrong of lying. Several problems arise, however, as to the degree of condemnation of untruth under certain circumstances. Sometimes even good men become enmeshed in lies, for example, ABRAHAM (Gen. 20:2), DAVID (1 Sam. 21:2), PETER (Matt. 26:72). This is no more excusable in their lives than in any life, but in their case it was the exception rather than the pattern. On the other hand, one notes that no word of condemnation is leveled at RAHAB for lying about the whereabouts of the Hebrew spies (Josh. 2:3–6; cf. Heb. 11:31; Jas. 2:25). MICAIAH explained to AHAB that God sent a lying spirit to speak lies through the false prophets (1 Ki. 22:23). PAUL wrote that God will cause the deceivers to be deceived in the last days (2 Thess. 2:11), but one should note that (1) God, who does not lie, allows others to use lies and at times applies this to further his own plans; (2) those who are used in this way are people who have already committed themselves to such a role in life.

These examples, however, point up ethical questions relevant to present conditions. Is there such a thing as a lie of expediency? Does the situation sometimes remove the stigma of sin from the lie? Can a physician in all good conscience give temporary relief to dying patients by telling them they will recover? Can a husband seek to protect his wife and family from the assaults of a marauding criminal by lying about their whereabouts? Do the conditions of war justify the soldiers' or the spies' use of untruth or the government's misrepresentation of the facts to the world or to its own people?

Those who maintain that truth is relative, shifting with the change of time and place, are naturally inclined to deny anything absolute about the condemnation of lying. Each instance, they insist, must be judged upon its own merits, whether it is acceptable or to be condemned. The law of LOVE and the impulse of self-defense can justify untruth in some situations is their claim. Contextual ethics (e.g., Dietrich Bonhoeffer, "What Does It Mean to Tell the Truth?" in *Ethics* [1955]) and *koinonia* ethics (cf. Paul L. Lehmann, *Ethics in a Christian Context* [1963], 124ff.) oppose the absolutist's position (see Immanuel Kant, "On a Supposed Right to Lie from Altruistic Motives," in *Kant's Ethical*

they attempt to assume the place of God in judging the intentions and principles involved in each situation.

The Scripture does teach the existence of absolutes, but under extenuating circumstances it allows for a middle ground between absolute right and absolute wrong where only God can declare the wrong or right of a deed. It seems obvious that he would take into consideration: (1) Is the statement of an untruth deliberate? (2) Is it given with a calculated intent to deceive? (3) Is it intended deceit for the malicious purpose of bringing misery upon another or for the selfish end of one's own advantage? (4) Are the character and intent of the one to whom untruth is directed basis for such measures in defense? (5) Can the polite untruth demanded by etiquette be differentiated from the morally unjustifiable lie? It is impossible to say that lying is ever right, but certainly the situation may make it less wrong on some occasions than others.

The penalties for lying are severe. At times there is the recoil of the evil upon the liar (Deut. 19:19; cf. GEHAZI and the leprosy of NAAMAN, 2 Ki. 5:20–27). The liar disqualifies himself from worshipful approach to God (Ps. 24:4). The liar forfeits any promise of eternal salvation (Rev. 21:27; 22:15). L. FOSTER

lieutenant. This English term is used by the KJV to render Hebrew *ăḥašdarpān* **H346**, which refers to a SATRAP (Ezra 8:36; Esth. 3:12; 8:9; 9:3; in the Aram. sections of Daniel, the KJV has "prince," Dan. 3:2–3, 27; 6:1–7).

life. It is apparent that the biblical concept of life moves in the framework of the grand cosmic conceptions of CREATION, FALL, REDEMPTION, and eschatological THEODICY. The idea frequently occurring in the Bible proves to be that of *eternal life*, with its special implications of a "quality of life" with rich ethical associations, as well as the implications of endless duration through the ages to come (SEE ETERNAL and ETERNITY).

I. The biblical idea of renewal and eschatological theodicy
   A. Basic orientation of immortality vs. biblical resurrection
   B. The death and resurrection of Jesus Christ as the basis of redemption-life
   C. The *palingenesis* of the individual
   D. The *palingenesia* of creation at the resurrection and the age to come
II. Life in the eternal state
   A. The delivering over of the kingdom
   B. Life triumphant in the eternal state of perfection

I. The biblical idea of renewal and eschatological theodicy

A. Basic orientation of immortality vs. biblical resurrection. Careful discussion by James Orr (*The Christian View of God and the World*, 3rd ed. [1897], 165–211) has made clear the uniqueness of the biblical concept of IMMORTALITY over against supposed pagan parallels. The biblical form of immortality is not merely the survival of the SOUL, but life of the whole person in body and soul. "It is said we have no doctrine of Immortality in the Old Testament. But I reply, we *have* immortality at the very commencement—for man, as he came from the hands of his Creator, was made for immortal life. Man in Eden was immortal. He was intended to live, not to die … it is not an immortality of the soul only that the Bible speaks of—that is left for the philosophers—but an immortality of the whole person, body and soul together. Such is the Christian hope, and such … was the Hebrew hope also" (ibid., 202–3).

Alexander Heidel, writing fifty years later than Orr, emphatically reiterates the latter's findings. "In Mesopotamia man was thought to have been created mortal, so that death was the natural result of his constitution; in Israel he was believed to have been created for never-ending life, wherefore death was something unnatural. … Even the latest Babylonian and Assyrian records reveal nothing of a resurrection of the flesh, a doctrine so clearly set forth in Daniel and Isaiah … These differences set the eschatology of the Mesopotamians and that of the Hebrews as far apart as the East is from the West" (*The Gilgamesh Epic and Old Testament Parallels*, 2nd ed. [1949], 137–223, esp. 222–23).

Thus the matrix of the biblical theology of life is already cast in the created constitution of human beings and the hope of a heavenly and gracious redemption from sin and death. There is a straight line from Eden and the fall to the appearance of the last ADAM and his redemptive work. Redemption-life must include the historic, space-time death, resurrection, and second advent of Christ, as well as the impartation of benefits to sinners in individual renewal and resurrection.

B. The death and resurrection of Jesus Christ as the basis of redemption-life. For the present purpose it is convenient to refer to the inspired philosophy of history given in Heb. 2. The divine purpose of redemption and triumph is found in the promise of Ps. 8 that all things will be put under man in the "inhabited earth" that is to come. To that end, the majestic Son of God, crowned with glory and honor, tasted death for everyone. Through death and the inseparable resurrection, he brought to nought him who had the power of death, and delivered those held in bondage. Having made the one sacrifice for sins forever, he resumed his place of sovereign sway at the right hand of God and now "waits for his enemies to be made his footstool, because by one sacrifice he has made perfect those who are being made holy" (Heb. 10:12–15).

C. The palingenesia of the individual

1. Life as connected with regeneration. This life which is connected with recovery from sin is basically an ethical and spiritual conception. The death that is its opposite is a death in trespasses and sins. Life involves *palingenesia* G4098, that is, REGENERATION, "a profound renovation and reorientation of personal nature and ethical alignments and loyalties, a new birth." A regenerate person is in the KINGDOM OF GOD (Col. 1:13), but there is also a future aspect of the kingdom into which he will enter (Jn. 3:3, 5; Matt. 7:21). These two aspects of the kingdom are called "life": the one who believes in Christ *has* life (1 Jn. 5:12) and he will *enter into* life (Mk. 9:43), which is the kingdom (9:47).

The HOLY SPIRIT imparts life in the new birth (Jn. 3:3–8; 1 Cor. 12:13). He will also make alive our mortal bodies (Rom. 8:11) that we may enter into "life" or "the world to come." It is the presence and work of the Spirit also which constitutes the kingdom: "The kingdom-making power is associated with the Spirit" (G. Vos, *Biblical Theology: Old and New Testament* [1948], 413). His work in the new birth admits one to the kingdom, and his work in the resurrection (and transformation of the living, 1 Cor. 15:51–54) prepares the regenerate to inherit the kingdom (v. 50). The two stadia of the kingdom correspond to the two stadia of life. They run parallel, and one is involved in the other. These events of the impartation of life and the entrance into life are gifts of God's grace (Rom. 6:23) and are based wholly on the redeeming work of Christ (Jn. 20:31; 1 Pet. 1:3–5; Tit. 3:5–8). This kingdom relationship in life through the Spirit is also a relationship to the new covenant of promise (Gal. 4:24, 28–29; Heb. 8:10–12; 9:15). The two stadia of life or the kingdom may also be thought of as present heirship (because we are sons, Gal. 3:29), and the resulting future entrance into the inheritance (Matt. 25:34; Acts 20:32; 1 Cor. 15:50; 1 Pet. 1:3–4; 1 Jn. 3:2–3; Rev. 21:7).

2. The transition from death to life in the Pauline epistles. The Pauline epistles show a special interest in the analysis of the transition from death to life in the individual experience. The impartation of faith and life by the Spirit takes place in the context of "calling" (or "effectual calling," in the language of the *Westminster Confession of Faith*). A classic statement of the order of the divine purposes is Rom. 8:29–30: the elect are called and justified, and, with logical certainty, will be glorified. This same point in the application of redemption passes under Paul's eye in Gal. 3:22–26. Before faith came, we were under the curse and penalty of the law, being shut up unto faith as the only hope for a person in his helplessness and guilt. There are striking parallels to these details in Rom. 7, if this chapter is read as the experience of a sinner under conviction, keenly recognizing the holiness of the law, and yet finding himself in bondage and without the liberating power of the Spirit of life.

In Eph. 4:1 Paul refers to effectual calling, while in 2:12–13 and 18 he speaks of access to the presence of God by faith, echoing in substance the words of Christ in Jn. 14:6 that he is the way of access to the Father. The whole concept seems to be drawn from the vivid application of the imagery of the access to the TABERNACLE set forth in classical fullness in Heb. 10:10–22. Another Pauline passage, Rom. 5:2 seems to reflect the same concept of having obtained access by faith into the grace wherein we have taken our stand, while Phil. 3:8–10 analyzes Paul's experience at the point where faith rests upon Christ in saving knowledge. In Col. 2:10–13 he describes the life-giving operation of the Spirit in OT and NT terms of CIRCUMCISION and BAPTISM, and a rising in new life. The letters to the Thessalonians lay emphasis on election, issuing in effectual calling (compactly stated in 2 Thess. 2:13–14), and Tit. 3:4–7 links together beautifully the life-giving work of the Spirit and the gracious JUSTIFICATION which is its necessary complement, and which makes the believer an heir according to the hope of eternal life.

3. Palingenesia in the NT. The last-mentioned passage (Tit. 3:5) introduces the striking word *palingenesia*, which is the organizing principle of the entire concept of redemption-life. The word occurs only here and at Matt. 19:28. Each of these occurrences serves as an organizing center for the two stages of the restoration of life. In the Titus context, the clear connotation is the regenerating work of the Holy Spirit in the soul of the individual. In the Matthew passage, the word refers to the time of resurrection and release of the creation from its groaning and will be further discussed below. "In one of the only two passages in which [the word] occurs in the NT (19:28) it refers to the repristination not of the individual, but of the universe, which is to take place at the end: and this usage tends to stamp upon the word the broad sense of a complete and thoroughgoing restoration. If in Tit. 3:5 it is applied to the individual in such a broad sense, it would be coextensive in meaning with the *anakainōsis* by the side of which it stands in that passage and would differ from it only as a highly figurative differs from a more literal expression of the same idea. Our salvation, the Apostle would in that case say, is not an attainment of our own, but is wrought by God in his great mercy, by means of a regenerating washing, to wit, a renewal by the Holy Spirit" (B. B. Warfield, *Biblical Doctrines* [1929], 454).

4. Johannine testimony to the transition from death to life. Johannine passages speak equally clearly of that momentous transition from death to life. In Jn. 5:24, Jesus posits FAITH as the inseparable concomitant of life; thus John comments, "He who has the Son has life; he who does not have the Son of God does not have life" (1 Jn. 5:12). In the Gospel of John, many of the personal confrontations of Christ with inquirers portray vividly the immediate circumstances of the impartation of faith and life, and this moment is actually the climax or turning point of the story. Examples are the royal official (Jn. 4:50) and the Samaritan woman (4:25, 26). In other instances the faith and assurance of believers are dramatically increased: Martha (11:23–27), John (20:8, 9), Thomas (20:27–29), and Peter (21:15–17). Always the emphasis falls on the interconnection of faith and life as in the climactic summary, "that by believing you may have life" (20:31).

5. The manifestation of life in good works. After the initial impartation of life and faith, the life and conduct of the believer come under close scrutiny in the Bible. It is constantly assumed that effectual calling will issue in good works. This intense ethical concern with practical HOLINESS and heart-conformity to the law of God is never blurred. The normal transition in the Pauline epistles is from a statement of doctrine to the ethical application and exhortation: Rom. 12:1–2 is typical of the whole series. The contrast of the works of the flesh and the fruit of the Spirit is clear in Gal. 5. The purpose of Christ's death is that we might be delivered from this present evil world (1:4; cf. 6:14). This triumph is actualized by the Spirit (5:5, 25).

The standard of ethical conduct is the law of God (Gal. 5:14; Rom. 13:8–10). The liberating power of the Spirit operates so that the righteousness of the law may be fulfilled in those who walk according to the Spirit (8:2–4). Thus, the "perfect law that gives freedom," the "royal law" (Jas. 1:25; 2:8) with sovereignty over every area of life, becomes a light and guide to the Christian. The law was "for life" (Rom. 7:10); that is, not to give life but to function as a rule and guide in a personality where the life-giving, liberating power of the Holy Spirit is operative. The present ethical manifestations of life by the enablement of the Spirit are constantly oriented toward a goal of perfection.

The Egyptian Tree of Life is depicted in this wall painting from the Beni Hasan tombs (Egypt, early 2nd millennium B.C.).

The present progress and the consummation are thus expressed by Paul: "May the Lord make your love increase and overflow for each other and for everyone else, just as ours does for you. May he strengthen your hearts so that you will be blameless and holy in the presence of our God and Father when our Lord Jesus comes with all his holy ones" (1 Thess. 3:12–13). Entire SANCTIFICATION and perfection in holiness are eagerly anticipated at the PAROUSIA of Christ (5:23) and the resurrection of believers.

6. The ethical nature of the new life. The life imparted to those dead in trespasses and sins is ethical and holy in every sense. Death came because man had corrupted the holy character God had given. For the Spirit of holiness to make his abode with sinners and lead them supernaturally to the triumphant issue envisioned in the Scripture, it was necessary that the Lamb of God should take away the sin of the world. The awesome spectacle of the Son of God bearing the sins of men and women surely shows that holiness is not compromised when God forgives the sinner. Justice is satisfied. The blood of Christ purges the conscience from dead works and gives peace. The life thus righteously purchased and bestowed by the Holy Spirit manifests itself in a conflict with sin and a striving for holiness without which no one shall see the Lord (Heb. 12:14). The resurrection is anticipated especially because it means the perfection of holiness, the entire SANCTIFICATION of the whole person. Heaven is not simply eternal existence, but there will appear a shining perfection of all God intended us to be: "his servants will serve him. They will see his face, and his name will be on their foreheads" (Rev. 22:3–4).

7. The palingenesia of the individual in the OT. The question of the spiritual state and privileges of believers before the cross has been widely discussed. It would probably be conceded by all that "the believing Israelite was born anew (cf. John 3:3, 5, with Luke 13:28)" (*Scofield Reference Bible*, 768 n. 1). This statement represents the understanding of Bible-believing people. The principal point gained here is that a new birth is admittedly characteristic of the redeemed of all ages. Discussion may continue concerning the content of the faith of believers before the cross, their spiritual privileges, and the fullness of their relation to the Holy Spirit. If it be conceded that all believers are born anew, it probably will also be admitted that such regenerate life could and can be sustained only by the constant presence and work of the Holy Spirit.

Further, it is the belief of this writer that in elaborating the scheme of recovery from sin and death, the apostolic writers of the NT look upon the OT as *fully spiritually normative for themselves*. Paul finds the blessedness of justification in the experience of ABRAHAM and DAVID (Rom. 4, quoting Gen. 15:16 and Ps. 32:1–2). Having reinforced the call to holiness of life (2 Cor. 6:14–18) with a mosaic of promises and exhortations drawn from the OT (Isa. 52:11; 43:6; Hos. 1:10), Paul says, "Since we have these promises, dear friends, let us purify ourselves" (2 Cor. 7:1). The author of Hebrew joins together God's ancient people and Christians, for we, too, are his house (Heb. 3:2, 6). Jesus brings Abraham, Isaac, Jacob, and all the prophets together in the kingdom of God, into which all the regenerate will enter (Lk. 13:28). Abraham "was looking forward to the city with foundations" (Heb. 11:10; 13:14; 11:40). It is the same city to which all aspire (13:14), for God has planned something better for all of us (11:40) than the opprobrium, persecution, and scorn of the world.

The OT has its own terminology for the renewal of the heart. CIRCUMCISION of the heart is required in Deut. 30:6; its ethical bearing is indicated in the resulting love for Yahweh with all the soul and with all the heart. Ezekiel links the work of the Spirit to the renewal of the heart, promising a "new heart" and ability to walk in God's law (Ezek. 36:25–27). Jeremiah's great prophecy of a new covenant is climaxed by the promise that God will write his law on the heart even as he forgives sins. See COVENANT, THE NEW. It is noteworthy in this latter passage that Jeremiah is rebuking his generation (Heb. 8:8) as is implied in the words, "No longer will a man teach his neighbor, or a man his brother, saying, 'Know the LORD' …" (Jer. 31:34). The implication is that Jeremiah was teaching and exhorting his self-righteous and rebellious generation. The inference is clear that the forgiveness and the writing of the law on the heart was contemplated as available to faith in Jeremiah's day.

The heroes of faith acknowledged that they were "aliens and strangers on earth" (Heb. 11:13). The simple exegesis of the following verses shows that they must have had a heavenly homeland in view, a city prepared by God. As G. Vos so well said, "It requires the assurance of the eternity of religion in the individual soul to secure the permanence of religion as such" (*Pauline Eschatology* [1952], 364–65). Christ said, "Because I live, you also will live" (Jn. 14:19). The presence of supernaturally imparted life in the soul carries the demand for and proof of eternal life with the soul's Savior. Hence the principal concern of the biblical thought with eschatology and especially resurrection. Vos eloquently says, "We encounter [in the Psalter] the ideas of peace, universalism, paradise restored, the dwelling of Yahweh's presence in the land, the vision of God, the enjoyment of glory, light, satisfaction of all wants, the outlook beyond death towards an uninterrupted contact with God and a resurrection" (ibid., 332).

The weightiest argument for the fullness of a supernatural renewal in OT believers is drawn from the efficacy of the cross of Christ. Whatever blessings of the goodness of God a sinful race has experienced must come because of the cross of Christ. Because it is the one sacrifice that actually atones for sin, it is absolutely unique: there is no other sacrifice for sin. If we grant that people in all ages have received countless blessings because of the one act of grace on Calvary, there is no reason why the Holy Spirit, because of the certainty that the atonement would be made, could not have applied its benefits in all ages from the beginning.

D. The palingenesia of creation at the resurrection and the age to come

1. Life in the intermediate state. Although spiritual life is imparted to believers in this life, physical DEATH still comes. The Bible has its adequate assurance for the believer: "to die is gain" (Phil. 1:21), and there is the calm assurance that "the Lord will rescue me from every evil attack and will bring me safely to his heavenly kingdom" (2 Tim. 4:18). Paul preferred "to be away from the body and at home with the Lord" (2 Cor. 5:8), though this state was less desirable than having the resurrection body (Phil. 3:20–21) and being "clothed upon" with immortality. Through this "intermediate state" the soul, made perfect in holiness, and enjoying communion with Christ, is preserved until the hour of resurrection. The swift tableau John gives of the souls beneath the altar (Rev. 6:9–11) clothed in white robes would suggest that God has made death itself the occasion of an advance in their perfection and holiness. Here are "the spirits of righteous men made perfect" (Heb. 12:23) awaiting the resurrection.

2. Life as related to resurrection. The concept of the RESURRECTION of the dead in Christ is necessary to the completion of the biblical scheme of our entire deliverance from sin and death. Through resurrection or instantaneous transformation of the living at the parousia (1 Cor. 15:51–52), believers are prepared to inherit the kingdom (15:50). So keenly is the resurrection felt to be related to full attainment of life that it is referred to as "coming to life" (Rev. 20:4) or "making alive" (Rom. 8:11). Modern alternative conceptions of resurrection as simply "spiritual" or "the persistence of the personality through death" do not approach the historic concreteness of the biblical view. Nor do they really solve the problem of death, the radical and unnatural rending apart of soul and body. For the healing of that stupendous rent in our being there is needed, as Christ said, the power of God in the resurrection of the dead (Matt. 22:29).

3. Palingenesia of creation. The *palingenesia*, then, of the individual issues in the resurrection. At this point in the analysis, Rom. 8:18–25 opens a further vista. Paul here logically connects with the resurrection of believers the deliverance of the creation itself. Since human beings are connected with the creation through their physical bodies, it is appropriate that when the BODY is made immortal, the creation should be raised to share the same glory and liberty, and itself experience a *palingenesia*.

The use of the word *palingenesia* in Matt. 19:28 provides a firm parallel from which to draw additional details about the creation's renewal. It is a time when the SON OF MAN shall sit on the throne of his glory. This statement, taken with Matt. 25:31 and Rev. 3:21, clearly distinguishes a special future reign of Christ from his present sharing of his Father's throne. His present session as contemplated in Ps. 110:1 (quoted in Matt. 22:44 et al.) is a continuation or resumption of his sovereign rule. The present imperative (*kathou*, "sit") may indicate, "maintain your place at my right hand," thus leaving room for the future reign in his own glorious throne. The parallel in Lk. 22:28–30 speaks of his "reign."

A further parallel (1 Cor. 15:25) touches this same point. This debated passage is minutely examined by G. Vos (*The Pauline Eschatology*, 235–46). His conclusion is that the "end" follows the parousia so closely that there is no room for a "kingdom." He thus concludes that the reign (for Christ must reign, 15:25) must have begun at Christ's resurrection and cannot be pushed into the future. We confidently dissent from Vos, though grateful for his masterly handling of eschatological issues generally. He has not accurately stated the three items in the series, nor has he dealt adequately with the resurrection of the unrighteous dead, who must be accounted for in accordance with the Pauline schema of a resurrection of the just and unjust (Acts 24:15), and the Johannine sequence of Rev. 20. When there are fitted into this picture the parallels of Matt. 19:28 and Rev. 20:4–6—where those who have come to life reign and judge (1 Cor. 6:2), and the defeat of the last enemy, death, is linked with the emptying out of Death into the lake of fire (Rev. 20:13–14)—the conclusion is irresistible that a third stage of resurrection is demanded (1 Cor. 15:24), following a reign of Christ which is the *palingenesia* of creation.

The conclusion is that an extended period of time when Christ and immortal saints reign is an integral part of the whole process of *palingenesia*, of renewal and fulfillment of the creation-purpose that humanity redeemed should have dominion through Christ, thus fulfilling the promise of Ps. 8.

II. Life in the eternal state

A. The delivering over of the kingdom. At the "end" (1 Cor. 15:24, 28) the Son delivers the kingdom to the Father, and death has been completely banished. The death contemplated in 1 Cor. 15:26 is to be distinguished from John's "second death." The unrighteous dead do not have part in the *palingenesia*, yet the unnatural separation of soul and body is mended ere they are handed over to their final doom. It is suggested that Satan's authority over death is done: Christ, the source of all life, in the sovereign exercise of judgmental authority, raises all the dead to life (Jn. 5:21–29) and thus shows that he has life "in himself" (5:26).

B. Life triumphant in the eternal state of perfection. The Bible scheme of recovery from sin and death thus reaches its goal as the redeemed enter, through resurrection and a triumphant *palingenesia*, into the everlasting kingdom of Christ, which is eternal life. Running through the splendid imagery of the heavenly scenes of the eternal state is the clear note: "And so we will be with the Lord forever" (1 Thess. 4:17). "Now the dwelling of God is with men, and he will live with them. They will be his people, and God himself will be with them and be their God" (Rev. 21:3).

The biblical keynote of *life* is never lost. The unrighteous enter their final doom, which is the second death (Rev. 21:8). The righteous enter into life, having their names written in the Lamb's book of life (21:27). They have access to the river of water of life and the TREE OF LIFE (22:1–2, 14). The light falls on the intensely ethical and personal features of the life of the redeemed. "No longer will there be any curse. The throne of God and of the Lamb will be in the city, and his servants will serve him. They will see his face, and his name will be on their foreheads" (22:3–4). (See further *NIDOTTE*, 2:108–13; *TDNT*, 2:832–75; *NIDNTT*, 2:474–83.)   W. B. WALLIS

life, author of. See AUTHOR.

life, book of. See BOOK OF LIFE.

life, tree of. See TREE OF LIFE.

light. This term (Heb. *ʾôr* H240, Gk. *phōs* G5890) often refers to physical illumination or brightness, but special interest attaches to its figurative, theological uses.

I. Introduction. According to the earliest biblical record concerning "the heavens and the earth" (Gen. 1:1), light was created by God and was therefore separate from him. He thereby challenged the DARKNESS, which engulfed the existing chaotic condition and which obstructed any possible ordered progress. This act opened the way to the great creative and growth processes that followed. To the prophets, God was the source of both light and darkness, of both good and evil (Isa. 45:7). Nevertheless, throughout the Bible light represents that which is compatible with God and darkness is symbolic of the evil forces that are opposed to God. Among the final scriptural references to the affairs of man on earth, BABYLON, the epitome of godlessness, is consigned to darkness (Rev. 18:23), while God's people (the city of God) are bathed in the light of his GLORY (21:23). In this city, the new Jerusalem, "There will be no more night. They will not need the light of a lamp or the light of the sun, for the Lord God will give them light" (22:5).

Light is superior to darkness (Eccl. 2:13) and is able to limit its scope and effects. This is especially evident in the NT. Light will triumph because darkness cannot overcome it (Jn. 1:5). Yet there is no indication in the Bible that darkness, literally or symbolically, will be finally or completely destroyed. The contest between light and darkness, between good and evil, is found outside the Bible in ZOROASTRIANISM and to a marked degree in the *Manual of Discipline* of the DEAD SEA SCROLLS.

II. Artificial light. The Bible briefly recognizes the necessity of artificial light because human activities do not always conform to the schedule of day and night, and natural light is not always sufficient for human needs (Exod. 25:6; Matt. 5:15; Lk. 15:8; Acts 20:8). A light was kept burning continually at night before the veil in the wilderness TABER-

Roman lamp from the 2nd cent. A.D., with an impression of four horses pulling a chariot in a race.

NACLE (Exod. 27:20–22; Lev. 24:2) as an emblem of the presence of God, "a lasting ordinance among the Israelites for the generations to come" (Exod. 27:20–21; cf. Lev. 24:1–4; 1 Ki. 7:49; 2 Ki. 4:7; 1 Macc. 1:21; 4:49).

III. Miraculous light. There are six references to miraculous light in the Bible, three in each of the Testaments: the BURNING BUSH by which God made himself known to MOSES (Exod. 3:2); the light that illuminated the Israelite homes while the Egyptians were left in darkness (10:23); the PILLAR OF FIRE in which God manifested himself as leader of Israel (13:21; a cloud in this incident is also said to be the vehicle of God's presence to his people); the light that accompanied the announcement of the birth of Jesus (Lk. 2:9); the light that engulfed Saul of Tarsus on the Damascus Road (Acts 9:3; 22:6; 26:13; see PAUL); and the light by which Jesus was transfigured (Matt. 17:2; see TRANSFIGURATION).

IV. Natural light. The poetry of the Hebrews is replete with references to light as opposed to darkness, which held a certain dread for them and power over them (Job 12:24, 25; Isa. 59:10; Jer. 13:16). Because God made both light and darkness, both are under his control. To those who trust him there is no fear of either the "terror" or the "pestilence" customarily associated with the darkness of night (Ps. 91:5–6). The reason is as simple as FAITH: "The LORD is my light and my salvation" (27:1). God "wraps himself in light as with a garment" (104:2), and darkness or dark clouds are "under his feet" (18:9). God also uses darkness. When nature is unfavorable or destructive, it is because God has covered himself with darkness (18:11–15). Morning is greeted with joy (30:5), for which the watchman has waited eagerly (130:6). This preoccupation with light and darkness can be attributed to the absolute control of the lives of the Hebrew people by the alternation of day and night, rather than to some religious motive. The religious emphasis they placed upon this natural phenomenon arose from the concept of God as creator of all things. So light very easily became the symbol for God and his concern for mankind, his highest creation.

V. Figurative uses

A. Revelation. God is known by human beings only because he has chosen to reveal himself, and this REVELATION is primarily for redemptive purposes. Light stands for the HOLINESS of God, the totality of his righteous character. "God is light" (1 Jn. 1:5) and the "Father of lights" (Jas. 1:17), whose dwelling is "in unapproachable light" (1 Tim. 6:16). The psalmist thought of God as being covered with light (Ps. 104:2), and the self-manifestation of God, both creatively and redemptively, is light for the guidance of mankind (119:105). "In your light we see light" (36:9). God's TRUTH and light are identified (43:3) as are his LOVE and light, for he is also manifested as love (1 Jn. 4:8). Light is identified with God as he has made himself and his will known to us (Isa. 10:17; 51:4; Hos. 6:5). Christ the Son of God is light (Lk. 2:32; Jn. 1:4, 9). It is only as men and women are enlightened that they can comprehend Christ, and God through Christ (Lk. 10:22). Light is synonymous with revelation, and enlightened believers themselves become light (Ps. 34:5; Eccl. 8:1; Matt. 5:14).

The CREATION of light (Gen. 1:3) suggests that one should look for the revelation of God in his activity more than in his verbal communication. What God has said supports what he has already done. The act of creating natural, physical light becomes prophetic of the entire sweep of God's self-revelation, both in nature and in redemption (2 Cor. 4:6). Revelation is light. Agents of revelation become light. The SUN, created apart from light as such (Gen. 1:16), came about by an act of God, and it has as its function to reflect the manifold GLORY of God in all of his creation (Ps. 19:1–6).

God's goodly favor toward the righteous is a lighted lamp in the darkness (Ps. 18:28). Hebrew orthodoxy held that LIFE always would be indicative of this principle. JOB had looked for reward because of his charitable regard for the afflicted, but only evil came to him: "when I looked for light, then came darkness" (Job 30:26). Yet Isaiah believed that eventually things would work out that way, that light would "break forth like the dawn" (Isa. 58:8). In anticipation of the coming restoration the prophet cried out, "Arise, shine, for your light has come, / and the glory of the LORD rises upon you" (60:1).

In the poetic parallelisms of the book of Job, light is synonymous with life (Job 3:16–20). In the fourth gospel Jesus is both life and the giver of life; also he is both light and the giver of light (Jn. 1:4–9). Christ, the LOGOS, the preexistent Son of God, is the source of all mankind's illumination, moral, intellectual, and spiritual (cf. 1:9). In Daniel's praise of the name of God who revealed to him the secret of the king's dream, the wisdom thus received was light (Dan. 2:22; 5:11–14). Jeremiah gives God's creation of natural light as the guarantee that God will keep his promise concerning the new covenant (Jer. 31:35, 36). To Paul the light of the gospel was the counterpart of the light of creation (2 Cor. 4:4–6). He would agree, however, with the book of Hebrews that the glory of God revealed in Christ is greater than that revealed in creation (Heb. 1:3).

B. Character. In the thought of Jesus, moral excellence is the product of the light he himself possessed, and it gives soundness and character to all of one's life (Matt. 6:22–23; cf. Lk. 11:34–36). The followers of Christ are lights because of the moral character they possess; and this display sheds light upon and reveals hidden defects in the lives of those around them (Matt. 5:14–16; Lk. 8:16;

11:34–36). People of light as opposed to people of darkness are aware and sober and prepared even for the apocalyptic DAY OF THE LORD (1 Thess. 5:4–8; cf. Rom. 13:11–14).

When Moses came down from Sinai after receiving the tablets of the commandments, his face shone so that the people were afraid (Exod. 34:29; cf. 2 Cor. 3:12–18). The revealed will of God is light to the heart, the soul, and the mind (Ps. 19:7–10). "The unfolding of your words gives light" (119:130; cf. v. 105). Light is given for a purpose (Eph. 5:8), and walking in the light is a walk of fellowship with God (1 Jn. 1:6), based upon pardon and cleansing (1:9). Both Isaiah and Paul saw that God's plan of redemption is light to be lived by (Isa. 62:1; Col. 1:12). If light is not followed, darkness ensues (Matt. 6:23) and judgment follows (Jn. 3:19; 12:48). Rejection of revealed light indicates an inner disposition that is contrary to the truth revealed (3:20), but a favorable response brings about a change in that disposition (1 Jn. 1:9). Paradoxically, John also says that acceptance of revealed light indicates an inner quality of character or disposition that is compatible with the light (3:21). Different personalities respond variously to light prior to actual acceptance or rejection.

The kingdom of Christ is a kingdom of light (Col. 1:12). God's people have been called out of darkness into light (1 Pet. 2:9). Christians are "the people of the light" (Lk. 16:8; Jn. 12:36; 1 Thess. 5:5). He who has been enlightened (Gk. *phōtizō* G5894) by the gospel has "tasted the heavenly gift" (Christ), has been a partaker of the Holy Spirit, has "tasted the goodness of the word of God and the powers of the coming age" (Heb. 6:4–5). The Christian life is an enlightened life, evincing knowledge and wisdom in regard to Christ and his work of salvation, both in the present and in the far-flung future (Eph. 1:17–21). The gospel does not make everything in one's environment light, but it does serve as a shaft of light through the darkness.

C. Influence. As a consequence of being enlightened, God's people themselves are lights (Matt. 5:14; 6:22–23). Israel as the servant of God was destined to be "a light for the Gentiles" (Isa. 42:6; 49:6). Nations will come to your light, / and kings to the brightness of your dawn" (60:3). Such prophetic statements have found their complete fulfillment in Christ (Lk. 2:32; Acts 26:23), also in Paul and Barnabas (Acts 13:47). This imposed parallelism between Jesus and the two men is rather astounding except that we read in the words of Jesus not only "I am the light of the world" (Jn. 9:5; 12:46) but also "You are the light of the world" (Matt. 5:14). Those who have entered the kingdom of God have lamps that shed light, and in the truest sense they are themselves lamps set on a stand—lighted cities on hills—where all may see and be guided by their lights (5:14). They are "children of light" (Eph. 5:8) who walk in love. To them Jesus said, "Let your light so shine before men, that they may see your good works and give glory to your Father who is in heaven" (Matt. 5:16).

(See C. Sheard, *Life-Giving Light* [1933]; E. Underhill, *Light of Christ* [1945]; B. Vassady, *Light against Darkness* [1961]; J. Pelikan, *The Light of the World* [1962]; L. Sibum, *The Bible on Light* [1966]; N. R. Peterson, *The Gospel of John and the Sociology of Light: Language and Characterization in the Fourth Gospel* [1993]; *NIDOTTE*, 1:324–29; *NIDNTT*, 2:484–96.)

H. J. S. BLANEY

lightning. The common biblical words for "lightning" are Greek *astrapē* G847 (Matt. 24:27 et al.) and Hebrew *bārāq* H1398 (Exod. 19:6 et al.; cf. also *ʾēš* H836 in Exod. 9:23–24, *ʾôr* H240 in Job 37:3, *bāzāq* H1027 in Ezek. 1:14, *lappîd* H4365 in Exod. 20:18). Lightning is used figuratively in various contexts: to symbolize God's awful and glorious majesty (Rev. 4:5; 11:19); to describe the brightness of Christ's countenance (Matt. 28:3); as an indication of Christ's quick and unexpected coming (Matt. 24:27; Lk. 17:24), the accompanying destructive judgments on the wicked (Rev. 8:5; 16:18), and the Lord's fighting for his people (Zech. 9:14).

Lightning refers generally to any and all of the various forms of visible electrical discharge produced by thunderstorms, that is, a flash of light in the sky caused by an electrical current. See THUNDER. The current may flow between a cloud and the earth, between two clouds, or between the charged surfaces of the same cloud. The electrical conditions of the earth's surface and atmosphere in normal fair weather and in stormy weather differ. The earth has a negative surface charge. In fair weather the electric potential of the atmosphere increases with elevation at the rate of about 100 volts per meter. The earth (negative) and atmosphere (positive—including upper atmosphere or ionosphere) thus form a vast electrical condenser. In a rapidly developing rainstorm, clouds become positively charged at the top and negatively charged below. Clouds consist of an immense number of tiny water droplets, each with a charge on its surface. Meteorologists believe that the clouds become charged due to the differential falling rates of large and very small drops.

Thunderclouds form at the tops of large, moist, rising air currents. Large drops in the cloud, which for some reason become negatively charged, fall due to gravity, whereas the smaller drops, which become positively charged, can be carried by updrafts to the top of the cloud. (A similar situation has been observed to exist in the spray droplets from a waterfall.) The large drops falling through the rising air currents in the cloud may split into smaller droplets and be carried upward again. The small drops will grow in size while traveling upward due to condensation and accretion. The cloud thus acts as a huge electrostatic machine with a continual process of charging taking place. Some flashes are several miles long with estimated cross-sections of four to six inches. Sheet lightning is merely the scattering of light, or reflection by clouds, of distant flashes.

W. AULT

lign aloes. See ALOES.

ligure. A precious stone. The term is used by the KJV to render Hebrew *lešem* H4385, which probably refers to the JACINTH (Exod. 28:19; 39:12).

Likhi lik´hi (לִקְחִי H4376, perhaps "[Yahweh] takes"). Son of SHEMIDA and descendant of MANASSEH (1 Chr. 7:19). The precise genealogical connection is not specified in 1 Chronicles, but elsewhere (Num. 26:32) Shemida seems to be regarded as a son of GILEAD. Some have suggested that Likhi is a scribal error for HEKEL, another son of Gilead (Num. 26:30).

lilies of the field. See LILY.

Lilith lil´ith (לִילִית H4327, derivation uncertain). This name is used by the NRSV and some other versions as a transliteration of a Hebrew word that occurs only once in a passage describing the terrible desolation that will befall EDOM (Isa. 34:14). The term is associated, probably by popular etymology, with Hebrew *laylâ* H4326, "night." Because most (or perhaps all) of the other creatures mentioned in the context are real animals or birds thought to inhabit waste solitudes, this word has been rendered variously as "screech owl" (KJV), "night hag" (RSV), "night-jar" (NEB), "night creatures" (NIV).

Its rendering as a proper name, "Lilith," reflects a derivation from Akkadian *lilītu* (itself derived from Sumerian *lil*, "storm-wind"), which was the name of a female demon or lesser deity about whom little is known. In the TALMUD (e.g., b. Šabb. 151b; b. ʿErub. 100b), Lilith is described as a long-haired witch who seizes people sleeping in a house alone. Later Jewish traditions develop these and other ideas in some detail (cf. R. Patai, *The Hebrew Goddess* [1967], 217–45). It must not be assumed that the prophet himself believed in the existence of Lilith. More likely, in a highly imaginative passage in which he describes the awful desolation of Edom, he simply mentions some creatures, real and unreal, which in the popular imagination are said to inhabit unpeopled solitudes. (See *ABD*, 4:324–25; *DDD*, 520–21.)

S. BARABAS

lily. Perhaps there is no flower about which more has been written or more conjectures made than the lily (*Lilium candidum*; Heb. *šûšan* H8808). It would seem that lilies were plentiful in the time of SOLOMON, but the cutting down of the forests and the subsequent soil erosion caused the plants to disappear. They have now been introduced again into Palestine, and are growing well.

When we read, "My lover has gone down to his garden, / to the beds of spices, / to browse in the gardens / and to gather lilies" (Cant. 6:2), does that mean that he went down to pick madonna lilies (*Lilium candidum*) to put in vases in the palace, or was he harvesting the bulbs of the lilies which in the E are considered delicious? The Hebrew verb for "browse" is *rāʿâ* H8286, which normally means

The red anemone is one of the flowers linked to the biblical "lily."

"graze, pasture [a flock]" (cf. KJV, "feed"). It could therefore easily be that "my lover" was feeding off lily bulbs, and if this is so, then the lily referred to was probably the tiger lily, *Lilium tigrinum*. In the case of the "lily of the valleys" (2:1), the plant may well be the *Hyacinthus orientalis*, which is common in Palestine; the flowers are fragrant and of a deep blue color, and in the spring, because of this hyacinth, the fields round about the Lake of Galilee can look blue.

It is only fair to consider seriously the madonna lily or *Lilium candidum*. It certainly was grown in Palestine, and Linnaeus, the greatest European botanist, stated that it was a Holy Land plant. The trouble was that in the 18th and 19th cent., the botanists were unable to find madonna lilies in their explorations. It was therefore wondered whether this lily was ever there. At last, in 1925, students of the Hebrew University of Jerusalem found a madonna lily growing wild in the N of Palestine, and more were found subsequently. Remember that the madonna lily is related to the lilies of the E.—far more so than to the Mediterranean lilies.

Another plant which has been considered as the Bible lily is the *Anemone coronaria*. It can be seen now on the MOUNT OF OLIVES in abundance. The Lord must have seen thousands of them when he was preaching on the shores of Galilee. This anemone is much admired today—the petals may be red, purple, blue, rose, or white—the stems being 12–15 in. high. The brilliant colors of the flowers would certainly surpass "Solomon in all his glory." *Lilium chalcedonicum* is considered still another possibility. It grows round about the Lake of Galilee, but is by no means as common as the anemone.

However, Jesus' reference to "the lilies of the field" (the Gk. noun is *krinon* G3211) is followed up by a comment about "the grass of the field, which is here today and tomorrow is thrown into the fire" (Matt. 6:28–30; Lk. 12:27–28; see GRASS). The fact that the plant was to be made into hay makes the writer believe that the lily referred to was the camomile, *Anthemis palaestina*, which has thin, scented leaves, and bears small white daisies. This plant is common in Palestine, and can be cut and dried as for hay. It is in flower at the time of hay-making, and would probably, therefore, have been growing around the feet of our Lord at the time he spoke. He was undoubtedly referring to some wild flower, and not to a tall lily. (See further *FFB*, 134–36.)

See also FLORA (under *Compositae* and *Liliaceae*); LILY-WORK. With regard to the use of the term "lily" as a musical superscription (Pss. 45; 60; 69; 80), see MUSIC VI.B.

W. E. SHEWELL-COOPER

lily-work. This term is used by several Bible versions with reference to the architectural ornamentation on the tops of the free-standing pillars, Jakin and Boaz, at the vestibule of Solomon's TEMPLE (1 Ki. 7:19, 22 [NIV, "in the shape of lilies"]; note also the description of the molten sea, 2 Chr. 4:5). It is thought likely that this lily-work was modeled after the Egyptian LOTUS, which was the staple ornament not only in Egyptian art, but also was widely used, as archaeological remains show, in Assyria, Persia, and Palestine. See FLORA (under *Nymphaeaceae*); JAKIN (PILLAR).

S. BARABAS

lime. A white caustic alkaline earth (calcium oxide or quicklime). The term also is loosely used to refer to calcium hydroxide (slaked lime) or calcium carbonate (limestone, CHALK, MARBLE). Calcium oxide is obtained by heating calcium carbonate to dull redness, 550°C (cf. Isa. 33:12; the Heb. term is *śîd* H8487). Carbon dioxide is given off and, if it is swept away in a current of air, as in a kiln, dissociation proceeds until the reaction is practically complete. The calcium oxide that is left looks like white ash (cf. the NEB rendering of 33:12). With the addition of water to quicklime, heat is evolved, clouds of steam are given off and the lime combines with the water, cracks, and after addition of sufficient water, crumbles down to a fine, dry, white powder (calcium hydroxide or slaked lime).

The chief use of lime is in the preparation of mortar, for building purposes, made from a thick paste of slaked lime together with three to four times as much sand as quicklime originally taken. In the hardening of the mortar there is no combination between the lime and the silica of the sand, the hardening consisting of the evaporation of the moisture, or by its absorption by the bricks and a slow reaction of the lime with atmospheric carbon dioxide producing calcium carbonate. (Note that *śîd* is rendered "plaster" in Deut. 27:2, 4.) The burning of bones produces a grayish-white ash, composed mainly of calcium phosphate, which resembles lime in appearance (cf. Amos 2:1). (See J. R. Partington, *A Textbook of Inorganic Chemistry*, 6th ed. [1950], 754–55.)   D. R. BOWES

line. This English term, with its different senses, is used variously to render a number of Hebrew words, especially *qāw* H7742, referring to a "measuring line," such as builders use (2 Ki. 21:13; Jer. 31:39; Ezek. 47:3; Zech. 1:16; sometimes used figuratively, as in Isa. 28:10, 17; 28:1; 34:11). The Greek word *kanōn* G2834, "[measuring] rod, ruler," is rendered "line" by the KJV in a passage where PAUL refers to a person's sphere of work or "territory" marked out by God (2 Cor. 10:16).   S. BARABAS

Linear A, Linear B. See LANGUAGES OF THE ANE III.

linen. A fabric woven from yarn made of the fine fibers of the stalk of the FLAX plant. The term also designates clothes and garments made of linen. Hebrew terms that can be rendered "[fine] linen" include *šēš* H9254 (Gen. 41:42 et al.), *bad* H965 (Exod. 28:42 et al.), and *bûṣ* H1009 (1 Chr. 15:27). The NT uses Greek *sindōn* G4984 (Matt. 27:59 et al.), *byssos* G1116 (Lk. 16:19; *byssinos* G1115 in Rev. 18:12 et al.), *othonion* G3856 (Lk. 24:12 et al.), and *linon* G3351 (Rev. 15:6). In some contexts these terms can be differentiated, but they often are used interchangeably. The term "fine linen" in the Bible refers to sheer, often almost translucent material of the expensive finely woven linen worn by royal and wealthy people or the priests of the temple.

The flax plant was common in Egypt, being cultured extensively in the fertile NILE Valley. Egyptian linen and WEAVING was considered the best of ancient times, so much so that some could not distinguish the fabric from SILK. Flax also was introduced into Palestine early and was grown in the Jordan Valley near JERICHO (Josh. 2:6) and also in GALILEE. The flax stalk grew quite tall and was cut or pulled out by the roots near full growth, dried for a time in the sun, then pounded vigorously to separate the fine fibers, washed, and bleached. The yarn, so fine at times as to be almost invisible, was then ready for the weaver.

Linen weavers were known in MOSES' day before the entrance into Canaan and were considered a gift of God to the people (Exod. 35:35; 38:23). Later we are informed of a guild of linen textile manufacturers at BETH ASHBEA (1 Chr. 4:21). Generally women did the spinning and weaving in the home; already during the exodus women were adept at this ancient art: "Every skilled woman spun with her hands and brought what she had spun — blue, purple or scarlet yarn or fine linen" (Exod. 35:25).

In biblical times linen was used for many purposes. It was popular material for clothing of many kinds and for sheets, curtains, sails of ships, for wrapping scrolls, etc. Fine linen always was used for the garments of the priests. Regarding AARON it is said, "Weave the tunic of fine linen and make the turban of fine linen. The sash is to be the work of an embroiderer. Make tunics, sashes and headbands for Aaron's sons, to give them dignity and honor. After you put these clothes on your brother Aaron and his sons, anoint and ordain them. Consecrate them so they may serve me as priests. Make linen undergarments as a covering for the body, reaching from the waist to the thigh" (Exod. 28:39–42). The tunic, headdress,

LINEN

Egyptian linen with fringes (from Saqqara, latter part of 2nd millennium B.C.).

and other articles of clothing the priests wore also were made of fine linen (39:27–29). Some of the fine linen woven in Palestine was the best in the world, even preferred by some to the linen manufactured in Egypt. The weavers in Palestine were able to make linen almost as fine as silk. It was so sheer and thin that it was diaphanous and cool in hot weather. The shirt people wore close to the body was made of fine linen. The material was also bleached white and the priests appeared in glittering white apparel.

Fine linen also was used much for dress in religious services, as in the case of the child SAMUEL (1 Sam. 2:18) and the singers in the temple (2 Chr. 5:12). Kings and other royal persons also wore much fine linen (2 Sam. 6:14). The Scriptures say that angels were dressed in white fine linen, as well as the multitudes of the redeemed with Christ in heaven (Ezek. 9:2; Rev. 19:14). Since fine linen with its extreme whiteness was used in a figurative sense for purity and righteousness of life (Rev. 19:8), one can easily understand why white garments are worn in special religious or significant ceremonies today such as weddings. When people used fine linen for ordinary purposes it was a sign of luxury and wealth (Isa. 3:23; Ezek. 16:10). This is the type of linen JOSEPH wore as prime minister in Egypt: "Then Pharaoh took his signet ring from his finger and put it on Joseph's finger. He dressed him in robes of fine linen and put a gold chain around his neck" (Gen. 41:42).

Linen material was used for the curtains, the veil, and other items in the TABERNACLE (Exod. 26:1–37). The "twisted" (KJV, "twined") linen mentioned here was made from yarn of which each thread was composed of many delicate strands. The Egyptians were experts in work of this kind, and HERODOTUS (*Hist.* 3.47) says that Amasis, king of Egypt (564–526 B.C.), sent someone a corselet, each thread of which consisted of 360 separate strands, all of them clearly visible.

Fine linen is such splendid cloth that sometimes translators of the Bible have rendered the term "silk." When the Lord speaks of punishing Israel, he includes the taking away of the finery of clothing, including linen garments (Isa. 3:18–23). In the same vein, the Lord speaks of his blessings to Israel in terms of beautiful cloth and clothing, "I clothed you with an embroidered dress and put leather sandals on you. I dressed you in fine linen and covered you with costly garments ... your clothes were of fine linen and costly fabric and embroidered cloth" (Ezek. 16:10, 13). DAVID and the Levites wore garments made of this fine linen when the ARK OF THE COVENANT was brought to Jerusalem (1 Chr. 15:27).

In the parable of LAZARUS AND DIVES, the latter is described as dressed in fine linen, considered the clothing of wealthy people (Lk. 16:19). It is possible that linen was also used for fishing nets (Isa. 19:8–9) and for drapes and beautiful hangings (Esth. 1:6). Linen material also was dyed in many brilliant colors.

The material was cheaper and less durable when the linen yarn or flaxen yarn was mixed with other yarn such as wool and cotton. The Hebrew word *šaʿaṭnēz H9122* signified garments or cloth made of two types of thread. God forbade the Israelites to wear garments made of such materials (Lev. 19:19; Deut. 22:11). Silk would have been difficult to obtain and very costly; it had to be imported by caravan from the Far East.

The use of linen for clothing among the people of the ANE was adopted by the Greeks. The Greek *sindōn* is the term used to describe the fine costly linen in which the body of Jesus was wrapped: "Joseph took the body, wrapped it in a clean linen cloth, and placed it in his own new tomb that he had cut out of the rock" (Matt. 27:59–60). Both John and Luke speak of linen cloths or clothes as the material in which Jesus' body was wrapped (Jn. 19:40; Lk. 23:53). The word used here is the plural of *othonion*, which refers to linen bands, large linen sheets torn into strips, used to wrap the body in a neat fashion. For centuries preceding, the Egyptians used strips of linen sheets to wrap Egyptian mummies. The Greek word *linon* is used to describe a linen garment (Rev. 15:6); this material may have been made of hemp as well as flax (the word is also used of the rag wick of ancient lamps, Matt. 12:20; Isa. 42:3). Without a doubt linen ranked with wool as one of the most common fabrics in the ancient world.

(See further L. M. Wilson, *Ancient Textiles from Egypt* [1933]; A. E. Bailey, *Daily Life in Bible Times* [1943]; G. M. Crowfoot, in *PEQ* no vol. [1951]: 5–31; F. H. Wight, *Manners and Customs of Bible Lands* [1953]; H. Daniel-Rops, *Daily Life in Palestine at the Time of Christ* [1962]; P. J. King and L. E. Stager, *Life in Biblical Israel* [2001].) See also CLOTH; DRESS; LEATHER. L. M. PETERSEN

linguistics. The scientific study of the nature of language. The discipline of *comparative linguistics*—the identification and analysis of languages that are genetically related—arose at the end of the 18th cent. and grew vigorously during the 19th. This approach was historical (or diachronic) in character: it focused on etymological connections among languages and sought to explain their evolution. In the 20th cent., however, a new (synchronic) approach developed that sought to explain the structure of language as such, without recourse to past developments. Known as *modern* or *general linguistics*, this discipline focused on the inner workings of human speech as it functions at any given time among those who use it.

Prominent names in the early development of modern linguistics include the Swiss scholar Ferdinand de Saussure (*Cours de linguistique générale* [1916]), the Danish Otto Jespersen (*Language: Its Nature, Development and Origin* [1922]), and the American Leonard Bloomfield (*Language* [1933]). The significance of general linguistics for the INTERPRETATION of the Bible was first explored systematically by James Barr (*The Semantics of Biblical Language* [1961]), and the last decades of the 20th cent. saw a vigorous attempt to integrate the two disciplines. (See further J. P. Louw, *Semantics of New Testament Greek* [1982]; P. Cotterell and M. Turner, *Linguistics and Biblical Interpretation* [1989]; M. Silva, *God, Language, and Scripture: Reading the Bible in the Light of General Linguistics* [1990], reprinted in *FCI*, 193–280; id., *Biblical Words and Their Meaning: An Introduction to Lexical Semantics*, rev. ed. [1994]; W. R. Bodine, ed., *Linguistics and Biblical Hebrew* [1992]; S. E. Porter, ed., *Diglossia and Other Topics in New Testament Linguistics* [2000]; *ABD*, 4:327–32.)

lintel. The head-piece of a DOOR, carrying the weight of the structure above it. The term is used by some Bible versions to render Hebrew *mašqôp* H5485 (Exod. 12:22–23). The Israelites were commanded to mark the top as well as the sides of the doorframe with the blood of the paschal lamb when the PASSOVER was instituted.

Linus li'nuhs (Λίνος G3352). A Christian who, along with others (CLAUDIA, EUBULUS, and PUDENS), was a friend of the apostle PAUL during his second Roman imprisonment and who sent greetings to TIMOTHY (2 Tim. 4:21). The 2nd-cent. church father IRENAEUS (*Ag. Her.* 3.3) says that this Linus was given the office of the episcopate of the church in ROME by the apostles PETER and Paul (Linus's successor, Irenaeus says, was Anacletus [Anencletus], and after him, in the third place from the apostles, Clement was given the bishopric). EUSEBIUS (*Eccl. Hist.* 3.2) similarly asserts that, after the martyrdom of Paul and of Peter, this Linus was the first who obtained the episcopate at Rome and that he served as bishop for twelve years (ibid., 3.13). Numerous church writers have recorded the type of tradition found in Irenaeus and Eusebius, and of course some elaboration has occurred. The APOSTOLIC CONSTITUTIONS (7.46) refers to Linus as the son (possibly the husband) of Claudia. (On "Early Roman Succession," see J. B. Lightfoot, *The Apostolic Fathers*, Part I, *S. Clement of Rome* [1890], 1:201–345.) J. H. SKILTON

lion. The Greek word for "lion" (*leōn* G3329) occurs six times in the book of Revelation (Rev. 4:7 et al.) and three times in other NT books (2 Tim. 4:17; Heb. 11:33; 1 Pet. 5:8). In the OT, however, there are well over one hundred references to lions, and several different Hebrew terms are

LION

used. The most general terms are ’ărî H787, which occurs over thirty times (e.g., Num. 23:24b), and its alternate form, ’aryēh H793, found almost forty times (e.g., Jdg. 14:8–9). Another common term, occurring thirty times, is kĕpîr H4097, which refers specifically to a "young lion" (e.g., Jdg. 14:5; note that this particular animal is also referred to with the more general term in vv. 8–9). A lion's cub is gûr H1594 (e.g., Deut. 33:22; cf. also gōr H1596, Jer. 51:38 and Nah. 2:12 [MT 2:13]), but this term can be applied to other animals (cf. Lam. 4:3). The word lābî’ H4233 refers specifically to a "lioness" (e.g., Num. 23:24a; alternate form lĕbiyyā’ H1231 only in Ezek. 19:2). Less frequent terms, which perhaps had special nuances, are layiš H4330 (e.g., Isa. 30:6) and šaḥal H8828 (e.g., Job. 10:16). This lexical richness, suggesting that lions were well known throughout the OT period, is exploited in a number of passages (cf. Gen. 49:9; Job 4:10–11; Nah. 2:11–13). The majority of references are figurative, yet it is clear that lions were sometimes common enough to be of some danger to both humans and stock.

The two giant cats—lion and tiger—are usually regarded as African and Asiatic respectively, but this is not wholly correct. The tiger's range is from the borders of Europe, in the Caucasus Mountains, to NE and SE Asia. The lion's main home is now in Africa S of the Sahara, yet it still has a small outlier in the Kathiawar Peninsula of NW India. The position was once very different. Lions lived in most parts of Africa, including Egypt and the N coast, outside the deserts, swamps, and jungles. In prehistoric times there were still lions in parts of Europe. During the reign of DAVID, lions were found more or less continuously from Greece through Asia Minor to India.

The African lion was generally reckoned to be long-maned, while the Asiatic or Persian form short-maned, but there is much variation and the black mane is found in individuals rather than in races. Thus the lion and tiger overlapped for much of their range, but the lion kept to grassland and dry open forest; the tiger to the dense forest and jungle, where its striped coat served as camouflage. Up to the 1900s humans had reduced the tiger's numbers more than its overall range, but by 1971 the tiger was on the danger list. Today the lion is confined to warm regions and shows less variation in color, size, and habitat than the tiger.

The lion began to lose ground as soon as humans made settlements and kept flocks and herds that needed protection. The cultivable parts of Egypt were occupied early and its lions disappeared many centuries before Christ. Elsewhere in Africa the pressure did not build up until recent years. The Cape lion was lost about 1865, and the Barbary lion of the N coast, in the early 1920s. Lions were extinct in Greece about the end of the 1st cent. A.D. and in Palestine during the time of the Crusades, the last probably being killed near Megiddo in the 13th cent. Lions were reported in Syria by Burton as late as 1851; they still survived in Persia and Iraq in the 20th cent., but these too had vanished before 1930.

The lion is the only plain-colored large cat, but the young, born in litters of two to five, have more or less obvious dark markings, sometimes not losing them until two years old. Unlike the rather solitary tiger, the lion is sociable and lives in family groups, called prides, so it is not surprising that Hebrew plural forms occur nearly fifty times. Lions normally feed on fairly large game, often combining in the hunt for it. They feed to capacity and then rest before killing again (cf. Num. 23:24, "like a lion that does not rest till he devours his prey").

Although there are occasional incidents in which humans are killed by lions, such events are unusual and are often provoked by the victims, for the habitual man-eating lion is rare. Such evidence

Male and female lion.

as the biblical record provides suggests that this pattern was true also at a time when lions were fairly familiar objects of the countryside. (1) In the case of the disobedient prophet (1 Ki. 13:24–25), it is interesting that the body was not eaten, for this is typical of the chance encounter where, on the human level, it can be said that the lion panics and kills. (2) The death of one of the sons of the prophets is a rather similar incident (1 Ki. 20:35–36). (3) The punishment of the pagan settlers in Samaria is stated clearly to have been God's judgment (2 Ki. 17:25–26). A modern parallel is seen in the notorious man-eaters of Tsavo, a group of lions that terrorized the labor force building the Kenya Railway (cf. P. Caputo, *Ghosts of Tsavo: Stalking the Mystery Lions of East Africa* [2002]). Numerous OT literal and figurative passages imply that lions often were common enough to be a potential danger to domestic stock.

The picture in the NT is so different that it seems reasonable to assume the lion had become rare. On the other hand, Diodorus Siculus, who wrote of events around the beginning of the Christian era but is not always reliable, reported that the NABATEANS had fertile plantations in the S NEGEV, where flocks had to be continually protected against lions and other beasts of prey (*Bibl. Hist.* 3.43). Of nine NT mentions, seven are purely figurative; one refers back to the prophets, and the single current one is 2 Tim. 4:17, where PAUL states that he was rescued from the lion's mouth. Some commentators see in this passage a reference to the devil (cf. 1 Pet. 5:8) or to NERO; others to a lion in the amphitheater, since by this time lions were being imported in great numbers for the games, mostly from the Upper Nile. Julius CAESAR gave shows involving 400 lions; Nero organized fights between cavalry, bears, and lions, and one of the standard sentences for Christians refusing to conform was being thrown to the lions.

Not all ancient rulers regarded lions in this brutal way. The book of Daniel pictures them being kept in captivity (Dan. 6:7; Aram. *ʾaryēh* H10069). In Egypt, 1,000 years earlier, lions were trained to help in the hunt; RAMSES II is reported to have had a tame lion that accompanied him to battle. At Nimrud (CALAH) lions regularly were bred by ASHURNASIRPAL II (883–859 B.C.). Lion hunting was a favorite pastime of these Assyrian kings, as is illustrated dramatically in reliefs on ASHURBANIPAL's palace at Nineveh c. 650 B.C. It is possible that a similar motive impelled these Assyrian kings as is found in African tribes today, whose young men kill lions in single combat and so are thought to acquire some of the lion's attributes.

The figurative mentions of the lion in OT are too many to analyze fully, but most commonly it is metaphorical for strength, as SAMSON asked, "What is stronger than a lion?" (Jdg. 14:18). Hence one of Christ's messianic titles—the Lion of the tribe of Judah (Rev. 5:5)—refers back to Gen. 49:9, where JUDAH is described as a lion's cub. (See further H. B. Tristram, *The Natural History of the Bible*, 9th. ed. [1898], 115–21; G. Loisel, *Histoire des ménageries de l'antiquité a nos jours* [1912]; G. S. Cansdale, *Animals and Man* [1952]; B. A. Strawn, *What Is Stronger Than a Lion? Leonine Image and Metaphor in the Hebrew Bible and the Ancient Near East* [2005]; *FFB*, 50–51; *ABD*, 6:1143.)

G. S. CANSDALE

lip. The fold of flesh that surrounds the opening of the mouth. The diverse usage of the Hebrew and Greek terms for "lip" illustrates the manner in which a primary organ of the body was employed to describe a number of widely variant phenomena. The Hebrew word *śāpâ* H8557 (cf. Akkadian *šaptu*) meant basically the physical lips of the mouth (e.g., 1 Sam. 1:13) or the lips as the organ of speech (e.g., Exod. 6:12; Ps. 106:33). By metonymy the lips became understood as the language or manner of speaking of individuals and nations alike (Gen. 11:1; Prov. 17:7), as well as the gossip of casual conversationalists (Prov. 17:4; Ezek. 36:3). It was used of an unknown language only once in the OT (Ps. 81:5).

The extension of the term by metaphorical usage naturally suggested the brink or shore of the sea or the bank of a river (Gen. 22:17; 41:3; Dan. 12:5, et al.). By further derivation the word was used to designate the border or edge of something, as with a garment or curtain (Exod. 26:4, 10; 28:26; et al.). The brim of the "molten sea" or cast bronze laver that occupied a conspicuous position in the courtyard of the Solomonic temple is described in 1 Ki. 7:23–26. It was employed also to describe the border of the altar mentioned in Ezek. 43:13, a reference in which Babylonian constructional terms for the design and building of ZIGGURATS occurred. Despite these extensions of meanings, however, the primary application of the term was to the human lips.

Another closely related Hebrew word, *śāpām* H8559, referred to the upper lip or the mustache (2 Sam. 19:4), and usually in the oriental sense of covering it with the hand or with some garment similar to a veil indicating shame or grief (cf. Lev. 13:45 [NIV, "lower part of his face"]; Mic. 3:7). Under special circumstances this procedure did not need to be observed—as in the case of EZEKIEL, who was forbidden to indulge in the customary mourning rites, having been informed that his wife was about to die (Ezek. 24:17, 22).

Because the ancients were deficient in their knowledge of the physiology of the nervous system, they assigned emotional and ethical qualities to bodily organs, including the lips. The lips not merely spoke but rejoiced (Ps. 71:23), quivered fearfully (Hab. 3:16), preserved knowledge (Prov. 5:2), offered praise (Ps. 63:3); and besides being righteous (Prov. 16:13) they could be lying (Ps. 120:2), uncircumcised (Exod. 6:12, 30), perverse (Prov. 4:24), and so on. Literary parallelism with the tongue or mouth was common in poetry (Pss. 34:13; 51:15). The close association between the thoughts and the lips was stressed in Prov. 16:23.

In the NT the Greek word *cheilos* G5927 was used both literally and metaphorically in the same sense as in the OT, almost always in quotations from the SEPTUAGINT (Matt. 15:8; Mk. 7:6; Rom. 3:13; 2 Cor. 14:21; 1 Pet. 3:10; cf. also Heb. 11:12; 13:15). R. K. HARRISON

literature, the Bible as. The term *literature* includes many aspects. Broadly it means a body of written works such as that of a people or nation in a certain period (e.g., Elizabethan literature) or throughout their entire history (e.g., English literature); more narrowly it may refer to writing that relates to some specific field of knowledge or endeavor (e.g., biblical literature, medical literature). The term also has an essential qualitative meaning relating to writing that is notable for excellence. Thus it denotes the written expression of what Matthew Arnold called "the best that has been known and said in the world."

I. The claim of the Bible to literary greatness
II. The literary study of the Bible
  A. In relation to inspiration
  B. Hermeneutical implications
III. Some important literary characteristics of the Bible
  A. General literary characteristics
  B. Specific literary forms and modes of expression
  C. Chapter and verse divisions
  D. The Bible as a translated book
IV. The influence of the Bible
  A. On the literature of the English-speaking people
  B. On other literatures
  C. The educating power of the Bible
V. The phenomenon of biblical unity

I. The claim of the Bible to literary greatness. The Bible has the highest claim to classification as great literature. It not only illustrates Thomas De Quincey's distinction between "the literature of knowledge" (that which aims to teach) and "the literature of power" (that which aims to move); it also fuses these two elements into living unity. It sets before its readers a wealth of knowledge, some of it of a nature obtainable only through divine REVELATION. At the same time, it moves its readers as does no other writing. In its effect upon human history and in its ability to reach people of all kinds, the Bible has no close competitor. More widely circulated and read than any other book, it is unique in world literature

II. The literary study of the Bible. The forty or so persons who wrote the Bible over a period of at least thirteen centuries varied greatly in literary ability. The literature called biblical includes the thirty-nine canonical books of the OT (plus twelve books of the APOCRYPHA in some communions) and the twenty-seven canonical books of the NT. These writings range in style from highly symbolic writing (as in the Apocalypse) through poetry of various kinds, many different forms of narrative, and closely reasoned discussion (as in certain epistles), to writing that is traditional and pedestrian (as in the genealogies and parts of the historical books). It is with this diversity of expression that the literary study of the Bible is concerned.

A. In relation to inspiration. Such study must take into account the divine INSPIRATION of Scripture, although its "God-breathed" character (*theopneustos* G2535, 2 Tim. 3:16) as the written Word must never be used to obscure or submerge its human aspect. To concentrate on the inspiration of Scripture to the neglect of its human quality, or to do the opposite, is as wrong as to consider the deity of Christ apart from his humanity or vice versa. Many theologians see an analogy between the fusion of the divine and human elements in the Bible and the union of God and man in the person of JESUS CHRIST.

B. Hermeneutical implications. Scholarly consideration of the Bible as literature has an essential place in the broad discipline of biblical studies. It goes beyond aesthetic insight, important though such insight is. It has hermeneutical implications, being directly related to the primary obligation of understanding the meaning of the written Word. Without a grasp of the basic literary characteristics of the Bible, the interpreter of its meaning is handicapped. For scholars to know the original languages, to make careful use of the grammatical-historical method of interpreting the text, to compare Scripture with Scripture, and to be competent in the findings of lower and higher criticism is not enough. Unless they are also alert to the literary aspects of the biblical text, they will be crippled in their hermeneutics and their theology may suffer. See INTERPRETATION.

In a posthumous essay entitled "Modern Theology and Biblical Criticism," C. S. Lewis said of radical theologians, such as Rudolf Bultmann and Alec Vidler, "Whatever these men may be as Biblical critics, I distrust them as critics. They seem to me to lack literary judgment, to be imperceptive about the very quality of the texts they are reading." Lewis had little patience with the critic who insists that certain incidents in the gospel records are legend or romance. Referring to the Gospel of John, regarded by some critics as "spiritual romance" or "a poem not a history," he speaks of the extraordinary reality of its dialogues and narratives and then says: "I have been reading poems, romances, vision-literature, legends, myths all my life. I know what they are like. I know that not one of them is like this" (C. S. Lewis, *Christian Reflections*, ed. W. Hooper [1967], 154–55). In a generation before Lewis, Richard G. Moulton made a similar point in his valuable work, *The Literary Study of the Bible* (1899). Referring to the marked contrast between Mic. 7:7–10 and the preceding context, he quoted Julius Wellhausen as taking this change of mood as evidence for the introduction of new material into Micah and thus saying that "between v. 6 and v. 7 there yawns a century." As Moulton dryly remarked, "What really yawns between the verses is simply a change of speakers" ("Preface to the Second Ed.," ix).

III. Some important literary characteristics of the Bible. These may be placed under two heads: those relating to the whole Bible or to large sections of it, and those relating to specific forms of literature or modes of expression within it.

A. General literary characteristics

1. Universality. Chief among the general literary characteristics of the Bible is its universality. No book reaches all kinds of people in all kinds of circumstances as does Scripture. To educated or uneducated, rich or poor, civilized or primitive, it communicates its message. Wherever people can read it, or, lacking ability to read, wherever they are taught it, there are some whose hearts it touches. According to the dictum of literary criticism that calls that great which on the basis of repeated examination is acknowledged as such by people of different nations, languages, and occupations throughout long periods of history, the perennial and universal appeal of Scripture clearly establishes its supremacy. (Cf. the Greek treatise by Longinus, *On the Sublime* 7.3–4, for the classic formulation of this dictum.) As A. S. Cook said of the Bible, it possesses "a universality which has placed it at the foundation, or head, or both, of all modern literatures" (*The Cambridge History of English Literature* [1907], 4:31).

The thought forms of the Bible are different from those developed by Greek philosophy (esp.

Aristotelianism), which have influenced civilization so profoundly. The biblical mode of thought is intuitive. It is more elemental than that of the Western world. By the same token it is more universal. For Scripture speaks directly to the human heart in the higher logic epitomized by Pascal's aphorism, "The heart has its reasons, which reason does not know.... It is the heart which experiences God, and not the reason" (*Pensées*, trans. W. F. Trotter [1931], nos. 277–78).

2. Sublimity. A second general characteristic of the Bible is its sublimity of thought and expression. Sublimity is a literary quality essential to ultimate greatness. No book reaches loftier heights than Scripture. Coleridge, the great poet and critic, said that "after reading Isaiah, or St. Paul's Epistle to the Hebrews, Homer and Virgil are disgustingly tame to me, and Milton himself barely tolerable" (quoted by R. M. Frye, *The Bible: Selections from the King James Version for Study as Literature* [1965], xxxi). Were the Bible not preeminent in sublimity, it would be strange, for as Longinus said, "Sublimity is the echo of a great soul" (*On the Sublime*, 9.2), and the chief biblical authors like Moses, David, Isaiah, Jeremiah, John, and Paul were indeed "great souls." And other biblical writers such as the minor prophet Habakkuk, the authors of certain non-Davidic psalms, and the author of Hebrews also attain sublimity. Indeed, this quality in Scripture is the echo not just of great human souls but of the Spirit of God.

3. Integrity. Integrity in its root sense of wholeness is a third general quality of the Bible. To speak of its literary integrity is another way of referring to the unique commitment of the Bible to TRUTH. Of all books it is the most truth telling. Its portrayal of humanity is unsparingly honest. Frankness pervades it even to the extent of plain statement of the sins of its great characters like ABRAHAM (Gen. 20:1–18), MOSES (Num. 20:7–13), DAVID (2 Sam. 11:1–12:23), and PETER (Matt. 26:69–75). No other writing so searchingly probes the innermost motives of human conduct. (Cf. esp. Christ's teaching in the SERMON ON THE MOUNT and in his parables.) In its manner of expression, Scripture, though varied, is never pretentious. And side

Tyndale New Testament (1534) open to the beginning of the book of Acts.

by side with what PAUL called "the depths of God" (1 Cor. 2:10 NRSV) are passages of utmost directness of expression. The reason for this is the "high seriousness" of the biblical writers. Whatever else they were, these authors were in earnest. It is this earnestness that is so profoundly reflected in John Bunyan, that most biblical of writers, who said, "God did not play in convincing of me, the devil did not play in tempting of me ... wherefore I may not play in my relating of them, but be plain and simple, and lay down the thing as it was" (preface to *Grace Abounding*, ed. R. Sharrock [1966], 3–4).

Truth in Scripture is not just a formal matter of correspondence with external reality. It is truth of heart and spirit as well as truth in fact. As *The Jerusalem Bible* says of the great verities that provide the foundation for the plan of salvation and that are set forth in the first eleven chapters of Genesis, "All these are truths which have their bearing upon theological doctrine and which are guaranteed by the authority of scripture; but they are also facts, and the certainty of the truths implies the reality of the facts" ("Introduction to the Pentateuch," 9).

B. Specific literary forms and modes of expression. Ancient writings in general use picturesque speech—simile, metaphor, metonymy, hyperbole, acrostic, puns (and other kinds of humor), irony, satire, proverbs, etc. Literatures contemporaneous with the Bible contain lyric, didactic, liturgical, and dramatic poetry, epic, law, history, genealogy, biography, shorter narrative, prophecy, apocalypse, parable, sermonic and other rhetorical discourse, and epistolary writing. Though the Bible uses such literary devices and forms, there is no reflection in it of a self-conscious "art for art's sake" attitude. All is subservient to the main purpose of the writers in communicating truth about God and his ways with man. "Neither of the two collections of books that make up the Bible is arranged from the point of view of art, but from that of religious value; they are collections not of national *belles-lettres* but of Sacred Writings" (*HDB*, 4:3).

1. Some examples of biblical use of literary forms. Limitations of space prevent discussion of the many literary devices and forms mentioned above, certain of which are treated in separate articles. However, examples of some of the important literary forms are as follows: *lyric poetry* (Exod. 15:1–18; Jdg. 5; Isa. 5:1–7); many psalms that may be classed as devotional lyrics or hymns (e.g., Pss. 1; 19; 23; 46; 90; 139; and the SONG OF SOLOMON, which is also dramatic); *dramatic poetry* (JOB, Song of Solomon); *liturgical poetry* (Pss. 120–134); *didactic poetry* (Ps. 119; cf. also WISDOM Literature); *epic* (Gen. 1–11; 37–50; the epic form is not necessarily incompatible with historicity); *law* (Exod. 20–23; the book of LEVITICUS; other parts of the PENTATEUCH); *history* (SAMUEL, KINGS, CHRONICLES, ACTS OF THE APOSTLES); *genealogy* (1 Chr. 1:1—9:44; Matt. 1:1–17; Lk. 3:23–38); *biography* (1 Sam. 16:1—1 Ki. 2:11; also biographical passages in the NT); *shorter narrative* (RUTH, ESTHER); *Wisdom Literature* (PROVERBS, ECCLESIASTES); *prophecy* (ISAIAH, JEREMIAH, AMOS; Matt. 24); *apocalypse* (Dan. 7–12; ZECHARIAH; REVELATION, BOOK OF); *parable* (Ezek. 17:1–10; Lk. 15); *sermonic and other rhetorical discourse* (Deut. 1:1—4:40; Matt. 5–7; Acts 7); *epistolary writing* (ROMANS to JUDE; Acts 15:23–29).

2. The Bible's transcendence of literary forms. A second observation about the kinds of literature within Scripture is that although the biblical writers employed literary forms of their times, they not infrequently transcended them. Just as the NT writers deepened and enlarged the meaning of familiar words like "love," "word," "life," and "grace," so the authors of both OT and NT books brought special dimensions to their writing of history, poetry, drama, and other kinds of literature.

In much of its narration the Bible achieves a living presentation of reality and power of expression unsurpassed elsewhere. The story of JOSEPH (Genesis), that of SAMSON (Judges), the extended account of DAVID (1 and 2 Samuel) are of epic quality. Among shorter narratives, the intricate story of ESTHER, the idyl of RUTH, and the vividly terse book of JONAH reach perfection. Of the latter, the English novelist Charles Reade, author of *The Cloister and the Hearth*, said, "Jonah is the most beautiful story ever written in so small a compass. It contains 48 verses and 1,328 English words. One does not get far in an English novel of 1,328 words. There is growth of character, a distinct plot worked out without haste or crudity. Only a great artist could have hit upon a perfect proportion between dialogue and narrative" (quoted by C. A. Dinsmore, *The English Bible as Literature* [1931], 256). Even more remarkable for succinctness are the PARABLES of Christ, which bring profound truth to life in the plainest of words.

While poetic passages in the Bible follow the forms of its times (see HEBREW POETRY; POETRY, NEW TESTAMENT), it rises to a kind of universality no other poetry has achieved (e.g., Ps. 23; Isa. 40; and Paul's hymn of love in 1 Cor. 13). As for poetic drama, JOB, called by Tennyson "the greatest poem of ancient or modern times," is preeminent in spiritual depth.

The opening of Genesis is not the only ancient COSMOGONY, yet in universal appeal and lasting relevance, it stands far above all others. PROPHETS and interpretations of DREAMS and visions were not peculiar to the Hebrew people, but no other nation had prophets of the order of ELIJAH and ELISHA, ISAIAH and JEREMIAH, and others. The concept of a God who cares so much for his people that he enters into personal dialogue with them in the "I-Thou" relationship set forth in both Testaments is distinctive. What R. G. Moulton aptly called "the prophetic rhapsody"—in which various literary forms are united as exalted communication between God and the prophet (or people)—mingles with lofty odes (e.g., Isa. 40–66; the book of Habakkuk), and has no real counterpart anywhere (*Literary Study*, 404–56).

As for the NT, here the epistolary form is lifted to new heights in books like ROMANS, EPHESIANS, and HEBREWS. Finally, APOCALYPTIC writing reaches its summit in the Apocalypse (see REVELATION, BOOK OF).

3. The Gospels—a unique literary genre. On a different level, however, from such instances in which the Bible transcends its literary forms are the NT GOSPELS. Here the message actually leads to a new and inimitable literary genre. Consider what the Gospels really are. In biographical material they are too incomplete to be classed as "lives" in the literary sense. Though their context and contents are certainly historical, they are more than history. To understand the special genre of a gospel, one must see the problem the four evangelists faced in dealing with the unparalleled event of the INCARNATION. How to tell the truth about Jesus the God-man in such a way as neither to slight his DEITY nor obscure his full humanity, and how at the same time to present him in living reality was their incredibly difficult task. That they solved it in the kind of memoir known as a NT gospel, and that they did this not once but four times while presenting in their own individual styles differing yet complementary portrayals of Jesus from the pages of which he stands out in his unique reality as the living Son of God—this is nothing less than a major literary miracle. As James Iverach said, to do this was "the greatest problem ever set to literature, and how the evangelists presented and solved it is found in the Gospels" (*ISBE* [1929], 2:1286).

Frye's comment is also apposite: "This task [that of the evangelists in writing the Gospels] had at least one further implication of great literary importance: on the basis of the New Testament, we cannot 'identify' ourselves with Christ as in other literary works we can identify ourselves with, say, Macbeth or Ophelia—or even as we can identify with such other Biblical characters as Ruth and David, or Martha, Peter, and even Pilate.

The inherent intent of the New Testament is to present Christ as *sui generis* uniquely human and divine" (*The Bible*, 156). That the evangelists—and the other NT writers also—succeeded in this great purpose of presenting Christ "as *sui generis*, uniquely human and divine," while indeed a literary miracle, is at the same time an unmistakable evidence of their divine inspiration.

C. Chapter and verse divisions. A major factor relating to understanding the literary forms of the Bible and thus linked to the comprehension of its contents is the way in which it has been and still is being printed. The chapter divisions, first made in the Latin and carried over into English versions, stem from Stephen Langton (d. 1228), or perhaps from Hugues de St. Cher (1262). The OT verse divisions are ancient, going back probably to the Masoretes (c. A.D. 500–1000; see MASORAH), and were used in the Latin translation of Pagninus (1528). The first English version to use them was the Geneva Bible (1560). The NT verse divisions first appeared in the Greek Testament of Robert Stephanus (1551 ed.), and their initial appearance in English was in 1557 in a NT translated by William Whittingham. (Cf. Josiah H. Penniman, *A Book about the English Bible* [1931], 370.)

While chapter and verse divisions are unquestionably essential for reference, the resulting sharp breaks in the Bible as commonly printed,

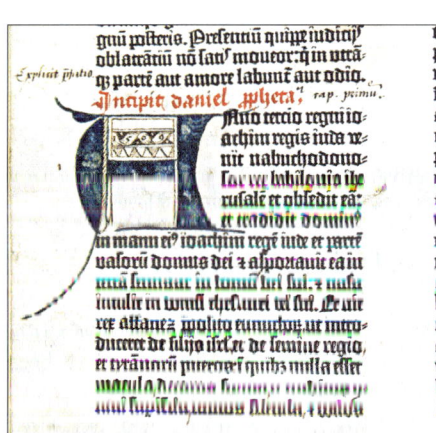

Detail of the Gutenberg Bible open to the beginning of the book of Daniel.

except in the newer versions, have certainly been a hindrance to the general reader's understanding of its meaning. These divisions are by no means consistently logical and have therefore led to a kind of piecemeal reading of the Bible that has obscured both its precise meaning and its literary structure. Yet, an impressive indirect tribute to the unquenchable vitality of Scripture is its survival of the way it is commonly printed.

The manner in which newer versions minimize through skillful typography the prominence of chapter and verse divisions, while at the same time retaining them for reference, is an immense help to the reader. Again, the practice of older versions not to make any distinction between the printing of prose and poetry has placed the reader under a handicap. The differentiation in newer versions between prose and poetry, though not without problems, also contributes greatly to the understanding of Scripture.

D. The Bible as a translated book. Literary study of the Bible must take into account that for the vast majority of its readers, it is a translated book. Few books, however, are so translatable as the Bible. This is particularly true of the OT, the vocabulary of which is so concrete and elemental, and so much of which is poetical. That Hebrew poetry depends not on rhyme but on parallelism of thought is of much aid to the translation. "Versification of this kind has the advantage that it can, without much loss, be translated into any language" (Émile Legouis and Louis Cazamian, *A History of English Literature* [1929], 378). And the Koine (common dialect) in which the NT is written, with its colloquial flavor and at times, as in the Johannine writings, a Hebraic cast, also lends itself to translation (see GREEK LANGUAGE).

IV. The influence of the Bible

A. On the literature of the English-speaking people. No influence in literary history has been more pervasive than that of the Bible. Directly or indirectly, it has affected most world literatures, but in none is its influence deeper and more extensive than in that of the English-speaking people. Many translations, among them the fragmentary Anglo-Saxon versions (c. 8th to 10th centuries) and the Wycliffite versions (1380–88), those of Tyndale (1525–31) and Coverdale (1535), and the Geneva (1560) and Bishops' (1568) Bibles, contributed to this influence and led up to the KJV of 1611.

1. The King James Version. It is the KJV that is so inextricably woven into the fabric of English and American literature. Moreover, this version, by common critical consent the greatest English classic, has left its impress not just upon the literature but upon the ordinary language of the people. Everyday speech and writing are studded with echoes of its diction, such as "clear as crystal," "root of all evil," "arose as one man," "the fat of the land," "thorn in the flesh," and "a soft answer." All great writers in English—in fact, lesser writers also—have in some way been affected by it, and its influence lives on.

One reason for this lasting influence is the condition of the English language in the first decade of the 17th cent., when the KJV was translated. After the comparative sterility of the 15th cent., during which the transition from Middle English was going on, there was the glorious creative outburst of the Elizabethan period, when Shakespeare, Spenser, Jonson, and Donne were writing. The language of the KJV, which was made in the early years (1604–11) of the reign of James I, was that used by men like these. Still fresh and flexible, open to new impressions, it was remarkably fitted for the subtle work of translation. This was a time of great English translations—North's Plutarch, Florio's Montaigne, and Chapman's Homer, for example—and of these the KJV is the climax.

2. Newer versions. Though its influence lives on, the KJV no longer stands alone, because in recent times the outburst of English translations of the Bible has far exceeded even that of the years from Tyndale's NT (1525) to 1611. It is no disparagement of the KJV to point out that this host of newer translations follow the lead of Moffatt (NT, 1913; OT, 1924), Goodspeed (NT, 1923), and others earlier in the 20th cent. who deliberately worked outside the KJV tradition. This new development, in which Roman Catholics as well as Protestants are active, evidences the living influence of the Holy Scriptures. See VERSIONS OF THE BIBLE, ENGLISH.

B. On other literatures. The literary influence of the Bible, so marked among the English-speaking people, extends also to other literatures and people. The nature of that influence has been and still is governed by the quality of the translations and ecclesiastical attitudes toward freedom to read them.

Consider several examples. In Martin Luther's translation, the German-speaking people have a classic version comparable in greatness to the KJV. The influence of Luther's Bible on the German language and literature and indeed upon the whole people has been crucial. As Roland H. Bainton says, "Their language was so far fashioned by his hand that the extent of their indebtedness is difficult to recognize.... And for sheer richness and exuberance of vocabulary and mastery of style he is to be compared only with Shakespeare" (*Here I Stand: A Life of Martin Luther* [1950], 384).

At the opposite pole is the Hispanic world. For the literature of both Spain and Latin America exhibits a great dearth of biblical influence — the result of ecclesiastical restrictions upon the translation, circulation, and reading of the Scriptures that have made a strong common version impossible. On the other hand, in the literatures of other traditionally Catholic countries, biblical influence, though less marked than in those of the predominantly Protestant countries, is much greater than in Hispanic literature. French literature, for instance, owes much to the profoundly biblical Pascal and reflects a less restrictive Catholicism than that of Spain and South America. To turn to Russian literature, there is a mystical and biblical strain (cf. Dostoevski and esp. Tolstoi), despite the absence of the central place of the Scriptures in Greek Orthodoxy.

C. The educating power of the Bible. An aspect of the continuing influence of the Bible that is in a different category from its effect upon great literature of the world is its educating power among illiterate peoples. The Scriptures are at the center of the missionary enterprise, and the history of missions is indissolubly united with Bible translation. When the pioneer missionary has gone to a primitive people and has reduced their language to writing, he or she has done so for the specific purpose of giving them the Bible in their own tongue. Thus the key to literacy and enlightenment has been placed, and continues to be placed, in the hands of multitudes who would otherwise have remained illiterate. The educational as well as spiritual implications of this are enormous — especially in view of the fact, as reported by the United Bible Societies, that by 1973 the whole Bible had been translated and published in 255 different languages and dialects and at least one book of the Bible had been translated and published in 1,500 languages and dialects. As of 2005, those figures had increased to over 420 for the complete Bible, and about 2,380 for at least some part of the Bible (out of approximately 6,500 languages spoken in the world today).

V. The phenomenon of biblical unity. Finally, no competent student of the Bible as literature can fail to be impressed by the phenomenon of its unity. That the sixty-six books comprising the two Testaments, and which were written by many authors over the period of nearly a millennium and a half, should be related together in living, organic unity, is a unique feature of the Bible. "One increasing purpose," said A. S. Cook, "runs through the whole, and is reflected in the widening and deepening thought of its writers; yet it is a purpose which exists germinally at the beginning and unfolds like a bud. Thus, all the principal books are linked and even welded together, and to the common consciousness form, as it were, but a single book, rather *to biblion* than *ta biblia*" (*The Cambridge History of English Literature*, 4:29).

What is the "one increasing purpose" that, as Professor Cook said, "runs through the whole" and binds the more than sixty books from Genesis to Revelation in such astonishing unity? The Bible itself leaves no doubt that its unity is essentially Christological. What makes it one book is the unfolding of God's sovereign purpose in JESUS CHRIST. From the protevangelium (Gen. 3:15), where he is seen at the dawn of history as the coming Deliverer, on through the OT presentation of him in type and prophecy as the MESSIAH, to his entrance into history as SON OF MAN and SON OF GOD, set forth in the Gospels, expounded in the Epistles, and revealed in his glorious, future manifestation in the Apocalypse, the Bible is centered in him.

What Paul said of Christ's cosmic significance, that "in him all things hold together" (Col. 1:17), applies to Scripture as to all else. Moreover, it was validated by the risen Lord himself when, "beginning with Moses and all the Prophets, he explained to them what was said in all the Scriptures concerning himself" (Lk. 24:27). The crowning literary characteristic of the Bible is its unity, and this points directly to its inspiration.

(In addition to the works cited in the body of this article, see L. Ryken, *How to Read the Bible as Literature* [1984]; T. Longman, *Literary Approaches to Biblical Interpretation* [1987], reprinted in *FCI*, 91–192; D. Norton, *A History of the Bible as Literature*, 2 vols. [1993]; J. B. Gabel et al., *The Bible as Literature: An Introduction*, 5th ed. [2006].)

F. E. GAEBELEIN

litter. This English term, in its meaning of an enclosed BED or COUCH used to carry a person, is used by some Bible versions to render the common Hebrew word *miṭṭâ H4753*, "bed," in Cant. 3:7 (NIV, "carriage"), and the rare term *ṣāb H7369*, "covered cart or wagon," in Isa. 66:20 (NIV, "wagons"; this Heb. term is used in only one other passage, Num. 7:3). According to 2 Macc. 9:8, ANTIOCHUS was carried in a litter (Gk. *phoreion*) after he had fallen from his chariot and severely injured himself.

Little Apocalypse. A term applied sometimes to Isa. 24–27, but more frequently to Jesus' eschatological discourse recorded in Mk. 13 and parallels. See ESCHATOLOGY III.B; JESUS CHRIST VI.B.2.

Lives of the Prophets. See PROPHETS, LIVES OF THE.

living creature. The usual translation of Hebrew *nepeš ḥayyâ* (*H5883* plus the adjective *ḥay H2645*, thus "alive soul, alive being") or simply the noun *ḥayyâ H2651* ("animal"). In Genesis and Leviticus, it is a nontechnical expression referring to animals (Gen. 1:21 et al.; Lev. 11:10, 14; see ANIMAL; BEAST; FAUNA). By using it technically, Ezekiel referred to the CHERUBIM (Ezek. 1:5, 13–15, 19–22). The four living creatures in his vision each had four faces (man, lion, ox, eagle).

In the NT, the corresponding Greek term, *zōon G2442* ("living being, animal"), refers simply to animals a few times (Heb. 13:11; 2 Pet. 2:12; Jude 10), but the special sense occurs only in Revelation, where it is applied to the four living creatures in the heavenly scene, always present in and around the throne of the Lamb (Rev. 4:6–9 et al.). Each had six wings (four in Ezekiel) and further differed from the OT description where the ox was replaced by an eagle, each creature having a single identity. The earliest interpretation was made by IRENAEUS (A.D. 170), who held that they represented four aspects of the work of Jesus, which in turn characterized in each instance one of the Gospels: the lion symbolized power (John); the calf as an animal of sacrifice symbolized priestly character (Luke); the man symbolized incarnation (Matthew); and the eagle symbolized the gift of the Holy Spirit (Mark). Subsequent interpretation most often has followed AUGUSTINE's identification of Matthew's gospel represented by the lion, Luke by the calf, Mark by the man, and John by the eagle.

H. L. DRUMWRIGHT, JR.

Livy li′vee. Titus Livius was born in N Italy, probably in 59 B.C. Not much is known of his personal life, but at some point he went to ROME and was befriended by AUGUSTUS. Although he wrote some philosophical works, he is best known as the author of an extensive *History of Rome* (the actual title was *Ab urbe condita libri*, "Books from the Foundation of the City"). Only 35 of the original 142 books have survived, but summaries (*Periochae*) of the work were composed by later writers, and these have been preserved (other fragmentary remains are also available). Livy depended primarily on previous literary histories, a feature that lessens somewhat the value of his record, but he is our primary (sometimes the only) source for much important information, and his writing style is regarded highly. Livy died in the city of his birth, Patavium (Padua), in A.D. 17 (according to some, A.D. 12). (See further P. G. Walsh, *Livy: His Historical Aims and Methods* [1961]; T. J. Luce, *Livy: The Composition of His History* [1977]; C. S. Kraus, *Latin Historians* [1997]; J. D. Chaplin, *Livy's Exemplary History* [2000]; J. P. Davies, *Rome's Religious History: Livy, Tacitus and Ammianus on Their Gods* [2004].)

lizard. A general term for reptiles (cold-blooded vertebrates) of various kinds other than snakes. Palestine has many lizards and they are the most conspicuous vertebrates other than birds. Some forty species have been identified, from the desert or land monitor, which reaches a length of over 4 ft., down to species of about 2 in., and they belong to a number of different families. Most languages commonly have at least one general name for such a group, and this is known by most people, also individual names for conspicuous or important genera or species, but these are less widely known.

Six of the eight Hebrew words in the list of unclean animals "that move about on the ground" (Lev. 11:29–30) are generally thought to refer to lizards. Since each of these terms occurs only once, some scholars believe it is not possible to identify the species referred to (cf. *FFB*, 52). Several comments may be made, however. The first item, *ṣāb* H7370 (NIV and NRSV, "great lizard") is not unlike Arabic *ḍabb*, the name given to spiny-tailed lizards of genus *Uromastyx* that are eaten by BEDOUINS. These reach a length of well over 1 ft. and are heavily built; they live in all types of desert and are partly vegetarian. The second term, *ʾănāqâ* H652, is identical in form to a Hebrew word meaning "groan," and this connection has led many scholars to identify this creature as the gecko (*Hemidactylus turcicus*), the only lizard that makes a vocal sound; it is commonly found in houses in Palestine (see *FFB*, 34–35).

A third term, *kōaḥ* H3947, derives from a root meaning "strength"; the expression "land crocodile" (cf. NRSV) is meaningless, unless it refers to the land monitor (cf. NIV, "monitor lizard"; the Vulgate *stellio* is interesting in that the most common large lizard in Palestine, seen on roadsides and old ruins, has the Latin name *Agama stellio*). The fourth word, *lĕṭāʾâ* H4321, has been variously understood as referring to the gecko (*HALOT*, 2:528) or the wall lizard (NIV), or as a general label (cf. NRSV). Also difficult is *ḥōmeṭ* H2793, often thought to be the skink (NIV), also known as the sand lizard (NRSV), which has a cylindrical body and small legs. The last item is *tinšemet* H9491, generally identified as the CHAMELEON (the same word form is used in Lev. 11:18 and Deut. 14:16 of a bird, probably some kind of OWL).

An additional term, *šĕmāmît* H8532, occurs in Prov. 20:38 and is translated "lizard" in most modern versions (though the KJV rendering "spider" has been supported by some scholars). Because the text says that this creature "can be caught with the hand," some think it refers to the gecko. If the above suggestions are correct, this list covers most of the major families of Palestine lizards, but it must be emphasized that they are largely conjectural. (See H. B. Tristram, *The Natural History of the Bible*, 9th ed. [1898], ch. 9.) G. S. CANSDALE

Grey lizard from Israel.

loaf. See BREAD.

Lo-Ammi loh-am´i (לֹא עַמִּי H4204, "not my people"). Also Lo-ammi. A symbolical name given by the prophet HOSEA to his second son and third child by his wife GOMER (Hos. 1:9). His firstborn son was called Jezreel, which means "Yahweh sows," an allusion to scattering or destruction (vv. 4–5); see JEZREEL (PERSON) #2. A previous daughter was given the name Lo-RUHAMAH, meaning "not pitied" (vv. 6–7). The names given to the children were symbolic of the fact that Israel, because of its disobedience, had forfeited the compassion and protection of Yahweh. Nevertheless, the passage immediately promises a reversal of this judgment: "Yet the Israelites will be like the sand on the seashore, which cannot be measured or counted. In the place where it was said to them, 'You are not my people,' they will be called 'sons of the living God'" (1:10 [Heb. 2:1]). And again, "Say of your brothers, 'My people,' and of your sisters, 'My loved one'" (2:1 [Heb. 2:3])." S. BARABAS

loan. See BORROW, LEND.

lock. In the sense of a device for securing doors, see BOLT; DOOR. In the sense of a length of hair, see BRAID; HAIR.

locust. This term is applied to a large number of grasshopper species that often migrate in immense swarms, destroying vegetation and crops.

I. Difficulty of identifying species.
The Greek term for locust is *akris* G210 (from which the insect's family name, *Acrididae*, is derived). The most common Hebrew term is *ʾarbeh* H746, which is used, for example, of the eighth plague in Egypt (Exod. 10:4 et al.), but at least eight other Hebrew words are rendered "locust" or "grasshopper" in one or more English versions. This rich vocabulary is evidence of the importance of these insects in the life of the Israelites.

There is little uniformity of translation among the English versions, and in some cases even within the same version. The terms are found in many different books and contexts, yet these provide almost no information. One possible exception is *ḥāgāb* H2506, which is used three times as a measure of smallness (e.g., Num. 13:33, "we seemed like grasshoppers"), once described as good for food, and only once as a potential danger to crops (2 Chr. 7:13). This could thus be a smaller grasshopper, perhaps nongregarious, of which there are many species (though some have suggested that the root from which the word is derived may indicate a swarming species). SOLOMON refers to the extraordinary coordinated mass movements of swarming locusts (Prov. 30:27), which is almost the only direct biblical comment on their biology and habits.

II. Are the Hebrew names species or phases?
Four insects are listed in Lev. 11:22: *ʾarbeh* H746 ("locust"), *solʿām* H6155 (NIV, "katydid"; NRSV, "bald locust"), *ḥargōl* H3005 (usually rendered "cricket"), and *ḥāgāb* H2506 (usually rendered "grasshopper"); they may represent separate species. From the striking description of the locust plagues in Joel 1:4, it seems at first that an additional three different insects are mentioned: *gāzām* H1612 (NRSV, "cutting locust"; NJPS, "cutter"), *yeleq* H3540 (NRSV, "hopping locust"; NJPS, "grub"), and *ḥāsîl* H2885 (NRSV, "destroying locust"; NJPS, "hopper"); but it is equally probable that these are all names for various phases of the migratory locust (cf. NIV, "great locusts ... young locusts ... other locusts"). Two other terms, both used collectively for swarms of locusts, are *gōbay* H1479 (Amos 7:1; Nah. 3:17) and *ṣĕlāṣal* H7526 (Deut. 28:42, perhaps cicadas or crickets).

Most of these Hebrew words may refer to the various attributes of locusts and may therefore be virtually synonymous. A similar usage is common today in some countries (e.g., in Ghana a ground squirrel can be a serious farm pest and is also eagerly killed for food; it has a precise name in each language, but is more often referred to as traveler, road-crosser, peanut thief, etc.). If such is true generally of "locust" in the Scriptures, there is no point in trying to identify words that may be largely nicknames.

III. Description of locust family.
In Europe locusts are often the larger members of the family and grasshoppers the smaller, but the criterion is sometimes that locusts swarm and migrate, while grasshoppers are more or less solitary. In America the connotation is different and the words are nearly interchangeable; even cicadas, of another insect order, may be called locusts. The name strictly belongs to a number of large insects of the family *Acrididae* (Greek *akris*) of the order *Orthoptera* (straight-winged).

The main characteristic of locusts is that from time to time they multiply at a frightening rate and move in huge swarms, often over great distances. Their antennae are short and the female has a short, stubby ovipositor. Locusts are entirely vegetarian, which is a reason they were allowed the Israelites as food, and they eat a wide range of green stuff. Much research work has been done on this major pest, and it is now known that all locusts exist in two phases, solitary and gregarious, with intermediate forms. These differ in appearance, and within each phase there is variation in color, size, and proportions. Swarming is in part a physiological response to conditions and is a way of colonizing new areas.

IV. Species now found in Palestine.

The migratory locust (*Locusta migratoria*), in many races, is found in most warm parts of the world except America. The other two likely to do damage in Palestine are the desert locust (*Schistocerca gregaria*) and the Moroccan locust (*Dociostaurus maroccanus*). Eggs are laid in small packets near the surface of the soil; hatching sometimes depends on moisture, and the eggs of some species, such as the South African brown locust, can survive for three and one half years in dry ground, but hatch in ten days if the soil is damp. The young that emerge have the same general shape as adults, but no wings, and they pass through five or six molts, growing larger after each and gradually acquiring wings. The narrow forewings are like parchment, while the hind-wings, which are folded like a fan when at rest, are broad and membranous, sometimes with a color pattern.

V. Locust control.

In their early stages locusts move only by crawling or hopping, being known as hoppers. These are less mobile and thus easier to destroy, and control organizations aim at forecasting swarm formation and movement in order to eliminate them. Many swarms fly out to sea or into true desert and so destroy themselves. Numbers can be astronomical; a desert locust swarm that crossed the Red Sea in 1889 was estimated to cover 2,000 sq. mi. Such swarms are like dark clouds and contain countless millions. Wind is the main factor in determining the direction taken by a swarm. Locusts usually approach Palestine from the Arabian deserts to the SE, but they may also come from other directions. Locusts have always been a scourge, especially in the Middle E, but modern materials and communications based on a degree of cooperation rare in that area, have greatly reduced the damage done annually.

VI. Locusts in the Bible.

Locusts appear mainly in three settings.

A. The eighth plague. The rendering "locust" is amply confirmed by the details in the narrative (Exod. 10): the complete stripping of all crops and green stuff; swarms dense enough to hide the sun; their arrival with the east wind (10:13) and then being carried away by a "very strong west wind" (10:19). Some see the locusts as part of a logical sequence, for the unusually heavy winds that began the series would create conditions likely to cause mass breeding and swarm formation. The divine element is seen in the complete control of the situation, with the swarms coming and going according to God's will. It is ironic that the cause of this devastating plague, with its long-lasting effects, should also have been a useful source of food to the Israelites on their desert journey.

B. Locust as a destroyer. From antiquity the locust has been almost synonymous with destruction. Joel 2:25 KJV, "the years that the locust hath eaten," is now a proverb. Soon after the Bible was translated into English by Tyndale (1546), a greedy, devouring man was known as a locust. To the inhabitants of Palestine and many lands to the NE, locust swarms were classed with drought and pestilence as utter calamities against which they could do nothing. It is not surprising that on nearly half the occasions where the words are used, it is in this connection. Many commentators see in Joel 1 the accurate description of an actual plague, but some take it as largely figurative. In at least three cases, apart from the plague, locusts are sent or threatened by God as a direct punishment for wrongdoing. In a list of the curses that will result from disobedience in Canaan, we read, "Swarms of locusts will take over all your trees and the crops of your land" (Deut. 28:42, see also 2 Chr. 7:13, Amos 5:9).

C. Locust as food permitted to Hebrews. The regulations about food in Mosaic law were not arbitrary rules such as one finds in food taboos among primitive tribes today, but divinely inspired laws for early recognition of safe and harmful kinds. Where distinction was hard, the good was forbidden along with the bad, as in Lev. 11:20: "All flying insects that walk on all fours are to be detestable to you." These would include beetles, cockroaches, crickets, etc., many of which feed on or live among carrion and domestic rubbish and are therefore liable to transmit filth diseases. All these must be avoided. Insects are, of course, six-legged, and "all fours" must be here regarded as a technical term for creeping or running as opposed to jumping, which characterizes the grasshopper tribe. So v. 21, "There are, however, some winged creatures that walk on all fours that you may eat: those that have jointed legs for hopping on the ground" (the hind pair of legs is greatly enlarged, and when at rest they reach far above the body).

VII. Value of locusts as human food. Except for termites in some areas, locusts are more important than any other insect as a source of food, and they have been used as such since antiquity. Stone carvings in the palace of ASHURBANIPAL (8th cent. B.C.) show locusts on sticks being carried to a royal banquet. Diodorus of Sicily (2nd cent. B.C.), among other Greek historians, refers to *acridiphagi,* or locust-eaters, of Ethiopia (*Bibl. Hist.* 3.2). Locusts are permitted food for Muslims, and tradition has it that Muhammad himself used to eat them. Some African tribes still largely depend on locusts for their protein for much of the year; after eating as many as possible roasted and boiled, they preserve large quantities by drying or grinding into flour.

Until recent years, the nomads of Algeria tried to store about 450 lbs. per tent. The recent influx of oil wealth into N Africa and other Arab lands has changed many old habits, but in poorer areas locusts are still a welcome and valuable addition to an often marginal diet. It is not stated directly that the Israelites ate locusts in the desert, but this can reasonably be assumed. The food laws were first given at Sinai, early in the journey, and, as for locusts, this permission probably codified a practice of long standing. Their routes must have crossed the lines taken by many swarms, and though the desert would offer no green food at most seasons, locusts cannot fly indefinitely and would be compelled to land at intervals, thus coming within reach of the travelers.

Locusts are a useful source of protein, fat, and calories; they also have a fair amount of mineral salts, but are not rich in vitamins. Dried locusts contain more than 50 percent protein and a variable amount of fat—up to 20 percent. When JOHN THE BAPTIST lived on "locusts and wild honey" (Matt. 3:4), he was enjoying a crude but fairly balanced diet; the honey would be basically sugar, but with some pollen and perhaps bee grubs as well, which would increase the protein content. (See H. B. Tristram, *The Natural History of the Bible,* 9th ed. [1898], 306–18; F. S. Bodenheimer, *Insects as Human Food* [1951]; *FFB,* 53–54; *ABD,* 6:1150.)

G. S. CANSDALE

Lod, Lydda lod, lid′uh (לֹד *H4254*; Λύδδα *G3375* [LXX, Λοδ]). A town said to have been built, along with ONO, by a Benjamite named SHEMED (1 Chr. 8:12); it is listed with Ono and HADID among the towns to which the Jews returned after the EXILE (Ezra 2:33; Neh. 7:37; 11:35). Its earliest mention is in the annals of the Asiatic towns and possessions held by Egypt from the time of THUTMOSE III (1502–1448 B.C.). These lists appear on the wall of the Amon temple at Karnak. Lod must have been in the area assigned to the tribe of BENJAMIN after the conquest, but it is not specifically mentioned in the Pentateuch or in the records of the conquest or the judges.

Lod is identified with modern el-Ludd, some 11 mi. SE of JOPPA. Its strategic position—on the two highways that led from Egypt to Babylon and from Joppa to Jerusalem—made it a prize of war throughout the centuries. In the Hellenistic period it came to be known as Lydda. During the era of Syrian rule it was part of SAMARIA, and it is mentioned

The earliest mention of Lydda occurs on the wall of the Temple of Amon at Karnak (15th cent. B.C.).

a number of times by Josephus, who states that Julius Caesar granted the town to the Jews and to the heirs of John Hyrcanus (*Ant.* 14.10.6 §208; see Hasmonean). During the period of political instability after Caesar's assassination, when Octavius and Antony were struggling for supremacy of the empire (36–31 B.C.), Antigonus, an Asiatic ally of Antony, quartered his troops in Lydda. By the close of the 1st cent. B.C., Lydda had grown to be a fair-sized town. Josephus reports that the Roman governor of Syria, Quadratus, traveled to Lydda to mediate the war then raging between the Jews and the Samaritans. He found Lydda, "a village that was in size not inferior to a city" (20.6.2 §130, LCL trans.). Peter cured a man with palsy there (Acts 9:32–35, the only NT reference to the town).

After the destruction of Jerusalem in A.D. 70, it became a center of Christian activity in N Palestine. It had been a center of rabbinic studies for a period even before the Roman overthrow of the rebellion. The town became known as Diospolis by the 3rd Christian cent. and was the center of a trade in purple dye. It was the site of the death of St. George, who was martyred there in 303. During the 4th cent. it was the episcopal seat of the Syrian church, and it served as the meeting place of the council that tried Pelagius for heresy in 415. The story of St. George so fascinated King Richard of England when he traveled there during the Third Crusade that George was ultimately made patron saint of England by edict of King Edward III. During the Renaissance and early modern period it was an Arab town, but has passed into the state of Israel. It is presently called Lod in Hebrew, but nearby its name is attached to the giant Lydda Airport so that again it serves travelers between E and W as in the days of Thutmose III. (See *NEAEHL*, 3:917.)

W. White, Jr.

Lo Debar loh-dee´buhr (לוֹ דְבָר *H4274* [2 Sam. 9:4–5], לֹא דְבָר *H4203* [2 Sam. 17:27], לֹדְבָר *H4203* [Amos 6:13], by popular etymology, "nothing"). Also Lo-debar. A town or city-state in Transjordan that was the home of Makir son of Ammiel (2 Sam. 9:4–5; 17:27). Jonathan's lame son, Mephibosheth, lived in Makir's house, and from that place David summoned him to the palace (9:1–13). Amos plays on the sound of the name Lo Debar (suggesting "nothingness") when he says, "But you have turned justice into poison / and the fruit of righteousness into bitterness— / you who rejoice in the conquest of Lo Debar / and say, 'Did we not take Karnaim by our own strength?'" (Amos 6:13). The conquest of the city, likely a place of pagan sacrifice and heathen idolatry, was apparently a subject of great satisfaction to the corrupt Israelite monarchy. On the basis of this passage, it is thought that Lo Debar (perhaps a vassal state under David) was lost in the Israelite wars with the Arameans and regained under Jeroboam II (see also Karnaim).

Some scholars think its original name was Lidbir (Lidebir), which may have been a town on the N boundary of the tribe of Gad in Gilead (Josh. 19:26 NJPS; cf. NRSV mg.). See Debir (place) #3. In any case, the location of Lo Debar is uncertain. It is often identified with Umm ed-Dabar, some 10 mi. SSE of the S tip of the Sea of Galilee. Others argue that the site should be sought N of the Yarmuk River, which served as the boundary of Gilead; if so, a likely candidate is Tell Dober, less than 2 mi. S of the Sea of Galilee (cf. *ABD*, 4:345–46).

lodge. This English verb is used often by the KJV, mainly as the rendering of Hebrew *lîn H4328*, "remain [through the night]" (Gen. 24:23 et al.), and Greek *aulizomai G007*, "to lie in the courtyard, to pass the night" (Matt. 21:17 et al.). The term is found less frequently in modern versions, which prefer such expressions as "stay" and "spend the night." As a noun, "lodge" occurs in the KJV as the rendering of *mělûnâ H4870* (Isa. 1:8; NIV, "hut"; NRSV, "shelter").

log. A Hebrew term used of the smallest liquid measure of capacity, about two-thirds of a pint. See weights and measures III.A.3.

logia loh´jee-ah. The Greek term *logia* (pl. of *logion G3359*) is used in nonbiblical literature for the utterances of deities. Such usage is also found in the Septuagint (e.g., Ps. 18:b Heb. [Eng. Ps. 119:] for Heb. *'imrâ H613*) and occasionally in the NT (Acts 7:38; Rom. 3:2; cf. Heb. 5:13; 1 Pet. 4:11). In the church fathers the term begins to be used for the sayings of Jesus (e.g., POLYCARP, *Philippians* 7.1) and in the present day is generally restricted to this usage.

However, the use of the term by PAPIAS (as quoted by EUSEBIUS, *Hist. Eccl.* 3.39.16) has been the subject of extensive discussion. Papias reports that Matthew compiled the Logia in the Hebrew dialect (*Hebraidi dialektō ta logia synetachato*). It seems that this term as used by Papias included some narrative material in addition to sayings of Jesus proper. Similarly, the content of "Q" (the material common to Matthew and Luke) apparently included narrative material and sayings—although it may have been an oral tradition rather than a written one. See GOSPELS III.B.1.

The existence and circulation of collections of Logia or sayings may be the source of possibly two AGRAPHA (sayings ascribed to Jesus in the NT, but not found in the Gospels)—Acts 20:35 and 1 Thess. 4:16–17. Luke may also have used such collections in his research in the preparation of his gospel (Lk. 1:1–3).

In modern times, actual collections of sayings dating from the early church have been discovered. Near the end of the 19th cent., B. P. Grenfell and A. S. Hunt began uncovering a vast collection of Greek papyri (see PAPYRUS) near ancient OXYRHYNCHUS on the NILE in Egypt. One of the first fragments found contained seven sayings of Jesus. This fragment is page 11 of a book and thus seems to be a part of a large collection of sayings. The document (POxy 1) is to be dated not later than about the middle of the 3rd cent., and the collection undoubtedly goes back at least to the 2nd cent. Each saying is introduced by the words, "Jesus says." In 1903 two more Greek papyri containing sayings ascribed to Jesus were found (POxy 654 and 655), also dating from the 3rd cent. Some of the sayings are found in the canonical Gospels, others only in the church fathers, and others were unknown prior to the discovery.

Included in the phenomenal discovery of Gnostic papyri in 1945 near modern NAG HAMMADI were two documents entitled *Gospel of Thomas* and *Gospel of Philip*. These are collections of sayings of Jesus in Coptic. The *Gospel of Thomas* contains 114 sayings and appears to be a 4th or 5th cent. Coptic version of a Greek original of about the middle of the 2nd cent. Strikingly close or substantial parallels to the sayings in the three Oxyrhynchus Papyri are found in the *Gospel of Thomas*. In comparison with the canonical sayings, this book shows some of the heretical tendencies of the Gnostic community where it circulated. The *Gospel of Philip*, a collection of 127 sayings purported to be revelations imparted by Jesus to a group (Hebrews) including Philip and dated about A.D. 400, is more heretical and esoteric than the *Gospel of Thomas*.

These discoveries reflect the early church's interest in the Logia of Jesus. That the early Christians thought it was appropriate to edit and interpret these dominical sayings is already evident in the way Jesus' teaching is reported in the inspired, canonical Gospels. In addition, there is the problem of translation from Aramaic to Greek in some cases. Nevertheless, although the identification of the *ipsissima verba* of Jesus (the exact words he spoke) is often doubtful, the canonical Gospels certainly contain the *ipsissima vox* (the very voice) of Jesus; that is, they faithfully transmit the Lord's teaching (cf. J. Jeremias, *New Testament Theology, Part One: The Proclamation of Jesus* [1971], 29–37). See also APOCRYPHAL NEW TESTAMENT I; GNOSTICISM; JESUS CHRIST IV.E; PHILIP, GOSPEL OF; THOMAS, GOSPEL OF. B. VAN ELDEREN

Logos loh′gohs. A transliteration of the Greek term *logos* G3364, which has a wide range of meanings, including "word, statement, conversation, speech," as well as "thought, opinion, reason," etc. In the Johannine writings, the term occasionally has a special Christological significance (e.g., Jn. 1:1–3, 14; 1 Jn. 1:1; Rev. 19:13).

  I. In Greek literature
     A. Classical writers
     B. The Stoics
 II. In Jewish authors
     A. The OT background
     B. Wisdom Literature
     C. Philo of Alexandria
III. NT usage
     A. Synoptic Gospels and Acts
     B. Pauline epistles
     C. Hebrews
     D. Johannine literature
 IV. Early Christian literature

I. In Greek literature

A. Classical writers. The term *logos* appears in Homer (*Iliad* 15.393) and Hesiod only in a nontechnical sense. Heraclitus of Ephesus (c. 500 B.C.) was among the first to use it in a distinctive philosophical sense. To Heraclitus the Logos is the continuum in an ever-changing cycle of renewal, the divine soul of the world. In a universe of flux the one stable factor is the Logos. In his thought, "all human laws are nourished by the divine law. Though this Word (*Logos*)—this fundamental law—existeth from all time, yet mankind are unaware of it" ("Fragment," 94). There was in Heraclitus no concept of a transcendent God; only an immanent "law" or "reason" in the world, the Logos. He recognized, however, that the world is a unity and that basic to all human institutions is a spiritual, all-pervasive principle with which they must deal.

Anaxagoras placed greater stress on the Creator's transcendence and thought of the Logos as intermediary between God and creation, the regulative principle in the cosmos, thus anticipating the Stoics. Plato made little direct contribution to the concept, but his doctrine of Ideas lent itself to later refinements of the doctrine. Platonic DUALISM, with its contrast between the ideal and the expression of the idea in a phenomenal world, has a parallel with thought and its verbalization which is the central idea in Logos. Also the world-soul which the Creator imparted to the cosmos (*Timaeus* 34) reappears in Jewish and Christian literatures of the early centuries (e.g., Wisdom of Solomon; *Epistle of Diognetus*). Aristotle reacted against Plato's dualism by stressing a monistic view of the universe, the transcendence of God and his noninvolvement in human affairs.

B. The Stoics. The STOICS, led by Zeno (c. 300 B.C.), revived the tenets of Heraclitus, especially the idea that the basic element in the cosmos is fire, or "seminal reason" (*logos spermatikos*), manifest in all of nature. They believed that Heraclitus and foo into were "inspired" because they adhered to this concept. Later Stoics distinguished between this germinal *logos*, the source of ideas, and its uttered expression (*logos prophorikos*), but agreed that the two are essentially one. Men, they said, participate in each other because of common participation in the common Logos. In the words of a later thinker, the "Logos is the soul of the world, it pervades the universe as honey fills the honey comb, and links time with eternity" (Cicero, *De natura deorum* 2.20).

The early Stoics believed the Logos to be an all-permeating fiery vapor, materialistic in nature. The later Stoics often resorted to allegorization, such as interpreting HERMES, messenger of the gods, as the Logos. But their Logos was a pantheistic world-soul, a materialistic abstraction rather than a hypostasis, hence had little in common with the biblical usage of the term. It did, however, help prepare the world for Christianity by its emphasis on the importance of the individual and the basic unity of all mankind, a variety in unity. It helped thoughtful persons to distinguish habitually between thought and the expression of thought in words. Most of all, it helped prepare the Greek world for the acceptance of a mediator between God and man. It also provided Christians with a means of explaining divine revelation via a unique Son.

II. In Jewish authors

A. The OT background. The Hebrew term behind the SEPTUAGINT was usually *dābār* דָּבָר, "word." Often it appears in the expression "the word of God." In the CREATION story (Gen. 1), God *spoke* and the world came into existence as a result. "By the word of the LORD were the heavens made" (Ps. 33:6). The word alone was the effective agent in creation: "For he spoke, and it came to be; / he commanded, and it stood firm" (33:9). Sometimes the word was regarded as possessing an entity and intrinsic authority apart from its source. Thus, ISAAC could not reverse his blessing of the FIRSTBORN, even though based on a misunderstanding (Gen. 27:37). In the same genre, perhaps, was the "law of the Medes and the Persians," which could not be altered, once it was uttered or written (Esth. 8:8).

The same term, *dābār*, was used to express the manner in which God's providence sustains the universe *after* its creation. In Pss. 147:18 ("He sends his word, and melts them") and 148:8 ("lightning and hail, snow and clouds, / stormy winds that do his bidding") the immanent word of God is seen as controlling nature. "His word," says the psalmist, "runs swiftly," both in nature and in the realm of moral law (147:15, 19). Sometimes the word was regarded as quasi-personal in nature: "so is my word that goes out from my mouth: / It will not return to me empty" (Isa. 55:11). God's word can also be a means of condemnation (Hos. 6:5) or of deliverance (Ps. 107:20).

The kinship between word and SPIRIT is indicated in Ps. 33:6, where the parallelism states, "By the word of the LORD were the heavens made, / their starry host by the breath [*rûaḥ* H8120] of his mouth," a passage prized by early defenders of Trinitarian doctrine. The kinship between deed, word, breath, and Spirit is obvious: the deed is the result of the word, the spoken word requires breath, and the same Hebrew term lies behind both "breath" and "Spirit." God's word in Hebrew thought was more than an expression of his thought; it was also an expression of his will in nature, in human life, and in history.

Preeminently, however, the "word of God" in the OT is a means of divine REVELATION. This is particularly true of the prophetic literature. Prior to the kingdom period, divine revelation was regarded as conveyed by DREAMS, by sacred LOTS (interpreted by the priest), and by the lawgiver. In the postexilic period APOCALYPTIC vision was a common mode of revelation. In the kingdom period the more prevalent mode of divine self-disclosure was by "the word of the LORD" (Amos 7:16).

God "sent a message [*dābār*] against Jacob" (Isa. 9:8) as a means of divine revelation through his prophets. The initiation of this phase of divine revelation was via SAMUEL, so much so that he was recognized as Yahweh's official spokesman (1 Sam. 3:1—4:1). For the Major Prophets this word or audition was almost irresistible; in the words of Jeremiah, it was like "a fire shut up in my bones. I am weary of holding it in" (Jer. 20:9; cf. Ezek. 33:7; Amos 3:8; Mic. 3:8). The audition ("word of God") was often equated with "vision" (cf. 1 Sam. 3:1; Isa. 1:1).

In the Major Prophets the "word of God" was the oracular disclosure of the mind of Yahweh. Later God's word was the equivalent of God's total revelation, the TORAH. It was a self-contained body of instruction, a way of life. "Your word," said the psalmist, "is a lamp to my feet" (Ps. 119:105); by it the young man would be able to "keep his way pure" (119:9). God's word in such contexts is the equivalent of God's LAW; it is parallel with and yet in contrast to the Logos of Jn. 1:17.

B. Wisdom Literature. Closely related to the concept of the word is that of WISDOM (*ḥokmâ H2683*), which is a form of divine revelation, often elusive (Job 28) and always invaluable. It comes not as a result of human achievement, but always as a gratuitous self-disclosure of God (28:12–28); it is a gift of grace (Dan. 2:21). It was given to craftsmen as manual skill for fabricating the TABERNACLE (Exod. 36:1); to JOSHUA was given "the spirit of wisdom" as essential to leadership (Deut. 34:9).

Best representative of this gift was SOLOMON, who was commended and rewarded because of his discriminating preference for wisdom as a means of service. This laid the foundation for the third most important portion of the OT, the Wisdom Literature. The sopherim (SCRIBES) and wise men came to be the most highly esteemed type of leadership in the nation. While Solomon was the most famous of them, the pioneer seems to have been AHITHOPHEL, a man whose judgment was considered on a par with the disclosures of prophet or priest (2 Sam. 16:23). In the book of Proverbs wisdom is the cardinal virtue, the possession of which assures God's favor.

Wisdom was sometimes personified. In what is probably the closest literary approximation to the prologue of John's gospel, wisdom appears in the role of a young woman, entreating young men, in competition with a prostitute (Prov. 1:20; 5:3; 7:10; 8:1–3; 9:4). Wisdom is personified as eternally existent and as sharing in the work of creation (Prov. 8:22–31; cf. Jn. 1:3; 5:17; Col. 1:16; Heb. 1:2). Another eloquent personification of wisdom is attributed to Jesus ben Sirach (c. 180 B.C.; see ECCLESIASTICUS). Probably under the influence of Prov. 8, he wrote of Wisdom, "I came forth from the mouth of the Most High, and covered the earth like a mist . . . . Those who eat me will hunger for more, and those who drink me will thirst for more.

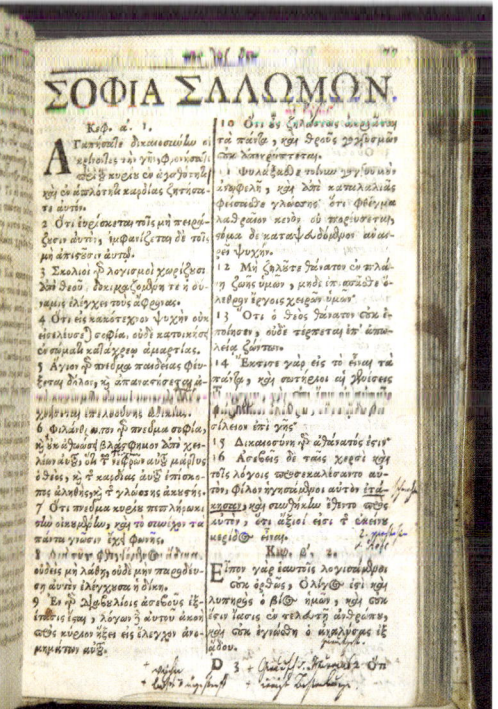

The Wisdom of Solomon (1715 ed.). The author of this apocryphal book artfully brings together the notions of Logos and wisdom.

Whoever obeys me will not be put to shame" (Sir. 24:3, 21–22; cf. Jn. 4:14; 6:35; 7:16; 17:8; Rom. 10:11).

In what is sometimes considered the first important attempt to achieve a synthesis between the Hebrew and Greek emphases, the author of the WISDOM OF SOLOMON (c. 100 B.C.?) thinks of wisdom as personalized. Wisdom is conceived as the quasi-personal agent in creation—"by your wisdom [you] have formed man" (Wisd. 9:2). The similarity and the contrast to the Johannine prologue are apparent in one notable passage, "your all-powerful word leaped from heaven, from the royal throne, into the midst of the land that was doomed, a stern warrior carrying the sharp sword of your authentic command" (Wisd. 18:15–16). The parallel is not with the incarnate word of Jn. 1:14 but rather with the conquering Word of Rev. 19:13. In this writer the Logos and Wisdom are personalized and are practically identical. Wisdom, like the "advocate" of 1 Jn. 2:1, is the believer's guide, defender, and deliverer. In alluding to Joseph the writer says, "When a righteous man was sold, wisdom did not desert him, but delivered him from sin" (Wisd. 10:13; cf. Gen. 39:10–15; Isa. 63:9; 1 Cor. 10:4).

The re-creating energy of the immanent Word-Wisdom is eloquently set forth by this author. "Wisdom," he says, "penetrates all things. For she is the breath of the power of God ... in every generation she passes into holy souls and makes them friends of God" (Wisd. 7:24–27). Wisdom is described as God's breath, emanation, reflection, mirror, and image (7:25–26; cf. Col. 1:15; Heb. 1:3). While this author comes closer than his predecessors to a personification of the Logos, he does not place God so far above the earth that no direct connection is possible. Because the God of the Bible is a living God, not the static deity of the Greek philosophers, there was no need of a second God to mediate between Creator and creature. Communication was by the Word.

By some writers the rabbinic concept of the word (Aram. *mêmrāʾ*, from *mêmar*) is viewed as the equivalent of the Logos. In the TARGUMS, the Memra was viewed as the intercessor before God and as the helper of the righteous. However, as G. F. Moore (in *HTR* 15 [1922]: 41–59) points out, Memra is a buffer word, not a mediating idea or person. It seems unlikely, therefore, that this term was any influence on Johannine usage of the term Logos.

C. Philo of Alexandria. The Hebraic and Hellenic concepts converged in PHILO JUDAEUS, the Jewish philosopher of ALEXANDRIA at the time of Christ. In Philo's voluminous writings may be traced the Greek emphasis on the Logos as reason and the Hebrew emphasis on communication by word and deed. Philo fused the all-pervasive energy stressed by Heraclitus, the metaphysical dualism of Plato, the transcendental monism of Aristotle, and the individualism characteristic of the Stoics. To him the Logos was common to these traditions and also to the OT. Under a great variety of titles, this impersonal Logos served an intermediate functionary between the remote God and the material universe.

Influenced by the Platonic doctrine of ideas, Philo spoke of the Logos as the realm of idea or pattern, yet his Hebrew heritage helped him see the Logos as also the embodiment or expression of the ideal. He speaks of the Logos as God's "firstborn son" and "ambassador" and as high priest. Common to all these various facets of the concept in Philo is the role of the Logos as intermediary between God and the world. This same emphasis on the transcendence of God and the nature of matter as evil reappeared, decades after Philo, in the various Gnostic systems of the 2nd cent. A.D. Philo differentiated between the *logos endiathetos* (ideas in God and reason in man) and *logos prophorikos* (the ideas projected in speech), as did the Stoics before him. The apparent complexity of the cosmos is therefore unified by the Logos or reason behind the phenomena. Like the Stoics and other Greeks, Philo would have recoiled at the idea of the Logos becoming incarnate; his Logos was a personification, never a person as in John. (The concept of word is not prominent in the DEAD SEA SCROLLS.)

III. NT usage

A. Synoptic Gospels and Acts. The seed in the parable of the soils is identified as the *logos*, "word" (Mk. 4:14) — in this instance the preaching of Jesus or the proclamation of God's truth (cf. Jn. 17:8). This is in harmony with the prevailing OT view that the word of God is the preaching of the prophets. It is also the revelation of the gospel of the Son of God; this word is the good news concerning Christ (Matt. 13:19, 21–23; Mk. 2:2; 4:14, 33; Lk. 5:1; 11:28; Acts 10:36), which includes also the preaching of the apostles (Acts 4:1–2, 29, 31; 6:2, 4, 7; 8:4, 14, 25; 10:36, 44; 11:1, 19). The term appears in Mk. 8:32, where after Peter's confession of faith Jesus began a new phase of his instruction, that of his approaching decease, and spoke the *logos* openly. The significance is that the word of the gospel culminates in the death and the resurrection of the Messiah.

The total Christian message is often termed "the word" (Lk. 1:2, 4; Acts 1:1; 2:41; 4:4; 6:2, 4, 7), especially as this message centers in Christ. Thus, the apostles asked and received boldness to "speak the word of God," that is, to preach the gospel, with courage (Acts 4:29, 31). The apostles determined to give priority to the ministry of the word (6:2, 4). The Samaritans were the first, other than Jews, to embrace "the word of God" (8:4, 14, 21, 25). CORNELIUS was among the first Gentiles to respond to "the word" (10:29, 36, 44). The message Paul brought to Jews and Gentiles of Asia Minor and Europe was the same "word of God" or "good news," as at ANTIOCH OF PISIDIA (13:5, 7, 15, 26, 49), later at EPHESUS (19:10, 20) and BEREA (17:11, 13). It is obvious that the authors of the Synoptic Gospels and Acts found it natural to regard the teachings of Jesus and the good news of the Christian preachers as in a continuum with the message of the OT prophets.

D. Pauline epistles. PAUL's usage is perhaps less distinctive than that of Luke-Acts and John. He continues the equating of the *logos* with the gospel. His presentation of Jesus Christ is essentially the same as that of John, but unlike John he does not link the person of Christ with the *logos* in any technical sense. When describing God's word, that is, the gospel message, he employs this term in a manner consistent with the Gospels (Rom. 9:6; 2 Cor. 1:18; 2:17; 4:2; 5:19; 6:7). Whether he was familiar with Philonic literature is debatable. Several passages in his epistles reveal Paul's awareness of the issues in Alexandrian speculation. The letter to the COLOSSIANS reflects Paul's concern with an incipient GNOSTICISM which stressed the contrast between Creator and creature and the necessity for intermediate beings. Paul insisted on the sole adequacy of Christ—he is the fullness (*plērōma G4445*) of the deity (Col. 2:9; see PLEROMA). The believers have their fullness in Christ alone without angels or other mediators (2:10–15). For Paul the gospel is good news concerning Jesus the Christ (1 Cor. 1:23; 2 Cor. 4:1–6; Gal. 3:1), who is both the power and the wisdom of God (1 Cor. 1:24; Eph. 3:10–12).

Paul's CHRISTOLOGY, moreover, is essentially the same as that of the fourth gospel and the epistle to the Hebrews. Paul repeatedly speaks of the uncreated Christ becoming incarnated—he voluntarily impoverished himself for others (2 Cor. 8:9), and he made himself nothing (Phil. 2:5–11) by assuming the "form of a servant." He existed with God the Father from eternity (Rom. 10:6; Gal. 4:4) and is re-creating man in his image or moral likeness

(1 Cor. 2:16; 15:49; 2 Cor. 3:18; Eph. 4:24; Phil. 2:5; Col. 3:9). Although Paul does not employ the term *logos* in a technical Christological sense, his corresponding term is *eikōn* G1635—God's image or likeness (Col. 3:10 et al.). See IMAGE OF GOD.

C. Hebrews. This anonymous epistle states that "the word of God is living and active" and that "it judges the thoughts and attitudes of the heart" (Heb. 4:12). The author is familiar with Alexandrian exegesis and nomenclature, as evidenced by the use of such concepts as angels, shadow, substance, pattern, and the paradox of seeing the invisible. The similarity to the prologue of John's gospel is especially apparent in the opening verses. Christ is present as the Son who is the effulgence of God's glory and who bears the stamp of God's nature—a relationship as intimate as that between die and matrix—also as God's heir and agent in creation (Heb. 1:1–3; cf. Jn. 1:1–3). By such language the author seeks to set forth the closest possible relationship to the Father without losing the Son's identity.

The *logos* in this letter is the apostolic preaching (Heb. 2:2–4), the illumination of the Spirit (4:2), the teaching of dedicated leaders (5:13; 13:7), and the epistle itself (13:22). In no Christian document is the paradox of Jesus' deity and humanity expressed more emphatically than here (1:1–3; cf. 2:14–18; 5:7–9). Although the relationship of the Son to the Father is essentially the same as set forth in Paul and in John, the term *logos* is not used to describe this relationship to the extent that it is in Philo and in John. The term occurs eleven times in the epistle as a designation of divine revelation, but is not explicitly related to the embodiment of that revelation in the Son.

D. Johannine literature

1. Epistles and Apocalypse. In the Apocalypse the messianic warrior with the "sword" in his mouth is called the *logos* of God (Rev. 19:13). It appears to be a symbolic presentation of the preaching of the good news, stated in numerous other places, as indicated above.

John's first letter speaks of the "word of life," in language strikingly similar to Jn. 1:1–18. In this

Detail of a 9th-cent. Greek minuscule MS of the Gospels open to Jn. 1:1.

context the expression could refer either to the preaching of the good news or to the incarnate Christ; it probably includes both. The former is consistent with the NT as a whole; the latter is consistent in the Johannine prologue, which it so closely resembles in other respects. (The best texts do not include the phrase "the Father, the Word, and the Holy Ghost" in 1 Jn. 5:7, but it at least reflects the sentiments of many in the ancient church.)

2. The fourth gospel. The term *logos* occurs forty times in this gospel but only in Jn. 1:1–3, 14 is the term explicitly equated with the Christ. With this term, however, is linked TRUTH (*alētheia* G237), "your word is truth" (17:17). Elsewhere Jesus says, "I am the way and the truth and the life" (14:6). Since "things equal to the same thing are equal to each other," the conclusion is clear—Jesus is the Logos. This, of course, is consistent with the prologue, where the identification is explicit and emphatic.

a. The relation of the Logos to the Father. The author goes back of the Genesis account to origins in eternity—"In the beginning was the Word." The Word was "with God" (*pros ton theon*). In God's presence, implying movement toward God and yet distinct from God); the language expresses perpetual intercommunion or fellowship. He is one with God in essence, yet distinct personally—"the Word was God." The relationship to God is as intimate as language can describe it and still retain individual identity. The thought is essentially that of Paul (Col. 1:15–20; cf. 1 Cor. 15:24) and of the author of Hebrews (Heb. 1:1–3). This usage marks an advance over the thought of the Pauline corpus and the letter to the Hebrews in that it was a successful synthesis of the prophetic doctrine of divine revelation, the later personification of wisdom, and the Alexandrian emphasis on reason and truth. The prologue expresses Christian revelation on a Hebraic background, using contemporary idiom to make it more appealing.

b. The relation of the Logos to the world is that of Co-creator to creation. The relation to the cosmos is not spelled out in the detail one sees in Paul (Col. 1:15–20 et al.), but it is embraced in John's all-inclusive affirmation—"Through him all things were made" (Jn. 1:3a). The following statement reiterates and emphasizes this point: "no single thing was created without him" (1:3b NEB). Just as the word of God spoke into existence every created thing in the Genesis account, so John affirms the same of the Logos. It is astonishing that the first-generation Christians who had known Jesus of Nazareth "after the flesh" could have become convinced that he was also the One who had caused the universe itself to have come into existence. The difference between Creator and creation is brought out by the contrast in the verbs "being" and "becoming." "The eternally existing One caused to come into existence in time everything else that exists."

c. The relation of the Logos to mankind is the main concern of John, as of the other evangelists. "The Logos became flesh" (Jn. 1:14) was an idea abhorrent to the Gnostics, as to holders of metaphysical dualism generally. Some hold with R. Bultmann that John's ideas are borrowed mainly from pagan ideologies, especially Iranian Gnostic systems, but the evidence is insufficient and the theory is rendered untenable by recent archaeological discoveries.

The Word is equated with the truth and with light in Johannine thought. As is characteristic of the fourth gospel, abstract ideas become concrete and personalized in Christ. The good news in this book becomes a person. Hence, the doctrine of the RESURRECTION becomes identified with Jesus—"I am the resurrection and the life" (Jn. 11:25). The same is true of "the way" (14:6), the manna from heaven (6:31, 50), the truth, and the word. What in the rest of the NT is the message of God's good news, in the fourth gospel is the person of Christ.

Yet this gospel is not different in its emphasis; it only makes the link between messenger and message more complete, expressed in an idiom that transcends national and sectarian boundaries and becomes universal in its appeal. The message becomes incarnate and personalized in Jesus of Nazareth, not only for a season but for all time. Boldly drawing upon contemporary nomenclature and yet defying one of the basic convictions of prevailing dualism, the evangelist declares that the eternal Logos became flesh in history (1:14) in what is perhaps the most characteristic affirmation of the gospel.

IV. Early Christian literature. At the close of the 1st cent., the Logos doctrine was the antidote to Gnostic dualism and docetic heresies (e.g., 2 Jn. 7). The apologists—including Justin, Tatian, Theophilus, and Athenagoras—sought to demonstrate that orthodoxy was opposed to pagan theosophies and yet at the same time was in agreement with elements of truth in such pagan ideologies as Stoicism, especially as represented by EPICTETUS. JUSTIN argued that Christ is the *Spermatic Logos* who issued from the Father as divine revelation. CLEMENT OF ALEXANDRIA emphasized the immanence of the Logos concept, that Christ was in the world before the historic incarnation preparing mankind for his advent. Additional strength was afforded this doctrine by Athanasius during the Trinitarian controversy. However, the Nicene Creed did not include the term, and later the Synod of Sirmium (A.D. 451) condemned the doctrine of *endiathetos* and *prophorikos logos*. The idea still holds its appeal for idealists and certain mystics.

In general, the Logos doctrine serves to indicate the power of the gospel to gather up and transform contemporary concepts that contain elements of truth. A weak and uncertain gospel would have avoided any use of alien symbols for fear of losing its distinctiveness. In much the same spirit Clement of Alexandria could refer to himself as a "Christian Gnostic." The genius of the author of the fourth gospel is that he did not disdain the use of a term that promised to extend the appeal of the Truth.

(See further G. Vos in *PTR* 11 [1913]: 557–602; W. R. Inge in *ERE*, 8:134–38; A. Alexander in *ISBE* [1929], 3:1911–17; G. Kittel et al.

in *TDNT*, 4:68–143; R. C. Burn, *The Fourth Gospel and the Logos Doctrine* [1942]; K. E. Lee, *The Religious Thought of St. John* [1950], 74–100; O. Cullmann, *The Christology of the New Testament* [1959], 249–69; J. N. Sanders in *IDB*, 4:868–72; B. Klappert et al. in *NIDOTTE*, 3:1081–1117; D. Winston, *Logos and Mystical Theology in Philo of Alexandria* [1985]; *ABD*, 4:348–56; *DDD*, 525–31.) See Christology; incarnation; Jesus Christ; word. G. A. Turner

loins. The Hebrew and Greek terms normally rendered "loins" in the KJV and some other English versions refer to the lumbar region or the hips in general. The Hebrew word *motnayim* H5516 (dual in form), often rendered "waist" in the NIV, describes the mid-portion of the back (Exod. 28:42) around which a belt could be fastened (2 Ki. 1:8) or a sword hung (2 Sam. 20:8). It was regarded as the thickest part of the body (1 Ki. 12:10), and the area where sackcloth was worn (Gen. 37:34; 1 Ki. 20:32). Throughout the ANE it was customary for the lower garments to be gathered or tied up around the hips when a person began to run (1 Ki. 18:46). In conformity with the Hebrew custom of assigning emotional qualities to organs of the human body, the loins were regarded as the locale of a man's physical strength (Nah. 2:1). They were deemed liable to attack by such noxious influences as disease or calamity (Ps. 66:11; Isa. 21:3), or to that kind of enervation that would "make their loins tremble" (Ps. 69:23 RSV) or would "ungird the loins" (Isa. 45:1 RSV).

A less frequent Hebrew word, also occurring in the dual form, *ḥălāṣayim* H2743, is used in a similar fashion to denote the mid-body area, with the same general range of meanings. However, it also symbolized the functions or organs of generation, and was used in that manner of a man's offspring as "those who come out of his loins" (cf. Gen. 35:11 KJV). A third term translated "loins" is *kesel* H4072, used always in the literal sense of physical tissue (Lev. 3:4 et al.).

The NT writers follow the general usage of the OT, but employ one word, *osphys* G4019, to cover the various meanings of the Hebrew terms. It indicates the waist (Matt. 3:4; Mk. 1:6), the place where garments were tied, but it is normally used in metaphors (Lk. 12:35; Eph. 6:14; 1 Pet. 1:13), including expressions that refer to "offspring" (Acts 2:30; Heb. 7:5, 10). R. K. Harrison

Lois loh′is (Λωΐς G3396). The grandmother of Timothy; she was probably the mother of Timothy's mother, Eunice (2 Tim. 1:5). The family lived at Lystra (Acts 16:1). Lois, a devout Jewish believer, likely was converted to Christianity during Paul's first missionary journey (Acts 14). Paul speaks of the unpretending faith of Timothy, and adds that this faith first dwelt in his grandmother Lois and his mother Eunice. S. Barabas

longsuffering. This English term, used rarely in modern Bible versions, occurs in the KJV seventeen times. In four OT passages (e.g., Exod. 34:6) it is the rendering of the Hebrew phrase *ʾerek ʾappayim* (from *ʾārēk* H800, "long, slow" and *ʾap* H678, "anger"), which the KJV also translates "slow of anger" (e.g., Ps. 103:8). The rest of the occurrences are in the NT, where the term renders Greek *makrothymia* G3429, "patience, forbearance" (e.g., Rom. 2:4; the cognate verb, *makrothymeō* G3428, is found in 2 Pet. 3:9 et al.).

God's longsuffering is that divine attribute (Exod. 34:6; Num. 14:18; Pss. 86:15; 103:8, 9; Joel 2:13) which delays the punishment of wicked and rebellious persons (Rom. 9:22; 1 Pet. 3:20). Divine justice would long ago have swept the ungodly into perdition, but Yahweh is "full of compassion, and gracious, longsuffering, and plenteous in mercy and truth" (Ps. 86:15 KJV). The purpose of God's longsuffering is to lead sinners to repentance (Rom. 2:4; 2 Pet. 3:9, 15); but when the wicked despise his patience (Rom. 2:4) and abuse it (Neh. 9:28–31; Eccl. 8:11; Matt. 24:48–49) they are punished (Neh. 9:30; Matt. 24:50–51; Rom. 2:5). The longsuffering of God is not infinite (Gen. 6:3; Jer. 44:22); it is tempered with justice (Prov. 1:24–27; 29:1; Isa. 42:14; Rev. 2:21–22).

The divine longsuffering is illustrated by the song of the vineyard (Isa. 5:1–7) and by two parables, namely, the wicked husbandmen (Matt. 21:33–41) and the barren fig tree (Lk. 13:6–9). Examples include God's treatment of (1) the antediluvian world (1 Pet. 3:20); (2) Pharaoh (Rom. 9:17, 22); (3) heathen nations (Acts 14:16), especially

(4) the Amorites (Gen. 15:16); (5) Manasseh (2 Chr. 33:10–13); (6) Israel (Neh. 9:31; Ps. 78:38; Isa. 30:18; 48:9, 11; Jer. 7:13, 23–25; 11:7; Ezek. 20:17; Matt. 19:8; 23:37; Acts 17:30); (7) Jerusalem (Matt. 23:37); and (8) Paul (1 Tim. 1:16). Christians ought to imitate God's longsuffering (Rom. 15:5) and plead it in prayer (Jer. 15:15). In the NT longsuffering is a virtue that enables the disciple to carry his cross patiently (2 Cor. 6:6; Eph. 4:2; 2 Tim. 4:2). See PATIENCE. R. E. PERRY

loom. An apparatus for weaving thread or yarn into cloth (Jdg. 16:14; Isa. 38:12). In Bible times three types of looms were in use. One was the horizontal loom, also called the ground loom, because it was laid out horizontally on the ground. It could be operated only in a stooping position. The other two types of loom were upright and were operated from a sitting or a standing position. They differed in that in one type the threads of the warp hung from a crossbeam and were kept taut with weights attached to their lower ends; while in the other type

Turkish woman working at a wooden loom.

the ends of the warp were attached to a revolving cloth beam, and therefore a much longer web could be woven. See WEAVING. S. BARABAS

loop. The TABERNACLE was covered with ten linen curtains, each measuring twenty-eight cubits by four. These were sewn along their length into two sets of five, which were draped over the frame of the tabernacle structure. Along one side of each set of curtains fifty loops (Heb. *lulāʾôt H4339*) of blue thread were sewn. Fifty gold clasps were attached to one side of the other set of curtains, and thus the two halves of the curtain were joined. The outer covering was made of goatskin in the same way, also with clasps and loops (Exod. 26:4–5, 10–11; 36:11–12, 17). S. BARABAS

lord. The English word *lord* (or capitalized, *Lord*) is used to translate various terms in the OT. As a title of men, it can designate governmental, religious, and military officials. The common Hebrew word *baʿal H1251* ("owner, husband," etc.) can be used in this sense (e.g., Isa. 16:8 NRSV; NIV, "rulers"), as can *ʾādôn H123* (Gen. 42:20 et al.), *seren H6249* (e.g., Jdg. 13:3 KJV) and the rare term *gĕbîr H1484* (only Gen. 27:29, 37). When applied to deity, the title *baʿal* came to be identified directly with a specific Canaanite god (see BAAL). In contrast, *ʾādôn* is used of the true God (e.g., Josh. 3:11), esp. in the form *ʾădōnāy H151* (lit., "my lords"; Gen. 15:2 et al.). Most English Bible versions use the form LORD (i.e., in small caps) to render God's special covenant name, Yahweh. See GOD, NAMES OF.

The Greek word *kyrios G3261*, which can also refer to human beings in positions of authority, is used by the SEPTUAGINT to render the Hebrew words applied to the true God. In the NT it occurs as a designation of the sovereign God in relationship to his creation (Matt. 1:20; 11:25; Lk. 4:18). But it is also the supreme title given to Jesus. "Jesus is Lord" was perhaps the earliest creedal statement formulated and recited (prob. chiefly at BAPTISM, Acts 8:16; 19:5) by the early Christians. Although found often in Paul's writings (Rom. 10:9; 1 Cor. 7:22; 12:3; 2 Cor. 4:5), this title was by no means original with him (but neither was it borrowed by him from the Hellenistic MYSTERY RELIGIONS, as suggested by W. Bousset, *Kyrios Christos*, 4th ed. [1935]). PETER knew and used it (Acts 1:21; 2:36).

The early Aramaic-speaking church, too, had worshiped Jesus as Lord, and its Aramaic prayer, MARANATHA, "Our Lord, come," still stands in the text as witness to this fact (1 Cor. 16:22). Indeed, if Phil. 2:6–11 is a primitive Christian hymn, as some have claimed, then PAUL was the recipient of an earlier tradition about the Lordship of Jesus rather than the originator of a new title to describe his own understanding of him. This title stood also in the tradition Paul had received concerning the LORD'S SUPPER (1 Cor. 11:23).

By referring to Jesus as Lord, the early church declared him as standing above the human level—an object of prayer (Acts 7:59, 60; 1 Cor. 12:8; 16:22) and trust (Acts 5:14; 9:42; 11:24; cf. also the fourth gospel), sharing with God in his sovereign rule (2:34), and ultimately sharing with God in his nature. For being conscious that the Greek OT regularly used *kyrios* to designate Yahweh, early Christians, even Jewish Christians, chose that term as the supreme title to convey their understanding of Jesus. By it, therefore, they intended to identify him with the God of the OT. This intent is seen most clearly in those NT passages where OT texts originally referring to Yahweh are now boldly quoted as referring to Jesus (Rom. 10:13; Heb. 1:10; 1 Pet. 2:3; 3:15). See CHRISTOLOGY; JESUS CHRIST.

The use of this title also meant that Jesus was master, worthy to receive power, glory, and blessing (Rev. 5:12). It meant he possessed all authority (Matt. 28:18), and was the One before whom every knee must bow in submission (Phil. 2:10), the universal sovereign (Rom. 10:12; 14:9; Phil. 2:11), King of kings and Lord of lords (Rev. 19:16). Especially was he Lord to the CHURCH (Jn. 20:28; Rom. 5:1; 2 Tim. 1:8). The term *slave* quite naturally, therefore, became a common designation of early Christians (Rom. 14:4; 1 Cor. 7:21–24). They served him (Rom. 12:11), ordered their lives in a manner worthy of him (1 Cor. 11:27), and paid him obeisance, OBEDIENCE being the only proper response of slave to master (Heb. 5:9). The will of this exalted Master was often communicated to the church through the revelatory word of his apostles and prophets (1 Cor. 14:37; Rev. 2; 3).

The ideas of firmness and strength inherent in this term were also important to the early church. When a Christian, therefore, called Jesus "Lord," he meant further that he had a foundation upon which to build his life. This idea is conveyed frequently by the phrase *en kyriō* (Rom. 8:39; 1 Cor. 7:22). See UNION WITH CHRIST.

The death, resurrection, and exaltation of Jesus were revelatory events. They alone brought the church to the unquestioned realization that Jesus was indeed the Lord (Matt. 28:18; Jn. 20:28; Acts 2:36; Rom. 10:9; Phil. 2:9–11; cf. also the frequent application of Ps. 110:1 to Jesus in Matt. 22:44; Mk. 12:36; Acts 2:34; Heb. 10:12–13). Hence, when *kyrios* is applied to Jesus in the Gospels prior to Easter, its meaning is generally limited to "sir," a title of respect, or to "master," in the sense of "rabbi" (Mk. 10:51, with Matt. 20:33 and Lk. 6:46; 18:41; Jn. 13:13; but contrast Matt. 7:21 and Mk. 12:35–36, where Jesus applies to himself the title in a more profound sense).

It is worth recalling, however, that the Gospels are postresurrection documents, whose writers wrote from the perspective of Easter. To them Jesus was a teacher par excellence, but more than that, he was their sovereign Lord. Perhaps, then, the evangelists chose *kyrios* as a title even for the historical Jesus because it could reflect both the superficial understanding of the masses who saw in him only a Jewish RABBI, and at the same time the later and more profound perception of the believing community who recognized in him God become man.

Although the church hailed Jesus as Lord, it also recognized that this role of his was a delegated one. They understood that he would bring all enemies under his feet and then surrender his lordship and subject himself to the One who subjected all things to him so that the triune God might be supreme (1 Cor. 15:27–28). (See further L. Cerfaux in *RSPT* 11 [1922]: 40–71; 12 [1923]:125–53; W. Foerster and G. Quell in *TDNT*, 3:1039–98; E. Schweizer, *Lordship and Discipleship* [1960]; L. W. Hurtado, *Lord Jesus Christ: Devotion to Jesus in Earliest Christianity* [2003].)

G. F. HAWTHORNE

Lord, day of the. See DAY OF THE LORD; LORD'S DAY.

Lord of hosts. The phrase "LORD of hosts" is used by the KJV and other Bible translations as a literal rendering of Hebrew *yhwh ṣĕbāʾôt*, which occurs well over two hundred times in the OT as a designation of the true God (it is esp. frequent in Isaiah, Jeremiah, Zechariah, and Malachi). The first word in the phrase is the divine name *Yahweh* (see GOD, NAMES OF). The second word is the plural form of the Hebrew noun *ṣābāʾ H7372*, which means "army" but also is applied to the stars (e.g., 2 Ki. 17:16) and to the heavenly attendants (1 Ki. 22:19). See HOST OF HEAVEN. In over sixty instances (mostly in Isaiah) the SEPTUAGINT renders the phrase with a transliteration, *kyrios sabaōth* (used twice in the NT, Rom. 9:29 [a LXX quotation]; Jas. 5:4). In a few instances (e.g., 1 Ki. 18:15), the LXX has *kyrios tōn dynameōn* ("Lord of the forces"), but in over one hundred passages it renders the phrase, with minor variations, as *kyrios pantokratōr*, "Lord Almighty," and this understanding has been followed by the NIV.

The exact reference of the Hebrew phrase has been debated for centuries. A military reference is clear in some contexts, as when DAVID exclaimed that he was coming against GOLIATH "in the name of the LORD of hosts, the God of the armies of Israel" (1 Sam. 17:45 NRSV; cf. also Isa. 13:4; 31:4). But many other passages are more general in character. The initial use of the concept of the "hosts" is found in Gen. 2:1, where it refers back to the totality of created beings in the "heaven and the earth." This would include all those self-conscious creatures that were brought into being under the creation ordinances of God. One use of the title "LORD of hosts" (Isa. 45:13) follows immediately upon a reference to the divine CREATION of the earth as well as the heavens and their hosts (v. 12). In Ps. 89:7–8, the title is in parallel with "the council of the holy ones," apparently based upon the concept of the "great congregation," that is, the gathering together of all the powers of the universe, heavenly and earthly, sacred or profane, at the command and summons of the Almighty (cf. Job 1:6).

W. WHITE, JR.

Lord's Day. This expression (Gk. *hē kyriakē hēmera*) is found in the Bible only in Rev. 1:10, where John states, "On the Lord's Day I was in the Spirit," when he received a divine commission to write the book of Revelation. The adjective *kyriakos G3258*, however, also occurs in 1 Cor. 11:20 in the expression, "the Lord's Supper." As will be shown, "the Lord's Day" is used frequently in other early Christian writings to designate Sunday, the first day of the week, observed from the time of the apostles as a day of Christian worship.

 I. The origin of the Christian Sunday
  A. The contribution of Judaism
  B. The influence of paganism
  C. The distinctive Christian elements
 II. The history of the Christian Sunday in the early church
  A. The apostolic period
  B. The Ante-Nicene period
 III. The history of the Christian Sunday in the medieval church
  A. The early medieval period
  B. The later medieval period
 IV. The history of the Christian Sunday in the modern church
  A. The Reformation period
  B. The modern period
 V. Conclusion

I. The origin of the Christian Sunday. Many people believe that the origin of the Christian Sunday is identical with the origin of the Hebrew SABBATH, and that the Sabbath was changed either by Jesus himself or by his apostles from the seventh to the first day of the week (Wilbur F. Crafts, *The Sabbath for Man* [1885], 376; R. L. Dabney, *The Christian Sabbath* [1882], 6–8; J. P. Hutchinson, *Our Obligations to the Day of Rest and Worship* [1916], 100). This belief has persisted even though no passage of Scripture can be found that teaches that the Hebrew Sabbath has been transferred from one day of the week to another.

The origin of the Christian Sunday is not as simple as those who hold this view would have us believe. The change from Sabbath to Sunday was gradual. Millgram describes it as follows: "The change from the Sabbath to Sunday was the result of a long historic process which is tied up with the formative years of Christianity. This process coincided with the drift of early Christianity from a messianic movement among the Jews to a religion of the Gentiles. When Christianity was predominantly Jewish, the Sabbath was the official Christian day of rest and worship. When Christianity finally became predominantly Gentile, the Sabbath was abandoned and Sunday became the official day of rest and worship. This change was not sudden. It was a slow process of more than three centuries' duration (A. E. Millgram, *Sabbath: The Day of Delight* [1944], 364).

In this process, which took place when Christianity was emerging from the confinement of JUDAISM, it was inevitable that JUDAISM should contribute a great deal to a Christian institution such as Sunday. During this period Christianity was also entering into conflict with paganism, which, especially in later ages, made its influence felt on the institutions of Christianity. At the same time, as the distinction between Christianity and Judaism, and between Christianity and paganism, came to be realized, it was certain that the observance of Sunday would contain some elements of a distinctively Christian character.

A. The contribution of Judaism. Christianity stands in debt to Judaism in at least three regards: (1) Judaism gave to Christianity its sacred Scriptures; (2) Judaism provided in the synagogue service a pattern for Christian worship; and (3) Judaism presented in the Hebrew Sabbath an example of a weekly day of rest and worship.

1. The Jewish Scriptures. The Jews regarded the writings now known as the OT as an authoritative divine REVELATION, and the Sabbath as a divine institution that rested upon the authority of that revelation. Jesus and the apostles likewise accepted the OT as the Word of God (Matt. 5:17–19; Jn 10:35; Rom. 3:31; 4:3; 2 Tim. 3:16; Heb. 1:1; 2 Pet. 1:21). Cotton asks the question, "How could Christianity, which accepted the Old Testament as authoritative, dare to set aside the Sabbath which was established as an institution within the very ten commandments, and set up as a kind of substitute the first day of the week to be observed as a sacred day?" (Paul Cotton, *From Sabbath to Sunday* [1933], 8). The answer to this problem lies in the interpretation the Christians gave to those Scriptures. PAUL, for example, following the principles set forth by Jesus and the Hebrew prophets, held that it was the spirit (or Spirit) and not the letter of the Scriptures that was applicable to the Christian believer (2 Cor. 3:6). This interpretation of the OT Scriptures enabled the early Christians to hold them as authoritative, and at the same time to regard the Hebrew Sabbath as no longer binding on them.

2. The Jewish synagogue. In every place where there was a sizable Jewish community, the SYNAGOGUE was the center of Jewish worship. Jesus made regular use of the synagogue to teach and preach (Matt. 4:23; 9:35; Mk. 1:21, 39; 6:2; Lk. 4:15–27, 44; 13:10; Jn. 18:20). The apostle Paul made it a practice to begin his ministry in any particular place by preaching in the synagogue (Acts 13:5, 14–47; 14:1; 17:1–3, 10; 18:4–7; 19:8–9). It was natural, then, that the weekly services in the Jewish synagogue should become a pattern for the Christian assemblies on the Lord's Day.

The general arrangement of the synagogue was followed in the Christian meeting places. The sexes were separated and the leader took his place on a raised platform in the center at one end of the building (A. Edersheim, *The Life and Times of Jesus the Messiah*, 2 vols., 8th ed. [1900], 2:434–39; Cotton, *From Sabbath to Sunday*, 91, 95). The order of worship, including the reading of the Scriptures, the singing of psalms, the preaching of a sermon, and the offering of prayers, was much the same in the Jewish synagogue and the Christian assembly. The Christian practice of reading the Scriptures consecutively week by week was borrowed from Judaism. Even the Christian postures in prayer were borrowed from the Jews. The close parallels between the features of worship in the Jewish synagogue and the Christian assembly become all the more significant when it is remembered that Sunday was the weekly day for Christian worship just as the Sabbath was the weekly day for Jewish worship.

3. The Jewish Sabbath. The Sabbath held a distinctive place in the life of the Jewish nation. The religious rites of the Jews centered on this one day. The early Christians had been reared in the traditions of Judaism. It was natural that many of these traditions should be retained and incorporated in the life of Christianity. Jews who had been accustomed to observe the Sabbath by resting from their ordinary labors and by worshiping in the synagogue would find it very difficult not to maintain the custom of observing a weekly day of rest and worship.

At first, Jewish Christians apparently observed both the seventh and the first day of the week. Later, however, when the Christian church became more Gentile in character, and when it was realized that Christianity was distinct from Judaism, the great majority of Christians observed only the first day of the week, but they transferred to it many of the features of the earlier institution, which had held such an important place in the heritage they had received from Judaism.

The character of the Jewish Sabbath was imitated in the Christian Sunday. Like the Sabbath, Sunday was regarded as a day of joy and festivity, and fasting was forbidden (Cotton, *From Sabbath to Sunday*, 92–93). The Sabbath began and closed with appropriate celebrations. Similarly, the early Christians met on Sunday early in the morning, and again in the evening to worship and to take food together (cf. esp. the letter of PLINY the Younger to the Emperor TRAJAN, in H. Bettenson, *Documents of the Christian Church*, 2nd ed. [1963], 4–5).

The Sabbath was, to the Jew, a memorial of God's rest after the six days of CREATION and a weekly reminder of the Israelites' deliverance from Egyptian slavery (Gen. 2:3; Exod. 20:11; Deut. 5:15). To the Christian, Sunday was a memorial of THE RESURRECTION OF JESUS CHRIST, a weekly reminder of the work of Christ and of his redemption from the bondage of sin. The most prominent feature of the Hebrew Sabbath was rest from all kinds of work. Although this feature of the Jewish sacred day was the last to be carried over into the Christian Sunday, as early as the beginning of the 3rd cent. there are indications that Christians abstained from work on the Lord's Day (Tertullian, *On Prayer* 23; see *ANF*, 3:689).

The fact that Sunday became a weekly day of rest and worship for the Christians (as opposed to a monthly or yearly observance) can be explained only by the weekly recurrence of the Jewish Sabbath. The Christian Sunday, both in its initial and more developed form, owed much to the Jewish Sabbath.

B. The influence of paganism. Paganism exerted little influence on early Christianity. Christianity took root not in the soil of paganism, but of Judaism. Judaism and Christianity alike stood in marked contrast to the ethics and ideals of the pagan world. In three respects, however, paganism influenced the origin and development of the Christian Sunday: (1) it gave to the Christian institution the name by which it is most commonly called; (2) it promoted the observance of Sunday by its adoption of the seven-day week; and (3) it prepared for the adoption of Sunday as the official weekly religious day by the prominence accorded to Sunday in the pagan religions.

1. The name "Sunday." This name for the first day of the week originated from the naming of the days of the week by the ancient Babylonians after the sun, moon, and five planets that were then known (R. J. Floody, *Scientific Basis of Sabbath and Sunday* [1906], 3; W. Rordorf, *Sunday: The History of the Day of Rest and Worship in the Earliest Centuries of the Christian Church* [1968], 24–25). Sunday was named in honor of the sun or the god of the sun. Although both Jews and Christians avoided the use of this pagan name in the 1st cent. of the Christian era, Christians began to use the name as early as the 2nd cent. (Justin Martyr, *First Apology* 67; see *ANF*, 1:186).

Ethiopian Christians worshiping at the Church of the Holy Sepulchre.

2. The adoption of the seven-day week. Although the Jews had observed a seven-day week for many centuries and there is some evidence that a seven-day planetary week was observed by the Babylonians, there is no conclusive evidence that such a week existed among the Romans until the 1st Christian century. The Roman historian Dio Cassius (*Roman History* 37.18–19), writing at the beginning of the 3rd cent., states that the planetary week (1) originated in Egypt, (2) was of relatively recent date, and (3) had by his time spread everywhere (cf. Rordorf, *Sunday*, 27, who also cites evidence from Pompeii). It would have been difficult, if not impossible, for Christians to have observed a weekly day of rest and worship if the Roman empire had not adopted the seven-day week.

3. The prominence of Sunday in pagan religions. One of the numerous oriental religions that became popular in the Roman empire at the beginning of the Christian era, especially among the Roman soldiers, was MITHRAISM, a religion that was imported from PERSIA. Mithra was the god of the sun. Consequently, Mithraism regarded Sunday as a sacred day. The veneration of this day by the adherents of this pagan religion no doubt contributed to the selection of Sunday by the Emperor Constantine as the imperial rest day. His edict, issued in the year 321, ordered all judges, city people, and craftsmen to rest on "the venerable day of the sun" (Bettenson, *Documents*, 26). Although the prominence given to Sunday in Mithraism and in other pagan cults did contribute to the acceptance of that day by the pagans as a national rest day, it did not account for the observance of the first day of the week as a day of worship by the early Christians.

The use of the name Sunday, the adoption of the seven-day week, and the association of Sunday with pagan religions all helped to make the observance of the Lord's Day more acceptable to the pagans, but in no way did paganism produce or modify the essential character of the Christian institution.

C. The distinctive Christian elements

1. Consciousness of a distinction from Judaism. The Christian Sunday, although manifesting a number of features borrowed from the Sabbath of Judaism, nevertheless was from the beginning a distinctive Christian institution. The first day of the week was observed because it was the day on which Jesus rose from the dead. The resurrection of Jesus, denied by Judaism, was foundational to the Christian movement. It was inevitable that Christians, even those who were Jews by race, would come to sense an essential difference between Christianity and Judaism. This consciousness of a distinction from Judaism demanded a separate day for WORSHIP.

The distinctiveness of Christianity from Judaism may be seen in (1) its universal character, (2) its internal character, and (3) its personal character. While Judaism was the religion of one people, even though other peoples were attracted to it, Christianity quickly became a universal religion transcending all racial bounds. The Hebrew prophets spoke of Israel's mission to the world (e.g., Isa. 42:6; 54:5), but Judaism was so closely intertwined with the social, economic, and political life of the Jewish people that it never became a universal religion. The emphasis on the observance of the law in normative Judaism tended toward an external observance of legal precepts, including those having to do with the Sabbath. The teaching of Jesus and of Paul and the other apostles, on the other hand, was that God demanded an internal righteousness effected by the HOLY SPIRIT in one's heart (Matt. 5:20; Mk. 7:21–22; Rom. 8:4, 9). Again, while Judaism emphasized the individual's personal relationship with God, it was tightly bound up with the national life of the Jewish people and was expressed in an elaborate system of worship. Christianity, on the other hand, at least in its early forms, was intensely personal. Christian believers from all races and strata of society formed a new community, based not on racial or national ties, but on personal faith in Jesus Christ. He was the One whom they worshiped as Lord on the day of the week which they came to designate as the Lord's Day.

2. The supernatural designation of Sunday. All four Gospels indicate that Jesus rose from the dead on the morning of the first day of the week (Matt. 28:1; Mk. 16:2; Lk. 24:1; Jn. 20:1). The resurrection of Christ on this day was reason enough for the Christians to observe it. Six of the eight appearances of Christ after his resurrection recorded in the Gospels took place on Sunday: (1) to MARY Magdalene (Jn. 20:11–18); (2) to the women who had brought spices to anoint his body (Matt. 28:7–10); (3) to the two disciples on the road to EMMAUS (Lk. 24:13–33); (4) to Simon PETER (24:34); (5) to the ten disciples when THOMAS was absent (Jn. 20:19–23; cf. Lk. 24:36–49); and (6) to the eleven disciples when Thomas was present (Jn. 20:24–29). These appearances of Christ on Sunday were sufficient to designate it as a day of peculiar significance.

If the CRUCIFIXION of Christ took place on Friday, as is traditionally held, then PENTECOST also occurred on Sunday that year. This Jewish festival received its name from the fact that it took place fifty days after the Passover. The latter was observed annually on the fifteenth of Nisan (Millgram, *Sabbath*, 339). Since the Jews were commanded to count the fifty days "from the day after the Sabbath ... to the day after the seventh Sabbath" (Lev. 23:15–16), and since the fifteenth day of Nisan, which was the first day of the Feast of Unleavened Bread (23:6), was considered a Sabbath, the feast of Pentecost would occur on Sunday only when this special Sabbath coincided with the regular weekly Sabbath. (The use of the plural form *sabbatōn* in Matt. 28:1 seems to support this view.) If Pentecost did occur on Sunday that year, then the outpouring of the HOLY SPIRIT also occurred on the Lord's Day (Acts 2:1–4).

These supernatural events, the resurrection of Christ, his appearances to his disciples, and the coming of the Holy Spirit at Pentecost, would serve to mark the first day of the week as a special day for the Christian. Jesus, when questioned about his authority, quoted an OT passage: "The stone the builders rejected has become the capstone; the LORD has done this, and it is marvelous in our eyes" (Ps. 118:22–23; Matt. 21:42). Peter, in his address before the Jewish Sanhedrin, quoted part of the same passage and applied it to the resurrection of Christ (Acts 4:11). Athanasius, in the 4th cent., added the succeeding verse and applied it to the resurrection day: "This is the day the LORD has made; let us rejoice and be glad in it" (Ps. 118:24; Athanasius, *Commentary on Ps. 118*, cited in J. A. Hessey, *Sunday: Its Origin, History, and Present Obligation* [1889], 69).

II. The history of the Christian Sunday in the early church

A. The apostolic period (A.D. 29–100). The NT is the only source of information concerning the observance of Sunday in the apostolic period, and it has little to say about it. This may be because its observance only gradually displaced that of the Jewish Sabbath and did not become prevalent until the close of the apostolic period. There are, however, three unmistakable references in the NT to the Christian observance of Sunday (Acts 20:7; 1 Cor. 16:1–2; Rev. 1:10).

1. Paul's command to the Corinthian church. The apostle PAUL, writing to the CORINTHIANS (c. A.D. 55) "about the collection for God's people"—a contribution that he had undertaken to gather from the churches in the four provinces where he had labored, for the relief of the poverty-stricken Christians in Jerusalem—gave them the following command: "Do what I told the Galatian churches to do. On the first day of every week, each one of you should set aside a sum of money in keeping with his income, saving it up, so that when I come no collections will have to be made" (1 Cor. 16:1–2; cf. Acts 24:17; Rom. 15:25–28; 2 Cor. 9:1–5). As early as the 2nd cent., a collection for the poor was a regular part of the worship service on the Lord's Day (Justin Martyr, *First Apology* 67; see *ANF*, 1:186). This custom may have had its origin from Paul's command to the Corinthian church.

Even though Paul's words seem to mean that each individual was to lay aside his contribution at home (Gk. *par' heautō*) on the first day of the week, it is clear that the apostle regarded Sunday as an appropriate day for the laying aside of that which was to be given to the poor. The verb translated "saving it up" (*thēsaurizō* G2564) is derived from a noun meaning "treasure box or chest" (*thēsauros* G2565), which some think might refer to the treasury or church box where the collection was to be deposited. If so, the money set aside was brought on that day to the church when it assembled for worship (J. Moffatt, *The First Epistle of Paul to the Corinthians* [1938], 271). Paul points out to the Corinthians that he had given the same instructions to the churches of Galatia. While this passage does not expressly say that there was an assembly of the church on that day, it does indicate that Sunday was viewed as an appropriate day for the performance of religious duties, and therefore regarded in some sense as a sacred day (G. C. Findlay in *EGT*, 2:945).

2. Paul's visit at Troas. Paul's stay at TROAS, recorded in Acts 20:5–12, took place about two years after the writing of 1 Corinthians, as the apostle was on his way to Jerusalem, bearing the contributions of the Gentile churches to the poverty-stricken Christians in the Jewish capital. Paul and his companions arrived in Troas after the close of the Feast of Unleavened Bread and remained there for seven days (v. 6). On Sunday evening the church gathered "to break bread" and Paul gave a farewell address to them which lasted until midnight (v. 7). After the miraculous resuscitation of EUTYCHUS, Paul broke bread with them and continued to converse with the believers until daybreak (vv. 8–11).

This passage is significant because it relates what seems to have been a customary weekly assembly of the Christians on the first day of the week for the purpose of breaking bread and listening to an exposition of the Word of God. Even though Paul was in Troas seven days, this is the only assembly reported. It would seem that Paul remained a full week, even though he was in a hurry to get to Jerusalem, in order to meet with the believers on Sunday. The "breaking of bread" refers to a simple meal that was taken together by members of a local church in token of their fellowship with one another and in memory of Christ's last supper with his disciples (Acts 2:42, 46; 1 Cor. 10:16–21; 11:20–34; Jude 12). The meal was followed by the eating of the bread and the drinking of the wine in obedience to the Lord's command and in remembrance of his death (Matt. 26:26–28; Mk. 14:22–24; Lk. 22:19–20; 1 Cor. 11:23–26). The assembly at Troas also included a public discourse. It is evident that the protraction of the address until midnight, or to daybreak, was not the usual practice. It is implied, however, that preaching had become a regular part of the Christian worship on the first day of the week.

Some have held that the service described in Acts 20:7–12 was on Saturday, rather than Sunday, evening (A. T. Robertson, *Word Pictures in the New Testament*, 6 vols. [1930–33], 3:338–39). However, since Troas was a Gentile community, it is quite probable that Sunday evening is meant. This becomes almost certain when the expression used here is compared with its use in Jn. 20:19, where "the first day of the week" cannot possibly refer to Saturday evening, but must refer to Sunday evening. Thus this passage provides a connecting link between the first meeting of Jesus with his disciples on the evening of the resurrection day (Jn. 20:19–23; Lk. 24:36–43) and the established custom of the church of the 2nd and 3rd centuries of assembling together for worship on the first day of the week. It is significant that the meeting of Jesus with the disciples on the first Lord's Day, the meeting of Paul with the disciples at Troas, and the meeting of the disciples in succeeding generations, each took place on Sunday evening; each was observed by the breaking of bread; and each was characterized by a discourse on the Holy Scriptures.

3. John's vision on Patmos. The first vision of the book of Revelation, written during the latter part of the reign of NERO (c. 66) or of the reign of DOMITIAN (c. 95), was given to John "on the Lord's Day" (Rev. 1:10; see REVELATION, BOOK OF). Although some have argued that this is merely an alternative designation for the DAY OF THE LORD, used repeatedly in the OT and NT for the day of judgment (cf. A. Deissmann in *EncBib*, 3:2815; F. J. A. Hort, *The Apocalypse of St. John, I–III* [1908], 13), most scholars conclude that it is a reference to Sunday (H. B. Swete, *The Apocalypse of St. John*, 3rd ed. [1909], 13; R. H. Charles, *A Critical and Exegetical Commentary on the Revelation of St. John*, ICC, 2 vols. [1920], 1:23). This conclusion is established by the subsequent, frequent use of "the Lord's Day" in early Christian writings to refer to Sunday (e.g., *Didache* 14.1; Ignatius, *Magnesians* 9.1; Clement of Alexandria, *Stromata* 7.12; Tertullian, *On Idolatry* 14).

It is remarkable that John received this vision of the risen Lord on the day that had become hallowed by the resurrection of Christ and his appearances to his disciples. As John fell before the "Living One," who had been "dead" but was "alive for ever and ever" (Rev. 1:18), he became an example for all those who, in succeeding generations, kept the Lord's Day as the day of the week sacred to the memory of that same risen, living Christ.

B. The Ante-Nicene period (100–321)

1. From Ignatius to Irenaeus. IGNATIUS, a disciple of the apostle John, and the bishop of ANTIOCH OF SYRIA, wrote to the Magnesians in the early years of the 2nd cent., describing Christians with a Jewish background as those who "have come to the possession of a new hope, no longer observing the Sabbath, but living in observance of the Lord's Day, on which also our life has sprung up again by him and by his death" (*Magn.* 9.1–3).

The DIDACHE, a manual of Christian worship written during the first quarter of the 2nd cent., contains the following instructions regarding worship on the Lord's Day: "But every Lord's day do ye gather yourselves together, and break bread, and give thanksgiving after having confessed your transgressions, that your sacrifice may be pure" (*Did.* 14.1).

In the pseudonymous *Epistle of Barnabas*, written in the early part of the 2nd cent. (see BARNABAS, EPISTLE OF), the author interprets certain OT passages (Gen. 2:2–3; Ps. 90:4; Isa. 1:13) to mean that God will bring the present world to an end at the conclusion of six days of a thousand years, each by ushering in the seventh day, or thousand years, of rest at Christ's SECOND COMING, after which God will make a beginning of another world on the eighth day. The writer then concludes: "Wherefore we keep the eighth day with joyfulness, the day on which Jesus rose again from the dead" (*Barn.* 15.9).

PLINY the Younger, Roman governor of PONTUS and BITHYNIA, wrote a letter to the Emperor TRAJAN around 112, in which he asked for an imperial ruling with regard to the treatment of Christians against whom accusations had been made. He says: "But they declared that the sum of their guilt or error had amounted only to this, that on an appointed day they had been accustomed to meet before daybreak, and to recite a hymn antiphonally to Christ, as to a god, and to bind themselves by an oath, not for the commission of any crime but to abstain from theft, robbery, adultery and breach of faith, and not to deny a deposit when it was claimed" (Bettenson, *Documents*, 4–5). Although Pliny does not state that the appointed day for the Christians' accustomed meeting was Sunday, his description of its observance is so accurate that it is certain that it was the Lord's Day.

JUSTIN MARTYR, around the middle of the 2nd cent., describes the order of worship in the Christian assembly "on the day called Sunday." It included the reading of the Scriptures, a sermon, prayers, the celebration of the Lord's Supper, and an offering. Justin then proceeds to give two reasons why Christians assemble for worship on Sunday: (1) because it was the day on which God began his work of creation; and (2) because it was the day on which Jesus Christ rose from the dead (*First Apology* 67). In his *Dialogue with Trypho* (ch. 19), Justin explains why Christians do not observe the Jewish Sabbath by asserting that true Sabbath observance under the new covenant consists in turning from sin. Later (ch. 41) he states that the command to circumcise children on the eighth day "was a type of the true circumcision, by which we are circumcised from deceit and iniquity through him who rose from the dead on the first day after the Sabbath, our Lord Jesus Christ" (ch. 41).

Other early testimonies include Dionysius, Bishop of Corinth, who in a letter to the church of Rome (c. A.D. 170) writes, "Today we have passed the Lord's holy day, in which we have read your epistle" (Eusebius, *Eccl. Hist.* 4.23.11); and IRENAEUS, Bishop of Lyons (c. A.D. 178), who wrote to the bishop of Rome with regard to the controversial question whether Easter should be celebrated on Sunday and commented, "The mystery of the Lord's resurrection may not be celebrated on any other day than the Lord's day" (Eusebius, *Eccl. Hist.* 5.24). All of these citations show that throughout the 2nd cent. Sunday was observed as a day of Christian worship in commemoration of the resurrection of Christ. There is no indication that

Sunday was observed during this time as a day of rest or that its observance was in any way connected with the observance of the Jewish Sabbath.

2. From Clement of Alexandria to Peter of Alexandria. CLEMENT OF ALEXANDRIA, at the close of the 2nd cent. and the beginning of the 3rd, was the first of the patristic writers to apply the spiritualizing method of ALEXANDRIA in support of the observance of Sunday. A passing reference in Plato's *Republic* to an eighth day is interpreted to mean that Plato spoke prophetically of the Lord's Day (*Stromata* 5.14). Later on in the same work, he speaks of a Christian as a true Gnostic: "He, in fulfillment of the precept, according to the Gospel, keeps the Lord's day, when he abandons an evil disposition, and assumes that of a Gnostic, glorifying the Lord's resurrection in himself" (7.12). In thus spiritualizing both Sunday and the Sabbath, he implies that the Lord's Day bears some analogy to the Hebrew Sabbath.

TERTULLIAN, the great apologist of the first quarter of the 3rd cent., in writing to Christians, insisted that "We have nothing to do with sabbaths or the other Jewish festivals, much less with those of the heathen. We have our own solemnities, the Lord's day, for instance, and Pentecost" (*On Idolatry* 14). In writing to pagans, however, Tertullian contrasts the Christian observance of Sunday with the pagan rites connected with the worship of the sun, and suggests that there is a resemblance between the Christian observance of Sunday and the Jewish observance of Saturday as a day of rest (*Ad nationes* 1.13). His most famous statement is found in another work addressed to Christians, where he says: "We, on the day of the Lord's resurrection, ought to guard not only against kneeling, but every office of solicitude, deferring even our businesses lest we give any place to the devil" (*De oratione* 23). Tertullian, then, was the first Christian writer to urge the cessation of labor on Sunday. He did not, however, base it on the Sabbath command, but on the need to preserve the Lord's Day as a day of worship.

ORIGEN, Clement's successor in the school of Alexandria, lived during the first half of the 3rd cent. Like his predecessor, he gave a spiritual interpretation to the observance of Sunday. In his famous defense of Christianity, he writes: "If it be objected to us on this subject that we ourselves are accustomed to observe certain days, as for example the Lord's day ... I have to answer that to the perfect Christian, who is ever in his thoughts, words, and deeds serving his natural Lord, God the Word,

Synagogue at Korazin (2nd–3rd cent. A.D.). Worship in the synagogues influenced both the style and setting of early Christian worship.

all his days are the Lord's, and he is always keeping the Lord's day" (*Against Celsus* 22). In spite of Origen's idealistic interpretation, he does bear witness to the Christian observance of the Lord's Day.

The Syriac document of the DIDASCALIA APOSTOLORUM, or *The Teaching of the Apostles*, probably written in the second half of the 3rd cent., affirms that the Lord's Day was appointed by the apostles as a day of Christian worship. The statement reads: "The Apostles further appointed: On the first day of the week let there be service, and the reading of the Holy Scriptures, and the oblation: because on the first day of the week our Lord rose from the dead, and on the first day of the week he ascended up to heaven, and on the first day of the week he will appear at last with the angels of heaven" (*ANF*, 8:668). Cyprian, Bishop of Carthage, in a synodical epistle from the third council of Carthage (A.D. 253), speaks of the Jewish practice of CIRCUMCISION on the eighth day as prefiguring the Christian observance of the Lord's Day (*Epistles* 64.4). Peter, Bishop of Alexandria, bears witness to the observance of Sunday at the beginning of the 4th cent. He writes: "We keep the Lord's Day as a day of joy, because of him who rose thereon" (*The Canonical Epistle*, canon 15). He concludes the testimony of the 3rd-cent. Christian writers to the continued observance of Sunday as a day of Christian worship based on the resurrection of Christ and the apostolic tradition.

III. The history of the Christian Sunday in the medieval church

A. The early medieval period (321–590). In 321 the Roman Emperor Constantine issued an edict that introduced a new era in the history of the Christian Sunday. Before this time Sunday had been observed by Christians as a day of worship, and, to some extent, also as a day of rest. It now became an officially recognized and prescribed day of rest. The edict permitted people living in the country to "attend to agriculture," but commanded that "all judges, city-people and craftsmen shall rest on the venerable day of the Sun" (Bettenson, *Documents*, 26).

1. Christian writings. EUSEBIUS, Bishop of Caesarea, argued in his *Ecclesiastical History* (5.23) that the decision to celebrate Easter on Sunday was based on apostolic tradition. He extolled Constantine for his pious observance of the Lord's Day and states that the emperor's appointment of Sunday as a day of rest for all his subjects was "to lead all mankind to the worship of God" (*Life of Constantine* 4.18). Although Eusebius does not base the observance of Sunday on the Sabbath commandment, he does draw an analogy between the Lord's Day and the Hebrew Sabbath (*Commentary on the 91st Psalm* [i.e., 92nd in Heb. Bible]).

Athanasius, Bishop of Alexandria at the same time as Eusebius, applies the words of Ps. 118:24, "This is the day the LORD has made; let us rejoice and be glad in it," to the Lord's Day (Hessey, *Sunday*, 69). In another work he declares that the Sabbath, the end of the old creation, has deceased, and the Lord's Day, the commencement of the new creation, has set in (*The Sabbath and Circumcision*, quoted in Hessey, *Sunday*, 68–69).

EPIPHANIUS, Bishop of Constantia, Cyprus, in the latter half of the 4th cent., contrasts the Sabbath of the law with "the Great Sabbath," which is Christ himself (*Against Heresies* 30.32). He asserts that the Lord's Day and the observance of Wednesday and Friday as fast days were established by the apostles (*Expos. fid. cathol.* 22).

Gregory, Bishop of Nyssa, and Ambrose, Bishop of Milan, speak of both the Hebrew Sabbath and the Christian Sunday as allegorical of rest from sin. Gregory calls them "sister days" (*De castig.* quoted in Hessey, *Sunday*, 72). Ambrose prohibited fasting on the Lord's Day (*Epistles* 13, quoted in William B. Trevelyan, *Sunday* [1902], 26).

AUGUSTINE, Bishop of Hippo, writing at the close of the 4th cent., condemns the practice of the MANICHEANS of fasting on the Lord's Day (*Ep. 36, To Casulanus* 11). In another epistle he distinguishes between the Jewish Sabbath and the Christian Sunday, but sees them both as typical days, the Sabbath of the repose of the dead, and Sunday of the resurrection of the dead (*Ep. 55*, 12–13). Similarly, CHRYSOSTOM, Bishop of Constantinople, warns Christians against sabbatizing with the Jews (*Comm. on I Cor.*, hom. 43), but maintains that Christian as well as Jewish ordinances have a spiritual interpretation (*Comm. on Matt.*, hom. 39).

JEROME, at the beginning of the 5th cent., describes the activities of certain Egyptian Christians on Sunday: "Every Lord's day they spend their whole time in prayer and reading" (*Letter* 22). Paula and her companions, however, are described as follows: "On the Lord's day only they proceeded to the church beside which they lived, each company following its own mother-superior. Returning home

The Byzantine Church of Hagia Sophia in Istanbul (Constantinople). Emperor Constantine officially declared Sunday to be a day of rest in A.D. 321.

in the same order, they then devoted themselves to their allotted tasks, and made garments either for themselves or else for others" (*Letter* 108).

The APOSTOLIC CONSTITUTIONS, a manual of church order written about this time, provides valuable information concerning the status of Sunday observance at the beginning of the 5th cent. After giving directions concerning daily worship, it enjoins Christians: "And on the day of the Lord's resurrection, which is the Lord's day, meet more diligently, sending praise to God that made the universe by Jesus, and sent him to us, and condescended to let him suffer, and raised him from the dead" (2.7.59). Fasting and labor were forbidden on both the Sabbath and Sunday (5.3.20; 8.4.33). Sunday has begun to be associated with other Christian festivals and with the Jewish Sabbath, which is observed in a similar way; and Sunday observance is now being enforced by ecclesiastical rules.

2. Church councils and legislation. During the 4th, 5th, and 6th centuries a number of church councils and imperial laws sought to enforce the proper observance of Sunday. The Council of Nicaea (A.D. 325) passed a canon to make uniform the custom of standing for prayer on the Lord's Day (20th Canon). The Council of Gangra (c. 350), condemned fasting on the Lord's Day and those who despised the House of God and frequented schismatic assemblies. The Council of Laodicea (363), commands Christians not to observe Saturday, the Jewish Sabbath, but Sunday as the day of rest. In 368, Theodosius the Great made an edict, repeating Constantine's permission of the manumission of slaves on Sunday and prohibiting trials before arbitrators, so that the sacred rites of religion should not be violated "on the day of the Sun, which our fathers rightly named the Lord's day" (quoted by Hessey, *Sunday*, 84).

The Fourth Council of Carthage (436) threatened excommunication for anyone who left church during the preaching, forbade fasting on the Lord's day, and discouraged attendance at the Games of the Public Circus on Sunday (Hessey, *Sunday*, 82). In 425, Theodosius the Younger had passed a law forbidding all games on Sunday and on other church festivals; in 469, another law was passed, forbidding the celebration of the games on Sunday even if that was the emperor's birthday (Hessey, *Sunday*, 83–84). In 538, the Third Council of Orleans forbade all agricultural work on Sunday, but condemned the practice of abstinence from journeys or of preparing meals as Judaistic (Trevelyan, *Sunday*, 46). The Second Council of Macon in 585, however, prohibited work and commanded worship on Sunday on the authority of the OT Sabbath regulations (Hessey, *Sunday*, 87–88).

During the period between Constantine and Gregory the Great, Sunday became a legalized day of rest, enforced by ecclesiastical and secular law; worship on the Lord's day was enjoined by church councils and imperial edicts; a number of other festivals came to be observed; and Sunday came to be less sharply distinguished from the Hebrew Sabbath.

B. The later medieval period (590–1517)

1. Christian writings. Among Christian writers during this period, the observance of Sunday gradually came to be based on the OT Sabbath commandments. As Christianity became more and more legalistic, it became quite natural for Christians to justify their legalism from the OT laws. So it was that, as Paul Cotton observes, "the Christian Sunday became a fixed and established institution with all the authority of the Roman government and the Hebrew Scriptures behind it" (*From Sabbath to Sunday*, 155).

Gregory the Great, who became Bishop of Rome in 590, wrote in most emphatic language against sabbatarianism, which he called a doctrine of Antichrist (*Epistles* 11.3). Similarly, Theodulphus, Bishop of Orleans in the 8th cent., pled for the observance of Sunday in accordance with its character as a day of Christian worship, not on the grounds of the Hebrew Sabbath law (Hessey, *Sunday*, 93).

The pleas of such men went unheeded. Alcuin, at the close of the 8th cent., based the observance of Sunday on the same foundation as the observance of the Hebrew Sabbath. He asserts: "Christian custom has transferred the observance of the Sabbath to the Lord's Day" (*Homily* 18, *post Pentec*.). Bernard of Clairvaux in the 12th cent. grounded both the Lord's Day and other holy days on the fourth commandment (Hessey, *Sunday*, 89–90). Peter Alphonsus, in the same century, was the first to use the term "Christian Sabbath" of the Lord's Day (Hessey, *Sunday*, 90).

Thomas Aquinas in the 13th cent. was the first to apply the distinctions of moral and ceremonial law to the observance of Sunday. He distinguished in the fourth commandment the moral element of an obligatory stated worship of God from the ceremonial element of the seventh day, and said: "The observance of Sunday under the new law follows the keeping of the Sabbath, not in consequence of a legal precept, but from the decision of the Church and the custom of Christians" (S. E. Warren, *The Sunday Question* [1890], 109). Tostatus, Bishop of Avila in the 14th cent., laid down a whole series of ordinances based on the regulations concerning the manna in Exod. 16:31–35, including prohibitions against hiring a musician, cooking a feast, washing dishes, traveling to places other than a shrine, or working for profit on the Lord's Day (Hessey, *Sunday*, 91–92).

2. Church councils and legislation. Both church councils and secular rulers imposed restrictions on the observance of Sunday similar to those imposed on the observance of the Jewish Sabbath. The Council of Clovishoff, held in England in 747, forbade traveling on the Lord's Day (Hessey, *Sunday*, 89). The Constitutions of Egbert in 749 forbade all work on Sunday under severe penalties (Hessey, *Sunday*, 89). In France, Charlemagne promulgated a decree in 789 that prohibited all ordinary labor on Sunday as a breach of the fourth commandment (Charles Huestis, *Sunday in the Making* [1929], 115). The exemption granted by Constantine to agricultural labor was repealed by the Emperor Leo Philosophus in 910, but he based his prohibition, not on the fourth commandment, but on apostolic appointment of Sunday (Hessey, *Sunday*, 94). The Archbishop of Canterbury, in the 14th cent., ordered "abstinence from secular works … on the sacred day of the Lord," but warned the people not to meet before Saturday evening for fear that they "partake in the Jewish profession" (ibid.).

There developed in the later medieval period an ecclesiastical sabbatarianism. Sunday became known as the Christian Sabbath; its observance was grounded on the fourth commandment or on the canons of the church; and its observance was enforced by severe ecclesiastical and secular restrictions. Other holy days with similar restrictions were imposed on the people, with the result that neither they nor the Lord's Day were observed as days of worship, but rather deteriorated into mere holidays devoted to idleness and dissipation (Warren, *The Sunday Question*, 121).

IV. The history of the Christian Sunday in the modern church

A. The Reformation Period (1517–1648)

1. The teaching of the Reformers. Martin Luther maintained that the believer in Christ was not subject to laws or ceremonies; for the believer all time was holy, so there was no need of festivals such as Sunday or the Sabbath. He realized, however, the benefits to be derived from a weekly day of rest and worship. In the *Larger Catechism*, he taught that the working classes needed a weekly day of rest so that there might be time for worship, but he insists that "no day is better or more excellent than another." In his *Table Talk*, he speaks out against making Sunday observance rest on a Jewish foundation: "If anywhere the day is made holy for the mere day's sake — if anywhere anyone sets up its observance on a Jewish foundation, then I order you to work on it, to ride on it, to dance on it, to feast on it, to do anything that shall remove this encroachment on Christian liberty."

Ulrich Zwingli shared Luther's view that the worship of God should not be tied down to any one day. He wrote: "If we would have the Lord's day so confined to a certain time, that it shall be thought wicked to transfer it to another time … this day, so scrupulously limited to a certain day, would impose on us a ceremony. For we are in no way bound to time, but time ought so to serve us, as to make it lawful, and permitted to each church, when necessity urges … to transfer the solemnity and rest of the Lord's day or sabbath to some other day" (Warren, *The Sunday Question*, 124–25).

John Calvin regarded the Hebrew Sabbath as typical of the entire rest and peace granted to Christians under the gospel. It was a part of the "shadow of things to come" (Col. 2:17 KJV) fulfilled in Christ, who is the body, the whole essence of the truth. He concludes: "This is not contented with one day, but requires the whole course of our lives, until being completely dead to ourselves, we are filled with the life of God. Christians, therefore, should have nothing to do with a superstitious observance of days" (*Institutes of the Christian Religion* 2.8). Calvin, however, saw the advisability of setting apart one day in seven as a day for Christian worship, but treats the observance of Sunday as a matter of expediency, and not an adherence to a shadowy ceremony.

John Knox agreed substantially with the opinions of Luther, Zwingli, and Calvin regarding the observance of Sunday. He did, however, advocate a greater strictness in keeping Sunday as a day of worship (*Book of Discipline*). All of the Reformers insisted that Sunday observance should not be based on the OT Sabbath commandment or in any way connected with the Hebrew Sabbath. The observance of Sunday was to be maintained as a matter of expediency, for it afforded rest for the body and an opportunity for united worship of God, especially in view of the fact that the day had been previously chosen for these purposes.

2. Creedal statements. The creedal statements produced in the post-Reformation period are significant, for they represent not simply the opinions of individual men, but the views of various groups with respect to the nature and obligation of Sunday observance.

The *Confession of Augsburg*, produced by Luther and Melanchthon in 1530, says in part: "For they that think that the observation [*sic*] of the Lord's Day was appointed by the authority of the Church, instead of the Sabbath, as necessary, are greatly deceived. The Scripture ... has abrogated the Sabbath. And yet, because it was requisite to appoint a certain day that the people might know when they ought to come together, it appears that the Church did for that purpose appoint the Lord's day" (Philip Schaff, *The Creeds of Christendom*, 3 vols., 6th ed. [1919], 3:69).

The *Second Helvetic Confession*, prepared by Henry Bullinger and edited by Theodore Beza in 1566, was a formulation of the faith of the Reformed churches in Switzerland. In an article relating to the observance of Sunday, it reads: "Although religion be not tied unto time, yet can it not be planted and exercised without a due dividing and allotting out of time. Every church, therefore, does choose unto itself a certain time for public prayers, and for the preaching of the Gospel, and for the celebration of the sacraments. In regard hereof, we see that in the ancient churches there were not only certain set hours in the week appointed for meetings, but that also the Lord's Day itself, ever since the apostles' time, was consecrated to religious exercises and to a holy rest; which also is now very well observed by our churches" (Schaff, *Creeds*, 3:899).

In an entirely different vein, the *Westminster Confession of Faith* (1643) states: "As it is of the law of nature, that, in general, a due proportion of time be set apart for the worship of God; so, in his word, by a positive, moral, and perpetual commandment, binding all men in all ages, he hath particularly appointed one day in seven for a Sabbath, to be kept holy unto him; which, from the beginning of the world to the Resurrection of Christ, was the last day of the week; and from the Resurrection of Christ was changed into the first day of the week, which in Scripture is called the Lord's Day, and is to be continued to the end of the world as the Christian Sabbath" (Schaff, *Creeds*, 3:658–59).

3. Puritanism. The *Westminster Confession* was the product of English Puritanism, which arose in England in the 17th cent. as a protest against the polity and practices of the Church of England that the Puritans regarded as contrary to Scripture. Since they held that only what was specifically commanded in Scripture should be believed or practiced, and since they did not find any command in the NT to observe the Lord's Day, they boldly identified it with the Sabbath of the fourth commandment and enforced its observance with all the rigor of the ancient Hebrew Sabbath (H. R. Gamble, *Sunday and the Sabbath* [1901], 121–22). A book entitled *The True Doctrine of the Sabbath*, written by Nicholas Bownd in 1595, was very influential in promulgating the Puritan doctrine of sabbatarianism. He not only based the observance of Sunday on the fourth commandment, which he regarded as moral and perpetual, but he set forth specific prohibitions of various kinds of labor on the Lord's Day.

The Puritan teachings affected other countries besides England. They were accepted by the Church and the Parliament of Scotland. They were introduced into Holland and became a part of the Synod of Dort held in Holland in 1618. Finally, the Puritans brought their Christian Sabbath to America, where it became the prevailing view for centuries.

B. The modern period (1648 to the present)

1. Sunday on the continent of Europe. Even though the Synod of Dort had adopted the view of the Puritans that Sunday was the Christian Sabbath, and persons such as J. L. Mosheim advocated the view that Sunday was an institution entirely distinct from the Sabbath and that it had been founded by the apostles of Christ under divine guidance, these views were never widely accepted on the continent of Europe. The view that prevailed was a purely ecclesiastical one, that is, that the observance of Sunday was based solely on the authority of the church. E. W. Hengstenberg, for example, maintained that the Sabbath was a Jewish institution that had been abrogated by Christ. The Sabbath may have suggested Sunday as a weekly day of worship. Sunday, however, was not instituted by Christ or by his apostles; it arose simply from the spontaneous feeling of the early church, guided by the Holy Spirit (Hessey, *Sunday*, 181–83).

The practical result of such a subjective view of the basis of obligation to observe Sunday was a widespread desecration of the Lord's Day on the continent of Europe. The teachings of the Reformers regarding Christian liberty, in spite of their exhortations to keep the day as a day of worship, led in many cases to antinomianism in practice as well as in principle. For a brief time at the close of the 18th cent., France abolished Sunday as a weekly day of rest. In other places Sunday was treated much like any other day. For the most part this condition has prevailed to the present time.

2. Sunday in England and Scotland. Due to the teachings of the Puritans in these countries, a fuller consideration of the subject of Sunday observance took place, which resulted in a more wholesome and Christian observance of the day, especially during the 17th cent. and the early part of the 18th. After a period of spiritual and moral decline in the first half of the 18th cent., the evangelical revival under John Wesley and George Whitefield brought about a better observance of the Lord's Day. During the century following the evangelical revival, sabbatarian and ecclesiastical views of Sunday observance vied with each other. Bishop Hessey's monumental work in the middle of the 19th cent. was an attempt to reconcile these two opposing views by basing the observance of the Lord's Day neither on the authority of the OT Sabbath command nor on the authority of the church, but on the authority of Christ and the teaching and practice of the apostles. In spite of such efforts to recover a proper observance of the day, there was a manifest decline in church attendance and in any spiritual observance of the day during the 20th cent.

Nearly the same state of affairs has been characteristic of Scotland, where for more than two centuries the Christian Sabbath of the Puritans was taught and enforced with a great deal of rigor. By the beginning of the 20th cent., a widespread reaction set in to these Puritan teachings and practices.

3. Sunday in the United States. The Puritans who came to America established their Christian Sabbath as an integral part of their social and religious life. To insure the due observance of their sacred day, they enacted laws, which came to be known as "Blue Laws," laws even stricter than those formulated by the ancient Jews to enforce the observance of their Sabbath. Beginning at sundown on Saturday evening, all forms of work or recreation were strictly forbidden under pain of severe penalties. Although such restrictions were regarded by many as altogether too strict, to those who gladly accepted them, the Sabbath must have been a welcome respite. As Alice M. Earle expresses it, "Sweet to the Pilgrims and to their descendants was the hush of their calm Saturday night, and their still, tranquil Sabbath—sign and token to them, not only of the weekly rest ordained in the creation, but of the eternal rest to come. The universal quiet and peace of the community showed the primitive instinct of a pure, simple devotion, the sincere religion which knew no compromise in spiritual things, no half-way obedience to God's Word, but rest absolutely on the Lord's Day as was commanded. No work, no play, no idle strolling was known; no sign of human life or motion was seen except the necessary care of the patient cattle and other dumb beasts, the orderly and quiet going to and from the meeting, and at the nooning, a visit to the churchyard to stand by the side of the silent dead. This absolute obedience to the letter, as well as to the spirit of God's Word, was one of the most typical traits of the character of the Puritans, and appeared to them to be one of the most vital points of their religion" (*The Sabbath in Puritan New England* [1893], 258).

The influence of Puritanism on American religious life cannot be overemphasized. The Christian Sabbath of the Puritans, so much a part of their religious life, worked itself into the hearts and minds of the American people and became a standard of the ideal Sunday of America for many generations. Beginning in the 19th cent., however, a marked reaction set in to the strict Sunday of the Puritans, especially to the laws that had been enacted to enforce its observance. This natural and inevitable reaction was augmented by the importation to America of the Continental Sunday. Crafts and Waffle, both writing in 1885, decry the growing desecration of the Lord's Day at that time. A report made in 1917 to the Federal Council of the Churches of Christ noted that while Sunday was being observed as a day of rest, its observance as a day of worship was declining (*Christian Cooperation and World Redemption*, 149). In 1933, R. H. Martin wrote: "America faces the peril of losing the Christian Sabbath. The holy day of our fathers is fast becoming a day for secular business and amusements, and little is being done to save it" (*The Day: A Manual on the Christian Sabbath* [1933], preface).

In spite of the efforts of individuals such as R. H. Martin, and of organizations such as the Lord's Day Alliance, to promote the due observance of Sunday as a day of rest and worship, the reaction to the strict observance of Sunday as characteristic of the Puritans has continued, and the observance of the day has continued to become more lax. This neglect of Sunday observance may be correlated with a general decline in spiritual matters. Even when renewed interest in spiritual things has been manifest, there does not seem to be any stricter observance of the Lord's Day. Sunday has, rather, become a day of business and recreation, with only an hour or two in the morning set aside for worship, and that only by devout Christians.

V. Conclusion. Many different views have been held regarding the nature of the Lord's Day and the Christian's obligation to observe it. These may be comprehended under three general classifications: sabbatarian, ecclesiastical, and utilitarian.

The sabbatarian view holds Sunday to be a Christian Sabbath and its observance to be based on the fourth commandment of the Decalogue. Its proponents, however, maintain that it is not the seventh day that is important in the Sabbath command, but the principle of one day in seven. Otherwise, the command is held to be moral and binding on all people. To be consistent, others have insisted that, if this command is binding on all people in all ages, then the seventh day should be observed. This is the view of Seventh-day Adventists and Seventh-day Baptists.

The purely ecclesiastical view holds that the Christian is to observe Sunday solely on the authority of the church. A modified ecclesiastical view is that Sunday was established by Christ through his apostles. They point to the NT references to the practice of observing the Lord's Day as a weekly day of worship in the early church.

The Reformers and modern dispensationalists have insisted that the Christian is not under obligation to observe any day, but for expediency it is good to observe the day.

The biblical view seems to incorporate some of each of these views. Christianity did have its roots in Judaism. It was, therefore, to be expected that Sunday would borrow many of its features from the Hebrew Sabbath. The divine institution of the Sabbath at the close of creation indicates the human need for a weekly day of rest. The fourth commandment was given specifically to Israel and applies in the strictest sense only to that nation. It does, however, contain principles that are moral and eternal. It recognizes the duty of man to worship his Creator, for which stated times for worship are needed. Jesus regarded the Sabbath as a provision for human need and not as a burdensome legal requirement. Neither he nor his apostles even enjoin the Sabbath on their followers. According to many expositors, Paul clearly indicates that the Sabbath was part of the old covenant that was done away in Christ. There is not the slightest hint that Christ or the apostles changed the Sabbath from the seventh to the first day of the week.

The NT shows that the first day of the week was made especially significant by the resurrection of Christ and his appearances to his disciples on that day. Other NT references to the first day of the week indicate that it was observed as a day of Christian worship in NT times. References in the writings of the early church fathers show its continued observance as a day of worship in the centuries following the NT age. Only gradually did it also become a day of rest, and this not before the 4th Christian century.

No specific command is given in the Bible to observe Sunday as a day of rest and worship. While ideally the Christian should observe every day as holy, and should need nothing except expediency and love to lead him to worship God, antinomian views have failed to motivate most people to observe regular times for worship. This writer believes that a true devotion to the Lord Jesus Christ will lead a Christian to observe the Lord's Day as a day when he turns from his ordinary weekday activities to worship the Lord in commemoration of Christ's resurrection from the dead and to engage in Christian service for his Lord.

(In addition to the works mentioned in the body of the article, see W. Thorn, *Eight Lectures on the Christian Sabbath* [1823]; F. Denison, *The Sabbath Institution Traced and Defended in Its History and Changes* [1855]; W. Milligan, *The Decalogue and the Lord's Day* [1866]; W. C. Wood, *Sabbath Essays* [1880]; M. Fuller, *The Lord's Day or Christian Sunday* [1883]; G. S. Gray, *Eight Studies of the Lord's Day* [1884]; W. W. Everts, *The Sabbath: Its Permanence, Promise and Defence* [1885]; W. D. Love, *Sabbath and Sunday* [1896]; S. W. Gamble, *Sunday, the True Sabbath of God* [1900]; J. D. Parker, *The Sabbath Transferred* [1900]; W. B. Dana, *A Day for Rest and Worship* [1911]; W. W. Mead, *The Modern Outcry against the Law* [1914]; A. A. Hodge, *The Day Changed and the Sabbath Preserved* [1916]; C. S. MacFarland, *Christian Cooperation and World Redemption* [1917]; United Lutheran Church, *The Sunday Problem* [1923]; V. J. Kelly, *Forbidden Sunday and Feastday Occupations* [1943]; S. Bacchiocchi, *From Sabbath to Sunday: A Historical Investigation of the Rise of Sunday Observance in Early Christianity* [1977]; R. T. Beckwith and W. Stott, *This Is the Day: The Biblical Doctrine of the Christian Sunday in its Jewish and Early Church Setting* [1978]; D. A. Carson, ed., *From Sabbath to Lord's Day: A Biblical, Historical, and Theological Investigation* [1982]; S. Bacchiocchi, *The Sabbath under Crossfire: A Biblical Analysis of Recent Sabbath/Sunday Developments* [1998]; B. A. Ray, *Celebrating the Sabbath: Finding Rest in a Restless World* [2000].)   H. WATERMAN

Lord's Prayer. The traditional name given to the prayer Jesus taught his disciples, as recorded in Matt. 6:9–13 and Lk. 11:2–4. Without a doubt this is the most widely known passage from the Bible and has been included in almost all of the Christian catechisms and liturgies since the days of the APOSTOLIC FATHERS. So familiar is it that in many languages it is usually known by its first line (e.g., Lat. *Pater noster*, Ger. *Unser Vater*, Dutch *Onze Vader*, Spanish *Padre nuestro*).

  I. The parallel texts
 II. Organization and outline
    A. Invocation
    B. First petition
    C. Second petition
    D. Third petition
    E. Fourth petition
    F. Fifth petition
    G. Sixth petition
    H. Seventh petition
    I. Doxology and close
III. The biblical theology of the prayer
IV. Its place in the church

I. The parallel texts. The text of the prayer is given in Matthew's narrative of the SERMON ON THE MOUNT, which Jesus preached to a large crowd on the N shore of the Sea of Galilee. There is strong indication that the original language of the prayer was ARAMAIC. The version of the prayer given by

Luke is not set in the same historical situation but included in that portion traditionally known as the Perean Period after Jesus' departure from Galilee. The Lukan version is shorter and incorporated in a general discourse on prayer (Lk. 11:1–13). There is no question that the Lord's Prayer was repeated by Jesus on any number of occasions, so the older critical argument against the authenticity of either passage is totally without merit.

A large number of MSS, including the late Greek minuscules of certain groupings and some VULGATE texts, end the prayer in Matthew with "Amen." Other phrases of an expanded doxology also are found, most of which appear to have begun as interpolations and insertions from liturgies. Sahidic versions of Upper Egypt (3rd cent. A.D.) and the DIDACHE read, "because yours is the kingdom." Four or five lesser versions omit the rest of the ending, but almost all the Vulgate and late Greek MSS continue with, "and the power and the glory unto the ages. Amen." This full doxology has been incorporated into almost all later translations of the text of the prayer.

Strangely enough, few extensive critical alterations in the body of the Matthew text have been proposed. However, there are a number of readings extant in the MSS that show attempts to bring the shorter Lukan version into agreement with the Matthean. The argument as to which form was original is without much validity, since each recorded his remembrance and the two are sufficiently similar to have been certainly repeated in variant forms. Many attempts have been made to justify and unite the two strands of the tradition, but so far unsuccessfully. The liturgical emphasis in the prayer has been overdone by a number of writers, but such a motivation does exist in many of the ancient prayers in both OT and NT. There is no doubt that the prayer was repeated as a devotional exercise and used in the corporate worship, and the two forms must have been dominant in various localities. Whether this is sufficient explanation for the two texts to exist seems irrelevant. The fact is that they did and that they were recorded in the inspired word.

II. Organization and outline

A. Introduction. The address or invocation of the prayer follows in both cases a discourse on PRAYER by Jesus. The early church seems to have adopted certain mixed liturgical phrases in Aramaic and Greek (cf. Rom. 8:15). Although there is evidence of the familiar form of address to God in Jewish

The Lord's Prayer written in Bariba, Cherokee, and Moore. From the Pater Noster Church in Jerusalem.

prayer, it is more likely that Jesus here utilized the common piety of the people. The specific sense in which God's FATHERHOOD is interpreted has been a source of some debate. The three primary opinions are that the address refers to God's creative fatherhood (Deut. 32:6 et al.), to God's special relationship to Israel (Jer. 3:4 et al.), or to God's fatherhood by virtue of redemption (Isa. 63:16). Suffice it to say that none of these forms of address appears to have been popular within rabbinic Judaism until after the Christian era began.

The additional phrase "who is in heaven" is characteristic of the qualifying usage of both Judaism and the Gospel of Matthew. It is quite probable that the usual form of the prayer as remembered in the early church was simply "Father," and Jesus may have used this simple vocative frequently. The Aramaic ABBA is found in early Christian liturgies. The MSS are practically unanimous in supporting the reading "Father." At one stroke the dual errors of pantheism and deism are rejected and the Christian's worship is directed toward a personal, objective, and living God. The phrase in Matthew does not detract from the force of this expression but simply qualifies it in the minds of the Jewish hearers.

B. First petition. "May your name be held in reverence" refers back to the giving of the COVENANT name Yahweh (Exod. 3:13–14; see GOD, NAMES OF) and to the third commandment of the Decalogue (20:7). God's name in the Bible is not merely his appellation but the characteristic REVELATION of himself to people. All the perfections and attributes he has disclosed in his covenant and his working in history are summarized in the knowledge of his name. To defile or deface, subvert or dishonor the divine name is to reject the SOVEREIGNTY OF GOD. In this and the two subsequent petitions the passive voice of the verbs is employed while the later petitions switch to the active. Appeals and exhortations for the "blessing of the name" were commonplace in Jewish prayers of the time. Although an eschatological aspect is involved, it is not the foremost one. The hallowing or sanctifying of the name implies no supernatural practice but simply refers to the recognition in every area of life in the cosmos of the sovereign presence and HOLINESS of God. The petition places no limit of time or space in which God's name is to be kept holy—the universality of the prayer is immediate and all encompassing.

C. Second petition. "May your kingdom come." Few biblical concepts are as all-pervasive as the KINGDOM OF GOD. The divine kingship in the OT has been carefully studied in contemporary theological works. The same importance is attached to it in the comprehension of the gospel narratives. Jesus was above all the heavenly exemplar, the King of the Jews, and as such his position as the final ruler of the house of David is emphasized repeatedly in the NT (Matt. 21). The wish invites the eschatological fullness, the final completion of the coming of the kingdom. The reference is to the messianic kingdom. It was brought to effect in Christ and will be completed wholly at the PAROUSIA.

The assertion that this was a specifically Jewish notion is without warrant, for God is rarely summoned as Israel's king either in or out of the rabbinical tradition. What the Jewish liturgies seek is the reformation and triumph of the Davidic kingdom. In some few versions and MSS the text of Luke is altered to read, "may your Holy Spirit descend upon us and cleanse us." The earliest substitution of this reading dates from the 3rd cent. Such an emphasis of the catharsis of the Spirit was popular during the high Middle Ages (e.g., St. Joachim of Floria, c. 1202), and the future often was portrayed as the Age of the Holy Spirit, a time of cleansing, renewal, and reformation of the monastic institution. Such interpolations were derived from liturgical phrases introduced into the text as glosses.

D. Third petition. "May your will be done." The will of God is the goal of Christian ETHICS and the norm of Christian OBEDIENCE. The will of God is revealed only in the Scriptures as inspired and pertains to the creation law order which God has ordained. The complete fulfillment of God's will on earth is an eschatological end. The perceptive teaching of the Scripture on God's will must be applied and reapplied in each situation by the people of God.

E. Fourth petition. "As in heaven so upon earth." This is a continuation and extension of the third request, and details the cases in which God's word and will are active. The idea of HEAVEN as a location is inextricable from the doctrine that it is the place and status where God's will is carried out perfectly in all respects. Thus earth, the sphere of human activity, would become the total environment of God's will. (The third and fourth petitions are lacking in Luke's version.)

F. Fifth petition. "Our daily bread, give us this day," is based on a common Semitic ideal, the royal or divine provision for the needs of the subjects (this and the remaining petitions have active rather than passive verbal forms). The term *epiousios* has been found only once in secular classical texts (F. Preisigke, *Sammelbuch griechische Urkunden aus Ägypten* [1915–1950], 5224, 20), and even that occurrence is doubtful. The word's etymology is disputed, and at least four major interpretations have been proposed: (1) "necessary for existence, needful for life" (as early as ORIGEN and CHRYSOSTOM); (2) "for this current day" (first proposed by A. Debrunner); (3) "for the following day," referring to a "daily" ration (H. Grotius and many after him); (4) "for tomorrow, the future" (as early as Cyril of Alexandria). The last of these derives the term from *eimi*, "to go, come" (rather than from *eimi*, "to be"), thus "the coming bread," and is popular among scholars who stress the eschatological thrust of Jesus' teaching in general and of the Lord's Prayer in particular (e.g., J. Jeremias, *New Testament Theology, Part One: The Proclamation of Jesus* [1971] 199–201, who interprets the petition as a request for receiving the bread of the time of salvation now, in the midst of a world enslaved by Satan).

The old rendering "required for our food," or the like, is to be preferred. The purpose of the petition is to relieve anxiety about material concerns and to rest in God's provision alone. The passage may also allude to the "bread of life," with its eschatological implications—the desire for participation in the heavenly feast as an integral part of the request. However, although there must be some fulfillment of this petition in the parousia, there is also the simple day by day providence of God which is in view. Both views gain some credence from the material of the DEAD SEA SCROLLS, in which the communal meal fills a central role. (See further *TDNT*, 2:590–99; E. M. Yamauchi in *WTJ* 28 [1966]: 145–56; BDAG, 376–77.)

G. Sixth petition. "And forgive us our wrongs as we forgive those who have wronged us." The Lukan version specifically has "sin" (*hamartia* G281) rather than the Semitic usage of "debt" (*opheilēma* G4052, reflecting the moral sense of Aram. *ḥôbā*ʾ). This request is clearly in opposition to any concepts of either sinless perfection or neutrality; the doctrine of total DEPRAVITY is one of the most maligned by modern culture, but it is the very basis of both prayer and redemption. There is some evidence in the versions that the secondary FORGIVENESS (from God) is in the future, but it does not greatly alter the meaning of the text. Although there is not the least comparison of degree between the two forgivenesses, they are related, and in this sense God's mercy is to be reciprocated by human compassion. Such sensitive moral relationships are simply avoided in the DSS and rarely mentioned in the later rabbinic literature. The concurrence of divine and human forgiveness involves sin and not mere intrusion. The importance of the two activities is made plain in a number of passages. (The translation "trespass," found in some liturgical forms of the Lord's Prayer, is totally without warrant in the Greek text.)

H. Seventh petition. "And lead us not into hard trials but deliver us from evil," has in view the humility of entrustment to God's perseverance. The difficulties of the passage have caused a number of variants, including the rendering, "Let us not fall to temptation," found in certain ancient versions. The key term is Greek *peirasmos* G4280, which means the sorest kind of testing or trial; nowhere, unless qualified, does it denote a solicitation to evil (Heb. 3:8). The text can be compared to Jas. 1:13, where the subject is not testing, but TEMPTATION. The notion at the heart of the petition is that of escape from such difficulty, deliverance from such trials. In this sense it is similar to Rom. 8:23 and other passages. Since this deliverance from the presence of evil, whether moral or physical, was based upon an eschatological state and would signify the satisfaction of all the other petitions, it logically comes at the end of the prayer. In the second phrase (found only in Matthew), *tou ponērou*, "the evil," can easily be read in the sense of "the evil one" (so NIV; cf. Jn. 17:15).

I. Doxology and close. "Because yours is the kingdom and the power and the glory unto the ages. Amen." This addition is found in no ancient commentator or exegete. It is totally and completely an intrusion from liturgical sources. There is also the singular fact that the Gospels contain no doxologies ascribed to Jesus and they are foreign to either Jewish or Aramaic prayers. It was probably an ancient response of the congregation. In both the *Didache* and the early 3rd and 4th cent. liturgies, a number of doxological phrases were said in the prayers, the congregation answering aloud antiphonally to the deacon or presbyter. For the reason that it is so much a part of the heritage of the church throughout the ages, it is not a detraction to the text as long as it is an acknowledged gloss of later origin. In both Matthew and Luke, the passages that follow continue points of issue raised in the prayer. The whole was not then a spiritual exercise but an instruction given to be followed.

III. The Biblical theology of the prayer. It has been stated repeatedly that the prayer is an epitome of all of Jesus' teachings. The assumption is that Jesus was teaching his disciples about his faith and conception of God. This does not take into consideration that there is no evidence that Jesus was actually praying this prayer. The context clearly indicates that he was teaching it. Jesus' messianic consciousness was such that he saw himself in a peculiar and unique relationship to the Father. This is made clear in his prayer in Jn. 17. In effect, this latter passage is "the Lord's Prayer," Jesus' intercession for the disciples, while the prayer of Matt. 6 and Lk. 11 was to be used by those who believed in him and the heavenly Father.

In this light the true eschatological meaning of the seven petitions becomes clear. Many modern authors have missed this central point by assuming a dialectic tension between Jesus' messianic expectation of the future and his immediate concern for the present. In such a tension the believer's prayer becomes an existential involvement, but this interpretation is totally unwarranted by the text. Life in the Christian covenant is an experiential and daily affair, but its basis and bounds are in Christ and it seeks to follow and expound its faith as revealed in the Word of God, of which this prayer is a part.

This belief means that the prayer is more than an epitome of our Lord's message, and more vital and significant than a mere set of propositions. It is a vehicle and means to the throne of God. Through it and by it we approach God's majesty and he provides for his children.

Of special importance is the fact that the pronouns of the prayer are plural. The church which prays this prayer is to be a community, a body of believers. The prayer was not formulated for singular, personal devotion; it was to be an act of corporate worship. The needs of the church and of its members are made more certain in regard to the coming of the kingdom. The character of the prayer is totally determined by the person and work of Christ in redemption, for it is by his act of atonement that any or all of the petitions are granted. The theme of the prayer is Christocentric. There are no tensions in its petitions as it summarizes its motives in the will of God—past, present, and future.

IV. Its place in the church. The Jewish synagogue and temple services were filled with rich liturgies; the Psalms, laws, and many responses were said in unison and antiphonally. There is much evidence that the early church kept this system of worship and added to it the prayers and phrases of the NT. There are many doxologies and liturgical phrases incorporated into the texts of the epistles (Jude 24–25).

How early the divine offices or stated prayers became fixed in the history of the church is conjectured, but certainly by the 4th cent. there was a clear set of hourly devotions. The prayer books from the early medieval period show the repetition of the Lord's Prayer at all six of the stated "hours": matins, lauds, terce, sext, none, and vespers. The wealth and welter of conflicting rituals led the Franciscans to shorten and condense as well as collate the services in the *Breviary*, and its companion the *Missal* for the communion. But the prayer was central in both. The Lutheran liturgy followed the custom of the Lollards and the Bohemian Brethren in merely translating the prayer from Latin into the colloquial speech.

The Reformed churches that followed Calvin and the Swiss Reformation dispensed with much of the medieval liturgy but retained the Lord's Prayer in a French version. Among the Reformed churches it was removed from the liturgy but placed in the catechism. It is discussed and demonstrated in questions 86 to 129 of the *Heidelberg Catechism*, and was an integral part of the Reformed doctrine of prayer. Although numerous revisions of creeds and standards have been effected in more recent times, the need for a common statement of conviction has forced the acceptance of a more common liturgy. Many ecclesiastical bodies have been forced to come to terms with mutual liturgies when the central cohesion of doctrine failed. The result has been a new interest in prayer. However, most recent studies lean heavily upon psychoanalytic insights and approach corporate worship as phenomena of group dynamics. Such attempts are far from the purpose of the Scriptures.

(A vast number of devotional, homiletic, and exegetical commentaries have been written on the text and numerous word studies are available; also commentaries on the catechisms in which the Lord's Prayer is included. Notable works include M. Margoliouth, *The Lord's Prayer No Adaptation of Existing Jewish Petitions* [1876]; H. J. Van Dyke, *The Lord's Prayer* [1891]; R. Rost, *The Lord's Prayer in 500 Languages* [1905]; P. Fiebig, *Das Vaterunser* [1927]; E. F. Scott, *The Lord's Prayer* [1951]; E. Lohmeyer, *The Lord's Prayer* [1965]; J. J. Petuchowski and M. Brocke, *The Lord's Prayer and Jewish Liturgy* [1978]; N. Ayo, *The Lord's Prayer: A Survey Theological and Literary* [1992]; D. L. Migliore et al., *The Lord's Prayer* [1992]; R. Pritchard, *And When You Pray: The Deeper Meaning of the Lord's Prayer* [2002]; G. O'Collins, *The Lord's Prayer* [2006]; *ABD*, 4:356–62.)　　　　　　　　　W. WHITE, JR.

Lord's Supper. This expression is found only once in the NT (*kyriakon deipnon*, 1 Cor. 11:20), where it refers not only to the special Christian rite of breaking the bread and drinking the cup, but also to the love feast that accompanied it. The expression "breaking of bread," which occurs frequently in Acts, may be another way the NT had of referring to the Lord's Supper. Certainly it became so in subsequent years of the church's history. But later names for this observance such as COMMUNION and EUCHARIST, are not used in the NT in any technical sense. The former, however, is derived from 1 Cor. 10:16 where Paul spoke of the *koinōnia* G3126 of the body and blood of Christ; the latter from Jesus' act of thanksgiving before he offered the cup to his disciples (*eucharisteō* G2373, Mk. 14:23).

　I. The Last Supper
　　A. Was the Last Supper a Passover meal?
　　B. The words of institution
　　C. The problem of the Lukan text
　II. The Lord's Supper
　　A. The scarcity of materials
　　B. When was the Lord's Supper observed?
　　C. How was the Lord's Supper observed?
　　D. Paul's understanding of the Lord's Supper
　　E. The Lord's Supper in the fourth gospel

I. The Last Supper. This institution, by whatever name it was called, began with that Last Supper Jesus had with his friends before his death. The principal texts dealing with this subject are: Matt. 26:26–29; Mk. 14:22–25; Lk. 22:14–20; and 1 Cor. 11:23–26.

A. Was the Last Supper a Passover meal? The Lord's Supper has been a subject of much recent scholarly debate, with the center of this debate being its relation to the PASSOVER meal. No consensus has been forthcoming. The problem arises from the differences existing between the Synoptic Gospels' account of the Last Supper and John's dating of Christ's CRUCIFIXION, on the one hand, and from the description of the supper itself and of the events surrounding it by the first three evangelists, on the other.

Seemingly the Synoptic Gospels claim that Jesus celebrated the Passover with his disciples and that the Last Supper grew out of the Passover meal (Matt. 26:17–29; Mk. 14:12–25; Lk. 22:7–20). John, however, has been understood to say that the Last Supper took place "before the Passover Feast" (Jn. 13:1–2, 21–30), and that Jesus, therefore, did not eat the Passover with his disciples, but was himself the supreme paschal sacrifice, put to death simultaneously with the slaughter of the Passover lambs (cf. Jn. 18:28; 19:12–14).

Some scholars assume the correctness of the Johannine account and explain the Last Supper of the synoptic narratives as an ordinary meal, or as a special meal such as those commonly shared by members of a religious association (rabbinic *ḥăbûrâ*), but not a Passover. They assume that the synoptics mistakenly linked it with the Passover because of the paschal nature of the supper. These scholars understand the words of Jesus, "I have eagerly desired to eat this Passover with you" (Lk. 22:15), to be an expression of intense desire on his part but not the satisfaction of a realized experience. They note that the synoptics never use the technical term for unleavened bread when they describe the Last Supper. Nor do they mention the lamb or the bitter herbs. The Gospels speak of a common cup shared by all the disciples, while, allegedly, only individual cups were used at the Passover. They refer to one or two cups of wine only, whereas the Passover ritual included four. It is also pointed out that Paul, although he writes about the Last Supper, does not describe it as a Passover in 1 Cor. 11:23–26, and that the early church celebrated the Lord's Supper once a week, or oftener, rather than once a year only, as might be expected had the Last Supper originated as the annual Passover meal (see below). Other objections to the Last Supper being a Passover meal have to do with events in the gospel narrative which seemingly could not have taken place on the festival day, Nisan 15, such as the session of the SANHEDRIN and condemnation of Jesus on the same night that the Passover meal was to be eaten. (A. H. McNeile, *The Gospel according to St. Matthew* [1915], 377ff.; G. Dix, *The Shape of the Liturgy* [1945], 50–52.)

Other scholars, however, side with the synoptics and assert that the fourth gospel is theologically motivated rather than historically accurate. John wished to present Jesus as the Passover lamb par excellence, put to death coincidentally with the other Passover lambs. Certainly the synoptic writers intended to say that the Last Supper was a Passover meal. This is most clearly presented in Luke, where the preparations for the supper are located precisely on the day on which the Passover lamb (*pascha G4247*) had to be sacrificed (Lk. 22:7). These evangelists also note that the Last Supper took place in the evening (Mk. 14:17), that Jesus and his disciples reclined at dinner (Matt. 26:20) in a day when Jewish people regularly sat at table for ordinary meals, that there was a dipping ceremony (Matt. 26:23),

and that the Supper concluded with the singing of a hymn (Mk. 14:26)—all of which are important characteristics of the Passover ritual (see below and J. Jeremias, *The Eucharistic Words of Jesus* [1955], 14–60, who gives detailed and convincing evidence for the Last Supper being a Passover meal).

Serious attempts have been made to harmonize the synoptic accounts with that of John so as to allow each to preserve its particular theological emphasis, and at the same time to be historically accurate. One of the more fruitful attempts is that based on information concerning Jewish calendars (see J. van Goudoever, *Biblical Calendar* [1959]). Apparently in Jesus' day there were two dates for celebrating the Passover. The people of Qumran as well as other groups followed an unofficial calendar according to which killing of the lambs and the Passover supper regularly fell on a Tuesday afternoon and evening, a time deliberately different from the date of the Passover according to the official calendar (Nisan 14–15 in both calendars).

If this is so, then it is possible that the high priest and the people ate the paschal lamb on the evening of the day of Christ's death, a Friday (*paraskeuē G4187*, as the Johannine account has it, Jn. 19:14 et al.), whereas Jesus and his disciples had already eaten it on the Tuesday before (as the synoptics relate, Mk. 14:12; Lk. 22:7), in each case on the 14th–15th of Nisan (Exod. 12:6; Lev. 23:5). Jesus' reason for celebrating the Passover in this way, apart from the possibility that he may have opposed the establishment at Jerusalem, may have been his desire to observe this ancient ritual of the Passover on a legal day before bringing it to an end by his death on the day of the official Passover. This explanation of the Passover provides additional time (which the synoptic writers telescope) between the Last Supper and the crucifixion—a factor that helps resolve some of the difficulties of the passion narrative, such as how the death of Jesus could take place on the same day as that of his trial, when Jewish law forbade this from happening. (See A. Jaubert, *The Date of the Last Supper* [1965], 102, 121.) See CHRONOLOGY (NT) I.B.5.

B. The words of institution. Assuming that the Last Supper was a Passover meal, then Jesus' words, instituting the new Christian supper, were spoken in a context of the Passover ritual and should be interpreted accordingly. The liturgy of the Passover began with the presiding person pronouncing a blessing (the *kiddush*) over the first cup of wine, which at the Passover meal was always red. This then was drunk by him and the others present, and was followed by bitter herbs dipped into *haroseth*, a fruit sauce, and eaten. Next came the explanation of the feast when the food for the main meal was brought in. The son first asked his father why this night differed from other nights, and he replied by saying that the Passover lamb is eaten because God passed over the house of our fathers in Egypt (Exod. 12:26–27), the unleavened bread because our fathers were redeemed from Egypt (12:39), and the bitter herbs because the Egyptians embittered the lives of our fathers in Egypt (1:14).

Afterwards the family or group sang the first part of the Hallel (Ps. 113 or both 113 and 114). Then came the drinking of a second cup followed by the president's taking unleavened bread and blessing God with these words: "Blessed art thou who bringest forth bread from the earth." He then broke it and handed it to the guests. Then came the meal proper, followed by another prayer from the president, a thanksgiving for the meal pronounced over a third cup of wine, "the cup of blessing" (cf. 1 Cor. 10:16). After supper the second part of the Hallel was sung, which ended with Ps. 118. Finally, a fourth cup of wine was taken to celebrate God's kingdom, and this concluded the liturgy. (See A. J. B. Higgins, *The Lord's Supper in the New Testament* [1952], for this summary; cf. also *m. Pesaḥim* 10:5; Str-B, 1:988–90; 4:41–76; D. Daube, *The New Testament and Rabbinic Judaism* [1956], 331.)

1. The form of the words of institution. It is not possible to know exactly what our Lord said when he returned over the bread and the cup of wine after supper from the Passover ceremony for special consideration and reinterpretation. The principal texts relating these words do not agree in every detail (see the texts above). But the bread-saying takes the following form when all of the sources are woven together: "Take [Matthew, Mark], eat [Matthew], this is my body [Matthew, Mark, Luke, Paul], which is given for you. Do this for my remembrance" [Luke's longer text, Paul]. The saying over the cup also is recorded variously by the different writers: "All of you drink from it, for [Matthew] this [Matthew, Mark, Luke, Paul] cup [Luke, Paul] is my blood of the covenant [Matthew, Mark; 'is the new covenant in my blood,' Luke, Paul], which is poured out [Matthew, Mark, Luke] for many [Matthew, Mark; 'for you,' Luke], for the remission of sins [Matthew]. Do this as often as you drink it for my remembrance" [Paul]. These cup-words are then immediately followed in Matthew and Mark by Jesus' promise never again to drink of the fruit of the vine until he drinks it new with his disciples in the kingdom of God. The same eschatological hope is found also in Paul, though worded differently, and he too places it after the cup-saying. Luke, on the other hand, couples the promise not to drink of the fruit of the vine with another similar promise not to eat again of the Passover until its real meaning is fulfilled in the kingdom, and places both of them before the sayings spoken over the bread and the cup.

There seem, then, to be essentially two accounts that are independent of each other: one represented by Mark, and the other by Paul. Which is the older is difficult to know and perhaps unnecessary, for there are "primitive" elements in both. And in spite of all the minor differences between the accounts, they are nevertheless in substantial agreement with one another. It is sufficient to say that each inspired writer was free to select and arrange the same traditional material so as to present adequately the theological significance of the Last Supper as he was led to understand it.

2. The meaning of the Last Supper. The Lord's Supper, composed of bread and wine, is a symbol of our Lord's body and blood, a symbol of his death: "This is my body given.... This is my blood poured out." One is not compelled by the present context nor usage elsewhere to give to the verb *estin* ("is") the meaning of "is equivalent to." Often it conveys merely the idea of "represents," or "means" (as in the interpretation of the parables, Matt. 13:38; cf. also Jn. 10:9, 14). Besides, it would have been almost impossible for Jesus to have equated the bread with his body and the wine with his blood and then to have asked his Jewish disciples to eat and drink. It is much more likely that his disciples saw him in the tradition of the OT prophets, and interpreted his words and actions accordingly. As those ancient prophets predicted future events by symbolic dramatic deeds (1 Ki. 21:11; Jer. 19:1–11; Ezek. 4:3), so Jesus broke the bread and took the cup as an acted parable to denote his coming death and point out its meaning.

Around this basic idea of the Lord's Supper as a symbol of the death of Christ there cluster several ideas. (a) First, the Lord interpreted his death as a substitutionary, vicarious self-giving event, universal in its scope: "This is my body given *for you*"; "this is my blood poured out *for many*." (Note: "many" is not to be understood as a limiting expression meaning, "some, but not all." Rather, it is a Semitic way of contrasting the many with the one, resulting in the meaning, "all"; cf. Matt. 20:28 with 1 Tim. 2:6, and Rom. 5:18 with 5:19. For other approaches see, e.g., T. R. Schreiner, *Romans*, BECNT [1998], 290–92; BDAG, 849a.)

(b) He further interprets his death as the means of ratifying the new covenant spoken of by Jeremiah (Jer. 31:31–34). This is observed in his words, "my blood of the covenant" (Mk. 14:24), which are almost identical with those of Exod. 24:8, where the ratification of the old covenant with Israel is recorded. But the addition of the pronoun "my" indicates that Jesus placed his blood in counterposition to that of the covenant-inaugurating animal of the OT, and that he viewed his death as bringing the old covenant to an end by fulfillment, and as the supreme sacrifice needed to introduce the new and give it permanent validity. See COVENANT, THE NEW.

(c) There are also elements in this Last Supper account which indicate that Jesus interpreted his death as the consummate act of the SERVANT OF THE LORD described by ISAIAH. This is particularly clear in Matthew, who adds the words, "for the forgiveness of sins," to the saying about Jesus' blood poured out (Matt. 26:28; cf. Isa. 53:12, "because he poured out his life unto death, / and was numbered with the transgressors. / For he bore the sin of many, / and made intercession for the transgressors").

(d) Perhaps the most obvious meanings attached to the Last Supper are those associated with the Passover. The Passover in Jesus' day was in reality a celebration of two events: it looked back in commemoration of Israel's deliverance from the oppression of Egypt (Exod. 12:14, 17; *m. Pesaḥim* 10:5); and it looked forward in anticipation of the coming messianic kingdom (*m. Pesaḥim* 10:6; cf. Rabbi Joshua ben Hananiah, *Mekilta* on Exod. 12:42; *Exodus Rabbah* on Exod. 15:1; see Higgins, *The Lord's Supper*, 47). These two themes are prominent in the narrative of the Last Supper. Selecting only two elements from the liturgy of the Passover—the unleavened bread and the cup after supper—Jesus seemed to say, "As Israel was spared from death at the hand of the destroying angel, and delivered from servitude to Pharaoh by the death of the passover lamb and the sprinkling of its blood, so you are spared from eternal death and freed from slavery to sin by my body broken and my blood poured forth." Hence, the original meaning of the Passover had now been superseded. Christ is the true paschal Lamb (1 Cor. 5:7), and by his death becomes the author of a new exodus, the Redeemer of an enslaved people. Such, at least, was the understanding of the early church, an understanding most beautifully expressed in a recently discovered sermon of Melito, Bishop of Sardis (d. c. A.D. 190):

> For this one, who was led away as a lamb,
> and who was sacrificed as a sheep,
> by himself delivered us from servitude to the world
> as from the land of Egypt,
> and released us from bondage to the devil
> and from the hand of Pharaoh,
> and sealed our souls by his own spirit,
> and the members of our bodies by his own blood.
>
> This is the one who covered death with shame
> and who plunged the devil into mourning
> as Moses did Pharaoh.
>
> This is the one who smote lawlessness,
> and deprived injustice of its offspring
> as Moses deprived Egypt.
>
> This is the one who delivered us
> from slavery into freedom,
> from darkness into light,
> from death into life,
> from tyranny into an eternal kingdom,
> and who made us a new priesthood
> and a special people forever.
> This one is the passover of our salvation.
>
> (*Homily*, 67–68)

The other theme of eschatological expectancy is also here. It is found in Jesus' promise not to eat the Passover or drink the fruit of the vine *until* the KINGDOM OF GOD shall have arrived. This promise is not a word of despair but a note of joy. Jesus sees beyond the darkness of Calvary to that time when he would share with his disciples the messianic banquet and enjoy with them the life of the age to come (cf. Isa. 25:6–8). "Thus Jesus offered his disciples in the Supper a full participation in the atoning benefits of his own self-offering on the cross—deliverance from the bondage of this world, remission of sins, incorporation in the new people of God, an inner obedience of the heart to the will of God, and the joy and benediction of his presence and fellowship in the age to come" (Massey H. Shepherd).

C. The problem of the Lukan text. There are questions concerning the correctness of the Greek text in all accounts of the Last Supper. (For complete information concerning these variants see the chapter on textual data by F. G. Kenyon and S. C. E. Legg in R. Dunkerley, ed., *The Ministry and the Sacraments* [1937], 272–86.) But the most difficult textual problem in these accounts is that posed by the chief witness of the "Western" text, CODEX BEZAE (D), supported also by some Old Latin and Syriac texts, which omits Lk. 22:19b–20 (a few of the texts rearrange the order of 22:17–20 so that v. 19 [or only v. 19a] comes before v. 17). The case for this shorter text is best set forth by B. F. Westcott and F. J. A. Hort (*The New Testament in the Original Greek: Introduction and Appendix* [1882], appendix, 63–64): (1) Since the chief characteristic of the "Western" text is to interpolate—i.e., include everything that looks authentic whether it is or not—the shorter text of Luke, therefore, must be very early, most likely original, for it is not found in the chief witnesses of this kind of text. (2) It is almost impossible to believe that these verses would have been stricken from the Lukan text at a later date. (3) It is conceivable, however, that they could be interpolated into Luke at a later time from 1 Cor 11:23–24 and Mk. 14:23–24 to eliminate the cup-bread order which exists when these verses are omitted.

There are some modern scholars who follow Westcott and Hort in rejecting the genuineness of the longer reading (see H. Chadwick in *HTR* 50 [1957], 257–70, R. Bultmann, *The History of the Gospel Tradition* [1963], 286 n.), and some modern translations (e.g., NEB) remove these verses from the text and give them a place in the margin. But the majority of scholars consider that the shorter text is secondary. It is difficult to believe that a later interpolation could find its way into *all* Greek MSS with the lone exception of Codex D. One notes too that the longer reading is cited by the church fathers as early as A.D. 150 (Justin, *1 Apology* 66). The omission of Lk. 22:19b–20 can be explained as due to a mechanical error on the part of a copyist, or to a desire to keep secret the inner meaning of Christian worship (although this is hard to believe since there is no evidence for the omission of v. 19a), or to avoid the inconsistency of having a second cup. (See further E. Schweizer, *The Lord's Supper according to the New Testament* [1967], 18–20; H. Schürmann in *Bib* 32 [1957]: 364–92, 522–41 [a very detailed textual analysis, concluding that the longer text is definitely original]; B. M. Metzger, *A Textual Commentary on the Greek New Testament*, 2nd ed. [1994], 148–50. For a recent defense of the shorter text, see B. D. Ehrman, *The Orthodox Corruption of Scripture. The Effect of Early Christological Controversies on the Text of the New Testament* [1993], 198–209.)

The interpretation of the Last Supper according to the shorter text of Luke would be quite different from that of the other synoptic writers and from that of Paul, omitting the cup-saying, preserving only the idea that the Last Supper was a foretaste of the coming eschatological banquet, and raising the question about whether the Lord's Supper always had been observed by the Christian church from the beginning in just the same way as it is presented by Mark and Paul (see below).

II. The Lord's Supper

A. The scarcity of materials. Apart from 1 Corinthians and the Synoptic Gospels, the rest of the NT is virtually silent on the subject of the Lord's Supper. There is no teaching on it anywhere else, although there are possible allusions in several books (Jn. 6:22–59; Acts 2:46; 20:7, 11; Heb. 6:4; 13:10; 2 Pet. 2:13; Jude 12). This paucity of material raises questions: Did the early church feel a need for liturgical secrecy? Was indeed the Lord's Supper central to the worship-life of the early church? Was there really general agreement in the apostolic age about the relation of the Last Supper to the death of Christ? These questions are not easy to answer, but suffice it to point out that if there had not been problems at CORINTH, one of which was disorders at the Lord's Supper, Paul himself might never have mentioned the subject. In other words, one should be careful about reading too much into silence. In this case the silence could mean that the Lord's Supper was so well-known and so central that mention of it was totally unnecessary except where disorders called for clarification.

B. When was the Lord's Supper observed?
One might expect that if the Lord's Supper grew out of a Passover meal, it would be celebrated only once a year, on the 14th–15th of Nisan. A study of early church history seems to support this speculation. EPIPHANIUS, for example, observed that the EBIONITES, an early Jewish-Christian sect, celebrated the Eucharist as an annual feast, like the Passover, in memory of Christ's death (*Haer.* 30.16.1). And Christians in Asia Minor in the 2nd cent. held a special Eucharist as a parallel to the Passover and at the same time as the Jewish Passover (see Higgins, *The Lord' Supper*, 56 n. 1).

The statement of the early chapters of Acts about the disciples "breaking bread" every day (Acts 2:42, 46) need not refute this idea. For it has been pointed out that the meals in Acts are very much like religious meals found elsewhere in Judaism (K. Stendahl, ed., *The Scrolls and the New Testament* [1957], 84–86), and their emphasis is quite different from that of the Last Supper as recorded in the Gospels. Whereas the Lord's Supper was a remembrance of Christ's death, these daily meals were joyful fellowships that celebrated his resurrection and continued presence in the church, and also anticipated the eschatological kingdom. They, thus, may not have originated in or been connected with the Last Supper, but may have had their source and meaning in the postresurrection meals that Jesus had with his disciples (Lk. 24:30–43; Jn. 21:1–14; Acts 1:4; 10:41; see O. Cullmann, *Early Christian Worship* [1953], 14–16).

Hence, in the early Jerusalem church it is probable that there were originally two kinds of fellowship meals: (1) the "breaking of bread," which occurred daily, and (2) the Passover, which occurred annually, each with its own peculiar emphasis. Only the latter "was directly related to the Last Supper, and only in it was the *meal* a specific remembrance of Messiah's death" (E. E. Ellis, *The Gospel of Luke* [1966], 250). Eventually, however, these two meals were combined into one new feast when the church moved outside of Jerusalem and the Jewish influence ceased to play a dominant role in the development of Christian worship. The joyful fellowship meal of Acts 2 became the *agape*-element of the Lord's Supper (1 Cor. 11:20–21), and the annual Passover meal became the Eucharist-element (11:23–26). By this time the new supper was celebrated neither daily nor annually, but weekly—on the first day of the week, the day of resurrection, possibly at night, pointing back to the Passover meal, which was partaken of in the evening (Acts 20:7; cf. 1 Cor. 16:2; Rev. 1:10; *Did.* 14.1).

C. How was the Lord's Supper observed?
This question, too, is difficult to answer, for little is said about it in the NT. But from 1 Cor. 11:20–34 it is possible to reconstruct the following order: (1) there was a full-blown dinner or love-feast to which participants brought their own food, and at which it was possible for some to be hungry or drunk (vv. 20–22). This practice was probably a carry-over from the Last Supper, when a complete meal took

In this model of 1st-cent. Jerusalem, the large flat-roofed complex in the center of the photo represents the upper room, where Jesus first celebrated the Lord's Supper with the apostles.

This aerial view of SW Jerusalem (looking NE) shows the area that is known today as Mount Zion. The traditional location of the upper room is marked by tower structures above the Hinnom Valley.

place between the bread and cup sayings. (2) Then came a period of self-examination (v. 28). The form this examination took is nowhere stated in the NT. It may have been strictly personal, or it may have involved individual public confession in the church, or corporate confession as part of a liturgical prayer (cf. *Did*. 6.14; 14.1). (3) Finally, there was the Lord's Supper proper, involving only the bread and wine, which recalled the death of the Lord Jesus (vv. 24–26). Acts 20:7–11 indicates that a sermon may have preceded the action outlined above and formed part of the liturgy of the Lord's Supper, but there is no indication what that sermon was about. There are no traces in the NT of Eucharistic prayers as are found in the later literature of the early church (*Did*. 9–10), nor is there evidence here for FOOTWASHING forming a part of the ceremony of the Lord's Supper.

D. Paul's understanding of the Lord's Supper. The Lord's Supper has been celebrated continuously by the church from the time of Jesus to the present day. Yet Paul's account of it is the earliest in the NT by several years. He says of it that he "received [it] from the Lord" (1 Cor. 11:23). This may mean that Paul learned of the events of the Last Supper and its real meaning in the same way he had earlier received the content of the gospel: not from man, nor by human teaching, but through revelation of Jesus Christ (Gal. 1:12).

Hans Lietzmann (*Mass and Lord's Supper* [1958], 204–8) made use of this interpretation to set up his antithesis between the Eucharist as celebrated in Jerusalem and the Eucharist as celebrated in the Pauline churches. The Jerusalem-type, he said, was a breaking of bread with no wine used. It was a continuation of the fellowship meals that the historical Jesus had shared with his disciples. It had no connection with the Last Supper and was marked not by any remembrance of Christ's death, but by a joyous ecstasy over his spiritual presence, and an expectancy of his return shortly. The idea of sacrifice was absent. Lietzmann saw the other type of celebration as coming from the Last Supper and from a special revelation to Paul in which he received new insight into the real meaning of the meal—a memorial of the sacrificial death of the Lord. By this revelation the original meaning of the Eucharist was radically transformed.

But Lietzmann's thesis is open to the following objections: (1) The "breaking of bread" in Acts, though certainly a Christian meal, may not have been Eucharistic in character (see above). (2) Paul's statement, "I received from the Lord what I also passed on to you," can also be interpreted to mean that he understood himself to be a person handing on in unaltered fashion that which had come to him as unaltered church tradition. The words he uses here for "receive" and "pass on" (respectively *paralambanō G4161* and *paradidōmi G4140*) are equivalents of rabbinic terms for the normal course of reception of tradition and its transmission (Higgins, *The Lord's Supper*, 25–26). Paul may have meant, then, that he received the story of the Last Supper and its meaning from the Lord *through the apostolic witness*. For the Lord was not simply a remembered historical figure but a living Presence in the church guiding the community into all truth (Jn. 16:13), and seeing to it that this truth was transmitted accurately to each succeeding generation. If this is what Paul meant, he cannot be charged with changing the meaning of the early Eucharist. He was authoritatively handing on what had been practiced in the church from its inception. (3) Eduard Schweizer has pointed out that from the start of Eucharistic celebration the two elements of eschatological joy, coupled with a sense of Christ's presence at the table and a hope for his return, and of the proclamation of his death as the means of salvation, belonged together (Schweizer, *The Lord's Supper*, 25). Paul combines both of these ideas in a single sentence: "You proclaim the Lord's death until he comes" (1 Cor. 11:26).

Illustration of Jesus celebrating the Lord's Supper in the upper room.

© Dr. James C. Martin. Illustration by Timothy Ladwig.

Paul's understanding of the Lord's Supper, therefore, is in essence identical with the traditional understanding of it, and what was said earlier about the meaning of the Last Supper will also apply here. But the disorders at the Lord's table in Corinth have given the apostle opportunity to provide teaching on the subject that appears nowhere else in the NT.

1. The Lord's Supper as a memorial feast. There is one word of the Lord in Paul (and Luke) which does not appear in Mark (and Matthew). It is, "do this in remembrance of me" (1 Cor. 11:24, repeated in v. 25). Paul therefore understands that the purpose of the Lord's Supper is to commemorate the death of the Lord Jesus, and that this purpose originated with the Lord himself. (J. Jeremias's view of this saying as meaning "that *God* may remember me" by bringing in the kingdom at the parousia has been convincingly answered by H. Kosmala, *NovT* 4 [1960]: 81–94.) Here again is seen a parallel between this new feast and the feast of the Passover. As the Passover was basically a remembrance celebration calling to mind the mercy and greatness of God in delivering his people from Egypt (Exod. 12:14; 13:8–10), so the Lord's Supper is designed to constantly remind the Christian of God's greatest act, that of deliverance from sin through the death (not the teachings) of the Lord Jesus.

But the biblical idea of "remembering" is more profound than our modern conception of it. It meant for the biblical writer more than simply having an "idea" about something that happened in the past. It also involved action, a physical response to the psychological process of recollection. For when the dying thief asked the Savior to "remember" him he meant more than have an idea of me in your mind; he meant, "Act toward me in mercy. Save me!" There was, then, this closeness of relation between thought and act. Thus when the Jew celebrated the Passover, he did more than just think about what happened to his forefathers. He in a sense reenacted that event and himself participated in the exodus. He was at one with his past (see B. S. Childs, *Memory and Tradition in Israel* [1962]).

There may also be this dimension to the word "remembrance" as used in 1 Cor. 11. When the Christian partakes of the Lord's Supper he not only has an idea in his mind about a past event, but in a sense he "reveals" that event and in such a way that it can no longer be regarded wholly as a thing "absent" or past, but present, and powerfully present. In the Lord's Supper, then, and uniquely in the Lord's Supper, the death of Christ is made so vivid that it is as if the Christian were standing beneath the cross. See MEMORIAL; REMEMBER.

2. The Lord's Supper a sacrifice? Did Paul regard the Lord's Supper as a sacrifice? Some interpreters answer this question in the affirmative, proposing to give to the words "do this" the meaning "offer this sacrifice." It is true that early on Christian writers began to call the Eucharist a sacrifice (*Did.* 14.1; cf. Ign. *Phil.* 4.1), and the church a place of sacrifice or altar (Ign. *Eph.* 5.2).

But Paul did not so understand the Lord's Supper, nor can his words "do this" be so construed: (a) the ordinary meaning of the verb "do" (*poieō* G4472) in the NT, the SEPTUAGINT, and Greek literature generally is opposed to such a translation. (b) The Greek church fathers, some of whom may have thought of the Eucharist as a sacrifice, never understood these words to mean "offer a sacrifice." (c) Finally, the witness of the LXX is also against this interpretation, for it never translates any of the many OT words for sacrifice in their frequent occurrence by the verb *poieō* (see A. Plummer, *The Gospel According to Luke*, 5th ed. [1922], 497–498). The words simply mean "perform this function." They are a command to remember.

3. The Lord's Supper as a proclamation. Paul also understood the Last Supper to be a proclamation: "For whenever you eat this bread and drink this cup, you proclaim the Lord's death" (1 Cor. 11:26). The verb "proclaim" found here (*katangellō* G2859) is used elsewhere in the NT of heralding the gospel (1 Cor. 9:14), and of making known one's faith (Rom. 1:8). Hence, it would seem that its action is directed manward rather than Godward. In performing the rite, the celebrant proclaims to all the Lord's death as victory. The Lord's Supper therefore becomes the gospel, a "visible word" as AUGUSTINE put it.

This idea of the Lord's Supper being gospel is helpful in understanding the Lord's presence in the observance. In the NT, proclamation has the character of event. As Schweizer puts it, the word is never "merely" something spiritual intended for the intellect. Christ himself comes in the word: "he who hears you hears me, and he who rejects you rejects me" (Lk. 10:16). In a similar way he comes in the Lord's Supper. Christ's presence is brought about not "magically by a liturgically correct administration of the sacrament.... It comes to pass where the Lord's Supper is understood as gospel, whether this gospel is believed or rejected.... This means, therefore, that the real presence in the Lord's Supper is exactly the same as his presence in the word—nothing more, nothing less. It is an event, not an object; an encounter, not a phenomenon of nature; it is Christ's encounter with his Church, not the distribution of a substance" (Schweizer, *The Lord's Supper*, 37–38).

4. The Lord's Supper as communion. The words of Paul in 1 Cor. 10:16 are not easy to translate, especially the expressions "communion of the blood of Christ" and "communion of the body of Christ" (KJV). The word translated "communion" (*koinōnia*) may also be translated "fellowship," meaning a group of people bound together in a COMMUNION or FELLOWSHIP by what they have in common with each other. And the preposition "of" does not exist in the Greek, but is an interpretation of the genitive case. It may also be interpreted to mean "brought about by" or "based upon." Translated in this way Paul is saying, "The cup of blessing which we bless, is it not (does it not represent) the fellowship which is brought about by the blood of Christ? The bread which we break, is it not the fellowship brought about by the body of Christ?" The Lord's Supper, then, is understood to witness to the fact that Christians belong to a special family which includes the Son and the Father (cf. 1 Jn. 1:3) and is marked by unity and love. It is a communion which required the death of Christ to create, and which is so close that it is as though believers were one body: "For we being many are one bread, and one body: for we are all partakers of that one bread" (1 Cor. 10:17 KJV). Perhaps, then, this was the great disorder in Corinth that prompted what little teaching there is on the Lord's Supper. The Corinthians' sin was that they did not discern or recognize the body (1 Cor. 11:29), that is, they failed to understand the oneness of the body of which each person was a part.

In Paul's day a fellowship meal preceded the breaking of bread and drinking of the cup. It was not an unimportant part of the Lord's Supper, and Paul had no desire to abolish it. What he was concerned to do, however, was to correct its abuses. For instead of symbolizing the unity its name intended, the fellowship meal at Corinth was the occasion for manifesting the opposite. The freemen despised the slave class, going ahead with the meal before the latter had opportunity to arrive (1 Cor. 11:21). The wealthy scorned the poor, feasting to the point of gluttony while the latter went hungry (vv. 21–22). Thus eating and drinking "in an unworthy manner" (v. 27) may have meant for Paul partaking of the Lord's Supper while holding each other in contempt and neither party striving to live up to the unity which took the Lord's death to bring about.

The word *communion* has still another meaning: "participation in." Hence, 1 Cor. 10:16 may be translated as the RSV does: "The cup of blessing which we bless, is it not a participation in the blood of Christ?" If this is so, then perhaps Paul understood the cup and bread to symbolize the Christian's participation in the death of Christ. Perhaps by borrowing his vocabulary from the MYSTERY RELIGIONS he showed that the Redeemer and the redeemed are so intimately bound up with each other that what happened to the Redeemer happened also to the redeemed. Thus when Christ died, the Christian died also, and partaking of the Lord's Supper symbolizes this participation in the body and blood of the Savior. Such a description of the Supper is Paul's way of stating what Christ already had said: "I am the living bread that came down from heaven. If anyone eats of this bread, he will live forever. ... I tell you the truth, unless you eat the flesh of the Son of Man and drink his blood, you have no life in you" (Jn. 6:51, 53).

The Lord's Supper, though of great importance to Paul, is not all-important. There are no magical qualities to it. It has no more power to communicate life and maintain it than did the spiritual food and drink provided Israel in the wilderness (1 Cor. 10:1–13). It cannot in and of itself debilitate or bring about death in spite of the fact that Paul says that many who eat and drink unworthily are weak and ill and some have died (11:30). Such sickness and death result from the judgment of the LORD (11:32), not from any magical power of the Supper. The importance of the Supper exists solely in the Person it points to, and whose redemptive acts it proclaims.

E. The Lord's Supper in the fourth gospel.
There is no specific reference to the Lord's Supper in the fourth gospel. John describes a final meal Jesus had with his disciples (Jn. 13), when he taught them the importance of humble service to others by himself washing their feet. But there is no bread or wine here, nor words of interpretation. Many, however, see the Johannine Eucharist in Jesus' discourse on the bread of life (ch. 6). It is here that Jesus says, "For my flesh is real food and my blood is real drink. Whoever eats my flesh and drinks my blood remains in me, and I in him" (6:55–56). If this is so, it would appear that for John the Lord's Supper is spiritual food (cf. v. 63), which nourishes and strengthens the life of the Christian (cf. *Did.* 10.4).

But perhaps John's primary aim was not to discourse on the Lord's Supper but on the meaning of FAITH. Certainly this is a subject that is continually being put forward in his gospel. What does it mean to have faith in Christ? When Jn. 6:47, "he who believes has eternal life," is juxtaposed with v. 54, "Whoever eats my flesh and drinks my blood has eternal life," it would seem that John, in searching for the way to answer this question, has at last found the model he needs. To believe on Christ is analogous to eating his body. As one would take food and eat it so that it is assimilated into the system and becomes one's very life, so faith is a similar appropriation of Christ, with the result that he is at the very center and is the energizing force of the Christian's life. But then, this is the very thing that the Lord's Supper is designed to remind us of in any case.

(In addition to the works mentioned in the body of this article, see I. H. Marshall, *Last Supper and Lord's Supper* [1980]; F. Chenderlin, *"Do This as My Memorial": The Semantic and Conceptual Background and Value of Anamnēsis in 1 Corinthians 11:24–25* [1982]; M. Barth, *Rediscovering the Lord's Supper* [1988]; W. Grudem, *Systematic Theology: An Introduction to Christian Doctrine* [1994], ch. 30; P. D. Molnar, *Karl Barth and the Theology of the Lord's Supper* [1996]; G. T. Smith, *Holy Meal: The Lord's Supper in the Life of the Church* [2005]; *ABD*, 4:362–72.)   G. F. HAWTHORNE

Lo-Ruhamah loh´roo-hah´muh (לֹא רֻחָמָה H4205, "she has not received compassion" or "she has not been loved"). Also Lo-ruhamah. A symbolical name given by the prophet HOSEA to his daughter and second child by his wife GOMER (Hos. 1:6). See LO-AMMI.

Lot lot (לוֹט H4288, derivation uncertain; Λώτ G3397). Son of Haran and nephew of ABRAHAM (Gen. 11:27, 31; 12:5). Born in UR of the Chaldees, Lot migrated to the city of Haran with his grandfather, TERAH, and Abram and Sarai. See HARAN (PERSON); HARAN (PLACE). Later, with Abram and Sarai, he migrated into Canaan. The biblical data regarding his life can be listed under five major episodes.

(1) When Lot's father died in Ur, Lot chose to accompany the portion of the family that was migrating from MESOPOTAMIA into CANAAN. Perhaps (as suggested by J. O. Boyd in *ISBE* [1929], 3:1930), a childless uncle and a fatherless nephew would find a mutual bond. In Canaan, stops were made and altars erected to sacrifice to Yahweh at SHECHEM and BETHEL before the wanderers finally settled in the NEGEV (Gen. 11:27–32; 12:4–10; 13:1). By inference from 13:1, it seems evident that Lot accompanied Abram and Sarai when they went down into Egypt to escape the famine in Canaan. This detail is attested in later tradition and is mentioned in the DEAD SEA SCROLLS (*Genesis Apocryphon* 20.11, 33–34). After the return from Egypt, Abram and his entourage, including Lot, settled near BETHEL.

(2) As flocks and herds multiplied, strife arose between Lot's and Abram's herdsmen over grazing and watering places. In addition to this struggle, Abram and Lot were faced also with the problem of relationships with the Canaanites and Perizzites who still possessed the land (Gen. 13:7b). At Abram's suggestion, Lot was given the choice of whatever territory he wanted. He chose "the plain of the Jordan" that "was well watered," a description usually interpreted to include the area around the place where the JORDAN River enters the DEAD SEA, extending 25 mi. N of the Dead Sea. At this period, Lot was still a nomad (13:12) and wandered as far as SODOM. He chose an area where wickedness was rampant (13:13). (See L. R. Helyer, "The Separation of Abram and Lot: Its Significance in the Patriarchal Narratives," *JSOT* 26 [1983]: 77–88.) In the choice Abram maintained the more

Byzantine chapel built over the "cave of Lot," on the SE side of the Dead Sea (view to the SW). Lot associated himself with the cities of the plain traditionally located in this area.

spiritual outlook (13:14–18). There is archaeological evidence that the plain of the Jordan was well populated as early as the 2nd millennium B.C. (J. P. Free, *Archaeology and Bible History* [1956], 56).

(3) This area near the Dead Sea became a target for a series of raids by four eastern kings (chieftains?). In one of these raids, KEDORLAOMER conquered the king of Sodom and his four allies (Gen. 14:1–16) at the Valley of SIDDIM. Sodom and Gomorrah were plundered, and Lot was taken captive. When Abram heard of his nephew's plight, he armed his retainers and pursued the invaders as far as DAMASCUS, and in a surprise attack rescued Lot and his goods.

(4) Lot was not content to dwell on the plain of the Jordan, but gradually entered into the orbit of the chief city of the Dead Sea area, Sodom. Eventually, he moved into the city and there settled down. Because of the great wickedness in the city, Yahweh had determined to destroy it. En route to Sodom, three angels stopped to see Abraham and tell him of Yahweh's intentions. Abraham prayed that the city might be spared, but not even ten righteous men were found in it, so it was doomed. Two of the angels proceeded to Sodom to warn Lot. In typical eastern fashion Lot welcomed them into his home. Officially, Lot was merely a sojourner in the city, and when he attempted to protect his visitors from the sensual lusts of the Sodomites, he was accused of seeking to rule (Gen. 19:9). To protect his guests, he was willing to give his daughters over to the foul desires of the Sodomites.

The men of the city, however, persisted and tried to take Lot's visitors by force. The angels smote the men with blindness as they attempted a forced entry into Lot's house. The angels warned Lot of the impending destruction of Sodom and persuaded him to leave the city while there was still time. Lot had no influence with his prospective sons-in-law when he sought to persuade them to leave the city, and they perished (Gen. 19:14). Even Lot was slow to leave until escorted from Sodom by the angels (19:15–16). His wife accompanied him, but when she looked back at the smoking city, she was turned into a pillar of salt (19:26; Lk. 17:29). Evidently, Lot was attached to the comforts and culture of Sodom (Gen. 19:16–22). His deliverance was credited to the fact that God remembered (i.e., had mercy on) Abraham. That Lot was saved by divine intervention is stated in Wisd. 10:6–8; Lk. 17:28–29; 2 Pet. 2:7–8. (See J. Penrose Harland, "The Destruction of the Cities of the Plain," *BA* 6 [1943]: 41–52, reprinted in *The Biblical Archaeologist Reader*, ed. D. N. Freedman and G. E. Wright [1961], 59–75.)

(5) Lot's final disgrace followed his leaving Sodom. At first, obtaining permission from the angels, he and his daughters stopped at ZOAR, near the SE end of the Dead Sea. This city did not share the ill repute of the other four CITIES OF THE PLAIN. Out of fear of further "fire and brimstone," Lot left Zoar and lived in a cave in MOAB with his daughters (Gen. 19:30–38). His daughters despaired of finding husbands, so to carry on Lot's line they devised a plan whereby they might become pregnant. On successive nights they made Lot drunk with wine, and each daughter, in turn, slept with him incestuously. From these unions Moab and BEN-AMMI were born (Deut. 2:9, 19; Ps. 83:8), from whom the Moabites and Ammonites (see AMMON) were supposedly descended. Some see in this unsavory story an etiological legend to explain the origin of these peoples. There is no reason, however, why the events may not have happened as recorded in Genesis. From the Moabites came RUTH, the ancestress of David and Christ.

Despite Lot's failings, the NT calls him "a righteous man" (2 Pet. 2:7–8).   A. K. HELMBOLD

Lotan loh´tan (לוֹטָן *H4289*). First son of SEIR the HORITE; he was a clan chief of EDOM (Gen. 36:20–22, 29; 1 Chr. 1:38–39). Because the name Lotan may derive from LOT, some have speculated that Abraham's nephew was the ancestor of this Edomite tribe (see *ABD*, 4:374–75).

Lothasubus loh-thah´suh-buhs (Λωθασουβος). One of those who stood on EZRA's side at the reading of the law (1 Esd. 9:44; called HASHUM in Neh. 8:4).

lots. Objects used for DIVINATION or for making a choice. In the history of the Bible, the casting of lots was used to determine the will of God. The method is not clearly defined. Some scholars believe that the URIM AND THUMMIM (Exod. 28:30; Deut.

33:9; Ezra 2:63) were objects, possibly two small round pebbles signifying "yes" or "no," that were placed in the EPHOD of the high priest. When the priest reached blindly into the ephod and took out one stone, the question was answered either affirmatively or negatively by the stone he found in his hand. There were, however, many instances recorded where lots were cast without the use of the Urim and Thummim.

Numerous passages in the OT indicate that the casting of lots was customarily employed for making important decisions. AARON, on the Day of Atonement, chose by lot one of the goats for a scapegoat to bear the sins of the people into the wilderness (Lev. 16:7–10, 21–22). The division of the land of Palestine after the conquest was accomplished by lot (Josh. 14:2; 18:6; 1 Chr. 6:54). The service of the TEMPLE, including the musicians (1 Chr. 25:7–8), the gatekeepers (26:13–16), and the supply of wood fuel for the altar, were regulated by casting lots (Neh. 10:34). The guilt of suspected criminals was established by lot (Josh. 7:14; 1 Sam. 14:42). The principle underlying this usage is stated in Prov. 16:33: "The lot is cast into the lap, / but its every decision is from the LORD." (Regarding the Feast of Lots, see PURIM.)

The same usage persisted in NT times. The soldiers at the foot of the cross cast lots for the clothing of Jesus (Matt. 27:35), thus fulfilling an OT prophecy (Ps. 22:18). Within the church, the successor of JUDAS ISCARIOT among the apostles was selected by lot (Acts 1:26). In the latter instance the choice was preceded by prayer. There is no explicit indication that this procedure was approved by God, and it never appears in the later activities of the church. The guidance of the HOLY SPIRIT seems to have been manifested in other ways.

F. E. HAMILTON

Lots, Feast of. See PURIM.

lotus. This English term is usually applied to the *Nelumbo nucifera* (a large aquatic plant with pinkish flowers) and to similar plants, such as the Egyptian water lily (*Nymphaea lotus*, see LILY-WORK). In modern Bible versions, however, the word is used as the rendering of Hebrew *ṣe'elîm* H7365, which occurs only in Job 40:21–22 in a description of the BEHEMOTH: "Under the lotus plants he lies / hidden among the reeds in the marsh, / The lotuses conceal him in their shadow [*ṣēl* H7503]; / the poplars by the stream surround him." The plant in view is apparently *Zizyphus lotus*, a deciduous small tree, bearing 3-veined leaves (elliptic-oblong in shape) and tiny flowers, followed by yellow, roundish fruits. The tree gives good shade (cf. KJV, "shady trees") and is well known in Palestine. See FLORA (under *Rhamnaceae*). W. E. SHEWELL-COOPER

love. A deep feeling of affection and solicitude for someone. Love is fundamental in true religion, harmoniously binding deity and worshipers. The revelation of deity as the God of love is a distinctive of the Hebrew and Christian religions. More than members of other religions, Christians consciously enjoy a mutual love between themselves and God.

The highest expression of love in the OT was commanded by MOSES in the Shema ("Hear," Deut. 6:4–5), quoted by Jesus (Matt. 22:39), and still today repeated twice daily by devout Jews. It is essentially the first commandment stated positively, which Jesus called "the great commandment." The Shema was a call to Israel to "Love the LORD your God with all your heart and with all your soul and with all your strength." Later, the PROPHETS—notably Hosea, Jeremiah, and Isaiah—declared God's "steadfast" and "everlasting love" for his people. Finally, God's supreme and immeasurable love was manifested in JESUS CHRIST. Consequently, it was revealed that God's love through his chosen people includes all mankind. Jesus condensed the TEN COMMANDMENTS by stressing two other commandments with "love" as the verb in both (cf. Deut. 6:5; Lev. 19:18). Then he said, "All the Law and the Prophets hang on these two commandments" (Matt. 22:40). And Paul said that "love is the fulfilling of the law" (Rom. 13:10).

Love is a dominant and indispensable virtue in both the OT and the NT. Through its impelling influence, the good news of God's care for human beings has ceaselessly expanded toward the remote corners of the world for two millennia. From the prophets of the OT to the preachers of today, the note of love has been sounded. Love in divine-human as well as interhuman relationships is at the heart of Christian life and teachings. Hymns, songs, literature, and poetry have been inspired and vitalized by the theme of love. PAUL declared love to be the greatest of the Christian graces (1 Cor. 13:13). JOHN THE APOSTLE stated that God himself is love, and that love emanates from God (1 Jn. 4:7–8). Jesus showed that love was the identifying badge of divine sonship (Matt. 5:44–45). Love is also a prerequisite to being a good citizen, a good neighbor, or a good husband or wife or parent.

   I. Definition
      A. Terminology
      B. Attributes
  II. The love of God
      A. Attribute of God's nature
      B. Expression of God's nature
      C. Extension of God's nature
 III. The love of Christ
      A. The donation of love
      B. The degrees of love
      C. The demands of love
 IV. Human love
      A. Family love
      B. Friendship love
      C. Spurious love
      D. Spiritual love
  V. The legacy of love
      A. A person—the Son of God
      B. A power—the Spirit of God
      C. A province—the kingdom of God
      D. A portrait—the nature of God
      E. A permanence—the City of God
 VI. Conclusion

I. Definition

A. Terminology. Love is an abstract quality and is therefore indefinable in precise terminology. It finds expression in both nouns and verbs, which occur throughout the Bible. Love is defined in one dictionary as "an emotion, sentiment, or feeling of pleasurable attraction toward, or delight in something, as a principle, or a person, or a thing, which induces a desire for the presence, possession, well-being, or promotion of its object"; it is also described as "strong feeling of affection … devoted attachment … great tenderness."

The term *love* in the OT is usually the rendering of the Hebrew verb *ʾāhab H170* or its cognate noun *ʾahăbâ H173*. The word is used for various types of love in the OT. Some examples of its use are: (a) sensuous, both legitimate and illicit, as shown respectively in JACOB's feelings for RACHEL (Gen. 29:30), and AMNON's lust for TAMAR (2 Sam. 13:4); (b) covenantal love between DAVID and JONATHAN (2 Sam. 1:26); (c) and spiritual love existing between God and Israel (Deut. 4:37; Mal. 1:2). In addition, the English word can be used to represent a variety of Hebrew terms, such as *ḥesed H2876* ("favor, grace, kindness"), and other expressions. (See further *NIDOTTE*, 1:277–99; 2:211–18.)

In the NT, Greek *phileō G5797* denotes an inclination prompted by sense and emotion. It means "to love" in the sense of being friendly, "to delight in or long for, to love to do, or to do with pleasure," and even "to kiss" (the cognate noun *philia G5802* occurs only in Jas. 4:4, but note *philadelphia G5789*, "brotherly love," and other compounds). This verb can also be used of divine love, however (Jn. 5:20; 16:27). Another verb, *agapaō G26*, properly denotes a love founded on admiration, veneration, and esteem. It means "to have a preference for, wish well to, regard the welfare of" (Matt. 5:43–44). It is to be full of good will both in thought and deed (Lk. 7:40–47). (This verb is used in a negative context in 2 Tim. 4:10; outside the NT, it is used of sexual love on a few occasions.) The noun form, *agapē G27* (first attested in the SEPTUAGINT and rarely found outside the Bible), is defined as "affection, good will, love, benevolence," as seen in numerous references (Jn. 15:13; Rom. 13:10; 1 Jn. 4:18). It is distinctively a biblical and ecclesiastical word, and the one commonly used in the spiritual sense. It is employed in expressing God's love to human beings (Jn. 3:16); human love for God (2 Thess. 3:5; 1 Jn. 2:5; 3:17); and spiritual love among human beings (Jn. 15:12–13; Rom. 13:8; Gal. 5:14). (Both the verb and the noun, however, can be used in negative contexts; e.g., LXX 2 Sam. 13:15 [lust]; LXX Isa. 1:23 [greediness]; Jn. 12:43 [vainglory]; 2 Tim. 4:10 [apostasy]; et al.)

AGAPE acquired special significance as the name applied to the love feasts of early Christians. This feast was a common meal in connection with and prior to the celebration of the LORD'S SUPPER. It was truly a love feast expressing and fostering mutual love. Therein poorer Christians mingled with the wealthier and partook in common with the rest of the food provided by the wealthier. This feast is mentioned by name or referred to in substance by three NT writers (Jude 12; cf. 1 Cor. 11:20–22; 2 Pet. 2:13).

Because there is of necessity some overlapping in the meanings of *agapaō* and *phileō*, they are in some instances used interchangeably (cf. Jn. 14:23 and 16:27). The use of the two verbs in 21:15–17 is thought by some to mark a semantic distinction, but others dispute this interpretation (see D. A. Carson, *The Gospel according to John* [1991], 676–77). One distinction may be seen in application. The verb *phileō* does not occur in commands to love, possibly because love as an emotion cannot be commanded. Contrarily, love as a choice may be commanded; hence, Jesus instructed his disciples, "Love [*agapate*] your enemies" (Matt. 5:44). (See further *NIDNTT*, 2:538–51.)

B. Attributes. Though love itself is an attribute (of God), it in turn consists of attributes. It is through these attributes, functional characteristics, and fruits, that love is portrayed in the Bible rather than through definitive terms. From the earliest patriarchal records (Gen. 24:12) the durability and permanence of love is portrayed in the continual recurrence of the word *ḥesed*, rendered "steadfast love" by the NRSV (see LOVINGKINDNESS; MERCY). It occurs in nearly every book in the OT, totaling well over two hundred times, and is particularly frequent in the Psalms and the later writings. It is repeated twenty-six times in Ps. 136. This is a thanksgiving psalm for the Lord's great deeds on behalf of his people, in which the response is, "For his steadfast love endures for ever" (NRSV). The same quality appears in Jeremiah when God promises joyful restoration from Babylonian exile, declaring to Israel, "I have loved [*ahab*] you with an everlasting love [*ʾahăbâ*]; / I have drawn you with loving-kindness [*ḥesed*]" (Jer. 31:3; here the NRSV has "faithfulness"). PAUL likewise subscribes to the eternal quality of love in declaring that "Love never fails" (1 Cor. 13.8a).

Another attribute of love is power. The maiden in the love song declares that "love is strong as death" (Cant. 8:6); and then with fire as a metaphor says, "Many waters cannot quench love; / rivers cannot wash it away" (v. 7). The power of love between the sexes sometimes forces one into unconventional ways, as in the case of SAMSON's love for the PHILISTINE women (Jdg. 14–16). The power of love holds the family together, binds church members together, and tethers believers to God.

Charity, in the broad sense of giving, is a primary quality of love. Certainly, giving is Godlike. "For God so loved the world that he gave" his dearest and best to save sinners (Jn. 3:16). Likewise, Jesus so loved people that he willingly died for them (Eph. 5:2). The Christian philosopher Thomas Aquinas said that CREATION itself sprang from God's love of giving. Love separates the givers from the getters. Consequently, eleven disciples left all that they had to give themselves to Jesus and his work, whereas JUDAS ISCARIOT grabbed thirty pieces of silver. The reward of the former was membership in the infinite kingdom of love; the reward of the latter, an untimely and ignominious death.

Other characteristics of love are compassion, tenderness, and sympathy. An old hymn says, "Love drew salvation's plan ... love brought God down to man." Love puts one in the other's place. Modern psychology has popularized the word *empathy*, but its meaning is as old as the Christian era, as God in Christ projected himself into human life. Jesus' own love was expressed in compassion and sympathy as "he bore the sin of many" (Isa. 53:12), and as he wept with those who mourned (Jn. 11:35).

The fullest biblical commentary is Paul's ode on love, 1 Cor. 13. It appears as the climax to his discussion on SPIRITUAL GIFTS in the preceding chapter (12:1–11). All these, he says, are worthless without love. Even if we have gifts of tongues, prophecy, faith, and make the supreme sacrifice, without love we gain nothing (13:1–3). Paul then lists the attributes and characteristics of love: "Love is patient, love is kind. It does not envy, it does not boast, it is not proud. It is not rude, it is not self-seeking, it is not easily angered, it keeps no record of wrongs. Love does not delight in evil but rejoices with the truth. It always protects, always trusts, always hopes, always perseveres" (13.4–7). In the succeeding verses he says, "Love never fails" (v. 8a); points up the perfection and maturity of love (vv. 10–11); and concludes, "And now these three remain: faith, hope and love. But the greatest of these is love" (v. 13). Paul was a beneficiary of God's love, and was therefore keenly aware of its necessity and effectiveness in his ministry as Christ's emissary.

II. The love of God. To experience love is to experience God; to know love is to know God. God is inseparable from his nature. It is significant that Paul wrote both of "the God of love" and "the love of God" (2 Cor. 13:11, 14). The former signifies the nature of God, and the latter, the expression of that nature. Both claim our noblest response. (On the attributes of God, see GOD, BIBLICAL DOCTRINE OF, III.C.)

A. Attribute of God's nature. Love is a part of the nature of God and has its ultimate origin in him. Every expression of love, therefore, whether divine or human, emanates from God. "God is love" (1 Jn. 4:8b), and consequently all love has its roots in the Godhead. To love is to be like God. The essence of God's nature is portrayed by John as "life" (Jn. 1:4), "spirit" (4:24), "light" (1 Jn. 1:5), "truth" (1:6), and "love" (4:8).

Although love is an eternal attribute of God, which always benefits his creatures, it was through the long process of revelation that people became more aware of this significant fact. It was not until the decline of the northern kingdom that the love of God, in Hosea's prophecy, was presented as a dominant theme (Hos. 11:1). Later, at the fall of the southern kingdom, Jeremiah portrayed the Lord as a God of love, compassion, and tenderness, not only to the Jews but to all mankind (Jer. 31:3). In the dark days of the Babylonian exile, Isaiah sang, "I will recount the steadfast love of the LORD ... his mercy, according to the abundance of his steadfast love" (Isa. 63:7 RSV).

B. Expression of God's nature. The love of God may be seen in all his creative works. At times and places, law and power are more in evidence in nature, but God's love is undergirding all (Rom. 1:20). Love is manifested in beauty and orderliness, and in the balance and sustenance of natural life. Nature in turn becomes an instrument of God's love for us in providing food in plants (Gen. 1:29–30) and in fish, birds, and animals (9:2–3). God's promise to NOAH after the flood summarizes his loving care for men and women through natural laws: "As long as the earth endures, seedtime and harvest, cold and heat, summer and winter, day and night will never cease" (8:22). God's love also transcends the area of ecology.

ENOCH and Noah experienced the personal love of God. ABRAHAM achieved divine favor and was chosen as the fountainhead of God's immeasurable redeeming love (Gen. 12:2; 22:15–18). Subsequently, God progressively revealed his love to the world until it reached its fullest measure in the gift of Jesus Christ. Early in his ministry, Jesus revealed to NICODEMUS, a ruler and teacher of Israel, that "God so loved the world that he gave his one and only Son, that whoever believes in him shall not perish but have eternal life" (Jn. 3:16). Luther called this verse "the Gospel in miniature." It reveals both the extent and power of God's love. It reveals the FATHERHOOD OF GOD and his compassionate care for his children on earth. Jesus' entire ministry expressed God's love.

C. Extension of God's nature. Christ is the foremost object of God's love (Jn. 17:24), yet long before Christ made his appearance in history God was manifesting his love. When MOSES returned from Mount Sinai with the two new tables of stone, God disclosed himself as "abounding in love and faithfulness, maintaining love to thousands, and forgiving wickedness, rebellion and sin" (Exod. 34:6–7). Subsequently, it became increasingly evident that Israel was the object of God's love.

Even in Israel's apostasy, God revealed to the prophet HOSEA his undying love for his chosen people. Divine compassion that would not let Israel go was realistically portrayed through HOSEA in the domestic drama of a faithful husband's love to an unfaithful wife (Hos. 1:2–3; 3:1–5). The prophet related God's consoling promise, "I will heal their waywardness / and love them freely, / for my anger has turned away from them. / I will be like the dew to Israel; / he will blossom like a lily" (14:4–5). When there was valid reason to reject Israel, God revealed himself as a husband whose persistent love ultimately reclaims his wayward wife. This advance in revelation portrays more of the love of God, and more of its availability to human beings. It becomes more intimate, more personal, and consequently more vital in human affairs.

In Judah's darkest hour — her beloved city ravaged, her sacred temple destroyed, her nobility deported to Babylon, and her land desolate and waste — God supported his people with his hand of love. Just before this dark hour, JEREMIAH acknowledged to God, "You show love to thousands" (Jer. 32:18). He delivered God's promise that restoration would occur and that his people would again sing their former song of praise, "Give thanks to the LORD Almighty, / for the LORD is good; his love endures forever" (33:11; cf. Ps. 136:1). "For I will restore the fortunes of the land as they were before, says the LORD" (Jer. 33:11).

God's love was never confined to the Hebrews, but was from their progenitor mediated through them (Gen. 12:3). In due time Jesus could declare that "salvation is from the Jews" (Jn. 4:22b). He said that "God so loved the world," not just Israel; that he provided eternal life for all who would believe (3:16). As God was fully revealed in Jesus Christ, his nature of extending and comprehending love became manifest. Henceforth it would be known that God loved Gentiles and Jews, sinners and righteous, aliens and neighbors, rich and poor, black and white — all people everywhere (Matt. 28:19; Acts 1:8), not just the favored ethnic or religious groups. In three parables — the lost sheep, the lost coin, and the lost son (Lk. 15:3–32) — Jesus illustrated God's love for an individual, its searching mission accomplished, and the consequent joy in heaven. This lends credence to Paul's assertion, "Love never fails" (1 Cor. 13:8).

III. The love of Christ.

The love of Christ is unique in that Jesus is both the personification and mediator of God's love. From this approach may be seen the donation, degrees, and demands of love.

A. The donation of love. Christ is the gift of God's love to us, and sufficient for all our needs: life, liberty, healing, happiness, fellowship with others and with God. Paul admonished the Roman Christians, "Let no debt remain outstanding, except the continuing debt to love one another" (Rom. 13:8). Love therefore is a personal product of supreme value, and a debt that every Christian owes his brother; but love is a free gift from God, unmerited by sinners. God does not owe it, but we do, because we are placed under obligation by the free gift from God to share it with others. When Jesus sent the Twelve on their initial tour of home missions, he said to them, "Freely you have received, freely give" (Matt. 10:8b).

Jesus specifically declared to his disciples his mediation of God's gift of love: "As the Father has loved me, so have I loved you. Now remain in my love. If you obey my commands, you will remain in my love, just as I have obeyed my Father's commands and remain in his love" (Jn. 15:9–10). Jesus' fourfold ministry of preaching, teaching, healing, and redeeming was God's love in action, as well as an expression of Jesus' own love (Matt. 4:23; 20:28; cf. 10:7–8).

B. The degrees of love. There are degrees of love as there are varieties of love. "For God so loved" implies degree, in this case the fullest degree. Sinners who love only those who love them (Matt. 5:43–48) limit their love to small degrees. Jesus admonished his disciples to do better than that. An example of degrees of love was pointed out by Jesus as he sat at table in the house of Simon the Pharisee. During the meal, a sinful woman poured ointment on Jesus, at the same time weeping and wiping his feet. The Pharisee inaudibly scorned the act because Jesus allowed a sinful woman to touch him. In response Jesus told Simon a parable of two debtors, with unequal debts, whose creditor forgave both, and asked Simon which one would love most. Then Jesus contrasted Simon's limited love with that of the woman, declaring, "Her many sins have been forgiven — for she loved much. But he who has been forgiven little loves little" (Lk. 7:47).

The postresurrection scene at the seaside provides another example of the degrees of love. Here Jesus asked PETER, "do you love me more than these?" (Jn. 21:15). The question recalled Peter's former boast when he implied that he loved Jesus more than the other disciples did (Mk. 14:29).

The Gospels record that Jesus stated the measure of love: "Love the Lord your God with all your heart and with all your soul and with all your mind", and "Love your neighbor as yourself" (Matt. 22:37–40). The law then was summarized in the expression of love as stated in these two commandments (cf. Deut. 6:5; Lev. 19:18). To these Jesus added a NEW COMMANDMENT of love by which his disciples were to be bound in spiritual brotherhood: "My command is this: Love each other as I have loved you. Greater love has no one than this, that he lay down his life for his friends" (Jn. 15:12–13). That was the supreme measure of love, the highest degree possible to human beings. Soon afterward Jesus laid down his life for his friends and challenged them to comparable devotion.

C. The demands of love. Paul wrote to the Corinthians, "Christ's love compels us" (2 Cor. 5:14). Christians are controlled, constrained, and motivated by the love of Christ. As Jesus faced the cross, he said, "The man who loves his life will lose it" (Jn. 12:25). Jesus was ready to lose his life to save it and others. Thus he also said, "But I, when I am lifted up from the earth, will draw all men to myself" (Jn. 12:32). Paul felt the pull of that love on the cross, and he saw its effects in Christian converts. Love like that could not end at the cross; it would find response in the hearts of people and make demands upon their lives.

The love of Christ placed Paul "under obligation both to Greeks and to barbarians, both to the wise and to the foolish" (Rom. 1:14 RSV). Throughout this masterful treatise, Paul made it clear that his impelling drive to share his spiritual blessings came out of his experience in Christ. His rejoicing, endurance, and hope, even in suffering, were "because God has poured out his love into our hearts by the Holy Spirit, whom he has given us" (5:5). This love he traced through Christ from God, climaxed in the CRUCIFIXION. "But God demonstrates his own love for us in this: While we were still sinners, Christ died for us" (5:8). All the commands of the Decalogue could not be as effective as this one act of supreme love. Paul was willing to live for it and to die for it. It was his drive and demand, in work and in death. "We know that in all things God works for the good of those who love him" (8:28). Triumphantly he asked, "Who shall separate us from the love of Christ?"; and answered that no power or person "will be able to separate us from the love of God that is in Christ Jesus our Lord" (8:35–39).

For clarity it may be seen that "the love of Christ compels" in three areas of the believer's life: his faith, his manner of life, and his ministry. All are evident in NT Christians, particularly in the boldness and persistence of the apostles in their preaching. Paul said, "Woe to me if I do not preach the gospel!" (1 Cor. 9:16). Peter and the other apostles deliberately disobeyed the Jewish council's order not to preach, and then boldly defied the council in court, declaring, "We must obey God rather than men!" (Acts 5:29). STEPHEN—a deacon, not an apostle—was so impelled by Christ's love that he gave his life after preaching one sermon to the SANHEDRIN (7:2–60). Thousands of men and women since have followed the examples of these early Christians for the love of Christ.

IV. Human love. When John exhorts his readers to "love one another," the reason he gives is that "love comes from God … God is love" (1 Jn. 4:7–8). Divine love is therefore the source of

The love between a husband and wife is artfully illustrated in this statue of Meryre (scribe of the Memphis temple) and his wife, Iniuia (from Saqqara, c. 1335 B.C.).

human love. Love is that essential, benevolent, and desirable reciprocal bond that binds a person pleasingly and favorably to the beings dearest to him or her—family, friends, and God. After listing a number of interpersonal virtues, Paul admonished, "And over all these virtues put on love, which binds them all together in perfect unity" (Col. 3:14). Such love finds expression in numerous ways in the home, community, and church.

A. Family love. Human love in the FAMILY forms a bond between husband and wife, between parents and children, and among siblings. A distinctive of the Hebrew race was its emphasis on family ties. Beginning with Abraham and increasing in importance, the home was sacred and held in highest esteem (Exod. 20:14, 17). Jacob's family, in spite of shortcomings, made an indelible impact on the history of the family. Hebrew records of genealogy is another example. Through Jesus' life and teachings, family love was enhanced and became a cherished Christian heritage. The holy family, Jesus' presence at a marriage, his parables related to marriages, his elevation of womanhood, and his tenderness for children formed a precedent for strong family love.

Matrimonial love was ordained of God (Gen. 2:18–25), and in three recorded biblical instances God specifically revealed in it his purpose to bless mankind. In the beginning God created "male and female" for the purpose of companionship, love, and increasing the human race (1:27–28; 2:18–24). God also chose the matrimonial love of Abraham and Sarah to produce a chosen people through which all nations could be blessed (12:1–3; 17:15–16). Also, God chose the home of Joseph and Mary to bring his own Son into the world to redeem it (Lk. 1:30–33; 2:47). Other examples confirm God's blessings on sexual love in marriage: Jacob and his wives Rachel and Leah (Gen. 29:20, 30, 32); Ruth and Boaz (Ruth 2–4); and David and Bathsheba (though tainted at first), whose son Solomon perpetuated the royal lineage (2 Sam. 11; 1 Ki. 1:28–30).

Therefore, matrimonial sexual love is legitimate, essential, and desirable. It has played a major role in human society from the beginning. The love lyrics in the SONG OF SOLOMON reflect the normal impassioned courtship love of young adulthood

Terra-cotta plaque from Ur showing an affectionate couple (early 2nd millennium B.C.).

as a prelude to marriage. After marriage, man is told to "Enjoy life with your wife, whom you love" (Eccl. 9:9). Paul encouraged matrimonial love and compared it to the love bond between Christ and his CHURCH. Consequently, he commanded: "Husbands, love your wives, just as Christ loved the church" (Eph. 5:25). To this he added the instruction, "In this same way, husbands ought to love their wives as their own bodies. He who loves his wife loves himself. After all, no one ever hated his own body, but he feeds and cares for it, just as Christ does the church" (vv. 28–29).

Reciprocally, he commanded that "the older women ... train the younger women to love their husbands and children" (Tit. 2:3–4). Jesus emphasized the sacredness and joy of the marriage bond both in his teachings (Matt. 5:31–32; 19:3–9) and by his presence at the marriage at CANA, where he performed his first miracle (Jn. 2:1–11). Paul recommended love as the unifying bond of the entire household, mentioning wives, husbands, children, fathers, and slaves (Col. 3:18–22). Jesus metaphorically spoke of the spiritual family, with God as the heavenly Father (Jn. 14:23).

B. Friendship love. There is an interhuman bond of love in which neither sex nor spirit is dominant. It exists between man and man, woman and woman, and man and woman (often called "platonic love"). One well-known classic example stands out in biblical history—that of JONATHAN and DAVID, one the king's son, the other the king's servant. When David's life was threatened by King SAUL, he informed his friend Jonathan (natural heir to the throne) of his father's intention. Jonathan then jeopardized his own life and his royal inheritance to save David. "And Jonathan had David reaffirm his oath out of love for him, because he loved him as he loved himself" (1 Sam. 20:17). Later, in David's lamentation over the death of Saul and Jonathan, he expressed, "I grieve for you, Jonathan my brother; you were very dear to me. Your love for me was wonderful, more wonderful than that of women" (2 Sam. 1:26).

Another biblical story of friendship love, hardly less known and loved, is that between RUTH and her mother-in-law NAOMI. Ruth, a young Moabite widow, voluntarily left her native land to go with Naomi, an Israelite, back to her home in BETHLEHEM in Judea. Her deep devotion is expressed in the well-known verse: "Don't urge me to leave you or to turn back from you. Where you go I will go, and where you stay I will stay. Your people will be my people and your God my God. Where you die I will die, and there I will be buried. May the LORD deal with me, be it ever so severely, if anything but death separates you and me" (Ruth 1:16–17).

Jesus set a beautiful example of personal human friendship. There were specific ones of whom it was said Jesus loved. John refers to himself as "the disciple whom Jesus loved" (Jn. 21:20). Earlier, in recording the sickness of LAZARUS and his subsequent death, John had quoted MARY and MARTHA as saying in their message to Jesus, "Lord, the one you love is sick" (11:3). To this he added his own comment, "Jesus loved Martha and her sister and Lazarus" (v. 5). It is common in human experience to have an inner circle of friends who are best loved. Jesus had his, and thereby endorsed friendship.

C. Spurious love. Love that is limited to selfish interest of a worldly and temporal nature is spurious. It expresses itself in a number of ways. One is extramarital sex indulgence, the prostitution of honorable members of the body by spurious love (1 Cor. 12:23–24). Two of the Ten Commandments, seventh and tenth, forbid adultery and sexual lust respectively (Exod. 20:14, 17). Jesus speaks strongly against illicit sexual desires (Matt. 5:28). In the Wisdom Literature, men are warned against the enticing flattery and seduction of a harlot or adulteress who says, "Come, let's drink deep of love till morning; let's enjoy ourselves with love! My husband is not at home; he has gone on a long journey" (Prov. 7:18–19). In the unfaithfulness of Hosea's wife, the heartbreaking effects of Israel's apostasy is illustrated (Hos. 3:1). With vivid metaphor, Ezekiel drew a sordid picture of Judah's apostasy: "Then the Babylonians came to her, to the bed of love, and in their lust they defiled her" (Ezek. 23:17).

Spurious love also takes the form of greed for material things—houses, lands, money, all kinds of worldly possessions. Jesus called these things MAMMON, and uttered strong warnings against their influence. He said, "No one can serve two masters. Either he will hate the one and love the other, or he will be devoted to the one and despise the other. You cannot serve both God and Money [*mamōnas* G3410]" (Matt. 6:24). He often warned against riches and, in two parables—the rich farmer (Lk. 12:16–21) and the rich man and Lazarus (16:19–31)—against the fatal consequences of being a slave to riches. Summarily, Paul said, "For the love of money is the root of all kinds of evils" (1 Tim. 6:10). Later he wrote to Timothy, "Demas, because he loved this world, has deserted me" (2 Tim. 4:10).

Jesus pointed out that even love for one's family could be selfish. "Anyone who loves his father or mother more than me is not worthy of me; anyone who loves his son or daughter more than me is not worthy of me" (Matt. 10:37). Moreover, the one "who loves his life loses it" (Jn. 12:25; cf. Rev. 12:11).

A fourth type of spurious love is vainglory. It is most prevalent and most tempting, making its appeal to the ego. It can destroy the effectiveness of religion by replacing God with self, as did the Jewish leaders in Jesus' day. Jesus called them hypocrites who "love to pray standing in the synagogues and on the street corners to be seen by men" (Matt. 6:5). His renunciation was strong: "Woe to you Pharisees, because you love the most important seats in the synagogues and greetings in the marketplaces" (Lk. 11:43). He warned against the scribes for the same conduct plus their love for "the places of honor at banquets" (20:46).

To these may be added the love of pleasure and the love of wine (Prov. 21:17; Isa. 47:8), and anything else that may come under the heading of "the world or anything in the world. If anyone loves the world, the love of the Father is not in him" (1 Jn. 2:15).

D. Spiritual love. The highest form of human love is spiritual. In the godly person it is both spontaneous and commanded. Jesus defined the bond of believers in a love sequence. "As the Father has loved me, so have I loved you. Now remain in my love. If you obey my commands, you will remain in my love, just as I have obeyed my Father's commands and remain in his love" (Jn. 15:9–10). With God and his kingdom as the focal attraction of human love, all other objects of love may properly and acceptably fall into subordinate categories. The kingdom of God and his righteousness, however, are to be sought first for a person to keep his love in proper perspective (Matt. 6:33).

Love on a lower plane is based on emotion and therefore prompted by feeling, whereas spiritual love can be commanded. Consequently, in NT righteousness, Jesus could and did make a threefold command to love. The believer must love God completely, his neighbor as himself, and his Christian brother as Christ loves him (Lk. 10:27; Jn. 15:12).

As Paul discussed various activities of the Christian life, he concluded by pointing out "the most excellent way" (1 Cor. 12:31b) with his immortal classic on love (1 Cor. 13). In it he virtually personified love, and this portrayal may very well be a picture of Jesus Christ. It is at once the greatest of the spiritual gifts, the attributes of Christ, and the example of perfection for Christians. It lacks jealousy, boastfulness, arrogance, rudeness, selfishness, and irritability; it rejoices in the right, bearing all things, believing, hoping, enduring; and never fails in any endeavor and ends in him as in circumstances. This is spiritual love—excellent and eternal—and attainable by human beings through the love of Christ.

On the same high plane, John emphasized brotherly love of believers. He is persuasive in his logical presentation: God's love is seen in sending his Son for the expiation for our sins; to love one another is the primary authentication that we know God, whom no man has ever seen; the testimony of the Holy Spirit, combined with our confession that Jesus is God's Son, insures our dwelling in God and God in us; and this perfected love allays any fear of judgment in us; and finally that love originates with God, and that love for a brother is essential to love for God (1 Jn. 4:7–21). According to the enlightening quality of love, John wrote, "Whoever loves his brother lives in the light, and there is nothing in him to make him stumble" (2:10). Thus Jesus, Paul, and John show the necessity, nature, and rewards of man's spiritual love.

V. The legacy of love. Love may be viewed from many standpoints, but no comprehensive view is possible without citing the benefits and blessings of God's love. Hosea stated the phrase, "fruit of unfailing love" (Hos. 10:12). It suggests the legacy of love. The multiple expressions of God's love may be summarized in five legacies to man.

A. A person—the Son of God. Jesus Christ is God's preeminent gift to human beings, since through him all others were and are administered. He is love in person, offering the rich legacies of love. He makes available not only eternal life, but abundant life with joy, gladness, peace, assurance of God's daily care, and hope (Matt. 5:12; 6:25–33; Jn. 10:10, 11:27). The person, works, and teachings of Jesus constitute the world's richest legacy. He set the perfect example of ethical love. In his brief and busy ministry, he supplied human need in tenderness and love: "he went about doing good and healing all who were under the power of the devil" (Acts 10:38). Finally he mediated God's love in its deepest expression by his voluntary death on the cross (Matt. 20:28; Jn. 10:17–18). He helped people live, and he gave life beyond death. Beyond the grave he gave them hope: "Because I live, you also will live" (Jn. 14:19b). He showed the world the immortality of love. Paul, like other believers, got the message and boldly asked, "Who shall separate us from the love of Christ?" (Rom. 8:35). Triumphantly, he answered his own question with the assurance that neither invisible powers "nor anything else in all creation, will be able to separate us from the love of God that is in Christ Jesus our Lord" (v. 39). The crowning gift of God's love is his Son.

B. A power—the Spirit of God. Someone has said that in the OT God was for man; in Jesus Christ God was with man; and in the Holy Spirit God was in man (cf. Jn. 14:17b). God not only sent Jesus, he sent his HOLY SPIRIT to dwell in those who love Jesus and keep his commandments (v. 15). "Whoever has my commands and obeys them, he is the one who loves me. He who loves me will be loved by my Father, and I too will love him and show myself to him" (v. 21). Thus Paul could rejoice in suffering, "because God has poured out his love into our hearts by the Holy Spirit, whom he has given us" (Rom. 5:5). In turn, Paul says, "The fruit of the Spirit is love …" (Gal. 5:22; cf. Col. 1:8).

Jesus identified the Holy Spirit as God's legacy to believers who love Christ and keep his commandments; a legacy given in response to Jesus' prayer. "And I will ask the Father, and he will give you another Counselor to be with you forever—the Spirit of truth. The world cannot accept him, because it neither sees him nor knows him. But you know him, for he lives with you and will be in you" (Jn. 14:16–17). This is a unique legacy for believers only, imparting to them Christ's life, uniting them to God, and giving peace of heart and guidance of mind (vv. 18–31). In Christ's service, the Holy Spirit is the source of power for the believer in sustaining him, in his preaching the gospel, and in his warfare against Satan (Acts 1:8; Rom. 15:13; 1 Cor. 2:4).

C. A province—the kingdom of God. The initial note in the preaching of JOHN THE BAPTIST and of Jesus was, "the kingdom of heaven is near" (Matt. 3:2; 4:17). In his teaching, Jesus sought, primarily through parables, to portray the image of the kingdom. It is in essence a spiritual kingdom (Lk. 1:33; 13:29; 17:21; Jn. 18:36) whose citizens are bound together by bonds of God's love.

In his SERMON ON THE MOUNT, sometimes called the Magna Charta of the kingdom of God, Jesus enumerated both the blessings to be received (Matt. 5:3–11) and the blessings to be given. Disciples were not only to receive the legacy of love, but they were also to convey it. It is not enough to "love those who love you": "Love your enemies … that you may be sons of your Father" (5:44–46). Jesus commanded the strongest kind of love for binding together members of the kingdom (Jn. 15:12–13). Paul wanted the Laodiceans and other believers to be "united in love" (Col. 2:2); and his prayer for the Philippians was that their love "may abound more and more" (Phil. 1:9). Similarly, Peter commanded believers: "Love the brotherhood of believers" (1 Pet. 2:17; cf. 3:8; 2 Pet. 1:7).

D. A portrait—the nature of God. In all the various aspects of God's self-disclosure, the most far-reaching and fruitful knowledge that ever came to human beings was the revelation that "God is love," demonstrated fully and magnificently in Jesus Christ. The portrait of God as a loving Father was revealed by Christ (Jn. 17:20–26). John was deeply impressed with this revelation of God. He exclaimed, "How great is the love the Father has lavished on us, that we should be called children of God!" (1 Jn. 3:1; cf. Jn. 1:12; Rom. 8:15). The writer, in his masterful sermon (1 John), portrays God so dominantly as love that other attributes are hardly seen. Thus Christ and the early Christians bequeathed to the church a glowing portrait of the God of love.

E. A permanence—the City of God. The final legacy of love is an eternal dwelling place with God. From that night in old Jerusalem when Jesus told NICODEMUS that God's love purchased eternal life for sinners (Jn. 3:16) to the closing scenes envisioning the new Jerusalem (Rev. 21:10—22:5), the NT shows that our eternal home is a gift of God's love. Jesus told his disciples that he was going to prepare a place for them, and return to take them home with him (Jn. 14:2–3). Paul said, "Now we know that if the earthly tent we live in is destroyed, we have a building from God, an eternal house in heaven, not built by human hands" (2 Cor. 5:1).

Venus de Milo, one of the best known pieces of ancient Greek sculpture (c. 130 B.C.), is thought to depict Aphrodite, called Venus by the Romans, goddess of love and beauty.

perseveres under trial, because when he has stood the test, he will receive the crown of life that God has promised to those who love him" (Jas. 1:12). Again, "Has not God chosen those who are poor in the eyes of the world to be rich in faith and to inherit the kingdom he promised those who love him?" (2:5). Furthermore, our assurance of eternal heritage lies in love on earth, "We know we have passed from death to life, because we love our brothers" (1 Jn. 3:14). Paul gave the assurance that "In love he predestined us to be adopted as his sons through Jesus Christ" (Eph. 1:4b–5). The ultimate destiny of the disciple's journey is his "Father's house" (Jn. 14:2), and the way is paved with love.

VI. Conclusion. The final word on love cannot be said, but a treatise may well be concluded with some scriptural highlights on the subject. Paul admonished believers to "Follow the way of love" (1 Cor. 14:1). There are three obvious reasons for doing so.

First, love is the essence of harmony. Without love there would be universal chaos. By it all other attributes of God are harmonized; by it all heavenly beings are in harmony; and wherever it prevails on earth there is harmony. "Above all, love each other deeply, because love covers over a multitude of sins" (1 Pet. 4:8). Love is spiritual healing of frictions and fractures in interpersonal relations. It makes possible the boundless reach of God's kingdom on earth. Love holds together and harmonizes various human elements. It binds the brotherhood. In the love of God (Jude 21) is peace and harmony. Without love, human beings are beastly, greedy, suspicious, selfish, murderous, and always at enmity with others. With love they build homes, churches, and communities, and live in harmony with God and others.

Second, love is the essence of life. "Anyone who does not love remains in death" (1 Jn. 3:14b). To love is to give, and to give is to live. Whoever loses himself in the love of God finds his life in the greatness of God (Mk. 8:35). Without love one does not risk the outward reach, but is driven by fear into the suffocating bonds of self until he dies. However, "There is no fear in love. But perfect love drives out fear" (1 Jn. 4:18). It alleviates all fear of punishment here and hereafter. It releases the life-giving

Final transaction, however, is made and possession secured when we reciprocate with love. "No eye has seen, / no ear has heard, / no mind has conceived / what God has prepared for those who love him" (1 Cor. 2:9; cf. Isa. 64:4). James gave the same conditional promise: "Blessed is the man who

forces in believers and enables them to grow toward Christian maturity. Love is an essential ingredient for human sustenance, and all people all the time need it.

Finally, love is the essence of occupational service. All occupations grow out of supply and demand in such areas as food, clothing, shelter, health, education, and spiritual welfare. The supply of God's love is abundant, and the demand is great. Agents are needed to deliver the goods. This constitutes an occupation in which there is no threat of unemployment. Every Christian is employed in the business of sharing love. Jesus closed his earthly ministry with this emphasis. Someone must take his love to the unlovely and the unloved, and keep his own supplied. At his postresurrection appearance by Galilee, after breakfast Jesus gave Peter a second test on love. Peter had failed the first in thinking that the sword was more powerful than love. Things were different now. Love had broken the bonds of death, to which he was witness. In reminiscence of his former boast of love (Mk. 14:29) and subsequent denial (Jn. 18:17, 25–27), Jesus asked him, "Simon son of John, do you love me more than these?" (Jn. 21:15). The question was repeated three times, providing the opportunity for three affirmative answers, to revoke the three denials. He passed the test, and Jesus gave him a special threefold assignment to express his love. "Feed my lambs.... Take care of my sheep.... Feed my sheep" (vv. 15–17). And this is the assignment of love for all Christians until the Lord of love comes again!

G. B. FUNDERBURK

love feast. See AGAPE.

lovingkindness. This term, apparently coined by Miles Coverdale in his translation of the Bible (1535; see VERSIONS OF THE BIBLE, ENGLISH) and rarely found in modern versions, is used by the KJV almost thirty times to render Hebrew *ḥesed* H2876, a theologically significant word that has a broad range of meaning. It signifies an attitude—either divine or human—born out of mutual relationship, for example, between relatives, friends, master/subject, host/guest. Primarily it is not a disposition but a helpful action; it corresponds to a relationship of trust. As exercised by a sovereign, it protects his dominion; it gives people security in their mutual dealings. (See *NIDOTTE*, 2:211–18.)

The term *ḥesed* also denotes "kindness" or "help" received from a superior. The meaning fluctuates: "[covenant] obligation," "loyalty," "love," "grace." Frequently it is associated with FORGIVENESS and is almost equal to MERCY (Exod. 20:6; 34:6, 7; Mic. 7:18). However, the principal connotation is "loyal love"—a love that is associated with the COVENANT (Deut. 7:12; 1 Sam. 20:8). Human beings could always rely upon the divine *ḥesed*. (The sense "covenant loyalty" was argued by N. Glueck *Ḥesed in the Bible* [1967; German orig. 1927] and has been widely accepted; this view has been criticized by S. Romerowski in *VT* 60 [1990]: 89–103.)

When the term refers to God, it indicates in general the divine love flowing out to sinners in unmerited kindness. On the divine side it comes to designate particularly GRACE. In a religious sense the *ḥesed* of God always signifies his merciful and faithful aid. The psalmist sees Yahweh as One whose *ḥesed* has been "from of old" (Ps. 25:6). He exclaims, "How priceless is your unfailing love! / Both high and low among men / find refuge in the shadow of your wings" (36:7). This divine faithfulness is extolled especially in Ps. 136. In Ps. 40 the faithfulness of God seems to imply the giving of Jesus Christ—the most convincing proof of divine mercy, kindness, and lovingkindness that could be given to a lost world (vv. 10–11). In Ps. 51 David prays, with a deeply penitent heart, for the remission of sins and expects God to grant it "according to your unfailing love" (v. 1). He is continually praising Yahweh for his love, which is good (69:16) and "better than life" (63:3). God's lovingkindness is that steadfast love that will not let Israel go. This essential and distinctive quality of God, however, should also characterize God's people (Hos. 4:1; 12:6; Mic. 6:8). See also FAITH, FAITHFULNESS; GOOD; LOVE.

R. E. PERRY

low country. See SHEPHELAH.

loyalty. See FAITH, FAITHFULNESS; LOVINGKINDNESS.

Lozon loh´zon (Λοζων). Ancestor of a group of "Solomon's servants" who returned from Babylon with ZERUBBABEL and his associates (1 Esd. 5:33; possibly the same as DARKON in the parallel passages, Ezra 2:56; Neh. 7:58).

Lubim loo´bim. See LIBYA.

Lucas loo´kuhs. KJV alternate form of LUKE (Phlm. 24).

Lucifer loo´si-fuhr. KJV rendering of Hebrew *hêlēl* H2122 ("shining one"), which occurs only once, in an oracle against the king of BABYLON (Isa. 14:12). The name comes from the VULGATE (Latin *lucifer*, "light-bringing"; cf. LXX, *eōsphoros*) and is applied to the MORNING STAR, that is, Venus (see ASTRONOMY II.D.). Some Latin church fathers, associating this passage with Lk. 10:18 (cf. also 2 Cor. 11:14), applied the name to SATAN, and this usage became common.

Lucius loo´shuhs (Λούκιος G3372 [Apoc. Λεύκιος], Lat. *Lucius*, from *lux*, "light"). **(1)** A Roman CONSUL who, in response to an embassy sent to Rome by SIMON MACCABEE, wrote a letter to PTOLEMY Euergetes of Egypt (1 Macc. 15:16–21) and other ANE rulers (15:22–23) supporting Simon in his struggles with the SELEUCIDS. That his title is imperfectly reproduced is evident in that only his praenomen is given and a date and mention of the senate are lacking. His identification is problematic. Some recent scholars think that the reference is to Lucius Caecilius Metellus Calvus, who was the consul in the year 142 B.C. This proposal assumes that there is textual or chronological confusion in the passage (see *HJP*, rev. ed. [1973–87], 1:195–97; J. A. Goldstein, *I Maccabees*, AB 41 [1976], 492, 496).

(2) A man from CYRENE, named third among the five "prophets and teachers" in the church at ANTIOCH OF SYRIA (Acts 13:1). This Lucius was apparently one of the Hellenistic Jewish Christians who had boldly preached to the Greeks in this city (11:20–21), where he remained to minister in the church.

(3) One of three "relatives" of PAUL (the others being JASON and SOSIPATER) who sent greetings to the Christians in Rome (Rom. 16:21). According to many scholars, however, the Greek term *syngenēs* G5150 here means "kinsman" (cf. RSV) and should be understood in the sense of "fellow-Jew" (cf. 9:3). It is possible, moreover, that this description applies only to Jason and Sosipater. The Lucius mentioned here is thought by some to be the same as #2 above, but that identification is not probable. (See C. E. B. Cranfield, *A Critical and Exegetical Commentary on the Epistle to the Romans*, ICC, 2 vols. [1975–79], 2:805.)

Inscriptional evidence shows that *Loukas* (LUKE) was used as an alternative form for Lucius or Lucanus, and this fact has been used to support a proposed identification of the author of the third gospel and Acts with either of the above companions of Paul. The suggested identification of Luke with #3 is as old as ORIGEN, whereas the fact that Cyrene was famous for its medical resources has been appealed to as support in identifying Luke with #2. Many believe that either identification is ruled out by Col. 4:12–14, which indicates that Luke was a Gentile rather than a Jew. Others argue that Rom. 16:21 is ambiguous regarding the ethnic identity of Lucius #3. (See A. Deissmann, *Light from the Ancient East* [1927], 435ff.; MM, 381; H. J. Cadbury in *BC*, 5:489–95; id., *The Book of Acts in History* [1955], 155–56; *ABD*, 4:396–97.)

D. E. HIEBERT

lucre. This English term is used by the KJV once in the OT to render Hebrew *beṣaʿ* H1299, "gain, profit," in a passage where the term has a negative connotation (1 Sam. 8:3; NIV, "dishonest gain"; NRSV, "bribe"). In the KJV NT it is always qualified by "filthy" as the rendering of *aischrokerdēs* G153 ("shameful gain") or a cognate expression (1 Tim. 3:3 [TR], 8; Tit. 1:7; 1 Pet. 5:2). The term *lucre* can mean simply "profit," but the rendering "filthy lucre," which goes back to Tyndale's translation, has given the word itself a bad name. A pejorative connotation, however, is already found in Middle English and even in the Latin term from which the word comes (*lucrum*, which could mean "avarice").

Lud luhd (לוּד H4276). Son of SHEM and grandson of NOAH (Gen. 10:22; 1 Chr. 1:17). Earlier in the Table of NATIONS, however, the Ludites (KJV "Ludim," Heb. *lûdîm*) are said to be descendants of Mizraim or Egypt (Gen. 10:13; 1 Chr. 1:11 [*Ketib*, *lûdiyyim*]). Since the Table of Nations is basically ethnographic in character and concerned chiefly with the origin and classification of certain of the nations of the ancient world, Lud and Ludim are to be regarded as eponymous ancestors of two different nations (one Semitic and the other Hamitic) that continued to bear their names.

The identification of Ludim/Ludites with Lydia is ruled out on the basis of the close geographical and ethnic association of Ludim with Egypt. It is probably better to regard it as a nation now unknown, as are the Anamites and Naphtuhites, which also descended from Mizraim. Lud, on the other hand, is almost certainly Lydia in several passages. The Assyrian inscriptions refer to the Lydians as *Luddu*, a cognate of Hebrew *Lud*. Josephus (*Ant*. 1.6.4) equates Lud in Gen. 10:22 with Lydia, and Herodotus speaks of Lydus, who was the traditional progenitor of the Lydians. Lud appears in association with Tarshish, Tubal, and Greece (Isa. 66:19), nations that were located along the N shores of the Mediterranean Sea. Since Lydia was in the same general area, its identification with Lud in this passage seems to be warranted. See Lydia (place).

In Ezek. 30:5 Lud probably refers to Ludim, the African nation (but see NIV). It occurs in association with Ethiopia and Libya in an oracle directed against Egypt. Some have suggested that Lud in this context may refer to Lydian mercenaries who were employed in the army of Egypt from the time of Psammetichus I, but the context seems rather to require the name of a place. In an oracle against Tyre, Ezekiel refers to mercenaries from Lud (27:10). The passage is of little help in locating Lud geographically because it is associated with Persia and Put, widely separated nations. It is quite probable, however, that Lydian mercenaries are intended, for their prowess in battle was lauded by Herodotus (*Hist*. 1.79), while the Assyrian Annals (Ashurbanipal, Rassam Cylinder) speak of Lydian mercenaries. In Jer. 46:9 a reference is obviously to the African Ludim because of its association with Ethiopian Put (but see NIV).

Egyptian inscriptions from the 13th to the 15th cent. B.C. refer to a people called Luden located near Mesopotamia. This information has led some to infer that the Lydians were displaced from their original home in Mesopotamia by the Assyrians and migrated to Asia Minor.

T. E. McComiskey

Ludim, Ludites loo′dim, loo′dīts. See Lud; Lydia (place).

Ludlul bēl nēmeqi. The first line and title of the greatest hymn to Marduk, the god of Babylon, yet discovered. The line means, "Let us praise the god of wisdom." The poem on four tablets, all in damaged condition, tells the personal lament of a pious man who is smitten by disease and later restored. It is in the most erudite dialect and form of Middle Babylonian and written in cuneiform. The superficial similarity to the theme of the biblical book of Job has brought the text to the attention of Bible students. It contains some of the finest self-conscious insights into the mood and philosophy of ancient paganism extant from the ANE. Of special interest are the lines expressing the suppliant's despair, "Who has learned the plan of the heavenly gods, Who knows the scheme of the Nether World, Where have mortals comprehended the way of the gods?" Such depths of agnostic melancholy are not equaled in ancient documents. (See W. G. Lambert, *Babylonian Wisdom Literature* [1960], 21–62; W. White, *A Babylonian Anthology* [1966], 30–34; *ANET*, 596–600.)

W. White, Jr.

Luhith loo′hith (לוּחִית *H4284*, "platform, terrace, shelf"). A city of Moab, associated with Horonaim (Isa. 15:5; Jer. 48:5). Refugees from ruined Moab are described as fleeing to Zoar by the ascent of Luhith and in the way to Horonaim. Luhith may therefore have been on a hill. Eusebius placed the town between Areopolis (i.e., Rabbath-Moab) and Zoar, but the precise location is unknown. One possibility is modern Katrabba, about 6 mi. E of the south tip of the Dead Sea.

S. Barabas

Luke look (Λουκᾶς *G3371*, a name used in inscriptions as an affectionate form of *Loukios* [see Lucius]; on the possible connection with other names, such as Lucanus, Lucianus, and Lucilius, see A. Plummer, *A Critical and Exegetical Commentary on the Gospel according to Luke*, ICC, 5th ed.

[1922], xviii, and J. A. Fitzmyer, *The Gospel according to Luke I–IX*, AB 28 [1981], 42–43).

I. Identity. Luke is mentioned by name only three times in the NT—all by PAUL while in prison (Col. 4:14; 2 Tim. 4:11; Phlm. 24). Although Luke never mentions his own name in his writings, his identity was certainly known to THEOPHILUS and, no doubt, to the reading public of that day. Luke does identify himself in a measure in the "we" sections of ACTS OF THE APOSTLES. All the leading associates of Paul (mentioned in the epistles) are eliminated from possible authorship by data in Acts, except TITUS and Luke. Since no case can be made for Titus, Luke implies his own authorship. This inference is supported by unanimous early tradition. There are, then, valid autobiographical references by Luke, particularly in Acts. His personality shows through in his gospel (see LUKE, GOSPEL OF). Luke was a Gentile, not "of the circumcision" (Col. 4:10–14). His skill in the use of Greek, along with his viewpoint and attitudes (e.g., *hoi barbaroi*, Acts 28:2, 4) mark him as such. He was a physician, a traveler, a missionary, and a writer.

II. Background. Luke probably was born in ANTIOCH OF SYRIA (so say JEROME, *De vir. ill. 7*, and EUSEBIUS, *Eccl. Hist.* 3.4.7). He shows unusual interest in this city (Acts 6:5; 11:19–27; 13:1; 14:19, 21, 26; 15:22–23, 30, 35; 18:22). Even W. M. Ramsay conceded that he was born in Antioch of a Macedonian family (*St. Paul the Traveller and Roman Citizen*, 14th ed. [1925], xxxviii). Some think he was the brother of Titus (2 Cor. 8:18; 12:18). If so, this connection would help answer the silence of Acts about Titus. D. Hayes conjectures that Paul may have known Luke at the university of TARSUS in student days (*The Most Beautiful Book Ever Written* [1913], 21). He also suggests that Luke may have known the family of the Latin poet Lucanus, the nephew of GALLIO and SENECA—a possible cause of Gallio's leniency toward Paul in Acts 18:12–17 (ibid., 7–12). Some have thought Luke may have been a freedman. Names with contractions ending in -*as* were particularly common among slaves. Greek and Roman masters often educated slaves as physicians and later freed them for their services (ibid., 46). It is even conjectured that he may have been born in the household of Theophilus, who was possibly a wealthy government official in Antioch (Lk. 1:3).

III. Medical missionary. If the reading of CODEX BEZAE in Acts 11:27–28 (which includes the pronoun "we") is correct, Paul may have known Luke in Antioch. At least by the time of Paul's visit to TROAS on the second journey, Luke joined the apostle and was with him intermittently until Paul's final imprisonment in Rome. The beloved physician not only bolstered Paul's frail health and perhaps added years to his life, but he also practiced medicine at times in their journeys. The word for "cured" in Acts 28:9 (from *therapeuō* G2543) can mean "medically treated." Luke shared the labor and the rewards. Luke also shared the call and labors of preaching (16:10–13). Perhaps he should be regarded as the first trained medical missionary.

IV. The historian. Luke was an able and deliberate historian, writing more than one-fourth of the volume of the NT—more than any other man. Modern research has vindicated the quality of his work. In legend, Luke was a painter. In fact, he was the recorder of truth that supplied the inspiration and subjects for religious art.

(See further W. Hobart, *The Medical Language of St. Luke* [1882]; W. M. Ramsay, *Luke the Physician, and Other Studies in the History of Religion* [1908]; A. Harnack, *Luke the Physician* [1909]; H. J. Cadbury, *The Making of Luke-Acts* [1927], 213–368; A. T. Robertson, *Luke the Historian in the Light of Research* [1930], 1–29; J. Baker, "Luke, the Critical Evangelist," *ExpTim* 68 [1956–57]: 123–25; I. H. Marshall, *Luke: Historian and Theologian*, 3rd ed. [1988].)

W. T. DAYTON

Luke, Gospel of. The third account of the gospel of JESUS CHRIST, according to the present common order of listing in the NT canon.

    I. Background
    II. Unity
    III. Authorship
    IV. Date
    V. Place of origin
    VI. Destination

VII. Occasion
VIII. Purpose
IX. Canonicity
X. Text
XI. Special problems
XII. Content
XIII. Theology

I. Background. The Gospel according to Luke has been called the most beautiful book ever written (E. Renan, *Les évangiles et la seconde génération chrétienne* [1877], 283). At its heart is the perfect life, Christ's teachings, redemption through him, and the lives of those who cluster around him. In this book and its counterpart, the ACTS OF THE APOSTLES, more knowledge is given of the apostles and leaders of the primitive church than is found in any other document. This author, in fact, wrote more pages of the NT than any other person.

The Greek style of this gospel is generally recognized as among the best in the NT. Though there are, of course, reflections of Semitic sources, the book is not a mere collection or compilation of fragments. It is a connected treatise by a capable and well-informed person. Whatever the author borrowed from oral or written tradition, he made it his own and cast it in his own style.

That the author had sources is evident. He made no claim of being an eyewitness of the things he described. Rather, he affirmed that the things recorded were delivered to him and to his contemporaries "by those who from the first were eyewitnesses and servants of the word" (Lk. 1:2). These words, however, also contain an important claim. While Luke was not in the apostolic group during the earthly ministry of Jesus, he does insist that the sources of his information were persons who had seen that which transpired from the beginning. Barring specific information to the contrary, the passage seems to imply not only that Luke wrote during or near the time of the apostles, but also that they were the obvious source of much of his information. In any case, he was no sketchy or casual inquirer. He had "carefully investigated everything from the beginning" so as to be able to write "an orderly account" (v. 3).

The majority of modern scholars have held that Luke had access to two main literary sources, Mark and "Q," to which he added certain materials from a source peculiarly his own, called "L." As the documentary theory was being developed in the 1860s by H. Holtzmann (*Die synoptischen Evangelien: ihr Ursprung und geschichtlicher Character*), it was not the canonical Mark, however, which was considered a source but rather an early form in which the material was cast as a protogospel that came to be called Ur-Marcus. It was B. H. Streeter, in 1924, who sought to show that Matthew and Luke used Mark (*The Four Gospels: A Study of Origins*, 157). The hypothetical document called "Q" has usually been described as a body of sayings or teachings of Jesus, much after the pattern of WISDOM Literature. Some identify it with the LOGIA that PAPIAS attributed to Matthew. In general, it is held to consist of the "double tradition," that is, the material found in both Matthew and Luke but not in Mark. See GOSPELS III.B.

On this view of sources, there was relatively little demand for originality laid upon the writer of the third gospel. The written documents furnished most of the content, much of the order, and a model for much of the form. Deviation from the models would be largely a matter of preference and of style rather than of necessity. He would be more of an editor than an author.

In spite of the repeated insistence that the documentary view no longer needs to be proved (e.g., J. Moffatt, *Introduction to the Literature of the New Testament* [1925], 180) and that "it is the one absolutely assured result of a century of learned discussion … that St. Mark's is the oldest Gospel which we possess" (A. E. J. Rawlinson, *St Mark* [1925]), there have always been dissenting voices. Germany had its Hilgenfeld, Zahn, and Schlatter. Sanday's famous seminar at Oxford had its dissentients, Allen and Bartlet. The voice of objection has not ceased in the United States from the days of E. D. W. Burton in 1904 (*Some Principles of Literary Criticism and their Application to the Synoptic Problem*) to the present. In 1964, W. R. Farmer wrote a major volume (*The Synoptic Problem: A Critical Analysis*) "to demonstrate that the idea of Markan priority is highly questionable." The debate was thus reopened but has reached no new consensus (cf. D. A. Black and D. R. Beck, eds., *Rethinking the Synoptic Problem* [2001]).

Meanwhile, it is possible to think in broader and more flexible terms of Luke's sources than would be indicated by the documentary hypotheses. Luke may well have interviewed persons related to the household of Jesus. Reports directly from eyewitnesses are probable, especially during Luke's stay in Palestine while Paul was in prison in Caesarea. Personal acquaintance with some of the apostles and other leaders of the early church is almost certain. He obviously had access to the information accumulated by Paul. Irenaeus (*Against Heresies* 3.1.1) says that Luke "recorded in a book the gospel preached by" Paul. Could not Luke have used a multiplicity of oral and written sources, possibly including another of the Synoptic Gospels, treated in the context of his own familiarity with the places and events of Palestine, governed by a strong historical sensitivity, influenced by a Gentile breadth of insight and viewpoint, and guided and inspired by the Spirit of God? How else could he have produced such a masterpiece? One thing is certain: he used his sources, but he was no slave to them.

II. Unity. Not only is the unity of the third gospel assured; there is also general agreement that its sequel, the Acts of the Apostles, is by the same author. On the basis of the same addressee (Lk. 1.3, Acts 1:1), the specific reference to the former in the latter (Acts 1:1), and the obvious similarities of style, method, and materials, it is common to refer to the two books as one compound volume of Luke-Acts.

The same distinctive literary excellence characterizes the whole. Renan called this the "most literary of the Gospels." It is the Greek of the educated man, characterized by a rich vocabulary, striking contrasts, breadth of interest, depth of insights, and intelligent concern for all types of people. His Gentile orientation is never narrow. It includes every son of Adam. The poor, the helpless, the infirm, and the sin-sick occupy his thought. He is ever a missionary and evangelist, as is his Lord.

A. Plummer says the author is the most versatile of all the NT writers (*A Critical and Exegetical Commentary on the Gospel according to Luke*, ICC, 5th ed. [1922], xlix). Though a learned Gentile (see Luke), he is sufficiently oriented in Hebrew society that he can be as thoroughly Hebraistic in describing it as he is Greek in describing his own culture. Accordingly, when Luke uses distinctly Semitic sources, as in the first two chapters of the gospel, he makes them so completely his own that they in no way mar the unity of the whole. With apparent ease, Luke moves from the classical Greek models of the prologue to a Septuagint type of Greek strongly flavored with Semitisms in the infancy narratives and on to a good literary Koine Greek in the body of the writing (see Greek language). There is no awkward piecing together of unrelated fragments. As A. B. Bruce says, "It does not matter what documents Luke used, he exercised his own judgment in using them" (*EGT*, 1:48). No part of Luke-Acts is without the distinctive and unifying stamp of the author's own genius and style.

Another mark of unity is the consistent historical interest and insight. Luke is called the first church historian. As D. Hayes says, "Mark and Matthew wrote memoirs. John wrote a philosophy of religion.... Luke the Gentile set himself to write a historical gospel, following Gentile models at certain points and connecting his account with Gentile history throughout" (*The Synoptic Gospels and the Book of Acts* [1919], 215). He alone of NT writers names the Roman emperors and uses a great many proper names to correlate times and events. From beginning to end, he is bent on relating the gospel

Latin MS of Luke with glosses or brief explanations (12th cent.).

to the world, to the empire, to all nations, and to all times. Luke raised sacred history from Israelitish nationality to universal humanity. The pattern is consistent throughout Luke-Acts.

A great deal has been said about the medical language of Luke. Whatever can be proved concerning the authorship of the gospel by it, a strong case can be made for the unity of Luke-Acts. Whether the author spoke as a physician or as an informed layman, there is a consistent pattern peculiar to these writings. No other NT book approaches the frequency of reference to medical needs, facts of diagnosis, descriptive details of the diseases and cures, psychological accompaniments, and marks of recovery. Nor does any other book contain so abundant casual use of medical vocabulary and reference to interests more particularly common to physicians. Whatever the reason, the phenomenon exists so persistently as to amount to a signature of the same author on the whole.

III. Authorship. The author never mentions his own name, but there was no difference of opinion in the early church as to his identity. No possibility was ever mentioned of questioning that the author was Luke the beloved physician, traveling companion and joint missionary with Paul. Plummer compares the certainty of the authorship of the third gospel with that of the four great epistles of Paul (*Commentary on Luke*, xvi). Irenaeus quotes from nearly every chapter of the gospel, often referring to Luke as the author. CLEMENT OF ALEXANDRIA, who had received the tradition handed down from father to son from the apostles (*Stromata* 1.1), quotes the gospel frequently and definitely assigns it to Luke. TERTULLIAN works through most of the gospel in his treatise against MARCION, often calling it Luke's. The MURATORIAN CANON not only refers to Luke but also calls him *medicus*.

Even A. Jülicher, who in modern times rejected the Lukan authorship, admitted that the ancients universally accepted it. Upon those who reject Luke as the author there rests the burden of explaining the universal voice of the church fathers in his favor. Certainly the name of Luke was not selected as a pseudonym to give prominence to the book. His name was quite unknown except as it was enhanced through his writings. As Renan says, "Luke had no place in tradition, in legend, in history" (*Les apôtres* [1866], xvii). The only reason for so universal an association of the name with the documents seems to be that Luke wrote them and thus became known.

Though Luke's writings are the source of more knowledge of the apostles, deacons, and evangelists of the early church than are the writings of any other person, Luke tells little or nothing directly about himself. He makes one reference to himself by a pronoun in the gospel (Lk. 1:3) and uses the pronouns "we" and "us" a number of times in Acts. Paul alone of NT writers refers to him by name (Col. 4:14; 2 Tim. 4:11; Phlm. 24). These references and the reflections of the author in his writings have made possible a fairly rich and authentic acquaintance with Luke. Legend has, of course, greatly elaborated the data and has led to the production of many imaginative biographies of Luke.

The strongest internal evidence for authorship stems from the "we" sections in Acts (Acts 16:10–17; 20:5—21:18; 27:1—28:16). The author was apparently a companion of Paul. The third-person phrasing in 20:4 eliminates, as possible authors, the names of Timothy, Sopater, Aristarchus, Secundus, Gaius, Tychicus, and Trophimus. Silas cannot be easily fitted into the "we" sections. There is neither external nor internal evidence for Titus. For the remaining person of Paul's associates, namely Luke, there are both kinds of evidence. The rest of Luke-Acts is by the same author as the "we" sections if style, vocabulary, and the usual marks mean anything. Therefore, it is reasonable that Luke should be considered the author of the third gospel.

W. Hobart devoted more than three hundred pages to a study of *The Medical Language of Luke* (1882). He considered four hundred terms that were used by Luke alone among writers of the NT or that were used more frequently by him than by others and that were found also in the Greek medical writers. The evidence seemed overwhelming that Luke was a physician. H. J. Cadbury argued that the data proved only that Luke was an educated man (*The Making of Luke-Acts* [1927]), and most recent scholars now consider the evidence ambiguous. Even when proper allowance is made for lay use of medical language, however, A. von Harnack's explicit statement of the case stands (*Luke the Physician* [1909]). He proves that Luke was a physician not only by his vocabulary but also by a variety of traces throughout his writings such as points of view, preference for the healing miracles, tendency to diagnose diseases, interests characteristic of physicians, and ways of reporting anecdotes. It is true that a few isolated instances prove little. But the overwhelming mass of data appears conclusive that the author was indeed a physician, presumably Luke, the only physician known to belong to Paul's missionary party.

IV. Date. The question of date is closely related to that of sources and of the order in which the Synoptic Gospels were written. If the popular view of the priority of Mark is correct and if, as is widely held, Mark's gospel was written near the time of the death of Peter and Paul (A.D. 68), Luke must have been written rather late. Streeter bridges the gap by positing a Proto-Luke—a combination of Q and the bulk of the material peculiar to the third gospel—to which Luke later added the infancy stories and materials from Mark (*The Four Gospels*, 217–18). The idea of a Proto-Luke is, however, challenged by some scholars (e.g., H. F. D. Sparks in *JTS* 44 [1943]: 129–38). Even if it should be necessary to concede that Luke wrote after A.D. 68, it is almost certain that he had been collecting sources for some years.

If, however, as a growing number of scholars believe, it is not necessary to accept the priority of Mark, or if Mark wrote earlier than the late 60s, a more natural date for Luke becomes possible. Luke says plainly (Acts 1:1) that his gospel was written before Acts. If the reason for the abrupt ending of the Acts account of Paul's life, and for the silence concerning the outcome of the Roman trial should, as many think, be simply that Acts was written while Paul was still in prison in Rome, this book must have been written early in the 60s. Then the gospel must have been written in the early 60s as well, or even in the late 50s. The fact that Luke spent two or more years in Palestine, while Paul was in prison in Caesarea, means that he was within easy walking distance of the places and people that could furnish all the data he needed. He would also have had the leisure to write at this time. On this basis, a date of A.D. 58 would be a good approximation, being near the end of Luke's residence in Palestine and before the strenuous events described in the latter part of Acts.

The objection that Luke is so commonly third in the lists of the Gospels is more apparent than real. Ancient lists appear not to have been arranged always according to date of writing. There was a strong tendency to list the two apostles, Matthew and John, first. Others, it is thought, put Mark second because he was writing as a disciple of Peter, the prominent apostle. In any case, the ancient lists present no uniform order. ORIGEN frequently cites the Gospels in the order Matthew, Luke, and Mark. CLEMENT OF ALEXANDRIA, before Origen, puts the Gospels that contain the genealogies first on the basis of the tradition he had received from the primitive elders (Euseb., *Eccl. Hist.* 6.14). Luke also stood in the second place in Ambrosiaster's list, in the Catalogue of the Sixty Canonical Books, in the Old African Latin codex, and in the cursives 90 and 399. If Luke was not an early gospel, it is remarkable that it, not being written by an apostle, was ever listed in second place, especially by such notable leaders. The preponderance of evidence tends toward A.D. 58, in the absence of any compelling reason for rejecting an early date.

V. Place of origin. JEROME, in the preface to his commentary on Matthew (see *PL*, 26:18), said that Luke wrote the gospel in ACHAIA and BOEOTIA, but the source of his information is not known. Modern guesses as to the origin of the gospel vary considerably. Plummer lists the following: Rome (Holtzmann, Hug, Keim, Lekebusch, Zeller), Caesarea (Michaelis, Schott, Thiersch, Tholuck), Asia Minor (Hilgenfeld, Overbeck), Ephesus (Köstlin), and Corinth (Godet). Then he adds, significantly, that there is no evidence for or against any of them. In the absence of any need to think otherwise, Hayes (*The Synoptic Gospels*, 203) conjectures that Luke made his first considerable gathering of material in Palestine while Paul was in prison in Caesarea.

If one accepts a relatively late date of the actual writing, one of the places mentioned above can be chosen according to the time and circumstances imagined. Or, if Acts was written during Paul's imprisonment in Rome, Luke was written either before Paul and Luke left Caesarea or soon after they arrived in Rome. As abundant as Luke's sources of information must have been among his apostolic acquaintances and others over a period of time, there is no reason why he could not have written the gospel before leaving Caesarea, unless one is bound by an opinion on the relationship between Luke and Mark that would make this view unacceptable. Wherever the gospel was written, there can be little doubt that it reflects much material that was collected personally in Palestine, and that the handling of the material reflects a broad Gentile background which includes both wide missionary vision and experience in sharing the gospel with the whole world.

VI. Destination. Both Luke and Acts are addressed, ostensibly, to an individual named THEOPHILUS. That the reference is indeed to a person and not simply to lovers of God everywhere is made clear from the epithet "most excellent" (Lk. 1:3; Acts 1:1), which Luke ascribes also to the governors FELIX and FESTUS (Acts 23:26; 24:3; 26:25). The name Theophilus was common among Jews and especially among Gentiles (Plummer, *Commentary on Luke*, xxxiii). According to the CLEMENTINE LITERATURE, Theophilus was a wealthy citizen of Antioch. The title in Luke and its absence in Acts may indicate that he held a position in the government before being established as a Christian believer. This wealthy Christian may have been Luke's literary patron, furnishing him the financial backing necessary for the publication of his two books (Hayes, *The Synoptic Gospel*, 194).

It is difficult, however, to believe that the writer of the gospel had only one reader in view. The book is too admirably suited to the whole Gentile world. While Matthew wrote with a Jewish point of view and Mark adapted that viewpoint to the action-conscious Romans, Luke wrote from a Gentile standpoint in the best Greek for the broad Greek-speaking world. Luke explained Jewish commonplaces to his Gentile readers, for example, that Nazareth was in Galilee (Lk. 1:26) and that the Feast of Unleavened Bread was called the Passover (22:1). The outlook is broad. The GENEALOGY OF JESUS CHRIST goes back to Adam (3:38). He is King not just of the Jews (Matt. 2:2). The good tidings are for all the people (Lk. 2:10). Prophecies are emphasized that include all flesh (3:5–6). Illustrations are given of God's ancient concern for Gentiles (4:25–30). Throughout the gospel, the Gentiles "belong" in God's plan of redemption and in the concern of Jesus. The companion of Paul shared the missionary vision and the arduous labors in order that all might know and believe. He wrote the Gentile gospel to the Gentile world in particular, and to the whole world in general.

VII. Occasion. The immediate occasion may well have been Luke's interest in the influential Theophilus, who had apparently made some move toward the Christian faith. The manner in which he is addressed places his needs in focus. If Luke was also of Antioch, and especially if his associations with Theophilus were particularly significant, Luke may have been greatly concerned that a full authentic account be presented to this discriminating leader. If further motive was necessary, Luke's missionary experience probably had taught him that a multitude of other discerning persons could use the same persuasive gospel.

The interruption of Paul's itinerant ministry by a prolonged imprisonment in Jerusalem and Caesarea provided the needed leisure. Luke's loyalty to Paul and perhaps Paul's recurrent need of a physician did not permit distant solitary campaigns. They did permit Luke to "carefully investigate all things" and "to write an orderly account" so that the reader or readers might "know the certainty of the things" they had been taught (Lk. 1:3–4). After participating in Paul's second and third missionary journeys, Luke did not find the data of the gospel new to him. He was in an excellent position to verify, arrange, and record the truths he had received from a variety of sources. The many attempts of others (1:1) seemed inadequate. With his superior scientific training and greater command of the Greek language, Luke no doubt felt an urge from God to do what others had only attempted. There had to be a better instrument for reaching the Gentile mind, especially among the cultured and influential.

Coin minted under Archelaus, ruler of Judea during Jesus' childhood (4 B.C. to A.D. 6).

VIII. Purpose. Though none of the Gospels reflects an aim to be complete and comprehensive in recording all the historical details of the life, ministry, and death of Jesus, history was definitely a specific aim of Luke in his work. He made no attempt to probe the silent years of Jesus' childhood and early maturity or to chronicle every event that could be reported. He did specifically investigate everything with care in order to give a perfectly reliable account of those important events and facts that constitute the gospel of Jesus Christ (Lk. 1:1–4), the historic foundations of the faith. Plummer observes that "Luke begins at the very beginning, far earlier than any other Evangelist; not merely with the birth of Christ, but with the promise of the birth of the forerunner. And he goes on to the very end: not merely to the Resurrection but to the Ascension" (*Commentary on Luke*, xxxv). Luke also has an unusually high proportion of material peculiar to himself, including many of the most beautiful treasures we possess (ibid.). Fullness of historically relevant data was an achieved goal.

While none of the Gospels is without historical interest, there is a new dimension in Luke's. He followed Gentile models at certain points and connected his accounts with Gentile history throughout. He has been called the first church historian. He did not write with a narrow controversial goal. His aim was not to depreciate the Twelve in the interests of Paul, nor to vindicate Paul, nor to reconcile the Judaizers with Paul's disciples (ibid., xxxvi). The document is no party paper under the cover of fictitious history. It is a carefully prepared research treatise on the facts of the gospel for the conversion and confirmation of readers in the salvation that is in Jesus Christ. The purpose is a gospel—a sure, historical gospel.

IX. Canonicity. The case for the Lukan authorship of the third gospel already has been discussed. While Luke was not one of the apostles, he was the companion of Paul and apparently was thought, in some sense, to have spoken for Paul. Tertullian said, "For even Luke's form of the gospel men usually ascribe to Paul" (*Against Marcion* 4.5). Irenaeus said, "Luke also, the companion of Paul, recorded in a book the Gospel preached by him" (*Against Heresies* 3.1.1). The general acceptance accorded the gospel in antiquity seems to indicate that any demand for apostolicity was met in the association with Paul and in the apostolic community. As H. N. Ridderbos says, "Apostolic authority and apostolic tradition in the New Testament must not be bound to the person of the apostle" (*The Authority of the New Testament Scriptures* [1963], 35). What is apostolic is not limited to the *viva vox* of the apostles nor to their writings. It acquires its own "unpersonal" existence. The apostolic witness, authorized by Christ and inspired by the Holy Spirit, belongs to the *depositum custodi*, the treasure with which the church is entrusted (1 Tim. 3:15; 4:6, 12; 6:20; 2 Tim. 1:14; 2:2). The apostolic and canonical significance of a book for the church depends in large measure on whether its content is a part of the basic apostolic tradition (ibid.).

That the third gospel was recognized early as authoritative is beyond reasonable question. Plummer said that it already had been recognized as authoritative before the middle of the 2nd cent. (*Commentary on Luke*, xvi). No abrupt shift is observed in the use or acceptance of the gospel. As soon as it appears, its authority seems to be assumed. No question is raised. As more time elapses since apostolic times, words of explanation are introduced to identify Luke and to clarify his relationship with Paul and the apostolic church. Such references were noted above in the section on authorship. The notes of Tertullian, Irenaeus, Clement of Alexandria, and the Muratorian Fragment come from the end of the 2nd and the beginning of the 3rd centuries, but the sources directly known to them cover easily an earlier half century. Particularly in the case of Clement of Alexandria, the claim is made that the tradition was handed down first from the apostles and then from father to son (*Stromata* 1.1).

Is there evidence from the period between the apostles and these writers of the existence and use of Luke's gospel? There is. As Plummer says, "We obtain a very imperfect idea of the early evidence in favor of the Third Gospel when we content ourselves with the statement that it is not attributed to Luke by any one before Irenaeus and the Muratorian Fragment" (*Commentary on Luke*, xv). Justin Martyr cites a variety of particulars that are found only in Luke (*1 Apol.* 34; *Trypho* 78, 88, 100, 103, 106). His pupil Tatian used the gospel in the DIATESSARON. Celsus knew the third gospel with its genealogy extending to the first man (Origen, *Contra Celsum* 2.32). The Clementine *Homilies* contain similarities that appear to be allusions (3.63, 65; 11.20, 23; 17.5; 18.16; 19.2). Marcion adapted this gospel to his purposes. Indeed, if Luke's gospel had not been in such common use for a long time, how could a scholar of Origen's breadth have listed it among the number of "those four Gospels admitted by all the churches under heaven"? F. Godet presents a good case for allusions by Clement of Rome in the 1st cent. to Luke's second document, Acts (*A Commentary on the Gospel of Luke*, 2 vols. [1893], 1:8–9). In the NT itself, he finds John's narrative alluding, even in expression, to Luke's and sees the long ending of Mark as "scarcely anything but an abridged reproduction of Luke's" narrative (ibid., 11).

Since no question of debate is raised to indicate a shift of attitude between the time of writing and the universal acceptance of the third gospel as reflected in the latter part of the 2nd cent.; since these early Christian leaders clearly believed that they had an original and firm tradition; since this belief is supported by various evidences of the existence and broad use of the document throughout the early church; and since no voice is raised against the authority of this Gentile nonapostle, it is reasonable to assume that the third gospel's position in the canon was firm and original. See CANON (NT).

X. Text. The third gospel has no lack of textual materials. The five primary uncials (ℵ A B C D) are the chief witnesses for the text. All of these but C (CODEX EPHRAEMI RESCRIPTUS) contain the whole gospel complete, while C has one long gap between Lk. 12 and 19 and a number of shorter gaps throughout the book. Of the complete MSS, B (CODEX VATICANUS) is, of course, king of the uncials, and ℵ (CODEX SINAITICUS) is next in rank. Where these two agree, the support for a reading generally is considered very strong. As Plummer indicates, "the Western element which sometimes disturbs the text of B is almost entirely absent from the Gospels" (*Commentary on Luke*, lxxii).

These primary uncials are reinforced by a number of others (including L, Δ, R, T, X, Ξ, and W). To these are added several hundred minuscules that contain the whole or part of the Gospels. Though these vary in importance, many of them are of considerable value. A variety of early Latin (from N Africa and Europe), Coptic (Egypt), and Syriac versions also are very useful. Many of these translations reflect texts that antedate the oldest uncials (which come from the 4th cent.) and represent wide geographical areas. Finally, the quotations from the church fathers reflect ancient text types that furnish a basis for comparison.

Relatively late discoveries have enriched the resources of the critic. Codex W (Washingtonensis), purchased in 1906 by Mr. Freer, could be listed as a sixth primary uncial. It contains only the four Gospels, but it comes from the late 4th or 5th cent.; its text of Luke is part Alexandrian and part Byzantine in type. The Koridethian Manuscript (Θ), an uncial of the four Gospels, was published in 1913. It is mostly Byzantine except in Mark, where it is akin to two groups of minuscules with which it has been grouped into the Theta or Caesarean family. Among the papyri, P[45] (CHESTER BEATTY Papyrus I), dating from the 2nd or 3rd cent., has been outstanding. Originally the codex contained all four Gospels and Acts, but the discovery c. 1930 included only certain leaves—seven in the case of Luke. In 1961, Papyrus BODMER XIV-XV (P[75]) was published. It contains most of Lk. 3–24 in its present form and is comparable to P[45] in many ways.

Godet mentions five or six thousand variant readings in the documents of Luke and says that "in general they are of very secondary importance and involve no change in the matter of Gospel history" (*Commentary on Luke*, 40). The critic's task is simplified by the tendency of certain MSS to go habitually together in opposition to others until two principal forms are established—often the older uncials grouping against the minuscules and the less ancient uncials. The exact scholar finds no substitute for careful analysis and exegesis in each instance. Even so, it is still proper to speak of the general agreement of the text with the most ancient versions and with the quotations of the fathers of the 2nd and 3rd centuries, and to speak of the general uniformity of the MSS in which the Greek text has been preserved. As Godet says, "A text so universally diffused could only proceed from the text which was received from the very first" (ibid., 46). See TEXT AND MANUSCRIPTS (NT).

XI. Special problems.

Since Luke's interest is so specifically historical, the most serious questions to be raised concerning his writings are charges of inaccuracy in reporting facts. These charges and detractions take four main forms: (1) the inference that a theological interest has displaced any genuine concern for historical accuracy; (2) the charge that Luke's facts are wrong as compared with secular history; (3) the assertion that Luke and Paul contradict each other in their reporting of facts and events; and (4) the theory that the speeches and songs allegedly reported by Luke are his own compositions, in which he uses the literary device of putting his own ideas into the minds and mouths of others. A fifth problem has historical overtones—the matter of alleged theological differences between Luke and Paul. These last would be serious only if they made impossible the traditional relationship between these men.

Many have been disturbed by the fact that nearly all that is known about Jesus is from the writings of theologians or at least of people who were committed believers in Jesus as the Christ. It is argued that the theological judgment about Jesus was the mother of the narratives of the Gospels rather than that the facts narrated demanded the theological conclusions. In other words, it is alleged that the Gospels are not sober historical witnesses to Jesus of Nazareth but are simply the theological opinions of the early church as embellished and illustrated by such items of fact, legend, and mythology as could be used to present their views. The impossibility, on this view, of distinguishing fact from myth or legend has led many to despair of ever recovering the historical Jesus. On the other hand, the major effort of *Formgeschichte* (see FORM CRITICISM) is to peel back the layers of theology in order to come as close as possible to the truth.

Of course, the whole assumption that theology and HISTORY are at odds is an unproved hypothesis of doubt. None of the apostles would have admitted such a bipolarity. They considered themselves witnesses of evident facts that had compelled them and many others to believe that Jesus is indeed the Christ. The "works" of Jesus were not inventions of the apostles and evangelists to illustrate their faith; their faith was, in part, dependent upon these "works" and "signs" (Lk. 5:24; Jn. 5:36). To say that Luke had a definite theological interest is not to say that the history has been conformed to the theology. Rather, as D. Guthrie says, "Luke brings out the theological significance of history" (*New Testament Introduction: The Gospels and Acts* [1965], 88).

Luke exposed himself to attack in the matter of reliability as a historian by the fact that he, more than any other evangelist, followed historical models, related the narrated events to major details of the empire and of world affairs, and claimed to give special effort to providing a reliable account. The chief point of attack in the gospel is the enrollment by order of AUGUSTUS in the time of QUIRINIUS (Lk. 2:1-3). Critics have denied that Augustus ever issued a decree ordering a universal CENSUS, that such a decree would have affected King Herod's Palestine, that Quirinius was governor when Jesus was born, that Jesus was born at the time of a census, and that a Roman census would have proceeded on a tribal basis.

Sir William M. Ramsay and others accepted the challenge. Particularly as a result of Ramsay's *Was Christ Born at Bethlehem?* (1898), the reputation of Luke for accuracy is greatly improved. Though no contemporary sources have confirmed this enrollment, the probabilities now lie on the side of Luke's account. Quirinius was twice the imperial legate in SYRIA. His first term seems to have been as military governor or legate at the same time that Varus was busy as governor over the internal affairs of Syria around 7–5 B.C. (ibid., 243ff.). It has been discovered that a general census was taken by the Romans every fourteen years. Luke distinguishes this "first" census from the well-known decree of A.D. 6 (Acts 5:37). This would imply a date of about 8 B.C. for

This rock inside the Church of All Nations (Jerusalem) is the traditional location of Jesus' struggle in prayer at the Garden of Gethsemane (Lk. 22:39–46).

the beginning of the first census. Where there was resistance, enrollment took a long time (e.g., forty years in Gaul; see F. Stauffer, *Jesus and his Story* [1960], 21–32). Perhaps HEROD followed the Jewish tribal custom to avoid resistance, even at the cost of two or three years' delay in the first census. E. F. Harrison suggests that the first census may have taken fourteen years, so that this first enrollment may have had its beginning date near the time of the birth of Christ and its end at the better known A.D. 6. To accomplish this task in so short a time may have been worthy of note (*Introduction to the New Testament* [1964], 194).

In any case, the probabilities are against Luke's having been careless of a point so easily checked when he was affirming to a prominent leader his own care for accuracy, and was using historical detail to substantiate his central message. Ramsay well inquires how, if Luke made such a glaring error in the facts surrounding the birth of Christ, did these inaccuracies escape the attention of the enemies of the gospel in Roman times? The probabilities, historically, lie on the side of Luke's accuracy. It is even possible that the most striking result in a century of NT research is the relative vindication of the historical accuracy of the author of Luke-Acts and his present standing as the first real church historian.

The charge of contradiction between Luke's writing and that of Paul applies more to Acts than to the gospel. According to Acts, for example, Paul appears to have visited Jerusalem three times after his conversion (Acts 9:26; 11:30; 15:2). Galatians mentions only two occasions (Gal. 1:18; 2:1). The problem is created by the assumption that Paul is listing all of his visits to Jerusalem and not just those in which he had contact with the apostles. Or, if Galatians was written before the COUNCIL OF JERUSALEM, as some think, there is no problem. Others point to Paul's circumcision of TIMOTHY (Acts 16:3) and his refusal to circumcise TITUS (Gal. 2:3), but Timothy was part Jewish and Titus was not. Luke tends to record Paul's concessions to Jewish practice and wishes, while Paul insists that he never sacrificed the principle of freedom in the gospel. Suffice it to say that no direct contradiction has been proved—only reflections of a different interest in the significance of the events.

The question of the origin of the recorded speeches is more often in relation to Acts than in the gospel. However, the words attributed in Lk. 1–2 to Mary, Elizabeth, Zechariah, Simeon, and Anna, as well as the discourses of Jesus himself, are notable exceptions. It is true that one option lying before the evangelist was to follow Thucydides and make the speakers speak in a way which seemed to be demanded by the occasion, though adhering as closely as possible to the general sense of what was actually said (*History of the Peloponnesian War* 1.22.1). That some Greeks used Thucydides' method without his conscientious care is admitted. Others were severely critical of speech invention and regarded the historian's task as recording what was actually said (R. M. Grant, *A Historical Introduction to the New Testament* [1963], 141).

There is no evidence that Luke departed from his careful historical method when he introduced speeches. Where it is possible to check (as between Mk. 13 and Lk. 21), the results are favorable to correct reporting. The intimate details concerning Mary, the prophetic utterances, and the hymns of praise are not invented to express Luke's tradition; they are set forth only because they illumine the significance of an event—the event about which the book is written—the coming of the Christ. Even the variations between the SERMON ON THE MOUNT (Matt. 5–7) and the Sermon on the Plain (Lk. 6:17–49) may indeed indicate only what they claim to present—two separate sermons of the Christ rather than the sermons of two evangelists. Is it not likely that Jesus, as other rabbis, repeated his principal teachings from time to time in different forms to suit a variety of occasions?

The fifth problem, that of the theological differences between the Acts and Paul, is related to the question of the authorship of Luke-Acts. It has been asserted that Luke's record of Paul's teaching differs so radically from Paul's own presentation that the author must not have been acquainted with Paul. In Acts there is no hint of the theological tension reflected in Galatians, where law is seen as leading into bondage from which Christ has freed sinners. Guthrie well says, however, that there is no ground for demanding that Luke must present Paul's theology in his historical book in precisely the same form as Paul presents it in his practical and didactic letters. Paul himself accommodated to circumstances. He circumcised Jewish Timothy but rejected circumcision as a means of salvation (Rom. 2:25). He agreed to concessions to Jewish culture patterns for the Gentiles who looked to Jerusalem for guidance (Acts 15:25–29), but later, in the distant mission fields, he demanded no such conformity (Rom. 14:2–3). It is really no harder to establish theological harmony between Luke and Paul than to demonstrate consistency in Pauline thought and action.

XII. Content. In a unique sense the third gospel depicts Jesus as the divine Redeemer who came to seek and to save those who were lost. The account begins before the annunciations to ZECHARIAH and to MARY, MOTHER OF JESUS, and ends with the ascension into heaven. Set in the context of full deity, the perfect humanity of Jesus is revealed in more detail than in any other gospel. Luke gives the fullest account of the birth, childhood, growth, and domestic and social life of Jesus, but emphasizes that he came as Savior and Redeemer. Christ is depicted not so much as the Messiah of the OT as the Redeemer of the whole world. Time and again the point is stressed that the kingdom is open to all races and conditions of people—Samaritans and pagans as well as Jews; poor as well as rich; outcasts, publicans, and sinners as well as respectable people; and to women as well as to men. It is the universal gospel of the Savior of all.

It is also the gospel of the HOLY SPIRIT. The Holy Spirit is the secret of Christ's own ministry (Lk. 4:18). The human spirit throbs with prayer, praise, joy, forgiveness, weeping, love, friendship, wisdom, understanding, glory, and authority. Notices of time and place are more frequent here than in the other Gospels. Biographical interest is more intense, but the uniting theme is Christ's saving purpose throughout.

Whatever may be said about sources or independence, Luke shares the "triple tradition" with Matthew and Mark and the "double tradition" with Matthew in the sense of using in his own way the general bodies of material to which they all had access and in which they were all interested. To these Luke adds significant materials peculiar to himself, arranging the whole "in order," sometimes chronologically and sometimes logically. The first two chapters, recording the birth of JOHN THE BAPTIST, the annunciation, the adoration of the shepherds, the circumcision of Jesus, his presentation in the temple, and the visit to Jerusalem at the age of twelve, are strongly Semitic in character. Ramsay makes a good case for Mary herself as the source of Luke's information (*Was Christ Born at Bethlehem?* 73–91). The long section that extends from Lk. 9:51 to 18:14, as well as a shorter passage in 19:1–28, are also peculiar to Luke. Together they contain sixteen of the twenty-three parables in Luke and many of the most interesting events in the life of Christ. The so-called Perean ministry occupies a prominent part in this section. The book may be outlined briefly as follows:

  A. Prologue (Lk. 1:1–4)
  B. Nativity narratives (1:5—2:52)
  C. Preparation for the ministry (3:1—4:13)
    1. Mission of John the Baptist (3:1–20)
    2. Baptism of Jesus (3:21–22)
    3. Genealogy of Jesus (3:23–38)
    4. Temptation of Jesus (4:1–13)

D. Galilean ministry (4:14—9:50)
  1. Early Galilean ministry (4:14—7:50)
  2. Later Galilean ministry (8:1—9:6)
  3. Journey northward (9:7–50)
E. Late Judean and Perean ministry (9:51—19:27)
  1. Way to Jerusalem (9:51—11:54)
  2. Mighty words and works (12:1—19:27)
F. Passion and triumph (19:28—24:53)
  1. Closing ministry in Jerusalem (19:28—21:38)
  2. Betrayal, trial, and death (chs. 22–23)
  3. Resurrection and appearances (24:1–49)
  4. Ascension (24:50–53)

XIII. Theology. Luke is first of all a historian of the gospel events and only secondarily a theologian (cf. E. F. Scott in *HTR* 19 [1926]: 143–44). The gospel as he knows it is full of theological data and implications, but he reports it as he received it rather than as an inventor or theoretician (J. M. Creed, *The Gospel According to St. Luke* [1930], lxxi). It is important to treat the "theology" of Luke in the light of this basic informality and not to impose one's own systems of theology upon it.

Luke may be called a Paulinist in the sense that he shares with great conviction Paul's position as the great apologist for the Gentile mission. Everything points to the fact that the gospel is for all. Otherwise, little or nothing is said in the Gospel of Luke that bears directly on the Pauline controversies. Christ must indeed have suffered, which the prophetic Scriptures had foretold, but no further theology of the cross is elaborated to explain redemption. Luke does not mention the death of the Son of Man as "a ransom for many" (as Mk. 10:45) or refer to the cup as the "blood of the covenant, which is poured out for many" (14:24). He is content with the implicit force of the reported events and the portrait of the Redeemer.

The KINGDOM OF GOD holds its central place in the gospel as the "reign of God," which also has its eschatological aspect with the sudden return of the Son of Man (Lk. 17:22–23 and 21:35–36). Jesus is the Christ, the Son of Man, the Redeemer, the Lord. The facts of his heavenly origin, his virgin birth, his divine person, his works, and the outcome of his passion speak for themselves. No elaborate CHRISTOLOGY need be added. He is Savior.

In the same informal way, Luke reveals an implicit "theology of the Spirit." Christ ministered in the power of the Spirit (Lk. 4:18) and promised the same to his followers (24:49)—a promise that was noted as fulfilled in the beginning of Acts (Acts 2:4) and which became a dominant theme of that book.

(Significant commentaries include F. Godet, *A Commentary on the Gospel of Luke*, 2 vols. [1893]; A. Plummer, *A Critical and Exegetical Commentary on the Gospel according to Luke*, ICC, 5th ed. [1922]; J. M. Creed, *The Gospel According to St. Luke* [1930]; N. Geldenhuys, *Commentary on the Gospel of Luke*, NICNT [1952]; W. Arndt, *The Gospel According to St. Luke* [1956]; I. H. Marshall, *The Gospel of Luke: A Commentary on the Greek Text*, NIGTC [1978]; J. A. Fitzmyer, *The Gospel according to Luke*, AB 28–29, 2 vols. [1981–85]; C. F. Evans, *Saint Luke* [1990]; D. L. Bock, *Luke*, BECNT, 2 vols. [1994–96]; J. B. Green, *The Gospel of Luke*, NICNT [1997]; F. Bovon, *Luke*, Hermeneia, 2 vols. [2002–].

(See also N. B. Stonehouse, *The Witness of Luke to Christ* [1951]; P. Parker, *The Gospel before Mark* [1953]; H. Conzelmann, *The Theology of St. Luke* [1960]; S. G. Wilson, *Luke and the Law* [1983]; I. H. Marshall, *Luke: Historian and Theologian*, 3rd ed. [1988]; L. Alexander, *The Preface to Luke's Gospel: Literary Convention and Social Context in Luke 1.1–4 and Acts 1* [1993]; J. Verheyden, ed., *The Unity of Luke-Acts* [1999]; B. Shellard, *New Light on Luke: Its Purpose, Sources and Literary Context* [2002]; D. S. McComiskey, *Lukan Theology in the Light of the Gospel's Literary Structure* [2004]; S. P. Kealy, *The Interpretation of the Gospel of Luke*, 2 vols. [2005]; F. Bovon, *Luke the Theologian: Fifty-five Years of Research (1950–2005)* [2006]; M. C. Parsons, *Luke: Storyteller, Interpreter, Evangelist* [2006]; and the bibliography by W. E. Mills, *The Gospel of Luke* [2002].)

W. T. DAYTON

lunatic. Meaning "insane," this term derives from the Latin *luna* ("moon"), indicating a person under the influence of the moon. The common idea that an individual could be affected mentally by the moon is reflected also in the Greek verb *selēniazomai* G4944, "to be moon struck" (from *selēnē* G4943, "moon"; thus KJV "lunatick" in Matt. 4:24 and 17:15). The insanity contemplated was thought to have recurring periods that corresponded to the lunar phases. The verb seems to be distinguished from *daimonizomai* G1227 (Matt. 4:24), and modern versions interpret it as a reference to epilepsy. However, the same symptoms described in Matt. 17:15 are attributed to spirits or demons elsewhere (cf. Mk. 9:17; Lk. 9:39). The word tended to be used inexactly, and while it included epilepsy it did not necessarily exclude demon-possession. See DEMON; DISEASE (under *epilepsy*), MADNESS. R. K. HARRISON

lust. This term (as a noun or verb), referring to an intense desire, most often has a negative connotation, being used especially of unrestrained sexual craving (see SEX). English Bible translations use the term variously to render a number of words and expressions, in particular Greek *epithymia* G2123. This Greek noun (as well as the cognate verb *epithymeō* G2121) can refer to DESIRE in a neutral or even positive context (e.g., Lk. 22:15; Phil. 1:23; 1 Thess. 2:17), but in the NT it is so frequently joined with such terms as "evil" (e.g., Col. 3:5) that the word by itself takes on a negative nuance ("covetousness, sinful passion," etc.). Another significant term is *pathos* G4079, which in extrabiblical Greek has a broad semantic range ("incident, experience, suffering, emotion"), but which is used in the NT only in negative contexts (Rom. 1:26; Col. 3:5; 1 Thess. 4:5; see PASSION). The consequences of evil lust are not only privation of good, but also enslavement, suffering, and death.

lustration. Purification by means of a propitiatory sacrifice or certain ceremonies. The word is not found in the English Bible, but other terms referring to PURIFICATION are found in both Testaments often. Ceremonial cleansing was an important part of Israelite religious life, for people regarded as ceremonially unclean were kept from the altar in the sanctuary and were kept from fellowship with their coreligionists.

The law of Moses made clear distinctions between CLEAN and unclean. UNCLEANNESS was primarily ceremonial defilement, not moral, and was contracted in several ways, some of them avoidable, some unavoidable, and provision was made for purification. A person was rendered ceremonially unclean in the following ways: (1) contact with a dead body, especially a human corpse (Num. 19:11–22); (2) leprosy (Lev. 13:14); (3) seminal emissions and childbirth (Lev. 12; 15); (4) eating the flesh of an unclean fish, bird, and animal (Lev. 11; Deut. 14:3–21); (5) physical defects or impairments (Lev. 21:16–24).

Israelites who had contracted uncleanness were required to separate themselves from the congregation, the length of time depending upon the nature of the uncleanness (Lev. 12; 15:11–13). Usually this was seven days; in the case of the birth of a male child it was forty days, and of a female child, eighty days. The mode of purification was bathing the body and washing the clothes in water (15:8, 10–11), but for the more serious forms of uncleanness sacrifice was necessary (12:6; 15:29–30). People rendered unclean by leprosy (Lev. 14) or by touching a corpse (Num. 19) were sprinkled with water mingled with blood or ashes. The penalty of refusing to be purified was execution (19:20).

In the NT there are references to ceremonial purification in connection with childbirth (Lk. 2:22), leprosy (17:11–19), and the Passover (Jn. 11:55; 18:28). In contrast with the PHARISEES, Jesus emphasized moral rather than ceremonial purity (Mk. 7:1–23). Although PAUL made clear that Christ repealed all the Levitical regulations on unclean meats and practices (Rom. 14:14, 20; 1 Cor. 6:13; Col. 2:16, 20–22), he himself, in order that his message might more readily be received, underwent the rite of purification (Acts 18:18).

H. A. HANKE

lute. See MUSIC, MUSICAL INSTRUMENTS IV.D.

Luz luhz (לוּז H4281, "almond tree"). (1) The earlier Canaanite name of the city better known as BETHEL (Gen. 28:19; 35:6). It was changed to the latter (meaning "house of God") by JACOB after the Lord appeared to him in a dream during his flight from home, and it became a holy place in the later history of Israel. According to the citations in Genesis, Luz is indistinguishable from Bethel, but JOSHUA, in delineating the S boundary of EPHRAIM and MANASSEH, speaks of it as going out "from Bethel to Luz" (Josh. 16:2), apparently regarding the two as distinct locations. It is possible that this reflects a distinction between the city and the nearby holy place. More probably, however, the reference is not to the city of Bethel but to a mountain range closely associated with the city which is mentioned as the previous boundary point (v. 1) and from which the line went out to Luz (the city of Bethel). In Josh. 18:13, which records the delineation of the boundary of the territory of BENJAMIN, Bethel and Luz are regarded as identical. The city continued to be known as Luz to the Canaanite inhabitants until the time of the judges (Jdg. 1:23).

(2) A town built in the land of the Hittites by a former inhabitant of Luz #1, apparently named after the Canaanite city (Jdg. 1:26). The expression "land of the Hittites" probably refers to SYRIA, but the term HITTITE is ambiguous, and some think that the phrase may designate the hill country W of Bethel (cf. Num. 13:29). The location of this town is unknown. T. McCOMISKEY

LXX. Abbreviation for SEPTUAGINT.

Lycaonia lik´uh-oh´nee-uh (Λυκαονία *G3377*; cf. Λυκαονιστί *G3378*, "in Lycaonian [language]"). A region in south central ASIA MINOR. Although its borders are not well defined, Lycaonia had GALATIA to the N, CAPPADOCIA to the E, CILICIA to the S, and PISIDIA to the W. It consisted for the most part of a high, treeless plateau, the land being fertile enough and productive where there was water, but good mainly for raising sheep and goats (Xenophon, *Anabasis* 4.2.23). The people who inhabited the region have been described as warlike and energetic. They emerge in about the 6th cent. B.C., already speaking a language of their own, and during the long rule of PERSIA in Asia Minor maintained themselves free from Persian domination. After the fall of PERSIA and the death of ALEXANDER THE GREAT, the region fell under control of the SELEUCIDS and so remained until 190 B.C., when the Romans handed Lycaonia over to PERGAMUM. When King ATTALUS died in 133 B.C. and the Pergamene kingdom was dissolved, the region was administered by the Romans as part of their settlement in Asia, and from 25 B.C. onward became part of Galatia or Galatia-Cappadocia.

The leading cities of Lycaonia were LYSTRA and DERBE. ICONIUM was evidently a Phrygian city (see PHRYGIA), for when the Jews stirred up trouble for PAUL and BARNABAS there, they fled to the Lycaonian cities for safety (Acts 14:5–6). As everywhere else in the Seleucid realm, the process of hellenization went on (see HELLENISM), but slowly in Lycaonia, for the people are described as being backward. The GREEK LANGUAGE was no doubt understood in the cities, but the people still retained their own speech, which they used in response to the miracle Paul worked upon the cripple in Lystra (14:11). They then proceeded to get ready to sacrifice to Paul and Barnabas as though they were gods, an act from which Paul barely restrained them. This whole incident indicates the strong hold of pagan religion upon the populace of the region.

The book of Acts speaks of aggressive groups of Jews both in ANTIOCH OF PISIDIA and in Iconium (Acts 13–14), but says little about any such groups in Lystra and Derbe. In fact, it was Jews from Antioch and Iconium who came and stirred up the people at Lystra against Paul and Barnabas (14:19–20). There must have been some Jews living in the Lycaonian cities, for TIMOTHY came from Lystra, and his mother was Jewish. Indeed, Paul decided to circumcise Timothy because of the Jewish element in the place (16:1–3).

In all, Paul made three visits to Lycaonia. The first was on his first missionary journey, accompanied by Barnabas, and they preached there with some success (Acts 14:21–22). On his second journey, Paul returned to the region with SILAS, found Timothy at Lystra and added him to the company, and ministered to the Christians in the cities there (16:1–5). When he set out from ANTIOCH OF SYRIA on his third journey, he again went through the region, encouraging and strengthening the churches (18:23). (See A. H. M. Jones, *Cities of the Eastern Roman Provinces*, 2nd ed. [1971], ch. 5.)

R. C. STONE

Lycia lish´uh (Λυκία *G3379*). A mountainous country in SW ASIA MINOR. This territory of about 3,500 sq. mi. protrudes southward into the Mediterranean Sea bounded on the NW by CARIA, on the N by PHRYGIA and PISIDIA, and on the NE by PAMPHYLIA. Lycia was shut in by rugged mountain

Lycian tomb monument from Xanthos (4th cent. B.C.).

ranges, and since the land jutted out into the sea, it would not have any important trade routes. Its climate rapidly fluctuated between the extremes of temperature. Its mountainous slopes afforded much excellent timber for the building of houses and ships, and were also suitable for grazing and for vineyards and olive farms. The valleys provided space for the cultivated grains.

Its main contact to the outside world was through its seaports, the main two being PATARA and MYRA. On the return of the third missionary journey, PAUL's ship stopped at Patara (Acts 21.1; some mss also include another stop at Myra) and then sailed to PHOENICIA. On his journey to ROME, Paul's ship went along the coast of CILICIA and Pamphylia, and at Myra he and the other prisoners were put on another ship that had come from ALEXANDRIA and was sailing for Italy. Due to prevailing W winds, it was common for Alexandrian grain ships to travel N along the Syrian coast and then move slowly E along the coasts of Cilicia and Pamphylia. Myra was a natural place for the grain ships (cf. Acts 27:38) to harbor and to be serviced before their journey to Italy, and hence it would not be unusual for the centurion to find one here for Paul and the other prisoners.

The traditions on the origin of the Lycian population would seem to point to an immigration from CRETE. In the 6th cent. they were the only people of W Asia Minor not subject to Croesus. However, they were not strong enough to withstand the Persian invasion in 546 B.C., though they did retain their national unity under the Persians. Although they were temporarily in the Delian confederacy in 446, it was not until the arrival of ALEXANDER THE GREAT in Lycia in the winter of 334/33 that the country finally came under the Greek influence. Upon the death of Alexander, Lycia became a part of Antigonus's domain, but it was invaded in 309 by Antigonus's enemy, PTOLEMY I of Egypt.

Egyptian control over Lycia continued until it was conquered by ANTIOCHUS III in 197 B.C. Antiochus was defeated by the Romans in the battle of Magnesia, and so in 189 the Romans placed Lycia under RHODES. The Lycians bitterly resisted the Rhodian rule, and after several complaints to Rome, the senate finally granted freedom to Lycia in 167 (cf. Appian, *The Syrian Wars* 44). This freedom was not revoked until A.D. 43 by CLAUDIUS when he established the province of Lycia-Pamphylia under a practorian legate (Dio Cassius, *Rom. Hist.* 60.17.3; Suetonius, *Claudius* 25.3). In A.D. 69 VESPASIAN detached Pamphylia from Lycia and combined Pamphylia with the Galatian province, at which time Lycia probably became a free country.

The existing Jewish community in many of the cities of Lycia is evident from a letter sent by the Romans c. 139 B.C. to the confederate cities that they should not harm the Jews (1 Macc 15:23). Evidence for Christianity in the first two centuries is lacking.

(See further W. M. Ramsay, *St. Paul the Traveller and the Roman Citizen*, 14th ed. [1925], 297–300, 316–320; J. Keil, "The Greek Provinces," *CAH*, 11 [1936], 590–97; D. Magie, *Roman Rule in Asia Minor* [1950], 1:516–39, 2.1370–96; B. Levick, *Roman Colonies in Southern Asia Minor* [1967], passim; J. A. O. Larsen, *Greek Federal States* [1967], 240–63; G. E. Bean, *Turkey's Southern Shore: An*

Archaeological Guide [1968], 151–73; A. H. M. Jones, *The Cities of the Eastern Roman Provinces*, 2nd ed. [1971], ch. 3; G. E. Bean, *Lycian Turkey* [1978]; A. G. Keen, *Dynastic Lycia: A Political History of the Lycians and Their Relations with Foreign Powers, c. 545–362 B.C.* [1998].)
H. W. HOEHNER

Lydda lid′uh (Λύδδα *G3375*). A town about 11 mi. SE of JOPPA where the apostle PETER healed a paralytic named AENEAS (Acts 9:32–35, 38). See LOD.

Lydia (person) lid′ee-uh (Λυδία *G3376*). A business woman from THYATIRA; she lived in PHILIPPI and was PAUL's first convert there (Acts 16:12–15, 40). Her name, while common for women (cf. Horace, *Odes* 1.8.1; 3.9.7ff.), may be an adjectival form, "the Lydian [woman]," as indicating her origin, since Thyatira was in the region of Lydia. See LYDIA (PLACE). She is identified as "a dealer in purple cloth." Like all of Lydia, Thyatira was noted for its dyeing industry and production of purple dyed garments, which were highly prized and costly. She doubtless was the agent in Philippi of a local firm in her native city. Her trade implies that she was a woman of some means. If a widow, she may have been carrying on the business of her deceased husband.

Lydia is further described as "a worshiper of God," the usual designation for a Jewish PROSELYTE. She probably had accepted the Jewish faith in her native city, for it had a strong Jewish colony. At Philippi she faithfully participated in the SABBATH services at the place of prayer by the riverside. After listening to Paul's message there she was converted. After Lydia and her household (presumably her servants and their dependents) were baptized, she urged Paul and his coworkers to make her home their headquarters. That all this occurred on the first Sabbath need not be assumed. Her home apparently became the meeting place of the local church (Acts 16:40). Lydia's own hospitality doubtless did much to foster the unique financial relations between Paul and the Philippian church (Phil. 4:15–16).

Lydia is not mentioned in the Philippian letter. The omission has been accounted for in several ways: that she had left Philippi; that she had died; that Lydia was not her personal name, but she was one of the two women mentioned in Phil. 4:2. The suggestion that she was the "loyal yokefellow" of 4:3, or even Paul's wife, is sheer fancy. (See W. M. Ramsay, *St. Paul the Traveller* [1909], 214–15; B. Witherington III, *Women in the Earliest Churches* [1988], 147–49.)
D. E. HIEBERT

Lydia (place) lid′ee-uh (Λυδία). A large territory in NW ASIA MINOR.

I. Geography. Lydia's borders are difficult to define accurately. It was bounded on the N by MYSIA, on the S by CARIA, on the E by PHRYGIA, and on the W by the AEGEAN SEA. The S boundary may have gone as far as the Maeander River (Strabo, *Geogr.* 12.8.15). The E boundary is confusing, for there is a dispute whether Catacecaumene, an inland volcanic area on the upper Hermus River, was a part of Lydia or Mysia (ibid., 13.4.11) and because some of the territories were claimed by both of these regions (ibid., 12.8.3; 13.4.12). It is a land mostly of fertile river valleys with the Hermus River in the N and the Cayster valley, which is between the Tmolus and Messogis mountain ranges, in the S part of Lydia. SARDIS served as Lydia's capital.

II. History. The earliest reference to Lydia is in Gen. 10:22 (cf. also 1 Chr. 1:17), where it refers to LUD as a son of SHEM; expounding on that passage,

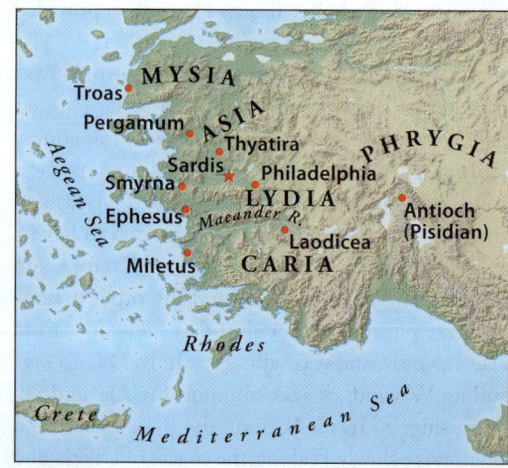

Lydia.

LYDIA (PLACE)

The artificial mound in this picture contains Lydian tombs dating to the 4th cent. B.C.

JOSEPHUS refers to the Lydians as Lud's descendants (*Ant.* 1.6.4. §144). HERODOTUS (*Hist.* 1.7) does not preclude a Semitic origin of the Lydians. In Isa. 66:19 Lud is listed with TUBAL (in Asia Minor), GREECE, and "the distant islands" (or "coastlands"), a context that would fit with the location of Lydia. In Ezek. 27.10 and 30.5 Lud is listed as an ally with TYRE and with EGYPT respectively. Lydia is mentioned also in the Neo-Babylonian annals.

The age of prosperity and strength for Lydia came with the Mermnad dynasty founded by Gyges (c. 685–657/52 B.C.), who murdered King Canduales and married his widow (Herodotus, *Hist.* 1.8–12). Gyges gradually subdued the coastal cities of Miletus, Smyrna, and Colophon and sent offerings to Delphi (ibid., 1.14–15). Gyges made a pact with ASHURBANIPAL (669–633) of ASSYRIA against the CIMMERIANS. Gyges defeated the Cimmerians and broke his alliance with Ashurbanipal and in fact made an alliance with Psammetichus I (c. 663–609) to help liberate the Egyptians from the Assyrian control. The Cimmerians made another attack on Lydia resulting in Gyges's death. It was not until Alyattes (c. 610–560), the fourth in the Mermnad dynasty, that the Cimmerians were finally driven out (ibid., 1.16). Alyattes made war against Cyaxares the Mede and finally established peace in 585, whereby the Halys River served as a border between Lydia and Media. Hence, Lydia had extended its borders. In the peace agreement, Alyattes's daughter Arvenis and Cyaxares's son Astyages were married, and from them a daughter was born named Mandane, who became the mother of CYRUS the Great (ibid., 1.74).

The best known and last king of Lydia was Croesus (c. 560–546 B.C.), son of Alyattes. He was friendly to the Greeks and encouraged hellenization (see HELLENISM), as seen by his contributions to Greek shrines, especially Delphi, and in the rebuilding of the temple of ARTEMIS in EPHESUS. However, with the rise of the Persian power, Croesus thought he could expand his borders and invaded Persian territories. It was a bad move, for Cyrus then attacked Lydia, captured Sardis, and overthrew Croesus in 546 (ibid., 1.75–86). Lydia lost its political independence and was a satrapy of Persia until the invasion of Asia Minor by ALEXANDER THE GREAT in 334. After Alexander's death, Lydia was under Antigonus for a while and then under the SELEUCIDS. When ANTIOCHUS II was defeated at Magnesia in 190, the Romans presented it to their ally EUMENES II, king of PERGAMUM (Appian, *The Syrian Wars* 38, 44; Polybius, *Hist.* 21.45; Livy, *Hist.* 28.39; 1 Macc. 8.8). In 133 B.C., Attalus III, son of Eumenes II, bequeathed Pergamum to Rome. Therefore, Lydia formed a part of the Roman province of Asia and remained so until it became a separate entity in Diocletian's reign (c. A.D. 316).

III. Inhabitants. The origins of the Lydian people are obscure, but as already noted there seems to have been an early Semitic influence. During Antiochus III's reign (223–187 B.C.), many Jews were settled in Lydia (Jos. *Ant.* 12.3.4 §§147–49). The Anatolian influence was quite strong early, with more Greek influence from the reign of Croesus reign onward. There was a constant tension between Greek and Anatolian influences. Inscriptions from the 4th cent. seem to indicate that the Lydian language was an idiom of the Indo-European family, but by the beginning of the Christian era Greek was the common language (Strabo, *Geogr.* 13.4.9, speaks of an ancient writing; see also LANGUAGES OF THE ANE IV).

IV. Industry. Lydia was rich in natural resources. It is told that during Croesus's reign gold was washed down the Pactolus River, and Strabo mentions the existence of gold mines that were exhausted in his day (*Geogr.* 14.5.28). Lydia was known for its rich fertile land, producing olives, figs, grapes, and grain. Its best known industry was the manufacture of textile fabrics; along with this THYATIRA was well known for its dyeing processes (cf. Homer, *Iliad* 4.141), and its guild of dyers was known to be prosperous. One of those in the industry was the Thyatiran woman who was converted to Christianity at PHILIPPI by Paul (Acts 16:14). See LYDIA (PERSON). One significant achievement of the Lydians was their invention of coinage (Herodotus, *Hist.* 1.94). The first Lydian coinage had alloys mixed with gold, and the gold content varied between 36 and 53 percent. Such significant variance shook the public confidence in coinage, and so this may be the reason for Croesus' introducing coinage of pure gold and pure silver. The new invention was accepted by the Greek cities of the coast and then by the whole world.

V. Importance in the NT. As noted above, Lydia the seller of purple was Paul's convert in Europe at Philippi (Acts 16). Also in Lydia is Ephesus, the place where Paul spent nearly three years (ch. 19). Moreover, out of seven churches addressed by John in Rev. 2–3, five of them were in Lydia (see EPHESUS, SMYRNA, THYATIRA, SARDIS, PHILADELPHIA). However, the NT writers never address the above churches as being in Lydia, but rather in Asia, in accordance with the Roman provincial classification.

(See further W. M. Ramsay, *The Cities and Bishoprics of Phrygia*, 2 vols. [1895–97], passim; D. Magie, *Roman Rule in Asia Minor* [1950], 1:45–50; 2:807–17; G. E. Bean, *Aegean Turkey: An Archaeological Guide* [1966], 259–72 et passim; B. Levick, *Roman Colonies in Southern Asia Minor* [1967], passim; A. H. M. Jones, *The Cities in the Eastern Roman Provinces*, 2nd ed. [1971], passim.)

H. W. HOEHNER

lye. KJV, "nitre." An alkaline substance used for cleansing purposes; it refers either to sodium carbonate, found in certain places as an incrustation on the ground or in certain saline lakes, or to potassium carbonate, which was obtained by leaching wood ashes or other vegetable matter. Both possess excellent detergent qualities. The term is used by the NRSV to render Hebrew *neter H6003* (Jer. 2:22 [NIV, "soda"]; the Hebrew term occurs also in Prov. 25:20) and *bōr H1342* (Job. 9:30 [NIV, "soap"]; Isa. 1:25 [NIV differently]). See SOAP.   S. BARABAS

lying. See LIE.

lyre. See MUSIC, MUSICAL INSTRUMENTS IV.D.

Lysanias li-say'nee-uhs (Λυσανίας *G3384*). The TETRARCH of ABILENE at the beginning of JOHN THE BAPTIST's ministry (Lk. 3:1), probably in A.D. 26. JOSEPHUS referred to a Lysanias who in 40 B.C. succeeded his father Ptolemy to the throne of Chalcis; he was put to death by Mark Antony in 36 B.C. at the instigation of CLEOPATRA, upon whom the dominion was bestowed (*Ant.* 14.13.3; 15.4.1). Josephus also recorded that among the regions assigned to Agrippa I (see HEROD VII) was the "tetrarchy of Lysanias" (18.6.10; 19.5.1). Some scholars hold that there was no one named Lysanias who later ruled in those parts and that Luke therefore was guilty of a gross chronological blunder in naming Lysanias as a ruler in A.D. 26.

Such an inference seems very improbable in view of Luke's established general accuracy.

It seems a necessary assumption that Josephus referred to two different men named Lysanias. One of them, the son of Ptolemy, bore the title of *king*, given him by Antony (Dio Cassius, *Rom. Hist.* 49.32); but Josephus, in agreement with Luke, also mentioned a *tetrarch*. Their territory was not the same. The first, with his capital at Chalcis, ruled over a considerable area that included Abila, but was not called Abilene. CLAUDIUS bestowed upon Agrippa II "the tetrarchy of Lysanias" but took from him Chalcis (Jos. *Ant.* 20.7.1; *War* 2.12.8); Josephus thus expressly distinguished Chalcis from the tetrarchy of Lysanias.

An inscription discovered at Abila established that there was a later "Lysanias the tetrarch" (*CIG*, 4521). The inscription related to the dedication of a temple contains the words, "on behalf of the salvation of the Lords Imperial and their whole household" by "Nymphaies, a freedman of Lysanias, the tetrarch." The mention of "the Lords Imperial" may refer to the joint rule of AUGUSTUS and TIBERIUS (A. R. C. Leaney, *A Commentary on the Gospel according to St. Luke* [1958], 48–50), placing the inscription as late as A.D. 11; more probably, the reference is to Tiberius and his mother Julia (W. M. Ramsay, *The Bearing of Recent Discovery on the Trustworthiness of the New Testament* [1915], 297–300), thus giving a time between A.D. 14 and 29. Clearly this establishes a tetrarch Lysanias at the very time that Luke mentions. Why Luke should mention the tetrarch Lysanias while omitting the ruler of DAMASCUS is not clear. For further details, see ABILENE.   D. E. HIEBERT

Lysias lis´ee-uhs (Λυσίας *G3385*). (1) A prominent Syrian general and official who served under Antiochus IV Epiphanes and Antiochus V Eupator. He is given considerable attention in 1 and 2 MACCABEES and in JOSEPHUS (e.g., 1 Macc. 3:32–38; 6:17; 7:1–4; 2 Macc. 10–11; Jos. *Ant.* 12 §§295–98, 313–15, 361, 367).

(2) See CLAUDIUS LYSIAS.

Lysimachus li-sim´uh-kuhs (Λυσίμαχος). (1) One of the Diadochi (Successors) of ALEXANDER THE GREAT. He was granted the province of THRACIA in 323 B.C. After SELEUCUS I defeated Antigonus in 301, Lysimachus received the northern parts of ASIA MINOR, which made him extraordinarily wealthy. Some years later he invaded and occupied MACEDONIA. He lost his life in battle in 281.

(2) Son of a certain Ptolemy, mentioned at the end of the Greek text of ESTHER (Add. Esth. 11:1). According to this passage, in the fourth year of the reign of Ptolemy and Cleopatra, Dositheus, who said that he was a priest and a Levite, and Ptolemy his son brought the letter about Purim (to Egypt), which they said had been translated by Lysimachus, son of Ptolemy of Jerusalem (see H. B. Swete, *An Introduction to the Old Testament in Greek* [1902], 25, 258; R. H. Pfeiffer, *History of New Testament Times* [1949], 310–11).

(3) Brother of MENELAUS, high priest in the days of ANTIOCHUS Epiphanes, who served in Menelaus's stead in the priesthood for a time (2 Macc. 4:29; 39–41). He is said to have committed many sacrileges with the consent of Menelaus, so that the people were aroused against him. When the multitude rose against him, and were filled with rage, Lysimachus armed about 3,000 men and began first to offer violence. The people retaliated, defeated the forces of Lysimachus, and killed him beside the treasury.   J. H. SKILTON

Lystra lis´truh (Λύστρα *G3388*, construed both as fem. sg. and neut. pl.). A town in the central region of S ASIA MINOR (Acts 14:6, 8, 21; 16:1–2; 2 Tim. 3:11). Lystra is an ancient village of the district of LYCAONIA that was c. 24 mi. S of ICONIUM (in PHRYGIA). Lystra was built upon a small hill suddenly rising c. 100–150 ft. above the surrounding plain located on the E of the mountain ranges that form the Pisidian triangle (see PISIDIA). It was not located on any significant road or trade route; in fact, it was located c. 8–10 mi from the great trade route. It is probable that the territory of Lystra was bounded in the N by Iconium, in the W by the mountains, and in the S by Isauria Vetus. The borders of the territory of Lycaonia are difficult to determine, especially in the E, because of the absence of towns in the area. It is thought that the territory of Lycaonia was not any larger than 100 sq. mi. The plain surrounding Lystra was fertile, with two small rivers passing by the village's mound.

LYSTRA

The region of Lystra as seen from the city acropolis. (View to the S.)

The history of Lystra is quite unknown. Lycaonia was under Persian control and later under Greek control (first under the SELEUCIDS [c. 280–189 B.C.] and second under the Attalids [c. 189–133 B.C.; see ATTALUS]), and finally under the Romans. In 36 B.C. Lycaonia was given to Amyntas, king of Pisidia, who was then made king of GALATIA. When in 25 B.C. Amyntas was killed in a campaign against the Homonadeis, the greater part of his kingdom, which included Lystra, was taken over by the Romans and made the province of Galatia. In 6 B.C. the Homanadenses were subdued, and AUGUSTUS planted five more military colonies around Homonadeis, one of which was Lystra.

Some scholars have been puzzled to know the reason why Rome made such an insignificant town as Lystra a Roman colony; a possible explanation is that it was located on the eastern side of the mountains and thus could be made a strong fortress in order to keep in check the mountain tribes S and W of it. Since it was the most eastern of the fortified cities, it would help in the pacification of Pisidia and Isauria as well as serve as a base for another attack from the E. Both Lystra and DERBE were under the direct control of Rome until c. A.D. 37/38, when it was put under the control of the client king Antiochus IV of Commagene. In A.D. 72 Antoninus Pius returned these two cities to the Roman provincial rule of CILICIA.

In becoming a Roman colony, Lystra sent (in the 2nd cent.) a statute of concord to its sister colony of ANTIOCH OF PISIDIA. When Lystra had become a colony, she acquired some Roman settlers, most of whom were veterans. Also, under the Roman influence roads were built during Augustus's rule; one of them went from Iconium through Lystra and then on to Derbe and Laranda and finally into Cilicia.

Regarding Lystra's inhabitants, the Roman element was a small group of the local aristocracy of soldiers; they were the ruling class. There were also the Greek-educated residents, called the Hellenes, who were not a racial group but an educated and generally well-to-do segment of the population. TIMOTHY, whose father was a Hellene and his mother a Jew (Acts 16:1), probably belonged to the educated and upper income bracket. Finally, the majority of the population was made up of the uneducated Lycaonians, who were a small Anatolian tribe. The Roman aristocracy spoke Latin, the educated were able to speak Greek, and the Lycaonians used their own vernacular (14:11), which continued to be spoken until the 6th cent. A.D.

On the first missionary journey, PAUL and BARNABAS arrived at Lystra (c. A.D. 49), having fled the hostility of the Jews at Iconium (Acts 14:6).

Upon arrival at Lystra, Paul healed a man who had been lame from birth and the crowd concluded that the apostles were the gods HERMES and ZEUS (vv. 6–18). On an earlier occasion, the same two gods, as the local legend relates, had come to that region to visit an aged and pious couple, Philemon and Bucis (Ovid, *Metamorphoses* 8.626–724). Afterward the Jews from Antioch of Pisidia and Iconium came and influenced the people against Paul and consequently stoned Paul dragging him out of the city as dead. Probably it was this visit of Paul during which Timothy was converted and undoubtedly helped to establish the infant church at Lystra (2 Tim. 3:10–11). Paul and Barnabas went on to Derbe but later on their return visited Lystra (Acts 14:19–23). On his second missionary journey Paul traveled through SYRIA and CILICIA (c. A.D. 50) and revisited the churches and Derbe and Lystra (Acts 15:41—16:2). A visit to Lystra on the third journey (c. A.D. 53) is implied in Acts 18:23.

(See further W. M. Ramsay, *The Historical Geography of Asia Minor* [1890], passim; id., *The Church in the Roman Empire before A.D. 170*, 5th ed. [1897], 47–54 et passim; id., *A Historical Commentary on St. Paul's Epistle to the Galatians* [1899], 223–27; id., *The Cities of St. Paul* [1907], 407–18; id., *The Social Basis of Roman Power in Asia Minor* [1941], 180–99 et passim; D. Magie, *Roman Rule in Asia Minor* [1950], 1:462–64; 2:1324–27; E. M. Blaiklock, *Cities of the New Testament* [1965], 31–34; B. Levick, *Roman Colonies in Southern Asia Minor* [1967], 51–53, 195–97 et passim; A. H. M. Jones, *The Cities of the Eastern Roman Provinces*, 2nd ed. [1971], 134–35.)   H. W. HOEHNER

We want to hear from you. Please send your comments about this book to us in care of zreview@zondervan.com. Thank you.

ZONDERVAN.com/
AUTHORTRACKER
follow your favorite authors